MACMILLAN
COMPENDIUM

LATIN AMERICAN LIVES

MACMILLAN
COMPENDIUM

LATIN AMERICAN LIVES

SELECTED BIOGRAPHIES FROM THE
FIVE-VOLUME

Encyclopedia of Latin American History and Culture

MACMILLAN LIBRARY REFERENCE USA

New York

Macmillan Library Reference USA
1633 Broadway, 5th Floor
New York, NY 10019

Manufactured in the United States of America.

printing number
1 2 3 4 5 6 7 8 9 10

Library of Congress Cataloging-in-Publication Data

Latin American lives.
    p.   cm. — (Macmillan compendium)
  "Selections from the five-volume Encyclopedia of Latin American history and culture."
  Includes index.
  ISBN 0-02-865060-3 (alk. paper)
  1. Latin America—Biography—Dictionaries.   I. Title.
II. Series.
CT502.E54   1998
920.08—dc21   98-41832
                                               CIP

This paper meets the requirements of ANSI/NISO Z39.48-1992 (Permanence of Paper).

Latin American Lives

Table of Contents

Preface   vi

A–Z Listings   1

Appendix: Biographies by Category   1099

Index   1135

Preface

As classrooms across the United States become ever more inclusive of the Western Hemisphere as a whole, students have become increasingly interested in the history and culture of Latin America in particular. The publishers and editors of Charles Scribner's Sons recognized this interest, and in 1996 published the five-volume *Encyclopedia of Latin American History and Culture*. For the purposes of this publication, Latin America is broadly defined to include South America, Central America, Mexico, the Caribbean Sea, and the historical Spanish borderlands north of the Rio Grande that are now part of the United States. Sweeping coverage spans the centuries from the earliest civilizations of the Olmec, Maya, and Chavin to the present day.

Students and library patrons have indicated a need for a single-volume biographical encyclopedia describing the lives of the individuals who played a part in the vast history and multifaceted culture of Latin America. *The Macmillan Compendium: Latin American Lives*, comprised of the 3000 biographies in the *Encyclopedia of Latin American History and Culture*, is designed to fulfill that need.

The *Encyclopedia of Latin American History and Culture* was lauded by the *Library Journal* as "among the best reference works published" in 1996. Foremost among the encyclopedia's accolades was the honor of being named an American Library Association Outstanding Reference Source for 1997. According to the *L.J.*, the "work's strongest features are the 3000 biographical entries, covering individuals across all classes, occupations, and times." All of these biographies have been reprinted in this single-volume *Macmillan Compendium: Latin American Lives*.

Grand in scope, *Latin American Lives* is organized in an A-to-Z format. Fascinating biographies explore the life and work of the people who had an impact on the history and culture of Latin America. In preparing this volume, it was agreed that articles would be excerpted in their entirety. Cross-references within articles will assist readers as they explore the compendium. A comprehensive index will provide further assistance.

FEATURES

To add visual appeal and enhance the usefulness of the volume, the page format was designed to include the following helpful features.

- Call-out quotations: These relevant, provocative quotations are highlighted to promote reader interest and exploration.
- Cross-references: Appearing within articles, cross-references will encourage further research.
- Photographs: Selected to complement the text, the photographs are chosen to further engage the reader.
- Index: A thorough index provides thousands of additional points of entry into the work.

ACKNOWLEDGMENTS

Macmillan Compendium: Latin American Lives contains over one hundred illustrations. Acknowledgments of sources for illustrations can be found in the captions. The articles herein were written for the *Encyclopedia of Latin American History and Culture*, edited by Barbara A. Tenenbaum, specialist in Mexican Culture at the Library of Congress in Washington, D.C. More than 800 scholars from twenty-nine countries contributed to the original set.

This book would not have been possible without the hard work and creativity of the staff at Macmillan Library Reference. We are grateful to all who helped create this marvelous work.

Editorial Staff
Macmillan Library Reference

A

ABAD Y QUEIPO, MANUEL

Manuel Abad y Queipo (*b.* 26 August 1751; *d.* 15 September 1825), bishop of Michoacán (1810–1814) and acute social commentator on late colonial Mexico. The illegitimate son of a noble Asturian family, Abad y Queipo was born in Santa María de Villarpedre, Asturias, Spain. He studied at the University of Salamanca for ten years before emigrating to the Americas, where he received a doctorate in canon law from the University of Guadalajara in 1805. He served in Michoacán from 1784 to 1814, rising through the ecclesiastical hierarchy to become acting bishop (unconfirmed by captive King Ferdinand VII) in 1810. An exemplification of the enlightened clergyman, Abad y Queipo strove to improve local economic conditions, in one instance by promoting the production of raw silk. He also advocated social reforms, such as the abolition of tribute, and he criticized many Bourbon policies, notably the Intendancy System and the sequestration of pious funds.

An exemplification of the enlightened clergyman, Abad y Queipo strove to improve local economic conditions.

Abad y Queipo, however, always favored reform within the imperial system. In 1810, when the rebellion led by his old friend Miguel HIDALGO Y COSTILLA broke out, he excommunicated the insurgent leader and unceasingly preached the social and economic evils of civil war. Nonetheless, he was suspected of harboring dangerously liberal views, and the restored Ferdinand VII recalled him to Spain in 1814. Abad y Queipo was finally confirmed as bishop of Michoacán but was never allowed to return to Mexico. In 1822 he resigned his hard-won bishopric to become bishop of Tortose. He also served in the provisional junta of 1820, which rekindled Ferdinand's doubts about the cleric's political loyalty; this led in 1824 to his arrest and imprisonment in the monastery of Sisla, where he died.

— R. DOUGLAS COPE

ABADÍA MÉNDEZ, MIGUEL

Miguel Abadía Méndez (*b.* 5 June 1867; *d.* 15 May 1947), Colombian president (1926–1930). Born in La Vega de los Padres (now Piedras), Tolima, Abadía was sent to Bogotá for his education. He attended various private schools and received his doctorate in law in 1889 from the Colegio del Rosario. He became a publicist for Conservative Party ideals and was editor of several Bogotá newspapers. He also taught history and law. Abadía's energy, dedication, and deserved reputation for probity won him election to several congresses. An expert in constitutional law, he served as minister in the cabinets of several Conservative regimes before becoming president in 1926. During his presidency, the last of the "Conservative Hegemony," there was further irresponsible borrowing abroad to support the country's infrastructure. The economic downturn at the end of the 1920s brought increasingly violent confrontations with newly organizing labor in the petroleum fields (Santander) and the bloody repression of the banana workers' strike (Magdalena, November–December 1928). These episodes in turn provoked further civil unrest, including popular and student demonstrations and deaths (8–9 June 1929) in Bogotá. As a result, Abadía was forced to fire his war minister and others, and the Conservative Party fragmented. His political life was over. He died at La Unión, Cundinamarca, after five years of severe mental illness.

— J. LEÓN HELGUERA

ABALOS, JOSÉ DE

José de Abalos, intendant of the province of Venezuela (1776–1783). Born in La Mancha, Spain, Abalos was chief official of accounting and of general administration on the island of Cuba and chief accountant in the province of Venezuela. When the intendancy of Venezuela was created by royal decree on 8 December 1776, he was appointed to the office of intendant by order of King Charles III.

By order of the crown, Abalos developed a program of instruction for the workings of the intendancy, which can be considered the first organic law for the administration of finance in Venezuela. While serving as intendant, he promoted numerous initiatives for the economic and commercial benefit of the province. He was inflexible in the collection of taxes; intervened in and confronted the Compañía Guipuzcoana; offered credits to landowners; stimulated the diversification of crops; reactivated the mining industry; fought contraband; and established the state monopoly on playing cards, spirits, and tobacco. By the time of his retirement from the post in 1783, Abalos had brought about important advances in the reorganization of the royal finances and in the recuperation of the economy of the province of Venezuela.

– INÉS QUINTERO

ABASCAL Y SOUZA, JOSÉ FERNANDO

José Fernando Abascal y Souza (*b.* 3 June 1743; *d.* 31 July 1821), viceroy of Peru (1806–1816). A native of Oviedo in northern Spain, Abascal pursued a military career and first visited America in 1767 as a junior officer assigned to the garrison of Puerto Rico. Following service in Spain, he returned to the empire with the 1776 expedition to the Río de la Plata, which captured the outpost of Sacramento on the eastern bank of the river from the Portuguese and established a new viceroyalty governed from Buenos Aires. After further service in Santo Domingo and Havana, he went to Guadalajara (Mexico) in 1799 as president of the *audiencia* (tribunal of justice). Appointed viceroy of the Río de la Plata, Abascal was transferred to Peru before he was able to take up his position in Buenos Aires; wartime complications delayed his arrival in Lima until 1806.

Abascal's fame derives primarily from his firmness in repressing conspiracies against continued Spanish rule in Peru during the period 1809–1810 (at a time when his counterparts in other viceregal capitals were meekly acquiescing to the demands of creole revolutionaries), and in raising expeditionary forces to put down the early independence movements in Chile, Ecuador, and Upper Peru (Bolivia). A firm royalist and absolutist, he obstructed the implementation in Peru of the Spanish Constitution of Cádiz, promulgated in 1812. Although disturbed in 1814–1815 by a serious insurrection in Cuzco, Peru remained a bastion of royalism when Abascal retired to the peninsula in 1816.

– JOHN R. FISHER

ABASOLO, MARIANO

Mariano Abasolo (*b.* ca. 1783; *d.* 14 April 1816), Mexican insurgent leader. A native of Dolores, in 1795 Abasolo entered the regiment of the Queen's Provincial Dragoons at San Miguel el Grande. He joined Miguel HIDALGO in Dolores when the priest led an uprising against the colonial regime in September 1810. Abasolo became a colonel in the insurgent forces and eventually

rose to the rank of field marshal. On 28 September 1810 he besieged Guanajuato and demanded its surrender, but he did not participate in the sack of the city. After the insurgents' defeat at Calderón Bridge in January 1811, he fled north with Hidalgo. He refused to remain in command of the troops when the principal insurgent leaders decided to continue to the United States. Captured at Acatita de Baján on 21 March 1811, Abasolo was taken to Chihuahua, where during his trial he denied all responsibility for the insurrection. Because of his denials and his wife's efforts he was condemned to perpetual exile rather than to death. He died in the fortress of Santa Catalina in Cádiz, Spain.

– VIRGINIA GUEDEA

ABBAD Y LASIERRA, ÍÑIGO

Íñigo Abbad y Lasierra (*b.* 17 April 1745; *d.* 24 October 1813), author of the first history of Puerto Rico, *Historia geográfica, civil y natural de la Isla de San Juan Bautista de Puerto Rico* (1788). Born in Lérida, Spain, Abbad was educated at the monastery of Santa María la Real in Nájera, Spain. A Benedictine, he went to Puerto Rico in 1772 as confessor to the bishop Manuel Jiménez Pérez. He died in Valencia, Spain.

In the nineteenth century, Abbad's history underwent two editions, in 1831 and 1866. The latter edition, corrected and annotated by the Puerto Rican scholar José Julián Acosta, is still considered a valuable source of information. In 1959, the University of Puerto Rico reissued Abbad's work with an introduction by the historian Isabel Gutiérrez del Arroyo.

– OLGA JIMÉNEZ DE WAGENHEIM

ABENTE Y LAGO, VICTORINO

Victorino Abente y Lago (*b.* 2 June 1846; *d.* 22 December 1935), Paraguayan poet. Abente published his first poems in his native town of Murguía, in the province

---

Abente y Lago began to write poems reflecting human solidarity in the face of total destruction while harboring a deep faith in man's ability to recover and rebuild.

---

of La Coruña, Spain. He went to Asunción in 1869, where he saw firsthand the sacking of the capital during the War of the Triple Alliance. Profoundly shaken by the devastation and ruin, he began to write poems reflecting human solidarity in the face of total destruction while harboring a deep faith in man's ability to recover and rebuild. Having developed a fondness for its land and people, he decided to remain in Paraguay and become a citizen. Abente was the first poet on record to sing of the Paraguayan woman in "Kygua Verá" (Lustrous Comb) and of her role in Paraguayan history in "La sibila paraguaya." He published most of his poems in Asunción dailies.

– CATALINA SEGOVIA-CASE

ABREU, DIEGO DE

Diego de Abreu (d. 1553), conquistador and early settler. Abreu was born in Seville, Spain, and came to the Río de la Plata with the expedition of Pedro de MENDOZA in 1536. After the original settlement of Santa María del Buen Aire was abandoned, and after Mendoza's death earlier that year, Juan de Salazar y Ezpinosa founded Asunción in 1537. When Alvar Núñez Cabeza de Vaca, the second *adelantado* of the Río de la Plata, and the settlers of Asunción came into open conflict over how the settlement should be run, Abreu supported Nuñez. He later protested the naming of Domingo Martínez de Irala as governor and was sent to prison. He escaped, and led a group of loyalists against Martínez. When Martínez left Asunción on an exploratory trip in 1547, Abreu demanded that his successor, Francisco de Mendoza, surrender command. Abreu had Mendoza imprisoned and executed. When Martínez returned in 1549, Abreu abandoned the governorship he had assumed by force and fled inland. He wrote a detailed report of these disputes in 1548. Abreu never returned to Asunción and died in an Indian hamlet.

– NICHOLAS P. CUSHNER

ABRIL, XAVIER

Xavier Abril (b. 1905; d. 1990), Peruvian poet and critic. A leading member of Peru's avant-garde movement from the mid-1920s, Abril helped introduce surrealism and other modernist movements in Peru and Latin America, particularly with his contributions, both poetry and criticism, to *Amauta,* the leading cultural journal of the period.

His early poetry, usually ascribed to surrealism, is collected in *Hollywood* (1931) and *Difícil trabajo: Antología 1926–1930* (1935). In these books of verses and short prose, oneiric images of natural elements and human anatomy present a self in the process of fragmentation, and a desire for reintegration.

Abril's literary criticism includes studies of the work of Stéphane Mallarmé and the Peruvian poet José María

EGUREN; he is best known for his works on the poetry of César VALLEJO: *Vallejo: Ensayo de aproximación crítica* (1958), *César Vallejo o la teoría poética* (1962), and *Exégesis trílcica* (1980).

Abril's focus on literary criticism, particularly his writings on Mallarmé, seems to coincide with a shift in his poetry to a more controlled use of imagery. Another factor in this change is the influence of Spanish medieval and Golden Age poets, which is reflected in his use of more conventional poetic forms, including traditional meters. Although this shift is apparent in his third collection, *Descubrimiento del alba* (1937), it is the determining element of his later poetry, which is marked by abstract symbolism.

– JOSÉ CERNA-BAZÁN

ACEVAL, BENJAMÍN

Benjamín Aceval (b. 1845; d. 25 July 1900), Paraguayan statesman and educator. Though born in Asunción, Aceval spent most of his youth in Argentina, where he finished his law studies in 1873. He returned to Paraguay a year later in order to assume the post of justice minister in the Juan Bautista Gill government. In 1875 the same government sent him to Washington, D.C., where he presented Paraguay's claims to the Chaco Region to President Rutherford B. Hayes, who had agreed to act as arbiter in Paraguay's land dispute with Argentina. Hayes upheld the Paraguayan claim, and Aceval returned to Asunción a much celebrated man. In 1877 he founded the Colegio Nacional of Asunción, with a subsidiary campus in Villarrica, and in 1886 he helped organize the Biblioteca Nacional. He continued to hold various ministerial and diplomatic posts until the end of the century. In 1887 he arranged a border treaty with Bolivia that provided a generous solution to the Chaco dispute but was rejected by the Paraguayan legislature, leaving the question open until it was resolved by war in the 1930s. Aceval died in Asunción.

– THOMAS L. WHIGHAM

ACEVEDO DÍAZ, EDUARDO INÉS

Eduardo Inés Acevedo Díaz (b. 1851; d. 18 June 1921), Uruguayan journalist and novelist, born in Montevideo. Connected from early on with his country's National (or Blanco) Party, Acevedo Díaz took up arms on three occasions between 1870 and 1897 to participate in revolutionary movements. As a journalist, he wrote tough polemics concerning party struggles in such periodicals as *La Democracia, La Razón,* and *El Nacional.* Due to his political militancy, he was imprisoned and exiled on several occasions, and it was during his exile in Argentina between 1876 and 1895 that he wrote his most representative works, the historical novels *Brenda* (1886), *Ismael* (1888), *Nativa* (1890) and his famous *Soledad* (1894), a series that would be completed in 1914 by *Lanza y sable.*

Acevedo Díaz is considered to be the first Uruguayan novelist as well as the founder of the historical novel in Uruguay. His entire work can be seen as an investigation into the origin of nationality, yet his effort occurred in the framework of the modernizing process carried out by the ruling class between 1870 and 1920. This process entailed the formation of a modern state, which required for its legitimacy the building of a nationalist sentiment in order to lend cohesion to the community. The work of Acevedo Díaz, like that of his contemporary Juan ZORRILLA DE SAN MARTÍN (*La leyenda Patria* [1879] and *Tabaré* [1888]), were significant contributions to this effort.

– MARÍA INÉS DE TORRES

ACEVEDO HERNÁNDEZ, ANTONIO

Antonio Acevedo Hernández (*b.* 1886; *d.* 21 September 1962), one of the founders of modern Chilean theater and the originator of social theater. His first plays date back to 1913–1914, a period in Chile marked by the influence of European theater and the Spanish *comedia.* His primary preoccupation as a dramatist was to define the creative options of an autochthonous theater that could express the social problems and existential dilemmas of the marginated strata—campesino sectors and lower-class urban settlements—of a society in the process of capitalist modernization.

A man of humble origins, Acevedo Hernández was forced to make a living moving from place to place working various jobs, such as farmhand, manual laborer, office worker, and free-lance journalist. This rich and diverse living experience became the main thematic source for his dramas and *comedias.* He wrote approximately thirty plays that include a variety of forms ranging from *sainetes* and *comedias* to political and social theater, and even biblical dramas. Durán Cerda provides a useful classification of Acevedo Hernández's plays. His most important works are *Arbol viejo* (1930; The Old Tree), which presents the dramatic conflict between the ancestral wisdom of the campesino's world and the changing values fostered by urban society, and *Chañarcillo* (1933), an epic drama of miners' struggles for social justice in nineteenth-century Chile. In his autobiography *Memorias de un autor teatral* (1982; Memories of a Playwright), Acevedo Hernández describes his literary formation through an intimate account of the

conflicts and challenges he was forced to confront in order to stage his works. He died in Santiago.

– J. A. EPPLE

ACHÁ, JOSÉ MARÍA

José María Achá (*b.* 8 July 1810; *d.* 29 January 1868), president of Bolivia (14 January 1861–28 December 1864). After coming to power via a coup, Achá shared power in a three-man junta from 14 January until 4 May after which he became constitutional president.

Achá's presidency was marked by intense internal political agitation. His chief of police of La Paz, Plácido Yáñez, was responsible for Bolivia's worst political massacre on 23 October 1861. Yáñez arrested and then executed more than seventy political opponents, among whom was former president Jorge CÓRDOVA. Yáñez was later lynched by a mob. Known as the "Massacre de Yáñez," this episode detracted from Achá's positive accomplishments in the areas of economic and administrative reforms. Achá's administration also faced Chile's first attempts at expansion on the Bolivian coast, actions that eventually precipitated the War of the Pacific (1879–1884), the conflict in which Bolivia lost its coastal area.

Achá's political career, which included an unsuccessful attempt to overthrow the government of Manuel Isidoro BELZÚ (1850), was ended by a military coup led by Mariano MELGAREJO.

– CHARLES W. ARNADE

ACOSTA, JOSÉ DE

José de Acosta (*b.* September or October 1540; *d.* 15 February 1600), Spanish Jesuit historian. Born in Medina del Campo, Acosta joined the Jesuit order while young and went to Peru in 1571. He lived there for fourteen years, and in Mexico City for one, before returning to his native Spain in 1587. His *Historia natural y moral de las Indias* (A Natural and Moral History of the Indies) was published in Seville in 1590. Widely read by educated Spaniards and quickly translated into most important European languages as well, Acosta's *Historia* enjoyed immediate success. Like other similar texts, the *Historia* places the entire American continent within a universal and providential Christian framework, implying a divine role for Spain as a conquering power. Many features of the natural American world, as well as indigenous religions, cultures, and governments, are described in great detail, making Acosta's work an invaluable source of information. Today it is considered by literary scholars and historians to be an elegantly written, classic example of sixteenth-century New World historiography.

— KATHLEEN ROSS

ACOSTA, TOMÁS

Tomás Acosta (*b.* 1744; *d.* 1821), governor of Costa Rica from 1797 to 1810. Born in Cuba, Tomás Acosta is considered one of the most beloved and capable of Costa Rica's colonial governors. As early as 1805, he exposed the harmful effects of the tobacco monopoly on Costa Rica's economy and instituted policies designed to diversify agricultural production. Under the general aegis of the Bourbon Reforms, Acosta removed some of the taxes from coffee production and greatly

---

Acosta removed some of the taxes from coffee production and greatly increased the growth of that important crop.

---

increased the growth of that important crop. His administration contributed to a growing sense of nationality among Costa Ricans in the pre-Independence era. Acosta, though a Spanish colonial official, was popular enough among Americans to have been considered as the intendant for Costa Rican economic affairs in 1812. He died in Cartago.

— KAREN RACINE

ACOSTA GARCÍA, JULIO

Julio Acosta García (*b.* 23 May 1872; *d.* 6 July 1954), president of Costa Rica (1920–1924). As a nephew of Braulio CARRILLO (president 1834–1841) and a descendant of the conquistador Juan Vázquez de CORONADO, Acosta was well positioned for public life. He held many posts in the Costa Rican government, including delegate to the Constitutional Congress of 1902–1906, governor of his home province of Alajuela (1907), and consul to El Salvador (1912–1915) before winning the presidency in 1920. Acosta, a Liberal, served as Costa Rica's delegate to the Central American Unionist Party. He engaged troops in a border conflict with Panama. After his term he received many national and international awards and was the chief of Costa Rica's delegation to the United Nations organizational meetings in San Francisco in 1945.

— KAREN RACINE

ACOSTA LEÓN, ÁNGEL

Ángel Acosta León (*b.* 1932; *d.* 1964), Cuban painter. Born in Havana, Acosta León attended the famous San Alejandro school of painting and sculpture on a scholarship. He worked at odd jobs, including train conductor, to support himself while pursuing a career in the arts. In 1958 and 1959 he won prizes at expositions in Havana and received another award in 1959 from the National Salon. In 1960 Acosta León won a poster contest sponsored by the new National Institute of Industry and Tourism, and his oil painting *Carruaje* earned him a prize at the Second Pan-American Biennial in Mexico. Images of wheels and modern technology dominate Acosta's paintings; his major works are *Cafetera, Carro,* and *El circo* (all 1959), and *Carruaje* (1960).

— KAREN RACINE

ADEM CHAHÍN, JOSÉ

José Adem Chahín (*b.* 27 October 1921; *d.* February, 1991), leading Mexican mathematician. A native of Tuxpan, Veracruz, Adem received his early education in his birthplace. He studied mathematics at the National University of Mexico from 1941 to 1945, after which he did graduate work at the Mathematics Institute (1946–1948). He traveled to the United States to complete a doctorate at Princeton University (1952). A researcher and educator, Adem taught at the National School of Engineering and Sciences and the National University, becoming a full-time researcher at the Mathematics Institute (1954–1961). His works on algebra have appeared in English. He directed the mathematics department at the National Polytechnic Institute from 1961 to 1973. He was a member of the National College, and received Mexico's National Prize in Sciences (1967).

— RODERIC AI CAMP

ADEM CHAHÍN, JULIÁN

Julián Adem Chahín (*b.* 8 January 1924), leading Mexican geophysicist and specialist in atmospheric sciences. Adem obtained an engineering degree from the National University (1948) and his doctorate in applied mathematics from Brown University (1953), after which he completed advanced studies in atmospheric sciences in Stockholm (1955–1956). After serving as a full-time researcher at the Geophysics Institute, he became its director and then founded the Center for Atmospheric Sciences. Invited to be a member of the prestigious National College, Adem received Mexico's National Prize in Sciences (1976). Brother of mathematician José Adem Chahín, he is known for his discovery of a long-range predictive thermodynamic model.

— RODERIC AI CAMP

AGRAMONTE Y LOYNAZ, IGNACIO

Ignacio Agramonte y Loynaz (*b.* 23 December 1841; *d.* 11 May 1873), Cuban general. Agramonte is known to Cubans as a man of irreproachable behavior in both his public and his private lives. His gallantry as a cavalry commander is legendary. Few Cuban military feats against Spanish forces are better known than the daring rescue of his friend, Colonel Julio Sanguily, from the Spanish column that had captured him.

In a renowned daring military feat, Agramonte y Loynaz rescued his friend, Colonel Julio Sanguily, from the Spanish column that had captured him.

Agramonte, born in Camagüey, in central Cuba, was a distinguished lawyer and cattle farmer who became one of the insurgent leaders in his region when the Ten Years' War (1868–1878) broke out. He espoused the radical liberal ideas that were supported by many Camagüeyans but were in opposition to the conservative views of the head of the revolt, Carlos Manuel de Céspedes. When the vicissitudes of war forced Céspedes to come to terms with the Camagüeyans, they hastily drafted a constitution for the insurgent provisional government. Agramonte was one of the two authors of this constitution, which was a solemn manifestation of Camagüeyan liberalism.

Agramonte's relationship with Céspedes, who had been proclaimed president of free Cuba, continued to be marred by serious conflicts, some of them of a personal nature. But the two men succeeded in burying their differences, and Céspedes finally put Agramonte in command of the insurgent forces in Camagüey, where he developed into an exceptional military leader, quickly becoming the soul of the rebellion. After Agramonte was killed by a stray bullet while deploying his troops, his body fell into the hands of the Spaniards, who took it to the city of Camagüey, where they put it on display. Later the body was cremated, and Agramonte's ashes were scattered to the wind.

— JOSÉ M. HERNÁNDEZ

AGUAYO, MARQUÉS DE

Marqués de Aguayo (marqués de San Miguel de Aguayo y Santa Olalla; *b.* ca. 1677; *d.* 9 March 1734), rancher, military governor of Coahuila and Texas. Born in Spain to a landed family of Aragon, Aguayo married Ignacia Xaviera Echeverz Subiza y Valdés, heiress to the marquisate of San Miguel de Aguayo, through whom he acquired his title. In 1712 the couple moved to Coahuila, where Aguayo took over the administration of the family estates, increasing holdings by over 3 million acres by the time of his death.

Aguayo served as governor of Coahuila and Texas from 1719 to 1722. In 1716 he had provided livestock to the Domingo Ramón expedition, which established the permanent occupation of Texas. Three years later, in response to a French attack on the Spanish in east Texas, Aguayo offered to mount an expedition to drive the French out. Receiving a viceregal commission to raise five hundred men, he proceeded in 1720 to San Antonio and then to Los Adaes (present-day Robeline, La.), where he restored the abandoned presidio and missions. He also founded Presidio de los Texas, near present-day Nacogdoches, and Presidio Bahía del Espíritu Santo (now Goliad, Texas). Soon after his return to Coahuila, Aguayo resigned the governorship, citing poor health. PHILIP V rewarded Aguayo for his services in Texas by naming him field marshal in 1724.

— JESÚS F. DE LA TEJA

AGÜERO ROCHA, FERNANDO

Fernando Agüero Rocha (*b.* 1918), Nicaraguan Conservative Party leader (1960–1972). Agüero assumed the leadership of a revived Conservative Party in 1960. The party's platform not only was anti-Somoza but also favored a "democratic revolution." Agüero stressed the need for economic and social reforms to prevent a Communist takeover in response to Somoza's entrenchment. In early 1963 he announced that the Conservative Party would boycott the forthcoming elections because the Somozas controlled the election machinery. True to Agüero's accusations, René SCHICK GUTIÉRREZ, the Somoza's handpicked successor, won the presidency.

In the presidential election of 1967, Anastasio SOMOZA DEBAYLE was a candidate himself. The opposition, consisting of Conservatives, Independent Liberals, and Christian Democrats, formed the National Opposition Union, (UNO) and coalesced behind their candidate Agüero. Somoza won by a three-to-one margin, prompting Agüero to charge Somoza with election fraud, claiming that ballot boxes were seized from Granada (an opposition center) and that intimidation at the polls and violation of voting secrecy were commonplace.

The unrest and scandal stemming from Somoza's election led to elaborate plans for his cession of the presidency without relinquishing his power. In 1971, the Kupia-Kumi Pact, arranged between Liberals and Conservatives, provided that Somoza would step down in favor of a three-man junta, comprised of two Liberals and one Conservative. Agüero joined the junta, calling the pact a "national solution," although he still opposed Somoza. The junta, commonly referred to as "The Three Little Pigs," split the opposition. Somoza controlled the junta and the National Guard; thus, the junta wielded no real authority. This lack of power was seen clearly in the aftermath of the 1972 earthquake, when Somoza appointed himself head of a national emergency council with special powers.

Agüero opposed Somoza's rule by decree, so Somoza removed him from the junta. By this time, Agüero had lost the popular backing of students and had been removed as Conservative Party leader anyway. In addition, Agüero's cooperation with Somoza resulted in the alienation and disillusionment of younger Conservatives and others, thereby splintering the Conservatives.

– SHANNON BELLAMY

AGÜEYBANA II

Agüeybana II (d. 1511), nephew of Agüeybana I and next in line to rule the political confederacy of Boriquén (Puerto Rico) when the Spaniards took over the island in 1508. Agüeybana was of the Taino culture. Given in *encomienda* to the settler Cristóbal de Sotomayor, Agüeybana II led a revolt against the Spaniards in 1511. He succeeded in destroying their settlement and killing Sotomayor, but also lost his own life in the struggle to defeat the Spaniards.

– OLGA JIMÉNEZ DE WAGENHEIM

AGUIAR, ADONIAS

Adonias Aguiar (Adonias Filho; Aguiar Filho; Adonias; b. 27 November 1915; d. 4 August 1990), Brazilian novelist. Set largely in the author's native state of Bahia, Adonias Filho's fiction blends the social themes of the regionalist novel of the 1930s and early 1940s with the existential and metaphysical concerns of the psychological novel that began to emerge at the same time. Such works as *Memórias de Lázaro* (1952), *Corpo vivo* (1962), and *O forte* (1965) juxtapose multiple levels of time and space in a dense, poetic, elliptical style, creating a dreamy atmosphere in which human beings fulfill their frequently tragic destinies.

– RANDAL JOHNSON

AGUILAR, JERÓNIMO DE

Jerónimo de Aguilar (b. ca. 1490; d. 1531), colonist and translator. Born in Écija, Spain, Aguilar was aboard a ship proceeding from Darién to Santo Domingo in 1511. When it struck shoals off Jamaica, he was among twenty men who escaped in a longboat that drifted to the east coast of the Yucatán Peninsula. The local cacique soon sacrificed thirteen of the men, but seven, including Aguilar, escaped into the territory of another ruler, who maintained them as servants. When Cortés's expedition arrived in 1519, Aguilar was one of only two Spaniards still surviving; the other chose to remain among the Mayas. Aguilar, fluent in Spanish and Maya, proved invaluable as a translator for CORTÉS. Unable to speak Nahuatl, the language of the Aztecs, he teamed up with Cortés's mistress Doña Marina (MALINCHE), who spoke Nahuatl and Maya, to translate from Nahuatl to Spanish once the expedition reached the Aztec Empire. Rewarded with an encomienda after the Conquest, Aguilar died without marrying.

– JOHN E. KICZA

AGUILAR, MARTÍN DE

Martín de Aguilar (d. January 1603), Spanish mariner, explorer of the Californias. Aguilar began his career of exploration as a sailor on the expedition of Sebastián VIZCAÍNO in the Gulf of California (June–November 1596). Subsequently he was an ensign on Vizcaíno's voyage that charted the coast of the Californias in 1602–1603. Next he served on the frigate *Tres Reyes*, the crew of which explored, made soundings, and obtained provisions along the coast to Monterey. From 17 December 1602 to 3 January 1603 he provisioned the *Tres Reyes*, which sailed north from Monterey. Separated from the flagship *San Diego* north of Point Reyes on 5 January, the *Santo Tomás* was forced beyond Cabo Blanco, Oregon. Aguilar discovered a large, raging river thought to be the Strait of Anián.

Aguilar and his pilot, Antonio Flores, died at sea; the pilot's aide, Esteban López, returned to Navidad, Jalisco, on 28 February 1603. The torrential river, first named the Santa Inés, was subsequently named the Martín de Aguilar (and was also known as the Antón Flores).

– W. MICHAEL MATHES

AGUILAR, ROSARIO FIALLOS DE

Rosario Fiallos de Aguilar (*b.* 29 January 1938), Nicaraguan novelist. Born in León, Nicaragua, Aguilar has lived her entire life in the same city except for her studies in the United States (1955–1956) and a brief period in Costa Rica during the turmoil of the Sandinista revolution. Her first novel, *Primavera sonámbula* (1964), is the story of a young woman tottering between sanity and insanity. *Aquel mar sin fondo ni playa* (1974) tells the haunting story of a stepmother's guilt and her rejection of a severely retarded child. *Siete relatos sobre el amor y la guerra* (1986) is a collection of stories linked thematically by the Sandinista fight to oust the dictatorship of Anastasio Somoza. Her 1992 novel, *La niña blanca y los pájaros sin pies,* re-creates the lost female voices of the Spanish conquest of Central America. While Aguilar denies she is a feminist writer, her novels all center around women, maternity, and the consequences of rejecting motherhood, the Latin American

---

Aguilar's novels all center around women, maternity, and the consequences of rejecting motherhood, the Latin American social imperative for women.

---

social imperative for women. The Latin American literary critic Raymond Souza called her "one of the best-kept secrets in contemporary Spanish American fiction."

— ANN GONZÁLEZ

AGUILAR VARGAS, CÁNDIDO

Cándido Aguilar Vargas (*b.* 12 February 1888; *d.* 19 March 1960), Mexican revolutionary, Constitutional, Convention leader, and politician. From modest origins in rural Veracruz, Aguilar signed the first revolutionary program in Veracruz, the Plan of San Ricardo, in 1910. A supporter of Francisco MADERO, he became a Constitutionalist in 1913 and was governor of his home state from 1914 to 1917. He was a deputy to the Constitutional Convention of 1917, of which he was elected first vice president, a position he used to publicize progressive issues. He served as secretary of foreign relations under Venustiano CARRANZA (1918), to whom he remained loyal until 1920. Aguilar went into exile in the early 1920s, after the rebellion led by Adolfo DE LA HUERTA, but returned to political activity as a federal deputy and senator in the 1930s and 1940s. He was expelled from the Mexican Revolutionary Party in 1944

for exposing corruption. He retired from the army as a division general. He spent his last years in self-imposed exile in El Salvador and Cuba and died in Mexico.

— RODERIC AI CAMP

AGUILERA MALTA, DEMETRIO

Demetrio Aguilera Malta (*b.* 24 May 1909; *d.* 29 December 1981), Ecuadorian novelist and playwright. Hailing from the Andes mountains and the coast, respectively, Jorge ICAZA (1906–1979) and Aguilera Malta are the two best-known Ecuadorian fiction writers. The latter's fiction spans several decades, beginning with *Don Goyo* (1933) and ending forty years later with *El secuestro del general* (1973). Early on, Aguilera Malta copublished a set of short stories, *Los que se van* (1931), that focused on problems of economic and ethnic exploitation of the coastal lower classes. His other novels take up many themes, among them, problems of economic development, the Cuban Revolution, the travels of Vasco de BALBOA, and indigenous beliefs and customs. An intriguing, well-crafted novel, *Siete lunas y siete serpientes* (1970) adeptly meshes legend, witchcraft, and modern superstition with the machinations of a local, lustful political boss bent on governing with an iron hand. In this work Aguilera Malta blends magic and realism to make an ironic commentary on Ecuadorian politics. In *El secuestro del general,* Aguilera Malta uses wordplay and irony to capture the way in which the power of language can sway and subjugate people to the absolute power of dictators. Language, myth, legend, fantasy, and concepts of power are the basic ingredients of the fictional worlds of Aguilera Malta.

— DICK GERDES

AGUIRRE, JUAN FRANCISCO DE

Juan Francisco de Aguirre (*b.* 1758; *d.* 17 February 1811), Spanish colonial naval officer and major geographer of Paraguay. Born in Asturias, Spain, Aguirre was a graduate of the Spanish Royal Naval Academy. He fought in several campaigns and was commissioned a lieutenant before being sent to South America in 1784. As part of the Madrid Treaty of 1750, Spain and Portugal had decided to readjust their frontiers in the Platine basin. To prepare the way for the arrival of Spanish and Portuguese border commissioners, Aguirre was dispatched to Paraguay. He spent twelve years in the colony, mapping its rivers and assembling a vast array of information in the form of a diary.

With the one possible exception of Félix de Azara's *Viaje,* Aguirre's work constitutes the most detailed extant account of life in eighteenth-century Paraguay. Aguirre was a keen observer. He visited almost every community in that isolated quarter of the empire and made a thorough study of its people and history. Since much of the original documentation from this period has been lost, Aguirre's diary remains one of the few reliable sources available to modern scholars. He was particularly interested in Paraguayan Indians, and the ethnographic materials included in the diary fill a major gap between the works produced by early Jesuit writers and those of the modern era.

After leaving Paraguay in 1796, Aguirre went first to Buenos Aires and then back to Spain, where he finished his naval career as a captain during the Napoleonic Wars. When the French invaded Spain, Aguirre went into hiding in the province of Asturias, where he died.

– THOMAS L. WHIGHAM

AGUIRRE, JULIÁN

Julián Aguirre (*b.* 28 January 1868; *d.* 13 August 1924,), Argentine composer and pianist. Born in Buenos Aires, Aguirre spent his formative years in Spain. At fourteen, he enrolled in the Madrid Royal Conservatory, where he studied composition with Emilio Arrieta, piano with Pedro Beck, harmony with José María Aranguren, and fugue with Cató. He was awarded first prize in piano, harmony, and counterpoint. In Madrid the celebrated Spanish composer Isaac Albéniz heard his music and predicted a brilliant career for the young musician. Aguirre returned to Argentina in 1886 and made a name for himself by giving concerts around the country. He spent a year in Rosario studying and experimenting with folk music before settling in Buenos Aires, where he played an important role in the artistic and musical life of the city. His early works drew their inspiration from European styles and forms, but from 1889 on, when he joined with Alberto WILLIAMS and others to create a distinctive nationalist style, his compositions for voice and piano—especially the *tristes* for piano—are based on the folk tunes, rhythms, and harmonies of his native Argentina.

Considered one of the best Argentine composers of his generation, Aguirre was also active in the field of music education, holding administrative and academic positions (professor of harmony) at Williams Conservatory. He founded the music department of the Athenaeum of Buenos Aires (1892) and the Argentine School of Music (1916). He wrote more than sixty piano pieces, two of which, the popular *Huella* and *Gato,* were orchestrated and performed by Ernest Ansermet in 1930. The remarkable *Rapsodia criolla* for violin and piano is a seminal work in the development of an Ar-

gentine nationalist style. Aguirre's output of nearly a hundred works includes chamber pieces, voice and piano works, and numerous songs and choral works, many for children. He died in Buenos Aires.

– SUSANA SALGADO

AGUIRRE, LOPE DE

Lope de Aguirre (*b.* 1518; *d.* 27 October 1561), self-proclaimed rebel leader of ill-fated descent of the Amazon River. Few sixteenth-century Spanish explorers have secured the notoriety of Lope de Aguirre. He was a soldier from Oñate, in the province of Guipuzcoa, Spain, who joined the Pedro de URSÚA expedition to the Amazon. Aguirre was one of the instigators of a plot to assassinate Ursúa, and at first supported Fernando de Guzmán to replace the slain Ursúa. As the group traveled against great odds downstream, discipline disintegrated, Indian carriers were abandoned, and an increasing number of men were killed in brawls. Aguirre captained Guzmán's militia, heading fifty Basque harquebusiers. Paranoid, filled with delusions of grandeur, he cowed followers and massacred Guzmán and all others suspected of disloyalty.

Challenging the authority of king and church, Aguirre argued that the land belonged to the conquerors. His unrealistic goal was to descend the Amazon, sail northwestward until he could attack Spanish authorities in Peru frontally, then assume the land's administration. Shortly after he reached the Venezuelan coast, however, royal supporters surrounded his encampment. He killed his own daughter to prevent her capture. His was one of the bloodiest and most controversial expeditions of the Age of Discovery.

– NOBLE DAVID COOK

AGUIRRE, NATANIEL

Nataniel Aguirre (*b.* 10 October 1843; *d.* 11 September 1888), Bolivian writer and politician. Born in Cochabamba, Aguirre was an important political figure during the period of the War of the Pacific (1879). He was a firm believer in liberal ideas and a great defender of federalism. But Aguirre's importance comes from his literary work. He is the author of plays, short stories, and a historical novel, *Juan de la Rosa: Memorias del último soldado de la Independencia* (1885), which is his most important work and is considered the national novel of Bolivia. He also wrote historical books and diverse political treatises.

Juan de la Rosa is the story of the uprising of Cochabamba between 1810 and 1812, at the beginning of the War of Independence. Its narrator and protagonist is a twelve-year-old boy who participates in the events leading to the emergence of nationalism in the future Republic of Bolivia. In this novel, Aguirre endorses the main ideas of liberalism and tries to blend them with the vital force of the mestizo (mixed-blooded) population, which is portrayed as the protagonist of these early battles.

— LEONARDO GARCÍA PABÓN

AGUIRRE CERDA, PEDRO

Pedro Aguirre Cerda (*b.* 6 February 1879; *d.* 25 November 1941), president of Chile (1938–1941). Born to a modest family in Pocuro, a village in Aconcagua Province, Aguirre Cerda graduated from the University of Chile with degrees in pedagogy and law. A member of the Radical Party, he served in the Chamber of Deputies from 1915 to 1921 and in the Senate from 1921 to 1924. He also held ministries in the administrations of Juan Luis SANFUENTES and Arturo ALESSANDRI PALMA. He was elected president in 1938 as the candidate of the Popular Front, a coalition of the Radical, Socialist, Communist, and Democratic parties and the Chilean Labor Confederation, narrowly defeating Conservative candidate Gustavo ROSS. Rightist strength in Congress and Aguirre Cerda himself, who had parlayed law and politics into a personal fortune, assured that Chile's first government of the working and middle classes would not pursue radical objectives. Aguirre Cerda had originally opposed the Popular Front concept, which originated in Moscow as an anti-Fascist strategy; Chile's was the only Popular Front government elected in Latin America.

Aguirre Cerda, who had parlayed law and politics into a personal fortune, assured that Chile's first government of the working and middle classes would not pursue radical objectives.

As president, Aguirre Cerda vetoed the efforts of his Marxist allies to unionize agricultural workers, thus preserving the overrepresentation of landowners in Congress. He faced the rebuilding of the south-central provinces in the wake of the devastating 1939 earthquake centered in Chillán. Among his major achievements were the founding of the Chilean Development Corporation (CORFO), the state agency charged with fostering industrialization, establishing the minimum wage for urban workers, reforming education, and recogniz-

ing Chilean territorial claims in Antarctica. A genuinely popular president, Aguirre Cerda died unexpectedly after less than three years in office.

— THOMAS C. WRIGHT

AGUIRRE Y SALINAS, OSMÍN

Osmín Aguirre y Salinas (*b.* 1889; *d.* unknown), president of El Salvador (1944–1945). A career military officer, Osmín Aguirre y Salinas was a member of the junior officers' clique which deposed President Arturo ARAÚJO in December 1931, establishing military control of El Salvador. During the regime of General Maximiliano HERNÁNDEZ MARTÍNEZ he was governor of the departments of Cuzcatlán, La Paz, and Usulután and chief of staff of the National Police, rising to the rank of colonel.

His brief tenure as president was part of the tumultuous era that followed the overthrow of Hernández Martínez. Fearing the fragmentation of the nation, an army coup removed Hernández Martínez's successor, the defense minister, General Andrés I. Menéndez, from the presidency in October 1944, installing Aguirre y Salinas. The Salvadoran Supreme Court declared his tenure unconstitutional, and the United States, which considered his regime profascist, withheld recognition.

Aguirre y Salinas maintained power despite protests, conducting elections during January 1945 installed the official candidate, General Salvador CASTAÑEDA CASTRO. Aguirre y Salinas's career ended when he led an unsuccessful coup against his handpicked successor.

— KENNETH J. GRIEB

AGUSTÍN, JOSÉ

José Agustín (*b.* 19 August 1944), Mexican novelist born José Agustín Ramírez Gómez. In his novel *La tumba,* a youth-centered narrative rejecting middle-class morality and the clichés of nationalism, and celebrating pleasure and self-exploration, Agustín uses street slang to create a lively, ironic narrative voice. With its publication in 1964, Agustín (together with Gustavo SAINZ) founded the literary movement known as "La Onda." In what is perhaps his best novel to date, *Se está haciendo tarde (final en laguna)* (1973), Agustín engages in a self-critique of the potential narcissism and alienation of such individualistic quests. In *Ciudades desiertas* (1982), based on his experiences in the University of Iowa's International Writing Program, the author advocates a return to the family and monogamy and to Mexican national culture, while lampooning the sterility of life in the United States. This reconciliation is extended to the family in *Cerca del fuego* (1986), in which the author attempts to fuse anti-imperialist and Jungian discourses.

As the preeminent enfant terrible of his generation, Agustín has maintained an irreverent, independent leftist stance (from his participation in the Cuban literacy campaign to his attacks on Mexican literary mafias and censorship). His history of contemporary Mexico, *Tragicomedia mexicana 1: La vida en México de 1940 a 1970* (1990), reflects this position.

– CYNTHIA STEELE

AGUSTINI, DELMIRA

Delmira Agustini (*b.* 24 October 1886; *d.* 7 July 1914), Uruguayan poet. Born in Montevideo, Agustini was a member of the Uruguayan group of writers of 1900—together with Julio HERRERA Y REISSIG, María Eugenia Vaz Ferreira, Alberto ZUM FELDE, and Angel Falco—and an innovative voice in Spanish American poetry. During her short life she published *El libro blanco (Frágil)* (1907), *Cantos de la mañana* (1910), and *Los cálices vacíos* (The Empty Chalices, 1913). The *Obras completas,* published posthumously in 1924, includes unpublished poems possibly belonging to a projected volume entitled *Los astros del abismo* (The Stars of the Abyss), which included a group of poems entitled "El rosario de Eros." Her early poetry, published in literary magazines, was very well received and showed the influence of *Modernismo.* In her later collections, she developed a more personal style and a voice that departs steadily from the canonical modernist poetics to which she subscribed. The language and imagery of her poetry was acclaimed for its erotic nature, an important foundational feature in Spanish American feminine poetics.

Agustini lived with her parents in Montevideo and spent long periods in Buenos Aires. Although she was well known in the cultural and social life of Montevideo, she was not an active member of the intellectual groups of her epoch. In 1913 she married Enrique Job Reyes, a common man with no intellectual interests, with whom she had had a long and formal relationship. She left him after a short period and returned to her parental household for comfort.

There are several unexplained mysteries regarding Agustini's short life. She was killed by her former husband, who then killed himself. This tragic event brought to Agustini's biography considerable sensationalism, which has colored the critical studies of most literary historians. It is fair to say that her life and her poetry are characterized by contradictory features that deserve much attention.

– MAGDALENA GARCÍA PINTO

AIZENBERG, ROBERTO

Roberto Aizenberg (*b.* 22 August 1928), Argentine painter and printmaker. Born in Villa Federal, province of Entre Ríos, Aizenberg studied architecture at the University of Buenos Aires, receiving a degree in 1954. He later studied painting with Juan Battle Planas. Aizenberg achieved a level of maturity quite early in life. His images relate to the subjective world of the unconscious and continue the surrealistic tradition exemplified in Argentina by Battle Planas. He received the Palanza Prize (Buenos Aires, 1967) and the Cassandra Foundation Award (Chicago, 1970).

– AMALIA CORTINA ARAVENA

ALAMÁN, LUCAS

Lucas Alamán (*b. 18* October 1792; *d.* 2 June 1853), Mexican statesman and historian. Born in Guanajuato, Alamán studied in Mexico City at the School of Mines. In January 1814 he traveled to Europe, where he observed politics in the Cortes in Spain and in other nations, met leading officials and men of science and learning, and studied mining and foreign languages. He returned to Mexico in 1820, beginning his political career in 1821 when he was elected deputy to the Cortes from Guanajuato. Alamán played an active role in the Spanish parliament, proposing programs to restore the mining industry as well as a project for home rule for the New World, taking Canada as its model.

In 1822, upon learning that Mexico had declared its independence, Alamán traveled to London, where he organized the Compañía Unida de Minas (United Mining Company), arriving in Mexico in March 1823. He served as minister of interior and exterior relations during the periods 1823–1825, 1830–1832, and 1853. Initially, he distinguished himself as a liberal and a strong critic of the Vatican for failing to recognize his nation's independence. As a result of the increasing radicalization of politics in the later 1820s, however, he became a conservative and a supporter of the church as the one institution that could help maintain order.

During his term as minister of the interior from 1830 to 1832, Alamán gained notoriety as an authoritarian but also as a strong fiscal conservative. He devoted much of his effort to rebuilding the nation's economy, particularly the mining and the textile industries. He founded the Banco de Avío, the hemisphere's first development bank, and served as director of the ministry of industry from 1842 to 1846. He also reorganized the Archivo General de la Nación and founded the Museo de Antigüedades e Historia Nacional.

In his later years, Alamán became a champion of conservatism and advocated the return to monarchy. He is best known for his writings, particularly his *Disertaciones sobre la historia de la República Méjicana . . .* , 3 vols. (1844–1849), and his *Historia de Méjico desde los*

In his later years, Alamán became a champion of conservatism and advocated the return to monarchy.

---

primeros movimientos que prepararon su independencia en el año 1808, hasta la época presente, 5 vols. (1849–1852), a magisterial work that remains the best and most distinguished account of the epoch.

— JAIME E. RODRÍGUEZ O.

ALAMBERT, ZULEIKA

Zuleika Alambert (*b.* 1924), Brazilian Communist Party leader and feminist activist. Born in the port city of Santos, Alambert joined the Brazilian Communist Party (PCB) during the political ferment that accompanied the end of World War II and the Estado Nôvo. She was elected to São Paulo's state legislature for the PCB at the age of twenty-four. When the party was banned in 1947 she went underground until 1954.

Alambert served as a member of the overwhelmingly male-dominated central committee of the Moscow-line PCB. Several years after the establishment of a military dictatorship in Brazil in 1964, she went into exile in Chile. Following Salvador ALLENDE's overthrow in 1973, she left Chile for France, where she participated in the organization of the European Committee of Brazilian Women. Returning to Brazil after almost ten years in political exile abroad, she, like some other female activists, encountered difficulties in channeling gender-specific claims through male-dominated political party organizations. She left the PCB and in 1986 published a theoretical criticism of Communist understandings of the "woman question." She served as president of São Paulo's State Council on the Status of Women, and then as special adviser to subsequent council presidents.

— JUNE E. HAHNER

ALARCÓN, MARTÍN, DE

Martín, de Alarcón (flourished 1691–1721), governor of Coahuila (1705–1708) and governor of Coahuila and Texas (1716–1719). Alarcón's expedition, in 1718 and 1719, to aid Spaniards on the Neches River in east Texas and monitor the French who entered Texas from Louisiana, led to the founding of the Mission San An-

tonio de Valero (the Alamo) and a *villa* (a Spanish town) at present-day San Antonio. These institutions became the nucleus of Spanish influence in the province of Texas. Before his service in northern New Spain, Alarcón was a soldier of fortune in Oran; he also served in the Spanish navy and was a sergeant major in the Guadalajara militia of New Spain (1691) and an *alcalde mayor* (a local appointed magistrate) and captain of Jacona and Zamora (Michoacán).

— ADÁN BENAVIDES, JR.

ALBÁN, LAUREANO

Laureano Albán (*b.* 9 January 1942), Costa Rican poet. Born in Santa Cruz de Turrialba, Costa Rica, Albán is best known for the poetry he wrote after leaving Costa Rica for Spain in 1978. That is especially true of *Herencia del otoño* (1980; *Autumn's Legacy,* 1982) winner of Spain's coveted Adonais Prize for poetry and the Costa Rican Prize for literature. *El viaje interminable* (1983; *The Endless Voyage,* 1984) was awarded the First Prize of Hispanic Culture by the Ministry of Spanish Culture. Albán's dedication to poetry began at fifteen when he and the Costa Rican poet Jorge Debravo formed the Turrialba group. In the 1960s he created the Costa Rican Writers Circle, published his first book of poems, *Poemas en cruz* (1962), and went on to establish the transcendentalist literary movement with his wife, the poet Julieta Dobles, and two younger Costa Rican poets, Ronald Bonilla and Carlos Francisco Monge. His English translator, Frederick Fornoff, describes his view of poetry as "a vehicle through which the poet carries his audience beyond the limited, circumstantial nature of human experience to the world of transcendent intuition that is universally confirmable through and only through poetry." Alban's work has been translated into French and Hebrew as well as English. He published *Infinita memoria de América* in 1991 and *Los nocturnos de Julieta* the following year.

— ANN GONZÁLEZ

ALBERDI, JUAN BAUTISTA

Juan Bautista Alberdi (*b.* 29 August 1810; *d.* 19 June 1884), Argentine diplomat, political philosopher, and constitution maker. Perhaps Alberdi's most salient trait was that he did not fit the usual image of the Latin American nation builder. He was a sullen and somewhat timid man who spent most of his adult life away from his native land and who was devoid of eloquence and leadership qualities. Yet because he had a powerful mind and an acute sense of reality, Alberdi was able to influence his contemporaries to such an extent that he is rightly considered one of modern Argentina's founding fathers. The constitution of 1853 is essentially a reflection of his political creed, and it was his ideas that largely prevailed when the process of national unification culminated in 1880 and the country began to transform itself into one of the wealthiest and most dynamic in Latin America. At this time, too, Argentina was on the way to becoming the most Europeanized nation in the region as a result of an uninterrupted flood of immigration. This was a key development with which the name Alberdi is inextricably associated.

HISTORICAL SETTING. This remarkable statesman was born the same year that the Argentine independence movement began. At that time the total area of the new nation (more than a million square miles) was populated by fewer than 400,000 people. For this reason, and because the population centers were isolated and remote from one another, Argentines referred to their land as the "desert." Long little-regarded by Spain, it had developed along a pattern of disunity. Originally it had been settled from different and unrelated points in the neighboring territories, and it had been further divided by the political and economic systems imposed by the metropolis. As a consequence, Argentina had grown up as a polarized colony. On the one hand, there was the port city of Buenos Aires, which after its opening to transatlantic trade late in the eighteenth century, was economically and culturally oriented toward Europe. On the other, there were the cities of the interior, which had remained satellites of other colonial economies such as that of present-day Bolivia. This cleavage reflected not only conflicting interests, but also diverse social arrangements and life-styles.

By setting up a "national" government in 1810 without first consulting the provinces, the porteños (people of the port city of Buenos Aires) further complicated the situation and so paved the way for the period of internal strife and anarchy that followed. Buenos Aires wanted unity, but only if the provinces accepted its supremacy. The provincial caudillos, for their part, rejected centralization under *porteño* rule, favoring instead local autonomy under a loose federal system. Total disintegration might have been Argentina's fate had it not been for the rise of a strong man, Juan Manuel de ROSAS, who governed with an iron hand between 1829 and 1852. He paid lip service to federalism, because in that way he would not have to share the income generated by the Buenos Aires customhouse with the provinces. But Rosas exercised authority over the country as a whole, more so than anyone before him. He also symbolized the traditionalist, nativist reaction that set in against the liberal and "exotic" ideas of Bernardino RI-

VADAVIA, who had attempted to modernize the country during the previous decade.

EARLY YEARS. Alberdi arrived in Buenos Aires from his native Tucumán in 1824. He was a weak, poor youngster who had lost both parents. But he had family connections and had been awarded a scholarship to study in the College of Moral Sciences of the University of Buenos Aires, recently founded by Rivadavia. Young Alberdi's ambition was to become a lawyer.

Alberdi was able to influence his contemporaries to such an extent that he is rightly considered one of modern Argentina's founding fathers.

Alberdi indulged in too much outside reading, however, and for this reason was a poor student; it took him a long time to achieve his professional goal. But the delay gave him the opportunity to witness the emergence of Rosas, develop personal contacts with him and other caudillos, and most importantly, join the "generation of 1837," a group of intellectuals largely born after 1810. These young men were strongly influenced by romanticism, the new literary and political movement that Esteban ECHEVERRÍA had introduced from France in 1830. They formed a literary salon in June 1837, at one of whose meetings Alberdi read his first important paper, an attempt to interpret Argentine reality in terms of romantic ideology. On this occasion he also dismissed Rivadavia as doctrinaire and proclaimed that Rosas's power was legitimate.

Nevertheless, when Rosas's dictatorship tightened shortly afterward, the salon had to go underground (under the name "May Association"), and its members later had to seek refuge in Montevideo, Uruguay. Here Alberdi was finally able to obtain his law degree and begin a profitable practice. Having turned against the dictator like most of his colleagues, he became involved in the literary warfare that the exiles waged for the liberation of their country. In addition, he supported the military campaign of the Uruguayan anti-Rosas faction and its French allies. But these activities led nowhere, and he felt increasingly disappointed. When a victorious pro-Rosas Uruguayan army laid siege to Montevideo in 1843, he realized that he had no taste for the life of a soldier. Alberdi left for Europe, where he met Argentina's most illustrious exile, General José de SAN MARTÍN, the hero of national independence. Upon returning to the Americas, Alberdi chose Chile as his haven, settling there in April 1844.

Juan Bautista Alberdi. (Archivo General de la Nación, Buenos Aires)

ALBERDI AND NATIONAL ORGANIZATION. By this time Alberdi was a man of note among Argentine exiles. His articles and pamphlets were well known, and his analyses and political opinions were widely commented upon and discussed. He had the opportunity to put them to work when, in 1852, a coalition led by provincial caudillo Justo José URQUIZA ousted Rosas and called a convention to draw up a new constitution. Alberdi wrote a book especially for the occasion, commonly called *Bases,* which rapidly turned into the most influential of its time. It was the convention delegates' chief source of information on constitutional matters.

Unsurprisingly, therefore, the new constitution, promulgated on 25 May 1853, largely followed Alberdi's recommendations. Seeking to reconcile Argentina's warring factions, it provided for a federal system of government similar to that of the United States, but it also included significant adaptations to Argentina's peculiar needs. According to Alberdi, Argentina had to set aside "its ridiculous and disgraceful mania for the heroic" and move forward along the path of material progress. It had to promote the advance of learning and instruction in general, build railroads and navigable canals, attract foreign capital, and encourage and facilitate the colonization of the lands of the national domain. Above all, there was Alberdi's most celebrated aphorism, "to govern is to populate." Argentina had to promote immigration (especially of hardworking Anglo-Saxons) in order to transform the "desert" into a source of wealth and abundance. All of this required writing into the constitution the fundamental principles of economic liberalism, which the delegates did, including a remarkable bill of rights guaranteeing liberty, equality, the right to work and trade, and the civil rights of aliens.

NATIONAL UNIFICATION. Another feature of the constitution was the stipulation that Buenos Aires should be the capital of the republic and that the income from customs was to belong to the nation. This was unacceptable to Buenos Aires, and as a result Argentina now split into two separate states: the city of Buenos Aires and its province and the inland Argentine Confederation. Urquiza remained as head of the latter, and Alberdi broke with his own Buenos Aires associates—including Domingo F. SARMIENTO and Bartolomé MITRE—in order to serve him through a diplomatic mission to Europe, to which he went without setting his foot in the territory of the confederation. He spent seven years as a diplomat and a writer, defending the integrity of Argentina against Mitre's policies. To him, *mitrismo* was *rosismo* in disguise, just as Rosas's dictatorship had simply been a prolongation of colonial practices.

In 1861 Mitre's forces defeated the Confederation at Pavón; Alberdi lost his position the following year. But although he remained in Europe, Alberdi did not retire to private life; rather, he continued to write about Argentine problems, albeit not always accurately, as was the case with the Paraguayan War (1865–1870). The criticisms that he directed against the Buenos Aires government on this occasion showed that he was not well informed; furthermore, he was dubbed a traitor to the fatherland. Because of this, and because he had to contemplate how his enemies rose to power while he aged perceptibly in exile, he lived through bitter days. This is clearly reflected in his writings, wherein he began to justify his actions with an eye on posterity.

By the late 1870s, however, things began to change in the distant fatherland. There was an upsurge of provincial opposition to *porteño* domination, and a native of Tucumán, Nicolás AVELLANEDA, was elected president. Alberdi's followers thought that the time was ripe for his political comeback and elected him to congress. He arrived in Buenos Aires in 1879. By this time, however, he was a tired man of sixty-nine who could not even read his own speeches. Therefore, he could not give a good account of himself. But he was able to witness the triumph of his ideas about national unification, for it was during his Buenos Aires sojourn that the port city finally became part of the Argentine federal republic as its capital, as the 1853 constitution had called for.

LAST YEARS. Defeat did not silence Alberdi's critics, who fiercely opposed the diplomatic appointment that the Argentine government proposed to bestow upon him in 1881. It was obvious that his compatriots would never give him the wide recognition that he deserved. Disillusioned and disappointed, Alberdi expatriated himself, living again in France. He died there three years later, surrounded by a few friends. He had never married.

In 1889, by popular request, his remains were brought back to Buenos Aires, where they were buried in an impressive ceremony. The most prominent representatives of the local and national government were not present.

— JOSÉ M. HERNÁNDEZ

ALBERNI, PEDRO DE

Pedro de Alberni (*b.* 1745; *d.* 11 March 1802), Spanish soldier and explorer. Alberni, a native of Tortosa, Catalonia, joined the Barcelona-based Catalonian Volunteers in 1767. Following the Sonora Expedition of 1767–1771 in Mexico, he served in Jalisco and Nayarit, where he married Juana Vélez of Tepic. In 1782, Alberni was promoted to captain of the First Company of Catalonian Volunteers. Between 1789 and 1793 he commanded his unit on several expeditions to the Pacific Northwest. He established a Spanish base for the expeditions at Nootka Sound on Vancouver Island. As troop commander, Alberni assigned Catalonian Volunteers to assist in the mapping of the Spanish claim to the coast of Alaska and the Pacific Northwest prior to the Nootka Sound Convention that led to Spain's loss of the area. He made friends with the Nootka Indians and compiled a small dictionary of 633 words in their language and their Spanish equivalents. While

---

Alberni established a Spanish base for the

expeditions at Nootka Sound on Vancouver Island.

---

military commander of California, Alberni died at Monterey and was buried at Mission Carmel. Port Alberni on Vancouver Island is named for him.

— JOSEPH P. SÁNCHEZ

ALBERRO, FRANCISCO DE

Francisco de Alberro, governor and commander in chief of the province of Venezuela (1677–1682). Alberro was appointed to both posts by the royal decree of 11 August 1675 after he gave 28,000 pesos to meet the needs of the monarchy. This marked the beginning of a series of appointments that were made in exchange for monetary gifts to help meet the colonial administration's economic needs. While in office he enforced the royal decree abolishing the use of Indians as personal servants. He also promoted wall-building and fortification projects in the cities of La Guaira and Caracas, both undertaken simultaneously after the French pirate François Grammont's attack on the port of La Guaira in June 1680.

At the end of Alberro's term, his successor, Diego de Melo Maldonado, convoked a trial of residence, as was the custom. In voluminous records Alberro is accused of abuse of power, illegal money collecting, unwarranted seizures, and carelessness and negligence in the performance of his duties.

— INÉS QUINTERO

ALBERTO, JOÃO

João Alberto (*b.* 16 June 1897; *d.* 26 January 1955), prominent Brazilian political figure. As a young artillery officer, Alberto participated in the Prestes Column that traversed Brazil's interior during much of the 1920s. Alberto eventually broke with Prestes, joining the Revolution of 1930 that brought Getúlio VARGAS to power. Appointed federal intervenor in São Paulo by Vargas in 1930, Alberto served less than a year in the post. In 1932 he was appointed chief of police in the Federal District, where he created the special police to repress groups and individuals opposed to Vargas. Alberto was elected to the National Constituent Assembly the following year as a representative from Pernambuco, affiliated with the Social Democratic Party (PSD). In 1935 Alberto entered the diplomatic service, discharging various duties in Europe and the Americas until 1942. With Brazil's entry in the Second World War, Alberto led the Coordenação da Mobilização Econômica, a newly created superministry tasked with wartime economic planning and industrial-policy formulation. Following the progressive weakening of Vargas's Estado Novo in 1944, Alberto once again led the Federal District police forces, until Vargas was removed from power in 1945. Vargas's return to the presidency in 1951 occasioned Alberto's return to government service in various positions, most prominently as the Brazilian representative to the General Agreement on Tariffs and Trade.

— WILLIAM SUMMERHILL

ALBIZU CAMPOS, PEDRO

Pedro Albizu Campos (*b*. ca. 12 September 1891; *d*. 21 April 1965), president of the Puerto Rico Nationalist Party in the 1930s and figurative head of the island's struggle for independence. Albizu Campos was born in Ponce, the illegitimate son of a black mother and a white, Spanish father. He excelled in his studies as a young man, obtaining a scholarship to attend college in the United States. While at Harvard, he was drafted to serve in the U.S. army, where he was placed in a segregated regiment. He returned to Harvard Law School after the war and obtained his degree in 1923.

Back on the island that year, Albizu became active in the Nationalist Party, founded in 1922. In the final years of the decade, he traveled to several Latin American and Caribbean countries, advocating the cause of Puerto Rican independence before government leaders and thus internationalizing "the colonial question." Upon his return, he took over a divided movement that weakly opposed the U.S. presence on the island, began to criticize the nature of existing relations between Puerto Rico and the United States, and committed himself to end U.S. colonial domination through the use of force. Under Albizu's leadership (he was elected president in 1930), the Nationalist Party of the 1930s was pro-Hispanic, militant, and violent. Its membership reached nearly 12,000.

The activities of the Cadets of the Republic, the paramilitary arm of the Nationalist Party, led to frequent clashes with government authorities. In 1936 chief of police Francis Riggs was shot to death, and shortly thereafter two nationalist supporters were seized and killed by police. Albizu and seven others were arrested in connection with the assassination and accused of conspiring to overthrow the government of the United States. The court sentenced Albizu to imprisonment in a federal penitentiary, where he remained until 1947.

In a climate of economic uncertainty following the Depression and political persecution promoted by U.S. colonial authorities, violent confrontations continued in the late 1930s. The "Ponce Massacre" gained the most notoriety, as 21 persons, including 2 policemen, were killed in what had been planned as a peaceful march. The commotion arose when Nationalists, shortly after Albizu's conviction, decided to hold a parade in Ponce, despite the last-minute revocation of their permit to march. The demonstrators apparently carried no arms, although a shot provoked the police into firing at the crowd. An American Civil Liberties Union investigation concluded that the ensuing violence was the result of extremist agitation and lack of police restraint.

Albizu returned to the political scene as Puerto Rico debated the benefits of permanent association with the United States, following the approval of Public Law 600, the precursor to local self-government. In 1950 from the mountain town of Jayuya he was involved in the declaration of independence. In a simultaneous move, police headquarters and the Puerto Rican governor's residence were attacked, as was Blair House, the temporary home of the U.S. president in Washington. Albizu was again arrested and found guilty of attempted murder, illegal use of arms, and subversion. Governor Luis MUÑOZ MARÍN granted him conditional freedom in 1953.

In 1954 three young nationalists fired their guns at U.S. representatives while the House was in session, wounding six people.

In 1954 three young nationalists fired their guns at U.S. representatives while the House was in session, wounding six people. Again, Albizu was jailed, until declining health required his transfer to a hospital in 1964. Governor Muñoz pardoned him on 15 November 1964; he died shortly thereafter. Although many have rejected Albizu's glorification of violence to achieve the lofty ideal of independence, his unequivocal actions and fiery rhetoric have inspired nationalists of all persuasions for many decades.

– TERESITA MARTÍNEZ-VERGNE

ALBUQUERQUE, ANTÔNIO FRANCISCO DE PAULA

Antônio Francisco de Paula Albuquerque (*b*. 1797; *d*. 1863), Brazilian imperial statesman, senator, and Liberal politician. Albuquerque was educated in Germany and began his career in the military, serving in Mozambique, in Macao, and in the 1824 revolt in Pernambuco. He retired with the rank of lieutenant colonel in 1832. Albuquerque represented his home state, Pernambuco, in both the Chamber of Deputies and the Senate. He ran unsuccessfully for regent in 1835 and 1838. Albuquerque served in eight different cabinets: as minister of the treasury in 1830, 1831, 1832, 1846, and 1852; as minister of the empire, in 1832 and 1839; as minister of justice in 1839; as minister of war in 1844; and as minister of the navy in 1840, 1844, and 1846. He was appointed counselor of the state in 1850 and was awarded the title of viscount.

– JUDY BIEBER FREITAS

ALBUQUERQUE, MATIAS DE

Matias de Albuquerque (*b.* 1595; *d.* June 1647), governor and *capitão-mor* of Pernambuco (1620–1626), thirteenth governor-general of Brazil (1624–1627), superintendent of war in Pernambuco and inspector and military engineer for the captaincies of the north (1629–1635). Born in Lisbon and baptized in the church of Loreto, Albuquerque was the younger son of Jorge de Albuquerque COELHO, third lord-proprietor of Pernambuco, and his second wife, Dona Ana, daughter of Dom Alvaro Coutinho, commander of Almourol. Later in life he changed his baptismal name, Paulo, to Matias in honor of his guardian, his father's first cousin, Matias de Albuquerque, viceroy of India (1591–1597), who was himself childless and named Matias as his heir. In 1604, after a papal dispensation was obtained because he was underage, young Albuquerque received a knighthood in the Order of Christ. In 1619, having served three years in North Africa, the Mediterranean, and the Straits of Gibraltar at his own expense, he was summoned to Madrid.

In March of 1620 Albuquerque was named governor and *capitão-mor* of his brother's (Duarte de Albuquerque Coelho) captaincy of Pernambuco, Brazil, and arrived there the following day. Three urgent problems awaited him in his new post. The first was the restoration of donatarial authority after almost a half-century of absenteeism on the part of the second, third, and fourth lords-proprietor of Pernambuco and after the last four governors-general had resided in his family's captaincy instead of in Bahia, the Brazilian capital. Second, there was the need to supply men, foodstuffs, and materials for the expanding Portuguese presence in northern and northeastern Brazil. Last, old defenses had to be rebuilt and new ones erected, and the local militias had to be trained to protect Pernambuco from threats of a Dutch attack. When the Dutch West India Company seized Bahia along with the governor-general, Diogo de Mendonça Furtado, in 1624, Albuquerque was named thirteenth governor-general of Brazil. From Pernambuco he helped wage war against the Dutch until the joint Spanish-Portuguese armada of 1625 succeeded in recapturing the Brazilian capital in May of that year. As governor-general, he continued to coordinate efforts to supply Bahia, put down Indian revolts in the interior of the northeast, and prevent Dutch reinforcements from establishing themselves in Baía de Traição in the neighboring captaincy of Paraíba.

On 18 June 1627, Albuquerque departed from Pernambuco for Portugal. During the next two years, while he was in that kingdom and in Spain, he penned a number of important memorials to the crown on such varied topics as navigation in the Atlantic and Brazil's fortifications, sugar industry, and lack of coinage. Because of reports of plans of another Dutch attack on Portuguese America, Albuquerque was sent back to Brazil in 1629, arriving there on 18 October. This time, he was given a new post, free from the control of the governor-general—that of superintendent of war in Pernambuco and inspector and military engineer for the captaincies of the north. Four months later, on 15 February 1630, the Dutch West India Company's force of approximately sixty-seven ships and 7,000 men attacked Pernambuco. By 3 March they had control of the towns of Olinda and Recife and the adjoining island of Antônio Vaz. Albuquerque rallied his outmanned and outgunned forces, and for the next two years, from his strategically located headquarters at the Arraial do Bom Jesus three miles away from both Olinda and Recife, he kept the Dutch, who were superior in numbers, hemmed in and unable to profit from the captaincy's rich sugar plantations. He was attempting to follow the successful policy that had enabled the Portuguese to recover Bahia from the Dutch in 1625.

But this time no Spanish-Portuguese armada arrived to challenge Dutch control of the sea. With the desertion by April 1632 of several important Brazilian soldiers and the arrival of substantial reinforcements from Europe, the Dutch soon expanded up and down the coast of Pernambuco and other captaincies to the north. The Portuguese fought back, but to little avail. By the end of 1634, the Dutch controlled the coast from Rio Grande do Norte to the Cape of Santo Agostinho, and a great number of Portuguese settlers had made peace with them. In 1635, Porto Calvo, the Arraial do Bom Jesus, and Fort Nazaré were captured, and much of the surrounding rich sugar land was in Dutch hands. Albuquerque and over 7,000 Portuguese settlers, their families, and slaves were forced to retreat to the southernmost part of the captaincy to what is now the state of Alagoas. In late 1635, Dom Luis de Rojas y Borgia, a former governor of Panama, landed with 2,500 soldiers in Alagoas, replacing Albuquerque as head of the forces fighting the Dutch. Albuquerque continued by land to Bahia before returning to Portugal in 1636. Blamed for the loss of Pernambuco, he was imprisoned in the Portuguese border town of Castelo da Vide. In late 1640, his place of incarceration was moved to Lisbon's Castelo de São Jorge. Soon after the acclamation of the Duke of Bragança as King João IV on 1 December 1640, Albuquerque was freed.

He pledged his loyalty to Portugal's new monarch and, because of his military background, was made a member of the newly established Council of War and given the post of *mestre de campo general* (commander in chief) of the army that was being raised to defend the Alentejo. In that province he continued to train the Portuguese troops and help with the fortifications. He was also active in the early fighting and was given the post of commander of the troops (*governador das armas*) in the Alentejo, the first of three times he held that position. However, Albuquerque was soon imprisoned again, suspected of treason because his brother, the fourth lord-proprietor of Pernambuco, had been in Madrid when the Portuguese revolution began and remained there and because Albuquerque was a close relative of several of those involved in the conspiracy of 1641 against King João IV. Eventually his innocence was established, and he was restored to full honors and made a member of the Council of State. On 26 May 1644, he led Portuguese troops to victory at the battle of Montijo in Spanish Extremadura—the first significant Portuguese victory in a war that lasted almost thirty years, until peace was finally signed in 1668. Soon after his victory, Albuquerque was named the first count of Alegrete. At about that time, he married Dona Catarina Barbara de Noronha, sister of the future first count of Vila Verde. They had no children. Albuquerque retired from active duty late in 1646 and died the following year.

– FRANCIS A. DUTRA

ALCARAZ, JOSÉ ANTONIO

José Antonio Alcaraz (*b.* 5 December 1938), Mexican composer. Alcaraz studied at the National Conservatory in Mexico and then pursued postgraduate studies at the Schola Cantorum in Paris, the summer courses for new music in Darmstadt, and the Opera Center in London. With his interest in music theater and mixed media, Alcaraz has composed some very significant works, including the aleatoric opera *Arbre d'or à deux têtes* for voice, piano, and toy instrument; an evening of theater music entitled *Qué es lo que faze aqueste gran roido, sol de mi antojo,* (1983); and a series of profane madrigals for voice and piano. *De Telémaco* for soprano, flute, and piano (1985); *Toccata* for piano (1957); *Otra hora de junio,* a two-voice madrigal (1988); *D'un inconnu* for violin and voice (1973); and *Cuanta consagración para tan poca primavera* (1981) and *Aubepine* (1984) for four mezzo-sopranos. His ballet *Homenaje a Lorca* (1963) received a prize from the University of the Theater of the Nations in Paris.

Alcaraz wrote *Hablar de música* (1982), *Suave teatro* (1984), and *Al sonoro rugir del telón* (1988). He founded the Micrópera de Mexico and the Opera de Cámara of the National Institute of Fine Arts (INBA).

– ALCIDES LANZA

ALCORIZA, LUIS

Luis Alcoriza (*b.* 1920; *d.* 1992), Mexican film director. Born in Badajoz, Spain, into a theatrical family, Alcoriza performed in various plays as a child. After the fall of the Spanish Republic in 1939, the Alcoriza family immigrated to Mexico, where Luis continued his acting career in films in the 1940s. He also worked as a screenwriter for director Luis BUÑUEL on the acclaimed films *El gran calavera* (1949), *Los olvidados* (1950), *El bruto* (1952), *El* (1952), and *El ángel exterminador* (1962). He made his directorial debut in 1960 with the film *Los jóvenes.* Throughout the 1960s, Alcoriza directed a number of noted pictures, which constitute the most important film productions of the era: they include *Tlayucan* (1961), *Tiburoneros* (1962), *La puerta* (1968), and *Mecánica nacional* (1971), for which he received the Mexican film academy award, the Ariel, for best director. Other Alcoriza films include *Las fuerzas vivas* (1979) and *Lo que importa es vivir* (1987).

– DAVID MACIEL

ALCORTA, DIEGO

Diego Alcorta (*b.* November 1801; *d.* 7 January 1842), Argentine philosopher, physician, and politician. Born in Buenos Aires and educated there at the Colegio de la Unión del Sur and the University (1823–1827), Alcorta was more successful as an educator than as a politician. He was a founder of the Sociedad Elemental de Medicina in 1824 and became one of the pioneering surgeons of the Hospital de Hombres in 1828, a year after completing his medical studies. Also named principal professor of philosophy at the university that year, he dominated the philosophy department for fourteen years. An entire generation of writers and intellectuals had their first brush with European liberal writings under Alcorta's tutelage. His favorite texts came from the French Enlightenment, a reflection of the vogue for rationalism and utilitarianism in Buenos Aires in the 1820s. Among his students were Juan Bautista ALBERDI, Juan María Gutiérrez, José MÁRMOL, Felix Frías, and Vincente Fidel LÓPEZ, the shining lights of the Generation of 1837. As a deputy in the Chamber of Representatives, Alcorta voted in 1832 against the reinstatement of the caudillo Juan Manuel de ROSAS as governor of Buenos Aires. In 1833 he became vice rector of the University of Buenos Aires, but was ousted by Rosas supporters a year later. This did not prevent him from helping to write a blueprint constitution, which was dismissed in the emerging caudillo order as too liberal. Alcorta died in Buenos Aires.

– JEREMY ADELMAN

ALDAMA Y GONZÁLEZ, IGNACIO DE

Ignacio de Aldama y González (*d.* 19 June 1811), Mexican insurgent leader. A lawyer who engaged in commerce, Aldama became magistrate of his native San Miguel el Grande. His brother Juan had joined Miguel HIDALGO, who launched an armed rebellion against the colonial regime on 16 September 1810. When Hidalgo

---

Taken to Monclova, Aldama was tried and

condemned to death. After submitting a disavowal

of his actions, he was shot.

---

reached San Miguel at the end of that month, Aldama signed an accord recognizing the authority of the insurgent leader. He subsequently joined the insurgent forces, eventually attaining the rank of field marshal. In February 1811, when Hidalgo and other insurgent leaders decided to retreat to the United States in search of aid, Aldama was sent, in the company of Friar Juan Salazar, as ambassador to Washington. Both men were captured in San Antonio Béjar, along with 100 bars of silver. Taken to Monclova, Aldama was tried and condemned to death. After submitting a disavowal of his actions, he was shot.

— VIRGINIA GUEDEA

ALDAMA Y GONZÁLEZ, JUAN DE

Juan de Aldama y González (*b.* 3 January 1774; *d.* 26 June 1811), Mexican independence leader and corevolutionary of Father Miguel Hidalgo. A Mexican creole *hacendado* anxious for recognition and social improvement, Aldama joined the Regimiento de Dragones Provinciales de la Reina, based in San Miguel el Grande, during the 1795 reorganization of the army of New Spain. Beginning service as a lieutenant, he had been promoted to the rank of militia captain by 1808. Involved in the Querétaro conspiracy (1810), Aldama traveled to the town of Dolores to inform Father HIDALGO and Captain Ignacio ALLENDE that the plot had been exposed. He was present during the first moments of the Hidalgo revolt, when prisoners were liberated from the Dolores jail and the district subdelegate was arrested.

From the beginning, Aldama attempted to maintain moderation among the rebels and opposed excesses such as property destruction and violence against Spaniards. Following the rebel capture of Guanajuato and the occupation of Valladolid, Morelia, he was promoted to lieutenant general. After the rebel defeat at Puente de Calderón (17 January 1811), Aldama retreated north with other principal rebel leaders. He was captured on 21 March 1811 and tried by royalist court-martial at Chihuahua. Despite his claims that he was a minor participant, Aldama was condemned to death and executed by firing squad.

— CHRISTON I. ARCHER

ALDANA, JOSÉ MARIA

José Maria Aldana (*b.* 1758; *d.* 7 February 1810), Mexican composer and violinist. Aldana began violin lessons while a choirboy at the cathedral in Mexico City. In 1775 he joined the cathedral orchestra but relinquished that post in 1788 when duties as violinist at Mexico City's Coliseo theater, begun two years earlier, conflicted. In 1790 he was named the Coliseo's orchestra director, a position he held concurrently, after 1808, with leadership of the Mexico City choir school. Compositions such as his vesper psalms for the Office of the Dead and other sacred and secular works (*Boleras nuevas; Minuet de variaciones*) place Aldana among the best native composers of his day.

— ROBERT L. PARKER

ALEGRE, FRANCISCO JAVIER

Francisco Javier Alegre (*b.* 12 November 1729; *d.* 16 August 1788), historian of the Jesuits in New Spain, latinist, and literary critic. A Jesuit priest and teacher born in Veracruz of Spanish parents, Alegre is best known for his *Historia de la Provincia de la Compañía de Jesús de Nueva España.* In this four-volume work, Alegre chronicles the history of Jesuit missionary activity in New Spain from their arrival in 1572 to shortly before the suppression of the order in 1767. Alegre was known to be a brilliant teacher and writer with broad interests. He wrote several poetic works as well as a prodigious multivolume treatise on theology, *Institutionum theologicarum,* published posthumously in 1789. After the Jesuits of New Spain were banished to the Papal States in 1767, Alegre, along with several of his colleagues, lived the rest of his life in Italy and made a living as a tutor and librarian. One of the more original works of this period is his *Arte poético del Mon. Boileau,* a translation and extensive commentary on Nicolas Boileau's *L'art poétique,* published posthumously by Joaquín García Icazbalceta in 1889. This is an early instance of literary criticism from a decidedly Latin American perspective.

— ALLAN FIGUEROA DECK, S.J.

ALEGRÍA, CIRO

Ciro Alegría (*b.* November 1909; *d.* February 1967), Peruvian novelist, essayist, and politician. A relative of the Argentine novelist Benito LYNCH, in his youth, Alegría had as his first-grade teacher the *mestizo* César VALLEJO, one of the most important Latin American poets of the twentieth century. Alegría lived for some time on his paternal grandfather's estate in Marcabal Grande, where he familiarized himself with the indigenous culture, camping with the natives at the edge of the jungle and listening to their tales.

Alegría was active in the American Popular Revolutionary Alliance (Alianza Popular Revolucionaria Americana—APRA), for which he was imprisoned in 1932–1933. Forced into exile from 1934 to 1960, he returned to Peru and was elected to the Peruvian Chamber of Deputies in 1963. While in exile Alegría lived and wrote in Santiago, Chile, winning prizes for his first three novels: *La serpiente de oro* (1935; The Golden Serpent), *Los perros hambrientos* (1938; The Hungry Dogs), and *El mundo es ancho y ajeno* (1941; Broad and Alien Is the World), which was honored by its American publisher Farrar and Rinehart. It subsequently was translated into twelve languages. In the 1940s Alegría lived in the United States, where he taught at several universities.

Revealing his concern for the marginalized members of Peruvian society, particularly the indigenous population, Alegría's novels demonstrate considerable artistic merit and are of great testimonial value. According to Mario VARGAS LLOSA, *Broad and Alien Is the World* is "the point of departure for modern Peruvian narrative literature and its author [is] our first classic novelist." Alegría cared little about novelistic structure and form, but was able to re-create with great skill the experiences and dialogue of indigenous peoples, achieving at his best considerable lyrical intensity.

— KEITH MCDUFFIE

ALEGRÍA, CLARIBEL

Claribel Alegría (*b.* 1924), Salvadoran writer. An outstanding poet, Alegría pioneered feminism as well as the modernization of the Central American novel with her masterpiece, *Cenizas de Izalco* (Ashes of Izalco, 1965). Her later works have been recognized for their testimonial writing about Salvadoran women.

Although she was born in Nicaragua, Alegría was taken to El Salvador at age one. She was only seven when the matanza (massacre) of 1932—in which dictator Maximiliano HERNÁNDEZ MARTÍNEZ assassinated 30,000 peasants in the space of a month—took place.

She swore that one day she would write down everything she had witnessed. She studied at Georgetown University in Washington, D.C., during the late 1940s and became one of the first Central American women to obtain a university degree. While in Washington she married Darwin Flakoll, with whom she wrote *Cenizas de Izalco,* which initiated a shift from poetry to narrative as the basic Central American literary form. Flakoll also translated this work in 1989. In the 1950s they moved to the small town of Deyá on the island of Majorca, Spain. They lived next to the English poet Robert Graves, and shared an expatriate life with well-known artists and writers. In 1980 Alegría moved to Nicaragua, where she worked on behalf of the Salvadoran people. She also cowrote with Flakoll her testimonial narrative about women, *No me agarrarán viva: La mujer salvadoreña en la lucha* (1983), translated by Amanda Hopkinson as *They Won't Take Me Alive: Salvadoran Women in the Struggle for National Liberation* (1984).

Besides *Cenizas,* her books include *Sobrevivo* (1978), winner of the Casa de las Américas Award; *Álbum familiar* (1984), translated by Amanda Hopkinson as *Family Album* (1991); *Pueblo de Dios y de mandinga* (1985); and *Luisa en el país de la realidad* (1987), translated by Flakoll as *Luisa in Realityland* (1987).

— ARTURO ARIAS

ALEGRÍA, FERNANDO

Fernando Alegría (*b.* 26 September 1918), Chilean writer and scholar. Born and raised in Santiago, Chile, he moved to the United States in 1940. His creative works (fifteen novels and four volumes of short stories) have centered primarily on the historical reality of his native country, but have also focused on the relationships and divergences between the Latin American and North American cultures. He began his academic career as professor of Latin American literature at the University of California, Berkeley (1947–1967), and later taught at Stanford University, where in 1990 he was awarded an endowed chair in the humanities.

Alegría wrote about Chileans who come to work in the United States where they are later forced to confront their true identities vis-à-vis the contradictions of American society.

Three thematic concerns dominate Alegría's narrative work. The first is the literary representation of the founding fathers of Chile's social history, found in the biographical novels *Recabarren* (1938), *Lautaro, joven libertador de Arauco* (1943; Lautaro, A Young Liberator, 1944), and *Allende* (1989). The second distinctive theme is the reevaluation of the historical and cultural experience of the Generation of 1938, developed in *Mañana los guerreros* (1964; Tomorrow the Warriors) and the autobiographical novel *Una especie de memoria* (1983; A Type of Memoir). Finally, he has written a trilogy focusing on the picaresque misadventures of Chileans who come to work in the United States where they are later forced to confront their true identities vis-à-vis the contradictions of American society: *Caballo de copas* (1957; *My Horse González,* 1964), *Amerika, Amerikka, Amerikka* (1970; *The Funhouse,* 1986), and *La rebelión de los placeres* (1990; The Rebellion of the Placeres).

– J. A. EPPLE

ALEIJADINHO

Aleijadinho (Antônio Francisco Lisbôa; *b.* ca. 1738; *d.* 18 November 1814), Brazilian architect and sculptor. Born in the provincial capital of Villa Rica do Ouro Prêto, Aleijadinho was a product of colonial Brazil, where the baroque and rococo art and architecture of minas gerais was a vehicle of nativist expression; here Saint Michael the Archangel appeared in a profusion of Indian feathers, and a dark-skinned Virgin Mary was portrayed as a *mestizo.* Contributing to this nativism was Antônio Francisco Lisbôa, known as Aleijadinho (the Little Cripple), whose prolific and distinctive work as an architect, sculptor, and decorator of Mineiro churches is emblematic of the era.

Aleijadinho was the son of Manuel Francisco Lisbôa and a slave named Isabel; he had two full siblings. The year Aleijadinho was born, his father married another woman, by whom he had four legitimate children. Although his father recognized Antônio Francisco as his son, gave him his name, and brought him into his profession of builder and artisan, little documentation illuminates their relationship. His father may have learned his craft from family members in Portugal, because his brother, Antônio Francisco Pombal, was also an architect who built Mineiro churches; on their mother's side they were presumably related to the celebrated Portuguese architect João Antunes. In addition to working under his father's direction, Aleijadinho was taught design by the painter João Gomes Baptista.

Aleijadinho executed his first pieces in wood and stone at age fourteen and worked steadily at his craft until close to his death in Ouro Prêto at the age of seventy-six. He made effective use of Brazil's native

The prophet Baruch. Sculpture by Aleijadinho, at the church of Bom Jesus de Matinhos (1796–1805). (Benson Latin American Collection, University of Texas at Austin)

soapstone, which is relatively easy to carve when freshly cut. He often worked in conjunction with the painters Francisco Xavier Carneiro and Manoel da Costa Ataíde.

The church was the center of Mineiro social life and Aleijadinho's main patron. Eighteenth-century Portuguese church architecture was influenced by that of Bavaria and Austria, in part due to the cultural interchange resulting from the marriages of King João V (reigned 1707–1750) and the Marquês of POMBAL to Austrian princesses. The Austrian-Bavarian influence is apparent in the churches of Minas, particularly those designed and decorated by Aleijadinho. Although Aleijadinho never left Brazil, printed engravings gave him a familiarity with European forms.

While Aleijadinho's body of work is immense, and he is known to have contributed to many projects as a subcontractor, his documented work is concentrated in Ouro Prêto, Sabará, São João del Rei, and Congonhos do Campo. His most important works are the churches of São Francisco in Ouro Prêto and São João de Rei, Nossa Senhora do Carmo in Sabará, and Bom Jesus de Matosinhos in Congonhos. This last church is a pilgrimage site graced by Aleijadinho's magnum opus, sixty-six wooden life-size figures that comprise an incomplete set of the stations of the cross (1796–1799) and twelve remarkable soapstone statues of the Old Testament prophets (1800–1805), arranged in a dramatic, ballet-like way on the entry terrace.

Much of this work was done under the handicap of a debilitating and painful disease that has been variously described as leprosy, syphilis, or a viral influenza contracted in 1777. It caused scarring, crippling, progressive loss of movement, and disfigurement, and gained for him the name by which he is best known. He lost his toes, his hands atrophied and shriveled, and he had to be carried to his work sites, where curtains shielded him from casual views. He executed the Congonhos prophets with chisel and mallet strapped to the stumps of his gnarled hands.

Details of Aleijadinho's life are provided by his mid-nineteenth-century biographer, Rodrigo José Ferreira Brêtas, who obtained information from Aleijadinho's daughter-in-law, Joana Francisca Lopes, in whose home the artist spent his last days. Among the known facts of Aleijadinho's personal life is that he had a son with a slave named Ana; Manuel Francisco Lisbôa was born circa 1775 and followed his father's profession.

More than a dozen Mineiro towns and Rio de Janeiro claim to possess statues, retables, pulpits, altars, doorways, windows, fountains, and buildings attributed to Aleijadinho. Some of the many items ascribed to him may have been done by his assistants and students. His most distinctive works are undoubtedly his sculptures, which Aleijadinho infused with his own suffering. Art historian Pál Kelemen wrote, "Aleijadinho carried Brazilian Rococo to its fullest flowering. . . . A rare human story lives in his masterpieces; his gift was genius."

– FRANK D. MCCANN, JR.

ALEM, LEANDRO

Leandro Alem (*b.* 25 February 1842; *d.* 1 July 1896), theoretician and founder of the Argentine Radical Party (Unión Cívica Radical—UCR). Profoundly opposed to the arranged politics of the ruling oligarchy in late-nineteenth-century Argentina, Leandro Alem founded and led the Unión Cívica (UC) between 1890 and 1896. Against a backdrop of economic depression, in 1890 Alem and his associates rebelled against the government and forced the resignation of President Miguel JUÁREZ CELMAN. But elements of the ruling elite succeeded in co-opting many of those affiliated with the Unión Cívica. Alem broke with the UC, created an intransigent splinter group, the Unión Cívica Radical, and played at revolution for the next five years. He failed, however, to generate the popular support necessary to challenge the government. In 1896 the UCR was a minor faction on the margin of the political spectrum. Frustrated and despondent, Alem committed suicide in 1896.

Born in Buenos Aires, Alem attended schools in his native city. His tumultuous public life began in 1868 in an independent political club called Equality, whose members advocated ethical and moral politics and effective suffrage (votes not compromised by corruption). In 1871 he entered the politics of Buenos Aires Province, and in 1874 he was elected a national deputy. A defender of provincial rights, Alem vigorously opposed the federalization of the city of Buenos Aires and warned against a dangerous centralization of politics.

Increasingly isolated, Alem resigned from Congress and assumed a new role as the intellectual leader of discontented pockets of the elite who were frozen out of national politics. Together with Aristóbulo del VALLE and Hipólito YRIGOYEN, Alem in 1877 formed the short-lived Republican Party, which was dedicated to federalism and to civic honesty rather than corrupt and arranged politics. In 1889 Alem and others organized the Unión Cívica de la Juventud (Youth Civic Union), which in 1890 evolved into the Unión Cívica as it attracted wider support.

"The conservative members of the Radical Party will go along with Don Bernardo; other Radicals will become socialists or anarchists; the Buenos Aires rabble, led by that perfidious traitor, my nephew Hipólito, will come to an agreement with Roque Sáenz Peña, and we intransigents, we will go to hell."

Alem was a primary leader in "El Noventa" ('90), an armed insurrection against the government in July 1890 that brought down the regime of President Juárez Celman, although the rebels failed to take power. A shaken government was forced to guarantee total amnesty to the rebels. As one politician stated: "The revolution is conquered, but the government is dead." But it was the politics of accommodation that deprived Alem of a victory. During 1891 the UC split into the National Civic Union (UCN), led by Bartolomé MITRE, and Alem's faction, the UCR. Mitre's UCN soon reached an arrangement with the oligarchy and won participation in the political process. Alem preached "relentless struggle," which became the motto of the UCR.

The UCR emerged in the 1890s as a party of vague ideals motivated more by emotion than by a carefully developed program. It was Alem who erected the two great principles of radicalism: an ethical conception of politics and a federal form of government. The UCR continued to flirt with revolution. In 1893 Alem led an insurrection in the province of Santa Fe and identified the party with the demands of agricultural colonists. Failure to generate a revolution on a broader scale precipitated division and crisis in party ranks and severely weakened the UCR. A bitter Alem surveyed the wreckage of the party in 1896 and predicted: "The conservative members of the Radical Party will go along with Don Bernardo [de Yrigoyen]; other Radicals will become socialists or anarchists; the Buenos Aires rabble, led by that perfidious traitor, my nephew Hipólito [Yrigoyen], will come to an agreement with Roque SÁENZ PEÑA, and we intransigents, we will go to hell" (José Luis Romero, *A History of Argentine Political Thought,* pp. 216–217). Alem had lost both influence and authority, which likely contributed to his suicide later in the year.

In a larger historical context, Leandro Alem not only led disaffected members of the elite but also represented traditional popular elements that earlier in the century had identified with the dictator Juan Manuel de ROSAS. Alem was a link between the federalism and populism of the early and mid-nineteenth century and the later reforms of Hipólito Yrigoyen and, some would argue, Juan Domingo PERÓN.

– PAUL GOODWIN

ALEMÁN VALDÉS, MIGUEL

Miguel Alemán Valdés (*b.* 29 September 1900; *d.* 27 September 1983), president of Mexico (1946–1952). Alemán represents a notable political generation in twentieth-century Mexico. He was the first civilian to hold the presidency for a full term after a series of revolutionary generals, a feat that marked the beginning of the dominance of the professional politician in Mexico. His administration is remembered for the young,

college-educated politicians appointed to his cabinet; for corruption in high office; for an emphasis on state-supported industrialization; for the reform of the government-controlled party, the Institutional Revolutionary Party (Partido Revolucionario Institucional—PRI); for the decline in the number of military officers in political office; for additions to the National University; and for increased ties between politicians and business elites. Alemán produced one of the two most influential political groups in contemporary politics (the Alemanistas), one that influenced decision making through the 1970s.

Alemán was born in the small rural community of Sayula, Veracruz, on Mexico's east coast, the son of a farmer who became a general during the Mexican Revolution (1910–1920). He studied in various towns before moving to Mexico City to enroll at the National Preparatory School. Alemán continued his studies at the National Autonomous University, where he received his law degree in 1928. Although he initially practiced law, specializing in labor disputes, he soon entered the political arena.

Alemán's first post was as an adviser to the Secretary of Agriculture and Livestock (1928–1930); he subsequently was appointed a judge of the Superior Court of the Federal District from 1930 to 1934. At the age of thirty-four, he represented his home state in the Senate, and two years later he achieved national recognition by winning election as governor of Veracruz (1936–1939). Before completing his term of office, Alemán was appointed head of General Manuel ÁVILA CAMACHO's presidential campaign in 1939. Following Ávila Camacho's successful bid for the presidency, Alemán was named minister of internal affairs (1940–1945), a position that he used to set his career on a course toward the presidency in 1946.

After leaving government, Alemán directed Mexico's tourism agency from 1961 until his death. He became a major figure in business circles, developing holdings in print and electronic media, including Televisa, Mexico's largest television network. The president's son, Miguel Alemán Velasco, has continued to be an important figure in Mexican television.

– RODERIC AI CAMP

ALENCAR, JOSÉ MARTINIANO DE

José Martiniano de Alencar (*b.* 1 May 1829; *d.* 12 December 1877), Brazilian writer, playwright, poet, and statesman. He was born in Messajana, state of Ceará, in northern Brazil. In 1850 he graduated from law school and founded the academic journal *Ensaios Literários,* of which he was the editor. Between 1851 and

1855, Alencar contributed to *Ensaios Literários* and other academic journals and also worked as a journalist on several daily newspapers. Most of his political career occurred between 1859 and 1877.

Alencar is considered to be one of the founders of Brazilian narrative writing. He cultivated Indianist and urban novels and introduced some of the most significant techniques observed in the Latin American narrative. As a romantic writer and an artist, he sought to underscore nationalistic themes and undermine Eurocentric aesthetics, which were so prevalent at the time. Before Alencar, Brazilian letters were characterized by gongoristic classicism. which also dominated Portuguese literature. In all of his work, Alencar demonstrated an acute concern for language and the establishment of a true Brazilian linguistic expression, one devoid of all Portuguese influence.

Some of his most significant works are *O marquês de Paraná* (1856), an autobiographical piece; *O guarani* (1857), an interpretation of Brazilian colonial history in which he depicts the relationship between native Brazilians and the Portuguese colonizers; *O demônio familiar* (1857), a two-act comedy; *A noite de São João* (1857), a musical comedy, with music by Elias Lobo; *As asas de um anjo* (1860), a comedy in one prologue, four acts, and one epilogue. His novel *Lucíola* was first published in Paris in 1862. *As minas de prata* (1862, 1865–1866) is another historical novel.

The novel *Iracema* (1865), subtitled by Alencar "the myth of Ceará," is considered to be his chief work. Its leitmotiv is the beauty of Brazil. It is seen as the most nationalistic of his books, a work that has merited translations in several languages and is acclaimed as one of the world's most important classics of romantic literature. Alencar's narrative displays the Portuguese language as it was spoken in the Americas, with its own dynamic linguistic expressions, and with creative images and symbols that capture in great detail the unique beauty of Brazil. It is a romantic love story between an Indian princess, Iracema, and the white Martim; from their love is born Moacyr, whose name means "the son of pain." Iracema is also considered to be the first heroine of the Brazilian novel, for her death is depicted in the narrative as the sacrifice of her love for Martim. Alencar died in Rio de Janeiro.

— ROSÂNGELA MARIA VIEIRA

ALESSANDRI PALMA, ARTURO

Arturo Alessandri Palma (*b.* 20 December 1868; *d.* 24 August 1950), president of Chile (1920–1925 and 1932–1938). Educated at the University of Chile as a lawyer, he entered politics as a candidate of the Liberal Party (PL). A bombastic orator and tireless campaigner, he served in the Chamber of Deputies, in the Senate, and as a cabinet minister. Running on a reformist ticket, he was elected president in 1920. Alessandri had the bad luck to become president when Chile was suffering from a massive economic dislocation caused by the postwar collapse of the nitrate market.

Alessandri hoped to introduce numerous economic and social reforms, but his political opposition refused to pass his legislative program. Caught between widespread social unrest and an entrenched parliamentary opposition, Alessandri's reforms languished. The president found an unexpected ally in disaffected field-grade army officers who, distressed by their own wretched economic situation and the nation's suffering, intimidated the legislature into passing the reform package.

While initially pleased with his newfound support, Alessandri discovered that the officer corps was demanding that the legislature resign. Aware that he could not control them, Alessandri quit in January 1925, and a conservative military junta began to rule. When it became clear that the junta would attempt to elect a conservative to the presidency, junior army officers seized power and requested Alessandri to return. Upon doing so in March, Alessandri, ruling under the newly written Constitution of 1925, managed to pass certain reformist legislation. He resigned a second time in October, when he realized that he could not control the minister of war, Carlos IBÁÑEZ DEL CAMPO, who would seize power in 1927.

Alessandri went into exile, joining the various plots to overthrow Ibáñez. After the dictator's fall, in 1931, Alessandri returned to Chile, where he unsuccessfully ran against Juan Esteban Montero Rodríguez for the presidency. In 1932, following the collapse of the Montero administration and the Socialist Republic, Alessandri became president for a second term.

Due to widespread unrest and the collapse of the economy, Alessandri's second term of office was only slightly less turbulent than his first administration. He nonetheless managed to govern the nation, stimulating the economy by encouraging the creation of national industries and supporting the construction of public and private housing. His brutal suppression of an abortive Nazi coup in 1938 alienated many people, contributing to the defeat of Gustavo Ross Santa María, Alessandri's candidate for the presidency.

An energetic and dynamic individual, Alessandri remained active in Chile's political life, serving as president of the Senate. A forceful leader, he may best be remembered as the man who appealed to the lower classes and who, using the powers provided by the 1925

Constitution, restored order to Chile and led it out of the Great Depression.

— WILLIAM F. SATER

ALESSANDRI RODRÍGUEZ, JORGE

Jorge Alessandri Rodríguez (*b.* 19 May 1896; *d.* 31 August 1986), president of Chile (1958–1964). The son of former president Arturo ALESSANDRI PALMA, Jorge was an engineer who entered politics in 1926. An industrialist, he served as a senator and, later, as cabinet minister in the government of Gabriel GONZÁLEZ VIDELA. A man without clearly defined political ideas, the conservative Alessandri became president in 1958, barely defeating his left-wing opponent, Dr. Salvador ALLENDE, in a bitterly contested election.

As a minority president, Alessandri attempted to revive the Chilean economy by stimulating the domestic industries, particularly the construction sector, and encouraging the American copper companies to increase production. His government was one of the first to institute a modified agrarian reform program. After some initial success, Alessandri's economic program foundered because the sluggish domestic economy could not satisfy consumer needs. When imports soared, Alessandri had to devalue the Chilean currency, precipitating another devastating round of inflation that led to widespread political unrest. Rather than expanding the role of the state, the austere Alessandri unsuccessfully attempted to cure Chile's deep-seated socioeconomic problems using traditional methods.

In 1970, supported by the conservative National Party (PN), Alessandri again opposed Salvador Allende for president. This time, unlike 1958, Allende triumphed, largely because his opposition was divided between Alessandri and the Christian Democrat, Radomiro Tomic.

— WILLIAM F. SATER

ALEXIS, JACQUES STÉPHEN

Jacques Stéphen Alexis (*b.* 22 April 1922; *d.* April 1961), Haitian novelist, story writer, essayist, and physician. Son of historian, novelist, playwright, and diplomat Stéphen Alexis, Jacques Stéphen was born in Gonaïves during the American occupation of Haiti. Successor to the Marxist nationalism of Jacques ROUMAIN, he eventually emerged to become the compelling exponent of his own lyrically infused, proletarian-identified vision of a uniquely Haitian "marvelous realism." Initially educated at the College Stanislas in Paris and the Institution Saint-Louis de Gonzague in Port-au-Prince, Alexis took an early, active part in Hai-

tian avantgarde cultural and political life. A member of the Communist Party at sixteen, he later also wrote regularly, as Jacques la Colère, for the radical journal *La Ruche*. With René DEPESTRE and other members of its editorial staff, he directly contributed to the success of the Revolution of 1946, which brought down the government of Élie LESCOT. While pursuing his medical studies in Paris, Alexis moved in radical, left-wing, surrealist, existentialist, and Antillean négritude circles. Thereafter, he traveled through Europe, the Middle East, Russia, and China. Returning to Haiti in 1954, Alexis published *Compère général soleil* (1955), the novel that established his reputation as one of his country's most important writers of fiction. *Les Arbres musiciens* (1957), *L'espace d'un cillement* (1959), and *Romancero aux étoiles* (1960), a collection of short stories, followed in quick succession to confirm that original assessment.

Representing a formal and thematic convergence between literary realism, Afro-Antillean cultural nationalism, Marxist anticolonialism, and a universalizing art that "is indissolubly linked to the myth, the symbol, the stylized, the heraldic, even the hieratic," Alexis's fiction strives for "a new balance . . . born of singularity and antithesis" (J. S. Alexis, "Of the Marvelous Realism of the Haitians," *Présence Africaine* [English edition], nos. 8–10 [1956]: 265). Extending the legacy of Jacques Roumain, it enlarges the settings, formal daring, thematic range, and visionary reach of the Haitian peasant and working-class novel. His influence among contemporary writers continues to be felt near the end of the twentieth century and is particularly evident in René Depestre's *Le mât de cocagne* (1979) and Pierre Clitandre's *Cathédrale du mois d'aout* (1982).

Alexis was the compelling exponent of his own lyrically infused, proletarian-identified vision of a uniquely Haitian "marvelous realism."

Radical opposition to the François DUVALIER regime forced Alexis to leave Haiti clandestinely in 1960. Attempting to land secretly at Mole Saint Nicholas a year later as part of a small guerrilla group, Alexis was apprehended, imprisoned, and finally stoned to death by his captors. In addition to published novels, stories, and essays bearing witness to his passionate devotion to Haiti's common folk and a historical materialist critique of essentialist versions of négritude, he left behind two unpublished works in progress, *L'Eglantine* and *L'étoile absinthe*.

— ROBERTO MÁRQUEZ

ALFARO, RICARDO JOAQUÍN

Ricardo Joaquín Alfaro (*b.* 20 August 1882; *d.* 23 February 1971), a Panamanian statesman who served as minister to the United States (1922–1930; 1933–1936), foreign minister (1946), and provisional president (1931–1932). A tireless advocate of Panamanian rights in the Canal Zone, Alfaro negotiated the Hull–Alfaro Treaty (1936) and served as an adviser during the treaty negotiations with the United States in 1947. He also protested the continued U.S. occupation of defense sites after World War II until the U.S. withdrawal in 1948. Alfaro presided over the 1932 presidential campaign with fairness and honesty, a rarity in Panamanian politics. Subsequently, he served as a member of the International Court of Justice at The Hague (1959–1964).

— THOMAS M. LEONARD

ALFARO DELGADO, JOSÉ ELOY

José Eloy Alfaro Delgado (*b.* 25 June 1842; *d.* 28 January 1912), president of Ecuador (interim 1896–1897, constitutional 1897–1901, interim 1906–1907, constitutional 1907–1911). Born in Montecristi, Manabí, Alfaro began his political career as a partisan of General José María Urvina, leading revolts in 1865 and 1871 against the conservative regime of Gabriel García Moreno (1869–1875). When the movements failed, he fled to Panama, where he developed a successful business and married. He subsequently used his wealth to finance liberal publications and insurrections against conservative governments in Ecuador and to support liberal causes throughout Latin America. By 1895, when he returned to Ecuador to lead the liberal forces, Alfaro had an international reputation as a revolutionary. With the support of wealthy coastal exporting interests, Alfaro's forces defeated the government troops. Alfaro convened a constituent assembly that wrote a new liberal constitution and elected him president. The liberals would retain power for the next three decades.

Despite a commitment to liberal principles, including the creation of a secular, activist state, Alfaro's political style was authoritarian and personalist. Until his death in 1912, he sought to maintain power by any means and was a principal cause of the political turmoil that characterized Ecuador in this period. He failed in his effort to prevent the inauguration of his successor Leonidas Plaza in 1901, but managed to oust Lizardo García, who took office in 1905. As in 1896, Alfaro convened the 1906 constituent assembly to legitimize his usurpation of power.

During Alfaro's second constitutional term, the Quito and Guayaquil Railroad was inaugurated, and real property held in mortmain by religious orders was nationalized. These accomplishments were partly eclipsed by Alfaro's harsh repression of political opponents and lack of respect for civil liberties.

Failing to prevent the inauguration of Emilio Estrada as his successor on 31 August 1911, Alfaro once again fled to Panama. However, when Estrada's untimely death in December 1911 unleashed a civil war, he returned from Panama to participate in the unsuccessful insurrection against the government. The public damned Alfaro and his supporters as unprincipled opportunists willing to destroy the nation to gain their ends and demanded that the rebels be punished. Alfaro was taken to Quito for trial. A mob burst into the prison and murdered the prisoners, including Eloy Alfaro.

— LINDA ALEXANDER RODRÍGUEZ

ALFARO SIQUEIROS, DAVID

David Alfaro Siqueiros (also Siqueiros; *b.* 29 December 1896; *d.* 6 January 1974), Mexican artist. Muralist, painter, printmaker, theoretician, labor organizer, soldier, and Communist Party leader, Siqueiros not only produced a sizable and influential body of political-artistic theory but was the most technically innovative of the *tres grandes,* the Big Three of the Mexican School, begun in 1922 with Diego RIVERA and José Clemente OROZCO. After returning in 1922 from studies in Europe, Siqueiros, along with Rivera and Xavier Guerrero, organized the Syndicate of Technical Workers, Painters, and Sculptors and began to publish the artist newspaper *El Machete* (1924).

In the search for materials and methods that could be used for outdoor murals that would be legible to spectators in transit, Siqueiros was the first artist, from 1932 on, to employ industrial synthetic paints (Duco or pyroxilyn, vinylite, etc.), an electric projector to transfer images onto the wall, and a spray gun (with stencils) to paint murals. He also used surfaces such as damp cement, masonite, and plywood, as well as more traditional grounds. He invented polyangular perspective, often on curved walls, to activate filmically a static surface. He also used blowups of documentary photographs as contemporary visual sources and *esculto-pintura* (sculptural painting). His painting style was dramatic and exuberant, even baroque, with simplified solid images thrusting forward, illusionistic destructions and re-creations of space (floors, walls, and ceilings), and the building up of surfaces with granular materials.

Far from being merely a formalist innovator, Siqueiros employed these means to strengthen and make more powerful his political content, an approach he called *pintura dialéctico-subversiva* (dialectic-subversive painting). He championed monumental rather than easel painting, street murals, collective artistic teams, a scientific and psychological knowledge of artistic tools and forms, multiple and portable paintings rather than unique ones. He wrote to Anita Brenner, explaining that "what we seek is not only technique and style in art that sympathizes with revolution, but an art that itself is revolutionary."

– SHIFRA M. GOLDMAN

ALFONSÍN, RAÚL RICARDO

Raúl Ricardo Alfonsín (*b.* 13 March 1926), president of Argentina (1983–1989). The son of a local storekeeper, Alfonsín was raised in Chascomús, Buenos Aires Province. His maternal great-grandfather was an Irishman named Richard Foulkes, who married Mary Ford, daughter of a family of Falkland Islands kelpers. Staggeringly different from most British residents of South America, Don Ricardo became a passionate Argentine patriot fighting alongside the famous Radical leader Hipólito YRIGOYEN in the abortive revolution of 1905. With such family traditions, Alfonsín grew up fiercely

Raúl Alfonsín at independence celebration, Buenos Aires, 9 July 1985. (Reuters/Bettmann Archive)

opposed to electoral fraud, dictatorship, and corporatism. But it was only after Ricardo BALBÍN's death in September 1981 that he attained power in the Radical Party by winning the presidency (his first government post) in October 1983. The Radicals, who normally polled about 25 percent, got 51.7 percent, while the Peronists, with 40 percent, suffered their lowest vote and first ever defeat. The Alfonsín government introduced heterodox economic shock treatment, dubbed the Austral Plan, organized the first human rights trials in Latin America, and withstood three military uprisings. Defeat came in the shape of a civilian challenge. The Peronist Carlos Saúl MENEM captured 47 percent in the May 1989 election, reducing Alfonsín to an opposition figure once again.

– ROGER GRAVIL

ALLENDE, IGNACIO

Ignacio Allende (*b.* 25 January 1769; *d.* 26 June 1811), Mexican independence leader and corevolutionary of Father Miguel HIDALGO. Born to a wealthy landowning family, Allende joined the militia of San Miguel el Grande as a lieutenant and was promoted in 1797 to captain. He participated in the meetings of creole societies that plotted for Mexican Independence, favoring independence under King Ferdinand VII or some other member of the Spanish royal family. When the regime discovered the Querétaro conspiracy in September 1810, Allende went to the town of Dolores to assist Father Miguel Hidalgo, who later named him captain-general of the American armies.

Many historians point to Allende's military background, but it should be remembered that he was a militia officer who had not commanded significant forces. A creole, he experienced difficulties with a rebellion that exploded rapidly into a mass movement dominated by Indians and mestizos. During and after the bloody occupation of Guanajuato, Allende attempted to restore order and to halt atrocities against Spaniards, uncontrolled pillaging, and other excesses. At Valladolid, Morelia, he ordered his troops to use force against insurgent looters. On many occasions, he opposed Hidalgo's apparent willingness to sanction violence as a means to attract supporters to the revolutionary cause.

After the battle of Monte de las Cruces (30 October 1810), Hidalgo rejected Allende's belief that the capital should be occupied, and the insurgents began the peripatetic wanderings that led to the occupation of Guadalajara. Even before the disastrous rebel defeat at Aculco (7 November 1810), many Indians and mestizos abandoned the rebel army. Allende was present in Guanajuato, but he did not play a major role in the battle of 25 November 1810 that resulted in the second major rebel defeat. Following the royalist victory at the battle of Puente de Calderón on 17 January 1811, the insurgent chiefs replaced Hidalgo, naming Allende supreme commander. Retreating to the north, Allende decided to regroup the insurgent forces in the United States. However, on 21 March 1811, the senior rebel commanders were surprised by treachery and captured north of Saltillo. Allende was taken prisoner, tried by court-martial at Chihuahua, and executed by firing squad.

— CHRISTON I. ARCHER

ALLENDE, ISABEL

Isabel Allende (*b.* 2 August 1942), Chilean novelist, born in Peru, where her father was a member of the diplomatic corps. After her parents separated, she was brought up in an old labyrinthine house surrounded by stories that eventually influenced her first novel, *La casa de los espíritus* (1982; *The House of the Spirits,* 1985), a work that brought Isabel Allende immediate international recognition. The novel is a melodramatic account of a patriarchal family saga whose story runs parallel to Chile's history in the twentieth century. Translated into several languages, it achieved remarkable success throughout the Western world.

From 1967 to 1974, Allende worked as a journalist for *Paula,* a woman's magazine in her native Santiago. In 1973 her uncle, Chilean president Salvador Allende, was assassinated by the Chilean military during a coup d'état that ousted his Socialist government. In 1975, fearing for her life, Isabel left Chile and went into exile. She settled with her family in Caracas, Venezuela, where she continued to practice journalism.

In *The House of the Spirits* she highlights the independent nature of the female characters, whose lives become increasingly entangled in the political process of their country, assumed to be Chile but never actually named. Her second novel, *De amor y de sombra* (1984; *Of Love and Shadows,* 1987), centers around a historical event, the discovery of the remains of a group of victims of a massacre by the military regime in a mine at Los Riscos, Chile. The novel can be interpreted as a denunciation of the military regime that ousted President Allende's government. Beginning with her third novel, *Eva Luna* (1987; *Eva Luna,* 1988), Allende's attention shifts from Chile's contemporary reality to a broader setting, where storytelling from a female viewpoint becomes the focus of her fiction. In 1989, after moving to California, she published *Los cuentos de Eva Luna* (*The Stories of Eva Luna,* 1991), tales told by the title character of her previous novel. Later works include

El plan infinito (1991; *The Infinite Plan,* 1993) and *Paula* (1994, trans. 1995). In 1994 she was awarded the Orden al Mérito Gabriela Mistral by the Chilean government.

— MAGDALENA GARCÍA PINTO

ALLENDE GOSSENS, SALVADOR

Salvador Allende Gossens (*b.* 26 July 1908; *d.* 11 September 1973), president of Chile (1970–1973). Born in Valparaíso of an upper middle-class family, Allende studied in the public schools and graduated from the University of Chile with a medical degree in 1932. He was an active Mason throughout his adult life.

Allende was attracted to socialist doctrine during his youth. He participated in university politics and in 1933 was a founding member of the Socialist Party. He was elected to the Chamber of Deputies in 1937, and he served as minister of health (1939–1942) in the Popular Front government of Pedro AGUIRRE CERDA. His long career in the Senate began in 1945 and continued until 1969. As a senator, he gained a reputation as an expert in parliamentary procedure and rose to the presidency of the Senate (1965–1969). Allende held various offices in the Socialist Party, serving twice as secretary-general.

Salvador Allende greeting miners during the first anniversary of the nationalization of the copper mines, 12 July 1972, Santiago, Chile. (La Nación)

Allende ran for the presidency of Chile four times. In 1952 he garnered only 5.4 percent of the vote. In 1958 and 1964 he ran as the candidate of the Popular Action Front (FRAP), which was founded in 1956 to unite the Communist, Socialist, and smaller leftist parties. With coalition support, Allende received 28.9 percent of the vote in 1958; he lost to Jorge ALESSANDRI RODRÍGUEZ by only 33,500 of 1,236,000 votes cast. The leftward movement of Chilean politics in the wake of the Cuban Revolution (1959) raised expectations of an Allende victory in the 1964 presidential election. To prevent that possibility, the rightist Conservative and Liberal parties broke their alliance with the Radical Party and threw their support to reformist Christian Democrat Eduardo FREI. After an intense campaign featuring Central Intelligence Agency (CIA) financing and scare tactics equating Allende with Fidel CASTRO, Frei won with 55.6 percent of the vote to Allende's 38.6. Throughout the Frei administration, Allende was the most visible spokesman of the opposition Left and advocate of more vigorous reform.

The 1970 presidential election offered Chileans clear choices. Reacting to Frei's reforms, the Right reorganized as the National Party and selected former president Jorge Alessandri as its candidate. The Christian Democrats ran Radomiro TOMIC of the party's left-center bloc. Allende was the candidate of Popular Unity (UP), a new coalition of the Socialists and Communists and four non-Marxist parties, including the historic Radical Party. Allende won a close race: he received 36.5 percent of the vote to Alessandri's 35.2 and Tomic's 28.0. After two months of U.S.-orchestrated attempts to block congressional ratification of the popular election and to foster a military coup, Salvador Allende took office on 3 November 1970.

Allende's election fixed the world's attention on Chile, which would provide the laboratory for testing the question: Is there a peaceful road to socialism? Allende had promised to move Chile rapidly toward socialism through the acceleration of agrarian reform and extensive nationalization in key economic sectors. His first year in office was highly successful in meeting these goals and in building popular support. Thereafter, mounting problems began to plague his government, compounding the difficulties imposed by opposition control of Congress and the judiciary. By the end of 1971, accelerating inflation, the exhaustion of foreign currency reserves, and disinvestment in the private sector had weakened the economy. Meanwhile, the Christian Democrats and the National Party formalized an anti-UP alliance, the Nixon administration stepped up its destabilization campaign, and critical divisions within the UP and Allende's own Socialist Party began to surface.

Although the pace of reform rose dramatically under the UP, popular expectations rose faster, resulting in widespread extralegal worker occupations of haciendas and factories. Torn between his legal obligations and his commitment to the *pueblo,* Allende vacillated on the wave of takeovers; he lost crucial middle-class support by appearing soft on the rule of law. The opposition struck a major blow in an October 1972 "bosses' strike." Called by the *gremio* (guild) movement, a broad coalition of business and professional groups, the strike paralyzed the economy, revealed the government's vulnerability, and forced Allende to bring military officers into his cabinet. From this point forward, confrontation escalated and much of the opposition embraced the goal of overthrowing the government.

Despite the growing polarization and the rise of violence, Allende achieved an impressive record of reform. Under his administration, the traditional rural estate virtually ceased to exist, the state took control of the "commanding heights" of the economy, and progress was made in income redistribution. The final test of UP popularity was the March 1973 congressional election. The UP received 44 percent of the vote, down from the 49.7 percent it had won in the April 1971 municipal elections but still 7.5 points above the 1970 presidential vote tally. Nonetheless, the UP's failure to achieve a congressional majority and the opposition's failure to attain the two-thirds majority necessary to impeach the president signaled three and a half more years of conflict before the 1976 presidential election. A second *gremio* strike took place in July and August 1973. With the

---

The overthrow and death of Allende marked the end of the transition to socialism and the beginning of a lengthy military dictatorship.

---

country in chaos and the government near collapse, the military staged a coup on 11 September. Salvador Allende, *compañero presidente* to Chile's poor, committed suicide in the Moneda Palace while it was under military attack. The overthrow and death of Allende marked the end of the transition to socialism and the beginning of a lengthy military dictatorship.

– THOMAS C. WRIGHT

ALLENDE-SARÓN, PEDRO HUMBERTO

Pedro Humberto Allende-Sarón (*b.* 29 June 1885; *d.* 17 August 1959), Chilean composer. Allende was born in Santiago and studied composition at the National Conservatory in Santiago (1899–1908). He studied piano and violin, the latter under the guidance of Aurelio Silva. Early in his career he taught violin and general musical subjects in secondary schools and later taught composition and harmony at the National Conservatory. He was a key figure in revitalizing the music education system in Chile, both at the primary and secondary school levels. After a trip to Europe in 1910–1911, Allende was elected to the Chilean Folklore Society. In recognition for his research and compositional efforts, as well as for his contribution to music education, in 1945 he received the Premio Nacional de Arte, becoming the first composer to be so honored.

Allende was the first important figure to promote Chilean musical nationalism by integrating in his works the songs and dances of the Araucanian and Mapuche Indians as well as mestizo folk music, which he orchestrated in a lavish French impressionist style. He wrote *Paisaje chileno* for chorus and orchestra (1913); *Escenas campesinas chilenas* (1913–1914), a symphonic suite; *La voz de las calles* (1919–1920), a symphonic poem; *Tonadas de carácter popular chileno,* for piano (1918–1922); *Concerto sinfónico* for cello and orchestra (1915); *Luna de la media noche* for soprano and orchestra (1937); Violin Concerto (1940); and *La Cenicienta* (Cinderella, 1948), a chamber opera for children.

Allende's writings include *Metodología original para la enseñanza del canto escolar* (1922); *Conferencias sobre la música* (1918); "La música popular chilena" in *Art populaire,* from the First International Congress of Popular Art, Prague (1928); and "Chilean Folk Music," in the *Bulletin of the Pan American Union* (September 1931).

— ALCIDES LANZA

ALMAFUERTE

Almafuerte (*b.* 13 May 1854; *d.* 28 February 1917), pseudonym of Pedro Bonifacio Palacios, Argentine poet and journalist. Born in San Justo in Buenos Aires province, Almafuerte was self-taught. Raised by an aunt in Buenos Aires, he remained in the capital, living in poverty and solitude.

Almafuerte cultivated an extravagant persona that bespoke his commitment to exemplifying attributes and values of a mystical, unsettled, and contradictory self-identity that transcended established middle-class conventions. To be sure, during this period Buenos Aires remained relatively sedate alongside its European models. Yet, Almafuerte was able to project a complex, idiosyncratic persona that gave him a unique status among the writers of the period as something of a prophet concerning the impact on the solitary individual of the multiple tensions of a society undergoing vertiginous modernization. In this sense, Almafuerte may be read as an antiphony to the vast sociopolitical undertaking of the Generation of 1880, who sought to impose a liberal hegemony on Argentine society.

In the worldly and often aggressively profane (or, at least, decidedly materialistic) context of the Generation of 1880, Almafuerte aligned himself with a traditional, humanitarian Christian sentiment that is reflected in titles like *Evangélicas* (1915), *Cristianas y Jesús, El drama del Calvario, Cantar de cantares, Lamentaciones* (1906), and *El misionero* (1905) and in the didactic, sermonizing tone of many of his compositions. Yet, despite this sort of catechistic focus, the structure of his poetry frequently reflects the innovative exercises of the more urbane and sensual modernists.

— DAVID WILLIAM FOSTER

ALMAGRO, DIEGO DE

Diego de Almagro (*b.* ca. 1475; *d.* 8 July 1538), conqueror of Peru and Chile. Almagro, illegitimate son of Juan de Montenegro and Elvira Gutiérrez, was born in Almagro, in New Castile. His first years were eco-

Diego de Almagro. Anonymous grabado from Antonio de Herrera, Historia general de las Indias, Islas y Tierra Firme del Mar Océano en VIII décadas, 1292–1554 *(Madrid, 1601–1615). (Library of Congress)*

nomically and socially difficult ones, and in 1514 he left for the Indies in search of fortune. He participated with some distinction in minor discoveries in Castilla del Oro and became a close associate of Francisco PIZARRO, another dynamic social-misfit soldier of fortune. With some financial assistance from cleric Hernando de LUQUE, who may have been representing a silent partner, the two men began making plans to explore South America's west coast, widely believed to be the seat of an empire of great riches.

Pizarro set sail southward from the Isthmus of Panama in the first expedition of 1524; Almagro, responsible for maintaining supplies, followed behind, covering much the same route and suffering hardships similar to those of the Pizarro group. In an encounter with the cacique (chief) of Las Piedras, Almagro lost an eye at Pueblo Quemado. On the second expedition (1526), which was jointly planned with Pizarro, neither the leaders nor their men got along well. When Almagro returned to the isthmus for more troops and supplies, he inadvertently carried notice of the discontent. When the governor of Panama got wind of the situation, he recalled both men. In the meantime, Pizarro was able to secure enough evidence of wealth to convince the official that a third and more massive attempt was warranted.

At this juncture Pizarro returned to Spain and procured an agreement with the crown that made him chief commander of the expedition, leaving Luque as bishop of Tumbes. Almagro, who received relatively minor offices in the north, remained on the isthmus ill, perhaps with syphillis, as Pizarro started the third expedition near the end of 1530. By the time Almagro and his men were able to reach Pizarro at Cajamarca, the Inca ruler ATAHUALPA had already been captured and much of the wealth allocated to Pizarro's men. Almagro did secure appointment as the chief commander of New Toledo, about 520 miles south of Pizarro's New Castile, and marched into Cuzco (Peru) on 15 November 1533.

Convinced that vast cities and wealth lay to the south, and perhaps encouraged by the duplicitous Pizarrists who wanted to be rid of him, he organized an expedition and marched southward on 3 July 1535. The group passed Lake Titicaca, crossed with great hardship and loss of life through frigid Andean passes, and entered Chile at Copiapó. The expeditionary force marched as far south as the Maule River in south-central Chile, but found no indication of the expected treasures. Instead, the Europeans were attacked by fierce Indian fighters who had eluded Inca rule.

Almagro and his men gave up and returned to Peru via the desert coastal route. The soldiers passed through what became Arequipa and marched into Cuzco on 8 April 1537, shortly after Pizarro supporters had broken

the siege led by MANCO INCA. Almagro and his men occupied Cuzco, believing it to be within the jurisdiction of New Toledo. Almagro, to ensure his control, imprisoned Francisco's brothers, Hernando and Gonzalo Pizarro, while Friar Francisco de BOBADILLA, a suspected Pizarrist, began negotiations to effect a peaceful settlement of the territorial dispute. Gonzalo Pizarro escaped jail, and Almagro freed Hernando on the condition that he return to Spain. Hernando, however, fielded a Pizarrist army that met and defeated Almagro on 6 April 1538 at Salinas, near Cuzco. Fearing an uprising of Almagro's supporters, Hernando Pizarro ordered him executed in his cell. He was buried in Cuzco's Mercedarian church.

Almagro's illegitimate mestizo son, Diego de Almagro, the Younger, born in Panama in 1520 (his mother was Ana Martínez, a native of the isthmus), would later head a movement to overthrow Pizarrist domination of Peru. After the assassination of Francisco Pizarro in Lima on 26 June 1541, he governed Peru briefly, but fell to the king's forces, led by Governor Cristóval Vaca de Castro, on 16 September 1542 in the battle of Chupas, near Huamanga. He was captured and executed in Cuzco. Only twenty-two years old when he died, he was buried alongside his father in the Mercedarian church.

– NOBLE DAVID COOK

ALMAZÁN, JUAN ANDRÉU

Juan Andréu Almazán (*b.* 12 May 1891; *d.* 9 October 1965), Mexican politician. Almazán, a general, was an important figure during and immediately following the Mexican Revolution (1910–1920). Noted for his candidacy in the Mexican presidential election of 1940, Almazán represented the Revolutionary Party of National Unification (Partido Revolucionario de Unificación Nacional—PRUN) in opposition to the government candidate, General Manuel ÁVILA CAMACHO, who was chosen to succeed President Lázaro CÁRDENAS. The campaign generated considerable electoral violence, and some observers expected Almazán to lead a rebellion against the government after losing. Instead he went into exile in Panama, Cuba, and the United States. He returned to Mexico in 1947, and was a businessman until his death in Mexico City.

– RODERIC AI CAMP

ALMEIDA, JOSÉ AMÉRICO DE

José Américo de Almeida (*b.* 10 January 1887; *d.* 10 March 1980), a leading Brazilian social novelist of the 1930s. Almeida was an important figure in both Northeastern and national Brazilian politics until his death.

A strong supporter of Getúlio VARGAS's 1930 revolution and a minister in Vargas's government, his own presidential candidacy was thwarted by Vargas's coup in 1937. Later he served as governor of his home state of Paraíba. These and other episodes of his political life were described in his memoirs *Ocasos de sangue* (1954).

Influenced by positivism and Euclides da CUNHA's *Os sertões*, Almeida wrote *A Paraíba e seus problemas* (1923), which documents his sociopolitical concerns about his state and region. Although he wrote three novels with similar economic and social themes and the same poetic style, *A bagaceira* (1928; *Trash*, 1978) is recognized as his most important work. A pioneering regionalist work within the nationalist ideology of Brazilian modernism, *A bagaceira* is primarily a literary exemplification of beliefs and ideas he expressed in *A Paraíba e seus problemas*. In this poetic novel replete with regionalist expressions, he describes the effects of the periodic droughts on the people of the Northeast and, specifically, the conflict between the *sertanejos* (frontiersmen) and the *brejeiros* (marshmen). Today, however, the novel is considered more of a monument of that period than a vibrant work of literature.

— IRWIN STERN

ALMEIDA JÚNIOR, JOSÉ FERRAZ DE

José Ferraz de Almeida Júnior (*b.* 8 May 1850; *d.* 13 November 1899), Brazilian painter best known for his *caipira* paintings. Born in Itú, São Paulo, Almeida Júnior enrolled in the Imperial Academy of Fine Arts in 1869. A disciple of Vítor MEIRELES, Almeida Júnior specialized in drawing and historical painting. Between 1871 and 1874 he won seven student painting awards. In 1874 he obtained the gold medal in historical painting, entitling him to compete for the academy's European travel award competition. Although he declined, he did accept a monthly stipend to travel in Europe offered by the emperor, PEDRO II, who took an active interest in supporting talented young artists.

The paintings of Almeida Júnior helped bring into focus the important historical role of the Brazilian backwoodsmen.

In Paris he studied with French academic artists and entered several Salon exhibitions. When he returned to Rio in 1882, he organized an exhibition to show the eight paintings he had completed while in Europe. They included religious paintings, figure studies, genre

paintings, and a new category, *caipira* painting. His *O Derrubador brasileiro,* the first in a series of *caipira* paintings, expanded the narrow thematic options then available to historical and genre painters. It remained faithful to the traditional academic aesthetic canons but depicted a scene in the daily life of the common people from the interior of the state of São Paulo. These paintings helped bring into focus the important historical role of the Brazilian backwoodsmen. His other *caipira* compositions include *Caipiras negaceando, Caipira picando fumo, Pescando, Amolação interrompida,* and *Caipira pitando.*

— CAREN A. MEGHREBLIAN

ALMEIDA, MANUEL ANTÔNIO DE

Manuel Antônio de Almeida (*b.* 17 November 1831; *d.* 28 November 1861), Brazilian novelist. Almeida is famous for a single text, the novel *Memórias de um sargento de milícias,* which was serialized in 1853 and published in two volumes in 1854–1855. It was rediscovered, after 1922, by the modernists, who celebrated it for its detailed and quite realistic descriptions of urban life in Rio de Janeiro in the years just before Independence in 1822—descriptions that include a broader range of social types than any other Brazilian novel of its time—and for its entertaining and highly unsentimental vision of life. Some critics endeavored to classify Almeida's *Memórias* as an early example of the realist novel in Brazil, but clearly its literary roots can be traced to such eighteenth-century British works as Henry Fielding's *Tom Jones.* It has also been suggested that the nineteenth-century Brazilian novel would have developed along quite different lines had Almeida not died in a shipwreck in 1861, but there is no evidence that he produced any prose fiction between 1853 and his death.

— DAVID T. HABERLY

ALMONTE, JUAN NEPOMUCENO

Juan Nepomuceno Almonte (*b.* 1803; *d.* 1869), regent of Mexico's Second Empire (1863–1864). The illegitimate child of José María MORELOS Y PAVÓN—a leader of Mexico's independence movement—Almonte was awarded the rank of brigadier general before the age of thirteen by the Congress of Chilpancingo. In 1815 he was part of the commission sent by Morelos to the United States, the first of many diplomatic posts he would hold. After serving as part of a commission to establish the border between Mexico and the United States (1834), Almonte fought against the rebellion in Texas at the battles of the Alamo and San Jacinto, where he was captured. Freed in 1836, Almonte served as minister of war (1839–1841) before returning to the United States as ambassador in 1842.

When the United States admitted Texas as a state, Almonte returned to Mexico to support the war effort. Originally a federalist, he became a conservative and a monarchist. He served as Mexico's minister to London and later to Paris. After the republican forces won the War of the Reform (1858–1861), Almonte openly sought European intervention to establish a monarchy in Mexico. He returned to Mexico with the support of the French army in 1862 and was selected as one of the executive triumvirate of the Council of Notables and later regent. Emperor MAXIMILIAN gave Almonte various honors, including a cabinet post, before naming him as the Mexican Empire's representative to Napoleon III (1866). On the fall of the Second Empire, Almonte remained in Paris, where he died.

– D. F. STEVENS

ALOMÍA ROBLES, DANIEL

Daniel Alomía Robles (*b.* 3 January 1871; *d.* 17 July 1942), Peruvian ethnomusicologist and composer. Born in Huánuco, Alomía Robles was sent as a child to Lima to study solfège with Cruz Panizo and piano with Claudio Rebagliati. From 1892 to 1894 he studied medicine in San Fernando. While doing research on the Campas Indians, he was encouraged by a Franciscan friar to study aboriginal music. He eventually dedicated more than twenty years of his life to the subject. His research took him to remote regions of Ecuador and Bolivia, where he collected and classified folk materials. In 1910 he gave a celebrated lecture on Andean melodies at the University of San Marcos in Lima. Alomía Robles's wife, the pianist Sebastiana Godoy, assisted in the harmonization of native music. Although he became a noted composer, he is best known for his research on Indian music. He died in Lima.

– SUSANA SALGADO

ALONSO, AMADO

Amado Alonso (*b.* 13 September 1896; *d.* 26 May 1952), Argentine writer and literary critic. Born in Lerín, Navarra, Spain, Alonso directed the Institute of Philology at the University of Buenos Aires from 1927 to 1946, a position that allowed him to exercise considerable influence on the introduction of European formalism and stylistics into Argentina, and from there into Latin American literary and linguistic scholarship. In 1938 Alonso, along with Pedro HENRÍQUEZ UREÑA, published *Gramática castellana,* one of the classic struc-

turalist analyses of the Spanish language. The *Gramática,* designed to be used in secondary-school courses, had numerous reprintings in subsequent decades. Alonso authored many important studies on Iberian and Latin American literature, including early studies on Jorge Luis BORGES. His most important text, however, remains *Poesía y estilo de Pablo Neruda* (1940), probably the first full-length monograph on a Latin American poet to be written from the point of view of formalist stylistics, in addition to being one of the earliest studies on the Chilean poet. In 1945, Alonso translated into Spanish Ferdinand de Saussure's *Curso de lingüística general* (1945), one of the founding texts of modern linguistics. Whether writing specifically about poetry or exploring the poetic dimension of prose, Alonso exemplified the importance accorded by the literary criticism of the period to the questions of the specific qualities of literariness.

– DAVID WILLIAM FOSTER

ALONSO, MANUEL A.

Manuel A. Alonso (*b.* 6 October 1822; *d.* 4 November 1899), Puerto Rican essayist, story writer, and poet. Son of a Spanish captain posted in Caguas, Alonso received his early education there. He went on to study medicine in Barcelona, Spain. Returning as a doctor in 1849, he assumed his place in colonial Puerto Rican society as one of the group of moderate liberal reformers that identified an authentic national purpose with the ascendency of the island's progressive white creole elite. As a writer, he was the first to give effective literary expression to its programmatic outlook and its defense of the existence of a distinctly Puerto Rican nationality. While studying in the Catalán metropolis, he joined other Puerto Rican students in compiling, contributing to, publishing, and sending home the *Aquinaldo puertorriqueño* (1843, 1846; Puerto Rican Christmas Carol), the *Album puertorriqueño* (1844; Puerto Rican Album), and *El cancionero de Borinquén* (1846; Puerto Rican Songbook) now generally regarded as the catalytic events promoting a self-consciously Puerto Rican literature.

Alonso synthesized the colonial, ethnic, and interclass drama of a historically evolved local culture.

After 1849, Alonso quickly emerged as the island's signal *costumbrista,* its preeminent writer on local idiosyncrasy, particularly peasant folkways, creole custom, lore, and traditions. Published in 1849, and in an expanded two-volume edition in 1882–1883, Alonso's signature collection of lyric vignettes and ethnographic prose sketches, *El jíbaro,* gave the titular metaphor of the independent rural mestizo peasant symbolic currency as the emblematic representation of the popular ethos and the recalcitrant obstacle to the creole elite's presumptively more enlightened, entrepreneurial notions of national progress. Impressively synthesizing the colonial, ethnic, and interclass drama of a historically evolved local culture during a crucial period of transition, *El jíbaro* established Alonso as the key figure of a nascent insular tradition of short narrative, literary criticism, and the essay of cultural commentary. After later visits to Spain (1858–1861 and 1866–1871), Alonso returned to Puerto Rico, serving in his later years as editor of the liberal reformist periodical *El agente* and as medical director of the Asilo de Beneficencia.

– ROBERTO MÁRQUEZ

ALONSO, MARIANO ROQUE

Mariano Roque Alonso (*b.* 1792?; *d.* 1853), Paraguayan consul (1841–1844) and military figure. Alonso emerged during the hectic months following the September 1840 death of José Gaspar Rodríguez de FRANCIA, Paraguay's first authoritarian dictator and leader of the country since 1814. Francia had left no formal provision for a successor, and when he died, power devolved to the four chiefs of the Asunción barracks, who proved to be ineffectual and corrupt administrators. In January 1841, they were replaced by a triumvirate headed by a sergeant and two former alcaldes of the city. This regime was itself displaced within a month by Alonso, then a junior officer with many years of service but with little real authority or talent. Evidently feeling himself inadequate to the task of governing, he made a fateful decision to appoint as his secretary Carlos Antonio LÓPEZ, a noted attorney from the interior. Alonso needed the latter's help in organizing a national congress that would create and legitimize a new government. When the congress met in March 1841, however, Alonso played the role of subordinate to López, and agreed to join with him in a two-man consular regime authorized by the congress. After the consuls took office, Alonso in effect abdicated his position, preferring to return to the barracks and the company of rustic soldiers like himself. He made sure that his military colleagues refrained from further interference in politics. This show of support brought him many rewards from López, who continued to favor him with a substantial annual pension after the consulate was replaced by a presidential regime in 1844.

In his later years, Alonso lived quietly on his cattle ranch in the interior, where he died in 1853.

– THOMAS L. WHIGHAM

ALONSO, RAÚL

Raúl Alonso (*b.* 24 January 1924; *d.* 31 July 1993), Argentine painter and printmaker. Born in Buenos Aires, the son of the distinguished Spanish artist Juan Carlos Alonso, Raúl was self-taught. In 1958 he traveled to Europe and settled in Paris for a while. He exhibited around the world. He was invited to the Universal Exhibition in Brussels and to the Ibero-American Biennials in Mexico City, São Paulo, Valparaíso, Cali, and Punta del Este. In 1991 he had a show at the Hammer Gallery in New York. He received several awards, including the honor prize at the National Salon (Buenos Aires, 1975). He illustrated several books, among them *The Ten Commandments, Amatoria,* and *Borradores.* Alonso's paintings combine nature and imagination, appealing not only to the mind but also to the emotions of the viewer.

– AMALIA CORTINA ARAVENA

ALSINA, ADOLFO

Adolfo Alsina (*b.* 14 January 1829; *d.* 29 December 1877), Argentine politician. Alsina was born in Buenos Aires, the only son of Valentín ALSINA and Antonia Maza. He received his early education in Buenos Aires and Montevideo, and a law degree from the University of Buenos Aires in 1854. After the battle of Caseros, he wrote articles attacking the commander, Justo José de URQUIZA, and plotted his assassination. As a member of the Liberal Party, to which his father belonged, he helped defend Buenos Aires when it was besieged by Urquiza. He subsequently fought at the battle of Cepeda, was one of the *porteño* (Buenos Aires) deputies denied admission to the congress that met in Paraná, and participated in the battle of Pavón.

In 1862 Alsina was elected deputy to the national Congress. During an internal party dispute over a proposal to federalize the city of Buenos Aires, he and his followers broke with the Liberal Party to form the Autonomista Party. The party, which consisted of important *estancieros,* Federal Party intellectuals, José HERNÁNDEZ, and Leandro ALEM, had little support outside the province of Buenos Aires. In 1866 Alsina became governor of Buenos Aires, with Nicolás AVELLANEDA as his minister of government. Among the accomplishments of his administration was the separation of the office of justice of the peace from that of the military commandant.

In 1867, Alsina was Domingo SARMIENTO's running mate in the latter's successful bid for the presidency. His relations with Sarmiento were never harmonious, but he did support Sarmiento's decision in 1870 to punish Ricardo LÓPEZ JORDÁN (h) for the assassination of Urquiza. He again was a candidate for the presidency in 1874, and in the congressional elections of that year he won in Córdoba and La Rioja but not in Buenos Aires, which his partisans controlled, because Sarmiento sent national troops to supervise the elections. Lacking support, Alsina withdrew his candidacy and endorsed the man Sarmiento had selected as his successor, Avellaneda, and his own supporter, Mariano Acosta, for the vice presidency.

President Avellaneda appointed Alsina his minister of war and the navy. Alsina was responsible for the suppression of the Revolution of 1874, a pro-Bartolomé MITRE movement, and for the campaign that built a new frontier line of forts from Carhué to Laguna del Monte and to Trenque Lauquén. He hoped to minimize Indian resistance to the advance by incorporating some tribes into the national guard, but as a precaution he supplied the national army with revolvers and telegraph lines. In 1877 he furthered the policy of "conciliation" by persuading Mitre to stop his partisans from starting a revolution; he was planning another advance of the frontier line when he died in Buenos Aires.

— JOSEPH T. CRISCENTI

ALSINA, VALENTÍN

Valentín Alsina (*b.* 16 December 1802; *d.* 6 September 1869), Argentine politician. Alsina was born in Buenos Aires, the son of Juan de Alsina and María Pastora Ruano. He studied at the University of Córdoba, where Gregorio Funes was one of his teachers, and received his law degree in Buenos Aires. From 1824 to 1827 he contributed articles to *El Nacional* and *El Mensajero Argentino* and was undersecretary of foreign affairs in the government of Bernardino RIVADAVIA. Alsina supported General Juan LAVALLE's revolution of 1 December 1828, and briefly served in his government. In 1829 he was the director of the public library in Buenos Aires. He was persecuted by Buenos Aires Governor Juan Manuel de ROSAS and was kept a prisoner aboard the lighter *Sarandí* until Colonel Enrique Sinclair, a relative, and Dr. Manuel Vicente MAZA, his father-in-law, arranged for his escape to Colonia in 1835. His wife, Antonia Maza, and their small child, Adolfo, fled from Buenos Aires with the help of Sinclair's friend Ricardo Haines, an Englishman. The family was reunited in Montevideo, where Alsina became a member of the Argentine Commission, which had as its aim the overthrow of Rosas. The commission sent his brother, Juan José Alsina, to represent it; he was later replaced by his relative, Governor Pedro Ferré of Corrientes. Unlike many members of the commission, Valentín Alsina never believed that Lavalle and his Ejército Libertador would overthrow Rosas.

In 1843 Alsina participated in the defense of Montevideo, then besieged by Manuel ORIBE, by enrolling in the Argentine Legion. His function was to contribute anti-Rosas articles to the local newspapers *El Moderador, El Nacional, El Grito Argentino,* and especially to *El Comercio del Plata.* In 1843 he wrote his famous "Notes" to the first edition of Sarmiento's *Civilización i barbarie,* (1845), in which he maintains that terror first appeared in Buenos Aires with Rosas.

In 1852 Alsina was appointed minister of government by Vicente López y Planes, governor of Buenos Aires. As minister he restored to their rightful owners the properties Rosas had confiscated. He represented the extreme wing of the Unitarian Party, opposing national organization and the Acuerdo de San Nicolás because representation in congress would be based on population. Elected governor of Buenos Aires Province 30 October 1852, Alsina made Bartolomé MITRE his minister of the interior, annulled the land grants Rosas had made to the veterans of the Indian campaigns and civil wars, organized an invasion of Entre Ríos, and appointed Hilario Lagos and Cayetano Laprida to the departmental posts of military commandant. When Lagos and Laprida revolted on 1 December 1852, he resigned as governor.

In 1853 Alsina was president of the Court of Justice, and in 1854 he was twice elected senator but did not serve. From 1855 to May 1856 he was minister of government and foreign affairs in the administration of Pastor Obligado. In 1857 he was again elected governor of Buenos Aires Province, approved the return to Buenos Aires of Rivadavia's remains, and evidently became involved in a plot to assassinate the military commander Justo José de URQUIZA. The legislature forced Alsina to resign after the provincial forces were defeated by the confederation armies at the battle of Cepeda. Three days later Buenos Aires and the Argentine Confederation signed the Pact of San José de Flores (11 November 1859), which was mediated by Francisco Solano López, whereby Buenos Aires agreed to join the confederation after a provincial convention examined the Constitution of 1853. Alsina participated in that convention.

In 1862, after the battle of Pavón, he was elected a senator of the national Congress that met in Buenos Aires and refused the presidency of the Supreme Court. That year he was entrusted with the task of writing the provincial rural code that became law in 1865. As the temporary president of the Senate, he proclaimed the election of Bartolomé MITRE and Marcos Paz as president and vice president in 1862, and of Domingo SARMIENTO and of his son Adolfo ALSINA as president and vice president in 1867. He died in Buenos Aires.

– JOSEPH T. CRISCENTI

ALSOGARAY, ALVARO

Alvaro Alsogaray (*b.* 22 June 1913), Argentine economist and political leader. A disciple of Ludwig von Mises and an ardent defender of the social market economy, Alsogaray has been one of Argentina's leading conservatives in the postwar period. He was born in Esperanza, in the province of Santa Fe, and first held public office as undersecretary of commerce and then as minister of industry (1955–1956) during General Pedro ARAMBURU's government. As Arturo FRONDIZI's economics minister (1959–1962), Alsogaray implemented a conservative, market-oriented reform program, unsuccessfully attempting to control inflation by reducing the public payroll and privatizing a number of deficit-ridden state corporations. From 1966 to 1968 he was Argentina's ambassador to the United States. In 1983 Alsogaray founded the Union of the Democratic Center (UCD), a conservative party whose economic program has largely been implemented by the Peronist government of Carlos Saúl MENEM (1989–).

– JAMES P. BRENNAN

ALTAMIRANO, IGNACIO MANUEL

Ignacio Manuel Altamirano (*b.* 13 November 1834; *d.* 13 February 1893), Mexican writer. Born in Tixtla, Guerrero, Altamirano learned Spanish and studied at the Instituto Literario de Toluca, a school for the education of indigenous scholars. Journalist, bureaucrat, statesman, and diplomat, Altamirano supported liberal causes in Mexico during the years of the Reform, the French Intervention, and thereafter. He founded the

---

Altamirano's articles constitute the first serious attempt to produce a systematic history of Mexican literature since Independence.

---

review *El Renacimiento* (The Renaissance), which lasted for one year (1869), in order to advocate and foment a national literary culture. His series of articles, *Revistas literarias de México* (Literary Reviews of Mexico [1868–1883]), constitutes the first serious attempt to produce

a systematic history of Mexican literature since Independence. In his criticism, he viewed the novel as the ideal genre for educating readers and establishing a national literary culture. His narrative production includes a collection of novellas, *Cuentos de invierno* (Winter Tales [1880]); and three novels, *Clemencia* (1869), *La navidad en las montañas* (Christmas in the Mountains [1871]), and *El Zarco* (written between 1886 and 1888, published posthumously in 1901). After years of public service as a teacher in Mexico and as a consul in Spain and France, Altamirano died in San Remo, Italy.

– DANNY J. ANDERSON

ALVARADO, ANTONIO

Antonio Alvarado (*b.* 1938), Panamanian abstract painter. Although he studied under the figurative painter Alberto DUTARY (*b.* 1932), Alvarado's early works showed a keen awareness of international trends such as abstract expressionism. A UNESCO grant in 1969 allowed him to travel to Japan, where he was influenced by oriental art, Zen, and Buddhism.

In his drawings, serigraphs, and bright acrylic paintings, Alvarado experiments with reducing art to its essential forms, and his work ranges from precise, hard-edge paintings like *Homenaje a Varèse* (1972) to such strong gestural compositions as *Buda No. 120* (1981). In the 1970s, he held the position of director of the Department of Visual Arts of Panama's Instituto Nacional de Cultura.

– MONICA E. KUPFER

ALVARADO, LISANDRO

Lisandro Alvarado (*b.* 19 September 1858; *d.* 10 April 1929), Venezuelan ethnologist, linguist, naturalist, and historian. At the age of twenty, Alvarado traveled to Caracas to study medicine at the University of Caracas; where he came in contact with the positivist and evolutionist ideas that were in vogue in Latin America in the latter part of the nineteenth century. The tenets of these schools of thought would serve as a guide to his diverse intellectual activities. Alvarado conducted investigations in the areas of ethnography, linguistics, and history and studied ancient and modern cultures, traveling throughout the country as part of his research. He was proficient in several languages and was one of the first Venezuelans to study the indigenous customs and languages of the country's aboriginal groups. Alvarado was a regular member of the academies of medicine, language, and history. His major works include: *Sobre las guerras civiles del país* (1894) and *Glosario de voces indígenas de Venezuela* (1921).

— INÉS QUINTERO

ALVARADO, SALVADOR

Salvador Alvarado (*b.* 1880; *d.* June 1924), military leader of the Mexican Revolution and social reformer. Alvarado, the son of a printer, was born in northwest Mexico. After opposing the Porfiriato in the anarcho-syndicalist Mexican Liberal Party (Partido Liberal Mexicano—PLM) and participating in the brutally suppressed workers' strike at Cananea in 1906, he transferred his allegiance in 1909 to the more moderate, broader-based movement of Francisco I. MADERO. His organizational and tactical skills elevated him rapidly in the military hierarchy during the revolutionary campaigns against Porfirio DÍAZ and Victoriano HUERTA. In 1914, Madero's successor, the Constitutionalist leader Venustiano CARRANZA, promoted him to division general. Then, following a brief stint as military commandant of the Federal District, he became Carranza's proconsul for the conquest and administration of the state of Yucatán.

Subduing a powerful regional oligarchy with his 7,000-man army in March 1915, Alvarado immediately attempted to make Yucatán a model of what the Mexican Revolution could accomplish, to transform the region into a social laboratory. His three-year governorship (1915–1918) was characterized by an effective blend of populist reform and authoritarian military rule. Buoyed by a swell in henequen revenues generated by World War I, Alvarado established more than a thousand new schools, the majority of them in remote, previously untouched hamlets and hacienda communities. He enforced an earlier, moribund decree "freeing" the debt peons who worked in slavelike conditions on the henequen estates and attempted to redress labor abuses through state-run tribunals. Under Alvarado's aegis, Mexico's first feminist congresses were convened, and special feminist leagues were organized. Alvarado was also responsible for the creation of a small but powerful urban labor movement, based in Mérida, the state's capital, and in Progreso, its principal port. In 1916, seeking to institutionalize his regional movement, Alvarado incorporated the workers and campesinos into a nascent state party, the Socialist Workers' Party (Partido Socialista Obrero). Its name was changed a year later to the Socialist Party of Yucatán (Partido Socialista de Yucatán). Many now regard it as a forerunner of Mexico's present-day corporatist edifice, the Institutional Revolutionary Party (Partido Revolucionario Institucional—PRI).

Carranza removed Alvarado as governor in 1918; although Alvarado harbored presidential aspirations, he never regained the renown he had known as Yucatán's revolutionary caudillo. In 1924, with fellow Sonoran Adolfo DE LA HUERTA and an important segment of the Mexican army, he rebelled against Carranza's successor, Alvaro OBREGÓN SALIDO, and was killed by Obregonistas in El Hormiguero, Chiapas, in June 1924.

— GILBERT M. JOSEPH

ALVARADO XICOTENCATL, LEONOR

Leonor Alvarado Xicotencatl (*b.* 22 March 1524; *d.* 1583), the first prominent *ladina* (child of Spanish and Indian parents) born in Guatemala.

Daughter of the conquistador Pedro de ALVARADO and of Luisa de Xicotencatl, a Tlascalteca Indian princess, doña Leonor was born at Utatlán, the capital of the Quiché, and was brought up by her godparents. Alvarado arranged her marriage to his friend and chief lieutenant, Pedro de Portocarrero, about 1541. She escaped death when a mudslide resulting from a flood and earthquake covered the capital at Almolonga and killed her stepmother, doña Beatríz de la Cueva, in 1541.

After the death of Portocarrero in 1547, doña Leonor married Francisco de la CUEVA, the brother of her stepmother. From this marriage were born the children who were Pedro de Alvarado's descendants in Guatemala. Her second husband died in 1576, and doña Leonor died seven years later, at the age of fifty-nine. Her remains were buried in the Cathedral at Santiago (now Antigua Guatemala), beside those of her father and her stepmother.

— DAVID L. JICKLING

ALVARADO Y MESÍA, PEDRO DE

Pedro de Alvarado y Mesía (*b.* 1485?; *d.* 29 June 1541?), a leader in the Spanish conquests of Mexico, Central America, and Ecuador. Born in Badajoz to a family of the minor nobility, Alvarado came to the Americas around 1510. He was a member of the Juan de GRIJALVA expedition to the Gulf coast of Mexico, and then accompanied Hernán CORTÉS as his chief lieutenant on his conquest of central Mexico (1519–1521). He was in charge of the garrison in Tenochtitlán (Mexico City) during the events that led up to the disastrous Spanish withdrawal from the city (the Noche Triste) and played an outstanding role in the final siege and Spanish victory.

Known to the native peoples as "Tonatiuh" (the Sun), Alvarado was sent south by Cortés in 1523 with

Pedro de Alvarado y Mesía, 1808. Known as the "Guatemala Portrait." (Organization of American States)

an army of 429 Spaniards and some 20,000 Tlaxcalans and other Indian allies. He led the Spanish conquests of Soconusco, Guatemala, and El Salvador, and pushed into Honduras, where he met conquistador groups coming from Nicaragua. His two letters of *relación* to Hernán Cortés are the only extant and immediate eyewitness accounts of the campaign. In all these events he showed his customary bravery, impetuousness, and cruelty.

After the Conquest he ruthlessly suppressed a major Cakchiquel revolt, and founded the first two Spanish capitals, Almolonga and Ciudad Vieja. (The latter was destroyed in 1541 by an avalanche of water and mud that killed his second wife shortly after he himself had died.) He seized the best *encomiendas* and slave *cuadrillas* for himself, his five brothers, and other relatives and associates. Many of his Indian slaves were put to work on gold panning or shipbuilding. At one time he allegedly owned 1,500 branded native slaves who worked in the gold fields.

Alvarado dominated much of Central America for about seventeen years (1524–1541). His life after he became governor of Guatemala was marked by ambition and restlessness. His frequent absences and predatory return visits were disruptive. Each new expedition deprived the region of Spaniards, native auxiliaries, and supplies.

Leaving his brother Jorge in charge, Alvarado returned to Spain via Mexico in 1526–1527 to defend himself against charges of wrongdoing. While there, he married Francisca de la Cueva, a member of the high nobility, won his case, and was named governor and captain-general of Guatemala. His new wife died in Veracruz (1528) during the return journey to Guatemala.

Alvarado immediately began to plan an expedition to the South Seas but was diverted from it by news of the wealth won in Peru by Francisco PIZARRO and Diego de ALMAGRO. Against royal orders, he set off for Quito in 1534, again leaving Jorge as lieutenant governor. This time he took some 500 Spaniards and 2,000 native auxiliaries with him. Penetrating inland, Alvarado met Almagro. Potential conflict turned to negotiations when Alvarado realized that his men were tired, and that some of them were being induced to change sides. He finally agreed to turn over most of his men, ships, and equipment in return for 100,000 gold pesos. After his return to Guatemala (1535) he complained to the crown about Almagro's conduct, and his anger was increased by the discovery that some of the payment he had received consisted of adulterated and even falsified coinage.

Again facing accusations, this time from Mexico, Alvarado boldly set off from the coast of Honduras to plead his case in Spain (1536). There, on 22 October 1538, Charles V absolved him of all blame, and reappointed him as governor of Guatemala for seven more years. Charles also obtained a papal dispensation so that Alvarado could marry Beatríz de la CUEVA, his deceased wife's sister.

Alvarado had been absent for over three years when he returned to Santiago de Guatemala in 1539. On his way from the coast he took over the governorship of Honduras from Francisco de Montejo and moved its main city inland to Gracias a Dios. In Guatemala he vigorously set about finding places for the large entourage that he and his new wife had brought from Spain. He also began to build ships and to collect men and supplies for yet another voyage of discovery to the Spice Islands.

He sailed with the new expedition in 1540, leaving Francisco de la CUEVA in charge. This time he took 850 Spaniards and many Indians with him. The fleet stopped for supplies at a port in Jalisco, where Alvarado met Viceroy Antonio de MENDOZA, made a series of agreements with him, and joined in the suppression of a native revolt in Nueva Galicia. In late June 1541, during a skirmish, he was crushed to death by a falling horse.

— MURDO J. MACLEOD

ÁLVAREZ, JUAN

Juan Álvarez (*b.* 27 January 1790; *d.* 21 August 1867), president of Mexico (1855–1856). The orphaned son of a landowner in Santa María de la Concepción Atoyac in coastal Guerrero State, Álvarez joined the insurgent army of José María MORELOS Y PAVÓN in 1810. After independence Álvarez commanded militia forces in Guerrero and participated in several federalist revolts of the 1820s and 1830s. He is best known for his strong relationship with Guerrero's peasantry. During widespread peasant revolts in the 1840s he mediated land claims and reduced taxes. He simultaneously recruited the peasant rebels for federalist movements and the war against the United States. His efforts and political connections led to the creation in 1849 of the state of Guerrero, of which he was the first governor. In 1854–1855 Álvarez led the Revolution of Ayutla against the conservative government of Antonio López de SANTA ANNA. This movement began the period of the Reform. Álvarez retired to Guerrero after a brief stint as president from October 1855 to September 1856. He remained politically active and supported the Liberal governments of Benito JUÁREZ against both the Conservatives and Maximilian's empire. He died at his hacienda on the Guerrero coast.

Álvarez was most important as a champion of the incorporation of Mexico's peasant masses into the polity of the young nation-state. Advocating universal male suffrage and municipal autonomy, he utilized the fundamental similarities between the peasant tradition of annual elections for village office and the basic tenets of popular sovereignty common to nineteenth-century political ideologies in Mexico and elsewhere. In promoting this model of state formation, Álvarez differed from both conservatives and many prominent liberals.

— PETER GUARDINO

ÁLVAREZ, LUIS HÉCTOR

Luis Héctor Álvarez (*b.* 25 October 1919), Mexican politician and opposition party leader. A native of Ciudad Camargo, Chihuahua, Álvarez received part of his education in El Paso, Texas. A businessman, he was first employed in the textile industry, after which he became director of the Río Bravo Industrial Company (1957). Selected by the National Action Party (PAN) as its presidential candidate, he opposed Adolfo LÓPEZ MATEOS in the 1958 presidential election. Although he remained out of the national political limelight for many years, he won election as mayor of Chihuahua in 1983. Upon completion of his term, he became president of the PAN in 1986. Under his leadership PAN ran its most successful presidential campaign, with Manuel CLOUTHIER as its presidential candidate, in 1988.

— RODERIC AI CAMP

ÁLVAREZ, MANUEL

Manuel Álvarez (*b.* 1794; *d.* 5 July 1856), fur trapper, merchant, and government official in New Mexico.

The life of Álvarez, a native of Abelgas, Spain, exemplifies the tremendous opportunities that existed in New Mexico during the first half of the nineteenth century for an enterprising and well-connected immigrant.

In 1818 Álvarez emigrated to Mexico; in 1823 he moved to Cuba after Mexican independence unleashed anti-Spanish sentiment. There he obtained a U.S. passport and sailed to New York, planning to work his way back to Mexico. By 1824, Álvarez had joined a trading group in Saint Louis and had reached New Mexico, where he became friends with Charles Bent. There he opened a store to sell goods imported from Missouri.

The contacts and commercial ties that Álvarez built during the 1820s enabled him to take up fur trapping in 1829, when Mexican authorities expelled all Spanish residents from the country. By 1831, Álvarez worked for the American Fur Company as the leader of a team of forty fur trappers hunting in an area that is now part of Yellowstone National Park. Álvarez managed his store in Santa Fe from a distance until 1834, when he returned there, his Spanish origin no longer a problem.

Álvarez exemplifies the tremendous opportunities that existed in New Mexico during the nineteenth century for an enterprising and well-connected immigrant.

While claiming Mexican citizenship, Álvarez used his U.S. passport to gain an appointment as U.S. consul for Mexico, based in Santa Fe. Forced loans that American merchants made to the New Mexican officials during the 1837 revolt in Taos and Río Arriba, and losses to Americans resulting from the Texan expedition against Santa Fe in 1841, prompted American claims for reimbursement. Even though he never received complete confirmation of his post, Álvarez represented these petitions to the New Mexican governor and Mexican officials. His success in this role came from his relationship with Governor Manuel ARMIJO, based in part on the information that Álvarez and Bent provided about Apache and Texan movements of concern to New Mexico.

Upon the U.S. declaration of war against Mexico in 1846, the Americans sent "spies" to speak to Álvarez. He appears to have provided reports about affairs in New Mexico and advice on how to proceed with its occupation. Álvarez met with Governor Armijo and probably contributed to his decision not to oppose Colonel Stephen Watts Kearny and his force when it arrived to occupy Santa Fe. Although his friend Charles Bent served as interim governor of New Mexico until his murder during the 1847 revolt against the Americans, Álvarez received no post in the administration.

In the wake of the military government imposed on New Mexico after the revolt of 1847, Álvarez began to use his political skills in defense of the Spanish-Mexican population of the territory. He came to lead a political party, arguing against the propensity of military rule to ignore the civil rights of the population and advocating immediate statehood for New Mexico in order to bring back civilian rule. After a brief stint as editor of one of the early New Mexican newspapers in order to gain support for the statehood faction, Álvarez won the post of lieutenant governor alongside Congressman William Messervy in the election of 1850. Because Messervy had to spend most of his time in Washington, D.C., lobbying for statehood, running the state fell to Álvarez. Opposition from the army and the territorial party hampered the new government's ability to function. Soon after, the Compromise of 1850, admitting California to the Union as a free state and organizing New Mexico and Arizona into a single territory, made the position of the Statehood faction untenable.

Álvarez was never again involved as prominently in the affairs of the territory, and withdrew to his commercial ventures during the last years of his life. His ambition, and his service as an advocate for various American and Spanish-Mexican constituencies, wove him into the fabric of the critical events of New Mexican history bridging the Mexican and American periods. He died in Santa Fe.

– ROSS H. FRANK

ÁLVAREZ ARMELLINO, GREGORIO CONRADO

Gregorio Conrado Álvarez Armellino (*b.* 26 November 1925), Uruguayan military leader and president (1981–1985). Álvarez played an important role from 1973 to 1985, when the armed forces governed the country. The press, including that of the Left, had already popularized the figure of "Goyo" Álvarez, a commanding officer with a nationalist orientation and sympathies toward

the leftist militarism of Peruvian General Juan VELASCO ALVARADO. Álvarez was appointed president by the military regime in 1981. He became one of the elements most opposed to the move toward democracy in Uruguay. After the election of Julio María SANGUINETTI to the presidency, the political parties refused to accept the transfer of power directly from General Álvarez. The president of the Supreme Court of Justice had to intervene as a transitional leader in order for the restoration of democracy to be completed.

– JOSÉ DE TORRES WILSON

ÁLVAREZ BRAVO, LOLA

Lola Álvarez Bravo (*b.* 3 April 1907; *d.* 31 July 1993), Mexican photographer. A pioneering modernist photographer, Álvarez Bravo's career spanned six decades. Born in Lagos de Moreno, Jalisco, she studied photography in the 1920s under the tutelage of Manuel ÁLVAREZ BRAVO, to whom she was married from 1925 to 1949. While some of her early imagery bears relation to his, by the 1930s she had developed a distinct pictorial language that evinces her deep interest in the cinema as well as her empathy for the Mexican people. Her oeuvre includes photographs documenting everyday urban and rural life; these compositions often emphasize the ironic, humorous, or poetic aspects of mundane events. Other bodies of work include landscapes, still lifes, portraits of Mexican artists and intellectuals, and innovative photomontages. Álvarez Bravo was active as a teacher, documentary photographer for governmental agencies, exhibition curator, and director of the prestigious Galería de Arte Contemporáneo in Mexico City (1951–1958), which mounted important exhibitions featuring the artists of the Mexican School. She died in Mexico City.

– ELIZABETH FERRER

ÁLVAREZ BRAVO, MANUEL

Manuel Álvarez Bravo (*b.* 4 February 1912), Mexican photographer. Self-taught in the art of photography, Álvarez has practiced the profession since 1923. In the 1930s, he began to capture on film the works of the Mexican muralists and other scenes of Mexican cultural life. Soon after his first exhibition, in 1932, his photographs were discovered by the international art community. Álvarez Bravo has exhibited his work in museums and galleries all over the world. He was awarded the National Prize for Art in 1975, and has been the recipient of numerous other national and international awards for photography. He is a member of the Mexican academy of arts.

Álvarez Bravo uses black and white film; his themes are creativity and beauty, and he is known for his portraits of famous as well as common people, and urban and rural scenes of a changing Mexico. He is one of the most renowned Latin American photographers.

— DAVID MACIEL

ÁLVAREZ DE PINEDA, ALONSO

Alonso Álvarez de Pineda (*d.* 1520), sailor. Little is known about Álvarez de Pineda, except that he was captain-general of the first European expedition to navigate systematically the entire coastline of the Gulf of Mexico from the Florida Keys to the Yucatán Peninsula. The voyage resulted in a hand-drawn map showing the peninsula of Florida as part of the mainland, not an island, as had been believed. The voyage also located the mouth of the Mississippi River (Río del Espíritu Santo), with its great discharge of fresh water.

The Alvarez de Pineda voyage resulted in a

hand-drawn map showing the peninsula of Florida

as part of the mainland, not an island,

as had been believed.

Made in 1519, the voyage was sponsored by the governor of Jamaica, Francisco de GARAY, who sought knowledge of the lands between those Juan Ponce de León had reached in 1513 (west of the Florida Peninsula) and the region west of Cuba (Yucatán and Central America). He also hoped to find a passage to the "South Sea" (the Pacific Ocean), discovered by Vasco Núñez de Balboa.

— JERALD T. MILANICH

ÁLVAREZ GARDEAZÁBAL, GUSTAVO

Gustavo Álvarez Gardeazábal (*b.* 31 October 1945), Colombian writer. A native of Tuluá, Valle, he studied chemical engineering at Medellín's Universidad Pontificia. About 1963 he published parts of his first novel, *Piedra pintada* (1965), and was expelled from the university. Álvarez returned to Valle and continued to write fiction. The Violencia in Valle remained a major theme of his work, but after 1977 his novels reflected other currents as well, including opposition to the Gran Cauca elite. Álvarez taught at the Universidad del Valle (Cali) and was elected in 1978 to the municipal councils of Cali and of Tuluá. Recognized as Valle's major writer,

he was a Guggenheim fellow in 1984–1985 and has won numerous other awards. His novels include *La tara del papa* (1971); *Cóndores no entierran todos los días* (1972); *Dabeiba* (1973); *El bazar de los idiotas* (1974); *El titiritero* (1977); *Los míos* (1981); and *Los sordos ya no hablan* (1991).

— J. LEÓN HELGUERA

ALVAREZ MARTÍNEZ, GUSTAVO

Gustavo Alvarez Martínez (*b.* 12 December 1937; *d.* 26 January 1989), Honduran general, chief of the armed forces. When Honduras resumed a civilian government in January 1982 with the election of Roberto Suazo Córdova to the presidency, the military coalesced under the leadership of Colonel Alvarez Martínez, appointed by the national assembly as commander in chief of the armed forces. Leading the armed forces as a "third party" of hard-liners in the Honduran political spectrum, Alvarez Martínez centralized and modernized the command structure, a feat that earned him a promotion from colonel to brigadier general. Then, with President Suazo Córdova, he forged a united front that stressed military subordination to the constitution as well as an alliance between the armed forces and the Liberal Party of Honduras. However, fellow officers, annoyed by his "high-handedness," ousted Alvarez Martínez and split decisively with Suazo in 1984. Five years later, the general was assassinated in Tegucigalpa by six men, an act for which the Popular Liberation Front claimed responsibility.

— JEFFREY D. SAMUELS

ALVEAR, CARLOS MARÍA DE

Carlos María de Alvear (*b.* 25 October 1789; *d.* 2 November 1852), Argentine soldier and politician. Alvear, born in Misiones, was the son of a Spanish naval officer and a creole mother. After service in the Peninsular War he returned to Buenos Aires in 1812 with José de SAN MARTÍN and other patriots to play a leading role in the military and political organization of independence. As president of the Assembly of the Year XIII (1813), he influenced its policy in the direction of liberal reform. The capture of Montevideo from the Spanish in 1814 strengthened Alvear's military base, and he was appointed supreme director of the United Provinces of the Río de la Plata to restore stability to the revolutionary government. His tendency toward dictatorship and centralism caused his overthrow and exile after less than four months in office (April 1815).

Alvear subsequently changed political direction and joined forces with the Littoral caudillos in an attempt to overthrow the Buenos Aires government and establish a federal system. But the caudillos' success at Cepeda (1820) failed to secure him the governorship he desired. He was recalled to office by Bernardino RIVADAVIA and, while minister of war, fought a successful military campaign against Brazil at Ituazingó early in 1827. He retired to private life until Juan Manuel de ROSAS appointed him minister to the United States in 1838. He died in New York.

– JOHN LYNCH

ALVEAR, MARCELO TORCUATO DE

Marcelo Torcuato de Alvear (b. 4 October 1868; d. 23 March 1942), Argentine political leader and president (1922–1928). Born into a prominent landed Buenos Aires family, Alvear became involved in the political reform activities of Leandro ALEM and the Radical Civic Union (UCR) as a law student at the University of Buenos Aires. Alvear supported the UCR's 1893 uprising, but in the wake of its failure and the UCR's declining fortunes, he undertook a self-imposed exile in Europe and was not present at the time of the Radicals' 1905 rebellion. Despite this, Alvear maintained close contacts with Hipólito YRIGOYEN and other prominent Radicals and was elected to Congress in 1912.

As Yrigoyen's ambassador to France (1916–1920), Alvear had his first serious differences with the Radical leader, specifically in his opposition to Argentina's neutrality in World War I. Alarmed by labor protests and the oligarchy's increasing hostility to his government, Yrigoyen chose Alvear as his successor, seeing his aristocratic credentials as an asset and his lack of a solid base within the party as leaving him open to manipulation. As president, Alvear tried to solve the problem of the national debt, a legacy, in large part, of Yrigoyen's patronage practices.

During Alvear's presidency, Yrigoyen's rivals within the UCR organized a separate party, the Antipersonalist Radical Civic Union, though Alvear himself was not a promoter of the *antipersonalista* movement. After the 1930 coup, he was forced into exile in Brazil but returned to assume control of the party, supporting its policy of electoral abstention until 1935 and then serving as the leader of the Radicals' loyal opposition to the nondemocratic governments of the period, losing as the 1937 Radicals' presidential candidate in an election characterized by widespread fraud.

– JAMES P. BRENNAN

ALVES, FRANCISCO

Francisco Alves (Francisco de Morais Alves; b. 19 August 1889; d. 27 September 1952), Brazilian singer and songwriter. Alves was born in Rio de Janeiro and raised in the Saúde district of São Paulo. He began his musical career in 1918 as a singer in the João de Deus-Martins Chaves Circus. The following year, Alves made his first recording with an interpretation of "Pé de anjo" (Angel's Foot) and "Fala, meu louro" (Speak, My Parrot), both by SINHÔ. He continued singing and recording while driving a taxi and occasionally performing in the circus or musical theater. In 1927 Alves began recording at the Odeon, where he took the stage name Chico Viola. Subsequently, he became a great success performing in Carnival celebrations, with the sambas "A Malandragem" (Gypsy Life) in 1928, "Amor de malandro" (A Scoundrel's Love) in 1930, "Se você jurar" (If You Promise) in 1931, and "Sofrer é da vida" (Life Is about Suffering) in 1932. At the Odeon, Alves made the first electronically produced record in Brazil with his interpretation of Duque's "Albertina" and "Passarinho do má" (Bad Little Bird) in 1927. In 1952 Alves was killed in an automobile accident; his funeral was attended by thousands. Known as the *rei da voz* (king of voice), Alves recorded the most 78 rpm LPs of any Brazilian singer: almost 500 records.

– LISA MARIC

ÁLZAGA, MARTÍN DE

Martín de Álzaga (b. 1757; d. 11 July 1812), Argentine merchant and political figure. A Basque of humble origins, Álzaga probably arrived in Buenos Aires in 1769. After serving a ten-year clerkship with the prominent merchant Gaspar de Santa Coloma, Álzaga launched his own mercantile career in 1780, becoming a successful merchant, a leading figure in the local *cabildo* (town council), and a spokesman for those merchants who worked to preserve the Spanish monopoly trade. Dismayed by the liberal trade policies enacted by Viceroy Santiago de LINIERS Y BREMOND, and convinced that Liniers was an agent of the hated French, Álzaga and his followers attempted a royalist coup d'état on 1 January 1809, which was defeated by an increasingly radicalized militia led by Cornelio de SAAVEDRA.

After independence in 1810, Álzaga continued to represent the concerns of Spanish loyalists. In July 1812 he again led a coup against a creole government that he viewed as inimical to the interests of Spain. No more successful than three years earlier, Álzaga and his followers were arrested by the government, now under the leadership of Bernardino RIVADAVIA, and were executed.

– SUSAN M. SOCOLOW

ALZATE Y RAMÍREZ, JOSÉ ANTONIO DE

José Antonio de Alzate y Ramírez (b. 21 November 1737; d. 2 February 1799), prominent figure in the

Mexican Enlightenment. Born in Ozumba (modern state of Mexico), Alzate studied at the Colegio de San Ildefonso, where he received a bachelor's degree in theology in 1756, the same year he took holy orders. From an early age, Alzate was also deeply drawn to secular studies, including mathematics, physics, astronomy, and the natural sciences; his wide-ranging interests earned him the sobriquet the "Pliny of Mexico." Alzate carried out his own research, such as conducting astronomical observations to determine the latitude of Mexico City. However, he made his greatest scientific contribution as an author and editor, promoting new scientific knowledge and the worldview of the Enlightenment through a series of publications, culminating in the *Gazeta de literatura de México* (1788–1795). Though sometimes marred by polemics, this journal informed readers of the latest scientific advances in both Europe—Alzate had become a member of the Royal Academy of Sciences in Paris in 1771—and the Americas. Alzate translated foreign materials and himself contributed numerous articles in which he described Mexico's rich natural and human resources and pointed out the practical benefits of new scientific methods for Mexican economic development.

— R. DOUGLAS COPE

AMADO, JORGE

Jorge Amado (*b.* 10 August 1912), perhaps the most widely known and most popular of all Brazilian novelists. A major figure of the generation that developed the social "novel of the Northeast" in the 1930s, Amado has been writing for six decades, completing more than twenty novels. His work has been translated into at least thirty languages and has inspired many films, television series, and even popular songs. A recipient of numerous international awards, Amado was elected to the Brazilian Academy of Letters in 1961.

From the 1930s until the 1950s Amado was both a political activist and a writer. He was a member of the Aliança Nacional Libertadora (1935) and the Brazilian Communist Party, of which he was an elected federal congressman during its brief period of legality (1945–1947). Because of his political activities, he spent several periods in exile. The trilogy *Os subterrâneos da liberdade* (1954) re-creates, in novelistic form, the political struggles against Getúlio VARGAS's authoritarian Estado Novo in the 1930s and 1940s.

Amado's literary production ranges from novels marked by social protest and denunciation, especially during his "proletarian" phase of the 1930s—for example, *Cacau* (1933), *Suor* (1934; *Slums*, 1938), *Jubiabá* (1934; *Jubiabá*, 1984)—to those notable for the colorful, humorous, and often picaresque chronicles of

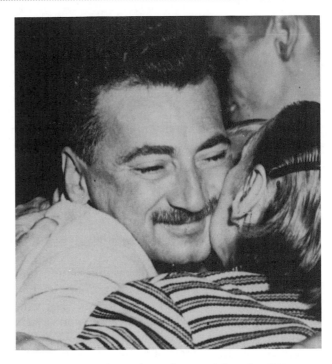

Jorge Amado greets his mother on his arrival from the USSR in 1952. (Iconographia)

the political customs and sexual mores of Brazilian society; these latter often have memorable female protagonists, for example, *Dona Flor e seus dois maridos* (1966; *Dona Flor and Her Two Husbands,* 1969), *Tereza Batista, cansada de guerra* (1972; *Tereza Batista, Home From the Wars,* 1975), and *Tieta do Agreste, pastora de cabras* (1977; *Tieta the Goat Girl,* 1979). Many critics have pointed to *Gabriela, cravo e canela* (1958; *Gabriela, Clove and Cinnamon,* 1962) as the dividing line between Amado's politically engaged narratives and his more exuberant, picturesque, populist tales that exalt the freedom to live and love outside the confines of bourgeois morality. The short *A morte e a morte de Quincas Berro d'Água* (1959) ingeniously and satirically contrasts bourgeois and "popular" culture and values.

Amado's novels and his occasional short narratives typically deal with different aspects of his home state, focusing primarily on the city of Salvador or the cacao region of southern Bahia. Novels such as *Terras do sem-fim* (1943; *The Violent Land, 1945*), *São Jorge dos Ilhéus* (1944), and *Tocaia Grande: A face obscura* (1984) recreate struggles for control of rich cacao lands, combining political intrigue and intertwined love affairs.

Those works set in Salvador often focus on the life and culture of the city's predominantly black lower classes, frequently portrayed as living in a sort of harmonious primitive communism (*Capitães de areia,* 1937) and spiritually sustained by the values of the Afro-Brazilian religion Candomblé. Amado's praise of miscegenation and Afro-Brazilian culture reaches its high point in *Tenda dos milagres* (1969; *Tent of Miracles,* 1971).

Amado's idealization of the lower classes has drawn harsh criticism from those who see him as exploiting, rather than celebrating, their culture. But his defenders have argued that his insistent focus on the poor, even if vitiated by the use of "exotic local color," has made him an eloquent spokesman for the downtrodden and the oppressed in Brazilian society.

— RANDAL JOHNSON

AMADOR, MANUEL E.

Manuel E. Amador (*b.* 25 March 1869; *d.* 1952), one of Panama's first modern artists, creator of the national flag (1903). Amador occupied the public posts of minister of finance (1903–1904) and consul in Hamburg, Germany (1904–1908) and in New York City, where he lived from 1908 to 1925. Later, he worked as an auditor in Panama's Contraloría General (1926–1940).

Amador produced most of his oeuvre between 1910 and 1914, and after 1940. His style of vigorous drawing, gestural brush strokes, and somber colors reflected the lessons of German expressionism and the American artist Robert Henri (1865–1929). He painted landscapes and still lifes, but his main subject was the human figure, as exemplified by *Cabeza de Estudio* (1910) and *Rabbi* (1948). The University of Panama holds an important collection of his drawings, watercolors, and prints.

— MONICA E. KUPFER

AMADOR GUERRERO, MANUEL

Manuel Amador Guerrero (*b.* 30 June 1833; *d.* 2 May 1909), physician and politician, first president of Panama (1904–1908). Born in Turbaco, Colombia, Amador Guerrero was a member of a distinguished Colombian family. In 1855 he began studying medicine and became a successful physician. Beginning his political career as a Conservative, he was named president of the department of Panama in 1867, but a revolution prevented him from assuming the post. After a year in exile, he returned to become chief physician of the Panama Railroad. In 1903 he traveled to the United States to secure support for the independence movement. (French engineer Philippe Jean Bunau-Varilla arranged for financial and military support for the cause in return for an appointment as ambassador to the United States.) The price Amador paid for support was the unfavorable Hay–Bunau-Varilla Treaty of 1903, which dominated U.S.-Panamanian relations for years to come. Amador became the first president of the independent republic of Panama in 1904 and immediately embarked on a vigorous public-works program. His term ended a year before his death.

— SARA FLEMING

AMAR Y BORBÓN, ANTONIO

Antonio Amar y Borbón (*b.* March 1742; *d.* 26 April 1826), viceroy of New Granada (1803–1810). Amar y Borbón had a distinguished career in Spanish military service before becoming viceroy of New Granada in 1803. A conscientious ruler, he was generally well liked during the first part of his administration. After 1808, however, he faced creole demands for the establishment of American juntas to assume rule during the captivity in France of King Ferdinand VII. When such a junta was created in Quito (1809), he was unable to suppress it, in part because he had to deal with the same demands in Bogotá. He first sought to head off the junta movement there, while the viceroy of Peru saw to Quito. But as conditions in Spain deteriorated further with further French advances, a junta was formed in Bogotá on 20 July 1810. Largely as a figurehead, the viceroy was made a member and then deposed five days later. Expelled from the colony, he returned to Spain and remained there until his death.

— DAVID BUSHNELL

AMARAL, ANTÔNIO JOSÉ AZEVEDO DO

Antônio José Azevedo do Amaral (*b.* 1881), Brazilian journalist. Born in Rio de Janeiro, Amaral earned a degree from Rio's Faculdade de Medicina in 1903, but he soon established himself in Carioca journalism, writing for *Jornal do Commércio, A Notícia,* and *Correio da Manhã.* Expelled from England for his pro-German reporting in 1916, he returned to Brazil. After becoming the editor of the *Correio da Manhã,* he went on to edit *O País* and founded *Rio-Jornal* (1918) with João do RIO and *O Dia* (1921) with Virgílio de Melo Franco. A translator of the corporativist Mihail Manoilesco, Amaral is most noted for the rightist nationalism of his own essays, which made him an influential spokesman for the nationalist authoritarianism and statist industrialization of the Estado Nôvo era.

— JEFFREY D. NEEDELL

AMARAL, TARSILA DO

Tarsila do Amaral (*b.* 1 September 1886; *d.* 17 January 1973), Paulista artist and salon leader whose paintings, sculpture, drawings, engravings, and illustrations helped to define, inspire, and stimulate the Brazilian modernist movement, especially the *Pau Brasil* (Brazilwood) and *Antropófagia* (Cannibals) avant-garde submovements. Her works are known for their cubist forms, Brazilian colors and themes. *A negra, A caipirinha, Abaporu, Floresta, Antropófagia,* and other works were shown at galleries and museums in Paris, London, Argentina, Chile, and Brazil from 1922 until 1970. Amaral also wrote poems and articles and illustrated books and periodicals. Other writers and composers dedicated works to her, and she was the subject of a film, books, articles, and interviews.

Amaral grew up on the family *fazenda* and attended *colégios* in Santana, São Paulo, and Barcelona. After her 1906 marriage to André Teixeira Pinto, she settled in São Paulo, where she studied sculpture with Zadig and Mantovani, and design and painting with Pedro Alexandrino and Georg Fischer Elpons. In Paris in the early 1920s Amaral attended the Académie Julian and studied at the studios of Émile Renard, Pedro Alexandrino, André Lhote, Albert Gleizes, and Fernand Léger.

She joined the "Grupo dos Cinco" (with Anita MAL-FATTI, Mário de ANDRADE, Oswaldo de ANDRADE, and Menotti del Picchia) in 1922. With other Brazilians, including Lucília Guimarães Villa-Lobos, Heitor VILLA-LOBOS, Victor Brecheret, and Emiliano DI CALVAL-CANTI, Amaral traveled annually between Europe and Brazil until 1928. In 1930 she briefly became diretora-conservadora of the Pinacoteca do Estado (State Painting Museum) in São Paulo. In 1931 she exhibited at the Moscow Museum of Modern Western Art, which bought one of her works (*O pescador*). Recognized by retrospective exhibits in Rio (1933, 1969), São Paulo (1950–1951, 1969), and Belo Horizonte (1970), Amaral's work is widely reflected in the literature on Latin American art and culture.

— MARY LUCIANA LOMBARDI

AMAT Y JUNIENT, MANUEL DE

Manuel de Amat y Junient (*b.* 1704; *d.* 1782), viceroy of Peru (1761–1776). Born in Varacisas into a noble Catalan family, Amat pursued a military career in Europe and North Africa until becoming captain-general of Chile in 1755. In Santiago he promoted higher education and public order, but his efforts to subdue the Araucanian Indians were unsuccessful.

As viceroy of Peru, Amat oversaw with ruthless efficiency the expulsion of the Jesuits in 1767, and, superficially at least, undertook a major overhaul of defenses, fortifying ports and organizing militia companies throughout the provinces. Although public revenues expanded considerably in this period, Amat's vice-regency was pervaded by corruption, according to his many crit-

ics, including Antonio de ULLOA (1716–1795), who served under him as governor of Huancavelica, in south-central Peru. Following his return to Barcelona in 1777, the aged bachelor married a young Catalán, leaving for both her and posterity the splendid Palacio de la Virreina, now a museum.

— JOHN R. FISHER

AMBROGI, ARTURO

Arturo Ambrogi (*b.* 19 October 1875; *d.* 8 November 1936), Salvadoran writer. Born in San Salvador, the son of an Italian-born Salvadoran army general, Ambrogi edited several literary reviews in San Salvador in the 1890s before traveling widely in South America, where he was much influenced by intellectuals in Chile and Uruguay, particularly by Rubén DARÍO in Buenos Aires. He became one of the leading Salvadoran modernist and impressionist writers of the early twentieth century, especially with his lyrical *Manchas, máscaras y sensaciones* (1901) and *Sensaciones crepusculares* (1904), *El libro del trópico* (1907), *El tiempo que pasa* (1913), and *Sensaciones del Japón y de la China* (1915). His frequent travels throughout the world are strongly reflected in his work, which also contains much folklore.

— RALPH LEE WOODWARD, JR.

AMEGHINO, FLORENTINO

Florentino Ameghino (*b.* 18 September 1854; *d.* 6 August 1911), Argentine geologist and paleontologist. The son of Italian immigrants, Ameghino was born at Luján

---

Ameghino was an avid collector of bones and fossils, and he continued this avocation while working as a schoolteacher and storekeeper.

---

in Buenos Aires Province. As a boy he was an avid collector of bones and fossils, and he continued this avocation while working as a schoolteacher and storekeeper. He never received formal scientific training, but his reputation as a man of learning spread, especially after he traveled to Paris in 1878 with part of his collection. He ultimately published almost two hundred articles and monographs, corresponded with foreign specialists, and served as museum director in La Plata and Buenos Aires. Ameghino won greatest notoriety for his hypothesis that humankind originated in and spread from South America. This was not generally accepted, yet he is recognized as a tireless investigator and a pioneer of Argentine science.

— DAVID BUSHNELL

AMÉLIA, EMPRESS

Empress Amélia (Amélia Augusta de Leuchtenberg; *b.* July 1812; *d.* January 1873), empress consort of Brazil (1829–1831). Milan-born daughter of Eugène de Beauharnais, Napoleon's stepson, and the Bavarian duchess of Leuchtenberg, Amélia became the second wife of Emperor PEDRO I of Brazil in 1829. A young woman of rare beauty and sensitivity, Amélia appeared in Rio de Janeiro at a critical time for the Brazilian monarchy—a time of recrimination over the loss of Uruguay, governmental deadlock, financial crisis, nativist ferment, and growing public dissatisfaction with the emperor.

Amélia's arrival in Rio was predicated on the banishment of Pedro's mistress, the marchioness of Santos, which cleared the way for the emperor's reconciliation with José Bonifácio de ANDRADA E SILVA, a bitter foe of the marchioness. Empress Amélia joined Andrade in advising Pedro to appoint a new cabinet headed by the marquis of Barbacena, who had been her escort from Bavaria to Brazil. The Barbacena ministry smoothed the emperor's relations with parliament and probably prolonged his reign. Pedro's dismissal of Barbacena a year later set off the chain of events that led to the abdication and exile of Pedro and Amélia in April 1831.

From Brazil they went to Paris, where Amélia bore the former emperor a daughter, Maria Amélia, and served as guardian of his eldest daughter, Maria da Glória, when Pedro left for Portugal to secure the Portuguese throne for Maria da Glória. Amélia rejoined Pedro in Lisbon in September 1833, a year before his death. She devoted most of the rest of her life to charity work in Portugal.

— NEILL MACAULAY

AMENÁBAR, JUAN

Juan Amenábar (*b.* 22 June 1922), Chilean composer. Born in Santiago, Amenábar was introduced to music by his father, a cellist and member of the Bach Society. At age thirteen he entered the Catholic Conservatory, where he studied harmony with Lucila Césped and choral techniques with Luis Vilches. In 1940 he enrolled at the University of Chile to study civil engineering. He attended the composition classes of Jorge Urrutia Blondel from 1948 to 1952 at the National Conservatory of Santiago. Amenábar joined the National Society of Composers (1953) and while chief of the music pro-

grams at Radio Chilena (1953–1956) he promoted contemporary Chilean composers and started to experiment with electronic music. From 1954 to 1957 he organized the concerts of the music department at the Catholic University in Santiago, where he founded the experimental sound workshop. His *Los peces* (1957), a study on the Fibonacci series, was the first tape composition made in Latin America. In 1958 he took electronic music courses given by Werner Meyer-Eppler at the University of Bonn. Upon his return to Chile, he worked with José Vicente ASUAR in the creation of an electronic music studio at the University of Chile.

Amenábar has taught composition and has served as president of the National Association of Composers. In addition to electronic music, he has written religious choral music, incidental music for theater and films, chamber music, and piano and organ pieces. He has also written and published musicological essays about new musical techniques, music for movies, folk music, etc.

— SUSANA SALGADO

AMERICO DE FIGUEREIDO E MELO, PEDRO

Pedro Americo de Figuereido e Melo (*b.* 29 April 1843; *d.* 7 October 1905), Brazilian painter. Americo's artistic career began at a young age. At the age of nine he was chosen to accompany the naturalist Louis-Jacques Brunet on a scientific mission through Northeastern Brazil. Soon after his return from the expedition, he moved to Rio, and in 1855 enrolled in the Imperial Academy of Fine Arts. By 1858 his artistic capabilities had captured the attention of the emperor PEDRO II, who personally awarded him a European travel stipend. In Europe, Americo studied painting with such masters as Ingres and Horace Vernet. But his interests and talents extended beyond the fine arts. He wrote a criticism of Ernest Renan's *Life of Jesus,* for which he received a commendation from Pope Pius IX, and obtained a doctorate from the University of Brussels in natural science and applied physics. When he returned to Brazil in 1864, he wrote a novel entitled *Holocausto.* The same year he won the competition for professor of figure drawing at the academy.

Although Americo lived a good part of his adult life in Europe, he nevertheless left an important artistic legacy in Brazil. Alongside Vítor MEIRELES, Americo was instrumental in producing visual images, which official institutions of the Second Empire sponsored and prized. His artistic repertory includes religious and allegorical compositions as well as court portraits and historical paintings. His most important historical paintings include two military paintings depicting battles from the

War of the Triple Alliance, the 1872 *Batalha de Campo Grande* and the 1879 *Batalha do Avaí*, and his 1888 homage to Brazilian independence, *Grito do Ipiranga*.

– CAREN A. MEGHREBLIAN

AMÉZAGA, JUAN JOSÉ DE

Juan José de Amézaga (*b*. 28 January 1881; *d*. 21 August 1956), president of Uruguay (1943–1947). Amézaga was born in Montevideo. After receiving his law degree in 1905, he was a professor of philosophy, director of the Labor Office, twice a representative for the department of Durazno, minister of industry, ambassador to Argentina (1916), adviser on secondary education, president of the State Insurance Bank (1918), and attorney for the Central Railroad of Uruguay. Amézaga was elected president as Uruguay emerged from a decade of institutional changes initiated in 1933 by President Gabriel TERRA's coup d'état and culminating with the coup of his successor, General Alfredo BALDOMIR, in 1942.

Amézaga's election guaranteed that Uruguay would be aligned with the Allied cause during the war.

Greatly influenced by international trends, Baldomir guaranteed free elections and a restoration of democracy. From that new electoral process, the Colorado Party and Amézaga emerged triumphant by promoting Batllismo, the ideology based on the political, economic, and social ideas of the former president, José BATLLE Y ORDÓÑEZ. With its exports of meat and wool, Uruguay prospered economically during World War II. And Amézaga's election guaranteed that Uruguay would be aligned with the Allied cause during the war.

Amézaga was the author of numerous legal texts, including *Enseñanza del derecho civil* (1908) and *Un capítulo de historia internacional* (1942).

– JOSÉ DE TORRES WILSON

AMORIM, ENRIQUE

Enrique Amorim (*b*. 25 July 1900; *d*. 1960), Uruguayan writer and educator. Born in Salto and educated in Buenos Aires, Amorim was named minister of education and foreign affairs of Uruguay in 1918. His early and most highly regarded novel, *La carreta* (1931), reveals the writer's attraction to the Criollista movement as well as the intimate knowledge, gained as a child, of the customs, problems, and people of the countryside. His participation in militant activities of the Communist Party influenced Amorim's socially oriented writing

during the 1930s and 1940s. Later novels, such as *Corral abierto* (1956), *Los montaraces* (1957), and *La desembocadura* (1958), continued to display the essential characteristics of his fiction: a dialogue between humans and the land, a strong ethical flavor, rural characters or themes, and a novelistic structure resembling multiple short stories. He focused above all on the new consciousness of the rural people, as seen in *El caballo y su sombra* (1941) (translated into English as *The Horse and His Shadow*, 1943) and in *La victoria no viene sola* (1952). Amorim also excelled as a poet, literary critic, movie scriptwriter, and film critic.

– WILLIAM H. KATRA

AMPÍES, JUAN DE

Juan de Ampíes (*d*. 8 February 1533), Spanish conquistador. Ampíes played an important role in the process whereby Spain established itself in the New World. In 1511 he became the first royal factor on the island of Hispaniola. An advocate of a peaceful Conquest, he defended the Indians on the Los Gigantes Islands (today Curaçao, Aruba, and Bonaire) and was partly responsible for their being declared *indios guaitiaos* (friendly Indians). When the Indians who inhabited Cumaná (the coastal region of northeastern Venezuela) put to death the missionaries who had come to evangelize the area, Ampíes opposed the use of retaliatory measures against them. When the first peaceful colonizing activities were undertaken with Indians considered to be friendly—activities that were consistent with the doctrines promoted by Fray Bartolomé de LAS CASAS— Ampíes was assigned in 1520 to populate Los Gigantes with a group of Caquetío Indians. He later established contact with the inhabitants of the South American mainland and was able to gain their confidence.

In 1526 Ampíes bought some captured Indians on Hispaniola and then freed them and made use of a commercial expedition to return them to their homelands. This gesture led to the organization of an expedition under the leadership of his son, whose object was to create a permanent settlement on the mainland. The result was the founding of Coro on 26 July 1527. Because of an agreement with the House of Welser banking firm, however, Ampíes had to abandon the settlement of Coro in 1528 and limit his authority and jurisdiction to the island territories.

– INÉS QUINTERO

AMPUDIA Y GRIMAREST, PEDRO DE

Pedro de Ampudia y Grimarest (*b*. 1805; *d*. 1868), Mexican military officer and minister of war (1859–

1860). Born in Havana, Cuba, Ampudia arrived in Mexico in 1821 as a lieutenant in the retinue of the last viceroy of New Spain, Juan o'DONOJÚ. He joined the Army of the Three Guarantees and supported the Plan of Iguala for Mexican autonomy and independence. Ampudia fought against the Spanish holding the fort of San Juan de Ulúa in the harbor of Veracruz, and later against the rebels in Texas. He served as governor of the state of Tabasco (1843–1844). During the war with the United States (1846–1848), Ampudia directed the defense of Monterrey and fought under General Antonio López de SANTA ANNA at the battle of Angostura. Ampudia also served during the war as governor of the state of Nuevo León, and he held that office again during several months in 1854. Elected to the Constituent Congress of 1856–1857, Ampudia fought on the republican side during the War of the Reform; during the Second Empire, he served MAXIMILIAN.

— D. F. STEVENS

AMUNÁTEGUI ALDUNATE, MIGUEL LUIS

Miguel Luis Amunátegui Aldunate (*b.* 11 January 1828; *d.* 22 January 1888), Chilean historian and public figure. Born and educated in Santiago, and one of the numerous disciples of Andrés BELLO, Amunátegui was a brilliant member of a brilliant Chilean generation. A devoted Liberal, he was eight times elected to the Chamber of Deputies and also served in the cabinet during the presidencies of José Joaquín PÉREZ, Aníbal PINTO, and (briefly) José Manuel BALMACEDA. In 1875 he was offered the chance to become the "official" candidate for the presidency. The government's control over elections would have ensured his triumph, but he declined.

Among the great nineteenth-century Chilean historians, Amunátegui can be ranked as second only to Diego BARROS ARANA. His chief works were *La reconquista española* (1851), *La dictadura de O'Higgins* (1853), *Los precursores de la independencia de Chile* (3 vols., 1870–1872), and *La crónica de 1810* (3 vols., 1876). His numerous other writings cover a range from philology to the Chilean frontier dispute with Argentina. His two-part work on the latter theme, *Títulos de la República de Chile a la soberanía y dominio de la extremidad austral del continente americano* (1853, 1855), was the first to give coherent shape to Chile's territorial claims.

— SIMON COLLIER

ANAYA, PEDRO MARÍA DE

Pedro María de Anaya (*b.* 1794; *d.* 21 March 1854), president of Mexico (1847, 1847–1848). A career military officer, Anaya served as deputy in the Mexican Congress (1829–1830) and as a senator (1844–1845). He was appointed minister of war in 1845 by President José Joaquín de HERRERA. He was substitute president for Antonio López de SANTA ANNA from 2 April 1847 to 20 May 1847 and later that year was elected interim president, serving from 13 November 1847 until 8 January 1848. As defender of the convent of Churubusco on the southern outskirts of Mexico City during the war with the United States, Anaya was forced to surrender by U.S. General David E. Twiggs. When Twiggs occupied Churubusco and asked him where the munitions were, Anaya answered, "Si hubiera parque, no estarían ustedes aquí" ("If we had any munitions, you would not be here"). Anaya served as minister of war in 1848 and again in 1852, and was governor of the Federal District in 1849. He was serving as director general of the Post Office at his death in Mexico City.

— D. F. STEVENS

ANCHIETA, JOSÉ DE

José de Anchieta (*b.* 19 March 1534; *d.* 6 September 1597) Jesuit missionary. An early Jesuit missionary known as the "Apostle of Brazil," José de Anchieta was skillful in teaching and evangelizing the native Indians. Of Spanish origin, he was born in Tenerife, in the Canary Islands, and studied at the University of Coimbra, where he entered the Society of Jesus as a brother in 1551. In 1553 he arrived in Brazil, where he taught at the Jesuit College of São Paulo. He was an accomplished writer and linguist. A master of Latin grammar and prose, he was one of the first missionaries to learn the Tupi language of the Indians well enough to write a Tupi grammar to augment the Jesuit missionary endeavors in Brazil. He served as the secretary to Manuel da NÓBREGA, the leader of the first group of Jesuit missionaries in Brazil. He was responsible for the founding in Brazil of the Jesuit educational system based on the *ratio studiorum,* which emphasized classes in Latin, grammar, philosophy, mathematics, cosmography, and astronomy. In 1577 he made solemn profession as a priest in the Jesuit order.

While Manuel da Nóbrega was working in northern Brazil, Anchieta concentrated his efforts on founding *aldeias,* or fortified missions, in the southern captaincies of São Vicente, Rio de Janeiro, and Espírito Santo. He founded a third regular college in 1554 in São Paulo, where he was a zealous teacher. He also composed a great number of hymns, sacred songs, plays, and a poem in praise to Our Lady. In 1563 he worked with Manuel da Nóbrega in a pacification mission among the Tamoios, who were allied with the French and attacking settlements in Santos and São Vicente. After serving as a teacher and missionary, he was appointed Jesuit provincial of southern Brazil from 1578 to 1587.

A saintly and dynamic missionary, Anchieta spent forty-four years laboring in South America, despite a painful back injury which often incapacitated him. His letters and sermons give glowing accounts of the natural beauty of Brazil and are an excellent chronicle of early Brazilian history. Various miracles were attributed to him and he is called the "miracle worker" of Brazil.

– PATRICIA MULVEY

ANDAGOYA, PASCUAL DE

Pascual de Andagoya (*b.* 1495; *d.* 1548), early Spanish explorer and chronicler of the Conquest. Andagoya arrived in the Caribbean in 1514 with Pedrarias Davila (Pedro Arias de ÁVILA), and in 1521 he became governor of Panama. The following year he led a group to explore to the south. Andagoya sailed down the Pacific coast to the San Juan River of southern Colombia,

---

Andagoya sailed down the Pacific coast to the San Juan River of southern Colombia, and he returned with tales of great riches to the south.

---

where, suffering from an injury and virtually out of supplies, he turned back. Andagoya returned with tales of great riches to the south. Inspired by these tales, Francisco PIZARRO utilized the information uncovered by Andagoya in subsequent forays south. In 1537 Andagoya became governor of the Pacific coast region of Colombia. However, his rival Sebastián de Belalcázar brought charges against him, believing that Andagoya had encroached on his domain. Andagoya was jailed and sent to Spain. According to some accounts, he died in Cuzco, Peru, in 1548; others maintain that he never returned to the New World.

As an explorer Andagoya enjoyed a special reputation for his humane regard for the natives. He is most remembered for his lively account of the deeds of conquest, *Narrative of the Proceedings of Pedrarias Davila in the Provinces of Tierra Firme or Castilla del Oro, and of the Discovery of the South Sea and the Coasts of Peru and Nicaragua* (translated by Sir Clements Markham, 2d ed. 1978).

– RONN F. PINEO

ANDERSON IMBERT, ENRIQUE

Enrique Anderson Imbert (*b.* 12 February 1910), Argentine critic, literary historian, fiction writer, and influential teacher. Born in Córdoba, he studied philology and literature at the University of Buenos Aires with Pedro HENRÍQUEZ UREÑA and Alejandro KORN. His novel *Vigilia* (1934) was awarded the Buenos Aires Municipal Prize for Literature. He wrote essays, fiction, and articles for major Argentine journals, such as *Sur*, and was literary editor of the newspaper *La Vanguardia*. After teaching at the University of Tucumán (1940–1947), he went to the United States, where he taught at the University of Michigan until 1965, returning briefly to Argentina in 1955 to teach at the universities of Buenos Aires and La Plata. From 1965 to 1980 he was the Victor Thomas Professor of Hispanic Literature at Harvard University. Since then he has divided his time teaching at various universities in Argentina, serving as president of the Argentine Academy of Letters, lecturing, and, primarily, writing creative fiction. In 1954–1961 he published his best-selling two-volume book on literature, *Historia de la literatura hispanoamericana* (Spanish-American Literature: A History, 1963).

Julio CORTÁZAR considered Anderson Imbert one of the most important short-story writers of Latin America. The author of more than thirty books of essays, fiction, and criticism, Anderson was awarded the Mecenas Prize in 1990 for *Narraciones completas*. He has written definitive critical essays about Henrik Ibsen, Domingo SARMIENTO, Rubén DARÍO and George Bernard Shaw. His major works of fiction included *El grimorio* (1961), *El gato de Cheshire* (1965), *La locura juega al ajedrez (1971), Evocación de sombras en la ciudad geométrica* (1989); his works of criticism include *Mentiras y mentirosos en el mundo de las letras* (1992) and *Teoría y técnica del cuento* (1979). An excellent selection of Anderson's short stories is translated into English in *Woven on the Loom of Time* (1990).

– GEORGETTE MAGASSY DORN

ANDRADA, ANTÔNIO CARLOS RIBEIRO DE AND MARTIM FRANCISCO RIBEIRO DE

Antônio Carlos Ribeiro de Andrada and Martim Francisco Ribeiro de Andrada, Brazilian statesmen and younger brothers of José Bonifácio de ANDRADA. Children of a merchant of Santos, they all graduated from Coimbra University and entered government service. All three were self-assured, quarrelsome, unscrupulous, and vindictive when crossed, confusing personal and family advancement with the public interest.

Antônio Carlos (*b.* 1 November 1773; *d.* 5 December 1845), then a royal judge, gave support to the 1817 revolt in Pernambuco, suffering three years' imprisonment. Elected from São Paulo to the Lisbon Cortes in

1821, he took the lead in asserting Brazil's rights. Martim Francisco (*b.* 27 June 1775; *d.* 23 February 1844) served as minister of finance in the cabinet headed by José Bonifácio from 1822 to 1823. The three brothers sat in the Constituent Assembly and, following the dismissal of José Bonifácio and Martim Francisco as ministers, launched a campaign of opposition to PEDRO I that contributed to the violent dissolution of the Constituent Assembly in November 1823. Deported to France, the brothers did not return from exile until 1829. After Pedro I's abdication in 1831, the brothers tried by various means, legal and illegal, to secure control of power. They were involved in the abortive coup of April 1832 and in the Caramurú movement for Pedro I's restoration. In 1834 and again in 1838 Antônio Carlos unsuccessfully sought election as regent. He and Martim Francisco played a leading part in securing the premature declaration of PEDRO II's majority in July 1840. The two brothers dominated the first cabinet appointed by the emperor, but their ambition and high-handedness brought about their dismissal from office in February 1841. Antônio Carlos, the most energetic and domineering of the three brothers, became a leader of the new Liberal Party, securing election to the Senate prior to his death.

— RODERICK J. BARMAN

ANDRADA, JOSÉ BONIFÁCIO DE

José Bonifácio de Andrada (*b.* 13 June 1763; *d.* 6 April 1838), statesman and geologist, known in Brazil as the patriarch of independence. A native of Santos, São Paulo, and the eldest of the Andrada Brothers, José Bonifácio settled in Portugal after graduating in 1788 from Coimbra University. In 1790 the Portuguese government sent him on a mission to study scientific topics in northern Europe. During a decade's absence, he established himself as an expert on minerals and mining. In 1801 he was appointed to several government posts in Portugal. The multiplicity of his new responsibilities and his impatient, imperious character reduced his effectiveness as a bureaucrat. Following the French invasion of Portugal in 1807, he did not accompany the government to Brazil but played a notable role in organizing resistance. His subsequent career in Portugal was stultifying. In 1819 he finally secured permission to retire to Santos, still drawing most of his salary.

The revolution that began in Pôrto in 1820 drew José Bonifácio to the center of Brazilian politics. He played a key role in the provisional government of São Paulo and publicly advocated the continuance of the kingdom of Brazil created in 1815. When the prince regent, Dom Pedro, decided in January 1822 to defy the Cortes and to stay in Rio, José Bonifácio was the logical choice to serve as the prince's chief minister and adviser. José Bonifácio's self-confidence, energy, and determination were indispensable during the next year and a half in establishing the prince's authority within Brazil. The flow of events forced José Bonifácio, not originally an advocate of political independence, to accept that outcome in September 1822. He preserved for the new emperor PEDRO I the traditional powers of the Portuguese monarchy.

José Bonifácio's very successes undercut his position. As the new nation state was consolidated, so his talents became less indispensable and his domineering character less tolerable. Intrigues at court achieved his dismissal as minister in July 1823. José Bonifácio and his brothers, as members of the Constituent Assembly, sitting at Rio since May, went into opposition, denouncing the Portuguese-born faction at court and thereby attacking the emperor himself. The outcome was the violent dissolution of the Assembly in November 1823 and the exiling to France of the Andrada brothers until 1829.

On his return, José Bonifácio again became a favored advisor of PEDRO I. When the emperor abdicated on 7 April 1831, he named José Bonifácio to be his son's guardian (*tutor*). Although the new regime refused at first to recognize this nomination, the legislature voted in June to make José Bonifácio guardian. His handling of his position was not successful. PEDRO II and his sisters did not flourish physically or psychologically. José Bonifácio used his position for political purposes, being involved in plots to overthrow the regime. The government forcibly removed him as guardian in December 1833. José Bonifácio spent his remaining years in quiet retirement on Paquetá Island, Rio de Janeiro.

— RODERICK J. BARMAN

ANDRADE, CARLOS DRUMMOND DE

Carlos Drummond de Andrade (*b.* 31 October 1902; *d.* 17 August 1987), considered Brazil's most important twentieth-century poet. Drummond (or "The Master," as he is best known) was an active poet and writer through several literary generations—from modernism through concretism—and influenced many contemporary Brazilian poets. Born in Minas Gerais and intimately associated with that state in his poetry, Drummond spent most of his life in Rio de Janeiro where, like many other Brazilian writers, he earned his living as a bureaucrat—in the education ministry—and a journalist. He contributed poetry to major literary re-

Carlos Drummond de Andrade. (Iconographia)

views and translated many of the classic writers of French and Spanish literature. He also wrote hundreds of *crônicas* (journalistic sketches) about daily life that reveal a genuine, kind soul.

Drummond was not an original member of the group that "founded" Brazilian modernism in São Paulo in 1922. Nevertheless, under their influence, he, along with other contemporary young *mineiro* (that is, of Minas Gerais) writers (e.g., Emílio Moura [1901–1971]), founded *A Revista,* the leading literary review of *mineiro* modernism in 1925. It was not until his 1928 collaboration on Oswald de ANDRADE's journal *Revista de Antropófagia* (Review of cannibalism) that he attained national acclaim. His poem "No meio do caminho" (In the middle of the road) established the characteristics he pursued in all his poetry: a rejection of traditional forms and structures; a conversational tone and a highly colloquial language reflecting actual Brazilian speech; and an interest in everyday affairs of life, often from a satirical point of view.

Collections of poems published in the 1930s and early 1940s reflected contemporary political upheavals.

He debated leftist ideologies and antibourgeois sentiments in *A rosa do povo* (1945), but the volume ends on a note of a search from within for resolution of these dilemmas. Later collections would turn to his sense of isolation from his small-town roots and a growing displeasure with big-city life. *A vida passada a limpo* (1959) reviews his perennial interests within a new light. Here, the elegy on the destruction of Rio's Hotel Avenida assumes several levels of symbolic meaning: society's change, the "endurance" of a work of art (be it one of architecture or poetry), and the role of the artist. Among his other important collections are *Lição das coisas* (1962), which includes experimental concretist verse, and *As impurezas do branco* (1973), which examines modern technology.

Drummond was a friend of the American poet Elizabeth Bishop, who spent some twenty years in Brazil. His reputation in the United States was a consequence of her translations of his works, often published in the *New Yorker,* and also of later translations by Mark Strand, among others. Drummond's influence on modern Brazilian poetry has been immense.

— IRWIN STERN

ANDRADE, GOMES FREIRE DE

Gomes Freire de Andrade (*b.* 11 July 1688; *d.* 1 January 1763), governor and captain-general of southern and western Brazil. A member of a distinguished family whose roots trace back in Galicia before 711, the year of the Moorish invasion, and in Portugal since the fourteenth century. For centuries the Freire de Andrades contributed senior officials to Portugal's army, navy, church, and civil service. Andrade, named after an uncle who served as governor of Maranhão during the Beckman Revolt, was born in Jeromenha, situated between Vila Viçosa and Badajóz. He attended the University of Coimbra and became fluent in French and Spanish. Along with his father, he served in the War of the Spanish Succession, after which he retained an appointment in a cavalry unit stationed in the capital. In 1733 he was appointed governor and captain-general of the captaincy of Rio de Janeiro, a post he retained until his death. It was the first of many administrative units for which he became responsible. By 1748 he governed all of western and southern Brazil, including Minas Gerais, Goiás, Mato Grosso, São Paulo, Santa Catarina, and Rio Grande do Sul. Among his notable responsibilities were the settlement of coastal Rio Grande do Sul, the definition of Brazil's southern boundary in accordance with the Treaty of Madrid (1750), commander of Portuguese forces in Rio Grande do Sul during the Guaraní

War (1752–1756), and the expulsion of the Jesuits (1760) from lands under his jurisdiction. Andrade never married; he died in Rio de Janeiro after an extended illness.

– DAURIL ALDEN

ANDRADE, JORGE

Jorge Andrade (*b.* 1922; *d.* 1988), Brazilian playwright. In his theater Jorge Andrade was the sensitive historian and understanding judge of a fast-disappearing society. He became in every sense the first completely successful modern Brazilian playwright, doing for São Paulo what the novelists and dramatists of the Northeast and Érico VERÍSSIMO in the South have been accomplishing for their regions, for Brazil, and for the world since the 1930s.

A moratória (1954), a play in three acts with two sets, demonstrates the dramatist's great maturity. The subject is essentially a continuation of that of *O telescópio* (1951), both chronologically and thematically, but reflects the considerable development of the author as a person and artist. Here, the slow, painful, and somehow inconclusive passage from one era to another is emphasized more sharply. Simultaneous use of two sets, one the *fazenda* in 1919, the other a city apartment in 1932, requires superior technical skills as well as literary sophistication for full realization and appreciation.

Employing carefully selected situations, emotions, and language, which appear simple and natural without naturalistic triviality, the author solves the age-old problems of classical tragedy with Flaubertian precision. The entire, balanced action turns on the past and its influence on the present through the use of graphic reminiscences that join the two times and places for the author and spectator, whereas the characters must rely on memory alone. With a view of both the past (1919) and the fictional present (1932), we in the actual present are afforded unique historic and dramatic perspective. Transitions from hope to despair on one level, underscored ironically or fatalistically on the other, grip the audience emotionally.

Having vindicated through its ancestors a society whose demise he had begun to record, Jorge Andrade now turned to another class of that society, the tenant farmers. *A vereda da salvação* (published 1957; produced 1964) has as its point of departure a tragic example of religious fanaticism in Minas Gerais, the details and analyses of which the playwright studied most carefully. During a long period of revision, Andrade reconsidered the events, the criticism of his work, and his own meditations on the human condition. More than ever, the new *Vereda da salvação* is neither *mineiro* nor *paulista,* but Brazilian and universal. In fact, it has enjoyed long successful runs in Poland.

The collection *Marta, a árvore e o relógio* (1970) is a very interesting anthology from several points of view. Not only does it contain two new plays, but it also presents Jorge Andrade's major works in a historico-fictional chronology, rather than in the chronology of their writing, to create his full cycle of São Paulo. Thus, the newest play, *As confrarias,* is the first in the collection, and *O sumidouro,* long in progress and the second newest, is the last. The other eight are inserted between these two in more or less fictional order and not in the order in which they were written. The title is comprised of symbols that recur throughout the series of plays.

Having in every way explored everything possible in the world of coffee barons and São Paulo and having realized that censorship made it virtually impossible to stage anything serious on current matters in Brazil, Jorge Andrade turned to television after 1970. When he did create another play, *Milagre na cela* (1977), which dealt with political oppression and torture, his public could receive it only in published form.

– RICHARD A. MAZZARA

ANDRADE, MÁRIO DE

Mário de Andrade (*b.* 9 October 1893; *d.* 25 February 1945), Brazilian writer. Mário Raul Moraes de Andrade was a man of multiple talents and immensely varied activities. From a relatively modest background, especially compared with his modernist counterparts, he was born in São Paulo and, after graduating from the Ginásio Nossa Senhora do Carmo, studied music and piano at the Conservatorio Dramático e Musical in São Paulo, and was professor of piano. Widely acknowledged as the leading figure—or "pope"—of the Brazilian modernist movement of the 1920s, he was arguably Brazil's most important and versatile literary personage during the first half of the century. He was involved in almost all of the literary, artistic, and cultural movements of the period. He wrote novels, short stories, and poetry; he was a literary, art, and music critic and theorist; he was also a musicologist, a folklorist, and an ethnographer. As director of São Paulo's Department of Culture from 1935 to 1938, he fostered many activities that promoted the development of modern social science in Brazil.

One of the governing concepts of Andrade's cultural and artistic activity, along with his insistence on freedom of artistic expression and experimentation, is what has variously been called his "sense of commitment" or his "quasi-apostolic consciousness." Especially important in this regard is his extensive research into the specific characteristics of Brazilian speech and popular culture, research intended to help forge a more authentic cultural identity. Andrade conceived of nationalism as the first step in a process of self-discovery that would eventually contribute to universal cultural values, to the extent that it was authentic and faithful to itself. His ultimate goal was the integration of Brazilian culture into universal culture, not the closure implied by the more xenophobic currents of nationalism that also found expression within the Brazilian modernist movement. Andrade recognized the difficulty of creating an authentic national culture in a country permeated by European values and standards. He expressed this theme as early as 1922 in the poem "Inspiração," which opens the collection *Paulicéia desvairada* (*Hallucinated City*), when he wrote: "São Paulo! comoção de minha vida . . . / Galicismo a berrar nos desertos da América!" (São Paulo! tumult of my life . . . / Gallicism crying in the wilderness of America!). In "O trovador" in the same volume, he wrote, "Sou um tupi tangendo um alaúde!" ("I am a Tupi Indian strumming a lute!").

"Sou um tupi tangendo um alaúde!"

("I am a Tupi Indian strumming a lute!").

Andrade's artistic answer to this dilemma was to use popular forms of expression structurally—not merely ornamentally—in elite cultural forms. He began by systematizing errors committed in everyday speech as a means of capturing an authentically national social and psychological character through language itself. By bringing those errors into educated speech and writing, he hoped to help in the formation of a Brazilian literary language. His interest in popular culture as a means of understanding Brazil evolved into the systematic study of Brazilian folklore and the re-creation of popular forms on an erudite level. Knowing and incorporating the foundations of Brazilian popular thought, he felt he could help lead Brazil to self-knowledge and contribute to its passage from nationalism to a universal level in the higher arts. The 1928 novel *Macunaíma*, which David Haberly has described as both an etiological myth of national creation and an eschatological myth of national destruction, represents the artistic culmination of Mário de Andrade's research in Brazilian folklore and popular forms of expression.

— RANDAL JOHNSON

ANDRADE, OSWALD DE

Oswald de Andrade (*b.* 11 January 1890; *d.* 22 October 1954), Brazilian writer and intellectual. As a theoreti-

cian of Brazil's social and aesthetic modernization, Andrade was a leading contributor to the Brazilian modernist movement in the arts and culture, initiated formally by the Modern Art Week held in February 1922 in São Paulo, which he helped to plan. His principal modernist contributions are the "Manifesto da poesia pau Brasil" (1924; Brazilwood Manifesto), whose ideas inspired the cubistic geometrism and "constructive innocence" of Tarsila do AMARAL's canvases of the mid-1920s—and the "Manifesto antropófago" (1928; Cannibal Manifesto), which led to the founding of a national vanguardist movement whose model of "devouring assimilation" of foreign influence under the totem of the cannibal tribes who devoured Europeans was summarized in the aphorism "Tupy or not Tupy, that is the question." The *Antropofagia* movement—again paralleled in the plastic arts by Amaral's paintings—created a paradoxical telluric and vanguardist model for resolving the dialectic between national and foreign cultural influences.

Andrade's early years reflect the transition from Brazil's belle époque aesthetic to modernism. A graduate of São Bento Seminary and the Largo de São Francisco Law School, Andrade began his literary career as a journalist and contributor to fin-de-siècle and premodernist magazines (*O Pirralho, Papel e Tinta*), in which he introduced Italo-Paulista dialect. With Guilherme de Almeida he wrote two plays in French in 1916. His premodernist life is fictionalized in *A trilogia do exílio,* later published as *Os condenados,* and in the collective diary *O perfeito cozinheiro das almas deste mundo.* During the 1920s he spent much of his time in Paris with Amaral and her circle. Influenced by cubism and the poetic prose of Blaise Cendrars, his early modernist work includes two "inventions" combining fragmented poetry with prose, *Memórias sentimentais de João Miramar* (1924) and *Serafim Ponte Grande* (1933); the poetry collection *Pau Brasil* (1925); and the two manifestos.

Andrade also wrote expressionistic drama (*O homem e o cavallo; O rei da Vela; A morta*), followed by the social mural novels in the series *Marco-Zero.* His works after 1945 include poetry ("Cântico dos cânticos para flauta e violão") and essays on literature, culture, and philosophy addressing utopian themes. In the 1960s his work began to receive critical reevaluation, culminating in the current recognition of his texts as foundations of Brazil's literary and intellectual modernity.

— K. DAVID JACKSON

ANDREONI, JOÃO ANTÔNIO

João Antônio Andreoni (pseud. of André João Antonil; *b.* 1649; *d.* 13 March 1716), Jesuit administrator and author of a seminal study of the economic roots of early eighteenth-century Brazil, *Cultura e opulência do Brasil por suas drogas e minas* (1711). Born in Tuscany and educated in law at the University of Perugia, he entered the Society of Jesus on 20 May 1667 and came to Bahia, Brazil, in 1681. There, after serving as secretary to Antônio VIEIRA, he became Vieira's rival and leader among German- and Italian-born Jesuits serving in Brazil. A proficient Latinist and a keen administrator, he held a succession of posts in the Society of Jesus, from minister of novices to rector of the college at Bahia, and served both as provincial Visitor and as provincial. Unlike Vieira, he sided with the settlers in their efforts to obtain Indian labor and, again unlike Vieira, he was anti-Semitic. But he is best known for his unique and outstanding treatise concerning the sources of Brazil's wealth—sugar, tobacco, gold, and cattle. He died in Bahia.

– DAURIL ALDEN

ANDRESOTE

Andresote (Andrés López Del Rosario), the *zambo* leader of the rebellion in Venezuela against the Compañía Guipuzcoana of Caracas in 1730–1733. Andresote dealt in contraband in the region of Yaracuy, mocking the controls which the Compañía Guipuzcoana sought to place on the commerce of the province of Venezuela. To protect his interests, the director general of the *compañía* ordered his arrest. Andresote and his followers clashed violently with the authorities and representatives of the *compañía* in their effort to continue their contraband operations with the island of Curaçao. Troops were sent from Caracas to put down Andresote's group, but when they failed to accomplish this in 1732, the commander in chief of Venezuela vowed to combat him personally. Andresote fled in 1733 to Curaçao, where he died a short while later.

– INÉS QUINTERO

ANDREVE, GUILLERMO

Guillermo Andreve (*b.* 1879; *d.* 1940), Panamanian journalist, intellectual, and politician. Andreve was one of the most influential liberal leaders in Panama in the early twentieth century. He held many government positions. He was a member of the National Assembly, secretary of public education, secretary of government and justice, and an ambassador in Latin America and Europe. Andreve wrote on many subjects, and his writings are an important source for the study of Panamanian politics in the 1920s. In his writings Andreve dwells on the inadequacies of the laissez-faire structure created by nineteenth-century liberalism and advocates a more interventionist state for Panama.

– JUAN MANUEL PÉREZ

ANDUEZA PALACIO, RAIMUNDO

Raimundo Andueza Palacio (*b.* February 1843; *d.* 17 August 1900), president of Venezuela (1890–1892). Andueza began his political and military activity after the Federal War (1859–1863) as aide-de-camp and secretary to the president of the Republic, Marshal Juan Crisóstomo FALCÓN (1863–1868). Having ties with the Liberal Party, he carried out important, and sometimes divisive, public duties during the administrations of Antonio GUZMÁN BLANCO (1870–1877) and Francisco LINARES ALCÁNTARA (1877–1878). After a brief period of exile, Andueza returned to Venezuela and became one of the political leaders of the Partido Liberalismo Amarillo (Yellow Liberalism Party).

With the end of the hegemony of Guzmán's policies during the administration of Dr. Juan Pablo ROJAS PAÚL (1888–1890), the Federal Council elected Andueza president for the 1890–1892 term. In an atmosphere of conflict between militarists and those favoring civilian rule, he declared himself a defender of the trend toward civilian rule and appointed a cabinet composed primarily of civilians. His administration is seen as having been blessed by a period of economic boom. Andueza saw the completion of various public projects begun before his regime and fostered a politics of clientele, with the object of creating a broad base of support that would allow him to remain in power. From within the state legislatures, he promoted a constitutional reform that included, among many other amendments, the lengthening of the presidential term from two to four years. Congress refused to launch this constitutional reform immediately, but the president declared that the new statute was in effect. The immediate result was the beginning of the Legalist Revolution led by General Joaquín CRESPO, who put an end to Andueza's term of office. When Crespo died in 1898, Andueza returned from exile and again took up political activity, becoming minister of foreign affairs under General Cipriano CASTRO, who became president in 1900.

– INÉS QUINTERO

ANGEL, ALBALUCÍA

Albalucía Angel (*b.* 7 September 1939), Colombian novelist. Angel is one of Colombia's most important writers since Gabriel GARCÍA MÁRQUEZ. Following an independent narrative style, she has produced four distinct novels. *Los girasoles en invierno* (1970) is an experiment in radical feminism, and *Dos veces Alicia* (1972) plays on the Lewis Carroll text of *Alice in Wonderland.* The later novels delve into deeper issues of Colombian history and cultural values. *Estaba la pájara pinta sentada en el verde limón* (1975), her most significant novel, deals with the period of Colombian history known as La Violencia (1948–1956) and intriguingly reconstructs the era through two parallel but opposing perspectives: on the one hand, the unseen violence perpetrated by a young female adolescent who is not allowed to leave her house, and on the other, the quoted firsthand descriptions of actual grotesque political killings as reported in journals and books.

Misiá Señora (1982) looks at the relationship of a daughter, mother, and grandmother. Through erotic imagery, soliloquy, and monologue, the novel captures what was once the ideal of femininity, which encompassed sensuality, decency, courage, inner strength, and a feeling of fulfillment. The four novels show not only

---

Angel writes of unseen violence perpetrated by a young female adolescent and firsthand descriptions of actual grotesque political killings.

---

the author's search for innovation through language and theme and creativeness in her early period but also her successful later efforts to transform the literary act into a profound social and cultural commentary on her native land.

– DICK GERDES

ÁNGELES, FELIPE

Felipe Ángeles (*b.* 13 June 1869; *d.* 26 November 1919), Mexican revolutionary. A well-educated career soldier, Ángeles was in France when the revolution broke out in 1910. He returned to Mexico in 1912. Sharing Francisco MADERO's liberalism, Ángeles soon became one of the new president's closest confidants within the military. Ángeles was arrested because of this association after the February 1913 coup that brought Victoriano HUERTA to power, but he was soon able to join the Constitutionalists in their fight against the Huerta regime. Within this camp he quickly found his most important revolutionary role as Pancho VILLA's close advisor and played a large part in the fighting that would eventually lead to Huerta's downfall. In 1914 Ángeles helped bring the Villistas and the Zapatistas together in an alliance against the followers of Venustiano CARRANZA. But after Villa lost the big battles of

Celaya and León de las Aldamas in 1915—often ignoring the tactical advice of Ángeles in the process—Ángeles fled the country in exile to the United States. Always ambitious, he tried to rejoin the revolutionary struggle by leading a small band of soldiers across the border into Chihuahua. In 1919, he was captured there and executed by forces loyal to Carranza.

– SAMUEL BRUNK

ANGELIS, PEDRO DE

Pedro de Angelis (*b.* 29 June 1784; *d.* 10 February 1859), essayist and scholar. Bernardino RIVADAVIA, former president of Argentina (1826–1827), persuaded Angelis, an Italian intellectual living in Paris, to take up residence in Buenos Aires and help develop the cultural life of the new nation. Angelis arrived in 1827 and became co-editor of Rivadavia's official paper, *La crónica política y literaria de Buenos Aires.* He also founded the Ateneo (an intellectual society) and edited the *Gaceta mercantil.* In 1828 Angelis edited the Latin text *Cornelli Nepotis . . . vitae excellentium imperatorum* for the university.

He attained prestige in the Argentine literary world and served Rivadavia's cause as well as that of Juan Manuel Ortiz de ROSAS. During the second Rosas dictatorship (1835–1852), Angelis became fascinated with history and began collecting original historical documents, many of which he included in his six-volume work *Colección de obras y documentos relativos a la historia antigua y moderna de las provincias del Río de la Plata. Ilustrada con notas y discertaciones* (1836–1837). He served as head of the government printing office and was head archivist. In 1852 Angelis sold his collection of over twenty-seven hundred books and twelve hundred manuscripts to the government of Brazil, where today they can be consulted in the National Library (in Rio de Janeiro) under *Colección de Angelis.*

– NICHOLAS P. CUSHNER

ÂNGELO, IVAN

Ivan Ângelo (*b.* 1936), Brazilian novelist, short story writer, and journalist. Born in Minas Gerais, Ângelo began his literary career in 1956 in Belo Horizonte, Minas Gerais, as an editor of the literary journal *Complemento.* Three years later he published a collection of short stories, *Homem sofrendo no quarto,* for which he was honored with the Prêmio Belo Horizonte. In 1966 he moved to São Paulo and began a career with the newspaper *Jornal da Tarde,* becoming editor in chief in 1984. Ângelo's very successful and highly political novel *A festa* (1976) details, in a fragmented style, life in Brazil under military rule in the early 1970s. *A Casa de vidro: Cinco histórias do Brasil* (1979) is a critical investigation of Brazilian society. A collection of dynamic short stories, *A face horrível* (1986), reveals the author's commitment to facing the social issues affecting the country.

– GARY M. VESSELS

ANTEQUERA Y CASTRO, JOSÉ DE

José de Antequera y Castro (*b.* 1693; *d.* 5 July 1731), governor of Paraguay (1721–1725) and leader of an anti-Jesuit uprising. In 1724 Antequera led Paraguayan forces into battle against a Jesuit-trained Guaraní militia from the missions who sought to remove him from office. Born in Panama, Antequera was the son of a Spanish bureaucrat. Educated first by Jesuits, he earned his licentiate in arts and doctorate in law in Charcas and Lima and went to Spain to seek employment. He became a member of the Order of Alcántara and secured an appointment for several years as protector of the Indians for the Audiencia of Charcas, where his father had once been a judge (*oidor*). As acting prosecutor (*fiscal*) in 1720, he took sides in a feud between Paraguayans and Jesuits that reached the *audiencia*. He undertook a judicial review of an unpopular governor, Diego de los Reyes y Balmaceda, an ally of the Jesuits, and simultaneously got the *audiencia* to name him next governor of Paraguay, a common but technically illegal combination, although the viceroy confirmed the appointment.

After Antequera arrived in Paraguay in 1721, he removed Reyes from office, took a Paraguayan mistress, and befriended an opponent of the Jesuits, José de Ávalos y Mendoza. In retaliation, the Jesuits had the viceroy reinstate Reyes, although he never again served. In 1722 the Jesuits helped Reyes flee to Corrientes, infuriating Paraguayans and from there threatening Antequera. The latter insisted that the Jesuits accept him as governor. Antequera argued that the dispute was a matter of justice, not government, and that the *audiencia,* not the viceroy, had jurisdiction. The *audiencia* agreed until 1724, when an aggressive viceroy, José de ARMENDÁRIZ, challenged the Charcas judges. He ordered an army of mission Guaranis led by Baltasar García Ros, lieutenant governor of Buenos Aires, to depose Antequera, but 3,000 Paraguayans with Antequera destroyed the smaller Guarani force in August 1724 at the Tebicuary River. They then expelled the Jesuits from Asunción.

Antequera's victory made his position untenable. The viceroy, the Jesuits, officials in Buenos Aires, and the new bishop of Paraguay, José de Palos, opposed him. His former colleagues in Charcas cut him adrift, and in 1725 he fled to Córdoba, where Franciscans sheltered him, and then moved to Charcas. He was apprehended and sent to Lima. From 1726 to 1731, he was jailed at the viceregal court, where he prepared his defense. Renewed rebellion in Paraguay in 1730 caused the viceroy to demand that the Audiencia of Lima find Antequera guilty of heresy and treason, and the judges complied. They ordered his execution and that of his principal lieutenant, Juan de Mena. The sentence was so unpopular that it provoked a riot in Lima, and the viceroy's troops shot Antequera on his way to the gallows. Four decades after Antequera's death, King Charles III, who had expelled Antequera's Jesuit enemies from Spain in 1767, posthumously exonerated Antequera. In Asunción, Antequera's legacies were the spirit of rebellion and José Cañete, his natural son and father of the noted jurist Pedro Vicente Cañete. Antequera's memory is honored by streets named for him in Asunción and Lima.

– JAMES SCHOFIELD SAEGER

ANTUÑANO, ESTEVAN DE

Estevan de Antuñano (*b.* 1792; *d.* 1847), Mexican industrialist. One of Mexico's first modern industrialists, Antuñano was born in Veracruz into a Spanish immigrant family. He was educated in Spain and in England, where he became familiar with industrial production. In the 1830s he led the modernization of the textile industry in Puebla, setting up Mexico's first mechanized spinning factory, La Constancia Mexicana, which produced cotton yarn on Arkwright spindles powered by the waters of the Río Atoyac. By the early 1840s, he owned four such factories in Puebla.

An enlightened entrepreneur, Antuñano recognized that the mechanization of spinning deprived women and children of employment and tried to alleviate the problem by turning La Constancia into a model experiment in the employment of family labor. He provided both housing and health care for his workers. Unfortunately, wages were low and people worked eleven to sixteen hours daily.

A vigorous propagandist, who authored over sixty pamphlets, Antuñano had a vision of national development. He wanted to see the traditional manufacturing center of Puebla wrest control of northern Mexican markets, then dependent on contraband. Trade with the north would revitalize Mexico's central cities and agricultural districts. Silver exports would bring in foreign exchange. His vision floundered on the realities of the scarcity of raw cotton and currency, the persistence of contraband, and national disintegration. Antuñano died of natural causes during the U.S. Army's occupation of

Estevan de Antuñano. Anonymous. (Benson Latin American Collection, University of Texas at Austin)

the city of Puebla. A French merchant, to whom he owed money, acquired most of his propertics.

— MARY KAY VAUGHAN

ANTÚNEZ, NEMESIO

Nemesio Antúnez (*b.* 1918; *d.* 19 May 1993), Chilean artist, whose work is characterized by optical and psychological effects achieved by means of perspective distortions and geometric configurations. Antúnez's work has been classified as surrealist, due to the unusual effects resulting from his manipulation of space. He studied architecture at Catholic University in his native Santiago from 1937 to 1943 and at Columbia University in New York City in 1945. A fellowship enabled him to study with Stanley W. Hayter of Atelier 17 in New York in 1947. In 1950 he followed Hayter to Paris. After returning to Chile in 1953, he organized *Taller 99,* an artists' collective. In the late 1950s his work anticipated op art effects, with an emphasis on expression. He executed a mural, *Heart of the Andes,* at the

United Nations (1966). A characteristic presentation of space in Antúnez's painting consists of rectangular boxes telescoping out of one another as though suspended in a void. Seemingly transparent planes and figures are used to create the illusion of endless expanses of space. Minuscule anthropomorphic figures often populate these spatial configurations (e.g., *New York, New York 10008,* 1967). His work consolidates the heritage of geometric art and surrealism, two strong movements in the art of Latin America.

Antúnez held several administrative posts, including director of the Museum of Contemporary Art, University of Chile, Santiago (1961–1964), cultural attaché at the Chilean embassy, New York City (1964–1969); director, National Museum of Fine Arts, Santiago (1969–1973).

— MARTA GARSD

ANZA, JUAN BAUTISTA DE

Juan Bautista de Anza (*b.* 1736; *d.* 19 December 1788), military officer, governor of New Mexico (1778–1788). One of the most effective instruments of the Bourbon Reforms on the northern frontier of New Spain, Anza was born at the presidio of Fronteras (Sonora), where his father, a member of the landowning-military-merchant elite, served as commander. While captain at Tubac (present-day southern Arizona), young Anza led an exploring party overland to southern California in 1774, and in 1775–1776, by the same route, he escorted the colonists who founded San Francisco. Appointed governor in 1777, Anza rode personally with the combined Hispano-Indian force that defeated Cuerno Verde, the Comanches' leading war chief, in New Mexico in 1779. His diplomacy resulted in treaties and alliances, first with the Comanches in 1786, and then with the Utes, Jicarilla Apaches, and Navajos. A generation of relative peace ensued, with steady growth of the Hispanic population and unprecedented territorial expansion. Anza died in Arizpe (Sonora).

— JOHN L. KESSELL

ANZOÁTEGUI, JOSÉ ANTONIO

José Antonio Anzoátegui (*b.* 14 November 1789; *d.* 15 November 1819), officer in the Venezuelan Emancipating Army. Anzoátegui was on the pro-independence side from the beginning of the independence movement in 1810. In his birthplace of Barcelona, Venezuela, he stood out as a leader of the Sociedad Patriotica de Caracas who was in favor of emancipation. Anzoátegui took part in the Guiana campaign of 1812, and when the First Republic fell, he was imprisoned in the vaults of La Guaira.

Anzoátegui returned to war in 1813 and fought in numerous battles. He helped Simón BOLÍVAR take the city of Bogotá in 1814; participated in the two Los Cayos expeditions financed by Alexandre Pétion, president of Haiti; was present at the taking of Angostura in 1817, in the Los Llanos campaign of 1818, and in the campaign for the liberation of New Granada in 1819. Bolívar placed him in charge of operations in Santa Marta and Maracaibo, but his death prevented him from carrying out his mission. For his military actions, he was decorated with the Order of the Liberators of Venezuela and the Boyacá Cross.

– INÉS QUINTERO

APOLINAR

Apolinar (Pablo Livinalli Santaella; *b.* 23 July 1928), Venezuelan artist. Although born in the small town of Guatire, Apolinar has spent his life in Petare, near Caracas. His preference for religious themes derives from years spent in a Catholic boarding school. He became an artist in 1965, when he produced his first painting, *The Bolivarian Neighborhood.* Since then his works have combined a primitive style with religious intimacy. In 1967 three of his paintings were included in the First Retrospective of Twentieth-Century Venezuelan Primitive Art, at the Musical Circle Gallery in Caracas. In the early 1970s he began a series of very imaginative books, the *Biblioteca de Apolinar,* which were first exhibited in 1972. The artistic and thematic complexity of these books gained him immediate recognition and inclusion in the 1977 Creadores al Margen show at the Museum of Contemporary Art in Caracas.

– BÉLGICA RODRÍGUEZ

APONTE-LEDÉE, RAFAEL

Rafael Aponte-Ledée (*b.* 15 October 1938), Puerto Rican composer. Born in Guayama, Puerto Rico, where he was educated, Aponte-Ledée left Puerto Rico in 1957 to study with Cristóbal Halffter at the Madrid Conservatory. He remained in Madrid until 1964, when he left to begin studies with Alberto GINASTERA and Gerardo GANDINI at the Torcuato di Tella Institute in Buenos Aires. After returning to Puerto Rico in 1965, Aponte-Ledée moved to the forefront of the new music movements of the 1960s. In San Juan he co-founded the Fluxus group (1967) with Francis Schwartz. He also spent several years teaching music composition and theory at the University of Puerto

Rico (1968–1973) and at the Puerto Rico Conservatory (from 1968).

Aponte-Ledée's works include *Tema y 6 diferencias* for piano (1963); elegies for strings (1965, 1967); *Presagio de pájaros muertos* (1966); *Impulsos . . . in memoriam Julia de Burgos* for orchestra (1967); *La ventana abierta* (two versions; 1968, 1969); *SSSSS²* (1971); and *El palacio en sombras* for orchestra (1977).

– SARA FLEMING

APPLEYARD, JOSÉ LUIS

José Luis Appleyard (*b.* 1927), Paraguayan poet. Born in Asunción, Appleyard studied law. He also taught literature and history at the Ateneo Paraguayo (Atheneum of Paraguay) and at the National University. He belongs to the poetry group that calls itself Academia Universitaria del Paraguay. Appleyard was awarded the First Prize in Poetry in 1943 and the Municipal Poetry Prize of Asunción in 1961. He is an aesthetic and nostalgic

---

Appleyard explores the "third language of Paraguay," the mixture of Spanish and Guaraní.

---

poet, with an oeuvre firmly rooted in the Paraguayan land and culture. In *Los monólogos* (1973) and *La voz que nos hablamos* (1983) he explores the "third language of Paraguay," the mixture of Spanish and Guaraní. Among Appleyard's lyrical works are *Tomando de la mano* (1981), *El labio y la palabra* (1982), *Solamente los años* (1983), and *Las palabras secretas* (1988). Other works by Appleyard are *Entonces era siempre* (1946); *El sauce permanece* (1947); and *Imágenes sin tierra* (1964).

– WILLIAM H. KATRA

ARAMAYO FAMILY

Aramayo Family, a wealthy silver and tin dynasty of the nineteenth- and twentieth-century Bolivian oligarchy. The first members in the New World were a Spanish silver miner, Diego Ortiz de Aramayo, from Navarre, and a Chichas landowner, Francisco Ortiz de Aramayo. Francisco's son, Isidoro Ortiz de Aramayo, was the father of José Avelino, born on 25 September 1809 in Moraya, a small town in the province of Sud Chichas. A mining industrialist, writer, and public servant, José Avelino founded the tin dynasty. A self-made man and a mining innovator, he bought silver mines in Potosí and, with European associates, began mechanizing Bolivian silver mining. As a writer and national deputy, he opposed the crude military despotism of Manuel Isidoro BELZU, Mariano MELGAREJO, and Agustín MORALES. At his death in Paris on 1 May 1882, he reportedly left more debts than riches to his descendants.

On 23 June 1846, José's son Félix Avelino was born in Paris. In the family tradition he became a mining industrialist, writer, and noted diplomat. In 1901, while serving as Bolivia's ambassador to London, he gave an Anglo-American company, the Bolivian Syndicate of New York, concessionary rights to the rubber-rich Acre region to prevent further Brazilian encroachments. War ensued, however, and Bolivia ceded the territory to Brazil in the 1903 Treaty of Petrópolis. As part of Félix Avelino's modernization of the family tin and bismuth mines, he incorporated the Aramayo, Francke Company in London in 1906. Before his death in 1929, he passed control to his son Carlos Víctor, who internationalized family holdings by founding the Compagnie Aramayo des Mines de Bolivie in Geneva in 1916.

Carlos Víctor was born in Paris on 7 October 1889, and died there in April 1981. One of Bolivia's three tin barons (with Simón PATIÑO and Mauricio HOCHSCHILD), he epitomized the Aramayo dynasty's zenith. Critics charged that the family's wealth, second in the country, benefited neither the state nor the Indian mine workers. Although their share of national tin output averaged only 7 percent, the Aramayos exerted enormous political influence. Carlos Víctor bankrolled the Republican Party and owned La Paz's reactionary newspaper, *La Razón.* He successfully plotted with Hochschild and Patiño against reformist governments of the 1930s and 1940s, but failed to prevent revolution and expropriation in 1952.

— WALTRAUD QUEISER MORALES

ARAMBURU, PEDRO EUGENIO

Pedro Eugenio Aramburu (*b.* 21 May 1903; *d.* ca. 1 June 1970), president of Argentina (1955–1958). During the 1950 coup against Juan D. PERÓN, General Aramburu remained on the sidelines. But menaced by a "Bring Back Lonardi" movement and by Perón's possible return from exile, he led the 13 November 1955 coup against President Eduardo LONARDI. After Lonardi's death Aramburu implored the United States to force Perón out of Latin America. When Peronist-inclined officers mutinied in July 1956, Aramburu ordered them killed in the first wave of political executions in twentieth-century Argentina.

Aramburu's régime reversed Lonardi's conciliation and launched a suppression of Peronism by declaring its functionaries ineligible for public service. In economic policy Aramburu was rigid on wage control, encouraged foreign investment, and denationalized Ar-

gentina's Central Bank in favor of membership in the World Bank and International Monetary Fund. With this course set, in 1958 he called elections. Even with Peronist candidates forcibly excluded, Aramburu lost the presidency to Arturo FRONDIZI. In July 1963 Aramburu again ran unsuccessfully for president, this time on the Argentine People's Union ticket. With resentment over the 1956 shootings and his concealment of Eva PERÓN's corpse still smoldering, the Montoneros, leftist Peronists, kidnapped and shot him in Timote, Buenos Aires Province.

— ROGER GRAVIL

ARANA, FELIPE DE

Felipe de Arana (*b.* 23 August 1786; *d.* 11 July 1865), Argentine landowner and official. Born in Buenos Aires to a merchant family, Arana took a law degree in Chile, then returned to Buenos Aires to participate in the revolution of May 1810. He was president of the House of Representatives in 1828 during the first government of Juan Manuel de ROSAS and was appointed minister of foreign affairs when Rosas returned to office in 1835. His policy was nationalist in tendency, and he negotiated treaties (1840 and 1850) that ended French intervention in the Río de la Plata. But Arana had few ideas of his own, and on domestic as well as foreign policy was little more than a mouthpiece of Rosas. During the terror of 1840–1842 he was deputy governor of Buenos Aires.

— JOHN LYNCH

ARANA, FRANCISCO J.

Francisco J. Arana (*b.* 1905; *d.* 18 July 1949), chief of the armed forces of Guatemala (1945–1949). A leader of the October revolution of 1944, Arana became a member of a three-man revolutionary junta that supervised the transition to the democratic and reformist government of Juan José ARÉVALO in March 1945. As Arévalo's chief of the armed forces, he suppressed a number of attempted coups by right-wing landowners and reactionary officers. Entertaining presidential ambitions of his own, he eventually courted the right-wing opposition to the revolution by promising to curb the growing influence of communism. The other presidential aspirant, Colonel Jacobo ARBENZ GUZMÁN, another hero of the 1944 revolution, pursued a left-wing agenda with the support of leftist labor unions. Political rivalry between Arana and Arbenz intensified in the summer of 1949. Arana was allegedly plotting the takeover of the government when he was shot resisting arrest by partisans of Arbenz. The suppression of the revolt that followed Arana's assassination cleared the way for Arbenz's election in 1950.

— PAUL J. DOSAL

ARANA, JULIO CÉSAR

Julio César Arana (*b.* 1864; *d.* 1952), a Peruvian businessman who exploited rubber and other jungle products in the Putumayo River lowlands of northeastern Peru. By 1903, after some twenty years of work, he had set up the largest natural rubber-gathering business of the era. He controlled Amazon lands totaling 25 million acres, importing men from the British Caribbean colonies as overseers and workers and using members of local tribes as actual rubber gatherers. The company demanded that the workers meet daily quotas. Many were beaten, and some were murdered if they did not comply. News of enslavement and terror in the rubber camps eventually reached human rights groups. An international scandal developed after British diplomat Roger Casement witnessed the abuses in 1910 and reported that the native population had been reduced by

---

Arana's company demanded that the workers meet daily quotas. Many were beaten, and some were murdered if they did not comply.

---

four-fifths. Pressure from the United States and England in 1910 led the Peruvian government to force Arana to stop the worst abuses, and his power declined as the natural rubber boom ended.

— VINCENT PELOSO

ARANA OSORIO, CARLOS

Carlos Arana Osorio (*b.* 17 July 1918), president of Guatemala (1970–1974). Born in Barbareña, Santa Rosa, Arana pursued a military career. Graduating from the Escuela Politécnica in 1939, he rose rapidly as a military officer, achieving the rank of lieutenant colonel in 1952. During the presidency of Julio César MÉNDEZ MONTENEGRO (1966–1970), he directed a counterinsurgency campaign that earned him the title "Butcher of Zacapa." Allegedly head of the Mano Blanca (White Hand), a right-wing terrorist organization, he was implicated in the plot to delegitimize the left by kidnapping archbishop Mario Casariego in 1968.

In 1970 Arana was elected president in a campaign marked by violence and fraud. His presidency was characterized by repression and economic nationalism. State

planning produced marked increases in public investment and economic growth. Since leaving office he has remained politically influential through the CAN (Central Auténtica Nacional).

— ROLAND H. EBEL

ARANGO, DÉBORA

Débora Arango (*b.* 1910), Colombian artist. Born in Medellín, Arango studied with Eladio Vélez in the Medellín Institute of Fine Arts, from 1933 to 1935, first displaying her works in 1937. Her bold and expressive use of color and contrast, often of exaggerated human forms, inspired heated debate over the morality of herself and her work, especially from the Roman Catholic church in Bogotá. Indeed, Arango's innovative and vibrant oil and watercolor paintings of provocative nudes shocked many sectors of Colombian society in the 1940s.

Arango then turned to social criticism, often from a feminist perspective, focusing upon such themes as prostitutes and popular culture. Her work of the late 1940s and 1950s, which retained its highly political and anticlerical character, much in the style of the caricaturist Ricardo Rendón (1894–1931), placed her in the vanguard of Colombian abstract art. In the 1950s, Arango traveled to England and Paris, where she added ceramics to her repertoire. She became professor at the Institute of Fine Arts in 1959.

— DAVID SOWELL

ARANGO Y PARREÑO, FRANCISCO DE

Francisco de Arango y Parreño (*b.* 22 May 1765; *d.* 21 March 1837), Cuban statesman, economist, and sugar planter. Educated in Cuba and Spain, Arango y Parreño graduated with a degree in law and spent his life in public service, including representing the city of Havana to the court in Spain and as one of two representatives from the island to the Cortes of Cádiz. In 1792 he wrote the *Discourse on the Agriculture in Havana and Ways of Developing It* that called for development of the sugar industry, utilizing massive slave labor, a position he modified after the Haitian Revolution. He returned to Cuba and, with the cooperation of Governor Luis de las Casas, shifted the focus of the island's economy to development of sugar. He also co-owned one of the five largest plantations on the island. He served as director of the Economic Society in 1795 but believed its function less important than that of the *consulado,* of which he was also a member. He contributed articles to the *Papel Periódico* favoring government intervention to develop the sugar industry and hinder the Spanish monopolies. His writings and his defense of Cuba in Spain helped form the liberal Cuban mind of the period. The major effect of his policies on the island, however, was the growth of the sugar industry, and its benefit to those who are now referred to as the sugarocracy.

– JACQUELYN BRIGGS KENT

ARANHA, OSWALDO

Oswaldo Aranha (*b.* 15 February 1894; *d.* 27 January 1960), Brazilian politician and diplomat. Aranha was part of the clique from Rio Grande do Sul that came to national prominence after the Revolution of 1930. A close friend of Getúlio VARGAS, Aranha was one of the architects of the Revolution of 1930. He served successively as minister of justice and minister of finance in the Provisional Government (1930–1934) and helped Vargas establish national authority by turning the blame for Brazil's economic crises away from the elite classes. From 1934 to 1937 Aranha served as Brazilian ambassador to the United States and became convinced that Brazil should ally itself with the United States, not with Germany. In 1938 he became foreign minister and moved Brazil into a clear pro-Allied role first as a supplier of raw materials, and later as a supplier of troops who fought in Italy.

Although often identified as a "liberal" member of the Estado Novo, Aranha viewed race, ethnicity, and class as determinants of intelligence and success, and he shaped Brazil's immigration laws to attract urban professionals at the expense of rural laborers. From 1947 to 1948 Aranha served as president of the General Assembly of the United Nations, where he increased Brazil's international presence and is best known for presiding over the partition of Palestine. In 1953 Aranha was appointed minister of finance in the democratically elected Vargas government. Aranha withdrew from public life following the suicide of Vargas in 1954 but remained an active member of the Partida Trabalhista Brasileiro until his death.

– JEFFREY LESSER

ARAUJO, ARTURO

Arturo Araujo (*b.* 1878; *d.* 1 December 1967), president of El Salvador (1 March–2 December 1931). Arturo Araujo's presidential campaign and brief presidency revealed fundamental changes that had occurred in Salvadoran politics by 1930. Himself a member of the landowning oligarchy, Araujo was educated as an engineer in England and returned to El Salvador with pro-union sentiments and admiration for the British Labour Party. In June 1918, Araujo was the keynote

speaker at the First Workers' Congress, held in the western town of Armenia, where he received the title of Benefactor of the Working Classes in General for his efforts on their behalf. The next year, Araujo made an unsuccessful bid for the presidency, then attempted to come to power through an invasion from Honduras in 1922. When Pío Romero Bosque declined to name his successor in the elections of 1930, Araujo and the Partido Laborista won with a platform based on Alberto MASFERRER's nine-point *mínimum vital* program. He guaranteed adequate food, clothing, housing, education, and work for all Salvadorans and held out the promise of agrarian reform to the dispossessed rural population. However, government corruption and the Great Depression prevented the fulfillment of these campaign planks, and Araujo was overthrown in a coup engineered by his vice-president, General Maximiliano HERNÁNDEZ MARTÍNEZ. Araujo's failed experiment with labor-based appeal resulted in fifty years of direct military rule in El Salvador and the elite's deep distrust of popular politics.

– KAREN RACINE

ARAUJO, JUAN DE

Juan de Araujo (*b.* 1646; *d.* 1712), Spanish composer active in Peru and Bolivia. Araújo was born in Villafranca de los Barros, Extremadura. He studied music in Lima, first with his father, and later at the University of San Marcos. It is possible that TORREJÓN Y VELASCO may have been Araujo's music teacher during the 1660s. For a while Araujo worked as choirmaster in churches in Panama, but around 1672 he was back in Lima, where he was ordained a priest and designated choirmaster of the cathedral of Lima, where he served until 1676. After spending some time in the area of Cuzco, in Peru, he traveled to Bolivia, where in 1680 he was appointed chapelmaster of the cathedral of La Plata, a position he retained until his death. In La Plata (now Sucre), one of the most influential and wealthy cities of the Viceroyalty of Peru, Araujo substantially expanded the musical library of the cathedral with Spanish and European religious music. He also formed several important boy choirs and during some celebrations conducted works for ten voices. He composed a number of pieces, including several religious works: a Passion, two Magnificats, three Lamentations, a Salve Regina, as well as religious hymns and other choral works, most of them now in the archives of the Sucre Cathedral and the seminary of San Antonio Abad in Cuzco. In more than 106 *villancicos* and *jácaras,* Araujo displayed a vivid wit in his adept utilization of the polychoral technique. The texts of the *villancicos* are taken from Spanish baroque poetry, usually accompanied by a harp. The collection of *villancicos* is now preserved at the Archives of the Musical Section of the Museo Histórico Nacional of Montevideo, Uruguay.

– SUSANA SALGADO

ARBENZ GUZMÁN, JACOBO

Jacobo Arbenz Guzmán (*b.* 14 September 1913; *d.* 27 January 1971), president of Guatemala (1951–1954). Born in Quezaltenango to a Swiss immigrant father and a Guatemalan mother, Arbenz completed his military education in 1935 at the Escuela Politécnica, where he excelled in athletics. In 1939 he married the daughter of a wealthy Salvadoran planter, María Cristina Vilanova, who was alleged to have Communist sympathies.

Arbenz participated in the movement to overthrow President Jorge UBICO in July 1944, going into exile when he became disillusioned with Ubico's successor, General Federico Ponce Vaides. He joined the October Revolution against Ponce and became a member of the

Jacobo Arbenz Guzmán delivers inaugural address, 15 March 1951. (AP/Wide World)

triumvirate that conducted the elections of December 1944, which brought Juan José ARÉVALO to power.

Named minister of defense by President Arévalo, Arbenz began to maneuver to succeed him. He also used his position to obtain the necessary bank loans to enable him to become a wealthy landowner. Faced with formidable political opposition from armed forces chief Major Francisco Javier ARANA, Arbenz conspired with Arévalo to have him assassinated while investigating an illegal arms cache on 18 July 1949. This provoked a military uprising that was put down when Arbenz distributed arms to students and workers. Now the undisputed head of the Revolution and backed by a coalition made up of the military, many peasants, the trade unions, government employees, and a number of centrist and left-wing parties (named the Unidad Nacional), he was overwhelmingly elected president in November 1950.

Although perceived in the United States as either Communist or under Communist influence, the Arbenz regime can best be understood as populist and nationalist. Arbenz's economic policies were directed toward creating a modern capitalist nation. In his inaugural address, President Arbenz stated that his economic policies would stress private initiative, but with Guatemalan capital in the hands of Guatemalans. To achieve that end, he adopted the proposals of the World Bank to begin construction of an Atlantic port and highway to compete with the port and railroad owned by the United Fruit Company; he also built a hydroelectric plant to compete with the U.S.-owned power plant.

Arbenz's populism was reflected in his support for the newly formed National Confederation of Guatemalan Campesinos (CNCG)—which gradually came under Communist influence—and its campaign to increase agricultural wages. Most important was the enactment of the famous Decree 900, the agrarian reform law that was designed to expand domestic purchasing power and put unused land under cultivation. Under the law, idle land on holdings above 223 acres could be expropriated and distributed to peasants for lifetime usufruct. Owners were to be compensated through twenty-five-year bonds for an amount equal to their self-declared tax valuation for 1952 and paid for by the peasants at a rate of 3 to 5 percent of their annual production. Under the program some one hundred thousand peasants received 1.5 million acres, for which the government issued over $8 million in bonds.

The United Fruit Company, which had only 15 percent of its land under cultivation, was particularly hard hit: 400,000 of its more than 550,000 acres were expropriated for $1,185,115—the amount of its own valuation for tax purposes. The company declared that the property was worth at least $16 million.

The agrarian reform law, the perceived radicalization of the peasantry by the now Communist-led CNCG, and the growing influence of a small cadre of Communists such as José Manuel FORTUNY, Carlos Manuel Pellecer, and Víctor Manuel GUTIÉRREZ, galvanized both upper- and middle-class opposition, even from many of the individuals and groups that had originally supported the Revolution. Intense lobbying by the United Fruit Company and the fear that Guatemala might become a Communist "bridgehead" in the Americas galvanized the Eisenhower administration into making common cause with the opposition, now led by the exiled Colonel Carlos CASTILLO ARMAS and General Miguel YDÍGORAS FUENTES. When a shipment of arms from Czechoslovakia arrived in Guatemala in May 1954, the CIA helped Castillo Armas invade from Honduras. Abandoned by the army, Arbenz resigned the

---

Although perceived in the United States as Communist, the Arbenz regime can best be understood as populist and nationalist.

---

presidency on 27 June. U.S. Ambassador John Puerifoy dictated a settlement that resulted in Castillo Armas assuming the presidency on 8 July. Arbenz went into exile, living in Cuba, Uruguay, France, Switzerland, and finally Mexico, where he died.

— ROLAND H. EBEL

ARBOLEDA, CARLOS

Carlos Arboleda (*b.* 1929), Panamanian sculptor and painter. Arboleda studied at the San Marcos Academy in Florence, Italy (1949–1954), and at the Real Academia de Bellas Artes in Barcelona, Spain (1955–1960). Upon his return to Panama, he became professor of sculpture at the Escuela Nacional de Artes Plásticas (1961–1964). He was the founder of and a teacher at the Casa de la Escultura, later renamed Centro de Arte y Cultura (1964–1990).

Although his early works included neoclassical nudes in marble, like *Serenidad* (1950), Arboleda also worked in wood, stone, ceramics, and metal, developing a less academic, more symbolic mature style. His talent is most outstanding in sculptures with indigenous themes such as *Piel Adentro*.

— MONICA E. KUPFER

ARBOLEDA, JULIO

Julio Arboleda (*b.* 9 June 1817; *d.* 12 November 1862), Colombian poet, politician, and presidential claimant (17 August–12 November 1862). Born to a family of aristocrats in Timbiquí, Cauca, he studied at Stoneyhurst College in England (1831–1834) and the University of Popayán (1837–1838). He lost part of his wealth while serving in the War of the Supremes (1839–1841). A gifted orator and an elegant essayist, Arboleda served as congressman (1844–1846). He opposed President José Hilario LÓPEZ in the press, was jailed, and led a revolt against López (1851). Fleeing to Peru, he remained in exile there until November 1853, when he was elected to the Senate. Back in Bogotá, in 1854 he escaped from the dictator José María MELO, against whom he had campaigned. Elected president designate [stand-in] in 1857, 1858, 1859, and 1860, Arboleda won the presidency (1860) for the 1861–1865 term but was not sworn in. During the Liberal revolution led by his uncle, Tomás Cipriano de MOSQUERA, he fought at Santa Marta (November–December 1860), moved his forces across Panama, and reached Pasto in May 1861. A year of bitter civil warfare that wracked southern Colombia ensued. Arboleda routed an invading Ecuadorian army (July 1862), and was killed at Berruecos (Nariño) four months later. Although Arboleda was celebrated for his literary genius, his greatest work, the epic poem *Gonzalo de Oyón,* survives only in fragments.

— J. LEÓN HELGUERA

ARCE, ANICETO

Aniceto Arce (*b.* 17 April 1824; *d.* 14 August 1906), president of Bolivia (1888–1892). Born in Tarija to an important merchant family, Arce was the largest shareholder of the Huanchaca Company, the most prosperous silver mining company in late-nineteenth-century Bolivia. He became one of the leaders of the Conservative (or Constitutionalist) Party and one of the most effective presidents of Bolivia during the period of hegemony of the Conservative oligarchy (1884–1899). He helped capitalize the Huanchaca Company through close association with the sources of Chilean capital. During the War of the Pacific (1879–1884), Arce favored a peace treaty with Chile, but he was exiled. His competition with Gregorio PACHECO in the 1884 elections, in which both candidates tried to outspend the other, signaled a new oligarchical electoral style. When Arce became president in 1888, he sponsored the building of a rail network that tied the Bolivian silver mines to the Pacific coast. He also improved the road system, reformed the military, and fostered the exploration of the Chaco frontier. According to a controversial biography by Ramiro Condarco Morales, Arce attempted to reform the hacienda labor system and bring Bolivia into the industrial age rather than, as other authors asserted, exploit the country for his personal profit. He died in Sucre.

– ERICK D. LANGER

ARCE, MANUEL JOSÉ

Manuel José Arce (*b.* 1 January 1787; *d.* 14 December 1847), the first constitutionally elected president of the United Provinces of Central America. Born in San Salvador to a creole family, he studied at the University of San Carlos in Guatemala but did not graduate. Much influenced by Doctor Pedro MOLINA and Father José Matías DELGADO, Arce participated in the Salvadoran insurgencies of 5 November 1811 and 24 January 1814, the latter of which resulted in his imprisonment until 1818. He led the Salvadoran forces who opposed Central American annexation to Agustín de ITURBIDE's Mexican Empire until his defeat at San Salvador by General Vicente FILÍSOLA on 7 February 1823, when he went into exile in the United States.

After Central American independence from Mexico (1 July 1823), Arce returned in February 1824 to join the governing junta of the new republic, serving briefly as provisional president. After a heated electoral campaign in 1825, the federal congress elected him Central American president over José Cecilio del VALLE by a vote of 22 to 5 (even though del Valle had won a plurality of 41–34 in the electoral college, only one vote short of the required majority). Arce's deals with conservative legislators cost him support among his liberal supporters, and his attempts to strengthen the Central American federation by interventions in the state governments led to the civil war of 1827–1829. Frustrated and disillusioned, he turned over power to his conservative vice president, Mariano Beltranena, on 14 February 1828. When Francisco MORAZÁN triumphed in the war, Arce went into exile in Mexico, where he wrote his memoirs, a valuable historical source for the 1820s.

Arce attempted to return to power in 1832, but, defeated at Escuintla by federal forces under the command of General Nicolás Raoul, he retreated to Soconusco, where he engaged in agriculture for several years. In 1843 he returned to El Salvador but soon was forced to flee to Honduras. In 1844 he appeared again in Guatemala, where he raised a force with the intention of ousting General Francisco MALESPÍN from power in El Salvador. Malespín dealt him another military defeat in May of that year, preventing Arce's return to his native

land until after Malespín's death in 1846. Arce died a year later, impoverished, in San Salvador.

– RALPH LEE WOODWARD, JR.

ARCE CASTAÑO, BAYARDO

Bayardo Arce Castaño (*b.* 21 March 1949), Nicaraguan leader and member of the Sandinista National Directorate. Arce was born in Managua. His father's career as a journalist led him to become a reporter for *La Prensa* while a student at the National Autonomous University in León. He came into contact with the Sandinista National Liberation Front through his work at the newspaper and joined the Student Revolutionary Front in 1969. Arce was responsible for rural logistical support in the northern highlands from 1974 to 1976. He belonged to the Prolonged Popular War faction of the Sandinistas. Tomás BORGE chose Arce to be his representative on the unified Sandinista National Directorate in March 1979.

After the fall of Anastasio SOMOZA in 1979, Arce became head of the Sandinista political commission. He greatly influenced the September 1979 meeting of the Sandinista leadership that set forth its short-term strategies in the "Seventy-two-Hour Document." In May 1980 he became president of the Council of State. As a leading radical theorist, Arce gave a speech in 1984 rejecting the need for elections and endorsing a one-party state. He organized the Sandinista presidential campaigns in 1984 and 1990. In 1993 Arce became president of the editorial council of the newspaper *Barricada*.

– MARK EVERINGHAM

ARCHILA, ANDRÉS

Andrés Archila (*b.* 24 December 1913), Guatemalan violinist and musical conductor. Archila was the son of Andrés Archila Tejada, director of a well-known marimba band. Recognized as a prodigy and violin virtuoso, Archila studied at the Santa Cecilia Academy in Rome. After returning to Guatemala in 1944, he promoted the organization of the National Symphony Orchestra, of which he was conductor until 1959, when he moved to the United States. For more than twenty-five years he was third violin in the National Symphony Orchestra as well as associate director of the Washington Symphonic Orchestra in Washington, D.C. He also founded and played first violin in the Pan American Union String Quartet.

– RALPH LEE WOODWARD, JR.

ARCINIEGA, CLAUDIO DE

Claudio de Arciniega (*b*. before 1528; *d*. 1592/93), the most important architect of sixteenth-century New Spain. Originally from Burgos, Spain, Arciniega was in the city of Puebla from 1554 to 1558; in 1559, the viceroy, Luis de VELASCO, called him to Mexico City and appointed him *maestro mayor de las Obras de Cantería de la Nueva España*. His 1559 monument commemorating the death of Emperor Charles V is known through an illustrated contemporary publication. In a sober Renaissance style sometimes called "purist," it provides some idea of what his many other works, known only through documents, may have been like. Arciniega was involved in most of the important construction projects of his time in Mexico City, including the cathedral (of which he was the first architect), the viceregal palace, and the churches of the principal religious orders. He also was called upon to give opinions about the cathedrals of Puebla and Pátzcuaro, the fortifications of Veracruz, and the mines of Taxco. In Mexico City elements in the cathedral and the facade of the Church of San Antonio Abad are ascribed to him or to his followers.

– CLARA BARGELLINI

ARCINIEGAS, GERMÁN

Germán Arciniegas (*b*. 6 December 1900), Colombian writer, diplomat, and political figure. Born in Bogotá of Basque descent, Germán Arciniegas became one of Latin America's most colorful and well-known writers. From an early age, he exhibited a talent for combining politics and journalism. In 1921, while attending the law faculty of the National University in Bogotá, he founded the journal *Universidad,* at which time he also attended a discussion group that included future Colombian reform leader Jorge Eliécer GAITÁN. In 1924 Arciniegas received an appointment to the faculty of sociology and continued to write for several newspapers and reviews throughout the next decade. He was director of *La revista de las Indias* in 1938 and *El Tiempo* in 1939. Both positions brought Arciniegas into collaboration with Latin America's leading intellectuals.

In 1939 Arciniegas was appointed Colombian chargé d'affaires in Buenos Aires. It was an exciting time to be in that city, and while there Arciniegas met with and was influenced by the community of exiles from Spain, a distinguished group that included José Ortega y Gasset, Ramiro de Maetzu, Ramón Pérez de Ayala, and also with the Argentines Alfredo PALCIOS and Victoria OCAMPO. Arciniegas was also influenced by the cultural elitism of José Enrique RODÓ, and he corresponded with such intellectual figures as Stefan Zweig, Alfonso REYES, and Gabriela MISTRAL.

Arciniegas was recalled to Colombia to serve as minister of education in 1941–1942, a position he held for a second time from 1945 to 1946. While in office he founded the Popular Library of Colombian Culture and a museum of colonial artifacts, both designed to enhance the public's awareness of Colombian history and culture. When domestic politics made it uncomfortable for Arciniegas to remain in Colombia, he relocated to the United States for a series of professorships at major universities: the University of Chicago (1942, 1944); the University of California at Berkeley (1945); and Columbia University (1943, 1948–1957).

In 1959 Arciniegas resumed his diplomatic career when he was named ambassador to Italy; the next year he was transferred to Israel, where he received an honorary degree from the University of Tel Aviv. He also became ambassador to Venezuela in 1967 and in the 1970s acted as Colombia's emissary to the Vatican. Arciniegas continued his editorial work throughout his life: he was the original force behind *La Revista de América* and subsequently donated his papers and books to the National Library in Bogotá.

Arciniegas has been a controversial figure, eliciting both praise and criticism. His hostility to Spain and the Conquest, coupled with his economic interpretation of history, have led many critics to condemn him as a spokesman for Moscow, but a closer reading reveals that Arciniegas's true vision of America was as a democratic continent free from the fanaticism of Europe. He glorified the nationalist and democratic spirit of America and praised the triple virtues of independence, democracy, and republicanism, an attitude that has appeared in the hundreds of books and articles he has written during his lifetime. Among his most notable works are: *Amerigo and the New World: The Life and Times of Amerigo Vespucci,* translated by Harriet de Onís (1955); *América es otra cosa: Antología y epílogo de Juan Gustavo* (1992); *Germans in the Conquest of America: A Sixteenth-Century Venture,* translated by Angel Flores (1943); *America in Europe: A History of the New World in Reverse,* translated by Gabriela Arciniegas (1986); *Biografía del Caribe* (1945); *Bolívar y la revolución* (1984); and *El caballero de El Dorado, vida del conquistador Jiménez de Queseda* (Caracas, 1959).

– KAREN RACINE

ARCOS, SANTIAGO

Santiago Arcos (*b*. 25 July 1822; *d*. September 1874), Chilean radical. The son of a Spanish father and a Chilean mother, Arcos was born in Santiago but grew up in Paris, where in 1845 he met his friend Francisco BILBAO (1823–1865). In 1847 he traveled in the United States (part of the time with the Argentine writer and politician Domingo Faustino SARMIENTO [1811–1888]) and from there went to Chile (February 1848). With Bilbao and others he formed the radical Sociedad de la Igualdad (Society for Equality) in April 1850. When the society was suppressed in November 1850, he was deported to Peru, from where he set out to visit the California goldfields. Back in Chile in 1852, he wrote (in prison as a subversive) his classic *Carta a Francisco Bilbao* (first printed in Mendoza, Argentina), an acute analysis of the defects of Chilean society. For this, he was swiftly banished to Argentina. In the 1860s he settled in Paris, where he remained for the most part. With the onset of fatal illness, he committed suicide by throwing himself into the Seine.

– SIMON COLLIER

ARDEN QUIN, CARMELO

Carmelo Arden Quin (*b.* 1913), Uruguayan abstract artist. Born in Rivera, Uruguay, Arden Quin was educated in Catholic schools in Brazil. He converted to Marxism in 1930 and began to study art in 1932. In 1935 he met the influential constructivist artist Joaquín TORRES GARCÍA in Montevideo. Moving to Buenos Aires three years later, Arden Quin studied philosophy and literature, and soon joined that city's artistic avant-garde, which included Edgar Bayley, Gyula KOSICE, Tomás Maldonado, and Lidy Prati. By the early 1940s, Arden Quin's early cubist style had given way to a geometric abstraction that tentatively rejected the convention of a rectangular frame by employing irregular and cut-out supports for paintings and collages; he pursued this direction in his art throughout the remainder of the decade, as did others in his milieu. He also experimented with sculptures and paintings with movable components, such as his *Coplanal* (1945), a square relief with manipulable geometric figures at each corner.

Arden Quin's early cubist style gave way to a geometric abstraction that employed irregular and cut-out supports for paintings and collages.

Along with Kosice and Rhod Rothfuss, Arden Quin was one of the chief contributors to the single issue of the review *Arturo,* published in 1944, and with them he initiated the Grupo Madí in 1946. He and the sculptor Martín Blaszko left the group in 1948, and Arden

Quin moved to Paris, where he began to associate with some of the leading figures of European abstract art, including Jean Arp, Auguste Herbin, Michel Seuphor, Constantin Brancusi, Serge Poliakoff, and Nicolas de Staël. One-man exhibitions of Arden Quin's art were held at the Galerie de la Salle, Saint-Paul de Vence, in 1978 and at the Espace Latino-Américain, Paris, in 1983.

– JOSEPH R. WOLIN

ARDÉVOL, JOSÉ

José Ardévol (*b.* 13 March 1911; *d.* 7 January 1981), Cuban composer. Born in Barcelona, Ardévol began composing as a boy. His father, Fernando Ardévol, conductor of Barcelona's Chamber Orchestra, instructed him in piano, composition, and conducting. At nineteen he studied conducting with Hermann Scherchen in Germany. In 1930 he moved to Cuba, where he taught history and aesthetics at Havana Municipal Conservatory (1936–1941); he also taught composition in the universities of Havana (1945–1950) and Oriente (1949–1951). Ardévol founded the Chamber Orchestra of Havana (1934), conducting it until 1952, and helped found the Grupo de Renovación Musical (1942), of which he was the spokesman and leader. He was very much committed to the Cuban Revolution, directing an underground group called the National Music Committee. In 1959 he was appointed director of the radio orchestras of the Ministry of Education and subsequently national director of music. He also served as editor of the musical magazine *Revolución* and as professor of composition at the Havana Conservatory (1965) and the National School of Music (1968). Ardévol's early music reflects a neoclassical influence mixed with nationalism; by the 1940s he had changed toward serialism and atonality, influenced by Anton von Webern. His works include *Música de cámara, Tres Ricercari, Suites cubanas,* several concerti and other orchestral works, plus a considerable amount of chamber and vocal music. He won the Cuban First National Music Award six times (1938–1953) and the International Ricordi Symphonic Award (1949). His *Música para pequeña orquesta* was a commission that premiered at the First Inter-American Musical Festival in Washington, D.C. in 1958. He died in Havana.

– SUSANA SALGADO

ARENALES, JUAN ANTONIO ÁLVAREZ DE

Juan Antonio Álvarez de Arenales (*b.* 13 June 1770; *d.* 4 December 1831), military and political leader of the Independence era. Born in Spain, Arenales entered on a military career that in 1784 took him to South America. He served in Upper Peru (later Bolivia) where he demonstrated a special interest in the welfare of the Indian population. His involvement in the 25 May 1809 revolution at Chuquisaca led to his arrest and imprisonment, but he escaped to collaborate first with Manuel BELGRANO in his campaigns in the Argentine Northwest and Upper Peru and then with José de SAN MARTÍN in his attempt to liberate Peru. Returning to Salta, where he had married, he became governor in 1823. Arenales sought to emulate the enlightened reformism of Bernardino RIVADAVIA and the Unitarist faction and also participated in the final mopping up of royalist resistance in Bolivia. However, in the general backlash against the Unitarists' effort to impose a centralist constitution, Arenales was deposed as governor early in 1827. He died in exile in Bolivia.

– DAVID BUSHNELL

ARENAS, REINALDO

Reinaldo Arenas (*b.* 16 July 1943; *d.* 7 December 1990), Cuban novelist, short story writer, poet, and essayist. Arenas was born in Perronales, a rural area in Oriente Province. His early experiences living in the country in a house full of what he terms "semisingle" women [as depicted in his novels *Singing in the Well* (1982) and *The Palace of the Very White Skunks* (1991)] shaped much of his work and character, as did the friendship and guidance of writers Virgilio PIÑERA and José LEZAMA LIMA when he was a young man. Although Arenas received little formal schooling as a child, his mother taught him to read and write, and he began writing while very young. In 1959 he joined Fidel Castro's rebel forces, and after the fall of the government of Fulgencio Batista he studied agrarian management in the Oriente town of Holguín and in Havana. His increasing disenchantment and unwillingness to compromise with the new Cuban regime, along with the unabashed homosexuality evident in both his life and his work, caused him to run afoul of the Castro government. Although both his novels *Singing in the Well* (1982) and *Hallucinations* (1971) received some attention in Cuba, he was persecuted, imprisoned, and censored there, even as his work was being published and acclaimed abroad. In 1969 *Hallucinations,* which had been smuggled out of Cuba, was honored in France as one of the best foreign novels. In 1980 he joined the Mariel Boatlift and left for the United States, where he settled in New York City until taking his own life in the final stages of AIDS.

Arenas's work takes the lyrical, ornate, baroque style of Cuban literary tradition and applies it to the themes of rebellion, repression, and the dehumanization that the subjugation of human beings brings upon both victims and perpetrators. Using the specific situations that he lived and knew intimately, he explores the universality of slavery and oppression. Particularly successful examples are his long poem *Leprosorio* (1990) and his novels *Arturo, la estrella más brillante* (1984) and *El asalto* (1991). Shortly before his death he finished his autobiography, *Antes que anochezca* (1992; translated as *Before Night Falls,* 1993). His work has been translated into many languages.

– ROBERTO VALERO

ARÉVALO BERMEJO, JUAN JOSÉ

Juan José Arévalo Bermejo (*b.* 10 September 1904; *d.* 7 October 1990), president of Guatemala (1945–1951). Born in Taxisco, Santa Rosa, he graduated from the Escuela Normal in 1922. After working for the Ministry of Education, he spent the duration of the UBICO administration in voluntary exile in Argentina,

Juan José Arévalo Bermejo on his inaugural day. (Life Magazine, © Time Warner, Inc.; Frank Scherschel)

where he completed his doctorate in philosophy in 1934. The leaders of the October Revolution of 1944 brought him back to campaign for the presidency, which he won overwhelmingly in December 1944.

Arévalo took office on 15 March 1945 with a broad, and ultimately contradictory, populist agenda: to pursue economic development while defending economic nationalism; to create a stable democratic order while greatly increasing political participation; and to expand social welfare while encouraging industrialization. Unable to achieve all of these objectives, the Arévalo administration, nevertheless, changed the legal and institutional structure of the country. Among its major accomplishments were a social security law (1946) guaranteeing workmen's compensation, maternity benefits, and health care; a labor law (1947) legalizing collective bargaining and the right to strike, and mandating a minimum wage (although peasant unions were forbidden); the Social Security Institute (IGSS), which built hospitals and clinics throughout the country; the National Production Institute (INFOP), which provided credit and expertise for small producers; and the creation of a national bank and a national planning office. Foreign investments were to be left intact but subject to government regulation. In 1949 the Congress enacted the Law of Forced Rental, which allowed peasants to rent unused land on large estates. The government also began to distribute lands confiscated from their German owners during World War II.

Arévalo's populist coalition began to unravel early in his administration. Among the causes were the establishment of diplomatic ties with the Soviet Union on 20 April 1945, the emergence of Communist leadership in the Confederación de Trabajadores de Guatemala (Víctor Manuel GUTÍERREZ GARBÍN) and the Partido de Acción Revolucionaria (José Manuel FORTUNY), the creation of the Communist-oriented Escuela Claridad (1946), and the passing of a Law on the Expression of Thought (1947) that expanded the definition of sedition to include anything urging "disregard of the laws or authorities."

The final blow to the legitimacy of the Arévalo administration was his connivance with his handpicked successor, Captain Jacobo ARBENZ, in the assassination of Arbenz's conservative presidential rival, Major Francisco Javier ARANA, on 18 July 1949. The assassination touched off a military rebellion that was put down by students and workers armed by Defense Minister Arbenz. However, stimulated by the "minute of silence" demonstrations commemorating the assassination, many students and professionals joined the conservative opposition. In all, President Arévalo had to contend with over twenty coup attempts against his government.

Although he left Guatemala at the end of his presidency and Arbenz was overthrown in 1954, *arevalismo* remained an important current in Guatemalan politics and was greatly feared by the supporters of the counterrevolution of 1954. His 1962 announcement (from Mexico) that he would once again run for the presidency in 1963 precipitated the demand that a "preventive coup" be launched by the army. On 29 March he secretly crossed the Mexican border, precipitating the overthrow of the YDÍGORAS FUENTES government. The military government that followed canceled the elections, thereby ending his bid for the presidency. He returned to Guatemala City in the 1980s, where he lived until his death.

– ROLAND H. EBEL

ARÉVALO MARTÍNEZ, RAFAEL

Rafael Arévalo Martínez (*b.* 25 July 1885; *d.* 1975), one of Guatemala's foremost literary figures. Born in Guatemala City, Arévalo Martínez attended the Colegio de Infantes, a school where children of the rich and the poor studied side by side. Along with other fathers of Guatemalan literature, such as Miguel Ángel ASTURIAS, Enrique GÓMEZ CARRILLO, and Máximo Soto-Hall, Arévalo Martínez is credited with introducing modernism to twentieth-century Guatemalan literature. Influenced by two of Latin America's foremost modernist poets, Rubén DARÍO and José MARTÍ Y PÉREZ, Arévalo Martínez exhibits the development of a distinct, yet confident, Latin American consciousness in his novels and poetry.

The ability of Arévalo Martínez to combine aesthetic concerns with a social commitment is undoubtedly his largest contribution to contemporary Latin American prose and poetry. Throughout his long literary career, his unique literary style balanced his personal search for identity with a need to discover his place in society. Among Arévalo Martínez's outstanding works are his 1915 masterpiece, *El hombre que parecía un caballo* (The Man Who Looked Like a Horse), which remains one of the finest pieces of literature in the first quarter of the twentieth century; the psycho-zoological utopian classics, *El mundo de los maharachíasa* (The World of the Maharachías [1939]) and *Viaje a Ipanda* (Journey to Ipanda [1939]); and his critical historical study of the Estrada Cabrera administration, *¡Ecce Pericles! La tiranía de Manuel Estrada Cabrera en Guatemala* (3d ed., 1983).

– WADE A. KIT

ARGUEDAS, ALCIDES

Alcides Arguedas (*b.* 15 July 1879; *d.* 6 May 1946), Bolivian writer, politician, and diplomat. Born in La

Paz, Arguedas studied in his native city, where he received a law degree, and in Paris. He served in Bolivian legations in Europe for twenty-five years. In these years he began to write for the press and, upon his return to La Paz, gained a measure of fame for his articles. In 1916 he was elected to the Chamber of Deputies, and in 1919 he became foreign agent in France and Spain. He also wrote historical novels, one of the earliest being *Pisagua* (1903), which dealt with the events of the War of the Pacific. His most highly regarded work, however, was his sociological study *Pueblo enfermo* (1909), in which he criticized his own people for defects in their character, brought on, he suggested, by their oppressive history. This theme carried over to other books, including his *Historia general de Bolivia* (1992). It was no wonder then that his works—novels, histories, articles—would all be controversial. At the same time, however, his histories have been praised by his countrymen and foreigners alike for the biting criticism of his nation's past.

– JACK RAY THOMAS

ARGUEDAS, JOSÉ MARÍA

José María Arguedas (*b.* 18 January 1911; *d.* 2 December 1969), Peruvian novelist, poet, and anthropologist. The most important Latin American writer of indigenous narrative, Arguedas, although born of white parents, saw indigenous culture from the inside, having been raised in his early years by Quechua Indians in various towns in the Peruvian Andes. He spoke Quechua before he learned Spanish. His mother died when he was three years old, and his father, an itinerant judge, was often away. Between 1931 and 1963 Arguedas earned degrees in literary studies and anthropology and held posts in various government cultural programs and museums of folklore and ethnology.

Arguedas admired the Spanish cultural heritage, but he feared its power to destroy the indigenous culture he valued so highly. In his folkloric and ethnological studies, Arguedas aspired to preserve the best of indigenous culture. He sought to attain a kind of cultural fusion, or *mestizaje,* in which the values of both of Peru's cultures could be joined. His novels and short stories reflect this most strikingly in their ability to re-create in Spanish the indigenous mentality and way of life.

In 1964 Arguedas became head of the department of ethnology and professor of Quechua at the Agrarian University. One day after his resignation, in December 1969, he shot himself. It was perhaps his doubt that *mestizaje* would ever be achieved—that in fact indigenous culture would not survive—which led to his suicide. Evidence for this exists in his final unfinished novel, *El zorro de arriba y el zorro de abajo* (The Fox

from Above and the Fox from Below), published posthumously in 1970.

– KEITH MCDUFFIE

ARGÜELLES, HUGO

Hugo Argüelles (*b.* 2 January 1932), Mexican playwright. Born in Veracruz, Argüelles studied at the School of Dramatic Arts of the Instituto Nacional de Bellas Artes (INBA) in Mexico City, where he later taught. He also founded the School of Fine Arts in Puebla. He won, among others, the Premio Nacional de Teatro in 1958 for his play *Los cuervos están de luto* (1958; The Crows Are in Mourning) and the Juan Ruiz de Alarcón award in 1961 for *Los prodigiosos* (1956; The Prodigies). His plays are characterized by black humor and a tone of mockery, capturing the essence of the Mexican spirit. Argüelles enjoys broad recognition for his extensive production of theatrical works, some of which he has successfully directed for television. Other major plays are *La dama de la luna roja* (1970; The Lady of the Red Moon), *El gran inquisidor* (1973; The Grand Inquisitor), *El cocodrilo solitario del panteón rococó* (1985; The Solitary Crocodile of Rococó Pantheon), and *Los gallos salvajes* (1986; The Wild Roosters).

– JEANNE C. WALLACE

ARGÜELLO, LEONARDO

Leonardo Argüello (*b.* 1875; *d.* 15 December 1947), Nicaraguan physician, writer, and politician. Born in León, the center of Nicaraguan liberalism, Leonardo Argüello participated in the revolutionary movement of 1911–1912. For his efforts Argüello was made a deputy in and the president of the Nicaraguan Congress. In 1925, Argüello was named minister of public instruction, a position in which he distinguished himself by attempting to broaden education to include the rural population and by allocating more money for schools and libraries. During the 1930s and 1940s, Argüello

---

Argüello, although already over seventy years old,

did not prove to be the puppet that Somoza has

anticipated.

---

occupied himself with his writing but was brought from academic life back to politics in February 1947, when Anastasio SOMOZA GARCÍA arranged to have Argüello succeed him as president of the nation. Argüello, although already over seventy years old, did not prove to be the puppet that Somoza has anticipated, rather, he began to increase the participation of anti-Somocistas in the government. Three months into his term, Argüello was removed from office by a May 1947 coup led by Somoza's National Guard and forced into exile.

— KAREN RACINE

ARGÜELLO, SANTIAGO

Santiago Argüello (b. 1791; d. 1862), Spanish military and civilian official in New Spain and Mexican California. Born at Monterey, California, he began his career as an officer in the Spanish army and later served the Mexican government until 1834. Described as tall, stout, and of fair complexion, Argüello was appointed *alcalde* of San Diego in 1836 and prefect of Los Angeles in 1840. He also served as administrator of the former mission at San Juan Capistrano from 1838 to 1840. Argüello's lands included Rancho Tia Juana, Rancho Trabuco, and the San Diego Mission estate, which were granted to him in 1829, 1841, and 1846, respectively. He and his wife, Pilar Ortega, of Santa Barbara, had twenty-two children, many of whom became influential in Mexican California society.

— IRIS H. W. ENGSTRAND

ARIAS, ARTURO

Arturo Arias (b. 22 June 1950), Guatemalan novelist and literary critic. Born in Guatemala City, Arturo Arias is considered one of the leading representatives of the Guatemalan "new" novel. His first novel, *Después de las bombas* (1979; *After the Bombs,* 1990), narrates the mythical and carnivalesque story of a boy's search for his father during the political unrest that followed the Guatemalan counterrevolution of 1954. His second novel, *Itzam Na* (1981), which won the prestigious Cuban Casa de las Américas Award for best novel, is a combination of voices and written documents depicting the social and political alienation of bourgeois Guatemalan youth of the 1970s. His third novel, *Jaguar en llamas* (1989), deals with the indigenous side of Guatemalan history from the Conquest to the present and is his most ambitious work to date. In 1990 he published his fourth novel, *Los caminos de Paxil,* which also looks at contemporary Guatemalan political history in light of the Mayan past. Arias has also published a collection of short stories, *En la ciudad y en las montañas* (1975), and a collection of essays, *Ideologías, literatura y sociedad durante la revolución guatemalteca: 1944–54* (1979), which won the Casa de las Américas Award for essays; he coauthored the screenplay for *El Norte* (1983). In 1988 he was elected president of the Con-

gress of Central American Writers. Arias has a doctorate in the sociology of literature from the École des Hautes Études en Sciences Sociales in Paris and teaches at San Francisco State University.

— ANN GONZÁLEZ

ARIAS, DESIDERIO

Desiderio Arias (b. 1872; d. 1931), military figure, politician, and president of the Dominican Republic (17 May 1916–June 1916). Born in Muñoz, Dominican Republic, Arias emerged as a key leader in the Liberal guerrilla movement led by Juan I. Jiménez in the 1910s. Assigned to the post of minister of war and the navy after Jiménez's election, General Arias consolidated his own power and moved against the president in a coup d'état in 1916.

Arias's coup and the civil disorder that followed provoked the United States to intervene, and Arias retired to private life under the watchful eye of the United States. Until the end of his life, Desiderio Arias played a role in his nation's political life as a symbol of the Liberal guerrillas. He died in a rebellion against President Rafael TRUJILLO MOLINA.

— TODD LITTLE-SIEBOLD

ARIAS CALDERÓN, RICARDO

Ricardo Arias Calderón (b. 1933), Panamanian philosopher and intellectual and leader of the Christian Democratic Party (PDC) known for his honesty. In the 1980s, Arias Calderón became one of the leading opponents of the dictator General Manuel Antonio NORIEGA MORENO (1983–1989). In 1984, he ran for second vice president on a ticket headed by Arnulfo ARIAS MADRID in a coalition with the latter's Authentic Panameñista Party (PPA). With the death of Arias in 1988, the opposition to Noriega was thrown into chaos. In 1989, in preparation for the May elections, the Christian Democrats joined with the majority faction of the Panameñistas, headed by Guillermo Endara Paniza, and other political parties to form a broad anti-Noriega coalition called CivicADO (Democratic Alliance of Civic Opposition). With Endara heading the ticket, Arias Calderón ran for vice president. The candidate for second vice president was Guillermo Ford.

The Noriega government claimed victory in the elections, but the opposition's count as well as that of independent observers indicated just the opposite. The government later annulled the results. During a demonstration against Noriega's rule, Arias Calderón and the other candidates were beaten by the dictator's "dignity battalions." CivicADO took over the government after the 1989 U.S. invasion. On 17 December 1992, Arias Calderón resigned from the vice presidency under pressure from his own party because of disagreements with Endara and because Endara had lost a referendum on constitutional and other issues two days earlier. (The PDC had already pulled out other members from the coalition in April 1991.)

– JUAN MANUEL PÉREZ

ARIAS DE SAAVEDRA, HERNANDO

Hernando Arias de Saavedra (Hernandarias; *b.* 1561; *d.* 1634), one of the greatest figures in Argentine history and the first creole to hold public office in Latin America. He was born in Asunción to Captain Martín Juárez de Toledo, a close associate of Álvar Núñez CABEZA DE VACA, and María Sanabria, daughter of the *adelantado* Juan Sanabria y Mencia Calderón. Following a common custom of the period, he was given his paternal grandfather's last name. From a very young age, Hernandarias participated in conquests and explorations and came in contact with important figures of the early history of the Río de la Plata region. He became known for his bravery and was severely wounded more than once.

In 1576, when he was only fifteen years old, he went to work for the governor of Tucumán, Gonzalo de Abrego. In 1577, he entered the service of Hernando de Lerma in Santiago del Estero, and three years later he accompanied Alonso de Vera y Aragón, cousin of the *adelantado* Juan Torres de Vera y Aragón, in a six-month cattle drive from Paraguay to Buenos Aires. In 1582, Hernandarias was with Juan de GARAY for the second founding of Buenos Aires. That year he married Garay's daughter, Jerónima Contreras. In 1588, he accompanied Juan Torres de Vera y Aragón in the founding of San Juan de Vera de las Siete Corrientes.

Hernandarias held public office a total of six times, three times between 1590 and 1597 as interim governor of the Río de la Plata, and another three times between 1597 and 1618 as governor. The first time he became governor he was only 29 years old. As governor, Hernandarias proved to be an enlightened administrator. He encouraged commerce among the different provinces; tried to curb the rampant contraband in the Río de la Plata region; protected the Indians and encouraged the creation of Jesuit missions in Paraguay; distributed land among Spaniards, creoles, and mestizos; built schools, churches, and hospitals; and promulgated laws designed to improve the living standards of the population.

Hernandarias's policies created resentment among powerful Spaniards, particularly those engaged in contraband. In 1618, his enemies prevailed against him, and the new governor, Diego de Góngora, had him imprisoned and most of his property confiscated. His wife sought refuge with her brother, General Juan de Garay. Hernandarias's friends took his case to the crown, which sent the *juez pesquisador* (investigating judge) Matías Delgado Flores to investigate. Hernandarias was set free, and he was absolved of any wrongdoing in July 1624 by the oidor Alonso Pérez de Sálazar, who had been sent by the Audiencia of Charcas. Hernandarias died in Santa Fe.

– JUAN MANUEL PÉREZ

ARIAS MADRID, ARNULFO

Arnulfo Arias Madrid (*b.* 15 August 1901; *d.* 10 August 1988), Panamanian politician and three-time president (1940–1941, 1949–1951, 1968). A medical doctor by profession and a graduate of Harvard Medical School, Arnulfo Arias was a controversial politician. Elected three times and overthrown on every occasion (the last time after just eleven days in office), Arias dominated Panamanian politics for fifty-seven years. He was highly nationalistic and anti-American. After joining the nationalistic organization *Acción Comunal* in 1930, he was leading it a year later in the revolution that overthrew the corrupt government of Florencio Harmodio ARO-SEMENA.

Arias's enemies, the U.S. in particular,

accused him of Nazi tendencies.

As a populist leader, Arias tried to ingratiate himself with the masses by promoting social revolution and using anti-establishment rhetoric. His platform was embodied in what he called *panameñismo,* translated as "Panama for the Panamanians." His policies against the Chinese and West Indians, whom he stripped of citizenship, and others, such as requiring people in some professions to wear uniforms, made people uneasy. His first presidency constituted a small revolution, challenging the oligarchy and the United States. He promulgated a nationalistic constitution, created a social security system, gave women the right to vote, attempted a land reform program, and involved the state more actively in the economy. His enemies, the U.S. in particular, accused him of Nazi tendencies. Arias did not allow the U.S. to acquire more land for military bases with long-term leases and full jurisdiction as the U.S. had requested. Arias was trying to avoid the creation of other areas in Panamanian territory over which Panama would not have control. His nationalism and anti-Americanism put him on a collision course with the U.S., which in 1941 was involved in his overthrow. In the mid-1980s, Arias became the major figure opposing the dictator General Manuel Antonio NORIEGA. His followers came to power after the 1989 U.S. invasion and renamed his party the Arnulfista Party of Panama.

— JUAN MANUEL PÉREZ

ARIAS MADRID, HARMODIO

Harmodio Arias Madrid (*b.* 3 July 1886; *d.* 23 December 1962), Panamanian politician and president (1932–1936). Harmodio Arias was a prominent and highly respected politician in the 1920s and one of the leaders of the 1931 revolution that overthrew the government of Florencio Harmodio AROSEMENA. He and his brother Arnulfo became the leaders of a new and more nationalistic generation of middle-class Panamanians. He was very popular for his opposition to the ratification of the 1926 treaty with the United States. Harmodio became president in 1932 after one of the freest and most honest elections the country had seen.

He came from a modest family. In 1911, he earned a doctorate in law and political science at the University of London. In 1912, President PORRAS appointed him to a commission charged with drafting a legal code. He was a professor at the law school (1918–1920), deputy to the National Assembly (1920–1924), and Panama's representative to the International Court of Justice at The Hague and the League of Nations. As a member of the National Assembly, he staunchly defended national sovereignty. He also had a very successful law practice.

As president, Harmodio Arias attacked corruption and incompetence, for which he incurred the wrath of those accustomed to using the government for personal gain. He presided over an honest administration. In 1935, Arias founded the University of Panama. In 1936, he negotiated a new treaty with the United States that ended the latter's right to intervene in Panama's internal affairs. As the editor of *El Panamá-América,* he continued to be an influential voice in Panamanian politics after he left the presidency.

— JUAN MANUEL PÉREZ

ARIAS SÁNCHEZ, OSCAR

Oscar Arias Sánchez (*b.* 13 September 1940), president of Costa Rica (1986–1990), awarded the Nobel Peace Prize in 1987 for designing a plan for peace in Central America. Arias Sánchez's father was an early follower of José FIGUERES FERRER and an active member of the

Oscar Arias Sánchez. Guatemala City, 7 August 1987. (Jason Bleibtreu/Sygma)

National Liberation Party (PLN). His mother's family is part of the Costa Rican coffee elite that emerged during the nineteenth-century coffee boom. Arias Sánchez came to international prominence shortly after his inauguration in 1986 when he took bold initiatives to propel Central America into a peace process. His proposals for peace and stability in the region led to an agreement, signed in 1987, between Honduras, Guatemala, Nicaragua, El Salvador, and Costa Rica.

The Arias plan, or Esquipulas II, established the framework for the pacification and democratization of Central America. It provided for the restoration of civil liberties, for amnesty for political prisoners, for free elections, and for genuine dialogue between governments and opposition forces. The plan contributed to the process that brought peace and free elections to Nicaragua and new hope for the eventual demilitarization of the region.

Even though Arias came to the international scene at a relatively young age, he had served a long apprenticeship in the highly competitive arena of Costa Rican party politics and in the rigorous intellectual environment of the University of Costa Rica (UCR). He received his law and economics degrees from the UCR, was awarded a master of arts degree in political science and economics from the London School of Economics (1967), and earned a doctor of philosophy degree from the University of Essex, England (1974). He joined the faculty of UCR in 1969 and served as a member of the ad hoc Commission of the National University (1972–1975). He was a director of the Costa Rican Technological Institute from 1974 to 1977.

Arias began his political career in the PLN and held high elected and appointed positions in the national government and in the party. He served as secretary to the president (1970–1972) during the last José Figueres Ferrer administration. From 1972 to 1977, he held a cabinet-level position as minister of national planning and economic policy. While serving as a member of the National Assembly (1978–1982), he also held other leadership positions. He was secretary of international affairs (1975–1979) and he was elected secretary general in 1979 on a reformist platform that brought a new generation of leaders to the fore. Arias ascended to the presidency chiefly by serving in positions of party leadership and in the administration of President Luis Alberto MONGE ÁLVAREZ. He won the PLN primary and then defeated Rafael Angel CALDERÓN FOURNIER in the general election.

Arias has received many awards and honorary degrees from universities in Europe, Central America, and the United States. Since his presidency he has lectured widely on the related questions of world peace and the environment, donating the proceeds from the lectures to the Arias Foundation, which was established to support research on these issues. He has also continued to be active in politics.

— JOHN PATRICK BELL

ARIDJIS, HOMERO

Homero Aridjis (b. 6 April 1940), Mexican writer. Like many of his contemporaries in Mexico, Aridjis has had a varied career, including journalism, diplomatic service, and teaching. Trained as a journalist, he was a member of a writing workshop directed by the noted Mexican short-story writer Juan José ARREOLA and was awarded fellowships by the Centro Mexicano de Escritores (Mexican Writers Center) and the Guggenheim Foundation.

Aridjis has written poetry and prose, much of it first published in Mexican literary journals and Sunday cultural supplements of newspapers and subsequently appearing in numerous collected works. His many volumes of poetry, among them *Antes del reino* (1963) and *Vivar para ver* (1977), focus on themes of love, life, and death, and are heavily charged with emotion. More re-

cently he has attempted to create the "poema nuclear" (nuclear poem), modifying his use of language and including social and historical themes. As a prose writer of stories and novels, he combines narrative and poetic elements (*Mirándola dormir*, 1964, and *Perséfone*, 1967), autobiography (*El poeta niño*, 1971), and the historical (*1492, vida y tiempos de Juan Cabezón de Castilla*, 1985). Much of Aridjis's writing has been translated into English and other languages. In recent years, he has been actively involved with other intellectuals in the Grupo de los Cien (Group of 100), Mexico's foremost ecological movement.

— GABRIELLA DE BEER

ARISMENDI, JUAN BAUTISTA

Juan Bautista Arismendi (b. 1775; d. 23 July 1841), officer in the Venezuelan Emancipating Army. Arismendi was born in La Asunción on Margarita Island. At the commencement of the movement for emancipation from Spain, Arismendi took the pro-independence side and participated in the 1812 expedition to Guiana. He returned to Margarita Island following the expedition only to find it under the control of Coronel Pascual Martínez of the Spanish government. Arismendi's pro-independence leadership led to his arrest and imprisonment first in La Guaira and later on Margarita Island. During his imprisonment, Spanish authority was forcibly ousted and Arismendi was named governor of the island in 1813. That same year he traveled to Caracas to place himself in the service of Simón BOLÍVAR, who put him in charge of the Barlovento campaign.

Arismendi returned to Margarita Island in 1814 and was named its commander in chief. In 1819 he served as vice president of the republic for a short time. Two years later he led his own armed contingent in the battle of Carabobo. He remained on Margarita Island and on more than one occasion during the Southern campaign resisted orders for his recruitment. In 1828 José Antonio PÁEZ appointed him second in command of the army, and in 1830 he was an active participant in the movement that dissolved Gran Colombia. Arismendi was elected senator in the National Congress for the province of Margarita in 1835 and was reelected in 1839.

— INÉS QUINTERO

ARISMENDI, RODNEY

Rodney Arismendi (b. 22 March 1913; d. 27 December 1989), leader of the Communist Party of Uruguay. Arismendi was born in the city of Río Branco in the department of Cerro Largo. He studied law in Montevideo, where he was a prominent student leader. During this period he joined the Communist Party, whose secretary general, Eugenio Gómez, had held the office since the party's inception. Arismendi took over for Gómez as secretary general in 1955 and held the office until 1989. As a journalist and director of the daily *Diario Popular,* he was forced into exile but was elected a representative to Parliament in 1946, and went on to serve a number of terms in the legislature. In 1973 Arismendi was imprisoned by the military regime and later deported; he lived for more than ten years in the Soviet Union. Returning to Uruguay in 1984, he was elected to the senate, an office he held until his death.

Arismendi was one of the principal pro-Soviet Marxist theorists in Latin America, publishing several books on ideological themes and playing an important role in the creation of the leftist Frente Amplio. After his death, he was replaced as secretary general of the Communist Party by Jaime Pérez, a former union leader.

— JOSÉ DE TORRES WILSON

ARISTA, MARIANO

Mariano Arista (*b.* 1802; *d.* 1855), president of Mexico (1851–1853). Arista enlisted as a cadet in the Provincial Regiment of Puebla at the age of fifteen. In June 1821 he joined the Army of the Three Guarantees under the leadership of Agustín de ITURBIDE to support the Plan of Iguala for autonomy and independence for Mexico. Arista continued to serve in the army, reaching the rank of brigadier general. On 8 June 1833 he rebelled against the radical reforms of President Valentín GÓMEZ FARÍAS, calling on General Antonio López de SANTA ANNA and the army to preserve the fueros (prerogatives) and properties of the regular and secular clergy. Exiled to the United States in November 1833, Arista was able to return to Mexico only after the triumph of the Plan of Cuernavaca, which provided the basis for Santa Anna's formation of a more conservative government. Arista served as a member of various military commissions before being named commanding general of the state of Tamaulipas in 1839. In 1846, Arista was called to lead the Army of the North. On 8 May 1846, at Palo Alto, Tamaulipas, Arista's forces were defeated by a U.S. army contingent under General Zachary Taylor in the first major battle of the war. The next day Arista retreated and turned over command to General Francisco Mejía. Arista served as minister of war from 12 June 1848 to 15 January 1851, on which date he assumed the office of president. He resigned on 6 January 1853 and moved to Europe. He died aboard a British ship en route from Portugal to France, where he hoped to ob-

tain medical treatment. He was buried in Lisbon; his ashes were returned to Mexico in 1880.

— D. F. STEVENS

ARISTIDE, JEAN-BERTRAND

Jean-Bertrand Aristide (*b.* 15 July 1953), president of Haiti, 1991. Following a period of violence and instability, Aristide won a popular democratic election and became the youngest president in Haitian history, succeeding provisional president Ertha Pascal Trouillot on 7 February 1991. A charismatic Roman Catholic priest who strongly supported the theology of liberation, Aristide had strong backing from the black peasant masses. A Vodun priestess participated in the inauguration ceremony as Aristide took the oath of office in the creole language of the poor peasants. Well educated and dedicated to the welfare of the poor, Aristide was an outspoken critic of the DUVALIER dictatorship and of the Tonton macoutes, who continued to threaten him after the ouster of Jean-Claude Duvalier in 1986. The *macoutes,* along with the oppressive poverty of Haiti, presented formidable obstacles to the popular Aristide as he began his administration. Resistance to Aristide's military reforms led to his ouster by the army on 30 September 1991 in a coup led by Brigadier General

---

A Vodun priestess participated in the inauguration ceremony as Aristide took the oath of office in the creole language of the poor peasants.

Raoul Cedras. The imprisoned former leader of the *Tonton macoutes,* Roger Lafontant, was reportedly executed during the coup. Late in 1994 Aristide was returned to office following lengthy U.S.-sponsored diplomacy and the virtual occupation of the country by an American military force.

— RALPH LEE WOODWARD, JR.

ARLT, ROBERTO

Roberto Arlt (*b.* 2 April 1900; *d.* 26 July 1942), Argentine writer. Born in Buenos Aires, Arlt's writing was one of the major critical (re)discoveries of the halcyon, countercultural period between the demise of Juan PERÓN (1955) and the military coup of 1966. One dimension of the interest in Arlt was a reaction against the emerging international monumentalization of Jorge Luis BORGES. Arlt evoked several components of Argentine culture that were judged to be absent in Borges:

he was of immigrant extraction; he was unlettered and unencumbered by an immense bookish learning; his literature centered on the urban proletariat, with a heavy emphasis on the socially marginal, misfits, and the aberrant; he was unconcerned by coherent ideologies and, indeed, often seemed to relish the incoherent and the contradictory; and he exemplified the practice of literature, not as an intellectual pastime, but as gainful employment. While today it may seem specious to promote a categoric disjunction between Borges and Arlt, Arlt was championed as an authentic voice of all of the gritty aspects of the Argentine sociopolitical body that the aloof Borges—at least in his world-literature embodiment—seemed to deny. Moreover, in novels like *Los siete locos* (1929; *The Seven Madmen,* 1984), dramas written for the populist theater, such as *Trescientos millones* (1932), and in the hundreds of newspaper columns that constitute a veritable mosaic of the underbelly of the Buenos Aires proletariat and petite bourgeoisie in the watershed years of the Great Depression, Arlt moved the literary registers of Spanish away from the rhetorical and poetic models of modernism and other European standards (including ossified academic norms) toward the beginnings of a true urban colloquiality in Argentine literature, one perhaps less sociolinguistically authentic than it is emblematically authentic. He died in Buenos Aires.

– DAVID WILLIAM FOSTER

ARMENDÁRIZ, JOSÉ DE

José de Armendáriz (*b.* 1670; *d.* ?) marquis of Castelfuerte and viceroy of Peru, 1724–1736. A native of Rivagorza, Spain, Armendáriz pursued a military career from a young age, serving in Flanders, Catalonia, Naples, Portugal, and Villaviciosa. Captain-general of Guipúzcoa when named viceroy of Peru in 1723, he was probably the most distinguished Spanish military officer to serve in South America.

Armendáriz proved energetic and firm, unlike his predecessor, Fray Diego Morcillo, but was neither an innovator nor a reformer. He stepped up surveillance along the Pacific coast to reduce smuggling by foreign vessels and limited the duration of the Portobelo fairs to deter contraband. Armendáriz also devoted great energy to strengthening colonial defenses throughout the continent. He captured and executed José de ANTEQUERA, the former *oidor* (judge) of Charcas, who had installed himself as an independent governor of Paraguay. The execution touched off a serious tumult in Lima, which Armendáriz crushed. Because the guards killed two Franciscan partisans of Antequera in suppressing the uprising, the clergy harshly criticized the

viceroy, but the crown fully supported him. He also acted swiftly and severely to defeat the mestizo rebellion of Alejo Calatayud in Cochabamba. Armendáriz attempted to curb the corruption of provincial governors (*corregidores*) and restrict the sale of *aguardiente* (distilled liquor), with little success.

Promoted in 1729 to captain-general, the highest Spanish military rank, Armendáriz received the great honor of membership in the Order of the Golden Fleece upon his return to Spain. He then commanded the regiment of royal guards.

– KENDALL W. BROWN

ARMENDÁRIZ, PEDRO

Pedro Armendáriz (*b.* 1912; *d.* 18 June 1963), Mexican actor. Born in Mexico City, Armendáriz attended school in San Antonio, Texas, and completed his studies at the California Polytechnic Institute. He worked as a journalist in the United States before returning to Mexico in 1934. Armendáriz debuted in the film *María Elena* (1935) and went on to appear in more than 100 movies. He was a leading actor with the famed team of director Emilio "El Indio" FERNÁNDEZ. Armendáriz's striking screen presence made him one of the most popular leading stars of Mexican cinema. His most memorable films are *Distinto Amanecer* (1943), *María Candelaria* (1943), *Maclovia* (1948), *La perla* (1946), and *Enamorada* (1947). He was also cast in several Hollywood films, including *Fort Apache* (1948) and *From Russia with Love* (1963). He died in Los Angeles.

– DAVID MACIEL

ARMIJO, MANUEL

Manuel Armijo (*b.* 1801; *d.* 1853), governor of New Mexico (1836–1846). Armijo's administration was notable mainly for its opposition to Anglo-American incursions. He sought to control the illegal activities of American trappers, and in 1841 he led the Mexican forces that defeated a group of Texans, led by General Hugh McLeod, who sought to conquer New Mexico. In 1846 Armijo led the Mexican army that opposed the invasion of the province by General Stephen W. Kearny. In the face of superior U.S. forces, he abandoned the defense of the territory and fled to Mexico, where he remained.

– RICHARD GRISWOLD DEL CASTILLO

ARNAZ, DESI

Desi Arnaz (*b.* 2 March 1917; *d.* 2 December 1986), Cuban bandleader, actor, and pioneer television producer. Born Desiderio Alberto Arnaz y Acha in Santiago de Cuba to an influential family, Arnaz and his father went into exile in Miami with the overthrow of President Gerardo MACHADO in 1933. Discovered there by Xavier CUGAT, he joined the Cugat band for a six-month tour. He then returned to Miami and, with his own band, introduced the conga line to the United States, and started a national dance craze. During the 1940s, he appeared on Broadway and made several feature films. While filming *Too Many Girls* in 1940, he met Lucille Ball, marrying her the same year. They were divorced in 1960.

Although popularly known for his role as Ball's husband in the television show *I Love Lucy,* his most important contributions came as the guiding force behind its production company, Desilu. His many innovations created the presentation and format of the situation (sitcom) comedy as it is known today and began the practice of "reruns." Desilu bought its own studio and became the most important independent production house in the industry, producing many of the successful 1950s television comedies. Arnaz retired in the early 1960s. He died in Del Mar, California.

– JACQUELYN BRIGGS KENT

ARNS, PAULO EVARISTO

Paulo Evaristo Arns (*b.* 14 September 1921), archbishop of São Paulo, Brazil (1970–). A Franciscan priest born in Forquilhinha, Santa Catarina, Arns was a relatively unknown figure until he was named auxiliary bishop of São Paulo in 1966. Like most of the hierarchy, Arns supported the 1964 military coup, but after being named archbishop in November 1970, he became a

---

The Vatican undertook an investigation of dioceses identified with liberation theology, including the archdiocese of São Paulo, which was admonished to avoid portraying Christ as a revolutionary.

---

trenchant critic of the military government and one of Brazil's outstanding voices on behalf of human rights. A venerated public figure, Arns denounced the widespread use of torture. In January 1972 he created the Archdiocesan Justice and Peace Commission, which became known for its efforts to defend human rights. In his pastoral work, Arns supported Christian base communities, which became controversial in the 1970s and 1980s because of some activists' support for the labor

movement and the Workers' Party. In 1973, he was named a cardinal.

After becoming one of Brazil's most prominent public figures in the 1970s, Arns fell out of favor with the Vatican and was less visible in the 1980s. When John Paul II became pope in 1978, Arns and the archdiocese of São Paulo came under careful scrutiny. In 1980, the pope asked Arns to write a report explaining and defending the church's overt support for a major strike that had taken place that year. Four years later, the Vatican undertook an investigation of seminars in dioceses identified with liberation theology, including the archdiocese of São Paulo, which was admonished to avoid portraying Christ as a revolutionary. In 1989, the pope dismantled and subdivided the archdiocese, which had previously been the largest in the world in terms of its Catholic population. Arns remained archbishop of São Paulo, but it was now a smaller archdiocese, from which most of the poor areas where base communities had flourished were excised.

– SCOTT MAINWARING

AROSEMENA, FLORENCIO HARMODIO

Florencio Harmodio Arosemena (*b.* 17 September 1872; *d.* 30 August 1945), a civil engineer and president of Panama (1928–1931). Arosemena presided over one of the most corrupt periods in Panamanian history. His only previous political involvement had been a brief period as a councilman in the Panama City government. He became president largely as a result of the manipulations of President Rodolfo CHIARI (1924–1928). He and his cronies lined their pockets and used their offices for their own personal businesses. He was overthrown on 2 January 1931 by the nationalistic organization *Acción Comunal.* It was the first time since its separation from Colombia that a constitutionally elected government of Panama had been overthrown.

– JUAN MANUEL PÉREZ

AROSEMENA, JUAN DEMÓSTENES

Juan Demóstenes Arosemena (*b.* 24 June 1879; *d.* 16 December 1939), jurist, teacher, journalist, member of the Panamanian Academy of History, and president of Panama (1936–1939). Arosemena had a long history of public service. In 1912 he was named chief justice by President Belisario PORRAS, who appointed him governor of the province of Colón in 1922. He became secretary of foreign relations in the administration of Florencio Harmodio AROSEMENA (1928–1931).

In 1936 he was the candidate for president of the National Revolutionary Party, which his younger brother, Arnulfo, had helped to organize. He was elected with the backing of President Harmodio ARIAS MADRID (1932–1936). He died before his term expired and was succeeded by Augusto S. Boyd. Arosemena's regime was basically a caretaker government, paving the way for Arnulfo ARIAS's ascension to power in 1940.

– JUAN MANUEL PÉREZ

AROSEMENA, JUSTO

Justo Arosemena (*b.* 1817; *d.* 1896), Panamanian intellectual and statesman. At sixteen he was awarded a bachelor's degree in humanities from the College of San Bartolomé, Colombia. In 1837 he was awarded a doctorate in law by the University of Magdalena. Arosemena spent most of his life in government, serving as minister of foreign relations (1848–1849), speaker of the Chamber of Deputies of the Colombian Congress (1852), senator, president of the Constitutional Convention of Río Negro (1863), and the first president of the Federal State of Panama (1855).

He wrote extensively on law and politics and was a prominent exponent of European liberal ideas. He belonged to the radical faction of the Liberal Party, the Golgotha. Arosemena believed that freedom had to reach everyone in society and that this required sovereignty. He favored autonomy for the isthmus. Arosemena envisioned the potential economic benefits that could be derived from an interoceanic canal, but he warned against foreign domination. Although he admired the U.S. political system, he spoke against U.S. intervention in other countries, particularly after the Mexican War (1846–1848). His most important works are *Examen sobre la franca comunicación entre los dos océanos por el istmo de Panamá* (1846), *Estudios constitucionales* (1852), and *El Estado Federal de Panamá* (1855).

– JUAN MANUEL PÉREZ

AROSEMENA, PABLO

Pablo Arosemena (*b.* 1836; *d.* 29 August 1920), Panamanian politician and president (1910–1912) and an ardent supporter of classical nineteenth-century liberalism. Arosemena held many important political posts during his long political life. He was attorney general, president of the Sovereign State of Panama in 1875 and 1885 (on both occasions overthrown by the Colombian army), and in 1880 he was elected second vice president to the Colombian presidency. Arosemena continued to be active in politics after Panama's separation from Colombia. In 1904 he became president of the National Constituent Assembly. He served as Panama's president

from September 1910 to October 1912, having been appointed by the National Assembly to finish the term of José Domingo de Obaldía following his death. (Arosemena succeeded Carlos Antonio MENDOZA, who temporarily had assumed the presidency immediately following Obaldía's death.)

– JUAN MANUEL PÉREZ

AROSEMENA GÓMEZ, OTTO

Otto Arosemena Gómez (*b.* 19 July 1925; *d.* 20 April 1984), president of Ecuador (1966–1968). A native of Guayaquil who received his law degree from that city's public university, Arosemena entered local politics. Serving as president of the Guayas provincial electoral tribunal (1952) and then as a deputy in the National Congress, he became a prominent businessman as well as a lawyer. He was twice chosen as senator representing coastal commercial organizations. Originally a Liberal, Arosemena broke away to organize his personalistic Coalición Institucionalista Democrática (CID) on 2 February 1965. He was one of three CID members in the 1966 Constituent Assembly, where he made a pact with the Right and was chosen provisional president of the nation (November 1967).

Arosemena remained in office for twenty months, during which a new constitution was adopted and national elections were held. His government was cautious in the area of domestic policy, although Arosemena was outspoken in foreign affairs. Hostility to U.S. policy led him to withhold his signature from the official declaration adopted by the 1967 conference of hemispheric presidents in Punta del Este, Uruguay. He subsequently criticized the Alliance for Progress and after a public exchange with the U.S. ambassador, ordered his expulsion from Ecuador. Once out of office, Arosemena sought to build the CID, but with limited success. His party backed the rightist presidential candidate León FEBRES-CORDERO in the 1984 elections, then swiftly dissolved upon the death of Arosemena.

– JOHN D. MARTZ

AROSEMENA MONROY, CARLOS JULIO

Carlos Julio Arosemena Monroy (*b.* 24 August 1919), president of Ecuador (1961–1963). Scion of a wealthy Guayaquil family, Arosemena received his law degree in 1945 from the University of Guayaquil and became active in Liberal politics. By the 1950s he was an ardent nationalist, loyal to José María VELASCO IBARRA. He was elected to the Chamber of Deputies in 1952 and 1958, and he became president of the Federación Nacional Velasquista in 1960. In the latter year he was the vice presidential candidate on the slate with Velasco and was swept to office by the Velasquista landslide victory.

Presiding over Congress in his role as vice president of the republic, Arosemena soon broke with Velasco and became an outspoken critic. When Velasco was overthrown in 1961, Arosemena, at age forty-two, succeeded him as president. A supporter of labor and an outspoken nationalist, he espoused moderate reforms while expressing sympathy for the Cuban Revolution. This position aroused traditional domestic interests and angered the United States. His public displays of drunkenness became increasingly frequent, and the opposition hardened. On 11 July 1963 Arosemena was overthrown by the armed forces, which set up their own junta.

Arosemena soon organized his personalistic party, the Partido Nacionalista Revolucionario (PNR), which carried his banner in elections for the 1966 Constituent Assembly and afterward. But the PNR was unable to generate significant popular support. By 1984 its congressional representation consisted of Arosemena himself, and since 1986 the PNR has been moribund.

– JOHN D. MARTZ

AROSEMENA QUINZADA, ALBACÍADES

Albacíades Arosemena Quinzada (*b.* 20 November 1883; *d.* 8 November 1958), Panamanian president (1951–1952). Arosemena was born in Los Santos. He was a cattleman and a businessman but was also very active in politics, having served as minister of the treasury, treasurer of the Panama City government, and ambassador to Spain and France. Arosemena Quinzada was president after the overthrow of Arnulfo ARIAS. His period in office was very chaotic, and he was unsuccessful in his attempts to calm the situation.

– JUAN MANUEL PÉREZ

ARRAIS, MIGUEL

Miguel Arrais (*b.* 15 December 1916), governor of Pernambuco (1963–1964, 1987–1991), mayor of Recife (1960–1962), federal deputy (1991–1994), and populist figure in Northeastern Brazil.

Miguel Arrais was born into a rural middle-class family in the interior of Ceará. He eventually settled in Recife and graduated from law school in 1937. A government job and his family provided him with political connections and led to his appointment as finance secretary of Pernambuco in 1947. By 1955, he had joined the Frente do Recife, a reformist left-center coalition that reached out to rural workers. Arrais won election

as mayor of Recife in 1960 and gained a reputation for courting poor voters with slum improvement programs.

In 1963 Arrais became governor of the state amid rising tensions throughout the country. He implemented a minimum wage for rural workers, expanded farm credit, and promoted unionization in the countryside. Although not an ally of President João GOULART, Arrais was accused of radicalizing politics in the Northeast and blamed for successive waves of strikes and lockouts. As a result, he was jailed for a year following the 1964 coup. He spent most of the period 1965–1979 in Algeria, representing petroleum exporters.

Arrais returned to Brazil in 1979 and three years later won election to Congress. Using his image as an elder statesman, he ran for governor in 1986 and took office the following year. He failed to make a large showing in the primaries for president in 1989 but was elected federal deputy that year. He was the leading candidate for governor of Pernambuco in 1994.

– MICHAEL L. CONNIFF

ARRAU, CLAUDIO LEÓN

Claudio León Arrau (*b.* 6 February 1903; *d.* 9 June 1991), Chilean pianist. Early recognized as a prodigy, Arrau became one of the most accomplished Latin American musicians of the twentieth century. As a youth from Chillán, Arrau was sent on a grant from the Chilean government to study at the prestigious Julius Stern Conservatory in Berlin under the tutelage of Martin Krause from 1912 until 1918. During his tenure in Germany he earned numerous honors, including the Liszt and Ibach prizes. Throughout the 1920s and 1930s Arrau toured Europe and the Americas before settling in the United States after the outbreak of World War II.

Arrau announced that he would no longer publicly perform any Bach, as he felt the piano could not do the composer justice.

Arrau was known for his slow tempos and lack of ostentation, a style that emphasized the inherent beauty of the music rather than the skill of the musician. In 1935, Arrau played a series of recitals in Berlin featuring the complete keyboard works of Bach. After this performance, he announced that he would no longer publicly perform any Bach, as he felt the piano could not do the composer justice.

In later years, Arrau brought his talents to Japan, Australia, and Israel, and recorded distinctive versions of major works by Beethoven, Brahms, Chopin, and others. He received many honors, including the UNESCO International Music Prize, and was named a commander in the French Legion of Honor. The cities of Santiago and Chillán both contain streets bearing Arrau's name.

— JOHN DUDLEY

ARREOLA, JUAN JOSÉ

Juan José Arreola (*b.* 21 September 1918), Mexican writer. Born in Ciudad Guzmán in the state of Jalisco, Arreola received the prestigious Premio Xavier Villaurrutía in 1963 for his only novel, *La feria* (The Fair, 1963). He has also written drama but is best known for his innovation in the short story and other short prose forms. His major collections of stories and prose pieces include *Varia invención* (Various Inventions, 1949), *Confabulario* (Confabulary, 1952), *Palindroma* (Palindrome, 1971), and *Bestiario* (Bestiary, 1972). Together with writers such as José Revueltas and Juan Rulfo, Arreola's works move Mexican literature beyond a parochial consideration of nationalistic themes and address Mexican identity in the context of universal human truths and archetypes. Through the use of humor, satire, irony, fantasy, and linguistic playfulness, he has explored themes such as religiosity, the absurd, materialism, the commercialism of the United States, and relations between the sexes. He has also played an influential role in Mexican literature as the director of writing workshops and as the editor of two important literary series in the 1950s, *Cuadernos del unicornio* (The Unicorn's Notebooks) and *Los presentes* (Those Present).

— DANNY J. ANDERSON

ARRIAGA, PONCIANO

Ponciano Arriaga (*b.* 1811; *d.* 1 March 1863), Mexican politician and cabinet minister, "Father of the Constitution of 1857." Born in the provincial capital of San Luis Potosí, Arriaga was an ardent federalist and radical liberal. He used his oratorical and writing skills in the movements against President Anastasio BUSTAMANTE in 1832 and later against President Antonio López de SANTA ANNA. Arriaga was deposed as *regidor del ayuntamiento* (president of the city council) of San Luis Potosí and jailed for these activities in 1841, but the following year he was elected to represent his home state in the national Congress.

During the war with the United States (1846–1847), Arriaga helped to supply the Mexican army in Coahuila and Nuevo Laredo. He opposed the Treaty of Guadalupe Hidalgo for conceding territory in order to gain peace. He served briefly (13 December 1852–5 January 1853) as minister of justice under President Mariano Arista. When Santa Anna regained the presidency, Arriaga was exiled. In New Orleans, he met Benito JUÁREZ, Melchor OCAMPO, and other liberals. With the triumph of the Revolution of Ayutla (1854), Arriaga returned to Mexico and was elected to the Constituent Congress of 1856–1857. As president of the congress, he was one of the principal authors of the Constitution of 1857. During the War of the Reform (1858–1861), Arriaga supported the Juárez government and later served as republican governor of the state of Aguascalientes (1862–1863) and the Federal District (1863).

— D. F. STEVENS

ARRIETA, JOSÉ AGUSTÍN

José Agustín Arrieta (*b.* 1803; *d.* 1874), Mexican painter. In an effort to explain the Mexicanism, the rustic provincialism, of Arrieta's work, it has been judged according to a single criterion, that of popular painting. It is often forgotten that as a student at the Academy of Fine Arts in Puebla under the direction of Julián Ordóñez and Lorenzo Zendejas, he was competent in genres typical of the academy, such as painting historical themes or representing the human figure, in full or in half, as well as torsos and heads. Although he was not a student at the Academia de San Carlos in Mexico City, he occasionally sent work there from 1850 to 1871.

Arrieta's extensive work stresses two themes: folkloric paintings and dining-room paintings or still lifes. He took pride in an impeccable technical control. His dining-room paintings, which became popular with collectors of rustic art, are full of allusions to European art in their details as well as in some elements of their harmonious composition. His folkloric paintings depict scenes inside homes as well as in public places, such as the street. His work is replete with subtle implications of popular culture.

— ESTHER ACEVEDO

ARRIETA, PEDRO DE

Pedro de Arrieta (*fl.* 1691–15 December 1738), Mexican architect. Born in Real de Minas, Pachuca, Arrieta passed the examination to become a master architect in Mexico City in 1691. Four years later he supervised the buildings of the Inquisition, and in 1720 he became *maestro mayor de la catedral y del real palacio,* the highest rank to which an architect in New Spain could aspire. Among the many public and private buildings ascribed to him are the Basilica of Guadalupe (1695–1709); the remodeling of the Jesuit church of the Profesa, contracted in 1714 and completed in 1720; and the Palace of the Inquisition with its peculiar suspended arches (1733–1737). His work is classicizing in that he insisted on the use of columns and rejected the surface movement of the salomonic baroque with its characteristic spiral columns. Also characteristic of Arrieta's buildings are polygonal arches and narrative reliefs.

— CLARA BARGELLINI

ARRIVÍ, FRANCISCO

Francisco Arriví (*b.* 24 June 1915), Puerto Rican author, dramatist, and theater director. Arriví was born in San Juan and graduated from the University of Puerto Rico in 1938. From 1938 to 1941 he taught at Ponce High School, where his students staged his first plays. After his return to San Juan in 1941, he wrote, directed, and translated dramas and was active in the radio productions of the School of the Air until 1948. He studied drama at Columbia University in New York under a Rockefeller grant in 1949 and was programming director for the Puerto Rican government radio station for ten years. A tireless organizer, Arriví established the Tinglado Puertorriqueño experimental theater company and developed the theater program of the Institute of Puerto Rican Culture, which he directed from 1959 to 1970. He launched the institute's yearly festivals, among them Puerto Rican Theater, International Theater, and the Theater of Ponce. He was instrumental in the creation of the Fine Arts Center in Santurce as a forum for the performing arts in 1981.

In 1959 the Institute of Puerto Rican Literature honored Arriví's *Vejigantes* (Carnival masks, 1958), a powerful drama about racial identity in Puerto Rico, which formed part of a trilogy of plays on the same theme that Arriví entitled *Máscara puertorriqueña* (Puerto Rican masquerade, 1959–1960). Other famous plays by Arriví are *María Soledad* (1947), *Caso del muerto en vida* (The case of a man dead in life, 1951), *Club de solteros* (Bachelors' club, 1953), and *Cóctel de Don Nadie* (The cocktail of Mr. Nobody, 1964). Arriví has also published books of poetry and collections of essays on theater and literature, including *Areyto mayor* (An indigenous festival, 1966) and *Conciencia puertorriqueña del teatro contemporáneo, 1937–1956* (Puerto Rican awareness of contemporary theater, 1967).

— ESTELLE IRIZARRY

ARROYO DEL RÍO, CARLOS ALBERTO

Carlos Alberto Arroyo del Río (*b.* 27 November 1893; *d.* 31 October 1969), president of Ecuador (nonelected 1939 and elected 1940–1944). Born in Guayaquil, Arroyo del Río studied law, entered private practice, and taught at the University of Guayaquil, eventually be-

---

Within a few months of Arroyo del Río's inauguration, Peru invaded territory claimed by Ecuador.

---

coming rector in 1932. He became active in the Liberal Radical Party, serving as a member of the *Junta de Beneficencia,* secretary of the Municipal Council (1917–1918), and president of the Municipal Council (1921–1922). In 1922–1923 he represented Guayas Province in Congress, serving as president of the Chamber of Deputies in 1923. Elected senator in 1924, he actively opposed the revolution of July 1925 and the Ayora administration, and ten years later (1934–1935) led the congressional opposition to President José María VELASCO IBARRA that resulted in the dissolution of Congress.

When Aurelio Mosquera Narváez died in office on 15 November 1938, Arroyo del Río assumed executive power as president of the Senate and presided over an extraordinary congress that abrogated the Constitution of 1938 and reinstated the Constitution of 1906. He resigned on 28 May 1944 to run for president. He was elected and took office on 1 September 1940. The supporters of his leading opponent, Velasco Ibarra, charged that the election was fraudulent and attempted a coup. The insurrection failed, and the leaders, including Velasco Ibarra and Carlos Guevara Moreno, were exiled.

Within a few months of Arroyo del Río's inauguration, Peru invaded territory claimed by Ecuador. In 1944, Arroyo del Río was removed from office as a result of the country's defeat in the 1941 border war with Peru, and Velasco Ibarra was recalled from exile to replace the discredited president. Arroyo del Río left the country, going first to Colombia, then to New York City; he returned to Guayaquil in 1948 to resume his legal practice. He remained the target of public attacks until his death.

— LINDA ALEXANDER RODRÍGUEZ

ARRUFAT, ANTÓN

Antón Arrufat (*b.* 14 August 1935), Cuban playwright and poet. Born in Santiago in Oriente Province, Arrufat studied in his native city as well as at the University of Havana. He has traveled to Czechoslovakia, France, Italy, and England and been very active in promoting literary activity in Cuba. He was editor in chief of the influential *Casa de las Américas* from 1960 to 1965 and has contributed to *Lunes de Revolución, Ciclón, Cuba en UNESCO, La Gaceta de Cuba,* and others. His work has attained such national acclaim as the honorable mentions he received for his play *El vivo al pollo* in the Casa de las Américas competition in 1961 and for his collection of poetry *Repaso final* in the 1963 competition. In 1968 he won the coveted prize given by the Cuban Union of Writers and Artists (UNEAC) for his play *Los siete contra Tebas,* which established him as one of Cuba's leading playwrights and at the same time brought him into temporary disfavor with the Castro regime. After a decade or so of being relegated to the periphery, he was rehabilitated and has become active again. Arrufat remained in Cuba, where he began publishing and participating in cultural activities once again. His most recent work is a novel, *La caja está cerrada* (1984).

— ROBERTO VALERO

ARTIGAS, JOSÉ GERVASIO

José Gervasio Artigas (*b.* 19 June 1764; *d.* 23 September 1850), Uruguayan caudillo and leader of the independence movement. Born into a prominent landowning family, Artigas received his early education in a school run by Franciscan friars in Montevideo. In his youth he developed a love for the common people and a firsthand practical knowledge of the country's resources by participating in the primary economic activity of the region—the roundup of unmarked cattle and the illegal sale of hides to Portuguese and British commercial agents. In 1799 he was appointed an official of the Blandengues, a militia regiment centered in Montevideo, which was charged with protecting rural settlers against Indian raids and countering the smuggling activities of the Portuguese in present-day Brazil.

Artigas was an early enthusiast of the independence movement against the Spanish viceregal government first announced in Buenos Aires in 1810. The following year, as head of the rural militia in the Banda Oriental (literally, "East Bank," or today's Uruguay), he commanded a brilliant military triumph in Las Piedras (18 May 1811). Months later, he refused to abide by the armistice negotiated by the elitist Ruling Committee in Buenos Aires, which would have returned his province to the Spanish. His army's march into exile along the banks of the Ayuí River in Entre Ríos—referred to as El Exodo Oriental (the Exodus of the Orientals)—was joined by nearly 16,000 people who were largely from the lower classes. In no other region of the insurgent provinces was the emancipation struggle waged with such a high degree of popular adhesion. Henceforth, Artigas's distrust of *porteño* (Buenos Aires) priorities would play a decisive role in his actions.

For the next decade, Artigas defended the territorial integrity of the Banda Oriental against military invasions and economic incursions by the Spanish, Portuguese, and British. Moreover, by providing firm leadership in the resistance to the centralist ambitions of Buenos Aires, he emerged as a defender of the confederation of provinces that included Entre Ríos, Córdoba, Corrientes, and Santa Fe. Styling himself the "Protector of Free Peoples," he issued a number of farsighted decrees from his military encampment at Purificación, near present-day Paysandú. Artigas's "Instrucciones del Año XIII," modeled upon the legal principles of the United States, set forth the tenets of a federal constitution to unite the provinces on an equal basis. His "Reglamento provisorio para el fomento de la campaña y seguridad de sus hacendados" (1815) aimed at subdividing large landholdings in order to create economic opportunity for the large class of "dispossessed" creoles, mestizos, zambos, and Indians, and at accelerating the resettlement of rural areas in order to restore regional prosperity. These measures, in addition to the priority he gave to the defense of Banda Oriental territory at the expense of the struggle in the north against Spanish royalist forces, earned him the wrath of Buenos Aires's Dictatorial Party. Artigas's Federalist League, in contrast with the Buenos Aires leadership, demanded assemblies and congresses, not kings; a democratic order with the participation of the rural masses rather than a patrician society governed by an urban elite; and protection for local agriculture, industries, and arts rather than the domination of American markets by European trading companies.

Simultaneous with Artigas's defense of Banda Oriental autonomy was his objective of establishing a loose confederation uniting all the provinces of the former viceroyalty. Between 1814 and 1820 there was continual conflict in the region between the armies commanded by the Buenos Aires elite and what they called the "Anarchists of the Littoral"—that is, the caudillos of the provinces, who supported Artigas. On several occasions Artigas himself fought shoulder to shoulder with the plebeian soldiers of Santa Fe and Entre Ríos in order to repel armies sent from Buenos Aires. He also organized the region's defense against Portuguese invasions from the east. In 1816 his vastly outnumbered forces suffered defeats in San Borja, Ibiracoí, Carrumbé, India Muerta, Arapey, Arroyo Catalán, and Aguapey, which led to the Portuguese occupation of Montevideo in January 1817.

Approaching the new decade, Artigas continued his struggle against the Portuguese and the Spanish despite his troops' lack of arms and the decimation of his fighting ranks. Conflict and dislocation had claimed the lives of half of the region's 50,000 inhabitants. His program of land confiscations and levies fueled local resistance. In 1819 Artigas rejected the constitution promulgated by Buenos Aires on account of its monarchist orientation and the central role ascribed to that city for governance of the region. In January 1820, his army of 3,000 troops suffered heavy losses to Portuguese troops in the battle of Tacuarembó. Fructuoso RIVERA (later Uruguayan president), until then a trusted lieutenant, deserted his ranks weeks later by signing an armistice with the Portuguese. In the battle of Cepeda in February 1820, Artigas's lieutenants, Pedro Campbell (of Irish ancestry), Francisco RAMÍREZ, and Estanislao LÓPEZ (strongmen of Entre Ríos and Santa Fe) inflicted heavy losses on the Buenos Aires army led by José RONDEAU, and ended for the time any pretense of *porteño* domination over the united provinces. The Treaty of Pilar, as negotiated by López and Ramírez with the leaders of Buenos Aires, created an important legal precedent for Argentina's future reconstruction according to federalist principles. Yet the intractable Artigas, who had no part in the negotiations, angrily accused Ramírez of treason for having made a pact with the enemy.

Artigas's military decline came rapidly. He led an army of 2,500—half of whom were mission Indians—in a series of inconclusive skirmishes against Ramírez, who then pulverized Artigas's troops in the battle of Avalos, Corrientes, in 1820. Artigas fled to exile in Paraguay, where the dictator Dr. José Gaspar Rodríguez de FRANCIA kept him virtually a prisoner. Confined and in humble circumstances, Artigas lived in obscurity until his death thirty years later.

Nineteenth-century Argentine historians—most notably Manuel BELGRANO, Bartolomé MITRE, Vicente Fidel LOPEZ, and Domingo F. SARMIENTO—treated the legacy of Artigas in most disfavorable terms: he represented in their eyes the paradigmatic example of a despotic caudillo at the head of "barbarous" rural masses who were intent upon destroying urban civilization. However, beginning in the 1880s, revisionist Uruguayan writers began propagating a benevolent image of Artigas as "father of the country," a view that prevails to this day.

— WILLIAM H. KATRA

ARZÁNS ORSÚA Y VELA, BARTOLOMÉ

Bartolomé Arzáns Orsúa y Vela (*b.* 1676; *d.* January 1736), Bolivian writer and historian. Born in Potosí of Spanish parents, Arzáns dedicated his life to the writing of his multivolume *Historia de la villa imperial de Potosí,* the most complex and fascinating text of the colonial period in Bolivia. Arzáns did not completely finish the work; his son Diego wrote the final 8 of its 322 chapters. The manuscript was lost for many years, and the first edition was not published until 1965.

In this work, Arzáns attempts to give a complete and detailed history of Potosí, one of the most prosperous cities of the New World during the sixteenth and seventeenth centuries. It was founded in 1545 next to the Mountain of Potosí, a rich silver mining site. In order to capture and convey the splendor and greatness of the city, Arzáns includes historical data, legends, short stories, Indian myths, descriptions of daily events, and details about various aspects of life in the city. The book is an exuberant and baroque depiction of Potosí, with history and fiction intertwined. The *Historia* is crucial to an understanding of Bolivia because of the historical, literary, and ideological information it provides; it can be seen to prefigure the nationalism in the country.

— LEONARDO GARCÍA PABÓN

ARZE, JOSÉ ANTONIO

José Antonio Arze (*b.* 13 January 1904; *d.* 23 August 1955), Bolivian intellectual and politician. Born in Cochabamba, Arze was the most influential Marxist intellectual and the leading leftist politician in Bolivia during the 1940s. In 1928 he helped found the National Student Federation (FUB), which demanded university reforms on the Argentine model. As the presidental candidate of the FUB in 1940, Arze received almost a fifth of the total vote. Thereafter, he was instrumental in organizing the first effective national leftist party, the Party of the Revolutionary Left (PIR), which rivaled in size and influence the National Revolutionary Movement (MNR) among the opposition parties of the 1940s. Arze again became a presidential candidate in 1951. He was a professor of sociology at the University of San Francisco Xavier in Sucre and founder of the Institute of Bolivian Sociology and its journal, the *Revista del Instituto de Sociología Boliviana.* The author of numerous books and translator of Louis

Baudin and Georges Rouma, Arze influenced several generations of leftist politicians in Bolivia.

– ERICK D. LANGER

ASCASUBI, HILARIO

Hilario Ascasubi (*b.* 14 January 1807; *d.* 17 November 1875), Argentine poet, journalist, politician, and entrepreneur. His adventurous adolescence took him through Portugal, France, England, and Chile. In 1824 he reorganized an old printing shop in the provincial city of Salta, renaming it Imprenta de la Patria, and began publishing the *Revista de Salta.* Thus began his journalistic career, which he never abandoned. In 1825 Ascasubi began a second career, this time in the army fighting the *caudillaje* (bossism). As a lieutenant he was in charge of recruiting and tasted defeat in two battles. Under General Juan LAVALLE, the hero of the fight against the tyrant Juan Manuel de ROSAS, Ascasubi became captain. A prisoner during 1831–1833 in a pontoon in Buenos Aires, he escaped to Montevideo and set up a bakery, becoming rich enough to help Lavalle and the Argentine refugees. At the same time, he managed to continue pursuing his poetic interests, achieving fame with this "gauchescos" *trovos* (popular ballads) published later under the title *Paulino Lucero* (1872).

Absorbed by the political events in his country,

Ascasubi was not only a chronicler, but an

exceedingly active participant.

Ascasubi joined the armies successfully fighting the Rosas dictatorship and, as a lieutenant colonel in the ensuing period (1843–1852), performed various jobs while continuing his writing. From 1853 to 1859 he published *Aniceto el Gallo, Gaceta Joco-Tristona y Gauchi-Patriótica* (Aniceto the Rooster, Humorous-Sad and Gauchi-Patriotic Gazette). Although retired, Ascasubi was sent to France in 1860 to recruit for the Argentine army. In Paris he finished and published his main work, the lengthy *Santos Vega, o Los mellizos de La Flor* (1872), a narrative poem that depicts the pampa, the idiosyncrasies of its inhabitants and their customs, the intimate life within the estancia, and the mythological figure of the payador (singer).

Absorbed by the political events in his country, Ascasubi was not only a chronicler, but an exceedingly active participant. As a writer, he transmitted the everyday happenings, the anecdotes that humanize and draw us near to historical events. As a publisher, he estab-

lished a number of important newspapers. As a businessman, he brought gas service to Buenos Aires, extended the railroad tracks, and helped erect the Teatro Colón (1857).

– ANGELA B. DELLEPIANE

ASPÍLLAGA FAMILY

Aspíllaga Family, Peruvian plantation owners. The matriarch of the family, Catalina Ferrebú de Aspíllaga, migrated to Lima from Chile in the 1820s. Sons Ramón (d. 1875) and Antonio went into the family's transport business, which operated between Lima and Callao. As partners of financier Julián Zaracondegui, they purchased a large property on the northern coast, Hacienda Cayaltí. Ramón managed the plantation with his sons Antero (1849–1927) and Ramón (1850–1940) and eventually took control of it. Earlier they had purchased a cotton farm in the Pisco Valley, Hacienda Palto. They stocked both enterprises with indentured Asians, whom they overworked with impunity. They then sank the profits into commercial urban real estate and developed close ties with English lenders. Younger brothers Baldomero and Ismael helped out, but the older sons Antero and Ramón ran the family business. The Aspíllagas became linked with other wealthy families of Lima through marriage, and they joined the prestigious Club Nacional.

In politics, the Aspíllagas helped organize the Civilista Party. The younger Ramón sat briefly in the national Chamber of Deputies. After 1906 Antero was elected to the Chamber of Deputies and then moved to the Senate, where he carefully guarded the interests of export planters. He lost as the candidate of the Civilista Party in the presidential elections of 1912 and 1919. On the eve of the ballot count in 1919, Augusto LEGUÍA, a contender for president, conspired with the army to nullify the vote, despite the fact that he probably would have won. Thereafter the family concentrated on its plantation and on mining and banking. Family members sat on the board of directors of the powerful Banco Popular, from which they received large low-cost loans in the 1930s. On the plantations they fiercely opposed all efforts to organize labor and became hated opponents of the American Popular Revolutionary Alliance (APRA), which tried to organize field workers into unions and teach them to read in night classes. The Aspíllagas supported Luís Sánchez Cerro for president in 1931 and General Oscar BENAVIDES thereafter. After World War II they withdrew from direct management of Hacienda Palto but continued in sugar despite shrinking returns. In 1968 the military reform government seized control of the Aspíllaga plantations, compensating the owners with government bonds.

— VINCENT PELOSO

ASSUNÇÃO, LEILAH

Leilah Assunção (*b.* 1943), Brazilian playwright, author, and actress. Born Maria de Lourdes Torres de Assunção in Botucatu, São Paulo, Assunção holds a degree in education from the University of São Paulo and has studied acting, fashion design, literary criticism with Antônio CALLADO, and theater at the Teatro Oficina. Besides writing, she has acted in several plays and worked as a fashion model. In her theater Assunção reveals a humorous sensitivity for the middle class and their problems, and especially for women restricted in their environment and confronting a man's world. Although some of her works were censored in the years of military rule, Assunção's first play, *Fala baixo senão eu grito* (1969), a critical analysis of the heroine's life, won a Molière Prize. Margot Milleret describes *Boca molhada de paixão calada* (1980), perhaps Assunção's most political play, as depicting "a couple in their forties who re-create their past by acting out previous sexual encounters." Assunção is considered one of the most important playwrights in Brazil today, and is one of the few to live exclusively on the earnings from her writing, due in part to the popularity of her television scripts.

— GARY M. VESSELS

ASTURIAS, MIGUEL ÁNGEL

Miguel Ángel Asturias (*b.* 19 October 1899; *d.* 9 June 1974), Guatemalan writer and Nobel Prize winner (1967). His country's greatest writer in the twentieth century, Asturias was also one of the forerunners of Latin America's Boom literature of the 1960s, along with Jorge Luis BORGES of Argentina and Alejo CARPENTIER of Cuba.

Asturias was born in the old district of La Parroquia in Guatemala City and spent his early years there. His father, a lawyer, fearing persecution by dictator Manuel ESTRADA CABRERA (1898–1920), moved the family to the small town of Salamá, where they lived from 1903 to 1907. In this town the young mestizo (mixed Mayan and Spanish heritage) came into contact with the Mayan life-style, something that would mark him for the rest of his life.

In Guatemala City, Asturias completed his secondary education at the nation's top public institution, Instituto de Varones, and enrolled in the law school of the University of San Carlos in 1918. In April 1920 he became active in the overthrow of dictator Estrada Cabrera, emerging as a student leader after this epic struggle. As a result, he traveled to Mexico City with a student delegation and met Mexico's minister of education, José VASCONCELOS, a well-known philosopher on ethnic issues and miscegenation. Young Asturias was greatly influenced by his thinking. Asturias received his law degree in 1923 but never practiced. Already the author of poems, short stories, and essays, he left for Paris in 1924.

In Paris, Asturias studied ethnology under Georges Raynaud, a Mayanist, and came to rediscover his own Mayan roots as a result. He was also a correspondent for *El Imparcial,* one of Guatemala's leading newspapers, and traveled extensively throughout Europe. His first published book was *Leyendas de Guatemala* (Legends of Guatemala, 1930), in which the prehuman forces and creatures of Mayan myth are given new life, and Mayans are placed in that landscape.

In 1933 Asturias returned to Guatemala, then under the control of another dictator, General Jorge UBICO (1931–1944). Unable to make a living as a writer, Asturias was forced to work for the official newspaper, *El Liberal Progresista.* Later he founded the first radio news program in Guatemala, "Diario del Aire" (Radio newspaper, 1937).

In 1944, when the Ubico dictatorship was overthrown, Asturias fled to Mexico, where he published his best-known novel, *El señor presidente* (The President, 1946). Of this work, critic Gerald Martin says that it "exemplifies more clearly than any other novel the crucial link between European Surrealism and Latin American Magical Realism" (1989). It remains the single most famous Latin American "dictator novel."

One year later the new democratic government of Juan José ARÉVALO (1945–1951) named Asturias cultural attaché in Mexico. Three years later he was appointed ambassador to Argentina, where he published his masterpiece, *Hombres de maíz* in 1949 (translated as *Men of Maize* in 1975). Soon after, he began his ideological transition toward leftist politics. *Men of Maize* is considered by some critics to be the first unmistakable Magical Realist Joycean novel in Latin America, the most ambitious to this day, and perhaps the greatest of the twentieth century. According to Chilean critic Ariel Dorfman (1992), the contemporary Spanish American novel begins with its publication. It anticipates by fifty years many issues popular at the end of the twentieth century, such as ecology, feminism, global consciousness, and a defense of native peoples. Gerald Martin describes it as "a profound meditation on the history of Guatemala, contained within a symbolic history of Latin America since the conquest, contained within the history of humanity's passage from so-called barbarism to so-called civilization since the

Greeks, contained within the novelist's own reflections on the human condition."

Asturias was ambassador to El Salvador in 1954 when the country was invaded by a mercenary army and the democratic process was interrupted. He went into exile in Argentina, then moved to Genoa, Italy, where he published his last truly memorable novel, *Mulata de tal* (1963), a work that, fusing the experience of Quetzal-coatl with that of Dante, anticipates Latin America's Boom literature.

In 1966 Asturias's old university friend Julio César MÉNDEZ MONTENEGRO was elected president of Guatemala and named Asturias ambassador to France. That same year Asturias won the Lenin Peace Prize, and the following year, the Nobel Prize for literature.

When General Carlos ARANA OSORIO gained control of Guatemala in 1970, Asturias resigned as ambassador and gave the Nobel Prize money to his son, Rodrigo, who apparently used it to found a guerrilla organization. Asturias died in Madrid and is buried in the Père-Lachaise Cemetery in Paris.

Asturias, essentially a novelist, also wrote poetry, plays, and journal articles. His books are *Leyendas de Guatemala* (stories, 1930); *Émulo Lipolidón* (play, 1935); *Alclasán* (play, 1940); *El señor presidente* (novel, 1946); *Sien de alondra* (poetry, 1949); *Hombres de maíz* (novel, 1949); *Viento fuerte* (novel, 1949); *El papa verde* (novel, 1954); *Weekend en Guatemala* (stories, 1955); *Soluna* (play, 1955); *Los ojos de los enterrados* (novel, 1960); *El Alhajadito* (novella, 1961); *Mulata de tal* (novel, 1963); *Clarivigilia primaveral* (poetry, 1965); *Letanías del desterrado* (poetry, 1966); *El espejo de Lida Sal* (stories, 1967); *Maladrón* (novel, 1969); *Tres de cuatro soles* (poetry, 1971); and *Viernes de dolores* (novel, 1972).

– ARTURO ARIAS

ASUAR, JOSÉ VICENTE

José Vicente Asuar (*b*. 20 July 1933), Chilean composer and acoustic engineer. Born in Santiago, Asuar began his musical studies with Jorge Urrutia-Blondel (composition) and Juan ORREGO-SALAS (orchestration) at the Santiago Conservatory. From 1952 to 1958 he studied engineering at the Catholic University of Chile, continuing his education in Germany, at the Technical University of Berlin (1959–1960). While in Germany, he studied with Boris Blacher at the Berlin Hochschule für Musik (1959–1960) and with Jacques Wildberger at the Baden Hochschule für Musik. He studied composition privately under Fritz Winckel and Werner Meyer-Eppler; at Darmstadt University he attended the summer seminars of Boulez, Ligeti, Stockhausen, and Maderna (1960–1962). Back in Santiago, Asuar was

director of the electronic music studio (1958–1959) at the Catholic University. In 1960 he returned to Germany to organize an electronic music studio at Karlsruhe. In Caracas from 1965 to 1968, Asuar created and directed the first Venezuelan studio of electronic music. In 1969 he became director of the Department of Sound Technology at the University of Chile. The following year he was awarded a Fulbright grant to study computer music with Lejaren Hiller at the State University of New York at Buffalo.

Asuar has written works for instrumental ensembles, chamber and vocal music, and a considerable number of electronic music pieces. Some of his compositions are *Variaciones espectrales* (1959), *Encadenamientos* (1957), *Preludio a la noche* (1961), *Estudio aleatorio* (1962), *La noche II* (1966), and *Kaleidoscopio* and *Catedral* (1967). He has also written several essays about electronic-music techniques.

– SUSANA SALGADO

ATAHUALPA

Atahualpa (*b*. ca. 1498; *d*. 26 July 1533), Inca ruler at the time of the Spanish Conquest of Peru. Little accurate information exists about the life of Atahualpa—even his date and place of birth are uncertain. Some suggest he was born in the imperial center of Cuzco; others, that he was from Tomebamba (Cuenca, Ecuador). His father was HUAYNA CAPAC, the last undisputed ruler of Tahuantinsuyu, the Inca Empire; his mother was a favorite secondary wife from the north. Huayna Capac died unexpectedly from smallpox that swept into the Andes ahead of the Spanish.

The Andean practice of succession was not based on primogeniture; any male child from the principal or from any of the secondary wives could become *último Inca* (ruler). The division of Cuzco into separate halves (*hanan* and *urinsaya*) with a divided government and the importance of the cults of the lineages (*panacas*) of previous Inca rulers complicated the question of succession. As he lay dying, Huayna Capac was repeatedly asked by elder advisers about the succession. It seems he favored his youngest child, Ninan Cuyochi, who, unfortunately, also contracted smallpox and died.

After realizing the European thirst for gold, Atahualpa offered to fill a room within two months with gold, and twice with silver.

Huayna Capac's second choice was probably HUASCAR, his son with Ragua Ocllo. Initially the Cuzco religious and political elite supported Huascar. Indeed, the Cuzco leadership proclaimed him heir after Huayna Capac's death. But as Huayna Capac shifted into and out of a coma in his last hours, he also named Atahualpa, a favorite from the north, who had promising military potential. Atahualpa, with the support of great military commanders, moved southward in an attempt to secure control of Tahuantinsuyu. Victorious, Atahualpa's forces captured Huascar outside Cuzco and imprisoned him. General Quizquiz went into Cuzco, attempting to obliterate completely the Huascar faction.

Such was the political scene in the realm when the handful of Spaniards under Francisco PIZARRO arrived on their third expedition of 1531. Atahualpa had left commander Rumiñavi in charge of Quito and Chalicuchima in control of the central Andes while he, along with a few thousand troops, traveled to Cajamarca to rest and enjoy the thermal baths nearby. There he was captured by the Spanish on 16 November 1532. After realizing the European thirst for gold, Atahualpa offered, as ransom, to fill a room within two months with gold, and twice with silver. Pizarro and the other Europeans were astounded, as shipments slowly began to make their way into Cajamarca from throughout the realm. With the completion of the ransom (a total of about 13,420 pounds of 22½-carat gold and 26,000 pounds of good silver), the quandary of what to do with the Inca ruler increased. Atahualpa began to mistrust the promise of release and had probably ordered his commanders Rumiñavi and Chalicuchima to move toward Cajamarca. But the Spanish convinced Chalicuchima to enter Cajamarca and took him prisoner.

Ultimately, a group that included royal officials and the recently arrived Diego de ALMAGRO persuaded Pizarro that it was dangerous to keep the Inca captive and that he should be executed. The principal Atahualpa defenders, Hernando de SOTO and Hernando PIZARRO, were away at the time the mock trial took place. Atahualpa was charged with ordering while in jail the execution of his half brother and preparing a surprise attack against the Spaniards, charges for which he was found guilty and sentenced to die at the stake. Friar Vicente de Valverde succeeded in converting Atahualpa to Christianity, and therefore the Inca was garroted instead of burned. In later years myths evolved (the *Inkarrí* cycle) that he would return and usher in a new age during which the yoke of the invaders would be overthrown.

– NOBLE DAVID COOK

ATAHUALPA (JUAN SANTOS)

Atahualpa (Juan Santos) (*b.* 1710?; *d.* ca. 1756), leader of an indigenous rebellion in the jungles and mountain slopes of east-central Peru from 1742 to 1752. Not much is known about the early life of Juan Santos, who later took the name Atahualpa. He was born either in Cajamarca or, more likely, Cuzco; he learned Spanish and Latin while studying with the Jesuits. A Jesuit may have taken him to Spain and Africa.

In 1742 Juan Santos appeared in the mountains of Chanchamayo, declaring himself the descendant of ATAHUALPA, the Inca captured and murdered in 1533 by Francisco PIZARRO at the outset of the Spanish conquest of Peru. A charismatic leader, Juan Santos combined Christian and Andean messianism. Raiding from the jungles of the Gran Pajonal, his followers destroyed the region's Franciscan missions. Juan Santos aimed to drive the Spaniards out of Peru but was unable to mobilize the populous central highlands. Nonetheless, several military expeditions against his stronghold failed to defeat him, and the government finally established forts along the frontier to prevent him from invading the highlands. In 1752 Juan Santos's forces seized Andamarca, threatening Jauja, but quickly withdrew. His hostilities then ceased. He probably died in Metraro. His uprising reflected mounting indigenous resistance to the colonial system. Revolts in Tarma (1744) and Lima (1750) supported his call for insurrection, and even after 1752 rumors about the new Atahualpa disturbed Peru.

– KENDALL W. BROWN

ATL, DR.

Dr. Atl (Gerardo Murillo; *b.* 1875; *d.* 1964), Mexican artist and participant in the Mexican Revolution. A native of Guadalajara, he became a noted landscape artist and volcanologist. After studying painting at Bellas Artes in Mexico City, he departed in 1896 for Rome, where he later received degrees in philosophy and law. His pseudonym, Dr. Atl (*atl* being the Nahuatl word for "water"), was suggested to him by the writer Leopoldo LUGONES in Paris in 1902, and he used this name on his works of art. Returning to Mexico, he hiked up Popocatépetl and Iztaccíhuatl, an experience that led to a lifelong interest, both scientific and artistic, in volcanoes.

After a second stay in Europe, Atl returned to Mexico in 1914 and joined the Constitutionalist movement under Venustiano CARRANZA. He became a member of the Revolutionary Confederation, a group of military and other Constitutionalist officials formed in 1914 that pressured Carranza to carry out social reforms. He was a close collaborator of General Álvaro OBREGÓN, and helped him attract the support of the Casa de Obrero Mundial and other workers' groups in Mexico City during the Constitutionalist occupation in early 1915. After the Revolution, he returned to painting and authored several books, including works on art and volcanology.

— LINDA B. HALL

AVELLANEDA, NICOLÁS

Nicolás Avellaneda (*b.* 10 October 1837; *d.* 25 November 1885), president of Argentina (1874–1880). Avellaneda, a native of Tucumán, established a regime that completed the formation of modern Argentina by consolidating national order. He represents a continuation of liberal policies that were adjusted to appease provincial interests. A friend of Domingo SARMIENTO and the minister of religion, justice, and public instruction in Sarmiento's regime, Avellaneda became president by imposition. When Bartolomé MITRE, the defeated presidential candidate, led a revolt in 1874, Sarmiento headed the government forces and crushed Mitre. Avellaneda, however, could not mold the interior and the *porteños* into an effective coalition. He sought to curb Buenos Aires province, for example, by allowing European immigrants, but not Argentine citizens, to settle Patagonia.

Throughout the 1870s financial difficulties limited Avellaneda's presidency. He angered major exporters who depended upon European markets by defaulting on payment of Argentina's foreign debt. Because of budgetary constraints, there were few public works projects in the provinces. During Avellaneda's presidency, the first wheat was shipped from Rosario to Great Britain (1878). Agricultural production increased, as did immigration. In 1876 the government enacted the first comprehensive public land law, mainly to facilitate the settlement of European farmers. Wool production increased to 50 percent of the value of all Argentine exports. The gaucho population declined rapidly. Cultural life flourished, and education became more widely available. Avellaneda signed boundary treaties to settle disputes with Paraguay (following the War of the Triple Alliance), Brazil, and Chile.

The government federalized the city of Buenos Aires in 1880, a decision that provoked a bloody revolt in Buenos Aires Province. Avellaneda and Congress crumbled under the pressure of this event, but a nationalist junta eventually suppressed the rebellion. The traditional parties began to fade away, paving the way for the rise of the Partido Autonomista Nacional. As if to indicate the triumph of an evolving liberal system, the remains of José de San Martín were brought from France to Argentina.

Avellaneda's interest in education, land, and unification formed the basis for his writings. At one time he was an editor of the influential newspaper *El Nacional.*

In addition to lecturing frequently, Avellaneda was a prolific writer of essays. He also produced a book, *Tierras públicas* (Public Lands, 1865). His collected writings, *Escritos y discursos* (1910), fill twelve volumes.

— DOUGLAS W. RICHMOND

ÁVILA, ALONSO DE

Alonso de Ávila (*b.* ca. 1539; *d.* 3 August 1566), leader of the so-called Cortés Conspiracy of 1565–1566. Ávila was a leading light of the second, native-born generation of *encomenderos* in Mexico. Less economically secure than their fathers, they grew increasingly resentful of the royal policies that progressively limited their power. They sought a champion in Martín CORTÉS, the conquistador's son and second marqués del Valle, who arrived in Mexico in 1563. Cortés soon clashed with the viceroy, Luis de VELASCO, and his pretensions to political influence increased when Velasco's death left an undersized, three-man *audiencia* as the highest authority in the colony.

In October 1565, Alonso de Ávila, Gil GONZÁLEZ DÁVILA (his older brother), and several other members of the colonial elite began actively plotting the overthrow of the government. They planned to assassinate the *audiencia* judges and other high officials and to proclaim Cortés king. But the marqués wavered, refusing explicitly to endorse the conspiracy. His indecision, along with the general indiscretion and ineptitude of the conspirators, allowed the *audiencia* to strike first. On 16 July 1566, the *audiencia* arrested the Ávila brothers and Cortés. After a brief trial, Alonso and Gil were condemned to death—a sentence clearly intended to deter any future conspirators. Both brothers were beheaded in Mexico City's central Plaza.

— R. DOUGLAS COPE

ÁVILA, JULIO ENRIQUE

Julio Enrique Ávila (*b.* 4 August 1892; *d.* 1968), Salvadoran poet and intellectual leader. A professor of chemistry and pharmacology, and later dean of the Faculty of Chemistry and Pharmacy at the National University of El Salvador, Ávila became known primarily as a literary figure. His first book, *Fuentes de alma* (1917), established him in the "modernist" school of Rubén DARÍO. Subsequent works, especially the poetic novel *El vigía sin luz* (1927) and an anthology, *El mundo de mi jardín* (1927), established him as one of the leading Salvadoran poets of his generation.

— RALPH LEE WOODWARD, JR.

ÁVILA, PEDRO ARIAS DE

Pedro Arias de Ávila (Pedrarias Dávila; *b.* ca. 1440; *d.* July 1531), Spanish soldier, governor of Panama (1514–

1526) and of Nicaragua (1527–1531), and founder of Panama City (1519). Pedrarias was a member of a prominent noble family of Segovia; his uncle was an archbishop and his older brother was the count of Puñonrostro. He was perhaps of *converso* origins.

In his boyhood Pedrarias was a page in the court of Juan II of Castile and León (1406–1454). In later life he distinguished himself in the war against the Moors in Granada (1482–1492) and as a colonel of infantry fighting in North Africa (1508–1511). Physically imposing and athletic, Pedrarias was nicknamed "the jouster" and "the gallant." After another had declined the honor, he accepted an appointment as captain-general and governor of Castilla del Oro in Darién (also known as Panama), offered in June 1513, despite his being seventy-three years of age.

Information had reached the king about the riches to be found in Panama, and owing to rumors of a great body of water to the south, a large fleet was organized under the command of Pedrarias. Among fifteen hundred or more passengers, the vessels carried a brilliant array of notables, including Pedrarias's wife, Isabel de Bobadilla y Peñalosa, the chronicler Gonzalo Fernández de OVIEDO Y VALDÉS, the historian Bernal DÍAZ DEL CASTILLO, and Hernando de SOTO. Altogether, it was perhaps the most distinguished passenger list of any fleet sailing to the New World. Pedrarias embarked for the Indies in April 1514 with orders to assume control of the colony; suspend the acting governor, Vasco Núñez de BALBOA; and to bring Balboa to justice on the charge of usurping authority from previous leaders.

Pedrarias led predatory entradas *in search of gold and slaves, undoing by their brutality much of the goodwill Balboa had established among the natives.*

The king learned of Balboa's discovery of the Pacific Ocean a few days after the departure of Pedrarias. Accordingly, the crown appointed Balboa adelantado, but he was subject to Pedrarias. It took six months for the commission to reach Panama, and Pedrarias withheld the information from Balboa. Initial contact between the two men was cordial, and Balboa freely shared his knowledge of the land and people of Panama with Pedrarias. Balboa was acquitted in his judicial review, but because of his prestige and popularity, Pedrarias seethed with resentment and jealousy. To help relieve the tension, Bishop Juan de Quevedo arranged the betrothal of Pedrarias's daughter María to Balboa. The aging governor doubtless welcomed a good political match for his eldest daughter, who was in a convent in Seville.

Meantime, lieutenants of Pedrarias led predatory *entradas* in search of gold and slaves, undoing by their brutality much of the goodwill Balboa had established among the natives. Balboa continued his project to build ships to sail down the Pacific coast to explore the rich land of "Biru," of which Indians had spoken. His plans were interrupted when a companion betrayed him, charging that he planned to overthrow the authority of Pedrarias, to whom he was still subject. Balboa was also accused of being more interested in his Indian mistress than in his betrothed. Pedrarias, his parental pride wounded, saw the opportunity to be rid of his rival once and for all. Balboa, apparently innocent of the charge of treason, was found guilty, denied appeals, and beheaded along with three of his friends at Acla in January 1519.

That same year Pedrarias founded the city of Panama, on the south coast of the isthmus. Under his aegis Pascual de ANDAGOYA made an exploratory voyage in 1522 to investigate the great civilization that was said to exist to the south. Later, Pedrarias was a partner in the expedition of Francisco PIZARRO that led to his conquest of Inca Peru. In 1522 Pedrarias also dispatched lieutenants northward, and in 1523 Francisco HERNÁNDEZ DE CÓRDOBA, who was welcomed by local Caciques, founded the cities of León and Granada in Nicaragua. When he plotted with others and renounced the authority of Pedrarias, Hernández de Córdoba was arrested and executed in 1526. Despite mounting criticism of Pedrarias, he was appointed governor of Nicaragua in 1527.

His daughter María was married to Rodrigo de Contreras, a nobleman of Segovia and later governor of Nicaragua (1534–1544); another daughter, Isabella, became the wife of explorer Hernando de SOTO, the future governor of Cuba. His extreme cruelty to Spaniards and Indians alike notwithstanding, Pedrarias enjoyed powerful support, including that of the influential Juan RODRÍGUEZ DE FONSECA. With such friends back in Spain, as well as extraordinarily good luck, he served as a governor in Central America for seventeen years, a remarkable career for the times. In 1531, at age ninety, the bitter old man died in León. By then he had justly earned the nickname "the wrath of God," bestowed upon him by a contemporary chronicler.

– WILLIAM L. SHERMAN

ÁVILA CAMACHO, MANUEL

Manuel Ávila Camacho (*b.* 24 April 1897; *d.* 13 October 1955), president of Mexico (1940–1946), remembered for his moderate leadership and for his consolidation and refinement of the achievements of his predecessor, Lázaro CÁRDENAS. His administration was crucial in the final transition from military to civilian political leadership, and in tempering government attitudes toward the Roman Catholic church after he declared himself a believer. He also moderated the nationalism and anti-Americanism of the Cárdenas administration, which had been symbolized by the 1938 nationalization of oil, and allied Mexico with the United States during World War II. As president Ávila Camacho reversed socialist tendencies in public education, repealing constitutional amendments stipulating adherence to that philosophy of education.

Ávila Camacho was born in Teziutlán, Puebla, the hometown of his lifelong friend, the notable labor leader Vicente Lombardo Toledano. (One source claims, however, that his birthplace was Martínez de la Torre, Veracruz.) He was largely raised by his mother, Eufrosina Camacho, and received some preparatory schooling and business training, but instead of continuing his education he joined the Constitutionalists under General Antonio Medina in 1914. He remained in the army as a career officer, serving his mentor, Lázaro Cárdenas, as chief of staff in 1920. Three years later he commanded the 79th Cavalry Regiment in Michoacán, where he opposed the rebellion of Adolfo DE LA HUERTA. Promoted to brigadier general in 1929, he again fought under General Cárdenas against the Escobar rebellion, the last major uprising of disgruntled Revolutionary generals against the government. Between 1929 and 1934 he commanded several important military zones, and when Cárdenas reached the presidency in 1934, Ávila Camacho was appointed *oficial mayor* (executive officer) of the secretariat of national defense, after which he rose to subsecretary and, ultimately, in 1937, to secretary of that agency. He resigned his position 17 January 1939 to run for president on the government party ticket in a heated electoral campaign against Juan Andrew Almazán.

– RODERIC AI CAMP

AVILÉS, GABRIEL

Gabriel Avilés (marqués de Avilés: *b.* 1735; *d.* 19 September 1810), viceroy of Peru (1801–1806). Like his predecessor, Ambrosio O'HIGGINS, Avilés served as captain-general of Chile (1795–1799) before his promotion to Peru, and also briefly as viceroy in Buenos Aires (1799–1801). Avilés played a prominent role in the repression of the Túpac Amaru rebellion (1780–1783), combining firmness as a military commander with denunciation of the social abuses and administra-

tive corruption that had provoked the insurrection. Before his transfer to Chile—as field marshal and second marqués de Avilés—he served as governor of Callao.

During his vice-regency in Peru, Avilés promoted public health, repressed a conspiracy in Cuzco, and oversaw the incorporation into the viceroyalty of Mainas and Guayaquil (in present-day Ecuador). He remained in Peru for four years under his successor ABASCAL, but refused the offer of appointment as viceroy of the Río de la Plata following the May 1810 revolution. Shortly thereafter he left Lima for Spain, but died in Valparaíso, Chile.

– JOHN R. FISHER

AXAYACATL

Axayacatl (*b.* ca. 1449; *d.* 1481), Aztec emperor from 1468/69–1481. The sixth Mexica Tlatoani (a "speaker" or ruler), Axayacatl ("Watery Visage") was the grandson of two previous rulers: MOTECUHZOMA I on his mother's side, and ITZCOATL on his father's side. According to one native history, he became ruler at age nineteen. His short reign was devoted to military campaigns. To the expanding Aztec empire he added Toluca, Malinalco, and other Matlatzinca polities west of the Mexica capital of Tenochtitlán; he also subdued the Tuxpan area on the Gulf coast. In 1473 a dispute between Axayacatl and his sister's husband Moquihuix, ruler of Tlatelolco, Tenochtitlán's neighbor to the north, led to Tlatelolco's military defeat. In 1478 Axayacatl led a disastrous campaign against the Tarascans in Michoacán; native histories state that all but 200 of Axayacatl's 20,000 or more soldiers perished in the worst Mexica defeat until the Spanish conquest. Axayacatl was succeeded by his brother, Tizoc. Axayacatl's son, MOTECUHZOMA II (1466–1520), was ruling when CORTÉS invaded Mexico.

– LOUISE M. BURKHART

AYALA, ELIGIO

Eligio Ayala (*b.* 1880; *d.* 24 October 1930), president of Paraguay (1924–1928) and educator. Born in Mbuyapey of humble parents, Ayala displayed considerable talent at an early age and rose rapidly in the ranks of the Partido Liberal. In the 1890s, he moved to Asunción, where he attended the Colegio Nacional and began teaching in 1904, giving courses in philosophy, civics, psychology, and logic. In 1908 he received a doctorate in law from the university.

At this time, Ayala embarked on a political career. He held office as attorney for the indigent, civil judge, and congressional deputy. After participating in the

1904 and 1911 revolutions as a Liberal stalwart, he left Paraguay and spent the next eight years in Europe.

Upon his return after World War I, Ayala dedicated himself to teaching and journalism. He regained his old congressional seat and in 1920 was appointed finance minister by President Manuel Gondra. Ayala quickly gained a reputation for honesty and level-headedness. Eschewing the jingoism of many Liberals, he took a stand in favor of negotiations with Bolivia over the disputed Chaco Region.

After serving as provisional president of Paraguay in 1923, he was elected to that office one year later. His administration brought the first spate of internal peace in more than twenty years. Bent on reforming the nation's archaic fiscal system, Ayala balanced the national budget, stabilized the currency, and paid off a considerable portion of the government's debt. With Paraguay's renewed access to international credit, Ayala purchased munitions for his fledgling army and two warships for the navy. His emphasis on the professionalization of the armed forces rescued the military from continued partisan strife and prepared it for the upcoming Chaco War, a conflict that Paraguay was unable to avoid after all. Indeed, in the last year of Ayala's administration there was a series of border incidents that overshadowed all the progress he had promoted.

In 1928 Ayala resumed the post of finance minister, this time in the government of his successor, José P. Guggiari. He also retained several key posts in the Partido Liberal. Two years later he was killed in Asunción, the victim of a tragic romantic involvement.

– THOMAS L. WHIGHAM

AYALA, EUSEBIO

Eusebio Ayala (*b.* 15 August 1874; *d.* 4 June 1942), intellectual, statesman, provisional president (1921–1923), and president of Paraguay (1932–1936). Ayala studied law and wrote essays on history, political economy, and international law. In 1900, he obtained his law degree at the National University in Asunción, subsequently teaching in various disciplines. As a diplomat, he displayed a profound knowledge of the major boundary dispute that existed with Bolivia. On 20 August 1920, Ayala was appointed to President Manuel GONDRA's cabinet, but because of factional fighting, Gondra was forced to resign. Ayala replaced him in November 1921 as provisional president, only to resign in 1923 in the middle of a civil war. He was elected president in 1932, leading Paraguay through the Chaco War against neighboring Bolivia. After the defeat of the Bolivians, Ayala's government was toppled on 17 February 1936 by a military coup that had civilian support. In

spite of his overthrow, Ayala has been regarded as one of the most capable national leaders of his generation.

– MIGUEL A. GATTI

AYALA, JOSÉ DE LA CRUZ

José de la Cruz Ayala (*b.* 1854; *d.* 29 January 1892), Paraguayan politician, journalist, and social critic. Better known by his pen name "Alon," Ayala was a Liberal firebrand who helped crystallize resistance to the Bernardino CABALLERO and Patricio ESCOBAR governments in the 1880s. Born in the interior town of Mbuyapey, Ayala witnessed the cruelties of Paraguayan politics as a child, when his father and older brother were assassinated in his presence. When he arrived in Asunción in 1877, he was already very much a confirmed rebel. He entered the Colegio Nacional, where he studied the Greek and Roman classics and received a bachelor's degree in 1882.

While at the *colegio*, Ayala cemented his friendship with the young historian Cecilio BÁEZ, who encouraged him to enter the then booming field of journalism. Following Báez's suggestion, he wrote for several newspapers, including *El Heraldo* and *La Democracia*. His editorial pieces, published pseudonymously, attacked the government's policy of selling public lands to foreign entrepreneurs. More generally, he denounced the corruption that had seeped into every level of the Paraguayan body politic. Deeply offended by Ayala's stinging criticisms, President Caballero had him drafted and sent to an isolated army outpost in the Chaco. Ayala managed to escape and, from hiding, smuggled out a

---

Ayala witnessed the cruelties of Paraguayan politics as a child, when his father and older brother were assassinated in his presence.

---

series of letters (tellingly entitled *Cartas del infierno*), which appeared in opposition dailies, vexing Caballero and Escobar still further. In 1891 Ayala momentarily came out of hiding to join the Liberals in a civil war, but he was forced to escape to Argentina, where he died one year later.

– THOMAS L. WHIGHAM

AYCINENA, JUAN FERMÍN DE

Juan Fermín de Aycinena (*b.* 7 July 1729; *d.* 3 April 1796), first *marqués* of Aycinena. He has been called the most powerful man in the history of Central America. Born in Siga, Navarra, in July 1729, he emigrated to New Spain in 1748 and began his commercial career as a mule runner, principally in Oaxaca, before arriving in Santiago de Guatemala (today Antigua) in 1753 or 1754. Subsequently he became the leading indigo exporter, wholesale merchant, and creditor in the Kingdom of Guatemala, and perhaps its only millionaire. He acquired several estates, especially Salvadoran indigo plantations, many through foreclosure. He was among the leading *trasladistas,* or supporters of the transfer of the capital city after 1773 to Guatemala City, and a generous benefactor of church and state. In 1783 he acquired the only Castilian title in late colonial Central America. In 1794 he became the first prior of the Consulado de Comercio of Guatemala City. Married three times, his numerous offspring became the center of the "oligarchy" in late colonial and early republican Central America.

– RICHMOND F. BROWN

AYCINENA, MARIANO DE

Mariano de Aycinena (*b.* 15 September 1789; *d.* 22 January 1855), chief of state of Guatemala (1827–1829). Aycinena was a leading figure in Central American independence. A younger son of Juan Fermín de Aycinena, first marquis of Aycinena, he was a patriarch of Guatemala's most prominent and powerful family in the late colonial and early republican era. As *síndico* (attorney general) of the *ayuntamiento* of Guatemala City, he helped lead the movement for independence. Afterward he promoted the annexation of Central America to the Mexican Empire of Agustín de ITUR-BIDE, with whom he had corresponded prior to independence. He became a leader of Central American conservatives in the early republic and an officer of the Consulado de Comercio while managing his family's international trading firm. He was involved in the negotiations that resulted in a British loan to Central America in 1824, the proceeds of which some contemporary politicians and later historians accused him of appropriating.

As chief of state of Guatemala during the presidency of Manuel José ARCE, Aycinena was a central figure of the civil war that disrupted the United Provinces of Central America from 1826 to 1829. Aycinena's faction was ultimately defeated by the forces of the Honduran general and unionist hero Francisco MORAZÁN. Exiled after the war, he returned to Guatemala in the late 1830s and lived there for the rest of his life. Although not a prominent participant in Guatemalan government during that time, he enjoyed informal influence through his family, whose members dominated government and society in the Conservative Era (1838–1871).

– RICHMOND F. BROWN

AYCINENA, PEDRO DE

Pedro de Aycinena (*b.* 19 October 1802; *d.* 14 March 1897), Guatemalan minister of foreign relations (1854–1871) and interim president of Guatemala (1865). Aycinena was a principal minister and adviser to the Conservative regimes of Rafael CARRERA (1851–1865) and Vicente CERNA (1865–1871). Son of Vicente Aycinena, second *marqués* of Aycinena, younger brother of Juan José de Aycinena, and nephew of Mariano de Aycinena, he belonged to one of Guatemala's most prominent families. In 1836 he married his first cousin, Dolores Aycinena y Micheo, daughter of José de Aycinena, Spanish Councilor of State and the Indies under Ferdinand VII. Their son Juan Fermín de Aycinena Aycinena was the eminent Guatemalan poet.

Graduating in civil and canon law from the University of San Carlos in 1821, Aycinena joined the Colegio de Abogados in 1823. He spent much of the 1820s in Europe representing his family's merchant house and returned to Guatemala to manage his family's affairs in the 1830s, following the family elders' expulsion after the civil war of 1826–1829. In the 1840s, with the return to Conservative rule in Guatemala (and most of his brethren to the country), he became involved in government. As foreign minister, he negotiated the controversial Wyke-Aycinena Treaty of 1859, which acknowledged British rights to Belize. He also negotiated Spanish recognition of Guatemalan independence in 1863. He was briefly exiled following the Liberal Revolution of 1871 and returned to pursue law and commerce until his death in 1897, the last of the Guatemalan *serviles* (conservatives).

– RICHMOND F. BROWN

AYCINENA PIÑOL, JUAN JOSÉ DE

Juan José de Aycinena Piñol (*b.* 29 August 1792; *d.* 17 February 1865), third marquis of Aycinena and titular bishop of Trajanópolis (1859). Juan José de Aycinena was the dominant figure of the conservative political faction in nineteenth-century Central America and the Guatemalan Republic, which he helped found. Born in Antigua Guatemala to a family of immense wealth and power, Aycinena trained as an attorney before entering the priesthood in 1817. Although a cleric, he was involved in virtually every area of Guatemalan public life. As a member of the Economic Society, he promoted the development of a Central American silk industry. Most important, he operated in the midst of Central American politics. A promoter of Central American independence from Spain (1821) and annexation to the Mexican Empire (1821–1823), Aycinena was sent into exile in the United States for most of the 1830s with his political faction's (and family's) defeat in the Central American civil war of 1827–1829.

A forceful advocate of constitutional monarchy and of a pronounced secular role for the Catholic church, Aycinena is perhaps best known for a series of political tracts written in exile in the early 1830s. The *Toros amarillos* (yellow-paged polemics) called for the dissolution of the United Provinces of Central America in the name of isthmian peace. Returning to Guatemala in 1837, Aycinena played a central role in the formal breakup of the United Provinces through his newspaper, *El Observador,* and as a delegate to the federal congress.

With the collapse of the federation, Aycinena exercised extraordinary power as Guatemala's minister of government, justice, foreign affairs, and ecclesiastical affairs (1842–1844). Subsequently, as vice president of Guatemala's Chamber of Representatives (1851–1865), as a councillor of state (1856–1865), and especially as rector of the University of San Carlos (1840–1854; 1859–1865), Aycinena helped set the tone of politics and society under Guatemalan strongman José Rafael CARRERA (1844–1849; 1851–1865). His biographer, David L. Chandler, asserts, no "single individual [was] more responsible . . . for the outlines of society and government that subsequently took shape in Guatemala. . . . Father Aycinena became the Conservative prophet of a new era."

– RICHMOND F. BROWN

AYLWIN AZÓCAR, PATRICIO

Patricio Aylwin Azócar (*b.* 26 November 1918), leader of the Christian Democratic Party (PDC) and president of Chile (1990–1994). One of the original founders of the PDC, he served as the head of the National Falange as well as of the party itself. As the leader of the PDC's more conservative wing, the *oficialistas,* and later, as head of the entire party, he doubted the Allende government's (1970–1973) commitment to respect the nation's constitution. Aylwin increasingly came to believe that President Salvador ALLENDE could not be trusted and, following last-minute negotiations, demanded that the president appoint only military men to his cabinet as proof of his honest intent. When Allende complied only partially, Aylwin apparently sided with the pro-coup forces, believing that the military would restore democracy to the nation.

Following Allende's overthrow in 1973, Aylwin, particularly after the death of Eduardo FREI, slowly emerged as the PDC's most viable spokesman. As the head of Chile's most popular party and one of the leaders of the anti-PINOCHET forces, Aylwin became a leader around whom the various diverse parties could unite. In 1989 he managed to forge a coalition of seventeen disparate elements, defeat two opponents, and win the presidency with 55 percent of the vote.

Following his election, Aylwin created a coalition government in an attempt to retain widespread public support. His economic programs consisted of attempting to build on the momentum generated by the Pinochet administration while implementing new laws, and passing new taxes, to protect the working class.

Aylwin's principal problem following his election, as well as before it, was General Augusto Pinochet. The former dictator, although no longer president, still controlled the army. He was intent, moreover, on ensuring that the newly elected government would not punish the armed forces for their activities in overturning Allende or in the succeeding years. Aylwin, however, had to attempt to heal the nation while bringing to justice those who had committed abuses. Aylwin's election marked the return of Chile to its democratic traditions.

– WILLIAM F. SATER

AYOLAS, JUAN DE

Juan de Ayolas (*b.* 1539?), Spanish explorer active in Argentina and Paraguay. Ayolas was born a HIDALGO in the Briviesca region of Spain. Thanks to his long-time friendship with Pedro de MENDOZA, he received a commission as *mayordomo* when the latter organized an expedition to explore the basin of the Río de la Plata in the early 1530s.

The voyage from Spain was not without its problems. Ayolas discovered a plot against Mendoza by dissident Spaniards while the small fleet was off the Brazilian coast. His quick action saved the adelantado and placed Ayolas in a good position to play a major role in the exploration of the Plata.

After the founding of Buenos Aires in 1536, Mendoza chose his friend to lead a new expedition inland to find a viable route to the silver districts of Upper Peru (what he optimistically termed the *Sierra de la Plata*). Ayolas ascended the Río Paraná with three vessels and two hundred men. He received succor along the way from various groups of Guaraní Indians, especially in the vicinity of what would one day become the city of Asunción. Proceeding upriver from that point, he finally halted in February 1537 at a spot some 120 miles to the north. There he divided his men, leaving behind forty under the command of Domingo Martínez de IRALA and setting out on foot with the remaining 160 to cross the inhospitable Chaco region to Peru.

What occurred on the expedition is not entirely clear

and is based exclusively on the testimony of a

converted Chané Indian boy named Gonzalo.

What occurred next is not entirely clear and is based exclusively on the testimony of a converted Chané Indian boy named Gonzalo. According to this eyewitness, after many tribulations, Ayolas and his party actually reached the Andes. He left a number of Europeans at an improvised camp in the hill country and, ferrying a quantity of silver taken from the resident Incas, recrossed the Chaco to the Río Paraguay, where the exhausted Ayolas expected to find Martínez de Irala and the three vessels awaiting his return. Irala, however, had gone south after a year in order to find provisions and to repair his ships. While Ayolas pondered his next move, a large band of Payaguá Indians invited the weary Spaniards to take refuge with them, and then, at a prearranged signal, fell upon them and killed them to a man. Only the Indian boy Gonzalo escaped to report what he had seen to Irala. The latter campaigned hard against these same Payaguáes over the next few years, but he never recovered the bodies of his comrades.

— THOMAS L. WHIGHAM

AYORA CUEVA, ISIDRO

Isidro Ayora Cueva (*b.* 31 August 1879; *d.* 22 March 1978), president of Ecuador (nonelected 1926–1929 and elected 1929–1931). Born in Loja, Ayora studied medicine in Quito, did postgraduate work in Berlin, and completed an internship in Dresden. After returning to Ecuador in 1909, he developed a private practice and taught obstetrics at Central University, where he accepted the post of director of maternity (1917). Elected deputy of Loja in 1916 and president of the cantonal council for 1924–1925, Ayora was appointed rector of Central University and director of the Civil Hospital of Quito in 1925. On 10 January 1926 he became a member of the provisional governing junta and minister of social welfare, labor, and agriculture. On 1 April 1926 he accepted the position of provisional president.

Ayora concluded an agreement with Princeton economist Edwin W. Kemmerer to head an advisory mission whose purpose was to propose solutions to the nation's financial problems. In October 1926 the mission drafted laws to modernize and strengthen Ecuadorian financial institutions and procedures to eliminate budget deficits. Ayora, with the backing of the military, was able to enact most of the sweeping reforms proposed by the Kemmerer Mission.

Ayora was elected to the presidency in 1929 but suffered increasing public criticism for his policies, many of them based on the recommendations of the Kemmerer Mission. Public dissatisfaction mounted as internal conditions deteriorated in response to disruptions in the world economy. Critics blamed the Ayora government for exacerbating the nation's problems. When popular discontent erupted in mass demonstrations in Quito, Ayora resigned on 24 August 1931. He returned to his medical practice and remained active in professional organizations and administrative positions.

— LINDA ALEXANDER RODRÍGUEZ

AZAR, HÉCTOR

Héctor Azar (*b.* 17 October 1930), Mexican playwright who founded the Centro de Arte Dramático (CADAC, 1975), a respected theater school. Azar, born in Atlixco, Puebla, studied in the United States under the direction of Max Reinhardt at Actors' Studio. His first plays (both 1958), *La Apassionata* and *El alfarero,* depicted social problems from a stylized point of view. *Olímpica* (1962), his best-known work, and *Inmaculada* (1963) are poetic dramas that deal mainly with feminine frustration. His collection of short pieces, *Juegos de azar* (1973), includes a religious mystery play, *La seda mágica,* and a Renaissance farce, *Doña Belarda de Francia.* A more traditional drama, *Los muros vacíos* (1974), contrasts with his later experimental works, such as the farcical trilogy *Diálogos de la clase medium* (1979–1986) and a poetic drama that pays homage to the Mexican painter Rufino TAMAYO, *Las alas sin sombra* (1980). His critical essays are collected in *Funciones teatrales* (1982).

— GUILLERMO SCHMIDHUBER

AZARA, FÉLIX DE

Félix de Azara (*b.* 18 May 1746; *d.* 20 October 1821), scientist and writer. Spanish military man and enlightened scientist, Azara spent twenty years (1781–1801) traveling throughout the Viceroyalty of the Río de la Plata, gathering information about the area and conducting experiments. He was born in Aragon, and after studying philosophy at the University of Huesca, entered the Military Academy at Barcelona. Commissioned as *alférez* (ensign) in the Company of Engineers, he participated as an officer in the Algiers campaign of

1775. By 1781, with the rank of lieutenant colonel, Azara was in America to participate in the boundary commission charged with fixing the limits between the Spanish and Portuguese dominions in South America. Upon returning to Spain in 1802, Azara wrote scientific treatises as well as general descriptions of the area. Best known are *Descripción é historia del Paraguay y del Río de la Plata* (1847) and *Viajes por la América meridional* (1809).

— SUSAN M. SOCOLOW

AZCÁRATE Y LEZAMA, JUAN FRANCISCO DE

Juan Francisco de Azcárate y Lezama (*b.* 11 July 1767; *d.* 31 January 1831), Mexican lawyer, writer, and leader of the struggle for Mexican independence. Azcárate studied jurisprudence and in 1790 became a lawyer of the Royal Audiencia. He taught courses at the University of Mexico and became a member of the Academy of Jurisprudence and the College of Lawyers. A distinguished lawyer, Azcárate was also interested in politics, becoming a member of the city council of Mexico City in 1803.

Azcárate played an important role during the imperial crisis provoked by Napoleon's invasion of Spain and the abdication of the Spanish monarchs, when the capital's city council, dominated by creoles, decided to promote autonomist interests. He was the author of the council's *representación* of 19 July 1808 to the viceroy against the recognition of any monarch but the legitimate one. An active participant in the meetings convened to discuss the creation of a governing junta, Azcárate was imprisoned during the coup d'état of 15 September. Freed in 1811, he rejoined the city council in 1814. He was a member of the governing junta in 1821 and one of the signers of the Declaration of Independence. Azcárate served in various diplomatic posts during the Augustín de ITURBIDE regime. In 1827 he was a member of the Committee of Public Education and the following year of the Tribunal of War and Marine.

— VIRGINIA GUEDEA

AZCÁRRAGA MILMO, EMILIO

Emilio Azcárraga Milmo (*b.* August 1930), prominent entrepreneur and chief executive officer of Televisa, Latin America's largest media network. He is the son of Emilio Azcárraga Vidaurreta, founder of Televisa, and Laura Milmo, members of prominent Mexican entrepreneurial families. Emilio Azcárraga Milmo and his family have a controlling interest in the Televisa media empire, which dominates Mexican programming. He

became president of Televisa in 1973 and, according to *Forbes* magazine, had a net worth of $1 billion in 1991. Azcárraga bought out his partners, Miguel Alemán and Rómulo O'Farrill, in 1990, giving his family exclusive control of the business. He has continued the family policy of generous support of the arts. Azcárraga was president of Friends of the Arts in Mexico, a major sponsor of "Mexico: The Splendor of 30 Centuries," an exhibit that appeared in New York, San Antonio, and Los Angeles in 1990 and 1991.

— RODERIC AI CAMP

AZCONA HOYO, JOSÉ SIMÓN

José Simón Azcona Hoyo (*b.* 26 January 1927), president of Honduras (1986–1990). Born and raised in Honduras, José Azcona received his degree in civil engineering from the National Autonomous University in 1963. He studied and worked in Mexico, Costa Rica, and the United States intermittently during the 1960s and 1970s but maintained his ties to the Liberal Party in Honduras. He served in a variety of political positions, including congressional deputy (1982–1985) and minister of communication (1982–1983). Azcona broke with incumbent president Roberto SUAZO CÓRDOVA in 1985 and led a faction of the Liberal Party known as the Rodista Dissent Movement, after his mentor Modesto RODAS. Under a new electoral system, in which the two main parties alternate terms in power, Azcona won the 1985 presidential race even though he did not receive a plurality. Despite this successful transition of power between civilian presidents, the strength of the Honduran military grew during Azcona's administration. Although he was widely viewed as responsible and trustworthy, Azcona was a weak president faced with increasingly complicated domestic and foreign issues: the presence in his country of Nicaraguan contras, rapidly expanding U.S. involvement in the area, Salvadoran refugees, and the appearance of a guerrilla threat.

— KAREN RACINE

AZCUÉNAGA, MIGUEL DE

Miguel de Azcuénaga (*b.* 4 June 1754; *d.* 19 December 1833), Argentine military man. Born in Buenos Aires, the son and grandson of prominent Basque merchants (Vicente de Azcuénaga and Domingo Basavilbaso), Azcuénaga was related by blood or marriage to many of the more conservative Spanish monopoly traders in Buenos Aires. After studying in Spain, he returned in 1773 to the city of his birth as a commissioned military officer. Between 1776 and 1800 he served as a member of the *cabildo,* a colonel in the militia, and the chief of militia in Buenos Aires. He was especially active as the commander of a volunteer infantry battalion during the English invasions of 1806–1807.

A participant in the *cabildo abierto* (open town council meeting) of 23 May 1810, Azcuénaga was a fervent supporter of the end of viceregal rule. He served in the first independence government and was especially active in organizing the military forces of the new government. Dismissed from the government as the result of political intrigue, Azcuénaga later held a variety of posts, including *gobernador intendente* of Buenos Aires (1813), president of the War Commission, and Buenos Aires deputy to Congress (1818). He died in Buenos Aires.

– SUSAN M. SOCOLOW

AZEVEDO, ALUÍSIO

Aluísio Azevedo (*b.* 14 April 1857; *d.* 21 January 1913), Brazilian novelist. Aluísio Azevedo was the major figure of Brazilian naturalism, a movement influenced by the novels of Émile Zola and other European naturalists, but also firmly grounded in the social and historical context of Brazil at the end of the Empire period. Azevedo appears to have seen literature as a way to get ahead in life, and his first naturalist novel, *O mulato* (1881) was a scandalous success. He published three more naturalist novels, including his masterpiece, *O cortiço* (1890), but simultaneously turned out a number of romantic potboilers. Azevedo abandoned fiction after he

---

Azevedo's Brazilian contemporaries were shocked and titillated by the heavy-handed treatment of sexuality in Azevedo's novels.

---

was appointed to the Brazilian diplomatic corps in 1895, at the age of thirty-eight. While his works exhibit his gift for describing places, from the provincial city that is the setting for *O mulato* to the Rio de Janeiro slums in *O cortiço,* all Azevedo's novels are weakened by their improbable plots and stereotypical characters. His Brazilian contemporaries were shocked and titillated by the heavy-handed treatment of sexuality in Azevedo's novels—the English translation of *O cortiço,* published in 1926 as *A Brazilian Tenement,* had to be drastically censored for North American audiences—but today's critics view his works primarily as historical documents. While he and his contemporaries saw these works as innovative attempts to modernize and renew the Brazilian novel, the underlying themes of his naturalism are pessimism about Brazil's future and fear of all the

changes that the future might bring: the family skeletons that abolition of slavery might uncover, the white population's prospect of increased competition from mulattos and immigrants, and the education and emancipation of women.

– DAVID T. HABERLY

AZEVEDO, FERNANDO DE

Fernando de Azevedo (*b.* 2 April 1894; *d.* 19 September 1974), Brazilian educator, editor, sociologist, and cultural historian. As city director of public education from 1926 to 1930, Azevedo led in the implementation of school reforms in Rio de Janeiro. Later he was secretary of education and culture in São Paulo. In 1934 he founded and then later directed the humanities faculty of the University of São Paulo. As editor of the Biblioteca Pedagógica Brasileira and Brasiliana series, he introduced new ideas and revived Brazilian classics.

Azevedo wrote on sports and physical education, classical Latin literature, educational sociology, and the sociology of sugar mills and railroads. His major work was *A cultura brasileira* (1943), published as a supplement to the 1940 census. This ambitious survey combines a social and psychological history of the development of the Brazilian people with an institutional history of the Catholic church, the professions, literary and artistic achievements, and the sciences. It interprets Brazilian culture through the history of education from colonial times through the 1930s, calling for a unified system of public education to build national unity.

– DAIN BORGES

AZEVEDO, THALES DE

Thales de Azevedo (*b.* 26 August 1904), Brazilian social scientist and first director of the Instituto de Ciências Sociais at the Universidade Federal da Bahia. Thales Olimpio Góis de Azevedo was born in the city of Salvador, Bahia. He studied medicine and later anthropology and ethnography. Dedicated to the creation of a center for social sciences at Universidade Federal da Bahia, he was one of the authors of the proposal calling for the establishment of such a center. In 1961 the president of the university founded the Instituto de Ciências Sociais and appointed Azevedo the first director.

Azevedo's publications include *Gaúchos, notas de antropologia social* (1943); *Uma pesquisa sobre a vida social no estado da Bahia* (with Charles Wagley and Luís de Aguiar Costa Pinto, 1950); *Civilização e mestiçagem* (1951); *Les élites de couleur dans une ville brésilienne* (1953); *O catolicismo no Brasil* (1955); *Atualidade de*

Durkheim (with Nelson Sampaio and A. L. Machado Neto, 1959); *Ensaios de antropologia social* (1959); *Social change in Brazil* (1963); *Cultura e situação racial no Brasil* (1966); *A evasão de talentos* (1968); *Integração intercultural* (1974); *Democracia racial, ideologia e realidade* (1975); *A religião civil brasileira: Um instrumento político* (1981).

— ELIANA MARIA REA GOLDSCHMIDT

AZUELA, MARIANO

Mariano Azuela (*b.* 1 January 1873; *d.* 1 March 1952), Mexican writer. Azuela wrote more than twenty novels, numerous short stories, three plays, biographies, and books of essays. He was born in Lagos de Moreno, Jalisco, and studied medicine in Guadalajara. From early on he alternated between practicing that profession and writing. He published his first book, the short novel *María Luiza,* in 1907, but did not receive international or even national recognition until the mid-1920s, when *Los de abajo* (*The Underdogs*) was "discovered" and praised as a great novel reflecting the cultural heritage of the Mexican Revolution. This book had originally appeared in serial form and then was published in one volume at the end of 1915 in El Paso, Texas, but the definitive edition was published by the author himself in 1920, when he moved to Mexico City. Azuela's narrative work is a vast mural on which appear the changes and critical characters of Mexican society in the first half of the twentieth century, beginning with the years immediately preceding the Revolution.

Honoré de Balzac and Émile Zola were decisive influences on his work. Latin American "modernista" literature (not to be confused with European and North American "modernism") was clearly imprinted in Azuela's style.

Two qualities distinguish Azuela as a twentieth-century artist: the acuity with which he captures his characters as social actors, and the lucid way in which he insists, throughout all of his work, that Mexico's social and political problems are rooted in the moral decay of society. No one was better than he at portraying the opportunism, social climbing, resentment, and greed that arose during the Mexican Revolution and later spread throughout all of Mexican society.

Azuela's vision, however, was static and prototypical. His characters are not psychologically complex or capable of dramatic change, and his moralistic clarity becomes at times an obsession. This gives his work the air not of a great human comedy, but of a gallery of scenes with vivid, precise, and incisive images that lack perspective and movement. This mixture of strengths and defects explains why critical judgment and history have almost unanimously declared *Los de abajo* Azuela's masterpiece. It is not by chance that the subtitle of the book is *Cuadros y escenas de la Revolución Mexicana* (Sketches and Scenes of the Mexican Revolution) by which the author himself clearly shows that his vision is more episodic than dramatic. With all its defects, *Los de abajo* continues to be the most intense description of the revolutionary masses and all their contradictions.

Azuela's intense and austere realism influenced other major works, such as Martín Luis Guzmán's *El águila y la serpiente* (1928), Nellie Campobello's *Cartucho* (1931), Rafael F. Muñoz's *Vámonos con Pancho Villa* (1931), and Juan Rulfo's *Pedro Páramo* (1955). His works are available in *Obras completas,* edited by Francisco Monterde, 3 volumes (1958–1960).

— JORGE AGUILAR MORA

B

BACA FLOR, CARLOS

Carlos Baca Flor (*b.* ca. 1865; *d.* 20 February 1941), Peruvian artist. Born in Islay, formerly Peruvian now Chilean territory, Baca Flor moved with his family to Santiago, Chile, in 1871. At age fifteen he entered the School of Fine Arts in Santiago, where he studied with Cosme San Martín and the Italian Giovanni Mochi. Awarded the Prix de Rome in 1887, he declined the prize rather than renounce his Peruvian citizenship. He moved to Lima shortly thereafter, where the government granted him a fellowship to study at the Royal Academy of Fine Arts in Rome. Three years later he went to Paris to study with Benjamin Constant and Jean-Paul Laurens at the Julian Academy. He never returned to Peru.

For many years Baca Flor lived in extreme poverty,

but his luck changed when he obtained first prize at

the Salon des Artistes.

For many years Baca Flor lived in extreme poverty, but his luck changed when he obtained first prize at the Salon des Artistes in 1907. Soon afterward, banker John Pierpont Morgan commissioned him to do his portrait. Subsequently, he obtained portrait commissions from major personalities in the financial world. He painted one hundred and fifty portraits, among them that of Cardinal Eugenio Pacelli, later Pope Pius XII. In 1926 he was elected a member of the Academy of Fine Arts in Paris.

Baca Flor died in Neuilly-sur-Seine, considering himself a Peruvian although he had spent only eight years in his native country. His impeccable technique, at times brilliant composition, and the amazing realism of his portraits are recognized even by those who perceive his academic style as anachronistic.

– MARTA GARSD

BACHILLER Y MORALES, ANTONIO

Antonio Bachiller y Morales (*b.* 7 June 1812; *d.* 10 January 1889), Cuban writer, historian, and archaeologist. Born in Havana, Bachiller y Morales became a lawyer and a university professor. He was persecuted and exiled by the Spanish authorities when the Ten Years' War (1868–1878) began because he favored Cuba's autonomy from Spain. He is best known for his extensive and tireless research, the basis of studies in which he brought together information that had not previously attracted attention. Perhaps the most important of these studies is his three-volume history of Cuban letters and education (*Apuntes para la historia de las letras y instrucción publica de la isla de Cuba*, 1859–1860), but he also made significant contributions on the period of the British domination of Havana (*Cuba: Monografía histórica . . . desde la perdida de la Habana hasta la restauración española*, 1883) and on the pre-Columbian inhabitants of Cuba (*Cuba primitiva*, 1880). Although Bachiller y Morales made quite a few mistakes in his haste to gather information, the efforts of modern historians would have been far less fruitful without his dedication and spadework. He died in Havana.

– JOSÉ M. HERNÁNDEZ

BÁEZ, BUENAVENTURA

Buenaventura Báez (*b.* 1812; *d.* 1884), five-time president of the Dominican Republic. Báez was born in Azua to a wealthy landowner and his African slave. During the Haitian occupation of Santo Domingo, Báez represented Azua in the Haitian Congress and Constituent Assembly. He distrusted the Dominican independence movement and refused to recognize its authority after the proclamation of independence on 27 February 1844. Throughout his political career, Báez sought to place his country under the protection of a major foreign power, believing that the Dominican Republic did not have the strength to maintain genuine independence. With the aid of his future archrival, General Pedro SANTANA, he assumed the presidency for the first time in 1849.

First Presidential Term (24 September 1849–15 February 1853) Báez negotiated with both France and England for their possible acquisition of the Dominican Republic. He became the champion of the interests of the upper and middle classes by promoting the development of industry and furthering the educational system through the opening of national colleges at Santo Domingo and Santiago de los Caballeros. Báez concluded a concordat with the Vatican by which the Roman Catholic church was permitted to provide religious instruction in Dominican public schools. During his first term, the country suffered frequent attacks by Haiti, all of which were repelled. In 1853 Báez was forced into exile by Santana.

Second Presidential Term (8 October 1856–12 June 1858) Báez began his second term by unleashing a fierce persecution of Santana and his followers. He issued paper currency, which led to a devaluation of the peso and the ruin of many landowners, particularly the tobacco cultivators of the Cibao. A revolt in that fertile agricultural region toppled Báez, who fled to Spain. While still in exile there, he advocated Spain's annexation of the Dominican Republic.

Third Presidential Term (8 December 1865–29 May 1866) During his third term, Báez established a truly despotic regime marked by his effort to crush all opposition. He antagonized Dominican patriots by negotiating a deal with U.S. Secretary of State William H. Seward, by which the Dominican Republic would allow the United States to acquire the Samaná Peninsula in return for economic aid. Once again, a revolt in the Cibao forced Báez to flee the country.

Fourth Presidential Term (2 May 1868–January 1874) Báez's fourth term was the bloodiest and the most anarchic of his five terms. It is known in Dominican history as the "Regime of the Six Years." After failing to sell Samaná to the United States for $2 million, Báez offered the entire country to Washington. This plan met with a positive response from U.S. President Ulysses S. Grant, but the determined resistance of Senator Charles Sumner of Massachusetts prevented the annexation. By 1874, revolutionary forces compelled Báez to flee to Curaçao.

Fifth Presidential Term (27 December 1876–2 March 1878) Báez began his final term by promising democratic, liberal reforms, but he was soon indulging in familiar repressive measures. He also renewed his efforts to incorporate his country into the United States. His final exile from Santo Domingo began in March 1878. He died in Puerto Rico.

— KAI P. SCHOENHALS

BÁEZ, CECILIO

Cecilio Báez (*b.* 1 February 1862; *d.* 18 June 1941), politician, intellectual, diplomat, public servant, and provisional president of Paraguay (1905–1906). Cecilio Báez was one of the founders of the Liberal Party in 1887 and later its president. He was a deputy in Congress for several terms, beginning in 1895. He might be remembered most as the party's leading theoretician.

Báez was also known for denouncing Francisco Solano LÓPEZ, the controversial leader who led Paraguay into disastrous War of the Triple Alliance in 1864. He was appointed provisional president on 9 December 1905 for eleven months. Because of his influence, he was often able to keep the Liberals somewhat united in spite of their tendency to splinter into factions. By profession a doctor of law and a historiographer, Báez was instrumental in shaping a national education program. His prolific writings dealt with Paraguayan history as well as literary, legal, and political issues. He was a great advocate of democracy as well as a strong critic of the Catholic church. Báez was the National University's rector throughout the 1920s and 1930s. After the Chaco War with Bolivia, Báez, as foreign minister, signed the peace treaty on 28 July 1938.

— MIGUEL A. GATTI

BALAGUER, JOAQUÍN

Joaquín Balaguer (*b.* 1 September 1907), Dominican author, lawyer, politician, and president of the Dominican Republic (1960–1961, 1966–1978, 1986–). Balaguer, a native of Villa Bisono, studied law at both Santo Domingo and Paris, receiving a doctorate of law from each. In 1930 he became involved in the conspiracy of

Joaquín Balaguer. (UPI/Bettman Archive)

Rafael Estrella Ureña against president Horacio Vásquez, which brought Rafael-Leónidas TRUJILLO MOLINA to power. Balaguer served the Trujillo regime in important ambassadorial posts abroad and as minister of education, vice president (1957–1960), and president (1960–1961) at home. Whereas most members of Trujillo's government used their positions for personal enrichment, Balaguer continued to lead his modest bachelor existence.

Whereas most members of Trujillo's government used their positions for personal enrichment, Balaguer continued to lead his modest bachelor existence.

In the wake of Trujillo's assassination in 1961, Balaguer served as an important transitional figure between the end of the era of Trujillo and the presidential elections in 1962. He initiated a number of reforms that were designed to persuade the Organization of American States to lift its sanctions against the Dominican Republic. Balaguer opposed the attempt of Trujillo's brothers José Arismendi and Héctor Bienvenido to resurrect Trujilloism without Trujillo. He presided over the Council of State that ruled the country until the inauguration of the new president in February 1963. As the nation's political situation became volatile in late 1962, Balaguer decided upon exile in New York City. Thus he was absent from the Dominican Republic during Juan BOSCH's ephemeral presidency (1963); the military coup and subsequent triumvirate headed by Donald Reid Cabral, and the 1965 revolution, civil war, and foreign intervention.

During the presidential elections of 1966, Balaguer was the candidate of the Reformist Party (PR), which he founded during his years in exile. He won 57 percent of the vote. Thus began the twelve-year era of Balaguer, which witnessed his reelection as president in 1970 and 1974. The era was marked by massive aid from the United States, an economic boom triggered by the rise in world sugar prices, and a large building program that included the restoration of the colonial part of Santo Domingo.

After an interlude of presidents belonging to the Dominican Revolutionary Party (PRD) from 1978 to 1986, Balaguer was elected to the presidency twice more (1986, 1990). It was Balaguer's desire to preside over the 1992 celebrations accompanying the five-hundredth anniversary of Christopher Columbus's arrival on Hispaniola. Balaguer will be remembered as the Dominican Republic's outstanding statesman of the twentieth century. His contributions to Dominican literature have also been significant, especially his critical history of Dominican literature, *Historia de la literatura dominicana* (1956), and his other literary criticism, his historical works on the Trujillo era, including *Memorias de un cortesano* (1989), and his work on Dominican relations with Haiti, *La isla revés: Haiti y el destino dominicano* (1983). Balaguer's intense rivalry with Bosch extended to literary as well as political pursuits.

– KAI P. SCHOENHALS

BALBÁS, JERÓNIMO DE

Jerónimo de Balbás (*d.* 22 November 1748), retablo master. Balbás was born in Zamora, Spain, and lived in Cádiz in the early eighteenth century; later he worked in Seville and in Marchena. In 1718 he was in New Spain. Reminiscent in design of his principal retablo for the Sagrario of the cathedral of Seville (1706–1709, destroyed 1824), his Retablo de los Reyes for the cathedral of Mexico City (1718–1737), with four large *estípites,* determined the direction that much of the art of New Spain was to take for the rest of the century. The final breakdown of the Renaissance grid scheme in retablo design and the introduction of the *estípite* along with a new vocabulary of motifs are due to Balbás's work in the cathedral of Mexico City. He stayed on in New Spain and executed numerous other retablos, including the altar of Pardon and the central free-standing retablo, or "ciprés," of the cathedral; only the first survives, reconstructed after a fire in 1967.

– CLARA BARGELLINI

BALBÍN, RICARDO

Ricardo Balbín (*b.* 29 July 1904; *d.* 9 September 1981), Argentine political leader and one of the principal Radical Party figures in the postwar period. Originally from Buenos Aires, Balbín was elected in 1930 as a Radical congressman from La Plata but was unable to serve because of the military coup of that same year. He was one of the leading *intransigentes* (Intransigent Radicals) who, with Arturo FRONDIZI, was cofounder of the Movimiento de Intransigencia y Renovación (MIR) in 1945. With Frondizi, Balbín (as party whip) led the Radicals in the Argentine Congress under Juan PERÓN until 1949, when the government began a campaign against him, which led to his forced resignation as congressman and imprisonment. In the 1951 election, he was the unsuccessful Radical presidential candidate against Perón.

Balbín broke with Frondizi and the *intransigentes* after Perón's ouster and in 1956 established the Radical Civic Union of the People (UCRP), a more conservative and decidedly anti-Peronist party, which nominated him in the election won by Frondizi in 1958. With the demise of the *intransigentes,* Balbín emerged as the principal leader of the Radical Party and was one of the country's most important political figures until his death. In 1970 he led his party in a broad civilian front, La Hora del Pueblo (The People's Turn), working on behalf of the restoration of civilian rule, and was again defeated in his bid for the presidency in the 1973 elections.

In the wake of the electoral defeat, a left-wing faction within the party, the Movimiento de Renovación y Cambio, led by Raúl ALFONSÍN, emerged to challenge his leadership, critical of both his backroom-style politics and conservative program. Following the 1976 coup, he was an outspoken critic of the military government and twice imprisoned.

— JAMES P. BRENNAN

BALBOA, VASCO NÚÑEZ DE

Vasco Núñez de Balboa (*b.* ca. 1475; *d.* January 1519), a Spanish conquistador from Jerez de los Caballeros in Estremadura, and the first known European to see the Pacific Ocean. A poor, illiterate hidalgo, he sailed for the New World in 1501 with the expedition of Rodrigo de BASTIDAS, exploring the northern coast of modern Colombia. After settling on Hispaniola, he failed as a farmer, and in 1510 he escaped his creditors by stowing away on a vessel bound for the coast of Urabá (Colombia). The expedition, led by Martín Fernández de ENCISO, sailed to relieve the settlement founded near Cartagena by Alonso de OJEDA, and now led by Francisco PIZARRO, which was in desperate straits. Balboa, accepted as a common soldier, advised moving the colony west across the Gulf of Urabá, a region he had visited with Bastidas. The wretched settlers took the advice and found a plentiful supply of food, much gold, and Indians without poisoned arrows.

Seen as the savior of the colony, Balboa quickly gained popularity and respect among the men. The settlement of Santa María de la Antigua del Darién was founded in 1510 in Panama (then called Darién and, later, Castilla del Oro) under the jurisdiction of Diego de NICUESA. Therefore, Balboa noted, Enciso had no authority. When Nicuesa appeared, the colonists of Antigua forced him aboard an unseaworthy ship, and he disappeared at sea. The pompous Enciso was then charged with usurping the authority of Nicuesa and was expelled from the colony. He returned to Spain, where

Vasco Núñez de Balboa. Anonymous engraving from Retratos de los españoles ilustres con un epítome de sus vidas *(1791). (Organization of American States)*

he leveled charges of usurpation against Balboa, who realized that he needed to counter them with a spectacular achievement. In late 1511 the king had named Balboa interim governor of Darién, and in 1513 he was appointed supreme commander of the colony. He also received word of an impending order directing him to return to Spain to face charges. Instead, Balboa moved with some urgency to find the great body of water south of the isthmus, of which a friendly cacique had spoken.

On 1 September 1513, Balboa set out with 190 Spaniards, 1,000 Indian porters, and some bloodhounds. After extreme hardships—cutting through dense jungle and swamps, crossing rough mountains, and fending off hostile natives—the expedition finally reached its objective. Advancing alone to a peak on 25 (or 27) September, Balboa gazed upon the vast "South Sea," subsequently called the Pacific. Four days later he waded into the surf, claiming for Spain the ocean and the shores washed by it. The enterprise succeeded brilliantly for Balboa because he had subjugated many tribes without the loss of a single Spaniard, and he returned triumphantly to Antigua in January 1514 with a fortune in gold, pearls, and slaves.

Balboa is often portrayed as having treated the Indians humanely, but this is true only in a relative sense. More than most conquistadores, he befriended Indians, enjoying good relations with some thirty caciques. He also kept various mistresses. Yet he did not hesitate to fight those whom he considered obstinate. He was a man of his time and circumstances, sometimes enslaving Indians and punishing them severely. Among other atrocities, he ordered Indian homosexuals burned at the stake, and dogs were set upon recalcitrant caciques.

Meanwhile, the king—ignorant of Balboa's great achievement, and persuaded by Enciso and others of his culpability—appointed a new governor of Darién. He was Pedro Arias de ÁVILA (Pedrarias Dávila), the aging scion of a prominent family. Sailing for Panama with a large fleet in April 1514, Pedrarias carried orders to suspend Balboa's authority and bring him to justice. Initial inquiry acquitted Balboa, and Pedrarias came to resent his popularity, especially after Balboa's deeds became known in Spain. Though still subject to Pedrarias, Balboa was appointed adelantado of the Southern Sea and captain-general of the provinces of Coiba and Panama in 1515. Relations between the two rivals appeared to improve when Pedrarias's daughter María was betrothed to Balboa in 1516. In fact, the rancorous old man nursed a grudge. While the "son-in-law" made plans to explore the Pacific coast of Panama on his own, he was betrayed by a friend, who accused him of ignoring Pedrarias's authority. Balboa was arrested on trumped-up charges of treason. Found guilty, and denied an appeal to Spain, he was decapitated at Acla.

— WILLIAM L. SHERMAN

BALBUENA, BERNARDO DE

Bernardo de Balbuena (*b.* ca. 1562; *d.* 11 October 1627), a major poet of colonial Spanish America. Balbuena was born in Valdepeñas, La Mancha, but emigrated to Mexico, possibly with his father, about 1564. He studied first in Guadalajara and then in Mexico City. In 1585 while at the University of Mexico, he won the first of several prizes for poetry. Beginning in 1586, he occupied a series of ecclesiastical posts in the Guadalajara region, where he composed most of the poetry that would bring him fame. Balbuena returned to the capital to oversee publication of his *Grandeza mexicana* (1604), an idealized description and eulogy of Mexico City that presaged and contributed to the development of creole patriotism. Thereafter, however, his career in the church took precedence. He went back to Spain to resume his studies, earning a doctorate in the-

ology from the University of Sigüenza in 1608. Appointment as *abad mayor* (abbott) of Jamaica soon followed, and in 1619 he was named bishop of Puerto Rico, an office he held until his death.

Balbuena also published *Siglo de oro en las selvas de Erífile* (1608), a pastoral romance, and *El Bernardo, o Victoria de Roncesvalles* (1624), an epic poem largely composed before 1600 glorifying Spain's past and present. His poetry displays a baroque mixture of erudition; fertile invention; vigorous, evocative language; and rich (perhaps excessive) ornamentation.

— R. DOUGLAS COPE

BALCARCE, MARIANO

Mariano Balcarce (*b.* 8 November 1807; *d.* 20 February 1885), Argentine diplomat. The son of Antonio González Balcarce, a military hero of the struggle for independence, Mariano Balcarce was born in Buenos Aires. He spent most of his life in diplomatic service in Europe. His first assignment, at age twenty-four, was as an assistant to the Argentine minister to Great Britain. He later moved to Paris, where he was living at the time of his death. Balcarce negotiated the treaty by which Spain recognized Argentine independence, and he assiduously publicized the attractions of Argentina for prospective immigrants. He befriended numerous Argentine and other Latin American visitors to France and established a particularly close relationship with José de SAN MARTÍN during the latter's years of exile in France; he married Mercedes de San Martín, the Liberator's daughter, in 1832.

— DAVID BUSHNELL

BALDOMIR, ALFREDO

Alfredo Baldomir (*b.* 1894; *d.* 1948), president of Uruguay (1938–1943). Baldomir was the brother-in-law of President Gabriel TERRA, who chose him as his potential successor. Baldomir had been chief of police in Montevideo at the time of Terra's 1933 coup.

The 1938 election was a family affair for the Colorado-backed president. Terra had the party offer two candidates: his brother-in-law, Baldomir, who received 121,000 votes, and his father-in-law, Eduardo BLANCO ACEVEDO, who received 98,000. The Colorado Party, with a total of 219,000 votes, thus defeated the Herrerist Blancos (National Party), which offered only one candidate, who had 114,000 votes.

With an economic upturn and a resurgence of the Batllist tradition, Baldomir felt that Terra's alliance with the Blancos, led by Luis Alberto de HERRERA, as defined in the 1934 Constitution, had outlived its usefulness.

The Blancos were opposed to much of Baldomir's domestic program and were critical of his cooperation with the United States at the start of World War II. Their guaranteed control of half of the seats in the Senate left them with a strong veto power. Consequently, on 21 February 1942 Baldomir postponed the upcoming March elections, dissolved Congress, and called for a constitutional plebiscite to restore the normal functioning of the electoral system. He created a Council of State, to which he submitted his constitutional proposal on 29 May. The new constitution did away with the division of the Senate between the 1933 coup leaders (Terra and Herrera) and restored full constitutional democracy. Baldomir is quoted as having said, "We have the costliest electoral system on the continent, but it is cheaper than revolution."

— MARTIN WEINSTEIN

BALDORIOTY DE CASTRO, RAMÓN

Ramón Baldorioty de Castro (*b.* 28 February 1822; *d.* 30 September 1889), a leading member of Puerto Rico's autonomy movement. Of humble roots, Baldorioty received his early education from Padre Rufo Fernández, who recognized the youth's superior intellect. In 1846, Fernández arranged for Baldorioty to study at the University of Madrid. After returning to Puerto Rico, Baldorioty taught at the School of Commerce, Agriculture, and Navigation (1854–1870).

A member of Puerto Rico's Liberal Reformist Party, Baldorioty served in the Constitutional Cortes of 1869 and as a deputy in the Cortes of 1870–1871. After the Spanish monarchy was restored in 1875, Baldorioty went into exile to Santo Domingo for four years.

As a Liberal Reformist, Baldorioty advocated basic civil rights, abolition of slavery, and administrative decentralization. However, the party split into two factions, one favoring assimilation into Spain's political system and the other seeking autonomy. Upon his return from exile in 1878, Baldorioty steered liberals toward the Republican Autonomist wing of the Liberal Reformist Party. He led efforts to reorganize the party along autonomist lines, and at the Assembly of Ponce, in 1887, he presided over the newly created Puerto Rican Autonomist Party. The Autonomists eventually secured Puerto Rican autonomy from Spain in late 1897, eight years after Baldorioty's death.

— JOHN J. CROCITTI

BALLAGAS Y CUBEÑAS, EMILIO

Emilio Ballagas y Cubeñas (*b.* 7 November 1908; *d.* 11 September 1954), Cuban poet and essayist. Born in Camagüey, Cuba, Ballagas's writing career began with a 1926 essay about Cuban patriot José MARTÍ, which won him a scholarship sponsored by the *Revista Martiniana* to study at the University of Havana. Better known as a poet, he published his first compositions in *Antenas* in 1928 and in the avant-garde *Revisita de Avance* the following year. While a student at the university, Ballagas published his much-acclaimed "Elegía de Mariá Belén Chacón" in *Revista de Avance* (1930). One year later he published *Júbilo y fuga,* which confirmed Ballagas's importance as a national and international poet and signaled the first of three stages in his poetry.

Although many of Ballagas's poems highlight the folkloric aspects of Afro-Cuban traditions, some speak to the economic and social conditions of blacks on the island.

Ballagas completed his Ph.D. in pedagogy in 1933 and taught at the Normal School for teachers in Santa Clara, becoming its director the following year. His *Cuaderno de poesía negra* (1934) and *Antología de la poesía negra hispanoamericana* (1935) exemplify the tradition of Afro-Cuban poetry. Although many of Ballagas's poems highlight the folkloric aspects of Afro-Cuban traditions, some speak to the economic and social conditions of blacks on the island.

During a trip to Paris in 1937 to research Amerindian languages at the Bibliothèque Nationale, Ballagas met many of the best-known poets of the period. In 1939 he published *Sabor eterno,* a collection of poems about love, written with the intense emotions that characterized the second stage of his poetry. Ballagas completed a second Ph.D. in 1946 and published his dissertation, "Situación de la poesía afroamericana," in the *Revista Cubana* and the anthology *Maps de la poesía negra americana* (1946). He traveled to New York and became associated with the Institute for the Education of the Blind.

Ballagas's religious feelings, which are expressed in the third stage of his poetry, are evident in *Nuestra Señora del Mar* (1943), dedicated to the patron saint of Cuba, the Virgen de la Caridad del Cobre. He continued his religious poems in *Cielo en rehenes,* which won the National Prize for Poetry in 1951, although it was not published until 1955, and *Décimas por el júbilo martiano en el centenario del apóstol José Martí,* a patriotic as well as spiritual book, which won the Centenario Prize in 1953, commemorating Martí's birth. Ballagas died in Havana.

— WILLIAM LUIS

BALLIVIÁN, JOSÉ

José Ballivián (*b.* 30 November 1805; *d.* 16 October 1852), president of Bolivia (1841–1847). Born in La Paz, he is perhaps best known as the victorious general in the 1841 battle of Ingaví, in which the Bolivian army beat the Peruvian invaders under the leadership of General Agustín GAMARRA, forever ending Peruvian plans to annex Bolivia. Ballivián was also a capable administrator and one of the best nineteenth-century Bolivian presidents. Although he joined the military early in life, having fought as a teenager in the Spanish and patriot armies, Ballivián was a self-taught man who fostered science and culture. He was fortunate that during his government the country enjoyed relative prosperity due to revenues from taxes on guano from the Pacific coast, quinine from the eastern foothills, and a silver boomlet. Most important was his attempt to consolidate Bolivia's eastern frontier regions. He founded the department of Beni in the Amazon basin of northeastern Bolivia, promoted the exploration of the Otuquis River region in Santa Cruz, and attempted but largely failed the exploration, military conquest, and settlement of the Chaco.

— ERICK D. LANGER

BALMACEDA FERNÁNDEZ, JOSÉ MANUEL

José Manuel Balmaceda Fernández (*b.* 19 July 1840; *d.* 19 September 1891), diplomat, politician, and president of Chile (1886–1891). The son of politically prominent and wealthy parents, Balmaceda briefly studied at a seminary, an experience that may have contributed to his anticlericalism. Although a large landowner, he also became involved in a variety of tasks: editor of various newspapers, private secretary to a president, and a diplomat. Not surprisingly, he won, at age twenty-four, the first of his many congressional elections. While serving as a deputy he also undertook certain diplomatic missions, arranging a border settlement with Argentina. During the administration of Domingo SANTA MARÍA (1881–1886), he held the posts of minister of foreign relations, minister of war, and the more important position of minister of the interior. Since he was hand-picked by Santa María, his election to the presidency was virtually assured, thanks to his mentor's massive intervention in the political process.

Balmaceda took over Chile at a transitional time. Increasingly, the nation's economy, and its revenue base, rested on the mining and exporting of nitrates. The new president had clear ideas of what he wanted to do with these funds: build railroads and public buildings, expand educational facilities, modernize the military, colonize the newly opened southern territories, and reward his political henchmen and their families with lucrative government positions and contracts.

Certain forces, however, stood in the way of Balmaceda's programs. The politicians wanted their place at the public trough. They particularly disliked the fact that the newly created ministry of public works seemed so powerful and that Balmaceda often used his executive powers to create jobs without consulting the legislature. The deputies and senators resented that the president alone seemed to have the power to dispense largess.

The second problem was the nature of the nitrate trade. Nitrates, while an essential component of fertilizers and explosives, were still a commodity whose value fluctuated with the state of the world economy. When prices fell, the nitrate producers, or *salitreros,* generally responded by limiting production, in hopes of driving up the mineral's value. While such production cutbacks proved beneficial to the mining interests, they hurt the government, which depended upon the export levy on nitrates to sustain the régime and its various public-works projects. Hence, Balmaceda viewed as an enemy anyone who could reduce production. His particular bête noire was John Thomas North, an English financier who owned much of what was worth owning in the nitrate-rich province of Tarapacá: a bank, a supply company, the local source of water, and the railroad that carried the *salitre* from the pampas to the port of Iquique.

The conflict between these two men became quite hostile. North, by keeping prices high for transport, increased the cost of the nitrate and hence limited its sale. Balmaceda, who resented the loss of potential income, tried to break North's monopoly on the nitrate-transportation network by offering railroad concessions to other foreign financiers. North deeply resented Balmaceda's efforts and tried to marshal his friends in the Chilean Congress to prevent the president from implementing his policies.

Balmaceda's principal problem was not North or his associates but his own methods of ruling. Although Balmaceda had initially enjoyed the support of a majority of the congress, he began to lose popularity. In part, various politicians, including some in his own party, disliked the way Balmaceda had been elected president. Others resented his seemingly unlimited control over patronage, particularly his willingness to appoint men to positions on the basis of talent, not political connections.

Legislative animus toward the president increased when he ruthlessly intervened in the 1888 congressional elections. Worse, Balmaceda lost his majority in Congress when the legislators concluded that he would select Enrique Salvador Sanfuentes to succeed him. It became obvious that if he wished to rule, Balmaceda would have to consult the legislature.

Balmaceda went on the offensive, demanding a strengthening, not a diminution, of presidential powers. Doubtless, these proposals shocked the Congress, which might have expected compromise. Clearly, the nation had reached an impasse: throughout 1890 the Congress demanded that the president create a cabinet to its liking before the legislature would approve the budget. Balmaceda refused. Since the president and the Congress seemed more intent on insulting each other than on addressing the Country's pressing problems, the nation stagnated.

Thanks to the intervention of Archbishop Mariano Casanova, Balmaceda succeeded in forming a new cabinet acceptable to the legislature. When it collapsed, Balmaceda formed one composed of his friends, further antagonizing the Congress, which still refused to pass a budget.

Increasingly, Balmaceda ruled by decree, which created more uncertainty than it solved problems. Believing that the president might act illegally, his legislative foes created a junta to coordinate their efforts should it be necessary to resist his government. They soon had a reason: in January 1891, Balmaceda, citing the legislature's earlier refusal to approve his request for funding, unilaterally declared that he would use the budget authorized for 1890 for 1891 instead. Considering this act a violation of the 1833 Constitution, the junta rebelled, thereby initiating the Revolution of 1891.

Balmaceda's military efforts seemed as ill-fated as his political programs. Since the rebels controlled the nitrate-rich north, they had more money than the legitimate government. Worse, the rebels, who enjoyed naval supremacy, successfully prevented Balmaceda from taking possession of two cruisers under construction in Europe. All the president could do was mobilize his army, whose morale seemed to have deteriorated as much, if not more than many of their weapons, and await the ultimate invasion.

The attacks came in August. By the end of the month, the rebels controlled Santiago. As the congressionalist mobs looted the homes of his supporters and killed his officers, Balmaceda took refuge in the Argentine embassy. He remained there until 19 September 1891, the day after his term of office expired. Then he shot himself.

It is easier to say what Balmaceda was not than what he was: his willingness to deal with foreign investors other than North indicated that he was not an economic nationalist; his cynical manipulation of elections demonstrated that he was not a democrat; his brutal suppression of strikes showed that he was not a friend of the worker. While he was perhaps a visionary, his political methods seemed more typical of a bygone era than of a nation groping its way toward democracy.

– WILLIAM F. SATER

BALSEIRO, JOSÉ AGUSTÍN

José Agustín Balseiro (*b.* 23 August 1900; *d.* 1992), Puerto Rican writer and professor. Balseiro earned a law degree from the University of Puerto Rico (1921), and an honorary doctorate from the Catholic University of Chile. His writings are varied. His three novels move from the biographical mode of *La ruta eterna* (1923) to the indictment of social ills in *La gratitud humana* (1969). His poetry began emphasizing love and wine (*La copa de Anacreonte,* 1924) and ended with love and transcendence (*El ala y el beso,* 1983). His best-known critical works are *Novelistas españoles modernos* (1933), *Expresión de Hispanoamérica* 2 vols. (1960–1963), and *The Americas Look at Each Other* (1969).

Balseiro's critical essays, his creative works, his teaching (at the University of Illinois–Urbana, Duke University, and elsewhere), and his many lectures throughout Latin America won him wide recognition, including membership in the Spanish Royal Academy, Madrid's Center of Historical Studies, Mexico's Academy of Letters, and Argentina's Sarmiento Institute. He received the Orders of Isabel la Católica (Spain) and Vasco Núñez de Balboa (Panama). Balseiro also served as Puerto Rico's senator-at-large.

– MARÍA A. SALGADO

BALTA, JOSÉ

José Balta (*b.* 1814; *d.* 26 July 1872), president of Peru (1868–1872). A soldier of common background and strong convictions, he led troops from Chiclayo on the northern coast against the government when President Mariano Ignacio PRADO issued decrees to curb the political power of Catholic bishops. With army support, Balta remained in power for a full presidential term. Convinced that Peru must escape its financial dependence on local guano consignees, he placed the Ministry of Finance in the hands of Nicolás de PIÉROLA and approved his policy of domestic spending of income earned by contracting for a guano monopoly with the Dreyfus Company of France. Thereafter military salaries and pensions rose, and public facilities improved. Contractors laid hundreds of miles of new rail lines throughout the country, including the famous Central Railway linking Lima with the mining center of La Oroya in the Andean highlands. But expenditures quickly outran income from all sources, and public sentiment soon associated the military with public waste.

At the end of Balta's term, Peru faced a foreign debt

of £49 million, a tenfold increase over what it had

been when he took office.

Balta and Piérola clashed repeatedly until Piérola resigned in 1871. Balta then incurred new debts to the Dreyfus Company. At the end of Balta's term, Peru faced a foreign debt of £49 million, a tenfold increase over what it had been when he took office. By the election of 1872 military leadership was in disrepute. Balta's secretary, Ricardo Palma, and North American entrepreneur Henry Meiggs, among others, persuaded him not to prevent the inauguration of his successor. In the military uprising that followed this decision, Balta was imprisoned and shot dead in his cell by guards.

— VINCENT PELOSO

BANDEIRA, MANUEL CARNEIRO DE SOUZA

Manuel Carneiro de Souza Bandeira (*b.* 19 April 1886; *d.* 13 October 1968), Brazilian poet. Born in Recife, Pernambuco, Bandeira moved to Rio at the age of ten. He planned to be an architect, but his studies were interrupted by tuberculosis. While ill, he wrote verses that filled his idleness and alleviated his suffering, but eventually he began to write great poetry. His health improved, and in 1917 he published his first volume of poetry, *A cinza das horas* (The Ashes of the Hours).

He lived for thirteen years in a working-class suburb of Rio and later taught literature at the Pedro II School and what is now the Federal University of Rio de Janeiro.

Bandeira's work has been divided into two not very distinct phases. The first comprises his three earliest collections of poems. *A cinza das horas* follows symbolist and Parnassian ideals. *Carnaval* (1919) reveals independent traits that depart from the literary conventions of the time and includes "Os Sapos," later a national anthem of the modernists. *O ritmo dissoluto* (Dissolute Rhythm, 1924) contains unconventional themes and forms.

Libertinagem (Libertinage, 1930) is the first volume of Bandeira's second phase. It reveals a transition to the modernistic aesthetic in several ways: the adoption of Portuguese as spoken in Brazil; prosaic themes; popular aspects of Brazilian culture; and humor, varying from fine irony to straight jokes. Additional works by Bandeira include *Estrela da manhã* (Morning Star, 1936), *Lira dos cinqüent'anos* (Lyrics of Fiftieth Birthday, 1940), *Belo, Belo* in his *Poesias Completas* (3d ed., 1948), *Mafuá do malungo* (2d ed., 1954), *De poetas e poesia* (1954), *A Brief History of Brazilian Literature* (1958), *Estrela da tarde* (Evening Star, 1963), *Estrela da vida inteira* (Whole Life Star, 1966), *Andorinha, andorinha* (1966), and *Poesia completa e prosa* (4th ed., 1983). *This Earth, That Sky: Poems by Manuel Bandeira,* translated by Candice Slater, appeared in 1988.

Bandeira continued to be open to new approaches, even having written concretist poems. He always remained, however, an essentially lyric poet. His poetry, often tinged with irony, melancholy, and tragic humor, betrays reminiscences of his own life. He is also recognized as a literary critic, anthologist, essayist, and translator.

— MARIA ISABEL ABREU

BANZER SUÁREZ, HUGO

Hugo Banzer Suárez (*b.* 1926), president of Bolivia (1971–1978). Born in the small town of Concepción, Banzer Suárez studied at the Military Colleges in La Paz and Argentina. Following the 1952 revolution led by the Nationalist Revolutionary Movement (MNR), his military career almost ended because the size of the armed forces was severely reduced.

Following the overthrow of the MNR in 1964 by General René BARRIENTOS ORTUÑO, Banzer's career took a decidedly political turn when he began a 22-month term as the military government's minister of education. From 1967 to 1971 he held a number of other posts, including military attaché in Washington.

In 1971, Banzer emerged as the leader of a conservative faction of the armed forces whose goal was the overthrow of the populist government headed by General Juan José TORRES GONZÁLEZ. The group's first attempt failed and Banzer was imprisoned and then exiled to Argentina. On 21 August 1971 a civilian-military alliance launched a second, successful coup that installed Banzer, then only a colonel, as president of Bolivia.

Banzer had a great deal of difficulty in maintaining the fragile coalition—dubbed the Nationalist Popular Front. By 1974, he had opted to eliminate political party support and ruled with the support of prominent members of the private sector and the military. In March 1979 Banzer and several prominent members of the private sector and dissident politicians founded the Nationalist Democratic Action (Acción Democrática y Nacionalista—ADN) mainly to establish a political mechanism to defend the former dictator against charges of wrongdoing. Banzer ran as the ADN's candidate in the 1979 and 1980 elections, in which, surprisingly, his party finished third, demonstrating that he still enjoyed a great deal of popular support.

In the July 1985 election, Banzer received the largest number of votes (28.6 percent), winning the first round by a small margin. Since he did not have the support in the congressional runoff to be named president, he gave his support to the MNR candidate, Victor PAZ ESTENSSORO, a move many have considered a significant act of statesmanship that contributed to the continuity of democratization in Bolivia.

Again the ADN candidate in the 1989 elections, Banzer ran a close second to the MNR candidate. Again the election was to be decided by Congress. When agreement with the MNR proved impossible, Banzer agreed to support the Movement of the Revolutionary Left (MIR) candidate, Jaime PAZ ZAMORA, as president. His health deteriorating, Banzer relinquished leadership of the ADN in the aftermath of its 1993 electoral defeat.

— EDUARDO A. GAMARRA

BAPTISTA, MARIANO

Mariano Baptista (*b.* 16 July 1832; *d.* 19 March 1907), president of Bolivia (1892–1896). One of the greatest political orators of Bolivia, Baptista is also considered the ideologist of the Conservative (or Constitutionalist) Party, which prevailed from 1884 to 1899. Dedicated to politics all his adult life, Baptista was a supporter of the dictatorship of José María LINARES (1857–1861). As a diplomat, Baptista represented Bolivia well in border negotiations with virtually all neighboring countries. Elected vice president during the Gregorio PACHECO administration (1884–1888), Baptista became one of the most important Conservative politicians. He wrote profusely in various newspapers in favor of the Catholic church, mining interests, and railroad development, and against the anticlerical Liberal Party. When Baptista was elected president in 1892 he had the misfortune of presiding over the collapse of international silver prices and the economic crisis it triggered in Bolivia. During his administration he fostered railroad construction and the exploitation of rubber resources in the Acre region of northeast Bolivia.

— ERICK D. LANGER

BAQUEDANO, MANUEL

Manuel Baquedano (*b.* 1826; *d.* 1897), Chilean military leader. Born in Santiago, Baquedano ran away at the age of twelve and sailed as a stowaway in the expedition sent to destroy the Peru-Bolivia Confederation. In 1839 he fought in the battles of Portada de Guias and Yungay. During the civil war of 1851 he fought in the battle of Loncomilla against his father. In 1854 he was separated from military service by the government of Manuel MONTT but was reinstated in 1859. Baquedano fought against the Araucanian Indians in 1868 and was a brigadier general when the War of the Pacific (1879–1883) broke out. In February 1880 he commanded 14,800 men during the campaign against Tacna and Arica. Following this series of victories, he commanded 26,500 troops in the attack on Lima. On 13 and 15 January 1881 he won the bloody battles of Chorillos and Miraflores, which led to the capitulation of Lima and drove Peru to accept defeat.

Baquedano ran away at the age of twelve and sailed as a stowaway in the expedition sent to destroy the Peru-Bolivia Confederation.

Following the war Baquedano was promoted to generalissimo. In 1881 the Conservative Party proclaimed him their presidential candidate, but he refused to accept. Between 1882 and 1894 he served in the Chilean Senate. In early 1891 the Chilean Congress asked Baquedano to support its position against President José Manuel BALMACEDA, but he declared neutrality and took no part in the revolution of 1891. Following Balmaceda's 1891 suicide, Baquedano took command of the nation until those opposed to Balmaceda could take charge.

— ROBERT SCHEINA

BAQUERIZO MORENO, ALFREDO

Alfredo Baquerizo Moreno (*b.* 28 September 1859; *d.* 20 March 1951), president of Ecuador (1916–1920). Baquerizo, a native of Guayaquil, first earned distinction as a writer of prose and poetry before embarking on a career in politics. He held various government posts—mayor of Guayaquil (1890–1896); secretary to the minister of the superior court in Guayaquil (1894–1901); minister of foreign relations (1902–1912); vice president of Ecuador (1903–1916); and senator from

Guayas province and president of the Senate (1912–1916)—before being elected president. In office he helped resolve Ecuador's lingering boundary dispute with Colombia (the Muñoz–Vernaza–Suarez Treaty, 1916). Baquerizo signed legislation in 1918 that legally ended the institution of forced labor (*concertaje*), although the law was seldom enforced. His adminstration did, however, implement a successful anti–yellow fever campaign in Guayaquil in 1919. During his term the Ecuadorian cacao export economy began to decline, due to rising competition from British and Portuguese colonies in Africa and to *Monilia*, a plant fungus that destroyed many Ecuadorian plantations. At age seventy-two, Baquerizo briefly served as interim president (September 1931–August 1932) following General Luis Larrea Alba's failed bid to establish a dictatorship. He died in New York City.

— RONN F. PINEO

BAQUÍJANO Y CARRILLO DE CÓRDOBA, JOSÉ DE

José de Baquíjano y Carrillo de Córdoba (*b.* 13 March 1751; *d.* 24 January 1817), Peruvian intellectual, educator, and high court judge. The precocious and ambitious son of a wealthy, titled family in Lima, Baquíjano obtained a doctorate in canon law from Lima's University of San Marcos at the age of fourteen. After an unsuccessful trip to Spain seeking a high court (*audiencia*) appointment (1773–1776), he returned to Lima and in 1778 joined the faculty at San Marcos.

In 1781 Baquíjano delivered the university's welcoming eulogy for Viceroy Augustín de Jáuregui. Royal censure of the published text, replete with references to prohibited literature, was followed by unsuccessful efforts to win either the rectorship of San Marcos or the senior chair of civil law.

Baquíjano's fortunes improved in the 1790s. He wrote articles for the *Mercurio peruano,* secured the senior chair in canon law at San Marcos, and again set off for Spain to pursue an appointment to Lima's audiencia.

Persistence paid off. After being named a criminal judge on the Lima court in 1797, an unusual accomplishment for a native son at the time, Baquíjano advanced to the civil chamber in 1806. Although he was named to the Council of State by the Cortes of Cádiz in February 1812, Baquíjano was never seated. By the time he reached Spain, Ferdinand VII had returned and nullified the Cortes' actions. Baquíjano died in Seville, still loyal to the Spanish monarchy.

— MARK A. BURKHOLDER

BARALT, RAFAEL MARÍA

Rafael María Baralt (*b.* 3 July 1810; *d.* 4 January 1860), Venezuelan writer and historian. After spending his childhood in Santo Domingo, Baralt returned to Venezuela in 1821. His first task as a historian was to accompany Santiago MARIÑO on the western campaign and organize and publish the documents pertaining to it. During the administration of José Antonio PÁEZ, he traveled to Caracas and mingled with the intellectuals of the city. He joined the Economic Society of the Friends of the Country and participated with Agustín CODAZZI in editing the *Resumen de la geografía de Venezuela* (1841) and the *Atlas físico y político de Venezuela* (1840). He also prepared one of his best-known works, the *Resumen de la historia de Venezuela,* published in Paris in 1841. The government placed Baralt in charge of studying the border disputes with British Guiana.

In September 1841 Baralt left for Europe, working in the Spanish archives and making connections in the Spanish literary world. He settled permanently in Spain, where he was intensely active intellectually and published numerous works. In 1853 Baralt was elected a regular member of the Royal Academy of the Spanish Language, and he held important public posts in Spain. He was director of the official periodical, *Gaceta de Madrid,* and administrator of the National Printing House.

— INÉS QUINTERO

BARBERO, ANDRÉS

Andrés Barbero (*b.* 28 July 1877; *d.* 14 February 1949), Paraguayan physician, scientist, and philanthropist. Born into a very wealthy Asunción family, Barbero decided at an early age to pursue a career in the sciences, despite the backwardness of his country's scientific establishment. Accordingly, he studied medicine, graduating in 1904. His practice lasted only a short time, however, and he soon abandoned it to dedicate himself to teaching and scientific research.

In 1921 Barbero founded the Sociedad Científica del Paraguay together with naturalists Guillermo Tell Bertoni and Emilio Hassler. He also established a journal, the *Revista Científica del Paraguay,* which he edited for many years and which he filled with his own erudite pieces on Paraguayan flora and fauna.

Barbero's greatest contribution came in the field of philanthropy. He almost single-handedly created and maintained the Paraguayan Red Cross, the School for Rural Obstetrics, the National Cancer Institute, and a dozen other institutions emphasizing public health. After his death in 1949, his family donated still more funds for a new foundation, La Piedad, which supported efforts in many fields, from investigations into the indigenous languages of the Chaco to the care of retirees in the capital city, to the maintenance of various museums.

– THOMAS L. WHIGHAM

BARBOSA, DOMINGOS CALDAS

Domingos Caldas Barbosa (*b.* 1738; *d.* 9 Nov. 1800), Brazilian poet, singer, and songwriter. The son of a slave woman and a Portuguese merchant, Barbosa studied at Jesuit schools in Rio. His early satires got him into trouble with the authorities and led to a military assignment in a distant province until 1762. He went to Portugal with the hope of entering the university, but his father's death prevented him from doing so. Introduced by family friends to the Lisbon court, he gained favor as a poet and performer of original songs. As a composer, he was a central figure in the emergence and dissemination of the *modinha* and Afro-Brazilian *lundu* song forms. With the aid of his protectors, Barbosa also took holy orders. His case is an example of the symbiosis of religious and secular spheres in his day.

Barbosa was a founding member and first president of the stylish Nova Arcádia literary club. His poems, collected in the two volumes of *Viola de Lereno* (1798, 1826), exemplify both neoclassicism and innovative applications of Afro-Brazilian language. Father Barbosa's work is both transitional, ranging from a strict continental style to a more flexible New World expression, and synthetic, drawing on erudite as well as popular sources.

– CHARLES A. PERRONE

BARBOSA, FRANCISCO VILLELA

Francisco Villela Barbosa (*b.* 20 November 1769; *d.* 11 September 1846), marqués of Paranaguá and minister of the Empire of Brazil. Born in Rio de Janeiro, where his father dealt in commerce, Barbosa graduated in 1796 with a degree in mathematics from the University of Coimbra, later becoming a professor of geometry at the Royal Navy Academy in Lisbon.

His political role was particularly important during the reign of Pedro I (1822–1831). After serving as Rio de Janeiro's representative to the Lisbon Cortes, he returned to Brazil in 1823 and was appointed minister of the empire and of foreign affairs. He also held, on various occasions, the post of navy minister (1823, 1825, 1826, 1829, 1831, and 1841). He supported the dissolution of the Constituent Assembly and participated in the framing of the Constitution of 1824. He was a

state councilor, and in 1825 he took part in the negotiations to recognize Brazil's independence. In 1826, Barbosa was appointed a senator, but his fidelity to PEDRO I forced him to withdraw, temporarily, from public life after Pedro's abdication in 1831. Later, he championed the project that advanced the coming of age of PEDRO II. He wrote several works, chiefly treatises on geometry.

– LÚCIA M. BASTOS P. NEVES

BARBOSA DE OLIVEIRA, RUI

Rui Barbosa de Oliveira (*b.* 5 November 1840; *d.* 1 March 1923), Brazilian statesman, jurist, writer, and diplomat. Barbosa was a leader in many of the great causes that transformed Brazil in the late nineteenth century, leading to the abolition of slavery, the fall of the empire, the creation of the republic, the development of a federal system, and the separation of church and state all within a period of two years. Born in Salvador, Bahia, Barbosa attended law school in Recife and São Paulo, returning to Salvador to practice law. He quickly turned to journalism, becoming a defender of civil rights and a proponent of abolition. Barbosa first served as a representative from Bahia in the imperial parliament, and later as a senator from 1891 to 1923. While he joined the republican cause only shortly before the fall of Dom PEDRO II in 1889, he became one of its greatest leaders, helping to consolidate the new government. Barbosa acted as the first minister of finance for the provisional government of the republic (1889–1891), in which capacity he instituted sweeping banking and monetary reforms, established high tariffs, and abandoned the gold standard. Credited by some historians with being the first minister of finance (and the only one up until the 1930s) to break with liberal economics in order to spur industrial development, Barbosa is characterized by others as doing so simply to curry favor with the elite banking community in order to appease criticism of the new regime. Industrial development and the beginnings of import-substitution were fortuitous by-products.

Barbosa was the principal author of Brazil's Constitution of 1891, which he based to an important extent on the United States Constitution.

Barbosa was the principal author of the Constitution of 1891, which he based to an important extent on the United States Constitution, especially in the design of federalism. This naturally gave to U.S.–Brazilian relations "an intimate approximation," in Barbosa's words, though he was not as ready as the great foreign minister, the baron of Rio Branco, to follow the lead of the United States in international matters as part of an "unwritten alliance." This reluctance became especially evident at the Second International Peace Conference at The Hague in 1907, which Barbosa attended at the foreign minister's request. Barbosa (and Brazil) gained international renown at the conference for his eloquent arguments in defense of the equality of all nations and, specifically, in favor of the right of small or weak nations to equal representation on an International Court of Justice. This position was at odds with that of the United States and other powers, which sought a smaller court dominated by them. The conference ended without a decision on the court but with Brazilian prestige and Barbosa's popular reputation significantly enhanced.

Barbosa ran for the presidency in 1910 and 1919, touring the provinces and taking issues directly to the voting public for the first time in Brazilian politics. Both bids for higher office were unsuccessful, however, undermined in part by the opposition of influential members of the military, whose involvement in government Barbosa had attacked repeatedly throughout his career. Barbosa was elected to the Brazilian Academy of Letters in 1908 and served as its president until 1919. His published works on finance, civil liberties, education, and the law number more than 150 volumes.

– ELIZABETH A. COBBS

BARBOSA Y ALCALÁ, JOSÉ CELSO

José Celso Barbosa y Alcalá (*b.* 27 July 1857; *d.* 21 September 1921), Puerto Rican politician and physician. Born in the town of Bayamón to a humble family of African descent, Barbosa rose to a position of prominence in the political life of Puerto Rico. He earned a medical degree at the University of Michigan (1880) and then returned to his homeland to become a fervent advocate of annexation to the United States, which he saw as the only way to free Puerto Rico from the bonds of Spanish colonialism. Barbosa joined the Liberal Reform Party in 1883, and he spent the rest of his life leading the movement for Puerto Rico's incorporation as an autonomous unit within the United States. In 1898 he formed what a year later became known as the Republican Party of Puerto Rico, which he led until his death. From 1900 to 1917, Barbosa served on an executive council arranged by the Foraker Act. This post allowed him further participation in Puerto Rico's early

attempt to settle its status after independence from Spain.

– TODD LITTLE-SIEBOLD

BARCO VARGAS, VIRGILIO

Virgilio Barco Vargas (*b.* 17 September 1921), president of Colombia (1986–1990). From a prominent Cúcuta family, Barco combined study in the United States (including doctoral work in economics at MIT) with politics in his home city. In the 1960s he held several cabinet posts and was highly regarded as mayor of Bogotá (1966–1969); he later served as ambassador in Washington, D.C. After an aborted candidacy for president in 1982 he won a landslide victory in 1986. The economy performed creditably under his administration, but the Barco years were better known for the upward spiral of violence propagated by guerrillas, right-wing death squads (which acted with suspicious impunity), and drug traffickers. Colombia's drug cartels stepped up their attacks on judges, journalists, and officials, culminating in the murder of Barco's presumptive successor, Luis Carlos GALÁN, in August 1989. Over the next several months hundreds were killed in cartel-ordered bombings, while the government's hard line produced few results. The definitive incorporation of the M-19 guerrilla movement into legal politics, near the end of Barco's term, brightened the scene somewhat.

– RICHARD J. STOLLER

BAREIRO, CÁNDIDO

Cándido Bareiro (*b.* 1838?; *d.* 4 September 1880), Paraguayan diplomat and president (1878–1880). Bareiro was one of a score of young Paraguayans sent to Europe for advanced study by the Carlos Antonio LÓPEZ government in the late 1850s. Bareiro's field was diplomacy, and within a few years he received an appointment as minister to Paris and London. His stay in the European capitals coincided with the War of the Triple Alliance (1864–1870), in which Paraguay faced the combined military might of Brazil, Argentina, and Uruguay. Bareiro's loyalty to the López regime and his unceasing efforts to counter Allied propaganda in Europe brought him some acclaim among those few Paraguayans then living abroad.

He finally returned to a wrecked and occupied Asunción in 1869. At once he became the focus of a Lopizta group that included Bernardino CABALLERO and Patricio ESCOBAR, both war heroes. Other conservatives, many with Brazilian connections, came to join this same group, which, after Bareiro's death evolved into the Colorado Party. Bareiro himself manipulated various Paraguayan factions, as well as the Brazilian occupiers, during the 1870s. In this, he worked hard to oppose the liberals who had tried to undercut the influence of the traditional rural elites.

Bareiro was elected president in 1878. Though his administration was short lived and his attempts to resuscitate the economy woefully inadequate, he did make an honest attempt to curb the corruption that had seeped into Paraguayan politics since the war. He also had the satisfaction of seeing Paraguayan claims over the Chaco Boreal upheld in an arbitration award.

Bareiro died suddenly of a stroke while working at his desk in the presidential palace.

— THOMAS L. WHIGHAM

BARNET, MIGUEL

Miguel Barnet (*b.* 28 January 1940), Cuban novelist, poet, essayist, and ethnologist. Born in Havana, educated in a local American primary school, and later a student of the distinguished ethnographer Fernando ORTÍZ, Miguel Barnet came of age during the final years of the Fulgencio BATISTA dictatorship. With the triumph of the Cuban Revolution, he became an active contributor to the process of literary experimentation and cultural reclamation it set in motion. Barnet first came to national attention as the poet of *La piedra fina y el pavorreal* (1963) and the much-praised *La sagrada familia* (1967), a lyrical autopsy of petit bourgeois domestic life. Publication of *Biografía de un cimarrón* (1966; *The Autobiography of a Runaway Slave,* 1968), the first in an ethnic tetralogy of documentary narratives, brought almost immediate international acclaim and established him as an innovating pioneer of the testimonial genre in contemporary Latin America. *La canción de Rachel* (1969; *Rachel's Song,* 1991), *Gallego* (1981), and *La vida real* (1986) confirmed his reputation as Cuba's premier exponent of the documentary novel.

Barnet explores the common ground between anthropology and literature, blending the methods and procedures of the novelist's and biographer's art—oral history—and the ethnographer's record of popular life and culture. Each work is a vivid textual re-creation of the spoken voice of ordinary, often-disdained or socially slighted Cuban citizens: a runaway black slave; a small-time mestizo female cabaret entertainer of the 1940s; a Spanish immigrant to the island; and a peasant migrant to the United States. The individuals usually absent from conventional history thus become emblematic personifications of Cuba's evolving historical experience and ethnocultural development; those lost to national recollection are reclaimed for the collectivity: "Memory,

as a part of the imagination," Barnet notes in the prologue to *La vida real,* ". . . [is] the essential key of all my work of testimony."

Barnet has been a professor of folklore at Havana's School for Art Instructors (1961–1966), a researcher for the Institute of Ethnology and Folklore of the Cuban Academy of Science, and most recently a member of the editorial board of *Unión,* the journal of the Union of Cuban Artists and Writers (UNEAC). His other collections of poetry include *Isla de Guijes* (1964), *Orikis y otros poemas* (1980), and *Carta de noche* (1982).

— ROBERTO MÁRQUEZ

BARNOLA, PEDRO PABLO

Pedro Pablo Barnola (*b.* 28 August 1908; *d.* 12 January 1986), Venezuelan writer and educator. As a student at the Academy San Ignacio de Loyola in Caracas, Barnola was the first Venezuelan to join the Jesuits after their reestablishment in the country. He completed his studies first in Europe (1925–1932) and later in the United States (1935–1940). Ordained a priest in 1938, he dedicated himself to teaching at the Academy San Ignacio. He was director of the magazine *SIC,* rector of the Andrés Bello Catholic University, editorial director of the *Obras completas de Andrés Bello* (1951), and member of the editorial commission for the *Obras completas de Rafael María Baralt.* He was a regular member of the Royal Academy of the Spanish Language and an outstanding defender of the purity of Castilian Spanish. He collaborated with Professor Ángel Rosenblat on the first volume of the *Diccionario de Venezolanismos* (1983). He is the author of numerous works of literary criticism. The principal ones include: *Altorrelieve de la literatura venezolana* (1970); *Estudios crítico-literarios* (1945, 1953, 1971); and *Raíz y sustancia de la civilización latinoamericana* (1953).

— INÉS QUINTERO

BARRADAS, RAFAEL

Rafael Barradas (*b.* ca. 4 January 1890; *d.* 12 February 1929), Uruguayan painter. Born in Montevideo, Barradas had a brief career as an illustrator and journalist for newspapers and magazines such as *El Tiempo, Bohemia,* and *La Semana;* in 1913 he founded the periodical *El Monigote* (The Bumpkin). Barradas traveled to Europe that year and settled in Spain, where he worked as an illustrator for the magazines *La Esquella de Torratxa,* in Barcelona, and *Paraninfo,* in Zaragoza. He exhibited at the Galerías Dalmau in Barcelona in 1916 and the following year in the Salón de los Humoristas in Madrid. In his first solo exhibition at the

Galerías Layetanas (1918), he introduced an aesthetic conception which he called *vibracionismo,* his interpretation of futurism and cubism.

Barradas introduced an aesthetic conception which he called vibracionismo, *his interpretation of futurism and cubism.*

During the early 1920s Barradas worked in Madrid as scenographer and toy and poster designer. He also illustrated editions of books by Charles Dickens, Alexandre Dumas, and Félix Lope de Vega and was costume designer for Federico García Lorca's *El maleficio de la Mariposa.* He frequented the *Ultraístas,* a group of poets that included Jorge Luis Borges, and collaborated with the latter on the magazine *Tableros.* He worked on *Los Magníficos,* portraits of popular Spanish types, rendered in monumental geometric forms. He devised *clownism,* an expressionistic style in which he painted picturesque details of busy urban areas. In 1924 he was awarded the Grand Prix at the International Exhibition of Decorative and Industrial Arts in Paris. Back in Barcelona, he painted a series of watercolors called *Estampones de Montevideo* (Prints of Montevideo), humorous views of that city.

In 1928 Barradas returned to Montevideo, where he died a few months later. His last work was a series of madonna and child images rendered in a postcubist style. Barradas, who produced his most significant work in Spain, is considered an innovative personality in the history of Uruguayan art.

— MARTA GARSD

BARRAGÁN MORFIN, LUIS

Luis Barragán Morfin (*b.* 9 March 1902; *d.* 22 November 1988), Mexican architect and landscape architect. Barragán trained as a civil engineer at the Escuela Libre de Ingeniera, in his native Guadalajara, Jalisco, and received his diploma 13 December 1923, after which he presented his admission thesis for the architecture program. Upon admission, he left for a year's study and travel in Europe (1924–1925). He returned to a Mexico radically changed by revolution and land reform and found his architecture program disbanded. As the youngest son of a landowning family, he joined his brother's construction firm in the development of urban Guadalajara. Without formal design training Barragán found the need to overlap architecture with civil engineering and, working with his brother Juan José Ba-

rragán, produced a number of projects, including the house for Enfraín González Luna (1929–1931).

At the invitation of architect-engineer José Luis Creixell and the primitive painter Jesús (Chucho) Reyes Ferreira, Barragán began work in Mexico City on several International Style buildings. Barragán's twenty-year design and intellectual collaboration with Reyes and the émigré sculptor Mathias GOERITZ was a major turning point in modern architectural design and theory. They worked separately or in consultation with one another, each taking the lead in their individual discipline. Barragán, the architect, treated a building site like a transparent solid defined by its light, natural configuration, and context. He moved through the site to find indications of forms and connections as a sculptor would explore the volume of a block of stone to find its contained figure. Program requirements and circulation then cut the volume, disciplined the light, and defined enclosures from a plan diagram sketched on the ground for workmen or on a scrap of paper for a client's information. Barragán, Reyes, and Goeritz took the indigenous architectural style of Mexico through the filter of the International Style into the intellectual abstraction and pragmatism of projects like the Towers of Satellite City and Casa Gilardi in Mexico City, then returned to the memory of Barragán's childhood home, Hacienda de Corrales, near Mazamitla, Jalisco, to design projects like the contemporary equestrian hacienda San Cristobal, near Mexico City (1967–1968). In the more than fifty international projects attributed to Barragán, the hacienda form always alludes to Mexico.

One of Mexico's most important architects and architectural design theorists, Barragán was a founding member of the Mexican Society of Landscape Architects and its honorary president for life (1973), a recipient of the Premio Nacional de Artes (first prize for architecture) (1976), and honorary fellow of the American Institute of Architects (1976), the second winner of the Pritzker Prize for Architecture (1980), and an honorary member of the American Academy and Institute of Arts and Letters (1984). His architecture was the subject of exhibitions at the Museum of Modern Art in New York (1976) and the Museo Rufino Tamayo in Mexico City (1985) and a traveling exhibition organized by *Montage Journal* of Boston (1989–1994). Luis Barragán's death in Mexico City was honored by a memorial exhibition at the Palacio de Bellas Artes.

— ESTELLE JACKSON

BARREDA, GABINO

Gabino Barreda (*b.* 1818; *d.* 1881), Mexican philosopher and educator. Born in Puebla, Barreda is credited with introducing Comtian positivism to Mexico. After studies in Mexico at the Colegio de San Ildefonso, he entered law school but later abandoned it to pursue his passion for the natural sciences in the Mining School and School of Medicine. After enlisting as a volunteer in the war against the United States, he left in 1847 for Paris, where he took courses with Auguste Comte. Returning to Mexico in 1851, he completed his degree as a medical doctor and taught in the School of Medicine.

In 1867 President Benito Juárez appointed him to preside over a commission to reorganize Mexican education. The resulting *Leyes orgánicas de la educación pública* in 1867 and 1869 made public schooling lay, free, and obligatory for the Federal District and territories. Professional school programs were reformed to eliminate speculative thinking and emphasize the positive sciences. Attention was focused on the founding of the Escuela Nacional Preparatoria for men in the old Colegio de San Ildefonso, with Barreda its director.

With a uniform curriculum based on Comte's interpretation of the physical and social sciences, the school addressed what Barreda believed were the causes of Mexican backwardness: a disdain for productive labor and entrepreneurialism; a proclivity for clericalism, which had inhibited the development of a scientific attitude; and a liberal preoccupation with abstract principle. Like Comte, Barreda believed in a hierarchical social order in which a team of social engineers would aid captains of industry to ensure orderly economic progress.

Opposition to Barreda's positivist ideas on the part of Liberals and Catholics led to his appointment in 1878 as ambassador to Germany. However, his intellectual contribution was great. He is credited with the formation of a generation of Mexican positivists, many of whom successfully combined statesmanship and business, among them Francisco BULNES, Francisco G. Cosmes, Joaquín Casasús, José Yves LIMANTOUR, Pablo Macedo, Justo Sierra, Roberto Núñez, Rafael and Emilio Pardo, Porfirio Parra, Rafael Reyes Spíndola, Rafael Hernández Madero, and Miguel Macedo.

– MARY KAY VAUGHAN

BARREDA Y LAOS, FELIPE

Felipe Barreda y Laos (*b.* 1888; *d.* 1973), Peruvian historian, lawyer, diplomat, educator. He was educated in a Jesuit school and at the University of San Marcos in Lima, where he became a professor. He was the author of several books, including treatises on intellectual currents in colonial Peru, Hispanic culture, and other diplomatic, educational, and historical subjects. Initially influenced by positivism, his view of the colonial past was critical of the influence of the scholastic tradition

in Peru. In later works, however, he emphasized the unity of the peninsular and American Hispanic tradition and the beneficial effects of Hispanic culture in America. He also assumed a continental view in his diplomatic works.

– ALFONSO W. QUIROZ

BARREIRO, ANTONIO

Antonio Barreiro (*b.* ca. 1780; *d.* after 1835), *assessor* (legal adviser) of New Mexico during the 1830s. Barreiro was sent by the Mexican government in 1831 to establish a judicial system. After a year in the territory, Barreiro published his report, *Ojeada sobre Nuevo-México.* The work synthesized data collected earlier in the century by Alexander von Humboldt, reports of soldiers of the presidio of Sante Fe, and the reports of the representatives to the first National Congress in Mexico.

Barreiro's *Ojeada* represents a plea for Mexico City to provide a modicum of investment in the rich territory he described. Government support to aid in the building of stone bridges, for example, would ease the difficult conditions for transport and export. Strengthening the powers of the governor and New Mexican courts of first instance could aid in the punishment of petty crime and greater deliberation on matters of import to the citizens. National warehouses, an adequate building in which to house the public treasury, and stronger defenses along the New Mexican frontier would increase and secure tariff revenues, encourage and streamline trade, and dissuade both the raids of "wild Indians" and the grasping Americans interested in extending "the boundary of Louisiana to the left bank of the Bravo or North River" (Rio Grande). Barreiro concluded, "Only the attention of the government toward this country, which is worthy of a better fate, will remove all the obstacles to its welfare. Only an extraordinary effort on the part of the government will develop the valuable elements which lie submerged there and which will some day raise it to the height of prosperity."

Partly due to the publication of his report, Barreiro won election in 1834 and 1835 as New Mexico's deputy to the Mexican Congress. With a printing press imported from Missouri in 1834, Barreiro published the first New Mexican newspaper, *El Crepúsculo de la Libertad.*

– ROSS H. FRANK

BARRETO DE MENEZES, TOBIAS, JR.

Tobias Barreto de Menezes, Jr. (*b.* 7 June 1839; *d.* 26 June 1889), Brazilian philosopher and jurist, founder of the Recife School. Born in Campos, in the province of Sergipe, to a family of very modest circumstances, Barreto learned Latin from a priest and, from the age of fifteen, made his living teaching humanities. He studied law in Recife and became known for his poetical disputes with Antônio de CASTRO ALVES. As a member of the Generation of 70 he fought for intellectual renewal in the Brazilian Empire.

Unlike most of his generation, who turned to French positivism, Barreto found inspiration in German authors. In the areas of religious criticism (Georg von Ewald, Ludwig Feuerbach), political ideas (von Gneist, Frobel), and law (von Ihring), they seemed to him to offer views more suitable to combat the spiritualist and neo-Thomist eclecticism then dominant in Brazil. His "Germanism" produced a model for solving Brazilian problems and enabled him to criticize the French-inspired Brazilian liberals, the francophile elite of the Southeast, and the dominant juridical conceptions.

In his lectures Barreto defended the view that law is neither divine nor natural, but a product of history.

Although he was married to the daughter of a Liberal *fazendeiro* (rancher), Barreto suffered social and racial discrimination as a result of his mixed heritage. After a brief and not very successful involvement in local and regional politics (he was a Liberal member of the provincial assembly in 1878–1879), he gained influence by becoming a professor at the law faculty of Recife in 1882. In his lectures he defended the view that law is neither divine nor natural, but a product of history. A supporter of philosophical monism, he was responsible for the wide dissemination of Ernst Haeckel's theories in Brazil and became famous for his polemics against ultramontanist and idealist positions.

Although Barreto was widely attacked, his views were supported by his friend, the literary critic Sílvio ROMERO, and by a group of students who played major roles during the Old Republic: Clóvis Beviláqua, Higinho Cunha, Benedito Leite, and Artur Orlando.

– MATTHIAS RÖHRIG ASSUNÇÃO

BARRETT, RAFAEL

Rafael Barrett (*b.* 1876; *d.* 17 December 1910), Anglo-Spanish anarchist writer who influenced an entire generation of Paraguayan radical intellectuals. Born in Santander, Spain, in 1876, Barrett moved to Asunción in 1904. Working days in the general statistics office, he devoted his nights to journalistic efforts, churning out article after article of social criticism, focusing especially on the plight of poor workers in the yerba plantations of eastern Paraguay. His principal writings, compiled in a volume entitled *El dolor paraguayo* (1910), have been favorably compared with the works of Peru's Clorinda MATTO DE TURNER, Ecuador's Jorge ICAZA CORONEL, and Bolivia's Alcides ARGÜEDAS. Afflicted with tuberculosis, Barrett left his Paraguayan wife and children behind at San Bernardino and returned to Europe, where he died at Arcachón, France.

– THOMAS L. WHIGHAM

BARRIENTOS ORTUÑO, RENÉ

René Barrientos Ortuño (*b.* 1919; *d.* 27 April 1969), army officer and president of Bolivia (1966–1969). Barrientos, a native of Cochabamba, graduated in 1943 from the military academy from which he had earlier been expelled for supporting the government of President Germán BUSCH (1937–1939). He played an active though very junior role in the 1944 peasant congress sponsored by the regime of President Gualberto VILLARROEL (1943–1946) and the Movimiento Nacionalista Revolucionario (MNR). Although he stayed in the army after the overthrow of Villarroel, he was retired for participating in an MNR insurrection against the conservative government.

He participated in the 1952 MNR revolution that launched the Bolivian National Revolution. While the MNR was in power, he became head of the air force and of the "military cell" of the MNR. In the 1964 election, as a result of military pressure, the civilian selected to run as the MNR candidate for vice president with President Víctor PAZ ESTENSSORO was forced to step down. René Barrientos was put in his place. Even before becoming vice president in August, Barrientos was leading a conspiracy to overthrow Paz Estenssoro, which came to fruition on 4 November 1964. For some time after Paz Estenssoro's overthrow, Barrientos and General Alfredo OVANDO were "copresidents." During that period, there were violent clashes between the regime and organized labor, particularly the miners. The mining camps were occupied by troops and many miners and members of their families were either killed or wounded.

In 1966 General Barrientos was elected president. Although his regime continued to rule in a high-handed fashion and was particularly hostile to organized labor, it did enjoy wide support among the peasantry. Barrientos spoke Quechua, and spent much time traveling in rural areas. He also continued to support the land redistribution that had taken place under the MNR government as well as extensive programs of extending technical help to the Indian peasants. Peasant support was of key importance in helping the Barrientos government to defeat the guerrilla effort launched in 1967 by Ernesto "Che" GUEVARA. Guevara was executed by the Bolivian army unit that captured him. Barrientos died in the mysterious crash of a helicopter he was piloting.

— ROBERT J. ALEXANDER

BARRILLAS, MANUEL LISANDRO

Manuel Lisandro Barrillas (*b.* 1844; *d.* 1907), president of Guatemala (1885–1892). Barrillas was appointed provisional president in 1885 after the death of Justo Rufino BARRIOS and was constitutionally elected the following year. Like Barrios, he was a coffee grower who participated in the Liberal Revolution that swept the Conservatives from power in 1871. His liberal credentials and vast coffee holdings in San Marcos and Retaluleu ensured a smooth rise to power. The Barillas administration rested largely on its ability to induce the nation's Indian majority to labor on large coffee fincas. When the Indians resisted, his government, with the aid of the military, resorted to a number of forced-labor schemes that included the mandamiento, debt bondage, and a vagrancy law.

The Barrillas government coincides with a tremendous expansionary period for Guatemala's coffee industry. In the late 1880s and early 1890s world prices for Guatemalan coffee reached record high levels. Coffee cultivation was introduced to large new tracts of land to take advantage of the favorable world market. It is in this period that Guatemala gained its reputation as a producer of one of the world's finest mild coffees.

— WADE A. KIT

BARRIOS, AGUSTÍN

Agustín Barrios (*b.* 23 May 1885; *d.* 7 August 1944), Paraguayan musician and composer. Born in San Juan Bautista in the Paraguayan Misiones, Barrios came from an impoverished background. He nonetheless attained fame early on as a local prodigy with the guitar. At the end of the century, he was discovered by Gustavo Sosa Escalada, the country's most famous guitarist, who helped Barrios to develop his skill with the instrument. After studying at the Colegio Nacional in Asunción, Barrios began a concert tour of South America in 1910. The tour lasted fourteen years, and included extended stays in Chile, Argentina, Uruguay, and Brazil.

In his presentations, Barrios often appeared in Indian costume, replete with feathers, and went under the stage name of *Cacique Mangoré.* Throughout this time Barrios also composed pieces for the guitar, a good many of which he attributed to obscure European composers in the belief that they would then be taken more seriously.

After a brief return to Paraguay in the mid-1920s, Barrios again left the country, this time in the company of a diplomat, Tomás Salomini, who served as his patron and who arranged recitals for him in Cuba, Mexico, and, in 1934, in several European capitals. Barrios was the first major Latin American musician to play before European audiences. He has frequently been compared to Andrés Segovia as an interpreter, and to Niccolò Paganini as a virtuoso. He evidently wrote over a hundred works, though many of these are now lost. His extant corpus includes *Danza paraguaya, El catedrál,* and *Rapsodia andaluza.* Starting in 1939, Barrios taught at the National Music Conservatory in San Salvador, El Salvador, where he died.

— MARTA FERNÁNDEZ WHIGHAM

BARRIOS, EDUARDO

Eduardo Barrios (*b.* 25 October 1884; *d.* 13 September 1963), Chilean novelist, short-story writer, and playwright. Known primarily for his psychological novels, Barrios subordinated action to character portrayal in his works. Many of his protagonists are will-less, alienated men destined to failure. His first collection of stories, *Del natural* (1907), reflects the tenets of nineteenth-century realism and Zola's naturalism. The unifying theme is love, which Barrios examines within the context of middle-class mores. The title story of his second collection, *El niño que enloqueció de amor* (1915), is a psychological study of a nine-year-old boy who becomes enamored of an older woman and goes mad when he discovers her with her boyfriend. The story re-creates the imaginary world of a child who is increasingly alienated from adults. Critics have seen precursors of modernism in the extreme delicacy of the boy's portrait. Barrios's novel *Un perdido* (1918) combines a subtle character analysis with a detailed description of the Chilean middle class. *El hermano asno* (1922), which deals with the repressed erotic yearnings of a friar named Lázaro, has been called anticlerical because Lázaro witnesses an apparent crime and Church authorities try to silence him. *Tamarugal* (1944) and *Gran señor y rajadiablos* (1948) are set in rural areas; the former deals with life in the nitrate mines in the north of Chile, while the latter portrays life on a typical Chilean farm around the turn of the century. *Los hombres del hombre* (1950) is a psychological portrait of a man who suspects his wife of infidelity. Barrios also wrote a number of plays, including *Lo que niega la vida* (1913), *Vivir* (1916), and *¡Ante todo la oficina!* (1925).

— BARBARA MUJICA

BARRIOS, GERARDO

Gerardo Barrios (*b.* 3 October 1813; *d.* 29 August 1865), general and president of El Salvador (1859–1863). Born to a wealthy, well-connected family in the department of San Miguel, Barrios remains a popular figure in the history of modern El Salvador. He was the first president in Central America to introduce reforms based on liberalism-positivism, and set the course for the modernization of Salvadoran society.

Barrios's family had extensive landholdings, on which they grew indigo. Young Gerardo felt a vocation for the military and joined the militia at a young age. By 1840 he had already participated in the overthrow of one president, José María Cornejo, and fought in battles at Mixco, San Miguelito, Espíritu Santo, Perulapía, and in Guatemala. He joined other Central American leaders in the struggle against the American filibuster William WALKER in Nicaragua in the 1850s. In this campaign Barrios earned a reputation as a skillful leader and formed a close relationship with the Guatemalan president Rafael CARRERA. In July 1858, Carrera decorated Barrios with the Cross of Honor. This friendly association was not destined to last long, however, for Barrios was more of an ideologue than Carrera, and friction developed after Barrios succeeded to the presidency of El Salvador when President Miguel de Santín de Castillo's health failed in 1858.

Barrios then embarked on a remarkable new course that revealed his deep admiration for the United States and Europe. In fact, Barrios often spoke of the perfection of the British and French political institutions. He undertook the modernization of the Salvadoran government: an expansion and centralization of the bureaucracy, the restoration of San Salvador as the national capital, and the transfer of the Supreme Court back to San Salvador. Barrios next overhauled the legal system by drafting new civil and penal codes and altering the process of justice. The right to collect taxes was removed from local jurisdiction and decreed a national responsibility. He repatriated the remains of the great Liberal leader of independence Francisco Morazán, who was actually Honduran, and buried them in San Salvador with much ceremony. Barrios extended the term of the presidency from two to six years, increased the role of the executive branch at the expense of the legislative, and upheld the democratic transfer of office. He returned office to Santín upon the latter's recovery late in 1859, but arranged to have himself elected the following year.

In 1860, Barrios began to promote the production of coffee on a large scale, by lowering production taxes on the new crop, exempting the coffee labor force from military service, and distributing land to those promising to grow coffee on two-thirds or more of the area. Barrios's government took an unprecedented, active role in the economy of the nation when it purchased a boat and attempted to export coffee to California itself. Furthermore, Barrios followed the French model and transformed the old-style Salvadoran militias into a modern national army; he also created a military academy with a Colombian as its head.

By 1862, Barrios's liberalism had begun to encroach on the privileged position of the Roman Catholic church. Although he was not an enemy of the church, as president Barrios stressed the ultimate authority of secular over religious authorities. He required all priests to declare obedience to the state, thereby provoking conflict with the Vatican and stirring up fears among other Central American leaders. In 1862, Barrios reached a concordat with the Holy See in which priests agreed to swear loyalty to the Constitution but not to the actual government. Barrios's main efforts were concentrated in education and the expansion of transportation and communication. By 1863, he had many enemies both within El Salvador and across Central America. He repelled a Guatemalan invasion in early 1863, but before the end of the year Carrera returned and conquered El Salvador. Barrios was caught in Nicaragua while trying to escape. He languished in jail and was executed in 1865. Thus ended the first liberal-positivist experiment in Central America.

— KAREN RACINE

BARRIOS, GONZALO

Gonzalo Barrios (*b.* 1902), Venezuelan politician. The son of a well-to-do family from Portuguesa State, Barrios studied law at the Central University of Venezuela, where he was a prominent member of the Generation of 1928. After returning from a European exile in 1936, he became a founder of the Venezuelan Organization (Organización Venezolana—ORVE), the National Democratic Party (Partido Democrático Nacional—PDN), and Democratic Action (Acción Democrática—AD). During the AD *trienio* (1945–1948) he served as a member of the revolutionary junta, secretary of the presidency, and governor of the Federal District. After 1958 he held a series of important positions in AD (including secretary-general) and in government (minister of the interior, senator). After running as AD's unsuccessful presidential candidate in 1968, he continued to play an active role in party and national affairs.

— WINFIELD J. BURGGRAAFF

BARRIOS, JUSTO RUFINO

Justo Rufino Barrios (*b.* 19 July 1835; *d.* 2 April 1885), president of Guatemala (1873–1885). Born in San Lorenzo, department of San Marcos, Guatemala, Justo Barrios was the son of Ignacio Barrios, a prominent dealer in horses and cattle and landowner, and Josefa Auyón de Barrios. He led the Liberal Reforma of 1871 and represented the shift in power from the Conservative elite of Guatemala City to the Liberal coffee interests of the western highlands.

Barrios received his elementary and secondary education from tutors and schools in San Marcos, Quetzaltenango, and Guatemala City, where he studied law and earned his certificate as a notary in 1862. In Guatemala City he came under the influence of leading Liberals, Miguel García Granados and Manuel Dardón, but he returned to his family lands in 1862 and especially developed his estate "El Malacate" along the Mexican border.

In 1867 Barrios joined the Liberal insurgency against President Vicente CERNA. When an attack on the barracks at San Marcos failed, Barrios fled into Chiapas, in southern Mexico, where in 1869 he organized a rebel force in collaboration with Field Marshal Serapio CRUZ. After Cruz's death in 1870, García Granados joined the movement and formed a provisional government early in 1871, with Barrios as military commander. They quickly gained control of the western highlands, and in a manifesto issued at Patzicía on 3 June 1871 they stated the goals of their revolution. The crucial battle came at San Lucas Sacatepéquez, on the heights above Guatemala City, where on 29 June, Barrios routed Cerna's army. On the following day he marched into the capital victorious. García Granados served as the first president under the Reforma. Barrios wanted more sweeping reforms, however, and in 1873 he won election as president of Guatemala.

Barrios quickly forged a strong dictatorship, eliminating the Conservative opposition and greatly strengthening the power of the state. He represented the coming to power in Guatemala of the liberal-positivist philosophy that would remain dominant until at least 1944. Barrios promoted strongly anticlerical legislation, suppressed the tithe, abolished the regular orders, expropriated church property, and greatly reduced the number of priests in the country; he also established religious liberty, civil marriage and divorce, and state

collection of vital statistics. He launched a public education system at all levels and took the University of San Carlos out of the control of the church, making it the state university and establishing other secondary and normal schools. His educational reforms, however, benefited primarily the upper and middle classes of Guatemala City and Quetzaltenango. Most rural Guatemalans continued to have little access to education and often now lost their village priests, who formerly had provided some education to parishioners. Barrios's restructuring of the university emphasized professional and technical education at the expense of the humanities and liberal arts, another reflection of positivist thinking.

Barrios put great emphasis on material progress. Coffee exports increased enormously as he encouraged the encroachment of ladino planters on Indian communal lands and made their labor more accessible to planters, began a railroad system, and developed ports and roads. He facilitated formation of banks and other financial institutions to provide credit for economic development and modernization. New ministries of agriculture, development, and education reflected this emphasis on economic growth as well as the increased role of the state. Barrios also attracted immigration and investment from overseas; German and U.S. influence increased notably. His administration codified the laws and promulgated a new constitution in 1879, under which he was reelected in 1880. His policies spurred substantial modernization of both Guatemala City and Quetzaltenango.

In foreign affairs Barrios played an important role in the neighboring states of El Salvador and Honduras, and in 1882 he settled differences with Mexico at the cost of giving up Guatemalan claims to Soconusco and other parts of Chiapas. He renewed the Guatemalan claim to Belize, however, repudiating the Wyke-Aycinena Treaty of 1859 with Great Britain. He also tried to revive the unionist spirit of Francisco Morazán and sought to reestablish the Central American federation by means of Guatemalan military power. That effort, however, ended abruptly in 1885 when Salvadoran forces defeated the Guatemalan army at Chalchuapa, where Barrios died in battle.

Barrios established a new "coffee elite" centered in the western highlands around Quetzaltenango, reducing the power of the Guatemala City merchant elite that had dominated the country since the late colonial period. At the same time, he greatly accelerated exploitation of the indigenous population and moved Guatemala more rapidly into an export-led economy dependent on foreign markets and investment. Although celebrated in Guatemalan history as the "Reformer" who ended the long Conservative dictatorships of Rafael Carrera and Vicente Cerna (1839–1871), his own dictatorial rule and strengthening of the military established a pattern of repressive government for subsequent Liberal governments even to the present. Barrios's personal wealth increased enormously during his rule, especially in comparison with earlier Guatemalan presidents. In this, too, he set a pattern that many of his successors would emulate.

— RALPH LEE WOODWARD, JR.

BARRIOS DE CHAMORRO, VIOLETA

Violeta Barrios de Chamorro (*b.* 18 October 1929), president of Nicaragua (1990–). Elected president as the representative of the fourteen-party National Opposition Union (Unión Nacional Opositora—UNO) coalition, Barrios de Chamorro seemed an unlikely candidate. She was born in the southern Nicaraguan province of Rivas to wealthy, landowning parents and attended Catholic schools. In 1950 she married Pedro Joaquín CHAMORRO CARDENAL, a leader of the middle-class opposition to the dictatorship of the SOMOZA family. Nonetheless, her political participation during the decades of the 1950s, 1960s, and 1970s was confined to that of supportive wife and mother.

In January 1978 Chamorro Cardenal was assassinated, probably by a member of the Somoza family. The assassination set off a wave of strikes and mass insurrection that helped carry the Sandinista Liberation Front (Frente Sandinista de la Liberación Nacional—FSLN) into power. Doña Violeta, as she is called, was named a member of the five-person ruling junta. She resigned from that body less than a year later.

For the remainder of the 1980s, her political participation was confined to criticizing the FSLN and supporting the Contra war from her position as owner of the daily newspaper *La Prensa*, which she inherited from her late husband. Other members of her family took more prominent roles in politics.

Barrios de Chamorro reentered formal politics when she ran for president in 1990. Running on the promises to end the Contra war and repair the economy, she portrayed herself as the traditional mother who would reconcile the Nicaraguan family just as she had reconciled her own politically torn family. She won the election with 55 percent of the vote.

Since Barrios de Chamorro's election, the civil war has ended, for the most part. Massive devaluations and cuts in real wages (now among the lowest in the hemisphere)

Violeta Barrios de Chamorro campaigning in the general elections of 1990. (Jason Bleibtreu/Sygma)

have eliminated hyperinflation. Her relative independence from the United States, whose support was essential in putting her into power, has come as something of a surprise to both her supporters and detractors. Her administration has often chosen to govern in coalition with moderates in the FSLN rather than with the far-right members of the UNO. This choice has hastened the disintegration of the inherently unstable fourteen-party UNO coalition.

— KAREN KAMPWIRTH

BARROS, ADHEMAR DE

Adhemar de Barros (*b.* 22 April 1901; *d.* 12 March 1969), three-time governor of São Paulo (1957–1961), and frequent populist candidate for president (1955, 1960, 1965).

The Barros family lived on its extensive coffee lands and owned businesses in the interior of São Paulo. Adhemar attended high school in the capital, completed his medical training in Rio, and interned in Europe. His political career began with Getúlio VARGAS's surprise appointment as state interventor in 1938. Adhemar seized the opportunity to build hospitals, roads, clinics, and schools, making a name for himself as a vigorous administrator.

In 1945 Adhemar formed the populist-style Social Progressive Party (PSP) and ran for governor in 1947. Finding his upper-class background a hindrance, he adopted the image of a rough-and-tumble provincial. Spending both his own and illicitly raised money, he hired publicity experts, conducted polls, purchased media exposure, and flew his own airplane to expand his following. In office he stressed building programs—schools, hospitals, highways, and dams—that glorified his image as "the manager." Tempted by the presidency in 1950, he withdrew in favor of Vargas with the understanding that the latter would support him in 1955.

Adhemar's flamboyant career was blocked by the meteoric rise of Jânio QUADROS, who defeated him in the 1954 gubernatorial election. An indictment for corruption stalled his campaign for president the following year. Absolved of the charges and vindicated by his mayoral victory in 1957 and his gubernatorial defeat of Quadros in 1963, Adhemar hoped to win the presidency in 1965. The military revoked his political rights because of graft, however, and he died three years later in self-imposed exile.

— MICHAEL L. CONNIFF

BARROS, JOÃO DE

João de Barros (*b.* ca. 1496; *d.* 21 October 1570), bureaucrat, humanist, lord-proprietor (*donatario*) in Brazil, historian. The son of a member of the lower nobility, João de Barros served as a page to Prince João, future king of Portugal. From 1525 to 1528 he was treasurer of the Casa da India, Mina, e Ceuta. In 1532 Barros became factor (*feitor*) of the Casa da India e Guiné (also called the Casa da India e Mina), a post he held until 1567. He was the author of *Clarimundo* (1522), a romance of chivalry, and *Ropica Pnefma* (1532), an allegory greatly influenced by Erasmus.

In 1535 Barros became the seventh of the twelve lords-proprietor to be awarded hereditary captaincies in Brazil between 1534 and 1536. He received several grants of land on the northern coast of Brazil along with two other lords-proprietor, Aires da Cunha and Fernão Álvares de Andrade. In 1535 the three lords-proprietor financed an expedition to explore and settle their lands, but most of the fleet was shipwrecked and little came of the effort. In 1555 or 1556, Barros sent another expedition that included his sons, Jerónimo and João, but this effort, too, was unsuccessful, leaving Barros in very serious financial straits. Many historians, unaware of the second expedition, have combined the two into one and have asserted, without evidence, that Barros's sons were on the 1535 voyage. After suffering a stroke in 1567, Barros retired to his country estate, São Lourenço do Ribeiro de Alitem, near Pombal, where he died.

Published between 1552 and 1615, Barros's most important literary work was the four-volume *Décadas de Asia,* modeled on Livy's *History.* Covering Portugal's overseas activity to 1538, the work is of great value to historians because of Barros's access to materials as factor of the Casa da India e Guiné, his incorporation of Portuguese translations of Asian chronicles and other documents that have since disappeared, and his use of eyewitness accounts of those Portuguese returning from overseas.

— FRANCIS A. DUTRA

BARROS ARANA, DIEGO

Diego Barros Arana (*b.* 16 August 1830; *d.* 14 November 1906), Chilean historian and diplomat. One of Chile's premier scholars, Barros Arana graduated from the Instituto Nacional, Chile's finest secular high school. As a liberal historian he tended to equate conservative ideology with backwardness; consequently, his works tended to flay both the Roman Catholic church and the authoritarian regime of Manuel MONTT. He was a professor at the University of Chile and later was the director of the Instituto Nacional. He enjoyed an active political life, serving as a deputy for the Liberal Party. Barros Arana's articles in various newspapers so incensed Montt that Barros Arana fled his homeland.

Upon his return, he took up once again a life of scholarship and public service. An extremely prolific historian, Barros Arana published a variety of biographies as well as a multivolume history of Chile. He also acted as Chile's minister to Argentina, where he negotiated a treaty resolving the question of the ownership of Patagonia. Rather than follow his instructions, Barros Arana gave up Chile's claim to the disputed territory, permitting the Argentines to occupy Tierra del Fuego. This act not only compromised Chile's claims to vast territory but also threatened Santiago's vital trade routes to Europe. Recalled in disgrace to Chile, he became an object of public scorn, although he continued in public life, serving as a deputy. Barros Arana's scholarship had a lasting impact on Chilean intellectual life, influencing subsequent generations.

— WILLIAM F. SATER

BARROSO, ARY

Ary Barroso (*b.* 7 November 1903; *d.* 9 February 1964), Brazilian songwriter. Barroso was one of his country's most influential composers of samba music; his songs were renowned for their beautiful melodies and picturesque language, and often celebrated Brazil, its people, and culture. Barroso's "Aquarela do Brasil" (known elsewhere simply as "Brazil") ranks among the world's best-known popular tunes of the twentieth century.

Born in Ubá, Minas Gerais, Barroso moved in 1920 to Rio, where he played for dance-hall orchestras and later became a successful writer of hit songs for Carnaval. He helped develop the genre called *samba-canção,* a softer, more sophisticated samba that emphasized melody more than rhythm and featured more complex harmonies. With "Aquarela do Brasil" (Watercolor of Brazil), Barroso created another style, *samba-exaltação,* so-called for its characteristic grand, epic songs with soaring melodies that "exalted" a particular subject. Among his other standards are "Na batucada da vida" (a strong indictment of poverty), "No tabuleiro da baiana" (On the Baiana's Tray), "Na baixa do sapateiro" (also called "Bahia"), "Rio de Janeiro," and "Inquietação" (Disquiet).

For the last fifty years, Barroso has been one of the most recorded Brazilian composers both inside and outside his country, and his songs have reached the world through the animated films of Walt Disney (such as *The Three Caballeros*), movies such as Terry Gilliam's *Brazil* (1985), and countless interpretations by world pop and jazz artists. "Aquarela do Brasil" rivals "The Girl From Ipanema" as the most internationally famous Brazilian tune of all time.

— CHRIS MCGOWAN

BARROSO, GUSTAVO DODT

Gustavo Dodt Barroso (*b.* 29 December 1888; *d.* 3 December 1959), Brazilian writer, journalist, and politician. Barroso was a pioneer of the Brazilian folklore movement known as Northeastern Regionalism. Under the pen name "João do Norte" he wrote *Terra de sol* (1912), in which he praised the backlands peasantry for hard work, devotion to family, religious zeal, and closeness to nature. In *Heróes e bandidos: Os cangaceiros de Nordeste* (1917), he adopted the view that backlands bandits such as Antonio Silvino were predisposed to crime because of their race, lack of education, and the "savagery" of their environment. In the 1930s he became a supporter and one of the most influential propagandists of *integralismo,* the Brazilian variant of fascism.

Born in Fortaleza, Ceará, Barroso studied in Ceará, attended the Law School of Fortaleza from 1907 to 1909, and graduated in 1911 from the Law School of Rio de Janeiro. In 1914 he was appointed secretary of justice and interior for the state of Ceará and later directed *Diário Oficial.* A prolific writer, he published 128 books, including folklore, short stories, history, biography, criticism, plays, poetry, essays, a dictionary, memoirs, translations, and children's readers. He founded and directed the National Historic Museum, edited the Rio magazines *Fon-Fon* and *Selecta,* and served on the 1919 Brazilian delegation to the Versailles Peace Congress. In March 1923 he was elected a member of the Brazilian Academy of Letters. Other writings include *O integralismo em marcha* (1933) and *O que o integralista deve saber* (1935).

— TERESA MEADE

BARRUNDIA, JOSÉ FRANCISCO

José Francisco Barrundia (*b.* 12 May 1787; *d.* 4 August 1854), proponent of Central American independence, ideological leader of the radical liberals during the early national period. The son of prominent Guatemalan creoles Martín Barrundia and Teresa Cepeda y Coronado, Barrundia was a brilliant lawyer, orator, and writer. Educated in Guatemala, he was among the intellectual elite of the late colonial period. In 1811 he translated John Milton's *Paradise Lost* and several classical Italian works into Spanish.

As a *regidor* (alderman) on the Guatemala City Council, Barrundia revealed his liberal political views. He participated in the ill-fated Belén Conspiracy of 1813 but escaped capture and a death sentence by hiding from the police of Captain General José BUSTAMANTE Y GUERRA for the next five years. As a member of the Tertulia Patriótica, along with José María Castilla, Pedro MOLINA, Manuel Montúfar, Marcial Zebadúa, and José Beteta, he plotted Guatemalan independence. He also joined with Molina in editing the pro-independence newspapers *El Editor Constitucional* and *El Genio de la Libertad.* When Barrundia opposed annexation to Mexico, Captain General Vicente FILÍSOLA branded him a terrorist and "dangerous subject." Upon the separation of Central America from Mexico in 1823, Barrundia served on the Council of Government (1823–1825) and was a co-author of the Constitution of 1824. In 1825 he was elected as the first vice president of the United Provinces of Central America but refused the office.

Barrundia's erudite writings in periodicals, several of which he edited, made him one of the most influential liberals of his era. His strident, uncompromising liberalism made him appear arrogant to some, but he was foremost among the so-called *exaltados,* or *fiebres,* of the early national period. He served briefly as president of the United Provinces (26 June 1829–16 September 1830), but it was in the legislatures of both Central America and Guatemala that his leadership was most prominent. In the election of 1830, Francisco MORAZÁN defeated him for the presidency of Central America, but the speech Barrundia delivered in turning over the office of president to Morazán was eloquent and gracious. He was elected governor of Guatemala in the same year, but he refused that office, preferring to remain in the legislature. His essays and other political writings formed a major part of the liberal polemic in Guatemala for the first thirty years of independence.

Under Governor Mariano GÁLVEZ (1831–1838) Barrundia served as minister of education, and he was also the major advocate for Guatemala's 1836 adoption of Louisiana's Livingston Codes of penal law, which he translated from English. Division among the liberals led him to oppose Gálvez in 1837 and collaborate briefly with Rafael CARRERA, the peasant guerrilla leader, to bring down Gálvez's government in 1838. He was unable to control the rebel caudillo, however, and spent much of the remainder of his life in exile, actively conspiring to overthrow the Conservative Carrera. He played a prominent part in the brief Liberal Revolution of 1848 in Guatemala but was once more forced into exile.

Barrundia spent his last years in Washington, where he served from 1852 until his death (in New York) as the Honduran minister to the United States. He was the leading ideologue and champion of the liberal cause in Central America and a strong supporter of Francisco Morazán and Central American union.

— RALPH LEE WOODWARD, JR.

BARRUNDIA, JUAN

Juan Barrundia (*b.* 8 October 1788; *d.* ca. 1843), first governor of the state of Guatemala (12 October 1824–6 September 1826) following its organization within the United Provinces of Central America in 1824. Like his better-known brother, José Francisco BARRUNDIA, he was among the radical liberals (*fiebres*) who supported the independence movement. In 1826 federal president Manuel José ARCE deposed and imprisoned him. After his release, Barrundia hid out in Suchitepéquez until Francisco Morazán's military triumph of 1829. MORAZÁN restored Barrundia as governor of Guatemala, and Barrundia served from 30 April 1829 until 30 August 1829, when the legislature elected Pedro MOLINA to succeed him. Doctor Mariano GÁLVEZ defeated Barrundia for the governorship in the election of 1831. In 1836 Barrundia presided over the federal congress in San Salvador. With a conservative change in government, he went into exile at San Cristóbal de las Casas, Chiapas, Mexico, where he died.

— RALPH LEE WOODWARD, JR.

BASADRE, JORGE

Jorge Basadre (*b.* 12 February 1903; *d.* 24 June 1980), Peru's most prolific twentieth-century historian. He was trained in the schools of Lima and the National University of San Marcos, where he earned the Litt.D. and LL.D. degrees. In 1928 he joined the Faculty of Letters at San Marcos as a professor of history and then, in 1931, the Faculty of Law. In addition to teaching, he administered the university library for two terms in the 1930s and 1940s, and during World War II he directed the National Library. There he launched a drive to make the library's treasures more accessible to scholars. At the end of the war he served as minister of public education in the national government (1945). Historians throughout the world recognized his work. He received honors from many academies and visiting appointments to the Carnegie Foundation (1931–1932), the Ibero-American Institution of Berlin (1932), the Universidad de Sevilla (1933), and the Universidad de Buenos Aires (1942). He wrote a prodigious number of historical studies, which began to appear in the 1920s and did not stop until after his death. Among the more widely known are *La iniciación de la república* (2 vols., 1929–1930), *La multitud, la ciudad y el campo en la historia del Perú* (1929), *Perú: Problema y posibilidad* (1931), and the renowned *Historia de la república del Perú, 1822–1933.* Begun in 1939 as a three-volume survey, a sixth edition (1968–1970) expanded the encyclopedic history of the republic to a monumental 17 volumes.

To complement this great work, Basadre compiled a two-volume *Introducción a las bases documentales para la historia de la república del Perú, con algunas reflexiones* (1971), an erudite evaluation of the sources used in the expanded history. With illustrations and introductory essays to each section, it stands as a major work in its own right. His numerous articles appeared in newspapers and historical journals in several languages. Many were collected in a single posthumous volume, *La vida y la historia* (1975).

— VINCENT PELOSO

BASALDÚA, HECTOR

Hector Basaldúa (*b.* 29 September 1895; *d.* 21 February 1976), Argentine painter, printmaker, stage designer, and illustrator. Basaldúa was born in Pergamino, Buenos Aires Province. In 1914 he studied in the capital city at the private academy of the Italian artist Bolognini, and later at the National Academy of Fine Arts under Pío Collivadino. Between 1923 and 1930 he studied in Paris under Charles Guérin, André Lothe, and Othon Friesz. Basaldúa received a gold medal for stage design at the Paris International Exhibition, in 1937, and first prize for painting at the Argentine National Salon of Plastic Arts. He visited the United States to study theater techniques in 1946, and was the designer of opera and ballet sets at the Teatro Colón, Buenos Aires. In 1980 the National Museum of Fine Arts, in Buenos Aires, held a retrospective of his works. A quick perception of reality and an unerring feeling for decorative effect are basic to Basaldúa's work. His activity as a stage designer and book illustrator gave to his work an artificial tone related to rapidly captured images.

— AMALIA CORTINA ARAVENA

BASSO MAGLIO, VICENTE

Vicente Basso Maglio (*b.* 22 December 1889; *d.* 15 September 1961), Uruguayan poet, writer, journalist, and editor. His career in journalism began when he was an editor for *La Reforma, El Día,* and *La Razón,* all in Montevideo. Subsequently he was director of *El espectador* and its subsidiary broadcasting system, Difusoras del Uruguay. Basso Maglio's most acclaimed poetry collection, *Canción de los pequeños círculos y de los grandes horizontes* (1927), features the poet's transcendental, mystical comprehension of the relationship between man and God. His dense, hermetic expression sometimes reveals an excessive confidence in abstract symbols to communicate the complex web of relationships linking inner and outer reality. Other works by Basso Maglio include the acclaimed *La expresión heróica* (1928) and *Tragedia de la imagen* (1930), a work on modern art.

— WILLIAM H. KATRA

BASSOLS, NARCISO

Narciso Bassols (*b.* 22 October 1897; *d.* 24 July 1959), Mexican intellectual and public official, a member of the intellectual generation of 1915, whose leaders, the "Seven Wise Men," included Alfonso CASO Y ANDRADE, Manuel GÓMEZ MORÍN, and Vicente LOMBARDO TOLEDANO.

Born in Tenango del Valle, Bassols was the great-nephew of President Sebastián Lerdo de Tejada and the son of a humble judge, Narciso Bassols. He attended the National Preparatory School in Mexico City (1911–1915), and graduated from the National School of Law on 29 May 1920, after which he taught at both institutions. At the law school he made his mark as a brilliant professor, and scores of his students went on to become leading public officials. As dean of the law school from 1928 to 1929, he attempted to introduce academic reforms, including a trimester system, which provoked a student rebellion. Meanwhile, in addition to his academic duties, he wrote the agrarian law of 1927. He continued teaching law, becoming professor of constitutional law and of writs and guarantees, but left teaching in 1931 to pursue a career in public life.

Bassols employed his multiple talents in reconstructing Mexico's modern banking system in 1930 and 1931. He also became a key cabinet member in the six-year interregnum between the presidencies of Plutarco Elías CALLES and Lázaro CÁRDENAS, serving as secretary of public education (1931–1934) and secretary of government (1934). He served as secretary of the treasury in the first cabinet of Cárdenas, but believing loyalty and integrity to be more important than political expediency, he resigned in 1935, when Cárdenas broke with Calles. Bassols later served as ambassador to London, Paris, and Moscow. Disenchanted with the direction of public policy, in 1941 he founded the League of Political Action with Vicente Lombardo Toledano, and in 1947 he was one of the founders of the Popular Party, the forerunner of the Popular Socialist Party, which for many years was the only leftist opposition party in Mexico.

— RODERIC AI CAMP

BASTIDAS, RODRIGO DE

Rodrigo de Bastidas (*b.* ca. 1460; *d.* 1526), early Spanish explorer. With a royal commission to explore and trade, Bastidas sailed from Cádiz in 1500 or 1501 with three ships carrying more than fifty people, including some women. He was neither a pilot, an adventurer, nor a man of arms; rather, he was a successful and respected notary in Triana (Seville). He was also unusual among leaders of early expeditions because of his relatively humane treatment of the Indians. Exploring regions not previously seen by Europeans, he discovered the Magdalena River, the Gulf of Urabá, and eastern Panama. By contrast with most later expeditions in the area, his was remarkable for its comparatively good relations with the local inhabitants, whose wealth of gold and pearls was willingly traded for Spanish trinkets. Though his ships were wrecked, Bastidas salvaged seventy-five pounds of gold and pearls, returning to Spain a rich man. He moved his family to Hispaniola, where he prospered as a cattleman. Made governor of Santa Marta in 1520, Bastidas was assassinated in Cuba by an ambitious lieutenant.

— WILLIAM L. SHERMAN

BASURTO, LUIS

Luis Basurto (*b.* 11 March 1920; *d.* 9 July 1990), Mexican playwright, actor, director, producer, and critic. A native of Mexico City, Basurto studied law, philosophy, and literature at the National Autonomous University of Mexico and began his career as a journalist. For many years he wrote film and theater reviews and a regular Thursday column in the *Crónica de México.* He was a tireless performer known throughout the Hispanic world. When he was awarded the Juan Ruiz de Alarcón Prize for literature shortly before his death, it was fitting tribute to a man who brought enormous talent and energy to the Mexican theater for more than fifty years.

Several of Basurto's twenty-six plays, some of which date from the 1940s, have become classics of the Mexican repertory. In more than 7,000 performances *Cada quien su vida* (1955) has shown with compassion and understanding the realities of Mexico's marginal classes during a New Year's Eve celebration. Other major works include *Los reyes del mundo* (1959), *Con la frente en el polvo* (1967), and *El candidato de Dios* (1986). At the time of his death Basurto was directing *Corona de sangre* (1990), the history of Padre Pro, who was executed for treason without trial in 1927 but had recently been beatified by the Vatican. Many of his plays have strongly Catholic themes. Basurto was adept at mixing sensational and often degenerate aspects of society with a strong social message.

— GEORGE WOODYARD

BATISTA, CÍCERO ROMÃO

Cícero Romão Batista (Padre Cícero) (*b.* 24 March 1844; *d.* 20 July 1934), Brazilian priest and political leader of Ceará. Born at Crato in Juàzeiro, in 1865 Cícero entered the seminary at Fortaleza and was one of its first graduates. Ordained in 1870, he began his clerical career as a teacher in Crato. Two years later he was appointed to the chaplaincy in Juàzeiro. In 1889, a communion wafer Cícero administered reportedly turned to blood in the mouth of one of his parishioners. This "miracle" gave him religious power, which he later converted into political strength; he became one of the most influential political bosses in the Northeast, and the village of Juàzeiro became a site for religious pilgrimages. Although the church disavowed the "miracle" and restricted his religious activities, it made no attempt to remove him, for the peasants of the interior regarded him as a saint. Although he clashed with both ecclesiastical and governmental authority, his movement did not seek to destroy political or religious order, but rather attempted to improve the social and economic conditions of his followers. Juàzeiro do Norte became the economic and industrial center of the backlands under

Padre Cícero. (Iconographia)

his leadership. His followers marched on Fortaleza, bringing about the downfall of its state government. Padre Cícero continues to be regarded as an unofficial saint in the Northeast, and each year large numbers of pilgrims gather at his grave in Juàzeiro.

– MICHAEL L. JAMES

BATISTA Y ZALDÍVAR, FULGENCIO

Fulgencio Batista y Zaldívar (*b.* 16 January 1901; *d.* 6 August 1973), the Cuban army's strongman in the 1930s, elected president in the 1940s, and dictator in the 1950s. The son of a farm and railroad laborer, Batista was born in Banes, Oriente Province. He spent his early years in poverty and attended a Quaker missionary school. At twenty he joined the Cuban army because it offered an opportunity for upward mobility. He attended evening classes at the National School of Journalism, from which he graduated. In 1928 he was promoted to sergeant and assigned as stenographer at Camp Columbia in Havana.

The deepening economic depression and the overthrow of Gerardo MACHADO's dictatorship in 1933 had released a wave of uncontrolled anger and anxiety. Unhappy with a proposed reduction in pay and an order restricting their promotions, the lower echelons of the army began to conspire. On 4 September 1933, Batista, together with anti-Machado student leaders, assumed the leadership of the movement, arrested army officers, and overthrew the provisional government of Carlos Manuel de CÉSPEDES. They appointed a five-man junta (the Pentarchy) to rule Cuba and, on 10 September, named Ramón GRAU SAN MARTÍN as provisional president. Grau's nationalistic and revolutionary regime was opposed by the United States, which refused to recognize it. Batista soon became a colonel and chief of staff of the army.

On 14 January 1934, the alliance between students and the military collapsed. Batista forced Grau to resign, thus frustrating the revolutionary process that had begun with Machado's overthrow. Batista ruled through puppet presidents until 1940, when he was elected president. Desiring to win popular support, he sponsored an impressive body of welfare legislation. Public administration, health, education, and public works improved. He legalized the Cuban Communist Party and in 1943 established diplomatic relations with the Soviet Union. Immediately following the Pearl Harbor attack, Batista brought Cuba into World War II on the Allied side. Air and naval bases were made available to the United States, which purchased all of Cuba's sugar production and provided generous loans and grants. In

1944 Batista allowed the election of his former rival, Grau San Martín.

Batista settled in Daytona Beach, Florida, where he wrote *Sombras de América* (published in Mexico in 1946). In 1948, while still in Florida, he was elected to the Cuban Senate from Santa Clara province. He returned to Cuba that same year, organized his own party, and announced his presidential candidacy for the June 1952 elections. On 10 March 1952, however, Batista, joined by a group of army officers, overthrew the constitutionally elected regime of President Carlos Prío Socarrás. Batista suspended Congress and the 1940 constitution, canceled the elections, and dissolved all political parties. University students soon began to show their opposition by rioting and demonstrating. On 26 July 1953, young revolutionaries led by Fidel CASTRO unsuccessfully attacked the Moncada military barracks in Oriente Province. Some of the attackers were killed and others, including Castro, were jailed.

In a rigged election in November 1954, Batista was reelected for a four-year term. Corruption in his administration reached unprecedented proportions, leading students to increase their protests. After his release from prison in 1956, the revolutionary leader Fidel Castro went to Mexico to prepare an expedition that landed in Cuba in December of that year and began guerrilla operations. On 13 March 1957, an attack on the Presidential Palace by students and followers of deposed President Prío nearly succeeded in killing Batista. The Batista government met terrorism with counterterrorism. By 1958 national revulsion against Batista had developed. Finally, defections from the army precipitated the fall of the regime on 1 January 1959. Batista escaped to the Dominican Republic and later to Madeira. He died at Guadalmina, near Marbella, Spain.

– JAIME SUCHLICKI

BATLLE, LORENZO

Lorenzo Batlle (*b.* 10 August 1810; *d.* 8 May 1887), general and president of Uruguay (1868–1872). When the Great War (Guerra Grande) began in 1839, Batlle became a captain on the side of the Colorado Party (Unitario) and played an active role in the circle associated with the *Defensa* of Montevideo. From 1847 to 1851, he was minister of war and the navy in the cabinet of Joaquín Suárez and became a central figure in the postwar period, which was characterized by political experimentation, efforts toward a stable peace, and the ongoing debate concerning political parties. First he joined the ranks of the so-called Conservative Party, a Colorado group with an oligarchic slant and strong support from the military and financial sectors. He subsequently became a member of the Liberal Union and then returned to the Colorados. He became minister of finance in the government of Gabriel Antonio Pereira (1856–1857) and minister of war and the navy again during the dictatorship of Venancio FLORES (1865–1868).

Batlle was elected president in 1868, introducing a "politics of partisanship" with a decided elitist bent. During his administration, he faced a grave economic crisis, permanent conflict with his party's regional caudillos, and the outbreak of the so-called Revolution of the Lances led by the Blanco caudillo Timoteo Aparicio. After his presidency, he went into a long period of retirement from public life, interrupted only in 1886 when he became a leader of the Quebracho Revolution against the dictatorship of General Máximo Santos. Batlle died in poverty a year later.

– GERARDO CAETANO

BATLLE BERRES, LUIS CONRADO

Luis Conrado Batlle Berres (*b.* 1897; *d.* July 1964), president of Uruguay (1947–1951). Luis Batlle Berres was the nephew of the great leader of the Colorado Party and founder of modern Uruguay, José BATLLE Y ORDÓÑEZ. He began his political career in the 1920s as a deputy in Congress for Montevideo. Elected vice president in 1946, he succeeded to the presidency upon the death of Tomás BERRETA. Smart and ambitious, "Lusito," as he was known, found himself constrained by the Batllist faithful, the adoring but increasingly conservative followers of José Batlle led by his sons Lorenzo and César. In 1948 Batlle Berres had signaled his independence by starting his own newspaper, *Acción,* as a voice separate from *El Día,* the Colorado newspaper founded by José Batlle and run by his sons. He thus distanced his own political movement, List 15, from his cousins' List 14. His faction proved to be dominant within the party in the 1950 elections.

Batlle Berres favored the continuation of a presidential system, even in the face of an almost religious demand by the Batllist faithful to create a Colegiado (collegial executive system). Batlle Berres's urban populist coalition had swept his faction to such a convincing victory in 1950 that the Blanco (National Party) leader, Luis Alberto de HERRERA, was willing to join with Lorenzo and César in support of a collegial executive in order to prevent a new political dynasty. Unable to withstand the List 14 and Herrerist calls for constitutional reform, Batlle Berres supported the 1951 plebiscite that gave Uruguay a collegial executive system under the new 1952 Constitution. Nevertheless, Batlle

Berres's List 15 continued to dominate Colorado voting, giving him the most powerful voice in Uruguayan politics through the mid-1950s. Following his death, the leadership of List 15 passed to his son Jorge Batlle, and this sector of the party became known as Radical Batllism.

– MARTIN WEINSTEIN

BATLLE Y ORDÓÑEZ, JOSÉ

José Batlle y Ordóñez (*b.* 21 May 1856; *d.* 20 October 1929), journalist and president of Uruguay (1903–1907, 1911–1915). One of the most important and influential personalities in Uruguayan history, José Batlle y Ordóñez's first avocation was philosophy rather than politics. With an initial Catholic education, he was influenced as a youth by the ideas of Karl Christian Friedrich Kraus. His transition to a rationalist, spiritualist philosophy would mark his later public career. Also early in his life, he began a lifelong journalism career,

José Batlle y Ordóñez. (Organization of American States)

writing for such periodicals as *La Razón, La Lucha,* and *El Espíritu Nuevo.*

FROM ANTIMILITARISM TO SOCIAL REFORM. Batlle y Ordóñez began his political life between 1876 and 1886, confronting the military dictatorships of Lorenzo LATORRE and Máximo Santos. He participated in the 1886 Quebracho Revolution against Santos, which, despite military defeat, marked the beginning of a political transition toward civilian rule. In this same year he founded the newspaper *El Día,* which served as a mouthpiece for the Colorado Party. From its pages, he led the opposition to the Santos regime. After its early financial problems and government repression, *El Día's* low price and street distribution caused it to become the foremost newspaper in Uruguayan history.

With Santos out of power, Batlle y Ordóñez—part of the group of allies of then Minister Julio HERRERA Y OBES—was appointed as political chief of the department of Minas by President Máximo TAJES. This was his first position as a public servant, and it lasted only six months. Already deeply involved in the political militancy of the Colorado Party, he was elected to the Chamber of Deputies in 1893 and the Senate in 1896. He opposed the oligarchic practices of President Herrera y Obes (1890–1894) and worked intensely on the organization of a popular faction within the Colorado Party. He adamantly opposed the presidency of Juan Idiarte Borda, who, assassinated in 1897, never finished his term.

Batlle y Ordóñez supported the rise to power of Juan L. CUESTAS, which began a dramatic political ascent that would win him the presidency of the Senate. He supported the 10 February 1898 coup led by Cuestas and formed part of the interim state council. He was considered a favorite to succeed to the presidency in 1903, but in 1901 he seemed to lose all chances when he strongly rejected the Blancos (Nationalists) and was displaced from the presidency of the Senate. Cuestas withdrew his support for Batlle y Ordóñez due to the latter's proven independence of character. Conservative Uruguayans also began to oppose Batlle. They saw him as a "war candidate," due to his growing ill-will toward the Nationalists and his doctrinaire defense of the "politics of partisanship," which threatened the system of *coparticipación.* They also mistrusted some of the reformist ideas he outlined in his critiques of the gold-supporting oligarchy in 1891 and in his editorials supporting workers' movements in 1895.

GOVERNMENT AND CIVIL WAR. With arduous effort, Batlle y Ordóñez won over the internal factions of the Colorados along with a group of dissident Blancos. This assured him a majority among the legislators. He was elected president by the General Assembly on 1

March 1903. His first presidency was marked by the Blanco uprisings of 1903 and 1904 led by the caudillo Aparicio SARAVIA. Batlle y Ordóñez was also confronted by two antagonistic visions of the political future of the country: the continuance and deepening of *coparticipación* versus the "politics of partisanship." Saravia's death in 1904 marked the end of the revolution and the consolidation of "partisanship."

El Día's low price and street distribution caused it to become the foremost newspaper in Uruguayan history.

Reformist measures adopted during the first administration of Batlle y Ordóñez included the abolition of the death penalty, legalization of divorce by mutual consent, a law of labor regulation, expansion of public education, creation of the Colleges of Commerce and of Agronomy and Veterinary Science, and a plan for public works and roads. At the end of his presidential term in 1907, Batlle y Ordóñez left almost immediately on a trip to Europe and the Near East that lasted almost four years. In 1907 he participated in the Second International Peace Conference in The Hague. While visiting many European countries, he studied their social conflicts and joined in ideological debates, thereby polishing many of the ideas and proposals that constituted the reformist plan he would implement during his second presidential term. He returned to Uruguay in February 1911 and on 1 March was again elected president by an overwhelming majority of legislators in the General Assembly. (The Blanco Party had abstained from the legislative elections in 1910 after another attempt at revolution failed.)

THE RISE AND FALL OF REFORM. The second presidency of Batlle y Ordóñez constituted the decisive period during which his reformist plan was implemented. The debate over a broad range of initiatives dominated the public stage. These reforms generated strong resistance from the Blanco Party (which abandoned its abstentionist posture in 1913), from management guilds, from foreign capital (especially British), and from the army.

The Batllist plan was organized around six major reforms. First, economic reform was based on the nationalization of strategic sectors and industrialization through protectionist legislation. Second, social reform centered on "critical support" for unions, "protective" social legislation for workers and other philanthropic

B

measures. Third, rural reform was aimed at the gradual elimination of large ranches, the promotion of a more balanced and automated livestock industry, and the transformation of rural poverty. Fourth, fiscal reform sought tax increases for the wealthy, a decrease in taxes on consumption, the use of economic pressure as an instrument of social justice, and the stimulation of economic development. Fifth, moral reform promoted the concept of a cosmopolitan nation, secular politics, and various feminist principles. Finally, political reform promoted public debate and supported proposals that the executive branch be organized in a collegiate system.

Not all of these reforms came to fruition, due in some cases to strong opposition and in others to ambiguity among the Batllists themselves. Also, proposals for political reform did not include essential democratic changes that the opposition demanded, such as the secret ballot, proportional representation, and guarantees against electoral fraud. The essence of the reform plan was implemented before the democratization of the political system, which occurred with the second constitution in 1919. Batllism suffered a defeat in the decisive elections of 30 July 1916 for members of the National Constituent Assembly. Batlle's successor to the presidency, Feliciano VIERA, adopted the so-called "halt politics," which drastically decreased proposals for reform. From 1916 to the end of the 1920s, the predominant atmosphere in public policy favored putting the brakes on reform. Batllism gradually lost its political initiative and strength.

THE LAST YEARS. Although with less power than earlier, Batlle y Ordóñez continued to be politically active throughout the last years of his life. He was one of the fundamental backers of the political accord from which sprang the new constitution. In 1921 and 1927 he served briefly as president of the National Council of Administration, the central component of the new collegiate executive branch. He was a major force behind the effort to attain electoral unity among distinct Colorado Party factions. He made exhausting tours of the country, seeking grassroots support for his reforms, and until his death he led the often acerbic debates in the inner recesses of the Colorado Party. Even in the midst of political uproar, he constantly promoted political debate from the pages of *El Día*.

Batlle y Ordóñez died just a few days before the great stock market crash on Wall Street. The Great Depression had its effects on Uruguay, among them putting a halt to a good part of the reformist projects of Batllism. Most of the first three decades of the twentieth century in Uruguay are referred to by historians as the Batllist Era. Whether in a spirit of polemic or agreement, the ideas and symbols associated with Batlle y Ordóñez remain present in the Uruguayan public debate.

— GERARDO CAETANO

BATRES JUARROS, LUIS

Luis Batres Juarros (*b.* 7 May 1802; *d.* 17 June 1862), Guatemalan politician and businessman. Born in Guatemala City, Batres Juarros received a law degree from San Carlos University in 1823. He fought against Francisco MORAZÁN in the civil war and then emigrated to the United States for a time. After 1839 he became a very important figure among supporters of the Guatemalan conservative regime. He served several terms as a representative in Congress and was a minister of war, of finance, and of the interior. He also held the positions of mayor of Guatemala City (1845), state advisor, and attaché to the consulate of commerce. He played a key role in the drafting of the Constitution of the Republic in 1851, reorganized the mint, and defended the reestablishment of the Jesuits in 1851.

— ARTURO TARACENA ARRIOLA

BATRES MONTÚFAR, JOSÉ

José Batres Montúfar (*b.* 18 March 1809; *d.* 9 July 1844), Guatemalan writer, soldier, and politician. Born in San Salvador, in 1824 he entered the Cadet School, and with the rank of second lieutenant of artillery, he participated in the Federal War at the side of President Arce. He was taken prisoner in the battle of Mexicanos in 1828. While in prison he learned English and began to read Byron, who inspired his later literary work. In 1829 he returned to Guatemala and began his career as a writer. Of primary note are his lyrical compositions in the romantic style, especially *Tradiciones de Guatemala*, which consists of three satirical pieces—the last unfinished—in which he describes the life-style and mentality of the dominant class in Guatemala at the beginning of the nineteenth century. These are written along the lines of the *Novelle galanti* of Giovanni Casti.

While in prison Batres Montúfar learned English and began to read Byron, who inspired his later literary work.

In 1836, Batres Montúfar graduated from the Academia de Estudios, and as a surveyor he participated in the 1837 engineering commission that, under the direction of John Baily, explored the San Juan River of

Nicaragua for the possible development of an inter-oceanic canal. His younger brother Juan died during this endeavor. He was named political head of Amatit-lán in 1839, and in 1840 fought as captain of artillery, defending Guatemala City against Francisco MORAZÁN. In 1842 he was elected as a representative to Congress from the department of San Marcos.

– ARTURO TARACENA ARRIOLA

BAZAINE, FRANÇOIS ACHILLE

François Achille Bazaine (*b.* 13 February 1811; *d.* 23 September 1888), French military commander in Mexico (1863–1867). Born near Metz, Bazaine joined the French Foreign Legion in 1832, serving in Algeria and Spain. He served with General Élie-Frédéric Forey in the Crimea (1854–1856) and in the Italian campaign (1859). Bazaine took North African troops with him to Mexico in 1863, and Napoleon III appointed him on 16 July 1863 as supreme commander of French Intervention forces, replacing Forey.

In Mexico, Bazaine's aim was to reconcile the various factions and win over moderate opinion to the empire. He disliked the Mexican Conservatives and followed Napoleon's policy of blocking any reversal of the Reform Laws. He became critical of Emperor MAXIMILIAN's indecision. The peak of Bazaine's career was the Oaxaca campaign of 1865. With 8,000 men he took the city on 9 February and captured Porfirio DÍAZ, Liberal military commander. He put into effect Napoleon's evacuation policy during 1866 and left Mexico on the last convoy on 12 March 1867, returning to France without military honors, since Mexico had already become an embarrassment to Napoleon.

At the outbreak of the Franco-Prussian War in 1870, Bazaine commanded the 103,000 men of the Third Army Corps, with headquarters at Metz. Although he held down a Prussian army in Lorraine, he was unjustly accused of treason for surrendering Metz in October 1870 after a seventy-day siege. After returning from captivity in Germany and seventeen months of house arrest, he was courtmartialed on 6 October 1873 and sentenced to twenty years on the prison island of Sainte Marguerite, from which he escaped on 10 August 1874. He spent the last years of his life in Spain.

– BRIAN HAMNETT

BAZÁN, JUAN GREGORIO

Juan Gregorio Bazán (*d.* 1570), conquistador of Tucumán province and lieutenant governor. Begun in 1549, the permanent occupation of Tucumán was characterized by jurisdictional conflicts between Spaniards. Bazán, born in Talavera de la Reina, Spain, was present at the founding of Santiago del Estero (1553) and of San Miguel de Tucumán (1565), and became governor of the town of Esteco in 1567. He unsuccessfully combed the countryside for Indians to serve as laborers for newly founded towns. The Lules Indians attacked him and his party on their return from Peru, where he had gone to meet his newly arrived family. Bazán was killed, as was his son-in-law, Diego Gómez de Pedraza, who uttered a phrase during the battle that has remained part of Argentine folklore: "Caballero soy y no voy huyendo" ("I am a gentleman, and I do not flee").

– NICHOLAS P. CUSHNER

BECERRA-SCHMIDT, GUSTAVO

Gustavo Becerra-Schmidt (*b.* 26 August 1925), Chilean composer. Becerra was born in Temuco and studied at the National Conservatory and at the Faculty of Musical Arts, University of Chile, under the guidance of Pedro Humberto ALLENDE and Domingo Santa Cruz. He taught composition and musical theory from 1953 to 1956. From 1958 to 1961 he was the director of the renowned Institute of Musical Extension and its research publication, *La revista musical chilena.* In 1969 he was elected to the Fine Arts Academy of Chile and two years later received the Premio Nacional de Arte. For a number of years he resided in Europe, serving as the cultural attaché at the Chilean embassy in Bonn. In 1974 he became a professor of composition at the University of Oldenburg (Germany).

At the beginning of his career Becerra cultivated a neoclassical style, but soon started using more contemporary techniques, including dodecaphonism. The pointillism he practiced during the late 1950s and the 1960s gave way to a more romantic *Klangfarbenmelodie* (tone-color melody) and the use of what Becerra called a "complementary polychordal system." His String Quartets nos. 4, 5, and 6 (1958, 1959, 1960) and his Symphony no. 2 (1955–1958) are good examples of those techniques. Becerra also tried to combine more accessible musical elements into his works, like Chilean folk music and Javanese music, which he used with very modern devices.

During the 1960s Becerra experimented with aleatoric techniques, as in his Symphony no. 3 (1960), the Guitar Concertos nos. 1 and 2 (1964, 1968), and his oratorio *Macchu Picchu* (1966), with words by Chilean poet Pablo Neruda. Becerra composed works of pure experimental theater, such as *Juegos* (Games) for piano, Ping-Pong balls, and live recording (1966). Other important works by Becerra include String Quartet no. 7 (1961); Quintet for piano and string quartet (1962); a leftist political composition *Chile 1973,* for voice and small orchestra (1973–1974); Trio for flute, violin, and piano (1958); *Saxophone Quartet* (1959); *Llanto por el hermano solo* for choir (1966); *Responso para José Miguel Carrera* for voice, wind quintet, piano, and percussion (1967); *Morula, gastrulay blastula* (1969), for piano and tape (1969); *Provocation* (1972), a minidrama; *Parsifae* (1973), an opera; and *Diez trozos para ocho solistas* (1977).

— ALCIDES LANZA

BEDOYA DE MOLINA, DOLORES

Dolores Bedoya de Molina (Bedoya González, María Dolores; *b.* 20 September 1783; *d.* 9 July 1853), Guatemalan politician. Like most of her brothers, she was from early on an advocate of Central American independence. She married the statesman Pedro MOLINA in 1804 and moved to Granada, Nicaragua, where he served as doctor for the fixed battalion until 1811. On returning to Guatemala in 1814, she lent her support to her brother Mariano, imprisoned as a result of the Belén Conspiracy against Captain General José de BUSTAMENTE in 1813. She supported Molina's campaign for independence in the pages of *El Editor Constitucional,* and during the proclamation of independence from Spain on 15 September 1821, she led a crowd of advocates for independence outside the Palace of Government. Emancipation brought with it the conflict between republicans and those who favored annexation with the Mexican Empire of ITURBIDE. This conflict resulted in the assassination of Mariano Bedoya by the government's annexationist forces on 29 November 1821 and the exile of the Molina-Bedoya family to Verapaz. Bedoya always supported the political career of her husband, whether it was as leader of the Liberal Party, chief of state, or political exile.

— ARTURO TARACENA ARRIOLA

BEDOYA REYES, LUIS

Luis Bedoya Reyes (*b.* 1919), Peruvian politician and lawyer, charismatic mayor of Lima for two terms (1964–1969), and a contender for the presidency of Peru in the elections of 1980 and 1985. His political activities started with his support of the civilian president José Luis BUSTAMANTE Y RIVERO (1945–1948). In 1956 he contributed to the formation of the centrist Christian Democratic Party (PDC) and became its first general secretary. His close links with Popular Action, headed by his friend Fernando BELAÚNDE TERRY, led to his nomination as minister of justice when Belaúnde was elected president in 1963. He renounced this ministerial post to run for mayor of Lima in 1964.

Clearly at odds with the PDC's leader, Héctor Cornejo Chávez, Bedoya formed the Christian Popular Party in 1966. Extremely popular in Lima, Bedoya headed the Right's feeble opposition to the military dictatorship between 1974 and 1980. In 1978, Bedoya received the second most votes as representative to the Constituent Assembly. He has since been associated with the political right, which suffered sound defeats in the presidential elections of 1985 and 1990.

— ALFONSO W. QUIROZ

BEDREGAL DE CONITZER, YOLANDA

Yolanda Bedregal de Conitzer (*b.* 21 September 1918), Bolivian poet, novelist, and artist. Probably the best-known Bolivian female poet, Bedregal is called simply "Yolanda of Bolivia." She has received the most prestigious literary awards of Bolivia, among them, the Erich Guttentag National Prize for her novel *Bajo el oscuro sol* (1971). Her poetry covers a variety of themes and styles, but its most prominent characteristic is a special sensibility for childhood—she has written several books of poetry for children. Another very important subject in her writing is the land and native people of Bolivia. Although at times Bedregal casts the Indian in a romantic light, she grasps the spirit of Indian culture (especially Aymara culture). In her latest poetry, such as the collection *Nadir* (1950), strongly religious (even mystical) motifs are evident.

— LEONARDO GARCÍA PABÓN

BÉJAR, HÉCTOR

Héctor Béjar, Peruvian author, journalist, and Castroist guerrilla leader in the 1960s. Involved in radical politics since his years as an art and law student, he formed and led the Army of National Liberation (ELN), which launched a guerrilla campaign in 1965. In prison after 1966, he contributed to the understanding of the character, limitations, and rigidities of the Peruvian guerrilla movement by writing a treatise prized and first published in Cuba. The guerrilla movement, he explained, developed out of the climate of rebellion and oppression after the end of General Manuel ODRÍA's dictatorship. Freed by the military government after the amnesty of 1970, Béjar accepted a government post to conduct official propaganda among peasants.

— ALFONSO W. QUIROZ

BELALCÁZAR, SEBASTIÁN DE

Sebastián de Belalcázar (also Benalcázar: *b.* 1490?; *d.* 30 April 1551), Spanish conquistador. Born probably as Sebastián Moyano, like many illiterate and humble folk, Belalcázar changed his name to that of his home town:

Belalcázar, province of Córdoba. His later fame and success demonstrated the possibilities for social mobility in the New World. Belalcázar came to Santo Domingo in 1507, joined Vasco Núñez de BALBOA in Darién in 1513, received an *encomienda* in Panama in 1519, and became first *alcalde* of León, Nicaragua, in 1523. Participating as captain in the capture of the Inca Emperor ATAHUALPA at Cajamarca, Peru, in 1532, he received 2.25 of the 217 shares of the booty amassed from Atahualpa's treasure and became rich.

Belalcázar was made governor of Popayán for life,

had his three mestizo children legitimized, and

married his son to a Spanish noblewoman.

Investing in new expeditions and freeing himself from the authority of Francisco PIZARRO, Belalcázar moved north and conquered southern Colombia. He helped found the cities of Quito in 1534, Guayaquil in 1535, and Cali and Popayán in 1536. In 1538 he pushed even farther north toward the gold and dense population of the Chibcha (Muisca) Indians, but Gonzalo JIMÉNEZ DE QUESADA and Nicolás FÉDERMAN and their expeditions from Santa Marta and Coro, respectively, had already arrived. They each claimed the Chibcha territory but agreed in 1539 to journey to Spain together to resolve the dispute there.

Although unsuccessful in his Chibcha claim, Belalcázar received many honors in Spain. He was made governor of Popayán for life, had his three mestizo children legitimized, and married his son to a Spanish noblewoman. Back in Cali in 1542, he found himself reluctantly drawn into the Peruvian civil wars; he survived even when on the losing side, as in Viceroy Blasco NÚÑEZ VELA'S defeat at Iñaquito in 1546. While others lost their heads, as Núñez Vela did, or were shunted aside, as Jiménez and Féderman were, Belalcázar successfully defended his governorship in southern Colombia against all comers from 1536 until his 1550 *residencia* (impeachment) and death sentence. That sentence, based on his 1546 execution of Jorge Robledo for encroaching on the Popayán territory, was being carried by Belalcázar to Spain for appeal when he died in Cartagena.

— MAURICE P. BRUNGARDT

BÉLANCE, RENÉ

René Bélance (*b.* 28 September 1915), Haitian poet. After graduating from the École Normale (Port-au-Prince), Bélance entered government service (departments of justice and commerce). He wrote for *Le nouvelliste*, *Conjonction*, and *Optique*, among other journals. In an interview in *Callaloo*, he says he was mistakenly labeled a surrealist because his *Luminaires* (1943) was published at the same time as the "hermetic" work of Magloire Saint-Aude. After spending several years in Puerto Rico, Bélance settled in the United States and taught at Brown University. Although he wrote some metrical verse, he favors free verse and poetic prose, with deep roots in African rhythms and dance. He writes with a deceptive simplicity—"Je sais des musiques sereines / au charme délicieux." L.-S. Senghor saw him as "the most gifted of the young Haitian poets" (*Anthologie de la nouvelle poésie nègre et malgache*, 2d ed., 1969). Other poetical works by René Bélance include *Rythme de mon coeur* (1940), *Pour célébrer l'absence* (1943), *Survivances* (1944), *Épaule d'ombre* (1945), and *Nul ailleurs* (1983).

— CARROL F. COATES

BELAÚNDE, VÍCTOR ANDRÉS

Víctor Andrés Belaúnde (*b.* 15 December 1883; *d.* 14 December 1966), Peruvian intellectual, educator, publisher, and diplomat. Born in Arequipa and educated as a lawyer at the universities of Arequipa and San Marcos in Lima, Belaúnde taught history at San Marcos and the Catholic University. In addition to his academic activities, he headed the Boundaries Section of the Ministry of Foreign Affairs during the crucial period of international disputes with Ecuador, Colombia, and Chile between 1907 and 1911. His main intellectual contributions address the issues of Peruvian nationality and its role in solving national problems. Belaúnde was initially influenced by positivism before embracing French idealist and Catholic philosophies. He believed in the need to integrate Peruvians of disparate historical backgrounds within a Peruvian national ideal. He named this ideal *peruanidad* ("Peruvianness"). Peruvian social problems should not lead to revolutionary changes, as proposed by José Carlos MARIÁTEGUI and Víctor Raúl HAYA DE LA TORRE, but to social and cultural conciliation. Only through a strong feeling of national unity and a deep understanding of the genuine contributions of Peruvian history would Peru be able to form part of the community of modern nations.

Belaúnde publicized Peruvian cultural contributions as the editor of a new and third version of the landmark *Mercurio Peruano*, first published in 1791–1795. The new *Mercurio Peruano*, which appeared with brief interruptions between 1918 and 1978, published articles on a wide variety of national and international subjects. It became the longest-lasting cultural journal in Peru.

Exiled for his political opposition to President Augusto LEGUÍA (1919–1930), Belaúnde taught in several U.S. universities, including Columbia, Virginia, Miami, and Chicago. On his return to Peru in the early 1930s, he helped successfully mediate the border dispute between Colombia and Peru. As president of the Catholic University and minister of foreign affairs in 1957, he achieved national stature as an intellectual eminence. In his later years Belaúnde held a high diplomatic post at the United Nations in New York City, where he died.

— ALFONSO W. QUIROZ

BELAÚNDE TERRY, FERNANDO

Fernando Belaúnde Terry (*b.* 7 October 1912), Peruvian politician, twice president of Peru (1963–1968, 1980–1985). Representing civilian centrist political forces opposed to militarism and the Peruvian Aprista Party's established influence, Belaúnde received enthusiastic initial support of his populist modernizing ideology. He was born in Lima to a family of intellectuals and politicians from Arequipa. His father, Rafael, brother of the distinguished nationalist intellectual Víctor Andrés BELAÚNDE, went into exile in France during Augusto B. LEGUÍA's regime in the early 1920s. Thus, Fernando was able to study mechanical and electrical engineering in Paris between 1924 and 1930 and later architecture at the universities of Miami and Texas, from which he graduated in 1935.

Upon his return to Lima, Belaúnde established in 1937 the professional journal *El Arquitecto Peruano,* which became an influential means of spreading modern ideas on urbanization. Belaúnde also became professor of urban studies and founder of the Institute of Urban Studies. In 1944, Belaúnde supported the successful bid for the presidency by José Luis BUSTAMANTE Y RIVERO's National Democratic Front. He consequently was elected congressional deputy for Lima. After Bustamante's ouster by a military coup in 1948, Belaúnde resumed his professional and teaching activities. With the return of democracy in 1956, Belaúnde's presidential candidacy was supported by the Front of Democratic Youth. Although he was not elected, Belaúnde was soon able to establish a new political party, Popular Action, which, together with the support of the Christian Democratic Party, would be the base for his second and successful candidacy for the presidency in 1962.

During his first presidency Belaúnde had to face the powerful opposition coalition of the Aprista Party and the Odriista National Union. He tried to carry out a program of extensive public works financed by foreign and domestic credit. However, between 1965 and 1968 inflation increased and political scandals (corruption, contraband, and unpopular agreements with a foreign oil company) were uncovered. Military pressure mounted as a consequence of the substantial authority ceded to the army to fight the guerrilla movement of 1965. The military ousted Belaúnde in 1968 and continued to govern until 1980. Reelected as president in 1980, Belaúnde again confronted daunting economic problems and the growth of a new rural and urban armed struggle led by Shining Path (Sendero Luminoso). His popularity, and that of his party, fell as a consequence of an overall inefficient government between 1980 and 1985.

— ALFONSO W. QUIROZ

Fernando Belaúnde Terry, ca. 1980. (René Pinedo/Archivo Caretas, Lima)

BELGRANO, MANUEL

Manuel Belgrano (*b.* 3 June 1770; *d.* 20 June 1820), Argentine independence leader. Born into a wealthy merchant family, Belgrano was educated in his native Buenos Aires and at the University of Salamanca in Spain. He was admitted to the practice of law and in the last years of the colonial regime also belonged to a circle of creole professional men, all influenced by enlightenment thought, who were eager to promote economic development and practical improvements in infrastructure. Becoming secretary of the Buenos Aires Consulado, or merchant guild, he worked to encourage new productive activities and to improve the system of education. He also served in the local militia forces opposing the British invasions of 1806–1807.

Belgrano's initial response to the Spanish imperial crisis of 1808 was to support a project for constitutional monarchy in the American colonies under Princess CARLOTA JOAQUINA, sister of King Ferdinand VII, a captive of Napoleon. She was currently in Rio de Janeiro as wife of the Portuguese prince regent. This scheme came to nothing, and following the May Revolution of 1810 Belgrano threw in his lot frankly with the patriot cause. He served on the Buenos Aires junta itself, but in early 1811 set off for Paraguay as commander of an expedition sent to bring that province under control of the new authorities. He was defeated militarily, but soon afterward Paraguayans carried out their own revolution against Spain, for which Belgrano's proselytizing efforts in Paraguay had helped prepare the ground.

In 1811 Belgrano assumed command of patriot forces in the Argentine northwest, facing the royalists in Upper Peru (later Bolivia). He won some victories, but his own invasion of the Bolivian Andes in 1814 ended in defeat. Having yielded his command to José de SAN MARTÍN, Belgrano traveled to Europe in 1815 as part of a diplomatic mission that hoped to negotiate an agreement with Spain for an independent Argentine monarchy under a prince of the Spanish royal family. The idea was flatly rejected by Spain. On his return to Argentina, Belgrano worked both to obtain a formal declaration of independence (as finally effected on 9 July 1816) and to create a constitutional monarchy under a descendant of the Incas. In his final years, he again served militarily on the northern front while trying to mediate in political quarrels among various bands of patriots.

Among the leaders of Argentine independence, Belgrano is second only to San Martín in the esteem of later generations, although no great military or political triumphs are associated with his name. None of the forms of constitutional monarchy that he backed ever took hold. However, he served his country steadily and disinterestedly, enjoying the respect if not always winning the agreement of his fellow revolutionaries.

– DAVID BUSHNELL

BELLEGARDE, LUIS DANTÈS

Luis Dantès Bellegarde (*b.* 18 May 1877; *d.* 14 June 1966), Haitian educator, politician, diplomat, and author. A native of Port-au-Prince, Bellegarde taught at the secondary and university levels before entering politics. He joined the Ministry of Foreign Affairs around 1905 and was minister of public instruction and agriculture in 1918–1921. In 1950 he was president of the Constituent Assembly. Bellegarde's diplomatic activity included service as ambassador to France and the Vatican (appointed 1921) and as ambassador to the United States (appointed 1931) and to the United Nations.

Bellegarde was coauthor of almost twenty books on Haitian history, politics, and sociology. Among them are *La nation haïtienne* (1938), written with Sténio Vincent, and *Haïti et son peuple* (1953), written with Mercer Cook.

Bellegarde remains controversial for his pro-French, Christian, and Western views. Nevertheless, his contributions to Haitian social thought; foreign, financial, and economic policy; and education are clear. He died in Port-au-Prince.

– ANNE GREENE

BELLI, GIOCONDA

Gioconda Belli (*b.* 9 December 1948), Nicaraguan poet and novelist. Best known for her autobiographical, erotic, and feminist celebration of sexuality and the female body, Belli has published four books of poetry: *Sobre la grama* (1974); *Línea de fuego* (1978), winner of the Cuban Casa de las Américas Prize; *Truenos y arcoiris* (1982); and *De la costilla de Eva* (1987; *From Eve's Rib*, 1993). In testimony to her rising reputation in Central America, all four books were republished together as *Poesía reunida* (1989). An ardent supporter of the Sandinista revolution, Belli wrote eloquently of the loss of friends and comrades in the fighting. Her first novel, *La mujer habitada* (1988; *The Inhabited Woman*, 1994), recounts the struggle of a Latin American woman to transcend the politics of individualistic bourgeois feminism and join the broader historical struggle of all oppressed peoples. Her second novel, *Sofía de los presagios* (1990), depicts the feminist struggles of a woman in contemporary Nicaragua. In addition to English, much of Belli's work has been translated into German.

– ANN GONZÁLEZ

BELLO, ANDRÉS

Andrés Bello (*b.* 29 November 1781; *d.* 15 October 1865), Venezuelan polymath and public servant, the most distinguished Latin American intellectual of his (and perhaps any other) century. Born and educated in Caracas, Bello accompanied Simón BOLÍVAR (1783–1830), whom he had briefly taught, as a member of the first Venezuelan diplomatic mission to Britain (1810).

Andrés Bello. (Benson Latin American Collection, University of Texas at Austin)

The collapse of the Venezuelan Republic stranded him in London, where he lived, often penuriously, for more than eighteen years. In the 1820s he coedited the influential Spanish-American journals *La Biblioteca Americana* (1823) and *El Repertorio Americano* (1826–1827), and worked as an official of the Chilean and Colombian legations. At the invitation of the Chilean government, he moved to Santiago in 1829. He was employed thereafter as senior official in the foreign ministry, as editor of the government gazette *El Araucano,* and as first rector of the newly founded University of Chile (1843–1865)— still colloquially known in Chile as *la casa de Bello* (Bello's house). He was a senator from 1837 to his death.

The extraordinary range of Bello's genius was reflected in prolific writings on international and Roman law, philosophy, literature, drama, grammar, and science. His poems, especially the two great "London poems," "Alocución a la poesía" (Allocution to Poetry, 1823), and "A la agricultura de la zona tórrida" (Agriculture in the Torrid Zone, 1826), have often been seen as the true starting point of all postcolonial Latin American literature. Bello's work as a jurist was crowned by his single-handed authorship of the classic Civil Code of the Republic of Chile (1855). His numerous writings on language culminated in the *Gramática de la lengua castellana destinada al uso de los americanos* (Grammar of the Spanish Language for the Use of Americans, 1847), which won him honorary membership in the Real Academia in Spain. He made radical proposals to modify the orthography of Spanish; several features of his scheme remained in use in Chile until around 1910. His guidance also shaped a school of Chilean historians.

Bello's influence on the intellectual life of nineteenth-century Chile is incalculable. At the heart of all Bello's work lay the belief that Latin America, now politically free, needed to create its own cultural and intellectual traditions, traditions that would be authentically Latin American, without repudiating the achievements of European civilization. At his funeral in 1865 the scientist Ignacio Domeyko (1801–1889) doubted "that one man, in one lifetime, could know so much, could do so much, could love so much." Bello's bicentennial in 1981 was extensively commemorated throughout Spanish America.

– SIMON COLLIER

BELTRÁN, LUIS

Luis Beltrán (*b.* 7 September 1784; *d.* 8 December 1827), Franciscan friar and chaplain of several Platine armies during the struggle against Spain. Born near Mendoza, Argentina, Fray Beltrán entered the Franciscan order when barely sixteen years old and soon moved to the convent in Santiago, Chile. His military career started after he joined José Miguel CARRERA's army as chaplain and took part in the battle of Hierbas Buenas in 1812. Although this battle was disastrous for the rebels, it allowed Beltrán to demonstrate his skills at military engineering. He later held, for example, the post of director of ordnance (1820–1824) for the Chileans and worked in that same capacity under Simón BOLÍVAR in Peru in 1824. An argument with Bolívar, however, led to a suicide attempt by Beltrán and dimmed his lifework and health thereafter. Lieutenant Colonel Beltrán left the army in 1827 and retired to Buenos Aires, where he renewed his interest in the religious life he had never formally abandoned. He was named "heroic defender of the nation" by Buenos Aires. He died in Buenos Aires.

— FIDEL IGLESIAS

BELTRÁN, LUIS (SAINT)

Luis (Saint) Beltrán (*b.* 1 January 1526; *d.* 10 October 1581), Spanish Dominican missionary and patron saint of Colombia. Born in Valencia and ordained in 1547, Beltrán arrived in Cartagena in 1562. After proselytizing among the Indians of the northern coast, he served for three years as *doctrinero* of Turbará, near present-day Barranquilla. A letter from Bartolomé de LAS CASAS warning him to be careful of how he confessed and absolved *encomenderos* of their sins may have led him to a more determined defense of the Indians. Appearing before one banquet table of *encomenderos,* Beltrán dramatically squeezed the corn *arepas* (pancakes), the fruit of Indian labor, so hard that blood supposedly trickled onto the white tablecloth. His conflicts with *encomenderos* and his fame as a holy man grew. Brought back to Cartagena as a preacher and fund-raiser, Beltrán addressed audiences all along the Caribbean coast from Nombre de Dios to Santa Marta. On his way to serve as prior of the Dominican friary in Bogotá, he was ordered back to Spain, where he arrived in 1569. Chosen to head several Spanish religious houses, he died in Valencia. He was beatified by Paul V in 1608 and canonized by Clement X in 1671.

— MAURICE P. BRUNGARDT

BELTRÁN, MANUELA

Manuela Beltrán (*b.* 1724; *d.* ?), Comunero insurgent. A heroine of the Comunero Revolt that swept through the uplands of New Granada in 1781, Manuela Beltrán remains an obscure figure. Born of Spanish ancestry in Socorro, province of Tunja, she appears to have been a woman of modest means. Her home, a prosperous agricultural, commercial, and textile manufacturing town, was hit hard by the ambitious, intemperately applied revenue measures of Regent Visitor Gutiérrez de Piñeres. Riots erupted in Socorro on 16 March 1781 following the promulgation of the decree separating the collection of the Alcabala and the Armada de Barlovento taxes, which people mistakenly believed to be a new tax. Emerging from the angry crowd, Manuela Beltrán, in the midst of riotous applause, dramatically tore

down the Armada de Barlovento ordinance, an act that at least symbolically marked the beginning of the Comunero revolt. Thereafter, Beltrán disappeared from history, but she is representative of the prominent role that women so often played in the popular protests of the eighteenth century.

— ALLAN J. KUETHE

BELTRÁN, PEDRO

Pedro Beltrán (*b.* 17 February 1897; *d.* 16 February 1979), Peruvian landowner, economist, publisher, and politician. Born in Cañete, he became a distinguished representative of liberal interests among the economic elite of coastal Peru. He studied at San Marcos University and in London at Kings College and the London School of Economics, from which he received a master's degree in economics in 1918. On his return to Peru, he promoted agricultural modernization and organized cotton and sugar producers. By 1929, Beltrán had become the president of the influential National Agrarian Society and a member of the board of directors of the Peruvian Reserve Bank.

After the fall of President Augusto B. LEGUÍA in 1930, Beltrán continued to exercise his influence as a leading exporter of agricultural goods through the daily newspaper *La Prensa,* which he bought in 1934. Between 1944 and 1946, Beltrán was the Peruvian ambassador to the United States and presided over the Peruvian delegation at the Bretton Woods conference. He vigorously opposed state controls over imports and foreign currency exchange under president José Luis BUSTAMANTE Y RIVERO (1945–1948). In 1956, Beltrán was imprisoned by Manuel ODRÍA for his opposition as head of the National Coalition, a civilian political group. In 1959–1960, during the second Prado administration, he served as minister of finance. In 1974 the military government expropriated his newspaper. He lived thereafter in exile in New York City, where he died.

— ALFONSO W. QUIROZ

BELTRÁN, WASHINGTON

Washington Beltrán (*b.* 7 February 1885; *d.* 2 April 1920), Uruguayan lawyer, journalist, and politician. While earning very high grades in Montevideo's National University, School of Law and Social Sciences, Beltrán published several articles of note in scientific and literary journals. Later, he extended his expertise into philosophical and legal terrains, with the publication of articles such as "Los filósofos del siglo XVIII," *"El contrato social,"* and "Fallos de la Alta Corte de Justicia en materia civil, penal, comercial, administrativa y de lo contencioso administrativo" in Buenos Aires's *Revista de Derecho* between 1908 and 1909. With Carlos Roxlo he directed the newspaper *El Civismo* and later wrote on political issues for *La Democracia* and other newspapers. He also served in the Justice Department. As codirector and principal writer of *El País,* he consistently opposed the socialist and populist program of Colorado Party leader José BATLLE Y ORDÓÑEZ, during Batlle's second term as president from 1911 to 1915. In 1914 Beltrán was elected deputy to the National Congress. Between 1916 and 1917 he served as a member of the National Constituent Assembly, which approved a two-party governing council, the Colegiado, to replace the presidency. Beltrán was killed in 1920 during a pistol duel with Batlle.

— WILLIAM H. KATRA

BELZU, MANUEL ISIDORO

Manuel Isidoro Belzu (*b.* 4 April 1808; *d.* 27 March 1865), president of Bolivia (1848–1855). Born into a poor artisan family in La Paz, Belzu was educated at the Franciscan monastery. At thirteen he ran away from the monks and joined an army fighting Spanish forces. He fought for various generals, including Agustín Gamarra of Peru and Andrés Santa Cruz, José Ballivián, and José Miguel de Velasco of Bolivia. He became minister of war in the Velasco government in February 1848.

At thirteen Belzu ran away from the Franciscan monastery and joined an army fighting Spanish forces.

Belzu seized control of the government in December 1848. Employing populist rhetoric, he was the first general to base his regime on the urban artisans and Cholos (people of mixed Indian and European heritage). Although he remained in power until 1855, when he "constitutionally" handed the presidency to his son-in-law, General Jorge Córdova, Belzu failed to consolidate control. He survived one assassination attempt in 1850 and forty-two revolutions against his authority. From 1855 to 1857, he represented Bolivia in Europe, where he remained until 1865. That same year he returned to Bolivia in order to prevent the assumption of power by Mariano MELGAREJO, who had him assassinated.

— ERWIN P. GRIESHABER
ERICK D. LANGER

BEMBERG, OTTO

Otto Bemberg (*b.* 1827; *d.* 1895), German-born businessman in Argentina. Bemberg arrived in Buenos Aires in the 1850s and established a prosperous import-export business. He married the daughter of the influential Senator Mariano Ocampo and served as Argentine consul in Paris during the War of the Triple Alliance (1865–1870). He became involved in the arms trade with Argentina, and following his return to Buenos Aires, he became an agent for many important French industrial companies, especially the Schneider firm, which exported railway and other heavy equipment to the Río de la Plata.

With offices in Buenos Aires and Paris, Bemberg began to specialize in financial dealings, and he was the agent for a large number of Argentine provincial loans issued on the Paris Stock Exchange in the 1880s. He was an agent to various French banks and helped arrange financing for a French-owned railway in Argentina and for the construction of the port works in Rosario.

In 1888 Bemberg established the Quilmes Beer Company, long the largest brewery in Argentina, which remains owned by the Bemberg family. The brewery expanded production spectacularly between 1900 and 1925 and also bought competing breweries to establish its dominance. The company was nationalized by the government of Juan D. PERÓN in 1947 and was returned to the Bemberg family in 1955.

— CARLOS MARICHAL

BENAVIDES, ALONSO DE

Alonso de Benavides (*b.* before 1579; *d.* ca. 1636), Franciscan missionary and propagandist in New Mexico. The personification of Christian spiritual conquest, Benavides acted in New Mexico in the seventeenth century with a zeal reminiscent of his sixteenth-century brethren. He was born at San Miguel, in the Azores, and entered the Franciscan order in Mexico City, serving subsequently in various capacities. Appointed superior of the New Mexico missions and agent of the Inquisition, Benavides presented his credentials to Governor Felipe de Sotelo Osorio at Santa Fe early in 1626. During his three-year term, Benavides labored actively not only among Pueblo Indians, but also among Apaches. When the ardent friar returned to Mexico City in early 1630, Franciscan authorities sent him to Spain to lobby at court. His sanguine report of missionary progress and potential in New Mexico, published the same year, and a revised version prepared for the pope in 1634 remain valuable ethnohistorical sources.

— JOHN L. KESSELL

BENAVIDES, OSCAR RAIMUNDO

Oscar Raimundo Benavides (*b.* 1876; *d.* 1945), Peruvian general and twice de facto president of Peru (1914–1915, 1933–1939). Born in Lima, he was one of the first professional officers to graduate from the Peruvian Military School in the 1890s. He completed studies in science at the San Marcos University in 1905 and his military training in France in 1907. In 1911 he became nationally known for his swift mobilization of an army he led to Iquitos during the military actions arising from a dispute between Peru and Colombia over a jungle area.

As chief of staff of the Peruvian army in 1913, he did not endorse President Guillermo BILLINGHURST's bid to enhance his executive power. Consequently, Benavides was temporarily ousted from the army. Soon, however, he led the first institutional military coup in Peruvian history against Billinghurst in 1914. In 1915 constitutional order was restored. Benavides continued his military service into the 1920s, when his opposition to President Augusto B. LEGUÍA resulted in his exile to Guayaquil, where he continued to conspire. When Colonel Luis M. SÁNCHEZ CERRO overthrew Leguía in 1930, he appointed Benavides ambassador to Spain and Great Britain and then called him back to Peru during the brief war with Colombia in 1932.

After Sánchez Cerro was assassinated in 1933, the Peruvian Congress designated Benavides president of the republic. During his administration he proscribed the APRA movement and in 1936 held elections which were nullified because of the electoral victory of the candidate supported by the APRA. He established the social security system and carried out a program of public works in the midst of a slow economic recovery after 1933. In 1939, Benavides handed over power to his relative, civilian Manuel PRADO.

— ALFONSO W. QUIROZ

BENEDETTI, MARIO

Mario Benedetti (*b.* 14 September 1920), Uruguayan writer. Along with Juan Carlos ONETTI, Benedetti is the most highly regarded member of the literary generation of 1945. In his most important works of fiction, the novels *La tregua* (1960), *Gracias por el fuego* (1965), and *El cumpleaños de Juan Angel* (1971), and a set of short stories titled *Montevideanos* (1959), he portrays Uruguay's mundane, hedonistic urban middle class. His characters are consumed by anguish without the means for self-realization. Many are frustrated public employees, incapable of taking important initiatives or expressing great passions, who listlessly await easy solutions to their economic and sexual problems. Benedetti treats with empathetic tenderness, and sometimes with irony, his countrymen's dissatisfactions with and resentment toward life, and their vague nostalgia for an unrecoverable past.

Benedetti has also published several important collections of essays. *Literatura uruguaya siglo XX* (1963; rev. ed. 1969), *Letras del continente mestizo* (1967), and *Sobre artes y oficios* (1968) qualify him as one of Uruguay's most authoritative cultural and literary critics. Notable works concerning politics and the national situation are the witty and penetrating *El país de la cola de paja* (1960) and *Terremoto y después* (1973), which analyzes the urban guerrilla war of the Tupamaros and the military's severe response; *El escritor latinoamericano y la revolución posible* (1974), which considers the role of culture in promoting radical social change across the continent; and *Primavera con una esquina rota* (1982), chronicle of the writer's years of exile during the military dictatorship from 1972 to 1986.

Among his works for the theater, the acclaimed *Pedro y el capitán* (1979) is about Uruguay's experience under military rule; it explores the existential situation of an incarcerated political activist and the self-justifications of his military torturer. Benedetti's considerable output of lyrical poetry—sixteen collections since 1945—received widespread recognition when the famed Catalán singer Joan Manuel Serrat featured his verse in the recording *El sur también existe*. In another recording, *Las dos voces,* Benedetti's poems are juxtaposed with short songs by Uruguayan protest singer Daniel Viglietti. The songs address issues such as exile, the Chilean coup of 1971, and the suffering resulting from military violence. Since 1980, Benedetti has emerged as perhaps Uruguay's most visible and respected intellectual.

— WILLIAM H. KATRA

BENÍTEZ, GREGORIO

Gregorio Benítez (*b.* 1834; *d.* 1910), Paraguayan diplomat and author. Born in the interior town of Villarrica, Benítez received his education there and at Asunción. In the early 1850s, he was noticed by officials of the Carlos Antonio LÓPEZ government, who decided to groom him for a career in the state bureaucracy. In 1856, he received an assignment to act as secretary to the president's son, General Francisco Solano LÓPEZ, who was at that time war minister. Benítez later accompanied the younger López to Buenos Aires on a mission to mediate a dispute between that province and the Argentine Confederation.

His position as a diplomat established, Benítez was designated secretary of legation at London in 1860. After the beginning of the War of the Triple Alliance in 1864, he went to the continent to solicit European support for the Paraguayan cause. He became his country's chief diplomatic representative in Prussia, France, and Britain before journeying to the United States in 1868. In Washington and other cities, Benítez tried to gain North American help in arranging peace negotiations with Argentina and Brazil, but these efforts were rebuffed by the two nations, who went on to defeat the Paraguayans in 1870.

Benítez reemerged on the diplomatic scene more than twenty years later when he negotiated an 1894 boundary agreement with the Bolivians that set limits on expansion in the Gran Chaco territory. Though this treaty, jointly issued with Bolivian diplomat Telmo Ichazo, was tragically short-lived, it nonetheless permitted some respite from the escalation of tensions between the two countries.

Benítez wrote several informative memoirs, including *La triple alianza de 1865: Escapada de un desastre en la guerra de invasión al Paraguay* (1904) and *Anales diplomático y militar de la guerra del Paraguay* (1906).

— MARTA FERNÁNDEZ WHIGHAM

BENÍTEZ, JAIME

Jaime Benítez (*b.* 29 October 1908), Puerto Rican intellectual, politician, and member of the United States Congress (1973–1977), and one of the architects of modern Puerto Rico, especially its system of higher education. He was born in Vieques and educated in public schools in Puerto Rico; he received a master's degree in law from Georgetown University in 1931 and a master of arts from the University of Chicago in 1938. From 1931 to 1942, Benítez taught political science at the

---

Benítez worked closely with Puerto Rican statesman Luis Muñoz Marín to establish the Commonwealth of Puerto Rico.

University of Puerto Rico and served as chancellor and then president of the university—and the entire university system—from 1942 until 1971. As president, he directed a complete reorganization of the university, publishing his plan in *La reforma universitaria* (1943). He established a university museum and a research library in the university's main campus at Río Piedras. Benítez attracted major intellectuals to teach at the uni-

versity, among them the Spanish poets Pedro Salinas and Juan Ramón Jiménez, and founded and contributed to the literary review *La Torre.*

Benítez wrote influential books on education, including *Education for Democracy on a Cultural Frontier* (1955), *Etica y estilo de la universidad* (1964), *Junto a la Torre: Jornadas de un programa universitario* (1963), and *La universidad del futuro* (1964). He wrote for *Sur* and *Cuadernos Americanos,* the most prestigious cultural journals of Latin America, was a member of the United States National Commission for UNESCO (1948–1954), and lectured at many universities around the world. Benítez worked closely with Puerto Rican statesman Luis MUÑOZ MARÍN to establish the Commonwealth of Puerto Rico. He was a member of the Constitutional Convention of Puerto Rico and served as chairman of the Committee on Bill of Rights (1951–1952). He was a delegate to the Democratic National Convention in 1976 and was elected as a Popular Democrat to the U.S. House of Representatives in 1972 for a four-year term. From 1980 to 1986 he was a professor of government at the Inter-American University in Puerto Rico, and in 1984 he became a professor of government at the American College in Bayamón, Puerto Rico.

— GEORGETTE MAGASSY DORN

BENÍTEZ-ROJO, ANTONIO

Antonio Benítez-Rojo (*b.* 14 March 1931), Cuban novelist, essayist, and short-story writer. Benítez Rojo was born in Havana, received bachelor's degrees from the University of Havana in literature and accounting, and studied statistics at American University in Washington, D.C. He has served as director of statistics for the Ministry of Labor and for the Theater Group of the National Council of Culture. He was editor in chief of the magazine *Cuba* and contributed articles to the magazines *El Caimán Barbudo, Bohemia, Casa de las Américas,* and others. He also published articles in foreign publications such as *Les Lettres Nouvelles* (France) and *Cuadernos del Ruedo Ibérico* and *Insula* (Spain). In 1967 he won the Casa de las Américas prize for a collection of short stories, *Tute de reyes* (1967). In 1968, Cuba's Union of Writers and Artists (UNEAC) gave him its short-story prize for *El escudo de hojas secas.* Prior to his leaving Cuba, he was a researcher at the Center of Literary Research at the Casa de las Américas.

Although Benítez-Rojo never came into direct conflict with the Cuban government, in 1980 he opted not to return to Cuba during a stay in Europe. A professor of literature at Amherst College in Amherst, Massachusetts, he has published many books of essays and novels, among them *El mar de las lentejas* (*The Sea of Lentils*, 1990), and *La isla que se repite* (*The Repeating Island*, 1992). His literary style is crisp and straightforward, his essays characterized by sharp insight. In general he has a historical approach to fiction. His work has been translated into several languages.

— ROBERTO VALERO

BENNETT, MARSHALL

Marshall Bennett (*b.* before 1775; *d.* 1839) Belize entrepreneur. Bennett was involved with every major enterprise in the Bay of Honduras. His foresight, enterprise, and success were unique for the time. A commanding figure in the oligarchy that ruled Belize, he was first elected magistrate in 1789 and served consecutively from 1813 to 1829. Besides being chief magistrate and the wealthiest merchant, Bennett was the senior judge of the Supreme Court, colonel commander in the militia, agent for Lloyds of London, a major shipowner, and the only Belize merchant to open a branch in Guatemala, where he spent most of his time after 1828.

The mahogany trade was Bennett's prime concern, and he had separate arrangements with Guatemalan chief of state Mariano GÁLVEZ and Central American Federation President Francisco MORAZÁN to control mahogany lumbering on the Caribbean coast. Although apparently trusted and respected by his many associates, he was accused of breaking up Gregor MacGregor's settlement at Black River, reneging on a colonization contract with Gálvez, and manipulating the Eastern Coast of Central America Company for his own purposes.

— ROBERT A. NAYLOR

BERBEO, JUAN FRANCISCO

Juan Francisco Berbeo (*b.* 17 June 1729; *d.* 28 June 1795), a leader (*capitán*) of the Comunero Revolt in New Granada (1781). Berbeo was a member of the second-tier elite of his native Socorro, politically well connected but economically in modest circumstances. In April 1781, after a month of popular protests against new taxes, he led the Socorro *cabildo* into an alliance with the protesters, thus confirming Socorro's leading role in the rebellion. With Archbishop Antonio CABALLERO Y GÓNGORA Berbeo negotiated the June 1781 agreement that led to the demobilization of the *comuneros'* army of several thousand—an agreement that Caballero soon nullified—and in 1782 Berbeo and almost all of the other participants were pardoned. Berbeo claimed that he joined the rebellion in order to moderate its course and to preserve Socorro's ultimate obedience to the crown, but the Socorro elite doubtless sympathized with many of the plebeians' complaints against the fiscal and administrative effects of recent Bourbon Reforms.

— RICHARD STOLLER

BERENGUER, AMANDA

Amanda Berenguer (*b.* 1921), Uruguayan poet. Born in Montevideo, she began her literary career in earnest with the publication of her third book of poems, *Elegía por la muerte de Paul Valéry* (1945). Her first two publications, *A través de los tiempos que llevan a la gran calma* (Through the Times That Lead to the Great Calm, 1940) and *Canto hermético* (1941), had very limited circulation. With *El río* (1952) and *La invitación* (1957), Berenguer begins to develop a personal and original poetic voice; *Contracanto* (1961) is a collection of brief poems. With *Quehaceres e invenciones* (Chores and Inventions, 1963), Berenguer reaches linguistic and lyrical precision in poems of oneiric and enigmatic landscapes.

She is considered a representative of a new and daring voice in Uruguayan poetry. In *Declaración conjunta* (Joint Statement, 1964), *Materia prima* (Raw Material, 1966), and *Composición de lugar* (To Lay One's Plans, 1976), the lyric voice searches for a vision of the world that rejects tradition through the creation of new poetic structures. Her *Poesía 1949–1979* (1980) includes her complete works up to that time, except for the first three books of poems. *Identidad de ciertas frutas* (The Identity of Certain Fruits, 1983) continues to construct peculiar and innovative imagery. In 1986 Berenguer received the Reencuentro de Poesía Award granted by the University of the Republic in Montevideo. She is considered one of the main poets of contemporary Uruguay by Angel Rama, Mario Benedetti, and others.

— MAGDALENA GARCÍA PINTO

BERGAÑO Y VILLEGAS, SIMÓN

Simón Bergaño y Villegas (*b.* 1784; *d.* 1828), Guatemalan journalist. Bergaño y Villegas was born in Escuintla, Guatemala. Biographers think that, due to his limited economic resources, he was self-educated. Owing to an accident in his youth, he had to use crutches throughout his life and to spend much time in a wheelchair.

Bergaño y Villegas was both an excellent journalist and a poet. From 1804 to 1807 he edited the *Gazeta de Guatemala*, which, at the time, was a sixteen-page weekly containing the writings of various intellectuals. Bergaño y Villegas's encyclopedic knowledge made his writings a threat to the conservative ideas of the time. Some of his writings in the *Gazeta de Guatemala* appeared under the pseudonym Bergoñer de Segiliú. Nevertheless he was tried for his writings by the Inquisition in 1808 and sentenced to exile in Spain. He was taken to Havana, where he fell ill and spent several months in a hospital, thus evading transport to Spain. In Cuba he founded the periodical *Correo de las Damas* (1811), which was shut down by the bishop of Havana. In 1812 he founded the *Diario Cívico*. He died in Havana.

– OSCAR G. PELÁEZ ALMENGOR

BERGES, JOSÉ

José Berges (*b.* late 1820s; *d.* 21 December 1868), Paraguayan diplomat and jurist. Berges was a charming, quick-witted man whose social skills and intelligence were early recognized by President Carlos Antonio LÓPEZ, who appointed him to the office of district judge in the mid-1840s. His success in this position was such that López soon transferred him to the diplomatic service, where he distinguished himself on several key occasions. In 1851 he negotiated an agreement in Montevideo whereby Paraguay agreed to support a military alliance against the Argentine dictator Juan Manuel de ROSAS. Five years later he went to Rio de Janeiro to work with Brazilian diplomats on a mutual trade and boundary treaty.

Berges's finest moment as a diplomat, however, came in 1860, when he journeyed to Washington, D.C., to argue Paraguay's case before an arbitration commission called to decide culpability in the Water Witch dispute with the United States. The decision of the chief arbitrator favored the Paraguayans, and when Berges returned to Asunción, his fame had grown so much that some even spoke of his succeeding the aging López.

When López died in 1862, he was instead succeeded by his eldest son, General Francisco Solano LÓPEZ. The new president, though in many ways an egomaniac, saw no reason to hold Berges's popularity against him and soon appointed him foreign minister. In this capacity, he sent notes of protest to Brazil when that country intervened in Uruguay in 1864. These protests were only a prelude to the six-year War of the Triple Alliance, which commenced shortly thereafter. During the course of the fighting, the Paraguayan army invaded northeastern Argentina, and Berges was named to organize a short-lived puppet regime at Corrientes.

After López abandoned his Argentine campaign in late 1865, Berges returned to Asunción, where he headed up virtually all public administration in the Paraguayan capital. Three years later he was accused of conspiring against the Solano López regime. After being subjected to merciless torture, he confessed and was then summarily shot along with other supposed plotters.

– THOMAS L. WHIGHAM

BERMAN, SABINA

Sabina Berman (*b.* 21 August 1952), Mexican dramatist, scriptwriter and short story writer. She studied psychology and, later, directing and play writing under the guidance of Héctor AZAR, at the Centro de Arte Dramático (CADAC), and with Abraham Oceransky and

---

One of Berman's best works is a modern interpretation of the Mayan legend of the founder of Uxmal.

Hugo Argüelles. Three of her plays received the national prize for drama: *Bill* or *Yankee* (1979), about a psychotic Vietnam veteran in Mexico, *Rompecabezas* (1981), about Trotsky's assassination, and *Herejía* (1982), a well-structured play about Judaism in colonial Mexico. One of her best works is the children's play *La maravillosa historia del Chiquito Pingüica* (1982), a modern interpretation of the Mayan legend of the founder of Uxmal.

– GUILLERMO SCHMIDHUBER

BERMEJO, ILDEFONSO

Ildefonso Bermejo (*b.* 1820; *d.* 1892), Spanish publicist and writer active in Paraguay. A budding journalist with experience in Madrid, Bermejo first came to Asunción in 1855 at the behest of the Carlos Antonio LÓPEZ government, which had hired him to help launch several projects of a cultural nature. Over the next few years, Bermejo was the main force behind such state-sponsored newspapers as *El Semanario de Avisos y Conocimientos Útiles, El Eco del Paraguay,* and *La Época.* More important, he trained a team of young Paraguayans in the field of journalism, and his flair and erudition appeared in much of their subsequent work. In 1860, for instance, they produced *La Aurora,* an ambitious literary and scientific review, the first publication of its kind in the still very isolated Paraguay.

Aside from his journalistic work, Bermejo founded several secondary-level educational institutions, including the Aula de Filosofía. He also wrote plays for the newly constructed Teatro Nacional.

Bermejo had an irascible character that all too often conflicted with the rather conservative members of the Asunción elite. After disagreements with officials of the Francisco Solano LÓPEZ regime in 1863, he returned to Europe, where he published a scathing account of his Paraguayan experiences, *Repúblicas americanas: Episodios de la vida privada, política, y social de la República del Paraguay* (1873), in which he lampooned the López family and the country he had left behind.

– THOMAS L. WHIGHAM

BERMÚDEZ, JOSÉ FRANCISCO

José Francisco Bermúdez (*b.* 23 January 1782; *d.* 15 December 1831), officer in the Venezuelan Emancipating Army. Bermúdez was involved with the cause of independence from 1810. In 1812 he participated in the Barcelona campaign, and with the fall of the First Republic that year, he left for Trinidad. With Santiago MARIÑO, he invaded Venezuelan territory in 1813 and participated in the liberation of eastern Venezuela. When the Second Republic fell in 1815, he went to Cartagena and the Antilles and joined the troops of Mariño to participate in the Guiana campaign (1816–1817). Simón BOLÍVAR appointed him commander in chief of the province of Cumaná in 1817 and later commander in chief of the Army of the East. He participated in the Battle of Carabobo in 1821 and in the battles which finally consolidated the liberation of Venezuelan territory. With the creation of Gran Colombia, he was appointed intendant and commander of the department of Orinoco. Between 1828 and 1830, he put down various insurrections in eastern Venezuela. The following year he retired from public life.

– INÉS QUINTERO

BERMÚDEZ VARELA, ENRIQUE

Enrique Bermúdez Varela (*b.* 11 December 1932; *d.* 16 February 1991), former colonel in the Nicaraguan National Guard and military commander of the Nicaraguan Democratic Forces (Fuerzas Democráticas Nicaragüenses—FDN), an anti-Sandinista counterrevolutionary organization. Educated primarily at the Military Academy of Nicaragua, Bermúdez entered the National Guard in 1952. As a military engineer, he occupied various positions within the Department of Transit and the Department of Roads. In 1965, Bermúdez served with the Inter-American Peace Force in the Dominican Republic and later obtained appointment as military attaché to the Nicaraguan embassy in Washington, D.C. In 1981, Bermúdez helped establish

the FDN, a radical group devoted to the overthrow of the Sandinista government.

– D. M. SPEARS

BERNAL JIMÉNEZ, MIGUEL

Miguel Bernal Jiménez (*b.* 16 February 1910; *d.* 12 July 1956), Mexican composer and musicologist. Born in Morelia, Michoacán, Bernal Jiménez started his musical career as a choirboy at the Morelia cathedral and began musical studies at the Colegio de Infantes with Mier y Arriaga and Aguilera Ruiz. Later he entered the Escuela Superior de Música Sagrada in Morelia. After his graduation in 1928 he went to Rome to study organ, composition, Gregorian chant, and musicology at the Pontificio Istituto di Musica Sacra, graduating in 1933. He returned to Morelia, where he began teaching at the Escuela Superior de Música Sagrada, where in 1936 he became director. While there, he started the magazine *Schola Cantorum*. During this period he toured Mexico and the United States, performing organ concerts, conducting choirs, and giving lectures. From 1954 to 1956 he was dean of music at Loyola University in New Orleans, where he taught until his death in León, Guanajuato, Mexico.

Bernal wrote several works for the stage, among them *Tata Vasco* (1941), an opera commemorating the fourth centenary of the arrival of Vasco de QUIROGA, first bishop of Michoacán, and two ballets: *Tingambato* (1943), based on a Tarascan legend, and *Los tres galanes de Juana* (1952). He also wrote the *Suite michoacana* (1940), and *Noche en Morelia* (1941), as well as a considerable number of major compositions and sacred vocal music. He has also written a number of important musicological essays based on his researches.

– SUSANA SALGADO

BERNAL Y GARCÍA PIMENTEL, IGNACIO

Ignacio Bernal y García Pimentel (*b.* 13 February 1910; *d.* 24 January 1992), Mexican archaeologist. Born in Paris, Bernal came from a family of illustrious Mexican historians: he was the grandson of Luis García Pimentel and the great-grandson of Joaquín GARCÍA ICAZBALCETA. In 1943 he joined Alfonso CASO in the Monte Albán excavations and began his lifelong interest in the archaeology of Oaxaca. Bernal received a doctorate from the Universidad Nacional Autónoma de México in 1949. His books *Urnas de Oaxaca* (1952, with Caso) and *La cerámica de Monte Albán* (1967, with Caso and Jorge Acosta) established the foundations of Oaxaca archaeology. From 1949 to the 1960s he directed excavations at seven sites in Oaxaca, including Yagul and

Dainzú. In 1962 he was chosen the first director of the Museo Nacional de Antropología e Historia; he retired in 1976. Despite a heavy schedule of teaching and administration, Bernal produced 270 publications.

— MICHAEL D. LIND

BERNARDES, ARTUR DA SILVA

Artur da Silva Bernardes (*b.* 8 August 1875; *d.* 23 March 1955), president of Brazil (1922–1926). Bernardes was born in Viçosa, Minas Gerais, the son of a Portuguese solicitor. He attended the Lazarist school in Caracas and studied law in Ouro Prêto, where he was a leader in the *Bucha,* a secret student society inspired by the German *Burchenschaft.* After completing his studies, he returned to Viçosa to work as a lawyer, and in 1903 he married Clélia Vaz de Melo.

Bernardes began his political career in the early 1900s, holding various posts in Minas Gerais, including president of the municipal chamber, chief executive of Viçosa, and state deputy. Between 1909 and 1915, he served as a federal deputy. As his political career advanced, Bernardes became the secretary of finances for the state of Minas Gerais in 1910, serving until 1914. Four years later, he was elected governor of Minas Gerais.

Elected president of Brazil in 1922, Bernardes, however, ruled the country under a state of siege during most of his presidency, with challenges coming from both the Right and the Left. The most celebrated opposition faction was led by the Communist revolutionary leader Luís Carlos PRESTES.

President Bernardes implemented constitutional reforms that strengthened executive powers and sought reductions in public expenditures. He withdrew Brazil from the League of Nations in 1926 because it refused to admit Germany as a member nation.

After his presidential term ended, Bernardes (a senator from 1929 to 1932) helped organize the unsuccessful Constitutionalist Revolution against Getúlio VARGAS in 1930. He was exiled to Portugal in 1932 for five years. Elected federal deputy upon his return to Brazil, Bernardes continued his nationalistic campaign in which he advocated exploitation of the country's natural resources solely by Brazilians. He lost reelection in 1937 but returned to politics in 1945, when he organized the political party União Democrática Nacional (UDN). Soon after, however, he broke with this party and founded the Partido Republicano (PR), of which he was president until his death in 1955.

— IÊDA SIQUEIRA WIARDA

BERNI, ANTONIO

Antonio Berni (*b.* 14 March 1905; *d.* 13 October 1981), Argentine painter. Berni was born in Rosario, where in 1916 he studied at the Centre Catalá under Eugenio Fornels and Enrique Munné. In 1925 he went to Madrid, and then to Paris, where he studied at the Académie de la Grande Chaumière under André Lothe and Othon Friesz. The influence of the surrealists Salvador Dali and Giorgio de Chirico is evident in his early works. Berni met the Mexican David ALFARO SIQUEIROS in Buenos Aires in 1933, after which he favored representation in his work. In the following decades Berni developed his style in neorealistic, narrative compositions. His creation of two folk figures, "Juanito Laguna" and "Ramona Montiel," constitutes the visual and conceptual synthesis of his attempts to incorporate decorative elements in his art. Berni's creative imagination and enthusiasm were manifest until his last days, when he created three-dimensional animals in assemblages with mannequins, a curious return to the surrealistic output of his early years. Berni received the first prize for painting at the National Salon of Buenos Aires (1937) and the Grand Acquisition Prize, also at the National Salon (1940).

— AMALIA CORTINA ARAVENA

BERRETA, TOMÁS

Tomás Berreta (*b.* 22 November 1875; *d.* 1 August 1947), president of Uruguay (1947). Berreta was from the department of Canelones, where he was a farmhand, cattle driver, policeman, chief of police (1911–1916), and quartermaster general (1917). He was elected to Parliament in 1923 and served as minister of public works (1943–1946) during the presidency of Juan José de AMÉZAGA before being elected president. He died five months into his term.

A man of humble background and a descendant of Italian immigrants, Berreta exemplified through his career the changing nature of Uruguayan society in his day. At age seventeen he met José BATLLE Y ORDÓÑEZ while delivering a report to the newspaper *El Día.* Their friendship helped launch Berreta's political career from a department that was still rural and in which the ideas of Batllismo were just beginning to blossom.

— JOSÉ DE TORRES WILSON

BERRÍO, PEDRO JUSTO

Pedro Justo Berrío (*b.* 28 May 1827; *d.* 14 February 1875), Antioquian (Colombian) statesman. A leader in the department of Antioquia's struggle for self-determination, Berrío, a native of Santa Rosa de Osos, received his doctorate in law at Bogotá in 1851. He subsequently served in the Antioquian Assembly (1852–1853), as a magistrate (1854), and in the national Congress (1856–1857). A Conservative, he led the partisan forces that in December 1863 overthrew the Liberal regime of Antioquia. Berrío's nearly universal support in the department won his government formal recognition from the national Liberal president, Manuel MURILLO TORO, on 18 April 1864. As governor (10 January 1864–7 August 1873), he actively promoted internal improvements such as the Antioquia Railroad. Berrío's importance derives from his success in keeping Antioquia out of the Colombian economic and social turmoil of the 1860s and early 1870s. Antioquia's economy and prosperity expanded considerably during his tenure. Berrío died in Medellín.

– J. LEÓN HELGUERA

BERRO, CARLOS

Carlos Berro (*b.* 17 January 1853; *d.* 15 October 1930), Uruguayan politician. Berro was born in Montevideo, but his family, exiled for belonging to the Blanco (National) Party, resettled in Santiago, Chile, where he received with honors his doctorate in jurisprudence. He returned to his homeland in 1873 and was named counseling judge of the department of Colonia. In 1885 he was elected national representative for the department of Lavalleja. In 1890 he was appointed Minister of justice, culture, and public education by President Julio HERRERA Y OBES. Between 1891 and 1896 he represented the department of Treinta y Tres in the Senate.

Berro participated in the transformation of the Blanco Party into a force that disputed power at the ballot box rather than through revolution.

In the uprisings of 1894 and 1897, Berro joined with the revolutionary forces of Aparicio SARAVIA, the military leader of the Partido Nacionalista. In 1898 he was elected national representative for the department of Montevideo and in 1907 he was elected first vice president of the Directorate. An active militant in the Blanco Party, he participated in the constituent assembly, which in 1917 enacted the first constitutional reform in the history of Uruguay.

Berro's career illustrates the evolution of the Blanco Party at the turn of the century. A student in exile, graduate of a foreign school, and noted lawyer, judge, legislator, revolutionary, and party boss, he later returned to civil activities and participated in the transformation of the Blanco Party into a force that disputed power at the ballot box rather than through revolution. In the elections for the constituent assembly of 30 June 1916 (the first elections in Uruguay to use the secret ballot and proportional representation), Berro was elected, and he helped to write the Constitution of 1917.

– JOSÉ DE TORRES WILSON

BERTONI, MOISÉS

Moisés Bertoni (*b.* 1858; *d.* 19 September 1929), Swiss-born naturalist active in Paraguay. A native of the Alpine cantor of Tessin, Bertoni left an indelible mark on scientific investigation in Paraguay. He attended the universities at Geneva and Zurich where he studied science before arriving in South America in 1884. Advised by the French geographer Elisée Reclus that the Misiones region of northeastern Argentina boasted flora and fauna found nowhere else, Bertoni relocated across the Paraná River to Paraguay in 1887. On the edge of the river, he built a fine home and laboratory at an isolated camp from which he conducted all manner of biological research. He published scores of articles and papers on such topics as yerba mate, ethnobotany, and the habits of aquatic mammals.

President Juan Gualberto González brought Bertoni to Asunción in the early 1890s to head the Jardín Zoológico and the newly established agricultural school. In 1893, while serving in that latter post, he recruited a number of Swiss colonists to settle at Colonia Guillermo Tell (later called Puerto Bertoni) in southeastern Paraguay. He acted as patron to these immigrants, a good many of whom stayed on in the country despite the fact that the colony did not prosper. For his part, Bertoni continued to edit scientific journals and write works on natural history, many of which were printed on a primitive press at Guillermo Tell. His magnum opus, *Descripción física y económica del Paraguay,* filled seventeen volumes, but Bertoni was only able to print four before his death.

– THOMAS L. WHIGHAM

BERTRAND, FRANCISCO

Francisco Bertrand (*b.* 1866; *d.* 1926), president of Honduras. Francisco Bertrand served as president of Honduras three times between 1911 and 1919. Through a policy of reconciliation and control, he imposed order on Honduras's traditionally unstable political system. His first term, 28 March 1911 to 31 January 1912, arose out of an agreement between the government of General Miguel DÁVILA and rebels led by General Manuel BONILLA. Under the Tacoma Pact of 1911, these parties agreed to end hostilities. Bertrand was appointed provisional president and oversaw elections that Bonilla won without opposition. In the succeeding administration, Bertrand became secretary of government and justice, and later vice president. Following Bonilla's death in 1913, Bertrand served as interim president from 20 March 1913 to 28 July 1915. Six months before the end of his presidency, he resigned to campaign for a third term. His third term, from 1 February 1916 to 9 September 1919, was one of relative stability. Bertrand's attempt to impose his own successor, however, led to a rebellion and a return to political chaos. On 9 September 1919, Bertrand resigned from office and left the country.

– PETER A. SZOK

BERUTI, ANTONIO LUIS

Antonio Luis Beruti (*b.* 2 September 1772; *d.* 3 October 1841), military officer in the struggle for Argentine independence. Born in Buenos Aires, Beruti studied in Spain but even before the 1810 revolution was involved with other creole patriots in conspiracy against the colonial regime. He became a strong supporter of the May Revolution of 1810 and of Mariano MORENO against rival revolutionary factions. Beruti held military positions in both Buenos Aires and the interior and accompanied José de SAN MARTÍN in his crossing of the Andes in 1817. After independence he was an active Unitarist and opponent of the dictatorship of Juan Manuel de ROSAS. As such he took part in the civil wars against Rosas, and following the Unitarists' defeat at Rodeo del Medio, Mendoza, in September 1841, he suffered an attack of delirium from which he soon died.

– DAVID BUSHNELL

BERUTTI, ARTURO

Arturo Berutti (*b.* 27 March 1862; *d.* 3 January 1938), Argentine composer. Born in San Juan, Argentina, Berutti studied composition with his father, a composer and pianist, and with Ignacio Álvarez. Later, in Buenos Aires, he was a student of Nicolás Bassi's. At twenty he published his fantasia *Ecos patrióticos* and began writing a series of articles in the *Revista Mefistófeles* to promote musical nationalism. After winning an official scholarship, Berutti traveled to Germany and enrolled at the Leipzig Conservatory (1884), where he studied with

Carl Reinecke and Salomon Jadassohn. In 1887 the Stuttgart Orchestra premiered his *Obertura Andes.* He composed two symphonies on Latin American subjects; *Rivadavia* and *Colombiana* (both in 1888). After traveling to Paris, he settled in Milan, where he wrote the *Sinfonía Argentina* (1890) and *Vendetta,* his first opera, which premiered at the Teatro Lirico in Vercelli. In 1893 his *Evangelina* was performed at Milan's Teatro Alhambra.

Berutti, like the Brazilian Antônio Carlos GOMES, was one of the few South American composers whose operas met with success in Italy. He composed *Pampa* (1897), the first Argentine opera based on the native drama of Juan Moreira. It was followed by *Taras Bulba* (1895), which premiered at the Teatro Regio in Turin, *Yupanki* (1899), *Khrysé* (1903), and *Los héroes* (1909), based on an incident of the de Rosas period. He also composed *Facundo Quiroga* and *El espectro,* both unpublished, and *Horrida Nox,* the first Argentine opera with a Spanish libretto. Although based on Latin American subjects, all of Berutti's operas—as was true of other Latin American operas of the time—were European and classical in style and musical structure. While he was a passionate promoter of nationalism, as a composer Berutti is aesthetically linked to the romantic tradition. With short trips to Argentina, he resided in Europe until 1903, when he returned to Buenos Aires, where he continued to compose until his death. In addition to operas and symphonies, he composed orchestral works and vocal and piano pieces.

– SUSANA SALGADO

BETANCES, RAMÓN EMETERIO

Ramón Emeterio Betances (*b.* 8 April 1827; *d.* 18 September 1898), Puerto Rican abolitionist and revolutionary. A physician, graduate of the University of Paris, Betances lived in exile most of his adult life due to his activism against the Spanish colonial government. During his last residence in Puerto Rico (1853 to 1867), he founded a secret abolitionist society to emancipate slave children in Mayagüez. Exiled again in 1867, he organized an armed expedition that resulted in the failed uprising against Spanish rule of 23 September 1868, known as the Grito de Lares.

– OLGA JIMÉNEZ DE WAGENHEIM

BETANCOURT, RÓMULO

Rómulo Betancourt (*b.* 22 February 1908; *d.* 28 September 1981), president of Venezuela (1945–1948, 1959–1964). The founder of contemporary Venezuelan democracy, Betancourt was also a hemispheric leader and symbol of democratic values and practices. A strong critic and opponent of both Marxist and right-wing authoritarianism, he personified enlightened democratic reformism in the Americas. He was also the founder and organizational genius of Venezuela's political party Democratic Action (Acción Democratica—AD), which he regarded as among his most important achievements. Betancourt's AD has remained a dominant force in Venezuelan politics for a full half-century and has survived his death.

A strong critic and opponent of both Marxist and right-wing authoritarianism, Betancourt personified enlightened democratic reformism in the Americas.

Born to a modest family in Guatire, a town east of Caracas, Betancourt became absorbed by politics during his student days. Emerging as a leader of the "Generation of '28," he was a major participant in the uprising which protested the government of long-time dictator Juan Vicente GÓMEZ. The February 1928 uprising led to the exile of Betancourt and other young Venezuelans until Gómez's death in 1935. It also nourished their intellectual and political hunger for democracy in Venezuela, and led to a search for new political and doctrinal solutions to national problems, especially those related to the overwhelming influence of petroleum on society and national life.

Betancourt assumed a major role in building a reformist political organization following his 1936 return to Caracas. (He returned again in 1941.) He built the nucleus for what later became AD, formally established in September 1941. Having purged Marxist elements from the organization, Betancourt stressed the need for open debate and discussion of petroleum policy and other major issues. When the AD and lesser opposition parties were effectively barred from meaningful participation in elections set for 1945, Betancourt and his colleagues joined with junior military officers to overthrow the existing regime. This so-called October Revolution (1945) introduced a three-year period, the *trienio,* which was marked by dramatic and far-reaching reforms.

For more than two years a seven-person junta headed by Betancourt led Venezuela toward an institutionalized open political system. The Constituent Assembly wrote a new constitution (signed into law 5 July 1947) and national elections held 14 December 1947 brought to office a government headed by the AD's Rómulo GA-

LLEGOS early in 1948. Betancourt and other members of the junta had pledged not to seek office in the next administration. When the government of Gallegos, an eminent writer but inexperienced politician, was overthrown less than a year after being inaugurated, Venezuela entered a decade of military authoritarianism dominated by Marcos PÉREZ JIMÉNEZ.

Betancourt spent a decade of exile in Cuba, Costa Rica, and Puerto Rico. Other prominent party leaders had similar experiences, and those in the underground were persecuted and killed. When a massive civic protest finally led to the collapse of the Pérez Jiménez government in January 1958, Betancourt and other democratic leaders returned home. They created a new arrangement of power sharing, and Betancourt won election to the presidency in December 1958. Although he took office with the support of other democratic parties, he experienced an extraordinarily difficult incumbency.

Remnants of rightist militarism instigated two substantial uprisings. An assassination attempt planned by the Dominican strongman Rafael Leónidas TRUJILLO killed a member of Betancourt's party; Betancourt's hands were burned and his equilibrium was affected. Meanwhile, young admirers of Fidel CASTRO and the Cuban revolution mounted an armed insurgency that brought violence and terrorism in the cities of Venezuela at a time when Betancourt was grappling with a depressed economy left by the corrupt military dictatorship.

Betancourt courted the private sectors, encouraged properly controlled foreign investment, and moved toward a meaningful program of agrarian reform. Labor was supported, education received special attention, and other measures sought to correct social injustices. Betancourt also established warm relations with the Kennedy administration in Washington. The personal friendship of the two presidents grew strong as Venezuela emerged as the model of democratic reformism in Latin America.

As required by the 1961 Constitution, Betancourt left office after his five-year term (1959–1964). Once power had been transferred to Raúl LEONI, another member of the AD's founding generation, Betancourt went into exile for nearly five years, during which time he recuperated from the serious injuries suffered during the attempted assassination. After returning, he declined to run for the presidency in 1973, instead backing Carlos Andrés PÉREZ.

In his final years Betancourt was still a powerful force in AD. A tenacious defender of democratic values, he brooked no opposition to his vision of representative government throughout the hemisphere. He died after suffering a stroke during a visit to New York City and was buried in Caracas.

— JOHN D. MARTZ

BETANCOURT CISNEROS, GASPAR

Gaspar Betancourt Cisneros (*b.* 28 April 1803; *d.* 20 December 1866), Cuban advocate of annexation to the United States. Born in Camagüey, Betancourt Cisneros, also known by his pen name El Lugareño, was a progressive businessman who sponsored the establishment of schools, built bridges, and promoted the construction of the first railroad in his native province of Camagüey. A firm believer in constitutionalism and deeply influenced by physiocratic ideas, he distributed a large portion of his estate to peasants at a minimal cost. He also rejected slavery as the worst evil. Always concerned with Cuba's future, in 1823 Betancourt Cisneros went in search of Simón BOLÍVAR in order to request his support for overthrowing the Spanish yoke. Later he advocated Cuba's annexation to the United States, although, in his view, "Annexation is not a sentiment but a calculation . . . it is the sacred right of self-preservation." Toward the end of his life, however, he returned to his advocacy of independence as he came to distrust U.S. intentions. Betancourt Cisneros died in Havana.

— JOSÉ M. HERNÁNDEZ

BETANCUR CUARTAS, BELISARIO

Belisario Betancur Cuartas (*b.* 4 February 1923), president of Colombia (1982–1986). The second of twenty-two children of a poor family from Amagá, Antioquia, Betancur received a law degree in Medellín in 1947 and worked in Conservative journalism there. In the 1960s he served in the congress and as minister of labor. In 1979 he was appointed ambassador to Spain. After two unsuccessful runs for the presidency, Betancur finally won in 1982. He inherited a banking crisis and a developing recession, which he handled with relative success. His major domestic initiative was an opening to Colombia's guerrilla groups, culminating in truce agreements with three of the four largest in May–August 1984. But by late 1985 these truces collapsed, as dramatically illustrated by M-19's seizure of the Palace of Justice in Bogotá in 1985. Increased pressure against cocaine traffickers, after years of official nonfeasance, led to the assassination of Betancur's minister of justice in April 1984. On the international front, Betancur's advocacy for developing countries at the United Nations in October 1983 won wide applause, as did his role in the Contadora peace process for Central America.

— RICHARD J. STOLLER

BETHANCOURT, PEDRO DE SAN JOSÉ DE

Pedro de San José de Bethancourt (also Betancur; *b.* 21 March 1626; *d.* 25 April 1667), founder of charitable institutions in Guatemala. Born in Villaflor, Canary Islands, Hermano Pedro (as he is known today) traveled to Guatemala in 1650–1651 by way of Cuba. He studied for the priesthood in Santiago de Guatemala but gave up after three years. While he was in nearby Petapa, a vision of the Virgin came to him. Newly encouraged, he returned to Santiago, where, upon relating his experience to his confessor, he was admitted to the Third Order of the Franciscans. Inspired to help the poor and sick, he established a primary school and hospital in a straw hut, becoming known as the "Servant of God." Through charity he raised funds to build a hospital and formed a group of followers whom he called Bethlehemites, in recognition of the importance he placed on the Nativity as a period of Christian devotion each year. When he died, leadership for his work passed to Rodrigo de Arias MALDONADO, known as Rodrigo de la Cruz. Hermano Pedro was buried in the Chapel of the Third Order in the San Francisco church in Santiago (now Antigua), where his tomb continues to be a much-visited shrine. Many miraculous healings have been attributed to him. The request for his beatification was considered from 1712 to 1771, when Pope Clement XIV granted him the status of "Servant of God." Beatification waited until 22 June 1980.

— DAVID L. JICKLING

BIANCO, JOSÉ

José Bianco (*b.* 21 November 1908; *d.* 24 April 1986), Argentine writer, editor, and literary critic. Born in Buenos Aires, Bianco served from 1938 to 1961 as editorial director of Victoria OCAMPO's influential literary and intellectual review *Sur*. After he broke with Ocampo over a visit he made to Cuba (the Cuban Revolution occasioned many partings in Argentine cultural life in the 1960s), Bianco played a major role in the development of the University of Buenos Aires Press, one of the significant axes of cultural development in Argentina until the university was taken over by the military regime in 1966. Throughout his life, Bianco published his critical essays in an impressively diverse array of forums, from the oligarchic daily *La Nación* to the Cuban revolutionary journal *Casa de las Américas*.

Ficción y reflexión (1988) is an anthology of Bianco's literary criticism.

Bianco's creative literature is most identified with early texts: *Sombras suele vestir* (1941), a novel that anticipates the formal experimentation of works twenty years later in its utilization of a fragmented point of view and the counterpoint between narrative shifts and the cruel human drama it chronicles; and *Las ratas* (1943), where a plot turning on murder-suicide displaces the traditional omniscience of the mystery story with the relativization of narrative knowledge. *Las ratas* was enthusiastically acclaimed by Jorge Luis BORGES at a time when the latter was particularly interested in detective fiction, a genre with a long record of influence in Argentine literature.

– DAVID WILLIAM FOSTER

BICALHO OSWALD, HENRIQUE CARLOS

Henrique Carlos Bicalho Oswald (*b.* 1918; *d.* 1965), Brazilian engraver and painter. The son of the painter Carlos Oswald, Bicalho Oswald enrolled in the mid-1940s in the National School of Fine Arts in Rio de Janeiro. While in Paris in 1958, he became acquainted with the printmaker Johnny Friedlaender. Upon his return from Europe in 1959, Henrique settled in Salvador and accepted a position as head of the printmaking department at the University of Bahia. Alongside Hansen-Bahia (Karl Heinz Hansen) and Mario Cravo, Bicalho Oswald helped popularize engraving in Bahia. Although he executed religious canvases and decorative and abstract works, Henrique is best known for figurative works documenting the landscape and daily life of Bahia, including *Inflation, Alone,* and *Northeastern Migrants.*

– CAREN A. MEGHREBLIAN

BIGAUD, WILSON

Wilson Bigaud (*b.* 1933), Haitian painter who has been an integral part of the renaissance of Haitian art. He is

---

Bigaud is hailed as an innovator of the vraiment naïf *genre with his paintings of pop-eyed rural folk and people with disproportionate bodies.*

---

hailed as an innovator of the *vraiment naïf* genre with his paintings of pop-eyed rural folk and people with disproportionate bodies. The renowned artist Hector Hyppolite took Bigaud as an apprentice when the latter

was only fifteen years old. Bigaud joined the Centre d'Art in Port-au-Prince in 1946 and shortly thereafter painted his masterpiece, *Miracle at Cana* (1950–1951), for the Holy Trinity Cathedral. In this work, all Bigaud's trademark elements are present: a jungle murder, a cemetery, drums, and voodoo images, all bathed in a rich yellow light. His *Adam and Eve* is considered the best of all Haitian primitive paintings. In the late 1950s Bigaud suffered a series of nervous breakdowns that interrupted and changed his style, after which he became a recluse.

– KAREN RACINE

BIGNONE, REYNALDO

Reynaldo Bignone (*b.* 21 January 1928), Argentine military leader and president (1982–1983). Born in Morón, province of Buenos Aires, he graduated from the Military Academy (Colegio Militar) in 1947. After attending senior military schools in Argentina and Spain, he became the director of the Military Academy in 1975. Throughout his career, Bignone led numerous missions to Europe. Between 5 December 1980 and 4 December 1981 he was the commander of the Campo de Mayo military base, Argentina's most important military installation and detention site for those suspected of being guerrillas. General Bignone retired on 4 January 1982. Following the disastrous Falklands/Malvinas War, Bignone was named provisional president by the outgoing military junta and given the task of overseeing the transition to civilian rule. The Bignone junta passed an amnesty law absolving military figures who had participated in the Dirty War, but it was voided by the new civilian government that took office on 10 December 1983.

– ROBERT SCHEINA

BILAC, OLAVO

Olavo Bilac (*b.* 16 December 1865; *d.* 18 December 1918), Brazilian poet. Declared in 1907 "the prince of Brazilian poets," Bilac was one of the greatest figures in Parnassianism. This movement in poetry, like naturalism in the novel, displayed the same antiromantic revolt that dominated the literary scene at the end of the nineteenth century. Bilac was born in Rio de Janeiro. His first book of poems, *Poesias* (1888), was warmly received, and the author was lauded by the leaders of Parnassianism. In the first poem of the collection, "Profissão de fé" (Profession of Faith), the author insists on the Parnassian ideal of language perfection. He viewed the poet's task as similar to that of a goldsmith fashioning delicate jewels: "When I write, I envy the goldsmith/I imitate the love/With which he, in golden relief/Creates his flowers." He expressed his love for the Portuguese language in "Língua Portuguesa": "I love your agrestic lushness and your aroma/Of virgin forests and large oceans!/I love your rude and dolorous idiom." He conserved this spirit throughout his life.

Bilac worked with a great variety of themes—personal and historical—the latter ranging from classical Rome to Brazilian history. His lyrical production diverges from exaggerated sentimentalism to sensualism. In "Ouvir estrelas" he converses with the stars, explaining, "Love and you will understand them./Only one in love is/Able to listen to and understand the stars." His love poems, the best of his work, are still very much alive. Part of the contemporaneous force of Bilac's lyrics lies in the plasticity of the universe created by his verse: forms, colors, textures, sounds, and movements breathe life into his imagined world.

Bilac had illustrious careers in government and literature. He was a founding member of the Brazilian Academy of Letters, and he was above all a revered poet whose verse resounds in the voice and heart of his people. Additional works by Bilac include *Poesias* (2d ed., 1902), *Conferências literárias* (1906), *Ironia e piedade* (1916), and *Últimas conferências e discursos* (1924).

– MARIA ISABEL ABREU

BILBAO BARQUÍN, FRANCISCO

Francisco Bilbao Barquín (*b.* 9 January 1823; *d.* 19 February 1865), Chilean radical. Born in Santiago and educated at the Instituto Nacional, Bilbao quickly revealed radical tendencies. His controversial article "La sociabilidad chilena" (The Nature of Chilean Society), published in the journal *El Crepúsculo* (June 1844), was immediately condemned by the authorities as blasphemous and immoral, though not subversive. In October 1844 Bilbao left for Europe, staying in Paris and making the acquaintance of the French thinkers Hugh-Félicité-Robert Lamennais (1782–1854), Jules Michelet (1798–1874), and Edgar Quinet (1803–1875). From autumn 1847 to summer 1848 he traveled in Germany, Austria, and Italy: he was in Paris in time to witness revolutionary activity there.

In February 1850 Bilbao returned to Chile where, with Santiago ARCOS and others, he formed the Sociedad de la Igualdad (Society for Equality) in April 1850. The society's leaders took nicknames from figures of the French Revolution: Bilbao's was Vergniaud, a testimony to his considerable talent for oratory. He went into hiding when the society was suppressed in November 1850. He fought in the Santiago insurrection of 20 April 1851 and later went into hiding and then into exile in Peru; he never returned to Chile. In 1855 he moved to Europe and in 1857 he made his final move to Argentina.

Bilbao's writings, liberal and democratic in content, are high-flown and often very lyrical. His works *La América en peligro* (America in Danger, 1862) and *El evangelio americano* (The American Gospel, 1864) highlight the contrast between the free and prosperous United States and the "disunited states" of Spanish America.

– SIMON COLLIER

BILLINGHURST, GUILLERMO ENRIQUE

Guillermo Enrique Billinghurst (*b.* 1851; *d.* 1915), Peruvian populist president (1912–1914), heir to the dictatorial tradition of civilian caudillo Nicolás de PIÉROLA. Born in Arica to a family whose wealth originated in the nitrate business, Billinghurst supported, financially and politically, Piérola's forceful actions to become president.

In 1894–1895 Billinghurst financed Piérola's forces fighting a civil war against General Andrés CÁCERES. Following Piérola's success in 1895, Billinghurst became first vice president and president of the Chamber of Senators. In 1898 he was in charge of negotiating a settlement over the Chilean-occupied territories of Tacna and Arica, which was turned down by the Chilean legislature. Failing to obtain official support due to Piérola's pact with the Civilista Party, Billinghurst lost the presidential elections of 1899. However, after reorganizing Piérola's former Democratic Party in 1908, Billinghurst became mayor of Lima (1908) and in 1912 was finally elected president of the republic. Attempting to establish stronger executive and protectionist changes, he faced a strong opposition by the Civilistas. When he tried to close the legislature in 1914, Billinghurst was ousted by a military coup led by General Oscar Benavides. Billinghurst died in Iquique.

– ALFONSO W. QUIROZ

BIOY CASARES, ADOLFO

Adolfo Bioy Casares (*b.* 15 September 1914), Argentine novelist, essayist, and short-story writer. Born in Buenos Aires, he studied law and philosophy and letters, but chose instead to run his family's estancia. In 1932 he became a close friend of Jorge Luis BORGES, with whom, under the pseudonyms of H. Bustos Domecq, B. Suárez Lynch, and B. Lynch Davis, he wrote several detective stories. He is chiefly identified as a writer of fantastic literature due to his novel *La invención de Morel* (1940; *The Invention of Morel and other Stories,* 1964), which was awarded the Municipal Prize for Literature in 1941. This book marks the beginning of the modern science-fiction narrative in Argentine literature. In the same year, he wrote and published, together with his wife, the writer Silvina Ocampo, and Borges, the now classic *Antología de la literatura fantástica*.

Bioy demonstrated a wide range of narrative interests, from thrillers to love stories, with existentialist, Gothic, and pseudoscientific themes, and displayed his ability for light humor as well as dark irony and hallucinatory fantasies. He has written about thirty books, many of which have been made into movies and television productions in Argentina and Italy, and he has received the Cervantes Prize (Spain, 1991), the Mondello Award (Italy, 1984), and the National Literary Award (Argentina, 1962 and 1967). In 1973 he was awarded the major literary prize of his country, the Grand Prize of the Argentina Society of Writers.

— ANGELA B. DELLEPIANE

BLANCO, ANDRÉS ELOY

Andrés Eloy Blanco (*b.* 6 August 1897; *d.* 21 May 1955), Venezuelan poet, journalist, and statesman. A prolific author of poetry, theater, stories and anecdotes, innumerable articles in periodicals, and political speeches, Blanco is chiefly remembered today for his very popular poems in a folkloric vein and for his humorous writings. He was also, however, a lifelong (and frequently imprisoned or exiled) opponent of successive dictatorships and an important figure in the evolution of what came to be the Acción Democrática party. He is credited with important contributions in the drafting of the 1947 Constitution, and he served as minister of foreign affairs during the brief presidency of Rómulo GALLEGOS (February–November 1948). In his poetry he was among the earliest in this century to reabsorb traditional Hispanic popular forms and themes into contemporary poetic practice; many of his works in this mode are charming, some are memorable. Juan Liscano and Efraín Subero note an underlying Christian attitude in his hopeful celebrations of common people and his vision of the nation. Subsequent generations of poets have turned away from Blanco's regionalist or nativist manner. Some of his verses have entered oral tradition, and he remains widely read by the general public, for whom he stands alone among modern Venezuelan poets as a national icon.

— MICHAEL J. DOUDOROFF

BLANCO, JOSÉ FÉLIX

José Félix Blanco (*b.* 24 September 1782; *d.* 18 March 1872), officer in the Venezuelan Emancipating Army,

politician, and historian. Blanco studied in the seminary of Caracas and was ordained a priest in 1809. At the beginning of the movement for independence in 1810, he joined the patriotic forces as an army chaplain. He participated in numerous campaigns from 1812 to 1817, when Simón BOLÍVAR assigned him to the administration of the missions of Caroní. Blanco attended the Congress of Cúcuta in 1821. Political and military activities distanced him from his priestly duties and, in 1833, he requested (of Rome) and was granted secularization. Over the next two decades, Blanco was commandant of Maracaibo, secretary of war and the navy, a candidate for vice president and president of the Republic, and secretary of finance and foreign affairs.

After leaving public life in 1854, Blanco repeatedly sought reordination, which was finally granted in 1863. From 1855 until his death, he dedicated himself to the compilation and organization, with Ramón Azpurua, of the documents and testimonies relative to the history of the emancipation. The voluminous collection was published after his death under the title *Documentos para la historia de la vida pública del Libertador* (1875–1877). Its fourteen volumes constitute, even today, one of the most important collections of documents on Latin American emancipation.

— INÉS QUINTERO

BLANCO, JUAN

Juan Blanco (*b.* 29 June 1920), Cuban composer. Born in Havana, Blanco began his traditional composition studies at the Municipal Conservatory in Havana and then studied at the University of Havana under the guidance of Harold Gramatges and José ARDÉVOL.

Blanco's Poema espacial, *no. 3 combines sound and light and requires the use of four tape tracks distributed among thirty-seven loudspeakers.*

During the mid-1950s he taught himself the techniques of *musique concrète,* electronic music, recording, as well as the use of sound for films. In 1969 he became the main musical adviser for the House of the Americas in Havana. Blanco is a prolific writer and critic who has published many articles and written criticism for several Cuban magazines and newspapers. Almost all his compositions since 1965 involve the use of electronic techniques and mixed media. Blanco has done extensive research with "spatial techniques," in some cases utilizing multiple loudspeaker networks. *Poema espacial,* no. 3 ("Viet-Nam," 1968), combines sound and light and requires the use of four tape tracks distributed among thirty-seven loudspeakers.

Other important compositions are *Canto a la paz* for soloists, mixed choir, and orchestra (1952); Elegy for orchestra (1956), a memorial to the fighters who died during the Cuban Revolution; *Divertimento* for string orchestra (1954); Quintet for winds, timpani, and piano (1972); *Música para danza* (1961); Études, nos. 1 and 2 for tape (1962–1963); *Texturas* for orchestra and tape (1963–1964); *Pirofonías* (1976); Episodes for orchestra (1964); *Contrapunto espacial,* no. 1 (1965–1966); *Erotofonías* for orchestra and tape (1968); and *Erotofonías,* no. 2 (1974) for tape. Blanco composed tape music for the Cuban Pavilion at Expo '67 and Expo '70 and for the São Paulo Biennial in 1988. For several years he has produced and directed the International Festival of Electroacoustic Music in Varadero, Cuba.

– ALCIDES LANZA

BLANCO ACEVEDO, EDUARDO

Eduardo Blanco Acevedo (*b.* 19 March 1894; *d.* 1971), Uruguayan politician. Born in Montevideo, Blanco Acevedo received his medical degree in 1908 from the Facultad de Medicina de Montevideo. After joining the diplomatic corps, he served as attaché to the Uruguayan embassy in France in 1909, undersecretary at the Uruguayan embassy in Belgium in 1912. From 1914 to 1919 he worked as a surgeon in various French hospitals; he was appointed chief surgeon of the Rothschild Hospital in 1915. The French government conferred on him the title of chevalier in the Legion of Honor. His family was historically associated with the Colorado Party and related to president and later dictator Gabriel TERRA, in whose regime, which began 31 March 1933, Blanco Acevedo participated. When Terra's mandate ended, according to the stipulations of the Constitution of 1934, Blanco Acevedo was one of the candidates who hoped to succeed him in the 1938 elections. Also running in the election was General Alfredo BALDOMIR, who won, it is said, due to the women's vote, which was exercised for the first time in Uruguay. Nevertheless, Blanco Acevedo's politics (Blanco Acevedismo) remained a conservative force within the Colorado Party, and Blanco Acevedo held the post of national adviser to the government from 1952 to 1955.

– JOSÉ DE TORRES WILSON

BLANCO ENCALADA, MANUEL

Manuel Blanco Encalada (*b.* 21 April 1790; *d.* 5 September 1876), first president of Chile, first commander of the Chilean navy, and longest-surviving hero of Chile's Wars of Independence. Born in Buenos Aires, he served in the Spanish navy before returning to South America to play his part in the struggle for independence, during which he fought in numerous actions in Chile. In June 1818 he was named commander of the newly formed Chilean navy, handing it over to Lord Thomas Alexander Cochrane at the end of that year; but when Cochrane left Chile in January 1823, Blanco Encalada resumed command.

As president of Chile from July to September 1826, he was the first Chilean head of state to be called President rather than Supreme Director. In 1837 he was given command of the first Chilean offensive against the Peru–Bolivia Confederation. His assent to the Treaty of Paucarpata (17 November 1837), entailing Chilean withdrawal from Peru, was repudiated by the government and led to his court-martial, but he was acquitted. He was later intendant of Valparaíso (1847–1852) and minister to France (1852–1858).

– SIMON COLLIER

BLANCO FOMBONA, RUFINO

Rufino Blanco Fombona (*b.* 17 June 1874; *d.* 17 October 1944), Venezuelan writer. One of the most widely read Latin American authors of his generation, Blanco Fombona began his career as a politician at the age of eighteen when he participated in a movement against President Raimundo ANDUEZA PALACIO. At twenty, he went to Philadelphia as Venezuelan consul. Two years later he moved to The Hague in the same capacity. Between 1900 and 1905 he served the government of Cipriano CASTRO as secretary general of the state of Zulia (1900), consul to the Netherlands (1901–1904), and governor of the Amazon Territory (1905). His political career ended in 1910, when Juan Vicente GÓMEZ forced him into exile in France and Spain until 1936. In exile, Blanco Fombona carried on an ardent campaign against Gómez, and fought despotism in his writings and through participation in a number of abortive anti-Gómez revolts.

Both before and during his exile, Blanco Fombona wrote a number of important essays and novels. His works reflected his life, often in an autobiographical manner, and his commitment to expressions of Spanish Americanism. Like Leopoldo LUGONES in Argentina and José VASCONCELOS in Mexico, he relied on creole themes that dealt with political corruption, anti-imperialism, and celebration of the best aspects of Spanish-American society. Several times nominated for the Nobel Prize in literature, he produced works that included a wide range of subjects and genres, from poetry to history, from literary criticism to political commentary.

— WINTHROP R. WRIGHT

BLANCO GALDÓS, HUGO

Hugo Blanco Galdós (*b.* 1934), Quechua-speaking agronomist, Trotskyist, and former student leader. Born in Cuzco, in 1958 Blanco organized the small tenant farmers of the coffee-growing valleys of La Convención in the high jungle north of Cuzco into a peasant federation that challenged the traditional landlord class. After a series of strikes, land invasions, and armed clashes with the police as well as the spread of such tactics into the southern and central sierra, the government of Manuel PRADO was compelled to establish a commission to study the possibility of agrarian reform. Imprisoned in 1963, Blanco was later released, served as an adviser to the government of Juan VELASCO on agrarian reform, and continues to be active in leftist politics.

— PETER F. KLARÉN

BLANCO GALINDO, CARLOS

Carlos Blanco Galindo (*b.* 12 March 1882; *d.* 3 October 1953), president of Bolivia (June 1930–March 1931). Born in Cochabamba to a patrician family with roots going back to the time of Bolívar, Blanco Galindo was an urbane scholar and army officer with a long history of public and international service. Upon the dissolution of the Hernando Siles Reyes government in May 1930, a military junta chaired by Blanco Galindo assumed power. As the new acting president, he was determined not to stay in power, however, and prepared the way for an elected civilian government, that of Daniel SALAMANCA, who was inaugurated on 5 March 1931. Blanco Galindo's short term was one of the most productive in Bolivia's history. Among its achievements was an educational reform that included university autonomy. After 1931 Blanco Galindo continued to serve the nation and Cochabamba but stayed aloof from the squabbles of the military during the tragic Chaco War. He died in Cochabamba.

— CHARLES W. ARNADE

BLANES, JUAN MANUEL

Juan Manuel Blanes (*b.* ca. 1 June 1830; *d.* 15 April 1901), Uruguayan artist, regarded as the founder of Uruguayan art. Born in Montevideo, Blanes abandoned school at age eleven to work and help his humble family. Around 1843 he moved with his mother and brothers to El Cerrito, returning to Montevideo in 1853, where he made his living as a typographer. In 1855 Blanes moved to the town of Salto, where he taught painting at the School of Humanities and painted commissioned portraits. In 1856 he painted eight pictures of Justo José de URQUIZA's military victories for the general's San José Palace. He returned to Montevideo at the outbreak of a yellow fever epidemic, which he documented in a now lost painting (1857). At Urquiza's request he painted the general's family as well as religious themes for the chapel at San José Palace. In 1860, on a grant from the Uruguayan government, he moved to Paris, then to Florence, where he studied at the Florentine Academy with Antonio Ciseri. From then on academic neoclassicism marked his artistic production.

In 1865 Blanes returned to Uruguay and for the next fifteen years received commissions to paint the portraits of famous Latin American personalities, including Paraguayan President Francisco SOLANO LÓPEZ. His historical paintings earned him prestige in Argentina and Chile. Blanes revealed a naturalistic approach to painting when dealing with subjects of contemporary significance (*Yellow Fever in Buenos Aires,* 1871) and in his series of gauchos (*Dawn*). From 1879 to 1883 he was living once again in Florence, where he painted *Paraguay: Image of Your Desolate Country* (ca. 1880), an allegorical image of Paraguay after the devastating War of the Triple Alliance. After returning to Montevideo in 1883, he worked on a portrait of Uruguayan general José ARTIGAS. The Argentine government commissioned his renowned *Review of Río Negro by General Roca and His Army.* Blanes moved to Pisa in 1898, where he died. He was buried at the Pantéon Nacional in Montevideo.

— MARTA GARSD

BLEST GANA, ALBERTO

Alberto Blest Gana (*b.* 4 May 1830; *d.* 9 November 1920), Chilean novelist and diplomat. One of the most important Latin American novelists of his period, Blest Gana studied engineering in France and taught mathematics in Chile before embarking on his first series of novels, the best known of which are *Martín Rivas* (1862) and *El ideal de una calavera* (A foolish ideal, 1863). The first of these, his most popular novel, depicts the fortunes of a provincial youth in the Santiago of 1850, with a wealth of precise social observation: it is as good a fictional account of mid-nineteenth-century Santiago as can be found. He greatly admired Honoré de Balzac (1799–1850) and regarded him as something of a model. In 1866 Blest Gana joined the staff of the Chilean embassy in Washington, D.C., and spent most of the rest of his life abroad as a diplomat, serving successfully as ambassador to both France and Britain.

A long hiatus in his creative work ended with the publication of *Durante la reconquista* (During the reconquista, 1897), a lengthy and somewhat ponderous historical novel portraying the years 1814 to 1817 in Chile. *Los transplantados* (The uprooted, 1904) scrutinizes rich South Americans in high-society Europe. In 1909 Blest Gana reverted to the theme of the Santiago of his youth in the charming *El loco Estero* (The madman Estero), whose opening pages evoke in superb fashion the victory parade at the end of Chile's war against the Peru-Bolivia Confederation. At its best, Blest Gana's style is lively, but his work is uneven in quality. His older brother Guillermo Blest Gana (1829–1905) was among the better-known poets of nineteenth-century Chile.

— SIMON COLLIER

BOBADILLA, FRANCISCO DE

Francisco de Bobadilla (*d.* ca. 1502), governor and judge of the island of Hispaniola. Bobadilla was probably from an Aragonese family, although the date and place of his birth are uncertain. Appointed on 21 May 1499, he was given authority superseding that of Christopher COLUMBUS. The purpose of the royal appointment was to end instability and strife in the colony. Arriving in Santo Domingo on 23 August 1500, Bobadilla might have seen the executed enemies of Columbus while disembarking. He had Columbus jailed upon his return from an expedition into the interior in September 1500. It was Bobadilla's intention to send him to the Spanish court for trial, where a powerful group rejecting the pretensions of the Italian explorer was active.

Appointed on 21 May 1499, Bobadilla was given

authority superseding that of Christopher Columbus.

As planned, both Columbus and his brother Bartolomé were returned under arrest to Spain. The crown, however, convinced that Bobadilla had exceeded the authority of his instructions, freed the Columbus brothers soon after their arrival in Spain. Bobadilla, disgraced for acting too strongly against Columbus, embarked for Spain in 1502. Unfortunately, that June his fleet was caught in a powerful hurricane in which almost all the ships were lost and much of the documentation involving the early administration of the island destroyed. The

historian Oviedo characterized Bobadilla as "honest and religious."

— NOBLE DAVID COOK

BOBO, ROSALVO

Rosalvo Bobo (*d.* 1929), Haitian populist leader of the Cacos rebellion of 1915. On 28 July 1915, U.S. Marines landed at Port-au-Prince in response to the orders of Admiral William B. Caperton to restore civil order following the death of President Jean Vilbrun Guillaume SAM. They were also to prevent Rosalvo Bobo, Sam's political opponent and critic of U.S. imperialism in Haiti, from assuming the presidency.

Bobo opposed the McDonald contract, an attempt by a U.S. company to build a railroad through northern Haiti that would have involved the seizure of Haitians' property through eminent domain. He was also against U.S. receivership of Haitian customs. Thus the United States blocked his election to the Haitian presidency in 1915, instead ensuring that of Philippe-Sudré DARTIGUENAVE, a puppet ruler. Bobo fled to Cuba, then to Jamaica and finally France, where he died.

— THOMAS O. OTT

BOCAIÚVA, QUINTINO

Quintino Bocaiúva (*b.* 4 December 1836; *d.* 11 July 1912), journalist and a founding father of the Brazilian Republic. Born Quintino Ferreira de Souza, Bocaiúva was the main author of the Republican Manifesto of 1870, in which he defended the idea of a Liberal and federalist republic to be engendered through pacific means, by "evolution" rather than "revolution." He also criticized the isolation of Brazil as a monarchy among the neighboring republics. "We belong to America and want to be Americans" is one of the most quoted phrases of the manifesto. Elected president of the Republican Party in May 1889, Bocaiúva was prominent among those who instigated the military question and, through it, promoted the alliance of the Republicans with the army, the "yellow button" as they termed it. For this reason he was called a militarist and even an opportunist by his fellow Republicans.

When the Republic was proclaimed, on 15 November 1889, Bocaiúva was the only civilian leader to head the military parade alongside Marshal Deodoro da FONSECA and Lieutenant Colonel Benjamin CONSTANT BOTELHO DE MAGALHÃES. A prominent figure of the new regime, he was Minister of Foreign Affairs until the collective resignation of the first Republican ministry on 20 January 1891 and senator for Rio de Janeiro, elected in 1890 and reelected several times until his death. From 1901 until 1903, he served as governor of the state of Rio de Janeiro.

— EDUARDO SILVA

BODEGA Y QUADRA, JUAN FRANCISCO DE LA

Juan Francisco de la Bodega y Quadra (*b.* 22 August 1737; *d.* 26 March 1794), Spanish naval officer, explorer of the Pacific Northwest. Born in Lima, Peru, Bodega became a Spanish naval officer and was posted to the department of San Blas in 1774. The following year he had command of the *Sonora* on its voyage to southern Alaska. Bodega was promoted to ship's lieutenant in 1776 and commanded *La Favorita,* which sailed to Alaska, in 1779. He remained in San Blas in 1780–1781, then went to Peru to obtain artillery in 1782. After serving in Spain from 1783 to 1789, Bodega returned to San Blas as its commandant in 1790. He was at Nootka in 1792 as the Spanish commissioner under the 1790 convention with Great Britain. With his British counterpart, George Vancouver, Bodega circumnavigated the island later named for both men. After returning to San Blas in 1793, he retired because of poor health. Bodega died in Mexico City.

— W. MICHAEL MATHES

BOERO, FELIPE

Felipe Boero (*b.* 1 May 1884; *d.* 9 August 1958), Argentine composer and teacher. Born in Buenos Aires, Boero studied with the composer Pablo Berutti until 1912, when, as a winner of the *Premio Europa* (Europe Prize) established by the Argentine Ministry of Culture, he traveled to France to study at the National Conservatory in Paris under Paul Vidal and Gabriel Fauré (1912–1914). Upon his return to Argentina he founded the National Music Society—later known as the Argentine Association of Composers—which was dedicated to the promotion of Argentine works. A high point in his pedagogic career came in 1934, when the National Council of Education commissioned Boero to create and direct a choral group of two thousand voices. In 1935 he became a member of the National Fine Arts Committee and was appointed music professor and choir director at both the Mariano Acosta Normal School for Teachers and the Manuel Belgrano Institute.

Boero's first opera, *Tucumán,* which premiered in 1918 at the Teatro Colón in Buenos Aires, was the first opera on a Spanish libretto to be composed in the nationalist style; it won the Municipal Prize. Boero wrote seven more works for the stage: the opera-ballet *Ariana y Dionysos* (1916) and the operas *Raquela* (1918), *Siripo*

(1924), *El Matrero* (1925), *Zincalí* (1933), plus two incidental works: *Las bacantes* (1925) and *El inglés de los "güesos"* (1938). *El Matrero,* premiered at the Colón in 1929 under the baton of Ettore Panizza, became the most performed, most popular Argentine opera of the first half of the twentieth century, and was recorded by RCA Victor. Boero composed several orchestral works, among them *Suite de danzas argentinas* (1920–1930), *Madrugada en la pampa* (1930), *Suite argentina* (1940), a Mass (1918) on Latin text, as well as works for vocal soloist and orchestra, for orchestra with choir, choral works, songs, many works for piano, and a collection of children's songs.

— SUSANA SALGADO

BOFF, LEONARDO

Leonardo Boff (*b.* 14 December 1938), Brazilian theologian. A Franciscan priest born in Concordia, Brazil, Boff is arguably Brazil's best-known theologian and is one of the world's foremost liberation theologians. He studied theology in Brazil and Germany, where he did his doctoral work, and was ordained in 1964. His book *Jesus Christ, Liberator,* which portrayed Christ as a liberator of the poor, brought him international visibility and acclaim after its publication in 1972 (English trans. 1978). Since then, Boff has published scores of books that deal with a wide range of themes. In 1972 he was named editor of Brazil's foremost theological journal, the *Revista eclesiástica brasileira.*

In the mid-1970s, the Vatican began investigating Boff's work on the grounds that it strayed too far from Catholic orthodoxy.

In the late 1970s, as Brazil's military regime began to show signs of unraveling and as the opposition conquered new spaces for contestation, Boff became more involved in writing about explicitly political themes. He expressed his support for the leftist Workers' Party and, in the mid-1980s, declared his admiration for the Soviet Union.

In the mid-1970s, the Vatican began investigating Boff's work on the grounds that it strayed too far from Catholic orthodoxy. Boff's life after the publication of *Church: Charisma and Power* (1981; English trans. 1985) was marked by increasing controversy as his work came under attack by conservative theologians and clerics. Calling for a church born from the faith of the poor, Boff's book criticized the Catholic church for being authoritarian and excessively concerned with power. Conservatives counterargued that Boff was unduly critical of the institution, and that the pope and bishops must assume responsibility for leadership in the church. In this view, popular religion therefore holds no special claim to truth in the church.

In September 1984, Boff went to Rome to defend his writings. After several months of deliberation, the Vatican formally criticized Boff's work in May 1985, imposing a silence that was lifted the following year. Because Boff was so prominent, this sanction was broadly perceived as an attack upon the liberation theology movement. In May 1991, Boff was again sanctioned by the Vatican, which required him to resign as editor of the *Revista Eclesiástica Brasileira* and ordered him not to publish any works for a year.

— SCOTT MAINWARING

BOLAÑOS, CÉSAR

César Bolaños (*b.* 4 June 1931), Peruvian composer. He was born in Lima and began his musical studies with Andrés Sas at the National Conservatory in Lima and then studied electronic music at the RCA Institute of Electronic Technology in New York City (1958–1963). His postgraduate studies took place at the Latin American Center for Advanced Musical Studies at the Torcuato di Tella Institute in Buenos Aires, where his mentors were composers Alberto GINASTERA and Gerardo GANDINI. Bolaños collaborated with the electronic music laboratory, founded in Buenos Aires in 1964. He taught the seminar on electroacoustic composition and gave classes on audiovisual theory. His main compositional efforts since 1970 have utilized computers, and many of his works were created at the facilities of Honeywell Bull Argentina. To refer to some of these works generically Bolaños used the acronym ESEPCO, for *estructuras sonora-expresivas por computación* (digital sonic-expressive structures). At the Di Tella Laboratories in 1964 he created his first electronic tape composition, *Intensidad y altura,* based on a poem by César VALLEJO. Other important compositions by Bolaños include *Ñacahuasu* for chamber orchestra and narrator (1970); *Ensayo* for string orchestra (1956); *Cantata solar* for orchestra, choirs, solo voices, and tape (1963); *Variaciones* for alto, flute, clarinet, bass clarinet, double bass, and percussion (1963), with text by César Vallejo; *Divertimento,* no. 1 for flute, clarinet, bass clarinet, trumpet, harpsichord, piano, double bass, and percussion (1966); and *Divertimento,* no. 3 for flute, clarinet, bass clarinet, piano, and percussion (1967). Among his most theatrical works are *I-10-AIFG/Mn1-1* for flute, violin, accordion, two percussionists, and three narra-

tors (1969); *Alfa-Omega* for two narrators, theatrical mixed choir, electric guitar, double bass, two percussionists, two dancers, tape, slide projections, and lights (1967), which utilizes biblical texts; and the celebrated *I-10-AIFG/Rbt-1* for three narrators, horn, trombone, electric guitar, two percussionists, two operators for keyboard controlled lights and six radios, nine slide projectors with automatic synchronization, tape, and instrumental amplification, with black lights for the reading of scores and "programmed conducting" using synchronized light signals (1968).

— ALCIDES LANZA

BOLAÑOS, LUIS DE

Luis de Bolaños (*b.* 1549; *d.* 11 October 1629), Franciscan missionary. Called the Apostle of Paraguay, Bolaños was born in Marchena, Spain, in Andalusia. He joined the Franciscan order as a youth and was ordained a deacon. In 1572 he volunteered to serve as a missionary in the Río de la Plata and left Spain with his mentor and friend Fray Alonso de Buenaventura. After arriving in Paraguay in 1575, the two friars preached to Guaranis near Asunción and then in the northern area of the Jejui Guazú River, where the followers of Cacique Overá were resisting Spanish pressure. There in 1580, the missionaries founded Altos, the first enduring reduction of Paraguay. Later, Bolaños and Buenaventura founded Ypané, Atyrá, Tobatí, Itá, Yaguarón, Yuty, and Caazapá, which all survive. Bolaños attempted to work in the part of Guairá that is now the state of Paraná in Brazil, but the Spanish colonists there expelled him for blocking their exploitation of Native American labor. After mastering the Guarani language, Bolaños wrote a Guarani grammar and vocabulary and became the primary translator into Guarani of the catechism of the Council of Lima of 1583, the basis for instruction in the Franciscan reductions and the later Jesuit missions of Paraguay.

In 1585 Bolaños was ordained a priest, and after 1600 he cooperated with Governor Hernando ARIAS DE SAAVEDRA, Bishop Martín Ignacio de Loyola, and colonizer Juan de GARAY to extend Spanish secular and religious authority. The more famous Jesuit reductions of Paraguay founded after 1610 were partly the fruition of the methods of Franciscans like Bolaños, who advised Father Manuel de Lorenzana and other members of the Society of Jesus. Though famous as a missionary, Bolaños was also an able administrator. At the end of his life, he retired to the Franciscan house in Buenos Aires, where he died. In 1979 his body was returned to Asunción, Paraguay, where he is a national hero.

— JAMES SCHOFIELD SAEGER

BOLÍVAR, SIMÓN

Simón Bolívar (*b.* 24 July 1783; *d.* 17 December 1830), foremost leader of Spanish American independence. Born in Caracas to a wealthy landed family with slave-worked cacao plantations, Simón Bolívar received little

Portrait of Simón Bolívar by José Gil de Castro, 1825. (Organization of American States)

formal education, although his private tutor, Simón Rodríguez, helped instill in him an admiration for the thinkers of the European Enlightenment. Bolívar traveled to Europe in 1799, and in Madrid in 1802 he married María Teresa Rodríguez de Toro, the daughter of a Caracas-born aristocrat. Upon her death soon after they returned to Venezuela, he made a second trip to Europe, during which he vowed to work for the liberation of Spanish America.

When the Napoleonic invasion of Spain triggered the crisis of the Spanish monarchy in 1808–1810, Bolívar played a minor role in the various attempts to set up a governing junta in Caracas. However, once a junta was created, in April 1810, he became an active participant in the revolutionary movement. After heading a diplomatic mission sent to London, he pressed for an outright declaration of independence, which was issued on 5 July 1811.

Having served as a colonial militia officer, though without formal military training, Bolívar was eventually given military command of the key coastal fortress of Puerto Cabello, whose loss in July 1812 served to hasten (though it hardly caused) the collapse of Venezuela's First Republic. When the Venezuelan dictator Francisco de MIRANDA accepted the inevitable and signed a capitulation to the royalists, Bolívar was one of those who angrily arrested him and by preventing his escape in effect turned Miranda over to the Spanish. Bolívar himself soon escaped to Curaçao and from there to Cartagena in New Granada, where he issued the Cartagena Manifesto (the first of his major political documents) and sought assistance for a new attempt to liberate Venezuela. With help from the United Provinces of New Granada, he invaded his homeland in 1813, and in less than three months swept into Caracas. This *campaña admirable* (admirable campaign), as it has been called, first earned Bolívar the title of "Liberator" and made him the acknowledged political as well as military leader of Venezuela.

Bolívar chose not to restore the federal constitution adopted in 1811 by the First Republic, believing that federalism was a dangerously weak form of government. The Second Republic that he then created, a frank military dictatorship, was no more successful than its predecessor, for it was soon being worn down by the assault of royalist guerrilla bands. Appealing to the Venezuelan masses to reject an independence movement whose principal figures (like Bolívar) were drawn from the creole elite, the royalists found a favorable response especially among the rough cowboy population (*llaaneros*) of the Orinoco plains. Before the end of 1814, Bolívar was again a fugitive in New Granada.

B Bolívar, Simón

Despite his distaste for federalism, Bolívar repaid the New Granadan federalists grouped in the United Provinces for the aid they had given him by helping them subdue Bogotá, whose leaders favored a strong central authority. But he had little desire to take part in this or other internecine conflicts of the New Granadan patriots, especially when the defeat of Napoleon in Europe and restoration of Ferdinand VII to his throne now permitted Spain to redouble its efforts to suppress colonial rebellion. In mid-1815 Bolívar left New Granada, shortly before the arrival of the Spanish expeditionary force that would reconquer most of it for the king. Bolívar went first to Jamaica, where in his "Jamaica Letter" he offered a keen analysis of the present and future state of Spanish America. He next moved to Haiti, where he obtained help from the Haitian government for a new attempt to liberate Venezuela—and for a second attempt when the first ended in failure. By the end of 1816, he had regained a foothold and made contact with revolutionary bands still active in northeastern Venezuela.

In July 1817, Bolívar's forces seized Angostura (today Ciudad Bolívar), on the lower Orinoco River. The port of Angostura gave Bolívar a link to the outside world, while the Orinoco River system facilitated contact with pockets of patriot resistance in other parts of the Orinoco Basin, including the Apure region, where José Antonio PÁEZ had won increasing numbers of llaneros over to the patriot cause. When Páez accepted Bolívar's leadership, the Liberator gained a critically important ally. As a llanero himself, Páez helped to give the independence struggle a more popular image. So did Bolívar's declaration (issued soon after his return to Venezuela in 1816) making abolition of slavery one of the patriot war aims. The mostly llanero cavalry of Bolívar and Páez could not dislodge the veteran Spanish troops occupying Andean Venezuela; but neither could the royalists make much headway on the Orinoco plains.

Bolívar sought to institutionalize the revolutionary movement by calling elections for a congress, which assembled at Angostura in February 1819 and ratified his leadership. Yet Bolívar's long-term objectives were not limited to Venezuela. In May 1819 he embarked on the campaign that took him westward across the llanos and over the Andes to central New Granada, where on 7 August he won the decisive battle of Boyacá. The victory opened the way to Bogotá, occupied three days later, and gave Bolívar control of an area with important reserves of recruits and supplies. It also gave him a victorious momentum that he never entirely lost.

Bolívar placed the New Granadan officer Francisco de Paula SANTANDER in charge of the recently liberated provinces and then returned to Angostura, where, at his urging, in December 1819, the congress proclaimed the union of Venezuela, New Granada, and Quito (Ecuador) a single Republic of Colombia (usually referred to as Gran Colombia). The following year Bolívar turned his attention to the part of Venezuela still under royalist control. Military operations were suspended temporarily by an armistice of November 1820, but the victory at Carabobo, in June 1821, brought the war in Venezuela to a close except for royalist coastal enclaves that held out for another two years.

Meanwhile Gran Colombia was given a constitution by the Congress of Cúcuta, meeting in 1821 on the border between Venezuela and New Granada. The document was not entirely to Bolívar's liking, but he agreed to serve under it when the Congress named him first constitutional president, with Santander as vice president. Since Bolívar intended to continue leading the military struggle against Spain, Santander became acting chief executive in the Colombian capital of Bogotá, charged with organizing the home front and mobilizing resources.

After a local uprising in Guayaquil threw off royalist control of that port city, Bolívar sent his trusted lieutenant Antonio José de SUCRE to Ecuador with a Colombian auxiliary force. While Bolívar fought his way through southern New Granada, Sucre penetrated the Ecuadoran highlands. After Sucre defeated the royalists at the battle of Pichincha (May 1822), on the outskirts of Quito, Bolívar entered Quito as well. Continuing to Guayaquil, he obtained its semivoluntary incorporation into Gran Colombia just before he met there with the Argentine liberator José de SAN MARTÍN. The exact substance of their discussions was never revealed, but it would seem that one thing they disagreed on was how to complete the liberation of Peru, where San Martín controlled the coastal cities but not the highlands. Soon afterward, San Martín abandoned Peru, and Bolívar accepted a call to take his place.

Once he reached Peru, in September 1823, Bolívar found Peruvian collaboration to be somewhat fickle, but by mid-1824 he was ready for his last great campaign. On 6 August he scored an important victory at Junín, in the central Peruvian Andes, and on 9 December, in the battle of Ayacucho, his army (commanded by Sucre) obtained the surrender of the main royalist army. In the following weeks Sucre mopped up remnants of royalist resistance in Upper Peru (modern Bolivia).

A few days before Ayacucho, Bolívar, from Lima, issued a call to the Spanish American nations to meet at Panama and create a permanent alliance. He did not have a Pan-American gathering in mind, for he failed to invite the United States, Brazil, and Haiti—even while hoping that Great Britain would send an observer.

154

The United States and Brazil were invited by the administration of Vice President Santander in Bogotá, though in the end they did not take part; and neither did the Panama Congress of 1826 produce the hoped-for league of Spanish American states. Bolívar's design for the congress, however, revealed his ambivalence toward the United States, whose institutions he admired in principle but considered unsuited to Latin American conditions and whose growing power he foresaw as a long-term threat. His interest in having British representation clearly reflected both his belief that British friendship was essential for the security and economic development of the new republics as well as his deep admiration for Great Britain and its system of constitutional monarchy.

Bolívar soon followed Sucre to Upper Peru, where he assumed provisional direction of the newly independent nation that was to name itself Bolivia in his honor. Bolívar did not stay there long, but when the Bolivians invited him to draft their first constitution, he gladly accepted. The proposal that he later submitted (in May 1826) had some progressive features, yet its centerpiece—a president serving for life with power to name his successor—aroused wide criticism as a disguised form of monarchy. Bolívar was gratified that both Bolivia and Peru adopted, at least briefly, the main lines of his scheme. However, his hope that Gran Colombia, too, would adopt some form of it was never realized.

Bolívar's interest in reforming Colombian institutions was heightened by the rebellion of Páez in April 1826 against the government of Santander. The Liberator returned home before the end of the year, settled Páez's rebellion with a sweeping pardon, and added his support to demands for an immediate reform of the constitution. These actions led to a conflict with Santander, who became a leader of the opposition to Bolívar at the constitutional reform convention that met at Ocaña from April to June 1828. When the sessions ended in deadlock, Bolívar's supporters called on him to assume dictatorial powers to "save the republic," and he agreed to do so.

As dictator, Bolívar rolled back many of the liberal reforms previously enacted in Gran Colombia, including a reduction in the number of monasteries and abolition of Indian tribute. He did not necessarily oppose the reforms in question; he merely decided they were premature. And he did not touch the free-birth law that Gran Colombia had adopted for gradual elimination of slavery.

Bolívar's dictatorship was bitterly opposed by the adherents of Santander, some of whom joined in the abortive September 1828 attempt to assassinate Bolívar. After that, political repression became harsher, and San-

tander was sent into exile, but scattered uprisings still broke out. Also, serious disaffection arose in Venezuela, which was ideologically the most liberal part of the country as well as generally resentful of being ruled from Bogotá. The last straw was an intrigue by Bolívar's cabinet to recruit a European prince to succeed him as constitutional monarch when the Liberator died or retired. Páez again rose in rebellion in late 1829, and this time Venezuela became a separate nation.

Another convention that met in Bogotá in January 1830 did produce a new constitution, but it could not stem dissolution of the union. Ailing and disheartened, Bolívar stepped down from the presidency in March 1830 and set off for self-imposed exile. He died at Santa Marta before he could board ship, though not before Ecuador seceded from the union and newly autonomous Venezuela prohibited its most famous son from setting foot on its soil.

Though at the end it seemed to Bolívar that his work had been in vain, he is revered today as the one person who made the greatest contribution to Spanish American independence. His contribution was not just military but also political, in the articulation of patriot objectives and the establishment of new states. Moreover, he has been claimed as a precursor by every ideological current, from the revolutionary Left (which admires him for his opposition to slavery and distrust of the United States) to the extreme Right (which approves his authoritarian tendencies): there is something about Bolívar to appeal to every taste and every age.

– DAVID BUSHNELL

BOLOGNESI, FRANCISCO

Francisco Bolognesi (*d.* 1880), Peruvian national hero and military commander in charge of the defense of the Peruvian garrison in Arica during the War of the Pacific (1879–1883). Together with Alfonso Ugarte, Bolognesi is considered the premier military hero. Both died in the battle of Arica (1880) and are credited with heroic self-sacrifice in defense of Peru. However, the battle and the war resulted in sound defeats for the Peruvian army. This legacy is a cornerstone of official Peruvian nationalism.

Bolognesi was typical of those military officers who were trained during the struggles among military chieftains during the mid-nineteenth century in Peru, as opposed to the professional military cadre that appeared in the 1890s. Bolognesi supported General Ramón CASTILLA against Generals José Rufino ECHENIQUE and Manuel Ignacio VIVANCO in 1853–1858. He studied artillery in Europe and became commander general of artillery in 1862. During the War of the Pacific he led the Third Division in the battles of San Franciso, Tarapacá, and Arica. Outnumbered by Chilean forces in Arica he refused to surrender and rallied his soldiers to "fight until firing the last bullet."

— ALFONSO W. QUIROZ

BOMBAL, MARÍA LUISA

María Luisa Bombal (*b.* 8 June 1910; *d.* 6 May 1980), Chilean novelist, born in Viña del Mar. Two highly original novels, *La última niebla* (1935) and *La amortajada* (1938), translated into English by the author herself as *The House of Mist* (1947) and *The Shrouded Woman* (1948), attest to María Luisa Bombal's outstanding position among Latin American writers. Educated in France, she lived most of her life away from her country.

An innovative novelist, Bombal was very influential in the development of contemporary narrative in Latin America, and she has had a profound effect on the development of a feminine perspective among Latin American women writers because of her treatment of the feminine characters in her work. Her novels are perfect narratives of fantasy and feminine sensitivity. She is a good representative of the feminist will to surpass the limitations imposed on women by society, and her works are an example of the stylistic experimentation of the period.

After having accomplished both an expression of women's views and the development of a new style, Bombal ceased to publish new works. In her old age she returned to her native country and enjoyed a brief recognition of her influence on younger writers, particularly women. Today, a literary prize for novels is given in her name.

— S. DAYDÍ-TOLSON

BONIFAZ ASCASUBI, NEPTALÍ

Neptalí Bonifaz Ascasubi (also Ascazubi; *b.* 29 December 1870; *d.* 1960?), was elected president of Ecuador in 1931 but did not serve. A wealthy sierra landowner, in 1925 he became president of Ecuador's newly created Central Bank. His successful election bid brought together an unlikely coalition of small businessmen, artisans, campesinos, and workers—conservatives, liberals, and socialists—all adversely affected by the Great Depression. His platform, the Compactación Obrera Nacional (National Workers' Compact, 1932), called for mildly progressive reform. Bonifaz defeated his Liberal opponent, Modesto Larrea Jijón, in Ecuador's first free election in nearly forty years. However, Liberals still controlled Congress, and they distrusted Bonifaz, be-

lieving that he would favor banking and landowning interests. Congress voted to disqualify president-elect Bonifaz in 1932 on the grounds that he was not born in Ecuador. The charge was true: the son of a diplomat, Bonifaz had been born at the Peruvian embassy in

Bonifaz Ascasubi brought together an unlikely coalition of small businessmen, artisans, campesinos, and workers all adversely affected by the Great Depression.

Quito—technically not Ecuadorian soil. More seriously, Bonifaz had listed his citizenship as Peruvian until he was forty-six years old. Following Congress's action, Bonifaz lost an ensuing military struggle over the presidency, the War of Four Days. Hundreds died in bitter house-to-house combat in Quito.

— RONN F. PINEO

BONIFAZ NUÑO, RUBÉN

Rubén Bonifaz Nuño (*b.* 12 November 1923), Mexican writer. Born in Córdoba, Veracruz, Bonifaz Nuño received a law degree from the National University but has devoted himself primarily to literature, mostly poetry, since the publication of *La muerte del ángel* (The Death of the Angel) in 1945. He won a scholarship from the Centro Mexicano de Escritores for the 1951–1952 academic year. In 1953 he published *Imágenes* (Images), a collection of poems that combined classical Greek and Latin influences with Nahuatl. He turned even more fully to the indigenous world in *Siete de espadas* (Seven of Spades), published in 1966, followed by *El ala del tigre* (The Wing of the Tiger) in 1969. In 1974 he was awarded the National Literature Prize. He is also known for his translations of the *Georgics* by Virgil (1963) and the *Eclogues* by Dante (1965), as well as for his essays.

Critics have placed Bonifaz Nuño in the "generation of the 1950s" with Jaime Sabines, Rosario CASTELLANOS, and Jaime García Terres. Whether he is addressing the themes of solitude, disillusionment, misery, immortality, or hopelessness, Bonifaz's poetry is defined by a preference for urban spaces, experimental innovations with traditional poetic forms, a unique mixture of high and popular cultures, and a profound belief in the power of language and poetry to unmask enigmas and reinvent the world. A member of El Colegio Nacional and the Mexican Language Academy, he currently directs the Instituto de Investigaciones Filológicas at the National University.

— NORMA KLAHN

BONILLA, POLICARPO

Policarpo Bonilla (*b.* 17 March 1858; *d.* 11 September 1926), president of Honduras, 1894–1899. Bonilla emerged as the Liberal Party's heir apparent during Céleo Arias's failed bid for the presidency in 1887. Upon Arias's death in 1890, the Liberals chose Bonilla to be their candidate against the Progressive Party's nominee, Ponciano Leiva, in the 1891 elections. The Progressives stole the election, then harried the opposition Liberals into exile. From his Nicaraguan asylum, don Policarpo invaded Honduras, unleashing that country's bloodiest civil war. Bonilla's forces, amply supported by Nicaraguan strongman José Santos ZELAYA, managed to overthrow the government after more than two years' struggle.

As diligent in office as he had been intransigent in the field, Bonilla rewrote the nation's constitution in 1894 to reflect his brand of doctrinaire liberalism, established in it the preeminence of the executive branch, and revamped public administration at every level. He firmly believed that disciplined political parties competing in honest electoral contests would cure much of what ailed Honduras, but he made little headway in persuading his fellow Hondurans to accept this Anglo panacea. Although mildly xenophobic (his legal practice exposed him to the seamy side of international capitalism), Bonilla continued his predecessors' efforts to foster development through mining and banana export, and he tried unsuccessfully to refund his country's enormous foreign debt.

A lifelong "Unionist," Bonilla took the lead in a misguided attempt to revive the Republic of Central America shortly before leaving office in 1899. Hoping to return to law or retail trade after his term in office, he instead spent much of his remaining years in jail, in exile, or abroad on diplomatic missions. He represented Honduras at Versailles after World War I, courageously speaking against trying German leaders as war criminals and challenging Woodrow Wilson to redefine the Monroe Doctrine to fit League of Nations principles. He ran for president in 1923 but lost. Three years later he died in New Orleans.

— KENNETH V. FINNEY

BONILLA CHIRINOS, MANUEL

Manuel Bonilla Chirinos (*d.* 21 March 1913), president of Honduras (1903–1907 and 1912–1913). The off-

spring of poor, country folk, Manuel Bonilla began his career as a soldier and Liberal partisan. He rose to brigadier general during Marco Aurelio Soto's regime (1876–1883) and served his party as commander during the 1892–1894 Liberal Insurgency. After serving part of a term as vice president and minister of war, General Bonilla broke with the Liberal Party and went into exile.

In 1902 he formed the National Party to run for president in 1903. Although he received more votes than the other candidates, he did not receive a majority, and Congress gave the presidency to Juan Ángel Arias. General Bonilla responded by ousting Arias and installing himself as president. When dissident Liberal legislators, led by Dr. Policarpo BONILLA, challenged the régime, General Manuel Bonilla sent his chief of police, Lee CHRISTMAS, to arrest the congressmen and close the Congress. During his first administration, he rewrote the constitution, gave a decided push to education and the North Coast banana companies, submitted the Nicaraguan border dispute to international arbitration, and tried to form peaceful alliances with his Central American neighbors.

In late 1906, dissident Hondurans invaded Honduras from Nicaragua to topple President Bonilla. The rebels occupied Tegucigalpa in March, 1907, sending Bonilla into exile. Four years later, General Bonilla, backed by Samuel Zemurray, unleashed a counterrevolution on the North Coast. After U.S. diplomatic negotiation with the belligerents, an election was held, which Bonilla won (1912). He died the next year.

— KENNETH V. FINNEY

BONNET, STEDE

Stede Bonnet (*d.* 1718), British pirate. A retired officer and successful Barbados planter, Major Bonnet was an unlikely, latecoming pirate. His decision to turn to piracy has been attributed both to the desire to flee a nagging wife and to Bonnet's own mental instability. Captaining the *Revenge* (later the *Royal James*), he plundered several ships along the Atlantic seaboard before briefly joining the infamous Blackbeard (Edward Teach) in August 1717. At Blackbeard's suggestion, he surrendered to the King's Pardon (offered by Britain's King George I) in September, only to find that Blackbeard had used the occasion of his capitulation to steal his loot. Abandoning plans to privateer in the war against Spain, he unsuccessfully pursued Blackbeard, then recommenced pirating off the Carolina coast. Captured twice (he escaped the first time) by Colonel William Rhet, he was brought to trial, sentenced, and hanged in Charleston.

— PHILIPPE L. SEILER

BONNY, ANNE

Anne Bonny, an early-eighteenth-century pirate. Born near Cork, Ireland, Anne Bonny was the illegitimate daughter of an adulterous lawyer and his maid. At first, her father attempted to disguise her as a young male relative. When this ruse failed, he openly took up residence with Anne and her mother. His law practice suffered as a result of this affair, and he decided to emigrate to South Carolina along with Anne and her mother. He became a successful merchant in Charleston and later purchased a sizable plantation.

Anne's potential inheritance attracted many suitors, yet she eloped with James Bonny, a sailor of questionable integrity. The couple moved to New Providence in the Bahamas, a well-known pirate's haven. As part of his campaign to impose royal authority on the island, Captain Woodes Rogers offered to pardon James Bonny for whatever past crimes he had committed. Bonny not only accepted the pardon, but also spied on his former shipmates.

Disguised as a man, Anne became infatuated with another sailor. The object of her affections turned out to be Mary Read, another woman impersonating a seaman.

In the meantime, Anne had fallen in love with Captain "Calico Jack" Rackam and sought a divorce by sale from her husband. When he refused, Rackam and Anne, who posed as a seaman, hijacked a ship and fled the island. Together they raided coastal areas from Jamaica to Cuba. Her continuing masquerade did not prohibit intimate contact with Rackam and at one point she remained ashore in Cuba to bear their child. She had rejoined Rackam when they accepted the royal decree of amnesty for pirates in 1717. They later enlisted on the *Griffin,* a privateering ship, on which they mutinied and returned to piracy. Still disguised as a man, Anne became infatuated with another sailor. The object of her affections turned out to be Mary READ, another woman impersonating a seaman. The triangle formed by the two women and Rackam naturally led to a complex set of accusations, relationships, and clandestine rendezvous.

Anne fought courageously as a pirate and vehemently resisted capture by authorities. At her trial on 28 November 1720, Anne suprised the court with the revelation that she was an expectant mother. Anne's condition saved her from the gallows and she even mocked Rackam on the day of his execution. Anne spent time in prison for her crimes, although she occasionally was granted leaves. Her life after prison passed without notoriety.

– JOHN J. CROCITTI

BONPLAND, AIMÉ JACQUES

Aimé Jacques Bonpland (*b.* 29 August 1773; *d.* 11 May 1858), naturalist. Bonpland was born in La Rochelle, France, and studied medicine at the University of Paris. However, his real interest was in natural science. From 1799 to 1804 he accompanied Alexander von Humboldt on his travels to South America, where he collected 60,000 plants. Bernardino RIVADAVIA invited Bonpland to visit Buenos Aires. In 1817, with his wife and two assistants, he did so, and stayed. In 1818 he was named naturalist of the Río de la Plata, and became deeply interested in the possibility of cultivating yerba maté in the former Jesuit reducciónes. Bonpland practiced medicine in Buenos Aires, and in 1821 was named to the chair of medicine of the Instituto Médico Militar. While traveling to the old Jesuit missions, he ran afoul of the dictator of Paraguay, José Gaspar Rodríguez de FRANCIA, who kept him in Paraguay from 1822 to 1831.

Bonpland spoke out against the ROSAS dictatorship and became involved in anti-Rosas activity. He remained in the provinces of Misiones and Corrientes, and in 1854 was named director of the Museo de la Provincia in Corrientes. Bonpland conducted numerous scientific expeditions, sending back to France and Germany flora and fauna of the Río de la Plata. He died in São Borja, Brazil.

– NICHOLAS P. CUSHNER

BORBA GATO, MANUEL DE

Manuel de Borba Gato (*b.* ca. 1628; *d.* 1718), explorer and administrator in Brazil's mining region. One of the most famous *bandeirantes* (São Paulo explorers who sought wealth and slaves in frontier regions), Borba Gato participated in expeditions, in search of gold and jewels, that crossed the frontier region between his native São Paulo and Bahia. From 1674 to 1681 he accompanied his father-in-law, Fernão Dias Pais, on one of the largest and best organized of these missions. Although it failed in its quest for emeralds, the expedition opened up new areas for other mining and for eventual settlement. Then, implicated in the 1682 murder of the general administrator of mines, Dom Rodrigo de Castelo Branco, near Sumidouro, Borba Gato fled to the

Rio Doce region. Never ceasing to look for mineral wealth, he remained in voluntary exile for nearly twenty years.

Borba Gato's exoneration of the murder charge came through the intervention of political allies in 1700. In that same year Borba Gato revealed that he had found gold in the Rio das Velhas area, a discovery that would make him one of the mining zone's richest men. With wealth came power, and he moved quickly into administrative posts. Beginning as the chief customs officer of Rio das Velhas, he rose in 1702 to general administrator of mines for the region.

When civil war flared up in 1708 between those who had come to the mines from São Paulo and the *emboabas* (outsiders), people from other areas, Borba Gato at first showed sympathy for his Paulista compatriots. Siding with two of his kinsmen in a dispute with the *emboabas'* leader, Borba Gato called the latter a thief and ordered his banishment from the area. He never carried out this order, however, and in fact tried to effect a reconciliation. Throughout the war he maintained a position of neutrality. After hostilities ended in 1709, Borba Gato received royal grants of land and the position of superintendent of mines as a reward for his loyal service.

– ROGER A. KITTLESON

BORDABERRY, JUAN MARÍA

Juan María Bordaberry (*b.* 1928), president of Uruguay (1972–1976). The constitutional period of his presidency ended in June 1973 with his dissolution of Congress. From then, until his deposition in 1976 for refusing to negotiate a return to constitutional government, he headed a military regime (1973–1985).

Bordaberry started his political career as a member of Benito NARDONE's populist *ruralista* movement, which played a major role in the National (Blanco) party's election victory of 1958. He later joined the Colorado party of Jorge PACHECO ARECO, was elected a senator (1969–1971), and was nominated for president by Pacheco Areco. In the 1971 elections Bordaberry's slate of candidates received only 22 percent of the total vote. The narrow Colorado victory over the Blanco candidate, Wilson FERREIRA ALDUNATE, is widely believed to have been the result of fraud.

Bordaberry's government was characterized by vigorous repression of all popular protest movements and the persecution of the Tupamaro urban guerrilla movement, which, according to military sources, was defeated in 1972. Following passage of the State Security Bill of 1972, arbitrary detentions, torture, and attacks by paramilitary groups became endemic. In 1973/1974

all opposition media were shut down, and all political and trade union activity was proscribed. In an essay titled "Las opciones" (1980) and during a speech at the National University in Santiago de Chile (1987), Bordaberry maintained that due to divine right, rulers are not obliged to seek legitimation by democratic vote. He has not held public office since 1976.

– DIETER SCHONEBOHM

BORGE, TOMÁS

Tomás Borge (*b.* 13 August 1930), Nicaraguan leader and cofounder of the Sandinista National Liberation Front. Tomás Borge was born into the family of a drugstore owner in Matagalpa. His political experience began in 1946 with the Independent Liberal Party's student arm, the Democratic Youth Front. He mobilized high school and university students in traditional Liberal areas against the SOMOZA family. He met Carlos FONSECA and Silvio MAYORGA in 1954, upon entering law school at the National Autonomous University in León. Two years later he was arrested in connection with the assassination of Anastasio Somoza García and convicted on the basis of false testimony. After being severely tortured, he escaped to Costa Rica in 1959. In 1960 he sought support from Fidel CASTRO for the nascent revolutionary movement in Nicaragua. He helped found the Sandinista National Liberation Front in July 1961.

In 1963 Borge led combatants in the attack on the National Guard post in Río Coco. Two years later he became an organizer of the short-lived Republican Mobilization movement. This venture failed in 1966, so he returned to guerrilla warfare, participating in the ill-conceived battle at Pancasán in 1967. Borge fled to Costa Rica, then spent time in Peru and Cuba before returning to Nicaragua in 1971. The National Guard captured him in 1976 and again subjected him to torture. The Sandinista takeover of the National Palace in August 1978 led to Borge's release from prison. He subsequently assumed the leadership of the Prolonged Popular War faction with Henry RUÍZ and Bayardo ARCE.

After the July 1979 Sandinista victory and Somoza's exile, Borge became minister of the interior, in charge of the police and security forces. He also managed the government's relations with the indigenous peoples on the Atlantic coast. In the 1980s he wrote on many subjects, including human rights, national sovereignty, and revolutionary ideology. While in power, Borge was considered the principal representative of the intransigent, Marxist-Leninist wing of the Sandinista regime. He was replaced as minister of the interior by the Chamorro government in April 1990. As of 1993 he was writing articles for Latin American, North American and European journals.

— MARK EVERINGHAM

BORGES, JACOBO

Jacobo Borges (*b.* 28 November 1931), Venezuelan artist. Born in a rural area near Caracas, Borges attended only primary school. In 1949–1951 he studied painting at the Cristóbal Rojas School of Fine and Applied Arts in Caracas while simultaneously working for an advertising agency and drawing comic strips. In 1952 he won a scholarship from Metro-Goldwyn-Mayer as part of a promotion of its film *An American in Paris* to study in Paris, where he joined the Young Painters' group and developed an expressionist style with social and political implications. Upon his return to Caracas in 1956, he became a very active artist and soon held his first solo exhibition. Selected as one of the Venezuelan entries to the São Paulo Bienal in 1957, he won an honorable mention. From 1957 until 1965 he was a member of the Round Table Group and Whale Group cooperative. From 1965 until 1971, Borges stopped painting and devoted himself to theater and film design. He returned to painting in 1971, and five years later an exhibition of forty-eight of his canvases, Magic of a Realist Critic, was presented in Caracas and Mexico City. He wrote and illustrated *The Mountain and Its Era* (1979). In 1988 he represented Venezuela at the Venice Biennale and was included in the Latin American Spirit show at the Bronx Museum, New York, and the Guggenheim Museum exhibit, Fifty Years: Anniversary Collection. Major retrospectives of his work have been held in the Staatliche Kunsthalle (Berlin, 1987) and the Museo de Arte Contemporáneo (Caracas, 1988).

— BÉLGICA RODRÍGUEZ

BORGES, JORGE LUIS

Jorge Luis Borges (*b.* 24 August 1899; *d.* 14 June 1986), Argentine writer. Born in Buenos Aires, Borges attended the Collège de Calvin in Geneva during World War I. In the period immediately after the war, he became involved with ultraism, an avant-garde movement in Madrid, and on his return to Argentina helped start an Argentine ultraist group. His earliest surviving poems are iconoclastic, showing concern with the trench warfare of the Great War and sympathy for the Bolshevik Revolution. In the 1920s Borges published three books of poetry (*Fervor de Buenos Aires, Luna de enfrente,* and *Cuaderno San Martín*) and three books of essays (*Inquisiciones, El tamaño de mi esperanza,* and *El idioma de los argentinos*); his writings of the period are imbued with cultural nationalism, in keeping with his support for the populist leader Hipólito YRIGOYEN.

In the early 1930s Borges worked for a time on the literary supplement of Natalio Botana's innovative daily *Crítica;* it was there that he first published the sketches of the lives of various gangsters, pirates, imposters, and murderers that became his first book of fiction, *Historia universal de la infamia* (1935). In 1937 he became an employee at the Miguel Cané Municipal Library in Buenos Aires, a job that afforded him abundant time for reading and writing. From 1939 to 1953 he produced his most famous stories, collected as *Ficciones* (1944) and *El Aleph* (1949). These years also saw the publication of the essays in *Otras inquisiciones* (1952), most of which were first delivered as lectures in Argentina and Uruguay after Borges was fired from his job in the municipal library for signing a petition against the alliance of the Argentine military with the Nazis. His lectures and essays were no doubt celebrated in part because he was viewed as a symbol of opposition to Juan Domingo PERÓN. When Perón fell in 1955, Borges was named director of the National Library, a job he held until the return of Peronism.

"La fiesta del monstruo" is a ferocious satire on the Peronist mass meetings in the Plaza de Mayo; the "Monster" of the story is Perón himself.

The final years of Borges's life were marked, or perhaps marred, by celebrity. Beginning in 1961 when he was awarded the Formentor Prize (an international publishers' prize, which he shared with Samuel Beckett), Borges's work was translated into many languages and became the subject of an ever more vast critical bibliography. Borges was also pursued by students of literature and by journalists; even one of Woody Allen's characters in *Manhattan* boasts of her intentions to interview him. As a result, we know Borges's opinions on soccer, politics, Richard M. Nixon, Argentina, blacks, the English language, Federico García Lorca, and so forth, and for a time these (often misinformed or bigoted) opinions seemed to eclipse Borges's own work. Even years after his death, the details of his life seem to have the power to fascinate or titillate the public, particularly the Argentine public; revelations on his love life, brushes with psychoanalysis, proxy marriage, and death in Geneva have all, rather improbably, been major news in Argentina and elsewhere.

Of greater interest in the long run, perhaps, are Borges's complex relations to Argentine culture, history, and politics. His initial populist nationalism (and enthusiasm for Yrigoyen) included a measure of intolerance for "low-brow" Argentine culture: he condemned the poet Alfonsina STORNI for what he termed her shrill sentimentality, and he made similar attacks on Carlos GARDEL's tangos in the 1920s and 1930s. The national tradition to which he was to prove most faithful was liberal and cosmopolitan, as defined in his lecture "The Argentine Writer and Tradition" in 1951 (later included in the second edition of *Discusión* in 1957); his version of the Argentine national tradition necessarily competed with a number of others, and one of them, that of Perón, was to prove rather more decisive.

Two stories written in the late 1940s illustrate Borges's complex relations to the time in which he lived. "La fiesta del monstruo," written (in collaboration with Adolfo BIOY CASARES) in 1947 but not published until after the fall of Perón, is a ferocious satire on the Peronist mass meetings in the Plaza de Mayo in the first years of the new regime; the "Monster" of the story is Perón himself, who inspires his followers from afar in their torture and killing of a Jewish passerby. The story is narrated by a brash young Peronist and is an obvious recasting of two crucial liberal texts of the nineteenth century by opponents of the government of Juan Manuel de Rosas: Esteban ECHEVARRÍA's short story "El matadero" and Hilario ASCASUBI's gauchesque poem "La refalosa."

In 1948 Borges's sister and mother were arrested for taking part in a demonstration against the new Peronist constitution (which among other things, of course, gave women the right to vote). A few months later, Borges wrote a curious story, "Historia del guerrero y de la cautiva," which (when compared to "La fiesta del monstruo") is a rather more nuanced reflection on the need for political action. The character Droctulft, the Germanic invader of Italy who changes sides to join the inhabitants of Ravenna in the defense of their city, is an unequivocal convert to "civilization" but is offset in the story by an English captive woman who chooses to remain with her Indian husband. The captive's story is retold later by Borges's English grandmother, Fanny Haslam de Borges, in a way that barely alludes to the two events that consolidate her feelings of solidarity with the captive woman she saw so many years before on the pampas: her husband, Colonel Francisco Borges, was killed in the civil war in 1874 when he chose to follow Bartolomé MITRE against Adolfo ALSINA; the English captive's husband was no doubt to be captured or killed in the "Conquest of the Desert" in 1879. Who is to know, Borges seems to be saying, whether one ultimately is taking the part of civilization or of savagery?

– DANIEL BALDERSTON

BORGES DE MEDEIROS, ANTÔNIO AUGUSTO

Antônio Augusto Borges de Medeiros (*b.* 19 November 1863; *d.* 25 April 1961), Brazilian statesman and political boss of Rio Grande do Sul (1903–1930). Born the son of an imperial judge in Capavaca, Rio Grande do Sul, Borges graduated from the Recife Law School in 1885 and agitated for the republic in his native province. A member of the federal Constituent Assembly, he supported Júlio de CASTILHOS's coup in 1892 and fought the rebels in the Federalist Revolt of 1893–1895. Picked by Castilhos as governor in 1898, Borges served the Riograndense Republican Party boss until Castilhos's death in 1903. Borges then became party leader and ruled the state until 1930, serving as governor a total of twenty-five years.

Like Castilhos, a Comtian positivist, Borges used the former's autocratic constitution to promote public education and rural property taxes; he also balanced the budget and practiced labor paternalism. With Senator Pinheiro MACHADO, Borges made the Riograndense Republicans contenders in national politics against counterparts in Minas and São Paulo. The gauchos opposed the Paulistas successfully in 1910, played arbiter in 1919, lost in 1922 and 1930, but then incited a revolt, overthrowing the regime. Riograndense economic interests, which were tied to the domestic foodstuffs market, often collided with those of the export-oriented Paulistas.

In 1928 Borges made Getúlio VARGAS governor, and he backed Vargas's revolution in 1930. He soon broke with Vargas, supporting São Paulo's Constitutionalist Revolt (1932). Following the defeat of that movement and his imprisonment in Pernambuco, Borges de Medeiros received the second largest number of votes for the presidency in the Constituent Assembly of 1933–1934, losing to his protégé Vargas. Elected to Congress in October 1934 on the opposition ticket, Borges advocated a parliamentary regime to preclude a presidential dictatorship. His fears were realized three years later, when Vargas declared the authoritarian Estado Nôvo regime and closed Congress, effectively terminating Borges's political career.

– JOSEPH L. LOVE

BORJA CEVALLOS, RODRIGO

Rodrigo Borja Cevallos (*b.* 19 June 1935), president of Ecuador (1988–1992). Born in Quito of a family descended from early Spanish settlers, Borja graduated with distinction from the law school of the Universidad Central in 1960. Already a member of the Liberal Party, he soon entered politics and was first elected to Congress in 1962. Borja was later a central figure among the young Liberals who broke with the traditional leadership to found a new political party, the Izquierda Democrática (Democratic Left—ID) in 1977. Borja was elected congressman from the province of Pichincha in 1970. When constitutional rule was suspended by military *golpe* (1972), he turned to building and developing the ID as Ecuador's first national, mass-based political party.

When military rule came to an end, Borja ran for the presidency in 1978, finishing fourth but establishing himself and his party as a major political contender. Subsequently seated in Congress in honorary office, Borja became a leading spokesman of Ecuador's center Left, and in 1984 he was narrowly defeated in the presidential race. Continuing as the leading opposition congressman, Borja was again the ID candidate in 1988 and won by a comfortable margin. Inaugurated in August 1988, he faced high inflation, economic recession, a huge foreign debt, and declining oil prices. Despite his prestige as a leader of Latin American social democracy, he was forced to adopt basically neoliberal policies, such as cutting subsidies and using free-market practices. Continuing austerity and economic hardship cost his party popular support, and the ID lost its majority in the 1990 congressional elections. Constitutionally prohibited from a second consecutive term as president, Borja continued to grapple with economic pressures as his administration drew to a close.

– JOHN D. MARTZ

BORJA Y ARAGÓN, FRANCISCO DE

Francisco de Borja y Aragón (Príncipe de Esquilache; *b.* 1583; *d.* 26 September 1658), twelfth viceroy of Peru. The prince of Esquilache, scion of a distinguished Spanish family related to Pope Alexander VI and Saint Francis Borja, was one of the most cultured of royal bureaucrats, an accomplished poet, patron of the arts, and administrator. Esquilache was appointed viceroy in 1614, when he was only thirty-two years old. His rule was marked by its concern with the practice of idolatry among the Indians and with the security of the empire in the face of continuing Dutch threats. His correspondence with the crown was copious and became a model for other viceroys. Nevertheless, there is debate over Esquilache's personal involvement in governing Peru, since it is possible that he left many details to his well-trained staff. Anxious to hurry back to the court to greet

the new monarch, Philip IV, he left the viceroyalty in 1621, before his successor arrived. He spent the last thirty years of his life writing poetry.

– JOHN F. SCHWALLER

BORNO, JOSEPH LOUIS E. ANTOINE FRANÇOIS

Joseph Louis E. Antoine François Borno (*b.* 1865; *d.* 19 July 1942), president of Haiti (1922–1930). Before becoming president, Borno served as minister of foreign affairs and ambassador to the Dominican Republic. He was an advocate of the U.S. intervention in Haiti, inducing the Haitian government to sign the 1915 treaty by which it pledged total cooperation with the United States.

On 12 April 1922, Borno was elected to his first term as president of Haiti. He was reelected in 1926. His first term was relatively stable, but the second ended in crisis with the United States. The combination of the poor economic conditions and the tensions arising from the U.S. occupation led to an uprising against the U.S. Marines in 1929. In 1930, he accepted President Herbert Hoover's investigating committee's recommendations that U.S. Marines be gradually withdrawn and that popular elections be held. He agreed to step down and supported the U.S. selection of Eugene Roy as provisional president until elections could be held. Roy was replaced by Stenio Vincent.

– DARIÉN DAVIS

BORRERO Y CORTÁZAR, ANTONIO

Antonio Borrero y Cortázar (*b.* 28 October 1827; *d.* 9 October 1911), president of Ecuador (1875–1876). A moderate politician, Borrero was selected by Conservative president Gabriel GARCÍA MORENO (1861–1865, 1869–1875) to run for the vice presidency in 1863. Borrero won in a landslide despite the fact that he did not want the job. He immediately resigned, disgusted by García Moreno's rigging of the election. When García Moreno was assassinated in 1875, Borrero won the subsequent election for president. He hoped to be a healer, peacemaker, and reconciler for a nation so often bloodied by regional and ideological battles. However, in seeking to find a middle road between Liberals and Conservatives, he managed only to antagonize both.

General Ignacio de VEINTIMILLA overthrew Borrero in 1876. After seven years in exile in Peru, Borrero returned to serve as governor of Azuay province (1888–1892). A man of laws, a well-read—if not well-traveled—intellectual, Borrero was known by contemporaries as the "Cato of Cuenca," or the "Washington of Azuay." Borrero is sometimes viewed by historians as the first Progresita, the grouping of pragmatic political moderates that governed Ecuador from 1883 to 1895. He died in Cuenca, his birthplace.

— RONN F. PINEO

BOSCH GAVIÑO, JUAN

Juan Bosch Gaviño (*b.* 30 June 1909), Dominican novelist, sociologist, historian, politician, and president of the Dominican Republic (1963). Bosch, a native of La Vega, published his first collection of short stories, *Camino Real,* in 1933. One year later, Rafael Leónidas TRUJILLO MOLINA arrested Bosch for conspiracy against his regime. Released in 1935, Bosch became literary editor of the Dominican Republic's most prestigious newspaper, *Listín Diario.* In 1936 he published one of his most popular novels, *La Mañosa.* Unable to live under the Trujillo dictatorship, he fled his country in 1938. During the next twenty-three years of exile, Bosch resided in Cuba, Costa Rica, Bolivia, Chile, and Venezuela. He was one of the organizers of the Dominican Revolutionary Party (PRD), which was founded in 1939 at Havana. Later, he served as secretary to Cuban President Carlos Prío Socarrás (1948–1952) and helped to organize the abortive attempt to overthrow Trujillo, known as Cayo Confite.

After Trujillo's assassination in 1961, Bosch returned to his native land in order to organize the PRD on Dominican soil. In December 1962, he won the first presidential elections held in the Dominican Republic since 1930. Inaugurated in February 1963, he was deposed after only seven months by a military coup backed by elements of the military (under General Elías Wessín y Wessín), the landowning and business elites, the hierarchy of the Roman Catholic church, and the military attachés of the United States. Bosch was once again forced into exile, from which he did not return until 1966.

Bosch has stated that FBI agents surrounded his residence in Puerto Rico in order to prevent his return to Santo Domingo.

The regime installed by the military coup in September 1963 proved to be most unpopular and was removed by a revolution that occurred on 24 April 1965. The chief aim of the revolutionaries, who called themselves Constitutionalists, was to return Bosch to the presidency of the nation. In order to prevent this possibility, U.S. President Lyndon Johnson dispatched U.S. Marines to Santo Domingo on 28 April. Some historians have claimed that Bosch was a coward for not returning to his country to lead the Constitutionalists in their battle against the Loyalists of Wessín y Wessín and the interventionist forces of the United States. Bosch has responded to this criticism by stating that agents of the Federal Bureau of Investigation surrounded his residence in Puerto Rico in order to prevent his return to Santo Domingo.

Both Bosch and his rival, Joaquín BALAGUER, returned from exile for the presidential elections of 1966, in which they were the candidates for the Dominican Revolutionary Party, and the Reformist Party, respectively. Balaguer possessed decisive advantages during the electoral campaign and won the election. In 1973 Bosch broke with the Dominican Revolutionary Party, which he had helped to found, and formed his own political movement, the Party of Dominican Liberation (PLD). When the PLD ran for the first time in 1978, it obtained only an insignificant number of votes, but by the elections of 1982, it was represented in the Dominican Congress by six deputies. In 1986 the PLD obtained 18.3 percent of the vote as well as sixteen deputies and two senators in the Congress. With the disintegration of the Dominican Revolutionary Party into various factions, the PLD emerged as the main challenger of Balaguer's Reformist Party.

During the presidential elections of 1990, Bosch and Balaguer faced each other once again, the latter winning by a narrow margin. Bosch accused his opponent of electoral fraud and threatened to take the dispute to the streets, a move from which he was dissuaded by former U.S. President Jimmy Carter, who mediated between the octogenarian rivals. Although deeply involved in Dominican politics for over five decades, Bosch will probably be remembered more for his literary achievements than for his accomplishments in the political realm.

— KAI P. SCHOENHALS

BOTERO, FERNANDO

Fernando Botero (*b.* 19 April 1932), Colombian artist. Born in Medellín, Botero began his career as a writer and illustrator for the Sunday literary supplement of *El Colombiano,* a Medellín newspaper, where his articles on Picasso and Dalí resulted in his expulsion from Jesuit secondary school. He moved to Bogotá in 1951, when he had had his first one-man show. The following year he went to Madrid, where he enrolled in the Real Academia de San Fernando and studied the works of Goya and Velazquez in the Prado. He then went to study art history and fresco painting at the Academia San Marco in Florence. In 1955 he returned to Bogotá, and exhibited at the Biblioteca Nacional. His work was not well received, however, and he moved to Mexico City the following year. From 1958 to 1960 he taught at the Escuela de Bellas Artes at the National University in Bogotá. Botero received the award for the Colombian section of the Guggenheim international exhibition in 1960. That same year he moved to New York, where he lived until 1973. In 1961 the Museum of Modern Art of New York acquired his painting *Mona Lisa at Age 12.* This period reflects his fascination with the Renaissance masters.

In 1973 Botero moved to Paris. Although his subject matter continued to center on small-town Colombia, as evidenced by satirical images of clerics, military men, politicians, and marginals, Botero soon turned to sculpting the images and figures that appeared in his paintings. He had retrospective exhibitions in Germany (1970), Colombia (1973), the Netherlands (1975), the United States (1979–1980), and Germany (1979–1980). After his retrospective at the Museum of Contemporary Art in Caracas in 1976, the Venezuelan government awarded him the Order Andrés Bello, reserved for outstanding figures in Latin American culture. The department of Antioquia honored him with the Cruz de Boyaca for services to his nation. Botero's work has appeared at exhibitions at the Bronx Museum (New York, 1988) and at the Indianapolis Museum, the Hayward Gallery (London), and Centro de Arte Reina Sofia (Madrid), all in 1989.

— BÉLGICA RODRÍGUEZ

BOUCHARD, HIPÓLITO

Hipólito Bouchard (*b.* 13 August 1783; *d.* 5 January 1837), naval hero of Argentine independence. Born in France, Bouchard had been active in his country's merchant marine and in privateering by the time he reached Buenos Aires in 1809. There he stayed, and after the May Revolution of 1810 he was one of the cadre of foreign sailors who gave the Argentine patriots a respectable naval force, especially for corsair operations. Bouchard was naturalized as an Argentine citizen in 1813. He sailed with Admiral Guillermo BROWN to the Pacific in 1815 and starting in 1817 commanded the frigate *Argentina* on a privateering voyage that took it around the world. He was a member of the expedition in 1820 that carried José de SAN MARTÍN to Peru. Thereafter he continued serving Peru, where he acquired a sugar estate and spent the last part of his life as *hacendado.*

— DAVID BUSHNELL

BOVES, JOSÉ TOMÁS

José Tomás Boves (*b.* 18 September 1782; *d.* 5 December 1814), officer in the Spanish army. A native of Spain, Boves received his nautical education in Asturias, obtained his pilot's license in 1803, and joined a mercantile business with interests in Venezuela. He was accused of smuggling, imprisoned in Puerto Cabello, and later confined in the town of Calabozo. When the War of Independence broke out, Boves declared himself to be on the side of emancipation. But he then became suspect when he supported the royalist leader, Domingo Monteverde, and was imprisoned in 1812 at Calabozo. That same year he joined the royalist ranks under the command of Eusebio Antoñanzas, who released him from prison, and was appointed commander in chief of Calabozo.

Boves rapidly attained great popularity among the inhabitants of the plains for his favorable attitude toward sacking and looting. His detailed knowledge of the plains territory brought him numerous victories over republican troops. In testimonies of the time and in the collected writings on Venezuelan independence, Boves stands out for his fierceness and cruelty to those he defeated. He rebelled against his immediate superior and ignored the authority of the royal *audiencia.* After his death at the battle of Urica, the royalist cause lost popularity among the people of the plains.

— INÉS QUINTERO

BOYER, JEAN-PIERRE

Jean-Pierre Boyer (*b.* 1776; *d.* 9 July 1850), ruler of Haiti (1818–1843). The regime of Jean-Pierre Boyer marked a vital watershed in the development of Haitian government and society in the nineteenth century. Born in Port-au-Prince, Boyer began his career when he joined the revolutionary forces led by Pierre Dominique Toussaint L'OUVERTURE that abolished slavery and freed Haiti from French colonial domination. In the power struggles dividing Haitians after independence, Boyer, himself a mulatto, sided with mulatto leader Alexandre Sabès PÉTION and, in March 1818, succeeded Pétion as head of the Republic of the South. In 1821, after the death of his major rival in the North, Henri CHRISTOPHE, Boyer unified the country. Under his auspices, Haiti began to consolidate its status as an independent nation. In 1822, out of fear of French plans for reprisal, Boyer sent his troops to the vulnerable eastern half of Hispaniola, which, with Boyer's encouragement, had recently declared its independence from Spain. He remained in control of the region for the remainder of his twenty-five-year reign. In 1825, Boyer obtained France's diplomatic recognition (by paying an indemnity of 150 million francs), an achievement that had eluded earlier leaders of the young nation and that marked the end of Haiti's status as an international pariah. Recognition from the British came in 1826, after which other countries followed suit.

Despite these successes on the international front, Boyer faced serious challenges at home. The most significant problem was trying to reconcile the needs and interests of two major sectors of the population: the mulatto elite and the black peasantry. During his early years in power, Boyer tried to win the loyalty of the peasantry through land distribution. This popular policy was started by Pétion and contributed to the predominance of small-scale, subsistence agriculture, especially in the South. Yet, Boyer also responded to the demands of mulatto landowners for a restoration of plantation agriculture. In May 1826, he implemented the Code Rural in an attempt to force peasants to work for the large estates. The code stipulated that all peasants were to contract themselves to an estate owner or be considered "vagabonds" liable to arrest and forced labor on public-works projects. It also provided for a rural police force to inspect plantations and keep order in the countryside. Yet, because of government laxness as well as lack of cooperation from some estate owners, it was impossible to enforce the code. Thus, Boyer witnessed the decline of Haiti's once-productive plantation system and the rise of subsistence farming as a way of life for most Haitians.

Boyer's regime also saw a hardening of social and class divisions based on skin color as well as property ownership. In general, government fell into the hands of the more educated, Westernized mulattoes while blacks dominated the military. This split helped undermine the success of Boyer's effort to entice free blacks from the United States to settle in Haiti. During the Boyer period, about 13,000 blacks arrived on the island with the hope of becoming property owners and living in a more egalitarian society; yet, due to problems created by language and cultural differences as well as mulatto social prejudice against blacks, little more than half that number stayed. The revolt of 27 January 1843 led to his exile on 13 March, first in Jamaica and later in Paris. In sum, Boyer not only brought about Haitian unity and consolidated his nation's claim to sovereignty but also oversaw the emergence of a society with color and class divisions that have continued to shape Haitian society and politics to this day.

– PAMELA MURRAY

BRAMUGLIA, JUAN ATILIO

Juan Atilio Bramuglia (b. 19 January 1903; d. 4 September 1962), Argentine labor lawyer, foreign minister, and supporter of Juan PERÓN. As legal counsel for the railroad workers' union, Bramuglia's strong initial support of Perón earned him appointments in the government. In 1944 he was named general director of social welfare, and from 1944 to 1945 he served as federal intervenor in the province of Buenos Aires. When Perón was elected president in 1946, Bramuglia became foreign minister. Bramuglia sought recognition of Argentine claims in Antarctica and the Falkland Islands (Malvinas) and achieved some success in presenting Perón's "third position" in international affairs. In 1948 he was provisional president of the Third Assembly of the United Nations in Paris, and in 1949 he was elected chairman of the United Nations Security Council. After incurring the displeasure of Evita PERÓN, Bramuglia resigned from government and pursued scholarly activities. His published works include *Jubilaciones ferroviarias* (1941) and *La previsión social Argentina* (1942).

– JAMES A. BAER

BRAÑAS GUERRA, CÉSAR

César Brañas Guerra (b. 13 December 1899; d. 22 February 1976), Guatemalan poet, journalist, and writer, and one of the founders of the influential Guatemalan daily *El Imparcial* (1922–1985). Born in Antigua, Brañas was the best-known of a family of important literary figures. His father was an immigrant from Galicia and his mother a schoolteacher in Antigua. His prolific output of poetry, novels, historical works, and critical essays was highly influential in mid-twentieth-century Guatemala. Like Miguel Ángel ASTURIAS, he contributed to a social consciousness among the Guatemalan intelligentsia. His large library, a part of the University of San Carlos, is especially useful for study of the nineteenth and early twentieth centuries.

– RALPH LEE WOODWARD, JR.

BRANCO, MANUEL ALVES

Manuel Alves Branco (Caravelas, Visconde de; b. 7 June 1797; d. 13 July 1855), Brazilian politician. Born in Bahia, he attended the University of Coimbra in Portugal, where he studied law. He returned to Brazil in 1824 and began a distinguished career in politics. Branco was elected a deputy from Bahia in 1830. In 1835 he was named minister of justice in the triumvirate regency (1831–1835). During his tenure as minister he was responsible for Lei no. 57 (6 October 1835), which abolished the civil and religious entailment (*morgados* and *capelas*), and Lei no. 4 (10 June 1835), which imposed a death penalty on slaves who physically hurt their owners. The latter law became one of the principal juridical foundations for imperial slavery legislation. In 1837 Branco was elected senator from Bahia. In 1842 PEDRO II named Branco as one of his first councilers of state. He became the first Brazilian to hold the post of president of the Council of Ministers, created in 1847. As the first prime minister of the Empire, Branco was a militant politician in the Liberal Party. Noted for his skills as an orator and his deep knowledge of the law, Branco was one of the most significant politicians during the period of the Brazilian monarchy.

— EUL-SOO PANG

BRANDÃO, IGNÁCIO DE LOYOLA

Ignácio de Loyola Brandão (*b.* 31 July 1936), Brazilian author. Brandão's writing career began at the age of sixteen, when he was a movie reviewer for a newspaper in Araraquara, his hometown, in the hinterland of the state of São Paulo. Soon after his twenty-first birthday, he moved to the state capital, where he became a journalist. The peculiarities and problems of urban life made a profound impression on him, and for the next eight years he witnessed the people's increasing mistrust in the government, and the resulting turmoil that led to a military coup in 1964. Being a reporter, Brandão had firsthand knowledge of the turbulence of the metropolis, intensified by a period of extreme violence between police and militants following the coup. This environment pervades his fiction. His first book, *Depois do sol* (1965, After the Sun), a collection of short stories, was followed by *Bebel que a cidade comeu* (1968, Bebel, Swallowed Up by the City). Both books portray the social and psychological crises of 1960s Brazil, resulting from political oppression and economic unrest. Brandão eventually abandoned his career as a journalist and devoted himself to his fiction, though his novels and short stories retain a journalistic feel, revealing the author's analytical mind and stylistic irreverence, which often extends to graphic layouts emulating newspapers. His criticism of the government led to censorship of his novel *Zero,* which was banned from publication in Brazil for six years (1969–1975). He became, then, the first Brazilian writer to resort to publication abroad; *Zero* was printed in Italy (1974) before its publication in Portuguese. The first English-language translation was published in the U.S. in 1984. Brandão also wrote travel logs, including *Cuba de Fidel: viagem à ilha proibida* (1978, Fidel's Cuba: Voyage to a Forbidden Island) and *O verde violentou o muro: visões e alucinações alemãs* (1984, The Greenery that Shook the Wall: German Visions and Hallucinations). Brandão is a prolific writer whose work has evolved with the times; he remains

faithful to his primary vision of a world unredeemable in its unfairness and cruelty.

— REGINA IGEL

BRANNON DE SAMAYOA CHINCHILLA, CARMEN

Carmen Brannon de Samayoa Chinchilla (pseud. Claudia Lars; *b.* 1899; *d.* 1974), Salvadoran modernist writer. The daughter of an Irish-American father and Salvadoran mother, Lars grew up on a *finca* (farm) in Sonsonate. She was educated by nuns in Santa Ana and exhibited a literary inclination from a very early age. In her youth she fell in love with the Nicaraguan poet Salomón de la Selva, who introduced her to the world of European romantic literature and served as her mentor. However, her father disapproved of the match and sent her to live with relatives in New York. Upon her return to El Salvador, Lars fell in with a group of modernist and humanist writers known as the Generation of the 1930s, which had assembled around Alberto MASFERRER's newspaper *La Patria* and included Serafín Quiteño and Salarrué. Lars emigrated to San Francisco in 1944, where she experienced the drudgery of working in a biscuit factory. In 1974 she returned to El Salvador. The theme of the mysteries of life and the cosmos dominates her major novels and poems. Lars is considered one of the first great modern female literary figures of Hispanic America.

— KAREN RACINE

BRÁS PEREIRA GOMES, WENCESLAU

Wenceslau Brás Pereira Gomes (*b.* 26 February 1868; *d.* 15 May 1966), president of Brazil (1914–1918). After serving as governor of the state of Minas Gerais (1908–1910) and vice president under Hermes da Fonseca (1910–1914), Brás was elected president of Brazil in 1914. The Brás presidency marked the end of the extreme federalism of Brazil's early republican years, as the federal government took an increasingly active role in directing state politics and the national economy. Under Brás, force and intimidation were used in several federal interventions into the internal affairs of politically weak states, as well as for the suppression of the Contestado Rebellion along the Santa Catarina-Paraná border. Brás's presidential policies favored the most powerful states. São Paulo and Minas Gerais, which were allied in a power-sharing arrangement known as the politics of *café-com-leite* (an allusion to the prominent coffee-growing and ranching economies of São Paulo and Minas Gerais, respectively).

Aside from declaring war on the Central Powers in 1917, thus making Brazil the only South American republic to join the Allies, Brás is best known for signing the Civil Code of 1917. The Brás presidency is also notable for a rise in domestic industrial production stimulated by the disruptions of international trade and credit brought on by World War I. In November 1918 Brás left office amid a Spanish flu epidemic that ravaged Rio de Janeiro. He subsequently returned to Minas Gerais to lead a private life out of the public spotlight.

— DARYLE WILLIAMS

BRASSEUR DE BOURBOURG, CHARLES ÉTIENNE

Charles Étienne Brasseur de Bourbourg (*b.* 8 September 1814; *d.* January 1874), French prelate, antiquarian, and pioneer ethnohistorian. Ordained in 1845, Brasseur enjoyed a variety of postings in the Americas, where he was able to make most of his lasting contributions. Among the countries he visited were Canada (1845–1846), the United States (on at least two occasions, in 1848 and 1854), Mexico (1848–1851, 1863–1866, and 1871), Nicaragua and El Salvador (1854), Guatemala (1855–1857 and 1863), and Honduras (1863).

Brasseur is significant today primarily for his discovery, translation, and publication of several important colonial sources concerning Mesoamerican Indians, principally the Maya. These include Diego de LANDA's *Relación de las cosas de Yucatán*, the Popol Vuh, the *Título de los señores de Totonicapán*, the Troano Codex, and the *Memorial de Tecpán Atitlán*, or *Annals of Cakchiquels*. He also compiled and published linguistic materials for both highland Maya (primarily Quiché, including the *Rabinal Achí* drama) and lowland Maya (Yucatecan) peoples that continue to be useful to scholars. Unfortunately, Brasseur's historical interpretations of the documents he worked so tirelessly to discover were judged even by his contemporaries to be seriously flawed. Of little use to present-day scholars on the region, his pronouncements retain only a documentary interest.

To his credit Brasseur did much to promote American studies in his native France, through cofounding the Société Américaine de France (1857) and participating in the subsequent Société d'Ethnographie and the Société de Géographie of Paris. He also raised popular consciousness concerning the indigenous peoples and civilizations of Mesoamerica through his publication of many episodes and discoveries made during his travels.

— ROBERT M. HILL II

BRATHWAITE, EDWARD KAMAU

Edward Kamau Brathwaite (*b.* 11 May 1930), Caribbean historian, poet, and critic. Born in Bridgetown, Barbados, Brathwaite attended high school at Harrison College in Barbados, and college at Cambridge University. He was a professor of history at the University of the West Indies and later became a professor of comparative literature at New York University. As a historian, Brathwaite's scholarly publications include the important works *The Folk Culture of the Slaves in Jamaica* (1969; rev. ed. 1981) and *The Development of Creole Society in Jamaica, 1770–1820* (1971). He is the author of ten collections of poetry and several plays. *The Arrivants: A New World Trilogy* (1973) secured his reputation as a major poet of the Caribbean. In *Roots* (1993), a collection of literary scholarship and criticism, and in other critical writings, Brathwaite shows himself to be foremost among the theorists of Caribbean literature and culture.

Major themes of Brathwaite's poetry are Caribbean history and identity; slavery and colonization are integrally connected to the themes of fragmentation and alienation. Brathwaite's poetry attempts to provide a "whole, living tradition" out of which can be derived a new consciousness.

— EVELYN J. HAWTHORNE

BRAVO, CLAUDIO

Claudio Bravo (*b.* 8 November 1936), Chilean artist. A virtuoso of realism in painting, drawing, and lithography, Bravo was born in Valparaíso into a wealthy family. He attended Miguel Venegas Cienfuentes's art school from 1947 to 1948. In 1961, he moved to Spain, where he earned his living painting realistic portraits of the Spanish aristocracy. In the mid-1960s, he turned to trompe l'oeil paintings of isolated objects, such as motorcycle paraphernalia, clothing, folded and crumpled pieces of papers, wrapped canvases (*Homage to St. Teresa*, 1969; oil on canvas), and packages (*Blue Package*, 1971). His emphasis on texture, angled lighting, and narrow foreground planes derived from his studies of Francisco de Zurbarán's *bodegones*. Bravo replaced the Spanish master's empty backgrounds with skyscapes and white walls. The realism of Bravo's painting contrasts with his avoidance of all contextual references. His rendering of commonplace objects, biblical themes, and kneeling figures in undefined places or empty space has been interpreted as a surrealist trait. In 1972 Bravo moved to Tangier, Morocco.

— MARTA GARSD

BRAVO, LEONARDO

Leonardo Bravo (*b.* 1764; *d.* 14 September 1812), Mexican insurgent leader. The Chilpancingo-born patriarch of a large family, Bravo joined the insurgent movement in May 1811, along with his son Nicolás and his brothers Miguel, Víctor, and Máximo, when Hermenegildo GALEANA came to his hacienda of Chichihualco. Bravo became one of José María MORELOS's most distinguished officers. He played a major role, first in the fortification, and later in the defense, of Cuautla, where the insurgents, besieged by the royalists, held out for seventy-two days despite a lack of supplies. When the siege was lifted at the beginning of May 1812, Bravo traveled to the hacienda of San Gabriel, where he was captured by partisans of the colonial regime. He was taken to Mexico City, where he was tried and executed despite the efforts of his relatives, and even of Morelos, to obtain a pardon in return for the exchange of a sizable group of royalist prisoners.

— VIRGINIA GUEDEA

BRAVO, MARIO

Mario Bravo (*b.* 27 July 1882; *d.* 17 March 1944), Argentine Socialist congressman and senator. Bravo, who was elected a national deputy from the city of Buenos Aires four times (1913–1914, 1914–1918, 1918–1922, and 1942–1946) and a senator twice (1923–1931 and 1932–1938), was one of the leading Argentine Socialist Party politicians of the early twentieth century. Born in the city of Tucumán, Argentina, he received his law

---

Bravo was best known for bringing attention to the conditions of sugar-plantation workers in his home province of Tucumán.

---

degree from the University of Buenos Aires and joined the Socialist Party soon thereafter. He rose rapidly through the party's ranks, becoming its general secretary in 1910, the same year in which he embarked on his career in public office. As a legislator, he was best known for initiating measures to democratize the selection process of the city council (*consejo deliberante*) of the federal capital, a change that took effect in 1918, as well as for bringing attention to the conditions of sugar-plantation workers in his home province of Tucumán. A well-regarded poet, his literary efforts focused primarily on social issues and themes. Collections of his poems include *Poemas del campo y de la montaña* (1909); *La huelga de Mayo* (1909) and *Canciones y poemas* (1918).

— RICHARD J. WALTER

BRAVO, NICOLÁS

Nicolás Bravo (*b.* ca. 1784–1792; *d.* 22 April 1854) Mexican independence leader and politician. Born in Chilpancingo, Bravo and his family joined the insurgency, in which he distinguished himself in a series of campaigns against the royalists. Captured in 1817, he was imprisoned until October 1820. He supported the Plan of Iguala in 1821, emerging as one of the major political figures of the new order.

Although Bravo served in the regency in 1822, he later opposed Emperor Agustín de ITURBIDE, eventually becoming part of the government that replaced the emperor. Elected vice president in 1824, he became the Grand Master of the "aristocratic" Escoceses (Scottish rite Masons), and in January 1828 joined a conservative revolt against the growing power of the radical Yorkinos (York rite Masons), which failed and led to his exile to South America.

Upon his return, Bravo served as commander of the Army of the North, deputy to Congress, and interim president in 1839, 1842–1843, and 1846–1847. During the U.S. invasion in 1847, Bravo commanded troops in battles in Puebla, the defense of the capital, and the last stand in Chapultepec Castle, where he was captured. Although invited to join the revolution of Ayutla, he declined because of illness.

— JAIME E. RODRÍGUEZ O.

BRAY, ARTURO

Arturo Bray (*b.* 1 April 1898; *d.* 2 July 1974), Paraguayan military figure and writer. Born in Asunción to an English father and a Paraguayan mother, Arturo Bray was educated in Asunción and departed for England in 1914 to study medicine. The next year he enlisted in Lord Kitchener's New Armies as a private. He served for two years on the Western Front during World War I, rising to the rank of lieutenant in the infantry. After the war, he returned to Paraguay and quickly received a commission.

During the 1922 military rebellion, Bray remained loyal to the government and held a number of posts in the 1920s. In 1930 he was named director of the Escuela Militar; the following year he was appointed interim chief of police of Asunción. At the outbreak of the Chaco War, Bray was promoted to lieutenant colonel, becoming a divisional commander in 1933. He commanded a unit of infantry at the battle of Boquerón that year. A failed military operation in late 1933 led to his detention until 1935 and left him permanently embittered against many Liberal colleagues within and without the army. Eventually he was cleared of charges and in 1936 participated as chief of the Paraguayan military delegation to the Chaco Peace Conference.

The *Febrista* coup of 1936 resulted in his dismissal from the army and his arrest. With the Liberal restoration in the late 1930s Bray again became chief of police of Asunción; he was promoted to colonel and in 1938 served as minister of the interior. Differences (dating back to the Chaco War) with José Félix ESTIGARRIBIA and other Liberals led to Bray's diplomatic "exile" as minister to Spain and Portugal (1939–1940) and minister to Chile (1940–1941). The 1941 seizure of power by Higinio MORÍNIGO after the death of President Estigarribia spelled the end of Bray's public career.

During his military career, Bray had published professional articles in Paraguayan and foreign newspapers and periodicals. As a private citizen after 1941, he devoted himself to writing. *Hombres y épocas del Paraguay* (1943) and *Solano López, soldado de la gloria y infortunio* (1946) are his best-known works. Later he added another volume to *Hombres y épocas*. He also translated several historical works from English to Spanish. He died in Asunción in 1974.

– JERRY W. COONEY

BRECHERET, VÍTOR

Vítor Brecheret (*b.* 22 February 1894; *d.* 17 December 1955), Brazilian sculptor. Born in Italy, Brecheret moved to Brazil with his sister in 1913 and began his formal artistic education at the Liceu de Artes e Ofícios de São Paulo in 1912. For the next six years he studied art in Europe, where he came to greatly appreciate the work of the French sculptor Auguste Rodin. While in Rome, he won first place in Rome's International Exhibition of Fine Arts for his *Despertar*.

When Brecheret returned to São Paulo in 1919, he set up a studio, and by January 1920 he had met fellow artists DI CAVALCANTI, Hélios Seelinger, Menotti des Picchia, and Oswald de ANDRADE, who recognized his importance for modernism. That same year he was selected to submit plans for a monument commemorating the participation of the bandeira in Brazil's early history. In 1921, after his *Eva* was acquired by the prefecture of São Paulo, Brecheret obtained a government stipend to finance a second trip to Europe. Before leaving for France, however, he selected twelve of his sculptures for exhibition during São Paulo's Modern Art Week in 1922.

Between his return to Brazil in 1930 and his death in 1955, Brecheret realized numerous exhibitions and founded the Sociedade Pró-Arte Moderna (1932). He received the French Legion of Honor and won the National Prize for Sculpture in the 1951 São Paulo Biennial. He also did several commemorative public monuments.

– CAREN A. MEGHREBLIAN

BRESSER PEREIRA, LUIZ CARLOS

Luiz Carlos Bresser Pereira (*b.* 30 June 1934), Brazilian economist. Born in São Paulo, Bresser Pereira received a law degree from the University of São Paulo (USP) in 1957. After joining the faculty of the Getúlio Vargas Foundation in São Paulo (FGV-SP) in 1959, he went to Michigan State University, where he earned an M.B.A. in 1961. Returning to Brazil, he continued his academic career at FGV-SP, becoming a full professor in 1972, the same year in which he earned a Ph.D. in economics from USP. A prolific writer, he has written more than fifteen books and hundreds of articles covering a broad array of subjects. Sometimes characterized as a neo-structuralist, he took the role of the state in the process of economic development as a major theme of research. In the early 1980s, together with Yoshiaki Nakano, he wrote seminal contributions to the formulation of the theory of inertial inflation. He also had a successful career in the private sector (as administrative director of a major Brazilian supermarket chain) and was politically active (as one of the leading economists of PMDB—the main opposition party to the military regime).

In 1983, Bresser Pereira was appointed president of the state-owned bank of São Paulo (BANESPA), and from March 1985 to April 1987 he served both the Montoro and the Quércia administrations as state secretary. Appointed by President José SARNEY, Bresser Pereira replaced Dilson Funaro on 29 April 1987 as Brazil's finance minister after the collapse of the Cruzado Plan. His stabilization program (the Bresser Plan) relied on a temporary price freeze and on measures of fiscal austerity. When the resistance of President Sarney to fiscal austerity became evident, Bresser Pereira resigned on 18 December 1987. He is also known for his attempts to persuade foreign creditors of the necessity for debt relief in developing countries.

– CARLOS ALBERTO PRIMO BRAGA

BRIERRE, JEAN-FERNAND

Jean-Fernand Brierre (pseud. Jean-François; *b.* 28 September 1909; *d.* 24 December 1992). Haitian writer

169

and government official in Haiti and Senegal. In 1932, after serving as secretary to the Haitian Embassy in Paris (1929–1930), Brierre founded the opposition newspaper *La Bataille*. The paper was suspended and Brierre was imprisoned. After an appointment as inspector of schools in Jérémie, Brierre finally became ambassador to Argentina under President Paul MAGLOIRE. Imprisoned again by President François DUVALIER in 1961, Brierre left for Jamaica. He settled in Dakar when Senegalese President Léopold Sédar Senghor offered him a position in the ministry of culture.

Brierre's writing has been characterized by a celebration of the suffering and the triumphs of black people, especially Haitians. Addressing both slaves and his contemporaries in "Black Soul," Brierre wrote that "the black serpent of pain ripples through the contortions of your body." A current of Christian ideology informs even his more erotic poetry. Brierre published copiously from his early twenties into his seventies in Haiti, Argentina, Paris, and Dakar. His name has been associated variously with the Haitian Indigenist poets as well as with the negritude poets.

Works by Jean-Fernand Brierre include: *Le drapeau de demain* (play, 1931); *Chansons secrètes* (poetry, 1933); *Nous garderons le dieu* (poetry, 1945); *Les aïeules* (drama, 1945); *Black Soul* (poetry, 1947); *Belle* (drama, 1948); *Dessalines nous parle* (poetry, 1953); *Au milieu des flammes* (drama, 1953); *Les horizons sans ciel* (novel, 1953); *Pétion et Bolivar, avec Adieu à la Marseillaise* (poetry, 1955); *La Source* (poetry, 1956); *La Nuit* (poetry, 1957); *Hommage au Maître Occilius Jeanty* (poetry, 1960); *Cantique à trois voix pour une poupée d'ébène* (poetry, 1960); *Or, uranium, cuivre, radium* (poetry, 1961); *Découvertes* (poetry, 1966); *Un autre monde* (essay, 1973); *Images d'argile et d'or* (poetry, 1977); *Un Noël pour Gorée* (poetry, 1980); and *Sculptures de proue* (poetry, 1983).

– CARROL F. COATES

BRIÓN, LUIS

Luis Brión (*b.* 1782; *d.* 27 September 1821), Venezuelan naval commander. The son of a successful Flemish Jewish merchant of Curaçao, Brión became commander of Simón BOLÍVAR's Venezuela squadron in 1813 and his most trusted naval adviser. He played a major role in the assault on Spanish maritime interests in the Caribbean during the Wars of Independence, bringing British arms to Bolívar's support and thwarting the reconquest campaign of General Pablo MORILLO. His commercial connections in the Caribbean, especially with Maxwell Hyslop at Jamaica, also helped secure credit for Bolívar's forces. Brión's bitter rivalry with

French privateer Louis-Michael Aury undermined the patriot naval effort when Aury refused to serve under Brión's command in 1816, but Brión's fleet, operating out of Margarita Island, continued to harass the Spaniards. In 1820 Brión took charge of the transition from a privateer fleet to a more formal Venezuelan navy, but when he became ill in the spring of 1821, his command was transferred to Lino de Clemente.

– RALPH LEE WOODWARD, JR.

BRITTO GARCÍA, LUIS

Luis Britto García (*b.* 9 October 1940), Venezuelan writer. Twice awarded the Casa de las Américas literary prize (*Rajatabla* [short stories], 1970; *Abrapalabra* [novel], 1979), Britto García engages in linguistic experimentation, in both prose and drama, that ranges from the poetic to the entropic (serving as his point of departure for the deconstruction of contemporary Venezuelan cultural and social phenomena).

Venezuelan culture is also the subject of Britto García's more recent nonfiction works, such as *La máscara del poder* (1988), a systematic investigation of the cultural aspects of populism in Venezuelan politics, and *El imperio contracultural* (1991).

– SHELLY JARRETT BROMBERG

BRIZOLA, LEONEL

Leonel Brizola (*b.* 22 January 1922), governor of Rio Grande do Sul (1959–1963) and Rio de Janeiro, Brazil (1983–1987, 1991–1995). Born into a poor family in rural Rio Grande do Sul, Leonel Brizola was raised by his mother. He worked hard to complete his education, moving to Pôrto Alegre at age fourteen. By taking different jobs, he managed to complete his engineering degree.

In 1945, as a recruiter for the Brazilian Labor Party (PTB), Brizola cultivated the working-class and socialist identity that helped him win election to the state legislature. His association with João GOULART led to his marriage to the latter's sister and to closer ties to Getúlio VARGAS. After several state posts, Brizola won election as federal deputy in 1954.

In 1955 Brizola's promises to improve the lives of the workers won him the mayoralty of Porto Alegre. For three years he developed his reputation as an engineer with a social conscience, speaking on the radio, writing newspaper columns, meeting with civic groups, and overseeing projects.

His success as mayor led to his victory in the 1958 gubernatorial election. Two controversial nationalizations—the American-owned electric power and telephone companies—projected Brizola onto the national scene. Moreover, he mobilized civilian and military forces in Rio Grande to compel the succession of Goulart to the presidency in 1961. A year later Brizola heightened his national prominence when he was elected Guanabara's federal deputy by the most votes ever cast. From his new political base he pressured Goulart and Congress to carry out major reforms, such as land distribution, rent control, and nationalization of utilities. Although popular among workers, Brizola's campaign alienated businessmen, the upper middle class, the U.S. government, and the military. His tendency to polarize issues contributed to the crisis of 1964.

Although popular among workers, Brizola's campaign alienated businessmen, the upper middle class, the U.S. government, and the military.

After the 1964 coup, Brizola fled in exile to Uruguay, where he organized guerrilla resistance and participated in various conspiracies; eventually he settled down and conducted business there. Deported in 1977, he traveled in the United States and Europe, making contacts and developing a democratic socialist image.

In 1979 he returned to Brazil under the amnesty and founded the Democratic Labor Party (PDT), with which he won election as governor of Rio in 1982. He was notable for founding integrated school centers for children, curbing police abuses, and pressuring Congress to hold direct elections for president in 1984–1985. Having run unsuccessfully for president in 1989, he was elected governor of Rio the following year. After a successful term as governor, he again ran an unsuccessful race for president in 1994.

– MICHAEL L. CONNIFF

BRIZUELA, FRANCISCO

Francisco Brizuela (*b.* 17 February 1879; *d.* 14 August 1947), Paraguayan soldier in the Chaco War and civil war of 1947. Born in Carapeguá, Brizuela entered the armed forces at an early age and participated in several of Paraguay's minor civil wars of the 1900–1920 period. Having advanced to the rank of major, he acted as chief of police for Asunción between June 1918 and September 1919.

Brizuela made little secret of his own political ambitions and therefore spent most of the 1920s out of uniform. At the end of the decade, however, he was called out of retirement to command a Paraguayan infantry division in the early stages of the Chaco War. The energetic defense he prepared at Fort Nanawa in 1933 prevented the Bolivians from advancing southward toward Asunción. Soon afterward, they began their long retreat to the Altiplano.

Brizuela later participated in the 1947 civil war. While attempting to fly munitions to rebel forces in Paraguay, he was killed in an airplane accident outside Montevideo.

– THOMAS L. WHIGHAM

BROQUA, ALFONSO

Alfonso Broqua (*b.* 11 September 1876; *d.* 24 November 1946), Uruguayan composer. Broqua was born in Montevideo, where he began his music studies. In 1894 he went to Paris and entered the Schola Cantorum, where he studied composition under Vincent d'Indy for six years. After spending some time in Brussels with Eduardo FABINI, he returned to Montevideo in 1904. His first nationalist work, *Tabaré,* based on a poem by Juan ZORRILLA DE SAN MARTÍN, premiered in 1910. Broqua set out to create a new musical aesthetic based on the use of vocal themes and dance forms and rhythms from Uruguayan folk music. *Tabaré,* a lyric poem for soprano, female chorus, and orchestra, was considered a major event at Montevideo. It was performed at the Teatro Solís on 30 June 1910 and conducted by the composer. That same year the National Orchestra presented his version of *El poema de las lomas,* originally a major piano triptych premiered by Ernest Drangosh in 1909. Two other works from this period are *Quinteto en sol menor* and *La cruz del Sud,* a never performed opera.

In terms of musical form and aesthetics, the Piano Quintet in G minor is the best written of his works; its last movement, *Variaciones sobre temas regionales,* shows a clear influence of the new nationalist style, which he, Fabini, and Luis CLUZEAU-MORTET helped to inaugurate. In 1922 Broqua settled in Paris, where he continued composing. His other major works include *Impresiones sinfónicas* (1912) for orchestra, *Preludios pampeanos* (1938) for guitar, *Evocaciones criollas, Estudios criollos,* and *Preludios* (1929), as well as three suites for guitar and numerous pieces for solo piano and for voice, piano, and guitar. He died in Paris.

– SUSANA SALGADO

BROUWER, LEO

Leo Brouwer (*b.* 1 March 1939), Cuban composer and guitarist. A student of Stefan Wolpe and Vincent Persichetti at the Julliard School of Music, Brouwer also studied at the Hartt College of Music under Isadore Freed. He was a music assistant with Radio Havana (1960–1961) and director of the music department at the Institute of the Film Industry and Art (IAIC) in 1960–1962. He taught theory and composition at the National Conservatory in Havana (1961–1967) and in 1969 he became director of the experimental branch of the IAIC. A guitarist of international recognition, he has made many recordings of classical and contemporary music. He has achieved similar success as a composer of orchestral and chamber music and has written music for film and for the theater. Brouwer used conventional styles at the beginning of his career. For example, in the more than fifty compositions he wrote from 1956 to 1962 he used mostly folkloric elements within a nationalistic and rather conventional style. Having had contacts in the 1960s with contemporary composers like Bogustaw Schäffer and Henyrk Górecki and also with Luigi Nono and Hans Werner Henze, Brouwer turned toward the avant-garde, chance, and experimental music. He has explored contemporary techniques and is probably among the first Cuban composers to successfully utilize the open forms and aleatoric techniques, frequently including graphic and proportional notation in his scores. He has also collaborated with pop artists and mass-media productions.

Among his more important works are *Danzas concertantes* for guitar and string orchestra (1958); *Variantes* for percussion (1962); *Sonograma I* for prepared piano (1963); *Sonograma II* for orchestra (1964); *2 Conceptos del tiempo* for ten players (1965); *Homage to Mingus* for jazz combo and orchestra (1965); *Tropos* for orchestra (1967); *Sonograma III* for two pianos (1968); *5 Epigrams* for cello and piano (1968); *Conmutaciones* for prepared piano and two percussionists (1966); *El reino de esto mundo* for woodwind quintet (1968); *Rem tene verba sequentur* for string quartet (1969); *Cantigas del tiempo nuevo* for actors, children's choir, piano, harp, and percussion (1969); *Exaedros,* for six players or multiples of six (1969–1970); *Anima Latina* (Madrigali guerrieri ed amorosi) for orchestra (1977); and *Es el amor quién ve,* for voice and chamber ensemble (1972). He has written for guitar *Canticum* (1972); *La espiral eterna* (1970); *Tarantos* (1977); *Per sonare a due* (1973); and *El decamerón negro* (1981).

— ALCIDES LANZA

BRULL, MARIANO

Mariano Brull (*b.* 24 February 1891; *d.* 6 August 1956), Cuban poet. Brull was born in Camagüey Province but spent his childhood in Spain. He returned to Cuba as an adolescent and began publishing his early poems. In 1913 he received a law degree from the University of Havana and worked as a lawyer until 1917, when he obtained a diplomatic post in Washington, D.C. He later served in Cuba's embassies in Peru, Belgium, Spain, Switzerland, France, Italy, Canada, and Uruguay. Brull was published in several key literary magazines, including *Clavileño* and the legendary *Orígenes,* founded by José LEZAMA LIMA. One of the most influential poets of the first decades of this century, he is well known for his *jitanjáforas,* poems constructed with words invented for the beauty of their sound and their rhythm, as the term *jitanjáfora* itself, the title of one of those poems. Well-known poets and critics of his time acclaimed Brull's poetry, among them Paul Valéry, Alfonso REYES, Gastón Baquero, Pedro HENRÍQUEZ UREÑA, and Cintio VITIER, and he exerted great influence upon the following generation of Cuban poets. Among his works are *La casa del silencio: Antología de su obra, 1916–1954* (1976) and *Una antología de poesía cubana* (1984).

— ROBERTO VALERO

BRUM, BALTASAR

Baltasar Brum (*b.* 18 June 1883; *d.* 31 March 1933), president of Uruguay (1919–1923). Brum was one of the most prominent politicians in the country from 1913 to 1933. As well as president of Uruguay, he was president of the National Council of Administration from 1929 to 1931 and served as minister of public education (1913–1915) and of foreign affairs (1914–1915).

The son of landowners of Brazilian origin, he subscribed to the beliefs of Batllism, specifically to its reformist tendencies. He began his political career young and by the age of thirty was minister of education. He was the first president to govern under the system of a collegial executive branch consisting of the president and the National Council of Administration, which had been approved in 1917. During his administration legislation for the benefit of the working class was promoted on issues such as a minimum wage for rural laborers, social security, workplace safety, weekly time off, and an attempt at regulating labor practices regarding women and children.

Brum's administration was followed by Riverista leaders who represented the conservative wing of the Colorado Party. Batllism regained the presidency in 1931 with the election of Gabriel TERRA, although he was more conservative than the original Batllistas. Brum belonged to the National Council of Administration, which confronted the president on more than one occasion. When Terra assumed dictatorial powers in 1933, Brum committed suicide in public as a symbolic gesture, even though his personal liberty was not at stake.

— FERNANDO FILGUEIRA

BRUNET, MARTA

Marta Brunet (*b.* 9 August 1897; *d.* 10 August 1967), Chilean feminist writer. Brunet was born in Chillán and raised in southern Chile but spent most of her life in other countries, living first in Europe (1911–1914) and later working as cultural attaché to the Chilean Embassy in Argentina (1939–1952), Brazil (1962–1963), and Uruguay (1963–1967). She wrote nine novels and ten collections of short stories. Her most important fictional works are *Montaña adentro* (1923; Deep into the Mountains), "Soledad de la sangre" (1943; "The Solitude of the Blood"), *Humo hacia el sur* (1946; Smoke Towards the South), *María Nadie* (1957; Maria Nobody), and *Amasijo* (1962; Dough for Baking). Her *Obras completas* were published in Chile in 1963.

Although Brunet initially followed the "criollista" tendency in fiction that was prevalent in Chile through the 1930s, she soon went beyond its nativist parameters to present universal concerns through the psychological and existential conflicts of her characters. Based primarily on the world of women, her work characterizes female desire for self-actualization. By means of the opposition between reality and dream, Brunet focuses at once on a woman's submission to the patriarchal forces of family and community and her possibility for spiritual empowerment through the realm of fantasy. In 1961 she became the second woman to receive the National Prize for literature. She died in Montevideo.

— J. A. EPPLE

BRYCE ECHENIQUE, ALFREDO

Alfredo Bryce Echenique (*b.* 19 February 1939), Peruvian novelist, short-story writer, and journalist. Bryce Echenique was born in Lima to an aristocratic family. He studied literature and law at the University of San Marcos in Lima, receiving a Ph.D. in 1964. He then studied at the Sorbonne in Paris. Beginning in 1968 he taught at the universities of Nanterre, Sorbonne, and Vincennes. In 1980 he relocated to Montpellier and taught literature at Paul Valéry University. In 1986 he moved to Spain.

An original combination of the oral tradition, memory, and humor is the basic feature of Bryce Echenique's entire body of literary work. *Un mundo para Julius* (1970; *A World for Julius,* 1992) was his first novel and

one of his most successful ones. It depicts a sector of the Lima oligarchy with authenticity, humor, and irony.

In his novels *Tantas veces Pedro* (1977), *La vida exagerada de Martín Romaña* (1981), *El hombre que hablaba de Octavia de Cádiz* (1985), and *La última mudanza de Felipe Carrillo* (1988), Bryce Echenique narrates the cycle of apprenticeship and maturity in the erotic experience of one Latin American character, of oligarchic origin, in Europe in the 1960s and 1970s. He has also published several short-story collections: *Huerto cerrado* (1968), *La felicidad ja, ja* (1974), *Cuentos completos* (1981), and *Crónicas personales* (1988). His journalistic work is equally extensive in magazines and newspapers.

— JESÚS DÍAZ CABALLERO

BUARQUE, CHICO

Chico Buarque (Francisco Buarque de Holanda; *b.* 19 July 1944), Brazilian singer, songwriter, and writer. The son of historian Sérgio Buarque de Holanda, Buarque has distinguished himself as an insightful artist in the field of entertainment. He studied in Rio and São Paulo but abandoned architecture to dedicate himself to music in the mid-1960s. His involvement in drama began in 1966 with the musical settings for a stage version of João Cabral de Melo Neto's verse play *Morte e vida severina* (Death and Life of Severina). Through the historic songwriters' festivals of the late 1960s, Buarque gained national attention as an incomparable songsmith of both traditional vocal samba and bossa nova. Also known for the social criticism in his lyrics, he went into voluntary exile in Italy in 1969 to escape the military regime, which censored an appreciable portion of his work in the 1970s.

Buarque gained national attention as an incomparable songsmith of both traditional vocal samba and bossa nova.

The composer's battles with government censors comprise a major chapter of the history of institutional intervention in the arts during that decade. His most controversial play, *Calabar,* a musical collaboration with Ruy Guerra, reexamined a Brazilian figure accused of treason during the Dutch occupation in the early seventeenth century. In 1974, Buarque published a novel, *Fazenda modelo: Novela pecuária* (Model Farm: A Bovine Novel), an allegorical sociohistorical critique inspired by George Orwell. He also wrote some children's literature. On a cultural mission in 1978, Buarque made his first of several visits to Cuba and introduced some new Cuban music to the Brazilian public. In the 1970s and 1980s, in addition to crafted sentimental songs and numerous masterpiece sambas of social observation, Buarque wrote many songs for films (e.g., *Bye Bye Brazil*) and for his own stage productions, including *Ópera do malandro* (Hustler's Opera), which later was adapted for film. Buarque is respected as one of the leading performing songwriters in the history of the nation and as one of her most perspicacious artists.

— CHARLES A. PERRONE

BUCARAM ELMHALIN, ASAAD

Asaad Bucaram Elmhalin (*b.* 24 December 1916; *d.* 5 November 1981), leader of the populist Concentración de Fuerzas Populares (1962–1981) in Ecuador. Born in Ambato to Lebanese parents and self-taught, Bucaram assumed leadership of the Concentration of Popular Forces (Concentración de Fuerzas Populares—CFP) after the resignation of Carlos Guevara Moreno. Elected mayor of Guayaquil (1962–1963) during a period of economic prosperity, he earned a reputation for personal honesty and administrative ability. He was deposed, jailed, and deported by the military government in 1963, when he attempted to mobilize the CFP to defend the government of Carlos Julio AROSEMENA MONROY (1963).

After returning to Ecuador, Bucaram headed the CFP delegation to the 1966 constituent assembly and was elected vice president of the assembly. Reelected as mayor of Guayaquil in 1967, he brought his party into the Front of the Democratic Left (Frente de la Izquierda Democrática—FID), which supported the candidacy of Andrés F. Córdova Nieto in the 1968 presidential election. Elected prefect of Guayas Province in 1970, he was subsequently exiled, a second time, by VELASCO IBARRA.

Bucaram was the leading candidate for president in 1972, but the military coup of 15 February 1972 prevented his election and exiled him a third time. Prior to the restoration of constitutional government in 1979, the military government disqualified his candidacy. Bucaram then selected Guayaquil lawyer Jaime ROLDÓS AGUILERA to run as the candidate of the CFP. Prior to the election of Roldós, however, relations between the two CFP leaders began to deteriorate, and the party subsequently divided into two factions. The conflict was ideological as well as personal. Bucaram was a populist whose power base was primarily regional. Thus, he favored government expenditures that provided patronage for his supporters and coastal public works projects at the expense of fiscal responsibility and projects se-

lected on the basis of national criteria. Bucaram was unsuccessful in his bid to prevent Roldós from taking office but cemented an agreement with the conservatives that allowed him to become president of the Chamber of Deputies, a position he used to obstruct presidential initiatives until his death.

— LINDA ALEXANDER RODRÍGUEZ

BUCARELI Y URSÚA, ANTONIO MARÍA

Antonio María Bucareli y Ursúa (*b.* 24 January 1717; *d.* 9 April 1779), captain-general of Cuba (1766–1771) and viceroy of New Spain (1771–1779). Born in Seville, Spain, to a noble family, Bucareli joined the Spanish army as a cadet and served in campaigns in Italy and Portugal. He achieved the rank of lieutenant general and was inspector general of cavalry and inspector of coastal fortifications of the Kingdom of Granada. In 1766, he was named governor and captain-general of Cuba, a difficult post which he occupied with distinction. Although Bucareli wished to return to Spain following his Cuban assignment, the crown wanted an experienced administrator in the Mexican viceregency who could deal with the reforms proposed by Visitor General José de GÁLVEZ.

Bucareli was conservative in his approach to change and, where possible, tended to support traditional solutions. He reorganized the militia units, rebuilt coastal fortifications, and oversaw the construction of the fortress of Perote, which was designed to prevent an enemy invasion inland. In the north of New Spain, Bucareli dealt with growing Indian depredations against frontier presidios and problems related to the exploration and settlement of Alta California. To verify the possibility of Russian penetration on the North American coast, Bucareli dispatched the maritime expedition of Juan PÉREZ, the first in a series of voyages that carried Spanish exploration into Alaskan waters.

As a colonial administrator, Bucareli rejected many of the reforms proposed by Gálvez. He criticized schemes for territorial reorganization and doubted the possible benefits of introducing a system of powerful provincial intendants. A zealous and capable bureaucrat, Bucareli was able to get the best results out of the cumbersome colonial regime. He is recognized as one of the best eighteenth-century viceroys of New Spain. Bucareli died in office, and his remains were interred at the shrine of the Virgin of Guadalupe.

— CHRISTON I. ARCHER

BUCARELI Y URSÚA, FRANCISCO DE PAULA

Francisco de Paula Bucareli y Ursúa (*d.* after 1770), governor of Buenos Aires (1766–1770), brother of Antonio María Bucareli, viceroy of New Spain. Bucareli, probably born in Seville, Spain, was a career army officer imbued with the ideas of the Spanish version of the Enlightenment. In 1776 he assumed the post of governor of Buenos Aires, where he immediately became involved in expelling the Portuguese from Rio Grande do Sul in May of 1767. In the same year he directed the expulsion of 345 Jesuits from the twelve colleges, residences, and missions of the Río de la Plata. As a result, over fifty estates with thousands of head of cattle, slaves, and real estate were auctioned and sold. In 1770 Bucareli ousted English settlers from Port Egmond in the Falkland Islands, reclaiming the islands for Spain. Soon afterward he returned to Spain, where he died.

– NICHOLAS P. CUSHNER

BULNES, FRANCISCO

Francisco Bulnes (*b*. 4 October 1847; *d*. 22 September 1924), Mexican political writer. Bulnes, a native of Mexico City, received a civil and mining engineering degree from the National School of Mines. After 1874 he turned to politics, journalism, and economic affairs. He was periodically a national deputy and senator for thirty years, and in 1893 and 1903 led in the effort of the Científico group to limit presidential power. He served on numerous committees devoted to banking, mining, and financial legislation, and in 1885 he wrote on the British debt.

Bulnes won notoriety for his polemical works attacking Benito JUÁREZ and the doctrinaire liberal (Jacobin) tradition in Mexican politics, including *El verdadero Juárez* (1904) and *Juárez y las revoluciones de Ayutla y de reforma* (1905). He later defended the regime of Porfirio DÍAZ in *El verdadero Díaz y la revolución* (1920). His intellectual orientation was positivist, and as a writer he was influenced by Hippolyte Taine. His critical insights have attracted many modern scholars to his work.

– CHARLES A. HALE

BULNES PRIETO, MANUEL

Manuel Bulnes Prieto (*b*. 25 December 1799; *d*. 19 October 1866), president of Chile (1841–1851). Born in Concepción, Bulnes became a soldier at the age of twelve. He distinguished himself in the Wars of Independence and he fought at the battle of Maipú (5 April 1818). Promoted to general in 1831, he was placed in command of the second Chilean expedition to Peru during the war against the Peru-Bolivian Confederation, and won the decisive battle of Yungay (20 January 1839). On the strength of his popularity as a war hero,

he was chosen to succeed Joaquín PRIETO (1831–1841) as Chile's president.

A bluff, amiable man with an enormous appetite, Bulnes served two consecutive terms; he displayed great tolerance in tranquil periods but used a firm hand at times of political agitation (1845–1846 and 1850–1851). He was the first Chilean president to use the late-colonial Casa de la Moneda as the presidential palace.

When he finished his second term in September 1851, Bulnes took charge of an army to quell a major revolt in the southern provinces, which was led by his cousin, General José María de la Cruz (1799–1875). Bulnes defeated Cruz in the bloody battle of Loncomilla (8 December 1851). In 1866, opponents of the reelection of President José Joaquín PÉREZ (1851–1871) proclaimed Bulnes a presidential candidate; had he won, he would have served only one month.

– SIMON COLLIER

BUNGE, ALEJANDRO

Alejandro Bunge (*b*. 8 January 1880; *d*. 24 May 1943), Argentine economist. Educated in his native Buenos Aires and in Germany, Bunge was the foremost intellectual representative of the 1920s and 1930s reaction against the open, agrarian, exports-led model of economic development that had spurred Argentina's expansion from the late nineteenth century on; he favored a more active role for the state in the promotion of local industries. A leader of the Social Catholic movement, he directed the Círculos de Obreros Católicos between 1912 and 1916, confronting both liberals and socialists in numerous debates about labor policies.

Bunge began his career in public administration as director of statistics of the National Department of Labor between 1913 and 1915, later becoming director of the Office of Statistics between 1915 and 1920 and 1923 and 1925. In 1918 he founded the influential *Revista de Economía Argentina,* a forum for the new economic ideas, which he directed for more than two decades. Bunge also taught economics at the universities of Buenos Aires and La Plata and wrote several books, among which *La economía argentina* (4 vols., 1928–1930) and *Una nueva Argentina* (1940) were the most significant.

– EDUARDO A. ZIMMERMANN

BUNGE, AUGUSTO

Augusto Bunge (*b*. 25 April 1877; *d*. 1 August 1948), Argentine hygienist and politician. After graduating with honors from the Medical School of the University of Buenos Aires in 1900, Bunge specialized in public health and in 1906 was sent to Europe by the national government to study the organization of public health and safety measures in factories and workshops. He was put in charge of the Industrial and Public Health Section of the National Department of Public Health, where he launched a campaign for the improvement of working conditions in local industries, as can be seen in his *Las conquistas de la higiene social* (1910–1911). He was a founder and member of the Independent Socialist Party (PSI) and was elected to Congress for five consecutive terms in 1916, 1920, 1924, 1928, and 1932. In Congress, he actively promoted social and labor legislation, drafting in 1917 a detailed system of social insurance based on the German and British models.

Bunge's thought was representative of the fusion of biological and social ideas with a strong racialist component that characterized much of the intellectual life

---

Bunge was a firm believer in the anthropological and moral inferiority of nonwhite races to Caucasians.

---

of turn-of-the-century Latin America. In several works he argued for a biological foundation of human ethics, and he was a firm believer in the anthropological and moral inferiority of nonwhite races to Caucasians, as stated in his book *El culto de la vida* (1915).

– EDUARDO A. ZIMMERMANN

BUNGE, CARLOS OCTAVIO

Carlos Octavio Bunge (*b.* 1875; *d.* 22 May 1918), Argentine author, educator, and positivist social critic. Born in Buenos Aires, Bunge studied law at the University of Buenos Aires. He later joined the faculty there. Author of numerous works, his most important include: *El espíritu de la educación* (1901), *Nuestra América* (1903), and a biography of Domingo Faustino SARMIENTO. In his work, he criticized the Spanish, American, and African elements of Latin American culture and society. While critical of tyrants, such as Juan Manuel de ROSAS (ruled 1829–1852), he appreciated such modernizing states as the Porfiriato (1876–1910) in México, which promoted order and progress. Reflecting on his own country in *Nuestra América,* he believed that European immigration would facilitate Argentina's efforts to become one of the world's leading nations. In these respects, he was typical of many Latin American

intellectuals of his generation who echoed the Eurocentric ideals of Social Darwinism and positivism.

– DANIEL LEWIS

BUÑUEL, LUIS

Luis Buñuel (*b.* 22 February 1900; *d.* 29 July 1983), surrealist film director and naturalized Mexican citizen. Born in Calanda, Spain, Buñuel studied at the University of Madrid, where his friends included Salvador Dalí and Federico García Lorca. Interested in film from a very young age, Buñuel moved to Paris in 1923 and worked as assistant to the film director Jean Epstein. Buñuel's first film, *Un chien andalou* (1928), a collaborative effort with Dalí, created a scandal and made both of them famous. Their second film, *L'âge d'or* (1930), attracted praise from literary figures, but the "respectable" press was deeply shocked. Fascist thugs took their criticism to the streets, viciously attacking theaters and moviegoers. The Paris prefect of police, believing surrealism to be more dangerous than fascism, banned the film. Buñuel returned to Spain for his third film, *Las hurdes—tierra sin pan* (1932), a documentary about rural misery.

Working for the Republican government of Spain during the Civil War, he produced documentaries and was sent on a diplomatic mission to Hollywood in 1938. After Franco's victory, Buñuel remained in the United States, working on anti-Nazi projects for the Museum of Modern Art in New York, and the U.S. Army during World War II. After the war, Buñuel worked in Hollywood (1944–1946) before moving to Mexico, where he began his most prolific period, directing twenty-one films (including nineteen in Mexico) between 1947 and 1962. His *Los olvidados* (1950) won the prize for the best direction and the International Critics' Prize at the Cannes Festival in 1951, reestablishing Buñuel's international reputation. The film combined elements of a neorealist study of juvenile delinquency and social protest with dream sequences and surrealistic violence that linked *Los olvidados* to his earlier work. Among the outstanding films Buñuel directed in this period are *Subida al cielo* (1951); *El bruto* (1952); *Él* (1952); *La ilusión viaja en tranvía* (1953); *Ensayo de un crimen* (1955); *Nazarín* (1958); *La fièvre monte à El Pao* (1959); *Viridiana* (1961); and *El ángel exterminador* (1962).

Making his first three films outside the film industry afforded Buñuel greater control over his work than he had while working as director for less imaginative producers during this middle period. Nevertheless, Buñuel was able to infuse these projects with his own style while appealing simultaneously to the uneducated audiences and the aesthetically sophisticated. In the words of Raymond Durgnat, Buñuel's films "have thrills galore at a lowbrow level, and a subtler meaning on a highbrow level, and a great deal of human meaning on all levels. But their sorts of aesthetic refinement, philosophical interest, and particularly, moral issues, tend to puzzle the bourgeois middlebrow, to leave him dissatisfied and perhaps a little contemptuous" (p. 13).

Commercial success permitted Buñuel greater artistic control over his French-made films in the late 1960s and early 1970s, including *La voie lactée* (1969), *Le charme discret de la bourgeoisie* (1972), and *Le fantôme de la liberté* (1974). Buñuel sought to portray social reality while undermining conventional ideas and destroying the illusion of the inevitability of the bourgeois world. He died in Mexico City.

— D. F. STEVENS

BURGOS, JULIA DE

Julia de Burgos (*b.* 17 February 1914?; *d.* 6 July 1953), Puerto Rican poet. Born to a poor family in Carolina, Puerto Rico, Julia Constanza Burgos García studied at the University of Puerto Rico's High School and Normal School. She taught at a small rural school while continuing her university studies. Her first work, a small, typewritten edition of *Poemas exactos a mí misma* (Poems exactly like myself, 1937), was followed by *Poemas en veinte surcos* (Poems in twenty furrows, 1938) and *Canción de la verdad sencilla* (Songs of simple truth, 1939), honored by the Institute of Puerto Rican Literature. In 1940 Burgos left Puerto Rico for New York, where she lived a bohemian life. Later that year she moved to Cuba, where she remained until 1942. A failed love affair brought her back to New York, where she suffered from ill health and the alcoholism that eventually caused her death. Two poems, "Welfare Island," written in English, and "Dadme mi número" (Give me my number) foreshadowed her death, alone and anonymous, in New York. Her body was later brought to Puerto Rico and buried near the Río Grande de Loíza, which she had glorified in one of her most famous poems.

Burgos's poems are about love, death, the passing of time, Puerto Rico, freedom, and justice. Images of rivers and the sea permeate her poetry, especially in *El mar y tú* (The sea and you), published posthumously in 1954.

— ESTELLE IRIZARRY

BURLE MARX, ROBERTO

Roberto Burle Marx (*b.* 1909; *d.* 4 June 1994), foremost landscape architect in Brazil. Roberto Burle Marx was born to a German businessman and his wife, a Brazilian pianist. Although he shared his mother's interest in gardening, Burle Marx originally intended to become a painter. It was while studying art in Berlin in 1928 that he discovered the beauty of Brazil's native plants, which were often neglected in the gardens of his own country.

Returning to Brazil, Burle Marx took up painting as his career and gardening as a hobby. One of his gardens attracted the attention of Lucio COSTA, an architect and longtime friend, who asked Burle Marx to design a garden for a private residence. This garden, containing a variety of Brazilian plants, as opposed to the formal, European-style gardens that had been the custom, was an immediate success and the first of many commissions. Among his many award-winning projects are Flamengo Park and the plant-lined mosaic sidewalks that run along Copacabana Beach in Rio. Not limiting himself to Brazil, he designed gardens for the UNESCO headquarters in Paris, public parks in Venezuela, a waterfront renovation project in Key Biscayne, Florida, and private gardens on three continents and numerous islands.

Burle Marx planned his gardens with a painter's eye. Sharp contrasts in color and shape characterize his style. "The garden must be linked to nature," appears to be his prevailing philosophy. Other Burle Marx hallmarks are his use of stone and water plants, which grace many of his gardens.

Working so intimately with plants, Burle Marx became an advocate for the preservation of Brazil's natural environment and frequently spoke out against the threat that development poses to his beloved plants. He, himself, discovered several of the country's native plants, some of which are named after him.

— SHEILA L. HOOKER

BUSCH BECERRA, GERMÁN

Germán Busch Becerra (*b.* 23 March 1903; *d.* 23 August 1939), president of Bolivia (July 1937–August 1939). Busch was born in Trinidad, in the eastern department of El Beni. His father was an eccentric German medical doctor, and his mother, Raquel Becerra, was a native of Trinidad. In his early youth Busch joined the army as a cadet. He became noted for his daring, physical fitness, and hot temper—characteristics that served him well in the Chaco War.

After participating in the overthrow of presidents Daniel SALAMANCA, José Luis TEJADA SORZANO, and David TORO, in July 1937 he assumed the presidency in the belief that all three previous presidents had been inept in their handling of the war. On 27 May 1938 Busch was elected constitutional president for the period 1938 to 1942. On 24 April 1939 he declared himself a dictator, proclaiming "military socialism" and undertaking radical reforms that included the nationalization of the Standard Oil holdings. He condemned the German-born tin magnate Mauricio HOCHSCHILD to death and nationalized the tin mines. Prevented by his cabinet from executing the sentence, in a fit of rage, Busch committed suicide in front of his aides, saying it "is best to terminate my life" to convince the Bolivian nation of the righteousness of his action. Although the

---

In a fit of rage, Busch committed suicide in front of his aides, saying it "is best to terminate my life" to convince the Bolivian nation of the righteousness of his action.

---

suicide is an accepted historical fact, there has been some talk of assassination. Just before Busch's death a permanent peace treaty with Paraguay went into effect, although hostilities had long since ended. Busch, considered a forerunner of Bolivia's great reforms of the next three decades, has become virtually a legendary figure in Bolivian history.

— CHARLES W. ARNADE

BUSTAMANTE, ANASTASIO

Anastasio Bustamante (*b.* 17 July 1780; *d.* 1853), Mexican military man and politician. Born in Jiquilpán, Michoacán, Bustamante studied medicine in Mexico City. During the struggle for independence, he joined the royal army, distinguishing himself in combat. Nevertheless, he supported Agustín de ITURBIDE (later emperor) in 1821. After the fall of the empire, he allied himself with the Escoceses (Scottish rite Masons), was elected vice president in 1829, and overthrew the government in January 1830. His administration (1830–1832) was noted for its conservatism, political repression, and the execution of President Vicente GUERRERO. Subsequently ousted and exiled, Bustamante returned to office as president in 1837–1839, 1840, and 1841, becoming one of the most important politicians of the early republic. He also served as senator and participated in various military campaigns, the last of which was the pacification of the Sierra Gorda insurrection in 1848.

— JAIME E. RODRÍGUEZ O.

BUSTAMANTE, CARLOS MARÍA DE

Carlos María de Bustamante (*b.* 4 November 1774; *d.* 21 September 1848), Mexican patriot, politician, and writer. Born in Oaxaca, Bustamante studied theology and law. He distinguished himself early as a champion of the poor, and during the Wars of Independence became defense counsel for various conspirators. One of the founders of the *Diario de Méjico* in 1805, he became famous in 1812 as the editor of the anti-government *El Jugetillo* (The Small Toy) and was chosen "elector" of the city of Mexico that year. Later he became an adviser to José María MORELOS and was instrumental in convincing the insurgents to hold a congress in Apatzingán and in writing the Constitution of Apatzingán (1814). After independence he served in nearly every congress from 1822 until his death.

A strong centralist, Bustamante grew increasingly conservative as the country he loved fell into anarchy. He was extremely influential as a journalist and a pamphleteer; over his lifetime he published many newspapers and hundreds of pamphlets. Following his intellectual mentor, Father MIER NORIEGA Y GUERRA, in recovering pre-Columbian and colonial manuscripts and in creating the political myth of the ancient "Mexican Empire," Bustamante also helped to create the "official history" of independence that persists to the present day. In addition, he was one of the principal chroniclers of the period, having written Mexico's history from independence until the U.S. invasion, an event that left him "sick of soul and body" and coincided with his death.

Bustamante's most important historical works are *Cuadro histórico de la revolución de la América mexicana* 3 (1823–1832), and *Continuación del cuadro histórico de la revolución mexicana* 4 (1953–1963). Perhaps the most significant of all his contributions was his personal diary, "Diario histórico de México," forty-eight volumes, which records the events of the period 1822–1848.

— JAIME E. RODRÍGUEZ O.

BUSTAMANTE Y GUERRA, JOSÉ

José Bustamante y Guerra (*b.* 1759; *d.* 1825), Spanish naval officer who served as captain-general and governor of Uruguay (1795–1810) and Guatemala (1811–1818). Bustamante distinguished himself in Spain's North African campaign in 1774 and was a member of the Malespina expedition that circumnavigated the globe between 1784 and 1791. He became governor of Uruguay in 1795 and later commanded Spanish naval forces in the Río de la Plata. He was transferred to Guatemala in 1811, where he served as captain-general until 1818. Unsympathetic to the Cádiz Constitution of 1812, Bustamante delayed implementing its reforms in Guatemala and concentrated instead on insulating Central America from the revolutionary events occurring in Mexico. He became notorious in Central American history for authoritarian rule, especially after the restoration of Ferdinand VII of Spain in 1814.

Although Bustamante subdued several revolts and maintained the loyalty of Central America when much of the rest of the Spanish Empire was in rebellion, his draconian policies stimulated animosities among the creoles and sentiment for independence, which erupted soon after his departure. He became director-general of the Spanish Navy in 1819 and died six years later in a shipwreck en route to Buenos Aires.

– SUE DAWN MCGRADY

BUSTAMANTE Y RIVERO, JOSÉ LUIS

José Luis Bustamante y Rivero (*b.* 1894; *d.* 1990), democratically elected president of Peru (1945) who was ousted in 1948 by a military coup led by General Manuel ODRÍA. Bustamante y Rivero, born in Arequipa, was educated as a lawyer at the universities of Arequipa and Cuzco. During his early political activities he expressed southern regionalist interests influenced by the local version of *pierolismo* (after the civilian caudillo Nicolás de PIÉROLA). He opposed President Augusto B. LEGUÍA's failed policies toward the provinces. In 1930, as political secretary of the Revolutionary Junta in Arequipa, Bustamante supported the military coup led by Colonel Luis M. SÁNCHEZ CERRO. Between 1934 and 1945 he held diplomatic posts in Bolivia, Paraguay, and Uruguay.

In 1945, a group of middle-class leaders of moderate populist ideology, supported by the illegal Aprista movement and the Communist Party, formed the National Democratic Front (FDN) in Arequipa. With the consent of the army, the FDN announced Bustamante's candidacy in the 1945 elections, in which he successfully defeated the right.

In several ways the Bustamante administration continued and enhanced protectionist measures introduced by the previous president, Manuel PRADO. These measures included exchange and price control and import quotas. As a result, the moderate inflation that had begun to rise under the Prado administration increased substantially under Bustamante. The floating internal debt also increased, contributing to inflation. President Bustamante was under the political pressure of the well-organized Aprista Party, which was strongly represented in the parliament. A failed Aprista armed uprising in 1948 precipitated the coup by Odría, who, with the help of U.S. financial advisers, reintroduced liberal economic measures. He died in Lima.

– ALFONSO W. QUIROZ

BUSTOS, HERMENEGILDO

Hermenegildo Bustos (*b.* 1832; *d.* 1907), Mexican painter. Bustos lived his entire life in the town of Purísima del Rincón, Guanajuato. The diverse types of jobs he held—ice vendor, sacristan, carpenter, maguey planter, and musician—allowed him to bring to his canvases a variety of themes, which were combined with the freshness of a small-town painter who worked by assignment.

Bustos's ex-votos depict tragic scenes from which the subjects felt they had been saved by the miraculous intercession of a saint.

The great majority of his work consists of ex-votos, a form of religious expression popularized in the eighteenth and nineteenth centuries. These small works, painted in lamina, depict tragic scenes from which the subjects felt they had been saved by the miraculous intercession of a saint, to whom the ex-voto was dedicated. The ex-votos of Bustos are distinguished by the individuality he gave to his subjects. His talent as a portraitist enabled him to capture with a rural flavor the features of his subjects—whom we know by name, thanks to an inscription on the ex-voto.

Bustos did more than paint models; he instilled his subjects with a character that went beyond physical features. Two of his dining-room paintings are outstanding for their iconography and extraordinary pictorial quality, recalling the botanical illustrations of the eighteenth century. The paintings must have been highly prized by Bustos, since they remained in his home until his death.

– ESTHER ACEVEDO

C

CAAMAÑO DEÑÓ, FRANCISCO

Francisco Caamaño Deñó (*b.* 11 June 1932; *d.* 16 February 1973), leader of the 1965 constitutionalist revolt in the Dominican Republic and president of the Dominican Republic (1965). Born in Santo Domingo, Caamaño began a career in the military in 1949, following in the footsteps of his father, Fausto Caamaño Medina, one of Rafael Leonidas TRUJILLO's most notorious generals. His father's influence enabled Caamaño to advance rapidly through the military ranks. When the April 1965 revolt split the military, Colonel Caamaño sided with the rebels in their efforts to reinstate the constitutional government of Juan BOSCH (elected December 1962; overthrown September 1963). Caamaño became the leader of the revolutionary troops, and in an emergency session on 4 May 1965, the Dominican National Assembly elected him constitutional president, a position lasting until 31 August. The United States intervened, installing Héctor GARCÍA-GODOY as interim president of the republic in September. In 1966, following the renewal of hostilities between the rebels and the conservatives, Caamaño was sent to London, effectively exiled, to assume a diplomatic post. A year later he abandoned the position and fled to Cuba, where he spent the next six years planning a campaign to overthrow the government of Joaquín BALAGUER (elected 1966). On 3 February 1973, Caamaño landed with a guerrilla band on Dominican soil. Less than two weeks later, he was captured and executed.

— SARA FLEMING

CAAMAÑO Y GÓMEZ CORNEJO, JOSÉ MARÍA PLÁCIDO

José María Plácido Caamaño y Gómez Cornejo (*b.* 5 October 1838; *d.* 31 December 1901), president of Ecuador (1884–1888). Caamaño, a wealthy coastal cacao grower from Guayaquil, was selected to follow President Gabriel GARCÍA MORENO (1861–1865, 1869–1875) in office in 1865. However, he refused. He also opposed the dictatorship of Ignacio de VEINTIMILLA (1876–1883), which led to his arrest and exile in Peru. In 1883 he returned and helped organize the overthrow of Veintimilla. Caamaño joined the provisional government; the subsequent National Convention elected him president. The first of three Progresista (1883–1895) presidents, Caamaño sought to remain independent of both Liberals and Conservatives; his family ties in both the sierra and the coast afforded a further measure of neutrality.

Accused of taking a bribe, Caamaño fled Ecuador when angry citizens laid siege to his home.

Caamaño had hoped to implement a program of public works but instead spent his term fighting efforts to throw him out of office, employing particular brutality in quelling the revolts of coastal guerrillas (*montoneras*). After his presidency he served as governor of Guayas province (1888–1895). Critics saw Caamaño as leader of a corrupt clique, "the ring" (*la argolla*), thought to be a conspiracy of coastal financial interests who secretly controlled the nation. Caamaño was implicated in the Esmeraldas affair (1894–1895), a scandal that involved the use of the Ecuadorian flag to cover the sale of a Chilean warship to Japan. Accused of taking a bribe (a charge he denied), the former president fled Ecuador when angry citizens laid siege to his home. Caamaño traveled to Spain, where he spent the rest of his life in poverty. He died in Seville.

— RONN F. PINEO

CABALLERO, BERNARDINO

Bernardino Caballero (*b.* 20 May 1839; *d.* 26 February 1912), Paraguayan military leader and president (1880–1886). Born in the interior town of Ybycuí, Caballero spent his early career in the cavalry and by the beginning of the War of the Triple Alliance in 1864, had risen to the rank of sergeant. He participated in almost every engagement of the war, from the Mato Grosso campaign to those of Humaitá and the Cordilleras. His success in harassing the advancing Brazilians, as well as his exceptional loyalty, drew the attention of President Francisco Solano LÓPEZ. Advancements for Caballero came rapidly, until 1869, when he achieved the rank of general and with it command over what was left of López's army. Even after the fall of Asunción, he continued the fight, until, in March 1870, the Brazilians cornered and killed López at Cerro Corá. Caballero was taken prisoner shortly thereafter.

Caballero's star rose much higher in the postwar period. As one of the only Paraguayan generals to survive the war, he naturally caught the eye of various contending factions, who sought to use him as a figurehead. A Conservative movement led by Cándido BAREIRO secured his appointment as war minister in 1878, but he proved to be his own man.

Caballero assumed the presidency in 1880 after the death of Bareiro. His administration made only limited contributions to the public welfare. It disposed of thousands of hectares of state land by selling them to foreign buyers. Caballero also founded the National Bank and the National Law School. The most important innovation of his tenure, however, was in the political realm. In 1887, with the help of José Segundo DECOUD, he founded one of the country's traditional parties, the Asociación Nacional Republicana, or Partido Colorado. He continued to direct this organization long after he left the presidency in the hands of his colleague Patricio Escobar. Caballero died in Asunción.

– THOMAS L. WHIGHAM

CABALLERO, PEDRO JUAN

Pedro Juan Caballero (*b*. 1786; *d.* 13 July 1821), Paraguayan soldier and politician of the independence era. Born in Tobatí, Caballero spent his early youth in the Paraguayan countryside, where he learned to ride and, like many men of his class, to command small bands of troops in the colonial militia. He evidently participated in the Indian campaigns of the first years of the nineteenth century and, by 1810, had attained the rank of captain.

The following year Caballero was catapulted into prominence. The revolutionary junta in Buenos Aires, seeking to gain Paraguay's adherence to the patriot struggle against Spain, had sent an expeditionary force to the province. Commanded by Manuel BELGRANO, this small army anticipated little resistance. The Paraguayans, however, had no desire to be controlled from Buenos Aires, and their militia proceeded to defeat Belgrano in two separate engagements.

In the aftermath of these battles, some Paraguayan officers, Caballero included, actively fraternized with the defeated *porteños,* who convinced them that some form of independence was desirable. Together with colonels Fulgencio Yegros and Manuel Atanasio Cavañas, Caballero organized a conspiracy against the royal government in Asunción. When the plot was discovered in May 1811, Caballero acted in the absence

of his associates, seizing the *cabildo* offices and arresting the governor at dawn on the fifteenth of the month.

The rebellion brought Paraguay independence but not political stability. Over the next three years a provisional junta composed of Caballero, Yegros, and three other notables ruled the country, though often in an erratic fashion. Their inability to govern effectively made possible the ascendancy of José Gaspar Rodríguez de FRANCIA, the one outstanding political figure in Paraguay, and a man whom Caballero detested. In 1814, when Francia became dictator, Caballero wisely retired to Tobatí, but six years later he was implicated in a major plot against the dictator. Jailed by Francia's police, he committed suicide in his cell.

– THOMAS L. WHIGHAM

CABALLERO Y GÓNGORA, ANTONIO

Antonio Caballero y Góngora (*b*. May 1723; *d.* March 1796), viceroy of New Granada (1782–1789). A native of Córdoba Province, Spain, Caballero y Góngora became bishop of Yucatán in 1776 and archbishop of Santa Fe de Bogotá in 1779. He later entered the secular realm when, after defusing the Comunero Revolt of 1781, he became viceroy on 15 June 1782. The archbishop-viceroy championed enlightened education and science, and secured the creation of a mining reform mission. He also imposed centralized control on the colonial army and, to sustain royal authority, gained approval to establish in Santa Fe a veteran regiment reinforced by a disciplined militia.

During much of his administration, Caballero y Góngora resided at Turbaco, near Cartagena, directing ambitious military operations to pacify the aboriginals of Darién. He enhanced treasury receipts impressively but spent huge sums on the military and the bureaucracy. In the name of economy, his successors would dismantle much of his program. Replaced by Francisco GIL DE TABOADA Y LEMOS in January 1789, Caballero y Góngora returned to Córdoba, serving as archbishop until his death.

– ALLAN J. KUETHE

CABALLERO Y RODRÍGUEZ, JOSÉ AUGUSTÍN

José Augustín Caballero y Rodríguez (*b*. 28 August 1762; *d.* 7 April 1835), Cuban priest, philosopher, and educator. Along with Francisco ARANGO Y PARREÑO, Caballero was a pioneer of reformism in Cuba. Born in Havana, he was ordained as a priest in 1785. He became professor of philosophy (1785) and later director at San Carlos Seminary, where he was able to influence the intellectual formation of Father Félix VARELA Y MO-

RALES, doubtless the most famous of his disciples. An eloquent orator and a gifted writer and critic, Caballero put his exceptional abilities at the disposal of Cuba's Patriotic Society, a respectable colonial institution where he pleaded constantly for a more flexible approach to human problems. Along with his newspaper articles and his speeches (some of which are magnificent rhetorical pieces), he left us a treatise on logic written in Latin, *Lecciones de filosofía electiva* (1796), the first text for the teaching of philosophy ever produced in Cuba by a Cuban.

Although he mentions in his work empiricist thinkers such as John Locke, Francis Bacon, and Étienne Bonnot de Condillac, Caballero was by no means a radical innovator. Basically he was a follower of the Spanish thinker Benito Jerónimo FEIJÓO, whose chief concern was to free philosophy from its submission to Aristotle and scholasticism, maintaining that all authorities were acceptable provided they taught the truth. Caballero's contribution to modernity, therefore, never went beyond trying to reconcile Cartesian rationalism with Aristotelianism. Faithful to the church, he never hesitated to place faith above reason, although he did favor the teaching of experimental physics and advocated greater freedom for university teachers and broader and deeper techniques of inquiry.

Caballero thought that slavery was an inevitable crime, although he wrote numerous articles urging slave owners to treat their slaves better.

Caballero was also a believer in self-government, and in 1811 he put forward a proposal for the establishment of quasi-autonomist rule in Cuba. Never favoring the separation of Cuba from Spain, he was a moderate, politically and socially. Moreover, he thought that, given the prevailing conditions, slavery was an inevitable crime, although he wrote numerous articles urging slave owners to treat their slaves better. Despite his moderation, Caballero must be credited with laying the groundwork upon which later Cubans built their more radical thoughts.

– JOSÉ M. HERNÁNDEZ

CABALLERO CALDERÓN, EDUARDO

Eduardo Caballero Calderón (*b.* 6 March 1910; *d.* 1993), Colombian novelist and essayist. Author of more than two dozen books, Caballero Calderón is one of Colombia's major novelists of the twentieth century. He has also published numerous essays on literary, cultural, political, and historical topics. Caballero Calderón began writing in the 1940s and rose to prominence in the 1950s and 1960s. His major novel, *El buen salvaje* (The Good Savage) appeared in 1966, receiving international acclaim in Spain and throughout the Hispanic world. His ten novels, four volumes of short stories, and eleven books of essays have placed him at the forefront of Colombian writers.

Caballero Calderón's earliest publications were essays. The first, a volume titled *Tipacoque* (1941), is a set of nostalgic portraits of rural, provincial life in Colombia. In his book of essays, *Breviario del Quijote* (1947), the author demonstrates the importance of Spanish literary tradition for him and for Latin American writers in general: he writes about his admiration for the *Poema del Cid, Don Quijote,* writings of the Spanish Golden Age, and other classic Spanish texts. For the remainder of his career, he remained closely aligned to the culture of Spain.

Caballero Calderón's early novels dealt with the Colombian civil war commonly known as La Violencia, a conflict that took place primarily from 1948 to 1958. Many interests were represented in this conflict, but the primary antagonists were the traditional Conservative Party and the Liberal Party. In his novel *El Cristo de espaldas* (1952; Christ on His Back) a son in the Liberal Party is accused of killing his father of the Conservative Party, and the town priest becomes the sacrificial victim when he attempts to justify the son's act. The protagonist of *Siervo sin tierra* (1954) is also a victim of *La Violencia.* The basic thesis of the novel *Manuel Pacho* (1962) is that each person has one opportunity in life to be a hero. In *El buen salvaje,* Caballero Calderón rises above local stories of violence and constructs a self-conscious fiction about a young Latin American intellectual in Paris.

– RAYMOND LESLIE WILLIAMS

CABAÑAS, JOSÉ TRINIDAD

José Trinidad Cabañas (*b.* 9 June 1805; *d.* 8 January 1871), military figure and president of Honduras (1852, 1853–1855). Born a creole, the son of José María Cabañas and Juana María Faillos, Cabañas was a Liberal politician whose role in Honduran history dates from his participation in the civil war of 1826–1829 as a follower of Francisco MORAZÁN. In 1844 he defended León, Nicaragua, against Francisco MALESPÍN's forces. In 1845 he led Salvadoran forces against the same Malespín. He served as constitutional president from 1 March 1852 to 28 October 1852 but was deposed by Conservatives in Guatemala (and within Honduras).

When war resumed between Honduras and Guatemala, he led Honduran forces to triumph at Chiquimula and Zacapa, in southeast Guatemala, in July 1853 but was unable to hold these positions. Guatemala's capture of the castle of Omoa on 24 August 1853 removed Honduras from the conflict.

Cabañas returned to power as constitutional president from 31 December 1853 to 6 October 1855. Among the important accomplishments of his second presidency were the ratification of a railroad contract with Ephraim George Squier and the formation of the Ferrocarril Interoceánico de Honduras (Interoceanic Railway Company) on 28 April 1854. Interference in Guatemalan affairs led to his overthrow once again, and this time he fled to El Salvador.

A prominent general as well as a politician, Cabañas took to the battlefield again. He was defeated by Guatemalan forces under Rafael CARRERA (1814–1865) at the Battle of Masagua on 6 October 1855. Although his successor, Santos Guardiola, was a Conservative, Cabañas remained active in Central American affairs and participated in a Salvadoran uprising in 1865. (In 1860 he had been connected with an abortive attempt by William WALKER to return to Central America.) His presidencies faced not only Guatemalan opposition but other challenges, such as British efforts to colonize the Bay Islands and frustrated attempts to reunite the Central American federal government. A unionist movement failed when a constituent assembly dissolved shortly after his first presidential term on 10 November 1852.

– JEFFREY D. SAMUELS

CABEZA DE VACA, ALVAR NÚÑEZ

Alvar Núñez Cabeza de Vaca (*b.* ca. 1490; *d.* 1564), Spanish explorer, conquistador, and author. Cabeza de Vaca was most likely born in Jerez de la Frontera, Andalusia. He was treasurer and marshal of Pánfilo de NARVÁEZ's expedition to Florida (1527–1537) and was appointed governor of the Río de la Plata, in present-day Paraguay (1540–1545). For different reasons, both enterprises proved disastrous for Cabeza de Vaca, the first beginning in shipwreck, the latter ending in political failure.

After accidentally landing south of Tampa Bay in the spring of 1528, the ill-fated expedition of Narváez progressively deteriorated. It was not until eight years later that Cabeza de Vaca, Andrés Dorantes de Carranza, Alonso del Castillo Maldonado, and an African slave named Estevanico, the only four survivors, encountered a party of Spaniards on the west coast of Mexico. Cabeza de Vaca's account, known in Spanish as the *Nauf-*

ragios (Shipwrecks), tells the story of his travails and coexistence with the Mariame, Avavare, and Opata peoples. He became a merchant and, with the three other survivors practiced shamanism with such success that hundreds of Indians formed a cult about them and traveled with them across the continent. The *Naufragios* is at once an account of an officer of the crown and the story of a European who penetrated and was penetrated by Native American cultures. On his return to Spain, he was given the governorship of Río de la Plata. The *Comentarios,* written by his amanuensis Pedro Hernández, tells of Cabeza de Vaca's journey from the island of Santa Catalina (Brazil) to Asunción (Paraguay), and the subsequent rebellion of Domingo Martínez de IRALA that ended with Cabeza de Vaca's return to Spain in chains in 1545. He died in Seville.

Although a pirated edition of *Naufragios* appeared in 1542, while Cabeza de Vaca was in Paraguay, the authorized version was published with the *Comentarios* in 1555. The *Naufragios* is the more compelling of the two in its narration of a complete loss of material civilization and total dependence on the Indians. In this regard the *Naufragios* manifests the dubious nature of Western civilization's claims to superiority, since it is the Spaniards who are naked and unable to feed themselves or build boats, who fall into anomie and resort to cannibalism.

Cabeza de Vaca's story is the antithesis to *Robinson Crusoe* as it testifies that the Western individual does not embody the knowledge of European civilizations and must learn from Native Americans to survive. His account of cannibalism among the Spaniards includes a condemnation of the act by the Indians and a description of a highly ritualized consumption of the ashes of dead shamans. Thus, Europeans come to embody the savagery conventionally attributed to Indians.

– JOSÉ RABASA

CABOT, SEBASTIAN

Sebastian Cabot (*b.* ca. 1474, *d.* 1557), Venetian or English navigator. Cabot was born in Bristol or Venice, the son of the explorer John Cabot. He served as cartographer to Henry VIII, accompanied an English force to Spain, and was appointed in 1518 by Holy Roman Emperor Charles V to the Spanish Council of the New Indies. He was named pilot major and in 1525 entrusted with an expedition to develop commercial ties with the Orient. Upon reaching South America and hearing tales from native inhabitants of enormous riches to be found upriver, Cabot chose to explore the Río de la Plata instead of continuing on to the Pacific. He also explored the Paraguay and Paraná rivers, but returned empty-handed to Spain in 1530. As punishment for the failure of his expedition, he was banished to Africa for two years, but he was then pardoned and regained his title of pilot major. In later life, he returned to England, where he organized an association of merchants to sponsor future expeditions. He died in London.

— HILARY BURGER

CABRAL, MANUEL DEL

Manuel del Cabral (*b.* 7 March 1907), Dominican poet and writer. Cabral is considered the greatest poet of his country and one of the best of Latin America. He is admired for the variety of his themes, which range from the African roots of Dominican culture to eroticism. His writings include short stories, novels, essays, plays, poems, autobiographies, epistolary confessions, and parables. Cabral has received prizes and awards from many hispanic countries, including the Premio de la Fundación Argentina para la Poesía. His published works include *Trópico negro* (1941), *Manuel cuando no es tiempo, Compadre Mon* (1942), *Sangre mayor* (1945), *De este lado del mar* (1949), *Los huéspedes secretos* (1951), *La isla ofendida* (1965), *Los relámpagos lentos* (1966), *Los anti-tiempos* (1967), *Egloga de 2,000* (1970), and *Obra poetica* (1987).

— KAI P. SCHOENHALS

CABRAL, PEDRO ÁLVARES

Pedro Álvares Cabral (*b.* 1467 or 1468; *d.* ca. 1520), Portuguese explorer, leader of the follow-up fleet to Vasco da GAMA's first voyage to India. His expedition made the first recorded sighting of Brazil by the Portuguese on 22 April 1500.

On 15 February 1500, King Manuel I of Portugal chose Cabral, a *fidalgo* of the royal household, to command a fleet of thirteen ships and 1,200–1,500 men to sail for India. The purpose of the voyage was to establish trade and diplomatic relations with the *samorim* of Calicut and other rulers in India.

Cabral left Lisbon on 9 March 1500. On 22 April, Monte Pascoal, a mountain in what is now Brazil, was sighted. Cabral thought he had discovered an island, which he called Ilha de Vera Cruz. Sailing northward, he reached a harbor that he called Porto Seguro (now known as Baía Cabrália). He remained there for eight days and was on friendly terms with the region's inhabitants. The first Catholic Mass in Portuguese America was officiated by Frei Henrique Soares de Coimbra, one of eight Franciscans accompanying Cabral. He also celebrated the second Mass, which was attended by fifty or sixty Amerindians.

On 2 May, Cabral continued on to India. To announce to King Manuel I the discovery of the new land, soon to be called Santa Cruz and then Brazil, he sent one of his supply ships carrying reports by Cabral and by his captains, pilots, and other members of the fleet. Only two of the documents survived: the reports of Pero Vaz de Caminha and Mestre João Faras. Both are addressed to King Manuel and dated 1 May 1500. These two documents are the original manuscripts and seem to have been unknown to all the great chroniclers of the sixteenth century.

After sailing around the Cape of Good Hope and then reaching Calicut on 13 September 1500, Cabral battled Muslim traders and bombed Calicut. However, he established friendly relations with the Hindu ruler of Cochin before beginning his return voyage to Portugal. The *Anunciada*, one of the ships in the Cabral expedition, arrived in Lisbon on 23 June 1501. Cabral himself did not arrive in Lisbon until the end of July.

Despite the importance of Cabral's visit to Brazil and India, relatively little is known about the man, the expedition, and the motives behind the sighting of Brazil and Cabral's brief stay there. In the past, there has been considerable debate over whether Cabral's visit to Brazil was intentional or accidental and whether the Portuguese were aware of its existence before 1500. Although the issue continues to be debated, most scholars now believe that Cabral was unaware of Brazil's existence until winds and currents brought him within sight of land.

— FRANCIS A. DUTRA

CABRERA, LYDIA

Lydia Cabrera (*b.* 20 May 1900; *d.* 19 September 1991), Cuban writer and anthropologist. Daughter of a well-known lawyer and historian, she was tutored at home, where she also became entranced by the tales of the black servants. After her father's death, she studied painting and Oriental art at L'école du Louvre in Paris (1927–1930). Her stay in France coincided with European interest in primitive cultures, a trend that reawakened her childhood fascination with African Cuban culture. She began her new studies at the Sorbonne and did her research in Cuba in 1930. In Paris again, she wrote *Cuentos negros de Cuba* (1934), published in French (1936) to great acclaim. In 1938 she moved back to Cuba, intent on continuing her studies in African Cuban folklore and conducting interviews among the black population. A second collection of short stories (*¿Por qué?... Cuentos negros de Cuba*), written in the same direct and colorful style, appeared in 1948. In 1954 she published her first anthropological work, *El* *monte: Notas sobre las religiones, la magia, las supersticiones y el folklore de los negros criollos y del pueblo de Cuba,* considered by some to be her most important contribution to African Cuban culture. In the 1950s Cabrera became a consultant to the National Institute of Culture and published three major works: *Refranes de negros viejos* (1955), *Anagó: vocabulario Lucumí* (1957), and *La sociedad secreta Abakuá* (1958).

Cabrera's stay in France coincided with European interest in primitive cultures, a trend that reawakened her childhood fascination with African Cuban culture.

The Cuban Revolution burst upon her whirlwind of activity, and Cabrera moved to Miami, losing most of her research. Slowly, she reestablished her career and in 1970 published *Otán Iyebiyé: Las piedras preciosas* and the fictional tales of *Ayapá: Cuentos de Jicotea* (1971). After a stay in Spain to research some of her lost sources, Cabrera returned to Miami. She received two honorary degrees—from Denison (1977) and the University of Redlands (1981)—and continued her anthropological research: *La laguna sagrada de San Joaquín* (1973), *Yemayá y Ochún* (1974), *Anaforuana: ritual y símbolos de la iniciación en la sociedad secreta Abakuá* (1975), *La Regla Kimbisa del Santo Cristo del Buen Viaje* (1977), *Trinidad de Cuba* (1977), *Reglas de Congo, Palomonte Mayombe* (1979), *Los animales en el folklore y la magia de Cuba* (1988), *La lengua sagrada de los Ñáñigos* (1988), and *Supersticiones y buenos consejos* (1988). She also published two collections of short stories: *Francisco y Francisca: Chascarrillos de negros viejos* (1976) and *Cuentos para grandes, chicos y retrasados mentales* (1983).

— MARÍA A. SALGADO

CABRERA, MIGUEL

Miguel Cabrera (*b.* 1695; *d.* 16 May 1768), Mexican painter. Although doubts exist about the authenticity of the document that gives his birth date and nothing is known about his training, Cabrera's will makes it clear that he was a native of Oaxaca. It is believed that by 1719 Cabrera was in Mexico City, where he became the most important painter of his day. With other artists he attempted to found an academy in Mexico City in 1753, and in 1756 he published *Maravilla americana,* an account of his examination of the original image of the Virgin of Guadalupe. Among his many works, those

for the Jesuits are outstanding in number and quality; but he had numerous other important patrons, including the archbishop of Mexico City and the miner José de la Borda in Taxco. His paintings display a sense of ample space and often brilliant, light coloring. Sweetness of expression is a hallmark of his religious figures, whose repetitive portrayal was much appreciated in his time and in the nineteenth century, but has occasioned twentieth-century criticism. Cabrere's reputation has also suffered because of the disparate quality of many paintings signed by or attributed to him, a number of them executed in what must have been a large workshop. He is also known for his portraits and for an extraordinary series of *casta* paintings, depictions of the mixed races that peopled New Spain.

— CLARA BARGELLINI

CABRERA INFANTE, GUILLERMO

Guillermo Cabrera Infante (*b.* 22 April 1929), Cuban novelist and essayist. Cabrera Infante was born in Gibara in Oriente Province. In 1947 he moved to Havana with his parents and began studying medicine at the University of Havana. After quickly deciding to take up writing, he abandoned medicine for journalism. In 1952 he was arrested and fined for publishing a short story that contained English profanities. In the late 1950s he began to earn prizes with his short stories.

Meanwhile, his passion for the cinema led him to film reviewing. With the pseudonym G. Caín [*Cabrera Infante*] he wrote film reviews and articles on the cinema for the weekly *Carteles,* becoming its editor in chief in 1957. He was the founder of Cinemateca de Cuba, the Cuban Film Society, over which he presided from 1951 to 1956. In 1959 he became director of the Cuban Film Institute and of the literary magazine *Lunes de revolución.* In 1962 he served the Cuban government as cultural attaché in Belgium. In 1964 he received the prestigious Biblioteca Breve prize for his novel *Tres tristes tigres* (1971). In 1965 he decided to break with the Cuban government, leaving his diplomatic post and permanently settling in London.

As of the mid-1990s, Cabrera Infante was the best-known living Cuban author. *Tres tristes tigres,* translated into English as *Three Trapped Tigers,* won him worldwide recognition. In this novel, as has been pointed out by such eminent critics as Emir Rodríguez Monegal, language itself is the main preoccupation. Here, too, as in all of Cabrera Infante's work, there is a great deal of humor, especially word games and puns. Because of this aspect of his work, he has been compared to Russian emigré writer Vladimir Nabokov. His mastery of the English language—one of his later novels, *Holy Smoke*

(1985), was written in English—has also begged comparison with Joseph Conrad. Cabrera Infante, who became a British citizen, has said ironically that he is as English as muffins and is a happy subject of the queen. Besides *Tres tristes tigres,* some of his best-known works are *La Habana para un infante difunto* (1984) and *Vista del amanecer en el trópico* (1974). His novels have been widely translated.

– ROBERTO VALERO

CABRERA LOBATO, LUIS

Luis Cabrera Lobato (*b.* 17 July 1876; *d.* 1954), leading Mexican intellectual remembered for a brilliant speech before the Chamber of Deputies advocating an agrarian reform law in 1912, for hundreds of political essays written under the pen name of Blas Urrea, and for his complete intellectual independence from successive post-revolutionary governments.

Cabrera, the son of a humble baker, Gertrudis Lobato, attended the National Preparatory School (1889–1893). He went on to complete his law degree from the National School of Law in 1901, after which he practiced law and taught. A cofounder of the Anti-Reelectionist Party in 1909, he became dean of the National School of Law and a federal deputy in 1912, later serving as an agent of the Constitutionalists in the United States and as Venustiano CARRANZA's treasury secretary. He retired from politics in 1920, and though he was twice offered the presidential candidacy by opposition parties—in 1933 and 1946—he declined to run.

– RODERIC AI CAMP

CÁCERES, ANDRÉS AVELINO

Andrés Avelino Cáceres (*b.* 1833; *d.* 1923), Peruvian military hero and president (1886–1890, 1894–1895), commander of the highland guerrilla resistance to the Chilean occupation of coastal Peru during the War of the Pacific (1879–1883). Like Francisco Bolognesi, Cáceres was drawn to military life in the 1850s in support of General Ramón CASTILLA against Generals José Rufino ECHENIQUE and Manuel Ignacio VIVANCO. During Castilla's second term in office, Cáceres served as military attaché to the Peruvian legation in France. Upon his return to Peru he supported Colonel Mariano Ignacio PRADO's 1865 revolution against General Juan Antonio PEZET's unpopular though legitimate government. When Manuel Pardo was elected as the first civilian president in 1872, Cáceres served as a faithful military officer. At this time he began to express political

differences with his life-long foe Nicolás de PIÉROLA, who conspired against Pardo.

Born in Ayacucho, Cáceres had extensive family and landowning interests in the south-central and central highlands of Peru, which provided him with the power base necessary to conduct his military campaigns against the Chilean army and to advance his own political ambitions. During the War of the Pacific, Cáceres fought in the battles of San Francisco and Tarapacá and in the 1881 defense of Lima in San Juan and Miraflores. Wounded in the latter battle, he hid in Lima and later went to the strategic central highland town of Jauja to initiate and lead his military and political resistance, the La Breña campaign. His guerrilla tactics earned him the name "Wizard of the Andes." The support his forces received from peasant communities fighting for their livelihood constituted the key factor of this protracted resistance.

However, Peruvian military and political leaders during the Chilean occupation were divided into several factions. Some, like Francisco García Calderón, had been imprisoned and exiled by the Chilean army. One such faction, led by General Miguel IGLESIAS, signed the Treaty of Ancón (1883), which allowed the Chilean army to withdraw from Lima. Cáceres opposed and fought Iglesias and assumed the presidency in 1886. During his term of office the Grace contract (1889), a costly settlement with foreign creditors, was signed to establish the bases for the economic recovery of Peru in the 1890s. In 1890, Cáceres handed power to General Remigio MORALES BERMÚDEZ, who died in office in 1894. Cáceres's subsequent attempts to regain power faced a popular insurrection led by Piérola, who succeeded in forcing Cáceres to resign and leave the country. After a long exile Cáceres returned to Peru and was awarded the honorific title of marshal in 1919. He died in Lima.

– ALFONSO W. QUIROZ

CÁCERES, ESTHER DE

Esther de Cáceres (*b.* 1903; *d.* 1971), Uruguayan poet and educator. After earning a degree in medicine (1929), Cáceres taught humanities at the Teacher Training Institute and the Institute of Advanced Studies, both in Montevideo. She belonged to a cohort of leading women intellectuals and literary figures. Her first book of poetry was *Las ínsulas extrañas* (1929), followed in rapid succession by *Canción* (1931), *Libro de la soledad* (1935), *Los cielos* (1935), and many others. Especially noteworthy is *"Concierto de amor" y otros poemas,* with a prologue by Gabriela MISTRAL (1951). In Cáceres's early poetry, the mood alternates between melancholy and joy, as felt through mystical communion with God and other religious experiences. Later works— *Los cantos del destierro* (1963), *Tiempo y abismo* (1965), and *Canto desierto* (1969)—focus more on the subjective anguish caused by metaphysical displacement and the poet's immersion in the turbulent social and political circumstances of the time.

— WILLIAM H. KATRA

CÁCERES, RAMÓN

Ramón Cáceres (*b.* 15 December 1866; *d.* 19 November 1911), president of the Dominican Republic (1906–1911). Born in Moca, in the north-central part of the country, to a distinguished and prosperous family, Cáceres, a landowner, was in the forefront of the opposition to president Ulises HEUREAUX (1882–1899). Cáceres earned national recognition when, on 26 July 1899, he assassinated the dictator during a public appearance in Moca. The ensuing political chaos resulted in several years of unstable regimes. Cáceres was forced into exile in 1903 but returned in 1904 to become vice president under Carlos Morales. When the latter abandoned his post in 1906, Cáceres assumed the office.

Cáceres earned national recognition when, on 26 July 1899, he assassinated the dictator during a public appearance in Moca.

Cáceres's presidency was one of the most peaceful and prosperous periods in Dominican history. He expanded federal power without debilitating local government, reformed the constitution, began an ambitious public works program, and transferred many privately owned utilities to the public realm. The shifts in economic power engendered by his reform earned him powerful enemies, and there were several unsuccessful plots against his government. In 1905, a United States customs receivership was established. Cáceres welcomed the prosperity it brought but remained concerned about financial dependence on the United States. Then in 1911, as he took his evening ride, Cáceres was assassinated. His death was followed by a resurgence of political and economic disorder and, ultimately, by the U.S. occupation of the Dominican Republic in 1916.

— SARA FLEMING

CAFÉ FILHO, JOÃO

João Café Filho (*b.* 3 February 1889; *d.* 20 February 1970), president of Brazil (1954–1955). Lawyer, strike leader, and popular opposition figure in his native state of Rio Grande do Norte, Café Filho helped the 1930 revolution that brought Getúlio VARGAS to the Brazilian presidency. Without completing the required course work for a degree, he passed an examination that admitted him to the bar. Elected to Congress in 1934, he opposed repression by Vargas. In 1937–1938 he spent six months in exile in Argentina to avoid arrest. He did not return to politics until 1945, near the end of the Vargas dictatorship, and, together with São Paulo's Ademar de BARROS, founded what became the Partido Social Progressista (PRP), which returned him to Congress.

Following Barros's 1950 alliance with Vargas, Café Filho became Vargas's running mate and was narrowly elected vice president despite Catholic objections to his leftist past. When Vargas committed suicide on 24 August 1954, Café Filho assumed the presidency. Members of his cabinet, regarded as conservative and anti-Vargas, opposed the inauguration of Juscelino KUBITSCHEK, elected in 1955, but war minister Henrique LOTT favored the inauguration and carried out a coup on 11 November 1955, while Café Filho was hospitalized for a heart ailment. When Café Filho was released from the hospital later in November, Lott's troops prevented him from resuming the presidency. Congress, favoring Kubitschek's inauguration, declared Café Filho unable to govern, a judgment upheld by the Supreme Court. Before his death, Café Filho served (1961–1969) on the accounts tribunal responsible for ruling on the legality of financial steps taken by the Guanabara State government.

— JOHN W. F. DULLES

CAJEME

Cajeme (José María Leyva; *b.* 1837; *d.* 21 April 1887), Yaqui Indian leader. After leaving the Yaqui valley in southern Sonora in his youth, he became a dependable volunteer member of the state forces backing the liberal *caudillo* Governor Ignacio Pesqueira whenever there was a crisis, including campaigns against his own people in the late 1860s. Rewarding Cajeme with the post of district administrator of the Yaqui valley (1874), the Pesqueira government assumed he would help obtain the Yaquis' total and permanent submission. Instead, he mobilized them (and neighboring Mayos) to achieve the status of separate nations which the two tribes had long claimed was rightfully theirs. Cajeme restructured and disciplined Yaqui society toward greater economic security and military preparedness: instituting a tax system; controlling external trade; reviving the mission practice of community plots and institutionalizing the tribal tradition of popular assemblies as decision making bodies; amassing war material. But by the early 1880s, the advantage of political instability from Pesqueira's fall had given way to national and state governments united in their zeal to colonize the rich lands of the Yaqui and Mayo valleys, employing a large, unrelenting, military force to do so. Though Cajame was defeated and captured by Ángel Martínez at San José de Guaymas, and executed, Yaqui guerrilla resistance continued through 1910.

— STUART F. VOSS

CALCAÑO, JOSÉ ANTONIO

José Antonio Calcaño (*b.* 23 March 1900), Venezuelan composer. Calcaño was born and educated in Caracas. After studying for a year at the Academy of Music in Bern, Switzerland, he returned to Caracas, where he had an outstanding career as a music teacher, music historian, and choir director. His compositions contributed greatly to giving Venezuelan music its particular character. His best-known work is the ballet *Miranda en Rusia*. Also well-known is his cantata "Desolación y gloria," written in honor of Simón Bolívar. Calcaño's book *La ciudad y su música* (1958) presents an overview of the musical life of Caracas from colonial times to the 1950s.

— OSCAR G. PELÁEZ ALMENGOR

CALCHAQUÍ, JUAN

Juan Calchaquí (*d.* ca. 1600), Indian chief. In the middle of the sixteenth century, Juan Calchaquí was the principal chief of the region of Tolombón, in the territory which today bears his name, the Calchaquí Valley. In the latter half of the sixteenth century he led the rebellion that spread across almost all of northwest Argentina and part of the southern high plateau of Bolivia. He gained control over the various indigenous groups in the area of the Calchaquí Valley as well as the Omaguaca of the Quebrada de Humahuaca; the Casabindo, the Apatama, and Chicha of La Puna; and the Jurí of Santiago del Estero.

The founding of the Spanish settlements at Córdoba of Calchaquí, Londres in the Hualfín Valley, and Cañete in Tucumán pushed the Indians to the point of war. In 1561, with Juan Calchaquí in the lead, they attacked these new European centers, causing their evacuation. The prestige of Chief Juan Calchaquí was such that his authority extended across all of the northwest of Argentina as well as the eastern plains and the south of La Puna in Bolivia. His reputation gained an almost sacred

air. In 1563 the Audiencia of Charcas reported to the king that "they honor him as if he were a burial mound."

— JOSÉ ANTONIO PÉREZ GOLLÁN

CALDAS, FRANCISCO JOSÉ DE

Francisco José de Caldas (*b.* 4 October 1768; *d.* October 1816), astronomer, cartographer, mathematician, and engineer in New Granada's proIndependence army. Born in Popayán, Caldas was urged by his family to practice law. Instead he became one of the most prominent creole scientists of the early 1800s, participating in the Royal Botanical Expedition of José Celestino MUTIS (1805) and later becoming director of the Royal Astronomy Observatory of Bogotá. His journal, *El Semanario del Nuevo Reino de Granada,* was one of the first scientific periodicals to be published in Latin America. As professor of mathematics at the progressive Colegio del Rosario in Bogotá, Caldas encouraged the dissemination of modern science, including Newtonian experimental physics and Copernican cosmography.

Although he benefited from his contacts with the influential German investigator Alexander von Humboldt, Caldas called on American scientists to end their dependence on Europeans. He discovered independently that the temperature of boiling water was proportional to atmospheric pressure and devised a formula to measure altitude with a thermometer. He also studied the properties and value of cinchona (quinine) bark and of cochineal.

Caldas personified the late colonial Latin American striving for scientific, economic, and, eventually, political independence. After 1810, he served the independence cause as coeditor of the official *Diario Político* and as captain of the newly created Corps of Engineers. Captured by the Spanish royalists in 1816, he was executed as a rebel. His death, and that of other creole insurgent scientists, dealt a near fatal blow to the continuity of scientific inquiry from the colony to the republic.

— IRIS H. W. ENGSTRAND
LOUISA S. HOBERMAN

CALDERA RODRÍGUEZ, RAFAEL

Rafael Caldera Rodríguez (*b.* 24 January 1916), president of Venezuela (1969–1974; reelected 5 December 1993). In 1936, Caldera helped found the National Student Union (Unión Nacional Estudiantil), an anti-Marxist Catholic student organization. He served as attorney general of the republic in 1946, and between 1959 and 1961 as president of the Chamber of Deputies. In 1946, he organized the Independent Political

Electoral Organization Committee (Comité de Organización Política Electoral Independiente, COPEI), which became the Social Christian Party (Partido Social Cristiano, COPEI). Elected president in 1968 on a "democratic progressive" platform, Caldera formed a government that addressed popular issues such as distribution of wealth, housing, and education. He also established an accord with leftist guerrillas that ended a decade of internal warfare. His foreign policy broke with his predecessors' anticommunism, accepted international social justice, and reflected a growing anxiety over the expansion of Brazil's power. Caldera also negotiated an agreement with Guayana in which both nations agreed not to claim each other's territory for twelve years.

– WINTHROP R. WRIGHT

CALDERÓN FOURNIER, RAFAEL ÁNGEL

Rafael Ángel Calderón Fournier (*b.* 14 March 1949), president of Costa Rica (1990–1994) and founder of the Social Christian Party. Rafael Ángel Calderón Fournier has spent virtually his whole life involved in Costa Rican partisan politics. He served as a leading member of the national legislature while still a law student at the University of Costa Rica—he received his law degree in 1977—and he has been deeply involved in public life ever since.

He shared with his father, Rafael Ángel CALDERÓN GUARDIA (1940–1944), the distinction of being the youngest presidents in Costa Rican history. They were both only forty years old when elected. (Since then, thirty-nine-year-old José María Figueres Olsen was elected in 1994.) From birth, Calderón Fournier's destiny has been politics, his life intertwined with that of his famous father. He was born in Managua, Nicaragua, while his father was in exile after the defeat of the progovernment forces in the 1948 civil conflict and later was reunited with his exiled father in Mexico, where he spent much of his early youth. When the family returned to Costa Rica, his father's many followers passed their loyalty to his son and namesake.

Following a term in the national legislature (1974–1978), he led the Calderónists into the Unidad coalition that elected Rodrigo CARAZO ODIO president in 1978. He then served as foreign minister from 1978 to 1982 and as a member of the board of the social security system.

After running unsuccessful presidential campaigns in 1982 and 1986, Calderón Fournier was elected for a four-year term in 1990 on a platform that emphasized privatization of the economy while maintaining intact the extensive national social welfare program, much of which his father initiated during his presidency.

– JOHN PATRICK BELL

CALDERÓN GUARDIA, RAFAEL ÁNGEL

Rafael Ángel Calderón Guardia (*b.* 10 March 1900; *d.* 9 June 1970), president of Costa Rica (1940–1944). Calderón Guardia was born in San José, Costa Rica, to a bourgeois, Catholic family. After completing secondary school, he went to Belgium to pursue his medical career. He studied at the Catholic University of Lovain, where he was influenced by Christian-socialist ideas. He then went to the Free University of Brussels, from which he graduated as a surgeon in 1927. In Belgium he married Ivonne Clays before returning to Costa Rica. He later married Rosario Fournier, with whom he had three children, including Rafael Ángel CALDERÓN FOURNIER (president of Costa Rica, 1990–1994). In Costa Rica he practiced medicine, dedicating himself to the poor, an experience that influenced his populist ideas.

Calderón Guardia recognized the urgency of making changes in Costa Rican society in order to attend to the needs of the working class.

Calderón Guardia began his political career in 1930, when he was elected councilman and president of the municipality of San José. In 1934 he was elected to Congress, and in 1936 he became third alternate (vice president) of the Republic. In 1938 he was reelected to Congress and was chosen as its president due to his gift as a political leader. In 1939 he was the presidential candidate of the National Republican Party, and with little opposition he was elected. Even though Calderón Guardia had the support of the oligarchy and the liberal politicians of the time, once in power, he decided to implement a series of social reforms. He recognized the urgency of making changes in society in order to attend to the needs of the working class and avoid serious future conflicts.

His vision and success were shaped by his Christian-socialist ideals, his medical profession, and the Costa Rican economic crisis brought on by World War II and a dependent economy. Domestically, a series of conditions made the country ripe for reformism. The Catholic Church, led by Monsignor Víctor Manuel SANABRIA and following papal encyclicals, supported laws in favor of the working class. The Communist Party under Manuel MORA was advocating state intervention on behalf of the proletariat and the peasants. The union movement had been growing since the beginning of the twentieth century. And several new reformist and revolutionary political parties were demanding reforms in the country. These factors allowed the government of Calderón Guardia to create the University of Costa Rica in 1941, establish a social-security system in 1942, and institutionalize a labor code in 1943. The reforms were made possible by an alliance between the government, the Catholic Church, and the Communist Party. For these reasons, Calderón Guardia is remembered as a statesman, a willful leader, and a social reformer. However, he also displayed a lack of fiscal planning and a tendency toward political favoritism, and he failed to confront Costa Rica's economic problems.

After his term as president, Calderón Guardia continued to exercise a strong influence in the administration of Teodoro PICADO (1944–1948). In 1948 he was again a presidential candidate but lost to the opposition, led by the journalist Otilio ULATE. Not accepting the defeat, Calderón Guardia demanded that Congress nullify the election, which it did. With a strong political opposition and an armed movement under the leadership of José FIGUERES, the country was thrown into civil war in April 1948. After the military triumph of Figueres, Calderón Guardia, Picado, and other leaders went to Nicaragua. Backed by Anastasio SOMOZA, Calderón Guardia invaded Costa Rica in 1948, but the mission failed. In 1955, again backed by Somoza, he undertook another invasion and failed. He lived in Mexico until 1958, when he returned to Costa Rica upon being elected to Congress. In 1962 he ran again for the presidency, but lost. From 1966 to 1970 he served as ambassador to Mexico, then returned to Costa Rica. He died in San José. In 1973 the Congress declared him a national hero in honor of his political legacy and work as a social reformer.

– JORGE MARIO SALAZAR

CALFUCURÁ

Calfucurá (*b.* late 1770s; *d.* 1873), Araucanian leader. Calfucurá headed the rise of an important intertribal confederation in the Argentinian pampas that flourished in the last half of the nineteenth century until subjugation by the Argentine army in the 1880s.

In 1835 a group of Araucanians (also called Mapuches) headed by Calfucurá moved east from Chilean homelands near Llaima, in the southern cordillera (in the region of the Imperial River and Cautín), to estab-

lish a permanent encampment near a large salt deposit called the Salinas Grandes. Following a struggle for power over control of the Salinas Grandes with the Voroganos—a loosely organized group of Pampas and Araucanian followers of Mariano Rondeau—Calfucurá emerged victorious, and Rondeau's followers joined Calfucurá's Araucanian settlement.

Calfucurá's leadership was derived primarily from personal charisma as well as from military knowledge and status within the Araucanian world. Under his leadership, this Araucanian confederation in the pampas expanded to enjoy relative prosperity and autonomy and to become a large, well-organized threat to Argentine lives and property. Between 1834 and 1856, Calfucurá negotiated temporary alliances between neighboring Pampas, Tehuelches, Ranqueles, and other Araucanian bands or tribes, and also entered into a structured alliance with the government of Juan Manuel de ROSAS in exchange for annuity payments in goods. Because of their control of the salt mines in the Salinas Grandes, Calfucurá's people escaped dependency on the payments and thrived on intratribal trade in salt—necessary for making charqui (salted meat)—and livestock (mostly cattle and horses).

When the annuity program ended after the fall of Rosas in the 1850s, the Araucanian followers of Calfucurá responded with raids called *malones* (also called *malocas*). In the next two decades in a series of highly organized raids against creole ranching interests in the southern Argentina frontier, Calfucurá's Voroganos acquired hundreds of thousands of head of cattle and horses and hundreds of *cautivos* (captives) to tend to these herds. When Calfucurá died of natural causes in 1873, he left a confederation of Araucanians that included over 224 tribes. This confederation, under the leadership of Manuel Namuncurá, Calfucurá's son, continued to resist Argentine subjugation until 1879.

– KRISTINE L. JONES

CALLADO, ANTÔNIO

Antônio Callado (*b.* 26 January 1917), Brazilian journalist, playwright, and novelist. Born in Niterói, Rio de Janeiro, Callado worked in London for the BBC from 1941 to 1947. He is best known for his novels dealing with religious and political themes. Perhaps his most famous work, *Quarup* (1967) describes the transformation of a missionary priest into a revolutionary who discovers his own sexuality in the process. *Bar Don Juan* (1971) relates the points of view of six would-be revolutionaries who plot to overthrow the military government. Callado has received literary prizes that include the Golfinho de Ouro, the Prêmio Brasília, and the Goethe Prize for Fiction for *Sempreviva* (1981). He has also written nonfiction.

— GARY M. VESSELS

CALLADO JUNIOR, JOAQUIM ANTÔNIO DA SILVA

Joaquim Antônio da Silva Callado Junior (*b.* 11 July 1848; *d.* 20 March 1880), Brazilian flute virtuoso, teacher, prolific composer of popular instrumental dance pieces, and key figure in the history of Brazilian music. Son of a bandmaster in Rio de Janeiro, Callado received an appointment to teach flute at the Imperial Conservatory of Music in 1870, during which time he organized a popular musical ensemble called "Choro carioca." The first of many Choro ensembles in Rio, the traditional group included a solo flute or other woodwind instrument, with various guitar-type and occasional percussion instruments. Repertoire consisted of polkas, quadrilles, schottisches, waltzes, *lundus* (Afro-Brazilian dance), and polka-*lundus*. With the addition of a singer, the performance was called a *seresta*. Callado became famous as the composer of *Querida por todos*, a polka dedicated to a well-known woman composer, Chiquinha GONZAGA.

Callado became famous as the composer of Querida por todos, *a polka dedicated to a well-known woman composer, Chiquinha Gonzaga.*

One of Callado's principal contributions was to establish the *choro* as a form of popular music and to develop an individualized style of popular composition that served as a model for later composers. The *choro* became the favored form of Heitor VILLA-LOBOS to express musical elements that were distinctively Brazilian.

— DAVID P. APPLEBY

CALLEJA DEL REY, FÉLIX MARÍA, CONDE DE CALDERÓN

Félix María, Conde de Calderón Calleja del Rey (*b.* 1757; *d.* 24 July 1828), commander of royalist forces in the War of Mexican Independence and viceroy of New Spain (1813–1816). Born in Medina del Campo, Castilla la Vieja, Spain, Calleja entered the infantry regiment of Savoy as a cadet in 1772. He saw wartime service in the abortive 1775 expedition to Algiers, served aboard the floating artillery platforms during the 1782 siege of Gibraltar, and was present at the siege of Menorca. Promoted to the rank of captain in 1789, Calleja accompanied his patron, Viceroy Conde de Revillagigedo, to Mexico. From 1790 to 1797 he held important commissions to inspect frontier districts, to raise militia units, and to conduct detailed geographical and resource studies. After promotion to colonel in 1798, he took command of the Tenth Militia Brigade, based at San Luis Potosí, in 1799. Calleja further strengthened his position in the Mexican north through marriage in 1807 to María Francisca de la Gándara, daughter of a wealthy landowner. He was promoted to brigadier in 1810 and to field marshal in 1811.

Although surprised by the Hidalgo revolt of September 1810, Calleja acted quickly to mobilize the militia brigade at San Luis Potosí, which formed the core of the effective royalist Army of the Center, and successfully dispersed the rebels at Aculco (7 November 1810), Guanajuato (25 November 1810), and Puente de Calderón (17 January 1811). In 1812, following the defeat of Hidalgo, Calleja led his army out of the Bajío provinces to raze the insurgent town of Zitácuaro and south to Cuautla, where his army besieged the defensive positions of José María MORELOS. Both sides suffered terrible hardships during the seventy-two-day siege, and starvation forced the insurgents to flee Cuautla.

Calleja introduced a controversial counterinsurgency system designed to mobilize the urban and rural populations and to free army units to chase major insurgent forces. On 4 March 1813, he was named viceroy of New Spain. By 1815 his forces had eliminated Morelos and fragmented if not defeated the insurgency. By the time he transferred command to Viceroy Juan RUÍZ DE APODACA on 19 September 1816, Calleja had come to believe his own propaganda that the royalists had won the war.

Calleja returned to Madrid, where he received the title of Conde de Calderón. In 1819, King Ferdinand VII named him captain-general of Andalusia, governor of Cádiz, and general in chief of the Spanish army that was being assembled to reconquer the Americas. In the military campaign of 1820 and the restoration of the constitution, Calleja was arrested and experienced political difficulties that continued until the return of absolutism in 1823. In 1825, he went to Valencia, where he remained until his death.

— CHRISTON I. ARCHER

CALLEJAS ROMERO, RAFAEL LEONARDO

Rafael Leonardo Callejas Romero (*b.* 14 November 1943), president of Honduras (1990–1994) who promoted economic development along neoliberal lines.

The son of a landowning family, Callejas earned B.S. (1965) and M.S. (1966) degrees in agricultural economics at Mississippi State University. Beginning in 1967 he was an economic planner in the Honduran government and a board member of several Honduran public and private corporations.

Callejas was an unsuccessful National Party presidential candidate in 1981 and 1985 before winning in 1989 as head of the MONARCA (Rafael Callejas National Renovation Movement) faction of the National Party. He favored development under U.S. president Ronald Reagan's Caribbean Basin Initiative and enjoyed strong U.S. support in his campaign. His popularity with conservative leaders in the industrial nations helped him gain favorable international financial agreements that contributed to economic gains early in his administration as he devalued the currency, privatized government enterprises, and pursued other structural adjustments favored by the U.S. Agency for International Development (AID). By 1993, however, Honduras was in serious financial difficulty and suffered severe shortages of foodstuffs, problems that contributed to a Liberal victory in the November 1993 presidential election. Although Callejas was the third elected civilian president to rule Honduras in succession since 1980, the armed forces, which remained autonomous under Callejas, continued to be a strong force in Honduran politics.

— RALPH LEE WOODWARD, JR.

CALLES, PLUTARCO ELÍAS

Plutarco Elías Calles (*b.* 25 September 1877; *d.* 19 October 1945), president of Mexico (1924–1928). The poor relation of a notable family in the northwestern state of Sonora, Calles was an aspiring young professional and entrepreneur who had met with only limited success before the Mexican Revolution. Initially on the periphery of Francisco MADERO's movement against the Porfirio DÍAZ regime, from a minor appointment in the new state government he rose steadily in the ranks of what became the constitutionalist army, becoming Alvaro OBREGÓN's principal political associate. As president, and then as *jefe máximo* (supreme chief) in the wake of the assassination of president-elect Obregón (1928), Calles dominated the national government for more than a decade and initiated the institutionalization of the Revolution.

Until the Revolution, Calles's life had been punctuated with misfortune and disappointments. He was the illegitimate son of Plutarco Elías, scion of one of the most prominent families in northeast Sonora in the nineteenth century. Following the death of his mother when he was four, he was raised by his stepfather, Juan

Plutarco Elías Calles, ca. 1924. (Benson Latin American Collection, University of Texas at Austin)

B. Calles, who owned a small cantina in Hermosillo (and from whom he took his second family name). After being educated in Hermosillo, Calles became a schoolteacher. The death of his first wife, Francisca Bernal, in 1899 prompted him to move to the port of Guaymas, where he began a decade-long search for economic success and social mobility. To do so, he relied on his connections with, and the support of, his father's family, the Elíases. First a school inspector and newspaper editor in the port, Calles next was appointed municipal treasurer (he lost the post when funds were discovered missing), followed by a stint as manager of his half brother's hotel until it burned. He moved in 1906 to Fronteras, where he managed his father's modest hacienda, was bookkeeper for and shareholder in a small flour mill, and served as municipal secretary—at last achieving modest success and some local prominence. But he then became embroiled in the Elíases' conflict with the local cacique (boss) and in a dispute with farmers over water rights. As a result he returned to Guaymas in 1910 to manage a hotel and open a commission business in partnership.

Though not an active participant in the local Maderista movement, Calles lent it some support—his store as a meeting place. He used this connection to run unsuccessfully for the state legislature in 1911. Again he returned to northeast Sonora, opening a general store (in partnership) in the border town of Agua Prieta, a most fortunate choice. The railroad running through the town connected Arizona with important mining districts in the interior of Sonora; and the new governor, José M. Maytorena, was looking for a loyal follower who, as the town's police chief, would secure customs revenues, quiet disgruntled former insurgents, and forestall a rumored invasion from Arizona by the radical Magonista revolutionaries. His choice of Calles proved to be the turning point of the latter's life. Calles proved to be a capable, diligent local official, against the Orozquista rebels (1912) and the Huerta coup a year later (being among the first to proclaim armed resistance in the state).

Calles soon developed a working relationship with Obregón, who was emerging as the leader of the revolutionary *jefes* in the northwest. While Obregón carried the constitutionalist movement beyond the state, Calles remained to manage the military and political affairs of Sonora. As governor of Sonora (1915–1916, 1917–1919) and working with Obregón's other principal Sonoran associate, Adolfo DE LA HUERTA (governor, 1917, 1919–1920), Calles set forth a radical program to promote education on a broad scale; break up monopolies (including the cancellation of all prior government concessions which had tax exemptions) and support small entrepreneurs; extend secularization (including the legalization of divorce and the expulsion of all priests); establish an agrarian commission to distribute the expropriated land of those deemed enemies of the Revolution; foster government patronage of workers, assisting in their organization and legislating rights and benefits; and limit foreign influence (principally, severe economic and social restrictions on Chinese immigrants, and cancelling contracts with some large foreign investors). This radical program put Calles at loggerheads with President Venustiano CARRANZA. Obregón sought to moderate these concepts, but failed in his efforts to establish singular control over the state. He was forced to work with Calles and de la Huerta, forming a triumvirate.

When Obregón announced his presidential candidacy, Calles resigned as secretary of industry, commerce, and labor (1919–1920). Soon after, he led the military forces and proclaimed the Plan of Agua Prieta against

Carranza's attempt to impose his successor, and then served as Obregón's interior secretary (1920–1923). When Obregón chose to support Calles over de la Huerta as his successor, and de la Huerta led a revolt, Calles commanded the troops in the northwest. As president, Calles pressed his radical anticlericalism in the face of the Catholic church's challenge to the restrictions of the 1917 Constitution and then of the Cristero Rebellion (1926–1929). But his support of agrarian reform and the workers' movement ebbed as he moderated his policies and concentrated on the development of the nation's infrastructure (especially irrigation, roads, air and postal service, a telephone network, national banking and investment institutions) and on the promotion of enterprise, even to the point of supporting large-scale domestic and foreign investors.

To retain control over the national government in the wake of the assassination of president-elect Obregón, Calles and his followers pursued a limited and expedient institutionalization of the hierarchical, personalist system that had bound the ruling coalition of revolutionary *jefes* together: the National Revolutionary Party. However, the *Maximato* (the oligarchic rule of the Callista political machine) increasingly lost a popular base, as it turned away from the Revolution's promises of reform and as the Great Depression deepened. Reformers in the party used its structure to institute a radical program and mobilize popular support, coalescing around Lázaro CÁRDENAS. Again employing expediency, Calles responded by acceding to some of the reformist demands and settling on Cárdenas for the 1934 presidential elections, as the best option to contain growing party dissidence and rising popular alienation. This time, however, his expedient adjustments set in motion forces he could not control. Cárdenas mobilized popular support and employed the institutional prerogatives of the party and the presidency to the fullest. When Calles resisted, he was deported (April 1936). He remained in California until Cárdenas's successor, Manuel ÁVILA CAMACHO, permitted his return in 1941 and accorded him full honors at his funeral four years later.

– STUART F. VOSS

CALÓGERAS, JOÃO PANDIÁ

João Pandiá Calógeras (*b.* 19 June 1870; *d.* 21 April 1934), Brazilian statesman, minister, and author. Educated as an engineer, Calógeras served as a federal deputy (1897–1899 and 1903–1914). He sponsored a law giving the government control over subsoil resources, and was active in boundary and military questions. Close to reformist army officers, who backed his appointment as minister of agriculture, industry, and commerce in 1914, he rose to minister of economy (Fazenda) in 1915–1917. He reorganized government finances and foreign loans, thereby preventing foreign creditors from gaining control over customs receipts.

At the Versailles Conference, he served as delegation chief after Epitácio PESSOA was elected president. In 1919, Pessoa named him the first and only civilian to serve as the republic's minister of war (1919–1922). He oversaw the reorganization of the army, the establishment of army aviation and the French Military Mission, the creation of new training schools, a re-armament program, the massive building of new barracks, and the development of a national defense policy. Military professionalization contributed to the revolt of July 1922 that began the cycle of rebellion leading to the Revolution of 1930. Calógeras backed Getúlio VARGAS in the 1930 election and was participating in the constituent assembly when he died in 1934. A convert to Catholicism, in 1932 he was president of the Liga Eleitoral Católica. His books and articles ranged from history and government to engineering and religion.

– FRANK D. MCCANN, JR.

CALVO, CARLOS

Carlos Calvo (*b.* 26 February 1822; *d.* 3 May 1906), Argentine diplomat and jurist. Born in Montevideo and educated in Buenos Aires, Calvo lived in the tumultuous early years after independence in the Río de la Plata region. In 1859, the president of Paraguay, Carlos Antonio LÓPEZ, appointed him Paraguay's representative to mediate a conflict between Great Britain and Paraguay. His mission was a success. Thereafter he retired from public life to write. In 1868, he published a book that gave him international recognition, *Derecho internacional teórico y práctico de Europa y América,* which contained the essence of what has come to be known as the Calvo Doctrine.

He argued that America as well as Europe consisted of free and independent nations and that their sovereignty not be ignored. He declared that sovereign states enjoyed the right to freedom from intervention by other states. Moreover, foreigners were not entitled to rights not accorded to nationals. Thus, the essence of Calvo's ideas were nonintervention and the absolute equality of foreigners with nationals. According to Calvo, European interventions in Latin America were a violation of the equality of sovereign nations, and no nation had the right to employ force against another for the enforcement of contracts or agreements between its citizens and those of the other. Many Latin American countries have incorporated this clause into contracts with international corporations.

Calvo enjoyed a long diplomatic career. In 1878, he served as a delegate to the International Congress of Geography that met in Paris. He was minister plenipotentiary to the postal congress of Paris (1878) and Vienna (1891). In 1883 he became special envoy and minister plenipotentiary to Berlin and to the Russian and Austrian emperors in 1889 and 1890, respectively. In 1899, Calvo was appointed minister to France and the Holy See. He died in Paris.

– JUAN MANUEL PÉREZ

CAMACHO ROLDÁN, SALVADOR

Salvador Camacho Roldán (*b.* 1 January 1827; *d.* 19 June 1900), Colombian Liberal politician, publicist, and businessman. Born in Nunchía, Casanare, Camacho received his doctorate in law and became a judge in 1848. His prominence brought him increasingly higher appointments during the 1850s, including the governorship of Panama (1852–1853). Camacho was elected to the House of Representatives in 1854 and served both there and in the Senate for the next thirty years. A fiscal expert, he served successively as minister of finance and development (1870–1872) and of foreign affairs (1878). He had been president designate (1868–1869) and acting president (December 1869) but never became president, except for one day in July 1871. Camacho's decades of public service left him poor until 1887, when he established the Librería Colombiana and the dry goods firm of Camacho Roldán y Tamayo, in Bogotá. He edited numerous important newspapers from 1849 to 1881. Camacho advocated a technologically oriented educational system as the means to economic growth. His *Escritos varios* (3 vols., 1892–1895, repr. 1983) were culled from his extensive corpus of economic and political works. His travels are recorded in *Notas de viaje* (1898). Camacho is best known for his *Memorias* (2 vols., 1894, 1924, repr. 1946). He died at "El Ocaso," his country house, at Zipacón, Cundinamarca, about thirty miles from Bogotá.

– J. LEÓN HELGUERA

CÂMARA, HÉLDER

Hélder Câmara (Dom Hélder; *b.* 7 February 1909), Brazilian Catholic archbishop. Born in the poor northeastern state of Ceará, Câmara was ordained as a priest at age twenty-two. As a young cleric, he joined Ação Integralista Brasileira, a movement that sympathized with fascism. In 1936, he went to Rio de Janeiro to work with archbishop Sebastião Leme. In the 1940s, when he served as national assistant to Brazilian Catholic Action, Câmara moved toward liberal theological and political positions.

In 1952, Câmara was named auxiliary bishop of Rio. That same year, he helped create the National Conference of Brazilian Bishops (CNBB), which became the most important organization within the Brazilian Catholic church. From 1952 until 1964, he served as secretary-general of the CNBB. In 1955, Câmara created the São Sebastião Crusade, a liberal organization whose objective was to improve the living conditions in Rio's *favelas* (slums).

Câmara repeatedly denounced Brazil's military regime for human rights abuses and for neglecting the poor.

On 12 March 1964, three weeks before the military coup, Câmara was named archbishop of Recife and Olinda. The new archbishop repeatedly denounced the military regime for human rights abuses, for neglecting the poor, and for imposing an economic model that concentrated wealth. His courageous statements in the face of constant intimidation made the diminutive cleric the most famous church leader in Brazil. At first relatively isolated in his criticisms of the military government, by the late 1960s Câmara had the support of a substantial part of the church hierarchy. He and many of his close associates in the archdiocese were frequently harassed by the military government; some were expelled from Brazil, tortured, and even killed. Câmara was a leading figure in the turn of the Brazilian church toward more progressive ecclesiastical and political positions in the 1960s and 1970s.

After retiring as archbishop in 1985, Câmara continued to work in Recife, mostly among the urban poor. His successor, José Cardoso Sobrinho, dismantled many of the programs Câmara had established and clashed with many who had worked with the retired archbishop.

– SCOTT MAINWARING

CAMARGO, SERGIO DE

Sergio de Camargo (*b.* 1930), Brazilian sculptor. A native of Rio de Janeiro, Camargo left Brazil in the 1940s. In 1946 he entered the Academia d'Altimira art school in Buenos Aires, where he studied with the artist Emilio PETTORUTI and one of the school's founders, the painter Lucio FONTANA. He went to Europe for the first time in 1948, and studied philosophy at the Sorbonne in Paris. Influenced by Constantin Brancuşi, Jean Arp, and Georges Vantongerloo, he began to sculpt. From 1948 to 1974, Camargo lived in Paris. In 1953, he traveled to Rio de Janeiro, where he exhibited several of his sculptural works in Rio's National Salon of Modern Art. He also made a brief trip to China.

Although figural sculpture predominated in his early years, Camargo experimented with wood reliefs, geometric abstractionism, and constructivism. Along with contemporaries Julio Le Parc and Carlos CRUZ DIEZ, Camargo is also one of the pioneers of kinetic art. Using a cylinder or cube, he arranges forms and explores the "madness of order." He received the International Sculpture Prize at the 1963 Paris Biennale. In 1965, he began sculptural pieces for Oscar NIEMEYER's Foreign Ministry Building in Brasília. In the same year, he was named best national sculptor in the São Paulo Bienal. He returned to Rio de Janeiro in 1974, and in 1977 he won the sculpture award given by the São Paulo Association of Art Critics. In the 1980s Camargo had solo exhibitions in both the Rio and São Paulo museums of modern art, and he participated in the 1982 Venice Biennale.

– CAREN A. MEGHREBLIAN

CAMBACERES, EUGENIO

Eugenio Cambaceres (*b.* 24 February 1843; *d.* 14 June 1889), Argentine novelist. Cambaceres was born in Buenos Aires into a wealthy landholding Argentine family of French heritage. Like other young Argentines of fortune, he frequently traveled to Europe, making his headquarters in Paris. There and in his native city he was known as a man-about-town, very fond of the ladies; he married an opera diva shortly before his death. During the 1870s, Cambaceres engaged unsuccessfully in politics, and only during middle age, in the 1880s, did he start writing novels. In six short years, he produced four volumes—*Sin rumbo* (1885) is his masterpiece. This promising literary career was cut short when he died of tuberculosis.

All of his novels—*Potpourri* (1882), *Música sentimental* (1884), *Sin rumbo,* and *En la sangre* (1887)—are cast in the naturalist mold, influenced by the French writer Émile Zola. Cambaceres bitterly attacks society, but unlike Zola fails to give moral guidance. In most of his work, we find a typical naturalistic stress on the sordid; the romantic love of earlier nineteenth-century Spanish American novels has given way to an obsession with sex. In its best moments, however, *Sin rumbo* transcends its naturalist theme and trappings and becomes a powerfully dramatic novel, written with intensity and great narrative art. It has become a classic, one of the most dynamic and significant works of nineteenth-century Spanish American literature.

— GEORGE SCHADE

CAMILLE, ROUSSAN

Roussan Camille (*b.* 27 August 1912; *d.* 7 December 1961), Haitian poet and journalist. Camille first wrote for *Le temps,* often publishing poems along with his regular columns. He was named editor in chief of *Haïti Journal* (1935) and director (1936), after the death of Charles Moravia. From 1947 to his death, he held several official positions: division head in the ministry of public instruction (during World War II), vice-consul of Haiti in New York City (1947–1948), secretary to President Dumarsais Estimé (1948–1950), and director of cultural affairs. Camille was imprisoned briefly after serving President Estimé. At the news of Camille's death, Franck Fouché published a poem to "celebrate the multiple presence of a great poet" (*Symphonie en noir majeur,* 1962).

Camille moved away from French poets toward the inspiration of Langston Hughes and Nicolás Guillén. He wrote with empathy for the victim—whether slave, prostitute, or child—and a sense of fraternity with his fellow poets. He was awarded the Dumarsais Estimé Prize for his collected poetry when he submitted the manuscript of *La multiple présence* in 1961. Among his other works are *Assaut à la nuit* (1940), and *La multiple présence, derniers poèmes* (1978).

— CARROL F. COATES

CAMNITZER, LUIS

Luis Camnitzer (*b.* 1937), Uruguayan artist. German born, Camnitzer emigrated with his family to Uruguay in 1939. He studied sculpture and architecture at the Universidad de la República Oriental del Uruguay in Montevideo in the 1950s, and at the Akademie der Bildenden Künste in Munich (1957). He received a John Simon Guggenheim Memorial Fellowship in 1964 and moved to New York City, where he was also granted a Memorial Foundation for Jewish Culture Fellowship (1965–1966). He was a founding member of the New York Graphic Workshop (1967). During this period he used text without images to describe spaces and objects in installations. He has taught at the Pratt Institute, Fairleigh Dickinson University, and the State University of New York (Old Westbury).

Using text, a site plan, and schematic representations, Camnitzer acknowledged the 1969 massacre in Puerto Montt, Chile. In an installation consisting of a wall of boxes, each wrapped in bloodstained gauze to symbolize anonymous political victims, Camnitzer presented the theme of political repression in Latin America (*Leftovers,* 1970). In the 1980s he addressed themes related to human rights and environmental decay in Latin America. An outsider to the art market system, Camnitzer has devoted a great deal of his time to writing about art and organizing noncommercial exhibitions.

— MARTA GARSD

CAMÕES, LUÍS VAZ DE

Luís vaz de Camões (*b.* 1525?; *d.* 10 June 1580), Portuguese poet. One of the most renowned figures of Portuguese letters, Luís de Camões authored a substantial corpus that includes the epic poem *Os Lusíadas* (*The Lusiads,* 1572), a cornerstone of his fame in world literature, lyric poetry (principal editions published in 1595 and 1598), plays, and familiar epistles. Little biographical information is known about Camões, although it's certain that he spent many of his adult years as a soldier in the Portuguese Empire. His poetry, written in both Portuguese and Spanish, was composed in the traditional style (the *medida velha,* as it was known in the poet's time) as well as in the *dolce stil nuovo,* introduced into Portugal by Francisco de Sá de MIRANDA. *Os Lusíadas* consists of 1,102 stanzas in ottava rima divided into ten cantos and reflects the epic imagination of the sixteenth-century Portuguese. The theme is nothing less than the history of Portugal—and it is the nation that emerges as the collective hero—articulated around the voyage of Vasco da GAMA to India in 1497. *Os Lusíadas* was the model for Bento Teixeira's *Prosopopéia* (1601), an encomiastic poem about Jorge de Albuquerque COELHO, governor of Pernambuco.

— JOSIAH BLACKMORE

CAMPA SALAZAR, VALENTÍN

Valentín Campa Salazar (*b.* 14 February 1904), Mexican labor union leader and presidential candidate, a controversial figure in the railroad workers' union and a longtime activist of the Mexican Communist Party while it was underground. Born in Monterrey, Nuevo León, Campa completed only his first year of secondary education before he began working for La Corona, a subsidiary of the Royal Dutch Company, in 1920. He was a labor activist and organizer, cofounding the Sindicato Unitario Mexicano. Imprisoned thirteen times for his labor organizing, first in 1927, Campa spent ten years in Lecumberri Prison after a 1958–1959 railroad strike. Campa ran for president on the legalized Mexican Communist Party (PCM) ticket in 1976 and served as a federal deputy for the PCM in the 1979–1982 legislature.

— RODERIC AI CAMP

CAMPERO, NARCISO

Narciso Campero (*b.* 29 October 1813; *d.* 12 August 1896), president of Bolivia (1880–1884). Campero was born in Tojo in the department of Tarija. Near the beginning of his military career, he fought in the battle of Ingavi in November 1841. He attended military school in Paris in 1845. From 1859 to 1879 Campero served in military, diplomatic, and administrative posts, usually under Liberal presidents. When the War of the Pacific began in 1879, he was appointed general of the Fifth Division. Because of their confidence in Campero, the Bolivian directors of the Huanchaca Silver Company sent provisions to the Fifth Division. When the inhabitants of La Paz overthrew President Hilarión DAZA on 27 December 1879, they named Campero as their new leader. Following the advice of the silver barons, Campero gradually removed Bolivia from the war by 1884. Meanwhile, to legitimize his new government, Campero called a constituent assembly, which met in 1880. The delegates not only confirmed Campero as president but also approved a new constitution for Bolivia that remained in force until 1938. By cooperating with the mining oligarchy, Campero brought an end to unstable caudillo rule and, through the Constitution of 1880, allowed a small elite of mine owners to open Bolivia to the industrial world.

— ERWIN P. GRIESHABER

CAMPISTEGUY, JUAN

Juan Campisteguy (*b.* 7 September 1859; *d.* 1937), president of Uruguay (1927–1931). Campisteguy, born in Montevideo, entered politics when he joined the revolutionary movement against the autocratic regime of Máximo Santos in 1886. His career within the ruling Colorado party was closely linked to José BATLLE Y ORDÓÑEZ, of whose newspaper *El Día* he was one of the founding editors.

After two terms as member of the House of Representatives (1891–1897), Campisteguy was minister of finance (1897–1898) during Juan Lindolfo CUESTAS's constitutional presidency as well as during his autocratic period following the 1898 coup. In 1903/1904, as minister of government under Batlle y Ordóñez, Campisteguy was one of the architects of the government victory over the Blanco rebellion led by Aparicio SARAVIA. He was subsequently a senator (1905–1911); a member of the Constituent Assembly for the Colorado party's Riverista faction, which opposed Batlle's plans for the introduction of a *colegiado* system (1917); a deputy (1920–1923); and a member of the National Council of Administration (1921–1927).

Important achievements of Campisteguy's presidency were the creation of the state-owned Frigorífico Nacional (National Meat Packing Plant, 1928) and the Comité de Vigilancia Económica (Committee of Economic Vigilance, 1929).

— DIETER SCHONEBOHM

CAMPO, ESTANISLAO DEL

Estanislao Del Campo (*b.* 7 February 1834; *d.* 6 November 1880), Argentine poet, legislator, journalist, civil servant, and officer of the Civic Guard. His admiration for Hilario ASCASUBI and the Gauchesca literature prompted him to write poetry in this style. He even adopted the pseudonym of Anastasio el Pollo (Anastasio the Chicken) as a sign of respect for Ascasubi's *Aniceto el Gallo* (Aniceto the Rooster). In 1866 del Campo wrote the gauchesca poem *Fausto,* in which one gaucho, chatting with another, tells the plot of the Gounod opera that he happened to see in Buenos Aires's Teatro Colón. The novelty of this text is that del Campo injected an urban, highly cultured subject into gauchesca literature. He erased the disparity between the popular language and the cult subject of the Faustian legend by reducing it to the concrete reality and perceptions of the gaucho. In spite of the hilarity of the text, the gaucho-narrator and his friend are never ridiculed. On the contrary, their deep friendship is emphasized. The poem is also famous for its romantic descriptions, without parallel in gauchesca literature.

In 1866 del Campo wrote the poem Fausto, *in which one gaucho, chatting with another, tells the plot of an opera he saw in Buenos Aires's Teatro Colón.*

Committed to the party of General Bartolmé MITRE, del Campo fought at the battles of Cepeda (1859) and Pavón (1861) for a Buenos Aires state separate from the Argentine Confederation. In the late 1860s del Campo was elected to the House of Representatives of the province of Buenos Aires as a member of the Liberal Party. In 1874 he was made lieutenant colonel of the Civil Guard. Del Campo took part in the Mitre revolution against Nicolás AVELLANEDA. He retired from public life in April 1880 and died six months later in Buenos Aires.

— ANGELA B. DELLEPIANE

CAMPO, RAFAEL

Rafael Campo (*b.* 24 October 1813; *d.* 1 March 1890), president of El Salvador (1856–1858). Educated at the University of San Carlos de Guatemala, Campo continued his father's successful agricultural and commercial enterprises in El Salvador and was among the first coffee planters in the country. He became politically active in the Conservative Party and was elected president on 30 January 1856, taking office on 12 February. He turned over power to his vice president, Francisco Dueñas, on 12 May of the same year, but resumed the presidency on 19 July. Regarded by many as a puppet of Guatemalan caudillo Rafael CARRERA, the conservative Campo allowed greater political freedom than in other Central American states of the period.

In July 1856 Campo joined the other Central American states in the National War against William WALKER, sending Salvadoran troops to Nicaragua under Ramón Belloso and Gerardo BARRIOS. Upon returning from the war in Nicaragua, Barrios failed in an effort to overthrow Campo in June 1857. Barrios gained power in 1858, however, when Campo stepped down on 1 February of that year, after the serious cholera epidemic of 1857 had exhausted the country. Campo later served as foreign minister under Francisco Dueñas, and was president of the Constitutional Convention of 1871. A critic of the Liberal governments that followed, Campo was in exile in Nicaragua for most of the decade following, but in 1882 he returned to Sonsonate, his birthplace, where he worked for the establishment of the hospital there. He died in Acajutla.

— RALPH LEE WOODWARD, JR.

CÁMPORA, HÉCTOR JOSÉ

Héctor José Cámpora (*b.* 1909; *d.* 1980), president of Argentina (1973). Although Alejandro LANUSSE allowed Juan D. PERÓN to return from exile in Spain to Argentina, a 9 July 1972 rule required that candidates be in residence by 25 August 1972. Whatever the reason, Perón did not return until November, thereby forfeiting his eligibility to run for president and enabling someone else, namely Héctor Cámpora, to risk defeat. Lanusse also ruled that the Peronists had to capture 50 percent of the vote to take office. Lanusse's rule notwithstanding, Cámpora was sworn in with 49 percent on 25 May 1973 but remained president only until 13 July 1973.

Born in 1909 in Mercedes, Buenos Aires Province, Cámpora trained in odontology and practiced as a dentist during his periodic political eclipses. He was national deputy for his province from 1946 to 1952 and served as president of the national Chamber of Deputies (1948–1952). He advised on Argentina's constitutional reform of 1949 and in 1951 assisted Brazil with the same issues of the presidential mandate and term in office. The following year he was returned for another six years as deputy. After the military coup of September 1955 Cámpora fled to Chile, where he remained until 1963, when the amnesty allowed him to return.

Though usually viewed as a puppet of Perón, Cámpora did not lack ideas of his own. His presidency showed conciliation to guerrillas, labor militants, and students. Such policies cost him Perón's support, so that he fell on 13 July 1973. Raúl Lastiri bridged the rest of the gap until Perón himself assumed the presidency on 12 October 1973. Following Perón's death on 1 July 1974, Cámpora opposed Perón's wife, Isabel. He ran for president on the Authentic Peronist Party ticket with Oscar Alende. After the military coup of 24 March 1976, Cámpora sought asylum in Mexico's embassy in Buenos Aires. He died of throat cancer, for which the military had denied him treatment, at the end of 1980.

— ROGER GRAVIL

CAMPOS, FRANCISCO LUIZ DA SILVA

Francisco Luiz da Silva Campos (*b.* 18 November 1891; *d.* 1 November 1968), Brazilian presidential adviser. The son of Jacinto Alves da Silva Campos and Azejúlia de Souza e Silva, Campos was born in Dores de Indaiá, Minas Gerais. A lawyer, politician, and educator, he married Lavinia Ferreira da Silva, with whom he had two children. The couple eventually separated; later he lived with Margarita Leite.

As an educator, Campos was a professor at the Faculty of Law in his home state and a tenured professor at the Federal University of Rio de Janeiro. As a politician, he held various posts, including state legislator, federal legislator, secretary of the interior for the state of Minas Gerais, and mayor of Belo Horizonte. He was also a leader in the Liberal Alliance, which supported the presidential candidacy of Getúlio VARGAS, a movement that culminated in the Constitutionalist Revolution of 1930.

As the country's first minister of health and education (1930–1932), Campos reformed the training procedures for primary school teachers and established a federal university educational system. He wrote a number of works on education, including *Educação e cultura* (1940). As a jurist, Campos authored case studies and opinions that still appear in constitutional, administrative, and civil law texts.

In 1932, as Vargas's interim minister of justice, Campos had a great impact on the implantation of the *Estado Novo* (New State) program and authored the 1937 *Estado Novo* charter, in which many corporatist features were outlined. In addition, he was the main author of the Institutional Act No. 1, which juridically incorporated the revolution in the spring of 1964. He died in Belo Horizonte in 1968.

— IÊDA SIQUEIRA WIARDA

CAMPOS, JULIETA

Julieta Campos (*b.* 8 May 1932), Mexican novelist, essayist, and translator. Born in Cuba, Campos has resided in Mexico since 1960 and is a naturalized Mexican. As writer-in-residence at the Centro Mexicano de Escritores (1966–1967) and on staff at the Instituto de Investigaciones Estéticas at the National University of Mexico (1969–1970), Campos has been active in the cultural politics of the country. She began as an essayist and translator in Mexican journals and cultural supplements in the 1950s and became a collaborator and member of the editorial board of *Vuelta* in 1977. She served as director of the *Revista de la Universidad de México* from 1981 to 1984. Campos won the Xavier Villaurrutia Prize for her novel *Tiene los cabellos rojizos y se llama Sabina* (1974), and in 1993 her novel *El miedo de perder a Euridice* (1979) was translated into English. Rejecting traditional narrative forms of plot, linearity, and spatial and temporal specificity, she elaborates in her writing a self-reflexive and imaginative perspective on identity, nostalgia, love, time, and death. Her critical work includes assessments of literary authors and periods, discussions of the nature and function of literature, and the study of Nahuatl stories within the problematics of oralism and literacy.

— NORMA KLAHN

CAMPOS, LUIS MARÍA

Luis María Campos (*b.* 1838; *d.* 1907), Argentine military leader. Born in Buenos Aires, Campos entered the army in 1859 as a sublieutenant in the national guard regiment. He fought in the battles of Cepeda and Pavón, which ended the long struggle among the provinces, earning the rank of sergeant major. Campos served throughout the War of the Triple Alliance (1864–1870), perhaps the bloodiest in Latin American history. He fought at Paso de la Patría, Estero Bellaco, and Curupayty. Seriously wounded at San Ignacio, Campos was sent to the province of San Juan to recover.

Returning to the war, he fought at most major engagements, including Lomas Valentinas and Angostura. Late in the war he was decorated by the commander in chief of Allied Forces, CONDE D'EU, for his bravery.

Between 1870 and 1873 Campos fought against Ricardo LÓPEZ JORDÁN, the rebellious caudillo of Entre Ríos. In 1875 he was named inspector general of arms, and in 1892 he was appointed chief of staff of the army and then minister of war and navy until 1896. In March 1896 he mobilized the national guard for a possible international conflict, and in 1898 he again became minister of war. At this time the Army War College was established under his supervision. He was promoted to lieutenant general in 1899 and retired in January 1906.

— ROBERT SCHEINA

CAMPOS, MANUEL JORGE

Manuel Jorge Campos (*b.* 22 April 1847; *d.* 15 December 1908), Argentine general who led troops in support of the Radical Party rebellion against President Miguel JUÁREZ CELMAN in July 1890. Born in Buenos Aires, Campos was a career military officer who saw service in the War of the Triple Alliance, fought to support the national government against regional caudillos, and served with General Julio ROCA in campaigns to conquer the Indians of Argentina's southern plains.

In 1890 the leader of the Radical Party, Leandro ALEM, sought assistance from expresident Bartolomé MITRE and General Campos in a revolt against the Conservative president. Campos led his troops in a desultory fashion while Mitre negotiated the resignation of the president and the assumption of Vice President Carlos PELLEGRINI, a compromise that angered Alem. In 1892 Campos became the chief of police in the federal capital, and he later served as a senator, then a national deputy, in Congress.

— JAMES A. BAER

CAMPOS, ROBERTO (DE OLIVEIRA)

Roberto (de Oliveira) Campos (*b.* 17 April 1917), Brazilian minister of planning and economic coordination (1964–1967). Diplomat, economist, professor, public official, and legislator, Campos has been a central participant in Brazilian economic affairs since joining the foreign service in 1939. He is known for his neoliberal (conservative) economic positions, including less state intervention and fewer restrictions on foreign capital investment. He attended many of the international economic conferences held in the 1940s, including the Bretton Woods Conference. As a government economic adviser in the 1950s, Campos helped found the National Economic Development Bank (Banco Nacional de Desenvolvimento Econômico—BNDE) to finance infrastructure and served as its director-superintendent (1955–1958) and president (1958–1959). He has held many posts in government, acting as ambassador to the United States (1961–1963) and to London (1975–1982), federal senator (1983–1991), and federal deputy (1991–).

As minister of planning and economic coordination (1964–1967), Campos was the principal architect of the Economic Action Plan of the Government (Plano de Ação Econômica do Governo—PAEG), which included budget-balancing and restrictions on money-supply growth to fight inflation and institutional reforms to provide the foundation for further economic expansion. Among the reforms enacted were indexed government bonds, called Readjustable Obligations of the National Treasury (Obrigações Reajustáveis do Tesoro Nacional—ORTN), and a general indexation system, termed *correção monetária* (monetary correction); a noninflationary and regressive wage policy; a weakening of job security; a housing finance system; limited, pro-production land reform; and a central bank. PAEG brought down inflation, but at the cost of an unpopular recession. The reforms established the basic institutional framework for subsequent Brazilian economic life and provided the foundations for the subsequent high-growth period called the Economic Miracle (1968–1974).

– RUSSELL E. SMITH

CAMPOS CERVERA, HÉRIB

Hérib Campos Cervera (*b.* 1905; *d.* 28 August 1953), Paraguayan poet. Widely considered to be Paraguay's finest poet of the post–Chaco War (post-1935) generation, Campos Cervera has left an indelible mark on the literature of his country. Descended from a well-known family of artists and writers, he began his life's work in poetry while teaching engineering at the Colegio Nacional and at the Escuela Normal de Profesores. Initially, his poems appeared only in student newspapers, but he soon gained a literary following in intellectual circles in Asunción.

Campos Cervera's earliest works were heavily influenced by the modernism of Rubén DARÍO and other turn-of-the-century writers. After a time, however, he became attracted to the *vanguardista* school and soon became its principal exponent in Paraguay. During the 1930s Campos Cervera was forced into exile because of his political associations. This stay outside of the country was actually helpful in developing his talent: in Buenos Aires, he discovered the writings of Federico

García Lorca (who became his personal friend), and he helped found the literary group *Vy'araity*, which counted among its members his aunt Josefina PLÁ, the novelist Augusto ROA BASTOS, and such figures as Hugo RODRÍGUEZ ALCALÁ and Oscar Ferreiro.

During the 1930s Campos Cervera was forced into exile because of his political associations; this stay outside of Paraguay was actually helpful in developing his talent.

Campos Cervera's finest work can be found in his poetic compilation *Ceniza redimida*. He also was among the first to popularize poetry in the Guaraní language. He died in Buenos Aires.

– MARTA FERNÁNDEZ WHIGHAM

CAMPOS-PARSI, HÉCTOR

Héctor Campos-Parsi (*b.* 10 October 1922), Puerto Rican composer, music critic, teacher, and concert manager. Campos-Parsi completed his early education in Ponce and then went on to study biology and psychology at the University of Puerto Rico. In 1945 he entered the school of medicine at the National University of Mexico, but ill health forced him to abandon this pursuit. He received a fellowship to the New England Conservatory from 1947 to 1950 and, while in New England, also studied with Aaron Copland who arranged for him to work in Paris under Nadia Boulanger from 1950 to 1953. He was named director of the music division of the Institute of Puerto Rican Culture in 1958 and in 1970 to the Academy of Arts and Sciences. A prolific composer in various styles, he is best known for his *Sonatina para piano y violín* for which he won the Maurice Ravel Prize in 1953, *Tres fantasías para piano* (1950), and *Juan Bobo y las fiestas* (1957). Copland's influence is most evident in Campos-Parsi's folkloric works such as *Yerba bruja* (1962) and *Arawak* (1970).

– JACQUELYN BRIGGS KENT

CAMPOS SALES, MANUEL FERRAZ DE

Manuel Ferraz de Campos Sales (*b.* 13 February 1841; *d.* 28 June 1913), president of Brazil (1898–1902). Born in Campinas, São Paulo, Campos Sales studied and practiced law before being elected a provincial deputy by the Liberal Party in 1867. He became an organizing member of the Republican Party of São Paulo in

1871, and was elected to the provincial chamber in 1881 and the national legislature in 1885 as a Republican and doctrinaire federalist. He was voluble, principled, and politically astute.

With the establishment of the Republic, Campos Sales served as minister of justice in General Manoel Deodoro da FONSECA's governments and built the administrative and judicial basis of the new republic. Weathering the political conflicts of the 1890s, he was elected president in 1898. His administration is best known for the reconstruction of the nation's finances and the creation of the political process that characterized the Republic until 1930.

In the economic crisis characterized by rampant inflation and speculation, known as the *Encilhamento*, Campos Sales made financial reconstruction the priority of the administration. Bolstered by the "funding loan" he negotiated with the Rothschilds, the government carried out deflationary currency policies, cut spending, abandoned public works, increased taxes and tariffs, and emphasized agriculture over industry. Notwithstanding considerable unpopularity for his policies, by 1902 Campos Sales had rehabilitated the national finances and international credit.

Elected in an atmosphere of regional revolts and fractious party politics, Campos Sales proclaimed himself above partisan politics. He articulated the Política dos Governadores, in which incumbent state governments supplied loyal federal congressional delegations in exchange for nonintervention in state affairs. Relying heavily on the larger states' economic and demographic strengths, the political system revolved around São Paulo and Minas Gerais. This reciprocity created a hierarchy of interlocking interests and loyalties down to the *coroneis,* the local bosses who delivered the votes for patronage and financial favors.

Sales died in Santos, São Paulo.

— WALTER BREM

CANALES, NEMESIO ROSARIO

Nemesio Rosario Canales (*b.* 18 December 1878; *d.* 14 September 1923), Puerto Rican writer and statesman. Nemesio R. Canales interrupted his studies of medicine in Saragossa, Spain, in 1898, when Puerto Rico came under United States sovereignty. He left the island two years later to study at the Baltimore School of Law. After graduating in 1903, he returned to Puerto Rico to practice law and began a career in politics. He wrote articles for the *Revista de las Antillas* and *La Semana,* and a column for the Ponce newspaper *El Día;* he also cofounded *Juan Bobo,* a weekly, and edited *Cuasimodo,* an inter-American journal on culture. Concerned with

politics and the economy as well as social, labor, and cultural issues, he served in the Puerto Rican Congress and in the Department of Justice. His most famous work is a collection of humorously ironic articles entitled *Paliques* (Chit-chat, 1913). Canales also published a novel, *Mi voluntad se ha muerto* (My will has died), in 1921, and a drama, *El héroe galopante* (The galloping hero), in 1923, the year of his death in New York.

— ESTELLE IRIZARRY

CAÑAS, JOSÉ MARÍA

José María Cañas (*b.* 1809; *d.* 30 September 1860), commander of the Central American army in the National War against William WALKER in Nicaragua. Born in El Salvador, Cañas was an officer in Francisco MORAZÁN's army and later rose to prominence in Costa Rica as an ally of his brother-in-law, President Juan Rafael MORA PORRÁS. After General Cañas distinguished himself at the battle of Rivas (11 April 1856), Mora named him inspector general of the Central American allied army in January 1857 and later commander in chief of the Central American forces. When Mora was ousted from the presidency of Costa Rica in 1859, Gerardo BARRIOS put Cañas in command of the Salvadoran army. In 1860, after supporting Mora's unsuccessful attempt to return to power in Costa Rica, Cañas and Mora were executed at Puntarenas. Cañas also represented Costa Rica in the intrigues relating to U.S. and British efforts to gain canal rights through Guanacaste in the border area between Nicaragua and Costa Rica during Mora's administration.

— RALPH LEE WOODWARD, JR.

CAÑAS, JOSÉ SIMEÓN

José Simeón Cañas (*b.* 18 February 1767; *d.* 4 March 1838), Salvadoran intellectual and politician. Born in Santa Lucía Zacatecoluca, El Salvador, to a wealthy family, Cañas was educated as a priest in Guatemala, where he received his doctorate in theology. He became rector of the University of San Carlos in 1802. He joined with José Matías DELGADO and Manuel José ARCE in supporting Central American independence in 1821. As a member of the Central American Congress, on 31 December 1823 Cañas made the motion to abolish slavery in Central America, enacted the following year. He subsequently supported the cause of Central American unity. He died, and is buried, in San Vicente, El Salvador.

— RALPH LEE WOODWARD, JR.

CANDAMO, MANUEL

Manuel Candamo (*b.* 1842; *d.* 7 May 1904), the son of one of the wealthiest merchants of mid-nineteenth-century Peru, whose fortune rested on shipping (especially the trade in indentured Asians), guano, and railroad construction. The family was typical of that group of merchants and entrepreneurs who replaced the aristocracy as the ruling elite of the country. The aristocracy had banned political parties as tasteless and dangerous. But Candamo was active in the Civilista Party and won election as the mayor of Lima. In 1902 he gained further public attention as an activist president of the Lima Chamber of Commerce. He became a candidate for president of Peru in 1903 as a moderate conciliator between two intransigent factions of the Democratic and Civilista parties. The Civilista Party disappeared briefly when leading members joined former Democrats in the Liberal Party. This action prompted another faction of Civilistas to form a surprise alliance with the Constitutionalist Party, the party of the military. Candamo remained the single Civilista trusted by and popular with all factions. Inaugurated in November after he won the election, he fell ill and died the following July. Thereafter mutual distrust sowed discord once again among party factions.

– VINCENT PELOSO

CANDANEDO, CÉSAR

César Candanedo (*b.* 12 May 1906), Panamanian writer. Candanedo was born in David, Panama. Self-taught, he was awarded a scholarship by the World Health Organization to pursue studies in the School of Public Health of the University of Chile. After completing his studies, he worked as a public health inspector for the Department of Public Health in Panama. This position gave him the opportunity to travel and to become familiar with the diverse regions of the country and, in particular, to become aware of the hopelessness that permeates every aspect of the daily existence of Panama's rural population.

In his first book, *Los clandestinos* (1957; The Clandestine Ones), he depicted the impact of the United Fruit Company and the Canal Zone on the living conditions of Panama's rural population. His later works, *La otra frontera* (1967; The Other Frontier), *El cerquero y otros relatos* (1967; The Encloser and Other Stories), *Memorias de un caminante* (1970; Memories of a Traveler), *Palo duro* (1973; Hard Truncheon), and *El perseguido* (1991; The Fugitive) reaffirm his reputation as both a writer of vigorous works of social protest and a writer of regional literature. *El perseguido* received first prize in the 1986 Ricardo Miró competition.

– ELBA D. BIRMINGHAM-POKORNY

CANDIOTI, FRANCISCO ANTONIO

Francisco Antonio Candioti (*b.* 1743; *d.* 25 August 1815), Argentine landowner and supporter of the independence movement. With large landholdings in the present-day provinces of Santa Fe and Entre Ríos, Candioti, "prince of the gauchos," generously provided arms and provisions for his friend Manuel BELGRANO at the outbreak of the independence movement in 1810. Responding to widespread provincial sentiment against the centralist ambitions of *porteño* (Buenos Aires) leaders, he sought out the support of José Gervasio ARTIGAS, whose federalist sympathies he largely shared. In 1815 Artigas loyalists led by José Eusebio Hereñú dislodged the *porteño* army under José Miguel Díaz Vélez, dissolved the provincial junta, and constituted the newly autonomous province of Santa Fe, with Candioti as its first governor. Aged and sickly, however, Candioti could contribute little to the province's defense against destructive Indian raids after the rapid departure of federalist forces. He died shortly after *porteño* troops reoccupied the city and put a temporary end to the newly won autonomy.

– WILLIAM H. KATRA

CANÉ, MIGUEL

Miguel Cané (*b.* 27 January 1851; *d.* 5 September 1905), Argentine writer and statesman. Cané's most enduring achievement remains *Juvenilia* (1884), a memoir of student days at the Colegio Nacional in Buenos Aires. He never abandoned literature and produced many essays and miscellaneous writings as a member of the generation of '80. His commentaries on national affairs in the newspapers *La Tribuna* and *El Nacional* earned Cané the appellation of chronicler of his generation.

Cané entered politics in 1874 and supported Adolfo ALSINA, who suppressed a revolution headed by Bartolomé MITRE. He held various positions, including congressman (1875), director of the postal and telegraph service (1880), municipal intendent of Buenos Aires (1892), minister of foreign affairs (1893), and the first dean of the School of Philosophy and Letters at the University of Buenos Aires (1900). He was also minister plenipotentiary to Colombia and Venezuela in 1881 and to Spain in 1886.

Although Cané professed liberalism, he had reservations about Argentine democracy. He distrusted the United States and its use of the Monroe Doctrine and supported protectionist economic legislation. He favored the residence law, which curtailed the growing influence of foreign labor by banning undesirable foreigners, and approved of other legislation upholding oligarchic interests and policies. Cané became more and more conservative in the last years of his life as a national senator (1902–1905).

— MYRON I. LICHTBLAU

CANECA, FREI JOAQUÍM DO AMOR DIVINO

Frei Joaquím do Amor Divino Caneca (*b.* 20 August 1779; *d.* 13 January 1825), Brazilian Carmelite friar, priest, journalist, and revolutionary. Born in Recife, Pernambuco, Caneca joined the Carmelite order in his native province and achieved prominence as a teacher of geometry and rhetoric. In 1817 he joined the Pernambucan republican revolt, for which he forfeited a nomination to be bishop of Maranhão and spent four years in prison in Salvador da Bahia. Freed after the 1821 liberal coup in Bahia, Frei Caneca returned to Pernambuco, where he became a member of the provincial junta. In 1822 he disavowed the regional republicanism of 1817 and advocated Pernambuco's adherence to the independent Brazilian monarchy proclaimed by Emperor PEDRO I in Rio de Janeiro. He founded a newspaper, *Typhis Pernambucano,* to propagate his liberal-federalist-constitutionalist ideology.

Frei Caneca and fifteen other confederation leaders were condemned for insurrection; he died before a firing squad in Recife.

Frei Caneca denounced the emperor's closing of the national Constitutional Convention of 1823 and led the fight in Pernambuco against the ratification of Pedro's centralist Constitution of 1824. After Pedro declared the constitution ratified, despite its rejection by the municipal councils of Recife and other northeastern cities, Frei Caneca declared it void in Pernambuco and called for the formation of an autonomous government for the Northeast. The result was the separatist Confederation of the Equator, which was crushed by imperial troops in 1824. Frei Caneca and fifteen other confederation leaders were condemned for insurrection; he died before a firing squad in Recife.

— NEILL MACAULAY

CAÑEDO, FRANCISCO

Francisco Cañedo (*b.* 1839; *d.* 5 June 1909), governor of the state of Sinaloa. One of many migrants from neighboring Tepic, Cañedo began work as an errand boy and then clerk in large merchant houses, first in Mazatlán and then in Culiacán. Aided by marriage into the notable Batiz family, by the patronage of Culiacán's leading political family (the Vegas), and by his cultivation of close ties with Porfirio DÍAZ, Cañedo rose to preeminence in Sinaloan politics through the 1870s. Serving as governor (1877–1880, 1884–1888, 1892–1909), he assumed sole control of the state government thereafter until his death. He incorporated Mazatlán's notables into his political circle, ending the bitter and destructive rivalry between the state's two cities. Cañedo followed Porfirista policies faithfully. He consolidated control by eliminating all *municípios* (municipalities) but the district seats, which were firmly controlled by the prefects he appointed.

— STUART F. VOSS

CAÑEDO, JUAN DE DIOS

Juan de Dios Cañedo (*b.* 18 January 1786; *d.* 28 March 1850), Mexican politician and diplomat. A scion of one of the great families of Jalisco, Cañedo studied law in Guadalajara. He was active in politics from 1811 until his death, distinguishing himself as a champion of legislative power and of federalism. Cañedo served in various elected positions: the *ayuntamiento* (city council) of Guadalajara (1811); the Cortes in Spain (1813; 1820–1821); the Mexican Constituent Congress (1823–1824); senator from Jalisco (1825–1828); deputy from Jalisco (1830–1831; 1849); and president of the *ayuntamiento* of Mexico City (1844). He also served as minister of foreign affairs from 1828 to 1829 and again from 1839 to 1840. He was Mexico's minister to South America (1831–1839); England (1846); and France (1847). A leader of the political opposition, Cañedo was brutally murdered in March 1850. Those responsible were never brought to justice.

— JAIME E. RODRÍGUEZ O.

CANEK, JACINTO

Jacinto Canek (*b.* ca. 1731; *d.* 14 December 1761), a Maya who led an Indian uprising in Yucatán. Born Jacinto Uc de los Santos, this Indian from Campeche led a Maya cultural revitalization movement that ultimately challenged Spanish rule in colonial Yucatán. In 1761 in the village of Cisteíl he proclaimed himself to be King Canek (the legendary name of Maya kings), whose coming had been foretold in Maya prophecy. Thousands of Indians joined his movement, which combined traditional Maya and Christian elements and sought both cultural and political autonomy. The Spanish colonial authorities, using their military might, finally defeated Canek's forces in battle, thus crushing the movement. Canek was captured, tried, and executed by being torn limb-from-limb.

— ROBERT W. PATCH

CANO, MARÍA DE LOS ÁNGELES

María de los Ángeles Cano (*b.* 12 August 1887; *d.* 26 April 1967), Colombian labor leader and feminist. An icon of the Colombian Left, Cano was born into a prominent family in Medellín. Small in stature, she had great energy combined with a deeply felt social conscience. Reared in a liberal-minded home, she absorbed secular literature, encouraged by her educator father. She became a journalist in Medellín, thereby gaining access to international wire services, which from 1922 on, reported on the Soviet Union. Cano came to admire that nation greatly and also began to meet with artisans and workers, who as part of May Day festivities proclaimed her the "Flower of Medellín Labor" in 1925. Over the next several months, Cano made seven nationwide tours in which she spoke out for socialism and workers' rights. Despite official persecution, workers' groups proclaimed her the "National Flower of Labor," in November 1926. She was among the founders of the Partido Social Revolucionario in September 1927. Although she was not a participant in the banana workers' strike against United Fruit Company (November–December 1928) at Santa Marta, her oratory on behalf of labor did help to create a climate favorable for such action. Cano was imprisoned and harassed, yet she continued her activities. After the mid-1930s, her health deteriorated, however, and her political activities ceased. Cano died in Medellín.

— J. LEÓN HELGUERA

CANTILO, JOSÉ LUIS

José Luis Cantilo (*b.* 6 February 1871; *d.* 11 October 1944), Argentine politician and journalist. First elected a provincial deputy for Buenos Aires in 1896, Cantilo rose through the ranks of the Unión Cívica Radical, participating in the Radicals' last armed protest in 1905. Cantilo was a close associate of Hipólito YRIGOYEN and joined the national Congress in the wake of the reform of the suffrage law in 1912. President Yrigoyen named him intervenor in the province of Buenos Aires in 1917,

in an effort to defuse the opposition of conservatives. Soon afterward, Cantilo returned to the capital as intendant (1917–1922); there he dealt with the social upheaval of 1917 to 1921. He did not stand out as either a great conciliator or an effective administrator, but he was a loyal follower of the Radical faction led by Yrigoyen. From 1922 to 1926, Cantilo served as governor of the province of Buenos Aires, where he was charged repeatedly by Conservatives and dissident Radicals with undiluted partisanship but nevertheless succeeded in displacing the Conservatives and consolidating a Radical hold. He was again intendant of the capital from 1926 to 1930. Had Yrigoyen not stood for reelection in 1928, Cantilo would have been the logical Radical candidate. With the coup d'état in September 1930, Cantilo was forced to leave politics. A decade later, with signs that the country would return to unobstructed democratic rule, he was elected to Congress in 1940. He served very briefly as a foreign minister until March 1941, when he was replaced by a Conservative Hispanophile. From 1941 until his resignation in June 1943, he was president of the Cámara (lower House of Representatives). As the country polarized between archconservatives and rising trade unions, and faced military rumblings, the political room for a liberal like Cantilo quickly contracted.

— JEREMY ADELMAN

CANTINFLAS

Cantinflas (Mario Moreno; *b.* 12 August 1911; *d.* 20 April 1993), Mexican comedian and film star. Cantinflas began studies in medicine at the National Autonomous University of Mexico (UNAM), but dropped out for a career as a popular stage comedian in *carpas* (traveling stage shows). From the onset, Cantinflas created a unique comic persona, dressing in ragged clothes, his pants close to falling off, and using a rapid, nonsensical manner of speech. He debuted in cinema with a small part in *No te engañes corazón* (1936). The two films that followed, *Así es mi tierra* (1937) and *Águila o Sol* (1937), marked Cantinflas as a rising star. His role in *Ahí está el detalle* (1940) assured his popularity and success. Cantinflas went on to star in over forty features. Among his best-known and praised films are *El gendarme desconocido* (1941), *El 7 machos* (1951), *El bombero atómico* (1952), *Ni sangre ni arena* (1941), *El señor fotógrafo* (1952), and *Abajo el telón* (1954). He also starred in two Hollywood productions, *Around the World in 80 Days* (1956) and *Pepe* (1960). Cantinflas, whose career spanned over fifty years, is Mexico's best-

Cantinflas in a scene from El siete machos *(1951). (Organization of American States)*

known film celebrity, both nationally and internationally.

— DAVID MACIEL

CANTÓN, WILBERTO

Wilberto Cantón (*b.* 15 July 1925; *d.* 5 March 1979), Mexican dramatist. Cantón was a prominent, popular playwright who wrote more than two dozen plays. He also was a director, translator, critic, and journalist, holding such posts as head of the theater department of Mexico's National Institute of Fine Arts. He wrote two basic types of plays: those employing historical Mexican settings for dramatic action and those treating contemporary Mexican social problems. Outstanding works include *El nocturno a Rosario* (1956), *Malditos* (1958), and *Nosotros somos Dios* (1963). The theater at the General Society of Mexican Writers in Mexico City is named for him.

— CARL R. SHIRLEY

CANTÚ, FEDERICO

Federico Cantú (*b.* 3 March 1908; *d.* 1989), Mexican painter. Born in Cadereyta, Nuevo León, Cantú studied at the San Carlos Academy of Fine Arts in Mexico City and later lived and worked in France between the world wars. While in Europe, he was exposed to the works of Botticelli, El Greco, and the English Pre-Raphaelites. Back in Mexico, Cantú became one of a group of painters who rejected the politics of muralism and returned to easel painting with an intimate and classicizing sensibility. As a devout Christian, Cantú made the central theme of his art a contemporary representation of Christian subjects, such as annunciations and crucifixions. A virtuoso engraver, he produced prints depicting the Passion and other devotional themes. He also executed many frescoes in churches, among them a monumental crucifixion in the Santísima Trinidad in Mexico City. For many years, Cantú was an instructor of drawing and painting at the Esmeralda School of Fine Arts. He died in Mexico City.

— ALEJANDRO ANREUS

CAPABLANCA, JOSÉ RAÚL

José Raúl Capablanca (*b.* 19 November 1888; *d.* 8 March 1942), Cuba's foremost chess player and world champion. Ever since 1894, when a world chess championship began to be recognized by most nations, only three non-Europeans have held the title—two Americans, Paul Morphy and Bobby Fischer, and the Cuban Capablanca. Having learned to play when he was not quite five years old, he soon amazed his father and the members of the prestigious Chess Club in Havana. In 1906 he made a name for himself when he participated in a lightning (speed chess) tournament at the Manhattan Chess Club in New York. Three years later he defeated the United States champion, Frank J. Marshall, and from then onward he achieved a series of brilliant successes that culminated when he ended Emanuel Lasker's long reign over the world of chess in March 1921. Capablanca held most of the world's chess records during his lifetime, and has been regarded by some experts as the greatest chess player of all time. He lost his crown in 1927 to the Russian Alexander Alekhine, who later always found pretexts to avoid Capablanca's repeated challenges for a rematch.

— JOSÉ M. HERNÁNDEZ

CAPELO, JOAQUÍN

Joaquín Capelo (*b.* 1852; *d.* 1928), Peruvian sociologist and engineer who was author of the three-volume *So-*

ciología de Lima (1895–1902). In it he employed an organic metaphor to suggest the institutional structure of society in Lima. Elected to the Senate to represent highland Junín in 1900, he later wrote *Los menguados* (1912), a novel that deplored the corrupt practices common in Peruvian elections. A reformer, he sought legal protection for exploited workers in the lead mines. Yet he believed that ultimately society must rely on the individual to improve his own conditions. Although he sought legislation to enforce basic fair treatment of plantation workers by the owners, he argued that the worker must be left to advance his own cause. If he did not, the government should no longer interfere. His favorite public works project was the construction of a trans-Andean roadway from the coast to the eastern town of Pichis near the Amazon lowlands, and he made several reports to various ministries of government on the subject. The best of his ideas appeared in a two-volume study, *La vía central del Perú* (1895–1896). Capelo later became a leader of the *indigenista* movement in Peru. Along with Pedro ZULEN and Dora Mayer de Zulen, he helped publish the *indigenista* organ, *El deber pro-indígena*. In the pamphlet *La despoblación* (1912), he argued that the slow rate of population growth in Peru was the measure of the country's loss of its "potential." He died in Paris.

– VINCENT PELOSO

CAPISTRANO DE ABREU, JOÃO

João Capistrano de Abreu (*b.* 23 October 1853; *d.* 13 August 1927), Brazilian historian, scholar, and journalist. A landowner's son born in Maranguape, Ceará, Capistrano's formal education stopped at the *colégio* (secondary school). Widely read in French, English, and German, he was profoundly influenced by Auguste Comte and Herbert Spencer. In 1875, Capistrano moved to Rio de Janeiro, where he lived until his death, and worked as a school teacher, journalist, and bureaucrat. His historical writings drew on a formidable talent for archival research and displayed an original, penetrating mind. However, this work was largely restricted to short articles and reviews that did not sustain the promise of his first book, *O descobrimento do Brasil e seu desenvolvimento no século XVI* (1883). A distrust of worldly success, deep pessimism about life, the premature death of his wife, and time spent on scholarly translations and ethnographic research explain Capistrano's failure to write what contemporaries expected of him: a definitive study of colonial Brazil. *Capítulos de história colonial, 1500–1800* (1907), a commissioned work, is no more than suggestive of such a study. Nonetheless,

his writings remain invaluable for their insights and analytical power, and Capistrano stands at the forefront of Brazilian historians.

– RODERICK J. BARMAN

CARAMURÚ

Caramurú (Diogo Álvares Correia; *d.* 5 April 1557). Born in Viana do Castelo, northern Portugal, Caramurú arrived in Bahia de Todos os Santos, Brazil, sometime between 1509 and 1511 under uncertain circumstances: he may have been a *degredado* (criminal), a shipwrecked sailor, or a deserter. Because of his skills with firearms, he was befriended by the local Tupinambá Indians, one of whom he married.

With his knowledge of Tupi and of the lands and waters around All Saints Bay, Caramurú, the "Man of Fire," as the Amerindians dubbed him, proved extremely useful to a succession of Europeans who came to Bahia, among them ship captains; a lord proprietor, Francisco Pereira Coutinho; Brazil's first two governors-general, TOMÉ DE SOUSA and Duarte da Costa; and the first members of the Society of Jesus. He became an adviser to the proprietor, though it remains unknown whether he ignited or defused an indigenous uprising against him. He also aided Tomé de Sousa in the selection of a site for the city of Salvador, Brazil's first capital. He left part of his estate to the Jesuits and became the first civilian to be interred in their church in Salvador, where he died.

– DAURIL ALDEN

CARAZO ODIO, RODRIGO

Rodrigo Carazo Odio (*b.* 27 December 1926), president of Costa Rica (1978–1982), founder of the University for Peace (1980). Born in Cartago, Rodrigo Carazo began his distinguished career in public service in the aftermath of the 1948 revolution, when he was named a city councilman in Puntarenas. Shortly after receiving his degree in economics and administration from the University of Costa Rica (1951), he served at the national level during the first elected presidency of José FIGUERES FERRER (1953–1958).

Carazo began his political career as a follower of Figueres and held high positions in his administration and in that of Francisco ORLICH BOLMARCICH (1962–1966). He broke with the National Liberation Party (PLN) and formed the Democratic Renovation Party, a group that later joined with other parties to form the Unity Party, which supported his successful candidacy in 1978.

Although he came to the presidency on a ground swell of popular support for reform, his administration became embroiled in logistical support for the Sandinista revolution in Nicaragua. Because of charges of arms trafficking against members of his administration and oil crisis–induced inflation, his administration came to be popularly identified with high inflation and declining living standards after a generation of sustained economic growth. Despite many positive programs and high initial popularity, Carazo could not overcome the twin blows of rising oil prices and falling coffee prices.

Despite many positive programs and high initial popularity, Carazo could not overcome the twin blows of rising oil prices and falling coffee prices.

Carazo has since become a private businessman, although in 1983–1984 he did briefly attempt to create a new political party, Partido Radical Democrático (Radical Democratic Party).

– JOHN PATRICK BELL

CARBALLIDO, EMILIO

Emilio Carballido (*b.* 22 May 1925), Mexican playwright. Carballido, a native of Córdoba, Veracruz, has been at the center of the Mexican theater since the 1950s. A prolific playwright with nearly 100 plays published and performed, he has set the standard of quality and originality in the contemporary theater while championing a younger generation of writers. Imbued with boundless energy, enthusiasm, and a superb sense of humor, Carballido is identified primarily with the theater, although he also has written several stories, novels, and movie scripts. His creative spirit has led him to experiment with virtually all forms of theater, including farce, children's theater, allegory, opera, and monologue, as he plays constantly with elements of tragedy, comedy, folklore, classical myth, satire, and politics.

Beginning with his earliest play in 1948, Carballido has mixed realism and fantasy in innovative ways, building a pattern of experimentation in his search for ways to express a Mexican reality deeply rooted in tradition. His provincial plays, such as *Rosalba y los Llaveros* (1950) and *La danza que sueña la tortuga* (1955), were surpassed by daring experiments with magic and symbolic figures such as those in *La hebra de oro* (1956). His farces, such as *¡Silencio, pollos pelones, ya les van a echar su maíz!* (1963), are entertaining and provocative. In 1966 *Yo también hablo de la rosa*, a dramatization of

the creative process built around the metaphor of the rose and the infinite ways of perceiving reality, became a classic of the Mexican theater. In recent years Carballido has continued to be experimental. *Tiempo de ladrones: La historia de Chucho el Roto* (1984) glorifies a Mexican-style Robin Hood in a complex play written for two settings (*dos tandas*). His *Rosa de dos aromas* (1987) has been particularly popular for its portrayal of two women "married" to the same man. Carballido has set the standards, then broken them, throughout his long and productive career.

– GEORGE WOODYARD

CARBALLO, AIDA

Aida Carballo (*b.* 1916; *d.* 19 April 1985), Argentine printmaker, illustrator, and ceramist. Carballo studied in Buenos Aires at the Prilidiano PUEYRREDÓN School of Fine Arts, at the Ceramics National School, and at the De la Cárcova School of Fine Arts. In 1959 the French government awarded her a grant to study in Paris. She also studied engraving and drawing in Madrid and Barcelona. Her engravings describe Buenos Aires life in its rich local color. She produced work of marked linear accent, which has a haunting, overwhelming effect, presenting a complex, ironic vision of the contemporary world.

– AMALIA CORTINA ARAVENA

CARBO Y NOBOA, PEDRO JOSÉ

Pedro José Carbo y Noboa (*b.* 19 March 1813; *d.* 24 December 1895), leading proponent of liberalism in nineteenth-century Ecuador. A persistent voice for coastal interests, Carbo, a native of Guayaquil, served in Congress and as a diplomat in the early decades of the republic. His fierce ideological battles against archconservative dictator Gabriel GARCÍA MORENO (1861–1865, 1869–1875) proved to be the defining struggles of Carbo's career. He led the opposition to García Moreno's concordat with the Holy See of 1862. Named president of the Senate in 1867, Carbo used his position to battle the figurehead presidents named by García Moreno. In 1869 Liberals supported Carbo in his bid for the presidency, but he was defeated and exiled to Panama.

During the dictatorship of Ignacio de VEINTIMILLA (1876–1883), Carbo accepted appointments as minister of the Treasury (1876) and supreme chief of Guayaquil province (1883). His anticlerical policies, including steps toward the secularization of education, greatly angered the Catholic hierarchy and led to armed revolts against the government. As Veintimilla grew increasingly corrupt and violent, Carbo left the government, ultimately joining the Liberal opposition. After Veintimilla's defeat in 1883, Carbo served as head of the provisional government. In the last years of his life Carbo wrote *Páginas de la historia del Ecuador* (1898), a work that brought together his liberal perspectives on nineteenth-century Ecuadorian politics.

– RONN F. PINEO

CÁRCANO, MIGUEL ÁNGEL

Miguel Ángel Cárcano (*b*. 18 July 1889; *d*. 1978), Argentine author and statesman. Born in Buenos Aires, Cárcano trained as a lawyer at the University of Buenos Aires. Beginning in 1913, with his thesis *Las Leyes agrarias argentinas,* Cárcano gained prominence as a historian. As a law professor at the University of Buenos Aires, he won his first national literary prize for the classic *Evolución histórica del régimen de la tierra pública, 1810–1916,* which describes the inequities of land alienation in Argentina.

Cárcano moved from academics to politics. He represented Córdoba province in the national Chamber of Deputies beginning in 1929. He remained active after the Revolution of 1930 and the formation of the Concordancia, and was reelected in 1931 and 1934. He served as a member of the diplomatic mission that negotiated the controversial Roca–Runciman Pact of 1933. Later, President José Agustín JUSTO named him minister of agriculture in 1935. While remaining active in national affairs, he completed his public service as ambassador to Great Britain from 1942 to 1946.

– DANIEL LEWIS

CÁRCANO, RAMÓN JOSÉ

Ramón José Cárcano (*b*. 18 April 1860; *d*. 2 June 1946), Argentine politician and historian. Born and raised in, and long-time political chieftain of, the province of Córdoba, Cárcano was a remarkably successful conservative politician. Educated at the University of Córdoba, he affiliated with governors Antonio del Viso and Miguel Juàrez CELMAN (the latter was elected president in 1886). Cárcano was elected to the national Congress in 1884 and two years later returned to Córdoba, where he occupied several key ministerial posts, including justice and education. Between 1890 and 1910 he devoted himself to teaching law and writing. Elected again to Congress in 1910, he returned to public life as one of the most respected politicians of the interior provinces. Cárcano was passed over repeatedly, though always in the running, as candidate for president. He was instrumental in the rise of President

Roque SÁENZ PEÑA, who promulgated the suffrage law of 1912. In 1913 he returned to Córdoba as governor and dominated the province for the next several decades. During his terms, he earned the reputation for sponsoring transportation and public works development. He also served as ambassador to Brazil (1933–1938). Cárcano wrote several classic accounts of mid-nineteenth-century Argentine politics and was twice president of the National Academy of History.

– JEREMY ADELMAN

CARDENAL, ERNESTO

Ernesto Cardenal (*b*. 20 January 1925), Nicaraguan writer and minister of culture (1979–1988). Born into a wealthy family in Granada, Cardenal received his early education from the Christian Brothers and the Jesuits. A precocious writer, he allied himself with Carlos Martínez Rivas and others of the Generation of 1940. As a student of philosophy at the Universidad Nacional Autónoma de México (1942–1947), Cardenal joined other Nicaraguan exiles opposed to the dictatorship of Anastasio SOMOZA GARCÍA. Reading T. S. Eliot and the Imagists (Ezra Pound and Amy Lowell, among others) during two subsequent years of study at Columbia University (1947–1949) shaped his emerging *exteriorista* poetics, which emphasized nonmetaphoric language and concrete (frequently historical) detail.

Cardenal's political, poetic, and critical abilities were evident in *La ciudad deshabitada* (1946), *Proclama del conquistador* (1947), and his introduction to *Nueva poesía nicaragüense* (1949; translated as *New Nicaraguan Poetry*). Following a year of study in Spain (1949–1950), he returned to Managua for seven years, where he operated a bookstore and formed a small publishing company (both called El Hilo Azul) with ex-*vanguardista* José CORONEL URTECHO. He continued to write poetry on romantic and, increasingly, political themes.

Influenced by the Chilean poet Pablo NERUDA and others, Cardenal explored Latin American indigenous culture and native resistance to domination, concerns that are prominent in *Con Walker en Nicaragua* (1952). His participation in the anti-Somoza April Rebellion of 1954 supplied themes for *La hora cero* or *Hora O* (1957–1959), especially that of the renewal of life through revolutionary activity. A religious conversion in 1956 led him to two years (1957–1959) of study with Thomas Merton at a Trappist monastery in Gethsemane, Kentucky, and two more years at a Benedictine monastery in Cuernavaca, Mexico; ultimately he went to Colombia to study for the priesthood (1961–1965). Cardenal's evolving political and religious views issued in the lyrical poems of *Gethsemani, Kentucky* (1960), *Epigramas* (1961), *Salmos* (1964; a recasting of the Psalms in terms of present-day political realities and language), and *Oración por Marilyn Monroe y otras poemas* (1965).

In 1966 Cardenal established on the island of Solentiname in Lake Nicaragua, an experimental Christian contemplative colony oriented to agricultural, social, political (anti-Somoza), and cultural work among the largely illiterate rural population. During the Solentiname years, Cardenal published the political poems of *El estrecho dudoso* (1966), *Homenaje a los indios americanos* (1969), and *Canto nacional* (1972) and the Christian-Marxist exegetical dialogues of *El evangelio en Solentiname* (1975). The Solentiname community was destroyed by Somoza's National Guard in 1977. Increasingly Marxist in orientation during the 1970s, Cardenal became a cultural ambassador for the anti-Somoza FSLN (Sandinista National Liberation Front) in 1976. Appointed minister of culture by the new Sandinista government in 1979, he projected a "revolutionary, popular, national, and anti-imperialist" cultural policy modeled substantially upon the earlier Solentiname experiments (especially the controversial *exteriorista* poetry workshops and primitivist painting). Ambitious plans for film production and a national system of centers for popular culture, libraries, museums, and theater and dance companies were frustrated by the post-1982 budget crisis, exacerbated by the Contra war financed by the United States. The Ministry of Culture ceased to exist as a separate entity in 1988.

– DAVID E. WHISNANT

CÁRDENAS, BERNARDINO DE

Bernardino de Cárdenas (*b.* 1579; *d.* 20 October 1668), bishop of Paraguay (1642–1651) and opponent of the Jesuits. Born in La Paz, Upper Peru, Cárdenas joined the Franciscan order at the age of fifteen. After ordination, he preached for twenty years in native languages to the Quechua and Aymara peoples of Peru and Upper Peru, who reputedly revered him. His reputation caused King Philip IV in 1638 to nominate, and Pope Urban VIII in 1640 to appoint, Cárdenas bishop of Paraguay. Consecrated in Santiago del Estero in 1641, Cárdenas then left for Asunción, where the bulls of his investiture were read in 1642.

Cárdenas allied himself with labor-hungry Paraguayan settlers who coveted the Guaranís in Jesuit missions as workers. He also insisted on visiting all curacies and parishes of his bishopric, including the Jesuit missions, a policy that Jesuits opposed. These disputes intensified friction between colonial Franciscans and Jes-

uits. The Jesuits challenged the validity of the bishop's consecration, hoping to remove him from the province. Cárdenas also fought with Governor Gregorio de Hinestrosa, a Jesuit ally, who brought Guaraní forces from the Jesuit missions to Asunción to shield the Jesuits from the Paraguayans, an action that the Paraguayans resented.

Cárdenas criticized Jesuit economic practices and accused the fathers of teaching false doctrine.

Cárdenas criticized Jesuit economic practices and accused the fathers of teaching false doctrine. In 1644 the governor expelled Cárdenas from Paraguay. Supported by Franciscans throughout South America, the exiled bishop spoke against his adversaries and persuaded the Audiencia of Charcas to order his reinstatement. He returned to Asunción in 1647 to face a new governor, Diego de Escobar Osorio, whose death in 1649 allowed the Paraguayans to name Cárdenas to the post. This right, they claimed, they had possessed since the Conquest. Applauded by the Asunción *cabildo*, the bishop-governor expelled the Jesuits from the capital, and a mob vandalized their property. Jesuit interests, however, finally prevailed; a mission army defeated the Paraguayan militia near San Lorenzo in 1650 and occupied and sacked Asunción. Although Cárdenas was then exiled from Paraguay, the king in 1660 ordered him reinstated as bishop. Old and feeble, he rejected further Paraguayan conflicts and instead accepted the bishopric of Santa Cruz de la Sierra, Upper Peru, where he served until his death. His legacy in Paraguay was an intensified anti-Jesuit feeling, and later rebellions in the 1720s (*see* ANTEQUERA Y CASTRO) and 1730s recalled his anti-Jesuit efforts.

– JAMES SCHOFIELD SAEGER

CÁRDENAS ARROYO, SANTIAGO

Santiago Cárdenas Arroyo (*b.* 4 December 1937), Colombian painter. Born in Bogotá, Cárdenas studied painting at the Rhode Island School of Design (B.F.A. in 1960). After traveling in Europe, he returned to the United States and enrolled in the School of Fine Arts at Yale University, where he studied with Alex Katz, Jack Tworkov, and Neil Welliver, receiving his M.F.A. in 1964. Even before graduation, his work had appeared in his native Colombia at the Asociación de Arquitectos Javerianos, Bogotá (1963). He won first prize for painting at the Art Festival of New Haven, Connecticut (1964). In 1965 he returned to Bogotá and began teaching painting and drawing at the National University, the University of the Andes, and the University of Bogotá. He continued exhibiting his work and won national first prize and regional first prize in painting, III Croydon Salon, Bogotá (1966). In 1967 he had solo exhibitions at the Museum La Tertulia, Cali, and the Belarca Gallery. In 1972 he won first prize at the III Biennale of Art Coltejer, Medellín, Colombia, and was named director of the School of Fine Arts of the National University of Colombia, Bogotá. The following year he had a solo show at the Center for Inter-American Relations, New York, followed by another at the Museum of Modern Art, Bogotá (1976), and the Art Museum, National University, and the Garcés Valásquez Gallery, Bogotá, in 1980.

– BÉLGICA RODRÍGUEZ

CÁRDENAS DEL RÍO, LÁZARO

Lázaro Cárdenas del Río (*b.* 21 May 1895; *d.* 19 October 1970), President of Mexico, 1934–1940. Born in the small provincial town of Jiquilpán, in the western state of Michoacán, Mexico, Cárdenas was the oldest son of a shopkeeper. He left school after the fourth grade and worked as a clerk in the local tax office. Following his father's death in 1911, Cárdenas, a quiet, serious, conscientious youth, became a surrogate parent for his many siblings; several of his brothers emulated him by pursuing careers in the military and politics. A fierce patriotism nurtured by the liberal school curriculum and a hungry though unfocused ambition lurked behind Cárdenas's stolid mien, and in 1913, three years after the Mexican Revolution broke out, the eighteen-year-old enlisted with rebels resisting the military regime of Victoriano HUERTA. After initial setbacks (he was captured in 1923, escaped, and had to lie low in Guadalajara for some months), Cárdenas began a rapid rise through the ranks, helped by the friendship and patronage of his commanding general, Plutarco ELÍAS CALLES. After campaigns against the Yaquis in Sonora, the Villistas in Chihuahua, and the rebel-bandit forces of Chávez García in his home state, Cárdenas became interim governor of Michoacán (1920) and military commander on the isthmus (1921) and in the oil country of the Huasteca (1925–1928), where he condemned the corruption and arrogance of the foreign oil companies. During these years he developed close political alliances with President Elías Calles (1924–1928), with his fellow Michoacano, the radical Francisco MÚGICA, and with his own chief of staff, Manuel ÁVILA CAMACHO, member of a powerful revolutionary clan in the state of Puebla. As a military leader Cárdenas was bold

to a fault, his impetuosity leading to defeats in 1918 and 1923, on which occasion he was severely wounded.

In 1928 Cárdenas was elected governor of his home state, where he undertook to accelerate agrarian reforms, develop education, and foster labor and peasant organizations, which he did through the radical anticlerical Confederación Revolucionaria Michoacana de Trabajo. His creation of a solid political base, however, was compromised by several leaves of absence, which he took in order to serve as president of the nascent National Revolutionary Party (PNR) (1930–1931), as minister of government (1932), and as minister of war (1933). Politically shrewd beneath a sphinxlike exterior, Cárdenas grasped—as some rival revolutionary caudillos, such as Adalberto Tejeda of Veracruz, failed to do—that the federal government, considerably strengthened and consolidated by the presidency and *maximato* of Calles, was the surest ladder of political advancement. Loyalty paid off, and in 1933 Cárdenas was chosen—in effect by Calles—as the PNR presidential candidate. Calles, who had governed through the medium of three relatively pliant presidents, no doubt expected that he could control his old protégé, in which respect, political opinion concurred. However, the onset of the Depression had undermined the broadly export-oriented economic project of the 1920s, and those who favored both a more interventionist state and a greater commitment to social legislation saw Cárdenas, known as a reformist governor of Michoacán, as the best hope within the party.

Cárdenas's radicalism—a practical, populist desire for social betterment rather than any bookish Marxism—was further stimulated by his extensive presidential campaign of 1934, which set the style for a peripatetic presidency: a quarter of his six years in office were spent on the road, touring Mexico, reaching remote villages, listening to local complaints, distributing patronage and public works, often by executive fiat. The rapport Cárdenas thus achieved with popular groups, which endured long after his presidency, served him in good stead when, in 1935–1936, he challenged Calles's authority, marshaling trade unions and peasant groups, generals and politicos, in order to force the dismayed *jefe máximo* (highest chief) into exile. By mid-1936, Cárdenas was emphatically master in his own house; the authority of the presidency had been reinforced, an assertion of presidential power that had been unusually bloodless.

During the middle years of his *sexenio,* Cárdenas enacted a raft of reforms that changed the political face of Mexico. Most important, he confiscated some 45 million acres of private land and distributed it in the form of *ejidos*—peasant communities in which the land was individually worked or, as on the big Laguna cotton estates, collectively farmed. With the *ejidos* came a rapid expansion of rural schools, now commited to a form of socialist education which sought to instill nationalism, class consciousness, and anticlericalism. Welcomed by some, this ambitious program of social engineering offended many, especially devout Catholics. In the face of protests, parental boycotts, and a good deal of local violence, Cárdenas, who had never shared Calles's dogmatic anticlericalism, reined in revolutionary anticlericalism, declaring that material betterment was the greater priority. Meanwhile, the president encouraged the political organization of the peasantry under the aegis of a national confederation which, in 1938, formally incorporated itself into the offical party as the National Campesino Federation (CNC).

A similar process of mobilization and incorporation affected the considerably smaller working class. During the *maximato,* the hegemony of the once-dominant Regional Confederation of Mexican Workers (CROM) was splintered, and the ravages of the Depression, though less severe and prolonged in Mexico than in some other Latin American countries, encouraged a new working-class militancy, upon which Cárdenas could capitalize, especially as the economy revived after 1933. Major industrial unions were formed in the leading sectors of industry—oil, mining, railways—and they began to press, strenuously and effectively, for national collective contracts. Meanwhile, the Mexican Federation of Labor (CTM), led by the flamboyant Marxist Vicente LOMBARDO TOLEDANO, arose from the ashes of the CROM; and, by virtue of a politically close alliance with the president, Lombardo and the CTM came to play a role in the 1930s similar to that of Luis N. MORONES and the CROM in the 1920s. The CTM benefited from sympathetic official arbitration in strikes and, in return, it backed the government, as did the Mexican Communist Party (PCM), which, pledged to a collaborationist popular-front strategy, now enjoyed a brief heyday as a political, ideological, and cultural force. In 1938 the CTM joined the CNC as corporate pillars of the new official party, the Party of Mexican Revolution (PRM).

The radical thrust of the Cárdenas administration was evident in a series of nationalizations. Several mines and factories that threatened closure became workers' cooperatives. In 1937–1938 the railways were nationalized and placed under a workers' administration (conservative critics pointed to the inefficiency of the operation; radicals contended that the workers—seeking to run a decrepit system at low cost—made the best of a bad job). Most dramatic of all was the petroleum nationalization of March 1938, the first major seizure of

oil assets by a developing country. Confronted by a long-runnning labor dispute, intransigent managers, and a perceived threat to Mexico's economic well-being and national sovereignty, Cárdenas expropriated the Anglo-American companies and established a state oil company, Petróleos Mexicanos (PEMEX). Two consequences followed. Relations with the United States, which had been tolerably cordial since the late 1920s, cooled. But Cárdenas reassured the United States that oil was a special case, that further nationalizations were not contemplated, and that an adequate indemnity would be paid. And President Roosevelt, pilloried by big business at home and alarmed by the rise of fascism overseas, was reluctant either to champion the companies or to offend a friendly, anti-fascist Mexico. Indeed, with his condemnation of fascist aggression in Europe, Abyssinia (now Ethiopia), and China and his vigorous support of the Spanish Republic (a policy that elicited strong criticism from pro-Franco Mexicans), Cárdenas now appeared as a stalwart ally of the democratic powers. The United States therefore refrained from political or military reprisals and entered negotiations over the proposed oil indemnity, which was agreed to in 1942.

Cárdenas was criticized by some as an authoritarian

populist and revered by others as the greatest

constructive radical of the Mexican Revolution.

The oil crisis, followed by an oil company boycott of PEMEX, harmed the Mexican economy. Exports, the peso, and business confidence declined. Inflation quickened. Workers in the nationalized industries were required to tighten their belts and Cárdenas spent much of his final two years in office wrestling with the problems of the oil and railroad industries. Meanwhile, the presidential succession began to absorb political attention. International tensions—in particular, the global fascist–popular front confrontation—affected domestic politics. Right-wing groups, on the defensive since the Depression, staged a comeback. The National Sinarquista Union (UNS), a popular, Catholic, quasi-fascist movement founded in 1937, inveighed against Cardenista collectivism and "atheism." Conservative elements also mobilized behind dissident caudillos, on the right of the PRM, and in the pro-business, pro-Catholic National Action Party (PAN), founded in 1939. Some working-class Cardenistas broke ranks. Fearing destabilization, Cárdenas tacked to the center, reining in his radical policies and opting for a right-of-center successor, Ávila Camacho, rather than the radical Francisco Múgica. In the July 1940 presidential election Ávila Camacho easily defeated the challenge of the conservative caudillo Juan Andréu ALMAZÁN, but did so amid scenes of fraud and violence. The Cárdenas presidency, which had indelibly marked Mexican political life, thus ended in dissent and controversy.

After 1940, the rightward drift of official policy was accelerated. Agrarian reform slowed, socialist education ended, détente with the church and the United States advanced. The structures set in place by Cárdenas—PEMEX, the corporate party, the collective *ejido*—remained, but they now contributed to a national project dedicated to industrialization and capital accumulation, goals that Cárdenas had neither set nor endorsed. The ex-president, however, remained loyal to the system he had helped create. He served as minister of war in 1942–1945, reassuring nationalist sentiment as Mexico collaborated increasingly closely with the United States. During the 1950s and 1960s he headed two major regional development projects, working, as in the past, for the material betterment of the poorer regions of southern and southwestern Mexico, thereby reinforcing his popular and populist reputation (a factor that would prove significant with the rise of "neo-Cardenismo" the leftist movement headed by Cárdenas's son, Cuauhtémoc CÁRDENAS, in the late 1980s). Loyalty to the system did not, however, prevent him from exercising significant influence: against the proposed reelection of President Miguel Alemán in 1951–1952; against the Vietnam War and U.S. policy toward Cuba in the 1960s; and in favor of political dissidents within Mexico. At the time of his death in 1970, Cárdenas was criticized by some as an authoritarian populist and a dangerous fellow-traveler, and revered by others, particularly in the Cardenista countryside, as the greatest constructive radical of the Mexican Revolution.

– ALAN KNIGHT

CÁRDENAS SOLORZANO, CUAUHTÉMOC

Cuauhtémoc Cárdenas Solorzano (*b.* 1 May 1934), Mexican politician and presidential candidate. Cárdenas's presidential candidacy, representing a coalition of opposition parties in the 1988 election, provoked the strongest support against the Institutional Revolutionary Party (PRI) since 1952. Cárdenas's parties, which included the Partido Popular Socialista, the Partido Auténtico de la Revolución Mexicana, the Partido Mexicano Socialista, and the Partido del Frente Cardenista de Reconstrucción Nacional, won four senate seats in Michoacán and the Federal District and captured most of the congressional seats in the key state of México,

the Federal District, Michoacán, and Morelos. Cárdenas himself received a reported 31 percent of the vote to Carlos SALINAS GORTARI's reported 51 percent. Most observers believe extensive fraud took place, and some analysts assert that Cárdenas actually defeated Salinas.

Born in Mexico City, Cardenas is the son of General Lázaro CÁRDENAS, without doubt Mexico's most popular president of the twentieth century. This fact accounts in part for his own political popularity, especially among the *campesinos,* who considered Cárdenas Senior an agrarian savior. The son studied at the Colegio de San Nicolás in Morelia and graduated from the National School of Engineering 22 January 1957. Cárdenas then studied abroad on a Bank of Mexico fellowship, interning in France and for Krupp in Germany (1957–1958).

Cárdenas got his first taste of electoral politics in 1951, when as a preparatory student he supported the candidacy of General Miguel Henríquez Guzmán, who—as Cárdenas would later do—left the government's fold to oppose the official party presidential candidate. Later he joined the Movimiento de Liberación Nacional, a loosely constituted leftist opposition movement supported by his father, serving on the national committee with Heberto Castillo, who would join him in the 1988 presidential campaign.

After engaging in private practice in the 1960s, Cárdenas began holding various public positions. In 1970 he became subdirector of the Las Truchas steel complex, a decentralized federal agency, and in 1973 served as director of the public trust fund of Lázaro Cárdenas City. In 1976 he was elected senator from his home state, but he left his post that same year to serve as undersecretary of forest resources and fauna in the secretariat of agriculture and livestock. In 1980 he resigned this position to run for governor of Michoacán as the PRI candidate. Elected, he served until 1986, when he began his efforts to reform the official party. He and other reformers advocated democratizing the internal structure of the PRI and the electoral system in general. Their economic policies were populist, focused on debt renegotiation, deficit spending, and an increased state role in the economy. When the government leadership refused to accept their views, Cárdenas, Porfirio Muñóz Ledo (a former president of the PRI), and other leaders bolted the party in 1987. Not all the reformists followed their lead. Some, who call themselves the Critical Current, remained within the PRI.

Following the 1988 elections, Cárdenas's coalition reorganized itself as the Partido de la Revolución Democrática and offered intensive opposition in races for mayor and state legislative and gubernatorial posts. The strength of Cárdenas's opposition movement, and its persistence after the 1988 presidential elections, contributed significantly to the pressure for electoral reform and internal change within the government party. Cárdenas used his personal stature within Mexico and abroad to appeal for honesty in the electoral process.

– RODERIC AI CAMP

CARDIM, FREI FERNÃO

Frei Fernão Cardim (*b.* 1540; *d.* 27 January 1625), Portuguese Jesuit and writer. Cardim accompanied the visitador Cristóvão de Gouveia to Brazil. Arriving in Bahia on 9 May 1584, Cardim described their activities in a report on the Jesuits entitled *Narrativa epistolar, ou Informação da missão do padre Cristóvão de Gouveia às partes do Brasil.* The two had visited the captaincies of Bahia, Ilhéus, Porto Seguro, Pernambuco, Espírito Santo, Rio de Janeiro, and São Vicente. Cardim was nominated dean of the Jesuit *colégio* in the city of Salvador, where he served until 1593, and then as dean in Rio de Janeiro in 1596. Returning from a 1598 mission to Rome, he was captured by Flemish pirates and kept in England until 1601.

By 1604 Cardim was provincial of the Jesuits in Brazil, and in 1607 he was nominated for the second time as dean of the Bahian *colégio,* the position he occupied when the Dutch attacked Salvador in 1624. The Jesuits took refuge in the Indian village of Espírito Santo, where Cardim died in 1625. He summarized his Brazilian experiences in two treatises: *Do princípio e origem dos índios do Brasil e de seus costumes e cerimônias* and *Do clima e terra do Brasil e de algumas coisas notáveis que se acham assim na terra como no mar,* both published anonymously in Samuel Purchas's *Purchas his Pilgrimes* (London, 1625).

– MARIA BEATRIZ NIZZA DA SILVA

CARDOSO, FELIPE SANTIAGO

Felipe Santiago Cardoso (*b.* 1 May 1773; *d.* 17 September 1818), Uruguayan politician. Cardoso played an important role in the period of the revolution of the Provincia Oriental, known today as Uruguay. He was elected representative for Canelones to the Congress of April 1813, which produced the famous Instructions of 1813—the first expression of federalist thought of the eastern caudillo José ARTIGAS. Cardoso acted as a confidential agent of Artigas in Buenos Aires, attempting to win the inclusion of representatives from the Provincia Oriental in the constituent assembly, which the government of Buenos Aires opposed. The representatives were finally rejected for technical reasons, the real reason being their federalist ideas, which ran contrary to the centralism of the capital. Cardoso was a member of the town council of Montevideo in 1815, a time during which Artigas, from his camp in Purificación on the Uruguay River, exercised a protectorate over the provinces of the Argentine littoral.

– JOSÉ DE TORRES WILSON

CARDOSO, FERNANDO HENRIQUE

Fernando Henrique Cardoso (*b.* 18 June 1931), Brazilian sociologist and politician. Cardoso studied sociology with Roger Bastide and Florestan Fernandes at the University of São Paulo and taught there until the 1964 coup. In exile in Santiago, Chile, Cardoso contributed signally to dependency analysis at a moment when import-substitution industrialization (ISI) seemed to have failed. The structuralist economist Celso FURTADO had already hypothesized the connection between development and underdevelopment and argued that economic phenomena had to be understood in a historical framework. In the mid-1960s Cardoso and his collaborator Enzo Faletto extended the analysis to social relations. Pessimistic about development directed by "national bourgeoisies" as a result of his earlier research, Cardoso saw dependency not solely as a historical situation determined by a dynamic capitalist "center," but one in which there also exists a complex internal dynamic of class conflict in dependent countries of the less-industrialized "periphery." He accepted the structuralists' argument that the center gains more from exchange than the periphery through the latter's deteriorating terms-of-trade. But he stressed mutual interests among social classes across the international system—in particular, those of the bourgeoisies of the center and periphery. Cardoso and Faletto linked the failure of populism with the stagnation of ISI, viewing authoritarian regimes as necessary to secure political demobilization of the masses.

But unlike some other contributors to dependency (notably Andre Gunder Frank and Ruy Mauro Marini), Cardoso emphasized shifting alliances and a range of historical possibility. For Latin American economies controlled by local bourgeoisies, he saw the option of "associated dependent" development. Like other dependency writers, he saw the international system, not the nation-state, as the proper unit of analysis; development and underdevelopment were *locations* in the international economic system, not stages. Cardoso also denied that dependency (for him, a region of Marxism) could be operationalized as a quantitative methodology but rather saw it as a framework for concrete historical analysis of a specific dialectical process.

Cardoso returned to Brazil in 1968, opposed the military dictatorship, and was elected to the Brazilian Senate in 1986. In 1988 he helped form the Partido da Social Democracia Brasileira (PSDB).

On the impeachment of President Fernando COLLOR DE MELLO, Cardoso became foreign minister in the cabinet of Itamar FRANCO, Collor's successor, in October 1992. In May 1993 Cardoso was named finance minister, the most powerful cabinet post. The following year he ran for the presidency. His campaign was helped greatly by the fact that the policies ("Plano Real"), which he had introduced as finance minister, were sharply reducing the rate of inflation. In October 1994 Cardoso was elected president by direct popular vote, but he publicly disavowed many of his theses about dependency. Cordoso was inaugurated in January 1995.

– JOSEPH L. LOVE

CARDOZA Y ARAGÓN, LUIS

Luis Cardoza y Aragón (*b.* 21 June 1904; *d.* 4 September 1992), Guatemalan poet, essayist, and art critic. Widely recognized for his book *Guatemala: Las líneas de su mano* (1955), Cardoza y Aragón was one of modern Guatemala's most important literary figures. Following the surrealist tradition of the 1920s, he used experiences in Europe to nourish his aesthetic and social preoccupations through poetic works such as *Luna Park* (1923) and *Maelstrom* (1926). With the French anthropologist Georges Raynaud he translated a pre-Columbian Maya-Quiché drama, *Rabinal Achí* (1928).

In 1931 Cardoza chose exile in Mexico over a return to Guatemala, which was entering one of the most brutal and repressive periods of its modern history under the dictatorship of Jorge UBICO Y CASTAÑEDA (1931–1944). He continued to publish his poetry—*Soledad* (1936) and *El sonámbulo* (1937)—and began to write critical essays on contemporary Mexican art, including the controversial volume *La nube y el reloj* (1940).

Cardoza returned to Guatemala in October 1944, on the eve of the revolution. He was cofounder of *Revista de Guatemala* (1945) and continued his artistic and political commitment to the revolution until its defeat in 1954.

Cardoza returned to Mexico, where he completed and published *Guatemala: Las líneas de su mano* (1955), in which he underscores his personal experiences through a presentation of Guatemala's cultural and political heritage. His poetic account of Guatemala, and the hopes of the October Revolution, establish this work as essential reading for understanding Guatemala and its people as well as Cardoza y Aragón's life. He died in Mexico City.

– SHELLY JARRETT BROMBERG

CARDOZO, EFRAÍM

Efraím Cardozo (*b.* 16 October 1906; *d.* 10 April 1973), Paraguayan diplomat and historian. Born in Villarrica, Efraím Cardozo was the son of noted educator and journalist Ramón I. Cardozo and Juana Sosa. Given his parents' interest in the study of history, it is little wonder that Cardozo became a professional historian, one of Paraguay's best. He received a doctorate in law and social sciences at the National University of Asunción in 1932, and set off immediately on a diplomatic career, participating in the cease-fire negotiations that ended the Chaco War (1932–1935) and in the 1938 signing of the final peace treaty with Bolivia.

Cardozo was a Liberal, and on several occasions, officially (1970–1972) as well as unofficially, was president of the Liberal Radical Party. His political affiliations brought him considerable hardships during the Higinio MORÍNIGO dictatorship (1940–1948), including exile to Argentina on eight occasions. He later served in the Chamber of Deputies and in the Senate, while simultaneously working as a professor at the National University and the Catholic University in Asunción.

Cardozo is best remembered for his many historical studies, which were scrupulously researched and which betrayed none of the partisan fanaticism so common in Paraguayan historiography. His thoroughly documented *El imperio del Brasil y el Río de la Plata: Antecedentes y estallido de la guerra del Paraguay* (1961) won the Alberdi-Sarmiento prize for its incisive analysis of South American diplomacy prior to the War of the Triple Alliance (1864–1870). His other publications include *Paraguay independiente* (1949), *Vísperas de la guerra del Paraguay* (1954), *El Paraguay colonial: Las raíces de la nacionalidad* (1959), *Historiografía paraguaya* (1959), and *Hace cien años: Crónicas de la guerra 1864–1870* (13 vols., 1967–1976).

– MARTA FERNÁNDEZ WHIGHAM

CARÍAS ANDINO, TIBURCIO

Tiburcio Carías Andino (*b.* 15 March 1876; *d.* 23 December 1969), president of Honduras (1933–1948).

Carías was born in Tegucigalpa, the youngest son of General Calixto Carías and Sara Andino de Carías. An excellent student, he received his law degree from the

Central University of Honduras in 1898; later he taught mathematics at the National Institute as well as night classes for poor children and workers. Standing six feet, two inches in height, unusually tall for a Central American, Carías developed natural leadership ability. As early as 1891 he was campaigning for the dominant Liberal Party, in which his father was active. Thereafter he became involved in the military conflicts related to Central American politics.

Standing six feet, two inches in height, unusually

tall for a Central American, Carías developed

natural leadership ability.

In 1903 Carías left the Liberals to support Manuel BONILLA in founding the National Party, a successor to the nineteenth-century Conservative Party. Although his part in a 1907 revolt earned him the rank of brigadier general, he was not primarily a military man but rather a skillful politician who used the military to build an effective political machine. As a congressman and governor of several departments, Carías became the National Party leader and in 1923 its presidential candidate. He won a plurality but lacked the required majority, and when the Congress failed to resolve the stalemate, his armed forces seized Tegucigalpa in 1924. Subsequent elections, assisted by United States mediation, elected Carías's running mate, Miguel PAZ BARAONA, as president. When, in 1928, Carías lost to the Liberals by twelve thousand votes, many of his supporters called for revolt, but Carías accepted the official results, a move that won him wide respect.

Honduran politics of the 1920s were closely related to the rise of the U.S. banana companies, which were responsible for much of the political turbulence of the era. Samuel Zemurray's Cuyamel Fruit Company supported the Liberals, while the United Fruit Company backed Carías's National Party. In 1932 Carías won a convincing victory over José Ángel Zúñiga Huete and took office in 1933 after putting down an opposition revolt. Revisions of the constitution in 1939 allowed Carías to remain in office, first to 1944 and later through 1949. When he finally stepped down on 31 December 1948, having ruled his country longer than any other president in Honduran history, he turned over power to his protégé and minister of war, Juan Manuel GÁLVEZ DURÓN, following the first presidential election in the country since 1932.

Carías has been compared to contemporary dictators in the other Central American states: Jorge UBICO in Guatemala, Maximiliano HERNÁNDEZ MARTÍNEZ in El Salvador, and Anastasio SOMOZA in Nicaragua. His regime had similar fascist tendencies, and he achieved order and a measure of economic growth at the cost of civil liberties and the general welfare. Ángel Zúñiga kept up a propaganda campaign against Carías from exile in Mexico and there was an occasional revolt attempted from within, but Carías's firm control of the military assured his continued rule. He also cooperated closely with American business and government interests, including support of the Allies in World War II. Although he promoted modernization and made his country the leader in the development of Central American commercial aviation, Honduras continued to be the least developed of the isthmian states.

Unlike his "Dictators' League" counterparts in one important respect, Carías abandoned the Liberal Party. Although he had come from a Liberal Party background, his National Party retained some of the nineteenth-century Conservative Party philosophy, which defended a curious alliance of the leading families of the elite with the masses and adopted a somewhat friendlier attitude toward the Roman Catholic church than had the Liberals. While all of the Central American dictators were repressive and often brutal, Carías was somewhat more benign than the others, and he was the only one of them to step down gracefully. The overthrow of Hernández and Ubico by popular uprisings in 1944 probably contributed to Carías's decision to leave the presidency in 1948, for he, too, began to face student and labor unrest in 1944. In reality, his National Party, still a force in Honduras today, represented a union of nineteenth-century Liberal and Conservative elitist attitudes, allowing the Honduran Liberal Party of today to become more closely identified with middle-class interests. The major role of the military in modern Honduran politics was another legacy of Carías's dictatorship.

In the election of 1954, the seventy-nine-year-old Carías sought unsuccessfully to return to the presidency. A subsequent coup reduced his political influence even more, although he continued to live in Honduras until his death.

– RALPH LEE WOODWARD, JR.

CARLÉS, MANUEL

Manuel Carlés (*b.* 30 May 1872; *d.* 25 October 1946), Argentine politician, teacher, and president of the anti-leftist Argentine Patriotic League (1919–1946).

Carlés was born in Rosario, Santa Fe, to a prominent family. Although he never joined the Radical Civic Union (Unión Cívica Radical), he favored efforts to reform politics and participated in the Radical revolt of 1893. He served as national deputy from 1898 to 1912 and supported President Roque SÁENZ PEÑA (1910–1914), who helped institute electoral democracy. After 1912 he devoted himself to the law and to his teaching at several schools, including the Colegio Militar de la Nación and Escuela Superior de Guerra, where he influenced many future military officers. He initially sympathized with the government of the Radical leader Hipólito YRIGOYEN (1916–1922, 1928–1930), who appointed him *interventor* (temporary administrator) in Salta in 1918. The next president, the Radical Marcelo T. de ALVEAR (1922–1928), appointed him *interventor* in San Juan in 1922.

Nevertheless, Carlés, like other middle- and upper-class Argentines, thought that the Yrigoyen government was not doing enough to repress leftism. During the Semana Trágica (Tragic Week) disturbances between labor and the forces of order in Buenos Aires in 1919, military officers and civilians, including Carlés, formed militias to protect bourgeois neighborhoods and attack worker areas. Militias spread throughout the country. On 20 January 1919 these groups united to form the Argentine Patriotic League and on 5 April, Carlés was elected its president, a post he retained until his death. In the early postwar years, the League violently suppressed strikes and leftist groups. In 1923 an anarchist unsuccessfully attempted to kill Carlés. Fearing a leftist resurgence and disorder, Carlés influenced the League and the public to turn against Yrigoyen in 1930 and thus helped inspire the coup of that year. General José F. URIBURU's (1930–1932) antidemocratic excesses, however, led Carlés to denounce this administration and return to his Radical roots. While he continued to criticize leftism, during the 1930s Carlés opposed electoral fraud and supported Marcelo Alvear's efforts to unite and strengthen Radical forces.

– SANDRA MCGEE DEUTSCH

CARLOS, ROBERTO

Roberto Carlos (*b.* 1943), Brazilian pop singer and songwriter. Carlos has been one of Latin America's most popular recording artists throughout his career. He started out singing rock and roll, cowriting songs with Erasmo Carlos (no relation), and gained fame singing the 1963 hits "Calembeque" and "Splish Splash" (a cover of the American hit). In 1965, he and Erasmo led the *jovem guarda* movement, a post–Bossa-Nova manifestation of domestic rock by several young Brazilian

musicians. Roberto and Erasmo hosted the "Jovem Guarda" show on the TV Record network from 1965 to 1968, and cowrote hit songs like "Parei na contramão" (I Parked the Wrong Way), "é proibido fumar" (No Smoking), and "Garota do baile" (Dance Girl).

In the 1970s, Roberto transformed himself into a romantic interpreter of ballads and boleros, although he and Erasmo continued their songwriting partnership. During that decade, Roberto was the top-selling recording artist in Brazil, selling an annual average of one million records (quadruple-platinum) with each new album. With recordings frequently hitting the top ten in numerous Latin American and European countries, he also became an international star. In the 1980s, Carlos recorded hits in Portuguese, Spanish, French, and English, but was supplanted as Brazil's number-one recording artist in the late 1980s by the children's music singer XUXA.

– CHRIS MCGOWAN

CARLOTA

Carlota (Carlota Joaquina de Borbón y Parma; *b.* 25 April 1775; *d.* 7 January 1830), Spanish princess, queen consort of Portugal, and royalist leader in South America. Daughter of King Carlos IV and Queen María Luisa of Spain, Princess Carlota Joaquina consummated her arranged marriage to Prince João, heir to the Portuguese throne, in 1790. The royal pair thoroughly disliked each other and were constantly at odds over political and personal matters; nevertheless, they produced nine children, including Pedro, who became emperor of Brazil, and Miguel, who usurped the Portuguese throne—although the paternity of the latter as well as that of two of his sisters is in doubt. Carlota reluctantly joined the emigration of the Portuguese court to Brazil in 1807, when Portugal was invaded by France in alliance with Spain.

In Rio de Janeiro, after the French had deposed her brother, King Fernando VII of Spain, Carlota in 1808 set out to establish herself as the regent of Spain's empire in the Americas in the name of her imprisoned brother. Carlota enlisted the aid of her good friend, British admiral Sir Sidney Smith, and initially had her husband's acquiescence in the regency project. But Prince João, regent of Portugal for the insane Queen Maria I, perceived a united Spanish America ruled by his wife as a threat to his own domains. His concern was shared by the British government, which, in 1809, recalled Admiral Smith and forestalled his scheme to sail with Carlota to Buenos Aires and install her there as Spanish regent.

A new opportunity for Carlota arose with the revolution in Buenos Aires in May 1810. From Rio she established contact with members of the Buenos Aires junta, offering herself as their leader. João was disconcerted by his wife's willingness to deal with revolutionaries to further her ambitions. In the end, however, Carlota's royal absolutism found few partisans in Spanish America and Fernando's return to the throne in Spain in 1814 obviated any need for a regency in his name.

In 1821 Carlota returned with her husband, now King João VI, to Portugal, where she continued to conspire against him. In 1824 she and her favorite son, Miguel, seized the government in Lisbon and forced João to seek refuge on a British warship. The British demanded and got João's restoration. After João's death in 1826, Carlota vigorously supported Miguel as king of Portugal, denying the claim of Maria II, Pedro's daughter. With Miguel seemingly secure on the Portuguese throne, Carlota died in 1830.

— NEILL MACAULAY

CARNEIRO DE CAMPOS, JOSÉ JOAQUÍM

José Joaquím Carneiro de Campos (Caravelas, Marquês de; *b.* 4 March 1768; *d.* 8 September 1836), Brazilian statesman. Campos first pursued a religious career as a Benedictine monk, but then abandoned the ecclesiastic life to study law in Coimbra, Portugal. After receiving a doctor of jurisprudence degree, Campos began his political career in the kingdom of Portugal. He followed the royal family into exile in Brazil in 1807, shortly before the Napoleonic invasion. As aide to Prince Regent Dom João (later João VI), Campos rose quickly within the court. After independence in September 1822, Campos was elected to the constituent assembly, where he was one of the principal authors of the constitution of the monarchy. By 1823 Campos was already a cabinet member. In 1826 he was elected to the Senate from Bahia and ennobled by Emperor PEDRO I. Subsequently, he served twice more in the cabinet during the First Empire (1822–1831).

José Campos and his brother Francisco, also a senator and cabinet officer, were as politically prominent as the ANDRADA BROTHERS of São Paulo and the Cavalcanti brothers from Pernambuco. In April 1831, when PEDRO I abdicated and retreated to Portugal, Campos was one of the three provisional regents elected to govern Brazil in the name of the child emperor, PEDRO II. In June 1831 Campos was elected one of the three permanent regents who ruled in Pedro's name until 1835.

— EUL-SOO PANG

CARNEY, JAMES "GUADALUPE"

James "Guadalupe" Carney (*b.* 28 October 1924; *d.* probably 16 September 1983), U.S. Catholic missionary in Honduras, revolutionary priest. Carney, a native of Chicago, entered the Jesuit seminary in 1948 and was ordained a priest in 1961. He was sent to Honduras, where he served as chaplain for the National Association of Honduran Peasants (ANACH), championed land reform, and helped establish Christian base

---

After declaring himself a Christian Marxist, Carney resigned from the Jesuits and then crossed into Honduras with ninety-six Honduran guerrillas.

---

communities in the department of Yoro. Expelled from the country in 1979, he was assigned to rural Nicaragua, where he was impressed by Sandinista social programs. After writing his autobiography and declaring himself a Christian Marxist, he resigned from the Jesuits and then crossed into Honduras in July 1983 with ninety-six Honduran guerrillas. Although U.S. and Honduran authorities claim he died in the jungle from starvation, subsequent investigations have led some scholars to conclude that he had been captured, tortured, and executed by the Honduran military. His body was never found.

— EDWARD T. BRETT

CARO, JOSÉ EUSEBIO

José Eusebio Caro (*b.* 5 March 1817; *d.* 28 January 1853), Colombian Conservative publicist and romantic poet. Caro was born in Ocaña, Norte de Santander. His mother's amorous relationships with Simón BOLÍVAR, Francisco de Paula SANTANDER, and José Ignacio de MÁRQUEZ shadowed his impoverished youth. He received his doctorate in law in 1837 and became a government clerk (1838). A political libertarian, Caro wrote articles for the press and started composing verse. Among his best-loved poems are "El bautismo" and "Estar contigo." The violence of the War of the Supremes (1839–1842), in which he served sporadically but with distinction, caused Caro to move to more conservative political ground. He rose in the bureaucracy to chief of a section in the Secretariat of Interior and Foreign Relations (1843), and expounded his increasingly authoritarian ideas in *El Granadino*, which appeared sporadically between 1840 and 1845. A partisan, he deplored the bipartisanship (after 1846) of Tomás Cipriano de MOSQUERA's administration, though he did serve briefly as finance minister (1848). Caro's vehement opposition to the Liberal José Hilario LÓPEZ (1849–1853) caused his removal from government service (September 1849). With Mariano OSPINA RODRÍGUEZ, he fashioned the first Conservative Party platform (1849) and was an editor of the newspaper *La Civilización* (1849–1850), whose editorials were a devastating indictment of López's presidency that resulted in Caro's exile (1850–1853) to New York. Upon returning to Colombia, Caro died of yellow fever in Santa Marta.

— J. LEÓN HELGUERA

CARO, MIGUEL ANTONIO

Miguel Antonio Caro (*b.* 10 November 1843; *d.* 5 August 1909), Colombian president (1894–1898). Miguel Antonio Caro lived his entire life in the area of Bogotá, where he was born, and was a staunch defender of traditional Catholic and Hispanic values. A professor of Latin at the Universidad Nacional and expert in Spanish grammar and linguistics, Caro achieved distinction as a scholar (collaborating with Rufino José CUERVO) but is chiefly remembered as one of the architects of the regeneration that put an end to Liberal hegemony in Colombia. He was the principal author of the centralist, proclerical Constitution of 1886. As a "Nationalist" Conservative he became vice president under Rafael NÚÑEZ in 1892 but in reality was acting president, completing the term (1894–1898) after Núñez's death. His doctrinaire rigidity alienated both Liberals and the "Historical" faction of Conservatives, thus contributing to the outbreak of the War of the Thousand Days that began shortly after he left the presidency.

— DAVID BUSHNELL

CARONDELET, FRANÇOIS-LOUIS HECTOR

François-Louis Hector Carondelet, Baron de (*b.* 27 July 1747; *d.* 10 December 1807), governor of San Salvador and Louisiana; president of the Audiencia of Quito. A prototype of the bureaucratic *ilustrados* who staffed the late eighteenth-century Spanish colonies, Carondelet trod an ambiguous path between progress and reaction. Born at Cambray or Flanders, in what is the present-day French department of Nord, he entered the military service of Charles III of Spain at fifteen and saw brief action at the conclusion of the Seven Years' War. After serving at Algiers in 1775 and writing a book on infantry training and strategy, he was assigned to the Carib-

bean, where he fought with Bernardo de GÁLVEZ against the British at Pensacola (1781).

In 1789 Carondelet became governor–intendant of San Salvador, an indigo-producing region on the Pacific coast of the Audiencia of Guatemala. He strove to rationalize dye production and marketing, and to establish settlements for those displaced by expanding commercial agriculture. Two years later, he was promoted to the governorship of Louisiana and West Florida.

The succeeding five years severely tested Carondelet's determination to keep the lower Mississippi watershed under permanent Spanish sovereignty. With paltry resources, he bluffed and badgered the local French Jacobins, the region's mercurial Indian groups, land-hungry American frontiersmen, free colored, a slave population equaling that of the free, including Europeans, and intriguers of many stripes. He deftly outmaneuvered a range of antimonarchical forces and challenged American use of the Mississippi and the right of deposit at New Orleans.

Carondelet was reassigned to the presidency of the remote Audiencia of Quito (where he was also governor-general) late in 1798. There he found a declining textile trade, widespread native unrest, and bickering among the clerical orders. Although at a loss to cope with internal issues of an unfamiliar society, Carondelet managed to complete a road to the north coast and to facilitate the expedition of Alexander von Humboldt. He died in Quito.

— THOMAS FIEHRER

CARPENTIER, ALEJO

Alejo Carpentier (*b.* 26 December 1904; *d.* 24 April 1980), Cuban novelist and short-story writer. Carpentier was born in Havana and studied music with his mother, through whom he developed a love of music that became central to his life and work. In 1921 he studied architecture at the University of Havana and that same year began writing for local newspapers and magazines. Together with the noted Cuban composer Amadeo ROLDÁN he organized concerts of "new music," bringing to Cuba the works of Stravinsky, Poulenc, Satie, and Malipiero. He also wrote the librettos for two ballets with music by Roldán.

In 1928, with the help of Cuban poet and then-diplomatic official Mariano Brull, Carpentier moved to Paris, where he met André Breton, Paul Éluard, Ives Tanguy, Arthur Honegger, and Pablo Picasso, among others. With the 1933 publication of his first novel, *¡Ecue-Yamba-O!*, in Madrid, he traveled to Spain, where he met the celebrated Spanish poets Federico García

Lorca, Rafael Alberti, Pedro Salinas, and José Bergamín. In 1937, along with fellow Cuban writers Juan MARINELLO, Nicolás GUILLÉN, and Félix PITA RODRÍGUEZ, he represented Cuba at the Second Congress for the Defense of Culture, held in Madrid and Valencia.

In 1939 Carpentier returned to Cuba to work for the Ministry of Education and to teach the history of music at the National Conservatory, where he later conducted research that led to the rediscovery of neglected Cuban composers Esteban Salas and Manuel Saumell. In 1945 he moved to Venezuela to work in radio and advertising. While there, he traveled extensively in 1947–1948 through the Amazon region, an area vividly evoked in his novel *Los pasos perdidos* (1953; *The Lost Steps,* 1956). After the Cuban Revolution in 1959 Carpentier returned to Cuba, where he was appointed vice-president of the National Council on Culture. He was also a vice-president of the powerful Cuban Union of Writers and Artists (UNEAC) and from 1963 to 1968 the director of the Cuban National Publishing House. He traveled widely as a representative of the Cuban government on both cultural and political missions. In 1968 he was named Ministerial Counsel for Cultural Affairs at the Cuban embassy in Paris, a post he occupied until his death in 1980.

Carpentier's novels and short stories have been greatly acclaimed both in Cuba and abroad. He received many national honors as well as the international prizes Cino del Duca and Alfonso Reyes (1975). His work frequently evokes a particular historical period and is characterized by an ornate, meticulous, and rhythmical prose in which his love of music and architecture is evident. Among his other well-known works are *El reino de este mundo* (1949; *The Kingdom of This World,* 1957); *El siglo de las luces* (1962; *Explosion in a Cathedral,* 1963); and *El recurso del método* (1974; *Reasons of State,* 1976).

— ROBERTO VALERO

CARPIO NICOLLE, JORGE

Jorge Carpio Nicolle (*b.* 1932), Guatemalan journalist and politician. Born in Guatemala City, he received his degree in political science from the University of San Carlos in 1980. In 1963, he began publishing the newspaper *El Gráfico,* which has the second largest circulation in the country, and in 1984 he founded the political party Union of the National Center (Unión del Centro Nacional—UCN), which he serves as secretary general. He belongs to the Liberal International and has been the Secretary General of its Central American branch. He has twice been a candidate for the presidency of Guatemala, finishing second in 1985 and

1990. He has long been an avid supporter of cycling and is the author of *La ideología centrista* (1989).

— FERNANDO GONZÁLEZ DAVISON

CARRANZA, VENUSTIANO

Venustiano Carranza (*b.* 29 December 1859; *d.* 21 May 1920), first chief of the Constitutionalist forces during the Mexican Revolution (1913–1917), president of Mexico (1917–1920), Carranza was born at Cuatro Ciénegas in the northeastern frontier state of Coahuila, son of a well-to-do landed proprietor who had supported Benito Juárez. After a conventional liberal education in Saltillo and Mexico City, Carranza returned to Coahuila, where, during the Porfiriato (1876–1911), he farmed and engaged in politics. After election as mayor of his hometown in 1887, Carranza was ousted by the autocratic state governor, José María Garza Galán, against whom he successfully rebelled (1893). Porfirio DÍAZ acquiesced in the installation of a state government congenial to the Carranza family and sympathetic to the great caudillo of the northeast, Bernardo REYES of Nuevo León. Carranza, a loyal Reyista, served as mayor, state deputy, and federal senator, combining cautious political advancement with the acquisition of land and other property.

During the 1900s, political opposition to Díaz mounted and Reyes became a major contender for power. As the Reyista movement boomed (1908–1909), Carranza ran for the governorship of Coahuila. However, Díaz, resentful of overly powerful subjects, froze Reyes out of national politics and ensured Carranza's defeat. In retaliation, Carranza then forged an alliance of expedience with fellow Coahuilan Francisco MADERO, who dared challenge Díaz for the presidency. Although he was linked to the Madero family by old political ties and shared Madero's liberal philosophy, Carranza lacked Madero's naïve optimism; he was, rather, a crafty and hardened practitioner of realpolitik. Thus, while Carranza supported the successful Madero revolution (1910–1911), he did so with typical caution, exercising his role as revolutionary commander of the northeast from the sanctuary of Texas. He also criticized Madero for being too generous to the defeated Porfiristas when he signed the Treaty of Ciudad Juárez (May 1911).

During Madero's presidency (November 1911–February 1913) Carranza served as governor of Coahuila, adhering to a moderate liberal program that stressed municipal democracy, educational and fiscal reform, and temperance. He also built an independent state military, which defended Coahuila against rebel incursions, afforded the state government a certain political autonomy, and gave rise to serious wrangles between himself and Madero. Indeed, there were rumors that Carranza and some like-minded northern governors—"hawks" who rejected Madero's dovish conciliation of conservative opponents—flirted with outright rebellion.

In February 1913, when military rebels ousted and killed Madero, installing General Victoriano HUERTA in power, Carranza refused to recognize the coup. While his admirers depict this as an act of immediate outrage, the truth was more complex. For two weeks after the coup the telegraph wires between Coahuila and the capital hummed. Carranza negotiated with Huerta, whose characteristic bullheadedness prevented a deal from being made. Instead, Carranza marshaled his forces and declared himself in revolt. His military fortunes soon faltered. A rebel attack on Saltillo was a costly failure; during the summer of 1913 he was forced to flee to the northwestern state of Sonora, where a similar rebellion had begun with greater success.

However, Carranza's stand was politically decisive. As the senior Maderista rebel, he became the figurehead—and to some extent the actual leader—of a broad anti-Huerta movement. On 26 March 1913, Carranza and his entourage drew up and promulgated the Plan of Guadalupe, in which they repudiated Huerta and promised the return of constitutional rule. (Hence Carranza became "First Chief of the Constitutionalist Army.") However—at Carranza's insistence and to the disgust of some young radicals—the Plan made no reference to broader socioeconomic reforms.

During 1913–1914, as the revolt against Huerta spread, Carranza established an alternative government in the north. He decreed, taxed, issued currency, dealt with foreign powers, and tried to control the heterogeneous Constitutionalist forces. He succeeded, to the extent that Huerta was forced from power; and he succeeded, too, in securing U.S. backing without ceding an iota of Mexican sovereignty. (Indeed, his prickly nationalism made him, in American eyes, a difficult ingrate.) But his relations with Emiliano ZAPATA, in the distant south, were tenuous and mutually suspicious. Francisco "Pancho" VILLA, the charismatic caudillo of Chihuahua, who was victorious in the campaigns against Huerta in 1914, chafed under Carranza's persnickety authority. He resented Carranza's interference in Chihuahua and applauded the U.S. occupation of Veracruz—which tightened the noose around Huerta's neck—even as Carranza outspokenly condemned it. Differences were patched up until the fall of Huerta in July 1914.

Thereafter, the Constitutionalist revolution fragmented. The Zapatistas of Morelos had little time for Carranza, an elderly Porfirian politico whose commitment to agrarian reform was suspect. Villa, too, regarded Carranza with suspicion and personal dislike; when Villa and Zapata met in December 1914, they broke the ice by trading insults about Carranza. More important, the grand revolutionary convention that met at Aguascalientes in October 1914 proved incapable of reconciling the major caudillos of the Revolution—Carranza spurned it, and Villa effectively hijacked it. Mexico's many lesser caudillos were forced to choose, and the forces that had been briefly united against Huerta now split apart and embarked on a bloody internecine conflict.

When Pancho Villa and Emiliano Zapata met in December 1914, they broke the ice by trading insults about Carranza.

The civil war resolved itself into a struggle between Villa, loosely allied to Zapata, and Carranza, whose chief ally was the Sonoran general Álvaro OBREGÓN. For some historians, this last great bout of revolutionary warfare was a clear-cut conflict between a popular and peasant coalition led by Villa and Zapata and the "bourgeois" forces of Carranza. However, this interpretation overlooks the sameness of the two sides' social makeup (nationwide, the Carrancistas included many "peasants," just as the Villistas included landlords and bourgeoisie) and political programs (the rival programs differed little).

But the struggle was not irrelevant to Mexico's future. For while a victory of Villa and Zapata would probably have resulted in a weak, fragmented state, a collage of revolutionary fiefs of varied political hues presided over by a feeble central government, a victory by Carranza and his Sonoran allies would—and did—lay the foundations of a more ambitious, centralizing state dedicated to national integration and nationalist self-assertion. In this respect, Carranza, a product of Porfirian politics, helped lend a "neo-Porfirian" coloration to the revolutionary regime after 1915; he served, as Enrique Krauze observes, as the bridge between two centuries.

Carranza's triumph over Villa and Zapata, like his previous successes, owed more to political shrewdness than to military prowess. During 1914–1915 he overcame his ingrained political caution and promised agrarian and social reforms, legitimizing the efforts of his more radical supporters and undercutting the popular appeal of his enemies. He allowed Obregón to form an alliance with the workers of Mexico City and dispatched "proconsuls" to the states of southern Mexico, compelling those states to enter the revolutionary fold and—in Yucatán—skimming off valuable export revenues.

All this would have been in vain had not Obregón triumphed on the battlefield, repeatedly defeating Villa in a series of battles between April and June 1915, forcing him to relinquish claims to national power. Carranza was therefore recognized as de facto president by the United States in October 1915, establishing his administration in Mexico City, and, following elections, inaugurated as constitutional president in May 1917.

Carranza's three years as president were difficult. Rebellion still simmered. Large areas of the country remained ungovernable. The economy was in disarray, the currency had collapsed, and 1917 became known, in popular memory, as the "year of hunger." Over two-thirds of government expenditures went to the military, on whose bayonets Carranza depended. Politics remained the preserve of the Carrancista faction (their enemies were proscribed) and elections, though boisterous, were rigged and unrepresentative. A constituent congress, summoned by Carranza, produced a new constitution (1917) embracing radical measures: labor and agrarian reform, anticlericalism, and economic nationalism. (Carranza probably wanted a more moderate document, but was content to go with the tide.) Implementation came slowly. Land reform remained minimal, while Carranza ordered the wholesale restitution of haciendas seized during the revolution. The brief alliance with the Mexico City workers ended and, in 1916, when he was de facto president, a general strike was ruthlessly crushed. When, in 1918, a new national labor confederation (the Confederación Regional Obrera Mexicana [CROM]; Mexican Regional Labor Confederation) was established, Obregón, rather than Carranza, was the chief political sponsor—and beneficiary.

As in the past, Carranza displayed more skill and consistency in the international arena. After Villa's defeat, the U.S. government grudgingly recognized the Carranza administration, without extracting any quid pro quo from the obstinate Mexican leader. When, in 1916–1917, U.S. troops entered Mexico in pursuit of Villa, Carranza demanded their unconditional withdrawal, ultimately successfully. He flirted with Germany, the better to keep the United States at bay; but he spurned the offer of an alliance, communicated in the notorious Zimmerman telegram. He also made a determined, if unsuccessful, attempt to enforce the provisions of the new constitution that claimed subsoil deposits (including petroleum) as the patrimony of the state. The booming oil companies were obliged to yield vital additional revenue to the penurious state, but they refused to acknowledge their new constitutional status. The impasse remained a source of serious contention into the 1920s.

Carranza thus stoutly defended the integrity of Mexico and the principles of the revolution in the face of foreign pressure. But domestically, Carranza soft-pedaled reform and displayed a poor grasp of the populist politics the Revolution had ushered in. After 1918 his authority waned. As the presidential election of 1920 neared, and Obregón launched a powerful campaign, Carranza attempted to impose a chosen successor, a little-known diplomat named Ignacio Bonillas. The military balked; the CROM backed Obregón; and the Sonoran leaders initiated a coup that swiftly drove Carranza from Mexico City into the Puebla sierra. There, in May 1920, he was killed at Tlaxcalantongo or, as Krauze hypothesizes, he committed suicide rather than give his enemies the satisfaction of killing him. This was to be the last successful rebellion of Mexico's revolutionary history. Obregón and the Sonorans, the architects of Carranza's rise and fall, shared his hard-headed opportunism, but they displayed a better grasp of the mechanisms of popular mobilization, allied to social reform, that would form the bases of a durable revolutionary regime after 1920. For this reason, Carranza has often been regarded as a conservative revolutionary who was overtaken by events and outflanked by younger, more "populist" revolutionaries. He did, however, forge a winning revolutionary coalition, defeating both Huerta and Villa and sponsoring the 1917 Constitution. In addition, most critics concede, he was a strenuous and successful defender of Mexican sovereignty against the United States.

— ALAN KNIGHT

CARRANZA FERNÁNDEZ, EDUARDO

Eduardo Carranza Fernández (b. 23 July 1913; d. 13 February 1985), Colombian poet, born in Apiay. Carranza started to achieve recognition in 1934 through the publication of his poetry and his collaboration on the journal *Revista de las Indias*. His first sonnets, written between 1937 and 1944 and collected in *Azul de ti* (1947), made him famous. Carranza was an important member of the Piedra y Cielo group, influenced by the poetry of Juan Ramón Jiménez and, to a lesser extent, Pablo NERUDA. The works of Jiménez, Rafael Alberti, and Gerardo Diego were the models for Carranza's poetry, which is metaphorical, musical, and reminiscent of traditional Spanish styles. In the early 1940s his aesthetic confronted the modernist poet Guillermo VALENCIA, who was then the model of Colombian poets.

While Valencia cultivates the perfection of the meter and shows preference for exotic landscapes, Carranza prefers intimate and vernacular landscapes. Carranza's work is also marked by a purity of language and faithfulness to love, Catholicism, and country, and is untouched by Colombia's political violence of the 1950s and 1960s. In the 1940s and 1950s, his poetry circulated widely in Spain and Chile, countries in which he traveled and resided because of his work in the Colombian diplomatic service. Other collections of his poetry are *Los pasos cantados* (1975), *Los días que ahora son sueños* (1973), and *Veinte poemas* (1980).

— JUAN CARLOS GALEANO

CARRASQUILLA, TOMÁS

Tomás Carrasquilla (*b.* 1858; *d.* 1940), Colombian fiction writer. One of Colombia's greatest classic prose writers, Carrasquilla is best known for two novels, *Frutos de mi tierra* (1896) and *La Marquesa de Yolombó* (1926); between the publication of these two novels and afterward, he published several other novels, short novels, and numerous short stories with folkloric, psychological, fantastic, and symbolic perspectives. Carrasquilla believed that themes of rural, provincial life in Colombia were enough to make for good fiction; as such, his writings fall within the category of *costumbrista* (local color), which consists of providing vivid descriptions of popular customs and recreating the language of the popular classes. Nevertheless, Carrasquilla's fiction transcends the moralizing tone and didactic goal of *costumbrista*.

Carrasquilla does not just extol the good life in the Colombian provinces but also exposes moral issues centered on bigotry and cruelty.

In one sense, his narrative success lies in his ability to draw upon such literary traditions of Spanish literature as the picaresque novel and stories portraying Spanish customs. While *Frutos de mi tierra* is a Cinderella story, it relies on local color, proverbs, legends, and the oral tradition to provide anecdotes that focus on hypocrisy in small, provincial towns. Carrasquilla does not just extol the good life in the provinces but also exposes moral issues centered on bigotry and cruelty. *La Marquesa de Yolombó* is Carrasquilla's most ambitious effort. The action takes place during the Spanish American colonial period of the late nineteenth century and criticizes the colonial government for inefficiency, corruption, and waste.

— DICK GERDES

CARREÑO, MARIO

Mario Carreño (*b.* 24 June 1913), Cuban-born painter. Born in Havana, Carreño trained at the Academy of San Alejandro in Havana, the Academy of San Fernando in Madrid, and the École des Arts Appliques in Paris. During the 1920s he worked as a political cartoonist for *Revista de Havana* and *Diario de la Marina,* both in Cuba. In the 1930s Carreño lived in Spain, where he designed revolutionary posters (1932–1935). After meeting the Mexican muralists in 1936, he returned to Paris, where he met the surrealist Oscar Domínguez and Pablo Picasso (1937). His paintings from the late 1930s combined traditional European painting techniques with the influence of the school of Paris and classical Picasso.

At the outbreak of World War II Carreño fled first to Italy, then to New York City, returning to Cuba in 1941. Influenced by David Alfaro SIQUEIROS, he experimented with industrial paint, a medium he had tried in the late 1930s (*Cane Cutters,* 1943). In 1946 he was appointed professor of painting at the New York School for Social Research and in the late 1940s turned to a late cubist vocabulary with distinctively Afro-Cuban themes (*Caribbean Enchantment,* 1949). He moved to Chile and became a citizen in 1951. For a brief period he worked on an abstract geometric style. In the late 1950s Carreño began to paint surrealist petrified and fragmented human figures in volcanic landscapes.

In the 1960s he collaborated with Chilean architects in the design of three-dimensional murals. The most distinguished examples are a freestanding, double-faced wall designed with glazed bricks for the Central Plaza of the University of Concepción (1962); an exterior wall for the Saint Ignatius Loyola School in Santiago (1960); and a freestanding wall and pool monument designed for the United Nations Regional Building, also in Santiago (1963–1964).

— MARTA GARSD

CARRERA, JOSÉ MIGUEL

José Miguel Carrera (*b.* 15 October 1785; *d.* 4 September 1821), Chilean patriot and revolutionary. Carrera came from an old and distinguished family. A troublesome youth, he was sent in 1806 by his father to Spain, where he fought in at least thirteen actions in the Peninsular War. In July 1811 he returned to Chile and immediately immersed himself in the struggle for independence, using his sway over the military to seize power (15 November 1811). Handsome and personable, Carrera was a popular leader. During his dictatorship Chile's first newspaper, *La Aurora de Chile,* was published and the first national flag created. However, no declaration of independence was forthcoming.

With the arrival of a royalist expedition from Peru early in 1813, Carrera took command of the patriot forces in the south, leaving the government in the hands of a junta, over which his adversaries later assumed control. Given his limited military success, the junta transferred command to Bernardo O'HIGGINS (1778–1842), thereby opening up a serious rift between the two men. Soon afterward Carrera was captured by the royalists, but he escaped and returned to Santiago, where he staged a second coup d'état 23 July 1814. Civil war between the followers of O'Higgins and Carrera was averted only by the arrival of a new and powerful royalist expedition under the command of General Mariano Osorio (1777–1819). Carrera's failure to send relief to O'Higgins's valiant defense against Osorio at Rancagua (1–2 October 1814), resulted in a complete royalist triumph and the collapse of patriot Chile.

Carrera and two thousand others fled across the Andes to Mendoza, where the governor of Cuyo, José de SAN MARTÍN, preferring the more reliable support of O'Higgins, ordered Carrera on to Buenos Aires. In November 1815 Carrera traveled to the United States, procured two warships, and then returned to Buenos Aires. Denied a part in the liberation of Chile now underway, he moved to Montevideo and launched a propaganda war against the new O'Higgins government.

Temperamentally incapable of remaining inactive for long, he next involved himself in the fighting then raging in the Argentine interior, lending support to various provincial caudillos. He was finally captured and executed at Mendoza, where his brothers Juan José (1782–1818) and Luis (1792–1818) had been shot three years earlier. These executions roused resentment against the O'Higgins regime in Chile. The remains of the three Carreras were repatriated in 1828. Following in his father's footsteps, Carrera's son, José Miguel Carrera Fontecilla (1820–1860), fought in the Chilean rebellions of 1851 and 1859.

– SIMON COLLIER

CARRERA, JOSÉ RAFAEL

José Rafael Carrera (*b.* 24 October 1814; *d.* 14 April 1865), chief of state of Guatemala (1844–1848, 1851–1865). Born to poor parents in Guatemala City, Carrera joined the Central American federal army as a drummer

at age twelve, and rose rapidly in the ranks during the civil war of 1826–1829. The army, dominated by the Guatemalan conservative elite, not only provided military training but also indoctrinated him in conservative ideology. After Francisco MORAZÁN defeated this army in 1829, Carrera drifted for several years, eventually settling in Mataquescuintla, where he became a swineherd. Father Francisco Aqueche influenced him there and was instrumental in Carrera's marriage to Petrona García, the daughter of a local landowner.

Carrera emerged as a natural leader of the peasants and landowners of eastern Guatemala against the liberal reforms of the Guatemalan governor, Dr. Mariano GÁLVEZ. The rural population, spurred on by the clergy, opposed his anticlericalism, taxes, judicial reforms, and land, labor, and immigration policies that appeared to favor foreigners over natives. With these grievances already strong, the Gálvez government's efforts to check the cholera epidemic that broke out in 1837 led to uprisings, especially in eastern Guatemala. Although Carrera did not instigate the 1837 revolt, and in fact had accepted assignment as commander of a government quarantine patrol, local residents soon persuaded him to join the revolt. At Santa Rosa, on 9 June 1837, he led a ragged band of insurgents to a stunning victory, sending government troops fleeing back to the capital.

Aided by serious divisions between Gálvez and José Francisco BARRUNDIA, Carrera's peasant army took Guatemala City on 1 February 1838, bringing down the Gálvez government. This resulted temporarily in a more liberal government under Lieutenant Governor Pedro Valenzuela, who succeeded in persuading Carrera to leave the capital in return for promised reform and military command of the district of Mita. Resurgent strength of the conservative elite of the capital, however, and failure of the Valenzuela government to move fast enough with the reforms caused Carrera to resume the war in March 1838. President Morazán brought federal troops from El Salvador into the struggle, but on 13 April 1839 Carrera once more took the capital, this time installing a conservative government under Mariano Rivera Paz. In March 1840 Carrera decisively defeated Morazán at Guatemala City, effectively ending the Central American national government. From this point until his death, except briefly in 1848–1849, Carrera was the military master of Guatemala. He consolidated the power of his army during the early 1840s, especially by the Convenio of Guadalupe on 11 March 1844.

In December 1844 Carrera assumed the presidency of Guatemala. Although his policies were conservative, during this period he sometimes supported moderate liberal political leaders as a check against the pretensions of the conservative ecclesiastical and economic elite of the capital. On 21 March 1847 Carrera completed the process of Guatemalan secession from the defunct Central American union by establishing the Republic of Guatemala.

Liberal opposition, combined with continued rebel activity in eastern Guatemala, led to Carrera's resignation and exile in Mexico in August 1848. The new Liberal government, however, failed to achieve unity or solve the country's problems, and Carrera reentered the country in March 1849 at the head of an "army of restoration" composed heavily of Indians. When Carrera took Quetzaltenango, several generals defected to him and an agreement was reached in June that made him a lieutenant general in the Guatemalan army, followed in August by his appointment once more as commanding general of the army. Thereafter he strengthened the army as he carried out campaigns against continuing rebellions within Guatemala and against the liberals' attempts to revive the Central American union in El Salvador, Honduras, and Nicaragua. He dealt those forces a major blow with a stunning victory against the "national army" at San José la Arada on 2 February 1851. This victory assured the dominance of the conservatives in Guatemala for many years to come.

After 1850 Carrera allied himself closely with the conservative and ecclesiastical elite of Guatemala City. His government restored close relations with Spain and signed a concordat with the Vatican guaranteeing the clergy a major role in the regime. Although Carrera was often described as reactionary by his opponents, Guatemala enjoyed considerable economic growth during the next twenty years as coffee began to replace cochineal as its leading export. Carrera once more became president of Guatemala on 6 November 1851. He consolidated his strength and greatly increased his power when he became president for life, a virtual monarch, on 21 October 1854.

As the most powerful caudillo in mid-nineteenth-century Central America, Carrera affected the development of neighboring states as well, frequently intervening to assure conservative rule in El Salvador and Honduras. When the North American filibuster William WALKER came to the aid of Nicaraguan liberals and subsequently became president of Nicaragua, Carrera provided substantial aid to the combined Central American force that routed Walker in 1857. Although he declined an invitation to command the Central American army, leaving that to Costa Rica's Juan Rafael Mora, Carrera sent more troops than any other state in the "National Campaign."

In 1863 Carrera challenged the rise in El Salvador of Gerardo BARRIOS, who had begun to pursue liberal, anticlerical reforms. Although initially repulsed at Coate-peque in February, he returned to conquer San Salvador later in the year, removing Barrios from office.

When he died in 1865, probably from dysentery, Carrera had achieved considerable stability and economic growth for Guatemala, but had also established a stifling political dictatorship that had reserved many of the benefits of the regime for a small elite in Guatemala City. At the same time, Carrera deserves credit for protecting the rural Indian masses of the country from increased exploitation of their land and labor and for bringing Indians and mestizos into positions of political and military leadership. Perhaps the most lasting legacy of his long rule, however, was the establishment of the military as the dominant political institution in the country.

– RALPH LEE WOODWARD, JR.

CARRERA ANDRADE, JORGE

Jorge Carrera Andrade (*b.* 18 September 1903; *d.* 11 November 1978). Possibly Ecuador's greatest poet of the twentieth century, Carrera Andrade was also a diplomat and anthropologist who traveled extensively both inside and outside his native land. In constant evolution throughout Carrera Andrade's life, his literary works comprise more than two dozen books of poetry spanning fifty years, numerous prose works, translations, and several literary studies of Ecuadorian, French, and Japanese literature. In his poetry, the luscious, diverse land of Ecuador and its strong telluric magnetism symbolize, in the vein of the European romantics and French symbolists, the origins of cosmic man and woman. Carrera Andrade's verse is a vehicle that constantly takes him back to the center of his poetic world: Ecuador.

In Carrera Andrade's poetry, the luscious, diverse land of Ecuador and its strong telluric magnetism symbolize the origins of cosmic man and woman.

Early on, his poetry reads like a carefully crafted, melodious song dedicated to his native land and the American landscape, and it continues to impart a musical quality to the land through innovative visual imagery and metaphor. Through his poetry, Carrera Andrade rediscovers his identity in the beauty and order of nature, which gives rise to certain constants in his poetry: optimism, despite growing world problems throughout his long career; social concern for the less fortunate in the world; and a search for ways to deal with solitude. *Hombre planetario* (1957–1963) is his best book of poetry, for in it he reconfirms his long-standing conviction concerning the need to understand our relationship with the land and with each other. Carrera Andrade also pioneered the adaptation of haiku to the Spanish language.

– DICK GERDES

CARRILLO, JULIÁN [ANTONIO]

Julián [Antonio] Carrillo (*b.* 28 January 1875; *d.* 9 September 1965), Mexican composer, theorist, conductor, violinist, and teacher. Born in Ahualulco, San Luis Potosí, Carrillo studied at the National Conservatory in Mexico City, where he took violin with Pedro Manzano, composition with Melesio MORALES, and acoustics with Francisco Ortega y Fonseca. He went to Europe in 1899, remaining there until 1905 and studying at the Leipzig Conservatory with Salomon Jadassohn (composition), Carl Reinecke (theory), Jean Becker (violin), and Arthur Nikisch and Sitt (conducting). He also studied violin with Albert Zimmer at the Ghent Conservatory. In Leipzig he led the Gewandhaus Orchestra. During that epoch Carrillo started to develop his new musical theory about dividing a violin string in such a way as to create a ratio of 1:1–007246. Carrillo divided the octave into microtones (intervals smaller than the semitone), calling his system "Sonido 13"—the "thirteenth sound." He also developed a method of music notation for the microtonal system. Carrillo's Symphony no. 1 (1902) was premiered under his baton by the Leipzig Conservatory Orchestra. In it he used what he called "ideological unity and tonal variety." He continued to experiment and began using an excessively complex musical vocabulary, even though one third of his works are written without microtones.

Carrillo returned to Mexico and was appointed professor of composition at the National Conservatory (1906), inspector general of music for Mexico City (1908), and director of the National Conservatory (1913–1915, 1920–1924). Beginning in 1926 Carrillo's musical works and theoretical writings were very much praised abroad, by the New York League of Composers, the Philadelphia Orchestra, in Belgium and in France. In 1961 the Lamoureux Orchestra of Paris recorded twenty of his microtonal and tonal works. A special piano for use with Carrillo's new system was built by the firm of Carl Sauter. Carrillo composed two operas as well as several symphonies, orchestral works, chamber music, and works for guitar, violin, and piano,

and published numerous essays about his musical theory. He died in San Ángel.

– SUSANA SALGADO

CARRILLO COLINA, BRAULIO

Braulio Carrillo Colina (*b.* 20 March 1800; *d.* 15 May 1845), president and later dictator of Costa Rica (1835–1837; 1838–1842). Carrillo was an opponent of the Central American Federation as led by Francisco MORAZÁN, in whose execution he was implicated. However, he followed essentially radical liberal policies in internal economic affairs. He was most strongly identified with the supremacy of coffee-growing interests and of the new national capital of San José. After studying law in León, Nicaragua, he returned to serve as deputy from his native city of Cartago (1827–1829), San José's principal rival as capital. He was chosen as a compromise chief of state in 1835 and then deposed his successor, Manuel Aguilar, to become virtual dictator in 1838. He was overthrown by Morazán's expeditionary force in 1842. Later, after engineering Morazán's capture and execution, he was forced into exile in El Salvador and assassinated near San Miguel.

During his first term Carrillo forcefully resolved the question of the site of the new capital by ending the system of "ambulatory," or rotating, capitals in favor of San José. When challenged in revolt (Guerra de la Liga) in 1835, he defeated the anti–San José forces despite his forces being outnumbered nearly three to one. This was followed by an abortive invasion of exiles (led by Manuel Quijano) from Nicaragua to Guanacaste, in June 1836, with even less success.

During his dictatorship Carrillo abrogated the 1825 Constitution and replaced it with the Ley de Bases y Garantías in 1841, which named him ruler for life. Although that provision was short-lived, the larger document proved more significant, greatly influencing the Constitution of 1871 in further strengthening the central government and liquidating the power of local municipal authorities. He also convened a Constituent Assembly in 1838 which declared Costa Rica's independence from the collapsing Central American Federation. Severely tested by Morazán's occupation, this policy was reaffirmed in 1848.

Carrillo's policies were consistently in favor of coffee exports and the city of San José, despite his origins in the rival city of Cartago. He ordered municipalities to provide coffee seedlings to all who would plant them, as well as terms for purchase or rental of public lands for coffee cultivation. He also abolished the collection of the tithe on coffee production after 1835, a policy of great importance in both stimulating production and undermining the power of the church thereafter.

— LOWELL GUDMUNDSON

CARRILLO FLORES, ANTONIO

Antonio Carrillo Flores (*b.* 23 June 1909; *d.* 20 March 1986), leading political figure in Mexican financial affairs since 1952. Born in Mexico City, he was the son of a famous musician Julián Carrillo. With Miguel Alemán, Carrillo Flores was a member of the 1929 law school graduating class at the National University. From 1946 to 1970 he held a succession of influential political posts, including secretary of the treasury (1952–1958), ambassador to the United States (1958–1964), and secretary of foreign relations (1964–1970). Through his public service and teaching careers he trained two generations of disciples who became mentors to Mexico's new political technocrats of the 1980s and 1990s. He was the brother of the distinguished scientist Nabor Carrillo Flores.

— RODERIC AI CAMP

CARRILLO FLORES, NABOR

Nabor Carrillo Flores (*b.* 23 February 1911; *d.* 19 February 1967), educator, scientist, and intellectual. Born in Mexico City, he was the younger brother of Antonio Carrillo Flores, and the son of the musician Julián Carrillo. He received a civil engineering degree from the National University in 1938 and a doctorate from Harvard in 1942. Internationally renowned for his work in subsoil mechanics, Carrillo Flores studied with Sotero Prieto before receiving a Guggenheim fellowship (1940). He directed various scientific research projects at the National University, and served as its rector from 1952 to 1961. He received the National Prize in Sciences in 1957 and pioneered the use of atomic energy in Mexico. He died in Mexico City.

— RODERIC AI CAMP

CARRILLO PUERTO, FELIPE

Felipe Carrillo Puerto (*b.* 8 November 1874; *d.* 3 January 1924), one of the Mexican Revolution's most radical agrarian leaders. During his short-lived governorship of Yucatán (1922–1923), Carrillo Puerto presided over what was arguably the Americas' first attempted transition to socialism. Assassinated in January 1924 by insurgent federal troops allied with powerful members of Yucatán's henequen oligarchy, he has since become one of the most enduring martyrs of Mexico's twentieth-century revolution.

Carrillo Puerto was born in Motul—the heart of Yucatán's henequen zone—the second of fourteen children of a modest mestizo retail merchant. As a young man he was a *ranchero* (small land-holder), mule driver, petty trader, and railroad conductor during Yucatán's henequen export boom, which descendants of the original Maya fieldworkers still recall as the *época de esclavitud* (age of slavery). Carrillo Puerto learned the Maya vernacular as part of his daily life, and developed close ties to Yucatán's rural underclass in the process. An autodidact who read a bit of Marx and other leftist European thinkers along with the more standard fare of mainstream Mexican liberalism, Carrillo Puerto was jailed several times for his political activities against the local oligarchical machine. Following the fall of the Porfiriato in 1911, his political aspirations within the state were frustrated by his backing of the wrong Maderista politician, and he left Yucatán for Morelos in late 1914 to volunteer his services to the celebrated agrarian movement of Emiliano ZAPATA. Six months later, however, he was back on his native soil, determined to work with the new populist governor, General Salvador ALVARADO, to bring agrarian reform to Yucatán.

Carrillo Puerto encouraged the teaching of Maya culture and art forms, and began earnest restoration of the great archaeological sites of Chichén Itzá and Uxmal.

Carrillo Puerto proved both too popular and too radical for the authoritarian Alvarado, who kept him on a short leash prior to departing the peninsula in 1918. Once Carrillo Puerto assumed control of Alvarado's Socialist Party of the Southwest (Partido Socialista del Sureste—PSS) later that year, the Mexican Revolution moved steadily to the left in Yucatán. Whereas Alvarado had been reluctant to let the rural masses participate in the political process, Carrillo Puerto encouraged them to accept responsibility for their political destiny. And while Alvarado had been prepared to initiate only a limited agrarian reform, under Carrillo Puerto's leadership, the pace of agrarian reform accelerated to the point that Yucatán distributed more land than any other state, save perhaps Zapata's Morelos. By the time of his death, Carrillo Puerto had made sure that virtually every one of the state's major pueblos had received at least a basic ejidal grant. His regime and life were snuffed out just as he seemed ready to initiate a more sweeping agrarian reform, one that would have expropriated the region's henequen plantations and turned them into collective farms owned and operated by the workers.

Under Carrillo Puerto the Mexican Revolution in Yucatán became a genuinely Yucatecan movement. He used locally trained cadres of agrarian agitators and activist schoolteachers, and allied with local Caciques (power brokers). Moreover, Carrillo Puerto reinforced the regional character of his revolution in a variety of symbolic ways, most of which sought to wean the Maya campesino away from the institutions and passive attitudes of the old regime and to develop a sense of ethnic pride as a prelude to class consciousness. He encouraged the speaking of Maya and the teaching of Maya culture and art forms, began earnest restoration of the great archaeological sites of Chichén Itzá and Uxmal, and made every effort to recall the great revolutionary tradition of protest to which the campesinos were heir.

Ultimately, Carrillo Puerto's homegrown variant of "Yucatecan socialism" proved threatening, not only to the regional oligarchy, but also to the more moderate regime then consolidating its control over the republic under the leadership of Sonoran caudillos Alvaro OBREGÓN SALIDO and Plutarco Calles. When, under cover of the DE LA HUERTA rebellion, insurgent federal troops were contracted by the henequen kings to expunge "bolshevism," Mexico City abandoned Carrillo Puerto. Yucatán's socialist experiment ended tragically when Felipe Carrillo Puerto and many of his closest supporters in Mérida were hunted down and summarily executed by a firing squad on 3 January 1924. Following the defeat of the de la Huerta rebellion, the remnants of the PSS were absorbed by the new corporatist structure in Mexico City. Only the outer trappings of the Americas' first attempted socialist transition—the red shirts, the radical slogans, the formal organization of the PSS—survived its leader's untimely death.

– GILBERT M. JOSEPH

CARRIÓN, ALEJANDRO

Alejandro Carrión (b. 11 March 1915; d. 1991), Ecuadorian writer. Born in Loja, Alejandro Carrión is known in Ecuador principally as a political journalist. Many of his writings were signed with the pseudonym "Juan sin Cielo." Carrión also wrote poetry and narrative fiction. Among his most cited works are La manzana dañada (1948), a collection of short stories that depicts the sordid aspects of a school system controlled by the Catholic church in southern Ecuador, and La espina (1959), a novel of solitude in which the protagonist tries to reconstruct the image of his mother, who had died during his birth. Because of his political views, which ran the gamut from socialism in his early life to

conservatism in his later years, Carrión was a controversial figure in Ecuador. During the government of León FEBRES CORDERO (1984–1988), many accused Carrión of being the president's principal apologist; in his journalism, Carrión defended the government's neoliberal economic policies and its conservative political agenda. In 1985, President Febres awarded Carrión the Eugenio Espejo Prize for Literature.

– MICHAEL HANDELSMAN

CARRIÓN, JERÓNIMO

Jerónimo Carrión (b. 6 July 1801; d. 5 May 1873), president of Ecuador (1865–1867). Carrión served as governor of Azuay province (1845–1847), deputy (1845, 1852) and senator (1847–1849) from Loja province, and vice president of Ecuador in 1859 during the administration of Francisco ROBLES (1856–1859). In 1865 he accepted the invitation of archconservative dictator Gabriel GARCÍA MORENO (1861–1865, 1869–1875) to succeed him. The retiring president arranged a landslide electoral victory for Carrión, who, to García Moreno's dismay, proved unwilling to be a puppet ruler. He chose his own cabinet, naming several liberals, and dispatched García Moreno on a diplomatic mission to Chile.

Yet on policy matters Carrión did not diverge significantly from the García Moreno agenda, save for his unwillingness to savage political opponents with violent repression. Under Carrión freedom of expression returned, bringing the reemergence of a lively—if often reckless and irresponsible—opposition press. In 1867 his leading minister, Manuel Bustamante, angered powerful Liberal elements then ascendant in Congress. In the ensuing political showdown with Senate president Pedro CARBO Y NOBOA, Congress censured Carrión. He was overthrown and replaced by Pedro José Arteta in 1867. Lacking support, Carrión agreed. Contemporaries generally regarded him as honest if not especially bright or energetic.

– RONN F. PINEO

CARRIÓN, MANUEL BENJAMÍN

Manuel Benjamín Carrión (b. 20 April 1897; d. 8 March 1979), Ecuadorian essayist. Originally from Loja, Benjamín Carrión spent his life writing about the major social, political, and cultural problems of both his native Ecuador and the rest of Latin America. During his youth, he was one of the early founders of Ecuador's Socialist Party (1925). His contributions to the continent's many democratic causes were formally recognized when the Mexican government awarded him in 1968 the prestigious Benito Juárez Prize. In 1944,

Carrión founded Ecuador's Casa de la Cultura Ecuatoriana (House of Ecuadorian Culture), which through the years has become one of the country's principal institutions charged with developing among all Ecuadorians the many forms of cultural and intellectual expression. In Ecuador, Carrión is revered for his efforts to stimulate and guide others in their creative endeavors. His most celebrated works are *Atahuallpa* (1934) and *Cartas al Ecuador* (1943). In 1975 he received the Eugenio Espejo Prize, Ecuador's highest literary and cultural honor.

– MICHAEL HANDELSMAN

CARVAJAL, LUIS DE

Luis de Carvajal (*b.* 1566; *d.* 8 December 1596), prominent crypto-Jew (secret Jew) in Mexico. Carvajal was born in Benavente, Castile, and studied at the Jesuit school in Medina del Campo. In 1580 he and his family emigrated to Mexico at the invitation of Luis's uncle, Luis de Carvajal y de la Cueva, conquistador and governor of Nuevo León, who was unaware that his relatives secretly practiced Judaism. Carvajal tried his hand at a variety of trades, raising sheep, and working as an itinerant merchant. The Carvajals established extensive contacts with other crypto-Jews and became the cynosure of the Inquisition's first major campaign against Judaizers. On 9 May 1589 agents of the Inquisition arrested Carvajal and his mother. While in prison, Carvajal had several dreams that convinced him that God had chosen him to sustain the Jewish community in Mexico. He therefore feigned repentance, formally abjured his heresy, and was reconciled to the Catholic church. But he continued to practice Judaism in secret and persuaded other members of his family to do the same.

While serving in the Colegio de Santiago de Tlatelolco as part of his penance, he used the library to further his knowledge of the Old Testament and correct Jewish practice. In early 1595 Carvajal wrote his *Memoirs,* a mystical autobiography in which he referred to himself as Joseph Lumbroso ("the Enlightened"). Shortly after, he was again arrested by the Inquisition and condemned as a relapsed heretic. He and several other family members were burned at the stake in the century's largest auto-da-fé. According to some reports, Carvajal made a last-minute conversion to Christianity and was garroted before being burned.

– R. DOUGLAS COPE

CARVALHO, ANTÔNIO DE ALBUQUERQUE COELHO DE

Antônio de Albuquerque Coelho de Carvalho (*b.* 1655; *d.* 25 April 1725), Portuguese colonial administrator.

Born in Lisbon and baptized on 14 September 1655, Carvalho was the son of the governor of Maranhão (1667–1671) of the same name; the nephew of Feliciano Coelho de Carvalho, the first lord-proprietor of the captaincy of Camutá (also known as Cametá); the grandson of Francisco Coelho de Carvalho, first governor-general (1626–1636) of the newly established state of Maranhão and Grão-Pará; and the great-grandson of Feliciano Coelho de Carvalho, Indian fighter and governor of Paraíba in the 1590s. He accompanied his father to America, leaving Portugal in 1666 and returning in 1671. In 1678 young Carvalho returned to Maranhão to serve as *capitão-mor* of his family's captaincy of Camutá until 1682. That same year, he fathered by Angela de Bairros, whose parents were said to be *pardos* from Pernambuco, the bastard Antônio de Albuquerque Coelho (1682–1746), who later gained fame as the one-armed governor and captain-general of Macau. From 1685 to 1690 Carvalho served as governor and *capitão-mor* of Grão-Pará. On 17 May 1690, he became governor and captain-general of the state of Maranhão, Grão-Pará, and Rio Negro, administering that vast territory until 1701.

After returning to Portugal, Carvalho served in the War of Spanish Succession. For his services in Portuguese America, Carvalho, already a knight in the Order of Christ, was awarded a commandery worth 300 milreis and the post of *alcaide-mor*. Since there was no single commandery available with annual receipts for that amount, he was given the commandery of Santo Ildefonso de Val de Telhas in the Order of Christ, two other commanderies in Setúbal, and the post of *alcaide-mor* of Sines—the latter three in the Order of Santiago.

In March 1709, Carvalho was named governor of Rio de Janeiro. He arrived in June 1709, departed for Minas Gerais in July, and spent the next few months pacifying the area in the wake of the War of the Emboabas, the civil conflict between the Paulistas who had discovered the area's mineral wealth and the newcomers from Portugal and coastal Brazil. In the late fall he returned to Rio de Janeiro, where he remained until his appointment as governor of the newly created captaincy of São Paulo and Minas do Ouro. Installed in São Paulo in June 1710, he remained in the captaincy, erecting new townships and strengthening crown authority, until late September 1711. Upon hearing that an armada of eighteen ships under the French corsair René Duguay-Trouin had arrived at Rio de Janeiro, he quickly mobilized six thousand men from the mining areas and marched to the city's rescue. But it was too late: Rio had already been occupied and plundered by the French, and most of the ransom they had demanded had been paid. After the French departed on 13 November 1711, Carvalho helped restore order and rebuild Rio de Janeiro, holding the post of governor (October 1711–June 1713) while he continued to hold his governorship of São Paulo and Minas do Ouro.

Late in 1713 he set sail for Portugal. Enroute he spent eighteen days in Recife's harbor in the aftermath of Pernambuco's War of the Mascates and, upon his return to Portugal, he lobbied for the planter faction.

Carvalho married Dona Luisa Antônia de Mendonça, daughter of Dom Francisco de Melo and Dona Joana de Abreu e Melo. From this marriage, a son, Francisco de Albuquerque Coelho de Carvalho, was born. On 22 March 1722, Carvalho took office as governor of Angola, where he died.

– FRANCIS A. DUTRA

CASADO, CARLOS

Carlos Casado (*b.* 16 March 1833; *d.* 29 June 1899). Born in Valencia, Spain, Casado emigrated to Argentina in 1857 and opened a business in the city of Rosario in Santa Fe Province. He also established a private bank that became one of the foundations for the offices of the Bank of London and the Río de la Plata that opened in Rosario in 1868. In 1870 he set up the Candelaria agricultural colony, promoting the immigration of European agricultural workers and realizing the first major export shipment of wheat to Europe. Casado organized a company of wheat mills, promoted the construction of docks in the Rosario port, and was a founder and president of the Banco de Santa Fe, a leading commercial bank. He was also elected counselor of the city government of Rosario.

– CARLOS MARICHAL

CASAL, JULIÁN DEL

Julián del Casal (*b.* 7 November 1863; *d.* 21 October 1893), Cuban poet who used the pseudonyms the Count of Camors, Hernani, and Alceste at times during his literary career. Casal was born in Havana and showed a great talent for poetry from an early age. His first poems were published in *El Estudio,* an underground publication that he founded with a group of friends. He began studies for a career in law in 1881 at the University of Havana but never finished them. Instead, he became finance minister while writing articles and working in diverse capacities for newspapers and literary publications, among them *La Discusión, El Fígaro,* and *La Habana Literaria.* Casal published a series of articles on Cuban society in the magazine *La Habana Elegante.* The first, a derogatory piece about the Spanish captain-general Sabas Marín, cost him his government post. In his short life Casal earned a place as one of the great

poets in Cuban history. Along with three other poets, fellow Cuban José MARTÍ, Colombian José Asunción SILVA, and Mexican Manuel GUTIÉRREZ NÁJERA, he was an initiator of modernism, the first literary movement to originate in Spanish-speaking America.

– ROBERTO VALERO

CASALDÁLIGA, PEDRO

Pedro Casaldáliga (*b.* 1928), bishop of São Félix do Araguaia, Brazil. Casaldáliga was born in Barcelona and raised on his family's cattle ranch in Catalonia. In 1952 he was ordained into the Claretian order, and sixteen years later he arrived in Brazil. By 1971 he had attracted the attention of Brazilian authorities by writing a critical report titled "Feudalism and Slavery in Northern Mato Grosso." In the following year Casaldáliga was consecrated as the first bishop of São Félix do Araguaia, a large but remote region in the states of Goiás and Mato Grosso.

In 1988 the Vatican issued an order that Casaldáliga not speak publicly, publish any further writings, or leave his diocese without explicit permission.

In subsequent years, however, the prolific writer and poet found himself in direct conflict with the landowners of Goiás and Mato Grosso, the Brazilian government, and the Catholic hierarchy because of his emphasis on developing community leadership among the peasants within his diocese, providing health care and education, and resisting the continued expansion of ranches at the expense of peasants' rights. In 1973, the same year that the Missionary Council to Indigenous Peoples was founded in Brazil, Francisco Jentel, a priest under Casaldáliga's authority, was tried under Brazil's National Security Law for inciting class warfare as the government sought resolutions to continuing conflicts at Santa Terezinha. In October 1976 Casaldáliga was present when Brazilian authorities shot and killed a Jesuit missionary, João Bosco Penido Burnier, for interfering with the interrogation and torture of two women. After 1973 public criticism began to surface from Archbishop Sigaud and Cardinal Joseph Ratzinger about Casaldáliga's pastoral work as well as his theological convictions.

In 1985 Casaldáliga began traveling extensively throughout Central America, including Nicaragua, El

Salvador, and Cuba, in "a ministry of borders and consolation." As a result of criticism for these trips, as well as for his writings supportive of liberation theologians and his characterization of Archbishop Oscar Romero as a martyr, in 1988 the Vatican issued an order that Casaldáliga not speak publicly, publish any further writings, or leave his diocese without explicit permission.

— CAROLYN E. VIEIRA

CASALS, FELIPE

Felipe Casals (*b.* 28 July 1937), Mexican film director. Born in Zapopán, Jalisco, Casals studied film in Paris. He is one of the leading directors of the generation of 1968, which contributed greatly to a brief flowering of Mexican cinema in the 1970s. Among the most celebrated of his films are *Canoa* (1974), *El apando* (1975), *Las poquianchis* (1976), *El año de la peste* (1978), *Bajo la metralla* (1982), *Los motivos de Luz* (1985), and *El tres de copas* (1986). Casals' films are characterized by hard-hitting, violent portrayals of Mexican national issues, particularly social strife and the underclass. Most of his films have been produced by the state. He received the Ariel from the Mexican film academy for best director for *El año de la peste* and *Bajo la metralla*. He has filmed other minor features for the video market, such as *Las abandonadas* and a musical biography of the popular singer Rigo Tovar, entitled *Rigo es amor.*

— DAVID MACIEL

CASANOVA Y ESTRADA, RICARDO

Ricardo Casanova y Estrada (*b.* 10 November 1844; *d.* 14 April 1913), archbishop of Guatemala (1886–1913). Casanova was born in Guatemala City and studied law at the University of San Carlos. He served in governmental positions until 1874, when he angered President Justo BARRIOS by deciding a case in favor of an abolished religious community. Being forced by Barrios to parade through the city in a cassock convinced the lawyer to become a priest. Ordained in 1875 and consecrated archbishop in 1886, he issued several pastoral letters defending the church against the Liberals. He was exiled by President Manuel BARILLAS in 1887 and returned to Guatemala in 1897, spending the rest of his life guiding the church during the dictatorship of Manuel Estrada Cabrera. Casanova was also a poet, writing under the pseudonym of Andrés Vigil.

— EDWARD T. BRETT

CASASOLA, AGUSTÍN

Agustín Casasola (*b.* 1874; *d.* 1928), Mexican photographer. Born in Mexico City, Agustín Casasola worked

as a reporter for numerous periodicals, including the Porfirian daily *El Imparcial.* There he began to collect illustrations, documents, books, and photographs which would eventually become the Casasola Archives, containing nearly one million photographs, the richest pictorial documents of twentieth-century Mexican history. The most prolific Mexican photographer of his day, Casasola captured the last years of the Porfiriato, the revolutionary struggle, and its aftermath. Like Matthew Brady, distinguished photographer of the American Civil War, he witnessed and recorded history; his photographs include figures such as Pancho Villa and Emiliano Zapata, rebels hanged from trees or executed by firing squads, and *soldaderas* riding atop boxcars and shouldering rifles. A collection of his photography, including some of what he collected from others, was published by his son Gustavo in *Historia gráfica de la Revolución Mexicana: 1900–1940,* edited by Luis González Obregón and Nicolás Rangel.

— MARY KAY VAUGHAN

CASÁUS Y TORRES, RAMÓN

Ramón Casáus y Torres (*b.* 1765; *d.* 10 November 1845), archbishop of Guatemala (1811–1845). Born in Jaca, Huesca, Spain, Casáus entered the Dominican order in Saragossa and later earned his doctorate in Mexico City. He was bishop of Oaxaca when appointed archbishop of Guatemala in 1811. As archbishop, he worked to improve educational facilities and donated his library to the University of San Carlos. He was especially interested in Indian languages and arranged for teaching Quiché and Cakchiquel at the university and the seminary. He opposed independence from Spain and Mexico and became closely associated with conservative political interests in the civil wars following independence. He strongly resisted establishment of a separate diocese for El Salvador.

Liberal victory in 1829 resulted in Casáus's exile from Central America by Francisco MORAZÁN. He spent the remainder of his life in Havana. The state of Guatemala declared him a traitor on 13 June 1830. After Rafael CARRERA came to power, in 1839, the Guatemalan government invited him to return, but the continuing turmoil on the isthmus deterred the archbishop from returning to his see before his death. His remains were brought to Guatemala for burial in 1846.

— RALPH LEE WOODWARD, JR.

CASO Y ANDRADE, ALFONSO

Alfonso Caso y Andrade (*b.* 1 February 1896; *d.* 30 November 1970), Mexican archaeologist, intellectual, and public figure who wrote numerous works on Middle American indigenous populations. From 1931 to 1943 he directed the explorations of Monte Albán, one of Mexico's major archaeological sites.

The son of the engineer Antonio Caso y Morali and Maria Andrade, brother of the distinguished intellectual Antonio CASO Y ANDRADE, and the brother-in-law of a leading intellectual and labor leader, Vicente LOMBARDO TOLEDANO, Caso was part of a significant generation of Mexican intellectuals. A longtime professor at the National University, he directed the National Preparatory School and, in 1944, after directing the National Institute of Anthropology and History, became rector of the National University. Caso briefly served (1946–1948) in Miguel Alemán's cabinet as the first secretary of government properties and in 1949 he founded and became director of the National Indigenous Institute, a position he held until his death. A member of the National College, an honorary society of distinguished Mexicans, Caso was awarded the National Prize in Arts and Sciences for his intellectual contributions.

– RODERIC AI CAMP

CASO Y ANDRADE, ANTONIO

Antonio Caso y Andrade (*b.* 19 December 1883; *d.* 6 March 1946), a leading Mexican philosopher who wrote numerous books on values and sociology but is more important for his contribution to the cultural emancipation of the Mexican and the destruction of positivism. He is also remembered for his notable debates on academic freedom in 1933 and for his impact on dozens of major intellectual and political figures who passed through the National University from 1910 through the 1920s.

The son of engineer Antonio Caso y Morali and Maria Andrade, and brother of Alfonso CASO Y ANDRADE, he became first secretary of the National Treasury in 1910 and was a founding member of the first graduate school in 1913. He was among the members of the distinguished intellectual generation of the Ateneo de la Juventud. Caso directed the National Preparatory School, the School of Philosophy and Letters, and, in 1921–1923, the National University. He served briefly as an ambassador in South America and was an original member of the prestigious National College, an honorary society of distinguished Mexicans.

– RODERIC AI CAMP

CASTAÑEDA, FRANCISCO DE PAULA

Francisco de Paula Castañeda (*b.* 1776; *d.* 12 March 1832), Argentine educator and journalist. Born in Buenos Aires, Castañeda studied at the College of San Carlos, became a Franciscan friar, and was ordained a priest in 1800. He taught moral theology for three years and staunchly supported the May Revolution of 1810. He was a firm advocate of public education and in 1815 founded a school of design and drawing. In the same year he became the superior of the Franciscans.

Castañeda opposed Bernardino RIVADAVIA's anticlerical measures (e.g. abolishing tithes, prohibiting persons under twenty-five from entering monastic life, and limiting the number of monks that could reside in monasteries), for which he was banished from Buenos Aires (1821–1823). He wrote prolifically and energetically against Rivadavia's reforms, characterizing his rule as "insane, heretical, immoral, and despotic." Among his publications are *La verdad desnuda* (1822), *Derecho del hombre,* and *Buenos Aires cautiva.* He founded schools for Indians of Paraná and San José de Feliciano. Castañeda died in Paraná.

– NICHOLAS P. CUSHNER

CASTAÑEDA CASTRO, SALVADOR

Salvador Castañeda Castro (*b.* 6 August 1888; *d.* 5 March 1965), general and president of El Salvador (1945–1948). Born in Chalchuapa to a well-connected family, Salvador Castañeda Castro received his education under the Chilean mission to El Salvador and had attained the position of lieutenant by age eighteen. He rose quickly through the ranks and served in a variety of political positions after 1931, the most important being director of the military school, minister of the interior under General Maximiliano HERNÁNDEZ MARTÍNEZ, and governor of various departments. Following the overthrow of Hernández Martínez in 1944, General Castañeda Castro ran unopposed in a presidential election marred by violence and intimidation. His victory represented the supremacy of the army's old guard and a return to *martinista*-style politics without Martínez. In December 1945 a group led by the aged liberal Miguel Tomás Molina invaded El Salvador from Guatemala, but the expected military rebellion against Castañeda Castro never materialized. Less than a year later, popular discontent manifested itself in the general strike of October 1946, which was effectively repressed.

Among the major events of Castañeda's presidency were visits by Chilean and French missions in 1945, the creation of a national tourism commission, and the dedication of both a major thoroughfare in San Salvador and the Pan-American Highway to Franklin Delano Roosevelt. During his administration, Castañeda brought the control of notaries under the direction of the Supreme Court and passed a so-called law of social majority designed to tighten the government's control over the population. His most significant undertaking, however, was the passage in 1945 of a new, regressive constitution that alienated even the younger cadres within the military. The latter, led by Colonel Oscar

---

During his administration, Castañeda passed a so-called law of social majority designed to tighten the El Salvadorean government's control over the population.

OSORIO, overthrew Castañeda in 1948 when it became clear he would seek to extend his rule through a second term. Castañeda continued to reside in San Salvador until his death.

– KAREN RACINE

CASTELLANOS, AARÓN GONZÁLEZ

Aarón González Castellanos (*b.* 8 August 1800; *d.* 1 April 1880), commonly regarded as the greatest promoter of agricultural colonization of nineteenth-century Argentina. Born in the city of Salta, as a young man he joined the cavalry forces led by a regional caudillo named Martín Güemes, who fought against the Spanish. After the conclusion of the wars of independence, he went to Peru, where he engaged in trade in the mining center of Cerro de Pasco. Subsequently he became involved in an ambitious colonization scheme on the Río Bermejo but was persecuted by Paraguayan dictator José FRANCIA, who held him prisoner from 1825 to 1830. Later Castellanos established himself in Buenos Aires Province, where he raised cattle. In the late 1830s he sold his properties and went to Paris, where he became known for writing several descriptive publications on Argentina. Castellanos returned to Argentina in 1853 and convinced the provincial government of Santa Fe to support his colonization scheme in the Chaco region. He helped finance the emigration of 200 families of agricultural workers from Dunkirk and Antwerp, then founded the agricultural colony of Esperanza in Santa Fe, which is still a prosperous grain-producing town. Castellanos also promoted the construction of docks in the port of Rosario and served in the municipal government of that city.

– CARLOS MARICHAL

CASTELLANOS, GONZALO

Gonzalo Castellanos (*b.* 1926) Venezuelan composer and conductor. Born in Caracas to a musical family,

Castellanos studied piano and organ with his father before apprenticing with the great Vicente Emilio Sojo at the National Modern School. This institution and its graduates initiated a new movement in Venezuelan music that was based on a postimpressionist aesthetic. Castellanos traveled to Paris, where he was active in the Schola Cantorum, and later received training from the European pianist Sergiu Celibidache. Upon his return to Venezuela, Castellanos conducted the Venezuela Symphony Orchestra and served at the collegium of the Museum of Caracas. Among his most famous pieces are *Suite caraqueña, Symphonic Fantasy,* and *Andelación e imitación fugaz.*

– KAREN RACINE

CASTELLANOS, JUAN DE

Juan de Castellanos (*b.* 9 March 1522; *d.* 27 November 1607), Spanish poet-chronicler, soldier, and priest. Born to farmers in Alanís (Seville province), Spain, as a teenager with some command of Latin, Castellanos went to Puerto Rico, where he continued his studies. In 1540, he traveled to Cubagua, an island off the Venezuelan coast, to work as a pearl fisherman, then joined the army and traveled to New Granada and Venezuela (1541–1545). From 1545 to 1554 he campaigned in the Bogotá and Pamplona regions, before being ordained a Roman Catholic priest in Cartagena (ca. 1554). Castellanos was curate and diocesan treasurer of Cartagena from 1557 to 1558, when he became curate of Riohacha, a position he served in until 1560. He moved to Tunja, in the highlands, as an assistant curate sometime after 1561; in 1568 he became curate. In Tunja, Castellanos devoted much of his time to writing. His *Elegías y elogios de varones ilustres de Indias* was composed between 1570 and 1590. Its nearly 114,000 verses narrate the discovery, conquest, and settlement of Spanish America, especially New Granada and Venezuela.

– J. LEÓN HELGUERA

CASTELLANOS, ROSARIO

Rosario Castellanos (*b.* 25 May 1925; *d.* 7 August 1974), Mexican author and diplomat. Born in Mexico City, Castellanos spent her youth in the state of Chiapas, a region with a high concentration of Indians and a history of conflict between the Tzotzil Indians and the wealthy landowners. In two prize-winning novels, *Balún-Canan* (1957; *The Nine Guardians,* 1960) and *Oficio de Tinieblas* (1962), and in the short stories of *Ciudad Real* (1960), Castellanos depicted the psychology and cosmology of the Chiapas Indians without romanticizing or stereotyping her characters, a marked departure from earlier "indigenist" writers.

Castellanos, educated at the National Autonomous University and in Madrid, also pioneered new territory in her exploration of gender relations. Her published master's thesis, *Sobre cultura femenina* (1950), provided the intellectual underpinnings for the contemporary women's movement in Mexico. Her essays, published regularly in Mexican periodicals and compiled in collections such as *Juicios sumarios* (1966) and *Mujer que sabe latín* (1973), as well as her dramatic works, particularly *El eterno femenino* (1975), and some thirteen volumes of poetry, often probed issues relating to the place of women in Mexican culture and history.

Castellanos was also a teacher and diplomat. She taught Latin American literature in Mexico, the United States, and Israel. From 1971 until her accidental death in 1974, she was Mexico's ambassador to Israel.

– VIRGINIA M. BOUVIER

CASTELLI, JUAN JOSÉ

Juan José Castelli (*b.* 19 July 1764; *d.* 12 October 1812), Argentine independence leader. The son of an Italian father and Spanish mother, Castelli was born in Buenos Aires and studied law at the University of Chuquisaca in Upper Peru (modern Bolivia). He practiced in Buenos Aires, where, along with his cousin Manuel BELGRANO and other creoles who had absorbed Enlightenment ideas, he worked to promote liberal reforms.

In 1810 Castelli took an active part in the May Revolution and was one of the secretaries of the revolutionary junta. That same year the junta sent him to accompany an expeditionary force to Upper Peru, where he proposed the elimination of monastic houses and other radical religious innovations, while also seeking to enlist the Indian population in the struggle. When Upper Peru was lost in mid-1811, Castelli's rivals sought to make him a scapegoat; he stood trial in Buenos Aires, but before a verdict could be handed down he died of cancer.

– DAVID BUSHNELL

CASTELLO BRANCO, HUMBERTO DE ALENCAR

Humberto de Alencar Castello Branco (*b.* 20 September 1900; *d.* 18 July 1967), president of Brazil (1964–1967). A *nordestino* (northeasterner) from Fortaleza, Castello Branco was born of a long line of military officers. After studying at the Military Preparatory School of Rio Prado in Rio Grande do Sul from 1912 to 1917,

he enrolled as a cadet in the Realengo Military Academy in Rio de Janeiro. Commissioned into the army in 1921, he married Argentina Vianna the next year. Devout Catholics, the couple formed a close union until her death in 1963.

As a young lieutenant devoted to professionalism and the rule of law, Castello Branco declined to participate in the various military uprisings of the 1920s. Instead he fought against the Luís Carlos PRESTES COLUMN in Mato Grosso and Bahia and remained loyal to the government during the Revolution of 1930.

Castello Branco was promoted to captain in 1932, and then named assistant director at Realengo, where he had previously served as an instructor. He was also attached to the French military mission. Subsequently he was sent to Paris to attend the Superior War College, which enhanced his academic reputation.

In 1940 Castello Branco, now a major, was posted to assist the minister of war, Eurico G. DUTRA, who later became president (1946–1951). In preparation for dispatching the Brazilian Expeditionary Force (FEB), Castello Branco was enrolled in the U.S. Army Command and General Staff College at Fort Leavenworth, Kansas, in 1943. As a lieutenant colonel he embarked the next year for Italy, where he was chief of operations (G-3) of the Brazilian Expeditionary Force. After advancing to colonel in 1945 for his effectiveness during that campaign, he returned to Brazil, where he alternated between general staff and field assignments. In 1952 he was named brigadier general and assumed command of the Tenth Military Region (Ceará). In 1954 he signed the General's Manifesto of 23 August calling for the resignation of President Getúlio VARGAS.

After commanding the army's general staff college in 1954–1955, Castello Branco moved on to the Escola Superior da Guerra (ESG), Brazil's Superior War College, as assistant commandant and director of the armed forces and command course in 1956–1958. As general of division he was transferred in 1958–1960 to head the Amazonia and Eighth Military Region headquartered in Belém, Pará, and went on to assume the directorship of army instruction, which allowed him to remain in close contact with the war college.

The ascension to the presidency of reformist Jânio da Silva QUADROS in 1961 and his subsequent resignation and replacement by populist João GOULART provoked a crisis in the officer corps that polarized into legalist and hard-line factions. In spite of Goulart's pro-Castro stance, nonaligned foreign policy, counterproductive economic policies, and support for a radical syndicalist republic, Castello Branco remained a legalist until early 1964.

Humberto de Alencar Castello Branco reviewing troops in 1965. (Iconographia)

Named a four-star general and posted to command the Fourth Army at Recife in 1962, Castello Branco found the Northeast unsettled by Peasant League–provoked turmoil, fomented, he believed, by Pernambuco governor Miguel ARRAES and President Goulart's brother-in-law, Leonel BRIZOLA, leader of one of the socialist parties. Once elevated to army chief of staff in mid-1963, Castello Branco sought to persuade President Goulart to abandon certain of his allegedly unconstitutional actions. Failing to do so, he agreed, in the name of legality, to head a long-prepared military-civilian conspiracy to oust the chief executive.

A well-planned coup led by the army, state governors, and opposition congressmen came off easily, with little loss of life on 31 March 1964. Discussions among the various governors, congressmen, business leaders, politicians, and high-ranking military men resulted in Castello Branco's selection as president. On 11 April 1964, by a wide margin the congress confirmed him as president to complete the remaining two years of Goulart's term. While pledging to respect the Constitution of

1946, Castello Branco appointed coconspirator General Artur da COSTA E SILVA as war minister.

The new chief executive hoped to turn this joint military-civilian coup into a revolution dedicated to controlling inflation, containing Communism, fomenting economic development, and promoting political, social, and educational reform. A team player, Castello Branco selected Roberto CAMPOS as minister of finance and Octavio Bulhões as minister of planning. Together they instituted an indexation system to neutralize economic distortions caused by a high rate of inflation, as well as a tax-reform structure that forced firms and individuals to adopt realistic accounting methods.

A long-term economic policy that endured for some fifteen years was launched under Castello Branco, who sought to promote capital formation, expand the market for durable consumer goods, reduce wages, foster industrial exports, and stimulate foreign capital investment. This growth strategy, however, was designed to perpetuate the country's basic economic and social structure, thereby permitting the traditional agricultural elite to support the regime while the industrial sector expanded. Hence, the nation's potential was developed while its agricultural and industrial sectors retained control. Because foreign as well as domestic stability was deemed essential to development, Brazil avoided being drawn into conflict with the United States, the dominant power in the hemisphere, and sought to associate itself with the United States in global affairs. The latter in turn reciprocated with generous financial aid and investment.

The Castello Branco regime further insured internal order by a series of measures known as Institutional Acts. The first, promoted by the hard-liners and enacted on 9 April 1964, actually prior to Castello Branco's inauguration, sought to purify the government. Three former presidents—Jânio da Silva Quadros, João Goulart, and Juscelino KUBITSCHEK DE OLIVEIRA—as well as seventy others were stripped of their political rights. In addition, the granting of tenure to civil servants was suspended for six months and military police courts, called IPMs, were established to investigate subversion.

The Second Institutional Act, effective 27 October 1965, was provoked by the reaction of hard-liners to state elections that went against the regime. Under this act all political parties were dissolved, indirect election of the president by congress was mandated, the government's right to dismiss civil servants was reinstated, citizens' political rights were canceled, and the Supreme Court was packed. The next month Brazil's political parties were re-formed. A government party, the National Renovating Alliance (Arena), and an opposition party, the Brazilian Democratic Movement (MDB), were established in congress.

Early in 1966, Castello Branco's presidential term was extended, against his wishes, for another year, to 15 March 1967. Protests against these measures then erupted, led by the National University Students Union and by certain socially sensitive Catholic clergy, notably Hélder CÁMARA, archbishop of Olinda and Recife.

Tensions increased as presidential candidates proliferated. Castello Branco favored a civilian successor. União Democrática Nacional leader Olavo BILAC PINTO, Senator Daniel Krieger of Rio Grande do Sul, and Foreign Minister Juracy Magalhães were his top choices. Nevertheless, the hard-liners prevailed. War Minister Costa e Silva, who was nominated and inaugurated on 15 March 1967, served as president until 1969.

In retirement, Castello Branco continued to exert a moderating influence on national affairs until his untimely death in an airplane accident.

— LEWIS A. TAMBS

CASTILHOS, JÚLIO DE

Júlio de Castilhos (*b.* 29 June 1860; *d.* 24 October 1903), Brazilian statesman and founder of the "positivist dictatorship" of Rio Grande do Sul. Born into a ranching family in the Serra region of Rio Grande, Castilhos graduated from the São Paulo Law School in 1882. As the director of the Riograndense Republican Party's newspaper *A Federação,* he agitated for a federal republican regime. Following the empire's collapse in 1889, he led the Riograndense delegation at the Constituent Assembly. After imposing an authoritarian state constitution, he was elected governor of Rio Grande do Sul in 1891, but was deposed for supporting President Marechal Deodoro da Fonseca's failed coup in which he closed Congress. In 1892 Castilhos engineered a countercoup and new election, provoking the Federalist Revolt (1893–1895), which claimed 10,000 casualties. He left office in 1898 but continued to rule through his highly disciplined Republican Party until his untimely death.

The *castilhista* Constitution, inspired by Auguste Comte, remained in effect till 1930 (though modified in 1923). It limited the legislature to budgetary matters, gave the governor decree power on all other issues, and allowed him to serve indefinitely. Despite his authoritarianism, Castilhos's policies on land taxation, public education, and secularization were progressive.

Castilhos's successor in 1898, Antônio BORGES DE MEDEIROS, used the *castilhista* regime to rule the state from Castilhos's death until 1930, serving as governor most of the time.

— JOSEPH L. LOVE

CASTILLA, RAMÓN

Ramón Castilla (*b.* 27 August 1797; *d.* 25 May 1867), military officer and twice president of Peru (1845–1851, 1855–1862), he contributed to the formation of the Peruvian republican state during the nineteenth-century struggle by military strongmen (*caudillos*) after independence from Spain. His efforts were aided considerably by the dawn of the Guano Age, which brought considerable income from export activities to the Peruvian state.

Castilla was born in Tarapacá. During his early military career he was trained by the Spanish colonial army and fought against the forces of independence led by the Argentine general José de SAN MARTÍN in Chacabuco, Chile (1817). Taken prisoner, he escaped to Brazil and then in 1818 to Peru. Castilla switched allegiances only in 1822, when he offered his military services to General San Martín in southern Peru. He fought in the army of Simón BOLÍVAR against the Spanish army in the decisive battle of Ayacucho (1824), which guaranteed Peruvian independence.

After independence in 1825, Castilla was named subprefect of his native province of Tarapacá. He started his career as a rather conservative and creole-patriotic military caudillo by opposing Bolívar's constitutional designs. In 1829, Castilla rejected General Andrés de SANTA CRUZ's liberal leanings, instead supporting the protectionist and conservative General Agustín GAMARRA. In 1833, Castilla fell from grace with Gamarra and transferred his support to generals Luis José de ORBEGOSO and Felipe Santiago SALAVERRY. When Santa Cruz seized power in 1836 for the second time, Castilla traveled to Chile and once again joined Gamarra in a successful Chilean military expedition against Santa Cruz's Peru-Bolivia Confederation. During Gamarra's second administration (1839–1841) Castilla was appointed minister of the treasury and in that capacity arranged the first guano export contracts with native businessman Francisco Quirós. In 1841, Castilla was taken prisoner at Ingaví, Gamarra's failed last adventure against Bolivian forces. Soon, however, Castilla was politically active again in Cuzco.

By 1845, Castilla had surfaced as supreme chief from the complex caudillo struggles that pitted Generals Juan Crisóstomo Torrico, Francisco Vidal, and Manuel Ignacio VIVANCO against each other. During Castilla's first administration his most important measure was the introduction of the first national budget. New contracts for guano marketing abroad were signed with local and foreign merchants. Eventually the British firm Antony GIBBS Y CÍA assumed the distribution of guano to Great Britain and the French firm Montané the distribution to France. Consequently, transportation began to improve (steamship lines, the first railway between Lima and Callao in 1851), and state finances, military facilities, and payroll became organized. Most important, Castilla regularized the service of the internal and external debts, introducing in 1850 the Law of Consolidation (amortization and repayment) of the floating national debt.

Castilla saw in General José Rufino ECHENIQUE a deserving successor and peacefully handed power to him in 1851. However, Echenique's supporters manipulated the consolidation of the internal debt to their own advantage through corrupt means. Politically, the archconservative Echenique began to drift away from Castilla's watchful eye. Sensing growing popular opposition, Castilla decided to lead a motley group of liberals and radicals who fought Echenique in a civil war (1854 1855). To obtain support, Castilla followed the advice of liberals Pedro Gálvez and Manuel Toribio Ureta and abolished slavery and the Indian tribute in 1854. Castilla regained power in 1855 after the battle of La Palma, in which Echenique was finally defeated.

During his second term of office, Castilla initially complied with the liberal faction that had supported him, pressing for the liberal constitution of 1856. However, after the defeat of the conservative reaction led by Vivanco in 1858, Castilla turned against his liberal supporters and promoted instead an executive-biased constitution that was enacted in 1860. His preoccupation with such constitutional matters earned him the name of "Soldier of the Law." A successful short war over boundaries with Ecuador in 1859 enhanced Castilla's conservative constitutionalist and nationalist stand.

At the end of his second term in 1862, Castilla once again peacefully handed power to elected General Miguel de San Román. However, San Román died in office and was succeeded by vice president Juan Antonio PEZET, who, like Echenique before him, disregarded the influential Castilla. The unpopular Pezet was deposed as a result of the nationalist movement led by Colonel Mariano Ignacio PRADO against the Spanish aggression of 1864–1866. Prado, however, was opposed by Castilla, who went into exile in Chile to organize yet another revolution. Castilla died in Tivilichi.

– ALFONSO W. QUIROZ

CASTILLO, JESÚS

Jesús Castillo (*b.* 9 September 1877; *d.* 23 April 1946), Guatemalan composer and student of native Indian music. Castillo was born in San Juan Ostuncalco, near Quezaltenango in the western highlands of Guatemala. As a young man he became interested in traditional Indian music. He composed his "First Indian Overture" based on the Dance of the Little Bulls, a traditional

dance at fiestas. Traveling from village to village in the highlands, he collected data about the music of the different Indian groups. Castillo used themes and melodies

---

Traveling from village to village in the Central American highlands, Castillo collected data about the music of the different Indian groups.

---

in a classical tradition to compose his symphonic poems, suites, operas, and ballets. He became a leading authority on Indian music and instruments. His writings include *La música Maya-Quiché* (1941) and *Legado folklórico a la juventud guatemalteca* (1944). He died in Quezaltenango.

– DAVID L. JICKLING

CASTILLO, OTTO RENÉ

Otto René Castillo (*b.* 1937; *d.* 19 March 1967), Guatemalan poet. He is the best known of Guatemalan contemporary poets because of his revolutionary militancy and his heroic death. Castillo is one of the "guerrilla poets" who flourished throughout the continent during the 1960s, and is the author of Guatemala's best-known contemporary poem, "Vámonos patria a caminar" ("Let's start walking").

Castillo was born in Quezaltenango, Guatemala's second city. He was a student organizer and led the Association of High School Students. As a result, when the country was invaded in 1954, he was exiled to El Salvador. In 1955 he shared the Premio Centroamericano de Poesía with the Salvadoran poet Roque DALTON. He returned to Guatemala in 1957 and enrolled at the University of San Carlos. In 1959 he left for East Germany, where he studied literature at the University of Leipzig. In the early 1960s he trained as a filmmaker with the well-known Dutch documentary directory Joris Ivens. Castillo returned to Guatemala in 1966 and joined the ranks of the Rebel Armed Forces (FAR). In March 1967, after eating nothing but roots for fifteen days, his guerrilla group was ambushed and captured. Four days of torture ensued, after which Castillo was burned to death. His books are *Vámonos patria a caminar* (1965), *Informe de una injusticia* (1975), and *Sabor de luto* (1976).

– ARTURO ARIAS

CASTILLO, RAMÓN S.

Ramón S. Castillo (*b.* 1871; *d.* 1944), president of Argentina (1942–1943). Born in Catamarca, Castillo was a wealthy landowner, a conservative politician, and a jurist, who served as a criminal judge (1895) and a commercial judge (1905) of the province of Buenos Aires. He was a justice of the criminal court (1910); dean of several law faculties (1923–1928); a member of the Constituent Convention in 1931; senator from Catamarca (1932–1935); minister of justice and public instruction in 1936; minister of the interior (1936–1937); and vice president under President Roberto M. ORTIZ in 1938. Castillo became acting president in 1940 upon the incapacitation of Ortiz, and president when Ortiz resigned in June 1942. During his controversial presidency, Castillo was supported by corrupt members of the oligarchy, disgruntled intellectuals, pro-Fascist elements, and pro-Axis military. While insisting on diplomatic ties with the Axis at the Rio Conference of January 1942 and suppressing pro-Allied demonstrations, he emphasized that the United States would continue to be considered a nonbelligerent. This policy, an attempt to receive military assistance from either side, was not successful. Apprehension about his chosen successor, a wealthy rancher, opposition by pro-Allied and pro-Axis elements, and his inability to secure arms for the military resulted in Castillo's overthrow on 4 June 1943 by General Arturo Rawson, who was replaced three days later by Castillo's minister of war and a member of the right-wing Group of United Officers (GOU), General Pedro Pablo RAMÍREZ.

– CHRISTEL K. CONVERSE

CASTILLO ARMAS, CARLOS

Carlos Castillo Armas (*b.* 4 November 1914; *d.* 26 July 1957), president of Guatemala (1954–1957). Born into a provincial Ladino family in the department of Escuintla, Castillo Armas pursued a military career, rising to the rank of colonel and director of the national military academy in 1947.

Obsessed by the July 1949 assassination of army chief and presidential candidate Colonel Francisco Javier ARANA (an act he attributed to Arana's political rival, Lieutenant Colonel Jacobo ARBENZ, who was elected president in November 1950), Castillo Armas launched a five-year rebellion against the Arbenz regime. In November 1949 he led an abortive attack on a Guatemala City military base. He was shot, but he revived while being taken to the cemetery. Sentenced to death, he tunneled out of the Central Penitentiary in June 1951 and took refuge in the Colombian embassy, which granted him political asylum. From Colombia he moved to Honduras, where, with a number of other Guatemalan political dissidents, he launched the National Liberation Movement. Supported by the Central

Intelligence Agency (CIA), this offensive succeeded in overthrowing Arbenz on 2 July 1954 and established Castillo Armas as leader of a five-man governing junta set up in San Salvador under the auspices of U.S. Ambassador John Peurifoy. On 10 October 1954 Castillo Armas was elected president in an unopposed plebescite.

The presidency of Carlos Castillo Armas followed three broad interrelated policies: the dismantling of most of the governmental programs and institutions established by the Cerezo ARÉVALO and Arbenz regimes during the so-called revolutionary decade (1944–1954); a socioeconomic strategy that can be termed "conservative modernization"; and close cooperation with the United States. The "liberationist" regime banned all existing political parties, labor federations, and peasant organizations; disenfranchised three-quarters of the electorate by excluding illiterates; annulled the Arbenz agrarian reform law; and restored the right of the Roman Catholic Church to own property and conduct religious instruction in the public schools.

Seeking to become a "showcase of capitalist development," the regime encouraged foreign investment by granting tax concessions and by repealing laws restricting foreign oil exploration and investments in public utilities. It secured substantial loans and credits from the United States for road building and beef and cotton production. It also sought to stimulate internal investment by maintaining low taxes and wage rates.

The July 1957 assassination of President Castillo Armas by one of his personal bodyguards in the National Palace has been attributed to a power struggle in his political party, the National Democratic Movement.

– ROLAND H. EBEL

CASTILLO LEDÓN, AMALIA

Amalia Castillo Ledón (*b.* 18 August 1902; *d.* 3 June 1986), prominent early feminist in Mexico. A native of San Jerónimo, Tamaulipas, and daughter of a schoolteacher, Castillo Ledón completed graduate studies in the humanities at the National University. After her marriage to the prominent historian Luis Castillo Ledón, she established herself as an early feminist in United Nations and Mexican organizations. She served as president of the Inter-American Commission of Women in 1949, and in 1953 she addressed the Mexican Senate on women's suffrage, the first woman to do so. The first female Mexican diplomat, she was minister plenipotentiary to Sweden (1953), Finland (1956), and Switzerland (1959). She was the first woman to serve as undersecretary of education (1958–1964).

– RODERIC AI CAMP

Castro, José Gil de

CASTILLO Y GUEVARA, FRANCISCA JOSEFA DE LA CONCEPCIÓN DE

Francisca Josefa de la Concepción de Castillo y Guevara (*b.* 6 October 1671; *d.* 1742), Colombian nun and author. The daughter of a Spanish official, Francisca Josefa was born in Tunja and entered the convent of Saint Clare in 1689. She remained there until her death, holding various offices in the community, including that of abbess.

Madre Francisca is remembered for two literary works, which she undertook upon the advice of her confessor. The first of these is her autobiography, known as the *Vida,* which was published in 1817. In this work she recounts her physical and spiritual travails, including her conflicts with fellow nuns and her visions of Jesus Christ, the Virgin Mary, and others. The second is the *Afectos espirituales,* also known as *Sentimientos espirituales,* which was published in 1843. The *Afectos* consists of 195 meditations on religious themes that express her longing for union with God. Because of their clear, forceful style and their spirituality, Madre Francisca's writings are often compared to those of other mystics, notably Saint Teresa of Avila.

– HELEN DELPAR

CASTRO, CIPRIANO

Cipriano Castro (*b.* 12 October 1858; *d.* 4 December 1924), president of Venezuela (1899–1908). Born and raised in Capucho, Táchira, Castro attended schools in Colombia. During the 1880s and 1890s he brought Colombian liberalism to his native Venezuela when he participated in Tachiran politics.

In 1899, Castro launched his Revolution of Liberal Restoration against the government of President Ignacio Andrade, whom he defeated in a campaign that lasted from 23 May to 22 October. He established a coalition government that even included some of the Caracas liberals whom he had overthrown. Basically, Castro attempted to continue the process of centralization begun by Antonio GUZMÁN BLANCO, but financial problems and a series of major conflicts with foreign powers restricted his government. His personal behavior further inhibited his effectiveness as a national leader.

During his reign, Castro adopted a highly nationalistic policy. In 1902, his belligerence led to a blockade of Venezuela by European powers. The intervention of the United States eventually ended the blockade, but Castro remained hostile to foreign governments, including that of the United States. In retaliation for the blockade, Castro closed most Venezuelan ports to trade from the Antilles and imposed a 30-percent surcharge on all goods shipped from the British West Indies.

As a dictator, Castro faced a number of revolts, most notably those led by Manuel Antonio Matos (1902–1903), José Manuel "El Mocho" HERNÁNDEZ (1900), and Antonio Paredes (1907). Over 12,000 died in the fighting. These struggles, and the nation's fiscal difficulties, meant that Castro accomplished very little in the way of reform. He enriched friends and allies through monopoly concessions but did little to improve the nation's transportation, sanitation, or education facilities.

Castro enriched friends and allies through monopoly concessions but did little to improve the nation's transportation, sanitation, or education facilities.

In December 1908, Castro left Venezuela to seek medical treatment in Europe for a urinary tract infection caused by his heavy drinking, use of aphrodisiacs, and venereal disease. Upon his departure, Juan Vicente GÓMEZ seized power. Castro died in exile in Puerto Rico.

– WINTHROP R. WRIGHT

CASTRO, JOSÉ GIL DE

José Gil de Castro (*b.* ca. 1785; *d.* ca. 1841), Peruvian artist and cartographer. Known as "El Mulato Gil," he was first to paint portraits of the heroes of the South American Wars of Independence. Born in Lima under Spanish viceroyal rule, he probably apprenticed with a master of the old colonial school. His *Portrait of Fernando VII* (1812) was influenced by Francisco de Goya. He accompanied Bernardo O'HIGGINS in his military campaign for Chilean independence. In Santiago he executed several portraits, including those of General José de SAN MARTÍN, O'Higgins, and their military collaborators. O'Higgins appointed him captain of the engineering corps of the revolutionary army for his expertise in engineering and cartography.

Gil de Castro returned to Peru via Argentina with San Martín's troops and in 1822 was named chamber painter of the Peruvian state. He became the Peruvian aristocracy's favorite portrait painter. In his several portraits of Simón BOLÍVAR, Gil de Castro displayed his fascination with military regalia. His portrayal of sitters in frontal and full-length images recall votive paintings. Craftsmanship, absence of perspective, and the incorporation of inscriptions into framed plaques in his paintings relate Gil de Castro to colonial painting traditions. A provincial neoclassicist, he was the first representative in Latin America of an independent and naive pictorial school.

— MARTA GARSD

CASTRO, JUAN JOSÉ

Juan José Castro (*b.* 7 March 1895; *d.* 5 September 1968), Argentine composer and conductor. Born in Avellaneda, Buenos Aires Province, Castro began his musical education in Buenos Aires, studying piano and violin under Manuel Posadas, harmony under Constantino Gaito, and fugue and composition under Eduardo Fornarini. As a winner of the Europa Grand Prize, he went to Paris to study composition with Vincent D'Indy at the Schola Cantorum, attending Edouard Risler's piano classes. Returning to Buenos Aires, he founded the Sociedad del Cuarteto in 1926 and performed there as first violin; two years later he started a conducting career with Orquesta Renacimiento. Castro was appointed conductor of the ballet season at the Teatro Colón in 1930 and traveled abroad conducting that ensemble. In 1933 he was named director of the Colón.

Parallel with extensive tours as principal conductor of several Latin American orchestras, Castro began a productive career in composition as a founder-member of the Grupo Renovación; nevertheless, his music was individualistic and he remained independent of group theories. His works exhibit three influences: nationalism, Spanish subject matter, and a free cosmopolitan style, the latter a product of his Parisian years. The last quality applies to the color and sonority of his orchestral works, in which he achieved a sort of American impressionism. He became internationally known when Ernest Ansermet conducted the award-winning *Allegro Lento e Vivace* (1930) at the International Society of Contemporary Music (ISCM) Festival. Among Castro's five stage works there are two operas after Federico García Lorca: *La zapatera prodigiosa* (1943), first performed in Montevideo in 1949, and *Bodas de sangre* (1953), which premiered at the Teatro Colón in 1956. *Proserpina y el extranjero,* a three-act opera, first performed at Milan's La Scala, was the recipient of the first International Verdi Prize in 1951. Among his orchestral pieces is *Corales criollos* No. 3, a first prize winner at the Caracas Interamerican Music Festival (1954). As a teacher, Castro was appointed by Pablo Casals as dean of studies and professor at the National Conservatory in San Juan, Puerto Rico, from 1959 to 1964.

— SUSANA SALGADO

CASTRO, JULIÁN

Julián Castro (*b.* 1815; *d.* 1875), provisional president of Venezuela from March 1858 to August 1859, during which time the Constitutional Convention of Valencia created the Constitution of 1858. Castro began his career as an officer in the republican army of Venezuela. As a captain he participated in the Revolution of the Reforms in 1835–1836. He joined the Liberal Party at its inception in 1840. Before being chosen as provisional president of the nation, he was governor of the province of Carabobo.

Castro assumed office on 18 March 1858 as the titular head of a coalition of Conservatives and dissident Liberals who conspired to overthrow President José Tadeo MONAGAS. His "gobierno de fusión" was doomed from the start. The only goal the Conservatives and Liberals shared was their desire to remove Monagas from office. Both groups jockeyed for Castro's approval. The Conservatives quickly alienated the Liberals by pushing through Congress a bill making government employees responsible for past embezzlements. The Castro government's refusal to free Monagas and other prominent Liberals who had sought refuge in the French embassy resulted in a blockade of Venezuela's two major ports by the French and British in 1858. Castro's attempts to placate rebellious Liberals through concessions, along with the fact that his government was weak and unpopular, led to the Federal War, a civil war that lasted from 1859 to 1864.

On 1 August 1859, Castro was overthrown by a Conservative-led coup known as the Federalist Revolution. He was imprisoned by government troops, then tried and convicted for treason but later absolved. He completed his career as a general in the Liberal armies of Antonio GUZMÁN BLANCO.

— DAVID CAREY, JR.

CASTRO, RICARDO

Ricardo Castro (*b.* 7 February 1864; *d.* 20 November 1907), Mexican pianist and composer. Castro was the leading piano virtuoso in Mexico when that tradition was in full flower at the end of the nineteenth century. After study and a debut in Europe, where his music and his pianistic prowess gained immediate success, he returned to Mexico, propagating a European style marked by his own formidable technique and clarity of expression. His orchestral works (two symphonies and two concertos) and operatic music (*La Légende de Rudel,* 1906) were favorably accepted in his own epoch but have not had the enduring appeal of his works for solo piano.

— ROBERT L. PARKER

CASTRO ALVES, ANTÔNIO DE

Antônio de Castro Alves (*b.* 14 March 1847; *d.* 6 July 1871), Brazilian poet. Castro Alves was the last and the greatest Brazilian romantic poet. He is also remembered as a playwright and an orator. Born on a large plantation in Bahia into a family of slave owners, he developed a passionate opposition to slavery; he is called "the poet of the slaves." Castro Alves is also known as the leader of the *condoreiros* (condor poets), who used the condor, strong and high flying, as their symbol. Their poetry is marked by ardent sentiment and grandiloquence, abounding in daring figures of speech.

Castro Alves led a tragic life. When very young, he fell in love with an actress, Eugênia Câmara. They had an amorous liaison, but after two years Eugênia left him. His mother's early death, the insanity and suicide of his brother, and the amputation of his foot after an accident deeply affected the poet. At sixteen he contracted tuberculosis, which killed him at the age of twenty-four. He loved life and did not want to die: "To die . . . when this world is a paradise," he wrote in "Mocidade e morte" (Youth and Death), which appeared in the collection *Espumas flutuantes* (Floating Foam, 1870). "Mocidade e morte" was written during a critical point in his illness, and it marks the beginning of his great art. Grief awoke in him the supreme accents that he later would extend to the sufferings of humanity.

Castro Alves became known through poems appearing in periodicals and recited at meetings. During his lifetime only one volume of his poetry was published, *Espumas flutuantes,* a collection of erotic, patriotic, and plaintive lyric verses. His antislavery poems appeared posthumously in *A cachoeira de Paulo Afonso* (The Waterfalls of Paulo Afonso, 1876) and *Os escravos* (The Slaves, 1883). The latter contains some of his most celebrated poems, such as "Vozes d'áfrica" (Voices of Africa), an oration from Africa imploring God's justice, and "O navio negreiro" (The Slave Ship), a dramatic composition picturing all the horrors of an African slaver. Additional works include *Obra completa* (1960) and *Gonzaga ou a revolução de Minas* (Gonzaga or the Revolution in Minas, 1875).

— MARIA ISABEL ABREU

CASTRO JIJÓN, RAMÓN

Ramón Castro Jijón (*b.* 1915), representative of the navy in the military junta that ruled Ecuador from 11 July 1963 until 1966. Born in Esmeraldas, Castro Jijón received advanced military training in Chile and the United States. He served as a naval attaché in Western Europe. When the military overthrew the government of Carlos Julio AROSEMENA MONROY, Commander Castro was the only member of the junta from the coast. The movement that overthrew Arosemena's government was the first institutional intrusion of the military into politics since the coup of 23 October 1937.

After suppressing Ecuador's leftist critics, the junta began to implement a program of structural reforms, including agrarian and tax reforms.

The junta, which had wide public support during its first year, announced that the armed forces had the responsibility to promote new socioeconomic structures that would provide a foundation for true democracy. After suppressing leftist critics and purging the government of Arosemena supporters, the junta began to implement a program of structural reforms, including agrarian and tax reforms, which quickly alienated important civilian groups. The junta created a personal income tax; rationalized taxation by suppressing hundreds of levies that directly financed public agencies and autonomous institutions; and transferred revenue collection from autonomous agencies to the Central Bank. The latter measure prompted widespread public criticism, against which the junta retaliated by imposing martial law. The Agrarian Reform Law of 11 July 1964, which abolished the huasipungo labor system, and the establishment of maximum limits for the size of landholdings, sought to redress one of the most unequal distributions of land in South America. Although the law was relatively weak and threatened only the most inefficient producers, its passage galvanized sierra elite opposition to the junta.

When the economy began to falter in 1964, government deficits burgeoned. The junta sought to stabilize public finances by increasing import duties, but was forced to back down in the face of widespread public criticism, which culminated in a general strike in Guayaquil. When the junta again sought to increase import duties in early 1966, a second general strike spread throughout the nation and resulted in the resignation of the junta on 29 March 1966.

— LINDA ALEXANDER RODRÍGUEZ

CASTRO MADRIZ, JOSÉ MARÍA

José María Castro Madriz (*b.* 1818; *d.* 1871), president of Costa Rica (1847–1849, 1866–1868). Born in San José, Costa Rica, Castro Madriz studied law in León, Nicaragua. In 1848 he severed Costa Rica's ties with the United Provinces of Central America and declared the country's independence. As a result of strong political pressure, he was obliged to leave the presidency in 1849. When reelected in 1866, he supported improvements in the public education system, opened the bay of Limón to trade, and inaugurated Costa Rica's first telegraph. Overthrown in a military coup in 1868, Castro Madriz served as minister in subsequent governments. He was given the title Benemérito de la Patria (National Hero) and is called the founder of the republic.

— OSCAR PELÁEZ ALMENGOR

CASTRO POZO, HILDEBRANDO

Hildebrando Castro Pozo (*b.* 1890; *d.* 1 September 1945), Peruvian intellectual and writer from the northern border state of Piura. Castro Pozo first entered the national arena after he had already written strong essays on the misery and extreme poverty of sharecroppers on the coastal plantations. In 1920, President Augusto LEGUÍA named him to head the section on Indian affairs in the national Ministry of Development, a post he held until 1923. He then became one of the most articulate and forthright defenders of the rights of Indians in the country. Quickly parting with Leguía, he understood *indigenismo* through the spectacles of socialism; stressing that the exploitative, capitalist plantation agriculture of the coastal valleys of Peru could be ended only by the imposition of socialism. He felt further that the Indians, who had been communal village farmers since Incan times, would be the group in society most likely to carry out such a transformation. With landowners opposing him, he was sent into exile in 1923; he returned in 1924. His *Nuestra comunidad indígena* (1924) is a long essay on the naturally socialist character of indigenous village traditions. This and other writings influenced José Carlos MARIÁTEGUI, his contemporary among Peruvian *indigenistas* and the founder of the Socialist Party. A pragmatic leader, Castro Pozo encouraged party members to take positions in the government to help indigenous villagers. The Socialists hoped the government would introduce technological improvements into the villages, thereby better equipping them to compete with the big landowners. Two years after he died, the government passed a new, comprehensive sharecropping law.

— VINCENT PELOSO

CASTRO RUZ, FIDEL

Fidel Castro Ruz (*b.* 13 August 1926), Cuban revolutionary leader and premier (1959–1976), president, Council of State (since 1976). In 1956 Castro led a small band of revolutionaries in a landing in southeastern Cuba to amass popular support for the overthrow of dictator General Fulgencio BATISTA. Two years later, on New Year's Day 1959, Castro's army marched triumphantly into the Cuban capital of Havana and established a revolutionary regime.

Castro's life can be divided into two distinct periods: his early years as a revolutionary, when he risked all to overthrow the corrupt Batista; and the second, as master politician, successsfully playing off the world's superpowers against each other. This second phase is not over: as the de facto dictator of Cuba since 1959, Castro has shown a remarkable ability to challenge the might of the United States, and even that of his ally, the former Soviet Union, without losing his grip on political and economic control. Castro is one of those rare individuals who has proven to be both a brilliant revolutionary leader and a master politician.

EARLY LIFE. Castro was born in Oriente Province (home of the Grito de Yara, which signaled the beginning of the Ten Years' War of 1868–1878) in the district of Birán to an affluent landowning family. His father, Angel Castro, was a native of Galicia, Spain, while his mother, Lina Ruz Castro, was born in Cuba. Castro attended a Catholic boarding school in Santiago de Cuba and graduated from Belén College, Havana, also a Catholic school. He entered law school at the University of Havana in 1945 and began practicing in 1950. At the university Castro became involved with political factionalism of the campus and even shot a political opponent. In 1947 he took part in a plan to invade the Dominican Republic and overthrow the dictator Rafael TRUJILLO. The invasion was never carried out, however. The following year, 1948, Castro attended an anti-imperialist conference in Bogotá, Colombia, during which the Colombian populist Jorge GAITÁN was murdered and riots broke out. While there, Castro became embroiled in a battle between liberals and conservatives, siding with the liberals. He was arrested for trying to incite mutiny in a police barracks and was released and returned to Cuba only upon the intervention of the Cuban ambassador to Colombia on behalf of him and other students.

While Castro is most often identified with other Communist leaders of the twentieth century, it was anti-imperialist nationalism, not socialism, that served as the driving force of his younger years. His hero was José MARTÍ, not Lenin or Marx. As a student, Castro had amply opportunity to join the Cuban Communist party (Partido Socialista Popular—PSP) as his brother Raúl did, but Castro steered away from socialist politics in favor of the long-suppressed nationalism that influenced so many of Castro's generation. Since Cuba was first subjected to the open imperialism of Spanish rule, and later treated as little more than a colony of the United States, many Cubans had hoped to establish a nation free of the colonialism and neocolonialism under which it had labored for so long. Castro, one such Cuban nationalist, joined the reform-minded Orthodox Party in 1947, and ran for Congress in 1952. In the midst of the campaign, however, Batista headed a coup that suspended the elections and left him dictator of the island. This coup convinced Castro of the futility of trying to transform Cuba's government through legal means and converted him into a revolutionary.

Now firmly committed to a revolutionary course, Castro led a number of attempts that failed to overthrow the U.S.-backed Batista regime before leading his victorious forces into the capital city in 1959. Castro responded to the coup of 1952 by organizing a guerrilla organization to launch attacks against the Batista government. On 26 July 1953, Castro led an assault on the Moncada barracks in Santiago. While this attack was noted mostly for its sheer folly and was easily defeated, Castro nonetheless became a nationally known figure for his prominent role in it. Castro was captured and stood trial, which he skillfully used to his advantage. In his testimony defending the attack, Castro gave his famous "History Will Absolve Me" speech in which he listed, with unique flair, the corruption and shortcomings of the Batista regime as well as his own solutions to the problems besetting Cuba. His message was liberal nationalism, with its call for a democratic government, better education and health care, a more diversified economy, and an end to the overbearing influence of the United States in Cuba's politics and economy. Not only were socialists drawn into Castro's camp but also members of the Cuban middle class resentful of both the alliance of U.S. businesses with Cuba's elite and the uneven development of the Cuban economy.

Castro was jailed for his role in the attack and released as part of a general amnesty two years later.

Fidel Castro addressing cement factory workers, Santiago, Cuba. (© 1964, 1994 Lee Lockwood)

Rather than remaining in Cuba under the watchful eye of Batista's police, Castro went to Mexico to plot his next move. There he joined forces with Ernesto "Che" GUEVARA, an Argentine by birth and a doctor by training. The Argentine's anti-Yankee nationalism quickly led Guevara to embrace Communism after witnessing firsthand a U.S.-backed coup in Guatemala in 1954. Along with Guevara and Castro's brother Raúl, Fidel plotted a new attack on the island nation. On 2 December 1956, eighty-one guerrillas led by Castro landed on the southeastern coast of Cuba in the boat *Granma.* Most of the force was captured or killed, but Castro, Che, and Raúl survived. It was this small, poorly equipped army that would soon rally broad popular support among the Cuban people and overthrow Batista.

As Batista's army continually failed to capture Castro, his image among the Cuban people grew. Starting from his base in the mountains of eastern Cuba, Castro quickly made contact with other groups disillusioned with Batista's rule. While most observers, including most of the leaders of the PSP, were startled at Castro's success, he himself never doubted the eventual outcome of his struggle. On 1 January 1959, Castro's forces marched triumphantly into Havana just hours after Batista had fled Cuba.

HEAD OF STATE. Once in power, Castro gained world attention for taking a defiant stand against the United States. As head of the government, Castro made a commitment to nationalizing the Cuban economy, especially the sugar industry, as well as refusing to bow to U.S. economic and political pressures, which led to a quick cooling of U.S.-Cuban relations. At the same time, the Castro government turned increasingly toward the Soviet Union to counter U.S. pressure.

On 17 April 1961, U.S.-backed Cuban exiles launched an invasion at the Bay of Pigs on the southern coast of the island. The offensive, ill-conceived and poorly planned during the Eisenhower administration and carried out under the newly elected Kennedy administration, was a conclusive failure. The local police force and militia alone were sufficient to defeat the counterrevolutionaries, and Castro was hailed both at home and abroad as one of the few leaders capable of standing up to the North American giant. It was after the failed invasion, on 2 December 1961, that Castro publicly declared himself a Marxist, a conversion whose sincerity has since been the subject of much debate. The timing of his "conversion" does suggest, however, that Castro's move was more pragmatic than heartfelt. Whatever his motives, Castro was left with little alternative: the U.S. government, which was patently hostile

to his rule, would be satisfied only with the continuation of a Batista-style government sans Batista.

In October 1962, U.S. intelligence detected Soviet nuclear missiles on the island, and a tense period known as the Cuban Missile Crisis followed. For days it appeared that the United States and the Soviet Union were headed toward war, and while the world anxiously waited, Premier Nikita Khrushchev gave an eleventh-hour order to recall the Soviet missiles. This crisis sealed Cuba's fate. From the early 1960s to the present, Castro has led the country, with varied success, on the path of Soviet-style socialism. As had the socialists of Stalinist Russia, the Cuban government nationalized all economic endeavors, no matter how small, in an effort to centralize the economy and the distribution of resources. Absent from Castro's socialism was any hint of the independent workers', peasants', or soldiers' councils argued for by Lenin and the Bolsheviks. Following the model of China and the Soviet Union, all political activities, the press, and education were—and are—closely monitored by the state.

Between 1956 and 1965, when he formally became the head of the Cuban Communist Party, Castro maneuvered deftly around the various factions vying for power in revolutionary Cuba. During his march to power, Castro successfully had manipulated varied political groupings within Cuba to help achieve his revolutionary goal without relinquishing any real power. In April 1958 Castro at first supported a general strike planned by the urban wing of the underground Twenty-sixth of July Movement. This strike was opposed by the PSP and backed by the liberal wing of the movement. But later, when the strike proved unsuccessful, Castro opposed it. From that time forward, Castro was the undisputed leader of the movement to oust Batista. Not only did the failed strike discredit the liberals of the movement, but it also allowed Castro to absorb many PSP members into his twenty-sixth of July Movement. While Castro always mistrusted the party faithful, he nonetheless recognized that their commitment to rank-and-file organization and their well-organized party structure could be useful to his own aims. This would not be the last time Castro would successfully maneuver to exploit the well-organized strength of the PSP.

With the triumph of the revolution, Castro designated Manuel URRUTIA LLEÓ president of the country, a post Castro would take over himself once he had consolidated the necessary power. To do this, he turned again to the well-disciplined PSP, whose members he placed in key positions within the government. Resignations of liberals and moderates quickly followed, accompanied by pro forma protests that Cuba's government was turning too far to the left. But the wave of resignations and dismissals, and the arrest of the popular anti-Communist guerrilla commander Major Hubert Matos, only allowed Castro to consolidate further his political and economic power.

As supreme leader, Castro similarly balanced competing forces in order to maintain his uncontested rule. With the dismissal, exile, and execution of the liberals and moderates of the anti-Batista movement, Castro turned increasingly to his brother Raúl and the charismatic Che Guevara for support. Guevara in particular played a crucial role in government economic planning in the mid-1960s. But while Guevara's lasting contribution as a revolutionary is undeniable, his role as economic planner was largely a failure. Seeking to shift Cuba's traditional reliance away from sugar production, Guevara embarked on a disastrous plan of diversification. When it became clear that sugar was still the only Cuban product of significant value on the world market, he "recruited" armies of workers to get out the sugar harvest. Despite his call for Cubans to build a "new man" (one who would presumably work sixteen-hour days with no days of rest), the sugar harvest continued to falter because of poor economic planning. Yet Castro took little direct blame for the serious economic decline of the middle and late 1960s. Ever the populist caudillo, Castro succeeded in directing most of the responsibility toward Guevara, the unyielding government bureaucracy, and the United States. While events leading up to Guevara's departure are poorly documented and little discussed even today, it is clear that the two revolutionaries had a parting of the ways. Guevara left Cuba, to die in Bolivia in 1967.

Over the years, Castro has relied increasingly on individuals more noted for their loyalty and lack of imagination than their governmental and leadership skills. Second in power to Castro is his brother Raúl, who is general of the army, defense minister, and Fidel's designated successor and second secretary of the Communist Party. Another powerbroker in Castro's ruling circle is Osmani Cienfuegos Gorriarán, a stereotypical bureaucrat as colorless as he is loyal. Conversely, Fidel's rivals, even those who fought with him at the Moncada barracks in 1953, are periodically dismissed. In 1986, Comandante Ramiro Valdés, who served as minister of the interior and a member of the party's politburo, was relieved of his duties. The only top leader besides Fidel to wear the olive-green uniform of the revolution, Valdés is one of only three veterans to carry the title Comandante de la Revolución, a position not even Raúl enjoys.

While Castro's political genius has allowed him to enjoy unchallenged power in Cuba despite tremendous internal and external pressures (the U.S. government

has tried every method conceivable to oust Castro, including some, like an attempt to plant a bomb in his cigar, that were simply childish), he has surrounded himself increasingly with sycophants too browbeaten to challenge his decisions. One exception is Carlos Rafael Rodríguez, an experienced politician and Castro's senior by thirteen years. Rodríguez was crucial to the fusion of the guerrillas with the PSP after 1958. A true intellectual, he is vice-president of both the Council of State and the Council of Ministers and enjoys Castro's close friendship.

As Castro has squelched all opposition within the country, so too has he been forced to rely on a charismatic rule that places personality ahead of practical programs. Castro is forever the advocate. A brilliant speaker, he is capable of convincing huge crowds to enthusiastically endorse programs they may have been opposed to minutes earlier. His speeches are legend, both for their length (he has been known to speak for up to nine hours straight) and their ability to persuade. In a country where the citizenry is not consulted on decisions important or otherwise, Castro places great importance on his ability to move massive crowds (and Cuba's television audience) to endorse with their shouts and cheers whatever programs or policy he might be pushing for at the time.

PERSONAL LIFE. While Castro is ever the public figure, there is little known about his private life. In 1948, Fidel married Mirta Díaz-Balart, with whom he had one son before divorcing in 1954. His old comrades have died off, and he lacks close personal friendships with all but a few. He is still in touch with his ex-wife and also keeps in contact with his son, Fidelito, who is married and has two children. Trained as a physicist, Fidelito has taken an increasingly public posture as head of the Cuban Nuclear Commission. Castro maintains varying degrees of cordiality with his siblings. He is closest to his brother Raúl, of course, from their unique shared experiences starting with the attack on the Moncada barracks. One sister, Juana, is actively hostile toward him, however, and attacks him without mercy from self-imposed exile in Miami. (The family landholdings were gradually turned over to government control starting in 1959.)

If Castro has a lover, her identity is unknown, and, since the death of Celia SÁNCHEZ MANDULEY, Castro has shown no interest in elevating another woman to this position. Sánchez was in fact the first lady of Cuba, despite their never marrying. In addition to her role as companion, she exercised considerable political power as secretary of the Council of State and member of the party's Central Committee. Perhaps her greatest role, however, was her courage in standing up to Castro's gigantic ego and bluntly declaring to his face what others had only thought in private—that the great Castro could at times be wrong. After her death in 1980, numerous monuments and parks were erected in her honor.

AN ASSESSMENT. With the collapse of the Soviet bloc, Castro faces still another challenge to his rule and the Cuban state he has built. It is widely accepted that Castro's days are numbered, even that after his death the government will revert to the control of the Cuban exile community based in Miami. Yet the political pundits have never given Castro his due. It was popularly regarded as folly to attack the Moncada barracks and launch a sea invasion of Cuba with the *Granma,* yet Castro silenced his critics. Since the establishment of his socialist regime in Cuba, many have counted by the day or week, not year, the time it would supposedly take for Castro to be ousted, yet he has clung to power for over thirty years.

It is also common to regard Castro as nothing more than a caudillo, and in fact he displays many of the traits associated with such Latin American strongmen. Yet if his only goal had been to replace Batista, certainly a man of Castro's considerable abilities and class background could have reached the pinnacle of power in Cuba through the accepted military and social channels. While Castro's early days in the mountains of eastern Cuba nearly cost him his life, they also established that he was fighting for more than just personal aggrandizement and perpetuation of the old order. From his earliest days as a student, Castro has been an ardent nationalist fighting to rid Cuba of foreign control and the humiliation of poverty and illiteracy. While the foreign influences remain, certainly Cuba enjoyed greater leeway with the Soviet Union than it did in its relations with the United States. And while poverty and illiteracy there have not been eliminated, Cuba far surpasses the rest of Latin America in education and the fulfillment of basic needs. Although he cannot claim sole responsibility for this, Fidel Castro can take partial credit.

— MICHAEL POWELSON

CASTRO RUZ, RAÚL

Raúl Castro Ruz (*b.* 3 June 1931), Cuban revolutionary and military leader, younger brother of Cuban premier Fidel CASTRO RUZ, and one of the original members of the Twenty-sixth of July Movement that organized the successful overthrow of Cuban dictator Fulgencio BATISTA in 1959. Castro was born in Oriente Province, in the district of Birán, to an affluent landowning family. His father, Angel, was a native of Galicia, Spain; his mother, Lina Ruz González, was Cuban. As a youth he attended Catholic schools in Oriente Province and went on to study at the University of Havana. Unlike his brother Fidel, Raúl was early attracted to Marxism, and while a student at the university he joined the Socialist Youth Branch of the Partido Socialisto Popular (PSP).

The two brothers found common ground, however, in their hatred of the Batista regime and the pervasive role the United States played in all aspects of Cuban life. Raúl stood alongside his brother during the struggle to overthrow the Batista regime. In 1953 he was imprisoned with Fidel for the attack on the Moncada barracks, and joined his brother in exile in Mexico after Batista declared a general amnesty in 1955. Raúl helped Fidel plan the 1956 landing of a small band of revolutionaries from the boat *Granma* in Oriente Province. This invasion culminated in the ouster of Batista in 1959. When the new revolutionary government took power, Raúl was named minister of Cuba's Revolutionary Armed Forces.

As hostilities with the United States grew after the revolution, both Raúl Castro and Che GUEVARA were instrumental in influencing Fidel Castro to turn increasingly to the Soviet Union for economic and military aid. Whereas Fidel denied he was a Communist until December 1961, Raúl openly courted the Soviets while attacking the United States. With the Bay of Pigs Invasion in 1961 and the Cuban Missile Crisis the following year, Raúl played an integral role in moving Cuba from the U.S. to the Soviet sphere of influence.

As a trusted adviser to Fidel, Raúl has increased his power considerably over the years; many have charged the Castro brothers, not without reason, of turning the Cuban government into a family-owned business. Fidel holds the title of Cuban premier; Raúl continues to be vice premier (commander of the armed forces), and was named first vice president of the Council of State and the Council of Ministries during the "institutionalization" process of the 1970s. He is also a member of the Politburo and second secretary of the Cuban Communist Party. He has been president of the Agrarian Reform Institute since 1965, and is responsible for the Council of Ministers, the Ministry of the Interior, the Secretariat of the President, the Ministry of Public Health, and the Children's Institute.

Raúl Castro and his supporters built a modern army capable of protecting Cuba's borders against U.S. aggression and of launching military forays abroad. With the collapse of the Soviet Union and economic crises at home, the Cuban military, led by Raúl, is increasingly prominent in Cuban industries such as manufacturing and tourism. Once regarded as an "ideologue" compared to his pragmatic brother Fidel, Raúl Castro has recently shown considerable flexibility, especially in his direction of Cuba's economy. He has endorsed limited capitalist foreign investment, as well as market incentives for Cuban producers, as a remedy for the nation's current economic ills. Although Raúl possesses considerable power, he lacks Fidel's charisma, and most Cuba-watchers doubt that he would be able to fill his brother's shoes if Fidel were to die.

While there has been much criticism of Raúl, he and his brother Fidel did lead a successful revolt against both a despised dictator and the overbearing economic and political hegemony of the United States. Although it was widely accepted that Cuba could not survive without massive Soviet military and economic support, since the collapse of the Eastern bloc Cuba shows few signs, so far, of internal turmoil. Raúl Castro can take part of the credit for that.

— MICHAEL POWELSON

CAUPOLICÁN

Caupolicán (*d.* 1558), Araucanian warrior and hero. The cacique of Palmaiquén, he was active in the Araucanian resistance to the Spanish conquistadores from early on. He rose to prominence among his people after the death of LAUTARO (April 1557), when he was chosen as *toqui* (chief). He was a principal adversary of the newly arrived Spanish governor García HURTADO DE MENDOZA (1535–1609). Caupolicán's attacks on the new governor's hastily constructed fort near Concepción were repulsed. The Spaniards, now reinforced, defeated the Araucanians at the battles of Lagunillas (or Bío-bío) and Millarapue in November 1557. Caupolicán rejected all Hurtado de Mendoza's offers of peace. In mid-1558 a Spanish captain, Alonso de Reinoso, organized a surprise raid on the *toqui's* encampment at Palmaiquén and succeeded in capturing him. A woman, presumably his wife, revealed his identity to the Spaniards by reproaching him for being taken alive and dashing her infant son to the ground. (The name traditionally given to her, Fresia, is probably an invention of the poet Alonso de ERCILLA Y ZÚÑIGA.) Reinoso took Caupolicán back to the newly founded settlement at Cañete, where he was executed by impalement. He is remembered as second only to Lautaro among the Araucanian heroes of the sixteenth century.

— SIMON COLLIER

CAVALCANTI, NEWTON

Newton Cavalcanti (*b.* 1930), Brazilian engraver and illustrator. Although born in Pernambuco and trained

Statue of Caupolicán, Santa Lucía, Chile. (Organization of American States)

in Europe, Cavalcanti moved in 1952 to Rio de Janeiro, where he met the Brazilian metal engraver Raimudo Cela. In 1954 he studied wood engraving at the National School of Fine Arts in Rio de Janeiro under Oswaldo Goeldi. Along with fellow Pernambucan Gilvan Samico, Cavalcanti dedicated himself to xylography, the art of wood-block printing. Cavalcanti's woodcuts and wood engravings focused mainly upon themes from the legends, myths, and stories of Brazil's Northeast. Lyrical, grotesque, and fantastic animals and saints drift in and out of his nearly monochromatic green and black compositions. Examples of this style include *The System of the Doctor* and *The Counselor.* In 1960 he accepted a position teaching printmaking at the Educational Center in Niterói. Although best known for his graphic art, Cavalcanti has also produced illustrated books and has worked on film projects.

— CAREN A. MEGHREBLIAN

CAVALLÓN, JUAN DE

Juan de Cavallón (*b.* 1524; *d.* 1565), first conqueror of Costa Rica during the early 1560s. Although largely unsuccessful on his own, his invasion from Nicaragua in 1561 both set in motion the process and established the mechanisms by which subordinates such as Juan Vázquez de CORONADO would conquer the province. Cavallón held a licenciate in law and came from Castillo de Garcimuñoz, Cuenca, New Castile. He married Leonor de Barahona, the daughter of one of CORTÉS's associates in the conquest of Mexico. He was named *alcalde mayor* of Nicoya in the 1550s. From this base he led 80 to 90 men, recruited in Guatemala in 1560, as an expeditionary force to claim the province of Costa Rica.

In January 1561 the force left its base and landed on the coast near the modern port of Puntarenas. They attempted to establish two settlements, Landecho as a port and Castillo de Garcimuñoz further inland, but both soon failed. Relations with the Indians deteriorated quickly as their leader, Garabito, organized resistance to Cavallón's requisitioning of corn supplies. Cavallón financed this expedition in association with the Franciscan priest Juan de Estrada Rávago, a native of Guadalajara, New Castile, long resident in the Salvadoran Indian parishes of the cacao-rich Izalco district. Cavallón claimed to have lost nine thousand pesos of his own funds in the enterprise, and Estrada may have invested six or seven thousand. Estrada also undertook an expedition along the Atlantic coast, in coordination with Cavallón's march from the Pacific side, but with even more dismal results.

Cavallón was named *fiscal* of the *audiencia* in Guatemala in 1562 and left Estrada in charge of a rapidly declining force. Estrada also left Costa Rica, returning eventually to Spain, but several members of the conquering band remained to claim positions and *encomiendas* after the more lasting conquest expedition of Vázquez de Coronado in 1563.

– LOWELL GUDMUNDSON

CAVIEDES, JUAN DEL VALLE Y

Juan del Valle y Caviedes (*b.* 1650?; *d.* 1697), Peruvian poet. Very little is known of the early life of this foremost writer except that he was born in Andalusia, migrated to Peru at an early age, and kept a small shop in Lima. Although manuscripts of his work circulated during his lifetime, no printed editions appeared until the nineteenth century.

Caviedes's early work consists primarily of love lyrics and religious and philosophical poems, but his best tal-

ent is revealed in his satirical verse, which ridicules the superstitious, irrational Peruvian society and in particular the pretentious pseudoscience of the medical profession, as well as the corruption of the viceregal court. He describes one collection of his poems as a revelation of "deeds of ignorance brought to light by a patient who miraculously escaped from the errors of the physicians," and another as dedicated to social climbers who profess saintliness, learning, or nobility in order to secure status and wealth. The directness of his satire contrasts strongly with the artificiality of most literature of the seventeenth century.

– JOHN R. FISHER

CAYMMI, DORIVAL

Dorival Caymmi (*b.* 1914), Brazilian songwriter. Beginning in the 1930s, Salvador-born Caymmi composed a wide variety of highly successful tunes that explored Bahian and Afro-Brazilian culture and were popularized by singers such as Carmen Miranda, Anjos do Inferno, Ângela Maria, João GILBERTO, Elis Regina, Gal Costa, Gilberto Gil, and Caetano Veloso, as well as by foreign interpreters such as Andy Williams and Paul Winter. Caymmi worked in many different musical styles, including *sambas, marchas, toadas, modinhas, canções praieiras* (fishermen's songs), *cocos, sambas de roda,* and *pontos de candomblé* (*candomblé* invocations). Like novelist Jorge AMADO, with whom he composed "é doce morrer no mar" (It's Sweet to Die in the Sea), he is closely identified with Bahian culture.

Caymmi gained fame with "O que é que a baiana tem?" (What Is It That the Baiana's Got?), sung by Carmen Miranda in the films *Banana da terra* (1938) and *Greenwich Village* (1944); Caymmi recorded a duet with the actress in 1939. Other Caymmi standards include: "Samba da minha terra" (Samba of My Land), "Marina," "Nem eu" (Me Neither), "Saudade de Itapoã," "Oração de mae menininha" (a tribute to a famed *mae-de-santo* in Salvador), "Rosa morena," "Saudade da Bahia," "João Valentão," "Requebre que eu dou um doce," "Doralice," "Das rosas," and "Promessa de pescador" (Promise of a Fisherman). His three children (singer Nana, singer-songwriter Dori, and flutist-composer Danilo) are also musicians.

– CHRIS MCGOWAN

CAZNEAU, WILLIAM LESLIE

William Leslie Cazneau (*b.* 5 October 1807; *d.* 7 January 1876), a wealthy Texan and supporter of William WALKER's filibustering scheme in Nicaragua. As an expansionist in the 1840s, Cazneau encouraged the annexation of Cuba and Mexico's northern states to the United States. Subsequently, he fought in the Mexican-American War (1846–1848), for which he received the rank of general. In 1853 Secretary of State William L. Marcy appointed Cazneau special minister to Santo Domingo to negotiate a commercial treaty and to obtain Samaná Bay as a coaling station. The mission failed, and Cazneau returned to the United States in 1855. In 1856, he contracted with Walker to send one thousand colonists to Nicaragua within a year to be established in settlements of not fewer than fifty families, each settler to be given title to eighty acres of land. In return, Cazneau was to receive a considerable land grant. The effort failed with Walker's ouster from Nicaragua in May 1857.

– THOMAS M. LEONARD

CEDEÑO, JUAN MANUEL

Juan Manuel Cedeño (*b.* 1914), Panamanian painter. Cedeño studied under Humberto IVALDI and Roberto LEWIS at the Escuela Nacional de Pintura in Panama and at the Chicago Art Institute (B.F.A., 1948). His role as an educator is one of his greatest contributions to Panama. He was director of his alma mater, in 1952 renamed the Escuela Nacional de Artes Plásticas (1948–1967) and professor at the University of Panama (1967–1978).

In his work with local folklore themes, Cedeño was one of the first Panamanian artists to experiment with the geometrization of forms derived from cubism and futurism, as in *Domingo de Ramos* (1955). Although he also paints landscapes and still lifes, he is best known for his many commissioned portraits, for example, *Octavio Méndez Pereira* (1950).

– MONICA E. KUPFER

CEDILLO MARTÍNEZ, SATURNINO

Saturnino Cedillo Martínez (*b.* 29 November 1890; *d.* 11 January 1939), Mexican politician and rebel leader. An important revolutionary general and the regional boss of the state of San Luis Potosí, Cedillo led the last military rebellion against the government in the post-Revolutionary period and was killed in battle.

Born at Rancho de Palomas, Ciudad del Maíz, San Luis Potosí, the son of landowning peasants, he obtained a primary school education. He joined the Maderistas, but later, with his brothers Magdaleno and Cleofas, he sided with Emiliano ZAPATA and fought against MADERO on the side of Pascual OROZCO in 1912. He was captured and imprisoned. He later joined the Constitutionalists, but abandoned Venustiano CAR-

RANZA to support the Plan of Agua Prieta in 1920. He remained in the army, holding top military commands, and supported the government against rebel causes in 1923 and 1929. After serving as governor of his home state, he provided decisive peasant support for Lázaro CÁRDENAS's presidential candidacy in 1934, for which he was rewarded with the post of secretary of agriculture (1935). He broke with the president in 1937, leaving the cabinet. He then organized his supporters into a small army and opposed the Cárdenas government.

– RODERIC AI CAMP

CENTURIÓN, CARLOS R.

Carlos R. Centurión (*b.* 1902; *d.* 1969), Paraguayan historian. Born into an old and established family, Centurión chose to enter the legal profession but also spent many years in academic pursuits. His first literary undertaking, a two-volume account of the Gran Chaco dispute, *El conflicto del Chaco: Gestiones diplomáticas,* published in 1937, was well received, and a year later, he produced a detailed examination of Paraguay's first constitutional convention, *Los hombres de la convención del 70* (1938).

These two early works gave Centurión excellent preparation for his magnum opus, *Historia de las letras paraguayas.* This study, which appeared in three volumes between 1947 and 1951, has long been regarded as the most complete and best-researched intellectual history of Paraguay. Perhaps its only rival is Efraím Cardozo's *Historiografía paraguaya,* which addresses only the colonial period. Centurión's work received considerable acclaim when it first appeared. Subsequent critics have nonetheless charged that it avoids in-depth analysis of Paraguayan writers in favor of a superficial thoroughness. Even these critics, however, have failed to duplicate Centurión's efforts.

– THOMAS L. WHIGHAM

CENTURIÓN, JUAN CRISÓSTOMO

Juan Crisóstomo Centurión (*b.* 1840; *d.* 12 March 1903), Paraguayan diplomat, journalist, and author. Born in Itauguá in 1840, Centurión received his early education in Asunción, where he studied literature with European tutors. In the late 1850s, the government selected him as one of several young Paraguayans sent abroad for further education at state expense. He went to Britain, where he learned English and French and studied international law. He returned to Paraguay in 1863 and immediately became a key adviser to President Francisco Solano LÓPEZ. Two years later, when his country became deeply involved in a war with Argentina and Brazil, Centurión contributed his part, acting as a military officer, magistrate, and state propagandist. Faithful to López to the end, he fought at Itá-Ybaté and, in 1870, was with his commander at Cerro Corá, where he suffered a painful face wound. His Brazilian captors took him to Rio de Janeiro after the war.

In the late 1850s, the Paraguayan government selected Centurión as one of several young Paraguayans sent abroad for further education at state expense.

Released a few months later, Centurión made his way to London, where he married a Cuban acquaintance. He and his wife then moved to Cuba, where he practiced law. In 1877 he published a short memoir in New York. In 1878 he returned to Asunción, where he edited a key newspaper, *La Reforma,* served as attorney general under President Bernardino CABALLERO, and began writing another set of memoirs. Centurión joined General Caballero in organizing the Partido Colorado in 1887 and served as foreign minister under Patricio Escobar. In 1895, Centurión was elected senator, a post he held until his death in Asunción. His three-volume *Memorias o reminiscencias históricas sobre la guerra del Paraguay* (Buenos Aires, 1894–1897) is still regarded as the best war memoir from the Paraguayan side.

— THOMAS L. WHIGHAM

CENTURIÓN, ROQUE MIRANDA

Roque Miranda Centurión (*b.* 1900; *d.* 1960), Paraguayan dramatist. Born in Carapeguá, Centurión completed his secondary education at the National College in Asunción and began his theatrical career in the capital city in 1926 as an actor in Félix Fernández's *Mborayjhú pajhú.* That same year, his first play, *Cupido sudando,* was performed. From 1926 to 1928, he lived in France and Spain. In 1932, he collaborated with Josefina PLÁ in the Spanish-Guarani play *Episodios chaqueños.* In 1933, his play *Tuyú,* in Guarani, was performed, and in 1942 and 1943, he again collaborated with Plá in *Desheredado* and *Sobre en blanco.*

Centurión was the founder of the Escuela Municipal de Declamación y Arte Escénico, which he directed until 1960. He was one of the founders of the Academia de la Lengua y Cultura Guaraní. A radio pioneer, in 1936, Centurión promoted "La Peña," a broadcast created to provide the airways with cultural programs. In 1939, with Plá, he initiated the radio series "Proal," and he created the program "La Voz Cultural de la Nación."

— THOMAS E. CASE

CEREZO ARÉVALO, MARCO VINICIO

Marco Vinicio Cerezo Arévalo (*b.* 26 December 1942), president of Guatemala (1986–1991). Vinicio Cerezo was born in Guatemala City into a politically prominent family. His grandfather was murdered for opposing Jorge UBICO (1931–1944) and his father served on the Guatemalan Supreme Court. In 1954 Cerezo's political inclinations were awakened by the U.S.-sponsored overthrow of Jacobo ARBENZ (1951–1954). He joined the Christian Democratic Party (DCG) while a law student at the University of San Carlos. After completing his degree in 1968, he studied at Loyola University in New Orleans, Louisiana, and in Chile, Venezuela, West Germany, and Italy. He was elected to the congress in 1974. During the repressive regime of General LUCAS GARCÍA (1978–1982), he survived at least three attempts on his life.

In 1986 Vinicio Cerezo became the first elected civilian president since 1970 and only the second since Juan José ARÉVALO (1945–1951). Cerezo faced a difficult situation in 1986: a troublesome insurgency on the left, an intransigent military on the right, an increasingly mobilized peasantry, and an economy in a state of crisis (declining GNP, escalating inflation, 40 percent unemployment, and scarce foreign exchange). To address these problems Cerezo launched a neoliberal program of export diversification, currency devaluation, removal of price controls, and increased taxes. The results were generally favorable for the national economy, but living standards for most people were reduced. This led to a series of massive strikes in 1987, 1988, and 1989.

Although supported by the military high command, Cerezo was opposed by field commanders who thought that domestic concerns were taking precedence over the government's counterinsurgency efforts. Coup attempts by disgruntled officers were launched in May 1988 and again in 1989.

In January 1987 Cerezo renewed the diplomatic relations with Britain that had been ruptured in 1981 by the granting of independence to Belize. In 1986 and 1987, he hosted the Central American peace talks in Esquipulas which led to the successful implementation of the Arias peace plan, whose goal was the settlement of the insurgency wars in Central America.

Although elected on a platform to bring peace to Guatemala, Cerezo made little progress in ending the leftist insurgency or improving the country's human rights record. The coalition of four major guerrilla groups, the Guatemalan National Revolutionary Union (URNG), expanded its operations, and the number of assassinations by alleged right-wing death squads increased in Guatemala City. The problem was exacerbated by the massacre of fourteen men and boys in the Indian village of Santiago Atitlan in December 1990, which resulted in the cutoff of U.S. military aid.

Plagued by charges of corruption and drug trafficking, Cerezo was unable to secure the election of his handpicked successor, but he did preside over the first successive democratic presidential election in 151 years. Jorge SERRANO ELÍAS (*b.* 1945) was inaugurated in January 1991.

– ROLAND H. EBEL

CERNA, VICENTE

Vicente Cerna (*b.* ca. 1810; *d.* 27 June 1885), field marshal and president of Guatemala (1865–1871). A military officer who became by 1847 a close associate of the dictator Rafael CARRERA (1840–1865), Cerna played an important role at the battle of Arada (1851). This battle established Carrera as the dominant military figure in Central America and as president for life (formally so in 1854). Outside Carrera's family no military man was closer to the dictator than Cerna, who was politically and militarily dependable and a devout Catholic, as was Carrera. Cerna later received the rank of field marshal for his performance in the difficult 1863 campaign against El Salvador's Liberal president Gerardo BARRIOS. Shortly before his death in April 1865, Carrera named Cerna to succeed him. In the close presidential election that followed in May this endorsement gave Cerna his margin of victory.

Carrera's regime had been in large measure reactionary but provided peace and encouraged development of coffee culture. Cerna continued most of Carrera's policies, seeking sufficient modernization for economic development under traditional institutions such as monopoly franchises (*estancos*) and the Consulado de Comercio, which favored a restricted circle of landowners, entrepreneurs, and merchants. Under Cerna Guatemala became more closely connected with the world trading system, which favored free trade. Cerna's regime improved the infrastructure of transportation and communication: the Pacific port of San José was built up; some roads and highways were improved; railroads were commissioned, though not built; and the telegraph was introduced, although it would not become effective until after 1871. In 1870–1871 an ambitious currency reform was introduced, a reform of land tenure sought, and a modern public market, which would stand for a century, was completed.

Despite some successes, pressures on the regime grew. A series of insurrections began in 1867 and Cerna's church-dominated government had poor relations with Benito JUÁREZ's victorious Liberal regime in Mexico. Both foreign and Guatemalan entrepreneurs associated with the expanding coffee culture became impatient with Cerna's policy. His reelection in 1869 involved manipulation, and in 1870 political repression ended parliamentary debate. Miguel GARCÍA GRANADOS, leader of the opposition, was forced into exile, from whence both Guatemalan and Mexican allies aided his organization of the Liberal revolution of 1871. Joined by those impatient for modernization in Guatemala, García Granados and Justo Rufino BARRIOS defeated Cerna's army on 29 June 1871 and took control of the government the next day.

– WAYNE M. CLEGERN

CERRUTO, ÓSCAR

Óscar Cerruto (*b.* 13 June 1912; *d.* 10 April 1981), Bolivian poet, novelist, and storyteller. One of the most important figures of contemporary Bolivian literature, Cerruto wrote his first group of poems, *Cifra de las rosas* (1957), within the aesthetics of modernism. This poetical composition is followed by *Patria de sal cautiva* (1958), *Estrella segregada* (1973), and *Reverso de la transparencia* (1975), wherein Cerruto explores the possibilities of avant-gardism. His imagery is harsh and in harmony with the high plateau landscapes of Andean Bolivia. Of great intensity and linguistic precision, Cerruto's works denounce the excesses of power and examine the topics of hate, solitude, fear, and death. His poetry, embedded in the Judeo-Christian notion of guilt, dissociates itself from his early revolutionary ideals of social transformation, admirably set forth in his novel *Aluvión de fuego* (1935). The absence of social redemption can be perceived in his later narrative, particularly in *Cerco de penumbras* (1958), a volume of short stories.

– JAVIER SANJINÉS C.

CERUTI, ROQUE

Roque Ceruti (*b.* ca. 1683; *d.* 6 December 1760), Italian composer active in Peru. Born in Milan, then under Spanish rule, Ceruti studied the violin there until 1706. When the Marquis Castell dos Ríus, viceroy of Peru, appointed him director of music, Ceruti settled in Lima, where he conducted the premiere of his opera *El mejor escudo de Perseo* at the viceroyal palace on 17 September 1708. In 1720 he moved to Trujillo and was named *maestro de capilla* of the cathedral there (1721–1728). In 1728 Ceruti succeeded Tomás de TORREJÓN

Y VELASCO as *maestro de capilla* of the Lima cathedral, remaining in that position until his death. During Ceruti's tenure the cathedral continued to be an active music center. Ceruti composed and published numerous works: mythological operas and pastorals, secular and religious music, some in Spanish, others on Latin texts. His manuscripts are kept in the Lima Archives, in the San Antonio Abad Seminary in Cuzco, in Sucre cathedral, in Santa Clara Conventín Cochabamba, in private collections, and at the archive of the church of San Francisco de Asís in Montevideo. He died in Lima.

— SUSANA SALGADO

CERVANTES, VICENTE

Vicente Cervantes (*b.* 1755; *d.* 26 July 1829), distinguished botanist of Bourbon Mexico. Born in Zafra, Badajoz, Spain, Cervantes began his career as an apprentice to an apothecary, studying pharmacy part-time. After passing the pharmacist's examination, he served as chief pharmacist at the general hospital in Madrid until Charles III chose him as a member of the royal botanical expedition to New Spain. The expedition arrived in New Spain in 1787; Cervantes, appointed professor of botany at the University of Mexico, began teaching the following year. His popular courses, which emphasized Linnaean principles, introduced a generation of Mexican creoles to the modern study of botany.

Cervantes also was a founder of the Royal Botanical Gardens, located in the viceregal palace, and its head from 1802. There, he and his assistants cultivated some 1,400 species of plants; the New World flora came mostly from central Mexico, though some species were imported from as far away as Havana. Cervantes, who remained in Mexico when the rest of the expedition departed, faced difficulties after 1810. The hard-pressed viceregal government progressively slashed the Royal Botanical Gardens' budget, and Cervantes was unable to prevent the institution's gradual deterioration. He died in Mexico City.

— R. DOUGLAS COPE

CERVANTES KAWANAGH, IGNACIO

Ignacio Cervantes Kawanagh (*b.* 31 July 1847; *d.* 29 April 1905), pioneer of Cuban musical nationalism. Cervantes, a native of Havana, was not the first Cuban nationalist musician, but it was in his *contradanzas* that this musical genre found its fullest expression. He benefited from the friendship of the American composer Louis M. Gottschalk, who in 1865 advised Cervantes's parents to send him to study in Paris, where he won numerous awards. Like José WHITE, another Cuban

musician, he was forced by the Spaniards to leave Cuba (to which he had returned in 1870) during the Ten Years' War (1868–1878). He later became a friend of José MARTÍ, whom he assisted in his revolutionary activities. As a composer his magnum opus was his series of Cuban dances (some forty of which are extant). Because of their richness and complexity, they became concert music. They have been described as "the soul of Cuba in full bloom." He died in Havana.

— JOSÉ M. HERNÁNDEZ

CERVETTI, SERGIO

Sergio Cervetti (*b.* 9 November 1940), Uruguayan composer. Born in Dolores, Cervetti studied piano in Montevideo with Hugo Balzo and counterpoint and harmony with Carlos ESTRADA and Guido Santórsola. He then studied composition at the Peabody Conservatory in Baltimore under the direction of Ernst Krenek and Stefan Grové. Later he worked in electronic music under the guidance of Mario DAVIDOVSKY, Vladimir Ussachevsky, and Alcides LANZA. He received the composition prize at the Caracas Festival in 1966. In 1968 he was artist-in-residence with the DAAD (German exchange program) for the city of Berlin and received important commissions from Baden-Baden and the Art Academy in Berlin. His music for ballet includes *Transatlantic Light* (1987) for the Dance Company of Nina Wiener and *40 Second/42 Variations* (1979) for the Holland Festival.

Until 1971 Cervetti's work was characterized by dodecaphonic tendencies with some incursions into aleatoric languages. Following his move to New York City, he became part of the minimalist movement. Even if his aesthetics separated him completely from other Latin American musical schools modeled after the European, particularly Polish, composers, Cervetti created his own version of minimalism, producing works with strong lyrical lines, thick counterpoint, and a hypnotic atmosphere.

Other important works by Cervetti include Five Episodes for chamber ensemble (1965); *Divertimento* for woodwinds (1964); *Plexus* for orchestra (1970), commissioned by the Fifth Inter-American Music Festival, Washington, D.C.; *Zinctum* for string quartet (1967); *The Bottom of the Iceberg* for solo guitar (1975); *Transatlantic Light* for electronic keyboard (1987); *Lucet in Tenebris* for choir (1970); *Bits and Pieces and Moving Parts* for chamber ensemble and tape (1970); Trumpet Concerto (1977); *4 Fragments of Isadora* for soprano and piano (1979); *Wind Devil* for electronic tape (1983); *Llanto, muerte y danza* for harpsichord (1984); *3 Estudios australes* for piano (1989); Concerto for harpsichord and eleven instruments (1990); *Leyenda* for soprano and orchestra (1991); and *Las indias olvidadas,* a concerto for harpsichord and chamber group (1992), commissioned by the Festival of Alicante, Spain.

— ALCIDES LANZA

CÉSAIRE, AIMÉ

Aimé Césaire (*b.* 25 June 1913), West Indian writer. Born in Martinique, Césaire graduated from the well-known Lycée Victor Schoelcher in Fort-de-France in 1931. He later studied in Paris at the Lycée Louis-le-Grand, where he met Léopold Sédar Senghor from Senegal and many other young black students from African and Caribbean countries. In 1934 Césaire invented the neologism négritude as an expression of pride in the African cultural heritage. Césaire helped found the black magazine *L'étudiant Noir* (1934–1936). In 1939, the same year that his now classic epic poem *Cahier d'un retour au pays natal* (1939; Notebook of a Return to the Native Land) came out in Paris, Césaire returned to Martinique.

In 1934 Césaire invented the neologism négritude as an expression of pride in the African cultural heritage.

During World War II, Césaire worked as a teacher and founded the magazine *Tropiques* (1941–1945) in order to maintain contact with French-language literature. In spring 1941, the famous surrealist poet André Breton payed Césaire a visit. This historic encounter not only confirmed the strong identification Césaire felt with the antirationalism of the surrealist movement but also inspired Bretón to write a preface to a new edition of the *Notebook* (1947), in which he described Césaire as the "Great Black Poet." In the meantime, Césaire, who had written about the Haitian hero of independence Toussaint L'OUVERTURE in his *Notebook,* undertook a trip to Haiti, where he remained from May to December of 1944.

Although Césaire's poetry is highly regarded, he is better known for his polemical essays and plays. In 1945 he was elected mayor of Fort-de-France and, after denouncing the French Communist Party in 1956, he founded his own independent socialist party, the Martinican Progressive Party, or PPM, two years later. His political ideas are reflected in his essay against colonialism, *Discours sur le colonialisme* (1950); the letters against communism, *Lettres à Maurice Thorez* (1956); and a historical interpretation of *Toussaint L'Ouverture* (1960). In his plays—such as *La Tragédie du roi Chris-*

tophe, Une saison au Congo (1967), and *Une tempête* (1969)—he concentrates on the problems of newly independent African countries against the background of Caribbean history.

— INEKE PHAF

CÉSPEDES, CARLOS MANUEL DE (THE ELDER)

Carlos Manuel de Céspedes (The Elder) (*b.* 18 April 1819; *d.* ca. 22 March 1874), nineteenth-century Cuban revolutionary. Son of a sugar planter in Cuba's Oriente Province, Céspedes received his baccalaureate degree in Havana in 1840. He then went to study law in Spain where he was exposed to the ideas of Freemasonry, participated in revolutionary activities for which he was exiled to France, and committed himself to opposing colonial repression. When he returned to Cuba, Céspedes joined with other like-minded eastern planters and cattle ranchers, including Ignacio AGRAMONTE, Salvador Cisneros Betancourt, Bartolomé Masó, Pedro Figueredo, and Francisco Vicente Aguilera, who were convinced that Cuba would only win its freedom through the military defeat of Spain. Hence, in the isolated and less-developed corners of the Oriente, Céspedes and the other conspirators used Masonic lodges to organize and coordinate their activities.

On 10 October 1868, without consulting the other leaders, Céspedes held a public meeting at his plantation, La Demajagua, at which he freed his slaves. He then encouraged his listeners to follow the path of such Latin American freedom fighters as Simón BOLÍVAR and José de SAN MARTÍN. Finally, he issued the GRITO DE YARA, in which he proclaimed Cuban independence from Spain.

But despite their commitment to independence, Céspedes and his co-conspirators envisioned independence as a transitional step in the process of union with the United States. Only weeks after the independence proclamation, Céspedes led a delegation of Cuban revolutionaries to Washington, D.C., to petition the American secretary of state to consider Cuba's admission to the Union. A year later the revolutionary Constituent Assembly of Guáimaro explicitly proclaimed annexation as the ultimate purpose of the Cuban rebellion.

Despite an initial setback, by 1869 Céspedes was the acknowledged leader of the insurrection and on 10 April he was chosen to be president of the republic declared by the Constituent Assembly. However, divided by petty regionalism, class origins, and conflicts over military strategy, the revolutionaries lacked the unity and discipline essential for victory. Céspedes's authoritarian disposition only intensified the centrifugal forces of the revolutionary movement. In 1873 Céspedes was deposed in absentia as president, and on 22 March of the following year he was killed in a skirmish with Spanish forces.

— WADE A. KIT

CÉSPEDES Y QUESADA, CARLOS MANUEL DE

Carlos Manuel de Céspedes y Quesada (*b.* 1871; *d.* 1939), Cuban diplomat and writer. Céspedes y Quesada was the son of Carlos Manuel de CÉSPEDES, the Elder, the Cuban revolutionary who was elected president in 1869 and who was killed in battle during the Ten Years' War. As a child he studied in the United States, France, and Germany, and in 1901 he received a degree in public and civil law from the University of Havana.

Like his father, Céspedes y Quesada played an active role in the movement for Cuban independence. He was among the leading participants of the 1895 Cuban Revolution. Prior to American involvement in the war, he served as governor of Oriente Province, representative of the Second Army Corps, secretary of the Assembly of La Yaya, colonel of the General Staff of the Inspector General, and secretary of the "junta consultiva."

During the two American interventions (1899–1902, 1906–1909), Céspedes y Quesada withdrew entirely from political life. But upon the creation of the republic, he initiated a long and fruitful diplomatic and political career that lasted for more than thirty years. Among the most important posts he occupied were congressional representative from Oriente; president of the Commission on Tariffs and Codes; ambassador successively to Italy (1909–1912), to Argentina (1912–1913), and to the United States (1913–1922); secretary of state (1922–1926); and ambassador to France (1930–1933). While minister in Washington he negotiated the sale of the Cuban sugar crops of 1917 and 1918 to the United States and the Allies. Upon the overthrow of Cuban dictator Gerardo MACHADO Y MORALES in 1933, Céspedes y Quesada, by virtue of his brief tenure as secretary of state, became president of the republic, a position he held from 12 August until 5 September.

Besides being a member of numerous learned societies and the recipient of countless Cuban and foreign honors, he also was a renowned writer. Among the many works he authored, the most noteworthy are *Cuba y el derecho de la fuerza, El problema de la haciendas comuneras, La oración fúnebre del Mayor General Bartolomé Masó,* and *Carlos Manuel de Céspedes y Loynaz.*

— WADE A. KIT

CEVALLOS, PEDRO ANTONIO DE

Pedro Antonio de Cevallos (*b.* 29 June 1715; *d.* 24 December 1778), governor of Buenos Aires (1756–

1766); viceroy of Río de la Plata (1777–1778). Born in Cádiz, the son of the general superintendent of customs of that city, Cevallos studied for a military career at the Seminario de Nobles in Madrid. Promoted to field marshal by 1747, Cevallos arrived in the Río de la Plata in 1756 as governor and chief of a sizable military expedition charged with containing the Portuguese. During his tenure as governor, Cevallos traveled extensively in the Misiones area. He returned to Spain in 1767, but in 1776 was again called upon to confront the Portuguese. Proving himself to be a fine strategist, he successfully ousted the Portuguese from Colonia in 1777, proceeding to Buenos Aires as first viceroy of the Río de la Plata. During his brief term of office, Cevallos promulgated free-trade ordinances. Shortly after taking office, he fell ill on a trip to Córdoba and died. A lifelong bachelor, Cevallos left at least one illegitimate son in Buenos Aires, born shortly after his father's death.

— SUSAN M. SOCOLOW

CHACÓN, LÁZARO

Lázaro Chacón (*b.* 27 June 1873; *d.* 1931), president of Guatemala (1926–1930). Lázaro Chacón was born in Teculután, Zacapa. His grandfather was a military officer and his father was a cattle rancher. A career army officer, General Chacón assumed the presidency of Guatemala on 27 September 1926, the day following the fatal heart attack of General José María ORELLANA, his boyhood friend. Chacón's critics charged that the new president "was a man of very little intelligence, less education and no experience in government affairs."

Upon assuming the presidency, Chacón committed his government to the continuation of the policies of his predecessor. Also, with the country in the midst of a remarkable economic boom, Chacón announced his intention to prevent all forms of social and political unrest. Supported by a large majority of Guatemalan liberals, Chacón easily won the December 1926 presidential election. From most reports, the outcome of the election was never in doubt. Most of Guatemala's traditionally powerful landed elite had little reason to oppose Chacón's promises of prosperity and stability. While the opposition Progressive Party candidate, future president Jorge UBICO Y CASTAÑEDA, ran a campaign that was vaguely reformist, Chacón capitalized on his links to the Guatemalan military and on the economic prosperity enjoyed by the nation's coffee elite to secure an easy victory.

When the Guatemalan economy was crippled by the effects of a worldwide depression in the late 1920s, Chacón's government was already unpopular with the Guatemalan upper and middle classes. Accused of mismanagement, corruption, and inept administration, the Chacón government appeared to be on the verge of anarchy. In December 1930, Chacón suffered a massive stroke. With Chacón incapacitated, the government wallowed in a sea of indecision until Jorge Ubico was elected president in early February 1931.

— WADE A. KIT

CHACRINHA

Chacrinha (José Abelardo de Barbosa Medeiros; *b.* 1918; *d.* 1989), Brazilian television variety show host. Born in Pernambuco, he was one of the longest-running stars of radio, starting in 1943, then of television, with a leading show on TV Rio by 1958. He was considered very innovative in developing one of the two major Brazilian television entertainment forms, the live variety show (*show de auditório*). (The other major form is the *telenovela*.) His programs were characterized by his dressing in a flamboyant clown costume, an outrageous style of comedy, and close interaction with his audience. His shows relied on amateur performances, comedy, music, guests, dancers, and games. His two best-known shows were *Buzina de Chacrinha* (Chacrinha's Horn) and *Discoteca de Chacrinha.* In the 1960s and 1970s, Chacrinha was identified with the movement, known as *tropicalismo,* to revive authentic Brazilian popular culture, particularly in music. He was mentioned in Gilberto GIL's salute to Brazilian tropical culture, the song "*Alegria, Alegria*" (Joy, Joy). While Chacrinha was considered in dubious taste by some, including TV Globo's management, which fired him in 1972, many popular culture experts, both Brazilian and foreign, considered his shows the best forum for authentic Brazilian popular culture. He was called one of Brazil's best communicators for his rapport with his audience. His programs, along with other live programs, were banned by the military governments from 1972 to 1979 because they were too difficult to control. In the 1980s, Chacrinha appeared on several competing Brazilian networks.

— JOSEPH STRAUBHAAR

CHAGAS, CARLOS RIBEIRO JUSTINIANO

Carlos Ribeiro Justiniano Chagas (*b.* 9 July 1879; *d.* 8 November 1934), Brazilian medical scientist. Chagas is remembered for discovering a new human disease, *Trypanosomiasis americana,* commonly known as Chagas' disease, which to this day afflicts millions of people in South America.

Chagas was born in Minas Gerais and trained in medicine in Rio de Janeiro, where he obtained his medical degree in 1902. In 1907 he joined the staff of the Oswaldo Cruz Institute, which later sent him to Lassance, 300 miles from Rio, to organize an antimalaria campaign. It was while he was in Lassance that Chagas took up the study of a biting insect commonly known as the *barbeiro* (a *triatoma*), which lived in the walls and thatched roofs of the local dwellings. Finding a trypanosome in the gut of the insect, he suspected that it might produce disease and that humans might be its natural host. Therefore, Chagas proceeded to test its pathogenic effects in animals. He went on to discover trypanosome in the heart and brain tissues of patients whose diverse clinical symptoms had escaped understanding until that time.

The announcement of a new human disease in 1909 initiated years of research into its insect vectors; the life cycle of the causative agent, the *Trypanosoma cruzi* (named after Oswaldo CRUZ, Chagas's friend and director of the Oswaldo Cruz Institute); and its clinical symptoms. The disease has acute and chronic forms and causes cardiac, gastrointestinal, and neurological symptoms.

In 1917, Chagas took over the direction of the Oswaldo Cruz Institute; in 1919 he also became director of the federal public health program, where he oversaw the extension of public health campaigns into the rural areas of Brazil. Nevertheless, Chagas was primarily known as a medical scientist. His work on *Trypanosomiasis americana* gave him an international reputation in medicine; he received the Schaudinn prize for protozoology in 1913 and several honorary degrees.

— NANCY LEYS STEPAN

CHAMBI, MARTÍN

Martín Chambi (*b.* 5 November 1891; *d.* 1973), Peruvian photographer. Although all biographical facts about Chambi are currently under scrutiny, it is safe to say that he was born into a modest peasant family of Indian stock in the village of Coaza, near Lake Titicaca, in the southern highlands of Peru. His first experience with photography occurred when his father was working for the British Santo Domingo Mining Company, near Carabaya. The curious boy eagerly sought to help the company photographer, who was taking survey views of the area. Around 1908, Chambi moved to Arequipa, where he allegedly pursued a high school education and until 1917 was an apprentice at the studio of the then famous photographer Max T. Vargas. That same year he married Manuela López Viza; they had six children.

In 1917, seeking to establish his own business, Chambi moved to the thriving town of Sicuani. Some three years later he moved on to Cuzco, where he sought out Juan Manuel Figueroa Aznar, a former pupil of Vargas. For a while Chambi and Figueroa shared a studio in Cuzco. At the time, that ancient capital of the Incas was undergoing a cultural renaissance and the beginning of an economic recession. INDIGENISMO became a major intellectual and political force in Cuzco. Chambi befriended such leading *indigenista* intellectuals as José Uriel García, Luis Valcárcel, Gamaliel Churata, Roberto Latorre, and Luis Valesco Aragón. Chambi's work was published in illustrated magazines like *Variedades*. Politically, he sympathized with the early APRA party and contributed to the radical avant-garde magazine *Kosko* by taking ads for his studio in it.

During the 1920s Chambi's prestige as a photographer peaked, and his clientele included wealthy families such as the Lomellinis and the Montes. Some of his most memorable images are commissioned portraits to which he added a social commentary. Yet, his ethnographic work and documentation of Cuzco's colonial and Inca architecture is probably his most systematic. Many of the images for which he is famous today were never shown in the exhibitions curated by Chambi himself. The American photographer Edward Ranney, largely responsible for Chambi's "rediscovery" in 1977, has played an important role in the appreciation and perception of his work.

– FERNANDO CASTRO

CHAMORRO, FRUTO

Fruto Chamorro (*b.* 20 October 1804; *d.* 12 March 1855), first director of state and first president of Nicaragua (1853–1855). Chamorro is considered one of the most influential and significant figures in the political life of Nicaragua. He restored order to the republic after the chaos of the incessant postindependence wars caused by friction between Conservatives and Liberals.

Born in Guatemala to a Nicaraguan father, Pedro José Chamorro, Fruto Chamorro left his homeland for Nicaragua in early 1827. Soon realizing that Nicaragua suffered from anarchy, factionalism, and militarism, he focused his energy on the fight for liberty and order. In 1836 Chamorro was elected deputy to the Granada state legislature, a position he used to establish public education in that state. He considered education basic

Photo by Martín Chambi depicting the Andes in Peru. (Courtesy of Julia Chambi)

to social progress and saw it as a way to mend the fatal localism afflicting the country. Chamorro also was instrumental in the establishment of elections to create a Constituent Assembly that would reform the constitution of 1838. From 1839 to 1842 he was a senator.

By the end of 1842 Chamorro was managing the first newspaper in Granada, *Mentor Nicaragüense,* an organ of the Universidad de Oriente in whose pages he revealed his moral personality. He was an intensely faithful Christian, a staunch supporter of public education, an enemy of ignorance, a concerned political activist, and a dedicated public servant who devoted himself to the preservation of order in Nicaragua. The maintenance of order was Chamorro's major objective upon his assumption of the office of supreme director on 1 April 1853. The new constitution, promulgated on 4 March 1854, provided that the State of Nicaragua be renamed the Republic of Nicaragua and that the title supreme director be changed to president of the republic; thus, Chamorro served as the first and only supreme director and the first president of Nicaragua.

On 1 June 1855, U.S. adventurer William WALKER landed fifty-seven men at Realjo in order to take over Nicaragua. After initial military setbacks, Walker captured Granada in October 1855 and was appointed armed forces chief. Patricio RIVAS served as a figurehead president. Although Walker himself was elected president in June 1856, Honduras, El Salvador, and Guatemala allied against him. Nicaraguan forces ousted Walker in May 1857, and he spent the next three years trying to incite other revolutions. British marines eventually captured Walker in Honduras. He was executed in Trujillo on 12 September 1860. Nicaragua returned to peace, which the Conservative presidents who followed Chamorro maintained until 1893.

Chamorro's legacy, then, rests on the fact that his administration provided the foundation for the orderly succession of mainly civilian Conservative presidents. In addition, Chamorro was responsible for the formation of political clubs that evolved into the Conservative Party. His family has been an active and integral element in the Conservative Party ranks for generations. The Conservatives posthumously honored Chamorro as the founder of their party in 1859.

— SHANNON BELLAMY

CHAMORRO CARDENAL, PEDRO JOAQUÍN

Pedro Joaquín Chamorro Cardenal (*b.* 23 September 1924; *d.* 10 January 1978), Nicaraguan political activist. Chamorro came from a prominent Nicaraguan family with a long history of participation in partisan politics (four of his ancestors held the Nicaraguan presidency). Chamorro's father, Pedro Joaquín Chamorro Zelaya, had founded the daily newspaper *La Prensa* in 1926; upon his father's death in 1952, Chamorro became editor in chief and owner of the paper, which became a vehicle for his opposition to the dictatorship of the Somoza family. Chamorro also condemned the government in a number of books he wrote. In 1948 he cofounded the short-lived National Union of Popular Action and Justice (UNAP). In 1954 he was a member of the Internal Front, which attempted to overthrow Somoza García. He participated in an invasion of Nicaragua from Costa Rica in 1959, the first air invasion in Latin American history and another failed attempt to overthrow the Somoza dictatorship. In 1974 he brought together much of the middle-class opposition to Somoza in the Democratic Union of Liberation (UDEL).

Chamorro paid a high price for his activism. He suffered repeated imprisonment, torture, house arrest, and exile before his assassination in 1978. The public response to his death was a series of general strikes leading to mass insurrection. His death closed off the option of a negotiated end to the Somoza dictatorship. Instead, guerrillas of the Sandinista Liberation Front (Frente Sandinista de la Liberación Nacional—FSLN) overthrew the dictatorship in July 1979.

Chamorro's legacy is still debated. His widow, Violeta BARRIOS DE CHAMORRO (who was elected president of Nicaragua in 1990), and two of his children, Pedro Joaquín and Cristiana, all favor a conservative interpretation of that legacy. They argue that Chamorro was a nationalist devoid of Communist leanings, and that he was a staunch and traditional Catholic. They believe he would have struggled against the Sandinistas, just as they have done.

But his brother Xavier and two other of Pedro Joaquín's children, Carlos Fernando and Claudia, claim that his legacy was far more radical. They note that his nationalism led him to oppose the imperialist aggression of the United States and that his Catholicism led him to work for social justice through what he called "Christian revolution." They claim he would have been a Sandinista revolutionary as they are.

— KAREN KAMPWIRTH

CHAMORRO VARGAS, EMILIANO

Emiliano Chamorro Vargas (*b.* 11 May 1871; *d.* 26 February 1966), president of Nicaragua (1917–1921; 1926). The Nicaraguan who led more revolutions than any other began his military career in 1903, when he commanded an uprising against the Liberal dictator José Santos ZELAYA. Although unsuccessful, this armed rebellion catapulted the Conservative Emiliano Chamorro into the forefront of Nicaraguan politics. Chamorro's animosity toward Zelaya seemingly stemmed not only from party politics and personal ambition but also from Zelaya's mistreatment of Chamorro's father. Chamorro became Zelaya's primary military rival when he joined forces with Juan José ESTRADA and José María MONCADA to overthrow the dictator. By 1909, Zelaya had resigned under pressure from Conservative and anti-Zelaya Liberal forces. Chamorro not only proved himself through this success but also solidified his position as leader of the Conservative Party, a position he maintained until his death.

After Zelaya's ouster, Chamorro served as head of the Constituent Assembly. He returned to the battlefield in 1912, when Minister of War Luis Mena revolted against President Adolfo DÍAZ. After Chamorro defeated Mena, he expressed his own presidential ambitions. The United States, however, supported Díaz and offered Chamorro the position of envoy to the U.S., thereby eliminating any potential challenge to its old friend Díaz.

After the completion of the Panama Canal, the U.S. wanted to ensure that no other country would build a canal in Nicaragua.

As envoy, Chamorro negotiated and signed the controversial Bryan–Chamorro Treaty, which gave the U.S. the option on a canal through Nicaragua. After the completion of the Panama Canal, the U.S. wanted to ensure that no other country would build a canal in Nicaragua. Besides the canal option, the U.S. received a ninety-nine-year lease on the Corn Islands in the Caribbean and on a naval base in the Gulf of Fonseca that would be under U.S. jurisdiction. In turn, the U.S. agreed to pay $3 million in gold to Nicaragua upon ratification. William Jennings Bryan, the U.S. secretary of state under President Woodrow Wilson, and Chamorro signed the treaty in 1914, and the U.S. Senate ratified it in 1916.

The treaty met with strong opposition, particularly from Costa Rica, El Salvador, and Colombia. Costa Rica argued that Nicaragua had violated an arbitral award by U.S. President Grover Cleveland (1888) that bound Nicaragua not to make a canal grant without consulting Costa Rica, because of their common San Juan River boundary. El Salvador expressed outrage at the casual treatment of its territorial rights in the Gulf of Fonseca. Colombia protested Nicaragua's usurpation of the Corn Islands because Colombia claimed sovereignty over them. Chamorro maintained that the treaty provided the best means of solving Nicaragua's economic woes. Not until 1938 did he recognize his mistake in supporting and signing the treaty, for it jeopardized the sovereignty not only of other Latin American countries but also of Nicaragua itself.

Chamorro resigned his position as envoy in 1916 and returned to Nicaragua in order to seek the presidency. The U.S. had previously expressed doubts about Chamorro's military background—it preferred civilian leaders—but after his service as envoy, the U.S. supported Chamorro during the 1916 election, which he won. Upon assuming the presidency, he faced an empty treasury, a national debt, and a foreign debt outstanding since the days of Zelaya. He therefore focused his efforts on obtaining payment of the $3 million in gold promised to Nicaragua upon ratification of the Bryan–Chamorro Treaty. The U.S., however, tied its payment to the settlement of Nicaragua's foreign debt; consequently, Chamorro spent most of his term embroiled in lengthy negotiations.

Chamorro was elected president a second time in 1926, after he overthrew the Conservative government of Carlos SOLÓRZANO. Ostensibly, the coup was intended to neutralize the Liberal influence of Vice President Juan Bautista SACASA, but Chamorro's own desire for the presidency was widely known. Once again, Conservatives and Liberals waged war against one another. Although Chamorro's forces performed well at first, he had fallen out of favor with the U.S. He therefore resigned on 30 October 1926.

During the dictatorship of Anastasio SOMOZA GARCÍA, Chamorro continued his political machinations in the form of abortive uprisings and assassination attempts against the Liberal dictator. Nonetheless, in 1950 Chamorro and Somoza signed the Pact of the Generals, which guaranteed Conservatives one-third of the seats in Congress and one seat on the Supreme Court. Thus, the Conservatives obtained positions within the government while Chamorro's action, as leader of the Conservative Party, gave a boost to the regime's image. These benefits, however, were reaped at great cost, for the Conservative Party ultimately became a mere appendage of the Somoza dictatorship. The consequences were monumental: younger Conservatives who were disenchanted with their party and its leadership sought new avenues for political expression. Their quest led to the creation of the Frente Sandinista de Liberación Nacional, which overthrew the Somoza dynasty on 19 July 1979.

Chamorro, as head of the Conservative Party during this period, failed to provide true leadership, for in reality he represented only his personal ambitions and the interests of a small, elite class. The perennial revolutionary was merely an opportunist.

— SHANNON BELLAMY

CHARRY LARA, FERNANDO

Fernando Charry Lara (*b.* 1920), Colombian poet, born in Bogotá. His love poetry is erotic and characterized by a sense of mystery inspired by the night. Charry Lara's importance lies in his occupying a transitional position between the poets of the Piedra y Cielo group and those of the Mito group, which is known for its universalist poetry. The members of Piedra y Cielo, following the style of Spanish poetry, concentrated on purity of forms, whereas the members of Mito, influenced by existentialism, worried less about form and meditated on reality, love, and poetry itself. Charry Lara became famous with the publication of his first poems in 1944 in the poetry magazine *Cántico*. In the 1950s he was a part of the Mito group, whose magazine is notable for its criticism of the Colombian literary and social situation. Charry Lara's poetry collections are *Nocturnos y otros sueños* (1949), *Los adioses* (1963), and *Pensamientos del amante* (1981). Of the Mito group members, Charry Lara contributed the most to the criticism of Colombian poetry with his essay collection *Lector de poesía* (1975). His poetry was influenced by such Spanish poets as Vicente Aleixandre, by Pablo NERUDA and Jorge Luis BORGES, and by the German Romantic poets.

— JUAN CARLOS GALEANO

CHAUVET, MARIE VIEUX

Marie Vieux Chauvet (*b.* 16 September 1916, *d.* 19 June 1973), Haitian novelist and playwright. Chauvet is the most widely known Haitian woman novelist, and yet her audience has remained restricted. She received early recognition for her first novel, *Fille d'Haïti* (1954; Prize of the Alliance Française). In *Danse sur le volcan* (1957), she brought a feminist perspective to bear on the Haitian Revolution, at a moment when women's movements were virtually nonexistent in Haiti. *Fonds des Nègres* (1960) depicts a young city woman who regains the taste for traditional culture when she is caught in a small town (France-Antilles Prize). *Amour, colère et folie* (1968) has received high critical acclaim for the combination of a lucid style and unadorned insights into the fearful grip of François DUVALIER and his Tonton Macoutes on the Haitian bourgeoisie and intellectuals. It was banned in Haiti, however, and the Chauvet

family bought back all rights. *Les rapaces* (1986) was published posthumously after the fall of Jean-Claude Duvalier.

Although the Haitian political situation and a faltering literary establishment have kept Chauvet from gaining wide readership, she is increasingly recognized as a powerful writer and an early Haitian advocate of women's rights.

— CARROL F. COATES

CHAVES, FEDERICO

Federico Chaves (*b.* 1882; *d.* 24 April 1978), Paraguayan political leader and president (1949–1954). The son of Portuguese immigrants, Federico Chaves spent his early life as a lawyer and judge in Asunción and other locales. His affiliation with the Asociación Nacional Republicana (or Partido Colorado) in the 1930s and 1940s brought him some national prominence, and by 1946, he was vice president of the party. In that year, the dictator Higínio MORÍNIGO brought Chaves into the government as a concession to the Colorados. This coalition regime did not last, however, and in the 1947 civil war that followed, Chaves clarified his position as chief of the "democratic" wing of the party. By so doing, he had placed himself in opposition to the violent Guión Rojo faction, led by Juan Natalicio GONZÁLEZ. In 1948 a coup d'état gave Chaves the chance to ally himself with the new president, Felipe Molas López, with whom he purged the government of González followers.

This housecleaning paved the way for Chaves's own accession to the presidency in 1949. During his administration the Paraguayan economy was plagued by inflation, which Chaves sought to relieve through a close economic union with Perón's Argentina. At home, his policies were repressive, but his arbitrary use of police power failed to curb the opposition of former Guionistas and army officers, one of whom, General Alfredo STROESSNER, launched a revolt in May 1954. After some fierce fighting, Chaves stepped down. A year later, Stroessner rewarded his predecessor's noninterference in the new government by making him ambassador to Paris. He died in Asunción.

— THOMAS L. WHIGHAM

CHAVES, FRANCISCO C.

Francisco C. Chaves (*b.* 7 June 1875; *d.* 1961), Paraguayan educator and statesman. Chaves was born in the city of Asunción in the period in which Paraguay was recovering from the disastrous War of the Triple Alliance. His well-connected family was involved in the country's reconstruction at many levels and contributed several sons and grandsons to serve in high office. Chaves was educated at the Colegio Nacional, graduating with a bachelor's degree in 1895, and at the National University, from which he received a doctorate in law in 1901. He spent the rest of his career teaching law to young students.

After receiving his doctorate, the government named him a justice of the Superior Court and a professor of civil law at the university. Over the next ten years, he held numerous offices, including minister of justice, national deputy, minister to Brazil, and rector of the university.

Chaves taught a generation of lawyers in Paraguay and added a great deal to the professionalization of that field within the country. In later life, he became special envoy to a dozen international conferences while simultaneously serving as a national senator and president of the central bank. He capped his legal career by being named president of the Supreme Court.

— THOMAS L. WHIGHAM

CHAVES, JULIO CÉSAR

Julio César Chaves (*b.* 1907; *d.* 20 February 1988), Paraguayan historian and diplomat. Born into an old and distinguished Asunción family, Chaves spent his early years in the Paraguayan capital, where he later studied international law. After receiving his law degree from the National University in 1929, he went on to hold various educational and diplomatic posts. Chaves was ambassador to Bolivia after the conclusion of the Chaco War (1932–1935), and in 1940 he became President José Félix ESTIGARRIBIA's ambassador to Peru. Two years later, political conditions at home forced him to leave the diplomatic service, and he relocated to Buenos Aires, where he remained eleven years.

In Argentina, Chaves began to pursue his interest in historical topics. He eschewed the blind nationalism of many of his contemporaries and made every effort to give his investigations a measure of empirical depth. To this end, he conducted extensive research in South American and European archives and incorporated his findings in many publications. These included *Historia de las relaciones entre Buenos Aires y el Paraguay* (1938), *Castelli: El Adalid de Mayo,* 2d ed. (1957), *San Martín y Bolívar en Guayaquil* (1950), *El presidente López: Vida y gobierno de Don Carlos* (1955), *La conferencia de Yataity-Corá* (1958), and *Descubrimiento y conquista del Río de la Plata y el Paraguay* (1968). By common consent, however, Chaves's greatest work was *El supremo dictador* (1942), the first modern biographical treat-

ment of the nineteenth-century Paraguayan dictator Dr. José Gaspar Rodriguez de FRANCIA.

Chávez became an unofficial spokesman for Paraguay's intellectuals, traveling to scores of international scholarly conferences.

After his return to Asunción in the mid-1950s, Chaves resumed his teaching career. His good relations with the STROESSNER government (his brother was longtime president of the Colorado Party) assured him freedom of action in the country as well as considerable prestige. He became an unofficial spokesman for his country's intellectuals, traveling to scores of international scholarly conferences and acting as head of the Paraguayan PEN Club and of the Academia Paraguaya de la Historia.

— THOMAS L. WHIGHAM

CHÁVEZ, CARLOS

Carlos Chávez (*b.* 13 June 1899; *d.* 2 August 1978), Mexican composer, conductor, educator, and administrator. Chávez began piano studies with his brother and continued with Manuel Ponce and Luis Ogazón. His penchant for improvisation led him to begin composing at an early age. He wrote his first symphony at age sixteen, but most of his early works were miniatures derivative of European styles or drawn from the Mexican song tradition. A concert of his works in 1921 brought public awareness of a new creative voice in Mexico. Travels in 1922 left him discouraged over the conservative state of music in Europe. Back in Mexico he produced new music concerts, but impatient for a better response, he moved to New York City (1926–1928) and received professional encouragement from the new music establishment, notably Aaron Copland, Roger Sessions, and Edgard Varèse. Chávez returned to Mexico in 1928 and was appointed director of the Symphony Orchestra of Mexico (remaining twenty-one years). Quick success led to directorships of the National Conservatory and fine arts department in the Ministry of Education. His conducting reputation grew rapidly through engagements with the New York Philharmonic and NBC Orchestras (1937–1938). In 1947 President Miguel Alemán named him founding director of the National Institute of Fine Arts with sweeping authority over all of the arts. Chávez was an active and productive writer, lecturer, conductor, teacher, and statesman, but claimed these activities were no more than a means for him to compose. His most widely accepted composition was the nationalistic work employing Mexican Indian themes, *Sinfonía india* (1935). His more abstract and cerebral style in later years signaled a move away from nationalism.

— ROBERT L. PARKER

CHÁVEZ, MARIANO

Mariano Chávez (*b.* 1808; *d.* ca. 1845), president of the New Mexico Assembly and interim governor (1844). Like many of the political actors of the Mexican period, Chávez became wealthy through his participation in the trade between Santa Fe and Missouri during the 1830s. His wealth and elevated social status brought Chávez the opportunity to demonstrate his leadership during the popular revolt of northern New Mexicans in 1837 against the centralist governor, Albino PÉREZ. Chávez exhorted those who chose to show their allegiance to Santa Anna and his centralist government to follow the leadership of General Manuel ARMIJO. The Plan de Tomé denounced the rebel governor, José González, and named Armijo as the New Mexican leader and Chávez as his lieutenant. Together Armijo and Chávez defeated the rebels, reoccupied Santa Fe, and apprehended and executed González.

Chávez's status as a *rico* and his family connections to Manuel Armijo aided his election in 1844 as president of the New Mexican Assembly and explains his appointment as interim governor shortly afterward by Armijo, who became ill. As Assembly president, Chávez swore loyalty to Santa Anna and his recently promulgated *bases orgánicas* while protesting the neglect of New Mexico by the central government.

During his brief tenure as governor, Chávez distinguished himself by becoming involved in a feud between Father Antonio José Martínez of Taos and Charles Bent and his business associates. In 1844, in response to a petition by Martínez, Chávez revoked the enormous Beaubien-Miranda grant made by Armijo, thereby adding to its already complicated history. The year before, the governor's brother, Antonio José Chávez, had been robbed and murdered by American bandits. Agreeing with Martínez that increasing foreign influence and interest in New Mexico threatened Mexican sovereignty, Chávez sought to enforce a ban on foreigners holding an interest in Mexican land grants, apparently believing that Charles Bent held a share of the Beaubien-Miranda grant. On 15 May 1844, Chávez was replaced by a Santa Anna appointee, General Mariano Martínez.

Known as a wealthy and educated political operator during his short career, Chávez used his moment in power to diminish the growing political and economic power that American expatriates were gaining in New Mexico. Just before sending his son José Francisco to school in Saint Louis in 1841, Chávez apparently said to him: "The heretics are going to overrun all this country. Go and learn their language and come back prepared to defend your people."

— ROSS H. FRANK

CHÁVEZ MORADO, JOSÉ

José Chávez Morado (*b.* 4 January 1909), Mexican painter and educator. Born in Siloa, Guanajuato, Mexico, Chávez Morado belongs to the "second generation" of Mexican mural painters. He studied engraving and lithography at San Carlos Academy in Mexico City. In 1937, together with Feliciano Peña, Francisco Gutiérrez, and Olga Costa, he painted the murals of the Escuela Normal. In one year alone (1948) he painted over fifteen public buildings, using various techniques. Later he painted frescoes at the Alhóndiga de Granaditas and the Exhacienda Minera (now called Pastita) in Guanajuato. He has exhibited his easel paintings in important galleries and museums throughout Latin America, Europe, Asia, and the United States.

— BÉLGICA RODRÍGUEZ

CHÁVEZ SÁNCHEZ, IGNACIO

Ignacio Chávez Sánchez (*b.* 31 January 1897; *d.* 12 July 1979), Mexican educator and cardiologist. Member of a distinguished generation of intellectuals and politicians from the Colegio Nacional de San Nicolás, Morelia, Michoacán, Chávez became one of the youngest figures ever to direct a major Mexican university, the Colegio Nacional de San Nicolás, in 1920. After obtaining medical and Ph.D. degrees from the National University, he studied in Europe. He served as dean of the National Medical School (1933–1934) and in 1944 founded the National Institute of Cardiology, which he directed for many years. He was rector of the National University from 1961 to 1966, a period of student unrest. Personal physician to many presidents, Chávez left an important legacy in institutionalizing Mexican heart research. He was awarded Mexico's National Prize of Arts and Sciences in 1961.

— RODERIC AI CAMP

CHIARI, RODOLFO E.

Rodolfo E. Chiari (*b.* 15 November 1870; *d.* 16 August 1937), Panamanian politician, president (1924–1928), and businessman. Born in Aguadulce, he held many government posts before and after the country's separation from Colombia. He was a deputy to the National Convention in 1904, treasurer of Panama City (1905–1906), deputy secretary of the treasury in the national government (1908), and manager of the national Bank (1909–1914). In 1910 he was elected third designate to the presidency, and in 1912 he briefly took charge of the executive. In 1914 he became the secretary of government and justice, and in 1922 he was appointed director general of the telegraph service. Chiari was a prominent member of the Liberal Party, perhaps second only to Belisario PORRAS. Following his election in 1924, Chiari substituted Porras's populist style with a more business-oriented administration, which led to a quarrel and ultimately to a split in the party.

In 1925 Chiari faced two serious crises. The first was a rebellion by the Cuna Indians on the San Blas Islands, which he quelled successfully. Then, the Tenants Revolt (*movimiento inquilinario*) paralyzed the city for two days. The strike was defeated only after Chiari requested the help of U.S. troops stationed in the Canal Zone.

Chiari negotiated a new treaty with the United States in 1926, but it was never ratified by the National Assembly because of concern over one article that made Panama an instant ally of the United States whenever the latter became involved in an armed conflict.

– JUAN MANUEL PÉREZ

CHIARI REMÓN, ROBERTO FRANCISCO

Roberto Francisco Chiari Remón (*b.* 2 March 1905; *d.* 1981), Panamanian president (1949, 1960–1964). A liberal and popular politician, he was the son of Roberto CHIARI, who had been president of Panama from 1924 to 1928. Before becoming president he was deputy to the National Assembly (1940–1945) and minister of health and public works (1945). In 1948 he was elected second vice president, and in the following year he was president for five days (20–24 November 1949) after the overthrow of Daniel Chanis. Chiari resigned after the Supreme Court declared him ineligible for the presidency. In 1952 he was the presidential candidate of a popular coalition called the Civilista Alliance, whose victory was not recognized because of the opposition's imposition of Colonel José Antonio ("Chichi") REMÓN CANTERA.

Chiari was elected president in 1960 as the candidate of a four-party coalition, the first opposition candidate to win an election in Panama. He entered office with a reformist attitude and was intent on breaking the oligarchy's grip on power. However, most of his reform measures were blocked by the National Assembly. Seeking better relations with the United States, Chiari trav-

eled to Washington, D.C., and won some concessions from the Kennedy administration, including the right to fly the Panamanian flag at certain sites in the Canal Zone. However, as a result of the 1964 flag riots, Chiari broke diplomatic relations with the United States and demanded the abrogation of the 1903 treaty. He was succeeded in 1964 by Marcos Aurelio ROBLES.

– JUAN MANUEL PÉREZ

CHIBÁS, EDUARDO

Eduardo Chibás (*b.* 26 August 1907; *d.* 5 August 1951), founder of the Cuban Orthodox Party. Born in Oriente, Chibás was one of the founders of the Directorio Estudiantil at the University of Havana in the mid-1920s. He studied law and then lived in exile in Miami, Florida (1927–1933), because of his sharp criticism of Gerardo MACHADO's government (1925–1933). Following Machado's downfall, Chibás returned to Cuba to support the candidacy of Ramón GRAU SAN MARTÍN, who became president on 10 September 1933. On 14 January 1934, Fulgencio BATISTA orchestrated Grau's removal from power. Chibás became strongly critical of the series of governments headed by puppet presidents, and particularly of Batista. In 1938, he joined the Authentic Party and in 1940 again backed Grau for the presidency. After Grau was elected president in 1944, Chibás became disillusioned with his nepotism and governmental corruption.

In 1947, Chibás broke away from the Authentic Party and founded the Orthodox Party. He was a candidate for the presidency in 1948, finishing third in the race. During Carlos PRÍO SOCARRÁS's tenure (1948–1952), Chibás used weekly radio broadcasts to attack government policies and corruption.

Chibás committed suicide by shooting himself during an emotional radio broadcast on 5 August 1951. His death created a political vacuum and rift in the Orthodox Party, facilitating Batista's coup on 10 March 1952.

– JAIME SUCHLICKI

CHIMALPAHIN

Chimalpahin (*b.* 26 May 1579; *d.* 1660), premier writer of Nahuatl prose. Don Domingo Francisco de San Antón Muñón Chimalpahin Quauhtlehuanitzin, who was born in Amecameca, Mexico, and was most active in the first two decades of the seventeenth century, produced a mass of historical writings on indigenous Mexico. Although he never lost his close identification with his homeland, his career unfolded in Mexico City. Chimalpahin wrote copiously about both Chalco and Mexico Tenochtitlán, covering both pre-conquest and post-conquest periods. His annals represent a large range of Nahuatl thought and expression.

— JAMES LOCKHART

CHIRINO, JOSÉ LEONARDO

José Leonardo Chirino (*d.* 10 December 1796), leader of the 1795 slave uprising in Coro, Venezuela. Chirino was a *zambo*, the freeborn son of a male slave and an Indian woman. He worked for a rich Coro trader named José Tellería, whom Chirino had accompanied on one of his commercial ventures to Haiti. While there, Chirino became aware of the early black and mulatto insurrectionary movements. In 1795, he and fellow conspirator José Caridad González, an African slave who had fled Curaçao for Coro, instigated an uprising of blacks in which they favored the establishment of a republic based on French law and proclaiming social equality and the abolition of privileges. Chirino was pursued, imprisoned, and condemned to death by hanging. He was executed in the central plaza of Caracas. His head was hung in a cage at the door of the city, and his severed hands were displayed in two towns in the area of Falcón.

— INÉS QUINTERO

CHOCANO, JOSÉ SANTOS

José Santos Chocano (*b.* 14 May 1875; *d.* 13 December 1934), Peruvian poet. Acclaimed as Poet of America, Chocano was born in Lima to a father whose origin can be traced to Don Gonzalo Fernández de Córdoba, a famous Spanish soldier known as the "Great Captain"; his mother was a wealthy miner's daughter. Nevertheless, Chocano was not a happy child; he made the motto of his family coat of arms his own: Either I find a way, or I make one. On entering the University of San Marcos, at age 16, he began three careers: student, poet, and politician. In politics he learned that in Peru, family

---

Chocano was not a happy child; he made the motto of his family coat of arms his own: Either I find a way, or I make one.

---

name means more than personal skills. His success as a poet was outstanding: he began writing before the age of ten and published his first book at twenty. His *Poesías*

completas was published in Spain in 1902. King Alfonso XIII received from Chocano's hand the book *Alma América* (1906); Spanish American countries demanded his presence and applauded his recitals; and, in 1922, the Peruvian nation crowned him National Poet.

Chocano did not achieve political power because his creed accepted the so-called organizational dictatorships. But as a diplomat, he scored resounding victories arbitrating disputes between Guatemala and El Salvador, Colombia and Peru, and Peru and Ecuador. Twice Chocano escaped the firing squad. Once he eluded an angry mob in Guatemala, and on another occasion, after receiving a slap in the face, he fatally shot his adversary. One biographer characterized Chocano's adventurous and colorful life as a "mixture of vigor, audacity, and the picaresque." Disheartened, he moved with his young wife, Margarita, and their son to Chile. The Chileans welcomed Chocano, who continued writing, reciting, and trying his hand at business ventures. He died when an assassin fatally stabbed him on a streetcar. One of his verses inadvertently became a prophecy: "He who took a life by assault/could only die by a sword thrust."

— BALBINA SAMANIEGO

CHOCRÓN, ISAAC

Isaac Chocrón (*b.* 25 September 1932), Venezuelan playwright, director, actor, critic, and novelist, was trained in the United States and England as an economist. One of the moving forces in the contemporary Venezuelan theater, along with José Ignacio Cabrujas and Román Chalbaud, Chocrón, a native of Maracay, founded the Nuevo Grupo in 1967 and pioneered a vanguard, independent theater in Caracas that set the standards of quality for a new generation. The Nuevo Grupo offered an international repertoire as well as original plays by Venezuelan authors.

Chocrón's theater is varied and polemical. His first play, *Mónica y el florentino* (1959), focused on problems of alienation and communication within an international guest house. His popular *Asia y el lejano oriente* (1966), about the selling of a nation, was revived in 1984 for the grand opening of the Venezuelan National Theater Company, which Chocrón was invited to head. Chocrón dealt with consumerism in *O.K.* (1969) and with homosexuality in *La revolución* (1972). Other plays include *El acompañante* (1978) and *Mesopotamia* (1979). *Simón* (1983) presents Simón Bolívar and his mentor Simón Rodríguez in a challenging encounter between the would-be hero and his wiser master, who obliges him to face up his potential and to the promise of his leadership. Chocrón has written a major book on American playwrights of the twentieth century.

— GEORGE WOODYARD

CHONCHOL, JACQUES

Jacques Chonchol (*b.* ca. 1926), Chilean political leader and agrarian reform expert. A member of the Christian Democratic Party (PDC), Chonchol advocated the creation of a communitarian society as the way to solve Chile's economic problems and to avoid the excesses of socialism and capitalism. A member of the PDC's left wing, he served as a functionary of Eduardo FREI's agrarian reform program. In 1968, distressed by what he considered Frei's conservative policies, he broke with the PDC, creating the United Movement of Popular Action (MAPU). Chonchol later served as Salvador Allende's minister of agriculture, accelerating the pace of agrarian reform. He subsequently bolted from MAPU, which he claimed had become too Marxist, to form the Christian Left. Later he resigned from Allende's cabinet over political differences.

— WILLIAM F. SATER

CHONG NETO, MANUEL

Manuel Chong Neto (*b.* 1927), Panamanian artist. Chong Neto studied painting at the San Carlos Academy in Mexico (1963–1965). He began his professional career as a high school art teacher and, after 1970, he also taught at the Casa de la Escultura, the Escuela Nacional de Artes Plásticas, and the National University.

A figurative artist, Chong Neto's compositions are characterized by formal balance and the contrast of darks and lights. His early renderings of human characters and urban landscapes show the influence of Mexican social realism. He is best known for the large, sensuous, and enigmatic woman who appears in most of his paintings. She is often accompanied by men, voyeurs, and symbolic birds or owls, as in his dramatic drawings series *Poemas Eróticos* (1976).

— MONICA E. KUPFER

CHRISTMAS, LEE

Lee Christmas (*b.* 22 February 1863; *d.* 24 January 1924), North American soldier of fortune in Honduras. Christmas was probably the most famous of a generation of North American adventurers and filibusters who migrated to Central America from the 1890s until World War I. He left New Orleans in 1894 and got a job railroading on the north Honduran coast. From then until his return to the United States after World War I, he was involved in the political turmoil of Hon-

duras and Guatemala. He served as national police chief of Honduras, fought in the Honduran-Nicaraguan war of 1907, and plotted with former Honduran president Manuel BONILLA and Guy "Machine-Gun" MOLONY to restore Bonilla to power, a plan that culminated in the attack on La Ceiba in January 1911. Christmas was rewarded with a sinecure at Puerto Cortés, and Sam "The Banana Man" ZEMURRAY gained valuable concessions for his Cuyamel Fruit Company on the north Honduran coast. In 1915 Christmas lost favor with the Honduran regime and joined Manuel Estrada Cabrera's secret service in Guatemala. He returned virtually penniless to the United States in March 1922 and died of tropical sprue.

— LESTER D. LANGLEY

CHRISTOPHE, HENRI

Henri Christophe (*b.* 6 October 1767; *d.* 8 October 1820), president of the State of Haiti (1806–1811) and king (1811–1820). In the inky darkness of a mountain night, an exhausted entourage of royalty and servants led by Queen Marie-Louise reached the outer gates of the fortress of Citadelle la Ferrière. Once inside the compound, two royal aides hurriedly looked for shovels and a place to dispose of their cargo, an unshrouded body in a hammock. Finally, unable to inter the cadaver in suitable fashion, they simply dumped their cargo into a pile of quick lime and left. Later Haiti would entomb the remains on this site with the occupant's own prepared epitaph: "I shall be reborn from my ashes."

Always the showman, Henri Christophe left Haitians with the fear that he just might return. He had cleverly built a personal mythology to buttress his tyrannical rule of the northern State of Haiti. Historian James Leyburn called Christophe Haiti's best nineteenth-century ruler, which he was. And Simon BOLÍVAR might have been thinking of Christophe when he stated in his Jamaica Letter (1815) that Latin America needed strong, paternalistic rulers who would govern for life and who would educate and guide their people to assume democratic responsibilities.

Born a slave on Grenada, Christophe became the property of a ship captain and then the chattel of Saint-Domingue sugar planter Master Badechi, who soon put him to work at Couronne, a hostelry in Le Cap François. In 1778 Christophe served as a slave orderly for the French at Savannah, Georgia, where he suffered injury. In 1790 in northern Saint-Domingue he rode with a dragoon unit that suppressed the rebellion of Vincent Ogé (1755?–1791). It is probable that by this time Christophe had become a free black. He cherished his

British origins, always gave the English spelling, "Henry," and chose George III for hero worship.

When Toussaint L'OUVERTURE joined the French in 1794, Christophe's military career had been languishing, as he had attained only the rank of captain of the infantry at the garrison of Le Cap François. But Toussaint recognized in the young officer the qualities of good leadership. Christophe served his commander well in the La Petite-Anse district, where he and Colonel Vincent introduced the *fermage* (system of forced labor and government management) to maintain the plantation system. Under this profit-sharing plan, laborers had to surrender a great deal of personal freedom and submit to corporal punishment. Toussaint was impressed and used the scheme widely across Saint-Domingue. In 1799 Christophe, by then a colonel, commanded the garrison at Le Cap François and would later join Toussaint in crushing the Moyse Rebellion (October 1801).

When the expedition of General Charles Leclerc reached Haiti from France, Christophe at first fought well by torching Le Cap François and moving to the interior. But then came an unexpected event, Christophe's surrender to the French on 26 April 1802, and his agreement to command a French unit under General Jean Hardy. Ralph Korngold has argued that Christophe betrayed Toussaint, but his belief is not shared by biographer Hubert Cole. Christophe himself defended his action by saying that he was tired of living like a savage. In October 1802, he deserted the French and joined the rising tide of black rebels opposed to the restoration of slavery.

In February 1807, Christophe was angered when the mulatto-dominated assembly at Port-au-Prince handed him a weakened presidency. There followed a civil conflict in which Christophe ruled the State of Haiti in the north and Alexandre PÉTION and a mulatto clique governed the Republic of Haiti in the south.

From the beginning of his rule, Christophe pursued an effective social policy. He hired English teachers to establish a system of national schools. He demanded that his subjects have church marriages. On this issue he often wandered about the countryside looking for wayward lovers. If they suffered his apprehension, their fate was an altar and a priest. He even tried to impose desirable personal habits upon his people. The Royal Dahomets, his special African police force, inspected Haitians for neatness and honesty. They tested this second quality by dropping a wallet and other valuables in a public place, hiding, and then arresting any culprit who found the items without making a police report. Public awe of Christophe grew as his subjects often sighted him attended by an aide with a telescope. Pop-

ular rumor maintained that Christophe saw all and punished all.

Economically, Christophe followed Toussaint's maintenance of the plantation system without slavery. But Christophe did break up some of the large estates late in his rule and sold the parcels to small farmers, a point Hubert Cole believes other historians may have missed. To further his economic plans, Christophe became King Henry I on 28 March 1811. Surrounding his crown was a new Haitian nobility. To them he gave generous land grants and pompous titles. To him they gave loyalty and maintained prosperous plantations.

On 8 October 1820 a dying Christophe committed suicide at his plush palace, Sans Souci. Faithful followers carried his body to Citadelle La Ferrière, the great monument to black work skills, which Christophe had constructed during his rule. Their monument was fittingly his last resting place.

– THOMAS O. OTT

CHUMACERO, ALÍ

Alí Chumacero (*b.* 9 July 1918), Mexican poet, editor, and essayist. Early in his career Chumacero was associated with the literary journals *Tierra Nueva* (1940–1942) and *El Hijo Pródigo* (1943–1946) and subsequently with *México en la Cultura* and *La Cultura en México,* among others. He has held important positions with the publisher Fondo de Cultura Económica, has edited works of nineteenth-century Mexican Romantic poets and of Alfonso REYES and Xavier VILLAURRUTIA, and has collaborated with Octavio PAZ, José Emilio PACHECO, and Homero ARIDJIS in the preparation of the influential anthology *Poesía en movimiento* (1966). His essays range across the fields of poetics, literary history and criticism, and contemporary Mexican art. Chumacero's poetry, almost all of it written before 1956, is a very carefully crafted, subtle exploration of existential desolation, solitude, and the inadequate consolations of love. The earlier poems (*Páramo de sueños* [1944] and *Imágenes desterradas* [1948]) are quite hermetic, bearing traces of his predecessors, the Contemporáneos (most notably José GOROSTIZA and Villaurrutia). The later poems (*Palabras en reposo* [1956]) are more accessible, though no less complex.

– MICHAEL J. DOUDOROFF

CIENFUEGOS, CAMILO

Camilo Cienfuegos (*b.* 1931; *d.* October 1959), Cuban revolutionary and chief of staff of the rebel army. Born to a poor family in the Layanó district of Havana, Camilo Cienfuegos nevertheless had a happy childhood. He managed to secure an eighth-grade education while selling shoes to support his family, and he displayed his social conscience at an early age, collecting money in 1937 to aid the orphans of the Spanish Civil War. Cienfuegos's father resisted formal education for his children, preferring instead that Camilo and his older brother Osmany receive private lessons from an old Communist acquaintance. Nevertheless, Camilo was drawn to more social forms of activity and joined the anti-Fascist student paper *Lídice* in 1945. He was a handsome, popular, and athletic young man with red hair and a quick laugh. In 1947 Cienfuegos won the national *pelota* championships and was the pride of his family.

Cienfuegos managed to secure an eighth-grade education while selling shoes to support his family.

After ending his formal education for good, Cienfuegos worked at odd jobs in Havana and took up sculpting. The on-air suicide of political activist and radio personality Eddy Chibás in 1951 prompted Cienfuegos to leave Cuba for the United States, where he hoped to make his fortune. In 1955 he was back in Cuba and participating in demonstrations against BATISTA and the police on behalf of Fidel CASTRO's Twenty-sixth of July Movement. With his forceful personality, Camilo Cienfuegos quickly caught Castro's eye, and he joined the exile group in Mexico that was preparing for an invasion of Cuba. He was one of the eighty-one men who set out with Fidel Castro in November 1956 on the *Granma* to start a revolution.

After the initial landing, Cienfuegos became one of the *comandantes* of the rebel forces. He appears to have been an avowed Marxist at a time when the revolutionaries had not yet declared an official ideology; in his districts Cienfuegos set up schools that taught literacy and socialist doctrine.

After the rebels' victory on 1 January 1959, Cienfuegos was appointed chief of staff of the armed forces and became the second most popular figure of the revolution after Castro himself. He disappeared mysteriously on a solo flight from Camagüey to Havana in October 1959; no trace of the wreckage was ever found, and the disappearance remained controversial.

— KAREN RACINE

CIEZA DE LEÓN, PEDRO DE

Pedro de Cieza de León (*b.* ca. 1520; *d.* 2 July 1554), "prince of the Peruvian chroniclers." Born in Llerena, Spain, the son of Lope de León and Leonor de Cazalla, Pedro had at least three sisters and one brother. Little is known of his early years. On 3 June 1535 he set sail for the Indies, heading for Santo Domingo. He first entered South America via Cartagena on the north coast of present-day Colombia and participated in minor expeditions in search of riches, some of which were little more than grave-robbing episodes. In 1536 he joined the Entrada of Juan de Vadillo to explore the Gulf of Urabá; the next year he followed the same leader in the discovery of the province of Abibe—both were financial disasters. In 1539 he set out to explore the Cauca and Atrato basin with a new force under Jorge Robledo that later founded Ancerma and Cartago (1540) in the rich Quimbaya region. It was in Cartago in 1541 that Cieza first began to keep copious notes on what he saw and experienced. The following year he was representing Jorge Robledo in the Audiencia of Panamá, where he probably met for the first time those escaping the conflict in Peru. The same year he helped found the city of Arma and received an Encomienda for his efforts.

With the rising of Gonzalo PIZARRO in Peru, Cieza traveled to serve the royalists under Pedro de la GASCA, president of the Audiencia of Lima. In September 1547 he crossed the Pacasmayo Valley with the king's forces, continued into highland Jauja, and marched southward toward Cuzco. He fought at the battle of Jaquijahuana (9 April 1548) and witnessed the execution of the rebels Gonzalo Pizarro and Francisco de Carvajal. Gasca must have been impressed by young Cieza's scholarly capabilities, for he seems to have appointed Cieza official chronicler of events in Peru. During 1549 the young chronicler traveled into southern Charcas (modern Bolivia) under the president's orders. For a few months in 1550 he resided in Cuzco, where he took oral testimony about the Inca past from several Indians, including Cayu Tupac, descendant of the ruler HUAYNA CAPAC. Cieza completed the first part of his multivolume history in Lima on 8 September 1550.

In 1551 Cieza voyaged back to Spain and was in Toledo by mid-1552 to present Philip II with a copy of the manuscript. Following his return to Spain, Cieza married Isabel López de Abreu, daughter of Maria de Abreu and the prosperous merchant Juan de Llerena. Cieza died before he could complete his massive narrative and was buried in Seville in the Church of San Vicente alongside his wife, who died at age thirty-four only two months earlier.

Cieza de León intended to publish a four-part history of Peru. Part one, the only section printed during the author's lifetime, was a geographical and ethnological account of South America's Andean region; part two, the "Señorío de los Incas," was a history of the Incas;

part three was the account of the Spanish discovery and conquest of the realm; and part four, made up of five book-length manuscripts, examined the civil wars: Las Salinas, Chupas, Quito, Huarina, and Jaquijahuana. Cieza became a sixteenth-century "best-seller" with the 1553 Seville edition of part one, which was quickly followed by three Spanish editions in Amberes in 1554 and seven Italian translations between 1555 and 1576.

– NOBLE DAVID COOK

CISNEROS, BALTASAR HIDALGO DE

Baltasar Hidalgo de Cisneros (*b.* 12 June 1755; *d.* 9 June 1829), viceroy of Río de la Plata (1809–1810). A military man and the last viceroy of the Río de la Plata, Cisneros was born in Cartagena, Spain, the son of a high-ranking naval officer. Following in his father's footsteps, Cisneros entered the navy, progressing through the ranks and serving in the Pacific, in Algeria, and in the Spanish campaigns against the revolutionary government of France. He arrived in Buenos Aires in June 1809, sent by the Seville junta that was ruling Spain in the name of the deposed king. His nine months in office were marked by a disintegration of the political scene and a worsening of economic conditions. He also was unable to bring the local militia, emboldened by their victories in repelling two British invasions (1804, 1806–1807), under his control. By May 1810, forced into an emergency created by the fall of Seville to the French, Cisneros decided to call an open town council meeting (*cabildo abierto*). Although the viceroy believed that he would be called upon to form a new government, the *cabildo abierto* voted to depose Cisneros; however, he was allowed to return to Spain.

Able to absolve himself of any blame for the loss of Buenos Aires, Cisneros was successively named commandant general of Cádiz, minister of the navy, and director general of the fleet. Appointed captain-general of Cartagena by the Constitutionist government during the 1820 uprising, he held this post until his death.

– SUSAN M. SOCOLOW

CISNEROS, FRANCISCO JAVIER

Francisco Javier Cisneros (*b.* 28 December 1836; *d.* 7 July 1898), transportation developer in Colombia. Cisneros was educated in his hometown of Santiago de Cuba and in Havana, where he received his civil engineering degree (1857). He studied at Rensselaer Polytechnic Institute in Troy, New York, then engaged in railway construction in Cuba from 1857 to 1868. His pro-independence activities (1868–1871) forced him into exile in New York City. Cisneros attempted to

work in Peru but in 1873 left for Colombia. There, the Antioquia Railroad (upon which he labored intermittently until 1885), the Cauca Railroad (1878–1883), the Barranquilla Railroad (1885–1895), plus dock construction at Puerto Colombia and the placement of steamboats on the Magdalena River (1877–1885; 1889–1898) all testify to Cisneros's developmental vision. Colombia's unsettled politics and weak economy were structural liabilities that Cisneros found insurmountable. He died in New York City.

– J. LEÓN HELGUERA

CISNEROS BETANCOURT, SALVADOR

Salvador Cisneros Betancourt (*b.* 10 October 1828; *d.* 28 February 1914), Cuban independence leader and legislator. Cisneros Betancourt was born in Camagüey, central Cuba, to a wealthy and noble family. After independence, people affectionately continued to call him by his title, Marqués of Santa Lucía. As a young man, he was imprisoned in Spain for his conspiratorial activities. Cisneros Betancourt was involved in Cuba's two wars of independence and was president of the insurgent provisional government in both. He also participated in the framing of the insurgent constitutions and was a delegate to the constituent assembly that approved Cuba's first constitution as an independent nation (1900–1901). Cisneros Betancourt strongly urged the rejection of the Platt Amendment, accusing the United States of exercising "the power of the strong over the weak." He was a member of the Cuban Senate from 1902 until his death. Cisneros Betancourt died in Havana.

– JOSÉ M. HERNÁNDEZ

CLAIR, JANETE

Janete Clair (*b.* 1925; *d.* 1983), Brazilian *telenovela* author, was born in Minas Gerais. She was the most prominent scriptwriter of *telenovelas* (prime-time serial dramas) for TV Globo from the late 1960s to 1983. She started as a radio actress in 1943 for Rádio Tupi in São Paulo, and turned to writing after she married playwright Dias Gomes, who also became a prominent scriptwriter for TV Globo. Clair's first major success came in 1956 with the *radionovela Perdão, meu filho* for Radio Nacional. She wrote a few *telenovelas*, such as *Paixão proibida* (Prohibited Passion), for TV Tupi in the mid-1960s, then moved to TV Globo in 1967, at the time it began to invest heavily in *telenovela* production, including hiring all the best talent available. After 1968, TV Globo began to dominate the market for *telenovelas*, in part due to Clair's writing. She was the most popular author for the most watched *telenovela* time slot, 8 P.M. Her personal popularity contributed to an unusual phenomenon in popular television: some of the major scriptwriters for Brazilian *telenovelas* became major public figures, as popular and well known as the most prominent actors and actresses. Clair wrote nineteen *telenovelas* for TV Globo from 1967 to 1983. Her first was *Anastácia, a mulher sem destino* (Anastasia, the Woman Without a Destiny, 1967). Two of her more popular *telenovelas* were for *Selva de pedra* (Jungle of Stone, 1972) and *Pecado capital* (Mortal Sin, 1975–1976). After her death in 1983, her writing style and popular touch remained standards by which *telenovelas* were judged by critics and public. The TV Globo Center for Production (Casa da Criação) was named for her.

– JOSEPH STRAUBHAAR

CLARK, LYGIA

Lygia Clark (*b.* 1920; *d.* 1988), Brazilian painter and sculptor. Clark began her artistic training in the late 1940s at the school of Fine Arts in Belo Horizonte, where she was born. Her first teachers were the painter Alberto da Veiga Guignard and the landscape architect Roberto BURLE MARX. Upon graduating, she traveled to Europe and studied in Paris for two years with Ferdinand Léger. In 1952 she returned to Rio de Janeiro, where she began to experiment with the geometric abstract language common to constructivist and concrete art. In 1954, with the concrete movement in full swing, Clark joined Lygia PAPE, Hélio OITICICA, Decio Vieira, and other concrete artists as members of Grupo Frente. Eschewing representation, these artists opposed the imitation of nature as well as lyrical nonfigurative art.

Clark's neoconcrete movement "emerged out of the need to express the complex realities of modern man with a new plastic language."

By 1959, with the fragmentation of the concrete movement, Clark, Ferreira Gullar, Lygia Pape, Hélio Oiticica, and others formed the neoconcrete group. In their manifesto they declared that the neoconcrete movement had "emerged out of the need to express the complex realities of modern man with a new plastic language." They rejected the scientific and positivist attitudes permeating the concrete movement and called for the incorporation of "new verbal dimensions" in art. Through painting and sculpture, Clark sought to create "real," kinetic space. Toward this end, she extended her canvases beyond the confines of the frame, searching for an organic dimension within geometry so that the spectator could enter the painting and participate, such as in *Animals,* a sculpture formed of metal surfaces, which the spectator can manipulate.

In the 1960s Clark experimented with other tactile artistic projects such as short films and body art. By the 1970s her interests ventured away from art into the psychological implications of spectator participation and in 1976 led her to declare herself a "nonartist."

– CAREN A. MEGHREBLIAN

CLAVÉ, PELEGRÍN

Pelegrín Clavé (*b.* 17 June 1811; *d.* 13 September 1880), painter. Trained in his native Barcelona and in Rome, Clavé was in Mexico between 1846 and 1867 as director of the reestablished Academia de San Carlos. In Rome he studied with Tommaso Minardi and, like the sculptor Manuel VILAR, he was sympathetic to the Nazarenes (a group of German artists who sought to revitalize Christian art). While in Mexico he executed many portraits reminiscent of those of Jean Auguste Dominique Ingres, with which he must have become familiar in Rome; these are considered his most significant work. With his pupils Clavé decorated the interior of the dome of the church of the Profesa (1860–1867; destroyed by fire in 1914). He was instrumental in the formation of the collection of colonial paintings in the galleries of the Academia de San Carlos. Political difficulties led Clavé to return to Barcelona in 1868. There he lectured and wrote about Mexican painting, and worked on plans to decorate the dome of the church of the Merced.

– CLARA BARGELLINI

CLAVER, PEDRO

Pedro Claver (*b.* 26? June 1580; *d.* 8 September 1654), Catalan Jesuit missionary in Colombia who became a saint. Born in Verdú, Spain, Claver joined the Jesuits in 1602. He arrived in Cartagena in 1610, then quickly went on to Bogotá and Tunja, where he studied until 1615. Ordained in Cartagena in 1616, Claver worked among the black slaves as a protégé of Father Alonso Sandoval. In 1622 he signed his final vows as "Pedro Claver, slave of the negroes forever." For the next three decades he met the slave ships coming to Cartagena, the main slave emporium in Spanish America, and ministered to the needs of their human cargo. Claver had black translators fluent in African languages who questioned, instructed, and aided the slaves in religious and health matters. He also sought out the destitute in hospitals and jails and provided them with medicine, food, and clothes. When asked how many he had baptized, he answered, "more than three hundred thousand." Claver died in Cartagena. He was beatified by Pius IX in 1851 and canonized by Leo XIII in 1888.

– MAURICE P. BRUNGARDT

CLAVIGERO, FRANCISCO JAVIER

Francisco Javier Clavigero (Clavijero; *b.* 9 September 1731; *d.* 2 April 1787), historian and promoter of the Mexican Enlightenment. Clavigero, a native of Veracruz, is noted for his role in introducing modern philosophy into Mexico (a modified Aristotelian cosmology influenced by eighteenth-century sciences with an emphasis on empirically based critical analysis). He taught in the Jesuit *colegios* in Valladolid (modern-day Morelia) and in Guadalajara, where he was residing when the Jesuits were expelled from the Spanish Empire in 1767. Exiled to Bologna in the Papal States, Clavigero turned to history to consolidate the record of pre-Hispanic Mexico and also to refute the so-called theory of American degeneracy that some European writers, like Corneille de Pauw, were propagating to the effect that America and her native inhabitants were far inferior to Europe because of America's wretched climate and other factors. The outcome was his *Storia antica del Messico* (1780–1781) that not only accomplished his purpose but also fostered a spirit of regionalism and neo-Aztecism among certain Mexican patriots which they used to justify their revolt against Spain. Noteworthy also is his posthumously published *Storia della California* (1789), written to counteract charges against the Jesuits and their California missions and to acquaint Europe with that peninsula and its inhabitants. He died in Bologna.

– CHARLES E. RONAN, S.J.

CLEMENTE WALKER, ROBERTO

Roberto Clemente Walker (*b.* 18 August 1934; *d.* 31 December 1972), Puerto Rican baseball player. Born in Carolina, P.R., near San Juan, Clemente signed out of high school with the Los Angeles Dodgers (1954) but played his entire major league career, beginning in 1955, with the Pittsburgh Pirates. In his 2,433 Pirate games, he had 3,000 hits and a .317 batting average; he won four batting titles and twelve Golden Gloves, was named his league's Most Valuable Player in 1966, as well as World Series MVP in 1971, and appeared in twelve Major League All-Star Games. Until 1971 he likewise repaid his countrymen by playing in the Puerto Rican winter league. To achieve all this and earn de-

served praise in the United States, he had to overcome racism and prejudice against blacks and Hispanics and persistent physical ailments that hampered him and brought cruel accusations that he was a hypochondriac and malingerer. He died in a plane crash while trying to deliver relief aid that he had raised for earthquake victims in Managua, Nicaragua. In 1973 a special election made him the first Latin to enter baseball's Hall of Fame. In life, as on the field, Clemente displayed a capacity for toughness and tenderness, aggressiveness and compassion, as appropriate for the situation. In Puerto Rico his widow Vera and others still operate the youth sports center named in his honor.

– JOSEPH L. ARBENA

CLOUTHIER DEL RINCÓN, MANUEL J.

Manuel J. Clouthier del Rincón (*b.* 13 June 1934; *d.* 1 October 1989), leading Mexican opposition politician and 1988 presidential candidate. A native of Culiacán, Sinaloa, Clouthier attended high school in the United States at the Brown Military Academy in San Diego, and graduated from Monterey's Institute of Higher Studies with a degree in agricultural engineering. A successful local businessman, he became active in a variety of regional business-interest groups, including the United Fresh Fruit and Vegetable Association and the Businessman's Coordinating Council. In 1981–1983, he presided over the national Businessman Coordinating Council, one of Mexico's most influential private-sector organizations. Known for his hard-line defense of powerful agricultural interests, Clouthier became politically involved in the National Action Party (PAN). After losing as a PAN candidate for Congress, he led the party's opposition by running against Carlos SALINAS in the 1988 presidential election, during which he ran an aggressive and charismatic campaign, endearing himself to many voters. He lost the election, but helped many congressional candidates from his party to win. Clouthier was killed in an auto accident in Sinaloa under disputed circumstances.

– RODERIC AI CAMP

CLUZEAU-MORTET, LUIS [RICARDO]

Luis [Ricardo] Cluzeau-Mortet (*b.* 16 November 1889; *d.* 28 September 1957), Uruguayan composer, violist, and pianist. Born in Montevideo, Cluzeau-Mortet studied piano, harmony, and composition with his maternal grandfather, Paul Faget, a winner of the Grand Prix of the Paris Conservatory. Later he studied violin and viola with María Visca. In 1914 he joined the Asociación Uruguaya de Música de Cámara, for whom he played viola until 1931, when he accepted the position as first viola in the Uruguayan state orchestra (OSSODRE), where he remained until his retirement in 1946. Cluzeau-Mortet received an invitation from the British Council to visit London in 1938, to which he responded by giving concerts of his vocal and piano works there and in Paris.

Cluzeau-Mortet's musicial output comprises nearly two hundred works. His career can be divided into three periods: a brief romantic-impressionist phase that produced songs based on French poetry; a nationalist period; and a universalist phase. It is for his nationalist works that he is best known; indeed, Cluzeau-Mortet, with Alfonso BROQUA and Eduardo FABINI, is considered a progenitor of Uruguayan nationalism. About half of his output, which includes several orchestral pieces, is made up of chamber music works. Among them the vocal and piano compositions are the masterpieces of his career. *Pericón* for piano (1918), premiered by Artur Rubinstein, and *Canto de chingolo* for voice and piano (1924), recorded by RCA Victor in 1930, are the most well-known and representative works from his nationalist period. Other important works are: *Llanuras* (1932); *Soledad campestre* (1936); *Rancherío* (1940), premiered by Jasha Horenstein in 1947 and winner of a SODRE composition competition; and *Sinfonía Artigas* (1951), all for orchestra. He died in Montevideo.

– SUSANA SALGADO

COBO, BERNABÉ

Bernabé Cobo (*b*. 1580; *d*. 1657), Spanish Jesuit scholar of the New World. Father Bernabé Cobo arrived in Lima from Spain in 1599. He spent the rest of his life in different locations in Peru and Mexico, working as a missionary, teacher, and writer. Of the original forty-three books making up his *Historia del nuevo mundo* (History of the New World, finished 1653, published 1890), seventeen are extant. The first fourteen comprise a study of New World natural history and the history of the Incas; the last three treat the foundation of Lima.

Cobo, like other historians of his era, based his writing on personal observations, interviews with native informants, and the chronicles of other Spanish historians. His views on Inca beliefs and practices are highly judgmental, condemning native religion as diabolical. He provides excellent information on many Inca monuments as they were in the early seventeenth century. The *Historia* also contributes to our knowledge of the customs of everyday life in Peru before and after the Conquest. The prose is straightforward and clear, tend-

ing toward observation and description rather than interpretation.

– KATHLEEN ROSS

COBOS, FRANCISCO DE LOS

Francisco de Los Cobos (*b*. ca. 1477; *d*. 10 May 1547), official under King Charles I. The son of an impoverished noble family of Ubeda, Francisco de los Cobos devoted his career to government service. Aided by Lope Conchillos, who in 1507 was given substantial authority over New World affairs, Cobos's fortunes rose and he ultimately became secretary, and thus a leading adviser, to King Charles I (Emperor Charles V). In the 1520s Cobos served as secretary of a number of councils, including the new Council of the Indies. He remained influential until his death.

Cobos used his position to advance relatives and clients and to build a fortune. He amassed numerous royal favors, including grants from Indies' revenues, and gifts from persons, including the conquistador Hernán CORTÉS, who sought royal favor. Cobos invested in commerce in the Indies, participating with conquistador Pedro de ALVARADO in sending black slaves to Guatemala. To guarantee the perpetuation of his fortune, Cobos established an entailed estate (*mayorazgo*). His career vividly illustrates the rewards available to a trusted servant of the monarch.

– MARK A. BURKHOLDER

CODAZZI, AGUSTÍN

Agustín Codazzi (*b*. ca. 12 July 1793; *d*. 7 February 1859), military officer and cartographer. Born in Lugo, on the northeastern coast of Italy near Ravenna, Codazzi was a veteran of the Napoleonic armies and one of the European volunteers who joined Simón BOLÍVAR's troops in the War of Independence. However, his main contribution to both Venezuela and New Granada was as a geographer, by charting the maps of both countries and by actually visiting many unknown territories of both nations. After the war he remained in the Venezuelan Army as a geographer and cartographer for almost three decades.

In 1848, Codazzi became involved in one of the many civil wars between Páez and Monagas. Ending up on the losing side, he was exiled to New Granada, where he was put in charge of the Comisión Corográfica, a group that studied in detail most of the Colombian provinces and territories known and unknown, producing maps and descriptions of the local economies and advising how to build needed roads. Codazzi died in Colombia in a town on the Caribbean coast. The town and the National Geographic Institute of Colombia now bear his name.

— JOSÉ ESCORCIA

CODESIDO, JULIA

Julia Codesido (*b.* 5 August 1883; *d.* 8 May 1979), Peruvian artist. Codesido, known as one of the *indigenistas sabogalinos* (close followers of painter José SABOGAL) was born in Lima. She, like other *indigenistas,* aimed at creating a Peruvian school of painting based on the exploration of native themes and the depiction of Andean local scenes and customs. She studied at the National School of Fine Arts, in Lima, where she later taught. In 1935, she visited Mexico to study the muralist movement. After this visit, the influence of SIQUEIROS became evident in her work.

Codesido aimed at creating a Peruvian school of painting based on the exploration of native themes and the depiction of Andean local scenes and customs.

Codesido abstracted some pictorial elements in her paintings—trees, architecture—although she always stayed within the boundaries of realism.

In 1936, Codesido participated in the First Congress of American Artists, held in New York City. She exhibited in Mexico City and New York (1935 and 1936). When in 1943 Sabogal was relieved of his position as director of the National School of Fine Arts over artistic differences, Codesido resigned in solidarity with him. Subsequently, she dedicated herself to forming, with other members of the *indigenista* movement, a collection of popular art and artisanal work for the National Museum of Peruvian Culture.

— MARTA GARSD

COELHO, JORGE DE ALBUQUERQUE

Jorge de Albuquerque Coelho (*b.* 23 April 1539; *d.* 23 April 1601), third lord-proprietor of Pernambuco (1582–1601). Albuquerque was born in Olinda in the captaincy of Pernambuco, a younger son of Duarte COELHO PEREIRA, Pernambuco's first lord-proprietor. He and his older brother, Duarte Coelho de Albuquerque, were sent for their education to Portugal, where Jorge soon gained a reputation for his military skills. In 1560, he accompanied his brother, second lord-proprietor of Pernambuco, to Brazil to deal with Native American threats to the family's captaincy. Albuquerque was placed in charge of the Portuguese offensive. After almost five years of fierce warfare, he managed to remove hostile Indians from the coastal region south to the Rio São Francisco as well as from much of the fertile interior. His task completed, he left Recife for Portugal in mid-1565 on the 200-ton *Santo Antônio,* never to return to the land of his birth. This four-and-a-half-month voyage, described by Frei Vicente do Salvador as "one of the worst and most dangerous seafarers had seen," was the subject of a famous Portuguese shipwreck narrative. By 1601, an account written by Afonso Luís had gone through at least two printings of a thousand copies each.

After recovering from the effects of the voyage, Albuquerque served at the court of young King Sebastian. In 1574 he was a participant in the first of that monarch's two expeditions to North Africa. In late November of that year, he returned to Sagres in the company of Dom Antônia, prior of Crato. The following year, he was captain of a galley patrolling the Algarve coast. He also served with his future father-in-law, Dom Pedro da Cunha, on a mission to Flanders. In June 1578, Albuquerque and his brother (who had returned from Pernambuco six years earlier) were part of King Sebastian's ill-fated second expedition to North Africa. Celebrated by chroniclers for offering his horse to the hapless king during the battle of Alcácer Quibir, Albuquerque was captured. Wounded badly, he and his brother, who was also a captive, were among the eighty nobles ransomed at great expense. He was back in Portugal by 1579. His brother, however, died in 1581 in Morocco on the journey home. Permanently crippled, Albuquerque officially succeeded him as lord-proprietor of Pernambuco in 1582.

By the mid-1580s, because of revenues from his captaincy, Albuquerque was considered one of the wealthiest of those men who gained their riches from Portuguese America. His captaincy of Pernambuco continued to prosper, especially from sugar. In 1591 a crown official reported that there were sixty-three sugar mills in that captaincy and tithes of 28,500 cruzados. Albuquerque encouraged the religious life of the captaincy and was generous to the Franciscans, the Benedictines, and the Carmelites. He was, however, an absentee lord-proprietor, and in his absence there were charges of corruption. From 1593 to 1595 a visitor from the Inquisition was stationed in Olinda taking testimony from the inhabitants. In 1595, the English pirate James Lancaster seized Recife, sacking the port for several months before sailing on. As a result, Albuquerque suffered great financial losses as well as the loss of confidence of Pernambuco's inhabitants in the security of their port city.

After the death of his first wife, Albuquerque married the daughter of Dom Alvaro Coutinho, commander of Almourol. From this union there were two sons. The first, born in 1591, was Duarte de Albuquerque Coelho, who became fourth lord-proprietor of Pernambuco and author of *Memorias diarias de la guerra del Brasil* (1654), the eyewitness account of the early years (1630–1638) of the struggle against the Dutch in Pernambuco. The second, Matias de ALBUQUERQUE, born in 1595, later became *capitão-mor* of Pernambuco and governor-general of Brazil. Jorge de Albuquerque Coelho died in Lisbon and was buried in the Church of São Nicolau.

– FRANCIS A. DUTRA

COELHO NETO, HENRIQUE

Henrique Coelho Neto (*b.* 21 February 1864; *d.* 28 November 1934), Brazilian writer. Born in Caxias, in the state of Maranhão, he was a prolific novelist as well as a journalist, essayist, short-story writer, and playwright. Some of his chief novels are *Miragem* and *O rei fantasma,* both published in 1895, *Inverno em flor* (1897) and *A capital federal* (1893). His principal work, *Turbilhão,* was published in 1906. He is best known for his narratives, in which he employed many innovative literary techniques for which Brazilian letters would become known following the introduction of its modernist movement to the world during Modern Art Week, held in São Paulo in 1922. His work, however, is classified as premodernist, for it exhibits many Parnassian and symbolist characteristics. He also proposed a return to Brazilian nationalistic themes and sentiments. In fact, according to critics, Coelho Neto spoke vehemently against the modernist direction Brazilian letters was taking during the last years of his life. Coelho Neto also had an active political career. He was a public lecturer, and in 1909 he was elected as a federal deputy. He was subsequently reelected to two more legislatures. In addition, he occupied several diplomatic and other government posts. In 1926, he was elected president of the Brazilian Academy of Letters.

– ROSÂNGELA MARIA VIEIRA

COELHO PEREIRA, DUARTE

Duarte Coelho Pereira (*b.* latter part of the fifteenth century; *d.* 1553 or 1554), first lord-proprietor of Pernambuco (1534–1553/54). Coelho was one of the most important figures in sixteenth-century Brazil. The circumstances surrounding his birth and early career are shrouded in mystery. It is known, however, that he was

the illegitimate son of a certain Gonçalo Coelho and that a brother, João de Azevedo, was a priest and chaplain. In 1509, Coelho joined an armada going to India under the leadership of Dom Fernando Coutinho. During the next twenty years, Coelho's actions in the Far East earned him deserved praise and mention in almost all the chronicles of the period. He also amassed an immense fortune that later served him well in his efforts to colonize Brazil. In 1521 he was made a fidalgo in the king's household. Sometime around 1529, he arrived back in Portugal. In the latter part of 1530, Coelho was sent on a diplomatic mission to France. He returned to Portugal by late April or early May of 1531 and shortly thereafter was named Capitão-Mor of the annual armada sent to the African fortress of São Jorge de Mina. On the return voyage, he rendezvoused in the Azores with ships arriving from India. Later in the year 1532, he was again in charge of an armada, this one on coast guard duty along the Malagueta Coast. On this voyage, Coelho captured a French galleon. Toward the end of January 1533, he and his armada were ordered to the Azores to await that year's armada from India. He was back in Portugal by the end of July or early August of 1533.

By 1534, Coelho was married to Dona Brites de Albuquerque, niece of Jorge de Albuquerque, twice captain of Malacca and a former comrade-in-arms. In that year he was one of twelve men awarded captaincies in Brazil. Because of his exploits in Asia and as one of King João III's most trusted and dependable military men, Coelho received the choicest grant of land in Brazil: territory with fertile soil, a good port, previous settlement, and proximity to Portugal. On 10 March 1534, he was granted sixty leagues of land, roughly the area from the Rio São Francisco northward to the southern banks of the Rio Igaraçu (including all of present-day Alagoas and most of Pernambuco) and a vast number of powers and privileges. On 24 September 1534, the king issued Coelho's charter (*foral*), a statement of the obligations of the lord-proprietor (DONATÁRIO) and his settlers. Like the other lords-proprietor, Coelho was granted extensive administrative, fiscal, and judicial powers by the crown in exchange for settling and defending at his own cost the land granted him.

Early in 1535, with his wife and her brother, Jerónimo de Albuquerque, plus a good-sized armada of personnel and supplies, Coelho left Lisbon for Pernambuco. The lord-proprietor took firm hold of his captaincy and brought it order and prosperity by leading the fight against hostile Indians and French interlopers and by providing the blueprint for a stable agrarian colony. Even though brazilwood had been the region's most important product before the era of the captaincies and continued to play a major role during the first lord-proprietor's lifetime, it was soon supplanted by sugar as the chief money crop. Exactly when the first sugarcane was planted in Coelho's colony is not known, but by April of 1542 the lord-proprietor was reporting to the king that much cane had been planted and that a large sugar mill was almost ready for operation. At the same time, Coelho requested permission to import black slaves from Guiné (Guinea). Eight years later, in 1550, there were five *engenhos* (sugar mills) in use and many others under construction. Thus, in less than twenty years, Coelho had set his captaincy on a path of agro-industrial development that it would follow for the remainder of the Portuguese colonial era and well into the national period of Brazilian history.

Coelho, who had been granted his own coat of arms in 1545, reacted strongly to the crown's program in 1548 to cut back on donatarial prerogatives and establish a system of royal and centralized government in Brazil. As he informed King João III in 1550: "All the people of this Nova Lusitania were and are very much upset with these changes" (Dutra, 438). In mid-1553 or 1554, Coelho returned a second time to Portugal to plead his case personally but died shortly after his arrival. He was buried in the tomb of Manuel de Moura in Lisbon's church of São João da Praça. He left as his heirs two teenage sons, Duarte Coelho de Albuquerque and Jorge de Albuquerque COELHO, who succeeded him as second and third lords-proprietor of Pernambuco.

– FRANCIS A. DUTRA

COICOU, MASSILLON

Massillon Coicou (*b.* 9 October 1867; *d.* 15 March 1908), Haitian writer. Coicou became secretary of the cabinet of President Tirésias Sam in 1897. He later

---

After becoming involved in clandestine opposition to

Haitian President Nord Alexis, Coicou was arrested

and summarily executed with his two brothers.

---

served as secretary and chargé d'affaires of the Haitian legation in Paris from 1900 to 1903. Several of his plays were produced in Paris, and he became known in literary circles. Several volumes of his poetry were also published in Paris. After returning to Port-au-Prince, Coicou founded the journal *L'oeuvre.* He taught philosophy at the Lycée Pétion from 1904 on and founded the "Théâtre Haïtien" during this period. After becoming involved in clandestine opposition to President

Nord Alexis, Coicou was arrested and summarily executed with his two brothers and eight other persons.

Coicou was the author of numerous plays—tragedies, comedies, and one-act plays—most of them unpublished. The historical drama *Liberté* (produced in Haiti, 1894; in Paris, 1904), on the Haitian revolution, was highly praised by Parisian reviewers. While his surviving dramas have been criticized for weak structuring, Coicou was a master of French versification, and his poem "L'alarme" was memorized by most Haitian secondary students.

– CARROL F. COATES

COLL Y TOSTE, CAYETANO

Cayetano Coll y Toste (*b.* 30 November 1850; *d.* 19 November 1930), Puerto Rican physician, politician, historian. Born in Arecibo, Puerto Rico, Coll y Toste was educated in both Puerto Rico and Barcelona, Spain. Although he practiced medicine and wrote articles in that field, Coll y Toste is best known for his historiographical contributions. After retiring from the practice of medicine, he wrote numerous biographies of distinguished Puerto Ricans, compiled legends, and published the *Boletín histórico de Puerto Rico,* a multivolume collection of documents on the island's history. In 1913 he was given the title of official historian of Puerto Rico. Coll y Toste died in Madrid, Spain.

– OLGA JIMÉNEZ DE WAGENHEIM

COLLOR, LINDOLFO

Lindolfo Collor (*b.* 4 February 1890; *d.* 21 September 1942), Brazilian statesman. Born in Rio Grande do Sul of German descent, Collor received a pharmacy degree in 1909, but his first professional endeavors involved journalism and literature. His career in politics began when Antônio Augusto BORGES DE MEDEIROS, virtual dictator of Rio Grande, asked him to direct the state Republican Party newspaper in 1919. Thereafter, Collor rose rapidly in Riograndense politics and entered congress in 1925. After fellow Riograndense Getúlio VARGAS was defeated for the presidency in 1930, Collor participated in the October revolution of that year, a movement which overthrew the Constitution of 1891. One of the first acts of Vargas's provisional government was to create a labor ministry, headed by Collor.

Collor legalized those unions approved by the labor ministry, which could also intervene in their internal operation. In addition, he introduced the so-called two-thirds law, which required that two-thirds of the work force of all industrial enterprises be Brazilian nationals. He also set up conciliation boards to settle labor disputes, regulated working conditions of women, and established a minimum wage.

Collor's labor system has expanded and survived all the regimes since 1930. Fundamentally corporative, it was also eclectic, inspired by Catholic social doctrine (though Collor was Protestant), the welfarism of Uruguayan José BATLLE Y ORDOÑEZ, the Comtian paternalism of Julio de CASTILHOS, and Vargas's new commodity syndicates in Rio Grande.

Collor resigned his ministry in 1932, protesting Vargas's continuing dictatorship, and remained an opponent of his former colleague. A grandson, Fernando COLLOR DE MELLO, became president of Brazil in 1990 but resigned at the end of 1992 following impeachment.

– JOSEPH L. LOVE

COLLOR DE MELLO, FERNANDO AFFONSO

Fernando Affonso Collor de Mello (*b*. 12 August 1949), president of Brazil (1990–1992). Collor was born in Rio de Janeiro. His father, Arnon de Mello, was a journalist, senator, and governor of Alagoas. His mother, Leda Collor de Mello, was the daughter of Lindolfo Collor, who served as minister of labor in the first administration of Getúlio VARGAS. After attending the Padre Antônio Vieira, São Vicente de Paulo, and São José schools in Rio de Janeiro, in 1966 he transferred to the Centro Integrado de Ensino Médio (CIEM) in Brasília. He studied economics at the University of Brasília, then attended the Federal University of Alagoas, and returned to Brasília to obtain a degree in social communication. In his youth, Collor was an avid athlete and attained a black belt in karate. In 1975, Collor married Celi Elizabeth Monteiro de Carvalho, with whom he had two sons. They divorced in 1981, and the following year he married Rosane Malta, a member of a prominent family from Alagoas and manager of Rosane Enterprises.

In 1979, the National Renovating Alliance (ARENA), a government party, named Collor mayor of Maceió, where he served until 1982, when he was elected federal deputy by the Social Democratic Party (PDS). After changing his party affiliation to the Brazilian Democratic Movement Party (PMDB), he was elected governor of Alagoas (1987–1989). As governor and an outspoken critic of then President José SARNEY, he attracted national attention for his anticorruption measures aimed at public servants who received exorbitant salaries, often without working full time. Collor fought against powerful sugar-mill owners who refused to pay their debts to the state bank, Produban, which was eventually closed by the federal government.

Rejected by the PMDB, Collor launched his presidential campaign almost single-handedly, preaching the need for a crackdown on political corruption and promising a clean, efficient government. For months he remained third in the national polls, but eventually began to take the lead. In November 1989, among twenty-one candidates, he received the highest number of votes during the first round of elections, and he went on to the second round in a two-way contest against Luís Inácio (Lula) da Silva. On 17 December 1989, Collor was elected president with 43 percent of the vote to Lula's 38 percent. At age forty, he became the youngest president in Brazilian history.

During his inauguration speech, Collor declared that the federal government could no longer continue to subsidize a bloated bureaucracy. Breaking with Sarney's Cruzado Plan II, the newly elected president announced economic policies of austerity and cutbacks. In May 1991 he revamped his economic team and formulated new economic policies signaling a greater flexibility in negotiations with international banks. In the spring of 1992, Collor again made major ministerial changes. During that year, Brazil hosted the United Nations Conference on Environment and Development (Earth Summit), which won praise from the international community. By that time, however, the president had become the target of corruption charges. Following Collor's impeachment by the Chamber of Deputies, Vice President Itamar FRANCO was named acting president on 2 October 1992. Collor was officially removed from office by the Senate on 29 December and was charged with corruption in June 1993.

– IÊDA SIQUEIRA WIARDA

COLMÁN, NARCISO

Narciso Colmán (*b*. 1876; *d*. 1954), Paraguayan poet and anthologist. Born in poor circumstances in the interior town of Ybytymí, Colmán relocated to Asunción in the late 1880s to study at the Escuela Normal. In search of better opportunities, he went to Buenos Aires, where for several years he worked as a telegraphist for the Argentine National Railways. He finally returned to Paraguay in 1901 to assume the post of chief telegrapher with the postal administration, and spent a good part of the rest of his life in that position and in various juridical posts.

Colmán's true interest, however, lay in developing a public interest in Guaraní, the native Indian language of Paraguay. He collected folklore in the *campo* (countryside) and popularized it for the generation of the 1920s and 1930s. Writing under the pen name Rosicran, he published his own poetry in Guaraní, including *Ocara Poty* (Wild Flowers), in two volumes, and, more important, *Ñande Ypy Cuera* (Our Forefathers), an evocation of Guaraní myths. In many ways, Colmán could take credit for rescuing Guaraní from the ignominy to which it had been relegated by Paraguayan writers who worked exclusively in Spanish and who, disdaining the Indian tongue, produced simple imitations of European styles.

– THOMAS L. WHIGHAM

COLOSIO MURRIETA, LUIS DONALDO

Luis Donaldo Colosio Murrieta (*b.* 10 February 1950, *d.* 23 March, 1994), assassinated Mexican political leader. Born in Magdaleno de Kino, Sonora, he graduated from the Instituto de Estudios Superiores in Monterrey. He received an MA in economics from the University of Pennsylvania and spent a year in Vienna before taking a position at the Secretaría de Programación y Presupuesto in 1979. In 1985 he was elected a federal deputy from Sonora, and during the presidential campaign of Carlos SALINAS, he served as Oficial Mayor of the Institutional Revolutionary Party (PRI). After a brief stint as senator in 1988, Colosio became party president and presided over the 1991 congressional elections and internal party returns. In 1992, President Salinas made him the first secretary of the newly reconstituted Social Development Secretariat, where he presided over the Solidarity program before he was designated by Salinas as the PRI's candidate for president. It was expected that he would win the August 1994 presidential elections, but he was assassinated in Tijuana in mid-campaign. Colosio's murder produced numerous consequences for the political system, and coming so soon after the indigenous uprising in Chiapas, contributed to political instability. President Salinas was forced to select a replacement candidate, Colosio's campaign manager Ernesto Zedillo, who did not generate equal support within the party. Although the Salinas administration claimed Colosio was killed by a single, deranged gunman, President Zedillo later reopened the investigation, which alleges a wider plot, involving the chief of security, a general in the army.

– RODERIC AI CAMP

COLUMBUS, CHRISTOPHER

Christopher Columbus (*b.* ca. 1451; *d.* 1506), Genoese explorer.

EARLY LIFE IN GENOA AND PORTUGAL. Christopher Columbus was born in the republic of Genoa. His father, Domenico Colombo, was a wool weaver, wool merchant, tavern keeper, and political appointee. Columbus's early education was limited, although he read widely after reaching adulthood. He went to sea at an early age and sailed the Mediterranean on merchant vessels, traveling as far east as the island of Chios. In the mid-1470s, he settled in Portugal, joining other Italian merchants in Lisbon. Columbus sailed north to England and Ireland, and possibly as far as Iceland. He also visited the Madeira and Canary Islands and the African coast as far south as the Portuguese trading post at São Jorge da Mina (in modern Ghana).

In 1478 or 1479, Columbus married Felipa Moniz, member of a prominent Italian-Portuguese family. Her father and brother were hereditary captains of the island of Porto Santo, and her mother came from a noble family. In 1480 Felipa bore Columbus a son named Diogo (Diego in Spanish), who would later have a bureaucratic career in the lands his father claimed for Spain. Columbus's marriage provided connections to the Portuguese court, important ties to Madeira and Porto Santo, and at least some wealth.

THE ENTERPRISE OF THE INDIES. Columbus based his ideas about the size of the world and the possibility

Christopher Columbus. Reproduced from Paulus Jovius, Eulogia Vivorum Illustrium *(Basel, 1575). (Courtesy of the John Carter Brown Library at Brown University)*

of a westward voyage to the fabled riches of Asia on rumors of unknown Atlantic islands, unusual objects drifting ashore from the west, and wide reading of academic geography in printed books. He was also influenced by the Italian humanist-geographer Paulo del Pozzo Toscanelli, who described the feasibility of a westward route to Asia. Although Columbus knew that the world was spherical, he underestimated its circumference and believed that Asia stretched some 30 degrees farther east than it really does, and that Japan lay 1,500 miles east of the Asian mainland. Columbus estimated that the Canary Islands lay only 2,400 nautical miles from Japan, instead of the actual distance of 10,600 nautical miles. Neither Columbus nor anyone else in Europe suspected that two vast continents lay in the way of a westward passage to Asia.

Probably in 1485, on the basis of his miscalculations, Columbus tried to interest Dom João II of Portugal in his scheme for a westward passage to Asia, his "enterprise of the Indies." After assembling a learned committee to examine Columbus's ideas, the king turned him down, for unrecorded reasons, although he licensed other westward probes.

SPAIN BACKS COLUMBUS. Columbus left Portugal for Spain in 1485. After meeting Columbus early in 1486 at Alcalá de Henares, Isabella I of Castile and her husband, Ferdinand II of Aragon, appointed a commission to investigate the details of Columbus's plan. The spherical shape of the world was never in question. Although the commission disputed Columbus's flawed geography, the monarchs suggested that they might support him once they conquered Muslim Granada, and they even provided him with periodic subsidies.

During his years of waiting, Columbus established a liaison with a young woman in Córdoba, Beatriz Enríquez de Arana. In 1488, they had a son named Hernando, whom Columbus later legitimized. Hernando accompanied Columbus on his fourth transatlantic voyage and ultimately wrote a biography of his father.

In January 1492, during the final siege of Granada, Queen Isabella summoned Columbus to court. In the Capitulations of Santa Fe, signed in April, the monarchs contracted to sponsor a voyage and to grant Columbus noble status and the titles of admiral, viceroy, and governor-general for any islands or mainlands he might discover.

THE FIRST VOYAGE, 1492–1493. Columbus secured the use of two caravels, the *Pinta* and the *Niña*, and a larger *nao*, the *Santa María*. With the help of Martín Alonso PINZÓN, a prominent local mariner and captain of the *Pinta*, Columbus gathered a crew of around ninety men, including three from the local jail. The three ships sailed from Palos on 3 August 1492.

After repairs and reprovisioning in the Canaries on 6 September 1492, the fleet headed west into the open ocean, propelled by the northeast trade winds. The voyage went smoothly, with fair winds and remarkably little grumbling among the crew. On 12 October, at 2 A.M., the lookout on the *Pinta* saw a light; shortly after dawn the fleet dropped anchor at an island in what are now the Bahamas that local people called Guanahaní and that Columbus renamed San Salvador. Believing they were in Asia, the Europeans called the islanders "Indians."

The fleet sailed through the Bahamas and visited Cuba, seeking the vast commerce and rich ports of Asia. From Cuba, Martín Alonso Pinzón, without permission, sailed off in the *Pinta* to explore on his own. The two ships remaining with Columbus sailed to the island they named Hispaniola and explored its northern coast. On Christmas Eve 1492, the *Santa María* ran aground and broke up. Columbus founded a settlement, Villa de la Navidad, for the thirty-nine men he had to leave behind. Afterward Pinzón rejoined Columbus, and on 16 January the *Niña* and *Pinta* set sail for home with six captured Indians.

Columbus first tried a course directly east, but contrary winds forced him northward until he found winds blowing from the west. After a stormy passage, during which the caravels were separated, and a stopover in the Azores, the *Niña* reached Lisbon on 4 March. Columbus paid a courtesy call to Dom João II and departed for Spain on 13 March 1493, arriving in Palos two days later. Pinzón brought the *Pinta* into port later that same day, having first landed at Bayona, on the northwest coast of Spain.

Isabella and Ferdinand received Columbus warmly in Barcelona in mid-April. They confirmed all his privileges and gave him permission for a second voyage. Columbus asserted that the Asian mainland lay close to the islands he had found.

THE SECOND VOYAGE, 1493–1496. The Spanish monarchs facilitated Columbus's colonizing effort, and the queen ordered that the native islanders be treated well and converted to Christianity. Columbus found 1,200 men to accompany him as settlers. On 3 November 1493, the fleet of seventeen vessels reached an island in the Caribbean that Columbus named Dominica, then sailed through the Lesser Antilles and the Virgin Islands, past Puerto Rico, to Hispaniola.

They found that the men left in La Navidad the previous January were all dead, most of them killed by the islanders. Columbus founded a new settlement, named Isabella for the queen, on a poor site without fresh water. He then began to enslave some of the islanders. According to Spanish law, if the local people peacefully accepted takeover by the Europeans, they were protected against enslavement as subjects of the Castilian crown, but if they made war, they could be seized as slaves. Some islanders were certainly at war against the Europeans, and Columbus used their resistance as a justification for outright conquest. He and his men marched through the island with horses, war dogs, and harquebuses, seeking gold through barter but conquering and taking captives when they met opposition.

In April 1494, leaving Hispaniola under the control of his brother Diego, Columbus took an expedition to explore the southern shore of Cuba, which he believed was part of the Asian mainland. He even made his crew members sign a document to that effect. Columbus's brother Bartholomew had arrived on Hispaniola during Columbus's absence and found the colony in chaos. Disappointed colonists returned to Spain on a fleet dispatched by Columbus in 1494 and spread stories about the Columbus brothers' misdeeds and ineptitude as administrators. The Spanish rulers sent out an investigator named Juan Aguado, who observed many deaths among the Amerindians, and disease and desertions among the Europeans. To defend his administration in person, Columbus departed for Spain on 10 March 1496, leaving Bartholomew in charge on Hispaniola. He reached Cádiz on 11 June.

THE THIRD VOYAGE, 1498–1500. Despite reports about Columbus's failings as an administrator, the monarchs confirmed his previous grants and gave him permission for a third voyage, with a *nao* and two caravels for exploration and three more caravels to carry provisions to Hispaniola, plus 300 men and 30 women as additional colonists, including 10 pardoned criminals.

Departing from Spain on 30 May 1498, Columbus took his three ships south to the Cape Verde Islands before heading west, reaching the island of Trinidad on 31 July. He then sailed to the mainland of South America, realizing from the vast flow of water from the Orinoco River that he had encountered an enormous landmass, which he believed to be in Asia and near the Garden of Eden described in the Bible. After briefly exploring the coast of Venezuela, Columbus sailed on to Hispaniola.

Although Bartholomew had moved the main settlement from Isabella to Santo Domingo, the situation was in crisis. Some of the colonists had mutinied, the Indians were increasingly hostile, and neither Bartholomew nor Diego Columbus had been able to maintain order. Columbus himself had little better luck. Ferdinand and Isabella sent out Francisco de BOBADILLA to investigate and restore authority. He arrested the three Columbus brothers, seized their money, and sent them home in chains in December 1500. Columbus was

summoned to court in Granada, but the monarchs delayed granting his request for reinstatement to his official posts.

Eventually Ferdinand and Isabella allowed Columbus to keep some of his titles and all of his property, but the titles were thereafter empty of authority. They also delayed granting him permission for another voyage. Instead, they began to establish a bureaucratic structure outside Columbus's control, appointing Nicolás de OVANDO governor of Hispaniola and dispatching a large colonization fleet. In March 1502 Ferdinand and Isabella finally granted Columbus permission for a fourth voyage.

THE FOURTH VOYAGE, 1502–1504. With Columbus and his son Hernando sailing on the flagship, a fleet of four rickety caravels with second-rate crews left Spain on 11 May 1502. Departing the Canaries on 25 May, they arrived at Hispaniola on 29 June, even though Columbus was specifically forbidden to land there. Columbus knew that Governor Ovando was about to send a fleet home and saw that a hurricane was brewing. He warned Ovando of the approaching storm and asked to anchor in the harbor. Ovando refused and ordered the fleet to depart, just before the hurricane struck. Twenty-five of the fleet's ships were sunk.

Thereafter, Columbus and his men spent much of the voyage sailing along the coast of Central America. Bad weather and adverse currents and winds kept the crews from learning much about the lands and peoples, and the hostility of local Indians forced them to abandon plans for a settlement in Panama. Unable to reach Hispaniola, Columbus landed in northern Jamaica and awaited rescue for a year. He sailed back to Spain, broken in health, and reached Seville on 7 November 1504, never again to return to the Indies.

LAST YEARS. Columbus struggled to have all his grants and titles restored. He remained a wealthy man, but he felt betrayed and slighted by his royal patrons. For their part, the Spanish sovereigns justified their withdrawal of support on the basis of Columbus's mismanagement. Colonial settlement had grown too complex for any one person to manage.

Surrounded by family and friends, Columbus died in Valladolid in 1506, rich but dissatisfied. With the perspective of five centuries, we can recognize the extraordinary changes that resulted from his voyages. Instead of finding a new route to Asia, Columbus made the lands and peoples of the Western Hemisphere known to Europeans and set in motion a chain of events that altered human history on a global scale. The origin of many characteristics of the modern world, including the interdependent system of world trade, can be traced directly to his voyages.

COLUMBUS IN HISTORY AND MYTH. The myths surrounding Columbus make it difficult to put his accomplishments into their proper context. Often he is depicted as a perfect hero in advance of his time who conceived the idea of a spherical earth and had to fight traditional religious beliefs and prejudice before succeeding, and who died poor and alone. None of this is true. A product of his times, Columbus was strongly influenced by the powerful religious and economic currents of his day. In pursuit of profits, he established a slave trade in Caribbean natives, arguing that such slavery would allow them to be converted and reformed. Far from being oppressed by Christian beliefs, he hoped that some of the profits from his ventures would be used to recapture Jerusalem from the Muslims, in fulfillment of Christian prophecy. Neither the simple hero portrayed by generations of textbook writers nor the unredeemable villain depicted by some recent writers, Columbus was a complex human being who exemplified the virtues and the flaws of his time and place in history.

— WILLIAM D. PHILLIPS, JR.

COLUNJE, GIL

Gil Colunje (*b.* 1831; *d.* 1898), Panamanian jurist who spent most of his life in Colombia, where he became a senator. In his writings he often speaks against government corruption and injustice, which gained the admiration and respect of the people. He was repeatedly harassed by the government because of his ideas. Colunje held many government posts throughout his life. He served as minister of foreign relations, member of the Supreme Court, president of the Bank of Bogotá, and rector of the Colegio Mayor del Rosario. In 1865 he occupied briefly the presidency of the Sovereign State of Panama.

— JUAN MANUEL PÉREZ

COMONFORT, IGNACIO

Ignacio Comonfort (*b.* 1812; *d.* 13 November 1863), president of Mexico (1855–1858). Born in the state of Puebla, he pursued a military career from the period of the 1830s onward. After the war against the United States (1846–1848), he became the chief customs official in Acapulco and a close associate of Juan ÁLVAREZ, the *caudillo* of Guerrero. Comonfort was one of the authors of the Plan of Ayutla (1 March 1854), which began the military movement to oust Antonio López de SANTA ANNA from the presidency and put in place a Liberal government. He then traveled to the United States to raise funds for the war effort.

Returning to Mexico, Comonfort became the general in charge of operations in Jalisco and Michoacán. His mentor, Juan Álvarez, led the Ayutla Revolution to victory, became president in late 1855, and appointed his protégé his minister of war. Álvarez governed only briefly; Comonfort replaced him on 11 December 1855. A moderate Liberal, Comonfort tried to harmonize the demands of the radicals for rapid implementation of a reform program with the more gradual approach advocated by the moderates. He signed and promulgated the famous Ley Lerdo (25 June 1856) calling for the alienation of church and municipal properties, written by his treasury minister Miguel LERDO DE TEJADA. He vigorously crushed a Conservative revolt in Puebla in early 1856 and he also promulgated the Constitution of 1857. By late 1857, however, he was concerned that the radicals were too influential and were leading Mexico into a civil war. He then conspired with Conservatives to bring them to power, an act that started the war he had hoped to avoid, the War of the Reform (1858–1860).

Comonfort left the presidency in early 1858, remained in exile in the United States until 1861, and then returned to Mexico. He was rehabilitated by the Liberals, given a commission, served in President Benito JUÁREZ's cabinet, and took an active role in confronting the French Intervention. He was killed in a skirmish.

— CHARLES R. BERRY

CONCHA, ANDRÉS DE LA

Andrés de la Concha (*b.* ca. 1554; *d.* after 1612), painter and architect. Born in Seville and trained there in the mannerist style, possibly under Peter Kempeneer, Concha went to New Spain in 1567, with a contract

Some experts believe that there were two artists named Andrés de la Concha, one a painter and the other an architect.

to execute the main retablo at Yanhuitlán. Among the many works by Concha referred to in documents, numerous paintings and altarpieces were for the Dominican order in Oaxaca and Mexico City. A good number survive, such as the panels at Yanhuitlán, Coixtlahuaca, and Tamazulapán. In addition, the paintings that were formerly attributed to the "Master of Santa Cecilia" are now credited to Concha. Concha was named *maestro mayor* of the cathedral of Mexico City in 1601, and most of his activity after that year was architectural.

This lends weight to a recent hypothesis that there were two artists of the same name, one a painter and the other an architect.

— CLARA BARGELLINI

CONCHA, JOSÉ VICENTE

José Vicente Concha (*b*. 21 April 1867; *d*. 8 December 1929), president of Colombia (1914–1918). A member of the Conservative Party's traditionalist, or "Historical" wing, Concha, a native of Bogotá, became a critic of the Nationalist regime of Miguel Antonio CARO (1892–1898). In 1900 he conspired with fellow Historicals and with members of the Liberal Party to overthrow Nationalist President Manuel Antonio Sanclemente. The plotters replaced Sanclemente with José Manuel MARROQUÍN, who headed the government until 1904. Concha served as Marroquín's minister of war, and in 1902 was sent to Washington, D.C., to conclude negotiations on the Hay–Herran Treaty.

Concha was a leader in the struggle against the authoritarian regime of President Rafael REYES, whose five-year term (1904–1909) is known in Colombian history as El Quinquenio. Concha's term as president coincided with World War I, during which Colombia remained neutral in the face of U.S. pressure to declare war on Germany. Philosophically committed to administrative decentralization, to laissez-faire economics, and to a nonpartisan political style, Concha was frequently praised by leaders of the opposition Liberal Party.

Following his presidency, Concha served in the Colombian Senate, taught university courses, wrote literary essays, and authored legal treatises, especially in the areas of penology and constitutional law. He served as Colombia's minister to the Vatican under President Miguel ABADÍA MÉNDEZ (1926–1930). He died in Rome.

— JAMES D. HENDERSON

CONDÉ, MARYSE

Maryse Condé (née Boucoulon; *b*. 11 Feb. 1937), Guadeloupean writer and teacher. After studying in Guadeloupe and Paris, Condé taught in Guinea, Ghana, and Senegal for twelve years. Returning to Paris in 1972, she began a doctoral thesis and helped produce her first play, "Le morne de Massabielle." Condé complained that her early novels were badly received in the Caribbean and Africa, but she enjoyed wide success with the first volume of her trilogy, *Ségou*, distributed by a French book club in 1984. *Moi, Tituba sorcière* . . . received the Grand Prix Littéraire de la Femme in 1987.

Condé writes of the search for Caribbean identity. She has become an influential commentator on questions of the triple colonization of Caribbean women in sexist, racist, and colonialist cultures. She also writes novels for young people.

— CARROL F. COATES

CONI, EMILIO R.

Emilio R. Coni (*b*. 1854; *d*. 3 July 1928), one of Argentina's pioneer public-health physicians. Born in Corrientes in 1854, he attended medical school at the University of Buenos Aires during the 1870s and became well known in the medical community for his many statistical articles about diseases and mortality rates. Coni also published numerous books, including his autobiography, *Memorias de un médico higienista* (1918), and a study of Buenos Aires's public and private social assistance agencies, *Asistencia y previsión social Buenos Aires caritativo y previsor* (1918). Coni was particularly interested in the control of venereal disease through medically supervised prostitution, the establishment of tuberculosis treatment centers, the regulation of wet nurses and milk supplies of all types, the treatment of alcoholics, and the creation of municipal medical facilities to shelter the indigent. He was also involved in efforts to improve sanitation in Buenos Aires. Many of these programs were implemented as a result of Coni's determination to have the medical facilities of Buenos Aires rival those found in contemporary Europe.

— DONNA J. GUY

CONI, GABRIELA LAPERRIÈRE DE

Gabriela Laperrière de Coni (*b*. 1866; *d*. January 1907), Argentine feminist and health-care activist. The public career of Gabriela Laperrière de Coni was intense but brief. Little is known about her early life except that she was born in Bordeaux, France, in 1866 and published a novel about a woman's efforts to help sick children. In her career, fiction mirrored reality. Once Laperrière became active in Argentina, she campaigned as a feminist socialist for improved working and health conditions for poor families. Her marriage in 1899 to Dr. Emilio R. Coni, a noted public-health physician, reinforced her commitment to health issues. One manifestation of this concern was the extensive lectures she gave about the dangers of tuberculosis.

Laperrière's Argentine career began in 1900, when she served as the press secretary for the Argentine National Council of Women. Two years later she was appointed Buenos Aires's first factory inspector by the city's mayor, Adolfo Bullrich. Her research led in April

1902 to recommend that legislation to protect workers be enacted. Such a law was enacted by the Argentine Congress in 1907.

A popular speaker on public-health issues, Laperrière also helped found the Centro Socialista Femenino (Socialist Women's Feminist Center). In one of her last public appearances she helped mediate a dispute between factory owners and working women in a shoe factory. Her death in January 1907 terminated her brief career, but her concerns about health and working conditions were implemented by others.

– DONNA J. GUY

CONSELHEIRO, ANTÔNIO

Antônio Conselheiro (*b*. 13 March 1830; *d*. October 1897), a late-nineteenth-century Brazilian Catholic mystic and lay missionary. His career is immortalized in Euclides da CUNHA's *Os sertões* (1902; *Rebellion in the Backlands*).

Antônio Vicente Mendes Maciel was born in Santo Antônio de Quixeramobim, deep in the Ceará backlands. His grandparents were *vaqueiros* (cowboys). His father, Vicente's, first marriage ended disastrously; he deserted his wife after cudgeling her so savagely that she nearly died. Vicente's common-law second wife, Maria Maciel, was the boy's stepmother during his formative years. Known in the village as Maria Chana, she compensated by imposing strict religious discipline within her household and meting out frequent punishments to her children and slaves. Gradually, Vicente's fortunes as a merchant and property owner began to slip away. He grew morose and sullen, and was frequently inebriated.

As a child, Antônio was unobtrusive and studious. The boy's complexion was tawny (*moreno*), later attributed to partial Calabaça Indian ancestry. His birth certificate listed him as *pardo* (dark), but chroniclers who saw him generally referred to him as "white." His first formal instruction came from his father, who wanted him to become a priest. He was then enrolled in a school taught by Professor Manuel Antônio Ferreira Nobre, where he studied arithmetic, geography, Portuguese, French, and Latin. Some of his schoolmates later took their places in the regional elite as police chiefs, newspapermen, and lawyers.

The Mendes Maciel clan was a "good family" in the eyes of local inhabitants and, in the language of the day, part of the "conservative classes" although not particularly wealthy. At the age of twenty-five Antônio found himself responsible for four unmarried younger girls (two of them half sisters). He took over his father's business and filed papers to back the outstanding loans with a mortgage. In 1857, when he was twenty-seven, he married his fifteen-year-old cousin, Brasilina Laurentina de Lima, the daughter of Francisca Maciel, his father's sister. When she ran away with a soldier, Maciel sold his house and struck off to wander the backlands. He dressed austerely, fasted, and spent weeks and even months in small backlands towns, rebuilding dilapidated churches and cemetery walls. By the 1880s he began to acquire a reputation as a *conselheiro*, or religious counselor.

His wanderings took him through the backlands of Ceará, Pernambuco, Sergipe, and Bahia, in the heart of Brazil's Northeastern drought region. In 1887 he reached the seacoast, at Vila do Conde; he then turned back toward the semiarid interior. He wore a blue tunic tied with a sash, a turned-down hat to protect him from the sun, and sandals. He carried a leather bag with pen and ink, paper, and two prayer books.

Antônio lived on alms and slept in the back rooms of houses and in barns, always on the floor. His nightly orations from makeshift podiums in public squares entranced listeners, although he was not a particularly forceful speaker. The sophisticated called him a buffoon, laughing at his mixture of dogmatic counsels, vulgarized precepts from Christian morality, Latinate phrases, and prophecies. But he exerted a charismatic hold on the humble, many of whom began to follow him as he walked from place to place. In 1893, after a skirmish between his disciples and troops sent from the coast to arrest him, he set out for a remote abandoned cattle ranch on the banks of the Vasa-Barris River in the state of Bahia, a hamlet of 500 or so mud-thatched wooden shanties. Here, protected by a ring of mountains surrounding the valley (and by friendly landowners in the region as well as some local priests), he established a religious community called Canudos, or Belo Monte. As many as 25,000 pilgrims of all racial and economic groups (most of them impoverished backlands *caboclos* of mixed origin) took up residence there, making it Bahia's second most populous urban center by 1895.

Conselheiro's theological vision inverted the harsh and austere reality of the impoverished backlands of Brazil: the weak, strengthened by their faith, would inherit the earth.

Conselheiro's theological vision inverted the harsh and austere reality of the impoverished backlands: the weak, strengthened by their faith, would inherit the earth. Nature would be transformed: rains would come to the arid *sertão,* bringing forth the earth's bounty. Canudos would be a "New Jerusalem." As community leader, he retained his personal asceticism and humility. He dissuaded others from calling him a saint, and he never assumed the powers of the clergy. Although he borrowed from a Catholic apocalyptic missal used widely during the late nineteenth century (*A missão abreviada*), his teachings never strayed from traditional church doctrine. Conselheiro admonished his disciples to live austerely, to renounce luxury, and to await the imminent coming of the Day of Judgment at the millennium. He was a misogynist, and avoided eye contact with women. But he was no religious fanatic. His preachments fell squarely within the tradition of backlands popular Catholicism, which, cut off from church influence by the paucity of available clergy, always had emphasized the presence of sin, the need for penitence, and the personal role of saints and other intermediaries.

Politically, he opposed the (1889) Republic because he revered the exiled emperor PEDRO II and because Brazil's Constitution of 1891, influenced by positivist ideas, ceded jurisdiction over the registry of births, marriages, and deaths to the state. His enemies accused him of sedition and of advocating the violent restoration of the monarchy, presumably with aid from monarchists elsewhere in Brazil as well as from monarchies in Europe. Opposition to Conselheiro and his community was led by backlands landowners threatened by the loss of their traditionally docile labor force as thousands abandoned their residences and streamed to Canudos.

Conselheiro's community at Canudos was destroyed by a massive and bloody assault by the Brazilian army in October 1897, following four attacks over the space of more than a year. He had died, probably of dysentery, some days before, and had been buried by pious villagers. His body was disinterred, the head severed and mounted on a pike, and displayed at the head of military parades in Salvador and in other cities on the coast.

– ROBERT M. LEVINE

CONSTANT BOTELHO DE MAGALHÃES, BENJAMIN

Benjamin Constant Botelho de Magalhães (*b.* 18 October 1836; *d.* 22 January 1891), one of the founders of the Brazilian Republic. The son of a schoolteacher and a seamstress, Constant was instrumental in Brazil's transition from monarchy to republic. The army gave him the opportunity to rise above his humble birth. Trained as an engineer at Rio de Janeiro's Military Academy, Constant later taught mathematics at his alma mater. In 1866 he participated briefly in the War of the Triple Alliance, but illness forced his return to Rio de Janeiro.

A more successful teacher than soldier, Constant nonetheless was part of the new military that emerged from the Paraguayan war committed to more active participation in political affairs of the empire. He became a convert to positivist doctrines and was influential in spreading them among his students at the Military Academy and later at the War College. By the late 1880s Constant demonstrated vocal support for republicanism and conspired to bring down the empire in 1889. His prestige among students brought many cadets to support the republican cause. In November 1889, as vice president of the Military Club, he urged its president, General Manuel Deodoro da FONSECA, to lead the military against the Emperor PEDRO II and proclaim the republic.

Under the Republican administration, Constant served first as minister of war, then as minister of public instruction and postmaster in 1890. The positivist slogan, "Order and Progress," emblazoned on the Brazilian flag is attributed to him.

– JOAN MEZNAR

CONTRERAS BROTHERS

Contreras Brothers (Hernando [*b.* ca. 1529; *d.* 1550] and Pedro [*b.* ca. 1531; *d.* 1550]), sons of Rodrigo de Contreras, governor of Nicaragua (1534–1544), and grandsons of Pedro Arias de ÁVILA; in 1550 they led one of the most serious revolts against Spanish royal authority during the colonial period. Their father, from a prominent Segovian family, was accused, among other abuses, of misappropriating to himself, his family, and his friends the best *encomiendas* in Nicaragua. When he was relieved of office, his sons and supporters faced the reduction or loss of their pueblos, along with diminished social and political influence. Emboldened by sulking *encomenderos* and malcontents from Peru, the brothers rebelled with some three hundred followers, a majority of the residents in Nicaragua.

In León, Hernando and others murdered Bishop Antonio de Valdivieso, a persistent critic of Rodrigo, after which other rebels proceeded to destroy livestock and crops, as well as surplus sailing vessels. They aimed to capture the silver fleet from Peru, commanded by the formidable Pedro de la GASCA, and take control of the city of Panama. Thereafter they planned to establish rule in Peru under Hernando Contreras, the "prince of liberty," spuriously claiming that kingdom because initial Spanish expeditions to the general region had sailed under the aegis of Ávila and that, accordingly, certain proprietary rights accrued to his grandsons.

Because of overconfidence, poor planning, and inept leadership, the uprising failed. Reared in luxury and enjoying the favor of the colonists, the leaders were inexperienced; Hernando, though a licentiate, was only twenty-one, and Pedro nineteen. They understood strategy very poorly, making the mistake of dividing their forces into small groups. After a clumsy attack on Panama City, the residents there fought back with unexpected skill and resolution. In disarray, the hapless rebels fled for their lives. Pedro was lost at sea, and Hernando drowned in a river. His head was displayed as a warning to would-be traitors.

— WILLIAM L. SHERMAN

COOKE, JOHN WILLIAM

John William Cooke (*b.* 14 November 1920; *d.* 19 September 1968), principal Argentine theoretician of revolutionary Peronism, or *justicialismo.* Cooke was elected to Argentina's Congress in 1946 as a member of the Radical Party. He quickly gravitated to the charismatic Juan Domingo PERÓN, whom he supported in the pages of *De Frente,* a publication that to many Peronists became the political and moral conscience of the movement. With Perón's ouster in September 1955, Cooke developed a plan of resistance that had as its focus guerrilla warfare followed by general insurrection. Arrested in October 1955, he clandestinely directed from prison the Peronist resistance against both military and civilian governments. A dramatic escape in 1957 was followed in 1959 by exile in Cuba, where he arranged for the training of Argentine guerrillas.

By 1962 Cooke, still in Cuba, and Perón, in exile in Spain, had moved to different political positions and adopted different strategies. Cooke remained on the violent extreme left of the Peronist movement and felt that Perón had become little more than a symbolic memory. Perón considered Cooke "too Cuban" and unrepresentative of *justicialismo,* Perón's political and social philosophy. Cooke returned to Argentina in the mid-1960s, where he died of cancer.

— PAUL GOODWIN

CORDERO, JUAN

Juan Cordero (*b.* 10 June 1822; *d.* 28 May 1884), Mexican painter. After having attended the Academia de San Carlos during what was probably its most difficult period, Cordero went in 1844 to Rome, where he came into contact with the Nazarenes (a group of German artists who sought to revitalize Christian art) and exe-

cuted religious and historical canvases as well as portraits. On his return to Mexico in 1853, Cordero was disappointed at not being named director of painting at the Academia de San Carlos, a post then occupied by Pelegrín CLAVÉ. Nevertheless, he produced numerous fine portraits and received important commissions. Contrasts in lighting characterize a good number of his works, and a realistic bent informs even his most idealized portraits. Cordero painted the vaults and dome of the Church of Santa Teresa and the dome of the Church of San Fernando. An allegorical mural for the Escuela Nacional Preparatoria, known only through a copy, has been considered an antecedent of twentieth-century muralism by nationalist historians.

— CLARA BARGELLINI

CORDERO, ROQUE

Roque Cordero (*b.* 16 August 1917), Panamanian composer and pedagogue. Born in Panama City, Cordero studied composition at Hamline University in St. Paul, Minnesota, and orchestral conducting at Tanglewood. Among his teachers were Ernst Krenek, Leon Barzin, and Dimitri Mitropoulos. He was the director of the National Institute of Music in Panama from 1953 until 1964 and artistic director and conductor of the National Orchestra of Panama from 1964 to 1966. He then became professor of composition at the Latin American Music Center at Indiana University. Cordero's compositional style evolved from a guarded nationalistic approach near the beginning of his career to an atonal language with twelve-tone procedures. His own version of a serially organized atonal language became his most prevalent compositional technique from 1950 on. It is applied to pitch classes and intervals but also determines the evolution of his complex rhythmic structures and the overall form of the piece. In 1976 he received the First Inter-American Composition Prize in Costa Rica. Cordero has been music adviser to Peer International Corporation in New York City and has been invited to judge many international composition competitions.

His more nationalistic works include *Capricho interiorano* (1939), *Sonatina rítmica* (1943), *Obertura Panameña* (1944), and *Rapsodia campesina* (1953). Those early works show Cordero expressing himself through elaborations of typical Panamanian dance rhythms, such as the *mejorana* and the *tamborillo.* His first twelve-tone composition is his 1946 Sonatina for violin and piano. Other important works are the Symphony no. 2 (1956); String Quartet no. 1 (1960); *Mensaja fúnebre* for clarinet and string orchestra (1961), written in memory of Dimitri Mitropoulos; Violin

Concerto (1962), written in a virtuoso style and full of intricate rhythms; Soliloquies for alto sax; Sonata for cello and piano (1963); Symphony no. 3 (1965), a work with one theme and five variations, commissioned by the Third Music Festival in Caracas, Venezuela; *Sonata breve* for piano (1966); *Circumvolutions and Mobiles* for fifty-seven instruments (1967); String Quartets no. 2 and no. 3 (1968, 1973); Cantata (1974); *Permutaciones* (1974); *Variations and Theme for Five* (1975); and *Paz, Paix, Peace* for chamber ensemble (1970).

– ALCIDES LANZA

CORDERO CRESPO, LUIS

Luis Cordero Crespo (*b.* 6 April 1833; *d.* 30 January 1912), president of Ecuador (1892–1895). Born into a prominent family of Azuay, Luis Cordero Crespo studied law at the University of Quito but chose to devote himself to letters and politics rather than jurisprudence. As a man of letters he was most noted for his *Poesías serias* (1895), *Poesías jocosas* (1895), and a Spanish-Quechua dictionary. He founded several newspapers, was a professor of literature at the National College in Cuenca, and helped to inaugurate the universities of Guayaquil and Cuenca. He served as rector of the University of Cuenca from 1911 to 1912.

In 1883, Cordero helped found the Republican Party. After serving in Congress as a deputy and then as a senator, he was elected president in 1892. He attempted unsuccessfully to conciliate warring Liberals and Conservatives. His declaration that church interests were superior to those of the state turned Liberals against him. Revelation of his government's secret involvement in the sale of a Chilean warship to Japan aroused public indignation and forced Cordero to resign. The fall of the government brought the Liberal general Eloy ALFARO to power, thus ending twelve years of civilian rule.

– MARK J. VAN AKEN

CÓRDOBA, JOSÉ MARÍA

José María Córdoba (also Córdova; *b.* 8 September 1799; *d.* 17 October 1829), Colombian military hero. Born in La Concepción, Antioquia, the son of the alcalde, Córdoba joined the patriots in 1814. His valor brought him a captaincy in 1817; he was named lieutenant colonel in 1819 and, after the battle of Boyacá (7 August 1819), commandant of Antioquia (1819–1820). He proceeded to eliminate royalist remnants from Chocó and the northern Cauca and Magdalena basins (1820–1821), and was promoted to colonel. He joined General Antonio José de SUCRE ALCALÁ in Ec-

uador, distinguished himself at Pichincha (24 May 1822), and became a general (3 January 1823). In Peru, Córdoba went on to win further laurels. He led the Colombian infantry's decisive charge at Ayacucho (9 December 1824), the apex of his career.

Although Córdoba was Bolívar's minister of war (1828), the two men became estranged over Bolívar's flirtation with monarchy.

Although Córdoba had killed one of his sergeants at Popayán on 28 December 1823, and had threatened the lives of two other subordinates in 1824, he was acquitted by a court-martial for murder and threats to murder (1827). Then he became engaged to Fanny Henderson, daughter of James Henderson, the British consul general in Bogotá. Although Córdoba was BOLÍVAR's minister of war (1828), the two men became estranged over Bolívar's flirtation with monarchy. Falsely accused of disloyalty by Tomás Cipriano de MOSQUERA, he rebelled against the government and attempted to raise Antioquia. Wounded and a prisoner, with his little force routed, he was cut down at El Santuario by Colonel Rupert Hand.

– J. LEÓN HELGUERA

CÓRDOVA, ARTURO DE

Arturo de Córdova (*b.* 8 May 1908; *d.* 1973), Mexican film actor. Born Arturo García Rodríguez in Mérida, Yucatán, Córdova studied in Argentina. Upon his return to Mexico in 1930, he worked in radio. He made his cinematic debut in Hollywood with a small part in the film *For Whom the Bell Tolls*. In Mexico, his first acting part was in *Celos* (1936). By the 1940s, he had become one of the most sought-out and popular leading men of the "golden age" of the Mexican cinema. He starred in over 300 films in Mexico, Hollywood, Brazil, Spain, and Venezuela, and received three Ariels from the Mexican film academy for best performance by an actor for the films *En la palma de tu mano* (1950), *Las tres perfectas casadas* (1952), and *Feliz año amor mío* (1955).

– DAVID MACIEL

CÓRDOVA, JORGE

Jorge Córdova (*b.* 1822; *d.* 23 October 1861), president of Bolivia (1855–1857). Córdova's parents remain unknown. He joined the army of Andrés de SANTA CRUZ as an ordinary soldier and rose rapidly in rank. Córdova's marriage to the daughter of President Manuel Isidoro BELZÚ facilitated his entrance into politics.

Córdova succeeded his father-in-law as president. The transferral of power from Belzú to Córdova was the first peaceful one in Bolivia's history. Although Córdova was elected, he was overthrown by a military revolt and escaped to Peru. He returned to Bolivia several years later as a private citizen and died violently in the Massacre de Yáñez, which marred the presidency of José María ACHÁ.

Córdova had a reputation as a man of pleasure. As president he was fair and unpretentious and desperately tried to foster internal peace, tolerance, and cooperation among the political factions. These activities consumed so much of his time that little of substance was accomplished during his tenure.

– CHARLES W. ARNADE

CÓRDOVA RIVERA, GONZALO S.

Gonzalo S. Córdova Rivera (*b.* 15 July 1863; *d.* 13 April 1928), president of Ecuador. Born in Cuenca, Córdova Rivera completed a law degree at the Universidad de Cuenca. He served as deputy from Cañar Province from 1892 to 1897 and as governor of that province from 1898 to 1902. He was minister of the interior from 1903 to 1906. In 1912 he served as senator from Carchi Province and as vice president of the senate. He was Ecuador's minister to Chile, Argentina, and the United States in the period 1911–1913, and minister to Venezuela in 1922. He was popularly elected to the presidency in 1924. On July 9, 1925, a group of young lieutenants overthrew the Córdova government.

– LINDA ALEXANDER RODRÍGUEZ

CORNEJO, MARIANO H.

Mariano H. Cornejo (*b.* 1873; *d.* 25 March 1942), one of a group of positivist social scientists in late-nineteenth-century Peru. In 1896 he was appointed to the first chair of sociology at the National University of San Marcos. Cornejo relied upon precepts and convictions learned from European thinkers and adapted them to the society around him. He expressed optimism that an open-ended Peruvian aristocracy that admitted "new blood," together with the nation's scientists, could discover the sociological laws necessary to carry out the task of national progress. He scorned revolutionary change, favoring universal education and gradualism as the keys to national improvement. He denied that either race or class antagonisms governed history and

foresaw utilitarian cooperation as a more useful framework of analysis.

– VINCENT PELOSO

CORONA, RAMÓN

Ramón Corona (*b.* 1837; *d.* 11 November 1889), Liberal military commander and governor of Jalisco. Born to a family of modest social position in the southern Jaliscan village of Tuxcueca, Corona was the administrator of some mining operations near the Sinaloa–Tepic border when the Reform war began in 1858. Over the next decade, he emerged as the leader of the migrants driven from Tepic who sought to restore white and MESTIZO dominance over that territory and its Indians, whom Manuel LOZADA had united and allied with the imperialist cause. Rising to command the Tepic Brigade, and then the Army of the West during the Intervention (1862–1867), Corona became the dominant military and political figure in west-central Mexico in the postwar years. His career culminated in his defeat of Lozada in 1873. After serving as ambassador to Spain and Portugal for twelve years, Corona returned as the elected governor of Jalisco in March 1887. An activist who promoted infrastructure and education, he acquired a growing national reputation and became a leading presidential candidate. Corona was assassinated in Guadalajara.

– STUART VOSS

CORONADO, JUAN VÁZQUEZ DE

Juan Vázquez de Coronado (*b.* 1523; *d.* October 1565), conquistador and governor of Costa Rica (1562–1565). Founder of the Costa Rican city of Cartago (1564), Coronado headed a series of expeditions that brought most of Costa Rica under Spanish control by 1565.

Born in Salamanca, Spain, of noble parents, Coronado left Spain in 1540 to seek his fortune. He traveled to Mexico, joining his uncle, conquistador Francisco Vázquez de CORONADO. In 1548, Juan Vázquez de Coronado departed for Guatemala with a *cedula real* (royal letters patent) recommending him to the *audiencia.* Upon his arrival he was named *alcalde mayor* (royal governor) of El Salvador and Honduras. In subsequent years Coronado distinguished himself as a capable administrator and an adept conquistador. He was made *alcalde mayor* of Nicaragua in 1561. One of his first acts in this post was to subvert a rebellion of Spanish soldiers led by Lope de AGUIRRE.

In 1562, King Philip II designated him *alcalde mayor* of the provinces of Nueva Cartago and Costa Rica. Coronado began an extended campaign, tending to administrative problems in the cities of León, Nicoya, and Garcimuñoz, and pursuing the rebel *cacique* (local ruler) Garabito. In interactions with caciques, he proved to be a skillful negotiator and was far more moderate in his treatment of the Indians than were many of his contemporaries.

Coronado journeyed to Quepo and through the Guarco Valley in 1563, encountering strong Indian resistance in the town of Cuoto. A prolonged and bloody battle there ended in a Spanish victory. Coronado remained in the valley briefly, negotiating a peace with neighboring caciques and founding the city of Cartago, which became the capital of Costa Rica. After overseeing the provisioning and settlement of the city, he headed north, taking possession of the valley of Guaymi and the provinces of Texbi and Duy. He discovered gold in the Estrella River and in 1564 organized a registry of mines to facilitate the exploitation of the river's wealth.

In 1565, Coronado traveled to Spain to give Philip II a personal account of his progress. The Spanish monarch named him *adelantado* (governor) in perpetuity of the province of Costa Rica. In addition, Coronado received an annual salary, royal recognition of Cartago, and a three-year appointment as governor of Nicaragua. He was never to enjoy these privileges, however; on the return voyage, his ship, the *San Josepe,* was wrecked in a storm, leaving no survivors.

— SARA FLEMING

CORONEL, PEDRO

Pedro Coronel (*b.* 25 May 1923; *d.* 23 May 1985), Mexican painter and sculptor. Born in Jerez, Zacatecas, Coronel left in 1940 for Mexico City, where he studied at the National School of Painting and Sculpture (La Esmeralda) until 1945. He taught sculpture there in 1945–1946. In 1946, Coronel traveled to Europe. While living in Paris he studied painting in the studio of Victor Brauner and sculpture with Constantin Brancusi. In later years he was a friend of Sonia Delaunay, the Ukrainian-born painter and designer who was married to Robert Delaunay. Throughout his life Coronel traveled extensively in Mexico, Europe, Africa, and Asia, assembling collections of artifacts from these countries. Coronel returned to Mexico in 1952 and in 1954 had his first important exhibition in the Proteo Gallery, Mexico City, which was very well received and reviewed. From that point on he exhibited regularly in Mexico, the United States, and Europe, most notably in Mexico City at the Gallery of Mexican Art.

Coronel's mature work draws heavily upon the tenets of abstraction while incorporating figural imagery derived from ancient artifacts of Mexico, Europe, Africa, and Asia. His works on canvas are heavily textured and aggressively colored. Sculptures are executed in marble, onyx, and bronze. In 1959, Coronel received the National Prize of Painting; in 1984, he was awarded the National Prize of Plastic Arts.

— CLAYTON KIRKING

CORONEL URTECHO, JOSÉ

José Coronel Urtecho (*b.* 28 February 1906; *d.* 1994), except for Rubén DARÍO considered to be Nicaragua's most important writer. Born in Granada and educated at the Colegio Centroamérica, Coronel Urtecho studied for several years in the United States before returning to Nicaragua in 1925, bringing back a passionate interest in the "new American poetry" of Ezra Pound and others. With Luís Alberto Cabrales in 1931 he founded the *vanguardia* movement, which included Pablo Antonio CUADRA, Luís Downing, Joaquín Pasos, and others, most of them disaffected from their conservative upper-class Granada families. Taking as a motto "Beside our ancestors we go against our fathers," the iconoclastic *vanguardistas* reacted against Darío's imitators, bourgeois culture, the academy, and U.S. intervention in Nicaraguan political affairs. They proclaimed support for the patriotism of Augusto César SANDINO and fomented a rediscovery of *"lo nicaragüense"* (that which is Nicaraguan). The best work of the *vanguardistas* revitalized interest in the indigenous roots of national culture, introduced vigorous new North American and European literature (much of which they translated into Spanish) into Nicaragua, and produced an influential body of innovative writing in a variety of genres. Unfortunately, their paradoxical fascination with the elitist and antidemocratic ideals of emerging European fascism led them into a naive attempt to put their ideas into practice by supporting and taking part in the embryonic Somoza dictatorship.

The iconoclastic vanguardistas *reacted against bourgeois culture, the academy, and U.S. intervention in Nicaraguan political affairs.*

Coronel Urtecho's own writing has embraced many genres: short stories and short novels, poetry, essays, translations, literary criticism, political commentary, and history. Loath to write books, he left the task of collecting his widely dispersed writings mostly to others. Major collections are *Rápido tránsito (al ritmo de norteamérica)* (1953), an account of his North American sojourn; *Pól-la d'ananta katanta paranta: Imitaciones y traducciones* (1970), a collection of his poetry edited by Nicaraguan poet Ernesto Gutiérrez; *Prosa* (1972), edited by Carlos Martínez Rivas; and *Prosa reunida* (1985), which includes portions of his influential *Panorama y antología de la poesía norteamericana* (1949). A major historical work is *Reflexiones sobre la historia de Nicaragua* (3 vols., 1962–1967). Both Coronel Urtecho's writings and his politics have evolved continuously. In *Mea máxima culpa* (1975), he publicly regretted having served in the Somoza regime, as subsecretary of external relations, from the 1930s into the 1950s. In the 1970s, he moved into sympathy with the emerging Sandinista movement, writing *exteriorista* poetry in the manner of Ernesto CARDENAL. His *Conversación con Carlos* (1986) praises FSLN (Sandinista National Liberation Front) founder Carlos FONSECA AMADOR.

– DAVID E. WHISNANT

CORRAL VERDUGO, RAMÓN

Ramón Corral Verdugo (*b.* 10 January 1854; *d.* 10 November 1912), Mexican politician and vice president (1904–1911). Influential figure in Sonoran state politics and a fixture of the Porfirio DÍAZ administration from 1900 to 1911, he was a prototypical political-financial leader of the Porfiriato.

Corral was born in the mining town of Álamos, Sonora, on the Hacienda de Las Mendes, where his father operated a small store in the Palmarejo mines and later became mayor of Chinipas. Sharing his father's interest in politics, Corral wrote for opposition newspapers in an attempt to oust a succession of governors. In 1876 he joined the political faction of Luis E. Torres, serving as vice-governor, then governor (1895–1899) of Sonora. Although Corral was responsible for many public works in Sonora, thousands of Yaqui Indians were killed or deported to Yucatán during his administration. In 1900 he served in cabinet-level posts, beginning with governor of the Federal District (1900–1903), and in the key agency of secretary of government (1903–1911) while simultaneously holding office as vice president. Corral had many financial investments in Sonora. He died in exile in Paris.

– RODERIC AI CAMP

CORREA, JUAN

Juan Correa (*b.* ca. 1645; *d.* 3 November 1716), Mexican painter. An almost exact contemporary of Cristóbal de VILLALPANDO, Correa is more sober and conservative but equally productive and uneven. His works are found throughout Mexico and even in Europe. His first known painting is *Saint Rose of Lima* (1671). Notable are the two great canvases for the sacristy of the cathedral of Mexico City (1689–1691) and many devotional images. The catalog of his work lists nearly 400 paintings. A mulatto, Correa had a large and successful workshop and numerous followers, many of them relatives. The extensive and detailed knowledge of this workshop gained through recent studies sheds much light on the practice of painting in colonial Mexico.

– CLARA BARGELLINI

CORREA, JULIO MYZKOWSKY

Julio Myzkowsky Correa (*b.* 1890; *d.* 14 July 1953), Paraguayan dramatist, poet, and short-story writer. Son of a Brazilian who fought against Paraguay in the War of the Triple Alliance and grandson of a Polish immigrant who fought for Paraguay in the same war, Correa was raised in the Guaraní-speaking countryside. He became known as the creator of the Guaraní theater as it is known today. At the time of the Chaco War, he began to write down his plays, and to perform them with the help of his actress wife. He also did the staging, costuming, and training of the actors. Although Correa did not have a formal education in the theater and his works are crude and lacking in technique, his powerful characterizations of national types and his ability to dramatize the political feelings of his countrymen in Guaraní guaranteed his success. A prevalent theme in his works is the injustice of the *latifundia* and the deprivation of land and opportunity for the Paraguayan peasant. His bold and poignant satire landed him in jail more than once. He also defended the poor Guaraní-speaking peasant in his poetry and short stories.

– CATALINA SEGOVIA-CASE

CORREOSO, BUENAVENTURA

Buenaventura Correoso (*b.* 1831; *d.* 1911), Panamanian educator and journalist. In 1856 he headed the investigation of an incident in Panama City known as the Watermelon Riot, which was caused by a dispute between a white American and a black Panamanian watermelon vendor that led to a riot between Americans and Panamanians in which seventeen people died. He was a populist leader, greatly admired by the lower classes. In 1868, with the support of the people of the lower-class neighborhoods in the capital, he led a successful uprising against the government. He was chief of state three times. Correoso founded numerous schools and the first public library in the country.

– JUAN MANUEL PÉREZ

CORTÁZAR, JULIO

Julio Cortázar (*b.* 26 August 1914; *d.* 12 February 1984), Argentine novelist, short-story writer, poet, and essayist. Born in Brussels, Cortázar returned with his family to Argentina when he was four. In 1951 he moved to Paris, where he lived until his death. With BORGES, SÁBATO, and BIOY CASARES, he was instrumental in renovating Argentine narrative. Although considered a writer of fantastic literature, Cortázar illuminated problems of the Argentine middle class as well as the metaphysical anguish of modern man. His works have aesthetic and metaphysical dimensions, but also social and political ones, since he was an ardent defender of the Cuban and Nicaraguan revolutions. Throughout his texts, Cortázar always sought "an exactness of expression that would enhance creative freedom." To that effect, he employed words from different languages, diverse linguistic styles, and even invented a jargon (*glíglico*) composed of phonetic analogies. He played "phonosemantic tricks" with words, parodied linguistic clichés, and used semiphonetic graphemes to make his discourse as "nonaesthetic" as possible.

Julio Cortázar in the 1930s. (Organization of American States)

Modern language has a transcendent, creative, even magical function, according to Cortázar. Chiefly in his famous novel *Rayuela* (1963; Hopscotch, 1966), but also in *62: Modelo para armar* (1968; 62: A Model Kit, 1972), he subverted the very structure of the novel. In an almost surrealistic vein, Cortázar substituted imagination and desire for inefficient "reason." He perceived the search for man's essence as an ascesis or a mandala and therefore his literary creations assumed the character of an ontological peregrination: "To write is to draw my mandala and, at the same time, to travel over it, to invent purification purifying myself; the task of a poor white shaman with nylon underwear." He rejected limiting taxonomies and everything conventional and academic, and focused his interest on the exceptional, singular, and disconnected. These ideas determined the apparent disorder and fragmentation in his fiction. Nevertheless, he tended to a totality that goes beyond consciousness and permits one to discover what he called the "figures," the constellation of which one is part without knowing it. In Cortázar's creations, times, places, and people are mysteriously related to each other in nonlogical associations. These "figures" were a culmination of the theme of the doppelgänger, a sort of "bridge" or "passage" (key words in his work) between the distant and different beings who form the figures. All this compelled Cortázar to demand that his reader become his "accomplice." Through dreams, absurd situations or characters, Jungian coincidences, premonitions, eroticism, humor, and gratuitous acts, Cortázar was fighting life's absurdity and a dehumanizing world.

— ANGELA B. DELLEPIANE

CORTÉS, HERNÁN

Hernán Cortés (Fernando, Hernando; *b.* ca. 1484; *d.* 2 December 1547), conqueror of Mexico. Hernán Cortés was born in Medellín, Spain, in the province of Extremadura. Best known for his conquest of the Aztecs (Mexica) of central Mexico, he is also renowned for his famous *Cartas de relación*. Cortés was often depicted as a psychological and tactical master, but his greatest achievement was neither military nor literary; instead, it lay in his understanding that successful conquest was dependent upon successful colonization.

Cortés studied law at the University of Salamanca. While he probably did not become a *bachiller,* his activities and writings betray legal knowledge, especially of the *siete partidas,* which aided him in the process of conquest.

Seeking wealth and power, Cortés sailed for Hispaniola in 1504. After briefly serving as a notary in Hispaniola, he joined Diego VELÁZQUEZ in the conquest of Cuba, where he assumed the position of *alcalde* and in about 1515 married Catalina Suárez Marcaida. By 1517, he had acquired both an *encomienda* and several gold mines. Having shown little interest in the early exploratory voyages of Hernández de CÓRDOBA and Juan de GRIJALVA, he was nevertheless chosen to lead an expedition to find Grijalva in late 1518. By the time Cortés was ready, Grijalva had returned. Cortés, nevertheless, set forth on what became a mission of trade and exploration to the Yucatán in November 1519.

With an army of 508 soldiers, Cortés set out on an expedition that was primarily intended for trade, but he also was instructed to evangelize the Indians and to take possession of any new lands discovered, two tasks he undertook with zeal. He was not instructed to colonize, however. In April 1519 Cortés reached what is now Veracruz, where he learned of a rich and powerful ruler, MOTECUHZOMA II, who was located inland but who held domain over a vast area extending to the coastal region. The subsequent events of Cortés's conquest of the Aztec king's domain were defined by Cortés's unshakable desire to deliver that empire to the kingdom of Castile.

Cortés also learned that Motecuhzoma and his army had many enemies who might be turned against the Mexica. But to carry out such a project, both to find Motecuhzoma and to make alliances with native groups, would take time and material resources. Expanding upon the orders of Pánfilo de NARVÁEZ, an ally of Velázquez, Cortés established a town with a *cabildo* (Villa Rica de la Vera Cruz) and placed the town directly under the king's authority.

Now in open rebellion against Velázquez, Cortés and his army destroyed their own ships to cut their means of connection to Cuba. Meanwhile, envoys carrying gold and examples of elaborate Mexica featherwork had been dispatched to Spain, seeking royal sanction of Cortés's actions. Velázquez sent a representative to Spain to brand Cortés a traitor and organized an army to move against him. By August 1519, Cortés and most of his army had set forth, moving west to find Motecuhzoma and the capital of his empire, the island city Tenochtitlán. By September, Cortés had reached Tlaxcala. He may have heard that the Tlaxcalans were longtime enemies of the Mexica and thus been motivated to find and make allies of them. It took fierce fighting to subdue the Tlaxcalans, but by late September, Cortés had formed a critical alliance with Tlaxcala. After next pacifying Cholula, Cortés was ready to march into the heart of the Valley of Mexico. Having negotiated with emissaries of Motecuhzoma several times during the march west, Cortés could not be persuaded against entering the heart of Mexica territory, and Cortés and Motecuhzoma met in early November.

While we can never know precisely what occurred during the first meetings of the representatives of these two very different societies, the ultimate outcome was the imprisonment of Motecuhzoma by the Spaniards. Cortés decisively beat back the forces of Pánfilo de Narváez sent by Velázquez and thereby gained needed reinforcements. The entire conquest project, however, was almost ruined by the slaughter at the Great Temple by Pedro de ALVARADO, Cortés's lieutenant, and his forces. Cortés, meanwhile, released Motecuhzoma's brother, CUITLAHUAC, who immediately rallied the Mexica in violent opposition to the Spanish.

The situation deteriorated so badly that Cortés decided that retreat was necessary. On the so-called Noche Triste many Spanish soldiers lost their lives. Revealingly, Cortés's accounts also lament the gold that was lost that night. Retreating to Tlaxcala in July 1520, Cortés prepared for a final siege of Tenochtitlán. He ordered the building of thirteen brigantines to blockade the island capital, and set forth for Texcoco on 28 December. Over the next months, the Spanish soldiers conducted a series of assaults on Indian towns surrounding Tenochtitlán to pacify the area and to increase the size of their allied Indian forces. Once the ships were ready, Cortés undertook the final assault, which was achieved by blockade, massive force, and great destruction of life and property. Tenochtitlán fell in August 1521.

Salvador de Madariaga, one of Cortés's biographers, says that he was conquered by his own conquest; the events of the sixteen years after it bear this out. While he was consolidating his leadership of New Spain, he received official recognition as its legitimate conqueror and governor. But many of his soldiers nursed grievances, other Spaniards were jealous and resentful, and his wife died under mysterious circumstances.

Cortés embarked on further territorial expansion, sending Pedro de Alvarado to conquer Guatemala and Cristóbal de OLID to conquer Honduras. Alvarado succeeded but with little gain; Olid, with Velázquez's encouragement, rebelled against Cortés's authority. Olid's betrayal prompted Cortés to set off on an ill-fated expedition to Honduras. Royal authorities became disturbed by his willingness to take the law into his own hands, and his absence from Mexico City provided an opening for his enemies to move against his followers, thus strengthening the royal conviction to bring New Spain under its own firm control.

In 1529, after personal entreaties from Cortés, who had traveled to Spain, Charles V granted him the title marqués del Valle de Oaxaca, twenty-two *encomienda* towns, and the right to entail his estate. While he returned again to Mexico in the mid-1530s, he never again held the governorship. Thus to others fell the task of solidifying the territorial gains and administrative structures Cortés had put in place. Dogged by lawsuits and investigations, the marqués spent much of his latter years defending himself. Brilliant, active, and cruel, Cortés was the conqueror of the largest single community pacified in the New World. He died in Spain still seeking the status and riches he believed he had been denied.

– SUSAN KELLOGG

CORTÉS, MARTÍN

Martín Cortés (*b.* 1532/1533; *d.* 13 August 1589), legitimate son of the conquistador Hernán CORTÉS and Juana de Zúñiga, born in Cuernavaca. Not to be confused with his stepbrother, also named Martín (son of Cortés and MALINCHE), this Martín was the second marqués del Valle de Oaxaca. In 1540, he went to Spain, where he joined Charles V's royal service and later became a favorite in the entourage of Philip II. His return to Mexico in 1562 to claim his father's titles and property coincided with the Spanish crown's attempt to revoke the extension of the *encomienda* to the sons and grandsons of conquistadores. Indignant at the crown's assertiveness and eager to protect their inheritance, the criollos naturally looked to Martín Cortés for leadership. Don Martín, however, had an arrogant disposition and had an ostentatious lifestyle that offended many; more important, he seemed to lack the natural leadership abilities of his father. Though he tacitly agreed to their plan to make him king of Mexico, he never fully pledged his support for criollo plans to assassinate royal officials and overthrow the government. The plot failed, and the leaders were severely punished. Cortés was apprehended and sent to Spain to face trial in 1567; he was fined and sentenced to military duty. Though pardoned by the crown in 1574, Cortés never returned to Mexico. This failed uprising represented the last serious challenge to the crown's authority in Mexico by the early conquistadores and their families. Cortés died in Madrid.

– J. DAVID DRESSING

CORTÉS CASTRO, LEÓN

León Cortés Castro (*b.* 8 December 1882; *d.* 2 March 1946), president of Costa Rica (1936–1940). After receiving a law degree from the School of Law in San José, León Cortés Castro held many elected and appointed positions beginning with his appointment by the military dictator President Federico Tinoco Gra-

nados (1917–1919), to the post of commander of the Alajuela Garrison (Comandante de Plaza de Alajuela). Cortés served as president of the National Assembly (1925–1926), as minister of education (1929–1930), and as minister of public works (1930; 1932–1936). His tour as minister of public works under president Ricardo JIMÉNEZ OREAMUNO consolidated Cortés's reputation as a no-nonsense and frugal administrator, which prompted the leaders of the National Republican Party to choose him as their standard-bearer in 1936.

During his administration Cortés was a proponent of fiscal responsibility, extending the nation's highway network and embarking on an ambitious construction program. His brick, mortar, and asphalt approach provided employment that helped ameliorate setbacks due to the Great Depression. He founded the National Bank of Costa Rica in 1936.

Although generally accredited even by his detractors with being an effective administrator, Cortés frequently was charged with arbitrary actions. While president he intervened in the 1938 and 1940 elections preventing opposition candidates from being elected; he also meddled in the presidential candidacy of three-time president Ricardo Jiménez.

Shortly after Rafael Angel CALDERÓN GUARDIA's inauguration in 1940, Cortés, as the most prominent leader of the opposition forces, openly broke with Calderón and formed a rival party. When Cortés lost the 1944 election to Teodoro PICADO MICHALSKI (1944–1948), there were widespread charges that Calderón had used his executive power to perpetrate electoral fraud on a grand scale.

Cortés remained the leader of the opposition until his sudden death following a heart attack in 1946.

– JOHN PATRICK BELL

CORTÉS DE MADARIAGA, JOSÉ

José Cortés de Madariaga (*b.* 8 July 1766; *d.* March 1826), priest and political activist in the Venezuelan independence movement. A native of Chile, Cortés de

At the fall of the republic in 1812, Cortés de Madariaga was sent to the military prison at Ceuta, in Africa, from which he escaped two years later.

Madariaga was ordained in 1788. He arrived in Venezuela by chance in 1802 and obtained a canonry in the Cathedral of Caracas. He played an active role in the events of 19 April 1810 in Caracas and was a member of the Junta Suprema of Caracas. Cortés de Madariaga traveled to New Granada in 1811 and signed the first treaty of alliance and federation between Cundinamarca and Venezuela. At the fall of the republic in 1812, he was sent to the military prison at Ceuta, in Africa, from which he escaped two years later. When Venezuela regained its independence in 1817, he returned and promoted the founding of a representative, federal government. This plan was disclaimed and condemned by Simón BOLÍVAR. Cortés de Madariaga later traveled to Jamaica, where he again worked for independence. In 1823 the Congress of Colombia granted him a pension for his services in the cause of independence.

– INÉS QUINTERO

CORVALÁN LEPE, LUIS

Luis Corvalán Lepe (b. 1916), politician and secretary general of Unidad Popular, the Chilean Communist Party. A professor by education, Corvalán worked his way up in the party to serve as a senator representing the south. Then, selected by his predecessor, he became head of the party in 1957. Always a supporter of Moscow, he was nevertheless willing to cooperate with progressive elements. Corvalán rationalized the Unidad Popular's policies, arguing that it was possible to achieve socialism in Chile without revolution. Captured in the 1973 coup that overthrew Allende, Corvalán suffered torture at the hands of the Pinochet government. In 1976 he was exchanged for the Soviet political prisoner Vladimir Bukovsky.

– WILLIAM F. SATER

COS, MARTÍN PERFECTO DE

Martín Perfecto De Cos (b. 1800; d. 1854), Mexican general. A native of Veracruz, Cos joined the Veracruz regiment in 1820. He became a lieutenant under Augustín de ITURBIDE during 1821, but supported the formation of a Mexican republic by 1823. After Cos became a general in 1833, President Antonio Lopéz de SANTA ANNA sent him to control unrest in the North. In December 1835 he lost San Antonio to the Texans. Cos fought at the Alamo (1836) before being captured at San Jacinto in early 1836. Federalists defeated him in battle at Tampico in 1838 and at Tuxpan in 1839. During 1847 he fought against the U.S. army at Tuxpan. Cos acted as government leader for Tehuantepec before his death.

– ALWYN BARR

COS Y PÉREZ, JOSÉ MARÍA

José María Cos y Pérez (d. November 1819), Mexican insurgent ideologue. Born in Zacatecas, he studied in Guadalajara, where he entered the Seminario Tridentino. A doctor of theology, he opposed the insurrection in 1810. When suspected of sedition, he joined Ignacio LÓPEZ RAYÓN (1773–1832) and became a writer and ideologue for the insurgency. In 1812 he wrote the *Plan de paz y plan de guerra,* and published the insurgent papers *Ilustrador Nacional* and *Ilustrador Americano.* He served as vicar general of the army and deputy for Zacatecas in the insurgent Congress. A signer of the Constitution of Apatzingán (1814), he became a member of the executive branch. When Congress reprimanded him for directing troops while serving in the executive, he disavowed that body in 1815. Although first condemned to death and later to life imprisonment, he was released by Rayón and later received amnesty from the colonial regime in 1817. He died in Pátzcuaro.

– VIRGINIA GUEDEA

COSÍO VILLEGAS, DANIEL

Daniel Cosío Villegas (b. 23 July 1898; d. 10 March 1976), Mexican intellectual figure and cultural entrepreneur. A graduate of the National Preparatory School and the National School of Law, he became a prominent student leader and began teaching before graduating with degrees in law and literature. He was a disciple of Pedro HENRÍQUEZ UREÑA and a political collaborator of José VASCONCELOS. He became one of the first members of his generation to study economics abroad. In 1938 he founded *El Trimestre Económico* and the leading publishing house Fondo de Cultura Económica, directing both until 1948. Known for his collaborative historical projects on the Porfiriato, he directed *Historia Mexicana* (1951–1961) and cofounded and directed the Colegio de Mexico, where he produced many distinguished disciples. He was awarded the National Prize in Letters in 1971, and was a member of the National College from 1951 until his death.

– RODERIC AI CAMP

COSTA, CLÁUDIO MANUEL DA

Cláudio Manuel da Costa (also Manoel; b. 5 June 1729; d. 4 July 1789), considered the father of Brazilian literature and its major neoclassic poet. He was born in Mariana, Minas Gerais, to a well-to-do family. After studying with the Jesuits in Brazil, he obtained a law degree in Coimbra, Portugal, in 1753. Returning to Brazil, he set up residence in Ouro Prêto, where he pursued a career as a lawyer and public servant. Through investments in gold mining and moneylending, he became one of the wealthiest men in the province. His collected poems were published as *Orbas* [sic] (1768), and he also wrote an epic poem on the history of his home town (published as *Vila Rica* in 1839). In 1789 he was arrested under the accusation of participating in a plot to declare Minas Gerais independent of the Portuguese crown (Inconfidência Mineira). After a month in jail, he compromised himself and several of his named co-conspirators. Broken and remorseful, he committed suicide. Without presenting serious documentation, some historians have tried to contest the official version of his death, accusing his jailer of murder.

– HEITOR MARTINS

COSTA, HIPÓLITO JOSÉ DA

Hipólito José da Costa (*b.* 25 March 1774; *d.* 11 September 1823), journalist. Born in the colony of Sacramento, Brazil, where his father served in the royal troops, da Costa graduated with a degree in philosophy (1796) and law (1798) from the University of Coimbra. He began his public career under the protection of minister of the colonies Rodrigo de Souza Coutinho, who placed him in charge of a visit to the United States and Mexico in 1798, and appointed him director of Royal Press.

Da Costa undertook a voyage to England in 1802 with the aim of acquiring books, machinery, and other typographical equipment. When he returned, he was seized by the Inquisition and accused of being a mason. He escaped to London (1805), where, in 1808, he founded the liberal newspaper *Correio Braziliense,* a publication that had a decisive influence at the time of Brazil's independence, even though it did not advocate separation from Portugal until February 1822. As a result of new freedoms of the press and the proliferation of numerous periodicals, da Costa believed that Brazil no longer needed news emanating from abroad. Publication of *Correio Braziliense* ceased in 1822. After independence, da Costa was appointed the Brazilian representative in London, but he died soon after his nomination.

– LÚCIA M. BASTOS P. NEVES

COSTA, LÚCIO

Lúcio Costa (*b.* 27 February 1902), Brazilian urban planner, best known for designing the city plan of Brasília. Born in Toulon, France, Costa was part of an extraordinary flowering of creative genius in Rio de Janeiro in the 1950s that included, among others, the architect Oscar NIEMEYER, the landscape architect Roberto BURLE MARX (Costa's neighbor), and the creators of Bossa Nova, such as Antônio Carlos JOBIM and Luís Bonfa. Twenty-six plans, some with elaborate models

labored over for months by entire architectural firms, were submitted in the 1955 design competition for the new capital. Costa produced his plan in sixty-four hours. His only expenditures were for paper, pencils, and an eraser. Disillusioned by Brasília's failure to catalyze social change, as he and Niemeyer had hoped, Costa said, "You don't solve the social problems of a country by simply moving its capital, and in Brazil the main problem is the huge base of poor in the country."

– ALEX SHOUMATOFF

COSTA E SILVA, ARTUR DA

Artur da Costa e Silva (*b.* 3 October 1902; *d.* 17 December 1969), president of Brazil (1967–1969). Born in Taquarí, Rio Grande do Sul, Costa e Silva attended the Realengo Military Academy and graduated at the head of his class. As a young second lieutenant in 1922, he took part in the Copacabana Fort Revolt in Rio de Janeiro, for which he was imprisoned for six months. For supporting Getúlio VARGAS in the Revolution of 1930, Costa e Silva was named to a federal government post. During World War II, he served as an officer in the Brazilian Expeditionary Force (FEB) in Italy, after which he joined a group of officers who removed Vargas from office in 1945. Costa e Silva became a brigadier general in 1952; six years later he was named a major general and commander of the second infantry division and of the armored vehicle division based in São Paulo.

In August 1969, while campaigning for a national referendum on revisions to the Constitution of 1967, Costa e Silva suffered an incapacitating stroke.

He turned down President João GOULART's offer to become army chief of staff in 1961, but the following year he accepted command of the Fourth Army, based in northeastern Brazil. Costa e Silva played a key role in the March 1964 coup against Goulart, seizing the War Ministry Building in Rio, the armed forces' communication and bureaucratic center. The Supreme Revolutionary Command, which engineered the coup, named him head of the 200,000-man army. Two years later the Army High Command elected him to succeed fellow officer (and academy classmate) Humberto CASTELLO BRANCO as president.

Costa e Silva's presidency was marked by the imposition of authoritarian rule. In December 1968, he recessed the National Congress when it refused to waive immunity for a member perceived to have criticized the military. Costa e Silva then issued a series of Institutional Acts that expanded executive and military powers, limited media freedom, and suspended federal, state, and municipal elections. He justified his regime with an improving economy. The government cut taxes on Brazilian businesses, attracted foreign investment, and provided incentives to ranchers. The gross domestic product rose 11 percent in 1968 and the World Bank approved a $1-billion development loan, marking the beginning of the Brazilian Economic Miracle.

In August 1969, while campaigning for a national referendum on revisions to the Constitution of 1967, Costa e Silva suffered an incapacitating stroke. A military junta composed of the three armed forces ministers assumed power, bypassed the constitutionally designated successor, Vice President Pedro Aleixo, and with the Army High Command named General Emílio Garrastazú MÉDICI in October 1969 to succeed immediately to the presidency. Costa e Silva died in Rio de Janeiro.

– ROSS WILKINSON

COTAPOS BAEZA, ACARIO

Acario Cotapos Baeza (*b.* 30 April 1889: *d.* 22 November 1969), Chilean composer. Born in Valdivia, Chile, Cotapos was one of the group of authors, poets, composers, architects, and visual artists known as Los Diez, the first group to comprise the Chilean cultural avantgarde. Initially self-taught, at the age of twenty-seven Cotapos moved to New York to study. For the ten years following, he counted among his associates Edgard Varèse, Aaron Copland, Henry Cowell, Ernest Bloch, and Darius Milhaud. In 1927, with Varèse and others, Cotapos founded the International Composers Guild, one of the first organizations with a mandate to perform new music. In 1927, Cotapos left New York for Paris and Madrid, where he composed a number of important works. Returning to his homeland in 1940, he served as secretary of the National Conservatory from 1940 to 1946. He was supervisor of the Instituto de Extensión Musical of the University of Chile from 1949 until his death in Santiago. His musical output includes works for voice, piano, orchestra, and chamber ensembles. Much of his music, characterized by a free and independent spirit, tends toward the dramatic and monumental.

– SERGIO BARROSO

COTEGIPE, BARÃO DE

Barão de Cotegipe (João Mauricio Wanderley; *b.* 23 October 1815; *d.* 13 February 1889), Brazilian politi-

cian. Cotegipe was identified with Bahian politics and slavocratic sugar interests throughout his life. After graduating from the Olinda Law Faculty in Pernambuco in 1837, Cotegipe set out on the path that eventually made him the archetypal imperial mandarin. He moved up steadily through the political ranks, holding a county judgeship and a variety of provincial elected offices before becoming a national deputy in the early 1840s. By 1856 he was a senator from Bahia, and a member of the cabinet. An important chieftain of the pro-slavery national Conservative Party, Cotegipe was himself a slaveowner and a holder of several sugar plantations, all inherited by his wife, a daughter of the Conde de Passé, perhaps the richest planter in Bahia Province. In 1875 Cotegipe, then serving as minister of finance, authored the landmark legislation (Decree no. 2687 of 6 November 1875) that created the agricultural credit guaranteeing 7 percent interest on all investments to create the modern sugar mill complex, or *engenho central.* In 1885 Cotegipe became prime minister. His Conservative government, finally facing up to the reality that slavery in Brazil could not continue forever, introduced the Saraiva-Cotegipe Law of 1885 that freed all slaves over sixty-five years old, thereby immediately manumitting 120,000 older slaves. Typical of many imperial mandarins, Cotegipe was a poor businessman when it came to looking after his own interests and died poor, months before the monarchy was overthrown by a discontented army.

– EUL-SOO PANG

COUTINHO, JOSÉ JOAQUIM DA CUNHA DE AZEREDO

José Joaquim da Cunha de Azeredo Coutinho (*b.* 8 September 1742; *d.* 12 September 1821), bishop of Olinda (1794–1806) and author. A child of the late Portuguese Enlightenment, Coutinho was born into a landowning family from the Rio de Janeiro captaincy. He graduated with a degree in canon law from Coimbra University in 1780. Twelve years later he was elected to the Royal Academy of Sciences. In 1798, he left Lisbon for Olinda, Pernambuco, where he founded a renowned seminary, whose "Estatutos" ("Ordinances") he wrote. Also serving as provisional head of Pernambuco's government, he took harsh measures against what he considered, given his enlightened outlook, abusive practices such as tax evasion, and private appropriation of funds from the royal treasury. By so doing, he offended powerful vested interests. In 1802, Coutinho was called back to Portugal, where he was nominated bishop of Elvas in 1806. He retired from his see in 1817, and was appointed the last general inquisitor of the realm the following year.

As an author, Coutinho was chiefly concerned with the economic policy of the crown. His *A Political Essay on the Commerce of Portugal and Her Colonies* was published in 1794, and was translated into English in 1801. Later, he wrote a number of important works in a polemic vein on religious and administrative matters. His physiocratic beliefs, shrouded in a conservative outlook, revealed his sympathies with the reform-minded officials of the times, but some extreme attitudes, such as the defense of the slave trade, kept him somewhat apart from the leading intellectuals of the period.

– GUILHERME PEREIRA DAS NEVES

COUTINHO, RODRIGO DOMINGOS ANTONIO DE SOUSA

Rodrigo Domingos Antonio de Sousa Coutinho (*b.* 3 August 1755; *d.* 26 January 1812), first count of Linhares (1808) and a Portuguese diplomat. From a noble family of important court and state functionaries, Coutinho was the son of Francisco Inocêncio de Sousa Coutinho, a governor and captain-general of Angola (1764–1772) and ambassador to Madrid (1774–1780).

After studying at the Nobles' College in Lisbon and at Coimbra University, Coutinho visited France and subsequently served at Turin as minister plenipotentiary from 1779 to 1796. In 1790 he published a discussion of the effects of the mining of precious metals on industry that implied the need for technological innovation in Brazil's Minas Gerais mining industry. Recalled to Lisbon in 1796 to succeed the deceased Martinho de MELO E CASTRO as state secretary for the navy and colonies, Coutinho developed the concept of a joint Luso-Brazilian imperial economic and political unit, declaring in 1798 that Portugal's vast overseas domains, especially those in the Americas, were the basis of the crown's power and that without them continental Portugal would be reduced to a province of Spain.

After a term as president of the treasury (1801–1803), Coutinho left Lisbon in October 1807 with the regent João and the court and government when the capital was transferred to Rio de Janeiro to escape French armies invading Portugal. In Brazil he served as secretary of state for foreign affairs and war (1808–1812) and advised the regent on the negotiations leading to the three Anglo-Portuguese treaties of February 1810, which opened Brazilian ports to international trade and committed the Portuguese never to establish a tribunal of the Inquisition in the New World.

– DAVID HIGGS

COUTO, JOSÉ BERNARDO

José Bernardo Couto (*b.* 1803; *d.* 1862), Mexican jurist, politician, and writer. Couto studied jurisprudence and humanities at San Ildefonso, Mexico City. In 1827 he became a lawyer, and in 1828 served in the Veracruz legislature. He was counselor of state in 1842 and minister of justice in 1845. Couto was one of the Mexican commissioners during the peace negotiations with the United States in 1847–1848. A distinguished jurist, he was known for his radical anticlerical views in his youth, particularly because of his *Disertación sobre la naturaleza y límites de la autoridad eclesiástica* (1825). Decades later he retracted his anticlerical position in *Discurso sobre la constitución de la iglesia* (1857).

Couto was a supporter of the arts, particularly painting and sculpture, and served as president of the governing committee of the Academy of San Carlos. In addition, he was a writer of note, translating Horace, publishing various novels and volumes of verse, and contributing to the *Diccionario universal de historia y geografía*.

– JAIME E. RODRÍGUEZ O.

COVARRUBIAS, MIGUEL

Miguel Covarrubias (*b.* 22 November 1904; *d.* 4 February 1957), Mexican artist. Miguel Covarrubias was extremely multifaceted, particularly in artistic and cultural endeavors. A native of Mexico City, he was a caricaturist, set designer, book illustrator, cartographer, painter, writer, art historian, ethnologist, and anthropologist. His work on the Olmec civilization made a major archaeological contribution, and his innovative museum installations forever changed the way exhibitions are designed. Toward the end of his life, as director of dance at the Instituto de Bellas Artes, he created a nationalist dance movement that initiated what has been termed the golden age of modern Mexican dance.

In everything that Covarrubias accomplished he remained an artist. He possessed a rare intuitive ability to capture and synthesize at a glance the essentials of character or situation, as demonstrated by his famous caricatures for *Vanity Fair* and his illustrations for his first books, *The Prince of Wales and Other Famous Americans* (1925) and *Negro Drawings* (1927).

Covarrubias married Rosemonde Cowan, a dancer and choreographer, in 1930. She became his collaborator as researcher and photographer for his next two books, *The Island of Bali* (1938) and *Mexico South* (1946). In the early 1940s, they returned to live permanently in Mexico, where they entertained many of the major intellectual and show-business figures of the time.

As he matured, Covarrubias immersed himself in studies of early historical happenings, peoples, folklore, and civilizations, principally on the American continent and in Polynesia. He wrote and illustrated *The Eagle, the Jaguar, and the Serpent* (1954) and *Indian Art of Mexico and Central America* (1957).

Terence Grieder has said, "In some ways, Covarrubias was a man out of his age. The typical thought of his day took mathematical or statistical form rather than the pictorial form which was his, and incidentally the Renaissance way of expressing thought. But he typified the best of twentieth-century humanism: its fascination with the visual arts, its openness to other cultures, and its desperate and doomed struggle to preserve the humane virtues of the traditional societies against technocratic commercialism."

Miguel Covarrubias was the encyclopedic artist of Mexico's rebirth. When he died in Mexico City, he had won a lasting place as a distinguished artist, scholar, teacher, and advocate of Mexican cultural studies. His final gesture to the Mexican people was the gift of his extraordinary pre-Columbian collection to the National Museum.

— ADRIANA WILLIAMS

CRABB, HENRY A.

Henry A. Crabb (*b.* 1827; *d.* 7 April 1857), filibuster. A schoolmate of William WALKER, a fellow filibuster, in Nashville, Tennessee, Crabb journeyed to California during the Gold Rush. After settling in Stockton in

---

Ambushed on 1 April 1857 by Mexican troops and besieged for six days, Crabb and fifty-nine of his men were captured and brutally executed.

1849, he led a brief expedition of adventurers to Nicaragua in 1855. Crabb returned to California the next year and married Filomena Ainsa, who came from a prominent Sonora, Mexico, family. Then, in 1857, he organized the American and Arizona Mining and Emigration Company in a bold attempt to colonize part of Sonora. Crabb outfitted a group of men and marched into Mexico. Ambushed on 1 April 1857 by Mexican troops and besieged for six days, Crabb and fifty-nine of his men were captured and brutally executed to serve

as a warning to Americans that Mexico was not open to further colonizing ventures.

— IRIS H. W. ENGSTRAND

CREEL, ENRIQUE CLAY

Enrique Clay Creel (*b.* 30 August 1854; *d.* 17 August 1931), Mexican banker, governor of Chihuahua (1904–1911). Born in Chihuahua, Creel was the son of the U.S. consul there. He married the daughter of General Luis TERRAZAS and subsequently headed the financial and industrial enterprises of the Terrazas family. He was the leading Mexican banker of the prerevolutionary era and was a founder and manager of the Banco Minero de Chihuahua and several other banks. He also had widespread interests in food processing, mining, textiles, and manufacturing. He served as the most prominent Mexican officer or board member of several foreign corporations. Creel also entered politics, serving in Chihuahua's state legislature in 1882–1885 and 1897–1900. He was an alternate federal deputy from Chihuahua in 1892–1894 and a full deputy from Durango in 1900–1902 and from Chihuahua in 1902–1906.

In 1904 the governor of Chihuahua resigned in Creel's favor. Creel was elected on his own in 1907 and served to 1911. Creel was a member of the Científicos, a positivist group led by José Y. LIMANTOUR, the secretary of the treasury (1892–1911) under dictator Porfirio Díaz. As governor he tried to implement positivist principles by streamlining and modernizing state government, which caused protests from fiercely independent municipalities. While serving as governor, he was also Mexican ambassador to the United States (1907–1908) and secretary for foreign relations (1910–1911).

During the Mexican Revolution, when he fled for his life, Creel suffered heavy financial losses. He returned to Mexico from exile in the early 1920s and served as a financial adviser to President Álvaro OBREGÓN SALIDO.

— MARK WASSERMAN

CRESPO, JOAQUÍN

Joaquín Crespo (*b.* 1845; *d.* 1898), Venezuelan president (1884–1886, 1892–1898). Crespo, a tough young *llanero,* joined the Liberal side in the FEDERAL WAR (1859–1863) and, as a loyal supporter of Antonio GUZMÁN BLANCO, became his minister of war (1877–1878). In 1879, as a reward for his loyalty to the dictator, Crespo was given the title "Hero of Duty Done." From 1884 to 1886 Crespo served as figurehead president for Guzmán Blanco, and in 1888 he ran unsuccessfully for president. From 1892 to 1894 he served as interim president after seizing power in a caudillo rebellion. His constitutional presidency (1894–1898) corresponded with an economic slump and with clashes with Great Britain over the border with British Guiana. Crespo is credited with initiatives to professionalize the national army. After his presidential term was completed, he led the forces of the new regime of General Ignacio Andrade against a rebellion headed by José Manuel ("El Mocho") Hernández. In one of its first engagements Crespo was killed in battle.

– WINFIELD J. BURGGRAAFF

CREYDT, OSCAR

Oscar Creydt (*b.* 1907; *d.* ?) Paraguayan Communist leader. Born in San Miguel, in southern Paraguay, Creydt was the scion of a wealthy family, and although trained as a lawyer, he dedicated his life and fortune instead to organizing the Paraguayan Communist Party.

During the early 1920s, Creydt was a leading figure in the University Students Federation, and in the Consejo Mixto de Obreros y Estudiantes. This latter group (not more than fifty individuals) formed the basis for the Paraguayan Communist Party (PCP), founded in 1928 and brought into the Comintern four years later.

At this time, the PCP could count on little meaningful support in Paraguay, even within the labor unions. After the Chaco War (1932–1935), the Communists found many of their social programs "hijacked" by the nationalist Febrerista Party, and, at the same time, the PCP itself was forced underground. Creydt, however, proved to be a talented clandestine organizer. Through discipline and hard work, he drove out the Trotskyists within the party and managed to weather the persecutions of the Morínigo dictatorship (1940–1948).

In 1947, Creydt got his only opportunity for a measure of national power. A civil war had erupted, and the Communists forged an alliance with disaffected soldiers, Febreristas, and Liberals, which came critically close to defeating the rival Colorados. The strength of the PCP at this juncture surprised many observers, but Creydt, who felt that the political work was finally paying off, was not surprised. Nonetheless, the victory of the Colorados and the subsequent terror sent him and most party members into exile.

Creydt retained his hold on the secretary-general's post for many years. In the 1960s, younger Paraguayan Communists accused him of mimicking Stalin in fostering a cult of personality. The PCP split over this issue in 1968, with a substantial minority shifting to Creydt's old associate, Obdulio Barthe, who now adopted a pro-Beijing line. In an attempt to heal the breach, Creydt

negotiated with the Maoists, but in the end this gesture resulted only in a split of his own pro-Moscow wing. Creydt himself was supplanted as party chief by the much younger Miguel Angel Soler, whose arrest (and probable murder) by General Alfredo STROESSNER's police in 1975 brought another round of factionalization from which the Communists did not recover.

– THOMAS L. WHIGHAM

CRISTIANI, ALFREDO

Alfredo Cristiani (*b.* 22 November 1947), elected president of El Salvador in 1989. His constitutional term of office ended in 1994. The scion of a family of coffee planters and a graduate of Georgetown University, Cristiani was elected president during El Salvador's civil war (1979–1992). Before his nomination as candidate for the presidency, he was a businessman with little political experience. Although his party, the National Republican Alliance (ARENA), was founded by Roberto D'ABUISSON, a cashiered army officer with alleged links to death squads, and represented the most conservative elements in Salvadoran society, Cristiani conveyed a moderate image. With his election ARENA won the presidency for the first time.

In November 1989 Cristiani had to face the first major crisis of his presidency, a guerrilla offensive that reached San Salvador. During the struggle for the capital, six well-known Jesuit priests were brutally murdered. The prosecution of the crime was seen as a test of the commitment of his administration to control the excess of the army. Two army officers were eventually convicted of the crime, but disagreements remained as to whether the investigation had uncovered the full extent of army involvement. The main priority of the Cristiani administration was to bring the civil war to a negotiated end. The negotiations between the government and the guerrillas, sponsored by the United Nations, culminated with a cease-fire agreement signed 16 January 1992 by Cristiani and the leaders of the guerrilla forces in Mexico City. His administration advocated free-market economic policies. Despite criticisms of the way in which his administration implemented the peace accords, when Cristiani's term ended in 1994, opinion polls ranked him as the most popular politician in El Salvador, thanks in part to the pacification of the country and a healthy rate of economic growth.

– HÉCTOR LINDO-FUENTES

CROIX, MARQUÉS DE

Marqués de Croix (*b.* 1699; *d.* 1786), viceroy of New Spain (1766–1771). Born in Lille, France, Carlos Francisco de Croix rose to the rank of general within the Spanish army. He was serving as captain-general of Galicia when he was designated viceroy of New Spain in 1766. His term overlapped the Visita of José de GÁLVEZ (1765–1771), who had been sent by Charles III to inspect and reform the colony. Croix presided over the efficient expulsion of the Jesuits in 1767. He supported Gálvez's suppression of the resulting riots in Guanajuato and San Luis Potosí the following year. A staunch regalist in ecclesiastical matters, the viceroy successfully defied the Mexican Inquisition when he was summoned before it. Croix undertook the colonization of Alta California in 1769 to defend the northern boundary of the empire. By the end of his term, four settlements had been founded. Croix urged the creation of the Interior Provinces jurisdiction in the north, which was accomplished five years after his departure. He sought improvement of the militias being formed in Mexico and encouraged the addition of regular Spanish army units to bolster the defense of the colony. He departed Mexico in 1771 to become captain-general of Valencia, where he died.

– JOHN E. KICZA

CROIX, TEODORO DE

Teodoro de Croix (*b.* 30 June 1730; *d.* 8 April 1791), viceroy of Peru (1784–1790). Born in Lille, Flanders, into a military family, Croix went to America with his uncle, Carlos Francisco, who served as viceroy of New Spain (1765–1771) and, following his recall to Spain, as captain-general of Valencia. Not surprisingly, this powerful patronage brought Teodoro rapid promotion in the Mexican military hierarchy. He succeeded JÁUREGUI as viceroy of Lima as Peru began its slow economic and political recovery from the TÚPAC AMARU I rebellion, the administrative confusion associated with the *visita general* (general inspection), and the indebtedness of the exchequer in the early 1780s.

Although overanxious to protect the dignity of his office against the authority of the first generation of intendants (installed in 1784), Croix succeeded in overseeing a period of stable government and economic and fiscal growth. He succeeded in 1787 in persuading the crown to restore the superintendency of exchequer affairs to the viceroy, thereby undermining a key feature of the intendant system.

– JOHN R. FISHER

CRUZ, ARTURO

Arturo Cruz (*b.* 18 December 1923), banker, Nicaraguan ambassador to the United States (1981), former Contra leader. Born in Jinotepe, Cruz attended Georgetown University and earned degrees in economics from the School of Foreign Service (B.S., 1947; M.S., 1971). Cruz joined the Conservative Party at an early age and helped form the National Union of Popular Action in 1948. In 1954, he participated in an unsuccessful effort by young Conservatives to overthrow Anastasio SOMOZA GARCÍA, for which he was jailed for eleven months.

In 1977, the Sandinistas convinced Cruz to join a prestigious group of Nicaraguans, known as "The Twelve," which supported the revolutionary movement.

Cruz joined the Inter-American Development Bank as a finance officer in 1959. He was one of the architects of the Central American Common Market in the early 1960s. In 1977, the Sandinistas convinced him to join a prestigious group of Nicaraguans, known as "The Twelve," which supported the revolutionary movement. Cruz was president of the Central Bank of Nicaragua from July 1979 to May 1980, when he became a member of the Governing Junta of National Reconstruction. In March 1981, the Sandinista government named him ambassador to the United States; he resigned at the end of that year. Cruz started to run for president against Daniel Ortega in 1984, but never registered as a candidate. In 1985, he helped found the Nicaraguan Opposition Union, the political arm of the counterrevolutionary force. He resigned his post in February 1987 and from 1990 to 1994 served as the alternate executive director of the Inter-American Development Bank's section for Central America.

– MARK EVERINGHAM

CRUZ, OSWALDO GONÇALVES

Oswaldo Gonçalves Cruz (*b.* 5 August 1872; *d.* 11 February 1917), Brazilian pioneer in medicine and public health. Cruz's careers in medicine and public health were closely intertwined. As director of public health for the federal government between 1903 and 1909, he led the campaign to eliminate yellow fever, smallpox, and the plague from the federal capital of Rio de Janeiro. As director of the Oswaldo Cruz Institute, he created the first important center in the country for microbiological research and tropical medicine.

The son of a doctor, Cruz obtained his medical degree at the Rio Medical School in 1892 and pursued further training in bacteriology in Paris between 1896 and 1899. On his return to Brazil in 1899 he joined the staff of the Serum Therapy Institute at Manguinhos, outside Rio, rising quickly to the position of director. In 1902, Cruz came to the attention of the newly elected president of Brazil, Francisco Rodrigues ALVES, who asked him to lead an ambitious campaign against yellow fever, smallpox, and the plague, all of which were epidemic in the federal capital.

The campaign was based on the newest techniques of the sanitation sciences, notably the destruction of mosquitoes and their breeding sites, fumigation of houses, and isolation of sick individuals. Despite considerable opposition from doctors, sections of the military, and the poor, who were the main targets of the campaign and who objected to its intrusive nature, Cruz and his teams of "mosquito killers" were successful in controlling the plague and yellow fever. However, resistance to compulsory smallpox vaccination meant that many people were not vaccinated; as a result, the city experienced a severe epidemic in 1908, with more than 9,000 deaths.

In 1909 Cruz resigned his position in public health in order to devote his attention to the Serum Therapy Institute, which was renamed the Oswaldo Cruz Institute in his honor. There he established the first modern school of experimental medicine in Brazil. In early 1916 Cruz retired to Petrópolis, where he died at the age of forty-three.

– NANCY LEYS STEPAN

CRUZ, SERAPIO

Serapio Cruz (d. 23 January 1870), Guatemalan military officer and revolutionary leader. Known by the nickname of "Tata Lapo," Cruz served under the command of José Rafael CARRERA in the Guatemalan revolt of 1837. Cruz broke with Carrera in 1848. Though a leader in the revolution of 1848, he refused to collaborate with the new liberal government and continued to resist until he reached an agreement with President Mariano PAREDES on 2 February 1849. Upon Carrera's return to power in August 1849, Cruz reestablished his relationship with Carrera. He was an important military leader at the Battle of Arada in 1851 and in the campaign against El Salvador in 1863. Carrera suspected Cruz of a plot against him in 1863 but retained Cruz's loyalty by promising to leave him the presidency. Infuriated by Carrera's deathbed designation of Vicente CERNA as his successor, Cruz launched a revolt in 1867 against Cerna's government. In a daring attack at Palencia, near the capital, early in 1870, he died, thus

becoming one of the principal martyrs of the Liberal Reforma of 1871.

– RALPH LEE WOODWARD, JR.

CRUZ, VICENTE

Vicente Cruz (d. 20 March 1849), one of the leading officers in José Rafael CARRERA's 1837 revolt in Guatemala. Once in control of Guatemala, Carrera appointed Cruz CORREGIDOR of the departments of Mita and of Guatemala. Cruz was Carrera's vice president in 1844–1848, and he exercised the office of president when Carrera stepped down briefly from 11 September to 31 October 1845 and again from 25 January to 4 February 1848. When Carrera resigned in August 1848, Cruz expected to succeed him. But because the legislature opposed Cruz, he resigned on 28 November 1848 and took up arms against the government. He accepted, however, the Convenio de Zacapa (2 February 1849) arranged by President Mariano PAREDES and returned to the government's army. Little more than a month later, he died fighting rebels led by Agustín Pérez.

– RALPH LEE WOODWARD, JR.

CRUZ DIEZ, CARLOS

Carlos Cruz Diez (b. 17 August 1923), Venezuelan artist. Born in Caracas, Cruz Diez studied at the Cristóbal Rojas School of Fine and Applied Arts. He began his career as a graphic designer, working as an art director at several advertising agencies. While his paintings display a taste for social realism with portrayals of daily life and common people, his graphic work reflects a fascination with color. During a visit to Barcelona and Paris in 1955, he began experimenting with the kinetic possibilities of color in his series *Physichromies*. He returned to Caracas in 1957 and opened a studio of art and industrial design. Later he designed publications for the Venezuelan Ministry of Education and taught art history and design at the School of Fine Arts and Central University in Caracas.

Shortly after his solo show at the Museum of Fine Art in Caracas, he moved to Paris with his family (1960). Three years later he joined the Nouvelle Tendence group in Paris and his work began to appear in international group exhibitions: The Responsive Eye (New York, 1965) and Soundings Two (London, 1966). He won the grand prize at the Córdoba Bienal (Argentina, 1966), and the international prize of painting at the São Paulo Bienal (1967). His large chromatic works are in the Caracas international airport and the Guri Dam powerhouse.

– BÉLGICA RODRÍGUEZ

CRUZ E SOUSA, JOÃO DA

João da Cruz e Sousa (*b.* 24 November 1861; *d.* 19 March 1898), Brazilian poet. Born in Santa Catarina to freed slaves, Cruz e Sousa became one of the most notable men of letters of his time. His protector, the former master of his parents, sent him through high school (1874) and tutorials. After brief experiences in teaching and journalism, Cruz e Sousa joined a touring dramatic troupe in 1881. His travels around Brazil revealed to him the abject conditions of his fellow blacks. From 1882 to 1889, he collaborated on a pro-republican, abolitionist periodical that he published. In 1884 he was appointed to a government post in a provincial city but was barred from assuming his duties because of his race. At that time he issued his first books of verse, which reflect the dominant realist rhetoric of the period. In 1890, he moved to Rio to work in journalism and later in the archives of the railroad company. He soon launched symbolism in Brazilian letters, becoming the leader of the new aesthetic movement.

Cruz e Sousa suffered several tragedies: two of his four children succumbed to tuberculosis while the two that remained died of other causes, his wife went mad, and he himself became consumptive. The poet retired to a country home in Minas Gerais but soon passed away. While personal misfortune is reflected in his verse, Cruz e Sousa's awareness of the condition of blacks is historically more significant. His leadership role in symbolism is outstanding and important in terms of black participation in elite cultural production.

– CHARLES A. PERRONE

CRUZ UCLES, RAMÓN ERNESTO

Ramón Ernesto Cruz Ucles (*b.* 3 January 1903; *d.* 1985), lawyer, president of Honduras (1971–1972). After a thirty-year career in law, much of it as a district judge and legal expert in Honduras's border disputes with Nicaragua, Cruz was nominated by the National Party as a compromise candidate in 1962. The elections were scuttled in 1963 by the coup of Oswaldo LÓPEZ ARELLANO. Cruz was again nominated for president of Honduras by the National Party when General López stepped aside to permit elections in 1971. Cruz won a bare plurality (49.3 percent) and took office on 7 June 1971. During his brief eighteen months in office, he concentrated on foreign affairs, traveling widely and winning the return of the Islas de Cisne (Swan Islands)

from the United States. This diplomatic master stroke, however, could not offset his rapid and total isolation from his own party. In the face of virtual economic collapse and the escalation of agrarian strife, cresting with the massacre of Olancho peasants at La Talanquera by angry cattle ranchers, President Cruz lost control. General López quietly removed him from office on 4 December 1972.

– KENNETH V. FINNEY

CUADRA, PABLO ANTONIO

Pablo Antonio Cuadra (*b.* 4 November 1912), Nicaraguan poet, essayist, journalist, playwright, professor, and director of the Nicaraguan Academy of the Language. Cuadra studied with the Jesuits and attended law school at the Universidad Nacional de Oriente y Mediodía. At age nineteen he cofounded the Vanguardia group and began his lifelong involvement in journalism. Through the years he edited and coedited several literary and political newspapers and journals: *Vanguardia* (1931–1933), *Trinchera* (1936–1939), *Cuaderno del Taller San Lucas* (1942–1944), *El Pez y La Serpiente* (1961–1979), *La Prensa Literaria* (1954–1987), and *La Prensa,* the influential newspaper he edited after Somoza forces assassinated its editor, Pedro Joaquín CHAMORRO, in 1978. Cuadra has been deeply involved in theater since 1936, when he founded the Lope Theater and wrote *Por los caminos van los campesinos.*

Cuadra's poetry and political ideology grew together. He participated in the original Sandinista struggle and published his first poems while still in school. At twenty-two he published *Poemas nicaragüenses* (1934), followed by *Cuaderno del Sur* (1934–1935), *Hacia la cruz del sur. Manual del navegante hispano* (1936), and *Canto temporal* (1943). In the 1940s, while teaching and traveling, Cuadra wrote some important essays: *Breviario imperial* (1940), *Promisión de México* (1945), and *Entre la cruz y la espada* (1946).

Upon his return to Nicaragua in 1950, he resumed his writing and his political commitment. He published *La tierra prometida* (1952) and *Libro de horas* (1954). Upon Somoza's assassination, Cuadra was persecuted and imprisoned, an experience he recorded in *América o el purgatorio* (1955). He was awarded the Central American Rubén Darío Prize in Poetry (1959) for *El jaguar y la luna* and Spain's Rubén Darío Prize for Hispanic Poetry (1964) for *Poesía: Selección (1929–1962).* Some of his most important poetic contributions were written in the 1970s and 1980s. The lyrical rendering of the lives of ordinary people in *Cantos de Cifar y del Mar Dulce* (1971), *Tierra que habla* (1974), *Esos rostros que asoman en la multitud* (1976), *Siete árboles contra el atardecer* (1980), and *La ronda del año: Poemas para un calendario* (1988) reveal his profound humanism. His *Poesía selecta* (1991) contains an excellent introduction and biobibliography by the editor, J. E. Arellano.

The triumph of the Sandinista revolution did not end Cuadra's political marginalization. His commitment to human rights provoked the Sandinistas to close *La Prensa* in 1986. In the late 1980s and early 1990s, Cuadra firmly established his international status. He traveled and lectured abroad, was awarded Fulbright (1987) and Guggenheim (1989) fellowships, published his complete works, and participated in congresses on Latin American literature as well as on his own.

– MARÍA A. SALGADO

CUAUHTEMOC

Cuauhtemoc (*b.* ca. 1494; *d.* 1525), last ruler of Tenochtitlán-Tlatelolco and leader of the final defense against the Spanish invaders. Nephew of Emperor Moctezuma II, Cuauhtemoc was elected to the post of *tlatoani* after Cuitlahuac, Moctezuma's immediate successor, died of smallpox. Around twenty-five years old when he took power, Cuauhtemoc married a daughter of Moctezuma who was a widow of Cuitlahuac. Later baptized as Isabel Moctezuma, she wed three Spaniards in succession.

Though the Mexica under Cuauhtemoc put up a spirited resistance to Spanish attacks, lack of water and food, and mounting deaths from disease and combat took their toll. Abandoned by most of his allies, Cuauhtemoc finally embarked on 13 August 1521 with a large canoe-borne force (or, according to some indigenous accounts, in one canoe with a small number of companions), either to flee or to mount one last offensive. The *tlatoani*'s canoe was captured by the captain of one of the Spanish brigantines used in the siege, and though Cuauhtemoc is reported to have pleaded for death, he was instead brought as a prisoner before a jubilant Hernán CORTÉS.

Cuauhtemoc was pressed to reveal the location of

the "lost" Mexica treasure by having his feet burned

with hot oil.

Early in his captivity, Cuauhtemoc was pressed to reveal the location of the "lost" Mexica treasure by having his feet burned with hot oil. This torture led to nothing, and Cuauhtemoc remained a prisoner until October 1524, when Cortés took him and a number of other indigenous rulers on an expedition to Honduras to subdue Cristóbal de OLID, who had declared against the conqueror. Cortés and others seem to have feared that the Indian leaders might rebel if left behind, but the Spaniards soon came to suspect that Cuauhtemoc was somehow plotting an uprising. Accordingly, during Lent of 1525 Cuauhtemoc and two other rulers were convicted of treason and hanged from a *cieba* tree beside the trail to Honduras. As in the later Peruvian case of the captured Inca ATAHUALPA, who was executed on a similar charge, the conquerors became convinced that Cuauhtemoc had outlived his usefulness.

Though defeated in life, Cuauhtemoc, and not Cortés, ultimately triumphed as an important symbol of Mexican nationalism. Evidence of his heroic stature includes such work as the later-nineteenth-century libretto of the heroic opera *Guatimotzín* (ca. 1872), by Mexican composer Aniceto ORTEGA DEL VILLAR. By the twentieth century Cuauhtemoc's valor was celebrated in everything from post-Revolutionary murals to a statue gracing a *glorieta* (traffic circle) on Mexico City's Paseo de la Reforma, and even in the name of Cuauhtémoc CÁRDENAS, opposition presidential candidate in the election of 1988.

– ROBERT HASKETT

CUERVO, RUFINO JOSÉ

Rufino José Cuervo (*b.* 19 September 1844; *d.* 17 July 1911), Colombian philologist. Rufino José Cuervo, born in Bogotá, was largely self-taught in his various specialties, which spanned ancient and modern languages and literature, including Native American tongues and American Spanish dialects. Among his earlier works are *Apuntaciones críticas sobre el lenguage bogotano* (1867–1872) and *Gramática de la lengua latina* (1876), a Latin grammar he wrote with Miguel Antonio CARO. Cuervo traveled extensively in Europe, and after 1882 settled permanently in Paris, where he taught at the Sorbonne and contributed to European specialized journals. He also produced, in collaboration with his brother Ángel, a historically important life of their father, *Vida de Rufino Cuervo y noticias de su época* (1946). Cuervo also undertook a massive *Diccionario de construcción y régimen de la lengua castellana* (1886–1893), which he completed only to the letter D.

– DAVID BUSHNELL

CUESTAS, JUAN LINDOLFO

Juan Lindolfo Cuestas (*b.* 6 January 1837; *d.* 21 June 1905), president of Uruguay (1899–1903). A veteran politician, Cuestas was president of the Senate between

1895 and 1898 and provisional president between 1898 and 1899. In his early career he subscribed to the collectivist Colorado group led by HERRERA Y OBES, which had overseen the transition from militarism to civilian government. As president of the Senate exercising executive power after the death of the constitutional president, he modified his politics in order to broaden his base of support within both the Colorado and the Blanco (National) parties. The preceding president, Juan Idiarte Borda, assassinated in 1897, had left a legacy of revolution in the Blanco Party, led by Aparicio SARAVIA. Cuestas made a pact with Saravia, accepting what amounted to a formula for cogovernment. In 1898, unable to assure his own election by the Parliament, he dissolved the assembly by decree and assumed dictatorial powers. During his provisional presidency, military and presumably collectivist factions attempted a coup d'état and an invasion, which ultimately failed. Cuestas's constitutional presidency deserves credit for bringing the peace and order so longed for. José BATLLE Y ORDÓÑEZ succeeded him as president, beginning a new era in Uruguayan politics and suppressing the cogovernment of Cuestas and Saravia.

– FERNANDO FILGUEIRA

CUEVA, FRANCISCO DE LA

Francisco de la Cueva (*b.* ca. 1501; *d.* 1576), Spanish governor of Guatemala. Cueva accompanied the expedition of Pedro de ALVARADO Y MESÍA to Guatemala (ca. 1524). Later, he married Alvarado's daughter Leonor, child of Alvarado's union with the Tlaxcalan princess Luisa Xicoténcatl.

Alvarado named Cueva acting governor and captain-general of Guatemala on two occasions. He was acting governor when news of Alvarado's death reached Guatemala in 1541. He was replaced by his cousin Beatriz de la CUEVA DE ALVARADO, who was Alvarado's second wife. After her death (10 September 1541), Cueva and Bishop Francisco MARROQUÍN were co-governors until a replacement, Alonso de Maldonado, was sent from Mexico, 17 May 1542.

– MURDO J. MACLEOD

CUEVA DE ALVARADO, BEATRIZ DE LA

Beatriz de la Cueva de Alvarado (*d.* 10 September 1541), second wife of Pedro de ALVARADO Y MESÍA and the only female governor during the Spanish-American colonial period. Niece of the duke of Albuquerque, she married Pedro de Alvarado, her deceased sister's husband, in Spain in 1538, after receiving a papal dispen-

sation, and accompanied him to Guatemala when he returned there as governor the following year.

When news of Alvarado's death arrived in Guatemala in June 1541, she demanded the governorship. Her cousin, the acting governor, Francisco de la CUEVA, gave it to her. The conquistador elite, already shocked by what it considered to be her excessive and sacrilegious mourning for her husband, resented her assumption of the governorship. She was killed on 10 September 1541 by the flood and mudslide that destroyed the city following rainstorms and earthquakes. Years later she was buried beside Alvarado in the cathedral of Antigua, Guatemala.

– MURDO J. MACLEOD

CUEVA ENRÍQUEZ Y SAAVEDRA, BALTÁSAR DE LA

Baltásar de la Cueva Enríquez y Saavedra (count of Castellar), viceroy of Peru (1674–1678). An experienced administrator, Castellar attempted to reform colonial administration and increase crown revenues by streamlining accounting procedures and investigating tax collectors and regional treasuries throughout the viceroyalty. Through his efforts, hundreds of thousands of pesos in back taxes and other revenues owed the crown were collected, many from the *consulado* (merchant guild). His anticorruption campaign resulted in the public execution of two treasury officials and sanctions against many others, one of whom attempted to assassinate Castellar in 1675. Disgruntled treasury officials and members of the powerful *consulado* of Lima complained so strenuously to the crown that Castellar was removed from office in 1678.

– ANN M. WIGHTMAN

CUEVAS, JOSÉ LUIS

José Luis Cuevas (*b.* 26 February 1933), Mexican artist. Cuevas's precocious talent became apparent in 1953, a crucial time in Mexican art when the hegemony of the Mexican School was in question. His pen and ink drawings of mad people, cadavers, freaks, and prostitutes brought him acclaim in 1954 at the Pan American Union under the tutelage of its director, José Gómez Sicre. Cuevas promoted himself with a publicity campaign that culminated in 1956 with his article "La cortina de nopal" (The Cactus Curtain) in the newspaper *Novedades,* in which he fulminated against the Mexican School. He initiated an expressive figurative and intimist drawing style based on monsters and the grotesque. His later work drew extensively from literary sources (Kafka, Dostoevsky, Quevedo) and from such artists as

Van Eyck, Rembrandt, Goya, Dürer, Picasso, and OROZCO. He did several thematic series, which include *The Worlds of Kafka and Cuevas* (1957), *Funerals of a Dictator* (1958), *The Spain of Franco* (1960), and *The Conquest of Mexico* (1961), as well as innumerable self-portraits. Cuevas has had a strong influence on neofigurative Latin American artists.

— SHIFRA M. GOLDMAN

CUEVAS, MARIANO

Mariano Cuevas (*b.* 1879; *d.* 1949), Mexican historian. Born in Mexico City, Cuevas studied there until joining the Society of Jesus in Loyola, Spain, in 1893. From 1902 to 1906, Cuevas taught literature and history in Saltillo and Puebla, Mexico. He went on to study theology in St. Louis, Missouri (1906–1910). Cuevas was ordained a priest but continued to study archaeology, paleography, diplomacy, and historical methods. He spent most of the rest of his life researching and writing historical works. He published collections of documents as well as the results of his own investigations. His principal works include *Documentos inéditos del siglo XVI* (1914), *Cartas y otros documentos de Hernán Cortés* (1915), *Historia de la iglesia en México,* 5 vols., (1921–1928), and *La historia de la nación mexicana* (1940).

— D. F. STEVENS

CUGAT, XAVIER

Xavier Cugat (*b.* 1 January 1900; *d.* 27 October 1990), Spanish musician and bandleader. Born near Barcelona, Spain, Cugat immigrated to Cuba with his family in 1904. At age six, he appeared as a guest violinist with the Havana Symphony and became a full-time member of that orchestra in 1912. Later that same year, he moved to the United States. Unable to find work as a classical musician, he drew caricatures of movie stars for the *Los Angeles Times* until Rudolph Valentino asked him to organize a band to accompany him in a film requiring tango music. He and his band, the Gigolos, appeared in several films of the 1940s and 1950s, making his name a household word. He introduced the rumba to American audiences in his movies and through his appearances at clubs like the Coconut Grove, the Hotel Chase, and Al Capone's Chez Paris in Chicago, and a ten-year run at the Waldorf Astoria. His full-time career as a big band leader spanned from the 1940s to the 1960s. In 1986, he formed his last band and began touring Spain. He was married and divorced five times and had no children.

— JACQUELYN BRIGGS KENT

CUITLAHUAC

Cuitlahuac (*b.* before 1467; *d.* 1520), Aztec ruler, son of Axayacatl and older brother of MOTECUHZOMA II. Cuitlahuac governed the disintegrating Aztec Empire for a brief period during the Spanish invasion. Ruler of the town of Iztapalapa and one of his brother's chief advisers, Cuitlahuac was already a seasoned warrior and statesman when the Spaniards entered Mexico. According to native histories, he advised Motecuhzoma against allowing Hernán CORTÉS and his army to enter Tenochtitlán, the Aztec capital. When Cortés occupied the city, he imprisoned Cuitlahuac along with Motecuhzoma. After the Aztecs turned against the invaders and laid siege to their headquarters, Cuitlahuac gained release on the pretense that he would reopen the market to allow food to reach the invaders.

Cuitlahuac's death is frequently attributed to smallpox, the first of many Old World infectious diseases to strike Mexico's native population.

Following Motecuhzoma's death and the flight of the Spaniards and their allies from the city on the night of 30 June/1 July 1520, Cuitlahuac was elected to succeed his brother (according to some accounts he assumed this role even before Motecuhzoma's demise). His leadership of the resistance to the ensuing Spanish-led siege was short-lived. Within a few months of his accession, he died. His death is frequently attributed to smallpox, the first of many Old World infectious diseases to strike Mexico's native population, but the early sources do not state this explicitly. He was succeeded by his young nephew CUAUHTEMOC.

— LOUISE M. BURKHART

CUMPLIDO, IGNACIO

Ignacio Cumplido (*b.* 20 May 1811; *d.* 30 November 1887), Mexican publisher. Born in Guadalajara, Cumplido, the son of a doctor and medical school professor, grew up in Mexico City. While an employee at the National Museum, he began publishing newspapers. In 1829 he became the manager of the shop that printed *El Correo de la Federación,* soon followed by *El Fénix de la Libertad.* In 1838 he went to the United States to buy the equipment necessary for a first-class printing establishment, but he lost everything when the French blockaded the port of Veracruz. Nevertheless, he continued to publish the most celebrated authors of the day in *El Museo Mexicano, La Ilustración Mexicana,* and other periodicals. Although associated with liberal politics, Cumplido was imprisoned in 1840 for printing José María GUTIÉRREZ ESTRADA's pamphlet advocating monarchy. Soon after he was named superintendent of prisons.

Cumplido is best known for founding *El Siglo XIX* on 8 October 1841; it became the foremost daily newspaper of nineteenth-century Mexico City and was published almost continuously through 1896. The list of its editors forms a who's who of Mexican intellectual life of the time and includes Guillermo PRIETO, Manuel PAYNO, Ignacio RAMÍREZ, Francisco ZARCO, Francisco Sosa, and Francisco BULNES. In 1842 he was elected to Congress first as deputy and then as senator, always giving his salary to charity. He founded a lithography school for orphans in his home. In 1847, during the war with the United States, Cumplido volunteered as head of a battalion of national guard and was subsequently promoted to captain.

In 1848 Cumplido went to Europe and purchased steam-powered presses. Following the French Intervention, Cumplido became a member of the 1873 Ayuntamiento of Mexico City in charge of boulevards. It was his idea to plant trees on both sides of the Paseo de la Reforma in emulation of the Champs-Élysées.

– BARBARA A. TENENBAUM

CÚNEO PERINETTI, JOSÉ

José Cúneo Perinetti (*b.* 11 September 1887; *d.* 19 July 1977), Uruguayan artist. Cúneo Perinetti studied at the Circle of Fine Arts in his native Montevideo; in Turin, Italy, with Leonardo Bistolfi and Anton Mucchi (1907–1909); and in Paris at the Académie Vity with the Spanish painter Hermenegildo Anglada Camarasa (1911). Early in his career, he painted naturalist gardens under the belated influence of the Italian Macchiaioli and the contemporary Spanish painter Santiago Rusiñol. Back in Uruguay, he painted landscapes in Treinta Tres Orientales. In 1917 he returned to Paris to study with Kees van Dongen. Upon his return to Uruguay, he began painting geometrical landscapes, including Uruguayan rural huts (*ranchos*) and Spanish colonial sites in the town of Maldonado, and portraits involving pure, extended areas of color. In the 1930s he started the series of his so-called moon landscapes, for which he is best known (*The Moon Over the Ranch,* 1934).

Cúneo Perinetti's work from this period is characterized by a low palette, thick pigment, and compositions based on diagonals and dynamic lines. Swirling strokes give the impression of dragging everything—trees, dwellings, earth—into a vortex. These turbulent paint-

ings reveal the influence of Vincent van Gogh and Chaim Soutine. Oversized moons give his expressionistic landscapes a cosmic quality. He won gold medals at the National Salon in Uruguay in 1941, 1942, and 1949. In the late 1940s he turned once more to naturalist landscapes. Despite his long career he had little influence on subsequent Uruguayan artists.

– MARTA GARSD

CUNHA, EUCLIDES DA

Euclides da Cunha (*b.* 20 January 1866; *d.* 15 August 1909), Brazilian writer. Cunha began his career in 1888 as a journalist for the prestigious *A Província de São Paulo* after interrupting his studies at the Military Academy of Rio de Janeiro and resuming his military education at the Escola Superior de Guerra (Superior School of War) from which he would graduate in 1892 with an engineering degree. His fame as a writer began with the publication of his first articles, both titled "A nossa Vendéia" (Our Vendée), suggesting a comparison between the French Revolution of 1793–1796 and its Brazilian counterpart, the messianic movement of 1874–1897 headed by Antônio CONSELHEIRO (Anthony the Counselor) in the northeastern backlands, (*canudos*). Positive responses from readers and his own fascination with the subject prompted his newspaper to assign Cunha to cover the battles between the republican army and Antônio Conselheiro's followers. By the time he arrived at the war zone, the latter had crushed three military expeditions sent by local and federal governments. Thousands of republican soldiers had died and, baffled by the turn of events, government officials began to seek a plausible explanation for the series of defeats that had led the young and already fragile Brazilian republic into chaos and confusion.

During some thirty days spent in the battlefield,

Cunha experienced scenes so tragic and horrifying

that he was compelled to reevaluate his own view

of Brazil's civil war.

During some thirty days spent in the battlefield, Cunha experienced scenes so tragic and horrifying that he was compelled to reevaluate his own view of the conflict. For Cunha, a confessed republican who had also been an ardent militant, it did not take long to realize that Canudos was not simply a clash involving primitive peasants and "civilized" men, but a brutal civil war.

Once home from the battlefield, Cunha began to write his most acclaimed book, *Os sertões* (*Rebellion in the Backlands*), a powerful account of the war at Canudos. In it he strives to show that a misunderstanding and a breakdown in communications were responsible for the war between the two groups. The republicans thought of Antônio Conselheiro's movement as a means to restore the monarchy with the help of the British crown. The poverty-stricken members of his flock believed, on the other hand, that they were fighting the forces of evil, Freemasonry, and heresy.

It may well be that no other Brazilian journalist before or since Cunha has acquired such a deep understanding of Brazil's tremendous social problems. His ambition in writing *Rebellion* was not only to analyze the war but also to provide an account of the formation of the national identity of Brazil. Thus, the book delves into geology, geography, sociology, anthropology, military and social history, literature, and philosophy. Cunha's language is precise, metaphorical, and, above all, oxymoronic. He takes liberties with the use of technical terminology to render clear, precise descriptions of the complex geography of Canudos.

Despite the reliable voice of the narrator at the beginning of *Rebellion*, when Cunha presents himself as an unbiased historian, the book is not a completely objective historical account of the war. A divergence between its literary achievements and its scientific accuracy is noticeable. In his quest for truth Cunha did some intriguing speculating and arguing, especially since he knew little of geology and botany and had never seen Canudos before the last thirty-five days of the war. While many are inclined to ascribe the difficulties in Cunha's book to his peculiar language, undoubtedly some of his theories, for example, on what he called "physical determinism" (the influence of the backlands upon the individual) and on genetic anthropology (degeneration of the white race through miscegenation), today sound arcane and obsolete, though expressed with vigor and intelligence. On the other hand, his sociological theory of cultural isolation is still viable.

Soon after its publication in 1902, *Rebellion* was enthusiastically received by critics and became a best-seller in Brazil. The success of the book guaranteed Cunha membership in the Brazilian Academy of Letters, which he joined in 1903. Following literary fame came opportunities to work with the Brazilian government. In 1906, after returning from an official trip to the Amazon, where he chaired a committee to survey the borders of northwestern Brazil, Cunha began to write a report that became his next most important book, *Contrastes e confrontos* (Contrasts and Comparisons), issued in 1907. Cunha spent the last two years of his life working on his third book, *À margem da história* (On the Margin of History), posthumously published in 1909. In this collection of essays he demonstrates his maturity as a writer and thinker, and replicates the artistic qualities of his masterpiece.

— LEOPOLDO M. BERNUCCI

CUNHA DOTTI, JUAN

Juan Cunha Dotti (*b.* 1910; *d.* 1985), Uruguayan poet. Born in Sauce de Illescas, Cunha left for Montevideo when he reached eighteen; his first book of poetry was published a year later. That volume, *El pájaro que vino de la noche* (1929), established his enduring fame through hermetic yet colloquial images that communicated well the nostalgia of the time for a less complicated and anguished existence. Other collections of poems—Cunha published twenty-six during his lifetime—demonstrated his agile versification skills in sonnets as well as free verse, in popular songs as well as difficult, esoteric verses. His poetry always registered subtle mutations of taste and concern with urgent social issues. During the 1940s he published little. Cunha's mature expression after 1951, in works such as *A eso de la tarde* (1961) and *Pastor perdido* (1966), communicates the poet's resentful solitude amid the silent streets and locked front doors of Uruguay's capital city. Additional works by Cunha include *Sueño y retorno de un campesino* (1951); *Hombre entre luz y sombra* (1955); and *Carpeta de mi gestión terrestre* (1960).

— WILLIAM H. KATRA

D

DALTON GARCÍA, ROQUE

Roque Dalton García (*b.* 14 May 1935; *d.* 10 May 1975), Salvadoran Marxist writer and activist. Born and educated in San Salvador, Dalton went to Chile to study law and there began his career as a poet, essayist, novelist, and biographer. Returning to El Salvador with strong leftist political leanings, he became part of the literary group known as the Committed Generation. His leftist views forced him into exile in 1961. After several years in Cuba, Dalton traveled extensively in Europe and became closely associated with the ideas of Che GUEVARA and Régis DEBRAY in defense of the Cuban Revolution. After returning clandestinely to El Salvador, where he was the effective founder of the leftist Armed Forces of National Resistance (Fuerzas Armadas de Resistencia Nacional), he was executed by members of the rival Revolutionary Army of the People (Ejército Revolucionario del Pueblo), from which his FARN had broken away, in San Salvador. In addition to his many poems and novels, Dalton wrote a biography, *Miguel Mármol: Los sucesos de 1932 en El Salvador* (1972).

— RALPH LEE WOODWARD, JR.

DANTAS, MANUEL PINTO DE SOUZA

Manuel Pinto de Souza Dantas (*b.* 21 February 1831; *d.* 29 January 1894), prime minister of Brazil (1884–1885). One of the leading Liberal politicians of the last decades of the Brazilian Empire, Dantas began his career soon after finishing law school in 1851. He held a number of local and provincial political posts, including provincial president of Alagoas and of his native Bahia. At the same time he was a member of various sessions of the national Chamber of Deputies from 1852 to

---

Moderate in his views, Dantas described the goals of his cabinet as "neither retreat, nor halt, nor undue haste."

1868 and was named minister of agriculture, commerce, and public works in the Zacarias de Góes cabinet in 1866. When that administration fell in 1868, Dantas retired temporarily from electoral politics.

Dantas gained his greatest recognition when he returned to politics as a senator in the 1880s. In a period when the abolition of slavery was increasingly seen as the nation's most pressing problem—it was abolished in 1888—the emperor asked Dantas in 1884 to form a new cabinet that would take steps toward emancipation. Moderate in his views, Dantas described the goals of his cabinet as "neither retreat, nor halt, nor undue haste." Nevertheless, the bill he presented, the central provision of which would free slaves over sixty years of age, set off a storm of opposition in Congress. After attacking the principle of liberating any slave without compensating the former master, his enemies finally forced Dantas's cabinet out of power in 1885. The Conservative ministry that followed then passed a watered-down version of Dantas's Sexagenarian Law that same year.

With the end of the Brazilian Empire in 1889, Dantas became director of the Bank of Brazil and then the Bank of the Republic, until his death.

— ROGER A. KITTLESON

DARIÉ, SANDU

Sandu Darié (*b.* 1908), Cuban artist and art critic. Born in Romania, Darié studied law at the University of Paris. While there he continued to write art criticism for Romanian newspapers and contributed humorous sketches to the French press. Darié emigrated to Cuba in 1941 and embraced Cuban life and culture; he subsequently became a full citizen. In 1949 he had his first solo exhibit, at the Lyceum in Havana, and another showing in New York. He exhibited at shows in Brazil, Mexico, Italy, Argentina, and Japan, and has pieces in the permanent collection of the Museum of Modern Art in New York. Darié's work is uniquely interactive: through his transformable constructions, such as *Estructura espacial transformable* (1960), the viewer is able to participate in the creative process.

— KAREN RACINE

DARÍO, RUBÉN

Rubén Darío (*b.* 18 January 1867; *d.* 6 February 1916), born Félix Rubén García Sarmiento in Nicaragua, he was the leading poet writing in Spanish between 1888 and 1916.

Life and Works   Darío was born in Metapa (now Cuidad Darío). After his parents separated, he was reared by his great-aunt Bernarda Sarmiento Ramírez and her husband. He studied with the Jesuits and at the National Institute, reading the classics and publishing poetry from age twelve. By age fourteen he had joined the editorial staff of the local newspaper. In 1883 he traveled to El Salvador, where President Rafael Zaldívar enrolled him in school. Upon his return to Nicaragua (1884), he worked as a journalist and read voraciously at the National Library. In 1886 he moved to Chile. Through his friendship with the president's son, Pedro Balmaseda, he became immersed in French poetry, especially the Parnassians, which is the most salient influence in his *Azul,* a collection of short stories and verse, published in Valparaíso (1888).

In 1889, Darío returned to Central America and worked feverishly on his poetry and newspaper articles. The following year he married Rafaela Contreras. They moved to Costa Rica in 1891. In 1892 he was named secretary of Nicaragua's delegation to Spain's celebration of the fourth centennial of Columbus's voyage of discovery. Upon his return, he learned of his wife's death and was named Colombia's consul to Buenos Aires. He married Rosario Murillo in 1893, but left alone for Argentina via New York and Paris. In Paris he met Jean Moreas, Théodore de Banville, and Paul Verlaine, and in New York, José MARTÍ. In Argentina, Darío discharged his consular duties, wrote for *La Nación* and other newspapers, and became the leader of a group of young and brilliant writers. With one of them, the Bolivian Ricardo Jaimes Freyre, he founded the literary journal *Revista de América.*

In 1896 Darío took over the leadership of the *modernismo* group. That same year, he published *Los raros*—a collection of essays on American and European writers—and *Prosas profanas*—a book influenced by French Symbolism, although rooted in the Spanish classics. *Prosas,* a deliberate break with Romanticism, became Darío's most imitated work for its innovative form, musicality, beauty, and exoticism. In 1898, *La Nación* sent him to Spain to report on the aftereffects of the Spanish-American War. The results of this endeavor were later collected in *España contemporánea* (1901). While in Madrid he reaffirmed his leadership of modernism and met the younger poets, among them Antonio and Manuel Machado and Juan Ramón Jiménez. He also met Francisca Sánchez, the woman who became his lifetime companion and the mother of his son. In 1900 he moved permanently to Paris.

In 1905, Darío published *Cantos de vida y esperanza.* Its first poem, "Yo soy aquél . . . ," rejected his previous "blue verse and profane songs," while continuing his revolutionary treatment of meter, rhythms, and poetic techniques. *Cantos* is perhaps Darío's most accomplished book. In it he also introduced a note absent from his earlier poetry: sociopolitical concerns for the future of Latin America and Hispanic culture. The Spanish defeat in 1898 and Theodore Roosevelt's policies in Central America had awakened Latin Americans to the fact that the United States could no longer be regarded as a trusted neighbor. Instead, it appeared as a menace capable of swallowing the southern half of the continent. *Cantos* manifests this new awareness and the new sense of allegiance to Spain as the mother country.

During the following years Darío maintained his residence in Paris, while visiting Spain and Latin America and publishing a number of important books: *El canto errante* (1907), *El viaje a Nicaragua* (1909), and *Poema del otoño* (1910). In 1911 he joined *Mundial* magazine in Paris. Its publishers took Darío on an advertising trip to the New World the following year. While in Buenos Aires, he wrote *Autobiografía,* a work serialized in *Caras y caretas.* He returned to Paris in 1913. When World War I erupted, Darío was ill and in serious economic straits, but he accepted another lecture tour throughout the Americas. He spoke at Columbia University in New York, where he contracted pneumonia. Taken to Nicaragua, he died in the city of León.

It has been said that Darío's poetry divides

Hispanic literary history into "before" and "after."

Significance   By the time Darío published his first book, *Epistolas y poemas* (1885), at age eighteen, he was the leading Central American poet. Three years later, with the publication of *Azul,* he became the leading poet of the Hispanic world. It has even been said that Darío's poetry divides Hispanic literary history into "before" and "after." His renovation of poetic expression was so thorough that he is still a leading force. In his quest for poetry, he broke away from traditional conventions and maintained no allegiance to any one set of esthetic norms. He learned from the primitives and the standard-bearers of Golden Age poetics—Góngora, San Juan de la Cruz, Saint Teresa d'Ávila, Cervantes, Quevedo—as well as from Gustavo Adolfo Bécquer and the Romantics. To their invaluable lessons he added what he learned from the French Parnassians and Symbolists. He acknowledged his debt and achieved a style unequaled by any other Spanish poet of his day. His range of expression, his inventiveness, and his flawless rendering of music into words are still refreshingly new.

— MARÍA A. SALGADO

DARTIGUENAVE, PHILIPPE-SUDRÉ

Philippe-Sudré Dartiguenave (*b.* 1863), president of Haiti (1915–1922). Installed as president by the U.S. Marines, he was the first Haitian president since 1879 to be from the south of Haiti and the first mulatto. Dartiguenave supported the U.S. occupation and customs receivership, and relied on the U.S. authorities for financial advice. Contrary to popular opinion, however, he did not surrender absolute control of the island to U.S. interests. In 1922 the vote of the mulatto elite in the south prevented his reelection.

— DARIÉN DAVIS

D'AUBUISSON, ROBERTO

Roberto d'Aubuisson (*b.* 23 August 1943; *d.* 20 February 1992), Salvadoran army officer and political leader. Roberto d'Aubuisson was a career intelligence officer who left the service when a new reformist government seized power in El Salvador on 15 October 1979. An outspoken anti-Communist who opposed social reforms and called for a hard line against leftist rebels in the country's civil war, d'Aubuisson was widely believed to be responsible for human rights violations. His name was frequently associated with the activities of death squads, most notably the assassination on 24 March 1980 of San Salvador's archbishop Oscar Arnulfo ROMERO, as well as with coup conspiracies against the reformist junta.

Youthful and charismatic, d'Aubuisson sought a political following. He founded the right-wing Nationalist Republican Alliance (Alianza Republicana Nacionalista—ARENA) in 1981 and served briefly as president of the Constituent Assembly (1982–1984), but his higher ambitions were discouraged by the armed forces and by the administration of U.S. president Ronald Reagan, which feared that his reputation would jeopardize congressional support for military aid to El Salvador. Following his defeat by José Napoleón DUARTE in the 1984 presidential election, d'Aubuisson yielded his party leadership post to Alfredo CRISTIANI, a less controversial politician. D'Aubuisson's political influence endured. When Cristiani was elected president in 1989, many observers believed that the charismatic former party leader would wield the real power, but d'Aubuisson's death of cancer three years later at age forty-eight brought a premature end to his career.

— STEPHEN WEBRE

DAVIDOVSKY, MARIO

Mario Davidovsky (*b.* 4 March 1934), Argentine composer who became a naturalized U.S. citizen. Born in Médanos, province of Buenos Aires, he was a composition student of Guillermo Graetzer in Buenos Aires, where he developed an atonal, abstract lyricism in his compositions, such as String Quartet no. 1 (1954), *Noneto* (1957), and *Pequeño concierto* (1957). He then moved to the United States under a Guggenheim Fellowship and studied with Varèse, Babbit, Ussachevsky, Luening, and Sessions. He was associated with the Columbia-Princeton Electronic Music Center in New York from its inception and was an assistant director from 1965 to 1980. He became director in 1981. Davidovsky has been particularly interested in the combination of acoustic instruments and electronically produced sounds on tape. He is celebrated for his series of Synchronisms, including no. 1 for flute and tape (1963), no. 2 for flute, clarinet, violin, cello, and tape (1964), which was commissioned by the Fromm Foundation for the Tanglewood Festival, and no. 3 for cello and tape (1965). If some of his earlier pieces were somewhat exploratory, Davidovsky's style and personality emerged strongly in his Synchronisms no. 5 for percussion and tape (1969) and no. 6 for piano and tape (1971), which in 1971 was awarded the Pulitzer Prize. In 1974 the series was continued with Synchronisms no. 7 for orchestra and tape and no. 8 for violin and tape.

Davidovsky has produced a remarkable series for solo tape called Electronic Studies. The first dates from 1960, and the third (1965) was written as a homage to Varèse. Other important works include Transients for orchestra (1972) and String Quartet no. 3 (1976).

— ALCIDES LANZA

DÁVILA, MIGUEL R.

Miguel R. Dávila (*d.* 1927), provisional president of Honduras (1907–1908), then elected president (1908–1911). Dávila, a member of the Liberal Party, headed a regime that exemplified the political instability prevailing in Central America at the beginning of the twentieth century. The legendary rivalry between the Nicaraguan dictator José Santos ZELAYA and Guatemala's Manuel ESTRADA CABRERA brought Dávila to power in 1907 when Zelaya engineered a coup against Estrada Cabrera's ally General Manuel BONILLA. During Dávila's term in office, Honduras participated in the 1907 Washington Conference sponsored by Mexico and the United States to restore stability to Central America. He had to deal with numerous rebellions organized by

Honduran exiles. Dávila's regime ended in 1911 when Bonilla, financed by banana interests, took advantage of the tensions created by the renegotiation of Honduras's debt with the United States (part of Secretary of State Philander Knox's Dollar Diplomacy) to regain power.

— HÉCTOR LINDO-FUENTES

DÁVILA ESPINOZA, CARLOS GUILLERMO

Carlos Guillermo Dávila Espinoza (*b.* 15 September 1887; *d.* 19 October 1955), Chilean political figure and newspaper publisher. After serving as ambassador to Washington, Dávila continued his education in the United States. Dávila was one of three men who led the Socialist Republic of 100 Days. More conservative than his colleagues, he eventually replaced them until he too was deposed, this time by a military coup under the leadership of General Bartolomé Blanche Espejo. Following the socialist republic's fall, Dávila resumed his newspaper career, working in the United States and eventually acting as editor of the government-owned journal *La Nación.* Having served as Chile's representative to various international organizations, he subsequently became secretary-general of the Organization of American States, a position he held at the time of his death.

— WILLIAM F. SATER

DAZA, HILARIÓN

Hilarión Daza (*b.* 14 January 1840; *d.* 27 February 1894), president of Bolivia (1876–1879). Born in Sucre, Daza was trained as a soldier and rose to the rank of colonel under Mariano MELGAREJO (1864–1871). In 1870 he defected to revolutionaries, who deposed Melgarejo on 15 January 1871. Gen. Agustín Morales, the leader of the revolution, died in 1872, and his civilian successors showed little ability to consolidate power. Daza, head of the elite Colorado battalion, seized power in 1876. In constant need of funds for his army, Daza imposed a new tax on the Chilean mining concessions along the Pacific coast (1878). This tax, which immediately provoked a Chilean attack against Bolivia's coastal territory, resulted in the War of the Pacific (1879–1884). Repeated Chilean victories led not only to Daza's downfall at the end of December 1879, but also to Bolivia's loss of the guano and nitrate-rich coastal area. Daza's major political accomplishment was the calling of the Constitutional Convention of 1878, whose work led to the adoption of the Constitution of 1880, the longest lasting in Bolivian history (1938).

Daza was assassinated in 1894 in Uyuni by persons who claimed he was trying to regain the presidency.

— ERWIN P. GRIESHABER

DE JESUS, CLEMENTINA

Clementina de Jesus (*b.* 1902; *d.* 1987), Brazilian samba singer who achieved national acclaim late in life. Born to a musical family in Valença, Rio de Janeiro State, Clementina, as she is called, was singing by age twelve with the Carnaval singing group Moreninha das Campinas. At fifteen, she frequented *samba de roda* sessions in the Oswaldo Cruz neighborhood, and later paraded with the Portela and Mangueira *samba* schools. For

---

For most of her life, Clementina had to work as a maid to support herself, even though she was a superb samba vocalist.

---

most of her life, Clementina had to work as a maid to support herself, even though she was a superb samba vocalist and a living archive of old musical forms such as *lundu, jongo,* and *partido alto* (a type of samba). Finally, at the age of sixty she was "discovered" by critic-impresario Hermínio Bello de Carvalho, who arranged numerous concert appearances for Clementina. She performed on stage with the likes of classical guitarist Turíbio Santos and in 1963 starred with Paulinho da Viola, Araci Cortes, and several others in the musical *Rosa de ouro.* In 1970, when she was sixty-eight, Clementina recorded her first album, "Clementina, cade você?" (Clementina, Where Are You?), and was celebrated as a national musical treasure. Many leading Brazilian artists, such as Milton NASCIMENTO, invited her to perform duets on their albums.

— CHRIS MCGOWAN

DE LA HUERTA, ADOLFO

Adolfo de la Huerta (*b.* 26 May 1881; *d.* 9 July 1955), interim president of Mexico in 1920 and an important figure among the Constitutionalists during the Mexican Revolution. De la Huerta was born to an important family of Guaymas, in the state of Sonora. His family supported his studies in Hermosillo, where he obtained a teaching certificate in music. In 1900 he abandoned a career in that field to maintain his family by working in a variety of bookkeeping posts. In 1908 he joined the Anti-Reelectionist Club, becoming secretary in 1910. In that year, however, his antigovernment activities cost him his managerial job. In 1911 he entered local politics, defeating Plutarco ELÍAS CALLES to become the local deputy to the state legislature.

Having joined the Constitutionalists under Venustiano CARRANZA on 20 February 1913, de la Huerta served as Carranza's *oficial mayor* (chief clerk) of government from 1915 to 1916. His other positions included interim governor of Sonora (1916–1917), consul general in New York City (1918), senator (1918), and governor of Sonora (1919–1920).

De la Huerta supported the opposition to Carranza that resulted in the Plan of Agua Prieta and, after Carranza's death, served as provisional president of the republic, from 1 June to 30 November 1920. On the election of Alvaro OBREGÓN he joined the cabinet as secretary of the treasury (1920–1923), but when Obregón supported Calles for the presidency, de la Huerta led the first major, and most important, rebellion against the post-Revolutionary government (7 December 1923). Despite the support of a large part of the army and the civilian political community, the rebellion failed, and de la Huerta went into exile in Los Angeles, where he survived by giving piano lessons until 1935.

President Lázaro CÁRDENAS appointed him inspector general of Mexican consulates in the United States, a post he held until 1946, when he retired. His son, Adolfo, also became a senator from his home state, and his brother Alfonso was a revolutionary general.

– RODERIC AI CAMP

DE LEÓN, MARTÍN

Martín de León (*b.* 1765; *d.* 1833), successful Mexican rancher, colonizer, and founder of Victoria, Texas. De León was born in Burgos, Tamaulipas, in Mexico, to Spanish parents. He became a muleteer and merchant, and in 1790 joined the Fieles de Burgos Regiment in Nuevo Santander, reaching the rank of captain. He married Patricia de la Garza in 1795 and had ten children who became community leaders in Texas and northern Mexico. In 1824, de León founded the colony of Victoria on the Guadalupe River with forty-one Mexican families from Tamaulipas. De León's cattle raising made Victoria one of the most prosperous of the Texas colonies. He died in the cholera epidemic of 1833.

– A. CAROLINA CASTILLO CRIMM

DEBRAY, [JULES] RÉGIS

[Jules] Régis Debray (*b.* 2 September 1940), French intellectual and Marxist philosopher. Debray was Ché GUEVARA's most articulate interpreter, but after Gue-

vara's death in the disastrous 1967 Bolivian revolution, he synthesized the Leninist traditional view of revolution and Guevarist *focoismo* (revolution from a rural guerrilla center, or *foco*).

Debray became a student of the French Communist ideologue Louis Althusser in the early 1960s. While traveling in revolutionary Latin America, he became convinced that only insurrection, conducted according to local conditions, could bring successful revolution. Debray's most influential book, *Revolution in the Revolution?* (1967), popularized the *foco* philosophy of Guevara.

Three years in a Bolivian prison (1967–1970) and Marxist successes achieved without *focoismo* caused Debray to admit strategic mistakes. Nonetheless, he never criticized Guevara, but did criticize Chilean president Salvador ALLENDE and Uruguay's urban guerrilla Tupamaros for not adhering to the Cuban position. Many insist that his novel of revolutionary alienation, *The Undesirable* (1975), is autobiographical.

– PAT KONRAD

DEBRET, JEAN-BAPTISTE

Jean-Baptiste Debret (*b.* 1768; *d.* 1848), French painter. Under the leadership of Joachim Lebreton (1760–1819), secretary of the fine arts class in the Institute of France, Debret left his country in 1816 and went to Rio de Janeiro with the French group known as the French Artistic Mission, which had been invited by the Portuguese government. The group was composed of Nicolas Antoine Taunay (1755–1830), a landscape painter; his brother, Auguste Marie Taunay (1768–1824), a sculptor; Auguste Henri Victor GRANDJEAN DE MONTIGNY (1776–1850), an architect; Charles S. Pradier (1768–1848), an engraver; Sigismund Neukomm (1778–1858), a composer; and François Ovide, a specialist in mechanics. Although Debret was classified as a history painter, his first works in Brazil were portraits of the royal family, decorative paintings for public festivities, and stage settings for the Royal Theatre São João in Rio de Janeiro. It took ten years to establish the Brazilian Academy of Fine Arts, where the members of the French group were supposed to teach. Meanwhile, Debret taught his students in a private house.

Debret's best-known work is a series of drawings depicting Brazilian life and culture, which was published in three volumes in 1834 and 1839 under the title *Voyage pittoresque et historique au Brésil*. The drawings and the explanatory texts that accompany them may be considered the most striking documents on Brazilian daily life in the first decades of the nineteenth century. Following what he calls a "logical order," Debret began his book with descriptions of Indians belonging to several tribes. Although he had not traveled outside Rio de Janeiro, various travelers gave him the information he needed to represent the Indian way of life in the interior. No one better than Debret depicted slave life in Rio de Janeiro, and his drawings shocked the members of the Brazilian Historical and Geographical Institute because of their realism.

As a history painter, Debret also depicted historical events of the late colonial period: Her Royal Highness Princess LEOPOLDINA disembarking in Rio de Janeiro, the coronation of King João VI, the baptism of Princess María da Glória, the oath to the Constitution, and the coronation of PEDRO I as emperor of Brazil.

— MARIA BEATRIZ NIZZA DA SILVA

DECOUD, HECTOR FRANCISCO

Hector Francisco Decoud (*b.* 1855; *d.* 1930), Paraguayan historian and journalist. Born in Asunción, Decoud was a mere youth when the disastrous War of the Triple Alliance began in 1864. Entering the army as a noncommissioned officer, he fought in several battles before being arrested, together with his mother, by the dictator Francisco Solano LÓPEZ. Though his imprisonment was brief, he was poorly treated, and this left him with a lifelong hatred of López, a hatred that was reflected in his historical writings.

After the war, Decoud dedicated himself to journalism, working for *La Regeneración* and other Asunción newspapers. In 1882, he was appointed district attorney, but he resigned that post the following year after having been elected a national deputy, a position he held until 1887.

Decoud found the time during subsequent years to produce many highly partisan historical works. He focused on the Triple Alliance War and on the figure of López, whom he regarded as the worst sort of tyrant. His many studies included *Sobre los escombros de la guerra: Una década de vida nacional, 1869–1880* (1925), *Guerra del Paraguay: La masacre de Concepción ordenada por el mariscal López* (1926), *La revolución del comandante Molas* (1930), and *Elisa Lynch de Quatrefages* (published posthumously in 1939). Decoud died in Asunción.

— THOMAS L. WHIGHAM

DECOUD, JOSÉ SEGUNDO

José Segundo Decoud (*b.* 1848; *d.* 4 March 1909), Paraguayan statesman. Born into a prominent Asunción family, Decoud began his studies in the Paraguayan cap-

ital before moving on to the Colegio Nacional of Concepción del Uruguay, in Argentina. At the beginning of the 1860s, he transferred to the University of Buenos Aires, where he studied law. At the beginning of the War of the Triple Alliance in 1864, Decoud joined with his brother Juan Francisco and other Paraguayan exiles to found the Legión Paraguaya, a military unit that fought with the Argentines against Paraguayan President Francisco Solano LÓPEZ. An ardent Liberal, Decoud was anxious to see a constitutional regime established in Paraguay. When the secret clauses of the Triple Alliance treaty were published, however, he denounced the territorial claims they made against Paraguay and resigned his position in the *legión.*

After the war, Decoud returned to Asunción, where he became editor of *La Regeneración* and a key member of the 1870 Constitutional Convention. Annoyed by in-fighting among the Liberals, he supported the rise of Conservative Cándido BAREIRO and, later, of generals Bernardino CABALLERO and Patricio ESCOBAR. From 1879 until the end of the century, he was a member of every cabinet except one and was generally regarded as the most influential politician in the country throughout this time. He provided the ideological argument behind Paraguayan conservatism, formulating the original party platform when the Caballeristas organized the Asociación Nacional Republicana (or Colorado Party) in 1887.

Decoud was also active in diplomatic and educational affairs. He attempted at one point to create new *colegios nacionales* in several communities of the interior, but his plans were vetoed at the last moment. His fluency in many languages and his superb private library made him the focus of much intellectual interest, not only for Paraguayans but also for foreign visitors to the Platine countries.

— THOMAS L. WHIGHAM

DEGOLLADO, SANTOS

Santos Degollado (*b.* 1811; *d.* 1861), Mexican liberal general and cabinet minister. Degollado was born in the city of Guanajuato during the wars for Mexico's independence from Spain. Since his father was a supporter of the insurgency, the Spanish government confiscated his property. On the death of his father, an uncle took Degollado to Mexico City. In October 1828, Degollado moved to Morelia, where he took a job as a notary's clerk and studied in his spare time. Recognizing Degollado's organizational skills, the governor of Michoacán, Melchor OCAMPO, named him secretary of the Colegio de San Nicolás, and in 1846 Degollado served briefly as a substitute for Ocampo.

As a foot soldier, Degollado dedicated himself to the struggle against SANTA ANNA and rose through the ranks to general. After the triumph of the Revolution of Ayutla (1854), he was elected to the Constitutional Convention of 1856–1857 as a representative of the

---

A talented and tireless organizer of armies,

Degollado was notably less successful as their

leader in battle.

---

state of Michoacán. In 1857, he was elected governor of that state but served only a few months before resigning to join the forces of Benito Juárez in the War of the Reform. On 27 March 1858, Juárez named Degollado his minister of war and general of the federal army. Degollado also served briefly as minister of foreign relations during the first months of 1860. A talented and tireless organizer of armies, Degollado was notably less successful as their leader in battle. After his subordinate, Manuel Doblado, confiscated silver from British mine owners, Degollado took responsibility and promised repayment. Then, without authorization, he sought a negotiated settlement to the war, with a British official, George W. Mathew, as mediator. Juárez reacted to this step by removing Degollado from his command and replacing him with Jesús GONZÁLEZ ORTEGA, who led the army Degollado had organized to victory over the conservatives in late 1860. González Ortega paid homage to Degollado when the liberal army marched into Mexico City. Degollado received another command in Michoacán to pursue the guerrillas who had killed Melchor Ocampo, but he was ambushed, captured, and executed by the conservatives.

– D. F. STEVENS

DEIRA, ERNESTO

Ernesto Deira (*b.* July 1928; *d.* 1986), Argentine artist. Born in Buenos Aires, Deira turned to pop art, expressionism, and informalism to define a style halfway between abstract and figurative painting. He studied with Leopoldo Torres Agüero and Leopoldo Presas in the 1950s. Early works were reminiscent of Goya's grotesque creatures. A member of the Argentine New Figuration group, in 1961 he received a fellowship from the Argentine National Fund for the Arts to study in Paris. In 1964 he won the Guggenheim International Award and two years later a Fulbright fellowship to study in New York City, where he was visiting professor at Cornell University.

Deira's work is characterized by gestural brushstrokes and harsh contrasts of color. He allowed paint to drip freely over the canvas to generate informalist structures which he accentuated with graphic signs and dribbles to define distorted figures. Some of his segmented figures, with exposed entrails, are erotic. His images became more serene after 1966, although they still tended toward ironic, nightmarish themes. In his later years he settled in Paris, where he died.

– MARTA GARSD

DEL PRADO, JORGE

Jorge del Prado (*b.* 15 August 1910), leader of the Peruvian Communist Party for much of the twentieth century. Del Prado was born in Arequipa, where in 1928 he helped form the "Revolution Group" that united radical writers, artists, and union leaders. The group maintained close ties to the "Amauta Group" in Lima led by José Carlos MARIÁTEGUI. In 1929 he traveled to Lima, where he collaborated closely with Mariátegui during the rupture with Víctor HAYA DE LA TORRE and the APRA party and the creation of the Socialist Party that would soon become the Peruvian Communist Party (PCP). In the early 1930s, he worked in the mines of Morococha as a union organizer. In the following decades, he held many positions in the Communist Party. He was repeatedly imprisoned and exiled.

Since 1961, Del Prado has been the secretary-general of the Communist Party (referred to as the PCP-Unidad since the withdrawal of pro-China factions in 1964). In 1978 he was elected to the Constituent Assembly. In 1980 he was a candidate for vice president for the United Left (IU). He served three terms in the Peruvian Senate (1980–1985, 1985–1990, and 1990–1992). He has written almost a dozen books on the Peruvian left and on Mariátegui.

– CHARLES F. WALKER

DEL RIO, DOLORES

Dolores Del Rio (Dolores Asunsolo; *b.* 1905; *d.* 11 April 1983), Mexican stage and motion picture star. Born in Durango, Del Rio was discovered by the American director Edwin Carewe, who cast her in the silent film *Joanne* (1925) in Hollywood. She subsequently starred in various other silent and early sound Hollywood films, such as *Journey into Fear,* directed by Orson Welles. In 1942, director Emilio "El Indio" FERNÁNDEZ convinced her to return to Mexico and become a central part of his film team. Del Rio thus had major roles in the most acclaimed of Fernández's films: *Flor silvestre* (1943), *María Candelaria* (1943), *Bugambilia* (1944), and *Las abandonadas* (1944). In later years, she continued her career in both Hollywood and Mexico, receiving numerous acting awards in Mexico and elsewhere.

– DAVID MACIEL

DELFIM NETO, ANTÔNIO

Antônio Delfim Neto (*b.* 1 May 1928), Brazilian minister of finance (1967–1974) and planning (1979–1985). Economist, professor, and legislator, Delfim Neto oversaw Brazil's substantial economic policy apparatus for two extended periods during the military regime of 1964–1985. Known as a pragmatist, he was professor of economics at the University of São Paulo (1952–1965), secretary of finance of the state of São Paulo (1966–1967), ambassador to France (1975–1978), minister of agriculture (1979), and federal deputy (1987–). From 1967 to 1974, Delfim Neto presided over the Economic Miracle, a period when Brazil experienced an average annual growth rate in excess of 10 percent. Building on economic stabilization and institutional reform (1964–1967) and with the backing of a strong military government, his policies stimulated the economy, in the presence of wage and price controls, through lower interest rates, loosening of credit, export promotion, expansion of public investment in transportation and energy, and strengthening of public administration. The period witnessed rapid expansion of production, while provoking criticism over the increasingly unequal distribution of income and controversy over manipulation of the price indexes in 1973 to mask rising rates of inflation.

Delfim Neto began his second period in power promising to avoid a recession while combating inflation. In spite of active management, inflation surged in 1980, and output fell markedly in 1981. After a slight improvement in 1982, a key election year in the redemocratization process, chronic problems in Brazil's balance of payments worsened into a debt crisis. The years 1983–1984 witnessed harsh stabilization and export-promotion programs that caused a major internal recession while generating a sizable trade surplus that mitigated the debt crisis and created the external preconditions for the Cruzado Plan of 1986. The plan was an attempt to fight inertial inflation by freezing prices; ending wage indexation; and generally deindexing the economy, including long-term contracts. Although it was unsuccessful, experience with the plan contributed to subsequent plans. Delfim Neto was elected to the nation's constituent assembly in 1986 and again in 1990.

– RUSSELL E. SMITH

DELGADO, JOSÉ MATÍAS

José Matías Delgado (*b.* 24 February 1767; *d.* 12 November 1832), Salvadoran cleric and leader of the independence movement. Born in the provincial capital of San Salvador, Father Delgado became a champion of the Kingdom of Guatemala's independence from Spain and his province's separation from the overbearing influence of neighboring Guatemala. Trained in canon law and jurisprudence at the University of San Carlos in Guatemala, Delgado was part of a generation of discontented creoles who passed through the university in these years. The Enlightenment ideas he learned at San Carlos and his provincial resentments of both Spanish and Guatemalan control over his native Salvador quickly bore fruit. Delgado, Manuel José ARCE, and other Salvadorans organized the uprising of 1811, in which they planned to seize the Spanish magistrate, the armory, and the treasury and gain independence. The conspiracy failed, as did a similar revolt in Nicaragua, in the face of strong royalist military action. The repression following these conspiracies helped to postpone independence for another decade but could not quell the unrest that was their root cause.

Delgado soon went to Guatemala to contact other independence activists and begin agitating for the establishment of a separate bishopric for El Salvador. By 1821 he was again in the thick of political intrigue. With many of the leading Liberals of the day, such as José Cecilio del VALLE, Pedro MOLINA, and José Francisco BARRUNDIA, Delgado played an instrumental role in convincing Captain-General Gabino GÁINZA to declare Central America's independence from Spain on 15 September 1821.

After the collapse of the Mexican Empire, Central America gained its independence in its own right, and Father Delgado presided over the assembly that promulgated the first constitution of the independent United Provinces of Central America in July of 1823. With union came the reward for Salvador's help in the cause of independence, the formation of a new bishopric of El Salvador in 1825, with Delgado as the first bishop. Seven years later he died while witnessing the bloodshed of the internecine fighting that would plague the former Kingdom of Guatemala for generations to come.

– TODD LITTLE-SIEBOLD

DELGADO CHALBAUD, CARLOS

Carlos Delgado Chalbaud (*b.* 20 January 1909; *d.* 13 November 1950), president of Venezuela's military junta (1948–1950). Son of a famous Venezuelan general, Delgado received a degree in military engineering in France. Upon his return to Venezuela, he entered the army and rose rapidly in the officer ranks. From 1945 to 1948 he served as a member of the revolutionary junta and as war minister. After the 1948 military coup, Delgado, now a lieutenant colonel, served as president of the military junta until his assassination in 1950. One of the best-educated Venezuelan military men of his generation, he was regarded as a voice of political moderation among his army colleagues.

— WINFIELD J. BURGGRAAFF

DELLEPIANE, LUIS J.

Luis J. Dellepiane (*b*. 26 February 1865; *d*. 2 August 1941), career army officer, engineer, minister of war (1928–1930). Dellepiane was born in Buenos Aires and attended the military college in his home city, graduating in 1884. A general by 1910, he established his reputation as the officer who did the most to foster the development of the engineering branch of the Argentine army. He was also closely involved in Argentine politics. Following the assassination of the Buenos Aires police chief, Dellepiane was named interim chief in 1909. During the quasi-revolutionary *Semana Trágica* (Tragic Week) in Buenos Aires in 1919, President Hipólito YRIGOYEN (1916–1922) placed him in command of all military and civilian forces to restore order. Dellepiane's loyal service to Yrigoyen was later rewarded when he was appointed minister of war during Yrigoyen's second term (1928–1930). Concerned about rumors of a coup, Dellepiane advised Yrigoyen to arrest officers believed to be involved in the conspiracy. When he refused, Dellepiane resigned on 2 September 1930, just four days before elements of the army drove Yrigoyen from power. Dellepiane remained in retirement until his death.

— PAUL GOODWIN

DENEVI, MARCO

Marco Denevi (*b*. 12 May 1922), Argentine writer. Born in Sáenz Peña, Denevi today is considered perhaps more a gadfly presence in Argentine literary circles than a major voice. His works are best known for the absurdist humor with which he narrates the seemingly trivial comedy of quotidian existence. This is the salient feature of *Rosaura a las diez* (1955), cast as detective fiction but with several features atypical of the classic genre that has had so much influence in Argentina. As a consequence, the novel deals more with *porteño* idiosyncrasies within a register of gritty neorealism than with the dynamics of the thriller. *Ceremonia secreta*

(1955; *Secret Ceremony*, 1961), an expressionistic tale of fatalistic human rituals reminiscent of Roberto ARLT, won a prize from *Life en Español* magazine and was

---

Ceremonia secreta, an expressionistic tale of fatalistic human rituals, was made into a movie with Elizabeth Taylor and Robert Mitchum.

---

made into a movie (*Secret Ceremony*, 1967) with Elizabeth Taylor and Robert Mitchum, in which the shift from a Buenos Aires to a London locale deprives the story of any of its Argentine significance. *Falsificaciones* (1966) is a series of microtexts that are parables of human foibles, the dehumanization of modern social life, and the unknown lurking beneath the surface of routine existence. Denevi has written on Argentine national characteristics in *La república de Trapalanda* (1989).

— DAVID WILLIAM FOSTER

DEPESTRE, RENÉ

René Depestre (*b*. 29 August 1926) Haitian poet, essayist and novelist. After the surprising sales of a first volume of poetry (*Étincelles*, 1945), Depestre participated in the movement to overthrow the Haitian president, Élie Lescot, in 1946. As a student in Paris (1946–1950), he collaborated with the Caribbean and African intellectuals—Aimé CÉSAIRE, Léopold Senghor, and Léon Damas—to found the négritude movement. Expelled from France for political activism in 1950, Depestre found asylum in Czechoslovakia as secretary to the Brazilian novelist Jorge AMADO. Years of wandering through South America finally brought Depestre to a long stay in Cuba (1959–1978).

Depestre's poetry ranges from a passionate yearning to affirm the humanity and freedom of Haitians to very personal love poetry and, at times, doctrinaire political verse. In early stories (*Alléluia pour une femme—jardin*, 1981), he created a unique blend of humor and eroticism to produce some of the most readable fiction in the tradition of "marvelous realism." His first novel, *Le mât de cocagne* (1979) (translated by Carrol F. Coates as *The Festival of the Greasy Pole*, 1990) deftly applied similar narrative elements to political satire of the François Duvalier dictatorship (1957–1971). With his second novel, *Hadriana dans tous mes rêves* (1988), Depestre continued to exploit his Haitian heritage by focusing on the tale of a young woman turned into a zombie on her wedding night in the lush tropical setting of Jacmel, where Depestre grew up. He returned to the erotic vein in the stories of *Érôs dans un train chinois* (1990).

— CARROL F. COATES

DERQUI, SANTIAGO

Santiago Derqui (*b.* 19 June 1809; *d.* 5 September 1867), Argentine president. Trained as a lawyer, Derqui took an active role in the politics of his home province of Córdoba until, in the mid-1830s, it came firmly under the control of the dictatorship of Juan Manuel de ROSAS. He then joined the Unitarist general José María PAZ in the struggle against Rosas. After Rosas fell, Derqui served in the Constituent Convention of 1853 and collaborated with Justo José de URQUIZA in the government of the Argentine Confederation. He succeeded Urquiza as president in 1860, just as rivalry between the Confederation and the secessionist province of Buenos Aires came to a head in armed conflict. Defeated, he resigned the presidency in November 1861.

— DAVID BUSHNELL

D'ESCOTO BROCKMANN, MIGUEL

Miguel D'Escoto Brockmann (*b.* 5 February 1933), Nicaraguan priest active in the Sandinista revolution; foreign minister of Nicaragua (1979–1989). Born in California to Nicaraguan parents, D'Escoto was educated in Managua, California, and New York. He studied theology, education, and political economy and became a Catholic priest in the Maryknoll Order. During the 1960s, he worked first for Maryknoll in New York, then in the slums of Brazil and Mexico. Returning to his own country, he established the Nicaraguan Foundation for Integral Community Development in 1973. In 1975 he became an active supporter of the Sandinista movement. He was a leader of the Group of Twelve (*Los Doce*), which organized resistance to the Somoza government. When the Sandinistas came to power in 1979 he was named foreign minister, a post he held for ten years. In 1980 he became a member of the party's political group, the Sandinista Assembly.

The Vatican made known in 1980 its desire that priests not be involved in politics. This policy was relayed to D'Escoto; Ernesto Cardenal, the minister of culture; and two other priests who were participating in the Nicaraguan government at the time. D'Escoto and the others proposed that they take a leave of absence from the church and continue with their work in the government. The Nicaraguan bishops accepted this compromise. Cardenal was subsequently expelled from the Jesuit order, but the Maryknollers did not expel D'Escoto. Throughout the 1980s, D'Escoto was a forceful spokesman for the Sandinista cause. Because of

his fluency in English and his understanding of the political system of the United States he was particularly successful in communicating Sandinista positions to audiences in that nation.

— DAVID L. JICKLING

DESNOES, EDMUNDO PÉREZ

Edmundo Pérez Desnoes (*b.* 2 October 1930), Cuban novelist, essayist, and poet. Desnoes was born and raised in Havana and lived in New York, where he attended college from 1956 to 1959. He then returned to Cuba, where he held several posts in national cultural institutions, such as editorial board member of the Casa de las Américas. In 1967 he and film director Tomás Gutiérrez Alea adapted his 1965 novel *Memorias del subdesarrollo* (*Memories of Underdevelopment*) into a highly successful film that brought him immediate recognition. Largely because of this adaptation, Desnoes became a prominent figure in the Cuban cultural world of the 1960s, but in subsequent years his importance diminished as his literary output failed to live up to its earlier promise. Other works by Desnoes include the novel *El cataclismo,* an essay "Lam: Azul y negro," and a controversial anthology of Cuban literature, *Los dispositivos en la flor* (1981).

— ROBERTO VALERO

DESSALINES, JEAN JACQUES

Jean Jacques Dessalines (*b.* 1758; *d.* 17 October 1806), emperor of Haiti (1804–1806). In the early hours of an October morning in 1806, a fierce-looking black commander was trying to force his mount through a crowd of mutinous but stunned soldiers. Finally a shot rang out, the commander's horse rolled over, breaking and pinning the rider's leg, and with cries of anguish and curses rolling from the commander's lips, the stunned soldiers knew that their hated victim was mortal after all. They shot him to pieces and dragged his mutilated body from Pont Rouge to Port-au-Prince for public display. There but one person mourned his death—she was Défilée, an insane black woman. The object of her tears and flowers was the emperor, Jean Jacques Dessalines. No man in Haitian history has been more hated by his contemporaries or loved and respected by future generations of his countrymen than Dessalines.

Born on the Cormiers Plantation in northern Saint-Domingue, young Jean Jacques Duclos (later Dessalines) experienced many of slavery's horrors. Master Duclos sold both his parents and a favorite aunt to neighboring plantation masters, a clear violation of the Code Noir (1685), which mandated that slave families

Jean Jacques Dessalines. (Organization of American States)

be kept intact. In the late 1780s a free black master named Dessalines acquired the now mature Jean Jacques Duclos. His new master often whipped him, leaving him only pain and a new last name. Small wonder that Dessalines despised whites, mulattoes, and authority by the time of the Haitian Revolution.

When the revolution began, Dessalines may have been a maroon (slave fugitive), but runaway or not, he soon joined the black rebels. When Dessalines joined Toussaint L'OUVERTURE is unclear, but he became indispensable to the "Black Spartacus" once he did. With a viciousness rare in Toussaint's generals, he figured heavily in crushing the rebellion of Theodore Hedouville at Le Cap (1798), in defeating and punishing the mulattoes of South Province, led by André RIGAUD, during the War of the Knives (1799), in suppressing the rebellion of General Moyse (1801), and in opposing the expedition of French General Charles LECLERC (1802–1804). Clearly Dessalines was a gifted field commander, who earned the title of "Tiger."

But Dessalines's brutal manner and greed often tainted these achievements. At one time Dessalines had thirty plantations and an income so large that he refused to join the Moyse rebellion on the grounds that plantation division, one of its demands, threatened his economic interests. When Toussaint sent him to South Province as an occupation governor following the War of the Knives, the Tiger murdered hundreds of mulattoes. He also slaughtered practically the entire white population of Haiti in 1804. And he enforced *fermage* (system of forced labor and government management on plantations), introduced by Toussaint, with a severity seldom seen in any of the old colonial masters.

C. L. R. James is among those historians who emphasize that Dessalines acted largely on his own. But others, among them Hubert Cole, believe that Dessalines usually acted with Toussaint's knowledge and approval, the War of the Knives providing their best argument. The brutal Dessalines served as a sort of alter ego for the gentle Toussaint. While Toussaint might have found Dessalines useful on the battlefield, he absolutely believed him unfit to rule the emerging black state. Toussaint was right.

Dessalines carried Haiti to independence on 1 January 1804 and himself to the emperorship at his coronation on 8 October 1804. That France might once again attack Haiti was his abiding fear and, as Hubert Cole indicated, may have triggered his mass slaughter of all whites in mid 1804. But his furious behavior extended to the mulattoes also. He once quipped that he murdered any mulatto who looked white during the massacres of 1804. Later he mellowed with regard to the mulattoes and remarked that blacks and mulattoes should intermarry and obliterate race lines. But rationality soon gave way to another volcanic eruption of rage in Dessalines. When the mulatto Alexandre PÉTION refused to marry his daughter, Dessalines once again turned on them, and by the end of 1806 had planned their destruction. The Haitian national historian Thomas Madiou has treated Dessalines's social policies as those of a liberal. But other historians outside Haiti disagree. James Leyburn believes Dessalines brought social disaster on Haiti and fixed the caste system on the new state.

A reckless economic policy finally brought Dessalines down. He challenged mulatto land titles, put most of Haiti's able-bodied men under arms, enforced a harsh labor system, and neglected education. On 17 October 1806 most of Haiti rejoiced over his assassination.

– THOMAS O. OTT

DEUSTUA, ALEJANDRO O.

Alejandro O. Deustua (*b.* 1849; *d.* 1945), Peruvian philosopher, educator, politician, and lawyer. Born in Huancayo, Deustua initially was an exponent of the positivist school of thought prevalent in Latin America in the late nineteenth and early twentieth centuries. Subsequently he espoused idealist concepts developed by the European philosophers Karl Krause and his followers and Henri Bergson. This transition was not uncommon among Latin American intellectuals after the Mexican Revolution. In his later works, *Ante el conflicto nacional* (1931) and *La cultura nacional* (1937), Deustua expressed the need for a renewed sense of humanist nationalism among the elites. Deustua was a founding member of the historical Civilista Party (1872), minister of justice (1895) and government (1902), senator for Lima (1901–1904), a diplomat, and president of San Marcos University (1928–1930). He died in Lima.

– ALFONSO W. QUIROZ

DI CAVALCANTI, EMILIANO

Emiliano Di Cavalcanti (*b.* 1897; *d.* 1976), Brazilian painter. In 1914 Di Cavalcanti initiated his artistic ca-

Di Cavalcanti paints a portrait of Marina Montini. (Iconographia)

reer with the publication of one of his drawings in a magazine entitled *Fon-Fon.* In 1916 he moved from Rio de Janeiro to São Paulo, where he studied law and worked as an illustrator and journalist. In 1918, one year after exhibiting a series of "antiacademic" Beardsley-inspired caricatures in São Paulo, he began studying painting with the German painter Elpons. His first exhibition of paintings took place in 1921. During this period, Di Cavalcanti, in collaboration with modernist Paulistas Anita Malfatti and Vítor BRECHERET, became one of the leaders of the Brazilian modernist movement. These three artists conceptualized and ultimately organized the 1922 Semana de Arte Moderna (Modern Art Week), a week-long series of poetry, dance, and fine arts exhibitions. It coincided with the centenary celebration of Brazilian independence and is regarded as a watershed for Brazilian cultural expression.

Di Cavalcanti's first trip to Europe in 1923 introduced him to the European avant-garde in art and literature. While the cubism and surrealism of Picasso, Braque, Léger, and Matisse influenced his own painting greatly, he remained devoted to national themes such as the bohemian life in Rio de Janeiro, mulatto women, and Carnival. In his memoirs he affirmed that "the mulata for me is a Brazilian symbol. She is not black or white, neither rich nor poor. Like our people, she likes to dance, she likes music and soccer. . . . The mulata is feminine and Brazil is one of the most feminine countries in the world."

Upon his return to Brazil, he settled in Rio. Between 1927 and his return to Paris in 1935, Di Cavalcanti received a commission to prepare two wall panels for the João Caetano Theater. During this same period he exhibited in Rio de Janeiro and São Paulo. By the 1950s he had attained international recognition as one of the greatest modernist painters. In the second São Paulo Biennial in 1954, he won the highest honor, Best National Painter, and in the seventh São Paulo Biennial there was a special room devoted exclusively to an exhibition of his paintings.

– CAREN A. MEGHREBLIAN

DI TELLA, TORCUATO

Torcuato Di Tella (*b.* 15 May 1892; *d.* 22 July 1948), Argentine entrepreneur. Until age thirteen Di Tella lived in Italy, at which time his family emigrated to Argentina. His entrepreneurial career was launched in 1910, when he linked his market study of the demand for dough-kneading machines to a mechanic who could build a machine capable of competing with imported technology. Operating from a converted garage, the fledgling business, which would eventually operate under the name S.I.A.M. (Sección Industria Amasadoras Mecánicas), expanded rapidly over the next five years.

Di Tella's entrepreneurial career was interrupted by service with the Italian army in World War I. In 1919 he returned to Argentina, where he confronted a stagnant economy, sluggish market, and volatile labor force. The protectionist economic policies of the government and a labor policy that ranged from firing troublesome personnel to co-opting others through promotion allowed Di Tella to overcome the difficulties. With an unmatched ability to take advantage of every opportunity and to anticipate markets, he expanded his operations. Gasoline pumps were added to bakery machinery, and by the end of the 1920s S.I.A.M.'s success was symbolic of the emergence of industry in Argentina. Management became the province of the extended Di Tella family, which could be trusted to administer and operate the company. Di Tella expanded his operations to Brazil, Chile, Uruguay, and, for a while, London. By the end of the 1930s, S.I.A.M. had diversified into household appliances. Operating in the style of a *patrón,* Di Tella the man became "an integrating symbol for the company."

As a successful businessman, Di Tella was sought for a variety of national and international roles. He fought against the spread of Fascism, both in Italy and Argentina, wrote several books, represented Argentina at important international meetings, and between 1944 and 1948 was a professor of economics and industrial organization at the University of Buenos Aires. He was a patron of the arts and owner of an experimental dairy farm.

– PAUL GOODWIN

DIANDA, HILDA

Hilda Dianda (*b.* 13 April 1917), Argentine composer. Born in Córdoba, she studied under Honorio Siccardi and did postgraduate work in Europe (1958–1962) under Gian Francesco Malipiero and Hermann Scherchen. Dianda wrote some electroacoustic works at the Studío di Fonologia Musicale in Milan, Italy, and attended the new music summer courses in Darmstadt, Germany. Her early works have traces of moderated modernism—dissonant chords and jagged melodies—and a lyrical style. This is true of *Concertante* for cello and orchestra (1952) and *Poemas de amor desesperado* for voice and six instruments (1942). Later her style became more experimental, and she was one of the leading figures of the musical avant-garde in Argentina. Dianda participated in numerous international festivals, including Florence, Caracas, Rio de Janeiro, Madrid, Washington, D.C., Mexico, Zagreb, and Donaueschin-

gen. Dianda has also written articles published in several publications around the world and one book, *Música en la Argentina de hoy* (1966). For several years Dianda collaborated as a composer-member and concert organizer with the Agrupación Música Viva in Buenos Aires. This organization, which also included composers Gerardo GANDINI, Armando Krieger, Antonio TAURIELLO, and Alcides Lanza, presented concerts in Buenos Aires consisting of their own compositions and contemporary music from other countries.

Other important compositions by Hilda Dianda are *Núcleos* for two pianos, vibraphone, xylorimba, eight percussionists, and string orchestra (1963); *Estructuras* nos. 1, 2, and 3 for cello and piano (1960); String Quartet no. 3 (1963–1964); *Percusión 11,* for eleven percussionists (1963); *Ludus* no. 1 for orchestra (1968); *Ludus* no. 2 for eleven performers (1969); *Idá-ndá's* for three percussionists (1969); *a7* for cello and five tapes (1966); *Resonancias* no. 3 for cello and orchestra (1965); *Resonancias* no. 5 for two choirs (1967–1968); *Ludus* no. 3 for organ (1969); *Impromptu* for string orchestra (1970); and *Cadencias* no. 2 for violin and piano (1986).

– ALCIDES LANZA

DIAS, ANTÔNIO GONÇALVES

Antônio Gonçalves Dias (*b.* 10 August 1823; *d.* 3 November 1864), Brazilian poet. An outstanding romantic poet, Dias was the founder of truly national Brazilian literature. Romanticism represented perfectly the ideals of freedom, patriotism, and nativism so fervent in Brazil in the time of Independence. These sentiments were well expressed by Dias, whose work dealt mainly with Brazil's landscape and Indians (Indianism). He wrote exultant hymns to the beauty of tropical nature. With great imagination he treated Indian themes. Besides being a lyric poet, he was a prose writer, historian, ethnologist, and dramatist.

Born in Caxias, Maranhão, Dias was the illegitimate son of a Portuguese shopkeeper and a Brazilian *cafuza* (of mixed Indian and African blood). When his father married another woman, the child was separated from his mother and taken to live with the new couple. After his father's death, he went to Portugal to study at the University of Coimbra, where he received a bachelor's degree in 1845. His years in Portugal were very valuable. In addition to university work, he studied languages and literature, wrote intensively, made contact with great writers, and was loved and admired. Because of economic difficulties, however, he returned to Maranhão. In 1846 he went to Rio, where he published *Primeiros cantos* (First Songs, 1847), which was favorably reviewed by Alexandre Herculano. Other publications followed, including *Leonor de Mendonça* (1847); *Segundos cantos* (Second Songs, 1848), which contains "Sextilhas de Frei Antão" (Friar Antão's Sextets), a poem in the Portuguese troubadour style; and *Últimos cantos* (Last Songs, 1851).

Besides teaching positions, Dias held important government posts in Brazil and Europe. He published in Leipzig the second edition of his poems, titled *Cantos* (Songs, 1857), as well as *Os timbiras* (The Timbiras, 1857), and *Dicionário da língua tupi* (Dictionary of the Tupi Language, 1858). Additional works by Dias include *Obras póstumas* (6 vols., 1868–1869) and *Poesia completa e prosa escolhida* (1959).

In 1858 Dias traveled to Brazil, but in 1862 he returned to Europe seeking a cure for his poor health. Feeling worse, he sailed again for Brazil; although his wrecked ship was rescued from sinking, because he was ill, he was the only passenger who perished.

— MARIA ISABEL ABREU

DIAS, HENRIQUE

Henrique Dias (*d.* 8 June 1662), black military leader during the seventeenth-century Portuguese campaign against the Dutch occupation of northeastern Brazil. Although it is unknown whether or not he had ever been a slave, Henrique Dias was a free and literate man when he volunteered for service in 1633. At that time the Dutch were expanding their occupation of Pernambuco beyond the coastal towns of Recife and Olinda and would eventually overtake large portions of the northeastern captaincies.

In Brazil, Portuguese commander the Count of Torre granted Dias a patent in 1639 that carried the title "Governor of All Creoles, Blacks, and Mulattoes."

Initially the captain of a small force, Dias later commanded over three hundred men of color, some of whom were slaves. By 1636 he was a master of the guerrilla tactics that were then the basis of the Luso-Brazilian strategy against the Dutch. His skills as a military tactician were evident in all of his engagements, which ranged from his participation in the defense of Salvador (the capital of Bahia) in 1638 to his role in the campaign to recover territory in Alagoas in 1639. Returning to Pernambuco in 1645, Dias resumed his

part in the fight against the enemy, eventually traveling to Rio Grande do Norte, where he and his men took a Dutch fort in 1647. By 1648 he was in Olinda, where his fighting prowess contributed to the defeat of the enemy. Finally, he fought in the front lines in the recapture of Recife in January 1654.

Though subject to racist treatment during his long career, Dias received many honors for his service. In 1638, for example, King Philip IV awarded him a knighthood, a highly unusual status for a man of African descent. In Brazil, Portuguese commander the Count of Torre granted him a patent in 1639 that carried the title "Governor of All Creoles, Blacks, and Mulattoes." Finally, in March 1656, he traveled to Portugal, where, in an audience with the court, Dias requested and received the freedom of all slaves who had served in his *têrço* (unit) and the continued existence of his force, which was to have the rights and privileges of white units. Though he later died much as he had been born, in relative obscurity, his memory was preserved in the name given to all subsequent black militia companies. They were called the "Henriques."

— JUDITH L. ALLEN

DIAS GOMES, ALFREDO

Alfredo Dias Gomes (*b.* 1922), Brazilian playwright. Born in Bahia, Dias Gomes has tried and mastered all forms of drama, whether on the stage, radio, or television, and his theater has continued steadily to evolve. Always he has been both artist and social commentator. With his play *O pagador de promessas* (1960), Dias Gomes gained national prominence as a playwright. The central theme of the play is the tragic uphill struggle of the strong individual for true personal freedom in a capitalist society. This theme, a recurring one in Dias Gomes's theater, is closely related to two others: the problems of communication and intolerance, particularly religious intolerance, in modern society. The willful priest, every bit as intransigent as Zé, the title character, stands as the play's principal antagonist, and although Dias Gomes describes him as the symbol of universal rather than merely religious intolerance, the priest's attitude and actions constitute a rather caustic commentary on religious dogmatism. Yet another strength of the play is the adroitness with which the dramatist parallels the "Afro-Catholic syncretism" that characterizes the religious views of Zé and several other characters with a similar syncretism in setting and symbol. *O pagador,* then, with a compelling plot, a carefully elaborated classical structure, and a protagonist who is perhaps the most memorable character of all Brazilian drama, deservedly ranks as one of the best plays of that country's theatrical tradition.

It is in *O berço do herói* (1965) that the satiric humor and the expressionistic techniques introduced in *A revolução dos beatos* (1962) and *Odorico, o bem amado* (1962) find their fruition. The work concerns itself chiefly with the problem of true individual liberty in a capitalist society, much as does *O pagador*. Various critics, in fact, have stated that *O berço* is a very pessimistic answer to the questions concerning individual freedom and liberty that are raised in *O pagador*. Both heroes experience one phase of Calvary—Zé the journey with the cross and Jorge the trial. The similarity between the plays is such, in fact, that they seem to comprise a dramatic experiment in which the same set of basic ingredients is poured into two distinct molds—one tragic and the other burlesque. The play, although long banned, is perhaps the best satire to be found in the contemporary Brazilian theater.

Dias Gomes's sixth major play, *O santo inquérito,* was first presented in Rio in September 1966. Based on the life of Branca Dias, it is the only one of his works whose setting is in the rather distant past: the year 1750, in the state of Paraíba. The major concerns or themes, just as in *O pagador,* are individual freedom within a tightly structured societal boundary (i.e., the church), existential communication, and religious fanaticism. The Inquisition is employed primarily as a metaphor to describe military and political repression in Brazil in the 1960s. Following *O santo inquérito* and representing yet another experiment in structure and technique is *Dr. Getúlio, sua vida e sua glória,* a piece in two acts in which verse and prose are mixed. It dramatizes the period of ultimate crisis in the life of the president-dictator Getúlio VARGAS—the crisis that precipitated his suicide in 1954.

In *Os campeões do mundo,* Dias Gomes tells the story of two lovers who are involved in terrorism during the World Soccer Cup in Rio in the 1970s. It is a story of political oppression and torture whose outcome is known to the public; the dialectic of how and why things happened takes precedence over plot. With little of the usual interest in the denouement, spectators can be more objective and better able to exercise critical judgment, which is the goal of the author.

– RICHARD A. MAZZARA

DÍAZ, ADOLFO

Adolfo Díaz (*b.* 1874; *d.* 27 January 1964), president of Nicaragua (1911–1916, 1926–1928). Previously a secretary for La Luz and Los Angeles Mining Company, a U.S. firm based in Bluefields, the Costa Rican–born

Díaz entered Nicaraguan politics during the Conservative overthrow of Liberal dictator José Santos ZELAYA in 1909. He served as a source of funds for the rebel leader Juan ESTRADA. After Zelaya's ouster, Estrada became president and Díaz, his vice president. On 8 May 1911, Estrada resigned in the face of a revolt led by Minister of War Luis Mena. Díaz succeeded to the presidency and quickly cultivated U.S. goodwill. One month into his presidency he signed a treaty with the U.S. that permitted the Nicaraguan government to negotiate a loan with U.S. private banks.

Díaz desired financial and political security, but his forging of closer ties between Nicaragua and the U.S. caused him to lose support at home. Mena declared that Díaz had sold out, and sought supporters in the National Assembly. In July 1912 Mena led a revolt against Díaz. Although Conservative Party leader Emiliano CHAMORRO defeated Mena, Díaz failed to control this tumultuous situation and finally turned to the U.S. for assistance. President William Howard Taft dispatched the marines on 4 August 1912.

Díaz was reelected president in 1926 after Chamorro's unsuccessful coup d'état. A reinstated national assembly acknowledged him as president, and the U.S. promptly recognized his government. The former Liberal vice president, Juan Bautista SACASA, however, claimed the presidency for himself, and with the support of José María MONCADA, rose against the Conservative administration. With the help of the U.S., Díaz was able to end the resulting civil war, and gain control of the government until 1928. During this period he cooperated with the U.S. in the development and training of the National Guard.

– SHANNON BELLAMY

DÍAZ, FÉLIX, JR.

Félix Díaz, Jr. (*b.* 17 February 1868; *d.* 9 July 1945), Mexican general, diplomat, and politician. He was the son of Félix Díaz (1833–1872), a general and governor of Oaxaca (1867–1871), and a nephew of Porfirio DÍAZ, the dictatorial president. Díaz is best known for his role in the overthrow of President Francisco I. MADERO in February 1913 during the so-called *Decena Trágica* (tragic ten days).

Born in the city of Oaxaca, Díaz graduated from the National Military College with a degree in engineering in 1888. By 1909 he had become a brigadier general. He served as alternate federal deputy from Oaxaca (1894–1896) and Veracruz (1896–1900) and federal deputy from Veracruz (1900–1912). In 1902 he was a candidate for governor of Oaxaca, and in 1910 he served as that state's interim chief executive. He was a member of the Exploratory Geographic Commission (1901); consul general in Chile (1902–1904); inspector of police, Mexico City (1904); chief of the presidential staff (1909); and ambassador to Japan (1913).

Díaz was separated from the army and jailed by President Madero, who overthrew Díaz's uncle, Porfirio. Díaz initiated, along with generals Manuel Mondragón (1859–1922) and Bernardo REYES (1850–1913), the February 1913 rebellion against Madero that, when joined by federal army commander General Victoriano HUERTA, successfully ousted the president. Díaz subsequently lost the power struggle he waged with Huerta, briefly served as ambassador to Japan, and then went into self-imposed exile in Havana and New York. In 1916 he returned to Mexico to head the National Reorganizing Army against revolutionary chief Venustiano CARRANZA. He remained active against the Carranza regime until 1920, when he was again exiled until 1937. He died in Veracruz.

– DAVID LAFRANCE

DÍAZ, GONZALO

Gonzalo Díaz (*b.* 1947), Chilean artist. Throughout his career Díaz has addressed what he has termed the conceptualization of Chile as "cultural landscape" and the troubled status of painting in contemporary Chilean art. Born in Santiago, he studied art at the Escuela de Bellas Artes, Universidad de Chile, Santiago, from 1965 to 1969. Like the conceptually minded artists associated with the Avanzada, he was strongly affected by the institution of General Augusto Pinochet's military dictatorship in 1973. However, while most of the Avanzada artists abandoned painting, Díaz remained captivated by its theory, practice, and history in the era of photography. In the late 1970s he began producing labyrinthine installations that incorporate paintings as well as objects. His painting *Historia sentimental de la pintura chilena* (1982) exemplifies his central thematic concerns: the troubled status of painting in contemporary Chilean art, which in the late 1970s and early 1980s was largely dominated by conceptual and photographic practices, and the relationship between painting and the construction of national identity. Díaz has taught at the Universidad de Chile (1969), the Universidad Católica (1974), and the Instituto de Arte Contemporáneo (1977–1986), all in Santiago.

– JOHN ALAN FARMER

DÍAZ, JORGE

Jorge Díaz (*b.* 1930) was born to Spanish parents in Rosario, Argentina, but raised in Chile. He graduated

in architecture and first entered the theater as a scenographer. The Latin American playwright most closely associated with theater of the absurd, he achieved early success with *El cepillo de dientes* (1961), a two-character play that in language and structure epitomizes the clichés of contemporary life. Although his linguistic dexterity creates an illusion of vacuous and sterile relationships and the difficulties of authentic communication, his plays are underscored by a strong social and political reality. His early pieces played with language, time, music, humor, and the stultifying effects of bourgeois society.

Díaz' early pieces played with language, time, music, humor, and the stultifying effects of bourgeois society.

In 1965 Díaz emigrated to Spain to escape the administrative responsibilities of ICTUS, a vanguard theater in Santiago. In Spain his plays became more aggressive, using mixed-media techniques to denounce greed and insensitivity, such as a massacre in a Brazilian *favela* and the ITT intervention in Chilean politics. After Franco's death in 1975 brought a new sense of freedom to the Spanish theater, Díaz began to experiment with two distinctly different styles, one focusing on the sociopolitical, the other more personal and intimate. He wrote about the archetypal qualities of sex and death, which he claimed was to write about life. Some plays were intended for a Madrid audience, others for Santiago. On two occasions Díaz has dramatized his compatriot, the Nobel laureate Pablo NERUDA, most recently in *Pablo Neruda viene volando* (1991). Díaz's trenchant style and playful language have earned him the epithet of "absurdist" writer, but he seeks only to express his view of contemporary human existence. Díaz is also a prolific writer of theater for children.

– GEORGE WOODYARD

DÍAZ, JOSÉ EDUVIGIS

José Eduvigis Díaz (*b.* 1833; *d.* 7 February 1867), Paraguayan soldier. Born in Pirayú, Díaz entered the military at age nineteen and showed sufficient promise as a soldier to receive several important appointments by the early 1860s. He was police chief of Asunción when the War of the Triple Alliance broke out in 1864. One year later, Díaz participated in the Corrientes campaign, during which he caught the eye of President Francisco Solano LÓPEZ for having ferried 100,000 head of cattle to the Paraguayan lines with the Allied armies in close pursuit. Díaz rose quickly to the rank of general and fought in engagements at Corrales, Tuyutí, and Boquerón. His greatest achievement, however, came in September 1866, when his troops, defending reinforced trenchworks at Curupayty, repulsed a massive Allied attack, killing 9,000 of the enemy and suffering almost no losses themselves.

For a short time, Díaz was feted as López's favorite, but in January 1867, while on a reconnaissance patrol along the Paraguay River, his canoe was hit by a Brazilian cannonball, which shattered his leg. Despite the ministrations of several army doctors, septicemia soon set in, and Díaz died at López's encampment at Paso Pucú.

– THOMAS L. WHIGHAM

DÍAZ, JOSÉ PEDRO

José Pedro Díaz (*b.* 1921), Uruguayan writer, literary critic, and educator. Uruguay's foremost critic of French literature, Díaz often writes about French as well as Uruguayan literature in the weekly *Correo de los viernes*. He is also one of Uruguay's most important novelists. His *Los fuegos de San Telmo* (1964), one of the best novels produced by the Uruguayan Generation of 1945, investigates the Italian origins of Uruguay's majority population. *Partes de naufragios* (1969) focuses on the complacent life in Montevideo of the 1930s and 1940s, a view that assumes ironic dimensions, given the productive and moral crisis affecting the country at the time of its publication. Also important are Díaz's conceptual essays treating the Spanish poet Gustavo Adolfo Bécquer (1953), the Uruguayan fantasy writer Felisberto HERNÁNDEZ, and the poet Delmira AGUSTINI.

– WILLIAM H. KATRA

DÍAZ, PORFIRIO

Porfirio Díaz (*b.* 15 September 1830; *d.* 2 July 1915), president of Mexico (1876–1880 and 1884–1911). In recognition of his prominence in Mexican politics and government, the period from 1876 to 1911 is called the PORFIRIATO. Much of the literature written about Díaz during his presidency reflects the sycophantic adulation of his biographers, while that dating from the Revolution of 1910 has tended to castigate him as a repressive dictator. His life, of course, was more complicated.

Porfirio Díaz was born in the city of Oaxaca, the sixth child of a modest innkeeper and his wife. His father, José de la Cruz Díaz, died before Porfirio reached the age of three. His mother, Petrona Mori, was unable to keep the business going. As soon as he was old enough,

Porfirio was sent to work for a carpenter, but he found time for his primary studies. At the age of fifteen, he began attending the seminary, apparently with the aid of his godfather, the canon and later bishop of Oaxaca, José Agustín Domínguez. Porfirio interrupted his studies to enlist in the national guard during the war of 1846–1847 with the United States but saw no fighting. After graduating in 1849, Díaz refused to be ordained and insisted on studying law at the Institute of Sciences and Arts, passing his first examination in civil and canon law in 1853.

President Porfirio Díaz at the horse races at the Hipódromo de Peralvillo, Mexico City, ca. 1903. (La Fototeca del Inah)

With the triumph of the Plan of Ayutla (1854), Díaz was named subprefect of Ixtlán, the beginning of his political career. He joined the Oaxaca national guard in 1856 and fought for the liberals during the War of the Reform. He was promoted to the rank of brigadier general in August 1861. Elected to Congress that same year, he served only briefly.

Porfirio Díaz first achieved fame as a result of his crucial role in the victory against the invading French troops at Puebla on 5 May 1862. The following year he was twice captured but managed to escape and return to the struggle, sustaining guerrilla warfare against the occupying French army throughout 1866 and taking the city of Oaxaca on 31 October of that year. The following year he led his Army of the East to victory at Puebla on 2 April and drove the imperial army from the national capital on 21 June.

Díaz opposed President Benito JUÁREZ's *convocatoria* of 1867, which attempted to increase presidential power and alter the constitution by referendum. Díaz regarded the *convocatoria* as both unconstitutional and a personal affront. The legislature of Oaxaca lauded him in recognition of his efforts against the French, gave him the hacienda of La Noria, and supported him for the presidency of the republic. After Juárez's reelection (1867), Díaz resigned from the army and turned his attention to agriculture, his investment in the telegraph connecting Mexico and Oaxaca, and the presidential election in 1871. With another reelection of Juárez, Díaz rebelled. His Plan of la Noria claimed the election had been fraudulent and demanded that the presidency be limited to a single term. Díaz failed to dislodge Juárez, who died in mid-1872. Sebastián LERDO DE TEJADA, head of the supreme court, ascended to the presidency and was soon elected to a four-year term. Díaz retired to his hacienda, made furniture, and prepared for another campaign.

Díaz rebelled against Lerdo in January 1876, charging that the elections scheduled for July of that year would be fraudulent. His Plan of Tuxtepec retained the principle of no reelection and insisted on municipal autonomy. An expert in guerrilla warfare from his days fighting the French, Díaz designed a military strategy for the revolt that called for the use of hit-and-run tactics to force the government to diffuse its forces. Contrary to traditional histories, the "battle" of Icamole on 20 May did not indicate that Díaz's effort was crumbling. Although portrayed by Lerdo's government as a great victory over forces commanded personally by Díaz, the rebel leader was not present and his subordinate in charge of the encounter was under orders only to reconnoiter and skirmish with the enemy, not to engage in a decisive battle.

In any case, Lerdo's reelection prompted José María IGLESIAS to charge fraud and refuse to recognize the results. As head of the Supreme Court and next in line for the presidency, Iglesias tried to assume that office himself. Faced with the opposition of both Iglesias and Díaz, Lerdo resigned and went into exile. Díaz offered to acknowledge Iglesias as president if new elections could be held soon. Iglesias refused, but soon resigned when his forces were unable to stop Díaz's advance. After holding elections, Díaz took formal possession of the presidency on 5 May 1877 for a term to end on 30 November 1881.

Although the image of a repressive Díaz has been pervasive in the post-Revolutionary literature, his first term was notable for his efforts to conciliate his rivals and opponents as well as foreign governments. Díaz sent the proposal for no reelection to Congress and supported efforts to increase political competition for state and municipal posts as well. He attempted to divide and rule the economic elite by creating rivals for political power and expanding economic opportunities.

When the Grant administration in the United States attached conditions to its recognition of his government, Díaz arranged for payments on Mexico's debt. Rutherford B. Hayes soon succeeded Grant and raised the stakes, ordering U.S. troops to cross into Mexico in pursuit of raiders, bandits, and rustlers. Díaz ordered Mexican troops to resist any invasion, and only forbearance on both sides prevented a major escalation. Díaz defused the crisis by wooing U.S. investors (among them former president Grant) with concessions, thereby ending the clamor for intervention and achieving formal recognition of his government in 1878. To balance the tremendous weight of the United States, Díaz sought to renew ties to France and other European powers, using similar efforts to attract investment and diplomatic recognition.

At the end of his first term, Díaz made good on his promise and did not run for reelection; he accepted the post of secretary of development under President Manuel GONZÁLEZ and served as governor of the state of Oaxaca. In 1884, Díaz was again elected president, losing his antipathy to reelection in 1888, 1892, 1904, and 1910. He provided stable government, balanced the budget, and assured economic growth but increased Mexico's reliance on foreign capital and the subservience of Mexican capital and labor to foreign control. His power became dictatorial; he prevented the election of his opponents and muzzled the press. But if his skills had been limited to repression, he would never have lasted as long as he did. Díaz blocked formation of political parties but encouraged rivalries between elite factions. The two major contenders for favor were the *cien-*

tíficos, led by his father-in-law, Manuel ROMERO RUBIO (and after his death by Díaz's finance minister, José Yves LIMANTOUR), and a cohort of military officers, led by Manuel González and later by Bernardo REYES. Recent research suggests Díaz was able to exercise a relative degree of autonomy from economic interests. He acted to limit the expropriation of Indian lands by surveying companies and was flexible in dealing with peasant and labor grievances until the turn of the century.

After 1900, the system began to fall apart as the result of economic depression, political organization, increasing nationalism, blatant repression, and the fundamental uncertainty generated by the president's age. Díaz was either unwilling or unable to maintain the complex system of rivalries and balancing of contending interests that had provided stability for decades. In 1908, in an interview with the U.S. newspaper reporter James CREELMAN, he appeared to announce that Mexico was ready for competitive elections and that he would not run for reelection in 1910. Later Díaz changed his mind, but not until after the published remarks had created a sensation.

As he neared the age of eighty, it was obvious to everyone else that Díaz could not remain president much longer. Every level of Mexican society clamored for more nationalistic policies, from the *científicos,* who resented the interventionism of the U.S. government and the increasing size and power of U.S. corporations, to the railroad workers and miners, who were paid half as much as foreigners for the same work. Díaz rejected economic nationalism, but U.S. interests saw him as increasingly anti-American while his domestic opponents accused him of selling out to the United States. Finally, Díaz lost power the way he first gained it, as a result of guerrilla warfare. On 21 May 1911, his representative signed the Treaty of Ciudad Juárez with Francisco MADERO. Díaz resigned the presidency on 25 May, and by the end of the month was on his way to exile in Paris, where he died.

– D. F. STEVENS

DÍAZ AROSEMENA, DOMINGO

Domingo Díaz Arosemena (*b.* 25 June 1875; *d.* 23 August 1949), Panamanian politician and president (1948–1949) and a member of one of the most prominent political families in the country. He spent many years in public service as a member of the Panama City Council and deputy to the National Assembly. After the revolution of 1931 Díaz Arosemena founded the Doctrinary Liberal Party, one of the many offshoots of the Liberal Party after the revolution. He was a candidate for president in the 1936 elections, one of the most

hotly contested elections in the history of the country, but lost to the official candidate, Juan Demóstenes AROSEMENA. In 1948, Díaz Arosemena won the presidency with the backing of the country's major political forces. He died the following year.

– JUAN MANUEL PÉREZ

DÍAZ CASTRO, EUGENIO

Eugenio Díaz Castro (*b.* 1804; *d.* 11 April 1865), Colombian author noted for his novels and local-color sketches (*cuadros de costumbre*). Born in Soacha, Díaz studied in Bogotá's Colegio de San Bartolomé but spent most of his life in agricultural endeavors. When he was over fifty, he became acquainted with José María Vergara y Vergara, who published his sketches of rural life in Vergara y Vergara's literary magazine *El Mosaico.* Díaz also wrote three novels: *Manuela* (1858), *Los aguinaldos en Chapinero* (1873), and *El rejo de enlazar* (1873), only the first of which is well regarded. Set in 1856 in a small town near Bogotá, it is partly a romantic love story centered around the simple but sharp-witted Manuela. The novel also effectively portrays the ideological disputes of the era and points up the gulf between recently enacted reform legislation and the realities of rural Colombia.

– HELEN DELPAR

DÍAZ DE GUZMÁN, RUY

Ruy Díaz de Guzmán (*b.* ca. 1558; *d.* June 1629), known primarily for being the first creole historian of the Río de la Plata. Díaz de Guzmán was born in or near Asunción (modern Paraguay) and spent most of his early adult years fighting Indian wars and settling towns in the Río de la Plata, Paraguay, and Tucumán.

Díaz de Guzmán spent most of his early adult years fighting Indian wars and settling towns in the Río de la Plata, Paraguay, and Tucumán.

Between the founding of Santa Fe in 1573, the recolonization of Buenos Aires in 1580, and the division of La Plata into two major jurisdictions in 1617, most littoral and interior towns had been permanently established. Díaz de Guzmán's history of the first half-century of Spanish rule is composed mainly of the accounts of town foundings and stories surrounding the early post-Conquest years. Known as the *Argentina Manuscrita,* it was first printed in 1835 and has had subsequent editions. Díaz de Guzmán died in Asunción. Ricardo Rojas (1882–1957), the Argentine writer and scholar whose pioneering *Historia de la literatura argentina* (4 vols., 1917) is a milestone in Argentine scholarship, traces influences of Díaz de Guzmán's history from the sixteenth to the twentieth century.

– NICHOLAS P. CUSHNER

DÍAZ DEL CASTILLO, BERNAL

Bernal Díaz del Castillo (*b.* ca. 1495; *d.* 3 February 1584), Spanish conquistador and author. In a passage from his *Historia verdadera de la conquista de la Nueva España* (True History of the Conquest of New Spain), Díaz establishes his birthplace as Medina del Campo and recalls his first journey to America in Pedro Arias de AVILA's expedition to the Darien in 1514. He subsequently participated in the explorations of the Yucatán by Francisco HERNÁNDEZ DE CÓRDOBA (1517) and of the Gulf of Mexico by Juan de GRIJALVA (1518), both of which preceded Cortés's conquest in 1519. After the Conquest, Díaz was awarded several *encomiendas* in Guatemala.

Like the other *encomenderos*, Díaz was adversely affected by a series of decrees in the mid-sixteenth century that eliminated *encomiendas* in perpetuity and personal services. However, his description of his poverty in the *Historia verdadera* should be taken as a rhetorical device. There are numerous documents that disprove his complaints about not having been sufficiently rewarded for his participation in the Conquest. Recently critics have insisted that his claims of "lacking letters" and his criticism of Francisco López de Gómara's elevated style in the *Historia de las Indias y la conquista de México* (1552) are a subterfuge to mask the fact that Bartolomé de LAS CASAS is the true target of his attacks. Díaz's and Gómara's styles are not as different as Díaz would lead us to believe; both cultivate a simple and clear language. Las Casas's condemnations of the colonial order, however, influenced the decrees against the *encomienda* system, and it was during the early 1550s that Díaz decided to write his *Historia verdadera*. He constantly revised the work until he finally finished it in 1568. The *Historia verdadera*, however, was not published until 1632. Although Díaz's expressed intent in writing the *Historia* was to better the lot of his children and grandchildren, his story is nevertheless a riveting account of the Conquest that ultimately constitutes a defense of the conquistadores. He died in Guatemala.

– JOSÉ RABASA

DÍAZ LOZANO, ARGENTINA

Argentina Díaz Lozano (*b.* 15 December 1909), Honduran novelist. Born in Santa Rosa de Copán, Honduras, Díaz Lozano moved to Guatemala, the setting for many of her novels, in 1912. She studied at the University of San Carlos and became the first woman to graduate in journalism. A prolific writer (translated into French and English), she published her first novel at age seventeen and has received many awards for both her fiction and her journalism, among them the National Prize for literature in Honduras (1968) and awards from Guatemala, Brazil, and Italy. In 1957 ex-president Juan José Arévalo nominated her for the Nobel Prize in literature.

Her fiction belongs to the regionalist school predating the "Boom" of the 1960s in Latin American letters. Her novels focus on local themes, often exposing the plight of the poor, especially the tragic circumstances of Guatemalan Indians. Nevertheless, she shows little willingness to explore underlying issues of race, gender, and politics which might threaten the status quo. Her portrayal of women and Indians, while compassionate, essentially reflects the romantic and patronizing perspectives of the Ladino.

– ANN GONZÁLEZ

DÍAZ ORDAZ, GUSTAVO

Gustavo Díaz Ordaz (*b.* 11 March 1911; *d.* 15 July 1979), president of Mexico (1964–1970). Díaz Ordaz was the last president to preside over a period of consistent, stable economic growth, but his administration was widely condemned for his handling of student unrest on the occasion of the 1968 Mexico City Olympics.

Díaz Ordaz was born in Chalchicomula, Ciudad Serdán, in the state of Puebla. His father was a government accountant, his grandfather was General José María Díaz Ordaz, and one of his direct ancestors was the conquistador and chronicler Bernal DÍAZ DEL CASTILLO. After studying in Oaxaca, he received his law degree from the University of Puebla on 8 February 1937. While still a student he had begun his public career, serving as a court clerk (1932). Upon graduation he became a prosecuting attorney, then a federal agent, and later director of the labor arbitration board in Puebla.

After serving briefly as vice rector of the University of Puebla (1940–1941), Díaz Ordaz became secretary-general of government in Puebla and then federal deputy from that state (1943–1946). He moved from the lower to the upper chamber, serving as senator (1946–1952), and then joined the government secretariat, first as director-general of legal affairs (1952–1956), then as *oficial mayor* (1956–1958), and, finally, as secretary of government (1958–1964) in the administration of Adolfo LÓPEZ MATEOS.

The successful PRI candidate for president in 1964, he held that office when the Olympic Games took place in Mexico City in the fall of 1968. His government then became entangled in a conflict with a student movement that, like such movements in many other countries, involved a number of issues. When students staged a demonstration in the Plaza of the Three Cultures in the Tlatelolco district, the government called out army troops, who fired on the demonstrators, leaving hundreds of students and bystanders dead. The repercussions of this event produced the generation of Mexican political and intellectual leaders of the 1990s, including former President Carlos SALINAS, and altered the relationship between intellectuals and the government. Even more, this event raised serious questions about the legitimacy of the Mexican political and economic model and introduced pressures for political liberalization, the effects of which were to be seen in the 1970s and 1980s, culminating in the 1988 presidential election.

Even before the debacle of 1968, Díaz Ordaz had discouraged the early efforts of PRI president Carlos A. MADRAZO to democratize the party in 1965. As a result of these political failures, the Mexican presidency suffered a loss of prestige. After his presidency, his successor appointed him ambassador to Spain (1977), but he was so unpopular, and the public outcry against him so intense, that he resigned the appointment before serving and remained out of the public eye until his death.

– RODERIC AI CAMP

DÍAZ SOTO Y GAMA, ANTONIO

Antonio Díaz Soto y Gama (*b.* 1880; *d.* 1967), leading precursor of the Mexican Revolution. With Camillo Arriaga and Ricardo FLORES MAGÓN, he founded the Club Liberal Ponciano Arriaga and was one of its four secretaries. This organization later served as an organizational base for the Liberal Party. Díaz Soto is also remembered for his lively participation in debates in the Chamber of Deputies in the 1920s and as one of the founders of the National Agrarian Party in 1920.

He was born into the middle-class provincial family of Conrado Díaz Soto and Concepción Gama, and graduated from the Scientific and Literary Institute of San Luis Potosí as a lawyer in 1900. He later taught at the National Preparatory School and University. While in exile for his opposition to Porfirio DÍAZ, he became a Liberal Party activist. During the Mexican Revolution he supported Emiliano ZAPATA and, although he was

named secretary of justice by the Convention government in 1915, he refused the post. In 1920, and again in 1927–1928, he gave his political support to Alvaro OBREGÓN. He ended his political career as vice president of the Mexican Democratic Party in 1945 and then returned to intellectual activities.

– RODERIC AI CAMP

DÍAZ VÉLEZ, JOSÉ MIGUEL

José Miguel Díaz Vélez (*b.* 1770; *d.* 1833), Argentine patriot. Born in Tucumán and trained as a lawyer, Díaz Vélez was military commandant of Entre Ríos province from 1810 to 1814. He later held various positions in Buenos Aires. In 1825 he was a member of a mission to Upper Peru that sought to treat with Simón BOLÍVAR concerning the future status of that region and collaboration in a possible war against Brazil. The mission was a failure, as Upper Peru was by then committed to becoming a separate nation-state and Bolívar proved ambivalent regarding an anti-Brazilian alliance. Díaz Vélez served in the Unitarist regime set up in Buenos Aires by Juan LAVALLE in 1828; when it collapsed, he emigrated to Uruguay, where he died at Paysandú.

– DAVID BUSHNELL

DICKMANN, ADOLFO

Adolfo Dickmann (*b.* 1882; *d.* 1 September 1938), Argentine Socialist councilman and congressman. Born in Finland, Dickmann immigrated as a youth with his family to Entre Ríos Province, Argentina, in the late nineteenth century. After joining the Socialist Party in 1900, he received his degree in dentistry from the University of Buenos Aires in 1905 and established a practice in Morón in the province of Buenos Aires. He served first on the city council of Morón, and then in 1914 was elected to the provincial legislature, where he introduced legislation to create a provincial department of labor, to modify the tax on inheritances, and to regulate child and female labor.

In 1919, Dickmann was elected to the city council of the federal capital and then served three terms as a Socialist representative to the national Chamber of Deputies (1922–1926, 1926–1930, and 1932–1936). A prominent member of the Socialist delegation in the national Congress, he was associated with legislation intended to improve the management of municipal administration and to better the living and working conditions of employees, workers, and rural laborers. Himself a naturalized citizen, Dickmann wrote several works on immigration and nationalism as well as on tax policy, collective bargaining, and state control of the petroleum industry.

— RICHARD J. WALTER

DICKMANN, ENRIQUE

Enrique Dickmann (*b.* 20 December 1874; *d.* 30 December 1955), Argentine Socialist congressman and party leader. Born in present-day Latvia, Dickmann settled in Argentina in 1890. He became a naturalized citizen in 1897 and graduated from the medical school of the University of Buenos Aires with a medal of honor in 1904. In 1905 he was appointed chief of the clinic in a local hospital. As with several other Socialists, however, he became better known as a politician than as a physician. He joined the Socialist Party in 1896 and soon became an important figure in that organization, serving as editor of the party newspaper, *La Vanguardia,* first in 1898 and then for several periods thereafter.

Dickmann was a vocal opponent of the rise of fascism in Europe and warned of its possible extension to and growing influence in Argentina.

Dickmann was elected for the first time to the national Chamber of Deputies from the federal capital in 1914 and served in that body for more than three decades (1914–1916, 1916–1920, 1920–1924, 1924–1928, 1932–1936, 1936–1940, and 1942–1946). An energetic and outspoken legislator, Dickmann was a prominent figure in the Socialist bloc of deputies. He had a hand in most of the Socialists' initiatives of these years, ranging from measures to promote and protect the rights of workers, including women and children, to opposition to what the Socialists viewed as overly favorable concessions to foreign investors. In 1931–1932, Dickmann played an important role in helping to form a joint presidential ticket with the Progressive Democratic Party, one of the few instances when the Socialists agreed to participate in a political coalition. In the late 1930s and early 1940s, Dickmann was a vocal opponent of the rise of fascism in Europe and warned of its possible extension to and growing influence in Argentina. He was close to party founder Juan B. JUSTO and remained steadfast in his loyalty to the central party until the 1940s, when, contrary to the stance of most Socialists, he expressed sympathy with the goals and achievements of President Juan PERÓN (1946–1955). The author of numerous books, his best-

known work is his autobiography, *Recuerdos de un militante socialista* (1949).

— RICHARD J. WALTER

DIEGO, ELISEO

Eliseo Diego (*b.* 2 July 1920; *d.* 2 March 1994), Cuban poet and essayist. Diego was born in Havana, where he studied law for two years at the University of Havana. He was part of the editorial board of the literary publication *Clavileño* and was one of the founders of the influential magazine *Orígenes,* where his first poems and short stories appeared between 1944 and 1956. He taught English and served as inspector of English instruction for the Ministry of Education. In 1959 he earned a degree in education from the University of Havana. In 1962 Diego was put in charge of the Department of Children's Literature at the José Martí National Library in Havana, a post he occupied until 1970. He was secretary of public relations for the Cuban Union of Writers and Artists (UNEAC), and served on juries for several important literary contests in Cuba, including those of the UNEAC and the Casa de las Américas. He traveled widely to represent Cuba officially at international cultural events.

In 1993 Diego was awarded Mexico's Juan Rulfo literary prize, among the most important in Latin America. One of the foremost Cuban poets of the century, Diego exerted great influence on the younger generation of Cuban poets, especially after the publication of his first book, *En la calzada de Jesús del Monte* (1949). There is one compendium of his poems in prose, essays, and short stories (*Prosas escogidas,* 1983) and another of his poetry up to 1983 (*Poesía*). Both were published in Havana in beautiful editions. Other works by Diego include *Entre la dicha y la tiniebla: Antología poetica, 1949–1985* (1986), and *Veintiséis poemas recientes* (1986). His poetry has been translated widely. Diego died in Mexico City.

— ROBERTO VALERO

DIEGO, JOSÉ DE

José de Diego (*b.* 16 April 1866; *d.* 16 July 1918), Puerto Rican poet. Born in Aguadilla, Puerto Rico, de Diego studied law at the University of Barcelona in Spain, where he began writing poetry and prose. After completing his degree in Havana in 1892, he returned to Puerto Rico and became a prosecutor, later serving as undersecretary of justice and government, congressional representative, and Supreme Court justice. A staunch autonomist, he advocated the primacy of the Spanish language and Puerto Rico's independence from the United States. He was Speaker of the House of Representatives from 1907 until his death, president of the Union Party from 1914 to 1916, and president of the Puerto Rico Athenaeum from 1916 to 1918. De Diego was famous as an orator and for his books of poetry, among them *Pomarrosas* (Rose apples, 1904), *Cantos de rebeldía* (Songs of rebellion, 1916), and *Cantos de Pitirre* (Songs of Pitirre, published posthumously in 1949). Patriotism, Puerto Rico's country life, Americanism, the Antilles, and romantic love are his major themes. He also published a volume of selected prose, *Nuevas campañas* (New campaigns) in 1916.

– ESTELLE IRIZARRY

DIOMEDE, MIGUEL

Miguel Diomede (*b.* 20 July 1902; *d.* 15 October 1974), Argentine painter. Diomede was born in La Boca, an Italian bohemian neighborhood on the outskirts of Buenos Aires, where he lived and worked all his life, except for a short trip to Italy in 1954. A self-taught artist, he earned a living in humble jobs (street photographer, stevedore, hospital orderly, ship painter). He received several awards, including the first prize at the Salón de La Plata in Buenos Aires Province, 1957, and the bronze medal at the International Exhibition of Brussels, 1958. In 1959 he had a show at the Organization of American States in Washington, D.C. He became a member of the National Academy of Fine Arts in Buenos Aires in 1973. In 1974, two months before his death, he had a retrospective exhibition at the Galería LAASA in Buenos Aires.

The Argentine critic Damián Bayón called Diomede "one of the great melancholics," comparing his style to that of Eugenio Daneri. Diomede's work is marked by soft tones and large-scale composition. The elegance of his still lifes is immediately suggestive of the Italian Giorgio Morandi. He had a refined perception of reality and a soft sense of rhythm.

– AMALIA CORTINA ARAVENA

DISCÉPOLO, ENRIQUE SANTOS

Enrique Santos Discépolo (*b.* 27 March 1901; *d.* 23 December 1951), Argentine radio commentator, movie director, and composer of tangos. Born in Buenos Aires and the brother of the neogrotesque dramatist Armando Discépolo, Enrique Santos was known as "Discepolín" to distinguish him from Armando. Discépolo participated fully in the enormous expansion of commercial popular culture based in Buenos Aires in the golden years following World War I and the 1930 watershed marked by economic collapse and the country's first

fascist-inspired military dictatorship. A radio personality of considerable note and a successful movie director, Discépolo also wrote some of the most famous tangos of the period, compositions that have become an integral part of the classical repertoire: "¿Qué vachaché?" "Esta noche me emborracho," "¿Qué sapa, señor?" "Chorra," and, perhaps one of the most famous tango lyrics of all time, "Cambalache." The latter was banned by the military dictatorship in the late 1970s because of its harshly pessimistic tone, which was interpreted as socially disruptive.

– DAVID WILLIAM FOSTER

DITTBORN, EUGENIO

Eugenio Dittborn (*b.* 1943), Chilean artist. Born in Santiago, Dittborn studied painting and printmaking at universities in Chile and Europe from 1962 to 1969. Like many Chilean artists of his generation, he rejects traditional painting and the conservative values he believes it embodies. In the 1970s Dittborn became a leading member of the Avanzada, a group of Chilean artists and critics who developed an artistic language of metaphor and analogy related to conceptual art, in part to criticize General Augusto Pinochet's military dictatorship. In 1983 he produced his first Pinturas Aeropostales (Airmail Paintings), the works for which he has become best known. Consisting of appropriated photographic images, as well as drawings, texts, and objects, applied to wrapping paper and—after 1988—synthetic nonwoven fabric, they are folded in envelopes and airmailed to exhibitions throughout the world. Quintessential examples of the political-conceptual art Dittborn helped pioneer, they address, among other issues, the peripheral condition to which Latin Americans are often subject. He lives in Santiago.

– JOHN ALAN FARMER

DOBLES SEGREDA, LUIS

Luis Dobles Segreda (*b.* 17 January 1891; *d.* 27 October 1956), Costa Rican educator, writer, and diplomat. Born in Heredia, Dobles Segreda attended the Liceo de Costa Rica high school where he was taught by well-known intellectual Joaquín García Monge. In 1910 he became professor of Spanish at the Liceo and began writing articles for the *Havana Post,* as well as other newspapers, and founded, with others, the journal *Selenia.* Subsequently he taught at the Normal School in Heredia and in 1917 became its director. He received graduate degrees in education (1918), geography (1925), philology and grammar (1929), and literature (1930) from that school. He had studied English in his youth and in 1927 taught at Marquette University, and also at the Louisiana State Normal College. He was General Director (1927) and Minister of Education of Costa Rica in 1926–1928, 1930–1932, and 1936. Dobles Segreda served as minister plenipotentiary in Chile, Argentina, Spain, France, Belgium, and the Vatican. In 1927 he served on the municipal council of Heredia, his hometown, and was Costa Rica's delegate to the International Congress of Education in Paris. He wrote fifteen books about Costa Rica, among them *Por el amor de Dios* (1918), *Rosa mística: Historia y tradiciones* (1920), *El libro del héroe: Documentos históricos* (1926), *Caña brava* (1926), and his nine-volume *Indice bibliográfico de Costa Rica* (1927–1935). He assembled a comprehensive collection of books about Costa Rica which the Library of Congress purchased in 1943 and microfilmed in 1995. Dobles Segreda wrote articles about education and language in the journal *Repertorio americano,* the newspaper *El Triunfo* (San José), and other major papers in Latin America. He served in Costa Rica's 1948 constitutional convention, published the newspaper *Fortín* (Heredia), and in 1950 again represented his country in Spain. He was a member of the Costa Rican Academy of Language and was awarded the Order of Isabel la Católica (Spain) and France's Legion of Honor. Dobles Segreda, one of the major Costa Rican intellectual figures of his times, died in Heredia.

– GEORGETTE MAGASSY DORN

DOBRIZHOFFER, MARTÍN

Martín Dobrizhoffer (*b.* 7 September 1717; *d.* 17 July 1791), Austrian missionary active in Paraguay. Born in the Bohemian town of Friedburg, Dobrizhoffer studied philosophy and physical sciences at the universities of Vienna and Graz. In 1748, after joining the Jesuits, he was sent to the Río de la Plata region in Argentina, where he finished his education at the University of Córdoba. He then went to work for four years among the Mocobí Indians of Santa Fe. From 1754 to 1762 Dobrizhoffer was stationed at the Jesuit settlements of Paraguay, at Santa María la Mayor on the Uruguay River, where he gained considerable fame as a learned man among his colleagues and among the Guaraní Indians.

In 1762, the royal governor at Asunción mandated the establishment of a new mission some fifty leagues to the west in the most inhospitable area of the Chaco. He ordered Dobrizhoffer to take charge of the mission, called Nuestra Señora del Rosario de Timbó. The Austrian's missionary goal there, the conversion of the "wild" Abipón Indians, eluded him. After many bitter experiences, he abandoned Rosario de Timbó in 1765

and was reassigned to San Joaquín, in northern Paraguay.

With the expulsion of the Jesuits two years later, Dobrizhoffer returned to Vienna. There he attracted the attention of the empress Maria Theresa, who begged him to write an account of his life in the New World. These memoirs, published in 1783–1784 as *Geschichte der Abiponer,* constitute the most detailed examination we have of Indian–Caucasian relations in the eighteenth-century Chaco.

– THOMAS L. WHIGHAM

DOMÍNGUEZ, MANUEL

Manuel Domínguez (*b.* 1869; *d.* 1935), Paraguayan historian and essayist. Domínguez is widely regarded as the most important revisionist historian of Paraguay after Juan E. O'Leary. Born in the river port of Pilar toward the end of the War of the Triple Alliance, Domínguez grew up in an Asunción that had been terribly affected by the fighting. Despite these difficulties, he made major intellectual strides and ended up teaching subjects as varied as zoology, anatomy, and Roman history at the National College and serving as rector of the university. He also held various political and diplomatic posts for brief periods.

Domínguez was instrumental in introducing Auguste Comte's positivism to Paraguayan historical studies, which meant applying more scientific methods to research. Domínguez himself put theory into practice in his *El Chaco Boreal,* a work that defended Paraguayan claims to the Gran Chaco region. He also wrote an influential series of essays entitled *El alma de la raza,* which argued for a portrayal of Paraguayan history in strongly nationalist terms; the book likewise championed the figure of Marshal Francisco Solano LÓPEZ, who had led Paraguay into the earlier war. In this respect, Domínguez broke with the virulently anti-López diatribes of earlier historians, particularly Cecilio BÁEZ.

– THOMAS L. WHIGHAM

DOMÍNGUEZ, MIGUEL

Miguel Domínguez (*b.* 20 January 1756; *d.* 22 April 1830), precursor of Mexican independence. A distinguished lawyer born in Mexico City, Domínguez was named *corregidor* of Querétaro in 1802. His opposition to the Law of Consolidation of *vales reales* (royal bonds) (1805) gained him the enmity of Viceroy José de ITURRIGARAY, who had him replaced, although he was eventually restored to his post. With his wife, Josefa ORTIZ, he took part in the Querétaro conspiracy of 1810 against the colonial regime. When the plot was discovered, Domínguez, constrained by his office, locked his wife in their house and arrested some of the plotters. But she managed to notify others, causing Miguel HIDALGO to begin the revolution on 16 September. Domínguez was detained the same day; shortly thereafter he was released and restored to his post, although he was

---

When the Querétaro conspiracy was discovered, Domínguez locked his wife in their house and arrested some of the plotters.

---

ousted again in 1820. He became a member of the Supreme Executive Power in 1823. At the end of 1824, he became president of the Supreme Court, a position he held for the rest of his life. He died in Mexico City.

— VIRGINIA GUEDEA

DONOSO, JOSÉ

José Donoso (*b*. 5 October 1924), Chilean writer. Donoso is one of the most distinguished contemporary Latin American writers belonging to the generation of Gabriel GARCÍA MÁRQUEZ and Carlos FUENTES. Born in Santiago, Donoso began writing at the age of twenty-five. In 1951 he received a scholarship from the Doherty Foundation to study English literature at Princeton University. Upon returning to Chile he began a period of increased creative activity, writing short stories and publishing in 1955 his first book, *Veraneo y otros cuentos,* which won the Municipal Prize. His first novel, *Coronación* (1957) (*Coronation* [1965]) won the William Faulkner Foundation Prize for the Latin American Novel in 1962. He moved to Buenos Aires in 1958. Upon his return to Chile in 1960, he wrote for the weekly *Ercilla* and married María Pilar Serrano, a Bolivian painter. By the mid-1960s, Donoso was recognized as a major literary figure and was invited in 1965–1967 to the University of Iowa Writers' Workshop. He published his novels *Este domingo* (1966) (*This Sunday* [1967]) and *El lugar sin límites* (1966) (*Hell Has No Limits* [1972]) and a book of stories, *Los mejores cuentos de José Donoso* (1966).

In 1967 he left for Spain, eventually settling in Barcelona, where he published in 1970 what it had taken him eight years to write, *El obsceno pájaro de la noche* (*The Obscene Bird of Night* [1973]). This acclaimed novel placed Donoso among the top Latin American writers of his generation. There followed a series of outstanding novels: *Casa de campo* (1978) (*A House in the Country* [1984]), which won the Critics' Prize in Spain,

La misteriosa desaparición de la marquesita de Loria (1980), *El jardín de al lado* (1981), and *La desesperanza* (1986) (*Curfew* [1988]), among others. In his 1972 *Historia personal del boom* (*The Boom in Spanish American Literature: A Personal History* [1972]) Donoso scrutinizes with humor and grace Emir RODRÍGUEZ MONEGAL's discussion of the publishing phenomenon of the 1960s. Donoso also created a series of masterful short story collections, among them *El charleston* (1960) (*Charleston and Other Stories* [1977]), *Tres novelitas burguesas* (1973) (*Sacred Families* [1977]), *Cuatro para Delfina* (1982), and *Taratuta* (1990). He has also written a book of poetry, *Poemas de un novelista* (1981) and dramatic versions of one of his short stories, *Sueños de mala muerte* (1985), and of his novel *Este domingo* (1990).

Donoso's fictional narratives stand out as the most important part of his production. His novels, *The Obscene Bird* and *House in the Country,* in particular, are the most valuable narratives of the contemporary period in Chile. They are also unique manifestations of the Spanish American novel, standing alongside García Márquez's *Cien años de soledad* (1967) and Carlos Fuentes's *Terra nostra* (1975). Donoso's literary expression represents the dark side of imagination, a grotesque recreation of myth, folklore, psychology, and the fantastic. The mixing of many voices constitutes the unmistakable stylistic feature of his narrative.

— CEDOMIL GOIC

DORREGO, MANUEL

Manuel Dorrego (*b*. 11 June 1787; *d*. 13 December 1828), Argentine military officer in the independence struggle and Federalist leader. Though born in Buenos Aires, Dorrego was studying law in Chile when the revolution against Spain began. He actively embraced the patriot cause, first in Chile and then in his own country, joining the 1811 campaign to liberate what is now Bolivia. Later still he fought in Uruguay with the forces of Buenos Aires against those of the Uruguayan leader José ARTIGAS. He gained a reputation as quarrelsome and undisciplined, but he also took a principled stand against the centralism and monarchist intrigues of the government of Juan Martín de PUEYRREDÓN (1816–1819), which exiled him in 1817.

Dorrego spent three years in the United States, an experience that strengthened his Federalist convictions. After his return he held a number of military and other positions and became an active publicist in opposition to the Unitarist regime of Bernardino RIVADAVIA. At the collapse of Rivadavia's government in 1827, Dorrego became governor of Buenos Aires Province, in which capacity he brought to a close the war fought with Brazil over Uruguay, agreeing to accept Uruguayan independence. In December 1828 he was overthrown by Juan LAVALLE, who by executing Dorrego made him a martyr in the eyes of Federalists and unleashed a round of bloody reprisals and counterreprisals between the two parties.

— DAVID BUSHNELL

DORTICÓS TORRADO, OSVALDO

Osvaldo Dorticós Torrado (*b.* 1919; *d.* 23 June 1983), president of Cuba from 1959 to 1976. Born in Cienfuegos, Dorticós Torrado graduated from the University of Havana Law School in 1941. He served as dean of the Cienfuegos Bar Association and subsequently as vice president of the Cuban Bar Association. After his release from a short imprisonment for anti-BATISTA activities, Dorticós joined Fidel CASTRO's Twenty-sixth of July Movement and soon became its Cienfuegos coordinator.

When President Manuel URRUTIA resigned on 17 July 1959, Dorticós ascended to the presidency, becoming at forty the youngest president in the nation's history. Real power remained in Castro's hands, but Dorticós nevertheless remained loyal, receiving additional appointments, including minister of the economy in 1976. He held positions in the National Assembly of the People's Power and Council of State, was vice president of the Council of Ministers, and was a member of the Political Bureau of the Central Committee of the Cuban Communist Party. Dorticós committed suicide in 1983.

— JAIME SUCHLICKI

DRAGO, LUIS MARÍA

Luis María Drago (*b.* 6 May 1859; *d.* 9 June 1921), Argentine jurist. A native of Buenos Aires, Drago was elected three times to the Chamber of Deputies and became one of Argentina's most eminent international jurists. In 1909, at the request of Britain and the United States, he arbitrated two major disputes between them; he also was a judge on the Permanent Court of International Justice (1912–1916). His major contribution was in the context of American international law and another important doctrine, the Drago Doctrine, which was a narrowing of the Calvo Doctrine. This contribution, made while he was minister of foreign affairs, was in response to armed European intervention against Venezuela. In 1902, three European states (Britain, Germany, and Italy) imposed a naval blockade in order to force their financial claims resulting from default on bonds. On 29 December 1902 Drago sent an official note to the heads of the American governments stating that such use of force was contrary to international law: "The collection of loans by military means implies territorial occupation to make them effective [and it is] the suppression or subordination of the governments." His note received strong support in Latin America and at the Second Hague Conference (1907), where the United States had his doctrine modified.

— LARMAN C. WILSON

DRAGÚN, OSVALDO

Osvaldo Dragún (*b.* 1929), Argentine playwright, achieved international status with his *Historias para ser contadas* (1957), a group of brief and dehumanizing vignettes that capture a pithy social reality with sparse language, minimal plot and scenery, and often grotesque elements. Dragún, a native of San Salvador, Entre Ríos, lacked formal training in the theater but learned quickly by acting, directing, and writing for community theater groups. His career was launched with the independent group Fray Mocho in 1956 and the production of two historical plays that underscored individual and political freedom, *La peste viene de Melos* (1956) and *Tupac Amaru* (1957). The writers of Dragún's generation (including Roberto Cossa, Carlos GOROSTIZA, and Ricardo Halac) sought to interpret an Argentine reality that was chaotic under Juan Perón but even more anarchic after his demise. This "new realism" found expression in the aesthetics of the grotesque, an honored tradition in Argentina with its dehumanization of the individual. Dragún wrote many full-length plays, including *Y nos dijeron que éramos inmortales* (1963), a study of the illusions of alienated generations, and *Milagro en el mercado viejo* (1964), a Brechtian play about crime and betrayal. Of his twenty or so theater pieces, the most successful are *El amasijo* (1968), an absurdist rendering of two lonely individuals who regularly miss the opportunities life hands them, and *Arriba corazón!* (1986), an expressionist piece with autobiographical overtones. Dragún spent many years outside Argentina, primarily in Cuba, where he has been greatly involved with the International Theater School. In Argentina he was instrumental in creating the Teatro Abierto in 1981, a daring and ambitious presentation of twenty new plays, by various authors, structured to challenge Argentine political reality at its most vicious and repressive stage, the military dictatorship.

— GEORGE WOODYARD

DRAKE, FRANCIS

Francis Drake (*b.* ca. 1545; *d.* 28 January 1596), English privateer who became, from 1570 to 1595, the central figure in attacks by privateers on the Spanish Indies. A maritime genius and fervent Protestant, Drake was a glorious hero to the English and a frightening monster in the eyes of the Spanish. He developed a coherent West Indian strategy to replace the established pattern of small, uncoordinated raids on the Spanish. Although Drake achieved much success, acquiring great booty and inflicting considerable damage to Spanish holdings, he failed to break Spain's monopoly on territorial possession in the Caribbean.

A maritime genius and fervent Protestant, Drake was a glorious hero to the English and a frightening monster in the eyes of the Spanish.

Originally an illicit trader, Drake was with John HAWKINS of Plymouth during the disastrous defeat at San Juan de Ulúa in late 1568. In 1571 he carried out reconnaissance activities and forged alliances with savage indigenous warriors, particularly on the Central American isthmus. A year later he led a voyage which attacked Nombre de Dios, Panama, and acquired a large booty of Peruvian treasure. After the English-Spanish peace of 1574, Drake remained active in the West Indies for eleven years, becoming the first captain to sail his own ship around the world (1577–1580).

In 1585, Drake resumed his naval efforts by carrying out a full-scale operation known as the Indies Voyage, with a fleet of over twenty sail, which aspired to attack Santo Domingo and Cartagena, Colombia, then Nombre de Dios and Panama (by land, in collaboration with runaway slaves), and, finally, Havana. In addition to establishing an English stronghold in the Indies, Drake hoped to disrupt the flow of Latin American resources, particularly Peruvian silver, to the Iberian Peninsula, thereby hindering Spain's military efforts in Europe. This plan proved to be too ambitious, however. After destroying much of Santo Domingo and Cartagena, Drake decided not to attack the isthmus, because of his depleted manpower, a result of shipboard health problems. When adverse weather also prevented him from attacking the Spanish treasure fleet, Drake sailed for home in June 1586. Despite its temporary successes and the great damage it caused Spain's possessions and prestige, Drake's Indies Voyage failed in its larger aims, for the Spanish maintained their territorial supremacy.

Spain's desire to destroy England's growing geopolitical power took the form of an enormous naval attack against England in 1588, in which Drake played a key role. Along with John Hawkins and others he contrib-

uted to one of the largest naval defeats in history, that of the Spanish Armada (1588). By 1595, however, the Spanish had clearly learned some lessons, particularly in regard to the activities of privateers. When another great fleet, under the direction of Hawkins and Drake, left England to attack Spain's possessions in the Indies, the Spanish were well prepared. They defeated the English at San Juan, Puerto Rico, and at Cartagena. Moreover, having established a more defensible harbor, Porto Bello, to replace Nombre de Dios, they emerged victorious on the isthmus as well. Sir Francis Drake died shortly thereafter, off the coast of Veragua, Panama.

– BLAKE D. PATTRIDGE

DUARTE, AUGUSTO RODRIGUES

Augusto Rodrigues Duarte (*b.* 1848; *d.* 1888), Portuguese-born history painter. Augusto Rodrigues Duarte came to Brazil in 1866 and entered the Imperial Academy of Fine Arts, where he studied under the painter Vítor MEIRELES. Upon completion of his academic training in the early 1870s, Duarte left Brazil to study in Paris. In 1874 he entered the atelier of the French history painter Jean-Léon Gérôme and shortly thereafter won a second prize in the Paris Salon. He was one of the few nineteenth-century painters in Brazil to portray the Indian as the subject of a monumental history painting, a role traditionally reserved for members of the royal family and military heroes.

His most important artistic achievement was the Indianist painting entitled the *Funeral of Atala,* which was exhibited at the 1878 Universal Exhibition in Paris. The subject matter of the work borrowed from Chateaubriand's 1826 novel *Les Natchez.* Duarte's paintings exhibit the influences of the European aesthetic formulas of impressionism, symbolism, and even art nouveau. Beyond history painting, he is also known for his landscapes and genre paintings. He was awarded the title of Knight of the Imperial Order of Roses at the 1884 academic exhibition, where he entered fourteen paintings.

– CAREN A. MEGHREBLIAN

DUARTE, JUAN PABLO

Juan Pablo Duarte (*b.* 26 January 1813; *d.* 15 July 1876), leader of Dominican independence. While studying abroad in Europe, Duarte was influenced by the French romantic literary movement. With his homeland under Haitian occupation (1822–1844), the ideals of liberty and equality became of great importance to him. In 1838, Duarte and two others, Francisco de Rosario Sánchez and Ramón Mella, formed La Trinitaria, a secret society whose goal was independence. The society proved very successful but resulted in

Duarte's exile. After the Haitian president Jean-Pierre BOYER was overthrown in 1844, Duarte returned to Santo Domingo to take part in the formation of a new and independent government. Imbued with the ideals of the French Revolution, his idealism soon alienated him from the more militaristic leaders, and strongman General Pedro SANTANA jailed and ultimately exiled him once more. After a brief stay in Germany, Duarte spent fifteen years as a recluse in the jungles of Venezuela.

When Santana agreed to the country's reassumption of colonial status in 1864, Duarte returned to the Dominican Republic to take up the cause of independence again. Once more, however, Duarte was unable to participate in the provisional government of the Dominican Republic. It has been said of Duarte that he could inspire but not lead. He was exiled for the third time in 1865 and he returned to Venezuela, where he lived the rest of his life in poverty and obscurity. Like many great men, Duarte's significance and value was recognized only after his death. He is now considered the father of Dominican independence.

– HEATHER K. THIESSEN

DUARTE, PEDRO

Pedro Duarte (*b.* 1829; *d.* 1903), Paraguayan soldier and statesman. At the beginning of the War of the Triple Alliance, Duarte, a relatively obscure officer, was chosen as second in command of an expeditionary force sent south to attack Brazil. As the Paraguayans approached the Brazilian frontier in June 1865, their commander, Colonel Antonio de la Cruz ESTIGARRIBIA, split his forces, sending one column of 2,500 men under Major Duarte down the right bank of the Uruguay River, while he himself led the bulk of the troops down the left bank, toward the Riograndense town of Uruguaiana. The Argentines and Brazilians were waiting for both columns. Unable to secure help from Estigarribia and unwilling to consider withdrawal, Duarte was effectively isolated, and, on 17 August, at a spot called Yatai, 10,000 Argentine troops struck his column, annihilating almost everyone. Gravely wounded, Duarte was taken to Buenos Aires, where he spent the rest of the war as a prisoner. After the Allied victory in 1870, he returned to Paraguay and subsequently served as minister of war and marine in the governments of Cándido BAREIRO, Bernardino CABALLERO, and Patricio ESCOBAR.

– THOMAS L. WHIGHAM

DUARTE FUENTES, JOSÉ NAPOLEÓN

José Napoleón Duarte Fuentes (*b.* 23 November 1925; *d.* 23 February 1990), president of El Salvador (1980–

1982, 1984–1989). A civil engineer trained in the United States, Duarte first became active in Salvadoran politics as a leader of the Christian Democratic Party (Partido Demócrata Cristiano—PDC), founded in 1960. Personable and skilled at organization, he developed a substantial political following, especially among urban and middle-class constituencies. He was elected mayor of San Salvador in 1964, and his six years in office witnessed a number of governmental reforms at the municipal level. Over the years he became the country's most successful opposition politician. In 1972, Duarte ran for president as the candidate of the National Opposition Union (Unión Nacional Opositora—UNO), a coalition that included the centrist PDC and two smaller leftist parties. Although the UNO claimed victory on the basis of the popular vote, the army tampered with the results and awarded the presidency to Colonel Arturo Armando MOLINA (1972–1977). Duarte joined with a faction of dissident officers in an unsuccessful coup d'état and was captured, tortured, and expelled from the country. He spent most of the 1970s in exile in Venezuela.

Duarte returned to El Salvador following the coup (15 October 1979) that overthrew the repressive regime of Molina's successor, General Carlos Humberto ROMERO. In spite of rapid political polarization, spreading civil warfare, and escalating human rights abuses by the military and right-wing death squads, Duarte joined the second provisional junta in March 1980 and became its president in December. His willingness to collaborate with the armed forces angered many of his former political allies and precipitated a split in the PDC, but he insisted that the junta's agrarian reform and bank nationalization measures justified his actions.

Ousted as provisional president in 1982 by the right-wing coalition that controlled the newly elected constituent assembly, Duarte returned to office as constitutional president in 1984 when he defeated his chief political rival, rightist demagogue Roberto D'AUBUISSON of the Nationalist Republican Alliance (Alianza Republicana Nacionalista—ARENA). As El Salvador's first elected civilian president in more than fifty years, Duarte sought to expand his reforms and to open a dialogue with the leftist rebels engaged in the country's five-year-old civil war. His options were limited, however, by a war-damaged economy heavily dependent upon aid from the United States, by the need to maintain the loyalty of the officer corps, and by the refusal of the Left to support his reforms or to participate in the political process.

Despite the optimism surrounding Duarte's first meeting with guerrilla representatives at La Palma in October 1984, little came of his efforts to forge a lasting peace. He lost more credibility when his government responded poorly to a major earthquake that struck San Salvador on 10 October 1986. Finally, terminal cancer, diagnosed in May 1988, compromised his effectiveness even further during his last year in office. His most significant achievement may have come in June 1989, a few months before his death, when he completed his term in office and transferred the presidency to a legally elected civilian successor, Alfredo CRISTIANI of ARENA.

> *Duarte's presence in office was essential both to the administration of Ronald Reagan and to the Salvadoran military.*

Duarte's role in the Salvadoran crisis of the 1980s remains controversial. While personal ambition may have led him to cooperate with military-dominated regimes, for his own part, Duarte always insisted that he accepted office only because he understood that change in El Salvador was impossible without the support of the officer corps, the real power in the country. Rightists considered him a Communist because he supported reforms to benefit the poor, while his enemies on the left, many of them former allies and supporters, blamed him for the corruption, violence, and ineffectiveness that characterized his governments. Duarte was an outspoken anti-Communist, but he was also a critic of U.S. policies in Latin America and a well-known advocate of democracy and social justice. As such, his presence in office was essential both to the administration of Ronald Reagan and to the Salvadoran military. In spite of his chronic inability to restrain the excesses of the armed forces, Duarte helped guarantee continued approval of economic and military aid by the U.S. Congress.

– STEPHEN WEBRE

DUEÑAS, FRANCISCO

Francisco Dueñas (*b.* 1817; *d.* 31 March 1884), last Conservative president of El Salvador (1851–1854, 1863–1871). Francisco Dueñas studied law and was active in letters, education, and public service before seizing power in 1851 and again in 1863 with the assistance of Guatemala's Rafael CARRERA. As president, Dueñas strengthened the Salvadoran armed forces and enacted a new constitution (1864), which consolidated military and political power in his hands. He persecuted his political rivals and had a number of them killed, including his Liberal predecessor, Gerardo BARRIOS. The Dueñas regime created a stable environment for the growth of the coffee industry, which it encouraged with incentives similar to those more commonly associated with Liberal governments. Dueñas also promoted physical improvements in the country's infrastructure and in the capital city, San Salvador. Congress reelected Dueñas in 1870, but he lost the following year to a Liberal revolt under Santiago González. Dueñas spent much of his later life in exile. A pioneer coffee grower himself, he founded one of El Salvador's wealthiest and most powerful families.

– STEPHEN WEBRE

DUPRAT, ROGÉRIO

Rogério Duprat (*b.* 7 February 1932), Brazilian composer. Born in Guanabara, Rio de Janeiro, Duprat studied philosophy at São Paulo University. He also studied music theory, harmony, and composition with Olivier Toni and Cláudio SANTORO and cello with Varoli at the Villalobos Conservatory in São Paulo (1952–1960). From 1953 to 1963 he was a cellist with the São Paulo Municipal Orchestra and took summer courses at Darmstadt, Germany. He also studied electronic music at studios in Cologne, Paris, and Karlsruhe under Stockhausen, Ligeti, Boulez, and Pousseur. Duprat returned to São Paulo, where he cofounded the Estadual Orchestra and the São Paulo Chamber Orchestra; for the latter he was the director of an experimental music group. His early style was nationalist but later he turned to twelve-tone, serial, and electronic music. In 1963 he formed the group Música Nova with Gilberto MENDES, Willy Correia de OLIVEIRA, and Damiano Cozzella, manifesting strict devotion to contemporary and avant-garde trends. He has composed music for television and collaborated with the musical group Tropicália; and he has also taught at the University of Brazil.

– SUSANA SALGADO

DURÁN, DIEGO

Diego Durán (*b.* 1537; *d.* 1588), one of the more important chronicler/ethnographers who lived in sixteenth-century New Spain. A Dominican friar born in Seville and raised in Texcoco and Mexico City, Durán wrote a three-part work, *Historia de las Indias de Nueva España islas de tierra firme,* on the pre-Hispanic history, religion, and calendar of the Aztecs, respectively. He based it on indigenous manuscripts—including the Crónica X, now lost—and hundreds of indigenous informants. He also had some assistants, probably monastery-trained Nahuas, who helped him gather, copy, and interpret information, and he interviewed Spanish eyewitnesses who had been on the scene of the Conquest. The three parts of the *Historia,* containing many descriptions not duplicated in any other chronicles, were written approximately during the period

1576–1581. Durán's goal, like that of many chroniclers of his time, was to improve the Christian instruction of the indigenous people by first gaining a better grasp of their beliefs.

— STEPHANIE WOOD

DURÁN, FRAY NARCISO

Fray Narciso Durán (*b.* 16 December 1776; *d.* 1 June 1846), Franciscan missionary. Durán was born at Castellón de Ampurias in Catalonia, where he entered the Franciscan order at Gerona in 1792. Ordained in 1800, Durán left Spain in 1803 for Mexico, arriving in the Alta California missions three years later.

Durán remained in the Alta California missions for forty years and died at the Santa Barbara mission in 1846. During most of this period (1806–1833) he was stationed at the San José mission in the San Francisco Bay region and at the Santa Barbara mission. In 1832 Durán became the *vicar forane* (foreign vicar) and ecclesiastical judge for Alta California. He was president of the missions from 1833 to 1838 and commissary prefect after 1838.

Durán tried to defend the missions against reforms initiated by Mexican politicians and was vocal in his criticism of these changes. For example, he criticized the emancipation of mission Indians in the late 1820s and early 1830s. Moreover, in the 1820s and 1830s he refused to take oaths of loyalty to Mexico. Despite his views, Durán, like the other Spanish-born Franciscans in Alta California, was not expelled. However, in 1833 the Mexican government sent Mexican-born Franciscans from the apostolic college in Zacatecas to staff its missions in the northern part of the province, which was especially sensitive politically because of the presence of the Russians at Fort Ross north of San Francisco Bay.

— ROBERT H. JACKSON

DURAND, OSWALD

Oswald Durand (*b.* 17 September 1840; *d.* 22 April 1906), Haitian writer, journalist, and politician. Durand began work as a tinsmith and studied at night. He became a lycée principal and went into politics in 1885. After being elected president of the Chambre des Députés in 1888, he traveled to France and was introduced to the "Société des Gens de Lettres" by François Coppée. Upon his death in 1906, he was given a state funeral and was praised as the greatest Haitian poet.

The poetry of Durand was often an erotic evocation of the women he loved (he was divorced for philandering by the poet Virginie Sampeur), but he also evoked simple people and the landscapes and traditions of Haiti. Some poems in Creole contributed to the recognition of the language's literary citizenship.

Other works include *Rires et pleurs* (1896); *Quatre nouveaux poèmes* (1900). *Mosaïques* and *Primes fleurs et ballades* are both unpublished.

— CARROL F. COATES

DURÃO, JOSÉ DE SANTA RITA

José de Santa Rita Durão (*b.* ca. 1722; *d.* 24 January 1784), Brazilian poet. Durão was born in Minas Gerais, Brazil, but left, never to return, at age nine. He grew up and was educated in Portugal, entering the Augustinian Order in 1738 and earning a doctorate in theology from the University of Coimbra in 1758. After serving as a papal librarian in Rome, he returned to Portugal and served as a professor of theology at Coimbra before becoming prior of the Gration convent.

Durão endorsed the ideal of a Christian empire served by Portuguese conquests, but he accepted eighteenth-century natural law and viewed the savage as innately noble.

In 1781 Durão published his major work, *Caramuru.* Modeling himself on Luís de CAMÕES's *Os Lusíadas* with its celebration of Portuguese accomplishments in the Orient, Durão produced an epic poem in ten ottava rima cantos celebrating similar accomplishments in Brazil. As Camões had elaborated his narrative around Vasco da GAMA's voyage to India, Durão used the discovery of Bahia by Diogo Álvares CORREIA (1510) and Correia's subsequent adventures. Caramurú, or Dragon of the Sea, is Correia's Indian name.

Again like Camões, and contrary to the rationalism of the age, Durão endorsed the ideal of a Christian empire served by Portuguese conquests, but he accepted eighteenth-century natural law and viewed the savage as innately noble. His accurate descriptions of Brazilian nature, moreover, together with those of native life and customs, make him an important precursor of both literary nationalism and Indianism.

— NORWOOD ANDREWS, JR.

DUTARY, ALBERTO

Alberto Dutary (*b.* 1932), Panamanian painter. Dutary studied at the Escuela Nacional de Pintura in Panama

(1950–1952) and in Madrid, at the San Fernando Academy (1953–1955) and the Escuela Nacional de Artes Gráficas (1956–1958). From 1962 until 1992, he was art professor in private schools and at the University of Panama, where he became the first director of the Fine Arts Career Program in 1987.

A notable draftsman and figurative painter, his works from the 1960s, including the "Santos" series, combined the surface textures of Spanish informalism with dramatic ghostlike figures. He later turned to more realistic, and at times surrealistic, still lifes. In the 1970s, he focused on mannequinlike female figures that play with the concept of reality in paintings such as *Figuras frente a la Bahía* (1979).

– MONICA E. KUPFER

DUTRA, EURICO GASPAR

Eurico Gaspar Dutra (*b*. 18 May 1883; *d*. 11 June 1974), president of Brazil (1945–1951). Son of merchant José Florêncio Dutra and Maria Justina Dutra, Dutra was born in Cuiabá, state of Mato Grosso. He married Carmela Leite, widow of Uchoa Cintra, on 19 February 1914; they had two children.

Dutra studied at the Escola Preparatória e Tática of Rio Pardo and completed his military studies at the Escola Militar do Brasil. After distinguishing himself during the Constitutionalist Revolution, Dutra became a general in 1932. In 1935 he was made commandant of Military Region I and put down the Communist rebellion of 27 November 1935 in Rio de Janeiro.

As minister of war (1936–1945) during the Getúlio VARGAS dictatorship, Dutra organized the Brazilian Expeditionary Force (FEB), which saw combat in Europe during World War II. During this period, he actively participated in the Golpe Integralista (Integralist Coup) of 1937, for which he laid the groundwork. Dutra was also deeply involved in Vargas's nationalistic campaign to maintain Brazilian ownership of the nation's petroleum under the banner of "O petróleo é nosso" (the oil is ours).

In 1946 Dutra was elected president of Brazil and served until 31 January 1951. Not known as a charismatic figure, Dutra was respected for his honesty and ability to complete a full presidential term. Two Brazilian municipalities were named in his honor. Pursuing a close relationship with the United States, Dutra received President Harry S. Truman in Brazil, made an official visit to the United States, and broke relations with the Soviet Union. During his presidency, Dutra implemented a number of reforms in the federal government, including the establishment of the Tribunal Federal de Recursos, the Conselho Nacional de Economia, and the regional planning commissions.

– IÊDA SIQUEIRA WIARDA

DUVALIER, FRANÇOIS

François Duvalier (*b*. 14 April 1907; *d*. 21 April 1971), president of Haiti (1957–1971). A *noir* (black), Duvalier was born in Port-au-Prince; his father was an elementary schoolteacher and his mother a bakery worker. His formal education included elementary and secondary school at the Lycée Pétion and a medical degree from the École de Médecine the same year that the U.S. occupation (1915–1934) ended. After his internship, he worked in a clinic and in 1939 married Simone Ovide Faine, a mulatto (*mulâtresse*) nurse whose father was a merchant. They had four children, three daughters and a son—Jean-Claude.

In the 1940s, Duvalier became involved in the campaign against yaws (*pian*), a contagious tropical disease caused by a parasite, and then went on to direct training in the U.S. Army's malaria program. In the mid-1940s, he assisted Doctor James Dwinelle in the U.S. Army Medical Corps' yaws program. During this time he had a year's fellowship and studied public health at the University of Michigan.

Duvalier's ideas about race and politics and his literary and political activities were developed and took place both before and during his medical studies and working with yaws. In the 1920s, he became important in an ethnology movement as one of its three Ds, *les trois D*, later known as the *Griots,* and was a cofounder of its journal, *Les Griots.* This movement was based upon black nationalism (*noirisme*), *indigénisme,* and *négritude,* stressing African roots, including *voudon* (voodoo, *vodun*). It opposed the control and rule of the mulattoes. Certain events also affected Duvalier's attitudes and values: the U.S. occupation; President Rafael TRUJILLO's anti-Haitian views and actions, particularly the 1937 massacre of Haitians in the Dominican Republic; foreign intervention; control of economic and political life by the mulattoes; army intervention in national politics; and the campaigns of the church against *voudon.*

François Duvalier became politically active in 1946, when presidential candidate Daniel Fignolé formed a new party and made him its secretary-general. After the army assured the election of President Dumarsais ESTIMÉ, in his "Revolution of 1946," he designed reforms that downgraded the mulattoes in government. President Estimé made Duvalier a part of his government, first as director of the yaws program, then as undersecretary of labor in 1948, which was followed the next

Presidential candidate Dr. François Duvalier, May 1957. (AP/Wide World Photos)

year by minister of labor and public health. The growing rift between blacks and mulattoes resulted in Estimé's overthrow in 1950, and the army brought in General Paul MAGLOIRE, who lasted until 1956. There ensued great instability and virtual civil war, with five provisional governments, and then rule by a military council. In his 1957 campaign for president against Louis Déjoie, Duvalier called for honesty in government, stressed his background as a country doctor, and organized a paramilitary group to deal with his opponents. The army also "managed" this election, assuring the defeat of Fignolé (the U.S. embassy count showed a victory for Fignolé).

Once he was inaugurated as president at the age of fifty, Duvalier began the transformation of "cultural *négritude*" into "political *négritude*" by destroying his critics; neutralizing the army; Haitianizing the church; legitimizing *voudon* and making it an instrument of

government; and establishing a black nationalist, xenophobic, and personalist regime. He became the state.

Duvalier first silenced the press and broadcasters, who were arrested, attacked, and killed; he then burned and bombed their offices and stations. The major instrument was the Tonton Macoutes (in *créole*, bogeymen), who were officially recognized by the creation in 1962 of the *Volontaires de la Sécurité Nationale* (VSN). Second, he neutralized the army by transfers and by politicizing it, and he created a separate palace guard, which was quartered there with their arsenal located in the basement. At the same time he invited a U.S. Marine Corps mission to train the army as a means of showing U.S. support; but the mission (1958–1962), commanded by Colonel Robert D. Heinl, withdrew when the VSN replaced the army. Third, he took on the church in 1959, expelling high officials, including the archbishop; arresting members of the clergy; closing the seminary; and expelling the Jesuits. The Vatican responded by excommunicating him and his entire cabinet. Then he "Haitianized" the church by increasing the number of Haitian clergy until they were in the majority. (He reconciled with the church in 1966, mainly on his own terms.) He openly favored and practiced *voudon,* used some of its priests (*houngans*) as advisers, and always dressed in black.

What was unique about Duvalier's rule was that he controlled everything and almost everyone by making them responsible to him—loyalty was more important than competence. He and his family and closest advisers got a financial cut from all government enterprises, thus, it was "government by franchise."

In relations with the U.S., Duvalier played the anticommunist game in order to get aid, but when the administration of John F. Kennedy cut off most aid in 1963, he turned inward and toward Africa, stressing *négritude.* He invited and welcomed Ethiopia's Haile Selassie I with great fanfare and at great expense in 1966. Although a *noirist,* he really did not care about the black masses. After paving the way for naming his son Jean-Claude as his successor as "president for life," he died of natural causes at the age of sixty-four.

— LARMAN C. WILSON

DUVALIER, JEAN-CLAUDE

Jean-Claude Duvalier (*b.* 3 July 1951), president of Haiti (1971–1986). An unsuccessful law student and playboy, Duvalier became "president for life" upon the death of his father, François DUVALIER, but was only the titular head for the first few years, since decisions were made by a council of state appointed by his father before he died. This arrangement assured the continuation of

Duvalierisme. The council members included his mother and his father's main advisers; Luckner Cambronne was the power behind the throne and also headed the Leopards, a counterinsurgency force created with U.S. aid in 1971. When Jean-Claude dismissed and exiled Cambronne in 1972, it marked the president's emerging control and influence.

Duvalier stated that his goal was to effect an "economic revolution" (he had little interest in *négritude* or *noirisme*), which he pursued by making some cosmetic and some real changes in reducing political repression. These changes plus some genuine economic incentives ended Haiti's isolation, brought about the resumption of U.S. aid, and attracted foreign investment and companies.

Duvalier's marriage in 1980 to a mulatto divorcée, Michèle Bennett, daughter of a wealthy exporterimporter, provoked criticism from the antimulatto blacks. Her life-style served as a catalyst—along with the corrupt and incompetent bureaucracy—for his downfall. Her shopping sprees in Paris and lavish parties in Haiti caused national revulsion, prompting riots and demonstrations, which began in rural cities in 1984. Supported by the church, these acts of opposition convulsed the country and led the U.S. to urge Jean-Claude's resignation and departure. He and his family along with several close advisers were flown out of Haiti on a U.S. cargo plane in early February 1986.

– LARMAN C. WILSON

E

ECHANDI JIMÉNEZ, MARIO

Mario Echandi Jiménez (b. 1915), president of Costa Rica (1958–1962). Mario Echandi, who received his law degree from the University of Costa Rica, first came to prominence in national affairs as the general secretary of the National Union Party (PUN), which backed Otilio ULATE BLANCO's successful presidential campaign (1948). Under Ulate, he served as ambassador to the United States (1950–1951) and as foreign minister (1951–1953).

While in the national legislature (1953–1958), he was a recognized leader of the opposition to President José FIGUERES FERRER's social democratic programs. His leadership in Congress served as a springboard for his political ascension.

With the support of the followers of Ulate and Rafael Angel CALDERÓN GUARDIA, Echandi led the PLN opposition to victory in the 1958 election. His administration emphasized fiscal restraint, the expansion of the highway network, and a program to foster industrial development. True to his conservative credentials, he opposed the proposed Central American Common Market. After his presidency Echandi remained a conservative leader, and in 1970 ran unsuccessfully for president against his old adversary José Figueres Ferrer.

– JOHN PATRICK BELL

ECHAVE ORIO BALTASAR DE

Echave Orio Baltasar de (b. ca. 1548; d. ca. 1623), painter. Echave was in New Spain by around 1573 and is the most important of the second generation of mannerist painters in colonial Mexico. It is not clear how much of his training was European, since he does not seem to have been famous when he arrived in the New World. In 1582 he married Isabel de Ibía, the daughter of the painter Francisco de Zumaya, reportedly an artist in her own right. Two sons, Baltasar and Manuel, were both painters. Among the works by Echave which survive is the earliest known copy of the Virgin of Guadalupe, signed and dated 1606, and some of the panels from the retablo of Tlatelolco. Also attributed to Echave are the paintings of the retablo of Xochimilco. Echave wrote a treatise on the Basque language, published in 1607.

– CLARA BARGELLINI

ECHEANDÍA, JOSÉ MARÍA DE

José María de Echeandía (d. after 1833), governor of Alta California (1825–1831), in control of the southern part of the territory from 1832 to 1833. His most important policies concerned the Franciscan missions. He refused orders to expel the Spanish-born Franciscans in 1828, because most of the missionaries were from Spain and the missions would thus have been left without priests. Echeandía also initiated a partial emancipation of more acculturated Indian converts living primarily in the southern missions, most of whom left the missions.

Echeandía refused orders to expel the Spanish-born Franciscans in 1828, because the missions would thus have been left without priests.

Internally, Echeandía faced several revolts, which he successfully repressed, but he took power in the south following a military uprising against then-governor Manuel VICTORIA. In foreign relations, Echeandía allowed the Russians at Fort Ross to hunt for otters in Mexican waters. Wounded in an 1833 uprising, Echeandía returned to Mexico.

– ROBERT H. JACKSON

ECHENIQUE, JOSÉ RUFINO

José Rufino Echenique (b. 1808; d. 16 June 1887), president of Peru (1851–1854). Chosen by the national congress, he had been a counselor to President Ramón CASTILLA. But he was politically naive and chose anti-Castilla ministers and counselors, some of them reputedly dishonest. He accepted fraudulent claims against the public treasury, leading to a tremendous increase in the internal debt. In 1853 he secretly converted nearly half of this debt into claims on Peru's foreign debt. Intended to strengthen domestic public bonds weakened by speculation and embezzlement, the debt consolidation was funded by huge foreign loans backed by guano. A great scandal ensued, which combined with the outrages of his ministers, encouraged a popular revolution. During the rebellion, Echenique decreed abolition of black slavery, apparently to generate an army. His opponent, former president Castilla, duplicated this decree. In 1855 Echenique was forced into exile, first in Panama and then the United States. His successors continued the policy of linking the national debt to foreign trade.

— VINCENT PELOSO

ECHEVERRÍA, ESTEBAN

Esteban Echeverría (b. 2 September 1805; d. 19 January 1851), Argentine poet and political essayist.

After five years of study in Paris, Echeverría returned to Buenos Aires in 1830 infused with the spirit of romanticism and liberalism. He soon gained recognition as the leading figure of a new generation of writers. Influenced by Victor Hugo and François René de Chateaubriand, Echeverría published *Elvira, o la novia de la Plata* (Elvira, or the River Plate Bride) in 1832 and then, in 1837, *La cautiva* (The Captive), a long narrative poem exalting the American scene. In 1838 Echeverría wrote "El matadero" (The Slaughterhouse), a classic short story denouncing the Juan Manuel de ROSAS dictatorship, but for political reasons the work was not published until 1871.

Although Echeverría was the first romantic poet in Hispanic America, his reputation rests as well on the impact of his political writings at a time when Argentina was under the iron rule of Rosas (1829–1852). In 1837 Echeverría organized the Asociación de Mayo, which espoused the principles of the May 1810 revolution upon which the nation had been founded and swore its opposition to Rosas. The aspirations of this association were codified by Echeverría and published in Montevideo in 1846 as the *Dogma socialista*. This document expounded the ideals of a free society and a national literature similarly free of traditional restraints. Its political and social implications for a new Argentina based on liberty and justice were quickly recognized.

— MYRON I. LICHTBLAU

ECHEVERRÍA ÁLVAREZ, LUIS

Luis Echeverría Álvarez (b. 17 January 1922), president of Mexico (1970–1976). To the surprise of most analysts, Luis Echeverría, though a disciple of Gustavo DÍAZ ORDAZ, turned out to be a president in the populist mold, reintroducing, in certain respects, a style similar to that of Lázaro CÁRDENAS.

Echeverría was born in the Federal District, as were so many leading politicians of his and succeeding generations. He attended school in Mexico City and Ciudad Victoria, then, after graduating from the National Preparatory School, he enrolled in the National Law School in 1940, completing his degree in August 1945. He married the daughter of José Zuno Hernández, a former governor of Jalisco and a member of an important political family. A political disciple of Rodolfo Sánchez Taboada, the president of the PRI, he first held positions in the party, including press secretary, before following his mentor to the navy secretariat. In 1954 he became *oficial mayor* of public education, after which he attached himself to the career of another mentor, Gustavo Díaz Ordaz, as undersecretary of the government secretariat (1958–1963). Upon his mentor's nomination as the presidential candidate of the PRI, he replaced him as secretary, a position in which he remained from 1963 to 1969, when he resigned to become himself a presidential candidate. He was the last official party presidential candidate to come from this cabinet agency.

Echeverría's regime was characterized by greater levels of economic and political uncertainty than were those of his immediate predecessors. Early in his administration, he faced strong internal opposition within his own cabinet, led by Alfonso Martínez Domínguez, the head of the Federal District. Martínez Domínguez used a paramilitary force in a 1971 incident, after which the president removed him from office. Echeverría also faced—for the first time in many years—well-organized guerrilla opposition groups in urban and rural settings, most notably the band of Lucio Cabañas in Guerrero, which the army eventually eliminated.

On the economic front, Echeverría was responsible for the rapid growth of state-owned enterprises and the alienation of many elements of Mexico's private-sector leadership. He exacerbated divisions between the state and the private sector by nationalizing agrarian properties in northwest Mexico immediately before leaving office and by presiding over the first devaluation of the peso in many years. He left the presidency further delegitimized than when he took office, passing on to his successor, José LÓPEZ PORTILLO, a difficult set of problems.

After leaving the presidency in 1976, Echeverría served as ambassador to UNESCO (1977–1978), then briefly to Australia. He also directed a Third World studies institute upon his return to Mexico in 1979. He subsequently retired from all public activities.

— RODERIC AI CAMP

ECHEVERRÍA BIANCHI, JOSÉ ANTONIO

José Antonio Echeverría Bianchi (b. 16 July 1932; d. 13 March 1957), Cuban revolutionary. Born in Cárdenas, Matanzas, Echeverría was educated in primary school at the Colegio Hermanos Maristas de Cárdenas and graduated from high school in the same city. He entered the University of Havana School of Architecture in

---

Echeverría directed the takeover of a Havana radio station, where he was killed in a gun battle with police.

1953, where he was elected president of the Federation of University Students (1954, 1955, and 1956). Echeverría, along with Fauré Chomón, founded the Revolutionary Directorate in 1956. In the same year he attended the Congress of Latin American Students in Chile. He and Fidel CASTRO were signers of the "Letter from Mexico." He participated in the organization that attacked the presidential palace in March 1957, and he directed the takeover of a Havana radio station, where he was killed in a gun battle with police.

— MARÍA DEL CARMEN ALMODOVAR

EDER, SANTIAGO MARTÍN

Santiago Martín Eder (*b.* 24 June 1838; *d.* 25 December 1921), Colombian agricultural entrepreneur. Born in Mitau, in present-day Latvia, Santiago emigrated in 1851 to the United States to join his brother Henry, who was engaged in various mercantile activities in California, Panama, and Chile. His Harvard law education sustained his later activities as U.S. consul in Buenaventura, but his family's commercial relations shaped his life.

In 1864 Eder purchased La Rita and La Manuelita plantations near Palmira to develop export agriculture. After spotty success with tobacco, indigo, coffee, and sugar, Eder devoted himself to the general economic development of the Cauca Valley. His investments in the Buenaventura-Cali railroad, the Cauca steamship company, and various banks in Cali placed him at the fore of regional developers. Eder's son Charles married the daughter of Italian entrepreneur Ernesto Cerruti and assumed control of the family's Cauca properties. Another son, Phanor, became active in international commerce and law. The Manuelita mill, completely modernized by 1903, became the country's leading producer of domestically consumed refined sugar.

— DAVID SOWELL

EDWARDS, AGUSTÍN

Agustín Edwards (*b.* 17 June 1878; *d.* 1941), Chilean politician, financier, and writer. At age twenty-two, Ed-

wards became one of the youngest members in Chile's House of Representatives. At the same time he became active in the Edwards Bank of Valparaíso. Elected vice president of the House and president of the Ministry of Finance in 1902, he negotiated a peace treaty with Bolivia and initiated the construction of a railroad from Arica to La Paz. In 1906 he began his diplomatic career, serving successively in Italy, Spain, and Switzerland. Upon his return to Chile, he served as finance minister under President Pedro MONTT. During World War I he was named envoy to Great Britain in charge of diplomatic and financial affairs and, in 1920, became special envoy to the Court of St. James. In 1921 he was named representative to the League of Nations. He received many honors in Chile and Europe.

While living abroad Edwards studied newspaper and magazine production, then utilized this knowledge in Chile, where he founded the newspaper *El Mercurio* and several magazines, including *Zig-Zag*. In the financial domain, he reorganized the Edwards Bank, founded several companies, and was involved in nitrate mining. In 1925 he resolved a conflict with Bolivia and reestablished peace. Among his writings are his *Memoria sobre el plebiscito tacneño* (1926), in which he opposes a plan to allow Tacna and Arica to determine their nationality; *My Native Land* (1928), a cultural history of Chile; *Peoples of Old* (1929), on the Araucanian Indians; *The Dawn* (1931), on Chilean history from Independence (1810) to the first elected president (1841); and *Cuatro presidentes de Chile* (1932), on the period from 1841 to 1932.

— BARBARA MUJICA

EDWARDS, JORGE

Jorge Edwards (*b.* 29 July 1931), Chilean writer and diplomat. Considering his writing merely a pastime, Edwards entered the diplomatic corps in the late 1950s. His early books include two collections of stories, *El patio* (1952; The Patio) and *Gente de la ciudad* (1961; City People). His first novel, *El peso de la noche* (1965; The Weight of Night), a semifinalist in the Seix Barral literary contest, was followed by another collection of stories, *Las máscaras* (1967; The Masks). In 1970 the Allende government sent Edwards to Havana to open a Chilean embassy. In spite of the official nature of his assignment, Edwards maintained contact with vehement critics of the Castro government such as José Lezama Lima and Heberto PADILLA. After retiring from the diplomatic corps, he wrote *Persona non grata* (1973), a scathing indictment of the Castro regime as well as of other authoritarian systems. Attacked by both the extreme Left and the extreme Right, the book launched

Edwards's international literary career. *Persona non grata* was banned in Chile by the Pinochet regime and boycotted by several European and American publishers. After a new edition was published in Spain, Edwards brought suit against the government to allow its sale in Chile. Although he lost, the case drew attention to his cause. Edwards's other books are less overtly political. They include *Desde la cola del dragón* (1977; From the Dragon's Tail), a collection of essays on Chilean culture; *Los convidados de piedra* (1977; The Stone Guests), a novel about the bourgeois intellectuals of his generation who became revolutionaries; *El museo de cera* (1981; The Wax Museum), a historical fantasy about a conservative aristocrat who tries to stop time; *La mujer imaginaria* (1985; The Imaginary Woman), another novel, *El anfitrión* (1987; The Host), a kind of Chilean Faust story; *Adiós poeta* (1990; Goodby, Poet), a memoir about Edwards's experiences with Pablo NERUDA; *Cuentos completos* (1990; Complete Stories); and *Fantasmas de carne y hueso* (1993; Flesh and Blood Ghosts), stories that draw on Edwards's experiences as a diplomat and writer.

– BARBARA MUJICA

EDWARDS BELLO, JOAQUÍN

Joaquín Edwards Bello (*b.* 10 May 1887; *d.* 1968), Chilean journalist and novelist. A prolific writer and memorialist, Edwards Bello created an extensive commentary on Chilean life from a personal perspective. As a *criollista*, he was interested in creating an autochthonous literature, using South American subjects and a literary style free of European influences. He was a harsh critic of Chilean society and its decadence. In many newspaper columns and in novels such as *El inútil* (1910), *El roto* (1920), and *La chica del "Crillón"* (1935) he studied, from a naturalist perspective which underlined the grotesque in everyday life, the human and social weaknesses of the system.

– S. DAYDÍ-TOLSON

EGAÑA FABRES, MARIANO

Mariano Egaña Fabres (*b.* 1 March 1793; *d.* 24 June 1846), Chilean lawyer, diplomat, and intellectual. The son of Juan EGAÑA, from whom he inherited his strong intellectual streak, Mariano Egaña qualified as a lawyer in 1811, and held office briefly in the patriot governments of 1813–1814. Like his father, he was confined to Juan Fernández (an island prison for exiled political prisoners) during the Spanish reconquest (1814–1817). In 1824 he was sent as Chilean envoy to London. His credentials were not accepted because Britain had not

yet recognized Chile's independence, so Egaña settled in Paris. He returned to Chile in 1829. It was as a result of his initiative that Andrés BELLO (1781–1865), a prominent Venezuelan intellectual, was offered government employment in Chile.

In the new Conservative regime of 1830, in which he was a key figure, Egaña served as minister of finance (1830), of the interior (1830), and of justice (1837–1841), as well as senator (1831–1846). He was a leading influence on the drafting of the Constitution of 1833, though his more reactionary proposals (such as indefinite re-eligibility of presidents and hereditary senators) were excluded. Egaña's death (he collapsed and died in the street) had a great impact on Santiago. His book collection, the best in Chile, was bought by the state for the National Library.

– SIMON COLLIER

EGAÑA RISCO JUAN

Egaña Risco Juan (*b.* 31 October 1768; *d.* 20 April 1836), Chilean patriot and intellectual. One of the most learned men of his time and place, Juan Egaña Risco was born in Lima, the son of a Chilean father. He studied at San Marcos University, Lima, from which he graduated in 1789, the year he moved to Chile. An active patriot after 1810, he was a member of the first national congress (1811), for which he was banished to Juan Fernández (an island prison for exile of political prisoners) during the Spanish reconquest (1814–1817). He served several times in the congresses of the 1820s, but his moment of greatest influence came in 1823, when he was the principal author of the idiosyncratically conservative constitution of that year. It proved unworkable and was swiftly abandoned. Egaña's cast of mind was conservative, moralistic, and steeped in admiration for classical antiquity, the Inca empire, and China. Several volumes of his writings were published in London in the 1820s, and another volume in Bordeaux in 1836.

– SIMON COLLIER

EGAS, CAMILO ALEJANDRO

Camilo Alejandro Egas (*b.* 1895; *d.* 1962), Ecuadorian artist. Egas was born in Quito and attended the Academy of Arts in that city. A disciple of Paul Bar and Víctor Puiz, he won first prize in a national competition in celebration of Ecuadorian independence (1909). With the aid of an Ecuadorian government grant he studied at the Academy of Rome (1918) and the following year continued his studies at the Academy of San Fernando in Madrid. On another trip to Europe, he met Picasso in Paris, where he studied at the Colorrossi Academy (1922). Egas exhibited at the Salon des Indépendents and Salon d'Automme (Paris, 1924–1925). His expressionist paintings of Ecuadorian Indians frequently depict women in mourning or tragic instances (*Desolation*). In 1929 he received an appointment to teach painting at the New School for Social Research and in 1935 became the director of the school's painting department, a position he held until his death. In 1938 he collaborated on a mural project for the Ecuadorian Pavilion at the New York World's Fair. Egas was influenced by the surrealist exiles in New York in the 1940s and by Mexican muralist José Clemente OROZCO. He died in New York.

— MARTA GARSD

EGUREN, JOSÉ MARÍA

José María Eguren (*b.* 7 July 1874; *d.* 29 April 1942), Peruvian poet. Eguren began writing poetry at the height of the Spanish American *modernismo* movement at the turn of the century. Ironically, however, he is the one Peruvian poet to break out of the mold and bring Peruvian poetry into the twentieth century. Both in personality and poetry, he was radically different from such contemporaries as José Santos CHOCANO. In fact, Eguren was something of a recluse, and in his poetry he created imaginary worlds in which to cocoon himself. Steeped in French symbolism, his poetry at first blush seems to imitate the *modernistas* because of certain typical motifs, among them, mystery, love, and dreams, but his language is a storehouse of creativity that had tremendous influence on later Peruvian poets. His works also lead Peruvian poetry into the modern age in their themes of alienation, skepticism, and imitation of earlier forms.

Eguren spiritualizes inspiration in the form of a small girl with a blue lamp who leads the poet into the spheres of the imagination and the spiritual.

Eguren produced three books of poetry: *Simbólicas* (1911), *La canción de las figuras* (1916), and *Poesías* (1929). Lyrical, telluric, symbolic, and imaginative, his poetry enriches the Spanish language with regionalisms, archaic terms, neologisms, and even foreign and invented words. Inspiration, for instance, is allegorized in the form of a small girl with a blue lamp who leads the poet into the spheres of the imagination and the spiritual. In his later poetry, Eguren draws on the work of

the European vanguard in his use of metaphor and dream imagery.

— DICK GERDES

EICHELBAUM, SAMUEL

Samuel Eichelbaum (*b.* 14 November 1894; *d.* 4 May 1967), Argentine playwright and short-story writer. When he was only twelve years old, Samuel Eichelbaum left the town of his birth, Domínguez, Entre Ríos Province, to travel to Rosario, where he tried to interest theater companies in producing his *sainete Un lobo manso* (1906). Although this early attempt met with rejection, it exemplifies his lifelong dedication to the theater. Eichelbaum's work reflects characters who are archetypes within Argentine society, yet critics frequently recognize in his works the presence of Dostoyevsky, Ibsen, and Strindberg rather than any direct influence from other Argentine writers. His plays are rooted in introspection, as for example in *Dos brasas* (1952); through a seemingly psychoanalytic approach to drama he explores the self and the nature of conflicts between the conscious and unconscious. Other major themes include the importance for Argentina of both rural and urban areas, the strength of women, individual tragedy found at all socioeconomic levels, and the need to survive as an individual against all adversity. The theater of Eichelbaum is clearly distinguished by the intellectual capacity of the characters and their ability to think and reason, as expressed through dialogue.

Although few of his plays are political in nature, Eichelbaum does direct his attention to social problems. In *El dogma* (1922) he alludes to the role of Jewish activists in the labor movement, and in *Nadie la conoció nunca* (1926) there is a reference to attacks on Jewish neighborhoods after the workers' strikes of 1910 and 1919 (the latter known as *La Semana Trágica*). More than twenty years later, *Un patricio del 80* (1948), written in collaboration with Ulises Petit de Murat, was subject to official opposition because it was considered to imply criticism of Perón's interest in supporting foreign exploitation of Argentine natural resources.

Un guapo del 900 (1940), Eichelbaum's best-known and most commercially successful play, explores the moral codes of the *guapo*, a bodyguard to a political boss. Individual freedom of choice and sacrifice are bound to machismo and self-destruction in the search for dignity among the lower classes of Argentine society. As in other plays, Eichelbaum concentrates on the internal turmoil of his characters and the psychological processes guided by honor and individuality that lead to sorrowful outcomes.

— DANUSIA L. MESON

ELCANO, JUAN SEBASTIÁN DE

Juan Sebastián de Elcano (*b.* ca. 1476, *d.* 4 August 1526), Spanish navigator. Elcano was born in Guetaria, Vizcaya. He completed the first circumnavigation of the world by sea, at a time of intense rivalry between Spain and Portugal over the spice trade. In 1519 he joined the expedition of Ferdinand MAGELLAN to the Orient via South America; it entered the Pacific in November 1520. When Magellan was killed in the Philippines in 1521, Elcano, one of his captains, assumed leadership of the expedition. The only remaining ship, *Victoria,* sailed for Spain via the Cape of Good Hope (May 1522). After a voyage fraught with deprivation and sickness, Elcano and the seventeen other surviving men reached Spain in September 1522. As chief navigator and guide of an expedition to claim the Molucca Islands for Spain in June 1525, Elcano died en route in the Pacific.

— HILARY BURGER

ELHUYAR, JUAN JOSÉ DE

Juan José de Elhuyar (*b.* 15 June 1754; *d.* 20 September 1796), Spanish chemist and mineralogist and director of mines in New Granada (1783–1796). Born in Logroño, Spain, to Juan D'Elhuyar and Ursula de Zubice, Juan José de Elhuyar studied medicine in Paris from 1772 to 1777. After he returned to Spain, the Ministry of the Navy sent him and his younger brother Fausto de ELHUYAR in 1778 to study at the Mining Academy of Freiberg. Elhuyar's main objective was to learn better techniques for manufacturing cannon, but he also studied geology, metallurgy, and chemistry and visited many mining operations in Central Europe. Back in Spain the two brothers isolated tungsten and published *Análisis química del volfram y examen de un nuevo metal que entra en su composición* (1783).

In late 1783 Minister of the Indies José de GÁLVEZ selected Elhuyar as director of mines for New Granada, a position he occupied for the remainder of his life. He adapted the baron von Born's barrel method for amalgamating silver ores to local conditions and worked to raise the technological level of the Mariquita silver district. Elhuyar also developed a means for isolating platinum and carried out geological explorations. His work met resistance from both colonial officials and the mine operators. He died in Bogotá.

— KENDALL W. BROWN

ELHUYAR Y ZÚBICE, FAUSTO DE

Fausto de Elhuyar y Zúbice (*b.* 11 October 1757; *d.* 6 January 1833), Spanish scientist and director general of the Mining Tribunal of New Spain (1788–1821). A native of Logroño, Spain, Elhuyar was educated in Paris and at the famous Mining School of Freiberg, Germany (1778–1781, 1787), and taught mineralogy at the Patriotic Seminary of Vergara, Spain (1782–1786). He and his brother Juan José discovered tungsten in 1783 while experimenting with wolframite.

In July 1786, while Elhuyar was in Austria to recruit mining experts for service in Spanish America and to study the Baron Ignaz von Born's method of amalgamating silver ores, Secretary of the Indies José de Gálvez appointed him director general of the Mexican Mining Tribunal. According to Walter Howe, "the renaissance of the Tribunal may be said to have begun with Elhuyar's arrival" in 1788. As director general he was an influential and energetic advocate for the mining industry, but his bureaucratic service hindered the promise of his early scientific achievements. Elhuyar established a school of mines in 1792, the first secular academy in the Spanish colonies. With Mexican independence, Elhuyar returned to Spain in 1821 and served as director general of mining, until his accidental death in 1833.

— KENDALL W. BROWN

ELÍAS DOMINGO

Elías Domingo (*b.* 19 December 1805; *d.* 3 December 1867), Peruvian plantation owner and statesman. Born to aristocratic parents in the Ica Valley, the wine-growing center of the southern coast, he was educated in elite Peruvian schools and in Spain and France. On returning home he married Doña Ysabel de la Quintana y Pedemonte, sister of the new archbishop of Lima. Beginning as a merchant and lender, he later became one of the largest landowners in the coastal valleys of Peru. He owned more than 600 slaves by 1850 and cultivated wine, *pisco,* and cotton on his plantations. Elías soon became politically active. A convinced liberal, he strongly favored free trade, and by 1843 he had formed a partnership with Ramón CASTILLA. After Castilla became president in 1845, Elías joined his council of state, a three-member body of presidential advisers who by serving as liaisons with the national congress, held a great deal of power. A philanthropist, he donated large sums to found a high school, the Colegio de Nuestra Señora de Guadalupe, which became the source of liberal thought in Peru for decades. Elías also sought to preserve black slavery in Peru.

A major scandal erupted when he tried to bypass the prohibition against the African slave trade with a purchase in Colombia. The purchase included children, who under Peruvian law were free. In 1849 he designed a law to regulate the importation of indentured Asian labor. When José Rufino ECHENIQUE became president in 1851, Elías strenuously opposed his debt consolidation program because it would overburden the state, and he called the program a fraud. Echenique resorted to censorship and terrorism to stop his opponents, and Elías rebelled. Soon he joined forces with the popular uprising led by Castilla. Returning to the private sector, probably by 1859, he converted most of his remaining vineyards to cotton and focused completely on international cotton commerce. His efforts in this trade foundered on inadequate marketing techniques, and by the time of his death his cotton empire was in ruins.

– VINCENT PELOSO

ELÍO, FRANCISCO JAVIER

Francisco Javier Elío (*b.* 4 March 1767; *d.* 4 September 1822), last viceroy of the Río de la Plata. Born in Navarre, Spain, he began his military career as a lieutenant in the defense of Oran and Ceuta in North Africa. Elío was sent to the Río de la Plata in 1805 with the rank of colonel, to command the Banda Oriental. Shortly after the first English invasion (1806), Viceroy Santiago de LINIERS Y BREMOND named Elío interim governor of Montevideo. After the second English invasion (1807), he became one of Liniers's chief opponents and assumed the post of viceroy. After Liniers's successor, Cisneros, was relieved of his post by the Cabildo Abierto in May 1810, Elío returned to Spain and convinced the Regency Council to appoint him viceroy. The junta established in Buenos Aires refused to recognize his appointment, however, so he governed from Montevideo until he was forced from power by an antiroyalist uprising in the Banda Oriental. Elío returned to Spain in 1812 and became involved in Spanish political life. He was executed at Valencia.

– SUSAN SOCOLOW

ELIZAGA, JOSÉ MARÍA

José María Elizaga (*b.* 27 September 1786; *d.* 2 October 1842), Mexican pianist, organist, and composer. Piano study in his native Morelia and in Mexico City prepared Elizaga for a position as assistant organist in the Colegio de San Nicolás in Morelia (1799). Among his piano pupils was Doña Ana María Huarte, the future wife of emperor Agustín de ITURBIDE; he eventually became music director of Iturbide's imperial court (1822). Elizaga started his own music publishing business and in 1825 founded a conservatory that later formed the basis of the National Conservatory of Music. He served as *maestro de capilla* of the Guadalajara cathedral from 1827 to 1830 and retired to Morelia in 1842. His works include sacred music for orchestra and chorus, two didactic music treatises, and *Vals con variaciones* for piano.

– ROBERT L. PARKER

ELIZONDO, SALVADOR

Salvador Elizondo (*b.* 19 December 1932), Mexican poet and author. This notable figure in Mexican letters had an eclectic interest in poetry, film, essays, and fiction that has given him a well-deserved reputation for experimental work.

Born in Mexico City of wealthy parents, Elizondo resided for several years in Europe, where he studied in Paris and Cambridge, as well as the University of Ottawa, Canada, and Mexico's School of Philosophy and Letters of the National University (1952–1953). As a fellow at the Center for Mexican Writers, he wrote *Farabeuf* (1965), which received the distinguished Villaurrutia Prize in 1965. He cofounded the magazine *S. Nob,* an exploration of eroticism in Mexican letters, and served as editor in chief of *Estaciones.* Twice a Guggenheim fellow (1968–1969 and 1973–1974), he was considered a leader in the Nuevo Cine group. He conducted the "Contextos" radio program for the National University (1968–1978) and wrote for *Vuelta* in the 1980s.

– RODERIC AI CAMP

EMPARÁN, VICENTE

Vicente Emparán (*b.* January 1747; *d.* 3 October 1820), the last Spanish general of Venezuela. With the rank of rear admiral, Emparán left the Spanish Royal Navy for his first major appointment in America as naval commander at Puerto Cabello, on the Venezuelan coast. In 1792 he was appointed governor of Cumaná, a post he held for twelve years. Emparán returned to Spain briefly in 1808 and was appointed captain-general of Venezuela. When he returned to Venezuela in May 1809, he was confronted with the conspiratorial movements of late 1809 and early 1810. News of French advances in Spain prompted the agitators to convoke a meeting with Emparán on 19 April 1810. By popular demand, Spanish authority was renounced and the Junta Suprema de Caracas was formed to take over the government, thereby effectively declaring Venezuela's independence. Emparán was taken prisoner and later exiled to Philadelphia. He returned to Spain in 1810.

– INÉS QUINTERO

ENCINA, FRANCISCO ANTONIO

Francisco Antonio Encina (*b.* 10 September 1874; *d.* 23 August 1965), Chilean deputy and intellectual. An attorney by education, Encina wrote the twenty-volume *History of Chile to 1891* describing the nation's past from precolonial days to 1891, as well as numerous

---

Encina believed that Chileans were biologically predisposed toward being warriors, and were ill prepared to compete in the world of commerce.

---

monographs. A believer in the ideas of Joseph-Arthur Gobineau, he, like his contemporary Nicolás Palacios, argued that Chileans were a combination of Araucanian Indian and German *conquistador*. This genetic mixture, Encina believed, handicapped Chileans who, while biologically predisposed toward being warriors, were ill prepared to compete in the world of commerce. Though entranced by racist philosophies, Encina presciently recognized the need for Chile to diversify and modernize its economy by encouraging land reform, industrialization, and the teaching of technical skills.

— WILLIAM F. SATER

ENCINAS, JOSÉ ANTONIO

José Antonio Encinas (*b.* 1886; *d.* 1958), a prominent leader of the *indigenista* movement of early-twentieth-century Peru. As a land commissioner, in 1918 he drew up a program to help native Peruvians regain lands that had been stolen by white aristocratic lawyers. After the revolutionary military government of Juan Velasco Alvarado issued the Agrarian Reform Law of 24 June 1969, Agrarian Reform officials turned to some of Encinas's findings to guide them in organizing the formation of agrarian reform zones. The section of the law creating peasant cooperatives reflected in part the writings of Encinas.

— VINCENT PELOSO

ENCISO, MARTÍN FERNÁNDEZ DE

Martín Fernández de Enciso (*b.* ca. 1470; *d.* ca. 1528), a lawyer and central figure in an early sixteenth-century Vasco Núñez de BALBOA venture. In the first years of the sixteenth century, Diego de NICUESA, a wealthy resident of Hispaniola, and Alonso de OJEDA, a prospector on the island, submitted to the Spanish crown a plan to divide the entire coast of South America into two governing areas. Ojeda would receive a concession to settle and exploit an area from Coquibacoa to the Gulf of Urabá in modern Colombia, and in return the crown would receive a fixed percentage of the settlement's profits. The crown sealed this contract in 1508.

After it became clear that Pizarro's first attempt at colonization in 1509 had failed, Ojeda contracted with a lawyer named Martín Fernández de Enciso to travel to present-day Central America in relief of PIZARRO. In return he promised Enciso the position of *alcalde mayor* (governor) in the new colonies. On 13 September 1510 Enciso's party sailed from Hispaniola with 152 new settlers bound for Urabá. Lacking supplies and facing innumerable difficulties, Pizarro's group was wandering hopelessly in Darién when Enciso's ships arrived in late September bearing supplies.

Meanwhile, Vasco Núñez de Balboa had secretly boarded Enciso's ship in Hispaniola to avoid creditors and bailiffs who were pursuing him for outstanding debts. On discovering the stowaway's presence aboard his ship, Enciso declared his intention to abandon Balboa on a deserted island. However, Balboa's popularity grew among the other passengers, who disliked the petty and temperamental Enciso. Once Enciso's group encountered the Pizarro contingent, despite the latter's protestations and a release order from Ojeda, Enciso forced them to stay in Urabá, hopeful that they would contribute to his pursuit of wealth.

As the expedition unfolded, it became clear that Enciso had many shortcomings as a frontier commander and lacked real authority, for Ojeda's poor health meant that he no longer really controlled the venture. Thus, the popular Balboa emerged from this power struggle as the natural leader of the early settlements in northern South America. Although Enciso's group took Darién (probably in November 1510), Balboa and his supporters forced them to leave the colony, thus triggering a series of events which led to Balboa's later execution.

Balboa erred in permitting Enciso to return to Hispaniola because he thereafter cleverly pursued legal action against Balboa. Contending that the king had given the territory to Ojeda, Enciso maintained that the area was therefore rightfully theirs. Enciso eventually returned to Spain, where he vociferously protested Balboa's actions and supposed abuses. He joined others opposing Balboa by incessantly pushing these charges until finally Balboa was beheaded in 1519.

Somewhat later, Enciso helped lead an ill-fated expedition to Cenu, in northwestern South America. This attempt to secure wealth, like the first, failed, and Enciso again returned to Spain. Enciso is remembered primarily for his role in the Balboa story.

— BLAKE D. PATTRIDGE

ENRÍQUEZ, CARLOS

Carlos Enríquez (*b.* 3 August 1901, *d.* 2 May 1957), Cuban artist. Born in Santa Clara, Cuba, Enríquez was sent by his parents to the United States to study engineering, but upon his arrival he instead entered the Pennsylvania Academy of Fine Arts. He was expelled from the school because of his rebellious personality and returned to Cuba. During a 1930–1934 sojourn in Europe, he became particularly attracted to the art of El Greco, Zurbarán, Velázquez, and Goya. During the 1930s he incorporated political and historical themes in his paintings. He won a prize at the National Salon in Havana in 1938.

His paintings depict nature in a state of turmoil, an effect achieved by swirling forms, translucid planes, and overlapping figures (*The Rape of the Mulattas,* 1937). Sensualism and the female body, to which he alluded even in the shapes of animals and vegetation, are characteristic of his work (*Cuban Outlaw,* 1943).

— MARTA GARSD

ENRÍQUEZ, MANUEL

Manuel Enríquez (*b.* 17 June 1926; *d.* 26 April 1994), Mexican violinist, composer, and music administrator. At age six Enríquez began violin study with his father in Ocotlán, Jalisco, and continued with Ignacio Camarena in Guadalajara. He directed the Guadalajara Symphony (1949–1955). A scholarship to the Juilliard School of Music (1955–1957) allowed him to study violin with Ivan Galamian and composition with Peter Mennin. With a Guggenheim Fellowship in 1971 he researched folk music in Spain and the same year enrolled in the Columbia-Princeton Research Center for Electronic Music. His music, written largely in nontraditional graphic notation, embraces, at times, serially recurring patterns of pitch, rhythm, and timbre, and free sections in which some elements of chance are left to the performers. He deliberately avoids nationalistic references. Enríquez taught composition at the National Conservatory of Mexico and has directed both the Carlos Chávez Center for Music Research and the music department of the National Institute of Fine Arts.

— ROBERT L. PARKER

ENRÍQUEZ DE ALMANSA, MARTÍN

Martín Enríquez de Almansa (*b.* ca. 1508; *d.* 1583), viceroy of New Spain (1568–1580) and of Peru (1580–1583). Although from a noble family of Castile, Enríquez did not inherit a title and little is known of his early life. Appointed viceroy of New Spain at the age of sixty, he brought a strong rule to the colony in the

aftermath of the Cortés-Ávila conspiracy. He was authoritarian and at times bad tempered, but he was also just and kindly toward the Indians. He refused to grant colonial demands for a total war against the wild Chichimecs of the north. That and his imposition of the

---

Enríquez refused to grant colonial demands for a total war against the wild Chichimecs of the north.

---

detested *alcabala* (sales tax) made him unpopular. A wise administrator, he is generally credited with having raised the prestige of the viceroy's office. He reluctantly accepted the viceroyalty of Peru in 1580 and died in Lima three years later.

— STAFFORD POOLE, C.M.

ENRÍQUEZ DE GUZMÁN, ALONSO

Alonso Enríquez de Guzmán (*b.* ca. 1501; *d.* ca. 1549), author of a picaresque account of Peru's conquest and civil wars. Born in Seville and related to one of Spain's most powerful noble families, he married Constanza de Añasco at eighteen. Duels and nighttime escapades led to difficulties with city authorities. He left to fight in the Italian campaigns and, later, to become a courtier in the service of the emperor, from whom he repeatedly requested induction into the Order of Santiago. He was inducted into the order in 1529.

Enríquez de Guzmán sailed without license to the Indies and convinced the Audiencia of Santo Domingo to appoint him to an administrative position in Santa Marta, but news of Peruvian gold led him to South America's western coast in 1534. He planned to get rich and return to Seville to enjoy his wealth. He was in Lima in August 1535 and continued to Cuzco. Diego de ALMAGRO invited him on the Chilean venture, but he remained in Cuzco, and fought during the great native uprising of MANCO INCA.

When the Chilean expedition returned, Enríquez de Guzmán helped the Almagrists retake Cuzco from the Pizzarists, for which he received ample reward. During the battle of Las Salinas, Almagro left him in charge of Cuzco, where the victorious Hernando PIZARRO captured him. Barely escaping with his life by offering ransom, Enríquez de Guzmán was returned to Spain (1539) and jailed, but connections at court led to his freedom. He became an older companion for young Prince Philip. Offered a military command by the duke of Alba, he fought in Germany against Lutherans (battle of Mühlberg).

Enríquez de Guzmán left two important manuscripts: a rambling autobiography, *Libro de la vida y costumbres de don Alonso Enriques, caballero...* (The Life and Acts of Don Alonso Enríquez de Guzmán, A Knight of Seville . . .), and a poem on the death of Diego de Almagro. Originally believed to be more fictional than true, the work reveals upon careful reading that the Peruvian sections at least are largely accurate.

— NOBLE DAVID COOK

ENRÍQUEZ GALLO, ALBERTO

Alberto Enríquez Gallo (*b.* 24 July 1894; *d.* 13 July 1962), military figure and president of Ecuador (nonelected 1937–1938). Born in Tanicuchi, León, Enríquez graduated from the Colegio Militar Eloy Alfaro in Quito (1912). He served as minister of defense from 1935 to 1937, using his position to reform and professionalize the military. Promoted to general in 1937, Enríquez took over the presidency in October, when the military ousted interim president Federico PÁEZ (1936–1937).

Enríquez's administration undertook a broad-based reform of juridical, educational, administrative, and financial structures and legislation. His government also enacted a number of social reforms, including an advanced labor code and laws to protect children. Enríquez relinquished power to Manuel María Borrero after calling the Constituent Convention of 1938. Ten years later (1948) he was an unsuccessful presidential candidate of the liberal socialist coalition. He served as senator for the province of Pichincha from 1956 until 1960.

— LINDA ALEXANDER RODRÍGUEZ

ENSENADA, CENÓN DE SOMODEVILLA, MARQUÉS DE LA

Marqués de la Ensenada, Cenón de Somodevilla (*b.* 2 June 1702; *d.* 2 December 1781), secretary of state of Spain (1743–1754). Termed the "secretary of everything," by a contemporary because he was secretary of state, finance, war, marine affairs, and the Indies, Ensenada was the most powerful minister in Spain during the early reign of Ferdinand VI. Early in his bureaucratic career he specialized in naval administration, and once in office he became firmly committed to increasing Spain's naval power. In an effort to increase the crown's revenues from the Indies trade, he encouraged the use of register ships rather than fleets and imposed strict trade regulations. However, Ensenada is best known for his domestic fiscal reform policies, which included a proposed single tax on income, based on ability to pay

and applicable to all citizens. A ministerial power struggle in 1754 brought about his dismissal and exile.

— SUZANNE HILES BURKHOLDER

ERCILLA Y ZÚÑIGA, ALONSO DE

Alonso de Ercilla y Zúñiga (*b.* 1533; *d.* 1594), Spanish poet. Although he was in Latin America for only a short period, Alonso de Ercilla can be considered one of the first writers of the New World. In *La Araucana* (1569, 1578, 1589), an exemplary Renaissance epic poem based on his brief experience as a soldier fighting the Araucanian Indians in southern Chile, he combines the imagination of the poet with the observations and commentaries of the historian. He began writing the poem during the campaign, but he completed it years later in Spain, adding several passages about other important Spanish triumphs in Europe. Dedicated to King Philip II, in whose court he served from an early age, *La Araucana* praises the glories of the empire while also offering a sympathetic and admiring view of the Araucanians. Lacking an individual hero, the poem stresses

Alonso de Ercilla y Zúñiga. Engraving by Juan Moreno Sepata. Reproduced from Blave, Geographia, *vol. 2. (Amsterdam, 1662). (Courtesy of the John Carter Brown Library at Brown University)*

the valiant defense by the Indians against the Spanish invasion and even criticizes some aspects of the war.

– S. DAYDÍ-TOLSON

ERRÁZURIZ ECHAURREN, FEDERICO

Federico Errázuriz Echaurren (*b.* 16 November 1850; *d.* 12 July 1901), president of Chile (1896–1901). Son of former president Federico ERRÁZURIZ ZAÑARTU, Errázuriz was a lawyer by education and a farmer by profession. He entered politics in 1876, serving three terms as a deputy. Although he served as a minister in José Manuel Balmaceda's government (1886–1891), he joined the Congressionalist forces in the 1891 Revolution. Reelected to the chamber of deputies, he later became a senator. Errázuriz apparently spent heavily—probably over a million pesos—to win the presidency in 1896. Despite this sum, he barely defeated his opponent, the highly principled Vicente Reyes, who possessed neither Errázuriz's funds nor his political connections.

Despite these inauspicious beginnings, Errázuriz did manage to resolve the nation's frontier problems with Argentina over the Puna de Atacama, preserve Chile's territorial gains from the War of the Pacific, and personally intervene to avoid war with Argentina. In 1899 he met with the president of Argentina at the Strait of Magellan, where they declared that their two nations would never fight each other.

Errázuriz's fellow countrymen seemed less pacific, however, attacking the partially paralyzed and increasingly ill president. Forced by poor health to turn over his government in 1900 to his vice president for four months, Errázuriz returned to rule, but in May 1901 he again transferred power to the vice president. Errázuriz died before completing his term of office.

– WILLIAM F. SATER

ERRÁZURIZ VALDIVIESO, CRESCENTE

Crescente Errázuriz Valdivieso (*b.* 1839; *d.* 1931), archbishop of Santiago, Chile (1918–1931), during a period when the Catholic church distanced itself from its traditional alliance with the Conservative Party and accepted the separation of church and state.

Born in Santiago, Errázuriz was educated as a diocesan priest but subsequently joined the Dominican Order (1884–1911). Also trained in law, he worked as a journalist directing both *El Estandarte Católico* and *La Revista Católica,* and became one of Chile's best-known historians.

In 1918 the seventy-nine-year-old Errázuriz was named archbishop of Santiago after then President Juan

Luis SANFUENTES, with the support of the Senate, convinced the Vatican that the appointment was essential for the maintenance of good relations with the new Liberal government. Throughout his term as archbishop, Errázuriz played a major role in the modernization of the church, as well as the maintenance of its influence with Chilean society. He believed that unless the church was adaptable, its power would be diminished. He was also concerned about the direct involvement of priests in politics, and in 1922 he issued a decree forbidding it. While Errázuriz did not himself support the separation of church and state, he pragmatically participated in the drafting of the relevant parts of the 1925 Constitution that mandated it. This document ended government involvement in the appointment of priests, as well as state subsidies for church purposes.

– MARGARET E. CRAHAN

ERRÁZURIZ ZAÑARTU, FEDERICO

Federico Errázuriz Zañartu (*b.* 25 April 1825; *d.* 20 July 1877), president of Chile (1871–1876). A lawyer, Errázuriz became president after serving numerous terms as a national deputy, provincial governor, and cabinet minister. Errázuriz broke with the Conservative Party when it opposed his attempts to secularize the cemeteries, permit non-Catholics to marry, and exempt non-Catholics from having to attend religious courses in public schools. After 1873, Errázuriz led a coalition known as the Liberal Alliance, which consisted of members of the Radical and Liberal parties.

Although Errázuriz was the first president to serve only one term, his administration nevertheless implemented numerous reforms, among which were those that limited the power of the state, altered voting procedures, and modernized the penal and mining codes. His term began during a period of prosperity, that allowed Errázuriz to finance railroad construction and purchase ironclads for the navy. However, a fall in metal prices as well as a decline in copper and silver production limited Chile's economic growth, devastated the national economy, and ushered in a period of budget deficits and trade imbalances.

– WILLIAM F. SATER

ERRO, ENRIQUE

Enrique Erro (*b.* 14 September 1912; *d.* 10 October 1984), Uruguayan politician and trade unionist. A journalist employed by *La Tribuna,* Erro was a founding member of the Uruguayan Press Association. He was subsequently a member of the House of Representatives

E

Erro, Enrique

(1953–1966), minister of industry and labor (1959–1960), and a senator (1971–1973).

Ideologically Erro followed the principles of a Latin American "Patria Grande"—the name of his slate of candidates within the Frente Amplio (Broad Front) in the 1971 elections—and a popular, revolutionary nationalism. He served on the Anti-imperialist Committee and was a member of the Blanco party. Erro was a founder of the Unión Popular in 1962, later formed a coalition with the Socialist party, then joined the newly founded Frente Amplio in 1971.

From 1973 to his death, Erro rejected all negotiations with the military regime and called for abstention from the 1980 constitutional referendum and the 1982 elections. He denounced Uruguayan human rights violations before European governments and the U.N. Commission on human rights.

– DIETER SCHONEBOHM

ESCALADA, ASUNCIÓN

Asunción Escalada (*b.* 1850; *d.* 1894, Paraguayan educator. At the time of Escalada's birth in the mid-nineteenth century, education in Paraguay was almost entirely limited to male students; women were rarely permitted to take part in education except occasionally at the primary level. Escalada dedicated her career to opening Paraguayan education to women at all levels.

The War of the Triple Alliance (1864–1870) provided Escalada and other women with an opportunity to teach when so many male teachers were called to the front. She herself worked at a small primary school in the interior hamlet of Atyra. During the final stages of the fighting, however, Escalada was forced to abandon the town and accompany her grandfather, the noted Argentine educator Juan Pedro Escalada (1777–1869), on the tragic retreat to Cerro Corá.

After the war, Escalada convinced the new provisional government to fund the Escuela Central de Niñas, which she directed until 1875. This institution served as the model for the Colegio Nacional de Niñas, the best-known school for young women in today's Paraguay.

Aside from her efforts in education, Escalada was also instrumental in fomenting culture and the arts in the country, donating time and money to advance the career of guitarist Agustín BARRIOS and many others. She died in Buenos Aires.

– THOMAS L. WHIGHAM

ESCALANTE, ANÍBAL

Aníbal Escalante (*b.* 1909; *d.*, 11 August 1977), secretary-general of the Partido Socialista Popular (Cuban Communist Party—PSP) and editor of the party's organ *Hoy.* Born in Oriente Province into an affluent family, Escalante graduated with a degree in law from the University of Havana in 1932, the same year he joined the Communist Party. During that year Escalante founded *Hoy,* the official organ of the Cuban Communist Party. He was the paper's editor from 1938 into the early 1960s as well as the party's elected representative in the lower house of the Cuban Congress from 1948 to 1952.

Escalante survived the Batista dictatorship and the Cuban Revolution of 1959 to play a key role in the reformed Communist Party under the leadership of Fidel CASTRO. In 1961 he was given the task of merging Castro's own Twenty-sixth of July Movement with the Revolutionary Student Directorate and the Cuban Communist Party. Escalante attempted to forge a single party, the Integrated Revolutionary Organizations, modeled after the Soviet Communist Party. Perceived as a threat to Castro's power, he was dismissed from the National Directory in 1962 and was forced out of Cuba that same year. After a brief exile, Escalante returned to Cuba in 1964, and once again became active in politics.

In 1968 Escalante, along with other members of the old PSP, was accused of forming a "microfaction" within the new, ruling Cuban Communist Party (PCP), and was sentenced to fifteen years in prison for "attempting to destroy the unity" of the Cuban Revolution. He died in Havana.

– MICHAEL POWELSON

ESCANDÓN, ANTONIO

Antonio Escandón (*b.* 1824; *d.* 1877), Mexican entrepreneur. The younger brother of the notorious Mexican moneylender Manuel ESCANDÓN, he was born in Puebla. He married Catalina Barrón, daughter of Eustaquio Barrón, another influential moneylender of the period. Escandón spent the years of the French Empire in Europe trying to raise funds for building a railroad from Mexico City to Veracruz, a project that was completed in 1873.

Escandón is also noteworthy for his commitment to the beautification of Mexico City following the fall of the empire. He believed that the national government should make the newly renamed Paseo de la Reforma into a Mexican version of the Champs-élysées with streets intersecting to form traffic circles. In 1877, to celebrate the completion of the railroad, Escandón presented the city with a statue of Christopher Columbus that still stands in the second *glorieta* (traffic circle) on the Paseo. Ironically, he died in Europe, on a train en route from Seville to Córdoba.

– BARBARA A. TENENBAUM

350

ESCANDÓN, JOSÉ DE

José de Escandón (*b.* 1700; *d.* 1770), founder of Nuevo Santander. Born in Soto la Marina, Santander, Escandón came to New Spain in 1715 and settled in Querétaro, where he participated in numerous campaigns against the northern Indian tribes, the most notable of which being the pacification of the Sierra Gorda. In

---

In 1749, Escandón led over 3,000 people to Tamaulipas and established twenty-one Spanish and Tlaxcalan communities and fifty-seven Franciscan and three Dominican missions.

---

response to Indian attacks around Nuevo León and the threat of English and French expansion from Florida and Louisiana into Texas, the viceroy, the first Count of Revillagigedo, selected Escandón to conquer and settle the region around Tamaulipas and both sides of the lower Rio Grande. In 1749, after extensive planning and exploring, Escandón led a colonizing force of over 3,000 people to Tamaulipas and established twenty-one Spanish and Tlaxcalan communities and fifty-seven Franciscan and three Dominican missions. To pacify rebellious tribes in the area, he granted land and agricultural supplies to them and assigned Tlaxcalan instructors to their communities. The new region, Nuevo Santander, became one of the most successful colonies on New Spain's northern frontier and the birthplace of the Texas cattle industry.

— AARON PAINE MAHR

ESCANDÓN, MANUEL

Manuel Escandón (*b.* 1808; *d.* 7 June 1862), Mexican entrepreneur. Son of an Asturian merchant and a mother linked to the military and agricultural families of Jalapa, Veracruz, Escandón was born in Orizaba, Veracruz. Educated partly in Europe, he returned to Mexico in 1826 and moved to the capital in the early 1830s. By 1833, he was operating an important stagecoach line from Veracruz to Mexico City and had become involved in political wheeling and dealing through his relationships with prominent generals like Antonio López de SANTA ANNA, Mariano ARISTA, and others. Escandón quickly took advantage of the precarious financial situation of the Mexican treasury by lending money to the government and by agreeing to provide important services to it. In 1848 he purchased the French-owned Cocolapam textile mill in Orizaba and gained even

greater wealth after he and a consortium purchased the British-owned Real del Monte silver mines just before it hit a bonanza. By 1853 he and other moneylenders offered to found Mexico's first bank, but were turned down by Treasury Minister Antonio de HARO Y TAMARIZ.

During the last years of his life Escandón turned his attention to building a railroad from Mexico City to Veracruz, a project his younger brother Antonio completed in 1873.

— BARBARA A. TENENBAUM

ESCOBAR, LUIS ANTONIO

Luis Antonio Escobar (*b.* 14 July 1925; *d.* 11 September 1993), Colombian composer and diplomat. Born in Villapinzón, Escobar studied at the Bogotá Conservatory (1940–1947). In 1947 he received a scholarship to study with Nicholas Nabokov at the Peabody Conservatory in Baltimore. He attended composition courses at New York's Columbia University (1950–1951) and took classes with Boris Blacher at the Berlin Hochschule für Musik (1951–1953) and the Salzburg Mozarteum (1951). Upon his return to his native land he was named secretary of the National Conservatory, where he taught harmony, composition, and instrumentation. Escobar received several awards, including the National Prize (1955) for his *Sinfonía Cero* and two Guggenheim fellowships. In 1960 the New York City Ballet commissioned his *Preludios para percusión*. Escobar presented his *Pequeña sinfonía* at the Third Latin American Music Festival, held in Washington, D.C., in May 1965. He was appointed director of musical programs for television in Colombia and served on the national board of the Colombian National Orchestra. He was also chairman of the National Music Council and director of the cultural division of the Ministry of National Education. Escobar also served as consul (1964–1966) and second secretary (1967–1970) of the Colombian embassy in Bonn, West Germany. He died in Miami while serving as Colombia's cultural chargé d'affaires.

— SUSANA SALGADO

ESCOBAR, PATRICIO

Patricio Escobar (*b.* 1843; *d.* 19 April 1912), president of Paraguay (1886–1890) and soldier. Born in San José, Escobar entered the army just before the outbreak of the War of the Triple Alliance and rose in rank from private to general during the course of the conflict. Like his mentor, the cavalry general Bernardino CABALLERO, Escobar remained loyal to the cause of President Francisco Solano LÓPEZ and doggedly resisted the Brazilians until he was captured at Cerro Corá, the war's last battle.

Returning to Paraguay after several years' captivity, Escobar attached himself to Caballero and to Conservative figures associated with President Cándido BAREIRO. After Caballero's accession to the presidency in 1880, Escobar received the portfolio of war minister. Six years later, he himself succeeded to the highest office and generally continued the conservative, paternalistic policies of his friend and predecessor, though Escobar was perhaps more tolerant of opposition criticism. He opened the National University in 1889 and helped to expand the Paraguay Central Railway and other public works. In partisan politics, Escobar collaborated in the organization of the Asociación Nacional Republicana (or Partido Colorado), one of the country's two traditional parties. Unfortunately, his administration was also marked by corruption.

Stepping down from office in 1890, the by-now-wealthy Escobar continued to influence Paraguayan politics through various surrogates and intrigues. He died in Asunción less than two months after the death of Caballero.

— THOMAS L. WHIGHAM

ESCOBEDO, MARIANO

Mariano Escobedo (*b.* January 1826; *d.* 1902), Mexican Liberal army commander. Born in Galeana, Nuevo León, Escobedo fought as an ensign in the national guard against U.S. forces in 1846–1847, becoming a lieutenant in 1852. He supported the Plan of Ayutla and fought under Santiago VIDAURRI in 1854–1855. He became a lieutenant-colonel in the cavalry in 1856. During the Civil War of the Reform (1858–1861), he again fought alongside Vidaurri in the north central states. During the French Intervention, he fought at Puebla in 1862 and 1863, when he was captured.

Escobedo opposed Vidaurri's defection to the empire in 1864. He played the major role in the resurgence of Liberal forces in late 1865, capturing MAXIMILIAN, Miguel MIRAMÓN, and Tomás MEJÍA at Querétaro in 1867 and convening the summary military tribunal that sentenced them to death. A close friend of Sebastián LERDO, he became a senator in September 1875 and minister of war in 1876. He fought against Porfirio DÍAZ in the rebellion of Tuxtepec (1876) and conspired to restore Lerdo in 1877–1878. He was a federal deputy at the time of his death.

— BRIAN HAMNETT

ESLAVA Y LAZAGA, SEBASTIÁN DE

Sebastián de Eslava y Lazaga (*b.* January 1685; *d.* 21 June 1759), military figure and viceroy of the New Kingdom of Granada (1740–1749). Born in Navarra, he studied at the Real Academia Militar in Barcelona and entered active military service. He reached the rank of lieutenant general of the royal armies.

Philip V named Eslava, brother of Rafael de Eslava, former president of the Audiencia of Santa Fe (1733–1737), the first viceroy of the reconstituted viceroyalty of New Granada in 1738. Unlike his predecessor, Jorge de VILLALONGA (1719–1724), Eslava put the colony on a firm footing. He disembarked at Cartagena de Indias in April 1740 and, because of the hostilities with England, stayed there throughout his tenure. English Admiral Edward Vernon's failed attempt to capture Cartagena (1741) made heroes of Eslava and the naval commander Blas de Lezo, a judgment widely supported by modern Colombian historiography. The pressures of wartime rule, however, took their toll; in 1742 the viceroy began to lobby the crown for reassignment. He subsequently declined the promotion to viceroy of Peru in favor of returning to Spain. Eslava served with distinction in New Granada until his appointment as captain-general of Andalusia and the arrival of his replacement, José Alonso Pizarro (1749–1753). He served as minister of war from 1754 to 1759.

— LANCE R. GRAHN

ESPAILLAT, ULISES FRANCISCO

Ulises Francisco Espaillat (*b.* 1823; *d.* 25 April 1878), president of the Dominican Republic (29 May–5 October 1876). A white *criollo* (creole) whose Spanish parents belonged to an old, well-established family, Espaillat was born in Santiago de los Caballeros, the main city in the fertile Cibao Valley in the north. A pharmacist by profession, he was an intellectual and a patriot who became involved in politics in an effort to stabilize and unify the country after the *restauración* from Spain in 1863. He served as vice president in the provisional governments of General José Antonio Salcedo (1863–1864) and General Gaspar Polanco (1864–1865).

Espaillat was an honest and liberal nationalist (author of the liberal constitution of 1858). Elected president in the spring of 1876 with the strong support of General Gregorio LUPERÓN, Espaillat appointed the best people to his cabinet (Luperón was minister of war) and stressed honesty, a balanced budget, and the end of foreign entanglements. His financial reforms were unpopular and the military, used to regular pay-offs, opposed his efforts to create a professional army. Two former presidents, Buenaventura BAEZ (1856–1857, 1865–1866, and 1868–1873), and Ignacio María González (1874–1876) organized uprisings against him. The capital, Santo Domingo, fell to supporters of González in October 1876; Espaillat took refuge in the French embassy and in December returned to his home in the Cibao.

— LARMAN C. WILSON

ESPEJO, ANTONIO DE

Antonio de Espejo (*b.* 1538?; *d.?*), Spanish explorer. From Córdoba, Spain, Espejo was a lay officer of the Inquisition and a wealthy cattleman, with properties in Querétaro and Celaya, Mexico. In 1582–1583 he financed and led an expedition with the Franciscan friar Bernadino Beltrán to New Mexico and Arizona. The men hoped to rescue Fray Agustín Rodríguez, who had remained in New Mexico after having accompanied Francisco Sánchez Chamuscado from Mexico in 1581. The small force left Santa Bárbara in New Biscay in 1582 and traveled north, up the Rio Grande valley. After learning of Rodríguez's death, Espejo decided to prospect for mines and went west to Acoma, Zuni, and Hopi, and then southwest into Arizona, where he found evidence of mineral deposits. After a failed mutiny at Zuni in 1583, Beltrán and the rebels went back to Santa Bárbara. Espejo, however, turned north and east from the Rio Grande, and returned to New Biscay by way of the Pecos River valley. An account of his experiences, published in 1586, contributed to a knowledge of and interest in New Spain.

— RICK HENDRICKS

ESPELETA Y GALDEANO DICASTILLO Y DEL PRADO, JOSÉ MANUEL DE

José Manuel de Espeleta y Galdeano Dicastillo y del Prado (*b.* June 1742; *d.* 23 November 1823), captain-general of Cuba (1785–1789), viceroy of New Granada (1789–1797).

Born in Barcelona of Basque parentage, Espeleta came to Havana in 1779 as colonel of the Regiment of Navarre. During the American Revolution, he commanded the advance on Pensacola from Mobile (1780–1781). Later, after serving with distinction as captain-general of Cuba, he was promoted to viceroy of New Granada. An enlightened, effective administrator, Espeleta ranked among the best of New Granada's viceroys. He faced the monumental tasks of soothing the political tensions that had lingered since the Comunero Revolt (1781) and reducing the colonial debt through curtailing the size of the army and eliminating unproductive programs.

He was acutely embarrassed when Antonio NARIÑO published the *Declaration of the Rights of Man and the Citizen,* obtained from his own personal library. Replaced by Pedro Mendinueta y Muzquiz at the end of his term, Espeleta returned to Spain, becoming gover-

nor of the Council of Castile and captain-general (1797–1798) and, later, councillor of state (1798), captain-general of Catalonia (1808), and viceroy of Navarre (1814–1820).

— ALLAN J. KUETHE

ESPÍN DE CASTRO, VILMA

Vilma Espín de Castro (*b.* 1930), Cuban revolutionary and feminist. Vilma Espín was part of the underground resistance that fought to overthrow Fulgencio BATISTA and offered intelligence assistance to Fidel CASTRO's 26 July 1952 attack on the Moncada Barracks. She studied chemical engineering at the University of Oriente,

After the overthrow of Cuba's Batista government, Espín rode into Havana with the triumphant revolutionary army.

graduating in 1954, and then attended the Massachusetts Institute of Technology. She left her studies to join Castro's movement in the Sierra Maestra mountains in 1956, where she married Raúl CASTRO. After the overthrow of Batista's government, Espín rode into Havana with the triumphant revolutionary army. She became president of the new Federation of Cuban Women in 1960. In 1969 she became director of industrial development in the Ministry of Food Industries, and in 1971 she was named president of the Institute of Child Care. Espín joined the Central Committee of the Cuban Communist Party in 1965. She became a member of the Council of State in 1976 and of the Politburo of the Communist Party in 1986. She was removed as a member of the Central Committee in 1989.

— K. LYNN STONER

ESPINOSA, JOSÉ MARÍA

José María Espinosa (*b.* 1796; *d.* 1883), Colombian artist. Born to an aristocratic and distinguished creole family in Bogotá, Espinosa began studying painting with artist Pablo Antonio García, but the revolution of July 1810 against Spain interrupted his training. He served in the army until independence was achieved in 1819 and then published his account of his experiences fighting under General Antonio NARIÑO from 1813 to 1816 in *Memorias de un abandero.* While on the southern campaign, he was taken prisoner and drew caricatures of fellow prisoners as well as landscapes and battle scenes.

At the conclusion of the war, Espinosa returned to Bogotá and took his position in the social and political life of the new republic. He painted many portraits of the heroes of the independence struggle, and of Bolívar in particular, in a style that marked a transition from the colonial to the republican period.

— BÉLGICA RODRÍGUEZ

ESPINOSA Y ESPINOSA, (JUAN) JAVIER

(Juan) Javier Espinosa y Espinosa (*b.* 20 January 1815; *d.* 4 September 1870), president of Ecuador (1868–1869). During Gabriel GARCÍA MORENO's domination of Ecuador (1861–1865, 1869–1975), Espinosa briefly served as figurehead president. The son of Quito notables, his prior government experience had been limited to a few relatively minor posts. Espinosa selected for his cabinet a group of moderate Liberals and Conservatives, a move that outraged García Moreno; he had fully expected to control Espinosa. In August 1868 a violent earthquake devastated the northern sierra, leveling the cities of Ibarra and Otavalo. Espinosa appointed García Moreno to oversee aid and reconstruction. These chores (and, critics allege, the theft of charity funds) kept the former president preoccupied for a time. However, in 1869, as Ecuador prepared to hold elections for a new presidential term, García Moreno staged a coup, removed Espinosa, and returned to office. Espinosa died in Quito.

— RONN F. PINEO

ESQUIÚ, MAMERTO

Mamerto Esquiú (*b.* 11 May 1826; *d.* 10 January 1883), Argentine Catholic spokesman and bishop of Córdoba. The son of a devout family of farmers in Callesita, Catamarca Province, at the age of ten he entered the Franciscan order. He taught at the Franciscan convent school in Catamarca and for much of his career was closely associated with Catholic educational institutions. Also a noted preacher, he first gained national renown for a sermon he delivered on the occasion of the swearing of allegiance to the 1853 Constitution. Esquiú criticized the liberalism that permeated many provisions of the Constitution, but he called on Argentines to obey it in a spirit of submission to the constituted authorities.

Esquiú at various times was a member of deliberative assemblies in his native province, even as he became increasingly disillusioned with the factional wrangling and civil warfare that afflicted the country as a whole. He spent the years 1862–1875 in Bolivia (except for one brief trip to Peru and Ecuador), where he again earned prominence as a Catholic educator and publicist. For the final years of his life he was mainly in Argentina, despite his dismay over political and cultural trends there. Nevertheless, in view of his prestige among Argentine Catholics and his reputation as "orator of the Constitution," Esquiú was nominated as archbishop of Buenos Aires (which he refused) and bishop of Córdoba (which he reluctantly accepted). From the time he took over the Córdoba diocese in January 1881 until his death, he set an example of apostolic simplicity and tireless energy in service to his flock. Though he was never formally canonized, his biography appears in a series of "Popular Lives of Saints" published in 1977. He died in Suncho, Catamarca province.

— DAVID BUSHNELL

ESQUIVEL, MANUEL AMADEO

Manuel Amadeo Esquivel (*b.* 2 May 1940), prime minister of Belize (1984–1989). Born in Belize City, Esquivel was educated at the Jesuit-run St. John's College. He received a bachelor's degree in physics from Loyola University of New Orleans and did postgraduate work at New York University. Returning to Belize in the early 1970s, he taught at St. John's until 1984.

A founding member of the UDP, an alliance of three former opposition parties, he served as party chairman from 1976 to 1982 and party leader after 1982. After two terms on the Belize City Council (1974–1980) he was appointed to the Belize Senate in 1979. In 1984 the United Democratic Party (UDP), led by Esquivel, won a landslide victory in national elections, capturing twenty-one of twenty-eight seats in the House of Representatives. With this majority, Esquivel became Belize's second prime minister.

During a five-year administration, in which he also served as minister of finance and defense, Esquivel's sound fiscal management and encouragement of foreign investment in tourism, agriculture, and manufacturing helped invigorate the economy. He achieved balance of payments surpluses for four consecutive years and left foreign exchange reserves at record levels. Despite these economic successes, the UDP was accused of selling out the country to foreign investors. A split in party ranks in 1989, allegations of ministerial corruption, and a series of contested party caucuses contributed to the party's narrow loss in the elections of 1989.

Just four years later, on 30 June 1993, in a stunning upset, Esquivel led his United Democratic Party to a narrow victory in the general elections. The UDP captured sixteen of twenty-nine seats in the new parliament. On 3 July 1993, Esquivel took the oath of office and began his second term as prime minister. Esquivel began to implement some of his campaign promises including free education for Belizeans from primary school to university level and an investigation into alleged registration of illegal immigrants. He faced a gauntlet of difficult problems including high unemployment and a rising tide of urban violence brought on by the drug trade.

— BRIAN E. COUTTS

ESTEBAN

Esteban (Estevan; *d.* May 1539), guide/explorer of New Spain. Esteban, a black Arab from the Atlantic coast of Morocco, traveled across Florida, Texas, and northern Mexico from 1527 until 1536 with his owner and Andrés Dorantes, Alvar Núñez CABEZA DE VACA, and Castillo Maldonado, all fellow survivors of Pánfilo de Narváez's ill-fated expedition to Florida. He was then purchased by the viceroy of New Spain, Antonio de MENDOZA, who was eager to take advantage of his knowledge of the largely uncharted north country. In 1539, Esteban guided Franciscan friar Marcos de NIZA in his search for the Seven Cities of Cíbola. The travelers departed from San Miguel de Culiacán in Sinaloa, Mexico, where they had been accompanied by Francisco Vásquez de CORONADO, governor of the province of New Galicia. On the journey north into Sonora, Arizona, and New Mexico, Esteban and a number of Indian allies ranged far ahead of Niza, sending back reports of their progress. Esteban apparently angered the Pueblo Indians by demanding women and turquoise. He was killed at Hawikuh, the southernmost of the six Zuni pueblos.

Niza's report of his travels with Esteban helped persuade Vásquez de Coronado to launch his 1540 expedition to find the great cities and untold riches implied in Niza's descriptions. Among the Zunis, Esteban is known as an ogre kachina, or evil spirit.

— RICK HENDRICKS

ESTIGARRIBIA, ANTONIO DE LA CRUZ

Antonio de la Cruz Estigarribia (mid-1800s), Paraguayan soldier. When the War of the Triple Alliance began in 1864, Estigarribia was one of the most highly respected officers in the Paraguayan army. He had been an adviser to war minister Francisco Solano LÓPEZ during the 1859 mediation of a dispute between Buenos Aires and the Argentine Confederation, and, thanks to Solano López's sponsorship, was promoted to full colonel and given command of a major Paraguayan column.

In mid-1865, Estigarribia and his force crossed the Alto Paraná into Brazil as part of a coordinated attack on Corrientes and Río Grande do Sul. As Estigarribia's troops moved south, they destroyed town after town in Brazil, but they also began to lose touch with their own supply bases. After taking the town of São Borja, Estigarribia split up his forces, sending Major Pedro Duarte and 2,500 men down the right bank of the Río Uruguay while he continued with the main body of 8,000 men down the left bank to the town of Uruguaiana. In early August, he occupied the town and awaited news from Duarte. The news was not good: on 17 August Duarte's entire command was obliterated in an Allied attack, leaving Uruguaiana surrounded and Estigarribia without much chance of resupply.

The Paraguayan colonel debated for some time what his next move might be. He was completely cut off and without clear instructions from López. Finally, on 18 September, he agreed to generous Allied terms for surrender, which stipulated that the rank and file would be treated as prisoners of war and that his officers would be allowed to take up residence in any of the Allied nations but not to return to Paraguay.

Estigarribia, whose action was bitterly denounced by López, chose to go to Rio de Janeiro. He then dropped from sight except for a brief, pathetic moment in March 1869, when he petitioned the Brazilian emperor to offer his services as a guide for the armies then advancing into the Cordillera of central Paraguay.

— THOMAS L. WHIGHAM

ESTIGARRIBIA, JOSÉ FÉLIX

José Félix Estigarribia (*b.* 21 February 1888; *d.* 5 September 1940), president of Paraguay (1940) and soldier. Born at Caraguatay, Estigarribia came from a poor but distinguished family of Basque extraction. His ancestors included Colonel Antonio de la Cruz ESTIGARRIBIA, who had surrendered his army at Uruguaiana during the War of the Triple Alliance.

Young José Félix passed his early years in the countryside, and there was reason to think he might choose farming as a career. In 1903 he enrolled in the Agricultural School at Trinidad and then moved on to attend the Colegio Nacional at Asunción. The revolutions of the first decade of the new century, however, propelled Estigarribia into the ranks of the army. In 1911, he was sent to Chile for further military training, from which he returned two years later, becoming a first lieutenant in 1914. Estigarribia remained loyal to the government during the disturbances of 1921–1922, a fact that provisional president Eusebio AYALA never forgot. As a partial reward, the young captain was sent to France for further military study under Marshal Foch.

When he returned to Paraguay in 1927, he became chief of the general staff.

During Estigarribia's absence, the dispute with Bolivia over the Chaco Region had provoked a series of ugly incidents. These, in turn, developed into a full-scale war by 1932. In August of that year Estigarribia was given command of 15,000 men, with which he forged a powerful fighting force.

Colonel Estigarribia went from victory to victory fighting on some of the roughest land in South America.

Estigarribia gained a legendary status in the Chaco. Though his troops were regularly outnumbered by the Bolivians, still they boasted certain advantages over their counterparts from the Altiplano: they were closer to home bases, they were more accustomed to the terrain and climate, and, in Estigarribia, they had a commander who had a clear goal, who was a master tactician, and who understood his men. Over the next three years, Colonel Estigarribia went from victory to victory fighting on some of the roughest land in South America. After his exhausted troops gained the foothills of the Andes in 1935, a truce was signed. It was affirmed three years later in a boundary treaty generally favorable to Paraguay.

Meanwhile, President Eusebio Ayala had been removed by restive army officers and young radicals. Ayala's ally Estigarribia went on an extended tour abroad, teaching for a time at the Montevideo War College. In 1938 he became ambassador to Washington, and in 1939, though still in the United States, he ran unopposed as the Liberal candidate for president. When he returned for his inauguration at Asunción, however, Estigarribia discovered that radicals were demanding more far-reaching action than the Liberal program called for. Compromising, the new president proposed a semiauthoritarian constitution that had socialist, democratic, and fascist elements. Despite some inner doubts as to the wisdom of this document, Estigarribia ruled under it as dictator. Two months after its ratification, he died in an airplane crash outside Asunción. By executive decree, the Chaco hero was posthumously promoted to field marshal.

— THOMAS L. WHIGHAM

ESTIMÉ, DUMARSAIS

Dumarsais Estimé (*b.* 1900; *d.* 20 July 1953), president of Haiti (1946–1950). A native of Verrettes and a for-

mer mathematics teacher at the Lycée Pétion, Estimé was a member of the National Assembly and secretary of education before becoming president. He came to power on 16 August 1946 with the support of elite blacks (members of the Noiriste Party) who had been excluded from government under the regime of Élie LESCOT.

Lasting until 10 May 1950, Estimé's government also drew support initially from young radicals and Communists who looked forward to a social revolution that would benefit Haiti's black masses, both workers and peasants. Although it never went far enough to satisfy leftist desires, the government did make use of its popular mandate to carry out genuine reforms. In addition to granting greater liberty of speech and the press, Estimé established a populist and nationalist program that embraced inclusion of blacks in the state patronage system; support for unions; social legislation recognizing workers' rights; public education; attempts to curb U.S. economic control of the country, in part by breaking up the Standard Fruit Company's monopoly on banana production; and the agreement with the Export-Import Bank to finance the Artibonite Valley irrigation project. Estimé also encouraged development of Haiti's tourist industry by granting credits to the hotel business and investing millions of dollars in an international fair celebrating the founding of Port-au-Prince (1949). He was exiled to the United States and died in New York City.

— PAMELA MURRAY

ESTRADA, CARLOS

Carlos Estrada (*b.* 15 September 1909; *d.* 7 May 1970), Uruguayan composer, conductor, and teacher. Born in Montevideo, Estrada studied there with Adelina Pérez Montero (piano), Carlos Correa Luna (violin), Father Pedro Ochoa (Gregorian chant), and Manuel Fernández Espiro (harmony, counterpoint, and composition). In 1938 he traveled to Paris and attended classes at the National Conservatory given by Jean-Jules Aimable Roger-Ducasse and Henri Busser (composition), Noel Gallon (counterpoint and fugue), and Albert Wolff, Paul Paray, and Philippe Gaubert (conducting). Contrary to the prevailing Uruguayan nationalist style, Estrada utilized modal harmonic systems and neoclassical forms, with a strong influence, initially, from the French school. In 1936 he founded the Orquesta de Cámara de Montevideo.

In the early 1940s Estrada began to work in the major forms, composing the oratorio *Daniel* (1942) and incidental music for Paul Claudel's play *L'Annonce faite à Marie* (1943). He premiered and conducted his first symphony in Paris in 1951, and his string quartet no. 1, a SODRE Composition First Award, was premiered at the First Latin American Music Festival of Montevideo in 1957.

Estrada was director and professor of harmony and composition at the National Conservatory of Montevideo (1953–1968) and also taught at the Institute of Musicology (University of Montevideo School of Humanities). He founded the Municipal Symphony Orchestra in 1959 and conducted it until 1970; he also conducted several European orchestras. The French government honored Estrada by making him Officier de l'Académie and Chevalier des Arts et Lettres. He died in Montevideo.

— SUSANA SALGADO

ESTRADA, JOSÉ DOLORES

José Dolores Estrada (*b.* 16 March 1792; *d.* 12 August 1869), Nicaraguan general and hero of San Jacinto. Born in Nandaime to an agricultural family descended from the Gonzalo de Sandoval group of conquistadores, Estrada showed an affinity for the military at an early age. During the independence movement, Estrada accompanied Argüello but achieved real fame only decades later, when he led a dramatic victory against the filibuster forces of William WALKER and Byron Cole. The battle of San Jacinto (14 September 1856) was fought on an old hacienda near Tipitapa. There 160 men led by Estrada barricaded themselves in the house and fought the North Americans bravely. Their successful effort convinced other Central Americans that Walker could indeed be beaten, and Estrada and his forces quickly became symbols of nationalism and patriotism.

— KAREN RACINE

ESTRADA, JOSÉ MANUEL

José Manuel Estrada (*b.* 1842; *d.* 1894), Argentine writer, law professor, director of the Argentine Colegio Nacional and congressman. As a member of the so-called Generation of 1880, Estrada typifies the polyfaceted man of letters in Argentine public and intellectual life in Buenos Aires, where he was born. In addition to serving as rector of the Colegio Nacional, an institution that has traditionally provided secondary-school training to the brightest of the nation's youth, Estrada played an energetic role in the burgeoning area of cultural journalism. He was the founding editor of the *Revista Argentina,* an excellent example of the sort of comprehensive cultural publications of the period that contributed to a sense of sophisticated nationalism by serving as a forum for the exchange of ideas among

privileged literati, most of whom had ties to the economic boom of the late nineteenth century. This exchange was abetted by the way in which such publications functioned as a channel for the intensive Western intellectual production of the day.

Estrada is notable for his identification with a conservative Catholicism that was opposed to what he viewed as an immoral and tyrannical capitalist expansion at the expense of traditional values. Estrada's antiliberalism is typified by his early *El catolicismo y la democracia* (1862) and in his work as leader of the high orthodox Unión Católica. His *Lecciones sobre la historia de la República Argentina* (1868), based on his lectures as a law professor, constitute a notable example of his overarching conservative Catholic point of view and typify the sort of grandiloquent rhetoric customarily found in militant writings of those who sought to shape national consciousness. Estrada died in Asunción.

— DAVID WILLIAM FOSTER

ESTRADA, JOSÉ MARÍA

José María Estrada. (*d.* 13 August 1856), acting president (1854) and president (1855–1856) of Nicaragua. President Fruto CHAMORRO turned over the presidency to José María Estrada on 27 May 1854 in order to give full attention to leading the Legitimist (Conservative) army against the Democratic (Liberal) insurgents headed by Máximo JEREZ. Estrada had earlier served as foreign minister and as a member of the Assembly. After Chamorro died (12 March 1855), the Assembly authorized Estrada to continue in office. When Granada fell to William WALKER, Estrada opposed the Walker-backed government of Patricio RIVAS, repudiating the treaty of 23 October 1855. He established a government first at Masaya, then at Somotillo, and later at Matagalpa, allying himself with the conservative governments of the other Central American states against Walker in the National War. Democratic guerrillas attacked and killed Estrada at El Ocotal.

— RALPH LEE WOODWARD, JR.

ESTRADA, JOSÉ MARÍA

José María Estrada (*b.* 1810?; *d.* 1862?), Mexican painter. Born in Guadalajara, Estrada signed his paintings sometimes as José María Estrada and sometimes as José María Zepeda de Estrada, which has caused some confusion about his work. He studied under José María Uriarte, director of painting at the Academy of Guadalajara, who had received his education at the Academy of Mexico City. Estrada did not, however, follow the path of academic painters. Specializing in portraits, he painted in a style typical of his native state of Jalisco. His portraits are enchanting and are characterized by meticulous detail, with subjects in sober dress, their faces in three-quarter position, and their hands always holding a fruit, a kerchief, or a fan. Estrada used unadorned backgrounds to emphasize his subjects, and his colors tended toward the cool end of the spectrum. Unlike his adult subjects, he portrayed children full-bodied.

Estrada's compositional style was typical of popular painters who paint what they know, as opposed to painting what "should be seen" according to the rules of illusionist perspective imposed in the academies. He also painted dead children, a custom common in traditional painting. Estrada died in Guadalajara.

– ESTHER ACEVEDO

ESTRADA, JUAN JOSÉ

Juan José Estrada (*b.* 1865; *d.* 1947), provisional president of Nicaragua (29 August 1910–9 May 1911). Estrada, governor of the Caribbean department of Mosquitia, launched an uprising against President José Santos ZELAYA, whose government fell in 1909. He continued the revolt against Zelaya's successor, José Madriz, and in 1910 established a provisional government at Bluefields, where he received assistance from U.S. marines. Madriz turned over power to Estrada's brother, José Dolores ESTRADA, on 20 August 1910, and Juan José Estrada formally became provisional president on 29 August. A new Constituent Assembly unanimously elected him for a two-year term on 31 December 1910, but the real power rested with General Luis Mena, who commanded the military. Under pressure, Estrada resigned on 9 May 1911, turning power over to his vice president, Adolfo DÍAZ.

– RALPH LEE WOODWARD, JR.

ESTRADA CABRERA, MANUEL

Manuel Estrada Cabrera (*b.* 21 November 1857; *d.* 24 September 1924), president of Guatemala (1898–1920). In 1898 Estrada Cabrera secured the Guatemalan presidency following the assassination of his protector and predecessor, President José María REYNA BARRIOS. A Quetzaltenango lawyer of limited ability and humble parentage, Estrada Cabrera has been described as one of the strangest personalities who ever raised himself to great power. Even though he served the Reyna Barrios administration (1892–1898) as minister of the interior and justice and first designate (vice president), upon his ascendency to the presidency as the constitutionally recognized presidential successor, Estrada Cabrera was largely regarded as an undistin-

Manuel Estrada Cabrera. (Library of Congress)

guished rural politician. The violence of Reyna Barrios's assassination, however, proved to be a fitting introduction to Estrada Cabrera's twenty-two-year reign of terror, which still ranks as the longest uninterrupted rule in Central American history. The president's renowned tendencies toward cruelty and corruption, combined with his legendary resourcefulness and invulnerability undoubtedly contributed to the longevity of his administration.

Like the father of Guatemalan liberalism, the revered Justo Rufino BARRIOS (1873–1885), Estrada Cabrera was a typical Latin American *caudillo.* Careful to cultivate the support of the coffee elite and dedicated to the Positivist watchwords of "order" and "progress," the dictator guided Guatemala on a course common in Latin America in the latter half of the nineteenth century. Throughout his presidency, Estrada Cabrera fostered the creation of a society typified by large landed estates, forced labor, an export-oriented economy, and highly centralized political power. Latin American caudillos rarely delegated political authority to subordinates and Estrada Cabrera was no exception to this rule. According to Dana G. Munro, a U.S. State Department representative in the first quarter of the twentieth century, the dictator "had no friends or personal followers except the army officers and government officials who supported his regime" and these only "for the sake of the license and graft" that he permitted.

During the Estrada Cabrera presidency, the exploitative and exclusive nature of Guatemalan society became increasingly obvious. Instead of real development, what emerged was a landed oligarchy, engaged primarily in the production of coffee, that utilized its economic might to construct a state that protected its dominant social and political status. Although economic growth and modernization proceeded at a moderate pace during the first two decades of the twentieth century, political and social problems associated with increased economic activity, lack of development, and the altered fabric of Guatemalan society arose. Significant among these were the rapid growth of the capital's middle class, the emergence of a significant labor element, and a vocal and politically conscious student population, all of which were refused a forum for political expression, not to mention an equitable share in the profits of the republic's lucrative coffee industry. The cumulative effect of these forces, augmented by the extremely repressive nature of Estrada Cabrera's administration, presented the republic with a rare opportunity to implement real and significant reform.

In late 1917 and 1918 general disenchantment with the political and economic status quo of the Estrada Cabrera regime was accelerated by a series of devastating earthquakes that left much of Guatemala City in rubble. Estrada Cabrera's apathetic response to the earthquakes, coupled with the student protests of the same years, aroused a heretofore unknown reaction in the capital. Awakened by the students' commitment to reform, other sectors of society, notably the Roman Catholic church, an incipient urban middle class, organized labor, and eventually the military and the landed elite, pledged their support to a new unified political coalition, the Unionist Party, to oppose the dictator. By April 1920, the president's inability to adapt to the republic's changing political and social conditions and the coalition's commitment to the dictator's unconditional surrender, prompted the Guatemalan National Assembly to impeach a physically weakened and politically alienated Manuel Estrada Cabrera.

— WADE A. KIT

ESTRADA PALMA, TOMÁS

Tomás Estrada Palma (*b.* 9 July 1835; *d.* 4 November 1908), Cuban patriot and politician, president of Cuba (1902–1906). Born in Bayamo, Tomás Estrada Palma grew up in Oriente, the center of Cuba's protracted struggle for independence. He was sent by his family to study in Havana and then pursued a law degree at the University of Seville in Spain. A family crisis required Estrada to return home and assume administration of the family estate before he had finished his studies; nevertheless, he retained his passionate belief in the value of education and tried to set up rural schools for the benefit of his community.

As a young and progressive man, Estrada Palma participated in the Ten Years' War (1868–1878), joining the rebels in 1868 and quickly rising to the rank of general. In 1876 Estrada was elected president of the Republic in Arms but fell prisoner to the Spanish the following year. He was transported to Spain and released in 1878, when the Pact of Zanjón ended the war. Estrada then moved to Paris, where he began a discussion group for political exiles and took an interest in the intellectual life of Europe.

Estrada Palma left Europe for America in the late 1880s, passing through New York, where he visited José MARTÍ, and continuing on to Central America. He settled in Honduras, where he met and married Genoveva Guardiola, the daughter of the Honduran president. At the insistence of Martí, Estrada moved his family to New York, where the two expatriates formed the Cuban Revolutionary Party in 1892. Following Martí's death in battle in 1895, Estrada Palma reluctantly accepted the title of provisional president of Cuba after the defeat of Spain. He was elected president in his own right in Cuba's first independent election for the office, held in 1902.

A decent, honest, and hardworking man, Estrada Palma's accomplishments as president were manifold.

A decent, honest, and hardworking man, Estrada Palma's accomplishments as president were manifold: expansion of public education; a treaty of reciprocity with the United States; the completion of a national railroad; and the repayment of debts and reconstruction after a decade of war. His reputation, however, has suffered from his preference that the island remain a protectorate of the United States rather than a fully independent state. Estrada's decision to employ government resources to support his reelection efforts in 1905 prompted the opposition Liberal Party to boycott the proceedings. In the ensuing crisis, Estrada invited in a U.S. military force, which remained on the island from

1906 until 1909. Estrada resigned in 1906 and returned to his humble family plot.

— KAREN RACINE

ETCHEPAREBORDA, ROBERTO

Roberto Etchepareborda (*b.* 19 December 1923; *d.* 10 April 1985), Argentine historian, educator, and diplomat. Born in Milan, Italy, where his father was serving as an Argentine diplomat, Etchepareborda was educated in Europe and Argentina. As a prominent figure of the Radical Party, he was a member of the City Council of Buenos Aires (1958–1962), over which he later presided. In 1962 President Arturo FRONDIZI, a short time before he was deposed by a military coup, appointed Etchepareborda his foreign minister. From 1962 to 1964 Etchepareborda served as Argentina's ambassador to India. He was also director of the National Archives and a member of the Argentine Academy of History, as well as of similar academies in other American countries and in Spain. He was professor (1966–1971) and president (1971–1973) of the National University of the South in Bahía Blanca, Argentina, and in the 1970s and 1980s he taught at the University of North Carolina in Chapel Hill, and at the School of Advanced International Studies of Johns Hopkins University, and American University, both in Washington, D.C. In 1974 he held a Wilson Fellowship at the Woodrow Wilson International Center for Scholars, also in Washington. From 1979 to 1984 he was director of the Department of Cultural Affairs of the Organization of American States. An authority on Argentine political and diplomatic history, his most important works are: *Hipólito Yrigoyen: Pueblo y gobierno,* a twelve-volume compilation (1956); *Tres revoluciones: 1890, 1893, 1905* (1968), for which he received the National Book Award in 1970; *Rosas: Controvertida historiografía* (1972); and *Zeballos y la política exterior argentina* (1982). From 1981 until his death he was a contributing editor of the *Handbook of Latin American Studies.*

— CELSO RODRÍGUEZ

EUCEDA, MAXIMILIANO

Maximiliano Euceda (*b.* 1891; *d.* 1987), Honduran portrait painter. Born in Caridad, Honduras, near Tegucigalpa, Euceda, like other members of Honduras's Generation of '20, studied art in Spain, where he was especially influenced by the naturalism and realism of Romero de Torres. Euceda returned to Honduras in 1927, and gave art lessons until 1940, when he joined the staff of the newly formed Escuela Nacional de Bellas Artes in Tegucigalpa, where he taught for several decades thereafter. He and Carlos ZÚÑIGA FIGUEROA were especially important in training the generation of Honduran painters that emerged in the 1940s.

— RALPH LEE WOODWARD, JR.

F

FABELA ALFARO, ISIDRO

Isidro Fabela Alfaro (*b*. 29 June 1882; *d*. 12 August 1964), Mexican public figure and international jurist who contributed numerous works on international politics and law and taught international law for many years at the National University. With expertise in international arbitration from his long career in foreign relations, he was appointed a judge of the International Court of Justice, The Hague (1946–1952).

Fabela was born in Atlacomulco, in the state of México, which subsequently produced many leading political figures. He was the son of Francisco Trinidad Fabela and Guadalupe Alfaro. In 1909, Fabela was one of the founders of the Ateneo de la Juventud, which included José VASCONCELOS and Antonio CASO Y ANDRADE. He began his public career in Chihuahua in 1911 and became a federal deputy under Francisco MADERO in 1912–1913. Under Venustiano CARRANZA he served as secretary of foreign relations (1914–1915), after which he held a variety of diplomatic posts, eventually representing Mexico in 1937–1940 at the International Office of Labor. He governed his home state of Mexico from 1942 to 1945.

– RODERIC AI CAMP

FABINI, [FÉLIX] EDUARDO

[Félix] Eduardo Fabini (*b*. 18 May 1882; *d*. 17 May 1950), Uruguayan composer and violinist. Born in Solís de Mataojo, Lavalleja, Fabini studied violin with Romeo Masi at the Conservatorio La Lira in Montevideo; he

---

Fabini began to compose works for piano and guitar based on tunes, rhythms, and dances from the folk traditions of Uruguay.

---

also received instruction under Virgilio Scarabelli and Manuel Pérez Badía. At the age of eighteen Fabini entered the Royal Conservatory in Brussels and enrolled in the classes of César Thomson (violin) and Auguste de Boeck (composition). In 1904 he was awarded the first prize with distinction in violin. Upon his return to Uruguay he gave recitals and performed chamber music

in Montevideo. During his years in Brussels Fabini began to compose works for piano and guitar based on tunes, rhythms, and dances from the folk traditions of his homeland. With Alfonso BROQUA and Luis CLUZEAU-MORTET, he became a major exponent of musical nationalism in Uruguay. His best-known work is the symphonic poem *Campo*. Premiered by Vladimir Shavitch on 29 April 1922, it is considered Uruguay's major nationalist work of the period. Richard Strauss conducted it in Buenos Aires in 1923. *Campo* and *La isla de los ceibos* (1924–1926), another symphonic poem, were recorded by RCA Victor in the United States. *Mañana de Reyes* (1936–1937), *Melga sinfónica* (1931), and the ballet *Mburucuyá* (1933) completed Fabini's symphonic production. He also composed several *tristes* for piano and voice. He died in Montevideo.

– SUSANA SALGADO

FACIO BRENES, RODRIGO

Rodrigo Facio Brenes (*b*. 23 March 1917; *d*. 7 June 1961), perhaps the most influential social and political thinker in twentieth-century Costa Rica. Facio, son of a Panamanian immigrant father, served as both national deputy (1948–1949) and rector of the University of Costa Rica (1952–1961), whose main campus today bears his name.

Facio earned his law degree in 1941, at the age of twenty-four, with the thesis *Estudio sobre economía costarricense* (1942), which was to have enormous influence on subsequent generations. He had already organized the Law Students Cultural Association in 1937 and was a key figure in the Center for the Study of National Problems (1940). This group became, after 1945, the Democratic Action and Social Democratic parties, which led eventually to the formation of the National Liberation Party after its victory in the 1948 civil war. He was an assembly deputy in 1949 and, subsequently, a director and vice president of the Central Bank. After many years of working with party leader José FIGUERES FERRER, Facio broke with him out of anger at not being chosen to succeed Figueres as the presidential candidate for 1962. He left Costa Rica to work for the Inter-American Development Bank. He drowned soon afterward in El Salvador.

Facio's other major historical works are *La moneda y la banca central en Costa Rica* (1947) and *La federación de Centroamérica: Sus antecedentes, su vida y su disolución* (1957).

— LOWELL GUDMUNDSON

FACIO SEGREDA, GONZALO

Gonzalo Facio Segreda (*b.* 28 March 1918), Costa Rican ambassador to the United States on three occasions, former president of congress, minister of justice, and foreign minister.

Gonzalo "Chalo" Facio was appointed ambassador to the United States in 1990 by the newly inaugurated president of Costa Rica, Rafael Angel CALDERÓN FOURNIER (*b.* 1949). His credentials included nearly one half-century of prominence in political, cultural, and economic affairs. His most salient contributions have been in international affairs.

Born in San José, Facio entered the national scene while he was still in law school and was a founding member of the Center for the Study of National Problems (March 1940). He graduated from the University of Costa Rica in 1941. During the social reform–oriented government of Rafael Angel CALDERÓN GUARDIA (1940–1944), the Center developed a social democratic alternative to the Calderón-led alliance between the National Republican Party and a communist party, the Bloque de Obreros y Campesinos (BOC), which was renamed the Popular Vanguard Party (PVP) in 1943.

He entered the direct action group under the leadership of José FIGUERES FERRER, which paved the way for the armed uprising that overthrew the Teodoro PICADO MICHALSKI administration (1944–1948) after the disputed election in February 1948. After the successful revolt, Figueres appointed Facio minister of justice in the Founding Junta of the Second Republic (1948–1949), where he played an active role in suppressing communists and Calderónist leaders who had held high-level positions in the previous two administrations (1940–1948) through the establishment of special courts, such as the Court of Immediate Sanctions, which tried public officials who served between 1940 and 1948 for offenses committed, and the Court of Probity, which intervened the property of public officials who served during that same period. The decisions of these courts could not be appealed.

After the return to constitutional government in 1949, he worked actively with Figueres to form the National Liberation Party (PLN), which represented the ideological position of the junta and the revolutionary movement that brought it to power. With Figueres's election to the presidency in 1953, Facio served as president of congress (1953–1958). He served as foreign minister under Figueres in his third presidency (1970–

1974) and also under Daniel ODUBER QUIRÓS (1974–1978). Facio later broke with the PLN and became active in the Unidad coalition that elected Rodrigo CARAZO ODIO (1978–1982) and Rafael Angel Calderón Fournier (1990–1994) to the presidency.

Facio has also been active in business, professional, and academic affairs and has served as an officer and board member for several organizations. He has published numerous articles on national and international politics. He holds a doctorate in law from New York University.

— JOHN PATRICK BELL

FAGES, PEDRO

Pedro Fages (*b.* 1734; *d.* 1794), Spanish soldier and explorer. Fages, a native of Guisona, Catalonia, joined the Barcelona-based Catalonian volunteers in 1767 and participated in the Sonora Expedition of 1767–1771 in Mexico. In 1769 Visitador General José de GÁLVEZ ordered him and twenty-five Catalonian Volunteers to join Governor Gaspar de PORTOLÁ's California expedition. Between 1769 and 1774, Fages participated in the founding of San Diego, the march to Monterey that named many sites in California, and the discovery of

---

Fages participated in the founding of San Diego, the march to Monterey that named many sites in California, and the discovery of San Francisco Bay.

San Francisco Bay. Nicknamed "The Bear" ("El Oso"), Fages was the European discoverer of the Central and San Joaquín Valleys. In 1774 he wrote *A Historical, Political, and Natural Description of California,* an important ethnographic account of the area featuring references to its flora and fauna. Between 1774 and 1778, Fages commanded the Second Company of Catalonian Volunteers in Guadalajara. In 1776 he married Eulalia Callis, daughter of Agustín Callis, captain of the First Company of Catalonian Volunteers. In 1778 Fages served in Sonora, where in 1781 he commanded troops in the Colorado River campaign against the Yuma Indians who had destroyed a Spanish outpost at the confluence of the Colorado and Gila Rivers. In 1782 he was the first European to reach San Diego by crossing the Colorado River. He served as governor of California from 1782 to 1791, a generally peaceful time of mission building. Fages died in Mexico City.

— JOSEPH P. SÁNCHEZ

FAGOAGA Y LIZAUR, JOSÉ MARÍA

José María Fagoaga y Lizaur (*b.* 1764; *d.* 1837), Mexican politician. Fagoaga was born in Villa de Rentería, Guipúzcoa, Spain, of a distinguished family, and educated in Mexico City. A determined autonomist, he was in contact with like-minded individuals, among them the marqués de San Juan de Rayas and Jacobo de VILLAURRUTIA. Fagoaga held several important posts, including magistrate of the criminal chamber (1808–1812) and member of the Ayuntamiento of Mexico (1812). As a member of the secret society of Los Guadalupes, he aided the insurgents and later took part in the electoral processes established by the Constitution of Cádiz. He was elected to the Provincial Deputation in 1813 and in 1820 and served as deputy to the Cortes in 1814 and in 1820. Well known for his dissatisfaction with the colonial regime, Fagoaga was imprisoned and prosecuted in 1815. He was deported to Spain, but returned in 1821, in time to sign the Declaration of Independence and to become a member of the Provisional Governing Junta. He was one of the founders of the Scottish rite Masonic lodges, the *escoceses,* and he distinguished himself as a parliamentarian. In 1822 Fagoaga was one of the deputies imprisoned by Agustín de ITURBIDE. When the Spanish were expelled in 1827, he was forced into exile. Although Fagoaga subsequently returned to Mexico, he no longer participated in politics. He died in Mexico City.

– VIRGINIA GUEDEA

FAJARDO, FRANCISCO

Francisco Fajardo (*b.* ca. 1524; *d.* 1564), conquistador in Venezuelan territory. Fajardo was the son of a Spanish male and a female Indian chieftain of the Guaquerí tribe. He undertook various expeditions from Margarita Island to the mainland beginning in 1555 and in 1557 obtained authorization from the governor of El Tocuyo to rule and settle the coast. During a 1559 expedition, Fajardo headed inland and reached as far as the Valley of La Guaire, site of present-day Caracas. He returned to the coast, where he founded the settlement of El Collado. On a second expedition to La Guaire Valley, Fajardo discovered gold in Teque Indian territory. When the governor learned of the discovery Fajardo was stripped of his authority and sent to El Collado as its chief justice. In his place, Pedro Miranda was sent to exploit the gold, but he quickly alienated the local *cacique,* Guacaipuro. There followed a series of clashes in which Fajardo aided the Spanish forces despite his dispute with the governor. By 1562 the Indians had driven the Spanish from the valley and forced Fajardo to abandon El Collado. As Fajardo was provisioning yet another expedition in the settlement of Cumaná in 1594, he was arrested by the local chief justice. Though the charges are unclear, he was tried and sentenced to death. In retaliation, his followers on Margarita Island went to Cumaná and seized the chief justice, Alonso Cobos, whom they tried before the Audiencia of Santo Domingo, where he too was sentenced to death.

– INÉS QUINTERO

FALCÓN, JOSE

Jose Falcón (*b.* 1810; *d.* 1883), Paraguayan archivist, historian, and government official. Born in Asunción in the year of Platine independence, Falcón was well placed to participate in many key events during his country's formative years. Educated in the capital, he lived in seclusion in the far south of the country with his wealthy *hacendado* uncle during the dictatorship of José Gaspar FRANCIA. In 1844, President Carlos Antonio LÓPEZ chose Falcón as Paraguay's first foreign minister. In this capacity, he convinced foreign powers—especially Brazil, Britain, and the United States—to recognize Paraguay's independence. After stepping down from the foreign ministry, Falcón served successively as justice of the peace, criminal court justice, and, finally, director of the national archive (from 1854), which he organized along modern European lines.

When Francisco Solano LÓPEZ succeeded to the presidency in 1862, he named Falcón to the posts of interior minister and foreign minister. Falcón also remained director of the archive, which he had to move several times during the War of the Triple Alliance (1864–1870) as Brazilian forces advanced into Paraguay. He also witnessed some of the worst scenes of the war, notably the massacres at San Fernando, where many of his colleagues in government were executed on López's orders.

Falcón's fortunes improved after the war. He again occupied many official posts: senator, high court justice, president of the Asunción city council, and, once again, foreign minister. He helped to establish the Colegio Nacional in 1877. During the mid-1870s he went to Argentina to negotiate boundary agreements with that country.

During his thirty-six years of government service, Falcón kept copious notes, which he always meant to weave into a series of historical studies and memoirs. Although evidently these were never published, they are available in manuscript in the Manuel Gondra Collection in the Nettie Lee Benson Library at the University of Texas, Austin.

– THOMAS L. WHIGHAM

FALCÓN, JUAN CRISÓSTOMO

Juan Crisóstomo Falcón (*b.* 1820; *d.* 29 April 1870), Venezuelan president (1863–1868). Born in Coro (now Falcón) Province to a wealthy landowning family, Falcón participated in the civil wars of the mid-nineteenth century and rose to the rank of general. He was the outstanding commander of the Federalist armies in Venezuela's bloody Federal War (1859–1863) and, as a reward for leading the victorious forces, he was named provisional president in 1863. Falcón's five years in office were marked by administrative ineptitude, corruption, civil turmoil, and rebellion. Uninterested in the day-to-day operations of government, he spent long periods of time in his home province of Coro. In 1868 a temporary coalition of liberals and conservatives raised the banner of the Blue Revolution and drove the largely discredited president into exile, from which he never returned.

— WINFIELD J. BURGGRAAFF

FALLAS SIBAJA, CARLOS LUIS

Carlos Luis Fallas Sibaja (*b.* 21 January 1909; *d.* 6 May 1966), the best-known and most widely translated Costa Rican author, primarily through his classic work *Mamita Yunai* (1941). Fallas was an indefatigable labor organizer and politician who played a key role in the formation of the Communist Party in 1931 and in the Atlantic Coast banana workers' strike of 1934. Often writing from an autobiographical perspective in his novels, Fallas had worked as a youth of sixteen in the banana plantations of Límon province and on the docks of the port of Límon, loading the fruit. He knew firsthand the oppressive and absurd conditions suffered by local residents at the hands of the United Fruit Company and corrupt local politicians.

Fallas returned to his native Alajuela in the Central Highlands in 1931 and joined in the newly formed Communist Party as a leader of his fellow shoemakers in that city. The court system "exiled" him to Límon in 1933 for an incendiary speech; he then took up the task of organizing the banana workers, whose 1934 strike was by far the largest labor mobilization in Costa Rican history to that date. He was imprisoned briefly but later served as national deputy (1944–1948) before assuming a major military leadership role on the losing side of the 1948 civil war. He was again jailed and spent a year in prison, being the last prisoner released owing to his refusal to request a pardon from the Figueres-led junta. Over the next nearly twenty years Fallas led the fight to regain formal political rights for the defeated Communist Party, serving finally as *regidor* of the San José municipal government (1966).

Although he completed only eight years of formal schooling, Fallas could count on a rich store of life experiences. His *Mamita Yunai* emerged from a report on the manipulation of the 1940 presidential voting in the Talamanca region in far southeastern Costa Rica. Likewise, his other major novels (*Marcos Ramírez,* 1952; *Gente y gentecillas,* 1947) are based on working-class life in his home town. Fallas received recognition abroad for his literary achievements long before local cultural authorities would challenge political conventions at home. *Mamita Yunai* was widely read, and the novel *Marcos Ramírez* won a William Faulkner Foundation Prize in 1963. Fallas was officially declared Benemérito de la Patria on 14 November 1967, but his life and work still remain polemical subjects in Costa Rica.

— LOWELL GUDMUNDSON

FANGIO, JUAN MANUEL

Juan Manuel Fangio (*b.* 24 June 1911; *d.* 17 July 1995), Argentine race car driver. Born in Balcarce, 220 miles south of Buenos Aires, of recent Italian ancestry, as a teenage soccer player Fangio received the lifetime nickname "el Chueco" because of his bow legs. While working as a mechanic in a shop he partially owned, he ran in unsanctioned races beginning in 1936, then inaugurated his official career in 1938, winning for the first time in 1940. Except for four years during World War II, he raced continuously: open road, dirt track, and Grand Prix, joining the European circuit in 1948. He retired after finishing fourth in the French Gran Prix in 1958. Overall he won 102 of 186 international races he entered, 24 of 51 linked to the Driver's World Championship, a competition he captured five times (1951, 1954–1957), along with the affection of Argentines. Accused by some of being too cooperative with Juan and Evita Perón, he nonetheless avoided persecution and maintained heroic status among his countrymen. A 1941 tango, revived as late as the 1980s, labeled Fangio "the king of the steering wheel" and "the champion of champions"; a 1980 survey designated him "the greatest sportsman in Argentine sports history." Other drivers considered him talented and uncompromising, but always helpful and never deliberately dangerous or mean. The Centro Tecnológico-Cultural and Museo del Automovilismo Juan Manuel Fangio opened in Balcarce in 1986.

— JOSEPH L. ARBENA

FAORO, RAYMUNDO

Raymundo Faoro (*b.* 27 April 1925), Brazilian jurist and essayist. Born in Rio Grande do Sul of Italian forebears, Faoro received his law degree in 1948 and practiced law in Rio de Janeiro. From 1977 to 1979 he was president of the Ordem dos Advogados (Brazilian Bar Association) during the military dictatorship. Faoro secured the reinstitution of habeas corpus and helped restore a constitutional regime through public advocacy and political journalism.

Faoro published his best-known book, *Os donos do poder* (The Masters of Power), in 1958, but it had a greater impact during the dictatorship, when it appeared in a revised and much-expanded edition in 1975. Faoro was the first to apply Weberian analysis to Brazilian history, and his book has joined a short list of celebrated essays on the nature of Brazilian society. *Donos* surveys the national experience, focusing especially on the political estate (*estamento*). For Faoro, this group controlled the state, which he saw as fundamentally unaltered from its Portuguese prototype.

Regarding civil society, Faoro broke with conventional historiography, which viewed nineteenth-century Conservatives as owners of large estates. Faoro viewed them rather as controllers of "mobile wealth," that is, slaves and credit. It was not Conservatives but Liberals, he held, who predominated among *latifundists*, merchants and creditors allied with the political estate after independence in 1822. Excepting the early Empire (1831–1837) and the Old Republic (1889–1930), when relative decentralization strengthened landed elites, the political estate and its commercial allies succeeded in dominating civil society through a centralized state.

According to Faoro, the political estate has shaped the stratified character of Brazilian society, and has been impervious to the needs of the people as well as inattentive to the demands of powerful economic interests. The state dominates civil society, but the ruling estate has no clear national project.

Donos is most obviously Weberian in its interpretation of bureaucracy, offering an explanation of the enormous power of the contemporary Brazilian state, authoritarian and heavily engaged in parastatal enterprises when the second edition appeared. The work challenged dominant Marxist currents, among which Nicos Poulantzas's interpretation of the "exceptional capitalist state" and its "relative autonomy" was then most popular in Brazil.

– JOSEPH L. LOVE

FARIÑA NÚÑEZ, ELOY

Eloy Fariña Núñez (*b.* 25 June 1885; *d.* 1929), Paraguayan writer. Probably the most respected author in Paraguay during the first quarter of the twentieth century, Fariña Núñez was born in the tiny hamlet of Humaitá, site of a major battle during the disastrous War of the Triple Alliance some seventeen years earlier. Perhaps owing to the isolated position of his hometown, Fariña Núñez chose to go to Argentina for his education. He graduated from the Colegio Nacional of Corrientes and later studied law at the University of Buenos Aires.

Fariña Núñez spent most of his adult life in Buenos Aires, where he worked as a clerk in the internal revenue administration. His true love, however, was literature and his prime subject Paraguay. In 1913, when the Buenos Aires daily *La Prensa* opened a literary competition, Fariña Núñez won it with a short story entitled "Bucles de oro" (Golden Curls). He later published volumes of poetry (*Canto secular; Poesias escojidas*), miscellaneous prose (*Las vértebras de Pan; La mirada de los muertos; Cuentos guaraníes*), philosophical treatises (*Conceptos estéticos; Asunción; Crítica*), an essay in economics (*El estanco del tabaco*), and even a novel on Graeco-Egyptian life and customs (*Rhódopis*). His death at age forty-four robbed Paraguayan letters of one of its chief practitioners.

– THOMAS L. WHIGHAM

FARQUHAR, PERCIVAL

Percival Farquhar (*b.* 19 October 1864; *d.* 4 August 1953), American entrepreneur and railroad magnate. Born in York, Pennsylvania, Farquhar graduated from Yale University in 1884 with a degree in mechanical engineering. His Latin American business ventures began in Cuba shortly after the end of the Spanish-American War. There he profited from connections with U.S. occupation officials, purchased the Havana tram system, and electrically equipped it at the turn of the century. Beginning in 1900 he organized, along with Sir William Van Horne (of Canadian Pacific fame), the construction of the Cuba Railroad across the eastern half of the island.

In 1904 Farquhar purchased a Guatemalan concession to build a railroad connecting United Fruit Company lands and the Caribbean port of Puerto Barrios. With Indian draft labor, the line was completed in 1908. In the meantime, Farquhar had moved to Brazil, where he resided for the rest of his life. He invested in public utility companies in Rio de Janeiro and Salvador, managed the construction of port facilities in the north of the country, and directed the construction of the Madeira-Mamoré Railroad through the Amazon jungle. He also created and presided over the Brazil Railway Company, a syndicate that in 1912 controlled one-half of all Brazilian railroad mileage.

Farquhar spent the last decades of his life building and managing the steel plant at Itabira, Minas Gerais. From the start, this project faced fierce opposition from

Brazilian nationalists. President Getúlio VARGAS nationalized Itabira in 1942, making it part of the Companhia Vale do Rio Doce. Farquhar died in Rio de Janeiro.

— TODD DIACON

FARRELL, EDELMIRO

Edelmiro Farrell (*b.* 12 August 1887), Argentine general, ally of Juan PERÓN, and leader of a military junta (1944–1946). Farrell rose to prominence as part of a military *golpe* (coup) that seized power on 4 June 1943. A fervent nationalist, Farrell joined with Juan Perón and other army officers in the Group of United Officers (GOU). Influential among Argentina's officer corps, the GOU promoted anticommunism and economic nationalism. When factionalism pushed General Arturo Rawson, the *golpe*'s organizer, from command, Farrell became the minister of war (1943) under General and acting President Pedro Pablo RAMÍREZ (1943–1944) immediately after the *golpe.*

Factional disputes worked in favor of Farrell, who became president in 1944. As the junta's leader, Farrell allied with Juan Perón in efforts to establish a popular base for the military government. Farrell closed his term in power by supervising the national elections of 24 February 1946, which resulted in the election of Juan Perón as president.

— DANIEL LEWIS

FEBRES-CORDERO RIBADENEYRA, LEÓN

León Febres-Cordero Ribadeneyra (*b.* 9 March 1931), president of Ecuador (1984–1988). Born in Guayaquil, Febres-Cordero began his education in his native city and completed his secondary education in the United States. He studied mechanical engineering at the Stevens Institute of Technology in New Jersey. Returning to Guayaquil in 1956, he developed a successful business career, working as a mechanical engineer, manager, and executive in a variety of public and private enterprises, including the Exportadora Bananera Noboa S.A. He was active in a variety of business and civic organizations, serving terms as president of the Guayaquil Chamber of Industries in the 1970s, the National Federation of Chambers of Industries of Ecuador, and the Association of Latin American Industries.

Febres-Cordero entered politics in the 1960s as deputy to the Constituent Assembly (1966–1967), and senator and president of the Economic and Financial Commission of the National Congress (1968–1970). He was principal spokesman for rightist critics of the military juntas that ruled Ecuador from 1972 to 1979 and led the opposition to the Constitution of 1979.

Elected deputy to Congress in 1979 as a candidate of the Social Christian Party, he emerged as the leading critic of the governments of Jaime ROLDÓS AGUILERO (1979–1981) and Osvaldo HURTADO LARREA (1981–1983), and a staunch defender of coastal business interests.

Febres-Cordero won the 1984 presidential election as the candidate of the Frente de Reconstrucción Nacional, a coalition of rightist parties. His administration sought to restructure the Ecuadorian economy by reducing government regulations, freeing exchange rates, promoting the export of manufactured items, and encouraging foreign investment. His ability to implement his neoliberal reform program was undermined by an opposition congress and a deteriorating economy. Falling petroleum prices and the subsequent loss of oil revenues after the destruction of the trans-Amazonian oil pipeline forced the administration to adopt austerity measures that quickly alienated labor and opposition political parties. The administration's problems mounted when it failed to control burgeoning budget deficits or to shield the working classes from the impact of the austerity program. Although Febres-Cordero completed his presidential term, his dictatorial style provoked a series of constitutional crises and increased political violence.

— LINDA ALEXANDER RODRÍGUEZ

FÉDERMAN, NICOLÁS

Nicolás Féderman (*b.* 1505/09; *d.* 21/22 February 1542), German conquistador. Born Nikolaus Federmann, probably in the free imperial city of Ulm, Féderman worked for the Welsers, a German commercial house. The Welsers had authorization for a trading depot in Santo Domingo by 1526, and in 1528 their agents in Seville signed an agreement with Spanish officials to conquer and settle Venezuela. Féderman was one of several Germans sent to explore, conquer, govern, and exploit the commercial possibilities of the Venezuelan concession.

In his *Historia indiana* Féderman recounts how he crossed the Atlantic to Santo Domingo in 1529 and reached Coro, Venezuela, the following January. In July the ailing governor, Ambrosio Alfinger (Ambrosius Dalfinger), retired to Santo Domingo, leaving him in charge. Féderman boldly organized a successful six-month expedition into the interior, returning to Coro on 17 March 1531. Alfinger, now recuperated, banished him for four years for this unapproved expedition.

In Augsburg in 1532, Féderman shrewdly composed his *Historia indiana,* touting his exploits and the richness of Venezuela, with an eye on his employers, the

Welsers. The *Historia,* with its keen analysis of Indian life and warfare, had its desired effect. Féderman signed a contract with the Welsers, and the Council of the Indies made him governor and captain-general of Venezuela.

Féderman organized a conquest of the Chibcha

Indians of highland Colombia, where some legends

located El Dorado.

After his return to Coro, Féderman and Jorge Espira (Georg Hohermuth) organized a two-pronged conquest of the Chibcha (Muisca) Indians of highland Colombia, where some legends located El Dorado. Espira was to approach from the east by crossing the llanos, and Féderman was to enter from the west by moving up the Magdalena River, but the plan went awry. Espira left Coro in 1535 and spent three ruinous years before struggling back without having penetrated Chibcha territory.

In the meantime, Féderman secured the western boundary of the Welser concession, but then rival and vastly superior forces from Santa Marta blocked movement up the Magdalena. He returned to Coro, where, to avoid an unexpected *residencia* (impeachment), he suddenly resumed his expedition. Following the route taken by Espira, he traversed the Venezuelan and Colombian llanos, always keeping the Andes to the west in view. The two expeditions never met.

Upon finding gold, Féderman turned west and climbed the Andes, but discovered that Gonzalo JIMÉNEZ DE QUESADA and his expedition from Santa Marta had arrived two years earlier (1537) and had already conquered the Chibchas. Then a group from Popayán, led by Sebastián de BELALCÁZAR, appeared. Each conquistador claimed the Chibcha territory, but they agreed to journey to Spain together to resolve the dispute there. Before departing, Féderman accepted seven shares of any future booty taken by the Jiménez group and the *encomienda* of Tinjacá. Most of his men joined Jiménez's forces and helped them establish new cities and colonize central Colombia. They sold their horses and armament at great profit to Jiménez's men, who were in desperate need of these resources.

Back in Flanders in 1540, Féderman disagreed with the powerful Welsers over his accomplishments and was jailed. Petitions to the Council of Flanders were to no avail. Desperate for a way out, Féderman denounced the Welsers before the Council of the Indies for de-

frauding the royal treasury. Since the council wanted to separate the Welsers from their Venezuelan concession, the case was transferred to the council's jurisdiction in Spain and Féderman was brought to Valladolid, where he died. The Welsers pursued their Venezuela claim before the council until 1557, when the bankruptcy of Philip II led them to abandon it.

– MAURICE P. BRUNGARDT

FEIJÓ, DIOGO ANTÔNIO

Diogo Antônio Feijó (baptized 17 August 1784; *d.* 10 November 1843), Brazilian statesman and regent. Feijó's upbringing, career, style of life, and outlook personified the nativist, anti-Portuguese current in Brazilian affairs in the years after independence. A foundling, born in São Paulo, Feijó was educated for the priesthood and ordained in 1808. A deputy from São Paulo province to the Lisbon Cortes in 1822, he made his mark in the Chamber of Deputies elected in 1826 and 1830 as a prominent opponent to PEDRO I.

Absent from Rio de Janeiro, Feijó played no role in the crisis preceding Pedro I's abdication in April 1831. In July 1831, he accepted the key portfolio of justice. Defeating several armed risings and organizing the National Guard, Feijó served as bulwark of the new regime. Losing patience, he resigned in July 1832. He was a prime mover in the ensuing and abortive parliamentary coup, designed to turn Brazil into a federation of states. Despite this failure, Feijó remained the preeminent figure in liberal, nativist politics, becoming senator from Rio province in 1833. In the elections for a single regent, instituted by the constitutional amendment enacted in 1834 (the Ato Adicional), he was the Moderado party candidate and gained a plurality of votes cast. Worsening health and his own doubts about his suitability delayed his taking office until 12 October 1835.

Feijó's two years as regent proved as barren as he had feared, due in part to his foes' unrelenting hostility but also to his intransigence, belligerence, and, above all, failure to take drastic action against regional revolts. Reduced to impotence, he resigned on 18 September 1837. He stayed active in politics but no longer played a central role. Despite a paralytic stroke in 1840, Feijó actively supported the São Paulo revolt of 1842. Deportation to Espírito Santo and then a trial before the Senate probably hastened his death.

– RODERICK J. BARMAN

FEIJÓO, BENITO JERÓNIMO

Benito Jerónimo Feijóo (*b.* 8 October 1676; *d.* 26 September 1764), Benedictine monk who popularized modern European ideas in Spain and the colonies. Feijóo studied in Galicia and Salamanca before becoming professor of theology at the University of Oviedo. Through reading foreign works, Feijóo became aware of his country's intellectual backwardness, which he attempted to correct with his nine-volume collection of essays, *Teatro crítico universal* (1726–1739) and five volumes of *Cartas eruditas y curiosas* (1742–1760). The wide range of subjects he covered included literature, art, philosophy, natural science, mathematics, geography, and history.

Feijóo questioned contemporary medicine, exaggerated devotion to the saints, and religious superstition. He tried to persuade his countrymen that scientific progress need not undermine religious belief. Although his enlightened skepticism aroused controversy, he remained devoted to the Catholic faith and found favor with Ferdinand VI, who silenced his critics with a royal order in 1750. While few of Feijóo's ideas were new, many were relatively unknown in eighteenth-century Spain and its colonies. His writings enjoyed enormous popularity at home and, in part because of his favorable view of creoles' abilities, in the Indies.

– SUZANNE HILES BURKHOLDER

FELGUÉREZ, MANUEL

Manuel Felguérez (*b.* 12 December 1928), Mexican artist. Born in San Agustín Valparaíso, Zacatecas, Felguérez is one of the most important exponents of abstract art in Mexico. From 1947 to 1952 he lived in Paris, studying at the Academy of the Grande Chaumière; he also studied sculpture with Ossip Zadkine and Constantin Brancusi. Upon his return to Mexico City in 1953, he studied with Francisco Zúñiga. Felguérez's work includes a number of highly abstract sculptures, stained glass, and murals that he created with found objects. Most of his geometric paintings preserve figurative elements pointing to the dualism between order and disorder that characterizes his entire oeuvre. Felguérez has also worked as a set designer for such plays as *La lección* (1961) and *La ópera del orden* (1961), directed by Alexandro Jodorowsky. His work has been the subject of numerous individual and group exhibitions in Mexico and Europe.

– ILONA KATZEW

FÉLIX, MARÍA

María Félix (*b.* 8 April 1914), Mexican film actress. Born near Alamos, Sonora, as a young girl Félix moved to Guadalajara, where she completed her early schooling. She made her film debut in 1942 in the classic *El penon de las ánimas*. One year later, she starred in *Doña Bárbara,* a screen adaptation of the famous Venezuelan novel. The character Félix portrayed in that film epitomized the dominant, self-assured, strong-willed, and seductive heroine that became the actress's screen persona. Among her greatest and best-known films are *Enamorada* (1947), *La diosa arrodillada* (1947), *Maclovia* (1948), *Río escondido* (1949), *Doña Diabla* (1951), *El rapto* (1954), *Tizoc* (1957), *La cucaracha* (1959), and *Juana Gallo* (1961). The Mexican film academy awarded Félix the Ariel for best actress for the films *Enamorada, Río Escondido,* and *Doña Diabla.* Known as *"La Doña,"* Félix is a living legend and symbol of Mexican beauty, femininity, and strength, and is arguably the greatest screen presence of twentieth-century Mexican cinema.

– DAVID MACIEL

FERNANDES, FLORESTAN

Florestan Fernandes (*b.* 22 July 1920), Brazilian sociologist and reformer who founded the São Paulo school of sociology, which studied capitalist modernization in Brazil. Fernandes began his career with theses on social organization and war among the Tupinambá Indians (1949, 1952). In the 1950s, after establishing himself at the University of São Paulo, he turned to topics in folklore and race relations. A UNESCO-sponsored project, conducted in collaboration with Roger Bastide and others, resulted in *Relações raciais entre negros e brancos em São Paulo* (1955; Race Relations Between Blacks and Whites in São Paulo), the first of his several revisionist studies of race relations in the context of São Paulo's twentieth-century transition to a competitive, class society, including *The Negro in Brazilian Society* (1964; English trans. 1969). Fernandes influenced a generation of sociologists, including Fernando Henrique CARDOSO and Octávio IANNI, through his studies of slavery and race relations. Fernandes was purged from the University of São Paulo in 1969 and exiled. Upon his return to Brazil, he wrote an analysis of Brazil's transition to modern capitalism, *A revolução burguesa no Brasil: Ensaio de interpretação sociológica* (1975; The Bourgeois Revolution in Brazil). In the 1980s he published treatises on political redemocratization, and in 1986 was elected to the Constituent Congress by the socialist Partido dos Trabalhadores (Workers' Party).

– DAIN BORGES

FERNANDES, MILLÔR

Millôr Fernandes (*b.* 1924), Brazilian humorist, poet, playwright, and artist. Brazilian society and politics are favorite themes of Fernandes's highly original and satirical views, and most of his works underscore his keen ability to expose the incoherence of everyday life. He often highlights his writings with his own illustrations. His critical but extremely creative irreverence is also found in his "fables"—*Fábulas fabulosas* (1964) and *Novas fábulas fabulosas* (1978)—and in his protest theater—*Liberdade, liberdade* (1965). Fernandes has published frequently in newspapers and journals (such as *O Cruzeiro, Tribuna da Imprensa, Correio da Manhã, Pif-Paf*), is an important contributor to *Veja,* and has worked in radio and television. His works of art have been exhibited in the major cities of Brazil. Fernandes has also translated drama, of special note being his translations of works by Shakespeare, Molière, Brecht, and Synge. He is perhaps Brazil's most famous humorist.

– GARY M. VESSELS

FERNÁNDEZ, EMILIO "EL INDIO"

Emilio "El Indio" Fernández (*b.* 26 March 1904; *d.* 6 August 1986), Mexican film director. Beginning his studies in the military academy, by the mid-1920s Fernández was in Hollywood, learning the craft of filmmaking. In the next decade, he returned to Mexico and worked as an actor in cinema. He debuted as a director with *La isla de la pasíon* in 1941. Among his most celebrated films are *María Candelaria* (1943), *Bugambilia* (1944), *Flor silvestre* (1944), *Pueblerina* (1946), *Enamorada* (1946), *Río escondido* (1946), *Salón México* (1954), and *La red* (1954). His films won numerous national and international awards and brought Mexican cinema to the attention of both Mexican and foreign audiences. Through a nationalistic and artistic treatment of subjects, Fernández extolled the beauties and virtues of Mexico and its people, particularly the *campesino* and the Indian. Fernández is not only one of Mexico's leading directors but a major figure of world cinema.

– DAVID MACIEL

FERNÁNDEZ, JUAN

Juan Fernández (*b.* ca. 1530; *d.* 1599), Spanish navigator and discoverer of the Juan Fernández Islands. Actively engaged in navigation between Peru and Chile by 1550, Fernández theorized that Chile could be reached much more quickly by sailing further offshore, west of the Humboldt Current. Testing this theory, he discovered the islands that later bore his name, about 400 miles west of Valparaíso, Chile, on 22 November 1574. He reached Chile only thirty days after leaving Callao,

Peru, a voyage that formerly took three months or more. Although MAGELLAN may have seen these islands earlier, Fernández's sighting gave them navigational significance and greatly improved communications between Lima and Chile. His efforts to colonize the islands failed, but his leadership in the Peru-Chile trade earned him recognition in 1589 as "chief pilot of the South Sea." Minor difficulties with the INQUISITION earned him the nickname "El Brujo" (the sorcerer). In 1592 he retired to his Chilean estate of Rautén, where he lived until his death seven years later.

– RALPH LEE WOODWARD, JR.

FERNÁNDEZ, MAX

Max Fernández (*b.* 1943), founder and leader of Civic Solidarity Unity (Unidad Cívica Solidaridad—UCS) and president of the Bolivian National Brewery (CBN). Very little is known about Fernández's background except that he was born in Quillacollo, Cochabamba, and worked as a delivery man for the brewery he now owns. In 1985 Fernández purchased a majority share of the stock of the CBN and has since developed a significant empire. The U.S. embassy accused him of making his fortune trafficking drugs, but that allegation has not been substantiated.

With considerable support in the La Paz, Beni, Pando, and Cochabamba departments, Fernández became a serious contender in the 1993 elections. His populist style of campaigning, which included donating everything from hospitals to soccer balls, endeared him with marginal sectors of the Bolivian electorate. Fernández has also managed to destroy all competition to his beer factory and has announced plans to build new factories in Beni and Santa Cruz.

Fernández lacks charisma, speaks lower-class Spanish, and is unable to articulate any party platform.

Fernández has run the UCS in an authoritarian manner and, in classic populist style, control over his political party has been determined by his capacity to deliver prebends. He has named the party leadership; in fact, no assemblies or elections have been held to elect the governing body of the UCS. Most striking, however, is Fernández's rather unappealing personality. He lacks charisma, speaks lower-class Spanish, and is unable to articulate any party platform. To overcome these shortcomings, Fernández has hired prominent members of the major political parties who generally present UCS campaign promises.

A pragmatic entrepreneur, Fernández is generally perceived as a man of action and few words. Most appealing to the working classes is Fernández's innovative employer-worker relations at his brewery. Workers in the CBN enjoy high wages and other benefits not available to blue-collar employees elsewhere in the private or public sector.

Dozens of dissidents from major and minor parties have flocked to the UCS. Fernández parlayed a fourth-place finish in the 1993 elections into an alliance dubbed the "governability pact" with the victorious National Revolutionary Movement. The UCS was granted the ministry of defense in exchange for support in Congress for the MNR.

– EDUARDO A. GAMARRA

FERNANDEZ, OSCAR LORENZO

Oscar Lorenzo Fernandez (*b.* 4 November 1897; *d.* 27 August 1948), Brazilian composer, best known for his art songs. His first works, written between 1918 and 1922, were principally songs and piano compositions, but in the early 1920s he became interested in the nationalist movement and began to write works based on Brazilian subjects. In 1924 he was appointed professor of harmony at the National Music Institute and in 1936 established the Brazilian Conservatory, which he directed until his death in 1948.

In 1946, in recognition of the importance of the work of Heitor Villa-Lobos, Fernandez wrote an article, "A contribuição harmonica de Villa-Lobos," which stressed the innovative quality of the harmonic practices of Villa-Lobos. Fernandez shared with him an interest in the Indian melodies collected by explorer Roquette Pínto and in the use of native percussion instruments in orchestral composition. Fernandez's principal contribution to the emerging nationalist movement in music in Brazil was his ability to capture authentic elements of the Afro-Brazilian tradition in art songs and operas based on folk songs. He is best known as the composer of "Batuque," a movement from the suite "Malazarte," taken from an opera of the same title. This piece has been frequently arranged for various band and orchestral ensembles.

– DAVID P. APPLEBY

FERNÁNDEZ ALONSO, SÉVERO

Sévero Fernández Alonso (*b.* 15 August 1849; *d.* 12 August 1925), president of Bolivia (1896–1899). Born in Sucre, Fernández Alonso was a silver-mine owner, lawyer, and minister of war (1892–1896). He was the last president of the Conservative oligarchy that ruled Bolivia in the last two decades of the nineteenth century. Despite his efforts at conciliation with the rival Liberal and Federalist parties, the Federalist War (1898–1899) broke out during his presidency and effectively ended Conservative Party hegemony. Unable to fashion a compromise between the Sucre-based Conservatives and the northern Federalists, Fernández Alonso personally led the national army in an effort to crush the rebellion by the La Paz-based Federalists and Liberals. By remaining in Oruro with his army and vacillating in his attack on the city of La Paz, Fernández Alonso assured the military defeat of his government and the rise to power of the Liberal Party.

– ERICK D. LANGER

FERNÁNDEZ ARTUCIO, HUGO

Hugo Fernández Artucio (*b.* 1912; *d.* 1974), Uruguayan professor and publicist, was political editor of *El Día* from 1941 to 1966. In 1966 he supported the presidential campaign of Oscar GESTIDO and became director of the University of Uruguay's Vázquez Acevedo Institute. Fernández Artucio gained public recognition through a series of interviews on the "Espectador" radio station in 1940, in which he revealed a Nazi plot to overthrow the Uruguayan government. His findings helped a parliamentary investigation commission, established in 1940, to analyze NSdAP (Nationalsozialistische Deutsche Arbeiter-Partei) activities in Uruguay and to prepare legal action against its members.

– DIETER SCHONEBOHM

FERNÁNDEZ CRESPO, DANIEL

Daniel Fernández Crespo (*b.* 1901; *d.* 1964), Uruguayan educator and political leader of the National (Blanco) Party. Fernández Crespo was born in a rural area of the department of San José. He received his teaching degree and worked in education until 1932. His political career included his election to the town council of Montevideo in 1928, five terms as representative (1931–1950), senator in 1950, and national adviser in 1954. Between 1959 and 1963 he presided at the departmental council of Montevideo and at the National Council of Government, a nine-member committee established in 1952 to institutionalize coparticipation in the exercise of executive power. He was also active as a sports director, being associated with the Liverpool soccer club and the Aguada basketball club. Concerned especially with social problems, he personified the popular forces of nationalism in an urban setting, in which the Colorado Party and particularly BATLLISMO usually predominated. In 1958, after ninety-three years of government controlled by the Colorado Party, the National Party triumphed in the general elections as well as in those in Montevideo.

— JOSÉ DE TORRES WILSON

FERNÁNDEZ DE CABRERA BOBADILLA CERDA Y MENDOZA, LUIS GERÓNIMO

Luis Gerónimo Fernández de Cabrera Bobadilla Cerda y Mendoza (Conde de Chinchón; *b.* 1590; *d.* 28 October 1647), viceroy of Peru (1629–1639). The fourth conde de Chinchón and member of the Council of State (Aragon and Italy) and War assumed his viceregal duties on 14 January 1629. Reputed to be penurious, austere, and abstemious, Chinchón focused much of his attention on fiscal matters, especially new taxes imposed during his tenure, such as the Media Anata, Unión de Armas, Mesada Eclesiástica, and Composición *de pulperías* (bar taxes). He also vigorously pursued donations from individuals and communities throughout the viceroyalty to meet exigencies in Spain. In fact, during the eleven years he was in office, Chinchón remitted over 4 million ducats to Spain despite the fall in silver production at Potosí. Fortunately, silver strikes at Cailloma and Pasco in part made up for the drop in output in Upper Peru.

Militarily, the viceroy strengthened the fortifications at Callao, built two new vessels for the Pacific fleet, reinforced garrisons in Chile, and counteracted both the Dutch corsairs plying the Pacific coast and Portuguese encroachments on the eastern part of Peru. When the usefulness of quinine for treating malaria was discovered in the Loja province of Ecuador in 1630, the viceroy enthusiastically endorsed its effectiveness, but when word reached Rome, church officials there called it a "pact of the Peruvians with the devil." In Lima, Chinchón certified guilds for hatmakers, tailors, ironworkers, locksmiths, and potters. Known for his social conscience, Chinchón vigorously defended Indian rights and provided basic necessities for newly arrived slaves and for orphans and abandoned children. Evidently, too, he had a strong sense of religious and moral propriety: during Lent he ordered men and women separated in the churches of Lima. Relieved of his duties on 18 December 1639, he returned to Spain, where he died.

— JOHN JAY TEPASKE

FERNÁNDEZ DE CASTRO ANDRADE Y PORTUGAL, PEDRO ANTONIO

Pedro Antonio Fernández de Castro Andrade y Portugal (Conde de Lemos; *b.* 1635?; *d.* 6 December 1672), viceroy of Peru (1667–1672). The tenth count of Lemos,

Pedro Fernández de Castro was born in Spain and was only thirty-three when he assumed his post in Lima in November 1667. Upon arrival his most immediate task was quelling a civil war in the mining area of Laycacota in the province of Paucarolla, where armed bands led by the Salcedo brothers, Gaspar and José, terrorized other miners. In 1668 Lemos personally led a force of soldiers and militia into the mountains to put down the revolt, ruthlessly executing forty-two rebels. Returning to Lima in 1669 after visiting Chucuito and Cuzco, Lemos attached himself to the Jesuits, supporting their missions in the interior at Mojos and on the Marañon River and the construction of a sumptuous new chapel for their church of Nuestra Señora de los Desamparados, dedicated in June 1672. At the same time the viceroy sponsored construction of a new convent for female penitents and the Betelmite Indian Hospital of Santa Ana. An outspoken critic of the forced labor system (MITA) that supplied workers for the silver mines at Potosí, Lemos advocated its elimination but was successful only in reducing the number of *mita* Indians by half to approximately 2,000 annually.

Devout, fervent, and somewhat pompous, Lemos loved the panoply surrounding rites and ceremonies, ordering thirty masses each for the forty-two rebels he executed and elegant celebrations whenever religious or state occasions called for them. After only five years in office, Lemos suddenly fell ill and died at the age of thirty-eight.

— JOHN JAY TEPASKE

FERNÁNDEZ DE CÓRDOBA, DIEGO

Diego Fernández de Córdoba (marqués de Guadalcázar; *b.* 1578; *d.* 1630), viceroy of Mexico and Peru. Born in Seville, Guadalcázar served as VICEROY of New Spain from 1612 until 1621, when he moved to Peru, serving as viceroy there until 1629. During his reign in New Spain he was noted for the establishment of the *tribunal de tributos* (tribute court) and for two important public works projects: the continuing effort to drain the Valley of Mexico and the construction of the castle of San Diego in Acapulco.

In Peru, Guadalcázar put down a civil war in Potosí between the "Vicuñas" (Creoles) and "Vascongados" (Peninsulars). A Dutch fleet threatened the coast in 1624–1625, forcing the viceroy to fortify the coastal towns of the kingdom. Because the mercury mines at Huancavelica continued to pose health problems to the Indian miners, Guadalcázar eliminated nighttime mine activity and reduced the number of Indians assigned to the mines in the MITA. He sought to improve communications through the construction and maintenance of bridges. Rather than depend on a legal adviser, he took an active role in supervising law suits dealing with Indians. Although he, like his predecessor, attempted to deal with the issue of the Potosí *mita,* no concrete changes were implemented. He died in Córdoba, Spain.

— JOHN F. SCHWALLER

FERNÁNDEZ (HERNÁNDEZ) DE CÓRDOBA, FRANCISCO

Francisco Fernández (Hernández) de Córdoba (*b.* 1475?; *d.* June 1526), conqueror of Nicaragua. (He is not to be confused with Francisco HERNÁNDEZ DE CÓRDOBA [*d.* 1518], a conquistador of the Yucatán.) Fernández de Córdoba was a Spanish soldier of fortune who came to Panama sometime between 1514 and 1517. In the service of Pedro Arias de ÁVILA (Pedrarias Dávila), he was captain of the guard at Panama City in 1519. Pedrarias sent him to Nicaragua in 1523 to check the pretensions of Gil GONZÁLEZ DÁVILA. There Fernández founded the cities of Granada and León in 1524, as well as the village of Bruselas, the first European settlement in what is today Costa Rica. He also tried to take control of the territory of Honduras and to establish a kingdom independent of Pedrarias, perhaps in alliance with Hernán CORTÉS. Learning of this in 1525, Pedrarias came to Nicaragua and captured Fernández. After a speedy trial, in which Fernández was convicted of treason, he was beheaded in León in late June 1526. The Nicaraguan unit of currency, the córdoba, is named for him.

— RALPH LEE WOODWARD, JR.

FERNÁNDEZ DE LIZARDI, JOSÉ JOAQUÍN

José Joaquín Fernández de Lizardi (*b.* 15 November 1776; *d.* 21 June 1827), Mexican writer. Born in Mexico City, Fernández de Lizardi began his education in

---

Fernández de Lizardi's El periquillo sarniento *is recognized as the "first" Spanish-American novel.*

Tepozotlán, where his father was a physician. He later went to Mexico City for further education and in 1793 entered the Colegio de San Ildefonso. After abandoning his studies in 1798 at his father's death, Fernández de Lizardi held various bureaucratic positions and initially opposed the independence movement, a stance that he soon reversed in support of Iturbide. As a journalist he is most remembered for the newspaper *El Pensador Mexicano* (The Mexican Thinker [1812–1814]), which he founded when the Spanish Constitution of 1812 estab-

lished freedom of the press. His writings reflect the Mexican social milieu at the time of the country's struggle for independence. His special concern was the place of Spaniards born in the New World. Because of newspaper censorship, he resorted to fiction and wrote *El periquillo sarniento* (The Itching Parrot [published serially 1816; complete version published posthumously 1830–1831]). This picaresque tale is recognized as the "first" Spanish-American novel. It achieves compositional complexity and development, and it treats contemporary New World themes. Fernández de Lizardi wrote three other novels—*Noches tristes y día alegre* (Sad Nights and Happy Day [1818, 1819]), *La Quijotita y su prima* (Quijotita and Her Cousin [1818]), and *Don Catrín de la Fachenda* (written about 1819, published posthumously in 1832)—before he returned to journalism and pamphleteering in 1820. By 1822 Fernández de Lizardi became disenchanted with Iturbide and began to advocate liberal causes, and his modest social position became increasingly precarious. He died of tuberculosis in Mexico City.

— DANNY J. ANDERSON

FERNÁNDEZ HIDALGO, GUTIERRE

Gutierre Fernández Hidalgo (b. 1553; *d.* after 1620), Spanish composer. Born in Andalusia, Fernández Hidalgo arrived at New Granada (Colombia) in 1584 as the *maestro de capilla* of the Bogotá cathedral. He became sixteenth-century America's most eminent composer. As chapelmaster, Fernández Hidalgo asked the Bogotá bishop to require the seminarians of the newly founded Seminario Conciliar de San Luis to sing under his direction every day at cathedral services. In 1585 he was appointed rector of the seminary, but a dispute with his students over his demanding teaching style led him to leave Bogotá in 1586. He moved to Quito, where he was music director at the cathedral and seminary until 1589. Again, he proved too demanding for his subordinates. On 13 July 1591, he was appointed *maestro de capilla* of the Cuzco cathedral, where he conducted the cathedral choir and taught polyphony and counterpoint while composing in his free time. In 1597 he accepted a new assignment with a better salary, as *maestro de capilla* of the La Plata cathedral (present-day Sucre, Bolivia). He remained there, presumably, until his retirement in 1620. It is believed he died in Cuzco.

Fernández Hidalgo was technically and stylistically the best representative in America of the Spanish polyphony initiated by Tomás Luis de Victoria, Cristóbal de Morales, and Francisco Guerrero. Among his works are nine Magnificats for four and six voices, ten four-voice psalms, three Salve Reginas for four and five voices, and *villancicos,* motets, and hymns.

— SUSANA SALGADO

FERNÁNDEZ MADRID, JOSÉ

José Fernández Madrid (*b.* 19 February 1789; *d.* 28 June 1830), president of the United Provinces of New Granada. Born in Cartagena and trained in law and medicine, José Fernández Madrid was a prominent figure of New Granada's intellectual scene in the last years of colonial rule. A leading spokesman for the federalist cause in the independence movement, he was made president of the United Provinces in 1816, shortly before its final collapse. During the Spanish reconquest he was exiled from New Granada. He lived for a time in Havana, but at his death in London was serving as envoy of Gran Colombia to England and France. Fernández Madrid is further remembered as a noted journalist and author of poetry and drama.

— DAVID BUSHNELL

FERNÁNDEZ OREAMUNO, PRÓSPERO

Próspero Fernández Oreamuno (*b.* 18 July 1834; *d.* 12 March 1885), president of Costa Rica (1882–1885). Born in San José, Fernández studied there and in Guatemala. His presidency marked a watershed in Costa Rican history, ending the political domination by the "coffee barons" and ushering in fifty years of steady progress toward democracy. Following Costa Rica's first brush with dictatorship under Tomás GUARDIA GUTIÉRREZ (1870–1882), a new generation of Costa Ricans, constituting a fiercely democratic emerging middle class, undertook to extend the suffrage and eliminate the influence of the Catholic church.

Identifying with this rising group, Fernández sponsored educational reform and tough anticlerical laws. He enacted the Liberal Laws of 1884, which established free, compulsory education, expelled the Jesuits, made marriage a civil contract, legalized divorce, and secularized cemeteries. Fernández died during a military campaign against the Guatemalan caudillo Justo Rufino BARRIOS, but he had set the course for the so-called generation of 1889 that dominated Costa Rican affairs until the mid-1930s. The Legislative Assembly awarded him the Benemérito de la Patria in 1883.

— CHARLES D. AMERINGER

FERNÁNDEZ RETAMAR, ROBERTO

Roberto Fernández Retamar (*b.* 9 June 1930), Cuban essayist and poet. Fernández Retamar was born in Havana and received a doctorate in philosophy and literature in 1954. In 1951 he was awarded the National Poetry Prize for his book *Patrias.* He studied linguistics in Paris (1955) and London (1956). After returning to Cuba in 1958, he wrote using the pseudonym David for the underground revolutionary publication *Resistencia.* After the Cuban Revolution of 1959, he continued his academic career until the following year, when he was named cultural adviser for the Cuban embassy in Paris. He was elected coordinating secretary of the Cuban Union of Writers and Artists (UNEAC).

As of the mid-1990s, Fernández Retamar was a frequent representative of Cuba in international cultural activities and was active also in his own country's cultural affairs. His essays are among the best examples of revolutionary aesthetics in literature that Cuba has produced. Among his best-known works are his collection of poems *Cuaderno paralelo* (1973) and the essay *Para una teoría de la literatura hispanoamericana* (1977). Other works include *Entrevisto* (1982).

— ROBERTO VALERO

FERNÁNDEZ Y MEDINA, BENJAMÍN

Benjamín Fernández y Medina (*b.* 31 March 1873; *d.* 1960), Uruguayan writer and diplomat. Born in Montevideo, Fernández y Medina held a large number of posts in public administration, especially in the diplomatic corps. He was secretary to the chief of police in Montevideo in 1897 and prepared a draft of the Police Codes. He was a member of the Departmental Commission on Elementary Instruction in the capital in 1898 and became the first official of the Interior Ministry in 1905 and chief official in 1906. During the second presidency of José BATLLE Y ORDÓÑEZ, he was appointed undersecretary of foreign affairs. He later joined the Foreign Service and was appointed plenipotentiary minister in Germany and Holland in 1916. In 1917 he took up the same post in Spain, which was expanded to include Portugal. He later was transferred to Cuba and Mexico and retired from the diplomatic corps on 26 December 1935.

— JOSÉ DE TORRES WILSON

FERNANDINI, EULOGIO E.

Eulogio E. Fernandini (*b.* 13 September 1860; *d.* 24 December 1947), a pioneering Peruvian mine owner and cattleman who upgraded his mining operations during the copper boom of 1897–1898. Importing an entire mill in parts on muleback, he built a highly modern smelter. Like his peers, he relied on local capital and initiatives. When copper prices and technology attracted foreign investment, Fernandini fought to maintain his independence, but Cerro de Pasco Corporation drove out local business. Cerro spent massively on improvements and government contracts. By World War I, Fernandini was a minor shareholder in Cerro, to which he supplied food. In the 1920s and 1930s he turned to gold mining in the Andes.

— VINCENT PELOSO

FERRÉ AGUAYO, LUIS ANTONIO

Luis Antonio Ferré Aguayo (*b.* 1904) businessman, politician, and leading advocate of Puerto Rican statehood. Born into a wealthy Cuban family in 1904, Ferré spent his early years achieving commercial success. Through ventures such as the Puerto Rican Cement Company of Ponce, his hometown, Ferré added significantly to his family's fortune. His experience in business convinced him that Puerto Rico's future rested in North American–style capitalism. He became a leader of Puerto Rico's statehood movement and closely allied himself with the mainland Republican Party.

In 1951 Ferré was elected to Puerto Rico's constitutional convention. After 1952 Ferré and his brother-in-law, Miguel A. García Méndez, assumed leadership of the Republican Statehood Party (PER). Business successes such as the Puerto Rican Cement Company and philanthropic endeavors such as Ponce's art gallery brought Ferré widespread respect. While cultivating friendships among Eisenhower Republicans, Ferré appealed to the Puerto Rican working and middle classes by touting the economic benefits of statehood. Although badly losing the 1956 gubernatorial election to his rival, Luis MUÑOZ MARÍN, Ferré continued to develop a mass following. His defeat notwithstanding, PER demonstrated respectable electoral strength in urban centers such as San Juan, where a new middle class was taking shape. Ferré again ran for governor in 1964, but lost to Muñoz's handpicked successor, Roberto SÁNCHEZ VILELLA.

In the 1967 plebiscite regarding Puerto Rico's status, Ferré led an alliance favoring statehood, the United Statehooders, and gained a respectable 38.9 percent of the vote. Again displaying urban electoral muscle in San Juan and Ponce, the statehooders had high hopes for the 1968 elections. They were not disappointed. Ferré and the statehooders organized a new party, the New Progressive Party (PNP), under whose banner Ferré won a narrow victory in the November 1968 gubernatorial race. Ferré served only one term as governor, but remained a leading PNP personality. He maintained close contacts with Republican presidents Nixon, Ford,

and Reagan, and in November 1991 received the Medal of Freedom from President George Bush.

— JOHN J. CROCITTI

FERREIRA, BENIGNO

Benigno Ferreira (*b.* 18 February 1840; *d.* 24 November 1920), president of Paraguay (1906–1908) and soldier. Born in Limpio, Ferreira moved with his family to Argentina at an early age. He studied law at the University of Buenos Aires, where he affiliated with a group of radical Paraguayan emigrés opposed to the government of Carlos Antonio LÓPEZ and his son, Francisco Solano LÓPEZ. With the outbreak of the War of the Triple Alliance in 1864, Ferreira helped convert this group into the Legión Paraguaya, which fought alongside the Argentines in their invasion of Paraguay. With the defeat of Solano López in 1870, Ferreira's prospects should have dramatically improved, but the chaos of the postwar era meant that he had to limit himself to temporary alliances with various political patrons. He was interior minister under Salvador Jovellanos and later vice president of the Partido Liberal.

During most of the late nineteenth century Ferreira was back in exile in Buenos Aires, but after the successful Liberal revolt of 1904, he was recalled to Asunción. Though he was without major popular support, he nonetheless was appointed president two years later. New revolts that threatened to oust him from that position quickly coalesced into full-scale civil war. In July 1908, having had little chance to do anything with his presidency, Ferreira was forced from office, and from Paraguay, this time for good. He died in Buenos Aires.

— THOMAS L. WHIGHAM

FERREIRA ALDUNATE, WILSON

Wilson Ferreira Aldunate (*b.* 1919; *d.* 1988), a Blanco (National Party) senator and presidential candidate and an outspoken critic of the military dictatorship that controlled Uruguay from 1973 to 1984. Wilson, as he was known by friend and foe alike, was a charismatic political leader and a modern caudillo within the National Party. His faction, Por la Patria, was the highest vote getter within the party in the 1971 and 1984 elections.

Ferreira was from a ranching family. He began his political career first as a deputy and then as a senator (1967–1972). He also served as minister of agriculture under a Blanco government in 1963. He was a presidential candidate in the 1971 elections and received more votes than any other candidate, but his party lost the presidency because the Colorado Party's candidates received more total votes than the Blanco candidates. Some observers believe that the Blancos did, in fact, receive more votes but that the Colorados and conservative Blancos, together with the military, were not prepared to see Ferreira as president.

Ferreira fled to London after barely escaping with his life in June 1976, when two fellow exiled politicians were kidnapped and murdered.

After the military coup in 1973, Ferreira went into exile in Buenos Aires. He was an outspoken critic of the regime and fled to London after barely escaping with his life in June 1976, when two fellow exiled politicians were kidnapped and murdered. Ferreira testified before the U.S. Congress later that year and was a valuable voice in achieving a cutoff of military aid to the Uruguayan dictatorship. While in exile he continued his criticism of the regime and let his supporters know that he was opposed to the military's 1980 constitutional project. With his image enhanced by the defeat of the proposed constitution in a plebiscite, Ferreira's faction proved the most popular in the internal party elections permitted by the military in 1982. It was clear at this point that if the military allowed a free presidential election, Ferreira would emerge the victor. By early 1984, with the military convinced it had to exit politics but unwilling to accept the possibility of a Ferreira presidency, the generals released from prison Liber SEREGNI, leader of the leftist political coalition known as the Frente Amplio (Broad Front). The strategy was to relegalize the Left so that its followers would not support Ferreira in an upcoming election.

By this time Ferreira had returned to Buenos Aires. Sensing that events were outracing him, he returned to Montevideo on 16 June 1984. He was promptly arrested and incarcerated in a remote military installation in the interior, where he remained until several days after the November elections. The military, the Colorado Party, and the Frente Amplio had agreed to the elections in negotiations known as the Pact of the Naval Club. Not unexpectedly, with Ferreira excluded from running, the Colorados won the presidential election. Ferreira supported the incoming Julio María SANGUI-NETTI administration but favored some accounting for the military's human-rights abuses. Nevertheless, two years later, when a constitutional crisis seemed probable over the military's refusal to participate in civilian trials concerning abuses during the dictatorship, Ferreira reluctantly supported an amnesty law. Some felt he did this so that the military would permit him to run in the November 1989 presidential elections. Ferreira was diagnosed with cancer in 1987, however, and died the next year. There was a massive turnout at his funeral, as Uruguayans buried their last modern caudillo.

– MARTIN WEINSTEIN

FERRER, RAFAEL

Rafael Ferrer (*b.* 1933), Puerto Rican artist. Ferrer, a native of Santurce, studied literature and music at Syracuse University. He received art training from Eugenio Fernández Granell at the University of Puerto Rico in 1953. A resident of the mainland United States since 1966, Ferrer has taught at the Philadelphia College of Art (1967–1977), the School of Visual Arts in New York (1978–1980), and the Skowhegan School of Painting and Sculpture in Skowhegan, Maine (1981). During the late 1960s and early 1970s, he created conceptual art pieces, installations, and mixed-media sculptures and contributed to the development of process art and body art. His more recent paintings and mixed-media sculptures evoke the Caribbean through expressionistic means. His work has been included in numerous solo and group exhibitions throughout the United States.

– MIRIAM BASILIO

FERRERA, FRANCISCO

Francisco Ferrera (*b.* 1794 or 1800; *d.* 1851), president of Honduras (1841–1845). Ferrera was born in Cantarranas (later renamed San Juan de Flores), Honduras. Orphaned at an early age, he was educated by the village priest, José León Garín.

Ferrera rose to prominence when he laid siege to the fortresses on Honduras's north coast that Honduran conservatives had seized with aid from Spanish Cuba in 1831. He served as vice chief of state under Governor Joaquín RIVERA (1833–1836) and then rose to power as he led conservative Honduran and Nicaraguan forces against Francisco MORAZÁN's Central American government in 1839, forming an alliance with José Rafael CARRERA in Guatemala. Although he suffered reverses at Morazán's hand, notably at Espíritu Santo (5–6 May 1839) and at San Pedro Perulapán (25 September 1839), he became identified with the separation of Honduras from the Central American federation. Elected president by the National Assembly on 30 December 1840, he took office on 1 January 1841 as Honduras's first constitutional president. Ferrera served two two-year terms, until 1 January 1845, and was closely allied with Guatemala's Carrera and El Salvador's Francisco MALESPÍN, who assisted him in resisting the liberal forces of José Trinidad CABAÑAS. Ferrera was elected to a third term in 1847, but declined to serve; however, he did continue to be the country's dominant caudillo as minister of war and as armed forces chief until 1848.

– RALPH LEE WOODWARD, JR.

FERREZ, MARC

Marc Ferrez (*b.* 7 December 1843; *d.* 12 January 1923), Brazilian-born portrait and landscape photographer. The son of a French sculptor who arrived in Brazil with the 1816 French Artistic Mission, Ferrez studied in Paris before returning to Rio de Janeiro to apprentice as a photographer with Franz Keller at the German-owned Leuzinger Studio. After a fire destroyed his first studio, he returned to Paris to order new equipment manufactured to his design to allow him to produce panoramic views. His most lasting photographs have as their subjects what he considered the wonders of the Brazilian landscape: natural features, such as mountains, waterfalls, and jungles, and man-made feats of engineering, such as railroads, bridges, and urban buildings. Ferrez also photographed members of the indigenous Botocudo tribe while serving as a member of the American Charles Fredrick Hartt's 1875–1876 geological and geographic expedition to the interior of the province of Bahia. Following late-nineteenth-century custom, he posed his Indian subjects against artificial backdrops. Highly skilled at neutralizing the effects of ship movement, Ferrez was named "photographer of the Royal Navy" by Emperor PEDRO II. Photographic historians consider him to be the equal of such late-nineteenth-century master photographers as William Henry Jackson (1843–1942) and Eadweard Muybridge (1830–1904). Ferrez's grandson, Gilberto Ferrez, a leading collector and scholar, has devoted his life to publishing and publicizing his grandfather's work.

– ROBERT M. LEVINE

FICHER, JACOBO

Jacobo Ficher (*b.* 15 January 1896; *d.* 9 September 1978), Argentine composer, violinist, and conductor. Born in Odessa, Ukraine, Ficher came from a musical family. He began violin lessons when he was nine years old with Pyotr Solomonovich Stolyarsky and M. T. Hait. He entered the St. Petersburg Imperial Conservatory at sixteen and studied under S. Korguyev and

Leopold Auer, finishing his studies in 1917. In a violin competition he won the position of leader of the Petrograd State Opera Orchestra but declined the assignment. In 1923 he immigrated to Argentina, where he became active in the musical life of Buenos Aires. In 1929 he was a founding member of the Grupo Renovación, which was committed to the study and promotion of new styles of composition; he was also one of the founders of the Argentine Composers' League (1947). Ficher taught composition at the University of La Plata as well as at the National Conservatory of Buenos Aires, the Municipal Conservatory, and the Instituto Superior de Arte of the Teatro Colón.

Ficher received numerous awards, including the Municipal Prize for his String Quartet no. 1 (1929), for the symphonic poem *Sulamita* (1931), and for his Sonata for Piano (1943); the Coolidge Prize for his String Quartet no. 2 (1937); and the first prize from the Comisión de Cultura de Buenos Aires for his Third Symphony (1940). Ficher's Concerto for Violin and Orchestra received honorable mention from the Free Library of Philadelphia (1942); his String Quartet no. 4 (1953) received the López Buchardo Prize; and his Seventh Symphony (1960) won first prize in an Argentine competition to celebrate the sesquicentenary of the May Revolution. The Indianapolis Orchestra commissioned the Suite for Strings (1954), which was performed under maestro Fabian Sevinsky. Ficher also composed two operas, *El oso* and *Pedido de mano,* both based on libretti by Anton Chekhov with Russian and Spanish texts, four ballets, several choral works, eight symphonies, concerti, piano works, and music for stage and film. He died in Buenos Aires.

– SUSANA SALGADO

FIERRO RIMAC, FRANCISCO

Francisco Fierro Rimac (*b.* 1803; *d.* 1879), Peru's foremost painter of everyday life and prevailing customs (*costumbrista* painter). A mulatto, Fierro Rimac was born into a humble Lima family. Most of what is known about "Pancho Fierro," as he was called, is contained in a letter by Peruvian author Ricardo PALMA dated 1885. Fierro Rimac was self-taught and began his career as an artist drawing maps and painting coats of arms of Peruvian cities. Among his popular subjects were *Zambos* (natives of Indian and black origin), artisans, water carriers, street vendors, fishermen (*Stream Fishermen,* 1850), dances, and bullfights (*Juanita Breña Challenging a Bull with a Cloak,* 1821). He painted the mentally ill living in the streets of Lima and left some of the earliest images of the *tapadas* (Peruvian women wearing a unique costume consisting of a cloak that covers the bust and most of the head, leaving only one eye uncovered). He also designed street posters advertising bullfights and decorated walls with *costumbrista* scenes, allegories, and bucolic landscapes, none of which have survived.

An intuitive and talented colorist, Fierro Rimac worked primarily in watercolor, favoring small formats. His drawing was rudimentary; he did not use perspective. His work has been compared to some of Goya's *The Caprices* because of his caricaturesque style and his penchant for writing comments on drawings.

— MARTA GARSD

FIGARI, PEDRO

Pedro Figari (*b.* 29 June 1861; *d.* 24 July 1938), Uruguayan painter. Born in Montevideo, Figari had no formal art training in his youth but later studied drawing and painting with Godofredo Sommavilla in Montevideo and with Virgilio Ripari in Venice (1886). His astonishing artistic career did not begin until 1921, at

---

Figari turned out some 3,000 cardboard designs consisting of social topics, landscapes, colonial patios, folk dances, black country women, horses, and gauchos.

---

age sixty, when he had his first exhibition in Buenos Aires at the Galería Müller. In 1925 he moved to Paris, where he remained for nine years. In the seventeen years following his first exhibition in Buenos Aires he turned out some 3,000 cardboard designs consisting of social topics, landscapes, colonial patios, folk dances, black country women, horses, and gauchos. His style displays an inner dynamism deriving from rapid strokes and a poetic vision of color. He received the grand prize at the Centennial of Uruguayan Independence Exhibition in Montevideo, and the gold medal at the Ibero-American Exhibition, Seville, Spain, both in 1930. He was one of the founders of Uruguay's school of arts (1898), as well as a founding member of the Sociedad Amigos del Arte in Buenos Aires (1924). Figari was the author of several books, including *Art, Aesthetics and the Ideal* (1912), in which he developed ideas taken from Herbert Spenser, and *La historia Kiria* (1930), the description of a Uruguayan utopia.

— AMALIA CORTINA ARAVENA

FIGUEIREDO, AFONSO CELSO DE ASSIS

Afonso Celso de Assis Figueiredo (*b.* 31 March 1860; *d.* 11 July 1938), Brazilian politician and man of letters. The son of a prominent Liberal politician and nobleman, the viscount of Ouro Prêto, Figueiredo left his native Minas Gerais to study in São Paulo. After earning a doctorate in law in 1881, he quickly embarked on his political career, winning election to the parliament four times. In contrast to his father, he showed himself to be reform-minded, most notably supporting proposals for the gradual abolition of slavery in Brazil.

Although he had embraced republican ideas as a student, Figueiredo had become a strident monarchist by the time his father headed the final cabinet of the Brazilian Empire in 1889. When the empire gave way to the new republic late in that year, Figueiredo chose to follow his father into European exile. Upon his return he practiced and taught law, and dedicated himself to political journalism and other writings. Although he also produced poetry and novels, his greatest literary fame came from his nonfiction works. Figueiredo's historical memoirs, *Oito anos de Parlamento* (1981), and biography *Visconde de Ouro Prêto* (1935), are important sources for the study of politics in the late nineteenth century. By far his most widely read literary work was *Porque me ufano do meu país* (1900, 1943), a celebration of all things Brazilian. Hailed by many as a model of civic pride, this book gave rise to the term *ufanismo* (facile, unthinking patriotism).

Honored by France with the Legion of Honor and by Pope Pius X with the title of count, Figueiredo became a central figure in Brazil's literary and intellectual organizations. One of the founding members of the Academia Brasileira de Letras, he served as president of the Instituto Histórico e Geográfico Brasileiro from 1912 until his death.

— ROGER A. KITTLESON

FIGUEIREDO, JACKSON DE

Jackson de Figueiredo (*b.* 9 October 1891; *d.* 4 November 1928), Brazilian writer and Catholic layman who founded the Centro Dom Vital, a major center for orthodox Catholic thought.

Born in Aracajú, Sergipe, Figueiredo was an atheist who converted to Catholicism in 1918 and thereafter dedicated his life to church affairs. Influenced by nineteenth-century and contemporary European conservatives, he saw in Catholicism "the most fundamental element of Brazilian heritage," which could serve as a bulwark against the forces of disorder.

In 1922 he founded the Centro Dom Vital in Rio de Janeiro. It became the Catholic hierarchy's vehicle to mobilize opinions among educated Brazilians and advocated liturgical piety, theological thought, personal austerity, and conservatism. Figueiredo used the Centro to spark a powerful Catholic political movement that sought to regenerate the country morally. His political passion and intolerance, however, contrasted with his private gentleness and bohemianism. He died in Barra la Tijuca.

– ROSS WILKINSON

FIGUEIREDO, JOÃO BATISTA DE OLIVEIRA

João Batista de Oliveira Figueiredo (*b.* 15 January 1918), president of Brazil (1979–1985). At the time of his inauguration, Figueiredo was largely unknown to the public, though he had been an early conspirator in the 1964 military coup that overthrew President João GOULART. After the coup, he rose to the rank of general and served as chief of the Military Cabinet, secretary-general of the National Security Council, and head of the National Intelligence Agency (SNI).

Born in Rio de Janeiro, Figueiredo grew up in the town of Alegrete in Rio Grande do Sul. His father, General Euclides Figueiredo, commanded anti-Getúlio VARGAS troops during the 1932 São Paulo Rebellion. João Batista chose a military career, graduating first in his class at the numerous military schools he attended, including the military academy at Realengo, where he graduated as a cavalry officer in 1937. One brother, General Euclides de Oliveira Figueiredo, also followed a military path. Another brother, Guilherme de Figueiredo, is a well-known playwright and essayist.

The last of the post-coup military presidents, Figueiredo supervised the transition to civilian rule. Bridging the gap between hard-liners and moderates, he continued the cautious relaxation (*distenção*) of military rule begun by Ernesto GEISEL and completed the process of opening the political system (*abertura*). Under Figueiredo, prisoners who lost their political rights (*cassados*) were granted amnesty. His government abandoned the two-party system and promoted the creation of multiple parties. In 1982, Figueiredo allowed direct elections of state governors for the first time since 1965. Figueiredo tried to foster a populist image, but resorted to the hard line when necessary, as he did in the 1979 labor strikes.

Figueiredo left politics with the return to civilian rule in 1985. According to 1993 opinion polls, Brazilians rated Figueiredo's presidency high. Though mentioned as a possible candidate for the 1994 presidential elections, Figueiredo claimed little enthusiasm for the idea.

– SONNY B. DAVIS

FIGUERES FERRER, JOSÉ

José Figueres Ferrer (*b.* 25 September 1906; *d.* 8 June 1990), president of Costa Rica. José Figueres, "Don Pepe," presided over the Costa Rican nation on three separate occasions: once as head of a junta government (8 May 1948 to 8 November 1949) and twice as constitutional president (1953–1958 and 1970–1974). He was one of Costa Rica's most important political figures, setting the economic and social course of his country following the 1948 civil war and creating the National Liberation Party (PLN), Costa Rica's dominant political party after 1953. Moreover, during the 1950s and 1960s, he stood almost alone as the champion of democracy and economic and social reform in Central America and the Spanish-speaking Caribbean.

Born in rural San Ramón shortly after his parents had emigrated from Spain, Figueres had little formal education beyond the secondary level. He came to the United States in 1924 intending to study electrical engineering at the Massachusetts Institute of Technology, but he never matriculated. Instead, with the Boston Public Library as his classroom, he acquired the social democratic philosophy that guided his future political career. In 1928, he returned to Costa Rica to become a farmer-entrepreneur on a *finca* (ranch) he named La Lucha Sin Fin (The Endless Struggle), where he raised *cabuya* (a Central American agave) and built a factory to manufacture rope and bags from the homegrown fiber. La Lucha was the model for Figueres Ferrer's later national programs, wherein he developed the region, creating new jobs and skills and providing an array of benefits and social services. In 1942, Figueres Ferrer's life changed abruptly when he was expelled from the country in a dispute with President Rafael Ángel CALDERÓN GUARDIA.

Figueres criticized Calderón publicly for failing to prevent a riot in San José after an Axis submarine had attacked Puerto Limón. Calderón Guardia, for his part, accused Figueres of revealing military secrets and of participating in a scheme to shelter the properties of German and Italian residents of Costa Rica. When Figueres returned from exile in Mexico two years later, he was greeted as a hero who had opposed the authoritarian Calderón.

During his exile, Figueres and other Caribbean exiles developed the CARIBBEAN LEGION, a plan to rid Costa Rica (and the entire region) of tyranny. Figueres put his plan into operation in March 1948, when Calderón tried to steal the presidential election from the clear winner, Otilio ULATE BLANCO. Though most politicians hoped for a peaceful solution to the crisis, Figueres and Calderón were on a collision course. With a citizen-

Costa Rican presidential candidate José Figueres Ferrer shows broom to indicate that he swept away the opposition in the 1970 election. (AP/Wide World)

volunteer army and the help of his Caribbean allies, Figueres waged a successful six-week "war of national liberation," and took control of the nation as head of the Founding Junta of the Second Republic in May.

During the eighteen months that the junta governed, Figueres made fundamental changes in the life of the nation. He abolished the army, nationalized the banking system, imposed a 10 percent tax on wealth, and held elections for a constituent assembly to draft a constitution. The new constitution (1949) embraced Figueres's socialist tendencies, providing for government regulation of the private sector and creating "autonomous institutions" to perform the economic and social functions of the public sector. With the constitution in place, Figueres turned over the presidency to Ulate.

In 1953, Figueres became constitutional president himself and resumed where he left off four years earlier. Figueres expanded the role of government through the creation of additional autonomous institutions to provide such services as the production and distribution of electrical energy, banking, health care, insurance, and telephones. He established the National Council of Production to stimulate agriculture and business through credits, price supports, and marketing facilities.

Despite the economic growth and social progress that Costa Rica experienced under Figueres, his presidency was not tranquil. The Figueres era was particularly troubled by foreign policy. Costa Rica's safe democracy attracted political exiles from throughout the region, and Figueres openly opposed the dictatorships of Anastasio SOMOZA in Nicaragua, Rafael TRUJILLO in the Dominican Republic, Fulgencio BATISTA in Cuba, and Marcos PÉREZ JIMÉNEZ in Venezuela. Though he made promises of military support to his Caribbean allies that he could not keep, he collaborated closely with Venezuelan exile Rómulo BETANCOURT and sought to influence U.S. policy against the dictators.

In 1954, Costa Rica was the only country to boycott the inter-American conference in Caracas, and in the same year Figueres aided Nicaraguan exiles in an attempt to overthrow Somoza. Figueres supplied arms to Fidel CASTRO after 1956. On two occasions, the dictators retaliated. In 1948, while Figueres was heading the junta, and again in 1955, Somoza sponsored "exile" invasions of Costa Rica. Both times, Figueres, with no army, appealed to the ORGANIZATION OF AMERICAN STATES for help. Though the OAS came to his rescue, it pressured him to expel the so-called Caribbean Legion from Costa Rica and to enter into agreements to reduce tensions in the region.

The U.S. State Department labeled Figueres a "troublemaker" in the 1950s, but during the 1960s, in the context of the Cuban Revolution, the attitude changed. The Central Intelligence Agency sought his assistance in covert action against Trujillo and secretly funded his efforts to strengthen the democratic Left. Figueres had criticized Castro in April 1959, advising him to remain on the side of the United States in the cold war, and he became an avid supporter of President John F. Kennedy and the Alliance for Progress. After Kennedy's assassination, Figueres's role in international affairs diminished. His decline was especially steep after 1967, when it became known that he had collaborated with the CIA.

With Figueres barred by the constitution from succeeding himself in 1959, and the party badly split in choosing a candidate, the PLN lost the presidential election. It did manage to reunite for victory in 1962, but lost again four years later, convincing Figueres to run in 1970.

Figueres's second presidency was no less controversial than his first, but had fewer accomplishments to claim. Needing to recharge the economy, Figueres established trade and diplomatic relations with the Soviet Union and proposed the creation of an international financial district in Costa Rica. Both measures bedeviled his presidency. There were street demonstrations against any sort of relations with the Soviet Union, and militant right-wing groups used the situation to agitate. The plan for the international financial district brought Robert VESCO to Costa Rica. Though Figueres argued that Costa Rica needed capital, Vesco's reputation as a swindler and his holdings in Figueres's La Lucha caused a crippling scandal. Figueres believed that he was acting in the best interests of his country, but the principal achievement of his second presidency was that its shortcomings paved the way for a new generation of PLN leaders to take charge.

During the remaining years of his life, Figueres permitted the institutions and party that he had created to take shape without him. Because of a near-even division in Costa Rica between pro-Liberation and anti-Liberation sentiment, an informal two-party system evolved through the process of coalition politics. Figueres himself enhanced his country's democratic traditions and formalized the nation's general commitment to economic and social well-being, which enabled Costa Rica to avoid the bloodshed of Central America in the 1980s.

– CHARLES D. AMERINGER

FIGUEROA, GABRIEL

Gabriel Figueroa (*b.* 26 April 1908; *d.* 1997), Mexican film photographer. Figueroa learned his trade in Mexico and in Hollywood. He was the principal photographer of *Allá en el Rancho Grande* (1938). Since then, he has filmed over 200 features for Mexican, North American, and European directors. Noted particularly for his work with black and white film, Figueroa was called "the greatest muralist of Mexico" by Diego RIVERA. His aesthetic style is characterized by contrasts of darkness and light and by the use of panoramic shots. He has worked for such acclaimed directors as Emilio Fernández, Luis Buñuel, John Ford, and John Huston. Figueroa has received more Ariels from the Mexican film academy than any other photographer in Mexican cinema. In addition, he has been awarded major international prizes in Venice, Cannes, Prague, Madrid, and San Francisco. In 1971 he received the National Award for the Arts in Mexico.

– DAVID MACIEL

FIGUEROA, JOSÉ

José Figueroa (*d.* 1835), governor of Alta California (1833–1835). General Figueroa was one of the most important Mexican governors of the territory. In 1833 he initiated a new emancipation of a limited number of Indian converts living in Franciscan-run missions. That same year he also established Indian towns at three sites in the southern part of the territory—the San Juan Capistrano mission, the Las Flores rancho, and the San

Dieguito rancho—with the hope of creating stable Indian villages with formal municipal governments. This scheme, however, failed when the Spanish government secularized the missions.

Figueroa also cooperated in implementing the secularization of the missions ordered by the Valentín GÓMEZ FARÍAS government by way of a bill signed on 17 August 1833, working with local politicians to craft the secularization decree to benefit the elite of the territory. On 9 August 1834, Figueroa approved the secularization plan. Prominent Californios received appointment as *mayordomos* of the former missions, many using their positions to enrich themselves. Most of the converts still living in the missions were not legally emanicipated.

After Figueroa died in office in 1835, a period of political chaos followed, and in 1836 local politicians seized control of the government.

– ROBERT H. JACKSON

FIGUEROA, PEDRO JOSÉ

Pedro José Figueroa (*b.* 1780; *d.* 1838), Colombian artist. Son of a wealthy Bogotá family and descendant of a notable group of seventeenth-century Colombian painters, Figueroa began his studies with Peruvian painter Pablo Antonio García (1744–1814). During the war for independence in Colombia, he painted scenes of some of the battles as well as at least ten portraits (1819–1822) of Simón Bolívar. He served as director of the construction of the Church of Las Nieves in Bogotá and painted the *Holy Trinity* mural for the Bogotá cathedral. He painted many portraits of influential Colombians including archbishops. Figueroa established a studio for his pupils, among whom were his sons José Celestino and José Miguel y Santos.

– BÉLGICA RODRÍGUEZ

FIGUEROA ALCORTA, JOSÉ

José Figueroa Alcorta (*b.* 20 November 1860; *d.* 27 December 1931), president of Argentina (1906–1910). With his presidency began the process of evolution toward a true democracy in Argentina. With the support of the followers of Bartolomé MITRE and Carlos PELLEGRINI, Figueroa Alcorta confronted head-on the old system created by Julio Argentino ROCA ("El Zorro"), president (1880–1886 and 1898–1904) and the most important political figure in Argentina since the 1890s. Figueroa Alcorta intervened in the provinces seven times and in the process dismantled the Roquista political machinery in the interior of the country. Figueroa Alcorta also confronted Congress, another Roquista stronghold. When Congress refused to consider Figueroa Alcorta's budget proposal and other measures, he closed it down on 25 January 1908. If President Roque SÁENZ PEÑA (elected to office in 1910) was able to implement political reforms later on, it was because Figueroa Alcorta had already purged the system.

— JUAN MANUEL PÉREZ

FIGUEROA GAJARDO, ANA

Ana Figueroa Gajardo (*b.* 19 June 1907; *d.* 8 April 1970), Chilean career diplomat, journalist, women's rights activist. After graduating from the Instituto Pedagógico, Universidad de Chile, in 1928, Figueroa was a high-school teacher and principal. In 1946 she attended Columbia University and a summer institute at Colorado State University. From 1947 to 1949, she was general supervisor of the Chilean high-school system. In 1948 she became president of the Federación Chilena de Instituciones Femeninas (FECHIF) and was appointed director of the Chilean Women's Bureau. In 1950 she served as Chilean delegate to the Inter-American Commission of Women; from 1950 to 1952 she was the Chilean minister plenipotentiary to the Third General Assembly of the United Nations; and from 1952 to 1959 she served on the Security Council, UNESCO, and the UN Commission on the Juridical and Social Condition of Women. From 1950 to 1967, Figueroa was the first woman to serve as director-general of the International Labor Organization. She was also on the board of directors of the international YWCA.

— CORINNE ANTEZANA-PERNET FRANCESCA MILLER

FIGUEROA LARRAÍN, EMILIANO

Emiliano Figueroa Larraín (*b.* 1866; *d.* 16 May 1931), lawyer, politician, diplomat, and president of Chile. A member of the Partido Democrático, he served as president twice. Following the death of President Pedro MONTT, he occupied the Moneda as interim president from September through December 1910, until the election of Ramón Barros Luco. He was elected to the presidency in 1925, following President Arturo Alessandri Palma's second resignation. His naive attempts to govern, however, were frustrated by the maneuverings of the minister of war, Carlos IBÁÑEZ DEL CAMPO, and in April 1927 Ibáñez forced him to resign his office. Figueroa later represented Chile as ambassador to Peru.

— WILLIAM F. SATER

FILÍSOLA, VICENTE

Vicente Filísola (*b.* ca. 1789; *d.* 23 July 1850), captain-general of Guatemala (12 June 1822–4 July 1823).

Born in Rivoli, Italy, Filísola emigrated to Spain at a young age and began his military career. By 1810 he had attained the rank of second lieutenant and had received honors for his valiant fighting. He was sent to Mexico with royalist forces in 1811, but by 1815 he had become a close friend of Agustín de ITURBIDE. In 1821 he gave his support to Mexican independence, proclaimed in Iturbide's Plan of Iguala. At the head of four thousand men, he was the first insurgent leader to enter Mexico City on 24 September 1821, securing it for Iturbide's triumphal entry. Iturbide promoted him to brigadier general and gave him the title of Knight of the Imperial Order of Guadalupe, then sent him on a mission to Central America. There he was to keep order while the region decided on annexation to Mexico. On 4 November 1822, after most of Central America had voted in favor of union with the Mexican Empire, Filísola published a decree splitting the captaincy-general of Guatemala into the three commandancies-general of Chiapas, Sacatepéquez, and Costa Rica, with their capitals at Ciudad Real, Nueva Guatemala, and León respectively. Later that month, on Iturbide's orders, he led about two thousand men against San Salvador, the only major city to resist union with the Mexican Empire. After routing Manuel José ARCE's troops, he entered the city on 9 February 1823. Upon learning of Iturbide's overthrow, he returned to Guatemala and convoked a congress of the provinces. Believing the basis for Mexican annexation to be gone, he accepted their declaration of independence.

In 1822, Filísola led about two thousand men against San Salvador, the only major city to resist union with the Mexican Empire.

After returning to Mexico, Filísola fought as a division general in the Texas Revolution in 1835 and ended his career as president of the Supreme Court of War. He also wrote extensively. He published his two-volume *Memorias para la historia de Tejas* in 1848–1849, and conducted a lively polemic with José Francisco BARRUNDIA. Most of the documents ended up in Central America and were burned, but Filísola's biographer, Don Jenaro García, was able to obtain copies of Filísola's papers from one of his descendants and published them in two volumes as *La cooperación de México en la independencia de Centro América* (1911). Filísola died in Mexico during a cholera epidemic.

— PHILIPPE L. SEILER

FINLAY, CARLOS JUAN

Carlos Juan Finlay (*b.* 3 December 1833; *d.* 20 August 1915), a Cuban physician and epidemiologist. After earning his medical degree at Jefferson Medical College in Philadelphia, Finlay pursued additional studies in Havana and Paris before beginning his medical practice in Cuba. He represented the Cuban government to a commission from the United States that arrived on the island in 1879 to study the transmission of yellow fever. In 1881, Finlay concluded that a mosquito, known as the *Aëdes aegypti,* was the carrier of the disease, but his theory was largely ignored by the medical community until 1900, when U.S. General Leonard Wood ordered Walter Reed to test Finlay's theory. Reed's experiments in Havana confirmed Finlay's findings, a discovery that led to the eradication of yellow fever in much of the tropics. Unfortunately, Reed, rather than Finlay, has received most of the credit for the elimination of yellow fever.

— THOMAS M. LEONARD

FLORES, JUAN JOSÉ

Juan José Flores (*b.* ca. 1800; *d.* 1 October 1864), president of Ecuador (1830–1835, 1839–1845). Born in Puerto Cabello, Venezuela, Flores received little formal education before he was swept into the Wars of Independence, first in a royalist army and then in the patriot forces of BOLÍVAR. He received rapid promotions: to colonel in 1821 and to general in 1826.

Assignment to the command of the difficult royalist region of Pasto (southern Colombia) prevented Flores from fighting in the campaigns to liberate Ecuador and Peru. In 1826 he assumed authority over the department of Ecuador and soon exercised authority over most of the territory later to comprise the Republic of Ecuador. Marriage to the aristocratic Mercedes Jijón y Vivanco facilitated his rise to regional prominence. Flores, who came to favor monarchism, urged Bolívar to convert Gran Colombia (Venezuela, New Granada, and Ecuador) into a monarchy.

In May 1830 an extraordinary assembly of officials and citizens in Quito decided to separate Ecuador from Gran Colombia and named General Flores supreme civil and military commander. He was elected president soon after the assassination of General Antonio José de SUCRE, which removed his only serious competitor for leadership.

Though endowed with a lively intelligence, Flores was poorly prepared intellectually to provide wise leadership. He attempted to make up for his shortcomings by engaging tutors, such as the poet José Joaquín OL-MEDO, but his basic inclinations remained those of a military man. As president he tried unsuccessfully to incorporate the Cauca region into Ecuador, but he defended Ecuadorian independence from New Granada and helped establish the Carchi River as the northern border. In domestic matters Flores pursued liberal policies by restricting the privileges of the clergy, creating a public education system with special schools for Indians, and reforming tax laws.

These reforms, along with treasury deficits and other financial problems, aroused opposition to the foreign-born president. Publishers of the anti-administration newspaper *El Quiteño Libre* organized a violent uprising that Flores quelled only after agreeing to allow Vicente ROCAFUERTE, a rebel leader, to succeed him to the presidency in 1835.

During Rocafuerte's administration (1835–1839), Flores exerted much influence as commander-in-chief of the armed forces, and he arranged his own reelection to the presidency in 1839. When his policy of cordiality toward opponents failed, Flores secretly decided to convert Ecuador into a monarchy. In league with Andrés SANTA CRUZ of Peru, he sought to monarchize Peru and Bolivia, too. He had himself reelected president in 1843 under the new, authoritarian constitution. He secured the backing of Spain to erect a throne in Quito, but an uprising in 1845 sent him into exile.

In Spain, Flores received official but secret support for an armed expedition to seize power and, presumably, to erect a monarchy in Ecuador. Public reports of the expedition, however, forced its abandonment before it could depart Spanish shores.

General Flores returned to Spanish America in 1847 and spent the next thirteen years conspiring in various countries to regain power. His plots seriously undermined the Ecuadorian government but did not topple it. Finally, in 1860, with Ecuador in near anarchy, the struggling regime of Gabriel GARCÍA MORENO invited Flores to return to the country, to take command of the army, and to put down the opposition to the government.

Playing the role of senior statesman thereafter, Flores was elected president of a constituent congress in 1860 and helped draft the conservative Constitution of 1861. He supported a fruitless effort by the president to secure French backing for yet another monarchical scheme. As general in chief of the armed forces, Flores was a mainstay of the administration and was expected by many to succeed to the presidency in 1865.

When New Granada threatened Ecuador's independence in 1863, General Flores, though in poor health, led a poorly equipped army to defend the northern border. Subsequently he helped crush a rebel invasion near

Guayaquil but fell ill and died aboard a warship invoking the "Supreme God of Battles."

— MARK J. VAN AKEN

FLORES, LUIS A.

Luis A. Flores (*b.* 1899; *d.* 1969), Peruvian politician, lawyer, and diplomat. Born in Ayabaca, Piura, he is best known for his leadership of the Revolutionary Union, a radical nationalist party adopted by Colonel and President Luis SÁNCHEZ CERRO (1931–1933). Flores had been imprisoned during the LEGUÍA regime but became deputy for Lima during the term of the Constituent Assembly (1931–1936). After the assassination of Sánchez Cerro in 1933, Flores assumed the leadership of the Revolutionary Union and espoused overt fascist principles, tactics, and organization, modeled after Benito Mussolini's party. Flores sought popular support and battled communism and populist *aprismo*. In the 1936 presidential elections, which were annulled by President Oscar BENAVIDES, Flores finished second behind the candidate supported by the Aprista Party. Flores was subsequently exiled by Benavides but returned to become senator for Piura (1947–1948) and ambassador to Italy (1948–1950) and Nicaragua and Paraguay (1956–1962). He died in Lima.

— ALFONSO W. QUIROZ

FLORES, VENANCIO

Venancio Flores (*b.* 18 May 1808; *d.* 19 February 1868), Uruguayan military and political leader (Colorado Party). Flores was born in the town of Porongos, today called Trinidad. He took part in the campaign to free Uruguay from Brazil in 1825. He was political chief of the department of San José and military commander of that department at the outbreak of the GUERRA GRANDE (1839–1852). A rising figure in the Colorado Party, he was appointed political chief of Montevideo and minister of war and the navy in 1852. Upon the resignation of President Juan Francisco Giró in 1853, Flores formed a triumvirate with General Juan Antonio LAVALLEJA and General Fructuoso RIVERA in an attempt to avoid another outbreak of civil war. When these two men died, both of natural causes, Flores became a preeminent figure in his party.

Political hostilities and a popular disdain of the caudillo tradition that he represented led Flores to withdraw to the Entre Ríos province of Argentina (1857–1863). While there, he played an active role in the civil wars of that country, supporting the Liberal Party led by Bartolomé MITRE. When Mitre became president of Argentina in 1862, Flores gained his support and that of Emperor PEDRO II of Brazil for his campaign to win back the government in Uruguay. The leaders of these two powerful, neighboring countries, who were already planning what would come to be called the War of the Triple Alliance against Paraguay, were motivated by their need for the port of Montevideo. This was especially true for Brazil.

Calling his revolution the "liberation crusade," in memory of the 1825 campaign of that name, Flores began his assault against National Party President Bernardo Prudencio BERRO in 1863, and, with the help of an army of 5,000 Brazilian soldiers who entered Uruguayan territory, marched into Montevideo triumphantly in February 1865. Immediately, Argentina, Brazil, and Uruguay made public the treaty of the Triple Alliance, which committed them to fighting Paraguay to the end. Under the leadership of Francisco Solano LÓPEZ, Paraguay had become an important economic and military power, which made the War of the Triple Alliance (1865–1870) one of the bloodiest in the history of South America. Although scholars disagree on the total casualties, they agree that Paraguay suffered huge demographic losses.

Returning to Uruguay from the war in 1866, Flores resigned in 1868 and called for new elections. Flores was slain four days later by unknown assassins.

— JOSÉ DE TORRES WILSON

FLORES DA CUNHA, JOSÉ ANTÔNIO

José Antônio Flores da Cunha (*b.* 5 March 1880; *d.* 4 November 1959), Brazilian politician. Born to an oligarchical family from Santana do Livramento, Rio Grande do Sul, Flores was an important political figure in the three decades following the Revolution of 1930. He was educated at the São Paulo Law School from 1898 to 1902, and completed his studies at the Rio de Janeiro Law School in 1903.

Flores was among the dissident oligarchs who supported the revolution against the dominant oligarchies of São Paulo and Minas Gerais. Indeed, his support of Getúlio VARGAS was crucial to the overthrow of the First Republic and Vargas's seizure of power. However, as governor of Rio Grande do Sul and a senator in the 1930s, he staunchly defended federalism and worked to limit the centralization of political power under Getúlio Vargas's regime (1930–1945). His federalist stance, often backed by his threat to use the nation's largest state militia, made him too dangerous for Vargas to ignore. After a near outbreak of civil war in 1937, Flores was exiled to Uruguay until 1942. When he returned to Brazil, he was imprisoned.

Flores saw reaction against centralization as the only means of assuring oligarchical elites political space in the post-1930 world. Despite his support for the Revolution of 1930, Flores gradually distanced himself from Vargas after 1935. As governor of Rio Grande do Sul from 1935 to 1938, he was a major force in the continuing influence of traditional politicians and regionalism after 1930. In 1945, Flores joined the National Democratic Union Party (UDN), which opposed Vargas, and he supported the military's successful ouster of the dictator. In 1950 he was elected to Congress on a UDN ticket. In 1955 he broke with the UDN because he opposed its *golpistas,* who had conspired to mount a coup against the government. He lost his final campaign for office in 1958, completing his term in Congress in January 1959. Flores died in Rio Grande do Sul.

— BRIAN OWENSBY

FLORES JIJÓN, ANTONIO

Antonio Flores Jijón (*b.* 23 October 1833; *d.* 30 August 1915), president of Ecuador (1888–1892). Born in Quito, Antonio was the son of Juan José FLORES, Ecuador's first president. Antonio Flores Jijón completed his secondary education in Paris. In 1845, he entered the University of San Marcos in Lima, where he completed a law degree and joined the faculty.

Flores Jijón returned to Ecuador with Gabriel GARCÍA MORENO (president, 1860–1865) in 1860. Thereafter, he represented Ecuador in various diplomatic posts in Colombia, France, England, the Vatican, Peru, Spain, and the United States.

An unsuccessful candidate for the presidency in 1875, he opposed the government of General Ignacio de VEINTIMILLA (1876–1883), for which he was exiled. He lived in New York from 1878 to 1883, then returned to Ecuador in 1883 to participate in the ouster of Veintimilla and in the writing of a new constitution. During the José María Plácido CAAMAÑO presidency (1883–1888), Flores Jijón represented Ecuador in Europe, and in fact was in Paris in 1888 when he was elected president.

During his term, Flores Jijón sought to implement a progressive program with the support of moderates within the conservative and liberal parties. His government emphasized improved and expanded public education and public works, respect for civil liberties, and administrative, financial, and tax reforms. His accomplishments in the area of public finances included the suppression of the tithe, a renegotiation of the internal and external debt, reform of the customs tariff, state monopolies, and taxes on real estate. Many of his initiatives met strong opposition from conservatives and

the clergy. After completing his term in 1892, Flores returned to Europe. He died in Geneva.

— LINDA ALEXANDER RODRÍGUEZ

FLORES MAGÓN, RICARDO

Ricardo Flores Magón (*b.* 16 September 1874; *d.* 21 November 1922), Mexican journalist and revolutionary. Born in San Antonio Eloxochitlán, Oaxaca, Flores Magón was the second of three sons; his older brother, Jesús, was born in 1872, and his younger brother, Enrique, in 1877. In 1900 he founded the newspaper *Regeneración* to oppose the tyranny of the government of Porfirio DÍAZ. Flores Magón was arrested in May 1901 and *Regeneración* was suppressed soon after, closing in September 1901. He became a writer for Daniel Cabrera's *El Hijo del Ahuizote* until its demise early in 1903. Arrested again, Flores Magón was prohibited from publishing in Mexico. In January 1904 he and his brother Enrique entered the United States at Laredo, Texas, and went to San Antonio, where they renewed the publication of *Regeneración.* They settled in Saint Louis between 1905 and 1906 to escape harassment from local legal authorities along the border and to join revolutionary and radical labor groups. Persecution— including activities of local spies, police seizure of the printing press, and imprisonment of local partisans of a revolutionary exile group Flores Magón had founded in Saint Louis—eventually forced them to move to Los

Photo of Ricardo Flores Magón signing document as brother Enrique looks on. (Archivo General de la Nación, Mexico)

Angeles, where they established a new organ, *Revolución*. Arrested in August 1907, Flores Magón was tried in Arizona in 1909, sentenced to eighteen months in the Florence territorial prison, and released in August 1910.

When World War I began in 1914, Flores Magón, now an anarcho-Communist and pacifist, was a vociferous critic. Arrested on 22 March 1918 and charged with sedition, he was eventually found guilty of violating the Espionage Act of 1917. Sentenced to twenty-one years at McNeil Island, he was transferred in November 1919 to Leavenworth penitentiary because of failing health. On the morning of 21 November 1922, Flores Magón was found dead in Cell House B at Leavenworth. Although several radical scholars claim that he was murdered, the most likely explanation is that he died of natural causes, probably a heart attack.

– W. DIRK RAAT

FLORES MALDONADO MARTÍNEZ Y BODQUÍN, MANUEL ANTONIO

Manuel Antonio Flores Maldonado Martínez y Bodquín (*b.* 27 May 1723; *d.* 20 March 1799), viceroy of New Granada (1776–1782) and of New Spain (1787–1789).

Born in Seville, Flores pursued a naval career, holding the rank of lieutenant general of the Royal Armada at the time of his assignment to New Granada in 1776. An enlightened man, strongly interested in science, he was an efficient, perceptive administrator. He urged Regent Visitor GUTIÉRREZ DE PIÑERES to show restraint when imposing administrative and fiscal reforms, at least until the armed forces could be readied to discourage potential unrest, but his warnings went unheeded. While Flores was on the coast commanding the viceregal defenses during the War of the American Revolution, the Comunero Revolt (1781) swept the interior, compelling him to order nearly a battalion of coastal troops to Santa Fe to bolster royal authority.

Becoming severely ill with arthritis, he resigned and was replaced by Cartagena's governor, Juan Pimienta. Flores later brought enlightened rule to New Spain, but, his health again failing him, he was soon replaced by the Segundo Conde de Revillagigedo. He died in Madrid.

– ALLAN J. KUETHE

FLORIDABLANCA, CONDE DE

Conde de Floridablanca (*b.* 21 October 1728; *d.* 30 December 1808), secretary of state in Spain (1776–1792). As secretary of state, Floridablanca was a conservative reformer and devoted servant of absolutism. After 1776, when he was appointed *fiscal* (crown attorney), his power and influence over the king, Charles III, were unparalleled, and he was accused of ministerial despotism by his opponents. The outbreak of the French Revolution (1789) horrified Floridablanca, and he tried to prevent revolutionary ideas from entering Spain.

Floridablanca found it impossible to sanction his monarch's approval of Louis XVI's acceptance of the French constitution. His inability to compromise on this issue resulted in his dismissal from office on 28 February 1792. Retirement in Murcia was interrupted by arrest and confinement to a fortress in Pamplona while his enemies investigated him for abusing his former powerful position.

In 1794 Manuel de Godoy, Charles IV's minister, released Floridablanca and allowed him to return to Murcia. He was recalled to government service as president of the central junta meeting at Aranjuez (1808) but died shortly after the group fled to Seville in the wake of the Napoleonic invasion of Spain.

– SUZANNE HILES BURKHOLDER

FLORIT, EUGENIO

Eugenio Florit (*b.* 15 October 1903; *d.* 1997), Cuban-Spanish poet. Florit was born in Madrid and lived in Spain until 1918, when his family moved to Havana. He received a law degree from the University of Havana in 1926. In 1936 Florit befriended the Spanish poet Juan Ramón Jiménez. In 1940 he moved to New York to work for the Cuban consulate there. From 1945 to 1969 he taught at Barnard College, then part of Columbia University, and during summers, at Middlebury College, Vermont. He was the first codirector and later the director of the New York literary magazine *Revista Hispánica Moderna.* Florit edited and introduced such anthologies of poetry as *La poesía hispanoamericana desde el modernismo,* on which he collaborated with the eminent critic José Olivio Jiménez. In 1982 he moved to Miami, where he continues to reside.

As of the mid-1990s, Florit was one of the best-known living Cuban poets. His work is noted for its muted tones, religious—almost mystical—themes and its mastery of traditional poetic forms. *Asonante final* (1955) and *Doble acento* (1937) are two of the most important of his books. Florit has also been an excellent translator of American poets.

– ROBERTO VALERO

FONSECA, GONZALO

Gonzalo Fonseca (*b.* July 1922), Uruguayan sculptor. Born in Montevideo, as a child Fonseca traveled widely with his family and was particularly impressed by visits to museums and archaeological sites in Europe. He was carving in stone by the age of fifteen and entered the school of architecture at the Universidad de la República Oriental del Uruguay, Montevideo, in 1939. He abandoned his academic studies in 1942 for painting and shortly thereafter joined the studio of the artist Joaquín TORRES GARCÍA. While a member of the Taller Torres García (TTG), Fonseca began to study pre-Columbian art and architecture, and painted several constructivist murals in Montevideo. During the first half of the 1950s, he traveled throughout the Mediterranean region. He settled in New York City in 1958 and began making reliefs in cement and wood that featured semiabstract motifs and objects; in the aggregate, these function as symbols or, almost linguistically, as signs. In 1959 he completed a glass mosaic for the New School for Social Research. A one-man exhibition of his work was held in 1962 at the Portland Art Museum in Oregon.

In the mid-1960s, Fonseca began to carve quasi-architectural stone sculptures that simultaneously evoke ancient ruins, ritual fetishes, and mysterious games.

In the mid-1960s, Fonseca began to carve quasi-architectural stone sculptures that simultaneously evoke ancient ruins, ritual fetishes, and mysterious games. He designed a cement *Tower* for the 1968 Olympic Games in Mexico City. In 1971 the Jewish Museum in New York City mounted an exhibition of his work; that same year he began to divide his time between New York and Italy, where he could create large-scale marble sculptures at his studio near Carrara. Fonseca represented Uruguay in the 1990 Venice Biennale.

– JOSEPH R. WOLIN

FONSECA, HERMES RODRIGUES DA

Hermes Rodrigues da Fonseca (*b.* 12 May 1855; *d.* 9 September 1923), president of Brazil (1910–1914). The nephew of Manoel Deodoro da FONSECA, the republic's first president, Marshal Fonseca advanced his army and future political career by adroitly quelling a cadet rebellion during the 1904 Vaccine Revolt (an uprising by citizens opposed to forced vaccination against smallpox). Nominated as war minister in 1906, Fonseca championed efforts to modernize the army, outlining recruitment reforms, sending officers to study in Ger-

many, and staging large-scale maneuvers. His victory as the conservative Republican Party's candidate marked the republic's first hotly contested presidential campaign.

The marshal's presidency was equally tumultuous. In his first week, the government was forced to negotiate an end to the Chibata Revolt, in which rebel sailors protesting barbarous corporal punishment commandeered newly purchased battleships and threatened to bombard Rio de Janeiro with impunity. This conflict was followed by Fonseca's "salvationist" campaigns, or his frequent use of federal troops to interfere in conflicts between political parties at the state level. After his presidential term Fonseca became a controversial military spokesman. President Artur BERNARDES arrested Fonseca in 1922 after the marshal openly advised an army colonel not to obey government orders to intervene in Pernambucan politics. The marshal argued ironically that the army should not be politicized. His arrest precipitated the first *tenente* (lieutenant) revolt in 1922, a coup intended to reinstate Fonseca as president. Shaken by imprisonment and weakened by inveterate smoking, Fonseca soon died of a stroke.

– PETER M. BEATTIE

FONSECA, JUAN RODRÍGUEZ DE

Juan Rodríguez de Fonseca (*b.* 1451; *d.* 4 March 1524), head of the Casa de Contratación, the Spanish House of Trade. Born in Seville to a noble family, Fonseca came to Queen Isabella's court as a page, became a priest and royal chaplain, and in 1514 the bishop of Burgos. He was entrusted with diplomatic missions, administering the sale of indulgences and the outfitting of Christopher COLUMBUS's second voyage in 1493. In 1503 he was instrumental in establishing the Casa de Contratación, which, merging into the Council of the Indies set up in 1524, was to retain exclusive control of the Indies trade for nearly 300 years. In 1518 Fonseca fitted out Ferdinand MAGELLAN's fleet. Reputedly tight-fisted, arrogant, and impatient, he was at odds with Columbus and, later, Hernán CORTÉS. He presided over the 1512 Junta of Burgos, which was concerned with the theology of the rights of the Indies. He died in Burgos.

– PEGGY K. LISS

FONSECA, MANOEL DEODORO DA

Manoel Deodoro da Fonseca (*b.* 5 August 1827; *d.* 23 August 1892), a career army officer who became the first president of the Brazilian republic (1889–1891). Born in Alagoas, in Brazil's poor Northeast, Fonseca and his seven brothers all followed family tradition and entered the army. He helped subdue the liberal Praieira Revolt in Pernambuco in 1848, and served in the War of the Triple Alliance (1864–1870), achieving the ranks of brigadier general in 1874 and marshal in 1884. Through personal bravery and steadfastness, he became one of the most popular and respected army officers under the empire. Fonseca was a major figure in the so-called Military Question, a series of political conflicts during the 1880s between members of the armed forces and representatives of the imperial government that served gradually to weaken the imperial government.

Although not a republican by conviction, Fonseca was persuaded to join and lead the military movement that brought about the overthrow of the monarchy on 25 November 1889 and the proclamation of a republic that afternoon. A successful revolt toppling the monarchy would not have been possible without the support of influential senior career officers like Fonseca, who assumed the position of provisional president of the new republic. Elected to a four-year term as president of the republic by the Constituent Congress in February 1891, he continually clashed with this largely civilian body that often protested what it perceived as infringements on civil liberties by military men. Unable to adjust to the give-and-take of politics and lacking political sophistication and astuteness, Fonseca judged legislative opposition to his policies to be personal insults and unconstitutionally dissolved Congress early in November 1891. A few weeks later, he was forced out of office by dissatisfied military factions, notably members of the navy. His resignation as president late in November 1891 permitted the vice-president, Marshal Floriano PEIXOTO, to assume office and reconvene Congress. Fonseca died several months later.

– JUNE E. HAHNER

FONSECA AMADOR, CARLOS

Carlos Fonseca Amador (*b.* 23 June 1936; *d.* 8 November 1976), Nicaraguan leader and cofounder of the Sandinista National Liberation Front. Born in the city of Matagalpa, Fonseca was an illegitimate son of Fausto Amador. His father was administrator of Anastasio Somoza García's rural properties in the department of Matagalpa. The family had a stable, middle-class lifestyle that enabled Fonseca to enter law school at the National Autonomous University in León in 1954. He immediately became involved in student politics and began studying the writings of Augusto César SANDINO. He joined a Conservative Party youth organization but left after a few months, complaining that it was "too perfumed." He then became a member of the Nicaraguan Socialist Party. In 1957 Fonseca toured eastern Europe and the Soviet Union as a delegate of the General Union of Nicaraguan Workers. After his return in 1958, the Socialist Party published the pamphlet "A Nicaraguan in Moscow," a compendium of Fonseca's impressions of the Communist world. Fonseca increased his activities in the student opposition to the Somoza regime and participated in the unsuccessful attempt, launched from El Chaparral, Honduras, to oust the dictatorship in June 1959. He recognized the futility of agitating within the restrictive ideology of the Socialist Party, and in 1960 started the New Nicaragua Movement, the basis for the creation of the Sandinista National Liberation Front in July 1961.

Fonseca was the principal thinker behind the revolutionary organization, but he was not a Marxist-Leninist theorist. Rather, he carefully refined Sandino's eclectic ideology in order to build popular support for revolution. From the early years of the Sandinista guerrilla army in Río Coco, Fonseca accepted the necessity of cooperating with diverse urban and rural social groups. The strategy of armed struggle through the gradual accumulation of forces was borrowed directly from Sandino.

Fonseca was captured by the National Guard in 1964 and deported to Guatemala. He returned clandestinely and participated in the failed attack at Pancasán in 1967. Two years later he was arrested for bank robbery in Costa Rica and spent more than a year in jail. Freed after Sandinistas hijacked a jetliner, Fonseca spent the early 1970s shuttling between Nicaragua and the safety of Cuba. He was responsible for developing the main objectives of the Sandinista program that guided the revolutionary government in the 1980s.

In November 1976 Fonseca was killed by the National Guard near Matagalpa. He is still considered the most important historical figure of the Sandinista National Liberation Front. After the victory over SOMOZA in 1979, his body was exhumed and reburied in the Plaza of the Revolution in Managua, where a monument was erected in his memory.

– MARK EVERINGHAM

FONSECA E SILVA, VALENTIM DA

Valentim da Fonseca e Silva (Mestre Valentim; *b.* 1750; *d.* 1813), Brazilian sculptor, wood-carver, and architect. Although he was born in Minas Gerais, Mestre Valentim lived most of his life in Rio de Janeiro. The mulatto son of a Portuguese diamond contractor and black mother, he was orphaned at a young age. While studying wood carving under the Portuguese master craftsman Luis da Fonseca Rosa, he began to receive numerous commissions for candelabras, altarpieces, statuary, and other religious decorative work for churches throughout the city.

Mestre Valentim's best-known commissions include the carvings for the Church of Santa Cruz dos Militares, the carving and main altar in the Church of São Francisco de Paula, and the chapel of the novitiate in the Church of the Third Order of Carmo.

Beyond religious wood carvings, Mestre Valentim was the first in Brazil to apply enamel to metal. He also devoted himself to secular projects such as public fountains and architectural design. His masterpiece, the plans for the Passeio Público, was undertaken in collaboration with the painter Leandro Joaquim and the designers Francisco dos Santos Xavier and Francisco Xavier Cardoso Caldeira. Viceroy Luiz de Vasconcellos commissioned the public park as part of the government's attempt at the beautification of Rio de Janeiro.

— CAREN A. MEGHREBLIAN

FONTANA, LUCIO

Lucio Fontana (*b.* 19 February 1899; *d.* 7 September 1968), Argentine sculptor. Born in Rosario, Sante Fe Province, the son of Italian parents, Fontana went to Italy when he was six. He studied at the Brera Royal Academy in Milan, graduating in 1922. The following year he returned to Argentina. In the mid 1920s he was back in Milan studying under Adolfo Widt. After that he lived several years in Paris. Fontana's repertory of forms includes figures that produce a sense of wonder and fascination in the viewer. His sculptures are in various museums and collections in Argentina and Europe. He wrote a series of manifestos on "spatialism," asserting the need to integrate all the physical elements (color, sound, movement, and space) in an ideal material unity. He died in Varese, Italy.

— AMALIA CORTINA ARAVENA

FORNER, RAQUEL

Raquel Forner (*b.* 22 April 1902; *d.* 10 June 1988), Argentine painter. Born in Buenos Aires, Forner studied at the National Academy of Fine Arts in Buenos Aires, graduating in 1923, and with Othon Friesz in Paris (1929–1930). In 1932 she helped found the first private school of fine arts in Buenos Aires. She became a member of the Royal Society of Arts (England) in 1951 and received the National Prize for painting (Buenos Aires, 1942) and the grand prize at the First American Biennial of Art (Córdoba, Argentina, 1962). Through her encounter with the surrealists in Paris, Forner discovered the cosmic character of experience and endeavored to give it structural expression. In later years her paint-

ings focused on a science-fiction interpretation of the cosmos, as exemplified in *Black Astrobeings.* From the technical point of view her compositions are highly un-

---

In later years Forner's paintings focused on a science-fiction interpretation of the cosmos, as exemplified in

Black Astrobeings.

---

usual in structure; color plays a secondary role, inclining toward the monochromatic. Forner's work reflects the image of the human soul amid the complexity of the world.

— AMALIA CORTINA ARAVENA

FORTUNY, JOSÉ MANUEL

José Manuel Fortuny (*b.* 22 March 1916), Guatemalan Communist leader. Fortuny was born in Cuilapa in the department of Santa Rosa to a middle-class family. He studied law at the University of San Carlos but never graduated. Beginning in 1938 he worked as a journalist, and the following year he began to write poetry and theatrical works for radio. In 1940 he won a national poetry prize. Until 1942 he was a journalist with the radio news program *Diario del Aire,* directed by the novelist Miguel Angel ASTURIAS.

Fortuny began his political career in the student struggle against the dictator Jorge UBICO (1931–1944) and participated in the revolution of October 1944. From 1945 to 1949 he was a representative to the National Constituent Assembly and to the Guatemalan Congress. He founded the leftist Popular Liberation Front (FPL) in 1944 and served as secretary-general to both the FPL and the Revolutionary Action Party (PAR) in 1947. In that same year he formed a faction within the PAR called the Democratic Vanguard, which gave rise in 1949 to the Guatemalan Communist Party (PCG), renamed the Guatemalan Labor Party (PGT) in 1952. He was the secretary-general of this group until 1954.

Fortuny played a key role in the administration of President Jacobo ARBENZ (1951–1954) as the president's friend, personal adviser, and member of the so-called "kitchen cabinet," writing many of his speeches. After the North American intervention and the fall of Arbenz, Fortuny went into exile. He continued as leader of his party, and between 1971 and 1974 lived clandestinely within Guatemala. He later moved to Mexico City and went to work for the newspaper *Uno Más Uno.* In the 1990s he remained a Marxist and followed the moderate evolution of the former Italian Communist Party.

– VÍCTOR ACUÑA

FRANCIA, JOSÉ GASPAR RODRÍGUEZ DE

José Gaspar Rodríguez de Francia (*b.* 6 January 1766; *d.* 20 September 1840), dictator of Paraguay (1814–1840). One of three major nineteenth-century rulers of Paraguay, Francia was viewed by his elite contemporaries and traditional historians as a ruthless dictator who isolated Paraguay from outside contact and whose iron rule destroyed all who opposed him—foreigners, intellectuals, and the Paraguayan elite. Revisionist historians perceive him as an honest, populist ruler who promoted an autonomous, social revolution within Paraguay and encouraged the economic development of the country.

Born in Asunción to a Brazilian military officer and his elite Paraguayan wife, Francia earned a doctorate in theology in 1785 at the University of Córdoba, Argentina. He then taught theology at Asunción's Real Colegio y Seminario de San Carlos. Upon his dismissal for his liberal ideas on religion and politics, he turned to law. He never married and did not use his political opportunities to amass wealth. He gained political experience by serving on the municipal council of Asunción from 1807 to 1809 and won enough respect for his legal and administrative knowledge to be given the responsibility of defining the qualifications for participation in the revolutionary junta. Eventually dominating the junta, he espoused Paraguayan independence from both Spanish and Argentine hegemony and wrote the first constitution of Paraguay, which the Congress adopted in October 1813. The dual consulship of Colonel Fulgencio YEGROS and Francia soon failed. Francia's popularity, personality, and political ability led the National Congress of 1814 to elect him supreme dictator. Even though there were periods of shared power as well as self-imposed exile between 1811 and 5 June 1816, when the Popular Congress elected him perpetual dictator, Francia was the most powerful and popular politician for the first twenty-nine years of Paraguayan independence.

Francia destroyed the traditional power of the Spanish elite and the church, strengthened the military, and appealed to the peasants. He did not abolish the municipal councils in small towns but did terminate those in Asunción and Villa Rica that were controlled by the elite. He promoted state-operated cattle ranches and state commerce, which competed with the private *estancias* and mercantile houses and undermined the elite's ability to increase its wealth. Francia dominated the operations of the Roman Catholic church by collecting tithes, paying the clergy's salaries, and constructing churches. Although he closed the seminary at which he had once taught, between 1815 and 1840 he had at least ten new churches constructed and increased the number of priests in the villages.

To promote the nation's self-sufficiency, Francia encouraged greater utilization of state lands through government enterprises and low rents for small farmers who produced food for local consumption. He promoted internal trade, controlled external commerce and immigration, increased industrial production in both the private and public sectors, improved communications and transportation, and reduced taxes. To limit government costs, he maintained only a small bureaucracy. His frugality and careful attention to detail resulted in governmental fiscal surpluses. A paternalistic ruler, Francia supported religious celebrations and paid for pauper burials and the care of orphans. The state helped pay soldiers' debts, provided food for indigent prisoners, and aided foreign exiles.

To maintain internal security, suppress banditry, protect against Indians, and define the nation's boundaries, Francia built border forts and established garrisons at the northern border with Brazil at the Apa River, in the south at Pilar on the Argentine border, and in the southeast, which expanded control over the Misiones region. To end Paraguayan political independence, Francia sought Argentine recognition and free trade on the border along the Paraná River. When Argentine caudillos disrupted trade between 1817 and 1822 and Buenos Aires refused to recognize Paraguayan independence, Francia closed Paraguay's borders in 1819 and again between 1823 and 1840, redirecting Paraguayan external trade through the department of Itapúa (Encarnación) to Brazil and Uruguay. The conduct of trade down the Paraná, although regulated by Francia, never entirely ceased, because small boats were able to get through Pilar to Corrientes. By maintaining neutrality in Río de la Plata affairs and using Brazilian commercial interests to balance Argentine political demands, Francia assured Paraguayan independence.

In contrast to other Spanish-American states after independence, Francia's government was stable, efficient, and honest. At his death Paraguay possessed a prosperous, independent national economy and a centralized political system. His economic and political power and willingness to use force created critics among the elite and laid the basis for autocratic rule in Paraguay. Even though military officers and civilians maneuvered for power after his death, the peaceful transfer of government that occurred testifies to the strength of his administration. A dedicated nationalist, popular with the masses, Francia was a dictator whose paternalistic policies benefited a large majority of Paraguayans.

— VERA BLINN REBER

FRANCO, GUILLERMO

Guillermo Franco (active mid-1800s), Ecuadorian military and political figure. Following the ouster of Juan José FLORES in 1845, Ecuador entered a period of extreme political instability that culminated in the country's splintering into four regions in 1859. General Franco assumed leadership of Guayaquil on 6 September 1859 and signed a treaty with Peru conceding El Oriente to that nation in return for recognition of his presidency of Ecuador. As a result of this agreement, he lost popular support on the coast. The following year, in September 1860, Franco's forces were defeated by the army of the provisional government commanded by former president Juan José Flores. Franco fled into exile.

— LINDA ALEXANDER RODRÍGUEZ

FRANCO, HERNANDO

Hernando Franco (*b.* 1532; *d.* 28 November 1585), Spanish-born composer who, after his training in the Segovia cathedral and brief service in Guatemala, was brought to Mexico by Spanish patron Arévalo Sedeño. Music flourished under his direction at the Mexico City cathedral from 1575 until financial problems prompted his resignation in 1582. He returned to the post as conditions improved, but died shortly thereafter. His sacred music style incorporates the alternation of simple unison and intricate polyphonic part singing in a manner typical of the cathedral practice that existed during his apprentice and journeyman years in Spain.

— ROBERT L. PARKER

FRANCO, ITAMAR AUGUSTO CAUTIERO

Itamar Augusto Cautiero Franco (*b.* 28 June 1931), president of Brazil (1992–). Franco was born on board the ship *Itamar,* along the coast of Bahia. His mother, Italia Cautiero, who had just lost her husband, a public-health doctor in the interior of that state, was returning with her children Augusto and Matilde to raise them in Juiz de Fora, Minas Gerais. Although his birth certificate gives Salvador, Bahia, as the birthplace, Franco has always considered himself a Mineiro, and many of his initial curricula vitae, once he was elevated to the presidency, erroneously gave Juiz de Fora as his birthplace. His cultural background and his accent are Mineiro, and he was influenced by such nationally known Mineiro politicians as José Maria Alkimin, Bias Fortes,

Carlos Luz, and former presidents Juscelino KUBITSCHEK and Tancredo NEVES.

Franco attended Colégio Granbery, a school established by American Methodist missionaries at the turn of the twentieth century. During a later visit to the school, then Vice President Franco declared that it was to his mother, to Granbery, and to the local engineering school that he owed his moral, intellectual, and professional training. As an engineering student from 1950 to 1955, he was twice elected president of the academic center and demonstrated great debating skills while advocating student concerns.

Two years after graduating, Franco ran for city councilman on the Brazilian Labor Party (PTB) slate and was defeated. Four years later he also lost an election for deputy mayor. He finally succeeded in becoming mayor as a candidate on the Brazilian Democratic Movement (MDB, later PMDB) slate. His administration was marked by public works and major improvements that changed the face of the city. While mayor, he married journalist Ana Elisa Surerus. The marriage lasted nine years and the couple had two daughters.

In 1975 he ran successfully for a seat in the federal Senate, where he served until he ran for vice president in 1990. When President Fernando COLLOR DE MELLO resigned from office because of malfeasance, Franco served as interim chief executive and then as president from 29 December 1992 on.

His cabinet reflected his nationalistic tendencies and his penchant to trust old and intimate friends. He postponed a number of initiatives that had been undertaken by his predecessor, notably in the area of privatization. His works include *O negro no Brasil atual* (The Blacks in Today's Brazil, 1980), an attempt at a sociological interpretation, and *Trabalho parlamentar* (Parliamentary Work, 1984), detailing his years in the senate.

— IÊDA SIQUEIRA WIARDA

FRANCO, RAFAEL

Rafael Franco (*b.* 1897; *d.* 1973), Paraguayan president (1936–1937), Chaco War military figure, and founder of the Partido Revolucionario Febrerista, or Febrerista Party.

In December 1928 Paraguayan forces led by Major Rafael Franco, a relatively unknown army officer, launched an unprovoked attack against Bolivian-held Fortín Vanguardia in the disputed Chaco region. This incident, though successful in its immediate aim, was repudiated by the Asunción government, which was seeking a diplomatic solution to the conflict. Now regarded as an uncontrollable hothead, Franco lost his command, only to be recalled in 1932 when the border dispute gave way to open war. Franco's military exploits in the conflict were noteworthy, though hardly more so than his open political maneuvering against the Liberal regime of Eusebio AYALA. With the conclusion of the fighting, Franco, now a colonel, made his own position clear: on 17 February 1936, he led the armed forces in a mutiny that swept Ayala from office and installed the colonel as dictator.

Regarded as an uncontrollable hothead, Franco lost his command, only to be recalled in 1932 when Paraguay's border dispute gave way to open war.

Franco had no intention of ruling in the manner of previous dictators. He announced a reform program that focused on land redistribution, workers' rights, and statist politics. Before he could implement these plans, his regime was overthrown in August 1937 by military leaders loyal to the Liberal Party. Franco went into exile, though he remained influential in revolutionary circles within Paraguay.

From exile, the former colonel organized the Febrerista Party, a curious movement that drew support from students, workers, some military officers, and both left- and right-wing ideologues. The Febreristas burst onto the Paraguayan political scene in 1946, when dictator Higínio MORÍNIGO invited Franco to return to the country to participate in a coalition government. This coalition failed to materialize, however, and one year later the situation degenerated into civil war with the Liberals, Communists, and Franco's Febreristas on one side and the Colorados (and the majority of the military) on the other. Franco commanded the rebel forces in the fighting but, after a short time, had to accept defeat and exile once again.

The Febreristas retained some of their influence in Paraguay, though, as the years went by, the movement abandoned its earlier radicalism and adopted a social democratic line. Franco returned several times from exile at the behest of Alfredo STROESSNER (president 1954–1989); the Febrerista Party was permitted, in a limited way, to contest several elections after 1964, with the understanding that they would present little more than token opposition to the governing Colorados. Franco accepted this as a necessary compromise, but his own death in 1973 left the Febreristas without viable leadership.

— MARTA FERNÁNDEZ WHIGHAM

FRANCO, WELLINGTON MOREIRA

Wellington Moreira Franco (*b.* 19 October 1944), Brazilian politician. Moreira Franco entered Brazilian politics in the early 1970s, just as the military regime, which had controlled the federal government since 1964, began to liberalize national political life in a process known as ABERTURA. While serving as a federal deputy for the state of Rio de Janeiro (1975–1977), mayor of the city of Niterói in the state of Rio de Janeiro (1977–1982), and governor of the state of Rio de Janeiro (1986–1990), he became well-known for his vocal advocacy of the return to and consolidation of democratic political processes. During his mayoral and gubernatorial tenures, Moreira Franco sought to build grassroots support through government-sponsored projects in the areas of social welfare and political participation.

Born in the northern city of Teresina, Piauí, Franco moved to Rio de Janeiro in 1955, where he was trained in economics and public administration at the Universidade do Brasil (1966); the Pontífica Universidade Católica of Rio de Janeiro (1968); and the École Pratique des Hautes Études in Paris. A member of the opposition Brazilian Democratic Movement (MDB) during the 1970s, Franco joined the Social Democratic Party (PDS) in 1980. The PDS candidate for governor of the state of Rio de Janeiro in 1982, he was narrowly defeated. He later joined the Brazilian Democratic Movement Party (PMDB), which supported him during his successful 1986 gubernatorial bid.

— DARYLE WILLIAMS

FREI MONTALVA, EDUARDO

Eduardo Frei Montalva (*b.* 16 January 1911; *d.* 22 January 1982), president of Chile (1964–1970). Frei was born in Santiago and entered politics as a law student, founding what later became the Christian Democratic Party. After graduation from the Catholic University of Chile (1933) he specialized in labor law, then turned to editing a newspaper in the nitrate region of Tarapacá, in Chile's extreme north. He entered the Chamber of Deputies in the late 1930s, eventually becoming minister of public works in the government of President Gabriel GONZÁLEZ VIDELA (1946–1952). For some years he represented the province of Santiago in the Chilean Senate, running unsuccessfully for president in 1958. In 1964, however, he ran again, this time in a two-way race, and defeated Socialist Salvador ALLENDE, who was also supported by the Chilean Communists.

Frei's campaign came at a time when the prestige of the Cuban Revolution was at its height in Latin America, and Allende its chief beneficiary in Chile. The

Christian Democrats neutralized the appeal of the Left by conceding profound changes were needed to address inequality and injustice, but proposed to implement them without tampering with the country's historic commitment to the rule of law and due process (Frei's successful slogan was "A Revolution in Liberty"). Frei defeated Allende by a decisive majority, but one that owed much to the tacit support of the Chilean Right, which chose not to run a candidate of its own.

During Frei's presidency serious efforts were made at agrarian reform, tax reform, and the nationalization of the copper industry. The Right managed to obstruct some of Frei's legislative projects in Congress, often joining hands with the Left, for whom they were too conservative. Meanwhile, the Christian Democratic youth movement was pulling Frei's own party to the left, even imposing a candidate of their own, Radomiro Tomic, for the 1970 presidential elections. The result was a three-headed race in which Socialist Salvador Allende emerged with a slight plurality.

At the time of Allende's election Frei predicted that the former's Socialist-Communist government (Popular Unity) would end in "blood and horror." At first these concerns were dismissed even by members of his own party. However, three years later, Chilean society was polarized to the point of civil war. The stalemate was broken by an exceptionally bloody military coup, which produced a sixteen-year political "recess," in which the country was ruled by the iron-handed Army commander General Augusto PINOCHET UGARTE. Frei's remaining years were spent resisting Pinochet and helping to rebuild the Christian Democratic Party. He also served on the Brandt Commission and other international bodies.

– MARK FALCOFF

FREIRE, PAULO

Paulo Freire (*b.* 19 March 1921), Brazilian educator and philosopher. After studies in law and philosophy, Freire became a teacher with a special interest in grammar and linguistics. Between 1947 and 1959 he instructed adult illiterates as director of the Department of Education and Culture of the Social Service in Pernambuco. In 1959 Freire completed his doctoral thesis on teaching adult illiterates and was appointed professor of history and philosophy of education at the University of Recife. In 1963, after successfully leading literary efforts in his native state, Freire was placed in charge of a national literacy campaign by the GOULART government, which initiated training programs in almost all the state capitals. When this government fell prey to a military coup in April 1965, Freire, along with many others, was

jailed, stripped of his citizenship rights, and finally sentenced to exile. Freire resettled in Chile, where for five years he worked as a UNESCO consultant with the Agrarian Reform Training and Research Institute. While in exile, he led a national literacy campaign that won Chile a UNESCO award, and he wrote his first two books, *Pedagogy of the Oppressed* (1970) and *Education for Critical Consciousness* (1973), which describe his practice and theory of literacy education.

After a year's stay at Harvard University, in 1970 Freire took a position as educational consultant to the World Council of Churches in Geneva. In 1971 he established the Institute for Cultural Action, which fostered experimentation with Freire's method of conscientization. From this position he took part in literacy education in a number of developing countries. *Pedagogy in Process* (1975) describes his literacy efforts in Guinea-Bissau.

With other political exiles, Freire was permitted to return to Brazil in June 1980 after President FIGUEIREDO granted amnesty to Brazilian exiles and dissenters. He has since devoted himself to educational projects throughout the world. Especially through *Pedagogy of the Oppressed,* which has been translated into numerous languages, Freire is one of the most influential educators of the twentieth century.

– JOHN ELIAS

FREIRE SERRANO, RAMÓN

Ramón Freire Serrano (*b.* 29 November 1787; *d.* 9 September 1851), Chilean patriot, supreme director of Chile (1823–1826, 1827). Freire enlisted in the patriot army in 1811 and fought with great valor in many actions of the Chilean Wars of Independence. (During the restored colonial regime of 1814–1817 he served in Admiral William BROWN's corsair squadron.) In 1819 he was named intendant of Concepción. The desperate conditions in that war-ravaged southern province turned Freire against the Bernardo O'HIGGINS government. His *pronunciamiento* was the main cause of O'Higgins's downfall (January 1823). Freire was the inevitable successor. During his supreme directorship, he expelled the Spanish troops still holding out on the island of Chiloé (January 1826). In domestic affairs, Freire's liberalism allowed politicians a free rein; their failure to organize stable institutions made this a frustrating period. Freire soon had enough. In July 1826 he resigned, returning to power briefly in 1827 to restore order after a military mutiny.

Early in 1830 Freire once again took up arms, to oppose the Conservative seizure of power then well under way. His small army was defeated at the battle of

LIRCAY (April 1830), after which he was arrested and exiled to Peru. From there, in mid-1836, he led an expedition to Chile in the vain hope of overthrowing the Conservatives. He was captured, put on trial, and exiled to Australia. (Diego PORTALES wished to have him shot, but did not get his way.) By the end of 1837 Freire was living in Tahiti (where he is said to have befriended Queen Pomaré). In 1839 he settled in the Bolivian port of Cobija. The amnesty of 1841 enabled the general to return at last to his native land: the remaining years formed a quiet coda to an adventurous life.

— SIMON COLLIER

FRESNO LARRAÍN, JUAN FRANCISCO

Juan Francisco Fresno Larraín (b. 26 July 1914), archbishop of Santiago, Chile (1983–1990), during the last years of the military government of General Augusto PINOCHET.

Born in Santiago, Fresno was educated in the diocesan seminary and at Gregorian University in Rome, where he received a bachelor's degree in canon law. Ordained on 18 December 1937, he served in the influential posts of vice rector of the minor seminary in Santiago and as an adviser to the reformist lay group Catholic Action, which was particularly active in Chile from the 1940s into the 1960s. In 1958 Pope Pius XII named him bishop of the recently created diocese of Copiapó, and in 1967 Pope Paul VI named him archbishop of the more important archdiocese of La Serena.

Fresno participated in the Second Vatican Council (1962–1965), supporting greater involvement of the Catholic church in social justice activities. He also influenced the deliberations of the second Conference of Latin American Bishops (CELAM) in 1968, which translated into Latin American terms the general mandates of Vatican II to promote peace, justice, and human rights.

While Fresno publicly justified the coup that brought Pinochet to power in 1973, he engaged in negotiations to speed the return of elected government in Chile.

On 3 May 1983 he was named archbishop of Santiago and two years later was elevated to the rank of cardinal. While he had publicly justified the coup that brought Pinochet to power in 1973, ten years later he engaged in negotiations to speed the return of elected

government. In addition, he traveled widely to generate pressure within and without Chile to encourage Pinochet to resign. While his efforts were not successful, they did contribute to the ultimate defeat of Pinochet in a 1988 plebiscite and to the return of democratic government in 1990. On 30 March 1990 Fresno resigned as cardinal archbishop of Santiago.

— MARGARET E. CRAHAN

FREYRE, GILBERTO (DE MELLO)

Gilberto (de Mello) Freyre (b. 15 March 1900; d. 18 July 1987), pivotal Brazilian cultural historian and essayist of the 1930s. His historical essay *Casa-grande & senzala* (*The Masters and the Slaves,* 1933) popularized Franz Boas's anthropological concept of culture as an antidote to pessimistic race science. Freyre argued that Brazil's "mixture" was psychic and cultural in addition to racial. Modern Brazilians were not doomed racial mongrels but rather the fortunate heirs of the colonial plantation's fusion of Portuguese, Indian, and African culture. This energetic and erotic essay became a bestseller. It eventually inspired Carnival samba pageants (1962) as well as nationalist political propaganda. For example, the claim that Brazil was a model of racial harmony became a theme of Brazilian diplomatic initiatives. Many of the ideas of *Casa-grande & senzala* and its two sequels, *Sobrados e mucambos* (*The Mansions and the Shanties,* 1936) and *Ordem e progresso* (*Order and Progress,* 1959), established themes for the next generation of social scientists in Brazil. These included the centrality of the patriarchal family as a social institution, Brazil's historical formation as a slave society, the sugar plantation as an institution, and the importance of folkways, especially those related to the house, food, and healing.

Outside of Brazil, Freyre's ideas had their greatest repercussion in the United States, where his studies at Baylor (1918–1920) and Columbia (1920–1922) universities, bohemian life in New York, and travels in the South had refined his sense of Brazil's uniqueness. In the 1940s scholars influenced by Freyre, such as Frank Tannenbaum, challenged Americans to measure themselves against the model of race relations presented in *Casa-grande & senzala.* Their debates developed into the contemporary fields of comparative race relations and comparative history of slavery. Freyre's impact was not limited to the United States. *Casa-grande & senzala* was translated into at least six languages. Freyre lectured, visited universities, and received honors throughout the world, including an honorary British knighthood in 1971.

Freyre's history of Brazil took a nostalgic and regional perspective, centering on the rise and decline of the sugar plantations of the Northeast. According to *Casa-grande & senzala,* Brazil was founded in a burst of energy by the "miscible" Portuguese, who were culturally suited to the task of building a multiracial tropical colony. During three centuries of near isolation from Portuguese government, Brazil's "patriarchal" society centered around the self-sufficient plantation big house. In its kitchens and bedrooms, a cultural and sexual fusion of peoples was accomplished. The result was a culturally "Oriental" society, in which the Jesuit religious order was the only disciplined, "European" counterweight to patriarchal whims. Plantation paternalism harmonized Brazilians and encouraged racial democracy; but plantation slavery, "like a great economic God," divided Brazilians into masters and slaves and encouraged authoritarianism.

Sobrados e mucambos chronicles the decline of this order. Upon the arrival of the exiled Portuguese king in 1808, Brazil centralized, urbanized, and "re-Europeanized." During the nineteenth century, plantation families moved from country big house to city mansion. Once there, urban social institutions—doctor, street, and school—destroyed patriarchalism. The woman and the child emerged as individuals, free from the father's tutelage. Ultimately, "white" planter fathers acceded to the marriage of their daughters to mulatto men of talent, forming a multiracial, "semipatriarchal" establishment. *Ordem e progresso* argues that the abolition of slavery in 1888 and the overthrow of the emperor in 1889 completed the dissolution of patriarchy. From 1890 forward, republican Brazil cast about for identity, having symbolically rejected its father. By 1914 the institutions of the republic had begun to forge a modern order that could accommodate the challenge of the "social question" of the working class while preserving the legacy of racial harmony.

A political interlude from 1946 to 1950 marked a watershed in Freyre's career. Previously, he had been secretary to the governor of Pernambuco (1926–1930) and had briefly gone into exile in 1930. During the dictatorship of Getúlio VARGAS, his sponsorship of two Afro-Brazilian congresses in 1934 and 1937 and the audacious reputation of *Casa-grande & senzala* placed him under political suspicion. With the fall of Vargas, Freyre was elected to the 1946 Constituent Assembly and the Chamber of Deputies by a União Democrática Nacional (UDN) coalition. While in congress, Freyre championed cultural causes, including the chartering of the Instituto Joaquim Nabuco de Pesquisas Sociais in Recife, which eventually became his institutional base. In 1949 he was Brazilian delegate to the General Assembly of the United Nations. Freyre left political office in 1950, but he remained an active voice in Brazilian politics, now generally from the right. He contributed to the platforms of the pro-government Aliança Renovadora Nacional (ARENA) in the 1960s and 1970s.

After 1950 Freyre proposed the creation of a discipline of "Lusotropicology" that would study common aspects of the adaptations of Portuguese culture and rule to tropical colonies in Brazil, Africa, and Asia. Because Lusotropicalism appeared to embrace a defense of modern Portuguese colonialism in Africa, many other currents of social science in Brazil avoided it. Lusotropicalism never became a widespread intellectual movement. Furthermore, during the 1960s and 1970s, historians revised and criticized Freyre's descriptions of the

Gilberto Freyre late in his life. (Photo by Claus C. Meyer/Pulsar Imagens e Editora)

supposedly benign components of slavery and race relations. Cultural anthropologists in the 1980s looked back to the insights of his early work but not to Lusotropicology.

Freyre's presence in Brazilian intellectual life was not confined to his roles as anthropologist, historian, or politician; he was also a distinctive literary voice. In the 1920s he urged the literary avant garde of his native Recife to explore regionalist themes in contrast to the futurist avant garde of São Paulo. Later, he published a sequence of two "semi-novels," *Dona Sinhá e o filho padre: Seminovela* (*Mother and Son,* 1964) and *O outro amor do Dr. Paulo* (1977), that portray the traditional family relations and religiosity of the Brazilian Northeast. It was the style of his historical essays, however, that was his major contribution to Brazilian prose. He sometimes invoked Proust as his model for the autobiographical tone and nonlinear style of *Casa-grande & senzala;* other critics have detected a baroque aesthetic with Brazilian roots.

– DAIN BORGES

FRÍAS, ANTONIO

Antonio Frías (*b.* 13 October 1745; *d.* 1824), Argentine-born astronomer. Frías was born in Santiago del Estero and entered the Society of Jesus in 1764, just three years before the Jesuits were expelled from the Río de la Plata. Exiled, he sailed on the *Venus* to the Papal States, where he was ordained to the priesthood. Frías became interested in astronomy as a seminarian and retained the interest throughout his life. He worked under the Jesuit astronomer and mathematician Roger Boscovich. Frías conducted research in the observatory of Brera, near Milan, and published his findings in the *Efemeridi astronomiche* of Milan. He left several unpublished manuscripts, which today are in the Jesuit archive of the Colegio Salvador in Buenos Aires. He died in Milan.

– NICHOLAS P. CUSHNER

FRIGERIO, ROGELIO

Rogelio Frigerio (*b.* 1914), Argentine industrialist, journalist, and politician. Born in Buenos Aires, Frigerio achieved business success in textiles, mining, and agriculture. He served as editor and political director of the newsmagazine *Qué Sucedió en Siete Días,* director of the Center for National Research (1956–1988), and secretary for Economic-Social Relations of the Nation (1958). In 1959 he became economic counselor to the presidency. As Arturo FRONDIZI's closest advisor, Frigerio was responsible for the accord between Frondizi's

Intransigent Radicals (Unión Cívica Radical Intransigente) and Juan D. PERÓN (then in exile), which had provided Peronist voting support for Frondizi's presidential victory in 1958. Frigerio influenced Frondizi's industrial strategy for national economic independence, which required large-scale involvement, on favorable terms, of foreign capital and technology. The strategy—particularly as it affected the petroleum industry, which Frondizi had until shortly before defended as the cornerstone of economic nationalism—outraged nationalists; moreover, it failed to achieve the intended results.

The president's attempt to bring the Peronist remnant into a permanent Radical-led coalition aroused increasing opposition among military anti-Peronists; in late March 1962 Frondizi was ousted by a military coup—the first of many as Argentina descended into chaos in the 1960s and 1970s. Once in power, the military charged Frigerio and his associates with "economic crimes." Thereafter, Frigerio remained close to Perón, but stayed out of public life until the 1980s. He became affiliated with the Movement for Integration and Development after 1975, and in 1983 he made an unsuccessful run for the presidency.

Frigerio has published a score of books on politics and political economy, including *Los cuatro años (1958–1962)* (1962), *Petroleo y desarrollo* (1962), *Historia y política* (1963), *Crecimiento económico y democracia* (1963; 2d ed., 1983), *Estatuto del subdesarrollo: Las corrientes del pensamiento económico argentino* (1967; 3d rev. ed., 1983), *Síntesis de la historia crítica de la economía Argentina* (1979), and *Diez años de la crisis Argentina: Diagnóstico y programa del desarrollismo* (1983).

– RONALD C. NEWTON

FRONDIZI, ARTURO

Arturo Frondizi (*b.* 27 October 1908; *d.* 18 April 1995), president of Argentina (1958–1962). Born in Paso de los Libres, Corrientes Province, Frondizi trained as a lawyer and received his degree from the University of Buenos Aires in 1930. He became active in politics as a member of the Radical Party. He served as a national deputy representing Buenos Aires (1946–1951). In 1951, he ran as the Radical Party's vice-presidential candidate.

Although the Radicals lost the election, Frondizi became one of the Peronist regime's more influential opponents. His speeches and publications concerning domestic development of Argentina's oil reserves won him support among nationalists. After the military coup and President Juan PERÓN's resignation in September 1955, Frondizi moved to take control of the Radical Party. His competition with Ricardo BALBÍN, the party's 1951 presidential candidate, split the Radicals into two groups: the Radical Civic Union of the People (Unión Cívica Radical del Pueblo), which followed Balbín, and the Intransigent Radical Civic Union (Unión Cívica Radical Intransigente).

When the military scheduled elections in February 1958, Frondizi ran for president. With the Peronist Party banned from participating, he tried to attract Peronist supporters with a prolabor, proindustry and anti-United States campaign. While the strategy helped him defeat Balbín, it put his administration between pro-Peronist unions and the anti-Peronist military. Conditions in late 1958 and 1959 forced him to abandon his populist rhetoric and adopt austere economic measures to control inflation and attract investment. Organized labor called strikes and demonstrations against the new regime. By 1962, his actions had cost him support among the voters and the military. With popular unrest rising and economic conditions worsening, the military moved against him in March 1962.

Frondizi retired from active politics until the 1970s, when he abandoned the Radical Party to become the leader of the conservative Movement of Integration and Development (Movimiento de Integración y Desarrollo). Later, he headed the right-wing National Movement (Movimiento Nacional) coalition.

– DANIEL LEWIS

FRONDIZI, RISIERI

Risieri Frondizi (*b.* 20 November 1910), Argentine philosopher and author. Born in Posadas, Misiones Province, and brother of President Arturo FRONDIZI, Risieri Frondizi studied at the National Secondary Teaching Institute and then accepted a teaching position at the University of Tucumán (1938–1946). He continued his training abroad while writing and translating the works of George Berkeley, Alfred North Whitehead, and others. He received a masters degree in philosophy from the University of Michigan in 1943 and a doctorate from the National University of Mexico in 1950. For political and intellectual reasons, he accepted positions at universities in the United States and Puerto Rico.

Through his research and writing, he gained an international reputation as an expert in the study of individuals within society and of the nature of value and value judgments. His work includes *Substancia y fundación en el problema del yo* (1952), published in 1970 as *El yo como estructura dinámica*. After the 1955 overthrow of Juan PERÓN, Frondizi returned to Argentina and became rector of the University of Buenos Aires in 1957. After political events forced him from his university position, he returned to his research and writing.

– DANIEL LEWIS

FRUGONI, EMILIO

Emilio Frugoni (*b.* 30 March 1880; *d.* 28 August 1969), Uruguayan lawyer, professor, writer, and founder of the Uruguayan Socialist Party. Frugoni promoted Marxist and socialist ideas in highly regarded works such as *Socialismo, batllismo y nacionalismo* (1928), *La revolución del machete* (1935), *Ensayos sobre marxismo* (1936), and *Génesis, esencia y fundamentos del socialismo* (1947).

Frugoni was a supporter of Colorado Party president José BATLLE Y ORDÓÑEZ, whose first term from 1903 to 1907 marked an end to the country's long civil wars and the beginning of peace, prosperity, and undisputed Colorado control of government. Frugoni supported Batlle's important moral legislation (permitting divorce and ending the death penalty), state enterprises (strengthening of the state-owned Bank of the Republic and the Montevideo Electric Power System), support of labor (police neutrality in strikes and the promotion of an eight-hour work day), public works, and school construction. He also approved of Batlle's opposition to the church and to intransigent conservatism. In 1910 he supported the government against the threat of the "October Revolution" led by Nepomuceno Saravia, son of Aparicio SARAVIA, the famous Nationalist (Blanco) Party caudillo, and Basilio Muñoz, military commander of the Radicals.

Beginning in 1904 Frugoni promoted the formation of a Socialist Party that would constitute the country's workers as a political force. The Socialist manifesto that he authored in 1910 supported the constitutional order, in contrast to the Anarchists' destabilizing politics. As Socialist deputy to the national congress (1911–1914), he again collaborated with Batlle, who had been elected to a second presidential term, by authoring several important legislative projects aimed at socioeconomic reform on behalf of the working class. Frugoni's Socialist Party never came to rival the country's two traditional parties; it did not attract a significant working-class membership, perhaps due to the successes of Batlle's Colorado Party in implementing the greater part of its social program.

In subsequent years Frugoni was dean of the National University (1933). While serving as Uruguay's ambassador to the Soviet Union (1945–1948), he wrote *La esfinge roja* (1948), which praised the significant transformations of that nation but raised a voice of alarm about its denial of individual rights in favor of an omnipotent state. Between 1900 and 1959 he published twelve collections of lyrical poetry.

— WILLIAM H. KATRA

FUENTES, CARLOS

Carlos Fuentes (*b.* 11 November 1928), Mexican writer, major literary figure, and spokesman not only for his country, but for all of Latin America. A prolific writer of novels, short stories, plays, and essays that possess intellectual brilliance and a powerful style, Fuentes is also a pioneer in narration and structure. A highly visible figure, he has been the subject of several television documentaries and interviews.

Son of Mexican diplomat Rafael Fuentes Boettiger and Berta Macías Rivas, Fuentes was born in Panama City and attended elementary school in Washington, D.C., and secondary schools in Buenos Aires and Santiago, Chile. He studied law at the Institut des Hautes Études Internationales (Geneva) and received a law degree from the National University of Mexico. He was named secretary to the Mexican delegation of the In-

Carlos Fuentes. (Photo by Lola Álvarez Bravo)

ternational Law Commission of the United Nations (Geneva) in 1950. He launched his literary career in 1954 with a collection of short stories, *Los días enmascarados* (Masked Days) and his first novel, *La región más transparente* (1958; *Where the Air Is Clear,* 1960) which brought him immediate recognition.

From 1956 to 1959 Fuentes served as director of international cultural relations at the Mexican Ministry of Foreign Affairs. In 1962 he published one of his major works, *La muerte de Artemio Cruz* (1962; *The Death of Artemio Cruz,* 1964), a novel that vividly depicts the corruption of the Mexican Revolution through the portrayal of a man in his last twelve hours of agony, during which he relives twelve crucial moments of his life. The main themes of his novella *Aura* (1962), found in most of Fuentes's works, are time, history, identity, desire, and civilization. *Cambio de piel* (1967; *A Change of Skin,* 1968) received the Biblioteca Breve prize in Barcelona the same year it was published. In an important book of literary criticism, *La nueva novela hispanoamericana* (1969; The New Latin American Novel) Fuentes analyzed the internationally acclaimed group of Latin American writers of the 1960s. While serving as ambassador to France (1974–1977), he published his essay *Don Quixote; or, The Critique of Reading* (1976), arguably the best guide to a full understanding of Fuentes's ideas.

Fuentes's most ambitious novel, *Terra nostra* (1975), published in English under the same title in 1976, is a powerful epic illustrating how the discovery of America provided a second opportunity for utopia that was defeated by human events. Among the many literary accolades Fuentes has received are Mexico's Javier Villaurrutia Prize (1975), the Rómulo Gallegos Prize of 1977 in Caracas for *Terra nostra,* and in 1987 Spain's prestigious Cervantes Prize. *Burnt Water* (1980) is a collection of Fuentes's best short stories written between 1954 and 1980. They depict the Spanish and Indian past with force and nostalgia. In *Cristóbal Nonato* (1987; *Christopher Unborn,* 1989), the tone is similar to that of *Terra Nostra,* offering an apocalyptic vision of Mexico's future in which he uses humor, as well as his trademark remarkable play of words.

During the 1992 year of the quincentenary of the meeting of the Old World with the New, Fuentes narrated a popular television series, *The Buried Mirror,* on the epic of "encounter" of the European and the indigenous world of Hispanic America. He continues writing, delving into Mexico's past, defining Mexico's national identity, and serving as Mexico's goodwill ambassador.

— MARTHA PALEY FRANCESCATO

397

FUENTES, MANUEL ATANASIO

Manuel Atanasio Fuentes (*b.* 1820; *d.* 2 January 1889), Peru's foremost statistician of the era, he also was an acute observer of Lima in the mid-nineteenth century. A census taker, journalist, administrator, social commentator, satirist, historian, and folklorist, he also delivered expert opinion on legal and medical questions. Fuentes drew notice as a journalist in the 1840s, when he began writing on the everyday life and customs of Lima. A traditionalist who feared that guano excesses would destroy Peru's subsistence highland village economy and thus alter traditional highland culture, Fuentes sought to awaken intellectuals to thinking about the primacy of Andean culture. He also documented the size and variety of the artisan population of Lima in *Guía histórico-descriptiva administrativa, judicial y de domicilio de Lima* (1860), a study carried out after the artisan uprisings of 1858. Between 1858 and 1878 he produced a series of statistical studies based on painstaking research. His voluminous *Estadística general de Lima* (1858) listed data on every aspect of urban life: population, architecture, customs, and industry. He updated this survey four times and issued editions in French and English. He also wrote street guides and almanacs on Lima. As a public administrator, he directed the organization of a new faculty of political science and administration at the National University of San Marcos, a task undertaken at the behest of President Manuel Pardo, and he undertook the country's first scientific national census (1876).

— VINCENT PELOSO

FUENTES Y GUZMÁN, FRANCISCO ANTONIO DE

Francisco Antonio de Fuentes y Guzmán (*b.* 9 February 1642; *d.* 1 August 1699), Central American historian, poet, bureaucrat, and soldier. He was born in Santiago de los Caballeros (now Antigua), Guatemala; little is known about his early life. At age eighteen he was named *regidor* of his native city, and later first (and then second) *alcalde* of Santiago de Guatemala. He also held the post of *alcalde mayor* in the town of Totonicapán and the province of Sonsonate. In the army he attained the rank of captain. Among his poems are "El Milagro de América" and "La vida de Santa Teresa de Jesús."

The work for which Fuentes y Guzmán is remembered today is his monumental history of Guatemala, the full title of which is *Recordación florida: Discurso historial y demostración natural, material, militar, y política del reyno de Guatemala.* He embarked on the project with a number of aims in mind. First, he wanted to take advantage of the deteriorating documents still at his disposal, especially those pertaining to the Spanish conquest of Guatemala. Second, he hoped to fulfill a request of the crown to provide a detailed history of the region. Finally, Fuentes y Guzmán hoped to answer some of the criticisms directed at Bernal DÍAZ DEL CASTILLO, a lieutenant under Cortés whose own *True History of the Conquest of New Spain* drew attacks from many Spaniards and creoles. Fuentes y Guzmán was a great-great-grandson of Díaz and thus may have hoped that writing the *Recordación florida* would clear his family's name.

The *Recordación florida* covers the history of Guatemala from antiquity to the end of the seventeenth century, and includes detailed studies of the topography, climate, population, minerals, and natural resources of the kingdom. In addition to published materials, Fuentes y Guzmán relied on documents stored, and long ignored, in the capital city, as well as on information he gathered as *alcalde* of Totonicapán.

Although by the standards of the day his work was a model of scholarship, Fuentes y Guzmán reflected many of the biases held by his contemporaries. In his work Spaniards were invariably depicted as heroes; Indians, generally as slothful and immoral. Amid sound scholarship Fuentes y Guzmán included fantastic stories and doctored historical fact in order to portray the conquistadores in the most favorable light. Nevertheless, the *Recordación florida* continues to be a standard work for scholars of the pre-Columbian and colonial periods in Guatemala. Its contributions on the religion, geography, history, and natural sciences of the region are still significant today. The writing is first rate, reflecting the highly educated and erudite individual who wrote the first secular history of the kingdom of Guatemala. Fuentes y Guzmán died in Santiago de Guatemala.

— MICHAEL POWELSON

FUJIMORI, ALBERTO KEINYA

Alberto Keinya Fujimori (*b.* 28 July 1938), Latin America's first head of state of Japanese origin (nisei). Born in Lima of Japanese immigrants who arrived in Peru in 1934 and worked as farm laborers, Fujimori was raised in a working-class neighborhood and educated in Peru's public school system. After attending the National Agrarian University (La Molina) and receiving a degree in agricultural engineering, he pursued graduate study in France and in the United States, where he received a master's degree in mathematics from the University of Wisconsin at Milwaukee. Upon his return to Peru he became a professor at La Molina and was elected rector (president) of the university. He also hosted a

Alberto Fujimori after swearing in new cabinet members, 7 April 1992. (AP/Wide World)

successful television talk show on public issues, which made him widely familiar.

In 1989 Fujimori and a group of professionals, small businessmen, and evangelical Protestants organized a political party named Change 1990 (Cambio 90). He ran for the presidency in April 1990 and finished the first electoral round a surprising second, with 24.6 percent of the vote; in the second round, in June, he easily won with 56.5 percent, and was inaugurated for a five-year term on 28 July 1990.

Fujimori presided over major initiatives to bring the economy back from the brink of disaster, to dramatically reduce the threat posed by generalized political violence, and to recentralize government authority in a new constitution. His drastic economic shock program caused inflation to drop from record highs of 7,650 percent in 1990 to about 20 percent by 1994 (138 percent in 1991, 57 percent in 1992, and 40 percent in 1993). Economic liberalization reduced the number of government employees by over 400,000, induced net capital inflows of over $2 billion, and generated economic growth of 7–8 percent by 1993–1994, although over half the population remained below the "critical poverty" line. Fujimori's campaign against political violence was less successful during his first two years in office, but then achieved rapid success after the capture of the principal leaders and master computer file of

Shining Path and the Tupac Amaru Revolutionary Movement (MRTA) by police intelligence, beginning in September 1992—political violence in 1994 was less than 25 percent of the 1992 levels.

In a surprising move supported massively by the populace, Fujimori suspended Congress and the judicial branch in a self-coup (*autogolpe*) on April 5, 1992. Over the next eighteen months, he masterminded new elections for a Constituent Assembly/Congress (January 1993) and referendum approval for a new constitution (53 percent yes, 47 percent no) that recentralized executive authority, set up a smaller and unicameral Congress, established the death penalty for terrorism, and allowed for reelection of a sitting president. In October 1994, Fujimori announced that he would be a candidate again; the next year he succeeded in becoming Peru's first president to be elected for two successive terms.

– DAVID SCOTT PALMER

FUNES, GREGORIO

Gregorio Funes (*b.* 25 May 1749; *d.* 10 January 1829), Argentine priest and statesman. Funes was born in Córdoba, educated at the College of Montserrat, and continued his studies at the University of San Carlos, where he received his doctorate in 1774. He studied in Spain at the University of Alcalá de Henares, where he received a law degree in 1778. After returning to Córdoba, he became dean of the cathedral in 1804 and was elected rector of the University of Córdoba (1808). Having become familiar with and sympathetic to the ideas of the Spanish Enlightenment while in Spain, he declared his support for the May Revolution in 1810.

The *cabildo* of Córdoba elected him representative to the Congress of the United Provinces of the Río de la Plata, where he became an ardent spokesman for the interior provinces, which felt alienated from Buenos Aires. In 1811, he supported a freedom of the press law, and in 1816, following the uprising of José Gervasio Artigas's supporters in Córdoba, Funes became governor of the province. A staunch supporter of public education, he was elected senator in General Juan Gregorio de Las Heras's national congress in 1820. In 1823 he edited the periodical *El Argos de Buenos Aires,* and in October of that year the minister of Colombia named him agent of that country in Buenos Aires, a post linking him to Simón Bolívar and Antonio José de Sucre, through whom he was offered the deanship of the cathedral of La Paz, Bolivia. Funes accepted Bernardino Rivadavia's reforms but protested what he thought were his anticlerical excesses. The best-known of his scholarly works is *Ensayo de la historia civil del Paraguay,*

Buenos Aires y Tucumán (1816–1817). In 1825 he published *Examen crítico de la constitución religiosa para el clero.* He was elected deputy to the Constitutional Assembly in 1826, participating in the deliberations and in the formulation of a new constitution. Funes died in Buenos Aires.

— NICHOLAS P. CUSHNER

FÚRLONG CÁRDIFF, GUILLERMO

Guillermo Fúrlong Cárdiff (*b.* 21 June 1889; *d.* 21 May 1974), Jesuit priest and prolific historian of Argentina and America. Fúrlong was born in the rural region just south of Rosario in Santa Fe Province, Argentina. He was educated in British schools before enrolling in the Jesuit Colegio de la Inmaculada in Rosario. He entered the Jesuit order at fourteen and traveled to Spain two years later. In 1911 Fúrlong moved to the United States and eventually obtained a Ph.D. from Georgetown University. He returned to Argentina and taught Greek and Latin in the Seminario Pontificio de Buenos Aires from 1913 to 1916, and then taught the English language and Argentine history at the Colegio del Salvador.

From 1922 to 1926 Fúrlong traveled to Europe and visited the principal archives of Spain, France, Belgium, England, and Germany. On his return, he continued at the Colegio del Salvador of Buenos Aires, punctuating his teaching with visits to libraries and archives in Montevideo, Chile, and Bolivia. He explored both official and well-known archives as well as little-known and previously closed archives, in the process bringing to light important new sources and manuscripts. Fúrlong's initial studies concentrated on the early missionary efforts of the Jesuits in Argentina. Subsequently, he published works on the cultural achievements of colonial Argentine society in general, covering topics such as architecture, mathematics, printing presses, music, the role of women, philosophy, and others. In 1969 he drew upon his forty years of research and incomparable archival experience to publish the comprehensive *Historia social y cultural del Río de la Plata, 1536–1810.*

— J. DAVID DRESSING

FURTADO, CELSO

Celso Furtado (*b.* 26 July 1920), public administrator, economic development theorist, economic historian, and educator. Born in Pombal, Paraíba, Brazil, Celso Furtado received an M.A. from the University of Brazil (1944) and a Ph.D. from the University of Paris (1948). As director of the Economic Development Division of the United Nations Economic Commission for Latin America (ECLA) from 1949 through 1953 in Santiago, Furtado argued that developing Latin American econ-omies required agrarian reform and import-substituting industrialization. In 1953 he was given the chance to advance these ideas when he became head of a Joint Study Group established by ECLA and the Brazilian National Bank for Economic Development. The group's seven-year plan for Brazil, reported in 1956 and 1957, became the structure of President Juscelino KUBIT-SCHEK's economic development program.

In July 1961, Furtado met with U.S. President John Kennedy and persuaded him that the Northeast could be a showcase for the Alliance for Progress.

After teaching at Cambridge (1958) and returning to Santiago, Furtado joined forces in Brazil with the Working Group for the Development of the Northeast. Furtado prepared a plan calling for colonizing frontier areas, boosting electricity supply, changing the agrarian structure, industrialization, and creating the Development Superintendency for the Northeast (Sudene). Sudene was established in 1959, with Furtado serving until 1964 as its superintendent. In 1961, at Furtado's prompting, President Jânio QUADROS initiated a system of fiscal incentives to encourage Brazilian companies to invest in the Northeast. In July 1961, Furtado met with U.S. President John Kennedy and, by some accounts, persuaded him that the Northeast could be a showcase for the Alliance for Progress. In 1962, the U.S. Agency for International Development pledged $131 million to develop the region.

Late in 1962, President João GOULART named Furtado Brazil's first minister of planning. The Goulart administration's attempts to slow inflation through fiscal reform failed, and in June 1963 Furtado resigned. Ten days after seizing power in 1964, Brazil's generals included Furtado on the list of those deprived of their political rights, causing him to leave the country.

Furtado was a visiting professor at Harvard, Cambridge (1973–1974), and Columbia (1977), a professor at the Sorbonne (1965–1979), and in 1980 became director of research at the College for Advanced Studies in the Social Sciences at the University of Paris. His principal books include *Formação econômica do Brasil* (1959; *The Economic Growth of Brazil,* 1963), *Formação econômica da América Latina* (1969; *Economic Development of Latin America,* 1970), *Teoria e política do desenvolvimento econômico* (1967), and *Um projeto para o Brasil* (1968).

— DAVID DENSLOW

G

GABEIRA, FERNANDO NAGLE

Fernando Nagle Gabeira (*b.* 1941), Brazilian political activist and a leading participant in covert, often violent opposition to military rule established in Brazil in April 1964. As a member of the 8 October Revolutionary Movement (Movimento Revolucionário 8 de outubro—MR-8) Gabeira participated in the September 1969 kidnapping of Charles Elbrick, U.S. ambassador to Brazil. The military response to the kidnapping included severe repression and counterintelligence, which led to the eventual capture, torture, and exile of many revolutionaries, including Gabeira. Following a general amnesty for all political exiles, Gabeira returned to Brazil in 1979 and reemerged politically as a cofounder and 1986 gubernatorial candidate of the Green Party (PV), a leftist political party dedicated to social justice, the expansion of citizenship rights, and ecological management and preservation. His writings include *O que é isso, companheiro?* (1978) and *Goiânia, Rua 57* (1987).

– DARYLE WILLIAMS

GAHONA, GABRIEL VICENTE

Gabriel Vicente Gahona (Picheta; *b.* 1828; *d.* 1899), Mexican engraver. Gahona's early artistic calling took him from his birthplace of Mérida, Yucatán, to Italy for study. In Italy, probably through magazines and newspapers, he came to know the lithographic work of Doré, Daumier, Gavarni, and Guy, whose work mirrored Gahona's inclinations and temperament and provided the inspiration for his next project.

Gahona returned to Mérida in 1847 and began publishing Don Bullebule, *a comical periodical "published for a society of noisy people."*

Gahona returned to Mérida in 1847 and, under the pseudonym of "Picheta," he began publishing *Don Bullebule*, a comical periodical "published for a society of noisy people." Its themes of satire and social criticism were illustrated with eighty-six xylographs. Although it ceased publication later that year, *Don Bullebule* stands out as one of the first examples of journalistic social criticism in Mexico. It is preserved in two volumes, the first consisting of fifteen issues and the second of seventeen, at the National Library of Newspapers and Periodicals in Mexico City.

In 1851, Gahona opened a lithography studio. In 1880 he served as city council president of Mérida, where he died.

– ESTHER ACEVEDO

GAÍNZA, GABINO

Gabino Gaínza (*b.* 26 October 1753; *d.* 1824), acting captain-general of Guatemala (1821–1822). Born in Pamplona, Spain, Gaínza joined the military at the age of sixteen and served in various posts throughout South America for most of his adult life. He commanded the Spanish force that reconquered Chile in 1814.

Gaínza arrived in Central America from Chile in early 1821 amidst the political turmoil of impending independence from Spain to assume the post of army inspector general. That March, the very ill captain-general of Guatemala, Carlos Luis de Urrutia y Montoya (1750–1825), delegated his authority to Gaínza. After independence on 15 September 1821, Gaínza, who had tolerated creole rebellion, remained in office as chief executive. He played an active role in the decision to annex Central America to Agustín de ITURBIDE's Mexican empire, and he often mediated between the polemical political factions of the era. He was relieved of his command on 22 June 1822 by the new captain-general, Vicente FILÍSOLA. Afterward, he went to Mexico to become an aide-de-camp to Emperor Agustín I (Iturbide).

– MICHAEL F. FRY

GAINZA PAZ, ALBERTO

Alberto Gainza Paz (*b.* 16 March 1899; *d.* 26 December 1977), Argentine newspaperman. Gainza Paz gained international attention in 1951 when his newspaper, *La Prensa*, was expropriated by the government of Juan Domingo PERÓN. *La Prensa*, founded in 1869 by the Paz family, had always maintained an independent conservative editorial position dedicated to the expression of "true public opinion." Between 1947 and 1951, Gainza Paz's views clashed with the policies and practices of the Perón government. The paper and its publisher became international beacons of democracy standing firmly against dictatorship. With the paper's expropriation, it was transformed into a trade union tabloid. Gainza Paz fled into exile, where he became a symbol of freedom of the press and received many honors for his battle. With the fall of Perón in 1955, *La Prensa* was returned to the Paz family, resumed publication under Gainza Paz's direction early in 1956, and regained its former stature.

— PAUL GOODWIN

GAITÁN, JORGE ELIÉCER

Jorge Eliécer Gaitán (*b.* 23 January 1898; *d.* 9 April 1948), Colombian political leader. The man who was widely expected to accede to the presidency of Colombia in 1950 was walking out of his law office in downtown Bogotá with a group of friends at 1:05 P.M. on Friday, 9 April 1948, when he was fatally wounded by a lonely drifter. In life Jorge Eliécer Gaitán commanded the attention of his compatriots through fear-inspiring oratory and masterful political performances. In death he incited uprisings in Bogotá and other cities by passionate followers desperate to bring about quick political change.

In part because he died before rising formally to power, Gaitán's legacy is uncertain. Some are convinced that he was a careful man with a profound sense of equanimity who would have brought peace to Colombia. Others describe him as an inveterate rabble-rouser who would have turned La Violencia bloodier still had he lived. The scholar Richard Sharpless sees him as a left-leaning socialist, while others describe him as a rather conservative man of lower-middle-class values.

Gaitán was born in Bogotá to parents who struggled to keep a hold on the middle class. His father sold books and his mother was a well-known schoolteacher. Both were rank-and-file members of the Liberal Party, and Jorge Eliécer grew up hearing about the heroic exploits of "progressive" Liberals against the "reactionaries" of the Conservative Party. Although Gaitán would antagonize the leaders of his party throughout his life, confounding them and others at every turn, he would never seriously depart from the ideals of the Liberal Party. At the time of his death, many leaders of the party, and many Conservatives as well, felt a sense of relief, for they could never quite be certain of his allegiance, or how they might manage to control him and his many followers, whom he had formed into disciplined urban crowds that seemingly did only his bidding.

Although his parents were always seeking to ease his way by drawing on their meager political connections, Gaitán strove mightily to rise in society through his own

merits. In 1924 he obtained his law degree from the Universidad Nacional with an unorthodox thesis titled *Las ideas socialistas en Colombia*. He then went to Italy to study with Enrico Ferri, and while there he became drawn to the closely knit crowds created by the fascists.

On his return to Colombia in 1928 Gaitán toured the nation, making inflammatory speeches with his trademark guttural voice on the massacre of the United Fruit Company banana workers. This massacre was the same one Gabriel GARCÍA MÁRQUEZ wrote about in the novel *One Hundred Years of Solitude*.

Regardless of what his ideology may have been, Gaitán was in a sense Colombia's first modern politician. Upon election to the House of Representatives, he worked assiduously to reach the masses and elicit their support. He developed basic programs and ideas that he believed even his most uneducated followers could and should understand. Beyond the lofty and abstract rhetoric of Colombia's traditional politicians, Gaitán referred incessantly to detailed aspects of the daily, personal lives of his followers. He traveled extensively throughout the country, moving electoral politics outside the narrow confines of the two traditional parties. He produced his own newspaper, and was the first to use the radio to reach his followers. When he appeared to be stymied by the Liberals in the 1930s, he briefly formed the Unión Nacional Izquierdista Revolucionaria (UNIR). When troubles continued to appear on the horizon, he could always fall back on his own Gaitanista movement. He went in and out of public office, serving briefly first as mayor of Bogotá in 1936 and 1937, then as minister of education and of labor in 1940 and 1943, until he ran unsuccessfully for the presidency in 1945 and 1946 as a Liberal against the official Liberal candidate. Upon his death he was poised to take over the Liberal Party and win the presidential election of 1950.

The huge riot following his death, in which Gaitán's followers destroyed much of downtown Bogotá and caused disturbances in many other cities as well, is known in Colombia as *el nueve de abril* (the ninth of April), and elsewhere as the Bogotazo. At the time, the eyes of the world were on Bogotá, for the Ninth Pan-American Conference was being held in the city. U.S. Secretary of State George Marshall was there, and so too was Fidel CASTRO, who had met with Gaitán days earlier and had another meeting scheduled with him for that very afternoon. For a few brief moments Gaitán became well known to the outside world. And during at least the next three decades in Colombia, Jorge Eliécer Gaitán remained a central and enigmatic force in politics, the source of countless passions, untold conversations, and sundry questions about whether his unfulfilled policies would have succeeded, the answers to which few Colombians have found satisfactory.

— HERBERT BRAUN

GAITÁN DURÁN, JORGE

Jorge Gaitán Durán (*b.* 12 February 1924; *d.* 22 June 1962), Colombian poet and essayist. Despite his death at a young age, Gaitán Durán exerted a lasting influence on Colombian letters. A native of Pamplona Kúcuta, he is remembered primarily as a talented poet who published several books of profound metaphysical poetry. They include *Insistencia en la tristeza* (1946), *Presencia del hombre* (1947), and *Si mañana despierto* (1961). Much of this poetry deals with love and death in an existential void. Love emerges in many of the poems as an attempt to forget the flow of time. Poets and critics in Colombia considered him extraordinarily talented, and a mature writer for his age. His most accomplished book was *Si mañana despierto.*

Gaitán Durán is also remembered as the founding director of the prestigious journal *Mito,* which was published from 1955 until his death in an auto accident at Pointe-a-Pitre, Guadeloupe, in 1962. *Mito* was a cosmopolitan periodical that published the best of European, Latin American, and Colombian writing, thus serving as the voice of a generation of intellectuals in Colombia. Latin American writers who later became internationally recognized, such as Octavio PAZ, Julio CORTÁZAR, and Carlos FUENTES, all appeared in *Mito,* as did the Colombian Nobel laureate Gabriel GARCÍA MÁRQUEZ. *Mito*'s most important impact was its modernization of a provincial literary scene in Colombia.

— RAYMOND LESLIE WILLIAMS

GAITO, CONSTANTINO

Constantino Gaito (*b.* 3 August 1878; *d.* 14 December 1945), Argentine composer and teacher. Born in Buenos Aires, Gaito began his musical studies with his father, a violinist. At age eleven he began to compose. He received a scholarship from the Argentine government and went to Italy, where he enrolled at San Pietro a Maiella in Naples, studying under Pietro Platania (composition) and Simonetti (piano). He traveled to Milan to meet Giuseppe Verdi, who helped the young Gaito in his career by conducting a concert of his music at the Milan Conservatory. Initially influenced by the Italians, Gaito returned toward the nationalist style upon his return to Argentina in 1900. He wrote eleven operas, among them *Flor de nieve* (1922), *Ollantay* (1926), and *Sangre de las guitarras* (1932), all of which premiered at the Teatro Colón in Buenos Aires. He also wrote two ballets, an oratorio, chamber music, and vocal and piano works.

Gaito was the most renowned music professor of his time, and taught a generation of eminent Argentine composers. He founded a conservatory and taught harmony at the National Conservatory in Buenos Aires. He was also director of the Teatro Argentino in La Plata. Gaito died in Buenos Aires.

— SUSANA SALGADO

GALÁN, JULIO

Julio Galán (*b.* 5 December 1959), Mexican painter. Galán, a native of Múzquiz, Coahuila, studied architecture in Monterrey from 1978 to 1982. At that time he abandoned architecture and dedicated himself to painting. In 1980, he had begun exhibiting in Monterrey at

---

Influences on Galán's work include Frida Kahlo, Andy Warhol, and David Hockney, as well as Mexican popular painting, comic books, and American kitsch.

---

the Galería Arte Actual Mexicano. Influences on his work include Frida KAHLO, Andy Warhol, and David Hockney, as well as Mexican popular painting, comic books, and both Mexican and American kitsch. Frida Kahlo was for many of the artists of the 1980s a symbol of freedom from the Mexican artistic status quo, giving young artists license to explore themselves and their *mexicanidad.* The traditional *ex-voto* and *retablo* formats of the nineteenth and twentieth centuries are echoed in Galán's work. His images are often autobiographical and surrealistic, frequently contain sexual references, and make use of unnatural perspectives. The artist often includes his own image in his pictures, sometimes juxtaposed with a female character, suggesting sexual ambiguities and alternatives. Since the mid-1980s Galán has lived in Monterrey, with frequent stays in New York and Europe. His work is collected and exhibited internationally.

— CLAYTON C. KIRKING

GALÁN, LUIS CARLOS

Luis Carlos Galán (*b.* 29 September 1943; *d.* 18 August 1989), Colombian politician. Born into a middle-class family in Bucaramanga, Galán was educated in Bogotá. In 1971, at the age of twenty-seven, he was named minister of education in the bipartisan administration of Misael Pastrana Borrero. As editor of the magazine *Nueva Frontera* and later as a senator, Galán inherited from former president Carlos LLERAS RESTREPO the banner of reformist opposition to the "officialist" Liberal regimes of the 1974–1982 period. His attacks on human-rights abuses and the vices of clientelist politics won him much admiration but limited electoral success. His New Liberalism movement peaked at 11 percent in the 1982 presidential election; in late 1986 he returned to the official Liberal fold. In the late 1980s Galán spoke out against the growing power of Colombia's drug cartels; he was considered the likely successor to Virgilio BARCO VARGAS in the presidency. His assassination in August 1989, presumably the work of the Medellín cartel, was the most dramatic moment of the Colombian crisis of 1989–1990.

— RICHARD J. STOLLER

GALEANA, HERMENEGILDO

Hermenegildo Galeana (*b.* 13 April 1762; *d.* 27 June 1814), Mexican insurgent leader. Like other members of his family, Galeana, born in Tecpan, joined José María MORELOS at La Sabana in January 1811. He proved valiant and able from the outset, and Morelos named him his lieutenant in May 1811. Galeana won victories in numerous important battles. He took Taxco in December 1811, and occupied Tenancingo the following January. From February to May 1812, he participated in the defense of Cuautla, where his aid proved to be of great importance. Morelos named him field marshal in September 1812, at Tehuacán. Galeana participated in the capture of Orizaba in October 1812 and in the taking of Oaxaca that November. He played a decisive role in the taking of Acapulco in April 1813, and in the capture of the fortress of San Diego four months later, when he convinced its commander to surrender. In December 1813 Galeana participated in the attack against Valladolid, where the insurgents were defeated. In January 1814, after the defeat at Puruarán, Galeana headed south, pursued by the royalists. After his death in combat at El Salitral, Galeana's head was exhibited in the plaza of Coyuca.

— VIRGINIA GUEDEA

GALEANO, EDUARDO HUGHES

Eduardo Hughes Galeano (*b.* 1940), Uruguayan writer. Born in Montevideo, his writing talents found their first expression in the form of articles on literature and culture published in Montevideo's *Marcha*. Between 1971 and 1984—the duration of Uruguay's military dicta-

torship—he resided primarily in Spain, returning in the last year to assume editorial responsibilities at the newly founded periodical *Brecha*. His early fiction includes *Los días siguientes* (1963) and *Los fantasmas de día del león y otros relatos* (1967). Later fiction, which depicts a personal encounter with the despised military dictatorship, includes *La canción de nosotros* (1975) and *Días y noches de amor y de guerra* (1978). Galeano's most important work is the widely read *Las venas abiertas de América Latina* (1971), with more than thirty editions since its publication. This work, based on the "dependency" theories popular during the 1960s, presents a history of Latin America as an exploited continent from the time of Columbus to the present. Also noteworthy are the three volumes (fifteenth to eighteenth centuries, eighteenth and nineteenth centuries, twentieth century) of *Memoria del fuego* (1982–1986), a chronology of historical and cultural events that provides a unique and comprehensive view of Latin American identity.

Translations of Galeano's works include *Open Veins of Latin America,* translated by Cedric Belfrage (1973); *Days and Nights of Love and War,* translated by Judith Brister (1983); *Memory of Fire,* translated by Cedric Belfrage (1988); and *The Book of Embraces,* translated by Cedric Belfrage and Mark Shafer (1991).

— WILLIAM H. KATRA

GALÍNDEZ, JESÚS DE

Jesús de Galíndez (*b.* 12 October 1915; *d.* 13/15 March 1956), a critic of the Trujillo regime in the Dominican Republic. A native of Amurrio, Spain, Galíndez held a law degree from the University of Madrid. He had fought against Franco in the Spanish Civil War and in 1939 fled to the Dominican Republic, where he taught in the Diplomatic School and worked as a lawyer in the Department of Labor. When some labor disputes he arbitrated were too favorable to the workers, he got in trouble with the dictator Rafael TRUJILLO. He therefore moved to the United States in 1946 and became a political activist among anti-Trujillo exiles. He enrolled in Columbia University's doctoral program and became a leading critic of Trujillo. In addition to writing a number of articles, he produced a dissertation on Trujillo. He was also a part-time instructor. Galíndez defended his dissertation at the end of February 1956 and disappeared after finishing an evening class on 12 March 1956. There is general agreement that Trujillo had him kidnapped and flown, drugged, to the Dominican Republic, where he was killed after being tortured. His degree was awarded in absentia in June. He had left a Spanish draft of his dissertation with a Chilean friend, which was published as *La era de Trujillo: Un estudio casuístico de dictadura hispanoamericano* (1956). In 1973 an English edition appeared, edited by Russell H. Fitzgibbon: *The Era of Trujillo, Dominican Dictator.*

The disappearance of Galíndez became a cause célèbre. The young pilot Gerald Murphy, who had flown the chartered plane from Amityville, Long Island, on the night of 12 March, with a drugged man aboard, had disappeared in the Dominican Republic in the previous December. Murphy was from the state of Oregon; his congressman, Charles Porter, and Senator Wayne Morse put great pressure on the U.S. Justice and State departments to investigate. The Justice Department turned the investigation over to a federal grand jury that indicted a man associated with the plane's rental on Long Island. He was tried and convicted for violation of the Foreign Agents Registration Act. The body of Galíndez was never found. That of Murphy was found months later hanged in a Dominican jail, reported to be a "suicide."

– LARMAN C. WILSON

GALINDO, ALEJANDRO

Alejandro Galindo (*b.* 14 January 1906), Mexican film director. Galindo was born in Monterrey, Nuevo León, and moved at an early age to Mexico City. He studied drama and photography at the University of Southern California and at the Palmer Institute of Photography in Los Angeles, and served as a film director's assistant in Hollywood. In the early 1930s, he returned to Mexico and worked in radio and film as a scriptwriter. He made his directorial debut in 1938 with the feature *Refugiados en Madrid.* Since then, Galindo has directed over eighty feature films and documentaries. Unquestionably one of the most accomplished directors of the "golden age" of Mexican cinema, Galindo focuses in his films upon questions of national identity and the oppressed. Among his most noted films are *Campeón sin corona* (1945), *Una familia de tantas* (1948), *¡Esquina bajan!* (1948), *Doña Perfecta* (1950), *Espaldas mojadas* (1953), and *El juicio de Martín Cortés* (1974).

– DAVID MACIEL

GALINDO, BLAS

Blas Galindo (*b.* 3 February 1910), Mexican composer, teacher, and administrator. A Huichol Indian, Galindo came to Mexico City in 1931 from San Gabriel, Jalisco, and began composition study with Carlos CHÁVEZ at the National Conservatory. He affiliated with three other Chávez students, labeled "Los cuatro," a group committed to the creation and performance of a genuine Mexican music, engendering pieces like his pic-

turesque *Sones de mariachi,* which was premiered at a Mexican exhibit in New York's Museum of Modern Art in 1940. In 1941 he studied composition with Aaron Copland at the Berkshire Music Center and returned to Mexico to complete his conservatory training. He taught at the National Conservatory from 1944, and became its director in 1947, the year in which he was also appointed head of the music department of the National Institute of Fine Arts. His output—encompassing works for piano, small ensembles, orchestra, voice, and chorus—ranges from folkloric to neoclassic to boldly dissonant.

– ROBERT L. PARKER

GALINDO, JUAN

Juan Galindo (christened John; *b.* spring or summer 1802; *d.* 30 January 1840), émigré Anglo-Irish activist in Central America. The eldest child of Philemon Galindo, an Anglo-Spanish actor–fencing master, and Catherine Gough, an Anglo-Irish actress, Galindo arrived in Guatemala in 1827 after service with Lord Thomas Cochrane in South American wars of independence. His varied activities brought him distinction as a scientist, Liberal propagandist, military and administrative officer, and amateur diplomat. Duty and travel provided him opportunity to survey topography, examine archaeological sites, and observe native populations and natural history phenomena that he described in articles published in European scholarly journals.

Galindo decried encroachments on Central American territory and involved himself in several defensive countercolonization projects.

Galindo decried encroachments on Central American territory and involved himself in several defensive countercolonization projects, the major one of which ignited the smoldering Belize boundary and sovereignty issue. His diplomatic mission (1835–1836) to secure British recognition of Central American sovereignty over Belize proved futile. He died while fleeing the site of the battle of El Potrero, near Tegucigalpa, Honduras.

– WILLIAM J. GRIFFITH

GALINDO, SERGIO

Sergio Galindo (*b.* 2 September 1926; *d.* 3 January 1993), Mexican writer. Born in Xalapa, Veracruz, Galindo first published a collection of short stories in 1951,

La máquina vacía (The Empty Machine), and in the following years produced a sizable corpus of narrative, mainly novels. They include *Polvos de arroz* (Rice Powder, 1958), *Justicia de enero* (Justice in January, 1959), *El bordo* (The Precipice, 1960), and *La comparsa* (Carnival, 1964). Galindo received the 1986 Premio Xavier Villaurrutía for his novel *Otilia Rauda* (1986). In his writing, Galindo explores the tensions in middle-class Mexican families and the dynamics of intimate relationships. In contrast to the predominant emphasis on national identity in Mexican literature, such psychological concerns emphasize widely shared human behaviors. In addition to his literary production, from 1957 to 1964 Galindo edited the journal *La Palabra y el Hombre* (Word and Man) and directed the publishing department of the University of Veracruz, where he inaugurated an influential fiction series. Between 1965 and 1976 Galindo served in a variety of positions for the National Institute of Fine Arts and the Secretariat of Public Education. Since 1975 he has been a member of the Mexican Academy of Language.

– DANNY J. ANDERSON

GALLEGO, LAURA

Laura Gallego (*b.* 9 February 1924), Puerto Rican poet and educator. Closely identified with her native Bayamón, a suburb of San Juan, Laura Gallego taught high-school Spanish and was an education professor at the University of Puerto Rico. Her published books of poetry are *Presencia* (Presence, 1952), *Celajes* (Clouds, 1959), and *Que voy de vuelo* (Flying away, 1980). A 1972 anthology of her work includes the prose poems of *Almejas de tu nombre* (Clams of your name, 1954) and the previously unpublished collections of verse *En carne viva* (In the flesh), *La red* (The net), and *La del alba seria* (The woman of serious dawn). Gallego often speaks of words and silence in her verses, and in poetic dialogue addresses nature, God, an unnamed presence, and love lost. In *Celajes* Gallego writes about the natural beauty of Puerto Rico and of its people. Wounding images of arrows, darts, daggers, knives, and spines yield in her later poetry to meditative contemplations of the world, mankind, life, God, and the past.

– ESTELLE IRIZARRY

GALLEGOS, RÓMULO

Rómulo Gallegos (*b.* 21 August 1884; *d.* 7 April 1969), president of Venezuela (1947–1948). Best known as author of *Doña Bárbara* (1929), Gallegos also made major contributions to Venezuela as a secondary teacher and a politician. As a teacher during the 1920s he influenced a significant number of important politicians, including Rómulo BETANCOURT and Raúl LEONI. As a politician he was elected senator from Apure in 1931, but went into voluntary exile until the death of Juan Vicente GÓMEZ, (1935). On his return he served as minister of education under Eleázar López CONTRERAS, won a seat in the House of Deputies in 1947, and in 1941 took part in the organization of the Democratic Action Party (Acción Democrática).

Among his literary accomplishments, in 1909 Gallegos founded a reformist magazine called *La Alborada* (Dawn of Day), which dealt with political as well as literary topics. His novels combined realism with a deep-seated conviction that civilization would overcome barbarism, that goodness would prevail over evil. Gallegos, never polemical or directly critical of the Gómez dictatorship, published his best work while in exile in Spain. *Doña Bárbara* reflected his positivist background, depicting in an optimistic manner the ultimate victory of the educated Santos Luzardo over the backward Doña Bárbara. Two other novels, both written in exile, also portrayed in beautiful language the reality of Venezuelan life. *Cantaclaro* (1931) was a fictional account of the *llaneros* (plainsmen). *Canaíma* (1935) described the life of Marcos Vargas in the jungle of the Orinoco River valley, where the forces of justice fought those of evil. Later novels, such as *Pobre negro* (1937), which treated a slave rebellion of the 1860s, *El forastero* (1942), and *Sobre la misma tierra* (1943), never reached the high quality of Gallegos's earlier work, probably because of his involvement in political activities.

Gallegos was elected president in 1947; after his overthrow in November 1948, he spent time in Cuba and Mexico. He returned to Venezuela in 1958 and received a hero's welcome. He was awarded many prizes for both his political activities in the past and his writing. Two late novels, *La brizna de paja en el viento* (1952) and *La tierra bajo los pies* (1971), dealt with Cuban and Mexican themes, respectively.

– WINTHROP R. WRIGHT

GALLET, LUCIANO

Luciano Gallet (*b.* 28 June 1893; *d.* 29 October 1931), Brazilian composer and musicologist. In 1913 Gallet enrolled in the Instituto Nacional de Música, where he studied piano with Henrique Oswald and harmony with Agnelo França. His first compositions were in a romantic or impressionistic style, but contact with Mário de ANDRADE resulted in serious studies of Brazilian popular and folk music. Some of Gallet's earliest works consisted of harmonizations and arrangements of folk songs. It is significant that Mário de Andrade, the most important figure in the emerging nationalist movement in music, considered Gallet's research and studies sufficiently significant to arrange for the publication of Gallet's *Estudos de folclore.* Although Gallet has never been considered a major composer, except possibly in the area of the art song, his influence on Brazilian musical life has been significant in numerous areas, including concerts, teaching, composition, discography, radio, journalism, and folk music. In each endeavor he gave evidence of keen analytical thought and contributed to the development of the musical life of Brazil.

– DAVID P. APPLEBY

GALLO GOYENECHEA, PEDRO LEÓN

Pedro León Gallo Goyenechea (*b.* 12 February 1830; *d.* 16 December 1877), Chilean politician. Born into a prosperous mining family at Copiapó, Atacama Province, Gallo took a lifelong interest in politics, strongly supporting President Manuel MONTT (to whom he was related by marriage) at the time of his election (1851) but later turning against his authoritarianism. In January 1859 he launched an armed rebellion against Montt (the Constituent Revolution), sinking much of his fortune into the cause. At his base, the mining town of Copiapó, he recruited an army and manufactured weapons, also issuing his own locally minted currency (constituent pesos). Although Gallo staged a brilliant march to capture La Serena (March 1859), his army was defeated at the battle of Cerro Grande, just south of the city, two weeks later in April. Gallo fled into exile, returning to Chile in 1863, when, with his friend Manuel Antonio Matta, he founded the Radical Party, often nicknamed *la tienda de los Matta y los Gallo* (The Matta and Gallo store). In his later years he served as a member of the Chamber of Deputies, and in 1876 he was elected to the Senate.

– SIMON COLLIER

GALTIERI, LEOPOLDO FORTUNATO

Leopoldo Fortunato Galtieri (*b.* 15 July 1926), military leader and president of Argentina (1981–1982). Born in Caseros, province of Buenos Aires, he graduated in 1945 from the Military Academy (Colegio Militar), where he studied military engineering. In 1949 he attended the U.S. Basic Engineering Course in the Panama Canal Zone, and in 1958 he became a professor at the Senior War College. The following year Galtieri was in charge of the advanced engineering course at the Engineering School, and in 1960 he took an advanced engineering course in the United States.

On 28 December 1979 Galtieri became the commander in chief of the Argentine Army. When General Roberto VIOLA fell ill, Galtieri had the military junta declare him president of the republic on 29 December 1981. Galtieri also retained the post of commander in chief of the army.

In 1982 Galtieri approved the plan to recapture the Falkland (Malvinas) Islands from Great Britain, last occupied by the Argentines in the early 1830s. The war, which raged from early April to mid-June 1982, was disastrous for Argentina, and Galtieri was forced to resign on 17 June.

In 1985, General Galtieri was tried for human-rights violations during the Dirty War and for incompetence and maladministration during the Falklands/Malvinas War. He was acquitted on the first issue but convicted on the second. Galtieri was sentenced to twelve years imprisonment. In December 1990 he was released under a general amnesty.

– ROBERT SCHEINA

GALVÁN, MANUEL DE JESÚS

Manuel de Jesús Galván (*b.* 1834; *d.* 1910), Dominican writer, politician, and jurist. Galván was considered the Dominican Republic's greatest writer for his book *Enriquillo,* which dealt with the confrontation between the indigenous Tainos and Spanish colonizers. Galván was also a member of the Dominican Congress and a justice of the Supreme Court. Considered a masterwork of Spanish literature, *Enriquillo* is a fictionalized account of the struggle of the last Taino cacique, Enrique, who fled his Spanish landlord into the Bahoruco Mountains and organized with his followers a thirteen-year resistance (1520–1533) to Spanish rule. While Enrique and his followers never surrendered, and while a peace agreement that moved the surviving Tainos to reservations was signed, by the 1550s the Taino population had been virtually wiped out. Galván's novel was not published until 1882 and contains considerable embellishment, including the oft-repeated nineteenth-century style of depicting the indigenous Americans as "noble savages." Despite its nostalgia for the vanquished, Galván's novel is considered one of the greatest novels produced by a Dominican.

– MICHAEL POWELSON

GALVÁN RIVERA, MARIANO

Mariano Galván Rivera (*b.* 12 September 1791; *d.* 1876), Mexican publisher. After becoming established in Mexico City as a bookseller, Galván, a native of Tepotzotlán, opened a print shop, with Mariano Arévalo as manager, in 1826. That year he began publishing his *Calendario manual,* which continues to appear under the name *Calendario del más antiguo Galván.* From 1827 to 1830 he published *El observador de la República Mexicana,* and from 1833 to 1834, *El indicador de la Federación Mexicana,* edited by José María Luis MORA. From 1838 to 1843 he published the *Calendario de las señoritas mexicanas.* Other works that he published include *Sagrada Biblia* in twenty-five volumes; *El periquillo sarmiento; Colección eclesiástica mexicana; Don Quijote; Dicionario razonado de legislación;* Count de Segur's *Historia universal; Nueva colección de leyes y decretos mexicanos;* and *Concilio III provincial mexicano.* His bookstore became a gathering place for literary and political figures. In 1862 Galván was a member of the Assembly of Notables who decided to establish a monarchy in Mexico. Although imprisoned after Maximilian's fall, he was soon freed. He died in Mexico City.

– VIRGINIA GUEDEA

GALVARINO

Galvarino (*d.* December 1557), Araucanian warrior and hero. Nothing is known about Galvarino's life before the events in which he figured during the Spanish invasion of Chile. At the battle of Lagunillas (or Bío-bío) during Governor García HURTADO DE MENDOZA's (1535–1609) advance into Araucanian territory in 1557, he was captured and had both his hands cut off. The fiery speeches he delivered following his mutilation rallied his people to resist the Spaniards. Soon afterward, at the battle of Millarapue (November 1557), Galvarino was again captured and later hanged with other Araucanian prisoners.

The events of Galvarino's demise were witnessed by the poet-soldier Alonso de ERCILLA Y ZÚÑIGA (1533–1594), who recounted them in memorable passages in his epic *La Araucana.* This more than anything else gave Galvarino the legendary status he enjoys in the pantheon of Araucanian heroism. While some of the speeches attributed to Galvarino in this poem must have been invented by Ercilla, the events themselves are confirmed by independent sources.

– SIMON COLLIER

GÁLVEZ, BERNARDO DE

Bernardo De Gálvez (*b.* 25 July 1746; *d.* 30 November 1786), Spanish military officer, governor of Louisiana (1777–1783), and viceroy of New Spain (1785–1786), Gálvez was born at Macharavialla, near Málaga, to a family that held many important posts under the Spanish Bourbons. He accompanied his uncle, José de GÁL-VEZ, to New Spain, where he gained valuable experience against the Apaches on the northern frontier in 1769. After a tour of training with the French Cantabrian Regiment, he served under General Alejandro O'REILLY in a campaign against Algeria (1774), after which King Charles III named him commander of the Louisiana Regiment in 1776.

Upon arriving in New Orleans, however, he received orders to relieve Luis de Unzaga as governor of Louisiana, which he did on 1 January 1777. His administration in Louisiana coincided with the American Revolution, in which he played a prominent role. He increased the population and military strength of the colony and promoted its economic growth in accordance with the instructions of his uncle José, who now served as president of the Council of the Indies. In collaboration with Oliver Pollock, he clandestinely channeled arms to American revolutionaries operating in the Mississippi Valley, significantly aiding George Rogers Clark. Once Spain declared war on England, he launched a successful military campaign, with major victories at Baton Rouge (21 September 1779), Mobile (March 1780), and Pensacola (8–10 May 1781). His forces were also instrumental in breaking British military power in the northern Mississippi Valley. Gálvez's victories enabled Spain to recover Florida under the Treaty of Paris (1783) and contributed significantly to the achievement of American independence. Promoted to captain-general, Gálvez governed Cuba from 4 February until 20 April 1785, after which he succeded his father, Matías de GÁLVEZ, as viceroy of New Spain. He died in Mexico City.

– RALPH LEE WOODWARD, JR.

GÁLVEZ, JOSÉ DE

José de Gálvez (*b.* 2 January 1720; *d.* 17 June 1787), a leading Spanish bureaucrat and statesman instrumental in the reform of eighteenth-century colonial administration. Born a poor hidalgo in Macharaviaya, an Andalusian hill village, Gálvez earned a law degree at the University of Salamanca. Later, he conducted a successful practice in Madrid, in which he handled many cases involving parties in the Americas. He attracted the attention of Abbé Béliardi, a French agent, and through him, gained the patronage of the marqués de Esquilache and the marqués de Grimaldi, enlightened ministers of King Charles III of Spain. Their favor secured him the risky opportunity to conduct a *visita,* that is, a thorough inspection and overhaul of the administration of Mexico, where he arrived in July 1765.

Gálvez carried out a speedy and ruthless reorganization of tax collection and accounting procedures. He jailed corrupt officials, changed the tax structure, instituted a highly profitable tobacco monopoly, and shifted the control of trade with Spain from Mexican to Spanish merchants. In so doing, he forced capital into mining, which he aided with tax reductions, cheap mercury, and technical assistance. In this way, he decisively redirected the Mexican economy.

The *visitador* proposed the introduction of the intendancy system (provincial governors) and the establishment of the Provincias Internas, which created a separate government for the northern region of the country. In addition, Gálvez dealt with the expulsion of the Jesuits, Indian revolts in Sonora, raids in Chihuahua, and orders to colonize Alta California all at the same time. He brutally suppressed the uprisings occasioned by the ban, reorganized government in the north, and got the colonization effort under way by 1769.

Then, the strain of work, the responsibility, and the exhausting and indecisive struggle with the Sonoran Indians broke Gálvez's health, and in late 1769 he suffered a physical and mental collapse. He recovered and returned to Spain in 1771, but the end of the *visita* was clouded.

In Spain Gálvez assumed his place on the Council of the Indies, to which he was appointed in 1767. He was gradually given more important assignments, and when Julián de Arriaga y Rivera died, Charles III made Gálvez minister of the Indies (February 1776).

As minister, Gálvez tried to institute the reforms he had instituted in Mexico throughout the whole Empire. *Visitadores* cast in Gálvez's mold were sent to Peru, New Granada, Venezuela, and Ecuador to increase revenue, establish intendancies, and invigorate government. The situation in Buenos Aires was complicated by the opportunity, offered by Great Britain's preoccupation with the American Revolution, to settle long-pending disputes with the Portuguese regarding boundaries and smuggling. Eventually Spain declared war and sent a military expedition to the area. The result was the establishment of a viceroyalty of Buenos Aires, organized according to Gálvez's program.

When Spain followed France into an alliance with the Americans against Britain in 1779, Gálvez's reforms were again shouldered aside. Moreover, the need for money and the errors and misfortunes of two *visitadores* produced the TÚPAC AMARU rebellion (1780–1781) in Peru and the Comunero Revolt (1781) in New Granada. Gálvez reacted to them with the same fierce repression he had unleashed in Mexico against those who questioned royal authority.

Nevertheless, when Gálvez became marqués de Sonora in 1785, he could claim an important role in winning back Florida and ejecting the British from the Mosquito Coast and Darién. Unfortunately, just as Gálvez sought to bring his full authority to bear on the completion of the internal reforms, he died.

The consequent reorganization of the ministry redirected the course of policy, but Sonora's reforms had been too extensive to be abandoned totally. Gálvez was a hard-working and hard-edged administrator, efficient but not noted for accommodation or suppleness. His legacy of a more rational administration and higher revenues was purchased with the political alienation of many Americans and not a few Spaniards, whom he pushed from their traditional places and powers.

— GEORGE M. ADDY

GÁLVEZ, JUAN MANUEL

Juan Manuel Gálvez (*b.* 1887; *d.* 19 August 1972), president of Honduras, 1949–1954. Gálvez succeeded the long-time dictator, Tiburcio CARÍAS ANDINO, whom he had served as minister of defense. As Carías's hand-picked successor, Gálvez perpetuated National Party dominance and many of his predecessor's policies. He launched a more vigorous program of public works, infrastructure development, economic diversification, and tax reform while also easing restrictions on civil liberties.

The United Fruit Company workers' strike in 1954 precipitated a political crisis at the end of Gálvez's administration. Gálvez, who had been a United Fruit attorney for many years, showed little sympathy for the strikers and was clearly annoyed by the encouragement that Guatemala's pro-labor government of Jacobo ARBENZ gave the strikers. He actively collaborated with Guatemalan exiles and the U.S. Central Intelligence Agency in the overthrow of the Arbenz government in June 1954. In the November 1954 elections, Carías sought to return to office, but Liberal candidate Ramón VILLEDA MORALES received a plurality of the votes, with no one receiving a majority. Before the Congress could decide the election, Gálvez's vice president, Julio LOZANO DÍAZ, seized power, ending Gálvez's administration. Gálvez, now in ill health, did not contest Lozano's seizure of dictatorial power, and Lozano later appointed Gálvez president of the Supreme Court.

— RALPH LEE WOODWARD, JR.

GÁLVEZ, MANUEL

Manuel Gálvez (*b.* 18 July 1882; *d.* 14 November 1961), Argentine novelist and essayist. Gálvez was born in the provincial capital of Paraná. When he was three years old, his family moved to Santa Fe, where he studied at the Jesuit school La Inmaculada. In 1897, he completed his secondary studies in Buenos Aires at the

Colegio del Salvador. He graduated from the University of Buenos Aires with a law degree in 1904, but never practiced his profession. His dissertation on the theme of white slavery, reveals an early interest in social problems that never abated in his long career as a novelist and essayist.

One of Argentina's foremost novelists from 1915 until 1950, Gálvez played an important role in his country's cultural life. He was conservative in his political ideology, although as a young man he espoused a form of anarchism and defended Tolstoy's Christian socialism. In Gálvez's concept of nationalism, certain ideas were dominant: the central role of the church in maintaining the spirit and traditions of Argentina; an adherence to law and order above individual freedom; a distrust of Anglo-Saxon civilizations; and doubts about the advisability of having a totally democratic government. Nowhere was this nationalism more evident than in Gálvez's biography of the dictator Juan Manuel de ROSAS (1829–1852), whom Gálvez defended on the ground that he unified the country and prevented it from succumbing to the economic and political pressures of the French and English. In *El solar de la raza* (The Birthplace of Our Race, 1913), Gálvez underscored the cultural and spiritual affinity between Argentina and Spain. In works like *La sombra del convento* (The Shadow of the Convent, 1917), Gálvez preached a return to the traditional moral and religious values that could still be found in the provinces and opposed the utilitarian values he associated with life in Buenos Aires.

For twenty-five years, Gálvez served as national inspector of secondary and normal schools, an experience he drew on to write *La maestra normal* (The Normal School Teacher, 1914), which many critics interpreted as an attack on the normal schools and secular education. In novels of social protest such as *Nacha regules* (1919), Gálvez became a social reformer, defending the poor and downtrodden against society's indifference to human suffering.

During his career, Gálvez did much to promote Argentine letters and to make the country's writers known throughout Hispanic America. In 1917, he established the Cooperative Publishers of Buenos Aires and in 1919 founded Pax Publishers to introduce European works in translation to Argentine readers.

– MYRON I. LICHTBLAU

GÁLVEZ, MARIANO

Mariano Gálvez (*b.* 26 May 1794; *d.* 26 May 1862), chief of state of Guatemala (1831–1838). Gálvez was adopted as a foundling by an influential family in Gua-

temala City and eventually received a royal dispensation from the legal disadvantages of his suspicious birth. He was educated in the law, and his enthusiasm for the Enlightenment ideas of his day led him to a career in politics. He was much involved in the negotiations and turmoil that preceded independence from Spain. Indeed, he voted in favor of independence, but promoted, in fear of instability, political union with the new Mexican empire. After the fall of Agustín de ITURBIDE, emperor of Mexico, in 1823 and the separation of Central America from Mexico that same year, Gálvez held public offices at both the state and federal level, and in 1831, after a devastating civil war that destroyed conservative power, he was elected chief of state of Guatemala.

Gálvez fervently sought to set an example in Guatemala that would eventually turn all of Central America into a modern, progressive republic.

With the leading conservatives in exile and with the power to squash opposition, Gálvez fervently sought to set an example in Guatemala that would eventually turn all of Central America into a modern, progressive republic through enlightened social and economic legislation. His attack on the clergy reduced drastically the wealth and power of the church. He proclaimed religious toleration and destroyed the hegemony of the clergy in education by establishing a system of free, public, lay instruction. He began a series of projects for economic development designed to bring new life to sparsely populated and neglected areas of the country, often using foreign colonization to achieve his goals. He attempted to impose a new and alien system of common law, the Livingston Codes, on a society accustomed to the civil law of Spain. Most important, he sought to promote economic competitiveness and prosperity by reducing the communal lands of municipalities to private property. During his term of office, Gálvez instituted the most radical liberal program of reform of nineteenth-century Guatemala.

Gálvez's reforms alienated, offended, and often threatened the livelihood of large sectors of the population, especially the impoverished peasantry. Liberal trade policy damaged native industry. A head tax of two pesos per capita excessively burdened peasants who found themselves landless after the agrarian reforms.

The liberal demand for forced labor on public works projects further increased resentment. Peasants also found burdensome the travel that jury duty required. Eventually, profound discontent became outright rebellion. Peasants formed an unlikely alliance with disgruntled conservatives and clergymen that relied on the leadership of a brilliant guerrilla fighter, José Rafael CAR-RERA. Gálvez tried desperately to amend the errors of his reform program, but his stopgap measures were too late to impede a revolutionary movement that had gained tremendous momentum. When he tried unsuccessfully to stop the growth of a cholera epidemic in 1837 by implementing the most modern controls, his measures were misinterpreted by peasants as deliberate poisonings. For these reasons, Gálvez's liberal program was destined to die. He was overthrown in February 1838 and later forced into exile in Mexico.

– MICHAEL F. FRY

GÁLVEZ, MATÍAS DE

Matías de Gálvez (*b*. 2 July 1717; *d*. 3 November 1784), captain-general of Guatemala and forty-eighth viceroy of New Spain. He was born in Macharaviaya, Málaga, Spain, the eldest of at least five sons. His younger brother José de Gálvez, minister general of the Indies from 1776 to 1787, made possible Matías's success. Matías's son Bernardo Gálvez (1746–1786) succeeded his father as viceroy.

After a military career characterized by devotion to duty, Gálvez was ordered to Central America as inspector general of the Spanish forces. He arrived at San Fernando de Omoa, Honduras, in July 1778. Gálvez's immediate duty was to prepare the defense of Central America against possible British attack. On 15 January 1779, Gálvez was appointed to replace Martín de Mayorga, who was named viceroy of New Spain, as captain-general and governor of Guatemala. His principal responsibilities were to speed implementation of the Bourbon reforms, to drive the British from the Caribbean coast of Central America, and to finish the construction of a new capital city.

Gálvez reformed the militia and led successful attacks against the British in Honduras in 1779 and in Nicaragua in 1781. He also negotiated successful treaties with the Miskito Indians on the coast. His successes earned him the accolades of the Ayuntamiento of Guatemala as a "true father" of the region and a promotion to field marshal.

As a Bourbon reformer Gálvez attempted to encourage the economy of the region by offering economic incentives and by weakening the economic domination by a clique of merchants in Guatemala City. He established a *banco de rescate* in Tegucigalpa, and granted *repartimientos* of Indians to increase mining production in Honduras. To stimulate indigo production, Gálvez created a *monte pío* (fund for widows and orphans) for the growers so they would not have to rely on the credit extended by Guatemalan merchants. Also to weaken the Guatemalan oligopoly over the prices paid at the annual indigo fair, Gálvez instituted a pricing board and moved the fair. To assure an adequate supply of cattle and full collection of taxes, he moved the annual cattle fair deeper into El Salvador. During his tenure, tax collections increased over 20 percent, but control of the local economy was never wrested from Guatemala City. Despite short-term success, within two decades most of the changes wrought by Gálvez, both military and administrative, were completely undone.

As a result of his accomplishments in Central America and his family connections, Gálvez was named interim viceroy of New Spain on 14 August 1782 and assumed that post in April 1783. Four months later he earned a full viceregal appointment. His term in Mexico was marked by the reconstruction of Chapultepec Palace, improvement of the drainage system of Mexico City through the construction of dikes and drainage canals, installation of a lighting system, establishment of a branch of the Banco de San Carlos, and tighter administration of the *real hacienda*. During his tenure there was a tripling of royal receipts, due more to external factors than to administrative changes by Gálvez. He died in Mexico City.

– WILBUR E. MENERAY

GAMA, JOSÉ BASILIO DA

José Basilio da Gama (*b*. 1741; *d*. 31 July 1795), Brazilian poet. Born in Minas Gerais, Gama studied in Rio de Janeiro under the Jesuits and then in Rome after 1759, when the order was banished from Portuguese possessions. Later, while living in Portugal, he was arrested as a Jesuit sympathizer but escaped exile by gaining favor with the marquês of POMBAL, the realm's chief minister. His most famous work, *O Uruguai*, was published in Lisbon in 1769.

A long poem in ten blank-verse cantos, *O Uruguai* is constructed around episodes from the War of the Seven Reductions (1752–1756), which the Portuguese and Spanish waged jointly against the Jesuits and their TUPI-GUARANÍ Indian mission congregations in Uruguay. Sometimes regarded as an epic, it has also been considered a lyrical narrative and a poetic drama. The original version had been openly pro-Jesuit, but the published version criticizes the Jesuits scathingly, in consonance with Pombal's policies.

O Uruguai is considered the most important literary work of Brazil's colonial period. It presents sympathetically the inevitable demise of indigenous culture before the advance of white men. Its Indian heroes contributed to its popularity among the romantics, who also admired the freedom of its blank verse and who viewed its pictures of Indian life and the Brazilian landscape as a precursor of the autonomous national literature they sought to create.

– NORWOOD ANDREWS, JR.

GAMA, LUÍS

Luís Gama (*b.* 21 June 1830; *d.* 24 August 1882), Brazilian poet, lawyer, and abolitionist. The son of a profligate aristocrat and a rebellious free African woman, Gama was born free in Bahia. At the age of ten he was sold into slavery by his father and shipped to São Paulo. In 1847, while serving as a household slave, Gama was befriended by a student and taught to read and write. Soon afterward, having become aware of the illegality of his enslavement, Gama fled his master's house. He served in the militia for six years and later established himself as a journalist, poet, and self-educated lawyer. In 1859, literate for scarcely a dozen years, he published his first and most successful book of verse, *Primeiras trovas burlescas de Getulino*. Ten years later, by then a noted author, he coedited with Rui Barbosa, Joaquim Nabuco, and others the journal *Radical Paulistano*, which supported the reformist program of parliamentary liberals led by José Tomás Nabuco de Araújo. As a lawyer, Gama specialized in defending persons kept illegally in slavery, especially Africans held in violation of the anti-slave-trade law of 1831. According to his own count, he thereby freed more than five hundred persons. At the time of his death, Gama was the undisputed leader of the antislavery movement in the province of São Paulo.

– ROBERT EDGAR CONRAD

GAMA, VASCO DA

Vasco da Gama (*b.* 1460s; *d.* 24 or 25 December 1524), Portuguese explorer, discoverer of the maritime route to India. Son of a member of the household of Prince Fernando, da Gama had been a *fidalgo* in the royal household of King JOÃO II and, at the time of his first voyage, a knight and commander in the Order of Santiago. About 1507 he transferred to the Order of Christ, and in 1519 he became first count of Vidigueira.

King Manuel I named da Gama leader of the armada that sailed from the Tagus River on 8 July 1497 in search of a maritime route to India. Two of the four ships, the *São Gabriel* and the *São Rafael,* were commanded, respectively, by Vasco and his brother, Paulo. After more than ninety days at sea—the longest known voyage out of sight of land by a European to date—da Gama dropped anchor in the Bay of Santa Helena, 100 miles north of the Cape of Good Hope. On 22 November 1497, da Gama rounded the cape and on Christmas Day reached what is now known as Natal. On 2 March 1498, he reached the island of Mozambique. After stopping at Mombasa and Malindi, da Gama—with the help of a Muslim pilot from Gujarat—departed across the Indian Ocean on 24 April, and on 20 May he anchored several miles north of Calicut.

Da Gama remained in India for over three months. Early in his stay, he met with Calicut's Hindu leader, whom the Portuguese called the samorim. But relations with him deteriorated, and da Gama sailed northward to Angediva Island, along India's west coast, south of Goa. Beginning the return voyage on 5 October, da Gama rounded the Cape of Good Hope on 20 March 1499. He arrived in Lisbon in very late August or during the first three weeks in September, though one of his ships, the *Berrio,* already had arrived on 10 July. Honored for his efforts, da Gama was made admiral of India, became a member of the king's council, and was given financial rewards.

Made leader of the fourth Portuguese expedition to India, da Gama set sail from Lisbon in February 1502. After exacting reprisals in Calicut from the natives for the massacre of the Portuguese stationed there, da Gama left India on 28 December 1502 and reached Lisbon on 1 September 1503.

In 1524 da Gama returned to India for a third and final time at the behest of King João III. Sent to clean up corruption and restore authority in Portuguese Asia, he was given the post of viceroy of India, the second to receive that title. Sailing from Lisbon on 9 April 1524, da Gama reached Chaul on 5 September. His administration was an energetic one, but it was also short, as he died in Cochin less than four months after his arrival.

– FRANCIS A. DUTRA

GAMARRA, AGUSTÍN

Agustín Gamarra (*b.* 1785; *d.* 1841), quintessential military caudillo of nineteenth-century Peru, born in Cuzco, and twice president of Peru (1829–1833, 1839–1841) during an unstable period in which there were more than thirty presidents in twenty years (1826–1846). Like Andrés de SANTA CRUZ and Ramón CASTILLA, Gamarra was initially trained by the Spanish colonial army. Under creole Generals José Manuel Goyeneche and Pío Tristán, Gamarra fought against independence movements in the regions of Upper and Southern Peru between 1809 and 1820. In 1820, however, the entire royalist Numancia battalion in which Gamarra served passed over to General José de SAN MARTÍN's independence forces, at the time active on the Peruvian coast. Consequently, Gamarra fought in the independence army in the battles of Junín and Ayacucho that finally removed Spanish colonial presence in Peru.

In his first presidency, Gamarra foiled at least

seventeen rebellions with the aid of his belligerent

wife Francisca Zubiaga de Gamarra.

Soon after independence Gamarra became prefect of Cuzco and military commander of the southern Peruvian armies. Gamarra was a zealous creole-patriot, politically conservative and protectionist in trading matters. He achieved renown in early "national" military campaigns against Colombian influence in Bolivia (1828) and in the dispute over the port of Guayaquil with Colombia (1829). In the middle of the latter, unsuccessful campaign in Ecuador, Gamarra forcibly exiled President José de la MAR to become president of Peru. In his first presidency, Gamarra foiled at least seventeen rebellions with the aid of his belligerent wife Francisca Zubiaga de Gamarra, but was finally defeated in a civil war by General Luis José Orbegoso in 1833.

Gamarra continued to conspire but did not seize power until 1839, after he led the opposition against General Santa Cruz's Peru-Bolivia Confederation (1836–1839). The Chilean army, employing Peruvian dissenters such as Gamarra himself, defeated Santa Cruz in the battle of Yungay (1839). Finally, Gamarra's attempt to incorporate Bolivia into Peru was soundly defeated in the battle of Ingaví (1841), in which Gamarra lost his life.

— ALFONSO W. QUIROZ

GAMARRA, FRANCISCA ZUBIAGA BERNALES DE (LA MARISCALA)

Francisca Zubiaga Bernales de (La Mariscala) Gamarra (*b.* 1803; *d.* 1835), Peruvian first lady and woman-at-arms. Gamarra was born in Cuzco, the daughter of a Basque merchant and a Cuzqueña. She abandoned a monastic career because of ill health and married the prefect of Cuzco, General Agustín GAMARRA, in 1825. While the former commander of Peruvian forces under Simón BOLÍVAR rose to the presidency of the country, the flamboyant Doña Francisca was making a reputa-

tion in her own right. Known as La Mariscala (the lady marshal) for her unusual martial skills, particularly precision shooting, use of the sword, and superb equestrianship, she was also known to lead troops into battle in the country's interminable civil wars. Her political acumen and daring were equally renowned, earning her the sobriquet "La Presidenta" while at her husband's side in the National Palace. Her picturesque career and life ended prematurely in exile and impoverishment in Valparaíso, where she died of tuberculosis at the age of thirty-two.

— PETER F. KLARÉN

GAMARRA, JOSÉ

José Gamarra (*b.* 12 February 1934). Uruguayan artist. Gamarra was born in Tacuarembó, Uruguay, and studied at the School of Fine Arts in Montevideo as well as with Vicente Martin (1952–1959). He studied engraving with John Friedlaender and Iberé Camargo in Rio de Janeiro (1959). In 1963 he was selected for the Biennial of Young Artists in Paris, after which he settled in Arcueil, France.

Gamarra's early works were abstractions inspired by pre-Conquest art motifs and Uruguayan vernacular ironwork. After moving to Paris, he began to paint tropical landscapes modeled after nineteenth-century European and North American visions of Central and South America as a primeval and exotic territory. Historical, mythological, and contemporary figures (Indians, conquistadores, guerrillas, nuns, and pre-Conquest idols) coexist in Gamarra's painted rain forests. War vehicles and artifacts disturb his paradisiacal settings. Objects and human figures have been interpreted as suggesting narratives and critical comments about Latin American history, such as the Spanish conquest or North American interventions (*Five Centuries Later,* 1986).

— MARTA GARSD

GAMBARO, GRISELDA

Griselda Gambaro (*b.* 28 July 1928); Argentine playwright, short-story writer, and novelist. In *El campo* (1967; *The Camp,* 1971), *El desatino* (1965; *The Blunder*), *Los siameses* (1967; *The Siamese Twins,* 1967), and other works, Gambaro uses symbolic constructions to depict the real nature of human beings and of their relationships, to open "an imaginary space that, in turn, discovers, invents or anticipates new dimensions of reality." For her, valid literature must have an anticipatory quality and should question what constitutes reality and reveal what reality could be. Gambaro, in all her works,

413

is preoccupied with the absurdity of the human condition, the schizophrenic nature of man, and the exercise of power by men and women alike. Her theater and, to some degree, her novels are absurdist constructions with elements of the theater of cruelty and black humor. Gambaro herself has related it to the *grotesco criollo,* a parodic genre rooted in the distortion of the traditional bourgeois drama: that of the love triangle. Her characters are isolated, defeated, and devastated in a brutal, hostile world. Her mostly nonverbal language and violent physical images underline a dramatic vision of life and bestow a nightmarish and Kafkaesque quality to her plays.

Although Gambaro's writings deal with universal problems, not limited to a specific place or time, they could be related to the Argentine reality of the recent past. She won the Drama Critics' Prize for best play of 1990 with *Penas sin importancia* (Unimportant Sorrows).

— ANGELA B. DELLEPIANE

GAMBOA IGLESIAS, FEDERICO

Federico Gamboa Iglesias (*b.* 22 December 1864; *d.* 15 August 1930), Mexican public figure and intellectual, a major essayist for Mexican and international newspapers. A multifaceted intellectual whose contributions ranged from fiction to plays, he documented Mexican intellectual life in his major five-volume memoir *Mi diario.* He also supported intellectual activities by providing important leadership to the prestigious Mexican Academy of Language from 1923 to 1939.

Born in the capital, the son of General Manuel Gamboa, the governor of Jalisco, and Lugarda Iglesias, the sister of the leading Liberal politician José María Iglesias, he studied in New York City and then attended the National School of Law. After joining the Foreign Service in 1888, he served in numerous posts in Latin America and the United States. He was a federal deputy from Chihuahua before representing Mexico as minister to the Netherlands (1911–1912). He became undersecretary of foreign relations (1908–1910) and rose to secretary under Victoriano HUERTA in 1913. Discredited as a public official for his service under Huerta, Gamboa was in exile from 1914 to 1919.

— RODERIC AI CAMP

GAMIO MARTÍNEZ, MANUEL

Manuel Gamio Martínez (*b.* 2 March 1883; *d.* 16 July 1960), a Mexican anthropologist considered the initiator of modern *indigenismo* studies in Mexico and an activist in Latin American and European societies pro-

moting the examination and preservation of indigenous cultures.

The son of Gabriel Gamio and Marina Martínez, wealthy landowners in the Dominican Republic and Mexico, Gamio was educated in private schools and the National Preparatory School before studying archaeology under Nicolás León and Jesús Galindo y Villa in the National Museum in Mexico City. A student of Franz Boas at Columbia University, he obtained his M.A. in 1911 and returned for a Ph.D. in anthropology in 1921.

Returning to Mexico, Gamio undertook the organization of and became director for the department of anthropology in the secretariat of agriculture (1917–1920). From 1917 to 1920 he also led the first comprehensive exploration of the Teotihuacán ruins in the center of Mexico City's commercial district, where he discovered the *templo mayor.* Before 1925 he led other explorations and restorations of archaeological sites, including ones in Yucatán and Guatemala. He was a leader of educational and government institutions devoted to archaeological research and served briefly as undersecretary of public education in 1925. Thereafter he gave up archaeology to devote himself to protecting contemporary Indian cultures.

While concentrating on his research and academic pursuits, Gamio also held positions in the secretariat of agriculture and at the Institute for Social Research of the National University during the 1930s. In 1942 he became director of the Inter-American Indigenous Institute, a position he held until his death. Francisco Goitia, a noted Mexican painter, was a close collaborator. Gamio left a prolific body of published works.

— RODERIC AI CAMP

GÁNDARA ENRÍQUEZ, MARCOS

Marcos Gándara Enríquez (*b.* 1915), ideological leader of the military junta that assumed power in Ecuador in 1963. Born in Latacunga, Colonel (later General) Gándara, former director of the war academy and functional representative of the armed forces in the Senate, justified the military's assumption of power not simply as the product of contemporary conditions, including the military's perception of a rising threat of Communist subversion, but as a product of a long series of mistaken policies. The military assumed the responsibility for establishing new socioeconomic structures that would permit the evolution of democratic structures dedicated to serving the interests of all citizens.

During its first year in office, the junta suppressed political dissent, announced a series of development projects financed by U.S. loans, adopted a ten-year development plan proposed by the National Planning Board, approved an income tax, and issued an agrarian reform program. Although public opinion toward the junta was generally favorable at the end of its first year in office, the junta refused to develop political alliances or mobilize popular sectors to support its moderate reform program. The junta's rejection of partisan politics was rooted in its image of the military as the only truly national institution whose nonpartisan decisions would naturally generate public support.

Mounting economic problems during the second year of military rule quickly translated into growing public opposition expressed as demonstrations, strikes, and antigovernment media campaigns. By early 1966 the government faced daily challenges to its authority, frequently from students. Civilian politicians forged multiparty alliances that pressed for a return to constitutional government. The government's vacillating response to challenges, particularly from coastal economic and political elites, eroded support for continued military rule within the higher officer corps. A national strike and violent confrontations between students and the military at the Central University in Quito resulted in the fall of the government on 29 March 1966. Gándara went to Bolivia but later returned to Ecuador.

– LINDA ALEXANDER RODRÍGUEZ

GANDAVO, PERO DE MAGALHÃES

Pero de Magalhães Gandavo (d. 1576), Portuguese historian. In 1576 Gandavo wrote and published the *História da Província de Santa Cruz, a que vulgarmente chamamos Brasil*. His *Tratado da terra do Brasil*, written before 1573, was not published until 1824 by the Royal Academy of Sciences in Lisbon. Gandavo justifies his enterprise in the prologue to his History, on the basis of the fact that although Brazil had been discovered several decades previously, no Portuguese writer had

---

Gandavo's writings gave Portuguese colonists some

hope of finding "much gold and precious stones."

---

written about its discovery, and on his intention to persuade people in Portugal to emigrate and settle in the rich and healthy new land. His conception of history made him select as relevant the following elements: the description of the captaincies, the form of government, the distribution of land under the traditional Portuguese *sesmarias* (conditional grants), and the need for slaves as a labor force. With descriptive and narrative elements, Gandavo adroitly mixes past and present in

each chapter. As other sixteenth-century writers, he dedicates part of his History to the description of plants and their uses; he also describes animals, real and mythical. In the last chapter, Gandavo gives the colonists some hope of finding "much gold and precious stones."

– MARIA BEATRIZ NIZZA DA SILVA

GANDINI, GERARDO

Gerardo Gandini (b. 16 October 1936), Argentine composer, pianist, and conductor. He was born in Buenos Aires. His principal teachers on piano were Pía Sebastiani and Roberto Caamaño and in composition, Alberto GINASTERA. In 1964 Gandini resided in New York City while on a fellowship from the Ford Foundation. In 1966 he obtained a fellowship from the Italian government that permitted him to study under Goffredo Petrassi at the Accadémia Santa Cecilia in Rome.

He was professor of composition at the Catholic University in Buenos Aires (1962–1970) and at the celebrated Latin American Center for Advanced Musical Studies at the Di Tella Institute in Buenos Aires (1963–1970). An eager participant of the avant-garde school as a composer, Gandini became an active organizer of contemporary music series. He became the director of the Experimental Center for Opera and Ballet (CEOB) sponsored by the Teatro Colón in Buenos Aires. At the CEOB, Gandini premiered many staged works and also commissioned a number of mini-operas, most of them by composers from Argentina. Gandini was a founding member of the Agrupación Música Viva (AMV), a Buenos Aires organization devoted to the promotion of new music. Other members included Antonio TAURIELLO, Armando Krieger, Hilda DIANDA, and Alcides LANZA. Besides his career as a composer and promoter of new music, Gandini is a renowned conductor and pianist who performs frequently in Europe and North America.

His early compositions include Concertino for piano and orchestra (1960); *Variaciones* for orchestra (1962); *Per Mauricio Rinaldi* for chamber orchestra (1963); Concertino no. 3 for harpsichord and ensemble (1964); *Hecha sombra y altura* for ensemble (1965); *A Cow in a Mondrian Painting* for flute and instruments (1967); *Fantasía impromptu* for piano and orchestra (1970); *L'adieu* for piano, vibraphone, three percussionists, and conductor (1967); *Piange e sospira* for flute, violin, clarinet, and piano (1970).

In his more mature style Gandini has written a number of almost impressionistic compositions, always with a strong poetic vein, such as . . . *e sará* for piano (1973); *7 Preludios* for piano (1977); *Concierto* for Viola and Orchestra (1979); *Eusebius* (1984–1985), five nocturnes for orchestra; *Paisaje imaginario* for piano and orchestra (1988), which was commissioned by the BBC for the Welsh Symphony Orchestra.

— ALCIDES LANZA

GANTE, PEDRO DE

Pedro de Gante (*b.* ca. 1480; *d.* 1572), Franciscan missionary and educational pioneer in Mexico. Gante was originally from Ghent, Belgium, where he absorbed the refined choral style of the Low Countries. One of the first three Franciscans (all Flemish-born) to arrive in Mexico in 1523, he brought this musical foundation with him, later training the Indian singers employed by the cathedral in Mexico City. Although Gante never took holy orders, remaining a lay brother, his accomplishments and example did much to shape the Franciscan missionary enterprise. Like other early friars, Gante combined Christian fervor with Renaissance humanism. He assumed the inferiority of the indigenous cultures but believed the Indians fully capable of mastering European learning, and he made native education his life's work.

In 1526, Gante founded San José de los Naturales to teach Indian boys reading, writing, music, and basic Catholic doctrine. In addition, the school instructed Indians in Spanish artisanal skills, producing a generation of painters and sculptors who embellished the rapidly proliferating Christian churches (many of them built under Gante's supervision), and trained Indian catechists to aid the Franciscans' Christianization efforts. This institution became a model for the Colegio de Santa Cruz de Tlatelolco, whose goal (later abandoned) was to create a native priesthood.

A superb linguist, Gante composed an early and influential Christian doctrine in Nahuatl (1528), the Aztec language. Gante also wrote regularly to the crown, condemning Spanish abuses and advocating reforms to benefit the Indians. Among other things, he successfully urged Charles V to found an Indian hospital in Mexico City.

— R. DOUGLAS COPE
ROBERT L. PARKER

GAOS, JOSÉ

José Gaos (*b.* 26 December 1900; *d.* 10 June 1969), Spanish-Mexican philosopher. Gaos was born in Gijón, Spain. He lived in Oviedo with his maternal grandparents until he was fifteen, then moved to Valencia where his parents were residing. While reading the philosophy of James Balmes, Gaos discovered the topic that became the focus of his later thought: the radical historicity of philosophy (i.e., the extent to which any philosophy is grounded in the thinker's historical circumstances). Gaos began to study philosophy at the University of Valencia, then transferred to the University of Madrid in 1921, where he studied with Manuel García Morente, Xavier Zubiri, and, most important, José Ortega y Gasset. He earned his bachelor's degree in 1923 and his doctorate in 1928, both from the University of Madrid.

A firm supporter of the Republican cause, Gaos was named rector of the University of Madrid in 1936. Shortly thereafter, he fled the regime of Francisco Franco, living briefly in Cuba before arriving in Mexico in 1938. He declared himself a *transterrado* (transplant) rather than an exile, and spent the rest of his career encouraging research on the history of ideas in Latin America. His teaching at the Colegio de México and the Universidad Nacional Autónoma de México decisively influenced a generation of major Mexican thinkers, including Leopoldo ZEA. His philosophical work, a unique blend of metaphysics and historicism, was published in Mexico between 1940 and 1972. Gaos died in Mexico City.

— AMY A. OLIVER

GARAY, BLAS

Blas Garay (*b.* 1873; *d.* 19 December 1899), Paraguayan historian. Born in Asunción, Garay was something of a prodigy, publishing scholarly articles in local newspapers while still a teenager. He was one of the first Paraguayan historians to make systematic use of archives and primary documents of all kinds. He was sent to Spain in 1897 to visit Seville's Archive of the Indies in order to fulfill a government commission to substantiate Paraguay's legal claim to the Chaco Boreal region. While in Europe, Garay held several minor diplomatic posts.

As a member of the governing Partido Colorado, there was little way that Garay could avoid the passionate politics of his day. His newspaper pieces in *La Prensa,* which he founded, freely attacked his opponents, one of whom challenged Garay to a duel at Villa Hayes on 19 December 1899. Garay was shot, dying at the age of twenty-six.

Among his works, all of which are still read today, are *Compendio elemental de historia del Paraguay* (1896), *El comunismo de las misiones* (1897), and *La revolución de la independencia del Paraguay* (1897).

— THOMAS L. WHIGHAM

GARAY, CARLOS

Carlos Garay (*b.* 1 April 1943), Honduran impressionist painter. Born in Tegucigalpa, Garay studied at the Escuela Nacional de Bellas Artes in that city and from an early age became one of Honduras's few internationally recognized painters. In his formative period he often painted the human figure, but he eventually became known for his impressionist scenes of the Honduran countryside, which reflect an unusual mastery of light and color and a strong sensitivity to Honduran folk culture. In 1981 the Venezuelan government awarded him the Andrés BELLO Prize.

— RALPH LEE WOODWARD, JR.

GARAY, EPIFANIO

Epifanio Garay (*b.* 1849; *d.* 1903), Colombian artist. Born in Bogotá, Garay was the son of the portrait painter and cabinetmaker Narciso Garay. He studied first with his father and then with José Manuel Groot (1800–1878) while also training at the Academia de Música. He became an opera singer as well as the most important portrait painter in Colombian history. In 1865 he sang in a production of *La Traviata* and in Spanish musical comedies. His paintings during this period included genre, nudes, as well as religious subjects. In 1871 he received honorable mention for his painting *Dolor* at the Anniversary of the Independence show.

Thanks to his skill as a singer, Garay was able to travel extensively, giving him a sophistication noticeable in his paintings. From 1871 to 1880 he toured with the Compañía de Zarzuela, performing at the Musical Academy of New York. He returned to Bogotá in 1880 and was appointed director of the Academia Gutiérrez, but two years later he received a grant from the government to study in Paris with Bouguereau, Boulanger, Ferrier, and Bonnat. When civil war in Colombia led to the cancellation of his grant, he went on a singing tour through the capitals of Europe. He returned to Bogotá and, disappointed with the reception of his work, tried farming and cattle ranching before opening an art school in Cartagena. In 1894 he was named acting director of the School of Fine Arts in Bogotá, becoming director in 1898. With the onset of the revolution of 1899, the school closed. He died in Bogotá.

— BÉLGICA RODRÍGUEZ

GARAY, EUGENIO

Eugenio Garay (*b.* 16 November 1874; *d.* April 1937), Paraguayan politician and military figure. Born in Asunción, Garay spent part of his early years in the interior town of Pirayú. He later attended the Colegio Nacional in Asunción, where he received a bachelor's degree. Shortly thereafter, he received a scholarship to attend the military academy in Chile, from which he graduated with honors in 1898.

Returning to Paraguay in 1902, Garay entered the army with the rank of captain. When the 1904 revolution removed him temporarily from military service, he entered the world of journalism, working as a reporter for *Los succesos.* In 1908 the government sent him to Europe as a diplomat, but within three years he was back in the country acting as a adviser to the war ministry.

The series of interparty conflicts in the 1910s and 1920s gave Garay the opportunity to rise rapidly through the ranks, but this process was frequently interrupted by reverses when the wrong party was in power. He served as commander at Barrero Grande, minister of war, and then ambassador to Bolivia.

When the Chaco War broke out in 1932, Garay was recalled to active service. He headed a regiment that opposed the Bolivian forces at Pampa Grande and then at Campo Vía. Suffering from overwork that bordered on combat fatigue, he was relieved from command at his own request in late 1933, only to be recalled once again by President Eusebio AYALA a few months later. Garay, now a full colonel, commanded the principal Paraguayan units at the battles of Carmen and Yrendagüe.

With the conclusion of the war, Garay was demobilized and returned to Asunción. His health now seriously deteriorated because of the intensity of the earlier fighting, he survived the end of hostilities by only two years. He died of a heart attack.

— MARTA FERNÁNDEZ WHIGHAM

GARAY, FRANCISCO DE

Francisco de Garay (*d.* 27 December 1523), governor of Jamaica (1515–1523) and rival of the conquistador Hernán CORTÉS. Garay arrived in the Americas in 1493 with the second voyage of Christopher COLUMBUS. On Hispaniola, Garay combined government service, as notary and later chief constable, with economic venture. By the time he became governor of Jamaica in 1515, he was one of the richest men in the islands. In 1519 he sent four ships under the command of Alonso ÁLVAREZ DE PINEDA to search the Mexican coast north of Pánuco for a westward passage. Pineda and his men were the first Europeans to explore the Gulf coast west of Florida, but, badly damaged in conflicts with the indigenous peoples, the expedition limped back to Veracruz, where most of the men joined Cortés's army.

It was rumored that Cortés poisoned Garay,

but this seems unlikely, since Garay no longer

posed a threat to the conquistador.

These mixed results notwithstanding, Garay obtained a royal decree making him *adelantado* (royal representative) and governor of this vast stretch of coastline. This created a conflict with Cortés, who also had claims to Pánuco. In 1523 Garay landed there with several hundred men to confront Cortés directly, but he was preempted shortly thereafter, when Cortés received royal recognition as conqueror of Mexico and governor of New Spain. His authority superseded, Garay quickly acknowledged his defeat and traveled to Mexico City, where he died three days after meeting with Cortés. It was rumored that Cortés had poisoned him, but this seems unlikely, since Garay no longer posed a threat to the conquistador.

— R. DOUGLAS COPE

GARAY, JUAN DE

Juan de Garay (*b.* 1528; *d.* March 1583), conquistador, explorer, and governor of Río de la Plata (1578–1583). Born in Vizcaya, Garay arrived in Peru at the age of fourteen in the company of his uncle. He soon joined in the conquest of Tucumán (northern Argentina), settling first in Santa Cruz de la Sierra, where he served as one of the city's *regidores* (councilmen). In 1568 he moved to Asunción, where, awaiting the confirmation of his kinsman Ortiz de Zárate as governor, he was named *alguacil mayor* (chief constable). A dynamic, intrepid, and peripatetic leader, Garay founded the city of Santa Fé in 1573. During his lifetime he engaged in several military campaigns against the Charrúa along the lower Río de la Plata and against the Guaraní in Paraguay. He was also involved in putting down uprisings of discontented settlers in Santa Fé and Asunción.

After the death of Zárate in 1576, Garay, as his lieutenant, became acting governor and captain-general of the Río de la Plata. From Asunción, he organized an expedition of approximately sixty families who reestablished the city of Buenos Aires in 1580. He also headed an expeditionary force that explored south to the region of present-day Mar del Plata. Three years later, Garay was killed in a Querandí Indian attack while attempting

to return to Buenos Aires to reinforce troops accompanying the newly arrived governor of Chile.

— SUSAN M. SOCOLOW

GARCÉS, FRANCISCO TOMÁS HERMENEGILDO

Francisco Tomás Hermenegildo Garcés (*b.* 12 April 1738; *d.* 19 July 1781), Franciscan missionary who traveled extensively in SONORA, Arizona, and California. Born in Morata del Conde, Spain, Garcés entered the FRANCISCAN order at age fifteen. In 1768 he joined the Franciscans in Sonora as a missionary to the Pima and Papago Indians. From his post at San Xavier del Bac, Garcés made several expeditions into the surrounding areas. In 1774 he joined Juan Bautista de ANZA in opening a route from Sonora to Monterey, establishing a vital supply line to the Spanish settlements of California. In 1775 Garcés again joined Anza in a colonizing expedition to San Francisco. On his return from California, Garcés became the first to break a trail from the Pacific Coast to the Hopi pueblos of northeastern Arizona. In 1779 Garcés journeyed to Yuma to establish missions among the Indians on the Colorado River. Two years later, he was beaten to death in an uprising of Yuma Indians.

— SUZANNE B. PASZTOR

GARCÍA, ALEIXO

Aleixo García (*d.* 1525), Portuguese-born explorer, the first European in Paraguay. A minor member of the 1515–1516 Juan Díaz de SOLÍS expedition to the Río de la Plata, García witnessed the murder of Solís at the hands of Charrúa Indians in Uruguay in mid-1516. Some months later, García and eighteen other Europeans were shipwrecked on the Brazilian island of Santa Catharina, where he remained several years, gaining a practical use of the local Guaraní language.

In 1524, he and several companions journeyed to the mainland. Traveling west, they discovered the massive Iguaçú Falls, crossed the Alto Paraná River, and made contact with the substantial Guaraní populations of Paraguay. Told of a fabulously wealthy "white king," who lived further west, García enlisted the aid of 2,000 warriors and immediately set off in that direction through the heavily forested Chaco region. Upon reaching the foothills of the Andes, the small army raided a score of Incan communities. García made off with considerable booty, including a quantity of silver, and returned to the area of the Paraguay River. He sent word of his adventures (along with a portion of the silver) to Santa Catharina. Before he himself could return to the coast, however, he was murdered by his Indian allies, evidently in late 1525. Some of the silver ornaments he had on his person at the time of his death were discovered a decade later by Spanish explorers entering Paraguay from the south.

— THOMAS L. WHIGHAM

GARCÍA, CALIXTO

Calixto García (*b.* 4 August 1839; *d.* 11 December 1898), general during Cuba's wars for independence. García rose through the ranks of the liberating army during the first Cuban war of independence, the Ten Years' War (1868–1878). Captured by the Spaniards and set free at the end of the war, García attempted to reignite the rebellion by launching what came to be known as the Little War (1878–1880). Once again taken prisoner, he was this time deported to Spain, where he lived until returning to Cuba to join the rebel uprising of 24 February 1895. García first became military chief of Oriente Province and was subsequently appointed second in command of the insurgent army. His troops rendered invaluable assistance to the U.S. expeditionary forces in the the Spanish–American War, but they were not allowed to march into Santiago de Cuba when the city was surrendered by the Spaniards in 1898. On this occasion García sent the U.S. military commander a letter of protest that is one of the high points of Cuban nationalism.

— JOSÉ M. HERNÁNDEZ

GARCÍA, DIEGO

Diego García (*b.* ca. 1471; *d.* ca. 1535), Portuguese navigator in Spanish service. After participating in Ferdinand MAGELLAN's circumnavigation of the globe, García returned to Spain in 1522, organizing an expedition to the Río de la Plata in 1526. He explored Uruguay and established a shipyard near Colonia. During his expedition up the Paraná, he encountered and then joined forces with Sebastián CABOT in 1528. After returning to Spain in 1530, García and his caravel *Concepción* joined the expedition of Pedro de MENDOZA, *adelantado* (royal provincial governor) of Río de la Plata, departing Spain in August 1535. While in the Canary Islands, García fell ill and died at Gomera.

— CHRISTEL K. CONVERSE

GARCÍA, GENARO

Genaro García (*b.* 17 August 1867; *d.* 26 November 1920), Mexican politician, women's rights advocate, and historian. Born in Fresnillo, Zacatecas, García first attended school in San Luis Potosí but continued his studies in the capital, where he received a degree in law. He served as a congressional deputy for several terms; as governor of Zacatecas (1900–1904); as director of the National Museum of Archaeology, History, and Ethnology; and as director of the National Preparatory School.

García published many didactic works. From his *Desigualdad de la mujer* (1891) and *Apuntes sobre la condición de la mujer* (1891), arguing for greater rights for women, to his *Carácter de la conquista española en América y en México* (1901), presenting a pro-Indian perspective, García consistently was ahead of his time. However, he is best known as the editor of the thirty-six-volume *Documentos inéditos o muy raros para la historia de México* (1905–1911), and seven-volume *Documentos históricos mexicanos* (1901–1911), and *Documentos inéditos del siglo XVI para la historia de México* (1914). His library of twenty-five-thousand volumes and manuscripts forms the heart of the Mexican holdings of the Benson Latin American Collection at the University of Texas in Austin.

— CARMEN RAMOS-ESCANDÓN

GARCÍA, JOSÉ MAURÍCIO NUNES

José Maurício Nunes García (*b.* 20/22 September 1767; *d.* 18 April 1830), the most notable Brazilian composer of the early nineteenth century. Son of Lieutenant Apolinário Nunes García and Victoria Maria de Cruz, a black woman, José Maurício (as he is called in Brazil) learned to play the harpsichord and viola and studied *solfeggio* with Salvador José, a local teacher. Religious brotherhoods played a significant cultural role in nineteenth-century Brazilian society, and in 1784 José Maurício was one of the founders of the Brotherhood of St. Cecilia. Having entered the Brotherhood of São Pedro dos Clérigos in 1791, he was ordained a priest the following year on 3 March. In July 1798 José Maurício was appointed to the most important musical position in the city, *mestre de capela* of the cathedral of Rio de Janeiro, where his duties consisted of serving as organist, conductor, composer, and music teacher. For twenty-eight years he taught a music course that was open to the public free of charge, in which he trained some of the most important composers and musicians of the following generation, including Francisco Manuel da SILVA, composer of the Brazilian national anthem.

The arrival of dom João VI in Rio de Janeiro in 1808 had a decisive influence on the professional career of Padre José Maurício. A member of the Bragança family, which had a remarkable history of musical patronage, dom João was soon informed of José Maurício's talents

Portrait of José Maurício Nunes García. Reproduced from his Matinas do Natal *(Rio de Janeiro, 1978). (Courtesy of Harvard College Library)*

and appointed him on 15 June 1808 *mestre de capela* of the royal chapel, where his official duties included acting as organist, conductor, and professor of music. He also composed music for numerous official occasions, thirty-nine musical works in 1809, a year in which dom João decorated him with the Order of Christ.

In 1811 Marcos PORTUGAL, the best-known Portuguese composer of his day, arrived in Rio and was appointed *mestre de capela* of the royal chapel, for practical purposes replacing José Maurício. Thereafter, José Maurício's standing in the royal musical establishment declined. However, his best-known and most significant work, a requiem mass, was written in 1816 after the death of Queen Maria. On 19 December 1819 José Maurício conducted the first performance of the Mozart *Requiem* in Brazil.

Accustomed to music composed and performed by Europe's best musicians, dom João was amazed at the abilities of the relatively unknown, native-born mulatto. In a period when musical excellence was judged by adherence to European styles, José Maurício, a devoted admirer of Haydn, made no attempt to deviate from European models.

After dom PEDRO I returned to Portugal in 1821, many of his splendid musical reforms languished from lack of funds. José Maurício's lifelong pension was discontinued, leaving him in difficult financial circumstances until his death in 1830.

– DAVID P. APPLEBY

GARCÍA, SARA

Sara García (*b.* 8 September 1895; *d.* 21 November 1980), Mexican actress. García began her acting career on the stage in 1913. She made her cinematic debut in 1933 in the film *El pulpo humano* and went on to star in over 300 films. Noted for her work as a leading lady, in *Los tres García* (1936) she was cast in the role of the grandmother; from that moment on, García was the film world's perpetual *abuelita*. In 1970 she parodied her familiar screen role in Luis ALCORIZA's *Mecánica nacional*. She is regarded as a national treasure and a leading member of the Mexican cinema.

– DAVID MACIEL

GARCÍA CALDERÓN, FRANCISCO

Francisco García Calderón (*b.* 1834; *d.* 1905), a Peruvian lawyer and legal historian. Author of a compilation of nineteenth-century Peruvian law, he was forced to resign as minister of finance in the administration of José BALTA when he could not end Peru's financial dependence on its guano consignees. He achieved prominence and notoriety during the War of the Pacific (1879–1883). A committee of wealthy Limeños elected him president in early 1881, when they anticipated high Chilean occupation taxes. He began the negotiations that eventually led to the Treaty of Ancón (1883) that ended the war. During the negotiations, García Calderón adamantly refused to cede the southern departments of Tacna and Arica to Chile. Yet he underwent severe criticism from former president Nicolás de PIÉROLA, who resisted the Chileans from his position in Ayacucho, and from General Andrés A. Cáceres, who fought on in the central highlands. Fearing a rally of resistance among Peruvians and interference from the United States on the issue of cession of territory, the Chileans seized the president and imprisoned him in Santiago until the end of the war.

– VINCENT PELOSO

GARCÍA CATURLA, ALEJANDRO

Alejandro García Caturla (*b.* 7 March 1906; *d.* 12 November 1940) Cuban composer, considered the most talented musical artist of Cuba. Born in Remedios, Caturla was a lawyer by profession and became a judge. He studied music with Pedro Sanjuán in Havana (1926–1927) and attended Nadia Boulanger's classes in Paris (1928). He was founder and first conductor of the Orquesta de Conciertos Caibarién, a chamber ensemble. Together with composer Amadeo ROLDÁN, Caturla became the leader of *Afrocubanismo,* a nationalist musical trend, which mixed elements of white and black culture, incorporating Afro-Cuban songs, rhythms, and dances. Later on he used advanced techniques and French Impressionist styles combined with primitive tunes; as a result, some of his works show surprising juxtapositions of chords and moods. He composed *Concierto de cámara, Obertura cubana, Danzas cubanas,* and a suite for orchestra (1938). Many vocal works were inspired by Cuban poets such as Alejo CARPENTIER and Nicolás GUILLÉN; other works include one string quartet (1927), *Bembé,* for fourteen instruments, and *Primera suite cubana* (1930) among others. He produced numerous piano works, among them *Danza lucumí* (1928) and *Sonata* (1939). Murdered by a criminal tried in his court, he left unfinished one opera, a ballet, his *Primera sinfonía,* one concerto for piano and orchestra, and several piano and vocal works.

– SUSANA SALGADO

GARCÍA CONDE, PEDRO

Pedro García Conde (*b.* 8 February 1806; *d.* 19 December 1851), Mexican soldier. Born in Arizpe, Sonora, he began his military career as a cadet in the presidio company of Cerro Gordo and later served as director of the Military College from 1838 to 1844. In 1842 he was deputy to the national legislature and Secretary of War from 1844 to 1845 in the José Joaquín de HERRERA (1792–1854) government. An ardent patriot, he helped plan and fought in the Battle of Sacramento (1847) against the invading U.S. forces.

An accomplished geographer, García participated in the first geographic survey of the state of Chihuahua in 1833 and in 1842 published *Ensayo estadístico sobre el estado de Chihuahua.* In 1848 he received appointment to the presidency of the Mexican Boundary Commission, which was charged with mapping the new border between Mexico and the United States. He held this position twice but died in Arizpe before finishing the survey.

– AARON PAINE MAHR

GARCÍA DE CASTRO, LOPE

Lope García de Castro (*d.* 1576), governor and captain-general of Peru (1564–1569). Born in the district of Astorga, in northwest Spain, García de Castro studied at the University of Salamanca (1534). He received the licenciate in law and taught at Salamanca until his appointment as *oidor* (justice) of the Audiencia of Valladolid (1541). In 1558, Philip II transferred him to the Council of the Indies.

In response to complaints against Viceroy Diego López de Zúñiga, conde de Nieva, the king sent García de Castro to Peru to investigate and replace the errant official. When García de Castro reached American shores, he learned the viceroy had been assassinated (20 February 1564).

In October 1564 he arrived in Lima, where he began five years of honest, effective, and dedicated administration. In 1565 he established the Casa de Moneda (Mint Office) of Lima. (It was transferred to Potosí in 1572.) Ordered to increase royal revenues and cut expenses, he began the following year to collect the *almojarifazgo* (import duty) and undertook to organize effective exploitation of the mercury mines at Huancavelica. He divided Peru into provinces and established the *corregimiento* system for the local administration of Indians. In 1567 he founded an audiencia at Concepción, in Chile. (Suppressed in 1573, it was reestablished in 1609 at Santiago.)

García de Castro faced continued pressure from the Araucanians on the Chilean frontier and the Chiriguanos in lowland Bolivia, opposition from the neo-Inca state at Vilcabamba, northwest of Cuzco, and a bothersome uprising in the central Peruvian highlands associated with the Taki Onqoy movement. For more effective administration of Lima, he created El Cercado, an Indian town. During his rule the Tridentine reforms were announced in Lima (1565) and the Second Lima Church Council (1567–1568), which improved the administration of Indian *doctrinas,* was convened. At this time, also, the Jesuits began their work in Peru. García de Castro provided support for Captain Juan Álvarez Maldonado's exploration of the Mojos territory in the upper Amazon basin and, under his nephew Álvaro de Mendaña, also organized a voyage of exploration in the Pacific (1567–1568) that led to the discovery of the Solomon Islands. García de Castro returned to Spain in November 1569, shortly after welcoming the new viceroy, Francisco de TOLEDO Y FIGUEROA.

– NOBLE DAVID COOK

GARCÍA DIEGO Y MORENO, FRANCISCO

Francisco García Diego y Moreno (*b.* 1785; *d.* 19 November 1846), bishop of California (1840–1846). The Mexican-born Franciscan was the first Catholic bishop of the Californias. Associated with the apostolic college of Guadalupe in Zacatecas, he arrived to serve in the Alta California missions in January 1833 with a contingent of Zacatecan Franciscans sent to replace their brethren from the college of San Fernando in the missions of southern Alta California.

García Diego y Moreno, a Mexican-born

Franciscan, was the first Catholic bishop of

the Californias.

The bishopric of the Californias was established by a Mexican law (19 September 1836) authorizing the president to negotiate with the papacy to establish the new bishopric. This initiative also allocated 6,000 pesos from public funds for the support of the new bishop and transferred the administration of the so-called Pious Fund, an endowment organized by the Jesuits to finance their activities in Baja California, to his jurisdiction, although the Mexican government later resumed control of the fund. The papacy approved the new bishopric on 27 April 1840.

President Antastasio BUSTAMANTE selected Diego y Moreno from a list of three candidates submitted by the papacy. After having sworn an oath of loyalty to the president of Mexico, Diego y Moreno was consecrated as bishop at the shrine of the Virgin of Guadalupe outside Mexico City on 4 October 1841. He served in Alta California for six years and died in Santa Barbara.

– ROBERT H. JACKSON

GARCÍA GODOY, HÉCTOR

Héctor García Godoy (*b.* 1921; *d.* 1970), Dominican provisional president (1965–1966). Born into one of the Dominican Republic's old elite families, García Godoy distinguished himself as a career diplomat whose skill, tact, and moderation prepared him for his role as provisional president after the overthrow of Juan BOSCH (1963) and subsequent U.S. military invasion of his country (1965). Offered the position of president by U.S. Ambassador Ellsworth Bunker, García faced the difficult task of reconciling opposing forces, the left-leaning Constitutionalists and the right-wing military elements, who had kept the country in a chaotic civil war since Bosch's fall. During his nine months in office, he faced pressures from both factions as well as the United States. He rose to the occasion by eliminating the most troublesome military leaders who had refused to negotiate. His presidency smoothed the way for elections in June 1966 and for the birth of a new Domin-

ican government led by Joaquín BALAGUER. Afterward, García served as Dominican ambassador to Washington. Many Dominicans hoped that, upon his return, he would run for president. In 1970, García founded the Movimiento de Conciliación Nacional (MCN) in preparation for the 1974 presidential campaign. Soon thereafter, however, he died of a heart attack.

– PAMELA MURRAY

GARCÍA GRANADOS, MIGUEL

Miguel García Granados (*b.* 29 September 1809; *d.* 8 September 1878), a leader in the Guatemalan liberal revolution of 1871. Born in Cádiz, Spain, García Granados went to Guatemala with his parents as an infant. While he was still a young man he became interested in military affairs and in liberal political philosophy, especially that of Voltaire and Rousseau. As Spaniards, his family was not involved in the independence movement, but they shared many of the new ideals. García Granados traveled to New York with his older brothers in 1823. He studied there and in Philadelphia and London before returning to Guatemala in 1826. When conflicts began developing with El Salvador, he followed his older brothers into military service.

García Granados participated in two invasions of El Salvador, where he was captured, held prisoner, and exiled to Mexico, not returning to Guatemala until 1840. During the following thirty years he became a leader in the movements for political change, a free press, public education, fiscal reform, and restrictions on the power of the church. He served as a leader of the liberal cause in the conservative-controlled National Assembly during the long dictatorship of Rafael CARRERA. While in exile in Mexico he had met Justo Rufino BARRIOS. Together they planned the overthrow of the conservative government. They invaded Guatemala in May 1871 and, after a series of battles, entered Guatemala City victorious on June 30. García Granados became interim president and served until 1873, when Barrios succeeded him as the constitutionally elected president. The revolution of 1871 led to the expulsion of religious orders, to professionalization of the military, to expanded public education and public works throughout the country, and to a concept of the state as a positive force for introducing change in the society and the economy.

– DAVID L. JICKLING

GARCÍA ICAZBALCETA, JOAQUÍN

Joaquín García Icazbalceta (*b.* 21 August 1825; *d.* 26 November 1894), Mexican historian and bibliographer.

One of the most recognized historians of Mexico, Joaquín García Icazbalceta dedicated a lifetime to collecting, editing, and publishing documents that centered on the Europeanization of Mexico in the sixteenth century. Born in Mexico City to a Spanish father and Mexican mother, he left with his family for exile in Spain, where they remained seven years (1829–1836). Though he received no formal education outside of tutoring in the home, early in life he showed a strong interest in literature. He joined the family business in Mexico City, where he successfully balanced a career in commerce with his literary interests.

In 1848, after participating in the war against the United States, García Icazbalceta began in earnest to collect original manuscripts of historical and linguistic value. He spent the remainder of his life compiling bibliographies, writing numerous books and articles, and publishing documents for use by future historians. Most notable among his works are the *Bibliografía mexicana del siglo XVI* (1954), the two-volume *Colección de documentos para la historia de México* (1971), and a four-volume biography of Juan de ZUMÁRRAGA, first archbishop of Mexico. At the time of his death, García Icazbalceta served as director of the Mexican Academy of Language.

— BRIAN C. BELANGER

GARCÍA MÁRQUEZ, GABRIEL

Gabriel García Márquez (*b.* 6 March 1927), Colombian novelist and short-story writer. The two most important years of García Márquez's career are 1967, when his masterpiece *Cien años de soledad* (1967; *One Hundred Years of Solitude,* 1970) brought him overnight fame, and 1982, when he was awarded the Nobel Prize.

García Márquez was born in Aracataca, a town near the Atlantic coast, where he spent the first eight years of his life. His law studies at the National University in Bogotá were interrupted in 1948 by El Bogotazo, an outburst of violence triggered by the assassination of a popular politician. The university was closed, and García Márquez returned to the Atlantic coast, where he worked for several years as a journalist. The symbiotic relationship between his journalism and his fiction is the hallmark of much of his work. An early example is the novella *Relato de un náufrago* (1970; *The Story of a Shipwrecked Sailor,* 1986), which is the result of interviews he held with a young Colombian sailor who spent ten days on a raft after being swept overboard in the Caribbean. Although the youth's narration, which reads like a novel, appeared in the press in 1954, it was not printed in book form until 1970.

In 1955 García Márquez published his first novel, *La hojarasca* (Leaf Storm, 1972), whose plot and style recall Faulkner's *As I Lay Dying* (1930). Six years later, having lived as a journalist in Europe, Caracas, and New York, he published his novelette *El coronel no tiene quien le escriba* (1961; No One Writes to the Colonel, 1986). It is the masterful portrait of an aging, poverty-stricken ex-military officer who waits for his pension while hoping that his fighting cock will win a fortune in an upcoming contest. This sparsely written volume (one detects Hemingway's influence) is enhanced by veiled allusions to a bloody civil conflict (La Violencia) and by the good-humored but tenacious protagonist, who embodies the Colombian people's struggle against oppression.

García Márquez moved to Mexico in 1961 and the next year published *Los funerales de la Mamá Grande* (Big Mama's Funeral), a collection of eight tales dramatizing the political and social realities of Colombia. In 1965, after several years of writer's block, the author was driving to Acapulco when he envisioned the fictional world he had endeavored to create for more than a decade. Eighteen months later he emerged from his study with the manuscript of *One Hundred Years of Sol-*

Gabriel García Márquez after learning he has been awarded the Nobel Prize for literature, 21 October 1982. (UPI/Bettmann Archive)

itude. This novel, perhaps the second best (after *Don Quijote*) ever to be written in Spanish, tells the story of Macondo (the author's native Aracataca) from Genesis to Apocalypse. Seven generations of the Buendía family, the leading characters of the saga, find themselves caught up in the totality of human experience, ranging from the historical and the mythical to the everyday, the fantastic, the tragic, the comic, and the absurd. Major sections of the novel, which has been seen as a rewriting of history designed to refute official lies, deal with Colombia's nineteenth-century civil wars, the banana boom, and gringo imperialism.

Soon after the publication of *One Hundred Years of Solitude,* García Márquez moved to Barcelona to write *El otoño del patriarca* (1975; *The Autumn of the Patriarch,* 1976). This portrait of a prototypical Latin American dictator represents a daring experiment in the use of poetic language and literary technique, which explains in part why it is often considered the author's most significant achievement to date. The protagonist embodies all the evils of despotism, but equally important is the solitude imposed on him by the absolute power he wields. Like its predecessor, *The Autumn of the Patriarch* is sprinkled with humor and fantasy, but its rambling style and shifting points of view make it far more demanding of the reader.

Since 1975 García Márquez has maintained residences in both Mexico and Colombia. *Crónica de una muerte anunciada* (1981; *Chronicle of a Death Foretold,* 1982) records the testimony of witnesses to the murder of Santiago Nasar, the youth accused of seducing Ángela Vicario prior to her marriage. When, on her wedding night, Ángela's husband discovers that she is not a virgin, he returns her to her parents. The following morning, her twin brothers kill Nasar on the doorstep of his home. A riveting mélange of journalism and detective story, the novel implicitly condemns not only the Catholic church but also the primitive code of honor endorsed by the town citizens.

Both of García Márquez's most recent novels rely on historical and geographical documentation to enrich setting and plot. *El amor en los tiempos del cólera* (1985; *Love in the Time of Cholera,* 1988) describes Cartagena between 1870 and 1930, a time when the decaying, historic city was plagued by a series of epidemics. The action focuses on the aging process of the protagonists, two of whom, Fermina Daza and Florentino Ariza, are patterned after the author's parents. Reviewers have described this novel as one of the best love stories ever written. The protagonist of *El general en su laberinto* (1989; *The General in His Labyrinth,* 1990) is Simón BOLÍVAR, the liberator of much of South America. In May 1830, mortally ill and disillusioned by his fruitless

efforts to unite the continent under a single leader, Bolívar traveled down the Magdalena River from Santa Fe de Bogotá to the Atlantic coast, hoping to spend his remaining years in Europe. He died shortly after arriving in the port city of Santa Marta. Although the foreground action is a lineal account of Bolívar's arduous journey to his grave, numerous flashbacks evoke remnants of his life, molding an intricate labyrinth of memories, dreams, and hallucinations.

García Márquez's most recent works are *Doce cuentos peregrinos* (1992; *Strange Pilgrims,* 1993) and *Del amor y otros demonios* (1994; *Of Love and Other Demons,* 1995). The former is a collection of short stories about Latin Americans living in Europe; the latter, a novel, is set in a Colombian coastal city during the eighteenth century. Based on a legend, it narrates the strange tale of a young girl, Sierva María de Todos los Angeles, who is bitten by a rabid dog, falls in love with a priest, and ultimately dies in a convent during the exorcism mandated by the Inquisition. This final episode, in addition to the vivid descriptions of decadence and poverty, dramatizes the negative impact of Spanish colonialism.

With his broad literary canvases laced with myths and fantasy, García Márquez has rescued the contemporary novel from its rigid laws of logic. In its totality, his oeuvre depicts the stark reality of an underdeveloped, strife-torn continent universalized by the humanistic elements of unfettered imagination and aesthetic perception. García Márquez is one of the world's most widely admired writers of fiction today. The end result of his prodigious enterprise is an original, comprehensive vision of human experience.

– GEORGE R. MCMURRAY

GARCÍA MEZA, LUIS

Luis García Meza, army officer and Bolivian dictator (1980–1981). Following the coup d'état by General Alberto Natusch Busch in November 1979, García Meza—a professional army officer—was named commander in chief of the armed forces of Bolivia. After Natusch's overthrow a few weeks later, his successor, President Lidia GUEILER TEJADA, demanded García Meza's resignation. After first refusing to resign, García Meza was finally removed, but he continued to control the armed forces. On 17 July 1980, he led an insurrection that overthrew Gueiler.

García Meza's regime was one of the most brutal dictatorships in the country's history. Political parties, labor unions, and many other organizations were suppressed and their headquarters destroyed. Several important political leaders were murdered. Leading figures in the García Meza government, including his ministers of interior and education, were involved in the international cocaine trade. Because of this involvement the United States refused to extend diplomatic recognition to the García Meza government, and the television program *60 Minutes* twice aired a segment devoted to the Bolivian "drug smugglers' government."

In August 1981, García Meza was forced to resign. He fled abroad and was convicted in absentia of serious crimes. In 1994, the Bolivian government was still trying to have García Meza extradited to Bolivia from São Paulo, Brazil.

– ROBERT J. ALEXANDER

GARCÍA MORENO, GABRIEL

Gabriel García Moreno (*b.* 24 December 1821; *d.* 6 August 1875), president of Ecuador (1861–1865, 1869–1875). Born in Guayaquil into a family of modest means, Gabriel García Moreno completed his early studies at home before going to Quito for his secondary and university studies. He received a doctorate in law at the University of Quito, and in 1846 married the aristocratic Rosa Ascásubi Matheu. In 1855–1856 he took courses in the natural sciences in France at the Sorbonne.

García Moreno entered politics as a liberal, an opponent of General Juan José FLORES, and an admirer of the enlightened Vicente ROCAFUERTE. He gained notoriety as a publisher of three polemical newspapers: *El Zurriago* (1845), *El Vengador* (1846–1847), and *La Nación* (1853). His vehement opposition to the government forced him into exile three times between 1850 and 1856. Life abroad induced him to turn conservative, to become a francophile, and to champion the cause of the Catholic church.

Upon completing scientific studies in Paris in 1856, he returned to Ecuador and was named rector of the University of Quito. Soon afterward he won a seat in the Senate. When the government became mired in a grave crisis with Peru, García Moreno took part in a campaign that toppled the government and precipitated a period of anarchy in Ecuador.

In May 1859 a *junta de notables* named García Moreno a member of a triumvirate. He quickly emerged as the dominant leader but soon suffered a military defeat that caused him to flee to Peru. After securing support from the Peruvian president, he managed in a few months to return to Quito and to take charge there. Desperate to pacify the nation, he secretly proposed to establish a French protectorate over Ecuador. France did not respond to the proposal.

By early 1861 the nation was sufficiently pacified for a national convention to elect García Moreno president

for four years. He completed his term of office, bullied two successors for the next four years, and then seized power by force. He remained president until his violent death in 1875.

During his first administration García Moreno held power by ruthless repression of the opposition. He reformed the treasury, increased revenues, turned public schools over to the clergy, allowed the Jesuits to return to Ecuador, and defended his nation from the aggressive intentions of Colombia and Peru. His efforts to modernize the university and improve the transportation system gave the impression of continued liberalism, but his repression of criticism and his espousal of unabashed clericalism revealed a shift to authoritarian conservatism. Most revealing was the negotiation in 1862 of a controversial concordat with the Vatican that surrendered the *patronato* (government authority over clerical appointments and revenues), permitted church censorship of school texts, and called for reform of corrupt religious orders. A subsequent campaign to spiritualize the clergy helped turn the church into a strong pillar of the state.

Non-Catholics were denied civil rights, substantial sums of money were donated to the Vatican, and in 1873 Ecuador was dedicated to the Sacred Heart of Jesus.

The authoritarian Constitution of 1869 allowed García Moreno to become a legal dictator and to press his religious fervor to surprising extremes. Non-Catholics were denied civil rights, substantial sums of money were donated to the Vatican, and in 1873 the nation was dedicated to the Sacred Heart of Jesus. In secular affairs, García Moreno founded an astronomical observatory, a new military academy, and a polytechnic school. Public works included many new roads, especially a good cart road from Quito to Guayaquil, initiation of railroad lines, and a large prison in Quito.

While García Moreno was arranging his own reelection in 1875, copies of Juan MONTALVO's *La dictadura perpetua,* an inflammatory indictment of the Ecuadorian dictator, arrived in Quito. Soon afterward a group of young liberals, probably incited by Montalvo's words, cut down the president with machete blows. This bloody act ended the dictatorship but turned García Moreno into a martyr of conservatism.

– MARK J. VAN AKEN

GARCÍA MORILLO, ROBERTO

Roberto García Morillo (*b.* 22 January 1911), Argentine composer and critic. He was born in Buenos Aires and studied at the National Conservatory of Music and Theater Arts under the guidance of Floro Ugarte, José GIL, José André, and Constantino GAITO. Garcia Morillo is noted for the absence of nationalistic elements in his music. His style evolved as atonal music, with modernistic, dissonant harmonies, and very contrapuntal lines but without harshly clashing sounds. Garcia Morillo evoked the Hispanic origins of his ancestors, using renovated archaic forms and textures in his works such as his cantata *Marín* (1948–1950). The municipality of Buenos Aires awarded a composition prize for his *Poema para orquestra* (1932) and for *Las pinturas negras de Goya* (1939). His ballets *Harrild* (1941) and *Usher* (1940–1941) were awarded distinctions from the National Commission on culture and the Wagnerian Society, as was his music for the film *Juvenilia*, which received the Municipal Prize for film music in 1943. In 1938 he began writing music criticism for the newspaper *La Nación* in Buenos Aires, and he has written other articles for *Modern Music, Musical Courier,* and the *Revista ARS.* He is the author of several books: *Mussorgsky* (1943), *Rimsky Korsakoff* (1945), *Estudios sobre la danza* (1948), with Dora Kriner, *Siete músicos europeos* (1949), and *Carlos Chávez* (1960).

Some of Garcia Morillo's earlier compositions contain traces of neoclassicism, like his Piano Sonata no. 3, op. 14 (1944–1945). Other works of the same period demonstrate his dexterity with rhythms and the use of engaging and intriguing melodies. Among his important works are *Tres pinturas de Paul Klee* (1944); *El tamarit* (1953), a chamber cantata for soprano, baritone, and orchestra; *Romances del amor y de la muerte* for bass (1959); *Música para oboe y orquestra* (1962); *Cantata de los caballeros* for soprano (1965); *Música para violin y cuerdas* (1967); Symphony no. 1 (1946–1948); *Obertura para un drama romántico* (1954); Symphony no. 2 (1954–1955); Symphony no. 3 (1961); *Divertimento sobre temas de Paul Klee* (1967); *Ciclo de Dante Alighieri* for chamber orchestra (1970); and *Variaciones apolíneas* for piano (1958–1959).

— ALCIDES LANZA

GARCÍA PELÁEZ, FRANCISCO DE PAULA

Francisco De Paula García Peláez (*b.* 2 April 1785; *d.* 25 January 1867), archbishop of Guatemala, with jurisdiction over all of Central America (1846–1867). Born into a ladino family of modest means in San Juan Sacatepéquez, Guatemala, García Peláez studied law and theology at the University of San Carlos, where he received his doctorate in 1819. Although regarded as somewhat liberal in the late colonial period, as archbishop during the long, conservative dictatorship of José Rafael CARRERA, he became known as an ultraconservative. He had offered the first course in political economy at the University of San Carlos in 1814.

In 1842 Pope Gregory XVI named García archbishop coadjutor, to succeed the archbishopric upon the death of Archbishop Ramón CASÁUS, after it was clear that Casáus would not return to Guatemala from his exile in Havana. Following Casáus's death in late 1845, García was formally installed as archbishop, although he had been acting archbishop since 1844. García's appointment was a setback for the Guatemalan elite and particularly for Juan José de AYCINENA, who had expected to be named. Jorge VITERI Y UNGO was especially influential in arranging García's appointment as part of a compromise to get papal approval of a separate diocese of El Salvador, of which Viteri was named bishop. In 1861 Pope Pius IX named García Peláez domestic prelate and attending bishop to the pontifical throne, essentially a step below cardinal.

García Peláez wrote a three-volume history of the colonial Kingdom of Guatemala, *Memorias para la historia del antiguo reino de Guatemala,* a work commissioned by Governor Mariano GÁLVEZ.

— RALPH LEE WOODWARD, JR.

GARCÍA PÉREZ, ALAN

Alan García Pérez (*b.* 23 May 1949), president of Peru (1985–1990). García, born in Lima to middle-class parents active in the American Popular Revolutionary Alliance (APRA), was seven years old when his father was released from political detention. He earned a law degree from San Marcos University and pursued graduate work in Madrid and at the Sorbonne, where he received a doctorate in sociology. He won election to the Constituent Assembly in 1978 and outpolled all APRA candidates in 1980 to gain a seat in the Chamber of Deputies. In 1985 he led APRA to its first presidential victory and at thirty-six became Latin America's youngest chief executive.

García's reformist policies limited foreign debt repayment to 10 percent of national export earnings, thereby stimulating economic growth through 1987. His efforts to provide economic resources to rural areas affected by the Shining Path insurgency and his strong human rights stand contributed to reductions in violence during the first months of his term. But García's reforms foundered after a prison massacre in which more than 270 Shining Path inmates were killed by the military and police in June 1986, while García was hosting the Socialist International convention in a bid for a leadership position. García's bank nationalization program failed in June 1987. The last three years of his term were marked by four-digit inflation, an economic decline of over 20 percent, and an escalation of violence and human rights abuses related to the Shining Path insurgency.

Upon leaving office in 1990, García assumed his seat in the Senate as a former president and regained leadership of APRA in party elections in early 1992. After the self-coup (*autogolpe*) of April 1992 by his successor, Alberto FUJIMORI, he evaded arrest and obtained asylum in Colombia. Allegations of corruption contributed to his expulsion from APRA in 1994.

– DAVID SCOTT PALMER

GARCÍA ROBLES, ALFONSO

Alfonso García Robles (*b.* 20 March 1911; *d.* 2 September 1991), Mexican foreign service officer and disarmament specialist. A native of Zamora, Michoacán, García Robles completed his studies in law at the University of Paris, where he was one of two laureates at the Institute of International Studies in 1936. He also received a diploma from the International Law Academy at the Hague (1938). He joined the diplomatic corps in 1939, serving in a number of foreign assignments and posts within the secretariat of foreign relations. He is considered to have been largely responsible for the Nuclear Arms Treaty of Tlatelolco in 1967, later serving as Mexico's permanent representative to the United Nations Committee on Disarmament. For his efforts in regional disarmament, he was awarded the Nobel Prize for peace in 1982. He culminated his professional career in 1975 as secretary for foreign relations, receiving the rank of ambassador emeritus (1981). He is the author of numerous books and articles.

– RODERIC AI CAMP

GARCÍA SALINAS, FRANCISCO

Francisco García Salinas (*b.* 1786; *d.* 1841), Mexican cabinet minister and governor of the state of Zacatecas. García was born on a hacienda in the state of Zacatecas. As a young man he was involved in the mining business in Zacatecas. In 1821, he was the *regidor* (president) of the *ayuntamiento* (city council) of Zacatecas and was elected to represent the state in the First Constituent Congress of Mexico in 1822. García continued to serve in the Congress as deputy and then as senator from Zacatecas from 1823 to 1827, taking a special interest in financial matters and helping to reestablish

Mexico's foreign credit. President Guadalupe VICTORIA selected García as his minister of the treasury, a post he held for only a few months (2 November 1827 to 15 February 1828) prior to his election as governor of the state of Zacatecas in 1828.

García's administration of Zacatecas was a model of liberal reform that made the state, with its strong militia, one of the bulwarks of the federal system. García attempted to use church property to create a bank for agricultural credit and to use state funds to redistribute agricultural land by dividing large properties for sale. His administration also sought to develop the mining industry and the manufacture of cotton, silk, and woolen textiles. The state of Zacatecas opened new schools under the Lancasterian system of "utilitarian" education and vaccinated thousands of children against smallpox. The defeat of the Zacatecas militia by conservative and centralist forces in 1832 and 1835 marked a turning point in the early republican history of Mexico. After stepping down as governor in 1834, García continued in command of the state's militia. He retired to his hacienda, where he died.

– D. F. STEVENS

GARCÍA Y GONZÁLEZ, VICENTE

Vicente García y González (*b.* 23 January 1833; *d.* 4 March 1886), Cuban general. General García was one of the regional military caudillos who emerged in Cuba during the Ten Years' War (1868–1878). A native of the district of Las Tunas, Oriente Province, he was something of a feudal lord. He led his guerrilla troops to some brilliant victories over the Spanish army, but he was unruly and inconsistent, and his ambition prompted him to launch seditious movements against the insurgent provisional government, finally contributing to its collapse and the ultimate failure of the insurgent effort. García participated in some obscure way in the negotiations with the Spanish that culminated in the end of the war. Afterward he sought refuge in Venezuela, where he spent the rest of his life. He died in Río Chico, Venezuela.

– JOSÉ M. HERNÁNDEZ

GARCILASO DE LA VEGA, EL INCA

El Inca Garcilaso de la Vega (*b.* 12 April 1539; *d.* 22/23 April 1616), Peruvian author and historian. Born in Cuzco, son of Captain Sebastián Garcilaso de la Vega and Inca princess Chimpu Oello, his original name was Gómez Suárez de Figueroa. He studied, along with other mestizo children, under the cathedral canon Juan de Cuellar. About 1552 his father married a wealthy

Spaniard, and Garcilaso's Inca mother and siblings were forced to leave the household. His father died in 1559, and the following year the young Garcilaso set sail for Spain, planning to live and study with the support of a small stipend provided by his father's will. He would never return to Peru.

After settling in Montilla, in southern Spain, under the patronage of his uncle, Alonso de Vargas, Garcilaso fought briefly (1570–1571) in Granada during the uprising of the Moriscos of Alpujarras. About 1591 he moved to nearby Córdoba and devoted much of the remainder of his life to writing. His first literary effort was the translation of the *Diálogos de amor* (Dialogues of Love) of Leon Hebreo (Madrid, 1590), which served as a model of stylistic accomplishment. His first history, *La Florida del Inca* (1605), tells the story of the famous Hernando de SOTO expedition to what became the southeastern part of the United States. Based on published sources and the oral account of soldier Gonzalo Silvestre, Garcilaso was able to weave a detailed and compelling picture of the trials and tribulations of the Spanish exploration of Florida. When facts were lacking, he created with vivid ingenuity. His next history, the *First Part of the Royal Commentaries of the Incas,* appeared in Lisbon in 1609. Based on recollections of what he learned as a youth in Peru and on written sources, including the chronicle of Blas Valera, this is an articulate and compelling, if not always accurate, account of Inca civilization. With a brilliant prose style, and with the authority of speaking in the native American voice, he attempted to bring Inca institutions and history to the Europeans.

Continued reliance on Garcilaso as a primary source clouds and blurs an authentic vision of Tahuantinsuyu (The Land of the Four Quarters), even in the twentieth century. Indeed, Marcelino Menéndez y Pelayo, in his *Historia de la poesía hispano-americana,* wrote that the *Royal Commentaries* was not really history but might best be classified as a utopian novel. The second part of Garcilaso's commentaries, published one year after his death under the title of *Historia general del Perú* (1617), outlines the Spanish conquest of the Incas to the execution of TÚPAC AMARU I during the administration of Viceroy Francisco de TOLEDO (1567–1581). That Garcilaso was the first native American writer to be widely read in Europe, and continues to be read with pleasure and profit in spite of lapses into historical fantasy, is a lasting testament to his superb literary skills.

— NOBLE DAVID COOK

GARDEL, CARLOS

Carlos Gardel (*b.* 11 December 1890; *d.* 24 June 1935), arguably Latin America's greatest twentieth-century popular singer and the supreme figure in the story of the Argentine tango. Born in Toulouse, France, he was taken at the age of two by his unmarried mother to Buenos Aires, where he grew up in tenement rooms and on the streets. A naturally gifted baritone, he won local renown in the modest barrios of Buenos Aires before forming a celebrated folk duo with a Uruguayan friend, José Razzano (1887–1960), that lasted from 1913 to 1925.

In the early 1920s, with the development of the tango as a form of popular song, a movement Gardel himself strongly pioneered, he concentrated mostly on the new genre, making hundreds of recordings. Successful visits to Spain in 1925–1926 and 1927–1928 were followed by spectacular triumphs in the cabarets and music halls of Paris in 1928–1929. By now a superstar in Argentina and Uruguay, Gardel went on to gain unrivaled popularity all over Latin America by starring in seven movies, shot in Paris (1931–1932) and New York (1934–1935). These were mediocre, low-budget productions that nonetheless memorably projected Gardel's exceptional vocal talent and winning personality.

While undertaking a tour of countries around the Caribbean in 1935, the star was tragically killed in an airplane collision at Medellín, Colombia. His repatriated remains were accorded a solemn funeral attended by enormous crowds in Buenos Aires. Gardel's memory

Carlos Gardel, ca. 1930. (Archivo General de la Nación, Buenos Aires)

has been the focus of an assiduously cultivated popular cult. The centennial of his birth, December 1990, was extensively celebrated throughout Latin America.

– SIMON COLLIER

GARIBALDI, GIUSEPPE

Giuseppe Garibaldi (*b.* 4 July 1807; *d.* 2 June 1882), Italian revolutionary and patriot. Garibaldi was born in Nice (then in Italy), son of Domenico Garibaldi, a sailor, and Rosa Ragiundo. A member of Giuseppe Mazzini's Young Italy, he was forced to flee the country because of his revolutionary activities. After arriving in Rio de Janeiro in 1836, he supported the revolutionary movement in Rio Grande do Sul as a privateer. Garibaldi was wounded during a naval engagement with Uruguayan lighters. After obtaining medical treatment at Gualeguay, Argentina, he returned to Rio Grande to fight alongside the rebels.

In 1841 Garibaldi and Ana María Ribeiro da Silva, a native of Santa Catarina, arrived in Montevideo, with their son Menotti. There they were married (16 June 1842) and had two more children, Riccioti and Teresita. For a few months Garibaldi was a business agent and a history and mathematics instructor; then he assumed command of President Fructuoso RIVERA's small navy of five ships. His attempt to challenge Buenos Aires's control of the rivers failed when his ships were destroyed at Costa Bravo by Admiral William Brown on 15 August 1842, marking the end of Rivera's naval power. Garibaldi escaped overland to Montevideo.

During Manuel ORIBE's siege of Montevideo, Garibaldi, who held the rank of colonel, organized the Italian Legion of 600 men and a small fleet to protect the port. He successfully kept the bay of Montevideo free of the enemy. In 1844 he commanded one of the three columns that General José María PAZ led in an assault on Oribe's position in Cerrito. In 1845 he commanded a fleet of three ships with a landing force of 700 men of the Italian Legion, 200 Montevideo infantrymen under Colonel Lorenzo BATLLE, and 100 cavalrymen. Escorted by an Anglo-French squadron, he took and sacked Gualeguaychú, Colonia, and Salto.

Upon returning to Montevideo, Garibaldi was promoted to general (16 February 1846), and briefly commanded the forces defending the city. In August 1847 he returned to Europe to resume his fight for Italian unification. After his defeat in Rome by French forces (1849), he lived in Tangier, New York, Sardinia, and finally Caprera. He resumed his struggle for Italian unification in 1856. Four years later, after the death of Ana María, he married the Marchioness Giuseppina Raimondi. That year, encouraged by the Sardinian minister Camillo Cavour, he went to the aid of the Sicilian rev-

olutionaries. Garibaldi landed at Marsala, and from there went on to capture Palermo and Messina and to establish a provisional government. His dream finally was realized when Italian troops entered Rome in 1870. His *I Mille* (1874) is an account of his campaigns. Garibaldi and his sons fought for France in the Franco-Prussian War. After a brief term as national deputy, he returned to Caprera, where he wrote two novels and his *Memorie Autobiografiche* (*Garibaldi: An Autobiography,* 1860). He married Francisca Armorino in 1880 and died at Caprera.

– JOSEPH T. CRISCENTI

GARIBAY, PEDRO

Pedro Garibay (*b.* 1729; *d.* 1815), viceroy of Mexico (16 September 1808–19 July 1809). A Madrid-born military officer, Garibay arrived in New Spain after service in Europe and the Caribbean, eventually being promoted to the rank of field marshal before he retired. When Napoleon intervened in Spain in 1808, José de ITURRIGARAY, viceroy of Mexico, was overthrown because of his pro-Mexican sentiments in a coup led by Spanish merchants and supported by the Mexico City *audiencia* (royal court). As senior military figure in the colony, and thought by the conservatives to be easily manipulatable, the elderly, infirm Garibay was appointed viceroy and eventually recognized by the caretaker government in Spain. Though his emasculated government lasted only ten months, he was honored in retirement and granted a large annual pension.

– ERIC VAN YOUNG

GARIBAY KINTANA, ÁNGEL MARÍA

Ángel María Garibay Kintana (*b.* 18 June 1892; *d.* 19 October 1967), Mexican scholar and priest who pioneered in the study and translation of the literary traditions of the ancient Mexicans. Garibay was born in Toluca. While at the Seminario Conciliar de México (1906–1917), he learned Latin and Greek (and later published works on Greek philosophers) and became interested in Nahuatl language and culture. In subsequent years Garibay added Hebrew, French, Italian, German, English, and Otomí, as well as Nahuatl, to his language repertoire. He was ordained in 1917; later (especially 1924–1941) he served as a missionary and became more and more focused on his Nahua and Otomí studies. In 1941 Garibay was named prebendary canon of the Basilica of Guadalupe. From 1956 he served as director of the Seminario de Cultura Nahuatl at the Universidad Nacional. In 1952 he was named extraordinary professor at the Faculty of Philosophy and Letters at the Universidad Nacional. Although he began publishing articles in 1913, his major works appeared from 1940 through 1965; they included *Poesía indígena de la altiplanicie, Llave del Nahuatl* (1940), *Historia de la literatura Nahuatl* (2 vols, 1940), and three important volumes on the songs and poetry of the ancient Mexicans. His numerous translations of Nahuatl prose, historical texts, epic hymns, religious and lyric poetry, *pláticas* (short lectures), and other texts opened new doors to understanding the pre-Hispanic cultures of Mexico, and stimulated intense scholarly and humanistic interest in these arenas. Garibay died in Mexico City.

– FRANCES F. BERDAN

GARMENDIA, FRANCISCO

Francisco Garmendia, nineteenth-century capitalist and early industrialist, Peruvian born in Argentina. In 1861, Garmendia established one of the first factories in Latin America, a textile factory in Lucre; he imported industrial machines from France and, in an impressive feat of entrepreneurship, transported them by mule across the southern Andes of Peru to the town of Quispicanchis, near Cuzco. The factory replaced the old colonial textile mills (*obrajes*) of that region. The woolen textile it produced was of a coarse quality targeted for purchase by the Indian population. The factory had chronic financial and technical problems and faced increasing competition by export-import commercial firms based in Arequipa, but remained in business as the only factory in Cuzco Department up to 1898.

– ALFONSO W. QUIROZ

GARMENDIA, SALVADOR

Salvador Garmendia (*b.* 1928), Venezuelan novelist and short-story writer. One of Venezuela's major fiction writers of the century, Garmendia has published more than a dozen books since the late 1950s. Although he is recognized by writers and critics alike, Garmendia has never been included among the writers of the Boom of Latin American literature in the 1960s and 1970s. Consequently, his fiction is far better known in the Hispanic world than in the United States, particularly his novels *Los pequeños seres* (1959), *Día de cenizas* (1963), *Los habitantes* (1968), and *El Capitán Kid* (1988).

The masterly use of a precise point of view makes Garmendia one of Latin America's best exponents of the narrative technique of the French *nouveau roman*. In his early novels, he portrays alienated characters in urban environments. The protagonist in *Los pequeños seres* becomes so desperate with his circumstances that he commits suicide. Protagonists in his other early fiction include such characters as an unemployed truck

driver and a frustrated writer. In his later fiction, such as *El Capitán Kid* (1988), *Crónicas sádicas* (1990), and *Cuentos cómicos* (1991), Garmendia's tone is less anguished and often ironic and quite humorous.

– RAYMOND LESLIE WILLIAMS

GARRIDO CANABAL, TOMÁS

Tomás Garrido Canabal (*b.* 20 September 1891; *d.* 1943), radical Mexican provincial politician who dominated political life in the Gulf state of Tabasco in the 1920s and early 1930s. He is most remembered for his fanatical persecution of Catholic priests during the church-state conflict in the 1920s.

Garrido is most remembered for his fanatical persecution of Mexico's Catholic priests during the church-state conflict in the 1920s.

Born in Catazajá, Chiapas, Garrido studied law in Campeche and Mérida before serving as interim governor in 1919. He was governor of Tabasco from 1923 to 1926, senator (1927–1930), and governor once again from 1931 to 1934. With the support of his own Red Shirt movement, he took such extreme steps against priests as to prompt an investigation by the English Roman Catholic novelist Graham Greene, which resulted in Greene's famous 1940 work *The Power and the Glory*.

Garrido joined General Lazaro CÁRDENAS's first cabinet as secretary of agriculture (1934–1935). He refused Cárdenas's offer of a continued post in the cabinet, shortly after which his mentor, General Plutarco CALLES, was forced to leave Mexico. Garrido went into voluntary exile in Costa Rica, from which he returned to Mexico in 1940.

– RODERIC AI CAMP

GARRIDO-LECCA SEMINARIO, CELSO

Celso Garrido-Lecca Seminario (*b.* 9 March 1926), Peruvian composer. Born in Piura, Peru, Garrido-Lecca was a student of Rodolfo HOLZMANN's until moving to Chile, where he studied under Free Focke and Domingo Santa Cruz. He also studied orchestration with Aaron Copland in the United States. Later, at the Theater Institute of the University of Chile, he served as musical adviser, composition teacher, and composer. After the fall of the government of President Salvador Allende in 1973, he returned to Peru. He has taught at the National Conservatory in Lima and has represented Peru at various international events, including the Second Encuentros de Música Latinoamericana (Cuba, 1972) and the First International Rostrum of Latin American Music (TRIMALCA) International Music Council (IMC; Colombia, 1979). The music of Garrido-Lecca is often aleatoric, and utilizes modern signs and methods of notation. Garrido-Lecca has composed works for orchestra, string quartet, and piano, as well as chamber music and incidental music for theater and films.

– SERGIO BARROSO

GARRO, ELENA

Elena Garro (*b.* 11 December 1920; *d.* 22 August 1998), Mexican novelist, short-story writer, and playwright. Although Garro has spent much of her adult life in Spain and France, her writing reflects Mexican society, which she views pessimistically. Her coupling of detailed realistic descriptions and nightmarish fantasies places her among the magical realists. In her first book, *Los recuerdos del porvenir* (1963), she re-creates her hometown, Iguala, which she sees as a microcosm of Mexican society: desperate, defeated, and doomed. Garro actually wrote the book in the 1950s and published it later, with the encouragement of Octavio Paz, her husband from 1937 to 1959. Her first collection of stories, *La semana en colores* (1964), draws on Indian beliefs. Her second, *Andamos huyendo Lola* (1980), combines childhood memories with fantasy to create a kind of hell in which characters are constantly fleeing and scrounging for food. *Testimonios sobre Mariana* (1981) captures the anguish of modern society and parodies the bourgeois intellectual. *Reencuentro de personajes* (1982) examines the sober themes of violence, sexual manipulation, and psychological torture. In *La casa junto al río* (1983), Garro returns to her childhood village, still steeped in pettiness and mediocrity. *Y matarazo no llamó,* written in 1960 but published in 1991, is a kind of political thriller with existential undercurrents: the main character, an alienated loner, is lured into a political snare that drives him mad and leads him to an absurd end. Garro wrote a number of one-act as well as full-length plays featuring avant-garde techniques. *Felipe Ángeles* (1979) is a three-act work that presents a negative view of the Mexican Revolution.

– BARBARA MUJICA

GARRO, JOSÉ DE

José de Garro (*d.* ca. 1702), governor of Buenos Aires (1678–1682). Garro was born in Guipúzcoa, in the Basque country of northern Spain. He saw intense action in the wars in Portugal and Catalonia. In 1671 he came to America to govern Tucumán, where he was outstanding for his role in public works and in Indian fighting. As governor of Buenos Aires, Garro was responsible for confronting the advance of the Portuguese, who in 1680 had founded the colony of Sacramento in the eastern territory. Garro stormed the colony and took its founder, Manuel Lobo, prisoner. Later he served for ten years as governor of Chile (1682–1691), where his rule was particularly notable for the conversion of Indians. He went on to become military commander of Gibraltar (1693–1702) and finally of his homeland, Guipúzcoa (1702), where he died.

– JOSÉ DE TORRES WILSON

GARVEY, MARCUS

Marcus Garvey (*b.* 17 August 1887; *d.* 10 June 1940), Pan-African nationalist. Garvey was born in Saint Ann's Bay, Jamaica, to a comfortable family, possibly descendants of maroons. He attended school until the age of fourteen, when a financial crisis in his family obliged him to go to work as a printer's apprentice. By the age of nineteen, he had mastered the skills of this trade, which he was able to use later in his career as a publicist and propagandist in the cause of black nationalism. Between 1910 and 1914 he traveled in the Caribbean and Central America and resided in London. It was during this period that his political ideas took shape. In 1914 he returned to Jamaica and founded the Universal Negro Improvement Association (UNIA), which was received with little enthusiasm. In 1916, Garvey decided to travel to the United States, where his ideas gave rise to an important mass movement for the dignity and independence of blacks. In 1918 he formed a branch of UNIA in New York City and began the publication of the weekly *Negro World,* which quickly attained a large, international circulation. With the hope of aiding communication between African Americans and Africans, and to help further his "Back to Africa" vision, he founded the Black Star shipping line in 1919.

In 1920 UNIA reached its high point when it held its first international convention in New York. As the organization grew in size and importance, it faced increasing repression from U.S. authorities and from the European colonial powers that controlled Africa and the West Indies. Moreover, problems within UNIA derailed Garvey's plans. By 1921 the Black Star Line was a fiasco, as were efforts to colonize Africa and other projects begun in the United States. In 1923 the U.S. government accused Garvey of fraud, and he was sent to prison in 1925. In 1927 his sentence was commuted and he was deported to Jamaica. Although he continued his fight there and in London, where he relocated in 1935, he never regained the international influence he had had at the beginning of the 1920s. By the time of his death in London, he was forgotten.

The importance of Garveyism is that it was the first movement of the black masses based on black pride and dignity. Its international character also was significant. UNIA had branches in the countries of the Caribbean and Central America and was well received by the migrant plantation workers of the West Indies and Jamaica. Garvey is remembered as the forerunner of black nationalism in Africa and in America.

— VÍCTOR ACUÑA

GARZA SADA FAMILY

Garza Sada Family, major Mexican entrepreneurial family. The original head of probably the single most influential and extensive capitalist family in Mexico was Isaac Garza Garza, the son of Juan de la Garza Martínez, mayor of Monterrey, and Manuela Garza, Jewish immigrants from Spain who had settled in the region of Monterrey, Nuevo León. After studying merchandizing in Santander, Spain, he went into the grocery business with José Calderón, who married his aunt. Isaac married Consuelo Sada Muguerza, daughter of Francisco Sada Gómez, and in 1899 founded with his father-in-law Fábrica de Vidrios y Cristales de Monterrey, of which he became president. With other partners, he established a number of major firms at the turn of the century, including Cervecería Cuauhtémoc (1890), whose partners, often related by marriage, included José A. Muguerza and Francisco Sada, and the Fundidora de Fierro y Acero, with Vicente Ferrara.

His union with Consuelo produced numerous children, among them Eugenio Garza Sada, Isaac Garza Sada, and Roberto Garza Sada. Eugenio, the oldest of this generation, took over the leadership of a major group of interlocking corporations, which became known popularly as the "Monterrey Group." These included the original brewery, Cervecería Cuauhtémoc; a bottling company, Hojalata y Lámina; and Empaques de Cartón Titán, a packaging firm. Another son, Isaac, took over another set of firms, and also developed his own businesses. These children, in turn, intermarried with other prominent Monterrey families, including the Laguera and Sepúlveda families.

The untimely death of Eugenio Garza Sada, who was murdered in September 1973, served as a catalyst in breaking up the beer, glass, and steel empire into four separate, but complementary, holding companies. All

of these conglomerates rank among the top fifty companies in Mexico. The most famous of these groups, the ALFA industrial group, the largest in Latin America in the early 1980s, was founded by Bernardo Garza Sada, grandson of Isaac and son of Roberto. The other components are led by VITRO, VISA, controlled by the Garza Laguera family, and the CYDSA group, presided over by the Sada Zambrano family. The Garza Sadas continue to be a dominant force among Mexican capitalists, as shareholders and board members of leading industrial firms, as members of entrepreneurial interest groups, as leaders of business organizations, and as managers of major industrial holding groups.

— RODERIC AI CAMP

GASCA, PEDRO DE LA

Pedro de la Gasca (*b.* August 1493; *d.* 10 November 1567), president of the Audiencia of Lima and bishop of Palencia and Sigüenza. Born in a hamlet in Ávila, Spain, Gasca briefly attended the University of Salamanca before leaving in 1508 to attend the recently founded University of Alcalá de Henares, where he received a master of theology. He continued in Alcalá as *colegial* in the Colegio Mayor of San Ildefonso. In 1522 he returned to Salamanca to complete a study of law and in 1528 served briefly as rector of Salamanca.

In 1531, Gasca became affiliated with the Colegio Mayor de San Bartolomé, where he assumed the duties of rector for two terms. He received a prebend in Salamanca's cathedral (1531) and was named *maestrescuela* (teacher of divinity). Returning to Alcalá in 1537 as *vicario* (vicar), he was placed under the tutelage of Francisco de los COBOS, secretary of Holy Roman Emperor Charles V. Shortly thereafter he became general inspector of Valencia and, in 1540, justice of the Council of the Inquisition. Gasca served well in both capacities, impressing Cobos, who saw in him the qualities necessary to pacify Peru, then in the throes of rebellion. In late 1545 Gasca accepted the royal commission naming him president of the Audiencia of Lima and giving him power to offer pardons and make grants. He also was empowered to revoke the onerous chapter 30 of the New Laws, which prohibited inheritance of *encomiendas,* and to authorize new *entradas.* In addition he had general power to grant all types of office and to conduct any business in the name of the monarch.

Gasca left Spain in April 1546. When he reached Santa Marta, Colombia, on 10 July he learned of the execution of Viceroy Blasco NÚÑEZ VELA after the battle of Añaquito (18 January 1546). In Panama he entered into negotiations with Pizarrists, convincing many to abandon the rebels. By April 1547, when he headed south, he had gained the support of the Pacific fleet under Admiral Hinojosa. When they first landed, they discovered that several important cities in the north already had declared for the royalist cause. On 30 June Gasca reached Tumbes, on Peru's north coast, with a substantial force. During their one-and-a-half month's stay, Lima declared for the royalists, and the Pizarrists left for the highlands.

Gasca established military headquarters at Jauja, by which time he had collected 700 harquebusiers, 500 pikemen, and 400 horsemen. News of a stunning defeat of the royalist force (20 October 1547) under Diego de Centeno at Huarina, to the south, failed to discourage Gasca's forces. The final battle between Gonzalo PI-ZARRO and Gasca (9 April 1548) on the plain of Jaqui-jahuana, not far west of Cuzco, ended in royalist triumph; most Pizarrists threw down their arms and surrendered. Gonzalo Pizarro and his leading commander Francisco de Carvajal, along with some 48 principal leaders, were executed; 350 rebels were sent to labor in the galleys; and 700 were exiled from Peru.

In July 1548, Gasca retired with his secretary and Archbishop Loaysa to the hamlet of Guaynarima to distribute the spoils (Indian *encomiendas*) to the victors. He then departed for Lima, leaving the archbishop to announce the awards in Cuzco. The results shocked most royalists, two-thirds of whom received no grants, while some rebels who returned to the crown at the last moment were well rewarded. In May 1548 Gasca ordered a general inspection and tribute assessment for the *encomiendas*. The first systematic census to be undertaken and largely completed, it began in March 1549, with two inspectors for each district. Gasca's purpose was to increase yet stabilize tribute collection and to protect the Native Americans as much as possible.

Gasca restored a rebellious colony and provided the treasure that would allow Charles V to continue his imperial religious and political policies.

Gasca restored the administration of justice under firm royal authority. He licensed new expeditions, one of which led to the foundation of the city of La Paz, Bolivia. He also named Pedro de VALDIVIA governor and captain-general of Chile, thus recognizing him as conqueror of that land. Most important for the crown, he carried back an enormous treasure. Shipment of the king's fifth had long been delayed as a result of Peru's civil wars. Gasca left Lima in January 1550 and reached Seville in September. In November he reported to the Council of the Indies in Valladolid, where he was ordered to inform directly Charles V, who was then in Flanders. On 6 April, while he was in Barcelona preparing to travel to Germany, Gasca became bishop of Palencia. He sailed to Genoa, then north to Mantua, where he met Prince Philip in June. Passing through Trent, where the church council was in session, Gasca finally met Charles V (Charles I of Spain) at Augsburg on 2 July 1551. The emperor received him with gratitude, for Gasca had restored a rebellious colony and provided the treasure that would allow Charles V to continue his imperial religious and political policies in the heart of Europe.

Gasca returned to Spain early in 1553 and assumed his post at Palencia on 6 March. He was asked to report to the Council of the Indies several times in following years, and in 1556 he was called on by Charles V to escort his sisters, Queen Leonor of France and Queen Maria of Hungary, to interview the Infanta Maria of Portugal in Badajoz. Named Bishop of Sigüenza in 1561, he served there until his death at the age of seventy-four.

Pedro de la Gasca is buried in a beautiful stone coffin bearing his effigy in the center of the church of Santa María Magdalena, which he built in Valladolid.

— NOBLE DAVID COOK

GASTÃO D'ORLÉANS

Gastão d'Orléans (Luís Filipe Maria Fernando, Conde d'Eu; *b.* 28 April 1842; *d.* 28 August 1922), husband to ISABEL, heir to the Brazilian throne. A member of the French royal family, the Conde d'Eu spent his early years in exile, first in England and then in Spain, where he trained as an army officer, fighting in Morocco. Family connections—his uncle married PEDRO II's sister—and personal qualities led to his marriage in 1864 to Isabel. Hard working, cultured, and liberal in political outlook, Conde d'Eu at first sought an active role in Brazilian affairs, which Pedro II denied him. In 1869 he was named commander in chief of Brazil's forces in the War of the Triple Alliance, and he secured total victory in 1870. His war experience left him psychologically insecure and subject to recurring depression, and he restricted himself thereafter to family affairs and to chairing a few army commissions. Despite his considerable talents, he did not shine in public life, in part owing to growing deafness. His lack of charisma and his erratic treatment of subordinates meant that he did not command support or sympathy. The Conde d'Eu never ceased to be an outsider in Brazil. After the empire's fall in 1889, he spent his final years in contented privacy in France.

— RODERICK J. BARMAN

GATÓN ARCE, FREDDY

Freddy Gatón Arce (b. 27 March 1920), Dominican poet. Born in San Pedro de Macoris, Gatón is the last surviving champion of La Poesía Sorprendida, a movement that in the 1940s set out to reform Dominican poetry by transcending the local reality and embracing new and regenerative influences from European and American literatures. His enigmatic prose poem Vlía (1944), a text credited with introducing to the country the poetic form of automatic writing, which makes no concessions to the reader's understanding, highlights the kinship of Gatón Arce to the poets of Dada and surrealism. Despite the hermetism of his early work, his subsequent texts are more accessible to the uninitiated reader, with themes that manifest a concern with love, the downtrodden, and the relationship between the matter and spirit. His poetry, partly collected in Retiro hacia la luz: poesía 1944–1979 (1980), has continued to evolve; a dozen volumes have appeared in print since 1980. A lawyer by profession, Gatón Arce has also been a professor, an administrator at the Autonomous University of Santo Domingo, and, since 1980, the director of the newspaper El Nacional. He is acclaimed for having enriched journalistic prose in the Dominican Republic.

— SILVIO TORRES-SAILLANT

GAVIDIA, FRANCISCO ANTONIO

Francisco Antonio Gavidia (b. 29 December 1864; d. 23 September 1955), Salvadoran romantic poet and writer, one of the originators of modernism in Spanish America. Gavidia was born in San Miguel. His Versos (1884) brought him great notice for their innovations in meter and imagery, and he is believed to have been an important influence on his friend Rubén DARÍO. A long career as leading literary figure in San Salvador followed, with perhaps his most significant poetic work being the epic and dramatic Sóteer o tierra de preseas (1920). Gavidia's classic ode A Centroamérica (1945) reflected his strong democratic conviction and belief in Central American union. His literary versatility was also reflected in dramatic works, critical essays, and historical works, among which his two-volume Historia moderna de El Salvador (1917–1918), focusing on the Sal-

vadoran independence movements of 1811 and 1814, was the most important. Gavidia died in San Salvador.

— RALPH LEE WOODWARD, JR.

GAVIRIA TRUJILLO, CÉSAR AUGUSTO

César Augusto Gaviria Trujillo (b. 31 March 1947), president of Colombia (1990–1994). Born in Pereira, Gaviria studied economics at the Universidad de Los Andes. At the age of twenty-three he began his political career with election to the Pereira Municipal Council in 1970. He was appointed mayor of Pereira in 1974 and later served as vice minister of development in the administration of President César TURBAY AYALA (1978). Gaviria combined his political activities with those of a journalist, first with the newspaper La Tarde in Pereira, of which he became editor in 1982, and then as political and economic correspondent for the newspaper El Tiempo. He was appointed deputy director of the Liberal Party in 1986 and then served as minister of the treasury and minister of the interior in the administration of President Virgilio BARCO. In 1989 he became the campaign director of presidential candidate Luis Carlos GALÁN SARMIENTO. After Galán's assassination in August of that year, Gaviria was selected to be the presidential candidate of the Liberal Party. He was elected president of Colombia in 1990, with 47 percent of the votes.

Gaviria's election marked a generational and, to a lesser extent, an ideological shift in Colombian politics. He was the first of the post-Violencia generation to become president, elected with the support of a coalition of traditional Liberal Party bosses and the followers of the reform-minded Galán. Gaviria confronted the problems of narcotics-linked terrorism and a general lack of confidence in the political system with youthful energy and a neoliberal vision. He was the youngest elected president of Colombia in the twentieth century, and many of those who were appointed to serve in his government were younger than he. Continuing the process of reintegration of guerrilla groups into the political life of the country, which Gaviria had directed as a member of the administration of President Barco, he appointed M-16 leader Antonio NAVARRO WOLF to his cabinet.

Perhaps the crowning achievement of the Gaviria presidency was constitutional reform, the first since 1886, which modernized the state structure and the judicial system. The Constitution of 1991 was generally viewed as opening the political arena to more than the two traditional parties and as guaranteeing democratic participation. The Gaviria administration also promoted a more open economy, with an emphasis on privatization and deregulation. Trade barriers were lowered, regional economic integration (particularly with Venezuela) was supported, foreign investment was encouraged, labor legislation was modernized, and the role of private enterprise was emphasized. For these reasons and for Gaviria's cooperation in the effort to suppress the drug traffic, his administration was lauded by the U.S. government. By the end of his term, Gaviria was seen as an "efficiency-seeking technocrat" who had effectively initiated political and economic reforms that enabled Colombia to break out of the cycle of political and drug-related violence, slow economic growth, and political dissatisfaction that had characterized it in the 1980s.

In March 1994 Gaviria was elected to a five-year term as secretary general of the Organization of American States (OAS), and upon completion of his presidential term, in September 1994, he assumed that position.

– JAMES PATRICK KIERNAN

GEFFRARD, FABRE NICOLAS

Fabre Nicolas Geffrard (*b.* 1803; *d.* 31 December 1878), Haitian general and president (1859–1867). Geffrard rose to the rank of general under Emperor Faustin SOULOUQUE (1785–1867). He was one of the few to emerge with credit from Soulouque's disastrous last invasion of the Dominican Republic (1856). As head of the army, Geffrard led a revolt against Soulouque in 1858 and restored the republican constitution. He became president the following year and sought to improve Haiti's international image, which had deteriorated under Soulouque's harsh and nationalistic regime. He signed a concordat with the Holy See in 1860, and he obtained U.S. recognition of the Haitian state in 1862. President Abraham Lincoln and Congress had proposed settling U.S. blacks in Haiti, but in spite of some cooperation from Geffrard, the scheme failed.

President Abraham Lincoln and Congress proposed settling U.S. blacks in Haiti, but in spite of cooperation from Geffrard, the scheme failed.

Internally, Geffrard favored the Catholic church and attacked vodun, which had grown under Soulouque. He also favored the mulatto class, which had suffered under the regimes since 1844. Early in his term he attempted to install a more open and less authoritarian government, but assassination attempts against him and his family and a revolt led by Sylvain SALNAVE (1827–1870) at Cap Haïtien in 1865 pushed him to the fa-

miliar pattern of repression and executions. Geffrard was overthrown by Salnave in 1867, and he left for exile in Jamaica, where he died.

– MURDO J. MACLEOD

GEGO

Gego (Gertrude Goldschmidt; *b.* 1 August 1912; *d.* 17 September 1994), Venezuelan artist. Trained as an architect, Gego emigrated to Venezuela from her native Germany in 1939. In the latter half of the 1950s, she began to create a geometric sculpture that explored perceptual aspects of planes and volumes. She taught at the Universidad Central de Venezuela from 1958 to 1967 and at the Instituto Nacional de Cooperación Educativa (INCE) from 1964 to 1977. Gego is best known for her innovative abstract works that extend a systematic approach to three-dimensional art into a poetic ineffability. Her *Reticuláreas* (1969), for example, comprise webs of wire segments that have been hooked together and hung from the ceiling; filling a room, the *Reticuláreas* confront the viewer with a quasi-geometric and semi-mobile linear articulation of space. Gego's architectural projects have included sculptures at the Banco Industrial de Venezuela, Caracas, in 1962 and (in collaboration with her husband, Gerd Leufert) on the facades of the Sede del INCE in 1969. Her one-woman exhibitions include those in Caracas at the Museo de Bellas Artes in 1961, 1964, 1968, 1969, and 1984; at the Museo de Arte Contemporáneo in 1977; and at the Galería de Arte Nacional in 1982. Gego died in Caracas.

– JOSEPH R. WOLIN

GEISEL, ERNESTO

Ernesto Geisel (*b.* 3 August 1908), president of Brazil (1974–1979). A career army officer of German Protestant parentage from Rio Grande do Sul, Geisel entered the army on 31 March 1925. After graduating from the military college of Realengo in Rio de Janeiro, he served with the Brazilian Expeditionary Force (FEB) during World War II. He attended the U.S. Army Command and General Staff College at Fort Leavenworth, Kansas, and went on to fill various command and general staff positions. As a colonel he directed the Brazilian National Petroleum (Petrobrás) Refinery at Cubatão, São Paulo, in 1955–1956, and the next year he joined the National Petroleum Council. After his promotion to general on 25 March 1961, he served a series of military presidents as chief of military household (1964–1967), minister of the superior military tribunal (1967–1969), and president of Petrobrás (1969–1973).

Geisel's presidential candidacy was initiated by the military high command (his brother, Orlando, held the post of army minister from 1969 to 1974), confirmed by the National Renovating Alliance (Arena), the government party, and certified by 400 out of 503 members of the electoral college. Once inaugurated (March 1974), Geisel was confronted with the collapse of the "Economic Miracle," brought on by the oil crisis of 1973. His administration launched a series of petroleum-substitution plans, including hydroelectric projects such as Itaipú and gasohol refineries to convert sugar to fuel. His initial efforts to come to terms with socially active elements of the Catholic church failed, but tentative attempts at relaxation (*distensão*) of the political process restricted after the 1964 coup were evident by the end of his term.

Also taking place during the Geisel years was the end of the "unwritten alliance" between the United States and Brazil that had endured for three quarters of a century. The U.S. defeat in Southeast Asia, Cuban military intervention in Angola, Communist involvement in Mozambique, U.S.–USSR détente, and U.S. economic decline were capped by U.S. allegations of human-rights abuses. Geisel responded by canceling the defense agreement with the United States and redirecting Brazilian foreign policy to encompass more productive partners who were also interested in containing Soviet expansion. These included Japan, West Germany, and, briefly, Iran, along with the outcast quartet of South Korea, Taiwan, Israel, and South Africa. Investments from these members of the New Inter-Oceanic Alliance were encouraged. Concurrently, Brazil launched a cultural and commercial campaign in Lusophone Africa—Angola, Mozambique, and Guinea-Bissau—then proceeded to initiate development (since canceled) of its own nuclear weapons under Project Solimões (1977–1991).

Geisel's efforts at a democratic opening domestically (*abertura*) and reorientation in foreign policy precipitated a crisis in the hard-line military that was not resolved by the closure of congress in April 1977. It resurfaced in October 1977, when Geisel fired army minister General Sélvio Frota and other officers who contested the new directions.

As his successor Geisel selected General João Baptista FIGUEIREDO, who promised to proceed with the democratic opening up of the country. After retiring from public office on 15 March 1979, Geisel dedicated himself to private entrepreneurial activities.

– LEWIS A. TAMBS

GELLY, JUAN ANDRÉS

Juan Andrés Gelly (*b.* 1790; *d.* 1856), Paraguayan diplomat and author. Born in Asunción, Gelly left at an early age to complete his education at the Real Colegio de San Carlos in Buenos Aires. After the Platine states gained their independence, he became involved in the Argentine civil wars as a partisan of Manuel Dorrego and the Unitario Party. With the defeat of that party in the late 1820s, Gelly left Argentina. Instead of returning to Paraguay, where the dictator José Gaspar Rodríguez de FRANCIA had already persecuted his family, Gelly went to Montevideo to continue his legal studies. He soon became a well-known figure in expatriate circles.

Gelly made his way back to Paraguay after Francia's death in 1840. Overcoming his initial suspicion of Gelly's intentions, President Carlos Antonio LÓPEZ decided to call him into government service. Gelly's considerable experience in Uruguayan journalism made him an obvious choice for editor of the new state newspaper *El Paraguayo Independiente*.

In 1846 Gelly was dispatched to Rio de Janeiro to negotiate a boundary and trade agreement with the Brazilian Empire. Though this agreement was stillborn, he remained in Brazil as agent and publicist for the Paraguayan government. During his stay, he wrote a laudatory account of Paraguay's progress under López, entitled *El Paraguay, lo que fue, lo que es, y lo que será* (1848). Acting as delegation secretary, he later accompanied the president's son, Francisco Solano López, on a mission to Europe (1853–1854). He died in Asunción two years later.

– THOMAS L. WHIGHAM

GELLY Y OBES, JUAN ANDRÉS

Juan Andrés Gelly y Obes (*b.* 20 May 1815; *d.* 19 September 1904), Argentine general. Born in Buenos Aires, Gelly y Obes took exile in Montevideo with the rest of his family during the dictatorship of Juan Manuel de ROSAS. In 1839 he joined the *unitario* forces fighting against Rosas. Returning to Argentina after the fall of Rosas, he held both military and political offices in the separatist government of Buenos Aires Province and in 1861 became minister of war for a united Argentina in the cabinet of Bartolomé MITRE. He became chief of staff of the Argentine army of operations during the War of the Triple Alliance as well as personally taking part in many of the battles.

After the war Gelly y Obes fought against rebellious *caudillos* of the interior, yet took part himself in Mitre's unsuccessful 1874 uprising and in the porteño rebellion of 1880 over the federalization of Buenos Aires. He continued to hold various political and military positions until his death.

— DAVID BUSHNELL

GELVES, MARQUÉS DE

Marqués de Gelves (Diego Carrillo de Mendoza y Pimentel; *b.* 1500s; *d.* 1600s), fourteenth viceroy of New Spain (1621–1624). The Gelves administration is an excellent example of the limitations of colonial reform in the seventeenth century. Gelves arrived in Mexico under orders to improve government efficiency, crack down on the widespread corruption in public administration, and increase tax revenue. He enjoyed some success, particularly in the last endeavor. But he also managed to offend nearly every important sector of colonial society, partly because of his high-handed and autocratic manner and partly because his reforms threatened the financial interests of merchants, the creole elite, and many government officials.

The viceroy's most serious feud, however, was with the equally proud and unbending archbishop of Mexico, Juan Pérez de la Serna. Their dispute quickly evolved into a contest between civil and ecclesiastical authority. Pérez de la Serna excommunicated Gelves; Gelves exiled the archbishop. En route to the coast, the archbishop placed Mexico City under interdict, which was to begin on the morning of 15 January 1624. The populace, already angry at the viceroy over high maize prices, sided with the archbishop. A riot broke out in the central plaza, and soon a crowd of some thirty thousand was shouting for the viceroy's blood. The rioters stormed the palace, but Gelves escaped, disguised in servant's clothing, and fled to the Monastery of San Francisco. The *audiencia,* claiming that Gelves had abandoned his post, assumed viceregal authority. Although the crown briefly reinstated Gelves before replacing him, the marqués was in effect the first Mexican viceroy overthrown in a popular revolt.

— R. DOUGLAS COPE

GERCHUNOFF, ALBERTO

Alberto Gerchunoff (*b.* 1 January 1884; *d.* 2 March 1950), writer and journalist, born in Proskuroff (Khmelnitski) Russia; he emigrated with his family to Argentina in 1889, settling in Moisés Ville, Santa Fe Province. After his father's murder, the family moved to Rajil in Entre Ríos Province. In his classic *Los gauchos judíos* (1910; *The Jewish Gauchos of the Pampas,* 1955), Gerchunoff envisioned the promised land based on the agricultural colonies founded by Baron Hirsch as a haven for Jews fleeing from pogroms in czarist Russia. He

moved to Buenos Aires in 1895, where he met Enrique DICKMANN and Alfredo L. PALACIOS—the major figures of the Socialist Party—and writer Leopoldo LUGONES and Robert J. Payró. He began writing for the journal *Caras y Caretas,* where he developed a following for his sharp wit and satirical portrayals. Gerchunoff would later serve as a model for Abrahan Orloff in Manuel GÁLVEZ's *El mal metafísico* (1916). In 1909 Gerchunoff joined the staff of *La Nación,* which for a young Jewish immigrant signaled acceptance into the literary establishment.

Gerchunoff dismissed as deviations anti-Semitic acts such as those that occurred during the semana trágica *("tragic week") in Buenos Aires.*

His most acclaimed work, *Los gauchos judíos,* was published during the centennial of Argentine independence. Gerchunoff considered Argentina a "new Zion" where Jews could become fully integrated and therefore forgo the notion of a return to Palestine. The impact of the Holocaust, however, about which he wrote in *El problema judío* (1945), persuaded him to advocate the establishment of the state of Israel. His faith in Argentina led him to dismiss as deviations anti-Semitic acts such as those that occurred during the *semana trágica* ("tragic week") in Buenos Aires in January 1919.

Gerchunoff achieved his own integration into Argentine culture through his assimilation of Spanish literary classics, such as *Don Quixote.* A superb prose fiction writer of twenty-six books, he was also an acclaimed journalist and lecturer: *Retorno a Don Quijote* (1951), *Enrique Heine: El poeta de nuestra intimidad* (1927), *Las imágenes del país* (1931), and *El pino y la palmera* (1952) demonstrate the broad range of his literary production.

— SAÚL SOSNOWSKI

GERZSO, GUNTHER

Gunther Gerzso (*b.* 17 June 1915), Mexican painter. Born in Mexico City, Gerzso considers himself a self-taught artist. From 1941 to 1962, while painting, he designed sets for the Mexican cinema. In 1974 he studied lithography at the Tamarind Institute, University of New Mexico. His works have been shown since 1955 in exhibitions such as "Latin American Art Since Independence" at the Yale University Art Gallery (1966). He represented Mexico at the eighth biennial exhibition in São Paulo (1965). The University of Texas Art Museum in Austin in 1976 and the Museum of Modern

Art in Mexico City in 1977 organized major retrospectives of his work. In 1978 he was awarded the national Fine Arts Prize by the Mexican government.

– BÉLGICA RODRÍGUEZ

GESTIDO, OSCAR DANIEL

Oscar Daniel Gestido (*b.* 28 November 1901; *d.* 6 December 1967), Uruguayan military leader and president (1967). Gestido was born to a middle-class family in Montevideo. He began his military career in 1917 in the artillery. Beginning in 1923, he played an active role in organizing the Uruguayan Air Force. Between 1951 and 1955 he held the post of inspector general of the army. He later retired from the military, beginning his political career at a time of profound crisis in Uruguay. During the nationalist governments, Gestido had demonstrated skill in the administration of public bodies such as PLUNA, the state airline (1949–1951), and AFE, the state railroad (1957–1959). From 1963 to 1966 he was a member of the National Council of Government.

Gestido's image was one of honesty, which contrasted with the ever-more tarnished reputations of most politicians at the time. In 1966, the Colorado Front of Unity (List 515) was formed to support Gestido's successful presidential campaign. However, he died only nine months into his term, which was completed by his vice president, Jorge PACHECO ARECO.

– JOSÉ DE TORRES WILSON

GHIOLDI, AMÉRICO

Américo Ghioldi (*b.* 23 May 1899; *d.* ca. 1979/80), Argentine Socialist councilman, congressman, and party leader. Born in Buenos Aires, Ghioldi was a secondary school teacher, university professor, and prominent figure in Argentina's Socialist Party. He had joined the party by the early 1920s, and was elected, at the age of twenty-five, to the city council of Buenos Aires, where he served for five years. Following the course of a number of his council colleagues, he served three terms as national deputy from Buenos Aires (1932–1936, 1936–1940, 1940–1943). In Congress, Ghioldi was a leading member of the Socialist opposition to the conservative majority, noted especially for spearheading the struggle against what was considered undue concessions to foreign capital and interests in the 1930s.

Like most Socialist congressmen, Ghioldi concurrently held important positions in the party hierarchy, including editor of the Socialists' main newspaper, *La Vanguardia,* as well as of other publications. In the 1940s and thereafter, Ghioldi became one of the loudest

Socialist voices in opposition to the regime of Juan PERÓN (1946–1955), publishing a number of books critical of Peronism. In the late 1970s, in a controversial decision, he accepted appointment from the military government of General Jorge VIDELA (1976–1980) as Argentina's ambassador to Portugal.

– RICHARD J. WALTER

GHIOLDI, RODOLFO

Rodolfo Ghioldi (*b.* 21 January 1897; *d.* 3 July 1985), Argentine political leader, born in Buenos Aires, brother of Américo GHIOLDI. In 1918, he helped establish the Internationalist Socialist Party (PSI), which was renamed the Communist Party (PC) in 1920. Ghioldi traveled several times to the Soviet Union in the 1920s and 1930s and was one of only two Latin Americans to sit as an alternate delegate on the Comintern's executive committee. He served as the Argentine party's president in 1930–1931 and, along with Victorio Codovilla, dominated the Argentine Communists for most of their history. Ghioldi was his party's unsuccessful senatorial candidate in 1946 and a presidential candidate in the 1951 elections, but he never held public office.

As with most Argentine communists, he was a strict disciple of the party's often slavishly pro-Soviet line. Ideologically, Ghioldi adhered to orthodox positions on the role of the party and the necessity of passing through historical stages in the movement toward socialism.

– JAMES P. BRENNAN

GIL, GILBERTO

Gilberto Gil (*b.* 3 March 1942), prominent and innovative Brazilian composer and musician. Gil, along with Caetano VELOSO and others, was a major figure in the late-1960s cultural and musical movement known as *tropicalismo,* and continues to be one of the nation's most influential performers, especially as an articulator of a distinctly black idiom in popular music. Through the utilization in the 1960s of highly stylized versions of folk forms in compositions such as "Louvação" (1967; Homage) and "Procissão" (1965; Processional), the cinematographic construction of lyrics, and the original use of folk instruments in "Domingo no parque" (1967; Sunday in the Park), the introduction of electric instruments in "Questão de ordem" (1968; Question of Order), and the parodic use of advertising jargon in "Geléia geral" (1968; General Jelly), this last written with Torquato Neto. Gil was largely responsible for redefining the parameters of *música popular Brasileira* (Brazilian popular music).

Born and raised in the state of Bahia, like his contemporary Veloso, Gil was influenced by backlands *forro* singer Luís GONZAGA, *samba canção* composer Dorival CAYMMI, and especially the major figure of Bossa Nova, João GILBERTO. He also incorporated popular styles from Spanish America and consciously adapted the British rhythm-and-blues style of the Beatles to a Brazilian mode, most notably in "O sonho acabou" (1972; The Dream Is Over), released after his forced exile in England from 1969 to 1972 (presumably because he was a visible proponent of *tropicalismo*).

Gil incorporated popular styles from Spanish America and consciously adapted the British rhythm-and-blues style of the Beatles to a Brazilian mode.

Two formal and thematic preoccupations that recur in Gil's numerous songs from the 1970s and 1980s are mysticism and the music and culture of the African diaspora. Of the latter type, the most significant work can perhaps be found on the albums *Refavela* (1977; an invented word meaning to "re-ghetto"), which prefigures the shift of primary identification among many young Brazilian blacks from being Brazilian to being of African descent, and *Raça humana* (1984; Human Race). This second album, which was partly recorded with the Wailers in Jamaica and popularized reggae as a style to be utilized in Brazilian popular music, simultaneously portrays the African diaspora as the epitome of a universal historical experience and implies that Gilberto Gil, as the logical heir to the legacy of Jamaican singer Bob Marley, is the bard of this diaspora.

— ROBERT MYERS

GIL, JERÓNIMO ANTONIO

Jerónimo Antonio Gil (*b.* 1732; *d.* 18 April 1798), engraver. Trained in painting and engraving at the Academia de San Fernando in Madrid, Gil arrived in New Spain in 1778 to take charge of the Royal Mint in Mexico City and was entrusted with establishing a school of engraving there. His efforts in artistic education eventually resulted in the Academia de San Carlos, formally established in 1785, of which he was director until his death. His works include medals, coins, and illustrations. Especially noteworthy is the commemo-

rative medal of Manuel TOLSÁ's equestrian statue of Charles IV.

— CLARA BARGELLINI

GIL DE TABOADA Y LEMOS, FRANCISCO

Francisco Gil de Taboada y Lemos (*b.* 1733; *d.* 1810), viceroy of Peru (1790–1796). A native of Santa María de Sotolongo (Galicia), Gil pursued a naval career before serving briefly as viceroy, first, of New Granada (1789) and, soon thereafter, of Peru. Despite the increasing political confusion in Madrid in the early 1790s, Peru experienced considerable cultural development during his term of office: the progressive journal *Mercurio Peruano* appeared regularly, and the Society of Friends of the Country of Lima, which published the journal, sought, with viceregal support, to promote economic growth. Gil oversaw the production of a detailed census of the population in 1791, and a program of public works, and sought to restore the prestige of viceregal authority at the expense of the provincial intendants (first appointed in 1784).

On his return to Spain, Gil joined the Supreme Council of War, becoming commander of the navy in 1799, minister of marine in 1805, and a member of FERDINAND VII's Junta de Gobierno by means of which the latter forced his father to abdicate and assumed the throne in March 1808. Following Ferdinand's own abdication several months later, Gil refused to recognize Joseph Bonaparte as king of Spain and retired from office.

— JOHN R. FISHER

GIL FORTOUL, JOSÉ

José Gil Fortoul (*b.* November 1861; *d.* 15 June 1943), Venezuelan historian, writer, and politician. Gil Fortoul obtained his early education in El Tocuyo. After his early training in philosophy at the Colegio La Concordia, he left for Caracas in 1880 to study law, but eventually earned a doctorate in political science from the Universidad Central de Venezuela in 1885. He came in contact with the intellectual elements of the city and quickly gravitated toward positivist circles. Gil Fortoul traveled to Europe to fill various diplomatic posts for the government and remained there for ten years, during which he was intensely active intellectually.

Returning to Venezuela in 1897, Gil Fortoul collaborated on *El Cojo Ilustrado*, an important cultural magazine of the era. By government order he was given the task of writing a history of Venezuela. In 1902 he was dispatched to Europe, again on a diplomatic mission, and there wrote *Historia constitucional de Venezuela* (2 vols., 1907–1909). Upon his return to Venezuela in 1910, he joined a circle of intellectuals close to General Juan Vicente GÓMEZ, and subsequently became engaged in important public duties. Over the next several years, he served as senator, minister of public education, and chargé d'affaires for the presidency. As plenipotentiary minister of Venezuela (1917–1924), he was responsible for, among other things, negotiating the border conflicts between Venezuela and Colombia. In 1932 Gil Fortoul became director of *El Nuevo Diario,* a government publication. He also served as president of the Venezuelan Society of International Law.

Gil Fortoul is the author of a dense intellectual opus. Among his most outstanding books are *El hombre y la historia* (1890), *Filosofía constitucional* (1890), *Cartas a Pascual* (1894), *El humo de mi pipa* (1891), and *Historia constitucional de Venezuela* (2 vols., 1907–1909).

– INÉS QUINTERO

GILARDI, GILARDO

Gilardo Gilardi (*b.* 25 May 1889; *d.* 16 January 1963) Argentine composer and teacher. Born in San Fernando, Gilardi began his musical studies with his father; later he studied with the composer Pablo Berutti. He was a founding member of the Grupo Renovación (1929), an adviser to the Argentine National Orchestra and the National Cultural Commission, and a member of the Argentine Cinematography Academy. In his early works, Gilardi composed in the nationalist style, but as he matured he turned to more sophisticated compositional languages, as evidenced by the universalist style of his religious works, which include *Misa de requiem* (1914/ 1918), *Te Deum* (1936), *Misa de Gloria* (1936), and *Stabat Mater* (1952) all for organ, orchestra, and chorus. He composed two operas, as well as symphonic music, chamber works, music for children's chorus, vocal and piano works, and film and stage music. His opera *Ilse* (1919) premiered at the Teatro Colón in Buenos Aires, 13 July 1923, and *El gaucho con botas nuevas* (1936), a symphonic humorous piece, premiered in the United States under the baton of José Iturbi. Gilardi was a music critic and lecturer, and an excellent teacher. He was professor of harmony, counterpoint, and composition at the National Conservatory in Buenos Aires and at the School of Fine Arts of the National University of La Plata, and a juror in musical competitions. He died in Buenos Aires.

– SUSANA SALGADO

GILBERTO, JOÃO

João Gilberto (*b.* 1932), Brazilian singer and guitarist. Along with Antônio Carlos JOBIM, Vinícius de Moraes, and Carlos Lyra, João Gilberto launched the bossa-nova musical movement in Brazil in the late 1950s. Born in Joazeiro, a small town in the interior of Bahia State, Gilberto moved in 1949 to Rio de Janeiro, where he performed initially with vocal groups such as Garotos da Lua. Gilberto's highly syncopated style of playing the acoustic guitar, which distilled complex samba rhythms into a simplified form while utilizing harmonically progressive chords, provided the basic beat of the emerging bossa-nova style. Meanwhile, he also mastered a low-key, precise, subtle, and highly rhythmic vocal style that would also mark the genre.

Gilberto's guitar playing was first heard on Elizeth Cardoso's 1958 album "Canção do amor demais"; his debut as a recording artist came later that year, when Odeon released his singles "Chega de saudade" and "Desafinado" (each cowritten by Antônio Carlos Jobim). In 1959, Gilberto launched his debut album, "Chega de saudade," considered the first bossa-nova album. He recorded several more bossa LPs in the next few years in Brazil and the United States, including the highly successful album "Getz-Gilberto," with American saxophonist Stan Getz in 1964. On it, João's then-wife Astrud dueted with him on "The Girl from Ipanema," one of the world's best-known songs of the late twentieth century.

Gilberto had a profound influence on the next generation of Brazilian musicians, but from the late 1960s on João has led a reclusive life, with only sporadic concert appearances and record releases. He recorded only a handful of records in the 1970s and 1980s, among them: "Brasil" (1981), "João Gilberto Interpreta Tom Jobim" (1985), "João Gilberto: Live in Montreux" (1987), and "João" (1991).

– CHRIS MCGOWAN

GILDEMEISTER FAMILY

Gildemeister Family, owners of sugar plantations in the Chicama Valley on the northern coast of Peru. In the early twentieth century they built a vast network of lands around Hacienda Casa Grande. Their successes led them to expand operations, and in the early 1920s they purchased Hacienda Roma, owned by the Larco family. The purchase signaled a trend toward centralization of land ownership that characterized the Peruvian sugar industry in the late nineteenth and early twentieth centuries. Centralization and heavy investment in technical improvements were accompanied by a search for cheap labor. Asian indenture had ended, and to expand the labor force with indigenous people, the Gildemeisters, Peruvians with strong German ties, sent labor agents to the highland villages, where they advanced money to young men. The highlanders became heavily indebted peons on the plantations. Later, this same labor force was set free through total conversion to wage labor. Proletarianization of the indebted workers signified that by World War I, Peruvian sugar had reached a period of major expansion. That is because the replacement of sharecroppers and tenants with a mobile labor force meant sugar agriculture was flexible enough to meet market fluctuations. Some scholars see the process as the beginning point in establishing links between anti-imperialism and anticapitalism in Peruvian politics. At this time the American Popular Revolutionary Alliance (APRA) emerged as a major political force in the sugar valleys of coastal Peru. Many of the party's earliest rank and file, formerly small sugar producers, were driven off the land and into artisanry and technical work for the big producers.

— VINCENT PELOSO

GILL, JUAN BAUTISTA

Juan Bautista Gill (*b.* 1840; *d.* 12 April 1877), president of Paraguay (1874–1877). Born into a well-connected Asunción family, Gill spent his earliest years in the Paraguayan capital, where, for a time, he worked as apprentice to his father, a high official of the Carlos Antonio LÓPEZ government. In 1854 the younger Gill journeyed to Buenos Aires, where he spent several years studying medicine. He returned to Paraguay just before the beginning of the War of the Triple Alliance in 1864. During the fighting he distinguished himself as a medical orderly and participated in several battles before being captured at Angostura in 1868.

Upon his release one year later, Gill immediately involved himself in the turbulent politics of the postwar period. His vociferous support for Conservatives Cirilo Antonio RIVAROLA and Cándido BAREIRO gave him some prominence on the Paraguayan scene, as did his friendly connections with the Brazilians, whose army occupied the country. These same connections, however, earned Gill many enemies in the liberal camp.

Between 1872 and 1874 Bareiro masterminded a series of revolts aimed at toppling the government of Salvador Jovellanos. Although Gill played only a minor part in these actions, he stood the most to gain when the Brazilians dropped their support of Jovellanos. With their help, he became president in 1874.

Gill has often been portrayed as a Brazilian puppet, but he sincerely wished to see foreign troops leave Paraguay and worked tirelessly to that end. In 1876 he signed the Machaín-Irigoyen treaty with Argentina, an agreement that provided for the arbitration of the border dispute involving the Gran Chaco territory and

thereby hastened the evacuation of the remaining Brazilian troops.

Gill had little opportunity to enjoy his laurels. In April 1877, a band of assassins led by Juan Silvano Godoi murdered the president on his way to government house.

— THOMAS L. WHIGHAM

GINASTERA, ALBERTO EVARISTO

Alberto Evaristo Ginastera (*b.* 11 April 1916; *d.* 25 June 1983), Argentine musician. Born in Buenos Aires, Ginastera began his studies at age twelve, at the Alberto Williams Conservatory, graduating in 1935 with a gold medal in composition. In 1936 he entered the National Conservatory of Music to study with Athos Palma (harmony), José Gil (counterpoint), and José André (composition). His career as a composer began in the early 1930s, while he was a student at the Conservatory. His first significant work in the Argentine national idiom was the ballet *Panambí* (1936), which premiered at the Teatro Colón, 12 July 1940; it later won both the Mu-

Alberto Ginastera. (Organization of American States)

nicipal and the National Prize for Music. The turning point of his career came with a commission from the American Ballet Caravan for which he wrote *Estancia* (1941), which earned him a place of distinction among young Argentine composers. That same year he was named professor of composition at the National Conservatory. In 1942 he received a Guggenheim fellowship, but he did not go to the United States until after World War II. He lived in New York from 1945 to 1947 and attended Aaron Copland's classes at Tanglewood.

In 1948 Ginastera returned to Buenos Aires, where he founded the Argentine chapter of the International Society for Contemporary Music (ISCM). He was appointed director of the Conservatory of the Province of Buenos Aires in La Plata. Over the years he attended concerts of his works in Frankfurt, Oslo, Rome, Stockholm, Paris, and London. He participated in the Latin American Music Festival of Caracas (1957), acting as juror for the composition competition. The following year he went to the United States to attend the premiere of his *Segundo Cuarteto* by the Juilliard Quartet at the First Inter-American Music Festival in Washington, D.C. During the Second Inter-American Music Festival (1961), Ginastera achieved world recognition with the premiere of the *Cantata para América Mágica* and the Piano Concerto No. 1, commissioned by the Fromm and Koussevitzky foundations, respectively. His opera *Don Rodrigo,* based on a libretto by Alejandro Casona, premiered at the Teatro Colón in July 1964. Soon there followed two additional operas, both commissioned by the Opera Society of Washington: *Bomarzo* (May 1967) and *Beatrix Cenci,* performed on 10 September 1971 during the inauguration of the Kennedy Center for the Performing Arts.

Ginastera was one of the most prominent Latin American composers of the twentieth century and much of his music has entered the international repertory. His works have an exuberant, dramatic quality, and they range in style from a subjective nationalism to a more objective, abstract mode, using advanced techniques: polytonality, microtonality, aleatory procedures, and twelve-tone writing. All of his compositions retain a lyrical, expressionistic aspect, involving the use of *Sprechstimme* (speech song) in the vocal works. He died in Geneva.

— SUSANA SALGADO

GIRIBALDI, (VICENTE) TOMÁS E.

(Vicente) Tomás E. Giribaldi (*b.* 18 October 1847; *d.* 11 April 1930), Uruguayan composer. Giribaldi was born in Montevideo, where he began his studies with Giuseppe Strigelli and the celebrated Italian bass player Giovanni Bottesini. Later, he studied with the Spaniard Carmelo Calvo and the Italian Giuseppe Giuffra, European composers who had settled in Montevideo. As a member of a family of musicians of Italian origin, Giribaldi became an active participant in the musical life of Montevideo at an early age. His first compositions were piano and vocal pieces; as he matured, he became attracted to the operatic forms. As the first opera written by a Uruguayan composer, *La Parisina,* which premiered at the Teatro Solís in Montevideo on 14 September 1878, earned for Giribaldi a place of honor in the music history of his country. The Italian libretto by Felice Romani was sung by the artists of the Italian Lyric Company Nazarino under the baton of maestro Leopoldo Montenegro. Giribaldi composed three additional operas: *Manfredi di Svevia, Inés de Castro,* and *Magda,* none of which achieved the success of *La Parisina.* In addition, he composed works for orchestra, band, and piano, as well as chamber music, including the symphonic poem *El Athenaeum,* and the suite *Scènes militaires.* He died in Montevideo.

— SUSANA SALGADO

GIRÓN, FRANCISCO HERNÁNDEZ

Francisco Hernández Girón (*d.* 7 December 1554), leader of the last major uprising against royal authority during the Peruvian civil wars. Born in Cáceres, he probably participated in the conquest of Veragua in 1535, before continuing to Peru. A relative of Captain Lorenzo de Aldana, he marched under orders of Francisco PIZARRO to remove Sebastián de BELALCÁZAR from the north in 1538. Largely successful, he became a *vecino* of Pasto. He was a supporter of Viceroy Blasco NÚÑEZ VELA during the uprising of Gonzalo PIZARRO, and was named a captain of a company of infantry pikemen. He served the viceroy as well, particularly in defense of the rear guard.

During the battle of Añaquito (January 1546), Girón was in charge of a group of harquebusiers but fell wounded and was captured by Gonzalo Pizarro. Pizarro forced the prisoner to negotiate with Benalcázar to gain his support. But with the arrival of Pedro de la GASCA (ca. 1547), both Benalcázar and Girón traveled to Andahuaylas to join the royal cause. Girón received substantial reward: la Gasca extended him the *encomienda* of Jaquijahuana. He was, nevertheless, dissatisfied. Realizing his disaffection, and hoping to rid himself of the malcontent, La Gasca appointed him leader of an expedition to conquer the fierce Chunchos Indians. At this juncture, however, Girón's disagreements with the *corregidor* of Cuzco got him charged and brought to the Audiencia of Lima for trial. Freed on bond, he returned to Cuzco, where on 12 November 1553 he organized another uprising, this time directed against authorities of the Audiencia of Lima, which had ordered a new tribute assessment and the end to personal service of the Indians. He and his forces left Cuzco on 4 January 1554.

Meanwhile, after learning of the uprising, Marshall Alonso de Alvarado amassed an army of 700 Spaniards and 7,000 native Americans in the name of the king. (In late December 1553 the *oidores* in Lima had revoked the order ending personal service and created a military force in Lima.) Both forces met and fought at Chuquinga on 21 May 1554. Victorious, Girón traveled to Cuzco; at the same time, royal forces were reorganized. The final battle took place 8 October 1554 at the Inca site of Pucará. There, Girón's fortunes ended. The majority of his soldiers deserted, but the rebel escaped capture and fled to Acarí, hoping to take flight to freedom. Unfortunately, the ship sailed out of the harbor as his weary soldiers arrived, so he marched northward to Chincha, then entered the highlands, taking refuge in Hatun-Jauja. It was there he was captured after a final skirmish. He was transported to Lima and beheaded as a traitor in the Plaza de Armas on 7 December 1554.

– NOBLE DAVID COOK

GIRÓN DE LEÓN, ANDRÉS DE JESÚS

Andrés de Jesús Girón de León (*b.* 14 February 1946), Guatemalan priest and peasant leader. Girón was born in Santa Cruz del Quiché and was raised in the municipality of Tecpán in Chimaltenango. He received religious training at the seminary of Santiago de Guatemala and later in the United States.

Girón received widespread media attention by leading 16,000 peasants on an 88-mile march from Escuintla to Guatemala City in May of 1986.

Girón became an important national political figure when he founded the National Peasants' Association for Land (Asociación Nacional Campesina Pro-Tierra) in 1986. He received widespread media attention by leading 16,000 peasants on an 88-mile march from Escuintla to Guatemala City in May of 1986. His organization acquired several large landholdings for campesinos to farm cooperatively, but the movement lost membership and importance after 1989.

– RACHEL A. MAY

GIRONELLA, ALBERTO

Alberto Gironella (*b.* 26 September 1929), Mexican painter and illustrator. Born in Mexico City, Gironella considers himself a self-taught artist. He is a very talented draftsman and sensitive colorist. In 1959 he received a prize in the Paris Biennial of young painters. Since that time, his work has appeared in many individual and group exhibitions in the United States, Latin America, Europe, and Japan. His most noted individual shows have been at the Galería Prisse in Mexico City (1959), the offices of the Organization of American States in Washington, D.C. (1959), the Galería Juan Martín in Mexico City (1963, 1964, 1968, 1977, and 1979), the Sala Nacional of the Palacio de Bellas Artes in Mexico City (1972), and the Museo de Arte Moderno in Mexico City (1977). Gironella tempers crude naturalism with formal elements derived from Spanish painters, resulting in sarcastic reinterpretations of seventeenth-century court life. He also draws on familiar figures in Mexican folk art, such as the skeleton.

– BÉLGICA RODRÍGUEZ

GIRRI, ALBERTO

Alberto Girri (*b.* 1919), Argentine poet. Born in Buenos Aires, Girri may best be described as one of the last of the prominent male modernist poetic voices of the turbulent mid-twentieth century in Argentina. Girri wrote against the backdrop of some of the most violent and unstable times in his country's history, and his poetry evinces the firm conviction that a humanistic cultural tradition is the best refuge from and bulwark against the insecurities of life. Girri's modernist aesthetic put him outside the sphere of committed literature that was central at the time, and his poetry is marked by an emphasis on the solitude of the poetic voice and by extensive elaborations on the hermetic surrealism of the period, often with an impressive sense of the terror of existential anguish. Girri also published many translations of English-language poets.

– DAVID WILLIAM FOSTER

GISMONTI, EGBERTO

Egberto Gismonti (*b.* 5 December 1944), Brazilian composer, guitarist, and pianist. Born into a musical family with many professional musicians, including a band-director grandfather and a band-director uncle, Egberto Gismonti enrolled for his first music lessons in the musical conservatory of Nova Friburgo in the state of Rio de Janeiro at age five. He studied fifteen years with Jacques Klein and Aurelio Silveira, and then was awarded a grant for study in Vienna. An arrangement of one of his compositions, *O sonho,* written for an orchestra of one hundred performers, was performed in Rio in 1968. Shortly thereafter he went to France, where he continued his musical studies and worked as a professional accompanist.

Gismonti is best known for his startlingly vivid settings of songs recorded on compact discs released in France, Germany, and Brazil. His use of electronic instruments, traditional percussion instruments, Brazilian percussion instruments, and Indian flutes have made recordings such as *Agua e vinho* (1972) and other song settings powerful expressions of Brazilian popular culture. He has also been active as a composer of film music in *A penúltima donzela* (1969), *Em familia* (1971), and *Confissões do frei Abóbora* (1971).

— DAVID P. APPLEBY

GLANTZ, MARGO

Margo Glantz (*b.* 28 January 1930), Mexican writer and critic. A professor of philosophy and letters at the National University of Mexico, Glantz was for a time director of the university's creative journal *Punto de Partida* and head of the department of literature at the National Institute of Fine Arts (1982–1986). Her work includes creative prose, literary and cultural criticism, and translations. Her memoir *Las genealogías* (1981), about her family of Ukrainian Jewish origin, won the Magda Donato Literary Prize in 1982. This was followed by the Xavier Villarrutia Prize for the prose poem *Síndrome de naufragios* in 1984. As a feminist, Glantz has defied the conventional "male" genres to render postmodern, innovative, and experimental texts where a woman's perspective necessarily alters the traditional forms. As a critic, she is recognized for her controversial critique of "la generación de la Onda" (wave), a group of young writers influenced by the U.S. counterculture of the early 1970s. Glantz has also translated the works of Georges Bataille, Jerzy Grotowski, and Thomas Kyd.

— NORMA KLAHN

GLISSANT, ÉDOUARD

Édouard Glissant (*b.* 21 September 1928), writer and teacher of Martinique. Aimé CÉSAIRE was Glissant's professor at the Lycée Schoelcher in Fort-de-France, Martinique. With the group Franc-Jeu, Glissant and Frantz Fanon worked for Aimé Césaire's election to the Constituent Assembly in 1945. Glissant went to France on a scholarship in 1946. Active in the Front Antillo-Guyanais pour l'Indépendance, Glissant was barred (1961) from returning to Martinique or traveling to Algeria. After the French government finally allowed

Glissant to return to Martinique in 1965, he founded the Institut Martiniquais d'Études and the journal *Acoma* in an effort to develop cultural consciousness among young Martinicans. Glissant later accepted a chair in Francophone literature at Louisiana State University.

Édouard Glissant has become the major proponent of "creolization," a concept that underscores acceptance of a decentered position in the world, the willingness to encounter the other rather than take one's own standpoint as central, and the will to take cross-breeding (*métissage*) as normal rather than exceptional and reprehensible. Purists are shocked by the contagious mixing of cultures in the language of the young. "Alert to the intermingling of world cultures," poets, according to Glissant, "are delighted." Glissant wants to build the Tower of Babel "in all languages."

— CARROL F. COATES

GODOI, JUAN SILVANO

Juan Silvano Godoi (*b.* 12 November 1850; *d.* 27 January 1926), Paraguayan historian, bibliophile, and political figure. Though born in Asunción, Godoi spent his early years in Buenos Aires, where he studied law. He interrupted his studies in 1869 to return to Paraguay to participate, at age nineteen, in the drafting of his country's first democratic constitution.

The defeat of Marshal Francisco Solano LÓPEZ a year later initiated a period of great political instability and foreign intervention in Paraguay; various factions vied for power. Godoi joined actively in a number of political intrigues, including the 1877 assassination of President Juan Bautista GILL, a Brazilian puppet. As a result of these activities, Godoi was forced into exile and went to Argentina, where he stayed eighteen years. While there, he remained active in emigré politics, however, and on several occasions helped to arm rebel groups who sought to invade Paraguay.

In the mid-1890s Godoi accepted a government compromise that permitted him to return to Asunción. While in exile, he had amassed a prize-winning library of 20,000 volumes, which he now used to form the nucleus of a new national library. From 1902 until his death, Godoi was director of the National Library, Museum, and Archive. He was also a historian of note, having written a dozen studies, including *Monografías históricas* (1893), *Últimas operaciones de guerra del General José Eduvigis Díaz* (1897), *Mi misión a Río de Janeiro* (1897), *La muerte del Mariscal López* (1905), *El baron de Río Branco* (1912), and *El Asalto a los acorazados* (1919). Godoi's personal diaries and manuscripts are now held in the Special Collections Library of the University of California, Riverside.

— THOMAS L. WHIGHAM

GODOY CRUZ, TOMÁS

Tomás Godoy Cruz (*b.* 6 March 1791; *d.* 15 May 1852), Argentine businessman, educator, and politician. Born in Mendoza to a patrician family, Godoy Cruz earned degrees in philosophy and law from the University of San Felipe, Chile, in 1810 and 1813. When Facundo QUIROGA invaded Mendoza in 1831, José Videla Castillo, de facto governor of the province, and his allies, of whom Godoy Cruz was one, were exiled to Chile. In exile during the 1830s, Godoy Cruz published a *Manual* (1838) on textiles, taught extensively in related fields, and invested in Argentine commerce, mining, and textiles. Aware of Godoy Cruz's expertise, Governor José Félix Aldao asked him back from exile and in 1846 appointed him to direct governmental policies regarding textile industries in the province. His most notable contribution, however, was in politics. A contemporary viewed him as someone "accustomed to the admiration and even respect of San Martín and O'Higgins, having a great appreciation for his own person and the conviction of his opinions." Godoy Cruz, a close collaborator of SAN MARTÍN and a supporter of Platine independence who donated his homestead to the cause early in the conflict, displayed this self-confidence in the Congress of Tucumán (1816–1819) and as governor of Mendoza (1820–1822), where he died.

— FIDEL IGLESIAS

GOERITZ, MATHIAS

Mathias Goeritz (*b.* 4 April 1915; *d.* 1990?), Mexican painter, sculptor, and teacher. Born in Danzig, Goeritz studied medicine, art, art history, and philosophy in Berlin. He arrived in Mexico in 1949 and began an active life in the arts as a teacher, artist, and founder of four art galleries between 1950 and 1952 in Guadalajara, Jalisco. He is primarily known for his experimental museum El Eco, constructed in Mexico City in 1953, and his great Plaza of the Five Towers, constructed in 1957–1958 in Satellite City, a suburb of Mexico City. The monumental size of the towers and the spatial integration of a sculpture with the floor and walls of El Eco influenced primary structure and minimalist sculptors of the United States and Mexico in the 1960s and 1970s.

In 1960 Goeritz distributed "Please Stop," a printed leaflet, in front of the Museum of Modern Art in New York City to protest the exhibition of Jean Tinguely's *Homage to New York,* a self-destructing machine, because it exemplified the loss of spirituality in art. In 1961 a manifesto by Goeritz inspired Petro Friedeberg, José Luis CUEVAS, and others to form a group in Mexico City called Los Hartos (Fed Up). Goeritz's other major works include Pyramid of Mixcose (1970) for a housing project in Mexico City; Centro del Espacio Escultorico (1979), sixty-four modules with sculpture near the ancient site of Cuicuilco; and Laberinto de Jerusalem (1973–1980), a community center in Jerusalem that is a wonderful example of sculpture combined with architecture.

— JACINTO QUIRARTE

GOICURÍA Y CABRERA, DOMINGO

Domingo Goicuría y Cabrera (*b.* 23 June 1804; *d.* 6 May 1870), Cuban independence figure. Goicuría, a native of Havana, was a rich merchant who became even richer during the U.S. Civil War running supplies from Mexico to Texas. He favored slavery and the colonization of Cuba by whites. A tenacious opponent of Spanish colonial rule, at first he advocated the annexation of the island to the United States, and in 1855 he supported a U.S.-backed expedition to Cuba that failed.

A tenacious opponent of Spanish colonial rule, Goicuría advocated the annexation of Cuba to the United States.

This led him to embrace the idea of independence, and a year later he joined forces with the American filibuster William WALKER for the invasion of Nicaragua. He expected that after taking over Nicaragua, Walker would invade Cuba. But Walker wanted to conquer the rest of Central America rather than Cuba, and the two men quarreled. Afterward Goicuría intensified his anti-Spanish activities until he finally succeeded in invading Cuba after the 1868 outbreak of the Ten Years' War. He was captured in February 1870 by the Spaniards and three months later was publicly executed by garrote in Havana.

— JOSÉ M. HERNÁNDEZ

GOLBERY DO COUTO E SILVA

Golbery do Couto e Silva (*b.* 21 August 1911; *d.* 18 September 1987), Brazilian military officer and political figure. Born in Rio Grande do Sul, Golbery graduated from the military command college. He attended the U.S. Army Command and General Staff College at Fort Leavenworth in 1944 before serving in the Brazilian Expeditionary Force (FEB) in Italy in 1944–1945. In 1952 he began teaching at the recently formed Higher War College (Escola Superior de Guerra—ESG). Through his writings and work in the ESG, he exerted enormous influence on the formation of the National Security Doctrine. Golbery became the head of the National Security Council under Jânio QUADROS in 1961 but resigned when João GOULART became president in the same year. Between 1961 and 1964 he headed the IPES (Instituto de Pesquisas e Estudos Sociais), a privately funded think tank and intelligence-gathering operation that played a notorious role in working for the overthrow of Goulart.

After the military coup of 1964, President Humberto CASTELLO BRANCO created the SNI (Serviço Nacional de Informações) and named Golbery to head the agency with cabinet-level status. Along with other "moderates," Golbery lost influence with the "election" of Artur COSTA E SILVA (1967–1969) and then Emílio MÉDICI (1969–1974) to the presidency. He served as the head of the civilian presidential staff during the administration of Ernesto GEISEL (1974–1979) and in the first two years of the presidency of João Baptista FIGUEIREDO (1979–1985).

Along with Geisel, Golbery was one of the principal figures in the shaky and tentative process of *abertura* (political opening). He resigned from the government in 1981 when he was unable to persuade the president to press an investigation of a political scandal implicating the hardliners in the government and the SNI.

– MARSHALL C. EAKIN

GOLDEMBERG, ISAAC

Isaac Goldemberg (*b*. 15 November 1945), Peruvian author. Goldemberg was born in the small town of Chepén. His father and his family, Russian Jews, had immigrated to Peru in the 1930s. His maternal grandmother, a mestiza medicine woman, was from Cajamarca. Goldemberg received a Catholic education under the supervision of the local parish priest and was unaware of his Jewish heritage for a number of years. Learning of his mixed religious background reinforced his sense of being different from both Catholics and Jews. It is not surprising that the question of identity and a sense of exile pervade his works.

Completely bilingual in Spanish and English, Goldemberg helped produce the English translation of *Hombre de paso,* which was published in a bilingual edition. Among authors and critics who have praised his

work are José Miguel Oviedo, Severo SARDUY, Marco Martos, and Mario VARGAS LLOSA.

Since 1984 Goldemberg has lived in New York City, where he is a director of the Latin American Writers Institute/Instituto de Escritores Latinoamericanos, which organizes exhibitions of Latin American fiction and criticism. He is also on the staff of *Brújula/Compass,* a bimonthly magazine of bilingual Latino and Latin American literature written in the United States.

Goldemberg's published works are *Tiempo de silencio* (1969), poetry; *De Chepén a La Habana* (1973), poetry; *The Fragmented Life of Don Jacobo Lerner,* translated by Robert Picciotto (1976); *La vida a plazos de don Jacobo Lerner,* 2d ed. (1980); *Hombre de paso/Just Passing Through,* translated by David Unger and Isaac Goldemberg (1981); *Tiempo al tiempo* (1984); *Play by Play,* translated by Hardie St. Martin (1985); *La vida al contado* (1989), poetry, with a preface by Marco Martos and a sketchy and selective autobiographical account by Goldemberg.

– GUIDO A. PODESTÁ

GOMES, ANTÔNIO CARLOS

Antônio Carlos Gomes (*b*. 11 July 1836; *d*. 16 September 1896), the first Brazilian musician to achieve considerable success in Italy as a composer of operas. Son of a bandmaster whose most notable achievement appears to have been fathering twenty-six children, Tonico (as Antônio Carlos was called as a boy) learned the fundamentals of music and an elementary knowledge of several instruments from his father at an early age. His *Hino acadêmico,* an early composition, was well received, and he went to Rio de Janeiro in order to enroll in the Imperial Conservatory of Music. His conservatory studies in composition with Joaquim Giannini reinforced his interest in opera, and two works, *A noite do castelo,* produced in 1861, and *Joana de Flandres,* in 1863, met considerable success, resulting in a government subsidy for study in Italy. The greatest success of Gomes's career was the performance of his opera *Il Guarany* at La Scala, in Milan, on 19 March 1870. *Il Guarany* was followed by *Fosca, Salvator Rosa, Maria Tudor, Lo schiavo,* and *Condor,* his last opera, but none of the later works achieved the success of *Il Guarany.*

Gomes chose Brazilian subjects for some of his operas, but his style of writing and approach was Italian at a time of rising musical nationalism in Brazil. Expecting unqualified and enthusiastic acceptance in his native country during a time of rising republican sentiments, he was instead considered an aristocrat out of touch with political realities. The fact that his family sought to forbid performances of his operas in the Portuguese language, insisting on Italian, did nothing to allay the suspicions of adherents of the new nationalist sentiments.

— DAVID P. APPLEBY

GOMES, EDUARDO

Eduardo Gomes (*b.* 20 September 1896; *d.* 13 June 1981), Brazilian Air Force officer and political leader. Born in Petrópolis, Rio de Janeiro, Gomes enlisted in the army in 1916. He was commissioned in 1919, and three years later he became a national hero as one of the *tenente* defenders and survivors of the Revolt of Fort Copacabana. Imprisoned for his role as an air observer during the revolt of 1924, he returned to active duty in 1927. His assignment to the army air corps included the task, in 1930, of establishing the Brazilian military air mail systems. With the creation of the Brazilian air force in 1941, Gomes served as commander of the First and Second Air Zones in the northeastern section of the country during World War II.

In 1945, Gomes helped to organize the anti-Vargas National Democratic Union (União Democrática Nacional—UDN) and ran unsuccessfully against General Eurico DUTRA as its presidential candidate that year, and in 1950 against Getúlio VARGAS. He was an official and elder statesman of the party until its dissolution in 1965. Appointed minister of the air force by President João CAFÉ FILHO in 1954, Gomes retired from active service in 1961 with the rank of air marshal. President Humberto CASTELO BRANCO recalled him to serve as air minister after the revolution of 1964. He died in Rio de Janeiro.

— MICHAEL L. JAMES

GÓMEZ, BENIGNO

Benigno Gómez (*b.* 1934), Honduran painter and sculptor. Gómez is a native of the department of Santa Barbara, Honduras. His woodcarvings of doves won him a scholarship in 1950 to study at the Escuela Nacional de Bellas Artes in Tegucigalpa, where he was strongly influenced by Max EUCEDA. In 1960 he won another scholarship to study in Rome, where he remained until 1966, when he returned to Tegucigalpa as a professor at the Escuela Nacional de Bellas Artes. By now his neorealist paintings of the human figure had won him much recognition, particularly for his innovative use of color, but later he became more noted for his surrealist paintings. A trademark of his work is the presence of doves in virtually all his paintings, symbols of Gómez's optimistic spirit.

— RALPH LEE WOODWARD, JR.

GÓMEZ, EUGENIO

Eugenio Gómez (*b.* 1890; *d.* 1963), leader of the Uruguayan Communist party. As a barber in Montevideo he came into contact with the labor movement and joined the port workers' Federación Obrera Marítima (Maritime Workers Federation) and the Partido Socialista del Uruguay (Socialist Party—PSU), led by Emílio FRUGONI. During the debate about PSU membership in the Third International and subscription to its twenty-one conditions (1920), Gómez, Celestino Mibelli, and Rodríguez Saraillé led the majority faction favoring acceptance. After a special party conference held on 16–18 April 1921, the PSU changed its name to Partido Comunista del Uruguay (PCU). Frugoni and his minority faction reestablished the PSU in 1923.

From 1921 to 1955 Gómez headed the party executive committee, serving as its general secretary from the time of party proscription during the dictatorship of Gabriel TERRA (1937). Under his leadership the PCU became one of the most active promoters of Uruguayan solidarity with the Spanish Republic and the Anti-Nazi Action, and achieved its best election results in 1946.

Gómez was deputy from 1942 to 1946 and was a member of the parliamentary Special Commission on Working Conditions in Uruguay. After 1946 his leadership was characterized by an increasing loss of popularity due to personality cult and power abuse. In 1955 PCU membership stood at about 5,000.

— DIETER SCHONEBOHM

GÓMEZ, INDALECIO

Indalecio Gómez (*b.* 1851; *d.* 18 August 1920), Argentine statesman and author. Born in Salta and trained as a lawyer at the University of Buenos Aires, Gómez began his political career as a national deputy representing Salta Province. He gained national prominence as director of the National Bank of Argentina during the administration of Carlos PELLEGRINI (1890–1892). He remained active in national politics, serving as Argentina's ambassador to Germany under President Manuel QUINTANA (1904–1906) and as the interior minister under President Roque SÁENZ PEÑA (1910–1913). As interior minister, he orchestrated the passage of the Sáenz Peña Law (1911), which granted universal male suffrage and established a secret ballot for elections. Gómez supervised its implementation in the national congressional elections of April 1912. In numerous books and articles, including *El episcopado y la paz* (1895), he established his reputation as a political and social traditionalist who defended the elite values of Argentina's

Generation of 1880 during an era of turmoil and reform.

— DANIEL LEWIS

GÓMEZ, JOSÉ MIGUEL

José Miguel Gómez (*b.* ca. 1720; *d.* 1805), best-known colonial painter of Honduras. Born in Tegucigalpa, Gómez painted mostly religious themes. He began his studies in Comayagua but later studied in Guatemala City. He returned to Comayagua, where his painting of San José de Calasanz for the Araque family brought him to the attention of Bishop Rodríguez de Rivera, who commissioned a series of works from him for the cathedral of Comayagua. Gómez's paintings were characterized by their natural realism. He later painted many religious canvases for churches in and around Tegucigalpa. His painting of Father José Simón Zelaya is especially notable, as was his final painting, in 1805, of *La Divina Pastora,* depicting the Virgin with Child and a lamb, a vivid painting that reflected the influence of his Spanish and Guatemalan teachers.

— RALPH LEE WOODWARD, JR.

GÓMEZ, JOSÉ MIGUEL

José Miguel Gómez (*b.* 1858; *d.* 1921), president of Cuba (1909–1913). General Gómez began his rise to prominence during the Ten Years' War and was governor of Santa Clara during the U.S. occupation under General Leonard Wood. An astute and clever politician, Gómez switched from the Conservative to the Liberal Party in 1906 when the former failed to support his bid for the presidency. He was also active in the insurrection against President Tomás ESTRADA PALMA in 1906.

Gómez's administration is known for expenditures that approached $140 million and for its 1912 campaign against a black military force, the Independent Party of Color.

Running again on the Liberal Party ticket in 1908, Gómez won. During his presidency, the government was accused of corruption, patronage, and suspending duties on the exports of sugar and other products. The administration is perhaps better known for its expenditures that approached $140 million and for the 1912 military campaign against a black military force and its supporters, the Independent Party of Color.

Gómez was defeated in 1912 but remained in the political limelight. In 1920, opposed to Liberal policies and increasing internal strife, he plotted an unsuccessful revolution.

— ALLAN S. R. SUMNALL

GOMÉZ, JOSÉ VALENTÍN

José Valentín Goméz (*b.* 8 November 1774; *d.* 20 September 1833), Argentine educator and diplomat. Born in Buenos Aires and educated as a cleric at the University of Córdoba, Goméz became an ardent supporter of the revolution and subsequently a diplomat of the new government. In 1813 he was elected to the National Assembly and thereafter was sent on several diplomatic missions. One of his most interesting illustrates the monarchist tendencies of the government he represented. Under Juan Martín de PUEYRREDÓN in 1819 he went on a secret mission to France in order to persuade the French minister of foreign affairs, the Baron Dessolle, to establish a monarchy in La Plata under a European dynastic family. The duke of Lucca was the favored candidate, but Dessolle changed his mind and the scheme was abandoned. Gómez became the rector of the University of Buenos Aires in 1823 and was responsible for introducing the Lancastrian system of education and attempting other educational reforms. He died in Buenos Aires.

— NICHOLAS P. CUSHNER

GÓMEZ, JUAN CARLOS

Juan Carlos Gómez (*b.* 1820; *d.* 1884), Uruguayan journalist and poet. The long siege of Montevideo by Blanco Party forces under Manuel ORIBE, who was supported by Argentina's dictator, Juan Manuel de ROSAS, provided Gómez with an incentive to move to Chile in 1843. While there he joined Argentines and fellow liberals Domingo SARMIENTO and Bartolomé MITRE in the struggle against Rosas, and then in the task of implementing a liberal program of institutional renovation. His defense of freedom of the press in Valparaíso's *El Mercurio* in the 1840s and his promotion of liberal reforms in Buenos Aires's *El Orden, La Tribuna,* and *El Nacional* in the 1850s—and for a brief period in Montevideo's *El Nacional*—earned him wide respect.

Between 1852 and 1863 Gómez divided his time between Montevideo and Buenos Aires. In Montevideo he served as a representative in the national legislature and as minister of foreign relations. In Buenos Aires he supported Mitre's Nationalist Party. His principled opinions often sparked angry polemic: he stridently promoted the union of Uruguay and Argentina in a

"United States of the Plata," and he was an outspoken critic, beginning in 1869, of Argentina's role in the War of the Triple Alliance. Following Juan Bautista ALBERDI, he argued that the war "against the people" had weakened the Spanish-speaking countries of the Plata relative to their historical rival, Brazil. Gómez promoted the liberal ideas of the period, including the need to attract a European population to the regions of the Plata, to combat the retrograde rural society that joined despotic caudillos with illiterate gauchos, and to modernize at whatever cost. Gómez also wrote poetry. His "La libertad" is one of the finest in Uruguay's romantic canon.

– WILLIAM H. KATRA

GÓMEZ, JUAN GUALBERTO

Juan Gualberto Gómez (*b.* 12 July 1854; *d.* 5 March 1933), Cuban independence figure, journalist, and politician. Gómez was born in a sugar mill in Matanzas Province, the son of black slaves who managed to purchase his freedom upon his birth. When Cuba's struggle for independence began, his parents sent him in 1869 to study in Paris, where he became a journalist. Afterward he traveled through the Caribbean and Mexico, returning to Cuba in 1878 when the Ten Years' War ended. At this time he met José MARTÍ, who would become his close friend and with whom he immediately began to conspire against Spain. Deported from Cuba on account of these activities, Gómez settled in Madrid, where he spent the next ten years working on various daily newspapers. He also became the secretary of the Madrid abolitionist society. When he finally was allowed to return to Cuba (1890), Gómez again worked as Martí's secret agent on the island, and when the 1895–1898 war of independence broke out, he was imprisoned and once more deported to Spain. Returning in 1898, he participated in the Cuban constituent assembly of 1900–1901, where he was one of the strongest opponents of the Platt Amendment. Afterward he became one of the editors of the daily *La Lucha,* and was elected to the Cuban Senate in the 1910s. Gómez died in Havana.

– JOSÉ M. HERNÁNDEZ

GÓMEZ, JUAN VICENTE

Juan Vicente Gómez (*b.* 24 July 1857; *d.* 17 December 1935), president and dictator of Venezuela (1908–1935). During his twenty-seven-year dictatorship, Gómez created the modern Venezuelan nation-state. Like Porfirio Díaz of Mexico (1876–1911), Gómez brought an end to internecine struggles for power, established a strong central government, began the construction of a nationwide transportation and communication system, and put the economy on a stable basis through the judicious use of petroleum revenues. Along with Rómulo BETANCOURT, he is one of Venezuela's major twentieth-century political figures.

Gómez achieved power at midlife. A former butcher and cattle rancher from Táchira, he became involved in politics in 1892 when he joined Cipriano CASTRO in an abortive political movement. Forced into exile in Colombia following the failure of that struggle, Gómez returned in 1899 as an officer in Castro's small Army of the Liberal Restoration. At the age of forty-two, he entered Caracas for the first time. There he served Castro as a loyal and trusted associate, and played an instrumental role in defeating the many groups who rose up against Castro's regime. Gómez risked his life on numerous occasions to put down major revolts. In so doing, he won support from the Venezuelan military establishment, which considered him both brave and honest. He also gained allies among the civilian elites, who saw Gómez as an efficient, if ruthless, military leader. Like most caudillos, he also had a large following among the nation's campesinos, who revered him, in part because they believed he possessed supernatural powers.

In 1908, Castro named Gómez as acting president while he sought medical treatment in Europe. Gómez took advantage of his chief's absence to proclaim himself president of Venezuela. His pronouncement met with immediate success, both at home and abroad. Castro's enemies thought that Gómez was an individual they could control. Foreign powers, which had suffered through the Castro years, also believed they could trust Gómez. Within weeks of his coup, the United States recognized the new government, and European powers quickly followed suit. As a result, Gómez enjoyed good relations with the United States and European nations, all of whom played an important role in the development of Venezuela's oil resources.

Recently, Venezuelan scholars have begun to revise part of the Gómez legacy. While continuing to condemn him for the torture and imprisonment of opponents; his monopolization of land and concessions for himself, his family, and his friends; his high-handed use of censorship and police violence to silence his critics; and his seeming surrender of Venezuelan petroleum to foreign economic interests, they now recognize Gómez and his associates as important contributors to Venezuela's modernization. Without the Gómez administration, they argue, Venezuela would have continued as a wartorn nation, with a predominantly agricultural economy that depended on the vagaries of international demand for its chief export crops, coffee and cacao.

Under Gómez, the nation enjoyed unprecedented economic stability and growth, as well as political calm. A close alliance with bankers, financiers, businessmen, and representatives of the United States assured the former. Constitutions of 1914, 1922, 1925, 1928, 1929, and 1931 guaranteed the latter.

From the outset of his administration, Gómez gave generous concessions to foreign interests. His oil policy followed a moderate course based on his desire to develop the industry rapidly, with the aid of foreign investment. Under the direction of Development Minister Gumersindo Torres (1918–1922), a mining law of 1918 and a petroleum code of 1920 limited the freedom of companies. But under pressure from the U.S. State Department, Gómez had Congress remove some of the most restrictive measures from the 1920 code. In 1922, a new law gave foreign oil companies what they wanted: low taxes and royalty payments to Venezuela, slow exploitation rates, and no restriction on the amount of land the companies held.

Gómez also made important changes in the organization of the national armed forces. In 1910, the first inspector general of the army, Félix Galavís, opened the Military Academy, which trained the next generation of professional officers. Military professionalization assured Gómez of an armed force that could defend the nation as well as put down domestic revolts. Since the officers often received higher salaries than their civilian counterparts, Gómez attracted candidates to the armed forces who had closer ties to the Caracas elites than did the older officers. Until his death, his brothers and fellow Táchiran officers comprised a separate and more powerful part of the officers, whereas the younger generation trained during his rule comprised the backbone of the post-Gómez generation of military leaders.

Perhaps as important as his reform of the military, his fiscal policies also had a long-term impact upon Venezuela. Gómez often showed his rancher background when it came to budgets. Like his minister of the Treasury, Román Cárdenas (1913–1922), he believed firmly in a balanced budget. Cárdenas's centralization of tax collection helped raise monies needed to run the government efficiently. Cuts in salaries and expenditures, along with amortization of foreign debts, turned Venezuela into a nation with no public debt by the mid-1920s. Vicente Lecuna [Salbach], who served as director of the Bank of Venezuela, also worked with Gómez on the national budget. His mastery of international monetary exchange placed Venezuela on a firm footing as the nation entered its oil boom. Gómez died in Maracay, Venezuela.

— WINTHROP R. WRIGHT

GOMÉZ, MIGUEL MARIANO

Miguel Mariano Goméz (b. 1890; d. 1951), Cuba's sixth constitutionally elected president (May–December 1936) and the son of José Miguel Gómez, the second president. Gómez's term lasted for less than a year because he was the first president to be removed from office by Congress. A conservative member of Cuba's traditional ruling elite, he served in the House of Representatives for twelve years. Goméz was elected mayor of Havana during the Gerardo MACHADO Y MORALES administration. However, he attacked the repressive measures of the Machado regime. In January 1936, backed by the Liberal Party and army chief Fulgencio BATISTA Y ZALDÍVAR, he was elected president.

Goméz's biggest political shortcoming was his refusal to acknowledge the paramount position of General Batista. Inaugurated in May 1936, his first mistake was to choose his cabinet without consulting the general. His downfall came in December, when he vetoed a bill, supported by Batista, to set up a system of rural schools operated by the military. Goméz was adamant about reasserting civilian control over the government, and he believed that army control over rural education would erode constitutional and civilian power. Three days after the veto, General Batista had him impeached by the Senate.

— DAVID CAREY, JR.

GÓMEZ CARRILLO, ENRIQUE

Enrique Gómez Carrillo (b. 27 February 1873; d. 29 November 1927), Guatemalan chronicler, novelist, and pioneer of modern journalistic reporting. As a child, Gómez Carrillo traveled with his parents to Spain, returning first to San Salvador and then to his birthplace of Guatemala City, where he studied. His mother

---

In Paris, Gómez Carrillo befriended Paul Verlaine and was Mata Hari's lover.

---

taught him French at home. As a youth, he wrote for the local papers, praising modernism and severely criticizing the style of such revered Guatemalan writers as José MILLA. Rubén DARÍO helped him travel to Spain, where he published his work in various literary magazines and edited the Madrid daily newspaper *El Liberal,* helping to modernize the Spanish press. In Paris, where he would reside until his death, he worked as a correspondent for several Latin American and Spanish periodicals. He befriended Paul Verlaine and was Mata

Hari's lover. He published *Esquisses* (1892), *Sensaciones de arte* (1893), and *Del amor, del dolor y del vicio* (1898). Gómez Carrillo's legacy is his exquisite prose, the cosmopolitan vision which liberated him from provincialism, and especially the journalistic style of his literary stories.

– FERNANDO GONZÁLEZ DAVISON

GÓMEZ CASTRO, LAUREANO

Laureano Gómez Castro (*b.* 20 February 1889; *d.* 13 July 1965), president of Colombia (1950–1953). Born in Bogotá to middle-class parents from Ocaña, Norte de Santander, Gómez attended the Colegio de San Bartolomé and studied engineering at the Universidad Nacional (1905–1909). He was drawn, however, to politics. At twenty, he became editor of *La Unidad*, a Conservative paper, and remained at its helm until its demise in 1916. In the same period, he was elected to Congress and to Cundinamarca's Chamber of Deputies (1911–1916). His oratory was usually vehement and often wounding. President Marco Fidel SUÁREZ resigned in 1921 rather than suffer Gómez's taunts. After serving as minister plenipotentiary to Chile and Argentina (1923–1925), Gómez returned home in 1925 to become public works minister. His ambitious infrastructure program was rejected by the Congress, and he left public service until 1931, when he was appointed envoy to Germany. Some months later he was elected senator, remaining in office until removed—for calumny—in 1943.

A Liberal victory in 1930 left a power vacuum among Conservatives that Gómez, through his editorials in Bogotá's *El País* (1932–1934) and *El Siglo* (1936–1948), sought to fill. He unremittingly opposed the regimes of Enrique OLAYA HERRERA, Alfonso LÓPEZ PUMAREJO, and Eduardo SANTOS. Gómez's enthusiasm for Franco's Spain reflected his authoritarianism. The collapse, in 1945–1946, of Liberal unity brought in Gómez's choice, Mariano OSPINA PÉREZ, a Conservative, as president (1946). The increasing political violence led to Liberal withdrawal from the cabinet, and as a result Gómez became foreign minister in 1948. Nearly lynched in the Bogotazo of 9 April 1948, he fled to Spain. Gómez returned in 1949, ran unopposed (the Liberals abstained from voting), and won the presidency. His term was marked by repression, extreme partisanship, and violence. Some infrastructural improvements were achieved, however, including stadia in Bogotá and Medellín, roads, and oil pipelines. With no Congress to answer to, Gómez sent a Colombian battalion to join United Nations forces in Korea (1951–1953). On 13 June 1953, he was overthrown by General Gustavo ROJAS PINILLA and exiled to Spain. In 1956, joined by Liberal politicians at Sitges, Spain, Gómez founded the National Front. He died in Bogotá.

– J. LEÓN HELGUERA

GÓMEZ-CRUZ, ERNESTO

Ernesto Gómez-Cruz (*b.* 7 November 1933), Mexican stage and screen actor. Born in Veracruz, Gómez-Cruz studied theater at his hometown university. In 1967 he debuted in the acclaimed film *Los caifanes,* and since then has starred or costarred in over eighty features. He has received more best actor or supporting actor awards than any other actor in Mexican cinema. Gómez-Cruz is known for his ability to play a wide range of roles. His noted films include *Actas de Marusia* (1975), *Cadena perpetua; La venida del Rey Olmos; La vispera; Auandar Anapu, El imperio de la fortuna* (1986), *El norte; Lo que importa es vivir* (1988), and *Barroco*. Gómez-Cruz has also had a successful television and stage career.

– DAVID MACIEL

GÓMEZ DE AVELLANEDA Y ARTEAGA, GERTRUDIS

Gertrudis Gómez de Avellaneda y Arteaga (*b.* 23 March 1814; *d.* 1 February 1873), Cuban poet, novelist and playwright. Gómez de Avellaneda has the rare distinction of being claimed by the literatures of two countries, Cuba and Spain. Born in the city of Puerto Príncipe (now Camagüey) to a Spanish father and a Cuban mother, she spent her childhood and youth in Cuba. In 1836 she left Cuba with her mother and stepfather and settled in Spain, where she embarked on a literary career and what was for the times a scandalous personal life: she had several love affairs and bore a child out of wedlock, who died a few months after birth.

Gómez de Avellaneda was a friend and peer of several of the most distinguished Spanish poets, writers, and politicians of the day. In June of 1845 she was the winner of the two top prizes given by the Liceo de Madrid (she submitted one of the entries using her brother's name). In 1846 she married but three months later was widowed. Afterward, she retired to a convent briefly, only to return with fervor to literary life. Between 1844 and 1858, several of her plays were staged in Madrid, some with great success. In 1852 she was denied membership in the Royal Spanish Academy because she was a woman.

In 1854 Gómez de Avellaneda married a powerful, well-known politician, Colonel Domingo Verdugo, who was later given an official post in Cuba. In 1859,

Gertrudis Gómez de Avellaneda. (Organization of American States)

she returned with him to her native land where she was warmly welcomed and awarded the highest official honors from the literary community, including coronation by Luisa Pérez de Zambrana, a renowned Cuban poet. She remained in Cuba until the death of her husband in 1863. In 1865 thereafter she left Cuba with her brother, and after touring the United States, London, and Paris, she settled in Madrid in 1864; she remaind there until her death.

Gómez de Avellaneda is regarded as one of the most important Cuban poets and a notable novelist. Many critics consider her a feminist, and her ideas about slavery, as depicted in her best-known novel, *Sab* (1841), were revolutionary at the time.

— ROBERTO VALERO

GÓMEZ FARÍAS, VALENTÍN

Valentín Gómez Farías, (*b.* 1781; *d.* 1858), liberal reformer, vice president and acting president of Mexico (1833–1834 and 1846–1847) during two of Antonio López de SANTA ANNA's presidencies. Born in Guadalajara, Gómez Farías received his degree in 1807 and practiced medicine in Aguascalientes. He began his po-

litical career as *regidor* (president) of the *ayuntamiento* (city council) of Aguascalientes and was later elected to the Spanish Cortes. After independence, the state of Zacatecas elected him to the First Constituent Congress (1822), and during the 1820s he served repeatedly in the national legislature. In early 1833 he was finance minister before serving as acting president during the absences of Santa Anna in 1833–1834.

During this period, Gómez Farías attempted to carry out radical changes in the social and political structure of Mexico. His government first advised the clergy to restrict themselves to religious matters when speaking from the pulpit. Prompted by Gómez Farías and his allies José María Luis MORA and Lorenzo de ZAVALA, Congress voted to end the monopoly of the Catholic church over education and founded the Directorate of Public Instruction to organize public education in the Federal District and the national territories. Gómez Farías's government asserted its authority over the church hierarchy as well, claiming the right under the Patronato Real to name bishops and archbishops. Congress also abolished mandatory payment of the tithe and gave priests and members of religious orders the freedom to renounce their vows.

But these liberal reforms did not include toleration of other religions. Anticlerical legislation was combined with official "protection" for the Catholic church. Although some church property was confiscated to pay for educational reforms, Gómez Farías supported Mora's plan to sell all nonessential church property and collect a 4 percent tax on the sales. The proceeds of the tax would be divided between the federal government and the states, and the proceeds of the sales would be used to pay the expenses of the church. Gómez Farías also sponsored reforms to limit the power of the national army by reducing its size and abolishing its *fuero,* thus requiring military officers to stand trial in civil courts. These reforms were aborted when the army, the church, and wealthy conservatives supported a rebellion for "Religion and Fueros," forcing Santa Anna to remove Gómez Farías from office in 1834.

Gómez Farías, his pregnant wife, and his three small children fled into exile with few resources, since Gómez Farías was unable to collect the pay due him. He returned to Mexico in 1838 and in 1840 supported an unsuccessful rebellion by General José de URREA. Exiled again, he spent time in New York, Yucatán, and New Orleans before returning to Mexico in 1845.

Gómez Farías exercised presidential power as vice president under Santa Anna during the war with the United States in 1846–1847. When he sought to nationalize church property to pay for the war, the militia of Mexico City launched the "Rebellion of the Polkos" (1847), and Santa Anna reassumed the presidency. Gómez Farías was a member of the national legislature, where he opposed the Treaty of Guadalupe Hidalgo and supported the Revolution of Ayutla. He was elected to the Constitutional Congress of 1856–1857 and died in Mexico City.

– D. F. STEVENS

GÓMEZ HURTADO, ALVARO

Alvaro Gómez Hurtado (*b.* 8 May 1919), leader of Colombia's National Salvation Movement, a splinter of the Social Conservative Party. Gómez, a native of Bogotá, was editor-in-chief and remains an owner of the Bogotá newspaper *El Siglo* (later *El Nuevo Siglo*). A candidate for president in 1974, 1986, and 1990, he has been active in national politics since the 1940s. He was elected to the House of Representatives twice in the 1940s and to the Senate six times from the 1950s through the 1980s. Gómez inherited leadership of the "doctrinaire" wing of Colombia's Conservative Party following the death in 1965 of his father, former Colombian president Laureano GÓMEZ CASTRO (1950–1953). A staunch anti-Communist in his youth, and a close collaborator of his father during Colombia's politically turbulent 1940s and 1950s, Gómez later advocated redistributive economic programs within a setting of economic liberalism.

Kidnapped by members of Colombia's M-19 guerrilla organization in June 1988, Gómez was released unharmed after six weeks.

Gómez has consistently defended traditional conservative social values, as defined in Roman Catholic doctrine. Kidnapped by members of the M-19 guerrilla organization in June 1988, he was released unharmed after six weeks. In June 1990, he joined his kidnappers, by then elected delegates of the newly formed M-19 Party, to participate in drafting Colombia's progressive Constitution of 1991.

– JAMES D. HENDERSON

GÓMEZ MORÍN, MANUEL

Manuel Gómez Morín (*b.* 27 February 1897; *d.* 18 April 1972), Mexican financial figure, intellectual, and opposition leader. Born in Batopilas, Chihuahua, the son of a miner, he completed a course of studies at the National Preparatory School (1913–1915) and legal studies at the National School of Law (1915–1918). He maintained close friendships with the "Seven Wise Men," including Alfonso CASO, Vicente LOMBARDO TOLEDANO, and Narciso BASSOLS. Appointed a professor in 1918, he went on to influence a generation of prominent political figures.

Gómez Morín quickly entered public life, serving as *oficial mayor* and undersecretary of the treasury (1919–1921), and as founder and first director (1925–1929) of the board of the federal reserve Bank of Mexico. In 1923 he secretly gave financial support to the rebellion of Adolfo de la HUERTA and later served as unofficial treasurer of José VASCONCELOS's presidential campaign. Following that, he retired from public life (1929), but in 1931 he was the author of the first reform of credit institutions.

Meanwhile, he maintained his academic career as director of the National Law School from 1922 to 1924 and rector of the National University in 1933 and 1934. He subsequently went into private law practice and invested wisely in many major corporations at their founding. In 1939, disenchanted with the direction of the state, he and Efraín González Luna founded the National Action Party (PAN), which became Mexico's major opposition party until 1988. He spent his last thirty years as an investor and practitioner of law.

– RODERIC AI CAMP

GÓMEZ PEDRAZA, MANUEL

Manuel Gómez Pedraza (*b.* 1789?; *d.* 14 May 1851), Mexican politician and general. Born in Querétaro to a prominent family, he fought for the royalist cause in the War of Independence and then supported the ITURBIDE empire. Gómez successfully managed the ideological switch to federalism in 1824 and held several government posts, civil and military, during the Guadalupe VICTORIA presidency (1824–1829). A Scottish Rite Mason, he was elected president of Mexico in 1828 but was prevented from taking office by the revolt of the Acordade. After returning from exile, he served the final three months of his presidential term in 1833. He was elected to later congresses and held various ministerial posts. Known for his oratory and personal eccentricity—he forgot his own wedding day—he became a prominent member of the social elite in the capital. As one of the leaders of the moderate liberal federalists, Gómez was a presidential candidate on more than one occasion.

– MICHAEL P. COSTELOE

GÓMEZ Y BÁEZ, MÁXIMO

Máximo Gómez y Báez (*b.* 18 November 1836; *d.* 17 June 1905), major military leader in the wars for Cuban independence (1868–1878, 1895–1898). Born in Baní,

Santo Domingo, into a middle-class family, he attended a local elementary school and a religious seminary. He began his military career at age sixteen, in the war against the Haitians and later served as a lieutenant in the Dominican army. After the 1866 civil war in Santo Domingo resulted in the loss of all his property, Gómez fled to Cuba. Settling in Bayamó, he became a fervent advocate of independence. When Carlos Manuel de Céspedes's El Grito de Yara (The Shout of Yara) inaugurated the Ten Years' War (1868–1878), he joined Céspedes, quickly proving himself to be an invaluable military strategist and leader. With his promotion to the rank of general, he began a close association with the rebel leaders Antonio MACEO and Calixto GARCÍA.

Gómez and Maceo came to believe that success in the war was unlikely without an expansion into the prosperous western provinces. They advocated the mass disruption of sugar production and the liberation of slaves, hoping that the damage to Cuba's economic base would bring a quick rebel victory. The revolution's civilian leaders opposed the plan, but in 1872 fear of defeat made them consent to a modified version of it. Gómez and Maceo marched west, burning sugar plantations and freeing slaves. After several months, heavy casualties and low provisions necessitated their return, but changes in the political climate made a renewal of the campaign impossible. Disillusioned and frustrated with the lack of progress, Gómez pressed for a truce with the Spanish. In 1878 the Pact of Zanjón ended the Ten Years' War, and the rebel leaders who were unwilling to accept the truce went into exile.

During his years in exile, Gómez joined Maceo and the poet José MARTÍ and began preparations for a second revolution against Spain. Gómez and Martí had frequent disputes over strategy, resulting in a brief break in 1884; nevertheless, by 1893 their differences had been put aside and Martí named Gómez military commander of the Cuban Revolutionary Party. On 25 March 1895, he and Maceo issued the Manifesto of Monte Christi, renewing the Cuban Revolution.

When Martí died in a skirmish on 19 May 1895, Gómez assumed the mantle of leadership, becoming the commander in chief of the movement. Under his leadership, the war was immediately extended into the western provinces. He issued a moratorium on sugar production, promising death and destruction of property to anyone in violation of his decree. Although these tactics seriously endangered Cuba's economic future, they proved effective in the war. By 1897 the rebels had moved into Matanzas and Havana.

A year later, a Spanish counteroffensive left the rebels struggling to maintain their positions, but U.S. entry into the war (1898) put an end to Spanish resistance.

Following a four-year occupation, during which time the rebel leaders were all but totally ignored, the United States withdrew. As the Republic of Cuba was being established (20 May 1902), Gómez was urged to run for president, but he declined to do so, saying, "Men of war for war, and those of peace for peace."

– SARA FLEMING

GONDRA, MANUEL

Manuel Gondra (b. 1 January 1871; d. 8 March 1927), Paraguayan scholar, statesman, and president (1910–1911, 1920–1921). Manuel E. Gondra's varied and distinguished career in education, the military, diplomacy, and politics established him as one of Paraguay's leading public figures of the twentieth century. Born of an Argentine father and Paraguayan mother, Gondra was educated in the schools of Asunción and the Colegio Nacional. It was at the Colegio Nacional that Gondra later built a reputation as a highly effective educational reformer. Entering public life in 1902, he served as Paraguay's minister to Brazil (1905–1908) before being elected president in 1920. Confronting escalating political violence, Gondra resigned within a year of assuming the presidency.

During the ensuing decade, Gondra served as minister of war, reorganizing Paraguay's army and clarifying his nation's legal claim to the disputed Chaco region. While serving as Paraguay's minister in Washington in 1920, Gondra was again elected to the presidency. He fell victim to civil strife once again, however, and resigned his office after only fifteen months. Achieving more as a statesman than as a politician, Gondra was awarded his greatest recognition for his sponsorship of a treaty to prevent war among the American states at the Fifth International Conference of American States at Santiago, Chile, in 1923. For this initiative, Gondra was lauded by the Pan-American Union soon after his death in 1927. An accomplished scholar, Gondra owned one of the finest libraries in South America. His collection, containing 7,283 books, 2,633 pamphlets, 20,000 pages of manuscripts, and 270 maps, is now housed in the Benson Collection at the University of Texas.

– DANIEL M. MASTERSON

GONZAGA, FRANCISCA HEDWIGES

Francisca Hedwiges Gonzaga (Chiquinha; b. 17 October 1847; d. 28 February 1935), a colorful key figure in the early history of Brazilian musical nationalism. Daughter of an imperial field marshall, José Basileu Neves Gonzaga, Francisca Gonzaga was married at the age of thirteen to an officer in the Merchant Marine at the insistence of her parents. She divorced her husband at the age of eighteen and left home with her children, whom she supported by giving music lessons. She was befriended by composer Joaquim Antônio da Silva CALLADO JUNIOR, who, in spite of her basically classical training, introduced her to the *chorões,* popular musicians composing in an improvisational style. Gonzaga proved to be such an apt apprentice that she soon improvised a polka, "Atraente," at a party honoring composer Henrique Alves de Mesquita. This song achieved widespread popularity and was followed by a flood of popular pieces called *valsas,* polkas, tangos, *maxixes, lundus, quadrilhas, fados, gavotas,* mazurkas, *barcarolas, habaneras,* and *serenatas.* She is best known, however, as composer of seventy-seven pieces for theater, which consisted of comedies, operettas, and incidental music for plays that captured the imagination of the public and defined popular styles in a manner that influenced composers of art music. Her independent spirit and disregard for convention made her a sensation in her day. In addition to being the first woman in Brazil to conduct a theater orchestra and military band, Gonzaga also was extremely active in antislavery and republican causes, even selling manuscripts and using royalty funds to contribute to these causes.

– DAVID P. APPLEBY

GONZAGA, LUIZ

Luiz Gonzaga (*b.* 13 Dec. 1912; *d.* 2 Aug. 1989), Brazilian singer, composer, and accordionist. Gonzaga transformed the rural folk music of the Northeast into a national urban popular music in the late 1940s and early 1950s. Born in the state of Pernambuco, he learned the traditional music of the Northeastern backlands and distinguished himself as an accordionist. After a stint in the military he moved south to Rio de Janeiro in the late 1930s and began performing contemporary popular music in clubs and on radio shows. Success came in the mid-1940s, when he teamed up with Humberto Teixeira, a poet from the state of Ceará, and incorporated Northeastern music into his repertoire. Together they adapted syncopated rhythmic figures used by Northeastern folk guitarists to create a new song-and-dance genre they called *baião.* In 1946 the pair co-authored the song entitled "Baião," which became a commercial success and ushered in a Northeastern phase in the history of Brazilian popular music. During the late 1940s and early 1950s, Gonzaga and his co-writers, Teixeira and Zé Dantas, released a string of hit recordings based on the *baião* and other Northeastern genres, such as *chamego, xote, xaxado,* and *forró.* The

songs spoke of the culture, history, and physical beauty of the Northeast, and Gonzaga became a spokesman for Northeastern culture. He was crowned "King of the Baião."

When the national *baião* craze waned in the late 1950s, Gonzaga returned to the Northeast to spend his time performing throughout the interior. In the late 1960s, Gonzaga's music found a new generation of Brazilian listeners when the contemporary popular musicians Caetano VELOSO and Gilberto GIL popularized new versions of his songs. During the 1970s and 1980s, Gonzaga performed with numerous Brazilian popular musicians, such as Gal Costa, Milton NASCIMENTO, Fagner, Elba Ramalho, and his own son, Gonzaguinha. At the time of his death Gonzaga had made more than 200 recordings.

– LARRY N. CROOK

GONZAGA, TOMÁS ANTÔNIO

Tomás Antônio Gonzaga (*b.* 1744; *d.* 1810), Brazilian poet. Born in Portugal to a Brazilian father from Rio de Janeiro and a mother of English background, Gonzaga went to Brazil as a child, where he studied in the Jesuit school in Bahia. After completing his law degree at Coimbra, Portugal, in 1768, he became a magistrate in Beja, Portugal, and later in gold-driven Vila Rica, in Minas Gerais province in Brazil. There, as both a *reinol* (that is, one born in Portugal and living in colonial Brazil) and a poet, he became involved in political and intellectual societies. Cláudio Manuel da COSTA (1729–1789) and Inácio José de Alvarenga Peixoto (1744–1793) were among his closest friends and conspirators in the failed Inconfidência Mineira, the Mineiran Conspiracy of 1789. Gonzaga's judicial career in Brazil suffered because of a bitter political feud with the governor of Minas Gerais, Luís da Cunha e Meneses, who accused him of opportunism and corruption. Tried as a participant in the Mineiran Conspiracy, Gonzaga was sent into exile in Mozambique, where he married a rich widow, gradually regained his official position, and, at his death, was the Mozambican customs magistrate.

Gonzaga dedicated his lyrics to his beloved Marília, a sixteen-year-old girl he had intended to marry.

Gonzaga's poetry belongs to the Arcadian school, which flourished in late-eighteenth-century Minas Gerais. Using the name "Dirceu," he dedicated his lyrics to his beloved Marília, a sixteen-year-old girl he had intended to marry. He continued to write love poems throughout his exile in Mozambique, even when all hope of this marriage had already been dashed. Because his work was published on two continents and in several volumes (1792, 1799, 1812), the exact corpus of his poetry, published under the title *Marília de Dirceu,* has yet to be definitively established.

Perhaps more significant than his poems are the *Cartas chilenas* (1863), now attributed to Gonzaga. A veiled attack on Cunha e Meneses's government, these thirteen free-verse satirical letters offer a fascinating view of life in colonial Minas, in particular of the societal conflicts that surfaced among government officials, nobles, merchants, gold prospectors, and slaves.

Gonzaga's life and writings have inspired works by many other Brazilian writers down to the present, including Casimiro de Abreu, CASTRO ALVES, and Drummond de ANDRADE.

– IRWIN STERN

GONZÁLEZ, ABRAHAM

Abraham González (*b.* 7 June 1864; *d.* 7 March 1913), governor of Chihuahua, Mexico (1911–1913), minister of internal affairs (1911–1912). González was a gunrunner for the insurgency of Francisco I. MADERO (1909–1910). As governor he instituted a number of political reforms, including the abolition of company towns and the hated office of *jefe político* (district boss). After an interlude in Madero's cabinet, González returned to Chihuahua to confront growing unrest that erupted in the rebellion of Pascual OROZCO, Jr., in 1912. He defeated the Orozquistas, only to die at the hands of the reactionary forces that overthrew Madero. González typified the Maderista, middle-class political reformers caught between the radical demands of their present and worker followers and the reactionary Porfirian oligarchy.

– MARK WASSERMAN

GONZÁLEZ, BEATRIZ

Beatriz González (*b.* 1938), Colombian artist. González studied fine arts at the Universidad de los Andes in Bogotá (1959–1962) and printmaking at the Academia van Beeldende Kunsten in Rotterdam (1966). Her first individual exhibition was held at the Museo de Arte Moderno in Bogotá in 1964. González employs both popular imagery and well-known artworks as departure points, taking images from such European masterpieces as Leonardo da Vinci's *Mona Lisa* and Jan Vermeer's *The Lacemaker* and placing them within the context of Colombian daily life. She is also known for her satirical portraits of prominent Colombian figures. Her works

of the 1960s and 1970s are generally characterized by strong colors and a sense of irony, thus bearing a relationship to pop art. González now explores social themes: questions of identity, the history of her culture, and the impact of these issues on the lives of contemporary Colombians. González was included in the Bienal de São Paulo (1971) and the Biennale di Venezia (1978). Retrospectives were held at the Museo de Arte Moderno La Tertulia in Cali (1976) and the Museo de Arte Moderno in Bogotá (1984).

– JUDITH GLUCK STEINBERG

GONZÁLEZ, CARLOS

Carlos González (*b.* 1 December 1905), Uruguayan artist, who specialized in woodcut. Born in Melo, in the department of Cerro Largo, González studied with Andrés Etchebarne Bidart. In his youth, he traveled throughout the Uruguayan countryside selling his family's wheatmill products; later he devoted himself to forestry. It was not until 1938 that he began to make woodcuts. He received gold medals from the National Salon of Fine Arts in Montevideo in 1943 and 1944. His subjects were local legends, traditional countryside scenes, and socially concerned testimonies to the poverty-stricken rural areas. In a typical González woodcut, the central scene is surrounded by a printed border filled with written messages and symbols representing rural work, leisure, and culture. The figurative elements on the margins complement the central scene. Together, both marginal and central illustrations narrate events from Latin American and Uruguayan history. His printing style was harsh and sketchy, often the result of carving wood with a common knife.

González wanted his art to have a didactic function, specifically, to tell the history and social reality of Uruguay as he interpreted it. This task, he believed, required a collective (or cooperative) effort. Feeling isolated, he abandoned artistic practice at the prime of his career, in 1944. In 1970 he was credited with the invention of Uruguayan printmaking at the Fourth American Biennial of Printmaking in Santiago, Chile.

– MARTA GARSD

GONZÁLEZ, FLORENTINO

Florentino González (*b.* 1805; *d.* ca. 1875), Colombian political figure of the Liberal Party. Born in Cincelada, Santander, González studied at the College of San Bartolomé, obtaining the degree of doctor of jurisprudence in 1825. One of the participants in the attempt against Simón BOLÍVAR's life in 1828, González barely escaped the firing squad. He went to Europe in 1841, remaining there until 1846.

González's claim to historical notoriety rests on his being widely credited as the foremost proponent of free trade, a position based on ideas he had picked up in Great Britain in the early 1840s. As minister of finance in the first administration of Tomás Cipriano de MOS- QUERA (1845–1849), he implemented policies that re- flected his ideas. In the ensuing Liberal Party split be- tween an elite faction (the *gólgotas*) and a more "popular" faction (the *draconianos*), González attacked the *draconianos* as dangerous socialist levelers. As he be- came ideologically closer to the Conservatives and be- cause he favored annexation to the United States to avoid political instability, he broke with his party and faded away from the political stage. In 1860 he left Colombia never to return. He died in Argentina.

– JOSÉ ESCORCIA

GONZÁLEZ, JOAQUÍN VÍCTOR

Joaquín Víctor González (*b.* 6 March 1863; *d.* 21 De- cember 1923), Argentine author, educator, diplomat, and statesman. Born in Chilecito, La Rioja Province, he received his law degree from the University of Cór- doba in 1886. He began his political career in 1886, when he was elected as a deputy representing La Rioja. He then served as the province's governor (1889–1891) and senator (1907–1923). President Julio ROCA (1898– 1904) appointed him interior minister (1901) and later foreign relations minister (1903). He continued his ser- vice under President Manuel QUINTANA (1904–1906), heading the Ministry of Justice and Public Instruction. He concluded his public service by representing Argen- tina in the League of Nations.

An authority on law and politics as well as education, he is best known for his literary and historical works, including *La tradición nacional* (1888) and *Mis mon- tañas* (1893). He taught law at the University of Cór- doba (1894), served on the National Education Council (1896), and became the first rector of the National Uni- versity of La Plata (1906).

– DANIEL LEWIS

GONZÁLEZ, JUAN NATALICIO

Juan Natalicio González (*b.* 8 September 1897; *d.* 6 December 1966), Paraguayan poet, historian, journal- ist, statesman, and president (1948–1949). González was born in Villerrica and studied at the Colegio Na- cional in Asunción. He began his literary career under the guidance of Juan O'LEARY, with whom he shared many stylistic and thematic traits. González later be-

came associated with many other Paraguayan apologists in the task of reconstructing the image of their country. In 1920, he founded the journal *Guaranía*, which went through several stages as a vital cultural vehicle and con- tinued to be published into the 1940s. In 1925 Gon- zález lived in Paris, where he was active in publishing. The dominant Colorado Party supported him in his bid for president and he assumed office on 15 August 1948. His own party quickly disagreed with some of his pol- icies and had him removed in February 1949, after which he resided in Mexico.

Throughout his life he dedicated himself to national themes. His *Solano López y otros ensayos* (1926) is his best-known work, followed by *Proceso y formación de la cultura paraguaya* (1938).

– CATALINA SEGOVIA-CASE

GONZÁLEZ, JUAN VICENTE

Juan Vicente González (*b.* 28 May 1810; *d.* 1 October 1866), Venezuelan politician, writer, and journalist. As- sociated with the Liberals in 1840, González subse- quently distanced himself from them to the extent that by 1845 he had become one of their most radical op- ponents, promulgating his politics through various newspapers: *Cicerón y Catilina, Diario de la Tarde,* and *La Prensa.*

González ceased political activity during the regime of José Tadeo MONAGAS, founded the El Salvador del Mundo school (The Savior of the World School) in 1849, and did an extensive and varied amount of lit- erary and historiographic work. His *Biografía de José Felix Ribas* (1858) is representative of what is known in Venezuela as romantic historiography. Later on he op- posed pro-federation propaganda and, together with de- fenders of civilian rule during the Federal War (1859– 1863), opposed the dictatorship of José Antonio PÁEZ. In 1863 González supported the regime of Juan Cri- sóstomo FALCÓN, and then left his public activities to dedicate himself primarily to literary work, founding the *Revista Literaria* in 1865.

– INÉS QUINTERO

GONZÁLEZ, MANUEL

Manuel González (*b.* 18 June 1833; *d.* 8 May 1893), president of Mexico (1880–1884). Born in the state of Tamaulipas, González began his career as a professional soldier in 1847. During the War of the Reform (1857– 1860), González fought on the losing Conservative side, but during the French Intervention (1862–1867), he served with Liberal general PORFIRIO DÍAZ and eventu- ally became Díaz's chief of staff. Promoted to brigadier general in 1867, González served as governor of the National Palace and military commander of the Federal District (1871–1873).

After supporting Díaz's unsuccessful Plan of La Noria in 1871, González played a prominent military role in Díaz's triumph under the Plan of Tuxtepec in 1876. In March 1878 González was appointed minister of war by President Díaz. Ineligible for reelection in 1880, Díaz worked secretly for the election of González, who took office in December 1880.

González eased long-standing border problems

with the United States by agreeing to permit

reciprocal crossing of troops.

As president, González adopted a policy of conciliation toward the national congress, the state governments, the Roman Catholic church, and the military. In foreign relations, he eased long-standing border problems with the United States by agreeing to permit reciprocal crossing of troops and settled a lingering boundary dispute with Guatemala. Relations with Great Britain, broken in 1867, were renewed in 1884.

González accelerated government promotion of economic development, especially in the areas of transportation and communications. Federal lands were opened for settlement, and efforts were made to promote colonization and immigration. In 1884, the government issued a new mining code permitting private ownership of subsoil resources for the first time. Unfortunately for González, who had inherited an empty treasury, his spending for economic development only exacerbated the country's ongoing financial problems. The introduction of new nickel coinage in 1882 provoked inflation and devaluation. Negotiations aimed at settling the long-standing debt owed to British creditors also discredited González.

González completed his term of office amid mounting political crisis; he returned the presidency to Díaz in 1884. González later served three terms as governor of Guanajuato.

– DON M. COERVER

GONZÁLEZ, PABLO

Pablo González (*b*. 5 May 1879; *d*. 4 March 1950), Mexican general and revolutionary. González is best known for his military exploits in the Constitutionalist army of revolutionary chief Venustiano CARRANZA and

his role in the death of agrarian leader and revolutionary Emiliano ZAPATA.

González was born in Lampazos, Nuevo León, and orphaned at age five. He attended primary school in Nadadores, Coahuila, and then tried to enter the National Military College, but was turned down. He worked in a flour mill in Lampazos (1893), served as a laborer and later foreman on the Santa Fe Railroad (1902), and worked in California (1903). He joined the liberal political movement headed by Ricardo FLORES MAGÓN (1873–1922) and in 1907 edited the Mexican Liberal Party (PLM) newspaper *Revolución*. Later he joined the Anti-Reelectionist Party and supported Francisco I. MADERO against long-time dictator Porfirio DÍAZ. He commanded Madero's forces in Coahuila, rising to the rank of colonel (1911). In 1912 he fought against the anti-Madero rebellion led by Pascual OROZCO.

After joining the forces of Carranza in 1913, González rose to the rank of general and commander-in-chief of the armies of the Northeast and West. He participated in the Convention of Aguascalientes (1914–1915); became the zone commander of Morelos, Puebla, Oaxaca, and Tlaxcala; and served as the governor of Morelos (1916, 1919). While commander in Morelos he carried out an especially vicious military campaign against the Zapatistas and is considered to be the perpetrator of Emiliano Zapata's assassination (1919). In 1920 González ran unsuccessfully for the presidency and, upon Álvaro Obregón's overthrow of Carranza, rebelled against the new regime in July 1920. Captured and sentenced to death, González was allowed to seek asylum in San Antonio, Texas, where he remained until 1940. He died in Monterrey, Nuevo León.

– DAVID LAFRANCE

GONZÁLEZ ÁVILA, JORGE

Jorge González Ávila (*b*. 10 December 1925), Mexican composer. Born in Mérida, Yucatán, González Ávila was a pupil of the Spanish composer Rodolfo HALFFTER at the National Conservatory of Mexico. Like a number of Halffter's pupils, González Ávila became a true believer in the twelve-tone and avant-garde serial techniques that the Spanish master had been promoting in Mexico City's musical circles since his arrival in 1939. No dogmatist, González Ávila, who was predominately a composer of piano works, did not follow Halffter's style strictly but took an independent approach to the use of serial elements. Between 1961 and 1964 he wrote a collection of twenty-four inventions for piano; he was also the author of several collections of piano études, some of which demonstrate dodecaphonic writing.

— SUSANA SALGADO

GONZÁLEZ CAMARENA, JORGE

Jorge González Camarena (*b.* 1908; *d.* 24 May 1980), Mexican artist. González Camarena is known for his murals and sculptures. He invented a system of geometric harmonies by fusing precise painting with subdued but vibrant color and textures. Among his public murals are *The Formation of Mexico* (1950), in the Instituto Mexicano del Seguro Social (in front of whose entrance stand his sculptures of *Man* and *Woman*); *Belisario Dominguez* (1956), in the Cámara de Senadores; and *Liberation* (1958), in the Palacio de Bellas Artes— all in Mexico City. Many of his other murals were commercial commissions.

— SHIFRA M. GOLDMAN

GONZÁLEZ CASANOVA, PABLO

Pablo González Casanova (*b.* 11 February 1922), Mexican social scientist and academic administrator. A rigorous scholar and theorist of internal colonialism, dependency, and other conceptual models of analysis of the Latin American historical and contemporary reality, González Casanova has authored and edited over 200 books and published nearly as many scholarly articles. His most important studies include the classic *La democracía en México* (1965) and *El estado y los partidos políticos en México* (1981). He has also held important academic-administrative positions, including director of the Escuela de Ciencias Políticas y Sociales (1957– 1965) and president of the National Autonomous University of Mexico (UNAM) (1970–1972). In 1984, González Casanova was awarded the National Prize in Mexico for Social Sciences and Humanities.

— DAVID MACIEL

GONZÁLEZ DÁVILA, GIL

Gil González Dávila (*b.* 1490; *d.* 1550), Spanish conqueror and explorer of Nicaragua. While still a young man, González achieved renown for his military exploits in Europe and won permission from the Spanish king to explore Central America. He left Spain in 1518, passed through Cuba, and reached Panama in 1519. Although holding a commission from the king himself, González fell afoul of the tyrannical governor of Panama, Pedro Arias de ÁVILA (Pedrarias), a circumstance that delayed his expedition for three years. These intervening years, however, enabled González to familiarize himself with New World conditions and gather information of use to his mission.

In 1522 González set out by sea with the fleet of the recently executed Vasco Núñez de Balboa and reached Costa Rica. Finding no easy riches there, González's interest in lands northward was aroused by a Costa Rican *cacique*. Abandoning his worm-eaten fleet, he continued inland on foot. Using his Costa Rican contacts, González obtained an introduction to Chief Nicarao, leader of a large settlement of Indians, and spent eight days with him in the area now known as Rivas. González subsequently claimed the entire region for the king of Spain and named it Nicaragua, a derivation of the chief's name. The Spaniards did not have much time to exploit their new acquisition, however; on 17 April 1522 a rival chief, Diriangen, attacked their group, forcing the would-be conquerors to withdraw.

Arriving in Panama, González recounted his accomplishments for the governor: the discovery of Lake Nicaragua, the addition of 224 leagues of land to the king's empire, the purported baptism of some 32,000 Indians, and the seizure of riches. González also claimed Nicaragua as his separate and independent authority, granted under the king's commission, something Pedrarias found unacceptable. A bitter competition for jurisdiction followed—a common occurrence among the Spanish conquerors—until Pedrarias stripped González of his right to primacy in the area and replaced him with Francisco FERNÁNDEZ DE CÓRDOBA. González managed to flee Panama with 112,524 gold pesos obtained during his Nicaraguan expedition. He remained in Santo Domingo for several years, all the while pressing his claims and plotting a military counterattack.

In 1525 González and his supporters defeated a detachment of Fernández's men and encouraged Fernández to rebel against Pedrarias. The three-way struggle for Nicaragua prompted a year-long civil war ending in 1526 and culminating in Fernández's execution when Pedrarias moved northward to assume the governorship himself.

González remained in exile and returned to Panama in 1532, the year after the death of his arch rival, Pedrarias. He continued to fight for his claims and formed an alliance with Hernán CORTÉS against Cristóbal de OLID, who was attempting to set up his own authority in Honduras. González was found guilty of the assassination of Olid. But he had won the gratitude of Cortés, who permitted him to return to Spain, where he spent the remainder of his days enjoying his reputation and his riches.

— KAREN RACINE

GONZÁLEZ DE ESLAVA, FERNÁN

Fernán González de Eslava (ca. 1534–ca. 1601), Spanish playwright in New Spain. González de Eslava was born in Spain, probably León, but his precise birthplace, along with many other details concerning his life, remain unknown. He arrived in Mexico around 1558, and within five years there were notices of his poetic activities. As a playwright he is known primarily for his *coloquios,* the first of which dates from about 1567. By 1572 he was preparing to be a cleric, but two years later he was jailed for seventeen days when his writing produced a conflict between the Viceroy Martín ENRÍQUEZ DE ALMANSA and Archbishop Pedro MOYA DE CONTRERAS. He became a priest, probably by 1575 or 1576, and wrote his last *coloquio* in 1600.

As a playwright in the New World González de Eslava is neither first (Juan Pérez Ramírez deserves that honor) nor American (having been born in Spain). His theater is religious with didactic aims. In the second half of the sixteenth century, theater was designed for the new, primarily creole, society being formed. His dramatic works consist of sixteen *coloquios,* four *entremeses,* and nine *loas.* The works tended to be light and facile, and to give a clear and honest vision of life in the colony. Without pretensions, they communicated a religious message (at least eleven of the *coloquios* are considered "sacramental") that was easily accessible to a wide public. González de Eslava had a gift for versification, and his plays are marked by a delightful use of language that incorporated New World structures. He is particularly known for an engaging sense of humor that pervades his language, his characters, and the situations. His *simple* is a likely precursor of the Siglo de Oro *gracioso.* On occasion González de Eslava revealed his disdain for the indigenous population, but for all his defects, he is still the major writer of Mexico who anticipated Sor JUANA INÉS DE LA CRUZ by a full century.

– GEORGE WOODYARD

GONZÁLEZ DE SANTA CRUZ, ROQUE

Roque González de Santa Cruz (*b.* 1576; *d.* 15 November 1628), Paraguayan Jesuit who founded many of the Jesuit missions (*reducciones*) in his native land, as well as in present-day Argentina and Uruguay. Born of Spanish parents in Asunción, he learned Guaraní as a child. He was ordained a priest around 1589 and worked among the Indians in the region of Jejuí, north of Asunción. In 1603 he was named rector of the cathedral in Asunción, and in 1609 he entered the Society of Jesus.

As a Jesuit he returned to work with the Indians. He helped build the first of the *reducciones,* San Ignacio Guazú, south of Asunción. In 1614 he wrote a letter to his brother Francisco, the lieutenant governor of Asunción, in which he denounced the *encomenderos* for their mistreatment of the Indians. He went on to found many other *reducciones* in southern Paraguay, in the province of Misiones in present-day Argentina, and in Uruguay. In 1627 he was appointed superior of all of the *reducciones* in Uruguay. At Caaró, in modern Rio Grande do Sul, Brazil, he and two other Jesuits were killed by Indian shamans who were hostile to his efforts to Christianize the Indians in their region.

González and two other Jesuits were killed by Indian shamans who were hostile to his efforts to Christianize the Indians in their region.

González was a skilled builder, leader, and organizer. Although he died at the hands of hostile Indians, he was greatly esteemed by the Indians in general, who appreciated his efforts to organize them in defense of their land and culture against Spanish exploiters. The first Paraguayan to be a missionary in his own land, he was also the first martyr born in the New World. He was canonized in 1988.

– JEFFREY KLAIBER

GONZÁLEZ FLORES, ALFREDO

Alfredo González Flores (*b.* 15 June 1877; *d.* 28 December 1962), president of Costa Rica (1914–1917). Born in Heredia, González Flores received a law degree in 1902. The Costa Rican Congress chose him to be president of the Republic in 1914. Ironically, Costa Ricans were supposed to elect their president directly for the first time that year, but none of the three candidates received a majority, sending the matter to Congress, which selected González Flores, who had not even been on the original ballot.

González Flores became president at a time when Costa Rica's population was growing dramatically and the price for its principal export, coffee, was falling precipitously. Costa Rica was beginning to experience the effects of monoculture, wherin its "golden bean" was leaving a bitter taste. González Flores courageously proposed an income tax to try to alleviate the suffering of the poor, but he was too weak politically for such bold action.

The outbreak of World War I compounded his difficulties. With exports curtailed and imported goods scarce, Costa Rica experienced inflation and declining revenues. Though González Flores attempted progressive economic measures by imposing exchange regulations, levying export taxes, and cutting salaries of public employees, he had little support. The minister of defense, General Federico TINOCO GRANADOS took advantage of the president's unpopularity to stage a coup on 27 January 1917, which established the second dictatorship in Costa Rican history.

González Flores persuaded President Woodrow WILSON not to recognize the Tinoco dictatorship. In recent years biographers have viewed him more favorably as a precursor of Costa Rican reform movements. He gave a lifetime of service to his native city, Heredia, and Costa Rica awarded him the Benemérito de la Patria in 1954.

– CHARLES D. AMERINGER

GONZÁLEZ GOYRI, ROBERTO

Roberto González Goyri (*b.* 1924), Guatemalan artist, inspired by pre-Conquest cultures. He studied with Rafael Yela Günther at the Academy of Fine Arts in Guatemala City, where he received academic training, and worked as a draftsman at the National Museum of Archeology. On a grant from the Guatemalan government, he studied in New York from 1948 to 1952. International recognition came in 1951, when he won a prize for a sculpture of the unknown political prisoner in a contest sponsored by the London Institute of Contemporary Arts. The Museum of Modern Art in New York acquired his semiabstract sculpture *The Wolf* (1951) in 1955. He was director of the National School of Plastic Arts in Guatemala City (1957–1958).

As a sculptor, González Goyri worked with terracotta, concrete, and metals combining an expressionist, symbolic style with abstract motifs. His mural and sculptural projects for public buildings, such as the Social Security Institute in Guatemala City (1959), and his monumental sculpture of the Guatemalan Indian hero Tecún-Umán (1963) symbolically depict Guatemalan history from the dawn of Maya civilization to independence. As a painter, he has worked primarily in a postcubist style, inspired by the strong colors found in Guatemalan crafts. His mural *Religion in Guatemala: Its Pre-Hispanic, Colonial, and Contemporary Roots* (1992) is a monumental interpretation of Guatemalan religious life, from the *Popol Vuh,* the sacred Maya book, to the present.

– MARTA GARSD

GONZÁLEZ LEÓN, ADRIANO

Adriano González León (*b.* 1931), Venezuelan fiction writer. One of Venezuela's most innovative and demanding writers, González León is the author of one of the most accomplished Venezuelan novels of the century, *País portátil* (1969). He also published the novel *Asfalto-infierno* (1963) and several volumes of short fiction. His first set of stories, *Las hogueras más altas* (1957), portrays solitary and violent characters. González León used Faulknerian narrative techniques to construct his historical and political novel *País portátil,* which tells the story of the Barazarte family through the mind of one of its members, a young revolutionary. At the same time, *País portátil* also recounts Venezuelan history since the nineteenth century. The young revolutionary, Andrés, carries a bomb on a bus through the city of Caracas. The reader is bombarded with images of modern urban chaos in the city and the conscious and subconscious thoughts of Andrés. González León has published short fiction in the 1970s and 1980s, but no other novels.

– RAYMOND LESLIE WILLIAMS

GONZÁLEZ MARTÍNEZ, ENRIQUE

Enrique González Martínez (*b.* 13 April 1871; *d.* 19 February 1952), Mexican poet. A central figure in the literary life of the nation from the beginning of the Revolution until his death at mid-century, González

The condition of solitude, a certain pantheistic urging, and a longing for lucidity and transcendent vision give shape to González Martínez' work.

Martínez was trained as a physician but spent most of his career in public service. His early poetry reflects the turn-of-the-century *modernista* techniques, and in the 1920s there are traces of *vanguardista* influences; he is noted, however, for his consistent, profound exploration of personal experience and metaphysical searching through his art. He is a master of traditional forms, especially of the sonnet; his language evolves toward simplicity; biblical and classical allusions are common, but never recondite. The condition of solitude, a certain pantheistic urging, a longing for lucidity and transcendent vision, the "resplendent moment," give shape to much of his work. An occasional trace of didacticism may also be found.

The early period culminates in the definition of his voice in *Silénter* (1909) and *Los senderos ocultos* (1911). The latter collection includes the sonnet "Tuércele el cuello al cisne" ("Wring the Swan's Neck"), his most anthologized poem, often misread as marking the end of *modernismo*. González Martínez is best understood as one of the most important exponents of the symbolist strain in *modernismo* as it has subsequently evolved. *Parábolas y otros poemas* (1918), *El romero alucinado* (1923), and *Las señales furtivas* (1925) are major collections of his middle period. His later poetry is marked by the death of his wife and of his son, Enrique González Rojo (1899–1939), also a poet. These works include *Ausencia y canto* (1937), *El diluvio de fuego* (1938), *Bajo el signo mortal* (1942), and *El nuevo Narciso y otros poemas* (1952). The "Estancias," twenty-one octaves and a concluding sonnet that open this last collection, are an exceptionally beautiful summing up of his life and art. He wrote an autobiography published in two parts, *El hombre del buho* (1944) and *La apacible locura* (1951). He was a fine translator of French poetry. In 1911 he was elected to the Mexican Academy, and he was a member of the Ateneo de la Juventud and a founding member of the Colegio Nacional (1943).

– MICHAEL J. DOUDOROFF

GONZÁLEZ ORTEGA, JESÚS

Jesús González Ortega (*b.* 1822; *d.* 1881), Mexican military officer and cabinet minister. Born on a hacienda near Teúl, Zacatecas, and educated in Guadalajara, Ortega held an office job in Teúl until the War of the Reform. Of liberal ideas, he was elected to the legislature of the state of Zacatecas in 1858 and soon after was designated the state's governor. Ortega began his military career by organizing and leading the Zacatecas militia. One of the most successful liberal generals, he was appointed by President Benito JUÁREZ to succeed Santos DEGOLLADO. After a series of victories over the Conservatives, Ortega led the victorious liberal army into Mexico City on 1 January 1861, ending the War of the Reform.

After Juárez named him minister of war on 20 January, Ortega resigned three months later over political differences with the president. Under the Constitution of 1857, as the congressionally elected interim president of the Supreme Court, Ortega was first in line of succession to the presidency of the republic. During the French Intervention, President Juárez reluctantly turned to Ortega to take command of the Army of the East. After the siege of Puebla in 1863, Ortega was forced to surrender, but he escaped his captors and fled to the United States. Juárez decreed the extension of his own presidential term and announced that Ortega had renounced his claim to the presidency by remaining in a foreign country without permission. When Ortega returned to Mexico in 1866, he was arrested and held without trial. He was released in August 1868 with the stipulation that the government reserved the right to prosecute him. Ortega resigned as president of the Court and retired from politics.

– D. F. STEVENS

GONZÁLEZ PRADA, MANUEL

Manuel González Prada (*b.* 5 January 1844; *d.* 22 July 1918), Peruvian writer. González Prada was born in Lima and studied law there. A cofounder of the Unión Nacional, a short-lived liberal party, in 1891, and author of twenty-one books and three pamphlets, he was the first ideological agitator of modern Peru. In his sociopolitical essays, written with cutting sentences and satirical in tone, his witty mordancy is softened by an expert application of literary devices that reveals a powerful will and a firm determination to invent, adapt, transform, and re-create a literary language to be used as a comfortable, swift, efficient, and suitable linguistic vehicle. His best-known books are *Pájinas libres* (1894) and *Horas de lucha* (1908).

– EUGENIO CHANG-RODRÍGUEZ

GONZÁLEZ SUÁREZ, (MANUEL MARÍA) FEDERICO

(Manuel María) Federico González Suárez (*b.* 12 April 1844; *d.* 1 December 1917), noted Ecuadoran historian and archbishop of Quito (1906–1917). González Suárez, a native of Quito, is most remembered for his multivolume *Historia general de la República del Ecuador* (1890–1903), based on extensive research in local archives and in Spain. González Suárez's goal had been to write a general history of America, but he completed only the eight volumes that dealt with Ecuador's pre-Columbian and colonial eras. He devoted most of his attention to the ecclesiastical history of the city of Quito, giving scant notice to Guayaquil or to economic matters. González Suárez's mild criticism of the colonial Ecuadorian clergy evoked bitter attacks from the church and from conservatives. Other works by González Suárez are *Estudio histórico sobre las Canaris* (1878), *Historia eclesiástica del Ecuador* (1881), *Nueva miscelanea o colección de opusculos publicados* (1910), and *Defensa de mi criterio histórico* (1937).

During the terms of the Liberal president Eloy Alfaro y Arosemena (1895–1901, 1906–1911) and the drive to secularize Ecuadorian society (principally through measures for civil marriage and divorce), Archbishop González Suárez played a critical role in depoliticizing the clergy. A peacemaker, he provided a calm voice for moderation in the clergy. His publications inspired a group of young disciples, most notably Jacinto Jijón y Caamaño.

– RONN F. PINEO

GONZÁLEZ VIDELA, GABRIEL

Gabriel González Videla (*b.* 22 November 1898; *d.* 22 August 1980), president of Chile (1946–1952). A lawyer who was born in the provinces, González Videla served as a diplomat before ruling Chile during the turbulent post–World War II era. As a member of the Radical Party's left wing, he promised to revive many of Pedro Aguirre Cerda's policies. Unable to win the popular vote in the 1946 election, he entered into a political alliance with the Liberal and Communist parties. When it became clear that he could not reconcile these two ideological foes, González Videla dismissed the Communists from his cabinet. The Communists retaliated by launching a series of violent strikes that paralyzed the nation, eventually forcing González Videla to use the military to restore order. Claiming to have discovered a leftist plot, he outlawed the Communist Party and broke off diplomatic relations with Eastern bloc nations.

As president, González Videla encountered substantial economic problems. A decline in world copper prices and the onset of powerful inflation—33 percent in 1947 alone—devastated the Chilean economy. When the government imposed an austerity program, it precipitated a series of violent public demonstrations.

While it was beset by economic and political problems, the González Videla government was not without its accomplishments: the state built a steel plant, organized a government oil company, encouraged hydroelectric projects, founded the Technical University, and enfranchised women.

– WILLIAM F. SATER

GONZÁLEZ VÍQUEZ, CLETO

Cleto González Víquez (*b.* 13 October 1858; *d.* 23 September 1937), president of Costa Rica (1906–1910, 1928–1932). González Víquez was born in Barba de Heredia, Costa Rica, to an aristocratic family. He was an eminent attorney, distinguished politician, and one of the most illustrious historians of his country. With his colleague, friend, and adversary Ricardo JIMÉNEZ, he dominated national politics for four decades in an era characterized by *caudillismo*. He published numer-

ous works on law and history, most notable of which are his investigations into historical geography and genealogy and his interesting studies of protocol, from which we can learn about colonial life in Costa Rica. He studied law at the University of St. Thomas, where his performance was outstanding. He took part in the commission that drew up the civil, penal, and legal codes.

González Víquez had an important political career, in which he served twice as a representative to the national Congress and once as minister of Government. He defended liberal principles and opposed the reformist movements of the era. In 1906, after a controversial election in which his rivals were expelled from the country, he was elected president of Costa Rica, an office he held until 1910. In Congress he led the opposition to President Alfredo GONZÁLEZ FLORES from 1916 to 1917 and supported the coup d'état that drove Flores from power. In the 1920s he maintained his liberal stance and continued to be influential in the National Republican Party. He was again elected president in 1928 in the last years of the liberal republic, and he was forced to face the effects of the economic crisis beginning in 1929.

– JORGE MARIO SALAZAR

GORODISCHER, ANGÉLICA

Angélica Gorodischer (*b.* 28 July 1928), Argentine writer. Born in Buenos Aires to an upper-middle-class Spanish family, Gorodischer began writing late in life in the port town of Rosario, where she settled with her husband and children. *Opus dos* (1967), her first novel, the short stories contained in *Bajo las jubeas en flor* (1973; Under the Jubeas in Bloom) and in *Casta luna electrónica* (1977; Chaste Electronic Moon), and particularly her tales of the intergalactic trips of a traveling salesman from Rosario, Trafalgar Medrano (*Trafalgar,* 1979), would permit classifying her as a writer of speculative science fiction. On the other hand, these stories, together with some others, constitute what could be labeled as "fantastic." Some could even be classed as thrillers, whodunits, and Gothic tales. She is interested in the absurd, monstrosities, dreams, myths; in the great themes that are a pretext for human beings to continue fighting to live; in the relationship between man and the universe, man and God, and power and death; in all that man does not know.

For Gorodischer, literature is a way of "unmasking" reality. In her works there is a counterpoint between the imaginary and the real worlds that gives transcendental meaning to her stories, so they end by being allegories, metaphors, or symbolic chronicles of the contemporary world and of the human condition, generally presented in a humorous vein.

— ANGELA B. DELLEPIANE

GOROSTIZA, MANUEL EDUARDO DE

Manuel Eduardo de Gorostiza (*b.* 1789; *d.* 1851), Mexican military officer, diplomat, cabinet minister, and dramatist. Gorostiza was born in Veracruz, but his family returned to Spain after the death of his father, a colonial governor, when he was five. Because of his liberalism, Gorostiza was forced to flee from Spain to Mexico in 1822. He served as a Mexican representative in London, where he kept the British Parliament and public well informed about U.S. designs on Texas in the late 1820s. In 1830 he was named Mexico's minister plenipotentiary in London and minister to all the European countries. In 1933 Gorostiza was recalled to Mexico, where he served on Gómez Farías's commission on educational reform and was named the first director of the National Library and the National Theater.

After the fall of Gómez Farías, Gorostiza wrote and produced plays to support himself, reviving the theater in Mexico and becoming famous for his comedies in Spain as well. He later served as Mexican minister in Washington (1836), treasury minister (1838, 1842–1843, 1846), and foreign relations minister (1838–1839). During the U.S. invasion of Mexico in 1847, Gorostiza organized and paid for a battalion, which he led at the Battle of Churubusco.

— D. F. STEVENS

GOROSTIZA ACALÁ, JOSÉ

José Gorostiza Acalá (*b.* 10 November 1901; *d.* 16 March 1973), Mexican poet and diplomat. He and his brother Celestino were major intellectual figures in Mexico and were members of the Contemporáneos intellectual circle with Jaime TORRES BODET. Octavio PAZ considered Gorostiza to be a major Latin American poet.

A native of Villahermosa, Tabasco, Gorostiza began teaching at the National Preparatory School in 1921 and published his first book of poems in 1925. Joining the foreign service, he became first chancellor in London in 1927, after which he served as head of the fine arts department in public education. He returned to the foreign service where, in the 1930s and 1940s, he held a series of posts abroad, including ones in Italy, Guatemala, and Cuba. In 1950 he became ambassador to Greece and, a year later, permanent representative to the United Nations. He culminated his career as un-

dersecretary of foreign relations (1953–1964), serving briefly as secretary in 1964. He won the National Literary Prize in 1968.

— RODERIC AI CAMP

GORRITI, JUAN IGNACIO DE

Juan Ignacio de Gorriti (*b.* June 1766; *d.* 25 May 1842), Argentine priest and independence leader. Born in Los Horcones, Gorriti's early education in Latin and philosophy was directed by the Franciscans in Jujuy. From 1781 to 1789 he studied theology and literature at the Colegio Nusetra Señora de Monserrat in Córdoba, and he obtained a doctorate in sacred theology from the University in Charcas in 1791. He briefly worked as a parish priest in Cochinoca and Casabindo, small villages in the altiplano of Jujuy, earning distinction for his sermons. He participated in Argentina's independence movement, arguing that the authority of the viceroys and other Spanish officials had expired when the French deposed the legitimate king of Spain. In September 1810, he was named representative of Jujuy to the revolutionary Junta de Buenos Aires. He remained in politics as Salta's representative to the Congress in 1824 but was exiled to Bolivia by political enemies in 1831. There he wrote "Reflexiones sobre las causas morales de las convulsiones interiores de los nuevos estadoes americanos y examen de los medios eficaces para remediarlas" (Valparaíso, 1836), an early attempt to solve the problems facing the newly formed nations of South America. Gorriti died in Sucre, Bolivia.

— J. DAVID DRESSING

GOULART, JOÃO BELCHIOR MARQUES

João Belchior Marques Goulart (*b.* 1 March 1919; *d.* 6 December 1976), Brazilian Labor Party (PTB) leader and president of Brazil (1961–1964), whose overthrow led to two decades of military rule.

João "Jango" Goulart was born in São Borja, Rio Grande do Sul. His family was allied politically and economically with that of Getúlio VARGAS. Jango, the eldest boy of eight children, spent his early years on the family ranches that produced cattle, sheep, and horses. From the age of nine, he attended schools in larger cities, finally receiving a law degree in 1939. He soon took over the family businesses and became a millionaire.

Jango befriended Getúlio Vargas when the latter returned to São Borja in 1945. A popular figure, Jango formed district chapters of Vargas's PTB. Eventually he became a confidant, aide, and spokesman for Vargas during his 1950 campaign for president. At about that time his sister married Leonel BRIZOLA, who would become his closest political ally.

After leading the PTB in Pôrto Alegre for a year, Jango transferred to Rio to help Vargas manage national labor politics, for which he was appointed labor minister in 1953. He showed great skill in handling workers, whom he favored with a 100-percent wage hike in 1954. The furor resulting from this decision forced Jango's resignation, but he continued to exercise great influence in labor matters through his leadership of the PTB.

In many ways Vargas's heir, Jango rode the PTB into the vice presidency in 1956 and again in 1961, allying with Juscelino KUBITSCHEK and Jânio QUADROS, respectively. He continued to use his position to help labor, and the PTB grew rapidly in Congress and the states—the only major party to do so.

Jango was in China when Quadros resigned in August 1961, creating a succession crisis. His many supporters—especially Brizola in Rio Grande—threatened civil war should the military attempt to deny the presidency to Jango. A compromise between Congress and the military chiefs allowed Jango to be titular president in a parliamentary system. The arrangement proved cumbersome, and when put to a plebiscite in early 1963, it was abandoned.

U.S. businessmen, abetted by increasingly cool diplomatic relations, worked to discredit Goulart, while Washington disallowed financial assistance.

Goulart took the restored presidential powers as a vote of confidence, yet his tenure proved controversial and stormy. Although he continued to enjoy popularity among the working class, he never captured (as Vargas had) the support of the middle and upper classes. The U.S. government treated him with aloofness, especially after Brizola nationalized a subsidiary of International Telephone and Telegraph. U.S. businessmen, abetted by increasingly cool diplomatic relations, worked to discredit Goulart, while Washington disallowed financial assistance. The country plunged into a depression, exacerbated by Goulart's erratic policies and mismanagement. Politics became dangerously polarized, and Goulart failed in several attempts to conciliate opposing groups. Finally, in March 1964 he decided to make a bold appeal to the workers, rural poor, and leftists by announcing a major reforms package, including redistribution of land near federal installations. This effort,

as well as his mishandling of two military revolts, led the army to overthrow him on 1 April 1964 in order to rid the country of a leftist president and restore economic order. Goulart flew into exile and lived in Uruguay and Argentina until his death from a heart attack.

– MICHAEL L. CONNIFF

GRAÇA ARANHA, JOSÉ PEREIRA DA

José Pereira da Graça Aranha (*b.* 21 June 1868; *d.* 26 January 1931), Brazilian writer of the premodernist social novel. Graça Aranha was born to an aristocratic Maranhão family and graduated from law school in Recife. While municipal judge in the German settlement of Porto do Cachoeiro in 1890, his observations of the immigrants' struggle inspired the plot for his first and most famous novel, *Canaã* (1902; *Canaan,* 1920). Previous to its publication he was elected to a seat on the Brazilian Academy of Letters. From 1900 to 1920 he held diplomatic offices and traveled through many parts of Europe. Upon his return to Brazil he published *A estética da vida* (1920). Graça Aranha's thesis novels are sociological studies of the contemporary Brazilian problem of assimilation of races and cultures, and philosophical explorations of his theory of universalism and humanitarian evolutionism. His documentary prose contains brilliant descriptions and abstract characters.

Aside from a modest literary production, Graça Aranha's most important contribution is his role in initiating the modernist movement in Brazil. He organized Modern Art Week in 1922 to promote among Brazilian artists a reformation of national thought and sensibility, launching the modernist movement in the arts, which sought to rediscover Brazil in its native elements. He broke with the Academy of Letters in 1924, calling on its members to create a national literature.

– LORI MADDEN

GRAEF FERNÁNDEZ, CARLOS

Carlos Graef Fernández (*b.* 25 February 1911), Mexican mathematician and educator. A disciple of Manuel SANDOVAL VALLARTA, Graef Fernández graduated from the National University with a degree in engineering before completing a Ph.D. at the Massachusetts Institute of Technology in 1940. He began teaching relativity at the National School of Science in Mexico in 1941 and then at Harvard from 1944 to 1945. He devoted many decades to teaching at the National University, serving as dean of the National School of Sciences (1957–1959) and director of the Institute of Physics. A leader in Mexico's efforts to harness nuclear energy, he coordinated its national commission in the 1960s, and served as a governor of the International Organization of Atomic Energy (1960–1961). Mexico awarded him its National Prize in Sciences in 1970.

— RODERIC AI CAMP

GRANDJEAN DE MONTIGNY, AUGUSTE HENRI VICTOR

Auguste Henri Victor Grandjean de Montigny (*b.* 15 July 1776; *d.* 2 March 1850), French architect. Grandjean de Montigny studied at the École des Beaux-Arts in Paris. He arrived in Rio de Janeiro with the French Artistic Mission, which was organized by Joaquim Lebreton (1760–1819) at the invitation of the Portuguese crown. After his arrival on 26 March 1816, he was asked to design the future Academy of Fine Arts, and he was nominated professor of architecture and given two assistants. The construction of the academy began, but financial difficulties delayed its completion.

Meanwhile Grandjean de Montigny looked for other jobs, such as the Praça do Comércio (1820), a structure in which merchants conducted business. He was also responsible for the old market of Candelária (1836) and for several private houses. Grandjean de Montigny and other French artists were in charge of decorating Rio de Janeiro's Palace Square with ephemeral structures for the coronation of João VI (6 February 1818). Greek temples, Roman arches, and obelisks were the fashion for this kind of urban decoration in public festivities, after which they were destroyed. Montigny operated a private school of architecture until 1824, when Emperor PEDRO I finally ordered that the construction of the Academy of Fine Arts, where Montigny held his lectures, be concluded.

— MARIA BEATRIZ NIZZA DA SILVA

GRAU, ENRIQUE

Enrique Grau (*b.* 18 December 1920), Colombian painter. Grau was born to a prominent family from Cartagena that encouraged his creative talents. His first exhibition, in 1940, preceded formal art studies, which he began at the Art Students League in New York City (1941–1942). Grau has worked in many media, including set design, costumes, and films. However, his reputation as one of the most important Colombian artists—along with Fernando BOTERO, Alejandro OBREGÓN, Edgar Negret, and Eduardo Ramírez VILLAMIZAR—was established in the early 1960s by his paintings. Although he was always a figurative artist, Grau's works of 1955–1962 show the influence of abstract geometry; his images—in painting, drawing, and sculpture from 1962—demonstrate the development of a style that combines refined mimetic skills with satire.

Retrospectives of Grau's work have been organized in Colombia by the Universidad Nacional, Bogotá (1963); the Museo de Arte Moderno, Bogotá (1973), and the Fundación Da Vinci, Manizales (graphic work, 1988). Grau's work also has been featured in international exhibitions focusing on contemporary Colombian and Latin American art: *Latin American Art Since Independence* (Yale University Art Gallery and University of Texas Art Museum, 1966); *Lateinamerikanisch Kunstausstellung* (Kunsthalle, Berlin, 1964); *El Arte Colombiano a Través de los Siglos* (Petit Palais, Paris, 1975); *Perspective on the Present: Contemporary Latin America and the Caribbean* (Nagoya City Art Museum, 1991).

— FATIMA BERCHT

GRAU, MIGUEL

Miguel Grau (*b.* 1834; *d.* 1879), Peru's greatest naval hero, renowned for his prowess as admiral of the Peruvian navy in command of the ironclad *Huáscar* during the War of the Pacific (1879–1883). Born in Piura, Grau started his career as a sailor on whaling ships. In 1856 he obtained the rank of lieutenant. He participated in the caudillo struggles of the time in support of General Manuel Ignacio VIVANCO against Ramón CASTILLA, a political decision that led to his ouster from the war navy in 1858. At the end of Castilla's second presidential term, however, Grau was back in the navy on a mission to Europe under Admiral Aurelio García y García to buy badly needed warships. In 1865, Grau supported Colonel Manuel Ignacio PRADO's uprising against compliance with a forced treaty with Spain, and in 1866 he fought the bellicose Spanish fleet in the battle of Abtao.

In 1868, Grau was appointed commander of the *Huáscar.* He opposed the coup attempt by the GUTIÉRREZ BROTHERS in 1872, after which he became commander in chief of the Peruvian navy as well as deputy for Paita (1876–1878). At the start of the War of the Pacific in 1879, Grau returned to the command of the *Huáscar,* one of two ironclads Peru sent against the far more numerous Chilean fleet. Grau performed legendary feats against Chilean vessels and ports trying to buy time for new warship purchases. He died in the naval battle of Angamos, which secured decisive naval superiority for Chile.

— ALFONSO W. QUIROZ

GRAU SAN MARTÍN, RAMÓN

Ramón Grau San Martín (*b.* 13 September 1887; *d.* 28 July 1969), Cuban physician and politician, president of Cuba (1933–1934, 1944–1948). Born into a privileged and well-known family, Grau San Martín received a first-class education in both the sciences and the humanities. He earned a medical degree and began a lifetime involvement with the University of Havana, where he served on many committees. Beginning in 1927, Grau actively and consistently opposed the dictatorship of Gerardo MACHADO; indeed, he was the only faculty member who refused to sign the edict authorizing Machado's honorary doctorate from the university. For his efforts, Grau was jailed and exiled from Cuba in the late 1920s.

In the early 1930s, the tide of anti-Machado sentiment in Cuba was swelled by the Depression and growing anti-American feeling. Progressive elements of the military and civilian groups banded together to force out Machado, who resigned through the mediation of U.S. representative Sumner Welles. A provisional government, headed by Carlos Manuel de CÉSPEDES, was itself quickly overthrown on 4 September 1933. This revolt brought to the forefront Sergeant Fulgencio BATISTA Y ZALDÍVAR as its chief and Grau as the most prominent member of a civilian pentarchy.

On 10 September 1993, Grau abrogated the hated

Platt Amendment, which had kept Cuba in a state

of dependence on the United States.

Events unfolded rapidly and, backed by his faithful students, Grau and Antonio Guiteras became the principals of a brief but extremely important political experiment. On 10 September, Grau abrogated the hated Platt Amendment, which had kept Cuba in a state of dependence on the United States. The revolutionary government effected other dramatic changes, including the requirement that at least 50 percent of a business's employees had to be Cuban, the granting of autonomy to the University of Havana and removal of restrictions for enrollment, the extension of the vote to women, compulsory trade unionization and the creation of professional associations, and an agrarian reform designed to benefit peasants. Not surprisingly, the government's activism spurred demonstrations for more radical reforms, earning it the enmity of the political Right and hostility from the United States. Furthermore, as the demands of the Left began to outpace the reforms, another potential support base for the Grau–Guiteras team was alienated. In January 1934 a military coup led by Batista, by then the army chief, toppled the government, although the legacy of the experiment lived on.

Grau remained active in politics and university life for the next decade. He founded the Authentic Party and won the presidential election in 1944. During his four-year term, Grau returned to many of his previous policies. This time, in the years of euphoria after World War II, Grau found a more fertile and sophisticated political climate for his ideas. Although he was an opportunist with a keen sense of symbolism and ceremony, Grau held to his basic principles of anti-imperialism, nationalism, and non-Marxist socialism throughout his life.

– KAREN RACINE

GRIJALVA, JUAN DE

Juan de Grijalva (*b.* ca. 1489; *d.* 1527), conquistador who first learned of the Aztec Empire and a nephew of Pánfilo de NARVÁEZ. Grijalva was born in Cuéllar and came to the Caribbean as a youth. He accompanied Diego VELÁZQUEZ, and later his uncle, on their first expeditions to Cuba in 1511, and subsequently resided in prominence on the island. In 1518, Governor Velázquez dispatched him to expand upon the discoveries made by Francisco FERNÁNDEZ DE CÓRDOBA along the coast of Yucatán. His fleet discovered Cozumel, the Grijalva and Banderas rivers, and San Juan de Ulúa. After his force was attacked at the latter site by a number of natives in canoes, he decided not to attempt to colonize and returned to Cuba, an action that greatly displeased Velázquez. The first Spaniard to learn of the Aztec Empire, Grijalva reported its existence to Velázquez, but he did not accompany CORTÉS. He was killed in battle against natives near Villahermosa.

– JOHN E. KICZA

GRILO, SARAH

Sarah Grilo (*b.* 1919), Argentine painter. Born in Buenos Aires, Grilo lived in Madrid and Paris (1948–1950) and traveled throughout Europe and the United States (1957–1958). According to Damián Bayón, among the Buenos Aires group comprising José Fernández Muro, Clorindo Testa, Kasuya Sakai, and Miguel Ocampo, Grilo "always represented the extreme sensibility to color." From 1960 she evidenced this sensibility in compositions whose right-angled structures were permanently altered by the inclusion of circular forms. Her chromatic modulations are suggestive of the tonal values of Pierre Bonnard and his concept of color as a continuous state of exaltation in which form loses all importance. Later Grilo introduced tachiste effects (graphic signs). Her right-angled structures disappeared, giving way to a surface freely dotted with spots of paint and sprinkled with texts, words, letters, and numbers backed

Sarah Grilo at Galería Bonino, Buenos Aires, with one of her paintings, 1961. (La Nación)

by radiant color, which created imaginary codices of great enchantment. Grilo has exhibited throughout North and South America as well as in Europe. She has received several awards, including the Wertheim Prize (Buenos Aires, 1961) and a Guggenheim Foundation Fellowship (New York, 1962).

— AMALIA CORTINA ARAVENA

GRIMARD, LUC

Luc Grimard (pseudonyms, Lin Dege; Marie Gérard; *b.* 30 January 1886; *d.* 24 October 1954), Haitian writer, educator, and diplomat. Luc Grimard finished a law degree at age nineteen. He taught classics, philosophy, and social science before serving as Haitian consul in Le Havre (1922–1927). During his directorship of the Lycée Philippe Guerrier in Cap Haïtien (1927–1932), Grimard's resistance to the American occupation (1915–1934) was exemplary to his students. In 1932 he went to Port-au-Prince as inspector of the École Normale des Instituteurs. He was named director of *Le Temps* (1938) and later of the Catholic daily, *La Phalange* (1941–1950). President Elie Lescot appointed him conservator of the Musée Sténio Vincent (1941). Grimard also served as rector of the University of Haiti (1951–1954) and was a member of the Cuban Academy of Arts and Letters.

His first volumes of poetry were published in France in 1927. His early verse has been compared to that of Paul Verlaine. Later he turned to Haitian history, nature, and women for inspiration. From his early poetry through his stories there runs a thread of fascination with mystery and the supernatural.

— CARROL F. COATES

GRIPPO, VÍCTOR

Víctor Grippo (*b.* 10 May 1936), Argentine artist. Born in the town of Junín, in the province of Buenos Aires, Grippo studied chemistry and design at the University of La Plata. In 1971, he became a leading member of a group of thirteen artists (known as *Grupo de los Trece*). Named *Grupo de Cayc* (for the Centro de Arte y Comunicación where they met), these painters wanted to generate radical changes in the practice of art through the exploration of the relation of art to science and the use of massive communication techniques and inexpensive materials.

In his installation *Analogy 1* (1971), sprouting potatoes were strung together with zinc and copper electrodes and connected with a voltmeter. By means of written descriptions, Grippo drew parallels between the germinating tubers' energetic power and the awakening of human consciousness: the potato, a staple food native to South America, symbolizes the potential of autochthonous resources. Manual labor, in its most rudimentary forms, was the subject of his installation *Crafts* (1976). Since the 1980s his work has consisted of assemblages of quasi-geometric forms that resemble spheres, artificer's lead pencils, and *crusets*.

— MARTA GARSD

GROUSSAC, PAUL

Paul Groussac (*b.* 15 February 1848; *d.* 27 June 1929), Argentine essayist, philosopher, and historian. François Paul Groussac was born in Toulouse, France, and finished secondary school in Brest. He settled in Argentina in 1866, during the War of the Triple Alliance (Paraguayan War), and went on to became a leading intellectual in his adopted country. Groussac taught mathematics at the Colegio Nacional in Buenos Aires and spent many hours in the national library broadening his intellectual horizons. He lived in San Miguel de Tucumán in northwestern Argentina, taught at the Colegio Nacional in Tucumán (1871–1874), became superintendent of education in that province (1874–1878), and was appointed director of the Teachers' College in 1878.

Keenly interested in Argentine history and Latin American thought, Groussac wrote for Argentine newspapers and authored important books in the field. His works include: *Los jesuítas en Tucumán* (The Jesuits in Tucuman [1873]), *Les îles Malouines* (The Malvinas [1910]), *Viaje intelectual* (Intellectual Voyage [1904]), *El pensamiento de América* (American, i.e., Latin American, Thought [1989]), *El Congreso de Tucumán* (1916), *Los que pasaban* (Some Who Passed Through [1919]), and *Del Plata al Niágara* (1897). Combative in his newspaper articles, Groussac was befriended by such influential intellectuals and politicians as Nicolás AVELLANEDA, José Manuel ESTRADA, Eduardo WILDE, Lucio V. MANSILLA, Aristóbulo DEL VALLE, and Carlos PELLEGRINI. Groussac's lasting contributions included the reorganization of the National Library, of which he became director in 1885; the publication of the scholarly journal *La Biblioteca* (1896), which became *Anales de la Biblioteca* in 1900 (it ceased publication in 1915); and participation in the founding of *El Sud Americano* and *La Nación*. He belonged to the influential group of educators and writers at the turn of the century who shaped modern Argentina. He died in Buenos Aires.

– GEORGETTE MAGASSY DORN

GROVE VALLEJO, MARMADUKE

Marmaduke Grove Vallejo (*b.* 6 July 1878; *d.* 15 May 1954), Chilean army officer and Socialist Party leader. Grove was born in Copiapó. He enrolled at the Escuela Naval in 1892, was dismissed in 1894, but two years later entered the Escuela Militar. Upon graduation in 1898, Second Lieutenant Grove entered the artillery. In 1901 he became a first lieutenant and was assigned to the staff of the Escuela Militar. Four years later he was sent to Germany and spent time in an artillery regiment and at the Charlottenburg Artillery Training School, where he received a diploma. In 1910 he returned to Chile a captain. He studied at the Academia de Guerra (staff school) from 1912 to 1914. He married Rebeca Valenzuela in 1915.

As a young officer, Grove was known for his advanced social and political ideas. In 1918 he was promoted to major, served on the Division I staff, then on the general staff, and the next year was appointed subdirector of the Escuela Militar in Santiago. For his outspoken criticism of war ministry activities in 1920, Grove was transferred out of Santiago, but he moved back to the Escuela Militar in 1921. He was a key figure in the military-political activities of 1924–1925. Then after quarreling with army strongman Carlos IBÁÑEZ DEL CAMPO (president, 1927–1931), he was posted to Europe on a mission for Chile's fledgling air corps, which he had helped found. There he plotted against Ibáñez and tried unsuccessfully to overthrow him, for which he was exiled to Easter Island. He escaped and,

following Ibáñez's ouster in 1931, was appointed air commodore. Grove became a key figure in the 1932 Socialist Republic, was exiled again, and was elected to the Senate (while in jail) soon after his return, serving from 1934 to 1949. He was an early leader of the Socialist Party, and the party's contender for the Popular Front presidential candidacy in 1938, before giving way to Radical Pedro Aguirre Cerda.

– FREDERICK M. NUNN

GUAMAN POMA DE AYALA, FELIPE

Felipe Guaman Poma de Ayala (*b.* ca. 1535; *d.* ca. 1615), one of the most polemic and most admired native authors of the colonial period. Guaman Poma wrote *Primer nueva corónica y bien gobierno* (ca. 1615), a long, illustrated history (1,188 pages with 398 pen-and-ink drawings) of ancient Andean times, Inca rule, and Spanish rule. The book was discovered in 1908 in the Royal Danish Library in Copenhagen and was first published in 1936. An abridged version, *Letter to a King,* translated by Christopher Dilke, appeared in 1978. Anthropologists consider the book a primary source of information on the pre-Columbian Andean world and on the first decades of Spanish colonization. Literary scholars, after ignoring the document for years, now regard it as a symbolic representation in which the author criticizes colonial rule while submitting a plan for "good government" to the Spanish king, Philip III, to whom the chronicle is addressed. Traditionally, historians have pointed out inaccuracies in Guaman Poma's work; however, recent research has explained how and why the author took advantage of information available from native and European sources to present an Andean version of history.

With the exception of what Guaman Poma says about himself in *Primer nueva corónica,* there is very little documentary evidence about his life. It is believed that he was born about 1535 in San Cristóbal de Suntunto (a small village in what is today the province of Ayacucho in Peru), lived for several years in Cuzco, and later moved (about 1562) to the city of Guamanga, now known as Ayacucho. According to Guaman Poma, his father was an ethnic lord of the Yarovilcas, a group conquered by the Incas and later incorporated into their empire; his mother was the daughter of the powerful Inca ruler Túpac Yupanqui. The historical evidence does not support Guaman Poma's claim to this distinguished lineage.

Educated in the Spanish language and culture, perhaps by missionaries, and well versed in Quechua, his native tongue, Guaman Poma became an interpreter in the campaigns against idol worship in the Andes (ca.

1568–1571). It is very probable that he also served as interpreter in the Third Council of Lima (1583–1584). In this regard, it has been speculated that it was through the library of the church inspector Cristóbal de Albornoz, as well as through books belonging to missionaries, that Guaman Poma became familiar with the writings of key religious, historical, and juridical authors and with engravings and illustrations of saints and biblical themes. These books and iconography, together with the Andean oral tradition and Guaman Poma's own experiences, became the sources of *Primer nueva corónica*.

Guaman Poma's work is the angry testimony of how a native Andean experienced and interpreted the cultural clash brought about by the Conquest and colonization.

Legal documents show that Guaman Poma served again as interpreter (1594) and, in addition, was the witness in a land claim presented by native Andeans (1595). He was later expelled from Guamanga (1600) and San Cristóbal de Suntunto (1611) for his defense of the native population and for claiming ancestral lands. Guaman Poma returned to Lima in 1601, to complain about the poor treatment that he and other Indians were receiving from colonial administrators, and in 1613, to present the manuscript of *Primer nueva corónica* to the viceroy. Even though he failed in this attempt, in a letter (Guamanga, 14 February 1615) to Philip III he states that his chronicle has been completed. After this date we lose all track of him.

Guaman Poma's encyclopedic work is the living and angry testimony of how a native Andean experienced and interpreted the cultural clash brought about by the Conquest and colonization. *Primer nueva corónica* exhibits the talents of an indigenous historian who took up the pen, thus bringing together European and Andean traditions, Spanish and Quechua, writing and painting, to praise the past, condemn colonial administrators, and demand a better society for his people.

— RAQUEL CHANG-RODRÍGUEZ

GUARDIA, RICARDO ADOLFO DE LA

Ricardo Adolfo De La Guardia (*b.* 14 June 1899; *d.* 29 December 1970), president of Panama (1941–1945). Minister of government and justice under president Arnulfo ARIAS MADRID, Guardia organized a movement to depose the dictator. He assumed the office of president

with the support of the National Guard, the oligarchy, and much of the Panamanian populace. The attack on Pearl Harbor brought fear that the Panama Canal would become a target, and Guardia endorsed controversial plans for the construction of U.S. bases in Panama. In 1944 the National Assembly rebelled against Guardia's authority, insisting that he name a constitutional successor. In response, he dissolved the assembly and abrogated the 1941 constitution. He called elections in 1945 that established a new assembly and installed Enrique A. JIMÉNEZ as provisional president. Arias returned to power in 1949, forcing Guardia to flee to the Canal Zone, where he remained until 1951.

— SARA FLEMING

GUARDIA GUTIÉRREZ, TOMÁS

Tomás Guardia Gutiérrez (*b.* 16 December 1831; *d.* 6 July 1882), president and dictator of Costa Rica (1870–1882). Guardia is often seen as the expression of triumphant liberalism in Costa Rica with his dictatorial style, the rewriting of the Constitution of 1871, and the hegemony of an entire generation of elitist Liberals in the 1880s and 1890s. However, Guardia was not the first to champion liberal policies, and his reign was more a reflection of severe intra-elite tensions within a liberal framework than of liberalism's ascendancy for the first time. Indeed, the Constitution of 1871 proved to be a highly presidentialist document, with Guardia and his relatives rigidly controlling political power for some twenty years while pursuing liberal economic transformation of the country.

Guardia, born in Bagaces, was the son of leading ranching families in Guanacaste and Alajuela provinces. Nevertheless, his power transcended particular regions. His father's family was originally from Panama, and the family remained active in the politics of that nation as well. As a colonel in the Costa Rican army, Guardia led a revolt against the government, taking the artillery barracks in San José on 27 April 1870. He became general commandant of an interim government headed by Bruno Carranza Ramírez. He was elected president in 1872 under a system that centralized the election procedures in the executive branch. He engineered the election of an ally, Aniceto Esquivel Sáenz, in 1876, but soon thereafter (1877) he reassumed the presidency as virtual dictator. He convened yet another Constituent Assembly in 1880 and reestablished the Constitution of 1871 by decree in 1882. Guardia died of natural causes in 1882, prior to the scheduled presidential election.

Guardia was something of an outsider in mid-nineteenth-century Costa Rican politics. He was not a leading member of the coffee oligarchy, dominated by the Mora and MONTEALEGRE clans, which had ruled for over twenty years before his coup. Many of his policies can best be seen as designed to wrest political power from the family-based cliques of the coffee barons of the Central Valley. He exiled former President José María Montealegre Fernández to the United States for life in 1872, and, although his own family would benefit enormously, much of his regime's support came from non-oligarchic forces in the coffee economy. Coffee elite members who were more ideologically and institutionally than personally oriented, as well as liberals of more modest social origins, tended to support Guardia, while the "old money" families more often felt his wrath.

Guardia's regime was most highly identified with the long-lasting (until 1949) Constitution of 1871 and the building of the railroad to the Atlantic coast. The latter endeavor was contracted with Minor Keith and led to both the first serious foreign debt and to the United Fruit Company dominance of much of the Atlantic coast province of Limón. Other major achievements included the abolition of the death penalty in 1882, the beginning of a major effort at mass primary education, and, curiously for an avowedly presidentialist regime, the strengthening of both the legislative branch and legal norms in public affairs. A substantial group of ideologically committed liberal deputies and magistrates came to power during Guardia's reign, as is suggested by the reformulation of the Civil Code in 1886.

In foreign affairs Guardia was able to deter Central American unification efforts led by the Guatemalan strongman Justo Rufino BARRIOS, preserving local independence and a special commercial relationship with Great Britain. Perhaps the overzealous pursuit of British loan capital and investment, brokered by Keith, is today seen as the most negative aspect of Guardia's admittedly authoritarian form of liberalism.

– LOWELL GUDMUNDSON

GUARDIA NAVARRO, ERNESTO DE LA

Ernesto De La Guardia Navarro (*b.* 30 May 1904; *d.* 2 May 1983), president of Panama (1956–1960). Born in Panama City, Guardia Navarro, a conservative businessman with a degree from Dartmouth, was the first Panamanian president since World War II to complete his term in office. Elected to the presidency in 1956 as a candidate of the National Patriotic Coalition, he furthered programs begun by President José Antonio REMÓN CANTERA (1952–1955). He created a minimum wage, sponsored housing projects, undertook minor educational reforms, and lowered unemployment levels.

In 1958 he began negotiations with U.S. President Eisenhower over the fine points of the Remón–Eisenhower Treaty, seeking an equal status for the Spanish language and the Panamanian flag in the Canal Zone.

In April 1959 a group of Cubans intending to overthrow Guardia Navarro's government landed in Colón. The conflict was quickly resolved and the invaders deported. In November of the same year, violence erupted when protesters marched into the Canal Zone carrying Panamanian flags. Eisenhower conceded, and the Panamanian flag was raised in the zone. In 1960, Guardia Navarro's term ended peacefully with the election of a member of the opposition.

– SARA FLEMING

GUARDIOLA, SANTOS

Santos Guardiola (*b.* 1812; *d.* 11 January 1862), military figure and president of Honduras (1856–1862). Guardiola established himself as a prominent Conservative and military leader during the National War against William WALKER's invasions. Known as "the butcher," Guardiola was considered a particularly ruthless and cruel commander. His forces defeated Walker and the latter's small force of fifty-five men at Rivas on 29 June 1855. Guatemalan Conservatives helped establish Guardiola as president of Honduras on 17 February 1856. He assumed a second term on 2 July 1860 and ruled until his assassination.

Guardiola's presidency had certain measurable successes at first but in the end was marred by violence and economic stagnation. After signing an alliance with Guatemala and El Salvador against Walker, Guardiola set out to assert Honduran sovereignty over the Bay Islands and Mosquito Coast, areas of permanent British incursions and long-standing dispute. British citizens were allowed to remain as inhabitants of the Bay Islands and were exempt from taxation. The Dallas-Clarendon Convention of 17 October 1856 removed the British protectorate over the Mosquito Coast but at the same time restricted Honduran sovereignty. Plans were made in January 1853 for an interoceanic railway with the founding of Ferrocarril Interoceánico de Honduras (Interoceanic Railway Company) on 28 April 1854, organized in Honduras with offices in New York and London. Walker's eventual capture and execution at Trujillo in 1860 represented the pinnacle of Guardiola's presidency.

Difficulties with Miguel del Cid, head of the diocese of Honduras, resulted in Guardiola's excommunication on 26 December 1860. Guardiola's rebuke and anticlericalism erupted in the *Guerra de los padres,* which pitted the church against its former Conservative ally in April 1861. The same month, Guardiola was forced by deteriorating economic conditions to authorize the issue of copper coins. The deteriorating economy, coupled with the violence of Guardiola's presidency, led to his assassination in early 1862 and, after several Conservative administrations, to the consolidation of power by the Liberal Party in 1876.

— JEFFREY D. SAMUELS

GUARNIERI, GIANFRANCESCO

Gianfrancesco Guarnieri (b. 6 August 1934), Brazilian dramatist and actor. Guarnieri has been a central figure in modern Brazilian theater and is particularly associated with the Arena Theater of São Paulo. His political orientation is Marxist, and his Brechtian theatrical technique requires the audience's direct emotional participation in the action to achieve a type of classical catharsis. *Eles não usam black-tie* (1958), his most celebrated play, presents the inevitable personal tragedy resulting from disunity in workers' struggles. Other dramas question the accepted truths of Brazilian history and the nation's contemporary reality. His *Ponto de partida* (1976) is an allegorical protest against the military regime's murder of journalist Vladimir HERZOG.

— IRWIN STERN

GUARNIERI, M[OZART] CAMARGO

M[ozart] Camargo Guarnieri (b. 1 February 1907), Brazilian composer, conductor, teacher, and leader of the nationalist school of composers. Guarnieri was the son of a Sicilian immigrant remotely related to the

---

Guarnieri's father had a lifelong passion for opera and named his four sons Mozart, Rossini, Bellini, and Verdi.

Guarneri family of violin makers (the name was accidentally changed due to the mistake of an immigration official) and a Brazilian mother. His father, Miguel Guarnieri, an amateur musician, played the piano, flute, and string bass. He had a lifelong passion for opera and named his four sons Mozart, Rossini, Bellini, and Verdi. When Guarnieri became aware of the significance of the name Mozart, he dropped it and signed his name M. Camargo Guarnieri, feeling that it was presumptuous to be called by the name of the great master. Aware that his son had musical talent, and that educational opportunities were limited in the town of Tieté,

Miguel Guarnieri moved to the city of São Paulo in 1922. In São Paulo, Camargo was placed under the tutelage of two teachers who exercised a decisive influence on his artistic and intellectual development: the Italian conductor and teacher Lamberto Baldi and Mário de ANDRADE, philosopher, teacher, and leader of the modernist movement in Brazil. Guarnieri studied with both teachers during the same period. Andrade undertook the direction of Guarnieri's studies in aesthetics and literature, and Baldi taught him counterpoint, fugue, and orchestration, while also gently guiding his efforts in composition. Guarnieri's first successful composition to exhibit obvious national characteristics was a sonatina for piano written in 1928. This work exhibited several characteristics of Guarnieri's mature style of composition: melodies that sounded folklike while avoiding direct quotations of folk melodies, use of typically Brazilian tempo and expression markings in Portuguese—*Molengamente* (indolently) and *Ponteado e bem dengoso* (with a plucked sound, coyly), contrapuntal writing, and use of layers of syncopated voices.

Guarnieri had a major influence on Brazilian music by his teaching of composition, by establishing a high level of craftsmanship in his own musical writing, and by providing a model of tonal and nontonal works with convincing national elements. Although Guarnieri did some writing in an atonal style, he soon came to the conviction that his style of writing was incompatible with what he regarded as the straitjacket of dodecaphony. He believed so strongly that atonality was incompatible with the development of national elements that he conducted a vigorous debate in Brazilian newspapers against what he regarded as the pernicious influence of atonality in the works of Brazilian composers.

Camargo Guarnieri wrote over six hundred musical works, many unpublished. The fifty *Ponteios* for piano are one of the most significant contributions to piano literature from any Brazilian composer and are a treasure of elements uniquely and distinctively Brazilian. Several orchestral works have won international acclaim, and his fourth and fifth sonatas for violin are masterpieces of the genre.

— DAVID P. APPLEBY

GUAYASAMÍN, OSWALDO

Oswaldo Guayasamín (b. July 1919), Ecuadoran painter. Born in Quito, to a humble Indian family, Guayasamín demonstrated his artistic talents at an early age. In 1932 he began studies at Quito's National School of Fine Arts, graduating with honors in 1941. In the following year he had his first solo exhibitions, in Quito and Guayaquil. In 1943, Guayasamín received an invitation through Nelson Rockefeller, who worked for the State Department, to visit the United States. This gave him the opportunity to study firsthand the works of masters like El Greco, Francisco Goya, and Pablo Picasso. The Mexican muralist José Clemente OROZCO, whom Guayasamín met and worked with for a brief period in 1943, had a major impact on the development of his painting, especially on the expressive distortions of the human figure. In fact, throughout decades of prolific work—in painting, drawing, and printmaking—Guayasamín's main pictorial subject has been the human figure, rendered in isolation or as a part of epic scenes, a symbolic carrier of the artist's quest for social and political justice.

From the late 1940s, the ideological and humanitarian appeal of his images, inspired by past and current struggles in Latin America, won Guayasamín commissions for large murals, created for public spaces like the Casa de la Cultura Ecuatoriana, Quito (1948); Centro Bolívar, Caracas (1954); Palacio del Gobierno, Quito (1958); and Barajas Airport, Madrid (1982). Exhibitions of his work outside Ecuador include those at the Museo de Bellas Artes, Caracas (1954); Pan-American Union, Washington, D.C. (1955); IV Bienal de São Paulo (1957); Palacio de Bellas Artes, Mexico City (1968); Museo Español de Arte Contemporáneo, Madrid (1972); Musée d'Art Moderne de la Ville de Paris (1973); the Hermitage, Saint Petersburg, Russia (1982); Museo Nacional Palacio de Bellas Artes, Havana (1985).

– FATIMA BERCHT

GUDIÑO KIEFFER, EDUARDO

Eduardo Gudiño Kieffer (*b.* 2 November 1935), Argentine writer. Born in Esperanza, he was the son of Luis Gudiño Kramer, who wrote on the legendary gaucho Judíos in Entre Ríos at the turn of the century. Gudiño Kieffer never emerged as a major novelist in Argentina, but he attracted some attention in the 1960s and 1970s for his trenchant satiric characterizations of the mentalities and personalities that emerged from the cultural effervescence before the military coup of 1966 and the resistant countercultures it fueled. The effective destruction of this milieu by the Dirty War in the 1970s, the concomitant pessimism the latter engendered, and the sober (if not postmodern) attitudes that accompanied the return to constitutional democracy in 1983 appear to have left Gudiño Kieffer without much material. Yet his most significant work, *Guía de pecadores en la cual se contiene una larga y copiosa exhortación a la virtud y guarda de los mandamientos divinos* (1972),

with all of its baroque counterreformation intertextualities, is both an acerbic denunciation of the moral righteousness of the Argentine neofascism of the period and a biting characterization of individuals more marked by libertinism than libertarianism. Published at the pivotal time of the brief and ultimately failed transition to a Peronista-led democracy (the 1973–1976 parenthesis between almost two decades of military rule), *Guía* can be read as a parable of the irresolvable ideological dilemmas of urban Argentine society at that time. Gudiño Kieffer's narrative style is also notable for the incorporation of multiple colloquial registers of urban, multimedia-oriented life. *Carta abierta Buenos Aires violento* (1970) is an essay denouncing the violence in Argentine social life, a recurring emphasis in contemporary Argentine fiction.

– DAVID WILLIAM FOSTER

GUEILER TEJADA, LIDIA

Lidia Gueiler Tejada (*b.* 1926), president of Bolivia (16 November 1979–17 July 1980). Born in Cochabamba, Gueiler, a graduate of the American Institute in La Paz, was trained as an accountant. She served as a deputy in Congress on two separate occasions and as ambassador to the Federal Republic of Germany, Colombia, and Venezuela. Her *La mujer y la revolución* (1957) was about the role of women in the 1952 Bolivian national revolution. She joined the Nationalist Revolutionary Movement (MNR) in the 1940s but went on to join the leftist Revolutionary Workers Party (POR) in the 1950s. In November 1979, Gueiler emerged as the compromise candidate between Walter GUEVARA ARZE and General Alberto Natusch Busch, who had ended the former's short-lived interim government on 2 November. On 16 November, she became the first woman ever to be elected president of Bolivia.

Gueiler presided over a particularly difficult time in Bolivian history when relations between the armed forces and civilians were at their lowest level. Her mission was mainly to hold power until a new round of elections on 29 June 1980 could determine the next constitutional president. The elections went off as scheduled, but Gueiler could do little to prevent disgruntled sectors of the armed forces tied to drug traffickers from launching a coup on 17 July 1980 that ended Bolivia's return to democracy. Gueiler spent the next two years in exile. When democracy returned to Bolivia in October 1982, Lidia Gueiler was named ambassador to Colombia and later served as ambassador to Venezuela.

– EDUARDO A. GAMARRA

GÚEMES, MARTÍN

Martín Gúemes (*b*. 7 February 1785; *d*. 17 June 1821), ruler of Argentina's northwestern province of Salta (1815–1821). Argentina's deep political divisions and Salta's peripheral location have combined to shroud Gúemes in controversial, often erroneous images. No one, however, denies his forceful military leadership in ejecting Spanish royalists from the north. *Salteños* revere him as a patriot and defender of provincial autonomy against centralist political forces. Born and educated in Salta, Gúemes joined the military as a cadet in 1799, at the age of fourteen. He first saw action during the English invasion of Buenos Aires in 1806. An aide to Santiago LINIERS, he received a promotion to the rank of lieutenant and later to general.

Gúemes joined the independence forces after the revolution of May 1810. He led a military unit into Upper Peru that gained intelligence on royalist movements and disrupted their communications. Gúemes then served in Montevideo and Buenos Aires. In March 1814, General José de SAN MARTÍN appointed him general commander of forces in Salta. The success of Gúemes's gaucho cavalrymen in expelling the royalists from Salta created great popular support. Thanks to his kinship ties to the *salteño* landed elite, he was elected governor of the province in May 1815.

Like Juan Manuel de ROSAS in Buenos Aires Province, Gúemes drew support from both the gaucho masses and elements of the landed elite. But he aroused strong opposition from political rivals and from some wealthy *salteños* with his taxation and land-reform proposals. He died ten days after being wounded by a royalist supporter, possibly with the complicity of local opponents. The anti-Gúemes Patria Nueva movement condemned him as a tyrant. Yet he effectively held royalist forces at bay and led his province through a period of brutal warfare and political conflict.

– RICHARD W. SLATTA

GUERRA, RAMÓN

Ramón Guerra (*b*. 1841; *d*. 1922), Venezuelan caudillo. Guerra began his political and military career during the Federal War (1859–1863), becoming a key figure in the Venezuelan political alliances of the era. He was an opponent of Juan Crisóstomo FALCÓN; both an enemy and temporary ally of Antonio GUZMÁN BLANCO; a successful military commander (1892) and later member of the Consejo Militar (1893) in the regime of General Joaquín CRESPO; and a crucial figure behind the victory of Cipriano CASTRO, whom he later opposed in La Libertadora Revolution of 1901–1903. He sup-

ported the accession to power of Juan Vicente GÓMEZ and was part of the Council of Government. When that body dissolved in 1914, Guerra retired permanently from public life.

– INÉS QUINTERO

GUERRA Y SÁNCHEZ, RAMIRO

Ramiro Guerra y Sánchez (*b*. 31 January 1880; *d*. 30 October 1970), Cuban historian. Because of the intrinsic value and influence of his writings, Guerra, a native of Batabanó, Havana Province, is arguably Cuba's foremost historian of the twentieth century. Starting as a teacher in a modest rural school, he rose to become professor and director of Havana's Normal School, school superintendent of Pinar del Río Province, and national school superintendent. In 1932–1933 he held the position of secretary to the president's cabinet. He also represented Cuba as technical adviser to numerous missions abroad. In his books Guerra severely criticized U.S. policies toward Cuba and Spanish America. Many of them are still classic studies, such as his *Guerra de los diez años, 1868–1878,* 2 vols. (1950). None, however, has had the impact of *Azúcar y población en las Antillas* (1927), originally a series of newspaper articles; many editions of it have appeared, including an abridged English translation as *Sugar and Society in the Caribbean* (1964). This volume, a sober indictment of the dangers of latifundism in Cuba, contributed greatly to shaping the views of the 1933 Cuban revolutionaries.

– JOSÉ M. HERNÁNDEZ

GUERRERO, VICENTE

Vicente Guerrero (*b*. 10 August 1783; *d*. 14 February 1831), Mexican independence leader and politician. Born in Tixtla in the present state that bears his name, he joined the insurgent Hermenegildo GALEANA in 1810 under José Maria MORELOS. He continued the struggle after Morelos's defeat and death in 1815. In 1821 he joined Agustín de ITURBIDE's movement, emerging as one of the major military leaders after independence, but soon broke with Iturbide.

In the 1820s Guerrero, now a prominent populist, became the Grand Master of the Yorkinos (York rite Masons) in 1826. After losing the bitterly contested presidential election of 1828, he joined his supporters in the Revolt of Acordada, and became president in 1829. Guerrero attempted to introduce democratic programs as well as to address the nation's fiscal crisis. While dealing with the emotional issue of the expulsion of the Spaniards and mass politics, he also faced a Spanish attempt to reconquer Mexico in the summer of

1829. Although victorious against the invaders, the president faced a revolt by conservatives led by his own vice president, Anastasio BUSTAMANTE. He abandoned office in December 1830. But the Bustamante administration proved to be repressive and threatened the autonomy of the states. As a result, Guerrero was enticed to lead a revolt against the government that had driven him from office. Unable to defeat him on the field of battle, the Bustamante administration managed to capture him by treachery, then to court-martial and execute him.

— JAIME E. RODRÍGUEZ O.

GUERRERO, XAVIER

Xavier Guerrero (*b.* 3 December 1896; *d.* 1975), Mexican artist. Xavier Guerrero learned painting from his house-decorator father. In 1921, he collaborated with Roberto MONTENEGRO on murals in the old Colegio de San Pedro y San Pablo and with Diego RIVERA in 1922–1923 on his mural in the Anfiteatro Bolívar in the National Preparatory School in Mexico City. Later he assisted Rivera with murals in the Secretaria de Educación, where he used a fresco technique. When David ALFARO SIQUEIROS was commissioned by the Mexican government to paint a mural for the Mexican-donated Escuela Mexicana in Chillán, Chile (1941), Guerrero joined him and painted murals in Chillán and Santiago. He also did murals in Chapingo, Cuernavaca, and Guadalajara.

— SHIFRA M. GOLDMAN

GUERRERO Y TORRES, FRANCISCO ANTONIO

Francisco Antonio Guerrero y Torres (*b.* February 1727; *d.* 20 December 1792), Mexican architect. Guerrero y Torres, born in Guadalupe, is the most famous of the last architects of New Spain to achieve maturity and success before the establishment of the Academia de San Carlos and the subsequent adoption of academic neoclassicism. After he passed the examination for master architect in 1767, he designed buildings in a neoclassical style proper to New Spain (generally called *neostilo*), retaining the materials, taste for color, and many of the motifs of *estípite* baroque (or Churrigueresque). Favored by wealthy criollos of Mexico City, he designed and built palaces, notably those of ITURBIDE and of the counts of Santiago de Calimaya. Criticized by the Academia toward the end of his life, Guerrero y Torres nevertheless built, at his own expense and in his characteristic manner, the Chapel of the Pocito near the

Basilica of Guadalupe, between 1777 and 1791. It is generally considered his masterpiece.

— CLARA BARGELLINI

GUEVARA, ERNESTO "CHE"

Ernesto "Che" Guevara (*b.* 14 June 1928; *d.* 9 October 1967), Marxist revolutionary and guerrilla. Guevara was born into a middle-class family in Rosario, Argentina. He attended medical school in Buenos Aires and received a medical degree in 1953. Guevara traveled widely throughout Latin America and arrived in December 1953 in Guatemala, where he became active in the Guatemalan revolution and met exiled Cuban revolutionaries. When U.S.-backed forces toppled the Guatemalan government in 1954, Guevara fled to Mexico.

Guevara's Cuban friends introduced him to Raúl and Fidel CASTRO in Mexico City during the summer of 1955. Guevara joined Castro's rebel group as one of the eighty-two revolutionaries who landed on the coast of Cuba on 2 December 1956. When Castro created a second rebel column in 1957, he promoted Guevara to commander. Guevara and his troops were among the rebel forces that entered Havana on 2 January 1959.

Guevara championed insurrection against dictatorship and U.S. imperialism throughout Latin America. His book *Guerrilla Warfare,* published in 1960, offered a practical guide for aspiring revolutionaries. Guevara recommended the creation of guerrilla *focos* in the countryside to serve as bases of operations. From the *foco* guerrillas would serve as a vanguard and eventually create an invincible people's army. Guevara stressed that there was no need to wait for revolutionary conditions to develop; the insurrection itself would create such conditions. Guerrilla fronts, inspired by the Cuban model and Guevara's call to arms, emerged throughout Latin America in the 1960s, but these groups had limited impact.

Guevara played a central role in the early government of revolutionary Cuba. As director of the Industrial Department of the National Institute of Agrarian Reform (INRA), president of the National Bank of Cuba, and Minister of Industry, Guevara shaped the early economic policy of the revolution. He favored extensive state ownership of productive enterprises and central economic planning. Guevara sought to create a "new socialist man" dedicated to the revolution and motivated by moral rather than material incentives. He hoped ultimately to abolish money altogether. Castro sided with Guevara against opponents who favored reliance on market forces within a socialist framework, and Guevara's economic policies enjoyed official sanc-

Ernesto "Che" Guevara in Havana, Cuba, 1963. Reproduced from Lee Lockwood, Castro's Cuba, Cuba's Fidel *(New York, 1969). (Lee Lockwood)*

tion until the late 1960s. Guevara also carried out numerous diplomatic missions abroad.

Eventually Guevara's influence in Cuban government waned. In 1965 he resigned his post as minister of industry. The reasons are obscure. Some scholars suggest a falling out between Guevara and Castro, while others claim Guevara left to engage in guerrilla activity. Guevara planned to use Bolivia as a base for continental revolution, and he set up a guerrilla *foco* there in 1966. They launched their first military action in March 1967. The movement, however, suffered numerous difficulties, including failure to win the trust of local peasants, inhospitable terrain, internal divisions, and poor relations with the Bolivian Communist Party. Bolivian troops, assisted by U.S. military advisers, inflicted serious losses on Guevara's forces. A Bolivian army unit captured Guevara and his last followers on 8 October 1967. These same troops murdered Guevara the next day. His image and political theory, however, have remained an inspiration for Latin American leftists into the 1990s.

— STEVEN S. GILLICK

GUEVARA ARZE, WALTER

Walter Guevara Arze (*b.* 11 March 1911), interim president of Bolivia (August 1979–November 1979). As a young lawyer, Guevara formed part of the post–CHACO WAR generation that founded the Nationalist Revolutionary Movement (MNR) in 1941. Guevara was the author of the 1944 *Ayopaya Thesis,* a manifesto that advocated sociopolitical rights for Bolivia's indigenous masses. He joined Víctor PAZ ESTENSSORO, Hernán SILES ZUAZO, and others in leading the MNR revolution of 1952. In 1959, owing mainly to the MNR's refusal to recognize his claim to the presidency, Guevara split with the party and founded the Authentic Revolutionary Party (Partido Revolucionario Auténtico—PRA). Several years later, in 1964, Guevara joined General René BARRIENTOS ORTUÑO to topple Paz Estenssoro and the MNR.

Guevara served several terms in Congress, was a cabinet officer for numerous governments between 1952 and 1974, and was Bolivia's ambassador to the Organization of American States, the United Nations, and France. The pinnacle of his career came in August 1979, when he was elected interim president of Bolivia following the failure of the nation's principal political parties to elect a head of state among the top three vote getters in the national elections.

Guevara was one of the principal opponents of military rule after the coup that toppled him on 2 November 1979. When democracy was reestablished in 1982, Guevara reclaimed his senatorship and played an important role as a frequent critic of the Siles Zuazo government. In the late 1980s, Guevara led a successful campaign to unite factions that had split away from the MNR. As a reward for his efforts, the MNR named him its vice-presidential candidate for the 1989 elections. His race was unsuccessful, however. In late 1993, he fell ill and ended most public appearances.

— EDUARDO A. GAMARRA

GUGGIARI, JOSÉ PATRICIO

José Patricio Guggiari (*b.* 17 March 1884; *d.* 1957), Paraguayan statesman and president (1928–1932). The son of Italian immigrants, Guggiari was born in Asunción, but as a young child moved to the interior town of Villarrica, where he received his early education. He returned to Paraguay to pursue legal studies and received a doctorate in law from the National University in 1910.

Guggiari began his political career by affiliating with the Liberal Party as early as 1903. At that time the Liberals were divided into various bickering factions unable to reach a consensus on overall policy for the country. Guggiari worked hard to reconcile these various groups. Though he was only partly successful, he gained a reputation as a level-headed and efficient democrat. He rose to the highest ranks within the party, as well as within the legislative branch of government. He was elected deputy in 1912, and in 1918 was chosen president of the Chamber of Deputies. Two years later, President Manuel GONDRA chose him to become interior minister.

The 1928 presidential election in which Guggiari defeated Eduardo Fleitas was widely regarded as the most honest up to that time. As president, he dedicated himself to the consolidation of Paraguay's democratic institutions after years of instability. These efforts, however, were eclipsed by the worsening dispute with Bolivia over the Gran Chaco region. The ensuing tensions indirectly brought about Guggiari's downfall. On 23 October 1931, university students protested his government's cautious response to Bolivian incursions by staging a rally in front of the National Palace. The police fired upon the assemblage, killing eight and wounding thirty. Mortified by these events, Guggiari resigned the presidency two days later. He died in Buenos Aires after a long exile.

– THOMAS L. WHIGHAM

GUIDO, BEATRIZ

Beatriz Guido (*b.* 1925; *d.* 4 March 1988), Argentine writer. Guido's fiction exemplifies the literary production of Argentina during the 1950s, which was deeply influenced by a postwar European sensibility of ethical despair and the imperative to manifest a social commitment, especially in the creation of fictional characters obliged to participate as fully conscious individuals in the dirty business of life. Many Argentine writers, including Guido, manifested their adherence to this imperative by addressing the historical upheaval produced in their country first by Peronism and then by the rabid reaction to it by the traditionalist oligarchy. A Rosario native, Guido was superbly skillful in portraying the alternately oblivious and cynical moral corruption at the core of the power elite (more the landed gentry than the nouveaux-riches capitalists who attracted the attention of a subsequent generation). Perhaps her two best works are her first, *La casa del ángel* (1954; *The House of the Angel,* 1957), of interest from a feminist perspective because of the dominant motif of the psychosexual abuse of the young female protagonist, Ana, and *El incendio y las vísperas* (1964; *End of a Day,* 1966), which centers on the torching in April 1953 by Peronista hoodlums of the Jockey Club, a legendary oligarchic bastion in Buenos Aires. The novel uses this event as an axis to portray the intersecting conflicts of two Peronista opponents: the decadent oligarchy and the emerging revolutionary left. Guido, whose novels provoked many outraged responses, saw several of her works filmed by her husband, Leopoldo Torre Nilsson, with whom she collaborated on numerous cinematographic projects.

– DAVID WILLIAM FOSTER

GUIDO, JOSÉ MARÍA

José María Guido (*b.* 1910; *d.* 1975), provisional president of Argentina (1962–1963). Born in Buenos Aires, Guido worked as a lawyer in Viedma, Río Negro Province. He became active in politics as a member of the Radical Party. In 1958, he was elected senator from Río Negro. In the Argentine Senate he served as president pro tempore. When economic and political conditions led to a military coup against President Arturo FRONDIZI in March 1962, the Azul (Blue) faction of the Argentine army convinced him to accept the office of president in accordance with the Argentine Constitution.

Guido served briefly as a figurehead for the military leadership. Not surprisingly, with Congress dissolved and the majority Peronist Party banned, his administration accomplished little. In accordance with the military's wishes, he issued an amnesty decree for rebellious officers of the army's hard-line Colorado faction in 1963. In July of that year, after the military approved new elections to maintain the semblance of civilian rule, he turned power over to Arturo ILLÍA (1963–1966).

– DANIEL LEWIS

GUILLÉN, NICOLÁS

Nicolás Guillén (*b.* 10 July 1902; *d.* 16 July 1989), Cuban poet. A contender for the Nobel Prize for literature, Nicolás Guillén was Cuba's national poet. He developed an early interest in poetry and published his first poems in *Camagüey Gráfico* in 1920. That same year he enrolled in the University of Havana to pursue a degree in law. For lack of interest and for financial reasons, Guillén left the university a few weeks later and returned to his native city, where he earned a living as a printer, a trade he learned from his father. With Vicente Menéndez Roque he edited the literary section of the newspaper *Las Dos Repúblicas* and contributed to *Orto* and *Castalia,* both literary reviews.

Guillén made a second attempt to continue his studies in Havana in 1921 but, as before and for similar reasons, he returned to Camagüey. That same year he gathered his poems under the title "Cerebro y corazón," which remained unpublished as a book until 1965. He also published his sonnets in *Alma Mater,* published the magazine *Lis,* and edited *El Camagüeyano.*

In 1926 Guillén went to work as a typist for the Ministry of the Interior in Havana, but continued to write and publish poetry. It was through Gustavo E. Urrutia, who invited the poet to write for a section he edited, "Ideales de una raza," in the *Diario de la Marina,* that Guillén began to compose poems about Afro-Cubans, which resulted in the publication of *Motivos de son* in 1930. These poems, along with others by José Zacarías TALLET, Ramón GUIRAO, and Emilio BALLAGAS, became part of the Negrista movement of the 1920s and 1930s. In his poems Guillén explored the exoticism and rhythm of the other poets, but also added a social and cultural dimension about the lives of Cuban people of African descent.

Guillen wrote poems about the subordinate conditions of blacks and their need to develop self pride not only in Cuba but throughout the Caribbean.

After the *Diario de la Marina* ceased to publish Urrutia's column, Guillén continued to explore Afro-Cuban themes in Lino Dou's "La marcha de una raza," in the newspaper *El Mundo.* Subsequently, he published *Sóngoro cosongo* (1931) and *West Indies, Ltd.* (1934), which were more expressive about the subordinate conditions of blacks and their need to develop self pride not only in Cuba but throughout the Caribbean. During this period, Guillén was editor of the newspaper *Información* and the weekly *El Loco.*

Guillén's political life and literary activities began to merge. In 1935, as a result of his political activities, he was forced from his job at the Department of Culture. He became a member of the editorial boards of *Resumen,* a publication of the Communist Party, and *Mediodía,* which he edited when it was transformed into a politico-literary weekly. In 1937, with other Cuban and Latin American notables, he attended the Congress of Writers and Artists in Mexico and the Second International Congress of Writers for the Defense of Culture in Barcelona, Valencia, and Madrid. That same year he joined the Cuban Communist Party and the following year two of his poems were published in its newspaper *Hoy.* Guillén's *Cantos para soldados y sones para turistas* (1937) and *España: Poema en cuatro angustias y una es-*

peranza (1937), completed before his trip to Spain, address conditions mainly in Cuba and Spain, respectively, and belong to a period of ideological commitment.

For Guillén, the 1940s were characterized by an internationalist consciousness and extensive travel throughout the world. After an unsuccessful candidacy for mayor of Camagüey in 1940, he traveled to Haiti in 1942 and Venezuela in 1945, and later to Colombia, Peru, Chile, Argentina, Uruguay, and Brazil. *El son entero: Suma poética, 1929–1946,* published while he was in Buenos Aires in 1947, gathers poems written both prior to and following his travels. Following an unsuccessful run in 1948 as senatorial candidate for the Cuban Communist Party he returned to Havana. Other trips included attending the World Peace conference in New York City and meetings in Paris, Prague, and Mexico; he later traveled extensively throughout Eastern Europe and the Soviet Union. Between 1948 and 1958, he wrote and compiled his *Elegías.*

An active opponent of the BATISTA dictatorship, after 1953 Guillén lived in exile for six years and continued to travel in Latin America and Europe, where he received the Lenin International Peace Prize in 1954. Guillén lived in Paris from 1955 to 1958 and then moved to Buenos Aires, where he resided until Fidel CASTRO's revolutionary triumph. *La paloma del vuelo popular,* which contains six elegies, is a product of this period and was published in Buenos Aires in 1958. Guillén returned to Cuba on 23 January 1959 as a hero of sorts. In 1961 he became a member of the National Council of Education and was named president of the National Union of Writers and Artists of Cuba; he later joined the Central Committee of the Communist Party. *Tengo* (1964), *El gran zoo* (1967), *La rueda dentada* (1972), *El diario que a diario* (1972), and *Sol de domingo* (1982) draw upon Guillén's social and political concerns as well as his inventiveness and creativity in developing further his poetic talents, particularly so with *El diario que a diario,* but these later collections do not reach the levels of literary quality, innovation, or importance he attained in his early work. *Prosa de prisa, 1929–1972,* a three-volume collection of newspaper articles, was published in 1975–1976. Guillén is buried in the Colón Cemetery in Havana.

Nancy Morejón, Keith Ellis, Ángel Augier, and others have suggested that Guillén's poetry is limited to an ideological or revolutionary perspective. Other critics, however, such as Vera Kutzinski, Roberto González Echevarría, Antonio Benítez Rojo, and Gustavo Pérez Firmat place Guillén within a broader literary framework. For example, Pérez Firmat points to Guillén's interest in writing Italian sonnets and madrigals, González Echevarría to his fascination for Baroque poetry, and

Benítez Rojo to the different stages in his career, shifting from Communist, to controversial, to subversive, and to philosophical positions. This more recent reading of Guillén confirms his greatness as a truly outstanding poet who appeals to a variety of readers.

– WILLIAM LUIS

GUIMARÃES, ULYSSES SILVEIRA

Ulysses Silveira Guimarães (*b.* 6 October 1916; *d.* 12 October 1992), Brazilian politician. Until his death in a helicopter crash off the coast of Rio de Janeiro, Ulysses Guimarães was one of Brazil's most prominent federal legislators. Although Guimarães suffered numerous setbacks during his lengthy career, including political repression, endemic legislative gridlock, and unsuccessful presidential bids in 1974 and 1989, his political persona symbolized a devout dedication to democratic principles in public service and national life.

As the long-standing president of the Brazilian Democratic Movement (MDB), which existed from 1966 to 1979, and its successor, the Brazilian Democratic Movement Party (PMDB), Guimarães led the party's legislative opposition to military rule and support of the restoration and extension of democracy. Guimarães played an instrumental role in the 1985 campaign for direct presidential elections, the 1987–1988 Constituent Assembly, and the 1992 impeachment proceedings against Fernando COLLOR DE MELLO. Toward the end of his political career, Guimarães's political influence faltered somewhat with the splintering of the PMDB into competing leftist and centrist parties.

A native of the state of São Paulo, Guimarães received a law degree from the University of São Paulo in 1940 and entered national politics in 1950 as a federal legislator for the Social Democratic Party (PSD). He served briefly as minister of industry and commerce (1961–1962) and represented the PSD in the Chamber of Deputies until 1966, when he joined the MDB. In 1974 Guimarães was the MDB "anticandidate" for president, running on a platform of opposition to repressive military rule. Although handily defeated by the military candidate, he remained a power broker throughout the 1970s and 1980s. Guimarães also represented Brazil in numerous international conventions.

– DARYLE WILLIAMS

GÜIRALDES, RICARDO

Ricardo Güiraldes (*b.* 13 February 1886; *d.* 8 October 1927), Argentine writer. Born in Buenos Aires into a patrician family of estancia owners, he spent the first three years of his life in Paris, speaking French before he learned his native language; an experience that permitted him to enrich his Spanish writings with bold transplants. His devotion to everything French and to his own land engendered a deep symbiosis of the European and Argentine heritages. A sophisticated European as well as a gaucho, skillful at tasks practiced by the cowboys of the Pampa, he was also a refined Argentine gentleman who helped to popularize the tango in Paris's café society. The First World War caused him to retreat into spiritualistic, existentialist, and oriental philosophies. In his yearly pilgrimages to Paris, he established deep friendships with the French writer Valéry Larbaud and the most important "decadent" poets of the time, who greatly influenced his literature. A man of authentic nationalistic feelings for Argentina, like many of his countrymen at the time, Güiraldes wanted to idealize his native roots while enriching them with the best European contributions. He had an ecumenical outlook and eagerness, although deeply rooted in his country and in his time. Güiraldes served as a board member of the influential literary magazines *Martín Fierro* and *Proa,* exercising a guiding role among younger writers. He published three volumes of poetry, two of short stories, and four novels; not a large body of work, but one of high quality and very avant garde. In 1926, a few months before his death in Paris, he won the National Prize for Literature for his novel *Don Segundo Sombra,* a classic of Argentine literature. Güiraldes found his voice, at once "gaucha," full of peasant imagery, but also very French. The book was innovative in the very personal style of his narrative; in being a bildungsroman, in which Güiraldes proposed a model for the education of his people with its hyperbolized figure of the gaucho; and in its depiction of a free, stoic, lonely, and silent life.

– ANGELA B. DELLEPIANE

GUIRAO, RAMÓN

Ramón Guirao (*b.* 1908; *d.* 17 March 1949), Cuban poet. A founding member of the *Sociedad de Estudios Afrocubanos,* Guirao first gained national attention with his poem "La bailadora de rumba," which appeared in the literary supplement of Havana's *Diario de la Marina* in 1928. From 1933 to 1940 he lived in Mexico, where he worked as a journalist. In 1937 he gained recognition for an essay on Cuba, which he presented to the secretary of education. He was the editor of the journal *Grafos.* Guirao played an instrumental role in the development of literature devoted to Afro-Cuban themes, as exemplified by such works as "Poetas negros y mestizos de la época esclavista," which appeared in *Bohemia* in 1934. He worked until the end of his life editing

Advance y Alerta, and contributed to several other literary journals.

— MICHAEL A. POLUSHIN

GUIRIOR, MANUEL

Manuel Guirior (*b.* 23 March 1708; *d.* 25 November 1788), viceroy of Peru (1776–1780). Born into a noble family in Aoiz (Navarre), Guirior pursued a distinguished naval career, primarily in the Mediterranean, before taking up in 1772 his appointment as viceroy of New Granada. During this first period of office, which ended in 1776 with his transfer to Lima, he acquired a reputation for firmness in dealing with frontier Indians, for progressive economic policies, and for the expansion and reorganization of university education. His service in Peru, by contrast, was blighted by the loss of Upper Peru (present-day Bolivia), high defense costs occasioned by the outbreak of war between Spain and Great Britain, and a prolonged conflict with the *visitador general* (inspector general), José Antonio de Areche, who arrived in Lima in 1777 to undertake a radical program of administrative, judicial, and fiscal reform. Although recalled to Spain in disgrace in 1780, Guirior was rehabilitated by the Council of the Indies in 1785 and given the title Marqués de Guirior.

— JOHN R. FISHER

GUTIÉRREZ, EULALIO

Eulalio Gutiérrez (*b.* 1880; *d.* 12 August 1939), Mexican revolutionary and convention president. Gutiérrez was born of a peasant family on the Hacienda Santo Domingo in the village of Ramos Arizpe, Coahuila, and was a shepherd in his youth. He later became a miner for the Mazapil Copper Company of Concepción del Oro, in Zacatecas.

Gutiérrez became a member of Ricardo FLORES MAGÓN's Liberal Party in 1906, and in 1909 he joined the group opposing the reelection of Porfirio DÍAZ to the presidency. With his brother Luis Gutiérrez, he supported Francisco MADERO in 1910. In 1913 he joined the Constitutionalists, rising to military commander of San Luis Potosí in 1914. On November 3 of that year, at the Convention of Aguascalientes, he was selected by the representatives of the leading military commanders to serve as their president, a post he held until 16 January 1915.

The Convention failed, however, to obtain the support of all the victorious revolutionaries, and the Constitutionalists split their support between Venustiano CARRANZA on the one hand and Francisco VILLA and Emiliano ZAPATA on the other. Gutiérrez opposed both Carranza and Villa during 1915, and the following year

went into exile. After returning to Mexico, he served as a senator from Coahuila in the 1920s, but left Mexico again after supporting the unsuccessful Escobar rebellion of 1929 by followers of the recently assassinated Álvaro OBREGÓN. He retired permanently from politics thereafter.

— RODERIC AI CAMP

GUTIÉRREZ, GUSTAVO

Gustavo Gutiérrez (*b.* 8 June 1928), Peruvian priest and founder of Liberation Theology. His attempt to interpret the meaning of Christianity within the context of the struggle for justice unleashed a revolution in Latin American theological inquiry. After training for the priesthood in Europe in the 1950s, Gutiérrez became part of a South and Central American network of Catholic church reformers seeking to apply the teachings of the Second Vatican Council (1962–1965) to Latin American conditions. Influenced by radicalized students, the Peruvian Marxist José Carlos MARIÁTEGUI, the author José María ARGUEDAS, and dependency theory, Gutiérrez came to champion the liberation of the Latin American poor. In 1968 he coauthored the central texts of the famous Medellín Latin American bishops' conference that denounced social and economic inequality. In his 1971 foundational text *Teología de la liberación: Perspectivas,* he proposed the new theological method of theology as reflection on the commitment of Christians to construct a just society.

Gutiérrez attempted to interpret the meaning of Christianity within the context of the struggle for justice.

The liberation theology movement that his ideas spawned committed some members of the Catholic church to defend the rights of the marginalized. Because of his use of certain aspects of Marxist theory, Gutiérrez's theology has attracted Vatican and conservative criticism. Nevertheless, he has continued to refine his ideas through conferences, international theological networks, and contact with the poor. In later works Gutiérrez has developed a spirituality of suffering.

— MATTHEW J. O'MEAGHER

GUTIÉRREZ, JOSÉ MARÍA

José María Gutiérrez (*b.* 20 June 1831; *d.* 26 December 1903), lawyer, journalist, and public figure deeply involved in issues concerning the character of Argentine nationhood, constitutionality, and administration. Gutiérrez served in numerous government positions, beginning in 1852 in the Ministry of Government of Buenos Aires Province, and as secretary of the Chamber of Representatives (1854–1857). He participated in the first Battle of Cepeda (1859) and in the Battle of PAVÓN, where the Confederation of Provinces was defeated in 1861. From 1862, Gutiérrez founded and edited *La Nación,* a paper devoted to defending Bartolomé MITRE, who became the first constitutional president of Argentina in 1862; in 1878, Gutiérrez founded another paper, *La Patria Argentina.* He was minister of justice and public instruction in 1877, was minister of state from 1890 to 1892, and from 1895 until his death, served on the National Council of Education.

— HILARY BURGER

GUTIÉRREZ BROTHERS

Gutiérrez Brothers, Peruvian insurrectionists. Persistent military rule of Peru since 1821 had spawned widespread antimilitarism, especially in Lima, in the late nineteenth century. Popular sentiment in the election of 1872, therefore lay with Manuel PARDO, the wealthy merchant who promised a severely reduced military budget and weakening of the military's grip on public offices. Most of the military agreed to stay clear of the election, but the minister of war, Colonel Tomás Gutiérrez, considered the election a direct challenge to the rightful preeminence of the military in Peruvian politics. Gutiérrez organized his brothers, fellow military officers Silvestre, Marceliano, and Marcelino, to seize President José BALTA and declared himself president of the republic on July 22, a week before the inauguration of Pardo. Local military garrisons received widespread public support to actively oppose the coup d'etat. The Gutiérrez brothers tried to organize a defense against the popular rejection of their actions, but armed civilians shot Silvestre in downtown Lima and beheaded him. When enraged mobs learned that the rebels had authorized the murder of Balta, they became uncontrollable. A mob killed Tomás and mutilated his body. The bodies of Tomás and Silvestre were then hung from the facade of the cathedral of Lima. Marceliano died fighting in Callao, and Marcelino escaped unharmed. The Gutiérrez uprising marked a nadir in the popular view of the military and may have undermined the confidence of the army and navy in preparing for the upcoming war with Chile.

— VINCENT PELOSO

GUTIÉRREZ DE LARA, JOSÉ BERNARDO

José Bernardo Gutiérrez de Lara (*b.* 20 August 1774; *d.* 13 May 1841), revolutionary during the Mexican War of Independence. Born in San Ignacio de Loyola, Tamaulipas, Gutiérrez de Lara was a blacksmith, merchant, and property owner, who participated in the independence struggle in Tamaulipas, served as an envoy from Miguel HIDALGO to the government of the United States, and led an invasion of Texas in 1812–1813. He later became involved in other military activities, including the expeditions of Francisco Javier MINA and James Long.

Following Mexican independence, Gutiérrez de Lara returned to Tamaulipas, where he was elected governor in 1824. He served until late 1825, when he became commandant general of the eastern Provincias Internas. Resigning the post in 1826, he did not again become involved in politics until 1839, when he opposed Antonio Canales's efforts to organize a Republic of the Río Grande.

— JESÚS F. DE LA TEJA

GUTIÉRREZ DE PADILLA, JUAN

Juan Gutiérrez de Padilla (*b.* ca. 1590; *d.* April 1664), Spanish-born Mexican composer. Educated at the cathedral choir school in his native city of Málaga, Gutiérrez served as music director in Jérez de la Frontera and at the Cádiz cathedral in Spain before emigrating to New Spain around 1622. He was employed as a musician in the Puebla cathedral and in 1629 became its *maestro de capilla.* This post, held until his death, placed him in charge of all music activities, including instruction of the choirboys at the Colegio de San Pedro. The position was considerably enhanced by the support of the wealthy Bishop Palafox y Mendoza. His Latin sacred music bears the early baroque traits of chromaticism and double choir antiphony that prevailed in Europe, but he also wrote popular, dancelike *chanzonettas* and *villancicos* in the vernacular to be used on special feast days.

— ROBERT L. PARKER

GUTIÉRREZ DE PIÑERES, JUAN FRANCISCO

Juan Francisco Gutiérrez de Piñeres (*b.* 25 August 1732; *d.* 7 October 1802), regent-visitor of New Granada (1776–1783). Born in Lebeña, León, Spain, Gutiérrez studied law in Seville, was appointed to the Audiencia of Valladolid in 1774, and two years later became oidor of the Casa de Contratación. In December 1776, José de GÁLVEZ named him visitor-general of New Granada and regent of the Audiencia of Santa Fe, bearing instructions to improve the administration of royal revenues.

With the outbreak of war in 1779 came authorization to raise taxes and royal monopoly prices. A technocrat lacking political skills, Gutiérrez pursued his mission with such zeal that Viceroy Manuel FLORES MALDONADO Martínez y Bodquín urged caution, but to no avail. When Flores assumed military command on the coast, he relinquished his civil powers to Gutiérrez. The Comunero Revolt of 1781, protesting his measures, forced the regent-visitor to flee Santa Fe for Cartagena. Thereafter, Gutiérrez saw his effective powers diminished, although he returned to the viceregal capital in 1782. Recalled to Spain in 1783, he assumed a position on the Council of the Indies, where he remained until his death.

— ALLAN J. KUETHE

GUTIÉRREZ ESTRADA, JOSÉ MARÍA

José María Gutiérrez Estrada (*b.* 1800; *d.* 1867), Mexican diplomat and politician. Born in the city of Campeche, Gutiérrez Estrada moved to Mexico City with his family when he was young. He was appointed minister of foreign relations by President Antonio López de SANTA ANNA (1834–1835) and later served as Mexico's diplomatic representative in several European countries. Upon his return to Mexico in 1840, Gutiérrez Estrada published an open letter to the president in which he called for free discussion of a liberal constitutional monarchy in Mexico, arguing that the monarchical form of government was more consistent with the traditions, needs, and interests of the Mexican people. He warned of the need for a strong government to defend Mexico against U.S. aggression, saying "If we do not change our ways, perhaps twenty years will not pass before we see the flag of the United States waving above our National Palace."

The pamphlet caused a sensation, and Gutiérrez Estrada was denounced by both liberals and conservatives. Although he was forced to flee to Europe, he continued his campaign for a Mexican monarchy. His fears were realized in 1847, when the U.S. army conquered Mexico and raised the Stars and Stripes above the National Palace, after which his proposal gained greater support among Mexican conservatives. Gutiérrez Estrada received various diplomatic commissions and was president of the commission that offered the crown of Mexico to Maximilian at Miramar. Each of his three wives was from a noble family.

— D. F. STEVENS

GUTIÉRREZ GARBÍN, VÍCTOR MANUEL

Víctor Manuel Gutiérrez Garbín (*b.* 10 January 1922; *d.* March 1966), Guatemalan educator and labor leader. Gutiérrez was born in the rural Guatemalan department of Santa Rosa. He was educated as a primary school teacher in Guatemala and taught at the National Boys' Institute in the western province of Chiquimula. After a short teaching stint in the capital, Gutiérrez was made the subdirector of the Industrial Institute for Boys in 1944.

During the revolutionary period (1944–1954), Gutiérrez became the most important and influential labor leader in the history of the country. His career as a labor leader began when he founded the Guatemalan Union of Educational Workers (Sindicato de Trabajadores en Educación de Guatemala, STEG) in 1944. After 1946, as president of the largest national workers' union, later the Confederation of Guatemalan Workers (Confederación de Trabajadores de Guatemala) and later the General Confederation of Guatemalan Workers (Confederación General de Trabajadores de Guatemala), he organized over 100,000 workers. He was known as a particularly honest and dedicated organizer who always maintained close ties to the rank-and-file of the labor movement. Gutiérrez was elected to Congress in 1950, and became first secretary of the Congress in 1954.

Because of his involvement with the Communist Party, Gutiérrez fled Guatemala in 1954. In March 1966, while attempting to return to Guatemala from Mexico, he disappeared, allegedly dropped from an airplane over the Pacific Ocean by Guatemalan security forces. His body was never found.

— RACHEL A. MAY

GUTIÉRREZ GONZÁLEZ, GREGORIO

Gregorio Gutiérrez González (*b.* 9 May 1826; *d.* 6 July 1872), Colombian poet considered the bard of his native Antioquia. After studying law in Bogotá, Gutiérrez held various judicial and legislative posts in Antioquia and represented the province in Congress. As a poet he is remembered partly for his romantic lyrics, such as the two poems entitled "A Julia" and the nostalgic and melancholy "Aures." His major literary achievement, however, is the *Memoria científica sobre el cultivo del maíz en Antioquia,* first published in 1866. A celebration of rural life in Antioquia, this long poem traces the cycle of corn cultivation from preparation of the field to the gathering of the crop. It also contrasts the delicious dishes made of corn with the "vile potato." The poem's bucolic imagery reveals the author's romantic roots yet its homely details impart a realistic flavor, as does the use of local dialect by Gutiérrez, who said that he wrote in *antioqueño,* not in Spanish.

— HELEN DELPAR

GUTIÉRREZ GUERRA, JOSÉ

José Gutiérrez Guerra (*b.* 5 September 1869; *d.* 3 February 1929), president of Bolivia (1917–1920). Born in Sucre, Gutiérrez Guerra was the last president of the period of Liberal Party domination (1899–1920). His administration was marked by rigged elections and government scandals. Gutiérrez Guerra initially included the main opposition party, the Republicans, in a cabinet of "national concentration" in an effort to sidestep a surge of nationalist fervor over recouping the Pacific coastal area lost during the War of the Pacific (1879–1884) with Chile. However, by 1919 party politics again turned acrimonious. The Liberal Party split over whether to fine Simón Iturri PATIÑO, the most important Bolivian tin-mine owner and important supporter of the party, who brought 80,000 cans of alcohol into the country after his contract to do so had expired. As a result, the Republican Party was able to organize an almost bloodless coup in July 1920 that toppled the government and ended twenty years of Liberal Party hegemony.

— ERICK D. LANGER

GUTIÉRREZ NÁJERA, MANUEL

Manuel Gutiérrez Nájera (*b.* 22 December 1859; *d.* 3 February 1895), Mexican writer. Gutiérrez Nájera was born in Mexico City. His father was a journalist and writer and his mother a devout Catholic. The middle-class family privately educated him and he developed a strong interest in reading classic literature and contemporary French works. He worked as a journalist and in 1888 was appointed to a political post. Gutiérrez Nájera was one of the progenitors of Spanish American *modernista* writing in Mexico. Through his poetry, essays, short stories, and journalistic chronicles, he explored in Spanish the stylistic and linguistic potentials associated with the French Parnassian and Symbolist movements.

Gutiérrez wrote under pseudonyms such as Mr.

Can-Can, El Duque Job, Puck, and many others.

He wrote under pseudonyms such as Mr. Can-Can, El Duque Job, Puck, and many others. Together with Carlos Díaz Dufoo, he founded *Revista Azul* (1894–1896; Blue Review), one of the principal *modernista* publications in Spanish America. He is frequently known only as a poet, but his prose writing in both the short story and chronicle genres is equally innovative and represents his aesthetic concerns and French cultural influences.

His short stories include the collections *Cuentos frágiles* (1883; Fragile Stories) and *Cuentos color de humo* (1898; Smoke-Colored Stories). His chronicles appear in series such as *Crónicas color de rosa* (Rose-Colored Chronicles), *Crónicas color de lluvia* (Rain-Colored Chronicles), *Crónicas color de oro* (Gold-Colored Chronicles), and *Crónicas de mil colores* (Myriad-Colored Chronicles). Gutiérrez Nájera died in Mexico City at the height of his career.

— DANNY J. ANDERSON

GUTIÉRREZ Y ESPINOSA, FELIPE

Felipe Gutiérrez y Espinosa (*b.* 26 May 1825; *d.* 27 November 1899), Puerto Rican composer. Gutiérrez is considered the best Puerto Rican composer of the nineteenth century and the main figure of Puerto Rico's musical life during that period. Born in San Juan, Gutiérrez received music lessons from his father when very young; thereafter he was self-taught. Starting as a battalion musician, he won the position of maestro de capilla of the San Juan Cathedral in 1858. Later he conducted the orchestra of the Teatro Municipal (later the Teatro Tapia). Around 1873 he traveled to Europe, studying in Paris for one year. Gutiérrez composed sacred music: masses, one oratorio, eight Salve Reginas, and other minor religious works. Of his three operas, *Guarionex, El bearnés,* and *Macías,* the last is the only extant opera of the nineteenth century in Puerto Rico. It was awarded a gold medal in 1871, but went unperformed in the twentieth century until 19 August 1977 at the Teatro Tapia, because its manuscript had been lost. Gutiérrez also composed one zarzuela and other orchestral and chamber music.

— SUSANA SALGADO

GUZMÁN, ANTONIO LEOCADIO

Antonio Leocadio Guzmán (*b.* 14 November 1801; *d.* 13 November 1884), Venezuelan politician and publicist. In 1825, Guzmán founded the newspaper *El Argos*. In 1830, he served as minister of interior, justice, and police. He helped organize the Liberal Party in 1840 and edited the party's newspaper, *El Venezolano,* which called for universal suffrage for males, emancipation of slaves, and the end of capital punishment. Guzmán served José Tadeo MONAGAS as minister of interior and justice and as vice president. In 1853, he went to Peru as ambassador. He joined the Junta Patriótica de Venezuela, led by Ezequiel Zamora, in 1858, and served as a propagandist. Guzmán's son Antonio GUZMÁN BLANCO became president in 1870.

— WINTHROP R. WRIGHT

GUZMÁN, AUGUSTO

Augusto Guzmán (*b.* 1 September 1903) Bolivian writer and historian. Guzmán was a prolific and diverse intellectual whose literary production includes novels, short stories, biographies, criticism, and literary history. He has centered his historical work on the region of Cochabamba. His novel *Prisionero de guerra,* based on his own experience as a soldier, is an important testimony of the Chaco War (1932–1935). Another major theme in his work is the condition of Indians and mestizos (those of mixed blood) in the countryside of Bolivia. His most popular work, "La cruel Martina" ("The Cruel Martina") is a short story that was made into a film in 1989. His literary criticism is a valuable source of information on Bolivian literature, while the biographies he wrote serve as a point of intersection between his literary and historical interests and are his best contribution to Bolivian studies. With the years, Guzmán has become one of the most respected representatives of Bolivian intellectual life.

– LEONARDO GARCÍA PABÓN

GUZMÁN, ENRIQUE

Enrique Guzmán (*b.* 2 August 1843; *d.* 23 May 1911), Nicaraguan intellectual and politician. Guzmán is renowned throughout Central America as a writer and a politician. In 1862 he published his first satirical essays. As a youth he was a member of the Liberal Party, but from 1886 to 1911 he was affiliated with the Conservatives. Guzmán first became politically active during his father's run for the presidency in 1867. In 1879 he served as a deputy in Congress. Among his friends was President Joaquín ZAVALA (1879–1883; 1893). Guzmán encouraged Zavala to maintain good relations with neighboring states in order to preserve Nicaraguan neutrality and peace. Under Zavala, he served as minister to Chile and Peru. During the ZELAYA dictatorship, he conspired against the government.

– SHANNON BELLAMY

GUZMÁN, MARTÍN LUÍS

Martín Luís Guzmán (*b.* 6 October 1887; *d.* 22 December 1976), Mexican literary figure and cultural entrepreneur best remembered for his post-Revolutionary novels *El águila y la serpiente* (1928) and *La sombra del caudillo* (1929). Based on personal experience, these works provide some of the best insights into the Revolution as well as a condemnation of the leading post-Revolutionary figures of the 1920s. Although he was part of the El Ateneo literary group in 1911, Guzmán largely abandoned his literary career in the 1930s, instead pursuing journalism and publishing.

The son of an army officer who died in combat during the Revolution, Guzmán joined the Constitutionalists. After founding many newspapers, he spent five years (1915–1920) of self-imposed exile in Spain and the United States. When his daily, *El Mundo,* was confiscated by the Obregón administration, he again exiled himself to Spain (ca. 1923–1936), where he directed several newspapers. In the 1940s he founded a number of publishing companies as well as the weekly magazine *El Tiempo* (modeled after *Time* magazine), which he directed until his death. He received the National Prize for Literature in 1958.

– RODERIC AI CAMP

GUZMÁN, NUÑO BELTRÁN DE

Nuño Beltrán de Guzmán (*b.* ca. 1485; *d.* 26 October 1558), governor of Pánuco (1527), president of New Spain's first *audiencia* (1528–1531), conqueror of Nueva Galicia (1529), and founder of Guadalajara (1531). Of the lower nobility of Guadalajara, Spain, Guzmán became noted for his corruption and brutality toward indigenous people. In Pánuco he earned the enmity of Hernán CORTÉS and other first conquerors by aggressively trying to expand his jurisdiction at their expense and, as *audiencia* president, by profiteering from the confiscation of their properties. Relations were not improved when in 1530 he tortured and then executed Cazonci, the Tarascan ruler of Michoacán, an ally of Cortés. In 1531, while Guzmán was still in Nueva Galicia, the first *audiencia* and its president were replaced, in part because of the complaints of such prominent figures as Bishop Juan de ZUMÁRRAGA. Guzmán continued as governor of New Galicia until January 1537, when he was arrested. After languishing in jail for eighteen months, he left Mexico in mid-1538, arriving in Spain in December (or perhaps in early 1539). He remained with the royal court under a kind of house arrest until his death in Valladolid.

The overwhelmingly negative picture of Guzmán that has come down to us is partly the result of his conflict with Cortés; with the exception of Guzmán's own correspondence, most of the primary information comes from the pens and testimony of Cortés's adherents, such as Francisco López de Gómara, who wrote that if "Nuño de Guzmán had been as good a governor as he was a warrior, he would have had the best place in the Indies; but he behaved badly both to Indians and Spaniards" (*Life of the Conqueror,* p. 394).

– ROBERT HASKETT

GUZMÁN BLANCO, ANTONIO LEOCADIO

Antonio Leocadio Guzmán Blanco (*b.* 1829; *d.* 1899), president of Venezuela (1870–1877, 1879–1884,

1886–1888). The son of Antonio Leocadio GUZMÁN, founder of the Liberal Party, Antonio Guzmán Blanco came to power as head of state upon taking Caracas by force on 27 April 1870. After more than a decade of civil war, he enforced order for almost two decades. Under his leadership, Venezuela made educational advancements, built many public works, and experienced economic progress.

Guzmán Blanco was not the typical nineteenth-century caudillo. He studied law and medicine, and lived and traveled abroad. In the 1840s, he served as consul in New York and Philadelphia, and as secretary of the Venezuelan embassy in Washington, D.C.

When General Juan Crisóstomo FALCÓN declared in 1859 in favor of a federal system, Guzmán Blanco joined him. As an agent of Falcón, he succeeded in ending the five years of civil war and anarchy when he negotiated the Treaty of Coche on 24 April 1863. The treaty called for the convening of a National Assembly, which appointed Falcón president and Guzmán Blanco vice president.

The peace thus established was short lived. Falcón governed from 1863 to 1868 amid constant political challenges and economic difficulties. Having inherited a nation which had experienced many years of civil conflict and economic disruptions, Falcón found that one of his most pressing problems was to negotiate with European creditors to reestablish Venezuela's credit and obtain a new loan.

This task was entrusted to Guzmán Blanco, who left for London in August 1863. He successfully contracted for a loan of £1.5 million, which was expected to raise 4.5 million pesos, but because of Venezuela's poor credit rating, only 1.5 million pesos were realized. Establishing a pattern he was to repeat often over the next three decades, Guzmán Blanco personally profited from this transaction.

The reign of Falcón saw a continuation of political anarchy, and, by 1867, Venezuela was again in flames. In 1868, José Tadeo MONAGAS captured Caracas; he died that November, leaving his son José Ruperto in control. Guzmán Blanco fled to Curaçao and established himself as leader of the Liberals. On 14 February 1870, he landed in Venezuela, marched to Caracas, and took the capital on 27 April. He assumed control of his nation and dominated it for the next eighteen years. Thus began one of the few extended periods of peace Venezuela was to enjoy in the nineteenth century.

Elections were held on 15 April 1873, and Guzmán Blanco arranged to win all but eighteen of the more than two hundred thousand votes cast. It was at this point that congress bestowed on him the title "Illustrious American and Regenerator of Venezuela." The president enjoyed his many titles and had numerous streets, boulevards, and plazas named for himself. Early in his rule his picture was placed in all public buildings, and many parks were adorned with a statue honoring him.

Guzmán had numerous streets and plazas named for himself, his picture was placed in all public buildings, and many parks were adorned with a statue honoring him.

Guzmán Blanco was aided in his efforts to improve the Venezuelan economy by his appointing able economic and financial advisers. One of the more challenging tasks was the ever-present public debt. Benefiting from the years of peace, Venezuela enjoyed a period of economic growth which contributed to an improvement in its credit rating. Agriculture in particular benefited from the president's attention, and wheat and coffee became the principal items of export.

The national economy also benefited from the extensive construction of highways, as communications between leading cities were improved. The main ports of La Guaira and Puerto Cabello were improved, and telegraph communication was established between Caracas and the state capitals. A rail link between Caracas and La Guaira was begun. Other public works included construction of a capitol, a federal court building, and a national theater, and expansion of the university. Education benefited under Guzmán Blanco's leadership. He instituted an extensive building program with the goal of making education free and available to all students for the first time in Venezuela.

One of the early challenges to Guzmán Blanco came from the Roman Catholic church. He and his party were seen as anticlerical and were opposed by the archbishop of Caracas. When asked for a *Te Deum* to celebrate the new government, Archbishop Silvestre Guevara y Lira refused, and was exiled. Soon after, Guzmán Blanco established civil marriages, prohibited the church from holding tracts of uncultivated land, and ended the practice, dating from the colonial period, of the state contributing to the church. An active Mason, the president saw to the building of the Masonic Temple in Caracas. After 1876, Guzmán Blanco made peace with the church but ensured that he kept it in its place.

In 1876, with a handpicked successor, Francisco LINARES ALCÁNTARA, as president, Guzmán Blanco left for Europe as Venezuela's representative to six governments. When Linares died in 1878, loyal Guzmancistas, Joaquín CRESPO and Pablo ROJAS PAÚL, took charge and recalled their patron from Europe. Guzmán Blanco stayed in Caracas from 1879 until 1884, when he returned to his luxurious life in Paris. Before leaving Venezuela, however, he oversaw the election of Crespo as president. The economy deteriorated, and congress called him home. He arrived in August 1886 to genuine demonstrations of support but, within a year, expressions of discontent began to surface. As some editors wrote about alternatives to Guzmán Blanco, their papers were confiscated and they were jailed, a practice followed earlier in his rule whenever it was felt necessary.

Rojas Pául was selected by Guzmán Blanco to take over when he again returned to the comforts of Paris in 1888. This time, however, the puppet did not follow the master, and Rojas Pául established himself as the real ruler of the nation. Since there was widespread anti-Guzmán Blanco sentiment, this was not so difficult to accomplish. The former president never returned to his native land. He died in Europe a decade later.

– CHARLES CARRERAS

H

HALFFTER, RODOLFO

Rodolfo Halffter (*b.* 20 October 1900; *d.* 14 October 1987), Spanish composer. Mainly self-taught, Halffter in 1929 sought advice from the eminent composer Manuel de Falla with whose spare, neoclassic style his music is frequently compared. He gained recognition in Europe in the mid-1930s but moved to Mexico in 1939. A permanent resident and citizen of Mexico from 1940, he held posts as professor at the National Conservatory (from 1940) and director of the composers' cooperative publishing firm, Ediciones Mexicanas de Música (from 1946). In 1969 Halffter was inducted into the Mexican Academy of Arts. He wrote some twelve-tone serial music, the first in Mexico, but his style retained its characteristic clarity and melodiousness with tinges of dissonance and without any Mexican influences. His students include Héctor QUINTANAR and Eduardo MATA.

— ROBERT L. PARKER

HALPERÍN-DONGHI, TULIO

Tulio Halperín-Donghi (*b.* 27 October 1926), Argentine historian. Born and educated in Argentina, Halperín-Donghi received his doctorate from the University of Buenos Aires in 1955. He taught at the universities of Rosario and Buenos Aires from 1955 until the military coup led by Juan Carlos ONGANÍA in 1966. Since then, he taught at Harvard, Oxford, and the University of California at Berkeley. Halperín-Donghi's work covers a wide range of topics in political history,

---

Halperín-Donghi's writings detail the breakdown

of the colonial order in Argentina.

---

economic and fiscal history, and social and intellectual history. His contributions on the crisis of independence, the fledgling efforts at national organization, and the social and economic continuities from the Bourbon to the post-Independence periods are particularly strong. His most important work is *Revolución y guerra: Formación de una elite dirigente en la Argentina criolla* (1972), which details the breakdown of the colonial order and the emergence of new elites in a context of

social and political crisis. Other works include *Tradición política española e ideología revolucionaria de Mayo* (1961), *Guerra y finanzas en los orígenes del estado argentino* (1982), and *José Hernández y sus mundos* (1985). He has also written such comprehensive histories as *Historia contemporánea de América Latina* (1969), *Hispanoamérica después de la independencia* (1972), and *El espejo de la historia: Problemas argentinos y perspectivas latinoamericanas* (1987). This last volume places Argentina in a Latin American context and reveals how Halperín's view of the region has been deepened by his years of life abroad. He retired from the University of California at Berkeley in 1994.

— IVÁN JAKSIĆ

HARO BARRAZA, GUILLERMO

Guillermo Haro Barraza (*b.* 21 March 1913), Mexican astronomer and physicist. Born in Mexico City, the son of José Haro and Leonor Barraza, Haro graduated from the National University and did postgraduate work at the Harvard University Observatory (1943–1944). A full-time researcher at the National University, he initiated an extensive fellowship program to train future Mexican scientists. He directed the National Astronomical Observatory for two decades (1948–1968) as well as the Tonantzintla Astrophysics Observatory. With Samuel RAMOS and Elí de Gortari, he cofounded the Seminar of Scientific and Philosophical Problems, which published dozens of works. His own work has appeared in English, and he has edited several scientific journals. He became a member of the National College in 1953, and Mexico awarded him its National Prize in Sciences (1963).

— RODERIC AI CAMP

HARO Y TAMARIZ, ANTONIO DE

Antonio de Haro y Tamariz (*b.* 1811; *d.* 1869), Mexican politician. Born in the city of Puebla, Haro y Tamariz studied law in Rome. He served as finance minister in 1844, 1846, and 1853 and was elected to the Senate in 1850 and 1852. During the war with the United States in 1846, Haro y Tamariz proposed that church property be sold and that the government collect taxes on the sales. Prices would be set on the assumption that annual rents represented 5 percent of the value of the property. Renters would have first preference in purchasing their homes. The church delayed implementation of the plan, and the government's desperate need for funds forced it to drop the disentailment plan, but it later served as a model for the Liberal reforms of 1856.

A lifelong associate of Antonio López de SANTA ANNA, Haro y Tamariz himself became more conservative, collaborating with Lucas ALAMÁN and serving in Santa Anna's cabinet in 1853. Unable to convince the church to make any further loans to the government and unwilling to borrow from *agiotistas* (moneylenders), Haro y Tamariz resigned only three months later. After the liberal Revolution of Ayutla overthrew Santa Anna, Haro y Tamariz launched a conservative rebellion in Puebla in December 1855 with the support of the army and the clergy. His Plan of Zacapoaxtla (1855) called for a restoration of the privileges of the church and the army and a return to the conservative Constitution of 1842. After a ferocious battle for the streets of Puebla, Haro y Tamariz was forced to surrender but managed to escape his captors. He supported the Conservative cause during the War of the Reform and the empire of MAXIMILIAN.

– D. F. STEVENS

HAWKINS, JOHN

John Hawkins (*b.* 1532; *d.* 12 November 1595), an Englishman active in the West Indies from 1562 to 1600 who was primarily interested in trading. In the early 1560s, a new group of interlopers, the English, were led by the ingenious John Hawkins of Plymouth, who organized four trading voyages to the Indies from 1562 to 1568, personally leading three of them. His purpose was trade: to exchange cloth and merchandise from England and slaves from Africa with the Spanish in return for sugar, hides, and silver. Hawkins wanted to legitimize his activities with the Spanish government by securing a license to trade freely. Even though he vowed to fight privateers if the Spanish would grant him the license he desired, the Spanish refused to do so, wishing to avoid setting a precedent.

Hawkins's earliest venture was successful in business terms, although his overall plan failed. The first voyage embarked in October 1562 and prospered greatly, as he traveled among the Caribbean islands trading English goods and African slaves for hides and sugar, returning to England in September 1563. Hawkins's first effort succeeded in the midst of relative peace between the English and Spanish. Relations between the two nations soured quickly, however, as the peace between England and Spain that was based on common opposition to

France broke down when France weakened from internal religious wars.

Thus, Hawkins's second and third voyages faced greater difficulties as Spain clamped down on its colonies and fervently attempted to prohibit foreign trade. Meanwhile, by the time of the second voyage (October 1564–September 1565), Hawkins had received more direct support from the English government. Nevertheless, the second and third voyages proved relatively unsuccessful in terms of trade, though each had its own accomplishments.

On his third and final voyage (October 1567–January 1569), Hawkins was bound for home in September 1568 when bad weather forced his fleet to dock at San Juan de Ulúa, the port of Veracruz. Later that month, a Spanish *flota* encountered his fleet there and destroyed most of it. In early 1569, after great hardships, he and fifteen remaining companions reached England. The Spanish, in fact, had proved unwilling to allow open trading, treating foreigners like Hawkins as pirates.

After aiding in the English defeat of the Spanish Armada in 1588, Hawkins and Francis DRAKE returned to the Caribbean in 1595 with a large fleet, attempting an Indies Voyage, a plan intended to break the territorial power of the Spanish in the New World. The well-prepared Spanish defeated this ill-fated effort at San Juan, Puerto Rico, and at Cartagena, Colombia. They also defeated the English on the Isthmus of Panama at Porto Bello. John Hawkins's career thus came to an ignominious end.

– BLAKE D. PATTRIDGE

HAYA DE LA TORRE, VÍCTOR RAÚL

Víctor Raúl Haya de la Torre (*b.* 22 February 1895; *d.* 2 August 1979), pivotal politician in Peruvian politics of the twentieth century, founder in 1924 of the Popular Revolutionary Alliance of America (APRA), a movement with continental ambitions, and in 1931 the local Peruvian Aprista Party (PAP). Haya developed an ideology that was initially anti-imperialist but gradually turned conciliatory. He was supported mainly by the lower middle classes of Peru, who were attracted by his charisma, his populist-nationalist views, and his syncretic-Indianist appeal.

Haya was born in Trujillo to a family of provincial distinction. However, his father, Raúl Edmundo, had to rely on his professional income as a journalist to support his family. Peter Klarén proposes that Haya's initial ideological positions were possibly minted in reaction to the expansion of land property by foreign companies in La Libertad at the turn of the century. Haya studied law in Trujillo (1915) and Lima (1917). After meeting

Víctor Raúl Haya de la Torre at political rally in 1931. (Latin American Library, Tulane University)

the intellectual Manuel GONZÁLEZ PRADA in the Peruvian capital, Haya added anarchistic elements to his provincial bohemian stance.

In 1919, Peruvian workers were fighting for the eight-hour workday. Haya's policy of solidarity with the workers allowed him to surface as student leader. He was president of the Student Federation in 1919 and 1920, leading a student congress in Cuzco, fighting for the reform of the university, and establishing the "popular universities" that constituted the bases of the future PAP. Haya was initially a fellow traveler of the rising socialist movement and collaborated in journalistic activities with socialist intellectual José Carlos MARIÁTEGUI.

By 1924, Haya had developed a strong opposition to President Augusto B. LEGUÍA and was imprisoned and exiled. Haya was invited by Mexican indigenist and minister of education José VASCONCELOS to Mexico, where he started his continental ideological movement. He broke politically with Mariátegui and became a stern opponent of communism.

After extensive travel and study in Europe he returned to Peru when Leguía fell in 1930. In the 1931 elections, Haya lost to the nationalist colonel Luis SÁNCHEZ CERRO. Apristas claimed fraud and organized an uprising in Trujillo in 1932 which was brutally repressed by the army. Haya was imprisoned but then freed after Sánchez Cerro's death in 1933. Thereafter he engaged in clandestine politics, and did not return

to open campaigning until 1945, with the election of APRA-supported Luis José BUSTAMANTE Y RIVERO. In 1948, however, another Aprista uprising, this time in Callao, led to repression by General Manuel ODRÍA and Haya's political asylum in the Colombian embassy in Lima (1949–1954).

By 1956 a more subdued Haya established with President Manuel PRADO a pact whose objective was an Aprista victory in the 1962 elections. However, once again Haya's presidential ambitions were thwarted by a military coup against Prado. Elections in 1963 resulted in the defeat of Haya by Fernando BELAÚNDE. During Belaúnde's regime, Haya's party formed a coalition of opposition with his former enemy Odría. The military coup of 1968 against Belaúnde further delayed Haya's ambitions. Only in 1978–1979 was Haya able to occupy the largely honorary post of president of the Constituent Assembly.

– ALFONSO W. QUIROZ

HEIREMANS, LUIS ALBERTO

Luis Alberto Heiremans (*b.* 14 July 1928; *d.* 25 October 1964), Chilean dramatist and writer. With the Chileans Egon WOLFF and Jorge DÍAZ, Heiremans shares international renown as a dramatist. He is an outstanding writer of his country's Generation of '50. He was an active member of the movement that began in the 1940s to reform drama in the university, which has had a great effect on the Latin American stage.

Aside from his highly praised brief narratives, collected in *Los mejores cuentos de Luis Alberto Heiremans* (1966), the critical world has identified three phases of his work. Outstanding in the initial phase is *Moscas sobre el mármol* (1958). The transitional phase includes *Los güenos versos* (1958), *Sigue la estrella* (1958), and *La ronda de la buena nueva* (1961), and the mature phase includes *Buenaventura* (1961), and his exceptional trilogy *Versos de ciego* (1961), *El abanderado* (1962), and *El Tony chico* (1964). His sensibility tended toward the existentialist, and he went beyond traditional literary realism. His works developed a poetic theater that symbolically codifies, sometimes through certain biblical correlations, the elements of custom and folklore in Chile, with the effect of making them universal.

– LUIS CORREA-DÍAZ

HENRÍQUEZ, CAMILO

Camilo Henríquez (*b.* 20 July 1769; *d.* 16 May 1825), Chilean patriot, revolutionary, and propagandist, "the father of Chilean journalism." Henríquez was born in Valdivia, but in 1784 he was sent for his education to

Lima, where he lived for the next quarter century, entering a minor religious order in 1787. He was three times investigated by the Inquisition because of his interest in prohibited books, such as those of Jean-Jacques Rousseau (1712–1778), Guillaume-Thomas-François de Raynal (1713–1796), and Louis-Sébastien Mercier (1740–1814).

Henríquez returned to his native Chile at the end of 1810 and threw himself into politics with enthusiasm. When the patriot government acquired its first printing press (from the United States), he was given the task of editing the first Chilean newspaper, *La Aurora de Chile* (13 February 1812 to 1 April 1813). The prospectus he issued prior to the first issue made a resonant claim: "After the sad and intolerable silence of three centuries—centuries of infamy and lamentation!—the voice of reason and truth will be heard amongst us." The newspaper contained many articles by its editor. On 6 April 1813 *La Aurora* was replaced by a second newspaper, *El Monitor Araucano,* which ran until the eve of the battle of Rancagua (1–2 October 1814) and the downfall of patriot Chile. Henríquez used these newssheets to spread his own revolutionary ideas. Between 1814 and 1822 he lived in exile in Buenos Aires, once again publishing newspapers for a time. In 1822 he returned to Chile at the invitation of Bernardo O'HIGGINS and played a minor role in public affairs for what remained of his life.

Henríquez's place as a publicist of patriot and revolutionary ideas during the Patria Vieja in Chile was unrivaled. His writing is always clear and direct. A brief flirtation with monarchism during his Argentine exile was no more than a temporary aberration from his liberal, democratic, and republican ideas.

– SIMON COLLIER

HENRÍQUEZ UREÑA, MAX

Max Henríquez Ureña (*b.* 16 November 1885; *d.* 23 January 1968), Dominican educator, writer, and diplomat. Henríquez Ureña, born in Santo Domingo, was the son of Francisco HENRÍQUEZ Y CARVAJAL, president of the Dominican Republic (1916), and the Dominican poetess and educator Salomé UREÑA DE HENRÍQUEZ. After receiving a law doctorate in 1913, he began his public career in 1916, as secretary to his father. This appointment was followed by twenty years of diplomatic service as his country's representative in various European capitals, the League of Nations, and the United Nations. During the first year of Rafael L. TRU-JILLO's reign (1930–1931), Henríquez Ureña was in charge of Dominican public education. Along with other Dominican intellectuals, he established the Do-

minican Academy of History. In Cuba, he founded the journals *Cuba Literaria* and *Archipiélago.* Henríquez Ureña contributed to important Hispanic magazines, such as *El Cojo Ilustrado* (Venezuela), *Cuba Contemporánea* and *El Figaro* (Cuba), and *Caras y Caretas* (Argentina). He taught at various universities in the Dominican Republic and abroad, including the Universidad Nacional Pedro Henríquez Ureña (UNPHU). Henríquez Ureña's most famous literary work is *Los Estados Unidos y la República Dominicana* (published in Cuba in 1919), in which he denounced the armed intervention by the United States in the Dominican Republic during 1916. Another well-known work is *Panorama histórico de la literatura dominicana,* a survey of Dominican literature published in Rio de Janeiro in 1945. Henríquez Ureña died in Santo Domingo.

– KAI P. SCHOENHALS

HENRÍQUEZ UREÑA, PEDRO

Pedro Henríquez Ureña (*b.* 29 June 1884; *d.* 11 May 1946), Dominican and Spanish American intellectual, educator, philologist, and literary critic. Born in Santo Domingo of a prominent family, he spent most of his lifetime outside his native country. His early schooling was in the Dominican Republic and in the United States (1902–1904), and he began his literary activities during a first residence in Cuba (1904–1905). He lived in Mexico from 1906 through 1914, where he completed a law degree, taught at the Preparatory School of the University of Mexico, and together with Alfonso REYES, Antonio CASO, and other young intellectuals took part in the founding of the Ateneo de la Juventud. He traveled to the United States again in 1914, and between 1916 and 1921 he both taught and did postgraduate work in Spanish literature at the University of Minnesota (his doctoral thesis, defended in 1918, was on versification in Hispanic poetry). In a second and shorter Mexican residence (1921–1924) he undertook a number of teaching and administrative responsibilities. In mid-1924 he left Mexico for Argentina, and for more than twenty years held secondary and university teaching positions in both Buenos Aires and nearby La Plata. He also carried on wide-ranging intellectual activities: a steady stream of books and articles on linguistics and literature, lectures, and consultations with journals and publishing houses. In 1931–1933 he served for a short time as General Superintendent of Education in the Dominican Republic, and in 1940–1941 he was invited to deliver the Charles Eliot Norton lectures at Harvard University.

Henríquez Ureña's influence was evident in several generations of well-trained students, but clearly his most significant contribution as a thinker and scholar has come in the expansiveness and persuasive clarity of his own writings. His publications are voluminous and contribute brilliantly to the study of language, literature, and culture in the Spanish-speaking world. As a linguist, Henríquez Ureña's best contributions are probably his *Gramática castellana* (1938–1939), his much reprinted grammar done with Amado Alonso, and his dialectal studies on American Spanish: *El español en México, los Estados Unidos y la América Central* (1938) and *El español en Santo Domingo* (1940). His most influential literary studies are the published doctoral thesis on versification, *La versificación irregular en la poesía castellana* (1920), and the Norton lectures from Harvard, *Literary Currents in Hispanic America* (1945; translated by Joaquín Díez Canedo and published in 1949 as *Las corrientes literarias en la América Hispánica*). As a cultural observer, his best-known work is *Seis ensayos en busca de nuestra expresión* (1928), a series of six persuasive essays on the possibilities of expressing an authentic American culture in Spanish.

— MERLIN H. FORSTER

HENRÍQUEZ Y CARVAJAL, FRANCISCO

Francisco Henríquez y Carvajal (*b.* 14 January 1859; *d.* 1935), provisional president of the Dominican Republic (1916). After the U.S. Marines invaded the Dominican Republic in 1916, Washington was unwilling to allow direct rule. The Dominican Congress reacted by meeting in secrecy and selecting Francisco Henríquez y Carvajal as provisional president. The United States was willing to allow Henríquez y Carvajal to take power under the conditions it determined. Unwilling to become a puppet of the United States, Henríquez y Carvajal resigned and left the country in November 1916. The Dominican Congress was dissolved and the United States imposed martial law by the occupying marines. These conditions prevailed until the marines were withdrawn in 1924.

— HEATHER K. THIESSEN

HENRY THE NAVIGATOR

Henry The Navigator (*b.* 4 March 1394; *d.* 13 November 1460), Portuguese prince noted for promoting the voyages of discovery that led to Portugal's creation of an overseas empire. Third son of King John I and Philippa of Lancaster, daughter of John of Gaunt of England, Prince Henry (Infante Dom Henrique) was duke of Viseu, governor of the city of Ceuta (captured in 1415 by the Portuguese from the Moroccans in an expedition in which Henry played a key role), the gov-

ernor of the Algarve, Portugal's southernmost province, where Henry established his own court at Sagres in 1419.

Prince Henry is one of the most controversial figures in Portuguese historiography, for historians differ widely in their assessments of the extent and motives of his leadership role in Portugal's voyages of discovery. In the *Crónica da Guiné,* Gomes Eanes de Azurara, a contemporary chronicler of the discoveries, portrays Prince Henry as a model crusader: a tireless fighter, a pious man, and a chaste saint who never married. Azurara's portrait does not, however, match other evidence concerning Henry's character, which suggests that he was a skilled politician with an acute sense of *raison d'état,* that he was a crafty courtier who knew how to employ court intrigue for his own advantage; or that he was a practical man of affairs whose preoccupation with overseas expansion reflected his purpose of serving both God and Mammon.

Prince Henry had been told about Saharan gold by the Moors of Ceuta and he vowed to find it by land or sea.

On several occasions Henry's actions put the lives of his own brothers or half brothers in peril. For example, his unsuccessful expedition to Tangiers in 1437 resulted in the capture of his younger brother, Dom Fernando, by the Moors. The Moors demanded the return of Ceuta as the price of Fernando's release. Hardliners in the Portuguese court, including Henry, opposed giving up Ceuta, and as a result Fernando died in captivity in Fez in 1443. Henry also supported the war against Dom Afonso, duke of Bragança, and his half brother, who was involved in a power struggle with Dom Pedro, his older brother. At the battle of Alfarrobeira in 1449 Dom Pedro was killed. Many Portuguese historians blame Dom Pedro's death on Henry's intrigues.

Concerning his role in overseas expansion, Azurar notes that João de Alenquer, the "vedor da fazenda," had convinced Prince Henry of the economic advantages of capturing Ceuta, then believed to be a bridgehead to the gold-producing lands south of the Sahara. Similarly, Diogo Gomes, one of the sea captains Henry supported, confided to Martin Behaim of Nürnburg that Prince Henry had been told about Saharan gold by the Moors of Ceuta and that he had vowed to find it by land or sea. This view of Henry's thirst for gold has been developed by a school of Portuguese historians led by Alexandre Herculano and presently is reflected in the writings of Vitorino Magalhães Godinho and others, who contend that the economic motive and maintaining the security of Portugal were the main reasons for the overseas expansion.

Nevertheless, in 1960 the Portuguese marked the five-hundred-year anniversary of Prince Henry's death by honoring him as the "saint of the Promontory of Sagres," a heroic visionary who initiated Portugal's overseas discoveries and was the fountainhead of its empire.

— TOMÉ N. MBUIA JOÃO

HEREDIA Y HEREDIA, JOSÉ M.

José M. Heredia y Heredia (b. 31 December 1803; d. 7 May 1839), Cuban Romantic poet. Heredia, born in Santiago de Cuba, was the most important literary figure of Latin American romanticism. His early education was directed by his father, José Francisco Heredia y Mieses, an important politician who traveled extensively in the colonies. Heredia graduated from the University of Havana Law School in 1823 and became an important member of the anti-Spanish movement on the island.

The Spanish authorities transferred Heredia's father to the Audiencia of Mexico in 1819. That year José followed him there and published his first book of poems, *Ensayos poéticos,* in Mexico. In 1821 he returned to Cuba, married, and published three books: *La inconstancia, Misantropía,* and *El desamor.* Also in 1822 Heredia was appointed rector of the Pontífica Universidad de la Habana. The following year he embarked for the United States, where in Boston he met Felix Varela and José Saco, Cuban liberals and advocates of independence. In 1824, he visited Niagara Falls, which inspired one of this best-known poems, "El Niágara." In December 1824 the Cuban government condemned him to perpetual exile for his involvement in revolutionary activities. Heredia died in Toluca, Mexico.

— DARIÉN DAVIS

HERMOSILLO, JAIME-HUMBERTO

Jaime-Humberto Hermosillo (b. 1942), Mexican film director. Born in Aguascalientes, Hermosillo studied film direction at the Center of Film Studies of the National Autonomous University of Mexico (UNAM). He began his career by producing short narrative films and documentaries. His first full-length film was *La verdadera vocación de Magdalena* (1971). Since that debut, Hermosillo has been one of the most consistent and dedicated directors of contemporary Mexican cinema. His main themes are the changing middle-class family,

sexuality and alternative life-styles, and the demise of tradition and values. Many of his leading characters are women or gay men. Among his most critically praised films are *La pasión según Berenice* (1976), *Matine* (1977), *Naufragio* (1977), *Amor libre* (1979), *María de mi corazón* (1979), and *La tarea* (1991). Hermosillo was awarded the Ariel for best direction by the Mexican film academy for *La pasión según Berenice* and *Naufragio.*

— DAVID MACIEL

HERNÁNDEZ, FELISBERTO

Felisberto Hernández (b. 20 October 1902; d. 1964), Uruguayan writer. During his adolescence he studied music and performed as a concert pianist. Along with the Argentine Jorge Luis BORGES, he is considered one of the foremost writers of fantasy literature in the Río de la Plata countries. Hernández's lifelong commitment to music can be seen in his work. In the short story "El balcón" ("The Balcony," 1947), the narrator is a concert pianist. The narrative exemplifies the author's deceptively simple but ingenuous prose style, which he uses to analyze sensations, turning them into metaphors.

Early works such as *Libro sin tapas* (1929), *La cara de Ana* (1930), and *La envenenada* (1931) are characterized by humor, the writer's power of observation, and an exuberance in the construction of fantasies. His most acclaimed works begin with *Por los tiempos de Clemente Colling* (1942) and *Nadie encendía las lámparas* (1947), novels of "evocation" in which the anecdotal takes second place to poetic reconstruction of reality and real people, on the basis of memory. *Las hortensias* (1949), *La casa inundada* (1960), and *El cocodrilo* (1962) mark the culmination of his fictional narrative, in which memory and fantasy constitute the dual pillars of narrative discourse.

Additional works by Hernández include *El caballo perdido* (1943); *Tierras de memoria* (1965); and *Obras completas,* 3 vols. (1983).

— WILLIAM H. KATRA

HERNÁNDEZ, FRANCISCO

Francisco Hernández (b. ca. 1517; d. 1587), medical doctor and botanist from Puebla de Montalbán, Toledo, Spain. While studying at Alcalá de Henares, Hernández learned of Erasmus of Rotterdam's doctrines and those of the most outstanding humanists of his time. He practiced medicine in Toledo and Seville and was King Philip II's court physician. Upon his appointment as *Protomédico de Indias* in 1570, he went to New Spain, where he became deeply interested in Nahuatl medicine, the therapeutic uses of American flora and fauna, and the Nahuatl cultural approaches to diseases.

Antagonized by the Mexican viceroy, Hernández returned to Spain in 1577. He was then dismissed as court physician and replaced by Nardo Antonio Recco, who severely abbreviated Hernández's written works, many of which were destroyed by fire in 1671. Nevertheless, a large number of Hernández's botanical and medical writings are extant. They include *Rerum medicarum Novae Hispaniae* (Rome, 1628), *Quatro libros de la naturaleza y virtudes medicinales de las plantas y animales de la Nueva España* (Mexico, 1615), and *De antiquitatibus Novae Hispaniae* (Mexico, 1926).

— CARMEN BENITO-VESSELS

HERNÁNDEZ, JOSÉ

José Hernández (*b.* 10 November 1834; *d.* 21 October 1886), Argentine poet, legislator, journalist, politician, soldier, and author of *Martín Fierro*. He exemplified the dual personality typical of the Argentine writer of the nineteenth century: a man of action and of thought. Paradoxically, although he created the most celebrated piece of Argentine literature, he was mostly a man of action. Endowed with great physical dexterity and well acquainted with the life-style of gauchos, Hernández enrolled in the army at age nineteen, fighting in the internecine wars between the central government and the provinces. He retired as assistant captain and in 1858 emigrated to the province of Entre Ríos, where he participated in the revolutions in that part of the country. There, Hernández began his journalistic career, but in 1859 he was back in the army as assistant to General Justo José de URQUIZA, taking part in the battles of Cepeda (1859) and Pavón (1861). An opponent of General Bartolomé MITRE and of President Domingo F. SARMIENTO, Hernández returned to Buenos Aires to found the newspaper *El Río de la Plata,* where he defended the gauchos and attacked Sarmiento. After participating in the Ricardo LÓPEZ JORDÁN rebellion, Hernández escaped to Brazil.

In 1872, back in Buenos Aires, he published the first part of *Martín Fierro;* the second appeared in 1879. He became a legislator (representative and senator) and was instrumental in founding the city of La Plata. His very active life illustrates his commitment to serve his country politically and militarily. It explains also the ideology of the heroic poem he created. Hernández wrote *Instrucción del estanciero* (1881; Education of the Rancher), and political and journalistic pieces that reflected his views as a public persona, citizen, and politician. In his ideology and language, Hernández epitomized the "interior" (provinces) of Argentina. His major work, the poem *Martín Fierro,* is a combative denunciation of social injustice and the virtual genocide of a social strata of the population, that of the gaucho. He adhered to the Argentine Confederation, a political alliance that confronted the Buenos Aires *estancieros* (ranchers) and defended the right of the provinces to share power with the domineering city. He defended the rights of the gauchos, unjustly and cruelly repressed by a government that reduced them to pariahs, without rights to possess land, real freedom, or a hopeful future.

— ANGELA B. DELLEPIANE

HERNÁNDEZ, JOSÉ MANUEL

José Manuel Hernández (*b.* ca. 1853; *d.* 1919), Venezuelan caudillo and politician. A native of Caracas and a perennial revolutionary, Hernández was injured in battle in 1870. After extensive travel in the West Indies and throughout Venezuela, and engaging in various business ventures, "El Mocho" (the maimed) became the president of Bolívar State, where he opposed attempts at centralization by the authorities in Caracas, and also served in Congress. One of three candidates in the 1887 presidential election, Hernández gained enormous popularity by waging Venezuela's first modern political campaign through appealing directly to the masses and campaigning throughout the country under the banner of the Liberal Nationalist Party. Losing in a grossly fraudulent election, the idealistic populist then led an unsuccessful rebellion against the new government of the official candidate, Ignacio Andrade. Hernández was imprisoned and later exiled, but returned to Venezuela in 1908 to accept a high post in the regime of Juan Vicente GÓMEZ.

— WINFIELD J. BURGGRAAFF

HERNÁNDEZ, LUISA JOSEFINA

Luisa Josefina Hernández (*b.* 2 November 1928), Mexican writer. Born in México City, Luisa Josefina Hernández is the most important woman author as well as one of the most innovative playwrights in Mexico. She has distinguished herself not only as a dramatist but as a novelist, translator, critic, and essayist. Her fictional works are noted for the range of their subject matter, their stylistic and structural variety, and their ironic tone and assiduous avoidance of sentimentality.

Hernández studied drama under Rodolfo USIGLI at the University of Mexico and was later appointed to the Rudolfo Usigli chair in dramatic composition there. She earned her doctorate with a study of the religious iconography of the colonial period and became the first woman to be awarded emeritus status by the University of Mexico. She has taught in the United States and in several other countries.

Hernández is known for her feminist critique of the "macho" mythologies of Mexican culture.

Hernández is known for her feminist critique of the "macho" mythologies of Mexican culture, and for her trenchant yet sympathetic portrayal of the plight of Mexican men. She has written approximately forty plays and twenty novels. Her most celebrated stage works are *La calle de la gran ocasión I* and *II* (1962; 1985); *El órden de los factores* (1983), *Escándalo en Puerto Santo* (1962), and *Los huéspedes reales* (1958). She translates from German, English, French, Latin, and Greek authors ranging from Shakespeare to Euripides to Arthur Miller to Brecht. She has won most of the major prizes for literature in Mexico, including the Villaurutía Prize (1983) for her novel *Apocalypsis cum figuris* (1982). Her most recent works are a novel, *Almeida* (1989), and a dramatic adaptation of this novel by the same name.

– WILLIAM I. OLIVER

HERNÁNDEZ COLÓN, RAFAEL

Rafael Hernández Colón (*b.* 24 October 1936), president of Puerto Rico's Popular Democratic Party and twice governor of Puerto Rico. As the son of Rafael Hernández Matos, associate justice of the supreme court of Puerto Rico, Hernández Colón began his education in local schools in Ponce and continued at the Valley Forge Military Academy in Pennsylvania. He graduated from Johns Hopkins University and received his law degree from the University of Puerto Rico, where he taught law from 1961 until 1966.

Hernández Colón entered politics in 1965 by appointment to the post of secretary of justice, where he wrote the Political Code, the Mortgage Code, and the Plebiscite Act of 1967. In 1968 Hernández Colón was elected senator-at-large and served as president of the Senate from 1969 to 1972.

At age thirty-six he was the youngest person to fill the post of governor when first elected in 1972. His inability to deal with growing economic problems led to his defeat in a 1978 reelection bid, but he won the office again in 1984.

– DAVID CAREY, JR.

HERNÁNDEZ (FERNÁNDEZ) DE CÓRDOBA, FRANCISCO

Francisco Hernández (Fernández) de Córdoba (*d.* 1518), Spanish navigator and conquistador from the province of Córdoba. (He is not to be confused with Francisco FERNÁNDEZ DE CÓRDOBA [*d.* 1526], the conqueror of Nicaragua.) A leading settler of Cuba under Governor Diego Velásquez, Hernández agreed to lead the first major effort to conquer the Mayas on the Yucatán Peninsula (1517). The Mayas defeated him, however, killing more than half his expedition. Hernández suffered thirty-three wounds, from which he died soon after his return to his home at Villa de Sancti-Spiritus. Although it failed, this expedition stimulated new interest in Mexico, which led eventually to the expedition of CORTÉS in 1519. News of the expedition also reached and worried the Aztec emperor, MOTECUHZOMA II.

– RALPH LEE WOODWARD, JR.

HERNÁNDEZ MARTÍNEZ, MAXIMILIANO

Maximiliano Hernández Martínez (*b.* 1882; *d.* May 1966), career army officer and politician, president of El Salvador (1931–1934 and 1935–1944).

Born in San Salvador and educated at the Guatemalan military academy, Martínez entered the army in 1899. Rising rapidly during the 1906 border war with Guatemala, he reached the rank of major three years after receiving his commission. By 1919 he held the rank of brigadier general. Highly regarded by his colleagues for his ability as a planner and strategist, Martínez spent most of his army career as a professor at the Salvadoran Military Academy and in the office of the chief of staff. His features were both Indian and boyish, and he always appeared considerably younger than his age. Despite a calm exterior, he was regarded as a stern commander and a strong-willed, ambitious man.

Martínez's political rise began in 1930. One of six candidates for the presidency, Martínez withdrew to become the vice-presidential candidate of Arturo ARAÚJO, a wealthy landowner who enjoyed labor-movement support. Receiving only a plurality of the votes in the January 1931 election, the pair was elected by the National Assembly. General Martínez was appointed minister of war in addition to his vice presidency. The regime proved controversial and was confronted with the economic and financial crises caused by the global depression.

The maneuvering resulting from a military coup on 2 December 1931 brought Martínez to power. Although Martínez was not directly involved in the coup and was apparently held prisoner by the junior officers who led the revolt during its initial stages, he was suspected of complicity. After several days of confusion, Martínez was released by the military directorate and installed as provisional president (5 December) in accordance with the constitutional provisions. While the junior officers apparently intended that he be a figurehead, he eventually outmaneuvered them to take full control.

Martínez's consolidation of power was facilitated by a leftist-led peasant uprising during January 1932. The bloody rebellion, which reflected peasant discontent, numbered Communists among its leadership. Attacks on landowners and towns in many areas of the country greatly alarmed the elite, which turned to the army for protection. The army put down the revolt after incurring extensive casualties, variously numbered from 10,000 to 30,000, in what became known as the matanza (massacre). The result changed the nation's political climate, solidifying the power of General Martínez, creating support for a military regime, and leaving the entire isthmus frightened of communism.

Initially other Central American governments, in particular that of General Jorge UBICO in Guatemala, supported the United States in opposing Martínez. Contending that the Washington Treaties of 1923 precluded recognition of anyone who came to power as the result of a coup, the United States insisted on Martínez's resignation. Martínez and Ubico became rivals in a diplomatic contest for support throughout the isthmus. When nonrecognition failed to topple Martínez because of his control of the internal government security apparatus and U.S. reluctance to intervene militarily, the United States recognized the Martínez regime in January 1934. The general arranged his own reelection in violation of the Salvadoran constitution in 1934, beginning his second term in March 1935. After a prolonged stalemate, the Central American Conference of 1934 was convened to modify the Washington treaties of 1923.

Martínez held the nation in the tight grip of a harsh dictatorship until 1944. A theosophist and spiritualist who believed in the transmigration of human souls into other persons, he was rumored to be involved in rituals and was often regarded as a witch doctor. The security apparatus controlled all aspects of Salvadoran life, including the press, ruthlessly suppressing dissent.

The general did stamp out corruption, cease foreign borrowing, and stabilize the currency. His regime was best known for its public works program, which though not as extensive as that of his Guatemalan contemporary, changed the face of the nation. His efforts included extensive road building as well as the construction of many government buildings. He was periodically reelected, save for a brief interim regime.

After a few years of continued rivalry, Martínez and Ubico joined the leaders of Honduras and Nicaragua in a détente in which each agreed to prevent rebel movements against his neighbors, thereby acknowledging that none could gain ascendancy. This agreement gave rise to the myth of a Central American Dictators League, which seemed to gain further credence when both Guatemala and El Salvador became the first governments to recognize the new Spanish regime of Generalíssimo Francisco Franco in Spain. In fact, however, there was no formal agreement and certainly no linkage to the Axis powers. Rather, the respective Central American military presidents merely adopted a mutual nonintervention policy.

Martínez was forced from office on 8 May 1944 by a general strike protesting a new effort to extend his tenure yet again. The revolution proved short-lived, but though the military regained control, Martínez's hour had passed, and he remained in exile in Honduras until his death.

– KENNETH J. GRIEB

HERNÁNDEZ MONCADA, EDUARDO

Eduardo Hernández Moncada (*b.* 24 September 1899), Mexican composer and conductor trained in the National Conservatory under Rafael Tello. He was Carlos CHÁVEZ's assistant conductor with the Mexican Symphony Orchestra from 1929 to 1935 and was named director of the new National Symphony Orchestra of the Conservatory, formed in 1947. He assisted Carlos Chávez's composition workshop briefly in 1960 and was well-known for his work as choirmaster of the National Opera Chorus. Mexican folk elements moderately imbue his music, such as the ballet *Ixtepec* and his only opera, *Elena*.

– ROBERT L. PARKER

HERRÁN, PEDRO ALCÁNTARA

Pedro Alcántara Herrán (*b.* 19 October 1800; *d.* 26 April 1872), president of New Granada (1841–1845). Born to gentry in Bogotá, Herrán served with the patriots from 1814 to 1816 and the royalists from 1816 to 1820, rising from private to captain. In the service of New Granada from 1821, he became a general by 1828. A partisan of BOLÍVAR, he left Colombia in mid-1830 for Europe, where he lived until 1834. During that sojourn, he forged ties to generals Francisco de Paula SANTANDER and Tomás Cipriano de MOSQUERA, and he married the latter's daughter in 1842. Back in

Colombia, Herrán served as minister of interior and foreign affairs (1838–1839), and commanded the army during the War of the Supremes (1839–1842). During his presidency, the regime sponsored education, recalled the Jesuits (1842), and centralized government via the 1843 Constitution. Herrán was minister to the United States from 1846 to 1848. He later worked for Mosquera and Company (1851–1854) in New York, then returned to Colombia to lead the constitutionalist army against General José María MELO (1954). He was Colombian envoy in Washington from 1855 to 1859. The following year he returned home; he was fired by Mosquera (1862). Again in Washington, he was Guatemalan minister to Peru (1863) and Salvadoran minister to Peru (1865). After being restored to Colombian military service (1866–1867) by Mosquera, Herrán returned to Colombia, where he was elected senator from Antioquia (1870–1872). He died in Bogotá.

– J. LEÓN HELGUERA

HERRÁN, SATURNINO

Saturnino Herrán (*b.* 9 July 1887; *d.* 8 October 1918), Mexican artist. Born in Aguascalientes, Herrán was one of the pioneers of the modern Mexican movement and is known primarily for a mural project for the National

Herrán emphasized the dual nature of Mexican identity by superimposing an image of the crucified Christ on the Aztec earth goddess Coatlicue.

Theater, *Our Gods,* for which he did numerous studies from 1914 to 1918. It was never completed, but his focus on issues of Mexican identity have assured him a place in the history of Mexican art. He emphasized the dual nature of Mexican identity by using the Aztec earth goddess Coatlicue as the central motif, on which he superimposed an image of the crucified Christ. The Aztec deity symbolizes the indigenous character of Mexico and the Christ figure its European aspect. Figures making offerings are shown on each side of the central motif, Indians on the left and Spaniards on the right. Easel paintings by Herrán on Mexican subjects (people at work, fiestas, traditions, and history) inspired the artists of the Mexican School of the 1920s through 1940s. In portraits and a series of paintings he called "the creoles," he used distinctive colonial churches in the background to identify the sitters as Mexican and the location as Mexico. Each of the criollas portrays a beautiful woman as a symbol of Mexico. In his early paintings of 1912

and 1914, Herrán placed elderly figures in thematic contexts that emphasized their hopeless condition, exhausted by a life of toil and suffering. In his later works of 1917, the elderly figures have a serenity and peace that reflects a spirituality or intense religiosity.

– JACINTO QUIRARTE

HERRÁN Y ZALDÚA, ANTONIO SATURNINO

Antonio Saturnino Herrán y Zaldúa (*b.* 11 February 1797; *d.* 7 February 1868), Colombian prelate. Born in Honda, Tolima, Herrán studied in Bogotá, where he received his doctorate in law. He was ordained in 1821, then served in various parishes around and in Bogotá until 1830, when he became a canon of the Bogotá cathedral. In 1833 he assisted in the escape of General José María SARDÁ, a conspirator against President Francisco de Paula SANTANDER. By 1840 Herrán was vicar general of Bogotá and a close associate of Archbishop Manuel José MOSQUERA. As second in command of the archdiocese, he became enmeshed in the church–state conflict during the presidency of José Hilario LÓPEZ (1849–1853). In October 1852 he was imprisoned by the government. The exile of Mosquera left him in charge of the archdiocese from 1853 to 1854, and he was elected its archbishop in January 1856. Herrán devoted his time (unsuccessfully) to re-creating his predecessor's reforms and to forming groups to aid the needy. The virulence of Tomás Cipriano de MOSQUERA's anticlericalism (1861–1863) brought rupture with the church. Herrán was exiled to Cartagena (1861–1864), was back in favor (1864–1866) during Manuel MURILLO TORO's presidency, then had to deal again with Mosquera's ill will (1866–1867). He died in Villeta, about forty miles from Bogotá.

– J. LEÓN HELGUERA

HERRERA, BARTOLOMÉ

Bartolomé Herrera (*b.* 1808; *d.* 10 August 1864), one of a group of Roman Catholic church leaders at the time of independence in Peru who sought to retain for the church the same privileged position it had held in colonial society. He was the leading advocate of the continuation of Rome's dominance over the Peruvian church. A man of humble origins who became an orphan at the age of five, Herrera later studied and taught philosophy. But he did his best work as a priest, among people in poor parishes. Basically he believed in leadership of republics by intelligent, moral elites, be they Inca or Spanish, and respect for faith and legitimate authority. He served the government of José Rufino ECHENIQUE (1851–1855) at the head of two ministries, and later he acted as Peru's ambassador to Rome. In 1860 he presided over a constitutional convention and was disappointed that the delegates did not restore to the church the privileges it had lost in 1855. He then served as bishop of Arequipa until his death.

– VINCENT PELOSO

HERRERA, BENJAMÍN

Benjamín Herrera (*b.* 1850, *d.* 29 February 1924), Colombian Liberal Party leader. Herrera was born in Cali of northern Colombian parents. He fought for the Liberal government in the revolution of 1876–1877 and was an officer in the Colombian army until the Liberals lost power in the mid-1880s. During the War of the Thousand Days (1899–1902), Herrera emerged along with Rafael URIBE URIBE as a top Liberal military leader. By late 1902 Herrera controlled most of Panama, but he was urged to make peace by Uribe Uribe, who himself took this step in October. When U.S. officials warned that they would not permit fighting near Panama City or Colón, Herrera signed a treaty with the Colombian government on 21 November 1902 that virtually ended the war.

In the postwar period Herrera often differed with Uribe Uribe regarding Liberal policy in the face of Conservative hegemony in government, but he remained a proponent of peaceful opposition. In 1922 he was the Liberal presidential candidate but was defeated by Conservative Pedro Nel OSPINA by a vote of 413,619 to 256,231 in what Liberals claimed was a fraudulent election.

– HELEN DELPAR

HERRERA, CARLOS

Carlos Herrera (*b.* 1856; *d.* 6 July 1930), interim president of Guatemala. Herrera assumed the Guatemalan presidency as leader of the Guatemalan Unionist Party on 8 April 1920 after the removal of the nation's longest reigning dictator, Manuel ESTRADA CABRERA. A member of one of Guatemala's premier families, and the owner of large sugar and coffee plantations, Herrera supposedly possessed no strong political ambitions. But in the wake of Estrada Cabrera's ouster, he acknowledged the nation's need for a fair and competent interim leader. Herrera was considered by his peers to be a cultured and learned gentleman. Of distinguished seventeenth-century Spanish heritage, he was widely respected for his qualities of honesty, incorruptibility, and administrative prowess.

After only twenty months in office, however, political instability and a severe economic crisis had over-whelmed Herrera's ill-prepared Unionist government. On the evening of 5 December 1921 a group of senior army officers headed by generals José María ORELLANA, José María Lima, and Miguel Larrave entered the residence of the president and demanded his resignation. He promptly complied with their request.

Although a member of the coffee elite himself, Herrera chose to govern in a manner that often disregarded the concerns of the dominant political and economic sector of the country. Although willing to suppress peasant unrest as severely as previous Liberal regimes, he occasionally permitted the lower classes to voice their concerns. Because of this, coffee growers, merchants, army officers, and some urban professionals were convinced that his administration jeopardized their interests and so they acted to undermine his authority.

– WADE A. KIT

HERRERA, DIONISIO DE

Dionisio De Herrera (*b.* 9 October 1781; *d.* 13 June 1850), chief of state of Honduras (1823–1827) and Nicaragua (1830–1833). Born to a wealthy creole family in Choluteca, Honduras, Herrera obtained a law degree in 1820. After serving as secretary to the municipal council of Tegucigalpa, Honduras, he became representative to the Cortes from Comayagua Province. He wrote the 28 September 1821 Declaration of Independence of Tegucigalpa and later represented Honduras in the Imperial Congress of Mexico (1822). After Central America separated from Mexico and formed the United Provinces of Central America in 1824, he became chief of state of Honduras and defended the country unsuccessfully against Federal president Manuel ARCE. Herrera was imprisoned in Guatemala until 1829, when the Liberal forces under Francisco MORAZÁN overthrew the Arce regime after a three-year civil war.

Herrera returned to politics and was elected president of the assembly of Honduras while also representing Choluteca. Later the government sent him as an envoy to Nicaragua, where he became chief of state from 1830 to 1833. He was elected by the Salvadoran assembly in 1834 to serve as chief of state in El Salvador, but he abandoned politics, except for a brief term as vice president of the Constituent Assembly of Honduras in 1839. He died in San Salvador.

– JEFFREY D. SAMUELS

HERRERA, FLAVIO

Flavio Herrera (*b.* 19 February 1895; *d.* 31 January 1968), noted Guatemalan romantic author and poet.

Born in Guatemala City, Herrera graduated in law from the national university. He traveled widely in Europe, Asia, Africa, and America. His first major collection of stories, *La lente opaca,* was published in Germany in 1921 while he lived there. Herrera served as ambassador for his country to Uruguay, Brazil, and Argentina. He established the first school of journalism in Guatemala at San Carlos University, where he also was a professor of law. His novels include *El tigre* (1934), *La tempestad* (1935), and *Caos* (1949). His poems were published in *Solera* (1962). An owner of coffee farms, he lived the last years of his life in Guatemala City with an elderly uncle.

— DAVID L. JICKLING

HERRERA, JOSÉ JOAQUÍN ANTONIO FLORENCIO

José Joaquín Antonio Florencio Herrera (*b.* 23 February 1792; *d.* 10 February 1854), Mexican general and politician. Born at Jalapa, Herrera was twice president of Mexico (1844–1845 and 1848–1851) and had a distinguished career in both the army and in political life. He fought for the royalists in the War of Independence, retiring in 1820 with the rank of lieutenant-colonel to Perote, where he opened a drugstore. After the publication of the Plan of Iguala, he joined the insurgency and was promoted to brigadier-general. A member of

---

Herrera was accused of being willing to negotiate the surrender of Texas to the United States.

---

the first independent congress, he opposed Agustín de ITURBIDE and was jailed. His subsequent career alternated between senior military commands and political posts as minister of war, member of congress, and governor of the Federal District. Known as a moderate liberal federalist, he was elected interim president in 1844 and president in 1845. Forced to resign as the result of a military revolt, he was accused of being willing to negotiate the surrender of Texas to the United States. He was elected to congress in 1846–1847 and was military commander of Mexico City during the U.S. invasion. In 1848, he was again elected president, and served until the completion of his term in 1851, only the second Mexican head of state up to that time to do so. Herrera was director of the national pawn shop (Monte de Piedad) after he left the presidency, and retired in 1853.

— MICHAEL P. COSTELOE

HERRERA, LUIS ALBERTO DE

Luis Alberto de Herrera (*b.* 22 July 1873; *d.* 8 April 1959), political leader of the Blancos (National Party) in Uruguay for much of the first six decades of the twentieth century. The only politician whose stature could be considered equal to that of the Colorado leader José BATLLE Y ORDÓÑEZ, Herrera was a political caudillo of enormous staying power, even though he was never elected president.

Herrera served as a deputy in Congress from 1905 to 1909 and from 1914 to 1918. He was a senator from 1938 to 1942 and from 1955 to 1959 and a candidate for president six times. A chief architect of the 1933 coup and of the 1934 and 1952 constitutions, Herrera engineered the Blanco electoral victory in 1958, which gave the party control of the executive (a plural executive at the time) for the first time in the century.

A conservative nationalist, Herrera founded in 1933 the newspaper *El Debate,* from which he expounded his opposition to much of the liberal, welfare-state agenda of the Colorado followers of José Batlle. Herrera opposed Uruguay's collaboration with and support for the Allies in World War II. By the 1950s, he had become a strident conservative anticommunist.

Herrera wrote volumes on Uruguayan history and foreign policy. His grandson, Luis LACALLE, was elected president of Uruguay in 1989.

— MARTIN WEINSTEIN

HERRERA, TOMÁS

Tomás Herrera (*b.* 21 December 1804; *d.* 5 December 1854), army officer and governor of Panama (1831–1840; 1845–1849). Born in Panama City, Herrera participated in the Wars of Independence, serving under Simón Bolívar. After rising to the rank of colonel in the armed forces of New Granada, he was named governor of Panama in 1831.

In the midst of the political chaos created by the liberal revolt in New Granada in 1839–1840, a Panamanian popular assembly declared its independence on 18 November 1840 and persuaded Herrera to assume the presidency. In 1841, however, discussions with negotiators from New Granada convinced Herrera to denounce Panamanian autonomy, and in December he signed an agreement that provided for the reintegration of Panama.

As a result of his participation in the act of secession, Herrera was forced into exile in 1841. But by 1845, Herrera was rehabilitated and that year was appointed as governor of Panama by the president of New Granada, Tomás MOSQUERA. After Herrera's term ended in

1849, he became minister of war in the cabinet of New Granada's liberal president José Hilario LÓPEZ. In 1854 Herrera took a leading role in the defense of New Granada against the dictator José María MELO (1854) and was mortally wounded in battle near Bogotá on 4 December.

— WADE A. KIT

HERRERA CAMPINS, LUIS

Luis Herrera Campins (*b.* 1925), Venezuelan president (1979–1984). A long-time leader of the Social Christian COPEI (Comité de Organización Política Electoral Independiente) Party of Venezuela, Herrera Campins began his political career as president of the (Catholic) National Union of Students in the 1940s and later became the head of COPEI's youth organization. While in exile during the military dictatorship (1948–1958), he received a law degree in Spain. In 1958 Herrera Campins returned to Venezuela and was elected first to the Chamber of Deputies and subsequently to the Senate on the COPEI ticket. During the 1960s and 1970s he served as president of COPEI, president of the party's congressional delegation, and secretary-general of the Latin American Congress of Christian Democratic Organizations. After a bitter primary battle Herrera Campins won COPEI's nomination for president in 1978 and was victorious in the general election. His presidency was marked by falling oil prices, rising foreign debt, and economic crisis. His leadership was regarded by many as weak and ineffective.

— WINFIELD J. BURGGRAAFF

HERRERA LANE, FELIPE

Felipe Herrera Lane (*b.* 17 June 1922), Chilean economist, lawyer, author, and leader of international organizations. Born in Valparaiso, Herrera studied law and philosophy at the University of Chile and then economics at the London School of Economics. He returned to teach economics and political economy at the University of Chile from 1947 to 1958, spending 1950–1951 teaching at the London School of Economics. At the same time, he served in various Chilean ministries, acted as a general director of the Chilean Central Bank from 1953 to 1958, and was a member of the boards of governors of the World Bank and the International Monetary Fund, where he acted as executive director from 1958 to 1960. Herrera's most important achievement was his involvement as one of the principal figures in the conception and establishment of the Inter-American Development Bank in 1959. He was elected first president of the new institution in 1960 and con-

tinued in that position until 1971. As one in charge of implementing the high ideals conceived for the bank, Herrera played the instrumental role in determining the initial thrust of development programs for Latin America. After his resignation, he returned to Chile to pursue his academic career. He briefly became involved in the Socialist politics of his past (he was defeated in a bid to become rector of the University of Chile in 1972), but ultimately rejected a cabinet position in the Salvador ALLENDE government in 1973. During much of the 1970s and 1980s, Herrera acted as executive of various international organizations, promoted international and Latin American development programs, and authored numerous books.

— J. DAVID DRESSING

HERRERA Y OBES, JULIO

Julio Herrera Y Obes (*b.* 9 January 1841; *d.* 6 August 1912), Uruguayan politician and journalist, president of Uruguay (1890–1894). Herrera y Obes came from a prestigious family of professionals affiliated with the Colorado Party. He served as secretary to General Venancio FLORES in the War of the Triple Alliance in 1865. He was minister of foreign affairs in 1872, representative to the national Parliament (*diputado*) from 1873 to 1875, and minister of government from 1886 to 1887 in the constitutional government of General Máximo TAJES. He was the principal inspiration behind the transition to civilian democracy from the militarism of Colonel Lorenzo LATORRE and General Máximo Santos. Elected president in 1890, Herrera y Obes immediately faced a serious financial crisis during which various banks failed, including the National Bank. He overcame the crisis by a consolidation of debts arranged in Great Britain and by maintaining the gold standard in Uruguay. These moves later brought enormous advantages for Urugayan public finance. A man of refined culture and from a wealthy landowning family, he represented an era of civil elitism in which little faith was placed in the idea of people governing themselves. He brought before the Parliament the notion of "directive influence," in which the president would be involved in all the actions of his administration.

Herrera y Obes was a romantic personality, for decades the beau of Elvira Reyes. He began visiting her by carriage in his days of splendor and ended as an old man taking the tramway to see her in her Prado villa. He retained his prestige among elite members of his party until the end of his days, but when he died, President José BATLLE Y ORDÓÑEZ denied him funerary honors. The term "oligarchic democracy" is used when referring to this period because the idea of "directive influence" implied the involvement of the president in the designation of his own successor.

— JOSÉ DE TORRES WILSON

HERRERA Y REISSIG, JULIO

Julio Herrera y Reissig (*b.* 9 January 1875; *d.* 18 March 1910), poet and essayist who belonged to the Uruguayan Generation of 1900. Herrera was born in Montevideo into a prominent family; he was the nephew of Julio HERRERA Y OBES, president of Uruguay (1890–1894). Suffering from a heart condition, his education was sporadic in private schools and from relatives. He resigned for health reasons from his job as clerk in the Customs Office and later from his position as assistant inspector-general of the National Board of Elementary Schools. Herrera flirted briefly with politics, but grew disenchanted. For the most part financially dependent on his family, after 1897 he devoted his life to literature and in 1899–1900 published the literary journal *La Revista.* A follower of modernism, Herrera stressed ideals of beauty and harmony and opposed the prevailing materialism of his age. Herrera was an important part of a brilliant decade in Uruguayan literature—the first decade of the twentieth century. After his worst heart attack in 1900, he wrote "La vida," first published in 1906, and "Las pascuas del tiempo," written in 1900 but not published until 1913. There followed *Los peregrinos de piedra* (1909), *Ópalos: Poemas en prosa* (1919), *Los parques abandonados* (1919), and *Las lunas de oro* (1924). Herrera's poetry was imbued with aestheticism, imagination, inventiveness, and irony. He also wrote essays and newspaper articles. His prose writings include *Epílogo wagneriano a la "política de fusión"* (1902) and *Prosas: Críticas, cuentos, comentarios* (1918). Important editions of his collected works are *Poesías completas* (1942), *Obras poéticas* (1966), with a prologue by Alberto Zum Felde, and *Poesía completa y prosa selecta* (1978), with an introduction by Idea Vilariño.

— GEORGETTE MAGASSY DORN

HERRERA Y TORDESILLAS, ANTONIO DE

Antonio de Herrera y Tordesillas (*b.* 1549; *d.* 1625), Spanish colonial historian and official chronicler of the Indies. Antonio de Herrera had a long and distinguished career in which he wrote one of the most encyclopedic accounts of Spanish activities in the New World. In his early years, he was appointed as secretary to Vespasiano Gonzaga, viceroy of Naples, where he began his history of the reign of Philip II. Herrera's loyalty to the cause of the crown attracted the attention of the court, and in 1596 he was appointed the official

historian of the Indies, with the task of providing a favorable account of the Conquest and settlement of the New World to combat the negative versions being written by Black Legend partisans in England and northern Europe.

Herrera's most famous work, the eight-volume *Historia general de los hechos de los castellanos en las islas y tierra firme del mar océano,* was published in Madrid from 1601 to 1615. As official historian, Herrera had access to persons and documents not available to other contemporary writers. He had never set foot in the New World and therefore relied upon information contained in the *relaciones geográficas* and other state-sponsored informational surveys and reports, the writings of Bartolomé de las Casas, Diego de LANDA, Gonzalo Fernández OVIEDO, and Francisco López de Gómara. Like others of his time, Herrera was obsessed with chronology and inclusiveness; his synthesis is remarkable, but the wealth of information renders his *Historia general* difficult for the modern reader.

> *Herrera's mission was to glorify the work of Ferdinand and Isabella by emphasizing their Christianizing mission and true concern for the Indians.*

Herrera's mission was to glorify the work of Ferdinand and Isabella by emphasizing their Christianizing mission and true concern for the Indians. As an imperialist historian, he sought to justify the empire as a unit and accordingly deemphasized the accomplishments of individual conquerors. Nevertheless, unlike Gómara and Oviedo, Herrera gave Columbus credit for his unique achievement. The chronicle is told from a clearly European perspective; it opens with a description of the Spanish Empire and continues with a discussion of official activities in the New World from 1492 to 1546. Herrera was intellectually honest enough to admit to some of the abuses that had occurred, but he refused to condemn the process of the Conquest in general. He did incorporate many of Las Casas's ideas and did much to restore his good name, but on the question of official policy toward Indians, Herrera took the side of Oviedo and Sepúlveda. Herrera's *Historia general* is a substantial and informative work, and it is a major example of the sophistication of the late imperialist school of colonial historiography.

— KAREN RACINE

HERRERABARRÍA, ADRIANO

Adriano Herrerabarría (*b.* 28 Dec. 1928), Panamanian painter. After completing a master of fine arts at the San Carlos Academy in Mexico City (1955), Herrerabarría returned to Panama, where he was an art professor and later director of the Escuela Nacional de Artes Plásticas.

Herrerabarría's early work reflected the influence of social realism and Mexican muralism. In his mature style, which can be described as a surrealism of organic forms, he combined sociopolitical and racial issues with a visionary mysticism, as in *Posesión* (1981). Unorthodox and rebellious, he published his radical views in numerous articles. In addition to his easel paintings, he created numerous murals.

– MONICA E. KUPFER

HERTZOG GARAIZABAL, ENRIQUE

Enrique Hertzog Garaizabal (*b.* 10 November 1897; *d.* 31 July 1981), Bolivian physician and politician, president of Bolivia (March 1947–October 1949). Hertzog, a native of La Paz, served as cabinet minister three times during the presidency of Daniel SALAMANCA. In the 1947 election Hertzog and his vice president, Mamerto URRIOLAGOITÍA, served as standard-bearers of the reconstituted Partido Unión Republicana Socialista. From the beginning of his administration, Hertzog faced severe labor unrest and a vocal political opposition. Concluding that his astute and tough-minded vice president was more adept in achieving results, Hertzog voluntarily left the office to Urriolagoitía, who completed the term in May 1951. Yet during Hertzog's two years in office, his government achieved improvements in education, social services, and communications. Hertzog returned to private life with the reputation of a dedicated citizen. He died in Buenos Aires.

– CHARLES W. ARNADE

HERZOG, VLADIMIR

Vladimir Herzog (*b.* 1937; *d.* 24 October 1975), a prominent victim of torture under Brazil's repressive military regime. Herzog was a widely respected São Paulo journalist who had worked for the newspaper *O Estado de São Paulo,* for the British Broadcasting Company, and in films. Herzog earned his degree from the University of São Paulo and later taught in its School of Communications. At the time of his death he was the news director of São Paulo's television station TV Cultura.

Brazilian security forces considered Herzog, a Yugoslavian Jew who had emigrated with his family to Brazil, a communist. In September 1975 he voluntarily presented himself for questioning to the local Center for Internal Defense–Department of Internal Order at the headquarters of the Second Army. The following day Herzog's body was returned to his wife with the explanation that he had hanged himself in his cell. Herzog's wife received the body in a sealed coffin and was warned not to open it. Military guards kept a watchful eye over the burial services to ensure that the coffin remained closed.

Herzog's death caused a swift, angry public reaction and became a symbol for supporters of the human rights movement to end state-sanctioned violence in Brazil. Despite government efforts to cover up the incident, Herzog's murder created a national and international scandal for the administration of Ernesto GEISEL because of its brutality and anti-Semitic undertones. Geisel, who was already in the process of moving the state apparatus away from brutal repression (*distensão*), took advantage of the scandal prompted by Herzog's death to neutralize the most repressive elements in São Paulo who were resisting *distensão*.

– SONNY B. DAVIS

HEUREAUX, ULISES

Ulises Heureaux (*b.* 21 October 1845; *d.* 26 July 1889), Dominican military officer and dictator (1882–1889). Known as Lilís, Heureaux was born at Puerto Plata to a Haitian father and a mother from the Lesser Antilles. Although raised in poverty, Heureaux acquired a good knowledge of economics, public finance, French, and English. He distinguished himself in the War of Restoration (1863–1865), during which he became the close friend of the leader of the insurrection against Spain, General Gregorio LUPERÓN.

After the restoration of Dominican independence, Heureaux became one of the outstanding leaders of the Partido Azul (Blue Party), on whose behalf he fought the Partido Rojo (Red Party) of the Dominican caudillo Buenaventura BÁEZ. During Báez's notorious Regime of the Six Years (1868–1874), Heureaux successfully opposed the caudillo's forces in the south of the country. In 1876 he defended militarily the presidency of Ulises ESPAILLAT. On orders of Luperón, Heureaux terminated the presidency of Cesareo Guillermo in 1879. He became minister of the interior and the police during the presidency of Archbishop Fernando Arturo de Meriño (1880–1882), whom he succeeded as president (1882–1884).

Heureaux became president again in 1887 and ruled the Dominican Republic as an iron-fisted dictator until his assassination on 26 July 1899 at Moca. The establishment of his dictatorship led to his complete break with Luperón, who was driven into exile in Puerto Rico. After decades of chaotic political strife, civil war, and fiscal irresponsibility, Heureaux's dictatorship provided the necessary climate for a great influx of foreign (especially U.S.) capital to the Dominican Republic and for the rapid development of the sugar industry. Heureaux's dictatorship served as a model for that of Rafael Leónidas Trujillo.

– KAI P. SCHOENHALS

HIDALGO, BARTOLOMÉ

Bartolomé Hidalgo (*b.* 24 August 1788; *d.* 28 November 1822), Uruguayan gauchesco poet, fervent defender of the independence of his native country, and a close friend of its liberator, José ARTIGAS. Hidalgo attended a Friars Franciscan school. He became a bookkeeper in the ministry of the royal public treasury in 1806 and then joined the militia. Hidalgo fought the English and the Portuguese and was declared *Benemérito de la Patria* (National Hero) for his *Himno oriental* (Oriental [Uruguayan] Anthem). He carried out a series of political functions in the newly liberated Uruguay, including administrator of the general post office, interim finance minister, and censor at the Casa de Comedias. In 1818 he went to live in Argentina, where he died in the village of Morón. He wrote "militant" poetry (*Cielitos y Diálogos patrióticos,* 1820–1822), inspired by his fervid participation in the civil movement for independence.

Hidalgo was the initiator of gauchesca literature, poetic compositions written from the point of view of the gauchos, recreating also their speech, an archaic form of Spanish (see the *Diálogos* as well as *Relación de las fiestas mayas de 1822*). A neoclassic poet, Hidalgo nevertheless was very successful in creating this form of *rioplatense* (Argentine and Uruguayan) popular poetry, which attracted the mass of the citizenry at a moment when it was necessary to impress on them the need for independence. His passion for freedom and concern for subjects that inspired the people ensured the success of this new kind of authentically American sociopolitical poetry.

– ANGELA B. DELLEPIANE

HIDALGO, ENRIQUE AGUSTÍN

Enrique Agustín Hidalgo (*b.* 28 August 1876; *d.* 27 September 1915), Guatemalan satirical writer. Born in Guatemala City, Hidalgo did not finish secondary school owing to family financial problems. He worked as a newspaper writer, businessman, and teacher. As a writer he used the pseudonym "Felipillo," the name of an Indian interpreter who had accompanied the Spanish

conquistadores. His most famous work of humor, the poem *Latas y latones,* was published posthumously in 1916.

– DAVID L. JICKLING

HIDALGO Y COSTILLA, MIGUEL

Miguel Hidalgo y Costilla (*b.* 8 May 1753; *d.* 30 July 1811), leader of the Mexican Independence movement (1810–1811). Born near Pénjamo, Guanajuato, the son of a hacienda administrator, Hidalgo distinguished himself as a philosophy and theology student at the Colegio de San Nicolás Obispo in Valladolid, Morelia, and at the Royal and Pontifical University in Mexico City. In 1778 he was ordained a priest. He gained recognition for his innovative thought and in 1791 became rector of the Colegio de San Nicolás. In 1792, however, his fortunes changed and he was appointed curate of the distant provincial town of Colima. Although the causes of Hidalgo's removal are not known, historians speculate that financial mismanagement, gambling, heterodox thinking, or his well-known affairs with women were responsible. He is known to have fathered several children.

Hidalgo was transferred to San Felipe near Guanajuato, and in 1803 to the prosperous town of Dolores. A landowner, educator, and restless reformer, Hidalgo devoted much of his time to stimulating industrial development at Dolores, introducing a pottery works, a brick factory, mulberry trees for silkworms, a tannery, an olive grove, apiaries, and vineyards. He knew the French language, which was unusual for a Mexican cleric, read modern philosophy, learned Indian languages, and loved music. He spent much of his time in the nearby city of Guanajuato, where he was highly respected in intellectual circles. Some of Hidalgo's activities brought him into conflict with colonial administrators, and he was investigated on several occasions by the Inquisition.

Although it is not known exactly where Hidalgo began to support the idea of independence, he knew Ignacio ALLENDE before 1810, had many contacts with the 1809 conspirators of Valladolid, and probably attended secret meetings of disgruntled creoles at Guanajuato and Querétaro. Many creoles in the Bajío region would not forgive the Spaniards for the 1808 overthrow of Viceroy José de ITURRIGARAY. As with the 1809 conspiracy in Valladolid and other plots, the creole leaders planned to achieve their goals by mobilizing the Indian and mestizo populations. The denunciation of the Querétaro conspiracy by some of its participants caught Hidalgo, Allende, and the other leaders by surprise. Although Hidalgo had manufactured some lances at Dolores and developed ties with members of the local provincial militia units, the exposure of the plot forced him to initiate the revolt prematurely.

The revolt commenced on 16 September 1810 with Hidalgo leading his brother Mariano, Ignacio Allende, Juan ALDAMA, and a few others to free prisoners held at the local jail and to arrest the district subdelegate and seventeen Spanish residents. After gathering some militiamen and others who possessed arms, Hidalgo marched on San Miguel el Grande and Celaya, arresting European Spaniards and threatening to execute them if there was armed resistance. Under the banner of the Virgin of Guadalupe, the rebellion recruited large numbers of Indian and mestizo villagers and residents of haciendas armed with lances, machetes, slings, bows, agricultural implements, sticks, or stones. They joined what became a triumphant if anarchic progress from town to town.

Hidalgo's revolutionary program remained unclear, but he sanctioned the confiscation of Spanish wealth at the same time he claimed to support King Ferdinand VII. The *ayuntamiento* of Celaya and the rebel chiefs named Hidalgo supreme commander. At Guanajuato on 28 September 1810, armed resistance by Intendant Juan Antonio RIAÑO at the fortified Alhóndiga led to the massacre of royalists and looting of the city by Hidalgo's followers and local plebeian elements. After taking some preliminary steps toward creating a new government, an organized army, a cannon foundry, and a mint, Hidalgo and his enormous force—estimated to be 60,000 strong—moved to the city of Valladolid, Morelia, which was occupied without resistance.

Declared generalíssimo, Hidalgo marched toward Mexico City by way of Toluca. On 30 October 1810, the inchoate rebel masses confronted a fairly well-disciplined royalist force commanded by Torcuato Trujillo. Following the battle of Monte de las Cruces, the royalists withdrew, granting a theoretical victory to the insurgents, but the green rebel troops had suffered such heavy casualties that many deserted. Hidalgo hesitated until 2 Novem-

Portrait of Miguel Hidalgo y Costilla. Oil on canvas by José Ines Tovilla, 1912. (Museo Nacional de Historia, Mexico)

ber before abandoning his plan to occupy the capital, realizing that his forces needed better military discipline, munitions, and weaponry. From this point, Hidalgo and Allende led a peripatetic march to disastrous rebel defeats by the royalist Army of the Center, commanded by Félix CALLEJA, at Aculco (7 November), Guanajuato (25 November), and Puente de Calderón, near Guadalajara (17 January 1811). After each battlefield defeat, the rebel forces dispersed, abandoning artillery, equipment, and transport.

Hidalgo did not fully formulate his ideas about independence or the form of government that was to replace the colonial regime, and he failed to develop a strategic plan to fight the war. At Guadalajara, however, he appointed ministers of justice and state, and he named a plenipotentiary to the United States. He abolished slavery, ended the unpopular tribute tax for Indians, and suspended the state monopolies of paper and gunpowder. The availability of a press at Guadalajara permitted the insurgents to publish a paper, *El Despertador Americano,* in which they disseminated their ideas and responded to royalist propaganda. Despite these advances, Hidalgo's dependence upon the lower classes and willingness to condone the cold-blooded slaughter of Spanish prisoners polarized the population and compelled the great majority of creoles to espouse the royalist cause.

Notwithstanding the continued popularity of Hidalgo and the rebellion, by the beginning of 1811 it was obvious that the military advantage rested with the royalist armies of Calleja and José de la Cruz. At Guadalajara, Allende opposed a definitive battlefield confrontation and proposed the division of the poorly armed and inexperienced rebel forces into several groups. This proposal was quite logical, but Hidalgo believed that the enormous numbers in the rebel force at Guadalajara—estimated by some historians at over 100,000 men—would overrun the royalists. However, in the six-hour battle at Puente de Calderón, the royalists annihilated the main force of the rebel army, freeing Calleja and other royalist commanders to pursue remaining rebel concentrations.

The senior insurgent leaders fled north with Hidalgo to Zacatecas. Differences between Hidalgo and the more moderate Allende had broken out previously, but even stronger denunciations followed in the wake of the disastrous military defeats. At the hacienda of Pabellón, near Aguascalientes, Allende replaced Hidalgo as the senior political and military chief of the rebellion. In the march across Coahuila to seek assistance in the United States, Hidalgo and his senior commanders were surprised and captured. Sent to Chihuahua for trial, Hidalgo was defrocked and executed by firing squad.

His head was sent with those of Allende, Aldama, and Mariano Jiménez to be displayed in iron cages at the four corners of the Alhóndiga of Guanajuato. Following independence, Hidalgo's remains were reinterred in Mexico City.

– CHRISTON I. ARCHER

HIPPOLYTE, DOMINIQUE

Dominique Hippolyte, (pseudonym, Pierre Breville; *b.* 4 August 1889; *d.* 8 April 1967), Haitian writer and lawyer. Hippolyte anticipated the themes of the Indigenist School. Besides nature and love, he demonstrated close knowledge of peasant beliefs. As a student, he acted in a play by Massillon COICOU and was deeply affected by the execution of the Coicou brothers in 1908. Patriotic disapproval of the U.S. occupation of Haiti (1915–1934) is to be found both in his poetry and in the drama *Le forçat* (1933). Hippolyte early introduced the poetry of the black American Countee Cullen in *La revue indigène,* helping to make the Harlem Renaissance known among Haitian intellectuals. He is the outstanding Haitian playwright of the first half of the twentieth century.

Hippolyte was trained in law and eventually was named *bâtonnier* of the attorneys in Port-au-Prince. He served at one time as a *commissaire* in the civil court. He headed the Haitian Commission of Intellectual Cooperation and the Alliance Française of Port-au-Prince. Laval University awarded him an honorary doctorate.

– CAROL F. COATES

HOCHSCHILD, MAURICIO

Mauricio Hochschild (*b.* 17 February 1881; *d.* 1965), Bolivian tin magnate. A naturalized Argentine citizen of Jewish ancestry who was born in Biblis, Germany, Hochschild emigrated to Chile in 1911. Twenty years later he was one of three tin barons of the Bolivian oligarchy (the Rosca) whose economic, social, and political privilege dominated the country until 1952. His mines, the second-largest tin producers, averaged 25 percent of Bolivia's total tin output after World War II and provided most of the ore sold to the United States. Hochschild influenced public opinion through his La Paz newspaper, *Última Hora.*

A mining engineer educated at Freiburg University, Hochschild was a metals broker until depressed tin prices after World War I enabled him to buy up bankrupt mines. By 1911 he had acquired the Minera Unificada del Cerro de Potosí; subsequently he consolidated the Compañía Minera de Oruro and the San José, Itos, Colquiri, and Matilde mines into the Hochschild

Group. He narrowly escaped the animosity of the military socialist governments of Germán BUSCH, who ordered him shot for opposing the 1939 mining law, and of Gualberto VILLARROEL, who had him kidnapped. The 1952 revolution nationalized his mining properties.

— WALTRAUD QUEISER MORALES

HOLANDA, SÉRGIO BUARQUE DE

Sérgio Buarque de Holanda (*b*. 11 July 1902; *d*. 24 April 1982), Brazilian historian. Born in São Paulo, Holanda was the son of a civil servant who had migrated there from the former Dutch colony of Pernambuco, a fact reflected by his surname. After completing his secondary education in São Paulo, Holanda left for Rio de Janeiro in 1921 to attend law school. In Rio he abandoned his legal studies for a precarious career as an essayist, literary critic, and free-lance journalist. He became part of the "modernist" movement, which rejected Portuguese formalism and exalted Brazilian popular culture. Holanda's writings attracted the attention of São Paulo press lord Assis Chateaubriand, who sent him to Germany as correspondent for his newspaper *O Jornal*. In Berlin in 1929–1930 Holanda familiarized himself with the main trends of German historiography and social science and developed a taste for the works of Max Weber. In Germany, Holanda felt the call to write a history of Brazil, to explain his country to the world. The result was *Raízes do Brasil* (Roots of Brazil) published in Brazil in 1936, after his return from Europe.

Holanda introduced the concept of the "cordial man"—the predominant Brazilian political type, the leader who prefers conciliation to confrontation.

In *Raízes do Brasil* Holanda introduces the concept of the "cordial man"—the predominant Brazilian political type, the leader who prefers conciliation to confrontation. The cordial interaction of its leaders, according to Holanda, enabled Brazil to survive and expand on a fragmented continent, but thwarted necessary social change. The book launched Holanda on an academic career that culminated with his tenure as professor of the history of Brazilian civilization at the University of São Paulo from 1957 to 1969. His other major works include *Monções* (Monsoons [1945]), a study of westward movement from São Paulo; *Caminhos e Fronteiras* (Roads and Frontiers [1957]), a cultural in-

terpretation of Brazilian colonial expansion; and *Visão do paraíso* (Vision of Paradise [1959]), an analysis of the images that drew colonists to the frontiers of Brazil. Holanda is the general editor of the first six volumes of the *História geral da civilização brasileira* (General History of Brazilian Civilization [1960–1971]) and the sole author of volume seven, *Do império à república* (From the Empire to the Republic [1972]).

— NEILL MACAULAY

HOLGUÍN, JORGE

Jorge Holguín (*b*. 30 October 1848; *d*. 2 March 1928), Colombian statesman who twice served as acting president (1909 and 1921–1922). Born in Cali, Holguín was well connected socially and politically. He was a nephew of Manuel María Mallarino (1808–1872), who was president from 1855 to 1857, and the younger brother of Carlos Holguín, who served as chief executive from 1888 to 1892. His wife, Cecilia, was the daughter of Conservative paladin Julio ARBOLEDA.

Like his kinsmen, Jorge became involved in Conservative politics, fighting in the revolution of 1876–1877 and serving as a party director in the 1880s. During the Conservative-dominated regeneration, he served in the senate and in the cabinets of Miguel Antonio CARO and Manuel A. Sanclemente. A long-time supporter of Rafael REYES, Holguín was a member of the commission headed by Reyes that unsuccessfully sought redress from the United States after the secession of Panama in 1903. During Reyes's presidency, Holguín negotiated an agreement with foreign bondholders (1905) that revived Colombia's international credit. When Reyes was forced from power in mid-1909, he designated Holguín to serve as president until a successor was chosen. Holguín again served as chief executive upon the resignation of Marco Fidel SUÁREZ in 1921.

— HELEN DELPAR

HOLZMANN, RODOLFO

Rodolfo Holzmann (*b*. 27 November 1910; *d*. 4 April 1992), Peruvian composer and ethnomusicologist. Born in Breslau, Germany, Holzmann began his music studies at age six and moved to Berlin in 1931 to study with Wladimir Vogel (composition), Winfried Wolf (piano), and Robert Robitschek (conducting). In 1933 he participated in the Session of Musical Studies organized by Hermann Scherchen in Strasbourg, taking conducting lessons with Scherchen. He later moved to Paris to study with Karol Rathaus (1934) and attended the twelfth festival of the International Society of Contemporary Music in Florence, Italy. He also studied oboe at the

Zurich Conservatory. In 1938 Holzmann moved to Lima, where he was professor of oboe at the Alzedo Academy of Music as well as the violinist for the National Symphony. In 1945 he became professor of composition at the National Conservatory of Music in Lima, later becoming professor of orchestral conducting. He also taught at the University of Texas at Austin (1957–1958). His ethnomusicological studies of Peruvian music are among the most important in the twentieth century and have received worldwide praise. Among his compositions are orchestral works, choral music, chamber music, and an extensive collection of songs based on Spanish and Peruvian melodies. He died in Lima.

— SUSANA SALGADO

HOMAR, LORENZO

Lorenzo Homar (*b.* 1913), Puerto Rican graphic artist. Homer, a native of San Juan, migrated to New York with his family in 1928. His early training was in design; he worked for Cartier from 1937 until 1950. He took courses at the Art Students' League (1931) and Pratt Institute (1940). In 1946, after military service, Homar attended the Brooklyn Museum Art School, where he studied with RUFINO TAMAYO and Arthur Osver and came into contact with Ben Shahn. Returning to Puerto Rico in 1950, Homar founded the Center for Puerto Rican Art (CAP) with Rafael Tufiño and José A. Torres Martinó. CAP was part of a movement to create a national art that was both accessible and contemporary.

In 1951 Homar began working with the Division of Community Education, which produced educational materials, including silk-screen posters, books, and films, for Puerto Rico's rural population. He became the director of its graphics workshop in 1952. Awarded a Guggenheim fellowship in 1956, Homar returned to New York. From 1957 to 1973, he headed the graphic arts workshop at the Institute for Puerto Rican Culture and trained many of the island's most prominent printmakers in xylography, silk screen, and other techniques. In 1970 Homar was one of the organizers of the first Bienal de San Juan del Grabado Latinoamericano. He established his own workshop in 1973. He has been awarded numerous prizes, and his work has been shown internationally.

— MIRIAM BASILIO

HOSTOS Y BONILLA, EUGENIO MARÍA DE

Eugenio María de Hostos y Bonilla (*b.* 11 January 1839; *d.* 11 August 1903), Puerto Rican philosopher, sociologist, educator, patriot, and man of letters. Born in Río Cañas, Hostos attended elementary school in San Juan, secondary school at the Institute of Balboa in Spain, and enrolled in law school in Madrid. He joined the Spanish republican movement and gained their promise of independence for Puerto Rico and Cuba. When the republicans abandoned that promise, Hostos moved to the United States in 1869.

In New York, he joined the Cuban Revolutionary Junta and became managing editor of its official periodical. Realizing that Cuban independence could not be fought from New York, he began a four-year journey in 1870 that would take him throughout South America to win support for the independence cause. Long an advocate of abolition of slavery and of Antillean federation after independence, Hostos involved himself during his travels with various social injustices. In Lima, his writings proved instrumental in turning public opinion against the mistreatment of Chinese laborers and against the Oroya railway project, despite the fact

Eugenio María de Hostos y Bonilla. (Library of Congress)

that its builders offered to donate $200,000 to the movement. In 1872, he taught at the University of Chile in Santiago, where his writings helped gain women the right of admission to professional programs. While in Argentina in 1873, he became a spokesman for a transandean railroad to Chile. In honor of his efforts, the first locomotive to complete the journey was named the *Eugenio María de Hostos.*

In 1875, he settled in Santo Domingo, where he founded a newspaper that echoed one of his strongest dreams, a federation of the Hispanic West Indies. After a brief trip to Venezuela where he married, he returned to Santo Domingo and revamped the education system, introducing the scientific method to the curriculum. He stated that the only revolution that had not taken place in Latin America was in education and he added the reformation of educational systems to his political agenda. After a disagreement with the Dominican dictator, Ulises HEUREAUX in 1888, he accepted an invitation from officials to return to Chile and reform its educational system.

Hostos returned to New York in 1898 and for two years unsuccessfully agitated for a plebiscite to determine the future status of Puerto Rico, even participating in a delegation that presented demands to President William McKinley. After the assassination of Heureaux, he returned to the Dominican Republic as inspector general of schools.

Hostos wrote fifty books and numerous essays. The impact of his novel, *La peregrinación de Bayoán,* is said to be as profound for Cuban independence as *Uncle Tom's Cabin* was for the abolitionist movement in the United States. His treatise on the scientific education of women made him a precursor of later feminist causes and his political writings made him a forerunner of the doctrine of self-determination in his homeland. It is said that no national literature evolved in the Dominican Republic until after his service to that country. His educational endeavors included founding schools, writing textbooks, and authoring the laws governing education. He wrote best of his own beliefs when he said in *La peregrinación,* "I wish that they will say: In that Island [Puerto Rico] a man was born who loved truth, desired justice, and worked for the good of men."

— JACQUELYN BRIGGS KENT

HOUSSAY, BERNARDO A.

Bernardo A. Houssay (*b.* 10 April 1887; *d.* 21 September 1971), Argentine physiologist, teacher, and researcher, Latin America's first Nobel laureate in science. Born to a French family in Buenos Aires, Houssay studied and, beginning in 1910, taught medicine at the University of Buenos Aires. In 1919 he was named professor of physiology and director of the Institute of Physiology. In 1933, at the initiative of the "Houssay group," the Asociación Argentina para el Progreso de las Ciencias was founded; it played a commanding role in obtaining and disbursing funding for Argentine scientific research. With his associates and hundreds of other intellectuals, Houssay was dismissed by the military government in 1943; he later clashed with President Juan PERÓN. Out of official favor, he continued his research under private auspices. By the late 1940s his writings on endocrinology, nutrition, physiology, pharmacology, diabetes, and medical education gained him an international reputation. Honors and awards culminated in 1947 in the Nobel Prize in physiology or medicine (shared with Carl F. and Gerty T. Cori), awarded to him in recognition of his research on the role of the pituitary gland in carbohydrate metabolism—research that pointed the way toward alternatives to insulin. Houssay served as president of the National Council for Scientific and Technical Research and remained professionally active until his death. His works include *Concepto de la universidad* (1940), *La crisis actual y bases para el adelanto de la universidad* (1943), *Human Physiology* (1965), and *La emigración de científicos, profesionales, y technicos de la Argentina* (1966).

— RONALD C. NEWTON

HUASCAR

Huascar (*b.* ca. 1495; *d.* 1532), son of Inca HUAYNA CAPAC. Huascar, born near Cuzco, had one of the most legitimate claims to leadership of Tahuantinsuyu at the time of the death (1525) of his father, for his mother was the primary wife Ragua Ocllo. In accordance with their customs, the Inca elite in Cuzco quickly performed the religious ceremonies acknowledging the assumption of power of the new ruler.

Half brother ATAHUALPA, who according to some had been named as one of the successors during the fevered last days of Huayna Capac, refused to come to Cuzco for the celebrations, preferring instead to remain in the Quito district with the large military force that had helped subjugate the area. The ill-treatment accorded the emissaries Atahualpa sent to Huascar led to open hostilities between the two factions. Atahualpa's army, under capable leaders Quizquiz and Chalicuchima, moved southward, and finally Chalicuchima succeeded in capturing Huascar outside Cuzco. By then the Cañaris, a northern ethnic group who strongly supported the Huascar faction, had been thoroughly beaten. General Quizquiz went on to march into the capital of Cuzco and attempt to destroy completely Huascar's supporters.

It was at this juncture that the Europeans under Francisco PIZARRO entered the Andean highlands and captured Atahualpa at Cajamarca on 16 November 1532. Atahualpa, fearing that the Spaniards might attempt to supplant him and rule through Huascar, ordered the execution of his half brother. The escort that was accompanying Huascar from Cuzco to Cajamarca carried out the orders at Andamarca, between Huamachuco and Huaylas. Huascar's demise was followed within months by the Spanish execution of Atahualpa on 26 July 1533, thus bringing to an end the effective independence of Tahuantinsuyu.

– NOBLE DAVID COOK

HUAYNA CAPAC

Huayna Capac (*b.* ca. 1488; *d.* ca. 1527), Inca emperor (ca. 1493–1527), the last undisputed ruler of the Inca empire. The son of the emperor Topa Inca and the grandson of the great Pachacuti, he ruled during the time of the first Spanish contact with Andean South America. During his reign the empire was extended northward to the Ancasmayo River, the present boundary between modern Colombia and Ecuador. Although the extent of Huayna Capac's conquests were substantially less than those of his father and grandfather, they took much longer; he was absent from the capital at Cuzco for nearly twenty years. His prolonged absence and his preference for maintaining his royal court in the city of Quito, far to the north of the imperial capital, eventually generated a schism within the Inca state.

Huayna Capac died suddenly during one of the great plagues brought to the New World by the Europeans. His presumptive heir, Ninan Cuyochi, also died about the same time, leaving the succession unclear. As a result, two of Huayna Capac's sons, HUASCAR, who was in Cuzco, and Atahualpa, who had been with his father in the north, initiated the civil war that greatly weakened the empire just prior to its conquest by Francisco PIZARRO.

– GORDON F. MCEWAN

HUERTA, VICTORIANO

Victoriano Huerta (*b.* 23 March 1845; *d.* 13 January 1916), general and president of Mexico (1913–1914). Huerta is best known for his role in the overthrow and death of President Francisco I. MADERO (1873–1913).

He was born in Colotlán, Jalisco, the son of a cavalry soldier and a Huichol Indian. He studied in the state capital, Guadalajara, before graduating from the National Military College as a construction engineer in 1876. As a career army officer he gained the rank of colonel in 1894, was promoted to brigadier general in 1901, and became division general in 1912. He headed the Third Infantry Battalion (1894–1901); fought Mayas in Yucatán under General Ignacio A. Bravo (1835–1918) in 1903; served as head of public works in the state government of General Bernardo Reyes (1850–1913) in Monterrey, Nuevo León (1905–1909); battled Zapatistas in Morelos and Guerrero in 1911; escorted President Porfirio DÍAZ into exile at Veracruz in 1911; and defeated the Pascual OROZCO rebellion in 1912.

In February 1913, upon the outbreak in Mexico City of the antigovernment rebellion led by Félix DÍAZ, Manuel Mondragón, and Bernardo Reyes, President Francisco Madero named Huerta military commander in charge of all progovernment forces. During the ensuing events, including the battle that devastated large portions of central Mexico City, known as the *decena trágica*, or tragic ten days (9–19 February 1913), Huerta conspired against Madero. With U.S. Ambassador Henry Lane Wilson acting as mediator, Huerta made a pact (El Pacto de la Embajada [Pact of the Embassy]) with the rebels in which he agreed to join forces with them in return for the provisional presidency. Subsequently, Huerta forced Madero and Vice President José María PINO SUÁREZ to resign. Although there is no direct evidence to substantiate it, he apparently ordered them shot on 22 February 1913.

Huerta's closing of the national congress, his persecution and killing of opponents, and his manipulation of the October 1913 vote all took their toll.

Huerta's call for recognition of his government met with three important opponents. One was Emiliano ZAPATA, whose followers continued their antigovernment struggle for land begun during the Madero administration. The second was the governor of Coahuila, Venustiano CARRANZA, who on 26 March 1913 issued his Plan de Guadalupe condemning Huerta's illegitimate rise to power and calling for his overthrow. Soon the Carrancistas and Zapatistas posed a significant challenge to Huerta in the north and south of the country, respectively. Huerta's third opponent was the newly elected U.S. president, Woodrow Wilson, who took office in early March 1913. He immediately removed pro-

Huerta Ambassador Henry Lane Wilson and refused to grant diplomatic recognition to the Huerta government.

The brutal and authoritarian nature of Huerta's rule undermined what support he had, except among hardcore conservatives and the Catholic church. His closing of the national congress, his persecution and killing of opponents, his manipulation of the October 1913 vote to elect himself constitutional president, and his militarization of society to combat Carrancistas and Zapatistas all took their toll. In April 1914 Woodrow Wilson ordered U.S. forces to occupy the port of Veracruz, thus substantially reducing Huerta's income and ability to import arms.

On 15 July 1914, with opposing armies led by Zapata, Álvaro OBREGÓN, Francisco "Pancho" VILLA, and Pablo GONZÁLEZ bearing down on Mexico City, Huerta fled the country. He lived in London, England, and Barcelona, Spain, before sailing for New York in March 1915. With the backing of anti-Carrancista Mexicans and the German government, Huerta hoped to raise a force in the United States that would return him to power. While traveling by train to El Paso, Texas, on 27 June 1915, U.S. agents arrested Huerta and fellow conspirator Pascual Orozco in Newman, New Mexico. Huerta was then incarcerated at Fort Bliss, Texas, where he died of cirrhosis of the liver.

Twentieth-century Mexican historiography generally portrays Huerta as the demon of the Mexican Revolution of 1910. His brutality, cynicism, and abuse of alcohol and allegedly of drugs are constantly cited. He is accused of ending the nation's experiment in democracy and of attempting to return it to the dark days of the Porfirio Díaz dictatorship (1876–1911). All revolutionaries and their actions are measured against Huerta's regime. In this way, Huerta has served as an important counterpoint, allowing for diverse political and socioeconomic factions to join under the banner of the Revolution. Nevertheless, at least one important study claims that Huerta's administration was not as conservative as the Díaz regime in several areas, including agrarian reform, labor, church policy, and foreign relations, and even more progressive in some of these areas than subsequent, so-called revolutionary governments.

– DAVID LAFRANCE

HUERTAS, ESTEBAN

Esteban Huertas (*b.* 1876; *d.* 1943), Panamanian general and a key figure in the independence of Panama. He was born in Umbita, Boyacá, Columbia, and went into the army at an early age. He was sent to Panama and participated in the War of the Thousand Days,

fighting in the province of Coclé. In October 1903 the Columbian government, nervous about the revolutionary activities in Panama, sent the Tiradores battalion, under the command of Generals Juan B. Tobar and Ramón G. Amaya, to relieve Huertas as military commander because they believed that he was conspiring with the revolutionaries. When General Tobar arrived in Panama City with his officers on 3 November, Huertas had them arrested. Once the news of the arrests reached the revolutionaries, they declared for independence. When the army was abolished after independence, Huertas was given the title of Hero of the Fatherland.

– JUAN MANUEL PÉREZ

HUIDOBRO FERNÁNDEZ, VICENTE

Vicente Huidobro Fernández (*b.* 10 January 1893; *d.* 2 January 1948), Chilean poet. The principal figure of the avant-garde movement in Latin American literature, Huidobro was born in Santiago to an aristocratic family; his privileged upbringing included education in Chilean private schools. In 1916 Huidobro moved to Paris, where he started publishing the most innovative poetry in the Spanish language. He was a cofounder, with the French poets Guillaume Apollinaire and Pierre Reverdy, of the literary review *Nord-Sud* (1917–1918), and along with Max Jacob, Paul Dermée, and the cubist painters Juan Gris and Pablo Picasso, helped design a new spatial poetry that used calligrammatic and ideogrammatic forms. His personal poetic style, which he called creationism, was a modality that emphasized the autonomy of poetic expression, a result of the transformation of external referents and of laws of grammar and "sense," and created its own images, descriptions, and concepts. In 1918 he brought fresh air to Spanish poetry with four volumes published in Madrid, *Poemas árticos, Ecuatorial, Tour Eiffel,* and *Hallali.*

The Spanish poets Gerardo Diego and Juan LARREA were his most faithful and direct disciples, but many other young poets imitated his creationist poetry. As a consequence of his influence, the literary movement Ultra was developed by Rafael Cansinos-Asséns and Guillermo de Torre. Ultraism was developed also in Buenos Aires by Jorge Luis BORGES, and Imagism arose in Chile, Simplicism in Peru, and Estridentism in Mexico. During the 1920s, Huidobro published three books in French: *Saisons choisies* (1921), *Tout à coup* (1925), and *Automne régulier* (1924). The most genial poetic expression of Huidobro is *Altazor; o, El viaje en paracaídas* (1931), a poem in seven cantos, which narrates a simultaneous flight and fall through seven regions, equating death with mystical experience. The work constitutes a poetic Babel, employing a variety of poetic languages that intimates both a plenitude of meaning and the gradual destruction of language. *Altazor* stands as an extraordinary example of the poetic avant garde. *Temblor de cielo* (1931), a prose poem written simultaneously with *Altazor,* deals with the meaning of life under the Nietzschean concept of the death of God. Huidobro's later poetic works include *Ver y palpar* (1941) and *El ciudadano del olvido* (1941). In these books his creative ingenuity manifests itself in whimsical as well as tragic visions of life and world. His last poems were collected in *Últimos poemas* (1948), published posthumously.

Huidobro's life in Paris, Madrid, and Santiago touched in various ways the literary cultures of these cities. Contacts with cubist poets and painters and with dadaists in Paris, with ultraists in Madrid, with the younger groups of Runrunists and Mandrágora in Santiago, all speak of his wide-ranging ability to disseminate the forms and concepts of the new poetry. The general content of *Nord-Sud, Índice de poesía americana nueva* (1926), and *Antología de poesía chilena nueva* (1935) marks the breadth and significance of his influence. In 1925 he published *Manifestes,* a collection of essays on creationism and poetic theory. Huidobro also contributed significantly to the renewal of narrative forms with his *hazaña* (heroic feat) *Mío Cid Campeador* (1929), his film-novel *Cagliostro* (1934), *Papá; o, El diario de Alicia Mir* (1934), *La próxima: Historia que pasó en un tiempo más* (1934), *Sátiro; o, El poder de las palabras* (1938) (*Satyr; or, The Power of Words,* [1939]), and *Tres inmensas novelas* (1935) in collaboration with the German poet Hans Arp. His collections of essays include *Pasando y pasando* (1914), *Finis Britannia!* (1923), and *Vientos contrarios* (1926). Huidobro also wrote two plays, *Gilles de Raíz* (1932), in French, and *En la luna* (1934).

– CEDOMIL GOIC

HURTADO DE MENDOZA, ANDRÉS

Andrés Hurtado de Mendoza (marquis of Cañete), viceroy of Peru (ca. 1556–1561). The marquis of Cañete arrived in Peru with the express purpose of strengthening royal authority, which had been lessened by four years of rule by the *audiencia*, the high court of Lima that held executive power within the colony in the absence of a viceroy. As part of this effort, a rival *audiencia* and administrative network for Upper Peru were established in Charcas in 1559. Committed to solidifying the crown's power over Peru's Indian population, Cañete sought to claim lands and reclaim labor service that had been granted to local elites through *encomiendas*

(grants of Indian labor). The opening of the mercury mines of Huancavelica in 1560 increased the demand for Indian labor, and Cañete became the first viceroy responsible for the production and transportation of Huancavelica mercury to the colony's silver mines, particularly Potosí.

– ANN M. WIGHTMAN

HURTADO DE MENDOZA, GARCÍA

García Hurtado de Mendoza (*b.* 1535; *d.* 1609), Spanish conquistador, governor of Chile, and viceroy of Peru. Hurtado de Mendoza was the second son of the marqués de Cañete (a title he eventually inherited). His father, then viceroy of Peru, appointed him governor of Chile. He arrived there in 1557 and almost immediately launched offensives against the Araucanians of the south, whom he defeated in the battles of Lagunillas (Bío-bío) and Millarapue. After founding the new settlement of Cañete, he ventured further south, where he discovered the archipelago of CHILOÉ and founded Osorno (1558). In December 1558 he won another victory over the Araucanians at Quiapo. The governor also sent ships to explore the Strait of Magellan and an expedition across the Andes to conquer Cuyo: the Argentine city of Mendoza (founded in 1561) is named after him.

Dismissed from the governorship by King Philip II (1527–1528) (his father was concurrently stripped of office), Hurtado de Mendoza left Chile in February 1561. The king later restored him to favor and made him viceroy of Peru (1588–1596). Hurtado de Mendoza was a celebrated figure in his own time: two plays were written to eulogize his exploits, one of them, *El Arauco domado,* by Lope de Vega.

– SIMON COLLIER

HURTADO LARREA, OSVALDO

Osvaldo Hurtado Larrea (*b.* 26 June 1939), president of Ecuador (1981–1983). After completing secondary education in Riobamba, Hurtado entered the Catholic University in Quito, where he became a political activist, eventually emerging as a leader of the Christian Democratic Party (PDC). After completing a doctorate, he taught political sociology at the Catholic University in Quito and published widely on the need for structural reform. In 1971 he drafted a detailed party program that emphasized structural and social reforms to promote national development and integration. In 1978 the military government appointed Hurtado chairman of the commission charged with revising electoral legislation in preparation for a return to civilian rule.

In the 1978–1979 presidential election, Hurtado, whose coalition was not allowed on the ballot, ran as the vice presidential candidate on the Concentración de Fuerzas Populares (CFP) ticket with Jaime ROLDÓS AGUILERA. Their successful issue-oriented campaign inaugurated a new phase in Ecuadorian electoral politics. They represented a new generation of political leaders, whose desire to expand the electorate, strengthen democratic institutions, and implement planned national development, threatened traditional political and economic elites.

When Jaime Roldós died in a plane crash on 24 May 1981, Hurtado became president. He inherited a severe budgetary crisis precipitated by the decline of the world price of petroleum and by growing opposition from organized labor—who opposed the government's commitment to fiscal restraint—and from business groups—who opposed the expansion of the state and its growing autonomy in economic policy-making. Although the domestic and international economic situation prevented Hurtado from achieving most of his reform program, he was able to complete his term and peacefully transfer power to a democratically elected successor.

— LINDA ALEXANDER RODRÍGUEZ

HYPPOLITE, HECTOR

Hector Hyppolite (*b.* 16 September 1894; *d.* 1948), Haitian painter and VODUN priest. Hyppolite led a simple, hard life in rural Haiti until he was discovered in 1944 by the European surrealist poet and art connoisseur André Breton and the Haitian art patron DeWitt Peters. Hyppolite's primitive paintings brought him immediate international attention and introduced the world to Haitian folk culture. His works were exhibited at a UNESCO show in Paris in 1947 and have spawned many imitators. The paintings of Hector Hyppolite are noted for their free, bold colors, their technical naïvete, and themes drawn from Haiti's unique, syncretic religion and vodun customs. Today his work hangs in many of the world's finest galleries.

— KAREN RACINE

HYPPOLITE, LOUIS MODESTIN FLORVILLE

Louis Modestin Florville Hyppolite (*b.* ca. 1827; *d.* 24 March 1896), president of Haiti (1889–1896). On 9 October 1889 the Haitian Constituent Assembly elected Florville Hyppolite to the Haitian presidency following his successful revolt against the government of François Denys Légitime. The United States had supplied weapons in support of Hyppolite against his French-backed opponent and expected the new president to reward its generosity with a naval station in Haiti. But Haitian national pride more than the resistance of Hyppolite blocked U.S. acquisition of the harbor at Môle Saint-Nicholas. Many U.S. newspapers of the time blamed U.S. Ambassador to Haiti Frederick Douglass rather than recognize this fact.

In 1893 Hyppolite scored a diplomatic triumph by appointing Frederick Douglass to represent Haiti at the World's Columbian Exposition of 1893 in Chicago.

Hyppolite, though a black and from the north, had leanings toward the mulatto-dominated Liberal Party. On the domestic scene, his greatest achievements were public-works projects, especially those involving communication and transportation. Hyppolite's biggest domestic problems, however, were heavy internal debt and French infringements on Haitian sovereignty. He found no solutions. He forced the French embassy to cease its practices of granting French citizenship to Haitians of proven Gallic ancestry. This had been a mulatto ploy to dodge Haitian law, but it became a Pyrrhic victory when Hyppolite borrowed 50 million francs from France to redeem his internal debt.

In 1893 Hyppolite scored a diplomatic triumph by appointing Frederick Douglass to represent Haiti at the World's Columbian Exposition of 1893 in Chicago. The old abolitionist had frequently expressed pride in Haiti but never to the extent that it confused his ambassadorial duties (1889–1891). Three years later Hyppolite died during a coup against his government.

— THOMAS O. OTT

I

IANNI, OCTAVIO

Octavio Ianni (*b.* 13 October 1926), Brazilian sociologist. Ianni, a native of Itu, São Paulo, taught at the university of São Paulo. In 1950 he worked with Florestan Fernandes and Fernando Henrique Cardoso, doing research on race relations sponsored by UNESCO. After teaching in the United States (1967), England (1969), and Mexico (1968–1973), Ianni returned to Brazil in 1977. He then taught at the Pontifical Catholic University of São Paulo and the State University of Campinas.

Ianni's writings include *Estado e capitalismo no Brasil* (1965), *Raças e classes sociais no Brasil* (1966), *Sociologia da sociologia latino-americana* (1971), *Sociologia e sociedade no Brasil* (1975), *Escravidão e racismo* (1978), *O ABC da classe operária* (1980), *A ditadura do grande capital* (1981), and *Origens agrárias do estado brasileiro* (1984).

— ELIANA MARIA REA GOLDSCHMIDT

IBÁÑEZ, ROBERTO

Roberto Ibáñez (*b.* 1902), Uruguayan poet, writer, literary critic, politician, educator, and husband of Sara de IBÁÑEZ. Among his important positions were director of the National Institute of Literary Investigations and Archives and editor of *Anden*. Although his poetry was published as early as 1925, in the work *Olas,* it is his 1939 collection, *Mitología de la sangre,* that is the most memorable, with its controlled technical virtuosity and vivid representation of psychological suffering, nostalgia for infancy, and horror of existence. In other collections Ibáñez treats the creative process and the sense of his own totality: "La poesía es el testimonio de mi ser" (Poetry is the testimony of my being). *La frontera* (1966) won the prestigious prize of Cuba's Casa de las Américas.

Other major works by Ibáñez are *La danza de los horizontes* (1927), *La leyenda patria y su contorno histórico* (1959), and *Americanismo y modernismo* (1968). With Esther de CÁCERES and Fernando de Pereda, Ibáñez is a major representative of the Ultraist school of literature.

— WILLIAM H. KATRA

IBÁÑEZ, SARA DE

Sara de Ibáñez (*b.* 1905; *d.* 1971), Uruguayan poet, literary critic, and educator. Born Sara Iglesias Casadei in Tacuarembó, she married Roberto IBÁÑEZ in 1928. In 1940 she produced her most important collection of poetry, *Canto*. With a prologue by Pablo NERUDA, it won the top prize in a Montevideo poetry competition in 1941 because of its wide range of vocabulary and its classical purity of form. Most distinguished among Ibáñez's eight other poetry publications is the epic poem *Canto a Artigas* (1952), which won a prestigious prize from Uruguay's National Academy of Letters.

Ibáñez in much of her work allows often dark symbolism, ornate expression, and attention to lyrical technique to predominate over human issues.

Some of Ibáñez's poems reveal nature and the inner soul as sources of inspiration. A poet's poet, Ibáñez in much of her work allows often dark symbolism, ornate expression, and attention to lyrical technique to predominate over human issues. A key theme of her verses is the anguished rift between physical and spiritual love. Additional sources of inspiration are historical themes and nature.

Ibáñez's major works include *Canto a Montevideo* (1941), *La batalla* (1967), and *Canto póstumo* (1973). She was acclaimed as a major poet by Gabriela MISTRAL, Carlos Drummond de ANDRADE, Manuel BANDEIRA, and Cecilia MEIRELES.

— WILLIAM H. KATRA

IBÁÑEZ DEL CAMPO, CARLOS

Carlos Ibáñez del Campo (*b.* 3 November 1877; *d.* 28 April 1960), Chilean army officer and president (1927–1931 and 1952–1958). Born in Linares, Ibáñez entered the Escuela Militar in Santiago in 1896. Two years later he was commissioned a second lieutenant and in 1900 he was promoted to first lieutenant. While a student at the Academia de Guerra, he was selected for the first El Salvador mission (1903) directed by Captain Juan Pablo Bennett. There he took charge of the new military school and formed the tiny nation's cavalry corps. Ibáñez won acclaim in the Central American country for his horsemanship and for taking part (against orders) in a minor battle between Salvadoran and Guatemalan forces in 1906, an adventure that made him the only Chilean officer to participate in a real war after 1883. He held the rank of colonel in El Salvador and made an advantageous marriage there to a young Salvadoran woman, Doña Rosa Quiroz Avila, with whom he returned to Chile in 1909.

Ibáñez served with the Cazadores cavalry regiment and then returned to the Academia de Guerra to complete his staff training. In 1914 he was on the staff of Division I, Tacna, and in 1919, now a major, was named police prefect in Iquique.

In 1921 President Arturo ALESSANDRI PALMA named Ibáñez director of the Cavalry School, where he came to know a number of political figures in the capital professionally and socially. He became involved with political affairs culminating in the military movements of 1924–1925 that resulted first in Alessandri's resignation and then his return. In 1925 Ibáñez became war minister, rising quickly from colonel to general. He quarreled frequently with Alessandri. In 1927, after brief stints as interior minister and vice president, he was elected president under the new 1925 Constitution. Then a widower, he married his second wife, Graciela Letellier, during his presidency.

Ibáñez's authoritarian administration (1927–1931) borrowed heavily from abroad to finance public works projects. He manipulated a spuriously elected Congress, brooked no political opposition, and applied the new constitution selectively, thus enhancing the powers of the executive branch. He involved the state in public health, communications, education, economic development, welfare, social security, and transportation more than ever before. His administration's economic policies made Chile vulnerable to the worldwide economic collapse, thus weakening his position and undermining his popularity by 1930.

Ibáñez resigned the presidency in 1931 during a general strike. He lived for a time in Argentina, returned to Chile, and was a contender for the Popular Front presidential candidacy of 1938 until his association with Chilean fascists became an embarrassment. He remained politically active in the 1940s and served as senator before being elected to a second term as president (1952–1958), as the candidate of a broad coalition of independent groups, small parties, and the corporativist Agrarian Labor Party. His repeated attempts to manipulate the army did not help him in any way and restored democratic processes precluded any return to the "good old days" of strong executive leadership. He died two years after turning the presidency over to Jorge Alessandri Rodríguez, son of his old nemesis.

— FREDERICK M. NUNN

IBARBOUROU, JUANA DE

Juana de Ibarbourou (Juana Fernández Morales; *b.* 8 March 1892; *d.* 1979), Uruguayan poet and fiction writer. Born in Melo, she was educated in a convent and later in the public-school system. In 1914 she married Captain Lucas Ibarbourou, with whom she had a child. In 1918 they moved to Montevideo, where she began to publish her poems in the literary section of *La Razón.* Her poems were so well received that the prestigious Argentine magazine *Caras y Caretas* dedicated an issue to her. *Las lenguas de diamante* was published in 1919 by the Argentine writer Manuel GÁLVEZ, then director of Editorial Buenos Aires.

Her poetry was first conceived within the modernist aesthetic, but with less ornamental language. *Raíz salvaje* (Wild Root, 1922) and *El cántaro fresco* (Fresh Pitcher, 1920) offer a more intimate tone, with themes of love, life, and the sensual pleasure of being alive. In 1929 the title of "Juana de America" was officially bestowed upon her by the Uruguayan public in a ceremony presided over by Juan ZORRILLA DE SAN MARTÍN, José Santos CHOCANO, and Alfonso REYES and attended by delegations from twenty Spanish American countries.

In *La rosa de los vientos* (Compass, 1930) Ibarbourou experiments with the language of earlier avant-garde writers. In 1934, two years after her father died, she published a volume of lyric prose with religious themes, *Loores de Nuestra Señora* (Praise to Our Lady), and another volume of works with similar concerns, *Estampas de la biblia* (Scenes from the Bible). She continued to be hailed throughout the continent. In 1944 she published *Chico Carlo,* a book of "memoirs" of her childhood, and in 1945 she wrote a children's play (*Los sueños de Natacha*). In 1947, Ibarbourou became a member of the Uruguayan Academy of Letters. *Perdida,* whose title came from D'Annunzio's chosen name for dancer Eleonore Duse, appeared in 1950. In this book, she renewed her seemingly diminished interest in poetry, and from then on she did not cease to write.

When her mother died, Ibarbourou became ill and depressed, a condition that lasted for some years and was a theme reflected in her poetry. At the same time, as Angel Rama has pointed out, she also continued to insist on frozen imagery, enabling the poetic voice to retain the past in an idealized construction, as shown in *Azor* (1953), *Romances del destino* (1955), *Oro y tormenta* (Gold and Storm, 1956), and *Elegía* (1967).

In 1957 a plenary session of UNESCO was organized in Montevideo to honor Ibarbourou. Attending as a representative of the poetry of Uruguay and of America, she presented her *Autobiografía lírica,* a recollection of some thirty-five years as a poet. Her *Obras completas*

Juana de Ibarbourou. Reproduced from Juana de Ibarbourou, *Estampas de la Biblia (Montevideo, 1934). (Courtesy of Harvard College Library)*

were first published in Spain in 1953 by Editorial Aguilar. Her other works are *La pasajera* (The Passenger, 1967) and *Juan Soldado* (Johnny Soldier, 1971).

Ibarbourou, who had enjoyed fame and a comfortable life, experienced considerable hardship in her later years. She died in Montevideo, poor and mostly forgotten by the very public that acclaimed her.

– MAGDALENA GARCÍA PINTO

IBARGÚENGOITIA, JORGE

Jorge Ibargúengoitia (*b.* 22 February 1928; *d.* 27 November 1983), Mexican novelist, playwright, and journalist. Ibargüengoitia was born in Guanajuato, studied engineering and drama at the National Autonomous University of Mexico (UNAM), and won scholarships from the Sociedad Mexicana de Escritors (1954, 1955) and the Rockefeller (1955) and Gusseheim (1969) foundations. Among his works are the imaginative novels *Los relámpagos de agosto* (1964), *La ley de Herodes*

(1967), and *Maten al león* (1969). His farcical comedies resemble those by Samuel Beckett and Harold Pinter: *Susana y los jóvenes* (1954), *Clotilde en su casa* (1955), and *Llegó Margo* and *Ante varias esfinges,* both in 1956. Later a disagreement with his mentor Rodolfo Usigli and some unfortunate stage productions alienated Ibargüengoitia from the theater. His last play, *El atentado* (1962), a historical farce about a presidential assassination, received the Casa de las Américas Prize in 1963. Two of his books are available in English translation: *Muertas* (*The Dead Girls,* 1983) and *Dos crímenes* (*Two Crimes,* 1984).

His sardonic sense of humor and imaginative techniques made him one of the best writers of his generation. He died in a plane crash in Spain.

– GUILLERMO SCHMIDHUBER

IBARGUREN, CARLOS

Carlos Ibarguren (*b.* 18 April 1877; *d.* 3 April 1956), Argentine statesman and nationalist intellectual. A distinguished lawyer, Ibarguren served as under secretary of finance and under secretary of agriculture during President Julio Argentino ROCA's second administration (1898–1904). He subsequently became secretary of the Federal Supreme Court (1906–1912) and minister of justice and education, under President Roque SÁENZ PEÑA (1912–1913). One of the founders of the Democratic Progressive Party in 1914, he was a candidate for the presidency in 1922. As a historian, he was awarded a national prize for his work *Juan Manuel de Rosas: Su vida, su tiempo, su drama* (1930). He supported General José Félix URIBURU's 1930 military coup and that same year was appointed *interventor* (delegate of the federal government) in the province of Córdoba, where he made it clear he shared Uriburu's belief in the need for a corporatist reorganization of the country's economic and political institutions. The corporatist leanings of the "nationalist revolution" were made even more explicit in Ibarguren's *La inquietud de esta hora* (1934), clearly inspired by the corporatist experiments of Italy, Germany, Austria, and Portugal, and by Pope Pius XI's encyclical *Quadragesimo anno* (1934). Although plans for a constitutional reform along those lines did not prosper, Ibarguren became one of the leading intellectuals of the nationalist reaction against the classical model of liberal democracy.

– EDUARDO A. ZIMMERMANN

IBARRA, DIEGO

Diego Ibarra (*b.* ca. 1510; *d.* 1600), Mexican miner. A HIDALGO from Guipúzcoa and a knight of Santiago, Ibarra came to New Spain in 1540 during the time of

Viceroy Antonio de MENDOZA and participated in the wars against the Chichimec tribes and the Caxcanes in Jalisco. Ibarra, Juan de Tolosa, Cristóbal de Oñate (1504/1505–*c.* 1570), and Baltazar de Temiño de Bañuelos (1530–1600) are credited with discovering and opening the great silver mines of Zacatecas and founding that city on 1 January 1548. After amassing a great fortune in the mines, Ibarra married Ana de Valasco y Castilla, a daughter of Viceroy Luis de VELASCO. In 1561 he loaned his nephew Francisco Ibarra 200,000 pesos to explore Nueva Galicia and Nueva Vizcaya. In 1576, Ibarra succeeded Francisco (*d.* 1575) as governor of Nueva Vizcaya. Ibarra organized an expedition of conquest into Sinaloa in 1583. He dedicated some of his fortune to constructing parish churches, the most notable of which being the parochial church at Pánuco. Ibarra moved to Mexico City later in life and finally to Tultitlán, where he died in 1600.

— AARON PAINE MAHR

IBARRA, JOSÉ DE PINEDA

José de Pineda Ibarra (*b.* 1629; *d.* 1680), first master printer of Guatemala. Ibarra was born in Mexico City to Diego de Ibarra and Juana Muñiz de Pineda. After a period of collaboration with noted printers of the metropolis, Ibarra moved to Puebla, where he married María Montez Ramírez. With the financial assistance of Payo Enríquez de Rivera, Bishop of Guatemala, he purchased a printing press and related equipment. Under contract with Enríquez, Ibarra set out for the Kingdom of Guatemala, arriving in the capital, Santiago de los Caballeros, in July 1660. In Santiago (present-day Antigua) he established a printing shop, the first of its kind in the country. Ibarra's only son, Antonio, who took over the business after his father's death, was born in 1661. Though granted a monopoly by Captain General Martín Carlos Mencos on the printing of religious and school materials, he was forced to engage in a variety of business ventures in order to supplement his meager earnings as a printer. He died, debt ridden, in Antigua.

— JORGE H. GONZÁLEZ

IBARRA, JUAN FELIPE

Juan Felipe Ibarra (*b.* 1 May 1787; *d.* 15 July 1851), Argentine military leader and Federalist governor of the province of Santiago del Estero (1831–1851). A native of Santiago del Estero, Argentina, Ibarra studied briefly for the priesthood before he began his military career in 1810. During the Wars of Independence, he served with distinction on the staffs of SAN MARTÍN and BELGRANO, rising to the high rank of graduate sergeant

major in 1817. In 1820, in response to an appeal by the local autonomists, he used the urban Abipone garrison to expel from the province of Santiago del Estero the occupying forces of Governor Bernabé Aráoz of Mendoza and subsequently was elected political and military governor by a *cabildo abierto* (open town council). He encouraged economic development by protecting local industries from competition with imports and by authorizing the minting of real and half-real coins. A Federalist, Ibarra admired the state system and the internal economic organization of the United States. He survived a plot by the Unitaristos to have the poet Hilario ASCASUBI assassinate him, but the Unitarists finally overthrew him. Other Federalists restored him to power, and in 1831 the legislature elected him governor and brigadier general, a post he held until his death.

Some saw Ibarra as a barbarian, ignorant and cruel; others, as a popular caudillo and Federalist.

A paternalistic ruler, Ibarra encouraged education, built churches, exercised the *patronato real*, banned imports that threatened the local economy, and condemned gambling, alcoholism, and other vices. Some see him as a barbarian, ignorant and cruel; others, as a popular caudillo and Federalist.

— JOSEPH T. CRISCENTI

ICAZA CORONEL, JORGE

Jorge Icaza Coronel (*b.* 10 July 1906; *d.* 26 May 1979), Ecuadorian novelist, playwright, and short-story writer. In general, Icaza's fiction has become linked to the regionalist movement of social protest of the 1930s; his best-known novel, *Huasipungo* (1934), attacks the exploitation of Indians in Ecuador. Written from the point of view of the dominant urban class in Ecuador, the novel highlights the ethnic and class gulf between Indians and whites by following, on the one hand, an idyllic love relationship between two young Indians and, on the other, the encroachment of foreign capitalism on an Indian community that is eventually destroyed. Grotesque, sordid descriptions of harsh living conditions and exploitation are meant to create a better awareness of the plight of the Ecuadorian Indians, most of whom lack the bare necessities of life in the novel.

In similar fashion, *En las calles* (1935) narrates a historical event in which an Indian soldier, assigned to quell a battle between rival political factions, ends up firing upon his own community. Icaza's next novels, *Cholos* (1937) and *Huairapamushcas* (1948), take a more complicated view of the struggle between Indians and whites. The *cholo*, or half-breed, works for the exploiter against the Indians until he realizes that his people are being oppressed. While no one survives the massacre in *Huasipungo*, in *Huairapamushcas,* an allusion to the survival of the *cholo* suggests the creation of a symbiotic relationship between Indians and whites. While not as well known as Icaza's first novel, by far his best is *El chulla Romero y Flores* (1958), a masterly recreation of the trials and tribulations of a marginalized *cholo* as he moves from a rural to an urban environment, thus complicating his life even more as he comes to grips with his mixed racial heritage. Icaza's last novel, *Atrapados* (1972), is more artistically rendered and contains autobiographical elements that portray the concerns of a writer whose creativity is vastly limited to the confincs of the sociopolitical world in which he lives.

— DICK GERDES

IGLESIAS, JOSÉ MARÍA

José María Iglesias (*b.* 1823; *d.* 1891), Mexican jurist and politician. Born in Mexico City and educated at El Colegio de San Gregorio, Iglesias began his political career in 1846 as a Mexico City councilman. As editor of *El Siglo XX* (1847–1850), he opposed the administration of SANTA ANNA and the Treaty of Guadalupe Hidalgo (1848). After the triumph of the Liberal Revolution of Ayutla in 1854, Iglesias served in the ministries of treasury and justice and was later elected to the Supreme Court. The War of the Reform (1857–1860) forced his return to private life, but he filled a variety of positions between 1863 and 1871 during the Benito JUÁREZ presidency: minister of justice (twice), minister of the treasury (twice), and minister of government. He was elected president of the Supreme Court in 1873.

As head of the Supreme Court, Iglesias fought against presidential-gubernatorial control of elections. He became part of a three-way contest for power in 1876, when President Sebastián LERDO DE TEJADA (1827–1889) ran for reelection. Iglesias maintained that the 1876 elections were fraudulent and that presidential power had devolved upon him as the constitutional successor to the president. Earlier, PORFIRIO DÍAZ had pronounced against Lerdo de Tejada in the Plan of Tuxtepec (1876). Repeated efforts to bring Díaz and Iglesias together failed. After Díaz dealt Lerdo's troops a major defeat at the battle of Tecoac on 16 November 1876, he turned on Iglesias.

As a professional soldier, Díaz's ability to attract military support proved crucial. Although supporters of Iglesias controlled over one-half of the country in December 1876, defections and military defeats forced Iglesias into exile in the United States in January 1877. He returned to Mexico in October 1877, but he did not resume his public career.

— DON M. COERVER

IGLESIAS, MIGUEL

Miguel Iglesias (*b.* 11 June 1830; *d.* 7 November 1909), provisional president of Peru (1884–1885). A wealthy landowner from the northern Peruvian department of Cajamarca, Iglesias was commander of Peruvian forces in the War of the Pacific (1879–1883). In August 1882, with Peru occupied by the Chilean army and beset by internal political divisions, Iglesias issued the Cry of Montán, in which he advocated pursuing peace with Chile even if it meant the loss of some Peruvian territory. In October 1882, he convened an assembly of northern Peruvian departments that proclaimed him supreme leader of the country.

Recognized as president of Peru by the Chilean government, Iglesias signed the Treaty of Ancón (October 1883), which ended the war between the two nations. Iglesias convened a constituent assembly in Lima that ratified the treaty and designated him provisional president of Peru (1 March 1884). General Andrés Avelino CÁCERES immediately opposed the Iglesias government, and after a long and bloody civil war, his forces occupied Lima in December 1885. Iglesias renounced his claims to the presidency and left the country. He died in Lima.

— WILLIAM E. SKUBAN

IGLESIAS CASTRO, RAFAEL

Rafael Iglesias Castro (*b.* 18 April 1861; *d.* 11 April 1924), president of Costa Rica (1894–1898, 1898–1902). After graduating from the Colegio de Cartago, Iglesias studied law at the University of Santo Tomás but left before obtaining his law degree. His first significant political experience came in 1889 when he supported the presidential candidacy of José Joaquín Rodríguez. When Rodríguez assumed the presidency in 1890, he named Iglesias minister of war. In 1893 Iglesias became minister of finance and commerce, and also married the president's daughter. As a presidential candidate in 1894 he enjoyed the support of the incumbent administration and took power after the government had suppressed his political opposition. In 1897 Iglesias secured congressional passage of a constitutional amendment that permitted his reelection and subsequently won a second presidential term when his opponents withdrew from the electoral process. During his two terms Iglesias placed the nation on the gold standard; inaugurated the National Theater; promoted railroads, highways, and port facilities; and oversaw the construction of a number of schools and hospitals. An authoritarian figure who often abused the political rights of the opposition, Iglesias nonetheless allowed freedom of the press. He stepped down from power in 1902 and ran unsuccessfully for the presidency in 1910 and again in 1914.

– RICHARD V. SALISBURY

IGLESIAS PANTIN, SANTIAGO

Santiago Iglesias Pantin (*b.* 22 February 1872; *d.* 5 December 1939), Puerto Rican labor leader. Born in La Coruña, Spain, Iglesias Pantin arrived in Cuba in 1886 as a stowaway and remained there until sailing for Puerto Rico in 1896. He began his political activities in 1898, being arrested for attempting to raise the "cost of labor." In 1900, he traveled to New York because of ill-health. While in New York, he became acquainted with members of the American Federation of Labor. The following year he was appointed union organizer for Puerto Rico and Cuba. In 1918, Iglesias Pantin organized the Pan American Federation of Labor and continued to participate and promote labor concerns until his death from malaria in 1939.

– ALLAN S. R. SUMNALL

ILLESCAS, CARLOS

Carlos Illescas (*b.* 19 May 1918; *d.* 1998), Guatemalan poet, considered one of the best in the "Generation of the 1940s" and the *Acento* literary circle. During the presidency of Jacobo ARBENZ GUZMÁN (1951–1954), he was the president's personal secretary. As a result, Illescas was forced into exile after the 1954 invasion of the country that led to the overthrow of the Arbenz government. He has lived in Mexico City ever since. Illescas is renowned not only as a poet but also as a radio and television scriptwriter, and as a distinguished professor of creative writing. His poetry is characterized by its mixture of classical Castilian language and powerful surrealist metaphor and imagery. His books are *Friso de otoño* (1958); *Ejercicios* (1960); *Réquiem del obsceno* (1963); *Los cuentos de Marsias* (1973); *Manual de simios y otros poemas* (1977); *El mar es una llaga* (1980); and *Usted es la culpable* (1983).

– ARTURO ARIAS

ILLIA, ARTURO UMBERTO

Arturo Umberto Illia (*b.* 4 August 1900; *d.* 1 January 1983), president of Argentina (1963–1966). A country doctor from Córdoba, Illia was born in Pergamino and entered Radical Party politics as a follower of Governor

Amadeo Sabattini (1935–1940). Throughout his political career Illia adhered to the nationalist principles that *sabattinismo* had resuscitated in the Radical Civic Union (UCR). He was elected president in 1963 on the Radical Civic Union of the People (UCRP) ticket with only 26 percent of the vote. His administration marked the first serious return to the economic nationalism of the 1946–1955 Peronist government. Illia rescinded the exploration agreements reached by his predecessor, Arturo FRONDIZI, with the foreign oil companies and undertook expansionary policies by liberalizing credit, increasing wages, and redistributing income to the working class. Price and exchange controls were also established. Despite his economic program, Illia's relations with the Peronist trade union movement were antagonistic and general strikes by the General Confederation of Workers (CGT) undermined the government and its policies. After Illia went on the offensive and attempted to oust the entrenched labor bureaucracy through a series of labor reform laws, including supervised union elections and tighter control of union monies, the labor movement began to openly encourage a coup d'état, which finally occurred in June 1966.

– JAMES P. BRENNAN

INCHÁUSTEGUI CABRAL, HÉCTOR

Héctor Incháustegui Cabral (*b.* 25 July 1912; *d.* 5 September 1979), Dominican poet. Born in Baní, Incháustegui Cabral wrote a sort of social poetry that ranges from raw identification with the disinherited to meditations on love, death, and mankind's relationship to God. He is best known for *Poemas de una sola angustia* (1940). His poetic texts appear in *Obra poética completa: 1940–1976* (1978), published by the Universidad Católica Madre y Maestra, where he taught literature for many years. The verse novel *Muerte en el Edén* (1951); the autobiography *El pozo muerto* (1960); two collections of essays on Dominican writers; three plays in verse based on ancient Athenian themes; and the novel *La sombra del tamarindo* (1984), which appeared posthumously, complete his vast production. A diplomat and public official during the dictatorship of his friend, Rafael TRUJILLO, Incháustegui Cabral held prestigious government positions throughout his life. Despite his association with the Trujillo regime, his literary legacy has been highly regarded by subsequent generations of Dominican writers.

– SILVIO TORRES-SAILLANT

INFANTE, JOSÉ MIGUEL

José Miguel Infante (*b.* 1778; *d.* 9 April 1844), Chilean patriot and politician. Infante played a number of important roles in the Chilean struggle for independence and in its aftermath. As *procurador* (attorney) of the *cabildo* (municipal government) of Santiago in 1810, he was active in putting forth the creole case for a national government. At the *cabildo abierto* (open town meeting) of 18 September 1810, he was given the task of making the keynote speech in favor of this change. He was a member of the first national congress (1811) and of the governing junta (1813–1814). He happened to be in Argentina at the time of the battle of Rancagua (1–2 October 1814), and remained there until 1817. Under Bernardo O'HIGGINS (1778–1842), Infante was briefly minister of finance (1818). He played one of the more important roles in the events of 28 January 1823, when O'Higgins relinquished power. As a senator in 1823 he was responsible for the law abolishing slavery in Chile.

As a senator in 1823 Infante was responsible for the law abolishing slavery in Chile.

Infante's moments of greatest influence came in the years 1824–1826, when his now strongly held "federalist" views dominated discussion in the Chilean congress. A federalist constitution, however, was never introduced, and Infante's influence quickly waned. Between 1827 and 1844 he published 206 issues of his own newspaper, *El Valdiviano Federal,* in which he continued to expound his increasingly dogmatic (and totally unfashionable) federalist views. He was widely respected as a man of great integrity. His death in 1844 made a deep impression on a new generation of Chilean liberals.

– SIMON COLLIER

INFANTE, PEDRO

Pedro Infante (*b.* 18 November 1917; *d.* 15 April 1957), Mexican actor and singer. Born in Mazatlán, Sinaloa, Infante learned the trade of carpentry, then made a guitar and taught himself music. In 1939, while in Mexico City, he began his singing career on the radio. He was "discovered" by the director Ismael Rodríguez and cast in the film *La feria de las flores* (1942). One year later he became a major star in *¡Viva mi desgracia!* He starred in a total of forty-five films, including *Nosotros los pobres* (1947), *Ustedes los ricos* (1948), *Escuela de vagabundos* (1954), *Dicen que soy mujeriego* (1948), *Las Islas Marías* (1950), *Ahi viene Martín Corona* (1951), and *Dos tipos de cuidado* (1952). A versatile actor who performed comedy and drama with equal

distinction, Infante has attained the status of a cultural icon in Mexico.

– DAVID MACIEL

INGENIEROS, JOSÉ

José Ingenieros (*b.* 24 April 1877; *d.* 31 October 1925), Argentine intellectual. Born in Buenos Aires, Ingenieros was one of early twentieth-century Argentina's most prolific and influential intellectual figures. A graduate of the medical school of the University of Buenos Aires, he was particularly interested in and wrote extensively on psychology, psychiatry, and criminology. Ingenieros was an early adherent of socialism, which he later abandoned, and was also active in the formation of the Unión Latino Americana, an organization of Latin American intellectuals and political leaders advocating continental solidarity against the growing influence of the United States in the region. In 1915, he took a teaching position in the school of philosophy and letters of the University of Buenos Aires and founded and edited two journals (the *Revista de Filosofía* and *La Cultura Argentina*), dedicated to literary and philosophical issues.

Ingenieros was the author of scores of articles and many books, his best-known publications being *El hombre mediocre* (1913), a discussion of the spiritually deadening effects of modern society, and *Evolución de las ideas argentinas* (1918–1920), a two-volume examination of Argentine history. Ingenieros was also a strong supporter of and inspiration for the university reform movement that began in 1918.

– RICHARD J. WALTER

IRALA, DOMINGO MARTÍNEZ DE

Domingo Martínez de Irala (Captain Vergara; *b.* 1509; *d.* 3 October 1556), Spanish explorer and conquistador. The youngest of six children, Irala was born in Vergara, Guipúzcoa, Spain, to a family of hidalgos. His father, Martín Pérez de Irala, was a royal office holder.

In 1534, Irala went on an expedition to the Río de la Plata, with the *adelantado* Pedro de MENDOZA. In 1535 he participated in the founding of Buenos Aires. The following year, he went on an expedition to the Paraná River with his friend Juan de AYOLAS. On 2 February 1537, Ayolas founded the port of Candelaria on the Paraguay River, and then continued north, leaving Irala in command.

In 1537 the *veedor* (colonial inspector) of the Río de la Plata, Alonso Cabrera, appointed Irala lieutenant governor. Soon after this appointment, Irala went to Asunción and founded several new settlements.

Irala participated in many other expeditions, such as an exploration of the Paraguay River and a region near Peru. In 1543 he participated in an Indian campaign under the second *adelantado* of the Río de la Plata, Alvar Núñez CABEZA DE VACA. He was also the main force behind the arrest of Cabeza de Vaca on 26 April 1544. When Irala sent him back to Spain one year later, he became the undisputed master of Paraguay.

In late 1547 and early 1548, Irala faced a rebellion in Asunción by some of Cabeza de Vaca's followers. He quelled the rebellion, and in order to ensure peace in the region, he gave his four daughters in marriage to four of the leaders. In 1555, the crown appointed him governor. He died the following year.

– JUAN MANUEL PÉREZ

IRIGOYEN, BERNARDO DE

Bernardo de Irigoyen (*b.* 18 December 1822; *d.* 27 December 1906), cattle baron and politician in Buenos Aires province and Argentina. Born in Buenos Aires, Irigoyen received his law degree from the University of Buenos Aires in 1843. He obtained his first important political position in 1844, when Federalist dictator Juan Manuel de ROSAS appointed him intervenor in Mendoza Province.

As a member of the National Autonomist Party, he was elected to the Buenos Aires Province Chamber of Deputies in 1873 and advanced to the provincial Senate two years later.

In the 1880s, he returned to national politics. Under presidents Nicolás AVELLANEDA (1874–1880) and Julio ROCA (1880–1886) he held various cabinet-level positions. Although he broke from the National Autonomist Party, helping form the Civic Union Party and the Radical Civic Union Party, he remained influential. In the final decades of his life he served as governor and national senator of Buenos Aires Province.

– DANIEL LEWIS

IRISARRI, ANTONIO JOSÉ DE

Antonio José de Irisarri (*b.* 7 February 1786; *d.* 10 June 1868), Spanish-American patriot, diplomat, historian, and journalist. Born in Guatemala, Irisarri settled in 1809 in Chile, where he played a prominent part in patriot politics during the *Patria Vieja*, among other things as editor of *El Semanario Republicano* from 1813 to 1814. His pen rarely idle, he also wrote many political works. Obliged to leave Chile in August 1814 because of his opposition to José Miguel CARRERA, he went to England, where, together with Andres BELLO, he published the pro-independence *El Censor Ameri-*

cano. Upon his return to Chile in 1818, he was appointed a diplomatic agent by Bernardo O'HIGGINS and sent back to Europe, where he contracted the £1 million Chilean loan of 1822. In 1826 he moved back to his native Guatemala, but in 1830 resettled in Chile. He was appointed Intendant of Colchagua in November 1835. He accompanied the first Chilean expedition to Peru in 1837, during the war against the Peru-Bolivia Confederation, and negotiated the Treaty of Paucarpata (17 November 1837) with Andrés de SANTA CRUZ. Seen as ignominious in Chile, the treaty was repudiated.

Finding it inadvisable to return to Chile, Irisarri spent the remainder of his life in Ecuador, Colombia, Venezuela, and the United States, finally settling in New York in November 1849. In 1855 he became ambassador of Guatemala and El Salvador to the United States, and was named as plenipotentiary for Nicaragua at the time of William WALKER's filibustering incursions. Irisarri died in Brooklyn.

– SIMON COLLIER

IRISARRI Y LARRAÍN, JUAN BAUTISTA

Juan Bautista Irisarri y Larraín (*b.* ca. 15 February 1740; *d.* 4 May 1805), Guatemalan merchant, banker, and planter. Irisarri was born in Aranaz, Spain. After coming to Guatemala he was successful in finance, commerce, and indigo production. By 1805 he was regarded as the wealthiest man in the kingdom. An active member of the Sociedad Económica de Amigos del País de Guatemala, he especially promoted the development of a Pacific coast port in the late colonial period. His second marriage linked him to the prominent creole Arrivillaga family. He also had family ties in Chile, where his illustrious son, Antonio José (1786–1868), migrated after independence.

– RALPH LEE WOODWARD, JR.

ISAACS, JORGE

Jorge Isaacs (*b.* 1 April 1837; *d.* 17 April 1895), Colombian poet, politician, and ethnologist. Born in Cali, to an English father—a Christian convert from Judaism—and a Catholic Spanish mother, Isaacs was also

"I have moved from shadow to light."

Indian, Catalan, and Italian. He epitomized the Spanish American quest for personal and cultural identity in his life and his works. Educated in Cali and Bogotá, he soon showed his strong, varied, and captivating personality. At seventeen he enlisted in a revolutionary army;

Antonio José de Irisarri. Reproduced from Carlos García Bauer, Antonio José de Irisarri: Diplomático de América *(Guatemala, 1970). (Courtesy of Harvard College Library)*

he later fought in several civil wars and summarized the history of one failed revolution in *La revolución radical en Antioquia* (1880). Although he entered politics as a Conservative, his rebellious nature pushed him to the Liberal Party, whereupon he declared "I have moved from shadow to light." Once involved in politics, he applied either democratic or authoritarian means to make good on his party's programs.

Isaacs traveled through La Guajira as secretary of a scientific commission for the study of natural resources. Lacking even experienced guides, the daring Isaacs began the exploration on his own and succeeded in finding coal mines and oil fields.

More than as a poet, explorer, politician, or ethnologist, Isaacs is known as a novelist for his only and unique novel. *María* (1867; *Maria,* 1890) won him a place in history and in the hearts of millions around the world. Published in every Spanish-speaking country and translated into many languages, *María* caused critics to proclaim it the "most exquisite sentimental novel" and "one of the most beautiful creations and . . . closest

to perfection" for its "clear aesthetic conscience." America, in its postindependence search for identity, found itself in *María*'s landscape and humane romantic soul. After a life dedicated to his country and in the midst of economic hardships, Isaacs died of a disease contracted during his exploratory treks.

— J. DAVID SUÁREZ-TORRES

ISABEL, PRINCESS OF BRAZIL

Isabel, Princess of Brazil (*b.* 29 July 1846; *d.* 14 November 1921), heiress to the Brazilian throne. Isabel was the daughter of PEDRO II and Empress Teresa Cristina Maria of Bourbon. Married to Gastão of Orléans, count d'Eu, on 15 October 1864, she assumed the regency in her father's absence in 1871, 1876, and 1887. Strong-willed, she displayed an uncommon ability to govern during her first regency. In Brazilian history her name is associated with emancipation and the abolition of slavery. In 1871 she signed the Law of the Free Womb (Free Birth Law), which freed newborn slaves. Her major achievement was the *Lei Aurea* of 13 May 1888, which abolished slavery. Her experience in government, combined with her abolitionist views, led Princess Isabel to evaluate correctly the chaotic political climate created by the abolitionist movement in the first months of 1888 and to decide that the crown had to intervene directly to end slavery. She disregarded some of the unwritten rules followed by her father for decades when she forced the resignation of the Cotegipe cabinet, selected the head of the cabinet that was to abolish slavery, and did not seek the advice of the plenary Council of State, the emperor's advisory body.

Despite her achievements, Princess Isabel was plagued by a degree of unpopularity caused by several factors. Her marriage to a Frenchman led to suspicion of foreign influence and dominance, and her husband's unpopularity had a ripple effect of its own. Her Catholicism was equally unpopular, for fear of papal influence in the affairs of state. Above all, the fact that she was a woman made her in the view of many unsuitable to govern. The adulation that surrounded her after she abolished slavery was ephemeral. With the fall of the monarchy on 15 November 1889, she was exiled with her family and spent the last part of her life in France.

— LYDIA M. GARNER

ISAMITT ALARCÓN, CARLOS

Carlos Isamitt Alarcón (*b.* 13 March 1887; *d.* 2 July 1974), Chilean composer and painter. Along with Carlos Lavín and Pedro Humberto Allende, Isamitt, who was born in Rengo, Chile, is noted for his extensive research on the native music of the Araucanian Indians. In 1932, he published a seminal classification of the Araucanian musical repertoire according to performance medium and function. In 1936, Isamitt became one of the founding members of the Asociación Nacional de Compositores de Chile. His early music could be described as nationalistic, expressed through the spirit and techniques of musical impressionism. Later, however, his work became more abstract through use of the twelve-tone technique, of which he was one of the first exponents in Chile. Isamitt is a major figure in the trend called "musical Indianism" in Chile, although he also explored creole folklore. For his use of indigenous folklore in his own compositions, he was awarded Chile's Premio Nacional de Arte in 1965. He held the posts of director of the Santiago School of Fine Arts and artistic director of the primary schools in Santiago. His large musical output includes music for orchestra, chamber groups, voice, piano, and ballet.

– SERGIO BARROSO

ITABORAÍ, VISCONDE DE

Visconde de Itaboraí (Joaquim José Rodrigues Tôrres; *b.* 1802; *d.* 1873). Born into a landowning family of Rio province, Itaboraí graduated from Coimbra University in 1825 and became an instructor at the Rio Military Academy. A doctrinaire Liberal, he served as a minister in 1831 and 1833. Converted to Conservative views, he was prominent in the Regresso movement (1835–1839) in favor of central authority and law and order. He was elected a deputy in 1834 and was named a senator in 1844. After PEDRO II's majority, Itaboraí served as minister in the Conservative cabinet of 1843–1844. On the Liberals' fall from office in 1848, he became minister of finance and, over the next five years, reorganized the fiscal system. He was prime minister from May 1852 to September 1853. Appointed president of the Bank of Brazil, he exerted considerable influence on monetary questions. In July 1868, Itaboraí formed a cabinet that, despite financial and political difficulties, brought the War of the Triple Alliance to a successful end. Himself a *fazendeiro* (plantation owner) and opposed to any meddling with slavery, Itaboraí voted but did not speak against the Free Birth Law of 1871. Very much the intellectual in politics, Itaboraí was perhaps the most capable and is certainly the most understudied leader of Pedro II's reign (1840–1889).

– RODERICK J. BARMAN

ITURBIDE, AGUSTÍN DE

Agustín de Iturbide (*b.* 27 September 1783; *d.* 19 July 1824), military figure and emperor of Mexico. Born

in Valladolid, Morelia, Iturbide entered the militia at age sixteen. Although vaguely involved with the Valladolid Conspiracy of 1809, he refused to join the revolt of Miguel HIDALGO Y COSTILLA in 1810. Instead, he served the royal government, distinguishing himself as an able officer and an implacable foe of the insurgents. In 1816 Colonel Iturbide was relieved of command because of charges of corruption. He spent the next years in Madrid defending himself. There he came into contact with important members of the elite who favored autonomy within the Spanish Empire. While New Spain's elite had reached a consensus regarding autonomy, only Iturbide acted decisively.

Restored to command, Iturbide negotiated in 1821 with the leading royalist officers as well as with the principal insurgents, convincing them to accept autonomy under the Plan of Iguala, which called for a constitutional monarchy with the Spanish king as sovereign, recognized the Constitution of 1812, and established equality among all groups. Independence was assured when Juan O'DONOJÚ, the newly appointed Spanish *Jefe Político Superior* (Superior Political Chief) ratified the plan by signing the Treaty of Córdoba (24 August 1821). Thereafter, the autonomists, New Spain's elite who had sought home rule since 1808, rapidly came into conflict with Iturbide. While they believed that the legislature should be dominant, he insisted on exercising his personal power resulting from the immense popularity that he had gained when he proclaimed independence. When Spain refused to ratify Mexican autonomy, Iturbide crowned himself emperor on 19 May 1822 with the backing of the army and strong popular support.

The new nation faced immense problems, among them the near bankruptcy of the government. Although there was a widespread national desire to form a strong and unified nation, the empire failed primarily because Iturbide proved unwilling to accept the figurehead role that the new Spanish-Mexican parliamentary tradition required. As a result, he and Congress were continually at odds. On 26 August 1822 he ordered the arrest of sixty-six persons, including twenty congressmen, for conspiracy, and on 31 October he dissolved congress. Discontent emerged in the provinces, but the military finally undermined him. The Plan of Casa Mata, which provided the provinces the opportunity to gain home rule, ultimately forced him to abdicate on 19 March 1823. He and his family were exiled to Italy, but supporters convinced him to return in July 1824 in an effort to regain the throne. He was captured, courtmartialed, and executed. Although he succeeded in emancipating his country, he failed, like his contemporaries throughout the region, to establish a stable regime and, thus, became an ambiguous figure in Mexican history.

— JAIME E. RODRÍGUEZ O.

ITURBIDE, GRACIELA

Graciela Iturbide (*b.* 16 May 1942), Mexican photographer. A native of Mexico City, Iturbide uses the camera to interpret the daily lives and rituals of indigenous peoples. She studied at the Center for Cinematographic Studies of the National Autonomous University from 1969 to 1972. Her most extensive body of work, executed in the 1980s, centers on the matriarchal culture of the Zapotecs of Juchitán, a town near the Isthmus of Tehuantepec on Mexico's southern Pacific coast. Among other projects, she has documented the singular manner in which the Mexican people approach death, and, in East Los Angeles, the daily lives of *cholos,* young Mexican American street gang members. Following in the tradition of her mentor, the photographer Manuel ÁLVAREZ BRAVO, Iturbide works in black-and-white; although her images are photojournalistic, they are characterized by a level of intimacy and candor not necessarily associated with the documentary tradition. Exhibitions of her work have been mounted internationally, and her photographs are included in the permanent collections of many major museums.

— ELIZABETH FERRER

ITURRIGARAY, JOSÉ DE

José De Iturrigaray (*b.* 27 June 1742; *d.* 1815), fifty-sixth viceroy of New Spain (1803–1808). A military man, he obtained the post of viceroy as a protégé of Spanish Prime Minister Manuel Godoy (1767–1851). He won the sympathies of New Spaniards with programs such as smallpox vaccinations. He organized the defense of the viceroyalty and stationed troops to protect the road to Mexico City. He took every opportunity to amass wealth, as evidenced by his implementation of the Royal Law of Consolidation (26 December 1804), from which he received a percentage of the amount collected.

When news arrived that King Charles IV (1748–1819) had abdicated in favor of Napoleon I (1769–1821), the Ayuntamiento (city council) of Mexico City proposed the establishment of a junta of authorities while an assembly of cities was convened. The Audiencia of Mexico, fearful that such action might lead to independence, proposed, instead, the recognition of one of the juntas formed in Spain. Backing the Ayuntamiento, Iturrigaray held several meetings, to which the Audiencia responded by encouraging a coup d'état. On the night of 15 September 1808, Gabriel de YERMO (1757–1813), at the head of 300 Spaniards, imprisoned the viceroy and detained several members of the Ayuntamiento as well as Fray Melchor de TALAMANTES (1765–1809). Thereafter, the conflict between *criollos* and *peninsulares* became acute. Removed from command, Iturrigaray was sent to Spain, where he was prosecuted for disloyalty, but his case was stayed. He underwent a *juicio de residencia,* which posthumously found him guilty of peculation. He died in Madrid in 1815.

— VIRGINIA GUEDEA

ITZCOATL

Itzcoatl (*b.* ca. 1380; *d.* 1440), Aztec ruler from 1426 to 1440. Itzcoatl ("Obsidian Serpent"), fourth Mexica ruler or *tlatoani* ("speaker"), was the son of Acamapichtli, the first *tlatoani,* and a slave woman. Itzcoatl led the rebellion against the Tepanec polity centered at Azcapotzalco, to which the Mexica had been tributaries.

According to Aztec tradition, Itzcoatl destroyed the manuscript records of Mexica history, thus obscuring its humble origins.

Itzcoatl's nephew (half-brother in some sources) and predecessor, Chimalpopoca (r. 1415–1426), died under mysterious circumstances. The accession of Itzcoatl, a mature man with a low-ranking mother, may have been engineered by Mexica leaders desiring to fight the Tepanecs. A skilled warrior and strategist, Itzcoatl joined forces with the Acolhua under NEZAHUALCOYOTL and the dissident Tepanecs of Tlacopan (Tacuba), forging the "Triple Alliance" that defeated Azcapotzalco's ruler, Maxtla, in 1428. According to native tradition, Itzcoatl then destroyed the manuscript records of Mexica history, thus obscuring the humble origins of the now-triumphant Mexica. To the nascent Aztec Empire, Itzcoatl added Coyoacan, Xochimilco, and Cuitlahuac. He was succeeded by his nephew, MOTECUHZOMA I.

— LOUISE M. BURKHART

IVALDI, HUMBERTO

Humberto Ivaldi (*b.* 1909; *d.* 1947), Panamanian painter. He trained initially under Roberto LEWIS and later at the San Fernando Academy in Madrid (1930–1935). In Panama, he became an art teacher and later director of the Escuela Nacional de Pintura, where he influenced a generation of Panamanian artists. A frustrated man, he left many unfinished works and his early death is presumed to have been a suicide.

Ivaldi's academic background stands out in his traditional still lifes and numerous portraits. However, his more "modern" genre paintings and landscapes, for example, *Viento en la Loma* (1945), are characterized by expressive brush strokes, dynamic compositions, and the rich atmospheric quality of his colors.

— MONICA E. KUPFER

IZQUIERDO, MARÍA

María Izquierdo (*b.* 1902; *d.* 2 December 1955), Mexican artist. María Izquierdo was largely self-taught. In the early 1930s she was the companion of Rufino TA-MAYO, with whom she shared stylistic affinities. Izquierdo's works include self-portraits, in which her Indian features are proudly evident, still lifes, and landscapes. "My greatest strength," she said about her work, "is that my painting reflects the Mexico that I know and love. . . . In the world of art, a painting is an open window to the human imagination." Along with her populism, she celebrated her passion for color, texture, and careful composition while maintaining a delight in spontaneity. Her palette changed over time from more obscure tones to contrasting and rich ones close to those of textiles, ceramics, and lacquered folk ware. Despite her often brilliant use of color, there is a tragic or melancholy undertone to many works along with a wry humor.

— SHIFRA M. GOLDMAN

J

JAAR, ALFREDO

Alfredo Jaar (*b.* 1956), Chilean artist. Born in Santiago, Jaar received degrees in filmmaking from the American Institute of Culture (1979) and in Architecture from the University of Chile in Santiago (1981). In 1982 he moved to New York, where he received fellowships

---

Employing photographs, light boxes, mirrors, and digital signs, Jaar addresses themes related to environmental decay and the inequality of human groups and nations.

---

from the Guggenheim Memorial Foundation (1985), the National Endowment for the Arts (1987), and the Deutscher Akademischer Austauschdienst Berliner Kunstlerprogram (1989). Employing over-life-size and close-up photographs, light boxes, mirrors, and digital signs in his installations, Jaar addresses themes related to environmental decay and the inequality of human groups and nations. The exportation of toxic industrial waste by developed countries to Nigeria was the subject of his *Geography = War* (1991), and the plight of the Vietnamese boat people was depicted in *(Un)Framed* (1987–1991). Jaar has traveled to and meticulously researched each site he selects as a theme. The simplicity of his installations has prompted comparisons with the minimalist artists Robert Morris and Donald Judd.

— MARTA GARSD

JAGUARIBE GOMES DE MATOS, HÉLIO

Hélio Jaguaribe Gomes de Matos (*b.* 1923), Brazilian political scientist. During the second half of the twentieth century, Jaguaribe distinguished himself as one of Brazil's foremost social scientists whose research interests and publications consistently presented innovative approaches to issues of political and social development in modern Brazil and Latin America. Best known for his studies on the role of political nationalism and social organization in Brazilian modernization, Jaguaribe's works are widely read among Latin Americanists in the Americas and Europe. Some of his most provocative

early writings include the controversial *O nacionalismo na atualidade brasileira* (1958), *The Brazilian Structural Crisis* (1966), and *Economic and Political Development: A Theoretical Approach and a Brazilian Case Study* (1968), as well as collaborations with the journal *Cadernos de nosso tempo.* His later works, including *Crise na república* (1993) and *Brasil: Reforma ou caos* (1989), concentrate on the institutional, social, economic, and political problems involved in the transition from authoritarian to democratic rule, particularly in Brazil.

A native of Rio de Janeiro, Jaguaribe received a law degree from the Pontífica Universidade Católica of Rio de Janeiro (1946) and a doctorate from Mainz University in Germany (1983). After receiving his law degree, Jaguaribe worked as a lawyer, entrepreneur, and industrialist in the states of Rio de Janeiro and Espírito Santo. After entering academics in the mid-1950s, Jaguaribe taught extensively in Brazil, serving as a faculty member of the Instituto Superior de Estudos Brasileiros (1956–1959) and the Universidade de São Paulo, and abroad, as visiting professor at Harvard (1964–1966), Stanford (1966–1967), and the Massachusetts Institute of Technology (1968–1969). In the early 1990s, Jaguaribe served as dean of the Instituto de Estudos Políticos e Sociais do Rio de Janeiro.

— DARYLE WILLIAMS

JAMES, CYRIL LIONEL ROBERT

Cyril Lionel Robert James (*b.* 4 January 1901; *d.* 31 May 1989), historian, philosopher, literary critic. C. L. R. James is well known outside his island home of Trinidad and Tobago as one of the twentieth century's leading intellectuals. His illustrious career as a writer spans several disciplines. His contributions to cultural studies, political philosophy, and West Indian creative and historical literature both predict and inform the late twentieth century's preoccupation with postcolonial studies and have earned him a place of high respect as an interpreter of both Marx's and Lenin's philosophies.

Throughout his life James was recognized as a brilliant student and teacher. When he emigrated to England in 1932, he established himself as a keen cricket commentator, writing for the *Manchester Guardian.* Later in his career he combined the history of cricket with autobiography to create a stunning cultural critique of the West Indies in *Beyond a Boundary* (1963).

His novel *Minty Alley,* written in 1927, is a foundational text in the Caribbean literary tradition. His historical work, *The Black Jacobins: Toussaint L'Ouverture and the San Domingo Revolution* (1938), remains a universally acclaimed account of the Haitian war for independence in relationship to the French Revolution.

James was a major figure in the Pan-African movement in the 1930s. The continual development of his political ideologies can be traced through his numerous and diverse essays, collected in several volumes. Both his essays and full-length works reflect a keen interest in and healthy skepticism for Marxism, Trotskyism, socialism, and notions of American democracy. In association with Trotsky's organization, with which he later broke, James spent fifteen years in the United States (1938–1953) lecturing and organizing black workers. A casualty of the McCarthy era, he was asked to leave the country because his activities were considered too radical. While awaiting deportation, James wrote *Mariners, Renegades, and Castaways: The Story of Herman Melville and the World We Live In* (1953), a literary critique of Herman Melville's novel *Moby Dick,* but also a political commentary on totalitarianism and American democracy. James periodically revisited the Caribbean and also traveled through Europe and Africa. In 1968, he was allowed to reenter the United States, where he taught at Federal City College for ten years. During the last decades of his life he continued to write and lecture widely, and received awards and accolades from around the world. He died in London, England, his adopted home.

— NICOLE R. KING

JARA, VÍCTOR

Víctor Jara (*b.* 28 September 1934; *d.* 14/15 September 1973), Chilean singer, songwriter, and theater director. One of the leading figures of the New Chilean Song

---

A loyal but undogmatic Communist, Jara became an immediate victim when the Chilean military seized power in September 1973.

---

movement of the later 1960s and early 1970s, Jara was born into a peasant family in Lonquén, near Talagante, in central Chile. After his military service (1952–1953), he studied acting at the University of Chile drama school, later acquiring a reputation as a theater director. Given his innate musical skill and his work with folk groups such as Cuncumén, with whom he toured Latin America and Europe, he soon found a place among the musicians gathering at the Peña de los Parra, an informal club founded in 1965 by Ángel and Isabel Parra, which was the focal point of New Chilean Song as it took shape. Several of Jara's songs (many pointed, some controversial) were to become true classics of the period, while his singing gained popularity.

A loyal but undogmatic Communist, Jara was a devoted supporter of President Salvador ALLENDE and became an immediate victim when the military seized power in September 1973. He was arrested, brutally beaten, and shot in one of the most tragic events of a tragic time.

— SIMON COLLIER

JARAMILLO LEVI, ENRIQUE

Enrique Jaramillo Levi (*b.* 11 December 1944), Panamanian writer, dramatist, and editor. Born in Colón, Jaramillo Levi attended La Salle High School and in 1967 received a degree in English from the University of Panama. He earned master's degrees in creative writing (1969) and in Latin American literature (1970) from the University of Iowa. In 1973, on a scholarship from the Center of Mexican Writers, he traveled to Mexico, where during the next twelve years he taught at Universidad Autónoma Metropolitana, founded *Editorial Signos,* and published several books, articles, and anthologies. From 1987 to 1990 he was a Fulbright scholar in the United States and also published the anthology *When New Flowers Bloomed: Short Stories by Women Writers from Costa Rica and Panama* (1991). His works include *Duplicaciones* (1973; *Duplications and Other Stories,* 1994), *El búho que dejó de latir* (1974; The Owl Who Stopped Throbbing), *Renuncia al tiempo* (1975; Renounce to Time), *Fugas y engranajes* (1982; Flights and Gears), *Ahora que soy él* (1985; Now That I Am He), *Extravíos: Poesía* (1989), and *El fabricante de máscaras* (1992; The Masks Maker).

Aside from enriching the innovative literary tradition started by Rogelio SINÁN, Jaramillo Levi's writings have opened new avenues of expression with emphasis on universality and aesthetic experimentation. He has received many literary prizes. He is founder and editor of *Maga* and director of Editorial Universitaria.

— ELBA D. BIRMINGHAM-POKORNY

JÁUREGUI, AGUSTÍN DE

Agustín de Jáuregui (*d.* 27 April 1784), viceroy of Peru (1780–1784). Although the date and place of Jáuregui's birth are uncertain, it is known that he was of noble Navarrese descent and served as equerry to Philip V before a period of military service in Cartagena, Cuba, and Honduras in the 1740s.

Following his return to Spain, he began a new period of service in America in 1773, with his appointment as captain-general of Chile, a post from which he was promoted to Lima in 1780 in succession to the disgraced Manuel de GUIRIOR. His period of office was complicated by widespread internal insurgency (notably the rebellion of TÚPAC AMARU I), the fear of British attack and the high costs of coastal defense occasioned by this fear, and the administrative reorganization that culminated in the introduction of the intendant system in 1784. Replaced as viceroy by Teodoro de CROIX on 3 April 1784, Jáuregui died later that month.

— JOHN R. FISHER

JAURETCHE, ARTURO M.

Arturo M. Jauretche (*b.* 13 November 1901; *d.* 25 May 1974), Argentine nationalist intellectual, born in Lincoln, in Buenos Aires Province. Along with Luis DELLEPIANE and Raúl SCALABRINI ORTIZ, Jauretche founded the Radical Orientation Force of Argentine Youth (FORJA) in 1935. The FORJA criticized the country's liberal order and especially its quasi-colonial relationship with Great Britain as part of a deep historical revisionism with political goals. Its members embraced a vitriolic anti-imperialism replete with epithets (e.g. *vendepatria*) that would become an integral part of Argentine political discourse over the next several decades. In its scorn for the oligarchy's cosmopolitan, antinational culture, its denunciations of the Roca-Runciman Pact, and criticisms of what it saw as U.S. pretensions to hegemony in Latin America, the FORJA helped contribute to the popular nationalism that would crystallize under Juan Domingo PERÓN. Jauretche was the most effective disseminator of the FORJA's ideas in books such as *Libros y alpargatas: civilizados o bárbaros* (1983) and *El medio pelo en la sociedad argentina* (1966).

The FORJA remained primarily an intellectual movement; expelled from the Radical Party, it never constituted an independent political force in its own right.

— JAMES P. BRENNAN

JEREZ, FRANCISCO DE

Francisco de Jerez (Xerez, Francisco de; *b.* 1497), Francisco PIZARRO's secretary at Cajamarca during the capture of Atahualpa in 1532 and author of one of the earliest and most widely read chronicles of the Conquest. Born in Seville, Jerez came to the New World in 1514 in the fleet of Pedro Arias de ÁVILA. He accompanied Pizarro on his three trips to Peru in 1524, 1526, and 1531, serving as the conqueror's secretary on all three. He witnessed the encounter with Atahualpa, as well as the Inca's subsequent kidnapping and execution at Cajamarca. While at Cajamarca, Jerez broke his leg, and used his convalescence to write his chronicle. He returned to Spain in 1533, a much wealthier man, and his chronicle was published a year later in Seville. Titled *True Relation of the Conquest of Peru,* and written in part to refute the chronicle of Cristóbal de Mena, it soon became the standard account of the Conquest. Written in dry and unembellished soldier style, it describes in detail Pizarro's march from Tumbes to Cajamarca, the Inca's entourage, his capture, the story of the ransom, and so on. Jerez used his new wealth to establish himself as an important merchant in Seville, but his business failed to prosper. He later petitioned the court to allow him to return to America. Whether he actually returned to the New World is not known, nor is the date of his death.

— JEFFREY KLAIBER

JEREZ, MÁXIMO

Máximo Jerez (*b.* 8 June 1818; *d.* 11 August 1881), Nicaraguan general and diplomatic figure. Jerez was born in León, the center of Nicaraguan liberalism. Political conditions forced his family to relocate to Costa Rica until 1825, when they returned to Nicaragua. Although his father had hoped he would join the family business as a painter, Jerez instead studied civil and canon law at León's university. He received his degree in 1837 and intended to become a priest; however, his scientific orientation led him to a second degree in philosophy the following year. In 1844 he worked for the noted jurist Francisco Calderón as a member of a diplomatic legation to European parliaments. Despite his youth, Jerez earned a reputation as a hard-working, honest, dedicated, and affable individual. His capabilities prompted President José León SÁNDOVAL to name Jerez to his cabinet in 1845. However, Jerez's liberal sympathies were becoming more pronounced, and he declined this position in a government led by a Conservative from Granada; instead, the ministry went to Fruto CHAMORRO.

Jerez joined the Liberal militia opposed to Sándoval and Chamorro and quickly distinguished himself in action. On 17 August 1845, Jerez was wounded in the battle of Chinandega; he was named colonel and major-general of the army. He recovered and took up the struggle with renewed vigor. In 1847 he was elected representative to the Central American Diet in Nacaome, where he formed an alliance with other Liberals and the pro-unionists José Sacasa and José Francisco BARRUNDIA and embarked on a lifelong friendship with the Honduran general Trinidad CABAÑAS. In 1848–1849 Jerez served as secretary of the legation to Great Britain, where he was very much affected by Lord Aberdeen's criticism of Nicaragua's inability to meet its treaty obligations. In 1853, Jerez was a Liberal delegate from León to the Constituent Assembly called by Fruto Chamorro to amend the 1838 Constitution. A crisis ensued when Chamorro overruled the Liberal opposition and exiled Jerez, Francisco Castellón, and José Guerrero on charges of conspiracy.

When William WALKER invaded Nicaragua in 1855, Jerez viewed him as the last hope of Central American liberalism and joined Walker's puppet government as cabinet minister for a short while until he grasped the true nature of Walker's designs. Jerez then defected to the opposition and led the Nicaraguan western army into Managua on 24 September 1856. Other Central American and legitimist troops followed. Jerez served as co-president in a provisional coalition with the Conservative Tomás MARTÍNEZ until November 1857, when Martínez alone was elected to continue. Jerez served in various diplomatic positions until his death in Washington.

– KAREN RACINE

JESUS, CAROLINA MARIA DE

Carolina Maria de Jesus (*b.* 1914; *d.* 1977), Brazilian writer. A fiercely proud black woman, Jesus spent most of her life in obscurity, raising her three children in São Paulo's Canindé Favela, and supporting herself and them by scavenging paper. Her diary, published in 1960 through the help of journalist Audálio Dantas, who discovered her accidentally, made her an overnight sensation. It described the misery of *favela* life and expressed her thirst to escape it and provide a better life for her children. Within a year, it had become Brazil's all-time best-selling book, and it ultimately was translated into thirteen languages and sold in forty countries. But her fame and fortune did not last. She moved out of the *favela* into a house in a middle-class neighborhood, where she was rejected by her new neighbors; she spent much of the money she received unwisely, giving large sums away to needy people she hardly knew; and because she was unwilling to control her outspokenness, she alienated the members of the elite for whom she had been fashionably chic. Even at the height of her fame, most Brazilians never took Jesus seriously. The Left rejected her because she did not speak out against the exploitation of the poor. The literary establishment rejected her writing as childlike; indeed, she enjoyed a much more positive reputation outside of Brazil, where her book was called "one of the most astonishing documents of the lower-class depths ever printed."

All of Jesus's subsequent books lost money, so that within a few years of her exceptional success, she was forced to move out of her house with her children. She became a recluse in a distant semirural district. Times were so hard for her that she had to walk back to the city to scavenge for refuse, and her family again suffered hunger. She died at the age of sixty-three, so poor that her children had to ask for charity to bury her. Her diary, translated into English as *Child of the Dark,* was still in print in many foreign countries, although it had been largely forgotten in Brazil.

– ROBERT M. LEVINE

JIMÉNEZ, ENRIQUE A.

Enrique A. Jiménez (*b.* 1888; *d.* 1970), president of Panama (June 1945–October 1948). Nicknamed "el submarino" for his apparent ability to fire on political opponents and to surface at the most opportune moment, Jiménez was supposed to be an interim president. He was supported by the Partido Renovador and Don Pancho Arias Paredes, who expected to succeed Jiménez but met an untimely death before elections were scheduled. With his support gone, Jiménez faced stiff opposition from Arnulfo ARIAS MADRID, who unsuccessfully attempted a coup d'état in December 1945, and was imprisoned for most of 1946. Although Jiménez negotiated an agreement with the United States regarding U.S. bases in Panama, anti-Yankee demonstrations led to its rejection by the National Assembly. Jiménez responded to the growing domestic agitation caused by students and labor with the iron fist of the National Police, which was under the leadership of José Antonio RÉMON CANTERA. Jiménez's political fortunes ended when his chosen successor, Domingo DÍAZ AROSEMENA, died of a heart attack (1946) and Remón installed Arias as president.

– MICHAEL A. POLUSHIN

JIMÉNEZ DE QUESADA, GONZALO

Gonzalo Jiménez de Quesada (*b.* 1509; *d.* 16 February 1579), Spanish conquistador. Jiménez was born into a Jewish converso family in Córdoba, which had moved to Granada by 1522. Both he and his father were lawyers who practiced before the Audiencia in Granada. His family's subsequent financial ruin, the result of a lawsuit, made emigration inviting. In 1535, Jiménez joined a New World–bound expedition led by Pedro

Fernández de Lugo, the experienced governor of the Canaries and at that time governor of the troubled colony at Santa Marta in what is now Colombia. As lieutenant to Governor Fernández, Jiménez was to oversee judicial and administrative procedures, not to command as conquistador.

The situation in Santa Marta was chaotic and grim: too many Spaniards and hostile Indians, and not enough food or gold. An expedition to the interior was an obvious solution, but Governor Fernández's son abandoned the project and returned to Spain. Suddenly, at the age of twenty-seven, unseasoned and inexperienced, Jiménez was given command as captain-general. Leaving Santa Marta on 5 April 1536, his force of 670 Spaniards made the difficult journey up the Magdalena and Opón rivers before reaching the Eastern Cordillera near Vélez in March 1537. The trek had taken its toll; fewer than 200 had survived.

Jiménez and his group seized more than 200,000 pesos in gold and 1,815 large emeralds.

But then their luck changed. They had reached the Chibchas (MUISCA), the largest group of Indians in Colombia. Jiménez and his group seized more than 200,000 pesos in gold and 1,815 large emeralds, distributed the Indians in *encomienda,* founded Santa Fé de Bogotá, and named the rich kingdom New Granada. The sudden appearance of Nicolás FÉDERMAN's and Sebastián de BELALCÁZAR's expeditions endangered this success, but Jiménez negotiated astutely. Leaving his brother Hernán in command, Jiménez traveled to Spain with Féderman and Belalcázar. There, however, he faced a hostile and pro-Indian Council of the Indies that ordered his imprisonment. He fled to France, Portugal, and Italy before returning to Spain in 1545. In the interval, the civil war in Peru and chaos in New Granada led the council to reconsider his merits.

Although he was not allowed to govern, Jiménez did return to New Granada in 1551 as *adelantado* (governor), marshal, senior *regidor* (alderman) in the Bogotá cabildo, and chief spokesman for the fast-disappearing conquistadores. He wrote at least four or five works, one running to more than 500 folios, of which only *El epítome* (1547) and *Antijovio* (1567) survive. The latter is an ambitious and complex work whose importance is still being debated.

In 1560 Jiménez exchanged his 2,000-ducat annual salary for *encomiendas* of equal value and joined the *encomendero* class. However, great wealth escaped him.

In 1569, at the age of sixty—some say seventy—hounded by debt and lawsuits, still mesmerized by the El Dorado legend, he organized and commanded a disastrous expedition into the llanos. Of 300 Spanish and 1,500 Indians, only 50 Spaniards and 30 Indians returned alive in 1572. Yet, at the request of the Bogotá *audiencia,* he was pacifying hostile Indians in the Central Cordillera near Mariquita in 1574. He died there in 1579, suffering from what was described as leprosy.

– MAURICE P. BRUNGARDT

JIMÉNEZ OREAMUNO, RICARDO

Ricardo Jiménez Oreamuno (*b.* 6 February 1859; *d.* 4 January 1945), president of Costa Rica (1910–1914; 1924–1928; 1932–1936). Born in Cartago, Costa Rica, Ricardo Jiménez earned his law degree from the University of Santo Tomás in San José in 1884. The following year he was named president of the municipality of San José and sent on a diplomatic mission to Mexico, where he successfully gained Mexican support for Costa Rica's battle against Justo Rufino BARRIOS, the Guatemalan general who was attempting to create forcibly one Central American republic. Upon completion of his mission, Jiménez left for Washington, D.C., where in January 1886 he published his most notable essay, "Colegio de Cartago," in which he condemned Jesuit control of schools and argued for complete separation of church and state. The essay not only established Jiménez as one of the leading liberal theorists of the Costa Rican Generation of '89, but served as that group's credo.

In the years that followed, Jiménez held several government posts. In November 1886 he was appointed secretary of state in the Office of the Interior, Police, and Public Works. In September 1889 he assumed the post of secretary of state in the Office of Foreign Relations, only to quit after eight days on the job. In November he was named secretary of the interior, foreign relations, and finance, and the following year he was named president of the Supreme Court. In 1892 he resigned his post in objection to the dictatorship of José Joaquín Rodríguez. In 1906 he was elected to the Costa Rican Congress and made a name for himself as the country's chief critic of the United Fruit Company's preferred economic status.

Jiménez was elected and served his first term as president from 1910 to 1914. After a brief retreat from politics he was elected representative of the provinces of San José and Cartago in 1921. He went on to serve as president of Costa Rica twice more (1924–1928 and 1932–1936). Jiménez was a highly accomplished leader best known for his foreign relations successes in protecting the sovereignty and neutrality of Costa Rica amidst Central American political strife. In 1939, at the age of eighty, Jiménez ran for a fourth term of office; however, he withdrew from the race due to a shortage of campaign funds. He remained an active voice in politics during his latter years and was honored as *Benemérito de la Patria* by a unanimous vote of Congress in 1942.

— DOUGLAS R. KEBERLEIN

JIMENO Y PLANES, RAFAEL

Rafael Jimeno y Planes (also Ximeno; *b.* ca. 1760; *d.* 1825), painter. Born into a family of artists, Jimeno was trained at the Academia de San Carlos in Valencia and also spent time in Madrid and in Rome absorbing the neoclassical style. In 1794 he arrived in New Spain to teach painting at the Academia de San Carlos; four years later he became its general director and continued to teach there for the rest of his life. His portraits of fellow academicians Jerónimo GIL and Manuel TOLSÁ are considered his best work, but just as significant were his paintings in the dome of the cathedral of Mexico City (1809–1810) and in the Capilla del Señor in the Church of Santa Teresa (1813), both lost. Important paintings in the chapel of Tolsá's Palacio de Minería (1812–1813) survive. Jimeno also did drawings for engravings, notably for illustrations of *Don Quixote* in Spain and of the Plaza Mayor of Mexico City after the installation of Tolsá's equestrian statue of Charles IV.

— CLARA BARGELLINI

JOAQUIM, LEANDRO

Leandro Joaquim (*b.* ca. 1738; *d.* ca. 1798), Brazilian painter and architect. Born in Rio de Janeiro, Joaquim studied with the painter João de Sousa and was a colleague of Manuel da Cunha. He collaborated with the sculptor Valentim da FONSECA E SILVA (Mestre Valentim) on the Passeio Público and designed sets for the Teatro de Manuel Luis. Although his oeuvre consists primarily of religious paintings and portraits of governmental dignitaries, his few secular compositions have received particular acclaim. They include *Incendio do Recolhimento do Parto* and *Reconstrução do Recolhimento do Parto* and six oval panels commissioned for a pavilion in the Passeio Público. The latter are aesthetically among his best works but are also iconographically significant because they document social life and urban transformation in late-eighteenth-century Rio.

— CAREN A. MEGHREBLIAN

JOBIM, ANTÔNIO CARLOS "TOM"

Antônio Carlos "Tom" Jobim (*b.* 25 January 1927; *d.* 8 December 1994), Brazilian composer. The most famous Brazilian songwriter, inside and outside of Brazil, Jobim was born in Rio de Janeiro. He studied with Lúcia Branco and Tomas Teran and was profoundly inspired by the works of Brazilian composer VILLA-LOBOS. As a young man, Jobim worked for a time as an architect but soon gave that up to pursue music as a full-time career. He began playing in nightclubs as a pianist around 1950, then got a job with the Continental record label in 1952 transcribing music, followed by a post with Odeon as artistic director, and then worked for various artists as an arranger. During the mid- to late-1950s, he would compose songs (alone and in collaboration with Newton Mendonça, Luiz Bonfá, and poet Vinícius de Moraes) that prefigured and then defined the bossa-nova style. Jobim wrote the music for such enduring songs as "Garota de Ipanema" (The Girl from Ipanema), "Samba de uma nota só" (One Note Samba), "Desafinado" (Off-Key), "Aguas de março" (Waters of March), "Dindi," "Corcovado" (English title: "Quiet Nights of Quiet Stars"), "Insensatez" (English title: "Foolishness"), and other standards often recorded by musicians in many countries. While singer-guitarist João GILBERTO provided the bossa-nova style with its beat, Jobim contributed its most important melodic and harmonic elements.

Jobim wrote the music for such enduring songs as "Garota de Ipanema" (The Girl from Ipanema) and "Desafinado" (Off-Key).

Jobim's compositions are warm and intimate and incorporate difficult harmonies even as the composer strove for a subtle simplicity. He sometimes wrote his own lyrics, but usually collaborated with songwriters such as Vinícius de Moraes, with whom he wrote the ground-breaking bossa standard "Chega de saudade" (No More Blues [1956]), songs for Moraes's play *Orfeu da conceição* (1956), tunes such as "A Felicidade" for the 1959 film *Orfeu Negro* (Black Orpheus), and later classics like "Garota de Ipanema" (1962). Jobim arranged João Gilberto's "Chega de saudade" (1959), considered the first bossa-nova album, and supplied several of its songs.

Jobim achieved international fame as a songwriter in the 1960s and recorded numerous albums over the next three decades as a singer-pianist. Some of Jobim's albums were strictly in the bossa vein, while others, such as *Urubu* (1976), which incorporated Brazilian regional music and evoked impressionistic classical music, ventured into other styles. Jobim (like João Gilberto) had a strong influence on succeeding generations of Brazilian musicians as well as on American jazz musicians in the 1960s and 1970s.

– CHRIS MCGOWAN

JOVELLANOS, SALVADOR

Salvador Jovellanos (*b.* 1833), Paraguayan president (1871–1874). The decade after the disastrous War of the Triple Alliance was a difficult period for Paraguay, with political factions shifting constantly and foreign armies in control of the streets of Asunción. Under such circumstances, obscure men sometimes achieved high political office. Salvador Jovellanos was one example. He had been chosen by President Francisco Solano LÓ-PEZ to study in Europe. After López was killed, Jovellanos was chosen as Cirilo Antonio RIVAROLA's vice president solely, it seems, on the basis of his charming manner. He in turn succeeded to the presidency when opponents forced out Rivarola in 1871. His charm notwithstanding, Jovellanos never gained the trust of any major faction. His administration was marred by four revolts and by two notorious loans negotiated in London in an effort to restore the country's wrecked economy.

– THOMAS L. WHIGHAM

JUAN DIEGO

Juan Diego (*b.* 1474?; *d.* 1548?), according to tradition, a neophyte Christian Indian who saw the Virgin Mary 9–12 December 1531. Details of his native town, time of marriage, and age at the time of the apparitions exist in various traditions. None of the information about him antedates the first published account in 1648. He inspired no cult, except for some hints in the 1660–1661 archdiocesan inquiry, and the place of his burial—today unknown—never became a place of devotion. He is inextricably linked with the apparition account, but there is no such evidence of this account prior to 1648. Because of the legendary nature of the tradition of the Virgin of Guadalupe, the existence of Juan Diego is dubious at best, and in all probability he was no more than a fictional creation. He was beatified by Pope John Paul II in 1989.

– STAFFORD POOLE, C.M

JUAN Y SANTACILIA, JORGE

Jorge Juan y Santacilia (*b.* 5 January 1713; *d.* 5 July 1773), Spanish scientist. Born in Novelda, near Ali-cante, Juan was orphaned at three but nevertheless received a first-rate education, first in Malta, then at the prestigious new Spanish naval academy (Guardia Marina) in Cádiz, and finally with the Spanish fleet plying the Mediterranean (1730–1734). In 1734 Philip V chose him and Antonio de ULLOA, another brilliant young naval officer, to join the French scientists Louis Godin and Charles Marie la Condamine on an expedition to the Indies to measure the exact length of a degree on the equator.

Finally reaching Quito in May 1736, the group immediately began their measurements, with Juan assigned to the ostensible leader of the expedition, Louis Godin, with whom he made observations at thirty-two sites. Juan's stay in Ecuador was not without controversy, however. Both he and Ulloa became embroiled with the president of the Audiencia of Quito and also with the French in a protocol dispute over whose names and royal coat of arms were to be placed on the pillars erected on the equator.

Called to Lima early in the War of Jenkins's Ear, the two officers advised the viceroy on military and naval matters before returning to Quito in January 1744 to make their own scientific observations. Late in October they left for Spain, where they began writing a four-volume descriptive work on their travels, *Relación histórica del viage a la América meridional* (Historical Report on the Voyage to America), published in 1748. In 1749 they completed a secret report for crown officials on conditions in the Indies.

Juan never returned to the Indies. After that last assignment, he became a royal troubleshooter in his native country, where he improved ventilation in the mercury mines at Almadén, strengthened the sea walls at Cartagena, built a new arsenal at El Ferrol, and served as ambassador to Morocco, among other duties. Spending his last days in Madrid as head of the Royal Seminary of Nobles, Juan was noted for his deep-seated attachment to Enlightenment ideas, confirmed by the posthumous publication of his book on astronomy in 1774.

– JOHN JAY TEPASKE

JUANA INÉS DE LA CRUZ, SOR

Sor Juana Inés de la Cruz (*b.* 12 November 1651 or 1648; *d.* 17 April 1695), the major poet of the Spanish colonies. Born in San Miguel de Nepantla, near the capital city of Mexico, Juana Inés de Asuaje y Ramírez was the illegitimate daughter of Isabel Ramírez de Santillana and Pedro Manuel de Asuaje y Vargas Machuca; her illegitimacy may explain the uncertainty about the year of her birth. Taken to the Spanish viceroy's court as a child prodigy, she became a nun in 1667, first with the Carmelites for a short time and then definitively, in 1669, in the Jeronymite Convent of San Jerónimo, where, with the religious name of Sor Juana Inés de la Cruz, she had her own collection of books and some free time for study and writing. Toward the end of her life she was more strictly ascetic. She died taking care of her sister nuns during a plague.

Almost all of Sor Juana's works were initially published in Spain in three different volumes (1689, 1692, and 1700). Her works include many different genres of poetry, dramatic works in verse, and prose works of a more doctrinal or autobiographical sort.

Personal Lyrics   Her secular lyric poetry is among her best-known work. We have, for example, such highly original works as her verse portrait of her beloved Marquise of Paredes (a viceroy's wife); her sonnet on a painted portrait of herself as a vain attempt to save her body from annihilation; several "carpe diem" sonnets centered on the image of the rose; and various poems on hope and the vanity of human illusions, on feminine fidelity, on absence and the sufferings of love, and on the imagination within which we can imprison the beloved.

Religious Writings and "Villancicos"   Among Sor Juana's devotional writings are the interesting prose *Ejercicios de la Encarnación* (Exercises on the Incarnation), in which she presents the Virgin Mary as a model of feminine power and wisdom, almost on the same level as God. Her *villancicos,* or carol sequences, written for

Sor Juana Inés de la Cruz. (Photo by Bob Schalkwijk)

festive performance in cathedrals, allow us a glimpse of her religious and social sensibility. This popular genre, with many different voices, permitted the poet to speak for marginal social groups such as black slaves, Indians, and women, and to make fun of masculine clerical types such as the student. These songs present women as intellectual as well as devout, as for example in the figure of Saint Catharine of Alexandria. Her black voices speak a special dialect of Spanish, and her Indians speak NAHUATL, to address God directly and to complain about how they are treated by Spanish representatives of the Church or State.

The "Sueño"   Sor Juana's lengthy *Sueño* (Dream) occupies a unique place among her works. In her highly significant autobiographical *Respuesta* (Reply), she refers to the *Sueño* as the only poem that she had written for her own pleasure. It is a compendium of contemporary scholastic and scientific knowledge, ranging from the ancient philosophers and church fathers to Florentine hermetic wisdom and the contemporary ideas of Athanasius Kircher and perhaps even of René Descartes. Literarily, the poem draws on Renaissance poetic commonplaces, recast in Spanish baroque forms. Its narrative structure is based on the arrival and departure of night, framing the dream itself, which is an adventure of the intellectual Soul in search of a complete understanding of the universe, a journey that represents the author's own crisis as a religious woman interested in the physical sciences. She seems to identify with Phaëthon, the illegitimate son of Apollo struck down by his father and thus made famous, and with other mythological figures, mostly feminine, such as Night. The Soul, who is the protagonist of the poem, comes back to earth in the final lines of the poem and is identified with the poet herself, who wakes up and, for the first time, asserts her feminine presence grammatically in the very last word of the poem.

The "Respuesta"   In 1690 the bishop of Puebla published Sor Juana's critique of a Portuguese Jesuit's sermon, along with a public letter of his own addressed to her over the pseudonymous signature of a nun. In her critique (*Carta atenagórica* or *Crisis sobre un sermón*), Sor Juana had refuted in a highly sophisticated and learned way the argument of Father Antonio de VIEIRA, in which he rejected interpretations by the fathers of the church and proposed his own. The bishop's letter, although somewhat ambiguous, reveals how much he admires her intellectually as he urges her to use her intelligence in the study of divine rather than secular matters. The bishop's critique provided Sor Juana with an excuse for a full-scale apologia in her *Respuesta a sor Filotea de la Cruz.* This eloquent and warmly human document fully explains the nun's intellectual vocation by recalling her childhood eagerness to learn to read and write and her adolescent rejection of marriage and choice of the convent as a place to study. She cites many famous women from the Bible and from classical antiquity in her defense of equal feminine access to study and to writing. She implies that women as scientists have empirical advantages when she asserts, "If Aristotle had done some cooking, he would have written even more." Such a feminist apologia is unique in the seventeenth-century Hispanic world. (In a letter, "Carta de Monterrey," discovered a few years ago, which Sor Juana wrote to her confessor long before her *Respuesta*, we find her defending her rights in even stronger terms.)

Neptuno alegórico (Allegorical Neptune) is, for the modern reader, a difficult work; it is an official *relación* or explanation of the triumphal arch erected in November of 1680 for the reception of the new viceroy, the Marqués of La Laguna, and his wife. The nun presents as an allegorical model for the viceroy the mythological figure of Neptune, in her poetic description of the arch. This is a highly learned text in which she displays her most arcane erudition and ingenuity.

Theater Sor Juana's theatrical works consist of several *loas* (short dramatic prologues) that are largely mythical and allegorical; three *autos sacramentales,* or allegorical dramatizations of sacramental theology in the tradition of Calderón, written, with their *loas,* for the feast of Corpus Christi; and two full-length "cape and sword" plays in the tradition of Lope de Vega. The *loas* that precede her *autos* are especially interesting for their presentation of Aztec feminine characters, who defend pre-Christian religious practices. Of the *autos, El cetro de José* (Joseph's Scepter) is based on a story from the Bible; *El mártir del Sacramento, San Hermenegildo* (The Martyr of the Sacrament . . .) is hagiographic; and *El Divino Narciso* (Divine Narcissus), the best of the three, is an ingenious allegorization of the pagan mythological Narcissus as the redeeming Christ. Narcissus (Christ), having rejected the advances of Echo (the Devil), who is the rival of Human Nature, sees the latter reflected in the Fountain of Grace, which unites God to Human Nature at the moment of the Incarnation; then Narcissus, in love with himself as reflected in Human Nature, falls into the fountain and drowns, allegorically crucified. One of the secular plays, *Amor es más laberinto,* was written in collaboration with Juan de Guevara; the other, *Los empeños de una casa,* has strong leading female roles, especially that of Leonor, which is a sort of autobiographical figure. The comic character Castaño, a mulatto servant from the New World, speaks satirically of the machismo of white Spaniards in a metatheatrical scene parodying the "cape and sword" comedy as a literary genre.

From the baroque intellectual world of her convent cell Sor Juana sends messages that intimate her deep concerns as a woman and a *criolla.* She is a key figure for understanding colonial Mexico.

– GEORGINA SABAT-RIVERS

JUÁREZ, BENITO

Benito Juárez (*b.* 21 March 1806; *d.* 18 July 1872), president of Mexico (1858–1872). Juárez led the liberals and Republicans during the War of the Reform (1858–1861) and the French Intervention (1862–1867). For many Mexicans, and in the official pantheon of national heroes, Juárez is a preeminent symbol of Mexican nationalism and resistance to foreign intervention. His critics, however, continue to charge that Juárez resorted to dictatorial methods to prolong his presidency, undermined the property rights of rural villages, and sacrificed Mexican sovereignty to the United States.

Juárez was born in the village of San Pablo Guelatao, Oaxaca. His parents were Zapotec Indian peasants who died before he reached the age of four. Juárez was raised by relatives and worked in the fields until the age of twelve, when, in hopes of getting an education, he left his village and walked the forty miles to the city of Oaxaca to live with his sister. There, he was taken in by Antonio Salanueva, a bookbinder and Franciscan monk, who immediately took Juárez to be confirmed and encouraged him to attend the seminary for his education. Still lacking a primary education and with no more than the rudiments of Spanish grammar, Juárez began studying Latin. After two years, Juárez convinced his patron to allow him to study the arts since he was still too young to be ordained a priest. Juárez completed his secondary education in 1827. Lacking the financial resources and the inclination to receive holy orders, he rejected an ecclesiastical career in order to study law at the newly established Institute of Sciences and Arts, where he received his degree in 1834.

Even before Juárez received his law degree, his political career had begun with election to the City Council of Oaxaca in 1831. Two years later he was elected to the state legislature. He made a living as a lawyer, and in 1841 he was appointed a civil judge. In 1843, he married Margarita Maza. The following year, he was appointed secretary of government by the state governor, Antonio León, and then to the post of prosecutor with the state supreme court. In 1845, Juárez was elected to the state legislature, but that body was soon dissolved in a conservative rebellion led by General Mariano PAREDES. Juárez was then named by liberal forces to the executive committee for the state. Elected to the national congress the following year, Juárez sup-

Portrait of Benito Juárez by Diego Rivera, 1948. (Archivo Cenidiap)

ported President Valentín GÓMEZ FARÍAS in his attempt to use church property to pay for the war with the United States. Organized opposition to these efforts, the Rebellion of the Polkos (1847), brought Antonio López de SANTA ANNA back to the presidency, ended the liberal government, and forced Juárez to return to Oaxaca.

In Oaxaca, liberals regained control of the state and elected Juárez governor in 1847. At the end of his term in 1852, he accepted the post of director of the Institute of Sciences and Arts. When Santa Anna returned to the presidency in 1853, he exiled Juárez and other leading liberals. Juárez eventually ended up in New Orleans, where he met Ponciano ARRIAGA, Melchor OCAMPO, and other opponents of Santa Anna, and where he earned his living making cigars.

With Juárez and his allies providing the political platform for the liberal Revolution of Ayutla in 1854, Juárez traveled to Acapulco to serve as a political aide. When Juan ÁLVAREZ forced Santa Anna into exile the following year, liberal exiles were able to return to Mexico. President Álvarez named Juárez his minister of justice and ecclesiastical affairs. Juárez wrote the Ley Juárez

(eliminating the right of ecclesiastical and military courts to hear civil cases), which President Álvarez signed in November 1855. Juárez resigned the following month, returning to Oaxaca, where he took office as governor in January 1856 and served for nearly two years. Juárez supported and swore to uphold the Constitution of 1857, but he took no direct role in drafting that document. President Ignacio COMONFORT designated Juárez minister of government in November 1857. Elected president of the Supreme Court (and first in line of succession to the presidency), Juárez took the oath of that office on 1 December 1857. Ten days later President Comonfort ordered Congress closed and Juárez arrested. Juárez was freed in January 1858 and escaped from the capital, just before conservative militarists overthrew Comonfort and declared Félix ZULOAGA president. The coup notwithstanding, in accordance with the Constitution of 1857, Juárez succeeded Comonfort in the presidency, taking the oath of office on 19 January 1858 in Guanajuato, thereby leaving Mexico with two presidents and civil war.

During the War of the Reform, or Three Years' War (1858–1860), Juárez fled to Guadalajara, where he was captured and nearly executed by conservative forces. Later he made his way to Colima, then Manzanillo, and by way of Panama, Havana, and New Orleans to Veracruz, where the liberal governor, Manuel Gutiérrez Zamora, allowed Juárez to establish his government. With the support of the radical liberals (known as puros) like Miguel LERDO DE TEJADA and Melchor Ocampo, Juárez issued the reform laws separating the church and state, establishing civil marriage and civil registration of births and deaths, secularizing the cemeteries, and expropriating the property of the church. The conservative forces held most of central Mexico but were unable to dislodge the Juárez government from Veracruz. Perennially short of funds to pay and provision the improvised forces that fought the conservatives, the liberal government expropriated and sold church property and negotiated with the United States.

During the war, Juárez authorized arrangements with the United States that have been the source of enduring controversies about his patriotism. The McLane–Ocampo Treaty, which Juárez's secretary of foreign relations Melchor Ocampo negotiated with the U.S. diplomat Robert M. McLane in 1859, permitted United States protection of transit over routes across Mexican territory in exchange for several million dollars. The treaty was rejected by the U.S. Senate. In what is known as the Antón Lizardo incident, President Juárez authorized U.S. ships to attack conservative vessels flying the Mexican flag at anchor in the port of Antón Lizardo, Veracruz, in 1860. Juárez's critics charge that he condoned foreign intervention and sold out to the United States.

Further concessions were not necessary before liberal forces under Jesús González Ortega defeated the conservative army and recaptured Mexico City in December 1860. At the end of Comonfort's term in 1861, there were new elections, which Juárez won. His government's suspension of payments on the foreign debt led to the intervention of Spain, France, and Great Britain. Spanish and British forces soon withdrew, but French forces, supporting the creation of a Mexican empire, advanced toward Mexico City in early 1862, and in 1864 the Austrian archduke MAXIMILIAN von Habsburg took the throne as Maximilian I.

The French Intervention (1862–1867) provides conflicting images of Juárez. A heroic Juárez led the Republican forces that tenaciously defended Mexico and its Republican constitution during desperate years of struggle against foreign and imperial armies. But Juárez's critics charge that he illegally extended his presidency when his constitutional term ended in 1865 and that he arbitrarily ordered the arrest and imprisonment of Jesús González Ortega, who ought to have succeeded to the presidency. The defeat of the imperial armies and the execution of Maximilian in 1867 provided a moment of unity for Mexican liberals, but Juárez's attempt to alter the constitution and strengthen the presidency by referendum again prompted critics to charge him with dictatorial methods. Many liberals opposed his reelection, but Juárez retained enough support to win the presidential elections of December 1867.

The liberals divided into three major factions backing Sebastián Lerdo de Tejada, Porfirio DÍAZ, and Juárez. The president repeatedly resorted to grants of extraordinary power to combat revolts and to maintain order. His critics maintained that Juárez was corrupted by power and increasingly dictatorial. By the time of the 1871 elections, Juárez could no longer count on a majority of votes, and the election passed to Congress, which elected him to another term. Porfirio Díaz resorted to rebellion, but Juárez was able to defeat him, again with an extension of extraordinary powers.

Not long afterward, on the evening of 18 July 1872, Juárez died. Controversial during his lifetime, he became a premier symbol of Mexican nationalism after his death. Ironically, Porfirio Díaz, as president, played a major role in creating the Juárez myth. As a national hero, Juárez has been most commonly invoked by presidents seeking to create an image of continuity with the past during times when stability and economic growth rather than reform have been the major concerns of government.

— D. F. STEVENS

JUÁREZ, JOSÉ

José Juárez (*b.* 1617; *d.* 1661), painter. The son of Luis Juárez, José was surely introduced to painting in his father's workshop. He has been considered by some to be the best painter of colonial Mexico. These claims are often accompanied by assertions that he must have received training in Spain. Others consider that the presence of Sebastián López de Arteaga and of original works by Francisco de Zurbarán in New Spain would have been sufficient for someone of his talent to develop as he did. Juárez's works show the influence not only of Zurbarán but also of compositions by Peter Paul Rubens, known in New Spain through prints. Probably his best-known painting is a complex composition depicting martyrdom and glorification, *Saints Justus and Pastor.*

— CLARA BARGELLINI

JUÁREZ, LUIS

Luis Juárez (*b.* ca. 1585; *d.* ca. 1635), Mexican painter. Juárez was the founder of an important dynasty of colonial Mexican painters. Although the place of his birth is unknown, his mannerist style can clearly be identified as Mexican—influenced, of course, by the Spanish masters who preceded him, particularly the Sevillian Alonso Vázquez, who came to New Spain in 1603 and died there in 1608. The works of Juárez are remarkably uniform in style and feeling, usually showing religious figures in an elegant yet subdued and direct manner. Scattered throughout Mexico are nearly one hundred paintings that can be attributed to Juárez, evidence that he was well and widely known.

— CLARA BARGELLINI

JUÁREZ CELMAN, MIGUEL

Miguel Juárez Celman (*b.* 29 September 1844; *d.* 14 April 1909), president of Argentina (1886–1890). Juárez Celman, born in Córdoba, took a strong anticlerical position in promoting secular education. After serving as a legal adviser, legislator, and provincial minister, he became an unconditional supporter of Julio Argentino ROCA. He married Roca's sister, and Roca married Juárez Celman's sister. In 1882, Roca decided that his brother-in-law should govern Córdoba. Impressed with Juárez Celman's political machine, Roca then imposed him as president of the republic.

As chief executive, Juárez Celman was self-serving and corrupt. His regime promoted European immigration, foreign investment, public works, and economic growth. Unfortunately, wild speculation, galloping inflation, and a tripling of the public debt occurred. A particularly irresponsible issue of paper currency resulted in the loss of political legitimacy. When Juárez Celman belatedly took measures to head off the financial crisis, his supporters refused to back him in Congress.

Angry investors and those who suffered a decline in their standard of living joined with Catholic activists and the Unión Cívica (Civic Union) in demanding honest government. Three days of rebellion, known as the 1890 Revolution, resulted in Juárez Celman's resignation on 6 August, 1890. Once worth over $30 million, he died in obscure poverty at Capitán Sarmiento Arrecites.

— DOUGLAS W. RICHMOND

JULIÃO, CARLOS

Carlos Julião (*b.* 1740; *d.* 18 November 1811), officer in the Portuguese army and artist. Born in Italy, Julião began a military career in Portugal in 1763 and by 1800 had been promoted to colonel. During his thirty-seven years in military service, he traveled to India, China, and South America. He recorded his travels in a pictorial travel account that was published posthumously in 1960 by the Brazilian National Library. One section of the account consists of forty-three watercolors without text. Entitled *Ditos de figurinhos de brancos, negros dos usos do Rio e Serro do Frio,* the watercolors depict diverse social and cultural aspects of the Portuguese colony of Rio de Janeiro during the late eighteenth century. They show members of the white elite at work and in their domestic life; slaves working in the mines, at festivals, and in the cities; and Indians. These watercolors are iconographically and sociologically significant because they document daily life in colonial Rio de Janeiro through the eyes of a Portuguese official.

— CAREN A. MEGHREBLIAN

JULIÃO ARRUDA DE PAULA, FRANCISCO

Francisco Julião Arruda de Paula (*b.* 16 February 1915), honorary president, Peasant Leagues of Brazil. Born to a once-prominent landowning family in Pernambuco State, Julião became a lawyer and politician who defended peasants and advocated land reform. He was twice elected state legislator in 1954 and 1958 and entered Congress in 1962. In 1964 the military imprisoned him, and in 1965 Mexico granted him asylum. Exiled, Julião returned to Brazil once in 1979 and again in 1986, when he ran unsuccessfully for Congress. Rejected by voters, he returned to Mexico.

Julião was a controversial figure in the rural labor movement. He believed that feudalism reigned in Brazil and only a bourgeois revolution could bring progress. He pushed for radical agrarian reform—the quick redistribution of large landholdings without compensat-

ing owners in cash—and the complete enfranchisement of the rural poor. Fiercely independent, he devised his own spiritually rich discourse of revolt and resisted the directives of organizations, even his own.

Key supporters of the rural movement, such as the Brazilian Communist Party, distanced themselves from Julião. Within the Peasant Leagues, his independence spawned factionalism, with some members forcefully seizing land and others supporting legal methods of change. All the same, Julião did more to popularize the cause of the rural poor in Brazil and abroad than any other individual.

— CLIFF WELCH

JUSTO, JOSÉ AGUSTÍN PEDRO

José Agustín Pedro Justo (*b.* 26 February 1876; *d.* 11 January 1943), general and president of Argentina (1932–1938); leader of the Concordancia. Born in Concepción del Uruguay, Entre Ríos Province, Justo gained national prominence as a member of the Argentine army. After graduating from the Military College of San Martín in 1892, he rose rapidly through the ranks. He gained

José Agustín Pedro Justo. (Organization of American States)

influence over a generation of military officers as the director of his alma mater between 1915 and 1922.

Having achieved the rank of brigadier general, he entered national politics in 1922, when President Marcelo T. de ALVEAR (1922–1928) appointed him minister of war. Along with other members of the Alvear administration, Justo joined the Anti-Personalist wing of the Radical Civic Union. In opposition to the second administration of President Hipólito YRIGOYEN (reelected 1928), he joined with the planners of the Revolution of 1930. When the military, led by General José Félix URIBURU, seized power, he participated in the provisional government as commander-in-chief of the army.

Justo became the leading spokesman for conservative politicians who hoped to impose limits on democracy and to use the government to protect their interests. When support for Uriburu faded in 1931, the provisional government sponsored elections engineered to favor the conservatives, and Justo, with the support of the National Democratic Party and the Anti-Personalist Radicals, was elected president. Serving from 1932 to 1938, he directed the consolidation of the Concordancia, a coalition of conservative political forces that controlled Argentine politics until 1943.

Justo's administration maneuvered Argentina through the Great Depression. The fiscal innovations initiated under Justo, including the Roca–Runciman Pact (1933), the Pinedo Plan, the establishment of a national income tax, and the creation of Argentina's Central Bank, were overshadowed by the growing reliance on electoral fraud, censorship, and repression that maintained the Concordancia in power.

— DANIEL LEWIS

JUSTO, JUAN B.

Juan B. Justo (*b.* 28 June 1865; *d.* 8 January 1928), Argentine Socialist congressman, senator, and party founder. Born in the city of Buenos Aires, Justo graduated from the medical school of the local university in 1888. After travel to Europe, he returned to Argentina in the early 1890s to serve as a surgical specialist at the head of a local clinic and as a professor at the school from which he had recently graduated. In these positions, he introduced modern sanitary and scientific techniques into Argentina's operating rooms.

In the 1890s, Justo's interests began to shift from medicine to politics. His concern with the many environmentally induced illnesses he was called on to treat made him determined to attack the social conditions producing them. In 1893 he began to meet with like-minded professionals and skilled workers to found a socialist newspaper. The result was the appearance in 1894 of *La Vanguardia,* destined to be the most influential socialist publication in Argentina. Soon thereafter, Justo helped found the Socialist Party of Argentina, which in 1896 began to participate in local and national elections on a regular basis.

As the Socialist Party evolved and expanded, Justo emerged as its principal leader and guiding force. A man of great intellectual ability, he molded the party in his own image and directed it along the path—mostly a moderate one—he believed best suited to Argentine conditions. One of the few Argentine Socialists well versed in Marxist theory (he produced the first Spanish translation of *Das Kapital*), he closely followed various European models of socialist theory, organization, and practice, adjusting them whenever necessary to local circumstances and conditions. Among his several publications, *Teoría y práctica de la historia* (1909) best describes and explains Justo's particular brand of socialism.

Under Justo's direction, the Socialist Party of Argentina grew in size, strength, and support. Justo himself was elected three times to the national Chamber of Deputies (1912–1916, 1916–1920, and 1920–1924) and once to the national Senate (1924–1928) from the federal capital. As a legislator, Justo was a forceful advocate for his party's programmatic agenda and an acerbic critic of the governments in power. His speeches were characterized by careful and often compelling reasoning, extensive documentation, frequent references to foreign examples, and sardonic wit. The acknowledged leader of his party, he also served as the head of its congressional delegation.

Justo's brilliance and leadership attracted many like-minded and able young men to the party. He developed a coterie of protegés, notably Nicolás Repetto and Enrique DICKMANN, who were closely tied to him not only by philosophy but also by marriage. Throughout the first three decades of the twentieth century, Justo and his allies dominated the editorial board of *La Vanguardia* as well as the main directive positions and candidate lists of the Socialist Party.

Although the party flourished under Justo's direction, there were many who chafed and occasionally rebelled against his tight discipline and the control he exercised from the top. Dissident reaction against the "family elite," a constant and repeated complaint, resulted in several serious schisms within the party in these years. Rarely, however, was open criticism directed against Justo himself, who remained the most widely respected, and by some revered, socialist in Argentina. The impact of Justo's ideas continued to have a substantial influence on the direction of Argentina's Socialist Party well after his death in 1928.

— RICHARD J. WALTER

K

KAGEL, MAURICIO RAÚL

Mauricio Raúl Kagel (*b.* 24 December 1931), Argentine composer who became a naturalized German citizen. He was born in Buenos Aires. At the University of Buenos Aires he studied literature and philosophy until 1955. He trained with private instructors, most notably with Juan Carlos PAZ. For a few years he worked as a pianist and conductor for opera preparation at the Teatro Colón in Buenos Aires. In 1957 he moved to Germany where he studied with Werner Meyer-Eppler at the Institute for Research in Phonetics and Communications in Bonn. His career developed rapidly as a composer, conductor, writer, and lecturer. He founded the Cologne Ensemble for New Music in 1961.

Kagel's 1974 work Bestiarium *is a sound fable for three actors, bird calls and other objects, and tape.*

Since 1965, Kagel has written for what is now called "musical theater," and he has written and directed his own films. His early compositions, written while he was still living in his native country, were very pitch conscious and precisely structured. The String Sextet (1953, revised 1957) uses polymetric rhythms and microtonal writing. His more experimental *Musique de tour* for tape with light projections (1953), required a light system projected from a steel tower and sound broadcast from twenty-four loudspeakers. Other influential compositions by Kagel include *Anagrama* for spoken choir, four soloists, and chamber orchestra (1957–1958), based on a palindrome by Dante; *Transición* no. 1 for electronic music (1958–1960); and *Transición* no. 2 for piano and tape recorder (1958–1959). Theatrical components became very important in his works *Sur scène* for instrumental theater (1959–1960); *Pandoras-box* for bandoneon, a type of accordion (1960–1962); *Ludwig van* (1970), a homage to Beethoven that appeared in several versions, including a German television film and a recorded version with Kagel's ensemble playing distorted music of Beethoven; and *Staatstheater* (1970), the prototype of a veritable anti-opera.

Other significant works by Kagel include *Match* for two cellos and percussion (1964); *Tremens,* instrumental theater for two actors and electronically amplified instruments (1963–1965); *Pas de cinq,* variable scenes for five actors (1965); *Music for Renaissance Instruments* (1965–1967); *Halleluja* for voices (1967–1968); *Atem* for one wind instrument, tape recorder, and two loudspeakers (1970); *Con voce* for three silent players (1972); *Zwei Mann Orchester* for two performers (1971–1973); *1898* for children's choir (1972); *Mare nostrum* for contralto, baritone, and chamber ensemble (1973); *Exotica* for non-European instruments (1972); *Die Mutation* for children's voices and piano obbligato (1971); *Siegfriedp* for cello (1971); *Bestiarium* sound fable for three actors, bird calls and other objects, and tape (1974); *Die Umkehrung Amerikas* (1975–1976), a radio play; *Unguis incarnatus est* for piano (1972); *Morceau de concours* for solo trumpet and tape (1971), a competition piece; *Variationen ohne Fuge* for orchestra and two actors, Brahms and Handel (1971–1972); *Tango alemán* for bandoneon (1978); *Vox humana?* cantata for narrator, choir, and orchestra (1979); *Rrrrrr....* a radio fantasy for different instrumental combinations (1982); *Pan* for piccolo flute and string quartet (1985); *Ein Brief* for mezzo-soprano and orchestra (1986); *Zwei Akte* for saxophone and harp (1988–1989); *Les idées fixes,* rondo for orchestra (1989); and *Der Windrose* for salon orchestra (1988).

Films written and directed by Kagel include *Antithèse* (1965); *Match* (1966); *Solo* (1966–1967); *Duo* (1968); *Halleluja* (1967–1968); *Sous tension* (1975); *Blue's Blue* (1981); and *Dressage* (1985). He also wrote the music for the film *MM51* (1977).

— ALCIDES LANZA

KAHLO, FRIDA

Frida Kahlo (*b.* 6 July 1907; *d.* 13 July 1954), Mexican artist. Kahlo was born in Coyoacán, the daughter of the Hungarian Jewish immigrant photographer Guillermo Kahlo and Matilde Calderón. She studied at the Escuela Nacional Preparatoria, one of thirty-five girls in a student body of two thousand. In 1925, she suffered a fractured spine and pelvis in a traffic accident that left her in constant pain. During her convalescence, she began to paint.

In 1929 Kahlo married the famed muralist Diego Rivera. Together they became international celebrities, honored by the art world and the political left. Among their friends, they counted Leon Trotsky, Max Ernst,

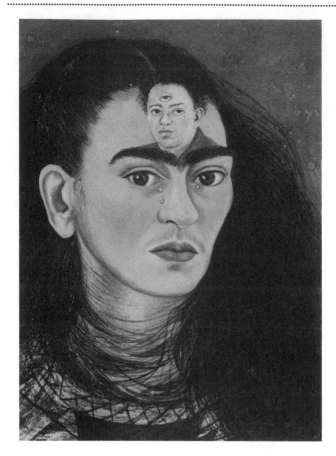

Diego y yo. *Oil on masonite by Frida Kahlo, 1949. (Mary-Anne Martin/Fine Art)*

Tina Modotti, Henry Ford, John D. and Nelson Rockefeller, Pablo Neruda, André Breton, and Isamu Noguchi. To complement Diego Rivera's extravagant character, Frida Kahlo created her own flamboyance. Drawing upon the Mexican cultural nationalist movement, she elevated Tehuana dress to haute couture and coiffed her hair in indigenous styles embellished with ribbons, bows, combs, and flowers. Necklaces, earrings, and rings completed her costume along with a prominent cigarette. A vivacious, engaging, and playful presence, Frida Kahlo was a living work of art, self-constructed to fight her constant physical agony and her sorrow at being unable to conceive a child and having to endure her husband's infidelities.

Most of Kahlo's paintings are small, intricately crafted self-portraits combining the real and the fantastic. They capture her spiritual and physical suffering in anatomical, surgical detail cast in traditional Mexican art forms like the *retablo,* using Catholic and pre-Colombian symbolism and imagery. Her subject matter is distinctly female: motherhood, fertility, the womb, childbirth, childhood, children, and family. Her art is precociously feminist in her concern with domestic violence, adultery, and her drive to control her own body. Often interpreted as surrealist, her depiction of flowing blood and wounded bodies in fact derives from Mexican popular culture. In her fantastic depiction of monkeys, prickly pears, and rainforest, she achieves a degree of sensual expression unequalled in Mexican art. André Breton wrote: "There is no art more exclusively feminine, in the sense that, in order to be as seductive as possible, it is only too willing to play alternately at being absolutely pure and absolutely pernicious. The art of Frida Kahlo is a ribbon about a bomb" (Herrera, p. 214).

Kahlo died in July 1954 at the age of forty-seven. By the 1980s, her art had received the international recognition that had eluded her in her lifetime.

— MARY KAY VAUGHAN

KINNEY, HENRY L.

Henry L. Kinney (*b.* 3 June 1814; *d.* July 1861[?]), U.S. filibuster and borderlands entrepreneur. A Pennsylvanian by birth, Kinney farmed and speculated in land in Illinois in the 1830s. Ruined in the Panic of 1837, he migrated to the Republic of Texas. In 1840, at the mouth of the Nueces River, within territory disputed by Texas and Mexico, he established a trading post/smuggler's nest that became known as Kinney's Rancho. Kinney, who became bilingual, survived border strife by providing information and supplies to Texan and Mexican forces alike, sometimes serving as intermediary between them. His ranch became the nucleus of a boomtown, Corpus Christi, after General Zachary Taylor stationed his army in its vicinity prior to the Mexican–American War. During that conflict, Kinney apparently was division quartermaster on the general staff of the Texas Volunteers and then agent of the U.S. Quartermaster Department, serving as supplier, scout, interpreter, and dispatch carrier.

Kinney served in the Republic of Texas's Ninth and Tenth congresses, as well as the Texas Constitutional Convention of 1845 (where he championed the interests of Spanish-speaking inhabitants). Although elected to the Senate of the first four Texas legislatures, he never took his seat in the second legislature and abandoned his seat in the fourth. After the Mexican–American War, he became involved in the publication of the *Corpus Christi Star* (later the *Nueces Valley*), Texas Ranger affairs, and promotion of Texas's first state fair (1852), held both to boost Corpus Christi and to raise aid for José María Carvajal's Republic of the Sierra Madre.

From 1854 to 1858 Kinney devoted himself to the Central American Land and Mining Company, designed to colonize—really filibuster—Central America's Mosquito Coast, on the basis of an invalid land grant. Kinney ruled Greytown (San Juan del Norte) as "civil and military governor" for part of this period. In 1859, Kinney served as Texas governor Sam Houston's agent to investigate Juan Cortina's raid on Brownsville. Elected a representative in Texas's eighth legislature, Kinney opposed secession and, in March 1861, was forced to give up his seat. Several undocumented accounts assert that he died at Matamoros, Mexico.

– ROBERT E. MAY

KINO, EUSEBIO FRANCISCO

Eusebio Francisco Kino (*b.* 10 August 1645; *d.* 15 March 1711), Jesuit missionary and explorer of northwestern New Spain. A native of Segno, near Trent, in the Italian Tyrol, educated in Austria and Germany, Kino was among the foreign-born Jesuit missionaries permitted by the Spanish crown under quota to serve in the Spanish Indies. He excelled in mathematics, astronomy, and cartography, and could have had a university chair in Europe. Instead, he put these skills to good use during a thirty-year career in New Spain, first as royal cosmographer of Admiral Isidro de Atondo's failed effort to occupy Baja California in the mid-1680s and then as the pioneer missionary of Pimería Alta (present-day northern Sonora and southern Arizona), capstone of the Jesuits' northwest missionary empire.

An irrepressible expansionist, Kino's restless nature better suited him for exploration and first contact with the Pimas and Pápagos (Tohono O'odam) than for everyday administrative routine at mission Dolores, which he established as his headquarters in 1687. On numerous expeditions, traveling the valleys of the San Pedro, Santa Cruz, Gila, and Colorado rivers, he introduced cattle, created demand for European goods, and mapped the country. His crowning cartographic achievement, which he drew the year before his death, showed California not as an island, a misconception of the seventeenth century, but as a peninsula.

In 1966, Kino's grave was discovered in Magdalena, Sonora, since renamed Magdalena de Kino. The Jesuits are promoting his cause for canonization. A mineral, a hospital, a table wine, and much else bear his name, and statues abound.

– JOHN L. KESSELL

KOELLREUTTER, HANS JOACHIM

Hans Joachim Koellreutter (*b.* 2 September 1915), German-born teacher and composer, who has lived in Brazil since 1937.

Koellreutter's effect on young Brazilian composers has been enormous. In 1939 he formed the group Música Viva Brasil and in 1940 began publishing a magazine of the same name. Through his group and his periodical, Koellreutter set out to introduce new music to Brazilian audiences. He championed the theories and music of Arnold Schoenberg, and encouraged his music students to employ the twelve-tone technique when writing music. Koellreutter's modernist agenda prompted Brazil's principal nationalist composer, Camargo GUARNIERI, to write the famous "Carta aberta aos músicos e críticos do Brasil" (Open letter to musicians and critics of Brazil), in which he attacked the idea that serial technique could be a suitable means of expression for nationalist music. Composers such as César Guerra PEIXE, Claudio SANTORO, and others who studied with Koellreutter went on to develop their own individual styles, but the ideas and teaching of Koellreutter made a major contribution to twentieth-century Brazilian music.

– DAVID P. APPLEBY

KORN, ALEJANDRO

Alejandro Korn (*b.* 3 May 1860; *d.* 9 October 1936), Argentine philosopher. Together with José VASCONCELOS and Antonio CASO in Mexico, Carlos VAZ FERREIRA in Uruguay, and Alejandro DEUSTUA in Peru, Korn belonged to a group of Latin American philosophers who were prominent at the end of the nineteenth and beginning of the twentieth centuries and who represented the beginning of a more professional approach to philosophy.

Korn was born in San Vicente, Buenos Aires Province, and educated in medicine at the University of Buenos Aires. He began his career as professor of philosophy at the University of Buenos Aires in 1906, while still engaged in his main profession as a psychiatrist. In the beginning, he was influenced by positivism, but he soon abandoned this position because of its naturalist determinism, which he felt made moral responsibility impossible. His Kantian-based philosophy was later influenced by the work of Europeans such as Wilhelm Dilthey and Henri Bergson.

Korn conceived of philosophy as a knowledge of the subjective, or the human, world, as opposed to science, which was the exact knowledge of the natural world. Philosophy was to him axiology, or the analysis of values and valuations as sources of all human action. Although it is not openly revealed in his philosophical writings, the base of his worldview is an intensely religious, but not dogmatic, feeling. His ethic is voluntarist and considers action as the way out of perplexities of theoretical antinomies. Although he considered Marxism an antiquated philosophy of the nineteenth century, he adhered to "ethical socialism," a form of socialism based on the moral reasoning of social justice.

Korn was the author of a classic work on the interpretation of the history of ideas in Argentina, *Influencias filosóficas en la evolución nacional* (1936). His philosophical writings have been collected in *Obras,* 3 vols. (1938–1940) and *Obras completas* (1949).

– JUAN CARLOS TORCHIA ESTRADA

KÖRNER, EMIL

Emil Körner (*b.* 10 October 1846; *d.* 25 March 1920), German army officer and founder of the modern Chilean army. Emil Körner Henze, as he was called in Chile, was born in Wegwitz, Saxony. He entered the army in 1866. He was a student and later taught at the Artillery and Engineer's School (Charlottenburg) and was decorated after Sedan. He graduated from the Kriegsakademie (staff school) in 1876 and served in Italy, Spain, and Africa. After nearly twenty years of service in the kaiser's army, Captain Körner had established a good record but, as a Saxon and a commoner, had a limited future as an officer of the imperial army. His military career took a sharp turn in 1885 because of the Chilean government's decision to professionalize its army. Impressed with what he had read of Chile's recent victory over Peru (War of the Pacific, 1879–1884), Körner accepted an offer to teach artillery, infantry, cartography, military history, and tactics; to serve as subdirector of the Escuela Militar; and to oversee establishment of a Chilean staff school. In Chile he ultimately rose to the rank of inspector general.

A year after his arrival he helped inaugurate the Academia de Guerra, and the Chilean army began a new life. Under Körner's direction the new staff school provided advanced training and the army adopted the general staff system in order to be prepared for war at any time. By 1889, the popular Körner was advocating wide-reaching reforms in military training. Two years later he helped the forces of the National Congress with the support of the Navy and some Army leaders to win a civil war against President José Manuel BALMACEDA. Subsequently Körner was given great latitude in the continual modernization of the army. He attracted several German missions to Chile in the last decade of the century, and by 1910, when he retired, Chile's army was superficially a creole copy of the kaiser's. Körner died in Berlin, but his remains were brought to Santiago in 1924.

– FREDERICK M. NUNN

KOSICE, GYULA

Gyula Kosice (*b.* 26 April 1924), Argentine painter and sculptor, born in Hungary. Kosice came to Argentina at age three. He studied at free academies from 1937 to 1942 and later at the School of Philosophy and Letters of the University of Buenos Aires and at the National School of Fine Arts. He founded the Grupo Madí art movement as well as the Asociación de Arte Concreto-Invención, a nonfigurative group. ("Madí," like Dada, is an arbitrary word.) Kosice designed the Hydrospatial City. He is the creator of hydrokinetic art and neon luminal sculpture. A member of the Argentine Writers' Society (SADE), Kosice wrote eight books, among them *Herbert Read* (1955), *Poème hydranlique* (1960), *Arte Hidrocinético* (1968), *Arte y arquitectura de agua* (1974), and *Arte Madí* (1980, 1982). His works are highly personal and imaginative, effecting a sense of tranquillity.

– AMALIA CORTINA ARAVENA

KRAUZE, ENRIQUE

Enrique Krauze (*b.* September 1947), Mexican historian and intellectual. Best known for his popular series of illustrated presidential biographies produced and marketed for the general public, Krauze has authored important historical works, most notably *Caudillos culturales en la revolución mexicana* (1976). His political essays in *Vuelta* often provoke critical discussion.

Born in the Federal District, Krauze graduated from the National University with an engineering degree and earned a Ph.D. from the Colegio de México. Awarded a Guggenheim fellowship for 1979–1980, he has collaborated closely with Nobel Prize winner Octavio PAZ as managing editor and subdirector of *Vuelta* since 1976. Krauze is the intellectual disciple of Daniel COSÍO VILLEGAS and Paz.

– RODERIC AI CAMP

KRIEGER, EDINO

Edino Krieger (*b.* 17 March 1928), Brazilian composer. Born in the state of Santa Catarina, Brazil, Krieger was the son of Aldo and Gertrudes Krieger. His father was a well-known violinist, conductor, and composer who undertook the musical instruction of his son when the boy was only seven. During the next seven years, Edino Krieger gave several recitals as a violinist, and at the age of fourteen received a scholarship to study violin at the Conservatório Brasileiro de Música in Rio de Janeiro. In 1944 he wrote an improvisation for solo flute and in 1945 became associated with a group of composers, Música Viva, under the leadership of Hans Joachim KOELLREUTTER, a pupil of Paul Hindemith. Three years later he won first prize in a competition sponsored by the Berkshire Music Center in Massachusetts. He later enrolled in the Juilliard School of Music in New York City, where he studied with Aaron Copland, Peter Mennin, and Darius Milhaud.

Krieger has combined a career as a composer of works of stylistic originality and powerful dramatic qualities with significant achievements as director of the music section of Brazil's National Foundation of the Arts. During his administration, the foundation contributed to a vitalization of musical performance throughout the nation and published scores of historical works by Brazilian composers, providing a heightened sense of the nation's cultural achievements. Important compositions by Krieger include his *Ludus symphonicus,* commissioned by the Instituto de Cultura e Bellas Artes of Venezuela, and his oratorio *Rio de Janeiro,* a dramatic narration of the birth of Brazil from its period of Portuguese colonization. Both these works were performed in Rio de Janeiro in 1988 at a special concert celebrating the composer's sixtieth birthday.

— DAVID P. APPLEBY

KRIEGER VASENA, ADALBERTO

Adalberto Krieger Vasena (*b.* 1920), a prominent Argentine economist. Educated at the University of Buenos Aires and in the United States, he received his doctorate in 1944 with a dissertation on "An Estimate of National Income." He has served on the faculties of the universities of Córdoba and La Plata and has held numerous posts. He served in the Ministry of the Treasury (1957–1958) and the Ministry of Economy and Labor (1967–1969). He is a member of the Economic Advisory Committee of the Stock Exchange of Buenos Aires and a member of the board of the Latin American Research Foundation and the board of the International Center for Economic Growth. He was chief of the Argentine delegation to the sixth meeting of the General Agreement on Tariffs and Trade (GATT) and has been an executive officer of numerous private companies. Dr. Krieger has written numerous articles and the book *Latin America: A Broader World Role.*

— ROBERT SCHEINA

KUBITSCHEK, MÁRCIA

Márcia Kubitschek (*b.* 23 October 1943), Brazilian cultural and political figure. The only natural daughter of President Juscelino KUBITSCHEK (another, Maria Estela, was adopted; he had no sons), she was born in Belo Horizonte, capital of Minas Gerais, while her father was its mayor. With the end of her first marriage, to a Bra-

zilian investment banker, she married the renowned Cuban American ballet dancer, Fernando Bujones, in New York City in 1980. Kubitschek has administered various cultural activities, including the Ballet of Rio de Janeiro, the Ballet of Brazil Foundation, the Brazilian Tourist Authority in New York City, and the Brasília 2000 Olympics Association. A political centrist, she was elected a member of the Brazilian Constituent Assembly of 1987–1988. The assembly reconstituted the country along civilian lines after the military dictatorship of 1964–1985, which had barred her father from campaigning for a second term as president. In the first direct gubernatorial elections held in the Federal District (Brasília), in 1991, she became lieutenant governor of the national capital built just over a generation before by her father. She lost a senatorial bid in 1994 although a record number of five women won seats that year to the Brazilian Senate.

— EDWARD A. RIEDINGER

KUBITSCHEK DE OLIVEIRA, JUSCELINO

Juscelino Kubitschek de Oliveira (*b.* 12 September 1902; *d.* 22 August 1976), president of Brazil (1956–1961), founder of Brasília (1960). Born in Diamantina, Minas Gerais, an impoverished colonial diamond-mining town, Kubitschek and his older sister were raised on the spare resources of their resolute and independent schoolteacher mother. Their father died when they were very young. A great-uncle had been prominent in early republican (late nineteenth century) state politics, favoring transfer of the capital from the baroque Ouro Prêto to a new, planned city, Belo Horizonte. Studying grade school with his mother and completing secondary education at a local seminary, Kubitschek entered the medical school of Belo Horizonte in 1922. Supporting himself as a telegraph operator, he became a doctor in 1927.

Income from his first years of medical practice allowed him to pursue specialized study in Europe during most of 1930. He established his own practice in Belo Horizonte the following year. That year he married Sarah Gomes de Lemos, member of a socially and politically prominent family. During an uprising in 1932 by the neighboring state of São Paulo against the federal government, Kubitschek was called to the borderline front as a medical officer. It was at this time that he met and impressed Benedito Valadares, a local politician serving as head of the military police in the region, who became Kubitschek's political mentor.

In 1933 President Getúlio VARGAS appointed Valadares interventor, or chief executive, of Minas Gerais. Valadares made Kubitschek his chief of staff. Actively

Juscelino Kubitschek de Oliveira. (Iconographia)

extending the political network of his boss, and building a base for himself in Diamantina, Kubitschek was elected a federal deputy the following year, occupying this position until the Vargas coup of 1937 closed Congress and established the authoritarian Estado Nôvo.

Uneasy about such a regime, he returned to his medical practice and profitably revived it. However, he entered public life again in 1940 when Valadares appointed him mayor of Belo Horizonte. His mayoralty gave singular impetus to the urban infrastructure of the still-developing city, augmenting streets, parks, water, and sewage systems; enhancing real estate; and encouraging commercial and industrial development. The model neighborhood of Pampulha became a signature of his administration with its dramatically modern church, designed by Oscar NIEMEYER and bearing murals by Cândido PORTINARI.

As the strength of the Estado Nôvo withered by 1945 under the victory of democratic forces in World War II, Vargas and his state interventors sought to maintain their political control in the emerging era of political liberty. They organized the Social Democratic Party (PSD) as a powerful opponent to the anti-Vargas forces, which had coalesced in the National Democratic Union (UDN).

Kubitschek became the organizing secretary of the PSD in Minas Gerais, the largest section of the party in the country, extending throughout the state his network of contacts. Removed from the mayoralty of Belo Horizonte with the ouster of Vargas near the end of 1945, Kubitschek was voted in by a substantial margin as a federal deputy that year and began his term in the Constituent Assembly in 1946.

Maneuvering himself within the factions of the PSD of Minas Gerais, Kubitschek ran successfully for the governorship of the state in the election of 1950. He obtained the tacit support of Getúlio Vargas, who won the presidential election the same year through another party he had founded, the trade-union-based Brazilian Labor Party (PTB).

With a campaign slogan of "energy and transportation," Kubitschek began in 1951 an intensive gubernatorial administration dedicated to activating the state's economy through industrialization. He expanded or inaugurated numerous hydroelectric plants; brought the West German steel company, Mannesmann, to the state; enlarged the road network by many hundreds of miles; and built many clinics, schools, and bridges. These projects were financed through federal funds, foreign capital, and mixed public and private enterprises, a pattern he would also apply at the federal level.

Using the success of his administration in Minas Gerais, Kubitschek prepared himself for the presidential succession of 1955. He launched his campaign in the shadow of the August 1954 suicide of Vargas, who had been charged with massive corruption by the military and the UDN. Attempting to acquire the power base of the fallen president, Kubitschek renewed the alliance of the PSD and PTB by selecting as his vice presidential running mate the political heir of Vargas, João GOULART. He thereby also acquired the ire of the anti-Vargas forces. Kubitschek campaigned with an extensive plan for national development, pledging himself to fulfill a series of economic targets that would culminate in the building of a new national capital, Brasília, on the central plateau of the country. He won the October election, however, with only one-third of the votes, the lowest in Brazilian history, since he was relatively unknown in national politics and bore the burden of anti-Vargas sentiment. Only a protective coup the following month allowed Kubitschek and Goulart to take office for their five-year term in January 1956.

Because Kubitschek entered the presidency under such bitter and delicate circumstances, diligent execution of his campaign promise of "fifty years of progress in five" became paramount for solidifying his national support. Campaign targets were achieved as the production of concrete, steel, energy, and other components of industrial expansion dramatically increased. The automobile industry was created, soon making the country almost self-sufficient in such production. The latter years of the Kubitschek government witnessed economic growth at annual rates averaging over 7 percent. In April 1960 he inaugurated the futuristic and controversial new capital, Brasília, with buildings by Niemeyer and an urban design of Lúcio COSTA, a bravura feat strikingly affirming national accomplishment.

The cost of such progress, however, was inflation. Kubitschek encouraged extensive foreign investment, and the vast market potential of a growing Brazil attracted it. However, declining income from Brazilian exports created a shortage of capital, pressuring inflation. Kubitschek was cooperative in international relations, suggesting Operation Pan American, a hemisphere-wide approach to Latin American problems, to U.S. president Dwight D. Eisenhower. But in 1959 Kubitschek rejected the International Monetary Fund's (IMF) efforts to make him reduce inflation by cutting his economic expansion program. As a result, inflation accelerated. This and charges of graft and favoritism, along with the fact that Kubitschek was constitutionally barred from succeeding himself, enabled the candidate of the opposition, Jânio QUADROS, to win the 1960 presidential election.

Still popular personally, Kubitschek was elected a senator from Goiás the same year. However, with the establishment in 1964 of a military regime, the political rights of Kubitschek were canceled for ten years, thereby ending his plans to return to the presidency in the election of 1965. He went into intermittent exile in Europe or the United States, supporting an unsuccessful Frente Ampla, a broad front of civilian leaders allied across the political spectrum. After 1967 he remained in Brazil, becoming an investment banking executive. He died in 1976 in an automobile accident on a highway between São Paulo and Rio de Janeiro. His funeral procession in Brasília produced one of the greatest popular outpourings of grief in the history of the city, and the military government was forced to decree three days of official mourning.

Although Kubitschek dominated the Brazilian national scene for a relatively brief period, his memory has proved lasting due to a concentration of exceptional personal, economic, political, and cultural factors. Possessed of great ambition and energy, he was able as an administrator to take advantage of economic opportunities resulting from increased Brazilian exports during World War II and then from the resurgence of international capital in the recovery from that war. He represented a generation of Brazilian elites that legitimized itself through modernization based on industrialization and accommodated itself to trade unionism growing from that development. During his presidency there occurred a rare combination of intensive economic production within a fully functioning democratic government. His administration bore, moreover, a cultural style, expressed in architecture, landscape design, sculpture, and even the rhythms of bossa nova, which projected itself as the embodiment of international modernism, giving Brazilians a sense of confidence and promise.

– EDWARD A. RIEDINGER

KUMATE RODRÍGUEZ, JESÚS

Jesús Kumate Rodríguez (*b.* 12 November 1924), Mexican health official and medical researcher. A native of Mazatlán, Sinaloa, Kumate graduated from Mexico's Military Medical School (1946), later obtaining a Ph.D. in biomedical sciences in 1963. Kumate taught at both the Military Medical School and the National University, and served as research coordinator of the Children's Hospital, Mexico City, an institution he later directed (1979–1980). In 1974 he was invited to become a member of the National College, and in 1983 the secretary of health appointed him coordinator of the National Institutes of Health for the entire country. He became assistant secretary of health in 1985, and in 1988 President Carlos SALINAS selected Kumate as his secretary of health.

– RODERIC AI CAMP

L

LA SALLE, RENÉ-ROBERT CAVELIER, SIEUR DE

René-Robert Cavelier, Sieur de La Salle (*b.* 22 November 1643; *d.* 19 March 1687), French explorer. A native of Rouen, France, La Salle was educated by the Jesuits but left the order and went to Canada in 1666 to enter the fur trade. In 1679 he built and launched the first sailing vessel to ply the Great Lakes. By canoe, he descended the Mississippi River to its mouth in 1682, claiming for France all the lands of its drainage.

By canoe, La Salle descended the Mississippi River to its mouth in 1682, claiming for France all the lands of its drainage.

La Salle envisioned a warm-water port on the Gulf of Mexico to serve his commercial aims and French designs of empire. Returning to France, he won royal support for a voyage to the Mississippi through the Gulf to establish a colony on the lower river. He sailed from La Rochelle on 24 July 1684. Because of geographical uncertainty, he missed the mouth of the Mississippi and landed his 280 colonists at Texas's Matagorda Bay on 20 February 1685. Realizing his error, he sought his post on the Illinois River by land, but was slain by a disenchanted follower near the Trinity River in eastern Texas.

La Salle was responsible for opening the Mississippi Valley for development. His Gulf of Mexico expedition sparked a renewal of Spanish exploration in the Gulf that led to Spanish occupation of eastern Texas and Pensacola Bay. Because of La Salle, the United States asserted a claim to Texas as part of the Louisiana Purchase, giving rise to a boundary dispute with Spain that lasted until 1819.

— ROBERT S. WEDDLE

LA SERNA, JOSÉ DE

José de La Serna (*b.* 1770; *d.* 6 July 1832), last viceroy of Peru and commander of the Spanish forces at the Battle of Ayacucho (1824). A native of Jerez de la Frontera, Spain, he was a professional soldier who fought in the defense of Ceuta in 1790, and later against England and France. He was sent to Peru in 1816 as one of the generals under Viceroy Joaquín de la Pezuela. He criticized the latter's decision to hold on to Lima at all costs, and in 1821, following Pezuela's overthrow, he was acclaimed viceroy by his fellow commanders. He negotiated briefly with General José de SAN MARTÍN, especially over the idea of placing Peru under a crowned head. The negotiations came to naught, and in July 1821, he abandoned Lima and took his army to the highlands, where he established his seat of command in Huancayo and later in Cuzco. On 9 December 1824, on a plain near Ayacucho, he led the last royal army in South America against General Antonio José de SUCRE, Simón Bolívar's chief lieutenant. La Serna was defeated, and with that loss Spain's empire in the New World, save its Caribbean possessions, disappeared. La Serna was taken prisoner and returned to Spain, where he received the title Count of the Andes. He subsequently held the post of captain-general of Granada (1831). He died in Seville.

— JEFFREY KLAIBER

LABARCA HUBERTSON, AMANDA

Amanda Labarca Hubertson (*b.* 5 December 1886; *d.* 1975), Chilean educator and feminist. Born in Santiago to Onofre and Sabina Pinto, Labarca studied at the Pedagogic Institute of the University of Chile in Santiago, at Columbia University in New York, and at the Sorbonne in Paris. She married educator and politician Guillermo Labarca Hubertson, a Radical Party activist who was minister of justice and education during the first presidency of Arturo Alessandri. Amanda Labarca taught most of her life and was active in the Radical Party. Her books on women's issues include *A dónde va la mujer?* (Whither Women?, 1934) and *Feminismo contemporáneo* (Contemporary Feminism, 1947). Labarca worked in the women's suffrage movement and was president of Mujeres de Chile (Chilean Women). A devoted secondary school teacher, she also served as director of a high school and later taught courses on education at the University of Chile. She wrote important books about education, including *Realidades y problemas de nuestra enseñanza* (Realities and Problems in Chilean Education, 1953), *La escuela secundaria en los Estados Unidos* (Secondary Schools in the United States, 1919), and *Historia de la enseñanza en Chile* (History of Chilean Education, 1939). Labarca also wrote essays and fiction during her early years, including *La lámpara maravillosa* (1921) and *Impresiones de juventud* (1909). With a handful of Latin American women, Labarca played a prominent role in focusing attention on women's issues and was an active participant in international feminist congresses during the first half of the twentieth century.

— GEORGETTE MAGASSY DORN

LABASTIDA Y DÁVALOS, PELAGIO ANTONIO DE

Pelagio Antonio de Labastida y Dávalos (*b.* 1816; *d.* 1891), bishop of Puebla, archbishop of Mexico, opponent of the Reform. Born in Zamora, Michoacán, Labastida was ordained in 1839. He became rector of the seminary in Morelia and governor of the diocese in the early 1850s, and was bishop of Puebla from 1855 to 1863. Labastida protested against President Ignacio COMONFORT's 31 March 1856 decree punishing the Puebla clergy for the rebellion of Zacapoaxtla, which he had not supported, and the loss of the city to the Conservatives. Banished from Mexico, he went to Rome and became a strong opponent of liberalism and the Reform movement. Labastida returned with the French Intervention, and on 21 June 1863 General Élie-Frédéric Forey appointed him to the three-man executive power. On 17 November Marshal François BAZAINE removed him as an obstacle to French efforts to find a compromise with moderate Liberals. Labastida opposed Maximilian's ecclesiastical policy, which sought to conciliate Liberal opinion by upholding the disamortization (the transfer of corporate properties to private ownership) policies of the period 1856–1863. Exiled in 1867 by JUÁREZ, he attended the First Vatican Council (1869–1870) in Rome. He was allowed to return to Mexico in 1871 and died in Oacalco, Morelos.

— BRIAN HAMNETT

LABRADOR RUÍZ, ENRIQUE

Enrique Labrador Ruíz (*b.* 11 May 1902; *d.* 1991), Cuban novelist, journalist, and short-story writer. Labrador Ruíz was born in Sagua la Grande in the province of Las Villas. Self-taught, he started out as a journalist for the newspaper *El Sol* in the city of Cienfuegos and eventually became one of its editors. When the paper moved to Havana, he, too, moved and once there, began to write for other newspapers and magazines. In 1946 he received the National Short Story Prize for "El conejito Ulán." In 1950 he was awarded the National Prize for

his novel *La sangre hambrienta,* and in 1951 he received the Juan Gualberto Gómez prize for journalism. His work appeared in publications all over the Americas, including *Orígenes* (Cuba), *The American News* (United States), and *Babel* (Chile).

After the Cuban Revolution of 1959, Labrador Ruíz became editor of the National Publishing House. Although he was initially supportive of the Cuban government, he eventually broke with it and emigrated to Miami, where he died in 1991. His work is considered to be a precursor of the modern Latin American novel.

Among Labrador Ruíz's most important works are the novels *El laberinto de sí mismo* (1933, repr. 1983), *Cresival* (1936), *Carne de quimera: Novelines neblinosos* (1947, repr. 1983), and *La sangre hambrienta* (1950), and the short stories *El gallo en el espejo* (1953) and *Cuentos* (1970).

— ROBERTO VALERO

LACALLE HERRERA, LUIS ALBERTO

Luis Alberto Lacalle Herrera (*b.* 13 July 1941), president of Uruguay, elected in 1989 and took office 1 March 1990. He was the first Blanco (National Party) president of Uruguay elected in the twentieth century. The grandson of the great Blanco leader Luis Alberto de HERRERA, Lacalle graduated from law school and gravitated toward a political career. He was elected a deputy to Congress in 1971 but lost his position in 1973 when Congress was closed in the coup that brought the military to power for the next twelve years.

In 1981 Lacalle founded a political group within the Blancos known as the National Herrerist Council, and by 1982 he was on the Blanco board of directors. In the national elections permitted by the military in November 1984, Lacalle was elected to the Senate. In 1987 he served as vice president to the Senate. In July 1988, Lacalle declared himself a presidential candidate. With the 1988 death of the last political caudillo, Blanco Senator Wilson FERREIRA ALDUNATE, Lacalle emerged as the leader of the party. On 26 November 1989, aided by infighting in the ruling Colorado Party and a stagnant economy, Lacalle was elected president, with his party receiving 39 percent of the vote.

Lacalle is an articulate, center-right politician who is attempting to steer Uruguay away from its welfare-state orientation. His major goals are to privatize, or at least to bring mixed ownership to, such state-owned operations as the airline and telephone company. He is also attempting to reform the social-security system, which is a heavy drain on government resources. On 26 March 1991 he signed an agreement with the presidents of Brazil, Argentina, and Paraguay for the creation by

1995 of a common market (*mercosur*) among these nations. Lacalle has written on political and economic matters, and he authored a book about his grandfather, *Herrera, Un nacionalismo oriental* (1978).

— MARTIN WEINSTEIN

LACERDA, CARLOS FREDERICO WERNECK DE

Carlos Frederico Werneck de Lacerda (*b.* 30 April 1914; *d.* 21 May 1977), famous for combative oratory and journalism that contributed to the fall of Brazilian presidents. According to historian José Honório Rodrigues, "No single person exerted as much influence on the Brazilian historical process" from 1945 to 1968.

Lacerda's journalistic work for communism ended in 1940 with his "expulsion" from the Communist Party, which he had in fact never joined.

Lacerda, born in the city of Rio de Janeiro, was a rebellious, intense youth who preferred to educate himself by reading instead of taking formal courses. In 1935 he dropped out of the Faculdade Nacional de Direito (Rio Law School) without obtaining a degree. His ardent oratorical and journalistic work for communism ended in 1940 with his "expulsion" from the Communist Party, which he had in fact never joined. Continuing to condemn the dictatorship of Getúlio VARGAS, he contributed to the achievement of democracy in 1945. His articles, such as those after 1949 in his own *Tribuna da Imprensa,* gained him admirers as an anticommunist and a courageous crusader against corruption. After his revelation of scandals in the final Vargas administration (1951–1954), supporters of the president killed a military officer while trying to assassinate Lacerda. Following Vargas's suicide (24 August 1954), mobs shouted "death to Lacerda." The latter, however, became the congressman who received the greatest number of votes.

Calling for a reform of the political system, Lacerda demanded in 1955 that President-elect Juscelino KUBITSCHEK be prevented from taking office. Kubitschek, inaugurated with the help of a military coup, in turn would not allow Lacerda, Brazil's most sensational orator, to broadcast, and tried unsuccessfully to have him removed from Congress. As congressional opposition leader, Lacerda secured passage of legislation to reform education and was active in advancing the campaign

that brought Jânio QUADROS to the presidency early in 1961.

When Quadros, attacked by Lacerda for harboring dictatorial plans, unexpectedly resigned in August 1961, the presidency went to Vice President João GOULART, despite Lacerda's wishes. Lacerda, who had been elected governor of Guanabara state, gave his state a brilliantly constructive administration while denouncing Goulart and the president's Communist allies in labor unions. During the military coup that overthrew Goulart in 1964, Lacerda dramatically prepared the governor's palace against a possible assault by Goulart's forces.

As a presidential candidate, Lacerda denounced the new military regime and its unpopular anti-inflation measures. After an institutional act ended direct presidential elections, he found allies in Kubitschek and Goulart for organizing an antidictatorial front. The increasingly repressive military regime jailed him for a week in 1968 and deprived him of his political rights for ten years. Lacerda then concentrated on business affairs, writing, and book publishing, activities to which he had turned in 1965 following a political setback. He died of a heart attack.

— JOHN W. F. DULLES

LACERDA, MAURÍCIO PAIVA DE

Maurício Paiva de Lacerda (*b.* 1 June 1888; *d.* 23 November 1959), popular politician and journalist who contributed to the collapse of Brazil's Old Republic in 1930 through his passionate oratory. Always attacking those in power, Lacerda stirred the masses in the streets and encouraged workers to strike. He named his son Carlos Frederico, after Marx and Engels.

Maurício de Lacerda was born in Vassouras, Rio de Janeiro State. He was the oldest son of Sebastião de Lacerda, a prominent politician of the state who became a cabinet minister and supreme court justice. Before the willful Maurício obtained his degree at the Rio Law School, he was a student leader, director of a newspaper in Vassouras, and participant in an ineffective antigovernment conspiracy. As a congressman (1912–1920) from his home state of Rio de Janeiro, Lacerda introduced labor legislation. The antigovernment revolts of 1922 and 1924 were insufficiently labor-oriented to attract him, but he was nevertheless arrested on both occasions. Following his imprisonment (1924–1926) he allied himself with the "Cavalier of Hope," Luís Carlos PRESTES, leader of the revolutionary Long March (1925–1927), but in 1929–1930 he angered Prestes by supporting the Liberal Alliance and its uprising, which brought Getúlio VARGAS to the presidency.

Lacerda denounced the economic policies and what he saw as the fascist viewpoints of the new Vargas regime, and in 1935 he joined the Aliança Nacional Libertadora, whose honorary president, Prestes, was by then a Communist in hiding. Following the unsuccessful uprising of Prestes and his followers that year, Lacerda was jailed, again without cause, for a year. During most of the Vargas dictatorship (1937–1945), he did legal work for the Rio de Janeiro municipality. He ran unsuccessfully for Congress when the dictatorship fell.

– JOHN W. F. DULLES

LACERDA, OSVALDO

Osvaldo Lacerda (*b.* 23 March 1927), Brazilian composer and teacher. Lacerda's formal music training started at age nine, when he began piano study in the city of São Paulo, where he was born. From 1945 to 1947 he studied harmony, and in 1952 he became a composition student of Camargo GUARNIERI. In 1963 he became the first Brazilian to win a Simon Guggenheim grant for study in the United States. He studied with Vittorio Giannini in New York City, and with Aaron Copland at Tanglewood. In 1965 he participated in the Inter-American Seminar of Composers at Indiana University and in the Third Inter-American Composers Seminar, held in Washington, D.C. In an era in which most Brazilian composers reject obvious national elements in their works, Osvaldo Lacerda remains an important spokesman for neonationalism with compositions such as nine *Brasiliana* suites for piano based on Brazilian themes and dances. He also excels in writing songs and choral works, such as *Poema da necessidade,* for four-part chorus, based on a poem by Carlos Drummond de ANDRADE.

– DAVID P. APPLEBY

LADRÓN DE GUEVARA, DIEGO

Diego Ladrón de Guevara (*b.* 1641; *d.* 9 November 1718), bishop and viceroy of Peru (1710–1716). Born in Cifuentes, Ladrón studied in Alcalá and Sigüenza before entering the church, serving as a canon in both Sigüenza and Málaga. He was sent to America in 1689 as bishop of Panamá and was subsequently promoted to Huamanga (Peru) in 1699, and Quito in 1703.

Following the death in office in 1710 of the viceroy of Peru, marqués de Castelldosríus, Ladrón, as the audiencia's third choice as interim successor, took office when the other two nominees died. Although recalled to Spain in 1713, he remained in office until 1716 and stayed in Lima for two further years to defend himself (unsuccessfully) against charges of corruption, permit-

ting contraband, and incompetence in defending shipping in the Pacific against English intruders. He left Peru for Acapulco in March 1718 and died in Mexico City later that year.

– JOHN R. FISHER

LAGOS, RICARDO

Ricardo Lagos (*b.* 2 May 1938), a leader of Chile's moderately socialist Partido por la Democracia (PPD) and minister of education (1990–) in the government of President Patricio AYLWIN AZCÓCAR. A lawyer who was once active in the Radical Party, Lagos staunchly supported the Popular Unity government of Salvador ALLENDE and taught in the United States following its overthrow in 1973. During the mid- and late-1980s, he was affiliated with the Socialist Party's Nuñez wing and helped to build the broad movement that opposed and ultimately forced from power the government of General Augusto PINOCHET. In a television appearance early in 1987, he issued a direct challenge to General Pinochet that helped to launch the eventually successful plebiscite campaign. Although he far outpolled all senatorial candidates in the 1989 general election except the Christian Democrat who was his ticketmate, Lagos was denied the second seat from Santiago because their combined totals fell just short of the requisite two-thirds of the votes cast.

– MICHAEL FLEET

LAGUERRE, ENRIQUE ARTURO

Enrique Arturo Laguerre (*b.* 3 May 1906), Puerto Rican novelist. Born in Moca, a rural community in the western part of the island, Laguerre is Puerto Rico's foremost novelist. Educated at the University of Puerto Rico, in 1924 Laguerre embarked upon a lifelong teaching career spanning from elementary to postgraduate education.

Laguerre's twelve novels form a saga of Puerto Rico's land, people, and history in the late nineteenth and twentieth centuries. Two of them, *El laberinto* (1959; The labyrinth, 1960) and *Los amos benévolos* (1976; Benevolent masters, 1976); are available in English. *La llamarada* (The blaze), a classic since its publication in 1935, deals with the exploitation of the sugarcane worker. *Solar Montoya* (Montoya Plantation, 1941) takes place in the coffee fields, and *Los dedos de la mano* (The fingers of the hand, 1951) in tobacco country. Other novels deal with the Puerto Rican in San Juan, New York, and abroad; university life, feminism, and the religious practices of Santería. Puerto Rican identity and values are central themes in *Cauce sin río* (Riverbed without a river, 1962), *El fuego y su aire* (Fire and its air, 1970), and *Infiernos privados* (Private infernos, 1986). Associated with the 1930s generation, Laguerre creates a historical consciousness by enriching the past with legends, folklore, and myths, especially in *La resaca* (The undertow, 1949) and *Los gemelos* (The twins, 1992). Laguerre's novels treat the plight of oppressed women, children, and workers; the effects of affluence and power on the individual; and conflicts of conscience. In his writing he has embraced both traditional and innovative forms.

— ESTELLE IRIZARRY

LALEAU, LÉON

Léon Laleau (*b.* 3 August 1892; *d.* 1979), Haitian writer, journalist, and diplomat. Léopold Sédar Senghor cited Laleau as "one of the best representatives among Haitian poets using the vein of blackness." Laleau made many contacts with European and Latin American writers during his diplomatic assignments in Rome, Paris, London, Lima, and Santiago de Chile. Influenced by French symbolism at first, he later became acutely conscious of the catastrophic effects of the U.S. occupation of Haiti (1915–1934). He began to move toward the writers of *La revue indigène* and to use Haitian themes in the volume of verse, *Musique nègre* (1931), and in his novel about the occupation, *Le choc* (1932). Laleau also managed *Haïti journal, Le nouvelliste,* and *Le matin* at different periods. He wrote for the *Mercure de France, Le divan, Le Figaro littéraire,* and *Paris soir,* among other French journals. A collective volume of Laleau's *Oeuvre poétique* ("À voix basse," 1919; "La flèche au coeur," 1926; "Le rayon des jupes," 1928; "Abréviations," 1929; "Musique nègre," 1931; "De bronze et d'ivoire," 1978) won the literary prize of Éditions Henri Deschamps for 1978.

Other works include *Amitiés impossibles* (theater, with Georges Léger, 1916); *Une cause sans effet* (theater, 1916); *L'étau* (theater, 1917); *La pluie et le beau temps* (theater, 1919); *La danse des vagues* (novel, 1919); *Le tremplin* (theater, 1921); *Maurice Rostand intime* (biography, 1926); and *Apothéoses* (essays, 1952).

— CARROL F. COATES

LAM Y CASTILLA, WIFREDO

Wifredo Lam y Castilla (*b.* 9 December 1902; *d.* 11 September 1982), Cuban painter. Born in Sagua la Grande of a Chinese father and mulatto mother, Lam received a scholarship from the town council in 1921 to study in Havana. From 1923 to 1937 he studied in Madrid, and from 1937 to 1939 he worked in Paris

with Pablo Picasso and rediscovered his African ancestry. The events of World War II forced Lam to Marseilles in 1939 and out of France in 1941 with a group of three hundred intellectuals who chose exile from the Vichy government. Seven months after leaving France,

---

Lam's works run the gamut from postimpressionist to surrealist to postcubist styles, yet he never lost his devotion to the African influence.

---

he returned to Cuba. In 1942–1943, he painted *The Jungle,* his best-known work. He lived in Paris, New York, and Havana from 1946 to 1964, finally settling in the Italian town of Albissola Marina. In 1966, he returned to Cuba and painted *The Third World* for display in the Presidential Palace. His works run the gamut from postimpressionist to surrealist to postcubist styles, yet he never lost his devotion to the African influence. His paintings are unique in depicting African Cuban VODUN spirits in a style based on Picasso and West Indian devices. Internationally acclaimed, he stands as Cuba's foremost modern painter.

— JACQUELYN BRIGGS KENT

LAMADRID, GREGORIO ARÁOZ DE

Gregorio Aráoz de Lamadrid (*b.* 28 November 1795; *d.* 5 January 1857), Argentine military and political leader in the Río de la Plata during the independence and early national periods. Born in Tucumán, Lamadrid entered the local militia in 1811. His revolutionary duties included fighting under Manuel BELGRANO, José RONDEAU, and José de SAN MARTÍN in 1812–1820. Lamadrid sided with the Unitarists of Buenos Aires against the Federalists of the interior and, accordingly, fought against Juan Facundo QUIROGA of La Rioja after assuming the governorship of Tucumán in 1825. He later fought against the dictatorship of Juan Manuel de ROSAS. In addition to his personal service in the struggles for Argentine independence and nation building, Lamadrid wrote two basic sources concerning these events: his autobiography and a work on José María PAZ that he completed shortly before his death in Buenos Aires.

— FIDEL IGLESIAS

LAMAR, MIRABEAU BUONAPARTE

Mirabeau Buonaparte Lamar (*b.* 16 August 1798; *d.* 19 December 1859), president of the republic of Texas (1838–1841). Born near Louisville, Georgia, Lamar founded (1828) and published the Columbus *Enquirer,* and served as secretary to Georgia governor George M. Troup and as state senator before moving to the Mexican province of Texas in 1835. Lamar was soon caught up in Texas's revolt against Mexico. His distinguished military service led to a succession of elected and appointed offices, including secretary of war, commander in chief of the army, vice president, and president of the Republic of Texas.

Lamar's presidency was characterized by many innovative, and often radical, programs. Texas became the first nation in the world to ensure that a person's home and livelihood could not be taken away because of debts. He also established a system of public education endowed entirely from the public domain. But improvident adventures, such as the Santa Fe Expedition, which tried to wrest that trade center from Mexico in 1841, and the republic's continued financial troubles overshadowed the positive aspects of Lamar's administration. Following his retirement from the presidency, Lamar spent much of his time writing poetry and history. He also served in the Mexican-American War (1846–1848) and as minister to Nicaragua and Costa Rica (1858–1859). He died in Richmond, Texas, two months after returning from Central America.

– MICHAEL R. GREEN

LAMARQUE PONS, JAURÉS

Jaurés Lamarque Pons (*b.* 6 May 1917; *d.* 11 June 1982), Uruguayan composer and pianist. Lamarque Pons was born in Salto, where he began his music studies with María Victoria Varela (piano). Later he moved to Montevideo and took advanced piano lessons with Wilhelm Kolischer. He took courses in harmony, counterpoint, and instrumentation with Tomás Mujica and Guido Santórsola. In 1949 he enrolled in the composition classes of the Spanish composer Enrique Casal-Chapí. His *Aires de milonga* premiered in 1943. Lamarque's earlier music was universalist in character and included piano pieces, chamber music, and vocal works. He later composed in the nationalist style, using popular urban melodies, such as old tangos and *milongas* and the rhythms of the Afro-Uruguayan *tamboril.* From that period came his opera *Marta Gruni* (1965), with a libretto from the Uruguayan playwright Florencio SÁNCHEZ. After its 26 February 1967 premiere at the Teatro Solís under his baton, it became one of the most frequently performed Uruguayan operas. Other important works of Lamarque Pons include the ballet *Suite según Figari* (1952), *Suite Rioplatense* (1954), and the ballet-pantomime *El encargado* (1956). He also composed music for stage and films. Lamarque Pons died in Montevideo.

– SUSANA SALGADO

LAME, MANUEL QUINTÍN

Manuel Quintín Lame (*b.* 31 October 1883; *d.* 7 October 1967), Colombian indigenous leader and author. The son of Páez sharecroppers, Lame organized the Indians of the departments of Cauca and Tolima. His efforts, which met with severe repression by Colombia authorities, revolved around the following demands: (1) defense of the *resguardo,* a communal landholding corporation of indigenous people; (2) consolidation of the *cabildo* (*resguardo* council) as a center of political authority; (3) reclaiming of lands usurped from the *resguardo;* (4) refusal by sharecroppers to pay rent; and (5) reaffirmation of indigenous cultural values.

Although Lame's program was obstructed in Cauca, where his 1910–1921 campaign provoked military occupation, police violence, and the eventual imprisonment of Lame and his associates, his efforts in Tolima were more successful. The pressure exerted by the growth of the coffee economy upon indigenous landholdings in Tolima resulted in the division of *resguardos.* Lame's campaign, which lasted from 1922 to 1939, restored the *resguardo* status of Ortega and Chaparral, thus reversing over a century of land loss under capitalist expansion.

Lame is best known for a 118-page manuscript, "Los pensamientos del indio que se educó dentro de las selvas colombianas" (The Thoughts of the Indian Who Was Educated in the Colombian Forests). Although it was completed in 1939, *Los pensamientos* was published only posthumously in 1971 as *En defensa de mi raza* (In Defense of My Race). This autobiographical treatise outlines Lame's political philosophy, offers an idiosyncratic vision of indigenous history, and denounces specific crimes against Colombian Indians. *Los pensamientos* is a philosophical attack on capitalism, called "civilization" by its author, and is strongly messianic in character.

– JOANNE RAPPAPORT

LAMPIÃO

Lampião (Virgulino Ferreira da Silva: *b.* 7 July 1897; *d.* 28 July 1938), Brazilian bandit. Brazil's best-known bandit of all time, Lampião was a world-class bandit as well. Son of a modest rancher and hauler in the backlands of Pernambuco, he went astray when he and his brothers began to feud with neighbors. As violence increased on both sides, the Ferreiras, of lower social status than their adversaries, were branded, not unjustly, as outlaws. After 1922, Lampião became the preeminent figure in the *cangaço,* the name given to the organized brigandage that flourished in the region from the 1870s to the 1930s. He seemingly verged on legality in 1926, when Father Cícero Romão Batista of Juàzeiro had him commissioned a captain in forces hastily raised to oppose Luís Carlos PRESTES's wandering revolutionaries. But the patent proved to be worthless, and he reverted to outlawry. For sixteen years, roaming over seven states; living from extortion, robbery, and abductions; and enjoying protection from sometimes reluctant ranchers, political bosses, and even for a time a state governor, he and his band so vanquished police and army forces sent against them that they virtually dominated portions of the backlands. Conscious of his image and ever catering to the press, he became one of the nation's most newsworthy figures, and the story of his exploits reached abroad. Partly the result of strengthened efforts, but largely by luck, the police killed him, his companion, Maria Bonita, and several others of his band in a surprise attack in Sergipe in 1938. Thus the *cangaço* ended. Lampião, whose preserved head long lay in a museum in Salvador, survives in folkore and history.

– BILLY JAYNES CHANDLER

LANDA, DIEGO DE

Diego De Landa (*b.* 1524; *d.* 1579), Castilian Franciscan missionary. Born in Cifuentes, Landa entered the monastery of San Juan de los Reyes in Toledo when he was sixteen. In 1549 he journeyed to Yucatán, where he learned the Maya language and ministered to the Maya people. Landa, one of the earliest Franciscans in Yucatán, helped convert the Maya to Christianity, only to discover that they refused to abandon their tradinal religion. Suspecting them of carrying out human sacrifice using Catholic ritual, he organized an inquisition (1562) that eventually led to the imprisonment and torture of 4,400 Indians. After extracting confessions, and after more than 170 people had died under torture or by committing suicide, Landa held an auto-da-fé (day of judgment, punishment, and penance) on 12 July 1562 and pardoned the survivors. He was later charged with misconduct in the affair but defended himself successfully and in 1564 returned to Spain, where he wrote his book about Maya history and culture (*Relación de las cosas de Yucatán*). He returned to Yucatán in 1573 as bishop and died there seven years later without further controversy.

– ROBERT W. PATCH

LANDALUZE, VÍCTOR PATRICIO DE

Víctor Patricio de Landaluze (*b.* 1828; *d.* 8 June 1889), Cuban painter and cartoonist who is considered the precursor of graphic political satire in Cuba. Born in Bilbao, Spain, Landaluze emigrated in the 1850s to Havana, where he founded the newspaper *Don Junípero* (1862). Between 1868 and 1878, he was the political cartoonist for *La Charanga, El Moro Muza* (under the pseudonym of Bayaceto), *Don Circunstancias,* and *Juan Palomo,* weekly journals through which he satirized the Cuban struggle for independence. He was both professor at and director of the Academy of San Alejandro in Havana.

In oil and watercolor paintings, he depicted popular Cuban stereotypes such as the *guajiro* (a rustic type), the landowner, the slave, and the *ñanigo* (a member of a secret black society), and illustrated the books *Tipos y costumbres* (Types and Customs) and *Cuba pintoresca* (Picturesque Cuba), both published in 1881.

His ironic attitude toward the Cuban independence movement earned him the antipathy of art critics. Ironically, his painting of the backward *campesino* Liborio became a Cuban national symbol. With the exception of an oil painting of a fugitive slave cornered by dogs and soldiers (*El cimarrón* [The Runaway Slave]), Landaluze's work is often considered biased in his presentation of blacks as lazy and lascivious. Much of his production, however, recorded with exactitude the costumes and rituals of the different nations of Cuban blacks. He died in Guanabacoa.

– MARTA GARSD

LANDÁZURI RICKETTS, JUAN

Juan Landázuri Ricketts (*b.* 19 December 1913), archbishop of Lima and primate of Peru (1955–1988), cardinal (1962–). Landázuri led the Peruvian Catholic church through a period of transformation in that institution's understanding of its mission in society. A Franciscan, and considered a church moderate, Landázuri championed the church's commitment to the reform of social and economic structures. Enjoying great prestige among fellow bishops, he copresided over the Second Conference of Latin American Bishops (CELAM) at Medellín, Colombia, in 1968 and served as the vice president of the Latin American Bishops' Council at the time of its third general conference in Puebla, Mexico (1979). Under his leadership, the Peruvian church distanced itself from the state and traditional elites, democratized church decision-making procedures, and turned its attention to organizing the poor. Though famous for his mediation skills, Landá-zuri's defense of the Liberation Theology of Gustavo GUTIÉRREZ, a Peruvian priest, culminated in the 1980s in clashes with the Vatican and division among an increasingly conservative Peruvian hierarchy.

– MATTHEW J. O'MEAGHER

LANDÍVAR, RAFAEL

Rafael Landívar (*b.* 27 October 1731; *d.* 1793), Guatemalan Jesuit priest and writer, born in Santiago de los Caballeros de Guatemala, today known as Old Guatemala City. He graduated from San Borja School and earned his Ph.D. in philosophy from the Pontifical University of San Carlos at the age of sixteen. Later he traveled to Mexico (1749) and in 1750 joined the Jesuit order. Five years later he was ordained a priest. In 1761 he returned to Guatemala, where he assumed the position of rector at the College of San Francisco de Borja.

When Charles III expelled the Jesuits from the American continent in 1767, Landívar and his colleagues roamed the ports of Europe for a year.

When Charles III expelled the Jesuits from the American continent six years later, Landívar and his colleagues roamed the ports of Europe for a year, an odyssey which finally ended when the Jesuits were allowed to settle in Italy. Though Charles III prohibited the members of the Jesuit order from performing priestly duties and writing books, this didn't prevent Landívar from writing in Bologna. His works include *Oración fúnebre a la muerte del arzobispo de Guatemala, Francisco Figueredo y Victoria,* two odes in Latin and one in Castilian, and the collection of poems entitled *Salva cara parens.* His most outstanding work, however, is *Rusticatio mexicana,* a mournful song of his native land in which he describes its natural attributes, its customs, and its disasters such as volcanic eruptions and earthquakes. The first edition was published in Modena in 1781 and the second in Bologna in 1782. It is the first ode to the Guatemalan homeland by a political exile and is considered the best verse about Latin America ever written in Latin.

– FERNANDO GONZÁLEZ DAVISON

LANUSSE, ALEJANDRO AUGUSTO

Alejandro Augusto Lanusse (*b.* 28 August 1918), president of Argentina (1971–1973). Born in the city of Buenos Aires, Lanusse became an officer in the cavalry. In 1956 he was special envoy to the Vatican and was the Argentine military attaché in Mexico from 1958 to 1960.

When Lanusse assumed the presidency on 26 March 1971, following a nonviolent coup, there were no fewer than five separate guerrilla armies; wildcat strikes were wrecking the economy; and there was student unrest. Although staunchly anti-PERÓN, Lanusse allowed the former dictator to return from exile, hoping to be bailed out of his predicament. Perón, in the meantime, allowed his subordinate, Héctor José CÁMPORA, to precede him in the presidency. The remainder of Lanusse's career was tarnished by his alleged involvement in the David Graiver affair and the murder of his daughter-in-law by left-wing guerrillas.

– ROGER GRAVIL

LANZA, ALCIDES

Alcides Lanza (*b.* 2 June 1929), Argentine composer. Born in Rosario, Argentina, Lanza studied composition with Julián Batista and Alberto GINASTERA. He continued his studies with Maderna, Copland, Messiaen, Loriod, and Malipiero at the Instituto Di Tella in Buenos Aires (1963–1964). From 1959 to 1965 he was a member of the artistic staff of the Teatro Colón in Buenos Aires, where he became one of the founding members of Agrupación Música Viva. Awarded a Guggenheim Fellowship in 1965, he studied with Ussachevsky and Mimaroglu at the Columbia-Princeton Electronic Music Centre in New York. Since 1971, he has been professor of composition and electronic music at McGill University in Montreal. From 1972 to 1973, he was composer in residence in Berlin. Director of the Electronic Music Studio at McGill since 1974, Lanza has also been artistic director and conductor of GEMS (Group of the Electronic Music Studio) at McGill and a member of the CEC (Canadian Electroacoustic Community) since its inception in 1987.

Showing the influence of his earlier architectural studies, his scores are based on ideograms, graphisms, and drawings, all intended to give a direct representation of his musical ideas. A substantial amount of Lanza's production includes electroacoustics either on tape, live processing, or both. Except for some mostly earlier solo tape pieces and a recent work for keyboard-controlled synthesizers with tape, this output consists of mixed compositions wherein an important role is assigned to some acoustic element. Notable are several pieces written for his life and artistic partner the actress-singer Meg Sheppard, with whom he has performed extensively in Canada and elsewhere promoting his music and that of many Latin American and Canadian avant-garde composers. Lanza's scores and recordings are published by Editions Shelan Publications in Montreal.

— SERGIO BARROSO

LAPLANTE, EDUARDO

Eduardo Laplante (*b.* 1818; *d. ?*), Cuban lithographer and painter. Born in France, Laplante was among the first to portray Cuban rural life as it existed in reality. He devoted particular care to details in his art, making his work useful for historians and students of mid-nineteenth-century Cuban planter society. Laplante is most famous for his collection of twenty-eight lithographs, *Los ingenios de Cuba* (1857), which provides detailed views of both external appearances and internal social conditions in Cuba's major SUGAR plants. With these lithographs Laplante achieved a realistic portrait of Cuban race and class relations as well as the operation of the rural sugar economy.

— KAREN RACINE

LAPRIDA, FRANCISCO NARCISO DE

Francisco Narciso de Laprida (*b.* 28 October 1786; *d.* 28 September 1829), Argentine patriot. Born in San Juan and educated in Buenos Aires and Santiago de Chile, Laprida returned to his native city in 1811 to practice law and participate in local politics. He was president of the Congress of Tucumán when, on 9 July 1816, it adopted the Argentine declaration of independence.

Laprida served briefly as acting governor of San Juan in 1818. As a liberal professional and eager to promote progressive innovations, he collaborated from 1822 to 1824 with the radical reformist government of Salvador María del Carril in his home province and then with the abortive national government of Bernardino RIVADAVIA and his Unitarist party. He was vice president of the Constituent Congress that issued the centralist 1826 Constitution. In the civil strife that followed adoption of the Constitution, he was a committed Unitarist. Laprida was killed by victorious Federalists in the immediate aftermath of the battle of Pilar, in Mendoza province.

— DAVID BUSHNELL

LARA, AGUSTÍN

Agustín Lara (*b.* 30 October 1900; *d.* 6 November 1970), renowned Mexican composer of popular songs. Lara was born in Tlacotalpan, Veracruz. He began composing in the mid-1920s, when the regional music of

Mexico had not yet become popular, and joined Radio XEW with his own program, "Hora Azul" (Blue Hour), on which he showcased his own compositions, often playing them on the piano. He wrote almost 600 songs, mostly in the International Latin style, including "Farolito," "Enamorada," "Mujer," "Cada noche un amor," and "Solamente una vez" ("You Belong to My Heart"), which achieved global fame. His choice to use an international rather than native Mexican styles brought extensive criticism from many Mexican musicians, scholars, and critics, who regarded his work as not truly Mexican. The song "Granada" became so popular in Europe and the Americas that he received honorary Spanish citizenship.

— GUY BENSUSAN

LAREDO BRU, FEDERICO

Federico Laredo Bru (*b.* 23 April 1875; *d.* 8 July 1946), president of Cuba 1936–1940. A veteran of the war of independence, Bru served as governor of Las Villas Province and as secretary of the interior under President José Miguel GÓMEZ. In 1923 he led an uprising of disgruntled veterans against President Alfredo ZAYAS. Bru was elected vice president of Cuba in January 1936, and when President Miguel Mariano GÓMEZ was impeached by a Senate subservient to army chief Fulgencio BATISTA, he was installed as the new figurehead president. He nevertheless discharged the duties of his office with great aplomb and dignity, counterbalancing military interference as much as possible. A law completely restructuring the sugar industry, one of the most important pieces of legislation of the period, was passed during his term in office. It was also under Laredo Bru that the 1940 constitution was framed by a freely elected constituent assembly.

— JOSÉ M. HERNÁNDEZ

LARRAZÁBAL UGUETO, WOLFGANG

Wolfgang Larrazábal Ugueto (*b.* 5 March 1911), Venezuelan naval officer and politician. Born in Carúpano, Larrazábal studied at the Escuela Naval (1928–1932). He became commander of the naval base at Puerto Cabello and held successively higher posts, finally rising to commander of the navy in 1957. As the senior navy officer, he joined forces with other military and civilian leaders to overthrow Marcos PÉREZ JIMÉNEZ in January 1958. When the dictator fled, Larrazábal headed the interim governing junta (23 January–13 November 1958) as provisional president. Prior to elections in December, he resigned from the military to run as a presidential candidate of the Democratic Republican Union and the Communist Party. His enormous personal popularity in Caracas and other cities enabled him to capture 34 percent of the popular vote. He lost to Rómulo BETANCOURT of Democratic Action, however, who received 50 percent. Larrazábal is noted for his support of democracy at a time when many military leaders preferred to rule. He backed the electoral process and encouraged the military to support the transition to civilian rule during his transition government. Larrazábal ran for president again in 1963 as the Popular Democratic Force candidate but won only 9.4 percent of the vote. He remained a political figure in the 1980s but broke with the Force to form a splinter group.

– KATHY WALDRON

LARREA, JUAN

Juan Larrea (*b.* 1782; *d.* 1847), Spanish-born merchant and member of the first Argentine patriot junta. Larrea arrived in Buenos Aires prior to 1806. He fought British invaders as a captain in the battalion of Volunteers of Catalonia. An early champion of independence, he was initially associated with the Spanish-dominated Partido Republicano, which controlled the *cabildo,* or town council. In 1810 Larrea joined Mariano MORENO and other creoles participating in the *cabildo abierto* on 22 May, and became a member of the first patriot junta. During the ensuing controversy between federalists and centralists, Larrea continued to support Moreno and was exiled to San Juan after Moreno's resignation and the revolt of May 1811. In January 1813 Larrea represented Buenos Aires at the constitutional assembly. Named minister of the treasury under Supreme Director Gervasio Antonio de POSADAS, Larrea and Carlos María de Alvear were charged to acquire a naval squadron. Larrea accomplished this with the aid of the North American merchants Guillermo Pío White and William Brown. The unraveling of the "united" provinces in 1815 forced Larrea, once again, into exile and obscurity. Reestablished as a merchant, he was appointed Argentine consul general in France several years later. Larrea eventually returned to Buenos Aires, where he died.

– CHRISTEL K. CONVERSE

LARRETA, ENRIQUE RODRÍGUEZ

Enrique Rodríguez Larreta (*b.* 4 March 1873; *d.* 7 July 1961), Argentine dramatist. Enrique Rodríguez Larreta was born in Buenos Aires of Uruguayan parents and belonged to the cattle-baron oligarchy; he earned a doctorate in law from the University of Buenos Aires. Larreta exemplifies the phenomenon of the gentleman literatus made possible by the enormous economic prosperity and international ties that characterized Argentine life in the federal capital of Buenos Aires and the province of Buenos Aires between 1880 and 1930. True to his class, Larreta specialized in a literature (basically narrative and lyrical dramas) that focused on questions of national identity from the perspective of the ruling creoles. This meant an emphasis on a chthonic definition of Hispanic roots, with or without the dimension of their forceful domination of indigenous elements. Larreta's most famous work, *La gloria de don Ramiro; una vida en tiempos de Felipe II* (1908), in the context of a decadent prose with important French parallels, explores contradictions of the Hispanic substratum of Latin American society and is most notable for its rereading of the Spanish racialistic obsession with the "purity of the blood." Larreta correlates Don Ramiro's nonpurity with his failure in the New World, a plot configuration that has strident ideological implications for early-twentieth-century political beliefs in an Argentina that opposed immigration (especially its Jewish components) and non-Hispanic liberalism, while at the same time calling for a reaffirmation of an authentic Hispanic heritage. Larreta, thanks in great part to the strains of literary decadence to which he was exposed, may not have been as facile in these matters as Leopoldo LUGONES (1874–1938) or the harsh-minded nationalists, but there is no question that his writing strikes a counterpoint to the dominant cultural liberalism of the modernists. One cannot help but be struck by the juxtaposition in Larreta of significant manifestations of an aesthetist posture and the mythmaking force of an austere Spanish traditionalism, a feature of his writing also evident in *Zogoibi* (1926), set in the legendary Argentine pampas.

– DAVID WILLIAM FOSTER

LAS CASAS, BARTOLOMÉ DE

Bartolomé de Las Casas (*b.* ca. August 1474; *d.* ca. 17 July 1566), Spanish bishop, defender of human rights, author. Bartolomé de Las Casas remains one of the most controversial figures in Latin America's conquest period. His exposé of Spanish mistreatment of Amerindians produced public outrage that was directed at both the conquistadores who were committing the atrocities and at the writer who had made them public. Las Casas's vast output of political, historical, and theological writing forms one of the basic sources for contemporary understanding of the conquest period and of some of the most important individuals involved in the initial colonization of the Spanish Indies.

The early years of Las Casas's life seemed destined to propel him toward the newly discovered Indies and its inhabitants. He was the son of a Seville merchant, Pedro de Las Casas. In 1493 the young Bartolomé saw Christopher COLUMBUS's triumphant return to Spain and the small group of Taino Indians Columbus brought with him. Las Casas remained at home in school while his father and other members of his family accompanied Columbus as colonists on the second voyage to the Indies. Five years later Pedro de Las Casas returned to Spain for a short period, bringing with him a Taino boy named Juanico. While his father was at home, Bartolomé declared his desire to become a priest and went to Salamanca to learn canon law. He also began to learn about the Indies from Juanico, with whom Las Casas struck up a lifelong friendship. In 1502 Las Casas quit school and sailed to the West Indies. His first years in Hispaniola were spent helping his father and aiding in the provisioning of Spanish military expeditions. At the same time, young Las Casas began learning several native languages and befriending local Indians; he had already begun deploring the violence he witnessed. He returned to Europe, first to Spain and then to Rome where, in 1507, he was ordained a priest.

In 1510 Las Casas returned to Hispaniola. These years were to be crucial both for Las Casas and for the

Fray Bartolomé de Las Casas. Reproduced from J. A. Llorente, Oeuvres de Don Barthélemi de Las Casas, évêque de Chiapa . . . *(Brussels, 1822). (Organization of American States)*

nature of Spanish-Indian relations. His return coincided with the arrival of the Dominicans. In 1511 the Dominican priest Antonio de Montesino represented his order in a highly public condemnation of the *encomienda* system that outraged the island's entire Spanish community. The message was not lost on Las Casas, who then held Indians as an *encomendero* (land grantee). Las Casas was ordained priest in 1512 or 1513, and in 1513 he joined Diego de VELÁZQUEZ and Pánfilo de NARVÁEZ in the conquest of Cuba. Las Casas preached to and converted the natives in preparation for the Spanish conquistadores, and those efforts largely succeeded. In reward for his services, Las Casas received land together with a grant of Indians and by all appearances had established himself as a typical *encomendero*.

The decimation of Cuba's native population by Spanish *encomenderos* through overwork, starvation, and murder made Las Casas realize that the real solution for Indian mistreatment lay not with challenging the conduct of individual *encomenderos* but by calling into question the entire system and its relationship to Christian morality. In 1514 he astonished his parishioners by condemning the *encomienda* in its entirety, freeing his Indians, and then vigorously interceding with local authorities on the natives' behalf. Failing to convert even a single *encomendero* to his position, he went to Europe in 1515 to plead his case with the king of Spain. Las Casas spent the next six years arguing that the period for military conquest of the Indians had passed. The time had arrived, he claimed, for peaceful conversion of natives and the promotion of agricultural colonization. He did not stand alone in condemning Spanish cruelties against Indians. Other voices had begun to sound in the Americas, and a small but influential group of royal ministers and Spanish churchmen supported the goal of protecting Indians. After heated debate, Emperor Charles V (Charles I of Spain) sided with Las Casas in 1519, ruling that the Indies could be governed without the force of arms. The ruling, however, had little practical effect in the distant Western Hemisphere.

During the next quarter century, Las Casas repeatedly suffered defeats in his efforts to defend the Americas' native populations. In 1520 he left Spain to establish a settlement in Venezuela, hoping to peacefully convert local Indians and create an economically self-sufficient community. But opposition from *encomenderos* and colonial officials helped to incite an Indian rebellion that wrecked the project. Despondent over its failure, he entered the Dominican order as a monk in 1523. The years that followed were ones of intellectual growth and personal frustration for Las Casas. He outlined his program for peaceful conversion, in opposition to military conquest, in *Del único modo de atraer a todos los pueblos a la verdadera religión* (1537; *The Only Way*). While in the monastery, he began his monumental *Apologética historia* (*In Defense of the Indians*) and the *History of the Indies* and continued a lifelong passion of collecting documents. One of Las Casas's critics charged that he once arrived in Tlaxcala, Mexico, "with twenty-seven or thirty-seven [Indian] carriers—and the greatest part of what they were carrying was accusations against the Spaniards, and other rubbish."

Although colonial Spaniards scorned any attempt to ameliorate the Indians' plight, moral encouragement arrived from Europe in the form of Pope Paul III's bull *Sublimis Deus* (1537), which proclaimed that American Indians were rational beings with souls, whose lives and property should be protected. During the same year Charles V supported an effort by Las Casas and the Dominicans to establish missions in Guatemala based on the precepts laid out in *Del único modo*. The high point of the crown's efforts came in 1542 with the so-called New Laws, which forbade Indian slavery and sought to end the *encomienda* system within a generation by outlawing their transference through family inheritance. Las Casas, who was in Spain at the time, directly influenced the direction of the New Laws in part by reading the first version of *The Devastation of the Indies* (a much longer text than the one he published in 1552) to a horrified royal court.

In 1544 he sailed to the Indies for a brief and tempestuous tenure as the bishop of Chiapas. Although he had been offered the Cuzco bishopric, the richest in the Americas, Las Casas instead accepted one of the poorest. When he tried to implement the New Laws in his see, local clergy who had ties to *encomenderos* defied him. After Las Casas denied final absolution to any Spaniard who refused to free his Indians or pay restitution, he received threats against his life. Proclamation of the New Laws brought outright revolt in parts of Spanish America and fierce antagonism everywhere. Even the Viceroyalty of New Spain and its high court openly refused to enforce them. In 1545 colonial opposition persuaded Charles V to revoke key inheritance statutes in the New Laws. Las Casas went to an ecclesiastical assembly in Mexico City and persuaded his fellow bishops to support a strongly worded resolution defending Indian rights. At the same time he publicly humiliated the viceroy, Antonio de MENDOZA, for attempting to silence him. But he left his most defiant act for last.

Just after arriving, Las Casas issued a confessor manual for the priests in his diocese that essentially reinstituted the inheritance statutes of the New Laws. His *Confesionario* produced public outrage by reiterating that all Spaniards seeking last rites must free their In-

dians and make restitution, even if the Indians were part of a deeded estate. Las Casas justified his decision by arguing that all wealth acquired through *encomiendas* was ill-gotten, declaring, "There is no Spaniard in the Indies who has shown good faith in connection with the wars of Conquest." This last statement put at issue the very basis of Spain's presence in the Americas. Las Casas contended that the Spanish had acquired all their wealth by unjustly exploiting Indians; if all of their activities since Columbus's landing were unjust, so too, logically, was the crown's American presence. Not surprisingly, the Council of the Indies recalled Las Casas to Spain in 1547 and ordered all copies of the *Confesionario* confiscated.

> *"There is no Spaniard in the Indies who has shown good faith in connection with the wars of Conquest."*

Colonial and Spanish opposition to Las Casas coalesced around Juan Ginés de Sepúlveda, one of Spain's leading humanists. Sepúlveda used Aristotle's doctrine of just war to defend Spanish conduct in the Americas. The vigor of Las Casas's counterattack led the Council of the Indies to call for a court of jurists and theologians to ascertain "how conquests may be conducted justly and with security of conscience." Charles V then ordered the two men to debate their positions before the court.

Much popular misconception has surrounded the 1550 "great debate" between Las Casas and Sepúlveda in the Spanish city of Valladolid. The two men never debated face to face but stated their cases individually before the court. Sepúlveda's three-hour defense of just wars against Indians rested on four points. First, the Indians had committed grave sins by their idolatry and sins against nature. Second, their "natural rudeness and inferiority" corresponded with Aristotle's view that some men were born natural slaves. Third, military conquest was the most efficacious method of converting Indians to Christianity. Finally, conquering Indians made it possible to protect the weak amongst them. In rebuttal, Las Casas took five days to read his *Apologética historia sumaria*. In the end, the majority of judges sided with Las Casas but, perhaps fearing controversy, refused to render a public decision. Legislation by the crown continued to move slowly toward the abolition of Indian slavery and some of the egregious features of the *encomienda* system.

Las Casas left Chiapas in 1547 and, in August 1550, resigned the Chiapas bishopric. He assumed residency in the Dominican San Gregorio monastery, where in 1552 he produced his most important work, *The Devastation of the Indies: A Brief Account. A Brief Account* was immediately translated into several languages and ignited a firestorm of controversy that continues today. Next came his two largest works. The first, *Apologética historia sumaria,* argued for the rationality of American Indians by comparing them favorably to the Greeks and Romans. After research in Hernando Columbus's library; he rewrote his three-volume *History of the Indies,* which remains a standard source on Columbus and Spain's first decades in the Americas.

Las Casas continued to champion Indian rights in the final phase of his life. His last great success occurred in 1555, when Peruvian conquistadores offered 8 million ducats to Philip II in exchange for perpetual *encomiendas.* Las Casas adroitly had the decision postponed while he gained the power of attorney, enabling him to act officially on the Indians' behalf. With their backing, he made a counteroffer that surpassed the conquistadores' bribe and led to its summary withdrawal. Despite that triumph, Las Casas's final years were characterized by urgent pleas about the Indians' circumstances and the belief that God might destroy Spain for its sins against them. On the day he died, Las Casas voiced regret for not having done more. He was buried in the convent chapel of Our Lady of Atocha in Madrid.

Today Las Casas is largely remembered for *A Brief Account* and his role in the controversy surrounding the Black Legend of Spanish conquest. Whether or not Las Casas exaggerated Spanish atrocities, as his critics claim, does not alter the fact that *A Brief Account* remains one of the most important documents ever written on human rights. The issues Las Casas raised in 1552 remain pertinent today. Modern scholarship has supported Las Casas's staggering toll of native deaths but assigns the principal responsibility to Afro-European diseases rather than Spanish cruelty. Recent work has also refuted the claim that Las Casas promoted the African slave trade as a substitute for Indian slavery, pointing out that his *History of the Indies* explicitly condemns African slavery. Although Las Casas never claimed to be an impartial historian, his historical texts continue to provide information on the conquest period. Ultimately, however, it is Las Casas as a crusader and symbol of the struggle for human rights that keeps him in our historical memory. Perhaps no one else in history has been more insistent or clear in articulating Western culture's moral responsibility to the oppressed.

– WILLIAM DONOVAN

LAS HERAS, JUAN GREGORIO DE

Juan Gregorio de Las Heras (*b.* 11 June 1780; *d.* 6 February 1866), Argentine general and hero of the wars of independence. Born in Buenos Aires and seemingly destined for a commerical career, he enrolled in the militia and fought against the British during the "English invasions" of 1806–1807. In 1813 he went to Chile with a force of Argentine auxiliaries and distinguished himself in the early campaigns of Chile's wars of independence. Following the collapse of patriot Chile (October 1814), he joined José de SAN MARTÍN's Army of the Andes, in which he commanded a division. He fought in many other actions, including the battles of Chacabuco (12 February 1817) and Maipú (5 April 1818), and later served as San Martín's chief of staff on the expedition to liberate Peru (1820–1821).

When San Martín withdrew from Peru, Las Heras returned to his native land. He became governor of Buenos Aires Province in 1824 and chief executive of Argentina in 1825. During his brief period in office, war was declared on Brazil. With Bernardino RIVADAVIA's assumption of the Argentine presidency (1826), Las Heras returned to Chile and resumed his military career. He was cashiered in 1830 for refusing to recognize the new Chilean Conservative regime. He was reinstated in 1842, after which he immediately retired. He spent the rest of his life in Chile. His remains were repatriated to Buenos Aires in 1906.

– SIMON COLLIER

LASO, FRANCISCO

Francisco Laso (*b.* 8 May 1823; *d.* 14 May 1869), Peruvian artist and writer. A painter influenced by the French romantic tradition who focused on Peruvian subjects, Laso was born in Tacna and studied at the Academy of Painting and Drawing in Lima, where he was assistant to Ignacio Merino, director of the academy. He went to Paris in 1842 to study with the painter Hippolyte Delaroche. On visits to Rome and Venice he was influenced by Titian and Veronese. In 1847 he returned to Peru and traveled throughout the countryside, sketching Indians. During a second trip to Europe he studied with the genre painter Marc Gabriel Charles Gleyre in Paris. In Gleyre's atelier, Laso finished his famous *El indio Alfarero* (The Indian Potter, also known as Dweller in the Cordillera, 1855), a painting of a young Indian holding a Mochica ceramic piece, which is considered a forerunner of Peruvian indigenist art in the twentieth century. Upon his return to Peru in 1856, he was commissioned to paint *The Four Evangelists* for the Cathedral of Lima and the *Saint Rose of Lima* (1866) in the municipal palace. Laso worked as a Red Cross volunteer during the yellow fever epidemic of 1868 in Peru and fell victim to it. He died at the height of his career.

– MARTA GARSD

LASTARRIA, JOSÉ VICTORINO

José Victorino Lastarria (*b.* 22 March 1817; *d.* 14 June 1888), intellectual and politician, the most active and brilliant mid-nineteenth-century Chilean Liberal. Lastarria had more than a touch of vanity. "Tengo talento y lo luzco" (I have talent, and it shows), he once told the Chilean congress. He *did* have talent. As a politician, his finest moments were in 1849–1850, when he was congressional leader of the resurgent Liberal opposition to the Conservative regime, a role for which he was arrested in November 1850 and briefly exiled to Peru. In 1851 he was expelled from congress. Later he held the office of minister of finance (1862) and minister of the interior (1876–1877). He was elected six times to the Chamber of Deputies (1849, 1855, 1858, 1864, 1867, 1870) and was a senator from 1876 to 1882. His many public services included diplomatic missions to Peru (1863), Argentina (1864), and Brazil (1879), and membership on the supreme court (1882–1887).

Lastarria's talent for active politics and diplomacy was limited. His true interests were intellectual and literary. He contributed to numerous newspapers and journals, serving as editor of *El Siglo* (1844–1845) and helping to found *La Revista de Santiago* (1848). An indefatigable "cultural entrepreneur," he was instrumental in founding the Sociedad Literaria (Literary Society) of 1842, an event regarded as the first real stirring of cultural life in postcolonial Chile. In a notable opening address to this society, Lastarria pleaded for an authentic national literature within the canons of modern romanticism. His own fiction, for example, *Don Guillermo* (1860), does not read well today, but his promotion of literature was tireless, and the several circles and academies he sponsored are vividly described in his *Recuerdos literarios* (1878), a remarkable intellectual autobiography. At his death, he left unfinished a prologue he had promised Rubén DARÍO (1867–1916) for his path-breaking *Azul* (1888).

Lastarria urged a "philosophical" approach to historical writing and engaged in a famous polemic on the subject with Andrés BELLO (1781–1865), whose ideas proved more enduring. Of greater positive influence was Lastarria's political-constitutional thought. Consistently liberal and democratic, it is best represented in his books *Elementos de derecho constitucional* (Elements of Constitutional Law, 1846), *Bosquejo histórico de la Con-*stitución chilena (Historical Outline of the Chilean Constitution, 1847), *Historia constitucional de medio siglo* (Constitutional History of Half a Century, 1853), and *Lecciones de política positiva* (Lessons in Positive Philosophy, 1874), the last of which reflects positivist influence, Lastarria having assimilated the thought of Auguste Comte (though not uncritically) in the 1860s.

– SIMON COLLIER

LASUÉN, FERMÍN FRANCISCO DE

Fermín Francisco De Lasuén (*b.* 7 June 1736; *d.* 26 June 1803), Franciscan missionary in California. Born in Victoria, Spain, Lasuén arrived in New Spain in 1759, posted first in Baja California and later in Alta California. While stationed at San Francisco de Borja mission in Baja California between 1768 and 1773, he directed the construction of a large adobe church and other buildings, the ruins of which still exist behind a later Dominican-constructed stone facade.

Between 1773 and 1803 Lasuén was stationed at the San Gabriel, San Diego, and San Carlos missions in Alta California. In 1785 he became the superior of the Alta California missions, directing the development of the missions until his death at San Carlos. During his tenure as superior, nine missions were established, including four in the summer of 1797 alone. As part of the maturation of the mission system, mission herds expanded and the Franciscans planted larger crops. The danger of food shortages passed, and the missionaries recruited larger numbers of Indians. To accommodate growing populations of converts, the Franciscans directed ambitious building projects, including the construction of larger churches. The stone structure that Lasuén began constructing at San Carlos in 1793 became the church that stands today.

– ROBERT H. JACKSON

LATORRE, LORENZO

Lorenzo Latorre (*b.* 28 July 1840; *d.* 18 January 1916), military leader and president of Uruguay (1876–1880). Latorre was the country's strongman after the uprising of 1875. His dictatorship from March 1876 until his resignation in March 1880 initiated the militarist period. The son of an immigrant warehouse-keeper, he began his military career as a soldier in Venancio FLORES's Colorado revolution and, later, as a professional soldier fought in the War of the Triple Alliance (1865–1870) against Paraguay. The Blanco caudillo Timoteo Aparicio's civil war between 1870 and 1872 created a power vacuum. The government that ruled until 1875 was one of cultured professionals, but lacked support from the military and the dominant economic groups—factors that provided the conditions for the establishment of militarism.

Latorre's program responded to the interests of the rural upper classes and to those of the financial and commercial classes who supported the gold standard and resisted the introduction of paper currency. His administration saw the escalation of fencing on the ranges that had begun in 1872, the reform of the Rural Codes, which tended to guarantee landownership and order in rural areas, and the extension of the authority of the army and the police. It sought balance in fiscal matters and guaranteed the continuation of the gold standard. Latorre was granted constitutional legitimacy in 1878.

Upon his resignation in 1880, Latorre was replaced by Francisco A. Vidal, president of the Senate. In 1882 another military leader, General Máximo Santos, assumed control of the government. Latorre, who settled in Buenos Aires after his resignation, was taken by surprise by a decree of permanent exile issued by the new dictator. Another military leader, Máximo TAJES, succeeded Santos and began the slow transition to civilian government.

— FERNANDO FILGUEIRA

LAUGERUD GARCÍA, EUGENIO KJELL

Eugenio Kjell Laugerud García (*b.* 25 January 1930), president of Guatemala 1974–1978. Brigadier General Kjell Laugerud García succeeded Carlos ARANA OSORIO as president of Guatemala in 1974. It is widely believed that the 1974 elections were fraudulent and that Efraín RÍOS MONTT was the actual winner.

Laugerud initially tried to implement a program of slight social and political reform. During his first years in office, membership in labor unions nearly tripled. Laugerud also inaugurated colonization programs for landless peasants in the Petén and along the Mexican border.

Laugerud's reform programs were cut short when a massive earthquake on 4 February 1976 caused enormous destruction and catalyzed social unrest. The last years of Laugerud's presidency were overshadowed by growing political violence. In May 1978, the army massacred one hundred civilians thought to be subversives in the village of Panzós, Alta Verapaz. One month later, Fernando Romeo LUCAS GARCÍA succeeded Laugerud as president of the republic.

— VIRGINIA GARRARD-BURNETT

LAUTARO

Lautaro (*b.* 1535?; *d.* 29 April 1557), Araucanian warrior and leader. Captured at an early stage of the warfare between the Araucanians and the Spaniards under Pe-

dro de VALDIVIA (1500–1553), Lautaro spent some time as a groom in the conquistador's entourage, where he learned much about Spanish military capacity. Escaping back to Araucanian territory, he emerged as a great military leader of his own people. Toward the end of 1553 his forces successfully attacked and destroyed the Spanish fort at Tucapel: a desperate counterattack by Valdivia himself led to the conquistador's death (December 1553). From this resounding victory, Lautaro went on to defeat the Spaniards at Marigueñu (February 1554) and to force the evacuation of Concepción. Re-founded by the Spaniards, the settlement was attacked and destroyed a second time by Lautaro in December 1555. The following year the brilliant Araucanian launched an offensive to the north of the river Maule. But the

Lautaro's deeds were frequently evoked as an inspiring precedent by creole patriots at the time of independence.

Araucanians were never as effective away from their own territory as they were on home ground. Repulsed by Pedro de Villagra (1508?–1577) near the river Mataquito in November 1556, Lautaro fell back on a safe position near the mouth of the Itata. On 29 April 1557 a second attack to the north of the Maule was countered by Francisco de VILLAGRA (1511–1563) at the battle of Peteroa (sometimes called the second battle of Mataquito), in which Lautaro received a fatal wound either from an arrow or a sword.

Lautaro's deeds were frequently evoked as an inspiring precedent by creole patriots at the time of independence. His name (like those of other Araucanian heroes of the period) has often been used as a given name for Chilean boys even in the twentieth century.

— SIMON COLLIER

LAVALLE, JUAN GALO

Juan Galo Lavalle (*b.* 17 October 1797; *d.* 9 October 1841), Argentine general. Born in Buenos Aires, Lavalle entered the military soon after the outbreak of revolution against Spain. He earned a reputation for valor tinged with rashness, distinguishing himself both in José de SAN MARTÍN's crossing of the Andes and in later service with Argentine expeditionary forces in Peru and Ecuador. He returned to Buenos Aires in 1824 and won further distinction in the war of 1825–1828 against Brazil.

Like most of the professional military, Lavalle was a supporter of the Unitarist faction against the Federalists.

He thus opposed the Federalist governor of Buenos Aires, Manuel DORREGO, whom he accused of inflicting a disorderly and arbitrary rule upon the province and of ending the Brazilian war on unfavorable terms. On 1 December 1828, Lavalle seized power in Buenos Aires by a coup. Twelve days later he had the former governor shot, thereby setting off a backlash of anger that in the end doomed Lavalle's government. Faced with counterrevolutionary uprisings throughout Buenos Aires Province, he held power less than a year.

For roughly ten years Lavalle lived as an exile in Uruguay, until in 1839 he launched a major invasion of Argentine territory, aiming to overthrow the Federalist dictatorship established by Juan Manuel de ROSAS. He penetrated deeply into Buenos Aires Province, but Rosas was able to assemble superior forces. In the meantime, Lavalle's alliance with the French forces intervening in the Río de la Plata made him vulnerable to charges of betraying national interests. He withdrew to the Argentine interior, where he suffered eventual defeat at the hands of Rosas's allies in 1841. Fleeing toward Bolivia, he was assassinated in Jujuy. Lavalle would remain a dashing hero in the middle of some; but the execution of Dorrego dogged his historical image just as it did his entire subsequent career.

— DAVID BUSHNELL

LAVALLE URBINA, MARÍA

María Lavalle Urbina (*b.* 24 May 1908; *d.* 1996), lawyer, public official, and early Mexican feminist. A native of Campeche, she grew up in an important political family. She graduated in law from the state university in 1945, and immediately entered public life. She became the first woman to serve as a state superior court justice (1947), after which she joined the federal bureaucracy. The first female senator to be elected from her home state (1964), she later served as undersecretary of education in 1976. She has written many articles on delinquency, human rights, and women; served on United Nations and national commissions in these areas; and presided over the Mexican Alliance of Women in the 1960s. She directed the Textbook Commission from 1982–1984.

— RODERIC AI CAMP

LAVALLEJA, JUAN ANTONIO

Juan Antonio Lavalleja (*b.* 20 June 1784; *d.* 22 October 1853), Uruguayan military leader and a hero in the struggle for Uruguayan independence. Born in Santa Lucía to a family of cattle ranchers, he began his military career in 1811 in José ARTIGAS's revolutionary movement for independence from the Spanish dominion. From 1816 to 1818 he fought against the invaders

from the Luso-Brazilian Empire, and in 1818 he was taken prisoner and confined for three years in Río de Janeiro. Once freed, he returned to his homeland, now called the Cisplatine Province, and joined the revolutionary movement for independence. Discovered, he was forced into exile in Buenos Aires, where he prepared the "liberation crusade." The final epic of national independence, Artigas's offensive was brought to a close in 1828 with a preliminary peace agreement and finally ended in 1830 with the establishment of a constitutional government.

Lavalleja's adherence to federalist ideals caused him on more than one occasion to favor forms of political unity with Argentina, but he finally renounced these to pursue an independent nation. The liberation crusade was the zenith of his career as well as the beginning of his rivalry with the other national caudillo, President Fructuoso RIVERA, against whom Lavalleja rose up in arms in 1832 and 1834. Defeated, he went into exile in Brazil. He returned in 1836 to fight against Rivera again, this time along with the constitutionalist forces of then President Manuel ORIBE. He defeated Rivera at the battle of Carpintería, where for the first time the colors symbolizing the traditional parties of Uruguay, red (*colorado*) for Rivera and white (*blanco*) for Oribe, were used. The war ended in 1851, and in 1853, Lavalleja joined the governing triumvirate—a short-lived one, since he died that same year.

— MAGDALENA GUTIÉRREZ

LAVISTA, MARIO

Mario Lavista (*b.* 3 April 1943), Mexican composer, editor, and administrator. Lavista was among the talented group of young musicians who in the 1960s matriculated at the Carlos Chávez composition workshop in the National Conservatory of Mexico. Others were Eduardo MATA and Hector QUINTINAR, the latter also one of Lavista's teachers. Study with leaders of Europe's avant garde—Karlheinz Stockhausen, György Ligeti, and Iannis Xenakis—and his own pioneering creative impulses led Lavista to discoveries of new sonorities coaxed from traditional instruments; however, he has not eschewed electronic sound synthesis, which he studied in Japan. Lavista has taught theory and composition at the National Conservatory, edited the music journal *Pauta,* and headed the music section of the National Council for Culture and the Arts.

— ROBERT L. PARKER

LAVRADIO, MARQUÊS DO

Marquês do Lavradio (Dom Luís de Almeida Portugal Soares Alarção Eça Melo Pereira Aguilar Fiel de Lugo

Mascarenhas Silva Mendonça e Lencastre; *b.* 27 June 1729; *d.* 2 May 1790), governor of Bahia and viceroy of Rio de Janeiro. Born in Lisbon, the son of an army officer who served as captain-general of Angola and briefly as the last viceroy of Brazil at Bahia de Todos os Santos, Lavradio became the forty-fifth governor and captain-general of Bahia (1768–1769) before being promoted to Rio de Janeiro, where he became the third viceroy to reside there (1769–1779). As had his predecessors, Lavradio found his authority far more circumscribed than his exalted title would suggest. His regime coincided with the climax of a century-long dispute between Spain and Portugal over the temperate lands between present-day São Paulo and the Río de la Plata. In spite of his best efforts, he was unable to prevent vastly superior Spanish forces from gaining control over the southern portions of that disputed territory. Acutely aware of the fact that Brazil's first gold boom was already over, Lavradio tried to stimulate new sources of royal income by encouraging the production of tobacco, cereals, fibers, whale products, and dyestuffs and to curtail illicit foreign trade with Brazilian ports. Toward the end of his viceregency he drafted an illuminating, markedly modest account of his administration, one of the few such terminal reports ever prepared by senior administrators of colonial Brazil. Subsequently, he became a member of the Council of War and president of the senior judicial tribunal of the kingdom, the Desembargo do Paço, but left no trace of his role in either body.

– DAURIL ALDEN

LE BRETÓN, TOMÁS ALBERTO

Tomás Alberto Le Bretón (*b.* 1868; *d.* 1959), Argentine politician and statesman. Born in Buenos Aires, Le Bretón trained as a lawyer at the university there and received his degree in 1891. He became a specialist in patent law and used this expertise to represent Argentina at the 1904 Berlin Industrial Property Congress as well as at a subsequent congress in Stockholm. Although Le Bretón is now remembered mostly for his dominant role in Radical Party politics after his election to the Chamber of Deputies in March 1914, he was also instrumental in promoting land colonization in the Chaco region as part of a process of government support for the nascent cotton industry there. He probably became interested in the matter as a member of the Administrative Commission of Land and Colonies in 1920, but he did not become officially active in this regard until 1923, following a term in the United States (1919–1922) as Argentine ambassador. As minister of agriculture from 1922 to 1925 he thoroughly reorganized the ministry, paying particular attention to the prospects of cotton cultivation. Le Bretón contracted with U.S. agronomist Dr. Ernest Tutt to provide the most modern agricultural and marketing information. These resources, along with the opening of government lands to settlers and provision by the government of free cotton seed to farmers, together served to promote the rapid development of this industrial fiber.

Le Bretón's links to the Antipersonalist Radical Civic Union led to his reentry into politics. In later years the conservative governments of General José Augustín P. JUSTO and Roberto M. ORTIZ appointed him to several important diplomatic posts. In 1936 Le Bretón was called upon to represent Argentina in commercial negotiations with Great Britain. He also served as Argentine ambassador to Great Britain from 1938 to 1941.

– DONNA J. GUY

LEAL, FERNANDO

Fernando Leal (*b.* 1896; *d.* 1964), Mexican painter. Born in Mexico City, Leal studied briefly at the San Carlos Academy of Fine Arts and at the Open Air Painting School in Coyoacán under Alfredo Ramos Martínez. He was a teacher of drawing and printmaking at the Open Air School for seven years. In 1921, together with Jean Charlot, he devoted himself to woodcuts, reviving the once popular medium with images of contemporary life. Leal was among the first Mexican painters to use subjects from the Mexican Revolution in his canvases, including *Zapatista Camp* (1922). Later that year, he was invited by Education Minister José Vasconcelos to paint on the walls of the National Preparatory School. The result was the large encaustic mural *The Feast of Our Lord of Chalma,* which depicted the Indian dances dedicated to the Black Christ of the village of Chalma. In 1927 Leal decorated, in fresco, the entrance to the laboratories of the Department of Public Health. In 1931, again using encaustic, he painted the vestibule of Bolívar Hall, incorporating various events from the Wars of Independence in South America.

Unlike many of his contemporaries, who were leftists and anticlerical, Leal was a devout Catholic, and in the late 1940s he was involved in mural decorations for the Church of Our Lady of Guadalupe in Mexico City. He also served as art critic for the newspaper *El Nacional Revolucionario* in 1934–1935. Although he ceased mural painting in the last decade of his life, he continued to produce many easel paintings of landscapes, figures, and still lifes, as well as woodcuts, until his death.

– ALEJANDRO ANDREUS

LEANTE, CÉSAR

César Leante (*b.* 1 July 1928), Cuban novelist and essayist. Leante was born in Matanzas and spent part of his childhood in Mexico. From 1944 to 1950 he was a member of the Socialist Youth Movement and later the Popular Socialist Party. In 1954 he began writing radio scripts and continued until 1959, the year he joined the staff of the newspaper *Revolución*. In 1961 he became an editor for the news agency Prensa Latina. He also taught theater at the National School for Instructors in the Arts until 1963, when he was named cultural attaché at the Cuban embassy in Paris. Leante went on to represent his country officially in international activities and to occupy prestigious posts at the Ministry of Foreign Relations and at the Cuban Union of Writers and Artists (UNEAC), which recognized his novel *Padres e hijos* with an honorable mention in 1965. He translated into Spanish the works of Simone de Beauvoir and Antoine de Saint-Exupéry.

Leante served as literary adviser to the National Council on Culture and enjoyed favorable treatment from the Cuban regime until opting not to return to Cuba while on an official trip to Europe. Since then he has published in Spain, his adopted home, and elsewhere in the Americas. One of his best-known works is the 1973 novel *Muelle de caballería*. Among his other works are *Tres historias* (1977), *Calembour* (1988), and *Fidel Castro* (1991). His novels have been translated into several languages.

— ROBERTO VALERO

LECHÍN OQUENDO, JUAN

Juan Lechín Oquendo (*b.* 19 May 1914), Bolivian labor leader. Born in the small mining town of Corocoro to an Arab father and a mestizo mother, Lechín studied at the American Institute in La Paz. He was a founding member of Bolivia's Federation of Miners (Federación Sindical de Trabajadores Mineros de Bolivia—FSTMB) and for over forty years (1944–1986) served as its permanent secretary. In 1952, Lechín joined the revolution of the Nationalist Revolutionary Movement (MNR) that nationalized the mining industry, declared universal suffrage, and carried out an extensive land reform program, playing a key role in the formation of the new regime. As minister of labor, Lechín was instrumental in the establishment of the Bolivian Workers Central (COB), an umbrella organization in which he presided as secretary general until the mid-1980s. He was also instrumental in securing worker cogovernment and comanagement in Comibol (the Mining Corporation of Bolivia).

In 1960, Lechín was elected vice president of Bolivia on the MNR ticket headed by Víctor PAZ ESTENSSORO. This relationship, however, was short-lived as Lechín resigned from the MNR to form his own Revolutionary Party of the Nationalist Left (Partido Revolucionario de Izquierda Nacionalista—PRIN) and then conspired with the military to topple Paz Estenssoro in 1964.

Lechín's support for the military coup did not prevent his joining the MNR leadership in exile while the new military government cracked down on labor. Ironically, between 1982 and 1985 Lechín was largely responsible for the erosion of labor's power. In an attempt to replay the 1950s, he demanded and obtained worker comanagement in Comibol; significantly, he rejected worker cogovernment. At the same time, however, Lechín launched numerous general strikes that crippled the government's attempts to stabilize the economy.

A year after the launching by the MNR of Bolivia's New Economic Policy in 1985, Lechín suffered a humiliating defeat when the miners he had served since 1944 refused to reelect him permanent secretary of the FSTMB. Earlier he had lost his position as secretary general of the COB. Since 1986, Lechín has become a marginal player in labor and in Bolivian politics.

— EDUARDO A. GAMARRA

LECLERC, CHARLES VICTOR EMMANUEL

Charles Victor Emmanuel Leclerc (*b.* 17 March 1772; *d.* 2 November 1802), commander of the French military expedition to Saint-Domingue in 1802. In December 1802 a French funeral ship docked at Marseilles. On board were the body of Leclerc and his grieving widow, Pauline. Napoleon officially declared his court in mourning and announced a state funeral for his brother-in-law.

Napoleon selected Leclerc to lead a French expedition against Toussaint L'Ouverture and the black rebels of Saint-Domingue.

Leclerc, a native of Pontoise, first served under Napoleon at the siege of Toulon (1793) and attained the rank of general in 1797 for his service in Italy. Leclerc married Pauline Bonaparte in 1797 and played an important role in Napoleon's coup against the Directory in 1799.

In 1801, Napoleon selected Leclerc to lead a French expedition against Toussaint L'OUVERTURE and the black rebels of Saint-Domingue. Leclerc encountered unexpected resistance from the rebels, attempted to restore slavery in the former colony, and arrested Toussaint L'Ouverture. He then contracted yellow fever and died at Cap Français. At the time of his death, Jean-

Jacques DESSALINES had organized the island's blacks for victory and independence from France.

— THOMAS O. OTT

LECONTE, MICHEL CINCINNATUS

Michel Cincinnatus Leconte (*d.* 8 August 1912), president of Haiti (1911–1912). Leconte was one of six Haitian presidents who ruled for very brief periods between 1911 and 1915, an era of chronic political instability that encouraged the U.S. military to intervene in Haitian affairs in 1915. Leconte staged a successful coup against President Antoine SIMONE. Lasting only from 14 August 1911 to 8 August 1912, Leconte's presidency was subject to the pressures produced by U.S. and German banking and commercial interests that were competing for control over Haitian economic life. With the support of the German merchants in Haiti, Leconte sought to appease native elite elements unhappy about the corruption that had occurred in Simone's dealings with U.S. bankers and railroad businessmen. U.S. diplomatic pressure, as epitomized by the visit of U.S. Secretary of State Philander Knox, encouraged him to impose order upon the country. Leconte reorganized the army and began developing a system of public education before he was killed in a mysterious explosion at the presidential palace in Port-au-Prince.

— PAMELA MURRAY

LECUONA Y CASADO, ERNESTO

Ernesto Lecuona y Casado (*b.* 6 August 1895; *d.* 29 November, 1963), Cuban pianist and composer. Lecuona, born in Guanabacoa, began to play the piano when he was barely four years old—he had to climb on a box to reach the keyboard. As the great Ignacy Jan Paderewski once noted, he gave the impression that "he had nothing to learn. Nature had made him a prodigious pianist." Thus pianists sometimes have difficulty playing many of his works because they were composed by an extraordinary master of the keyboard. He had the same natural gift for composing. Many times his works went straight to the publisher without Lecuona's having played them even once.

In this somewhat undisciplined fashion Lecuona's creative genius produced three groups of works. The first encompasses the bulk of his early *boleros, guarachas,* and *criollas*—Cuban music with European roots. The second is made up of Afro-Cuban compositions, which he began to write around 1920, the best known of which is probably the elegant and sensuous dance "La Comparsa." The third, less numerous group is his

Spanish-style works, among which the seven pieces that form his suite *Andalucía* stand out. It is said that the celebrated French musician Maurice Ravel believed that the semiclassic "Malagueña," one of these Spanish-style works, was more melodic and beautiful than his own "Bolero." Lecuona also wrote a number of works for the theater, from frivolous revues to tragic zarzuelas (Spanish operettas). Many of his best-known songs come from his stage work, among them "Siboney," one of his most popular pieces outside Cuba.

Plácido Domingo, the world-acclaimed tenor, won the 1985 Grammy Award for Latin American songs for his performance of "Always in My Heart," the theme song that Lecuona wrote for the film of the same title, released in the early 1940s. Lecuona died in Santa Cruz de Tenerife, Spain.

— JOSÉ M. HERNÁNDEZ

LEDUC, PAUL

Paul Leduc (*b.* 11 March 1942), Mexican film director. Leduc was born in Mexico City, where he attended the National Autonomous University of Mexico (UNAM) before receiving a scholarship to study film direction at the Institute of Graduate Film Studies in Paris. Upon his return to Mexico, he organized numerous film clubs and began his career as an assistant director and producer of various important documentaries. He debuted as a director of feature films with the acclaimed *Reed: México insurgente* (1970). A series of noted and controversial films followed. One of the most creative and original directors of current Latin American cinema, Leduc is equally adept at narrative film and documentary. He has consistently preferred to work as an independent film director. Leduc's other films are *Historias prohibidas de Pulgarcito* (1981), *La cabeza de la hidra* (1983), *Frida, naturaleza viva* (1985), *Como vas* (1989), *Barroco* (1990), and *Latino Bar* (1991).

— DAVID MACIEL

LEGUÍA, AUGUSTO BERNARDINO

Augusto Bernardino Leguía (*b.* 19 February 1863; *d.* 7 February 1932), Peruvian politician, businessman, and landowner, and twice president of Peru (1908–1912, 1919–1930) at a time of distressing economic modernization and social upheaval. Initially an important representative of the Civilista political elite, and an example of the rise of the more business-oriented sector of the Peruvian agro-export elite, Leguía broke with the Civilista Party over issues of executive initiative and state interventionism. In his second presidential term, Leguía used both popular and elite support to enhance the role of the state aided by foreign loans which became excessive after 1925.

Leguía was born in Lambayeque and studied accounting in a British school in Valparaíso. After the War of the Pacific he was tied through marriage to agro-exporting landed interests. He also developed financial ties with foreign and local banks and insurance companies. He established the British Sugar Company in 1896 and the South America Insurance Company in 1900. He rose meteorically in politics, first serving as finance minister under Presidents Manuel CANDAMO and José PARDO. As a presidential candidate with the official Civilista Party blessing, Leguía was elected president in 1908. His first term of office was traumatic. In an attempted coup in 1909, Leguía almost lost his life but also demonstrated considerable courage. His attempts at modernizing the state lost him favor among the Civilistas. From 1908 to 1910 Leguía also had to face international crises with neighboring Ecuador, Colombia, and Chile. In his second term Leguía was able to settle most of these old boundary disputes.

After 1913 Leguía lived abroad, mainly in London. In 1918 he returned to Peru with strong popular support. Leguía won the presidential elections of 1919, but fearing congressional opposition by his political enemies, he rallied military support for a coup to reinforce his presidential powers. Subsequently, his efforts to establish a New Fatherland (*Patria Nueva*) resulted in rigged reelections in 1924 and 1929. He exiled or imprisoned many of his political adversaries. His public works in Lima and the provinces (road construction, urbanization), state modernization, and encouragement of local capitalist interests seriously floundered during the financial crisis that led to the depression of the 1930s. He was ousted by a military coup led by Colonel Luis SÁNCHEZ CERRO and died in prison in Callao.

– ALFONSO W. QUIROZ

LEIGHTON GUZMÁN, BERNARDO

Bernardo Leighton Guzmán (*b.* 16 August 1909), Chilean politician. Bernardo Leighton Guzmán served as minister of the interior during the first half of Christian Democrat Eduardo FREI's presidency in the mid-1960s. Along with Frei, Radomiro TOMIC, and Rafael Agustín Gumucio, he was among the many young, middle-class Chilean Catholics attracted to the liberal currents of Catholic social thought that emerged during the 1920s and 1930s. After several years of burrowing from within the country's traditional Conservative Party, this group left the party in 1938 to establish the Falange Nacional, which in 1957 became the Christian Democratic Party (PDC).

Known affectionately as Hermano Bernardo (Brother Bernard), Leighton was one of the most congenial and widely respected of the Christian Democrats. He served in the cabinets of Liberal (Arturo ALESSANDRI) and Radical (Gabriel GONZÁLEZ VIDELA) governments, and throughout his career maintained cordial relationships with virtually all political forces, particularly those of the Left. Although one of the most trusted confidants of the strongly anticommunist Frei, he was among the minority of Christian Democrats who condemned the 1973 military coup and publicly criticized those who encouraged and supported it. He and his wife were attacked and left for dead by unknown assailants in Rome in 1978. He eventually recovered, but remains partially paralyzed.

– MICHAEL FLEET

LELOIR, LUIS F.

Luis F. Leloir (*b.* 6 September 1906; *d.* 2 December 1987), Argentine scientist and winner of the Nobel Prize in chemistry in 1970. Born in Paris to a wealthy Argentine landowning family, Leloir was brought to Argentina when he was two years old. He received an M.D. from the University of Buenos Aires in 1932, after which he briefly practiced medicine. In 1934 he joined the research team at the Institute of Physiology under the leadership of Dr. Bernardo A. Houssay, the pioneering Argentine scientist and 1947 Nobel Prize winner in physiology and medicine. From 1936 to 1937, Leloir pursued his interest in the young field of biochemistry at Cambridge University, England, with Sir Frederick Gowland Hopkins, another Nobel Prize winner (1929). He returned to Buenos Aires and rejoined the Institute of Physiology (1937–1943), where he studied the oxidation of ethanol and fatty acids, and later worked on the mechanism of renal hypertension.

In 1944, disagreements with the Juan PERÓN government led Leloir (and many other scientists) to pursue research abroad. Initially, he worked on the formation of citric acid as a research associate at Washington University in Saint Louis, and later joined the Enzyme Research Laboratory at the College of Physicians and Surgeons in New York City. In 1947, he returned to Argentina and became the first director of the Biochemical Research Institute in Buenos Aires, a research group formed and led by Leloir and financed by businessman Jaime Campomar. On Campomar's death in 1957, the U.S. National Institutes of Health provided a grant that allowed the institute to continue its research.

Leloir was awarded the 1970 Nobel Prize for the work he and his staff did at the institute in the late 1940s and early 1950s that led to the discovery of sugar nucleotides and their role in the biosynthesis of carbohydrates. His more than seventy scientific articles have been published in international scientific journals. Leloir's dedication and many scientific successes, despite an often astonishing lack of financial support for even basic equipment and laboratory space, attest to his genius and contradict the image of Latin American disinterest in science.

— J. DAVID DRESSING

LEMUS, JOSÉ MARÍA

José María Lemus (*b.* 22 July 1911), president of El Salvador (1956–1960). Born in La Unión of humble origins, Lemus attended the National Military Academy. He served as El Salvador's undersecretary of defense (1948–1949), and as President Oscar OSORIO's (1950–1956) minister of the interior (1950–1955); in the latter post he antagonized his colleagues by fighting corruption. Lemus was Osorio's choice to succeed him, and in 1956 he won a disputed election.

A man of democratic impulses, Lemus offended the press by requiring newspapers to print replies to news stories and editorials.

A man of democratic impulses, he brought a number of distinguished civilians into government. He repealed Osorio's antisedition law and permitted political exiles to return to El Salvador, thereby antagonizing the military. He also offended the press by requiring newspapers to print replies to news stories and editorials.

The use of production controls to combat the 1958 drop in coffee prices infuriated the growers, while rising prices and unemployment alienated the workers. A disputed congressional election in 1960 exacerbated tensions. Lemus responded by announcing reforms in health, education, and minimum wages. With the support of the Roman Catholic church, he organized a mass rally in support of the government. This was followed by student demonstrations praising the Cuban revolution. The subsequent roundup of students and other dissidents led to Lemus's arrest and exile on 26 October 1960.

— ROLAND H. EBEL

LENCINAS, CARLOS WÁSHINGTON

Carlos Wáshington Lencinas (*b.* 13 November 1889; *d.* 10 November 1929), Argentine caudillo. Born in

Rivadavia in the province of Mendoza, Argentina, Lencinas studied law at the University of Córdoba. Upon returning to Mendoza, he followed in the political footsteps of his father, José Néstor Lencinas, who in 1918 became the first governor from the Radical Civic Union (UCR) to rule the province. When his father died in office in 1920, Lencinas, who that year had been elected a representative to Congress, took the reins of the party and eventually formed a new one, the Lencinista UCR. In 1922 he was elected governor of Mendoza and ruled in a populist fashion. He was popularly called "el gauchito Lencinas." In 1924 his government was "intervened," an Argentine constitutional device that under specific conditions allows Congress or the central government to assume administrative control of a province; thus ended Lencinas's short-lived governorship. Two years later Lencinas was elected national senator by Mendoza's legislature, but his credentials were rejected by Congress. On 10 November 1929, Lencinas was assassinated while addressing a crowd in Mendoza. As his assailant was also shot and killed, the motivation for the crime was never clearly determined. A popular and charismatic leader, Lencinas established pioneer social reforms such as the minimum-wage salary, the eight-hour workday, and an employee pension system. These provincial measures were the harbinger of national social reforms instituted a generation later by Juan Domingo Perón.

— CELSO RODRÍGUEZ

LEÑERO, VICENTE

Vicente Leñero (*b.* 9 June 1933), Mexican writer and journalist. Leñero was born in Guadalajara, Jalisco. He earned a degree in engineering, which he practiced very briefly. During the early 1960s Leñero was a full-time journalist, and subsequently he continued working in that profession. He has produced short stories, novels, dramas, and cultural reports, and he has made decisive contributions to some of the most important journalistic and cultural enterprises in recent Mexican history. Since 1976 he has been assistant director of the magazine *Proceso.*

Inspired by the exemplary works of Juan RULFO and Juan José ARREOLA, Leñero published his first book, *La polvareda y otros cuentos,* in 1959. Published two years later was his first novel, *La voz adolorida,* a revised version of which later appeared under the definitive title *A fuerza de palabras.* This work began a novelistic career unique in Mexican literature. Perhaps because of his engineering background, Leñero is very conscious of the structure of his novels and in each of them displays a will to master a radically different and complex structure. This formal preoccupation has produced at least one masterpiece, *Los albañiles* (1964), winner of the Biblioteca Breve prize for a novel in 1963, at that time the most prestigious recognition that existed in the Spanish language.

Although some critics consider the spontaneity of Leñero's works excessive and even detracting, his approach has led him to explore the most diverse novelistic subgenres while reflecting with clarity and honesty on some of the most critical moral problems of our time.

— JORGE AGUILAR MORA

LENG, ALFONSO

Alfonso Leng (*b.* 11 February 1894; *d.* 11 November 1974), Chilean composer. Born in Santiago, Leng was largely a self-taught composer, he attended the conservatory in Santiago for less than a year (1905). Leng was a member of the *Grupo de los diez* (Group of the Ten), which had been formed by fellow composers Próspero Bisquertt, García-Guerrero, Acario COTAPOS, and Carlos Lavín, whose works introduced the concept of modernism into the Chilean cultural aesthetic. By about 1906 Leng had acquired his definitive style, as shown in such compositions as *Preludio no. 2* (1906) and his five *Doloras* for piano (1901–1914). In 1921 he composed *La muerte de Alsino,* a symphonic poem. Leng's style was strongly connected with German late romanticism. He wrote a considerable number of works for voice and piano as well as choral works. He was awarded the National Art Prize in Music in 1957. A noted dentist, he wrote several major papers on odontology. He died in Santiago.

— SUSANA SALGADO

LEÓN, ALONSO DE

Alonso de León (*b.* 1637; *d.* ca. 25 March 1691), first governor of Coahuila (1687–1691) and leader of early colonization efforts in Texas. The son and namesake of an important chronicler of Nuevo León, León was born in León, Spain. He grew up on Mexico's northern frontier, earned a reputation as an explorer and soldier, and rose to the rank of general in 1687. That same year, León became the first governor of the newly created province of Coahuila, which was intended to serve as a bulwark against the threatening French presence in the Gulf of Mexico. At first, he concentrated on internal affairs, distributing land grants and mining licenses, reorganizing the presidio system, and attempting to pacify the indigenous population. But imperial matters soon took precedence. In 1689 and 1690, León led expeditions to Texas. The first came across the remains of a French fort built by Sieur de La Salle, already destroyed

by Indians. On the second, León's party founded the first Texas mission, San Francisco de los Tejas. However, such missionary activity—underfinanced, poorly supplied, and insufficiently defended—could not be sustained in the face of a hostile Indian response and was abandoned within a few years. Spain would not establish a permanent base in Texas until 1716. León died in Santiago de Monclova, which he had founded in 1689.

— R. DOUGLAS COPE

LEÓN DE LA BARRA, FRANCISCO

Francisco León de la Barra (*b.* 16 June 1863; *d.* 22 September 1939), president of Mexico (26 May 1911– 6 November 1911). The son of a Chilean immigrant who fought for the Liberals in the War of the Reform, León de la Barra was a native of Querétaro. He graduated in 1886 from the School of Jurisprudence that was later absorbed into the National University. An outstanding international lawyer and career diplomat, León de la Barra was Mexico's ambassador to the United States when the Revolution of 1910 began. After being elevated constitutionally to the presidency by the Treaty of Ciudad Juárez, he presided over the most democratic elections held until that time.

Nicknamed the "White President" because of his apolitical behavior, León de la Barra walked with some success the slippery tightrope between demands for peace and order and the quest for social change. Although some interpretations have made his presidency the scapegoat for Francisco MADERO's inadequacies, more recent studies have been more favorable, pointing out that he allowed a free press and initiated labor and agrarian reforms. León de la Barra served Victoriano HUERTA briefly as secretary of foreign relations (1913), was ambassador to France in 1913–1914, and then retired to Europe, where he played a role in the post–World War I settlement. He died in Biarritz, France.

— PETER V. N. HENDERSON

LEÓN-PORTILLA, MIGUEL

Miguel León-Portilla (*b.* 22 February 1926), leading Mexican scholar of ancient Mexican literatures, philosophy, and culture. Born in Mexico City, León-Portilla received B.A. degrees at the Instituto de Ciencias in Guadalajara (1944) and Loyola University in Los Angeles (1948). In 1951 he graduated with an M.A. from Loyola and received a Ph.D. from the National University of Mexico in 1956. León-Portilla has held several positions since then, including professor in the Faculty of Philosophy and Letters at the National University of Mexico; director of the Inter-American Indigenist Institute (1960–1963); director of the Institute of Historical Research of the National University of Mexico (1963–1975); and delegate of Mexico to UNESCO.

Among León-Portilla's major contributions has been his willingness to grapple with questions of Aztec worldview and philosophy.

His honors include Mexico's 1981 National Prize in the Social Sciences, History, and Philosophy. León-Portilla's revised Ph.D. dissertation, *La filosofía Nahuatl estudiada en sus fuentes,* first published in 1959, set the stage for his lifelong scholarly endeavors. His more than 40 monographs, over 200 professional articles, instrumental involvement in the publication of numerous primary sources, and his editorships of *Estudios de cultura Nahuatl* and *Tlalocan* demonstrate his pivotal role in developing and furthering Aztec studies.

Among León-Portilla's major contributions has been his willingness to grapple with questions of Aztec worldview and philosophy, based on documentary sources that are incomplete and subject to interpretation. His translations of primary Aztec documentation have made a large and complicated corpus accessible to intensive study; his interpretations and analyses have stimulated scholarly research and debate; and his numerous syntheses of Aztec literature and culture have extended an understanding of ancient Mexico to a worldwide audience.

— FRANCES F. BERDAN

LEONI, RAÚL

Raúl Leoni (*b.* 26 April 1906; *d.* 5 July 1972), Venezuelan president (1964–1968). Raúl Leoni was one of the founding fathers of Venezuela's most important twentieth-century political party, Acción Democrática (AD). He began his political career when, as president of the Venezuelan Students Federation, he organized a Students' Week in February 1928 to protest the repressive regime of Juan Vicente GÓMEZ. Although the protest sparked a more general outcry against the regime, including an aborted rebellion led by young army officers, it also forced Leoni and his colleagues into exile for eight years. While in Barranquilla, Colombia, Leoni and other exiles plotted their return and drew up the *Plan de Barranquilla,* a nationalist reform document that foreshadowed the program of the AD. The plan stressed the need for political democracy and social justice in Venezuela and sought to curb the virtually unbridled power of the country's foreign-owned petro-

leum companies. Leoni returned to Venezuela after the death of Gómez, and in 1936 he was elected to the Venezuelan Chamber of Deputies as a member of the Partido Democrático Nacional (PDN), precursor of AD. However, Leoni was deported by President Eleazar LÓPEZ CONTRERAS in 1937 and was unable to take his seat.

After earning a law degree at the Universidad Nacional de Colombia in Bogotá, Leoni returned to Venezuela, where he became one of the main organizers of AD, which was legally recognized in September 1941. Leoni and Rómulo BETANCOURT led the party into power for the first time by cooperating with dissident army officers who, in 1945, overthrew dictator General Isaías MEDINA. As minister of labor during the heady years that followed, Leoni oversaw the unionization of Venezuelan workers and supervised the first collective bargaining agreement between the oil companies and their workers in 1946. When AD fell victim to its own mistakes and a military coup against President Rómulo GALLEGOS in November 1948, Leoni left the country again, this time to work for the International Labor Organization of the United Nations and with fellow AD exiles who formed part of a larger community of exiled Caribbean democratic-left leaders.

With the fall of the dictatorial General Marcos PÉREZ JIMÉNEZ in January 1958, Leoni returned to Venezuela to help his party regain power. After becoming president of AD the following year, he succeeded his old ally Rómulo Betancourt as president of Venezuela between 1964 and 1968. Relying initially on support from the AD-affiliated labor groups, Leoni largely continued the nationalist, reformist policies inaugurated by Betancourt. These included promotion of industrialization, agrarian reform, and expansion of public education. Leoni also proved to be an innovator by seeking conciliation with the radical Left which had launched a guerrilla war several years earlier, and by legalizing the Communist Party in 1968. Finally, by proposing a law to levy an excess profits tax on the oil companies, he goaded the latter into accepting a compromise arrangement that increased the industry's benefit to the national government. This step paved the way for future efforts to increase the government's share of Venezuelan oil wealth.

— PAMELA MURRAY

LEOPOLDINA, EMPRESS

Empress Leopoldina (Maria Leopoldina de Hapsburg; *b.* 22 January 1797; *d.* 11 December 1826), empress consort of Brazil (1822–1826). Daughter of Emperor Francis I of Austria, Archduchess Leopoldina married Pedro, prince of Brazil and heir to the Portuguese throne, in ceremonies in Vienna and Rio de Janeiro in 1817. The marriage became a factor in the acceptance of Brazil's independence from Portugal—declared by Pedro with Leopoldina's strong support in 1822—by Austria and the "Holy Alliance" of conservative European monarchies. Pedro and Leopoldina were proclaimed emperor and empress of Brazil on 12 October 1822.

Intelligent and well educated, especially in the natural sciences, Leopoldina came under the intellectual influence of her husband's chief minister, José Bonifácio de ANDRADA E SILVA, though she retained her innate political conservatism. Pedro's banishment of José Bonifácio in 1823 distressed her, and subsequent revelations of her husband's infidelities added to her unhappiness. While the emperor's political enemies publicly sympathized with his long-suffering wife, Leopoldina remained devoted to the unfaithful Pedro. She bore him four daughters, including the future Queen Maria II of Portugal, and two sons, one who died in infancy and one who became Emperor PEDRO II of Brazil. Barely a year after the birth of her second son, Leopoldina died of complications following a miscarriage.

– NEILL MACAULAY

LEPE, DIEGO DE

Diego De Lepe (*d.* before 1513), Andalusian explorer, possible discoverer of the Orinoco River in present-day Venezuela. A native of Palos, in southwest Spain, Lepe was one of several leaders of a series of minor expeditions from Spain's southern Atlantic ports that led to important advances in geographic knowledge of New World coasts. Leading a small fleet of two boats, Lepe left Seville in mid-November 1499, pursuing the course set two weeks earlier by Vicente Yáñez PINZÓN, who commanded four ships. Lepe followed the route of Pinzón, passing the Cape Verde Islands, then sailed to Cape San Agustín (Pinzón reached it on 26 January 1500) on the Brazilian coast. Pinzón seems to have been the first European to discover the Amazon estuary and enter the great river; he sailed upstream for a time and made contact with peoples along its banks. Diego de Lepe and his men followed within days.

At this point the account becomes confused. Some say Lepe sailed southward along Brazil's coast as far as the Río de la Plata; others argue he went northwestwardly, encountering several important rivers, including the Orinoco, of which he took possession in the name of the Spanish monarchs, calling it the Marañón. In skirmishes he lost eleven men but captured thirty-six Native Americans, whom he later presented as slaves to Bishop Juan de Fonseca in Seville. Given that Lepe's fleet and that of Pinzón came together in the Gulf of

Paria, the second version of Lepe's voyage seems most likely.

From the north coast of South America, Lepe's boats headed to the Isla de San Juan (Puerto Rico) in May 1500, while the Pinzón group sailed to Hispaniola's north coast in June of the same year. From Puerto Rico, Lepe sailed directly to Spain, reaching Seville several weeks earlier than Pinzón. He had an audience with the monarchs in Granada on 15 November 1500, and later secured an agreement for a new voyage on 14 September 1501. It is unclear if this expedition ever took place. Lepe died in Portugal sometime before 1513.

Both Pinzón and Diego de Lepe came upon Brazil several months prior to the official Portuguese discovery of Pedro Alvares CABRAL on 22 April 1500. Their logs, maps, and reports were used by cartographer Juan de la Cosa for his famous world map of 1500.

– NOBLE DAVID COOK

LERDO DE TEJADA, MIGUEL

Miguel Lerdo de Tejada (*b.* 1812; *d.* 22 March 1861), Mexican politician, author of the Ley Lerdo, and brother of Sebastián Lerdo de Tejada. A native of the city of Veracruz, Lerdo was elected to the Mexico City *ayuntamiento* (city council) in 1849 and became its president in 1852. Lerdo was a close associate of many of the *agiotistas* (moneylenders) of Mexico City and Veracruz and a consistent advocate of infrastructure development. Lerdo was deputy minister and later minister of development during the last presidency of Antonio López de SANTA ANNA (1853–1855). As finance minister for Ignacio Comonfort, Lerdo issued the Law Disamortizing Urban and Rural Property, commonly called the Ley Lerdo, on 25 June 1856. Lerdo served Benito JUÁREZ as finance minister (1858–1859, 1859–1860) and as minister of development (1859, 1860). On 12 July 1859, after Lerdo had threatened to resign, the liberal government issued a decree nationalizing all property of the regular and secular clergy, suppressing religious orders, and separating the church and the state. Lerdo hoped to use church property as collateral for a loan from the United States to adequately fund the liberal government and its war against the conservatives. He traveled to New Orleans, New York, and Washington, D.C., in 1859, but was unsuccessful in acquiring funds. Lerdo resigned in June 1860, when Juárez rejected his proposal to suspend payment on the foreign debt, but the real difference between the two men was Lerdo's position in favor of either negotiating peace with the conservatives or inviting U.S. intervention, neither of which Juárez would accept. After the liberal victory, Lerdo became a candidate for the presidency of the republic. During the campaign he died of typhus in Mexico City.

— D. F. STEVENS

LERDO DE TEJADA, SEBASTIÁN

Sebastián Lerdo de Tejada (*b.* 1823; *d.* 1889), president of Mexico (1872–1876). The younger brother of Mexican politician Miguel Lerdo de Tejada, Sebastián Lerdo was born in Jalapa, Veracruz. After renouncing an ecclesiastical career, he moved to Mexico City in 1841. Lerdo took a teaching post at the Colegio de San Ildefonso in 1849 and became rector in 1852. President Ignacio COMONFORT appointed him minister of foreign relations in 1857, but Lerdo remained in Mexico City as the rector of San Ildefonso and took no part in the War of the Reform. In 1861, he was elected to the national legislature, where he served as president of the Congress on three occasions. During the French Intervention, Lerdo accompanied President Benito JUÁREZ as a representative of the Congress. Juárez appointed Lerdo to head the ministries of government and foreign relations.

Along with Juárez and José María IGLESIAS, Lerdo was among the most prominent politicians in the Republican government. He wrote decrees (8 November 1865) explaining the extension of Juárez's presidential term until the end of the war and eliminating the possibility of succession for Jesús GONZÁLEZ ORTEGA. According to some sources, Lerdo convinced Juárez not to pardon MAXIMILIAN. Lerdo wrote the *convocatoria* of 1867, which sought to increase presidential power through an unconstitutional plebiscite.

Despite increasing opposition to him, Lerdo was elected vice president. He inherited the presidency on the death of Juárez in July 1872 and later that year was elected to a constitutional term. His presidency was marked by the completion of the Mexico City–Veracruz railroad (1873), the elimination of several regional caciques, and anticlerical reforms. As minister of foreign relations, Lerdo had consistently resisted U.S. encroachments on Mexican territory. As president, he delayed railroad construction in the north, saying "Between strength and weakness, the desert," but finally granted a concession to a U.S. firm. After announcing his intention to seek reelection in 1876, Lerdo faced two opposition movements, one led by José María IGLESIAS, the other by Porfirio DÍAZ. Although Lerdo was reelected, he was not able to defeat his armed opponents. He resigned the presidency on 20 November 1876 and fled into exile on 25 January 1877. He died in New York City.

— D. F. STEVENS

LESCOT, ÉLIE

Élie Lescot (*b.* 1883; *d.* 1974), Haitian dictator (1941–1946). Lescot, a native of Saint-Louis-du-Nord, was educated in Cap Haitien and received his doctorate from Laval University in Québec. Subsequently he was secretary of public education, justice, and the interior; envoy to the Dominican Republic; and a diplomat in the United States. His regime was known for its tyranny and corruption as well as for its close cooperation with U.S. government and business interests. Lescot established his dictatorship, in part, by taking advantage of circumstances produced by U.S. national and hemispheric security concerns after the outbreak of World War II. In the name of protecting Haiti from the Axis powers, he not only confiscated the property of Germans and Italians within the country, but also suspended the Haitian constitution. The regime also benefited from an influx of U.S. military and economic aid during the war period. U.S.-sponsored development projects went to enrich Lescot's family and friends. These included a project to grow sisal financed by the U.S.-controlled Société Haïtienne-Américaine du Développement Agricole (SHADA), to which Lescot made huge land concessions and which, in turn, led to the displacement of thousands of peasants.

Lescot's regime was known for its tyranny and corruption as well as for its close cooperation with U.S. government and business interests.

Lescot's policies favored members of the country's mulatto elite and, generally, denied the aspirations and interests of blacks. Lescot excluded blacks from important positions in his government. He also attacked black folk culture by supporting the Roman Catholic church's campaign against the vodun religion. Although this attack proved short-lived, it helped provoke widespread nationalist opposition to the regime. Lescot altered the constitution in order to extend his term of office and postponed elections, ostensibly because of World War II. By the end of 1945, students, workers, and intellectuals openly demanded an end to the dictatorship. Following the Revolution of 1946, Lescot was forced to resign on 11 January 1946. He was exiled to Canada.

— PAMELA MURRAY

LETELIER DEL SOLAR, ORLANDO

Orlando Letelier del Solar (*b.* 13 April 1932; *d.* 21 September 1976), Chilean ambassador to the United States and cabinet minister under President Salvador AL-LENDE. Born in Temuco to an upper-class family, Letelier graduated from the University of Chile with degrees in law and economics. After several years in the government's Department of Copper, he worked for Felipe Herrera at the Inter-American Development Bank in Washington, D.C., from 1960 to 1971. A long-time Allende supporter, he was appointed Allende's ambassador to the United States, a post in which he faced a hostile Nixon administration committed to subverting the Chilean government. During Allende's hectic final four months in office, Letelier served in his cabinet as minister of foreign relations, interior, and defense, successively. He was arrested in the 11 September 1973 coup and, with other ranking officials and supporters of the fallen government, he was sent to the prison camp on Dawson Island in the frigid Strait of Magellan. Exiled a year after the coup, Letelier went to Venezuela before accepting a position as associate fellow at the Institute for Policy Studies in Washington, D.C., where he was prominent among Chileans attempting to rally opposition to the Augusto PINOCHET regime. Agents of the Dirección Nacional de Inteligencia (DINA) blew up his automobile on 21 September 1976, killing him and his assistant Ronni Moffitt. U.S. courts tried and sentenced five DINA agents: Michael Townley (a U.S. citizen) and four Cuban exiles. Chile rejected extradition requests for three of its citizens indicted for the crime, straining relations with the Carter and Reagan administrations. In November 1993, a Chilean court sentenced former DINA head Manuel Contreras Sepúlveda and his assistant, Pedro Espinoza Bravo, to seven to ten years of prison; an appeal was pending in 1994.

— THOMAS C. WRIGHT

LETELIER MADARIAGA, VALENTÍN

Valentín Letelier Madariaga (*b.* 16 December 1852; *d.* 20 June 1919). Chilean thinker and political figure, often considered the chief Chilean disciple of positivism. Born in Linares City, he qualified as a lawyer in 1875 and later held a number of official jobs, including the secretaryship of Chile's legation in Germany (1880–1885). He was a deputy in the Congress of 1888–1891 and, as a leader of the Radical Party, was one of the signers of the act deposing President José Manuel BALMACEDA in January 1891 (for which he was later imprisoned and exiled by Balmaceda). In 1906 Letelier became rector of the University of Chile, where he instituted important reforms. At the third Radical Party convention in 1906, Letelier successfully advocated "socialist" (i.e., social reform) principles that were the di-

rect opposite of the "individualism" espoused by his chief adversary, the brilliant speaker Enrique MAC IVER RODRÍGUEZ. Letelier's pen was rarely idle; his numerous works, which incline to the ponderous, cover history, law, sociology, and philosophy.

— SIMON COLLIER

LETELIER VALDÉS, MIGUEL FRANCISCO

Miguel Francisco Letelier Valdés (*b.* 29 September 1939), Chilean organist and composer. Born in Santiago, Letelier Valdés is the son of composer Alfonso Letelier Llona. He received his early musical education at the National Conservatory of the University of Chile. Later studies included work in France with Max Deutsch, André Jolivet, and Jean-Jacques Grünenwald. In Argentina, where he eventually took up residence, he studied with Alberto GINASTERA. Letelier Valdés, who has given recitals throughout South America and Germany, has composed for orchestra, piano, chamber groups, and voice. The originality of his work makes it difficult to identify him with a particular style or tendency, but his later music shows an affinity with the work of György Ligeti and Luciano Berio.

— SERGIO BARROSO

LEVINGSTON, ROBERTO MARCELO

Roberto Marcelo Levingston (*b.* 10 January 1920), president of Argentina (18 June 1970–March 1971). With the fall of Juan Carlos ONGANÍA, Alejandro LANUSSE stayed in the background while the military junta recalled Levingston from the post of military attaché in Washington, D. C., to assume the presidency. The first item on his agenda after taking office was to salvage Onganía's stabilization plan. When that attempt failed, Levingston brought in Aldo Ferrer as economic minister. By October 1970 he and Ferrer had expanded credit, initiated a 6 percent pay hike, and promoted exports through a "buy Argentine" campaign.

Levingston's reform program notwithstanding, unrest burgeoned among labor, guerrillas, and political parties, with the latter forming a broad coalition, including Peronists, called the "Hour of the People." When Córdoba's governor, José Luis Camilo, dubbed some political agitators "vipers," he sparked the *viborazo,* a guerrilla insurrection. Alarmed, the military deposed Levingston and installed Lanusse as president, marking the end of the "Argentine Revolution."

— ROGER GRAVIL

LEVINSON, LUISA MERCEDES

Luisa Mercedes Levinson (*b.* 5 January 1914; *d.* 4 March 1988), Argentine writer. Born in Buenos Aires,

Levinson was part of the *La Nación* dynasty, the oligarchic Buenos Aires daily whose literary supplement continues to be a powerful voice in Argentine letters. Perhaps best known as the mother of writer Luisa VALENZUELA, Levinson exemplifies one literary alternative in Argentina during the turbulent 1950s and 1960s: the projection of an internationalist commitment to contemporary themes such as the individual against the "massification" and cultural commodification of society, the problematics for a woman of sustaining an intrinsic dignity and integrity in the wasteland of modern life, and the psychological depth of solitary lives. *La pálida rosa de Soho* (1959) deals in a highly poetic fashion with the experiences of a London prostitute, while the stories of *La hermana de Eloísa* (1955) were written in collaboration with Jorge Luis BORGES, with whom she was long associated. *El último zelofonte* (1984) is especially notable for its psychopathic eroticism and the possibilities it presents as a political allegory of contemporary Argentina.

— DAVID WILLIAM FOSTER

LEVY, ALEXANDRE

Alexandre Levy (*b.* 10 November 1864; *d.* 17 January 1892), Brazilian composer, pianist, conductor, and critic. A composer of French and Swiss descent, he enjoyed the musical advantages of being a member of one of São Paulo's most renowned musical families. His father was a clarinetist and owner of Casa Levy, a music store as well as a recital hall in which concerts of local and visiting artists took place. Alexandre Levy performed in public for the first time at the age of eight in a concert in which he and his brother played the piano, and his father the clarinet. Since his father owned a publishing business, several of the compositions he wrote as a teenager were published.

The last two decades of the nineteenth century in Brazil were marked by rising republican sentiment which culminated in the end of the empire and the establishment of the republic in 1889. The importance of Levy's work as a composer consisted of the fact that a respected Brazilian musician with excellent European training began to employ systematically the use of Brazilian folk and popular music in his compositions at a time when Brazilian musicians were attempting to break the bonds of European artistic domination. Levy also introduced Brazilian audiences to a significant number of European works unknown to them in his programming of works for the Haydn Club, of which he was program director and frequent conductor. Two of Levy's best-known works are *Variations on a Brazilian Theme* (Vem cá, Bitú [1887]), and *Suite brésilienne* (1890). On

17 January at a dinner on the country estate of his family, he complained of feeling unwell and died before the family was able to summon a physician. He was only thirty-one years old.

— DAVID P. APPLEBY

LEWIS, ROBERTO

Roberto Lewis (*b.* 1874; *d.* 1949), Panamanian painter. In the 1890s, Lewis studied under Albert Dubois and Leon Bonnat in Paris, where he was later named Panamanian consul (1904–1912). Upon returning to Panama, he became director of the Academia Nacional de Pintura from its founding until the late 1930s.

Lewis is well known for the official neoclassical paintings with which he decorated the interiors of public buildings such as the Teatro Nacional, the Palacio de Gobierno, and the Presidencia. He also painted many portraits, including all of the national presidents from 1904 to 1948. Unlike the academic portraits, Lewis's landscapes, including the famous *Tamarindos de Taboga* (1936), are characterized by the luminous colors and lively brushwork which reflect the influence of post-impressionism on his style.

— MONICA E. KUPFER

LEY, SALVADOR

Salvador Ley (*b.* 2 January 1907; *d.* 21 March 1985), Guatemalan composer and pianist. Ley was born of German parents who had settled in Guatemala City. At the age of fifteen Ley won a scholarship to study music in Berlin. He remained in Germany from 1922 until 1934, when he returned to Guatemala to teach and serve as the director of the National Conservatory of Music. In 1937, Ley moved to New York City, where he made his North American debut in January 1938. His subsequent tour of the United States included a performance at the White House. Ley returned to Guatemala and resumed the directorship of the National Conservatory from 1944 to 1953. In the latter year he returned to the United States and taught at the Westchester Conservatory of Music in White Plains, New York. Ley has composed orchestral works, including *Copla triste* and *Danza exótica,* the opera *Lera,* and works for piano and voice.

— STEVEN S. GILLICK

LEYVA SOLANO, GABRIEL

Gabriel Leyva Solano (*b.* 1871; *d.* 13 June 1910), precursor of the Revolution in Sinaloa. From northern Sinaloa, educated at the state *colegio* (preparatory school) in Culiacán, Leyva became a schoolteacher on a large rural estate. There, and in neighboring villages, he observed the misery and the atrocities of local political authorities which the country folk suffered. This, combined with reading of Porfirian abuses in the nation, led him to cultivate opposition sentiment among peasants. In time, as a lawyer's assistant, Leyva began representing the dispossessed in legal proceedings. An avid follower of Francisco MADERO, after the latter's tour of the state in 1909, Leyva espoused the Maderista cause among peasants and workers in northern Sinaloa. Harassed by authorities, he gathered a revolutionary band around him in May 1910. But within a month he was betrayed, captured, and executed without trial, an early martyr of the Revolution.

— STUART F. VOSS

LEZAMA LIMA, JOSÉ

José Lezama Lima (b. 19 December 1910; d. 9 August 1976), Cuban poet and novelist. Possibly the greatest Cuban novelist and one of the greatest Cuban poets of all time, Lezama Lima was born in Havana. He graduated from the law school of the University of Havana in 1929 and worked as a lawyer until 1941, when he received a post at the cultural office of the Ministry of Education. Aside from his own arduous literary creations, he promoted literature in Cuba by founding and directing four literary publications that were pivotal to the development of Cuban literature: Verbum, while he was a law student; Espuela de Plata, with Guy Pérez Cisneros and Mariano Rodríguez (1939–1941); Nadie Parecía, with Ángel Gaztelu (1942–1944); and Orígenes, with José Rodríguez Feo (1944–1956). This last

Lezama Lima became an internationally known author, receiving many invitations to cultural events abroad, but the Cuban government repeatedly denied him permission to travel.

publication became the center of Cuban literary and artistic life. It published only previously unpublished material and provided a forum for the work of Cuban writers of merit, both known and unknown, including Alejo CARPENTIER, Virgilio PIÑERA, Lydia CABRERA, Eliseo DIEGO, and Eugenio FLORIT. It also published the graphic work of great Cuban artists, among them Wilfredo LAM and Amelia PELÁEZ, as well as a section of reviews. Aside from attracting the best talent in Cuba, Orígenes also published the work of varied figures

of international renown, such as Albert Camus, Gabriela MISTRAL, Juan Ramón Jiménez, Octavio PAZ, Paul Valéry, giving Cuban cultural activity an unprecedented entry into the international scene.

Lezama Lima's official standing after the Cuban Revolution of 1959 was initially good. He was almost enthusiastic about the new regime, and he occupied several key posts in the Cuban cultural establishment: he was one of the vice presidents of the National Union of Cuban Writers and Artists (UNEAC), director of the Department of Literature and Publications of the National Council of Culture, and researcher and consultant at the Institute of Literature and Linguistics at the National Academy of Sciences. Although he never publicly dissented from the government, in his later years he was harassed and marginated because he failed to be actively supportive of official aims and policy.

Lezama Lima's best-known work, the novel Paradiso, was published in Cuba in 1966 to immediate acclaim there and abroad. Yet its distribution in Cuba was extremely limited, and shortly after its publication it mysteriously disappeared from bookstores and became very difficult to obtain. He became an internationally known and revered author, receiving many invitations to cultural events abroad, but the Cuban government repeatedly denied him permission to travel. He lived in Cuba until his death.

Lezama Lima is one of the most complex, baroque authors in the history of the Spanish language. An unabashed proponent of "art for art's sake" in a milieu that favored art as an instrument for social change, he spurned references to reality and sought to create a hermetic and self-referent world through language. His best-known works include Oppiano Licario (1977), the sequel to Paradiso; the essay Las eras imaginarias (1971); and a volume of his poetic work, Poesía completa, published in 1975. His novels and poetry have been translated into many languages.

— ROBERTO VALERO

LIAUTAUD, GEORGES

Georges Liautaud (b. 1899; d. after 1988), Haitian artist and sculptor. Liautaud, who has been described as Haiti's most consistently original artist, did not begin his career until middle age. He received an above-average education but also expressed an early interest in mechanics. He spent several years in the Dominican Republic working as a repairman for the railroads before returning to Haiti as a blacksmith and manufacturer of hardware. In 1953 DeWitt Peters, the director of the Centre d'Art in Port-au-Prince, discovered Liautaud's metal crosses and began to commission more such works of pure art. After this Liautaud shifted to one dimensional figures, especially representations of a half-woman, half-fish spirit known as Maîtresse La Sirène. Today his unique pieces can be found in galleries in Paris, New York, and Rotterdam.

— KAREN RACINE

LIDA, RAIMUNDO

Raimundo Lida (*b.* 15 November 1908; *d.* 20 June 1979), Argentine literary scholar. Born in Lemberg, Austria (Lvov, Poland), Lida arrived with his family in Argentina at the age of two and was educated at the University of Buenos Aires, as a student of Amado ALONSO and Pedro HENRÍQUEZ UREÑA. His literary scholarship represented the best of the philological tradition, while displaying a strong interest in aesthetics, philosophy of language, and newer critical methodologies. Lida became secretary of the Institute of Philology at the University of Buenos Aires under the directorship of Alonso. In 1948 Alfonso Reyes appointed him director of the Center of Linguistic and Literary Studies of the Colegio de México, where he also became the founding managing editor of the *Nueva Revista de Filología Hispánica (NRFH)*. Lida's distinguished career as professor at Harvard University began in 1953; in 1968 he became Smith Professor of Romance Languages. His *Letras hispánicas: Estudios, esquemas* (1958) is a collection of essays on philosophy, Latin American literature (Rubén DARÍO, Gabriela MISTRAL, and Jorge Luis BORGES, among others), and the prose works of Francisco de Quevedo, to which he dedicated much of his scholarly career. Nine of his later articles on Quevedo were collected posthumously as *Prosas de Quevedo* (1981). *NRFH* published a special issue titled *Homenaje a Raimundo Lida* (vol. 24, no. 1) in 1975. Known for his scholarly precision in addressing historical contexts and stylistic questions, and for the economy and subtle wit of his own critical style, Lida placed great emphasis on his role as mentor to several generations of Hispanists who shaped U.S. scholarship on the literature of medieval and early modern Spain and present-day Latin America.

— EMILIE BERGMANN

LIENDO Y GOICOECHEA, JOSÉ ANTONIO

José Antonio Liendo y Goicoechea (*b.* 3 May 1735; *d.* 2 July 1814), Central American educator and scientist, founding member of the Economic Society of Guatemala. Born to a creole family in present-day Cartago, Costa Rica, Goicoechea was instrumental in introducing the Enlightenment to late colonial Central America.

He entered the Franciscan order in his native Costa Rica, and it was during his studies to enter the order that he was first exposed to scientific training. In 1767 he earned a bachelor's degree from the University of San Carlos. He moved to Guatemala sometime during the late 1760s, and in 1769 he published a paper on experimental physics. In the 1780s Goicoechea visited Spain, where he was exposed to the "new learning" so popular at the time. He examined the libraries, botanical gardens, and natural history exhibits of Spain, an experience that provided him with the basis for his later work in Guatemala. He returned to Guatemala in 1788.

Along with other "enlightened" figures, on 20 November 1794 Goicoechea signed a petition to the crown calling for the establishment of an economic society modeled on those existing in Europe. He and his associates hoped that the society could help to enliven Guatemala's moribund economy, so backward in comparison with what Goicoechea had seen in Spain. But economic revival threatened many entrenched interests, and the crown ordered the suppression of the society in 1800, ostensibly because Goicoechea and another member, Antonio Muró, argued that Indians should be allowed to wear European-style clothing.

Goicoechea taught a generation of Guatemalans destined to lead the former Spanish colony as an independent nation. In addition to his article on Indian clothing, he wrote articles on indigo cultivation, the Indians of Comayagua, and poverty in the capital city. He died in Santiago de Guatemala.

— MICHAEL POWELSON

LIHN, ENRIQUE

Enrique Lihn (*b.* 3 September 1929; *d.* 10 July 1988), Chilean poet. Lihn was the prominent Chilean poet of his generation and one of the most original voices of contemporary Latin American poetry. *La pieza oscura* (1963) (*The Dark Room and Other Poems* [1978]) marks the initial maturity of his poetry of biographical experience and the manifestation of the strange and ominous. *Poesía de paso* (1966) develops a poetry of circumstance, which emanates from visits to art museums and famous cities and travel to foreign countries. It parodies art criticism and the language of travelogues. *Escrito en Cuba* (1969) and *La musiquilla de las pobres esferas* (1969) present an ironic vision of life and poetry, which marks a new stage of Lihn's work.

During the military dictatorship Lihn produced a series of books, which included *Por fuerza mayor* (1974), *París, situación irregular* (1977), *A partir de Manhattan* (1979), *Estación de los desamparados* (1982), *El paseo Ahumada* (1983), *Pena de extrañamiento* (1986), *Al bello aparecer de este lucero* (1983), *La aparición de la Virgen* (1988), and *Album de toda especie de poemes* (1989), published posthumously. These books played with all kinds of allusions to social, cultural, and political circumstances. Lihn also wrote three novels of parody, a collection of short stories, *Agua de arroz* (1964), plays, and numerous essays, and he did a number of original drawings. *Diario de muerte* (1989) is a collection of poems written when the author was suffering from cancer.

— CEDOMIL GOIC

LIMA, ALCEU AMOROSO

Alceu Amoroso Lima (*b.* 11 December 1893; *d.* 14 August 1983), Brazilian writer, publicist, and Catholic leader, whose career started in 1919 as a literary critic for the recently founded Rio de Janeiro newspaper *O Jornal.* Cautious that his activities as a writer could detract from the respectability of his position as an industrialist, he chose the pen name Tristão de Athayde, which was destined to make him famous. As an intellectual and a writer, he embraced many different roles simultaneously. These included social activist on Catholic issues, political doctrinaire, essayist at large, professor of literature and, of course, literary critic, which was his main persona throughout his life, with only sporadic interruptions.

His life was marked and divided by the year 1928, when, hitherto religiously indifferent, he converted not only to Catholicism but to militant Catholic causes. For a long time he was an intellectual of the rightist, conservative, ideology, but, after the military political coup of 1964 in Brazil, he identified himself progressively with left-of-center positions. As a matter of fact, he eventually belonged to the so-called Catholic Left, not going so far, however, as to join the Theology of Liberation.

Lima's influence was enormous, although it abated somewhat after his death. In any case, he personified the traditional Catholic thinker par excellence. Although he wrote hundreds of books and essays, the five volumes of his *Estudos* (1927–1933) may be taken as a largely representative introduction to the whole of his work.

— WILSON MARTINS

LIMA, JORGE DE

Jorge de Lima (*b.* 23 April 1895; *d.* 16 Nov. 1953), Brazilian poet, physician, politician. Lima was born in the northeastern state of Alagoas, where he completed secondary school. While drawn to the priesthood, he chose medicine as a career and went to Salvador to study. Having specialized in public health, he returned in 1915 to practice in Alagoas. In 1926, he became involved in public affairs, winning election to the state chamber of deputies as a candidate of the Republican Party. In 1930 he moved to Rio, where he was active in political causes while continuing his medical career. In 1946, he served on the governing council of the Federal District, and in 1949 he began to teach at the University of Brazil and the Catholic University.

Lima was born into a family that had been active in the abolition movement, and a concern for the black experience marks his writing.

Like many well-known intellectuals of the period, he participated in the Catholic movement of renovation. While the first poetry he published followed Parnassian models, Lima achieved recognition only in the second phase of modernism as a member of a spiritually oriented group in Rio. His poetry, inspired by his Christian faith, gave way to surreal verse of self-searching abstraction. In literary circles, Lima's most admired single work is *Invenção de Orfeu* (Invention of Orpheus, 1952), a dense ten-canto lyrical epic.

In terms of cultural nationalism, Lima's cult of northeastern regionalism, especially of the black cultural presence, is noteworthy. He was born into a family that had been active in the abolition movement, and a concern for the black experience marks his writing from the 1920s on. One of his most noteworthy works is *Poemas Negros* (1947), which invokes African deities. In addition to eighteen books of verse, Lima wrote five works of long fiction, but they are not of the same distinction as his verse. He also produced children's literature, biography, and art criticism.

— CHARLES A. PERRONE

LIMA, PEDRO DE ARAÚJO

Pedro de Araújo Lima (Marquis of Olinda; *b.* 22 December 1793; *d.* 7 June 1870), Brazilian politician. He received a degree in canon law from Coimbra University in Portugal. His career covered the last part of the colonial period, independence, the First Empire, Regency, and most of the Second Empire. In 1821 he was a member of Pernambuco's delegation to the Portuguese constitutional convention in Lisbon, and in 1823 he was Pernambuco's delegate to the Brazilian constitutional convention. Lima was minister of empire during the First Empire; president of the Chamber of Deputies, and last regent of the empire (1837–1840) during the minority of PEDRO II; senator for Pernambuco; four times president of the Council of Ministers in the Second Empire; and councillor of state.

Lima's political views and actions were influenced by the excesses of the theoretic parliamentarism he witnessed in the Portuguese and Brazilian constitutional conventions; by the solid English parliamentarism of Lord Liverpool, George Canning, and Robert Peel; and by the unconstitutional actions of Charles X of France. They were also profoundly marked by the chaos and disorder that engulfed Brazil during the Regency (1831–1840). He developed a marked distaste for parliamentary demagoguery and theories, advocated strict adherence to the constitution, called for a strong central government as an antidote to disorder and chaos, developed a willingness to share power with the opposition, and acquired an ingrained fear of political and territorial fragmentation of the state.

Lima's regency signaled the end of Liberal experiments in political and administrative decentralization, promoted the prestige of the monarchy, and strove to regain the prerogatives lost by the executive power during the period of decentralization. In 1841, he was among the first to be appointed to the Council of State, the emperor's advisory body. As councillor of state for twenty-eight years, he strongly defended political and administrative centralization and governmental control over the church. He served mostly in the Section of Empire, where he advised the ministers of empire and of agriculture. He specialized in the incorporation of Brazilian joint-stock companies, whose bylaws he scrutinized with the utmost care, and thus molded the commercial legislation affecting companies. As president of the Council of Ministers he was gifted in his ability to select as his ministers men of recognized talents and prestige, regardless of their political affiliation. As a result, important pieces of legislation were approved during his stewardships.

One of the Conservative national political leaders and the undisputed Conservative leader in the province of Pernambuco, he later became one of the founders of the Progressive Party, a league of moderate Conservatives and Liberals. In 1854 he was granted the title of marquis of Olinda. His position as former regent, as well as his political, institutional, and administrative knowledge of the life of the empire made him one of the most powerful and influential politicians of the Second Empire.

– LYDIA M. GARNER

LIMA BARRETO, AFONSO HENRIQUES DE

Afonso Henriques de Lima Barreto (*b.* 13 May 1881; *d.* 1 November 1922), Brazilian author. A fin-de-siècle realist writer, memorialist, and journalist from Rio de Janeiro, he produced novels, stories, and essays containing scathing critiques of the Brazilian plutocracy, the bureaucratic state, racism, and social injustice. The grandson of African slaves on both sides, he was for decades compared—almost always unfavorably—with Joachim Maria MACHADO DE ASSIS. Although both wrote urban fiction set in Rio, Machado's style was generally considered more sophisticated in form, whereas Lima Barreto's fiction was seen as a poorly articulated paraphase of his own life.

His fictional works, including his four major novels—*Recordações do escrivão Isaías Caminha* (1909; Memoirs of the Clerk Isaías Caminha), *O triste fim de Policarpo Quaresma* (1915; *The Patriot,* 1978), *Vida e morte de M. J. Gonzaga de Sá* (1919; *The Life and Death of M. J. Gonzaga de Sá,* 1979), *Clara dos Anjos* (1923; *Clara dos Anjos,* 1979)—were based on an aesthetic in which literature is seen as "liberating from all forms of prejudice." Initially devalued as romans à clef or autobiographical recollections, these works have more recently received favorable critical reappraisals for their antiliterary attitude and direct prose style.

A fierce opponent of the highly rhetorical, French-inspired "literature of the salons" promoted by his contemporary Henrique COELHO NETO, Lima Barreto was also a self-proclaimed anarchist who espoused virulent anti-Americanism. His best-known novel, *O triste fim de Policarpo Quaresma,* is a utopian novel and an overt attack on the Republican government of Floriano PEIXOTO. The hero, a fanatic nationalist obsessed with Brazil's redemption, dies a madman. In his diaries, Lima Barreto, who died at age forty-one, describes his own life as a tragic one, marked by alcoholism, discrimination, and economic hardship.

– MIRIAM AYRES

LIMA E SILVA, LUÍS ALVES DE

Luís Alves De Lima e Silva (duque de Caxias; *b.* 25 August 1803; *d.* 7 June 1880), patron of the Brazilian army and Brazil's most famous soldier. Caxias began his military career at age five as a cadet. His father, Francisco de Lima e Silva, was prominent in national politics and served as a member of the Regency from 1831 to 1835. Caxias saw action in the struggle for independence. During the Regency period (1830–1841), in which three political parties were grappling for power following the abdication of Dom PEDRO I, he served the goals of the moderate Chimango Party by dissolving the unruly army created by the former ruler. Then, with a corps of four hundred loyal officers (the Sacred Battalion) heading up units of the newly created National Guard, Caxias suppressed various regional uprisings. In 1840 he was appointed president of Maranhão Province, which was in rebellion. The seizure of the town of Caxias was crucial in bringing that area under control, and he was given the title of baron (later viscount, count, marquis, and duke) of Caxias. Subsequently, he was able to suppress revolts in the provinces of São Paulo, Minas Gerais, and Rio Grande do Sul.

Caxias is remembered as the providential figure in establishing and maintaining political stability for the empire and as a very active member of the Conservative Party, serving as minister of war, deputy, senator, and, on two occasions, as prime minister. He characterized himself as being "more of a soldier than a politician." Others described him as "the most civilian soldier." Although he demonstrated his military abilities in the campaign to topple the Argentine dictator Juan Manuel de ROSAS in 1852, it was as commander of Allied forces during the Paraguayan War (1865–1870) that Caxias met his greatest test both militarily and politically. Certain Liberal Party leaders in power at that moment subjected Caxias to a constant barrage of criticism in Parliament and the press, to which Caxias responded with a threat to resign. Dom PEDRO II removed the Liberal regime and, although the episode was complicated by other factors, Liberal leaders blamed the whole affair on "militarism."

Caxias, his health broken, and bitter over the way civilian leaders had allowed partisan considerations to affect their obligation to support him and the army in the war, returned home to further evidences of ingratitude. No hero's welcome was arranged, he continued to be criticized in Parliament, and the size of the army was cut drastically against his wishes. Although he subsequently served in various governmental positions, Caxias died disillusioned with the treatment accorded him and the army by civilian political leaders of the empire.

In the view of Brazilian military leaders, Caxias stands as the example of how the army, under the leadership of patriotic officers, could serve as the principal institution for maintaining the national unity needed for governing an essentially undisciplined society whose civilian leaders purportedly have lacked an adequate sense of patriotism. Thus, the term *Caxiasism* becomes synonymous with the term *civics.*

– ROBERT A. HAYES

LIMANTOUR, JOSÉ YVES

José Yves Limantour (*b.* 26 June 1854; *d.* 26 August 1935), Mexican secretary of the treasury (1892–1911), a leader of the *científicos.* In 1892 Limantour became secretary of the treasury in the government of Porfirio DÍAZ after serving for a year as *oficial mayor* of the ministry under Matías ROMERO. Faced with a severe eco-

nomic crisis, he initially was forced to secure a series of foreign loans at disadvantageous terms, to maintain Mexico's solvency, but eventually he reformed government finances to the extent that he produced a surplus in 1895 and for years thereafter. In 1899 he renegotiated the nation's foreign loans at significantly better rates.

His most pressing dilemma, however, was the decline in the value of silver during the 1890s. He determined that the best solution was to convert Mexican currency to the gold standard, and he did so in 1904.

After 1900, Limantour became increasingly concerned about the vast economic presence of U.S. investors in Mexico.

Limantour presided over the period of Mexico's most dynamic economic development until after 1940. His policy was based on the encouragement of foreign investment. After 1900, however, Limantour, like Díaz, became increasingly concerned about the vast economic presence of U.S. investors in the country. In 1902, worried by the likelihood that the two largest U.S.-owned railroad companies, the Mexican Central and the Mexican National, would swallow up other lines, Limantour initiated the government purchase of two railroad companies, the Interoceanic and the National. When this jeopardized the delicate financial situation of the Mexican Central, Limantour engineered its takeover by the government in 1906. Two years later, he merged all these lines together to form the Ferrocarriles Nacionales de Mexico. In 1908 Limantour sponsored a new banking law that reined in the unfettered growth of banks and attempted to curb abuses and corruption that marked the banking system.

Despite his reforms, the Mexican economy experienced a severe downturn in 1907 due to the decline in mineral prices on the world market. Foreign investment temporarily dried up and the country plunged into a depression, which, when coupled with a series of disconcerting political developments, badly destabilized the Díaz regime.

Between 1900 and 1910 Limantour led the *científicos,* one of two major factions within the Díaz dictatorship. Technocrats who sought to modernize the nation through positivist principles, they believed fervently in rational decision making. The opposing faction was a group of Porfirian generals, the most notable of whom was Bernardo REYES OGAZÓN, the political boss of Nuevo León. Their politics centered around personal relations with those who depended on their goodwill.

The rivalry between Limantour and Reyes took in more importance in 1904, when the aged dictator agreed to run for president for another term with a vice president for the first time. Two years earlier the finance minister had won a cabinet struggle that resulted in Reyes's ouster as minister of war and he triumphed again when Díaz chose *científico* stalwart Ramón CORRAL VERDUGO as his vice president. During this period, the *científicos* obtained the governorships of several key states. The division in *Porfirista* elite ranks badly weakened the government when it confronted the challenge of rebellion in 1910.

On 25 May 1911 Limantour resigned his post as finance minister and went into exile in France, where he lived for the next twenty-four years.

– MARK WASSERMAN

LINARES, JOSÉ MARÍA

José María Linares (*b.* 10 July 1808; *d.* 6 October 1861), president of Bolivia (1857–1861). Linares was born in Tilcala into an important Spanish family from colonial Potosí. Heir to one of the largest fortunes in Bolivia, he became the first civilian president in Bolivia's history. After the death of General José BALLIVIÁN in exile, Linares became the undisputed champion of the enemies of Manuel Isidoro BELZÚ (president, 1848–1855), who had mobilized Bolivia's lower classes to remain in power. A widely read and charismatic man, Linares, with his supporters, known as the "Rojo," conspired ceaselessly to overthrow the government. When they finally did so, he quickly established a dictatorship because he felt that this was the only way to reform Bolivian society. In particular, Linares attempted to rid the government of the corruption inherent in previous military regimes. Although a devout Catholic and proclerical, on other issues Linares was a precursor to later liberal administrations, fostering the mining industry and free trade and trying to inculcate European culture into Bolivian society. He tried to do this through dictatorial means, however, and ultimately failed. He was overthrown by members of his own administration in 1861.

– ERICK D. LANGER

LINARES, PEDRO

Pedro Linares (*b.* 29 June 1906; *d.* 26 January 1992), a Mexican papier-mâché artist (*cartonero*) who developed an expressive, one-of-a-kind style from folk art forms and traditional, ephemeral fiesta accoutrements. He is best known for two genres—the *alebrije* (fantastic animal) and the *calavera* (animated skeleton)—based on Holy Week Judas and Day of the Dead *calavera* miniatures.

Trained as a child by his father, Linares passed the family métier on to his three sons—Enrique, Felipe, and Miguel—who extended the imaginative possibilities of the medium. Grandsons Leonardo, Ricardo, and David have also taken up the work.

Alebrijes, a term coined by Linares, combine the body parts of serpents, scorpions, lions, reptiles, and butterflies and accentuate a playful outlook on reality. Intricate surface patterning in an array of bright colors and detailed tactile textures (spikes, bumps, curves) add dimension. Linares's *calaveras* touch on a pre-Hispanic rooted belief that death is an extension of life. Thus, *calaveras* engage in a wide variety of activities, such as guitar-playing, picture-taking, and skateboarding. Many of Linares's *calavera* scenes are inspired by the prints of José Guadalupe POSADA, most notably La Catrina, El Panteón, Don Quixote, and revolutionary figures.

– SUSAN N. MASUOKA

LINARES ALCÁNTARA, FRANCISCO

Francisco Linares Alcántara (*b.* 13 April 1825; *d.* 30 November 1878), president of Venezuela (1877–1878). Linares Alcántara began his political and military career before the Federal War (1859–1863). He participated in that as a proponent of liberalism and remained a prominent figure in the Liberal Party. In 1873 President Antonio GUZMÁN BLANCO named him first appointee of the republic, and as such he took on the duties of the first magistracy on various occasions.

With Guzmán's support Linares Alcántara was elected president in 1877. He brought together a cabinet composed mostly of civilians, promoted the politics of reconciliation by declaring a general amnesty, and supported freedom of the press and an administrative decentralization of funds destined for construction of public works. During his administration, a reaction against Guzmán, which Linares Alcántara tacitly encouraged, gained strength, and there were calls for a return to the Constitution of 1864. After Linares Alcántara's sudden death, his followers continued to participate in the reaction against Guzmán. The reinstatement of the Constitution of 1864 and the nullification of General Guzmán Blanco's statutes resulted in the Revolución Revindicadora (Revindicating Revolution) of December 1878, by which power was returned to Guzmán.

– INÉS QUINTERO

LINDLEY LÓPEZ, NICOLÁS

Nicolás Lindley López, one of the important Peruvian army leaders of the institutional military coup of 18 July 1962. The coup was officially justified by the allegation that the contested elections of that year had been fraudulent. None of the three main contenders in the elections, Víctor Raúl HAYA DE LA TORRE, Fernando BELAÚNDE, and Manuel ODRÍA, had been able to obtain the number of votes necessary to become president. The formation of a coalition between the Aprista Party and Odría's party and the congressional designation of Haya as president prompted the anti-Aprista forces in the military to stage the coup.

Together with generals Ricardo PÉREZ GODOY (army) and Pedro Vargas Prada (air force) and Vice Admiral Juan Francisco Torres Matos, Lindley López formed the executive of an interim government that held new elections in 1963, which were won by Belaúnde. After the forced retirement of Pérez Godoy, Lindley López became the de facto president. The military government restored constitutional guarantees, attempted a localized agrarian reform, and confronted strikes and armed insurrections led by Hugo BLANCO and Javier Heraud. The new technocratic attitude among the military was the basis for the far more consequential coup of 1968.

– ALFONSO W. QUIROZ

LINDO ZELAYA, JUAN

Juan Lindo Zelaya (*b.* 1790; *d.* 24 April 1857), president of Honduras (1847–1852) and El Salvador (1841–1842). Lindo was born in Comayagua, Honduras, the son of Joaquín Fernández Lindo and Barbara Zelaya. He studied in Mexico as a youth and later was appointed interim colonial governor of Honduras by Governor José Gregorio Tinoco de Contreras (ruled 1819–1821). The Constituent Assembly of Honduras, then reappointed him to the post, at which he served from 21 November 1821 to 11 February 1824. While president of El Salvador, he established in 1841 the Colegio de la Asunción, which was later elevated in status, becoming the University of El Salvador in 1847. He also raised the Honduran Academía Literaria in status and renamed it the University of Honduras (1847). Its curriculum, under his direction, included law, philosophy, and Latin.

On 12 February 1847, Lindo became president of Honduras with the support of Honduran Conservatives and the approval of neighboring Guatemala. Technically, his term expired on 16 July 1848, when the 4 February 1848 constitution took effect, and his second term began on the same date and lasted until 1 January

1852. Domestic unrest due to disputes with Great Britain over loan agreements marred his term of office, as did Liberal revolts in Tegucigalpa on 4 February 1849 and 12 February 1850, which forced him to flee. Liberal forces under General Santos GUARDIOLA, his successor, were eventually suppressed with the aid of Guatemala and El Salvador. Lindo's refusal to run for reelection and his belief in the 1848 constitution led him to allow a Liberal to take office unopposed.

– JEFFREY D. SAMUELS

LINIERS Y BREMOND, SANTIAGO DE

Santiago de Liniers y Bremond (*b.* 25 July 1753; *d.* 26 August 1810), viceroy of Río de la Plata (1807–1809). Born in Niort, France, Liniers was the son of a French naval officer from the Poitou region. At age twelve, he joined the Order of Malta as page to the grand master. He entered the service of the Spanish king in 1774 as an army officer in the Moroccan campaigns. Liniers first arrived in the Río de la Plata with the CEVALLOS expedition (1776) and returned in 1788. Married to María Martina de Sarratea, daughter of Martín de Sarratea, a prominent Spanish-born merchant, Liniers served as the head of the naval squadron charged with the protection of Montevideo, and then as interim governor of Misiones.

Present at the time of the second British invasion (1806–1807), Liniers was instrumental in reorganizing the militia that defeated the British invaders. Awaiting the arrival of a new viceroy to replace the discredited SOBREMONTE, who had fled during the invasions, Liniers was named interim viceroy and given the title of count of Buenos Aires. He was instrumental in putting down the ÁLZAGA rebellion of January 1809 and ruled until replaced by the newly arrived Viceroy Cisneros in August 1809. He then retired to Alta Gracia, Córdoba.

Upon hearing of the dramatic action of the *cabildo abierto* (open town council meeting) of Buenos Aires, Liniers helped organize the royalist opposition to the Buenos Aires revolutionary troops. He was captured and executed as a traitor to the revolutionary cause.

– SUSAN M. SOCOLOW

LINS, OSMAN DA COSTA

Osman da Costa Lins (*b.* 5 July 1924; *d.* 8 July 1978), Brazilian writer. A prolific author whose body of work includes short stories, drama, essays, and teleplays, Lins is best known for several novels exemplifying an important existentialist trend in Brazilian literature between the 1950s and the early 1980s. Lins's themes concerned the moral and ethical issues that must be confronted in everyday life, while the formal aspect of his fiction steadily evolved from simplicity to complex experimentation in language. His efforts to create innovative narrative techniques stand out in one of his best novels, *Avalovara* (1973; Eng. trans. 1980).

— PEDRO MALIGO

LINS DO REGO, JOSÉ

José Lins Do Rego (*b.* 3 June 1901; *d.* 12 September 1957), Brazilian writer. Author of numerous volumes of speeches, personal and travel memoirs, and children's literature, Lins do Rego is known principally as a novelist, most notably for the six volumes of the Sugarcane Cycle. Critics have traditionally included him in a group referred to as the Northeastern Generation of 1930, a half dozen novelists whose fiction came to dominate the Brazilian literary scene during the 1930s and 1940s. Indeed, he and another member of the group, Jorge AMADO, took turns writing many of the bestsellers at the time, and both had a sufficiently high profile to merit the attentions, generally unfavorable, of the government of Getúlio VARGAS. He was also affiliated

José Lins do Rego. (Iconographia)

with the Region-Tradition movement founded in 1926 by Brazilian sociologist Gilberto FREYRE, at least in the sense that his novels seemed to be the most faithful to the tenets of the regionalist movement.

Lins do Rego was born into the rural aristocracy and thus had a unique insider's perspective on the society he depicted in his works. He was born on his grandfather's plantation in Paraíba, was raised by his maiden aunts after his mother's death when he was only eight months old, and attended both a boarding school and law school in Recife. Each of these episodes is the theme of one of the novels of the cycle. A common criticism of his work as a novelist, in fact, is that he was more of a memorialist than a creator, but this perceived shortcoming is an advantage from the perspective of social history, for his novels provide perhaps the most complete, and certainly the most readable, portrait of the rural Brazilian society of the period. Lins do Rego is regarded as one of the masters of the "sociological novel," a rather vague category referring to his portrayal of characters who are at once affecting and convincing.

Freyre's notion of regionalism, detailed in his *Manifesto regionalista de 1926,* grew out of his opposition to the modernists of Rio de Janeiro and São Paulo, whom he considered too citified, too cosmopolitan, and too European to qualify as spokesmen for a still essentially rural Brazil. Today the manifesto sounds almost quirky, with its praise for regional cuisine and such things as palm thatch roofing, but it was at the time as much at the center of intellectual debate as the political question of left versus right, a matter rendered nearly moot by the Vargas coup of 1930 and utterly so by the declaration of the Estado Novo in 1937.

The modernists became urbane vanguardists, and the regionalists of the Generation of 1930 defined themselves as chroniclers of that "other," more real Brazil with its mansions and shanties, a Brazil in which the heritage of a colonial past lay just beneath the surface. Regionalism versus modernism was at the center of intellectual ferment of the period, although in hindsight it is clear that both groups were attempting, by quite different avenues, to accomplish the same end—to create a literature that could be clearly identified as truly Brazilian. The unstated agenda, and the factor that made Lins do Rego such an important writer of the time, was that the regionalists were consciously writing social documents, a posture that whether intentional or not, made the creation of art a secondary part of the exercise. There is no doubt that the public preferred such artlessness, but it is a factor that inhibits such documents from translating well into subsequent decades. From a historical perspective, however, this unadorned memorialism has its positive value, because the appeal of these works at the time of their publication was based in large degree on the fact that the Brazilian reading public *recognized* the characters and scenes and stories, which meant that their fidelity to the realities of Brazilian society was the key to their success.

It is not clear why the Vargas government regarded such writing as a threat to its well-being, but perhaps the very accuracy of the social portrayals made the government edgy. There is also some suspicion that Lins do Rego's works were targeted simply as a matter of guilt by association, because he was associated in the minds of many with other members of the generation who were in fact also members of the illegal Communist Party and whose works often made these sympathies more than evident. But the clearest sentiment evident in his works themselves is probably nostalgia, hardly a subversive quality.

The Sugarcane Cycle is largely a chronological account of the life of Carlos de Melo, who, like Lins do Rego, is the scion of a wealthy planter family. The first novel, *Menino de Engenho* (1932), deals with the early years of the timid and lonely young man, and the second, *Doidinho* (1933), continues with his trials at boarding school. *Bangüê* (1934) chronicles the years spent in Recife in law school, and *O Molegue Ricardo* (1935) tells the similar story of the black childhood companion of Carlos, who moves to the city and becomes involved in a union movement. *Usina* (1936) recounts the death of Ricardo and the transformation of the Santa Rosa plantation from the old labor-intensive plantation system into a modern, mechanized (and dehumanized) factory.

The final novel, not originally included in the cycle by its author, is also universally regarded as his best—*Fogo Morto* (1943). This volume, a tripartite narrative centering on three very different people, contains not only the best-drawn characters but also the fullest insights into a society on the verge of decadent collapse. The first central character is a saddle maker who lives on the plantation of Seu Lula, the second character, a member of the hereditary aristocracy who is the central character of the second part of the novel. The final segment features the third character, a local eccentric and his manic and misdirected exploits. Although each character is from a different social stratum and each has his own foibles and strengths, the narrative is in essence the story of a social system in which the fabric seems to be unraveling, where all assumptions about outcomes are thwarted. Lins do Rego also wrote fiction about other uniquely Brazilian and mostly rural issues, such as messianic movements and banditry, but his best works remain those most closely drawn from his own experiences. It is certainly this latter body of work that assures his place as one of the most important Brazilian writers of the century.

– JON S. VINCENT

LISBOA, JOAQUIM MARQUES

Joaquim Marques Lisboa (Almirante Tamandaré; *b.* 13 December 1807; *d.* 20 March 1897), patron of the Brazilian navy. Tamandaré graduated from the Naval Academy in 1826. He was appointed to noble status (baron, viscount, count, and marquis Tamandaré) by Dom PEDRO II for suppressing various rebellions, including the Confederation of the Equator (1824), the Balaiada Rebellion (1838–1841), and the Praieira Revolt (1848–1849). As commander of Brazilian naval forces in the Rio de La Plata in 1864, Tamandaré was involved in bringing pressure on the Uruguayan regime of Atanásio Cruz Aguirre by leading the attacks against Salto and Paissandú. He supported the mission of Counselor José Antônio SARAIVA, who was seeking satisfaction of Brazilian claims against the Uruguayan government. Tamandaré's testy, impulsive nature created problems for himself and the Brazilian government. He incurred the displeasure of the diplomatic corps when he tried to impose a blockade on Montevideo during a time of peace. He quarreled bitterly with other leaders of the high command of the forces of the Triple Alliance, and, despite numerous minor victories, he was strongly criticized for hesitating to attack the Paraguayan stronghold of Humaitá. He was finally relieved of his command in December 1866 and returned to Brazil, where, because of his long service, he was maintained on the active list until shortly after the creation of the Republic (1889). Tamandaré carried out an endless campaign to exonerate his name, a goal that was finally achieved via the Supreme Military Tribunal a few days before his death. His birthday is celebrated as Sailors' Day.

– ROBERT A. HAYES

LISCANO VELUTINI, JUAN

Juan Liscano Velutini (*b.* 7 July 1915), Venezuelan poet, folkorist, literary critic, essayist, and editor. Following early studies in Europe, Liscano returned to Venezuela, where he has been a central figure in national literary and intellectual life and founder and director of several journals, most notably the literary supplement of *El Nacional* (1943–1950) and *Zona Franca* (1964–1984), and of the publishing houses Monte Avila (1979–1983) and Mandorla. He participated in resistance activities during the dictatorship of Marcos PÉREZ JIMÉNEZ and spent the years 1953–1958 exiled in Europe. An independent thinker of greater erudition, he has written extensively, often polemically, on literature and art and on cultural, social, philosophical, and political issues. He is one of the most important literary critics of Venezuela. Although he won the Premio Nacional de Poesía in 1952, his best work is found in the more than a dozen books of poetry published since that date. In his early poetry, which culminates in the neoepic *Nuevo Mundo Orinoco* (1959), the themes of American nature, history, and experience predominate. His later work explores individual perception, metaphysics, and universal myth. More modern essays reflect his interest in the erotic, psychology, esoterica, and historical cultural patterns.

— MICHAEL J. DOUDOROFF

LISPECTOR, CLARICE

Clarice Lispector (*b.* 10 December 1925; *d.* 9 December 1977), Brazilian writer. After nine novels, six collections of stories, four children's books, translations, interviews, and a wealth of *crônicas* (newspaper columns), Lispector's literary reputation rests on three features, all of which, from the early years of her career, were a positive influence on Latin American narrative: a lyrical and metaphoric style conveying her philosophical subject matter; a structure based chiefly on interior monologue and stream of consciousness; and themes concerning anxiety, isolation, and the need for self-realization. A writer of greatly refined poetic prose, but one with a strong social conscience, Lispector is one of Latin America's most original and powerful authors of the post–World War II era.

The youngest of three daughters of Ukrainian immigrants, she read avidly, doing little else in her spare time, whether as a student or journalist. In general, her life seems to have paralleled the content, themes, and style of her works. Existential and mystical in nature, they reveal her innermost self acting upon more than reacting to exterior reality. Never very methodical, she finally learned at least to jot down her ideas and feelings as they came to her and before they were lost forever. Later she could piece them together as she understood them, and, except for *A maçã no escuro,* all her works were composed in this rather unstructured manner.

Never a popular author in the sense that great numbers of people read her works, she was from the beginning of her career in 1942 an important author, one whose achievements had already attracted a discerning international audience as well as a national one. Lispector was less interested in events than in the repercussions these events produced in the minds of her characters— an approach to fiction writing that put her largely at odds with what was then current in the Brazilian novel and short story. Not surprisingly, then, very little hap-

pens in a typical Lispector tale: plot, if defined in terms of the traditional realistic novel, is virtually nonexistent. The conflict of the work is based, almost invariably, in the mind of the character most centrally involved, the character whose hermetic and at times even claustrophobic point of view dominates both the telling and the structuring of the story. More than anything else, Lispector's narratives, her novels and her shorter pieces, are philosophical and poetic exercises that probe the complex and shifting inner realities of modern men and women. Her work has been praised for its brilliant use of language, its structural inventiveness, and its depiction of the alienated and frustrated modern human condition.

As a Brazilian writer, Lispector is best remembered for having opened new roads for Brazilian narrative, for having helped to lead it away from the productive but ultimately limiting kind of regionalism that had dominated the literary scene in Brazil for several decades. Lispector's first novel, *Perto do coração selvagem* (1942), broke radically with this deeply rooted tradition and established a new set of criteria that would help internationalize Brazilian literature and end its cultural and linguistic isolation.

The storm center of *Perto do coração selvagem,* and a character who, in her inner verisimilitude and complexity, can be taken as the prototype for later protag-

Clarice Lispector. (Iconographia)

onists of Lispector, is a young woman, the first of a series of striking female characters the author would create. Ranging from timid Ermelinda (*A maçã no escuro*), to the middle-class housewife Ana ("Amor"), to the hopelessly crippled refugee Macabéa (*A hora da Estrela*), to the existential voice of *Um sopro de vida,* Lispector's characters, whether female or male, all relate in one way or another to the issues of feminism, fulfillment, courage, freedom, and love.

Although many critics find her stories superior to her novels, because of the striking dramatic intensity that characterizes them, there can be no doubt that Lispector was a major precursor of the "new novel" in Latin America.

– RICHARD A. MAZZARA

LLERAS, LORENZO MARÍA

Lorenzo María Lleras (*b.* 7 September 1811; *d.* 3 June 1868), Colombian politician. As an educator, publicist, and politician, Lleras's moderate liberalism characterized an important current in early national Colombian politics. Born in Bogotá, Lleras received his education in his native city. His activity as a lawyer facilitated his political activity with General Francisco de Paula SANTANDER and Florentino GONZÁLEZ in the 1830s, especially as editor of *La Bandera Nacional.* Lleras was rector of the Colegio Mayor de Nuestra Señora de Rosario (1842–1846) before establishing the Colegio Mayor de Espíritu Santo, where he trained numerous influential Liberals. His *El Neo-Granadino* promulgated Draconiano Liberalism in the 1850s, an ideology he championed in the congress and in the cabinet of President José María OBANDO.

Lleras's association with members of the Democratic Society of Artisans led to his brief incarceration after the 1854 coup of José María MELO. He backed anti-Conservative forces in the 1859–1862 civil war and was a delegate to the Rionegro Convention (1863). Lleras and Clotilde Triana, his second wife, parented fifteen children, establishing a lineage that included Liberal presidents Carlos LLERAS RESTREPO (1966–1970) and Alberto LLERAS CAMARGO (1958–1962).

– DAVID SOWELL

LLERAS CAMARGO, ALBERTO

Alberto Lleras Camargo (*b.* 3 July 1906; *d.* 4 January 1990), president of Colombia (1945–1946 and 1958–1962). Born into a middle-class Bogotá family, Lleras Camargo briefly attended university but was quickly drawn into Liberal journalism and politics. Elected to Congress in 1930, he became the youngest interior minister in Colombian history during the first term of Alfonso LÓPEZ PUMAREJO (1934–1938). In López's troubled second term (1942–1945), Lleras was ambassador to the United States; he completed López's term upon the latter's resignation in July 1945, a period of severe political and labor unrest. He served as secretary general of the Organization of American States (1948–1954) and rector of the University of the Andes in Bogotá (1954). In 1956–1957 he negotiated with exiled Conservative leader Laureano GÓMEZ the agreements that formed the basis for the bipartisan National Front; in May 1958 he was elected president under that agreement. Lleras's regime faced serious problems of pacification and rehabilitation after more than a decade of violence; the western department of Caldas, plagued by murderous *bandoleros,* proved especially intractable. Reform projects inspired by the Alliance for Progress, such as a 1961 Agrarian Reform Law, produced indifferent results. After leaving office, Lleras edited the magazine *Visión;* in 1978 he retired from public life, though not before expressing dissatisfaction with the Liberal leadership of the late 1970s.

– RICHARD J. STOLLER

LLERAS RESTREPO, CARLOS

Carlos Lleras Restrepo (*b.* 14 April 1908; *d.* 27 September 1994), president of Colombia (1966–1970). The son of a prominent but poor Bogotá scientist, Lleras Restrepo was already a rising Liberal politician when he received his law degree in 1930. He served as comptroller and finance minister during the regimes of Alfonso LÓPEZ PUMAREJO and Eduardo SANTOS (1934–1942). A leader of the Liberals' "civil resistance" during the Conservative regime of Mariano OSPINA PÉREZ (1946–1950), he was forced into exile in 1952, during the presidency of Laureano GÓMEZ. A leading backer of the bipartisan National Front, he reached the presidency in 1966 promising an analogous "national transformation" on the social and economic fronts. A technocrat by temperament, Lleras Restrepo organized "decentralized institutes" in fields as diverse as sports and scientific research. In 1968 he forced through a constitutional reform increasing the executive's budgetary and planning powers. In the late 1970s, through his influential magazine *Nueva Frontera,* Lleras Restrepo was a vocal opponent of the Liberal regime of Julio César TURBAY. Lleras Restrepo's writings include the multivolume autobiography, *Historia de mi propia vida* (1983–).

– RICHARD J. STOLLER

LLORENS TORRES, LUIS

Luis Llorens Torres (*b.* 14 May 1876; *d.* 16 June 1944), Puerto Rican poet. Born into a comfortable family in Juana Díaz, in southern Puerto Rico, Llorens began writing verse at the age of twelve. He studied law in Barcelona and Granada, Spain, where he also wrote articles on Puerto Rican and Caribbean history for several periodicals. Llorens practiced law in Puerto Rico, while at the same time engaging actively in journalistic writing. In 1913 he founded and directed the journal *Revista de las Antillas,* which established new directions for the poetry of Puerto Rico, and two years later established the satirical weekly *Juan Bobo* (with Nemesio R. CANALES). He published articles under the pseudonym Luis de Puerto Rico and in 1914 wrote a historical drama, *El grito de Lares* (The cry of Lares, 1927). Llorens defined his philosophy of art as "everything is beauty" and "everything is poetry." Llorens wrote poems of intense patriotic sentiment about Spanish American history and the Caribbean; about Puerto Rico's towns, women, customs, heroes, history, folklore, natives, and landscape, and verse both admiring and protesting the United States. He was also a member of Puerto Rico's House of Representatives from 1908 to 1910, and was a supporter of self-determination for Puerto Rico. When Llorens became gravely ill in New York in 1944, President Franklin D. Roosevelt arranged to have him flown to Puerto Rico, so that he could die in his homeland.

His major works are *América* (1898), *Al pie de la Alhambra* (At the foot of the Alhambra, 1899), *Sonetos sinfónicos* (Symphonic sonnets, 1914), *"La canción de las Antillas" y otros poemas* ("Song of the Antilles" and other poems, 1929), *Voces de la campana mayor* (Voices of the great bell, 1935), and *Alturas de América* (Heights of America, 1940).

— ESTELLE IRIZARRY

LLORENTE Y LAFUENTE, ANSELMO

Anselmo Llorente Y Lafuente (*b.* 1800; *d.* 1871), bishop of Costa Rica (1851–1871). In 1850 Pope Piux IX created the diocese of Costa Rica, separating it from the diocese of León, Nicaragua. On 7 November 1851 Llorente, a native of Cartago, was consecrated its first bishop. Aside from failing to convince the legislature to provide funds for a seminary, Llorente's relationship with the government was harmonious until 1858, when the legislature, supported by President Juan Rafael Mora, passed a hospital tax. Since clergymen were not exempt from the tax, Llorente publicly opposed it, or-dering his priests not to pay it. Consequently, he was expelled from the country. He went to Nicaragua but was able to return in August 1859, when Mora was overthrown, largely due to outrage at the bishop's banishment. From then until his death, Llorente maintained a cordial relationship with civil authorities.

— EDWARD T. BRETT

L'OLONNAIS, FRANCIS

Francis L'Olonnais (*b.* 1630; *d.* 1670), notorious French buccaneer who preyed upon Spanish shipping in the Caribbean and terrorized settlements along the Spanish Main and the coast of Central America. He was born Jean David Nau but known as L'Olonnais after his birthplace, Sables d'Olonne in Brittany. L'Olonnais came to the West Indies as an indentured servant but on gaining his freedom, he quickly earned respect as a successful and unusually murderous buccaneer. With the support of the governor of Tortuga, L'Olonnais used that island as his base of operations, equipping his expeditions there and drawing his crew from its unsavory population. His greatest achievement was the capture and plunder of treasure from the relatively well-defended towns of Maracaibo and San Antonio de Gibraltar in the Gulf of Venezuela. L'Olonnais died at Islas Barú, Darién, Panama at the hands of a group of Indians allied to the Spanish. The natives tore his body apart and threw it, limb by limb, into a fire.

— J. DAVID DRESSING

LOMBARDO TOLEDANO, VICENTE

Vicente Lombardo Toledano (*b.* 16 July 1894; *d.* 16 November 1968), Mexican labor leader, intellectual, and opposition party leader. Along with Manuel GÓMEZ MORÍN and Alberto Vázquez del Mercado, Lombardo was a member of the important intellectual generation known as the "Seven Wisemen," which founded the Society of Conferences and Concerts. His intellectual orientation began with Christian Democracy and early in his adult life moved toward socialism. He was a labor activist best remembered as an organizer and secretary general of the Mexican Federation of Labor (CTM), Mexico's most powerful union. He lost control over this union to a group that included Fidel Velásquez, who dominated it from the mid-1940s to the 1990s. In 1948, disenchanted with the government, Lombardo Toledano founded his own opposition Partido Popular, which predated the Popular Socialist Party (1960), later an ally in Cuauhtémoc CÁRDENAS's 1988 electoral front.

Born in Teziutlán, Puebla, he was a childhood friend of Manuel ÁVILA CAMACHO. His grandparents were Italian immigrant peasants, and his father, who married into an old Spanish family, served as mayor of his hometown. Two of his sisters married leading intellectual contemporaries, Alfonso CASO and Pedro HENRÍQUEZ UREÑA. Lombardo Toledano completed his preparatory studies at the National Preparatory School and went on to obtain a law degree and an M.A. from the National University in 1919 and 1920, respectively. A professor

---

Lombardo was a member of the important intellectual generation known as the "Seven Wisemen."

---

for many years, he founded and directed the night-school program at the National Preparatory School (1923) and the Workers University of Mexico (1936–1968). A student leader in college, he worked for the Federal District, and at the age of twenty-nine, became interim governor of his home state, Puebla. He served in the Chamber of Deputies from 1924 to 1928 and again from 1964 to 1966, and held major union posts as secretary general of the National Federation of Teachers and secretary general of the Federation of Workers of the Federal District. When he lost his influence as the government co-opted labor unions after 1940, he founded and presided over the Federation of Latin American Workers from 1938 to 1963. He also organized and served as secretary general of the Socialist League (1944). He contributed many essays to popular magazines and newspapers.

— RODERIC AI CAMP

LONARDI, EDUARDO

Eduardo Lonardi (*d.* 22 March 1956), president of Argentina (September–November 1955). General Lonardi ruled for only fifty days and would have been forgotten but for the fact that he managed to oust Juan D. PERÓN when all others had failed. Lonardi had previously promoted an abortive revolt, which resulted in his own forced retirement in 1951. Terminally ill with cancer, Lonardi planned the coup while a patient at the Buenos Aires Military Hospital.

Though his presidency was brief, there were nevertheless distinguishing features. Once Perón was exiled (September 1955), Lonardi was magnanimous toward the Peronists, launching the slogan "neither victors nor vanquished." On the economic front, he appointed

Raúl PREBISCH to prepare a "what is to be done?" report.

Though ailing, Lonardi did not die in the presidency. Pedro Eugenio ARAMBURU ousted him on 13 November 1955 only to be confronted with a "Bring Back Lonardi" movement, but Lonardi died four months later.

— ROGER GRAVIL

LONGINOS MARTÍNEZ, JOSÉ

José Longinos Martínez (*b.* ca. 1755; *d.* 1803), naturalist in New Spain (1787–1803). A native of Calahorra, Spain, Longinos studied botany at the Royal Botanical Garden in Madrid before traveling to Mexico in 1787. Longinos preferred the study of animals and spent his time in Mexico studying birds, butterflies, fish, and mammals. He traveled through Lower and Upper California in 1791 and 1792, and kept a detailed journal on Indian life and customs, geography, and fauna and flora. Following his assignment in California, Longinos went to Guatemala, where he opened a small museum and gave lessons in botany. He died of tuberculosis on a trip to Campeche in Yucatán.

— IRIS H. W. ENGSTRAND

LÓPEZ, AMBROSIO

Ambrosio López (*b.* 1809; *d.* 19 June 1881), Colombian artisan and political activist. Ambrosio López illustrates the potential social mobility afforded by nineteenth-century patron-client relations. Born in Bogotá to the tailor Jerónimo López and the *chichera* (brewer) Rosa Pinzón, López used political associations with, first, General Francisco de Paula SANTANDER, and then Tomás Cipriano de MOSQUERA to secure various appointments. López helped found the Democratic Society of Artisans in 1847, only later (1851) to quit the organization because he thought that Liberal anti-Catholicism had corrupted it. Ambrosio supported Mosquera in opposing the 1854 revolt of José María MELO, for which he was rewarded with the post of director of waters for Bogotá during the 1860s. He participated in several Catholic mutual aid organizations, favored a more traditional political economy, and opposed Liberalism on most points. In the 1870s, Ambrosio ran the distillery Los Tres Puentes, owned by the SAMPER brothers. His association with the Sampers later enabled his son, Pedro, to become an important banker; his grandson, Alfonso LÓPEZ PUMAREJO, served as president of the country in the 1930s.

— DAVID SOWELL

LÓPEZ, CARLOS ANTONIO

Carlos Antonio López (*b.* 4 November 1792; *d.* 10 September 1862), president of Paraguay (1844–1862). López was the second of the three major nineteenth-century, post-Independence rulers of Paraguay, after José Gaspar Rodríguez de FRANCIA. Elite contemporaries and traditional historians have viewed him as a benevolent despot who discouraged opposition but was less ruthless, more self-interested, and more receptive to foreigners and the elite than was Francia. Revisionist historians see López's administration as having modernized Paraguay and developed commerce and foreign ties.

Born and educated in Asunción, López graduated from the Real Colegio y Seminario de San Carlos. He won a competition in 1814 for the chair of arts and another in 1817 for the chair of theology. A lucrative law practice served to introduce him to influential clients and friends. When Francia gained control of the elite, López retired to his family home in Recoleta. In 1826 he married Juana Pabla Carillo, who had an *estancia* in Olivares, southeast of Asunción. They had five children.

In February 1841, when Colonel Mariano Roque ALONSO, an uneducated soldier, won the power struggle that ensued at the death of Francia, López became his secretary. On March 12 a national congress appointed Alonso and López to a three-year joint consulate and elected López president in 1844, 1854, and 1857.

During his first term, López continued many of Francia's foreign and domestic policies. Paraguay, continuing its isolation from the countries along the Río de la Plata, regulated foreign commerce and migration. In his second and third terms, López sought to modernize Paraguay. The bureaucracy grew and taxes increased, but the budget was balanced. The government strengthened its army, developed a river navy, and improved internal transportation and communication. In 1852 the López government established steamship service between Asunción, Paraná, Rosario, Buenos Aires, and Montevideo. In 1853, López signed commercial treaties with Great Britain, France, and the United States that brought Paraguay international recognition. Although government regulation of major exports—yerba maté, lumber, and hides—continued, commercial treaties signed with Brazil in 1850 and with Argentina in 1856 defined borders, permitted free navigation of the Paraguay and Paraná rivers, and increased trade. In 1861, López inaugurated a railroad from Asunción to Santísima Trinidad, which was extended almost to Areguá before his death.

Pursuing his program of modernization further, López expanded rural primary schools, reopened the seminary that Francia had closed, and encouraged European immigration. He also contracted with European and North American technicians, engineers, educators, and advisers who, among other things, carried out a national geological survey; established medical services; developed industries such as a gun factory, iron foundry, and shipyard; and encouraged education and artistic endeavors. Although López limited free expression, he supported publication of Paraguay's first newspapers: *El Paraguayo Independiente* (1845–1852) and *El Semanario de Aviso y Conocimientos Útiles* (1853–1868). Under López agricultural production expanded and the government helped improve the quality of Paraguay's export cotton and tobacco. López ended the African slave trade, recognized Indian villagers as Paraguayan citizens, and used the army to end indigenous border raids.

Although López's vision for Paraguay was more self-serving than Francia's, his administration ensured that the Guaraní peasantry remained the basis of Paraguayan society. López bequeathed a unified, prosperous nation without foreign debt to his eldest son, Francisco Solano LÓPEZ.

– VERA BLINN REBER

LÓPEZ, ENRIQUE SOLANO

Enrique Solano López (*b.* 2 October 1859; *d.* 19 November 1917), Paraguayan journalist, teacher, and politician who left a large library and archives. Son of Francisco Solano López and Elisa LYNCH, he worked ceaselessly to revive his late father's reputation, which had been shattered due to his haste in bringing Paraguay into the bloody and disastrous War of the Triple Alliance in 1864. López traveled throughout Europe, and directed the conservative Colorado Party newspaper *La Patria*. He served as the national superintendent of primary schools (1897–1899) and was a Colorado Party senator (1912–1917) and mayor of Asunción in 1912. He ended his illustrious political and writing career as a professor at the National University.

– MIGUEL A. GATTI

LÓPEZ, ESTANISLAO

Estanislao López (*b.* 22 November 1786; *d.* 15 June 1838), governor of the province of Santa Fe (1818–1838). Born in the city of Santa Fe, Argentina, López studied in the local convent school. At the age of fifteen he joined the Blandengues who patrolled the northern frontier, where he learned the hit-and-run tactics that his *montonero* soldiers would later use. He participated in the reconquest of Buenos Aires (1806) and in the struggles for independence in the littoral. SAN MARTÍN early won him over to his ideas. On 23 July 1818, López separated the province of Santa Fe from Buenos Aires by proclaiming himself its interim governor; the following year, he was elected governor, and remained so until his death. In 1819 he gave the province its first constitutional statute. He joined José Gervasio ARTIGAS and Francisco RAMÍREZ in their war against Buenos Aires. He and Ramírez defeated Buenos Aires at Cepeda (1 February 1820) and compelled its *cabildo* to dissolve the national congress and to sign the Treaty of Pilar (23 February). Peace was reestablished between Buenos Aires and Santa Fe with the Treaty of Benegas (24 November). With the death of Ramírez in 1821, López became the dominant leader in the littoral. On 22 January 1822 he signed the Quadrilateral Treaty, and on the eve of the Brazilian invasion of Uruguay he approved an alliance with Montevideo (13 March 1823).

In 1828, López presided over the national convention in Santa Fe that approved the peace treaty with Brazil and appointed him commander of the national army to fight the unitarian José María PAZ. At his initiative, the Federalist Pact was negotiated and signed in Santa Fe (4 January 1831). As governor, he encouraged trade and economic development, pushed the provincial borders farther into the Chaco, improved the administration of justice, and established elementary schools, including one in an Abipón village, and a secondary school. His influence diminished as that of Juan Manuel de ROSAS increased.

— JOSEPH T. CRISCENTI

LÓPEZ, FRANCISCO SOLANO

Francisco Solano López (*b.* 24 July 1826; *d.* 1 March 1870), president of Paraguay (1862–1870) and the third of its three major nineteenth-century post-Independence administrators. Paraguayans traditionally have viewed López as a national hero, whereas revisionists have judged him to be an ambitious nationalist who overestimated the economic significance and military strength of Paraguay and involved it in the disastrous War of the Triple Alliance.

Born in Asunción as the eldest son of Carlos Antonio LÓPEZ, raised on the family *estancia* in Olivares, and privately educated by tutors, López became his father's principal adviser, confidant, and heir apparent. When Carlos Antonio López declared war on Juan Manuel de ROSAS of Argentina in 1845, he made eighteen-year-old Francisco Solano a brigadier general. From 1853 to 1854, the younger López negotiated contracts for technicians and arms in Europe, where he met Elisa Alicia

Francisco Solano López. (Organization of American States)

Lynch, who became his mistress and bore him five sons. As commander of the army and vice president, he dominated the triumvirate that ruled at his father's death. On 16 October 1862 a congress elected him president of Paraguay for a ten-year term.

General López continued the political system and economic policies of his father. He sought to make Asunción similar to European capitals—socially vibrant and culturally stimulating, with regular theater performances and fashionable events. He encouraged trade and provided government loans for commercial enterprises, railroad expansion, and telegraph construction. His administration increased the number of doctors, engineers, teachers, and skilled workers and also centralized education and the economy. Although López accumulated his own land and wealth, he was well accepted by both the peasantry and the elite.

When López sought to increase Paraguay's international role in the Río de la Plata area, he clashed with Argentina and Brazil. After leading the armed forces in the War of the Triple Alliance (1864–1870) for more than five years, he was killed at the battle of Cerro Corá.

— VERA BLINN REBER

LÓPEZ, JOSÉ HILARIO

José Hilario López (*b.* 18 February 1798; *d.* 27 November 1869), president of Colombia (1849–1853). Born in Popayán, López joined the patriots in 1814 and was imprisoned by the royalists from 1816 to 1819. Freed, he fought in Venezuela and in southern Colombia, becoming a colonel in 1826. He rejected Simon BOLÍVAR's dictatorship, and at the Ocaña Convention in 1828 he remained antidictator. Later that year, López and Colonel José María OBANDO defeated Bolívar's surrogate, Colonel Tomás Cipriano de MOSQUERA, and won control of Cauca. In 1830 López was promoted to general, and with Obando he raised an army that ousted General Rafael URDANETA in May 1831. López served in key gubernatorial posts from 1833 to 1837 and was the Colombian chargé d'affaires to the Vatican (1839–1840).

López did not join Obando in the War of the Supremes (1839–1842). Having married into the Neiva elite, he devoted himself to managing his estates until he was elected president. As chief executive, he carried out a liberal agenda. Education was made more secular, the clergy put on salary, the Jesuits expelled, tithe collection secularized, the ecclesiastical *fuero* abolished, clerical posts made elective, and Archbishop Manuel José MOSQUERA exiled. Also, slavery was abolished and legislation aimed at improving the status of women was enacted. López fought against the Melo Revolt (1854). He joined the Liberal Revolution (1860–1862) late, but contributed to its victory. He participated in the Rionegro Convention (1863).

– J. LEÓN HELGUERA

LÓPEZ, NARCISO

Narciso López (*b.* 19 October 1797; *d.* 1 September 1851), Cuban revolutionist. A native of Caracas, Venezuela, López joined the Spanish army in his mid-teens, participated in campaigns against Simón Bolívar's independence movement, and achieved the rank of colonel. When Spanish forces withdrew to Cuba in 1823, López accompanied the army to the island. There he married the sister of a creole planter, and acquired landholdings and mines. In 1827 López went to Spain, where, during the Carlist wars, he served as aide-de-camp to General Gerónimo Valdés in support of the queen-regent, María Cristina, and her daughter, Isabella, against the claims to the succession of Don Carlos, brother of the late Ferdinand VII. While in Spain, López rose to the rank of brigadier general. López returned to Cuba when Valdés became captain-general of the colony in 1841. During Valdés's tenure, López served as president of the Executive and Permanent Military Commission and governor of Trinidad Province—posts which he lost when General Leopoldo O'Donnell replaced Valdés in 1843. This loss of patronage, as well as financial setbacks, may have contributed to López's conversion to anticolonialism in the mid-1840s.

López's overt revolutionary activities commenced in 1848 with a plot named after his mines—Conspiracy of the Cuban Rose Mine. Set to erupt in late June, the uprising was postponed until mid-July in deference to the wishes of the Havana Club, which favored annexation of Cuba to the United States. Alerted by the U.S. government to the pending revolt, Spanish authorities took preemptive action. Having escaped arrest in the resultant crackdown, López reached the United States, where he organized a private military—or "filibustering"—expedition to liberate Cuba. In 1849 the Zachary Taylor administration thwarted this effort, which, like all filibustering expeditions, violated U.S. neutrality statutes, by blockading López's troops assembled at Round Island, off the Gulf coast, and by seizing his ships and supplies in New York City.

Undaunted, López and associated exiles announced a junta based in New York City but with a Washington, D.C., address. On 19 May 1850, López and some 520 followers captured Cárdenas, on Cuba's northern coast. His forces outnumbered by Spanish reinforcements, López fled to Key West, Florida. He was indicted in June 1850 for violating American neutrality laws but never stood trial (charges were dismissed after three juries failed to convict a coconspirator).

Federal authorities upset his next invasion scheme when, in April 1851, they seized the vessel *Cleopatra* in New York and arrested several filibuster leaders. However, that August, López eluded federal authorities and invaded Cuba with some 453 men. His force debarked the coasting packet *Pampero* near Bahía Honda, west of Havana. López mismanaged the ensuing military campaign, which was doomed to failure because Spanish authorities repressed developing resistance prior to the landing. Many of López's followers died in battle. The rest, except for a couple of officers who had returned to the United States for reinforcements, were captured. Spanish authorities released a few, but executed fifty invaders on 16 August and later sent some 160 captives to imprisonment in Spain. López was garroted in Havana on 1 September, in a public display. News of the 16 August executions sparked riots in New Orleans, Mobile, and Key West that did thousands of dollars' worth of damage to Spanish property. Disputes arising from the López invasions complicated for years diplomatic relations between the United States, Spain, and

Great Britain and France—the latter two seeking to dominate the Gulf-Caribbean region economically—and left a legacy of fear of American intentions among Spanish officials ruling Cuba.

In 1848, López reached the United States, where he organized a private military—or "filibustering"—expedition to liberate Cuba.

Some authorities, noting the disproportionate number of Americans in López's filibuster armies, his flag modeled upon the banner of the Republic of Texas, and his contacts with both Americans and Cubans favoring the annexation of Cuba to the United States as a new slave state, portray López as a conservative who intended to integrate Cuba into the United States. A few scholars, however, view López as a liberal nationalist—an early martyr to the cause of Cuban independence.

– ROBERT E. MAY

LÓPEZ, VICENTE FIDEL

Vicente Fidel López (*b.* 24 April 1815; *d.* 30 August 1903), Argentine historian and political figure. Born in Buenos Aires and the son of Vicente López y Planes, who wrote Argentina's national anthem, López as a young intellectual became involved during the 1830s in Esteban ECHEVERRÍA's Asociación de Mayo. Fearing possible persecution by the Juan Manuel de ROSAS dictatorship, López fled to Chile, where he worked as an educator and liberal publicist. Returning to Buenos Aires after the fall of Rosas in 1852, he served briefly in the provincial government, then emigrated to Uruguay until national unity was finally effected.

Once permanently reestablished in Buenos Aires, López served as university rector, finance minister, and in other capacities, as well as practicing journalism. However, he is best known for his work as a historian. That career began in Chile with the publication of historical novels and essays, and it culminated when he both published historical documents and authored a series of major works of Argentine history, notably his ten-volume *Historia de la República Argentina* (1883–1893). His writing was highly partisan and made use of a lively imagination rather than depending on rigorous documentation, a trait that drew him into a bitter polemic over historical method with Bartolomé MITRE. He was, however, a skilled writer and enjoyed a wide following in his time.

– DAVID BUSHNELL

LÓPEZ, WILEBALDO

Wilebaldo López (*b.* 3 July 1944), Mexican playwright. Born in Queréndaro, he studied acting, received a Writers' Guild Fellowship, and was the first dramatist of his generation to achieve recognition. Two of his early plays were widely staged in Mexico: *Los arrieros con sus burros por la hermosa capital* (1967) and *Cosas de muchachos* (1968). His others include *Yo soy Juárez* (1972) and *Malinche Show* (1977), adaptations of Mexican history in modern terms. His recent works have not enjoyed the same popularity as the earlier ones with audiences and critics.

– GUILLERMO SCHMIDHUBER

LÓPEZ ARELLANO, OSWALDO

Oswaldo López Arellano (*b.* 30 June 1921), the dominant military officer in Honduras from 1957 until 1975. Born in Danlí, López Arellano joined the armed services in 1939 and was schooled in military aviation in the United States. As commander of the armed forces beginning in 1956, he was installed as provisional president after the coup of 3 October 1963. This coup, carried out ten days before scheduled elections, reflected the Conservatives' and the military's displeasure with the prospect for a victory by the Liberal candidate, Modesto Rodas Alvarado. López continued as provisional president until a new constitution confirmed him as president in 1965. During his presidency the poor performance of the military in the war with El Salvador (1969) brought discredit on the armed services. López maintained a mild military dictatorship during his term, which continued until 1971. The National Party became his personal political vehicle.

In 1971 Ramón Ernesto CRUZ was elected president, but López, as chief of the armed forces, remained in control. In 1972, López again seized power and acted as president until he was toppled by his fellow officers in 1975. At that time, he was charged with corruption in accepting a bribe from United Brands (formerly United Fruit) to obtain lower banana export taxes. López subsequently became the president of the national airline, Servicio Aereo de Honduras, S.A. (SAHSA).

– DAVID L. JICKLING

LÓPEZ BUCHARDO, CARLOS

Carlos López Buchardo (*b.* 12 October 1881; *d.* 21 April 1948), Argentine composer and teacher. Born in Buenos Aires, López Buchardo began his musical studies with Héctor Belucci and studied piano with Alfonso Thibaud. He studied harmony with Luis Forino and Constantino GAITO. Later he moved to Paris to attend the composition classes of Albert Roussel. Returning to Buenos Aires, López Buchardo founded the eponymous Conservatorio López Buchardo (1924) and directed it until his death.

López Buchardo began to compose as a young man, starting with pieces for the stage, some musicals, and an early opera, *Il sogno di Alma,* which premiered in Buenos Aires on 4 August 1914. He was an excellent melodist with an extraordinary gift for vocal works, and his numerous song cycles, which are based on Argentine folk tunes and themes, were popular worldwide. Among his symphonic works is the *Escenas argentinas* (1920), in which he utilized two popular dances, the *milonga* and *gato;* it premiered under Felix Weingartner with the Vienna Philharmonic Orchestra in Buenos Aires in 1922. The following year López Buchardo received the Municipal Prize in Music. He was founder and director of the school of fine arts at the University of La Plata, where he was professor of harmony. He was also president of the Wagnerian Association, twice member of the board of Teatro Colón, and director of music and art for the stage for the Ministry of Public Instruction. He died in Buenos Aires.

— SUSANA SALGADO

LÓPEZ CAPILLAS, FRANCISCO

Francisco López Capillas (*b.* ca. 1615; *d.* ca. 18 January 1673), Mexican composer and organist. López Capillas may have been born in Andalusia and was probably a pupil of Juan de Riscos, the *maestro de capilla* of Jaén. Ordained a priest, he was named organist and bassoonist for the Puebla cathedral in December 1641. In 1645 he became first organist and singer. In May 1648 he went to Mexico City, where he was hired by the cathedral organist Fabián Ximeno, who had heard López Capillas on a visit to the Puebla cathedral and been impressed with his talent. He presented a volume of his choir compositions to the Mexico cathedral in April 1654, and on 21 May he was appointed *maestro de capilla* and organist of the cathedral. He was supervisor of the musical services and presented the cathedral with several excellently illuminated choirbooks. López's compositions are considered among the best written in New Spain; his eight Masses, eight Magnificats, and numerous other religious works are composed with extraordinary artfulness. His use of the polyphony, canon, and difficult mensural practices were remarkably competent. The arrival in Madrid of some of his choirbooks generated a court decree (1672) to bestow him a full prebend, but he died in Mexico City before the order became effective.

— SUSANA SALGADO

LÓPEZ CONTRERAS, ELEÁZAR

Eleázar López Contreras (*b.* 5 May 1883; *d.* 2 January 1973), president of Venezuela (1936–1941). Having completed high school in 1898, López Contreras joined the army of Cipriano CASTRO in 1899. In 1908, he left the army with the rank of colonel, but in 1913 he returned as commander of the barracks of Ciudad Bolívar, and in 1914 assumed command of an infantry regiment at Caracas. In 1919 he became minister of war and marine, and undertook the acquisition of war matériel from Europe and the United States. As a loyal supporter of Juan Vicente GÓMEZ, he used military force against students, workers, dissident army officers, and other opposition groups. For his reward, he rose through the ranks during the 1920s, taking over as commander in chief in 1930. From 1931 until December 1935, he again served as minister of war and marine.

López used military force against students, workers, dissident army officers, and other opposition groups.

Following Gómez's death López became president of the republic. He quickly ended popular demonstrations by students and workers. In so doing, he became the first Venezuelan president to speak to the nation by radio. In February 1936, he introduced a broad reform program aimed at appealing to everyone. On the one hand, he checked the power of the army. On the other, he followed Arturo USLAR PIETRI's call to "sow the petroleum" by using oil revenues to finance educational and institutional reforms. The government established a new teacher training institution, the Instituto Pedagógico (1936), and gave further assistance to child care by creating the Consejo Venezolano del Niño (1939), the Instituto Preorientación para Menores (1939), and the Casa de Maternidad Concepción Palacios (1938). New cabinet departments included the Ministry of Agriculture and Livestock and the Ministry of Labor and Communications.

López's administration guided Venezuela toward a more democratic government. He tolerated opposition movements, although he exiled Communists and radicals. Like Gómez, he followed an anticommunist policy and limited the activities of labor organizations. The government also imposed more control over the economy by creating the Industrial Bank and the National Exchange Office, as well as the Central Bank of Venezuela.

In 1938, the López government enacted petroleum legislation aimed at giving the nation more control over the industry and a larger share in the revenue, but for various reasons, including corruption, little was done to enforce the laws. In 1941, López stepped down from power, the presidential term having been reduced from seven to five years, and turned the government over to his chosen successor, Isaías MEDINA ANGARITA. Following the overthrow of the latter, López Contreras went into exile and effectively dropped out of politics.

– WINTHROP R. WRIGHT

LÓPEZ DE ARTEAGA, SEBASTIÁN

Sebastián López de Arteaga (*b.* 15 March 1610; *d.* 1652), painter. Born in Seville, López de Arteaga was examined as a painter in 1630. In 1638 he was in Cádiz; around 1640 he embarked for New Spain, where in 1642 he erected and decorated an arch with mythological subjects to celebrate the arrival of Viceroy García SARMIENTO DE SOTOMAYOR y Luna. López de Arteaga is credited with introducing into New Spain the tenebrist style of Francisco de Zurbarán, who some scholars claim had been his teacher. He sought, and with some success won, the patronage of the Inquisition. Although documents attest to López de Arteaga's considerable activity, only eight paintings can be ascribed to him with certainty, and even some of those are problematic. One of the most famous is the *Incredulity of Saint Thomas* (1643). More difficult is the *Marriage of the Virgin,* quite dissimilar and the subject of much discussion over what constitutes this master's style.

– CLARA BARGELLINI

LÓPEZ DE CERRATO, ALONSO

Alonso López de Cerrato (also Cerrato, Alonso López; *b.* ca. 1490; *d.* 5 May 1555), president of the Audiencia of Santo Domingo (1543–1547); president of the Audiencia de los Confines, later Guatemala (1548–1555). Of obscure origins but educated and enjoying royal favor, Cerrato was appointed to serve in Santo Domingo and then Guatemala to enforce the New Laws of 1542 and other proindigenous legislation. Stern and uncompromising, he freed Indian slaves in both jurisdictions, lowered tributes, and corrected abuses in Central America. Supported by Bartolomé de LAS CASAS (1474–1566) and other reformers and indifferent to local public opinion, he earned the enmity of Spanish settlers, who accused him of nepotism. He died while serving his *residencia.*

– MURDO J. MACLEOD

LÓPEZ DE COGOLLUDO, DIEGO

Diego López de Cogolludo (*b.* ca. 1612; *d.* ca. 1665), Franciscan historian and missionary. Born in Alcalá de Henares, Spain, Friar López de Cogolludo arrived as a missionary in Yucatán in 1634, and after years of work among the Maya he rose to be the chief (provincial) of the Franciscan province. In the 1650s he wrote *Historia de Yucathan,* a major source not only for the history of Yucatán but also for the study of Maya culture. The book was published posthumously in Madrid in 1688; later editions appeared in 1842 (Campeche), and 1846 and 1867–1868 (Mérida). Reprints and new editions also appeared in the twentieth century.

– ROBERT W. PATCH

LÓPEZ DE LEGAZPI Y GURRUCHÁTEGUI, MIGUEL

Miguel López de Legazpi y Gurruchátegui (*b.* 1510; *d.* 1572), *escribano mayor* (senior clerk of the Mexico City *cabildo* (municipal council) from January 1542 to 3 June 1557. López perhaps epitomizes the career of a sixteenth-century bureaucrat who, arriving late in a conquest area, had to work to achieve upward mobility. An *hidalgo* (nobleman) from Zumárraga, Guipúzcoa, in the Basque country, López departed for New Spain in 1528. On 19 January 1530 he became the *escribano de cabildo* of Mexico City, serving in that capacity until the end of 1541. For a period after 1535 he was secretary in the government of Viceroy Antonio de MENDOZA. After serving as *escribano mayor* of the *cabildo,* he transferred his rights to his son, Melchor de Legazpi.

López's offices, while not providing the opportunity to acquire an *encomienda* (grant of tribute from an indigenous polity) in New Spain, did permit the development of contracts, status (his wife, Isabel Garcés, was the sister of Julián Garcés, first bishop of Tlaxcala), and other assets that he parlayed into a license to settle the Philippine Islands. On 21 November 1564 his armada of 5 ships, 150 sailors, 200 salaried employees, some 25 settlers, and 4 Augustinian friars left Mexico. The navigator for the expedition was the Augustinian friar Andrés de URDANETA. López was governor of the Philippines when he died in Manila.

– ROBERT HIMMERICH Y VALENCIA

LÓPEZ DE QUIROGA, ANTONIO

Antonio López de Quiroga (*b.* ca. 1620; *d.* late January 1699), silver mine owner in Potosí. López de Quiroga was born near Triacastela in the province of Lugo, in northwestern Spain. He was the leading silver producer of Potosí (and possibly of all Spanish America) in the seventeenth century, owning mines and refineries at Potosí itself as well as at other sites widely scattered over its district. Between 1661 and 1699, these operations provided about 14 million ounces of silver, a seventh or an eighth of the Potosí district's total output in that period.

About 1648 López came to Potosí, where he used his prior commercial experience to set himself up as an importing merchant. He quickly married Doña Felipa Bóveda y Savavia, daughter of a prosperous local family from Galicia, close to his own birthplace in Spain. He benefited from an investigation of coinage adulteration at the Potosí mint, which led to the removal of most of the existing *mercaderes de plata* (silver traders and coinage supervisors) thereby paving the way for his eventual entrance to that profession in the 1650s. From this position, he moved into silver production about 1660, and in that decade rapidly expanded his holdings of mines and refineries in Potosí. In the 1670s and 1680s he extended his activities to Porco, Ocurí, San Antonio del Nuevo Mundo, and other sites in the district, often reviving old mines through the excavation of deep drainage galleries. To expedite this process, about 1670 he introduced the technique of blasting with gunpowder, probably for the first time in Spanish-American silver mining.

López placed many relatives in governmental positions in the Potosí district during the 1670s and 1680s, thus safeguarding his own interests. He became a large landowner and used his estates to supply goods useful in mining. Though he was unsuccessful in acquiring a title of nobility, he ended his days an already quasi-mythical figure in Potosí.

– PETER BAKEWELL

LÓPEZ DE ROMAÑA, EDUARDO

Eduardo López de Romaña (*b.* 1847; *d.* 1912), president of Peru from 1899 to 1903. When President Nicolas de PIÉROLA created the post of minister of development, he chose López de Romaña to fill it. López de Romaña successfully undertook an ambitious public works program and pledged to continue Piérola's progressive plans if the president in turn agreed to support him as the next president. On the basis of that agreement and with an alliance formed between Democrats and Civilistas, López de Romaña became president in 1899. In 1901 he began to reorganize the nation's schools to give more emphasis to technical skills in higher education. But his political naïveté made him susceptible to Civilista manipulation, and other progressive programs had less success. By the 1903 election the coalition of parties had split, some members joining the new Liberal Party and others returning to the Civilista Party. Even Piérola had abandoned him in favor of an old friend, Manuel CANDAMO, the Civilista candidate who won the election. The elite political machinations of the post-Piérola years thus kept power in the hands of the national oligarchy.

– VINCENT PELOSO

LÓPEZ JORDÁN, RICARDO

Ricardo López Jordán (*b.* 30 August 1822; *d.* 22 June 1889), military leader and staunch defender of provincial autonomy. Born in Paysandú, Uruguay, López Jordán was a nephew of Francisco RAMÍREZ and Justo José de URQUIZA. He attended the Colegio de San Ignacio in Buenos Aires, and began his military career at the age of nineteen as a soldier in the escort of Urquiza. He served in the forces of Urquiza and the Uruguayans Manuel ORIBE, Eugenio Garzón, Lucas Moreno, and César Díaz. Twice military commandant of Concepción del Uruguay, he became extremely popular when he stopped an invasion of his jurisdiction by General Juan Madariaga. He later taught military science at the Colegio del Uruguay, where among his students was Julio A. ROCA (who later defeated him in battle and became president of Argentina). He represented Paraná in the national congress (1858) and accompanied Urquiza to Asunción to settle an international dispute (1859). López Jordán served as minister of government in the provincial government of Urquiza (1860) and as president of the provincial legislature (1863–1864), but was unsuccessful in his candidacy for governor because of Urquiza's opposition (1864).

During the War of the Triple Alliance, López Jordán's troops were the only ones not to disband at Basualdo, and he escorted Urquiza home. The day after Urquiza was assassinated, an act for which he assumed responsibility, he was elected governor (12 April 1870). When President SARMIENTO refused to recognize the election and ordered the intervention of the province, the legislature authorized López Jordán to defend provincial autonomy. Sarmiento then besieged the province. Warships patrolled the Uruguay and Paraná rivers, and federal troops, eventually armed with imported Remington rifles, advanced into the province from Gualeguaychú and Corrientes.

López Jordán was supported by the people, many young intellectuals, and the partisans of Adolfo ALSINA. His secretary at the time was José HERNÁNDEZ, author of the epic poem *Martín Fierro*. Defeated at Naembé (26 January 1871), he fled to Brazil. Following an unsuccessful invasion in 1873, he returned to Brazil. His secretary now was Francisco F. Fernández. In 1876, in his last attempt at revolution, which received weak support, López Jordán was captured in Corrientes, but he was able to escape to Montevideo. In 1888, President

JUÁREZ CELMAN granted him a pardon. He returned to Buenos Aires, where he was assassinated. Some view him as the last defender of provincial autonomy.

— JOSEPH T. CRISCENTI

LÓPEZ MATEOS, ADOLFO

Adolfo López Mateos (*b.* 26 May 1910; *d.* 22 September 1969), president of Mexico (1958–1964). The accession of López Mateos to the presidency in 1958 represented the control of a postrevolutionary generation of politicians who, for the most part, were born in the first two decades of the twentieth century. López Mateos also represented politicians who had opposed the Mexican establishment in the 1929 presidential campaign, in which he and a prominent group of students joined forces with José VASCONCELOS in a bitter and unsuccessful campaign. During the transitional period of his presidency, from 1958 to 1959, López Mateos faced a most difficult labor strike, that of the railroad workers' union, led by Valentín Campa. This strike revealed the union leadership's failure to represent the rank and file and demonstrated the willingness of the new, untried president, who had achieved the office largely on the basis of his skill as labor secretary in avoiding such confrontations, to apply force when necessary. As a result of his use of army intervention, government-dominated union leadership strengthened its hold over this and other unions. In 1960 López Mateos briefly risked his early political successes by refusing to join the United States and most of the rest of Latin America in breaking relations with Castro's Cuba. In fact, he only succeeded in reinforcing Mexico's independent course in foreign affairs—a strategy followed by most of his successors.

López Mateos refused to join the United States and most of the rest of Latin America in breaking relations with Castro's Cuba.

On the economic front, López Mateos inherited a devalued peso, but in spite of pressures to devalue once again, he pursued a moderate economic philosophy, promoting the stabilization of the peso and the gradual, steady expansion of the economy. He appointed as treasury secretary Antonio ORTIZ MENA, who became the financial architect of an unprecedented twelve years of growth and continued at the helm of the treasury in the next administration. The López Mateos administration's repressive control of the urban working classes

extended to the countryside, as exemplified by the notorious execution of peasant leader Rubén Jaramillo while in the hands of government troops. The forced sacrifices of the Mexican working class were what made possible the economic growth of the 1958–1964 period. This expansion in turn produced a growing middle class and the beginnings of an important industrial infrastructure. There is probably no president in recent times who inherited a better economic and political situation than López Mateos's successor, Gustavo DÍAZ ORDAZ.

López Mateos was born in Atizapán de Zaragoza, México. His father, a dentist, died when he was quite young, leaving his mother to support five children. He attended the Colegio Francés in Mexico City on a scholarship, and completed his secondary and preparatory studies in Toluca, México. A student activist at a young age, he joined the Anti-reelections movement in 1929, working as a librarian to support himself. He attended law school at the National University (1929–1934). Disenchanted with Vasconcelos's failure to win the presidency, he attached himself to the president of the ruling National Revolutionary party (1931–1933). In 1934, he began working for the government printing office, becoming a labor representative of the National Workers Development Bank in 1938 and later serving in the secretariat of public education. President Miguel ALEMÁN VALDÉS, whom López Mateos represented on numerous assignments abroad, selected him as one of the PRI's candidates for senator from his home state in 1946. In 1951, while still a senator, he became secretary general of the party, organizing the campaign committee for Adolfo RUIZ CORTINES's presidential bid (1951–1952). Ruiz Cortines rewarded him for his efforts by appointing him secretary of labor, a position he served in successfully until his own candidacy for the presidency in 1957. He became the only person in the history of the party to win the presidential office from the labor post. After he left the presidency in 1964, president Díaz Ordaz asked him to organize the 1968 Olympic Games in Mexico City. Severe illness prevented him from fulfilling this assignment, and he died after a stroke.

— RODERIC AI CAMP

LÓPEZ MICHELSEN, ALFONSO

Alfonso López Michelsen (*b.* 30 June 1913), president of Colombia (1974–1978). The son of Alfonso LÓPEZ PUMAREJO (president 1934–1938 and 1942–1945), López Michelsen was educated in Bogotá, the United States, and Europe, and received his law degree in 1936. In 1958 he organized the leftist Liberal Revolutionary

Movement (MRL) in opposition to the bipartisan National Front. A decade later López rejoined the official Liberal fold, becoming governor of Cesar Department in 1967, and later foreign minister. In 1974 he won the first post-Front presidential election; his program included a series of fiscal reforms and an opening to the nonviolent left. Growing popular discontent fueled by rising inflation turned violent in the general strike of September 1977. The resurgence of guerrilla activity led López, once a critic of emergency powers, to impose a state of siege in June 1975. Running again in 1982 López was defeated by the Conservative Belisario BETANCUR CUARTAS. López's writings include *Cuestiones colombianas* (1955) and the novel *Los elegidos* (1953).

RICHARD J. STOLLER

LÓPEZ PORTILLO, JOSÉ

José López Portillo (*b.* 16 June 1920), president of Mexico (1976–1982). López Portillo took office at a time when Mexico first began undergoing a series of political and economic crises, beginning a long cycle of problems extending to the 1990s. When his predecessor, Luis ECHEVERRÍA, left office, he also left a legacy of devaluation, an unstable peso and inflation (for the first time in recent history), the distrust of the private sector, and a populist political heritage. Those disenchanted with the Echeverría administration were hopeful when López Portillo was inaugurated. The new president, with some intellectual credentials, and without a long career in the federal government, seemed to offer something new to expectant Mexicans. To mend fences with the alienated business leadership, the president made it clear that he would need its assistance to reverse the economic deficits created by his predecessor and that the government wanted to reestablish a cooperative relationship with the business community. With the participation of many of Mexico's leading capitalists, he succeeded in creating the Alliance for Production. Initially, this association enjoyed considerable success, and until the last year of his administration, the economy appeared to be growing steadily. But by 1982, after another devaluation, and the near bankruptcy of Mexico's leading industrial enterprise, Grupo Industrial AIFA, confidence in the government declined precipitously and capital flight rose to new highs. Mexico's foreign debt reached an estimated $83 billion. In desperation, the president took the extraordinary measure in his 1 September 1982 State of the Union address of nationalizing the domestically owned banking industry, blaming the bankers and, indirectly, the private sector for Mexico's economic woes. The president's decision to nationalize the banks not only failed to restore public confidence in the econ-

omy but also raised doubts about his ability to govern. His political decisions brought Mexico to the point of its lowest political legitimacy in modern times, leaving his successor, Miguel de la MADRID, with nearly insurmountable political and economic problems.

Politically, López Portillo, under the direction of Jesús Reyes Heroles, briefly flirted with serious party and electoral reforms, but failed in his attempts. The president, perhaps fearful of internal instability as well as problems caused by the presence of Central American refugees in Mexico, increased the size and budget of the Mexican military, beginning a pattern of increasing modernization. On the intellectual front, he further alienated support when, in the last year of his administration, he censored his most vociferous critic, the leftist weekly *Proceso,* publicly announcing in April that he would require all government agencies to withdraw advertising from the magazine. His actions produced a pall over the media, underlining their dependency on government goodwill. The level of popular dissatisfaction with his political and economic legacy was reflected in the vote tallies for Miguel de la Madrid in the 1982 elections, in which he obtained 71 percent, leaving López Portillo with the lowest figure up to that date for a government party candidate.

López Portillo is the son of engineer José López Portillo y Weber, a military officer, and Margarita Weber y Narváez, and the grandson of a prominent political figure in the administration of Victoriano Huerta (1913–1914). He was born in Mexico City, where he completed all of his schooling. He and his predecessor, Luis ECHEVERRÍA, were high school classmates. After graduating from the National University in 1946, he became a professor of general theory of the state there and founded the course in political science and government policy in Mexico. He obtained a doctorate in law from the University of Santiago, in Chile. During these years he also practiced law.

López Portillo did not hold his first public office until 1960, when he became director general of the federal board of material and moral improvement of the secretariat of national properties. In 1965, he served as director of legal advisers to the secretariat of the presidency, and three years later, became the assistant secretary of the presidency. In 1970, in the administration of Luis Echeverría, he became assistant secretary of national properties. During a mid-term cabinet shuffle, the president appointed him secretary of the treasury 29 May 1973, and he served in this capacity until his 22 September 1975 nomination as the official party presidential candidate. With at least half a dozen potential candidates, López Portillo was considered a dark horse. Since leaving the presidency he has lived abroad, largely because of his unpopularity in Mexico.

— RODERIC AI CAMP

LÓPEZ PUMAREJO, ALFONSO

Alfonso López Pumarejo (*b.* 31 January 1886; *d.* ca. 20 November 1959), president of Colombia (1934–1938, 1942–1945). One of the most influential presidents in the history of Colombia, López's impact can be measured by the fact that almost all legislation that "modernized" Colombia was passed during his first term in office.

Born in Honda (Tolima), López studied at the College of San Luis Gonzaga and then at the Liceo Mercantil (Mercantile Lyceum) in Bogotá, specializing in business. Afterward, he took courses at Bright College in England and worked in New York before returning to Colombia.

López began pushing a "New Deal" type of economic, social, labor, and educational legislation to which Colombia's patriarchal society was unaccustomed.

The 1929 world depression exposed the weakness of the Conservative Party—in power since 1886—which had no program to cope with economic collapse and social unrest. López became president in 1934 and, accompanied by an energetic group of young Liberal reformers, began pushing a "New Deal" type of economic, social, labor, and educational legislation to which the patriarchal society was unaccustomed. The most controversial of López's reforms, the Land Law 200 of 1936, has been misnamed the Agrarian Reform Law. In essence, what this law tried to accomplish was the legalization of titles to land and the affirmation of the "social function" of property, particularly landed property.

Reelected for a second term (1942–1946), López was forced to resign in 1945 because of the opposition of both the Conservatives and a sizable fraction of his own party, which together effectively blocked most of his initiatives.

— JOSÉ ESCORCIA

LÓPEZ REGA, JOSÉ

José López Rega (*b.* 17 October 1916; *d.* 9 June 1989), retired police corporal, onetime singer, spiritist, and dis-

ciple of the occult. López Rega rose from humble beginnings in Buenos Aires to become Isabel Perón's private secretary in the 1960s in Madrid and eventually to be the most powerful, and sinister, figure in Argentina during the 1973–1976 Peronist governments. He personally organized and, out of the Social Welfare Ministry, oversaw the activities of the infamous right-wing death squad, the so-called Triple A (Alianza Anticomunista Argentina), which committed political assassination and created a climate of terror in the country. After Perón's death in July 1974, he emerged as the power behind the throne and convinced Isabel to abandon the "Pacto Social" and to adopt a hard line toward organized labor. Protests by the latter and demands for his removal led to his resignation in July 1975.

— JAMES P. BRENNAN

LÓPEZ TRUJILLO, ALFONSO

Alfonso López Trujillo (*b.* 8 November 1935), Colombian churchman who as president of the Council of Latin American Bishops (CELAM) led a conservative movement against Liberation Theology and other progressive tendencies in the Latin American Catholic church. Born in Villahermosa, department of Tolima, he entered the seminary in Bogotá and was ordained a priest in 1960. He received a doctorate in philosophy at the University of Saint Thomas Aquinas, Colombia. In 1971 he was appointed auxiliary bishop of Bogotá. He became archbishop of Medellín in 1978 and was raised to the rank of cardinal in 1983. From 1987 to 1990 he was president of the Colombian episcopal conference. He was elected secretary-general of CELAM in 1972 and served as its president from 1979 to 1983. As secretary of CELAM he was in charge of the third meeting of the Latin American bishops, held in Puebla, Mexico, in 1979. In 1990 he was named president of the Pontifical Commission on the Family, in Rome.

— JEFFREY KLAIBER

LÓPEZ VALLECILLOS, ITALO

Italo López Vallecillos (*b.* 15 November 1932; *d.* 9 February 1986), Salvadoran journalist, historian, playwright, poet. As leader of the Generación Comprometida (Committed Generation) that emerged about 1950, López called for revision of Salvadoran literary values. His early poetry, most notably *Imágenes sobre el otoño* (1962), expressed the Committed Generation's sensitivity to the need for social change and relevance in literature. López raised Salvadoran historiography to a higher level of professionalism with his *Biografía de un hombre triste* (1954); *El periodismo en El Salvador*

(1964), articles on the independence of El Salvador; *Gerardo Barrios y su tiempo* (1967); and many articles on twentieth-century El Salvador. As director of the press of the Universidad Centroamericana and as a frequent contributor to *ECA—Estudios Centro Americanos,* he was an important intellectual leader of the country in the difficult period after 1972. The versatile López also wrote plays, notably *Las manos vencidas* (1964), *Burudi Sur* (1969), and *Celda noventa y seis* (1975).

– RALPH LEE WOODWARD, JR.

LÓPEZ VELARDE, RAMÓN

Ramón López Velarde (*b.* 15 June 1888; *d.* 19 June 1921), Mexican poet. López Velarde was born in Jerez, Zacatecas, and died in Mexico City. He was educated in the Seminarios Consiliares of Zacatecas and Aguascalientes and the Instituto Científico y Literario de Aguascalientes and received a degree from the Law School in San Luis Potosí. A lawyer, literary historian, and militant in the National Catholic Party, he occupied posts in revolutionary governments. As a poet, he abandoned Latin American modernism and in some respects moved toward the avant garde. *La sangre devota* (1916) expresses the conflict of provincial people, forced from their towns by the Revolution of 1910–1917, and the drama of a young Catholic who confronts his sexuality and a world that has rejected traditional beliefs. The great poetry of López Velarde springs from his relationships with two women with whom he never became intimate: Fuensanta (Josefa de los Rios), who represents childhood and the idyllic, and Margarita Quijano, symbol of the city and a woman of high culture who introduced him to French poetry. *Zozobra* (1919) carries rhyme and free verse beyond the point at which Leopoldo LUGONES had left them and speaks of death and passion in a way that is both diaphanous and mysterious. His celebrated poem "La sauve patria," written in 1921 during the period of nationalist renewal associated with José VASCONCELOS, was included posthumously in *El son del corazón* (1932). His prose poems and chronicles are collected in *El minutero* (1923), *El don de febrero* (1952), and *Prosa política* (1953). The best critical edition of his *Obras* is that of José Luis Martínez (2d ed., 1990). Several of his poems appear in *Mexican Poetry* (1985), translated by Samuel Beckett. López Velarde died in Mexico City.

– J. E. PACHECO

LÓPEZ Y FUENTES, GREGORIO

Gregorio López y Fuentes (*b.* 1892; *d.* 1966), Mexican novelist and journalist. As a young man, López fought in the Mexican Revolution. In the post-Revolution period, he began a distinguished career as a journalist at *El Universal,* becoming general editor of the newspaper in 1948 and serving in that capacity until the 1960s. Considered one of the major exponents of the "novel of the Revolution," López addressed in his works the principal social issues of his time. His novels include *Acomodaticio; Arrieros; Campamento; Cuentos campesinos de México; El Indio; Entresuelo, Huasteca; Los peregrinos inmoviles; ¡Mi general!; En Milpa, potrero y monte;* and *Tierra.* He also wrote a series of short stories for children entitled *Cartas de niños* and *El campo y la ciudad.* His fiction is distinguished by the anonymous nature of the characters; representation of types takes precedence over the individual.

– DAVID MACIEL

LORENZANA Y BUITRÓN, FRANCISCO ANTONIO DE

Francisco Antonio de Lorenzana y Buitrón (*b.* 22 September 1722; *d.* 17 April 1804), Spanish intellectual, archbishop of Mexico (1766–1772), and cardinal-archbishop of Toledo, Spain (1772–1804). Born in León, Spain, Lorenzana studied under the Jesuits in that city. He served as bishop of Plasencia (1765–1766), then as archbishop of Mexico, where he founded the Home for Abandoned Children in 1767. Among his accomplishments was the Fourth Mexican Provincial Council, held in 1771. Known as a promoter of culture and charity, Lorenzana was elected a cardinal in 1789 and was named envoy extraordinary to the Holy See by CHARLES IV of Spain in 1797. He organized the conclave at Venice that in 1800 elected the successor to Pope Pius VI. He then accompanied the new pope, Pius VII, to Rome, where he resigned his archbishopric. Lorenzana died in Rome.

Lorenzana's writings include *Concilios provinciales primero, y segundo* (1769); *Cartas pastorales y edictos* (1770); *Concilium mexicanum provinciale III* (1770); *Historia de Nueva España escrita por su esclarecido conquistador Hernán Cortés* (1770); *Missa gothica seu mozarabica* (1770); and *SS. PP. Toletanorum,* 3 vols. (1782–1783).

– W. MICHAEL MATHES

LORENZO TROYA, VICTORIANO

Victoriano Lorenzo Troya (*b.* 1864; *d.* 15 May 1903), native leader in the Panamanian province of Coclé during the War of the Thousand Days (1900–1903). In 1891, Lorenzo was accused of murder and the following year was sentenced to nine years in prison. He remained in jail until 1898. When the war broke out, he joined the liberal side and fought with Belisario PORRAS in Panama (then a department of Colombia) hoping that a liberal victory would end the abuses against the Indians. Lorenzo and his Indian followers made a formidable fighting force, practically unbeatable in the mountains. Their exploits became widely known during the war. After the failure of the liberals to take Panama City with their defeat at the Calidonia bridge (24 July 1900), Lorenza went back to Coclé, where he organized a guerilla group and rejoined Porras. In 1902 he was betrayed by the liberal general Benjamín HERRERA, who handed him over to the government. Despite the fact that he should have been protected under the terms of the peace of 21 November 1902, which ended the civil war between liberals and conservatives, the government executed him by a firing squad.

He execution was considered by many a great miscarriage of justice and there are many theories as to why he was executed. First, General Herrera, a Colombian liberal always looked with disdain to the Panamanian liberal leaders and wanted to impose his own authority on them. The fact that Lorenzo was only loyal to Porras—who at the time of his execution was in El Salvador—may have contributed to his arrest by Herrera. Second, the conservative government feared him a great deal and he was seen by them as an obstacle to a permanent peace. During the war, the conservatives had sent an expeditionary force to Coclé to capture him, but failed. Many Panamanian historians speculate that during the peace negotiations between liberals and conservatives, a secret agreement was reached by which the liberals would hand Lorenzo to the conservatives. In 1966, the Panamanian National Assembly, as a tribute to this popular leader, invalidated the proceedings in Lorenzo's trial, indicating that it was a violation of the peace treaty.

– JUAN MANUEL PÉREZ

LOSADA, DIEGO DE

Diego de Losada (*b.* 1511; *d.* 1569), Spanish conquistador and founder of Caracas, Venezuela. Losada traveled to America as part of the conquistador armies. He passed through Puerto Rico and later, in 1533, joined Antonio Sendeño's expedition on the Meta River. When Sendeño was assassinated, Losada moved on to the city of Coro. From there he was sent eastward with Juan de Villegas in 1543 to search for provisions and men.

Losada later traveled to Santo Domingo and returned to Venezuela in 1546 in the company of Juan PÉREZ DE TOLOSA, governor and captain-general of the province.

He took part in the founding of Nueva Segovia de Barquisimeto, received various Indian *encomiendas,* and performed diverse duties within the colonial administration.

In 1565 Losada was assigned the mission of subduing the Caraca Indians, a task at which others had failed. After heavy fighting, he occupied the valley of El Guaire, where he founded the city of Santiago de León de Caracas on 25 July 1567. Losada attempted to win the post of governor and captain-general of the province of Venezuela. To this end he traveled to Santo Domingo to send his petition to the king, but his attempt was unsuccessful.

– INÉS QUINTERO

LOTT, HENRIQUE BATISTA DUFFLES TEIXEIRA

Henrique Batista Duffles Teixeira Lott (*b.* 16 November 1894; *d.* 19 May 1984), Brazilian minister of war (1954–1960), politician, and presidential candidate (1959). A native of Sítio, in Minas Gerais, Lott attended the military school of Realengo in Rio de Janeiro. Upon graduation he enlisted in the army in 1911 and was commissioned five years later.

A dedicated professional, Lott remained loyal to the government during the military upheavals of the 1920s and on through the Revolution of 1930, the São Paulo constitutional revolt of 1932, the Communist uprising of 1935, and the 1938 Fascist putsch.

Lott studied abroad at the Superior War College in Paris and at the U.S. Army Command and General Staff College in Fort Leavenworth, Kansas. These courses further enhanced his well-deserved reputation as an instructor at the general staff school and other Brazilian military academies, where he became known for strong opinions and stern discipline. Posted to Italy with the Brazilian Expeditionary Force (FEB) during World War II, he was denied command, thus widening the split with the so-called Sorbonne Group of military reformers. Promoted to general at the age of fifty, he commanded the Second Military Region in São Paulo.

The suicide of President Getúlio VARGAS in 1954 brought Lott into politics with his appointment by acting president João CAFÉ FILHO, who named him minister of war because of his reputation for being apolitical. Café Filho's resignation in November 1955, ostensibly for health reasons, brought in Carlos Luz, president of the chamber of deputies, as chief executive. Allied with the Sorbonne Group, he soon resigned when Lott pronounced in favor of Nereu Ramos, the senate's president.

This institutional crisis coincided with the disputed presidential election of Brazilian Labor Party candidate Juscelino KUBITSCHEK. Lott favored Kubitschek's inauguration as the legitimate candidate, thus easing unrest and ensuring his own reappointment as war minister. He held this post until February 1960, although he retired, with the rank of marshal, in 1959 to run for president on the Labor Party ticket. Defeated by reformist Jânio QUADROS, Lott nevertheless remained a powerful figure, opposing both the military interventions against Vice President João GOULART in 1961 and his ousting as acting president in April 1964. Lott's 1965 attempt to present himself as a candidate for the governorship of the state of Guanabara was vetoed by the revolutionary military regime.

— LEWIS A. TAMBS

L'OUVERTURE, TOUSSAINT

Toussaint L'Ouverture (*b.* ca. 20 May 1743; *d.* 7 April 1803), leader of the slave rebellion in Saint-Domingue (Haiti) (1794–1802). As the sounds of martial music intermingled with the gentle tropical breezes that floated across the Palace d'Armes, the central square of Le Cap François, a small, ornately clad black man led a military procession of 2,000 smartly dressed troops into the city under an arch of triumph. He was Toussaint L'Ouverture, and this day, 22 November 1800, marked his greatest moment. He had defeated both his foreign and domestic enemies. More important, he had governed Saint-Domingue well, rebuilt its economy, and sought a program of racial harmony. The swell of pride must have been his when, at the end of his triumphant military procession, a beautiful woman from one of the colony's most prestigious white families greeted him. The mixed crowd of whites, mulattoes, and blacks burst forth with the "Marseillaise." In just over two years from this moment, this victorious "Black Spartacus" would be coughing and dying of pneumonia in a French prison.

François Dominique Toussaint was the first of his parents' eight children. His grandfather had been an Arada chief. Pierre Baptiste Simon may have been his father or his godfather. For the next forty-seven years Toussaint lived on the Bréda plantation and went through two name changes—Toussaint Bréda and finally Toussaint L'Ouverture. The significance of this last name change is unclear but may refer to his ability to move quickly to openings on the battlefield.

Toussaint lived about as well as any slave ever did in Saint-Domingue. He had a lifelong friendship with one of the plantation managers (Bayou de Libertad), had read books from the big house, married Suzanne Simon-Baptiste when he was forty, and settled down to the life of a coachman. He knew smatterings of ancient history, Stoic philosophy, and a few Latin phrases taught to him by his father.

The slave rebellion in Saint-Domingue swept up the Black Spartacus and set him ablaze with revolutionary fervor.

Just what Toussaint's role was in the great slave rebellion that exploded in Saint-Domingue on 22 August 1791 is unclear, despite biographer Ralph Korngold's contention that he actively participated in igniting the conflict. It is clear, however, that once under way, the conflagration, as Saint-Domingue sugar planters liked to call it, swept up the Black Spartacus and set him ablaze with revolutionary fervor. He saw to the safety of his old friend Bayou de Libertad and joined the armies of generals Jean-François and Georges Biassou already fighting for the Spanish. Third in command, Toussaint had the rank of "Doctor of the King's Armies" because of his knowledge of medicinal herbs.

After three years of service with Biassou and François, Toussaint defected to France and on 25 June 1794 joined forces with the embattled General Etienne Laveaux. The abolition of slavery by the French National Convention undoubtedly prompted his action, as did his own greed for power. Both C. L. R. James and Thomas O. Ott have recognized the complexity of these motives in their histories of the Haitian Revolution. Dedication to his people's freedom, though, was Toussaint's main consideration.

Over the next eight years, Toussaint enjoyed a mercurial rise from lieutenant governor to dictator of Saint-Domingue. And over that period he gave special emphasis to the domestic problems of a devastated land. He attempted to maintain the large plantations, invited former planters to return as "managers," and parceled out vast amounts of land to favorite generals to hold their loyalty. At one time, Jean Jacques DESSALINES owned thirty plantations. On these estates, Toussaint and his generals enforced *fermage* (a system of forced labor not unlike sharecropping). The laborer could not leave his plantation assignment without permission and was subject to severe corporal punishment for lazy habits. By 1800, Saint-Domingue had regained two-thirds of its economic prosperity of 1791. Most historians have joined Ralph Korngold to acclaim this a triumph, but biographer Pierre Pluchon labeled the Black Spartacus's program a failure.

Toussaint also gave attention to his people's religious training. He suppressed voodoo, made Catholicism the religion of state, and appointed Father Mainville the Catholic bishop for Saint-Domingue. Never reticent about interfering in their personal lives, he demanded the participation of "colonials" in compulsory religious parades and made divorce illegal. Though he kept many mistresses, Toussaint demanded monogamy and marital fidelity in his subjects.

Failure to incorporate the mulattoes into his revolutionary state constituted Toussaint's greatest domestic failure. Emotionally, he hated them, and sometimes he let this attitude break through his rational attempts to include them in his state. Finally he squared off against the mulattoes, led by André RIGAUD, in the War of the Knives (1799–1800). When he won, Toussaint encouraged Dessalines to bathe himself in their blood in South Province.

On the foreign front, Toussaint scored notable victories by defeating the British invasion (1793–1798) and by maintaining good relations with the United States. But France proved too delicate an operation for him. While swearing loyalty to the First Republic, Toussaint ever so gently removed the agents of France and sent them home. But he committed a major blunder when he proclaimed the Constitution of 1801 and himself governor-general for life with the right to appoint his successor. He had, moreover, proclaimed the constitution without the First Consul's approval. Napoleon was not fooled; he knew that Toussaint intended to make Saint-Domingue independent.

Historian Shelby McCloy believed Toussaint's highhanded acts alone prompted Napoleon to send the expedition of General Charles LECLERC to Saint-Domingue. But Napoleon's imperial ambitions for a Western empire and planter influence were probably more persuasive factors in his decision, according to historians J. Christopher Herold and Thomas O. Ott.

After holding his own against Leclerc for a few months, Toussaint suddenly surrendered to France on 6 May 1802. Korngold argued that Toussaint capitulated as a trick. Once yellow fever did its deadly work, Toussaint would come out of retirement and lead Saint-Domingue to independence. Ott, however, saw the surrender as the best deal Toussaint could make to ensure the freedom of his people. A month later, 7 June, Leclerc arrested the Black Spartacus and deported him to France to die. Leclerc believed that Toussaint was his main obstacle to the restoration of slavery in Saint-Domingue. Dessalines and the Haitians proved him wrong.

— THOMAS O. OTT

LOZADA, MANUEL

Manuel Lozada (*b.* 1828; *d.* 19 July 1873), Mexican cacique and rebel leader. Considered by some to be a precursor of later agrarian reformers, Lozada was a mestizo bandit whose extreme violence and invincibility earned him the attribute "El Tigre de Alica." Although still a controversial figure, he led one of the most serious uprisings of the nineteenth century.

Cacique of the Cora and Huichol Indians of western Jalisco, Lozada worked as a peon on the Hacienda de Mojarras. After a dispute with the administrator, he fled to the sierra. In his absence, the administrator was said to have maltreated Lozada's mother, misconduct for which Lozada returned to kill him. A self-designated general, he assumed leadership of the ongoing Indian resistance to European penetration of the Nayarit zone.

Armed conflict broke out in 1847 and reached a climax after the disamortization law of 1856. In his defense of community lands against privatization and hacienda penetration, he received the private support of the San Blas-based Barron and Forbes Company, which was heavily involved in contraband. His tacit support of the Conservative cause during La Reforma (the Civil War of the Reform, 1858–1861), together with his control of western Jalisco, threatened the Liberal position in Jalisco and Sinaloa. In March 1864, however, Lozada rallied to the empire, received a cash subsidy, and was decorated with the Legion of Honor. He abandoned the imperial cause in December 1866 and was thereafter virtually protected from his enemies by JUÁREZ.

Lozada's circular of 12 April 1869 had a distinctly agrarian character and provided for direct action by villages for the recovery of land. His power was broken at Mojonera, near Guadalajara, by General Ramón CORONA, after an ill-considered invasion of central Jalisco. Betrayed, he was executed on 19 July 1873.

— BRIAN HAMNETT

LOZANO, PEDRO

Pedro Lozano (*b.* 16 September 1697; *d.* 1752), JESUIT historian. Lozano was born in Madrid, and a year after entering the Society of Jesus (at fourteen years of age), he was sent to the Province of Paraguay. It was fairly common at the time to send young Jesuits to America for their novitiate training. In theory, they adapted more readily to the customs of the place and learned the local languages more easily. Lozano was assigned for most of his life to the College of Córdoba, where he taught philosophy and theology. He traveled extensively throughout the province, visiting missions and consulting Jesuit records in Santa Fe, Esteco, and Buenos Aires.

In 1730 Lozano began writing the first of the histories for which he became known, *Descripción corográfica del Gran Chaco Gualamba* (1733). He also wrote *Historia de la Compañía de Jesús en la Provincia del Paraguay* (2 vols., 1754–1755), and five volumes of the *Historia civil del Río de la Plata,* as well as two volumes titled *Historia de las revoluciones de la Provincia del Paraguay (1721–1735).* His most famous history, now a classic, is *Historia de la conquista de la Provincia del Paraguay, Río de la Plata y Tucumán* (1905). In 1750 he was given the task of preparing a report on why the Treaty of Limits (1750) would be harmful to the Indians. Lozano died in Humahuaca.

— NICHOLAS P. CUSHNER

LOZANO DÍAZ, JULIO

Julio Lozano Díaz, president of Honduras (November 1954–October 1956). Vice president under Juan Manuel GÁLVEZ, Lozano Díaz seized the presidency at a time of political ferment and trade-union agitation in Honduras. In 1954 a strike against the United Fruit and Standard Fruit and Steamship companies coincided with a three-way contest for the presidency between the Liberal Party candidate Ramón VILLEDA MORALES, Abraham Williams of the Movimiento Nacional Reformista, and Tiburcio CARÍAS ANDINO of the Partido Nacional. Although Villeda Morales had garnered nearly 50 percent of the vote, the Carías-controlled Congress refused to sanction a Liberal presidency and Lozano Díaz settled the issue by declaring himself interim president in November 1954. He successfully warded off an attempted coup on 1 August 1956 and orchestrated the victory of his party, the Partido Union Nacional, in the 7 October congressional election. The three opposition parties declared the election fraudulent, and on 21 October members of the Honduran military, led by General Roque J. Rodríguez, brought down the Lozano Díaz dictatorship and established a military junta.

— MICHAEL A. POLUSHIN

LOZZA, RAÚL

Raúl Lozza (*b.* 27 October 1911), Argentine painter, craftsman, and illustrator. Lozza was born in Alberti, Buenos Aires Province, and was self-taught. He was a founding member of the Asociación de Arte Concreto-Invención, a nonfigurative group, as well as the creator of *perceptismo,* a theory of color and open structure in painting that he called "cualimetría de la forma plana." Lozza's two- and three-dimensional works reveal an almost scientific concern for the intelligent use of technology, and the tonal values in his paintings are inten-

sified or reduced with mathematical precision. Lozza has had numerous exhibitions, including a retrospective in 1985 at the Fundación San Telmo in Buenos Aires. He is the recipient of several awards, including the Palanza Prize (1991) and the Konex Award (1992).

— AMALIA CORTINA ARAVENA

LUCAS GARCÍA, FERNANDO ROMEO

Fernando Romeo Lucas García (*b.* 24 July 1924), president of Guatemala (1978–1982). Brigadier General Lucas García succeeded Kjell LAUGERUD as president in June 1978. It is widely believed that the 1978 election was fraudulent, and that Enrique PERALTA AZURDIA was the real winner.

Romeo Lucas García presided over an administration that was generally perceived to be riddled with corruption, cronyism, and violence. During Lucas's tenure the Guerrilla Army of the Poor (EGP) gained significant support and territory from the mainly indigenous inhabitants of the western highlands. Political violence from the Far Right increased, particularly in urban areas, where students, union members, and professionals were regularly "disappeared" by death squads. During this period, the U.S. government under Jimmy Carter refused military aid to Guatemala because of human rights violations.

By 1980, Guatemala's once-vital economy had begun to weaken, due to world recession and a decline in tourism. Dissatisfaction with Lucas García within the military became acute, and on 23 March 1982 he was overthrown in a coup. Lucas was succeeded by a three-man junta consisting of General Efrain RÍOS MONTT, General Horacio Maldonado Schad, and Colonel Francisco Gordillo.

— VIRGINIA GARRARD-BURNETT

LUGONES, LEOPOLDO

Leopoldo Lugones (*b.* 13 June 1874; *d.* 18 February 1938), Argentine poet and social historian.

Lugones occupies a central position in the history of Hispanic-American modernism for his perfection of form and rich, original imagery in works such as *Los crepúsculos del jardín* (Garden Twilights, 1905). Lugones used his prodigious intellect and formidable learning to make his ideas known in literature, education, politics, government, and public affairs. He began his career as a journalist at the age of sixteen, writing articles for a newspaper in his native Córdoba. He came to Buenos Aires in 1896 and there published his first book of poems, *Las montañas de oro* (The Golden Mountains, 1897). In 1897, he cofounded *La Montaña* as a forum for his socialist—and at times anarchist—ideas. In

1899, he became director of the General Archives of the postal services and in 1904 general inspector of the secondary schools.

Lugones attacked democracy and was convinced that the use of force was necessary to secure social order and progress.

Lugones strongly opposed the ultraliberal revolutionary activities of 1904 and in 1907 launched a virulent attack on President Figueroa Alcorta from the columns of *El Diario*. When the Argentine Congress passed an electoral reform bill in 1912, Lugones protested strenuously. His views, which were frequently self-contradictory, suffered radical changes throughout his life. After World War I, he extolled the Versailles Treaty and was critical of German military leadership. Yet he also attacked democracy and was convinced that the use of force was necessary to secure social order and progress. Lugones supported the Argentine university reform laws enacted in 1918, but he opposed universal suffrage and populist solutions to national problems. With the reelection of Hipólito YRIGOYEN as president in 1928, Lugones's militarism became more extreme, and he participated actively in the September 1930 revolution that overthrew that regime. In his later years he began using a religious approach in his writing. He took his own life on 18 February 1938.

Best known as a poet and prose writer, Lugones is also the author of numerous books revealing his ardent nationalism, his profound insights into Argentine history, and his identification with the people and traditions of Argentina's provincial regions. Such works as *El imperio jesuítico* (1904), *Historia de Sarmiento* (1911), and *El estado equitativo* (1932) have had a strong impact on the way Argentines view themselves and have contributed to Lugones's stature as one of the foremost intellectual figures of his time.

— MYRON I. LICHTBLAU

LUÍS PEREIRA DE SOUSA, WASHINGTON

Washington Luís Pereira de Sousa (*b.* 26 October 1870; *d.* 4 August 1957), president of Brazil (1926–1930). Although known as the consummate defender of the political and economic interests of the state of São Paulo, Luís was born and schooled in the state of Rio de Janeiro. After moving to São Paulo in 1888, Luís steadily rose within São Paulo's political circles, serving as state deputy (1904–1906, 1912–1913), state secretary of justice (1906–1914), mayor of the city of São Paulo (1914–1919), governor of the state of São Paulo (1920–1924), and senator (1924–1926). In 1926 Luís was elected president of Brazil. He remained president until October 1930, when he was forced from office and into exile during the one-month civil war later known as the Revolution of 1930.

Luís was one of the most prominent members of the Partido Republicano Paulista (PRP), and his political career was representative of the oligarchic-led politics of Brazil's First Republic (1889–1930). He was a fiscal conservative who promoted state autonomy (particularly for the state of São Paulo) and economic policies favorable to coffee cultivation, nascent industrialization, and infrastructural improvements (especially in rail and roads). An advocate of stricter policing and opponent of organized labor, Luís coined the republican elite's dictum that the social question was a police question. However, his close association with the oligarchic interests of the First Republic also proved to be his downfall, as Luís failed to convince the reformist interests from Minas Gerais and Rio Grande do Sul supporting Getúlio VARGAS's 1930 presidential candidacy that Luís's hand-picked successor, *paulista* Júlio PRESTES, could best manage Brazil's extremely precarious position amidst the onset of the Great Depression. During the Revolution of 1930, Luís and President-elect Prestes were stripped of their political powers and Vargas became chief of the provisional government. Exiled, Luís lived in Europe and the United States. Upon returning to Brazil in 1947, Luís remained far from politics, concentrating his energies on his personal life and his interest in *paulista* history and culture.

— DARYLE WILLIAMS

LUISI, LUISA

Luisa Luisi (*b.* 1888; *d.* 1940), Uruguayan poet, critic, and educator; her work is grouped with the generation of Uruguayan "realist poets" between 1885 and 1935. Luisi's books of poetry include *Sentir* (1916), *Inquietud* (1921), *Poemas de la inmovilidad y canciones al sol* (1926), and *Polvo de dias* (1935). Her early poetry was conceptual and based on philosophical ideas, but an illness that left her without the use of her legs brought forth in her later poetry an anguish over her immobile state. Her tone became melancholic and reflected a spiritual restlessness and dismay that she was unable to realize her full potential. Luisi's critical prose include *A través de libros y autores* (1925).

Luisi was educated in Montevideo in both private schools and at the Normal Institute for Girls, qualifying to teach in the first, second, and third grades. She later became a school principal, taught reading and declamation in the Normal Institute for Girls, and remained active in Uruguayan education her entire life, despite retiring from teaching in 1929. Luisi, along with her two remarkable sisters, Clotilde and Paulina, broke down many barriers in Uruguayan society for female intellectual activity and for the advancement of women in other areas. Clotilde Luisi distinguished herself as the first woman lawyer in Uruguay and as professor of moral philosophy and religion at the Normal Institute for Girls. Paulina LUISI, one of the few and among the earliest Uruguayan women to become a doctor, held teaching posts and headed the gynecological clinic at the Faculty of Medicine.

– J. DAVID DRESSING

LUISI, PAULINA

Paulina Luisi (*b.* 22 September 1875; *d.* 17 July 1950), physician, educator, feminist, diplomat, social reformer. Luisi was the first Uruguayan woman to receive a medical degree. Her lifelong work on behalf of children (president of the Uruguayan delegation to the First American Congress of the Child, Buenos Aires, 1916) and women's health (Uruguayan delegate to the International Congress on Social Hygiene and Education, Paris, 1923; member of the League of Nations consultative committee on the Treaty to End Traffic in Women and Children, 1922, 1923, 1924, 1925) was paralleled by her commitment to woman suffrage and female education. She founded the Uruguayan branch of the National Women's Council in 1916 and represented Uruguay at the International Congresses of Women in Geneva and Cristiana, Norway, in 1920 and Rome in 1925. She was the first woman in the Western Hemisphere to represent her government as an officially appointed delegate to an intergovernmental conference (Fifth International Conference of American States, Santiago, 1923). Luisi also served as head of the Uruguayan delegation to the League of Nations. With her colleague, Argentine feminist and socialist Alicia MOREAU DE JUSTO, Luisi believed that female education and equal political rights were crucial to improving working conditions and health care for women and children.

– FRANCESCA MILLER

LUNA PIZARRO, FRANCISCO JAVIER DE

Francisco Javier De Luna Pizarro (*b.* 1780; *d.* 9 February 1855), Peruvian Roman Catholic priest. Born in Arequipa, in his youth he admired liberal ideas and found politics as practiced in the United States to be

worthy of emulation. After the protectorate of José de SAN MARTÍN ended in 1822, Luna Pizarro organized the liberal leadership in the national congress that formulated the constitutions of Peru from 1823 through 1834. This leadership favored free trade, administrative decentralization, a carefully restricted electorate, establishment of Roman Catholicism as the religion protected by the state, and the prohibition of all other views. Churchmen and the military retained the special privileges awarded them in the colonial era. Luna Pizarro later abandoned his support of the government's right to protect the church and appoint its priests. Regaining the favor of Rome, he then became a conservative archbishop of Lima (1845–1855).

– VINCENT PELOSO

LUNA Y ARELLANO, TRISTÁN DE

Tristán De Luna Y Arellano (*b.* ca. 1500/10; *d.* 16 September 1573), soldier and governor of La Florida (1559–1561). Born in Aragón, Luna came to New Spain with Hernán CORTÉS around 1530, returned to Spain, and came back to New Spain in 1535. In 1558 Luna, a veteran of the Coronado expedition to the American Southwest as well as of military exploits in Oaxaca, received a charter to establish a colony on the Gulf coast. Planned and outfitted in Mexico, the expedition of eleven vessels, five hundred soldiers, and a thousand colonists and servants (including Mexican natives) sailed from San Juan de Ulúa on the Gulf coast of Mexico on 11 June 1559 for the port of Ochuse (Pensacola Bay).

A hurricane sank most of the ships with their supplies before they could be offloaded. The colony quickly fell into disarray, a process hastened by Luna's illness, which at times incapacitated him. Colonists and scouting parties sent into the interior to seek food and shelter from native peoples were largely unsuccessful. In March 1561, Luna was relieved of the governorship and ordered to Spain; the colony was withdrawn.

– JERALD T. MILANICH

LUPERÓN, GREGORIO

Gregorio Luperón (*b.* 8 September 1839; *d.* 21 May 1897), president of the Dominican Republic (6 October 1879–1 September 1880). A black, born in Puerto Plata in the north, Luperón won great distinction as a general during the War of Restoration (1863–1865) and the defeat of Spain. He became a leading soldier-statesman and patriot dedicated to ending turmoil and uniting the country. For many years, he was a strong supporter of Ulises ESPAILLAT, who urged Luperón to become president in 1876. He regularly resisted assuming the office but finally agreed to serve as a provisional president in 1879. As president he reorganized the army and local administration, paid government workers their back pay of three years, and adjusted all foreign claims. In the early 1880s, he served as a diplomat in Paris, representing the democratically elected government of his successor, Father Fernando Arturo de Meriño.

— LARMAN C. WILSON

LUQUE, HERNANDO DE

Hernando de Luque (d. 1534), an early-sixteenth-century Spanish cleric who accompanied Pedro Arias de ÁVILA (Pedrarias) in 1514 on an expedition to colonize Panama. When Pedrarias took command at Darién, de Luque's friendship with the governor allowed him to establish a number of influential contacts. In Panama, de Luque joined in a business partnership with the conquistadores, Francisco PIZARRO and Diego de ALMARGO. In the early 1520s, the three men embarked on a plan to explore the regions south of Panama and to undertake the conquest of Peru. De Luque was instrumental in raising the necessary funds for the 1524 and 1526 expeditions into the Andean region. Acting as an agent for wealthy investors, including the judge Gaspar de Espinosa, who condemned BALBOA, de Luque raised two hundred pounds of gold bars. He was nicknamed "Fernando de Loco," the mad priest, for undertaking the venture. Later scholars have suggested it was de Luque who planned and organized the expeditions as well as arranged for the necessary financial backing. He did not accompany Pizarro and Almargo on the expeditions, remaining instead in Panama to manage their business affairs. De Luque died before the conquest was completed.

— HEATHER K. THIESSEN

LUSINCHI, JAIME

Jaime Lusinchi (b. 1924), Venezuelan president (1984–1989). While studying medicine at the Central University of Venezuela and the University of the East, Lusinchi became active in Venezuela's Democratic Action (Acción Democrática—AD). From 1952 to 1958 he was exiled by the military dictatorship. After his return, the young pediatrician became a member of the national executive committee of AD. He also served in the Chamber of Deputies and the Senate. From 1980 to 1983 he was the party's secretary-general. In the 1983 presidential election he defeated Rafael Caldera, the

candidate of the Social Christian COPEI (Comité de Organización Política Electoral Independiente) Party. As president, Lusinchi presided over a period of low oil prices and rising discontent; scandals also plagued his administration.

— WINFIELD J. BURGGRAAFF

LUTZ, BERTHA MARIA JULIA

Bertha Maria Julia Lutz (b. 2 August 1894; d. 16 September, 1976), the principal leader of the Brazilian woman's suffrage movement. Bertha Lutz was born in São Paulo to a Swiss-Brazilian father, Adolfo Lutz, a pioneer in the practice of tropical medicine in Brazil, and an English mother, Amy Fowler, a former volunteer nurse who cared for lepers in Hawaii. Lutz was educated first in Brazil and then in Europe, receiving her licencié

Bertha Lutz campaigning for women's suffrage, early 1930s. (Iconographia)

ès sciences from the Sorbonne in 1918. Later, in 1933, she earned a degree from the Faculty of Law in Rio de Janeiro.

Following seven years of study in Europe, Lutz returned to Brazil and helped to initiate a formal woman suffrage movement. Unlike many of her contemporaries, she felt that this was the time to organize, rather than just inform and educate, women. In 1920 she founded her own woman's rights organization. Two years later, immediately after Lutz's return from the United States, where she had served as Brazil's official delegate to the first Pan American Conference of Women, this small local group was transformed into the Brazilian Federation for Feminine Progress (Federação Brasileira pelo Progresso Feminino—FBPF), affiliated with the International Woman's Suffrage Alliance. Lutz served as its president from 1922 to 1942. The main suffrage organization in Brazil, the FBPF led the campaign for the vote, because no other suffrage association attained a similar size, geographic range, or network of personal contacts. In 1932, it achieved its major goal when a new civil code enfranchised women under the same conditions as men (illiterates of both sexes were still denied the vote).

More than other leaders of the FBPF, Lutz linked women's economic emancipation with their political and social emancipation. She repeatedly warned women that the franchise was not an end in itself, and she understood that without access to education and jobs, political rights would remain mere abstractions. In print and in public, she spoke out against the exploitation of the working class, and particularly of its lower-class women. But even though the professional women leading the FBPF tackled problems of concern to the working class, such as salaries, shorter working hours, working conditions, and maternity leaves, interclass linkages were not very strong.

Following the promulgation of the 1932 civil code that enfranchised women, Bertha Lutz served on the committee that drafted a new constitution for Brazil. The Constitution of 1934 confirmed the women's 1932 victory by specifically guaranteeing women the vote and equal political rights with men. Lutz ran twice for Congress; elected as an alternate deputy, she entered the Chamber of Deputies late in 1936 to fill the vacancy created by the death of the incumbent. During her year in Congress, she helped create the Commission on the Code for Women, which she headed. Through the commission, she pushed vigorously for enactment of a statute on women, a comprehensive law concerning women's legal status and social rights. But the establishment of the dictatorial Estado Nôvo in 1937 ended electoral politics and women's participation in them until 1945.

Although Lutz, like the FBPF, never regained a preeminent position as a voice for Brazilian women, she continued to work for woman's rights in Brazil while also pursuing her own scientific work in botany and herpetology. In 1973 she published a major work on Brazilian species of hyla. She also participated in international woman's rights activities, attending numerous women's conferences abroad, including the International Women's Year conference held in Mexico City in 1975, a year before her death at the age of eighty-two.

— JUNE E. HAHNER

LUTZENBERGER, JOSÉ ANTÔNIO

José Antônio Lutzenberger (*b.* 17 December 1928), Brazilian ecologist. Lutzenberger served as Brazil's first secretary of the environment (1990–1992), a cabinet-level post created by President Fernando Collor de MELLO in part to address growing international criticism of Brazil's Amazon policy as articulated during predecessor José SARNEY's presidency. Lutzenberger, an agronomist with a special interest in the Amazon region and a native of Rio Grande do Sul, had long been a critic of government development policies. He accepted the cabinet post only after Collor de Mello guaranteed that his administration would halt expansion of the controversial BR-364 highway across the southern Amazon, respect the rights of the indigenous peoples of the Amazon, and end all economic incentives to environmentally destructive development projects. Lutzenberger also supported debt-for-nature swaps, unlike the Sarney administration.

Lutzenberger was known for making bombastic gloom-and-doom pronouncements and was often criticized for his adherence to the scientifically unproven "Gaia" theory, which held that the Earth is a closed physiological system capable of altering the planet's climate at will. In late 1991, the Brazilian Chamber of Deputies, along with conservative politicians and the military, complained that Lutzenberger was "internationalizing" the Amazon to the point of compromising Brazilian national sovereignty and hence called for his resignation. Color de Mello replaced him in March 1992.

Lutzenberger enjoyed an international reputation, initially based on his active opposition to the use of pesticides. In 1971 he was a founder of the Association for the Protection of the Natural Environment of Rio Grande do Sul (Associação Gaúcha de Proteção Ambiente Natural—AGAPAN), the first ecological entity organized in Brazil. He was the 1988 recipient of the Swedish government's Right Livelihood Award, the environmental equivalent of the Nobel Prize.

– LAURA JARNAGIN

LUZ Y CABALLERO, JOSÉ DE LA

José de la Luz y Caballero (*b*. 11 July 1800; *d*. 22 June 1862), Cuban philosopher and educator. Luz y Cabellero was one of the three most influential Cuban thinkers of the nineteenth century, the other two being Father Félix VARELA Y MORALES and José Antonio SACO. A native of Havana, he initially studied for the priesthood but ended up a lawyer, although he never practiced law. Instead, he traveled extensively in Europe and the United States, becoming acquainted with most of the important writers of his time. He was influenced by the work of Francis Bacon, Étienne Bonnot de Condillac, and René Descartes, and came to embrace John Locke's nominalism, the denial that abstract entities or universal principles have real existence.

In Cuba, Luz y Caballero was a respected and popular teacher at the San Carlos Seminary (Cuba's most prominent institution of higher learning at the time) and later at the Colegio El Salvador, which he founded. His ideas and his teaching methods involved him in ardent polemics that provoked the hostility of the Spanish authorities, especially when he was accused of participating in the Conspiracy of la Escalera (1844), an attempted slave revolt. Luz y Caballero opposed violence, however, and held that Cuba was not prepared for self-government. His approach to the problem of slavery was cautious; he believed it should end gradually, by means of the suppression of the slave trade. Despite his timidity, however, he represented a progressive tendency in Cuban society; through his lectures and writings he helped to develop strong nationalistic feelings in a whole generation of Cubans. Luz y Caballero died in Havana.

– JOSÉ M. HERNÁNDEZ

LYNCH, BENITO

Benito Lynch (*b*. 25 July 1880; *d*. 23 December 1951), Argentine journalist and writer. Lynch came from an old, distinguished family of *estancieros* (ranchers) and spent his childhood on an *estancia* in Buenos Aires Province. In 1890 he settled in La Plata, where he later worked for the conservative newspaper *El Día*. From 1904 to 1941 he devoted himself to writing fiction. His novels *Los caranchos de la Florida* (1916; *The Vultures of La Florida*) and *El inglés de los güesos* (1924; *The English Boneman*), both later adapted for stage and film, made

him one of the most prominent Hispanic novelists. However, to preserve his privacy, Lynch shunned the trappings of success, refusing royalties and academic honors. A member of the generation presided over by Leopoldo LUGONES and Ricardo ROJAS, Lynch maintained his reclusiveness, his keen loyalty to his social class, his conservatism, and his divorce from contemporary political and literary life even when confronted with the innovative Martín Fierro group. His narratives almost exclusively concern life on the *estancias* of Buenos Aires Province around the beginning of the twentieth century, contrasting city life with the sedentary, stable life of the peasantry. An admirer of Zola, his naturalism contrasts with a sentimental vision of love and friendship, despite his basic distrust of the human race. Lynch's novels are considered models of linguistic frugality and well-adjusted plots.

– ANGELA B. DELLEPIANE

LYNCH, ELISA ALICIA

Elisa Alicia Lynch (*b*. June 1835; *d*. 27 July 1886), Irish mistress of Paraguayan dictator Francisco Solano LÓPEZ.

Born into impoverished circumstances, Lynch left Ireland at age fifteen when she married Xavier Quatrefages, a French military surgeon. Theirs was evidently a loveless marriage, and within a few years Lynch was on her own in Paris. In 1853, after having lived with several lovers, she met Solano López, son of the Paraguayan president Carlos Antonio LÓPEZ, who was then on an official tour of Europe.

President López installed Lynch in a sumptuous residence in Asunción, where she attempted to re-create in Paraguay a French-style salon.

Unable to marry López because of her then undocumented marital status, Lynch nonetheless accompanied him back to Paraguay. She was less than well received by the Paraguayan elites, who regarded her in a scandalous light. López installed her in a sumptuous residence in Asunción, however, and there she attempted to re-create in Paraguay a salon that included musicians, literary figures, and interesting foreign visitors. She introduced the piano in Paraguay, and popularized Parisian fashions. She had five children with López. Upon his accession to the presidency in 1862, Lynch became de facto first lady.

The outbreak of the War of the Triple Alliance in 1864 found Lynch at the front, together with her consort. Detractors later claimed that she was responsible for many of López's excesses, particularly the mass executions at San Fernando in 1868. Two years later, after a long and sanguinary retreat, López was killed in the northeastern region of Cerro Corá. Lynch witnessed his death, as she did that of their firstborn son, an army colonel.

At the end of the war, the Brazilian authorities deported Lynch, but after a few years she returned to Asunción to try to lay claim to lands that had been transferred to her name during the fighting. These legal efforts failed and she returned to Paris, where she died penniless in 1886. In the 1960s, the Stroessner government repatriated her remains.

— MARTA FERNÁNDEZ WHIGHAM

LYNCH, MARTA

Marta Lynch (*b.* 8 March 1925; *d.* 8 October 1985), Argentine writer. Born in Buenos Aires, Lynch was the daughter of an important political figure and the wife of a powerful corporate director. She is notable for making use of the circumstances of her socioeconomic privilege to portray a complex network of cultural oppressions in Argentina, with special reference to the victimization of middle-class women whose lives project a facade of passive comfort. *La señora Ordóñez* (1967) may be the first Argentine treatment of a woman's explicit sexual discontent, while *Al vencedor* (1965) centers on class conflict and its humiliations in Argentina during the so-called Argentine Revolution that followed the Peronist period. But Lynch's best writing focuses on the devastating social and personal price paid by Argentines for the Dirty War of the late 1970s, especially in the short stories of *Los dedos de la mano* (1976), *La penúltima versión de la Colorada Villanueva* (1978), and *Informe bajo llave* (1983). With her death, Lynch joined a line of notable Argentine women authors who have committed suicide.

— DAVID WILLIAM FOSTER

M

MACCIÓ, RÓMULO

Rómulo Macció (*b.* 24 March 1931), Argentine artist. Born in Buenos Aires, Macció was trained as a graphic designer and worked as an illustrator in advertising agencies. He took up painting in 1956, joining the New Figuration group in 1961. His early work consisted of paintings of anthropomorphic fragments, halfway between abstraction and figuration. After 1964 he began to paint distorted figures in expressionistic and surrealistic styles. He consciously sought to generate visual and thematic contradictions, such as the overlapping of planar and volumetric structures and the coexistence of two different subjects in the same painting. In 1967 he won the International Di Tella Prize. A rational and orderly composition characterized his paintings of the mid-1970s, although surreal traits remained present in melancholic portraits of lonely figures, often self-portraits (*Self-Portrait with Easel,* 1976; *At Seven O'Clock in Highbury Place,* 1976). In the late 1970s, he painted human figures as stylized silhouettes with spiritual and mystical connotations (*Amalfi,* 1980; *Adriatic,* 1979). Macció's tendency to expressionism became more evident in the 1980s (*Castel Sant' Angelo,* 1980). His most recent paintings are views from his atelier and subjects with some classical mythological overtones. He participated in the Venice Biennale in 1988 and exhibited in Paris, Milan, and Rome in 1991.

— MARTA GARSD

MACEDO, JOAQUIM MANUEL DE

Joaquim Manuel de Macedo (*b.* 24 June 1820; *d.* 11 April 1882), Brazilian novelist. Joaquim Manuel de Macedo was not the first Brazilian to publish novels, but

---

Macedo's sentimental tales of adventure and romance never challenged established social norms.

---

he was the great popularizer of the genre in the nation's literature. His two earliest novels, *A moreninha* (1844) and *O moço loiro* (1845), achieved enormous popularity; indeed, *A moreninha* is still widely read and enjoyed in Brazil, particularly by adolescent readers. Macedo's sentimental tales of adventure and romance never challenged established social norms; after a good many implausible plot devices, his aristocratic young heros and heroines always manage to find precisely the mates society and family would have chosen for them. The primary value of his texts today is their detailed documentation of upper-class mores in Imperial Rio de Janeiro. (Macedo was tutor to the children of Princess ISABEL.) Macedo continued to publish fiction after *O moço loiro,* but his skills as a novelist did not develop and his reputation as a writer was increasingly overshadowed by that of José de ALENCAR. The most interesting of Macedo's later works, none of which attracted the audience his earliest novels had enjoyed, is *As vítimas-algozes* (1869), a collection of three antislavery novellas.

— DAVID T. HABERLY

MAC ENTYRE, EDUARDO

Eduardo Mac Entyre (*b.* 20 February 1929), Argentine artist. A self-taught painter, Mac Entyre was born in Buenos Aires, where he still lives.

In 1959 Mac Entyre, with Ignacio Pirovano and Miguel Angel Vidal, founded a movement called Generative Art, which they defined as "engendering a series of optical sequences which are produced by the evolving of a given form." Mac Entyre uses geometrically precise sequences of exquisitely colored lines that give the canvas a magical effect of depth and appear to generate their own movement as they glide or whirl through space. In liberating his paintings from a static state, he achieved an important goal of twentieth-century avant-garde artists.

A pillar of geometric art in Argentina, Mac Entyre still adheres to the same principles while creating a tremendous variety of forms of his poetic geometry. In 1986 the Organization of American States and the Museum of Modern Art of Latin America honored Mac Entyre for his contribution to the development of the modern art of the Americas.

— IDA ELY RUBIN

MACEO, ANTONIO

Antonio Maceo (*b.* 14 June 1845; *d.* 7 December 1896), second in command of Cuba's independence army. Maceo was one of the greatest guerrilla fighters of the nineteenth century and certainly the most daring soldier ever born on Cuban soil. Cubans familiarly refer to him as the Titan of Bronze, as he was dubbed by an admiring speaker at a patriotic rally in New York City in 1895.

"Now, tomorrow, and always there shall exist in

Cuba men who will do justice to the people

of my race."

Maceo was the son of a Venezuelan mulatto émigré and a free Cuban black, Mariana Grajales, the mother of thirteen children, all of whom swore at her behest to free their country from Spanish domination or die in the attempt. When Cuba's Ten Years' War began in 1868, Maceo enlisted in the rebel army as a private; five years later he achieved the rank of general. From the outset he showed a superior ability to outsmart and outmaneuver the Spanish commanders and occasionally inflicted heavy losses on them. He also displayed extraordinary leadership and determination. Throughout his military career, which spanned the Ten Years' War and the 1895–1898 war, it is estimated that he fought in more than 900 actions. Since he never sought the safety of the rear guard, he sustained twenty-six wounds. Perhaps his greatest military feat was to lead an invasion of western Cuba in 1895–1896, a brilliant operation during which he covered more than a thousand miles in 92 days while engaging the Spanish army in 27 battles or skirmishes and capturing more than 2,000 rifles and 80,000 rounds of ammunition. When Maceo was killed, in a scuffle of little consequence, he had risen to the rank of second in command of the Cuban liberating army.

Maceo's place in Cuban history is as a symbol of tenacity and unwavering patriotism. On 11 February 1878 most of the generals of the Cuban liberating army realized that it would be impossible to defeat the Spanish forces and thus accepted the Pact of Zanjón to end the Ten Years' War. At this juncture Maceo refused to capitulate. He held a historic meeting, known as the Protest of Baraguá, with Spanish marshal Arsenio Martínez Campos, at which he demanded independence for Cuba and the total abolition of slavery. When Martínez Campos rejected these conditions, Maceo resumed fighting. Since the situation of the liberators was truly hopeless, Maceo eventually had to desist and ultimately leave Cuba. But his gesture remained a source of inspiration for future combatants and earned him the acclaim of Cubans and foreigners alike. The American

and Foreign Anti-Slavery Society was among the groups praising him warmly for his stand on slavery.

Maceo identified closely with the predicament of the men and women of his race. Although he himself suffered the attacks of racists within the Cuban liberating army, who accused him of attempting to create a black republic in Cuba, his defense of the rights of blacks was based on the theoretical notion of the rights of men rather than any ethnic affinity. "The revolution has no color" was his indignant rejoinder to his accusers. He trusted that "Now, tomorrow, and always there shall exist in Cuba men who will do justice to the people of my race." For this reason, he wrote, "I enjoin my own people not to ask for anything on the basis of the color of their skin."

This confidence in the ability of Cubans was probably the key to Maceo's attitude toward the United States. He favored the recognition of Cuban belligerency by the powerful republic to the north, but he did not think that American intervention was needed to defeat Spain. He believed that Cubans should depend on their own efforts, adding that it was better to rise or fall without help than to contract debts of gratitude with a neighbor as powerful as the United States. He wrote to the *New York World:* "I should not want our neighbor to shed their blood for our cause. We can do that for ourselves if, under the common law, we can get the necessary elements to overthrow the corrupted power of Spain in Cuba." And on another occasion he said: "Do you really want to cut the war down? Bring Cuba 25,000 to 35,000 rifles and a million bullets. . . . We Cubans do not need any other help."

– JOSÉ M. HERNÁNDEZ

MACHADO, GUSTAVO

Gustavo Machado (*b.* 1898), leader of Venezuelan Communist Party. Born into a wealthy Caracas family, Machado, while still in high school, became a revolutionary in opposition to the dictatorship of Juan Vicente Gómez (1908–1935). Over the course of his political career, he spent many years in exile and in prison for his revolutionary and Communist activities. During the Democratic Action *trienio* (1945–1948), the Communist Party now legalized, he was a vocal member of the Constituent Assembly and later of the Chamber of Deputies. In 1947 Machado ran for president on the Communist ticket, finishing third and last. After the military dictatorship (1948–1958) Machado returned from exile and was again elected to the Chamber of Deputies (1958), where he served as head of the Communist delegation. He was subsequently imprisoned (1963–1968), however, for allegedly fomenting guerrilla insurgency. After his release he resumed command of the Communist Party, but he renounced armed violence and instead stressed the peaceful road to socialism.

— WINFIELD J. BURGGRAAFF

MACHADO DE ASSIS, JOAQUIM MARIA

Joaquim Maria Machado de Assis (*b.* 21 June 1839; *d.* 29 September 1908), the greatest figure in Brazilian letters. Machado was a novelist, short-story writer, poet, essayist, playwright, and literary critic; fiction, however, gave him eminence in Brazilian literature. A contemporary of the romantics, who to some extent influenced him in his formative years, Machado developed a highly personal style.

Machado was born in a slum of Rio de Janeiro, the son of a black house painter and a Portuguese woman from the Azores Islands. At an early age, he became an orphan and began to earn his own living. He did not receive much formal education. He worked as a typesetter, proofreader, editor, and staff writer. In 1869 he married Carolina, the sister of his friend the Portuguese poet Faustino Xavier de Novais. At thirty-five he joined government service.

When still very young, Machado entered the field of letters, writing poetry, plays, opera librettos, short stories, newspaper articles, and translations. Active in artistic and intellectual circles, he was, however, a man of restrained habits who spent thirty-five years as a civil servant. Some of his biographers believe that the bureaucratic routine permitted Machado to devote himself completely to letters. Others view his hardships as having benefited his literature. Machado's anxieties regarding his race and social origin, the epilepsy that tortured him, and his stuttering all had powerful influences on his art. Literature was his relief.

Machado's first volume of poems, *Crisálidas* (Chrysalis), was published in 1864. Other publications followed: *Falenas* (Moth, 1870), *Contos fluminenses* (Tales of Rio de Janeiro, 1870), his first novel, *Ressurreição* (Resurrection, 1871), *Histórias da meia-noite* (Midnight Tales, 1873), *A mão e a luva* (The Hand and the Glove, 1874), *Americanas* (American Poems, 1875), *Helena* (1876), and *Iaiá Garcia* (1878).

In spite of this substantial accomplishment, Machado had not yet defined his identity, still searching for his own creative principles. At thirty-nine, sick and exhausted, he was granted a leave of absence, which he spent in the resort city of Nova Friburgo, near Rio. This period marks a turning point in his work. After his return to Rio he began one of the masterpieces that characterize the second part of his writing career, *Me-*

mórias póstumas de Brás Cubas (1881; *Epitaph of a Small Winner*, 1952).

This rise to greatness has been explained in different ways. Most modern critics, however, interpret his achievement as the consequence of a long desire for perfection and as the result of the struggle between romantic ideals and Machado's creative intuition with which they conflicted. There was not a sudden change between the two phases; the first phase prepared the second. It was a maturation process. After 1875 the technique of his short stories improved. As a result, the collections published after 1880 include several true masterpieces, such as "Missa do galo" (Midnight Mass), "Noite de almirante" (An Admiral's Evening), "A causa secreta" (The Secret Cause), "Uns braços" (A Pair of Arms), "O alienista" (The Alienist), "O enfermeiro" (The Male Nurse), "A cartomante" (The Fortune Teller), and "O espelho" (The Mirror).

Machado's first novel of the second phase, *Memórias póstumas de Brás Cubas,* is a fictional autobiography written by the dead hero. Starting with his death and funeral, the novel represents a complete break with the literary conventions of the time and Brazilian literature,

Joaquím Maria Machado de Assis, 1864. (Organization of American States)

which allowed an exploration of themes not utilized before. With psychological acuity, the author observes people in trivial, cynical, and egocentric conditions. He also portrays Brazilian society at the end of the empire.

The next novel is *Quincas Borba* (1891; *Quincas Borba: Philosopher or Dog?*, 1954). Rubião, a teacher from Minas Gerais, inherits from Quincas Borba a huge amount of money and a crazy philosophy. As he leaves for Rio, Rubião meets a pair of crooks, Christiano Palha and his beautiful wife, Sofia, with whom he falls in love. The couple, who become Rubião's close friends, slowly steal everything from him. Many other people belonging to a marginal and mobile society are involved. Rubião ends up poor and insane. The conclusion proclaims universal indifference in the face of human suffering and the abandonment of man by supernatural forces.

Machado reached the highest expression of his art in *Dom Casmurro* (1890; *Dom Casmurro*, 1971). This masterpiece is artistically superior to his other works; novelistic elements such as narrative structure, composition of characters, and psychological analysis are employed with incomparable genius. Bento Santiago wanted to join the two ends of life and restore youth in old age. For this purpose he had a replica of his childhood home constructed. Because the plan did not work, he decided to write about his past. Bento and Capitu are in love, but he must become a priest to comply with his mother's vow. Capitu's plotting convinces Bento's mother to allow him to leave the seminary. Bento receives his law degree, and finally the couple are united in a blissful marriage. They have only one child. Escobar, Bento's best friend, has married Capitu's best friend, and the two couples live in perfect friendship. As Escobar dies, Bento becomes convinced that his friend and Capitu have committed adultery. Bento tells his own story, which seems smooth on the surface. Implicitly, however, this is a tragic tale of evil, hatred, betrayal, and jealousy. This content, along with the outstanding artistic qualities of the book, makes *Dom Casmurro* Machado's most powerful work.

In *Esaú e Jacó* (1904; *Esau and Jacob*, 1965), Machado adds a new dimension to his treatment of symbolic and mythical elements. The novel contains more political allegories than do any of his other works. Two identical twins, Pedro and Paulo, differ from each other in every respect but their love for the same girl, Flora. The political atmosphere of the newly proclaimed Brazilian Republic is incorporated into the narrative.

Also in 1904, Machado was overwhelmed by the death of his wife. He wrote a very touching poem, "À Carolina," which appeared as an introduction to a new collection of short stories, *Relíquias da casa velha* (Relics

of an Old House, 1906). *Memorial de Aires* (1908; *Counselor Ayres' Memoirs,* 1972), his last novel, is a love story and reminiscence of his life with Carolina. Very ill and frail, Machado died the same year.

Machado de Assis was a powerful writer who impresses us intellectually and emotionally. His writing is predominantly psychological, but the best of his fiction combines the social, philosophical, and historical dimensions with the psychological to make a whole. His extraordinary ability to evoke the past is one of the secrets of his success. His stylistic traits include a simple, exact, and clear syntax and short, discontinuous sentences without rhetorical effects. Metaphor and simile are evident in his writing, but conciseness marks his style and is responsible for its greatness. The underlining philosophy is a pessimistic one that envisions man as solitary, depraved, and lost. Compatible with his tragic view of life, his themes embrace death, insanity, cruelty, ingratitude, disillusion, and hate. Machado found refuge for his nihilism in beauty. His heaven is the aesthetic ideal.

Additional collections of short stories included *Papéis avulsos* (1882), *Histórias sem data* (1884), *Várias histórias* (1896), *Páginas recolhidas* (1899), and *Outras relíquias* (1910). Many of these stories have been published in English. A three-volume collection of his complete works is *Obra completa* (1959).

— MARIA ISABEL ABREU

MACHADO Y MORALES, GERARDO

Gerardo Machado y Morales (*b.* 28 September 1871; *d.* 29 March 1939), president and dictator of Cuba (1925–1933). A man of humble origins, Machado joined the rebels during Cuba's second war of independence (1895–1898), rising to the rank of brigadier general. After peace returned, he became a prominent politician and businessman. In association with American capitalists, he invested in public utilities. He had become wealthy by the early 1920s, when he managed to win control of the Liberal Party and, with a platform of national "regeneration," was elected president in 1924 in a relatively fair election.

Although Machado is usually condemned by historians for eventually turning into a dictator, in his first presidential term not only did he appear to be genuinely concerned with "regenerating" the nation, but he also embarked on an impressive public works program that included the completion of a much-needed central highway and the construction of a national capitol building. In addition, he made a serious attempt to regulate sugar production and became the first president to promote Cuban sovereignty vis-à-vis the United

States. His most important step in this direction was a tariff reform bill he sponsored in 1927 that provided protection to emerging Cuban industries.

Betraying his electoral promises, however, Machado did contract several loans with U.S. banks to finance his public works program. He also showed a disposition to resort to force in order to solve problems, so that striking workers, restless students, and other dissidents at times suffered from his actions. On the whole, however, in 1928–1929 he was still popular and had a grip on the political situation.

> Machado showed a disposition to resort to force in order to solve problems, so that striking workers, restless students, and other dissidents at times suffered from his actions.

Ironically, this control proved to be Machado's undoing, for through bribes and threats he brought all the opposition parties under his influence and subordinated the Congress and the judiciary to his will. He was consequently able to push forward a change in the constitution that allowed reelecting himself virtually unopposed for a new six-year term. At the time of his second inauguration, 20 May 1929, he was still being hailed as the savior of the fatherland. But after that the number of people forced into active opposition increased considerably, and when shortly afterward the shock waves of the worldwide depression reached Cuba, the anti-Machado movement assumed the characteristics of a revolutionary upheaval.

In 1930 there were several antigovernment demonstrations, the most serious of which culminated in the closing of all the schools in the country. The following year, the leaders surviving from the wars of independence staged a full-scale military uprising in the countryside. Machado succeeded in crushing these revolts because he could count on the army, which he had transformed into the overseer of the civil government. But not even the full resources of the army could prevent the revolutionary struggle from degenerating into a vicious fight (as it did from 1932 onward) between the government's brutally repressive forces and clandestine opposition groups such as the so-called ABC movement and the Student Directorate, which were bent upon overthrowing the regime through sabotage and terrorism.

When Franklin D. Roosevelt became president of the United States in 1933, political stability was seen as essential for the successful development of New Deal Cuban policy. Thus, Sumner Welles was sent as ambassador to Havana for the purpose of finding a peaceful solution to the Cuban imbroglio. At first he tried to mediate between the Machado government and its opposition, but as the negotiations went on, he began to push Machado toward making concessions to his enemies. Playing for time, Machado accepted some of the conditions, but he soon drew the line and refused to yield to further pressure, paradoxically assuming the same nationalistic stand as radical opposition groups such as the Student Directorate, which had earlier rejected Welles's good offices. Thus the attempted mediation ended in a deadlock that was resolved only when a general strike paralyzed the nation. Machado then offered favorably disposed Communist labor leaders legal recognition and official support if they would use their influence to end the strike. This maneuver failed, however, and on 12 August 1933 Cuba's armed forces, fearing U.S. armed intervention, moved against the president.

Thus the defiant Machado, who even at the last minute sought to arouse the populace to defend Cuba against a U.S. landing, was finally forced to take a plane to Nassau in the Bahamas. He eventually settled in the United States, where he died, six years later, in Miami Beach. Cuban governments since have refused to authorize the transfer of his remains to his native soil.

– JOSÉ M. HERNÁNDEZ

MAC-IVER RODRÍGUEZ, ENRIQUE

Enrique Mac-Iver Rodríguez (*b.* 15 July 1845; *d.* 21 August 1922), a prominent Chilean lawyer, political figure, intellectual, and journalist. As a deputy to Congress, Mac-Iver supported the rebellion against President José Manuel BALMACEDA FERNÁNDEZ in 1890–1891. He also served as a senator (1900–1922) and as a government minister, and was a grand master of the Masonic Order. An astute social critic, he lamented the decline in Chile's political morality, the nation's international reputation, and the quality of its leaders. In a 1906 convention of the Radical Party, Mac-Iver unsuccessfully argued against Valentín LETELIER MADARIAGA that the state should not become involved in developing the economy and backing social reforms. At the same time, he questioned the capacity of the lower classes to participate in political life.

– WILLIAM F. SATER

MADERO, FRANCISCO INDALECIO

Francisco Indalecio Madero (*b.* 30 October 1873; *d.* 22 February 1913), revolutionary leader and president of

Mexico (1911–1913). Madero is best known for his key role in the overthrow of the dictator Porfirio DÍAZ in 1911 and his forced resignation and assassination in February 1913 by antirevolutionary elements headed by Victoriano HUERTA.

Madero was born on the Hacienda de El Rosario, Parras de la Fuente, Coahuila, to one of the wealthiest industrial and landowning families in Mexico, headed by his grandfather, Evaristo Madero, and his father, Francisco Madero Hernández. He studied in Parras, Coahuila, and at the Jesuit Colegio de San Juan, Saltillo, Coahuila, before taking business courses at Mount Saint Mary's College near Baltimore, Maryland (1886–1888). In France he attended the Liceo de Versailles and the Higher Business School in Paris (1887–1892). Subsequently he took classes in agriculture at the University of California at Berkeley (1893). Upon his return to Mexico, Madero founded a business school in San Pedro de las Colonias, Coahuila, where he also administered a family business and practiced homeopathic medicine, spiritism, and vegetarianism.

While working in rural Mexico, Madero came into direct contact with many of its problems, which he attributed to the lack of a liberal, democratic political system. When Porfirio Díaz claimed in the Creelman interview that he would be willing to step down and allow free and open elections, Madero published *La sucesión presidencial en 1910* (The Presidential Succession of 1910 [1908]), which called for freedom of suffrage, nonreelection of high public officials, and rotations in office. The book's appeal (the initial run of 3,000 copies sold out in three months) and its author's dogged determination and persuasive powers led to the formation in May 1909 of the Anti-Reelectionist Center of Mexico.

Within a few months, Madero's anti-reelectionist movement, and then party, had attracted a large enough following to pose a serious threat to the dictatorship. Madero traveled constantly throughout the country, dedicating himself to propagandizing, recruiting, and helping establish political clubs for the cause. The party's national convention, held in Mexico City in April 1910, attracted nearly 200 delegates from all the states and territories but four.

In early June 1910 authorities arrested Madero in Monterrey, Nuevo León, and then transferred him to the city of San Luis Potosí. He was incarcerated in order to remove him from the political scene until after the 26 June 1910 election, which Díaz and his vice-presidential running mate, Ramón CORRAL VERDUGO (1854–1912), using fraudulent means, won handily. During that summer in San Luis Potosí, Madero made the decision to escape and challenge the Díaz regime

with arms. In early October he fled north to San Antonio, Texas, where he and others drew up the Plan of San Luis Potosí, which called for revolution on 20 November 1910.

The arrests of Madero agents resulted in the confiscation of documents outlining the revolutionary plans for all of central Mexico, thus forcing the conspirators' hands. As a result, Aquiles Serdán (1877–1910) prematurely and futilely raised his revolt on 18 November in the state of Puebla, thus ending any chance of catching the government by surprise. The rebellion sputtered and nearly died, and Madero fled back to Texas for safety.

Only in the state of Chihuahua did any significant rebel activity continue, principally under the leadership of Pascual OROZCO. His successes, along with others in the northwest part of the country, convinced Madero to return to Mexico in mid-February 1911. Within weeks the insurgency spread to many areas of the nation and involved thousands of fighters, including followers of Emiliano ZAPATA (1879–1919) in Morelos. On 10 May 1911, the important border city of Ciudad Juárez, Chihuahua, fell. On 21 May Díaz signed the Treaty of Ciudad Juárez, thereby relinquishing power to an interim government headed by his ambassador to Washington, Francisco LEÓN DE LA BARRA. Madero's revolutionaries took control of the country.

Following elections, Madero assumed the constitutional presidency on 6 November 1911, but much of the popular support he had enjoyed the previous May had already disappeared. Once in office Madero proved incapable of stemming the disintegration of his movement.

Madero's difficulties arose from several complex and interrelated factors. First, Madero's social and political outlook had little in common with that of the majority of his followers. He came from a moderately conservative upper-class family that believed in elite rule and a paternalistic relationship with the lower classes. Madero felt comfortable with the upper classes and barely related to the peasants and workers in his movement, most of whom had rural, traditional backgrounds.

Madero's social values in turn shaped his political ideas. He believed that the establishment of a liberal, constitutional, democratic political system would ensure the free election of good men who then would deal with such problem areas as labor, land, education, and taxes. He therefore rejected many of his lower-class and rural supporters' calls for rapid and far-reaching socioeconomic reforms and advocated the more conservative positions of middle- and upper-class elements, many of whom were former supporters of the Díaz regime.

Second, the heterogeneous and disorganized nature of Madero's movement contributed greatly to its demise. The revolution between November 1910 and May 1911 mobilized several thousands of mainly radical, rural, and lower-class fighters throughout the country. The vast majority took advantage of Madero's call to arms to seek redress of local and sometimes personal grievances; they were unaware of or indifferent to Madero's pronouncements. This large, dispersed, and varied movement wanted immediate satisfaction of its demands. Incapable of satisfying his more radical supporters, Madero lost control in the rural areas where they were mainly based.

Third, Madero made a series of political decisions in the weeks following Díaz's surrender that quickly alienated his more radical adherents (and some moderates) and gave his conservative opponents a chance to regroup. Although professing a policy of nonintervention in state and local affairs (he left the Porfirian-era state legislatures intact), Madero intervened in the selection of many other state and local officials. For example, he named governors who generally were middle-aged, educated, and urban-oriented rather than the revolutionary leaders who fought to put him into power.

Madero also alienated many of his followers when he created a new political party, the Constitutionalist Progressive Party (PCP) to replace the Anti-Reelectionist Party. They felt that Madero was discarding an important symbol of the revolution and betraying a loyal supporter, Francisco Vázquez Gómez (1860–1934), whom Madero replaced as his vice presidential running mate. At the same time, Madero compounded the ill feeling toward him by agreeing to the ouster from his cabinet of Emilio Vázquez Gómez (1858–1926), Francisco's brother and one of the staunchest defenders of the left wing of the movement.

Maderista officers and troops also chafed over Madero's decision to demobilize them and maintain the Porfirian army as the only official force in Mexico. When they resisted and clashed with federal units (most notably in Puebla City in mid-July 1911), Madero resorted to the hated draft to build up the regular army and converted newly demobilized insurgents into *rurales* (rural police during Díaz's regime) to fight their former colleagues.

Finally, Madero proved slow to implement the reform program he had promised. The federal government could and did undertake some measures, such as the creation of a labor department and the construction of schools. However, the lack of resources, Madero's belated assumption of the presidency, his selective reluctance to interfere in nonfederal governmental affairs, and the fact that most reforms directly involved state and local levels of administration meant that Madero mostly had only an indirect say in what reforms were implemented.

Beginning in the summer of 1911, the disillusionment of much of his left wing and the continued adamant opposition of the conservatives, supported in part by backsliding moderate Maderistas who feared the increasingly violent masses, led to a series of rebellions, two of which most seriously threatened the regime.

After Díaz's fall, the Zapatistas waited for Madero's government to fulfill its promises, especially those regarding the restitution and protection of communal lands. They became especially angered when federal authorities demanded their demobilization. Zapata tried to reason with Madero, but President León de la Barra, who considered the Zapatistas rural bandits, sent General Victoriano HUERTA to subdue them. Thus provoked into rebellion in August 1911, the Zapatistas were soon operating over a wide area of south-central Mexico. In November 1911, they issued the Plan of Ayala, their formal declaration of rebellion, which called for agrarian reform and the overthrow of Madero. Although never able to topple the national government during the Madero period, the Zapatistas made life miserable for provincial authorities and elites, sapped the government's resources, and undermined its military and political credibility.

> *Madero has been portrayed as a well-meaning, progressive democrat who was betrayed by the dark forces of dictatorship and foreign intervention.*

The second major rebellion occurred in Chihuahua, where Pascual Orozco, financed by the conservative Terrazas-Creel clan, rebelled in early March 1912. His defeat of the federal army at Rellano, Chihuahua, on 23 March forced Madero to turn to Huerta to save the regime. Huerta defeated Orozco's forces at Rellano on 23 May 1911. The Orozquistas fled to the mountains from where they, too, carried on guerrilla warfare, thus also sapping the limited resources of the regime and forcing Madero to focus on a military solution to his problems.

In early 1913, with his movement in tatters, his credibility gone, and his government bankrupt and besieged, Madero faced a rebellion (whose events are referred to as the *decena trágica*, or tragic ten days [9–19 February 1913]) within the federal army, which was led by Félix DÍAZ, Manuel Mondragón, and Bernardo

Reyes. The seriousness of the revolt forced Madero once again to turn to Huerta to save his government. During the ensuring battle, Huerta, with the aid of U.S. Ambassador Henry Lane Wilson (1857–1932), plotted with the rebels against Madero. On 19 February, Huerta forced Madero to resign and assumed the interim presidency. On 22 February, government agents executed Madero and his vice president, José María PINO SUÁREZ (1869–1913), probably upon Huerta's orders.

Madero became a martyr, and his name entered the pantheon of revolutionary heroes as the father of the Mexican Revolution of 1910. He has been portrayed as a well-meaning, progressive democrat who was betrayed by the dark forces of dictatorship and foreign intervention. A more recent assessment, however, depicts him as the person who catalyzed the heterogeneous and dispersed revolutionary movement that managed to overthrow the Díaz regime, yet who did not have the ability or vision to institutionalize that movement and carry out the fundamental socioeconomic reforms necessary to meet the demands of the vast majority of his followers who put him into power. In fact, he oftentimes used autocratic methods to keep those very followers in check to the benefit of Mexico's more conservative and economically privileged groups.

– DAVID LAFRANCE

MADRAZO, CARLOS A.

Carlos A. Madrazo (*b.* 1915; *d.* 4 June 1969), Mexican political leader. Born in Villahermosa, Tabasco, Madrazo pursued his early education there before attending preparatory and law school at the Universidad Nacional Autónoma de México in Mexico City. Associated with Left, progressive groups, he was a spellbinding orator and leader in the Bloc of Revolutionary Youth of the Red Shirts (1933–1935) under Tabasco's radical governor Tomás GARRIDO CANABAL. He served as private secretary to Luis I. Rodríguez during the latter's tenure as governor of Guanajuato and later as president of the Party of Mexico Revolution (PRM), forerunner to the Institutional Revolutionary Party (PRI). His friendship with Gustavo DÍAZ ORDAZ, later president of Mexico (1964–1970), dated from the time when both served in the national Chamber of Deputies. Madrazo served as governor of Tabasco during 1959–1964.

A controversial figure, Madrazo's significance for modern Mexican political life stems from his failure as president of the PRI in 1964–1965 to make the party more democratic and independent of the presidency. Defeated by an alliance of state governors and cabinet

ministers, Madrazo remains a symbol for the still-unrealized renovation of the party.

– JOHN BAILEY

MADRID HURTADO, MIGUEL DE LA

Miguel de La Madrid Hurtado (*b.* 12 December 1934), president of Mexico (1982–1988). Miguel de la Madrid took office at the Mexican presidency's lowest level of legitimacy in modern times. Confronted with a major economic crisis consisting of rapidly increasing inflation, a downturn in growth, high rates of unemployment, extraordinary capital flight, and massive external debt, the president pursued an orthodox strategy of economic austerity. Having achieved only moderate economic success, de la Madrid is likely to be remembered more for having provided the groundwork for his successor's liberalization and privatization programs. However, de la Madrid's administration did bring inflation under relative control, renegotiate the debt, and begin the process of selling off state-owned enterprises.

Politically, de la Madrid restored the shattered relationship between the private and public sectors, a step necessary for the success of his economic strategy. While he initially attempted moderate electoral reforms, the government's mishandling of earthquake rescue efforts in 1985 provoked the development of numerous popular opposition movements. Worse still was the electoral fraud in Chihuahua in 1986, which brought, for the first time in four decades, formal denunciations from the church hierarchy and encouraged a more activist church posture in politics. In 1986, de la Madrid introduced a new electoral code mandating an increase in the number of proportional seats in the Chamber of Deputies from 100 to 200 (raising the total number of seats from 400 to 500), and thus setting the stage for the extraordinary representation of the opposition in the 1988 chamber.

Internally, de la Madrid reinforced the growing tendency of the two preceding administrations toward the dominance of political technocrats: younger, bureaucratically experienced, highly educated (often abroad), urban decision makers with few ties to the PRI or the electoral scene. The control of these leaders continued to exacerbate internal disputes between the more traditional leadership and reform-minded younger technocrats. Finally, de la Madrid's designation of Carlos SALINAS as his party's candidate and the unbending treatment of party dissidents Cuauhtémoc CÁRDENAS and Porfirio MUÑOZ LEDO, who formed their own party, led to the most disputed presidential election in the party's history, in which it captured only a bare majority of the votes cast.

Miguel de la Madrid was born in Colima, Colima, the son of Miguel de la Madrid Castro, a lawyer and government employee murdered by wealthy landowners after he defended peasant rights. His mother, Alicia Hurtado, took Miguel and his sister to Mexico City, where he attended the Colegio Cristóbal Colón and the National Law School, from which he graduated with an honorary mention 8 August 1957. An outstanding student, de la Madrid had the second-highest grades of his 732 law school classmates. In 1965, on a fellowship from the Bank of Mexico, de la Madrid obtained an M.A. degree in public administration from Harvard University, the first Mexican president with a graduate degree as well as the first with a degree from abroad. He also taught constitutional law at the National University from 1958 to 1967. As a student, he worked in the National Foreign Trade Bank under Ricardo J. Zevada, his professor, to support himself at school. After graduation, he obtained his first government post at the Bank of Mexico as an adviser to Mario Ramón Beteta through his professor, Daniel J. Bello. Beteta became the president's early mentor, and when he moved to the secretariat of the treasury, he took de la Madrid along as his subdirector general of credit (1965–1970). In 1970, de la Madrid became assistant director of finances for the government oil company, Pemex, but moved back to his mentor's agency as director general of credit (1972–1975). When Beteta became treasury secretary in 1975, he appointed de la Madrid as assistant secretary of credit, a post he continued to hold in the next administration. On 17 May 1979 President José LÓPEZ PORTILLO appointed him secretary of programming and planning. Although considered a dark horse candidate for the presidential nomination, he became the party's candidate on 25 September 1981. His ties to José López Portillo, who chose him as his successor, extended back to law school, where he studied under his predecessor. After de la Madrid left the presidency in 1988, his successor, Carlos Salinas, appointed him director of the government-funded publishing firm Fondo de Cultura Económica.

– RODERIC AI CAMP

MADUREIRA, ANTÔNIO DE SENA

Antônio de Sena Madureira (*b.* 1841; *d.* 1889), Brazilian military leader. Sena Madureira graduated from the military academy with a degree in science and mathematics. He was training in Europe when the War of the Triple Alliance (1864–1870) broke out, and served in the war with distinction. An abolitionist and a republican, Madureira's historical significance stems from his launching, in 1884, of the famous "military question,"

concerning the civil rights of the military. This occurred when his command gave a hero's welcome to the celebrated abolitionist Francisco de Nascimento. The minister of war labeled the episode a breach of discipline and censured Madureira. A related incident followed when a liberal colonel cited some irregularities in a command headed by a captain of conservative leanings. The captain felt aggrieved and turned to a conservative deputy, who verbally attacked the colonel in the Chamber of Deputies. The colonel responded in the press and was censured by the minister of war. Madureira joined in the debate by writing provocative articles in a republican newspaper. The minister of war sought to administer discipline but found that Madureira was under the direct command of General Deodoro da FONSECA, the most prestigious military officer in the army. Fonseca refused to censure his subordinate, since the matter involved Madureira's criticism of civilian authority, and not a breach of military hierarchy. The affair centered on the rights of the military to express their political views publicly. The Supreme Military Tribunal ruled in favor of the officers, and Madureira's punishments were revoked. The split between military and monarchist leaders remained, however, and the monarchy was overthrown by a military coup in 1889.

– ROBERT A. HAYES

MAGALHÃES, DOMINGOS JOSÉ GONÇALVES DE

Domingos José Gonçalves de Magalhães (*b.* 1811; *d.* 1882), considered the "father" of Brazilian romanticism. Magalhães was a doctor, a poet, and an influential diplomat of the empire who enjoyed the favor of Emperor Dom Pedro II. While living in Paris he fell under the influence of the European romantics. In 1836, along with the romantic painter and poet Manuel de Araújo PORTO ALEGRE (1806–1879) and Alberto Torres Homem, he cofounded a literary review, *Niterói: Revista Brasiliense.* While his early poetical works reflected the conservatism of the neoclassical literary canon, they also contained slight echoes of nascent liberalism.

His first collection of poems, *Suspiros poéticos e saudades* (1836), offered a pantheistic view of life: nature is omnipresent in, and consequently the major influence on, the poetic art. That same year, influenced by the romantic concept of nationalism, he published the first "history" of Brazilian literature, "Discurso sobre a história da literatura do Brasil." Romantic nationalism is also evident in his most notable drama, *António José; ou, O poeta e a inquisição* (1839), about the eighteenth-century Luso-Brazilian writer condemned by the Inquisition. Although he continued to write throughout his lifetime, his last major work (and the one for which he remains best known today) is the epic poem *A confederação dos Tamojos* (1856), in which he legitimizes the total destruction of an Indian tribe in the pursuit of independence and the establishment of the empire.

— IRWIN STERN

MAGAÑA, SERGIO

Sergio Magaña (*b.* 24 September 1924; *d.* 23 August 1990), Mexican dramatist and novelist. Magaña contributed to the formation of a new generation of playwrights with his first play, *La noche transfigurada* (1947), and mainly with his popular play *Los signos del zodíaco* (1951), which depicts the lower class in Mexico City through the simultaneous staging of various scenes. With the collaboration of Emilio CARBALLIDO, he founded a literary group called Atenea, which later became the School of Philosophy and Letters theater group, and exerted a great deal of influence on the avant-garde scene. Both *Los argonautas* (1953) and *Moctezuma II* (1954) concern the Spanish Conquest, while *Santísima* (1980), a stylized musical about a prostitute's life, uses characters from Federico GAMBOA's novel *Santa*. He has also written novels, such as *El molino del aire* (1953).

— GUILLERMO SCHMIDHUBER

MAGDALENO, MAURICIO

Mauricio Magdaleno (*b.* 13 May 1906; *d.* 30 June 1986), Mexican writer. Born in Villa del Refugio, Magdaleno wrote drama, novels, and movie scripts, most of which address the achievements, failures, and contradictions of the Mexican Revolution. In the 1930s Magdaleno founded the theater group Teatro de Ahora in partnership with Juan Bustillo Oro; he also published his most important novel, *El resplandor* (Sunburst, 1937). In the 1940s Magdaleno wrote many successful screenplays for the growing Mexican film industry. Named to the Mexican Academy of Language in 1957, Magdaleno later held a variety of bureaucratic and political offices, including a period as senator for the state of Zacatecas (1958–1964).

— DANNY J. ANDERSON

MAGELLAN, FERDINAND

Ferdinand Magellan (*Port.* Fernão de Magalhães e Sousa; *Span.* Fernando de Magallanes; *b.* 1480 [?]; *d.* 27 April 1521), Portuguese navigator who, under the service of the king of Spain, discovered the westward route to the Orient and initiated the first voyage to circumnavigate the globe.

Ferdinand Magellan was born near Oporto, Portugal, and in 1504 entered service to the Portuguese throne under Francisco de Almeida, viceroy of the Portuguese East Indies. Magellan served in Mozambique under Nuño Vaz Pereira before fighting in battles with the Muslims in India and later taking part in successful attacks on Goa and Malacca in 1511.

In 1519, Magellan set sail with five ships from Sanlúcar de Barrameda in search of a western passage to the Indies.

After service in Morocco, Magellan returned to Lisbon, where he was denied a promotion in the Portuguese military. Dissatisfied with his status in Portugal, Magellan sought support from King Charles I of Spain in 1517, the same year in which he married Beatríz Barbosa, daughter of an important official in Seville. Magellan persuaded the king to send him in search of a westward route to the Indies, whose islands Spain claimed as its rightful territory. On 20 September 1519, Magellan set sail with five ships from Sanlúcar de Barrameda in search of the western passage.

The vessels stopped briefly in Madeira and, after reaching the shores of Brazil, headed south along the coast of South America. In January 1520, Magellan entered the Río de la Plata and explored the region, finding the site that would later become Montevideo and discovering the Uruguay River. In March, Magellan entered the Bay of San Julián, where he chose to stay for the winter. During this time, a mutiny among some of his captains threatened Magellan's command, but it was successfully suppressed.

On 21 October 1520, the voyage entered the straits between the mainland and Tierra del Fuego that were to bear Magellan's name and, after a difficult passage, emerged on 28 November in the Pacific. Heading northwest, Magellan landed at Guam on 6 March 1521, after spending months on the open sea without encountering inhabited islands.

Soon after, the ships reached the Philippines, where Magellan made the mistake of taking part in a territorial dispute with local chieftains and was killed in a battle on the island of Mactan on April 27. The voyage continued, with only one ship, under the command of Juan Sebastian de ELCANO, returning to Spain on 8 September 1522, thus achieving the first circumnavigation of the globe.

— JOHN DUDLEY

MAGLOIRE, PAUL EUGÈNE

Paul Eugène Magloire (*b.* 1907), president of Haiti (1950–1956). Born in Cap Haitien into a family of the country's black elite, Magloire received an education at the Lycée Philippe Guerrier, at the military academy, and at the National University, where he earned a law degree. As commander of the Palace Guard, he and two mulatto officers organized the coup that toppled the dictatorship of Élie LESCOT in January 1946. After serving as minister of the interior under President Dumarsais ESTIMÉ, Magloire again conspired against his superior: when Estimé sought to prolong his rule in violation of Haiti's constitution, Magloire joined in the coup to overthrow him.

Supported by the Roman Catholic church, the Haitian military, and the U.S. government, Magloire's presidency, from December 1950 to December 1956, represented a return to power of Haiti's mulatto elite in cooperation with blacks like Magloire himself. Instead of continuing the social reforms started by his predecessor, Magloire focused on economic modernization with the help of private, foreign (mainly U.S.) investments, U.S.-government aid programs, and U.S.-backed international agencies like UNESCO. While lavishing money on showy development projects such as the Point Four–sponsored irrigation project in the Artibonite Valley, the regime did little for the bulk of the country's population. It not only suppressed civil

Paul Eugène Magloire (right) and Rafael Trujillo. (Organization of American States)

liberties and independent unions, but also aggravated conditions for the peasantry by allowing the country's best land to be taken over by foreign-owned agro-export industries. By increasing Haiti's dependence on agro-exports, Magloire contributed to the ecological and human disaster that explains the poverty of most Haitians today as well as the heavy migratory overflow that has characterized the country since his time.

– PAMELA MURRAY

MAÍZ, FIDEL

Fidel Maíz (*b.* 1828; *d.* 1920), Paraguayan cleric and figure in the War of the Triple Alliance. Born in the tiny hamlet of Arroyos y Esteros, Maíz was little more than an obscure country priest until the late 1850s, when he gained the attention of the all-powerful López family. One story has it that Maíz was the only Paraguayan priest willing to baptize the offspring of Francisco Solano LÓPEZ (the future president) and his Irish mistress Eliza Lynch. In any case, Maíz went on to officiate at the September 1862 funeral of President Carlos Antonio LÓPEZ, and to participate in the subsequent congressional meetings called to choose a new government. Some ill-chosen words at the latter assembly put Maíz in prison for several years, but in 1866, he was reprieved by Solano López and named army chaplain.

Two years later, Maíz played an infamous role in one of the ugliest episodes of the war: he acted as government prosecutor at a series of conspiracy trials, often referred to as the *tribunales de sangre*. Convened at San Fernando, the trials were characterized by their expediency and, more particularly, by the use of torture to obtain confessions. In this fashion, Maíz elicited confessions from scores of men said to be plotting against López. Many were condemned and bayoneted to death on the same day. In fact, however, historians today question whether any conspiracy ever existed.

After the war, Maíz was imprisoned for a time by the Brazilians and then censured by the Roman Catholic church. He traveled to Rome to appeal his case to the pope, was absolved, and returned to Arroyos y Esteros, where he spent the remainder of his life composing polemical tracts, memoirs, and textbooks for the little church school he ran.

– THOMAS L. WHIGHAM

MAJANO, ADOLFO ARNOLDO

Adolfo Arnoldo Majano (*b.* 1938), Salvadoran army officer and member of the provisional junta (1979–1980). Majano was briefly the most visible representative of reformist forces within El Salvador's officer corps. A participant in the coup d'état that overthrew the regime of Carlos Humberto ROMERO on 15 October 1979, Majano later served as one of two military members on the junta that replaced him. Considered honest and progressive, Majano supported the junta's reforms and urged greater respect for human rights and an opening to the Left. But he was not an effective leader, and rightist forces within the military eventually outmaneuvered him. Ousted from the junta in December 1980, Majano went into exile the following year.

— STEPHEN WEBRE

MALASPINA, ALEJANDRO

Alejandro Malaspina (*b.* 5 November 1754; *d.* 9 April 1810), Spanish naval officer and explorer. Alejandro Malaspina, a Spanish subject born in Mulazzo, in the Duchy of Parma, Italy, entered Spain's navy in 1774 as a midshipman and rose quickly through the ranks. After serving in Gibraltar, he circumnavigated the earth from 1786 to 1788 as commander of *La Astrea*. As a captain, Malaspina was given command of a five-year around-the-world scientific exploratory mission departing from Cádiz on 30 July 1789. The expedition sailed around the tip of South America and surveyed various Spanish ports. From Acapulco, Malaspina explored northward to the sixtieth parallel, visiting Alaska, Nootka Sound (Vancouver Island), and Monterey, California. His men gathered scientific data and charted the coastline before returning to Mexico. The ships sailed for the Philippines and Australia before recrossing the Pacific to South America and Spain. Prior to publishing his materials, Malaspina fell victim to court intrigue in 1795; he was imprisoned and stripped of his rank. After about eight years in jail, Malaspina was exiled to Parma, where he died.

Not until 1885 did a one-volume account of his expedition appear in print. Today, however, Malaspina's work has added valuable scientific and visual data to existing knowledge about the natural history of New World areas during the late eighteenth century.

— IRIS H. W. ENGSTRAND

MALDONADO, FRANCISCO SEVERO

Francisco Severo Maldonado (*b.* 1775; *d.* 1832), Mexican politician and reformer. Born in Tepic, Nayarit, Maldonado studied in Guadalajara and became a priest and a scholar. Joining HIDALGO's movement when the insurgent army arrived in Guadalajara in 1810, he published the revolutionary *El despertador americano* and began drafting a constitution. After the battle of Calderón, Maldonado was put on trial. He renounced his

earlier views and began to write for a royalist periodical, *El telégrafo de Guadalaxara* (1811). He supported both the Constitution of 1812 and the Plan of Iguala, and served in the early congresses. His social and political ideas, expressed in various editions of a work he called *Nuevo pacto social* and *Contrato de asociación* (1823), may have influenced Mariano OTERO. Maldonado's plans are, in the words of Charles Hale, "an odd blend of liberal individualism, utopian socialism, and traditional corporate theory." His views on land reform and corporate society have been seen by some as presaging the Constitution of 1917.

— D. F. STEVENS

MALDONADO, RODRIGO DE ARIAS

Rodrigo de Arias Maldonado (*b.* 25 December 1637; *d.* 23 September 1716), the moving force behind the organization in Guatemala of the religious order of Bethlehemites to serve the poor. Born into the Spanish nobility, Maldonado went with his parents as a child to Costa Rica, where his father served as governor. He took over the governorship when his father died in 1662. As governor of Costa Rica he subdued the Talamanca Indians, and he was expected to go on to higher posts. He moved to Santiago de Guatemala, opened a great house, and lived ostentatiously. He then came under the influence of Hermano Pedro de BETHANCOURT, who had established a hospital and was extending services to the poor. The king appointed Maldonado marquis de Talamanca, but he refused the honor and turned to a life of service. When Hermano Pedro died, leadership of the group known as the Bethlehemites passed to Maldonado, called Rodrigo de la Cruz within the church. Maldonado went to Rome in 1674 and again in 1685 to gain authorization to establish the order of the Bethlehemites. He then traveled to Mexico and Peru, founding hospitals and churches in the name of the new order. Upon his death he was buried in one of the churches that he had established in Mexico City.

— DAVID L. JICKLING

MALESPÍN, FRANCISCO

Francisco Malespín (*b.* 1790; *d.* 25 November 1846), president of El Salvador (1844–1845). Following Rafael CARRERA's defeat of Francisco MORAZÁN, Carrera imposed Malespín as commander of El Salvador's army in March 1840. Regarded as Carrera's puppet, Malespín effectively resisted Morazán's attempt to return to El Salvador in 1842. Collaborating with Bishop Jorge VITERI Y UNGO, Malespín broke with Salvadoran President Juan José Guzmán in December 1843 and took over the presidency on 1 February 1844. He stopped ex-President Manuel José ARCE's attempt to return to El Salvador to regain office, but his involvement in the liberal-conservative intrigues of the period led him into war with Nicaragua in October 1844. He captured LEÓN on 24 January 1845, but Gerardo BARRIOS and Trinidad CABAÑAS meanwhile pressured Acting President Joaquín Guzmán to depose Malespín on 2 February 1845. When Malespín ordered a priest executed later that year, Bishop Viteri y Ungo excommunicated him. Malespín's efforts to regain power led to war between Honduras and El Salvador in mid-1845. Malespín launched a new invasion of El Salvador in November 1846, but was murdered in a personal dispute at San Fernando, Chalatenango.

— RALPH LEE WOODWARD, JR.

MALFATTI, ANITA CATARINA

Anita Catarina Malfatti (*b.* 2 December 1889; *d.* 6 November 1964), Paulista artist who helped ignite the Brazilian modernist movement. Her oils, drawings, engravings, pastels, and watercolors were exhibited for fifty years in museums in Brazil, France, the United States, Argentina, and Chile.

Malfatti's Italian-born father died before she was thirteen. Her mother, a North American of German descent, was her first art teacher. Born with an atrophied right arm and hand, Malfatti received extensive training to use her left hand. After attending the Escola Americana, Malfatti graduated from Mackenzie College, and later taught at both institutions. Her uncle, Jorge Krug, sent her to Berlin (where she studied with Fritz Burger, Lovis Corinth, and Bischoff-Culm from 1910 to 1914). From 1914 to 1916 she took classes in New York at the Art Students League and at the Independent School of Art with Homer Boss. In 1915 her illustrations appeared in *Vogue* and *Vanity Fair* and she also painted some of the oils (*O japones, O homen amarelo, A boba, A mulher de cabelos verdes*) that led to the "Anita Malfatti Affair."

After returning to São Paulo in 1916, Malfatti painted two other controversial oils, *Tropical* and *O saci*, which were shown at her "Exposicão de pintura moderna" in São Paulo from December 1917 through January 1918. At first the exhibit was a success. But then an influential newspaper critic's hostile remarks led to demands for refunds and a flood of articles pro and con. Following this "Anita Malfatti Affair," a small group of young writers, other artists, and musicians began planning an event, the Modern Art Week, held in São Paulo in 1922, to vindicate her "martyrdom" and to modernize the Brazilian arts. The event did not change public opinion, however. With other members of the "Grupo dos Cinco" (Mario de ANDRADE, Tarsila do AMARAL, Oswaldo de ANDRADE and Menotti del Picchia) and other Brazilians, including Lucilia Guimarães Villa-Lobos, Heitor VILLA-LOBOS, Victor Brecheret, and Emiliano DI CALVALCANTI, Malfatti traveled to Europe, where she stayed until 1928.

Malfatti had many exhibitions in Brazil, including major shows at the Salão Paulista de Arte Moderna (1932), the Salão de Arte de Feira Nacional de Indústrias (1941), the Salão Bahiano de Belas Artes (1949), and the Bienales do Museu de Arte Moderna (1951, and retrospective 1963). She was president and director of the Sindicatos dos Artistas Plásticos from 1941 to 1946.

— MARY LUCIANA LOMBARDI

MALINCHE

Malinche (Marina; Malintzin; *b.* ca. 1504; *d.* 1527), Indian interpreter for Hernán CORTÉS. According to the Indian historian Domingo Chimalpahin Cuauhtlehuanitzin and Francisco Javier Clavijero, Malinche's complete indigenous name was Malinali Tenepal. She was baptized Marina and given the nickname Malinche, perhaps a distortion of Malintzin. (The termination *tzin* denotes nobility.) Several places of birth are given. Some historians, following Francisco López de Gómara, say she was born in the present-day state of Jalisco, while the more accepted version, based on Bernal DÍAZ DEL CASTILLO, locates her birthplace in the vicinity of Coatzacoalcos, in southern Mexico, probably in Painala but possibly in Oluta or Jaltipán. These historians also provide different accounts of her life before the arrival of the Spaniards. According to Gómara, she was stolen by some merchants during a war and then sold as a slave. Díaz's account lends her the semblance of a Greek tragic figure or the heroine of an Old Testament story.

Marina's knowledge about the political structures of central Mexico was indispensable to Cortés's alliances with traditional enemies of Tenochtitlán.

According to Díaz, Malinali's parents were caciques of the town of Painala. After her father died, her mother married another cacique, with whom she had a son. To keep Malinali from succeeding them as cacique, one night they sold her to some merchants from Xicalanco and proclaimed her dead. At that time the child of one of their slave women had died, and they passed the dead girl off as Malinali. The merchants from Xicalango sold Malinali to other Indians in Tabasco, who in turn gave her to Cortés along with nineteen other women sometime in the spring of 1519.

After the twenty women were baptized, Cortés distributed them among his officers. He gave doña Marina, who was barely fifteen at the time, to Alonso Hernández Portocarrero. After Portocarrero returned to Spain on 26 June 1519, she became Cortés's interpreter and lover. The language skills of Marina, who spoke Nahuatl and Maya, complemented those of Jerónimo de AGUILAR, who had learned Maya during his captivity in the Yucatán. One can hardly exaggerate the importance of her role in the conquest of Mexico. In addition to her function as a translator, Marina possessed information about the Aztecs as well as the political structures of central Mexico. This knowledge was indispensable to Cortés's alliances with traditional enemies of Tenochtitlán. Her presence in numerous indigenous portraits of Cortés testifies to this fact.

In 1522, Marina gave birth to a son, whom Cortés named Martín Cortés and eventually recognized as legitimate. From November 1524 to June 1526 Marina served as Cortés's interpreter in the expedition to the Hibueras (present-day Honduras). During the expedition, Cortés married her to Juan Jaramillo. It was also during this expedition that, according to Díaz, she encountered her mother and half brother. They feared she would punish them for having sold her, but she consoled them and gave them gifts. She also told them that she was fortunate to be a Christian, to have a son by her master, Cortés, and to be married to a gentleman like Juan Jaramillo.

Marina had a daughter named María with Juan Jaramillo. As dowry, Cortés gave Marina and Jaramillo the *encomiendas* of Olutla, and Jilotepec, near Coatzacoalcos. She died, still very young, most likely from smallpox, probably in Mexico City. Today in Mexico, as in most of its history, Malinche is identified as a prostitute or a traitor, as someone who sold out to the invaders. Thus, the term *malinchismo* names the tendency to prefer what is foreign. More recently, however, Mexican and Chicana (Mexican American) women writers and artists have sought to rescue Malintzin from the misogynist perceptions that have prevailed in the past.

– JOSÉ RABASA

MALLEA, EDUARDO

Eduardo Mallea (*b.* 14 August 1903; *d.* 12 November 1982), Argentine novelist and essayist. Of a distinguished colonial family, Eduardo Mallea was born in Bahía Blanca, a wind-swept seaport 300 miles south of Buenos Aires. His father, an eminent physician whose integrity and patriotism were beyond question, strongly influenced the young Mallea during his intellectual and artistic development. The Mallea family moved to Buenos Aires in 1916, and in 1920 Eduardo entered law school at the university, but never completed his studies. Instead, he devoted himself completely to literature, publishing his first book in 1926, a collection of short stories entitled *Cuentos para una inglesa desesperada* (Stories for a Desperate Englishwoman).

Mallea was Argentina's intellectual novelist; in him Argentina found the spokesman for its most authentic values and beliefs. Influenced by Jean-Paul Sartre and Martin Heidegger, Mallea was Hispanic America's most important existential fiction writer. In novels such as *La bahía de silencio* (The Bay of Silence, 1940) and *Todo verdor perecerá* (All Green Shall Perish, 1941), Mallea portrayed the emotional crisis of contemporary man seeking to find reason in an irrational and chaotic world. If Mallea's predecessors, the *criollista* novelists, portrayed the spirit of America as a physical presence, Mallea captured the spirit of man as an individual, in his fundamental essence, of man not necessarily in conflict with nature or his environment, but in a more basic conflict with himself and his emotions.

Mallea's life was his writing. In 1914 he began a long-time association with *Sur*, one of the most influential literary magazines in the Americas. He also contributed regularly to other journals and newspapers and in 1923 founded the magazine *Rivista de América*. Mallea also had close ties to *La Nación* as editor of that newspaper's literary supplement from 1934 to 1955.

In 1937, Mallea published *Historia de una pasión Argentina* (History of an Argentine Passion), a book-length essay that is both his spiritual autobiography and Argentina's most influential biography of the 1930s. In this work Mallea's stance is that of the liberal intellectual who saw this period as dominated by a repressive oligarchy subverting the truth and moral order on which the country had been built. Revealing Mallea's anguish over the destruction of Argentina's basic values and the bankruptcy of its ideals, *History of an Argentine Passion* contains many themes that appear later in his novels, notably the concept of a visible Argentina—the materialistic, ostentatious false veneer that the country (especially Buenos Aires) lives with from day to day—versus an invisible one—the genuine soul of the country, its true being, which lies submerged beneath the crass surface.

In 1940, Mallea became president of the Argentine Association of Writers. In 1955, he served as Argentina's delegate to UNESCO in Paris, and in 1956 he traveled to New Delhi to represent his country at a UNESCO conference. His fiction writing never abated. In 1957, he published *Simbad;* in 1967, *La barca de hielo* (The Ice Ship); in 1971, *Triste piel del universo* (Sad Skin of the Universe); and in 1982, *La mancha en el marmol* (The Stain on the Marble).

— MYRON I. LICHTBLAU

MALUF, PAULO SALIM

Paulo Salim Maluf (*b.* 3 September 1931), Brazilian politician. Maluf was born in São Paulo, the son of Salim Farah Maluf and Maria Estefano Maluf. He married Silvia Luftalla, with whom he had four children. Although trained as an engineer, Maluf has been a long-time political figure both locally and nationally. Owner of Eucatex and other enterprises, Maluf started his political career in 1967, when President Costa e Silva appointed him president of the Caixa Econômica Federal (Federal Savings Bank) of São Paulo, a post he held for two years. In 1969, he was appointed *prefeito* (mayor) of his hometown and served until 1971, when he was appointed secretary of transportation for the state of São Paulo. In 1979, Maluf was indirectly elected under the ARENA Party banner as state governor. In spite of corruption charges, the politician was elected federal deputy in 1982, having received more than 600,000 votes.

Maluf ran for the presidency in 1984, but in spite of military backing, was defeated in the electoral college by Tancredo de Almeida Neves. Later, he suffered additional defeats in his campaigns for governor of São Paulo state in 1986 and mayor of São Paulo in 1988, and in his candidacy for the presidency in 1989. The former governor attempted to regain the São Paulo governorship in 1990, but without success. He has remained politically active.

— IÊDA SIQUEIRA WIARDA

MAÑACH Y ROBATO, JORGE

Jorge Mañach y Robato (*b.* 14 February 1898; *d.* 25 June 1961), Cuban writer, born in Sagua la Grande. Mañach was learned in Cuban history and culture and participated in Cuban political life as senator of the Cuban republic (1940–1944) and as minister of state (1944). After studying in Cuba and going to Spain in 1907, where he attended Escuelas Pías in Getafé from 1908 to 1913, he was educated at Harvard, from which he graduated in 1920. In France he studied law at the Sorbonne and experienced the rich cultural and artistic life of Paris during the 1920s. Back in Cuba, Mañach took up a career in journalism (1922) on the famous journal *Diario de la Marina*. His first book, *Glosario* (1924), is a collection of the chronicles of his European and Cuban travels. This work comprises three genres: travel chronicles, *cuadros costumbristas* (works of local color), and essays of literary and art criticism. His essay *Indagación del choteo* (1928), which brought him recognition, deals with the humorous peculiarities and irreverent spirit of the Cuban personality. In *Martí: El apóstol* (1933), a biography in novel form, praise for the Cuban patriot José Martí is based on historical facts rather than on the subjective view of Martí given by the first republican generation. Exalting Martí as a hero, Mañach sought to restore political health to Cuba, which was then under the dictatorship of Gerardo MACHADO (1925–1933). Mañach rejected autocratic systems and considered the individual's inalienable right to freedom to be the foundation necessary for a social and political regime. And though his writings in the magazine *Bohemia* supported Fidel CASTRO, Mañach ultimately rejected the tenets of both Castro and Fulgencio BATISTA. Other important works by Mañach are *Examen del quijotismo* (1950), a phenomenological study of *Don Quijote,* and *Teoría de la frontera* (1970), which synthesizes the values of North American and Latin American culture, and suggests the potential for a good relationship between the two.

— JUAN CARLOS GALEANO

MANCO CAPAC

Manco Capac, founder of the Inca dynasty (the dates of his reign are unknown). In Inca myth Manco Capac emerged, together with his three brothers and four sisters, from three caves at Pacariqtambo, the Inca place of origin in the Peruvian highlands, a few miles southwest of the valley of Cuzco. Manco married his sister Mama Ocllo, founding the Inca bloodline, and led his siblings into the valley of Cuzco, establishing the city of Cuzco and the Inca dynasty around 1200. According to the legend, at the end of his life, Manco Capac turned into a stone that became one of the most sacred *huacas* of the Incas.

— GORDON F. MCEWAN

MANCO INCA

Manco Inca (*b.* ca. 1516; *d.* 1545), Inca emperor during the early colonial period (reigned 1533–1545). Manco Inca was one of the sons of the emperor HUAYNA CAPAC. After the deaths of his brothers Atahualpa, HUASCAR, and the first Spanish puppet Inca, another brother named Topa Huallpa, Manco Inca was chosen by the Spanish conquistadores to rule as Inca emperor under their control. Crowned in 1533, he was treated badly by the Spanish, who abused him and his family and publicly insulted them. As a result, in 1536 he rebelled and fled with a large group of followers into the *montaña* region of eastern Peru, where he formed the rump state Vilcabamba. Leading a vigorous resistance to the Conquest, he was killed by the Spanish.

— GORDON F. MCEWAN

MANDU LADINO

Mandu Ladino (*d.* 1719), leader of one of the largest Indian rebellions in the Brazilian colonial period. Mandu Ladino was a "civilized" (ladino means "latinized" or "civilized") Indian, who had been educated by the Jesuits. The revolt began in 1712 because of Tapuia resentment of forced labor in support of a Portuguese garrison. The Tapuia also wanted to avenge Indian killings committed by the Portuguese commander, Antônio da Cunha Souto-Maior, and his men, whose brutality including decapitating Indians for sport.

The Tapuia wanted to avenge murders committed by Portuguese soldiers whose brutality included decapitating Indians for sport.

Mandu's 400 men sacked military garrisons, burned ranches, and killed Portuguese soldiers and settlers in Ceará, Piauí and Maranhão, but they spared missionaries. When Portuguese troops attacked a group of Tupi Indians, they too joined the rebellion and killed 88 people. Rebels destroyed at least 100 ranches, causing substantial losses.

Several Portuguese military expeditions against Mandu failed. The governor of Maranhão led one expedition in 1716 and surrounded Mandu's village, but a premature shot alerted the Indians and allowed them to escape. A rival group of the Tapuia, the Tobajara, defeated Mandu Ladino in a series of engagements, reducing his force to about 50 men. They killed him as he attempted to escape across a river.

— ROSS WILKINSON

MANRIQUE DE ZÚÑIGA, ALVARO

Alvaro Manrique de Zúñiga (marqués de Villamanrique; *d.* ca. 1593), seventh viceroy of New Spain. Villamanrique is thought by some to have been the low point of viceregal government in Mexico in the sixteenth century. Governing from 1585 to 1590, Villamanrique is credited with having begun the process whereby the northern frontier was pacified. He sought to increase royal control over the distribution and sale of mercury, WINE, and meat. In keeping with royal legislation of 1574, Villamanrique helped strengthen royal control over the Catholic church. Because of these and other policies many residents of New Spain opposed the viceroy. In 1588 a jurisdictional dispute with the neighboring Audiencia of New Galicia was portrayed in Madrid as approaching a civil war, a prospect that prompted the crown to remove Villamanrique and to subject him to a judicial review. In 1589 he was arrested by the bishop of Puebla, don Diego Romano, and returned to Spain, suffering the sequester of his personal possessions.

— JOHN F. SCHWALLER

MANSILLA, LUCIO VICTORIO

Lucio Victorio Mansilla (*b.* 23 December 1831; *d.* 8 October 1913), Argentine soldier, explorer, diplomat, and author. The second of four children, Mansilla was an undisciplined student and, as a consequence, his father pulled him from school and sent him as his representative on business trips to India, Egypt, and Europe. Mansilla's lasting influence lay in Argentina, however. Properly speaking, Mansilla was more of a tutor to than a member of the Argentine Generation of 1880, the group that secured the liberal hegemony responsible for the modernization of the country following the tyranny of José Manuel de ROSAS, which ended in 1852. (Mansilla's mother was Rosas's sister.) Nevertheless, Mansilla is in many respects an emblematic figure of 1880. Published in 1888, his *Entre-nos, causeries del jueves* (note the Francophile title) first appeared in the newspaper *Sud América,* important as an ideological platform during the period. Mansilla's underscoring of the urbane dilettantism, the drawing room and café society, and the emphasis on public, oral performance characteristic of the period makes these sketches undoubtedly a principal sociocultural document.

Nevertheless, Mansilla is most known for his *Una excursión a los indios ranqueles* (1870), for many generations of Argentines (typically, Argentine boys) one of the first works of national literature to be read. Mansilla recounts with attention to detail—backed up by extensive European learning that made him a symbol of Argentine cultural sophistication—the expedition he led in mid-1870 to indigenous settlements in an attempt to establish boundaries that would put an end to Indian raids against the creole settlers encroaching on those settlements. Based on the belief that an understanding of Indian society and culture would enhance pacification, *Una excursión* is of undeniable value as a sort of protoanthropolitical document and a predecessor of

Claude Lévi-Strauss's *Tristes tropiques*. This protoanthropolitical quality is relevant to what Mansilla's text cannot relate: how the 1879–1880 Conquest of the Desert imposed a violent military solution to indigenous opposition to white settlement of the pampas.

– DAVID WILLIAM FOSTER

MANSO DE MALDONADO, ANTONIO

Antonio Manso de Maldonado (*b.* ca. 1670; *d.* 5 November 1755?), military figure and president of the Audiencia of Santa Fe de Bogotá (1724–1731). Drawn from the officer corps of the Barcelona garrison, Manso went to America as *audiencia* president and governor and captain-general of the New Kingdom of Granada in order to conduct the *residencia* (end-of-tenure review) of the first viceroy of New Granada, Jorge de VILLALONGA (1719–1724), under whose leadership viceregal rule had failed to meet royal expectations, and to oversee the reestablishment of political order in the colony. Manso arrived in New Granada in February 1724 and immediately began to gather testimony on Villalonga. Although faced with voluminous contradictory reports, he largely absolved the former viceroy of wrongdoing. The difficulties of rule, the opposition to his authority, and his scandalous private life left the president bitter and anxious to return to a military post in Spain. Manso's administration is generally considered to have been ineffective or even inept. Returning to Spain in 1731, he served as governor of Cueta and then as inspector of Spanish and foreign infantry.

– LANCE R. GRAHN

MANSO DE VELASCO, JOSÉ ANTONIO

José Antonio Manso de Velasco (*b.* 1688; *d.* 5 January 1767), count of Superunda and viceroy of Peru, 1745–1761. Born in Logroño, Spain, Manso followed a military career from an early age, rising to lieutenant general. From 1737 to 1745 he governed Chile with vigor and ability, founding a number of settlements.

On 24 December 1744, King PHILIP V named Manso viceroy of Peru, the first of the military officers who governed the viceroyalty in place of the traditional noblemen and diplomats. After the earthquake and tidal wave that devastated Lima and Callao in 1746, Manso rebuilt the city and port. He put down an Indian rebellion in Huarochirí but had less success with that of Juan Santos. For his services, King Ferdinand VI named him count of Superunda in 1748. Manso established the royal tobacco monopoly (*estanco de tabaco*) in 1752 and reformed the mints in Lima and Potosí. His sixteen-year tenure, until 12 October 1761, was the longest of any Peruvian viceroy.

Returning to Spain, he was in Havana when the British captured the port in 1762. As the senior official present, although in transit, Manso was blamed for the debacle. Sentenced to exile in Granada, he died there in 1767, a sad end to a distinguished career.

– KENDALL W. BROWN

MANZANO, JUAN FRANCISCO

Juan Francisco Manzano (*b.* 1797; *d.* 19 July 1853), Cuban poet, narrator, and playwright. The only slave in Spanish American history to become an accomplished writer, Manzano is one of the founders of Cuba's national literature. Born to Toribio Manzano and María Pilar Infazón and slave to Doña Beatriz de Justiz, Marquesa de Justiz de Santa Ana, Manzano published his first collections of poems, *Poesías líricas,* in 1821, and *Flores pasageras* [*sic*] in 1830.

In 1835, at the request of the literary critic and opponent of slavery Domingo DEL MONTE, Manzano wrote his autobiography. In it, Manzano tells of his good and bad moments under slavery: he was treated as a privileged slave by his first mistress and was punished as a common one by the marquesa de Prado Ameno. Manzano concludes with his escape from his last mistress in 1817. Manzano learned to read and write on his own and his autobiography contains numerous grammatical errors. To make it more presentable, it was corrected but also altered by Anselmo Suárez y Romero, who made the slave's antislavery stance even stronger than Manzano intended. This version was translated into English by Richard Madden as "Life of the Negro Poet," and published in London in 1840. The original was lost until 1937.

Manzano learned to read and write on his own and his autobiography contains numerous grammatical errors.

After writing his autobiography and reading his autobiographical poem "Thirty Years" in the Del Monte literary circle in 1836, Del Monte and other Cuban intellectuals purchased Manzano's freedom for 800 pesos. Manzano continued to write poetry, publishing much of it in periodicals of the period, and he wrote a continuation of his autobiography, which was lost by Ramón de Palma. In addition, Manzano published his only play, *Zafira,* in 1842. In 1844 Manzano and Del

Monte were falsely accused by the mulatto poet Gabriel de la Concepción VALDÉS (Plácido) of participating in the antislavery Ladder Conspiracy. Manzano was imprisoned for one year. Once released, and fearful that his writing might implicate him in other liberal activities, he never wrote again.

— WILLIAM LUIS

MAR, JOSÉ DE LA

José de la Mar (*b.* 1778; *d.* 1830), one of the first military presidents of Peru (1827–1829). Born in Cuenca, Ecuador, he was trained as a royalist officer in Spain. He was appointed governor of the Callao fortress in 1816. After initially fighting against the naval attacks led by Lord Thomas Cochrane, La Mar capitulated to General José de SAN MARTÍN's independence forces in 1821. In 1822, La Mar received the title of grand marshal and, when San Martín left Peru, he was put in charge of the government until his dismissal because of his lack of success against the loyalist resistance. However, Simón BOLÍVAR later recruited La Mar to fight in the definitive battles of Junín and Ayacucho against the remaining Spanish forces. In 1827, La Mar was elected president but, while in a campaign against Colombian forces, a coup in 1829 forced him out of office and into exile. He died in San José, Costa Rica.

— ALFONSO W. QUIROZ

MARECHAL, LEOPOLDO

Leopoldo Marechal (*b.* 11 June 1900; *d.* 26 June 1970), Argentine novelist, poet, playwright, and essayist. Born in Buenos Aires, Leopoldo Marechal re-creates in his works his life experiences: his childhood in Buenos Aires, the countryside of Maipú, years spent as a teacher, and trips to Europe are revealed through the written word. His first book, *Los aguiluchos* (1922), is a poetic vision of enjoyment found in the beauty of nature. *Días como flechas* (1926), a second book of poetry, alludes to the biblical story of creation and shows greater structure and harmony in the platonic world constructed by the poet. Marechal collaborated on *Martín Fierro* (1924), a seminal literary review that reflected experimental and stylistic changes in literature as they occurred in Europe, and he also contributed to *Proa,* an avant-garde literary journal.

In his longest, most complex, and highly influential novel, *Adán Buenosayres* (1948), Marechal explores themes that remained constant throughout his works. As an effort to reinterpret biblical themes symbolically through a protagonist simultaneously representing Adam and a contemporary resident of Buenos Aires, the novel oscillates between the symbolic and the realistic, examining the transformations of Argentine society brought about by massive immigration and industrialization. In spite of a favorable review by Julio CORTÁZAR, then a critic and aspiring writer aligned with Victoria OCAMPO's *Sur,* the novel was coolly received and left unattended for more than twenty years. This has been attributed, in part, to Marechal's identification with the Peronist Party. More recent writers consider the novel as one of their primary influences and as a precursor to the technical and thematic literary experimentation of the 1960s.

El banquete de Severo Arcángelo (1965), considered to be Marechal's most important experimental novel, reflects the interplay of illusion and reality also found in plays such as *Antígona Vélez* (1951) and *Las tres caras de Venus* (1966), as well as in his essays, including *Cuaderno de navegación* (1966). Marechal is best known for his use of religious and mystical motifs, for the poetic qualities interwoven throughout his narrative and essays, and the epic narrative style of his poetry. He died in Buenos Aires.

— DANUSIA L. MESON

MARGIL DE JESÚS, ANTONIO

Antonio Margil de Jesús (*b.* 18 August 1657; *d.* 6 August 1726), missionary and founder of missionary colleges in Guatemala and New Spain. A native of Valencia, Spain, Antonio Margil was ordained a Franciscan priest in 1682 and the following year volunteered for service in New Spain. Shortly after his arrival in the New World, he was sent to Central America, where he served in Yucatán, Guatemala, Costa Rica, and Nicaragua from 1684 to 1697. In 1701, during a second tour in Guatemala, he founded the Colegio de Cristo Crucificado, a missionary college.

Following his appointment as guardian of the new missionary college of Nuestra Señora de Guadalupe de Zacatecas in 1706, Margil spent the remainder of his life working in northern New Spain. From his base at the college, he conducted missionary activity among both Spanish and Indian populations of Nayarit, Nueva Galicia, Zacatecas, Nuevo León, and Coahuila. He participated in the permanent occupation of Texas, founding three missions in the eastern part of the province in 1716–1717 and another in San Antonio in 1720.

— JESÚS F. DE LA TEJA

MARIÁTEGUI, JOSÉ CARLOS

José Carlos Mariátegui (*b.* 14 June 1894; *d.* 16 April 1930), Peruvian essayist and political thinker. Born in

Moquegua to a poor family, he was able to obtain only a primary education. In 1909, Mariátegui began as copy boy at the Lima daily *La Prensa;* four years later he was promoted to reporter. He worked as a columnist at several newspapers until his departure for Europe in 1919. There, he broadened his education and married an Italian girl. Won over by Marxism, Mariátegui returned to Peru in 1923, where he became an outstanding leftist personality while earning his livelihood as a free-lance writer. His house became a meeting place for avant-garde intellectuals and artists, university students, and labor leaders before and after both his legs were amputated because of an illness dating from his childhood. In 1925 he and his brother established a publishing house that printed two of his books. Mariátegui's prestige rests primarily on his *Siete ensayos de interpretación de la realidad peruana* (1928), translated into several languages; his editorship of the journal *Amauta* (1926–1930), the organization of the Peruvian General Federation of Workers (1929), and the founding of the Socialist Party of Peru (1928).

Traditionally, more emphasis has been placed on Mariátegui's contributions to politics than on his literary writings of his early youth (1914–1919) and mature publications (1920–1930). Lately, however, his articles on cultural events, short stories, poems, and plays, all written before 1920, have been reappraised because certain constant elements of this period remained in his later works: profound religiosity, romantic antipositivism, antagonism toward academia, exaltation of heroism, and heterodoxy. During the last seven years of his life Mariátegui molded European ideological and aesthetic currents in order to conform them to his own preferences and originality.

As a Marxist, Mariátegui viewed art as an

economic superstructure, conditioned by

class struggle.

Just as Mariátegui's perception of Marxism exerted influence on his religious ideas, so his religiosity in turn modified his political outlook; he added a mystical dimension to his interpretation of socialism. Religion acquired a new meaning: it became a belief in the supreme good, translated into revolutionary action. At the same time his eclectic-Marxist approach to literature led him beyond a strict analysis of a work. Mariátegui felt the need for a global perspective that would blend previously utilized points of view with the Marxist position

on art. He was a Marxist when he viewed art as an economic superstructure, conditioned by class struggle and subject to the changes in the market of intellectual work. He was an eclectic when, compelled by his basic precepts, he adopted heterodox ideas to check dogmatism, arbitrary authority, and the presumed infallibility of the high priests of intelligence, art, and politics. Mariátegui's open-ended ideology and his eclectic methodology of analysis presaged for him the ushering in of a new art, consonant with the socialist society he envisioned.

– EUGENIO CHANG-RODRÍGUEZ

MARIGHELA, CARLOS

Carlos Marighela (Marighella; *b.* ca. 1904; *d.* 4 November 1969), Brazilian architect of Latin American urban guerrilla warfare. Marighela was born in Salvador, the son of an Italian immigrant and, on his mother's side, the descendant of African slaves. He studied engineering at the Salvador Polytechnic but dropped out. He joined the Brazilian Communist Party (PCB) in 1927 and was imprisoned after the party's attempted armed revolt of 1935. Released in 1937, Marighela moved to São Paulo.

Disenchanted with the party's conservatism, he urged violent revolution and a guerrilla struggle. He was elected a deputy from the state of São Paulo to the new Congress in 1946, but was forced underground following the ban on the PCB in 1947. His 1960 acceptance of an invitation to Havana extended to the PCB leadership, which they refused, initiated a break with the party that was complete by 1964. Having rejected the revolutionary theory made popular by Ernesto (Che) GUEVERA as too spontaneous, and therefore doomed to failure, Marighela founded the Action for National Liberation (ALN) in 1968. His "Minimanual of the Urban Guerrilla," written in 1969 as a training manual for the ALN and other guerrilla groups, is a mechanistic theory of urban guerrilla warfare and the most famous document to emerge from the urban struggle in Brazil. Marighela was killed in a police ambush in São Paulo.

– MICHAEL L. JAMES

MARINELLO, JUAN

Juan Marinello (*b.* 2 November 1898; *d.* 27 March 1977), Cuban poet and essayist. Marinello was born in Jicotea in Las Villas Province and received degrees in public and civil law from the University of Havana, where he was an outstanding student, receiving a scholarship for a year at Madrid's Central University (1921–1922). He was politically active from his student days, organizing and taking part in student protests and groups. He was among the founders of the Hispano-Cuban Culture Institution (1926) and the publication *Revista de avance* (1927). He was imprisoned repeatedly for his political activities, especially during the regimes of Cuban presidents Gerardo MACHADO and Fulgencio BATISTA. A life-long dedicated Communist and political activist, he embraced the Cuban Revolution of 1959 and in turn was wholeheartedly supported and promoted by the CASTRO regime until his death. Marinello became president of the University of Havana in 1962 and Cuban ambassador to UNESCO in 1963; he was elected by the Central Committee of the Cuban Communist Party to help draft the constitution of the Cuban socialist state. He also received such international honors as the Lenin Medal (1970) and was a part of the executive council of UNESCO in 1974. Although Marinello cultivated poetry in his youth, he is mostly known today for his essays and literary criticism. He compiled several anthologies on Cuban literary giant José MARTÍ, whose prose deeply influenced him. His best-known works are the essays *Españolidad literaria de José Martí* (1942), *Creación y revolución* (1973), and *Escritos sociales* (1980).

— ROBERTO VALERO

MARIÑO, SANTIAGO

Santiago Mariño (*b.* 25 July 1788; *d.* 4 September 1854), Venezuelan Independence leader. From 1811 to 1821 the aristocratic General Mariño led patriot forces against Spanish rule, especially in his native eastern Venezuela, where he was the most powerful caudillo. Although he several times sought to assert his independence from Simón BOLÍVAR, Mariño served under him for many years and was Bolívar's chief of staff at the battle of Carabobo (1821), which assured Venezuela's independence from Spain. Later he was elected vice president of the ill-fated Gran Colombia confederation. After he lost the 1834 election for president of Venezuela, he rebelled unsuccessfully against the government of José María VARGAS (1835–1836). Defeated for the presidency again in 1850, Mariño closed his career as a caudillo by participating in the Revolution of May (1853) that sought to overthrow José Gregorio MONAGAS.

— WINFIELD J. BURGGRAAFF
INÉS QUINTERO

MARISOL

Marisol (Marisol Escobar; *b.* 1930), Venezuelan pop art sculptor. Born in Paris to Venezuelan parents, Marisol traveled with them in Europe until 1935; the family subsequently commuted between the United States and Venezuela. She moved to Los Angeles in 1946 and then to New York City, where she studied with Yasao Kuniyoshi and Hans Hofmann. In 1954 she turned from painting to terra-cotta sculpture inspired by pre-Columbian art. Since 1960 she has been best known for her portrayals of modern life and famous people in multifigure ensembles that blend media images, found objects, and blocky materials. Her statues use painted wood figures with other items, such as doorknobs, locks, or plaster. All of her works combine fantasy with reality, the grotesque with the humorous.

Self-Portrait *by Marisol in wood, plaster, marker, paint, graphite, human teeth, gold, and plastic. 1961–1962. (Collection Museum of Contemporary Art, Chicago)*

— WINTHROP R. WRIGHT

MARKHAM, CLEMENTS ROBERT

Clements Robert Markham (*b.* 20 July 1830; *d.* 30 January 1916), British writer, translator, geographer, and historian. Born in Stillingfleet, Yorkshire, Markham was the son of the Reverend David F. and Catherine Markham. He studied at Westminster School and then, in 1844, he entered the navy.

Markham traveled and studied widely in Latin America and Asia. He spent a year in Peru (1852–1853), where he examined Inca ruins, learned the Quechua and Spanish languages, and translated some materials into English. He served as secretary (1858–1886) and later president (1889–1909) of the Hakluyt Society and translated and edited twenty-two books for that organization. He was also elected secretary (1863–1888) and president (1893–1905) of the Royal Geographical Society. In 1892, Markham wrote his *History of Peru.* Meanwhile, he sought to use some of what he learned in Peru to assist British development in India. In addition, he studied the irrigation systems of southeastern Spain. Critics claimed that while he had a remarkable career and eventually was knighted by the British government, his interests were too diverse and his work sometimes weakened by spreading himself too thin over too wide an academic area.

– JACK RAY THOMAS

MÁRMOL, JOSÉ PEDRO CRISÓLOGO

José Pedro Crisólogo Mármol (*b.* 2 December 1817; *d.* 9 August 1871), Argentine poet, novelist, and journalist. Born in Buenos Aires, Mármol became one of the main literary figures of his time in the fight against the tyranny of General Juan Manuel de ROSAS. His works include *El poeta: Drama en cinco actos en verso* (1842), *A Rosas el 25 de mayo* (1843), *Amalia* (in two parts, 1844, 1850), and *Cantos del peregrino* (1846–1847). Most of his works were published in Uruguay. His complete works, including *Armonías* and *El cruzado, drama en cinco actos,* were published posthumously. His novel *Amalia* is considered one of the classics of Spanish American literature. It portrays life in Buenos Aires during the dictatorial regime of Juan Manuel de Rosas from the viewpoint of the opposition (the Unitarios).

Mármol suffered financial hardship during his childhood (the years he lived in Montevideo, his mother's city of origin) and after his mother's death in Brazil. His father distanced himself from his son, who returned to Buenos Aires and began his studies at the University of Buenos Aires.

In 1839, Mármol was jailed by the Rosas regime. In 1840 he was back in Montevideo, where he joined Esteban Echeverría's group of patriots in their fight against the Rosas government in Buenos Aires. His literary mentor was Juan Cruz VARELA, who also became his friend and supporter. Works from this period deal with the political battles against the tyranny of Rosas as well as with disagreements among the three political groups fighting Rosas: the Unitarios, the older political theoreticians among the Federales, and Echeverría's group, the Young Argentine Generation. In Rio de Janeiro, Mármol met Juan Bautista ALBERDI, who was returning from a trip to Europe. Alberdi convinced Mármol to go to Chile, where he could be more effective in the fight against Rosas, but Marmol's ship was not able to reach Chile. This experience is the source of his *Cantos del peregrino* (Songs of the Pilgrim).

After his abortive trip to Chile, Mármol returned to Brazil, where he remained until 1846. His exile, as well as that of his peers, ended in 1852, when Rosas was defeated by General Justo José de Urquiza's army in the battle of Caseros. During the years that followed, he wrote many articles on political issues, but he never completed the unfinished cantos of the *Cantos del peregrino.* Appointed director of the Public Library of Buenos Aires in 1858 (a post he held until his death), Mármol was much admired as the heir to the political ideas of Esteban ECHEVERRÍA. He is an important writer of the generation of the Romantics, whose life and work centered on beliefs in liberty and democracy for Argentina and South America.

– MAGDALENA GARCÍA PINTO

MARQUÉS, RENÉ

René Marqués (*b.* 4 October 1919; *d.* 22 March 1979), Puerto Rican author. René Marqués showed an early interest in theater and cinema as a child in his native Arecibo. While studying drama at Columbia University, he wrote *Palm Sunday* (1956) in English; the book deals with a tragic episode in Puerto Rico's history. After returning to his homeland, Marqués began a seventeen-year association with the Department of Education's community education program in 1950 as a writer and head of the publishing section. In 1958 the Puerto Rico Athenaeum awarded him first prize in four genres: short story, novel, essay, and drama. Marqués taught courses and theater workshops at the University of Puerto Rico, in Río Piedras.

Marqués's first staged work was *El sol y los MacDonald* (The sun and the MacDonald Family, 1950), a tragedy set in the southern United States. His most celebrated work is *La carreta* (The oxcart, 1952), about the trials of a family displaced from rural Puerto Rico to the island's capital and then to New York. Another masterwork of intense national and poetic symbolism is *Los soles truncos* (The truncated suns), staged in the First Puerto Rican Theater Festival in 1958. Historical events are featured in *La muerte no entrará en palacio* (Death shall not enter the palace, 1958) and *Mariana o el alba* (Mariana or the dawn, 1965); biblical events in *Sacrificio en el Monte Moriah* (Sacrifice on Mount Moriah, 1969) and *David y Jonatán. Tito y Berenice* (1970); and futuristic events in *El apartamento* (The apartment, 1965).

Marqués's writings, which include essays and criticism, theater, movie scripts, short stories, poetry, and a novel, show deep concern with the destiny of Puerto Rico and its dependence on the United States. The problem of national identity and cultural conflict is likewise central to his innovative books of short stories, *Otro día nuestro* (Another day, 1955), *En una ciudad llamada San Juan* (In a city called San Juan, 1960 and 1970), and *Inmersos en el silencio* (Immersed in silence, 1976).

– ESTELLE IRIZARRY

MÁRQUEZ, JOSÉ IGNACIO DE

José Ignacio de Márquez (*b*. 7 September 1793; *d*. 21 March 1880), president of New Granada (1837–1840). Born in Boyacá, Márquez received a law degree from the Colegio de San Bartolomé in Bogotá at age twenty. In 1821 he served in the Congress of Cúcuta and was elected presiding officer. In 1830–1831, Márquez served as finance secretary, and his 1831 *Memoria de hacienda* stands as the classic statement of protectionist thought in nineteenth-century Colombia. From March to October 1832, Márquez served as acting president pending the return to New Granada of Francisco de Paula SANTANDER, whereupon he assumed the vice presidency. In 1837 he was elected president by the Congress after a bitterly divisive three-way contest against José María OBANDO and Vicente Azuero. Although Márquez was a sound administrator with some mildly progressive ideas, his presidency was poisoned by the rivalry between his ministerial grouping and the defeated *progresistas* gathered around Santander. Márquez's purge of *progresista* officials further exacerbated political tensions. In 1839 a rebellion erupted in the southwestern Pasto region, initially directed against a Márquez decree on the suppression of small convents, but which soon came under the leadership of Obando. Throughout 1840 other regional rebellions, known collectively as the War of the Supremes and led by quasi-retired military men and disgruntled local elites, snowballed into a major crisis for the Márquez regime, especially after Santander's death in May 1840 removed a major

brake on *progresista* intrigues. On 7 October 1840, after receiving news of a government defeat at Polonia (near Socorro in the northeast), Márquez temporarily stepped down from the presidency—ostensibly for health reasons—but resurfaced in Popayán two weeks later, rallying government forces. Márquez never returned to office, but by early 1842 the rebellions were defeated. He later served as representative for Tunja (1842–1845), interior secretary (1845–1846), and senator for Bogotá (1847–1850).

– RICHARD STOLLER

MÁRQUEZ, LEONARDO

Leonardo Márquez (*b*. 1820; *d*. 1913), Mexican general. His military career began in the 1830s in the Texas campaign. During the War of the Reform (1858–1860), he fought on the side of the Conservatives and later to support the monarchy of MAXIMILIAN during the period of the French Intervention (1862–1867). He is best known for three episodes: his order to execute captured Liberal officers and some doctors and medical students after the battle of Tacubaya (11 April 1859), an act that earned him the nickname of "Tiger of Tacubaya"; his 1861 orders to execute Melchor OCAMPO, leading Liberal statesman, and General Leandro Valle; and his role in the mid-1867 siege of Querétaro, where he left Maximilian to find reinforcements and never returned, thus leaving the emperor to his fate. After the fall of the Empire, Márquez went into exile in Cuba. He returned to Mexico in the 1890s, but upon the ouster of Porfirio DÍAZ, he went back to Havana, where he died three years later.

– CHARLES R. BERRY

MARROQUÍN, FRANCISCO

Francisco Marroquín (*b*. ca. 1499; *d*. 9 April 1563), first bishop of Guatemala (1537–1563). Probably a native of Santander, Spain, Marroquín was a diocesan priest and a protégé of Francisco García de Loaysa, bishop of Osma and president of the Council of the Indies. In 1528, when Juan de ZUMÁRRAGA was named bishop of Mexico, Marroquín accompanied him to the New World. At the invitation of Pedro de ALVARADO, he settled in Guatemala in 1530 and served as a parish priest there. In 1532, Marroquín was appointed bishop of the new diocese of Guatemala, and following papal approval, he was consecrated at Mexico City in 1537. Marroquín spent the rest of his life in Guatemala. During his long episcopacy, he showed great interest in the conversion of the Indians, in the settlement and development of the colony, and in education, especially for the Spanish population. He served briefly as co-governor of Guatemala (1541–1542) and thereafter collaborated closely with the presidents of the Audiencia of Los Confines, which was established in 1542. From his earliest days in Central America, Marroquín had a long and stormy relationship with Bartolomé de LAS CASAS, with whom he disagreed regarding the best method of dealing with the native population.

– STEPHEN WEBRE

MARROQUÍN, JOSÉ MANUEL

José Manuel Marroquín (*b.* 6 August 1827; *d.* 19 September 1908), acting president (7 August 1898– 3 November 1898), president of Colombia (31 July 1900– 7 August 1904). Marroquín, a member of the upper class, is better remembered for his literary achievements than for his political performance. As a writer, he was concerned with form as well as substance, and published works on Spanish poetics and rhetoric. His poetry has been hailed as charming and assured. He was a charter member of the Mosaico group of *costumbristas* ("sketch of manners" writers) and probably was the best of them, employing gentle satire to prod and instruct his readers. He was also a novelist; his best-loved work in that genre, *El Moro* (1897), is a sentimental tale about a horse. As president and nominal head of a disintegrating faction of the Conservatives, Marroquín had the ill fortune to preside ineffectually over a Colombia being torn apart by the War of the Thousand Days (1899–1903) and dismembered by the U.S.-sponsored secession of Panama (1903).

– J. LEÓN HELGUERA

MARTÍ, AGUSTÍN FARABUNDO

Agustín Farabundo Martí (*b.* 1893; *d.* 1 February 1932), Salvadoran Communist leader and labor organizer. Martí's father, a moderate landholder in Teotepeque, reputedly adopted his surname in honor of the Cuban patriot José MARTÍ. Young Farabundo grew up surrounded by poor campesinos, with whom he identified later in life. His biographers describe him as a precocious, sensitive child who could not understand the differences between men. When his father decided against dividing the family land among his sons, Martí enrolled in the Faculty of Jurisprudence and Social Sciences at the National University. From the beginning, however, he felt frustrated by the lack of open discussion in his college and began independently reading anarchist and communist texts in the library. He became involved in the nascent labor movement and participated in the first strikes held in El Salvador (1920). At

this same time, he provoked a duel with his professor, Victoriano López Ayala, over the nature of cognition. For this, Martí and his friend José Luís Barrientos were exiled to Guatemala in 1920.

There are only fragmentary records of Martí's movements for the period from 1920 to 1925, but it is generally believed that he spent this time living among the Quiché Maya and making contacts among the rural salaried workers of Guatemala. He traveled frequently, working as a baker and bricklayer and doing other odd jobs in Guatemala and Honduras; he also served with the Red Battalions in Mexico, becoming a sergeant. Martí apparently took a pessimistic view of the latter country's still-young revolution, for he once remarked, "Disgracefully, the workers of Mexico have been captured by the bourgeoisie." In 1925, Martí and a few other dissident intellectuals founded the Central American Socialist Party in Guatemala City, which pledged to work for the unity of the isthmus. They had some brief success in persuading the legislatures of Guatemala, El Salvador, and Honduras to sponsor a tripartite republic but lacked support in Costa Rica and Nicaragua, and the party disintegrated.

Martí then found his way back to El Salvador, where he tried to raise the class consciousness of the rural workers. In 1928, President Alfonso QUIÑONES MOLINA exiled Martí to Nicaragua. This move allowed Martí to

Agustín Farabundo Martí arriving for detention in Los Angeles, 1931. (Bettmann Archive)

link up with Augusto César SANDINO and serve as personal secretary to the Nicaraguan patriot. Martí failed to convert Sandino to Marxism-Leninism and returned to El Salvador in 1929, but Martí retained the highest personal regard for Sandino. Shortly before his execution in 1932, Martí declared that there was no greater patriot in all of Central America than General Sandino. For his own part, Martí was a hardened internationalist and a devout admirer of Leon Trotsky; throughout the 1920s he wore a lapel pin that featured an image of Trotsky within a red star.

Martí spent the closing years of the 1920s in and out of Salvadoran jails, with intermittent periods of exile. He spent some time in California, where he met several sympathetic members of the International Labor Defense and secured a position as Salvadoran representative of the Socorro Rojo (Red Aid), a socialist labor organization. He made his way back to El Salvador in time for the December 1930 election campaign. That year, Martí and a few close associates, including Miguel Mármol, founded the Communist Party of El Salvador. Contrary to the established Moscow-directed approach, the Salvadoran Communists refused to participate in elections and instead concentrated their efforts on organizing the dispossessed rural peasantry. The Communists initially lost ground to the reformist experiment of President Arturo ARAUJO, but gained strength after a coup in December 1931 brought the military to power. A mass uprising was planned for 22 January 1932, but the government uncovered the plot and executed Martí, along with two student accomplices, on 1 February. The period of repression that followed is known as the Matanza, or massacre. In 1980 several guerrilla groups joined forces and christened their umbrella organization the Farabundo Martí Liberation Front (FMLN) in honor of their model.

— KAREN RACINE

MARTÍ Y PÉREZ, JOSÉ JULIÁN

José Julián Martí y Pérez (*b.* 28 January 1853; *d.* 19 May 1895), father of Cuba's independence. Even if he had done nothing for his native land, Martí would have gone down in history as a great literary figure. But besides being a poet, journalist, and orator of genius, Martí was a revolutionary and a politician, the architect and organizer of Cuba's 1895–1898 war against Spanish colonialism. For this reason he is best known as the apostle of Cuba's independence. Cubans today revere his memory and regard his teachings as the living gospel of the fatherland.

EARLY CAREER. Born in Havana of poor Spanish immigrants, Martí was able to go to high school owing to the support of Rafael María Mendive, an enlightened schoolmaster whose influence outweighed all others on his early youth. Martí was still in school when the first Cuban war of independence, the Ten Years' War, broke out in 1868. Like many of his classmates, he embraced the cause of freedom. In January 1869, aged sixteen, he founded his first newspaper, which he appropriately named *La Patria Libre* (Free Fatherland). Shortly afterward he was arrested and sentenced to six years of hard labor in a rock quarry, merely because he wrote a letter denouncing a pro-Spanish fellow student as an "apostate." After serving only a few months, however, Martí's sentence was commuted to banishment to Spain, where he arrived early in 1871. That same year he published his celebrated essay *El presidio político en Cuba,* a passionate indictment of conditions in Cuba's prisons.

After this, his first exile (during which he completed his schooling at the universities of Madrid and Saragossa), Martí revisited Cuba only twice before 1895: in 1877 for less than two months, and again from 31 August 1878 to 25 September 1879. Altogether Martí spent twenty-three years away from the land of his birth, during which period he worked as a journalist in Mexico, the United States, and Venezuela, and as a professor in Guatemala. Nevertheless, for the most part he made his home in New York, which was the center of his activities from 1881 until just before his death in 1895.

LITERARY WORK. It was during this period that Martí gained recognition throughout the hemisphere, partly as a chronicler of life in the United States. He was a keen observer of the grandeur and miseries of the nation during the Gilded Age, and he reported what he saw in his columns for the *Opinión Nacional* of Caracas, *La Nación* of Buenos Aires, and more than twenty other Spanish American newspapers. In 1884 Martí was famous enough to be appointed vice-consul of Uruguay in New York. By this time he had become one of the forerunners of literary modernism in Spanish with the publication of *Ismaelillo* (1882), a collection of poems for his only son. In 1889 Martí delighted Spanish-speaking youngsters with his *Edad de Oro,* a magazine for children written entirely by him, and in 1891 he published his *Versos sencillos,* which in many ways marks the culmination of his poetic career. Martí's literary output at this point of his life was enormous and included several translations from English, a not very successful novel, and a romantic play. Nowhere is his genius revealed, though, as in the highly personal style of his articles and essays, his mesmerizing speeches, his political documents, and even his private correspondence. His prose is among the best in the Spanish language.

CUBAN INDEPENDENCE. Martí spent many of his years in exile plotting the independence of Cuba, a Herculean task. Not only did he have to hold in check those who favored the autonomy of the island under Spain or who endorsed its annexation to the United States, but he also had to cope with the threat of American expansionism and the authoritarian proclivities of the veteran generals of the Ten Years' War. Martí maintained that in order to avoid these pitfalls, Cuba's struggle for independence would have to be brief (so as to minimize the chances for U.S. intervention) and conducted with "republican method and spirit" (in order to prevent the island from falling prey to a military dictatorship after independence). Somewhere around 1887 he concluded that he would have to assume political leadership if these ends were to be attained. For this purpose, in 1892 Martí formed the Cuban Revolutionary Party, an essentially U.S.-centered organization through which he subsequently channeled his efforts to overthrow Spanish domination in Cuba. For more than three years, he worked untiringly until, by early 1895, he was ready to launch a new and more formidable rebellion on the island. The veteran generals would still be in command of the expeditions to sail from Fernandina, Florida, but they were now under the authority of the party and its leader.

At the last minute, however, U.S. authorities seized the boats and the war materials that Martí had clandestinely procured, and he could only join the fighting that had already started in Cuba on the sufferance of the military leaders. His leadership role declined as a result of the Fernandina fiasco. Once in Cuba, the generals challenged the principle of civil supremacy so dear to him, and he began to think of returning to the United States in order to cope with the threat of military authoritarianism that he had long feared. Thus, he was in a somber mood when he was killed in a skirmish of little consequence. The struggle continued, but his political doctrine had very little influence on subsequent developments. After the war ended, there were very few who thought that his statue should be erected in Havana's Central Park.

INTELLECTUAL AND POLITICAL LEGACY. Gradually, however, Martí became better known in Cuba. When the island was swept by a shock wave of nationalism in the late 1920s and early 1930s, he was vindicated, emerging as the political, moral, and spiritual mentor of a new generation of Cubans. It was at this time that the cultlike Cuban attitude toward Martí and his preachings took on its present form and substance.

Martí was so prolific that it is nearly impossible to offer an adequate insight into his thought. Often what may be considered as representative ideas are offset by completely different or even contradictory ones. For this reason he appears to be ambivalent on many subjects, while in other cases it seems that he simply refused to record an opinion. We look in vain, for example, for a passage stating his political program, the political system he preferred, or his constitutional doctrine.

Martí was not anti-American, nor did he ever intend to make an enemy of the United States, despite his well-known anti-imperialist stance.

It is not surprising, therefore, that leftist scholars and politicians should have found a Marxist slant in his writings. But Martí rejected the notion of the class struggle as well as the high level of violence employed by some of the labor leaders of his time. Furthermore, he condemned the idea of entrusting to the state the satisfaction of man's material needs. Therefore, while Martí may have sympathized with Marx's concern for the worker, he certainly was no Marxist.

Martí was not anti-American, nor did he ever intend to make an enemy of the United States, despite his well-known anti-imperialist stance. If anything, his view of the country, which he chose as his haven in exile, was critical, in the strictest sense of the word. He was aware of the sordid facets of life within its boundaries—and denounced them. But Martí also proclaimed his admiration for the dynamism and industry of Americans as well as his esteem for American thinkers and writers and "the wonderful men who framed the constitution of the United States of America." As Martí himself once said, he loved the land of Lincoln as much as he feared the land of Francis Cutting (a nineteenth-century adventurer who once tried to annex northern Mexico to the United States).

Although Martí was a pugnacious nationalist, when he worried about Cutting-like predators he was thinking not only about Cuba, but about Spanish America as well. He envisioned Spanish America as forming, from the Rio Grande to Patagonia, one single, colossal nation, which he called "our America," and which in his view would have a great future, "not as a conquering Rome but as a hospitable nation." Like Simón BOLÍVAR, therefore, he thought in hemispheric terms, and that is no doubt the reason why Rubén DARÍO, the great Nicaraguan poet, said that he belonged not to Cuba alone, but to "an entire race, an entire continent."

— JOSÉ M. HERNÁNDEZ

MARTÍNEZ, ANTONIO J.

Antonio J. Martínez (*b.* 1793; *d.* 1867), Roman Catholic priest, publisher, and political leader of New Mexico under Spanish, Mexican, and U.S. rule. Born in Abiquiu, New Mexico, Martínez was widowed after only one year of marriage. He subsequently studied for the priesthood in Durango, Mexico. As a pastor in Taos, Padre Martínez founded schools and published books and a newspaper called *El Crepúsculo de la Libertad* (The Twilight of Liberty). His was the first printing press west of the Mississippi River. Martínez's labors were characterized by a deep conviction about the importance of education for his people. He is best known for the often bitter controversies between himself and the first archbishop of Santa Fe, Jean-Baptiste Lamy, which exemplified the cultural conflicts between New Mexico (Hispano) Catholics and the European, especially French, priests sent to work in New Mexico after the territory passed to the United States in 1848. The clash revolved around the efforts of the Europeans, who viewed their ministry as being both religious and social, to Americanize the New Mexico Hispanics. They urged the New Mexicans to abandon their "old-fashioned" Catholicism for a more "modern" Jansenist Catholicism appropriate for Catholics in a Protestant nation. The Europeans, who were trained for the ministry in the austere seminaries of France, knew little about the deep cultural roots of New Mexican Catholicism. Padre Antonio J. Martínez has come to be viewed as a hero of New Mexico history and a forerunner of the Hispanic or Latino civil rights movement of the 1960s.

— ALLAN FIGUEROA DECK, S.J.

MARTÍNEZ, ESTEBAN JOSÉ

Esteban José Martínez (*b.* 9 December 1742; *d.* 28 October 1798), Spanish naval officer, explorer of the Pacific Northwest. Born in Seville, Martínez studied at the Real Colegio de San Telmo. He was second pilot in the Department of San Blas in 1773 and sailed as provisional ensign with Juan Pérez to southern Alaska the following year. From 1775 to 1785 he commanded supply ships that sailed to Loreto, San Diego, Monterey, and San Francisco. Martínez was promoted to first pilot in 1781; commanded the *Princesa* and the *Favorita,* and met the expedition of Jean François de La Pérouse at Monterey in 1786; and became an ensign in 1787. With González López de Haro he searched the Northwest Coast for foreign encroachment as far as Unalaska and Kodiak islands. Martínez was commandant of Nootka in 1789 and, after fortifying it, returned to San Blas in December of that year. Subsequently, the British captain James Colnett was arrested for encroachment upon assumed Spanish territory, an event that led to conflict and to the convention of 1790. Martínez was posted to La Coruña in 1792 and returned to San Blas, as a lieutenant, in 1795. He died in Loreto. Among the proposals he had made to the crown were the occupation of the Sandwich Islands (modern Hawaii) and the establishment of a sea otter trade in the Californias.

— W. MICHAEL MATHES

MARTÍNEZ, JUAN JOSÉ

Juan José Martínez (*b.* ca. 3 January 1782; *d.* ca. 25 July 1863), a hero of Mexican independence whose existence has been widely questioned. When Miguel HIDALGO besieged Guanajuato in September 1810, the Spaniards fortified themselves in the Alhóndiga de Granaditas granary. According to the legend, Martínez, a miner nicknamed Pípila (Turkey), joined the insurgents in their attack on the Alhóndiga. In the heart of battle he reached the great door of the granary by crawling under the protection of slab and set fire to the building, thus allowing the insurgents to enter. Lucas ALAMÁN, the greatest historian of the epoch, doubted that Martínez had existed, but his critic, José María de Liceaga, insisted on the veracity of the tale. In recent years, the Guanajuato historian Fulgencio Vargas has published articles claiming to possess documents that prove the existence of the hero.

— JAIME E. RODRÍGUEZ O.

MARTÍNEZ, TOMÁS

Tomás Martínez (*b.* 21 December 1820; *d.* 12 March 1873), president of Nicaragua (1859–1867). In his early life Martínez was involved in commerce and agriculture, only later turning to the military. He became president in 1859, after the ouster of U.S. filibuster William WALKER during the National War (in which Martínez emerged as a central figure). His administration developed a program that included the reorganization of agriculture, increased coffee cultivation, state support for secular schools, industrial growth, limitations on government monopolies, separation of church and state, abolition of the death penalty, establishment of trial by jury, and a plan for direct elections.

Ironically, although his administration ushered in thirty years of Conservative Party rule, his plan for direct elections ultimately caused the Conservative Party to split into four factions, creating a tumultuous situation that led to the installation of Liberal José Santos ZELAYA as president in 1893.

— SHANNON BELLAMY

MARTÍNEZ DE HOZ, JOSÉ ALFREDO

José Alfredo Martínez de Hoz (*b.* 10 July 1895), Argentine business magnate and former finance minister. Born in Buenos Aires to one of the wealthiest and most traditional families in Argentina, Martínez de Hoz occupied important economic posts during the governments of Arturo FRONDIZI and José María GUIDO. Former president of the National Grain Board and head of the country's largest steel company, Acindar, he was an important member of a giant conglomerate, the Roberts Group. He is infamous as the architect of the last military regime's (1976–1983) economic plan. As its finance minister from April 1976 to March 1981, Martínez de Hoz dismantled the protection for domestic industry, deregulated the financial sector, and curbed the power of Peronist trade unions. Convinced that state controls were the primary obstacles to economic growth, he deindustrialized the country, increased unemployment rates to unprecedented levels, and soon overvalued the currency, provoking massive balance-of-trade deficits and capital flight. The combination left Argentina with a $40 billion external debt. Martínez de Hoz was subsequently charged and convicted under the government of Raúl ALFONSÍN (1983–1989) for corruption and fraud.

– JEREMY ADELMAN

MARTÍNEZ ESTRADA, EZEQUIEL

Ezequiel Martínez Estrada (*b.* 14 September 1895; *d.* 5 November 1964), Argentine writer. Born of Spanish parents in San José de la Esquina, province of Santa Fe, Martínez Estrada was one of the most important Argentine writers of the twentieth century. Some consider him as influential as Domingo Faustino SARMIENTO had been for the nineteenth century. His reputation is even more remarkable considering that he had little formal schooling and no university education.

With Martínez Estrada an intellectual movement began in Argentina, the major preoccupation of which was the reassessment of the country's character following the political decadence that began after the military coup of 1930. His book *Radiografía de la pampa* (1933; The X-Ray of the Pampa) is a condemnation of the elite for trying to impose European modes on the Argentine reality, rejecting what Martínez Estrada considered native traits. In this book he dissected Argentine society and searched for its true nature, as it struggled between urban and rural models. When he raised these questions, he brought everything into the open; he criticized those who emphasized only fragments of Argentine life. Basically, his works represented a search for the essence of Argentina's soul, and, therefore, he called on the Argentines not merely to evaluate their past but also to change the way in which they assessed it.

His literary work is characterized by a great sense of pessimism about the country's future as a result of the political decadence that had come about since 1930. His pessimism grew with the military revolts of the 1940s and with Juan Domingo PERÓN's anti-intellectual attitude. Martínez Estrada went into self-imposed exile from Buenos Aires to Bahía Blanca and from there to Mexico and Cuba. He wrote two other important books, *The Head of Goliath* (1940) and *Sarmiento* (1946), which also deal with social and political thoughts about Argentine society.

– JUAN MANUEL PÉREZ

MARTORELL, ANTONIO

Antonio Martorell (*b.* 18 April 1939), Puerto Rican artist. Martorell received his early training with Julio Martín Caro in Madrid (1961–1962). He studied printmaking with Lorenzo HOMAR from 1962 to 1965 at the Institute of Puerto Rican Culture's graphics workshop in New York City. In 1968 he founded the Taller Alacrán (Scorpion's Workshop). Martorell has also worked as a set designer, book illustrator, caricaturist, textile and graphic designer, art critic, and writer. Since 1985, he has worked collaboratively with Rosa Luisa Márquez as performer and set designer for graphic-theatrical performance pieces. He has taught at the National School of Fine Arts in Mexico City, the Institute of Puerto Rican Culture, and the Universidad Interamericana in San Germán, Puerto Rico. His posters, paintings, and installations have been exhibited internationally, and he has won numerous awards.

– MIRIAM BASILIO

MASFERRER, ALBERTO

Alberto Masferrer (*b.* 24 July 1868; *d.* 4 September 1932), Salvadoran journalist and political figure, most famous for his *mínimum vital,* a nine-point program designed to provide a minimum standard of living to his countrymen. As a youth Masferrer displayed exceptional sensitivity to the social problems he encountered throughout Central America. He objected to the outmoded, restrictive system of education and the appalling conditions in which many Salvadorans, particularly those in rural areas, lived. His basic ideas, present in their most rudimentary form in his first work, *Niñerías* (1892), were refined over the next four decades.

In 1895, President Rafael Gutiérrez appointed Masferrer consul to Costa Rica. Here he also began to dabble in journalism and forge links with the nascent labor movement, two interests that were to continue throughout his life. He was reassigned to Chile in 1901 and Belgium in 1911 but left the diplomatic corps in 1914 to pursue a career in journalism. Masferrer returned to El Salvador in 1916 and quickly espoused the cause of the working classes. In 1918 he organized the First Workers' Congress, which featured the future president Arturo ARAUJO, a landlord, as its keynote speaker. Throughout the 1920s, Masferrer continued to campaign for an improved standard of living and to achieve official respect for the working classes. He served as the editor of several short-lived journals before founding *La Patria* in 1928. In his opening editorial, Masferrer pledged that his newspaper would describe the life of Salvadorans as it actually was and committed himself to working for "the health, welfare, prosperity, culture, liberty, peace and contentment of all." He wrote a series of articles known collectively as "El mínimum vital" (1928–1929) which called for adequate food, housing, clothing, education, work, recreation, and justice for all Salvadorans. In the 1930 campaign for the presidency Masferrer endorsed Arturo Araujo, who borrowed Masferrer's concept of *vitalismo* as his platform. Araujo easily won office after General Maximiliano HERNÁNDEZ MARTÍNEZ withdrew from the race, but his term lasted less than a year. Masferrer quickly realized that the Araujo administration was corrupt and powerless to effect real reforms, and left for self-exile in Guatemala. Upon hearing of the 1932 Matanza, wherein thousands of Salvadorans were killed by government troops, Masferrer became despondent and sank into deep depression. He died of a cerebral hemorrhage later that year.

Masferrer was a reformer who did not seek to tear down the whole social order; he merely wanted to rid it of its worst abuses.

Masferrer is an important figure in the intellectual history of Central America. His thought is part of a broad anti-positivist movement that flourished in Latin America in the early decades of the twentieth century. Though his writings shied away from addressing directly the need for political reform, Masferrer's ideas included a clear social and economic agenda which implied that such changes were needed for a more smoothly functioning society. In his mind any truly national culture had an obligation to provide for its people their minimum spiritual and material well-being. His

ideas reveal a strong affinity with the Roman Catholic church after *Rerum Novarum,* the 1891 papal encyclical that rejected both capitalism and socialism as paths for human development. His notion of an organic, harmonious nation that was hierarchical in organization and functioned along the lines of Christian charity and the dignity of all work is clearly typical of the intellectual flirtation with fascism that characterized so many thinkers of his generation. Masferrer was a reformer who did not seek to tear down the whole social order; he merely wanted to rid it of its worst abuses. Thus his ideas led directly into the Salvadoran Christian Democratic movement that flourished in the 1960s and similarly sought to improve general conditions through cooperation and conciliation rather than revolution. Masferrer remains a popular figure in El Salvador today.

– KAREN RACINE

MASSERA, JOSÉ PEDRO

José Pedro Massera (*b.* 1866; *d.* 1942), Uruguayan philosopher, professor, and politician. From 1887 to 1927 Massera taught philosophy at the University of the Republic in Montevideo. His only published work during his lifetime was *Reflexiones sobre Rodó* (1920), but various of his essays were published posthumously, on subjects such as the works of Carlos Vaz Ferreira and Ribot, moral values, and moral philosophy. In 1937 he gave up teaching to pursue a political career in the national Senate.

– WILLIAM H. KATRA

MASTROGIOVANNI, ANTONIO

Antonio Mastrogiovanni (*b.* 26 July 1936), Uruguayan composer. Born in Montevideo, Mastrogiovanni began musical studies with Nieves Varacchi and Héctor TOSAR. He studied composition under Carlos ESTRADA at the National Conservatory of Music (1963–1968), and was technical director of the music-publishing project at the conservatory. His *Monotemáticas* for violin and piano was well received at its premiere during the Second Latin American Festival of Montevideo (1966). He was awarded several prizes by the SODRE, the Association of Music Students, and the National Conservatory, and was honored by the Uruguayan Ministry of Culture (1960, 1961, 1963). *Sinfonía de Cámara* for orchestra (1965) and the piano concerto (1967) belong to that period. With *Contrarritmos* (1967), for two string orchestras and percussion, Mastrogiovanni shifted toward new composition techniques, in recognition of which he received a scholarship at the Latin American Center of Advanced Music Studies of the Di

Tella Institute in Buenos Aires, where from 1969 to 1970 he studied under Gerardo GANDINI (analysis), Francisco Kröpfl (composition), and von Reichenbach (electronic music). He received grants from the Organization of American States that enabled him to travel to Rome and Mexico to explore new composition techniques. His *Reflejos* and *Secuencial I* both won the Dutch Gaudeamus Foundation Prize (1970; 1971) and were premiered by the Utrech Symphony Orchestra. Other works of his include *Secuencial II* for tape (1970) and *Maderas* for ensemble (1974).

Since 1971, Mastrogiovanni's works have premiered throughout South America and Europe and have earned the composer awards both at home and abroad. He has taught at several prestigious institutions, including the Conservatorio Nacional de Música in Montevideo (1972–1973), the Conservatorio Nacional Juan José Landaeta in Caracas (1979–1988), and Montevideo's Escuela Universitaria de Música (1986–1993), where he also has served as director since 1988. In addition to composing commissioned works and conducting vocal and instrumental ensembles in Venezuela and Uruguay, he founded and organized an annual competition for advanced music students in Montevideo.

– SUSANA SALGADO

MATA, EDUARDO

Eduardo Mata (*b*. 5 September 1942; *d*. 4 January 1995), Mexican-born composer and conductor. His studies at the National Conservatory of Mexico focused on percussion and composition (with Carlos CHÁVEZ and Julian Orbón). He studied conducting with Max Rudolf and Eric Leinsdorf at the Berkshire Music Center in 1964. Mata has concentrated less on composition since his meteoric rise as a conductor, beginning in 1965 with orchestras at Guadalajara and the Free University of Mexico, and followed with Phoenix (1971–1977) and Dallas (1977–1991). He was appointed Fine Arts Opera director in Mexico City (1983) and was a guest conductor of the London Symphony Orchestra.

– ROBERT L. PARKER

MATAMOROS Y GURIDI, MARIANO

Mariano Matamoros y Guridi (*b*. 14 August 1770; *d*. 3 February 1814), Mexican Independence leader and corevolutionary of Father Miguel HIDALGO. Born in Mexico City, Matamoros studied theology at the Colegio de Santa Cruz de Tlatelolco. In 1811, he was interim curate of Jantetelco. He offered his services to the insurgent chief José María MORELOS, who named him a colonel and commissioned him to raise military forces. Mata-

moros accompanied Morelos to Taxco and was at Cuautla during the siege by the royalist army of Félix CALLEJA. Ordered to obtain provisions, on 21 April 1812, Matamoros and 100 dragoons broke through the royalist lines. When Morelos fled Cuautla, he dispatched Matamoros to reorganize the insurgent forces at Izúcar. A gifted military commander, Matamoros was a close adviser of Morelos during the Oaxaca campaign and was promoted to field marshal and later to lieutenant general. He was with Morelos at the abortive attack on Valladolid, Morelia, in 1814. Later, at Puruarán, Matamoros was captured by the royalists and executed.

– CHRISTON ARCHER

MATIENZO, BENJAMÍN

Benjamín Matienzo (*b*. 9 April 1891; *d*. May 1919), pioneer Argentine aviator. Born in San Miguel de Tucumán, son of a Bolivian-born jurist of the same name, Matienzo followed a military career. He became an aviation enthusiast at an early age and attended the Escuela de Aviación Militar in Palomar. In May 1919 he and two companions set out to fly over the Andes to Chile. Bad weather caused his companions to return to Mendoza; Matienzo, however, pushed ahead. His plane was forced down near Las Cuevas. While attempting to walk into the town, he froze to death. A monument commemorates his determination and sacrifice.

– RONALD C. NEWTON

MATIENZO, JOSÉ NICOLÁS

José Nicolás Matienzo (*b*. 4 October 1860; *d*. 3 January 1936), Argentine jurist and statesman. Matienzo, a native of San Miguel de Tucumán, specialized in constitutional law. He was a professor at the universities of Buenos Aires and La Plata, wrote extensively on constitutional matters (see his *Cuestiones de derecho público argentino,* 1924, and *Lecciones de derecho constitucional,* 1926), and served as a member of the Supreme Court of the province of Buenos Aires (1910–1913) and as attorney general (*procurador general*) (1917–1922). He also drafted a project for a criminal code, in collaboration with Norberto Piñero and Rodolfo RIVAROLA. A liberal of reformist inclinations, he was the first president of the National Department of Labor (1907–1909). In 1910 Matienzo published *El gobierno representativo federal en la República Argentina,* a detailed study of the workings of the country's political system, which he described as oligarchical. He shared with other members of his generation, particularly his friend Rivarola, editor of the *Revista Argentina de Ciencias Políticas,* a passionate interest in the reform of the country's political system. In 1922 he was appointed minister of the interior by President Marcelo ALVEAR, and in 1931 he was a candidate for the vice presidency on the ticket headed by Augustín Pedro JUSTO. He was elected to the National Senate in 1932, where he remained until his death in 1936.

— EDUARDO A. ZIMMERMANN

MATOS, GREGÓRIO DE

Gregório de Matos (*b.* 20 December 1636; *d.* 1696), Brazilian poet and satirist. Born in Salvador, Bahia, the son of a rich Portuguese immigrant and a lady of the local aristocracy, Matos was educated in Jesuit schools and then sent to law school in Coimbra, Portugal, in 1652. He graduated in 1661 and, after a period in Brazil, took up practice in Portugal as a guardian of orphans and as a criminal judge. He remained in the metropolis until his return to his native city in 1681. After taking minor religious orders, he was appointed by the archbishop to positions in the bishop's office and the treasury department.

His calling notwithstanding, Matos led a notorious bohemian life and earned a reputation locally as a poet and social observer. His verse was of three fundamental types: devotional, amorous, and satirical. He was especially sensitive to moral decay, corruption, exploitation, and injustice. Many of his poems are quasi-journalistic in nature, commenting on local events and personages. His biting verse earned him the nickname "Boca do Inferno" (Mouth of Hell) and the disfavor of powerful citizens. His unrelenting critical writing led to his exile in Angola (1686–1695). He died in Recife, Brazil, one year after his return from banishment.

Matos is generally considered the most important poet of the baroque period in Brazil. His work is an excellent example of the literary practice of his time, a style of conceit and formal play involving liberal borrowing and imitation. He did not publish a book in his lifetime; his poems circulated in manuscript form or were recited. It was not until the late nineteenth century that his work became widely known. The Brazilian Academy of Letters published his works in six volumes (1923–1933); a later commercial edition (1969) has seven volumes. The attribution of many texts, however, remains in dispute.

— CHARLES A. PERRONE

MATTA ECHAURREN, ROBERTO SEBASTIÁN ANTONIO

Roberto Sebastián Antonio Matta Echaurren (*b.* 1912), Chilean painter and printmaker. Known simply as "Matta," he was born in Santiago, Chile, and received his early education from French Jesuits. He went on to earn an architectural degree in 1933 from the Catholic University in Santiago, Chile. He took drawing classes in Santiago at the Academia de Bellas Artes. Matta left Chile in 1935 for Paris, where he worked for the architect Le Corbusier until 1937, by which time he had become a member of the surrealist group. He lived and worked in New York from 1939 to 1948. Shunned by the artistic community upon his return to Paris, he went to Rome. In the late 1950s he slowly regained acceptance in Paris, where, having become a French citizen, he spends part of each year. Matta resists being labeled a Latin American artist; rather, he sees himself in a universal context, as one who has integrated into his art elements of the many cultures with which he has come into contact.

— KATHERINE CLARK HUDGENS

MATTO DE TURNER, CLORINDA

Clorinda Matto de Turner (Grimanesa Martina Matto Usandivaras; *b.* 11 November 1852; *d.* 25 October 1909), Peruvian novelist and journalist. She was born and raised in the ancient city of Cuzco. The family lived in the city as well as in the Hacienda Paullu Chico. Her mother died when she was ten years old, and she was sent to a Catholic school to be educated. At age eighteen she left school to look after her younger brothers. She learned English to prepare herself for study in the United States, but failed to travel to that country. She married Joseph Turner, an Englishman, in 1871. The couple first settled in the small town of Tinta, in the province of Canchis, which later served as the model for the imaginary Killac, the city of her most widely read work, *Aves sin nido* (Birds Without Nest). While living in Tinta she developed two of her major intellectual preoccupations: defending the rights of women and protesting the cruel exploitation of the Indians.

In 1876 Matto returned to Cuzco, where she directed the literary magazine *El Recreo del Cuzco* (Cuzco's Entertainment). As an active journalist during these years, she became a well-known celebrity in Peru. She traveled to Lima in 1877 and was warmly received by the intellectual elite. She attended the *salón literario* organized by Juana Manuela Gorriti and was hailed as an important literary voice of Peruvian letters.

When Matto's husband died in 1881, leaving her in dire economic straits, she returned to Tinta to manage her hacienda personally. During this time Chile and Peru were engaged in the War of the Pacific, which left the defeated Peru devastated. Matto aided her compatriots by raising funds for military equipment and do-

Clorinda Matto de Turner, Lima, 1890. (Photo by Eugène Courret/ Archivo Caretas)

ustrado, of which Matto was appointed director in 1889. She insisted that the magazine reflect Peruvian concerns above all others. Together with writer Manuel GONZÁLEZ PRADA, she became known as a defender of the Indians. In 1889 she also published her best-known novel, *Aves sin nido.* It was the first indigenous novel that portrayed the life and social condition of the Indian population of Peru and the first favorable literary representation of the Indian cause, including a partial history of the abuse of the Indian by whites, mestizos, and the clergy in Spanish America. In 1892, Matto published her only play, *Hima sumac.* In 1893 she published *Leyendas y recortes.* Her other novels, *Indole* (1891) and *Herencia* (Inheritance, 1895), continue the Indian theme. *Boreales, miniaturas y porcelanas,* published in Buenos Aires in 1902, documents the difficult years of political turmoil in Peru and how they affected Matto. In 1895 she left Lima for Buenos Aires, where she wrote for *La Nación* and *La Prensa.* She founded the magazine *El Búcaro Americano* in 1897 and traveled to Europe in 1908. Her memoirs are collected in *Viaje de recreo* (Vacation Trips, 1910). She died in Buenos Aires of pneumonia, and her remains were returned to Peru in 1924.

– MAGDALENA GARCÍA PINTO

MAUÁ, VISCONDE DE

Visconde de Maúa (Irineu Evangelista de Souza; *b.* 28 December 1813; *d.* 21 October 1889), Brazilian merchant, banker, industrialist, railroad magnate, rancher, and national politician who rose from obscure beginnings to become a major protagonist in imperial Brazil's banking, transportation, and industrial infrastructure. Born in Rio Grande do Sul, Maúa initiated his business-entrepreneurial career in Rio de Janeiro at age eleven as a cashier in a cloth store and was later employed in a British firm, where he learned British business methods and successively held the positions of partner and sole manager by the 1830s, when the firm's founder returned to England.

Maúa invested in a variety of modernizing endeavors, most of which initially were aimed at improving Brazil's transportation and industrial infrastructure. From the establishment of an iron foundry that supplied pipes for a new water system in Rio de Janeiro, Maúa acquired concessions for a tramway line, the first gas-lamp system built in the country, and the first steamship company to operate on the Amazon River. An investor in the Second Bank of Brazil, he founded the Bank of Maúa in 1854, the same year he constructed Brazil's first railroad line from the port of Maúa on Guanabara Bay in Rio de Janeiro to the interior highlands, where coffee production for the foreign market was the mainstay of

nating her farmhouse for medical assistance to the troops. In 1883 she lost her hacienda and she went to Arequipa, where she again worked as a journalist. In 1884 she published *Tradiciones cusqueñas: leyendas, biografías y hojas sueltas* (Cuzco's Traditions: Legends, Biographies, and Other Writings), a volume of articles published in newspapers and literary magazines between 1870 and 1882, with a preface by Peruvian writer Ricardo PALMA. In 1886 she published a second volume, *Tradiciones cusqueñas: crónicas, hojas sueltas,* with a preface by José Antonio Laval. These short stories (*tradiciones*) follow the model of the genre created by Palma.

In 1887, Matto returned to Lima and organized a *salón literario* that became an important meeting place for Peruvian intellectuals. She joined the Ateneo de Lima and Círculo Literario literary groups. Connected to these groups was the literary publication *El Perú Il-*

the Brazilian economy. That year he also received the title of baron.

Mauá represented his native province of Rio Grande do Sul in the Chamber of Deputies from 1856 to 1873, and he received the title of viscount in 1874 after laying the first submarine cable between Brazil and Europe.

Mauá's widespread banking network extended to London, and his business ventures expanded to Argentina and Uruguay, where he held control over Uruguayan railroads, shipyards, gasworks, livestock farms, and meat-processing plants. His economic liberalism was not popular among conservative economic sectors in Brazil and Uruguay, and his creditors were not sympathetic to the losses he suffered in the Río de la Plata region during the War of the Triple Alliance (1864–1870). His finances declined in the 1870s, and in 1878 he was forced into bankruptcy. His "Exposition to the Creditors of Mauá and Company and to the Public," written in that year, attributed the reversal of his fortunes to his placing the well-being of the country before personal concerns, rather than to mismanagement or misdeeds. Mauá spent the remainder of his life managing a modest investment business.

– NANCY PRISCILLA SMITH NARO

MAURITS, JOHAN

Johan Maurits (John Maurice, Count of Nassau-Siegen; *b.* 17 June 1604; *d.* 20 December 1679), governor-general of Dutch Brazil (1637–1644). Born in Dillenburg in what is now Germany, Maurits was the eldest son of Johann VII, count of Nassau-Siegen (1561–1623), and his second wife, Margaretha, princess of Holstein-Sonderburg. Johan's paternal grandfather was Johann VI (1536–1606), younger brother of William the Silent of Orange. Maurits served with distinction in a number of campaigns in the Thirty Years' War with the army of the Dutch States-General. In August 1636, Maurits formally accepted an offer from the Dutch West India Company to be governor-general of Netherlands Brazil. Soon after his arrival in Recife on 23 January 1637, he successfully ousted the Portuguese military forces from the region north of the Rio São Francisco and forced them to retreat across the river to the captaincy of Sergipe del Rey. The entire captaincy of Pernambuco fell into Dutch hands.

Maurits then returned to Recife to restore order and encourage the Portuguese inhabitants to settle down and continue sugar production. As incentive, he allowed both Catholics and Jews to worship publicly and promised them good treatment. At the same time, he improved fortifications, formed alliances with the neighboring Indians, and tried to encourage more northern European immigration. Later that year, he sent an expedition under Colonel Hans Coen to capture São Jorge da Mina (Elmina) on Africa's Gold Coast. Another expedition, under Admiral Jan Corneliszoon Lichthart, sailed along the coast of Brazil to intercept Portuguese shipping and raided the captaincy of Ilheus, south of Bahia. In November of 1637, Colonel Sigismund von Schoppe attacked the captaincy of Sergipe del Rey. By the end of Maurits's first year in Brazil, the northern captaincy of Ceará was also in Dutch hands.

On 17–18 May 1638, Maurits attempted to capture the Brazilian capital of Bahia, but failed even though he had a force of 3,600 Europeans and 1,000 Indians. In 1640, he successfully defended Dutch Brazil from the count of Torre's large Spanish-Portuguese armada. In reprisal for the damage done by Portuguese troops to plantations in Dutch Brazil, Maurits sent another expedition under Lichthart to attack Portuguese sugar mills in the region around Bahia, and twenty-seven of them were destroyed. Other raids were made along the Brazilian coast, but not all were successful. After the Portuguese overthrow of Spanish rule (December 1640) and while a treaty between Portugal and the Netherlands was being negotiated, Maurits sent 3,000 men, including 240 Indians, to capture Luanda and Benguela in Angola, the islands of São Tomé and Ano Bom, and the fortress of Axim on the coast of Guinea, a task successfully completed during the second half of 1641 and early 1642. In November of 1641, São Luis do Maranhão was captured, giving the Dutch control over more than a thousand miles of Brazilian coastline. At this point, the Dutch West India Company reached its greatest territorial extension in the Atlantic world.

Maurits brought with him to America a large entourage of scholars, artists, and craftsmen.

During his seven-year stay in Brazil, Maurits rebuilt Recife and founded a new town (Mauritsstad) on the neighboring island of Antônio Vaz. He also built two country houses (Vrijburg and Boa Vista) on the island. On his properties he collected a wide variety of Brazilian flora and fauna. Maurits brought with him to America a large entourage of scholars, artists, and craftsmen. The most important were Georg Marcgraf (1610–1644), the German naturalist and astronomer; Willem Piso (1611–1678), the governor-general's personal physician, who published on tropical medicine and diseases; the landscape painter Frans Post (1612–1680); and Albert Eckhout (ca. 1610–1665), whose paintings depicted Brazilians and the country's animals and plants. Also of interest are the paintings by the amateur Zacharias Wagener, a German soldier in the service of the Dutch West India Company.

After more than seven years of rule, Maurits, greatly beloved by the populace of Dutch Brazil, was recalled by the directors of the Dutch West India Company. He left for Europe in May of 1644. He became stadholder of Cleves (1647–1679) and was made a prince of the Holy Roman Empire in 1652. He served in various Dutch military posts, distinguishing himself in battle as late as 1674.

– FRANCIS A. DUTRA

MAXIMILIAN

Maximilian (*b.* 6 July 1832; *d.* 19 June 1867), emperor of Mexico (1864–1867). Born in the Schönbrunn Palace in Vienna, Maximilian was the younger brother of Emperor Francis Joseph. He served as Austrian governor of Lombardy and Venetia from February 1857 until April 1859, when his liberal policies caused a breach with the Vienna authorities. In July 1857, he married Charlotte (known in Mexico as CARLOTA), daughter of Leopold I of the Belgians, who had earlier declined the Greek throne and the offer of a Mexican crown on the grounds that financial support had been lacking. Carlota, however, fervently believed in the Mexican imperial idea.

Rather than a politician, Maximilian was a romantic who wanted to do something for humanity. Before Napoleon III's suggestion of the Mexican crown, he had traveled the Mediterranean, and by the end of 1859, had also visited Madeira and Brazil. Francis Joseph, reluctant to be drawn into the Mexican scheme, left the matter of the crown to Maximilian, who verbally accepted the offer on 3 October 1863. Following Maximilian's acceptance, Napoleon, in the secret convention of Miramar, agreed to maintain an army of 20,000 men in Mexico until 1867 and the Foreign Legion until 1873, while in exchange, Mexico would cover the entire cost as well as pay back its past debts. In September-October 1863, he was apparently studying Lucas Alamán's *Historia de México,* a pro-monarchy tract. On 10 April 1864, Maximilian formally accepted the crown offered to him by a delegation of Mexican monarchists. Four days later he and Carlota set sail, by way of Rome, where they received the blessing of Pope Pius IX, reaching Mexico City on 12 June, after a *Te Deum* celebrated at the shrine of Our Lady of Guadalupe by Archbishop LABASTIDA. Maximilian had no intention of restoring the position of the church to that held before the Reform Laws, an attitude that led to intense conflict with the bishops and the papal nuncio. He ignored the pope's request to suspend Liberal measures, which he himself had ratified, and issued imperial decrees confirming purchases of ecclesiastical properties (28 December 1864) and continuing sales—though providing for division of rural properties (26 February 1865).

Maximilian also was determined to free himself of the French and disliked Marshal François BAZAINE, the French commander in chief in Mexico, who had abandoned the attempt to create a Mexican army late in 1864. The French army encountered fierce guerrilla resistance across Mexico. At the same time, Maximilian made the serious mistake of sending Miguel MIRAMÓN and Leonardo MÁRQUEZ, the best Conservative generals, on missions in Europe.

Maximilian's Council of State and cabinet consisted in the main of moderates, since there existed little basis of support for the empire among Conservatives and the clergy. The emperor's competition for the middle ground was undermined further by Napoleon III's determination from late 1866 to evacuate all French forces. After Miramón's return to France in November, Maximilian for the first time became dependent on the Conservatives for his survival. He had in the meantime withdrawn to Orizaba for one month to ponder the question of abdication and indulge his passion for catching butterflies. Meanwhile, Carlota went to France to appeal to Napoleon III to save the empire by committing more funds. She reached Paris in August 1866, but to no avail.

Maximilian's decision to remain on the throne was made public on 30 November 1866. A junta of notables voted on 14 January 1867 in Mexico City to uphold the empire by one vote, in spite of Bazaine's reservations concerning the empire's military position. Maximilian refused to abandon Mexico City with the last French troops and departed for the interior to take personal command of his army. He was captured by forces loyal to President Benito JUÁREZ and was summarily tried and executed at Querétaro on 19 June 1867. The case against him rested on JUÁREZ's decree of 25 January 1862 for the execution of all collaborators, and the death sentence, which Juárez refused to commute, was determined by the imperial decree of 3 October 1865, which had established the death penalty for all members of rebel bands or bandit groups. Juárez refused all appeals for clemency and delayed sending the corpse to Europe.

Maximilian had attempted to alleviate agrarian problems in his imperial decrees of 26 June 1865, which vested communal ownership in village inhabitants in reversal of Liberal policy, and in those of 1 November 1865, which granted laborers the right to leave employment at will. He did not consider himself to be the dupe of Napoleon III or the pawn of the French army. His decision to remain in Mexico after February 1867 reflected his determination to uphold his honor as a Hapsburg. He had sought to identify with Mexico and believed that the country could attain peace under his rule. Anxious to rally moderate opinion to the throne, he alienated Mexican Conservatives and the Catholic hierarchy. Moreover, Maximilian was hampered by his own lack of political skill.

– BRIAN HAMNETT

MAYORGA, SILVIO

Silvio Mayorga (*b.* 1936; *d.* 27 August 1967), Nicaraguan leader and cofounder of the Sandinista National Liberation Front. Mayorga was born in Matagalpa at approximately the same time as Carlos FONSECA. They grew up together and in 1954 entered law school at the National Autonomous University in León. Mayorga immediately became a student leader and joined the Nicaraguan Socialist Party in 1955. Like Fonseca, he soon rejected the passive character of the Socialists and encouraged more aggressive student radicalism. He became active in the Nicaraguan Patriotic Youth organization in the late 1950s and joined Fonseca's New Nicaragua Movement in 1960. In July 1961 Mayorga founded the Sandinista National Liberation Front with Fonseca and Tomás BORGE.

Mayorga was one of the principal commanders of guerrillas based in the village of Walaquistan. There he cooperated closely with Borge in planning the first Sandinista attack at Río Coco in 1963. He was gravely injured in an attack at San Carlos in the same year and spent several months recuperating. He reappeared in 1964 as a student organizer in León and Managua. For the next three years, Mayorga encouraged students and the urban poor to support the Sandinistas. In 1967, he led an expedition to explore Quinagua as an alternative guerrilla base in the mountains of Las Segovias. Mayorga's forces had little military experience, and some of his soldiers were teenagers. This proved disastrous when they attacked Pancasán in August 1967. Mayorga and fifty combatants were killed by the National Guard. His death and the Pancasán fiasco forced the Sandinista leadership to suspend frontal attacks on the Guard and seriously reevaluate its political and military strategy over the next two years. Mayorga was the first original Sandinista to fall in combat.

– MARK EVERINGHAM

MAZA, MANUEL VICENTE DE

Manuel Vicente de Maza (*b.* 1779; *d.* 27 June 1839), Argentine patriot and public official. Maza studied in his native Buenos Aires and in Chile, where he became a lawyer. After being imprisoned at Lima in 1810 as a patriot sympathizer, he returned in 1815 to Buenos Aires, where he held a number of government positions. A friend of Juan Manuel de ROSAS, he was a Federalist, and in 1829 he was deported by the Unitarist regime of Juan LAVALLE, returning the same year. However, he was a moderate who, as acting governor of Buenos Aires in 1834–1835, dismissed some of Rosas's strongest military supporters. He resigned the governorship in the aftermath of the assassination of Juan Facundo QUIROGA, but continued to serve in the legislature and as special judge of those accused of the murder. In 1839, after his son was involved in a plot against Rosas, Maza was assassinated in Buenos Aires.

– DAVID BUSHNELL

MEDEIROS DA FONSECA, ROMY MARTINS

Romy Martins Medeiros da Fonseca (*b.* 30 June 1921), Brazilian women's rights activist. Daughter of José Gomes Leite da Fonseca and Climéria da Fonseca Martins, Medeiros da Fonseca was born in Rio de Janeiro. She married the jurist and law professor Arnoldo Medeiros da Fonseca, with whom she had two children. A graduate of the law school at the Federal University of Rio de Janeiro, Romy Medeiros served as counselor to the State Council on the Rights of Women and has been a leader of the Brazilian Lawyers' Organization (OAB). In addition, she has served as president of the National Council of Brazilian Women (CNMB), an organization founded by Jeronyma Mesquita, a pioneer for women's suffrage.

Medeiros was a coauthor of the Married Woman's Statute, a law that defined social and family rights and supplanted civil code stipulations, which considered married women as "relatively incompetent." In 1972, she organized the First Congress of Women, in which national and international participants debated women's roles in political development. She has served as Brazil's delegate to the Inter-American Commission for Women at the Organization of American States and has been a formal and informal presidential adviser on women's issues since 1947. As a stalwart defender of women's rights, Romy Medeiros has long promoted women's integration into the country's military services and was instrumental in the passage of Brazil's divorce statute.

– IÊDA SIQUEIRA WIARDA

MÉDICI, EMÍLIO GARRASTAZÚ

Emílio Garrastazú Médici (*b.* 4 December 1905; *d.* 9 October 1985), military leader and president of Brazil (1969–1974). Médici was born in Bagé, Brazil, a village in southern cattle country close to the Uruguayan border. He entered a military school in Pôrto Alegre when he was twelve and enlisted in the cavalry nine years later. In 1934 he joined the Command and General Staff School in Rio de Janeiro. He was serving as an intelligence officer in Rio Grande do Sul in 1953 when Artur da COSTA E SILVA, commander of the Third Military Region, named him chief of staff. Eight years later Médici was promoted to brigadier general and appointed commander of the National Military Academy in Agulhas Negras.

Médici was the military attaché at the Brazilian Embassy in Washington, D.C., at the time of the military coup against President João GOULART in 1964. He left the army in 1966 to become civilian head of the National Intelligence Service, returning three years later to take command of the Third Army.

When President Costa e Silva suffered a stroke in August 1969, a three-man junta composed of the military service chiefs assumed control of the government. They bypassed the successor designated in the Constitution of 1967, Vice President Pedro Aleixo, who was perceived as being too much of a politician. After consulting 100 generals, the 10 generals of the Army High Command settled on Médici as the next president. He was then nominated by the government party, the National Renovating Alliance (ARENA), elected by the Brazilian National Congress, and sworn in 30 October 1969.

According to the Brazilian Amnesty Committee,

170 political opponents were killed during

Médici's presidency.

Médici promised a move toward democracy but instead practiced political repression. He permitted federal elections to Congress in November 1970, but allowed only one opposition party, the Brazilian Democratic Movement (MDB), to compete against ARENA. Before the election, the military carried out a mass crackdown of dissidents and arrested about 5,000 people. According to the Brazilian Amnesty Committee, 170 political opponents were killed during Médici's presidency.

The military considered suppression of dissent necessary for maintaining the stability needed to achieve economic growth. Médici's administration also helped to sustain the "economic miracle" that began in 1968. It attracted foreign loans for large-scale economic development projects and spent heavily on roads, railways, and utility projects—the infrastructure for heavy industry. Government-owned enterprises dominated steel, mining, and petrochemical industries. In 1974, 74 percent of the combined assets of the country's 100 largest firms belonged to state enterprises; state banks accounted for 56 percent of total deposits and 65 percent of loans to the private sector. This created further inequality of wealth among people and regions. Médici attempted to correct this imbalance in 1970 with construction of the Transamazon Highway, which was intended to encourage immigration and development in northeastern Brazil, the nation's poorest region. High government spending, along with the infusion of foreign capital, boosted economic growth rates to between 7 percent and 11 percent during Médici's years in office, but 80 percent of the population remained mired in poverty. Médici died in Rio de Janeiro.

– ROSS WILKINSON

MEDINA, HUGO

Hugo Medina (*b.* 29 January 1897), Uruguayan general and politician, was a key figure in the transition to civilian rule in Uruguay that took place in the mid-1980s. Commander of the Third Military Region in 1984, he was considered a staunch professional soldier who favored following the timetable established by the military for their withdrawal from executive power. Medina was a member of the military's Political Affairs Commission (COMASPO) from 1980 to 1981. On 7 June 1984, with the retirement of General Hugo Arano, he assumed command of the army. His working relationship with Julio Maria SANGUINETTI of the Colorado Party would prove crucial to the talks that resulted in the Naval Club Pact that led to the November 1984 elections. Medina retired from the army in January 1987, after having staunchly defended the armed forces against any trials for human rights violations. Late in 1987, President Sanguinetti appointed Medina minister of defense, a position from which he continued to pressure public opinion against overturning the amnesty law for the military that had been passed in 1986. The referendum on the amnesty law took place in April 1989. The law was upheld, giving Medina excellent credibility with his former military comrades. He continued to serve as minister of defense until the end of the Sanguinetti government.

– MARTIN WEINSTEIN

MEDINA, JOSÉ TORIBIO

José Toribio Medina (*b.* 21 October 1852; *d.* 11 December 1930), Chilean historian and bibliographer, and the most remarkable Latin American scholar of his time.

Although he was offered a seat in Congress and (in 1871) the secretaryship of the National (*Montt-Varista*) party, Medina preferred the life of scholarship. It was interrupted only by two short-term diplomatic jobs, in Peru (1875–1876) and Spain (1884–1886), and by public service during the War of the Pacific as military adviser and judge. Medina's support for President José Manuel BALMACEDA in the 1891 civil war made it advisable for him to live abroad until 1895. In fact he always enjoyed travel, making five extended journeys to Europe (always with Spain as his most cherished destination) and twice visiting the United States. In 1928, aged nearly seventy-six, he presided at the opening of the Twenty-third International Congress of Americanists in New York. He was honored by a wide variety of learned societies in America and Europe.

Medina was the author or editor of 408 books, essays, and articles. Some 185 of these publications were printed (1888–1919) on his own private presses. His copious writings embrace history, bibliography, biography, literary criticism, geography, cartography, palaeography, numismatics, and many other subjects. Of particular note are the series of books he wrote on the Inquisition in colonial Spanish America (he discovered the Inquisition papers in the Simancas archive in Spain), and the extraordinary sequence of bibliographical studies covering the output of colonial printing presses in more than thirty Spanish-American cities. His devotion to ERCILLA Y ZÚÑIGA yielded the classic modern study of that poet. Both Harvard University and the John Carter Brown Library offered Medina large sums for his magnificent collection of books and manuscripts. He donated it to the Chilean National Library, where it is kept in the beautifully appointed Sala Medina on the upper floor over the main entrance.

– SIMON COLLIER

MEDINA ANGARITA, ISAÍAS

Isaías Medina Angarita (*b.* 6 July 1897; *d.* 15 September 1953), president of Venezuela (1941–1945). In 1941, Medina became the hand-picked successor of President Eleázar LÓPEZ CONTRERAS, whom he had served briefly as minister of war in 1936. Medina, who entered the Military School in 1912, represented the new professional army officers who emerged during the Juan Vicente GÓMEZ era (1908–1935). During his military career he taught at the Military School, served as secretary to the Ministry of War and Marine, and headed military delegations to Ecuador (1930) and the United States (1940).

As president, Medina introduced a number of political reforms. Constitutional revisions instituted direct elections of national deputies and suffrage for women in municipal elections. Medina also introduced the first income tax law. In 1943, a petroleum law gave the government higher revenues through new taxes and royalties, and the petroleum companies gained more security. An agrarian reform law of 1945 addressed some of the nation's basic rural labor problems. Medina had success in negotiating border settlements with Colombia and Great Britain. In 1943 he headed his own party, the Venezuelan Democratic Party (Partido Democrático Venezolano), which advocated moderate reforms. In October 1945, a military-civilian coalition overthrew Medina.

– WINTHROP R. WRIGHT

MEIRELES, CECÍLIA

Cecília Meireles (*b.* 7 November 1901; *d.* 9 November 1964), Brazilian poet and educator. Born in Rio de Janeiro, Meireles lost her parents at an early age and was raised by her Portuguese Azorian grandmother. She studied in public schools and became a schoolteacher, later completing a graduate degree. In 1919 she published her first book, *Espectros,* sonnets in a Parnassian mold. In 1922, year of the Modern Art Week in São Paulo, she married a Portuguese artist who committed suicide in 1935. From 1930 on, she was a regular contributor to the Rio cultural press, and in 1934 she founded the first library of children's literature in Brazil. An authority on national folklore, she was professor of Luso-Brazilian literature at the University of the Federal District from 1936 to 1938. Following a second marriage, she visited the United States, teaching in one of the earliest programs for Brazilian literature (the University of Texas).

While thematic and linguistic nationalism became dominant in Brazil, Meireles remained close to the Portuguese lyrical heritage.

Meireles matured during the modernist period, but her work always maintained a very personal character, influenced above all by symbolism and Portuguese traditions. While thematic and linguistic nationalism became dominant in Brazil, she remained close to the Portuguese lyrical heritage. She published twenty books in her lifetime, the most noted of which, *Romanceiro da inconfidência* (1953), is a cycle of ballads about colonial conspirators for independence. She is one of the outstanding names in Brazilian literary history and is generally considered the nation's most important woman poet. Posthumously, she received the highest prize of the Brazilian Academy of Letters.

– CHARLES A. PERRONE

MEIRELES DE LIMA, VÍTOR

Vítor Meireles de Lima (*b.* 18 August 1832; *d.* 22 February 1903), Brazilian painter. Along with Pedro AMÉRICO, Meireles is one of Brazil's most important historical painters of the Second Empire. Born in the southern province of Santa Catarina, Meireles commenced his formal artistic formation in 1847 at the Imperial Academy of Fine Arts in Rio de Janeiro. In 1852 he won a travel stipend, the academy's top student honor. During his eight years in Europe, he produced his first important historical painting, and one of his greatest works, *A primeira missa no Brasil.*

Upon his return to Brazil, Meireles devoted his life to painting whether working as the academy's professor of history painting, fulfilling governmental commissions, or readying canvases for presentation in the academy's exhibitions. Between 1866 and 1879, he received three important governmental commissions to produce paintings with military themes. Sought to bolster the Second Empire's image after Brazil's participation in the victorious but draining War of the Triple Alliance (1864–1870), these military paintings represent his most celebrated works. They include *Combate naval do Riachuelo* and *Passagem de humaitá* (1872), which recreate events from the war, and *Primeira Batalha dos Guararapes* (1879), which documents a 1648 battle in which black, Indian, and Brazilian troops fought against Dutch colonial domination. Beyond these historical compositions, Meireles produced numerous portraits, an Indianist painting, *Moema,* and various landscapes and panoramas.

– CAREN A. MEGHREBLIAN

MEJÍA, TOMÁS

Tomás Mejía (*b.* 1820; *d.* 19 June 1867), Mexican general. Born in Pinal de Amoles, Querétaro, Mejía became an important military officer while retaining his ethnic ties to the Indian villagers of the Sierra Gorda. An Indian cacique, he led troops from his native region in support of the conservative cause during the Revolution of Ayutla, the War of the Reform, and in support of MAXIMILIAN's empire.

Mejía began his career in 1841 as a second lieutenant in the militia, engaging migratory Indians in the North in his first campaigns. He fought against the invading U.S. troops in Monterrey, Angostura, and Buena Vista

in 1847 and was promoted to squadron commander in 1849. He reached the rank of lieutenant colonel during the Revolution of Ayutla and division general during the Three Years War. Defeated by Jesús GONZÁLEZ ORTEGA in 1860, Mejía later became one of Emperor Maximilian's most trusted generals, and one of the most feared by his republican counterparts. As Maximilian's empire collapsed, Mejía chose to join the emperor in Querétaro, where he was captured, tried, condemned to death, and executed by firing squad alongside Maximilian and Miguel MIRAMÓN.

– D. F. STEVENS

MEJÍA DEL VALLE Y LLEQUERICA, JOSÉ JOAQUÍN

José Joaquín Mejía del Valle y Llequerica (also Lequerica; *b.* 24 May 1775; *d.* 27 October 1813), spokesperson for the rights of colonial Americans under Spanish imperialism. Mejía, a native of Quito, served as a substitute delegate of the Viceroyalty of New Granada to the Cortes of Cádiz (1810–1814). He ably led the American delegation in their struggle for equal representation in both the congress and the subsequent new constitution. The problem was population: that of Spain at this time was about 10.5 million, whereas that of Spain's overseas holdings totaled about 15–16.9 million. However, only whites enjoyed full citizenship in Spain and its colonies, and the New World had far fewer whites (2.5–3.2 million) than did Spain (10.5 million). Naturally, Spain was utterly unwilling to surrender political control of its empire to overseas whites.

During the Cádiz debates, Mejía advanced a proposal that the New World's free blacks and Indians, if not its slaves, be counted for purposes of proportional representation. The Cortes agreed to include creoles, Indians, and mestizos, but not Africans and mulattoes. Most historians agree that Mejía was the best orator in Cádiz. He died during a yellow fever epidemic in Cádiz.

– RONN F. PINEO

MEJÍA VICTORES, OSCAR HUMBERTO

Oscar Humberto Mejía Victores, chief of state of Guatemala (1983–1985). Brigadier General Mejía Victores served as minister of defense under Efraín RÍOS MONTT (1982–1983). After taking part in the 9 August 1983 coup d'état that ousted Ríos Montt from power, Mejía became chief of state, but declined to name himself president of the republic.

Guatemala's economy declined precipitously under Mejía's administration. However, Mejía oversaw the "transition to democracy" under which the military permitted the creation and promulgation of a new national constitution and the election of a civilian to the presidency. In 1986, Mejía stepped down to allow Marco Vinicio CEREZO ARÉVALO, a civilian and member of the Christian Democratic Party, to become president of the republic.

— VIRGINIA GARRARD-BURNETT

MELÉ, JUAN N.

Juan N. Melé (*b.* 15 October 1923), Argentine painter and sculptor. Born in Buenos Aires, he studied at the Prilidiano PUEYRREDÓN School of Fine Arts. In 1948–1949 he received a grant from the French government and studied at the Louvre under Georges Vantongerloo, Cesar Domela, Robert Delauney, and Constantin Brancusi, among others. Melé has had a distinguished career in abstract painting and sculpture. In Argentina he joined the Asociación Arte Concreto-Invención, a group of nonfigurative artists. His work is a fine example of highly personal abstract art combining purely plastic form and a sensitive treatment of color.

— AMALIA CORTINA ARAVENA

MELÉNDEZ CHAVERRI, CARLOS

Carlos Meléndez Chaverri (*b.* 3 June 1926), Costa Rican historian, diplomat, and university professor.

Carlos Meléndez Chaverri is recognized as the most productive and insightful twentieth-century Costa Rican historian. He has focused his research and writing on the colonial period in Costa Rica. His works on the colonial period culminated in the valuable monograph *Conquistadores y pobladores* (1982). He has published general histories of Costa Rica for different educational levels, biographies, a study of blacks in Costa Rica, monographs on other Central American topics, and a scholarly work on the national hero, Juan Santamaría.

Heredia-born Meléndez is a scholar-teacher in the full sense of the term, having taught at two high schools before joining the faculty of the University of Costa Rica (1958). There he served as the director of the School of History and Geography and was responsible for the formation of a more professional generation of Costa Rican historians. In addition to these academic functions, he held other public positions such as head of the anthropology and history section of the National Museum (1953–1966), president of the Academy of History and Geography, and Costa Rican ambassador to Spain.

Among his many honors are national literary awards, election to geographic and historical societies through-out Central America, and an honorary doctorate from Tulane University (1979).

— JOHN PATRICK BELL

MELÉNDEZ FAMILY

Meléndez Family, a Salvadoran family that held the presidency for three consecutive terms (1913–1927) during the period known as the Meléndez-Quiñónez dynasty era. The Meléndez presidents' fourteen-year occupancy of the nation's highest office is the most obvious example of the restrictive, elitist nature of Salvadoran politics. The Meléndez clan was part of the original Salvadoran landowning oligarchy dating from the early nineteenth century. Originally producers of indigo, they were among the first to grow coffee on a large scale.

President Carlos Meléndez (*b.* 1 February 1861; *d.* 8 October 1918) took office in 1913 following the assassination of Manuel Araujo. He had made many trips to the United States and wished to promote industrialization and the diversification of El Salvador's agrarian economy into henequen and cotton. However, his tenure in office is most notable for two policies: his decision to keep El Salvador neutral in World War I, despite heavy pressure from the United States, and his claim to the Gulf of Fonseca as a condominium territory. The latter resulted in the issuing of the so-called Meléndez Doctrine, which challenged Nicaragua's right to grant the United States a naval base in the Gulf of Fonseca as stipulated by the Bryan–Chamorro Treaty of 1913. Meléndez took his case to the Central American Court of Justice in 1914 and won a judgment in his favor.

Carlos Meléndez passed the presidency to his younger brother Jorge (*b.* 15 April 1871; *d.* 22 November 1953) when his health failed in 1918. Jorge ruled for four turbulent years punctuated by military uprisings, urban labor protests, and demonstrations in San Salvador. Of these, the most serious were a February 1922 revolt of students at the Military Polytechnic School and a popular demonstration in December of that same year which was put down by the army and police. Jorge Meléndez continued his brother's program of modernization by opening the first airport, announcing a campaign to eradicate illiteracy, and creating a monetary commission. However, Jorge Meléndez is remembered also for his increased usage of the Liga Roja (Red League), a shadowy paramilitary group designed to thwart labor organization.

The Meléndez's brother-in-law Alfonso QUIÑONES MOLINA was president from 1923 to 1927 and continued the same form of elite-dominated politics as his predecessors. The Meléndez-Quiñónez dynasty governed El Salvador during a crucial period in its modern history. In the 1980s, their descendant, Jorge Antonio Meléndez, fought with the People's Revolutionary Army (ERP) as part of the FMLN–FDR coalition against the government.

– KAREN RACINE

MELGAREJO, MARIANO

Mariano Melgarejo (*b.* 15 April 1820; *d.* 23 November 1871), president of Bolivia (1864–1871). Born in Tarata, Cochabamba, General Melgarejo was the archetypical bad caudillo during whose disastrous administration Bolivia gave up large territories to its neighbors, the first systematic assault on the Indian communities occurred, and the public financial system was ransacked. Melgarejo, a mestizo who had risen through the ranks of the army, achieved power after overthrowing General José María ACHÁ and later killing former president Manuel Isidoro BELZÚ. Extremely corrupt and with the government always in deficit, Melgarejo and his cronies

Mariano Melgarejo. Reproduced from Alcides Arguedas, Los caudillos bárbaros *(Barcelona, 1929). (Courtesy of Harvard College Library)*

took advantage of the prosperity of the peripheral regions of Bolivia by selling them to its more powerful neighbors. Thus, in the Chilean treaty of 1866, Melgarejo agreed to all Chilean territorial claims in the nitrate-rich Mejillones region of the Atacama Desert. In 1868, Melgarejo signed a treaty in which he ceded 40,000 square miles to Brazil in the Amazon region.

General Melgarejo was the archetypical bad caudillo during whose disastrous administration the first systematic assault on the Indian communities occurred.

In a desperate attempt to gain more revenue, Melgarejo also further debased Bolivian silver coinage. The dilution of the silver content in coins, though practiced by virtually every Bolivian administration, was so massive under Melgarejo that it led to difficulties in trade, especially in regions of adjacent countries that heavily used Bolivian coinage for circulation. Melgarejo's sales of Indian community lands in 1866 and 1868 also were tainted by corruption. The terms were exceedingly onerous for the Indians; if they did not purchase their own land within ninety days, it was put on the auction block for the highest bidder. Purchasers bought many lands with government bonds and others were given to friends and relatives, thus depriving the government of needed cash revenue. Most affected by these laws were community lands in the La Paz altiplano and the Cochabamba region.

Although his regime continuously had to combat movements against the government, Melgarejo was ousted in 1870 only when the creole opposition allied itself with the altiplano Indians. A massive Indian revolt forced Melgarejo to flee to Peru, where he died the following year. As a result of the revolt, Indian rebels retook many of their community lands.

– ERICK D. LANGER

MELGARES, FACUNDO

Facundo Melgares (*b.* 1775; *d.* ca. 1835), Spanish governor of New Mexico. Born in Villa Carabaca, Murcia, Spain, Melgares, nephew of a judge of the Audiencia of New Spain, entered military service in 1803 as a second lieutenant at the presidio of San Fernando de Carrizal, 75 miles south of El Paso del Norte, New Mexico. When a number of Spanish detachments marched from New Mexico and Texas to intercept American explorers in 1806, Melgares brought reinforcements from Carrizal and led his troops into Pawnee territory. After a party headed by Zebulon Pike, sent by the new governor of the Louisiana Territory to find the sources of the Red and Arkansas rivers, had become lost, a Spanish detachment rescued and arrested the men in 1807. Melgares and his soldiers accompanied Pike from Taos to Santa Fe and then down the Rio Grande to Chihuahua for further interrogation.

During Miguel HIDALGO's revolt of 1810, Melgares led royalist troops from Carrizal against the insurgents at Saltillo, Coahuila. Later he commanded an unsuccessful attack against Ignacio ALLENDE, then participated in Allende's capture near Monclova, Coahuila, on 21 March 1811. By 1817, Melgares was commander of the Santa Fe presidio. In July 1818 he brought troops from Chihuahua to defend New Mexico against Comanche-American attacks, taking over as acting governor. He received permanent appointment to the post one month afterward, and spent the rest of the period of Spanish rule defending the territory against periodic reports of American moves and leading numerous retaliatory campaigns against the Navajos. In August 1819, Melgares successfully concluded a formal peace between Navajos and Spanish.

After Mexico became independent, Melgares refused to allow the colonists in New Mexico to swear allegiance to the new republic until he received a direct order from the commandant general. As a result, he was relieved as governor in April 1822, after citizens of the province brought charges against him on 5 July 1822.

— ROSS H. FRANK

MELLA, JULIO ANTONIO

Julio Antonio Mella (*b.* 1905; *d.* 10 January 1929), cofounder and first secretary-general of the Cuban Communist Party. Mella received his early political training in the 1920s as a leader of the movement for university reform. He helped organize the first National Student Congress in 1923, the same year he took part in the famous "Protest of the Thirteen," in which thirteen of Havana's young intellectuals walked out of the Academy of Science when President Alfredo ZAYAS's minister of justice entered the hall.

Mella was also the editor of *Juventud,* a student literary journal, and it was his efforts as a student reformer that brought him in contact with Cuban Marxists, especially Carlos Baliño, a supporter of the Bolshevik Revolution. Along with Baliño, Mella cofounded the Cuban Communist Party in 1925 and was elected the party's first secretary-general. After the founding of the party, Mella gave weekly classes in politics for Havana labor unions, and he also led efforts to organize students

in opposition to the Cuban dictator Gerardo MACHADO. Mella was arrested that same year when he led a student strike that shut down the University of Havana. In prison Mella organized a hunger strike that gained international attention.

In 1927 Mella was deported to Mexico, where he continued his work against the Machado regime and where he also served briefly in 1928 as the secretary-general of the Mexican Communist Party. On 10 January 1929, Mella was assassinated in Mexico City. Fidel Castro's government later claimed that Mella was killed by agents of the Machado government. But it is also possible that internal squabbles may have led to Mella's death, since two weeks before his assassination Mella was expelled from the Mexican Communist Party.

— MICHAEL POWELSON

MELLA, RAMÓN MATÍAS

Ramón Matías Mella (*b.* 25 February 1816; *d.* 4 July 1864), Dominican revolutionary, active in the nationalist movement that led to the establishment of the Dominican Republic in 1844. In 1822 the island of Hispañola fell under the control of Haitian bureaucrats and soldiers. In 1838 Mella and other Dominican nationalists organized a secret society, La Trinitaria (The Trinitarian), for the purpose of overthrowing the corrupt Haitian dictator, Jean-Pierre BOYER. Mella and the Trinitarians aligned themselves, for tactical reasons, with La Réforme, a Haitian reform movement led by Charles Hérard.

Once Boyer was defeated in 1843, however, Hérard turned on his Dominican allies and had Mella and other Trinitarians arrested and incarcerated at Port-au-Prince. A revolt against Hérard that broke out in 1843 in Port-au-Prince was quelled only with the help of Mella and his Dominican troops. As a reward Mella and his Dominican regiment were released by Hérard. Soon after their arrival in Santo Domingo, the eastern part of the island of Hispañola, Mella and his followers began the process of retaking it and proclaiming independence. On 27 February 1844, Mella and his forces secured the city of Santo Domingo and declared independence from Haiti. Mella was named a member of the new ruling junta that was given the task of organizing the new government. But even after the defeat of the Haitians, Mella's life was not safe, since bitter fighting broke out among the new rulers of the republic. By the summer of 1844, the powerful rancher Pedro SANTANA took over the ruling junta and had Mella imprisoned. In 1848 Mella accepted a general amnesty and was released from prison.

— MICHAEL POWELSON

MELLO, ZÉLIA MARIA CARDOSO DE

Zélia Maria Cardoso de Mello (*b.* 20 September 1954), Brazilian minister of economy (1990–1991). The daughter of Emiliano Cardoso de Mello and Auzélia Cardoso de Mello, Mello was born in São Paulo. An economist by training, she was an analyst at the Banco Auxiliar de São Paulo in 1977 and an analyst at the Dumont Assessoria e Planejamento in 1978. She taught at the school of economics and business administration at the University of São Paulo until 1991, when she married television personality and comedian Chico Anísio.

Mello held her first political post in 1983, during the administration of André Franco Montoro, governor of the state of São Paulo. She also served as adviser to the executive board of the Companhia de Desenvolvimento Habitacional do Estado de São Paulo. In 1985, during the administration of President José SARNEY, Mello was invited by Minister of the Treasury Dilson Funaro to work with André Calabi on negotiations regarding the debts owed to the federal government by the states and municipalities. At that time she became acquainted with Fernando COLLOR DE MELLO (no relation), the governor of Alagoas and later president of Brazil (1990).

In 1990, Mello was appointed Brazil's minister of economy, treasury, and planning, the first woman to hold such a position.

In 1987, at the time of Minister of Treasury Dilson Funaro's resignation, she left the Sarney administration and founded the firm ZLC-Consultores Associados, which advised public and private enterprises in business negotiations. One of the firm's first major clients was Governor Fernando Collor de Mello. Upon his decision to run for the presidency, Mello joined his campaign. In 1990, she was appointed minister of economy, treasury, and planning, the first woman to hold such a position. She was in charge of implementing economic strategies outlined in the Brasil Novo (New Brazil) plan. Mello's affair with a fellow, married cabinet member led to her resignation, and she left the government on 9 May 1991 to resume her teaching and consulting career.

– IÊDA SIQUEIRO WIARDA

MELO, CUSTÓDIO JOSÉ DE

Custódio José de Melo (*b.* 9 June 1846; *d.* 15 March 1902), Brazilian veteran of the Paraguayan War and principal figure in a naval revolt during the civil war of 1893. Melo, whose father was a career army officer, distinguished himself in numerous battles during the Paraguayan War. In the Brazilian military he held various positions of command, mostly on ships. Bahian delegate to the Constitutent Assembly of 1890–1891, Melo opposed the dissolution of Congress by President Manoel Deodoro da FONSECA on 3 November 1891 and launched a rebellion of the fleet that produced Fonseca's resignation. Vice President Floriano PEIXOTO took control and named Melo minister of the navy.

A debate over interpretation of the constitution concerning whether Peixoto should have called new elections plus his clash with the Federalists of Rio Grande do Sul brought on the civil war of 1893 and a second revolt of the fleet under Melo. Peixoto resisted and Melo found himself facing a test of arms. Shore batteries at the military forts challenged the naval ships, some of which escaped, one with Melo aboard, and sailed to Santa Catarina, where they made contact with the Federalist rebels. Agreement between Melo and the rebels proved impossible, and Melo sailed toward Buenos Aires. By March 1894 Vice President Peixoto had acquired warships from Europe and the United States, and his superior naval strength, coupled with the support of five large U.S. naval vessels in the harbor, made the position of the rebel ships in Guanabara Bay untenable. Melo took refuge aboard a Portuguese ship and sailed into exile. He was eventually pardoned and returned to Rio to write his memoirs.

– ROBERT A. HAYES

MELO, JOSÉ MARÍA

José María Melo (*b.* 9 October 1800; *d.* 1 June 1860), Colombian military leader. A consummate professional military officer, Melo revolted in 1854 in defense of a permanent military institution. Born in Ibagué in west-central Colombia, Melo entered the patriot army in 1819 and participated in the battle of Ayacucho. He served in the Venezuelan military from 1830 to 1835, when he was expelled for his role in the Revolution of the Reforms. Melo served for three years at a Bremen military academy, after which he joined the WAR OF THE SUPREMES (1840–1842) against the Colombian government. President Tomás Cipriano de MOSQUERA restored his military rank in 1849. José María López appointed Melo commanding general of the department of Cundinamarca in 1849. The efforts of the Gólgotas to eliminate the permanent military led Melo to found the promilitary *El Orden* in 1852. Melo's ill-fated 17 April 1854 revolt failed to attract the support of leading Draconian Liberals. In exile, Melo continued his military career in Central America and Mexico, only to be killed in service to Benito JUÁREZ.

– DAVID SOWELL

MELO, LEOPOLDO

Leopoldo Melo (*b.* 15 November 1869; *d.* 6 February 1951), Argentine politician, lawyer, and university professor. Melo was born in Diamante, in the province of Entre Ríos, and graduated from law school in 1891. An expert in maritime and business law, he taught these subjects for over thirty years at the University of Buenos Aires. He served as a national deputy to Congress from Entre Ríos from 1914 to 1916, and as a senator from 1917 to 1930. In the 1928 elections he was the presidential candidate of the conservative wing of the Radical Civic Union (UCR), but he was defeated by Hipólito YRIGOYEN, the candidate of the Personalist faction. Melo served as minister of the interior (the political arm of the executive power in Argentina) under the conservative president Agustín P. JUSTO from 1932 to 1936. He presided over the Argentine delegations to the Inter-American conferences in Panama (1939) and Havana (1940), and wrote extensively on juridical matters. Melo died in Pinamar, in the province of Buenos Aires.

– CELSO RODRÍGUEZ

MELO E CASTRO, MARTINHO DE

Martinho de Melo e Castro (*b.* 11 November 1716; *d.* 24 March 1795), Portuguese diplomat (1751–1770), overseas minister (1770–1795). Born in Lisbon, Melo e Castro was a younger son of Francisco de Melo e Castro, Governor of Mazagão in North Africa (1705–1713), and Dona Maria Joaquina Xavier da Silva. His older brother, Manuel Bernardo de Melo e Castro, became the first and only viscount of Lourinha in 1777, after having served as governor and captain-general of Grão Pará and Maranhão (1759–1763). In his youth Melo e Castro followed an ecclesiastical career and studied at Évora and Coimbra. At what time he changed careers is not clear. From 1753 to 1755 he served as envoy to the Netherlands. The following year he was transferred to London, where he held the post of envoy extraordinary and minister plenipotentiary from 1756 to 1762. In that latter year he traveled to France, where he represented Portugal as minister plenipotentiary at the peace talks at Fontainebleau (1762) and Paris (1763) that ended the Seven Years' War (1756–1763). Following the signing of the treaties, Melo e Castro briefly visited Portugal before returning to England,

where he continued to serve as envoy extraordinary and minister plenipotentiary until 1770.

On 4 January 1770, he was named secretary of state for naval and overseas affairs, a post he held until his death in 1795. His correspondence during that twenty-five-year tenure is of great importance for understanding Brazil during some of the most critical years of its history. Jacome Ratton, the French-born but naturalized Portuguese merchant, industrialist, memoirist, and contemporary of Melo e Castro, described him as honest, though very stubborn and pro-English. He was well aware of the importance of Portuguese America. In 1779 he wrote: "Portugal without Brazil is an insignificant power." A strong opponent of mercantilism, Melo e Castro was in favor of monopoly companies, against "workshops and manufactories" in Brazil, and greatly concerned about the defense of Portuguese America and the extensive illegal trade carried on there. However, he was outvoted regarding the fate of Brazil's commercial companies, and the Company of Grão Pará and Maranhão lost its monopoly status in 1778, as did the Company of Pernambuco and Paraíba two years later. Melo e Castro was minister during the difficult period of adjustment in Minas Gerais in the aftermath of the gold boom. The Minas conspiracy of 1788–1789 was uncovered while he was in power.

– FRANCIS DUTRA

MELO FRANCO, AFONSO ARINOS DE

Afonso Arinos de Melo Franco (*b.* 27 November 1905; *d.* 27 August 1990), Brazilian constitutional lawyer, politician, writer, and diplomat. The son of diplomat Afrânio de MELO FRANCO, Afonso Arinos was born into a distinguished family of the state of Minas Gerais. A lawyer, he initially devoted himself to legal and historical writing, leaving politics to his father and brother, Virgílio Martins de Melo Franco. At the death of his father in 1943, Afonso Arinos joined the Friends of America to continue his father's opposition to the Estado Novo. He advocated economic and political liberalism and, in 1945, helped found the União Democrática Nacional (UDN), the opposition party to Getúlio VARGAS and later Juscelino KUBITSCHEK. He served as a federal deputy (1947–1959), a senator (1959–1961), and as minister of foreign relations under Jânio QUADROS (1961) and, briefly, João GOULART (1962). Melo Franco was an architect of Brazil's increasingly independent foreign policy vis-à-vis the United States. Under Quadros, he declined to support U.S. pressure on Cuba, advocated seating the People's Republic of China in the United Nations, and sought to restore diplomatic ties with the Soviet Union. However, as Goulart allied with the left, Melo Franco supported the president's overthrow. Only after the military indicated its intention of staying in power did Melo Franco oppose the regime, leading the congressional debate against the Constitution of 1967. When it passed, stripping the Congress of its powers, Melo Franco declined to run again for office, returning to academia (his works on history and law total nearly forty) until asked by President José SARNEY in 1985 to organize the drafting of a new, democratic constitution. He later served again as a senator.

— ELIZABETH A. COBBS

MELO FRANCO, AFRÂNIO DE

Afrânio de Melo Franco (*b.* 25 February 1870; *d.* 1 January 1943), Brazilian politician and diplomat. Afrânio de Melo Franco was born into a prominent family of the state of Minas Gerais. Trained as a lawyer, he joined with other students in 1889 to support Brazil's transition to a republican government dominated by powerful states ("Rule of the Governors"). During the First Republic he served as secretary of the legation to Uruguay, a federal deputy (1906–1929), and eventually as Brazil's representative to the League of Nations (1924–1926). As a leading *mineiro,* Melo Franco benefited from the political power of Minas Gerais and São Paulo, known as the "café com leite" (coffee with milk) alliance. In 1929 Melo Franco threw his support to Getúlio VARGAS in the national contest for power leading to the Estado Novo. Vargas made Melo Franco his first minister of foreign relations (1930–33), giving him a relatively free hand in the running of Itamaraty. Melo Franco reorganized the ministry, emphasizing foreign trade and, in light of growing world tensions, Pan-Americanism. Along with Oswaldo ARANHA, Melo Franco viewed cooperation with the United States as the surest road to national security and the key to Brazil's growing power within Latin America. Melo Franco represented Brazil at the Inter-American Conference of 1938, where he helped induce Argentina to join in the Declaration of Lima. He broke with Vargas in 1933 over a question of political patronage and, just before his death, joined the Friends of America, a group seeking democratization and an end to the Estado Novo.

— ELIZABETH A. COBBS

MELO NETO, JOÃO CABRAL DE

João Cabral de Melo Neto (*b.* 9 January 1920), Brazilian poet. Born in Recife, Pernambuco, Melo Neto spent his childhood on a sugarcane plantation and attended Catholic schools. In 1942 he published his first collection of poems and moved to Rio de Janeiro to study for the foreign service. During his long diplomatic career, he resided in England, France, Switzerland, and Senegal, as well as in Spain and Spanish America. From the late 1940s his literary reputation grew steadily, and near the end of the twentieth century he was widely regarded as the most important Brazilian poet of the century's second half.

A unique figure in the cultural sphere, Melo Neto has commanded respect both for pure aesthetic principles and for the social perspectives of his work. He has influenced such diverse genres as concretism, regional verse, literature of commitment, and the poetry of song (Música Popular Brasileira). His is not a conventional lyricism of self-expression but rather a controlled objective discourse, often connected to the actual settings and human realities of the northeastern region. In 1968, he was elected to the Brazilian Academy of Letters. He received the prestigious Camões prize in 1990 for lifetime literary achievement in Portuguese and two years later the Twelfth Neustadt International Prize for Literature (sponsored by *World Literature Today*).

— CHARLES A. PERRONE

MELVILLE, THOMAS AND MARGARITA (MARJORIE)

Thomas and Margarita (Marjorie) Melville, U.S. Catholic missionaries in Guatemala who became revolutionaries. Margarita Bradford (*b.* 19 August 1929) was born in Irapuato, Mexico, and studied at Loretto Academy

---

Frustrated by what they felt was a lack of commitment to the poor by Catholic church leaders, they decided to join the guerrilla movement.

---

in El Paso, Texas. She became Maryknoll Sister Marion Peter and was assigned in 1954 to teach at an upper-class school in Guatemala City. Influenced by the *cursillo de capacitación social* (short course of social empowerment) movement, she began to spend time teaching the urban poor and organizing vacation projects for affluent students in poverty-stricken rural areas. Thomas Melville (*b.* 5 December 1930), from Newton, Massachusetts, joined the Maryknoll order and, after ordination in 1957, was sent to work with Indians in the Guatemalan highlands. He helped them form cooperatives. Later he organized an Indian resettlement program in the Petén.

Both missioners became involved with radical university students, some of whom had contact with guerrillas. Frustrated by what they felt was a lack of commitment to the poor by church leaders, they decided to join the guerrilla movement, in order to give it a "Christian presence." Their plan was discovered, and they were expelled from Guatemala in 1967. Soon both left Maryknoll, and they were married in 1968. They later earned doctoral degrees in anthropology and wrote *Guatemala: The Politics of Land Ownership* (1971).

— EDWARD T. BRETT

MENCHÚ TUM, RIGOBERTA

Rigoberta Menchú Tum (*b.* 9 January 1959), recipient of the 1992 Nobel Peace Prize. Menchú is a Maya-Quiché Indian woman from Guatemala and the first indigenous Latin American so honored. She is a member of the Coordinating Commission of the Committee of Peasant Unity (CUC) and a founding member of the United Representation of the Guatemalan Opposition (RUOG). She was born in Chimel, near San Miguel de Uspantán, to Vicente Menchú and Juana Tum, Maya peasants and Catholic lay leaders. Self-educated, from the age of eight she accompanied her parents to harvest export crops on south coast plantations, and later worked for two years as a domestic in Guatemala City. She participated with her parents in local pastoral activities.

In the 1970s, expropriation of Indian land in El Quiché threatened Maya subsistence and prompted her family's political activism and involvement with the CUC. In the late 1970s, Menchú organized local self-defense groups, armed with rocks and machetes, in response to the government's escalated counterinsurgency war in the highlands. In January 1980, her father was burned to death in the occupation of the Spanish embassy in Guatemala City by campesinos with the support of trade unionists and students. Menchú continued organizing efforts in local Maya communities until forced to flee in 1981; since then she has lived in Mexico City.

A powerful speaker, Menchú has continued to work for peace and the rights of indigenous people in Guatemala in international forums. She has participated in the U.N. Working Group on Indigenous Populations, the U.N. Subcommission on Prevention of Discrimination and Protection for Minorities, and the U.N. Conference on the Decade of Women. She is a credentialed observer of the U.N. Human Rights Commission and the General Assembly. She serves on the board of

the International Indian Treaty Council and was a member of honor at the Second Continental Gathering of the "500 Years of Resistance" Conference. Among other awards, she has received the 1988 Nonino Prize special award, the 1990 Monseñor Proaño Human Rights Prize, the 1990 UNESCO Education for Peace Prize, and the 1991 French Committee for the Defense of Freedoms and Human Rights prize.

— MARILYN M. MOORS

MENDES, GILBERTO

Gilberto Mendes (*b.* 13 October 1922), Brazilian composer, teacher, critic. Gilberto Mendes has been associated with experimental movements in Brazilian music, most notably the Música Nova group. The *Manifesto música nova,* published in 1963, expressed a commitment to explore every aspect of contemporary musical language, including concertism, impressionism, polytonalism, atonality, serialism, phono-mechanical sound, and all aspects of electronic media. Composers associated with the Música Nova group included Willy Correia de OLIVEIRA, Rogério DUPRAT, Damiano Cozzella, and Júlio Medaglia.

Mendes studied composition with Henri Pousseur, Pierre Boulez, and Karlheinz Stockhausen. One of his best-known compositions, "Beba Coca-Cola" (Drink Coca-Cola), is a satire on a Coca-Cola commercial. In 1970 his composition "Blirium a-9" was chosen by the International Council of Composers of UNESCO for broadcast in Europe. In 1974 his composition "Santos Football Music" won an award from the Associação Paulista de Críticos de Artes as the best experimental work. In 1973 "Pausa e Menopausa" (Pause and Menopause), a composition based on a poem of Ronaldo Azeredo, explored the idea of indeterminacy, in which music could be written as poetry without text, music without sound, and visual impressions without sound. In 1978–1979 Mendes accepted an appointment at the University of Wisconsin–Milwaukee. During this period numerous performances of his works were given in the United States.

— DAVID P. APPLEBY

MENDES FILHO, FRANCISCO "CHICO" ALVES

Francisco "Chico" Alves Mendes Filho (*b.* 15 December 1944; *d.* 22 December 1988), Brazilian union leader and ecologist. Mendes, from Xapuri, Acre, began his career as a rubber tapper at the age of eight, when he assisted his father in gathering rubber. After working twenty-eight years in this profession, Mendes founded the Xapuri Rural Workers' Union in 1977. As its quietly persuasive president, he sponsored education for members and their children, and he helped establish health posts in Acre. Ten years later, Mendes assisted by anthropologist Mary Allegretti, formed the National Council of Rubber Tappers (CNS). Through the CNS, Chico helped organize *Projeto Seringueiro* (Rubber Tapper Project), which promoted cooperatives whose literate members learned to manage their own finances. Mendes also led the Xapuri Rural Workers in their tactic of *empate* (standoff). Large landowners who hired workers to clear the Amazonian rain forest were faced with groups of rubber workers who assembled en masse and barricaded the area to be cleared. Although large landowners often removed them at gunpoint, the union achieved success through *empates* about one third of the time. *Empates* brought worldwide attention to the rubber workers' social and environmental battles. Mendes won international recognition for his efforts and became a consultant to the World Bank and to the U.S. Senate on matters of investments in Amazônia.

Mendes promoted extractive reserves, the union's innovative alternative to deforestation, which allows workers to live on and extract products from the rain forest while leaving it intact. In 1988, when the Brazilian government expropriated land from powerful owners for three extractive reserves, Mendes began receiving death threats. He was shot to death on 22 December 1988. News of his death made headlines throughout the world, and he became a martyr in the fight to preserve the Amazonian rain forest. In December 1990, a jury found landowner Darly Alves da Silva and his son, Darci, guilty of Chico's murder.

– CAROLYN JOSTOCK

MÉNDEZ BALLESTER, MANUEL

Manuel Méndez Ballester (*b.* 4 August 1909), Puerto Rican dramatist. Born in Aguadilla, Puerto Rico, Méndez Ballester began his career in theater as an actor with the Teatro Rodante (Traveling Theater). His first publications were *Isla cerrera* (Wild island, 1937), a historical novel about the resistance of the Puerto Rican Indians to the Spanish conquest, and *El clamor de los surcos* (1940), a rural drama. In 1939 he studied under a Rockefeller grant in New York, where he penned his famous *Tiempo muerto* (Dead time, 1940), a tragedy about the sugarcane worker during the idle season. His 1958 drama about Puerto Ricans in New York, *Encrucijada* (The crossroads), was staged at the First Puerto Rican Theater Festival. *El milagro* (1957), an avantgarde metaphysical play, debuted the next year in English in New York as *The Miracle*. Two of his well-known satirical works are *Bienvenido, don Goyito*

(Welcome, Mr. Goyito, 1966) and *Arriba las mujeres* (Long live women, 1968).

In addition to writing, producing, and directing theatrical productions, Méndez Ballester served as assistant secretary of labor from 1954 to 1962 and subsequently, until 1968, as a member of the House of Representatives, where he initiated environmental reforms. A versatile dramatist, Méndez Ballester has cultivated classical tragedy, historical theater, the theater of the absurd, social satire, farce, and zarzuela (operetta). The conflict of material and spiritual values is an abiding theme in his writing, which in addition to novels and drama includes stories, essays, and a humorous column in *El Nuevo Día*. In 1992 the Institute of Puerto Rican Culture published a two-volume collection of his plays.

– ESTELLE IRIZARRY

MÉNDEZ FLEITAS, EPIFANIO

Epifanio Méndez Fleitas (*b.* 1917; *d.* 22 November 1985), Paraguayan political leader. An early associate of President Federico CHAVES (1949–1959), Méndez Fleitas first rose to a position of prominence when the latter came to power in 1949. As chief of police, Méndez Fleitas worked to defend Chaves's interests. He was named director of the Agrarian Reform Institute and later president of the Central Bank. At the same time, he rose rapidly within the "leftist" faction of the ruling Colorado Party, in part because of Chaves's patronage but also because of his own exceptional energy and forceful oratorical style.

Wishing to rise still further, Méndez Fleitas organized a plot with the help of General Alfredo STROESSNER, head of the artillery section of the army. In early May 1954, the coup was carried out, but shortly thereafter, Stroessner exiled his fellow conspirator to Buenos Aires and went on to impose a dictatorship that lasted until 1989.

In the Argentine capital, Méndez Fleitas published polemical writings and composed folk music. He also established the Movimiento Popular Colorado (MOPOCO), an emigré group composed of Colorados who had turned against Stroessner. MOPOCO continued to be a major center of opposition to the dictator, though its founder encountered a loss of prestige when it was alleged in the 1970s that he had accepted money from the Central Intelligence Agency. Méndez Fleitas died in Buenos Aires.

– THOMAS L. WHIGHAM

MÉNDEZ MONTENEGRO, JULIO CÉSAR

Julio César Méndez Montenegro, (*b.* 23 November 1915), president of Guatemala (1966–1970). Born in

Guatemala City, Méndez Montenegro interrupted his legal studies at the University of San Carlos to participate in the 1944 October Revolution. He was the first president of the Frente Popular Libertador (FPL), which supported Juan José ARÉVALO for president in 1945. After receiving his *licenciatura* in 1945, he taught at the National University until 1965, rising to dean of the law school.

After the mysterious death of his brother, two-time Partido Revolucionario (PR) presidential candidate Mario MÉNDEZ MONTENEGRO (1912–1965), he agreed to substitute for him in the 1966 elections. He defeated the military-backed PID (Institutional Democratic Party) candidate by 45,000 votes but, because he did not receive an absolute majority, had to bargain with the military and its legislative supporters to secure the confirmation of the Congress. As a result, Méndez gave the military both a free hand in conducting the war against the guerrillas in the eastern departments of the country and virtual control of the countryside.

The Méndez Montenegro administration is remembered primarily for the "scorched earth" rural pacification campaigns led by Colonel Carlos ARANA OSORIO (his successor in office [1970]), the kidnapping of Archbishop Mario Casariego (1968), and for the emergence of the Mano Blanca (White Hand) and other right-wing terrorist organizations. However, his government pushed through some reform measures, most notably the nationalization of the railroad owned by the United Fruit Company. Schools, public hospitals, port facilities, and a major hydroelectric plant were constructed. Some *campesino* organizing and limited land distribution were attempted, but the regime was frustrated in its agrarian reform efforts. Attempts to overhaul the tax code were defeated by street demonstrations.

After leaving office, Méndez Montenegro held a law professorship at the University of San Carlos.

– ROLAND H. EBEL

MÉNDEZ MONTENEGRO, MARIO

Mario Méndez Montenegro (*b.* 30 November 1912; *d.* 31 October 1965), mayor of Guatemala City (1944–1948) and founder of the Partido Revolucionario (PR). Born in Santa Rosa, he interrupted his law studies, which he completed in exile, to participate in the October Revolution (1944). He served as undersecretary of the junta and as secretary general of the presidency under Juan José ARÉVALO (1945–1951). In 1947 he broke with the radicals in the Revolutionary Action Party (PAR) and reconstituted the center-left Popular Liberation Front (Frente Popular Libertador—FPL), which he had helped found in 1944.

In 1957 Méndez Montenegro organized the PR from among the moderate supporters of Arévalo. When the PR was denied legal registration for the elections of 1957, Méndez Montenegro supported the street demonstrations led by General Miguel YDÍGORAS FUENTES (president, 1958–1963) that annulled them. He became the legal PR candidate for the January 1958 electoral rerun and received 28 percent of the vote. Opposed both ideologically and politically to the Ydígoras Fuentes regime, he backed the 1963 military coup that overthrew Fuentes. He died from a gunshot wound in October 1965, shortly before being nominated as the PR presidential candidate for the elections of 1966. Whether Méndez Montenegro was assassinated or committed suicide remains unclear.

– ROLAND H. EBEL

MÉNDEZ PEREIRA, OCTAVIO

Octavio Méndez Pereira (*b.* 1887; *d.* 1954), prominent Panamanian educator. He was born in Aguadulce and graduated from the University of Chile in 1913. He taught at and was president of the National Institute, served as minister of education, and became the first president of the University of Panama when it was founded in 1935. Méndez Pereira founded numerous schools and learned journals. He published essays on literature, education, and a variety of historical subjects. He wrote biographies of Vasco Núñez de BALBOA and Justo AROSEMENA, and he founded the Panamanian Academy of Language and the Panamanian Academy of History.

– JUAN MANUEL PÉREZ

MENDIBURU, MANUEL DE

Manuel De Mendiburu (*b.* 20 October 1805; *d.* 21 January 1885), considered Peru's foremost historian of the early republic and the forerunner to Jorge BASADRE. He was in fact a man of many careers—diplomat, government minister, and military officer. Mendiburu was involved in the highest levels of government for most of his adult life. No doubt the apex of his political accomplishments came when at the height of his political influence as the prefect of Tacna, he vigorously opposed the Peru-Bolivia Confederation of Andrés SANTA CRUZ (1829–1836). He briefly was minister of finance and war in the early years of Ramón CASTILLA's presidency and later was president of the council of state. He served the government of José Rufino ECHENIQUE as minister of finance and then as ambassador to London while the government was negotiating a settlement of the external debt. For the first five months of the War of the Pacific

(1879–1883), he served as minister of war. Between these assignments he compiled the invaluable *Diccionario histórico-biográfico del Perú* (8 vols., 1874), a descriptive catalog of colonial Peruvian public figures with heavy emphasis on the sixteenth century. He wrote many other studies, numbers of them unpublished, focusing primarily on diplomatic events of his own era.

– VINCENT PELOSO

MENDIETA, SALVADOR

Salvador Mendieta (*b.* 24 March 1882; *d.* 28 May 1958), Nicaraguan literary figure and Central American unionist leader. Born in Diriamba to a well-liked, hardworking merchant family, Mendieta grew up to become an ardent Central American unionist. Alejo Mendieta was committed to securing a good education for his sons and, when health problems threatened to intervene, sent young Salvador to Guatemala to finish primary school. He completed his baccalaureate in 1896 with a thesis entitled "The Constituents and the Federal Constituent Assembly of 1824." His doctoral thesis in law, titled "Organization of Executive Power in Central America" (Honduras, 1900) further underscores Mendieta's early commitment to the idea of union.

Mendieta's early activities were not confined to the classroom. In 1895 he organized the Minerva Society, a literary-scientific salon with marked unionist sentiments. In 1899 he cofounded another discussion group, El Derecho, which sponsored a journal of the same name. That same year Mendieta ambitiously declared the existence of the Central American Unionist Party, in response to political upheavals throughout the isthmus. He quickly aroused the animosity of Guatemalan dictator Manuel Estrada Cabrera, his lifelong nemesis, who then expelled Mendieta to Honduras in 1900. Nevertheless, the determined young man refused to be dissuaded and set about extending the Unionist Party to other Central American countries.

Mendieta established a newspaper, *Diario Centroamericano,* in Managua, which led President José Santos Zelaya to imprison Mendieta in 1903. During the first decade of the twentieth century, Mendieta traveled throughout the isthmus and began to write some of his most important works: *Páginas de Unión* (1902), *La nacionalidad y el Partido Unionista Centroamericano* (1905), *Partido Unionista Centroamericano* (1911), and *Cómo estamos y qué debemos hacer* (1911). Mendieta's most famous and enduring work was *La enfermedad de Centro América* (1906–1930), in which he focused on the obstacles to Central American development. Mendieta pointed to the lack of education, poor health and hygiene, unequal distribution of wealth and power, and the generally low level of public consciousness as the roots of the isthmus's infirmities.

Mendieta's ideas of union and social justice did not endear him to the oligarchical political elites of Central America, and he found it difficult to get his masterwork published. He traveled to Europe in search of support and finally reached an agreement with Maucci in Barcelona. Back in Nicaragua, Mendieta served as rector of the Universidad Nacional, but he resigned in protest of his inability to effect needed reforms. Seriously ill with a liver ailment, Mendieta nonetheless continued to head the Unionist Party, for which efforts he was sentenced to jail in 1955 by Anastasio SOMOZA. Fleeing on horseback, the aging Mendieta escaped Somoza's secret police and lived in San Salvador until his death.

– KAREN RACINE

MENDIETA Y MONTEFUR, CARLOS

Carlos Mendieta y Montefur (*b.* 4 November 1873; *d.* 29 September 1960), president of Cuba (1934–1935). A colonel in the war of independence and afterward a congressman for more than twenty years, Mendieta was also a vice-presidential candidate in 1916. Three years later he became editor of *Heraldo de Cuba,* where he achieved considerable fame as a combative political journalist. He was generally regarded as an honest man, and for a long time he was held by many to be the "hope of the Republic," until army chief Fulgencio BATISTA appointed him Cuba's provisional president on 18 January 1934.

Mendieta proved to be an inept and weak president whose main administrative skill was the ability to organize ephemeral compromises among party leaders. For this reason he was quickly dubbed Batista's puppet. During his brief term in office the revolutionary impetus that had begun the previous year came to an end when a general strike against the government was harshly repressed by the military. Mendieta's administration, however, was not altogether counterrevolutionary, for it confirmed much of the social legislation passed by the preceding revolutionary regime. It was also under Mendieta that women were enfranchised, and the Platt Amendment (1901), peceived by many Cubans as an infringement on their sovereignty, was finally abrogated by a treaty signed with the United States on 29 May 1934. Mendieta resigned on 10 December 1935.

– JOSÉ M. HERNÁNDEZ

MENDINUETA Y MÚZQUIZ, PEDRO DE

Pedro de Mendinueta y Múzquiz (*b.* 7 June 1736; *d.* 17 February 1825), viceroy of New Granada (1797–

1803). Born near Pamplona, Navarre, Spain, Mendinueta pursued a military career. He served as subinspector general of the army of New Spain (1785–1789), held a successful command during the French War (1793–1795), and had secured promotion to lieutenant general by the time of his assignment to New Granada. A leader of good ability and sound judgment, Mendinueta ruled during difficult times, facing a plethora of conspiracies inspired by the French Revolution and the threat of invasion during the First British War (1796–1802). Rather than assume personal command on the coast, which was the normal wartime practice for viceroys, he remained in Santa Fe to address questions of domestic security. Mendinueta is well remembered for his strong dedication to public health and the establishment of a school of medicine in Santa Fe. He was replaced by Antonio AMAR Y BORBÓN and returned to Spain, where he assumed a position on the Supreme Council of War and later became councillor of state. He died in Madrid.

– ALLAN J. KUETHE

MENDOZA, ANTONIO DE

Antonio de Mendoza (*b.* 1490/94; *d.* 21 July 1552), count of Tendilla, Spain's ambassador to Hungary, and viceroy of Peru (1551–1552). Mendoza, probably born in Granada, was also the first viceroy of Mexico (1535–1549). Chosen to represent the king and the Council of the Indies as well as to provide a check on the personal power of Hernándo CORTÉS, he brought to the office the prestige of the high nobility. Mendoza reached New Spain fourteen years after the military conquest of central Mexico had been completed. Typically, Spanish institutions arrived on the scene as the viability of new colonies became obvious and greater crown control

---

Mendoza's direct tie to the crown was relatively

loose, considering that fleets containing official letters

and orders sailed once a year.

---

seemed necessary. Yet, once in the colony, Mendoza's direct tie to the crown was relatively loose, considering that fleets containing official letters and orders sailed once a year. Mendoza, like other viceroys, occasionally avoided complying with royal pronouncements, such as his delay in enforcing the New Laws of the Indies that sought to limit *encomiendas* (grants of Indian labor and tribute). (The first viceroy of Peru lost his life in a rebellion following the implementation of the New Laws in that colony.)

Judicial matters and many ecclesiastical ones fell outside Mendoza's domain, but he administered nearly all other social, political, territorial, and economic concerns of the colony. Enhancing revenues through legislation covering taxation, trade, and transportation was probably one of his more pressing goals. Mendoza also supervised matters relating to the indigenous people of the new colony, ironically seeking to protect their rights and to see that they were subjugated and Hispanicized.

– STEPHANIE WOOD

MENDOZA, CARLOS ANTONIO

Carlos Antonio Mendoza (*b.* 1856; *d.* 1916), Panamanian lawyer and politician and author of Panama's declaration of independence. He headed the radical wing of the Liberal Party. A mulatto, he was very popular with the lower classes. Mendoza served as deputy to the National Assembly and was a member of the Panama City Council. He was also president of the national directorate of the Liberal Party. In 1910 he occupied the presidency for seven months after the death of President José Domingo Obaldía and prior to Pablo AROSEMENA, who completed Obaldía's term.

– JUAN MANUEL PÉREZ

MENDOZA, PEDRO DE

Pedro de Mendoza (*b.* 1487; *d.* 23 June 1537), first *adelantado* (frontier military commander) of Río de la Plata (1536–1537). Born in Guadix, Spain, Mendoza probably served in the Italian campaigns of Charles V. As part of an attempt by the Spanish crown to control Portuguese expansion in the New World, he was charged with populating the Río de la Plata area in 1534. Although he fell seriously ill before departing Sanlúcar da Barrameda, he had recovered sufficiently by August 1535 to embark on the expedition, which was composed of eleven ships and more than 2,000 men (and a few women) drawn primarily from the Basque region, Andalusia, and the Low Countries.

In February 1536, Mendoza founded a fortified city on the banks of the Río de la Plata, a city that he christened Santa María del Buen Aire. Within a year he and his men were forced to abandon their settlement because of the hostility of the Querandí Indians and the resultant lack of food. Suffering from hunger, recurring sickness, and Indian attack, Mendoza decided to return to Spain in early 1537; he died at sea. Those who had remained in Buenos Aires were compelled to abandon it in 1541 and to withdraw 1,000 miles upstream to the city of Asunción.

– SUSAN M. SOCOLOW

MENDOZA CAAMAÑO Y SOTOMAYOR, JOSÉ ANTONIO DE

José Antonio de Mendoza Caamaño y Sotomayor (Marqués de Villagarcía; *b.* ca. March 1668; *d.* 14 December 1746), viceroy of Peru (1736–1745). A grandee of the illustrious Mendoza family who had served Philip V as Spanish ambassador to Venice and as viceroy of Cataluña, Villagarcía took office in Lima on 4 January 1736. Described as a person of limited intelligence and little administrative ability with a certain pious perversity because of his great pleasure in presiding over the *autos de fe* of the Lima inquisition, Villagarcía's overweaning task as viceroy was that of bolstering the Pacific fleet and shoring up coastal defenses against the onslaughts of British naval forces. In 1742 he subdued a serious Indian uprising led by Juan Santos (Apu Inca) in Jauja and Tarma. So great were his military expenditures that Villagarcía ran up a debt of almost 3 million pesos, most of which was unpaid salaries for soldiers, sailors, and militiamen.

In Lima the contentious Villagarcía was constantly at odds with the town council (*cabildo*), merchant guild (*consulado*), royal treasury officials, and the Jesuits, and in the interior, with provincial administrators (*corregidores*). Besides his successful defense of Peru during the War of Jenkins' Ear, his other principal achievement was eliminating the practice at the University of San Marcos of awarding university degrees for gifts of money rather than for academic merit. Accused of mismanagement he was summarily relieved of office on 12 July 1745. He died off Cape Horn on a vessel taking him back to Spain.

– JOHN JAY TEPASKE

MENDOZA Y LUNA, JUAN MANUEL DE

Juan Manuel de Mendoza y Luna (marquis of Montesclaros), viceroy of Peru (1608–1615). Facing a sharp decline in state revenues, Montesclaros sought to rejuvenate the silver and mercury mining industries and increase remittances to Spain. His main efforts were directed at increasing Indian tribute and labor. The first viceroy to attempt radical changes in the Toledo resettlement system, Montesclaros proposed that Indian migrants be forced to pay taxes and participate in the state labor system. More important, Montesclaros tried to end the colonial practice of issuing licenses to those who employed yanaconas, Indians who effectively escaped state demands. Montesclaros also denounced the crown's policy of selling *juros,* annuities that depended on colonial revenues both as security for the purchasers' investments and as the source of interest payments. Although the sale of *juros* was halted in 1615, Montescla-

ros left office that same year still awaiting crown approval of his policies on Indian labor, which had been bitterly contested by Peru's agricultural and mining elites. His successor, the prince of Esquilache, would reverse most of the Montesclaros program.

– ANN M. WIGHTMAN

MENEM, CARLOS SAÚL

Carlos Saúl Menem (*b.* 2 July 1930), president of Argentina (1989–). Menem is the son of Syrian immigrants who settled in the northern province of La Rioja. Active in politics from university days, he was elected to the legislature of his native province on the Peronist ticket in 1955, and subsequently elected and re-elected its governor (1973, 1983, 1987). His career was interrupted by the military regime that deposed President Isabel Perón in March 1976, during which time he spent five years in prison. In 1989, defying all predictions, he defeated Antonio Cafiero for the presidential nomination of the Peronist Party, and won a relatively easy victory in the national elections.

Menem's presidency has been a revolutionary one, for Argentina and for Peronism. He reversed a fifty-year-old trend toward statism-populism, opening up the economy by drastically reducing taxes and tariffs, and wiping out huge budgetary deficits by privatizing large state-owned industries. A "convertibility plan" established a stable exchange rate for the Argentine peso in relation to the dollar and permitted the peso's free exchange for foreign currencies. Formerly politically sensitive areas like oil and hydrocarbons have been opened to foreign investments.

At the same time, Menem has reversed historic trends in Argentine foreign policy, openly aligning the country with the United States and offering cooperation with United Nations efforts at peacekeeping. Though frequently criticized for his rather haphazard style of administration, as well as for the corrupt practices of family members and immediate aides, such has been Menem's popularity that he has been able to convince the opposition Radical Party to support changes in the Argentine Constitution that would allow him to run for another term—for four, rather than six years—in 1995.

– MARK FALCOFF

MENÉNDEZ DE AVILÉS, PEDRO

Pedro Menéndez de Avilés (*b.* 1519; *d.* 17 September 1574), Spanish naval officer. Menéndez, a native of Avilés, Asturias, was appointed captain-general of the Indies fleet by PHILIP II in 1560. In a 1565 patent, he was named *adelantado,* governor, and captain-general of Florida; he agreed to settle and pacify the area at his own expense. In return, Menéndez received tax exemptions, a large land grant, and, in addition to those listed above, the title of marqués. At that time, Florida extended from Newfoundland to the Florida Keys; it was enlarged in 1573 to include the Gulf coast. When Philip II learned of the French establishment at Fort Caroline, he furnished royal support for the Menéndez expedition.

Menéndez sailed to Florida and defeated the French, killing many of them. He founded Saint Augustine on 8 September 1565, and established garrisons at San Mateo (the renamed Fort Caroline) and elsewhere in the Florida peninsula. In 1566, Menéndez established the city of Santa Elena on Parris Island, in present-day South Carolina; he left garrisons there and in Guale (present-day Georgia). Menéndez planned a line of fort-missions from Santa Elena to present-day Mexico, and sent Captain Juan PARDO on an expedition that reached as far as the Appalachian Mountains. First Jesuit and then Franciscan missionaries went to Florida to evangelize the Native Americans. Despite this and the coming of more than 200 settlers, Menéndez's Florida enterprise failed, largely due to difficulties between the Native Americans and the Spaniards. After the death of Menéndez in Santander, Spain, and the abandonment of Santa Elena, only Saint Augustine remained—the oldest permanent European settlement in the present United States.

— EUGENE LYON

MENININHA DO GANTOIS, MÃE

Mãe Menininha do Gantois (Maria Escolástica da Conceição Nazareth; b. 10 February 1894; d. 13 August 1986), the fourth priestess of Ilê Iya Omin Axé Iya Massé, known popularly as the Terreiro do Gantois. Born in Salvador, Bahia, Menininha was the great-niece of Maria Julia da Conceição Nazareth, who founded the Terreiro de Gantois in 1849 after a divergence with Engenho Velho, one of the oldest Candomblé communities in Bahia. The women of the Conceição Nazareth family, who have led Gantois since its foundation, trace their lineage to the city of Abeokuta in Nigeria and preserve many of their cultural traditions through Candomblé. Menininha was initiated as a devotee of the ORIXÁ Oxum at eight months, and named senior priestess of Gantois at the uncharacteristically young age of twenty-eight; hence, her nickname, which means "little girl." For sixty-four years she was spiritual counselor and inspiration to many well-known politicians, artists, and scholars, including Jorge AMADO, Carybé, Caetano VELOSO, Maria Bethania, and Antonio Carlos Magalhães. Mãe Menininha's openness helped to dispel widespread prejudice against the Afro-Brazilian Candomblé tradition. By the time of her death, she was the most beloved and widely venerated Candomblé priestess in Brazil. Her home in Bahia is now a memorial and museum.

— KIM D. BUTLER

MENOCAL, MARIO GARCÍA

Mario García Menocal (b. 17 December 1866; d. 1941), president of Cuba (1913–1921). Born in Jaguey Granada, Cuba, Menocal attended Cornell University in New York, receiving an engineering degree in 1888. Upon completion of his studies, Menocal went to work with his uncle, Ancieto G. Menocal, a noted canal engineer. Both men worked in Nicaragua, then a proposed trans-isthmian canal route.

Menocal participated in the Cuban War of Independence, he was appointed assistant secretary of war in the revolutionary government (1895), and fought with General Calixto GARCÍA in the Oriente campaign. In 1897, after a strategic success at Tunas he was promoted to general. Menocal cooperated with the U.S. intervention and was named Havana's chief of police. He ran for president on the Conservative Party ticket in 1908 but was defeated by the Conservative turned Liberal José Miguel GÓMEZ. Renominated in 1912, Menocal won, serving two terms. His presidency was fraught with corruption (including 372 indictments against public officials) and disrespect for the law. Indictments of government officials were rarely taken seriously and convictions were often negated through presidential pardons or congressional declarations of amnesty. Menocal's third attempt for the presidency in 1924 met with failure.

— ALLAN S. R. SUMNALL

MÉRIDA, CARLOS

Carlos Mérida (b. 2 December 1891; d. 22 December 1984), artist. Although born in Guatemala, Mérida is most often associated with the modern art movement in Mexico. In 1910 he traveled to Paris to study with Kees van Dongen (1877–1968) and Hermen Anglada-Camarasa (1873–1959), becoming closely associated with Pablo Picasso and Amadeo Modigliani. In 1914, Mérida returned to Guatemala to begin experimenting with folkloric themes in his painting. He exhibited his work in the National Academy of Fine Arts in Mexico in 1920, and his uniquely Latin American themes made him one of the pioneers of the Mexican artistic revolution.

The mural renaissance in Mexico in the 1920s greatly influenced his work. He was commissioned in 1921 to do two murals in the Ministry of Education in Mexico City. After a New York exhibition, Mérida again traveled to Europe, where he exhibited his work in Paris (1927). He returned to Mexico in 1929 to continue his work with plastic painting, gradually developing the abstract and plastic-surrealist style for which he is best known. Among his better-known works are mosaic murals in the Benito Juárez housing development in Mexico City (1952) and in the Municipal Building in Guatemala City (1956).

— SARA FLEMING

MERINO CASTRO, JOSÉ TORIBIO

José Toribio Merino Castro (*b.* 14 December 1915), Chilean naval officer. Born in La Serena, Merino entered the Chilean Naval Academy in 1931 and graduated as a midshipman in 1936. He specialized in gunnery and fire control. During the last year of World War II he served as an anti-aircraft battery officer on board the U.S. cruiser *Raleigh.* During his career he commanded the corvette *Papudo,* the transport *Angamos,* and the destroyers *Almirante Williams* and *Almirante Riveros.* Between 1956 and 1957 Merino served in the Chilean naval mission to Great Britain.

Merino and other naval officers initiated a plot to overthrow the government of Salvador Allende.

In 1963 Merino became chief of staff of the fleet. For the next four years he served as the assistant chief of the General Staff and the director of the Bureau of Weapons. In 1970 he became commander in chief and the naval judge of the fleet, the senior naval command afloat, and in 1973 he was named commander in chief and naval judge of the First Naval Zone.

Merino and other naval officers initiated a plot to overthrow the government of Salvador ALLENDE, informing General Augusto PINOCHET, commander of the Chilean army, that the navy would act on 11 September 1973. This forced Pinochet to advance a plot of his own from 14 to 11 September. With the overthrow of the Allende government, Admiral Merino served as a member of the junta and the commander of the navy until his retirement on 8 March 1990.

— ROBERT SCHEINA

MESSÍA DE LA CERDA, PEDRO DE

Pedro de Messía de la Cerda (Messía de la Zerda, Marqués de la Villa de Armijo; *b.* February 1700; *d.*

1783), military figure and viceroy of the New Kingdom of Granada (1761–1772). Born in Córdoba, he pursued a naval career upon completion of his schooling and took part in the Spanish "reconquest" of Sicily and in Mediterranean battles with the English. In 1721 he made his first cruise to the Americas. He was promoted to captain in 1745. He became a knight commander of the Order of Malta. Messía de la Cerda served in the southern Caribbean (1750s). He thus came to his viceregal post with firsthand knowledge of the defense and commercial difficulties that he would face. Important, too, with regard to Messía's qualifications and mandate as viceroy, he was concurrently the commandant general of the Caribbean squadron in charge of the fight against contraband traffic.

In the 1760s the viceroy authorized José Celestino MUTIS to introduce the academic study of mathematics and the sciences at the *colegio mayor* of Nuestra Señora del Rosario in Santa Fe de Bogotá, established the tobacco monopoly, and oversaw the expulsion of the Jesuits. By 1767, Messía complained of failing health and sought to return to Spain, which he did in 1772, when Manuel de Guirior (1772–1776) relieved him. He died in Madrid.

— LANCE R. GRAHN

MICHELINA, SANTOS

Santos Michelina (*b.* 1 November 1797; *d.* 12 March 1848), Venezuelan politician who became Venezuela's first secretary of finance in 1830. After briefly participating in the War of Independence, Michelina was imprisoned, then freed and expelled from the country. He settled in Philadelphia, where he studied economics, law, and business. In 1821 he returned to Venezuela and took up various public posts connected with financial affairs. In 1830 he became secretary of finance and foreign affairs and established the foundation for the financial organization of the republic. He took charge of managing the Venezuelan foreign debt and served as negotiator for the country in the working out of diverse international treaties. Later he filled other important public posts. He was elected representative to Congress and was wounded in the assault on Congress of 24 January 1848. He died in Caracas seven weeks later.

— INÉS QUINTERO

MICHELINI, ZELMAR

Zelmar Michelini (*b.* 24 March 1924; *d.* 20 May 1976), Uruguayan senator and founder of the Movement for a People's Government, a splinter faction of the Colorado Party, known as List 99, which later became the

Party for a People's Government (PGP). Michelini abandoned his law school studies and position as general secretary of the Federation of University Students (FEUU) to become an organizer in the Bank Employees Union (AEBU). An active member of the Colorado Party, he was elected to the Chamber of Deputies in 1953 as a close associate of Luis BATLLE BERRES. Michelini was reelected as a deputy in 1958 and 1962. Growing disagreements with the leadership led Michelini and others to form List 99 within the Colorado Party. With the party's return to the presidency in 1966, Michelini was given the post of minister of industry and commerce. On the death of President Oscar Daniel GESTIDO and the ascension of Jorge PACHECO ARECO to the presidency amid ongoing social tension and political conflict, Michelini, now a senator, took his group out of the Colorado Party in December 1970. In February 1971, Michelini's group, later known as the PGP, joined the Christian Democratic and the Socialist and Communist parties to form the Frente Amplio (Broad Front), a coalition modeled after Unidad Popular in Chile.

Michelini was reelected a senator in 1972 but this time as a member of the Frente Amplio. From this position he protested eloquently against the increased authoritarianism of President Juan María BORDABERRY and the growing role of the armed forces. The 27 June 1973 coup found Michelini in Buenos Aires, where he went into permanent exile. He spent the next three years fighting the dictatorship and denouncing its violations of human rights. He testified on these matters before the Bertrand Russell War Crimes Tribunal in Rome in March 1974. His tireless efforts on behalf of political prisoners and his work with other exiles led to his abduction by Uruguayan and Argentine security forces on 18 May 1976. His body was found two days later along with that of a fellow Uruguayan, Héctor Gutiérrez Ruíz. In the 1990s Michelini's PGP, as an independent party, was the dominant force in a social-democratic political movement known as the Nuevo Espejo (New Model). Michelini's son Rafael was a PGP deputy to the Chamber of Deputies.

– MARTIN WEINSTEIN

MIER NORIEGA Y GUERRA, JOSÉ SERVANDO TERESA DE

José Servando Teresa de Mier Noriega y Guerra (*b.* 18 October 1765; *d.* 3 December 1827), Mexican political theorist and independence leader. Born in Monterrey, Nuevo León, Mier entered the Dominican order, obtained a doctorate in theology, and became notorious on 12 December 1794 when he delivered a sermon questioning aspects of the account of the Virgin of Guadalupe and arguing that the Apostle Thomas had introduced Christianity to America before the arrival of the Europeans, thus questioning the Spanish mandate to govern the New World. Exiled to Spain by the archbishop, he traveled through Europe. After the 1808 coup in New Spain, he became the paid defender of the ousted viceroy José de ITURRIGARAY in Spain. As a result, he published the first history of the struggle for independence, *Historia de la Revolución de Nueva España* (1813).

An avid polemicist, Mier wrote extensively in support of independence, alleging that the New World had possessed an unwritten constitution since the sixteenth century. In 1817 he joined the ill-fated Mina expedition to free New Spain and was captured and jailed until 1820 when he managed to escape. He traveled to the United States, where he sought support for his country's independence.

Returning to Mexico in 1822, Mier was elected to Congress and numbered among those congressmen opposed to Emperor ITURBIDE. Subsequently he distinguished himself in Congress as the champion of a strong federal system. He died in 1827, a patriot and an honored legislator.

By exalting Indian society, Mier created the myth of an ancient Mexican empire, thus establishing the foundations of Mexican nationalism. He was also a brilliant political thinker who integrated the Indian past with Hispanic constitutionalism to form a unique Mexican political ideology.

– JAIME E. RODRÍGUEZ O.

MIER Y TERÁN, MANUEL

Manuel Mier y Terán (*b.* 18 February 1789; *d.* 3 July 1832), Mexican military figure and independence leader. Born in Mexico City, Mier studied at the School of Mines. In 1812 he joined the insurgents, distinguishing himself in combat. After the death of José María MORELOS in 1815, he tried, but failed, to assume unified command of the insurgent movement. Later, he served as minister of war and marine. He was subsequently appointed inspector general of the army.

In 1827 Mier assumed command of the commission to define the boundary between Mexico and the United States, a task that highlighted the dangers that Anglo-American immigration posed to Texas. Although he successfully participated in the 1832 revolt against the regime of Anastasio BUSTAMANTE and was widely considered the leading candidate for the presidency, he became deeply depressed by the situation in Texas and took his life in a vain effort to galvanize his countrymen to action.

— JAIME E. RODRÍGUEZ O.

MIGNONE, FRANCISCO

Francisco Mignone (*b.* 3 September 1897; *d.* 19 February 1986), Brazilian pianist, composer, conductor, and leading figure in the nationalist movement in music. Son of an Italian immigrant musician, he studied piano and flute with his father. At an early age he played both instruments in local dance orchestras and demonstrated an amazing facility for improvisation and the ability to absorb the various styles of popular music. His first compositions date from the year 1917 and display a romantic improvisational style as well as an interest in national subjects. In 1920 Mignone received a scholarship for European study from the São Paulo Committee of Artistic Grants and left Brazil in August to study composition at the Giuseppe Verdi Conservatory in Milan, Italy. Most of his teachers had received their musical training in France (Vincenzo Ferroni, his composition teacher, had been a pupil of Massenet). Following the completion of his formal studies in 1922, Mignone stayed for several years in Europe, occasionally conducting, presenting programs of his own works, and studying opera repertoire. His first opera, *L'innocente,* received its premiere in Brazil in 1928, shortly after Mignone's return to his native country. A review of the performance by Mário de ANDRADE, leader of the nationalist movement, praised the musical qualities of the work while at the same time challenging Mignone to reconsider his position and abilities as a national composer. Mignone accepted the challenge and embarked on a serious period of writing works on national subjects and works based on urban musical ideas.

"Mignone's is a singular spirit, practical and shrewd, capable of perceiving and adapting itself to the subtle variations of popular taste."

The period from 1929 to 1959, his most productive period of composition, revealed an intense interest in folk and popular traditions. Mignone's facile pen, improvisational facility, and keyboard skills have produced a large number of works of uneven quality. His compositional style is perhaps best described by Luiz Heitor Correa de Azevedo, who wrote: "His [Mignone's] is a singular spirit, practical and shrewd, capable of perceiving and adapting itself to the more subtle variations of popular taste. The enormous musical facility he possesses gives to all his works a quality of improvisation which takes its path through many diverse positions" (*Música e músicos,* p. 301).

In works such as his *Festa das igrejas* (1940), Mignone demonstrates a brilliance and originality of conception which have charmed audiences in Brazil, Europe, and the United States. His twelve *Valsas de esquina* (Streetcorner Waltzes) give the listener sophisticated moments of sounds of bygone days in Rio de Janeiro when popular musicians roamed the streets in night-long revelries. His four *Fantasias brasileiras* represent some of his best writing. Although Mignone had a lifelong attraction to opera, he is at his best in short piano works. A great admirer of Heitor VILLA-LOBOS, he wrote *Sexta missa,* a mass honoring the eightieth anniversary of the birth of Villa-Lobos in 1967. Mignone is remembered by his colleagues and friends for his gracious spirit of generosity.

— DAVID P. APPLEBY

MILLA Y VIDAURRE, JOSÉ

José Milla y Vidaurre (*b.* 4 August 1822; *d.* 30 September 1882), Guatemalan writer. Born in Guatemala City, the son of Honduran Colonel Justo Milla and Mercedes Vidaurre, a daughter of one of the city's leading families, "Pepe" Milla was the leading literary figure of nineteenth-century Guatemala and the principal intellectual supporter of the conservative regime of Rafael CARRERA (1839–1865). After Francisco MORAZÁN exiled his father in 1829, Milla grew up in the care of his uncle, Santiago Milla. He was educated under the guidance of Father José María Castilla, who had been a leader in the Central America independence movement. His literary talent, much influenced by European Romanticism, was recognized early, and he abandoned legal training to devote his time to editing and writing essays, novels, poetry, and history. He also abandoned a youthful attachment to liberalism and, as editor of the government's gazette (*Gaceta oficial,* later *Gaceta de Guatemala*) and of several independent newspapers, he eloquently defended the Guatemalan conservatives and Rafael Carrera's regime. He also served on the Council of State, in the legislature, and on several diplomatic missions throughout the period of conservative control.

Milla wrote under the anagrammatic pseudonym Salomé Jil. His novels, history, poetry, and descriptions of customs reflected his Romantic ideals but also drew heavily on Guatemalan themes, and in this sense he was a forerunner of Miguel Ángel ASTURIAS. He was Guatemala's most popular novelist well into the twentieth century, his best-known works being *Los nazarenos*

(1867), *El visitador* (1869), *La hija del adelantado* (1866), *Historia de un Pepe* (1882), *Memorias de un abogado* (1876), *Cuadros de costumbres* (1865), and *Viaje al otro mundo pasando por otras partes* (1875).

After the Liberal Reforma of 1871, Milla left public service, traveled widely in the United States and Europe, and retired to his hacienda at Quezada, near Jutiapa, in eastern Guatemala, where he wrote the first two volumes of his projected *Historia de la América Central* (1879), commissioned by the Guatemalan government. These volumes, covering the period 1502–1686, reflected his romantic attachment to Hispanic tradition as well as his sensitivity to the indigenous peoples of Guatemala.

– RALPH LEE WOODWARD, JR.

MILLAS JIMÉNEZ, JORGE

Jorge Millas Jiménez (*b.* 17 January 1917; *d.* 8 November 1982), Chilean philosopher. Jorge Millas was born and educated in Santiago, where he studied philosophy and law in the 1930s. He also studied psychology at the University of Iowa and held teaching appointments at Columbia University and the University of Puerto Rico. Millas's first major work was *Idea de la individualidad* (1943), a book in which he affirmed the essential individuality of human nature and followed Enrique MOLINA GARMENDIA's tradition of separating philosophy from politics. He became one of the founders of Chilean philosophical professionalism in the 1950s, a period in which the study of the discipline became highly specialized and responsive to European, especially German, philosophical currents. In response to social and political change in the 1960s, Millas defended spiritual and humanistic values against the pressures of mass society. His most important works during this period are *El desafío espiritual de la sociedad de masas* (1964) and *Idea de la filosofía* (1970). A philosopher who argued that both philosophy and the university should be free from external pressures, Millas produced an influential set of essays collected under the title *Idea y defensa de la universidad* (1981). During the period of military rule in the 1970s and early 1980s, his articulate defense of the rights of the university gave him great public prominence. He became a leader of the academic organization Andrés BELLO and an outspoken opposition voice until his death.

– IVÁN JAKSIĆ

MINA Y LARREA, JAVIER

Javier Mina y Larrea (*b.* 1 July 1789; *d.* 11 November 1817), Mexican insurgent leader. Born in Otano, Spain,

he fought against the French in Spain until he was captured and sent to France. After Napoleon's defeat in 1814, he returned to Spain, then under the absolutist rule of Ferdinand VII (1784–1833), to lead a conspiracy to restore the Constitution of 1812. When the movement failed, he fled to London, where he met Lord Holland, an Englishman sympathetic to the Mexican insurgency, and Fray Servando Teresa de MIER (1765–1827). Together the three planned an expedition to New Spain to fight there against absolutism. In May 1816 he departed for the United States, where he obtained credit, money, and men. He landed in Soto la Marina in April 1817. Leaving some of his forces there, he continued inland to join the insurgents. Although he threatened the regime and was successful in several actions, his enterprise was doomed because the organized insurgency had disappeared with the death of José María MORELOS Y PAVÓN (1765–1815). Mina then joined José Antonio Torres (1770–1818) at the fortress of El Sombrero. After El Sombrero fell, he attacked the convoys that laid siege to the fortress of Los Remedios. He was captured at the ranch of El Venadito on 27 October 1817 and shot at Los Remedios.

– VIRGINIA GUEDEA

MINDLIN, JOSÉ E.

José E. Mindlin (*b.* 8 September 1914), Brazilian entrepreneur and bibliophile. Mindlin was born in São Paulo, the son of Ephim Henrique Mindlin and Fanny Mindlin, both Russians who had come to Brazil in 1910. He married Guita Kaufman Mindlin, with whom he has had four children. In 1936, Mindlin graduated from the faculty of law at the University of São Paulo. Mindlin has served as president of the board and CEO of Metal Leve, S.A.–Indústria e Comércio, and as vice president as well as director of the department of technology of the Federation and Center of Industries for the state of São Paulo (FIESP). He presides over the council of the school of management of the Getúlio Vargas Foundation and served on the board of directors of the Instituto Brasileiro do Patrimônio Cultural, of several major museums in Brazil, and of VITAE, an institution that supports educational and social activities.

From 1975 to 1976, Mindlin was secretary of culture, science, and technology in São Paulo and he served twice as director of the Museu de Arte of São Paulo. His many positions and titles include charter member of the Botanical Foundation Margaret Mee, member of the board and president of the Conselho de Administração da Sociedade de Cultura Artística de São Paulo, honorary member of the Instituto Histórico e Geográfico Brasileiro, member of the University of São Paulo Press, honorary member of the international council of the Museum of Modern Art of New York, member of the board of governors of the John Carter Brown Library, member of the International Association of Bibliophiles, and fellow of the Pierpont Morgan Library.

In 1988, Mindlin was chosen by the magazine *Isto É Senhor* as "Man of the Year" and has been honored by the governments of Brazil, Chile, Japan, and Portugal. Mindlin has promoted the publication of facsimile editions of classic and modern Brazilian works. A lifelong bibliophile, his collection is perhaps the largest private library of Brasiliana, with some 25,000 volumes ranging from incunabula to modern works.

— IÊDA SIQUEIRA WIARDA

MINUJIN, MARTA

Marta Minujin (*b.* 30 January 1940), Argentine sculptor and painter. Born in Buenos Aires, Minujin studied at the School of Visual Arts from 1953 to 1959. She received a Guggenheim Fellowship in 1966. Her bronze and plaster sculptures find their inspiration in Greek art. Liberated from traditional rules and stripped of context, they constitute a new spatial conception that proposes the possibility of linking sculpture with architecture through a different idea of movement through the use of constructive kinetics. She has exhibited in New York City as well as throughout Latin America.

— AMALIA CORTINA ARAVENA

MIR, PEDRO

Pedro Mir (*b.* 3 June 1913), Dominican poet, novelist, short-story writer, essayist, and teacher. The popular and critically acclaimed dean of contemporary Dominican poets, Mir was born in San Pedro de Macoris, the son of a Puerto Rican mother and a Cuban father. He earned a law degree from the University of Santo Domingo in 1941. Mir's radical opposition to the Rafael Leónidas TRUJILLO dictatorship led, in 1947, to long years of exile. Effectively assuming a collective voice and condition, the intimate, politically charged poetry of *Hay un país en el mundo* (1949; There Is in the World a Country), *Contracanto a Walt Whitman: Canto a nosotros mismos* (1952; Countersong to Walt Whitman: Song to Ourselves), *Seis momentos de esperanza* (1953; Six Moments of Hope), *Amén de mariposas* (1969; Amen to Butterflies), and *Viaje a la muchedumbre* (1971; Journey to the Multitude) offer lyrically powerful testimony to the patriotic constancy of that exile and the years of crisis and struggle immediately after.

Mir's vigorous denunciation of the cruel realities of the Trujillato and an American imperial presence throughout the hemisphere includes contrapuntal emphasis on the epic historical journey of the common people in a Latin America where the conceit and miscarried promise of the Whitmanesque "I" "is no longer/. . ./the word fulfilled/the touchstone word to start the world anew./ . . ./[where] now the word is/us" (*Viaje a la muchedumbre,* p. 62). Mir returned to the Dominican Republic for two years in 1963, and he reestablished himself there definitively in 1968.

The Whitmanesque "I" "is no longer/. . ./the word

fulfilled/the touchstone word to start the world

anew./. . ./[where] now the word is/us."

A poet of great complexity, technical skill, and intellectual authority, his work combines an elegiac mood with a prophetic vision of hope; in 1982, its compelling immediacy and evocative force earned him the official designation of National Poet. An exacting stylist and multifaceted chronicler of his country's social and cultural history, his writings include two other books of verse; a poetic historicist novel, *Cuando amaban las tierras comuneras* (1978); and the elegant narratives of *La gran hazaña de Limber y después otoño* (1977); and *¡Buen viaje, Pancho Valentín!* (1981). His works of historical interpretation, aesthetic philosophy, and art criticism include the two-volume *La noción de período en la historia dominicana* (1981–1983), *Tres leyendas de colores: Ensayo de interpretación de las tres primeras revoluciones del nuevo mundo* (1969), *Las raíces dominicanas de la doctrina Monroe* (1974), *Apertura a la estética* (1974), *Fundamentos de teoría y crítica de arte* (1979), and *La estética del soldadito* (1991). Mir currently holds a faculty and research appointment at the Universidad Autónoma de Santo Domingo.

— ROBERTO MÁRQUEZ

MIRAMÓN, MIGUEL

Miguel Miramón (*b.* 1832; *d.* 19 June 1867), Mexican Conservative general and president, executed with Maximilian. Born in Mexico City, Miramón defended Chapultepec as a cadet in 1847. As lieutenant colonel, he fought with Santa Anna in 1854–1855 against the revolution of Ayutla. He played a major part in Puebla's resistance to the Comonfort administration in 1856, for which he was imprisoned in April 1857. After escaping, he became the principal Conservative general in the Civil War of the Reform (1858–1861). Victorious at Salamanca (10 March 1858), Barrancas de Atenquique (2 July 1858), Ahualulco (29 September 1858), and Estancia de las Vacas (12 November 1859), he failed twice to take the Liberal seat of government, Veracruz, in the spring of 1859 and again in February–March 1860.

He was president within the Conservative zone from 15 April 1860 until his defeat at Calpulalpán on 22 December. Following the Liberal victory, he went into exile in Europe, but declined to participate in the French Intervention. After returning to Mexico in July 1863, his relations with Marshal François BAZAINE deteriorated, since the French commanders found the presence of a former Conservative leader an embarrassment. This initial trust in MAXIMILIAN evaporated after he was consigned to Berlin in November 1864 to study artillery tactics. Miramón's absence (along with that of Leonardo MÁRQUEZ) delayed the formation of a Mexican imperialist army.

Against his wife's pleading, he returned to Mexico late in 1866, believing he could save the empire after the evacuation of French forces. A swift thrust at Zacatecas late in January 1867 nearly led to the capture of Juárez and his ministers, but Mariano ESCOBEDO trapped Maximilian, Miramón, and Tomás MEJÍA in Querétaro, where in June 1867 they were captured, summarily tried, and executed. The plea of Miramón's wife and children for clemency was unheeded by an implacable Juárez.

Still a controversial figure, Miramón combined military skill with political miscalculation. Although a Conservative, he was neither specifically monarchist nor imperialist and he remains a legendary figure for Conservatives.

– BRIAN HAMNETT

MIRANDA, CARMEN

Carmen Miranda (*b.* 9 February 1909; *d.* 5 August 1955), Portuguese-born Brazilian singer and entertainer. Flamboyantly dressed and gifted with a comic personality, Miranda is best remembered as the international "Ambassadress of the Samba." Born Maria Do Carmo Miranda da Cuhna, near Lisbon, Miranda arrived with her family in Rio de Janeiro in 1910. She attended Catholic schools, where she sang and appeared in plays. After singing sambas and tangos at local engagements, Miranda met Josue de Barros, a composer and guitarist who helped prepare her for professional appearances and radio broadcasts.

Signing with RCA Victor in 1930, Miranda emerged as a recording and stage star across South America. Dur-

ing the decade she recorded 281 songs, many of which were also performed by the famous sambista PIXINGUINHA. In 1939 producer Lee Shubert signed Miranda to star in the hit Broadway show *Streets of Paris.* Billed as the "Brazilian Bombshell," she appeared in numerous American films, including *Down in Argentine Way* (1940) and *That Night in Rio* (1941). As her film career waned, she found success in nightclubs in New York, Las Vegas, and London. In 1955, after taping a number for the Jimmy Durante Show, she died in Hollywood, California.

– JOHN COHASSEY

MIRANDA, FRANCISCO DE

Francisco de Miranda (*b.* 28 March 1750; *d.* 14 July 1816), leader of the First Venezuelan Republic (1811–1812). Miranda was born and raised in Caracas. His father was a successful merchant from the Canary Islands who shared with many of his countrymen a scorn for the local planter aristocracy. In order to enhance his status and power, Miranda opted for a career as an officer in the Spanish army. Unable to secure a commission in the local Caracas Battalion—the officer slots were reserved for peninsulars—in 1771 he migrated to Spain and purchased a commission in the army. He served in North Africa and in the Caribbean during the American Revolutionary War. Although he rose to the rank of colonel by his early thirties, there is nothing in the record to indicate Miranda was blessed with a great military mind. In 1783 he fled to the United States to avoid charges of misuse of funds brought against him by the Spanish military. For the rest of his life Miranda promoted the political independence of Spanish America.

For the next two decades following his departure, Miranda traveled widely in the United States and Europe, during which time he became increasingly convinced that Spanish America should follow the example of British North America and become independent. For two years Miranda traveled in the United States, examining the newly independent country and meeting many influential figures. In 1785 he returned to Europe, touring the Continent and Great Britain and observing firsthand the wide variety of rulers and the consequences of their political philosophies. In Russia, for example, Miranda spent nearly two years attempting to convince the Empress Catherine the Great to invest 20,000 rubles in his liberation plans. Although he was unsuccessful, Catherine did grant him 1,000 rubles and ordered Russian embassies to assist him. His writings from the period are a rich source for comparative history. By the time of his return to London in 1789,

Miranda had become an active plotter against the crown in Spain. Until 1805, with time out to fight in the French Revolution and obtain the rank of general in the French army, he tried unsuccessfully to obtain backing to revolutionize Spanish America.

Unable to obtain sufficient support in London, Miranda returned in 1805 to the United States, where he found another government unwilling to support his cause. He did, however, succeed in raising a volunteer force of approximately two hundred men, with which he sailed from New York for Venezuela in February 1806. En route he chartered two schooners in Santo Domingo, and the British navy in the Caribbean lent some support to the enterprise. Well aware of Miranda's intent, Spanish military leaders in the captaincy general were fully prepared when he arrived off the Venezuelan coast. With a force comprising three ships and one hundred fifty men, Miranda first attempted to land in April 1806 just west of Puerto Cabello. It was a total fiasco, with Miranda losing two ships and sixty men. Miranda then fled to Barbados, where he was assisted by the

Francisco de Miranda. Portrait by Georges Rouget. (Organization of American States)

British admiral Thomas Cochrane. In August 1806 Miranda returned with a force of ten ships and approximately five hundred men, landing just north of the city of Coro. This time the population fled inland and allowed Miranda and his force to enter the town. He spent a few days trying to convince local leaders to join in rebellion against the Spanish crown, but found no support among the people of Coro. When he and his invasion force were attacked by the local militia, he fled to Trinidad, and from there he returned to England in late 1807.

Miranda's failure in 1806 to spark a general revolt against the Spanish crown is an important event when analyzing the wars for independence that would break out in Venezuela within a few years. The very people who would be the primary actors in the call for Venezuelan independence—namely the local planter and merchant elite—contributed heavily to his defeat. Miranda was seen as being linked to the ideals of the French Revolution, and in 1806 this was not the road down which the reform wing of the Caracas elite wanted to travel.

Nevertheless, Miranda had cast his lot with those wanting separation from Spain, and when revolution did break out in Venezuela in 1810, he returned to lend his support and leadership. Independence was declared on 5 July 1811, and Miranda was selected to suppress the loyalist counterrevolutionaries in Valencia. He was successful in this mission, but he was unable to convince the patriot leaders of the Venezuelan Congress to form a strong centralized government with himself as the leader. In 1812, after a number of royalist victories under General Juan Domingo Monteverde and a disastrous earthquake in Caracas had brought the patriot cause to naught, Miranda was given dictatorial powers. The royalist forces under Domingo Monteverde were too strong for Miranda and his followers. Miranda capitulated to Monteverde on 25 July 1812, ending the First Republic. This capitulation is a source of considerable historical controversy in Venezuela. Many patriot leaders, including Simón BOLÍVAR, suspected Miranda's action bordered on treason. Bolívar, in fact, prevented Miranda's departure, which caused Monteverde to charge that the patriots had violated the terms of the capitulation. The royalists arrested Miranda and sent him to prison in Cádiz, Spain, where he died four years later.

As an international revolutionary activist, Francisco de Miranda is perhaps best remembered for doing more than anyone else to lay the groundwork outside South America for the continent's separation from Spain. He was not a great military leader, however, and the heroes of the Venezuelan independence movement would be those who made their mark on the battlefield. This was, perhaps, as much a condition of his age—he was in his sixties—as of his misunderstanding of the revolutionary cause due to his long absence from Venezuela. But Miranda was no mere footnote in the independence struggle. By the beginning of the nineteenth century, revolutionary struggle was an international undertaking. Miranda realized this reality and promoted his revolution internationally.

— GARY MILLER

MIRÓ, CÉSAR

César Miró (*b.* 1907), Peruvian novelist, poet, composer, and essayist. A professor of art history at San Marcos University for many years and a graduate in journalism, Miró began his literary career with a revolutionary book of poetry, *Cantos del arado y de las hélices* (1929). While he was influenced by the romance of Federico García Lorca's work—especially by its short, eight-syllable verse, vivid imagery, and narrative style— his poetry maintained a Peruvian perspective. In *Nuevas voces para el viento* (1948), the romance evolved to include new themes and language. Miró enters the political arena with such novels as *Teoría para la mitad de una vida* (1935), *El tiempo de la tarántula* (1973), and *La masacre de los coroneles: Sinfonía barroca en tres tiempos* (1982), which deal with themes of political oppression and rebellion. At age twenty, Miró, imprisoned because of political protest, declared a hunger strike, which demonstrated his commitment to fighting political dictatorship. The tarantula symbol in his work represents world threats against humankind: atomic explosions, the war in Vietnam, cataclysm in Peru. Miró stands out for his journalism and critical essays. *Mariátegui: El tiempo y los hombres* (1989) is a collection of essays that reconstruct the political world during and after which José Carlos MARIÁTEGUI, the first Latin American essayist to use a Marxist framework of analysis, lived (1894–1930), from Pablo NERUDA to the Sendero Luminoso. Miró also wrote travel literature describing the city of Lima. *La ciudad del río hablador* (1944) captures from a modern perspective the mystique and nostalgia of Lima during colonial times.

— DICK GERDES

MIRÓ CARDONA, JOSÉ

José Miró Cardona (*b.* 28 July 1907; *d.* 10 August 1974), Cuban political leader, lawyer, and professor. Miró Cardona graduated from the University of Havana Law School in 1938. He held numerous positions throughout his life, including chief of the archives of the Liberation Army, librarian of the National Institute of Criminology in Havana, professor of penal law and dean of the law school at the University of Havana, secretary of the Democratic Revolutionary Front, and professor of penal law at the University of Río Piedras in Puerto Rico.

In 1959 he became the first prime minister in the revolutionary government and was Cuba's ambassador to Spain in 1960. He subsequently broke with the CASTRO regime and became president (1961–1963) of the Cuban Revolutionary Council in Miami, which helped prepare the Bay of Pigs Invasion in 1961.

— MARÍA DEL CARMEN ALMODÓVAR

MIRÓ QUESADA FAMILY

Miró Quesada Family, a wealthy and notable Peruvian family, owner of the daily newspaper *El Comercio* since 1876, and very influential in twentieth-century politics in Peru. Through intermarriage with other wealthy families of Peru, the Miró Quesadas' interests have been an important part of the coastal elite groups that dominated Peruvian economic activities during and after major export boom cycles. Under the leadership of merchant and journalist José Antonio Miró Quesada (1845–1930), the family consolidated its wealth and reputation by the 1890s through its strong involvement with the Civilista Party. José Antonio's eldest son, Antonio Miró Quesada de la Guerra (1875–1935), was elected congressman between 1901 and 1912 and took charge of *El Comercio*. During the second regime of Augusto B. LEGUÍA (1919–1930), Antonio lived in Europe as a political oppositionist. Upon his return to Peru, he and his wife were assassinated by an Aprista follower in 1935.

Aurelio (1877–1950) and Luis Miró Quesada de la Guerra (1880–1976), brothers of Antonio, shared thereafter the management of the newspaper. In 1974 the military government of Juan VELASCO ALVARADO, as part of its Plan Inca, expropriated the family's newspaper business and assigned it formally to peasant organizations. In 1980, however, *El Comercio* was returned to the Miró Quesada family, represented by Aurelio Miró Quesada Sosa (*b.* 1907) and Alejandro Miró Quesada Garland (*b.* 1915).

— ALFONSO W. QUIROZ

MISTRAL, GABRIELA

Gabriela Mistral (*b.* 7 April 1889; *d.* 10 January 1957), Chilean poet. The first female Latin American writer of international stature, Mistral won the Nobel Prize for Literature in 1945. Born Lucila Godoy Alcayaga, in Vicuña, in the province of Coquimbo, Mistral began her career as a teacher and administrator; she directed various secondary schools in different regions of the country from Antofagasta to Punta Arenas. In 1922 Mistral left Chile, not to come back again except for short visits. Invited by President Álvaro OBREGÓN SALIDO of Mexico to contribute to the educational reforms of Minister José VASCONCELOS, she resided in Mexico until 1924. Her official and unofficial trips to South America and the Caribbean brought her public acclamation and the recognition of her peers. She served numerous diplomatic functions as consul in Rome, Marseilles, Guatemala, Nice, Aix-en-Provence, Madrid, Lisbon, Paris, Veracruz, Niterói, Petrópolis, Los Angeles, Naples, Miami, and Roslyn Harbor. She was a Chilean delegate to the First Assembly of the United Nations Subcommittee on the Juridical Status of Women in San Francisco, and she took part in the creation of UNICEF. In 1953 Mistral represented Chile in the United Nations General Assembly, and in 1955, at the request of Secretary-General Dag Hammarskjöld, she addressed the U.N. on human rights. During the Cold War, her essay "La palabra maldita" (The Damned Word [peace]), denouncing the tensions between East and West, circulated widely. Mistral kept in contact with the Spanish American world through her journalistic pursuits, publishing articles in the main journals of Caracas, Buenos Aires, Santiago, and other major cities. Her poetic works were widely featured in the literary magazines of Chile, Spain, and Latin America before she published her first book.

The poetry of Gabriela Mistral is comprised of five major works: *Desolación* (1922), *Ternura* (1924), *Tala* (1938), *Lagar* (1954), and the posthumously published *Poema de Chile* (1967). *Desolación* is divided into four sections: "Vida" (Life), "La Escuela" (The School), "Dolor" (Pain), and "Naturaleza" (Nature). The best-known section is "Dolor," which has served, somewhat inadequately, as a foundation on which to build a biography of the poet. The section is a sequence of twenty-seven poems loosely narrating a story of love and tragedy that describes a couple's first meeting, followed by the glowing experience of romantic love, the fears and insecurities of the enamored woman, the lover's betrayal and his unexpected suicide, the unbearable pain that followed, the healing period, and ultimately, serenity. The intense poetic tone and expression of unbridled passion are unique in Spanish poetry. The language is natural, showing only traces of modernist style; its allegiance is to the spoken language rather than to literary or poetic forms. The personal, intimate mood the poems evoke is also a reaction against the distancing quality of elegant literary expression. In the last section,

Mistral aligns herself with the new poetry of the avant garde, with its imagistic and creationist style. One of the section's poems is a close imitation of Vicente HUIDOBRO's poetry of those years.

> *"These letters carry with them my very tone, the most recurrent, the rural lilt in which I have lived and in which I will die."*

Mistral's second book, *Ternura*, contains a section of the first edition of *Desolación* and, in its 1945 edition, a section from *Tala*. It is a collection of poems for children: cradle songs, rhymes, *albricias* (rewards), and *jugarretas* (playful tricks). The compositions are full of charm and verbal creativity. The third book, *Tala*, is the definitive example of Mistralian poetry, with selected emphasis on simple matters, nocturnal elegies, and American hymns. The language is particularly close to colloquialism. Many cultural directions are represented, from biblical and classical to modern European and American Indian. Especially notable is a section called "América," which includes the hymns "Sol del trópico" (Tropical Sun) and "Cordillera" (The Andes Mountains). *Lagar* develops the themes of the previous book and builds upon forms introduced in *Tala*, among them the famous *recados* (messages) of which Mistral said, "These letters carry with them my very tone, the most recurrent, the rural lilt in which I have lived and in which I will die." The posthumous *Lagar II* (1991) is a collection of Mistral's theretofore unpublished poems, most of them unfinished or lacking the final approval of the poet. *Poema de Chile*, also published posthumously, was not reviewed by Mistral for final publication, but it is believed that the poem itself was conceived as an open form, constantly to be changed by subtraction or addition. The poem tells the story of a journey, from north to south along the Chilean territory, of an old woman's spirit accompanied by the phantoms of a child and a small deer. The tone is one of nostalgia. Familiarity with and praise of nature and ordinary things is a major theme. The flowers, herbs, fruits, birds, mountains, and rivers described refer to different regions of Chile. Mistral's extensive journalistic articles, letters, and essays have been collected in many volumes. Her poetic work makes her one of the most universal as well as one of the most singular and distinctive voices in Chilean and Spanish American literature.

— CEDOMIL GOIC

MITRE, BARTOLOMÉ

Bartolomé Mitre (*b.* 26 June 1821; *d.* 19 January 1906), president of Argentina (1862–1868) and one of the modern nation's founders. Along with Domingo Faustino SARMIENTO, Mitre best represents the liberal reformism that infused Argentina after the overthrow of Juan Manuel de ROSAS in 1852. Mitre acted simultaneously as statesman, soldier, journalist, and historian in order to set in motion and later consolidate the program laid out in the Constitution of 1853–1860.

Exile and Rise to Power From early on, Mitre was a member of the opposition to Rosas, and in 1837 he and his family were exiled to Montevideo, Uruguay. For the next fifteen years he worked intensively as a soldier and publicist in Montevideo; La Paz, Bolivia; and Santiago, Chile. He served as an artillery officer in the defense of Montevideo against the troops of Manuel ORIBE, and it was then that he began his historiographical labors, work he would continue until the end of his days. He

Bartolomé Mitre. (Archivo General de la Nación, Buenos Aires)

spent a brief time in La Paz in order to organize a military academy, and he brought his years of exile to a close as a journalist in Chile.

When the uprising against Rosas began, Mitre participated in the campaign of Justo José de URQUIZA, governor of Entre Ríos, which ended 3 February 1852 at the battle of Caseros. From that moment on, Mitre played a decisive role nationally. He disagreed with Urquiza in June 1852 by opposing the ratification of the accord of San Nicolás and by participating in the revolution of 11 September, which separated the province of Buenos Aires from the confederation of governors who supported Urquiza. Against the most extreme localist positions of the *porteño* (Buenos Aires) leaders, Mitre defended a conception of national liberalism that, after the defeat at Cepeda on 23 October 1859, brought about on 11 November the signing of the Pact of San José de Flores. As a result, Mitre was elected governor of the province of Buenos Aires in 1860, and the National Convention for Constitutional Reform accepted his anticentralist ideas, which resembled the North American constitutional model. Despite this success, during the rule of Urquiza's successor, Santiago DERQUI, there arose new complications in San Juan which led to a definitive confrontation, ending in Mitre's victory at the battle of Pavón on 17 September 1861.

Presidency In 1861 Mitre's leadership was recognized throughout much of the country. With Urquiza defeated, Mitre's intellectual vision for Argentina joined with his control over military resources and a constitutional organization that was finally recognized by all the provinces. Derqui resigned after Pavón left Mitre to carry out a complete reorganization of the executive, legislative, and judicial powers. On 12 October 1862 Mitre assumed the presidency, unanimously elected by the electoral college. That began a regular succession of constitutional presidents every six years in Argentina, interrupted only by the coup d'état of 6 September 1930.

Three major concerns dominated Mitre's presidency. The first was programmatic. By 10 June 1865 (when power was handed to Vice President Marcos Paz because of the war with Paraguay—the War of the Triple Alliance), Mitre's administration had established the basis for the organization of the three components of state power, to which was added a rigorous fiscal policy, with funds from customs at the port of Buenos Aires becoming part of the national treasury. Likewise, Congress passed a commerce code, and civil, penal, and judicial codes were recommended. The grant for the railway from Rosario to Córdoba was authorized and special attention was paid to the development of educational policy. National secondary schools were founded in Buenos Aires, Concepción del Uruguay (previously established by Urquiza), Catamarca, Salta, Tucumán, San Juan, and Mendoza. An exiled French republican, Amédée Jacques, was the first rector of the Buenos Aires school.

The second concern facing Mitre was institutional. With Urquiza withdrawn to the province of Entre Ríos, the national government could not declare the city of Buenos Aires capital of the republic because of the division in that province brought about by the followers of Adolfo ALSINA. Thanks to a compromise, the national government resided in Buenos Aires even though the city could not be federalized. Similarly, the rest of the provinces, with the exception of Entre Ríos and Santiago del Estero, were shaken by violent insurrections and by the reappearance of the *montoneras*. All these rebellions were drastically suppressed through federal intervention by the national government.

The third concern before Mitre was the War of the Triple Alliance. In April 1865, because of the invasion of the province of Corrientes by the troops of Marshal Francisco Solano LÓPEZ during a forced march to Brazil, the Argentine government declared war on Paraguay and a state of siege in all the territory. With the signing of the Treaty of the Triple Alliance with Uruguay and the Brazilian Empire, President Mitre was designated commander in chief of the Allied forces. The war ended with the death of Solano López in 1870. It reduced the population of Paraguay (from 1.1 million to 220,000).

From Opposition to Political Accord At the end of his term as president, Mitre resolved not to intervene in the designation of his successor. The election of 1868, although divided, turned the office over to Domingo F. Sarmiento, another important member of the group to which Mitre belonged. The following year Mitre was appointed national senator, and in 1870 he founded the newspaper *La Nación*. During Sarmiento's presidency, relations between the provinces and the national government changed. A new coalition of governors, allied with Adolfo Alsina, defeated Mitre in the presidential election of 1874. Mitre and his party did not accept the victory of Nicolás AVELLANEDA and revolted. They were defeated that same year by the national army in the battles of La Verde and Santa Rosa.

Mitre was tried and removed from his senatorial office and stripped of his military rank. With this defeat the political center shifted to the interior, although it did so by strengthening the authority of the national government. Halfway through the presidency of Avellaneda, Mitre communicated a policy of conciliation to Alsina, through which his military rank was restored. This underscored the style of compromising with his adversaries that he had exercised earlier with Urquiza.

In the election of 1880, Julio A. ROCA ran against Carlos TEJEDOR, governor of Buenos Aires and one of the most extreme proponents of *porteño* localism. Mitre had been elected national representative in 1878. In the conflict that arose between Tejedor and Avellaneda when the former rebelled against the national government, Mitre defended Buenos Aires and later negotiated a peace agreement. With the city of Buenos Aires federalized, a strong coalition over which Mitre had no control was consolidated under the leadership of Roca.

The government that came to power in 1880 was shaken by the economic crisis of 1889–1890. Mitre actively participated in opposing Roca's successor, Miguel JUÁREZ CELMAN, and in forming a new group, the Civic Union, but he traveled to Europe to avoid the civil and military uprising of July 1890. In 1891 the Civic Union announced the presidential ticket of Mitre–Bernardo de IRIGOYEN, which was supported by Leandro ALEM. For his part, Mitre urged an understanding with Roca, which resulted in a Mitre–José Evaristo URIBURU ticket. This caused a split in the Civic Union. Given the lack of consensus, Mitre renounced his candidacy and along with Roca supported the Luis SÁENZ PEÑA–Uriburu ticket in the presidential election of 1892.

Again elected national senator in 1894, Mitre maintained his stance as a nationalist until he retired from public life in 1901, never diminishing his demands for a free vote or his criticisms of electoral corruption. When he died in Buenos Aires in 1906, Carlos PELLEGRINI affirmed that "Mitre's thoughts and actions are so intimately tied to our national life that his biography will be the history of the politics of the Argentine people during the second half of the nineteenth century."

As Historian Mitre's work as a historian, publicist, critic, author, and literary translator was far-reaching. He was the founder of the historiography of Argentina's revolution and the nation's subsequent independence. Two great biographies crown this achievement: *Historia de Belgrano y de la independencia argentina* (1858–1859) and *Historia de San Martín y de la emancipación sudamericana* (1887). Mitre worked with methods based on documentary criticism and introduced his findings into a historical synthesis that emphasized the roles of individual actors as well as the profound effects of social, economic, and institutional factors. His polemic with Vicente Fidel LÓPEZ, summarized in *Comprobaciones históricas* (1882), reveals this orientation and the republican philosophy that inspired it.

— NATALIO R. BOTANA

MOGROVEJO, TORIBIO ALFONSO DE

Toribio Alfonso de Mogrovejo (*b.* 16 November 1538; *d.* 23 March 1606), also known as Santo Toribio, second archbishop of Lima. Born in Mayorga, in the province of León, Spain, he studied law at the universities of Valladolid and Salamanca. In 1574 he was named president of the Tribunal of the Inquisition in Granada. Even though he was a layman, he was named archbishop of Lima in 1578, where, after his ordination as priest and bishop, he arrived in 1581. He convoked the third of the Lima church councils (1582–1583). The council, which brought together bishops from all over South America, as well as the leading theologians of colonial Peru, aimed to systematize the evangelization process and to lay down norms for Christianizing the Indians more effectively.

Toribio considered himself primarily a missionary bishop called to reach the Indians, and secondarily a pastor for the Spanish population. He spent seventeen of his twenty-five years as archbishop outside of Lima, visiting his vast archdiocese. The longest of his four trips, 1584–1590, took him through the Callejón de Huaylas in the north central Andes. He preached to the Indians, baptized, confirmed, and married them. He wrote to the king criticizing local Spanish officials who abused the Indians. In 1584 he founded the seminary in Lima that bears his name. He died in the *villa* of Saña. In 1726 he was canonized.

– JEFFREY KLAIBER

MOJICA, JOSÉ DE JESÚS

José de Jesús Mojica (*b.* 14 September 1896; *d.* 20 September 1974), Mexican operatic tenor, film actor, and singer. Born in San Gabriel, Jalisco, Mojica attended the Escuela Nacional de Agricultura; when it closed during the Revolution, he entered the Conservatorio Nacional de Música. He then trained with Alejandro Cuevas and made his solo debut in *La Traviata*. After touring the republic, he sang his first lead role in *The Barber of Seville* in 1916 (Teatro Arbeu, Mexico City).

In 1930 Mojica went to Hollywood and began a career in musical films with One Mad Kiss.

Mojica appeared with Enrico Caruso when the latter visited Mexico City (1919). Caruso's recommendation resulted in an invitation to perform with the Chicago Opera, where Mojica acquired a notable reputation, especially in French operas, with the famed soprano Mary Garden, and in the world premiere of Sergei Prokofiev's *Love for Three Oranges* (1921). During the 1920s Mojica sang in Chicago and Mexico. He was a favorite tenor of Thomas Edison, for whose company he recorded arias and Hispanic folk songs.

In 1930 Mojica went to Hollywood and began a career in musical films with *One Mad Kiss,* followed by some dozen other movies, made in both the United States and Mexico. Following his mother's death, Mojica abandoned his career to become a Franciscan friar (1943). In order to build a training center for priests in Peru, he raised funds through additional films and concerts. He last appeared in Mexico City's Bellas Artes Theater (1969), celebrating his fifty years as a singer. He died in Lima, Peru.

– RONALD H. DOLKART

MOLINA, ARTURO ARMANDO

Arturo Armando Molina (*b.* 6 August 1927), Salvadoran military officer and president (1972–1977). Born into a military family, Molina began his primary education in Sonsonate and graduated from the military school in San Salvador in 1949 as a sublieutenant of infantry. He advanced through the ranks on schedule and served in a variety of positions: comandante of Santa Ana, subdirector of the military school, and professor of tactics, strategy, and military history until Fidel Sánchez Hernández chose him as his successor in 1972. The 1972 "stolen elections" were a milestone in Salvadoran history as the government's Party of National Conciliation denied the victory to the civilian UNO slate led by José Napoleón DUARTE. As president, Colonel Molina was distrusted by both the oligarchy and the right-wing military, as well as resented by the opposition from whom he had stolen power. Molina dubbed his presidency a period of "national transformation," a slogan that reflected his commitment to making visible changes not only in roads and ports but also in foreign investment incentives and administrative reforms. Molina's tenure saw the polarization of Salvadoran society as the Left began to form guerrilla groups and the Right countered with paramilitary "death squads." His attempts to silence opposition included the 1972 military occupation and closure of the university, violence directed against those protesting the 1975 Miss Universe pageant in San Salvador, and overt attacks on the church, including the assassination of priests. Molina's presidency set the stage for the civil war of the 1980s in El Salvador.

– KAREN RACINE

MOLINA, JUAN RAMÓN

Juan Ramón Molina (*b.* 17 April 1875; *d.* 2 November 1908), Honduran modernist poet. Born in Comayaguela, twin city of Tegucigalpa, Molina studied in Guatemala, where he met Rubén DARÍO, the great modernist poet, in 1891. Molina began writing at age seventeen and later edited several journals and newspapers. He served as undersecretary of public works for the government of Dr. Policarpo BONILLA (1895–1899). In 1900 he went to prison for criticizing President Terencio Sierra. In the revolution of 1903, Molina fought and earned the rank of colonel. In 1906 he participated along with Rubén Darío in the Pan-American Conference in Rio de Janeiro and for the first and only time experienced the creative environment of a large urban center. Another revolution in 1907 defeated Bonilla, and Molina was exiled to El Salvador. Throughout his life Molina felt stifled by his surroundings and suffered depression augmented by alcohol abuse. In 1908, at age thirty-three, he died from an overdose of morphine, an apparent suicide. After his death his poems and short prose pieces were collected by his friend and fellow writer, Froylan Turcios, in *Tierras, mares y cielos* (1911). Miguel Ángel ASTURIAS called Molina the greatest Central American modernist poet after Darío.

– ANN GONZÁLEZ

MOLINA, MARCELO

Marcelo Molina (*b.* 19 February 1800; *d.* 20 May 1879), Guatemalan lawyer, political leader, and first governor of Los Altos, the sixth state of the Central American Federation. The son of a notable Quetzaltenango family, Molina obtained a degree in 1821 from the Tridentine College and a law degree from the University of San Carlos in 1824. After a year of law practice in his hometown, he began his career in public service as syndic for Quetzaltenango and as a provincial judge, participating in 1831 in the unsuccessful experiment with trials by jury espoused by the Liberal government of Dr. Mariano GÁLVEZ. When Los Altos proclaimed its secession from Guatemala in 1838, Molina resigned his post as attorney general of the State of Guatemala and returned to Quetzaltenango to become governor of the new state in 1839. His political and diplomatic efforts on behalf of Los Altos proved fruitless, however, and the sixth state was forcibly restored to Guatemala by the Conservative dictator Rafael CARRERA in January 1840. Following a brief period of detention in Guatemala City, he went into exile in Mexico, where he remained until 1847. Back in Guatemala, he resumed his public service career, serving as member of the Supreme Court of Justice from 1847 to 1849. Molina then worked as a teacher of Latin in Quetzaltenango before being reappointed to the Supreme Court in 1856, where he served until his retirement in 1874.

– JORGE H. GONZÁLEZ

MOLINA, PEDRO

Pedro Molina (*b.* 29 April 1777; *d.* 21 September 1854), Guatemalan scholar, revolutionary, and statesman. Born in Guatemala City of illegitimate parentage, Molina studied humanities at an early age under the tutelage of one of the great Guatemalan scholars of the late eighteenth century, Fray Antonio de LIENDO Y GOICOECHEA (1735–1814). Never abandoning the Enlightenment ideas of his teacher, he later studied medicine and surgery, and received his degree on 11 June 1798. In the first decade of the nineteenth century, Molina served as a surgeon in Nicaragua. He returned to his native Guatemala in 1811 to assume the chair of professor of medicine at the University of San Carlos. In 1819, the colonial government awarded him the degree of doctor and the office of *protomédico*, or chief surgeon general, of the province of Guatemala.

In the years prior to independence from Spain, Molina became increasingly involved in politics. He eventually came to lead an unlikely alliance of conservative oligarchs and middle-class elements. Born out of opposition to the captain-general, José de BUSTAMANTE Y GUERRA, this political faction later became the most radical one of the era, actively urging independence. Molina had no close ties to the oligarchy but was an ardent and capable representative of the creole professional classes. The elite, especially the influential Aycinena family, supported Molina, only because the return to power of the Spanish liberals threatened its position of prestige and monopoly. Both factions of the coalition, the professionals and the aristocrats, viewed the opposition to their political dreams as a conspiracy of *peninsulars*.

The voice of this nascent political party, known derisively by its opponents as the *cacos,* or thieves, was the newspaper *El Editor Constitucional*, edited by Molina, who also wrote the column on physical and moral education. On the eve of independence (14 September 1821), Molina, a talented political activist and rabble-rouser, and the aristocratic Mariano AYCINENA (1789–1855) worked through the night to ensure that a mob would gather at the palace the next morning. Molina scattered his supporters throughout Guatemala City to stir up the masses to clamor for independence. After independence, however, the elite broke its alliance with Molina and the radical liberals and formed a truly conservative party.

Molina nonetheless continued to play an active role in politics and government. In 1825, as plenipotentiary to Bogotá, he signed the first treaty concluded by the newly created United Provinces of Central America, ensuring a defensive alliance with Colombia. In 1826 he served in another diplomatic post as one of the representatives of the Central American republic to the Panama Conference called by Simón BOLÍVAR. After the bloody civil war between conservatives and liberals from 1826 to 1829, Molina was elected chief of the state of Guatemala and almost immediately clashed with the federal government, under the leadership of Francisco MORAZÁN, over the question of reconstituting Guatemala City as a federal district and over Molina's project to reform the confederation. Molina favored the model of the Swiss republic, abolishing the expensive machinery of a federal government that was often in conflict with the different states. He called for a federal congress that would wield power in only foreign affairs.

The provinces showed little interest in these proposals, and many powerful men who either held or aspired to hold federal offices, the most prominent being Morazán, actively opposed the latter. In retribution, Molina was suspended as chief of state on false charges and actually brought to trial. Although he was acquitted, he was never allowed to return to his post. The failure of the reform scheme and Molina's inability to counter successfully his political enemies dealt a terrible blow to his political career.

Although less influential during the last two decades of his life than he had been, Molina remained an important political force. He supported the radical liberal administration of Guatemalan chief of state Mariano GÁLVEZ until Gálvez formed a coalition with conservatives in an effort to avert a popular insurgency. Thereafter, until the end of his life, Molina wrote political commentary, often under the pseudonym Liberato Cauto.

– MICHAEL F. FRY

MOLINA BEDOYA, FELIPE

Felipe Molina Bedoya (*b.* 30 April 1812; *d.* 17 February 1855). Central American politician and diplomat. He was born in Granada, Nicaragua, into the family of the independence heroine Dolores Bedoya and the prominent Guatemalan patriot and statesman Pedro Molina. As a member of the Liberal government that was deposed in April 1839, Molina was forced to emigrate to Quetzaltenango. In 1843 he joined his father and brother, José, in Costa Rica. A more stable political climate allowed the family to return to Guatemala in 1845. Molina was able to obtain his law degree before a new political crisis compelled him to leave Guatemala once again in 1847. He traveled in Chile and Peru before settling in Costa Rica. In 1849, President José María CASTRO appointed him to serve as Costa Rican ambassador to Nicaragua and then to England.

Through his efforts, Costa Rica was able to secure an advantageous commercial treaty with England. He then spent some time in France and Spain before moving to the United States in 1851, the year in which his *History of Costa Rica* was published. He died in Washington, D.C.

– JORGE H. GONZÁLEZ

MOLINA ENRÍQUEZ, ANDRÉS

Andrés Molina Enríquez (*b.* 30 November 1868; *d.* 1 August 1940), Mexican land reformer and lawyer. Portrayed in Mexico as the "Father of Agrarian Reform" and the "Rousseau of the Mexican Revolution," Andrés Molina Enríquez made important contributions, both ideologically and politically, to the official land-reform program of the Mexican Revolution. Molina Enríquez studied Mexico's agrarian problems in depth during the fifteen years prior to the Revolution while working as a land notary and judge in various rural locations in the state of Mexico. As early as 1905 he had arrived at the legal basis for land reform in Mexico in a proposed water law that mandated national control of natural resources for the common good and regulated foreign ownership of Mexican resources. He included these principles in his seminal book, *Los grandes problemas nacionales,* written on the eve of the Mexican Revolution in 1909, warning the *hacendados,* or large landowners of Mexico, that they faced land reform or revolution. Molina Enríquez appeared in Querétaro at the 1917 constitutional convention and wrote the first draft of Article 27, which followed his pre-Revolutionary land-reform ideas. The provisions limited foreign ownership of Mexican land and resources, called for the restitution of Ejido lands despoiled during the Porfiriato, and directed state governments to establish laws limiting the size of individual landholdings.

– STANLEY F. SHADLE

MOLINA GARMENDIA, ENRIQUE

Enrique Molina Garmendia (*b.* 4 August 1871; *d.* 8 March 1964), Chilean philosopher and educator. Enrique Molina graduated in 1892 from the University of Chile's Instituto Pedagógico, a leading teacher-training institution that launched a generation of secularly oriented secondary school teachers. Their aim was to further undermine the influence of the church in education. Molina, however, became critical of both Catholicism and the dominant secular school of positivism. He developed a philosophical approach that emphasized secular spiritual values. His most important work was *De lo espiritual en la vida humana*

(1937), which brought to Chile the emphasis on human values that changed the philosophical landscape in several Latin American nations. In this and other

---

Molina's writings brought to Chile an emphasis on human values that changed the philosophical landscape in several Latin American nations.

---

writings he introduced a distinction between spiritual and materialistic concerns that had a significant impact on the nature of philosophical studies in Chile: spiritual values came to be seen as the proper emphasis of philosophy. Molina was also a historian of Chilean philosophy. In his *La filosofía en Chile en la primera mitad del siglo XX* (1953), Molina reviewed the development of philosophy and advanced an interpretation of the discipline as removed from social and political concerns. An institution builder, Molina presided over the University of Concepción, the first private secular university, for nearly forty years (1919–1956). He also founded the journal *Atenea* and was instrumental in the creation of the Sociedad Chilena de Filosofía in 1948. Despite his antipolitical stands, he served as minister of education during the increasingly anti-Communist administration of Gabriel GONZÁLEZ VIDELA (1946–1952). He gave philosophical expression to the rejection of Marxism but retained a commitment to the reform of society through education.

– IVÁN JAKSIĆ

MOLINA SOLÍS, OLEGARIO

Olegario Molina Solís (*b.* 6 March 1843; *d.* 28 April 1925), governor of Yucatán, Mexico (1902–1909), Mexican minister of development (1907–1911). Born and raised in Bolonchenticul, in present-day Campeche, Molina moved with his family to Yucatán's capital, Mérida, in 1857, after the Caste War of Yucatán ravaged his family's properties. After securing degrees in law and topographical engineering, Molina served as secretary to Liberal General Manuel Cepeda Peraza, who defeated Emperor Maximilian's forces in the peninsula in 1867. During the 1870s Molina became an engineer, superintendent, and later a partner in the first railroad built in Yucatán, the Mérida–Progreso railway, which he helped complete. Later he established a profitable import-export company, O. Molina y Compañía, that largely exported Yucatán's principal crop, henequen, a fiber used by North American cordage and binder twine manufacturers. Some scholars contend

that in 1902, Molina y Compañía became the International Harvester Company's agent—at the time Harvester was the largest buyer of fiber in the United States. It is believed that Molina and his son-in-law, Avelino Montes, worked to depress fiber prices to benefit their North American partners (and themselves). Molina and Montes used their dominant position in the fiber trade to expand the investment base of their company dramatically. Ventures in real estate, import/exports, and speculation in local industry, commerce, and infrastructure made Molina and Montes, and their extended network of family and friends, an economic octopus in turn-of-the-century Yucatán.

It is noteworthy that Molina's financial success coincided with his political rise to Yucatán's statehouse. Driven by the desire to make his native state a dynamic partner in the modernization of Mexican society, Governor Molina is best remembered in the peninsula as "the builder." An indefatigable public servant, he is lionized for the number of schools he built, the paving and draining of Mérida's streets, and a spate of capital improvement projects in Mérida, including the O'Horan Hospital, the Juárez Penitentiary, the Peón y Contreras Theater, and the Ayala Asylum. (O. Molina y Compañía received lucrative contracts for many of these capital projects.) He also reorganized the property registry, rewrote the state constitution, reformed the penal and civil codes, and reorganized the state National Guard and Mérida police force.

The embodiment of nineteenth-century positivism, Yucatán's own *científico* (technocrat), Molina reasoned that, to the extent that he and his affluent class prospered, so would Yucatán. His regard for Yucatán's Maya Indians might best be described as paternalistic; he did little to provide education or other services to the tens of thousands of peons who lived on haciendas throughout the countryside. In 1906 President Porfirio DÍAZ visited Mérida, and after marveling at all of the impressive physical changes, rewarded Molina by bringing him to Mexico City to serve as minister of development. After Díaz was ousted in 1911 by revolutionaries, Molina, like many of Díaz's *científicos,* went into exile, living out his life in Cuba.

– ALLEN WELLS

MOLINA UREÑA, JOSÉ RAFAEL

José Rafael Molina Ureña (*b.* 1921), provisional president of the Dominican Republic (1965). The president of the Chamber of Deputies, José Rafael Molina Ureña was installed as provisional president of the Dominican Republic by the "constitutionalist" group of the Dominican Revolutionary Party (PRD) in 1965. The PRD government of Juan BOSCH had been overthrown by the military after just seven months in office in 1963. The civilian triumvirate under Donald Reid Cabral that replaced it then fell victim to a coup in 1965. Meeting in secret, the dissolved Dominican Congress declared Molina Ureña the constitutional president of the republic. As a result, Molina Ureña was arrested and exiled to Puerto Rico by anti-Bosch and anti-PRD "loyalists." After the constitutionalists ousted the military triumvirate, Molina Ureña returned from exile and was sworn in as the interim president until Juan Bosch could return from exile in Puerto Rico.

The fighting between the Bosch and Molina Ureña constitutionalists and the anti-PRD loyalists caused great concern in Washington, which considered the PRD a Communist-influenced party. As the constitutionalists made headway against the loyalists and looked to win the struggle, the U.S. Marines arrived on 28 April 1965 to suppress the constitutionalists and establish order.

– HEATHER K. THIESSEN

MOLINARI, RICARDO E.

Ricardo E. Molinari (*b.* 20 May 1898), Argentine poet. Born in Buenos Aires, Molinari began writing poetry in the 1920s, making him a contemporary of Jorge Luis BORGES and the postwar *ultraístas* who sought to initiate a vanguard movement against neoclassicist monumental poetry by implanting in Argentina a movement that would be both culturally nationalistic and internationalistically modernist. While Borges's ironic postmodernism *avant la lettre* quickly led him to abandon such a project, Molinari went on to establish himself as a major voice in Argentine poetry, for poetry as an objective art in which national cultural material is always a constant, as is especially to be noted in the key collection *Mundos de la madrugada* (1943). Molinari's poetry can be studied as virtually an academic showcase of the modernist lyric, with its utilization of complex metaphors, a hermetic style, the romantic nostalgia of the lone poetic voice, and the image of poetry as privileged expression.

– DAVID WILLIAM FOSTER

MOLONY, GUY

Guy Molony ("Machine Gun" Molony; *b.* 1884; *d.* 13 February 1972), North American soldier of fortune. Molony ran away to South Africa during the Boer War. He fought alongside Lee CHRISTMAS in the Honduran invasion of January 1911 and subsequently returned to New Orleans and became police chief in 1921. Four years later, he abruptly resigned and went back to Honduras, where he served as bodyguard to the president. He acquired plantations, an automobile dealership, and a post in the national brewery. In the mid-1930s, he fought rebels trying to overthrow President Tiburcio CARÍAS ANDINO. He operated a rice plantation in Honduras until the early 1960s, then retired to New Orleans, where he died.

– LESTER D. LANGLEY

MOMPOX DE ZAYAS, FERNANDO

Fernando Mompox de Zayas (*b.* ca. 1690; *d.* ca. 1745), Spanish-born revolutionary and participant in the Paraguayan Comunero Revolt of 1721–1735. Of shadowy origins, Mompox had been imprisoned in the late 1720s by inquisitorial authorities in Lima. In jail, he made the acquaintance of José de ANTEQUERA Y CASTRO, former leader of the anti-Jesuit faction of the Spanish residents of Paraguay. Shortly thereafter, Mompox escaped, and in 1730, armed with letters of introduction from Antequera, made his way to Asunción, where he began to resuscitate the popular opposition to the Jesuits. Passing himself off as a lawyer, he soon gained fame for his loud oratory in the streets of the town.

> *Mompox claimed that only the* común,
>
> *the "free-born" residents of Asunción,*
>
> *could speak for Paraguay.*

Though an outsider, Mompox quickly became the most important actor in Paraguayan politics, taking Antequera's movement in a new, radical direction. Mompox denounced the entire artifice of absolute government, claiming that only the *común*, the "free-born" residents of Asunción, could speak for Paraguay. This declaration threatened not only the power of the Jesuits, but also that of the king's representatives. When word came that a new governor, Ignacio Soroeta, was due to arrive, Mompox organized a plot against him. Armed Comuneros took over the Paraguayan capital and made it clear to Soroeta that they intended to retain power no matter what. Shortly thereafter, however, Mompox was betrayed and handed over to loyal officials. Later, while en route back to Lima, the prisoner escaped and managed to get across the Brazilian frontier. Mompox spent the rest of his life as a retailer in Rio de Janeiro. His Comunero associates, however, went down in defeat by early 1735.

– THOMAS L. WHIGHAM

MON Y VELARDE, JUAN ANTONIO

Juan Antonio Mon y Velarde (*b.* August 1747; *d.* 1 September 1791), *oidor* of the Audiencia of Guadalajara (1775–1778) and the Audiencia of Santa Fe (1781–1790), *visitador* of the province of Antioquia (1785–1788), and president of Quito (1790–1791).

Born into Asturian aristocracy in the town of Mon, Mon studied law at the universities of Oviedo and Salamanca. In 1778, after serving three years as *oidor* on the Audiencia of Guadalajara, he was assigned to Santa Fe, although he did not assume his position on the audiencia until three years later. Mon is best remembered for his work as judge-visitor of the province of Antioquia.

Commissioned by Viceroy Antonio CABALLERO Y GÓNGORA to impose order on the royal administration and treasury and to foment mining, agriculture, and commerce, he discharged his obligations with uncommon energy and enlightened vision. He also championed education and public works and founded towns. Mon was promoted to president of the Audiencia of Quito in 1790 but soon thereafter was recalled to Spain to assume a position on the Council of the Indies. His promising career ended prematurely owing to a fatal bout with food poisoning soon after his arrival in Cádiz.

— ALLAN J. KUETHE

MONAGAS, JOSÉ GREGORIO

José Gregorio Monagas (*b.* 1791; *d.* 15 July 1858), president of Venezuela (1851–1855). Monagas owed his presidency to his brother, José Tadeo MONAGAS. In 1848 the latter, a military chief, or caudillo, from eastern Venezuela, seized power from the Conservative coalition headed by José Antonio PÁEZ and put the Liberal Party in power. In 1851, José Gregorio succeeded his brother and ran a basic caretaker government, which, like his brother's, was characterized by widespread corruption.

On 25 March 1854, José Gregorio Monagas achieved a permanent place in Venezuelan history when he emancipated the nation's slaves by a presidential proclamation. That act, like most of his decisions, owed as much to political expediency as anything.

— WINTHROP R. WRIGHT

MONAGAS, JOSÉ TADEO

José Tadeo Monagas (*b.* 28 October 1785; *d.* 18 November 1868), president of Venezuela (1847–1851, 1855–1858). Monagas, who fought in the wars of independence, became a powerful regional leader in eastern Venezuela. In 1831, he led an abortive rebellion against President José Antonio PÁEZ. Four years later, he took part in the failed Revolution of Reform.

Despite rifts with Páez, the latter allowed Monagas to succeed Carlos SOUBLETTE as president in 1847. In 1848, Monagas shifted to the Liberal faction when he dismissed Conservatives from his cabinet. The National Congress attempted to censure Monagas, but on 24 January 1848 violence broke out and several deputies died in the fighting. Monagas immediately assumed dictatorial powers.

In 1851, Monagas chose his brother, José Gregorio, as his successor. The latter met one Liberal objective in 1854 when he emancipated the slaves. In 1855, José Tadeo returned as president. A revolt in 1858 led by moderate Liberals and Conservatives under General Julián CASTRO ended the Monagas dictatorship. Monagas fled to the French embassy. Threats to remove him from the embassy led to an international crisis. French and British gunships eventually guaranteed international protocol, and enabled Monagas to leave Venezuela under a safe conduct pass issued by the Minister of Foreign Affairs, Wenceslao Urrutia.

In 1864, Monagas returned to Venezuela, and as a leader of the unsuccessful Blue faction, tried to restore his power. In 1868, he entered Caracas and proclaimed a short-lived presidency that lasted one month. He died shortly after his defeat.

— WINTHROP R. WRIGHT

MONCADA, JOSÉ MARÍA

José María Moncada (*b.* 1871; *d.* 23 February 1945), president of Nicaragua (1929–1933). Moncada rose to fame as one of the principal Conservative generals responsible for the overthrow of the Liberal dictator José Santos ZELAYA in 1909. He was not, however, a professional military man; he had begun his career in Nicaraguan politics as a journalist for a Conservative newspaper published in Granada. During the Zelaya dictatorship, Moncada published a pro-government newspaper, but by 1906 he had fallen out with the dictator and had fled to Honduras. There he served as under secretary of the interior until the Conservative revolt against Zelaya began. After Zelaya's ouster, Moncada served as secretary of the interior in the Conservative government from 1910 to 1911. Moncada, however, fell out with the Conservatives and switched his allegiance to the Liberal Party. He was elected to the Senate in 1924. In 1926 Moncada supported the return from Mexico of former Liberal vice president Juan Bautista SACASA, not only by supplying arms and ammunition but also by serving as Sacasa's minister of war in his campaign against the Conservative government headed by Adolfo DÍAZ. The ensuing civil war led to increased U.S. intervention. As a consequence Moncada and his generals accepted the terms of the Tipitapa Agreements (1927) that Moncada and U.S. representative Henry L. Stimson negotiated to end hostilities.

In 1928, Moncada won the presidential election supervised by the U.S. The reemergence of Augusto César SANDINO, the only one of Moncada's generals who had refused to accept the terms of the Tipitapa Agreements and to lay down his arms, however, overshadowed the Moncada presidency. Nonetheless, the U.S. entrusted Moncada to hold elections in 1932. Sacasa was elected president, and the U.S. Marines left Nicaragua on 2 January 1933.

– SHANNON BELLAMY

MONCAYO GARCÍA, JOSÉ PABLO

José Pablo Moncayo García (*b.* 29 June 1912; *d.* 16 June 1958), Mexican composer. Born in Guadalajara, Moncayo García studied piano with Eduardo HERNÁNDEZ MONCADA and composition with Candelario Huízar and Carlos Chávez at the National Conservatory in Mexico City (1929–1935). He was pianist and percussionist for the Mexico Symphony Orchestra (1932–1944) and from 1949 until his death conductor of the Mexico National Orchestra. He studied composition with Aaron Copland at Tanglewood in Massachusetts (1942). With Blás GALINDO, Salvador Contreras, and Daniel Ayala he formed the Grupo de los Cuatro (Group of the Four) to promote new music styles. Moncayo's works are built on diatonic and polytonal harmony with the use of parallel chords of impressionist influence. He also used impressionist orchestral timbres. Moncayo's most important works are *La mulata de Córdoba,* an opera, which premiered at the Mexico City Palacio de Bellas Artes (October 1948); and *Amatzinac* (1935), *Huapango* (1941), based on three folk dances, Symphony (1944), and *Tres piezas* (1947), all for orchestra. He died in Mexico City.

– SUSANA SALGADO

MONGE ÁLVAREZ, LUIS ALBERTO

Luis Alberto Monge Álvarez (*b.* 1926), president of Costa Rica (1982–1986). Of humble origin and little formal education beyond the secondary level, Monge Álvarez, at age twenty-three, served in the constitutent assembly that drafted the Constitution of 1949. Two years later he was a founding member of the National Liberation Party (PLN), Costa Rica's dominant political party. He became secretary-general of the Inter-

American Regional Organization of Workers (ORIT) in 1952.

During the 1960s, Monge Álvarez almost gave up politics. In 1959 he and PLN leader José FIGUERES FERRER established the Inter-American Institute of Political Education, a collaborative effort of Latin American social-democratic parties. Monge Álvarez was dismayed by the disclosure that the institute was secretly funded by the U.S. Central Intelligence Agency. His disillusionment grew during the presidency of Francisco José ORLICH BOLMARCICH (1962–1966) because he believed that Orlich Bolmarcich was abandoning PLN goals. Figueres Ferrer managed to pull Monge Álvarez out of the doldrums and in 1966 encouraged him to become PLN secretary-general, a post he held for twelve years.

Monge Álvarez was dismayed by the disclosure that the Inter-American Institute of Political Education was secretly funded by the CIA.

Monge Álvarez used his position to build a solid base within the PLN. During Figueres Ferrer's presidency (1970–1974), he gained additional stature as president of the Legislative Assembly. In 1978, challenging the party's old guard, he ran for president, but lost. Four years later, he won by the highest percentage in Costa Rican presidential elections.

Monge Álvarez's policies as president surprised those who knew his politics and his attitude toward U.S. intervention. He assumed office amid an economic crisis. Working with the International Monetary Fund, Monge Álvarez instituted a stabilization program that brought inflation under control and restored economic growth. But he did it by raising rates charged by government-owned utilities, cutting social programs, trimming the public sector, and reducing the huge bureaucracy. He did it also by cooperating with U.S. efforts against the Sandinista government of Nicaragua.

– CHARLES D. AMERINGER

MONSIVÁIS, CARLOS

Carlos Monsiváis (*b.* 4 May 1938), Mexican writer. One of the leading cultural essayists and editorialists in Latin America, Monsiváis completed studies in economics and literature at the National Autonomous University of Mexico (UNAM). His works include the editorship of *Antología de la poesía mexicana* (1966), and the authorship of *Díaz de guardar* (1971), *Amor perdido* (1977), *Escenas de pudor y liviandad* (1981), and *En-*

trada libre (1987). He has published numerous interpretative articles on a multitude of cultural subjects in Latin America, the United States, and Europe. Widely respected and influential, he is regarded as one of the most authoritative, insightful, and independent voices of Mexico and Latin America. Monsiváis is a regular contributor to *La Jornada* and *Proceso*.

— DAVID MACIEL

MONTALVO, JUAN

Juan Montalvo (*b*. 13 April 1832; *d*. 27 January 1889), Ecuadorian writer. Juan Montalvo was born in Ambato, Ecuador. His formal schooling ended after two years at the University of Quito. Subsequently he educated himself by extensive reading and travel. He lived in Europe, chiefly France, from 1857 to 1860 and from 1881 until his death.

Montalvo dedicated himself primarily to fighting for liberal, democratic causes. Though he wrote some minor dramatic works, a few poems, and a novel, he made his fame as an essayist. In his journalistic work he crusaded against corruption, injustice, and tyranny. His style was often combative, polemical, and hyperbolic. After publishing a caustic denunciation of President GARCÍA MORENO entitled *La dictadura perpetua* (1874), Montalvo claimed that his pen had killed the dictator.

Montalvo's most notable works were *Las catilinarias* (1880–1882); *Siete tratados* (1882–1883), *El espectador* (1886), and a novel, *Capítulos que se olvidaron a Cervantes* (1895). In addition he published two periodicals, *El Cosmopolita* (1866–1869) and *El Regenerador* (1876–1878), that made him famous for vehement attacks on the despot Gabriel García Moreno and other public figures, including prominent liberals.

— MARK J. VAN AKEN

MONTALVO Y AMBULODI ARRIOLA Y CASABENTE VALDESPINO, FRANCISCO

Francisco Montalvo y Ambulodi Arriola y Casabente Valdespino (*b*. 18 May 1754; *d*. 1822), viceroy of New Granada. A Cuban-born noble, Francisco Montalvo had an active military career before being named captain-general of New Granada in 1812. He reached a royalist-held section of the Caribbean coast of New Granada in mid-1813. Following the arrival of the expeditionary force under Pablo MORILLO in 1815, Montalvo entered Cartagena, which remained his headquarters even after the position of viceroy was reestablished and he was named to it. Montalvo sought to limit the rigors of repression imposed on the defeated by Morillo and by Juan Sámano, whom Morillo established as military governor in the interior. However, Montalvo had scant success, for his authority in most of the colony was little more than nominal. Succeeded as viceroy by Sámano in March 1818, Montalvo departed for Cuba and then Spain, where he died.

— DAVID BUSHNELL

MONTE, DOMINGO DEL

Domingo del Monte (*b*. 4 August 1804; *d*. 4 November 1853), Cuban literary critic and poet. Domingo del Monte y Aponte was the most important literary critic in nineteenth-century Cuba. A humanist and respectable poet in his own right, Del Monte was the initiator of Cuba's national literature. Born in Maracaibo, Venezuela, Del Monte and his family emigrated to Santiago de Cuba in 1810 and later lived in Havana, where he studied philosophy at the university from 1816 to 1820 and received an advanced degree in civil law in 1827.

Having developed an interest in literature, Del Monte promoted a Cuban-based form of education on the island. With the Spanish writer J. Villarino, Del Monte founded and published the weekly *La Moda o Recreo Semanal del Bello Sexo* (1829–1831), a magazine about culture and literature. He was a member of the prestigious and powerful Sociedad Económica de Amigos del País and was in charge of the education section from 1830 to 1834. He was also named secretary and, in 1842, president of the Comisión de Literatura of the Sociedad Económica. With other Cuban intellectuals, Del Monte helped to make the Sociedad Económica's *Revista Bimestre Cubana* (1831–1834) one of the most important publications in the Spanish language. He and others supported a national culture and transformed the Comisión de Literatura into the Academia Cubana de Literatura. Literature became a vehicle for expressing a national culture and changing society. Supporters of slavery and others hostile to Cuban-born nationals suppressed the academy, but this did not stop Del Monte from pursuing his literary interests.

Del Monte, who married Doña Rosa de Aldama of the powerful Aldama family, is better known for his famous literary circle, which he began in his hometown of Matanzas in 1834 and continued in Havana after 1835. At his home, young and progressive writers gathered and looked to him for inspiration and guidance. Del Monte encouraged his writer friends to abandon romanticism, accept realism, write about Cuban society and culture, and condemn the evils of slavery. His ideal of Cuban literature was reflected in the antislavery narratives written between 1835 and 1839 by himself, Anselmo Suárez y Romero, and Félix Tanco y Bosmeniel, among others.

Due to his friendship with the British abolitionist David Turnbull, Del Monte traveled to Philadelphia in 1842. In his absence, he was falsely accused by the mulatto poet José de la Concepción VALDÉS (Plácido) of participating in the Ladder Conspiracy of 1844, a failed slave rebellion. Refusing to go before the military tribunal, Del Monte was never allowed to return to Cuba and died in exile in Madrid, Spain.

— WILLIAM LUIS

MONTE ALEGRE, JOSÉ DA COSTA CARVALHO, MARQUIS DE

José da Costa Carvalho, Marquis de Monte Alegre (*b.* 7 February 1796; *d.* 18 September 1860), Brazilian statesman. Monte Alegre was one of the Coimbra-trained magistrates central to the early monarchy. In the opposition to PEDRO I, he represented Bahia in the Constituent Assembly of 1823 and in the legislatures that obstructed Pedro I to the point where he chose to abdicate in 1831. As president of the Chamber of Deputies, Monte Alegre was a natural choice of the *moderados* for one of the three "permanent" regents during PEDRO II's minority (1831–1840). Like many Moderados he shifted to the right under the subsequent regency of Diogo Antônio FEIJÓ and emerged as a São Paulo deputy in the Conservative-majority Chamber of Deputies of 1837, whence he was elevated to the Senate (for Sergipe) in 1839. As provincial president, he was the Conservatives' point man during the 1842 Liberal revolt in São Paulo, the province where he had served as a judge (1821–1822), edited the periodical *Farol Paulistano* (1827–1831), directed the faculty of law (1835–1836), and married (twice) into the planter elite. A councillor of state in 1842, he also served (1849–1852) as the prime minister and minister of the empire in an administration dominated by the Saquarema reactionaries. That cabinet is credited with internal peace, reforms, and stability; the end of the slave trade; and the war against Juan Manuel de ROSAS.

— JEFFREY D. NEEDELL

MONTEAGUDO, BERNARDO DE

Bernardo de Monteagudo (*b.* 1789; *d.* 28 January 1825), prominent Argentine political leader at the time of independence. Monteagudo became involved very early in the movement for independence and was arrested several times. In 1808, he wrote *Diálogo entre Atahualpa y Fernando VII,* in which he criticized the colonial system. Monteagudo talked about the need for independence and favored the use of terror and the death penalty for those who opposed it. He also favored the installation of a dictatorship responsible to a popular assembly to ensure independence and freedom. As a consequence of his radicalism, Monteagudo was opposed by other independence leaders and was sent into exile several times. In 1817, he went to Chile, where José de SAN MARTÍN gave him an important governmental position. He accompanied San Martín on his expedition to Peru. There, he became minister of war, following a hard-line policy against the Spaniards and those suspected of opposing independence. His policies created such resentment that a rebellion broke out on 25 July 1822. He was murdered in Lima, Peru.

— JUAN MANUEL PÉREZ

MONTEALEGRE FERNÁNDEZ, JOSÉ MARÍA

José María Montealegre Fernández (*b.* 19 March 1815; *d.* 26 September 1887), president of Costa Rica (1859–1863). Montealegre was brought to the presidency as a consequence of the overthrow of his former brother-in-law, Juan Rafael MORA PORRAS. He served until 1863 as the representative of the wealthiest coffee planters and traders. His father, Mariano Montealegre Bustamante, had been the colonial-era tobacco administrator and one of the first coffee planters. The younger Montealegre continued the large-scale development of coffee plantings begun by his father, in the 1830s, to the west of San José in former municipal lands. One of the largest coffee producers of the day, he was also a leading export merchant and processor, as was common among the wealthiest growers of the time.

As part of a long political career Montealegre was deputy from the province of Guanacaste (although he never lived there) seven times (Chamber of Representatives, 1846–1848; Senate, 1863–1868). His partisan activities eventually led to his exile by strongman Tomás GUARDIA in 1872. He died in San José, California, 26 September 1887.

Montealegre was the son of Jerónima Fernández Chacón and Mariano Montealegre Bustamante. He was the first Costa Rican to study medicine in the United Kingdom (1827–1838), graduating from the University of Edinburgh in 1838. He returned home in 1839 and married Ana María Mora Porras in 1840; they had ten children prior to her death in 1854. He then married the tutor of his children, Sofía Matilde Joy Redman, with whom he had two children.

— LOWELL GUDMUNDSON

MONTEIRO, PEDRO AURÉLIO DE GÓIS

Pedro Aurélio de Góis Monteiro (*b.* 12 December 1889; *d.* 26 October 1956), Brazilian general. Born into an influential family of planters in the northeastern state of Alagoas, Góis spent about a decade in Rio Grande do Sul (1906–1916) as a young officer. In the 1920s he taught in the army's Command and General Staff College and served in the forces pursuing the Prestes Column throughout the Brazilian interior. Family ties (through marriage) and his long experience in Rio Grande do Sul led to his involvement in the uprising against the administration of Washington LUÍS in October 1930. Head of the triumphant rebel forces, Góis was promoted to general in 1931. He then led the government siege of rebel forces in São Paulo in 1932 and served as minister of war in 1934–1935.

Góis played a key role in the military coup of November 1937 that imposed the Estado Novo dictatorship, following which he served as the chief of staff of the Brazilian army (1937–1943). While serving a second tour (1945–1946) as minister of war, he personally organized the forced resignation of Getúlio VARGAS in October 1945 and oversaw national elections in December. From 1947 to 1951 he served as senator from Alagoas, failing in a reelection bid in 1950. During his second term, President Vargas appointed him chief of staff of the armed forces in 1951, a position he held until 1952.

– MARSHALL C. EAKIN

MONTEIRO, TOBIAS DO RÊGO

Tobias do Rêgo Monteiro (*b.* 29 July 1866; *d.* 3 August 1952), Brazilian historian. Born in Natal, Monteiro abandoned studies at Rio's Faculdade de Medicina in 1889 for journalism and key bureaucratic sinecures in the 1890s. He became an editor of the *Jornal do Commércio* (1894–1907), where he championed the emergent Paulista republicans at the century's turn. He also served as President Manuel Ferraz de CAMPOS SALES's secretary and apologist. His public life was crowned by election as a senator for Rio Grande do Norte (1920–1922). He began publishing history in 1913, studying the monarchy's decline; he is celebrated, however, for his work on the early monarchy. He remains noteworthy for his use of primary sources and his research in Brazilian and European archives.

– JEFFREY D. NEEDELL

MONTEIRO LOBATO, JOSÉ BENTO

José Bento Monteiro Lobato (*b.* 18 April 1882; *d.* 4 July 1948), Brazilian writer. He was born in Taubaté, São Paulo State, and graduated from law school in 1904. Between 1914 and 1917 Monteiro Lobato wrote prolifically for the newspaper *Estado de São Paulo*, where

he expressed many of his ideals and nationalistic concerns. In 1921 he began publishing children's books, in which he sketched the utopian world he envisioned, but could not build, for the Brazilian nation as a whole: a world devoid of inequalities and foreign influences, truly free and multidimensional in its visions and opportunities for all. Through the seemingly simplistic narrative structure of his children's books, Monteiro Lobato conveyed profound criticism of the way Brazilian society was undermined and subdued by its leaders. He introduced a discourse that blurred the lines dividing reality and fantasy. He was also very interested in Nietzschean philosophy, which supported his rebellious and independent spirit. His literary aesthetics, engendered from an individualistic mentality, remained apart from any group or literary movement, hence his reluctance to become associated with the Brazilian modernist movement. In his lifetime, Monteiro Lobato declined invitations to join both the Brazilian Communist Party and the Brazilian Academy of Letters.

Monteiro Lobato published children's books, in which he sketched the utopian world he envisioned, but could not build, for the Brazilian nation as a whole.

Monteiro Lobato was one of the first Brazilian writers to incorporate modernist ideals into his work. Still, his work is classified as symbolist, exhibiting realist and naturalist characteristics as well. Through his prolific literary production, Monteiro Lobato denounced Brazilian elitism and the hypocrisy and corruption of political officials. He spoke against the poverty that was widespread in rural Brazil, its interior, and backlands. Many consider him to have founded the book publishing industry in Brazil.

His main works are *Urupês* (1918), a collection of short stories in which the author introduces most of his literary innovations (such as an essentially Brazilian Portuguese language, with its many vernacular expressions), which would later be embraced by Brazilian modernists. In *Urupês,* Monteiro Lobato also cultivates nationalistic themes through the depiction of rural Brazilians, their world and economic deprivation. Other works of significance are *Problema vital* (1918), *Cidades mortas* (1919), *Idéias de Jeca Tatú* (1919), and his first children's book *Narizinho arrebitado* (1921).

– ROSÂNGELA MARIA VIEIRA

MONTEJO, FRANCISCO DE

Francisco de Montejo (*b.* 1479; *d.* 1553), conquistador, important associate of Hernán CORTÉS, and conqueror of Yucatán and Honduras. Born in Salamanca, Montejo came to America in about 1514 and served as a conquistador under Pedro Arias de ÁVILA, Diego de VELÁSQUEZ, and Juan de GRIJALVA (in 1518) before joining Cortés as one of the latter's most important lieutenants. On the eve of the conquest of Mexico, Cortés sent Montejo to Spain to represent him before Charles V in order to legalize the expedition. After several years Montejo accomplished his mission, and in return Cortés rewarded him with a large share of the booty of the Conquest, including the *encomienda* (landed estate) of Atzcapotzalco in the valley of Mexico.

In 1526 the crown granted Montejo the title of governor-captain-general adelantado (*gobernador capitán general adelantado*) and the right to conquer Yucatán and Honduras. Montejo undertook the conquest of Yucatán the same year, but failed because of Maya resistance. He then passed the Yucatán expedition on to his son, Franciso Montejo y León (1507–1565), whose 1537 expedition also failed. That same year, Montejo succeeded in conquering Honduras. The family's third attempt in Yucatán succeeded in 1542. In 1548 the crown, as part of an attempt to reduce the power of the original conquistadors throughout America, stripped Montejo of his political offices and encomiendas in Yucatán and Honduras. In 1551 he returned to Salamanca, Spain, where he died two years later.

— ROBERT W. PATCH

MONTENEGRO Y NERVO, ROBERTO

Roberto Montenegro y Nervo (*b.* 19 February 1887; *d.* 1968), Mexican artist. Montenegro, a native of Guadalajara, began his artistic studies at an early age in his hometown. Later, he traveled to Mexico City and enrolled in the Academy of San Carlos. In 1905, he was given a fellowship for European study by the Education Ministry and stayed, initially in Paris, later in Madrid, until 1920, becoming friends with the most important artistic and literary figures of the time, some of whom he met through his cousin, the poet Amado NERVO.

Upon his return to Mexico, Montenegro y Nervo developed a strong interest in folk art, in pursuit of which he published *Pinturas mejicanas 1800–1860;* painted murals in such important locations as the Colegio de San Pedro y San Pablo, the Ministry of Education, and other distinguished venues; and in 1921, along with DR. ATL and others, he held the first exhibit of folk art in Mexico. Throughout his adult life he gathered a superb collection of masks, which he donated to the Ministry of Education. In 1934 he became director of the Museum of Popular Art and head of the department of plastic art at the National Institute of Fine Arts. At the same time, Montenegro pursued an interest in the ballet, designing scenery for the screen version of *Coppélia* and helping Marc Chagall with the sets for the ballet *Aleko*. In 1958 he completed a mosaic, "Apollo and the Muses," for the Teatro Degollado in Guadalajara. Throughout his career he was also known as a distinguished portraitist, capturing such celebrities as Diego Rivera, Carlos Chávez, Lázaro Cárdenas, and Alfonso Reyes. In 1967 he won the National Prize for the Fine Arts. He died on a train traveling between Mexico City and Pátzcuaro.

— BARBARA A. TENENBAUM

MONTERROSO, AUGUSTO

Augusto Monterroso (*b.* 21 December 1921), Guatemalan short-story writer, considered one of Latin America's contemporary masters of the genre. Completely self-taught, Monterroso had no more than elementary schooling in his native country. He moved to Mexico City in 1944, where he has lived ever since, except for a brief period as Guatemalan consul in La Paz, Bolivia (1951–1954), and a short stay in Santiago, Chile (1954–1956). A very exact, demanding, precise, and well-read writer, Monterroso published his first book, *Obras completas y otros cuentos,* in 1959. A ten-year silence followed, during which he worked as an editor for Editorial Universitaria, then published a contemporary renewal of the fable genre in *Oveja negra y demás fábulas* (1969). This book won the Magda Donato Award in 1970 and was translated into English as *The Black Sheep and Other Fables* (1971). In 1972 Monterroso won the Xavier Villaurrutia Award for *Movimiento perpetuo*. Monterroso organized a creative writing workshop for the Instituto Nacional de Bellas Artes (National Institute of Fine Arts) and has had a hand in training most young Mexican writers. He became a best-selling author in Spain in the 1980s. Additional books by Monterroso are *Lo demás es silencio* (1978); *Viaje al centro de la fábula* (1981); *La palabra mágica* (1984); and *La letra E* (1987).

— ARTURO ARIAS

MONTES, CÉSAR

César Montes (*b.* 1941), Guatemalan guerrilla leader. Nicknamed "El Chirís," a Mayan term meaning "kid," Montes began to rebel at the age of thirteen, when he was expelled from a Catholic school for his reaction to the overthrow of the Jacobo ARBENZ government. Montes later attended law school and was imprisoned for his role in a student demonstration. At the age of twenty he became an active member of the Communist PGT (Guatemalan Labor Party) youth wing. By the time he was twenty-five, he had succeeded Luis Augusto TURCIOS LIMA as the leader of the Rebel Armed Forces (FAR). After breaking with the PGT on 10 January 1968, the FAR declared its total and definitive unification with the 13th of November Revolutionary Movement (MR-13), led by Marco Antonio YON SOSA (February 1968). The new group based its operations in the Sierra de las Minas.

– DOUGLAS R. KEBERLEIN

MONTES, ISMAEL

Ismael Montes (*b*. 5 October 1861; *d*. 18 December 1933), president of Bolivia (1904–1909 and 1913–1917). Born in La Paz, Montes was the most important leader of the Liberal Party, which he dominated during much of its twenty years in power. As prosperity reigned during his first term because of the boom in tin exports, Montes continued a railroad building program and provided money for other infrastructure projects. During his first term the most liberal land-grant policy in Bolivian history was put into effect; during his second term, however, he oversaw the cessation of land grants on the frontiers. His banking reforms of 1917 and the creation of a state bank based in La Paz undermined Sucre's role as the financial center of the nation. Montes's intransigence led to a split in the Liberal Party in 1914 and the creation of the Republican Party, which in 1921 took over the government in a coup.

– ERICK D. LANGER

MONTES DE OCA, CONFUCIO

Confucio Montes de Oca (*b*. 1896; *d*. 1925), Honduran painter of the Generation of '20. Montes de Oca painted scenes of his native La Ceiba. Largely self-taught, his paintings of the tropical scenes of the north coast of Honduras were especially noteworthy. In 1919 he went to Paris, where he perfected his style, and in 1921 his best-known painting, *The Blacksmith,* won international acclaim. In the same year he moved to Rome, where his romantic paintings of both urban and rural scenes were recognized for their beauty, harmony of forms, and forceful use of color. In Italy his style became more impressionistic with little trace of his early Honduran style remaining. In 1925 he returned to Honduras, but died two months after his arrival there. His brother, Zoroastro Montes de Oca (*b*. 1893), who

survived him, was also a popular painter in Tegucigalpa, but he never received the international recognition of Confucio.

– RALPH LEE WOODWARD, JR.

MONTESINOS, ANTONIO DE

Antonio de Montesinos (Montesino, Montezinos; *d*. ca. 1530), a Dominican priest who was the first public exponent of the rights of the Indians in the New World. Montesinos criticized Spanish treatment of the indigenous inhabitants on Hispaniola during the early sixteenth century. In his Christmas sermon of 1511, he denounced the maltreatment of the Indians, refused communion to the Spaniards he viewed as most responsible for such activities, and threatened them with damnation.

On 20 March 1512, King Ferdinand of Spain ordered Governor Diego Columbus to silence Montesinos and other Dominicans. On 23 March an official communication from the Dominican superior in Spain, Alonso de Loaysa, was received. It reprimanded Montesinos and ordered him to cease his public criticism. Should Montesinos refuse, he would be returned to Spain and no further Dominicans would be sent to the New World.

It is known that Montesinos spoke at the royal court in Spain in defense of the Indians. Most important, he convinced Bartolomé de LAS CASAS to renounce his *encomienda* and commercial interests on the island. Ordained as a Dominican priest, Las Casas undertook the most famous defense of the New World's indigenous population. Montesinos died in Venezuela while working to protect the Indians of that region from Spanish abuses.

– HEATHER K. THIESSEN

MONTT ÁLVAREZ, JORGE

Jorge Montt Álvarez (*b*. 22 April 1846; *d*. 8 October 1922), Chilean admiral and president of Chile (1891–1896). A career naval officer, Montt entered the navy at twelve. He served with distinction in the war with Spain of 1865–1866 as well as in the War of the Pacific. During the 1891 revolution he commanded the congressionalist flotilla and served as the head of the insurgent movement's governing board. Montt led the fleet during the key battles of Concón and Placilla.

Following the victory of the congressionalists over José Manuel BALMACEDA, the legislature unanimously elected Montt president of Chile. An apolitical supporter of the parliamentary cause, Montt did not want the post but was prevailed upon to take it in the interest of fostering national unity. He may have regretted giving up the simple life of a naval officer for the tumultuous one of ruling a nation beset by domestic problems and besieged by foreign enemies such as the United States and Argentina.

As president, Montt nonetheless managed to quell unrest, integrate the forces of Balmaceda into the country's political life, oversee honest elections, resolve the Baltimore Incident, and avoid war with Buenos Aires. He tried but failed to return the nation to the gold standard. This former admiral, perhaps out of deference to the new political system, did not rule Chile but left its administration in the hands of the eight cabinets that governed the nation.

After the completion of his presidential term, Montt returned to the fleet, where he labored to reform the navy's administrative system. Following his retirement from active duty after more than fifty years of naval service, he directed the Chilean Red Cross and served as an alderman in Valparaíso, where he attempted to reform municipal politics. An honest man who, unlike other parliamentary regime politicians, did not use public service to enrich himself, he died virtually penniless.

— WILLIAM F. SATER

MONTT TORRES, MANUEL

Manuel Montt Torres (*b.* 5 September 1809; *d.* 21 September 1880), president of Chile (1851–1861) and key political figure of his period. The relative poverty of his upper-class family meant that he had to make his own way in life. He became deputy rector of Santiago's prestigious Instituto Nacional in 1832 and rector in 1835, also serving as senior official in the Ministry of the Interior. He was minister of the interior in 1840–1841 and again in 1845–1846, winning a deserved reputation for toughness toward opposition. His reputation was undoubtedly enhanced by his own austere and rather inflexible character—although his numerous enemies always acknowledged his intelligence and administrative talent.

Montt's presidential candidacy for the ruling Conservative party provoked political agitation on a scale unseen in Chile since 1830. His election was marked by the outbreak of civil war, the most serious feature of which was a menacing revolt in the southern provinces. The government won, but Montt's repeated use of emergency powers thereafter gradually alienated many of his Conservative supporters. His administration, much of which coincided with a commercial boom, was noted for its industriousness. During Montt's two terms, Chile's first railroads were built, gaslights appeared in the streets of Santiago, banking developed,

the mail system was modernized, and the number of schools greatly increased. Material progress, however, did little to reconcile the Liberal opposition. With the Question of the Sacristan in 1856, it became impossible for Montt to contain political tensions. A large section of his Conservative party now defected, joining forces with the Liberals in the Liberal-Conservative Fusion (1858). Montt's own reduced following formed the new National Party.

In 1858 political agitation once again intensified. In the end, as usual, Montt imposed emergency powers. This was followed early in 1859 by rebellion in the northern provinces and rural guerrilla attacks in the Central Valley. The guerrillas were soon crushed, but in the north, where the rich miner Pedro León Gallo (1830–1877) improvised an army of a thousand soldiers, the outcome was only decided four months later at the battle of Cerro Grande (29 April 1859). Military victory was followed by political stalemate. Montt could not secure the presidential succession for his closest associate, Antonio Varas (1817–1886: minister of the interior, 1850–1856 and 1860–1861). The man selected, the easygoing patrician José Joaquín PÉREZ (1800–1889), soon called the Fusion into government (1862), thus displacing the Nationals (or *Montt-Varistas,* as these were now nicknamed).

Montt's main job after his decade of power was as president of the Supreme Court. His enemies tried, in vain, to impeach him in 1868–1869, proving that the strong passions Montt had aroused in the 1840s and 1850s were still very much alive. Montt also represented Chile at the American Congress held in Lima in 1864–1865, and did so with great dignity.

— SIMON COLLIER

MONTÚFAR, LORENZO

Lorenzo Montúfar (*b.* 11 March 1823; *d.* 21 May 1898), Guatemalan author, diplomat, educator, and government minister. Montúfar was the quintessential nineteenth-century Central American liberal. Deeply committed to isthmian union, anticlericalism, and the modernization of education and the law, and a proponent of constitutional government, he nevertheless supported authoritarian rule when it served his purposes. Son of Sergeant-Major (later General) Rafael Montúfar y Coronado, and nephew of Colonel Manuel Montúfar y Coronado, the author of *Memorias para la historia de la revolución de Centro-América* (*Memorias de Jalapa*), Lorenzo Montúfar received the standard, church-dominated education available to members of the elite at the time and was graduated with a law degree in 1845. Anticlerical writings and active opposition to the dictator Rafael CARRERA, however, quickly forced him into exile in Costa Rica.

In what became his second home, Montúfar practiced law and served in various government positions and in the university. Drawn back to Guatemala following the Liberal Revolution of 1871, he held ministerial posts and the rectorate of the University of San Carlos. In 1876, as a member of the Constituent Assembly, he made his famous defense of dictatorship, successfully recommending that rather than create a document the caudillo would violate, and thus weaken respect for the law, the assembly should allow Justo Rufino BARRIOS four more years of unfettered rule.

In 1878 Montúfar began his most influential scholarly work, the seven-volume *Reseña histórica de Centro-América* (1878–1887), which offered a spirited argument for Central American unification and a defense of Liberal rule. Montúfar held the post of minister of foreign affairs from 1877 to 1881 and served as special envoy to Washington, D.C., but broke with Barrios over the question of Guatemala's boundary claims against Mexico and again went into exile in Costa Rica. A brief return in 1885 provoked a confrontation with the church and expulsion, but Montúfar soon returned and ended his public career in 1891 as the unsuccessful Liberal Party candidate for president.

— DAVID MCCREERY

MONTÚFAR MONTES DE OCA, LORENZO

Lorenzo Montúfar Montes de Oca (*b.* 1743; *d.* 7 May 1808), Guatemalan soldier and politician. Montúfar was born in Santiago de Guatemala and earned his bachelor's degree in philosophy from San Carlos University in 1763. He served as provisional magistrate of Quezaltenango, magistrate of Tecpán-Atitlán and of Verapaz, and first mayor of Guatemala City in 1783. As lieutenant field marshal and magistrate of Sacatepéquez, he was a major figure in the Terronistas, who between 1773 and 1776 opposed moving the capital of the realm to Valle de la Ermita after the destruction of Santiago de los Caballeros (Antigua) by earthquakes. In 1793, as mayor of Antigua, he firmly opposed the order of the Royal Tribunal to destroy the ruins of the former capital, in gratitude for which his portrait in oil has hung in the chapter room of city hall in Antigua since 1936. He was the father of historian, soldier, and conservative politician Manuel Montúfar y Coronado.

— ARTURO TARACENA ARRIOLA

MONTÚFAR Y LARREA, JUAN PÍO DE

Juan Pío de Montúfar y Larrea (*b.* 20 June 1759; *d.* 31 July 1816), leader of an uprising against Spanish au-

thority in Quito. Montúfar, son of the marquis of Selva Alegre, who was president of the Audiencia of Quito (1753–1761), was born in Quito. He served in 1809 as the leader of a small group of antiroyalist conspirators who organized a Sovereign Junta of Quito on 10 August with Montúfar as president. The junta opposed French rule over Spain, declaring its loyalty to jailed Spanish monarch Ferdinand VII. Few in Quito or elsewhere in the *audiencia* supported these actions. The rebellion ended in October 1809 when Spanish troops arrived from Lima. Royal authorities executed all involved except for the noblemen on the Sovereign Junta of Quito.

> *The tenth of August is celebrated as Ecuadorian independence day, the uprising remembered as the "first cry of independence."*

Montúfar left for exile in Cádiz, Spain, where he died. The tenth of August is celebrated as Ecuadorian independence day, the uprising remembered as the "first cry of independence." However, most historians now depict the movement as one for greater autonomy from Spain, not complete independence.

— RONN F. PINEO

MOOG, CLODOMIRO VIANNA

Clodomiro Vianna Moog (*b.* 28 October 1906; *d.* 16 January 1988), Brazilian intellectual, novelist, and diplomat. His comparative study of national characters in the Americas, *Bandeirantes e pioneiros* (1954; *Bandeirantes and Pioneers,* 1964), contrasted the predatory style of Brazilian colonizers with the settler style of American pioneers.

Moog's experience of contrasts within the nation led him to define Brazil as a "cultural archipelago." After political exile in the Amazon, from 1932 to 1934, he published *O ciclo do ouro negro* (1936; The Cycle of Black Gold), depicting the challenge of nature to colonization of the Amazon. Upon return to his native Rio Grande do Sul, he directed the newspaper *A Folha da Tarde.* His novel *Um rio imita o Reno* (1939; A River Imitates the Rhine), reflecting on Brazil's assimilation of German immigrants, won him election to the Brazilian Academy of Letters in 1945. Thereafter, his career was that of a diplomat and man of letters, representing Brazil on economic and social commissions at the United Nations and the Organization of American States.

— DAIN BORGES

MORA, FERNANDO DE LA

Fernando de la Mora (*b.* 1785; *d.* 23 August 1835), Paraguayan statesman. One of the most highly educated and influential Paraguayans of his time, de la Mora failed to gain the fame he deserved only because he stood in the shadow of José Gaspar de FRANCIA, the country's first great authoritarian dictator of the nineteenth century. Born in Asunción, de la Mora attended school at the University of Córdoba, Argentina. He later aided in the defense of the viceregal capital during the English invasions of 1806–1807.

Returning to Asunción some time before 1810, de la Mora operated a successful distillery, dabbled in commerce, and held a seat on the *cabildo* of the province. With independence in 1811, he joined the first revolutionary junta alongside Francia. Unlike his isolationist colleagues, de la Mora openly favored some confederal arrangement for Paraguay with the other Platine states, especially Buenos Aires. This attitude drew much criticism at the time, however, and with increasing tensions along the rivers, it grew more unpopular as the months passed.

In 1812, the other junta members sent him as a civilian representative on a punitive expedition against hostile Mbayá Indians. During his absence, de la Mora's administrative powers were stripped from him at Francia's specific request. Then, in August 1813, he was forced to resign from the junta, again at the behest of Francia, who went on one year later to establish a "supreme dictatorship" that lasted until 1840.

De la Mora withdrew from politics to devote himself to his business affairs. He was not, however, permitted to enjoy his retirement. Branded as pro-*porteño* in sympathy, he was the object of constant police scrutiny. In 1820, though they had no clear proof of wrongdoing, the police accused him of complicity in an antigovernment plot. He was arrested and all his property confiscated. De la Mora died wretchedly in prison, forgotten by all save his family.

– THOMAS L. WHIGHAM

MORA, JOSÉ MARÍA LUIS

José María Luis Mora (*b.* 1794; *d.* 14 July 1850), Mexican politician and political theorist. Born in Chamacuero, Guanajuato, Mora studied theology, and was ordained a priest in 1829 when he obtained a doctorate. A moderate constitutionalist, Mora became a journalist and politician after independence. Elected to the legislature of the state of Mexico, he participated in writing that state's constitution. However, he became more significant as a journalist, a publicist for the *escoceses* (Scot-

tish rite Masons), and an apologist for Nicolás BRAVO and the rebels against the government in 1828.

A supporter of the repressive administration of Anastasio BUSTAMANTE (1830–1832), Mora nevertheless emerged as an advocate of reform in 1834 during the vice presidency of Valentín GÓMEZ FARÍAS, achieving distinction when he synthesized widely published criticisms of the church and when he joined liberals in favoring education reform. When that regime fell Mora traveled to Paris and subsequently represented his country in France and in England. He remained in France until his death. There he published three volumes of his projected four-volume *Méjico y sus revoluciones* (1836) and his *Obras sueltas* (1837), in which he claims to have played a key role in his country's politics. His works which criticize the excesses of the independence era and favor moderate liberalism, exerted great influence in the late 1840s and 1850s among a new generation of liberals who sought an antidote to the powerful conservative arguments of Lucas ALAMÁN. As a result, although a minor political figure, Mora has become known as the "liberal theorist" of early Mexico.

– JAIME E. RODRÍGUEZ O.

MORA FERNÁNDEZ, JUAN

Juan Mora Fernández (*b.* 12 July 1784; *d.* 16 December 1854), first president of Costa Rica (1824–1833). He was chosen head of state of Costa Rica by the Constituent Assembly of 1824 and reelected in 1829. His major achievement was survival amid the turbulence of the Central American Federation civil wars. His administrations kept as much distance as possible from Guatemalan authorities while seeking British commercial and political support.

Mora was able to convince Central American Federation leaders to provisionally accept the annexation of Guanacaste province (1825) over Nicaraguan opposition. Costa Rica's first formal constitution was enacted under his rule in 1825. Mora's ability to negotiate compromises on the conflict-laden issue of the location of the nation's capital helped prevent the collapse of constitutional authority locally, despite the repeated civil wars in the rest of Central America.

The son of San José residents Mateo Mora Valverde and Lucía Encarnación Fernández Umaña, Mora studied in Léon, Nicaragua, before returning to Costa Rica in 1806. He married Juana Castillo Palacios in 1819. He continued to be active in politics throughout his life, serving as a member of Congress eleven times between 1821 and 1848, representing San José and outlying Pacific coast districts of Boruca/Térraba. He served as vice president in the brief presidency of Manuel Aguilar and was exiled along with Aguilar by the revolt of 27 May 1838 led by CARRILLO. He returned to political life after Carrillo's fall, as a congressman (1842–1848).

— LOWELL GUDMUNDSON

MORA OTERO, JOSÉ ANTONIO

José Antonio Mora Otero (*b.* 22 November 1897; *d.* 26 January 1975), Uruguayan diplomat. Mora Otero had an extremely active international career, especially in Pan-American organizations. He was born in Montevideo, where he received his law degree in 1925. He joined the foreign service in 1926 and served in the Ministry of Foreign Affairs from 1933 to 1941. He was appointed minister to Bolivia in 1942. Starting in 1945, he played an active role in meetings that gave rise to the United Nations. In 1946 he was appointed minister to Washington and Uruguayan delegate to the United Nations. In 1951 he remained in Washington, now in the post of ambassador. In 1954 he was appointed chair of the Organization of American States (OAS) and from 1956 to 1968 served as secretary general of that organization. Returning to his country, he served as minister of foreign affairs from 1971 to 1972 before retiring. His writings include *Sentido internacional del Uruguay* (1938) and *From Panama to Punta del Este* (1968).

— JOSÉ DE TORRES WILSON

MORA PORRÁS, JUAN RAFAEL

Juan Rafael Mora Porrás (*b.* 8 February 1814; *d.* 30 September 1860), president of Costa Rica (1849–1859). Mora is best remembered for his leading role in defeating the filibuster William WALKER in the National Campaign of 1856. Along with his brother, José Joaquín (1818–1860), Mora was the primary military commander of the expeditionary force which engaged Walker in southern Nicaragua and northern Costa Rica. Some 9,000 troops were raised in Costa Rica and, along with local, British, Peruvian, and Guatemalan financial assistance, they were instrumental in the eventual collapse of Walker's puppet state in Nicaragua.

The impact of the military campaign on Costa Rica was enormous, in terms of both political mythology and material life. In purely demographic terms perhaps 10 percent of the nation's nearly 100,000 inhabitants died in the cholera epidemic which broke out with the return of the troops. As a tribute to Mora's leadership the border province of Guanacaste was briefly renamed Moracia (1854–1860). Subsequent generations have referred to him by the diminutive of "Don Juanito" and

have considered him perhaps the true founder of Costa Rican sovereignty.

Mora was one of the few early political leaders in Costa Rica without a university education. By the time his father died in 1836, Mora was already embarked on a business rather than an academic career. By the late 1830s Mora had become a significant property owner and one of the leading wholesale traders. He was also one of the first to undertake large-scale coffee plantings, west of San José on former municipal lands.

He was elected deputy from San José province (1846–1847) and assumed the presidency in 1849. He engineered his reelection in 1853 over semipublic military conspiracies against him. A similar reelection was staged in April 1859, but on 14 August 1859 he was deposed by a barracks revolt and exiled to El Salvador. He returned, leading an exile invasion force, on 17 September 1860, but after they landed at Puntarenas and secured a small coastal strip, the campaign fizzled. He was taken prisoner and ordered shot by the government headed by his former brother-in-law, José María MONTEALEGRE, in Puntarenas.

Opposition to Mora was led by rival coffee planter-merchants fearful of a state bank intended to provide smaller growers with crop loans, as well as to heighten Mora's control of finance and export activities. Mora and his associate in this endeavor, the Spaniard-Argentine Crisanto de Medina, were the targets of intense criticism by commercial competitors after the decree of 1 July 1858 established the Banco de Medina.

The Mora regime had also angered the church hierarchy by not responding to the creation of an archdiocese for Costa Rica in 1850 with a willingness to negotiate the application of the tithe to coffee production, disregarded locally since the beginnings of the industry in the 1830s. Church-state tensions reached new heights with the December 1858 expulsion of Archbishop Anselmo LLORENTE Y LAFUENTE for too vigorously defending family members involved in political disputes with the president.

A final element of discontent with the Mora regime was based on his ill-advised campaign to auction certain of the remaining common lands, often close associates. This decree, of 6 August 1859, threatened lands surrounding San José and Alajuela long occupied by farmers paying nominal annual rents. Public protests broke out and were used as justification by the military forces who deposed Mora the following week. In this, as in other areas, Mora followed classically liberal policies in Costa Rica's internal economic affairs, despite his identification in Central America with the conservative forces opposed to Morazán and later to Walker.

Juan Rafael Moras Porrás was the son of San José residents Camilo Mora Alvarado and Ana María Porrás. He married Inés Aguilar de Coeto, who survived him by several decades and successfully administered the couple's many properties. She was subsequently one of the major suppliers of sugarcane to the state liquor monopoly established by her husband while he was president. Their children were Camilo and Juana Mora Aguilar.

– LOWELL GUDMUNDSON

MORA VALVERDE, MANUEL

Manuel Mora Valverde (*b.* 1910), the leading figure and one of the founding fathers of communism in Costa Rica, elected to five terms in the national congress (1934–1948, 1970–1974), and twice candidate for the presidency (1940, 1974).

Mora capitalized on the deteriorating economic conditions during the Great Depression to bring the Communist Party to the forefront of labor-union organization.

Manuel Mora's life and career have been intertwined with the communist movement in his native Costa Rica. His active political career began while he was still a young law student at the School of Law in San José. In 1930 he played a leading role in the organization of the Workers and Peasants Bloc, which rather quickly evolved into the Costa Rican Communist Party (PC).

Along with Carlos Luis FALLAS SIBAJA, Jaime Cerdas Moran, and others, Mora capitalized on the deteriorating economic conditions during the Great Depression to bring the Communist Party to the forefront of labor-union organization. With his segment of the labor movement as a voting base, he made the Communist Party a force to be reckoned with in national politics. Never a true contender for power, it has been a militant and influential minority party.

Mora contributed to his country through his dedication, writings, austerity, and ability to change the agenda of Costa Rican politics. Political leaders from León CORTÉS CASTRO (1936–1940) through Rafael Angel CALDERÓN GUARDIA (1940–1944), Otilio ULATE BLANCO (1949–1953), and José FIGUERES FERRER (1948–1949, 1953–1958, 1970–1974) felt it necessary to respond ideologically to the communist challenge. Even though they rejected Mora's party and its links to the Soviet Union, most respected him as a national leader. Mora's program did not become the nation's program; however, the challenge that he posed led his political opponents to formulate their own responses to the socioeconomic problems of Costa Rica. He thus contributed to the great progress that has characterized Costa Rica since 1940.

Mora reached the apex of his power and influence during the administrations of Calderón Guardia (1940–1944) and Teodoro PICADO MICHALSKI (1944–1948). After changing the name of his party to the Popular Vanguard (PVP) and receiving the approval of Archbishop Víctor M. SANABRIA MARTÍNEZ, he entered into a political alliance with the governing National Republican Party. This alliance, which called itself the Victory Bloc, enacted wide-ranging social legislation, which has been maintained and enhanced by subsequent administrations.

With the overthrow of Picado by the Figueres-led revolution in 1948, Mora was forced into exile and his party was outlawed. He later returned to Costa Rica and renewed his political activities, but neither his own party nor the various leftist coalitions in which it participated ever achieved the strength and influence that the Popular Vanguard enjoyed during its alliance with the government between 1942 and 1948.

– JOHN PATRICK BELL

MORA Y DEL RÍO, JOSÉ

José Mora y Del Río (*b.* 24 February 1854; *d.* 22 April 1928), archbishop of Mexico, 1908–1928. A native of Pajcuarán, Michoacán, Mora y del Río studied in Rome and rose rapidly to become bishop of Tehuantepec (1893), a poor rural area. As bishop, he supported Catholic Social Action to benefit the peasantry. He was sympathetic to the presidency of Francisco MADERO (1911–1913), the collapse of which threw Mexico into a period of civil strife in which the Catholic church became identified with conservatism.

After five years in exile, Mora y del Río returned to Mexico in 1919 to confront growing anticlericalism. In 1926 he openly rejected the restrictions on the church in the Mexican constitution which President Plutarco Elías CALLES energetically enforced through closure of church primary schools and required registration of priests. The archbishop called a church strike which ended public religious services. Calles exiled Mora y del Río, who died in San Antonio, Texas, barely a year before the conflict ended through a negotiated settlement.

– JOHN A. BRITTON

MORAIS, VINÍCIUS DE

Vinícius de Morais (*b.* 19 October 1913; *d.* 9 July 1980), Brazilian writer and songwriter. Born in Rio, Morais studied in Jesuit schools. He graduated from law school with a bachelor's degree in 1933, when he published his first book of poetry. Influenced by Catholic intellectuals, his first efforts were in the Christian mystical vein of the second generation of Brazilian modernism. He wrote film criticism and worked as a government film censor before spending an academic year at Oxford (1938–1939), where he studied English literature. In the 1940s, with increasingly secular and material texts, he established a literary reputation. He entered the diplomatic corps in 1943. Serving in Los Angeles, he was able to cultivate further interests in film and jazz. On assignment in Paris, he wrote his widely read books of sonnets and the verse play *Orfeu da conceição* (1955), whose film adaptation by Marcel Camus, *Black Orpheus* (first place award, 1959 Cannes Film Festival), brought worldwide attention to Brazil, to Brazilian popular music, and to Morais as a lyricist.

In the early 1960s, Morais participated in a movement for sociopolitical awareness in poetry and began to perform as a vocalist. He gained wide public attention as the leading cowriter of bossa nova compositions, including "Garota de Ipanema" (The Girl from Ipanema). While his increasing involvement in popular music and bohemian life-style led to his departure from diplomatic service (he served in Montevideo until 1969), his application of his literary skills to songwriting and his support of song as an essential manifestation of national culture helped impart a new status and dignity to popular music. In the 1960s and 1970s, he published new books of poetry and *crônicas* (journalistic prose pieces) and made two dozen recordings. His standing as a cultural hero was enhanced by his criticism of the military regime.

— CHARLES A. PERRONE

MORAIS BARROS, PRUDENTE JOSÉ DE

Prudente José de Morais Barros (*b.* 4 October 1841; *d.* 3 December 1902), president of Brazil (1894–1898). Morais rose to political prominence as a distinguished provincial legislator representing São Paulo's Partido Republicano Paulista, the most important Republican party of the Brazilian Empire. As a legislator, Morais was a strong advocate of coffee planters' rights and foreign immigration. Following the proclamation of the Republic on 15 November 1889, Morais served as the first republican governor of São Paulo, subsequently rising to national distinction as the president of the Constituent Assembly of 1891. In March 1894 Morais became the first civilian president of the fledgling republic. While serving as president, Morais promoted the economic and political interests of São Paulo.

The Morais presidency was characterized by the slow and painful consolidation of the decentralized, federalist political system sought by the most powerful state Republican parties. The consolidation of stable civilian rule was hampered by a civil war in Rio Grande do Sul (1893–1895) and several revolts. By far, the most famous armed insurrection centered in Canudos, Bahia, where state and federal troops experienced enormous difficulties in subduing the ragtag *sertanejo* followers of the self-proclaimed prophet, ANTÔNIO CONSELHEIRO. Morais himself narrowly escaped death in a failed assassination attempt made by a disgruntled federal soldier returning from Canudos. Morais later used the attempt on his life to justify clamping down on political opponents.

Amid these political upheavals, a serious economic crisis prompted the federal government to secure the 1898 funding loan, which primarily aided the powerful coffee interests of São Paulo and Minas Gerais. Nevertheless, inflation, high prices, and low wages meant that few Brazilians prospered under Morais. But, despite these political and economic difficulties, when Morais stepped down from office in 1898, he was celebrated as the leader who pacified the Republic. In poor health, Morais returned to São Paulo, where he died four years later.

— DARYLE WILLIAMS

MORALES, AGUSTÍN

Agustín Morales (*b.* 11 May 1808; *d.* 27 November 1872), president of Bolivia (1871–1872). Morales's military career exemplified *caudillismo* in Bolivia. Born in La Paz, Morales at age twenty-two joined the army under Andrés de SANTA CRUZ and participated in the wars of the Peru-Bolivian Confederation. After Santa Cruz was deposed in 1839, Morales fought alongside José BALLIVIÁN and occupied the posts of commandant of Potosí and Cochabamba. When Ballivián's rival, Manuel Isidoro BELZU, seized power in 1848, Morales's commercial house in Cochabamba was sacked by the victorious troops. Vowing revenge, Morales attempted to assassinate Belzu in 1850. Failing to kill him, he fled into exile.

Returning a decade later, Morales joined with another caudillo, José María LINARES, in 1859 and then another, Mariano MELGAREJO, in 1865. Driven into exile again in 1865, Morales returned in 1870 and led a popular movement in La Paz that deposed Melgarejo.

After Morales became president in early 1871, he supported the newly emerging silver barons of southern Bolivia. He legalized free trade in silver, thereby ending a government monopoly in force since the beginning of the colonial era. His intemperate behavior toward his subordinates, however, led to his assassination by his nephew, Frederico Lafaye, in 1872.

— ERWIN P. GRIESHABER

MORALES, ARMANDO

Armando Morales (*b.* 1927), Nicaraguan painter. Born in Granada, Morales studied under Rodrigo Peñalba at the School of Fine Arts in Managua (1948–1953). He received the Ernest Wolf Award for best Latin American artist at the Fifth Biennial in São Paolo (1959). With a Guggenheim Fellowship he studied engraving at the Pratt Institute Graphic Center in New York City (1960) and in 1965 he won a gold medal for painting from the Association of American Writers and Artists in Managua. He taught at the Cooper Union in New York City from 1972 to 1973, and in 1982 he moved to Paris.

Even in Morales's most abstract paintings there are allusions to the landscape—forest, sea, sky, and beach. Some of his paintings incorporate animate and inanimate forms, frequently architectural. His work became more figurative, focusing on the depiction of the female figure, for example *Woman About to Return* (1972). Since then he has painted jungle scenes of overlapping trees (*Tropical Forest II,* 1984) and female figures, often with segmented limbs. He painted *Farewell to Sandino* (1985), an iconic image of the Nicaraguan revolutionary surrounded by other militants.

Morales's carefully crafted technique, consisting of glazes and polished brushstrokes, endows his images with a patina of archaic fragility, often reinforced by the inclusion of painted architectural fragments, reminiscent of Central American pre-Conquest architecture. Morales's work is particularly distinguished by his refined control of tonal variation.

— MARTA GARSD

MORALES, BELTRÁN

Beltrán Morales (*b.* 1945; *d.* 1986), Nicaraguan poet. Born in Jinotega, Nicaragua, Morales formed part of the so-called Betrayed Generation of the 1960s. His first book of poetry, *Algún sol* (Guatemala, 1969), consists largely of humorous and cynical love poems. His second collection, *Agua regia* (Costa Rica, 1972), is increasingly cynical, political, and experimental. *Juco final/ Andante* (Nicaragua, 1976) collects his later poetry (1966–1975), which is often short, cryptic, and contemplative

of the artistic process itself. Morales studied education and Spanish at the Universidad Nacional Autonoma de Nicaragua and was sent to Madrid (1964–1965) by the Instituto de Cultura. His prose and critical articles were collected in 1975 in *Sin páginas amarillas* and republished posthumously (1989) along with previously unpublished essays on poetry and poets. His reputation in Nicaragua is such that shortly after his sudden death in 1986 his complete works were collected and republished as *Poesía completa* (1989).

— ANN GONZÁLEZ

MORALES, EUSEBIO A.

Eusebio A. Morales (*b.* 1865; *d.* 1919), Panamanian lawyer and politician and one of the leading figures in the Liberal Party. He served in many government posts, including minister to the United States and secretary of the treasury. He wrote many essays on contemporary politics, which were later published in the book *Ensayos, documentos y discursos* (1977). Morales had presidential aspirations, but he had to abandon them after his supporters failed to change an article in the constitution that required presidents to be Panamanians by birth (he was born in Colombia).

— JUAN MANUEL PÉREZ

MORALES, FRANCISCO TOMÁS

Francisco Tomás Morales (*b.* 20 December 1781; *d.* 5 October 1845), officer in the Spanish army during the War for Independence. The proprietor of a tavern in the town of Piritu, Venezuela, Morales joined the royalist ranks under the command of José Tomás BOVES in 1813. On Boves's death he proclaimed himself commander of the royalist forces, joined the troops of Pablo MORILLO, and accompanied him in operations into New Granada. Morales later participated as troop commander in various campaigns against the republican forces. He was commander of the Spanish offensive against Venezuela after the republican victory at Carabobo in 1821. Meeting with no success, he returned to Spain after being defeated in the naval battle of Maracaibo in 1823. On his return to Spain, he was appointed commander in chief of the Canary Islands and subsequently president of the royal *audiencia* in 1827.

— INÉS QUINTERO

MORALES, MARIO ROBERTO

Mario Roberto Morales (*b.* 5 September 1947), Guatemalan novelist. Morales came of age during the first cycle of the armed revolutionary struggle in Guatemala in the 1960s and 1970s. His participation in the guerrilla movement resulted in his arrest in Mexico in 1982 and subsequent deportation to Costa Rica, where he lived until 1991. Improved political conditions have allowed him to reestablish residency in Guatemala. His

---

Morales' participation in the guerrilla movement resulted in his arrest in Mexico in 1982 and subsequent deportation to Costa Rica.

---

prize-winning novels combine autobiographical experiences with the linguistic, temporal, and structural experimentation found in Latin American "Boom" fiction. He is ranked by Seymour Menton as one of the leading representatives of the Guatemalan "new" novel. His experimental first novel, *Obraje* (1971), won the Floral Games Competition for Novel in Quetzaltenango; *Los demonios salvajes* (1978; 2d ed., 1993), which recounts his growing political awareness, won Premio Unico Centroamericano de Novela: "15 de septiembre"; *El esplendor de la pirámide* (1985), about a love affair between a Mexican girl and a Guatemalan guerrilla, won the Latin American EDUCA prize for the novel; and *El ángel de la retaguardia* (unpublished), about a Guatemalan expatriate in Italy, was a finalist for the Nueva Nicaragua Prize for Novel. His most recent works, *Señores bajo los árboles,* a novelized testimony of Guatemalan Indian voices, and *La ideología y la lírica de la lucha armada,* a critical study of Guatemalan literature during the two decades of the armed struggle, were published in 1994. Several of his short stories and his *Epigramas para interrogar a Patricia* (1982) have been translated into English.

– ANN GONZÁLEZ

MORALES, MELESIO

Melesio Morales (*b.* 4 December 1838; *d.* 12 May 1908), Mexican composer. Morales was born in Mexico City and began his studies with Felipe Larios, Agustín Caballero, Antonio Valle, and Cenobio PANIAGUA. He began composing operas to Italian libretti while in his teens; his first, *Romeo e Giulietta,* was premiered in 1863 by an Italian company. His second opera, *Ildegonda* (1865), was produced under the sponsorship of Emperor Maximilian. Morales spent three very successful years in Italy composing and attending performances of his operas. Upon his return, he established his own opera department "alla Napolitana" at the National Conservatory in Mexico City, training many of the composers of the next generation. Morales was the first

to conduct Beethoven's symphonies in Mexico. He himself wrote a symphonic fantasy entitled *La locomotora,* celebrating the inauguration of the Puebla railroad service (November 1869). Most of his works were published in Italy. He died in Mexico City.

– SUSANA SALGADO

MORALES BERMÚDEZ, REMIGIO

Remigio Morales Bermúdez (*b.* 1836; *d.* 1894), president of Peru (1890–1894). His death before the end of his term in office led to a civil war between caudillos Andrés A. CÁCERES and Nicolás de PIÉROLA. Morales Bermúdez was born in Tarapacá and worked in his father's nitrate business in what was Peruvian territory before the War of the Pacific (1879–1883). Trained for a career in the military beginning in 1854, Morales Bermúdez participated in several struggles for power among military chieftains. During the War of the Pacific he fought at the side of Cáceres in the resistance campaign in the Peruvian highlands. Supporting Cáceres's bid for power against Miguel IGLESIAS, Morales Bermúdez became vice president and, at the end of Cáceres's term in 1890, president until his sudden death in Lima. His son, Lieutenant Colonel Remigio Morales Bermúdez, army commander in Trujillo, was allegedly killed by Aprista militants in 1939.

– ALFONSO W. QUIROZ

MORALES BERMÚDEZ CERRUTI, FRANCISCO

Francisco Morales Bermúdez Cerruti (*b.* 4 October 1921), military president of Peru (1975–1980) who took power from ailing nationalist General Juan VELASCO ALVARADO and led the military government, in power since 1968, through a gradual transition—the so-called second phase—to a revived democracy, inaugurated in 1980. Son of Remigio Morales Bermúdez, commander of Trujillo who was killed in 1939, Francisco graduated with the highest honors from the Chorrillos Military Academy and specialized as an engineer. Promoted to general in 1968, he was minister of finance during the first term of Fernando BELAÚNDE (1963–1968). After the 1968 coup against Belaúnde, Morales Bermúdez was again minister of finance in charge of refinancing Peru's foreign debt and, in 1975, prime minister. In 1975, he led the coup that ousted Velasco Alvarado. In 1978, after intense labor and social protests, Morales Bermúdez devised a schedule for the return of democracy through elections to a constituent assembly (1978–1979) and general elections in 1980. He was an unsuccessful candidate for president in 1985.

– ALFONSO W. QUIROZ

MORALES CARRIÓN, ARTURO

Arturo Morales Carrión (*b.* 16 November 1913; *d.* 24 June 1989), Puerto Rican historian, teacher, diplomat. Morales Carrión was born in Cuba and came to Puerto Rico as a child. Trained in political science and in the history of Latin America at the universities of Puerto Rico, Texas (Austin), and Columbia, he excelled in various fields. He taught both in Puerto Rico and the United States and also served both governments. In the 1950s, Morales Carrión was Puerto Rico's undersecretary of state, and in 1961 President John F. Kennedy named him deputy assistant secretary for Inter-American Affairs. He wrote various books on Puerto Rico, most of which are considered classics and are still in use in Puerto Rico and the United States. He died in San Juan, Puerto Rico.

– OLGA JIMÉNEZ DE WAGENHEIM

MORALES LEMUS, JOSÉ

José Morales Lemus (*b.* 2 May 1808; *d.* 13 June 1870), Cuban independence figure. A wealthy lawyer and businessman born in Gibara, Morales Lemus professed moderate liberal ideas. He freed his own slaves but was only a qualified abolitionist. He disliked Spanish domination, and for a time favored Cuba's annexation to the United States. However, after the U.S. Civil War made this impossible, he joined the reformists, a group of prominent creoles who advocated constitutional reforms within the framework of Spanish rule. In 1866 he led the group of reformists who went to Madrid to negotiate with the Spanish government. After this effort failed, he cast his lot with the planters who initiated the Ten Years' War (1868–1878). As a result he had to seek refuge in New York, where he became president of the Cuban junta in exile. Later he served as minister of the Cuban Republic in Arms to the U.S. government. Because his properties were confiscated when he fled Cuba, he died penniless in New York City.

– JOSÉ M. HERNÁNDEZ

MORAZÁN, FRANCISCO

Francisco Morazán (*b.* 3 October 1792; *d.* 15 September 1842), president of the Federation of Central America (1830–1834, 1835–1839). The armed conflict between Central American Liberals and Conservatives after 1826 brought Morazán, a native of Tegucigalpa, Honduras, from provincial obscurity to leadership of the Liberal cause. In a military campaign (November 1827–April 1829) he drove the Conservative federal armies from Honduras and El Salvador, invaded Guatemala, and overthrew the "intrusive" governments there.

Temporarily assuming power as chief executive of both state and federation, he restored to office the "legitimate" Liberal state and federal authorities displaced in 1826, imprisoned the deposed officials, and exiled the principal prosecutors of the war. He was elected president (16 September 1830), and continued for a second term when in 1834 death removed José Cecilio del VALLE, chosen to succeed him. Until the federation collapsed, Morazán commanded the federal forces and either occupied the presidency or exercised the power that sustained it.

Morazán's victory temporarily established Liberal ascendancy, but it provided neither a working consensus nor an atmosphere of mutual toleration that enabled him to govern. As Liberal leader he championed reforms intended to restructure traditional Central American institutions to emulate the most advanced contemporary models, and sought to maintain Liberal regimes that would promote such reforms in each state. Mariano GÁLVEZ, for example, inaugurated in Guatemala a notably comprehensive restructuring of society for which Morazán shared responsibility. Tensions generated by a growing body of Liberal innovations that forced accommodation to unfamiliar institutions and draconian measures, such as the exile of leading Conservatives, including the archbishop of Guatemala and friars of three regular orders, drove offended and scandalized citizens into the domestic opposition and created a body of aggrieved and resentful exiles plotting invasion from abroad.

The outbreak of cholera in 1837 was a fatal blow to the Central American Federation, already threatened by dissolution.

Grave operational defects in the political structure of the Central American Federation restricted Morazán's options. The federal constitution was not universally accepted as appropriate to Central America, and modification or abandonment of the system was widely sought but never accomplished. Chronic financial exigency hampered both federal and state governments, and states not infrequently withheld federal revenues collected within their jurisdictions. Some states dared to nullify federal laws and, in the absence of legal penalties for counterfeiting, to mint spurious coins. Frictions generated by regional jealousies and rivalries between and among states subverted unity and severely strained the federal structure. Particularly destructive was a provincial distrust of Guatemala. The traditional seat of power, its population (which entitled it to overwhelming representation in the federal Congress), wealth, and economic suzerainty enabled it to dominate the federation. Guatemala successfully resisted an attempt to diminish its influence by creating a federal district around Guatemala City, and Morazán's attempt (1834) to achieve a more equitable balance among states by transfer of the capital to San Salvador produced little improvement. States frequently threatened revolt and occasionally seceded.

The outbreak of cholera in 1837 was a fatal blow to the federation, already threatened by dissolution. Terrorized by the advance of the disease and distrustful of the control measures, the peasants of eastern Guatemala erupted in a popular revolt from which José Rafael CARRERA emerged the natural leader. Divided counsels among Liberals paralyzed action, and when Morazán assented to a dissident faction's proposal to negotiate with Carrera rather than respond to an urgent appeal from Gálvez for military intervention, a Carrera force entered Guatemala City (30 January 1838). Gálvez resigned (1 February 1838), the federation lost its major source of support, and the unpredictable Carrera kept the state and the union in turmoil until Morazán entered the war (November 1838). To buy time, Carrera accepted peace, only to resume the offensive to displace the Liberal government Morazán had installed.

Recognizing that the federation was approaching the final stages of disintegration, the federal Congress formally released the states (30 May 1838) to adopt regimes of their choosing, and held the final session (30 July 1838) of the last federal Congress. When Morazán's second term expired (1 February 1839), no competent authority existed to call an election to choose a successor, so he transferred power to his brother-in-law, Vice President Diego Vijil (10 February 1839).

Elected head of state of El Salvador (June 1839), Morazán attempted with such troops as he could muster to force together the fragments of the broken union. He first had to defeat the allied armies of Nicaragua and Honduras (September 1839), sent to deprive him of his base of power. Then he invaded Guatemala to confront Carrera, and occupied the plaza of Guatemala City (18 March 1840), only to be routed by Carrera the following day. He fled into exile but, refitted in Peru, he returned to Central America (1842) and usurped the government of Costa Rica. He soon fell victim to a popular uprising, and in San José a firing squad ended his career.

As president, Morazán hoped to achieve the domestic stability and order necessary for sustained progress. Circumstances, however, determined that his energies went principally to sustain Liberal regimes, put down civil wars, remove opposition leaders who seized state governments, and cajole or coerce state authorities to honor their federal obligations. These activities provided the basis for his admirers to construct a portrait of an unswervingly loyal champion of the federation, unselfishly dedicating his life and sterling talents to its development and protection, and devoting his broad-visioned statesmanship and his unmatched prowess as a military leader to its defense.

As Morazán's tenure lengthened, criticism of the federal regime focused increasingly on the person of the leader rather than on institutional deficiencies or Liberal ideology. Critics charged that Morazán maintained a nepotistic monopoly of positions of power, that his zeal in sustaining the federation reflected determination to preserve his monopoly of privilege rather than loyalty or devotion to the union, that he manipulated office to his personal profit in such instances as sale of ecclesiastical properties. They charged that for profit Morazán sold out his country to the British by fueling the increased British presence and renewed assertion of suzerainty on the Mosquito Coast through his sales to Belize cutters of mahogany trees within the extensive tract the government of Honduras (1835) granted him there.

These disparate characterizations of Morazán's career and character rest largely on contemporary intuitive interpretations of his public life. Natural disasters and, if partisan allegations are credited, partisan purges of archives have so truncated the sources that the prospect that objective scholarship will be able significantly to resolve the discrepancy or flesh out the portrait is not promising.

— WILLIAM J. GRIFFITH

MOREAU DE JUSTO, ALICIA

Alicia Moreau de Justo (*b.* 11 October 1886; *d.* 1986), Argentine physician, socialist, and feminist. She was born in London to French parents, who were exiled in England for their activities in the Paris Commune. The family emigrated to Buenos Aires in 1890, where her father worked for progressive causes and the Socialist Party, founded by Juan B. JUSTO (1896). At fifteen Alicia Moreau helped to establish the Socialist Women's Center with Fenia Cherkov, believing that the fight for women's education should take precedence over civil or political equality. She taught child care and hygiene at the Socialist Women's Center in Buenos Aires and fought against prostitution. She wrote for the journal *Humanidad Nueva* and the socialist daily *La Vanguardia,* which she directed from 1956 to 1962. Moreau studied medicine, taught anatomy, graduated from the University of Buenos Aires in 1914, and practiced in working-class clinics. A lifelong socialist, Moreau put the fight for social-justice issues above individualistic goals. After the death of Juan B. Justo's first wife (Mariana Cherkov), Moreau married him in 1922, despite the objections of Justo's sister Sara, a dentist and prominent feminist. Moreau wrote influential books, including *La emancipación civil de la mujer* (1919), *El feminismo en la evolución social* (1911), *El socialismo según la definición de Juan B. Justo* (1946), and *¿Qué es el socialismo en la Argentina?* (1983). The influence of the Socialist Party declined in the 1930s after the defeat of the de la Torre–Repetto presidential ticket, splits in the party, and political repression. Although they belonged to different political camps, Moreau and the writer Victoria OCAMPO led the women's movement in the 1930s and fought proposed changes in the Civil Code. Moreau opposed Peronism and said in a 1977 interview that she never understood completely the importance of nationalism to Argentines. In 1984 she was named Woman of the Year and Physician of the Century, and her one-hundredth birthday was celebrated throughout the nation.

— GEORGETTE MAGASSY DORN

MOREIRA DA COSTA RIBEIRO, DELFIM

Delfim Moreira da Costa Ribeiro (*b.* 7 November 1868; *d.* 1 July 1920), president of Brazil (November 1918–July 1919). Moreira was a native of Minas Gerais, one of the most influential states of Brazil's First Republic (1889–1930). In the years following graduation from the São Paulo School of Law, the premier training ground for the Republican elite, Moreira garnered the support of the Partido Republicano Mineiro in several successful campaigns for state office. From 1914 to 1918 Moreira served as *presidente* (governor) of Minas Gerais, where he gained a national reputation as a skillful leader of the state's powerful political and economic interests.

In 1918 Moreira was elected vice president of Brazil on a ticket with *Paulista* presidential candidate Rodrigues Alves. However, Moreira was sworn in as interim president when Alves was too ill to assume the presidency on the day of inauguration. Alves died on 18 January 1919, and Moreira's interim presidency was extended pending the appointment of a new president. During his eight-month presidency, Moreira himself fell ill and the majority of daily presidential duties were carried out by the minister of the interior, Afrânio de MELO FRANCO. In July 1919 the federal legislature voted Epitácio PESSOA president and Moreira resumed his position as vice president, which he held until his death a year later.

— DARYLE WILLIAMS

Nancy Morejón. (Center for Cuban Studies, New York)

MOREJÓN, NANCY

Nancy Morejón (*b.* 7 August 1944), Cuban poet. Born in Havana to Angélica Hernández and Felipe Morejón, she received a degree in French from the University of Havana. A translator, journalist, editor, and director of the Centro de Estudios del Caribe at Casa de las Américas, Morejón has published four critical studies and eleven collections of poetry. Her lyrical verse, shaped by an Afro-Cuban sensibility and a feminist consciousness, evokes the intimacy of family, the ephemerality of love, and the significance of Cuban history. Poems like "Black Woman" and "I Love My Master" have been widely anthologized and translated.

— MIRIAM DECOSTA-WILLIS

MORELOS Y PAVÓN, JOSÉ MARÍA

José María Morelos y Pavón (*b.* 30 September 1765; *d.* 22 December 1815), foremost Mexican insurgent leader in the struggle for independence. Born in Valladolid, he worked as a scribe and accountant from 1779 to 1790, when he began ecclesiastical studies at the College of San Nicolás, where he met Miguel HIDALGO Y COSTILLA (1753–1811). In 1795 he entered the Tridentine Seminary and presented his bachelor of arts exam at the University in Mexico City. In 1796, he went to

Uruapan as an auxiliary priest. He was ordained presbyter in December 1799 and served as parish priest of Churumuco and La Huacana and later of Carácuaro and Nocupétaro. Upon learning of the Hidalgo revolt, he joined the insurgent leader in Charo and Indaparapeo in October 1810. When Hidalgo commissioned him to raise troops in the south, Morelos solicited leave from the See of Valladolid, returned to Carácuaro, and began his first campaign. With twenty-five men, he moved through Nocupétaro, Huetamo, Coahuayutla, Zacatula, and Petatlán, where he obtained men and weapons. In Tecpan, he was joined by Galeanas, including Hermenegildo GALEANA (1762–1814), who later became his lieutenant. After obtaining his first cannon there, he then marched toward Acapulco. En route, in Coyuca, he was joined by Juan ÁLVAREZ (1790–1867).

In addition to organizing troops, Morelos addressed political and social questions. On 17 November 1810, he issued an order abolishing slavery, the caste system, and *cajas de comunidad* (community treasury). He also engaged the royalists in battle in various places, among them El Veladero and La Sabana. Unable to capture Acapulco in February 1811, Morelos laid siege to the port. He returned to Tecpan, where he organized the government of that province. He then headed toward Chilpancingo and while still en route sent two commissioners to the United States to seek aid. Joined by the Bravos (Leonardo, Víctor, Máximo, Miguel, and Nicolás) at the Hacienda of Chichihualco, Morelos entered Chilpancingo on 24 May and two days later took Tixtla, where Vicente GUERRERO (1783–1831) joined him. There he ordered the creation of a national copper currency and wrote Ignacio RAYÓN (1773–1832) about forming a governing junta. In August 1811, Morelos sent José Sixto Verduzco as his representative to a meeting convened by Rayón to establish such a junta. At that time he took Chilapa, leaving the south, with the exception of Acapulco, in insurgent hands.

In mid-November, he marched toward Tlapa, thereby initiating his second campaign. He took Chiautla de la Sal and Izúcar, where he was joined by Mariano MATAMOROS (1770–1814). He proceeded to Cuautla and then to Taxco and Tenancingo. In February 1812, he returned to Cuautla, where he was besieged by Félix María CALLEJA (*c.* 1755–1828). He successfully defended the town, despite the royalist assault, lack of supplies, and lack of assistance from other insurgents. Forced to break the siege on 2 May, he left for Chiautla, from where he initiated his third campaign on 1 June.

Later that month, La Suprema Junta appointed Morelos captain-general and the fourth member of the body. After assisting Valerio Trujano (1760–1812) in

Huajuapan de León, he moved to Tehuacán, where he reorganized his troops. He named Matamoros second in command and appointed Galeana marshall. He also worked on the political organization of the insurgent movement. In October he marched to Ozumba, but was repulsed by the royalists in Ojo de Agua. On 29 October he took Orizaba. Upon his return to Tehuacán he was once again defeated and lost his artillery. But on 25 November he captured Antequera de Oaxaca, where he organized the government of that province, established a mint, and published the paper *El Correo Americano del Sur*. His fourth campaign began in February 1813 when he marched to Acapulco, which he captured on April 12, and then laid siege to the fortress of San Diego, which capitulated on August 20.

Concerned about the disagreements among the members of the junta, Morelos sought to mediate among them. After realizing that the governing body of the insurgency needed to be completely restructured, he instructed the provinces under insurgent control to designate representatives to the Supremo Congreso Nacional Americano. Meeting in Chilpancingo on 14 September 1813, the body structured itself following the guidelines Morelos set forth in his *Reglamento* and his *Sentimientos de la nación*.

After the Congress elected him *generalísimo* in charge of executive power, he initiated his fifth campaign. On 23 December Ciriaco de Llano and Agustín de ITURBIDE (1783–1824) defeated him in Valladolid. On 5 January 1814, he suffered defeat once again in Puruarán, where Matamoros was captured. In February, Congress removed him as *generalísimo* in Tlacotepec, where he was defeated once more and where he also lost his equipment and papers. Congress then sent him to Acapulco to save the artillery at San Diego, and the following March, removed him from the executive. After burning Acapulco, Morelos marched to Tecpan, Petatlán, and Zacatula. He then moved on to Atijo and to Ario, joining the Congress at Tiripitío. From there they moved to Apatzingán, where the Congress proclaimed the Constitution on 22 October 1814 and named an executive consisting of Morelos, José María de Liceaga (1785–1870) and José María COS Y PÉREZ (*d.* 1819). During 1815 Morelos remained with the Congress while it wandered, pursued by the royalists. In September Congress decided to move to Tehuacán and charged Morelos with its defense. On 5 November Manuel Concha captured him in Temalaca. He was then taken to Atenango, Cuernavaca, and Mexico City, where he was imprisoned first in the Inquisition and then in the Ciudadela. He was tried, found guilty, and condemned to death after first being defrocked from the priesthood. He was shot in San Cristóbal Ecatepec.

José María Morelos y Pavón. (Archivo General de la Nación, México)

His imprisonment and death were the worst blows the insurgent movement received and marked the end of the organized insurgency. In 1823, Morelos was declared *Benemérito de la Patria*. His native city was named Morelia in 1828; the state that bears his name was formed in 1869.

— VIRGINIA GUEDEA

MORENO, FULGENCIO

Fulgencio Moreno (*b.* 9 November 1872; *d.* 1935), Paraguayan journalist, diplomat, and historian. Moreno was descended on his maternal side from several of the founders of the Paraguayan republic, and much of his most important historical work centered on the early period of Paraguay's independence. Born in Asunción, he early decided on a career in journalism and served on the staffs of four major newspapers between 1893 and 1901. Journalism, however, turned out to be a stepping-stone to important political and diplomatic posts. In 1901 he became finance minister, and in 1903, senator. Four years later, the government appointed him to a technical commission to study the rights of Paraguay in the Chaco boundary dispute with Bolivia. Afterward, Moreno turned his efforts to diplomacy more narrowly defined: he served as minister first to Chile and Peru (1913), then to Bolivia (1918), and then back to Chile (1919).

These experiences gave Moreno ample material for his historical pursuits. He was prolific in his production of articles, pamphlets, and books. Among the latter were several works that are still read and admired in Paraguay today. These include *Diplomacia paraguaya-boliviana* (1904), *Estudio sobre la independencia del Paraguay* (1912), *Paraguay-Bolivia,* 3 vols. (1917–1920), and *La ciudad de la Asunción* (1926). Unlike many Paraguayan historians of his era, Moreno concentrated less on military heroes than on literary figures and movements— and thus his work is noteworthy for its appealing cultural emphases.

— THOMAS L. WHIGHAM

MORENO, MARIANO

Mariano Moreno (*b.* 23 September 1778; *d.* 4 March 1811), one of the leading figures of Argentina's independence movement. He studied theology and law in Chuquisaca (now Sucre), Upper Peru, and wrote his dissertation on Indian service, in which he favored their freedom. He was sickly, but what he lacked in physical strength he made up for in a powerful intellect. He became the Jacobin of the May 1810 revolution in Argentina. In 1809 he wrote the *Representación de los hacendados y labradores,* in which he criticized colonial policy and defended free trade. The book represented creole aspirations, and in a way it was written as a criticism of the new viceroy, Baltasar Hidalgo de CISNEROS, who had replaced Santiago de LINIERS and had repealed many of the latter's liberal policies.

Moreno was appointed secretary to the First Junta, headed by Cornelio de SAAVEDRA. He favored a tough policy toward Spaniards and toward anyone engaged in counterrevolutionary activities. In July 1810, Liniers and his followers rose in revolt against the revolutionary government. The revolt was crushed by Buenos Aires, and as a result of Moreno's insistence, the leaders, including Liniers, were executed. This action led to much criticism against Moreno because Liniers was still considered a hero by many for his contributions to the defense of Buenos Aires against the invading British armies in 1806–1807. Moreno was a firm believer in democratic government, but his radicalism and uncompromising attitude earned him many enemies, even in the junta itself. The showdown occurred when Saavedra imposed reactionary delegates from the provinces on the junta in face of Moreno's opposition. This may very well have been the first confrontation between *unitarios* and *federales.* Faced with a growing Federalist opposition, Moreno resigned from the junta at the end of 1810. His resignation almost caused a rebellion, and to avoid bloodshed, he accepted a diplomatic mission to England and died at sea en route. While in office he helped found the national library and a census bureau and published the *Gaceta de Buenos Aires*.

— JUAN MANUEL PÉREZ

MORGA SÁNCHEZ GARAY Y LÓPEZ, ANTONIO DE

Antonio de Morga Sánchez Garay y López (*b.* 29 November 1559; *d.* 21 July 1636), *oidor* (civil justice) of the Audiencia of the Philippines (1593–1603), *alcalde del crimen* (criminal judge) of the Audiencia of Mexico City (1603–1615), and president of the Audiencia of Quito (1615–1636). Born in Seville to a wealthy merchant family, this energetic jurist received his doctorate at the University of Salamanca in 1580. After holding several minor judicial posts in Spain, Morga attained first the governorship of the Philippines and later a judgeship in the Audiencia of Manila. He served with some distinction in the Philippines and in 1603 received a coveted promotion to the position of *alcalde del crimen* in the viceregal capital of Mexico City. He escaped blame in the numerous scandals surrounding that court, and in 1615 the crown named him president of the Audiencia of Quito.

During his presidency, Morga battled with the viceroys in Lima to secure more autonomy for the Audiencia in legal and political affairs. He sponsored an unsuccessful effort to build a road from Quito to the coast, through the frontier province of Atacames, to facilitate the export of highland foodstuffs and textiles. He also supported efforts to reorganize the labor and management systems of the highland *obrajes* (textile mills) and to reform Spanish–Native American relations.

Despite Morga's accomplishments, disturbing rumors of dissension on the court and of the president's illegal activities and personal immorality prompted a *visita general* (general investigation) in 1624. The visitor-general, Juan de Mañozca, and his successor, Juan Galdós de Valencia, charged Morga with seventy-three infractions, including illicitly introducing Chinese silks in 1615, carrying on disreputable gambling operations, engaging in unauthorized business ventures, living a scandalous personal life, and failing to observe the normal procedures and regulations governing the audiencia. In 1636 the Council of the Indies found Morga guilty on fifty-six of the charges, levied fines of 31,300 ducats, and suspended him from office for six years. The disgraced president was spared this final indignity, for he had died earlier in the year.

— KENNETH J. ANDRIEN

MORGAN, HENRY

Henry Morgan (*b.* ca. 1635; *d.* 25 August 1688), the most famous buccaneer of the West Indies from the mid- to late seventeenth century. A bold and brilliant tactician, Henry Morgan, a Welshman, assumed the leadership of the Port Royal, Jamaica, buccaneers after 1665. He first came to the New World, to Barbados, as an indentured servant (ca. 1655–1660). Later, Morgan escaped and joined the buccaneers, becoming a prominent leader by his late twenties. A heavy drinker, Morgan acquired wealth and land, was knighted, and after his buccaneering activities ended became lieutenant governor of Jamaica and helped suppress buccaneering.

Morgan's fame reached its height in the late 1660s and early 1670s. In 1668 the governor of Jamaica, Sir Thomas Modyford, commissioned him to carry out a reconnaissance mission in Cuba and then to attack Porto Bello with four hundred buccaneers. After arriving in Cuba, Morgan moved on toward Porto Bello, on the Isthmus of Panama. Although the port was well fortified, with 300 men defending it, Morgan successfully surprised the Spanish by entering at night from a swampy, forested area behind it. In killing the 300 defenders he solidified his reputation for brutality. His followers pillaged and debauched the town.

Instead of moving on to attack Cartagena, Colombia, the center of Spanish naval power, Morgan chose to assault Maracaibo, Venezuela, instead. The booty there was minimal, as the town had been pillaged only a year earlier. Upon leaving, however, he encountered three Spanish ships carrying silver, which he and his men plundered and destroyed or beached.

Morgan mounted his third, final, and biggest expedition, which was also commissioned by Governor Modyford, in 1670. With 1,500 men, one third of whom were Frenchmen from Tortuga, Morgan sacked Santa Marta and Río Hacha, Colombia, and Porto Bello. In December 1670 he marched across the isthmus to attack Panama, where he tortured and murdered most of the inhabitants and destroyed the city.

Following the Treaty of Madrid (1670) peace agreement between England and Spain, the two Jamaican governors, Lord John Vaughan and the Earl of Carlisle, employed Morgan in 1674 as their lieutenant governor, giving him the responsibility of suppressing buccaneers. The lack of military support meant that it was not until 1685, with the arrival of a new naval squadron, that Morgan was able to achieve much success in his effort to combat buccaneering. Morgan died three years later. Despite his later efforts against the buccaneers, in his earlier career, Morgan had carried out a reign of terror and brutality hitherto unsurpassed in the Caribbean.

— BLAKE D. PATTRIDGE

MORILLO, PABLO

Pablo Morillo (*b.* 5 May 1778; *d.* 27 July 1837), Spanish general. General Pablo Morillo was sent to northern South America by Ferdinand VII in 1815 with the title of Pacificador de Tierra Firme. His orders included the charge that he replace General Juan Manuel de Cajigal as captain-general of Venezuela. Morillo's career and meteoric rise to the rank of general paralleled that of many of the generals serving in Ferdinand's army. From the lower class, young Morillo became an officer in 1808 at the age of thirty due to leadership and loyalty displayed against the French at the Battle of Bailén. He was made a general just three years later.

The 1815 expedition to Venezuela under his command included ten thousand men and a fleet of sixty ships. The end of the Napoleonic Wars allowed the metropolitan authorities to confront the Venezuelan insurrection with considerably more manpower. The first military confrontations between Morillo's forces and those of the Venezuelan patriots in April 1815 changed

Portrait of Pablo Morillo. Oil on canvas by Pedro José Figueroa, 1818. (Museo Nacional de Colombia)

the nature of the war. No longer a civil war between factions of Venezuelans, the hostilities became more directed toward complete separation from Spain. Morillo allied himself with the wealthy planter class that had called for the break with Spain in 1811. Unfortunately for Morillo, too much had changed between 1811 and 1815. The forces unleashed in 1811, especially the *castas,* were too powerful to be ignored, and Morillo's vision of a royalist Venezuela—perhaps a realistic alternative in 1811—was no longer possible. In effect, the arrival of this expeditionary force ended royalist government in Venezuela. The lack of efficient bureaucracy forced Morillo to confiscate property to supply his army of pacification. Relying on terror and the military prowess of his experienced corps, Morillo conquered Venezuela and most of New Granada. He is perhaps best remembered today in Venezuela as a tyrant who ordered the execution of such men as Dr. Camilo TORRES and the scientist Francisco de CALDAS.

It soon became clear that the final chapter in the war between Spain and Venezuela would be settled by force of arms. The patriot victory at the battle of Boyacá in August 1819 caused Morillo to see the end was at hand. After the liberal rebellion in Spain in 1820, he was ordered to negotiate with the patriots on the basis of the Constitution of 1812. In November 1820 representatives of Símon BOLÍVAR and Morillo signed a six-month armistice. Morillo then returned to Spain, where he was granted the titles of conde de Cartagena and marqués de la Puerta and during the next decade held a number of government offices.

— GARY MILLER

MORÍNIGO, HIGÍNIO

Higínio Morínigo (*b.* 1897; *d.* 1983), Paraguayan president (1940–1948) and military leader. Born into a middle-class family in the interior town of Paraguarí, Morínigo decided early on a military career. In 1906 his family moved to Asunción, where he later entered the national military academy.

As a young junior officer in the early 1920s, Morínigo received orders to intervene in a civil conflict then raging between rival groups within the ruling Liberal Party. Though he obeyed these orders, he did so with much resentment—and this experience embittered him toward civilian politicians and their penchant for embroiling the army in their various power struggles. Perhaps because he failed to cater to such politicians, Morínigo soon found himself posted to a series of obscure frontier forts, most of them in the disputed Gran Chaco region.

The Chaco War fought with Bolivia over this same territory (1932–1935) gave Morínigo the chance for rapid promotion. A brief assignment as a regional field commander earned him the rank of major, and in 1936, the Rafael FRANCO government promoted him to colonel and gave him command of the important garrison of Concepción. By this time, Morínigo had developed considerable popularity among the growing *revolucionario* faction of the officer corps, a base that he used to advance to the post of army chief of staff in 1938 and then to interior minister in 1939 under Félix Paiva. Finally, in May 1940, radicals in the army pressured José Félix ESTIGARRIBIA to accept Morínigo as war minister. It was from this position that he was forced upon the Liberals as the new president when Estigarribia died in an airplane crash four months later.

As president, Morínigo erected a repressive police state with clear pro-Axis overtones. Despite Paraguay's official neutrality, the government permitted Nazi agents to work more or less openly in the country. At the same time, the United States attempted to woo Morínigo with the promise of aid for highway construction and other projects. In the end, Paraguay declared war on Germany, but only in February 1945.

By that point, Morínigo had chosen to compromise in domestic politics and had begun to ease out the far-right members of his wartime cabinet. He compromised still further in 1946, when he called for a coalition government that included Colorados and Febreristas. This coalition lasted only a few months before radical elements among the Colorados (especially the Guion Rojo group) were battling the Febreristas, Liberals, and Communists in the streets of Asunción.

Unable to control events any longer, Morínigo watched Paraguay slip into the bloody civil war of 1947. Aided by Colorado militias and arms sent from Perón's Argentina, he managed to defeat the rebels, but in so doing became little more than a figurehead for the Colorados. Their own infighting, in turn, made Morínigo's continued presence in the country inconvenient. In 1948, he agreed to retire from politics and went to live in permanent exile in Buenos Aires.

— THOMAS L. WHIGHAM

MORONES, LUIS

Luis Morones (*b.* 11 October 1890; *d.* 6 April 1964), Mexican labor leader of the 1920s. Morones experienced a meteoric rise from electrical worker to the nation's most powerful labor leader within a period of fifteen years. Born in the Federal District, he joined the anarchist-led House of the World Worker (Casa del Obrero Mundial), but ambition soon drove him in another

direction. Morones founded a small group within this splintering organization which then formed a separate union, the Regional Confederation of the Mexican Worker (Confederación Regional Obrera Mexicana) in Saltillo, Coahuila, in May 1918.

Morones's accomplishments were marred by his flagrant displays of personal wealth and persistent accusations of corrupt and violent methods.

Using a pragmatic approach in politics through alliances with key figures, Morones supported Álvaro Obregón in the maneuvering which led to the overthrow of President Venustiano CARRANZA (1917–1920). Morones organized strikes against the Carranza administration and sent armed workers into combat. During the Obregón presidency (1920–1924) Morones headed Mexico's vital government-operated munitions industry. During the administration of Plutarco Elías CALLES (1924–1928), Morones reached the pinnacle of his career. He continued as head of the Confederation, by then the nation's largest labor organization, at the same time that he was minister of industry, commerce, and labor. He made decisions in his government post that favored his union and weakened its rivals.

Morones's accomplishments were marred by his flagrant displays of personal wealth and persistent accusations of corrupt and violent methods. Critics also charged that he undermined the autonomy of the labor movement when he tied it to the national government.

Morones fell from power quickly. His opposition to Obregón's successful campaign for the presidency in 1928 factionalized his organized support. Political enemies wrongly accused him of complicity in Obregón's subsequent assassination. Morones's career as a labor leader was effectively ended. He became conservative in later years but had limited influence in labor and political affairs.

— JOHN A. BRITTON

MOSCOTE, JOSÉ DOLORES

José Dolores Moscote (*b.* 1879; *d.* 1958), Panamanian legal scholar. Moscote gained notoriety in the 1920s for his influential writings on the nature of the state. He opposed the classical tenets of nineteenth-century liberalism and favored a state more active in the life of the country. He participated in the drafting of the highly regarded 1946 constitution. Moscote was rector of the National Institute and vice rector of the National University. His most important works are *Introducción al estudio de la constitución* (1929), *Orientaciones hacia la reforma constitucional* (1934), and *Estudios constitucionales* (1938).

– JUAN MANUEL PÉREZ

MOSHINSKY BORODIANKSKY, MARCOS

Marcos Moshinsky Borodianksky (*b*. 20 April 1921), Mexican nuclear physicist. A native of Kiev, Ukraine, his father emigrated to Mexico in 1928 and became a naturalized citizen five years later. Moshinsky received most of his education in Mexico City, graduating with a chemistry degree from the National University in 1944 before studying physics as an Allen Nun fellow at Princeton University (1946–1949). He became a professor at the National University and a research scientist at the Institute of Geophysics. Moshinsky directed the theoretical nuclear physics section at the National University and edited the Mexican physics review. He was awarded the National Prize in Sciences in 1968 and named a member of the National College in 1972. He often writes for the popular media, including *Excélsior*.

– RODERIC AI CAMP

MOSQUERA, MANUEL JOSÉ

Manuel José Mosquera (*b*. 11 April 1800; *d*. 10 December 1853), Colombian prelate and reformer. Born in Popayán into southern Colombia's most distinguished family, he studied at its seminary until 1819. He later received his bachelor's degree and his doctorate at Quito, and was ordained in 1823. He served successively as vicar general of the diocese of Popayán (1828), a canon of the Bogotá cathedral (1829), and rector of the University of Cauca (1829–1835). A domestic prelate from 1832, Mosquera was elected archbishop of Bogotá in 1834 and assumed office in September 1835. His erudition and prideful manner combined to alienate many of his subordinates, since he demanded strict canonical behavior of them.

Mosquera revitalized the seminary (1841–1850) and sponsored the Jesuits' return to Colombia (1844). The presidency of his brother Tomás (1845–1849) further politicized his image, already compromised in Liberal eyes. The regime of the Liberal José Hilario LÓPEZ (1849–1953) expelled the Jesuits (May 1850), secularized tithe collections (January 1851), and ended the seminary's autonomy (January 1852). It then demanded archepiscopal acceptance of secular election of the clergy. Mosquera refused. Thereupon the Senate voted his exile (May 1852). In poor health, he left for Rome (September 1852). After visiting New York and Paris, he died in Marseilles.

– J. LEÓN HELGUERA

MOSQUERA, TOMÁS CIPRIANO DE

Tomás Cipriano de Mosquera (*b*. 26 September 1798; *d*. 7 October 1878), Colombian president (1845–1849, 1861–1863, 1863–1864, 1866–1867). Born into the Popayán elite, Mosquera had served only briefly in the military (1815–1816) before becoming a captain in 1820. He was a lieutenant colonel by 1822, and colonel by 1824. Severely wounded at Barbacoas, Cauca, in 1824, Mosquera lost most of his left jaw and as a result suffered from a lifelong speech defect. His ambition, dedication, and family connections brought him the intendency of Guayaquil, where in August 1826 he proclaimed BOLÍVAR's dictatorship. He became intendant of Cauca in 1828. His forces routed by Colonel José María OBANDO in November 1828 at Popayán, he was publicly humiliated by General José María CÓRDOBA before leaving, now a general, as envoy to Peru (1829–1830). Mosquera was in Europe and the United States from 1831 to 1833. Back in Colombia, he was elected to Congress, where, from 1834 to 1837, he opposed Francisco de Paula SANTANDER's administration while sponsoring initiatives for material improvements.

Mosquera's political importance began in 1839, when he became minister of war and, from 1840 to 1842, played a major part in the War of the Supremes. His military reputation secured, he won the presidency in 1845. His term was marked by fiscal, political, and educational reforms and infrastructural advances. Mosquera lived in New York (1851–1854); when his business failed, he returned to Colombia and helped defeat General José María MELO. After being elected senator (1855–1857), Mosquera espoused federalism and founded Cauca State, of which he became governor in 1858. He also organized Bolívar State. By 1860, now a Liberal, he led a revolution against the regime of Mariano OSPINA RODRÍGUEZ and captured Bogotá in July 1861. Mosquera decreed a harsh program of anticlerical measures, culminating in the abolition of mortmain. The Rionegro Convention of 1863 elected him president once again. He defeated an Ecuadoran army (6 December 1863) at Cuaspud, Nariño.

After a diplomatic mission to Europe (1864–1865), Mosquera was again elected president. His authoritarianism and grandiose military schemes clashed with the Liberal-dominated Congress. Mosquera dissolved it and, a month later, was overthrown by a coup (23 May 1867). He spent 1868–1870 in Peruvian exile. Cauca again elected him governor in 1871, and he served as senator from Cauca in 1876–1877. He died at "Coconuco," his estate, about thirty miles from Popayán.

— J. LEÓN HELGUERA

MOSQUERA Y ARBOLEDA, JOAQUÍN

Joaquín Mosquera y Arboleda (*b.* 14 December 1787; *d.* 4 April 1878), Colombian president (1830), vice president, diplomat, and educator. The eldest sibling of southern Colombia's leading family, Mosquera studied in his native Popayán and in Bogotá, where he received his law doctorate in 1804. After supporting independence in 1810–1814, he traveled in Europe (1815–1817) and engaged in trade in Jamaica and Cartagena (1817–1818) before returning home. He and his father, forced to emigrate to Quito by royalists (1819–1820), became supporters of BOLÍVAR (1821). Mosquera was named minister plenipotentiary for Colombia by Bolívar and negotiated treaties of alliance and friendship with Peru (6 July 1822), Chile (21 October 1822), and Buenos Aires (10 June 1823). He served in the Senate (1825–1826). In 1828 he was a moderating influence in the Ocaña Congress between the forces of Bolívar and SANTANDER and was chosen president, succeeding Bolívar, by the 1830 ("Admirable") Congress. Mosquera proved to be a vacillating president (12 June–5 September 1830) and he was overthrown by General Rafael URDANETA. He spent 1831–1832 and part of 1833 in Europe and the United States. His intercession with Bolívar (1828–1830) probably saved the life of General Francisco de Paula Santander, and may explain Mosquera's election as Santander's vice president (1833–1835). In that office, he promoted primary and secondary education. Back in Popayán, he served as rector of Cauca University (1835–1836). Mosquera died in Popayán.

— J. LEÓN HELGUERA

MOTECUHZOMA I

Motecuhzoma I (Motecuhzoma Ilhuicamina; *b.* ca. 1397; *d.* 1468/69), Aztec emperor from 1440 to 1468. The elder Motecuhzoma ("He Becomes Angry Like a Lord") was the fifth Mexica ruler, or *tlatoani*, and the first who can be called an emperor: his conquests extended Aztec rule beyond the Valley of Mexico and ensured a luxurious tribute supply. He was the son of Huitzilihuitl, the second *tlatoani*, and Miahuaxihuitl, a Cuauhnahuac (Cuernavaca) princess; the legend of his birth reflects Huitzilihuitl's temporary control over Cuauhnahuac, later reestablished by Motecuhzoma. Miahuaxochitl's sorcerer father sent scorpions and other vermin to guard her. Huitzilihuitl attached a precious

greenstone to an arrow he shot over the wall; when Miahuaxihuitl swallowed the stone Motecuhzoma was conceived. The name Ilhuicamina, "He Shoots Arrows at the Sky," by which he was probably known during his lifetime, may have suggested the tale.

According to native histories, Motecuhzoma sent envoys to the mythical origin-places of the Mexica and their deity Huitzilopochtli. With his half-brother Tlacaelel, he codified Aztec law and instituted the Flowery Wars, periodic skirmishes that provided sacrificial victims. The worst crisis of Motecuhzoma's reign was the famine of 1450–1454, which emptied the imperial granaries and forced people to flee to the humid lowlands; intensification of agriculture helped to prevent further famines.

— LOUISE M. BURKHART

MOTECUHZOMA II

Motecuhzoma II (Moctezuma, Montezuma; *b.* ca. 1466; *d.* ca. 30 June 1520), ninth Mexica ruler (ca. 1502–1520). Motecuhzoma Xocoyotl (or Motecuhzoma the Younger, often designated Motecuhzoma II) was described by an early chronicler as "a man of medium stature, with a certain gravity and royal majesty, which showed clearly who he was even to those who did not know him" (Cervantes de Salazar). Also described as deeply religious, very aware of his status as head of the Mexica ruling hierarchy, and rigid and elitist in his application of law and custom, Motecuhzoma was leader of the Mexica and their empire when, bent on conquest and colonization, Hernán CORTÉS led an army of Spaniards into Tenochtitlán in 1519.

Motecuhzoma II has long been depicted as superstitious, weak, and vacillating in contrast to the "determined" and "bold" Cortés.

Motecuhzoma II has long been depicted as superstitious, weak, and vacillating in contrast to the "determined" and "bold" Cortés. This picture is overdrawn and does not accurately portray the multiple, though ultimately ineffective, ways that Motecuhzoma II sought to protect his people and empire in the face of an enemy far different than any he had faced before.

He was chosen as his uncle Ahuitzotl's successor in about 1502. Almost every Mexica *tlatoani* (or supreme ruler) had enlarged the territorial holdings of the empire. Motecuhzoma II did so, though he did not gain as much territory as his immediate predecessor. His conquests followed the general geographic patterns of Ahuitzotl's conquests and lay largely to the east and south of the Valley of Mexico, concentrating especially on central and southern Oaxaca and northern Puebla and adjoining areas of latter-day Veracruz. He ignored areas lying to the west and north of central Mexico, and left the southern regions of the empire still only loosely tied. Continuing warfare with Tlaxcala—and the inability of the Tenochca Mexica and their allies to subdue it—created a political wedge that the Spanish were later able to use to their advantage during the Conquest.

While Motecuhzoma II is reported to have believed that Cortés was the returning deity Quetzalcoatl, it is unlikely that Motecuhzoma or his advisers still thought this when the Spaniards reached Tenochtitlán. Motecuhzoma tried to discourage the Spaniards from their inland march in search of the center of his empire. Unfortunately, one of Motecuhzoma's means of discouraging them was to send gifts such as gold, which only further excited Spanish interest. As the Spaniards moved closer to Tenochtitlán, the Mexica leader attempted to have them captured but to no avail.

When Motecuhzoma II and Cortés finally met, Motecuhzoma again tried to discourage Spanish interest in his empire. But in his much quoted address to Cortés, he acknowledged Spanish military skill and apparently stated that the Mexica would obey the Spanish. Inexplicably, Motecuhzoma allowed himself to be taken captive by Cortés and some of his soldiers. Although Motecuhzoma II sought to form an alliance with Pánfilo de NARVÁEZ while imprisoned, he had lost control of events and died in 1520. The Spanish sources generally state that he was stoned by other Mexica and died from his wounds. There is disagreement among Indian sources, though some, such as Chimalpahin, state that the Spaniards killed him. It was left to his successors, Cuitlahua (CUITLAHUAC) and CUAUHTEMOC, to mount a military opposition, which ultimately failed.

— SUSAN KELLOGG

MOTOLINÍA, TORIBIO DE

Toribio de Motolinía (also Toribio de Paredes and Toribio de Benavente; *b.* ca. 1487; *d.* 1569), one of the first twelve Franciscan friars ("Los Doce") who arrived in New Spain in 1524. Born in Paredes, near Benavente, León, Spain, he proudly took "Motolinía," (Nahuatl for "poor") as his name after hearing the indigenous people use it to describe the barefoot Franciscans in their tattered habits as they walked from Veracruz to Mexico City. Converting the local people to Christianity was his primary aim, but he studied and wrote at length about their culture before and after European

contact in order to be more effective in his evangelical task.

During the years 1524–1540, Motolinía wrote either three large religious chronicles or three different versions of the same chronicle. Two survive today in modified form as the *Historia de los indios de la Nueva España* and *Memoriales;* the third has been referred to as the *De moribus indorum.* Read and quoted by other colonial chroniclers, these works are valuable to modern ethnohistorians for their depth of detail on indigenous society, religion, food and artisanal production, modes of transportation, and calendrics. In volume and detail, as early firsthand accounts, Motolinía's writings are possibly second only to those of Bernardino de Sahagún.

— STEPHANIE WOOD

MOYA DE CONTRERAS, PEDRO

Pedro Moya de Contreras (*b.* 1530?; *d.* December 1591?), first inquisitor (1570–1573) and third archbishop of Mexico (1573–1591?), interim viceroy (1584–1585), and president of the Council of the Indies (1591). Moya was born in the village of Pedroche, in the province of Córdoba, Spain. After studies at Salamanca (1551–1554) he came under the patronage of Juan de Ovando, later the president of the Council of the Indies. In 1570 he was appointed first inquisitor of Mexico and in 1573 he was named archbishop of Mexico. From 1583 until 1586 he conducted a VISITA of the civil government of New Spain, the most exhaustive of the colonial period. His most important achievement was the Third Mexican Provincial Council of 1585, which established the organization of the church in New Spain. After his return to Spain in 1586, he acted as unofficial adviser to Philip II. He died in Madrid.

— STAFFORD POOLE, C.M.

MOZIÑO, JOSÉ MARIANO

José Mariano Moziño (*b.* 24 September 1757; *d.* 19 May 1820), natural scientist, theologian, and author. Moziño, born in Temascaltepec, Mexico, to Spanish parents, received a bachelor of philosophy degree from the Seminario Tridentino in 1776 and was awarded an academic degree in scholastic theology and ethics in 1778. Turning his attention to other fields, Moziño earned his bachelor of medicine from the Royal and Pontifical University in 1787 and completed the course in botany at the Royal Botanical Garden in Mexico City in 1789. In 1792 he joined the expedition of Juan Francisco de la Bodega y Quadra to the Pacific Northwest, where he wrote a description of the Nootka Sound area of Vancouver Island that included a detailed history of the native peoples. Upon returning to Mexico in 1793, Moziño conducted field trips throughout southern Mexico and Guatemala before traveling to Spain in 1803. He served as president of Spain's Royal Academy of Medicine and director of the Royal Museum of Natural History. Caught up in the problems of the French invasion, Moziño was exiled to France in 1812. He received permission to return to Madrid in 1817, but he died en route in Barcelona. Moziño was a dedicated scientist who, under different circumstances, could have brought international recognition to Spain and Mexico in the fields of botany and ethnography.

– IRIS H. W. ENGSTRAND

MÚGICA, FRANCISCO JOSÉ

Francisco José Múgica (*b.* 3 September 1884; *d.* 12 April 1954), Mexican revolutionary and presidential candidate. Múgica served as a deputy to the constitutional convention of 1916–1917, where he established his reputation as a radical ideologue. A close friend of Lázaro CÁRDENAS, he joined his cabinet as secretary of public works (1935–1939) and became a precandidate in 1939 for the presidential nomination of the government party against Manuel ÁVILA CAMACHO. Because Múgica was so strongly identified with radical elements in the party, Cárdenas, despite their close friendship, chose the moderate Camacho to succeed himself.

Born in Tinguindín, Michoacán, Múgica studied in the Zamora seminary until 1904, after which he taught school. Politically active in his home state, he joined Francisco MADERO's forces as a second lieutenant in 1910. He served as an assistant to Venustiano CARRANZA and in 1913 joined the Constitutionalists. Becoming a career officer in the new revolutionary army, he commanded numerous military zones in the 1930s. He served as governor of his home state (1920–1922) and of Baja California del Sur (1940–1946). In 1952 he supported the presidential bid of General Miguel Henríquez Guzmán.

– RODERIC AI CAMP

MUNGUÍA, CLEMENTE DE JESÚS

Clemente de Jesús Munguía (*b.* 23 November 1810; *d.* 14 December 1868), bishop and later archbishop of Michoacán, opponent of the Reform Laws. Munguía, reputedly born in Zamora, Michoacán, represented the new breed of mid-nineteenth-century bishops determined to defend the rights and independence of the church from state encroachments. Ordained in 1841, he became rector of the seminary in Morelia in 1843, and was consecrated bishop of Michoacán in 1852. He

wrote thirty-six pastoral letters during his time as bishop. He managed only a partial diocesan visit and recommended the establishment of new dioceses and parishes.

During SANTA ANNA's last régime (1853–1955) Munguía was president of the Council of State, a position that led him in November 1855 to oppose the Ley Juárez and argue for the church's right to the *fuero*. He believed that the government had exceeded its powers and should first have consulted the Holy See. He protested against the Ley Lerdo (1856) and the Ley Iglesias (1857), and denounced the government requirement of an oath to the 1857 Constitution. Munguía protested against General Epitacio Huerta's sack of the cathedral in Morelia on 22 September 1858 and occupation of the seminary building on 10 May 1859. He was the principal author of the 30 August 1859 bishops' manifesto condemning the Veracruz Reform Laws and refuting Liberal claims that the episcopate consisted of subversives. Expelled from Mexico by Juárez in 1861, he returned with the French Intervention in September 1863. When Pope Pius IX raised Michoacán to an archdiocese in January 1863, he appointed Munguía its first archbishop. An opponent of MAXIMILIAN's ecclesiastical policy, Munguía was exiled to Rome in June 1865, where he died in poverty.

– BRIAN HAMNETT

MUÑOZ, JOSÉ TRINIDAD

José Trinidad Muñoz (*d.* 18 August 1855), Nicaraguan military officer. Muñoz, a veteran of the Central American civil wars of the 1840s, received military training in Mexico under Antonio López de SANTA ANNA. He established a military academy in León, Nicaragua, and gained a reputation as the best tactician in Central America. On 4 August 1851 Muñoz overthrew the government of José Laureano Pineda in León but was subsequently ousted and left Nicaragua.

This large, handsome, but egotistical officer was generally on the Democratic (Liberal) side, but he was less ideologically committed than many of his contemporaries. After Máximo JEREZ retreated from Granada in early 1855, Francisco Castellón, head of the Democratic government at León, brought Muñoz back to relieve Jerez as commander of his army. William WALKER arrived to support the Democrats soon afterward. Seeing Walker as a rival for power, Muñoz took an instant dislike to him. They argued over strategy and tactics, and Walker accused Muñoz of sabotaging his campaign.

Some Nicaraguan historians have viewed Muñoz as a defender of Nicaraguan sovereignty in his efforts to undermine Walker while also opposing the Conservative forces that came from the other Central American states to fight against Walker. Muñoz sought a peaceful settlement between the *legitimistas* (Conservatives) and *democráticos* (Liberals). His death in August 1855 at the battle of El Sauce, where he had defeated Santos GUARDIOLA, opened the way for Walker to become the Democrats' leading general.

— RALPH LEE WOODWARD, JR.

MUÑOZ LEDO LAZO DE LA VEGA, PORFIRIO

Porfirio Muñoz Ledo Lazo de la Vega (*b.* 23 July 1933), Mexican politician and leader of the Democratic Revolutionary Party (PRD). An important political figure since the 1970s, Muñoz Ledo abandoned the government party after he and Cuauhtémoc CÁRDENAS failed to reform it from within. A key organizer of Cárdenas's campaign in the 1988 presidential elections, he was elected as one of the first opposition senators in modern times. In 1993, he became president of PRD.

Born in Mexico City, Muñoz Ledo graduated from the National School of Law and obtained an L.L.D. degree at the University of Paris. After working at various teaching positions, he entered public life, serving in the secretariats of public education and the social security institute, before rising to the post of under secretary of the presidency (1970–1972) and then secretary of labor (1972–1975). He became president of the Party of the Institutional Revolution (PRI) in 1975 and briefly served as secretary of education (1976–1977) before being fired by President José LÓPEZ PORTILLO. He later served as ambassador to the United Nations (1979–1985).

— RODERIC AI CAMP

MUÑOZ MARÍN, LUIS

Luis Muñoz Marín (*b.* 18 February 1898; *d.* 30 April 1980), the first elected governor of Puerto Rico (1948–1964). Muñoz Marín, the son of political leader Luis MUÑOZ RIVERA, spent much of his young life in the United States as a student, a writer, and an advocate of Puerto Rican independence. His political outlook gradually underwent a transformation, however, and he came to believe that economic development was more vital than immediate independence. In 1938, alienated from the political parties dominant in Puerto Rico, Muñoz Marín founded the Popular Democratic Party (PPD), whose motto was "Bread, Land, and Liberty." Following a strong PPD showing in the 1940 elections, Muñoz became president of the Puerto Rican Senate in 1941. He immediately pushed through basic reforms in land tenancy, natural resources, transportation, and

education. The PPD, with Muñoz Marín as its president, swept the 1944 elections, but the independence issue ultimately divided the party. Muñoz Marín remained with the less radical PPD, favoring economic and social reform with U.S. assistance.

In 1938, Muñoz Marín founded the Popular Democratic Party (PPD), whose motto was "Bread, Land, and Liberty."

The first gubernatorial elections took place on 2 November 1948, and Muñoz Marín won with a clear majority, becoming the first Puerto Rican to be elected governor of the island. He vigorously promoted industrial development as part of his program Operation Bootstrap, but eventually he rejected independence as an option for Puerto Rico, favoring instead a permanent union with the United States. After holding the office of governor for four terms, he declined to run again in 1964, though he remained an active figure in Puerto Rican politics for many years.

— SARA FLEMING

MUÑOZ RIVERA, LUIS

Luis Muñoz Rivera (*b.* 17 July 1859; *d.* 15 November 1916), Puerto Rican journalist, poet, and political leader. Born in Barranquitas, Puerto Rico, Muñoz Rivera completed his primary schooling in local schools and began his career in politics in 1887. He rose to prominence as a leader of the Autonomist Party. In 1890 he founded the newspaper *La Democracia*, which became the voice of the autonomist movement. He successfully negotiated a pact with the Spanish Liberal Fusionist Party in 1896 that ultimately resulted in the granting of autonomy to Puerto Rico. Muñoz Rivera and the autonomists won the first elections, but U.S. occupation in 1898 prevented the new government from assuming office. Renewing his struggle to procure political rights for Puerto Rico, Muñoz Rivera founded the Federalist Party in 1898 and became Puerto Rico's resident commissioner in Washington (1910–1916). He was instrumental in formulating the Jones Act (signed 4 March 1917), which increased Puerto Rico's powers of self-government, but he did not live to see its passage.

— SARA FLEMING

MURILLO TORO, MANUEL

Manuel Murillo Toro (*b.* 1 January 1816; *d.* 26 December 1880), Liberal president of Colombia (1864–1866 and 1872–1874). Murillo was born in Chaparral, Tolima, and received his law degree in Bogotá in 1836; he became a protégé of Francisco de Paula SANTANDER. Murillo served as secretary of the interior and as finance secretary during the regime of José Hilario LÓPEZ (1849–1853), and was the first president (i.e., governor) of Santander (1857–1858). After the Liberal triumph of 1861 he served as minister to France, the United States, and Venezuela. During his first presidency Murillo achieved tenuous reconciliations with the church and the defeated Conservatives and recognized the Conservatives' dominance in Antioquia. During his second term he pushed for railroad development and other infrastructure projects, giving rise to serious interregional rivalries. Ideologically, Murillo shifted from radical popular sovereignty (ca. 1850) to laissez-faire libertarianism (ca. 1858); by the late 1860s he espoused a government role in economic development and a moderated role for popular participation.

— RICHARD J. STOLLER

MURTINHO, JOAQUIM DUARTE

Joaquim Duarte Murtinho (*b.* 7 December 1848; *d.* 19 November 1911), minister of finance of Brazil (1898–1902). As minister of finance under Manuel Ferraz CAMPOS SALES, Murtinho, a native of Cuiabá, Brazil, based his economic policies upon the reestablishment of the gold standard of 1846. He pursued this policy in reaction to the inflation surrounding the financial crisis of 1891, following the financial market reforms of 1890 (the *encilhamento*). Since the mil-réis had depreciated 257 percent between 1855 and 1896, the necessary deflation (and depression) to achieve this parity was dramatic (around a 72 percent fall in the price level). Some historians feel that Murtinho's motivations were more than economic. According to Carlos Peláez and Wilson Suzigan (1981), Murtinho believed that the racial inferiority of the inhabitants of Brazil (compared with those of the United States and Western Europe) rendered industrialization an untenable policy goal. Murtinho also argued that the overabundant coffee production at the time was due to market inefficiencies and too many producers. The appreciation of the currency would rid Brazil of the small industry developed since 1886 and weed out inefficient coffee producers by making imports cheaper and coffee exports more expensive. Murtinho's restrictive monetary policies contracted economic activity to an extent only seen in the depressions of 1981–1982 and 1990. Murtinho's other credentials include that of medical doctor (to Marshal Deodoro da FONSECA), campaigner for the Republic, senator from Mato Grosso (1890), member of the Constituent Congress (1891), senator (1903–1906), and vice president of the Senate (1905–1906). He died in Rio de Janeiro.

— JOHN H. WELCH

MUTIS, ALVARO

Alvaro Mutis (*b.* 29 August 1923), Colombian novelist and poet. Known as a poet most of his life, Mutis, a native of Bogotá, blossomed as one of Colombia's major novelists during the 1980s and 1990s. He has published more than fifteen books of poetry and fiction. Mutis began publishing poetry in the 1940s, and continued in the 1950s and 1960s, describing a decaying world, often in a satirical tone. Many of his prose poems are narrated in the bitter and ironic voice of a character named Maqroll el Gaviero. One of Mutis's major books of poetry is *Los trabajos perdidos* (1965). He has lived most of his adult life in Mexico.

In 1986, at the age of sixty-three, Mutis published his first novel, *La nieve del almirante,* followed by *Ilona llega con la lluvia* (1987). Following the pattern and tone established in his prose poems, Mutis made Maqroll el Gaviero the protagonist of these two novels. Maqroll travels by ship to several countries, and the reader follows his spiritual voyage. Maqroll's mysterious and secretive travels continued in *Un bel morir* (1989), *La última escala del Tramp Steamer* (1989), and several other works of fiction. In all of his writing, Mutis tends to portray failure as a form of triumph.

— RAYMOND LESLIE WILLIAMS

MUTIS, JOSÉ CELESTINO

José Celestino Mutis (*b.* 6 April 1732; *d.* 11 September 1808), distinguished figure of the Spanish American Enlightenment. Born in Cádiz, one of the cities in Spain most receptive to the new ideas of the Enlightenment, Mutis studied first at the Colegio de San Fernando in his hometown and later at the University of Sevilla. Mutis concentrated on botany—he evidently had some correspondence with Linnaeus—although he also studied physics, mathematics, astronomy, and medicine. A licensed physician, he went to the Indies in 1760 as doctor to the new viceroy of New Granada, Pedro de MESSÍA DE LA CERDA.

Immediately after his arrival in Bogotá, Mutis began collecting and studying New World plants for their medicinal value. As the premier physician in New Granada—there were only two licensed in the realm—he became *protomédico* (medical examiner) in Bogotá, dedicating himself to improving public health and controlling epidemics. In 1773 he entered the clergy. Like the first *protomédico* of New Spain (Francisco HERNÁN-

DEZ) two hundred years earlier, Mutis combined his medical training with his botanical expertise.

Mutis headed a team of scientists who traversed Colombia, collecting samples of the flora, making drawings, and ascertaining the practical uses of 130 families of plants.

Late in 1783, with the title of First Botanist and Astronomer of the King from Charles III, Mutis headed a team of eighteen distinguished scientists who traversed virtually all of what is now Colombia, collecting samples of the flora, making drawings, and ascertaining the practical uses of the 130 families of plants and twenty thousand herbs they studied. To disseminate the findings of his expedition, Mutis planned a series of thirteen volumes, including color drawings, but he never saw his prodigious labors put into print. Overwhelmed by a multitude of scientific, clerical, and medical responsibilities in New Granada, he had no time to see to publication. Fortunately, however, after his death, almost seven thousand of his drawings and four thousand pages of manuscripts were shipped to the archive of the Real Jardín Botánico (Royal Botanical Garden) in Madrid.

A typical figure of the Spanish American Enlightenment, Mutis was interested in promoting all useful knowledge: the effectiveness of quinine against malaria, Spanish dictionaries of Indian languages, barometric pressure as it affects the growth of plants, and ways to control epidemics. When the renowned German scientist Alexander von Humboldt came to Bogotá during his travels in Spanish America, he was greatly impressed by Mutis's breadth of learning, referring to him at one point as the "patriarch of botanists" and later dedicating one of his scientific treatises to the Spanish American scientist. In 1803, engaging in yet another intellectual enterprise, Mutis established an astronomical observatory in Bogotá, the highest in the world at the time. He died in Bogotá at seventy-six.

— JOHN JAY TEPASKE

N

NABUCO DE ARAÚJO, JOAQUIM

Joaquim Nabuco de Araújo (*b.* 19 August 1849; *d.* 17 January 1910), Brazilian abolitionist and diplomat. Nabuco was born in Recife. His mother came from Pernambuco's planter elite, and his father, José Tomás Nabuco de Araújo, was a deputy, senator, Progressive League chieftain, Liberal leader, minister, councillor of state, and jurist. Nabuco was expected to assume his place. As a student at the Colégio D. Pedro II (1857–1866) and at law school in São Paulo and Recife (1866–1870), Nabuco was drawn to both literature and sociopolitical reform. He spent the 1870s indecisively, writing, touring Europe, and serving as a diplomatic attaché in London and New York. Upon his father's death in 1878, his family pressed him to seek election in Pernambuco as a deputy.

Nabuco conceived of himself as an English Liberal reformist. He found his cause in abolition, an issue that had attracted him since his student days. Slavery's destruction, he argued in *O Abolicionismo* (1883), was the most important of the reforms necessary to the empire's survival and progress. The abolition movement (1879–1888) involved sustained mobilization of the urban middle class and worker elements paralleled by plantation agitation, slave resistance and revolt, and flight.

Nabuco, using and attacking traditional politics, was an indispensable leader. A superb speaker and propagandist, charismatic and well-connected, he led the movement in parliament, public meetings, and international conferences. His commitment and political moralism cost him defeats, European self-exile, and party ostracism, but they also brought him romantic glory and a commanding position among reformists. Abolition was realized in 1888 by a Conservative cabinet, which completed the disarray of the traditional parties, produced reaction, and encouraged republicanism. Nabuco sought the monarchy's survival through further reform, but he was unsuccessful.

Nabuco interpreted the 1889 Republic as the reactionary work of the planters. He refused to participate in the new regime, and turned to journalism, law, and literature (1889–1899). In these years, he completed *Um estadista do império* (1897–1900), a biography of his father and the classic study of the monarchy, and *Minha formação* (1900), an intellectual autobiography. Nabuco helped found the Brazilian Academy of Letters in 1897.

When the Republic had painfully reconstructed political consensus, Nabuco allowed himself to be wooed into diplomacy to defend Brazil in an imperialistic era that he thought threatened his much weakened nation. His first mission, an arbitration with Britain over the Guyana border (1899–1904), ended in failure. Nonetheless, Nabuco, who was appointed minister to Great Britain (1900–1904) during the arbitration, was subsequently appointed Brazil's first ambassador to the United States (1905–1910). Nabuco was very successful; he lectured widely, and he secured a hemispheric partnership with the United States. His crowning achievement was the Pan-American Conference held in Rio (1906). This was his last, triumphant return to Brazil before his death in Washington, D.C., four years later.

– JEFFREY D. NEEDELL

NAIPAUL, V. S.

V. S. Naipaul (*b.* 17 August 1932), West Indian author. Vidiadhar Surajprasad Naipaul was born in Trinidad, of East Indian parents, and raised a Hindu. Considered one of the most important and prolific West Indian writers, he has written extensively about Trinidad and the colonial experience, being both critical of and criticized by his birth country. His early works present the local color of Trinidad and chronicle the colony in transition. In his later works he transcends regionalism, writing about India, Africa, the Islamic countries, British society, and the southern United States. Expressing the third world view, he deals with race, class, and colonialism as issues beyond national confines.

Educated at Oxford, Naipaul has lived in England since, though he travels extensively to gather material for his books. He published his first book, *The Mystic Masseur*, in 1957. His novel *A Turn in the South* was published in 1989.

– JOYCE E. NAYLON

NALÉ ROXLO, CONRADO

Conrado Nalé Roxlo (*b.* 15 February 1898; *d.* 2 July 1971), Argentine journalist, poet, and dramatist. Born in Buenos Aires, Nalé Roxlo contributed to a wide array of literary genres, but for the most part only his epigrammatic poetry and his works for the theater continue to be read. As a journalist and literary critic, he wrote for *La Nación, El Mundo,* and other such journals. His dramatic efforts corresponded to the enormously significant developments in theatrical activity in Buenos Aires in the 1930s, 1940s, and early 1950s known as the Teatro Independiente, a movement that affirmed a noncommercial (but very public) art theater in the tradition of Pirandello, O'Neill, and Shaw. (Nalé Roxlo's play *Judith y las rosas* [1954] won the Primer Premio Nacional de Comedia for 1954–1956.) Nalé Roxlo brought to his theatrical efforts the dominant emphases of his multifaceted poetry: a concern for the human comedy seen in often markedly farcical terms, the contradictions of fragile and transient individual endeavor, the interplay between illusion and anguished uncertainty, and a jocose manipulation of language that underscores life's existential ambiguities. The result is a highly original form of literary humorism that reveals a profound preoccupation with the human condition during a period of intense international and national moral, social, and political turbulence.

El grillo (1923), Nalé Roxlo's first book of poetry, possesses a significant metapoetic dimension that evokes the literary vanguard of the period and the emphasis on the privileged, primordial voice of the poet even when dealing with mundane reality and unpretentious natural elements. Other works by Nalé Roxlo include *Antologías apócrifas* (1943), *De otro cielo* (1952), and *El pacto de Cristina* (1945).

— DAVID WILLIAM FOSTER

NAMUNCURÁ, CEFERINO

Ceferino Namuncurá (*b.* 1888, *d.* 1905), Argentine ARAUCANIAN (MAPUCHE) proposed as a candidate for beatification. Descendant of the great Araucanian military leaders CALFUCURÁ and Manuel NAMUNCURÁ, Ceferino was educated in Salesian missions established near *reservas* set aside for subjugated Indians in Argentina in the 1880s. Ceferino Namuncurá's excellence as a student attracted the attention of his teachers, and he was sent to Rome for seminary studies. He died there of tuberculosis while in his early twenties.

— KRISTINE L. JONES

NAMUNCURÁ, MANUEL

Manuel Namuncurá (*d.* 1908), leader of Araucanian confederation in the Argentine pampas from 1873 until final defeat in 1883. Namuncurá assumed leadership of the confederation of the Araucanian and Pampas tribes in the Argentine pampas after the death of his father, CALFUCURÁ, in 1873. Originally chosen to serve as one of a triumvirate elected by Araucanian elders, Manuel

Namuncurá emerged as the most effective leader in achieving Araucanian hegemony in Argentina. In the five years following his ascendance, Namuncurá's followers maintained a strong line of defense against creole expansion and conducted highly organized and effective *malones* against their enemies. Following the military operations of Argentine generals Adolfo ALSINA (1877) and Julio A. ROCA (1878–1879), Araucanian resistance crumbled, and the last straggling forces under the leadership of Namuncurá finally surrendered in 1883.

— KRISTINE L. JONES

NAÓN, RÓMULO S.

Rómulo S. Naón (*b.* 17 February 1876; *d.* 29 December 1941), Argentine politician and diplomat. Having served in the cabinet of José FIGUEROA ALCORTA, Naón in 1910 began an eight-year diplomatic posting in Washington, D.C., first as envoy extraordinary and, after 1914, as Argentina's first ambassador to the United States. Naón represented Argentine interests in Washington in a time of rapid changes in U.S.-Argentine relations. Naón was a supporter of increased bilateral trade and financial ties, and his expertise in international law helped facilitate the growing American dominance of many Argentine commercial markets.

During the First World War Naón began to influence Argentine foreign policy, exceeding the normal ambassadorial role. In 1917 and 1918, as relations between the United States and Argentina deteriorated over the issue of Argentine neutrality, Naón worked hard to convince American officials that the nationalist rhetoric of President Hipólito YRIGOYEN and Foreign Minister Honorio PUEYRREDÓN was of little practical significance. For a time, and on the basis of his success in negotiating an important wheat sale agreement between Argentina and the Allied powers, Naón succeeded in defusing this antagonism. But in 1918, after having played a major role in the strengthening of U.S.-Argentine economic ties, Naón resigned his post in a rejection of what he regarded as Yrigoyen's intransigent anti-Americanism.

— DAVID M. K. SHEININ

NARANJO, CARMEN

Carmen Naranjo (*b.* 30 January 1928), Costa Rican writer, born in Cartago. Naranjo introduced existentialist themes and innovative narrative techniques into Costa Rican prose. She obtained a doctorate in Spanish philology and has held several positions in public administration while also writing novels, short stories, poems, and essays. During the second presidency of José

FIGUERES, Naranjo was the assistant administrative manager of the Costa Rican Bureau of Social Security cashier's office and ambassador to India (1972–1974). Naranjo was also the director of the Museo del Arte Costarricense, was the only woman to hold a cabinet position, and served as secretary-general of the Bureau

---

Naranjo's first novel focuses on the modern world's bureaucratic system, in which monotony and selfishness give rise to pessimism in the human being.

---

of Social Security. She became known with her first novel, *Los perros no ladraron* (1966), which focuses on the circumstances of the modern world's bureaucratic system, in which monotony, selfishness, and lack of fraternal feeling give rise to pessimism in the human being. Naranjo's other novels include *Memorias de un hombre palabra* (1968), *Responso por el niño Juan Manuel* (1971), *Diario de una multitud* (1974), *Mi guerrilla* (1984), and *Sobrepunto* (1985). Her short-story collections include *Ondina* (1985) and *Otro rumbo para la rumba* (1989). Her poetry anthologies are *Idioma del invierno* (1972) and *Homenaje a don Nadie* (1981). Her essays are collected in *Cinco temas en busca de un pensador* (1977) and *Cultura* (1978).

– JUAN CARLOS GALEANO

NARDONE, BENITO

Benito Nardone (*b.* 1906; *d.* 1964), Uruguayan radio personality and political figure who rose to political prominence in the late 1960s. His political vehicle was the Federal League of Rural Action (LFAR), the official name for the political movement known as *ruralismo*. The LFAR was an interest group ostensibly representing small farming and ranching interests even though its founder, Domingo R. Bordaberry, was a large ranch owner. Bordaberry started the newspaper *Diario Rural* in 1940 and hired Nardone, then a young journalist, as its editor. In 1951 Bordaberry and Nardone founded a radio station, Radio Rural, which quickly thrust Nardone into the public eye. He became the first important media personality in Uruguay.

By the mid-1950s, Nardone held mass public rallies in Montevideo, which he called *cabildos abiertos,* a reference to the rural protests of the past. *Ruralismo* was basically a conservative, nonpartisan movement until the 1958 election, when, disenchanted with the politics of Colorado President Luis Conrado BATLLE BERRES, Nardone joined the Herrerist (*see* Luis Alberto de HER-

RERA) faction of the Blancos (National Party). Nardone's support proved crucial to the Blanco victory and thrust him into an even more prominent role in national life. His writings under the name Chico-Tazo (Crack of the Whip) became more strident, reflecting a virulent anticommunism and a championing of the "little guy." In this respect, the movement can be compared to Poujadism in France. He attacked Batllism and all the liberal, urban values it represented while extolling the virtues of the small farmer and of rural society.

Nardone and a new close collaborator, a rich wood producer named Juan José Gari, continued to support the Blancos in their successful 1962 campaign, publishing the magazine *Mundo Americano,* whose slogan was "with democracy and against communism." The magazine echoed Nardone's attacks on liberalism and the Left. Nardone's movement dissipated quickly following his death. Radio Rural remained on the air, utilizing Nardone's widow as a symbol of continuity, but with rapidly diminished appeal and influence, *ruralismo* was not a factor in the 1966 elections.

– MARTIN WEINSTEIN

NARIÑO, ANTONIO

Antonio Nariño (*b.* 9 April 1765; *d.* 13 December 1823), Colombian independence leader. A member of the creole upper class of Santa Fe de Bogotá, Nariño was a prosperous merchant who served as *alcalde* and as royal treasurer of tithes. He also headed a group that met to discuss the issues of the day in the light of new intellectual currents emanating from the European Enlightenment, whose principal authors were represented in Nariño's extensive personal library.

When Nariño first toyed with the idea of independence is unclear, but he gained political notoriety when he was arrested in 1794 for having printed and secretly distributed a Spanish translation of the French revolutionary Declaration of the Rights of Man. He was tried and convicted of subversive activity and sentenced to exile in Spanish North Africa. However, Nariño escaped his captors on reaching Spain. From there he traveled to France and ultimately to England, where he attempted to sound out the British concerning possible help in case a revolution broke out in Spanish America. In 1797 he returned to New Granada, where he boldly surrendered to the authorities. He was not sent back to exile, but over the following years he was in and out of jail on suspicion of revolutionary activities; Nariño was in the dungeon of the Inquisition at Cartagena when the independence movement began in 1810.

By the end of 1810, Nariño was again in Santa Fe. He plunged into revolutionary politics, first as journalist—calling in the pages of his newspaper, *La Bagatela,* for outright separation from Spain and for creation of a strong centralist regime in New Granada. From September 1811 he was president-dictator of Cundinamarca, comprising Santa Fe and its surrounding area but not the outlying provinces, which were either committed to federalism or under royalist control. Conflict between Nariño's Cundinamarca and the federalist United Provinces of New Granada soon degenerated into civil war. Fortunes swung back and forth until in May 1814 Nariño, having led an army south to overcome the royalist bastion of Pasto, was taken prisoner by the enemy and shipped to Spain.

The Spanish liberal revolution of 1820 led to Nariño's freedom. He returned home to aid the cause of independence and served briefly in 1821 as provisional vice president of Gran Colombia, by appointment of Simón BOLÍVAR. However, he was defeated for a full term by Francisco de Paula SANTANDER, who became acting chief executive in Bolívar's absence and waged a campaign in Congress and the press to undermine the influence of his older rival. Although Nariño is revered today as "Precursor" of Colombian independence, he died in bitter disappointment at Villa de Leiva.

– DAVID BUSHNELL

NARVÁEZ, PÁNFILO DE

Pánfilo de Narváez (*b.* ca. 1478/80; *d.* 1528), Spanish soldier. Born in Valmanzano, Segovia, Spain, Narváez came to the New World around 1498. A veteran of military engagements in Jamaica, he helped to lead the bloody conquest of Cuba in 1510–1514. In 1520 he vied with Hernán CORTÉS in Veracruz for the opportunity to raid portions of Mexico. He lost, and was imprisoned for two and a half years.

In 1526 Narváez received a royal contract to explore La Florida. After landing near Tampa Bay in April 1528, he and three hundred men marched north to Apalachee, where they suffered illness and were attacked by natives. Retreating, they moved to the nearby coast to build vessels in which they could sail to Mexico. The Spaniards tried to follow the coastline west but were either swept out into the Gulf or washed ashore, where some lived among native groups. Four survivors, including Alvar Núñez CABEZA DE VACA, who wrote an account of the expedition, eventually walked westward nearly to the Pacific Ocean and were rescued near the Río Yaqui in 1536.

– JERALD T. MILANICH

NASCIMENTO, ABDIAS DO

Abdias do Nascimento (*b.* 14 March 1914), Brazilian playwright, educator, and political activist. Nascimento was born in Franca, São Paulo, and received a degree in economics from the University of Rio de Janeiro in 1938.

Among his first political actions was his participation in the Frente Negra Brasileira, which he joined in the late 1930s. In 1944 Nascimento founded the Teatro Experimental do Negro (TEN), initiating a twenty-four-year career as a theater director and playwright. TEN won critical acclaim with its productions of such works as Eugene O'Neill's *The Emperor Jones* and Nascimento's own play, *O sortilégio.* TEN also served as a vehicle for Nascimento's political activism. As a complement to TEN, Nascimento formed the Comité Democrático Afro-Brasileiro in 1945, to lobby the Brazilian Congress for the enactment of antidiscrimination legislation. Nascimento's efforts in this regard presaged the passage of the Afonso Arinos Law of 1951, Brazil's first law against racial discrimination. Nascimento also displayed leadership in the Brazilian arts by establishing the Museu de Arte Negra in 1968.

In 1969 Nascimento established residence in the United States, where he held several academic posts. He was visiting professor at Yale and Wesleyan universities, and subsequently was named professor in the department of Puerto Rican Studies at the State University of New York, Buffalo.

During the 1970s Nascimento traveled widely in the United States and Africa, speaking on behalf of blacks in Brazil and the Pan-African movement. He was instrumental in organizing several conferences of Afro–Latin American intellectuals under the banner of the Congress of Black Cultures in the Americas. Nascimento was elected President of the Third Congress of Black Cultures, which was held in São Paulo in 1982.

After returning to Brazil in 1979, Nascimento was named professor of black studies at the Pontifical Catholic University in São Paulo. While there, he created the research institute known as IPEAFRO (Afro-Brazilian Studies and Research Institute). In 1982 he was elected to Congress as a candidate of the Partido Democrático Trabalhista (PDT), led by Leonel BRIZOLA, with whom Nascimento had been closely associated.

Nascimento has written or edited some fourteen books, plays, and collections of essays on Afro-Brazilian culture and politics. His wife, Elisa Larkin Nascimento, has collaborated with him in several of these enterprises.

– MICHAEL MITCHELL

NASCIMENTO, MILTON

Milton Nascimento (*b.* 1942), Brazilian singer and songwriter. Born in Rio de Janeiro, Nascimento moved with his adoptive family at the age of three to Três Pontas, Minas Gerais, where he spent his formative years. He became a leading figure of the post–bossa nova musical generation and one of Brazil's most popular composers and performers in the 1970s and 1980s.

Nascimento's voice is rich in timbre and wide in range, and many critics consider him the greatest Brazilian vocalist of his time. His music merges influences from rural *toadas,* Minas church choral music, bossa nova, *nueva canción,* the Beatles, jazz, and classical music; his songs feature strong melodies, elaborate harmonies, unusual rhythms, and a pronounced lyricism. He collaborated on songwriting with fellow Minas musicians Wagner Tiso, Beto Guedes, Lô Borges, Márcio Borges, Tavinho Moura, and Fernando Brant.

Nascimento gained national fame at the 1967 International Song Festival in Rio, when he was named best performer and his "Travessia" took the second-place song award; his debut album "Milton Nascimento" appeared that year. Important later albums include: "Clube da esquina" (with Lô Borges, 1972), "Minas" (1975), "Native Dancer" (with Wayne Shorter, 1975), "Geraes" (1976), "Clube da esquina 2" (1978), "Sentinela" (1980), "Missa dos quilombos" (1982), and "Miltons" (with Herbie Hancock and Naná Vasconcelos, 1989). His songs have been recorded by Paul Desmond, Wayne Shorter, Paul Simon, Quincy Jones, Sarah Vaughan, Herbie Mann, the Manhattan Transfer, George Duke, and dozens of other musicians outside of Brazil.

— CHRIS MCGOWAN

NAVARRA Y ROCAFUL, MELCHOR DE

Melchor de Navarra y Rocaful (duke of Palata), viceroy of Peru (1681–1689). One of the most energetic and innovative but ultimately unsuccessful administrators of colonial Peru, Palata focused on reorganizing indigenous communities in order to increase tribute income and to maximize the *mita,* the state labor levy. Concerned with the continued decline in the mining industry, Palata initiated a series of proposals to stimulate production. He also undertook a major review of labor practices within the viceroyalty aimed at stabilizing the work force and combating the chronic shortfalls in the *mita.* Palata ordered a comprehensive census of indigenous society that would include individuals living within or outside of the communities through which their tribute and labor should be paid. Palata issued a series of orders designed to eliminate the protected status of various groups of Indians (such as forasteros and vanaconas) who were avoiding their obligations to the crown. Under the Palata reforms, the *reducción* (resettlement) system of the 1570s was effectively abandoned and Indians then required to pay tribute and

serve *mita* duty through the communities in which they currently resided.

Palata focused on reorganizing indigenous communities in order to increase tribute income and to maximize the mita, *the state labor levy.*

Palata's efforts were ultimately frustrated by resistance from those who benefited from private arrangements with these Indians—employers (particularly miners in Upper Peru), clergy, and some indigenous community leaders—and from Indian communities as well. When the Palata reform proposals threatened these arrangements and increased indigenous migration from areas subjected to *mita* demands, he was forced to abandon his program. The new tribute and labor assessments were first reduced and then revoked by Palata's successor, the count of Monclova.

— ANN M. WIGHTMAN

NAVARRO, MARTÍN ANTONIO (FÉLIX)

Martín Antonio (Félix) Navarro (*b.* 20 November 1738; *d.* 26 May 1793), soldier and first intendant of Louisiana. Born in La Coruña, Galicia, Spain, Navarro accompanied the first Spanish expedition to Louisiana on 5 September 1765 and remained there for the next twenty-two years. During the war against Great Britain, Navarro oversaw supplies and munitions for Governor Bernardo de GÁLVEZ's victorious expeditions against Baton Rouge (1779), Mobile (1780), and Pensacola (1781).

In 1780 Navarro became the first intendant in Louisiana; on 29 August of that year he wrote "Political Reflections on the Current Condition of the Province," recommending increased population and free trade. Consequently, the crown approved a new commercial code in 1782 permitting Louisiana direct trade with France and the Spanish West Indies as well as with designated ports in Spain. When Navarro granted licenses to Panton, Leslie, and Company to trade, critics protested his giving such rights to foreigners. In 1784 he and Governor Esteban Miró went to Pensacola and Mobile, where they met with the Creek, Choctaw, Alibamone, and Chickasaw Indians and drew up tariff arrangements for the pelt trade. Navarro left Louisiana on 10 May 1788 and returned to Spain. The following year he was appointed special commissioner of the crown and visited factories throughout Europe. His report concluded that Spain could manufacture most of the goods traded in Louisiana. Navarro died in Madrid.

— BRIAN E. COUTTS

NAVARRO WOLFF, ANTONIO

Antonio Navarro Wolff (*b.* ca 1948), Colombian political leader. After training as a sanitary engineer at the Universidad del Valle in Cali, Navarro joined the M-19 guerrilla movement, participating in a number of its operations against government and private targets over the next dozen years. In May 1985, Navarro was badly wounded, losing his left leg and suffering some speech impairment. Following Carlos Pizarro Leongómez's assassination in April 1990, leadership of the M-19 passed to Navarro, who brought it into open political participation. He was the Left's presidential choice in the 1990 elections and won 700,000 votes, better than 10 percent of the total. Navarro served for a few months as President César GAVIRÍA's health minister before resigning to enter the Constituent Assembly elections of December 1990. M-19 garnered 27 percent of the vote, and Navarro became a major force in the Assembly, helping to shape the constitution adopted in July 1991. His party did not fare well in the October 1991 congressional elections, but Navarro's potential as a presidential candidate in 1994 remains strong.

— J. LEÓN HELGUERA

NAZARETH, ERNESTO

Ernesto Nazareth (Júlio de Nazareth; *b.* 20 March 1863; *d.* ca. 2 February 1934), Brazilian salon pianist and composer. Nazareth's father, Vasco Lourenzo da Silva Nazareth, was a customs official, and his mother, Carolina Augusta Pereira da Cunha, a pianist who gave her son his first piano lessons. After his mother's death in 1873, Nazareth continued his musical studies with Eduardo Madeira and Lucien Lambert. An early intense interest in the music of Chopin continued to grow and became an important factor in the development of his compositional style. From 1920 to 1924 he played daily in the Cinema Odeon in Rio de Janeiro, where one of the cellists, Heitor VILLA-LOBOS, admired Nazareth's salon style of playing. When describing the *choro* as a musical genre, Villa-Lobos frequently spoke of his own compositions as music in the style of Nazareth and other salon musicians of the late nineteenth and early twentieth centuries.

Although Nazareth's compositions are exclusively piano pieces in salon style, Nazareth was the most important composer of popular music of his time. His approximately 220 compositions were an important source of ideas for composers in the emergent nationalist school of music. His works often bore a sophisticated or whimsical title of subtle meaning comprehensible only to a "carioca" (urban resident of Rio de Janeiro), such as *Odeon, Espalhafatoso,* and *Esta chumbado.* Subtitles were names of dances, provided in what often appeared to be a haphazard fashion, resulting in a fusion of dance forms such as maxixe, polka, polkamaxixe. During his lifetime Nazareth's music was performed only for entertainment in salon settings, but his music achieved a much wider audience after his death, often appearing on concert programs.

— DAVID P. APPLEBY

NEGRETE, JORGE

Jorge Negrete (*b.* 30 November 1911; *d.* 5 December 1953), Mexican actor and singer. Born in Guanajuato, Negrete began his studies in a military academy, but dropped out to pursue a music career. Throughout the 1930s he had a series of successful singing engagements in Mexico and the United States. In 1937 Negrete debuted in the film *La madrina del diablo.* His good looks, deep masculine voice, and self-assurance quickly propelled him to stardom. Negrete, along with Pedro INFANTE, dominated the *ranchera* films. Known as the "immortal *charro mexicano*," he starred in over forty films. Among his classic features are *El peñón de las ánimas; El cementerio de las ánimas; La Valentina; ¡Ay, Jalisco, no te rajes!; Historia de un gran amor; El rapto;* and *Dos tipos de cuidado.* He was also a founder and president of the cinema workers' union.

— DAVID MACIEL

NEPOMUCENO, ALBERTO

Alberto Nepomuceno (*b.* 6 July 1865; *d.* 16 October 1920), Brazilian composer and conductor, the "Father of Brazilian music." In an era in which the most important Brazilian music critic, Oscar Guanabarino, championed the Italian language as the language of art songs, Nepomuceno frequently stated that "a people who do not sing in their own language have no native land." In spite of fierce resistance from Guanabarino and other critics, Nepomuceno wrote arts songs in Portuguese now recognized as some of the finest works of the genre. Nepomuceno's wide range of musical activities were not confined to championing works by Brazilian composers. He helped Heitor VILLA-LOBOS, a young and very controversial composer at the time, get his works published by Sampaio Araújo, a Brazilian publisher, but he also conducted the first Brazilian performance of Debussy's *Prélude à l'après-midi d'un faune;*

he not only arranged to have Arnold Schoenberg's *Harmonielehre* translated into Portuguese but also had it adopted at the National Institute of Music, in spite of the fierce resistance of members of the faculty and critics. One of Nepomuceno's most significant contributions in providing Brazilian musicians with a historical sense of their heritage was his revival of the works of Padre José Maurício Nunes GARCIA, the most important Brazilian composer of the early nineteenth century. Nepomuceno's contributions as a composer included several operas; string quartets and chamber music; instrumental, vocal, and piano music. His orchestral composition *Série brasileira* greatly offended Brazilian critics by utilizing the reco-reco, a percussion instrument commonly employed only in popular music. The incorporation of rhythmic patterns previously used only by salon composers was, moreover, an important element in the emerging nationalist music.

— DAVID P. APPLEBY

NERUDA, PABLO

Pablo Neruda (*b.* 12 July 1904; *d.* 23 September 1973), Chilean poet. Born Neftalí Eliecer Ricardo Reyes Basoalto in Parral, southern Chile, Neruda is the most renowned poet of modern Latin American literature and one of the major poets of the twentieth century. Winner of the Nobel Prize for literature in 1971, Ne-

Pablo Neruda, 1970. (Photo by Sara Facio)

ruda's fifty-some books, produced in as many years, established his reputation as a writer of prodigious output and creative power, as well as a poet of remarkably varied styles. His work reflects in many ways the twentieth-century history of poetry in the Spanish language, moving from *modernismo* to more traditional verse forms and meters as well as free verse, only to plunge deeply into vanguard tendencies, especially surrealism. He employed a baroque, hermetic style as well as an epic stance with elements of the chronicle, and wrote in a lyrical mode as well as a conventional style. These movements did not necessarily coincide with nor were they limited to specific periods of his life. Some critics have assigned his work to the categories of nature poetry, public poetry, erotic poetry, and personal poetry; again, these are poetic stances rather than chronological designations. Neruda himself eschewed all such critical classifications, but they are not without validity in establishing his range.

Neruda's life reflects a constant series of voyages from his native Chile, with his country providing a constant geographical and emotional center for his poetic and political concerns. At the age of twenty-three, he was appointed consul in Rangoon, Burma. From 1928 to 1936 he filled consular posts in Sri Lanka (Ceylon), Indonesia (Java), Singapore, Buenos Aires, Barcelona, and Madrid. Because of his sympathy with the Republican cause in the Spanish Civil War and his support of the Communist Party, he lost his position as consul in Madrid and traveled to Paris to edit with Nancy Cunard the magazine *The Poets of the World Defend the Spanish People.* In 1937, after founding the Spanish American Society to Aid Spain with César VALLEJO he returned to Chile and Buenos Aires. In 1939 he was named consul for Spanish emigration in Paris, and in 1940 he was appointed consul to Mexico. Following several short trips to Cuba (1942), The United States (1943), and Colombia (1943), Neruda's visit to Inca ruins in Peru in 1943 inspired one of his most celebrated poems, "The Heights of Machu Picchu" (1945). In 1949, as a Communist Party member since 1945 and a senator in the Chilean government, he was forced into exile by the GONZÁLEZ VIDELA regime. He returned to Chile in 1952, and continued to travel extensively while maintaining his base there. He had three homes, in Valparaíso, Santiago, and Isla Negra.

In 1971, the government of Salvador ALLENDE named Neruda ambassador to France. He returned to Chile in 1973, and died in Santiago, only twelve days after the Chilean army overthrew Allende's Popular Unity Government in a coup d'état supported by elements of the U.S. government and business community. Though Neruda had bitterly criticized U.S. involvement in Latin American affairs, in his poetry and prose he was deeply influenced by Walt Whitman in both the thought and form of his poetry, and he was a great admirer of Abraham Lincoln, who he believed represented the finest aspects of the American democratic tradition.

Neruda's first published work, *Crepusculario* (1920; Twilight Book), was written in the received aesthetics of Hispanic *modernismo* (not yet the vanguard aesthetic implied by the Anglo-American term "modernism"), but he moved immediately, in the most popular book of poems ever published in Spanish, *Veinte poemas de amor y una canción desesperación* (1924; *Twenty Love Poems and a Song of Despair,* 1969, 1976), to a more individual style that moved between elaborate structures and imagery, and free verse. Here his two lifelong obsessions, nature and sex, are clearly revealed. With the first two volumes of *Residencia en la tierra* (1933; *Residence on Earth,* 1935), he achieved international recognition. Written during the Spanish Civil War, Neruda's *España en el corazón* (1937; Spain in My Heart) demonstrated a profound commitment to political concerns.

Tercera residencia (1947; Third Residency), the third volume in the *Residencia en la tierra* series, and *Canto general* (1950; General Song) were his next important books. The latter, his longest and most ambitious work, is an attempt to write the epic, both historical and mythical, of Latin America from a Marxist perspective. In the 1950s his work underwent another notable change as he turned from the epic style to the ode to express joy in the simple things of life. His four volumes in this form include *Odas elementales* (1954; Elementary Odes), *Nuevas odas elementales* (1956; New Elementary Odes), *Tercer libro de odas* (1957; Third Book of Odes), and *Navegaciones y regresos* (1959; Voyages and Homecomings). This series demonstrates Neruda's tendency to write in cycles, as do the *Residencia* volumes and *Canto general.*

Neruda continued to publish new volumes of poetry with extraordinary regularity, producing during his last years a number of notable works, including *Estravagario* (1958; *Extravagaria,* 1974), a word coined by Neruda to suggest extravagant, even eccentric, poetic moves and modes: "Of all my books, *Estravagario* is not one that sings the most, but rather the one that skips about the best. . . . Because of its irreverence it is my most personal book." The work's impudence, eclecticism, and humor make it his most individualistic work.

Between *Estravagario* and his death in 1973 Neruda produced nineteen books. Eight volumes of posthumous verse and his prose memoirs were released in 1974. Some of these works are varied in subject (*La*

barcarola, 1967; *Las piedras del cielo,* 1970), others develop only one theme (*Arte de pájaros,* 1966, translated as *The Art of Birds,* 1985; *Las piedras de Chile,* 1961). Introspection is a dominant note in his later work, and his most ambitious work after *Estravagario* is the autobiographical *Memorial de Isla Negra* (1964; *Isla Negra: A Notebook,* 1981) whose five volumes, another cycle, constitute a long nostalgic look back at his life.

Neruda's final major work was his prose autobiography *Confieso que he vivido: Memorias* (I Confess That I Have Lived: Memoirs, translated as *Memoirs,* 1977) written in the last decade of his life and published posthumously in 1974. The twelve *cuadernos* (notebooks) that comprise the work essentially take the form of confessions united by the perennial passions of the poet's life: his love of women and nature, his interest in politics, his affection for simple things, his devotion to life. As in much of his later poetry, there is humor, nostalgia, and a constant introspection joined to a profound commitment to the world about him. In various ways, Neruda's life exemplifies many aspects of the historical, literary, and cultural process of the political left in Latin America in the twentieth century.

– KEITH MCDUFFIE

NERVO, AMADO

Amado Nervo (*b.* 27 August 1870; *d.* 24 May 1919), Mexican writer. Born in Tepic, Nayarit, Nervo excelled as a student at the Colegio de San Luis Gonzaga in Jacona, Michoacán. In 1886 he began seminary in Zamora, Michoacán, but soon abandoned this path in order to help support his family. He moved to Mexico City in 1894 where he launched his literary and journalistic career. Nervo began his literary career writing in a romantic style with naturalist tendencies, but he soon fell under the influence of the *modernista* movement at the turn of the century. In this vein, he coedited the important cultural journal *Revista Moderna* (Modern Review [1898–1911]) with Jesús Valenzuela. He traveled internationally as a journalist. He was an associate of the Nicaraguan *modernista* poet Rubén DARÍO in Paris. After 1905, Nervo worked as a member of the diplomatic service. Although extremely popular at the turn of the century, Nervo's poetry and narrative have been disparaged by subsequent generations because of its overly sentimental and anti-intellectual characteristics. Nervo's first novel, *El bachiller* (The Student, 1895), attracted much attention because of its sexual theme. In 1898 he published his first important collections of poetry, *Perlas negras* (Black Pearls) and *Místicas* (Mystical Poems). Although the Mexican Revolution interrupted diplomatic services in 1914 and left Nervo in a financially difficult position in Madrid, in 1918 the Mexican government recalled him from Spain and then sent him to Argentina and Uruguay on a diplomatic mission. He died in Montevideo.

– DANNY J. ANDERSON

NEVE, FELIPE DE

Felipe De Neve (*b.* 1728; *d.* 21 August 1784), Spanish governor of California. Born in Bailén, Spain, Neve entered military service as a cadet in 1744, subsequently serving in Cantabria, Flanders, Milan, and Portugal. He came to New Spain in 1764, and saw duty in Querétaro and Zacatecas as a captain; he was promoted to lieutenant colonel in 1774. Neve assumed the governorship of the Californias 4 March 1775 at Loreto, and on 3 February 1777 he moved to establish a separate government for Alta California at Monterey. He founded the civilian towns of San José (29 November 1777) and Los Angeles (4 September 1781). He launched an attack against the Yuma Indians after they had massacred the party of Fernando de RIVERA Y MONCADA at the Colorado River, 18 July 1781. In 1782 Neve was named inspector general of the Provincias Internas del Occidente, and commandant general in 1783. He died at the Hacienda Nuestra Señora del Carmen de Peña Blanca, Chihuahua.

– W. MICHAEL MATHES

NEVES, TANCREDO DE ALMEIDA

Tancredo de Almeida Neves (*b.* 4 March 1910; *d.* 21 April 1985), president-elect of Brazil (1985). Neves, the son of Francisco de Paula Neves and Antonina de Almeida Neves, was born in São João del Rei, Minas Gerais. In 1928, he moved to Belo Horizonte and enrolled in law school. He and his wife, Risoleta Tolentino Neves, had three children.

Having completed his studies, Neves returned to his hometown in 1932 and opened a law office. In that same year, the lawyer was appointed public prosecutor for the local judicial district, a post he held for one year. In 1934, Neves was elected city council member and acceded to the office of president of the municipal legislature.

Following the 1937 coup that mandated the closing of all legislative bodies, Neves lost his position on the city council and resumed practicing law. In 1947, however, his political career was launched anew when he was elected state deputy on the Social Democratic Party (PSD) ticket. As his political career advanced, the politician took a seat as a federal deputy in 1950 and served on the committee for transportation, communication,

and public works from 1951 to 1953. Neves, nevertheless, gave up his seat to head the ministry of justice for one year until 1954, at which time he reassumed his post as a federal deputy.

Supported by a center-labor coalition of the PSD-PTB, Neves won the governorship of Minas Gerais in 1960. The following year, Neves was appointed prime minister of Brazil by President João GOULART and held this post until 1962. The following year, the prime minister resumed his position as a federal deputy for the Social Democratic Party and was elected majority leader.

In the elections of 1966, Neves, now affiliated with the Brazilian Democratic Movement (MDB), was elected to Congress. He served for many years as both a federal deputy and senator of Minas Gerais. In 1982, he was elected vice president of the new centrist Brazilian Democratic Movement Party (PMDB) and in the same year once again became governor of Minas Gerais. A consummate politician with a unique ability to bring together factions from the Right and the Left, Neves, defying all odds, prevailed against the handpicked candidate of the military administration and in 1985 was declared president by the electoral college.

On the eve of taking office in March 1985, Neves became ill and underwent surgery. In view of his condition, the office of the presidency was assumed by his running mate José SARNEY. Neves underwent seven operations, but his respiratory and kidney functions deteriorated, causing his death.

– IÊDA SIQUEIRA WIARDA

NEZAHUALCOYOTL

Nezahualcoyotl (*b.* ca. 1402; *d.* 1472), ruler of Texcoco, Mexico (1431–1472). Nezahualcoyotl ("Fasting Coyote") ruled the Nahuatl-speaking Acolhua polity centered at Texcoco, on the eastern shore of the Valley of Mexico lake system. Though he is one of the most renowned pre-Conquest Mexican rulers, part of his fame undoubtedly results from post-Conquest revision. According to native histories, Nezahualcoyotl witnessed the assassination of his father, Ixtlilxochitl, in 1418, during a conflict between the Acolhuas and their Tepanec overlords. He fled to his mother's people, the Mexica royal dynasty at Tenochtitlán. In 1428 he became a key player in the alliance of Mexicas, Acolhuas, and rebellious Tepanecs that defeated the Tepanec ruler Maxtla. Installed by the Mexica in his father's place and with a Mexica princess as his principal wife, Nezahualcoyotl remained a junior partner in the Aztec Empire. He became a wise judge and lawgiver, a master builder, a poet, and a philosopher, while fathering over one hundred children by his forty wives. Claims that he was a monotheist and that he composed several Nahuatl songs recorded in the sixteenth century are probably unfounded. He was succeeded by his seven-year-old son, NEZAHUALPILLI; his line continued into the colonial period and included the historian Fernando de Alva Ixtlilxochitl (1578–1650).

— LOUISE M. BURKHART

NEZAHUALPILLI

Nezahualpilli (*b.* 1465; *d.* 1515), ruler of Texcoco, Mexico (1472–1515). Nezahualpilli ("Fasting Child" or "Fasting Noble") succeeded Nezahualcoyotl as ruler of Texcoco, one of three polities heading the Aztec Empire, which was dominated by the Mexica of Tenochtitlán. Son of a Mexica noblewoman, Nezahualpilli was seven years old when his father died, having designated him as heir. His right to the office protected by his

---

In a famous (though likely legendary) episode,

Nezahualpilli predicted to Motecuhzoma II that

Mexico would soon be ruled by foreigners.

Mexica relatives from jealous older brothers, Nezahualpilli matured into a capable statesman and lawmaker, master builder, and renowned diviner. In a famous (though likely legendary) episode, Nezahualpilli predicted to MOTECUHZOMA II that Mexico would soon be ruled by foreigners. Motecuhzoma's own diviners claimed otherwise. Nezahualpilli challenged Motecuhzoma to a series of ball games in order to settle the argument; Nezahualpilli won the match. He died without naming an heir. The ensuing dispute between his sons Cacama and Ixtlilxochitl left the polity divided. Motecuhzoma installed Cacama; a few years later Ixtlilxochitl became one of Cortés's principal allies.

— LOUISE M. BURKHART

NICUESA, DIEGO

Diego Nicuesa (*d.* ca. 1 March 1511), Spanish explorer. Born in Balza, Spain, and raised in the house of Don Enrique Enríquez, uncle of Ferdinand V, Nicuesa was appointed on 9 June 1509 as governor of the reportedly rich Veragua, or Castilla del Oro (between Cape Gracias a Dios, at the border of Nicaragua and Honduras, and the middle of the Gulf of Darién). He left Hispaniola in November 1509 with 700 men, but shipwreck and hunger quickly reduced their numbers. Nicuesa continued on foot from a river near Carreto, eventually estab-

lishing a small fort at Nombre de Dios. He departed upon learning that Martín Fernández de ENCISO had encroached on his territory to establish the colony of Santa María la Antigua de Darién. Initially welcomed by the colonists to settle a dispute between Enciso and Vasco Núñez de BALBOA, Nicuesa lost his popularity by ordering the surrender of all gold. He was forced to leave for Santo Domingo on an unseaworthy vessel on 1 March 1511, the last time he was seen.

— PHILIPPE L. SEILER

NIEMEYER SOARES FILHO, OSCAR

Oscar Niemeyer Soares Filho (*b.* 15 December 1907), Brazilian architect. Niemeyer was born in Rio de Janeiro and attended the National School of Fine Arts there from 1930 to 1934. He began to work with Lucio COSTA and Carlos Leão, leaders of the modern movement in Brazilian architecture, in 1934. From 1937 to 1943, he collaborated with and ultimately succeeded Costa as head of the design team for the Ministry of Education and Health building in Rio, which brought Niemeyer into contact with Le Corbusier, the Swissborn French architect who consulted on the design. The raised peristyle design of the building infuses many of the characteristic Corbusian elements (rooftop garden, sun roof, and inverted roof) with Brazilian baroque expression.

In the late 1930s, Niemeyer once again worked with Costa. The Brazilian Pavilion for the 1939 New York World's Fair catapulted Costa, Niemeyer, and the whole Brazilian movement into the world spotlight. A fluid plan centers around an exotic garden layout, the work of the painter Roberto BURLE MARX. In 1947, Niemeyer was asked to represent Brazil on a commission in the planning of the United Nations buildings in New York City. In the 1940s, the architect Walter Gropius named Niemeyer the "bird of paradise" of the architectural world.

Niemeyer's first major solo project was the plan for a group of buildings in Pampulha, a new suburb in Belo Horizonte, the capital of the state of Minas Gerais. The project was commissioned in 1941 by Juscelino KUBITSCHEK de Oliveira (1902–1976), then mayor of Belo Horizonte and later president of Brazil (1956–1961). It incorporates the use of free forms, the interplay of light and shade, painting, and sculpture into the architectural formula. The complex includes the Casino, which some have called Niemeyer's masterwork. It is a "narrative" building with ramps, elliptical corridors, promenades, and labyrinthine accessways to direct the flow, while colorful stones, glass, and textures paint the mood. The building has served as an art museum since the inter-

Oscar Niemeyer Soares Filho. (Organization of American States)

diction on gambling. The other buildings in the Niemeyer group are a circular restaurant with a sun roof, the Yacht Club with an inverted slope roof, and the São Francisco de Assis Chapel adorned with parabolic shells.

Niemeyer's 1955 design for the Museum of Modern Art in Caracas serves as an aesthetic watershed in his career. Borrowing design elements and forms, such as pyramidal shapes, reminiscent of neoclassicism, he distances himself somewhat from the informal functional focus of his earlier free-form designs. To the detriment of function and social need, this tendency is reiterated and extended further in the free-form modernism of the new capital city, Brasília, the plans for which were initiated following the election of Kubitschek to the presidency in 1956. Niemeyer served as chief architect for Novacap, the government building authority, between 1956 and 1961. Responsible for designing the public buildings, Niemeyer helped fulfill Lucio Costa's master plans for the new city. Between 1958 and 1961, he designed the president's residence of Alvorada Palace, the Supreme Court building, the Presidential Chapel, the Three Towers Square, the National Theater, a group of buildings for the University of Brasília, the Arches Palace, and the Ministry of Justice.

Niemeyer returned to private practice in 1961 and has since engaged in civic, commercial, and governmental projects, on large and small scales. In the mid-1960s, he designed urban redevelopment plans for Grasse, France, the Algarve in Portugal, and Algiers. In 1966 he designed the French Communist Party headquarters in Paris. He returned to Brazil in 1968 to lecture at the University of Rio de Janeiro. While there, he designed Satetyles, a telecommunications complex in Rio, Cuiabá University in Mato Grosso, and the Ministry of Defense in Brasília. In the 1970s and 1980s, he designed the Hotel Nacional in Rio, the cathedral in Brasília, numerous office buildings in Brazil and in France, the Anthropological Museum in Belo Horizonte, a zoo in Algiers, a samba stadium, sixty schools in the state of Rio de Janeiro, and a project for a convention center in Abu Dhabi in the United Arab Emirates.

Niemeyer has always lived in Rio de Janeiro, except for international commissions that take him abroad. Niemeyer resides in an apartment overlooking Copacabana. The house he designed in São Conrado, a suburb of Rio, has been named a city landmark. There are plans to redesign it as a museum for his work. More recently he designed a theater in São Paulo, an annex to the Supreme Court in Brasília, and a theater complex for the state of São Paulo. He plans to design a music school in France.

Beyond his architectural planning and teaching, Niemeyer was the founder of the magazine *Modulo* in the 1950s. He has also received many international awards. They include the Lenin Peace Prize in 1963, the Benito Juárez Award for the Mexican Revolution Centennial in 1964, the Medal of the Polish Architectural Association in 1967, a gold medal from the American Institute of Architects in 1970, and a gold medal from the Parisian Académie d'Architecture in 1982. In 1988 he split the Pritzker Architecture Prize with Gordon Bunshaft of Skidmore, Owings, and Merrill.

His membership affiliations include honorary member of the American Academy of Arts and Sciences, Legion of Honor officer, commander of the Ordre des Arts et Lettres, honorary member of the Academy of Arts of the USSR, member of the European Academy of Arts, Sciences, and Humanities, and member of the Comitate Internazionale dei Garanti.

— CAREN A. MEGHREBLIAN

NIMUENDAJÚ, CURT

Curt Nimuendajú (*b.* 17 April 1883); *d.* 10 December 1945), German-born immigrant who devoted his life to the study and defense of Brazil's indigenous peoples.

Though not formally trained as an anthropologist, Nimuendajú is recognized for his prolific contributions to Brazilian ethnology and for his ability to immerse himself in indigenous cultures. Born Curt Unkel, he came to Brazil in 1903 at the age of twenty. Two years later he took up residence with the Apopocuva Guaraní, among whom he lived as an adopted member until 1908 and from whom he acquired the name Nimuendajú. His first significant ethnological publication (1914), dealing with Guaraní religion, resulted from these years.

Throughout his life, Nimuendajú lived among and visited numerous Brazilian indigenous groups. He received financing from foreign institutions such as the University of California at Berkeley and the Carnegie Institute through his collaboration with the American anthropologist Robert Lowie and from European museums for artifact collection. His collaboration with Lowie, initiated in the early 1930s, stimulated a period of intensive study of social organization among Gê groups and produced several scholarly publications, among them three monographs (*The Eastern Timbira; The Apinayé; The Šerente*). He was also occasionally employed by the Indian Protection Service (SPI) where he left copious ethnographic documentation in field reports, and for whom, from 1921 to 1923, he led the team that established peaceful contact with the Parintintin of the Madeira River. In his later years, he received support from the Museu Goeldia (Belém) and the Museu Nacional (Rio de Janeiro). In Belém, a year before his death, Nimuendajú completed his monumental *Ethnohistorical Map of Brazil and Adjacent Regions* and the accompanying *Guide*. He died among the Tukuna Indians of the Solimões River.

— LAURA GRAHAM

NIÑO, PEDRO ALONSO

Pedro Alonso Niño (*b.* late fifteenth century; *d.* early sixteenth century), Spanish explorer. A native of Moguer, Spain, Niño acted as pilot of the Santa María during the first voyage of Christopher COLUMBUS. In 1499 Niño and Christopher Guerra received permission from Bishop Juan RODRÍGUEZ DE FONSECA to explore the Gulf of Paria. On the island of Margarita they bartered for a considerable quantity of pearls and then made their way to the Cubagua Islands, which they believed to be part of Tierra Firme. There they traded for a substantial amount of pearls and returned to Spain in April 1500 only to be imprisoned for allegedly concealing part of the wealth they had acquired in the New World. Niño was exonerated of all charges, was set free,

and gained fame for participating in one of the most lucrative voyages to the New World.

— MICHAEL POLUSHIN

NIZA, MARCOS DE

Marcos de Niza (*d.* 25 March 1558), Franciscan explorer and chronicler who searched for the Seven Cities of Cíbola. From the French Franciscan province of Aquitaine, Niza arrived in the Americas by 1531, serving in Peru and Guatemala before going to New Spain. In 1539, following his guide, ESTEBAN, Niza traveled north from San Miguel de Culiacán in Sinaloa as far as Arizona and New Mexico, perhaps to within sight of the Zuni pueblo of Hawikuh. His *Relación del descubrimiento de las siete ciudades* (Report of the Discovery of the Seven Cities) told of seven magnificent cities on the order of Mexico City and Cuzco and of vast quantities of gold and turquoise. The account was influential in kindling interest in the exploratory expedition undertaken by Francisco Vázquez de CORONADO in 1540. Though serving as minister provincial in Mexico City, Niza accompanied Coronado, but when his claims about Cíbola proved false, he returned to New Spain. Ill and depressed, Niza completed his term as minister provincial, which concluded in 1543, at San Francisco de México. For the next few years he spent time in Jalapa, Xochimilco, and Mexico City, where he died and was buried.

— RICK HENDRICKS

NOBOA Y ARTETA, DIEGO

Diego Noboa y Arteta (also Novoa; *b.* 15 October 1789; *d.* 3 November 1870), president of Ecuador (1850–1851). A wealthy Guayaquil-born merchant and landowner, Noboa joined the governing Liberal triumvirate after the 6 March 1845 overthrow of President Juan José FLORES. He was a candidate in the 1850 presidential election, which ended in a deadlock, with support in Congress evenly divided between Noboa and General Antonio de Elizade. When Vice President Manuel de Ascásubi assumed authority, Noboa's ally General José María URBINA led a revolt that placed Noboa in power. In 1851 Congress ratified the coup. Largely ineffectual during his brief tenure in office, Noboa is chiefly remembered for allowing the Jesuits to return to Ecuador. In July 1851 his erstwhile friend Urbina (president, 1851–1856) staged a coup, sending Noboa into exile in Costa Rica. He died in Guayaquil.

— RONN F. PINEO

NOBRE, MARLOS

Marlos Nobre (*b.* 18 February 1939), Brazilian composer, conductor, and pianist. At the age of five, Nobre began his musical studies in the Pernambuco Conservatory in Recife and graduated in piano and theory in 1955. For his piano work *Nazarethiana,* he won an award and a scholarship for study in Teresópolis in the state of Rio de Janeiro, where he studied composition with Hans Joachim KOELLREUTTER. Subsequent studies with Camargo GUARNIERI, Alberto GINASTERA, and Aaron Copland proved decisive in the development of his compositional style.

In 1962 Marlos Nobre established residence in Rio de Janeiro, where for several years he was director of the Radio Ministério Educação e Cultura, whose broadcasts showcased the works of Brazilian composers, including his own. Nobre's work with various major musical organizations within Brazil and in Europe has made him one of the best-known contemporary Brazilian musicians. His most significant major commissioned work is *Cantata del Chimborazo,* written for the celebration of the bicentennial of the birth of Simón Bolívar. Works such as *Rhythmetron* and *Ukrinmakrinkrin* have demonstrated enormous rhythmic vitality and a powerful creative imagination. In 1992 he led the Royal Philharmonic in the premiere of his *Columbus* oratorio, commemorating the quincentennial of the discovery voyage.

— DAVID P. APPLEBY

NÓBREGA, MANUEL DA

Manuel da Nóbrega (*b.* 18 October 1517; *d.* 18 October 1570), Jesuit missionary. Manuel da Nóbrega was the leader of the first Jesuit mission to Brazil in 1549. Born in Minho in 1517 to a noble Portuguese family, he joined the Society of Jesus in 1544, after being educated at the universities of Salamanca and Coimbra. He spent more than twenty years in Brazil, dedicating his life to founding missions among the Indians and schools for the children of the white population.

Arriving in Brazil on the fleet carrying the first governor, Nóbrega headed a group of six Jesuit missionaries. He concentrated on learning the Indian languages and gathering small tribes into segregated missions, or *aldeias,* where they were converted and protected from enslavement. In 1553 Nóbrega was selected as the first provincial general of the Jesuits in Brazil. In 1554, in the captaincy of São Vicente, Nóbrega helped to found a mission and *colégio* near the village of Piratininga, modern São Paulo.

Nóbrega's greatest accomplishment was the founding of local schools, missions, and the College of São Paulo. In 1560, after Nóbrega was relieved of his duties as provincial general, he helped the Portuguese regain control of Rio de Janeiro by securing valuable Indian allies to expel the French pirates from Guanabara Bay. In 1567, in the newly established city of Rio de Janeiro, he founded another Jesuit *colégio* to educate the sons of Indian chiefs and white settlers. Nóbrega served as rector of the *colégio* until his death.

Nóbrega concentrated on gathering small tribes into segregated missions, or aldeias, *where they were converted and protected from enslavement.*

Nóbrega's letters and his two works, *Informação das Terras do Brasil* (Information about Brazil [1550]) and *Diálogo sobre a Converso do Gentio* (Dialogue about the Conversion of the Heathen [1556])—the first true literary works on Brazil—give glowing descriptions of the natural beauty of the New World, the "simplicity" of the Indians, and their "receptivity" to Christianity. As the first superior of the Jesuits in Brazil, he supervised the missionary activities in the south of Brazil and throughout the colony. A good diplomat and politician as well as an organizer of missions and schools, he left colonial Brazil a rich legacy.

— PATRICIA MULVEY

NOÉ, LUIS FELIPE

Luis Felipe Noé (*b.* 26 May 1933), Argentine artist. Born in Buenos Aires, Noé studied with Horacio Butler. Preoccupied with the chaotic modern world, Noé expressed his concerns by making figure and background hardly distinguishable from each other by using gestural brushstrokes, accidental painting, collage, and fragmented canvases. He was a cofounder of the New Figuration group in 1961, the same year that he painted his *Federal Series,* which includes *Agonic Image of Dorrego* and *General Quiroga Travels to His Death,* a depiction of the anarchy that characterized the Federal period in Argentine history. In these paintings he used primarily black and red to convey a climate of passion and death.

In 1964 Noé moved to New York City, where he had a Guggenheim Fellowship (1965–1966). During this period he wrote *Antiestética* (Antiesthetic), in which he argued that artists must focus on the act of creation rather than on traditional composition and techniques. At this time he began to experiment with concave mirrors to create chaotic environments but abandoned art in 1968 and devoted his time to teaching and organizing public painting experiences. In 1971 he published *Una sociedad colonial avanzada* (An Advanced Colonial Society), a satirical view of Argentina and Latin America. He resumed painting in 1975 with *Nature and Myths* and *Conquest and Destruction of Nature,* two series of colorful natural landscapes populated by mythical creatures in a state of metamorphosis. In 1976 he moved to Paris, where he lived until 1986, exhibiting frequently in Buenos Aires. After he made a trip to the Amazon in 1980, nature prevailed over mythical references in his work.

— MARTA GARSD

NORD, PIERRE ALEXIS

Pierre Alexis Nord (*b.* 1820; *d.* 1 May 1910), president of Haiti (1902–1908). Nord came to power after the abdication of Simon SAM and the subsequent civil war between forces led by Nord and those led by Antenor Firmin. After the victory of Nord's forces, he became president in December 1902. Nord's introduction of reforms such as punishment of looters of the national treasury made him unpopular.

In March 1908 an uprising resulted in almost fifty deaths. The government responded with a reign of terror. Four nations sent warships to Port-au-Prince to protect their citizens. In November 1908, Nord ordered General Antoine Simon, commander of the army in the south, to come to the capital to confer on the political situation. Instead Simon led a revolt, taking possession of Port-au-Prince on 2 December. Nord fled to Jamaica, where he died. Simon succeeded him as president (1908–1911).

— DARIÉN DAVIS

NORIEGA MORENO, MANUEL ANTONIO

Manuel Antonio Noriega Moreno (*b.* 11 February 1936), commander in chief of the Panamanian National Guard (1983–1989) and a highly controversial figure of the late twentieth century.

A street-wise native of a poor Panama City neighborhood, he attended public school, graduating in 1955 near the top of his class. He then attended the Peruvian Military Academy, graduating in 1962, the same year he became a National Guard Officer. He completed his education in 1967 at the U.S. School of the Americas in Panama, where he received counterintelligence training. An associate of fellow officer Omar TORRIJOS HERRERA, Noriega was instrumental in suppressing a December 1969 coup attempt, thereby enabling Tor-

rijos to return from Mexico to put down the revolt. As a reward, Torrijos promoted Noriega several ranks to lieutenant colonel and placed him in command of the guard's Intelligence Division G2.

Torrijos's death in an airplane crash on 31 July 1981 provided Noriega his opportunity. A participant in the 1983 coup that removed Colonel Rubén DARÍO PAREDES, Noriega signed an agreement with several colonels, each of who would resign at specified times, thus rotating the guard command among them. Professing loyalty to the revolution of General Torrijos, he continued projects benefiting urban labor and rural peasants and promoted their integration into the political system.

After becoming guard commander on 12 August 1983, Noriega established complete control of the nation. Concentrating power in his own hands and using tactics of intimidation perfected during his days as intelligence chief, he ruthlessly eliminated rivals, installed presidents at will, and rigged the 1983 election. He used the National Assembly to impeach a president who dared suggest his removal in 1988, appointed and dismissed several provisional presidents, and finally annulled the elections of 1989.

It is evident that during his career Noriega served as an intelligence operative for a number of causes, though specifics are hard to obtain. He was a paid informant of the U.S. Central Intelligence Agency for many years, apparently beginning as early as his days as a cadet in Peru. After involvement in the transit of arms from Cuba to the Sandinista rebels in Nicaragua, at one point Noriega aided U.S. arms shipments to their enemies, the Contras, although he later reversed himself and prevented further arms shipments through Panama. He provided intelligence to both Israel and Cuba in return for training his personal bodyguards. He was accused

Manuel Noriega saluting supporters, 10 April 1989. (Bettmann Archive)

of working with the Medellín drug cartel, allegedly facilitating international drug smuggling and money transfer and laundering through Panama. A U.S. grand jury in Miami indicted him on narcotics charges, and he was convicted in 1992.

The combination of Noriega's annulment of the 1989 elections (an act condemned by the Organization of American States [OAS]), the drug indictment, and his support of the Sandinistas in Nicaragua led to a break with Washington. In support of deposed president Eric Arturo Delvalle, the United States initiated a financial and economic boycott, while Noriega engaged in intimidating U.S. military personnel in Panama. After the failure of several attempted coups in Panama, the United States intervened militarily on 20 December 1989. Noriega took refuge in the Papal Nunciate, later surrendering to U.S. troops on 3 January 1990 to be taken to Miami for trial on the narcotics indictment. He was convicted in 1992 and sentenced to 40 years in prison. The United States then installed a new government, headed by Guillermo Endara.

– KENNETH J. GRIEB

NORONHA, FERNÃO DE

Fernão de Noronha (*b.* ca. 1460; *d.* after 1505), a Portuguese nobleman of Jewish descent who held the first royal concession to develop trade with Brazilian Indians. A wealthy merchant, he was an important investor in Portugal's far-flung empire, operating outlets in Africa, India, and Belgium. In 1502, he headed a group of financiers who leased a three-year monopoly contract to exploit Brazil. The consortium sponsored at least two voyages to Brazil, the second of which built the first European settlement there. The fortified trading post (*feitoria*) was located on an island near Cabo Frio; stories of the island's inhabitants are said to have inspired Thomas More's *Utopia*. The venture also inspired Portuguese Jews, then suffering from persecution, to envision the establishment of a safe haven in the Brazilian northeast. In 1504, Noronha was made captain of the coastal islands near Natal, which were later named for him. Although his contract expired in 1505, the trade in brazilwood, Indian slaves, and exotic animals was profitable enough to entice his continued investment.

– CLIFF WELCH

NOVÁS CALVO, LINO

Lino Novás Calvo (*b.* 22 September 1905; *d.* 24 March 1983), Cuban short story writer, novelist, translator, and essayist. Born in Spain, Novás Calvo emigrated to Cuba as a young boy and lived there until 1980, when he moved to the United States. His works often reflect the plight of people trapped by events beyond their control. In spite of their usual regional setting, his works ascend always to a universal level because of his themes of the basic loneliness of the individual and the uncertainties of human life. His narratives, while usually written in the first person and characterized by colloquial language, nonetheless avoid narrow regionalism. His best known novel is *El negrero* (1933; The Slave Trader). However, it is his short stories, collected mainly in *La luna nona y otros cuentos* (1942; The Ninth Moon and Other Stories), *Cayo Canas* (1946; Palm Key), and *Maneras de contar* (1970; Narrative Manners), that place him among the great writers of Latin America. They are characterized by magical realism, a deceptively simple narrative style, varied perspective, and unexpected developments and imagery.

– OTTO OLIVERA

NOVO, SALVADOR

Salvador Novo (*b.* 30 July 1904; *d.* 13 January 1974), Mexican writer. Born in México City, Salvador Novo was one of the first Mexican authors to demonstrate that a Mexican writer could earn a living by the pen. Novo entered the world of letters as a poet at a time when artists supported themselves by means of government appointments as teachers or bureaucrats. He led the way in breaking this dependence on the government when he became a professional essayist and editoral writer, as well as a playwright/director. Throughout most of his writing career his journalistic fee was "cinco centavos la palabra." He estimated that by the time he was fifty he had earned 425,250 pesos at this rate. He is known today primarily for his theater direction and for the incisive wit of his several plays, as well as for his autobiographical travel books and his essays.

With characteristic self-mockery, Novo described his youthful artistic posture as that of "an old, world-weary author whose writings deliberately betrayed the youth of the penman." He contrasted this with the creative stance he assumed during his middle years which he described as "a youthfulness only half-trying to disguise the venerable mind of the penman."

Along with Xavier VILLAURRUTÍA and Rodolfo USIGLI, Salvador Novo is one of the pillars of contemporary Mexican theater. His first work for the stage was *El Tercer Fausto* (1934, French; 1956, Spanish), and his best-known plays include *La culta dama* (1951), *Yocasta, o casi* (1961), and *La guerra de las gordas* (1963). He also wrote a collection of dialogues and short plays. Novo directed well over fifty stage productions and even wrote a text on acting, *Diez lecciones de técnica de ac-*

tuación (1951). Novo's best-known works of poetry are *XX poemas* (1925) and *Nuevo amor* (1933); his travel book is *Return Ticket* (1928). His critical writings have been collected in several anthologies.

— WILLIAM I. OLIVER

NUFIO, JOSÉ DOLORES

José Dolores Nufio, one of the principal leaders of the 1848 *montaña* revolt of the Lucíos in Guatemala. As military commander of Chiquimula, Nufio's defection to the liberals at the end of July 1848 was important in bringing about CARRERA's resignation on 15 August. Nufio promised to place his forces under the orders of the new assembly but separated himself from Guatemalan authority until that body covened, allying himself with rebels in Los Altos. Nufio then seized Izabal, where his control of the port and customs house made Carrera's position untenable.

Nufio's "National Army" raided and attacked Guatemala from sanctuaries in El Salvador and Honduras through 1850.

Following Carrera's departure, however, the liberal assembly failed to meet the demands of Nufio and other rebel commanders, who in turn refused to submit to the new government and continued the revolt. This division among the liberals helped Carrera eventually to return in 1849. In collaboration with José Francisco BARRUNDIA, Gerardo BARRIOS, and Trinidad CABAÑAS, Nufio joined forces with liberals in Los Altos, El Salvador, and Honduras. His "National Army" raided and attacked Guatemala from sanctuaries in El Salvador and Honduras through 1850. These activities eventually led to a showdown at San José la Arada, Guatemala, on 2 February 1851, where Carrera dealt the liberal allies a stunning defeat, thus assuring the security of conservative rule in Guatemala.

— RALPH LEE WOODWARD, JR.

NÚÑEZ MOLEDO, RAFAEL

Rafael Núñez Moledo (*b.* 28 September 1825; *d.* 18 September 1894), president of Colombia (1880–1882, 1884–1886, 1887, 1888). As the dominant political leader of Colombia from 1880 until his death in 1894, Rafael Núñez left a major imprint on his nation's history by bringing to a close a period of Liberal hegemony, inaugurating an era of Conservative rule lasting until 1930, and imposing the Constitution of 1886 (which remained in force until 1991). A native of Cartagena, Núñez received a law degree in the mid-1840s from the University of Cartagena. He remains an intriguing figure in Colombian history because of his apparent betrayal of a lifelong devotion to liberalism, his impressive intellect, his voluminous writings, including *Ensayos de crítica social* (Rouen, 1874) and *La reforma política en Colombia* (Bogotá, 1945–1950), and a private life that left him vulnerable to political attack.

The Liberal and Conservative parties had achieved clear definition by mid-century, and after a turbulent decade marked by liberal reform, dictatorship, and intermittent civil war, Liberals gained control of the government and held it from 1863 to 1885, a period characterized by extreme federalism, severe limitations on the church, free trade, and provisions for wide-ranging individual freedom. During this period there was also a division in Liberal ranks that deepened in 1875, when Núñez returned to his homeland after twelve years in the United States and Europe, where he served as Colombian consul and as a writer for Latin American newspapers. He launched an unsuccessful bid for the presidency as a Liberal representing the interests of the coastal region against the incumbent Liberals of the interior.

Upon his election as president in 1880, Núñez, concerned over a weakening federal system, civil turmoil, and a worsening economy, began moving against key elements of the Liberal program and calling for constitutional reform. Following his election again in 1884, Núñez, faced with rebellion by the bulk of the Liberal Party, summoned Conservatives to the aid of his administration, the Regeneration. Following the success of Núñez and his adherents in the war of 1884–1885, Núñez presided over implementation of the unitary Constitution of 1886, restoration of government protection of the church, and the undoing of the Liberal program.

— JAMES WILLIAM PARK

NÚÑEZ VARGAS, BENJAMIN

Benjamin Núñez Vargas (*b.* 1915), Catholic priest, sociologist, labor organizer, cabinet minister, diplomat, educator.

Father Benjamin Núñez Vargas entered public life as a protégé of Archbishop Víctor M. SANABRIA MARTÍNEZ, who had both encouraged and facilitated his sociological studies in the United States, first at Niagara University and then at the Catholic University in Washington, D.C. At Sanabria's request Núñez returned to Costa Rica to form the labor union federation Rerum

Novarum, named for Pope Leo XIII's encyclical that dealt with social problems, an activity that placed him in direct competition with the existing communist-oriented unions.

Núñez's social concern and activism propelled him into political action. His early commitment to the National Liberation Movement and the 1948 revolution catapulted him into political leadership, where he remained for over thirty years. He served as labor minister in the revolutionary junta (1948–1949). He took part in the formation of the National Liberation Party (PLN), which quickly became the dominant force in Costa Rican politics. He served in many party and national capacities, including ambassador to Israel and to the United Nations, as well as representative to UNESCO.

His special concern for the development of new leaders inspired a career in education that included a distinguished position as a professor at the University of Costa Rica, appointment as the first rector of the National University, and his establishment of a political training institute in San Isidro de Coronado for rising Latin American democratic leaders. Throughout his career he has been a confidant of all PLN presidents from José FIGUERES FERRER through Oscar ARIAS SÁNCHEZ.

– JOHN PATRICK BELL

NÚÑEZ VELA, BLASCO

Blasco Núñez Vela (*d.* 18 January 1546), ill-fated first viceroy of Peru. From Ávila de los Caballeros, Núñez Vela had served as *veedor general de las guardias de Castilla* before his appointment as first viceroy of Peru. A large fifty-ship fleet carrying the viceroy and justices (*oidores*) of the first Royal Audiencia of Lima sailed from Sanlúcar on 3 November 1543 and reached Nombre de Dios, on Panama's coast, on 10 January 1544. Entrusted with the application of the famous New Laws of 1542 for the protection of the Indians, the newly appointed viceroy quickly set out to enforce the legislation to the letter, in spite of vocal opposition from settlers. He freed Indian slaves in Panama, and on 24 January headed for Peru, arriving relatively quickly at Tumbes on 4 March 1544. From there he marched overland toward Lima.

Encomenderos and previous royal officials began to grow wary of Núñez Vela's seemingly intransigent character. He announced a full *residencia* (official inquiry) to examine the tenure of Governor Cristóbal VACA DE CASTRO. In Piura he ordered the *tambos,* the old way stations manned by natives, closed. In Trujillo he removed Indians from some *encomenderos* and mandated that natives could not be used to transport Europeans.

As he entered Lima, the royal factor, Illan Suárez de Carbajal, asked the viceroy to respect city rights. Tension rose between the viceroy and other officials. The viceroy ignored and insulted his chief advisers, the *oidores*. Meanwhile Gonzalo PIZARRO, the Peruvian rebel leader who had been proclaimed governor by the Audiencia in Lima, slowly moved toward the city, his ranks swelling with disaffected settlers. The turning point came when the viceroy, in a fit of anger, assassinated Suárez de Carbajal. The *oidores* decided that by this act the viceroy had threatened the stability of royal government in Peru, and they imprisoned him on 18 September 1544. They asked the crown for review of the New Laws and a trial for Núñez Vela, whom they planned to return to Spain to face charges before the Council of the Indies.

He was imprisoned for a time on an island off Lima, before his opponents shipped him to Panama. During the voyage north, however, the crafty viceroy convinced the ship's captain to land him at Tumbes, where he began to collect men and weapons to retake the viceroyalty. Hoping to engage quickly and defeat the still weak and disorganized Núñez Vela, Gonzalo Pizarro set out from Lima in March 1545. The viceroy retreated northward as far as Pasto, in modern Colombia, trying to unite with Sebastián de BELALCÁZAR, an old Pizarro enemy. A final engagement of rebel and royalist forces took place not far from Quito, in Ecuador. The viceroy was finally defeated and killed by the rebels at the battle of Añaquito on 18 January 1546.

– NOBLE DAVID COOK

NUSDORFFER, BERNARDO

Bernardo Nusdorffer (*b.* 17 August 1686; *d.* 18 March 1762), German missionary and writer. Nusdorffer, one of several non-Spanish Jesuits who worked as a missionary (in the Paraguay reductions), was born in Plattling, Bavaria, and entered the Jesuit order in 1704. He arrived with eight other German missionaries in the Río de la Plata in 1717 and spent most of his life in Paraguay as a missionary among the Indians. From 1732 to 1739 he was in charge of all of the Jesuit Guaraní reductions. In 1745, when he was the superior of the reduction of San Nicolás de Loreto, he wrote about the effects of alcohol among the Pampas Indians. He thought that its easy availability was leading to their destruction as a people. In 1747, again the provincial superior of the reductions, he wrote a lengthy account of the effects of the Treaty of Limits (1750), which transferred seven Guaraní missions to the Portuguese. In his *Relación de todo lo sucedido en estas Doctrinas en orden a las mudanzas de los Siete Pueblos* (1750–1756), Nusdorffer wrote that after receiving the order of transfer, he immediately took steps to find other land for the thousands of Indians who were being moved from their towns. Among Nusdorffer's writings are accounts of theatrical productions in Jesuit colleges of Paraguay, descriptions of the Indians within and outside the reductions of Paraguay, and several reports of the proceedings surrounding the opposition of the Indian towns to their forced evacuation. He died in San Carlos reduction in 1762.

— NICHOLAS P. CUSHNER

O, GENOVEVO DE LA

Genovevo de la O (*b.* 3 January 1876; *d.* 12 June 1952), Mexican revolutionary. The leader, in 1910, of an autonomous rebellion in the northwestern corner of the state of Morelos, de la O joined the movement of Emiliano ZAPATA shortly after the promulgation of the Plan of Ayala in 1911. He soon became one of Zapata's fiercest fighters and most important generals. Because he frequently struck north to the mountainous fringes of Mexico City, de la O was one of the Zapatistas most feared in the capital. In particular, he developed a reputation as a destroyer of trains. After the revolution he pursued a more conventional military career before retiring to his farm in 1941.

— SAMUEL BRUNK

OBALDÍA, MARÍA OLIMPIA DE

María Olimpia de Obaldía (*b.* 9 September 1891; *d.* 15 August 1985), Panamanian poet. Obaldía was born in Dolega, Panama. She completed her high school studies in a small school in the city of David. In 1913 she was awarded a teaching certificate by the Normal de Institutoras, and shortly after, was appointed to teach in Dolega by the mayor of the city. She returned in 1915 to her alma mater to occupy the position of superintendent, remaining in this post until 1917.

With the appearance of her first book of poems, *Orquídeas* (*Orchids*) (1926), and with the publication three years later of *Brevario Lírico* (*Lyrical Breviary*), she attained recognition and a distinguished place in Panamanian letters as a representative poet of the postmodernist movement. Her greatest contribution to Panamanian letters is not only the development of the theme of conjugal, maternal, fraternal, and filial love in Panamanian literature, but also the creation of a new space for the feminine voice in Panamanian poetry. The universality of her poetic message is another one of her major contributions to Latin American literature.

Obaldía was a distinguished member of the Panamanian Academy of the Spanish Language and a delegate at international conferences. Her works have appeared in anthologies published in Latin America and abroad.

— ELBA D. BIRMINGHAM-POKORNY

OBANDO, JOSÉ MARÍA

José María Obando (*b.* 8 August 1795; *d.* 29 April 1861), acting president (23 November 1831–10 March 1832) and president of Colombia (1853–1854). The illegitimate son of a member of an elite Popayán family, Obando was adopted by members of the Pasto gentry but educated in Popayán. He was a royalist guerrilla officer (1819–1822) in the Pasto-Popayán region, forming networks of personal friendship through his charismatic personality. In 1822, he joined the patriots as a lieutenant colonel and eventually emerged as the caudillo of southern Colombia. Obando led populist rebellions in 1828, 1831, and 1840–1842 (the latter War of the Supremes), then fled into exile in Peru and Chile (1842–1849). General Tomás Cipriano de MOSQUERA attempted, unsuccessfully, to extradite him. Obando, a hero to Colombia's Liberals, was elected president in 1853. Caught between their doctrinaire agenda and his own populist sympathies, and hamstrung by the Constitution of 1853, his presidency foundered. When, in April 1854, General José María MELO rebelled, Obando remained passive. He was removed from office by the Senate on 4 April 1855 and returned to Popayán. He joined his former enemy, Mosquera, in the Revolution of 1859–1861. He died in an ambush near Bogotá.

— J. LEÓN HELGUERA

OBANDO Y BRAVO, MIGUEL

Miguel Obando y Bravo (*b.* 2 February 1926), archbishop of Managua, Nicaragua from 1970. A member of the Salesian religious congregation, Obando was consecrated auxiliary bishop of Matagalpa in 1968 and became archbishop of Managua in 1970. In 1985 he was named a cardinal, a decision that many considered an effort to strengthen Obando's hand against the Sandinista revolutionary government.

During the 1970s Obando and other bishops criticized the SOMOZA dictatorship, but the National Guard's dubbing him "comandante Miguel" was not accurate; he was more aligned with the oligarchy's opposition to Somoza than with the Sandinistas' revolutionary struggle. During hostage-taking actions by the Sandinistas in 1974 and in 1978, Obando served as mediator between the Sandinistas and the government.

He continued this role in the late 1980s as mediator between the Sandinista government and the U.S.-supported contras, and in the early 1990s as verifier of the peace accords between the Violeta BARRIOS DE CHAMORRO government and groups that were continuing paramilitary activity.

During Obando's tenure as archbishop there have been bitter conflicts within the church: many Christian base communities, which supported the Sandinista revolutionary government as a means toward greater justice for the poor, identified Obando as a support of the violent counterrevolution. His supporters consider him a champion of freedom.

– JOSEPH E. MULLIGAN

OBIN, PHILOMÉ

Philomé Obin (*b.* 1892; *d.* 1985), Haitian painter. Obin was the head of an extensive family of artists in Haiti whose brothers Othan and Senêque and their children continue the tradition. Obin founded the school of northern realists in Haiti and is linked stylistically and thematically with the naïfs movement. His bright colors, voodo-inspired scenes, and tropical lighting share much with the later works of Wilson Bigaud. Obin became a Mason in 1918 and subsequently abandoned Catholicism for the Baptist church. He considered himself to be both a historian and an artist, because many of his best works deal with historical events and people: the revolutionary epoch, King Christophe, and the building of the Citadelle. Obin's masterpiece is *The Funeral of Charlemagne Péralte* (1947).

– KAREN RACINE

OBREGÓN, ALEJANDRO

Alejandro Obregón (*b.* 4 June 1920; *d.* 11 April 1992), Colombian artist. Born in Barcelona, Spain, Obregón always considered himself self-taught although he studied art in England, the United States, and France. His career was difficult at its inception because of his inability to master pictorial techniques. In 1943 he had his first solo show and launched his career. He developed special symbols—like the falcon and colorful flowers—to depict the Colombian landscape and its inhabitants. His figures are painted in large and strong brush strokes.

In 1948–1949 Obregón served as director of the School of Fine Arts at the National University of Bogotá. In the following decades he participated in group shows: the Bienal Hispanoamericana (Madrid, 1958), receiving first prize; the Gulf Caribbean International Exhibition (Houston, 1959); the Salon of National Artists (Bogotá, 1962 and 1966); and the São Paulo Bienal (1967), where he received the grand prize. In 1981 a retrospective of his work was held at the Avianca Cultural Center in Barranquilla, Colombia, and in 1985 another large retrospective traveled from Bogotá to Paris and Madrid.

– BÉLGICA RODRÍGUEZ

OBREGÓN, JOSÉ

José Obregón (*b.* 1832; *d.* 1902), Mexican painter. Obregón received his education at the Academia de San Carlos, where he was a student of Pelegrín CLAVÉ for more than fifteen years. In his youth, his pictorial themes corresponded with his desire to appreciate universal culture through biblical themes. In the 1860s, Obregón was the first painter to use themes involving early national episodes. His *The Discovery of Pulque,* a painting of undoubted historical significance, took its place in the moralist line of historical paintings. Its novelty lay in that, rather than being derived from a biblical or Greco-Roman episode, its theme sprang from a national event. This work interested other figure painters at the academy in the idea of using Mexican historical themes.

By order of Maximilian, Obregón painted the portrait of General Mariano Matamoros, as well as that of José María Morelos, for the Gallery of Heroes in the National Palace. He was likewise commissioned for the portraits of Maximilian and Carlota, which served as models in Europe for the coining of currency that bore their effigies. He enjoyed much success as a portraitist of Mexican society. He remained as a master at the academy until 1891, when the loss of his eyesight forced him to leave his post.

– ESTHER ACEVEDO

OBREGÓN SALIDO, ÁLVARO

Álvaro Obregón Salido (*b.* 19 February 1880; *d.* 17 July 1928), president of Mexico (1920–1924). The poor relation of one of southern Sonora's most prominent families, Obregón struggled to achieve a modest prosperity by 1910. Though he initially withheld active support of the Revolution, Obregón soon rose to national prominence through his military exploits outside the state. He built a wide base of popular support through much of the country and joined it to the alliance of revolutionary chiefs in northwestern Mexico in order to challenge successfully the attempt by Venustiano CARRANZA to establish hegemony over the national government. He was elected president in 1920, and again in 1928, but was assassinated before taking office.

Obregón's birth (he was the last of eighteen children) coincided with the culmination of the gradual loss of his father's small fortune. Francisco Obregón's business partner's affiliation with the empire of MAXIMILIAN had resulted in the confiscation of all his holdings in the interior of the country. The great flood of 1868 and Yaqui Indian raids thereafter had ruined his hacienda in the Mayo Valley. His death three months after Álvaro's birth left the family with only one important resource: his wife's family, the Salidos.

The Salidos owned the most important haciendas in the Mayo Valley. Through their close ties to the political circle that controlled the state government as subordinate allies of the Porfirio DÍAZ regime, the Salidos occupied the posts of district political prefect, state legislator, and state school inspector. Three of Obregón's sisters and a brother secured teaching positions in the emerging town of Huatabampo, to which the family moved. Obregón received his schooling from his siblings and from a Salido relative in the district seat of Álamos. As a boy, he worked at odd jobs to help support the family, developing mechanical interests and abilities. He began work as a mechanic at the flour mill of his uncles. In 1898, he moved to central Sinaloa to work in a similar capacity at the largest sugar refinery in that state, owned by an in-law of the Salido family. Two years later he returned to the Mayo Valley, briefly teaching school, then became mill manager on his uncles' hacienda. In 1904, recently married, he struck out on his own. After renting land for a year, he purchased a farm of nearly 450 acres, in part with a loan from the Salidos. He concentrated on chick-peas, a rapidly emerging export crop; and in 1909 he invented a chick-pea planter that eventually was manufactured and marketed by a Mazatlán foundry. He also worked on the extension of railroad lines and irrigation works.

Obregón's years of working closely with small farmers, rural workers, and industrial laborers had cultivated in him a concern for their plight.

Obregón did not participate in the Maderista movement in Sonora, though his cousin Benjamín Hill urged him to do so. His years of working closely with small farmers, rural workers, and industrial laborers had cultivated in him a concern for their plight. But, finally, after years of struggle, he and his family had achieved a measure of prosperity and stature in Huatabampo. They were considerably beholden to the Salidos for their suc-

cess. Moreover, he was then a widower with two small children. Though he did not sign an act of adherence to the Porfirista regime, as two of his brothers had done under pressure, he chose not to risk the personal interests of his family. Nevertheless, with the Revolution's triumph and his brother's appointment as interim municipal president, Obregón challenged the candidate of the ruling clique for the town's top office. He won the disputed post (the election was decided by the legislature), largely through the support of small farmers and agricultural workers. They included many Mayo Indians, whose language he spoke and with many of whom he had been friends since boyhood. These groups also formed the majority of armed recruits who enabled Obregón to establish himself in the revolutionary movement. In response to the Orozco Revolt (1912), he raised a local force of 300, the largest in the state and one of the few willing to serve wherever needed. Having distinguished himself militarily, Obregón was named chief of the state's forces to oppose the Huerta coup against Francisco MADERO in early 1913. Some of the more veteran Maderista commanders disputed this appointment, but Benjamín Hill proved a valuable intermediary.

Bypassing the Revolution's political struggles in Sonora, Obregón used his military success beyond the state as a springboard to national power, as one of Venustiano Carranza's three leading constitutionalist commanders. He sought to mediate the growing divisions between Carranza, Pancho VILLA, and Emiliano ZAPATA, most notably at the Aguascalientes Convention (1914). But when forced to choose, he allied with Carranza and was named commander in chief. He led a decisive series of battles in the Bajío region (1915), during which the Villistas' military power was broken. The following year he was named secretary of war in response to Villa's raid into New Mexico and the subsequent U.S. military expedition led by General John Pershing. At the same time, Obregón had been working to secure a power base of his own. Unable to establish singular control over Sonora, he was forced to ally with Plutarco ELÍAS CALLES and Adolfo DE LA HUERTA. But he was successful in mobilizing support among labor and agrarian movements, young professionals, and revolutionary chiefs across the country, who were joined in the Revolutionary Confederation and the Liberal Constitutional Party in support of major reform. In the Constitutional Convention of 1917, Obregón lent his military protection and accumulated prestige—as the Revolution's most noted military hero, as international negotiator (with the U.S. officials), and as a charismatic supporter of popular grievances—to the more radical group of delegates who prevailed on the major points of the Constitution of 1917.

With Carranza's election as constitutional president, Obregón retired to private life to mend his health (still suffering from the severe wound in 1915 that had led to the amputation of an arm and from mental fatigue); to expand his agricultural interests in southern Sonora; and to consolidate political support within the state and the nation for his candidacy in the 1920 presidential elections. As Carranza increasingly concentrated political control and ignored the reforms promised in the new constitution, Obregón's candidacy (announced in June 1919) rose in popularity. Carranza's attempt to impose a successor provoked the Agua Prieta Revolt, which brought the revolutionary faction headed by the Sonoran revolutionary chiefs to power, and Obregón to the presidency (1920–1924).

Throughout his revolutionary career, Obregón had almost always opted for moderation over radical change. Moreover, as president, he, more than the other Sonoran chiefs, recognized that the national regime they now headed possessed neither the internal cohesion, the fiscal capacity, nor the political control to pursue aggressively the reform options which the 1917 Constitution empowered a strong interventionist state to undertake. Obregón pursued with firm resolve only education (and, to a lesser extent, the agrarian option). Instead, he focused his efforts on political consolidation. He made significant strides in depoliticizing the regional armed forces and professionalizing the army. Through the Bucareli Treaty with the United States (1923), he secured diplomatic recognition. The financial and economic instabilities of a decade of civil war and the post–World War I depression were mitigated. However, Obregón's support of Calles as successor galvanized a rebellion led by de la Huerta in 1923.

That revolt was a serious but unsuccessful challenge to Obregón's forging of a personalist governing coalition that to a large degree reestablished the centralized state apparatus of the Díaz regime. And like Díaz, Obregón could not abide the no-reelection principle. By 1928, with Calles's official leadership, Congress reintroduced the six-year term and unlimited (but not immediate) reelection. Though successful, Obregón's candidacy provoked another rebellion and led to his assassination before taking office. Obregón's death initiated the demise of the Sonorans' personalist coalition. To retain control, Calles moved expediently toward the institutionalization of the governing coalition through the National Revolutionary Party.

— STUART F. VOSS

OCAMPO, MELCHOR

Melchor Ocampo (b. 1813; d. 3 June 1861), Mexican liberal politician and cabinet minister. Ocampo was born to unknown parents on the hacienda of Pateo in the state of Michoacán. He was raised by the owner of the hacienda, Doña Francisca Xaviera Tapia, from whom he later inherited the property. After his return from a trip to Europe in 1840, Ocampo turned to politics and was elected to represent Michoacán in the national legislature in 1842. As governor of Michoacán during the war with the United States, Ocampo supported the Mexican forces and offered more troops to continue resisting the invaders, arguing that the Treaty of Guadalupe Hidalgo should be rejected. In 1851, Ocampo was involved in a bitter dispute with the church over the refusal of a parish priest to bury a man whose widow could not pay the clerical fees for burial. He then began a campaign to reform parochial fees but was deposed as governor of Michoacán and exiled by Santa Anna in 1853. In New Orleans, Ocampo met Benito JUÁREZ and other exiled liberals.

With the triumph of the Revolution of Ayutla, he returned to Mexico. He served as President Juan ÁLVAREZ's first minister of foreign relations (October 1855) but resigned over differences with Ignacio COMONFORT. Ocampo was elected to the Constitutional Convention of 1856–1857 and served on the committee that drafted the constitution. When Juárez assumed the presidency in 1858, Ocampo served as minister of foreign relations (1858–1859, 1859–1860, 1860–1861) as well as minister of other departments. In 1859 Ocampo bitterly denounced the Ley Lerdo for inhibiting the transfer of property to those of modest means and for actually strengthening the church and increasing its wealth. He also feared that the wars between liberals and conservatives would make it impossible to pay Mexico's foreign creditors, thereby encouraging foreign intervention. To raise capital, Ocampo negotiated the controversial McLane-Ocampo Treaty, signed on 14 December 1859. The treaty has been criticized for giving the United States the right to transport troops and merchandise across the isthmus of Tehuantepec and from Matamoros to Mazatlán, and to use its own troops to protect U.S. citizens and their property in those areas in return for a payment of $4 million to Mexico. Others argue that the McLane-Ocampo Treaty only reaffirmed U.S. transit rights already conceded under the Treaty of Guadalupe Hidalgo and the Gadsden Purchase agreement. Although the McLane-Ocampo Treaty was eventually rejected by the U.S. Senate, it increased dissension in Juárez's cabinet, principally between Ocampo and Miguel LERDO DE TEJADA. On 22 January 1860, Ocampo resigned his post as minister of foreign relations and traveled to the United States to determine what help that nation might provide should the Mexican liberals be unable to defeat the conservatives on their own. He returned to the cabinet as minister of foreign affairs on 27 September 1860. Although the liberals had defeated the conservatives by December 1860, Ocampo's increasingly bitter disputes with Lerdo led to him to resign from the cabinet again on 17 January 1861. Ocampo retired to his hacienda, from which he was kidnapped by conservative guerrillas in May. A few days later he was shot on the orders of Leonardo MÁRQUEZ, who had his corpse hung from a tree. His murder led the liberals to take more extreme measures to repress the conservatives and carry out their reforms.

– D. F. STEVENS

OCAMPO, VICTORIA

Victoria Ocampo (*b.* 7 April 1890; *d.* 27 January 1979), Argentine essayist, critic, publisher, and promoter of cultural activities. Born in Buenos Aires into a well-

Victoria Ocampo behind the wheel of her late-model Packard in Buenos Aires in 1922. (Collection of Doris Meyer)

established, aristocratic family, Ocampo inherited a considerable fortune, which she used mainly to promote literature and art. In 1931, at the insistence of her friend, the Spanish philosopher José Ortega y Gasset, and with the help of two other friends, Waldo Frank and Eduardo MALLEA, Ocampo founded the cultural journal *Sur.* To help defray the expenses of the review, she also started a publishing house, also called Sur. A believer in universalist culture, she befriended the most distinguished literary figures of her time, invited them to her home, and had their work translated and published in her journal or by her publishing house. Rabindranath Tagore, Graham Greene, Albert Camus, and Aldous Huxley are the most important writers whose work she published. In 1953 Ocampo was imprisoned for her steadfast opposition to the authoritarian regime of President Juan PERÓN; protests were published in newspapers all over the world. She was the first woman to become a member of the Argentine Academy of Literature. In 1967, Harvard conferred upon her an honorary doctor of letters degree.

Although Ocampo was treated with respect and admired for her opposition to the Nazi and Fascist governments during World War II and for her support of feminism and women's suffrage, she was also bitterly criticized for her literary taste, considered elitist by leftists, as well as for her strong dislike of Castro's Cuba and Communism in general. Many thought her eccentric and *extranjerizante* (a lover of the foreign). A great believer in translation and a supporter of translators, Ocampo published numerous translations herself, as well as twenty-six volumes of essays, nine of which are called *Testimonios.*

– ROLANDO COSTA PICAZO

ODIO, EUNICE

Eunice Odio (*b.* 18 October 1919; *d.* 15? March 1974), Costa Rican poet. Overlooked by her compatriots during her lifetime, Odio, a native of San José, was later recognized as one of Costa Rica's greatest poets. Because she lived in several countries, including Guatemala and Mexico, she became a citizen of each. Her work as a journalist appeared in magazines throughout Latin America and France. Odio's books of poetry are *Los elementos terrestres* (1948), for which she won the Central American "15 de septiembre" prize; *Zona en territorio del alba* (1953); and *El tránsito de fuego* (1957); her poetry has been compared to the biblical Song of Songs in its tone and images. Odio also published the essays *En defensa del castellano* (1972) and *Los trabajos de la catedral* (1971) and a short story, "El rastro de la mariposa" (1970). She died in Mexico.

— SUSAN E. CLARK

O'DONOJÚ, JUAN

Juan O'Donojú (*b.* 1762; *d.* 8 October 1821), Spanish army officer and politician. Born in Seville, O'Donojú became a liberal Mason, serving as minister of war during the first constitutional period (1801–1814). Unique among Spanish liberals, O'Donojú supported Spanish Americans in their quest for home rule. When the constitution was restored in 1820, leading Mexican liberals such as Miguel RAMOS ARIZPE arranged to have him appointed *Jefe Político Superior,* the office that replaced the viceroy in the new system.

When he arrived in Veracruz in July 1821, O'Donojú discovered that most of the country was in the hands of the insurgents. As a liberal, he attempted to ensure that constitutional rule was firmly implanted in Mexico; as a Spaniard, he sought to retain whatever ties were possible with the mother country. Therefore, on 24 August 1821 he signed the Treaty of Córdoba, which recognized Mexican independence. He became a member of the new regency and entered Mexico City peacefully in September. Unfortunately for his new land, he died of pleurisy shortly thereafter.

Besides assuring Mexican independence, O'Donojú was also responsible for consolidating and expanding Masonry in Mexico.

— JAIME E. RODRÍGUEZ O.

ODRÍA, MANUEL APOLINARIO

Manuel Apolinario Odría (*b.* 26 November 1897; *d.* 18 February 1974), military dictator and president of Peru (1948–1956) who represented the rise to power of technocratic forces among the Peruvian army. Born in Tarma, he was educated in the military academy of Chorrillos (1915–1919) and trained in the Peruvian Advanced War School and in the United States. He rose to notoriety through his leadership as lieutenant colonel in the victorious battle of Zarumilla during the war between Peru and Ecuador in 1941, which was settled by international agreement in 1942.

Because of his military training, Odría was vehemently opposed to the populist Aprista Party. In 1946, Odría became the chief commander of the army. General Odría performed briefly as minister of government under President José Luis BUSTAMANTE Y RIVERO (1945–1948) before his resignation in opposition to the Apristas' growing influence. Odría led the coup d'état that overthrew Bustamante's beleaguered regime in 1948. By 1950, Odría maneuvered his "election" as constitutional president. He adopted the economically liberal recommendations of U.S. adviser Julius Klein, resumed servicing Peru's foreign debt, which had been in default since 1931, and enticed foreign (mainly U.S.) investment by liberalizing the mining and petroleum codes. This coincided with the favorable position of Peruvian export prices in the early 1950s to produce an economic boom.

In the domestic terrain Odría combined severe repressive measures, especially against the Aprista Party and its leader, Víctor Raúl HAYA DE LA TORRE, who sought a long asylum in the Colombian embassy, with demagogic acts and public works. His wife, María Delgado de Odría, became the leading figure of the regime's social charity. Housing, school, and health insurance projects were carried out, and concessions granted to slum dwellers. However, the growing opposition, even among the social elite led by Pedro BELTRÁN, resulted in the need to call elections in 1956. Odría handed power to Manuel PRADO (1956–1962). Odría partici-

Manuel Odría during a demonstration in Huancayo prior to the 1961 presidential elections. (Archivo Caretas)

pated in the elections of 1962 with his own party, the Odriista National Union, which paradoxically established an alliance with Odría's former foe, the Aprista Party, in opposition to the election and regime of Fernando BELAÚNDE (1963–1968). He died in Lima.

— ALFONSO W. QUIROZ

ODUBER QUIRÓS, DANIEL

Daniel Oduber Quirós (*b.* 25 August 1921; *d.* 1992), president of Costa Rica (1974–1978), founding member of the Center for the Study of National Problems and the National Liberation Party (PLN).

San José–born Oduber began his political career as a young law student and participated actively in the epoch-making events of the revolutionary decade (1940–1950). He helped organize and sustain the Center for the Study of National Problems (1940), the Social Democratic Party (1945), the United Opposition in the 1948 election, the inner circle of the FIGUERES FERRER–led revolution, and the PLN. He became nationally prominent when he was named general secretary of the revolutionary junta (1948–1949) and has played a prominent role in party and national affairs ever since.

Oduber has held many positions in government and the PLN, including president of the legislative assembly (1970–1973), president of the PLN (1970–1977), foreign minister (1962–1964), vice president of the Socialist International, and president of Costa Rica (1974–1978).

In addition to his law degree, he earned a master's degree from McGill University and a doctorate from the Sorbonne.

— JOHN PATRICK BELL

OGÉ, JACQUES VICENTE

Jacques Vicente Ogé (*b.* 1755; *d.* 25 February 1791), Haitian revolutionary. Ogé, a coffee merchant and owner of half a plantation in the northern parish of Dondon, was in Paris when the French Revolution broke out. The leader of the free mulattoes who fought for the civil rights of the *gens de couleur* (people of color), he was a vociferous member of Les Amis des Noirs.

When Ogé's requests for funds for the Haitian revolutionaries were rejected by the French, he turned to the British abolitionist Thomas Clarkson, who arranged for cash and letters of credit to be used to buy arms and ammunition in the United States. His forces landed on Haiti on 21 October 1790. After their defeat, Ogé fled to the Spanish part of the island. He was captured by the Spanish authorities and extradited by the French, who subsequently executed him.

— DARIÉN DAVIS

O'GORMAN, CAMILA

Camila O'Gorman (*b.* 1828; *d.* 18 August 1848), a national heroine. Born to an aristocratic *Rosista* family of Buenos Aires, Camila lived in a society dominated by the rules of the dictatorial regime of General Juan Manuel de ROSAS, who later ordered her execution in the name of "law and order." At nineteen, she fell in love with Uladislao Gutiérrez, a young and attractive priest from Tucumán, then serving her Parish of the Virgen del Socorro. After some hesitation and knowing that they were defying the moral and civil codes of their time, they decided to elope on 12 December 1847, thus confronting family, political authorities, and the Catholic church. Their action threatened to provoke a major scandal that had the potential of tearing apart the Rosas regime. Using assumed names, the couple ran away to San Fernando in order to reach Goya, Corrientes province, where they settled and opened an elementary school, thus becoming part of that community. They were discovered by chance and were taken to Buenos Aires in August 1848.

While they were in jail in Santos Lugares, the Rosas government, in compliance with the request of Camila's father, ordered their immediate execution. The tragic end of these young lovers was made even more dramatic by the fact that, according to most accounts, Camila was pregnant. This government action transformed a much-debated social transgression into one of the major crimes of Argentine history. Much has been written about the fatal journey of these lovers. Among the most interesting accounts in recent times are *Una sombra donde sueña Camila O'Gorman* (A Shadow Where Camila O'Gorman Dreams, 1973), a novel by the Argentine poet Enrique MOLINA, and the film *Camila* (1984), directed by Argentine filmmaker María Luisa Bemberg.

— MAGDALENA GARCÍA PINTO

O'GORMAN, EDMUNDO

Edmundo O'Gorman (*b.* 24 November 1906; *d.* 1996), Mexican historian of ideas and institutions. Born in Mexico City, O'Gorman was the grandson of the third commissioner of the first British mission to Mexico, Charles O'Gorman. Edmundo O'Gorman spent the first ten years of his professional life as a lawyer following completion of his degree at the National University (UNAM) in 1928. After working at the Archivo General de la Nación, he received his Ph.D. in history from

UNAM in 1951. He has published extensive original research on colonial Mexico, historiography, and intellectual history as well as editions of the writings of sixteenth-century historians such as Bartolomé de LAS CASAS, José de ACOSTA, and Fr. Toribio de MOTOLINÍA. O'Gorman's major subjects include the Conquest of the New World and America as a European cultural creation. He has debated these topics extensively with the highly regarded social theorists Silvio ZAVALA, Marcel Batallion, Georges Baudot, Miguel LEÓN-PORTILLA, and Octavio PAZ. He has served as a member of the governing board of the National University and as director of a seminar at the Archivo General de la Nación. Since 1967 he has been professor emeritus at UNAM.

O'Gorman argues that America was not discovered but rather constructed by its early chroniclers.

O'Gorman's most important works include *La idea del descubrimiento de América* (1951), which argues that America was not discovered but rather constructed by its early chroniclers, a proposition continued in *La invención de América* (1958). Some of his other important contributions include *La supervivencia política novo-hispana* (1969), a look at monarchism as a political concept in nineteenth-century Mexico, and *Destierro de sombras* (1986), an analysis of the devotion to the Virgin of Guadalupe.

— CARMEN RAMOS-ESCANDÓN

O'GORMAN, JUAN

Juan O'Gorman (*b.* 6 July 1905; *d.* 8 January 1982), Mexican painter and architect. A great admirer of Frida KAHLO and the nineteenth-century landscape artist José María VELASCO, Juan O'Gorman came from a wealthy and aristocratic Irish family with relatives in Mexico. His father, who arrived in Mexico at age twenty-four, was an amateur portrait painter and taught his son drawing and painting; his mother was Mexican born. Trained as an architect, O'Gorman introduced the functional international style to Mexico and built a number of schools and residences in this mode until he turned to the mosaic ornamentation of surfaces. His best-known buildings are the house-studio for Diego RIVERA in San Angel, Mexico City (1931), his own organic mosaic-covered home in San Angel (1949, destroyed 1969), and the narrative mosaic-covered library at the University of Mexico (1950–1951), which has been compared to a codex.

In 1931, O'Gorman began a series of murals in tempera and fresco, the most important of which are *The History of Aviation* (1937–1938; partially destroyed), the *History of Michoacán* (1941–1942), and *Altar of Independence* (1959–1961). Several of his murals were destroyed for political or anticlerical imagery. O'Gorman also produced a large body of easel paintings, many in tempera, which include portraits and imaginary landscapes with surreal qualities.

O'Gorman's mural style was strongly influenced by Diego Rivera but was even more complex and layered, though carefully organized for legibility. He frequently used textual references, reproducing lines from manuscripts, or injecting his own commentaries. His imaginary landscapes, however, are freer and more flowing in design, though painted with the same minute attention to detail as the murals.

— SHIFRA M. GOLDMAN

O'HIGGINS, AMBROSIO

Ambrosio O'Higgins (*b.* 1720; *d.* 18 March 1801), viceroy of Peru (1796–1801). Although best known as the father of Bernardo O'Higgins, Chile's first president, Ambrosio was an important figure in his own right, particularly as captain-general of Chile from 1789 until his promotion to Peru.

The details of O'Higgins's early career are obscure. Born in Ireland, he was taken to Spain as a child and initially pursued a commercial career—in Cádiz, Lima, Buenos Aires, and Santiago—before making a name for himself in the 1760s as an officer leading campaigns against the Araucanians on Chile's southern frontier. He secured rapid promotion, becoming intendant of Concepción in 1786 and field marshal in 1789. His term as viceroy of Peru was complicated by the financial and commercial difficulties arising from Spain's declaration of war against Britain in 1796, but he was able to undertake a number of major public works, including the improvement of the Callao–Lima road, before dying in office.

— JOHN R. FISHER

O'HIGGINS, BERNARDO

Bernardo O'Higgins (*b.* 20 August 1778; *d.* 24 October 1842), liberator and national hero of Chile. Born at Chillán, he was the natural son of a Chilean mother, Isabel Riquelme, and an Irish father, Ambrose Higgins (later O'Higgins, 1720–1801), a colonial official who later rose to be governor of Chile and viceroy of Peru. It is doubtful if Bernardo saw his father more than once, and he was separated from his mother at ten, when he was taken to Lima to start his education. In 1795 he was sent to England, where he continued his studies under tutors at Richmond-on-Thames. A decisive influence on the young creole's life was his meeting, in London, with Francisco de MIRANDA (1750–1816), from whom he eagerly imbibed subversive ideas of independence. In 1802 he returned to Chile and inherited Las Canteras, his father's large estate near the Araucanian frontier. He also petitioned to be allowed to assume his father's surname and titles of nobility; the surname was allowed, the titles were not.

An active and enterprising *hacendado* (landowner), O'Higgins became friendly with the tiny handful of separatists in the south of Chile. The crisis of the Spanish empire and the installation of a patriot government in Santiago (September 1810) gave him a chance to further his ideas. As a representative of the radical minority, he was elected to the first national congress (1811), but José Miguel CARRERA's (1785–1821) seizure of power (November 1811) soon compelled him to return to Las Canteras.

The outbreak of the Wars of Independence in 1813 drew O'Higgins into action at the head of militia forces he himself organized. He distinguished himself in a number of battles, including that at El Roble on 17 October 1813, in which he was wounded. When Carrera was dismissed as commander in chief early in 1814, O'Higgins assumed his role. Faced with another royalist offensive, he signed a peace treaty with the royalist commander, General Gabino GAÍNZA, at Lircay (May 1814), but this treaty was repudiated by the viceroy of Peru. Meanwhile, Carrera had seized power in Chile once again (23 July 1814), but O'Higgins refused to recognize the new regime. Civil war would have broken out had not a new royalist expedition launched a strong offensive. O'Higgins chose to make his stand at the town of Rancagua (1–2 October 1814), where his forces were totally overwhelmed. Patriot Chile collapsed.

O'Higgins himself escaped from the carnage and took refuge across the Andes in Argentina. There he became a close associate of José de SAN MARTÍN (1771–1850), who selected him for a key role in the liberation of Chile. When San Martín's Army of the Andes undertook its epic crossing of the Cordillera, O'Higgins was a divisional commander. His audacious cavalry charge secured victory at Chacabuco on 12 February 1817. In Santiago, four days later, he was appointed supreme director of Chile.

O'Higgins's first three years in power were dominated by the need to prosecute the war of independence. Only after the decisive battle of Maipú (5 April 1818) was Chile finally secure from the royalists. However, the struggle for independence was not over yet. Great efforts had to be made to create a navy and to mount the expedition San Martín was to lead to the Viceroyalty of Peru. With Argentina descending into chaos, most of the burden of organizing and financing the expedition fell on O'Higgins's government. The expedition's departure in August 1820 was probably his supreme personal moment. From then on, he was obliged to give full attention to domestic issues.

O'Higgins's government was commendably vigorous. It restored those patriot institutions abolished during the Spanish reconquest, such as the Instituto Nacional and the National Library. It abolished titles of nobility and the public display of coats of arms. It completed the San Carlos Canal, a public works project dating from colonial times and designed to irrigate the land to the south of Santiago. It made plans to convert a sheep track running down one side of the city into a tree-lined avenue—today the Avenida Bernardo O'Higgins. O'Higgins also launched a number of diplomatic missions, though his envoy in London failed to secure British recognition of Chile's independence. (The United States extended recognition in 1822.)

While O'Higgins retained much of his personal prestige, his government provoked increasing antipathy. In some quarters, the supreme director was suspected of being under excessive Argentine influence. His support for the execution of the three Carrera brothers alienated a powerful faction. Some of his ecclesiastical measures (prohibition of burial in church, temporary banishment of the bishop of Santiago, approval of a Protestant cemetery) aroused clerical hostility. His appointment of José Antonio Rodríguez Aldea (1779–1841) as finance minister in 1820 also incurred disapproval from those who distrusted this slippery ex-royalist.

More serious, perhaps, was the personal and somewhat cliquish nature of the regime, which seemed to discourage the bulk of the creole elite from taking an active part in public life. O'Higgins's first constitution (1818) was minimal, and allowed no element of popular election, although its nominated senate was by no means a subservient body. Pressure for political reform eventually compelled O'Higgins to summon a constituent convention. This body produced his second constitution (October 1822), which provided for elections, a congress, and similar liberal desiderata. It also included a clause that would have enabled O'Higgins to remain in office for another ten years, a prospect most creoles found unacceptable. The final blow to the regime came from the war-ravaged south, where a desperate economic situation breeding frustration and resentment toward the capital prompted General Ramón FREIRE (1787–1851), intendant of Concepción, to launch a rebellion against O'Higgins. The northern province of Coquimbo followed suit. In Santiago, leading creoles conspired against the dictator. On 28 January 1823, in a scene of compelling drama, he was persuaded to abdicate. Six months later he was finally permitted to leave the country, never to return.

Abandoning a plan to visit Ireland, the land of his forebears, O'Higgins settled in Peru. In 1824 he accompanied Simón BOLÍVAR (1783–1830) during part of the final patriot campaign in the highlands, but soon afterward doffed his uniform forever. The Peruvian government had awarded O'Higgins a couple of haciendas in the fertile Cañete Valley, to the south of Lima. Here and in Lima the exiled liberator lived out his final years in tranquillity, enjoying the company of his mother (until she died in April 1840), his half-sister Rosa, and his own natural son Pedro Demetrio, the fruit of a brief love affair that took place during the patriot campaigns of 1817.

O'Higgins was an amiable man with a simple, straightforward, unsubtle character. His many friends were devoted to him, and his followers very loyal. O'Higgins himself probably entertained few hopes of restoration to power. In 1826 he gave halfhearted support to a military insurrection in Chiloé, an ill-advised gesture that led the Chilean congress to strip him of his rank. In 1830 the successful Conservative rebellion led by his old protégé Joaquín PRIETO (1786–1854) may have briefly revived his aspirations. He was touched by the attentions of Chilean soldiers occupying Lima during the war between Chile and the Peru-Bolivia Confederation. In 1842 the Manuel BULNES government (1841–1851) restored his rank and emoluments, news of which reached O'Higgins shortly before his death. He was buried in Lima, and in January 1869 his remains were repatriated to Chile. Just over three years later, in May 1872, an equestrian statue of the hero was inaugurated in Santiago. Appropriately, it shows him in desperate action at the battle of Rancagua.

— SIMON COLLIER

O'HIGGINS, PABLO

Pablo O'Higgins (*b.* 1904; *d.* 1983), American artist who worked primarily in Mexico. Born Paul O'Higgins in Salt Lake City, Utah, he was raised and educated in the United States. In 1924 O'Higgins traveled to Mexico, where he was attracted to the muralist movement, then in its early years. He became a studio assistant of Diego RIVERA, and from 1925 to 1927 participated in the creation of Rivera's murals at Chapingo and Mexico City. In 1927 he joined the Communist Party, and from 1931 to 1932 he studied at the Moscow Academy of Arts. Upon returning to Mexico, he began to create his own murals, the first in 1933. His major public work, *La explotación del campesino y del obrero,* was executed at the Mercado Abelardo Rodríguez, Mexico City, in 1934–1936. He also produced murals in the United States, including one for the Ship Scalers' Union Hall, Seattle, in 1945. O'Higgins was a founding member in 1933 of the leftist artists' group Liga de Escritores y Artistas Revolucionarios, and in 1937 of the graphics collaborative Taller de Gráfica Popular. He died in Mexico City.

— ELIZABETH FERRER

OITICICA, HÉLIO

Hélio Oiticica (*b.* 26 July 1937; *d.* 22 March 1980), Brazilian painter and sculptor. Born in Rio de Janeiro, Oiticica began his artistic training as a student at Ivan Serpa, a pioneer in the Brazilian concrete art movement. In 1954 he joined Grupo Frente, whose members included Serpa, Lygia PAPE, Lygia CLARK, and other neoconcrete artists. Like his friend and colleague Clark, Oiticica was preoccupied with color and real space. In both *The Penetrables,* a series of tunnels, and a sculptural garden made of sand and color, he used diverse materials and objects to create an environment allowing spectator participation. Intrigued by the visceral effect achieved by color, he experimented with three-dimensional, solid, penetrable objects of color. In his *Fireball Box,* the red color mass has an energy field drawing the spectator into it.

In 1967 Oiticica participated in a neoconcrete exhibition entitled "New Brazilian Objectivity." His other exhibitions included the 1967 Paris Biennial, a 1969 retrospective of his work at London's Whitechapel Gallery, a 1970 exhibition at the Museum of Modern Art in New York, and a traveling retrospective in 1992.

— CAREN A. MEGHREBLIAN

OJEDA, ALONSO DE

Alonso de Ojeda (*b.* ca. 1466; *d.* 1516), Spanish navigator and conquistador. Ojeda traveled with Christopher COLUMBUS on his second voyage in 1493 and partook in explorations of Guadalupe and Hispaniola. Years later he obtained permission to travel to the mainland following the route of Columbus's third voyage. Ojeda set sail in 1499, accompanied by Amerigo VESPUCCI. They arrived near the equator, explored the coast of Trinidad and the entire Venezuelan coast, the mouth of the Orinoco, and the island of Margarita. After Ojeda returned to Spain, information from his expedition was incorporated into Juan de la Cosa's map of 1500, on which the name *Venezuela* appeared for the first time.

Ojeda made other expeditions in 1501 and 1509. In 1501 he was appointed governor of Coquivacoa, and in 1502 he explored the area of La Guajira. Francisco PIZARRO accompanied him on his 1509 voyage, in which Juan de la Cosa and one hundred other Spaniards perished in a skirmish with natives near Cartagena Bay.

Ojeda and Vespucci explored the coast of Trinidad and the entire Venezuelan coast, the mouth of the Orinoco, and the island of Margarita.

Ojeda finally occupied the Gulf of Urabá and founded the city of San Sebastián, but the expedition was chaotic overall and had little commercial success. Nevertheless, Ojeda was among the most important navigators and discoverers of the New World.

– INÉS QUINTERO

OLAÑETA, JOSEF JOAQUÍN CASIMIRO

Josef Joaquín Casimiro Olañeta (*b.* 3 March 1795; *d.* August 1860), Bolivian politician, who is often considered the real father of the country. Olañeta was the key figure in the creation of independent Bolivia and the most influential politician in the new nation's first decades. Born in Chuquisaca (now Sucre) into the small colonial elite of Upper Peru, he studied in Córdoba, Argentina, and at the University of San Francisco Xavier, where he received a degree in law. He became the secretary of the fierce royalist general Pedro Antonio de Olañeta, his uncle, whom he adroitly manipulated. In 1824, when it became apparent that the Spanish cause was doomed, he deserted and encouraged Antonio José de SUCRE and Simón BOLÍVAR to establish an independent Bolivia. Later he conspired against Sucre's Bolivarian government.

Never wanting to be president, Olañeta preferred to exercise power by Machiavellian means. During seven presidencies he held a variety of government posts in the executive, legislative, and judicial branches as well as that of diplomat. His shifty behavior earned him the sobriquet of Dos Caras (Two-faced).

– CHARLES W. ARNADE

OLAYA HERRERA, ENRIQUE

Enrique Olaya Herrera (*b.* 12 November 1880; *d.* 18 February 1937), president of Colombia (1930–1934). Born in Guateque, Boyacá, Olaya received his law degree in 1903. During the administration of Carlos E.

RESTREPO (1910–1914), he was foreign minister and later minister to Argentina. From 1922 to 1929 he was Colombian minister to the United States, a delicate position for a Liberal in a Conservative regime. In 1930, with the Conservatives divided, Olaya won the presidency under a "National Concentration" banner, promising a coalitionist government. His regime was faced with serious partisan violence, particularly in the northeast. He faced the Great Depression with orthodoxy; only in April 1933 did he suspend interest payments on Colombia's foreign debt. In social matters Olaya was weakly reformist, as seen in the 1931 Labor Code. He responded to the Peruvian seizure of the Amazon port of Leticia with a large-scale mobilization, but the matter was settled by negotiation. After his term, Olaya was minister to the Vatican; before his death he was a likely Liberal candidate for the presidency in 1938.

– RICHARD J. STOLLER

O'LEARY, DANIEL FLORENCIO

Daniel Florencio O'Leary (*b.* 1801; *d.* 24 February 1854), Irish officer in the Venezuelan Liberating Army and close aide of Simón BOLÍVAR. In 1817, at the age of sixteen, O'Leary traveled to Venezuela as a member of the British volunteers who united to fight for the cause of independence in America. He came to Venezuela by way of the town of Angostura and rapidly gained the confidence of Simón BOLÍVAR, who included him in his honor guard in 1818. O'Leary participated in the New Granada campaign in 1819, and in 1820 Bolívar appointed him as his aide-de-camp. He took care of Bolívar's correspondence and records, and remained very close to him throughout the Southern campaign. In the November 1820 negotiations that concluded with the Trujillo armistice, O'Leary acted as Antonio José de SUCRE's secretary. When Bolívar and Pablo MORILLO, leader of the royalist armies, met on 27 November 1820 in the town of Santa Ana to ratify the treaty, O'Leary acted as Bolívar's emissary in arranging the details of the meeting. O'Leary participated in the liberating campaigns of Venezuela (1821) and Ecuador (1822) and closely collaborated with Bolívar in his political projects concerning the integration of the Americas. He accompanied the leader until the latter's last days in Cartagena.

After Bolívar's death, O'Leary organized and compiled his voluminous archive, augmenting it with a great number of documents solicited from men who had been involved in the War of Independence. In Spain he visited Morillo, who handed over the documentation in his possession for inclusion in the collection. After O'Leary's death, his family gave the archive to the Venezuelan government. It was published in thirty-two volumes under the auspices of the Antonio GUZMÁN BLANCO administration and was known as the *Memorias del General Daniel Florencio O'Leary* (1879–1888).

After 1833 O'Leary undertook various diplomatic missions as Venezuelan minister to England, Spain, France, and the Vatican. As a diplomat in the service of the British government, he was named chargé d'affaires in Caracas in 1841 and in Bogotá in 1843.

– INÉS QUINTERO

O'LEARY, JUAN EMILIANO

Juan Emiliano O'Leary (b. 13 June 1880; d. 1968), Paraguayan historian, poet, and polemicist. Born in Asunción of mixed parentage, O'Leary received his education at the Colegio Nacional and the university, where he specialized in history. He later went on to teach history and geography at the *colegio* and the normal school. He was also for many years director of Paraguay's Archivo Nacional and Biblioteca Nacional.

As a historian, O'Leary saw as his particular goal the rehabilitation, even glorification, of Francisco Solano LÓPEZ, nineteenth-century field marshal and president of Paraguay during the War of the Triple Alliance and the object of heated criticism in its aftermath. Despite the fact that some members of his family had suffered under Marshal López, O'Leary spent years developing a portrait of the dictator as the supreme hero of the Paraguayan nation. Under the pseudonym Pompeyo González, O'Leary frequently wrote articles for the Partido Colorado's daily newspaper, *Patria*. His nationalist polemics were especially significant in channeling patriotic feelings in Paraguay during the Chaco War (1932–1935).

O'Leary lived to see his right-wing version of Paraguayan history adopted as official dogma during the Alfredo STROESSNER regime (1954–1989). On several occasions O'Leary participated more directly in government as a Colorado deputy. Still, it is for his historical works that O'Leary is chiefly remembered. They include *Páginas de historia* (1916), *Nuestra epopeya* (1919), *El libro de los héroes* (1922), *El mariscal López* (1925), and *El héroe del Paraguay* (1930). He died in Asunción.

– THOMAS L. WHIGHAM

OLID, CRISTÓBAL DE

Cristóbal De Olid (b. 1488; d. 12 May 1524), conquistador of Mexico and Central America. A trusted captain of Hernán CORTÉS, Olid later betrayed him in order to claim for himself regions he had explored in Honduras.

Born in Baeza, in the Andalusian region of Spain, Olid left for America in 1518 to search for gold and other wealth. Arriving in Cuba, he joined Cortés's expedition to Mexico. Olid was made quartermaster of Cortés's army, and in 1519 participated in the founding of Veracruz and in campaigns to Tlaxcala and Tenochtitlán (the capital city). Cortés appointed Olid captain of the guard in Tenochtitlán, and when the Spaniards captured MOTECUHZOMA II, Olid became the ruler's personal guard.

In 1524 Cortés sent Olid south to take possession of Honduras, which was believed to contain great wealth.

During the siege of Tenochtitlán, Olid became one of Cortés's most trusted captains. He distinguished himself as a loyal and capable soldier, rising quickly to the rank of camp commander, a position of both administrative and judicial power. In addition, he was given the command of a large company of his own, heading campaigns in Texcoco, Chapultepec, and Coyoacán. Following the conquest of Tenochtitlán in 1521, Olid led an expedition to Michoacán, extending Spanish control outward from the Mexican capital.

In 1524 Cortés sent Olid south to take possession of Honduras, which was believed to contain great wealth. He was also instructed to capture Gil GONZÁLEZ DÁVILA, a conquistador who had claimed for himself the area surrounding Lake Nicaragua. After gathering provisions in Cuba, Olid sailed down the coast, arriving in the Gulf of Honduras in May 1524. He claimed the land in Cortés's name and established the town of Triunfo de la Cruz. Soon after, he renounced Cortés's authority and claimed the region for himself. When Cortés learned of his captain's betrayal, he sent out an expedition under the leadership of Francisco de las Casas with instructions to capture Olid. Cortés began his own journey south in November 1524 to handle the matter.

Olid moved west into the Valley of Naco, where he encountered González Dávila. The arrival of Francisco de las Casas in the Gulf of Honduras, however, prevented an immediate pursuit. Olid tried to stall de las Casas's landing by proposing a truce. The ploy proved successful. A storm decimated de las Casas's forces, giving Olid the chance to capture both de las Casas and

González Dávila. The two men later managed to escape, attempting unsuccessfully to assassinate Olid, who fled, seriously wounded, to the mountains. He soon was found, however. After a perfunctory trial, Olid was sentenced to death and beheaded.

— SARA FLEMING

OLIVARES, CONDE-DUQUE DE

Conde-Duque de Olivares (Gaspar de Guzmán y Pimental; *b.* 6 January 1587; *d.* 22 July 1645), Spanish statesman and chief minister of Philip IV (1621–1643). Unlike the monarch he served, Olivares intimidated contemporaries with his tireless energy spent in pursuit of victory in European conflicts and centralization of the Spanish state. Of primary concern in European affairs was the defense of the Low Countries, which drew Spain into costly participation in the Thirty Years War (1618–1648). Although Spain lacked the revenue to support such military involvement, Olivares never allowed fiscal limitations to deter him from an aggressive foreign policy aimed at fulfilling Spain's destiny as a world power. He undertook the Mantuan war in Italy (1628–1631) to prevent the French successor from claiming the throne and to maintain Spain's control over northern Italy, but was unable to accomplish either. In 1626 he inaugurated the Unión de Armas in an effort to get the non-Castilian provinces in Europe and the New World to contribute to imperial defense.

Olivares's attempt to force Catalonian participation in the war between Spain and France resulted in the revolt of the Catalans in 1640. A revolt against Spanish rule in Portugal later in the year coincided with a collapse in transatlantic trade and sealed Olivares's fate. He willingly resigned for health reasons on 24 January 1643 and died two years later.

— SUZANNE HILES BURKHOLDER

OLIVEIRA, GERALDO TELES DE

Geraldo Teles de Oliveira (*b.* 1 January 1913), Brazilian sculptor. Rarely leaving the state of Minas Gerais where he was born, Oliveira began to experiment with wood sculptures in 1965. Although he works in relative isolation, in 1975 a commission from the French government threatened to end his obscurity. With only one exception, a gilded head of Tiradentes, which was a commission for the town of São João del Rey, his sculptures integrate African art and the Brazilian popular ex-voto tradition. All signed with the acronym of Oliveira's full name, "GTO," they almost exclusively depict human figures carved and interwoven within an architectural form, such as a wheel or column. In his *Living*

Wheel, done in 1968, human figures serve as spokes and fill in the empty spaces of a circular form. He participated in the 1969, 1971, and 1975 São Paulo Bienals. Belo Horizonte's Salão Global presented him with a travel grant to France in 1975, to be on hand for the exhibition of his sculpture for the French government. While in Europe, Oliveira exhibited works in the 1978 Venice Biennale and in group shows in Paris and Brussels.

— CAREN A. MEGHREBLIAN

OLIVEIRA, MANUEL BOTHELHO DE

Manuel Bothelho De Oliveira (*b.* 1636; *d.* 5 January 1711), Brazilian writer and politician. Born to a wealthy plantation family that belonged to the petty aristocracy, Oliveira studied law at the University of Coimbra in Portugal, where he knew Gregório de MATOS. He practiced law on his return to Bahia, and eventually entered politics and held several important offices. Oliveira's importance comes largely from his being the first Brazilian to publish his poetry in book form. His *Música do Parnasso* (1705) contains a variety of poems written in Spanish, Italian, and Latin, as well as Portuguese. Its emphasis on linguistic and formal virtuosity, including both cultism and conceptism, identifies it aesthetically as a late baroque work in the European tradition. Only the 325-line *silva* "Ilha da mare" is notably Brazilian in content. (A collection of poems on religious themes, *Lira sacre,* was posthumously published in 1971.)

Admitting that Oliveira is a minor though skillful poet, Wilson Martins has nevertheless identified him as the writer who, given his dates, consciousness of his profession, and responsiveness to a specific literary theory, became the founder of the Brazilian literary tradition. He also wrote two plays in Spanish, both imitative of contemporary Spanish *comedias.* Although lightly regarded today, they secure him a place in the history of Brazil's secular theater.

— NORWOOD ANDREWS, JR.

OLIVEIRA, WILLY CORREIA DE

Willy Correia de Oliveira (*b.* 11 February 1938), Brazilian composer and teacher. Oliveira has been associated with the Santos-based group of composers Música Nova (notably Gilberto MENDES, Rogério DUPRAT, Damiano Cozzella, and Julio Medaglia). The works of Pierre Boulez and Karlheinz Stockhausen were the focus of intense discussion within the group, which rejected the prevailing nationalist trends. Oliveira became interested not only in providing a unique formal structure for each work but also in forming a unique conceptual framework in which the actual sounds are of secondary importance. In the *Five Kitschs* (1967), for example, a series of pitches and a harmonic progression form the basis for all five pieces ("Background," "Nocturne," "Make It Yourself," "Jazztime," and "Narcissus"). The manner of repetition of the series is serialist in nature. The striving for maximum unity of structure and harmonic tension is minimalist in conception. Oliveira's approach to composition belongs to the postnationalist generation of composers who reject the idea of writing works with a clearly identifiable national element.

– DAVID P. APPLEBY

OLIVEIRA LIMA, MANUEL DE

Manuel de Oliveira Lima (*b.* 25 December 1867; *d.* 24 March 1928), Brazilian historian and diplomat. Although he was born in Recife, Oliveira Lima received most of his education in Portugal, where he began his diplomatic career in 1890 as an appointee of the new republican government. He later occupied many posts in Europe, the Americas, and Asia. A notable speaker and an engaging but outspoken conversationalist, he acted on several other occasions as an ambassador of Brazilian culture abroad. In 1920, he retired from public service and established himself in Washington, D.C., where he taught at the Catholic University of America. He donated over forty thousand books and manuscripts, which he had collected from his many travels, as a token of international peace and friendship to found the Oliveira Lima Ibero-American Library at the Catholic University. Most of the works focus on the history and culture of Portugal, Spain, and their American domains.

Oliveira Lima published a historical drama and several works on his diplomatic experience and many conferences on Brazilian history and literature, some of which he wrote in French. His first historical study, *Pernambuco, seu desenvolvimento histórico* (The Historical Development of Pernambuco [1895]) is a remarkable history of the province from its beginnings to 1848. Still useful are the notes he appended in 1917 to Francisco Muniz Tavares's *Historia da Revolução de Pernambuco em 1817* (History of the 1817 Revolution in Pernambuco, [1840]). It is in his masterpiece, *Dom João VI no Brasil* (*King John VI in Brazil*, 1908), that scholarship, literary skill, and sociological insight are matched to a degree rarely attained in Brazilian historical writing.

– GUILHERME PEREIRA DAS NEVES

OLMEDO, JOSÉ JOAQUÍN

José Joaquín Olmedo (*b.* 19 March 1780; *d.* 17 February 1847), Ecuadorian poet, liberal politician, and lawyer. Born in Guayaquil, Olmedo completed a law degree from the University of San Marcos in Lima. He was elected to the Spanish Cortes in 1810, served as secretary of the assembly, and participated in the writing of the liberal Constitution of 1812.

Olmedo returned to Ecuador at the end of 1816 and headed the provisional government formed at Guayaquil in October 1820 to liberate the Audiencia of Quito (1822). He was elected vice president of the republic and prefect of Guayas in 1830, president of the 1835 constituent congress, and member of the triumvirate of liberals that ousted Juan José FLORES in March 1845.

Olmedo was one of the great lyric poets of the nineteenth century. Among his most famous works is *La victoria de Junín*. In addition, he is considered, along with Andrés BELLO, one of the outstanding members of the Spanish American Enlightenment.

– LINDA ALEXANDER RODRÍGUEZ

OÑA, PEDRO DE

Pedro de Oña (*b.* 1570; *d.* 1643?), Chilean poet. The son of a Spanish captain killed in the Araucanian wars in Chile, Oña was born at Angol (Los Infantes). At around the age of twenty he went to Lima to study at the University of San Marcos. Encouraged by the viceroy, García HURTADO DE MENDOZA (1535–1609), who had been offended by ERCILLA Y ZÚÑIGA's (1533–1594) portrayal of him in *La Araucana*, Oña composed an epic poem to recount the Viceroy's earlier exploits as governor of Chile (1557–1561). The resulting work, *Arauco domado*, in nineteen cantos, was published in Lima in 1594. The first poem published by a Chilean creole author, it covers some of the events already narrated in Part 2 of *La Araucana*, but fails to carry the story through, and the bulk of the poem is based on episodes (such as a revolt in Quito and the viceroy's actions against English sea dogs) that are irrelevant to the Araucanian wars. Oña promised a second part, which never appeared.

Oña was not a truly talented poet, and *Arauco domado* does not bear comparison with *La Araucana*, which it sought to emulate and perhaps imitate: its meter is similar but not identical. However, Oña cannot be denied his rightful place as the first Chilean poet.

– SIMON COLLIER

OÑATE, JUAN DE

Juan de Oñate (*b. ca.* 1551; *d. ca.* 3 June 1626), founder and first governor of New Mexico (1598–1609). Son of the Basque Cristóbal de Oñate, developer of Zacatecas silver mines, Oñate negotiated a contract with Viceroy Luis de VELASCO in 1595 for the pacification of New Mexico, receiving the privileges of *adelantado* in return for the heavy investment of his family consortium. He led his colonizing caravan of several hundred people, among them ten Franciscan missionaries, north across the Chihuahua desert, striking the Rio Grande downriver from present-day El Paso, where he took formal possession of the colony on 30 April 1598. Some 350 miles up river, he established a settlement near San Juan Pueblo. When the Indians of Acoma killed his nephew in an open challenge to the Spaniards, Oñate dispatched seventy armed men to punish them, which, even though outnumbered, they succeeded in doing. Hoping to discover an exploitable resource to help support his colony, he ventured far out into the Great Plains and to the Gulf of California; he failed in his mission. Oñate resigned in 1607, leaving New Mexico two years later to a royal governor.

Subjected to the usual trial of a failed *adelantado,* Oñate eventually traveled to Spain, where, on a tour as royal inspector of mines, he died.

— JOHN L. KESSELL

ONETTI, JUAN CARLOS

Juan Carlos Onetti (*b.* 1 July 1909), Uruguayan novelist and short-story writer. Onetti's semantic and technical experimentation place him among the inaugurators of the "new novel" in Latin America. His anguished, alienated characters are archetypes of the existential novel. Onetti settled in Buenos Aires when he was twenty-one. His first novel, *El pozo* (The Pit, 1991), appeared in 1939. The protagonist, Eladio Linacero, expressed his estrangement from a bizarre, hostile world through a long, interior monologue. *El pozo* marks a significant transition from the telluric to the urban novel, in which the city is viewed as hostile and dehumanizing. *Tierra de nadie* (1941; *No Man's Land,* 1994), which won second place in the Losada competition, expressed resentment toward both reality and existential absurdity. In *La vida breve* (1950; *A Brief Life,* 1976), which catapulted him into the international limelight, Onetti uses a fragmentary structure to express the existential anguish of his character, Brausen, who, through his imagination, flees from Buenos Aires to the fictitious world of Santa María. Onetti's attitude is extremely pessimistic, for he rejects traditional values, while offering only an unsatisfying, absurd alternative. The short novel *Los adioses* (1954; *Farewells,* 1992) also expresses existential alienation, this time through a love story.

In *Para una tumba sin nombre* (1959; *A Grave with no Name,* 1992), set once again in Santa María, Onetti suggests that objective reality is impossible to know. In *El astillero* (1961; *The Shipyard,* 1968) and *Juntacadáveres* (1964; *Body Snatcher,* 1964) the author returns to

Juan Carlos Onetti. (Jesse Fernández)

Santa María. Onetti's later works include *La novia robada y otros cuentos* (1963), *Las máscaras del amor* (1968), *La muerte y la niña* (1973), *Tiempo de abrazar y los cuentos de 1933 a 1950* (1974), *Tan triste como ella y otros cuentos* (1976), and *Dejemos hablar al viento* (1979).

— BARBARA MUJICA

ONGANÍA, JUAN CARLOS

Juan Carlos Onganía (*b.* 17 March 1914; *d.* 8 June 1995), president of Argentina (1966–1970). Born at Marcos Paz in Buenos Aires Province, Onganía studied at the National Military College and trained for the cavalry. Internecine struggles in the army in the early 1960s found him leading the Blues faction against the Whites. He traveled abroad, visiting Nationalist China, Japan, West Germany, Spain, and England, and delivered a paper at the U.S. Military Academy on civil-military relations. On 28 June 1966 he launched a coup against President Arturo ILLIA.

Onganía pursued top-down social change, an "economic miracle," and an end to corporatism. His reforms, called the "Argentine Revolution" and the "Community of Solidarity," provoked popular uprisings in Córdoba in May and in Rosario in September 1969. Concerned for their own personal safety in the wake of Pedro ARAMBURU's 1 June 1970 murder, the military ousted Onganía in favor of Roberto Marcelo LEVINGSTON on 13 June 1970.

— ROGER GRAVIL

ORBEGOSO, LUIS JOSÉ DE

Luis José de Orbegoso (*b.* 1795; *d.* 1847), military leader and president of Peru (1833–1835). Orbegoso was born to a notable family of northern Peru. At the time of independence he was an officer of the royalist army, but he offered early support to José de SAN MARTÍN. Promoted to colonel and then general by Simón BOLÍVAR, Orbegoso was appointed prefect of Trujillo in 1824 and 1827. As an active and popular participant in one of the most complex struggles for power among nineteenth-century Peruvian military leaders, Orbegoso fought under the banner of the constitutional resistance to military caudillismo. Having been elected president of the republic by the National Convention in 1833, Orbegoso withstood attempts by Generals Augustín GAMARRA and Pedro Bermúdez to oust him in 1834. A civil war ensued that was initially favorable to Orbegoso. However, General Felipe Santiago SALAVERRY rebelled against Orbegoso in 1835. Orbegoso responded by allying himself with Bolivian General Andrés de SANTA CRUZ. The alliance defeated Salaverry and established the Peru-Bolivia Confederation (1836–1839), in which Orbegoso performed as president of the newly created state of Northern Peru. However, Orbegoso rebelled against the confederation in 1838, an action that led to his exile.

— ALFONSO W. QUIROZ

ORBIGNY, ALCIDE DESSALINES D'

Alcide Dessalines d' Orbigny, (*b.* 6 September 1802; *d.* 30 June 1857), French naturalist and explorer. Orbigny, a native of Couëron, France, was commissioned by the Paris Museum of Natural History to explore much of South America between 1826 and 1834. He spent the first year collecting plants and animals in Brazil and Uruguay. From 1827 to 1828, Orbigny traversed the Paraná River through Brazil, Paraguay, and Argentina. In 1828 the government of Argentina commissioned him to study the pampas in order to determine the region's agricultural value. After completing this assignment, Orbigny went to Patagonia to continue his studies in natural history. During his stay, he spent time with a native tribe and took part in an intertribal war. Afterward, he investigated the land, plants, and animals of Bolivia and Peru.

In 1834 Orbigny returned to France, where he won the grand prize of the Paris Geographical Society for his work. The French government published his research in nine volumes titled *Voyage dans l'Amérique méridionale* (1834–1847). In addition to its description of flora, fauna, and geography, it provides important ethnographical data on various Indian populations. Orbigny's travels through South America enabled him to produce a comprehensive map of the area in 1842. He died at Pierrefitte-sur-Seine, France.

— JOSEPHINE DELORENZO

ORBÓN, JULIÁN

Julián Orbón (*b.* 7 August 1925; *d.* 20 May 1991), Cuban composer, essayist, and educator. Orbón received his musical education in Spain, Cuba, and the United States, where he studied with Aaron Copland. In Havana he was a member of the Grupo Renovación Musical (1942–1949) and director of the Orbón Conservatory from 1946 until 1960, when he left Cuba. After teaching in Mexico from 1960 to 1963, he moved to New York City, where he taught composition at Columbia University. A composer of orchestral, piano, and choral works, he received commissions from various foundations. His compositions earned numerous prizes and were selected for inclusion in international festivals. Although he occasionally employed Cuban elements, his wide musical interests, originally rooted in the Spanish tradition, ranged from neoclassic to a restrained romantic expression.

— OTTO OLIVERA

ORDÓÑEZ, JOSÉ

José Ordóñez (*d.* 8 February 1819), Spanish army officer. Ordóñez fought in the Peninsular War and was briefly a prisoner of war in France. During the Spanish reconquest of Chile, he served as intendant of Concepción, arriving there in August 1815. When Chile was liberated, he successfully defended Talcahuano against stubborn assaults from the patriots. In 1818, with the arrival of General Mariano Osorio's expedition from Peru, Ordóñez took part in the final Spanish offensive in the Chilean Central Valley. He masterminded the surprise attack at Cancha Rayada (19 March 1818) that nearly destroyed the patriot army, and fought tenaciously at the battle of Maipú (5 April 1818). He was the last senior Spanish officer to surrender. With other royalist prisoners Ordóñez was sent across the Andes to San Luis in Argentina. He and a number of accomplices were executed after a daring but frustrated attempt to assassinate the provincial governor, Vicente Dupuy.

— SIMON COLLIER

ORÉ, LUIS GERÓNIMO DE

Luis Gerónimo de Oré (*b.* ca. 1554; *d.* 30 January 1630), Peruvian Franciscan, linguist, and first American-born bishop of Concepción, Chile. Luis Gerónimo was born in Guamanga. His father, Antonio de Oré, was one of Peru's early settlers; his mother, Luisa Dias de Roxas y Rivera, inherited the *encomienda* of Hanan Chilques. The family's fortune was based on Indian tributes and labor and on silver mines in the Guamanga district. Luis Gerónimo had several brothers and sisters; four brothers became Franciscans; three sisters were founders of the Poor Clares Convent in Guamanga. At fourteen Oré journeyed to Cuzco to become a Franciscan novice. He continued his studies in Lima at the University of San Marcos and was ordained by Archbishop Toribio de Mogrovejo on 23 September 1581.

At fourteen Oré journeyed to Cuzco to become a Franciscan novice.

Oré was fluent in Latin, Quechua, and Aymara and probably participated in the preparation of a Peruvian catechism ordered by the Third Church Council of Lima and published in 1584. In the mid-1580s Oré was assigned to the Collaguas Doctrina near Arequipa, where he perfected his translation skills and finished important dictionaries and grammars in Quechua and Aymara (now lost), as well as the *Symbolo Cathólico Indiano* (1598) and the *Rituale seu Manuale Peruanum* (1607). By 1600 he was preaching in the mining center of Potosí, Bolivia, and later received an Indian parish in Cuzco. Cuzco's Bishop Antonio de la Raya appointed Oré to represent the diocese in Europe in a jurisdictional dispute with Charcas. Oré spoke before the Council of the Indies in Valladolid, Spain, in the spring of 1605. By winter Oré was in Rome, where the massive *Rituale,* a manual for the administration of the sacraments in Andean America, was published.

In 1611 Oré was back in Spain, and was appointed to lead a group of missionaries to Florida. While collecting a contingent of friars, he met Peruvian historian El Inca GARCILASO DE LA VEGA in Córdoba in early 1612. The two discussed Peru's past and Florida's prospects. Unable to set out on his mission in 1612, Oré helped collect another group of Franciscan friars for the Venezuelan missions later that year. He also was ordered to conduct an inquiry into the Andalusian years of Francisco SOLANO, a Franciscan whose beatification was advocated by many. Oré quickly finished the *Relación de la vida y milagros del Venerable Padre Fr. Francisco Solano de la Órden de San Francisco* (1614).

Oré reached Saint Agustine, Florida, in the latter part of 1614, and again for a second inspection in November 1616. He conducted a thorough inspection of the province and held the first general chapter of the order in Florida. Before completing his work as general commissioner, he collected material for his *Relación de los mártires de la Florida* (1619). Perhaps during his return voyage to Spain he composed a long poem dedicated to the Virgin: *Corona de la sacratíssima Virgen María . . .* (1619).

On 17 August 1620 he was appointed bishop of La Imperial (Concepción, Chile). He traveled to Chile via Panama and Peru. When he arrived there in 1623, Concepción was a modest garrison on the Araucanian frontier. Oré's last years were troubled by conflict with both secular and religious authorities. He conducted an inspection of the distant Chiloé missions and established a seminary at Concepción. He consistently required solid training for mission clergy, stressing knowledge of native languages. He advocated peaceful Indian-European relations. His death in Concepción in early 1630 ended a period of peaceful coexistence on the Bío-bío frontier.

– NOBLE DAVID COOK

OREAMUNO, YOLANDA

Yolanda Oreamuno (*b.* 8 April 1916; *d.* 8 July 1956), Costa Rican writer. Born in San José, Yolanda Oreamuno was one of the initiators of the contemporary Costa Rican narrative. Her psychological novel *La ruta de su evasión* (1950) won the Guatemalan 15 de Septiembre Prize. Finding it difficult to establish herself as a writer and intellectual in her own country, which she outspokenly criticized for its provincial attitudes and overly folkloric literature, from 1943 on she resided alternately in Guatemala, where she became a citizen in 1948, and in Mexico, where she died. In 1933, she composed a fiery essay on the role of women, which was later published in the literary journal *Repertorio Americano,* as were most of her essays and stories. The existence and location of her other novels, possibly as many as four, remain uncertain. Some of her stories have been translated into English and are included, with critical comments, in Victoria Urbano, editor, *Five Women Writers of Costa Rica* (1978), and Enrique Jaramillo Levi, editor, *When New Flowers Bloomed* (1991). Other writings are in her collection *A lo largo del corto camino* (1961) and in Alfonso Chase, editor, *Relatos escogidos* (1977).

– SUSAN E. CLARK

O'REILLY Y MCDOWELL, ALEJANDRO

Alejandro O'Reilly y McDowell (Alexander; *b.* 24 October 1723; *d.* 23 March 1794), governor of Louisiana (1769–1770) and inspector general of the Spanish Army. A native of Beltrasna, county Meath, near Dublin, Ireland, O'Reilly was schooled in Spain at the Colegio de las Escuelas Pías de Zaragoza. His military career began at the age of ten, when he became a cadet in the Hibernian Infantry Regiment. He took part in the Italian campaigns of Isabella, queen consort of Philip V, from 1734 to 1736 and again from 1740 to 1748, and was seriously wounded in the latter affair.

Following service in two European wars, O'Reilly studied Austrian, Prussian, and French military organization. As a military consultant, he introduced Prussian tactics to the Spanish army. He was promoted to brigadier and then to inspector general and field marshal of the army. In his role as inspector general he accompanied Spain's captain general of Cuba, the Conde de Ricla, to Cuba and Puerto Rico in 1763 and 1765. Reaching Havana on 30 June 1763, O'Reilly participated in the restoration of Havana to Spanish control following the Treaty of Paris (10 February 1763) in which Havana, under British occupation, was exchanged for Florida. He reformed the Cuban militia, setting up a system that endured for nearly a century. Returning to Spain, O'Reilly won favor with King Charles III when he commanded troops accompanying the king in his flight to Aranjuez during the riots of March 1766 against Esquilace.

Three years later, on 16 April 1769, while in La Coruña, he was appointed to head an expedition to put down a revolt in Louisiana, where dissident elements had expelled the Spanish governor, Antonio de ULLOA, in 1768. Arriving in Havana on 24 June 1769, O'Reilly commanded a force of 2,056 men and twenty-one ships. The fleet sailed on 6 July, reaching New Orleans on 18 August to take control of the colony. An immediate investigation and trial of the conspirators took place and on 24 October the ringleaders of the revolt were condemned to death.

The rapid conclusion of the trial enabled O'Reilly to devote his remaining months in the colony to a thorough reorganization of Louisiana's administration, including political, military, and fiscal reforms, the promulgation of a new legal code, the Code O'Reilly, as well as religious and commercial reforms. The most important of O'Reilly's reforms was his integration of Louisiana into the Spanish commercial system.

O'Reilly departed New Orleans in March of 1770, and in April returned to Spain, where he established a military academy at Ávila for infantry, cavalry, and engineers. On 28 January 1772 Charles III bestowed on him the title of Conde de O'Reilly y Vizconde de Cavan.

O'Reilly's later career was marked by failure. He commanded the ill-fated expedition to Algiers in 1775, which historian John Lynch has called "a model of military incompetence." Uninformed about the strength of the enemy, and following an ill-advised battle plan, some 5,000 Spanish troops were killed or wounded. When O'Reilly later blamed this defeat on the cowardice of his troops, protests took place in several cities. O'Reilly was subsequently referred to as "general disaster."

In 1780 he was appointed captain-general of Andalusia and governor of Cádiz. With the death of Charles III in 1788, he lost much of his support, resigning his post in 1789 and retiring to Valencia. When the French National Convention declared war against Spain in 1793, he was called back to service to command the Spanish Army in the Eastern Pyrenees. He died en route at Murcia and was buried in Cádiz.

— BRIAN E. COUTTS

OREJÓN Y APARICIO, JOSÉ DE

José de Orejón y Aparicio (*b.* 1706; *d.* ca. 7–21 May 1765), Peruvian composer and organist. Born in Huacho, Orejón was considered to be a child prodigy; at the age of nine he replaced an adult singer at the Lima Cathedral Choir. He was probably a pupil of Tomás de TORREJÓN Y VELASCO, the Lima cathedral's *maestro de capilla,* and studied organ with Juan de Peralta. After Orejón was ordained a priest, he became chief organist at the cathedral in 1742. Gifted with extraordinary technical proficiency and musicality, Orejón was named alternate *maestro de capilla* at Lima upon the death of Roque CERUTI in December 1760, becoming full *maestro de capilla* in 1764.

As a composer Orejón wrote in the Neapolitan style, with an affinity for Giovanni Battista Pergolesi's sacred works. His natural talent and excellent technical skills surpassed those of any other colonial composer born in the Americas during his lifetime. His most significant piece is the *Passion* [sic] *del Viernes Santo* (Good Friday Passion) for triple chorus and orchestra (1750). Written in a homophonic style, it has thirteen segments, with the voices moving in thirds and doubling. The *Cantata al Santísimo Sacramento "Mariposa de sus rayos"* for soprano, continuo, and two violins is in the baroque style. Among his duets are *A del día, Enigma divino,* and *Jilguerillo sonoro.* Although Orejón's compositions never reached Spain in his lifetime, they were widely heard in South America, reaching as far as the La Plata cathedral in Sucre (Bolivia). Orejón's works are kept in two archives: the Archivo Arzobispal de Lima and the Catedral de La Plata (Sucre). He was without question the finest composer in the Americas during the eighteenth century. He died in Lima.

— SUSANA SALGADO

ORELLANA, FRANCISCO DE

Francisco De Orellana (b. ca. 1511; d. November 1546), leader of the first European descent of the AMAZON River. Born in Trujillo, Spain, Orellana was in Panama in 1528 and probably joined Alonso de Alvarado's expedition to Peru in 1535. He fought against the native inhabitants in the siege against Lima in 1537 and two years later was one of the founders of Guayaquil, in present-day southwest Ecuador.

During this period, following the battle of Salinas (west Ecuador) on 6 April 1538, Gonzalo PIZARRO made his way to Ecuador and organized an expeditionary force to find the wealthy kingdom of El Dorado, the "Land of Cinnamon." Orellana joined as second in command. The 1541 expedition (about 180 Spaniards and 4,300 Indian auxiliaries) entered the upper Amazon basin through the province of Quixos, descending tributaries of the great river. The men failed to encounter Indian groups worthy of note and suffered great hardships, exhausting both food and other supplies. Realizing that a vast jungle stretched before them and that return upriver was daily becoming more difficult, Pizarro sent Orellana downstream in a brigantine that had been constructed earlier to search for supplies, expecting him to return within twelve days. Orellana's group consisted of fifty-seven men, including the Dominican friar Gaspar de Carbajal, who would become the chronicler of the expedition. They left the main camp on 26 December 1541, but did not find an Indian village with food for eight days. Swift currents had carried them so

---

Orellana and his men engaged in combat with a powerful force that included women fighters whom they compared to the Amazons of classical mythology.

---

far downstream that they believed it impossible to return to the Pizarro camp within the allotted time. After waiting briefly for Gonzalo Pizarro's forces to descend, they decided to continue on. They reached the mouth of the Napo near present-day Iquitos in Peru on 14 February 1542 and stopped in a village they called Aparia la Mayor, where they constructed a second brigantine.

On 1 March, Orellana and his men signed a document declaring their independence from Pizarro. Setting sail in mid-April, they passed through the Omaguas territory, where from 12 May on they faced almost continuous attacks by Indians until they reached the mouth of the Purus River on 23 May. For three months they sailed downriver, passing many large villages with hostile warriors. On 24 June they engaged in combat with a powerful force that included women fighters whom they compared to the Amazons of classical mythology. Carvajal's account of these warriors and of a nearby kingdom where women ruled prompted European cartographers to name the river the Amazon. The group reached the broad mouth of the river on 8 August but no salt water until the 26th. From here they sailed northwesterly along the coast, reaching the island of Cubagua in September and continuing on to Santo Domingo.

Orellana returned to Spain and in May 1543 reported directly to Prince Philip and the Council of the Indies. Meanwhile, Gonzalo Pizarro had managed to struggle back to Quito, losing most of his men to hunger and disease. Complaints of treason were lodged against Orellana, but he secured an appointment (13 February 1544) to return and conquer the vast new land.

With his new wife, Ana de Ayala, Orellana left Spain in May 1545, leading a small fleet. Two of the four ships were lost in the crossing, and illnesses took a severe toll. About half the group sailed up the Amazon, with fifty-seven companions dying of hunger and another ship lost. Orellana himself came down with "fevers" and died in the arms of his wife. The remnants of the expedition sailed to the island of Margarita, off the coast of present-day Venezuela.

— NOBLE DAVID COOK

ORELLANA, JOAQUÍN

Joaquín Orellana (b. 1933), Guatemalan composer and violinist. Born in Guatemala City, Orellana studied with the distinguished Guatemalan composer Castañeda. Although his productions have not been extensive, Orellana's compositions include orchestral, chamber, and choral music. Particularly well-known is a string trio he wrote for an Inter-American Music Festival held in Washington, D.C., in 1965.

— WADE A. KIT

ORELLANA, JOSÉ MARÍA

José María Orellana (b. 11 July 1872; d. 26 September 1926), president of Guatemala (1921–1926). Born to humble rural parentage in El Jícaro, in the eastern department of Zacapa, Orellana was a military man for most of his life. As a youth, according to legend, Orellana attracted the attention of Guatemalan president Manuel ESTRADA CABRERA, who became the boy's mentor and sent him to Guatemala's military academy, the Escuela Politécnica. After Orellana graduated as an officer and an engineer, he served his mentor in several military and political capacities. Although Orellana remained close to the dictator during his rule, he was still highly respected for his honesty and fairness as an officer and a politician. He was described as broad minded, tolerant, hard working, and sincere.

At the time of the overthrow of Cabrera in 1920, Orellana was a member of the Guatemalan National Assembly and the dictator's minister of public instruction. In his capacity as minister, Orellana opposed many of Estrada Cabrera's actions, contributed to the momentum of the uprising, and, thereby, was recognized as a friend and supporter of the Unionists—the coalition opposing Estrada Cabrera.

Nonetheless, Orellana, like many senior military officers, became disillusioned with the Unionists' experiment with democracy and the unrest that was associated with their government (1920–1921). Consequently, with the support of several senior members of Guatemala's Liberal Party, he agreed to participate in the coup that ousted the government of Carlos Herrera on 5 December 1921. Early in 1922, General Orellana achieved an overwhelming victory as the Liberal candidate in the presidential election and served as president until a fatal heart attack resulted in his death.

— WADE A. KIT

ORFILA, WASHINGTON ALEJANDRO JOSÉ LUIS

Washington Alejandro José Luis Orfila (*b.* 9 March 1925), Argentine diplomat; secretary general of the Organization of American States. Born in the city of Mendoza, Orfila's father was then governor of Mendoza Province. In 1946, when Federico Cantoni became the first Argentine ambassador appointed to the USSR, Orfila was assigned to Cantoni's staff. This early experience was followed by consular posts in Varsovia (1947), San Francisco (1948) and New Orleans (1949). Orfila's diplomatic career began in the Argentine embassy in Washington. In 1960 he was appointed ambassador to Japan; as such he returned to Washington in 1973. On 17 May 1975 Orfila was elected secretary general of the Organization of American States, and reelected for the period 1980–1985, but resigned in 1984. During his tenure as secretary general of the OAS, the treaties between Panama and the United States were signed (1977), by

which full sovereignty over the Panama Canal reverts to Panama in 1999. He authored *The Americas in the 1980s* (1980).

— CELSO RODRÍGUEZ

ORIBE, EMILIO

Emilio Oribe (*b. ca.* 1890s; *d.* 1975), Uruguayan poet, writer, literary critic, and educator. After completing his medical studies in Montevideo, Oribe was posted to Brussels as scientific attaché at the Uruguayan embassy. While there, he published his first book of poetry, *Alucinaciones de belleza* (1912). He never practiced medicine, but taught philosophy and worked for the National Council of Education of Uruguay. Oribe's poetry and essays were informed by the work of classical Greek and medieval philosophers, as is shown in *Transcendencia y platonismo en poesía* (1948) and *Tres ideales estéticos* (1958).

Essayistic works such as *Teoría del nous* (1934) and *El mito y el logos* (1945) focus primarily on topics relevant to the process of writing poetry and on "eternal" concerns such as time, death, and immortality. Characteristic of most of Oribe's thirty-seven published collections is an intellectual or metaphysical focus. Other poems, however, treat more earthy topics, such as the emotion experienced in the countryside, personal confidences, nature, history, customs, and the mystery of life.

Other important works by Oribe include *Fugacidad y grandeza* (1941), *La medusa de Oxford* (1950), *Ars magna: Poemas* (1950), and *Antología poética* (1965). He is considered one of the outstanding intellectuals of his generation.

— WILLIAM H. KATRA

ORIBE, MANUEL

Manuel Oribe (*b.* 26 August 1792; *d.* 12 November 1857), second president of Uruguay (1835–1838) around whom the Blanco party was formed, one of the two traditional political parties in Uruguay. The name Blanco derived from the white ribbons worn by Oribe's men. Oribe became involved very early in the military. In 1812, when he was just twenty years old, he participated in the second siege of Montevideo by patriot troops. The following year he went to Buenos Aires to study as a cadet at the Escuela de Matemáticas. He went back to Montevideo in 1814 during the last stage of the siege. In September, several months after the fall of the city, he was promoted to lieutenant in the First Grenadier Regiment, and a few days later he became an aide to the governor. Oribe was growing increasingly uncomfortable with the way Buenos Aires was treating Montevideo. In February 1815, the city passed into the hands of José Gervasio ARTIGAS, and Oribe remained there and accepted his authority. In 1817, when Montevideo was in the hands of the Portuguese, who had invaded the country in 1816, Artigas named Fructuoso RIVERA commander of the irregular forces to the south of the Río Negro to fight the Portuguese in guerrilla warfare. Oribe did not like this appointment and left for Buenos Aires, where he remained until 1821.

In Buenos Aires, Oribe became associated with a society called the Caballeros Orientales, founded in 1819 to promote Uruguayan independence. This group came to be dominated by the *cabildo* of Montevideo. It took advantage of the divisions in the enemy ranks caused by the Brazilian declaration of independence in September 1822. In 1823, Oribe led an unsuccessful revolt and returned to Buenos Aires in 1824.

In 1825, he organized an invasion force that has come to be known in Uruguayan history as La Cruzada de los Treinta y Tres. By the end of the same year the Brazilians were being engaged in battle by the Uruguayans. The conflict evolved into a regional one when Buenos Aires entered the war on the side of the Uruguayans. Oribe fought the Brazilians successfully in various campaigns during 1825 and 1826. In 1828, he was sent to arrest Rivera, who had invaded the Misiones Orientales at the time when a peace treaty was being negotiated, and the rivalry between the two men began. In 1832, Oribe was appointed chief of staff and the following year minister of war.

In March 1835, Oribe was elected president and tried to initiate a period of national reconstruction. His administration was in sharp contrast with that of Rivera (1830–1835), who paid very little attention to the affairs of government. Oribe's problems began when he attempted to bring the interior under Montevideo's control, an area that Rivera considered his own. On 16 July 1836, Rivera rose in rebellion against him. Oribe had some initial success, but in 1838 he was totally defeated and was forced to resign in October. He went to his ally, Juan Manuel de ROSAS of Argentina, for help, and in 1839 Rivera declared war on Rosas, initiating the Guerra Grande (1839–1852), which started out as a political dispute and turned into a regional war with the involvement of Brazil and Argentina and later into an international conflict joined by France and England. Oribe defeated Rivera in December 1842, and in February 1843 he laid siege to Montevideo, which lasted until October 1851. When an agreement was reached with Justo José de URQUIZA, Oribe retired to private life,

but in 1853 he was forced into exile, not returning until 1855.

– JUAN MANUEL PÉREZ

ORLICH BOLMARCICH, FRANCISCO JOSÉ

Francisco José Orlich Bolmarcich (*b.* 1907; *d.* October 1969), president of Costa Rica (1962–1966). Born in San Ramón, a member of one of Costa Rica's wealthiest families, "Chico" Orlich Bolmarcich studied accounting and business administration in New York in the 1920s. Orlich, along with José FIGUERES FERRER, his close friend and collaborator since childhood, dominated Costa Rican politics for two decades following the 1948 civil war. He and Figueres founded Costa Rica's principal political party, the National Liberation Party (PLN), in 1951. During Figueres's presidency (1953–1958), Orlich served as party leader in the Legislative Assembly. He lost the election for president in 1958, but ran successfully four years later.

Regarded as the more conservative of the two, particularly in the area of government intervention in the economy, Orlich nonetheless tackled the difficult issues of agrarian reform and housing for the poor that Figueres had avoided. He sponsored Costa Rica's membership in the Central American Common Market. Orlich's presidency was hampered by the eruption of the volcano Irazú (1963–1965), which caused grave economic hardship for over two years and led to charges of mismanagement of disaster relief, which contributed to the PLN's defeat in the presidential election of 1966.

– CHARLES D. AMERINGER

ORO, JUSTO SANTA MARÍA DE

Justo Santa María de Oro (*b.* 3 September 1772; *d.* 19 October 1836), Dominican priest, patriot, first bishop of Cuyo. In 1789 Oro, a native of San Juan, Argentina, entered the Dominican order. He was ordained to the priesthood in 1794 and went to Spain in 1809 for further studies and to get permission to establish schools in Argentina. The next year, after the May Revolution broke out, he returned and worked with José de SAN MARTÍN in the formation of the Army of the Andes. Oro was a member of the Congress of Tucumán and adamantly opposed any form of monarchy that did not have the approval of the people. He supported the Chilean independence movement under Bernardo O'HIGGINS. In 1818 he was made superior of the Dominicans in Chile. Oro was sent to Juan Fernández Island in 1825 because of his suspected involvement in a movement against the government of General Freire.

Permitted to leave Chile in 1828, he returned to San Juan, Argentina, where he was named apostolic vicar by Pope Leo XII. In 1834, he was named bishop of the newly formed diocese of Cuyo.

— NICHOLAS P. CUSHNER

OROZCO, JOSÉ CLEMENTE

José Clemente Orozco (*b.* 23 November 1883; *d.* 7 September 1949), Mexican muralist. Orozco grew up in Mexico City, where he attended the Escuela Nacional de Agricultura, the Escuela Nacional Preparatoria, and the Escuela Nacional de Bellas Artes (San Carlos). His first exhibit in Mexico City in 1916 showed the influence of the popular engraver and illustrator of Porfirian broadsides, José Guadalupe POSADA. Because of its popular inspiration and controversial subject matter (he depicted several prostitutes), it was not well-received by the public.

José Clemente Orozco. (Cenidiap / Inba)

In 1917, Orozco worked in a doll factory in New York City, where he tried to establish himself as an artist. A declared enemy of the decorative folk nationalism then in vogue among young Mexican artists, Orozco sought an art that would address the emotional intensity of Mexico's cataclysmic revolutionary reality. Called upon in 1922 by Education Minister José VASCONCELOS to paint the walls of the Escuela Nacional Preparatoria as part of the artistic Renaissance, Orozco emerged as a major artist of the twentieth century, depicting the agony of war from a peasant perspective and initiating the pictoral history of Mexico as an interracial drama of struggle and sorrow. In 1923, with Diego RIVERA, David Alfaro SIQUEIROS, and others, Orozco formed the Syndicate of Revolutionary Painters, which declared war on "bourgeois individualism" and committed itself to the creation of a monumental art for and about the Mexican people to capture "the moment of transition from a decrepit order to a new one."

Painting in the early 1930s at Pomona College in California, the New School for Social Research in New York City, Dartmouth College, and Mexico's Palacio de Bellas Artes, Orozco developed New World historical themes with an outraged sense of tragedy over the destructiveness of the contemporary world, an interpretation at odds with his fellow muralists' Marxist optimism about progress. Between 1936 and 1939, he painted in Guadalajara. His work in the university auditorium displays a stinging critique of political leaders. In the Palacio de Gobierno, he painted his famous image of Miguel Hidalgo. His most outstanding work, and one of the greatest works of twentieth-century art, is in the Hospicio Cabañas in Guadalajara, where he synthesizes his understanding of human history and nature in the Promethean figure of a man consuming himself by fire.

Additional murals by Orozco are in the Palacio de Justicia, the Hospital de Jesús Nazareno, the Jiquilpán revolutionary museum, the Escuela Nacional de Maestros, and the Museo Nacional de Historia in Chapultepec. When he died in Mexico City, he was buried in the Rotonda de los Hombres Ilustres in the Panteón de Dolores, the first artist to have had this honor.

— MARY KAY VAUGHAN

OROZCO, OLGA

Olga Orozco (*b.* 17 March 1920), Argentine poet. Born in La Pampa, she began her career as a student of literature in the Faculty of Philosophy and Letters at the University of Buenos Aires. She joined a group of writers that published their work in the literary magazine *Canto*, which later would be identified with the Generation of 1940. Her first publication was *Desde lejos* (1946; From Far Away), followed by *Las muertes* (1951; The Deaths), and *Los juegos peligrosos* (1962; Dangerous Games). In 1964 she won the first Municipal Prize for Poetry. *La oscuridad es otro sol* (1967; Darkness Is Another Light) won the second Municipal Prose Award, and in 1971 she received the Grand Prize of Honor from the Argentine Foundation for Poetry. Her next works were *Museo salvaje* (1974; Wild Museum), *Cantos a Berenice* (1977), and *Mutaciones de la realidad* (1979).

In 1979, in recognition of her poetic development, the first collection of her complete poetry was published, establishing her as one of the main voices in Argentine poetry. *Obra poética* was awarded the Grand Prize of the National Fund of the Arts in 1980 and the Esteban Echeverría Award in 1981. Two later books are *La noche a la deriva* (1983; Night Adrift) and *En el revés del cielo* (1987; In the Underside of Heaven). Among the themes that characterize Orozco's poetry are the religious concerns of a poet searching for primordial unity and the incorporation of elements from astrology, witchcraft, alchemy, and the tarot, which in combination create metamorphic imagery that displays uncanny perceptions of reality.

– MAGDALENA GARCÍA PINTO

OROZCO, PASCUAL, JR.

Pascual Orozco, Jr. (*b.* 28 January 1882; *d.* 30 August 1915), guerrilla army leader in the state of Chihuahua during the early years of the Mexican Revolution. Born near San Isidro, Chihuahua, Orozco learned to read and write at a local public school. Working as a muleteer for various mining companies, he gained a reputation as a good worker and honest man.

His popularity as a leader in his home state, his ability to recruit and secure the allegiance of his followers, his knowledge of the local terrain, and his tactical ability in guerrilla combat made Orozco a key figure in the Revolution. He was one of the early leaders of the antireelectionist movement against General Porfirio DÍAZ and part of the initial group that rallied around Revolutionary leader Francisco I. MADERO. When Madero launched his rebellion after escaping from prison following the fraudulent elections of 1910, Orozco immediately rose to support Madero's Plan of SAN LUIS POTOSÍ (5 October 1910).

Orozco was responsible for some of the initial successes of the movement, including the first Revolutionary victory over federal troops at Pedernales (27 November). He later led the attack against Ciudad Juárez, which resulted on 10 May 1911 in the capture of that

city, the key victory of the uprising. As a result, Orozco enjoyed prominence as a hero of the Revolution. He was also responsible for putting down several revolts against the Madero regime.

Impatient with Madero, Orozco disavowed the administration and launched his own rebellion on 3 March 1912. Gaining control of much of the north, his movement constituted the strongest threat to the Madero administration, and his troops repelled an attack by a federal army led by the minister of war, General José González Salas. A few months later, however, Orozco was defeated by a federal army commanded by General Victoriano HUERTA in a series of battles at Rellano (23 May) and Bachimba (3 July).

When Huerta deposed Madero (February 1913), Orozco supported the Huerta regime and commanded troops opposing Madero's successors. His controversial campaigns on behalf of the Huerta regime gained him several promotions, carrying him ultimately to the highest rank in the Mexican Army, general of division, and also earning him the enmity of his former Revolutionary colleagues, who felt he had betrayed their movement.

After the fall of Huerta (15 July 1914), Orozco opposed both the interim regime and the Revolutionary government of General Venustiano CARRANZA. Forced to flee to the United States, Orozco joined with Huerta and other exiles in seeking to launch a new rebellion. The rebellion was forestalled when Orozco and Huerta were arrested by U.S. marshals on 27 June 1915. Escaping from custody, Orozco was shot by a U.S. posse in Culberson County, Texas.

– KENNETH J. GRIEB

OROZCO Y BERRA, MANUEL

Manuel Orozco y Berra (*b.* 1818; *d.* 27 January 1881), Mexican historian, engineer, and statistician. Born in Mexico City, the son of an insurgent captain who served under Mariano MATAMOROS during the Mexican War of Independence, Orozco attended the Colegio de Minería as an engineer topographer. While in Puebla as *maestro mayor* of public works, he received his licenciate in law (1847). His friend José Fernando Ramírez secured a post for him at the Archivo General de la Nación, of which he later became director. In 1856, he became senior official in the Secretaría de Fomento.

A contributor to literary and political journals since his youth, he wrote on geographical and historical subjects for the seven-volume *Diccionario universal de historia y geografía* (1853–1856). Between 1853 and 1857, he edited the *Documentos para la historia de México* in twenty volumes. A minister of the Supreme Court of

Justice (1863), he declined appointment to the Assembly of Notables but in 1864 he accepted membership in the Scientific Commission of Mexico.

Under the empire, he again worked at the Secretaria de Fomento and became director of the National Museum created by Emperor MAXIMILIAN, who appointed him to the Council of State in September 1865. Rehabilitated by 1870 (he had never been a Conservative), he rejoined the Society of Geography and Statistics and the Academy and Literature and Sciences. His last years were dedicated to his magnum opus, the four-volume *Historia antigua de la conquista de México* (1880). His interest in the pre-Columbian era distinguished him as part of the Mexican historiographical revival of the latter part of the nineteenth century.

— BRIAN HAMNETT

ORPHÉE, ELVIRA

Elvira Orphée (*b.* 1924), Argentine writer. Born in Tucumán, she is considered one of the most original authors in contemporary Argentine literature. She grew up in Tucumán and in Buenos Aires. She suffered health problems that affected her as a child, an experience from which she drew frequently to build her fictional world. When she was sixteen her mother died and she was sent by her father to live in Buenos Aires with relatives. There she enrolled at the University of Buenos Aires. Later she studied in Madrid and in Paris, where she met the Argentine painter, Miguel Ocampo, whom she married.

Orphée's La última conquista de El Angel *describes a member of the Buenos Aires secret police in charge of torture and abuse of political prisoners.*

Orphée published her first collection of short stories, *Dos veranos* (Two Summers), in 1956. In 1961 she published *Uno,* a novel, followed by *Aire tan dulce* (When the Air Is Soft, 1966), which is considered her best work for its innovative language and her treatment of love and hate. *En el fondo* (1969; At the Bottom) received the first Municipal Prize for the Novel. She divorced her husband and went to live in Caracas, Venezuela, for some time. In 1973 she published a collection of short stories, *Su demonio preferido,* followed in 1977 by *La última conquista de El Angel,* a novel in episodes whose main character is a member of the Buenos Aires secret police in charge of torture and abuse of political prisoners. Later works include *Las viejas fantasiosas* (1981;

The Old Ladies' Tales), *La muerte y los desencuentros* (1990), and *Ciego de cielo* (1990; Blind of Heaven), a collection of short stories that deal with justice.

— MAGDALENA GARCÍA PINTO

ORREGO-SALAS, JUAN ANTONIO

Juan Antonio Orrego-Salas (*b.* 18 January 1919), Chilean composer, born in Santiago. His composition teachers at the National Conservatory of Music in Chile were Humberto ALLENDE and Domingo Santa Cruz. He received degrees in arts and letters and in architecture. With fellowships from both the Rockefeller and Guggenheim Foundations he studied in the United States from 1944 to 1946 with Paul Henry Lang, Randall Thompson, and Aaron Copland. From 1949 to 1961 he edited the well known *Revista musical chilena.* He wrote articles on music folklore and theoretical topics and essays on Copland, VILLA-LOBOS, and the Chilean composers LENG and Santa Cruz. He was the director of the Latin American Music Center and professor of composition at Indiana University from 1961 to 1987.

Orrego-Salas's early musical language had influences of Spanish popular dances with their characteristic rhythms and harmonies. He utilized more experimental techniques and atonality in his larger works. Beyond some stylistic similarities with works of de Falla and Hindemith, the composer has done significant work with rhythmical relationships characterized by polyrhythms and multimetric layers. Nevertheless, Orrego-Salas's use of dodecaphonic techniques has never attained the level of strict twelve-tone writing. From his first period: *Cantata de Navidad* (1945) and *Canciones castellanas* (1948), both for soprano and chamber orchestra; Symphony no. 1 (1949); *El retablo del rey pobre* (1949–1952), an opera-oratoria. He began experimenting with more contemporary languages in *Serenata concertante* for orchestra (1954); *Dúos concertantes* for cello and piano (1955); and particularly with his Symphony no. 2 (1954). Among his piano works are Suite no. 1 (1946); *Variaciones sobre un pregón* (1954); *Rústica* (1952); *Sonata* (1967); and *Rondo-Fantasia* (1984).

In his *Missa "In Tempore Discordiae"* (1968–1969), a large work for chorus, tenor, and orchestra, he uses spoken effects, whispering, quasi-parlando and aleatoric procedures. A prolific composer, Orrego-Salas created *Biografía mínima de Salvador Allende* for voice, guitar, trumpet, and percussion (1983); Concerto for violin and orchestra (1984); Fantasia for piano and wind orchestra (1986); and *Partita* for alto saxophone and piano trio (1988). He wrote the opera *Widows* (1987–1990), based on the novel by Ariel Dorfman.

— ALCIDES LANZA

ORTEGA DEL VILLAR, ANICETO

Aniceto Ortega del Villar (*b.* 1825; *d.* 17 November 1875), Mexican composer and physician. Born in Tulancingo, Hidalgo, the son of a statesman, Ortega was educated in Mexico City at the Seminario Conciliar de México (1837), the Seminario de San Ildefonso (1840), and the School of Medicine (1841–1845). He founded the Sociedad Filarmónica Mexicana in 1866. In 1867 his march *Zaragoza* was published; later it became, unofficially, Mexico's second national anthem. Two other marches, *Republicana* and *Potosina*, premiered at the Gran Teatro Nacional. His nationalistic opera *Guatimotzin*, based on a libretto by José Cuellar, told the story of the defense of Mexico by the Aztecs. It was first performed on 13 September 1871, at the Gran Teatro Nacional, with the Mexican soprano Angela PERALTA and the tenor Enrico Tamberlik in the leading roles. This opera is generally considered the first in Mexico to incorporate indigenous elements into the Italian format then prevalent. Ortega also wrote several piano pieces, among them *Invocación a la Beethoven, op. 2* (1867). This work, performed in 1867 and published by Wagner and Levien, created an interest in that composer that resulted in a Beethoven Festival, held in Mexico City in 1871. Ortega died in Mexico City.

— SUSANA SALGADO

ORTEGA SAAVEDRA, DANIEL

Daniel Ortega Saavedra (*b.* 11 November 1945), Sandinista leader and president of Nicaragua (1985–1990). Ortega was born in the small town of La Libertad in the department of Chontales. His father was an accountant for a mining firm and fought with Augusto César SANDINO's army in the 1920s. Both of his parents were arrested by Anastasio SOMOZA GARCÍA in the 1940s. The family moved to Managua when Ortega was still a boy. He attended private church schools and met Jaime WHEELOCK at the Christian Brothers' Pedagogic Institute. He studied briefly for the priesthood in El Salvador, under the direction of the Nicaraguan bishop Miguel OBANDO Y BRAVO. However, Ortega soon returned to Nicaragua and increased his activities in the Nicaraguan Patriotic Youth organization in the early 1960s. For a short time he attended law school at the University of Central America, where he focused on organizing student protests.

Ortega made contact with the Sandinista leadership and was recruited into the guerrilla ranks in 1963. He generally operated out of Managua and did not have much experience with jungle warfare in the northern countryside. He was arrested for trying to seize a National Guard post and for bombing vehicles at the U.S. embassy. In 1964 Ortega was detained in Guatemala for illegal political activity and turned over to the Nicaraguan government. He was severely tortured, which led to his involvement in the assassination of a National Guard officer in October 1967. The following month, he was charged with bank robbery and sentenced to eight years in prison. While in jail, he studied law, history, and geography. He also wrote poems, one of which was titled "I Never Saw Managua When the Miniskirt Was in Style." A Sandinista raid on the Christmas party of a wealthy landowner freed Ortega in a prisoner-hostage exchange (December 1974). He joined the Sandinista National Directorate in 1975 and helped his brother Humberto develop the Tercerista insurrectionist strategy that was successful against the National Guard in the late 1970s. He rarely made statements for attribution before the victory and allowed Humberto to speak for the Terceristas. He was part of the reunified guerrilla leadership that directed the final offensive from March to July 1979.

After the fall of the Somoza regime, Ortega became a member of the Governing Junta of National Recon-

Daniel Ortega Saavedra after being sworn in as president, 10 January 1985. (Wide World)

struction. He emerged as the principal representative of the junta and the Sandinistas and traveled frequently in Latin America, Europe, and Asia as Nicaragua's chief diplomat. After the resignation of two non-Sandinista members of the junta in April 1980, Ortega and Sergio RAMÍREZ became the dominant political figures of the revolution. They were selected as the Sandinistas' presidential and vice presidential candidates for the November 1984 election. The ticket won by a landslide, with 67 percent of the popular vote.

Ortega assumed the presidency in January 1985 for a six-year term. One of his first acts was to centralize economic planning in the Executive Committee of the President. This created some tension among the normally collegial group of revolutionary commanders. The foremost tasks of his government were creating a new constitution and defending the country from the counterrevolutionary threat. Ortega divided his time between the constitutional debate, national economic planning, and international diplomacy. He gained the reputation of a pragmatist with a knack for political gamesmanship. His good relationship with Mikhail Gorbachev brought economic and military aid to Nicaragua from the Soviet Union at the height of the war with the contras. Ortega frequently traveled to eastern Europe to consult with heads of state and secure support for Nicaragua against the United States. Moreover, he played a key role in the negotiation of the Central American peace plan that was initiated by Costa Rican President Oscar ARIAS in February 1987.

Toward the end of his term, Ortega implemented a severe economic austerity plan designed by his economic adviser, Alejandro Martínez Cuenca. It was intended to control hyperinflation, encourage greater productivity, and reduce public spending. At the same time, Ortega opened lines of communication with the internal opposition and business community in a process known as *concertación*. Much of his political behavior in the late 1980s was in anticipation of the presidential election of February 1990. Ortega and the Sandinistas had to confront the military threat of the contra force and the electoral challenge of a fourteen-party opposition coalition, the Nicaraguan Opposition Union (UNO).

Once again, Ortega headed the Sandinista ticket. During the campaign, he portrayed himself as a stalwart revolutionary, a strong male figure, and a competent administrator. However, a large part of the female population, particularly housewives, and many peasants and young males rejected Ortega in favor of Violeta BARRIOS DE CHAMORRO. In the wake of defeat, Ortega promised supporters that they would "govern from below" and that the Sandinista revolution would continue. Executive power was passed to Chamorro in April 1990 after

two months of intense negotiation that culminated in the signing of the Protocol of Transition.

Ortega retained his place on the Sandinista National Directorate and his title of Commander of the Revolution. At the first party congress in July 1991, he was elected general secretary by a unanimous vote. This was the first time the Sandinistas had chosen a party secretary to oversee day-to-day activities. Ortega delivered a three-hour speech at the meeting that recognized the mistakes of the Sandinista revolutionary government but called on the members to defend their right to rebellion. In September 1991, he replaced Sergio Ramírez as leader of the Sandinista deputies in the National Assembly. This was attributed to Ortega's role as head of the party and his more aggressive political style. He has traveled widely as a self-proclaimed emissary of peace, most notably during the Iraqi occupation of Kuwait in late 1990. He has come under heavy criticism from political opponents for his frequent trips and for keeping his spacious residence, which has been claimed by its former owner.

– MARK EVERINGHAM

ORTEGA SAAVEDRA, HUMBERTO

Humberto Ortega Saavedra (*b.* September 1942), Nicaraguan leader and chief of the Sandinista Popular Army. Ortega, brother of Daniel ORTEGA, was born in the department of Chontales in central Nicaragua. He attended private Catholic schools and later taught catechism classes in Managua. He joined the radical student movement in the late 1950s and became the leader of the Nicaraguan Patriotic Youth organization in 1962. He joined the Sandinista National Liberation Front in 1965. After participating in the Sandinista defeat at Pancasán in 1967, Ortega fled to Cuba, where he remained for two years. He contributed to the refinement of the Sandinista strategy and objectives during this time. In December 1969, he was captured after trying to free Carlos FONSECA from a Costa Rican jail. He was handed over to the Nicaraguan National Guard and severely tortured. As a result, he partially lost the use of his right arm and some motor skills. He was freed in October 1970 after Sandinistas hijacked an airplane in Nicaragua.

Ortega became a prominent intellectual force in the revolutionary movement in the 1970s. He argued for a strategy of popular armed revolt throughout the country and worked closely with Carlos Fonseca. After Fonseca's death in 1976, Ortega emerged as the primary advocate of an urban-based insurrection. This plan was the basis for the "General Political-Military Platform of the Struggle of the Sandinista National Liberation Front," published in May 1977. The document coincided with the ascendancy of Ortega's Tercerista faction and efforts to recruit business, religious, and professional figures into the revolution. Tactical alliances with the middle and upper classes were critical factors in the Sandinistas' success during the civil war of 1978 and 1979. Ortega directly coordinated guerrilla attacks on the National Guard with business strikes and urban demonstrations until the July 1979 victory.

Ortega was named commander in chief of the Sandinista Popular Army in October 1979. He became minister of defense in January 1980, a post giving him control over the air force, air defense, navy, and Sandinista militia. He held the title Commander of the Revolution and was the only four-star general in the Nicaraguan military. He managed the military buildup and recruitment process during the war against the counterrevolutionary force. He established excellent relations with the officer corps and was popular among the soldiers.

After the Sandinistas' electoral defeat in February 1990, President Violeta BARRIOS DE CHAMORRO named herself minister of defense but retained Ortega as head of the military; in return he promised not to participate in partisan politics while head of the armed forces. This decision was harshly criticized by the far right of the fourteen-party coalition that backed Chamorro's candidacy. Ortega supported Chamorro's desire to eliminate obligatory military service and to reduce the armed forces to one-third of their size at the height of the conflict with the contras. In September 1991 Ortega officiated at the celebration of the twelfth anniversary of the Sandinista Popular Army, accompanied by President Chamorro and Cardinal Miguel OBANDO Y BRAVO.

At the Sandinista Party congress in July 1991, Ortega gave a strong speech in support of the neoliberal economic stabilization plan for Nicaragua. He also reiterated his assurances that the army would remain behind the administration under any circumstances. The Sandinista Assembly unanimously reelected him to the National Directorate during the congress, but he refused to reassume the post he had held since 1975. On account of political pressure from opponents in the National Assembly and legal difficulties linking him to the murder of the son of a wealthy family, Ortega agreed to step down as army chief in late 1994.

— MARK EVERINGHAM

ORTIZ, FERNANDO

Fernando Ortiz (*b.* 16 July 1881; *d.* 10 April 1969), Cuban scholar, public servant, and political activist. No three words can describe the life and activities of this multifaceted Cuban intellectual. He studied law in Ha-

vana, completed his studies in Barcelona, and began his career as a criminal law specialist. His interests soon broadened to include sociology, archaeology, history, philology, anthropology, musicology, and ethnology. He served as a consular official in Italy, as public prosecutor for Havana, as a professor of law and, later, anthropology at the University of Havana, and as a representative for several terms in Congress. A tireless political agitator, he directed the *Junta Cubana de Renovación Nacional* against governmental corruption in 1923 and organized the Cuban Alliance for a Free World Against Fascism in 1945. In answer to the fascist claim of Aryan superiority, he wrote *El engaño de las razas* (*Deception of the Races*) in 1945.

Ortiz introduced the term "afro" as a prefix in sociological and anthropological studies.

Ortiz is best known for his studies on African-Cuban culture and as a prosecutor of sugar monoculture. His studies of the African contribution to Cuban life have marked him as the "greatest definer of the Cuban identity." In his first study of colonial blacks, *Hampa afrocubano: Los negros brujos* published in 1906, he introduced the term "afro" as a prefix in sociological and anthropological studies. He further initiated use of the term "transculturation" to replace the many other terms used to describe the symbiosis of cultures. He founded the Society of Afro-Cuban Studies as a forum to promote awareness of the importance of Africans to the Cubans. His works span the colonial period to the modern, slavery to music and dance, and he laid the foundation for the unique national identity of the Cuban people.

His book best known to North Americans is *Cuban Counterpoint: Tobacco and Sugar* in which he condemns the sugar industry and describes its evils and calls for promotion of the Cuban tobacco industry. He strongly opposed the United States' growing influence on Cuba and accused it of using sugar to increase its dominance over Cuban people. His criticisms brought to light the political and economic dependence of Cuba on the United States.

— JACQUELYN BRIGGS KENT

ORTIZ, RAFAEL MONTÁÑEZ

Rafael Montáñez Ortiz (Ralph Ortiz; *b.* 30 January 1934), Puerto Rican artist. Ortiz, a native of Brooklyn, New York, received a B.S. and an M.F.A. from Pratt Institute, and a master's and a doctorate in education from Columbia University Teachers College. He has worked in sculpture, installation, performance, and computer-laser video. During the 1960s, he was involved in the Destruction Art movement. "Destructivism: A Manifesto," written in 1962, was the first of his many theoretical writings. Ortiz was also a member of the Art Workers' Coalition and one of the founders of New York City's Museo del Barrio, established to promote the culture of Puerto Ricans and other Latin Americans. His mixed-media performances incorporate ritual and shamanistic elements with audience participation. Ortiz has held performances and shown his mixed-media pieces and videos throughout North America and Europe. He has taught at New York University (1968), Hostos Community College (1970), and Rutgers University (1971).

– MIRIAM BASILIO

ORTIZ, ROBERTO MARCELINO

Roberto Marcelino Ortiz (*b.* 24 September 1886; *d.* 25 July 1942), cabinet minister and president of Argentina (1938–1942). Born in Buenos Aires, Ortiz received a law degree from the University of Buenos Aires in 1909. After establishing a successful law practice in the Argentine capital, he sought public office. He first served as a city councilman in Buenos Aires between 1918 and 1920. He then advanced to the Argentine Chamber of Deputies, where he represented Buenos Aires until 1924. In 1925, President Marcelo T. de ALVEAR (1922–1928) appointed him minister of public works.

Active in national politics through the 1920s, Ortiz became one of the leading Anti-Personalist Radicals. He returned to public service during the Concordancia, when President Agustín P. JUSTO (1932–1938) named him minister of finance (1935). Justo selected him as his successor, and in 1938 he was elected president. In office, Ortiz tried to curtail the fraudulent electoral practices that had undermined Argentine democracy after 1930. Before substantive changes were introduced, diabetes forced him to delegate power in 1940 to Ramón CASTILLO and then to resign in June 1942.

– DANIEL LEWIS

ORTIZ DE AYALA, SIMÓN TADEO

Simón Tadeo Ortiz de Ayala (*b.* 18 October 1788; *d.* 18 October 1833), Mexican entrepreneur and diplomat. Born in Mascota, Jalisco, Ortiz de Ayala visited Spain, where in 1810 he became a champion of independence and initiated a decade of travels in search of aid for his country that took him to the United States, much of South America, and England. In 1822 he published *Resumen de la estadística del Imperio Mexicano.*

After a mission to Guatemala in 1822, Ortiz de Ayala became a land speculator in Texas as well as in Coatzacoalcos in the south. Although he developed a number of schemes to colonize both areas, none was successful. While the Mexican consul in Bordeaux he published another important analysis, *México considerado como nación independiente y libre* (1832).

– JAIME E. RODRÍGUEZ O.

ORTIZ DE DOMÍNGUEZ, JOSEFA

Josefa Ortiz de Domínguez (*b.* 5 September 1768; *d.* 1829), Mexican insurgent heroine, known as "la Corregidora." Born in Morelia, she was the wife of Miguel DOMÍNGUEZ (1756–1830), who became corregidor (provincial magistrate) of Querétaro. She was in contact with various autonomists and participated in the conspiracy of 1810. When the conspiracy was denounced, Domínguez apprehended several of the participants and locked up his wife to prevent her from informing the others. But Josefa was able to send word of the danger to Ignacio ALLENDE (1769–1811). Upon receiving the news, Miguel HIDALGO Y COSTILLA (1753–1811) initiated the rebellion of 16 September. Confined to the convent of Santa Clara, Josefa was freed shortly thereafter. She continued aiding the insurgency. In 1813 the authorities initiated proceedings against her, believing her to be the "Anne Boleyn" of the movement, and she was imprisoned in Mexico City in the convent of Santa Teresa until 1817. When Agustín de ITURBIDE (1783–1824) proclaimed himself emperor in 1822, she refused to be a maid of honor of the empress. She died in Mexico City in 1829. In 1878, the Congress of Querétaro declared her *Benemérita de la Patria.*

– VIRGINIA GUEDEA

ORTIZ DE ZÁRATE, JUAN

Juan Ortiz de Zárate (*b.* 1521; *d.* 26 January 1576) and Juana (*d.* 1584), Adelantado of Río de la Plata and heir thereof. Ortiz de Zárate was born in Vizcaya, Spain, to a prominent family. He went to America with the first viceroy of Perú, Blasco NÚÑEZ DE VELA, and became a wealthy man in Chuquisaca.

In 1567, Diego López de Zúñiga y Velasco, count of Nieva, viceroy of Peru, gave Ortiz de Zárate a temporary *adelantazgo* (governorship) of the Río de la Plata. He returned to Spain to be confirmed by the crown, and disembarked again on 17 October 1572, arriving in the Río de la Plata in November of the following year. After suffering many hardships, he finally reached Asunción in February 1575 to take charge of the government. He died the following year.

Ortiz de Zárate named Juana, his daughter with the Inca Princess Leonor Yupanqui, his universal heir. The government of the *adelantazgo* would be in the hands of the person whom his daughter married, granted he follow all the capitulations made between Ortiz de Zárate and Philip II.

Juana had many suitors, and finally married *licenciado* Juan de Torres de Vera y Aragón in December 1577. She died seven years later.

– JUAN MANUEL PÉREZ

ORTIZ MENA, ANTONIO

Antonio Ortiz Mena (*b.* 22 September 1908), Mexican and international financial figure. As secretary of the treasury (1958–1970), Ortiz Mena presided over the longest period of consistently high rates of economic growth in Mexico and was the only Mexican in recent decades to hold this position consecutively under two administrations. He is considered to be the architect of the economic model, known as "stabilizing growth," that Mexico adopted during this period, and is regarded by leftist intellectuals as the true organizer of the new bourgeoisie.

Born in Parral, Chihuahua, Ortiz Mena is a member of a third generation of important political figures, his grandfathers having been active in politics and his father treasurer of the Federal District. Ortiz Mena is the political disciple of President Adolfo RUIZ CORTINES (1952–1958) and the uncle of President Carlos SALINAS (1988–1994). He attended the National Preparatory School and the National School of Law, where, along with future president Miguel Alemán (1946–1952), he was a member of the distinguished Generation of 1925–1928. Early in his career he was associated with the Guanajuato political group, led by José Aguilar y Maya. Aided by his mentor in the 1930s, he held a number of minor positions in the federal bureaucracy before joining Ruiz Cortines's cabinet as director general of the Mexican Institute of Social Security (1952–1958). After leaving the treasury secretariat in 1970, he headed the Inter-American Development Bank from 1971 through 1988. In 1988, Salinas appointed him director general of Banamex, one of Mexico's largest banks. He was twice considered as a possible precandidate for the official party nomination for president in 1963 and in 1969. His son, Antonio Ortiz Salinas, has also held political office.

– RODERIC AI CAMP

ORTIZ RUBIO, PASCUAL

Pascual Ortiz Rubio (*b.* 10 March 1877; *d.* 4 November 1963), Mexican president. He was elected in a hotly contested presidential race with José VASCONCELOS in 1929, after president-elect Álvaro OBREGÓN was assassinated before taking office. Some analysts believe he actually lost to Vasconcelos. During his administration (5 February 1930 to 4 September 1932), former president Plutarco ELÍAS CALLES (1924–1928) remained so powerful behind the scenes and his influence so openly pervasive that Ortiz Rubio resigned in protest against his lack of presidential sovereignty and authority. Ortiz Rubio was the second of three presidents to fill out the first six-year presidential term, 1928–1934.

Ortiz Rubio was born in Morelia, Michoacán, the son of lawyer Pascual Ortiz, from a landowning family, and Leonor Rubio. He was related by marriage to President José LÓPEZ PORTILLO. He attended preparatory school at the famous Colegio de San Nicolás in Michoacán, and as a student leader opposed the reelection of Porfirio DÍAZ in 1896. He completed his topographical engineering degree at the National College of Mines (later the National School of Engineering) in 1902 and returned to Morelia, where he soon involved himself in local politics. Elected to the 1912–1913 federal legislature after MADERO's victory, he became a member of the "Renovation Group." After Madero's murder, Victoriano HUERTA imprisoned him in 1913.

After his release, Ortiz Rubio joined the Constitutionalists as a colonel of engineers. In 1914, he was in charge of enemy properties for the Mexican government and directed the federal stamp bureau. By 1915, he had risen to the rank of brigadier general, responsible for engineering supplies. He later directed the department of military engineers for the secretariat of war before becoming governor of his home state (1917–1920). He served presidents Adolfo de la HUERTA and Obregón as secretary of communications and public works (1920–1921) and president Calles appointed him ambassador to Germany and then Brazil. He became the National Revolutionary Party's presidential candidate in 1929. After resigning the presidency in 1932, the only Mexican to do so since 1913, he went to the United States. He returned to Mexico in 1935.

– RODERIC AI CAMP

OSÓRIO, MANUEL LUÍS

Manuel Luís Osório (*b.* 10 May 1808; *d.* 4 October 1879), Brazilian military hero and politician. The son of a modest rancher, Osório overcame his relatively humble origin and almost complete lack of formal education to become one of his country's greatest military figures and leading Liberal politicians. His military career began with his participation as a low-ranking officer in the Cisplatine War (1825–1828). In the Farroupilha

Revolt (1835–1845), his distinguished service on the Loyalist side caught the attention of the military commander and sped his rise through the ranks. By 1852 he was entrusted with the command of the Brazilian division sent to Argentina to combat Juan Manuel de ROSAS. He also led the Brazilian force that occupied Montevideo in 1864. When the War of the Triple Alliance broke out the following year, Osório was in charge of the Brazilian military contingent, coordinating the first wave of attacks on Paraguayan forces with the Argentine Bartolomé MITRE. After leading his troops to a series of victories, Osório was wounded twice and left the front. On both occasions he returned to battle after short periods of recovery. In the midst of that war, he uttered his famous phrase: "It is easy to command free men; it is enough to show them the path of duty."

"It is easy to command free men; it is enough to

show them the path of duty."

As reward for his service, he received titles of nobility, being named first baron, then viscount, and finally marquês de Erval. At the close of the Farroupilha Revolt he served in the provincial legislature of his native Rio Grande do Sul. In 1862 he helped found a reformulated Liberal Party in that province and later won a seat in the national Senate. A year after achieving his country's highest military rank in 1877, Osório assumed the post of minister of war in the Sinimbú cabinet, a position he held until his death.

— ROGER A. KITTLESON

OSORIO, OSCAR

Oscar Osorio (*b.* 1910; *d.* 6 March 1969), president of El Salvador (1950–1956). A graduate of the Escuela Politécnica Militar, he rose through the ranks until exiled to Mexico for conspiracy in 1945. Returning in 1948, he joined the young officers who overthrew President Salvador CASTEÑEDA CASTRO in 1948. An admirer of the Mexican PRI (Partido Revolucionario Institucional), he organized the military-civilian coalition that, through the PRUD–PCN (Revolutionary Party of Democratic Unification–National Coalition Party), dominated Salvadoran politics for thirty-one years.

Osorio led the military junta of 1948–1949 and was elected to the presidency in 1950. As president he launched what Charles Anderson termed the "controlled revolution," namely, a strategy in which the government would seek to satisfy growing middle-class demands for change by enacting a moderate program of socioeconomic reforms without seriously disrupting the existing social and economic structure. Limited political opposition would be allowed by permitting a few accepted political parties to participate in elections.

— ROLAND H. EBEL

OSPINA, PEDRO NEL

Pedro Nel Ospina (*b.* 18 September 1858; *d.* 1 July 1927), Conservative Party leader and president of Colombia (1922–1926). Ospina was born in Bogotá's presidential palace, the son of President Mariano OSPINA RODRÍGUEZ. He spent much of his childhood in Guatemala and received a degree in mining engineering from the University of California. Settling in Antioquia, Ospina joined his brothers in managing the family businesses, which were concentrated in coffee but also included mining. Elected to Congress in 1892, he allied himself with the Historical wing of the Conservative Party. He distinguished himself as a Conservative commander during the War of the Thousand Days and was named minister of war in 1901 by Vice President José Manuel MARROQUÍN, who had seized power from President Manuel A. Sanclemente. Ospina's participation in an abortive plot to restore Sanclemente led to his banishment. While in exile, he studied cotton cultivation and textile manufacturing in Mexico, the United States, and Europe. He was later a founder of the country's first modern textile factory, established near Medellín in 1906.

In the presidential race of 1922 Ospina defeated Liberal Benjamín HERRERA. The most important achievement of his administration was the adoption of banking and fiscal reforms recommended by Edwin W. Kemmerer, who spent six months in Colombia in 1923. The reforms included establishment of a central bank, the Banco de la República; modernization of the budgeting process; and the creation of the office of national comptroller. Ospina was the father of the economic historian Luis Ospina Vásquez (1905–1977).

— HELEN DELPAR

OSPINA PÉREZ, MARIANO

Mariano Ospina Pérez (*b.* 24 November 1891; *d.* 14 April 1976), president of Colombia (1946–1950). From a prominent Medellín family, and grandson of the Conservative president Mariano OSPINA RODRÍGUEZ, Ospina received an engineering degree in Medellín and later studied in the United States. As head of the powerful coffee-growers' federation in the 1930s, Ospina often clashed with the Liberal government; but as a Conservative moderate he opposed the extremism of that party's leader, Laureano GÓMEZ. Elected president in 1946 over the divided Liberals, Ospina proclaimed a "National Union" government with Liberal participation; but as the partisan violence known as the *Violencia* spiraled out of control in much of Colombia, the accord collapsed. Ospina only narrowly survived the uprising that followed the assassination of Liberal leader Jorge Eliécer GAITÁN on 9 April 1948. On 9 November 1949 Ospina dissolved the Congress and imposed rigid press censorship, installing a Conservative dictatorship that lasted until the military coup of 13 June 1953. Ospina, like other protagonists of Colombia's political breakdown, supported the bipartisan National Front accord of 1957. In 1954 he founded the Bogotá financial newspaper *La República*.

– RICHARD J. STOLLER

OSPINA RODRÍGUEZ, MARIANO

Mariano Ospina Rodríguez (*b.* 18 October 1805; *d.* 11 January 1885), Colombian president. Born to a family of provincial landowners near Bogotá, Mariano Ospina Rodríguez was educated as a lawyer at the Colegio de San Bartolomé. As a young liberal activist he took part in the plot against Simón BOLÍVAR's life in 1828. When the plot failed, he was exiled to Antioquia, where he ultimately settled. Ospina's political views became steadily more moderate until the 1840s, when he founded the Ministerial (Conservative) Party. As interior minister in the government of Pedro ALCÁNTARA HERRÁN (1841–1845), he reformed the educational curriculum and was instrumental in bringing the Jesuits back to Colombia. Elected president in 1856, he accepted a federalist constitution in 1858, but was accused by Liberals of violating states' rights and became the only Colombian chief executive ever overthrown (in 1861) by full-scale civil war. He then spent ten years in Guatemala. Ospina died in Medellín, Colombia.

– DAVID BUSHNELL

OTERO, ALEJANDRO

Alejandro Otero (*b.* 7 March 1921; *d.* 13 August 1990), Venezuelan artist. Born in El Manteco, Otero was the son of a rubber worker who died soon after the artist's birth. He grew up in the small provincial town of Upata and then in Ciudad Bolívar. Although he began to study agriculture, he also took courses in art at the Cristóbal Rojas School of Fine and Applied Arts, in Caracas, where he taught painting and stained glass from 1943–1945. In 1945, on a government fellowship, he traveled to Paris, where he studied cubism and the Dutch neo-

plasticist artists. He completed a series of forty still lifes entitled *Las Cafeteras,* and exhibited them at the Organization of American States in Washington, D.C. (1948) and the Museo de Bellas Artes in Caracas (1949), where they produced a critical uproar among the conservative Venezuelan art world. In 1950 Otero along with other Venezuelan artists in Paris formed the group *Los Disidentes,* which published five issues of an art review promoting geometrical abstraction as the way to reach a universal art.

In 1952 he returned to Caracas, where he taught at the School of Fine and Applied Arts (1954–1959), and joined with the artists Calder, Vasarely, Arp, Léger, and Soto in designing the University City. In 1959 and 1975 he participated in the Venezuelan group show at the São Paulo Bienal. In 1960 he returned to Paris, where he produced a series of assemblages and collages. Back in Caracas he became vice president of the Instituto Nacional de Cultura de Bellas Artes (1964). In 1966 he began his famous series *Coloritmo,* an experiment with a striped pattern of industrial color on rectangular pieces of wood to produce a moving visual interaction of vertical lines of color. That year, and again in 1982, he represented Venezuela at the Venice Biennale.

In the mid-1960s, Otero began work on large-scale outdoor kinetic sculptures like *Delta solar* (Washington, D.C.), *Ala Solar* (Bogotá), and *Terra solar* (Guri Dam, Venezuela). In 1971 he received a Guggenheim Memorial Fellowship to research sculptural ideas at the Center for Advanced Visual Studies at the Massachusetts Institute of Technology. He participated in international group shows such as the Hayward Gallery's Art in Latin America (London, 1989) as well as many solo shows at the Museum of Contemporary Art (1985) and the National Gallery of Art (1990) in Caracas.

– BÉLGICA RODRÍGUEZ

OTERO, MARIANO

Mariano Otero (*b.* 1817; *d.* 1850), Mexican politician and cabinet minister. A native of Guadalajara, Jalisco, Otero studied law there and received his degree in 1835. His intelligence, eloquence, and energy soon attracted the attention of local liberals, and in 1841 Otero was elected to the Junta de Representantes de los Departamentos. As a deputy for Jalisco to the special national congress in 1842, he opposed the projected centralist constitution. That year he also published one of the most important analyses of Mexico's postindependence trauma, *Ensayo sobre el verdadero estado de la cuestión social y política que se agita en la República mexicana.*

Otero believed that Mexico was essentially different from European countries. The Mexican aristocracy had not exercised civil jurisdiction and had no political influence. Mexico's colonial experience was a "true despotism, without intermediate classes, and this power [colonial despotism] was essentially foreign." This despotism created a society in which each corporation, group, and class sought only its own prerogatives, thereby making coherent political action impossible. Otero proposed that Mexico's condition was the result of its historical development, and he stressed the underlying property relationships as the root of the problem. Otero's thought shows the influence of utopian socialism.

Otero believed that Mexico was essentially different

from European countries.

Otero wrote frequently for the newspaper *El siglo XIX* and other periodicals. After the liberal revolt of 1846, he returned to Congress, where he led the effort to pass the Reform Acts, which restored the federal Constitution of 1824 with some alterations. After the United States invasion, Otero was one of four deputies in Querétaro who opposed the Treaty of Guadalupe Hidalgo. He resigned from the senate in 1848 to become minister of foreign relations in the government of President José Joaquín de HERRERA. He died in the cholera epidemic of 1850.

– D. F. STEVENS

OTTONI, TEOFILO BENEDITO

Teofilo Benedito Ottoni (*b.* 27 November 1807; *d.* 17 October 1869), Brazilian statesman and entrepreneur, perhaps the foremost radical Liberal ideologue of his time. As a student at the Naval Academy, Ottoni associated with many of the leaders of the opposition to PEDRO I. He began his apprenticeship as a liberal polemicist and a journalist in the 1820s. In the early regency, he separated from his *moderado* mentors as a radical, calling for constitutional reform; as a Minas Gerais provincial deputy in 1835, and a national deputy for Minas Gerais after 1838, his star in the emergent Liberal Party rose high. Ottoni was a stalwart of the Majority movement (1840) and the Liberal Revolt of 1842, and was seen as the party chieftain in the Chamber of Deputies during the failed Liberal interregnum of the 1840s.

As a merchant and entrepreneur, Ottoni had called for infrastructural development since 1832; by the mid-1840s, he had begun to shift his interest from the dis-

appointments of Liberal politics to steamship and road linkage between northern Minas Gerais and the coast. From 1846 to 1858, he devoted himself to this Mucuri project, which brought him both failure and success. His subsequent return to politics quickly restored him to prominence, again on the party's left. By 1860 he was widely considered the most popular chief of the Liberals, and his campaign writing enjoyed general renown. A senator for Minas Gerais by 1864, he led the party's radical wing in the era of renewed ideological definition, figuring in the rebirth of the Liberal Party in 1868 and influencing the Liberal Manifesto of 1869, which defined the party's program in opposition.

– JEFFREY D. NEEDELL

OVANDO, NICOLÁS DE

Nicolás de Ovando (*b.* 1451; *d.* 1518), governor of Hispaniola. Born in Cáceres, in Extremadura, Spain, Ovando was a member of the military Order of Calatrava. On 3 September 1501 the crown ordered him to HISPANIOLA to investigate the administration of Francisco de BOBADILLA and to reestablish order. Ovando arrived in April 1502; his large fleet had departed Sanlúcar de Barrameda, Spain, with some twenty-five hundred colonists, including Bartolomé de LAS CASAS, a man who would later achieve fame as the Protector of the Indians. Using ample force and authority, Ovando completed the "pacification" of the island, subduing both native Americans and Spanish malcontents, and returning unruly colonists to Spain in chains.

Ovando also exercised some more positive imperatives. He sought to establish new towns and cities, following a general gridiron pattern that later came to characterize town planning in Spanish America. Santo Domingo was refounded on the opposite bank of the Ozama River. Ovando also ordered continued exploration of Hispaniola and nearby islands: Andrés Morales prepared a detailed map; Sebastián de Ocampo completed the circumnavigation of Cuba; Juan PONCE DE LEÓN was authorized to explore Puerto Rico. Ovando was generally interested in protecting Amerindians and experimented to see if they could live freely as Europeans. By a royal cedula of 20 December 1503, he instituted a division (*repartimiento*) of Indians, which was the foundation for the *encomienda* system.

On the outgoing fourth expedition of COLUMBUS, Ovando refused the explorer safe admission to the port of Santo Domingo. Had it been possible for Columbus to refit and repair ships and perhaps purchase better ones, the Jamaica disaster might have been averted. In 1508 Ovando was replaced by Diego Colón.

– NOBLE DAVID COOK

OVANDO CANDÍA, ALFREDO

Alfredo Ovando Candía (*b.* 1917; *d.* 1982), army officer and president of Bolivia (1964–1966, 1969–1970). Ovando graduated from the Bolivian Military Academy in 1936, after having been in active service during the Chaco War. He pursued further military studies in Bolivia and Argentina. He rose regularly in rank, before and after the Bolivian National Revolution of 1952. He became a division general in 1952 and was named army chief of staff in 1957 and commander in chief of the armed forces in 1962.

When President Víctor PAZ ESTENSSORO was overthrown in November 1964, the deposed president was confident of Ovando's loyalty, but Ovando was, in fact, the major co-conspirator with General René BARRIENTOS in Paz Estenssoro's ouster. Ovando and Barrientos became copresidents from 1964 to 1966, when Barrientos resigned to become a candidate for election as president. During Barrientos's administration, Ovando continued as commander in chief of the armed forces. When Barrientos died in April 1969, Vice President Luis Adolfo Siles Salinas took over, but late in September, Ovando ousted Siles and assumed the presidency.

In his second presidential term, Ovando launched a "nationalist" program, the centerpiece of which was the nationalization of the Gulf Oil Corporation's holdings in Bolivia, for which he promised to compensate the company. He also encouraged the reorganization of the labor movement and patronized several new leftist parties. He extended diplomatic relations to, and received a loan from, the Soviet Union.

In October 1970 a right-wing military coup resulted in Ovando's resignation. He had second thoughts and attempted to resume his office, but it was too late. After several days of confusion, a more leftist-oriented general, Juan José TORRES, became president. Ovando was named ambassador to Spain. After Torres's own overthrow in August 1971, Ovando resigned.

– ROBERT J. ALEXANDER

OVIEDO Y VALDÉS, GONZALO FERNÁNDEZ

Gonzalo Fernández Oviedo y Valdés (*b.* August 1478; *d.* 26 June 1557), chronicler of the Indies. Born in Madrid, Oviedo was one of the earliest and most astute chroniclers of the Indies, combining a critical understanding of the historical method with first-hand experience. In 1490 he entered the service of Alfonso de Aragon, duke of Villahermosa, who presented him to the court. He witnessed the surrender of Granada. In 1493 he entered the service of Prince Don Juan, who was his own age. After the prince's untimely death six years later, Oviedo participated in the Italian campaigns. In 1500 he was admitted to the court of Don Fadrique, king of Naples. Oviedo returned to Madrid in 1502 and married Margarita de Vergara, who died within ten months of the union. In 1503 Oviedo entered the service of the duke of Calabria and fought in Rousellon. He remarried in 1509 and had a son.

King Ferdinand named Oviedo secretary to Gonzalo Fernández de Córdoba, the Great Captain, in Italy. Oviedo and others, frustrated by lack of action and tardy pay, returned to Spain and joined an expedition to Castilla del Oro. With two thousand men on twenty-two vessels, the group departed Spain on 11 April, reaching Santa Marta on 12 July 1514, and continued on to Santa María de la Antigua. There, within a few weeks, with insufficient food and supplies and suffering illness, many settlers died. Oviedo returned to Spain to give full account of the disastrous expedition. In the meantime, King Ferdinand had died, so Oviedo traveled to Flanders to report to the young Charles. The question of inheritance in Spain led to long delays at Darién in the review of what happened, but Oviedo was vindicated and given fresh assignments in the Indies (1519). He also received royal support to complete a general history that he had already begun.

Within a few weeks, with insufficient food and supplies and suffering illness, many settlers died.

Oviedo returned to the Indies with his wife, two children, and eight servants, to assume administrative duties at Santa María de la Antigua. Conflict led to a *residencia* (investigation) of his activities. Although he was not found guilty of improprieties, he decided to return to Spain to give account of his services. Gravely ill, he left Panama for Cuba on 3 July 1523. While recuperating in Santo Domingo, he met Diego Colón. After reaching Sanlúcar, Spain, on 5 November, he journeyed north to Vitoria, where he held an audience with Charles, now emperor. At this time he secured fresh information from Juan Sebastián de EL CANO on the circumnavigation begun by MAGELLAN. Although granted a position in Darién, Oviedo remained at court, pressing claims against Dávila.

In 1525 he returned to the Indies a third time, stopping first in Castilla del Oro and then Nicaragua before finally settling in Santo Domingo. At the end of 1530 he returned to Spain again. It was then that Charles V named him "cronista general de Indias." In 1532 he returned to Santo Domingo, where he was *alcaide* of the city's fort. On his fourth return to Spain in mid-1534, he carried the completed first part of the *Historia general y natural de las Indias,* which was published in September 1535. Oviedo returned to Santo Domingo, where he remained from 1536 to 1546 while he finished the second and third parts of the history. He also collected a series of important new documents, including Diego de ALMAGRO's report on the Chilean expedition. He returned again to Spain (late 1546 to early 1549), carrying to court important reports on the Peruvian civil wars. Oviedo then returned to Santo Domingo, where he remained until his death. In addition to his *Historia general y natural de las Indias* and the *Sumario de la historia natural de las Indias,* he prepared several other histories.

— NOBLE DAVID COOK

P

PACHECO, GREGORIO

Gregorio Pacheco (*b.* 4 July 1823; *d.* 20 August 1899), president of Bolivia (1884–1888). Born in Livilivi, Potosí, Pacheco was a merchant who invested in silver mines and later became one of the wealthiest mine owners in the country. He was the first civilian president during the Conservative era (1880–1899), when the southern silver-mining oligarchy, based in Sucre, controlled the destiny of Bolivia. Although he ran on the ticket of the Democratic Party, the Conservative Party's Mariano BAPTISTA became vice president, and Pacheco's organization was later absorbed by Baptista's party. Pacheco's term was unusual for its political tranquility, with no major uprising during his term. Pacheco signed a truce with the Chileans after taking office, officially ending the War of the Pacific. During his tenure, efforts were made to guard the nation's eastern frontiers, and Puerto Pacheco was founded on the Paraguay River. After his presidency, Pacheco returned to managing his silver mines and haciendas, dying just when silver mining had become unprofitable.

– ERICK D. LANGER

PACHECO, JOSÉ EMILIO

José Emilio Pacheco (*b.* 30 June 1939), Mexican poet, novelist, short-story writer, literary critic, editor, translator, and journalist. Pacheco, a native of Mexico City and a graduate of the National University, stands out for both his creative singularity and the versatility of his cultural activities. Like two distinguished predecessors, Alfonso Reyes and Octavio Paz, he is able to create both highly imaginative works and remarkable scholarly studies.

Pacheco is a poet of desolation, obsessed with the destructive effect of time and moved by apocalyptic flashes.

Pacheco is a poet of desolation, obsessed with the destructive effect of time and moved by apocalyptic flashes, who has gradually abandoned an intimate and introspective poetic voice to acquire, from *No me pre-*

guntes cómo pasa el tiempo (1969), a diction in tune with contemporary sensibilities—conversational, epigrammatic, impersonal, and ironic. He considers writing to be a social act that belongs to no one in particular. Thus, the importance in his poetry of translations ("approximations"), of parodic rewriting of other works, of apocryphal masks, and of intertextuality (the process of creating literature from literature). In many ways his poetry is a palimpsest of readings, a dialogue between his own words and those of others, from which his authentic poetic voice emerges. *Tarde o temprano* (1980) collects his poetry to 1980. His subsequent books of poetry—including *Ciudad de la memoria* (1989)—show him to be one of the most accomplished poets of our age.

Like his poetry, Pacheco's narrative is tinged by the dominant presence of the passing of time, but it also reveals other dimensions, particularly the betrayal of childhood and innocence, the appearance of the fantastic in daily experiences, and the persistence of cruelty and injustice throughout history. His short-story collections (*El viento distante,* 1963; *El principio del placer,* 1972; and *La sangre de Medusa,* 1990) and his novels (*Morirás lejos,* 1967, and *Las batallas en el desierto,* 1981) exemplify his ability to respond to the many crises of society with innovative literary creations.

– HUGO J. VERANI

PACHECO, MARÍA LUISA

María Luisa Pacheco (*b.* 22 September 1919; *d.* 21 April 1982), Bolivian artist. Pacheco studied at the National Academy of Fine Arts in her native La Paz with nativists Cecilio Guzmán de Rojas and Jorge de la Reza. She pursued further studies at the Royal Academy of San Fernando in Madrid, and with the Spanish cubist Daniel Vásquez Días (1951–1952). Back in Bolivia, she founded Eight Contemporaries, a modernist group. She expressed her social consciousness in themes such as idol-like figures and women miners (*Idols,* 1956; *Palliri,* 1958), rendering them as fragmented planar structures (1953–1958). In 1956 she moved to New York, where she received a Solomon R. Guggenheim Memorial Foundation fellowship (1958–1960).

After 1959 Pacheco eliminated all figurative and ethnic elements in her painting. Her late style consisted of broad areas of brilliant hues and somber colors, penetrating one another in a constructivist manner. Under the general influence of international expressive abstraction, she emphasized texture and explored some accidental methods of execution (*Anamorphosis,* 1971, and *Catavi,* 1975). Although some have perceived her paintings as interpretations of the Andean environment, she claimed that subjective expression was her primary motivation. She was influential in the acceptance of abstraction in Bolivia. She died in New York City.

— MARTA GARSD

PACHECO ARECO, JORGE

Jorge Pacheco Areco (*b.* 1920), president of Uruguay (1967–1972). A right-wing Colorado Party politician and little-known editor of *El Día,* Pacheco became vice president in 1966. He became president less than a year later upon the death of President Oscar GESTIDO. A former boxer, Pacheco proved to be a stubborn politician. Faced with rising social unrest, strikes, inflation, and a budding guerrilla movement, he invoked a limited State of Siege (Medidas Prontas de Seguridad) during most of his term as president. As civil liberties became increasingly restricted, opposition voices rose within Congress, but Pacheco would not back down. As the struggle with the Tupamaro guerrillas become more dramatic and bloody, Pacheco actually received more support for his heavy-handed measures and his increased reliance on the military. In 1971, he tried to succeed himself by promoting a change in the constitution. Although this strategy ultimately failed, he was able to pick his successor, an even more conservative rural rancher named Juan María BORDABERRY.

Pacheco spent the years after his presidency as an ambassador, first in Spain and later in the United States and Switzerland. He never denounced the military government and appeared to be marginalized as party leaders struggled to restore democracy in the early 1980s. Nevertheless, Pacheco's faction of the Colorado Party, the Colorado and Batllist Union (UCB), did well in the 1984 elections, helping the Colorados to win the presidency. In the 1989 elections Pacheco's faction, with him running for president, received about 50 percent of the Colorado vote in a losing effort.

Pacheco continued to have a surprisingly large following among the urban poor in Montevideo as a no-nonsense law-and-order politician. In 1992 his faction was the only non-Blanco (National Party) group to offer parliamentary support to Blanco president Luis Alberto LACALLE HERRERA.

— MARTIN WEINSTEIN

PACHECO DA SILVA, OSVALDO

Osvaldo Pacheco da Silva (*b.* 4 September 1918), Brazilian national trade union leader. In 1945, as a candidate of the Communist Party (PCB), Pacheco was elected a federal deputy by the dockworkers of the famous "Red Port" of Santos, São Paulo. Ousted from office in 1948, he served as a national PCB organizer until 1957 when he returned to Santos. Respected for his honesty and courage, Pacheco was elected in 1959 president of the National Federation of Stevedores and in 1961 helped form the Pact of Unity and Action (PUA), which united dockworkers, seamen, and railroad workers. He played a key role in the formation of the General Strike Command that in 1962 became the General Labor Command (CGT), serving as secretary general (1962–1963) and first secretary (1963–1964). After the military coup of 31 March 1964, the CGT and PUA were outlawed. Pacheco was arrested; after his release he went into exile. Returning clandestinely in 1967, he continued his PCB activities until his arrest in April 1975. Sentenced to seven and a half years in prison, he was released in December 1978 and subsequently amnestied.

— JOHN D. FRENCH

PADILLA, HEBERTO

Heberto Padilla (*b.* 20 January 1932); one of the greatest Cuban poets and novelists. Padilla was born in Puerta de Golpe in the province of Pinar del Río. He was supportive of the Cuban Revolution of 1959 and enjoyed a favorable position among the cultural elite of his country until 1968, when he won first prize in the prestigious literary contest of the Cuban Writers and Artists Union (UNEAC) for his book of poems *Fuera del juego* (1969). This book, which brought him immediate national and international acclaim as a poet, also made him an object of intense political controversy. Published with a prologue decrying the "counterrevolutionary" nature of some of the poems, the book provoked what came to be known as El Caso Padilla, or the Padilla affair, now seen as a turning point in relations between the Cuban government and intellectuals, Cuban or otherwise. In 1971, Padilla was arrested, tortured, and forced to retract his stand publicly at an assembly of UNEAC. Receiving worldwide attention, his case prompted the drafting of a letter in his defense signed by intellectuals the world over, including Gabriel GARCÍA MÁRQUEZ and Simone de Beauvoir. Ultimately Padilla was allowed to emigrate with his wife, the outstanding poet Belkis Cuza Malé, but his case marked the end of a period of relative artistic freedom for Cuban intellectuals. Padilla eventually settled in Princeton, New Jersey, and later in Miami, Florida, and continued to write.

Other works by Padilla include bilingual editions of his poems *Legacies* (1982) and *A Fountain, A House of Stone* (1991). His poetry has been translated into many languages.

– ROBERTO VALERO

PADILLA PEÑALOSA, EZEQUIEL

Ezequiel Padilla Peñalosa (*b.* 31 December 1890; *d.* 6 September 1971), leading Mexican diplomat and public figure. A native of Coyuca de Catalán, Guerrero, Padilla graduated from the Sorbonne in constitutional law in 1914 and studied at Columbia University in 1916. A cofounder of the Free Law School in Mexico City, he served in the Revolution under Francisco VILLA, leaving Mexico in 1916. On his return to Mexico, he entered politics, becoming a federal deputy in 1922. In 1928 he joined Emilio PORTES GIL's cabinet as secretary of education. After his 1930 appointment as minister to Italy, he returned to the Chamber of Deputies in 1932 and to the Senate in 1934. From 1940 to 1945 he was secretary of foreign relations, playing a key role in promoting continental unity during World War II. He provided leadership at the 1942 Rio De Janeiro Conference, a benchmark in wartime inter-American relations. In 1946 he resigned his post to run as the opposition presidential candidate of the Mexican Democratic Party after failing to obtain the nomination of his own party. He remained politically inactive for the next two decades, serving once again as senator shortly before his death.

– RODERIC AI CAMP

PÁEZ, FEDERICO

Federico Páez (*b.* 6 June 1876; *d.* 1974), president of Ecuador (nonelected, 1935–1937). Born in Quito and educated at the École Supérieure des Mines in Paris and the École des Hautes Études Sociales in Brussels, Páez served as deputy of Pichincha (1916–1918) and became minister of public works in 1935 when the military named him interim president. During his administration there were reforms in a number of areas, including the organization, administration, and education of the military; the creation of the Institute of Social Security; and the founding of the Inspection of Public Works. These accomplishments were tarnished by restrictions on civil liberties, an expansion of the secret political police, the suppression of dissent, the persecution of leftists, and rumors that the government favored foreign business interests. Public discontent and divisions within the officer corps led to the resignation of Páez in 1937, turning over the office to General Alberto ENRÍQUEZ GALLO.

– LINDA ALEXANDER RODRÍGUEZ

PÁEZ, JOSÉ ANTONIO

José Antonio Páez (*b.* 13 June 1790; *d.* 6 May 1873), officer in the Venezuelan Liberating Army, president of Venezuela (1831–1835, 1839–1843, and 1861–1863). Páez began his public life in the Liberating Army. He stood out early as a good soldier and attained great popularity among the people of the plains. In 1816, he was named commanding officer of the region, and as such led numerous campaigns which consolidated control of the plains. He met with Simón BOLÍVAR in 1818 and recognized him as supreme commander of the Liberating Army. From the plains, Páez supported the New Granada campaign and took part in the preparations that culminated in the victory at Carabobo in 1821. He

José Antonio Páez. (Grupo Anaya)

was named commander in chief of one of the military districts into which the territory of Venezuela had been divided, and in that position defeated the armed factions that were still operating within Venezuela.

Through his military post and his personal prestige, Páez gradually became a key figure in the political process that evolved in Venezuela after adoption of the Constitution of Gran Colombia in 1821. The conflicting interests and fragile ties that characterized the unstable entity that was Gran Colombia finally led in 1826 to the outbreak of the separatist movement called La Cosiata, whose supporters ignored the authority of the government in Bogotá, recognized Páez as chief civil and military leader of Venezuela, and called for the dissolution of Gran Colombia. From that moment, Páez served as a unifying symbol of independence for the leading groups in Venezuela.

In December 1826 Bolívar returned from Peru and assumed the presidency of Gran Colombia. He traveled to Puerto Cabello, Venezuela, on 1 January 1827 and issued a decree which forgave all those who participated in La Cosiata. Bolívar recognized Páez as military governor of Venezuela and Páez recognized Bolívar as president of Gran Colombia. Between 1827 and 1829, Páez continued consolidating his power and when separatist sentiment returned among both the elites and the popular classes, Páez was well positioned to take advantage. In November 1829 the Assembly in the San Francisco Convent in Caracas disregarded Bolívar's authority, convened a constituent congress, and handed over all power to Páez, thus completing the dissolution of Gran Colombia.

The Constituent Congress named Páez provisional president of Venezuela, ratified a new constitution, and held an election, which Páez won. His political and military prestige brought a period of consensus during which the bases for the republic were established; the intense process of judicial, political, and economic organization was carried through; and the building of a nation state was initiated. His personal authority did not dissipate at the end of his term in 1835, and his influence continued to be felt in the country's politics. In 1838 he was reelected president. During his second four-year term, differences and confrontations within the ruling elite were becoming more and more evident. In 1846 he supported the election of General José Tadeo MONAGAS, who afterwards distanced himself from Páez and formed an alliance with the Liberal Party. This caused a rupture in the Conservative Party, with which Páez was associated. In 1847 Páez rose up in arms and was defeated, imprisoned, and exiled.

Páez remained abroad until the overthrow of Monagas in 1858, when he was called back to take charge of the pacification of the country. At the outbreak of the Federal War in 1859, he was appointed chief of operations against the federalists. After a brief absence from the country, he was named supreme chief of Venezuela with dictatorial powers in 1861. The war ended in 1863 with a victory for the federalists. Páez handed over power and again left the country. He spent his later years in the United States, where he wrote his autobiography, published in New York in 1869. He traveled to various Latin American countries, spent three years in Argentina, and then returned to the United States, where he died.

– INÉS QUINTERO

PAÍS, FRANK

Frank País (*b.* 1934; *d.* 30 July 1957), Cuban revolutionary leader during the BATISTA dictatorship. Born in Santiago de Cuba, País is best remembered as the leader of the 1956 Santiago uprising that coincided with the landing of Fidel CASTRO and his followers in Oriente Province on 2 December on the boat *Granma*. Under

---

"Che" Guevara asked to take the deceased País's place as leader of the Santiago revolutionary movement.

---

the Batista dictatorship, País built his reputation as a guerrilla fighter and member of Acción Nacional Revolucionaria. In 1955 País and his followers agreed to merge with Castro's Twenty-Sixth of July Movement and to coordinate the Cuban operations with Castro's landing from Mexico. On 30 November 1956, País led an uprising in Santiago that was briefly successful, with the insurrectionists taking control of the city. Stormy weather delayed Castro's landing, however, giving Batista's forces time to quell the País uprising before turning their attention to the landing of the *Granma*. While País escaped capture, he was killed less than a year later, on 30 July 1957, by the Santiago police. Páis's death was a great blow to the *llano* wing—the lowland and urban wing, as opposed to Castro's Sierra group—of the Cuban revolutionary movement. His role was so important that Ernesto "Che" GUEVARA asked to take the deceased País's place as leader of the Santiago revolutionary movement.

– MICHAEL POWELSON

PALACIO FAJARDO, MANUEL

Manuel Palacio Fajardo (*b.* 1784; *d.* 8 May 1819), diplomat and political activist in the Venezuelan independence movement. From early on Palacio Fajardo belonged to the independence movement. He was a member of the Constituent Congress of 1811. After the fall of the First Republic in 1812, he traveled to New Granada and was sent on a diplomatic mission to the United States and France. He later passed through London, where he devoted himself to garnering support for the cause of Venezuelan independence. While there, he published his book, *Outline of the Revolution in Spanish America* (1817), which was translated into French and German. He returned to Venezuela in 1818 with men and supplies for the war and was a participant in the Angostura Congress of 1819. On Simón Bolívar's request he revised and made suggestions for the speech that the former would present to that gathering. Palacio Fajardo also collaborated in *El Correo del Orinoco*, a newspaper dedicated to the independence cause, and in 1819 was designated the infant republic's secretary of finance.

– INÉS QUINTERO

PALACIOS, ALFREDO L.

Alfredo L. Palacios (*b.* 10 August 1880; *d.* 1965) Argentine Socialist congressman and senator. Born in the city of Buenos Aires, Palacios received his law degree from the local university in 1900. Soon thereafter he joined the Socialist Party, with which he had a long and frequently difficult relationship. Running on the party ticket in the federal capital in 1904, he became the first socialist in the Americas to be elected to a national congress. He served two terms in the Chamber of Deputies (1904–1908 and 1912–1916), during the second of which he was ousted from his party for dueling. He rejoined the party in 1930 and was twice elected to the national senate (1932–1935 and 1935–1944) from the federal capital, at a time when conservatives controlled the national administration. A vigorous opponent of the regime of Juan PERÓN (1946–1955), he was named ambassador to Uruguay for the two years following Perón's overthrow. After an unsuccessful bid for the presidency in 1958, he won a stunning election to the national Senate from the city of Buenos Aires in 1961 after campaigning as a champion of the Cuban revolution of Fidel CASTRO.

A charismatic orator and effective legislator, Palacios was a consistent proponent of social justice, especially for women and children, and a vociferous opponent of what he considered the undue influence of foreign investors in the country. He was the author of numerous essays and books, such as *La justicia social* (1954), many of which were collections of his parliamentary speeches.

– RICHARD J. WALTER

PALACIOS, ANTONIA

Antonia Palacios (*b.* 13 May 1904), Venezuelan writer and poet. From a very young age, Palacios was associated with the literary circles of the city. In 1936, she traveled to Europe, where she met César VALLEJO, Luis Aragón, and Pablo NERUDA. Her account of these contacts is contained in her first work, *París y tres recuerdos* (1945). Upon her return, she joined the Women's Cultural Society and presided at the first Venezuelan Women's Congress. She contributed to the newspaper *El Nacional* and devoted herself to writing *Ana Isabel, una niña decente* (1949), which was declared obligatory reading material for secondary students by the Venezuelan Ministry of Education in 1962. After the publication of *Viaje al frailejón* (1955), Palacios maintained a prolonged silence until *Crónica de las horas* was published in 1964. She pursued her literary activities, and in 1976 coordinated the literary workshop at the Rómulo Gallegos Center. That same year she became the first woman to receive the National Literature Prize. In her home she founded the literary workshop Calicanto, a forum for young poets and writers. The results of this experience were published in the magazine *Hojas de Calicanto*. Her career and her work are outstanding components of Venezuelan literary life in the twentieth century.

– INÉS QUINTERO

PALAFOX Y MENDOZA, JUAN DE

Juan de Palafox y Mendoza (*b.* 1600; *d.* 1659), bishop of Puebla (1640–1654), visitor-general, and seventeenth viceroy of New Spain. Palafox, born in Fitero, Navarra, was the illegitimate son of an Aragonese noble. After studying law at Salamanca, he rose rapidly in both the church and the royal bureaucracy, serving on the Council of the Indies while still in his thirties. In 1639, he was named visitor-general of New Spain and bishop of Puebla. A moralist with mystical leanings, Palafox believed strongly in the Christian mission of the Hapsburg monarchy, and sought to rectify the colonial administration, thereby making it a fit instrument for the reformation of society. He therefore never hesitated to employ the full extent of his authority: most notably, as bishop he engineered the removal of New Spain's viceroy, the duque d'Escalona, in 1642 because of the latter's supposed pro-Portuguese sympathies. During Palafox's ensuing term as viceroy (June–November 1642), the Inquisition launched a massive persecution of Mexican crypto-Jews (secret Jews), which culminated in the great autos-da-fé of 1646–1649.

P

As bishop, Palafox sponsored an impressive program of ecclesiastical construction, building some fifty churches and a seminary (to which he donated his personal library of more than 5,000 volumes), founding the convent of Santa Inés, and completing the imposing Puebla cathedral, which was consecrated in 1649. To strengthen episcopal power, he transferred control of thirty-six parishes from the mendicant orders to the secular clergy. Beginning in 1641, Palafox became embroiled in disputes with the Jesuits concerning tithes on their landed estates and episcopal authority over Jesuit priests. As the conflicts deepened, the new viceroy, García SARMIENTO DE SOTOMAYOR, conde de Salvatierra, sided with the Jesuits, putting Palafox in an increasingly precarious position. In 1647, to avoid arrest, he fled Puebla and went into hiding until the crown announced its verdict in his favor. However, this triumph was short-lived: in 1649 royal authorities ordered the disputatious bishop back to Spain, where he was named bishop of Osma (in Soria); he was forced to surrender the see of Puebla in 1654. Palafox's ultimate failure, like that of the marqués de GELVES, the reform-minded viceroy who was ousted by a riot in 1624, demonstrated the Spanish crown's inability to challenge entrenched power holders and make significant alterations in the colonial status quo. Palafox died in Osma.

— R. DOUGLAS COPE

PALENQUE, CARLOS

Carlos Palenque (*b.* 28 June 1944), founder of Conciencia de la Patria (Conscience of the Fatherland—CONDEPA), presidential candidate, and owner of Radio Metropolitana and Channel 4 (Radio y Televisión Popular—RTP). A native of the department of Tariya who has long been considered a powerful figure among La Paz's underclass because of his radio and television programs, Palenque was courted by nearly every major political party for the mayoralty of La Paz. In June 1988 he broadcast an interview with Roberto Suárez, until then considered the principal narcotics trafficker in the country, in which the latter accused the Nationalist Revolutionary Movement (MNR) government of involvement in the drug industry. The MNR responded by closing down the television station. Palenque then founded CONDEPA, through which he was able to rally a great deal of support for the reopening of his television station from the marginal sectors in La Paz that constituted his audience.

Since 1989 CONDEPA has consistently won local elections in the La Paz Department. Its support is drawn from marginal and displaced sectors, especially El Alto and the slums surrounding La Paz. Palenque and CON-

DEPA have played a crucial role in the stability of Bolivian democracy and may be a mitigating force that has prevented the emergence of radical groups among the marginal sectors. CONDEPA is primarily a populist party that employs patrimonial rewards to attract and keep followers.

At the national level, Palenque has fared poorly. He was soundly defeated in the 1993 presidential election. In December 1993, however, CONDEPA won the La Paz municipal elections, and Palenque's wife, Mónica, was sworn in as the first female mayor of the capital city.

— EDUARDO A. GAMARRA

PALÉS MATOS, LUIS

Luis Palés Matos (*b.* 20 March 1898; *d.* 23 February 1959), Puerto Rican poet, journalist, and essayist. Founding figure of the *negrista* movement and one of its most important exponents within the wider Hispanic Caribbean, Palés Matos is perhaps Puerto Rico's most significant modern poet. He was born in Guayama, the son of poets. A precocious talent, he published his first book of verse, *Azaleas* (1915), under the influence of the romantics, symbolists, and *modernistas*. In his early twenties he served as director of the newspaper *El Pueblo* (1919–1920), and he later became a regular contributor to the newspapers *El Imparcial, El Mundo,* and *La Democracia,* and journals such as *La Semana* and *Puerto Rico Ilustrado.* In 1921 he joined José I. de Diego Padró in inaugurating the short-lived *diepalismo* movement (a term formed from the initial syllables of their patronymics). Its nonconformist insistence on the search for novelty, the need for insular aesthetic renewal, and highlighting of onomatopoeic and musical effects as key elements of poetry were, despite *diepalismo*'s brief moment, suggestive of things to come. In 1918 and 1926 Palés published the first examples of his *negrista* poetry, which culminated in *Tuntún de pasa y grifería: Poemas afroantillanos* (1937). The embodiment of a mestizo middle class's more congregationally inclusive vision of a defining national ethos, this collection reflected an important shift of emphasis in island cultural politics. It pointed to the inevitably syncretic character of Puerto Rican life. Persisting elements of a conventional exoticism and an objectionable racial stereotyping notwithstanding, Palés's Afro-Antillean poems challenged a reigning Hispanophilic disregard of the African ancestor. Palés's metaphorical, thematic, lexical, historical, and powerfully rhythmic invocation of that neglected legacy dramatized its importance and his conviction that "The Antillean is a Spaniard with the manner of a mulatto and the soul of a black." By the

1950s the poet's central image of a *"mulatta antilla"* (mulatto Antilles) had itself become ideologically dominant and Palés was generally regarded as the island's unofficial "national poet." In his later years Palés's poetry, included in *Poesía, 1915–1956* (3d ed., 1968), turned increasingly inward and metaphysical and assumed a less celebratory, more skeptical and intimate tone of existential anguish. Other collections of his works include *Obras, 1914–1959,* 2 vols. (1984), and *Poesía completa y prosa selecta* (1978). Lesser-known works include the unpublished poems of "El palacio en sombras," written in 1919–1920, and "Canciones de la vida media," written between 1922 and 1925, and the novel *Litoral: Reseña de una vida inútil,* an unfinished work published serially in newspapers, mostly in 1949 and 1951.

— ROBERTO MÁRQUEZ

PALMA, RICARDO

Ricardo Palma (*b.* 7 February 1833; *d.* 6 October 1919), Peruvian diplomat, politician, writer, and historian. Born in Lima, Palma was the illegitimate son of Pedro Palma. He began writing as a very young man, as early as 1848. From 1861 to 1863 he lived in Chile. Then in 1864 he journeyed to Europe, living briefly in Paris and traveling to England and Venice.

Upon his return to Peru (1865), Palma served in a number of government posts, including secretary to President José BALTA in 1868. In addition he was elected to three terms in the Peruvian Senate. At the same time he worked as assistant librarian of Lima and contributed to the prestigious Buenos Aires newspaper *La Prensa.*

Palma waged such a tenacious campaign to rebuild Peru's National Library that he became known as bibliotecario mendigo *(the begging librarian).*

Palma is best remembered, however, for his own written work. He adopted romanticism, which came to Peru from Europe, and became the foremost advocate of that literary movement in his country. He wrote poems and articles but is known primarily for his *Tradiciones peruanas* (Peruvian Traditions, 4 vols., 1893–1896), short stories that combined history with his own imagination. This was a genre of romanticism that Palma acquired from Spain, where it combined the romantic legend with *costumbrismo* (articles about customs). Many of his traditions dealt with Inca themes, and he wrote exten-

sively about colonial Peru, to the point that some critics referred to him as "colonialist Palma." Whatever his subjects, he gained for himself and Peru a wide literary reputation outside the nation and the region.

Palma also popularized history for the reading public. Critics, however, complained that he bound literature so tightly with history that people could not extricate fact from fiction, and that therefore he was deficient as a historian.

Also a political activist, Palma tried to overthrow President Ramón CASTILLA in 1860, but he failed and was exiled to Chile for two years. When the War of the Pacific with Chile began in 1879, Palma enlisted in the reserves, but the invading Chileans destroyed his personal library of several thousand books and manuscripts. Peru's National Library also suffered looting at the hands of the Chileans. After Palma became director of the library in 1883, he spent the next twenty-eight years rebuilding the collection. He catalogued more than twenty thousand books in less than four years and waged such a tenacious campaign to rebuild the library that he became known as *bibliotecario mendigo* (the begging librarian).

While his library and archival activity was critical to the preservation of Peru's literature, Palma's own written work expanded the historical knowledge of Peru and made the public aware of the nation's past.

— JACK RAY THOMAS

PALOU, FRANCISCO

Francisco Palou (*b.* 22 January 1723; *d.* 6 April 1789), Franciscan missionary in Baja and Alta California. Born in Palma, Mallorca, Palou was a student and lifelong friend of Junípero SERRA, the Franciscan architect of the Alta California mission system. Palou went to New Spain in 1749 with Serra, then worked in the California missions under Serra's direction between 1768 and 1784.

Palou, stationed in the Baja California establishments between 1768 and 1773, became the superior of the missions when Serra joined a 1769 expedition that occupied Alta California. When the Franciscans transferred the Baja California missions to the jurisdiction of the Dominicans in 1773, Palou went to Alta California and served in the missions until 1786. During this period, he temporarily served as superior of the Alta California missions in 1784 and 1785, following which he returned to the apostolic college of San Fernando in Mexico City to serve as its superior from 1787 until his death. While there Palou wrote a hagiography of Serra and an important account of the early Franciscan years in Baja California (1768–1773) and Alta California

(1769–1786) (*Palou's Historical Memoirs of New California,* trans. and ed. by H. E. Bolton, 4 vols. [1926]).

— ROBERT H. JACKSON

PANDO, JOSÉ MANUEL

José Manuel Pando (*b.* 25 December 1848; *d.* 15 June 1917), president of Bolivia (1899–1904). Born in Araca, La Paz, Major General José Manuel Pando was the military leader of the Liberal and Federalist forces during the Federalist War (1898–1899). He became the first president of the era of Liberal Party dominance (1899–1920), which coincided with the beginning of the TIN-export boom. Pando was a professional military man who fought in the War of the Pacific (1879–1884) and later explored the Bolivian Amazon region for the government. Astutely allying himself with the La Paz Federalists and the Aymara Indian communities in 1898, Pando managed to overthrow the Conservative administration of Sévero FERNÁNDEZ ALONSO in 1899. After the Conservative defeat, Pando turned against both the Federalists and the Indians, thereby establishing the dominance of the Liberal Party for the next two decades. In 1903, Pando led Bolivian forces in the Acre campaign in the rubber-rich Bolivian Amazon against Brazilian-supported separatists. Bolivia lost and had to cede the region to Brazil the same year. Pando was assassinated under mysterious circumstances in 1917.

— ERICK D. LANGER

PANE, IGNACIO ALBERTO

Ignacio Alberto Pane (*b.* 1883; *d.* 1920), Paraguayan sociologist, literary critic, and politician. Born in Asunción, Pane was part of an intellectual movement dedicated to the revindication of Francisco Solano LÓPEZ, the dictator who had taken the country into the War of the Triple Alliance (1864–1870), and whose memory had been reviled by liberal Paraguayans ever since. Pane's polemic on the López era graced the pages of several Asunción newspapers and put him in the company of Juan O'Leary and other nationalist writers. He introduced sociology to Paraguay as a separate university discipline, and wrote many volumes of poetry, geography, social theory, and conservative polemics. Several of his works were published under the pseudonym Matías Centella. Pane died in Asunción.

— THOMAS L. WHIGHAM

PANI ARTEAGA, ALBERTO J.

Alberto J. Pani Arteaga (*b.* 12 June 1878; *d.* 25 August 1955), Mexican public figure and entrepreneur. He is considered to have been a critical influence on government financial policies as secretary of the treasury in the postrevolutionary era. As rector of the popular university, he contributed to expanded public education. He held the position of treasury secretary under more presidents than any other Mexican since 1920 and he was an intimate associate of President Plutarco ELÍAS CALLES, who recommended him to Congress as one of three candidates for the presidency after Pascual ORTIZ RUBIO resigned in 1932.

The member of a prominent family from Aguascalientes, Aguascalientes, he married Esther Alba, granddaughter of President Manuel de la PEÑA Y PEÑA. He is also the uncle of Mario Pani, a notable Mexican architect. Pani graduated from the National School of Engineering in 1902. In 1911, as a teacher there, he founded a student group to support Francisco I. MADERO's presidential candidacy and became subsecretary of education in his administration, after which he served as director of public works for the Federal District. A supporter of Venustiano CARRANZA, he turned down the post of secretary of education in his cabinet but later accepted the post of secretary of industry and commerce in 1917. He also served as Carranza's minister to France (1918–1920), a position he held again from 1927 to 1931. He served as secretary of foreign relations from 1921 to 1923, and became secretary of the treasury, first under President Álvaro OBREGÓN, (1923–1924), and again under Calles (1924–1927 and 1932–1933). He built a number of major buildings in Mexico City with his own construction firm.

— RODERIC AI CAMP

PANIAGUA Y VASQUES, CENOBIO

Cenobio Paniagua y Vasques (*b.* 30 October 1821; *d.* 2 November 1882), Mexican composer. Born in Tlalpujahua, Paniagua began his musical career as a violinist in the orchestra of the Morelia cathedral, under the direction of his uncle. He later joined the orchestra of the Mexico City cathedral, where he made contact with European musicians who had settled in Mexico, such as the Italian double-bass virtuoso Giovanni Bottesini, who also conducted opera in several cities of the new world. With Bottesini's help, Paniagua's first opera, with Italian libretto, premiered in September 1859. *Catalina de Guisa* (1845) was the first opera written and staged in Mexico, and created an appreciation for opera in the country. Paniagua's second opera, *Pietro d'Abano,* premiered in 1863, around the time he organized an opera company to tour the country. The enterprise failed, and in 1868, Paniagua moved to the city of Córdoba, Veracruz, where he composed religious works, among them the cantata *Siete palabras* (1869), the oratorio *To-*

bías (1870), a requiem (1882), and about seventy masses. He died in Córdoba.

— SUSANA SALGADO

PAPE, LYGIA

Lygia Pape (*b.* 1929), Brazilian painter, illustrator, engraver. One of the forerunners of the neoconcrete movement, Pape, along with Hélio OITICICA, Lygia CLARK, and other Brazilian artists, broke from both the constructivists and the concretes during the 1950s. A member of Grupo Frente from 1953 to 1955, she participated in the national exhibitions of concrete art in 1956 and 1957 and in the first neoconcrete shows in 1959. Pape favored abstraction over the imitation of nature. She began working with xylography, an engraving technique using a wooden block but quickly moved away from the two-dimensional medium and focused her attention on sculpture and other experimental formulas.

Pape is best known for her neoconcrete "book poems" and "box poems." Her *Book of Creation* (1959) serves as a neoconcrete standard-bearer. Geometric shapes serve as pages of a book, each one a metaphor for episodes in the Creation story. Spectators may participate in the experience and test their own creativity by manipulating the forms. Pages from the *Book* were placed around Rio de Janeiro, on benches, on the beach, and on rocks. Interested in working with the different possibilities of light, she put together a film project entitled *Brasília.* In 1967 she joined the New Brazilian Objectivity exhibition at the Museum of Modern Art in Rio, where she exhibited her "box poems" and projects incorporating live insects. In 1968 she took participatory art to its extreme with *The Divider,* which consisted of a huge white sheet cut with holes for people's heads. Spectators became part of the medium, their movements and voices determining the shape and structure of the piece.

— CAREN A. MEGHREBLIAN

PARANÁ, HONÔRIO HERMETO CARNEIRO LEÃO, MARQUÉS DE

Honôrio Hermeto Carneiro Leão, Marqués De Paraná (*b.* 11 January 1801; *d.* 3 September 1856), Brazilian statesman and diplomat—the preeminent political figure of the 1850s. A Coimbra-trained magistrate, Paraná's ascent as a jurist was rapid but was soon eclipsed by his political success in the early regency. As a *moderado* deputy for Minas Gerais, he was celebrated for turning back Diogo Antônio FEIJÓ's 1832 attempt to reform the Constitution of 1824; though he was quickly taken up by the regents as minister of justice

(1832), his party enemies brought him down. In the Chamber of Deputies, however, Paraná worked with Bernardo de VASCONCELOS and the Saquaremas to organize a majority and form the Conservative Party in opposition to Feijó's regency (1835–1837); by 1842 he was a member of the Senate and Council of State.

Minister of justice, then minister of foreign affairs, in the Conservative administration of 1843–1844, Paraná also defended Conservative goals in repressing the Liberal revolts of 1842 and the Praieira Revolt of 1848 (as provincial president of Rio de Janeiro and of Pernambuco, respectively) and in effecting the Platine diplomacy that led to the war that toppled Argentina's Juan Manuel de ROSAS in 1852. In 1853, PEDRO II asked Paraná to lead an administration that would terminate the partisan domestic strife in which Paraná had triumphed. He did so, as prime minister of the Conciliação cabinet, which he composed of willing veterans and able new protégés from both parties. He broke with the Saquarema chieftains to establish a climate of nonpartisan patronage and statism, constructive reform, and more representative elections. He thus closed the era of the monarchy's consolidation.

— JEFFREY D. NEEDELL

PARDAVÉ, JOAQUÍN

Joaquín Pardavé (*b.* 30 September 1900; *d.* 20 July 1955), Mexican film and stage actor, director, and songwriter. Born in Penjamo, Guanajuato, of theatrical parents, from an early age Pardavé displayed a natural talent, composing popular songs and acting in his uncle's theater company. He debuted in a supporting role in the film *Jalisco nunca pierde,* and became a major star with his role in *México de mis recuerdos,* in which he created his most memorable character, Don Susanito Peñafiel y Somellera. One of the most versatile and popular Mexican actors of his time, Pardavé was equally at ease with comedy and drama. In his later career he directed many of his own films. Among his best features are *El baisano Jalil, Ahí está el detalle, Arriba el norte, Yo baile con Don Porfirio, La barca de oro,* and *Los hijos de Don Venancio.* Pardavé also composed such popular songs as "La Panchita," "Caminito de la sierra," "Ventanita morada," and "Negra consentida."

— DAVID MACIEL

PARDO, JUAN

Juan Pardo, sixteenth-century Spanish soldier. Between 1566 and 1568, Pardo was commissioned by Pedro Menéndez de Avilés, governor of La Florida, to explore and to discover a route to Mexico. He twice led expeditions into the interior of La Florida from the town of Santa Elena (on Parris Island, South Carolina).

On the first journey, Pardo and 125 soldiers marched into western North Carolina. On the second, he followed the same route and then continued farther west, crossing the Appalachian Mountains and reaching Tennessee, probably south of present-day Knoxville. A portion of his route followed that taken by Hernando de SOTO in 1540. Pardo established several forts, but they were soon abandoned. Accounts from the expeditions are an important source of information about native societies.

— JERALD T. MILANICH

PARDO LEAL, JAIME

Jaime Pardo Leal (*b.* 1941; *d.* 11 October 1987), Colombian politician. Born in Ubáque, Cundinamarca, the son of a farmer, Pardo was sent to Bogotá to study. From the age of thirteen, he was involved in student protests and political action. At twenty, while a law student at the National University, he became vice president of the Federation of Colombian Students and was expelled from the university. In 1963, having nearly completed his law studies, he became a court clerk in Bogotá. A university amnesty in 1966 enabled Pardo to receive his law doctorate. He secured a judgeship in 1969. He organized Asonal, the national association of judicial workers in 1974, and led it in several nationwide strikes. From 1979 to 1985, Pardo was a magistrate on Bogotá's Superior Court. As Unión Patriótica's presidential candidate in the March 1986 elections, he polled 4.5 percent of the vote. From 1986 to 1987, more than 450 Unión Patriótica members were killed. Among them was Pardo, who was assassinated at La Mesa, Cundinamarca.

— J. LEÓN HELGUERA

PARDO Y ALIAQA, FELIPE

Felipe Pardo y Aliaqa (*b.* 1806; *d.* 1868), Peruvian writer. The foremost literary figure of the post-Independence period in Peru, Pardo was a journalist, *costumbrista* (member of a nineteenth-century literary movement that sought to depict local manners and beliefs), poet, and dramatist. He was born into an aristocratic *limeño* family and received a classical Enlightenment education in Spain, returning to Peru in 1828 to become a prominent member of the Conservative Party. His literary work, which had a didactic quality and was European in orientation, satirized the disorders of the new republic, the narrow provincialism of his compatriots, and the generally low level of Peruvian culture. Ideologically his writings expressed a general con-

servatism and stressed orderly progress through discipline, industry, civic virtue, and respect for culture. The

> *Pardo's literary work, which was European in orientation, satirized the narrow provincialism of his compatriots, and the generally low level of Peruvian culture.*

best of his work is represented in the *costumbrista* sketch "El paseo de Amancaes," his play *Frutos de la educación* (1830), and a poem, "El Perú."

— PETER F. KLARÉN

PARDO Y BARREDA, JOSÉ

José Pardo y Barreda (*b.* 1864; *d.* 3 August 1947), president of Peru (1904–1908; 1915–1919). The son of Peru's first full-term civilian president, Manuel Pardo y Alliaga, José Pardo inherited the mantle of leadership of the Civilista Party in 1904 when Manuel CANDAMO died suddenly in office. Supported by the younger, reform-minded wing of the party, his presidency has been called the golden age of Civilista rule. For the next four years he increased school expenditures by 250 percent, extended major rail lines, and created a merchant marine. He served a second term as president (1915–1919), when, at military urging, the Civilista, Liberal, and Constitutionalist parties supported a common candidate. In his last term, responding to various pressures he unenthusiastically raised the minimum wage for farm workers and supported religious toleration. But the first general strike ever carried out in Peru (1 January 1919), uniting workers and university students, demanded student power in university administration and a universal eight-hour workday. Half-hearted Civilista reforms failed to stem growing student and labor political unrest.

— VINCENT PELOSO

PARDO Y LAVALLE, MANUEL

Manuel Pardo y Lavalle (*b.* 9 August 1834; *d.* 16 November 1878), Peru's first full-term civilian president (1872–1876).

Son of the famed conservative writer Felipe PARDO, he was educated in Chile, Lima, and the universities of Barcelona and Paris. He returned to Peru in 1853 to launch a career in commerce and writing. His essays gained him a reputation as a champion of Peruvian nationalism. Already wealthy and well connected from ventures in banking, insurance, and commerce, he served as minister of the treasury in 1866, when guano was controlled by national merchants and the government borrowed heavily in Europe to fight a war with Spain (1864–1866). Two years later he served as president of the prestigious Lima Public Beneficence Society. After a brief, successful term as mayor of Lima (1869–1870), Pardo, a founder of the Civilista Party, was elected president in 1872 by the national electoral college. As president, Pardo sought to institute a program of reduced military expenditure, decentralization of government, restriction of clerical involvement in government, expanded public education, and state-planned economic development.

To carry out these plans under curtailed government spending, Pardo severely cut back the size of government bureaucracy and the army. In the meantime, the government raised taxes and printed paper money. In education, Pardo created public vocational schools, including one for indigenous youth, and founded national colleges to train teachers (men and women), miners, and engineers. New faculties of political and administrative sciences were established at the National University of San Marcos. He also organized a civilian national guard to counterbalance the professional army.

Pardo stepped down in favor of a military candidate in 1876, when party leaders were convinced that political anger was centered on the military; the purpose was to calm the military's fears of political isolation. This tactic did not stem the growing antagonism between the followers of Nicolás de PIÉROLA and the Civilistas. Rebellions by both groups were barely suppressed, and in this tense atmosphere an embittered army sergeant blamed his failure to win a promotion on Pardo. The sergeant assassinated the former president, and his partisans long afterward blamed the assassination on Piérola, who in the days before the murder had delivered a series of bitter anti-Pardo speeches.

– VINCENT PELOSO

PAREDES, MARIANO

Mariano Paredes (*b.* ca. 1800; *d.* 2 December 1856), president of Guatemala (1849–1851). Paredes began his military career as an officer in the army of Governor Mariano GÁLVEZ and later served with distinction under José Rafael CARRERA.

Because he was reputed to be relatively apolitical, the Guatemalan National Assembly named him president of Guatemala after the resignation of Bernardo Escobar on 1 January 1849. He served as a transition between the Liberal revolutionaries of 1848 and the return of Conservative Rafael Carrera as president in 1851. Paredes initially resisted Carrera's return but in June 1849

agreed to it and in August commissioned Carrera as commander of the armed forces. The Conservative rule that would last until 1871 was thus established under Paredes. He also permitted the Jesuits to return to Guatemala and promulgated a new, conservative constitution, under which Carrera returned to the presidency. General Paredes was a key officer in Carrera's army and commanded the Guatemalan forces in Nicaragua during the National War against William WALKER in 1856 until his death from cholera during the siege of Granada.

– RALPH LEE WOODWARD, JR.

PAREDES Y ARRILLAGA, MARIANO

Mariano Paredes y Arrillaga (*b.* 6 January 1797; *d.* 7 September 1849), Mexican general and politician. Born in Mexico City, Paredes was briefly president of Mexico in 1846. He had fought for the royalists in the War of Independence and supported Agustín de ITURBIDE's Plan of Iguala in 1821. A career army officer, he held various military posts in the 1820s but was slow to rise through the ranks. Favored by the regime of Anastasio BUSTAMANTE, Paredes was promoted to colonel in 1831 and the following year, at the age of thirty-five, to general. He served as minister of war for a few days in 1838. For the next several years, his base became Guadalajara of which he was made commander general. From 1841, Paredes participated in several rebellions on the side of General Antonio López de SANTA ANNA, but in 1844 he backed a successful revolt against him. The next year, he rebelled against President José Joaquín de HERRERA and assumed the presidency on 4 January 1846. On 28 July he was forced from office. He participated or was otherwise involved in further revolts until his death in Mexico City.

Paredes, who married into a wealthy Guadalajara family, was both an ardent centralist, supporting the restoration of a monarchy at one point in his career, and a fervent reactionary conservative, once warning Santa Anna of the dangers posed by "los terribles y perniciosos proletarios" (the dreadful and pernicious proletariat). Strongly proclerical, he believed that a liberal democracy and federal structure were inappropriate for Mexico in its then state of development, and that the country could be governed only by the army in alliance with the educated and affluent elite.

– MICHAEL P. COSTELOE

PAREJA DIEZCANSECO, ALFREDO

Alfredo Pareja Diezcanseco (*b.* 12 October 1908), Ecuadorian novelist and historian. Born in Guayaquil, Pareja had to interrupt his education after primary school because of the untimely death of his father when the young author was just thirteen. Later he attended the University of Quito, after which he became involved in several business activities. Only later did he turn to journalism and literature.

Throughout his long career, Pareja not only wrote extensively both fiction and nonfiction, but he also participated in diplomacy and politics. He represented Ecuador in Mexico, Argentina, and Chile, and he served as the administrator of the United Nations Relief Agency for Central America. In domestic politics, Pareja became elected deputy to the Constituent Assembly of Ecuador in 1944, and a leader in the Democratic National Front in 1956 and 1960. On occasion his impassioned opposition to dictatorial regimes cost him his freedom and forced him into exile.

It is Pareja's written work, however, that has built a solid reputation for him within and outside his country. He wrote several realistic novels in the 1930s and 1940s on the harsh life endured by the working Ecuadorian people. Later he turned to biographies and then to histories, culminating in his well-received *Historia del Ecuador* (2 vols., 2d ed. [1958]).

— JACK RAY THOMAS

PARRA, AQUILEO

Aquileo Parra (*b.* 12 May 1825; *d.* 4 December 1900), president of Colombia (1876–1878). Born in Barichara, Santander, to a family of modest means, in the 1840s Parra pioneered the jungle route between Vélez and Mompós, slowly accumulating a modest fortune.

The outbreak of the War of the Thousand Days in October 1899 represented the failure of Parra's presidency.

A reluctant defender of the Radical Liberal regime in Santander, Parra was imprisoned after the Liberal defeat at Oratorio in 1860. In 1874 he was elected president of Santander. In the 1875 elections for the national presidency, Parra represented the establishment Liberal bloc known derisively as the Radical Olympus, and his victory was widely ascribed to fraud. His administration, weakened by budget disputes and renewed conflict with the church, was soon faced with a Conservative rebellion. Despite suppressing the rebellion, Parra left office discredited. In the 1890s Parra attempted to strengthen the vanquished Liberals' organization, hoping to limit the appeal of more bellicose Liberals such

as Rafael URIBE URIBE. The outbreak of the War of the Thousand Days in October 1899 represented the failure of this effort; Parra died shortly thereafter. His informative *Memorias* (1912) confirm Parra's ideological place somewhat to the right of his contemporary Salvador Camacho Roldán, but to the left of many other figures of the "Olympus."

— RICHARD J. STOLLER

PARRA, FÉLIX

Félix Parra (*b.* 1845; *d.* 1919), Mexican painter. In 1861 Parra entered the school of drawing and painting at the College of San Nicolás in Morelia. In 1864 he moved to the Academy of San Carlos in Mexico City, which was occupied by French troops awaiting the arrival of Maximilian. Most of his education was under Mexican masters, since foreigners were not to Maximilian's liking. By this time the academy had already produced a generation of Mexicans trained under Spanish masters.

The themes that Parra presented in different exhibitions demonstrate the changes occurring at the time in the academy as well as in the critical world. In 1871 he presented a tender nude within the theme of the hunter, following the logic of European schools. In 1873 in the school of Padua he presented *Galileo,* which demonstrated the new astronomical theories. This is without a doubt one of his greatest works. In 1875 he unveiled a canvas of great dimensions, *Fray Bartolomé de las Casas,* and in 1877 he presented *La Matanza de Cholula,* whose historical component was taken from the book *Historia general de los Indios* by Fray Bartolomé de LAS CASAS. In it the Spanish missionary protests to his fellows the massacre of thirty thousand Cholultec Indians. This painting won Parra a scholarship from the academy to study in Europe.

Parra spent four years in France and Italy and returned to Mexico in 1882 as professor of ornamentation at the National School of Fine Arts. Beginning in 1909, another of his occupations was as sketcher at the National Museum, where he developed his skill with watercolor. He retired from his classes in 1915, by which time the school was no longer the center of artistic education.

— ESTHER ACEVEDO

PARRA, NICANOR

Nicanor Parra (*b.* 5 September 1914), Chilean poet. A former science teacher, Parra, who published his first collection of poems, *Cancionero sin nombre,* in 1937, describes himself, adopting a term coined by Vicente HUIDOBRO, as an antipoet. Like Huidobro, Parra demonstrates in his poems a freedom of experimentation and an irreverence toward traditionally held poetic values. Parra gained immediate popular acclaim with his second collection, *Poemas y antipoemas* (1954). With subsequent books, such as *La cueca larga* (1958), *Versos de salón* (1962), *Artefactos* (1972), *Sermones y prédicas del Cristo de Elqui* (1977), and *Hojas de Parra* (1985), Parra received international recognition. His innovative style of poetry combines wordplay, humor, the vernacular, and elements of literary tradition and popular culture to formulate an ironic commentary on human nature and society. Parra avoids personal involvement in his writing; his poems reflect a critical skepticism toward social conformism. A self-styled nihilist, Parra offers no escape from the absurdities and inconsequence of human values and beliefs. His sobering, if cynical, view of reality and his simple, direct style have made a lasting impact on Hispanic lyrical verse.

— S. DAYDÍ-TOLSON

PARRA, TERESA DE LA

Teresa de la Parra (Ana Teresa Parra Sanojo; *b.* 5 October 1890; *d.* 23 April 1936), Venezuelan novelist. She was born in Paris into Venezuela's plantation-owning class. When her father died in 1898, her mother took the family to Spain. As a member of an aristocratic Spanish family, she was sent to a convent to obtain a traditional education. At the age of eighteen, she returned to Caracas and lived in the Hacienda Tazón, where she read constantly. The Caracas society to which she belonged exposed Parra to the prejudice and discrimination that women faced. This awareness of differences in social standing between men and women led her to writing.

Parra's first work was "Mamá X," which later became part of her first novel, *Ifigenia*. This story won her an award that served as an incentive for further development. In 1923, Parra returned to Europe and settled in Paris, where she organized a *salón literario* at which Latin Americans met. Parra was invited to lecture in Cuba and Colombia, but she lived most of her life outside of Venezuela. She died in Madrid. In 1948 her remains were repatriated to her country of origin.

Parra's literary works are *Diario de una señorita que se fastidia,* (1922; Journal of an Upset Young Woman); *Ifigenia: diario de una señorita que escribió porque se fastidiaba* (1924), published in Paris with a preface by Francis de Miomandres; and *Las memorias de la Mamá Blanca* (1929), also published in Paris. Her letters and her unpublished lectures were included in *Obras completas* (1965). Her novels represent life in nineteenth-century Venezuela from the viewpoint of female protagonists, thus constituting a profound reflection on a passing way of life.

— MAGDALENA GARCÍA PINTO

PARRA, VIOLETA

Violeta Parra (*b.* 4 October 1917; *d.* 5 February 1967), Chilean folklorist, singer, and composer. Parra was the mother of the musicians Ángel and Isabel Parra and sister of the poet Nicanor PARRA. Born in San Carlos, in the province of Nuble, she moved to Santiago in her teens and scraped together a living by singing in bars, cafes, and restaurants. In the early 1950s she found her vocation as collector and performer of folk songs, and later made some memorable recordings. She soon began writing her own songs in folk idiom as well as developing her talents for weaving, pottery, and painting.

Parra lived for two periods (1954–1956 and 1961–1965) in France. Finally returning to Chile, she recorded her classic "Last Compositions of Violeta Parra," several of whose tracks are of exceptional quality, and established a folklore center in a circus tent in the Santiago suburb of La Reina.

A passionate, direct, sometimes tempestuous woman—Pablo NERUDA called her "a saint of pure clay"—she shot herself, partly in despair over a broken love affair. The music of this extraordinary woman was a key inspiration for the New Chilean Song movement of the late 1960s and early 1970s.

— SIMON COLLIER

PASCAL-TROUILLOT, ERTHA

Ertha Pascal-Trouillot (*b.* 13 August 1943), provisional president of Haiti (13 March 1990–7 February 1991). A lawyer, Pascal-Trouillot served as a lower court judge, and in 1986 she was the first woman appointed to the Supreme Court. Shortly after General Prosper Avril was forced out as de facto ruler, she was the only one among the twelve court judges who was acceptable or willing to become provisional president, as provided in the 1987 Constitution. When inaugurated, Pascal-Trouillot committed herself to oversee the preparation for a political campaign and national elections and "accepted this heavy task in the name of the Haitian woman." She remained in office—surviving one attempted coup—until the election (December 1990) and inauguration (February 1991) of Father Jean-Bertrand ARISTIDE as president.

— LARMAN C. WILSON

PASO, FERNANDO DEL

Fernando Del Paso (*b.* 1 April 1935), Mexican novelist. Born in Mexico City, Paso studied economics and medicine at the Universidad Nacional Autónoma de México. He then worked in advertising and for the BBC in London from 1970 to 1984, and since then has served as cultural attaché, then consul general, to the Mexican embassy in Paris.

Although he has published two volumes of poetry and has gained recognition for his paintings and drawings of whimsical castles and creatures, Paso is best known for his three monumental novels. *José Trigo* (1966) uses experimental techniques to evoke a working-class neighborhood of Mexico City and the railroad workers' movement of 1958. *Palinuro de México* (1977) is the saga of a medical student who, swept up in the student movement of 1968, dies in the government massacre at the Plaza of Tlatelolco. *Noticias del imperio* (1987) is a historical novel about the French Intervention in Mexico, which imposed the Hapsburg monarchy of Maximilian and Carlota (1864–1867); much of it is narrated from the point of view of the mad empress.

— CYNTHIA STEELE

PASO, JUAN JOSÉ

Juan José Paso (*b.* 2 January 1758; *d.* 10 September 1833), Argentine educator, journalist, lawyer, and public official in the Río de la Plata. Born in Buenos Aires, Paso studied law and theology (through 1779) at the universities of Chuquisaca and Córdoba. Returning to his birthplace, Paso taught philosophy at the Colegio de San Carlos (1781–1783). He was a member of the first patriot government of Argentina in 1810. During the early 1800s he edited, with Mariano MORENO, another secretary of the revolutionary junta, *La Gaceta de Buenos Aires,* the official newspaper of the new regime. Paso held the positions of assistant prosecutor of the Royal Treasury in 1803 and advisor to the government during Carlos María de ALVEAR's directorate in 1815. He also served on the triumvirates of 1811–1812 after the dissolution of the junta and as representative in the Congress of Tucumán in 1816. In addition, Paso was the Santiago-based diplomat of the United Provinces in 1814. Mariano BALCARCE, describing him as "the illustrious son of the nation who knew how to provide important services to the cause of independence, skillfully and with talent, and was a jurist known for his integrity and zeal," ordered the construction of a monument in his honor after his death.

— FIDEL IGLESIAS

PASO Y TRONCOSO, FRANCISCO DEL

Francisco Del Paso y Troncoso (*b.* 8 October 1842; *d.* 30 April 1916), Mexican historian. Born in Veracruz,

Paso y Troncoso originally studied for a career in business. In 1867 he journeyed to Mexico City in order to pursue a career in medicine, a course of studies which led him to investigate the history of science in Mexico under the Aztecs. He never completed his degree in medicine, turning his attention completely to the study of native history and linguistics. He gathered together major chronicles and other texts and codices on the precontact and colonial periods, and mastered Nahuatl, the language of the Aztecs. Appointed director of the National Museum in 1889, he sailed for Europe in 1892 in order to search for documents relating to Mexico. He scoured archives in Spain, England, Russia, Germany, Austria, France, and Italy, where he spent the last period of his life. Though he did not return to Mexico, he was in constant contact with government officials, including President Porfirio DÍAZ, who were funding his projects. After the outbreak of the Revolution funding became increasingly more difficult.

Paso y Troncoso scoured archives in Spain, England, Russia, Germany, Austria, France, and Italy, searching for documents relating to Mexico.

After his death the repatriation of the documents collected by this major investigator proved problematic, and his complete collection was never fully restored. Nonetheless, as a result of his exhaustive labors he brought to light a corpus of works by the sixteenth-century Franciscan ethnographer Bernardino de SAHAGÚN (ca. 1499–1590). He also prepared a monumental collection of documents known as the *Papeles de Nueva España,* consisting of bibliographies, geography and statistics, histories, letters, and dictionaries of native languages. Such were the volume of his findings and the detail of his inquiry that many of these projects were not published until after his death.

— BRIAN C. BELANGER

PASSARINHO, JARBAS GONÇALVES

Jarbas Gonçalves Passarinho (*b.* 11 January 1920), Brazilian military officer who became a prominent civilian leader of the military regime that ruled Brazil from 1964 to 1985. Named governor of the state of Pará shortly after the coup in 1964, Passarinho served in that post until 1966. In 1967, after being elected to the Senate, he was appointed minister of labor and social welfare by President Artur da COSTA E SILVA. In December 1968, Passarinho signed Institutional Act 5, which marked the beginning of Brazil's most repressive phase of military rule. One of the few politicians to enjoy confidence among the competing military factions, he served as minister of education and culture (1970–1973) under President Emilio Garrastazu MÉDICI. Elected to the Senate from Pará in 1975, Passarinho served for eight years. In 1983, Passarinho was appointed minister of welfare and social assistance by President João Baptista FIGUEIREDO. He demonstrated his remarkable resiliency by winning a third eight-year Senate term in 1986, under civilian rule, on the Partido Democrático Social ticket. Appointed minister of justice in 1990 by President Fernando COLLOR DE MELLO, Passarinho retained that post until 1992.

— SCOTT MAINWARING

PASTA, CARLO ENRICO

Carlo Enrico Pasta (*b.* 17 November 1817; *d.* 31 August 1898), Italian composer. Born in Milan, Pasta studied there and in Paris. In 1855 he settled in Lima, where he was active in the musical life of the city. A musical pioneer, he composed *zarzuelas* and operas using texts from Peruvian writers; Pasta was the first composer to take as his subject matter Peruvian folklore and Peru's pre-Columbian history. He was a member of the fraternity of Santa Cecilia. His first opera, *I tredici,* premiered in Turin's Teatro Sutera (1851). *La fronda* (1872) and *Una tazza di thé* (1872) premiered in Lima, and *Atahualpa* (1875), based on a libretto by Antonio Ghislanzoni, was first performed at Genoa's Teatro Paganini. *Atahualpa,* based on an Indian theme, received its first performance in America under maestro Francesco Rosa at Lima's Teatro Principal on 1 November 1877. Pasta's *zarzuelas* include *El loco de la guardilla, Rafael Sanzio, El pobre indio,* and *Placeres y dolores,* the last three with libretti by the Peruvian writer Juan Cosio. Pasta's most successful work was the *zarzuela La cola del diablo,* performed at Lima's Teatro Principal in 1865. He died in Milan.

— SUSANA SALGADO

PASTORA GÓMEZ, EDÉN

Edén Pastora Gómez (*b.* ca. 1937), Nicaraguan revolutionary. On 22 August 1978, Edén Pastora Gómez, "Commandante Cero," led a successful raid of the Nicaraguan National Palace by Sandinista forces—an event that proved to be a major catalyst in the Nicaraguan Revolution. Pastora had been a longtime member of the Sandinista National Liberation Front (FSLN). After the Sandinistas gained power, however, Pastora quickly became marginalized from the decision-making

process within the FSLN National Directorate, and in 1981 he quietly resigned. In 1982 he appeared in Costa Rica criticizing the FSLN leadership for subverting the revolution. Pastora formed the Revolutionary Sandinista Front (FRS) in Costa Rica and eventually joined other dissident groups to form the Revolutionary Democratic Alliance (ARDE). Pastora opposed a formal union with Somocista and ex-National Guard elements of the Honduran-based CONTRA group Nicaraguan Democratic Forces (FDN). The Costa Rican government deported Pastora to Venezuela in 1984. Pastora pulled the FRS out of the ARDE when the ARDE leadership joined with the FDN.

— HEATHER K. THIESSEN

PASTRANA BORRERO, MISAEL

Misael Pastrana Borrero (*b.* 14 November 1923), president of Colombia (1970–1974). Born to a prominent family in Neiva, Huila, and educated in Bogotá, he took his doctorate in law at Javerian University in 1945. As a teenage Conservative, he was perceived as having a promising future. He served in the Colombian embassy at the Vatican from 1947 to 1949, then was President Mariano OSPINA PÉREZ's secretary (1949–1950) and counselor at the Colombian embassy in Washington, D.C. (1950–1952). Pastrana worked in corporate private finance from 1956 to 1959, then returned to government (1960–1961). He was in the private sector again from 1961 to 1966, and became minister of development, then of public works, and then of finance and credit over sixteen months of the Carlos LLERAS RESTREPO presidency (1966–1970). In 1968, he returned to Washington, D.C., as Colombia's ambassador. Pastrana was elected president in 1970, after a bitter political campaign, winning by less than 64,000 votes out of 3,250,000 cast. One of the best-prepared, in terms of administrative experience, of any Colombian chief executive of the twentieth century, Pastrana had to overcome virulent opposition before being able to achieve some of his goals in the last two years of his term. These included tax reform, foreign petroleum company buyouts by the government, enlarged social services, and improvements in the infrastructure.

— J. LEÓN HELGUERA

PATERSON, WILLIAM

William Paterson (*b.* April 1658; *d.* 2 January 1719), the central figure behind an unsuccessful attempt to establish a Scottish colony at Darién (now Panama) at the end of the seventeenth century.

William Paterson was the key person in an ill-fated effort to establish a great international trading center for future generations, New Caledonia, at Darién from 1698 to 1700. Paterson, the Scot who was the founder of the Bank of England in 1694–1695, and the director of the African Company, was a believer in Scottish unification with England and an advocate of open trade with the Indies. Paterson's leadership of the African Company ensured that by 1696 the Darién project represented the focal point of the company's efforts. The company made two attempts at settlement, both of which failed.

The first settlers landed in New Caledonia in November 1698. These colonists faced poor trading conditions, a lack of leadership, a shortage of supplies, and periodic attacks by the Spanish, who considered them pirates. In June 1699, the first attempt at settlement was abandoned. Paterson protested the colonists' decision but was too ill to prevent their departure. The settlers then went to Belize, New York, and New England, hoping to find temporary refuge.

In November 1699, they returned to Darién in another attempt to establish a colony and found that the Spanish had pillaged their first settlement. Some left for Scotland but many stayed to try and rebuild the colony. They encountered ongoing health problems and a persistent lack of supplies, however. Moreover, Spanish attacks, from 23 February to 17 March 1700, eventually forced the total capitulation of the settlers, who abandoned the colony on 11 April 1700.

Spain never in fact accepted the colonizing group's claims to their small piece of land on the isthmus. And England failed to support the venture because the king wished to forestall the company's settlement of land and instructed colonial governors not to trade with or assist the Darién colony. Paterson thus underestimated the importance of Spain's claims to the territory, and with the forced dissolution of the colony, he lost a substantial sum of his own money. He was later indemnified by the British Parliament.

– BLAKE D. PATRIDGE

PATIÑO, JOSÉ DE

José de Patiño, (*b.* 1666/70; *d.* 3 November 1736), secretary of state for the Indies, navy, and treasury (1726–1736) during the reign of Philip V of Spain. Patiño's goal was to restore Spain's power in Europe by strengthening American trade through a strong navy and a fiscal policy designed to stimulate exports. He entered higher administration as intendant of Extremadura (1711) and then Catalonia (1713), where he applied the *Nueva Planta* (a wholesale reorganization of Castilian Spain in order to bring power to the crown of Aragon; 1716) and introduced the *catastro* (a property and income tax). In 1717 he became intendant general of the navy, the superintendant of Seville, and president of the House of Trade, newly located in Cádiz.

A master of bureaucratic compromise who was able to balance the demands of the crown and the needs of the state, Patiño combined expert knowledge of the Indies with administrative talent and proved that careers would be open to talent under the new Bourbon regime. In foreign policy, he took into account the interests of his Italian patron, the queen, Isabella Farnese of Parma, and tried to keep peace with Britain while building up the Spanish navy. In colonial affairs his goal was simply to increase Spain's profits in America and reduce the drain of revenues by British interlopers and American Spaniards.

– SUZANNE HILES BURKHOLDER

PATIÑO, SIMÓN ITURRI

Simón Iturri Patiño (*b.* 1 June 1860; *d.* 20 April 1947), Bolivian tin miner. Born in Santivañez, Cochabamba, Patiño spearheaded Bolivia's transition from silver to tin producer and in the process became one of the wealthiest men in the world, powerful enough to influence Bolivian politics greatly in the early twentieth century. Working first for Bolivian and German merchant houses and the Huanchaca Company, Bolivia's foremost silver-mining concern, Patiño purchased his own share of La Salvadora tin mine in 1894. After striking a rich vein in 1900, Patiño continuously modernized mining production and began purchasing other tin mines. He also began buying shares in German and, later, in partnership with U.S. venture capitalists, British tin-smelting operations in Europe. In 1924 he established Patiño Mines and Enterprises in the United States. He also bought into Malaysian tin mines. By the 1920s his Bolivian holdings were only a small fraction of his total business empire, although he continued to produce at least one-third of all Bolivian tin. With his Banco Mercantil, he was one of Bolivia's leading bankers; he also owned a majority share in the Sociedad Agrícola é Ganadera de Cinti, the largest agro-industrial enterprise in Bolivia.

Given his financial clout, Patiño was a major figure in Bolivian politics. His actions led to the splintering of the Liberal Party in 1919 and so aided in the revolution that brought the Republicans to power the following year. The Catavi Massacre in 1942, in which the army killed hundreds of unarmed miners and women and children in a labor dispute with Patiño, raised nationalist fervor against the mine owner. Since Patiño

Simón Iturri Patiño. (Benson Latin American Collection, University of Texas at Austin)

had lived in Europe from the 1920s and controlled so much of the Bolivian economy, many Bolivians resented him. This resentment ultimately led to the expropriation of his mines during the 1952 revolution and the creation of Comibol, the state mining company.

— ERICK D. LANGER

PATROCÍNIO, JOSÉ DO

José do Patrocínio (*b.* 8 October 1853; *d.* 1 February 1905), Brazilian abolitionist, journalist, orator, and poet. The son of a Catholic priest and planter in Rio de Janeiro Province and a black fruit vendor, Patrocínio was brought up in the vicarage of Campos and on a nearby estate, where he acquired an intimate knowledge of slavery. After serving an apprenticeship at Misericórdia Hospital in Rio de Janeiro, he completed the pharmacy course at the Faculty of Medicine. However, lacking funds to establish himself in his profession, he joined the staff of the capital's daily, *Gazeta de Notícias,*

and soon gained prominence as an opponent of slavery. In 1881, aided by his wealthy father-in-law, he acquired the *Gazeta de Tarde,* which under his leadership became the principal antislavery journal in Brazil until it was replaced by his equally effective *A Cidade do Rio* in 1887. Patrocínio advanced the antislavery cause as a powerful orator, as author of fiery articles and editorials, as organizer of antislavery groups, as an abolitionist emissary to Europe, and as an effective promoter of regional movements (Ceará in 1882, his native Campos in 1885, and the port of Santos in 1886). With the end of slavery in 1888, he organized the Guarda Negra (Black Guard), an association of black militants dedicated to protecting Princess Isabel, whose succession to the throne was threatened by a growing republican movement. After the military revolt of 1889 and the beginning of the federal republic, Patrocínio suffered persecution from President Floriano Peixoto's government, including exile in 1892 to the state of Amazonas and suspension of his newspaper, *A Cidade do Rio.* He was again active as a journalist at the time of his death.

— ROBERT EDGAR CONRAD

PATRÓN COSTAS, ROBUSTIANO

Robustiano Patrón Costas (*b.* 5 August 1878; *d.* 1953), Argentine sugar baron and conservative political boss. An old-regime provincial oligarch, Patrón Costas took a law doctorate at the University of Buenos Aires in 1901, then returned to his native Salta to rise through the political ranks to the governorship (1913–1916). In 1916 he was elected as a National Conservative to the federal Senate, where he served from 1916 to 1925 and again from 1932 to 1943; during the latter period he was the Senate's provisional president. Simultaneously he founded and managed the sugar *ingenio* (mill) San Martín del Tabacal at Orán in Salta, which gave him great wealth and power. The *ingenio* was known for its abuse of labor, particularly of Bolivian migrants. In 1943 it was learned that Patrón was the favorite of President Ramón S. CASTILLO, a provincial politician of similar stripe, to succeed him in office. Patrón was believed to be pro-Allies; his election would have meant a less rigid neutralism than Castillo's. It would also have required the military to supervise the necessary electoral frauds. Patrón's unsavory reputation as a sugar operator and as an exemplar of the corrupt, stagnant politics of the "década infame" (1932–1943) made him unacceptable to broad military and civilian sectors. Thus his nomination by Castillo was a contributing cause to the military coup of 4 June 1943, which ended oligarchic politics in Argentina.

— RONALD C. NEWTON

PAVÓN AYCINENA, MANUEL FRANCISCO

Manuel Francisco Pavón Aycinena (*b.* 30 January 1798; *d.* 19 April 1855), leader of the conservative elite that managed the Guatemalan government and developed the corporatist structure of the state during the regime of Rafael CARRERA (1839–1865). The son of Manuel José Pavón, a prominent Guatemala City creole, and Maria Micaela Aycinena Nájera, he was closely related to the powerful Aycinena clan. Educated as a lawyer at the University of San Carlos, he served as a lieutenant colonel in the federal army during the civil war of 1826–1829. In exile from 1830 to 1837 in New York, Paris, and Havana, he returned to Guatemala and between 1838 and 1854 served as secretary of the assembly, editor of the government gazette, diplomat, prior of the *consulado,* and minister of finance, foreign relations, war, justice, ecclesiastical affairs, and interior. He formulated major reforms in finance and promoted good relations with Great Britain through his friendship with British Consul Frederick Chatfield (1834–1852). His Ley Pavón of 16 September 1852 gave responsibility for elementary education to parish priests. He played a key role in engineering Carrera's elevation to president for life in 1854.

– RALPH LEE WOODWARD, JR.

PAYNO Y FLORES, MANUEL

Manuel Payno y Flores (*b.* 21 June 1810; *d.* 4 November 1894), Mexican government official and novelist. Son of treasury official Manuel Payno y Bustamante and cousin of President Anastasio BUSTAMANTE, Payno y Flores was a native of Mexico City.

As public servant, Payno is most remembered as the treasury minister who negotiated the 1850 settlements of the foreign (14 October) and internal debts (30 November). However, his subsequent service was equally, if not more, significant. Because he was implicated in the coup that overthrew President Ignacio COMONFORT in January 1858, Payno never again held the post of treasury minister. He nevertheless remained an active participant in discussions of fiscal matters, particularly those concerning the foreign debt. He wrote major tracts on the debt settlements that provoked the English-French-Spanish invasion of December 1861 and on the internal debt, and produced the only accounting of the expenditures of the imperial government. His views often formed the intellectual rationale for the policies of the JUÁREZ government on those issues.

Beginning in the 1830s, Payno wrote for the daily press. In 1845–1846, he published the first of his two *costumbrista* novels, *El fistol del diablo,* which detailed the everyday life of the period. In the 1870s, he wrote important school texts on Mexican history, geography, and law. Near the end of his life, while consul for the Mexican government in Spain, he published his masterpiece, *Los bandidos del Río Frío* (1889–1891), full of descriptions of local color and famous people. He died in San Ángel, D.F.

– BARBARA A. TENENBAUM

PAZ, JOSÉ MARÍA

José María Paz (*b.* 9 September 1791; *d.* 22 October 1854), Argentine general and unitarist. Born in Córdoba, Paz abandoned law studies to join the army during the War of Independence. He served in the Army of the North and lost an arm at the battle of Venta y Media. In January 1820, with Juan Bautista Bustos, caudillo of Córdoba, Paz revolted against Buenos Aires. He subsequently declared himself a unitarist and fought to establish a league of provinces under a central government. He was one of a number of military leaders who returned from the war against Brazil (1825–1828) determined to oppose the rise of Federalism. This brought him into conflict with Juan Manuel de ROSAS and his allies. Victories over Bustos and Juan Facundo QUIROGA in 1829–1830 enabled him to make Córdoba the center of the Liga del Interior with a centralized structure in opposition to federalist Buenos Aires.

For the next two decades Paz combined military and political action. In 1831 he was taken prisoner by Estanislao LÓPEZ, who saved him from the execution ordered by Rosas. As his league collapsed in the interior, he moved his base to Corrientes. But he was frustrated by the political rivalries in the Littoral and the rise of the federalist Justo José de URQUIZA. In 1846 he resigned his military command and retired to Brazil. There he remained until 1852, when he returned to Buenos Aires after the defeat of Rosas, in time to take part in the defense of the city against the excesses of its liberator Urquiza. He was briefly minister of war, and in 1854 was elected to the legislature.

Paz was a humane and educated man, regarded as a model general and a representative of "civilization" against the barbarism of the caudillos.

Paz was a humane and educated man, regarded by Domingo SARMIENTO as a model general and a representative of "civilization" against the barbarism of the caudillos. His *Memorias* are rich in detail and perception, and a prime source for the history of the period.

– JOHN LYNCH

PAZ, JUAN CARLOS

Juan Carlos Paz (*b.* 5 August 1897; *d.* 25 August 1972), Argentine composer, teacher, and writer. Paz was born in Buenos Aires, where he studied piano and composition with Alphonse Thibaud and harmony with Constantino GAITO but recognized a main influence in the figure of Eduardo Fornarini, an itinerant Italian musician. Fornarini initiated Paz in the analysis of the works of César Franck, Debussy, and the early works of Schönberg and Stravinsky. In 1924, Paz went to Europe and entered the Schola Cantorum in Paris, where he worked with Vincent d'Indy. In spite of all his studies, Paz considered himself largely self-taught. On returning to Buenos Aires he joined in 1929 with composers Juan José and José María CASTRO, Gilardo GILARDI, and Jacobo FICHER to create the Renovation Group to promote their music. Later, Paz withdrew from it due to a lack of agreement on the methods to achieve their goals and on aesthetic differences. Soon he began to teach composition privately, and he introduced twelve-tone techniques to his students and to the public at large. In 1937 he created the Agrupación Nueva Música (ANM), which performed in concert featuring works by Schönberg, Webern, Varèse, Cowell, Cage, Messiaen, and many others.

Paz's works were neoclassical well into the mid-1930s, characterized by linear, contrapuntal writing, with some harmonies within an atonal style, as in his *Tres piezas para orquesta* (1931) and Octet for wind instruments (1930). *Tres invenciones a dos voces* (1932), *Tres movimientos de Jazz* (1932) and his Piano Sonatina no. 3 (1933) show his angular, neoclassical writing and jazz influences. The abstract phrasing of these pieces introduced the strict atonal writing that Paz would favor in later years.

In 1934, Paz began to explore twelve-tone writing, a technique he applied in a very personal way in his *Primera composición en los doce tonos* for flute, English horn, and cello (1934); *Segunda composición en los doce tonos* for flute and piano (1934–1935); *Diez piezas sobre una serie de los doce tonos* for piano (1935); *Passacaglia* for orchestra (1936); and *Tercera composición en los doce tonos* for clarinet and piano (1937); and *Cuarta composición en los doce tonos* for solo violin (1938). Paz continued in this phase into the mid-1950s, although he tried something different in his *Rítmica ostinata* for orchestra (1942). In this work, a large toccata in fast tempo with sixteenth- and eighth-note values as a constant figura-

tion, the many pedal points and ostinatos are orchestrated brilliantly. During the 1960s, Paz explored other styles and techniques but favored what he had called the "return to intuition." He wrote only a few works after that, in a free style that offered him a greater freedom of language. During the 1960s he wrote *Continuidad* (1960) for orchestra; *Música* for piano and orchestra (1963); *Invención* for string quartet (1961); *Concreción* for woodwind and brass instruments (1964); *Galaxia* for organ (1964); and the series *Núcleos* for piano (1962–1964). Other important works by Paz include *Dédalus* for flute, clarinet, violin, cello, and piano (1950); *Transformaciones canónicas* (Canonical transformations) for orchestra (1955–1966); and his monumental *Música 1946* for piano (1945–1946).

His books left a mark on many young composers, not only in Argentina but throughout South America and Europe. They included *La música en los Estados Unidos* (1952; revised in 1958); *Introducción a la música de nuestro tiempo* (1955); *Arnold Schoenberg, o el fin de la era tonal* (1958); *Alturas, tensiones, ataques, intensidades* (1972).

– ALCIDES LANZA

PAZ, OCTAVIO

Octavio Paz (*b.* 31 March 1914; *d.* 19 April 1998), Mexican poet and essayist. Recipient of the Nobel Prize for literature in 1990 and one of the leading Mexican poets and intellectuals of the twentieth century, Octavio Paz was born and raised in Mixcoac, now part of Mexico City. His father, Octavio Paz Solórzano, was a political journalist who wrote a biography of Emiliano ZAPATA and helped found agrarian reform. Paz attended French and English language schools and read widely in the library of his grandfather, the novelist Ireneo Paz, before transferring to public schools, and ultimately the National Preparatory School, where he studied law. He founded the magazine *Barandal* (Balustrade) in 1931–1932, followed by *Cuadernos del Valle de México* (Notebooks from the Valley of Mexico) in 1933–1934. Paz abandoned his legal studies in 1937 to visit Yucatán, where he helped establish a progressive school for workers and discovered Mexico's pre-Columbian past. That same year he went to Republican Spain to attend the Second International Congress of Anti-fascist Writers, where he met most of the great poets writing in Spanish, as well as English and French writers, including André Breton, the founder of surrealism. As a result of this trip, he developed a philosophy of poetry that sought to create language anew, with the dual purpose of revealing human fragmentation and solitude and demonstrating how language prevents the modern world

Octavio Paz. Photograph by Sara Facio, 1971. (Organization of American States)

from understanding itself and its "real reality." In this way Paz tried to resolve the tension between pure poetry and art committed to social progress.

In 1938 Paz returned to Mexico and helped found the journal *Taller* (Workshop) to explore his new ideas. When that magazine folded, he helped found *El Hijo Pródigo* (The Prodigal Son) in 1943, a periodical representing the Mexican vanguard, poets who believed that writing had a special mission. In 1944 Paz was awarded a Guggenheim fellowship and spent the next ten years of his life away from Mexico. He went first to San Francisco and then to New York City, where he studied the life and work of José Juan TABLADA and published an important critical essay on that poet. Tablada's influence led him to his lifelong fascination with Asian literature and culture. In 1944 he taught at the Middlebury College Spanish Summer School in Vermont, where he met the poet Robert Frost and became reacquainted with Jorge Guillén. In 1945 he joined the Mexican diplomatic service and went to Paris, where he was strongly influenced by the surrealist movement. In 1952 he served as Mexican ambassador in India and Japan, furthering his interests in Eastern art and archi-

tecture and in the classics of Buddhism and Taoism, influences felt subsequently in his poetry. He returned to Mexico in 1953.

Paz's work reached maturity in the late 1940s. Appearing in 1949 was his *Libertad bajo palabra* (Freedom on Parole), championing the Latin American critical avant-garde. In 1950 he published a classic analysis of the Mexican people, *El laberinto de la soledad* (The Labyrinth of Solitude). These works inaugurated his most productive and complex period. He published poetry and essays, lectured on and presented new poets and painters, founded journals and a theatrical group, translated ancient and modern poetry, and participated in literary and political polemics. In 1956 he published *El arco y la lira* (The Bow and the Lyre), an important work examining the function of poetry itself. Paz returned to Paris in 1959 and subsequently was renamed ambassador to India in 1962, a post he resigned in 1968 in protest over the 2 October massacre of students in Tlatelolco Square. He displayed his outrage in *Posdata* (1970; Postscript), a critical reevaluation of the *Labyrinth of Solitude*. He expanded on the ideas in this book in *El ogro filantrópico* (1979; The Philanthropic Ogre). During the 1970s, he founded two significant magazines, *Plural* (1971) and *Vuelta* (1977), which he continued to edit in the 1990s, demonstrating his strong commitment to cultural journalism and his anticipation of the "postmodern."

Paz is primarily important as a poet and essayist, but he has also written unpublished short stories and a play. His published works in Spanish include nearly thirty volumes of poetry, over thirty volumes of essays, numerous anthologies of poetry in Spanish, as well as anthologies of poetry in translation from the French, English, Portuguese, Swedish, Chinese, and Japanese. His own poetry and essays have been translated into English, French, Italian, and numerous other languages. Paz is also important as an art critic and promoter.

Paz has taught at major universities in the United States and Europe. He is a member of the Colegio Nacional (Mexico) and the Consejo Superior de Cooperación Iberoamericana (Spain), and has won the International Prize for Poetry (Brussels, 1963), the Cervantes Prize (Spain, 1981), the International Prize for Literature (1982), and the Menéndez Pelayo Prize (Spain, 1987).

In the late twentieth century, Paz remained the leader of the generation that emerged toward the end of the 1930s, which was largely responsible for establishing the outlines of contemporary Mexican literary criticism and cultural thought. His work has been fundamental in bringing the Spanish language and Mexican literature and culture into the modern and postmodern age, as well as in opening them up to other cultures. Further, he has become one of the principal contemporary theorists of Mexican history and what he sees as the crisis of present-day Mexican culture. As he noted when he received the Nobel Prize, a writer has two loyalties, first to literature and second to his native culture.

– KEITH MCDUFFIE

PAZ BARAONA, MIGUEL

Miguel Paz Baraona (*b.* 1863; *d.* 1937) president of Honduras (1925–1929). Dr. Miguel Paz Baraona, a civilian member of the Nationalist Party, was elected president almost unanimously in 1925 (the Liberals abstained from voting). His election, which marked the final phase of the bloody civil war between multiple bands of rival warlords that had erupted in Honduras in 1924, gradually restored domestic tranquillity to Honduras. Peace enabled the banana companies to resume their expansion, which within a few years made Honduras the premier banana exporter in the world. An even more auspicious breakthrough was the Lyall Plan, which Paz negotiated with the British bondholders association for the reduction and repayment of the country's crippling foreign debt.

– KENNETH V. FINNEY

PAZ ESTENSSORO, VÍCTOR

Víctor Paz Estenssoro (*b.* 2 October 1907) president of Bolivia (1952–1956, 1960–1964, 1964, and 1985–1989). Born to a well-known landowning family in the southern department of Tarija, Paz Estenssoro graduated from high school at fifteen in the city of Oruro and went on to obtain a law degree from the national university in La Paz. In 1929, he became the *redactor de la camara de diputados* (official records keeper of the Chamber of Deputies), the first of numerous government posts he would hold in his long political career. A year later, when a military junta closed down Congress, he became an employee of the housing ministry's national statistics office.

In 1932, Paz Estenssoro joined thousands of Bolivian conscripted soldiers in the ill-fated Chaco War against Paraguay that resulted in Bolivia's loss of the Chaco territory and precipitated the collapse of the old tin-mining oligarchy. After the war, he joined prominent middle-class intellectuals in calling for sweeping social and political reform. In line with his political instincts, Paz Estenssoro took a post as a low-ranking official in the Ministry of Housing during the government of Colonel David TORO (1937). A year later he was elected deputy to the 1938 constitutional convention that re-

wrote the Bolivian constitution, enshrining a more active state intervention in both the economy and redressing social grievances.

Paz Estenssoro was catapulted to the forefront of Bolivia's political scene by two crucial events. In 1941, he joined Augusto Céspedes, Carlos Montenegro, Hernán SILES ZUAZO, Rafael Otazo, and Walter GUEVARA ARCE to found the Nationalist Revolutionary Movement (MNR). As a deputy in Congress, Paz Estenssoro delivered scathing indictments of the military government headed by General Enrique Peñaranda, perceived by the MNR as merely a puppet of the three largest tin-mining companies. It was the congressional speech he delivered in 1942, following the infamous Catavi Massacre of miners and their families by government troops, that had the most far-reaching effect. It enabled him to rally support for the MNR and forge an alliance between the MNR and a group of colonels and lieutenant colonels who advocated taking a more direct role in political affairs. This civil-military alliance was responsible for toppling Peñaranda and installing Colonel Gualberto VILLARROEL as president of Bolivia.

As the minister of finance, Paz Estenssoro became the architect of Bolivia's first flirtations with import-substitution strategies and a state-centered development strategy. Fortuitously, Paz Estenssoro resigned two weeks before a mob of university students, members of the Stalinist Party of the Revolutionary Left (Partido de la Izquierda Revolucionaria—PIR), and members of conservative parties stormed the government palace and lynched President Villarroel. Paz spent the next six years in exile, mainly in Argentina, witnessing the best years of the Peronist experiment. From Argentina, Paz fought an intense battle to maintain himself at the helm of the MNR while simultaneously attempting to broaden the appeal of the party to labor and other social sectors.

Paz returned triumphantly to Bolivia following the 9 April 1952 revolution that ended the monopoly of tin production by HOCHSCHILD, Patiño, and ARAMAYO, the country's so-called tin barons. During his first term as president (1952–1956), Paz nationalized the nation's tin-mining operations, downgraded the military institution, approved a major land-reform decree, and granted universal suffrage to all adult Bolivians. Paz returned to office in 1960. Seeking a third term in 1964, he was overthrown by a military coup orchestrated by General René BARRIENTOS ORTUÑO, his own vice president, who had been imposed on the MNR ticket by a restructured military institution.

Paz spent the next seven years in exile but returned to Bolivia in August 1971 to support General Hugo BANZER SUÁREZ's coup. Along with his faction of the MNR, Paz governed Bolivia with the military through the Popular Nationalist Front (FPN) until 1974, when he was again exiled. He returned to Bolivia in 1978 to run as the MNR's presidential candidate, placing second in the elections of 1979, 1980, and 1985. In 1985 he was elected president by Congress after entering into an informal agreement with the Movement of the Revolutionary Left (MIR). On 29 August 1985 he issued Decree 21060, introducing the New Economic Policy (NPE) that ended Bolivia's worst economic crisis. The NPE diminished the economic role of state enterprises and enlarged the role of the private sector. When Paz left office in August 1989, he enjoyed a 70 percent popularity rating, the highest ever for an outgoing Bolivian president.

— EDUARDO A. GAMARRA

PAZ GARCÍA, POLICARPO

Policarpo Paz García (*b.* 1932; *d.* 1991), president of Honduras (25 July 1980–27 January 1982). Paz was commander of the armed forces under President Juan Melgar Castro (1975–1978). Leader of the military junta that overthrew Melgar Castro on 7 August 1978, he acted as chief of state and chief of the armed forces until the Constituent Assembly elected him provisional president of Honduras. Under Paz, land reform slowed and external debt accelerated. His government was reputedly corrupt, and rumors persisted of his mafia and drug trafficking ties. The United States liberally supplied aid to Honduras under Paz, considering his government a bulwark against the communist regime in Nicaragua.

— JOYCE E. NAYLON

PAZ SOLDÁN FAMILY

Paz Soldán Family, an aristocratic Peruvian family active in government throughout much of the nineteenth century. With roots in the early colonial period, the family

---

Paz Soldán wrote bitterly against obvious signs of ethnic and cultural change, especially the Chinese influence, in an aristocratic Peru he hoped would remain unspoiled.

---

helped shape the national government and intellectual life in Peru through the major heads of its household. One of the more notable descendants of the line was Mariano Felipe Paz Soldán (1821–1886), who wrote

one of the earliest and most caustic histories of the struggle for independence in Peru. In the 1860s he also planned a model prison in Lima, where inmates were to be trained in useful trades. José Gregorio Paz Soldán (1808–1875), a leader among liberals before the era of Ramón CASTILLA, voiced these views as editor of the newspaper *El Constitucional,* and later he served as rector of the National University of San Marcos. As minister of foreign relations under President Castilla, he organized short courses in international law, protocol, and foreign languages, upgrading Peru's foreign service to one of the most respected in Latin America. Pedro Paz Soldán y Unanue (1839–1895), a poet and essayist, wrote bitterly against obvious signs of ethnic and cultural change, especially the Chinese influence, in an aristocratic Peru he hoped would remain unspoiled. The essay, published under the pseudonym Juan de Arona, appeared as *La inmigración en el Perú* (1891). Other members of the Paz Soldán family also left their mark in letters and public administration.

— VINCENT PELOSO

PAZ ZAMORA, JAIME

Jaime Paz Zamora (*b.* 15 April 1939), president of Bolivia (1989–1993). Born in the department of Cochabamba, Paz Zamora studied for the priesthood at Louvain University in Belgium in the 1960s but changed his course of studies to political science. One of the founders of the Movement of the Revolutionary Left (MIR) in 1971, he was imprisoned in 1974 by General Hugo BANZER SUÁREZ's government for conspiring to overthrow it. He escaped from jail and sought asylum in Venezuela. In 1978 he returned to Bolivia after the democratic opening as one of the founders of the Popular and Democratic Union (UDP) coalition and served as vice president in the government of Hernán SILES ZUAZO (1982–1985).

In the mid-1980s the MIR began to attract middle-class intellectuals, professionals, and young voters who were discontented with the traditional parties and politicians. This coalition, dubbed the Nueva Mayoría, and a strategic alliance with General Banzer's Nationalist Democratic Action (Accíon Democrática y Nacionalista—ADN) catapulted Paz Zamora to the presidency in August 1989. Abandoning his party's rhetoric about improving social policy, he concentrated on Bolivia's foreign relations. Domestically, he focused on maintaining the coalition and ensuring compliance with austerity measures. His image with the electorate fell considerably. While the MIR lost its popular appeal, Paz Zamora managed to maintain the confidence of international financial institutions and the United States.

When Paz Zamora stepped down as president in 1993, the general perception was that the MIR and ADN had presided over the largest increase in corruption since 1982. The most serious charge of corruption was the alleged ties of prominent members of the MIR to drug trafficking.

Paz Zamora remained politically active, serving as a member of the international peace commission in Chiapas, Mexico, in 1993.

– EDUARDO A. GAMARRA

PEÇANHA, NILO PROCÓPIO

Nilo Procópio Peçanha (*b.* 2 October 1867; *d.* 31 March 1924), president of Brazil (June 1909–November 1910). Although born to a modest family of the imperial province of Rio de Janeiro, Peçanha enjoyed a rapid rise through the elite-dominated political system of Brazil's First Republic. Peçanha earned political stature while participating in the abolition and republican movements, and in the years following the 1889 Proclamation of the Republic he rose to serve as federal senator (1903) and governor of the state of Rio de Janeiro (1903–1905). He was elected vice president of Brazil in 1906; in 1909 Peçanha assumed the presidency upon the death of President Afonso PENA.

A fiscal conservative, but also a strong advocate of a diversified economy, Peçanha was a noted proponent of the establishment of steel production, technical education, agronomics, and the early repayment of the 1898 funding loan. In spite of his calls for diversification, however, coffee production remained the prime motor of the Brazilian economy throughout Peçanha's political career. As president, Peçanha ordered federal intervention into political crises in Bahia and Amazonas. In 1910 he stepped down from the presidency amid charges that President-elect Marshal Hermes da Fonseca defeated *civilista* candidate Rui Barbosa through electoral fraud. Peçanha remained in politics, serving as governor of Rio (1914–1917), foreign minister (1917–1918), and senator (1918–1924). In 1921 he led the unsuccessful Reação Republicana (Republican Reaction) presidential campaign against Artur da Silva Bernardes.

– DARYLE WILLIAMS

PEDREIRA, ANTONIO S.

Antonio S. Pedreira (*b.* 13 June 1899; *d.* 23 October 1939), Puerto Rican poet. Pedreira's literary works focus on Puerto Rican identity and personality. He proposed the docility thesis of Puerto Ricans and expounded an insular theory of government. Pedreira's travels to Spain brought him into contact with Antonio Machado, Federico García Lorca, Rafael Alberti, Pedro Salinas, and Luis Cernuda. Influenced by Spanish modernism, Pedreira became more protesting and reformist in his writing. Pedreira also analyzed Puerto Rican culture and its intellectual movements.

– CHRISTOPHER T. BOWEN

PEDRO I OF BRAZIL

Pedro I of Brazil (*b.* 12 October 1798; *d.* 24 September 1834), emperor of Brazil (1822–1831). Born in Queluz palace, Portugal, Prince Pedro de Bragança e Borbón was nine years old when he fled with the Portuguese royal family to Brazil to escape an invading French army. The Braganças settled in Rio de Janeiro in 1808 and Pedro spent the next thirteen years in and around that city. Though he was the elder son and heir of the Portuguese regent, later King João VI (r. 1816–1826), Pedro received little formal education and spent much of his youth hunting, horse racing, bullfighting, brawling, tavern hopping, and wenching—often in the company of the Falstaffian Francisco Gomes da Silva, a native of Portugal commonly known as the *Chalaça* (Joker). Intellectually, the prince was most influenced by the count dos Arcos, former viceroy of Brazil and a proponent of enlightened despotism, and by his tutor and confessor, the liberal Friar António de Arrábida. In his quieter moments, especially after his marriage in 1817 to Princess Leopoldina de Hapsburg, Pedro read extensively in political philosophy.

In February 1821 Pedro persuaded his father to accept publicly in Rio the constitutionalist principles proclaimed by the revolutionary regime in Portugal. Two months later Pedro played a major role in suppressing a movement led by Portuguese-born radicals to set up a revolutionary government in Rio. In April 1821, when King João VI obeyed a summons from the Portuguese Cortes to return to Lisbon, he left Pedro in Rio as regent of Brazil with the advice not to resist Brazilian independence should it seem inevitable but to take control of the separatist movement and make himself king of the new nation.

As regent of Brazil, Pedro disregarded orders from the Cortes that he dismantle his government in Rio and embark for Europe. Fearing the return of Brazil to colonial status if Pedro left, various city and town councils in southern Brazil petitioned him to stay. In Rio in January 1822, Pedro publicly declared "Fico" (I am staying). Following his announcement, Pedro installed a new ministry headed by the Brazilian savant José Bonifácio de ANDRADA E SILVA, and events marched swiftly toward Brazil's declaration of independence, which Pedro issued near São Paulo on 7 September 1822. With the support of José Bonifácio and the major municipalities of the south, Pedro was proclaimed emperor of Brazil in Rio in October 1822.

Overcoming token opposition from the Portuguese garrison in Rio and fierce resistance from Portuguese army and navy units in Bahia province, Pedro's forces extended the emperor's control over virtually all of Portuguese America by the end of 1823. That same year a dispute arose between the emperor and his chief minister over the latter's persecution of his political enemies, which led to José Bonifácio's resignation from the government. A confrontation between the emperor and a constitutional convention he had summoned ended when Pedro forcibly dissolved the assembly and exiled José Bonifácio. Pedro then produced his own constitution, which he promulgated in March 1824. While in some respects more authoritarian than a draft the convention was considering, Pedro's constitution also was more liberal in providing religious toleration and enumerating civil rights.

The promulgation of Pedro's constitution sparked a major revolt in northeastern Brazil, which imperial forces suppressed in 1824. In the South, however, Pedro's army and navy were unable to prevent the loss of the empire's Cisplatine Province (present-day Uruguay), which was invaded by forces from Buenos Aires in 1825.

The loss of Uruguay (conceded in 1828), the emperor's hostility toward slavery and his attempts to end the African slave trade, his employment of European mercenaries in the Brazilian armed forces, his involvement in Portuguese dynastic affairs, his unconcealed marital infidelities, and his uncouth Portuguese companions contributed to Pedro's growing unpopularity among influential Brazilians. Reconciliation with José Bonifácio and marriage to the admirable AMÉLIA Augusta Leuchtenberg in 1829 (Leopoldina had died in 1826) slowed but did not halt the erosion of his support. In the midst of nativist riots in Rio, Pedro refused to make ministerial changes demanded by the mob and, on 7 April 1831, abdicated the Brazilian throne in favor of his five-year-old son PEDRO II.

Pedro returned to Europe and concentrated on removing his reactionary brother Miguel from the Portuguese throne and replacing him with his own daughter, Maria. Shortly after achieving these goals, Pedro died of tuberculosis in Queluz on 24 September 1834.

— NEILL MACAULAY

PEDRO II OF BRAZIL

Pedro II of Brazil (*b.* 2 December 1825; *d.* 5 December 1891), the second and last emperor of Brazil (1831–1889). A central figure in Brazil's development as a nation state, Pedro II was a man of complex personality and considerable abilities. His actions first consolidated and ultimately undermined the monarchical regime. Born in Rio de Janeiro, the son and heir to the emperor PEDRO I and the empress LEOPOLDINA, Pedro II was set apart by both ancestry and nurture. Related to almost all the monarchies of Europe, he grew up surrounded by a rigid etiquette and omnipresent deference inherited from the royal court at Lisbon. His destined task was to command, the role of all others to obey. His formal education gave him a love of knowledge and instilled a sense of self-restraint and a devotion to service.

Pedro II's early years were disturbed and psychologically cramping. His mother died before his first birthday, and he lost his father, his beloved stepmother, and his eldest sister when they sailed for Europe following Pedro I's abdication in his favor on 7 April 1831. As guardian of Pedro II from 1831 to 1833, José Bonifácio de ANDRADA failed to protect his ward's physical and emotional health. An epileptic attack in August 1833 nearly proved fatal. Pedro II's health and conditions of life did improve markedly after José Bonifácio's dismissal, but the psychological pressures remained. Pedro II's approaching adolescence and his intellectual precocity made him credible as a possible savior for Brazil, which was mired in crisis in the late 1830s. Deference and adulation fed his sense of indispensability and intensified his isolation from ordinary life. He offered no resistance to the political campaign that prematurely declared him of age, at fourteen years and seven months, on 23 July 1840.

The trappings of authority did not, Pedro II soon discovered, denote real power. Courtiers and politicians cooperated to manipulate his views, exploit his prerogatives, and determine his life, as he realized in October 1843 when the bride chosen for him, TERESA CRISTINA, proved to be plain and not an intellectual. Coldness, arbitrariness, and brevity of speech increasingly characterized Pedro II's public conduct. In 1845 the birth of a son (to be followed by three more children) and a long tour through the far south of Brazil provided the catalyst that brought maturity and unleashed his capacities as a ruler. By 1850, Pedro II had ended the power of court factions, learned the efficient management of public affairs, and established his public image as a beneficent, highly cultured, and dedicated sovereign. His success as ruler was facilitated both by a boom in coffee production and by an eclipse of radicalism and republicanism following the Praieira Revolt of 1848–1850.

During the 1850s and 1860s, Pedro II embodied, as monarch, the only legitimate source of authority. He exemplified the European civilization that Brazilians desired for their nation. His talents as ruler were formidable: inexhaustible energy, remarkable memory for faces and facts, iron control of speech and action, firmness in purpose, freedom from petty resentments, acute sense of tactics, and utter indifference to the trappings of power. Politicians came and went. He alone remained entrenched at the center of affairs, ultimately determining both the political agenda and the personal characteristics requisite for political success.

Pedro II's skill as ruler played a part in securing long-term political stability for Brazil. He worked tirelessly to promote the development of the nation's infrastructure. Two particular achievements must be mentioned. He pursued the War of the Triple Alliance for five years until Paraguayan President Francisco SOLANO LÓPEZ was eliminated in 1870. Initiating in 1865 a campaign to force the eventual elimination of slavery, Pedro II brought it to fruition in 1871 with the enactment of the Free Birth Law.

After 1871 new factors—a shift in the intellectual climate toward republicanism, greater confidence among Brazilians in their capacity to rule themselves, and growing resentment against a highly centralized administration—undermined the regime's legitimacy. Pedro II's innate conservatism in thought and behavior,

his staleness in mind and body induced by three decades of rule, and his unwillingness to surrender any part of his powers inhibited him from meeting this challenge. He held no intellectual belief in monarchy as such. Both his sons had died in childhood and, much as he loved ISABEL as a daughter, he did not perceive her as a credible successor. He therefore felt no duty to assure her future as monarch, an obligation that would have restricted his freedom of action. His antediluvian court, shabby palaces, and distaste for ceremony destroyed the emotional appeal of monarchy.

The growth in the size and complexity of government made Pedro II's insistence on personally supervising every detail of public business a clog on effective administration. His love of knowledge and concern for culture appeared increasingly as superficial, amateur, and antiquated. His dominance of public life and elimination of all competing centers of power produced a vacuum at the heart of the system. Among younger Brazilians his monopoly of power bred feelings of impotence and futility and a resentment against his tutelage.

From the middle of the 1880s diabetes increasingly deprived Pedro II of the qualities that had made him so

Pedro II and the imperial family, Petrópolis, Rio de Janeiro, November 1889. (Collection of Prince Dom Pedro de Orléans e Braganca; Photo by Otto Hees)

effective as a ruler. Still respected and even loved, he had ceased to be indispensable or even present in the country. During his prolonged absence in Europe in search of better health (1887–1888), Isabel used her powers as regent to secure the immediate abolition without compensation of slavery (13 May 1888). The disposal of one long-established institution could only suggest similar treatment for another that, for many Brazilians, had become an anachronism.

The army uprising that overthrew the monarchy on 15 November 1889 was as unexpected as it was decisive. Pedro II had no wish nor the ability to contest his dethronement and banishment to Europe. He conducted himself during exile with unwavering dignity, pursuing, as far as ill health would permit, his quest for knowledge. He died in Paris.

– RODERICK J. BARMAN

PEDROSA Y GUERRERO, ANTONIO DE LA

Antonio De La Pedrosa y Guerrero (b. ca. 1660; active late seventeenth and early eighteenth centuries), president of the Audiencia of Santa Fe de Bogotá (1718–1719). Pedrosa's public career in New Granada began in the mid-1680s when he served as the *fiscal protector de indios,* an official charged with the oversight of Indian policy, in the Audiencia of Santa Fe. He then rose to high-level metropolitan posts. Pedrosa's chief fame, however, rests on his role as the official sent to New Granada to establish the machinery of viceregal government that followed the royal decision in April 1717 to create a third Spanish American viceroyalty.

Acting with the authority of a viceroy and even called viceroy, Pedrosa largely concerned himself in 1718 and 1719 with administrative affairs, including the decision to establish the viceregal capital in Santa Fe instead of Cartagena, and policy regarding contraband trade. The frugal president clashed with the ostentatious first viceroy, Jorge de VILLALONGA (1719–1724), and the two remained political enemies even after Pedrosa returned to Spain in 1720.

– LANCE R. GRAHN

PEIMBERT, MARGARITA

Margarita Peimbert (b. 1795; d. before 1900), a member of the autonomist secret society Los Guadalupes. Peimbert was the daughter of the lawyer Juan Nazario Peimbert y Hernández, who was also a member of the Guadalupes and who held *tertulias* (gatherings) in his home in Mexico City at which politics was discussed. Margarita was in charge of distributing the group's correspondence. She was betrothed to the lawyer José Ig-

nacio Jiménez, who joined Ignacio RAYÓN's forces at the beginning of 1812. In May of that year, the royalists captured the correspondence that Rayón had sent to the capital, including letters to Peimbert from various insurgents. She was detained and interrogated in June, but revealed nothing. The same month, the royalists defeated Rayón at Tenango, and Jiménez was killed. Later, Peimbert married José Ignacio Espinosa, another lawyer and member of the Guadalupes.

– VIRGINIA GUEDEA

PEIXE, CÉSAR GUERRA

César Guerra Peixe (often listed as C. Guerra-Peixe; b. 18 March 1914; d. 26 November 1993), Brazilian composer, violinist, conductor, and musicologist. Born in Petrópolis, Peixe began to study music theory and solfeggio at the age of nine. Two years later, he enrolled in the Escola de Música Santa Cecília in Petrópolis. After completing studies in theory and solfeggio in 1929, he began to do arranging for instrumental ensembles. He wrote his first piece, a tango, *Otilia,* in 1930 and that same year was appointed professor of violin at the Escola de Música Santa Cecília.

In 1934 Peixe moved to Rio de Janeiro, where ten years later he began the study of composition with Hans Joachim KOELLREUTTER, a former student of Paul Hindemith. Koellreutter introduced him to serial techniques of writing and with Peixe and several other contemporary composers formed the Música Viva group in 1939 to explore serial techniques and promote concerts of recent works by group members and their European counterparts.

Peixe took a job at a radio station in Recife, a city with rich folk music traditions in the northeastern part of Brazil.

Gradually, Peixe became less interested in serial writing and more interested in exploring Brazilian folk traditions and native music. He took a job at a radio station in Recife, a city with rich folk music traditions in the northeastern part of Brazil, where he wrote a series of twenty articles, "A Century of Music in Recife," and a book, *Maracatus do Recife,* a study of a traditional folk festival. Respected for his extensive knowledge of Brazilian folk and traditional music, Peixe has won several awards in Brazil. His Symphony no. 1, a serial composition of 1946, was performed in London by the British Broadcasting Corporation as well as in Brussels, and his Divertimento no. 2 was performed in Zurich in 1947. A set of piano pieces, *Preludios Tropicais,* won the Golfinho de Ouro trophy in 1980.

— DAVID P. APPLEBY

PEIXOTO, FLORIANO VIEIRA

Floriano Vieira Peixoto (*b.* 30 April 1839; *d.* 29 June 1895), Brazil's "Iron Marshal" and second head of the Brazilian republic (1891–1894). Born in Alagoas, in Brazil's poor Northeast, Peixoto achieved a distinguished army career, serving in the War of the Triple Alliance (1864–1870), and rising to the rank of brigadier general in 1883.

Peixoto's role in the crucial days prior to the military overthrow of the monarchy and the establishment of the republic on 15 November 1889 has long been a subject of debate. Both sides in the impending clash, republicans and monarchists alike, felt that they could trust this popular army officer who occupied the key post of adjutant general. But the monarchists had misjudged Peixoto. On 15 November he refused to obey repeated orders to fire on the advancing rebels, thus sealing the fate of the monarchy. He then began to serve as a member of the military-dominated provisional republican government established on that same day. In February 1891 the Constituent Congress elected Marshal Deodoro da FONSECA, the so-called Proclaimer of the Republic, president, and Peixoto vice president.

Peixoto, noted for his personal honesty, unpretentiousness, and astuteness, kept out of the squabbles and struggles between President Fonseca and a basically civilian and hostile congress that often protested what it regarded as Fonseca's infringements on civil liberties. But Peixoto played a crucial role in the military movement that overthrew Fonseca following his unconstitutional dissolution of Congress in November 1891, and thereby ensured his own succession to the presidency.

More than any other chief executive of the Old Republic (1889–1930), Peixoto has been held up as a friend of the "people." But his major supporters, middle-class nationalists and army officers, derived far greater benefits from his regime than did the lower classes. His government did much more to aid industry than did his immediate successors. Regarded as a forceful, capable leader by his admirers, he was denounced as a dictator by his opponents. Cleverly using rising anti-Portuguese sentiments to strengthen his own position, Peixoto succeeded in maintaining himself in office despite very difficult times for the infant republic. Not only was a civil war, the Federalist Revolt, raging in Rio Grande do Sul, Brazil's southernmost state, but

a naval revolt under the leadership of Admiral Custódio de MELO against Peixoto's army-dominated government broke out in Rio de Janeiro's harbor late in 1893, and took six months to quell. Peixoto's success in restoring order earned him the title "Consolidator of the Republic." Less than a year after he completed his term of office and turned over the presidential palace to his elected civilian successor, Prudente de MORAIS of São Paulo, Peixoto died, and his funeral drew large crowds.

— JUNE E. HAHNER

PEIXOTO, JÚLIO AFRÂNIO

Júlio Afrânio Peixoto (*b.* 17 December 1876; *d.* 12 January 1947), Brazilian author and physician. A polymath whose more than fifty books range from medical texts to regionalist novels to literary studies to history and folklore, he epitomized the spirit of his premodernist generation with the phrase "Literature is the smile of society." His novel *A esfinge* (1911; The Sphinx), written to justify his election to the Brazilian Academy of Letters in 1910, documents life in Rio's high society. Like his other novels, such as *Maria Bonita* (1914), it explores female psychology and the contrasts between city and country life.

Trained in forensic medicine, Peixoto centered his career on health education and public administration. He was director of the national asylum (from 1904), professor of hygiene and legal medicine at the Rio de Janeiro medical school (from 1906) and at the law school (from 1915), director of public education in Rio de Janeiro (from 1916), and professor of the history of education at the Instituto do Rio de Janeiro (from 1932). He represented Bahia as a federal deputy from 1924 to 1930.

— DAIN BORGES

PELÁEZ, AMELIA

Amelia Peláez (*b.* 5 January 1896; *d.* 8 April 1968), Cuban painter. The niece of the Cuban symbolist poet Julián del Casal, Amelia Peláez is one of the most respected Cuban artists of the twentieth century. She graduated from the National School of San Alejandro, where she trained in academic impressionism, but she continued to modify her style throughout her life. Peláez studied in Paris under the Russian cubist Alexandra Exter and later experimented with modernist painting, ceramics, and stained glass. Her art evokes the Cuban creole spirit with its values of home, family, and a serene, glorious past. Devoted to her life-style and neighborhood, Peláez remained in Cuba after the revolution. Among her most famous works are *Gundinga* (1931);

an illustration for her uncle's poem "The Agony of Petronius" (1935); *Las dos hermanas* (1943); and *Las muchachas* (1943).

— KAREN RACINE

PELÉ

Pelé (Edson Arantes do Nascimento; *b.* 23 October 1940), Brazilian soccer player. Born in Dico (now Três Corações), Minas Gerais, Pelé grew up mainly in Bauru, São Paulo, where, inspired by the soccer skills of his father, João Ramos do Nascimento (Dondinho), he excelled at versions of street soccer, *peladas,* thus acquiring his future nickname. He played his first professional game with the Santos Football Club on 7 September 1956. The following year he became a member of the Brazilian national team, and in 1958 scored six goals in helping Brazil win its first World Cup. Although Brazil retained its title in 1962, Pelé was hurt and contributed little. In 1966 injuries kept Brazil from reaching the second round, but in his last World Cup (Mexico, 1970) Pelé led a creative team to permanent possession of the Jules Rimet Trophy. Scoring some 1,300 career goals, Pelé also played on clubs that won state and national championships, the Copa Libertadores de América, and the world interclub competition. His style was often more impressive than his numbers.

In 1974 Pelé retired from the Santos club, then surprised the world by joining the New York Cosmos (1975–1977) of the fledgling North American Soccer League. Despite the league's eventual demise, Pelé gained popularity in the United States and inspired a younger generation to try his sport. After leaving competition, Pelé worked in films, music, public relations, journalism, and volunteer coaching. He also coauthored a mystery novel and several pieces about his life and soccer. Through an emotional divorce, temporary economic setbacks, and criticism for failing to denounce Brazil's military regimes, Pelé retained his outward optimism and charm. A unique talent who epitomized the culture and aspirations of his countrymen, "the king" remains for most the world's best soccer player ever and a national hero.

— JOSEPH L. ARBENA

PELLACANI, DANTE

Dante Pellacani (*b.* 6 March 1923; *d.* 6 August 1981), Brazilian trade unionist and president of the Commando Geral dos Trabalhadores (CGT). Born and educated in São Paulo, Pellacani went to work in a printing plant at age fourteen. Swept up in the political opening of 1944–1946 while in the army, Pellacani led São Paulo's printers in 1948 to demand the end of government intervention in their union. That same year he joined the Brazil Communist Party (PCB) from which he was expelled ten years later. A key figure in the state labor movement, he was elected president of the National Federation of Printing Workers. Allied with the PCB and the Brazilian Labor Party (PTB), Pellacani created a ticket-splitting "Jan-Jan movement" (Jânio QUADROS and Jango Goulart) in the 1960 presidential elections. In 1961, he was named to the National Social Welfare Department and served as director general from 1962–1963. Elected president of the CGT in 1963, he simultaneously held office in the National Confederation of Workers in Industry (CNTI). A strong supporter of President Goulart's "basic reforms," he played a key role in the general strikes and popular mobilizations of March 1964. After the 31 March military coup outlawed the CGT, and "intervened" (restricted) the CNTI, Pellacani went into exile in Uruguay. Returning in 1969, he rededicated himself to union and political activities.

— JOHN D. FRENCH

PELLEGRINI, CARLOS

Carlos Pellegrini (*b.* 11 October 1846; *d.* 17 July 1906), president of Argentina (1890–1892). Pellegrini was born in Buenos Aires province to an English mother and an Italian father, a background which exemplifies the cosmopolitan nature of Argentina. He had little interest in religion and was convinced that economic, financial, and political interests were interchangeable. A successful businessman, a veteran of the war with Paraguay, and a skilled orator, Pellegrini fit easily into the upper class. A fervent supporter of European immigration, he made the first of several trips to Europe in 1876. After his election to Congress, he forged an alliance with Julio Argentino ROCA. As war minister during Roca's first presidency, Pellegrini played a vital role in establishing Buenos Aires as the national capital. His skill in negotiating foreign loans enabled him to become head of the Partido Autonomista Nacional and vice president (1886). It was no secret that Pellegrini was contemptuous of Miguel JUÁREZ CELMAN's abilities and policies.

Pellegrini became president in October 1890, after Juárez Celman fled the 1890 revolt. Pellegrini's leadership enabled the elites to keep their opponents out of power while his followers reformed the country. He was Argentina's leading financial representative and a nationalist. He moved to restore fiscal sanity and economic growth. Determined to restore Argentine credit, he began to reduce the foreign debt. The government revived the currency by establishing reserves. When Pellegrini discovered that many banks were fraudulent, he founded a new national bank in 1891. He reduced imports of luxury goods and established the first favorable trade balance in many years. Long a champion of national industries, Pellegrini continued to support the development of sugar, wine, rice, and tobacco. Citizens respected him because he cut waste, frustrated corruption, and prohibited the use of gold in the stock market.

In many ways, Pellegrini challenged the dependency theory that Latin American elites were subservient to U.S. or British influence. He criticized British investments, taxed foreign capital, and clashed repeatedly with the British over the taxation of their businesses and the freezing of the rates that their railroads and tramways could charge in Argentina.

Pellegrini challenged the dependency theory that Latin American elites were subservient to U.S. or British influence.

Pellegrini wielded great influence once he left the presidency. He opposed jingoistic calls for war with Chile and opposed an arms race with Brazil. He broke with Roca and urged a better system of labor relations, and until shortly before his death, Pellegrini continued to attack corruption and campaign for electoral reform. His writings are collected in his five-volume *Obras* (1941), with a two-volume introduction by the editor, Agustín P. Rivero.

— DOUGLAS W. RICHMOND

PELLICER CÁMARA, CARLOS

Carlos Pellicer Cámara (*b.* 16 January 1897; *d.* 16 February 1977), Mexican poet. Born in Villahermosa, Tabasco, Pellicer moved with his family to Mexico City in 1908. However, his native state, particularly its tropical scenery and its pre-Hispanic past, was to be a lifetime presence. In 1921 he published his first book of poetry, *Colores en el mar*. Pellicer was a prolific writer, and many more volumes followed. *Hora de junio* (1937), *Subordinaciones* (1949), and *Práctica de vuelo* (1956) are counted among his best. Although he is often grouped with the "Contemporáneos," Pellicer's explicit religiosity, his humor, and his interest in the external world, in nature, and in the epic dimension set him apart. Noteworthy is the incorporation of music and painting into his work, achieved by thematic

choices and by transpositions of the techniques and processes of these other arts into poetry.

Besides also writing prose, often on literature and art, Pellicer exercised his acute sense of the visual as a museographer. Particularly significant is the outdoor archaeological-ecological museum of La Venta in Villahermosa, where OLMEC sculpture alternates with tropical animals and plants. An admirer of Simón BOLÍVAR and Francis of Assisi, Pellicer was also an active participant in political and humanitarian causes. In 1922 he began his association with José VASCONCELOS, which nearly cost him his life in 1930, after the philosopher's unsuccessful bid for the presidency of Mexico. In 1937 Pellicer was one of a group of intellectuals who traveled to Europe to express sympathy for the Spanish Republic, and he visited Cuba on numerous occasions. Between 1943 and 1946 he was the director of what is now the Instituto Nacional de Bellas Artes, and at the time of his death he was senator for the state of Tabasco.

— CLARA BARGELLINI

PENA, AFONSO AUGUSTO MOREIRA

Afonso Augusto Moreira Pena (*b.* 30 November 1847; *d.* 14 June 1909), president of Brazil (1906–1909). Born in Santa Bárbara, Minas Gerais, Pena attended the Lazarist Colégio do Caraça and received a doctorate in law at the University of São Paulo, where he was a colleague of Rodrigues Alves, Rui BARBOSA, and Castro Alves. He married Maria Guilhermina de Oliveira, with whom he had one son, Afonso Augusto Moreira Pena Junior.

Pena's political career straddled both the imperial and republican years of Brazil's history. He served as a provincial deputy (1874–1878) and became a national deputy in 1879, serving for four successive legislatures. A novelty at the time, he held the post of minister of war as a civilian (1882–1883). Later, he served as both minister of agriculture in 1883 and minister of justice in 1885. In addition, he served as a member of the Civil Code Commission in 1888 and as a member of the Constitutional Convention from 1890 to 1891. Pena returned to Minas Gerais, where he served as governor from 1892 to 1895. During his administration, he moved the state capital from Ouro Prêto to Belo Horizonte and founded a school of law in the new capital city, where he also taught.

From 1894 to 1898, Pena was the president of the Bank of the Republic. He was elected vice president of Brazil in 1903, and in 1906 he was elected president, an office he held until his death. Among his more noteworthy contributions to the nation were reforms that made possible the exchange of different monetary units, expansion of the national railroad system, and establishment of telegraphic connections between Rio de Janeiro and Acre.

— IÊDA SIQUEIRA WIARDA

PEÑA, ANTONIA

Antonia Peña, (*fl.* early 1800s), a member of the secret society of Los Guadalupes. Her hacienda of León in Tacuba was one of the society's meeting places, and a location where correspondence from the insurgents was received and sent. Antonia and her husband, Manuel Díaz, a distinguished Mexico City lawyer and also a Guadalupe, helped José Mariano Martínez Lejarza and José María Gallegos to join the insurgents in January 1812, an act which led to her detention by the authorities. She also helped to take a press out from the capital and sent it to Rayón in April and she maintained correspondence with the insurgent Miguel Arriaga Díaz under the pseudonym "Serafina Guadalupe Rosier." Upon the death of Díaz, she married Juan Bautista Raz y Guzmán, another Guadalupe.

— VIRGINIA GUEDEA

PEÑA, LÁZARO

Lázaro Peña (*b.* 29 May 1911; *d.* 11 March 1974), Cuban Communist Party leader and secretary-general of the Cuban Labor Federation. Peña, a black tobacco worker who was born of extremely poor parents but grew up to become a prominent labor leader, became a member of the Communist Party in 1930. Because of his activism, participation in strikes, and denunciation of the Gerardo Machado dictatorship (1925–1933), he was forced to serve a number of jail sentences. When army chief Fulgencio BATISTA sought for political reasons to woo organized labor as well as gain the support of the Communist Party, Peña was unanimously elected as the first secretary-general of the Confederación de Trabajadores de Cuba (CTC), a new labor confederation established in January 1939. He remained in control of the CTC for some eight years until he was ousted by the anti-Communist government of Ramón GRAU SAN MARTÍN (1944–1948). Peña fled first to Mexico, then to the Soviet Union, returning to Cuba when Fidel CASTRO RUZ took over in 1959. Although he once again became the leader of the Cuban labor movement, he was merely an instrument chosen by the revolutionary government to implement its policies.

— JOSÉ M. HERNÁNDEZ

PENA, LUÍS CARLOS MARTINS

Luís Carlos Martins Pena (*b.* 5 November 1815; *d.* 7 December 1848), considered the founder of Brazilian comedy and cofounder, with Gonçalves de MAGALHÃES, of Brazilian theater. Pena began writing plays as a student in his native Rio de Janeiro between 1832 and 1834. The first to be staged, the comedy *O juiz de paz na roça* (1842; *A Rural Justice of the Peace*, 1948), opened successfully on 4 October 1838. That year Pena received the first of many civil service appointments.

Pena mastered the romantic comedy of manners, initially in rural settings with abundant local color, later in urban settings with an almost helter-skelter movement on stage as his works became more outrightly farcical. His characters are often caricatures but they ring true, especially linguistically. Usually pillorying the lower-middle class, he portrayed penetratingly Brazilian society at the time of King João VI's residency in Brazil (1807–1821).

Usually pillorying the lower-middle class,

Pena portrayed Brazilian society at the time of

King João VI's residency in Brazil.

Enormously popular during his lifetime, Pena wrote prolifically. His known plays include twenty-two comedies—ten new ones in 1845 alone—and six dramas. The former are still played to enthusiastic audiences. The dramas, five of them set outside Brazil, lack authenticity and appeal. He died in Lisbon.

— NORWOOD ANDREWS, JR.

PEÑA, MANUEL PEDRO DE

Manuel Pedro de Peña (*b.* 1811; *d.* 1867), Paraguayan publicist and revolutionary pamphleteer. Although born in Asunción in the first year of his country's independence, Peña chose to live for many years in Buenos Aires, where he moved in expatriate circles that were made up of men and women opposed to the regimes of Carlos Antonio LÓPEZ (1841–1862) and of his son, Francisco Solano LÓPEZ (1862–1879). Peña, who had once worked as a minor official in the government of the elder López in the late 1850s, began acting as spokesman for various Paraguayan revolutionary groups residing in the Argentine capital. He made eloquent, though bitter, attacks on the López family in the Buenos Aires press, especially in the daily *La Tribuna* and in *Nación Argentina*. These attacks appeared all the more poignant because Peña claimed an unproven family relationship with the Lópezes.

Peña's editorial efforts had the greatest impact after the beginning of the War of the Triple Alliance (1864–

1870), when he wrote a regular column, "Cartas del ciudadano paraguayo dirijidos a su querido sobrino," that appeared in several newspapers. The men of the Paraguayan Legion who fought in the war under Argentine command, were said to have carried his pamphlets into battle. Peña died in Buenos Aires.

— THOMAS L. WHIGHAM

PEÑA GÓMEZ, JOSÉ FRANCISCO

José Francisco Peña Gómez (*b.* 6 March 1937), leader of the Dominican Revolutionary Party (PRD) since 1965. The son of Haitian victims of the 1937 massacre, Peña Gómez trained as a lawyer. He was recruited by the PRD and received political training in Venezuela and Peru. His rise to prominence in the party was due to his oratorical skills and charismatic presence. After Juan BOSCH's overthrow in 1963, Peña Gómez was responsible for the reorganization of the party and for establishing advantageous contacts in the Dominican military. In 1966 he was elected secretary general of the party, a position he maintained despite pursuing advanced law studies in Paris from 1970 to 1973. His increasing popularity led to conflict with the aging Bosch and to Peña Gómez's resignation as secretary general in August 1973. Bosch, however, overestimated his own popularity and soon found himself resigning from the PRD in light of overwhelming support for Peña Gómez. Peña Gómez regained the position of secretary general and became the driving force behind the party.

Representing the democratic left, Peña Gómez led the PRD to membership in the Socialist International in 1976, and he became a vocal spokesman within the International. His popular base of support among the urban poor made him the bête noir of the Dominican armed forces. Because of his Afro-Haitian parentage, Peña Gómez has often been accused by the traditionally dominant white minority of being anti-Dominican. As illustrated in the 1994 federal elections, the issue of race has played a pivotal role in Dominican politics. Despite the populist and leftist tendencies of his party, Peña Gómez provided a moderating influence on its membership and encouraged a collegial style of leadership, allowing members to rise in the party. In 1978 he was elected mayor of Santo Domingo.

During the 1980s the PRD split in a bitter rivalry between Peña Gómez and Jacobo Majluta. Majluta served as vice president under the first PRD president, Antonio GUZMÁN (1978–1982). Peña Gómez withdrew from the PRD ticket in 1986 rather than run as Majluta's vice presidential candidate. The conflict between the two men resulted in Majluta splitting from the PRD to form the Independent Revolutionary Party (PRI).

Peña Gómez, hoping to be the Dominican Republic's first black president, led the PRD into the 1990 and 1994 federal elections. His presidential aspirations were stymied by the continued domination of the presidency by the aging Joaquín BALAGUER.

— HEATHER K. THIESSEN

PEÑA Y PEÑA, MANUEL DE LA

Manuel de la Peña y Peña (*b.* 1789; *d.* 1850), interim president of Mexico (September 1847–June 1848). The apex of Peña y Peña's career coincided with Mexico's nadir when he, as chief justice of the Supreme Court, succeeded Antonio López de SANTA ANNA on 16 September 1847. Peña y Peña, a native of Tacuba, maintained a moderate course between radical and reactionary voices from September 1847 to June 1848, during which time the Treaty of Guadalupe Hidalgo was negotiated, signed, and ratified.

Peña y Peña unknowingly spent his life in preparation for this service. He studied civil and ecclesiastic law at the Seminario Conciliar in Mexico City, graduating in December 1811. Two years later he was named *síndico* (receiver) of the Mexico City Municipal Council. In February 1820 Peña y Peña declined an appointment as *oidor* on the *Audiencia* of Quito, in the Viceroyalty of Peru, out of a sense of duty to Mexico at the time of independence. His age, education, experience, and connections brought a succession of public offices, primarily in the Supreme Court. Appointments not in the court included minister of the interior (1837) and minister of foreign relations and government (1845). In 1841 he was concurrently president of the Academia de Jurisprudencia and rector of the Colegio de Abogados. His writings include the four-volume *Lecciones de práctica forense Mexicana* (1835–1839). Ironically, one of the questions treated in this work was the exaggerated pretensions of a foreign power. Peña y Peña died in Mexico City.

— ROBERT HIMMERICH Y VALENCIA

PEÑALOSA BRICEÑO, DIEGO DIONISIO DE

Diego Dionisio De Peñalosa Briceño (*b.* 1621/22; *d.* 1687), governor of New Mexico from 1661 to 1664. Born in Lima, Peñalosa held several posts in Peru, Mexico, and Cuba before being appointed governor of New Mexico. Peñalosa was determined to use this office for personal gain, and his scheming strained relations between church and state. At the height of a jurisdictional dispute, Peñalosa arrested the Franciscan superior in Santa Fe. Charged with blasphemy and numerous other offenses by the Inquisition, he was banished from New

Spain. Peñalosa traveled to England and France, where he proposed an invasion of New Spain. Although neither country adopted his plans, Peñalosa's intrigues encouraged the 1685 expedition of LA SALLE to the Gulf coast.

— SUZANNE B. PASZTOR

PEÑALOZA, ÁNGEL VICENTE

Ángel Vicente Peñaloza (*b.* 1799; *d.* 12 November 1863), Argentine leader. Peñaloza was born in Guaja, La Rioja, Argentina, and received little education before he enrolled in the militia, where he developed a long-lasting relationship with Juan Facundo QUIROGA. He served as a trusted officer during Quiroga's anti-Unitarist campaigns. Popular, especially among the poor, he succeeded Quiroga as a leader after the latter's assassination in 1835. Convinced by the Unitarists that Juan Manuel de ROSAS was responsible for the death of Quiroga, Peñaloza turned against Rosas and fought the Federalists in the 1840s. He withdrew to his home once Governor Nazario Benavídez of San Juan promised to protect him. He did not participate in the Acuerdo de San Nicolás, but he was on good terms with Justo José de URQUIZA. When Benavídez was assassinated (23 October 1858), Peñaloza invaded San Juan to punish the guilty. In 1862, while Peñaloza was away mediating a dispute between Santiago del Estero and Catamarca, Governor Marcos Paz of Córdoba, a Unitarist, invaded La Rioja, and the governor turned against his followers. The popularity with which Peñaloza was received on his return convinced President Bartolomé MITRE and General Wenceslao Paunero to sign a peace treaty with him on 30 May 1862. Angry Liberal leaders objected and persuaded Mitre to reopen the war.

Peñaloza, allied now with the Federalists, or *"rusos,"* of Córdoba, urged Urquiza to resume leadership of the Federalist party. Mitre wanted the montoneros destroyed, and when Paunero defeated them at Las Playas (28 June 1863), he killed them without mercy. Peñaloza thrice sought peace before surrendering to his pursuers, who killed him despite a promise to spare his life. His body was mutilated; Domingo SARMIENTO humiliated and robbed his wife. Mitre officially disapproved of the assassination, but he promoted the assassin.

— JOSEPH T. CRISCENTI

PEÑARANDA DEL CASTILLO, ENRIQUE

Enrique Peñaranda del Castillo (*b.* 17 November 1892; *d.* 8 June 1969), president of Bolivia (April 1940–December 1943). Born in Larecaja, La Paz Province, Peñaranda spent most of his life in the military, where he rose in rank from cadet to full general. During the Chaco War he was supreme commander of the military forces. When the younger and more radical officers seized power in 1937, the next year he took a leave of absence from the military. With their fall from power following the death of President Germán BUSCH in 1939, Peñaranda emerged rapidly as the main Bolivian leader, first as minister of defense and eventually as elected president. He was overthrown three and a half years later by officers with pro-German sympathies who resented Peñaranda's military accomplishments, his conservatism, and his pro-Allies sympathy during World War II.

Peñaranda's strong pro-U.S. foreign policy brought Bolivia much U.S. attention and aid. During Peñaranda's presidency, democratic reforms were undertaken, the legislative branch was strengthened, and the administration was modernized. He spent his postpresidential years in modest circumstances and died in Cochabamba.

— CHARLES W. ARNADE

PERALTA, ÁNGELA

Ángela Peralta (*b.* 6 July 1845; *d.* 30 August 1883), Mexican operatic soprano and composer. Born in Mexico City, Peralta showed a natural gift for singing; she is supposed to have impressed the great German soprano Henrietta Sontag in 1854. Thereafter she became a student of Agustín Balderas, who sponsored her debut at fifteen in Verdi's *Il Trovatore* and then took her to Europe, where she made a notable impression. Peralta returned to Mexico during the Second Empire and became a favorite of Maximilian and Carlotta, appearing in the premiere of Melesio Morales's *Ildegonda*.

Ostracized in Mexico City, Peralta took her company to remote towns, including Mazatlán, where she contracted yellow fever and died at age thirty-eight.

The decade 1865–1875 was the period of Peralta's greatest activity. She toured Mexico and Europe, with performances in Havana and New York. A celebrated season followed her homecoming in 1871, because she brought with her the famous tenor Enrico Tamberlick and sang with him in another Mexican opera, *Guatimotzín,* by Aniceto Ortega del Villar. She formed her own opera company and acted as the impresario. Although best known for her bel canto singing, Peralta adopted a more dramatic style when she played the lead in her company's first Mexican production of Verdi's *Aida,* a role closely identified with her. Another facet of her later career was composition of popular songs.

Peralta's husband, Eugenio Castera, died in 1877; Peralta subsequently formed a scandalous liaison with her manager, Julián Montiel y Duarte. Ostracized in Mexico City, she took her company to remote towns, including Mazatlán, where she contracted yellow fever and died at age thirty-eight. In 1937 her remains were moved to the Panteón in Mexico City.

– RONALD H. DOLKART

PERALTA AZURDIA, ENRIQUE

Enrique Peralta Azurdia (*b.* 17 June 1908), head of government in Guatemala (1963–1966). Born in Guatemala City, Peralta graduated in 1929 from the National Military Academy, which he later headed. He became minister of defense in December 1960 after supporting Miguel YDÍGORAS FUENTES (1958–1963) against an attempted military coup. However, when Ydígoras allowed former president Juan José ARÉVALO BERMEJO (1945–1951) to return to Guatemala to campaign for the presidency in 1963, Peralta led the coup that overthrew Ydígoras Fuentes.

Peralta, who served as head of government from 1963 to 1966, launched the military-civilian alliance that ruled Guatemala from 1963 to 1986. His administration strengthened military control in the countryside and, through constitutional revisions, reduced the potential power of left-wing parties. Peralta permitted elections to be held in 1966, but the Institutional Democratic Party (PID), which he formed, split, allowing a civilian, Julio César MÉNDEZ MONTENEGRO (1966–1970), to capture the presidency.

Peralta remained an active player in Guatemalan politics during the next two decades by organizing the National Unity Front (FUN), originally a coalition between the Christian Democrats and two smaller center-right parties. FUN supported General Ángel Guevara for the presidency in 1982, and his fraudulent election led to the military coup of that year. In 1990 it supported the candidacy of José Efraín RÍOS MONTT.

– ROLAND H. EBEL

PERALTA BARNUEVO Y ROCHA, PEDRO DE

Pedro de Peralta Barnuevo y Rocha (*b.* 26 November 1664; *d.* 30 April 1743), Peruvian polymath. Peralta was born in Lima and educated at the University of San Marcos. An acountant, lawyer, mathematician, and cos-

mographer who taught mathematics at San Marcos and served as its rector, he was considered by contemporaries to be a "monster of erudition" and was recognized for his learning in both France and Spain.

Poet and historian, Peralta wrote numerous comedies and poems as well as the epic *Lima fundada* (1732). This history of Lima eulogized Francisco PIZARRO and underscored the accomplishments of Lima's creole nobility in the offices of church and state.

Several viceroys relied upon Peralta's mathematical abilities and supported his proposal to fortify Callao. The marquis de Castelfuerte (1724–1736), moreover, asked Peralta to prepare his final report. Peralta used the opportunity to argue for maintaining Lima as it had been under Hapsburg rule and to decry the viceroy's loss of authority to name provincial officials and the resulting reduction of Peruvian appointees.

– MARK A. BURKHOLDER

PÉRALTE, CHARLEMAGNE MASSÉNA

Charlemagne Masséna Péralte (*b.* 10 October 1886; *d.* 30 October 1919), Haitian rebel leader during the 1915–1934 U.S. occupation of Haiti. Charlemagne Masséna Péralte came from a rural, middle-class family in Hinche and was educated at a Catholic secondary school in Port-au-Prince. Afterward, he joined a rebel (CACO) group led by Oreste Zamor, his brother-in-law, who became president in February 1914. Péralte was made commander of Léogane, then of Port-de-Paix (1914).

When the U.S. Marines occupied Haiti, Péralte was forced to leave office. In October 1917, he was implicated in a robbery of the U.S. commander in Hinche. Péralte was convicted and sentenced to five years hard labor in Cap Haitien but escaped in September 1918.

After Péralte announced his intention to "drive the invaders into the sea and free Haiti," he formed a provisional government in the north, appointed himself its chief, and mobilized several thousand peasant irregulars. He attacked outlying military establishments, and then, on 7 October 1919, Port-au-Prince itself. A Marine order to "get Charlemagne" led Sergeant Herman H. Hanneken to trick Péralte into revealing his whereabouts. Hanneken shot him dead near Sainte Suzanne. When a Péralte associate, Benoît Batraville, was killed on 19 May 1920, armed opposition to the occupation dwindled.

Péralte is the best-known rebel leader of the 1915–1920 Caco Revolt, in which Haitians militarily resisted the occupation (which continued until 1934). Although Péralte did not espouse an economic or social program, his reputation as a Haitian hero and resistance leader has grown since the 1980s. He has appeared on stamps and in popular art, and he figures in political speeches.

— ANNE GREENE

PEREIRA, JOSÉ CLEMENTE

José Clemente Pereira (*b.* 22 February 1786?; *d.* 12 March 1854), Brazilian politician. Pereira was born in Castello Mendo, Portugal, to a humble family. He graduated in law from the University of Coimbra in 1809. In 1815 he arrived in Brazil, where he began his public career as a magistrate. In 1821 he assumed the post of foreign judge in Rio de Janeiro, which provided him a position of influence over events leading up to Brazilian independence. As president of the Senate of Rio de Janeiro, he delegated the representation of that city of Prince Pedro in the famous *Manifesto do fico* of 1822, which requested that the prince disregard the orders of the CORTES and remain in Brazil.

After helping to consolidate independence, Pereira was accused of republicanism because of his being a Mason and his defense of more radical liberal ideas. José Bonifacio had him arrested and deported to France. He returned to Brazil in 1824 and occupied various public posts during the empire, including representative in several legislatures, senator (1842), minister of the empire (1828), minister of war (1841), and adviser of state (1850). Besides his activities as a public figure, he stood out in the area of social assistance founding the Hospital of Mercy and the Peter II Hospice. Through his outstanding role in the struggle for Brazilian independence and his political activities, he became one of the builders of the Brazilian nation.

— LÚCIA M. BASTOS P. NEVES

PERERA, VÍCTOR

Víctor Perera (*b.* 12 April 1934), Guatemalan writer. Born in Guatemala of Sephardic Jewish parents who had immigrated from Jerusalem, Perera emigrated to the United States at age twelve. Educated at Brooklyn College (B.A., 1956) and the University of Michigan (M.A., 1958), he became a reporter, writer, and editor for the *New Yorker,* the *New York Times Magazine, Atlantic, Harper's,* and many other journals. His articles, short stories, and essays, often dealing with Latin America and Jewish themes, are noted for their sensitivity and perceptiveness. His first novel, *The Conversion* (1970), was followed by works of nonfiction, including *Last Lords of Palenque: The Lacandon Mayas of the Mexican Rain Forest* (with Robert D. Bruce, 1982), *Rites: A*

Guatemalan Boyhood (1986), and *Broken Promises: The Guatemalan Tragedy* (1991).

— RALPH LEE WOODWARD, JR.

PEREYNS, SIMÓN

Simón Pereyns (*b.* ca. 1535; *d.* 1589), painter. Apparently trained in his native Antwerp in the style of northern mannerism, Pereyns traveled in 1558 to Lisbon, where he worked as a painter, and then to Toledo and Madrid. In 1566 he arrived in New Spain with the viceroy Gastón de Peralta, for whom he painted frescoes of battle scenes (now lost). In 1568 Pereyns was tried before the Inquisition and sentenced to paint at his own expense a retablo of Nuestra Señora de la Merced, which may have been the *Virgen del Perdón,* destroyed by fire in the cathedral of Mexico City in 1967. The records of this trial provide information about the painter's life. Other documents attest to his prolific activity and to his central role in introducing Italianate Flemish mannerism to New Spain. Pereyns executed the paintings of the principal retablo of the cathedral of Mexico City as well as many others. He worked in collaboration with Francisco de Morales, Andrés de la CONCHA, Luis de Arciniega, and others. His only surviving works, however, are the paintings of the main altar at the Franciscan church in Huejotzingo (1856), possibly done with Concha, and a signed and dated *Saint Christopher* in the cathedral of Mexico City (1588).

— CLARA BARGELLINI

PÉREZ, ALBINO

Albino Pérez (*d.* 9 August 1837), governor of New Mexico from 1835 to 1837. The first Mexican governor of New Mexico, Pérez was appointed by the government of Antonio López de SANTA ANNA. As part of Mexico's shift away from federalism under Santa Anna, Pérez attempted to impose the authority of the central government through a new system of direct taxation and other measures. The Pérez administration alienated many New Mexicans, and in 1837 the governor's policies sparked a short-lived rebellion of Hispanics and Indians in northern New Mexico. While attempting to end the profederalist, antitaxation revolt, Pérez was captured, executed, and beheaded.

— SUZANNE B. PASZTOR

PÉREZ, CARLOS ANDRÉS

Carlos Andrés Pérez (*b.* 27 October 1926), president of Venezuela (1974–1979, 1988–1993). Andrés Pérez was a founder of Venezuela's Democratic Action (AD), inspired by Peru's Popular American Revolutionary Alliance (APRA). During his two presidential terms Pérez completed oil nationalization, was a spokesman for the Third World, and led efforts to influence U.S. policy through the Contadora organization of eight Latin American nations.

Carlos Andrés Pérez was born in Rubio, a Venezuelan Andean village. Dictator Juan Vicente GÓMEZ's repression of *campesinos,* as well as the forced sale of the Pérez family's coffee ranch, led Carlos into populist politics. The protégé of Democratic Action founders Leonardo Ruiz Pineda, Rómulo GALLEGOS, and Rómulo BETANCOURT, at eighteen Pérez was a delegate to the party's first convention. On the overthrow of the dictatorship of Eleazar LÓPEZ CONTRERAS in 1945, Pérez became secretary to Betancourt, the president of the revolutionary government junta. The junta was promptly overthrown by a military coup, and Pérez eventually joined Betancourt in Costa Rica, where they published an antimilitary newspaper. At the end of the dictatorship of Marcos PÉREZ JIMÉNEZ in 1958, Pérez returned to Venezuela as Betancourt's minister of the interior.

Pérez, one of Venezuela's most charismatic politicians, is known popularly as "CAP." During his first presidency, he completed the nationalization of Venezuela's petroleum industry and instigated state welfarism, engendered by the rise in international oil prices. Internationally, he championed wealth redistribution to the Third World through commodity power.

The inability of Perez' conservative coalition to maintain the illusion of easy wealth led to riots in February 1989.

When oil prices fell in the 1980s, Pérez pushed austerity moves. In 1988 he was the first president re-elected to a second term after a constitutionally mandated ten-year wait. However, the inability of the conservative coalition to maintain the illusion of easy wealth and permanent subsidized programs led to riots in February 1989. Two unsuccessful coup attempts in 1992 indicated that Pérez's program was no more popular than that of his predecessor, Luis HERRARA CAMPÍNS.

– PAT KONRAD

PÉREZ, JUAN

Juan Pérez (*d.* 1775), Spanish explorer. Juan Pérez, a native of Mallorca, was already an experienced pilot when he first sailed as part of the Manila Galleon before participating in the founding of California in 1769. In 1773, Viceroy Antonio María de BUCARELI of Mexico ordered him to lead a maritime expedition to explore the northern coast of California to check on Russians rumored to be in the area. Departing from the Pacific coast port of San Blas on the frigate *Santiago* on 24 January 1774, he reached San Lorenzo (present-day Vancouver Island) in August, as well as Nootka Sound and Cerro Nevado de Santa Rosalía (Mount Olympus). His expedition, the first to sail to 55 degrees north latitude, led to the subsequent Spanish exploration of the area as far as the Alaska Peninsula by the 1790s and formed the basis for its claims to that area. Pérez died of scurvy while piloting the *Santiago* along the California coast.

– JOSEPH P. SÁNCHEZ

PÉREZ ACOSTA, JUAN FRANCISCO

Juan Francisco Pérez Acosta (*b.* 1873; *d.* 1967), Paraguayan historian. Although his early career was limited to writings published in such opposition newspapers as *La Democracia* and *El Independiente*, Pérez Acosta was eventually recognized as the "dean of contemporary Paraguayan letters." He owed his success to his thorough and painstaking research in primary materials, especially the document collections in Paraguay's national archives. The results, as exemplified in his masterpiece, *Carlos Antonio López: Obrero máximo* (1948), placed him in the first rank of modern scholarship in Paraguay.

After the Liberal Party came to power in 1904, Pérez Acosta accepted various official posts: chief of police, director of the central bank, diplomat, jurist, and educator. He also edited several Asunción newspapers, including *El Diario* and *El Liberal*. With the defeat of the Liberals and the consolidation of Colorado Party rule in the late 1940s, Pérez Acosta retired to private life. Though he continued to write articles, his scholarly work slowly tapered off. He died in Asunción.

– THOMAS L. WHIGHAM

PÉREZ AGUIRRE, LUIS

Luis Pérez Aguirre (*b.* 1941), Uruguayan human rights activist. Pérez Aguirre was born to a patrician family. He had his primary education at the Richard Anderson School and his secondary education under the Jesuit fathers at Sacred Heart in Montevideo. He later studied civil aviation and in 1959 joined the Jesuits. While becoming a Jesuit priest, he undertook further studies in Chile, Argentina, and Canada in psychology, humanities, philosophy, and theology. He returned to his country in 1970 and threw himself into social work, concentrating primarily on the phenomenon of prostitution, but as the political situation worsened, he became more and more involved in the struggle for human rights.

After he was arrested for "subversive behavior," Pérez Aguirre was forced to leave the country and, under the direction of his superiors, undertook further studies at the University of Comillas in Spain. Returning to Uruguay around the late 1970s, he worked with groups of youths in the city of Las Piedras, in the department of Canelones, where he founded SERPAJ (Service for Peace and Justice) in 1984. This work gained him the support of Adolfo PÉREZ ESQUIVEL, the Argentine Nobel Peace Prize laureate. From Las Piedras, Pérez Aguirre involved himself in the intense political activity surrounding the plebiscite of 1980, with which began the country's movement toward democracy. With that work complete and a SERPAJ team established in Montevideo, Pérez Aguirre began directing La Huella, a home for abandoned children and young people in Las Piedras. He also publishes books on educational and cultural themes and continues his social work with prostitutes. His work is also associated with liberation theology.

– JOSÉ DE TORRES WILSON

PÉREZ DE TOLOSA, JUAN

Juan Pérez de Tolosa (*d.* 1548), governor and captain-general of the province of Venezuela (1546–1548). Pérez de Tolosa was the first governor of the province of Venezuela after the termination of the administration of the WELSERS, a group of Germans who were granted permission to settle and exploit the province of Venezuela. Their abuses of native peoples eventually resulted in a rescinding of the original grant and a trial. Pérez de Tolosa was the judge for this trial as well as that of Juan de Carvajal, a Spanish conquistador and colonizer of the Venezuelan interior, who ran afoul of Spanish authorities. He set up his government in the city of El Tocuyo and carried out diverse expeditions to the Andes, placing his brother, Alonso Pérez de Tolosa, and Diego de Losada in charge of them.

During Juan Pérez de Tolosa's rule, the system of the *encomienda* was initiated in Venezuela and the first looms were installed in El Tocuyo. At the end of his two-year mandate, the king extended it indefinitely. However, Pérez de Tolosa died shortly thereafter. His experience as an administrator in Venezuela is recorded in his book *Relación de las tierras y provincias de la gobernación de Venezuela, año 1546.*

– INÉS QUINTERO

PÉREZ ESQUIVEL, ADOLFO

Adolfo Pérez Esquivel (*b.* 26 November 1931), Argentine sculptor, peace activist, and coordinator of the Service for Peace and Justice (SERPAJ), Latin America's principal organization promoting societal change through nonviolence. In 1980 he received the Nobel Peace Prize for his work with SERPAJ.

Born in Buenos Aires, Pérez Esquivel was educated in Catholic schools and was deeply influenced by the writings of St. Augustine and Thomas Merton, as well as by the pacifist example of Mohandas Gandhi. Trained in sculpture at the National School of Fine Arts, he later taught there for fifteen years. He abandoned his successful career as a sculptor in the early 1970s to promote nonviolence as the most appropriate response to the violence that was afflicting Latin America as a result of increasing pressures for change.

In 1974 Pérez Esquivel joined with other Catholic activists to form Serpaj, an agency for the dissemination of knowledge of nonviolent strategies and for the promotion of greater observance of human rights, participatory models of economic development, greater political participation especially among the poor, disarmament, and demilitarization. That year Pérez Esquivel became the general coordinator of Serpaj, traveling throughout Latin America and elsewhere to promote nonviolence. As a result of his work, he was jailed for fourteen months in 1977–1978 by the Argentine military government. Upon his release, he resumed his work promoting nonviolence as the most effective way of creating a democratic and liberating social order.

– MARGARET E. CRAHAN

PÉREZ GODOY, RICARDO

Ricardo Pérez Godoy (*b.* 9 June 1905; *d.* 27 July 1982), commander in chief of Peru's armed forces, army general, and senior officer of the four-man junta that governed Peru from 18 July 1962 to 28 July 1963. After inconclusive presidential elections in June 1962 resulted in a virtual three-way tie among the leading contenders, the military took power by an "institutional act" of the armed forces. As commander in chief of Peru's armed forces, Pérez Godoy assumed the ceremonial duties of chief of state.

During the first months of junta government, several reformist initiatives concerning agrarian issues were promulgated. These anticipated the 1968–1980 military government's more sweeping reforms. The junta's reformist phase ended in January 1963 with the countrywide crackdown on Communist organizations and activists. Pérez Godoy was forced to retire in March

1963, amid allegations that he did not share his authority sufficiently with his copresidents. He lived quietly in retirement until his death.

— DAVID SCOTT PALMER

PÉREZ JIMÉNEZ, MARCOS

Marcos Pérez Jiménez (*b.* 1914), Venezuelan professional army officer and President (1942–1958). Pérez Jiménez was the dominant political figure in Venezuela from 1948 to 1958 and was the last of a series of army officers from the state of Táchira who ruled Venezuela in the late nineteenth and early twentieth centuries. A 1934 graduate of the Venezuelan Military Academy, Pérez Jiménez was a central figure in the 1945 overthrow of President Isaías MEDINA ANGARITA. Pérez had organized the revolutionary Patriotic Military Union (Unión Patriótica Militar—UPM) in 1944 and when he was arrested on 18 October 1945, the UPM overthrew the government. The junta that emerged the next day, however, headed by Rómulo BETANCOURT of the Democratic Action Party (Acción Democrática—AD), did not include Pérez Jiménez. Instead, Betancourt sent Pérez Jiménez abroad on an extended diplomatic mission. Alienated, Pérez Jiménez eventually organized the overthrow of the Venezuelan government of Rómulo GALLEGOS on 24 November 1948, restoring the military to power after three years of civilian rule. Pérez Jiménez was a member of the governing junta through the election of 1952, which appeared to be won by the opposition Democratic Republican Union (Unión Republicana Democrática—URD). Colonel Pérez Jiménez, however, suspended the election and seized power himself. His military dictatorship continued until 23 January 1958, when he was removed by other military officers, opening the way for the return of the AD and more democratic rule. Repression, corruption, and electoral fraud characterized his administration. The new government exiled the former dictator to the United States, but in 1963 extradited him and tried him for corruption during his administration. Convicted, in a five-year trial during which he was imprisoned, he was once more exiled and has lived in Spain since that time.

Supporters, however, in 1968 organized a political party supporting him. Although he won election as a senator from Caracas, his absence from the country led to his disqualification. His continued popularity, especially in Caracas, led to speculation that he might be a candidate in the 1973 presidential election until a constitutional amendment barred all ex-officeholders who had been convicted of felonies related to their tenure in office from running for any government post.

— RALPH LEE WOODWARD, JR.

PÉREZ MASCAYANO, JOSÉ JOAQUÍN

José Joaquín Pérez Mascayano (*b.* 6 May 1801; *d.* 1 June 1889), president of Chile (1861–1871). Pérez's early manhood was spent largely abroad, in Chile's diplomatic missions in the United States, France, and Argentina. A member of the Chamber of Deputies from 1836 to 1852 and then the Senate (1852–1861 and 1873–1882), he also served as minister of finance (1845–1846) and of the interior (1849–1850). Although he supported the Manuel MONTT administration (1851–1861) for its whole duration, his own temperament was averse to Montt's authoritarianism. In 1861, when public opinion fiercely rejected the presidential candidacy of Antonio VARAS, Pérez emerged as a suitably conciliatory figure to succeed Montt.

Pérez's presidency marked a genuine turning point in Chilean affairs. His own tolerant, patrician style did much to foster a new, more liberal atmosphere after the upheavals of the 1850s. In July 1862, abandoning Montt's National Party, Pérez invited into the cabinet the opposition Liberal-Conservative Fusion, which supported him for the remainder of his two presidential terms.

Pérez has never been well regarded by the admirers of strong government. Yet a persuasive case can be made for seeing him as *the* vitally important nineteenth-century president, the one head of state who truly consolidated the Chilean "idiosyncrasy" of civilized politics.

— SIMON COLLIER

PÉREZ SALAS, FRANCISCO ANTONIO

Francisco Antonio Pérez Salas (*b.* 1764; *d.* 10 November 1828), Chilean patriot politician. Pérez was named municipal *procurador* (attorney) in 1801, and was several times a member of the *cabildo* (municipal government) of Santiago in the last years of the colonial period. He was one of the more obdurate creole opponents of the last Spanish governor, Francisco Antonio García Carrasco (1742–1813). In 1810 he became an adviser of the first national junta, and figured thereafter in a number of public roles.

Pérez played his most important political part in 1813, following the departure of José Miguel CARRERA (1785–1821) to take command of the patriot forces in the south at the start of the wars of independence. In April 1813 he was appointed a member of a three-man governing junta, and remained so until September of that year, when, much afflicted by the death of his wife, he withdrew. The junta's reforms during this period included the establishment of a new Instituto Nacional (for secondary and higher education) and the National

Library. When Carrera seized power again in July 1813, he confined Pérez to San Felipe de Aconcagua.

During the Spanish reconquest of Chile (1814–1817) he was banished to Juan Fernández (an island prison for exiled political prisoners). After the liberation of Chile in 1817, Pérez served as a member of Bernardo O'HIGGINS's nominated senate (1818–1822).

– SIMON COLLIER

PERI ROSSI, CRISTINA

Cristina Peri Rossi (*b.* 12 November 1941), Uruguayan poet and fiction writer. Born in Montevideo, she studied literature at the University of the Republic in Montevideo. Her first book of short stories, *Viviendo* (Living), was published in 1963. The protagonists are marginal and indecisive female characters, immersed in solitude. In this first collection, Peri Rossi's fictional world began to develop. With the publication in 1969 of *Los museos abandonados,* a collection of short stories, and *El libro de mis primos* (The Book of My Cousins), her first novel, both built on an existentialist vision of reality, Peri Rossi began to be acknowledged as one of the most significant writers of her generation. The writers she recognizes as "mentors" are Uruguayans Juan Carlos ONETTI and Felisberto HERNÁNDEZ together with Jorge Luis BORGES, Julio CORTÁZAR, Ray Bradbury, and Dino Buzzati. She explores peculiar aspects of human beings who find themselves in ambiguous situations and in the middle of mysterious happenings. Peri Rossi published *Indicios pánicos* (Frightening Signs) in 1970 and, in 1971, her first book of poems, *Evohé: Poemas eróticos.* Two years later, after being expelled from her country for political reasons, she chose Spain as her home.

Further poetic works include *Descripción de un naufragio* (Description of a Wreck, 1975), *Diáspora* (1976), *Lingüística general* (1979), and *Europa después de la lluvia* (Europe After the Rain, 1987). Between 1976 and 1980, Spanish institutions awarded her three important literary awards. She wrote several works of fiction: *La tarde del dinosaurio* (1976), *La rebelión de los niños* (1980), *Cartas de Abelardo y Heloísa* (1982), *El museo de los esfuerzos inútiles* (The Museum of Useless Efforts, 1983), *La nave de los locos* (The Ship of Fools, 1984), *Una pasión prohibida* (1986), *Cosmoagonías* and *Solitario de amor* (1988), *Acerca de la escritura* (About Writing, 1990), *Babel bárbara* (Barbaric Babel, 1991), *Fantasías eróticas* (1991), and *La última noche de Dostoievski* (1992). A prolific writer, Peri Rossi, like other Romantics, finds her themes in nature.

– MAGDALENA GARCÍA PINTO

PERÓN, JUAN DOMINGO

Juan Domingo Perón (*b.* 8 October 1895; *d.* 1 July 1974), president of Argentina (1946–1955, 1973–1974). In June 1943 an infantry colonel named Juan Domingo Perón suddenly entered the Argentine political stage as the mastermind behind a successful military coup. For the next thirty years, whether in power or in exile, he remained at the center of that stage, a charismatic and controversial figure around whom all of Argentine politics revolved.

Perón's political base was primarily in the urban and rural lower classes, "the shirtless ones" (*descamisados*), whom he organized into powerful trade unions. Those unions were then consolidated into a national labor federation, the 2-million-strong General Labor Confederation (Confederación General de Trabajadores; CGT), which in turn was the backbone of the Peronist Party, now known as the Justicialist Party. The CGT and the party constitute part of Perón's legacy to his nation, along with a tradition of class conflict that has kept Argentina politically unstable and economically stagnant. Though Perón died in 1974, his party retained power into the 1990s, and the CGT continued to be a major political factor.

Perón's political genius lay in the fact that he was the first important Argentine leader to perceive labor's potential power and to make it his personal political vehicle. He succeeded so thoroughly in capturing the labor movement that he used its mass voting strength to win three presidential elections, in 1946, 1951, and 1973. Even in exile, from 1955 to 1972, labor's continuing loyalty to him allowed Perón to undermine every Argentine administration and force his opponents to agree to his return to power.

Despite his appeal to the lower classes, Perón himself came from a bourgeois background. His paternal grandfather had been a prominent Buenos Aires physician, professor, and public servant. His father, Mario, however, failed to maintain the family's fortune and social position, and was forced to accept a position as the manager of a Patagonian sheep ranch. Perón and his older brother, Mario, were born out of wedlock to a young Indian girl, Juana Sosa Toledo, barely past puberty. Although their parents later married, this branch of the family was socially ostracized.

The young Perón's quick intelligence won the sympathy of his widowed grandmother, whose social connections brought him acceptance into an elite polytechnic boarding school and then into the national military academy. He graduated as an infantry second lieutenant in December 1913, at the age of eighteen. Until 1930 he rose slowly through the ranks. Neither as a cadet nor as a young officer did Perón display any exceptional ability. Sports were his one outstanding area, especially boxing and fencing. An appointment as instructor at a noncommissioned officers' training school finally won Perón some recognition. Growing up on a sheep ranch had made him more at home with the lower classes and given him more of a popular touch than was the case with most army officers. That and his ability at sports made him extremely popular with the sergeants. Glowing reports about his success finally earned him, in 1926, a crucial appointment to the Superior War School. He applied himself to his studies and graduated near the top of his class. His reward was an appointment to General Staff Headquarters in 1929.

In 1930, soon after Perón arrived at his new post, he became deeply involved in a plot led by General José F. URIBURU to overthrow the civilian government headed by President Hipólito YRIGOYEN, but at the last minute he became convinced it would fail and switched his allegiance to a more broadly based movement led by General José Agustín P. JUSTO. Uriburu struck first, however, and succeeded. Perón was punished with a stint on the Bolivian frontier, but when Justo's faction got the upper hand in 1931 and began edging out Uriburu, Perón was made an instructor at the Superior War School in Buenos Aires. There he developed into a military intellectual, advocating in a number of books, including *Apuntes de Historia Militar* (1932) and *Las operaciones en 1870*, 2 vols. (1935), the need for national military power, a state-regulated economy, and strong leadership.

Perón studied Mussolini's fascist experiment closely and found that it conformed to his own ideas of good government.

From 1936 to 1938 Perón served as military attaché in Chile, where he is reputed to have acted as a spy. Shortly after his return to the Superior War School in 1938, his superiors posted him as military attaché to Rome. For the next two years Perón studied Mussolini's fascist experiment closely and found that it conformed to his own ideas of good government. He also visited NAZI Germany and described it afterward in glowing terms. Upon his return to Argentina, in January 1941, he involved himself in right-wing nationalist plots to prevent the pro-British conservative government from bringing Argentina into World War II on the Allies' side. He formed the United Officers Group (Grupo de

Oficiales Unidos; GOU), composed mostly of colonels and majors, which pulled off the successful coup of 4 June 1943 and helped him become the real power within the government.

Working through figurehead presidents, first General Pedro RAMÍREZ and then General Edelmiro FARRELL, Perón concentrated power in his own hands. As under secretary of war he put his own followers into key army positions. As secretary of labor and social welfare he built up the labor union movement, winning higher pay and better benefits for workers. As vice president of the Republic, by 1945 he was within reach of the highest office. In early October, however, envious army rivals joined to strip him of his offices and place him under arrest; but just as Perón's career seemed at an end, his supporters in the labor movement held a huge rally in downtown Buenos Aires, on 17 October, that forced the military to reverse themselves. A triumphant Perón appeared that evening on the balcony of the Presidential Palace to proclaim himself a candidate for the presidency. Free elections held in February 1946 resulted in a smashing victory for him and his supporters. Peronists controlled both houses of Congress, all provincial governorships, and all the provincial legislatures save one.

Though he had been democratically elected, Perón's rule was increasingly authoritarian. The Supreme Court was purged, as were the lower courts. Congressional opponents faced loss of immunity or arrest if they criticized the government or its policies too vigorously. All radio stations were government-owned, and opposition newspapers were closed down. It was necessary to belong to the Peronist Party to get a government job or contract. Opposition parties often saw their rallies broken up by storm troopers from the Peronist "National Liberating Alliance." In 1949 Perón rewrote the Constitution to permit his election to a second consecutive term. Two years later he won a second term in elections that were marred by widespread fraud and intimidation.

Perón's aim was a corporate state like Mussolini's, and to this end he sought to force every important social and economic group into a state-controlled organization. All workers had to join the CGT; all businessmen and farmers were in the CGE (General Economic Confederation); all professionals, schoolteachers, and intellectuals were forced into the CGP (General Confederation of Professionals); and all university students and professors had to belong to the CGU (General University Confederation).

Economic policy aimed at self-sufficiency and the redistribution of wealth in labor's favor. Foreign capital was discouraged, and wages rose faster than productivity. An industrialization program was to be financed by a state monopoly over the export of agricultural products. All went well for the first two years, because Argentina emerged from World War II with large currency reserves, but from 1949 on, the economy rapidly deteriorated. Farmers refused to produce at the government's fixed prices, the currency reserves were squandered on buying obsolete foreign properties such as railroads, trade and budget deficits got out of hand, and inflation negated wage increases. The vast network of bureaucratic regulations and restrictions encouraged widespread corruption.

Growing discontent eventually reached even the military and the Catholic church, previously supporters of Perón. Revolts in September 1951 and June 1955 reflected unease among officers at attempts to "Peronize" the military, especially the sergeants. The church, alarmed at the personality cult growing up around Perón and his flamboyant wife, Evita, fell out of favor in 1954 when it tried to organize Christian Democratic trade unions independent of the CGT. Perón's escalating war with the Catholic hierarchy, climaxing in the burning of several historic churches in June 1955, hurt him further with the military and gave all of his opponents an issue around which to rally. In September 1955 he was ousted by a military coup.

For the next seventeen years Perón was an exile, the guest of right-wing governments in Paraguay, Panama, Venezuela, the Dominican Republic, and Spain. Refusing to admit defeat, he gradually built up a network of contacts, set up an underground operation in Argentina, regained control of the labor movement, and was able to influence the votes of more than a million Argentines. When terrorist movements appeared in the late 1960s, the most important of them, the Montoneros, placed itself under his orders. Prevented from ruling himself, Perón was able to frustrate every government that tried to succeed him, whether civilian or military. Finally, in 1972, the military agreed to allow Perón to return from exile and to let his party field candidates in elections the following year. In May 1973 Perón's stand-in, Héctor CAMPORA, became president, but soon stepped aside for his master. New elections in September made Perón president for the third time. It was a storybook comeback, but he died ten months later.

During his brief third presidency Perón had to deal with the forces of anarchy he had helped to unleash. He reimposed the same corporate state scheme as before, but failed to reverse the runaway inflation and falling production that had already made a shambles of the economy. The young terrorists who helped him to power were disenchanted at his failure to embrace radical socialism, and resumed their violence. Argentines who had waited so long for their leader's return as a panacea had become aware by the time of his death that charisma is not enough.

– PAUL H. LEWIS

PERÓN, MARÍA ESTELA MARTÍNEZ DE

María Estela Martínez de Perón (Isabel; *b.* 4 February 1931), third wife of General Juan Domingo PERÓN and president of Argentina (1974–1976) and vice president (1973–1974). Born in La Rioja, María Estela was the youngest of six children born into a middle-class family. In 1934 the family moved to Buenos Aires, where María Estela attended elementary school. In 1951, when she was twenty, she entered the National School of Dance.

Known as Isabel, a name she adopted when she was a professional dancer with a touring nightclub company, she met the exiled Perón in Panama and became his companion/secretary in December 1955. They were married in Spain in November 1961. Since Perón had been forbidden to return to Argentina, she acted as his emissary on three different occasions. After his return on 17 November 1972, he became a candidate for a third term in office. In an attempt to neutralize Peronist factionalism, he selected Isabel as his running mate. They received 62 percent of the vote in the September 1973 presidential election. As violence among his supporters increased, Perón's economic recovery plan fell apart. On 1 July 1974, he died, and Isabel was sworn in, thus becoming the first female head of state in the Americas. Less than two years later, on 24 March 1976, as the country seemed to drift into anarchy, she was deposed by a military coup. Tried and convicted of corruption charges, she was kept under house arrest until 6 July 1981. After her release, she settled once again in Spain.

– MARYSA NAVARRO

PERÓN, MARÍA EVA DUARTE DE

María Eva Duarte de Perón (Evita; *b.* 7 May 1919; *d.* 26 July 1952), Argentine politician and actress and the second wife of President Juan Domingo PERÓN during his first term in office (1946–1952). Born on an estate near Los Toldos in Buenos Aires Province, Evita, as she was known, was the fifth illegitimate child of Juana Ibarguren and Juan Duarte, a local landowner. After his death, the family moved to Junín, in eastern Argentina, where Evita attended school and dreamed of becoming an actress. At fifteen, she decided to try her luck in Buenos Aires. Success eluded her in the theater and films, but she was very successful as a soap-opera radio actress. Her life changed substantially after January 1944, when she met Colonel Perón, then undersecre-

María Eva Duarte de Perón. (Archivo General de la Nación, Buenos Aires)

tary of war and secretary of labor, and soon-to-be-minister of war and vice president. To the consternation and shock of his fellow officers and Buenos Aires's sociopolitical elite, not only did Perón and Evita become lovers, but, contrary to accepted norms, they began to live together.

The transformation of the dark-haired young starlet into the elegant, blond, and fiery Evita, the charismatic leader of the *descamisados* (shirtless ones), was a gradual process that began after the 17 October 1945 crisis. On that day, thousands of workers went on strike to demand the release of Perón, who had been forced to resign from his three posts and was imprisoned. Although Peronist and anti-Peronist mythology credits Evita with a leading role in the workers' demonstration, she only tried to obtain a writ of habeas corpus for Perón's release. However, he wrote to her from jail and promised to marry her.

Shortly after their 21 October 1945 wedding, Perón began his campaign for the presidency. In a society where women could not vote and first ladies remained in the background, Evita sat in on strategy meetings and accompanied Perón on his tours of the provinces. After his inauguration, her interest in politics and her influence increased as she began to meet daily with union leaders and represented Perón at numerous functions. Invited by General Francisco Franco to visit Spain in an official capacity, she toured Spain, France, and Italy as if she were a glamorous movie star.

By 1948, Evita was clearly established as an influential member of Perón's government. Until her death, she played a crucial, though informal, role within the Peronist structure. Her only attempt to formalize her activities and become a vice presidential candidate in the 1951 elections generated too much opposition from the military. Officially, she was only Argentina's first lady, but, together with Perón, she was the leader of the *descamisados,* his liaison with organized labor, and his most effective publicist. She was also president of the Eva Perón Foundation, a wealthy social-welfare organization whose funds she used to build hospitals, low-income housing, schools, and youth hotels and to buy thousands of goods that she distributed to the needy. Finally, while her participation in the campaign to obtain women's suffrage was limited, she was instrumental in the massive incorporation of women into the political process and the organization of the women's branch of the Peronist Party. She presided over the party with a firm hand, and though she was already very sick when Perón ran for a second term, he was elected with an overwhelming female vote.

Evita's death transformed her into a powerful myth, but it also shook the stability of the Peronist structure at a time when Perón's economic policies strained the support of the *descamisados.* In September 1955 he was deposed by a military coup and forced into exile. Evita's myth became essential to the survival of Peronism during the following eighteen years and to Perón's own reelection in 1973.

— MARYSA NAVARRO

PERRICHOLI, LA

La Perricholi (Micaela Villegas, Miqueta; *b.* 1739; *d.* 17 May 1819), actress. Immortalized in legend, opera, and film, and reputed for her great beauty, La Perricholi was born in Peru and began her career on the Lima stage in 1760 as a comic actress. The next year she caught the attention of the newly arrived viceroy, Manuel de AMAT Y JUNIENT, then over sixty, who brought her to court and provided her with a palatial residence on the Lima Alameda. In 1773, however, they had a falling out. One story is that La Perricholi accepted an offer from a Lima theater manager to return to the stage, but when he criticized her for not learning her lines properly, she stabbed him in a violent rage, scandalizing residents of Lima and forcing Amat to break with her. Another version is that she appeared at the ceremony inducting the viceroy into Charles III's Order of San Jénaro in a golden coach that was exclusively reserved for titled nobility, creating an outcry that forced Amat to give her up. In 1775, however, a year before the viceroy left his post, they reconciled. According to legend, La Perricholi went through a religious change about this time, spending most of the rest of her life until her death dispensing alms and assisting the Carmelites.

One story maintains that when a theater manager

criticized La Perricholi for not learning her lines,

she stabbed him in a violent rage.

Versions of her life story constitute the basis of Jacques Offenbach's opera *La Périchole* and Jean Renoir's film *The Golden Coach*.

— JOHN JAY TEPASKE

PESSOA, EPITÁCIO DA SILVA

Epitácio da Silva Pessoa (*b.* 23 May 1865; *d.* 13 February 1942), president of Brazil (July 1919– November 1922). Orphaned son of a Paraíban landowner, Pessoa was raised by relatives in Pernambuco, where he later graduated from the Recife Law Faculty. After his arrival in Rio de Janeiro in 1889, Pessoa steadily rose among the elite of the young republic, serving as minister of justice (1898–1901), Supremo Tribunal Federal justice (1902–1912), and senator (1912–1919). In 1919 Pessoa led Brazil's delegation to the Versailles Peace Conference, winning fame while negotiating German war reparations and participating in the creation of the League of Nations. While in Versailles, Pessoa was chosen to become president of Brazil through a closed-door compromise struck among the political elite of Brazil's most powerful states, Minas Gerais and São Paulo, to fill out the term of deceased president Rodrígues Alves.

As president, Pessoa strongly supported federal investment in roads, railways, electrification, northeastern drought relief, and higher education. Pessoa contended with political discord among northeastern elites and disgruntled members of the Clube Militar. The final year of Pessoa's presidency, 1922, was a watershed in the steady destabilization of the First Republic, as São Paulo's Modern Art Week, the first *tenente* (lieutenant) revolt, and the Centenary Exposition of Brazilian In-

dependence all challenged the purported vision of republican peace and prosperity. Upon stepping down from the presidency, Pessoa remained active in federal politics, and also served for many years on the International Court of Justice.

— DARYLE WILLIAMS

PESSOA CAVALCANTI DE ALBUQUERQUE, JOÃO

João Pessoa Cavalcanti de Albuquerque (*b.* 24 January 1878; *d.* 26 July 1930), Brazilian politician, vice-presidential candidate (1930). Offspring of elite intermarriage in Brazil's northeastern state of Paraíba, Pessoa is best known for his 1930 death by assassination—an event which served as catalyst to the outbreak of the Revolution of 1930. Educated in military school and the Recife Law School, Pessoa moved to Rio de Janeiro in 1909 to begin a career in federal public service. During the 1920s, Pessoa served on various military tribunals, including the courts that judged the rebellious cadets and young officers involved in the decade's *tenente* revolts.

With the support of his uncle, former Brazilian president Epitácio PESSOA, and his home state's Partido Republicano da Paraíba, Pessoa was elected governor (*presidente*) of Paraíba in 1928. The fiscal and administrative reforms undertaken during his governorship often faced stiff opposition, particularly from political bosses (*coronéis*) of the state's interior. Pessoa faced even stronger opposition from the federal government when he refused to support the official presidential candidacy of Júlio PRESTES. Siding with a Rio Grande do Sul-Minas Gerais–supported opposition party, the Aliança Liberal, Pessoa accepted the nomination to run as vice president on the reformist Aliancista ticket headed by Getúlio VARGAS.

During the presidential campaign, Paraíban CORONEL José PEREIRA led a regional rebellion, known as the Princesa Revolt, in an effort to undermine Pessoa's regional and national credibility. Soon after the Aliança Liberal's electoral defeat, Pessoa was assassinated by personal and political rival João Dantas. This incident sparked civil and political unrest, as Dantas was linked to factions which supported the Prestes candidacy. Even though Pessoa had declared his opposition to armed insurrection, his assassination became a rallying cry for the defeated Vargas party. With Pessoa's death-cum-martyrdom still fresh in mind, the civil war that would be known as the Revolution of 1930 broke out in early October 1930. The capital of Paraíba was renamed João Pessoa to honor the slain governor.

— DARYLE WILLIAMS

PÉTION, ALEXANDRE SABÈS

Alexandre Sabès Pétion (*b.* 2 April 1770; *d.* 29 March 1818), President of Haiti (1807–1818). Born in Port-au-Prince of a mulatto mother and a wealthy French father, Paschal Sabès, Pétion belonged to the *liberto* (free colored) class of Port-au-Prince. He was despised by his father, perhaps partly because of Pétion's dark skin color. It is unclear why he used the name Pétion instead of Sabès. (Pétion is from the patois Pichoun, meaning "my little one," a nickname given to him by a foster mother.) At age eighteen, after serving as an apprentice to a blacksmith, Pétion enlisted in the colonial army. By age twenty-one, he had distinguished himself and risen to the rank of captain. Later, in the ranks of Toussaint L'OUVERTURE, he proved to be a skilled soldier and an excellent leader. In 1791 he joined the mulattoes in the uprising led by Boukman, a fugitive slave from Jamaica, and later was among Toussaint's troops who fought the British.

Pétion's alliance with Toussaint did not last, for he chose to fight in the ranks of General Charles LECLERC, sent by Napoleon in 1802. He soon realized, however, that victory for Leclerc and the French would mean a loss of rights for Haitians, both blacks and mulattoes. It was then that he joined ranks with Jean Jacques DESSALINES. He was one of the first to declare the rights of the members of his class, both political and civil equality with the whites, in accordance with the French Constituent Assembly's "Declaration of Rights of Man and Citizen." During the civil war of 1800, Pétion was exiled to France. In 1801, he returned to Haiti, where he began to actively fight for its independence. Pétion and Dessalines are credited with creating the Haitian flag.

In 1806, Pétion founded the Republic of Haiti and was the main force behind the country's constitution. Elected to the presidency by the Haitian Senate in 1807, Pétion was reelected in 1811 and in 1815. He never reconciled himself to the idea of Haiti as a black state. His hope was for a republic governed by an oligarchy of mulattoes. As a result, racial tensions intensified during his presidency. Nevertheless, he is remembered as a great leader of the independence movement and was praised by many of his Latin American contemporaries, including Simón BOLÍVAR, who visited him in 1815–1816. Pétion supplied Bolívar with troops and support for the liberation movement in Venezuela. Pétion is also remembered for his role in the distribution of land to the veterans of the War of Independence. Nonetheless, he did not achieve his economic and political goals. At his death Haiti had gone from the most productive colony in the hemisphere to the poorest.

— DARIÉN DAVIS

PETTORUTI, EMILIO

Emilio Pettoruti (*b.* 1 October 1892; *d.* 16 October 1971), Argentine painter, pioneer of abstract art in South America, who developed a style incorporating synthetic cubism, futurism and early Renaissance painting. Born in La Plata, Pettoruti was self-taught. In 1913 he went to study in Florence, Italy. Influenced by the futurists and kinetic figuration, Pettoruti painted symbolic abstractions of wind and light (e.g., *Lights in the Landscape,* 1915). From his study of quattrocento painting, he derived a halftone palette, painting quasi-geometrical portraits and landscapes (e.g., *Woman in the Café, Sunshine and Shade,* both 1917). He met Juan Gris in Paris in 1923 and returned to Argentina the following year. He was director of the Museum of Fine Arts, La Plata, from 1930 to 1947. In 1941 he exhibited at the San Francisco Museum of Art. His conception of art polarized traditionalists and avant-gardists. Influenced by cubism, he used dissected forms but did not employ simultaneous presentation of different profiles. In 1953 he moved to Paris, where he lived until his death.

After 1950 Pettoruti returned to pure, dynamic abstractions with a metaphysical bent (e.g., *Quietness of the Beyond,* 1957). Classified by some as an academic cubist, he was considered a classical modernist by others.

— MARTA GARSD

PEZET, JUAN ANTONIO

Juan Antonio Pezet (*b.* 1809; *d.* 1879), military leader who became president of Peru (1863–1865) upon the death in office of General Miguel de San Román. Born in Lima, Pezet had to confront a difficult international conflict with Spain resulting from the Talambo Affair (August 1863) and the Spanish government's renewed hostility toward its old colonies. The Spanish fleet, off the Peruvian coast at the time, seized the guano-producing islands of Chincha to press a settlement that included an apology for the deaths of two Spanish nationals killed on the Talambo estate, as well as the repayment to Spain of the public debt dating back to 1820. The Pezet government opted for a peaceful solution to the conflict with the signing of the Vivanco-Pareja Treaty (January 1865), which was seen by many Peruvians, including some military leaders, as a submission to Spanish demands. The still influential caudillo Ramón Castilla and Colonel Mariano Ignacio PRADO led the opposition to Pezet that caused his ouster in November 1865 and the rejection of the treaty by the new government of Prado. In 1866 the allied forces of Peru, Chile, Ecuador, and Bolivia fought several naval battles with the Spanish fleet, forcing the Spanish contingent to withdraw from the South American Pacific coast. Pezet died in Chorrillos.

— ALFONSO W. QUIROZ

PHELPS, ANTHONY

Anthony Phelps (*b.* 25 August 1928), Haitian writer, journalist, photographer, filmmaker, and ceramicist. After finishing his secondary schooling in Haiti, Phelps studied chemistry at Seton Hall University in New Jersey. He then studied plastic arts and photography in Montreal and New York. Together with several fellow writers (Davertige, Serge Legagneur, Roland Morisseau, René Philoctète), Phelps founded a literary group, Haïti Littéraire, and a journal, *Semences* (1962). Phelps was forced to flee Haiti in 1964 because of criticism of the Duvalier regime in his print and radio journalism. In Quebec he worked in television and theater and continued to write. Phelps achieved a level of popular appeal with his live poetry recitals and a number of records. Some of his videos have been broadcast by Radio Québec and in Haiti since the fall of Jean-Claude Duvalier in 1986.

Phelps participated in numerous writers' congresses in Africa and in Latin America and has maintained contacts with Latin American writers. His volume of poetry *Orchidée nègre* (1985, 1987) won the 1985 prize of Casa de las Américas and was first published in Cuba.

— CARROL F. COATES

PICADO MICHALSKI, TEODORO

Teodoro Picado Michalski (*b.* 10 January 1900; *d.* 1 June 1960), president of Costa Rica (1944–1948), educator, and legislator.

Teodoro Picado Michalski came to the presidency after one of the more violent electoral campaigns in Costa Rican history. Although he won election by an ample margin, his victory and his presidency were marred by charges of fraud and the consequent questioning of his right to govern.

Picado brought to the presidency a distinguished record as legislator, educator, public servant, and a truly gifted individual. Born in San José, he spent his early years in rural schools. After his graduation from the Liceo de Costa Rica in 1916, he taught high school history; in 1922 he received his law degree from the School of Law in San José. In 1930 he was appointed director of the Instituto de Alajuela, a secondary school. His involvement at all levels of education, from school administrator to law professor, helped in his role as sec-

retary of education under President Ricardo JIMÉNEZ OREAMUNO (1932–1936). He was elected to Congress in 1936 and served as president of that body from 1941 to 1944.

As the standard bearer of the Victory Bloc (Bloque de la Victoria), the political alliance between the Calderónists and the Communists in the 1944 election, Picado's candidacy was controversial from the beginning. The opposition to his government took many forms, from newspaper attacks to terrorism, and Picado's administration was largely reduced to the task of surviving until the next election.

The opposition to Picado's government took many

forms, from newspaper attacks to terrorism.

When Congress nullified the results of the 1948 election, Picado was overthrown by an armed uprising led by José FIGUERES FERRER. He remained in exile in Managua, Nicaragua, until his death.

— JOHN PATRICK BELL

PICÓN SALAS, MARIANO

Mariano Picón Salas (*b.* 26 January 1901; *d.* 1 January 1965), Venezuelan essayist, teacher, and diplomat. After publishing his first book, *Buscando el camino* (1920), Picón left the Venezuelan dictatorship of Juan Vicente GÓMEZ in 1923, seeking intellectual freedom in Chile. He completed his education at the University of Chile, where he taught and wrote until Gómez's death. Upon his return to Venezuela in 1936, Picón worked to improve national intellectual life. He held posts in Venezuela's Ministry of Education between 1936 and 1940, founded and directed the *Revista Nacional de Cultura* (1936), founded and was first dean of the Faculty of Philosophy and Letters of the Central University of Venezuela (UCV) (1946), and taught at UCV and in Mexico, Argentina, and the United States. Although he was uncomfortable with political activism, Picón admired and enjoyed a warm friendship with social democrat Rómulo BETANCOURT, founder of the Democratic Action Party (1941).

In his numerous publications, Picón stressed the importance of spiritual and cultural progress, preferring the universal humanistic values of the eighteenth century to the materialistic tenets of communism or positivism. His historical works, *Pedro Claver, el santo de los esclavos* (1950), *Miranda* (1946), and *De la conquista a la independencia: Tres siglos de historia cultural hispanoamericana* (1944) emphasize humanistic values, as does his autobiographical novel *Viaje al amanecer* (1943). Picón served as Venezuelan ambassador to Colombia, Mexico, Brazil, and UNESCO; as secretary-general in the Venezuelan cabinet (1963–1964); and at the time of his death as president-designate of the National Institute of Culture and Fine Arts.

– JUDITH EWELL

PIÉROLA, NICOLÁS DE

Nicolás de Piérola (*b.* 1839; *d.* 13 June 1913), president of Peru (1879–1881; 1895–1899) and a dominant figure in Peruvian politics from the 1870s through 1910. The scion of an aristocratic Arequipa family, Piérola won a following among Peruvians who sought government protection for Roman Catholicism and encouragement of democratic and regional politics. He became minister of finance in 1869 and angered national guano consignees by issuing a monopoly contract to a French firm, the Dreyfus Company, to market guano in Europe in return for a large cheap loan, a promise of annual payments, and debt relief for the government. A few years later he was severely critical of the government of Manuel PARDO and was blamed when Pardo was assassinated. When the Chileans invaded Peru during the War of the Pacific (1879–1883), the government collapsed, and a brief rebellion resulted in Piérola's election to the presidency. At the battles of San Juan and Miraflores in 1881, Chilean invaders crushed his untrained defense forces. Under heavy criticism, Piérola retreated to mountainous Ayacucho. After the war Piérola's partisans organized the Democratic Party and sought a return to civilian electoral politics.

When the generals staged fraudulent elections in 1894, Piérola's forces rebelled in Peru's last major popular militant uprising. In 1895 Piérola was elected president for four years. Little different from the Civilistas, his government respected the rights of the courts and congress. New taxes and stricter financial rules meant higher revenue and improved public services. He put the country on the gold standard and established a ministry of development. He hired French military advisers to professionalize the army; merit became the basis for military promotions. In 1899 Piérola turned the presidency over to civilians, but he continued to have an avid interest in national politics, helping to keep the Democratic Party a lively force in Peruvian politics for some years.

– VINCENT PELOSO

PINEDA-DUQUE, ROBERTO

Roberto Pineda-Duque (*b.* 29 August 1910; *d.* 1977), Colombian composer. Born in Santuario, Antioquia,

Pineda-Duque took music courses at Medellín's Institute of Fine Arts under Joaquín Fuster (piano) and Carlos Posada-Amador (harmony). In 1942 he moved to Cali to study with Antonio María VALENCIA (choral technique). In the early 1950s he studied composition, fugue, counterpoint, instrumentation, and the twelve-tone technique with Carlo Jachino, director of the National Conservatory of the University of Colombia. Two of his major works are the cantata *Edipo Rey* (1959) and the oratorio *Cristo en el seno de Abraham* (1961). His *Concierto para piano* (1960) was awarded the Colombian Sesquicentennial of Independence Prize. In 1961 he became professor of organ, harmony, and composition at the National Conservatory. He has composed primarily church music and has served as *maestro de capilla* at the church of Nuestra Señora de las Nieves in Bogotá. He died in Bogotá.

– SUSANA SALGADO

PINEDO, FEDERICO

Federico Pinedo (*b.* 1895; *d.* 1971), Argentine politician and political economist. Born in Buenos Aires, Pinedo graduated from the National University of Buenos Aires in 1915 with a degree in law and social science and then pursued a career in law and politics. He joined the reformist Socialist Party and was later a founder of the Independent Socialist Party. As such he was elected deputy for the Federal Capital in 1920–1922 and again in 1928–1933; he supported the overthrow of President Hipólito YRIGOYEN in 1930. A leading figure of the Concordancia, he served as minister of finance under presidents Agustín Pedro JUSTO (1933–1935) and Ramón S. CASTILLO (1940–1941). He is best known for the "Pinedo Plan" of 1940, which represented a notable turn away from Argentina's classic economic liberalism. The plan envisioned massive state investment in industry, to be financed by public bonds sold through private banks; an industrial credit bank would make the resultant capital available to industrialists. It emphasized housing construction and envisioned a state agency to purchase surplus primary products for resale overseas as well as state purchase of the British-owned railways, with wartime credits accumulating in London. Radical deputies defeated the plan in Congress but it won wide political support; PERÓN later adopted its leading proposals. As a democrat, however, Pinedo opposed Perón and was imprisoned.

Following Perón's overthrow in 1955 Pinedo advocated stern measures to restore the Argentine economy but came to believe that Argentina's problems were political in nature. During 1962 acting president José María GUIDO named him minister of finance. Pinedo believed congressional and judicial authority should be restored but held that the Peronist Party—a totalitarian party, in his view—should remain banned. His stand was unacceptable either to Peronists or to military hardliners, who soon imposed harsh demands on Guido. When the latter acceded to them, Pinedo, the spokesman for moderation, resigned after only two weeks in office. Pinedo had already achieved fame as a journalist and author; his major works include *En tiempos de la república y después* (5 vols., 1946), *El fatal estatismo* (1956), *La CEPAL y la realidad económica en América Latina* (1963), *La Argentina en un cono de sombra* (1968), and *La Argentina* (1971). Pinedo died in Buenos Aires.

— RONALD C. NEWTON

PIÑERA, VIRGILIO

Virgilio Piñera (*b.* 4 August 1912; *d.* 18 October 1979), Cuban poet, playwright, short-story writer, and novelist. Piñera was born in Cárdenas in Matanzas Province. He received a doctorate in philosophy and letters from the University of Havana in 1940. In 1942 he founded and managed the magazine *Poeta*. He lived in Buenos Aires for fourteen years, working on the staff of the Cuban consulate and eventually as a translator for the Argos publishing house. In Buenos Aires he befriended the Polish novelist Witold Gombrowicz, whose 1961 novel *Ferdydurke* he later helped translate into Spanish; he also published in the highly regarded magazine *Sur*. After returning to Cuba in 1955, Piñera and José Rodríguez Feo founded the literary publication *Ciclón*. In 1968 he won first prize in the Casa de las Américas contest for his play *Dos viejos pánicos*.

Piñera was always at odds with the Cuban Revolution, and upon his death many of his unpublished works were confiscated.

One of the most original and unique writers in all of Cuban history, Piñera excelled in the genres of poetry, drama, and the short story. His writing style is detached and concise; his work is noted for its black humor and use of the absurd. Piñera was always at odds with the Cuban Revolution, and upon his death many of his unpublished works were confiscated. Of these, two collections of short stories have been published posthumously (*Un fogonazo* and *Muecas para escribientes,* both 1987). Among his best works are *Cuentos fríos* (short stories, 1956), *Dos viejos pánicos* (drama, 1968), *Electra garrigó* (drama, 1960), *La isla en peso* (poem, 1943), *La vida entera* (poetry, 1969), and *Teatro completo* (drama, 1960).

— ROBERTO VALERO

PINGRET, ÉDOUARD HENRI THÉOPHILE

Édouard Henri Théophile Pingret (*b.* 30 December 1788; *d.* 1875), French painter. Pingret was born in Saint-Quentin, France. At the age of fourteen Pingret's father sent him to the studio of Jacques-Louis David, where he excelled as an apprentice. Two years later he went to Rome and frequented the Academy of San Lucas. In 1831 he received his first gold medal at an exhibition, and in 1839 he was awarded the rank of chevalier in the Legion of Honor. He spent time in Tripoli, Morocco, and Algeria, and in 1850, under the advice of Prince Joinville, Pingret traveled to Mexico as a representative of the American Maritime Transportation Company, a French firm, to resell stock belonging to Joinville and the Pignatari family, heirs to the marquisate of Oaxaca. At age sixty-two, Pingret met in Veracruz the printer Ernst Masson, who instilled in him an interest in archaeology. He gathered an interesting collection of pre-Hispanic and colonial pieces, which he later took back with him to Europe.

While in Mexico in 1852, Pingret exhibited for the first time at the Academia de San Carlos a group of paintings with European themes, and the following year demonstrated what he had seen and appreciated in Mexico by exhibiting a series of folkloric works. His scenes of the interiors of kitchens were rapidly copied by his students and exhibited at the academy. Pingret's work also includes landscapes and contemporary historical paintings, making him one of the visual editors of life in the middle part of the nineteenth century. He died in Saint-Quentin.

— ESTHER ACEVEDO

PINHEIRO, JOSÉ FELICIANO FERNANDES

José Feliciano Fernandes Pinheiro (*b.* 9 May 1774; *d.* 6 July 1847), viscount of São Leopoldo and minister of the Empire of Brazil (1825–1827). Born in Santos of a family of tradesmen, he graduated with a degree in law from the University of Coimbra in 1798. He was employed as a translator at the Arco do Cego Typography in Lisbon. There, he drew the attention of Rodrigo de SOUSA COUTINHO, who in 1800 appointed him minister of the colonies, to establish the Customs of Rio Grande de São Pedro do Sul Captaincy. He was elected representative to the Lisbon Cortes for São Paulo in 1821, and in 1823 he became a representative to the Brazilian Constituent Assembly.

PEDRO I appointed Pinheiro president of the province of São Pedro do Rio Grande do Sul (1824–1826), where he established the important immigrant colony of São Leopoldo. He was a senator from 1826 until his death and a member of the Council of State in 1827–1830.

Pinheiro played an important part in academic and cultural life. He was one of the founders of the Brazilian Historical and Geographical Institute, and a member of various foreign cultural institutions. He wrote several works, including *Annals of the São Pedro Province,* the first significant history of the region. He contributed to the creation of the Brazilian nation not only as a politician and administrator but as a memorialist and historian as well.

– LÚCIA M. BASTOS P. NEVES

PINHEIRO MACHADO, JOSÉ GOMES

José Gomes Pinheiro Machado (*b.* 1851; *d.* 8 September 1915), the most powerful figure in the Brazilian Senate from 1905 to 1915 and head of the congressional delegation from Rio Grande do Sul. Pinheiro Machado built a national political machine through which he controlled Brazil's weak northern states, played a key role in presidential successions, and brought his home state to the forefront of national politics. Scion of a ranching family, he graduated from São Paulo Law School, fought in the Paraguayan War (War of the Triple Alliance), joined the Riograndense republican conspiracy against the empire in 1889, rose to the rank of general in the Federalist Revolt (1893), and served continuously in the Constituent Assembly and federal Senate, which elected him vice president (1902–1905, 1912–1915). He wielded his extensive personal power through control of the credentials committee and his national Partido Republicano Conservador, constructed of state political machines in 1910. Armed with his hold over weak President Hermes Rodrigues da FONSECA, he outmaneuvered salvationist army officers who challenged his power in 1911–1912, and he initiated interventions in the smaller states in 1913–1914. Reaction against his corruption, strong-arm tactics, and efforts to control the presidential succession in 1914 led to the breakdown of his political machine and his assassination by an unemployed baker in Rio de Janeiro.

– JOAN BAK

PINHO, JOSÉ WANDERLEY DE ARAÚJO

José Wanderley de Araújo Pinho (*b.* 1890; *d.* 1967), Brazillian historian and politician. Born in Santo Amoro, Pinho graduated from the Faculdade de Direito da Bahia. His career began in local law and proceeded to the state's judicial hierarchy and politics. He became a minister of the Tribunal de Contas, a federal deputy, and municipal prefect of Salvador. His avocation for history, signaled by a later post at the Universidade da Bahia and his membership in local and national historical institutes, was first evident in early publications related to the career of his great grandfather, the barão de COTEGIPE (1815–1889). His work, based on careful archival research, remains important for an understanding of Second Empire politics and elite society in Bahia and Rio.

– JEFFREY D. NEEDELL

PINILLA, ENRIQUE

Enrique Pinilla (*b.* 3 August 1927; *d.* 1989), Peruvian composer. Pinilla was born in Lima and studied at the National Conservatory until 1946. For the next two years he studied with Nadia Boulanger in Paris. He completed his education at the Royal Conservatory of Music in Madrid where he lived until 1958. He became a student of Boris Blacher at the Berlin School of Music. In 1966–1967, Pinilla studied electronic music at Columbia University under the direction of Vladimir Ussachevsky and Alcides LANZA. Pinilla was the head of the music and film department at the Casa de la Cultura and director of the television and film department at the University of Lima.

Among his principal compositions are Sonatina for flute (1950); *Once canciones populares* for voice and piano (1952); and Six Pieces for strings and woodwinds (1958). A very effective use of shifting meters can be seen in his *Estudio sobre el ritmo de la marinera* for piano (1959). His interest in rhythmic structures evolved further during the 1960s in Four Pieces for fourteen wind instruments (1960); Three Movements for percussion ensemble (1961); Four Pieces for orchestra (1961); Canto no. 1 for orchestra (1963); Collages nos. 1 and 2 for piano (1966); *Festejo* for orchestra (1966); *Prisma* for tape (1967); Canto no. 2 for orchestra (1968); Piano Concerto (1970); Peruvian Suite for orchestra (1972); *Evoluciones* no. 2 for percussion and orchestra (1976); and *Cinco piezas para percusión* (1977). He also wrote *Tres piezas para guitarra* (1987); *La niña de la lámpara azul* for choir (1981); and *Diez piezas infantiles* for piano (1987).

– ALCIDES LANZA

PINO SUÁREZ, JOSÉ MARÍA

José María Pino Suárez (*b.* 8 September 1869; *d.* 22 February 1913), vice president of Mexico (1912–1913).

Pino Suárez was a prominent prerevolutionary politician and anti-reelectionist who became the only truly popularly elected Mexican vice president, the last individual to occupy that post in the twentieth century. Born on a hacienda in Tenosique, Tabasco, of a modest family, Pino Suárez completed his studies in law in Mérida, Yucatán, graduating 12 September 1894. In 1904, he founded *El Peninsular,* which he directed. He became active in opposing the government of Porfirio DÍAZ, and directed the anti-reelectionists in Yucatán, Campeche, and Tabasco. He supported MADERO in 1909, and became president of the National Independent Convention of Anti-reelectionist Parties and National Democratic parties in 1910. His role in opposing Díaz was dangerous and caused him to flee the country in 1910–1911. After returning in 1911, he served as a member of Madero's provisional government in Ciudad Juárez and as provisional governor of Yucatán. He served as secretary of public education while vice president. He and President Madero were murdered at the order of Victoriano HUERTA.

– RODERIC AI CAMP

PINOCHET UGARTE, AUGUSTO

Augusto Pinochet Ugarte (*b.* 25 November 1915), Chilean army officer and chief of state and president (1973–1989). Pinochet was born in Valparaíso. At the

Augusto Pinochet Ugarte waving to his troops, 10 March 1990. (Wide World)

age of seventeen he entered the Escuela Militar, graduated in 1936, and was promoted to second lieutenant in 1938. He and his wife, Lucía Hiriart, had three daughters and two sons.

In his professional career Pinochet distinguished himself as a specialist in military geography and geopolitics. His 1968 book *Geopolítica* went through several editions. He held several staff and command posts and was a member of the Chilean military mission in Washington, D.C., in 1956. He taught at the Escuela Militar, at the Academia de Guerra, and at Ecuador's national war college in the 1950s and 1960s.

By 1970, Pinochet had risen to the rank of division general, and the next year he became commandant of the Santiago garrison, the most sensitive and influential of Chilean army assignments. By this time, by his own admission, Pinochet had become very critical of politics in general and Marxism specifically. As Santiago garrison commandant he was an eyewitness to the social, economic, and political turbulence accompanying the administration of Socialist Salvador ALLENDE GOSSENS. When the army commander in chief, General Carlos PRATS GONZÁLEZ, became interior minister during a serious trucking strike in late 1972, Pinochet became acting commander in chief, and held this position again on the eve of the 11 September 1973 putsch. Pinochet became president of the military junta, a body composed of military commanders in chief. A year later he became president of the Republic of Chile. His term of office was formally extended later through the adoption of a constitution giving him an eight-year term (1981–1989).

From late 1973 until late 1976 the country was in an economic depression, the aftermath of Allende's policies and economic pressures applied by both foreigners and Chileans between 1970 and 1973. This was also a period of harsh authoritarian rule, during which Pinochet consolidated his control of the armed forces and the government. By 1978, however, Chileans, especially those of the middle and upper sectors, and some foreigners were talking of an "economic miracle" based on free enterprise, foreign loans, and "denationalization" of the economy. Pinochet's own popularity peaked in 1978, when a questionably legitimate plebiscite confirmed his leadership and policies. A steadily growing opposition, however, vociferously denied the validity of the vote. In the early 1980s his popularity plummeted as Chile suffered from the world recession, and the government resorted to stricter controls of the press, exile of some dissidents, curfews, and repression characteristic of the early years of Pinochet's rule.

From the beginning of his administration supporters of Pinochet considered him the one figure capable of both controlling the armed forces and politicians and suppressing Marxism. But he also became the figure toward whom the ever growing opposition, ultimately composed of church leaders, labor, politicians, human-rights advocates, centrists, and leftists, would direct its energies. The United States and other foreign governments were cautious in relations with his government until the mid-1980s, when the United States, especially, began to work for a return to democratic government. Throughout his administration he was a resolute opponent of Marxism.

In 1983 opposition leaders organized mass demonstrations against the regime's economic, political, and social programs. Beginning in May of that year, miners, students, workers, and dissident political leaders took to the streets to register their discontent. Pinochet used armed force to quell the demonstrations, then began talks aimed at political compromise. When talks stalled, he again used strong-arm tactics, claiming again that politicians and Marxists were to blame for Chile's problems. He employed such tactics for the rest of the decade.

In 1986 Pinochet survived an attempted assassination with only minor injuries. But by this time the international outcry against his alleged violations of human rights was growing louder week by week. Two years later, with the economy once again on the rebound, his bid to remain president of Chile until 1997 was thwarted when a plebiscite (5 October 1988) repudiated him. He did not run in the presidential election of December 1989 and turned over the sash of office to Patricio AYLWIN AZÓCAR in March 1990.

Following his unprecedented sixteen and a half years in office (the longest term of any chief executive in modern Chilean history), Pinochet retained the post of army commander in chief. He made it clear that he would protect the army's (and his own) institutional (and political) interests in this capacity. Blunt, normally humorless, and always military in bearing, Augusto Pinochet became the new prototype of the Latin American military dictator.

– FREDERICK M. NUNN

PIÑOL Y AYCINENA, BERNARDO

Bernardo Piñol y Aycinena (*b.* 2 November 1806; *d.* 24 June 1881), archbishop of Guatemala (1867–1881). Born in Guatemala, Piñol entered the Franciscan order and became a priest in 1830. After the suppression of religious associations in the 1830s, he joined the secular clergy. He obtained a doctorate in philosophy from the University of San Carlos, where he held a chair and served as rector during the Rafael Carrera presidency.

In 1854 he accepted the bishopric of Nicaragua and served in that post until his appointment as archbishop of Guatemala in 1867. He became embroiled in the church and state conflict after the Liberals assumed power in 1871. His defense of the church against anticlerical writings, his opposition to the government's expulsion of the Jesuits, and his refusal to honor the state's request to issue a pastoral letter calling for an end to Conservative rebellions led to his banishment in 1871 to Havana, Cuba. He remained archbishop of Guatemala until his death, while a series of apostolic administrators governed the archdiocese.

– HUBERT J. MILLER

PIÑOL Y SALA, JOSÉ

José Piñol y Sala (*d.* ca. 1780), a powerful merchant in late colonial Central America. A native of Barcelona, he emigrated to Guatemala in 1752. There he served as the factor of the Real Asiento de Negros, while conducting trade on behalf of his family's Cádiz firm, dealing primarily in slaves and indigo. In 1760 a vessel belonging to his family's company carried over 200,000

In 1760 a vessel belonging to Piñol's family's company carried over 200,000 pesos worth of indigo, roughly one-third of Central American indigo exports for the year.

---

pesos worth of indigo, roughly one-third of Central American indigo exports for the year. Piñol served as *alcalde ordinario* (city magistrate) of Santiago de Guatemala (today Antigua) in 1774, following the devastating earthquakes of 1773, which ultimately prompted the removal of the Central American capital to the present site of Guatemala City. Like many *peninsulares* (natives of Spain) Piñol married into a prominent creole family, the Muñoz clan. His offspring established especially close relations with the powerful Aycinena family—two daughters and a son joined the fellow peninsular clan—and became part of the core of Central America's late colonial and early independence aristocracy.

– RICHMOND F. BROWN

PIÑON, NÉLIDA

Nélida Piñon (*b.* 3 May 1935), Brazilian author. Born in Rio de Janeiro into a family of devout Catholics,

Piñon received a traditional education in Catholic schools. These events may have produced a paradoxical effect in her fictional construct, which possesses a mystical atmosphere while simultaneously challenging religious dogma and tradition.

Many of Piñon's life experiences have found their way, if transformed, into her fiction. At an early age she was sent by her family to spend some time in a village in Galicia, Spain, where her father and his parents had been born. That period became indelible in her literary memory and infused itself into the plot of *A república dos sonhos* (1984; *The Republic of Dreams,* 1989). Interested in ballet and opera, she imbues her fiction with the scenic arts, as in *A força do destino* (1978), a parody of the opera *La Forza del Destino,* and in *A doce canção de Caetana* (1987; *Caetana's Sweet Song,* 1992), which takes as its backdrop an itinerant Brazilian theater group.

Piñon tends to focus her work on unconventional topics, and has experimented with the linguistic possibilities of Portuguese. On both fronts, her literary expressivenes is regarded by critics as compelling, innovative, and resourceful.

— REGINA IGEL

PINTO, JOAQUÍN

Joaquín Pinto (*b.* 18 August 1842; *d.* 1906), Ecuadorian artist. One of the first Ecuadorian artists to paint local landscapes, Pinto was born in Quito and revealed a talent for art at an early age. He studied with Ramón Vargas, Rafael Vanegas, Andrés Costa, Tomás Camacho, Santos Ceballos, and Nicolás Cabrera. He mastered watercolor technique with Juan Manosalvas, who had studied in Rome. Pinto married fellow artist Eufemia Berrío in 1876; they lived at San Roque, an art colony in Quito.

Pinto painted religious and mythological subjects as well as portraits and scenes from daily life. He favored the small format and was influenced by the French artist Jacques Callot. At the suggestion of Bishop González Suárez, he documented the archaeological treasures of Ecuador. From 1903 to 1904 he was director of the Academy of Painting and Drawing in Cuenca and was a founding member of the New National School of Fine Arts in Quito (1904).

— MARTA GARSD

PINTO DÍAZ, FRANCISCO ANTONIO

Francisco Antonio Pinto Díaz (*b.* 1775; *d.* 18 July 1858), patriot general and Liberal president of Chile (1827–1829). An early adherent of the national cause,

Pinto Díaz was sent to Buenos Aires in 1811 as Chilean representative and to England in 1813 on a similarly fruitless mission. Once back in South America, he took part in campaigns in Upper Peru and Peru, returning to Chile in 1824 with the rank of brigadier general. Politics swiftly claimed him: after holding ministerial office (1824–1825), he took over from Ramón FREIRE SERRANO as acting president in May 1827.

Pinto's administration saw the most serious attempt yet made in Chile to consolidate a stable, liberal political order. Important administrative changes were instituted, and a new constitution (drafted with the help of Spanish liberal José Joaquín de Mora) went into effect in August 1828. A year later, at a time of mounting political tension, Pinto resigned, on grounds of ill health. Though reelected president in September 1829, he returned to power for no more than two weeks, sensing that there was no way of stopping the Conservative revolt then under way. The victorious Conservative regime in fact cashiered him in May 1830 in a spiteful measure that was only rescinded nine years later. Pinto Díaz was persuaded to run as the Liberal candidate in the presidential contest of 1841, but there was no chance he would win. In fact, he became largely reconciled to the Conservative regime, during which he served as a senator from 1846 until his death. Both his son-in-law, Manuel BULNES PRIETO, and his son, Aníbal PINTO GARMENDIA, also served as presidents of Chile.

— SIMON COLLIER

PINTO GARMENDIA, ANÍBAL

Aníbal Pinto Garmendia (*b.* 15 March 1825; *d.* 9 June 1884), president of Chile (1876–1881). The son of former president Francisco Antonio PINTO DÍAZ, diplomat and university professor, Pinto served in the Chamber of Deputies, in the Senate, and as minister of war before being elected president in 1876.

Misfortune marked Pinto's tenure in office. Chile's mining economy suffered catastrophic losses because of falling silver and copper prices; alternating drought and floods devastated agriculture; and an overexpansion of credit left all but one of the nation's banks without funds and the country without specie. After traditional methods of resolving the economic crisis proved unsuccessful, Pinto imposed direct taxes on income, gifts, and estates, and changed the tariff law to stimulate the creation of domestic industries.

Economic woes constituted only part of his problems: political infighting as well as conflicts with the Roman Catholic church undermined Pinto's authority. Worse still, in early 1879 a border dispute with Bolivia that was thought to have been settled led to Chile's involvement in the War of the Pacific. Happily, by the time Pinto retired in 1881, the war had turned in Chile's favor. Almost penniless, Pinto spent his last years living on a *fundo* (farm) purchased by public subscription.

— WILLIAM F. SATER

PINZÓN, MARTÍN ALONSO

Martín Alonso Pinzón (*b.* mid-1400s; *d.* ca. 31 March 1493), navigator, captain of the *Pinta.* A shipowner and commercial agent from Palos, on Spain's south Atlantic coast, Martín Alonso and his brother Vicente Yáñez PINZÓN proved invaluable to the success of the first expedition of Christopher COLUMBUS. From the mid-1470s he and his brother commanded trading voyages from Palos to the central Mediterranean, the Canaries, and probably the Guinea coast.

Pinzón piloted the *Pinta* on the 1492 expedition and was instrumental in maintaining discipline among the crew of the three ships, especially those on Columbus's flagship, the *Santa María,* as threat of mutiny increased in the days immediately preceding the sighting of land on 12 October. Off the coast of Hispaniola, however, Pinzón broke ranks and sailed ahead, leaving Columbus behind with his brother Vicente Yáñez to face the tragic shipwreck of the *Santa María.* Pinzón rejoined the principal force after many days' absence, reporting gold and other important discoveries. Columbus chafed, planning to charge him for insubordination after safely returning to Spain.

Columbus sailed back to Spain on the *Niña,* along with Vicente Yáñez. The ships were separated during a terrible storm off the Azores. Pinzón reached port at Bayona in Galicia, while Columbus was driven into Lisbon. Pinzón's son and other family members were in Bayona, returning with goods from Flanders. From there, Pinzón penned a report of the expedition and sent it overland to the Catholic monarchs, then resident in Barcelona. Ill, he set sail for Palos, and by coincidence, arrived the same day (15 March 1493) as Christopher Columbus. Admiral Columbus initiated action against him, but Martín Alonso's death in late March avoided a legal imbroglio. Some suspect that Martín Alonso was one of the first Europeans to fall victim to the New World epidemic—syphilis.

— NOBLE DAVID COOK

PINZÓN, VICENTE YÁÑEZ

Vicente Yáñez Pinzón (*b.* mid-1400s; *d.* ca. August– September 1514), captain of the *Niña* on the first Columbus expedition, "discoverer" of the Amazon River.

A navigator and shipper of the Andalusian port of Palos, Pinzón, along with his brother Martín Alonso PINZÓN, conducted trade from the mid-1470s with ports in the central Mediterranean, Canaries, and probably Guinea. He commanded the *Niña* during the first voyage to America in 1492, and after the loss of the *Santa María,* he acted as pilot, returning to Spain with Christopher COLUMBUS. Conflict between Columbus and Pinzón's brother Martín Alonso led to a break in their relations. The untimely death of Martín Alonso probably caused Pinzón to travel separately to Barcelona, after Columbus, to report to the Catholic monarchs on the fleet's discoveries.

Pinzón commanded the Niña *during the first voyage to America in 1492.*

In 1499 Pinzón received an agreement (6 June) to explore the coast of South America. He left Seville in mid-November, sailing to the Canaries, then to the Cape Verde Islands. Leaving the island of Santiago on 1 January, he reached the Brazilian coast on 26 January 1500. He named the Cape Santa María de la Consolación, and although exact identification is disputed, it was south of the Amazon River. From here, Pinzón explored northerly, tending west, from the mouths of the Amazon to what is now Venezuela, around the Gulf of Paria, where his small fleet united with Diego de LEPE. He returned via Hispaniola, exploring islands off the north coast before reaching Spain on 30 September 1500. He reported to the monarchs in Granada and in September 1501 was granted governorship of the lands he had discovered, but he was unable to conduct a new expedition that year.

In 1504 Pinzón returned to the Brazilian coast, sailing from roughly Recife to the Gulf of Paria, returning this time via Puerto Rico. In 1505 he attended the famous meeting in Toro with other experienced pilots-cosmographers and was authorized to head an expedition to the Spice Islands (not undertaken). He was named *corregidor* as well as *alcaide* of a fortress of San Juan (Puerto Rico) that was to be constructed. In 1508 he was in service in the Casa de Contratación in Seville and was named a "pilot," along with Juan de la Cosa and DÍAZ DE SOLÍS. In 1508–1509 he sailed with Díaz de Solís from Costa Rica past the Yucatán, and perhaps to the middle Gulf Coast of Mexico. Some dispute the exact route of this venture, while others reject the authenticity of the excursion altogether. Pinzón was ill in Seville in March 1514 and died later that year.

— NOBLE DAVID COOK

PITA RODRÍGUEZ, FÉLIX

Félix Pita Rodríguez (*b.* 18 February 1909; *d.* 1988), Cuban poet and short-story writer. Pita Rodríguez was born in Bejucal in the province of La Habana. Somewhat of an adventurer, he traveled through Mexico and Guatemala in 1926 and 1927 as an assistant to a snake-oil salesman. In the 1930s, while traveling through France, Italy, Spain, and Morocco, he wrote poems, which he published in *Revista de Avance.* After returning to Cuba in 1940, he joined the staff of *Noticias de Hoy,* the official publication of the Popular Socialist Party. He also wrote scripts for radio novels and in 1943 was voted best dramatic author of the year by the Radio and Press Association. In 1944 his play *El relevo* opened to much acclaim. He also translated Vietnamese literature from French.

After the Cuban Revolution of 1959, Pita Rodríguez became a full-fledged member of the cultural establishment, serving as a juror for some of its most important literary contests, including those of the Casa de las Américas and the Cuban Union of Artists and Writers (UNEAC). He was also president of UNEAC's literature section.

Among Pita Rodríguez's best-known works are *El relevo* (drama, 1944), *El corcel de fuego* (short stories, 1948), and *Tobías* (short stories, 1955). *Cuentos completos* is a collection of his short stories to 1963.

— ROBERTO VALERO

PITOL, SERGIO

Sergio Pitol (*b.* 18 March 1933), Mexican writer. Born in Puebla, Pitol has published short stories and novels, beginning with the volume *Victorio Ferri cuenta un cuento* (Victorio Ferri Tells a Tale, 1958). His later works include a collection of short stories that received the Premio Xavier Villaurrutía in 1981, *Nocturno de Bujara* (Bujara Nocturne, 1981), and a trilogy of novels: *El desfile del amor* (Love's Parade, 1984), *Domar a la divina garza* (To Tame the Heavenly Heron, 1988), and *La vida conyugal* (Married Life, 1991). His narrative work is associated with the cosmopolitan writings of Inés Arredondo, Juan García Ponce, Juan Vicente Melo, and José de la Colina, authors who contributed to the *Revista Mexicana de Literatura* in the late 1950s and early 1960s and revealed the influence of such foreign writers as Henry James, Thomas Mann, Cesare Pavese, Maurice Blanchot, Georges Bataille, and Pierre Klossowski. Pitol has also held diplomatic positions in Rome, Peking, and, most important, in Warsaw. He has translated into Spanish numerous critical and creative works, especially contemporary Polish literature.

— DANNY J. ANDERSON

PIXINGUINHA

Pixinguinha (Alfredo da Rocha Viana Filho; *b.* 23 April 1889; *d.* 17 February 1973), Brazilian songwriter. Born in the Rio de Janeiro suburb of Piedade, Pixinguinha, whose name was a blending of two childhood nicknames, grew up in a musical atmosphere encouraged by his stepfather, a flutist and collector of traditional *chôros.* Pixinguinha made his first flute recordings soon after initiating his study of the instrument in 1911, and in 1914 performed at Carnival with the Grupo de Caxangá, organized by João Pernambuco. In 1926 he conducted the Cine Rialto orchestra, which accompanied the Companhia Negra de Revista.

In 1928, with the guitarist Donga, Pixinguinha organized the Orquestra Típica Pixinguinha-Donga and recorded one of his most famous samba *chôros,* "Carinhoso" (Darling). One of the high points of his career came in 1930, when Pixinguinha recorded the *chôros* "Agüenta, seu Fulgêncio" (Suffer, Mr. Fulgêncio) and "Urubu e o gavião" (Vulture and the Falcon). Together with "Segura êle" (Hold Him) by Lourenço Lamartine, these songs demonstrate his clear execution and extraordinary ability to improvise. The following year Pixinguinha organized the Grupo da Guarda Velha, uniting some of the greatest Brazilian instrumentalists of the era. In 1945, Mayor Negrão de Lima honored him by naming a street in Olaria, Rio de Janeiro, the Rua Pixinguinha. After Pixinguinha's death in 1973, his body lay in state at the Museum of Image and Sound and was then buried, accompanied by over two thousand mourners singing "Carinhoso."

— LISA MARIĆ

PIZARNIK, ALEJANDRA

Alejandra Pizarnik (Flora Alejandra Pizarnik; *b.* 16 April 1936; *d.* 26 September 1972), Argentine poet. Born in Buenos Aires of Russian Jewish origin, Pizarnik had an intense and difficult life that ended in suicide at age thirty-six. She grew up in Avellaneda, near Buenos Aires, which she left in 1957 to live in Buenos Aires. She studied literature at the University of Buenos Aires, but did not finish. Instead, she began painting under the mentorship of the Argentine artist Juan Battle Planas. Seeking the artistic unity of poetry and painting, she produced in 1955 her first book of poems, *La tierra más ajena,* under the name Flora Alejandra Pizarnik, later to be shortened to Alejandra Pizarnik. *La última inocencia* (1956) included one of her most important compositions, "árbol de Diana." Her third book was *Las aventuras perdidas* (1958). Various feelings of loss (alterity, nostalgia, exile, silence, and orphanhood) became recurring themes in Pizarnik's poetry.

In 1960 Pizarnik moved to Paris, where she lived until 1964. The Parisian experience was hard, both materially and spiritually. She began to fear becoming insane. She confessed in a letter to a friend that she moved between a troubling feeling of wanting to be dead and of wanting to be alive. In 1962 she wrote several critical essays on Antonin Artaud, H. A. Murena, André Breton, Julio CORTÁZAR, Silvina Ocampo, and others in literary magazines of Latin America and Europe: *La Nouvelle Revue Française, Les Lettres Nouvelles, Tempo Presente, Humboldt, Mito, Sur, Diálogos, Temas, Zona Franca, Mundo Nuevo, Imagen,* and *Papeles de Son Armadans.* She also translated poems by Hölderlin, Artaud, Yves Bonnefoy, Aimé CÉSAIRE, Léopold-Sédar Senghor, and others.

In 1962 Pizarnik published *Árbol de Diana,* with an introduction by the Mexican poet Octavio PAZ. The brief but intense poems illustrate the maturity of her poetic thought as well as her tendency toward condensation. Silence and the night now became constants in her poems, as can be seen in *Los trabajos y las noches* (1965). This book signaled a new height in Pizarnik's poetic development.

Pizarnik's father died in 1966 and this intensified her fear of insanity. *Extracción de la piedra de la locura* (1968; Extraction of the Stone of Madness) was the outcome of this period, with its title taken from the Hieronymous Bosch masterpiece. In 1969 she published a *plaquette* of poems in prose, *Nombres y figuras,* with illustrations by Catalonian Antonio Beneyto. In 1969 she received a grant from the Guggenheim Foundation, and in 1972 she was granted a Fulbright scholarship to participate in the International Writers Workshop at the University of Iowa, which she decided not to accept. That same year she published the essay *La condesa sangrienta* (1971; The Bleeding Countess), a recreation of Erzsébet Báthory's life, followed by *Los pequeños cantos* (1971) and *El infierno musical* (1971).

Pizarnik committed suicide by ingesting an overdose of barbiturates. She is considered one of the main poetic voices of Spanish American literature in the twentieth century. Posthumously published works include *El deseo de la palabra* (1975), edited by the author with Antonio Beneyto and Martha I. Moia, and *Textos de sombra y últimos poemas* (1978), edited by Olga Orozco and Ana Becciú.

– MAGDALENA GARCÍA PINTO

PIZARRO, FRANCISCO

Francisco Pizarro (*b.* ca. 1478; *d.* 26 June 1541), conqueror of Peru. Pizarro was born in Trujillo, in Estremadura, Spain, the illegitimate son of the young hidalgo Gonzalo Pizarro and a peasant woman, Francisca González. Never recognized by his father, Pizarro seems to have grown up in the household of his mother or her relatives, although he did visit frequently the home of his grandfather, Hernando Alonso Pizarro. He never received a formal education. As a youth he probably traveled to Italy, where he may have served in the Spanish forces. In 1502 he joined the large fleet of fellow Estremaduran Governor Nicolás de OVANDO that set sail for Hispaniola.

Pizarro experienced a long apprenticeship in the Caribbean area, serving with Alonso de OJEDA in the exploration of the Gulf of Urabá (1509/1510). He helped found Nuestra Señora la Antigua del Darién with Martín Fernández de ENCISO and was a leader of Vasco Núñez de BALBOA's 1513 trek across the Isthmus of Panama in search of the South Sea. He was one of the founders of Panama (1519). He served under Governor Pedro Arias de ÁVILA in other minor expeditions that set out from the isthmus, receiving an *encomienda* for his services to the crown. He acted as lieutenant governor, chief magistrate, and council member of the city of Panama.

Pizarro, along with Diego de ALMAGRO (1480–1538) and cleric Hernando de LUQUE (*d.* 1532), began to plan the exploration of lands along the west coast of South America, rumored to be rich. He was by then one of the most experienced explorers in the Caribbean region. Largely in control of the enterprise, with Almagro securing supplies and recruiting men and Luque providing additional financial backing, Pizarro moved south on the first expedition in 1524. The group, facing contrary winds and currents, reached as far as the territory controlled by the Cacique de las Piedras, with little success.

Pizarro, according to some, took out his sword and drew a line on the sand.

The second expedition, beginning in 1526, ended in near disaster at the Isla del Gallo in 1527. Here, some of Pizarro's men returned to Panama for reinforcements, taking along a secret message calling for the rescue of those remaining. When a ship offering to return the men to Panama appeared, Pizarro, according to some, took out his sword and drew a line on the sand, declaring that all who crossed to the south side of the line and stayed with him would be rewarded with vast riches. The famous "thirteen" of the Isla del Gallo who remained with Pizarro ultimately became the heroes of Peru's conquest. They were transferred to the Isla de la Gorgona, and continued exploration southward. When they reached the city of Tumbes, on the edge of the Inca empire, in 1527, they knew then that their quest would bear fruit. After sailing as far south as the Santa River, they returned to Panama to announce the discovery and exhibited gold objects as proof.

Francisco Pizarro returned to Spain to secure backers and soldiers, as well as authority to continue as leader. The Agreement of Toledo (26 July 1529) placed Pizarro in full control of the venture and alienated Almagro, whose resentment ignited a civil war in Peru. Pizarro returned from Spain with a fleet and recruits, including half brothers Hernando, Juan, and Gonzalo, and other soldiers mostly from Estremadura. Near the end of 1530 the group left Panama. Sailing southward, they reached the Bay of San Mateo, where some of the men disembarked and marched overland, facing difficult conditions; others continued by sea. By early 1532, they were in the city of Tumbes. From there they continued southward and founded the first Spanish city in Peru, which they named San Miguel. On 24 September 1532 Pizarro and a large group set out from San Miguel for the highland city of Cajamarca, where it was rumored the Inca ruler was staying. Pizarro met the Inca leader ATAHUALPA at the central plaza of Cajamarca on 16 November 1532. Friar Vicente de Valverde read the *requerimiento* demanding submission to Spain, and the Inca was handed a religious book, which fell or was thrown to the ground. The Spanish, enraged by the insult, rushed out of hiding and massacred thousands of unarmed retainers, capturing Atahualpa.

The Spanish had in their hands a puppet they could manipulate to control an empire. The tactical maneuver was not unlike the taking of Aztec ruler MOTECUHZOMA by Hernán CORTÉS a few years earlier. In this case, Atahualpa offered to fill a room with gold and silver as ransom. Pizarro accepted, and for several months a vast treasure was collected from all parts of the realm and later distributed among the Spaniards present at Cajamarca; the crown also received a large portion. Rather than release their captive after the gold and silver was amassed, the Spanish charged Atahualpa with planning a surprise attack and executed the Inca ruler on 26 July 1533. Pizarro then marched toward the Inca capital of Cuzco, fighting several skirmishes along the way. He had named another captive member of the royal family, TUPAC AMARU, as Inca, and hoped to rule through him.

There were a number of reasons why a handful of outsiders were able to establish control over a vast empire of up to 14 million people: the recent devastation caused by smallpox; the subsequent civil war between half brothers Atahualpa and HUASCAR; the many ethnic entities of the Andes who were ready to assert independence from the Incas; the superior weaponry and astute

diplomacy of the Spaniards; and the initial hesitation about what type of creatures the outsiders really were (were they gods, Viracocha?). Francisco Pizarro entered the city of Cuzco, established a Spanish municipal corporation, chose officials, and distributed lots and nearby lands to followers. Pizarro also issued grants of Indians (*encomiendas*) as soon as a region was under Spanish control. Cuzco's location, isolated far from the coast at an elevation of about 11,000 feet, made the small number of Spaniards uneasy. An administrative center nearer the north, and the coast, was needed. After a first attempt at highland Jauja, Pizarro founded Lima (18 January 1535) on the central coast. The Spanish conquerors quickly founded other cities and distributed lands, offices, and Indians. Simultaneously, the first Christian missionaries began their work.

In the meantime, the conflict with Diego de Almagro intensified. Almagro reached Cajamarca too late to share in the ransom of Atahualpa. He had received the governorship of New Toledo to the south of Pizarro's jurisdiction, however. Unfortunately, the exact boundaries dividing the territories were imprecise. Almagro was at Cuzco and in 1535 left in search of rumored treasures to the south, in Chile. While the Almagrists were absent, a massive Indian uprising under MANCO INCA broke out; the Inca besieged Cuzco, and even the Spanish in the Lima area suffered major Indian resistance. As the uprising faded away in 1537, Almagro and the survivors of the Chilean fiasco returned and wrenched Cuzco from the Pizarrists. This, however, was only a temporary setback. With cunning diplomacy, military victory at Salinas (6 April 1538), and the execution of Diego de Almagro, Francisco Pizarro secured his position.

During the next three years Pizarro traveled extensively, founding several other Spanish cities. The king even made Pizarro a marquis, but on Sunday, 26 June 1541, a group of malcontents, claiming to act in the name of Diego de Almagro the Younger, broke into the house of Francisco Pizarro in Lima and assassinated him. Several others, including Francisco's half brother, Francisco Martín de Alcántara, was killed in the fray. Francisco Pizarro was survived by four mestizo children: doña Francisca and don Gonzalo by doña Inés Yupanqui Huaylas; and don Francisco and don Juan by doña Angelina Yupanqui.

– NOBLE DAVID COOK

PIZARRO, GONZALO

Gonzalo Pizarro (*b.* ca. 1506; *d.* 10 April 1548), conqueror of Peru and leader of the rebellion of *encomenderos*. Gonzalo, illegitimate son of Captain Gonzalo Pizarro and María de Biedma, was the youngest of the Pizarro brothers. He traveled with the third expedition to the Andes in 1531, was literate, and enjoyed the pastimes associated with the hidalgo: he was a good horseman, an excellent lancer, and a fine marksman. His position was minor during the first years of Peru's conquest, probably because of his youth. He was said to have been with DE SOTO at the interview with ATAHUALPA and accompanied Hernando Pizarro to Pachacamac, just south of Lima. He did receive a large share of Atahualpa's ransom as Francisco Pizarro's half brother and was named to a seat on the Cuzco council when that Inca city became a Spanish municipality.

Gonzalo's military abilities were first recognized during the Indian siege of Cuzco (1536–1537). Named captain of horse, he gained a reputation for brashness and impetuosity. When Hernando Pizarro left for Spain, Francisco began to groom Gonzalo for leadership in Peru. Commander of the expedition into Charcas and founder of La Plata, he received major *encomiendas* in the districts of Charcas, Arequipa, and Cuzco. In 1540 Francisco appointed him governor of Quito, where he organized and directed the famous search for the "Land of Cinnamon." His second in command, Francisco de ORELLANA, was the first European to travel the course of the Amazon River to the Atlantic. Gonzalo marched back to Quito from a base camp on one of the tributaries of the Amazon, suffering great hardship and loss of men, but securing fame as a tenacious leader against tremendous odds.

In Quito, Gonzalo learned of his brother's assassination in Lima and the naming of a new governor, Cristóbal VACA DE CASTRO. Angry and resentful (Francisco had appointed him governor of Peru in his will), Gonzalo retired under protest, by order of Vaca de Castro, to his estates and mines in Charcas. The arrival in 1544 of Peru's first viceroy, Blasco NÚÑEZ VELA, an unbending and arrogant administrator dedicated to the literal enforcement of the New Laws that would have destroyed the power base of the Peruvian *encomenderos*, provided Gonzalo the opportunity he needed. Proclaimed captain-general in city after city, he entered Lima in October 1544. The *audiencia* had already imprisoned the viceroy and sent him back to Spain to face numerous charges. But Blasco Núñez Vela had escaped during the voyage and amassed troops loyal to him and the monarch. After a series of maneuvers, loyalist and rebel forces clashed on 18 January 1546 not far from Quito in the battle of Añaquito (Inaquito), in which the viceroy was killed.

Meanwhile, the crown had sent Pedro de la GASCA with authorization to repeal sections of the New Laws and to reestablish royal authority in the rebellious colony. An adept diplomat, Gasca was able to gradually weaken support for Gonzalo and build an army. He effectively played on the fears and dislikes of Francisco de Carvajal, Pizarro's notorious military commander. After a defeat of the royalists at Huarina (21 October 1547), Gonzalo Pizarro established himself in Cuzco and waited for the forces of Gasca, missing, however, several opportunities to block the southward advance of the royalist army. By the time the two forces met on the plain of Jaquijahuana, not far from Cuzco, Gasca not only had gained a superior force, but, with subtle diplomacy, had suborned Pizarro's men. On 9 April 1548, the greater part of Pizarro's army melted away as he watched. Gonzalo Pizarro surrendered, and the following day he, Carvajal, and forty-eight leaders of the rebellion were executed. His body was interred in the Church of la Merced in Cuzco, while his head was sent to Lima to be nailed to a post and at last put to rest in the Franciscan convent there.

Gonzalo was one of the most attractive of the Pizarro brothers. According to James Lockhart, he "was well proportioned and graceful, with a handsome dark face and a beard that grew black and full as he matured." His death brought to an end the most important of the Peruvian civil wars.

— NOBLE DAVID COOK

PIZARRO, HERNANDO

Hernando Pizarro (*b.* ca. 1503; *d.* 1578), conqueror of Peru. Born in Trujillo, Estremadura, Spain, he was the only legitimate son of Captain Gonzalo Pizarro; his mother was Isabel de Vargas. He received a competent education and entered military service. As a youth he fought alongside his father in the wars in Navarre and then served in Spanish campaigns in Italy. He returned to Spain in 1528 and helped half brother Francisco PIZARRO secure from the crown the famous Agreement of Toledo, which placed Francisco fully in charge of the Peruvian venture. In Trujillo, Hernando helped organize the third expedition, in which all four Pizarro brothers participated.

Hernando's difficulties with Francisco's close associate, Diego de ALMAGRO, first began in Panama and would have grave consequences for both Francisco and Almagro. After helping to found the city of San Miguel, Hernando marched into the highlands of Peru with Francisco Pizarro. Hernando was a member of the first delegation to meet ATAHUALPA at Cajamarca on 6 November 1532, and, after the Inca's imprisonment, he was the one who led the expedition to the shrine of Pachacamac to collect the gold promised as ransom. This first European reconnaissance (5 January to 14

April 1533) of Peru's heartland and the magnificent pyramid of Pachacamac revealed to the outsiders the extent of Inca wealth. Francisco put Hernando in charge of transporting the royal fifth of the treasure from Atahualpa's ransom to Spain, where the wealth of the Incas stimulated the interest of other Europeans. Hernando became a member of the Order of Santiago, and Francisco gained new honors from the crown.

After Atahualpa's imprisonment,

Hernando was the one who led the expedition

to the shrine of Pachacamac to collect the gold

promised as ransom.

Hernando returned to Peru in 1535 and assumed charge of Cuzco, just as the Native American uprising led by MANCO INCA began. Hernando fought with great valor; as the siege at Cuzco was lifted, Diego de Almagro returned from Chile, claimed the city, and jailed Gonzalo and Hernando Pizarro. Gonzalo fled, while Almagro held Hernando captive and negotiated Peru's future with Francisco Pizarro. To win release, Hernando promised to return to Spain, but instead he led an army that destroyed the Almagrists at the battle of Salinas (6 April 1538). Hernando was largely responsible for Almagro's execution in Cuzco.

In July 1539 Hernando returned to Spain via Mexico. He lived briefly in Madrid, then Valladolid, but Almagrists filed charges against him in the Council of the Indies. Ordered imprisoned in the spring of 1540, he was jailed in 1541 in the castle of La Mota in Medina del Campo. He paid heavy fines and remained in prison until 17 May 1561. Throughout his long imprisonment, with the help of able agents, he conducted business in Spain and the Indies. He also maintained ample staff and was allowed female companions. Isabel de Mercado bore him several children, but ultimately he married (1551) his young niece, Francisca (1534–1598), daughter of his brother Francisco and Inca princess Inés Yupanqui Huaylas. They had three boys and two girls. Hernando built a great palace on the main plaza of Trujillo. Urban and rural properties and investments made the family one of the wealthiest in Estremadura, and in 1578 an entailed estate was established. Between July and August 1578, ill and bedridden, nearly blind, and too weak even to sign, Hernando Pizarro modified his will for the last time and soon died.

– NOBLE DAVID COOK

PIZARRO, JOSÉ ALONSO

José Alonso Pizarro (Marqués del Villar; *d.* 1755), viceroy of the New Kingdom of Granada (1749–1753). A respected naval officer, Pizarro received the mantle of viceregal authority from Sebastián de ESLAVA (1740–1749) in Cartagena de Indias in November 1749. Shortly thereafter, Pizarro fell ill in Santa Fe de Bogotá. Because of inadequate medical care, his condition did not improve over the next several months. Consequently, the viceroy began in 1751 to request that he be replaced. The crown acceded to his request two years later and named José SOLÍS FOLCH DE CARDONA (1753–1761) to succeed him.

As an administrator, Pizarro sought to develop the colony and enhance its viability. His policy initiatives focused on developing commerce and mining, colonizing the Magdalena River valley and Santa Marta province, promoting Jesuit evangelization and education, and pacifying the Chimila and Guajiro Indians. He did not leave a *relación de mando* (an official end-of-tenure report). He returned to Spain shortly after stepping down as viceroy.

– LANCE R. GRAHN

PLÁ, JOSEFINA

Josefina Plá (*b.* 1909), Paraguayan artist, dramatist, poet, and historian. Plá is generally considered to be the most influential woman in Paraguayan cultural matters in the twentieth century. Yet she was born not in Paraguay but in Spain's Canary Islands and only came to the inland republic in 1927 after having married the noted sculptor Andrés Campos Cervera (better known as Julián de la Herrería), who died ten years later. She gained fame for her earliest poetry, which was part of the *vanguardista* school and included such pieces as "El precio de los sueños" (1934), "La raíz y la aurora," (1960) and "Invención de la muerte" (1964).

During the 1932–1935 Chaco War with Bolivia, she helped operate a radio theater that presented dramas and comedic pieces to soldiers in the field. As part of this effort, she brought together poets and actors who later came to dominate the Paraguayan literary scene after the conclusion of the war.

As a sculptor and plastic artist, Plá has exhibited works all over South America. Several of her murals and mosaics can be seen on important buildings in today's Asunción. Her historical work includes *El barroco Hispano-guaraní* (1975), *Las artes plásticas en el Paraguay* (1967), and *Los británicos en el Paraguay* (1984).

As of 1992, Doña Josefina still contributed weekly columns on cultural issues to several Asunción newspapers.

– MARTA FERNÁNDEZ WHIGHAM

PLAZA, VICTORINO DE LA

Victorino de la Plaza (*b.* 2 November 1840; *d.* 2 October 1919), president of Argentina (1914–1916). De la Plaza, a native of Cachi, Salta, was a University of Buenos Aires–trained lawyer and a financier. He became president upon the death of Roque SÁENZ PEÑA on 9 August 1914. He had been interim president since September 1913 and had also served for several shorter periods because of the president's ill health. He had been chosen for the vice presidency because of his support for the establishment of fair voting procedures, his ties to the political establishment, and his lack of clear identification with political factions. He had been active in government service, serving three presidents as a cabinet minister.

As president, de la Plaza faced two challenges: World War I and the voting reforms of Sáenz Peña. He maintained Argentine neutrality and attempted to meet a growing economic crisis by taking Argentina off the gold standard. Although not enthusiastic about the reformed electoral code or the Radical Party, he oversaw fair elections that resulted in a Radical victory. De la Plaza died in Buenos Aires.

– JOEL HOROWITZ

PLAZA GUTIÉRREZ, LEONIDAS

Leonidas Plaza Gutiérrez (*b.* 18 April 1865; *d.* 18 September 1932), military figure and president of Ecuador (constitutional, 1901–1905 and 1912–1916). Born in Charapoto, Manabí Province, of Colombian parents, Plaza began a military career at age eighteen. After participating in the failed 1883–1884 liberal uprising in Manabí Province, Plaza escaped to Central America. During the next decade, he served in various administrative positions in El Salvador, Costa Rica, and Nicaragua, and earned an international reputation as a liberal revolutionary. He returned to Ecuador to participate in the liberal revolt that triumphed in August 1895. Plaza remained in Ecuador, and subsequently served as a member of the constituent assembly of 1896–1897, military commander of the coastal provinces, and deputy for Tungurahua Province at the 1900 and 1901 congresses, where he was president of the Chamber of Deputies.

At the end of his first presidential term, Eloy ALFARO selected Plaza as the candidate of the Liberal Party, but subsequently withdrew his support. Plaza, who retained substantial support within the military, won the presidency. The division between the two liberal leaders was one of the major causes of the turbulence of the ensuing decade. During his first administration, Plaza encouraged moderate conservatives to participate in his government, prompting his rivals to accuse the president of betraying liberalism. Plaza was a capable administrator who sought to build consensus, foster respect for civil liberties, including freedom of the press, and develop a secular, activist state. He supported Lizardo García for president in 1905.

Plaza was out of the country when Eloy Alfaro ousted García and convened a constituent assembly to ratify his usurpation of power in 1906. Plaza served as minister of finance in the short-lived government of Emilio Estrada. Estrada's death in December 1911 precipitated a struggle between the alfarista and plazista factions of the Liberal Party. The defeat of Alfaro, and his subsequent murder by a Quiteño mob, allowed the election of Plaza to a second presidential term in 1912. As arbiter of national politics between 1912 and 1925, Plaza used his influence to strengthen political institutions and the peaceful transfer of political power.

– LINDA ALEXANDER RODRÍGUEZ

PLAZA LASSO, GALO

Galo Plaza Lasso (*b.* 17 February 1906; *d.* 28 January 1987), president of Ecuador (1948–1952). The son of the former Liberal president Leónidas PLAZA GUTIÉRREZ, he received his university education in the United States and was named attaché at the Ecuadorian legation in Washington, D.C., in 1929. Upon later returning to Ecuador, he was active as gentleman farmer, diplomat, and politician. He served as minister of defense (1938–1940), ambassador to the United States (1944–1946), and senator from Pichincha (1946–1948). In 1948 he became the presidential candidate of the Movimiento Cívico Democrático Nacional (MCDN). Backed by the Liberal Party and by a group of independents and young professionals, he defeated the Conservative opposition.

Plaza sought a modernization of the economy and expanded the role of the state. His active promotion of the banana industry led to a boom that provided an important new economic resource. Plaza also devoted constant attention to the nurturing of his nation's fledgling democracy, insisting upon the basic importance of constitutional rule. Despite the unbridled partisanship of domestic opponents and the devastating impact of the worst earthquake in the nation's history, he served out his term—the first time in twenty-eight years any leader had served a full term.

Eight years later Plaza sought a second presidential term, once again putting together a coalition that included moderate reformers and progressives. However, he was soundly defeated in 1960 by José María VELASCO IBARRA. Plaza, however, remained one of the nation's most respected figures and was called upon for advice in times of crisis, as when a provisional president had to be named in 1966 following the swift withdrawal of the military junta of the day.

Although his candidacy was marred by a long and cordial relationship with the United States, Plaza was nonetheless chosen as secretary-general of the Organization of American States (OAS); he served two terms before stepping down in 1975. In his later years he was active in such efforts as the Inter-American Dialogue. He continued to espouse the cause of democracy until his death at the age of eighty.

– JOHN D. MARTZ

POBLETE POBLETE DE ESPINOZA, OLGA

Olga Poblete Poblete de Espinoza (*b.* 21 May 1908), Chilean women's rights and peace activist and historian. Poblete received her degree in history, geography, and civic education from the Instituto Pedagógico de la Universidad de Chile in 1929 and held the chair in contemporary history at the Universidad de Chile in 1952–1970. She was active in national and international summer school programs, including the one at Columbia Teachers College, New York, in 1945. Poblete traveled widely on behalf of her work in the international peace movement, cofounded the Movimiento Chileno de Partidarios de la Paz (1949), served as Latin American representative to the World Council of Peace from 1960 to 1966, and was president of the Chilean Peace Committee until 1973. In 1962 she received the Lenin Peace Prize and in 1988 was awarded the Eugenie Cotton Medal from the International Democratic Federation of Women. A member of the Movimiento Pro- Emancipación de la Mujer Chilena (MEMCH), Poblete took over leadership of that organization in 1947. In the early 1980s she joined the efforts of MEMCH83 to coordinate protest against the Pinochet regime.

– CORINNE ANTEZANA-PERNET
FRANCESCA MILLER

POINSETT, JOEL ROBERTS

Joel Roberts Poinsett (*b.* 2 March 1779; *d.* 12 December 1851), first U.S. ambassador to Mexico (1825–1829). In 1822, Poinsett, a native of Charleston, South Carolina, accepted a commission as special agent to Mexico, then ruled by Emperor Agustín de ITURBIDE. He returned to Mexico in May 1825 as U.S. minister plenipotentiary. During these missions he sought, without success, to acquire northern Mexican territory for the United States.

The struggles for influence in Mexico between the U.S. and British ministers were acrimonious. To pro-

vide a counterweight to the Scottish Rite Masonic lodges linked to the British ambassador, Henry George WARD, Poinsett helped to establish and regularize York Rite Masonic lodges in Mexico. After the York Rite Masons organized a successful revolt led by Vicente GUERRERO, Mexican public opinion could no longer tolerate the U.S. ambassador's blatant interference in Mexico's internal affairs. President Guerrero requested that Poinsett be replaced as U.S. minister, and in January 1830 Poinsett returned to the United States.

He was elected U.S. senator in 1836 and named President Martin Van Buren's secretary of war in 1837. He supported the independence and annexation of Texas but opposed the war of 1846–1847. He introduced the Mexican plant called *nochebuena* to the United States, where it is popularly known as poinsettia.

– D. F. STEVENS

POMBAL, MARQUÊS DE (SEBASTIÃO JOSÉ DE CARVALHO E MELLO)

Pombal, Marquês de (Sebastião José de Carvalho e Mello) (*b.* 13 May 1699; *d.* 8 May 1782), Portuguese diplomat and initiator of reforms in Brazil. Pombal, the eldest of twelve children, came from a family of modest gentry who had served as soldiers, priests, and state functionaries within Portugal and occasionally in its extensive overseas empire. He studied law at Coimbra University and served as ambassador to England (1739–1745) and envoy to Austria (1745–1749). His father had served in both the army and the navy, and had been an officer of the court cavalry. An uncle, an archpriest of the Lisbon patriarchy, managed an entailed estate consisting of a mansion on the present-day Rua do Sécolo in Lisbon (Pombal's birthplace) and an estate in Oeiras, a small town overlooking the Tagus estuary near Lisbon. Pombal inherited both properties; and it was at Oeiras, after his return from diplomatic service in Vienna in 1750, that he built an impressive country house and accumulated further landholdings.

Pombal's noble status was not hereditary but a reward for service to the monarch and to the Portuguese state. His background was neither as grand as his title might imply nor as modest as his enemies claimed. In fact, it was much like that of many ministers the absolutist monarchs chose to strengthen their power and enhance that of the state. His honors came late in life: he was made count of Oeiras in 1759 and was granted the title of marquês de Pombal in 1769. During that time he was secretary of state and foreign affairs (1750–1776), which meant he virtually ruled Portugal. In 1777, however, Queen Maria I stripped him of all power.

His brothers Paulo and Francisco were close collaborators in his administration. Paulo, a priest, was elevated to cardinal by Pope Clement XIV and subsequently became inquisitor general and president of the Municipal Council of Lisbon (a post to which Pombal later appointed his eldest son, Henrique, following the death of Paulo). Francisco served as governor and captain general of the Brazilian provinces of Grão Pará and Maranhão (an area that essentially covered the vast Amazon Basin); later, in Lisbon, Pombal appointed him secretary of state for the overseas dominions. Since neither Francisco nor Paulo married, they pooled their financial resources and property in Pombal's interest.

– KENNETH MAXWELL

POMPÉIA, RAÚL

Raúl Pompéia (*b.* 12 April 1863; *d.* 25 December 1895), Brazilian writer. Pompéia was born in Angra dos Reis, in Rio de Janeiro State. He lived a very solitary and repressed life, having to yield constantly to his parents' strict and exigent ways. A kind soul, he also possessed a depressed and morbid personality, having gone through many existential conflicts throughout his entire life. He committed suicide, by shooting himself in the heart, at the age of thirty-two.

A kind soul, Pompéia possessed a depressed and morbid personality, having gone through many existential conflicts during his life.

Upon his family's relocation to the city of Rio de Janeiro, Pompéia was sent to the Abílio Boarding School, run by the baron of Macaubus, where he experienced neglect and abuse at the hands of school officials and classmates. Most of his critics agree, however, that while attending this school Pompéia found the inspiration to write his realist-naturalist, existentialist masterpiece *O Ateneu,* published in 1888. This novel inspired authors from all over the world, including Sartre in his *Huis-clos* (1944; *No Exit,* 1947). Through his limited literary production, Pompéia captured the psychological agonies of modern man and expressed them in a literary discourse that was universal in nature. His other works include *Uma tragédia no Amazonas* (1880), his first novelistic essay, published in the newspaper *Gazeta de Notícias; Canções sem metro* (1881), prose poems; and *As joias da coroa* (1883), also published in *Gazeta de Notícias* in 1882.

– ROSÂNGELA MARIA VIEIRA

PONCE, MANUEL

Manuel Ponce (*b.* 8 December 1886; *d.* 14 April 1948), composer and pianist, born in Fresnillo, Mexico. Ponce studied at the National Conservatory in Mexico City, at Liceo Rossini in Bologna, and the Stern Conservatory in Berlin. He taught piano at the Mexican Conservatory (1909–1915 and 1917–1922), founded the periodical *Revista Musical de México* (1919), and directed the National Symphony Orchestra briefly in 1917. He spent a year as professor of folk music at the National Free University of Mexico (1933–1934), promoting Mexican criollo and mestizo music and the native Cuban music he absorbed during his stay there from 1915 to 1917. In Paris (1925– 1933) he worked with Paul Dukas and founded the music journal *Gaceta Musical;* after returning to Mexico he published the journal *Cultura Musical.* He served brief terms as director of the National Conservatory and of the music department of the Free University. Ponce's music reveals, in addition to native influences, leanings toward the impressionism of Debussy, Ravel, and Dukas. His best-known composition remains the popular song "Estrellita," but he is also known for his Mexican symphonic poem *Chapúltepec* (1921), a violin concerto, and salon pieces for solo piano.

– ROBERT L. PARKER

PONCE DE LÉON, FIDELIO

Fidelio Ponce de Léon (*b.* 24 January 1895; *d.* 19 February 1949), Cuban painter. Born in Camagüey, Ponce attended the National School of San Alejandro, where he fell under the influence of Leopoldo Romañach. Ponce had an artist's temperament and refused to work on subjects that did not interest him. He disappeared from public record in 1918 but reappeared in 1923 in Havana, where he lived cheaply and gave art lessons to poor children. As part of the burgeoning Cuban vanguard movement in the 1930s, Ponce began to exhibit his works and won a prize at the national salon of 1935 for his painting *Las beatas.* Typical of Ponce's style are pale colors, a fascination with light, and melancholy reflection on the animalistic nature of the human race. Unfortunately, his work suffers from deterioration and age and has lost much of its original brilliance.

– KAREN RACINE

PONCE DE LEÓN, JUAN

Juan Ponce de León (*b.* ca. 1460; *d.* July 1521). Spanish soldier, governor of San Juan, and leader of the first Spanish expedition to La Florida. He explored the island colony of San Juan (Puerto Rico) beginning in 1508 and served as its governor in 1509–1511.

Ponce de León was born in San Tervás del Compo, Valladolid, Spain. In 1512 he received a royal charter to explore and settle Bimini, an island rumored to be north of the Lucayos (Bahamas). He set sail from Puerto Rico in March 1513 on a course through the Bahamas that took him to the east coast of Florida. Because his arrival coincided with the Feast of Flowers (Easter Holy Week), he named the land La Florida. Ponce then sailed southward past Cape Canaveral and what is now Miami before rounding the Florida Keys and traveling up the Gulf coast to Charlotte Harbor and perhaps beyond. His was the first sanctioned Spanish voyage to the mainland of the United States.

In 1521 Ponce returned to Florida to establish a colony. That attempt failed when the Spaniards were driven off by native peoples and Ponce received a fatal wound.

– JERALD T. MILANICH

PONCE ENRÍQUEZ, CAMILO

Camilo Ponce Enríquez (*b.* 31 January 1912; *d.* 14 September 1976), president of Ecuador (1956–1960). A member of a traditional highland family, Ponce received his law degree from the Central University in Quito in 1938 and soon combined politics with his legal career. Conservative in outlook, he founded the Movimiento Social Cristiano (MSC) in 1951. It was to be his personal political vehicle for the next three decades.

After serving as the key minister to José María VELASCO IBARRA during the latter's third term as president (1952–1956), Ponce became the rightist candidate in 1956 and won a disputed victory by a bare 3,000 votes. The first Conservative president since 1895, Ponce survived his term despite a weak political base, economic difficulties, and bitter opposition from labor, which was subdued by stern police action. Eight years after leaving office Ponce sought his second term, running under the Alianza Popular label at the head of a rightist coalition. He finished third in a tight race that was won by Velasco.

Ponce remained influential as an elder statesman in later years and never relinquished hopes of returning to office once again. However, the intrusion of the military into politics in 1972 helped thwart these hopes. He gradually withdrew from politics, and by the time of his death in 1976 his personalist party had reorganized as the Partido Social Cristiano.

– JOHN D. MARTZ

PONIATOWSKA, ELENA

Elena Poniatowska (*b.* 19 May 1932), Mexican writer and journalist. A direct descendant on her father's side of the last king of Poland, Estanislau Poniatowski, and on her mother's side of an aristocratic Mexican family, Elena Poniatowska is a passionate advocate of dispossessed segments of Mexican society and of the democratic movement in her adopted country.

After moving from Paris, where she was born, to Mexico in 1942, she attended the Convent of the Sacred Heart in Torresdale, Pennsylvania, and then a secretarial academy in Mexico City. She was hired by the newspaper *Excelsior* in 1954 and quickly gained recognition for her innocent yet penetrating interviews of celebrities and her prizewinning political and social chronicles.

Poniatowska joined the ranks of Mexico's leading contemporary writers with the publication of *Hasta no verte Jesús mío* (1969), a testimonial narrative based on the oral history of Josefina Bórquez, a feisty washerwoman who participated in the Mexican Revolution and then struggled to survive in the shantytowns of Mexico City, and *La noche de Tlatelolco* (1971; *Massacre in Mexico,* 1975) a masterful oral-history collage of the student movement of 1968 and its brutal repression. Other major works include *Querido Diego, te abraza Quiela* (1978; *Dear Diego,* 1986), an epistolary novel based on actual letters of the painter Angelina Beloff to the husband who had abandoned her, Diego RIVERA; *Fuerte es el silencio* (1980), social chronicles; *Nada, nadie: Las voces del temblor* (1988), a testimonial narrative of the 1985 earthquake; and *La "Flor de Lis"* (1988), an autobiographical novel.

– CYNTHIA STEELE

POPENOE, FREDERICK WILSON

Frederick Wilson Popenoe (*b.* 9 March 1892; *d.* 20 June 1975), Honduran agriculturalist. Born in Topeka, Kansas, Wilson Popenoe accompanied his father at an early age to Central America and had a long career in the scientific development of the region's agricultural resources. Early in the twentieth century he was instrumental in promoting U.S. avocado production from Mexican budwood. From 1913 to 1925 he was a plant explorer in Latin America for the U.S. Department of Agriculture. Beginning in 1925 he established the United Fruit Company's Agricultural Research Station and botanical garden at Lancetilla, near Tela, Honduras. In 1941 he founded, in collaboration with Samuel ZEMURRAY and the United Fruit Company, the Escuela

Agrícola Panamericana at Zamorano, Honduras, which Popenoe directed until his retirement in 1957.

Popenoe was also an active promoter of Central American culture, and was, for example, responsible for bringing the great Honduran primitivist painter José Antonio VALÁSQUEZ to world attention. He and his wife also restored a beautiful colonial house in Antigua, Guatemala, the Casa Popenoe, which is still a major tourist attraction there. Popenoe published extensively on tropical horticulture and other subjects from 1911 to 1971.

— RALPH LEE WOODWARD, JR.

PORRAS, BELISARIO

Belisario Porras (*b.* 1856; *d.* 1942), Panamanian politician and three-time president (1912–1916, 1918–1920, 1920–1924). One of the most popular figures in Panama's history, Porras was born in Las Tablas. He headed the Liberal revolution in 1901, but he opposed Panamanian independence in 1903 under U.S. auspices, fearing that Panama would become a colony of the United States. As a result, he was stripped of his citizenship for one year (15 November 1905–13 September 1906).

Porras opposed Panamanian independence under U.S. auspices, fearing that Panama would become a colony of the United States.

He remained in Panama City for a while, but as his enemies made his life more and more difficult, he moved to Colón and later to his ranch in his native Las Tablas, where he remained until his rights were reinstated. He was first elected president in 1912. In 1918, with the death of his successor, Ramón Maximiliano Valdés, Porras, as first vice president, assumed the presidency once again to finish Valdés's term amid charges of fraud. The United States intervened to maintain order. In 1920 he was elected to another term.

Porras was a populist leader with both an urban and a rural following. He maintained his leadership through the system of *compadrazgo*. It was believed that he had as many as 757 *compadres* throughout the country.

Porras helped to build modern Panama. He organized a civil registry, the national archives, and the national bank; built the Chiriquí Railroad; and nationalized the lottery. On 6 November 1913, Porras had organized a national commission for the drafting of a Panamanian legal code. Prior to his election, the country was still governed by Colombian law. The commission included people like Carlos Antonio MENDOZA, Harmodio ARIAS, and Ricardo J. ALFARO. Its work was completed in 1916 when by Law 1 of 22 August 1916, the Administrative Code was approved. Law 2 of 22 August 1917 approved the penal, commercial, mining, civil, and judicial codes.

— JUAN MANUEL PÉREZ

PORRAS, DIEGO

Diego Porras (also Porres; *b.* 19 November 1677; *d.* 25 September 1741), Guatemalan architect. The most important architect in the kingdom of Guatemala during the first half of the eighteenth century, Porras won renown for designing and building the monastery and church of the Escuela de Cristo, the Santa Clara convent and church, the Archbishop's Palace, the Royal Mint, the San Alejo Hospital, and the City Hall, all monuments in Antigua, Guatemala. He helped design the following churches: Los Remedios, San Agustín, the Cathedral, la Recolección, Santa Teresa, and la Compañía de Jesús in Antigua, and the well-known church of Esquipulas, the Church of Concepción in Ciudad Vieja, and the churches in Patzicía and Escuintla.

Porras also was in charge of hydraulic engineering and planning. Under his direction, water was brought to the towns of San Bernardino Patzún and to San Juan Comalapa. He was the architect for the famous siren fountain in the central plaza in Antigua. In addition, he is credited with being the first architect in Guatemala to use the serliana balustered pilaster.

— JANE EDDY SWEZEY

PORRAS, JOSÉ BASILIO

José Basilio Porras (*b.* 14 June 1794; *d.* 9 November 1861), Guatemalan politician. Born in Guatemala City, Porras was the illegitimate son of Micaela Porras, from a notable creole family, and Mario Álvarez de las Asturias y Arroyve. A prosperous indigo merchant and owner of a printing business, he also rose to the rank of colonel in the army. Porras was a leading proponent of independence from Spain in 1821, and he thereafter served in both federal and state legislatures and in several other government positions, and briefly as minister of war in 1848–1849. Although a liberal ideologically, he served both liberal and conservative governments until 1849, when he retired from public life. Unlike many liberal politicians, Porras remained in Guatemala throughout the CARRERA dictatorship.

— RALPH LEE WOODWARD, JR.

PORRAS BARRENECHEA, RAÚL

Raúl Porras Barrenechea (*b.* 23 March 1897; *d.* 27 September 1960), one of the most important historians of the Peruvian colonial period. Born in the coastal city of Pisco, Porras studied at San Marcos in the Faculty of Letters (1912–1915). From 1915 to 1922 he read law at the same university and was one of the leaders of the Student University Reform Movement (1919). Porras also published several essays and shorter works during this period. From 1922 to 1926 he was librarian at the Ministry of Foreign Relations. Interested in Peru's claims in boundary disputes with Bolivia, he published many documents in defense of those claims. In 1928 he received a doctorate in history at San Marcos and began teaching history the following year.

Porras focused his attention on the primary accounts of the early Andean world, the chroniclers, the biography of Francisco PIZARRO, the Quechua legacy, the era of the Spanish conquest, and liberalism in the early republic. In 1945 his *Los cronistas del Perú* won the Inca Garcilaso de la Vega Prize for history, and it has since been used by generations of Peruvianists.

Porras, a well-respected teacher, also had a distinguished diplomatic career in Europe. His most important writings include: *Historia de los límites del Perú* (1926); *El Congreso de Panamá, 1826* (1930); *El testamento de Pizarro* (1936); *Las relaciones primitivas de la conquista del Perú* (1937); *Cedulario del Perú (1529–1534)*, 2 vols. (1944, 1948); *El Inca Garcilaso de la Vega (1539–1616)* (1946); *Crónicas perdidas, presuntas y olvidadas sobre la conquista del Perú* (1951); *Fuentes históricas peruanas* (1954); *El Inca Garcilaso en Montilla (1561–1614)* (1955); and *Cartas del Perú (1524–1543)* (1959).

– NOBLE DAVID COOK

PORRES, MARTÍN DE

Martín De Porres (*b.* 9 December 1579; *d.* 3 November 1639), Peruvian saint. Porres was the son of a union between Juan de Porres, knight of the Order of Calatrava, and Ana Velázquez, his black servant from Panama. At first the father failed to recognize his son or daughter Juana. He did so later, and took Martín to Guayaquil to be educated. When Juan de Porres was named governor of Panama, he returned with his children to Lima to get orders from the viceroy. There, the young Martín was confirmed by Archbishop Alfonso de Toribio de Mogrovejo. Juan de Porres left the boy in the care of his mother when he traveled to Panama to assume office.

Apprenticed to a surgeon at the age of twelve, Martín learned the basics of healing. He worked in the store of Mateo Pastor, who sold spices and medicinal herbs, and served the barber-bleeder Marcelo Rivero. Entering the Dominican convent in Lima at age fifteen as lay helper, he professed as a lay brother of the Dominican order on 2 June 1603. He experienced visions and ecstasies, did penance, and at the same time achieved renown for his healing powers and ability to control animals. Moreover, he gained fame for charity and humility. According to one observer, there was "a flood of beggars always awaiting him at the entrance of the convent."

Martín's funeral was attended by a mass of people; the archbishop and viceroy carried his bier. In 1668 there began a long apostolic process that would ultimately lead to canonization. In 1763 his virtues were declared "heroic." He was beatified in 1837; and finally, on 6 May 1962, Pope John XXIII canonized him. The popular festival of San Martín de Porres is celebrated on 3 November.

– NOBLE DAVID COOK

PORTALES PALAZUELOS, DIEGO JOSÉ PEDRO VÍCTOR

Diego José Pedro Víctor Portales Palazuelos (*b.* 15 June 1793; *d.* 6 June 1837), Chilean political leader and architect of his nation's political stability. Portales was one of more than twenty-three children of a Spanish colonial official who directed the mint. Originally destined for the church, he switched to more secular pursuits. A graduate of the University of San Felipe, he abandoned the study of law to become an assayer in the mint.

Both of Portales's parents participated in the struggle for independence and suffered for their political beliefs: his father was exiled to the Pacific island of Juan Fernández and his mother incarcerated. In 1819, Portales married his first cousin, Josefa Portales y Larraín, who died two years later. Her death, as well as that of his infant son, deeply affected Portales, who went through a religious crisis, vowing never to marry again. Although Portales's religious fervor subsequently subsided, he never did remarry. Still, while he eschewed matrimony, it is clear that he did not lead a celibate life.

After these events, Portales moved to Peru, where in 1821 and 1822 he established a business in partnership with José Manuel Cea. This experience apparently was pivotal in shaping Portales's political philosophy. Peru's political environment became so chaotic that Portales had to close his business, at great personal cost. In 1824 he returned to Chile, where he and Cea purchased from the government a concession giving them the exclusive right to sell tobacco, playing cards, and liquor. However, the same problems that had plagued Portales in Peru dogged his footsteps in Chile: domestic violence made it impossible for him to make a profit from his government concession. For a second time, political turmoil cost Portales his investment.

Portales concluded that because Latin America's citizens lacked the requisite civic culture or education, its countries could not function under democracy.

Portales concluded that because Latin America's citizens lacked the requisite civic culture or education, its countries could not function under democracy. He felt that years would pass before the Latin nations would be ready for this form of government. Not surprisingly, Portales concluded that Chile desperately needed internal order if it were to survive and prosper. Hence, he became involved in a political bloc called the *estanqueros,* which advocated the creation of a strong central government that would guarantee property rights and restore domestic stability. Portales allied himself with the Conservatives, who defeated the Liberal forces at the 1830 battle of Lircay. This victory provided Portales with the opportunity to implement his ideas.

Portales feared and loathed the prospect of political instability. Consequently, he worked strenuously to ensure that the government possessed the necessary political powers. He backed the 1833 Constitution, which virtually delivered control of the nation's political system to the oligarchy. Moreover, he moved to eradicate his political opposition, depriving the supporters of Bernardo O'HIGGINS and the old Liberals of their power and, in some cases, their lives. Portales also purged the army of any officers who might possibly threaten the government, founded a military academy to train professional—and, hopefully, apolitical—subalterns, and created a national guard, which could, in an emergency, subdue military conspirators. Although he was not religious, he gave the Catholic church a privileged position, even requiring government officials to attend mass in return for the church's support of his regime.

Few of Portales's innovations were unique, but unlike his contemporaries he went one step further—to create a disinterested government of laws rather than a personal dictatorship. Portales struck a Faustian bargain with the nation's oligarchy: the same constitution that granted the aristocrats control of the government also expected them to obey the laws they had enacted. Once established, this principle, backed up by the government's bayonets, ensured order, out of which perhaps prosperity might come.

Consistent with Portales's ideas was his desire to limit partisan activity to a minimum, not because he personally lusted for power but because, like Henry VIII, he saw bending the rules as a means of guaranteeing political order. Presidential campaigns, Portales rightly believed, revived vendettas which the recently established republic could not withstand. Hence, he insisted that President Joaquín PRIETO remain in office rather than subject Chile to a campaign which, he correctly feared, would plunge the nation into the maelstrom of civil war.

Although Portales wielded enormous power, he never held elective office, preferring to be Prieto's *éminence grise.* He did serve in various capacities, including minister of the interior, the second most important position after president, and as minister of war, navy, and foreign relations, as well as governor of Valparaíso. Portales never actively sought office. Indeed, in 1833 he quit public service to retire to his hacienda, *El Rayado.* There he remained in touch with the government, which often consulted him.

In September 1835, when a struggle between ministers Joaquín TOCORNAL and Manuel RENGIFO threatened to disrupt the national political balance, Portales reentered public life, first as minister of war and the navy and then as minister of the interior and foreign relations. For all intents and purposes, Portales was running Chile. But as before, he preferred to remain outside the seat of power, from where he choreographed Prieto's reelection to the presidency.

While he was politically innovative, Portales did not deviate substantially from his predecessors' economic policies. Fortunately for Chile, the War for Independence did not damage the nation's mines, located in the north. Consequently, this most valuable of Chile's natural resources continued to contribute mightily to the economy. Gold production slowed, but silver mining, fueled by discoveries at Chañarcillo, increased by 60 percent in the period of 1830 to 1840, while the output of copper almost doubled. The mining of these metals attracted substantial foreign investment, which provided the state with substantial revenues.

In conjunction with the Minister of Hacienda Pública, Manuel Rengifo, Portales developed Valparaíso into the hemisphere's premier port on the Pacific. In order to attract international shipping en route to the Orient and the Pacific coast of the Western Hemisphere, the state spent large sums improving Valparaíso's facilities, building new wharfs as well as secure warehouses. An 1832 law permitted the storage of cargoes in Valparaíso, at very low tax rates, for up to three years. A combination of innovative laws and modern facilities made Valparaíso the ideal place for merchant vessels to drydock for repairs and to revictual. The government also modernized the ports of Coquimbo and Huasco. In addition, it promulgated a new *aduana* (customs) code, which attempted to encourage the creation of a merchant marine and reserved coastal traffic to Chilean nationals.

If not an economic innovator, Portales did forge new foreign policy goals for Chile. Officially, he stated that Chile, while zealously defending its sovereignty, would remain aloof from hemispheric squabbling. In fact, however, Portales seemed willing to impose Chile's will on its neighbors, as its national motto stipulated, either "by reason or force." Fundamentally, Portales sought to ensure that no hemispheric nation could threaten Chile's territorial integrity. Consequently, he disdained the United States and its Monroe Doctrine, warning all his Hispanic neighbors to beware of Washington's evil intentions.

The creation of the Peru–Bolivia Confederation in 1836 by Bolivia's General Andrés SANTA CRUZ threatened Portales's vision of the Pacific. Clearly, this new nation, whose combined land mass and population dwarfed that of Chile, posed a potential military threat to the government in Santiago. Moreover, the confederation early on demonstrated an unhealthy independence, one example of which was the Santa Cruz government's abrogation of an 1835 treaty granting Chilean wheat access to Peru's markets. Worse still was Santa Cruz's wish to restore the port of Callao to its colonial preeminence. In pursuit of this goal he imposed special taxes on all imports entering the confederation via Valparaíso. Clearly, the Bolivian leader, whom Portales deprecated for being an "Indian," was challenging Valparaíso's attempt to secure commercial hegemony. Fearful that Chile's northern neighbor might eventually turn on it, Portales launched a preemptive war in December 1836 to destroy the confederation before it could jeopardize Chile's economic and political domination of the region.

The onset of this unpopular conflict—the masses did not want to serve in the army and had to be impressed into the military—threatened to destroy Portales's government. Political conspirators hoped to take advantage of the popular discontent to overthrow the government of Joaquín Prieto. Portales responded by organizing flying courts-martial, which tried and executed individuals suspected of plotting against the regime. This tactic had only limited success. A mutinous army unit captured Portales after he had come to visit the garrison at Quil-

lota. The rebels took Portales to Valparaíso, where they hoped to entice other military units to join in a revolt. When the loyal garrison refused, the rebels murdered Portales, mutilating his body with more than thirty stab wounds and stripping him of his clothes, which they divided among themselves.

The political system that he established survived Portales's death. Though harsh, this form of government imposed the order necessary for economic development and progress. Thus, while other Latin American nations seemed convulsed in internal upheavals, Chile, largely thanks to Diego Portales, prospered.

– WILLIAM F. SATER

PORTER, LILIANA

Liliana Porter (*b.* 6 October 1941), Argentine artist. Since the late 1960s, Porter has created prints, paintings, and wall installations in which she explores the relationships between illusion, artistic representation, and reality—a theme that has captivated many Argentine artists and writers. (Her major influences include the writer Jorge Luis BORGES and the artist René Magritte.) Born in Buenos Aires, she studied printmaking at the Universidad Iberoamericana, Mexico City, in 1960; she graduated from the Escuela Nacional de Bellas Artes, Buenos Aires, in 1963. A year later Porter moved to New York City, where she attended the Pratt Graphic Art Center. In 1965 she, Luis CAMNITZER, and José Guillermo Castillo founded the New York Graphic Workshop, where she began to create prints utilizing the techniques of photoetching and photo–silk screen. She simultaneously became a member of the conceptual art movement. Though still a prolific printmaker, Porter has produced numerous mixed-media paintings since the early 1980s. Porter lives in New York City.

– JOHN ALAN FARMER

PORTES GIL, EMILIO

Emilio Portes Gil (*b.* 3 October 1890; *d.* 10 December 1978), president of Mexico (1928–1930). The youngest person to become president of Mexico in the twentieth century, Portes Gil was the first of three Mexicans to serve out a six-year term won by General Álvaro OBREGÓN, who was assassinated before he could take office in 1928. A favorite of President Plutarco ELÍAS CALLES, he was selected by Congress to serve as interim president while new elections were held in 1929. Although many historians consider him to have been subservient to Calles during his brief administration, he pursued many of his own policies. He is best remembered for having settled a university strike that led to the autonomy of the National University in 1929, and even more so for secretly negotiating the resolution of the violent civil war between church and state known as the Cristero Rebellion, thereby paving the way for the church-state relationship that has lasted up to the 1990s.

A native of Ciudad Victoria, Tamaulipas, Portes Gil attended the National University before joining with fellow students to form the Free School of Law in 1912, from which he graduated in 1915. He worked for the department of military justice before becoming a member of the Chamber of Deputies from 1917 to 1918, a post he held again in 1920 and 1924. He became governor of his home state in 1925, and continued to influence politics there well into the 1950s. During the administrations of his two successors, he served as ambassador to France and to the League of Nations, and in 1932 became attorney general of Mexico. When Lázaro CÁRDENAS became president in 1934, Portes Gil served in his first cabinet as secretary of foreign relations. An important leader of the National Revolutionary Party, he served twice as its president, initially in 1930 and then from 1935 to 1936. He held a number of minor or ambassadorial posts until 1970, having achieved the stature of a senior statesman.

– RODERIC AI CAMP

PORTILLO, EFRAÍN

Efraín Portillo (*b.* 18 December 1941), Honduran modernist painter and sculptor. Born to a poor family in Choluteca, Portillo demonstrated extraordinary artistic talent, which won him a scholarship in 1966 to study at the Academy of Fine Arts in Rome. Portillo's creative style has combined Honduran and Italian influences in a unique expression that joins the abstract with realism. Portillo's work is characterized by geometric forms and straight, parallel black lines, but thematically Portillo reaches back to Honduras's Maya heritage in its emphasis on human and religious forms. A frequent winner of prizes in European and American exhibitions, together with other noted Honduran painters—including Benigno GÓMEZ, Joel Castillo, Mario Padilla, and César Rendón—he has initiated programs to encourage and assist younger Honduran painters.

– RALPH LEE WOODWARD, JR.

PORTINARI, CÂNDIDO TORQUATO

Cândido Torquato Portinari (*b.* 29 December 1903; *d.* 6 February 1962), Brazilian genre painter. Born in Bródosqui, São Paulo, the second of twelve children of Italian immigrants, Portinari was raised in an impoverished working-class environment. His experiences as a youth

on coffee and cotton plantations made him aware of the harshness of plantation work.

Considered by many to be the only Latin American painter outside Mexico able to create a national epic through his work, Portinari revealed an interest in painting at an early age, while assisting in the decoration of a local church. At fifteen, he began study at the National School of Fine Arts in Rio de Janeiro. In 1928, he received an award from the National Salon that enabled him to travel and study in Europe, where he was influenced by the works of Pablo Picasso, Marc Chagall, and Joan Miró.

In the 1930s Portinari, known as a social realist painter, was involved in an art movement in which Latin American social themes and a rejection of European forms predominated. Using both mural and easel painting, he concentrated on depicting the harsh working conditions and poverty of the coffee plantation workers and miners. His first international recognition came in 1935 with the exhibition of a painting titled *Coffee* at the Carnegie International Exhibition in Pittsburgh. Having won second prize at the exhibition, the painting established Portinari in the art world. Combining traditionalism, lyricism, realism, and nationalism, his portraits of both common people (like *The Mestizo*) and Brazilian celebrities (like poet Olegário

Cândido Torquato Portinari. (Iconographia)

Mariano) reflected a keen awareness of the ethnic diversity in Brazilian society.

In 1941 he was commissioned by the Hispanic Foundation of the U.S. Library of Congress to produce four murals titled *Discovery of the New World.* The individual murals were *Discovery of the Land, The Entry into the Forest, The Teaching of the Indians,* and *The Mining of Gold.* Two of his most significant projects were completed in 1945: the *Way of the Cross* murals for Brazil's first modern church, the Church of São Francisco in Pampulha, and the *Epic of Brazil* murals for the Ministry of Education and Health Building in Rio de Janeiro, which depicted the cultivation of sugarcane, tobacco, cotton, coffee, and rubber; cattle raising; and gold prospecting. He completed the *War and Peace* murals for the United Nations Building in New York City in 1953, and in 1957, he received the Guggenheim National Award. In 1961 he returned to Rio de Janeiro, where he died the following year from paint poisoning.

— MARY JO MILES

PÔRTO ALEGRE, MANUEL ARAÚJO

Manuel Araújo Pôrto Alegre (*b.* 29 November 1806; *d.* 29 December 1879), Brazilian painter, poet, and playwright. In 1827, soon after arriving in Rio de Janeiro from his home province of Rio Pardo, Pôrto Alegre enrolled in the Brazilian Imperial Academy of Fine Arts. He studied under the French history painter Jean-Baptiste Debret, who had come to Brazil in 1816 as part of the French artistic mission. After studying painting in Paris for five years, Pôrto Alegre returned to Rio de Janeiro, where he was appointed the academy's professor of history painting.

In 1840, the year of PEDRO II's acclamation, Pôrto Alegre was named official court painter and produced court portraits and canvases depicting important imperial events. In 1854 Pôrto Alegre was appointed the academy's fifth—and first Brazilian-born—director. That same year, as part of Pedro II's program to encourage nationalism and overhaul imperial cultural and economic institutions, the emperor asked his new director to carry out a thorough reform of the academy. But in 1857, with a new organizational structure in place, Pôrto Alegre resigned. He blamed irreconcilable differences with the academic faculty and imperial ministers. He spent the last years of his life as a foreign diplomat.

In addition to his artistic contributions, Pôrto Alegre was also a celebrated poet, journalist, and playwright. His most important literary work was a poem about the discovery of America, entitled *Columbo.* Emperor Pedro II conferred on him the title of *barão* in 1874.

— CAREN A. MEGHREBLIAN

PORTOCARRERO, RENÉ

René Portocarrero (*b.* 24 February 1912; *d.* 7 April 1986), Cuban artist. Born on the outskirts of Havana, Portocarrero was a child prodigy, mostly self-taught, except for a brief period of study at the Academy of San Alejandro in Havana. Initially he painted domestic interiors, later incorporating images of Cuban festivities and religious practices. Socially conscious, he taught drawing to prison inmates and claimed to have been influenced by them. Critics characterized Portocarrero's style as "baroque" for its exuberant ornamentation and multiple-foci compositions, characteristics that reached a peak in his painting between 1946 and 1947. In 1956 he worked on a series of imaginary urbanscapes reminiscent of Havana, and won the national prize for painting at the Eighth National Salon of Painting and Sculpture in Cuba. Four years later he helped found the National Union of Sculptors and Artists of Cuba. He worked on *The Color of Cuba,* scenes of Carnival celebrations on the island (1962–1963), for which he received the International Samba Prize at the Seventh Biennial in São Paulo, Brazil, in 1963. He painted a series called *Portraits of Flora,* emblematic images of a Cuban woman (1966) and executed several murals in public buildings throughout Cuba.

Portocarrero received the Félix Varela Order from the Cuban government in 1981 and was awarded the Aztec Eagle from the Mexican government the following year. He illustrated several of José LEZAMA LIMA's books as well as publications such as *Orígenes, Carteles, Bohemia, Revolución y cultura, Signos, Islas, La gaceta de Cuba,* and *Juventud rebelde.*

— MARTA GARSD

PORTOCARRERO Y LASSO DE LA VEGA, MELCHOR

Melchor Portocarrero y Lasso de la Vega (the count of Monclova), viceroy of Peru (1689–1705). As successor to the controversial duke of Palata, Monclova sought to increase the revenue base and labor pool of the colony without increasing the colonists' resentment and Indian resistance. Monclova enacted various measures that reversed earlier decrees: he reduced the number of Indians assigned to *mita* service (forced labor) at the silver mines of Potosí, he encouraged the use of wage labor, and he issued a new labor code that superseded the Palata regulations. In spite of persistent problems with tax collection and *mita* quotas, Monclova also reaffirmed the primacy of the Toledo *reducción* (resettlement) system, avoiding a fundamental reorganization of Peru's Indian community. His reversal of the Palata reforms postponed but could not prevent the major labor crises of the eighteenth century.

— ANN M. WIGHTMAN

PORTOLÁ, GASPAR DE

Gaspar De Portolá (*b.* ca. 1717; *d.* 10 October 1786), commandant-governor of the Californias. A native of Balaguer, Cataluña, Portolá rose from infantry ensign (1734) to lieutenant (1743), and to captain (1764). After serving in campaigns in Italy and Portugal, he arrived in New Spain in 1764. Three years later he was sent to Baja California to effect the expulsion of the JESUITS. In 1768 Portolá was commander of the Catalan Volunteers and led the expedition to settle Alta California that had been ordered by Visitor General José de GÁLVEZ. With the Franciscan Junípero SERRA he marched overland from Loreto to San Diego, where he aided in the founding of the mission and presidio (3 July 1768). On 14 July 1769 he led an expedition in search of Monterey; he discovered San Francisco Bay in November of that year, and returned to San Diego in January 1770. By that August, Portolá was back in San Blas, and as a lieutenant colonel of dragoons he returned to Spain later that year. As a colonel, he served as governor of Puebla de los Angeles, New Spain, from 1777 to 1785. In the latter year he returned to Spain in the Numancia regiment of dragoons. In February 1786 Portolá was named royal lieutenant of the city and castles of Lérida. He died in Lérida.

— W. MICHAEL MATHES

PORTUGAL, MARCOS ANTÔNIO DA FONSECA

Marcos Antônio da Fonseca Portugal (*b.* 24 March 1762; *d.* 7 February 1830), Portuguese composer and conductor. Born in Lisbon, Marcos Antônio, as he was called in Portugal, was admitted at the age of nine to Lisbon's Seminário Patriarchal, where he studied composition with João Souza de Carvalho. His first composition, a *Miserere,* was written at the age of fourteen. On 23 July 1783 he was admitted to the fraternity of musicians, the Brotherhood of Saint Cecilia, and between the years 1785 and 1792 wrote six comic operas.

A royal grant in 1792 made it possible for him to go to Italy, where he wrote twenty-one operas. Performances of his more successful operas in Italy, Germany, Austria, Spain, France, England, and Russia established Marcos Antônio Portugal, as he called himself at this time, as a prestigious composer with an international reputation. Appointed in 1800 as *mestre de capela* of the royal chapel and director of the São Carlos opera in

Lisbon, he produced his own operas as well as adaptations of Italian operas.

When Napoleon invaded Portugal and the royal court fled to Brazil in 1807, Marcos Antônio Portugal remained in Lisbon and composed a work honoring Napoleon on his birthday, which earned him the title of "turncoat." After the French left Lisbon, Marcos Antônio Portugal sailed to Brazil and received an appointment as *mestre de capela* of the royal chapel in Rio de Janeiro. He contributed to the rich musical life of the city during the period preceding Brazilian independence in 1822, after which the economic problems of the new nation severely limited funds for musical activities. Portugal died in Rio de Janeiro in 1830, the same year as Padre José Maurício Nunes GARCIA, the Brazilian composer who had also served as *mestre de capela.*

— DAVID P. APPLEBY

POSADA, JOSÉ GUADALUPE

José Guadalupe Posada (*b.* 2 February 1852; *d.* 20 January 1913), Mexican printmaker. Posada grew up in Aguascalientes, Mexico, where he attended drawing classes for a short time. Otherwise, he was a self-taught artist. In 1868 he joined the local lithography shop of José Tinidad Pedroza, where the opposition newspaper *El Jicote* was printed. In 1872 Posada and Pedroza moved to León to open a print shop, and there they produced illustrations for documents, cigar wrappers, religious images, caricatures, and the like. Posada moved to Mexico City in 1888 and soon joined forces with editor Antonio Vanegas Arroyo, with whom he would work until his death. By this time Posada had begun to work in the simple, free-flowing style for which he would posthumously become known. He also changed medium, to a kind of print that could be quickly created and easily combined with text.

The images for which Posada is now best known are the calaveras *(skeletons) he created for the Day of the Dead celebrations.*

Posada illustrated flyers, sensational news stories, books of magic tricks, new songs, recipes, and numerous other items for the popular penny press, many of which were printed on colored tissue paper and haphazardly hand tinted. The images for which Posada is now best known are the *calaveras* (skeletons) he created for the Day of the Dead celebrations. Though he produced well over twenty thousand images in print, in his lifetime Posada was not well known. He considered himself a printmaker and craftsman, not an artist. Posada died in Mexico City and was buried in a pauper's grave. Later, his works were discovered by the Mexican muralists, who made him their artistic mentor and teacher (though he had had little, if any, contact with them) and a political hero (though there is no evidence that he had any particular political affiliation). Posada made prints that satirized everyone and did not single out any one group. His prints do reflect the everyday life and concerns of the people of his time.

— KATHERINE CLARK HUDGENS

POSADAS, GERVASIO ANTONIO DE

Gervasio Antonio de Posadas (*b.* 19 June 1757; *d.* 2 July 1833), Argentine political leader of the independence period. Born in Buenos Aires to Felipe Santiago de Posadas and María Antonia Dávila, Posadas studied languages, philosophy, and theology in the Franciscan convent of that city. Despite his initial ambivalence about the revolutionary cause, an uncertainty that landed him in jail in 1811, Posadas eventually held various high-level positions in the patriot regime. They included membership in the general assembly and the triumvirate in 1813 and the supreme directorate the following year. Bartolomé MITRE described him as an "objective observer with common sense in whom seriousness and humor were combined." Posadas was not seen in that light, however, by his enemies. In 1815 he was exiled for almost six years after the revolt against Carlos María de ALVEAR, his relative and a political ally. His autobiography was completed before his death. An 1833 order for a monument honoring Posadas to be erected in the Recoleta Cemetery of the capital has yet to be implemented.

— FIDEL IGLESIAS

PRADO, JOÃO FERNANDO DE ALMEIDA

João Fernando de Almeida Prado ("Yan"; *b.* 8 December 1898; *d.* 23 October 1987), Brazilian historian and essayist. Born in Rio Claro in the state of São Paulo, Prado studied music and composition in Paris and Italy under several teachers, and took a degree at the São Paulo Law School. He also participated in the Brazilian modernist movement of the 1920s, an aesthetic and cultural reaction against European cultural dominance. Between 1928 and 1938 he wrote for major newspapers and literary magazines, among them *O Estado do São Paulo, Diário da Noite,* and *Correio da Manhã;* the literary magazines *Klaxon* and *Antropofagia;* and foreign publications such as *Recueil Sirey* and *Revue de synthèse.*

Prado was a lifelong student of Brazilian colonial history, one of the first to systematically study that era. His many published works, considered obligatory for students of colonial Brazil, are known primarily for their inclusion of important documents from the period. In the course of his life Prado amassed an enormous and important collection of Braziliana, including many rare books written by European travelers in Brazil. This collection as well as his personal library of 30,000 volumes are now housed at São Paulo University's Instituto de Estudos Brasileiros (Brazilian Studies Institute).

Prado's works include *Primeiros povoadores do Brasil* (1935); *Pernambuco e as capitanias do norte do Brasil* (1939); *O Brasil e o colonialismo europeu* (1955); *A Bahia e as capitanias do centro do Brasil* (1964); *Historia da formação da sociedade brasileira: D. João VI e o início da classe dirigente do Brasil* (1968).

— BRIAN OWENSBY

PRADO, MARIANO IGNACIO

Mariano Ignacio Prado (*b.* 1826; *d.* 1901), a general in the Peruvian military. Early in his career he was exiled for his opposition to the government of José ECHENIQUE but jumped ship, swam to freedom, and returned to Peru in 1854 to help overthrow his enemies. As dictator in 1866, he declared war on Spain and stood off a Spanish invasion. Later he oversaw a far-reaching program of constitutional reform aimed at curbing the power of the Roman Catholic church and the army. He halted dissident military rebellions against his rule, but then, in 1868, he decided to retire, leaving the field to the liberals. Eight years later civilians persuaded him to return to politics as the candidate of the Civilista Party.

Early in his career Prado was exiled but jumped ship, swam to freedom, and returned to Peru to help overthrow his enemies.

As president he disliked political maneuvering, and his enemies constantly plotted uprisings against him. When the economy deteriorated in the late 1870s, he fueled inflation by printing worthless paper money. At that point Peruvian diplomats feared for Peru's nitrate fields in the south, and the country headed toward war with Chile. In the early stage of the War of the Pacific (1879–1883), he watched as Peru's navy was destroyed by Chile. Losing confidence in his ability to rule, Prado sailed for exile in Europe in 1879.

— VINCENT PELOSO

PRADO, PAULO

Paulo Prado (*b.* 20 May 1869; *d.* 3 October 1943), Brazilian businessman and historian. Scion of an influential coffee-planting family, Paulo Prado was a native of São Paulo and the son of Antônio Prado, one of the last ministers of agriculture under the monarchy. He graduated from the São Paulo law school two weeks before the fall of the empire, in November 1889, and soon departed his uncertain homeland for a grand tour of Europe. Returning to Brazil during the period of Paulista ascendancy, he joined the family coffee-exporting firm and, in 1897, became its president. Under his direction, the company attained new levels of wealth and power. Prado served briefly as president of the National Coffee Council after the 1930 Revolution.

A patron of arts and letters, Prado made large donations to the São Paulo Municipal Library and supported the 1922 Modern Art Week celebration. He befriended some of the most talented Brazilian historians of his time and facilitated their work. His own major publications consist of two collections of historical essays: *Paulística* (São Paulo–like, 1925), in which the theme is regional, and the broader *Retrato do Brasil* (Portrait of Brazil, 1928). Prado's historical writings are strongly influenced by the work of João Capistrano de ABREU.

— NEILL MACAULAY

PRADO, PEDRO

Pedro Prado (*b.* 8 October 1886; *d.* 31 January 1952), Chilean writer. His earlier poetic work, beginning with *Flores de cardo* (1908; Thistle Flowers) and *El llamado del mundo* (1913; The Beckoning World) established a departure from modernism in vogue in Chile that marked the inauguration of free verse, the poem in prose, and antirationalist experimentation in the poetic endeavor. In his later poetry, *Camino de las horas* (1934; Path of the Hours), *Otoño en las dunas* (1940; Autumn in the Dunes), *Esta bella ciudad envenenada* (1945; This Beautiful Poisoned City), and *No más que una rosa* (1946; Only a Rose), he adopted the sonnet as a preferred form of esthetic expression.

Santiago-born Prado published three novels, *La reina de Rapa-Nui* (1914; The Queen of Rapa Nui), *Alsino* (1920), and *Un juez rural* (1924; A Country Judge). His masterpiece *Alsino,* an allegorical novel about a hunchback boy who wants to fly, has attracted much critical attention as well as continuous editorial success. In 1949 he was awarded the National Prize for literature in recognition of his overall creative production. He died in Viña del Mar.

— J. A. EPPLE

PRADO, VASCO

Vasco Prado (*b.* 1914), Brazilian sculptor and engraver. Born in Rio Grande do Sul, Prado received a grant from the French government that allowed him to study in Paris under the French painters Fernand Léger and Étienne Hadju. Upon his return to Brazil in 1950, Prado, along with Carlos Scliar, Glenio Bianchetti, Danúbio Gonçalves, and Glauco Rodrigues, founded the Clube de Gravura (Engraving Club) in Pôrto Alegre in 1950. This group supported social realism, an artistic movement rejecting romanticized and idealized subject matter and favoring an unadorned art with a political content.

Prado's repertory draws heavily from regional themes, focusing primarily on the life and customs of the gaucho from the southern state of Rio Grande do Sul. One of his best-known engravings, *Dead Soldier,* was executed for the Third Gaucho Congress in Defense of Peace (1951). In 1962 he won first prize in a competition for a monument to the composer Heitor VILLA- LOBOS. In 1965 there was a one-man exhibition of his sculpture at the Galería de Arte in São Paulo.

— CAREN A. MEGHREBLIAN

PRADO DA SILVA JÚNIOR, CAIO

Caio Prado da silva Júnior (*b.* 11 February 1907; *d.* 23 November 1990), Brazilian writer and editor. Caio Prado da Silva Júnior, a pioneer in historical materialist interpretation in Brazil, was born in São Paulo. He was a founder of the Partido Democrático (1926) and received a law degree from the University of São Paulo (1928). He joined the Communist Party in 1931, and Marxism guided both his life and his work. He expressed his political views in his first book, *Evolução política do Brasil* (1933), a summary of Brazilian history, and in his masterpiece, *Formação do Brasil contemporâneo* (1942), he analyzed the colonial period, especially at the turn of the nineteenth century. The enlargement of the latter book resulted in *História econômica do Brasil* (1945), which, with Roberto Simonsen's *História econômica do Brasil* (1937) and Celso Furtado's *Formação econômica do Brasil* (1959), led to emphasis on economic factors in Brazilian history.

Prado Júnior also wrote books on economics, philosophy, and politics. He was editor of the *Revista Brasiliense* (1955–1964) and founder of the traditional publishing firms Gráfica Urupês and Editôra Brasiliense.

Prado Junior combined intense political activity with profound intellectual work for which he suffered political repression. He was imprisoned twice (1935–1937 and 1971) and went into exile in France for two years

(1937–1939). He died in São Paulo, where his family had and still has an important cultural role.

— ELIANA MARIA REA GOLDSCHMIDT

PRADO Y UGARTECHE, JAVIER

Javier Prado y Ugarteche (*b.* 1871; *d.* 25 July 1921), a Peruvian sociologist with extremely anti-indigenous, pro-European cultural views. In *Estado social del Perú durante la dominación española* (1894), he argued that drunkenness and coca leaf addiction were signs of the cultural inferiority of the indigenous population of the country. He saw such practices as an outgrowth of frustration at not being able to rise to the level of Europeans. He attributed to Afro-Peruvians the genetic qualities of thievery and lasciviousness, traits he argued they had inherited from Africans. The son of former president Mariano Ignacio PRADO, Prado finished a doctoral dissertation at age twenty and in public competition won a chair of modern philosophy at the National University of San Marcos. He condemned the Spanish past of Peru for its deleterious effect upon the masses of people. To counter these ills, he argued that the national educational system should teach Peruvians a sense of social solidarity, civic virtue, and technical awareness. These qualities would awaken a desire in the citizen to acquire material wealth and thus would benefit the entire nation. Like many social scientists of his day, he was largely unaware of the local sources of investment and banking that had begun to tap the economic potential of Peru.

— VINCENT PELOSO

PRADO Y UGARTECHE, JORGE

Jorge Prado y Ugarteche (*b.* 1887; *d.* 29 July 1970), Peruvian politician. Exiling himself early in the dictatorship of Augusto LEGUÍA as a protest against tyranny, he was a Civilista and son of past president Mariano Ignacio PRADO. He opposed President Guillermo BILLINGHURST in 1914. In 1933 he served briefly as prime minister to Oscar BENAVIDES and formed a cabinet that sought to conciliate opponents. Politically moderate with democratic views, Prado wooed both socialists and fascists at various times. By 1936 it seemed that Benavides had chosen him as successor. During his presidency, Benavides formed the Frente Nacional to voice his views and banned the rival Aprista Party (APRA) from political activity. Fragmentation weakened other groups, yet in the election of 1936 Prado came in third behind the candidates of reform. Benavides nullified the election and extended his own term as president until 1939. He was succeeded by Jorge Prado's brother, Man-

uel. Jorge faded into obscurity. His candidacy symbolized the political malaise that gripped Peru when a dictatorship banned APRA from politics for fear of its ability to carry out popular economic reforms.

— VINCENT PELOSO

PRADO Y UGARTECHE, MANUEL

Manuel Prado y Ugarteche (*b.* 1889; *d.* 14 August 1967), son of former president Mariano Ignacio PRADO, president of Peru (1939–1945; 1956–1962). During his first term Prado completed many projects begun under the preceding dictatorship of Oscar BENAVIDES, including the national census of 1940, only the second in the country's history. His budgetary management encouraged a literacy campaign that led to the building of many schools and the training of new teachers, the establishment of a social security system, new medical facilities, and the extension of roads by 2,400 miles. During his second term Prado raised new public funds through indirect taxes on gasoline and other oil products. After 1955 Peruvian products found new markets abroad and the country imported more goods. Indeed, imports outweighed exports, adversely affecting the balance of payments. The numbers of wealthy and well off increased in these years, but with Peru experiencing a population increase, the numbers of poor also increased dramatically. Demands for new housing and land reform went unmet. To blunt criticism from the wealthy, Prado appointed Pedro BELTRÁN, the sharply critical editor of the influential *La Prensa,* as prime minister. Beltrán unsuccessfully sought to meet government needs through indirect taxes on oil products. Meanwhile, the legalization of APRA after 1956 allowed the leaders of that party to increase their popular support by campaigning against Beltrán and in favor of land reform. Prado had nearly completed his second term when military officers, fearing the rise to power of APRA through a deal among presidential contenders, seized control just after the 1962 vote count.

— VINCENT PELOSO

PRAT ECHAURREN, JORGE

Jorge Prat Echaurren (*b.* 24 April 1918; *d.* 1971), Chilean politician and well-known Conservative. Prat, the grandson of Chile's supreme naval hero Arturo Prat, never sat in Congress, though he served as minister of finance (1954–1955). A man of strong nationalist convictions, he mounted a campaign for the presidency in 1964, for which he formed his own party, the Acción Nacional (November 1963), but later withdrew his candidacy. Failing to win election to the Senate in March

1965, he subsequently led the Acción Nacional into the newly formed National Party in June 1966.

– SIMON COLLIER

PRATS GONZÁLEZ, CARLOS

Carlos Prats González (*b.* 2 February 1915; *d.* 30 September 1974), Chilean army officer and minister during the Salvador ALLENDE government (1970–1973). A professional officer, Prats assumed control of the armed forces in the turbulent times following the October 1969 death of General René SCHNEIDER. Prats attempted to insulate the military from the competing forces of the Left and the Right. A believer in the subordination of the military to civilian control, the general directed the crushing of an abortive army coup, referred to as the *Tancazo,* in June 1973.

Considered Allende's stooge by many, Prats became

the object of civilian disdain.

Largely against his will, Prats was drawn into politics. In 1972 he served as Allende's minister of the interior, resolving a teamsters' strike which had crippled the nation's economy. He later returned to the government as minister of defense. Considered Allende's stooge by many, Prats became the object of civilian disdain as well as hostility from the army's officer corps. Recognizing that he did not enjoy the confidence of his brother officers, he resigned as head of the army and minister of defense. Following the 1973 coup that overthrew Allende, which he did not support, he and his wife left for Argentina, where they both were brutally murdered, apparently by agents of the PINOCHET government's secret service, who may have feared that Prats would spearhead a movement to unseat the junta.

– WILLIAM F. SATER

PREBISCH, RAÚL

Raúl Prebisch (*b.* 17 April 1901; *d.* 29 April 1986), Argentine economist. Considered one of the third world's leading economists, Prebish was born in Tucumán, and died in Las Vertientes, near Santiago, Chile. After graduating in economics from the University of Buenos Aires in 1923, he was lecturer in political economy there (1925–1948), and director of Argentina's Central Bank (1935–1943). From 1949 to 1963 he was the executive secretary of the Economic Commission for Latin America and the Caribbean, and later he joined the United Nations Conference for Trade and Development, from which he resigned in 1969. At the time of his death he was director general of the Latin American Institute for Economic and Social Planning. Prebisch had a significant influence on Latin American economic policies, especially during the 1960s, with his views on the role played by the developed nations ("the center") in the economic and social progress of the underdeveloped countries ("the periphery"). Prebisch believed that to view the peripheral nations as mere suppliers of raw materials to the developed world resulted in the deterioration of the terms of trade, and the concentration of technical progress in the center. Prebisch promoted the theory of comprehensive industrialization for the periphery, in order to, in the words of Chilean economist Aníbal Pinto, "foster the growth of labour productivity, the expansion of employment opportunities and the establishment of new forms of insertion into the international economy capable of transcending mere specialization in exports of primary commodities." Although Prebisch's ideas evolved as the world economy evolved, they are subject to a lasting controversy, and have been questioned in view of the unresolved problems faced by the Latin American economies at the close of the twentieth century. His major works are: *Introducción a Keynes* (1947), *Change and Development: Latin America's Great Task* (1971), *Problemas teóricos y prácticos del crecimiento económico* (1973), *Capitalismo periférico: crisis y transformación* (1981), *La obra de Prebisch en la CEPAL* (1982), and *La crisis del desarrollo argentino* (1986).

– CELSO RODRÍGUEZ

PRESTES, LUÍS CARLOS

Luís Carlos Prestes (*b.* 3 January 1898; *d.* 7 March 1990), secretary-general of the Brazilian Communist Party (PCB) (1943–1980). Prestes was born in Porto Alegre, Rio Grande do Sul. He was in Rio de Janeiro in 1908 when his father, an army captain, died, leaving the family (Prestes had four sisters) with an insufficient pension. Prestes's mother gave lessons in French and music. Later Prestes occasionally tutored classmates in mathematics while attending the military school in Rio de Janeiro and the military academy, where, as an outstanding student, he earned a degree in engineering.

Prestes achieved fame in 1925–1927 as chief of staff of the revolutionary column that made what became known as the Long March in the interior. However, Prestes, the "Cavalier of Hope," condemned as insufficiently radical the objectives of the 1930 revolution that brought Getúlio VARGAS to power. After working with Dmitri Manuilski in the Comintern in Russia, Prestes returned clandestinely to Brazil, where he helped

Luís Carlos Prestes makes a speech during the Fifth Congress of the Brazilian Communist Party, 1960. (Iconographia)

prepare the uprising of 1935. Its failure was followed by anticommunist repression and torture. Prestes was arrested in 1936 and sentenced to 16.5 years of prison for having led the uprising. In 1940 the sentence was extended by 30 years because he was found guilty of having persuaded Communist leaders, before his arrest, to murder Elza Fernandes, a young woman accused by Communists of aiding the police. Olga Benário, a German Jewish Communist whom Prestes had married while abroad, was deported from Brazil to Germany, where she died, a prisoner of the Nazis, after giving birth to their daughter, Anita Leocádia.

A prisoner in Rio de Janeiro, Prestes supported the war effort of President Vargas. His "alliance with Vargas," which arose after his release in April 1945, was accompanied by Communist penetration of labor unions. The growing PCB espoused a moderate program and became legal until outlawed during a new presidential administration at the beginning of the cold war. Prestes then lost his Senate seat. From hiding he issued thunderous manifestos calling for uprisings.

During the administration of Jusceiino KUBITSCHEK, whom the Communists helped elect in 1955, Prestes emerged from hiding and campaigned for candidates who purchased PCB support in the local elections of 1958. Adhering to the Moscow line, he welcomed any ally who would oppose "United States imperialism." In the early 1960s, Prestes sought legality for the PCB and advocated achieving socialism by a peaceful path. But the very strength of the PCB in labor and student organizations, combined with the activities of violence-minded leftists, provided public support for the 1964

military coup that deposed left-leaning President João GOULART.

Prestes, forced again into hiding, was criticized by those advocating violent struggle against the new military regime. Following a party schism and the emergence of guerrilla groups and minor Communist parties, he denounced terrorism and went abroad. An amnesty decree of 1979 allowed Prestes to return to Brazil, where he accused PCB leaders of betraying the working class by cooperating with the government in the quest to legalize the party. He lost his post of secretary-general and sought, unsuccessfully, to have another party name him its senatorial candidate. Separated from the PCB, he spent his last days supporting the political aspirations of Leonel BRIZOLA.

– JOHN W. F. DULLES

PRESTES DE ALBUQUERQUE, JULIO

Julio Prestes de Albuquerque (*b.* 15 March 1882; *d.* 9 February 1946), president-elect of Brazil at the time of the 1930 coup that brought Getúlio VARGAS to power. Son of a traditional São Paulo family, Prestes served in both the state legislature and the national Congress before being elected governor of the state of São Paulo in 1927. As majority leader in the Chamber of Deputies at the start of Washington LUÍS PEREIRA DE SOUSA's presidential term (1926), Prestes won the confidence of the president, who selected him to run as his successor in the 1930 election. This decision ignored the "governor's politics," whereby the governor of the state of Minas Gerais should have been the preferred candidate for the presidency in 1930. Disgruntled *mineiros* joined the Liberal Alliance supporting the candidacy of Getúlio Vargas. In the meantime, the 1929 stock market crash highlighted the president's inability to mitigate his supporters' economic troubles. Although official election results confirmed Prestes as Brazil's new president, the widespread disenchantment with Pereira's final year in office cemented the success of Vargas's challenge. The armies of the Northeast and of the South marched on Rio de Janeiro and deposed Pereira, who went into exile as did Prestes. Upon his return from exile, Prestes retired to his ranch in the interior of the state of São Paulo, no longer interested in politics.

– JOAN MEZNAR

PRICE, GEORGE CADLE

George Cadle Price (*b.* 15 January 1919), prime minister of Belize (1981–1984 and 1989–1993). With the exception of a brief five-year period in the 1980s, George Price has been the dominant figure in Belizean politics since 1956. From 1954, when universal adult suffrage was first granted to British Hondurans, until 1993 his People's United Party (PUP) won every election in the pre-independence period.

Of Scottish and Maya extraction, Price was born in Belize City in 1919, the third of eleven children of William and Irene Price. His father was an auctioneer. After primary school, he graduated from the Jesuit-run St. John's College of Belize. In 1936 he enrolled in St. Augustine's College in Bay St. Louis, Mississippi, to pursue a religious vocation, transferring to Guatemala's National Seminary in 1941. He returned to Belize in 1942 before completing studies because of his father's illness. For the next thirteen years he served as private secretary to Robert Turton, a creole chicle millionaire and member of the legislative council.

Price entered politics in 1943 and lost his first bid for the Belize Town Board (City Council). In 1947 he won the first of his many political victories in his second bid for the City Council, on which he served until 1965, at one point (1958–1962) also serving as mayor of Belize City. On the national front, Price was a founding member of the People's United Party in 1950 and served successively as party secretary, party leader, member of the Legislative Council, member of the House of Representatives, first minister, and premier (1965–1981).

Price survived charges of sedition by the British in the 1950s for discussions with the Guatemalans. For his independent foreign policies, he has also withstood the opposition's charges of prosocialist views and charges of corruption against members of his cabinet, as well as numerous factional splits and defections within his own party.

Price was the chief architect of Belizean independence, secured in 1981, and is widely revered as the father of his country. An ascetic, charismatic bachelor who attended 6:00 A.M. mass every morning, he seemed to know virtually every family in Belize—a familiarity born of dozens of trips around the country in his personal Land Rover and years of citizens' day meetings each Wednesday in Belize City, where any citizen could discuss problems personally with the prime minister. He wrote poetry and musical theater, read voraciously, and was very knowledgeable about foreign affairs.

Severe economic problems, internal party wrangling, and the feeling by a majority of Belizeans that it was "time for a change" contributed to a landslide victory by the opposition United Democratic Party in the national elections of 1984. Price lost his own seat, Belize North. Out of office for the first time in thirty-seven years, he spent the next five years rebuilding the PUP and the *Belize Times,* the party-dominated weekly news-

paper. In the national elections of 1989 he led the PUP to a narrow victory, winning fifteen of twenty-eight seats, and reassumed the office of prime minister.

An ascetic, charismatic bachelor who attended

6:00 a.m. mass every morning, Price seemed to

know virtually every family in Belize.

Price has wisely chosen to continue some of the successful economic policies of his predecessor, Manuel ESQUIVEL. However, in contrast to the large-scale foreign investment policies of his predecessor, the PUP Manifesto for 1989–1994 promoted smaller-scale investments by Belizeans in the tourist and agricultural sectors.

Following a successful by-election victory in January, 1993 and landslide victories in local elections in April 1993, Price decided to call for an early election on 30 June 1993. However, a series of events beyond his control contributed to his government's defeat. These included a May decision by Great Britain to pull all troops out of Belize by January 1994, followed by a coup in Guatemala on 25 May, which reopened Belizean fears of Guatemalan intervention. Promising suspension of a Maritime Areas Act granting Guatemala access to the Atlantic Ocean through Belizean territory, the UDP won sixteen seats, to thirteen seats for Price's PUP. Price retained his Belize City constituency and became leader of the opposition in the new parliament.

— BRIAN E. COUTTS

PRICE-MARS, JEAN

Jean Price-Mars (*b.* 15 October 1876; *d.* 1 March 1969), Haitian teacher, diplomat, writer, and ethnographer. Price-Mars served as secretary of the Haitian legation in Washington (1909) and as chargé d'affaires in Paris (1915–1917). In 1922 he completed medical studies that he had given up for lack of a scholarship. After withdrawing as a candidate for the presidency of Haiti in favor of Stenio Vincent in 1930, Price-Mars led Senate opposition to the new president and was forced out of politics. In 1941, he was again elected to the Senate. He was secretary of state for external relations in 1946 and, later, ambassador to the Dominican Republic. In his eighties, he continued service as Haitian ambassador at the United Nations and ambassador to France.

Through his lectures and writing, Price-Mars brought popular culture, the Creole language, and the religion of Vodun into respectable focus. He laid the groundwork for the formation of the Indigenist movement and the important literary journals, *La revue indigène* and *Les griots*. Among his important doctrines was his opposition to the concept of "race" applied to human beings. He returned to the very sources of Haitian folklore in demonstrating parallels and resemblances with other early cultures (European and African). Berrou and Pompilus wrote that *Ainsi parla l'oncle* (1928) was "the condemnation of the bovarysm of the Haitian middle class." Depestre criticized Price-Mars for not early repudiating François DUVALIER, but Hoffman takes a more balanced view, that Price-Mars maintained a distance from Duvalier and the "Griots."

— CARROL F. COATES

PRIETO, GUILLERMO

Guillermo Prieto (*b.* 1818; *d.* 1897), Mexican cabinet minister, poet, dramatist, and author. Born in Mexico City, Prieto lived at Molino del Rey, near Chapultepec, where his father managed the mill and a bakery. When his father died in 1831 and his mother lost her sanity, Prieto worked in a clothing store until his poetry attracted the attention of Andrés QUINTANA ROO, who got him a post in the customs house and enrolled him in the Colegio de San Juan de Letrán.

Prieto's first poems were published when he was nineteen. The same year, President Anastasio BUSTAMANTE named Prieto his personal secretary and brought him to the presidential palace to live. Prieto's first theatrical work, *El alférez*, was produced in 1840, and others followed in 1842 and 1843. Prieto edited the *Diario Oficial* until Santa Anna overthrew Bustamante in 1841. He then wrote for *El Siglo XIX* and *El Monitor Republicano,* and in 1845 founded *Don Simplicio* with Ignacio RAMÍREZ. He was elected to the national legislature in 1848, 1850, and 1852.

Prieto published his analysis of Mexico's fiscal circumstances, *Indicaciones . . . ,* in 1850, and President Mariano ARISTA appointed him minister of finance in 1852. Although he recorded in his memoirs that he had sought attention and ostentation, Prieto also envisioned himself as a reformer. He favored lifting prohibitions on trade and reducing the costs of administration.

Arista's administration was soon overthrown, however, and Prieto was subjected to house arrest on orders from Antonio López de SANTA ANNA. A supporter of the Revolution of Ayutla, Prieto was appointed minister of finance by President Juan ÁLVAREZ. Prieto was a delegate to the Constitutional Convention of 1856–1857 and served on the finance committee. Benito JUÁREZ, who assumed the presidency in 1858, selected Prieto as

his first finance minister. In March 1858, when conservative troops captured Juárez in Guadalajara during the War of the Reform, Prieto's eloquence saved the president from a firing squad. Prieto again headed the finance ministry in 1859 and 1861, but he broke with Juárez when the president refused to turn power over to Jesús GONZÁLEZ ORTEGA in 1865.

Prieto remained active in politics, however, favoring congressional authority over that of the executive. He supported the efforts of José María IGLESIAS against President Sebastián LERDO DE TEJADA's abuse of executive authority in the 1876 elections and served as Iglesias's minister of government for several months before Iglesias was overthrown by Porfirio DÍAZ. Prieto remained a popular poet and continued publishing on such subjects as travel, history, and political economy. His *Memorias de mis tiempos* (1906) records his impressions of the years from 1828 to 1853.

— D. F. STEVENS

PRIETO FIGUEROA, LUIS BELTRÁN

Luis Beltrán Prieto Figueroa (*b.* 1902; *d.* after 1978), Venezuelan political leader. Founder and head of the Venezuelan Teachers Federation, Prieto subsequently was one of the founders and principal leaders of Democratic Action (Acción Democrática—AD). A leader of the revolution that overthrew President Isaías MEDINA ANGARITA (1945), he later was a member of the revolutionary junta, serving as education minister. In exile during the military dictatorship (1948–1958), Prieto returned to Venezuela to become, first, secretary-general and, later, president of AD. He also held a Senate seat. In 1968 he left AD to form the Electoral Movement of the People. He lost bids for the presidency in 1968, 1973, and 1978.

— WINFIELD J. BURGGRAAFF

PRIETO RODRÍGUEZ, SOTERO

Sotero Prieto Rodríguez (*b.* 25 December 1884; *d.* 22 May 1935), Mexican mathematician and scientist. Son of engineer Raúl Prieto and nephew of writer Isabel Prieto, Sotero Prieto came from a prominent intellectual family in Guadalajara, Jalisco, where he completed his primary and secondary studies. He graduated from the National School of Engineering with a specialty in mathematics, and in 1912 began teaching mathematics and geometry at the National University, where many future political and intellectual leaders were his students. He founded and directed the mathematics section of the Antonio Alzate Science Society from 1932 to 1935, and contributed significantly to the expansion of science in general in Mexico. He also influenced the progress of mathematics research in Mexico, and is remembered for his expertise in the Spanish language.

— RODERIC AI CAMP

PRIETO VIAL, JOAQUÍN

Joaquín Prieto Vial (*b*. 20 August 1786; *d*. 22 November 1854), president of Chile (1831–1841). Born in Concepción, and a soldier from his youth onward, Prieto was sent as a patriot auxiliary to Buenos Aires in 1811, but returned to fight in Chile's wars of independence (1813–1814). After exile in Argentina during the Spanish reconquest (1814–1817), he took part in the battles of Chacabuco (12 February 1817) and Maipú (5 April 1818), following which he took charge of patriot operations in the south. A member of several of the congresses of the 1820s, he was appointed commander of the army in the south in 1828. In 1829–1830 he led the successful Conservative rebellion in the hope (soon frustrated) of securing the restoration of Bernardo O'HIGGINS (1778–1842). He commanded the Conservative troops at the battle of Lircay in April 1830.

Diego PORTALES (1793–1837) persuaded Prieto to assume the presidency from September 1831. During his two consecutive terms, he saw the stabilization of Chile, the Constitution of 1833, the war against the Peru-Bolivia Confederation, the murder of Diego Portales, and, at the end of the decade, political relaxation.

Prieto was a pious, rather serious figure. Portales used to make fun of him, calling him "Isidro Ayestas"—the name of a deranged man who wandered the streets of Santiago during that time.

— SIMON COLLIER

PRIMO DE VERDAD Y RAMOS, FRANCISCO

Francisco Primo de Verdad y Ramos (*b*. 19 June 1760; *d*. 4 October 1808), lawyer and early martyr of the Mexican independence movement. Born in Ciénega del Rincón, Aguascalientes, Primo de Verdad studied law in Mexico City, where he became a representative in the *cabildo*. The *cabildo* was a stronghold of nationalist sentiment in New Spain and a leading institution in the independence movement. Shortly after Napoleon invaded Spain and forced the abdication of the Bourbon king, Ferdinand VII, Primo de Verdad called for a meeting of New Spain's regional *cabildos* and other authorities in July 1808. Acting as spokesman for the criollos, he delivered a speech that effectively called for New Spain's autonomy. The region's loyalty, he reasoned, was never to Spain or the Spanish people but rather to the

monarchy and the legitimate king, Ferdinand VII. In the king's absence, civil authority reverted to the Mexican people. His speech failed to convince powerful peninsular interests, whose sentiments still rested with Spain. In September 1808, Primo de Verdad was thrown into jail, where he died under questionable circumstances. Had Primo de Verdad and the other criollo leaders succeeded, Mexican independence could have occurred as early as 1808.

— J. DAVID DRESSING

PRÍO SOCARRÁS, CARLOS

Carlos Prío Socarrás (*b*. 1903; *d*. 1977), Cuban lawyer and politician, president of Cuba (1948–1952). From a middle-class family outside Havana, Prío Socarrás moved to the capital city to further his education and quickly became embroiled in the university reform movement of the 1920s. As a student of law, he upheld constitutionality and led the student protest when Gerardo MACHADO decided to run for a second term as president in 1927. In response, Machado abolished the student federation and briefly closed the university itself. Prío and other student leaders were banned from campus, but Ramón GRAU SAN MARTÍN, a professor-activist and future Auténtico president, permitted Prío to read his manifesto out loud in Grau's class; this was the beginning of a close political relationship between the two men.

In 1930 Cuban students organized opposition to dictator Machado. They were young, middle-class idealists, who naively thought all Cuba's ills could be solved merely by removing Machado.

In 1930 Cuban students organized opposition to dictator Machado, with Prío serving as a leader of the student Directorio. The generation of 1930 viewed themselves as the heirs of José Martí and the legitimate representatives of the Cuban national will. Its members were young, middle-class idealists, usually from rural regions where people naively thought all Cuba's ills could be solved merely by removing Machado. In August 1933 their wish was fulfilled when a military coup and general strike forced Machado into exile. Prío, as a Directorio leader, wielded great power and supported the civilian-dominated Pentarchy of Grau over the military elements during the subsequent struggle for control. Grau's reform experiment lasted only four months before, he, too, was ousted by the military under Fulgencio BATISTA Y ZALVÍDAR. In February 1934 Prío and like-minded Cubans founded the Auténtico Party and named Grau, now in exile, its leader. Their platform pledged economic and political nationalism, social justice, civil liberties, and greater Cuban control of the island's natural resources. Prío attended the Constitutional Convention of 1940 as a delegate and won recognition for university autonomy, a long-held student goal.

Carlos Prío Socarrás served in many government positions during the 1940s. He was a senator from 1940 to 1948, prime minister from 1945 to 1947, and labor minister under Grau from 1947 to 1948. In 1948 the electorate chose Prío as president, and he continued the moderate reformist policies of his Auténtico mentor, Grau San Martín. Prío managed to reduce political gangsterism, but his administration was plagued by charges of corruption and ineptitude. The 1940s were afterward generally seen as the high-water mark of constitutional liberalism in Cuba, although they failed to legitimize politics or entrench a system of loyal opposition and regular transfers of power. The Cuban public increasingly lost confidence in politicians, and the ensuing instability led Batista to oust Prío in a coup on 10 March 1952, less than three months before elections were to be held.

— KAREN RACINE

PUENTE UCEDA, LUIS DE LA

Luis de la Puente Uceda (*d.* 1965), radical politician in Peru, founder of the Rebel APRA and the Movement of the Revolutionary Left (MIR) in the early 1960s. Puente Uceda, a former student leader, led a group of Aprista dissidents who were disillusioned with the increasingly conservative character of the Populist Party, especially after the establishment in 1962 of a political alliance with the former dictator Manuel A. ODRÍA. In 1965 the MIR launched a seriously flawed armed insurrection in the interior provinces of Cuzco and Junín. Lacking a sound strategy and coordination with other guerrilla movements, such as the Army of National Liberation led by Héctor BÉJAR, the MIR was defeated and its main leaders, Puente Uceda and Ernesto Lobatón, killed by counterinsurgency forces of the Peruvian military.

— ALFONSO W. QUIROZ

PUEYRREDÓN, HONORIO

Honorio Pueyrredón (*b.* 9 July 1876; *d.* 23 September 1945), Argentine lawyer, university professor, political leader, and diplomat. Born into a prominent Argentine landholding family, Pueyrredón studied and taught law at the University of Buenos Aires before winning a political appointment in 1916. In recognition of Pueyrredón's strong support for the recently formed Unión Cívica Radical, newly elected president Hipólito YRIGOYEN named him agriculture minister

Pueyrredón served as foreign minister between 1917 and 1922, during which time he led his government's diplomatic efforts to chart a leadership role for Argentina in Latin America. Under Pueyrredón's stewardship, Argentina remained neutral after 1916 despite mounting U.S. pressures on Yrigoyen to enter the war. In addition, the foreign minister tried to organize an association of Latin American neutrals, which directly challenged U.S. political influence in the region.

In domestic politics Pueyrredón represented the interests of cattle raisers and other elites within the multiclass-based Unión Cívica. When the movement split in 1922, Pueyrredón sided with the more conservative antipersonalists and was named ambassador to the United States in the administration of President Marcelo T. de ALVEAR. During the 1920s Pueyrredón abandoned his antagonism toward Washington. He encouraged the growth of U.S. commercial interests in Argentina and offered to assist Washington in negotiating a favorable peace in Nicaragua.

In 1928, however, Pueyrredón did an about-face. As Argentine delegation chief to the Sixth Pan-American Conference, he gained international fame by contravening his government's instructions and publicly attacking U.S. intervention in Latin America. As a result, Pueyrredón was recalled to Buenos Aires. He remained active in politics and private legal practice during the 1930s.

— DAVID M. K. SHEININ

PUEYRREDÓN, JUAN MARTÍN DE

Juan Martín de Pueyrredón (*b.* 18 December 1777; *d.* 13 March 1850), one of the most important figures in Argentina's wars of independence. Pueyrredón was born in Buenos Aires of French and Spanish ancestry and became one of the leaders in the defense of Buenos Aires against the British invasion in 1806. He played an important role in recruiting men and matériel for the defense effort, and his own squad of Hussars fought brilliantly. Santiago de LINIERS, then the military governor, promoted him to lieutenant colonel. After the British were driven out, secure in the prestige and influence that he enjoyed, Pueyrredón demanded that the *cabildo* remove Viceroy Rafael de Sobremonte and replace him with Liniers. In recognition of his contributions, the *cabildo* sent Pueyrredón to Madrid.

He was in Spain when the French invaded the Iberian peninsula in 1808, and seeing what was happening, he became convinced that Argentine independence was necessary to prevent the country from being dominated by a Spanish junta or by the French. Disillusioned with the turn of events, Pueyrredón wrote to the *cabildo* advising it not to accept the appointments of viceroys that any junta would probably make. This act was considered treasonable, and when he returned to Argentina in 1809, he was arrested. He soon escaped to Brazil with the help of Manuel BELGRANO and others.

Pueyrredón returned to Argentina after the May 1810 revolution and was appointed governor of Córdoba. In January 1811, he was sent to the northern regions as governor and president of the Audiencia of Charcas. In 1812, Pueyrredón was elected to the first triumvirate to govern the United Provinces of Río de la Plata. He was overthrown in the October revolution and moved to San Luís.

In 1816, Pueyrredón was elected supreme director of the United Provinces. His tenure brought stability, which enabled him to concentrate on the war effort against Spain. His total support for José de SAN MARTÍN's expedition to Chile was crucial to its success. Pueyrredón favored a centralized form of government dominated by Buenos Aires, for which he often faced rebellions by the provinces. He resigned in June 1819 and soon left for Europe, where he remained for most of the next thirty years. He went home to Buenos Aires in 1850, where he died.

– JUAN MANUEL PÉREZ

PUEYRREDÓN, PRILIDIANO

Prilidiano Pueyrredón (*b.* 24 January 1823; *d.* 3 November 1870), Argentine painter and architect. Pueyrredón was born in Buenos Aires, the son of the former Supreme Director Juan Martín de PUEYRREDÓN. From the time he finished grammar school at age twelve until 1849, he spent more time in Europe than in Argentina. He earned an engineering degree from the Institut Polytechnique in Paris and began his painting career during his early European travels.

As an architect, Pueyrredón designed both public and private structures, including the mansion that is now the presidential residence at Olivos in the suburbs of Buenos Aires. He also undertook projects of architectural restoration. However, he was above all a portraitist in the neoclassical tradition. He has left portraits of Manuelita Rosas and his own father, as well as of other politically or socially prominent figures. Pueyrredón also painted landscapes and realistic country scenes, in both oil and watercolor. Like the portraits,

these have documentary value over and above their artistic merit (which is probably greater in the watercolors). He is remembered today as Argentina's outstanding nineteenth-century painter.

– DAVID BUSHNELL

PUGA, MARÍA LUISA

María Luisa Puga (*b.* 3 February 1944), Mexican writer. Born in Mexico City, Puga has published literary criticism, essays, short stories, and novels. She is most widely known for her first novel, *Las posibilidades del odio* (The Possibilities of Hate, 1978), about Kenyan society, and for *Pánico o peligro* (Panic or Danger, 1983). The latter novel, which received the Premio Xavier Villaurrutía in 1983, explores social relations in contemporary Mexico City through the experiences of a middle-class secretary. Puga's other works include three collections of short stories, *Inmovil sol secreto* (Immobile Secret Sun, 1979), *Accidentes* (Accidents, 1981), and *Intentos* (Attempts, 1987), and four other novels, *Cuando el aire es azul* (When the Air Is Blue, 1980), *La forma del silencio* (The Form of Silence, 1987), *Antonia* (1989), and *Las razones del lago* (The Reasons of the Lake, 1991). Puga's concern with the implications of racial, class, and gender differences constitutes the basis of her social criticism. Her critical view of Mexican society is shared by a generation of Mexican writers marked by the tragic results of the Mexican student movement in 1968.

– DANNY J. ANDERSON

PUIG, MANUEL

Manuel Puig (*b.* 28 December 1932; *d.* 22 July 1990), Argentine novelist. Born in General Villegas, Buenos Aires Province, he was educated at a U.S. boarding school in Buenos Aires. Puig had such a childhood passion for American movies that he learned English in

Puig had such a childhood passion for American movies that he learned English to enjoy them more thoroughly.

1942 to enjoy them more thoroughly. He also was very interested in French and Italian movies and studied filmmaking in Italy on a scholarship during the mid-1950s. Returning to Argentina in 1960, Puig began writing film scripts and working as an assistant director in the Argentine film industry. He then moved to New York City to devote himself to writing.

Under the disguise of pop literature, Puig built a complex narrative oeuvre, in which, paradoxically, he used film techniques. Both *La traición de Rita Hayworth* (1968; *Betrayed by Rita Hayworth,* 1971) and *Boquitas pintadas* (1969; *Heartbreak Tango,* 1973) examine the narrow world of alienated human beings who find refuge in the massive consumption of movies and soap operas. These initial novels, together with the rest of his production, including *The Buenos Aires Affair* (1973) and *El beso de la mujer araña* (1976; *Kiss of the Spider Woman,* 1979), implicitly attack the stratified and conventional realism of the traditional novel and the cultural foundations of the experimental and vanguardist novel, and they demystify modern Argentine conventions. He used sexual frustration as a literary tool for his task of demolition both at the individual and social levels.

One of the major interests of Puig's books resides in the kind of clichéd speech used by his characters, a speech canonized by the mass media. It is a euphemistic language that reveals the aberrant character of the linguistic codes of the mass culture, which confers a "subversive" dimension to his literature. He published a total of eight novels, two plays, and two movie scripts. He received the Curzio Malaparte Award (Italy) in 1986 for his novel *Sangre de amor correspondido* (1983; *Blood of Requited Love,* 1984).

— ANGELA B. DELLEPIANE

PUIG CASAURANC, JOSÉ MANUEL

José Manuel Puig Casauranc (*b.* 31 January 1888; *d.* 9 May 1939), Mexican politician-diplomat of the 1920s and 1930s. Born in Campeche and educated as a physician, Puig emerged in national politics as manager of Plutarco Elías CALLES's successful presidential campaign in 1924. Calles appointed him to head the prestigious Ministry of Education in his cabinet. In the uncertainty following the 1928 assassination of Álvaro OBREGÓN, Puig was a leading power broker and a presidential contender. The apogee of his public career was his confrontation with U.S. Secretary of State Cordell Hull at the 1933 Pan-American Conference in Montevideo, Uruguay. Cognizant of the leftward shift in Mexican politics, Puig criticized international bankers and U.S. dominance of the Mexican economy. In spite of his political adaptability, Puig became a peripheral figure during the Lázaro CÁRDENAS presidency.

— JOHN A. BRITTON

Q

QUADROS, JÂNIO DA SILVA

Jânio da Silva Quadros (*b.* 25 January 1917), president of Brazil (1961), mayor (1953–1954, 1986–1988) and governor (1955–1959) of São Paulo.

Born in Mato Grosso, Quadros soon moved with his family to Paraná, where his father practiced medicine and dabbled in politics. In 1930 the family moved to São Paulo, where Quadros completed his education and received a law degree. While practicing law and teaching, he became active in local politics. As a campaigner and later as a councilman, he gained a reputation as a bohemian, unpredictable, and quixotic figure.

Promising to "sweep out corruption," Quadros won broad support from the working and middle classes.

In 1950 Quadros won a seat in the state legislature, and his notoriety grew because of his constant questioning of officials and demands for rectitude. In 1953, with the backing of Paulista influentials, he ran for mayor on a platform that stressed cleaning up graft and curbing expenditures. He adopted the broom as a campaign symbol. His victory over veteran politicians brought national attention, and the following year he took on Adhemar de BARROS in the gubernatorial election. Promising to "sweep out corruption," he used unorthodox appeals that won broad support from the working and middle classes. His victory confirmed his image as a dragon slayer and quintessential populist.

From the moment of his election, Quadros turned his attention to the presidential succession, maneuvering for influence and federal patronage. São Paulo prospered from business expansion, and Quadros plowed growing taxes into infrastructure. São Paulo surpassed Rio in population as it became an industrial megalopolis.

In 1959 Quadros began campaigning for president, accepting the nomination of the National Democratic Union (UDN). His fresh image, unusual methods, and promises of national prosperity attracted a plurality of the voters, who also returned João GOULART to the vice presidency. As the first president inaugurated in Brasília, Quadros made headlines in early 1961 with an ambitious program of reforms while retaining his reputation for moralism and eccentricity. He pursued fiscal austerity, an activist and neutral foreign policy, closer relations with the Third World, and industrial growth. Soon, however, relations between the president and Congress soured, and in August Quadros abruptly resigned. He hoped to be recalled because Goulart was unpalatable to conservatives and the military, but Congress accepted his resignation and Goulart eventually succeeded him.

Failing to make a comeback as governor of São Paulo in 1962 and again in 1982, Quadros remained on the sidelines throughout the military years. Then he surprised critics by winning the mayoralty of São Paulo in 1985. His decision not to run for president in 1989 marked the end of his active career.

– MICHAEL L. CONNIFF

QUEIRÓS COUTINHO MATOSO DA CÂMERA, EUSÉBIO DE

Eusébio de Queirós Coutinho Matoso da Câmera (*b.* 27 December 1812; *d.* 7 May 1868), Brazilian statesman. Born in São Paulo Luanda, Angola, Queirós was the son of a Portuguese magistrate who rose to the highest Brazilian judicial elite. He took his law degree at Olinda in 1832 and was immediately appointed a judge. Shortly thereafter, he became chief of police in Rio de Janeiro (1833–1844). Queirós's fierce defense of order, underwritten by marriage into a powerful merchant and political family (1835), helps explain his rise in the Conservative Party (1837). With Joaquim José Rodrigues Torres and Paulino José Soares de Sousa, Eusébio formed the *trindade saquarema,* the party's most powerful, reactionary leadership. Eusébio took up crucial political responsibilities early on: provincial deputy in Rio de Janeiro (1838); national deputy for that province (1842–1844, 1848–1854); *desembargador da relação* in Rio (1842–1848); minister of justice (1848–1852); senator for Rio de Janeiro Province (1854); and member of the Council of State (1855). Responsible for developing the *Código Comercial* of 1850, he is better known for suppressing the African slave trade (1850) when he was minister of justice and for maintaining the power of the *saquarema* "oligarchy" in the Senate.

– JEFFREY D. NEEDELL

QUEIROZ, DINAH SILVEIRA DE

Dinah Silveira de Queiroz (*b.* 9 November 1910; *d.* 1983), Brazilian fiction writer. From the 1940s to the

1960s Queiroz was one of Brazil's most popular novelists. She was the second woman to be elected to the Brazilian Academy of Letters (1980). From a São Paulo literary family, Queiroz was a diplomat and a diplomat's wife; she lived for a time in Europe and in Russia. A journalist, she wrote technically skillful and sensitive stories, thus helping innovate Brazilian fiction. She also wrote *crônicas* (sketches), drama, children's literature, and science fiction. Queiroz received important literary prizes, including the Academy's Machado de Assis Prize for her complete works in 1954. Her fame, however, derived from novel serializations in popular magazines. Her novels *Floradas na serra* (1939; Blossoms on the Mountain) and *A muralha* (1954; The Wall) also became successful cinema and television vehicles.

– MARIA ANGÉLICA LOPES

QUEIROZ, RACHEL DE

Rachel de Queiroz (*b.* 17 November 1910), Brazilian novelist and journalist. Born in Fortaleza, Ceará, and reared on her father's ranch in the *sertão*, Rachel de Queiroz returns to the Northeastern region of Brazil in her literature. Educated in a convent school to be a teacher, she became a journalist in 1927 and has written for several newspapers and magazines. Her career as a novelist began when she published *O quinze* (1930) at age twenty. Although she is also a dramatist, chronicler, translator, and writer of children's literature, *O quinze* remains her most noted work. It placed her in the mainstream of the Northeastern regional novelists who documented the human, social, and geographical complexity of the Brazilian *sertão*. *O quinze* is a realistic drama told through one family's struggle to survive the disastrous consequences of the drought of 1915, which had in fact caused Queiroz's family to flee to Rio de Janeiro.

Other novels include *João Miguel* (1932), *Caminho de pedras* (1937), *As três Marias* (1939; *The Three Marias,* 1963), and *Dôra, Doralina* (1975; *Dora, Doralina,* 1984). Much of Queiroz's fiction addresses social problems associated with banditry and religious fanaticism in the *sertão,* such as in the dramas *Lampião* (1953) and *A beata Maria do Egito* (1958). Her special talent is illustrated in her portrayals of feminine characters who question their traditional roles in society and the family, but these sociological aspects form only a backdrop to situations and individual characters. Her literature incorporates simplicity of style and language.

Her limited political activity included a diplomatic mission to the United Nations on the Commission for Human Rights in 1966. Throughout her journalistic career, Queiroz has continued to write *crônicas* (short prose pieces), published in several collections. In 1957 she received the Machado de Assis award for her body of work, and she was the first woman to be admitted to the Brazilian Academy of Letters, in 1977.

– LORI MADDEN

QUERINO, MANOEL RAIMUNDO

Manoel Raimundo Querino (Manuel; *b.* 28 July 1851; *d.* 14 February 1923), Brazilian folklorist and reformer. His essays on religious cults, artists and artisans, cuisine, folk customs, and other topics celebrated skilled artisans and the Afro-Brazilian achievement.

Querino's works challenged racism by means of objective documentation. Those collected posthumously in *Costumes africanos no Brasil* (1938; African Customs in Brazil) and *A raça africana e os seus costumes* (1955; The African Race and Its Customs) assemble a gallery of black heroes and assess the African contribution to colonial Brazil. They describe Bahia's Candomblé religion without the social Darwinist theorizing of his contemporary, Raimundo Nina RODRIGUES.

Querino's works challenged racism by means of objective documentation.

Querino championed the arts and skilled trades in Bahia. He was founder (1872) and teacher at the Liceu de Artes e Ofícios, a vocational arts school, and founder (1877) of the Escola de Belas Artes. He represented Salvador's workers in cooperatives, at the 1892 Rio labor congress, and on the city council.

– DAIN BORGES

QUESADA, ERNESTO

Ernesto Quesada (*b.* 1 June 1858; *d.* 7 February 1934), Argentine scholar and diplomat. Quesada, the son of Vicente G. Quesada and Elvira Medina, was born in Buenos Aires. He studied at the Colegio San José, then went to Europe to continue his education. Upon his return, he enrolled in the Colegio Nacional, and from there went to the University of Buenos Aires, where he received a law degree in 1882. Quesada taught foreign literature at the Colegio Nacional from 1881 to 1884. When his father was Argentine ambassador to the United States (1885–1892), Quesada and his wife, Eleonora Pacheco, spent most of 1885 sightseeing there, and he studied American literature before leaving for Europe at the end of the year.

Quesada was devoted to his father, accompanying him on his numerous trips abroad and often serving as his interpreter and secretary. Father and son collaborated on many publications; thus, the works of each contain references to those of the other. Quesada's articles on contemporary intellectuals relied on notes made after hearing them at informal gatherings. He helped his father publish *Virreinato del Río de la Plata, 1776–1810* (1881), and together they edited the *Nueva revista de Buenos Aires* (1881–1885). The son was not active in politics, but he briefly was a supporter of Miguel JUÁREZ CELMAN before joining the Unión Cívica Radical. From 1893 to 1895 he was editor of the newspaper *El Tiempo,* in which many of his essays first appeared.

Quesada was not only a journalist and polemicist but also a distinguished lawyer and public servant. A strong supporter of Pan-Americanism, he was elected president of the Argentine delegation to the Pan-American Scientific Congress in 1915. That year Harvard University appointed him professor of history and Latin American economy, beginning in 1916, but for an unexplained reason he never appeared in Cambridge. He became professor of international law and treaties at the University of Buenos Aires in 1919.

From 1904 to 1923 Quesada was professor of sociology at the University of Buenos Aires. In 1907 he was named professor of political economy at the Law Faculty of the University of La Plata. In his lectures he stressed the need for social legislation and an examination of labor conditions. In 1908, at the request of the Law Faculty, he examined the methods of faculty promotion and history teaching at twenty-two German universities. During this investigation he met Karl Lamprecht, head of the Institute of World History and Civilization at the University of Leipzig. Lamprecht's institute probably was Quesada's model for the Institute of Historical Investigations, which he helped establish at the University of Buenos Aires. Quesada's second wife, Leonore Niessen Deilers, undoubtedly was instrumental in his decision to give his library—consisting of 60,000 books, 18,000 manuscripts, and the thirty unpublished volumes of his father's memoirs—to the University of Berlin. The university created the Ibero-American Institute to house it, and began publishing a journal, *Ibero-Amerikanische Archiv.* Quesada retired to Spiez, Switzerland, where he spent the rest of his life.

— JOSEPH T. CRISCENTI

QUIJANO, CARLOS

Carlos Quijano (*b.* 1900; *d.* 10 June 1984), Uruguayan journalist, writer, and political activist born in Montevideo, where he received a degree in law in 1923. He left Uruguay to study economics and political science at the Sorbonne in Paris. There he acted as a correspondent for the Uruguayan newspaper *El País* and cofounded the General Association of Latin American Students (AGELA). Intellectually, he came under the influence of the theoretical socialism of thinkers such as Gramsci, Sorel, and Croce, which greatly motivated his subsequent political committment when he returned to Uruguay in 1928. After returning to Uruguay, he was elected to Congress as a member of the National (or Blanco) Party from 1928 to 1931.

But Quijano's greatest influence on Uruguayan culture was through his role as founder and director of the weekly *Marcha,* through which he truly became mentor to a generation. For thirty-five years (1939–1974) *Marcha* served as a cultural reference throughout Latin America and a forum for writers and thinkers of different countries. In its pages appeared the work of Juan Carlos ONETTI, Angel RAMA, Emir RODRÍGUEZ MONEGAL, Carlos REAL DE AZÚA, Idea VILARIÑO, Joaquín TORRES GARCÍA, Arturo Ardao, Mario BENEDETTI, Mercedes Rein, Cristina PERI ROSSI, and Jorge Ruffinelli, among many others. In 1974, *Marcha* was shut down by the dictatorship, and after a brief period of imprisonment, Quijano left for Mexico along with other members of the weekly's staff. In exile he continued to work incessantly until his death, editing *Cuadernos de Marcha* and teaching classes at the National Autonomous University in Mexico City.

— MARÍA INÉS DE TORRES

QUIÑONES MOLINA, ALFONSO

Alfonso Quiñones Molina (*b.* 1873; *d.* 1950), president of El Salvador (1914–1915, 1918–1919, and 1923–1927). Alfonso Quiñones Molina belonged to the Quiñones–MELÉNDEZ FAMILY dynasty that controlled the presidency of El Salvador. Members of the dominant civilian landowning elite, these families used rigged elections to maintain governmental control from the 1890s until the Great Depression brought military control in 1931. The landowners facilitated the emergence of coffee as the dominant agricultural crop during an era characterized by peace, prosperity, and the concentration of land ownership among a few families.

Quiñones Molina held the presidency three times. He governed briefly in 1914 during the election that installed his brother-in-law, Carlos Meléndez (acting president, 1913–1914). After organizing the first official party, the Liga Roja (Red League) in 1918, he again held office during a transition that allowed the election of Jorge Meléndez (president 1919–1923). Quiñones Molina became president in his own right in 1923, serving until 1927. His controversial foreign borrowing to secure funds for street paving in San Salvador caused a rejection of external debt by the populace, a situation that was exploited by later military regimes, particularly that of General Maximiliano HERNÁNDEZ MARTÍNEZ.

– KENNETH J. GRIEB

QUINQUELA MARTÍN, BENITO

Benito Quinquela Martín (*b.* 1 March 1890; *d.* 28 January 1977), Argentine painter and muralist. Quinquela Martín was born in Buenos Aires and adopted by a humble family. He attended a night drawing academy in La Boca, a picturesque Italian neighborhood on the outskirts of Buenos Aires, and was fond of painting the harbor by the Riachuelo bank. He was discovered by Master Pío Collivadino, who decided to support him in his career. In 1920 he received second prize in the National Salon of Buenos Aires; the same year he had his first individual exhibition in Rio de Janeiro with great success. He visited Europe and the United States and exhibited in Paris, Madrid, Rome, London, and New York. In 1970 he was invited to Cuba, where he had a one-man show in Havana.

On large canvases, Quinquela Martín painted views of the port and dockyards, showing the bustling life of La Boca in scenes that are a hymn to human effort. He was a colorist of exceptional talent, creating high contrasts with strong spatula strokes. His masterpieces are in the great American and European museums. He is the founder of the Fine Arts School and Museum of La Boca. The National Museum of Fine Arts had a retrospective of his works in 1990.

– AMALIA CORTINA ARAVENA

QUINTANA, MANUEL

Manuel Quintana (*b.* 19 October 1835; *d.* 12 March 1906), president of Argentina (1904–1906). Born in Buenos Aires, Quintana received his law degree from the University of Buenos Aires in 1858. He entered public service and in 1860 was elected a deputy in the Buenos Aires provincial Congress. He rose rapidly, representing Buenos Aires Province first as a national deputy (1862–1864 and 1867–1870) and then as a senator (1870–1874). In 1889, Quintana represented Argentina at the first Pan-American Conference in Washington, D.C. Soon after, in 1892, he served as President Luis SÁENZ PEÑA's (1892–1895) minister of the interior. In the years that followed, Quintana became an important opponent of the reformist Radical Civic Union Party. In the wake of the Radicals' 1893 "revolution," he served as federal interventor in Tucumán, Santiago del Estero, and Santa Fe Provinces. In 1904, he

succeeded Julio ROCA (1880–1886, 1898–1904) as president. During his administration, Quintana maintained his conservative stand against the Radicals, who rebelled again unsuccessfully in 1905. He died in office and was succeeded by José FIGUEROA ALCORTA.

– DANIEL LEWIS

QUINTANA ROO, ANDRÉS

Andrés Quintana Roo (*b.* 30 November 1787; *d.* 15 April 1851), Mexican political theorist and statesman, who helped lay the groundwork for Mexico's nineteenth-century liberal reforms. Born in Mérida, on the Yucatán Peninsula, Quintana Roo moved to Mexico City in 1808 to complete his education. In 1812 he joined the insurgent struggle for Mexican Independence. His future wife, Leona VICARIO, whom he had met in Mexico City, joined him in 1813. Not a military man, Quintana Roo provided intellectual leadership, writing for the rebel newspapers *El Ilustrador Americano* and the *Semanario Patriótico Americano* and serving in the Congress of Chilpancingo.

For several decades following Independence in 1821, Quintana Roo held executive posts under federalist governments, such as minister of justice in 1833. During centralist-conservative regimes, he played an important role as an opposition legislator. Throughout the era, he continued his work as a trenchant political commentator, most notably in the 1830s for the periodicals *El Federalista* and *El Correo de la Federación*.

– RICHARD WARREN

QUINTANAR, HÉCTOR

Héctor Quintanar (*b.* 15 April 1936), Mexican composer, conductor, and founder of the first electronic music studio in Mexico (1970). He studied composition with Rodolfo HALFFTER and Carlos CHÁVEZ and assumed leadership of Chávez's composition workshop at the National Conservatory in 1965. His experimental interests took him to New York for electronic music study and Paris to explore *musique concrète* (the use of nonmusical recorded sounds in music scores). He has also pursued other styles such as nonrepetition, twelve-tone pointillism, and new sounds derived from traditional instruments. Quintanar has conducted the orchestras of the Free University of Mexico and the city of Morelia.

– ROBERT L. PARKER

QUINTERO, ÁNGEL

Ángel Quintero (*b.* 1805; *d.* 2 August 1866), Venezuelan politician. Quintero earned a doctorate in law from the University of Caracas in 1835. He began his political activity as a member of the Constituent Congress of 1830. Associated with the Conservative Party, he became secretary of the interior and of justice in 1839. Quintero opposed the government of José Tadeo MONAGAS, founded the periodical *El Espectador*, and joined José Antonio PÁEZ in his revolution against Monagas. The revolution defeated, he was seized and expelled from the country. Quintero returned shortly after the outbreak of the Federal War (1859–1863) and again joined Páez, but when Páez proclaimed his dictatorship, Quintero again left the country. He returned after the war and remained at the margin of political activity until his death.

– INÉS QUINTERO

QUIROGA, HORACIO

Horacio Quiroga (*b.* 31 December 1878; *d.* 19 February 1937), Uruguayan writer and one of Spanish America's greatest narrators. Quiroga was born in Salto; his father died in a hunting accident when he was three months old. Quiroga's life had more than its share of violent personal tragedies—his stepfather and one of his

Horacio Quiroga, 1917. (Museo Histórico Nacional, Montevideo, Uruguay)

two wives committed suicide and Quiroga killed one of his best friends in a gun accident—which explains his interest in death and the monstrous. His earliest literary influence was Edgar Allan Poe.

Quiroga attended the University of Montevideo for a short time. In 1903 he went to Misiones, the following year to the Argentine Chaco. When the farming venture failed, he went to Buenos Aires, taught school, and married. In 1915 his wife committed suicide. During the ensuing decade, he wrote some of his best stories, including *Cuentos de amor, de locura y de muerte* (1917), the haunting *Cuentos de la selva* (1918; *South American Jungle Tales, 1941*), and *Los desterrados* (1926); he also published in the journal *Caras y Caretas*.

To make ends meet, he served as Uruguay's consul in Buenos Aires from 1917 to 1926, and he married again in 1927. In 1932 he returned to San Ignacio, Misiones, with his second wife and children as Uruguay's consul. When the consulate closed, Quiroga returned to Buenos Aires, plagued by lifelong asthma and neurasthenia. He was diagnosed with cancer and in 1937 took his own life. Many of his more than 200 powerful stories, written with great economy of style, are set in the spectacular Argentine wilderness—the jungle, the plantations, the powerful Paraná River. Although his early writings tend to deal more with the extraordinary, the monstrous, and talking animals, his later production drew more on his own rich experience with people. *The Exiles and Other Stories* (1987) and *The Decapitated Chicken and Other Stories* (1976) represent some of his best writings translated into English.

– GEORGETTE MAGASSY DORN

QUIROGA, JUAN FACUNDO

Juan Facundo Quiroga (*b.* 1788; *d.* 16 February 1835), Argentine caudillo known as "The Tiger of the Llanos." Born in La Rioja to a family of landowners and regional officials, Quiroga began his own ascent in 1816 as a militia officer, serving the revolutionary government in Buenos Aires by mobilizing men and supplies for the Army of the North. As delegate of the center, he added military and political credentials to his landed power, and from this it was a short step to independent authority. In 1820 La Rioja proclaimed its "provisional independence" of neighboring Córdoba and became in effect a personal fiefdom of Quiroga. From this power base he waged war on Bernardino RIVADAVIA's centralized constitution, and in spite of defeat at the hands of General Gregorio Aráoz de La Madrid, he went on to extend his control over the provinces of the west and northwest from Catamarca to Mendoza. Recovering from losses to General José María PAZ in 1829 and

1830, he furthered his reputation as a federalist by defeating the unitarist forces under Aráoz de La Madrid in 1831. Thus, as Juan Manuel ROSAS was establishing his power in Buenos Aires, Quiroga was consolidating his control in the interior. But Quiroga went further. He moved to Buenos Aires and attempted to secure the calling of a constituent congress to give Argentina a federal republic, a proposal which was anathema to Rosas. He further challenged the idea of Rosas by demanding that the customs revenue of Buenos Aires be nationalized. In 1834 Quiroga was sent by the government of Buenos Aires on a peace mission to the northwest, in the hope that his influence could prevent a threatened civil war between Salta and Tucumán. Returning from successful negotiations, he was ambushed and assassinated at Barranca Yaco on 16 February 1835. The death of Quiroga removed a challenge to Buenos Aires and an irritant to Rosas, and among the possible assassins Rosas himself was suspected. The official judgment, probably correct, convicted the caudillos of Córdoba, all four Reinafé brothers, and their henchmen.

Quiroga, whom Juan Bautista ALBERDI regarded as an obscure guerrilla and a common killer, survives in history largely through the exposure he received in Domingo SARMIENTO's *Facundo* (1938), a classic of Argentine literature. There he not only was described as a tyrant and a terrorist but also was elevated to a thesis—the conflict between civilization and barbarism—which was widely invoked to explain the state of Latin America. He was the model of the provincial caudillo, his life a series of outrages, his rule the epitome of personal power.

– JOHN LYNCH

QUIROGA, VASCO DE

Vasco de Quiroga (*b.* ca. 1477/79; *d.* February/March 1565), judge of the second *audiencia* of Mexico (1530) and consecrated as the first bishop of Michoacán (1538). Born in Madrigal de las Altas Torres, Spain, Quiroga was sent by the Spanish crown to Mexico where, as both judge and bishop, he devoted most of his energy and resources to bringing an idealized, European lifestyle to the indigenous people. He organized utopian communities emphasizing religious instruction, encouraging the development of crafts, and promoting agricultural self-sufficiency, self-government, and care for the sick and needy, including an unusual plan for an infirmary for each town. Quiroga also brought indigenous youths raised in monasteries to his towns to help priests instruct other Indians in the Christian doctrine. One observer referred to Santa Fe de la Laguna, Michoacán, as a monastery. Quiroga's communities have also been called pueblo-hospitals and hospital-schools.

Quiroga devoted most of his energy and resources to bringing an idealized, European lifestyle to Mexico's indigenous people.

Most scholars agree that the utopian vision of "Tata Vasco," as his admirers called him, was influenced by St. Thomas More, but some controversy lingers regarding questions about Quiroga's communal intent and his perspectives on conquest. Sixteenth-century critics included some Indians who charged him with unremunerated labor and neighboring Spaniards who were jealous of his land and his residents' exemption from tributes and labor drafts. Both groups complained about his harboring of runaway slaves. Quiroga spent his last years making pastoral visits to the rural communities of Michoacán.

– STEPHANIE WOOD

QUIROGA SANTA CRUZ, MARCELO

Marcelo Quiroga Santa Cruz (*b.* 13 March 1931; *d.* 17 July 1980), founder and leader of the Socialist Party-One (PSU). Born in Cochabamba, Quiroga Santa Cruz was the intellectual leader of the Bolivian Left from 1970 until his death. In the 1960s he switched from the right-wing Bolivian Socialist Falange (FSB) to the socialist cause, becoming leader of the PSU in 1971. As minister of hydrocarbons, he effected the nationalization in 1970 of the Bolivian holdings of Gulf Oil Company. In 1979, Quiroga Santa Cruz began a congressional inquiry into the responsibility for human rights abuses during the General Hugo BANZER regime (1971–1978). He was assassinated in 1980 on the first day of the infamous "cocaine coup," in which General Luis GARCÍA MEZA (1980–1981) took power.

The most effective public speaker of his generation, Quiroga Santa Cruz was unable to translate his personal popularity into a popular political base. Nevertheless, he served as an important political gadfly and the conscience of the Bolivian Left during his lifetime.

– ERICK D. LANGER

QUIRÓS, CESÁREO BERNALDO DE

Cesáreo Bernaldo de Quirós (*b.* 29 May 1881; *d.* 29 May 1968), Argentine painter. Quirós was born in Gualeguay, Entre Ríos Province, and began to paint while very young. In 1899 he received the Prix de Rome, and the following year he won a scholarship and traveled to Italy. In 1901 he won a prize at the Venice Biennale. He also traveled in Spain, Italy, and Sardinia. In 1906 he returned to Argentina, where he had his first one-man show at the Salon Costa. The Modern Art Museum in Barcelona bought one of his paintings. He won the grand prize and the gold medal at the international art exhibition held in Buenos Aires in 1910. That year he returned to Europe, where he lived until 1915. Back in Argentina, he lived in his native province until 1927, working on a series of paintings dealing with gaucho life, which were later exhibited in Europe and North America. Quirós was a professor at the National Academy of Decorative Arts and chairman of the National Academy of Fine Arts. In 1963 he made an endowment of his works to the National Museum. In 1981 the Museo Pedro Martínez, in Paraná, Entre Ríos, inaugurated a hall in his honor, and in 1991 the Salas Nacionales de Exposiciones in Buenos Aires exhibited more than 150 of his paintings.

– AMALIA CORTINA ARAVENA

R

RABASA, EMILIO

Emilio Rabasa (*b.* 22 May 1856; *d.* 25 April 1930), Mexican novelist. Rabasa, a native of Ocozocuatla, Chiapas, studied law at the Instituto de Ciencias y Artes in Oaxaca and began his career as a deputy in the state legislature in 1881. In 1886 he went to Mexico City, returned to Chiapas as governor from 1891 to 1894, and then served as its senator from 1894 to 1913. He represented the government of Victoriano HUERTA at the Niagara Falls Conference in Canada (20 May–15 July 1914), alongside the envoys of Venustiano CARRANZA, to discuss the U.S. occupation of Veracruz and the incident at Tampico. Huerta fell in 1914, and Rabasa and his family remained in New York City until 1920.

Rabasa has been hailed as the father of

"Mexican realism."

Rabasa was known as one of Mexico's outstanding constitutional lawyers. He also distinguished himself as a novelist and journalist. In 1887 he cofounded *El Universal,* still in publication. In that year and the following one, he published four novels using the pseudonym of Sancho Polo, *La bola, La gran ciencia, El cuarto poder,* and *Moneda falsa.* A novel, *La guerra de tres años,* published serially in *El Universal* in 1891, appeared in 1931. Rabasa has been hailed as the father of "Mexican realism," and his work is frequently compared with that of his Spanish contemporary, Benito Pérez Galdós.

— BARBARA A. TENENBAUM

RADA, MANUEL DE JESÚS

Manuel de Jesús Rada (early 1800s), priest, politician, and author. Rada was pastor of the parish of Villa de Santa Cruz de la Cañada, northwest of Santa Fe, New Mexico, in 1821. Santa Cruz, the seat of regional government, incorporated the Indian pueblos of Santa Clara, San Ildefonso, Pojoaque, Nambé, San Juan, Taos, Picuris, and Abiquiú, with a population of just over 6,500. As the community leader, Rada delivered a trapping license from Governor Bartolomé Baca to William Becknell, establisher of the Sante Fe Trail, on 29 October 1824.

Rada was pastor of San Juan pueblo and vicar of Río Arriba from 1826 to 1828. He was elected as a deputy to the national Congress in October 1828; his report to New Mexico constituents in Chihuahua, dated 13 November 1828 and printed in Zacatecas, was later used by Deputy Diego Archuleta in 1845 to promote development of New Mexico. In January 1829, Rada presented *Proposición hecha al Soberano congreso general de la unión,* which called for increased spending on defense and education; development of industry; foreign investment; efficient, qualified government; abolition of taxes on tobacco and gunpowder; and abolition of tithes.

— W. MICHAEL MATHES

RAMA, ANGEL

Angel Rama (*b.* 30 April 1926; *d.* 27 November 1983), Uruguayan literary critic, journalist, publisher, and educator. Rama was born in Montevideo to Spanish immigrants. While studying humanities at the University of Uruguay he worked for Agence France Presse in 1945, and in 1950 he and Carlos Maggi founded the publishing house Fábula, which brought out Rama's first two books, *Oh sombra puritana* (1951) and *Tierra sin mapa* (1961). He married the poet Ida Vitale in 1950 and joined the influential journal *Marcha* (1958–1968), directed by Carlos QUIJANO, remaining a regular contributor until the dictatorial government of Uruguay closed it down in 1973.

Rama edited twenty-eight volumes in the collection of Clásicos Uruguayos, served as director of the Biblioteca Artigas from 1951 to 1958, and managed the journal *Entregas de la Licorne* (1953–1956). With his brother Germán Rama he established the publishing house ARCA in 1962; wrote for Uruguay's major newspaper, *El País;* held posts at the National Library of Uruguay (1949–1965); and taught literature at the University of Uruguay (1966–1974). He served on the editorial board of the Cuban publication *Casa de las Américas* from 1964 to 1971, when he resigned over the political trial in Cuba of the poet Heberto PADILLA.

Having divorced Vitale, Rama married Argentine art critic and essayist Marta TRABA in 1969 and moved to Puerto Rico. In 1974 they went to Caracas, where he directed the publication of Latin American classics entitled Biblioteca Ayacucho and taught at the Central University of Venezuela. He became a tenured professor at the University of Maryland in 1981. Rama and Traba died in a plane crash near Madrid.

In thirty books and numerous articles Rama examined literature from all periods of Latin American cultural history. In addition to his work on gaucho poetry, he also wrote about José Martí, Rubén Darío, Horacio Quiroga, Juan Carlos Onetti, and Gabriel García Márquez. Among his major works are *Los gauchopolíticos rioplatenses* (1976), *Rubén Darío y el modernismo* (1970), and *Transculturación narrativa en América Latina* (1982).

– SAÚL SOSNOWSKI

RAMALHO, JOÃO

João Ramalho (*b.* ca. 1490; *d.* ca. 1580), earliest permanent Portuguese resident of southern Brazil. Born in Vouzela, Portugal, Ramalho was stranded on the coast near São Vicente around 1513 and lived for many years among the Tupinikin, marrying Chief Tibiriçá's daughter Bartira. Wielding extraordinary influence among the Indians, Ramalho "could assemble five thousand warriors in a single day," according to contemporary traveler Ulrich Schmidl. With these attributes of an Indian headman, Ramalho played a central role in guaranteeing the European occupation of São Vicente, as he persuaded his indigenous relatives to form an alliance with the Portuguese against their mortal enemies, the Tupinambá (Tamoio). Ramalho's village on the interior plateau was one of the nuclei that later formed São Paulo, where he died.

– JOHN M. MONTEIRO

RAMÍREZ, FRANCISCO

Francisco Ramírez (*b.* 13 March 1786; *d.* 10 July 1821), Argentine caudillo of Entre Ríos and leader of provincial federalism against Buenos Aires. Born in Concepción del Uruguay, into the colonial elite of land and office, he joined the independence movement in 1810. The following year he supported José Gervasio ARTIGAS against the Spanish regime in Uruguay, and in 1816 against Portuguese invaders from Brazil. But Ramírez represented the interests of the *estancieros* of Entre Ríos and distanced himself from the agrarian populism of Artigas. He also resisted the centralism of Buenos Aires and its demands for resources. In 1819 he joined the caudillo Estanislao LÓPEZ of Santa Fe, and in 1820 he led a force of federalist *montoneros* (gaucho cavalry) to victory over Buenos Aires at the battle of Cepeda;

Buenos Aires was forced to agree to the Treaty of Pilar (23 February 1820), which recognized the jurisdiction of the provinces in a loose federal structure. In a decree of 29 September 1820 Ramírez styled himself *jefe supremo* of the Republic of Entre Ríos. The caudillo alliance was short-lived. Disputes between Ramírez and López over political leadership in the Littoral and strategy toward the Portuguese in Uruguay caused violent conflict which culminated in the defeat of Ramírez at Río Seco in July 1821. Returning to rescue his woman, the legendary Delfina, who had fallen into the hands of the enemy, Ramírez was killed. His head was exhibited in public by López.

– JOHN LYNCH

RAMÍREZ, IGNACIO

Ignacio Ramírez (*b.* 1818; *d.* 1879), Mexican journalist and cabinet minister. Ramírez was born in San Miguel de Allende, Guanajuato, and educated in Querétaro and Mexico City, where he received his degree in law. In 1845, with Guillermo PRIETO and Vicente Segura, he began publishing the satirical journal *Don Simplicio*. Using the pseudonym "El Nigromante" (The Necromancer), Ramírez denounced the wealthy and the church with a wicked sense of humor. For example, El Nigromante proposed that "The Ten Commandments shall be retained in all their vigor, except the seventh, as long as citizens lack another honorable means to maintain their subsistence." Ramírez extended this social analysis more directly in other articles: "We the workers say to the hacendados: Why without the sweat of your brows do you eat bread, or toss it to your prostitutes and lackeys? If you say because God made you rich, show us the deeds."

"Why without the sweat of your brows do you eat bread, or toss it to your prostitutes and lackeys?"

Ramírez may have been the most radical journalist and politician of his day and Mexico's most prominent atheist. Elected to the Constitutional Congress of 1856–1857, he advocated religious toleration. He argued that juridical equality was not sufficient and would not improve the standard of living for the majority of Mexico's people. Ramírez was criticial of the Ley Lerdo because it would make property available only to the middle class and the wealthy, who already owned some property and had the money to buy more.

President Benito JUÁREZ selected Ramírez to serve as minister of justice (21 January 1861–9 May 1861) and minister of development (18 March 1861–3 April 1861). Ramírez believed that the Constitution of 1857 gave Congress supremacy over the presidency and came to regard Juárez as a dictator. He spent much of the second empire in exile in California. After the restoration of the republic, Ramírez returned to Mexico and served as a justice of the Supreme Court from 1868 to 1879. He supported Porfirio DÍAZ's Plan of Tuxtepec and served as Díaz's first minister of justice (29 November 1876–7 May 1877).

– D. F. STEVENS

RAMÍREZ, JOSÉ FERNANDO

José Fernando Ramírez (*b.* 5 May 1804; *d.* 4 March 1871), Mexican political figure. Although born in Hidalgo del Parral, Chihuahua, Ramírez represented Durango in the federal Congress in 1833–1834 and was rector of the State College of Lawyers. He helped formulate the Bases Orgánicas of 1843 and served as secretary of foreign relations three times: December 1846–January 1847, September 1851–March 1852, and June 1864–October 1865 under the empire. A moderate Liberal, he rallied to the Plan of Ayutla in 1854. In Europe from mid-1855 until spring 1856, he continued research, which he had begun in the previous decade, on the pre-Columbian era. He declined to participate in the Assembly of Notables of 1864, but served on MAXIMILIAN's Council of State until March 1866. Tainted by collaboration with the empire, he died in exile in Bonn.

A collector of rare books and manuscripts, Ramírez championed the idea of a national library. His *Vida de Fray Toribio de Motolinía* (1858) formed volume one of Joaquín García Icazbalceta's *Colección de documentos para la historia de México.*

– BRIAN HAMNETT

RAMÍREZ, PEDRO PABLO

Pedro Pablo Ramírez (*b.* 30 January 1884; *d.* 11 June 1962), president of Argentina (1943–1944). Ramírez, born in Laz Paz, Entre Ríos, became president on 6 June 1943 in the wake of the 4 June coup that overthrew Ramón CASTILLO. A major general, he had been minister of war. Ramírez's first cabinet was sharply divided on World War II, and while pledging to eliminate corruption and restore democracy, it severely harassed Communists and restricted unions.

Ramírez lacked a strong personality and clear opinions. Into this vacuum stepped a military lodge, the G.O.U. (Grupo Obra de Unificación or United Officers Group), controlled by colonels, among whom was

Juan Perón, which quickly began to push its own objectives: the defeat of communism and preservation of neutrality. Beginning in October 1943, ultrarightists dominated the government. Repression increased drastically; Communist organizations went underground; political parties were abolished; and the press was strictly censored.

Using Argentine involvement in a Bolivian coup and an aborted weapons deal with Germany, the United States convinced Ramírez to break relations with Germany on 26 January 1944. Furious officers called for Ramírez's resignation. But when he tried to comply on 24 February 1944, Ramírez was persuaded the following day to delegate his authority to his vice president, Edelmiro FARRELL, because of fears that a resignation would complicate diplomatic recognition. On 9 March, Ramírez resigned.

– JOEL HOROWITZ

RAMÍREZ MERCADO, SERGIO

Sergio Ramírez Mercado (*b.* 5 August 1942), vice president of Nicaragua (1984–1990). Ramírez was born in the town of Masatepe in the rich coffee region of Nicaragua. His father was a coffee planter and member of the Somoza-dominated National Liberal Party. His mother was director of a small school called the Anastasio Somoza García Institute. In his youth, Ramírez defended the SOMOZA dynasty in his writings for a rightwing magazine. He attended law school at the National Autonomous University of Nicaragua in Managua with the support of the Somoza family. He also studied at the University of Kansas and in West Germany.

By the early 1960s, Ramírez opposed the Somoza dictatorship. He helped Carlos FONSECA form the Student Revolutionary Front in 1961. After moving to Costa Rica in 1964, he established a literary career as editor of the leftist journal *Ventana*. Ramírez lived in West Berlin from 1973 to 1975. He returned to Costa Rica to serve as secretary-general of the Central American Council of Universities.

Ramírez joined the Sandinista National Liberation Front in 1975. The Sandinista strategy for recruiting members of the upper classes grew out of conversations between Ramírez and Humberto ORTEGA. They formed the Tercerista faction in 1975 and in 1977 assembled a group of prominent Nicaraguans known as "The Twelve." Ramírez represented The Twelve in the Broad Opposition Front in 1978 but resigned after a few months.

Ramírez was a member of the Governing Junta of National Reconstruction from June 1979 until November 1984. He then became vice president of the republic after the first free election in the revolutionary period. He held this post until the Sandinistas lost the presidential election of February 1990. He was leader of the Sandinista opposition in the National Assembly from April 1990 to October 1991. Ramírez was elected to the Sandinista National Directorate at the first party congress in July 1991. He was the founding editor of the journal *Semanario* in September 1990.

— MARK EVERINGHAM

RAMÍREZ VÁZQUEZ, PEDRO

Pedro Ramírez Vázquez (*b.* 16 April 1919), leading Mexican architect and public figure. Internationally renowned for his architectural designs of private residences and public buildings, he designed Mexico's Secretariat of Foreign Relations and Aztec Stadium. But he is best known outside of Mexico for the imaginative and modern National Museum of Anthropology. A native of Mexico City, Ramírez Vázquez graduated from the National University with a degree in architecture in 1943 and taught architectural composition and urbanism at the National School of Architecture for fifteen years. A long-time public servant, Ramírez Vázquez began his career as head of building conservation in the educational secretariat and worked many years in the school building program. He became president of the Olympic Games Organizing Committee in 1966 and served as secretary of public works from 1976 to 1982. He then returned to private practice.

— RODERIC AI CAMP

RAMÍREZ VILLAMIZAR, EDUARDO

Eduardo Ramírez Villamizar (*b.* 1923), Colombian sculptor. Ramírez studied architecture and fine art at the National University in Bogotá. Upon graduation in 1945, he began his career as a painter. His later work amalgamated architecture, painting, and sculpture. From 1949 to 1952 and 1954 to 1956, he lived in Paris. While there, he abandoned expressionism and began to create paintings, murals, and sculptures based on the abstract geometric principles of constructivism. His later forms, however, are increasingly inspired by the pre-Columbian art of Mexico and Peru.

In 1956 Ramírez had his first one-man show at the Pan-American Union, and the Museum of Modern Art purchased his painting *Blanco y Negro*. In 1971 he participated in the International Sculpture Symposium at the University of Vermont, where he showed his first monumental sculptures (*Cuatro Torres*). When the Kennedy Center opened in 1973, Colombia presented as its gift Ramírez's *De Colombia a John Kennedy*.

In 1990 the Colombian government established the Ramírez Villamizar Museum of Modern Art in Pamplona, his birthplace.

— IDA ELY RUBIN

RAMÍREZ Y BLANCO, ALEJANDRO

Alejandro Ramírez y Blanco (*b.* 25 February 1777; *d.* 20 May 1821), Intendant of Puerto Rico (1813–1816) and of Cuba (1816–1821). Born in Alaejos, Spain, and educated in Valladolid and at the University of Alcalá de Henares, Ramírez immigrated to Guatemala in 1795. He became secretary to the consulado in 1798 and to the captain-general in 1802. For his work as a member of the economic society and as editor of its newspaper, he was the only Latin American of his time named a member of the American Philosophical Society.

As intendant of Puerto Rico, Ramírez retired an inflationary issue of paper money and opened vocational schools for women and night schools for artisans.

In Havana on 14 December 1812, he took the oath as intendant of Puerto Rico. He found a bankrupt colony and began reformation of its tax structure and diversification of its economy. He retired an inflationary issue of paper money, founded an economic society and edited its newspaper, and opened vocational schools for women and night schools for artisans. Despite efforts from peninsular officials to thwart his reforms, the island became self-sufficient during his tenure.

On 3 July 1816, he became superintendent of Cuba and intendant of Havana and pursued his policies of economic diversification and tax reform, doubling royal revenues by 1820. Recognizing the problems of monoculture, he introduced new crops to be utilized by small landowners. He obtained abolition of the tobacco monopoly, thus invigorating the industry. He also created a school of chemistry and a botanical garden and school of botany, and his efforts led to public education programs and support of charitable institutions for women and orphans. Due to opposition from sugar interests and peninsular Spaniards, he became the first colonial official to utilize the press to defend his actions. In early 1821, he accepted appointment as *jefe político* of Guatemala, but he died before leaving Cuba.

Ramírez showed that a liberal official, cooperating with creole interests, initiated outstanding successes utilizing Bourbon Reform policies. His legacy was the economic success in the colonies he served and a reputation for outstanding honesty.

— JACQUELYN BRIGGS KENT

RAMOS, ARTUR

Artur Ramos (Arthur Ramos; *b.* July 1903; *d.* 31 October 1949), Brazilian anthropologist, psychiatrist, and educator. Trained as a physician, Ramos first wrote psychiatric studies. In 1934 he moved to Rio de Janeiro to establish the psychiatric service of the Department of Education. That year he published *O negro brasileiro,* primarily a study of religion, and in 1935, *O folk-lore negro do Brasil: Demopsychologia e psychanalyse,* a study of dance, music, religion, and folktales. These studies explore psychoanalytical interpretations of Afro-Brazilian culture, but his later works emphasize processes of acculturation.

During World War II, Ramos's public career turned toward the application of anthropological research to antiracist propaganda. He founded the Brazilian Society of Anthropology and Ethnology in 1941 and became professor of anthropology at the Faculdade Nacional de Filosofia in Rio de Janeiro in 1946. Ramos died in 1949 while serving as director of the social science department of UNESCO in Paris, where he promoted the postwar UNESCO study of race relations.

— DAIN BORGES

RAMOS, GRACILIANO

Graciliano Ramos (*b.* 27 October 1892; *d.* 20 March 1953), Brazilian novelist. A member of the literary generation of 1930, Ramos is one of Brazil's most eminent writers. His works have been widely translated and have received international critical acclaim. Three of his narratives have been made into highly successful films.

Ramos was born into a modest family in a small town in Alagoas and spent much of his childhood on a farm in the *sertão* (backlands) of Pernambuco. There he witnessed the poverty and misery caused by unequal patterns of land ownership and by the periodic droughts that afflict the region, all of which would later be incorporated into his narratives with masterful artistry. Ramos never finished secondary school and began his adult life working in, and subsequently managing, his father's dry goods store. In 1928 he was elected mayor of the small Alagoan town of Palmeira dos Índios, following which he held numerous appointed posts in the state bureaucracy, notably as director of the government printing office and head of the Department of Education.

In March 1936, following the unsuccessful revolt of the Aliança Nacional Libertadora, a popular front organization, Ramos was arrested because he was suspected of being a Communist, and thereafter was held in various prisons until February 1937. Formal charges were never brought against him. Ramos recounted the humiliation and degradation of this experience in *Memórias do cárcere* (1953), one of the most eloquent condemnations of authoritarianism written by a Brazilian.

In "Os bichos do subterrâneo," Antônio Candido suggests that the actual events of 1936–1937, plus their subsequent fictional elaboration, made Ramos go from a view of the world as a prison to one of prison as the world. All of Ramos's major fictional works focus on his characters' inability to escape from or transcend the limitations imposed by their own psychological makeup and social situation. His first three novels offer a complex exploration of the dark corners of the human psyche, which has led some critics to see Ramos primarily as a psychological writer. Yet his characters are always portrayed in terms of the social situation of the Brazilian Northeast in a period characterized by the onset of modernization, a technique that identifies him as a social novelist. Ramos thus combines psychological and social analysis as few other Brazilian writers since Machado de ASSIS have been able to do.

The first three novels, all written in the first person, take the form of fictional memoirs. Set largely in a boardinghouse in a small town, *Caetés* (1933) deals with self-interest and the relativity of human moral values. The narrator-protagonist, João Valério, seduces his boss's wife, an act that eventually drives his boss to suicide. Valério is writing a novel about the Caeté Indians, who, through explicit comparison, serve as a metaphor for humanity's underlying primitive, egotistical, and barbarous self. Ramos's second novel, *São Bernardo* (1934), is structured as the memoirs of Paulo Honório, who has risen from worker to owner of a large *fazenda.* The story of his violent rise to wealth and power is also the story of his fall as a human being, for his ultimate financial, ethical, and psychological failure exposes the reification of human beings under capitalism, then rapidly expanding in Brazil. In its dense soundings, reminiscent of Dostoyevsky, Ramos's third novel, *Angústia* (1936), published while he was in prison, reconstructs the psychological disintegration of petit-bourgeois intellectual Luís da Silva, the scion of a decadent fraction of a previously dominant class of rural landowners. Together, these three novels constitute a complex portrait of what Valentim Facioli has called the contradictory and chaotic dynamism of a dependent capitalist Brazil.

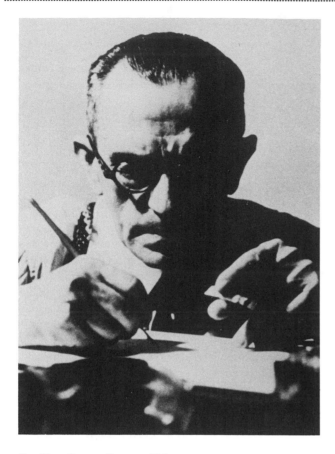

Graciliano Ramos. (Iconographia)

Many critics see *Vidas secas* (1938), Ramos's only novel written in the third person, as the high point of his career. The novel, circular in structure, portrays the suffering of an impoverished family during a period of drought. Through their strength and determination in the face of overwhelming odds, the family—composed of the cowherd Fabiano, his wife Vitória, their two sons, and the memorable dog Baleia—reveals a level of human dignity that is largely absent from Ramos's previous work. With his economical, harsh style, in a literary tour de force Ramos manages to penetrate the minds of his illiterate characters, and even of Baleia the dog, providing a haunting and moving portrait of the personal impact of environment and social tragedy.

With the exception of a few short stories, after *Vidas secas,* Ramos turned almost exclusively to journalistic and memorialistic writing.

– RANDAL JOHNSON

RAMOS ARIZPE, JOSÉ MIGUEL

José Miguel Ramos Arizpe (*b.* 1775; *d.* 1843), Mexican political theorist and politician. Born in Valle de San Nicolás, Coahuila, Ramos was ordained in 1803 and subsequently became professor of canon and civil law in Monterrey. Elected deputy to the Spanish Cortes in 1810, he became a leading champion of American rights and was the architect of the provincial deputation, an organization that provided home rule to the provinces. Arrested in 1814, when Ferdinand VII returned from France and abolished the constitutional system, he remained in prison until 1820, when the consitution was restored. Elected to the Cortes once again, he, together with other American deputies, proposed commonwealth status for the New World. After Independence Ramos returned to Mexico in 1822 in time to join the opposition to ITURBIDE; he was instrumental in mobilizing the provinces and in drafting the Plan of Casa Mata. Elected to the Second Constituent Congress, he was an advocate of moderate federalism and the principal author of the Constitution of 1824.

One of the founders of the Yorkino Masonic lodges in 1825, Ramos sided with the moderates in opposing the expulsion of the Spaniards and in supporting the presidency of Manuel GÓMEZ PEDRAZA in 1828. He served as minister of justice and ecclesiastic affairs in the VICTORIA and GÓMEZ FARÍAS administrations, distinguishing himself as a champion of national control of the church, while also continuing his clerical career, becoming dean of the cathedral chapter of Puebla. He was elected delegate from Puebla to the 1842 Congress shortly before he died.

– JAIME E. RODRÍGUEZ O.

RAMOS MEJÍA, EZEQUIEL

Ezequiel Ramos Mejía (*b.* 15 December 1853; *d.* 7 November 1935), Argentine politician who actively participated in the removal of President Julio Argentino ROCA's political machinery from power during the first decade of the twentieth century. Elected a provincial deputy in Buenos Aires in 1880, and a national deputy in 1900, Ramos Mejía was appointed minister of agriculture by President Roca in 1901. A native of Buenos Aires, his political allegiance was with Carlos PELLEGRINI rather than the provincial forces led by Roca. When Roca and Pellegrini parted ways in 1901, Ramos Mejía resigned and became a member of the growing opposition within the liberal-conservative forces. Under President José FIGUEROA ALCORTA (1906–1910) he served as minister of agriculture and minister of public works, continuing in the latter office under President Roque SÁENZ PEÑA until 1913. He was, therefore, at the forefront in the battle for power that developed during the Figueroa Alcorta administration between *roquistas* and the group of former *juaristas* (followers of former president Miguel JUÁREZ CELMAN), such as

Roque Sáenz Peña and Estanislao ZEBALLOS, who supported the president. His memoirs thus provide an invaluable source for the analysis of the political conflicts of the period.

Ideologically, Ramos Mejía evolved from a moderate nationalism to a growing disillusionment with democratic institutions. By the 1930s, influenced by his firsthand knowledge of the fascist experiment in Italy, where he served as ambassador between 1933 until his death, he was advocating the abandonment of the classical model of liberal democracy for a new type of political and economic organization.

— EDUARDO A. ZIMMERMANN

RAMOS MEJÍA, JOSÉ MARÍA

José María Ramos Mejía (*b.* 24 December 1849; *d.* 19 June 1914), Argentine physician, statesman, and intellectual. After studying medicine at the University of Buenos Aires, from which he graduated in 1879, Ramos Mejía promoted the creation of the Asistencia Pública de Buenos Aires, a municipal system of medical care for the needy, becoming its first director in 1883. Appointed professor at the Medical School at the University of Buenos Aires, he specialized in the study of mental pathologies, becoming one of the precursors of scientific psychiatry in Argentina. His first works reflected this interest: *Las neurosis de los hombres célebres en la historia argentina* (1878–1882); *Estudios de patología nerviosa y mental* (1893); and *La locura en la historia* (1895). Elected to Congress, he served as a national deputy (1888–1892) and was subsequently appointed director of the National Department of Health (1893–1908).

The profound social transformations that were taking place in early-twentieth-century Argentina awakened Ramos Mejía's interest in social psychology, as reflected in his works *Las multitudes argentinas* (1899), influenced by the work of Gustave Le Bon, and *Los simuladores del talento* (1904). Between 1908 and 1913 Ramos Mejía was in charge of the Consejo Nacional de Educación, where he launched an aggressive campaign to introduce the concept of "patriotic education" (emphasis on civics) in the schools, as a means of strengthening what he thought was a weakened sense of national identity, threatened by the impact of massive immigration.

— EDUARDO A. ZIMMERMANN

RAMOS Y MAGAÑA, SAMUEL

Samuel Ramos y Magaña (*b.* 8 June 1897; *d.* 20 June 1959), Mexican intellectual and educator. A student of Antonio CASO and collaborator of José VASCONCELOS and Pedro HENRÍQUEZ UREÑA, Samuel Ramos wrote a seminal work of Mexican philosophy and culture, *Profile of Man and Culture in Mexico* (1934), in the "lo mexicano" line of intellectual thought, continued by Octavio Paz in the 1960s. Although criticized for its lack of "empirical" evidence, this work continues to provoke significant discussion in the intellectual community.

Growing up in Michoacán, where he attended the Colegio de San Nicolás in Morelia, Ramos attended medical school before switching to philosophy his third year. He studied in Rome and in Paris, at the Sorbonne. He taught logic and the history of philosophy at the National Preparatory School and the National University. Ramos founded and edited *Ulises,* and managed José Vasconcelos's intellectual journal *Antorcha.* He entered public life briefly as *oficial mayor* of public education (1931–1932) under his friend Narciso BASSOLS, and in the 1940s represented Mexico at UNESCO. He was appointed a member of the National College in 1952.

— RODERIC AI CAMP

RAOUSSET-BOULBON, GASTON RAUL DE

Gaston Raul de Raousset-Boulbon (*b.* 2 December 1817; *d.* 12 August 1854), French filibuster. Scion of a French noble family, adventurer in the new colony of Algeria, and supporter of the 1848 Revolution, Raousset saw in the California gold rush the next opportunity to make his fortune. But the ambitions of most French immigrants there were frustrated. Encouraged by Mexican officials who sought European colonists on the northern frontier as an impediment to further U.S. expansion, three expeditions of French colonists from California to Sonora were attempted in the early 1850s, the last and most audacious led by Raousset. It was caught up in the struggle between two powerful foreign banking houses for the right to exploit the fabled mines of Arizona, on the present northwest border of Sonora.

Raousset saw in the California gold rush the next opportunity to make his fortune.

Raousset was the colonizing partner of Jecker de la Torre y Cia; state officials supported Barron, Forbes and Company. When Raousset ignored state regulations and the company cut off his supplies, he tried to foment an independence movement on the frontier. Defeated by state forces, he was deported. Undaunted, he returned two years later. Xenophobic feelings were now growing and Raousset's expedition of 400 men was met and defeated at the port of Guaymas on 13 July 1854. He was executed; his men were deported.

– STUART F. VOSS

RAVIGNANI, EMILIO

Emilio Ravignani (*b.* 15 January 1886; *d.* 8 March 1954), the founder of modern historical studies in Argentina. He was known for his objectivity and impartiality, his minute analysis of a document, his rejection of the anecdote, and his insistence on the complete and accurate publication of a document. He was a born teacher, always ready to help native and foreign students who sought his guidance.

A native of Buenos Aires, Ravignani attended the National University of Buenos Aires, where he received a law degree in 1906 and joined its recently created but short-lived history section. At the time, interest in historical studies was reviving, and scholars like Juan Agustín García, Ernesto QUESADA, and Clemente L. Frageiro were demanding that previously ignored documents on the post-ROSAS period, especially those in the provinces, be located and consulted. Ravignani was a founding member and head of a second history section in 1915 and then the director of the newly organized Institute of Historical Investigations, which replaced it in 1921. Under the energetic and erudite Ravignani, the institute became a model for other Latin American countries. It collected documents found in national, provincial, foreign, and private archives on a wide variety of subjects, for Ravignani believed a historian should be deeply grounded in the documents and spirit of the period he studied. It published scholarly monographs and assumed editorial responsibility for *Documentos para la historia Argentina,* a rich source of documents pertaining to before 1824.

Ravignani himself wrote numerous works but is most remembered for his *Historia constitucional de la República Argentina* (1926; 2d ed., 1930) and *Asambleas constituyentes argentina* (1937–1939). He had a remarkable ability to obtain congressional funding for the institute. In 1950 he organized the Institute of Historical Investigations in Montevideo. He was the dean of the Faculty of Philosophy and Letters at the National University of Buenos Aires from 1927 to 1931 and 1940 to 1943. Politically, he was an influential member of the Radical Civic Union and a national deputy for the Federal Capital (1936–1942, 1946–1947, and 1952–1953).

– JOSEPH T. CRISCENTI

RAWSON, GUILLERMO

Guillermo Rawson (*b.* 25 June 1821; *d.* 2 February 1890), Argentine medical doctor and statesman. The son of a New England physician who settled in Argentina during the Independence era, Guillermo Rawson was born in San Juan. He practiced medicine in his native city and later Buenos Aires, ultimately becoming a professor of medicine at the University of Buenos Aires. He took a special interest in matters of public health and in 1880 was the principal founder of the Argentine Red Cross.

Rawson's political career began in the 1840s in San Juan, where as a member of the legislature he took a cautious yet public stand against the dictatorship of Juan Manuel de ROSAS. Privately he worked for the overthrow of Rosas, in cooperation with his fellow *sanjuanino* Domingo SARMIENTO (from whom he subsequently became estranged despite their shared liberal ideology). After the fall of Rosas, Rawson served in the Congress and held other positions, of which the most important was minister of the interior during the presidency of Bartolomé MITRE (1862–1868). As minister he coped with a rash of provincial uprisings, and worked vigorously to promote immigration and infrastructural development.

– DAVID BUSHNELL

RAYÓN, IGNACIO

Ignacio Rayón (Ignacio [López] Rayón; *b.* 1773; *d.* 2 February 1832), Mexican insurgent leader. Born in Tlalpujahua, he studied at Valladolid, and became a lawyer in 1796. He joined Miguel HIDALGO Y COSTILLA (1753–1811) in Maravatío in October 1810 and became his private secretary. In Guadalajara, Hidalgo named him secretary of state. In March 1811, in Saltillo, he was named acting chief of the army while Hidalgo traveled to the United States and became the principal leader after the first insurgent chiefs died. Rayón reorganized his troops in Zitácuaro and, in August 1811, formed a government, the Suprema Junta Nacional Americana, which he headed. He drafted a plan for a constitution and attempted several times to establish relations with the United States.

Insurgent defeats and divisions among the members of the Suprema Junta cost him the leadership of the movement. Against his wishes, José María MORELOS Y PAVÓN (1765–1815) then convened a congress (El Supremo Congreso Nacional Americano), in September 1813, in which Rayón represented Michoacán. So ordered by Congress, he took charge of the province of Oaxaca. After the loss of its capital to the royalists, he moved on to Puebla, and in Zacatlán suffered a serious defeat in September 1814. He joined his brother Ramón (1775–1839) in Cerro del Cóporo, where he helped in its defense and where he stayed until September 1816. When he disavowed the insurgent government of the Junta de Jaujilla, the junta ordered his arrest, and Rayón was taken prisoner by Nicolás BRAVO. In December 1817 he was captured by the royalists and condemned to death, but he requested amnesty and won his freedom in 1820. After independence, Rayón served as treasurer of San Luis Potosí, commanding general of Jalisco, and president of the Military Tribunal. He died in Mexico City.

– VIRGINIA GUEDEA

READ, MARY

Mary Read (*b.* late 1600s; *d.* ca. 1720), early-eighteenth-century pirate. Read was born out of wedlock in England in the late seventeenth century. Her mother had been married to a sailor who either died or abandoned her and their young son while at sea. Shortly thereafter, the son died and Read was born. As a ruse to receive financial support from her deceased son's grandmother, Read's mother disguised the young girl as a boy and claimed that the imposter was the sailor's offspring. Such trickery proved successful and would become Read's modus operandi throughout her life. She went on to serve in the British army in the Low Countries and married a fellow trooper.

When Read's husband died, she resumed her masquerade as a man and joined a Dutch vessel bound for the West Indies. Pirates raided the ship and took on Read, still in disguise, as a fellow pirate. Read and her companions took advantage of the king's proclamation of 1717, which offered amnesty to pirates who turned themselves in. They later joined the British privateering ship *Griffin* with the intention of raiding the Spanish. However, Read and her crewmates mutinied and resumed their piracy under the leadership of Captain "Calico Jack" Rackam. During this period, Read and Anne BONNY met and began a close friendship.

By all accounts, Read displayed enthusiasm, skill, and fortitude in her trade. In one incident, she dueled to the death with another pirate who had threatened her lover. Read was brought to trial in 1720, but escaped the hangman's noose because she was pregnant. Shortly thereafter, fever overtook Read and she died in prison.

– JOHN J. CROCITTI

REAL DE AZÚA, CARLOS

Carlos Real de Azúa (*b.* 15 March 1916; *d.* 16 July 1977), Uruguayan intellectual, historian, and essayist.

Real de Azua was one of the most brilliant essayists of the so-called Generation of '45. His work consists of over 180 publications and in its breadth is typical of this avidly intellectual and political generation. Writings on travel, literature, Spanish-American culture, political science, history, and historiographical criticism are only some of the areas included in his multifaceted intellectual life. His works are essential references to understanding the spiritual trends in the arts during the nineteenth century: romanticism, classicism, and modernism. Through his first book, *España de cerca y de lejos* (1943) and his critique of the work of José Enrique RODÓ, he contributed to the debate over Spain's legacy in Latin America and especially Uruguay. His work is a fundamental part of the political science of Uruguay. *El patriciado uruguayo* (1961), perhaps his most successful book, analyzes what was a recurring preoccupation of his work: the formation of the Uruguayan nation-state and the role of the elite. Other works include *El impulso y su freno* (1964), *La clase dirigente* (1969), *Uruguay: Una sociedad amortiguadora?* (1984), and "Política, poder y partidos" in Luis Benvenuto et al., *Uruguay Hoy* (1971). Real de Azua was a professor at the University of the Republic, where he taught a variety of courses.

– CARLOS FILGUEIRA

REBOUÇAS, ANDRÉ

André Rebouças (*b.* 13 January 1838; *d.* 9 May 1898), Brazilian abolitionist, engineer, teacher, and advocate of land reform. A mulatto, Rebouças was the son of Antônio Pereira Rebouças, a national deputy from Bahia. Educated at the military school in Rio de Janeiro as a mathematician and engineer, he became a close friend and adviser to many influential Brazilians, including Emperor Dom PEDRO II. After travel and study in Europe in the early 1860s, he returned to Brazil in time to play an important role in the War of the Triple Alliance (1864–1870) as an adviser and strategist. Later, having supervised major engineering projects, including the construction of railroads and docks in Rio de Janeiro, he became a teacher at the Polytechnical School, where he influenced many students. As an abolitionist in the 1880s he wrote articles, pamphlets, and manifestos; helped create immigrationist and antislavery organizations; advised fellow reformers; and donated his wealth to the cause. With slavery's collapse in 1888, Rebouças and other major abolitionists worked for additional reforms, including popular education and a program of land reform he called "rural democracy." Forced to leave Brazil during the military revolt of 1889, he accompanied the imperial family into exile.

He spent the rest of his life in Europe, Africa, and on the island of Madeira, where he died mysteriously ten years to the day after the Brazilian Chamber of Deputies voted to end slavery. Rebouças was the author of many polemical articles, an informative diary, and *Agricultura nacional* (1883), an antislavery work calling for the democratization of Brazil's agriculture for the benefit of ex-slaves, immigrants, and the rural poor.

— ROBERT EDGAR CONRAD

RECABARREN SERRANO, LUIS EMILIO

Luis Emilio Recabarren Serrano (*b.* 6 July 1876; *d.* 19 December 1924), Chilean labor leader, newspaper editor, and politician. Born into modest circumstances in Valparaíso, Recabarren began work as a printer, which provided him with the means to educate himself. A newspaper editor of numerous journals, he also organized workers in the north, particularly the nitrate miners, to protest their horrible living and unsafe working conditions. His organizing efforts, as well as his newspaper editorials, led to his arrest and incarceration for sedition.

Recabarren joined the Democratic Party, then Chile's most left-wing party. Although he was twice elected to the Chamber of Deputies, the opposition refused to seat him, arguing that he advocated ideas that would lead to social discord. After serving more than a year in jail for inciting a strike of railroad and dock workers in 1906, he left for Argentina and Europe.

Extremely puritanical, Recabarren opposed alcoholism and prostitution and emphasized individual hygiene and education.

After denouncing the Democratic Party for its willingness to compromise and to support reformist tactics, in 1912 Recabarren created the Partido Obrero Socialista (POS), a working-class party dedicated to bringing socialism to Chile. Extremely puritanical, Recabarren preached a combination of personal morality, opposing alcoholism and prostitution and emphasizing individual hygiene and education, and dedication to the class struggle as a means of uplifting the masses. Recabarren traveled throughout Chile, personally preaching this message and founding countless newspapers.

Disenchanted with Europe's Social Democratic parties because they had supported their nations' participation in World War I, Recabarren became an early supporter of the Communist revolution. Elected a deputy in 1921, he led the Partido Obrero Socialista to join the Third Communist International. After visiting the Soviet Union in 1922, he returned to Chile to continue his legislative battle to improve the lot of the working class and to oppose the incumbent bourgeois government. Recabarren refused to run for a second congressional term. Apparently despondent over infighting within the Communist Party, in ill health, and perhaps depressed over a failed love affair, Recabarren committed suicide in 1924.

— WILLIAM F. SATER

REEVE, HENRY M.

Henry M. Reeve (*b.* 4 April 1850; *d.* 4 August 1876), cavalry commander in Cuba's Ten Years' War of independence. Cubans dubbed Reeve, the Brooklyn-born son of a preacher, "El Inglesito" because he was tall, blond, and, at first, spoke no Spanish. He came to Cuba in 1869 in an expedition commanded by the former Confederate general Thomas Jordan. Having been taken prisoner shortly after the landing, he soon found himself facing a Spanish firing squad. Having miraculously survived the experience, he joined the forces of the insurgent leader Ignacio AGRAMONTE, who came to hold him in high esteem. Because of his bravery and prowess, Reeve rose rapidly through the ranks, and eventually succeeded Agramonte as chief of Camagüey (1874). When the Cubans began a march toward the west, invading the province of Las Villas, Reeve was appointed to spearhead the offensive. He had gone beyond Las Villas and reached the rich sugar region of Colón, in the neighboring province of Matanzas, when he was killed near Yaguarma, fighting against superior Spanish forces. By then he had participated in about 400 war actions, and been wounded ten times, and had lost the use of one of his legs.

— JOSÉ M. HERNÁNDEZ

REGALADO, TOMÁS

Tomás Regalado (*b.* 7 November 1861; *d.* 11 July 1906), president of El Salvador (1898–1903). As president of El Salvador, the flamboyant Tomás Regalado withdrew El Salvador from the Republic of Central America, effectively terminating that union. He also involved his country in numerous plots and skirmishes.

Regalado, a native of Santa Ana, seized the presidency in November 1898 after a period of political chaos and economic decline. He reduced the national debt, adjusted the tariff structure to help commercial agriculture, and expanded the railroad and port system. Through strong executive authority he ended the threats of invasion by political exiles and restored domestic peace, often suppressing individual liberties. Regalado opposed President Manuel ESTRADA CABRERA of Guatemala, leading a military campaign against him in 1899 and aiding Guatemalan exiles throughout his presidency. President José Santos ZELAYA of Nicaragua, in turn, supported Regalado's enemies.

Regalado is criticized for favoring the coffee oligarchy, of which he was a member. In 1903, for the first time in twenty-six years, El Salvador inaugurated an elected president. Nevertheless, Regalado exercised strong influence over his successor. General Pedro José Escalón, whom Regalado selected because he could be easily controlled.

In 1906 Regalado encouraged Guatemalan expatriates to organize a military campaign against Manual Estrada Cabrera from Salvadoran territory. Hoping to install his own man as the Guatemalan president, Regalado apparently also provided the rebels with arms and personally led the attack on Guatemala. His death occurred during this invasion, near Yupiltepeque, Guatemala.

— PATRICIA A. ANDREWS

REGO MONTEIRO, VICENTE DO

Vicente Do Rego Monteiro (*b.* 1899; *d.* 1970), Brazilian painter and poet. Born in Recife into a family of artists, Rego Monteiro manifested artistic talent at an early age. He began his training at the age of twelve at the Académie Julien in Paris. Two years later, in 1913, he exhibited in the Salon des Indépendants. In 1919, two years after returning to Brazil, he had his first exhibition. He returned to Paris in 1922. Before his departure, he left the poet and art critic Ronaldo de Carvalho with ten of his paintings for inclusion in the 1922 Semana de Arte Moderna (Modern Art Week).

Rego Monteiro's work remained virtually unknown in Brazil until the mid-1960s, because of his long absences from Brazil and a devastating fire in the late 1920s that destroyed most of his best works. When he returned to Brazil in 1964, he became closely identified with the modernist movement. National and biblical themes predominate in his paintings. At the same time, eclectic artistic influences punctuate his repertory: futurism, cubism, Japanese prints, black art, the School of Paris, Brazilian baroque, and especially Amerindian art from the island of Marajó.

In addition to painting, Rego Montiero devoted his talents to other cultural pursuits. In the 1950s he or-

ganized the First International Congress of Poetry in Paris and founded a literary magazine in Recife entitled *Renovação*.

— CAREN A. MEGHREBLIAN

REJÓN, MANUEL CRESCENCIO

Manuel Crescencio Rejón (*b.* 1799; *d.* 1849), Mexican politician and cabinet minister, creator of the writ of *amparo* (protection). Rejón was born into a poor family in Bolonchenticul, Yucatán, and educated in Mérida. At an early age he entered politics and agitated for independence. Elected to the national legislature in 1822, Rejón spoke against ITURBIDE and for liberalism, federalism, and republicanism. Iturbide dissolved Congress and jailed Rejón in 1822. After the fall of Iturbide, Rejón served in the Constituent Congress and was one of the authors of the Constitution of 1824. Repeatedly elected to represent Yucatán in Congress from 1827 to 1834, he attempted to organize popular resistance to Bustamante's overthrow of Guerrero, and was jailed again.

Rejón returned to Yucatán in 1840 and wrote a constitution that included guarantees of individual rights and a writ of *amparo* to protect them. Soon afterward he returned to Mexico City, where he was first arrested and then named to a diplomatic post in Caracas. Rejón served as minister of domestic and foreign relations in 1844 and 1846 before he was exiled and fled to New Orleans. Upon returning to Mexico, he attempted to organize resistance to the United States annexation of Texas and opposed the Treaty of Guadalupe Hidalgo. Rejón served his final term in Congress in 1848 and died the following year.

— D. F. STEVENS

REMÓN CANTERA, JOSÉ ANTONIO

José Antonio Remón Cantera (*b.* 1 June 1908; *d.* 2 January 1955), president of Panama (1952–1955). Born into a prominent Panamanian family, Remón received a scholarship to attend the Military Academy in Mexico. After graduating third in his class in 1931, he returned to Panama and was made a captain in the National Police. Remón's attempts to reform and modernize the force were well received, and in 1947 he was made commandant. Under Remón, the National Police became the arbiter of Panama's political fate, making or breaking presidents at the will of the commandant.

In 1951, Remón made a bid for the presidency and, endorsed by a party of his own creation, won the 1952 elections with nearly half the votes. He immediately began a domestic campaign to bring order and prosperity to the country. During Remón's administration there were advances in education, health care, and commerce, but severe restrictions on political parties and labor unions earned him the reputation of dictator. Remón's greatest achievement while in office was the renegotiation of the 1903 Hay–Bunau-Varilla Treaty. The result of his efforts was the Eisenhower–Remón Treaty (1955), which gave Panama additional rights to Canal Zone revenues, ended discriminatory wage practices in the zone, and increased the annuity paid by the United States for the canal. Remón was assassinated in Panama City before the treaty was finalized.

– SARA FLEMING

RENGIFO CÁRDENAS, MANUEL

Manuel Rengifo Cárdenas (*b.* 29 December 1793; *d.* 16 March 1846), Chilean trader and politician. At the age of fifteen he went to work for a Spanish trading house in Santiago, later undertaking numerous commercial ventures of his own. In the late 1820s he became a close associate of trader and politician Diego PORTALES (1793–1837). With the Conservative triumph in 1830, he served as the new regime's finance minister (1830–1835). Rengifo systematically reorganized Chilean finances and implemented policies to promote the commercial predominance of Valparaíso in the Pacific. His presidential aspirations were ruthlessly checkmated by Portales in 1835. Rengifo returned to the finance ministry for a second period (1841–1844), during which his main achievement was the settlement of the long-standing debt arising from the London loan of 1822. His brother Ramón Rengifo (1795–1861) was the author of the still-popular patriotic "Canción de Yungay" (Song of Yungay).

– SIMON COLLIER

RESTREPO, CARLOS EUGENIO

Carlos Eugenio Restrepo (*b.* 12 September 1867; *d.* 6 July 1947), president of Colombia (1910–1914). Born into a prestigious but poor family in Medellín, he studied law in his hometown. Restrepo began a bureaucratic career in his early twenties. His diligence and honesty brought him important posts. He served in the War of the Thousand Days, then returned home to the rectorship of the University of Antioquia (1901–1902). Later he became professor of constitutional law there. Elected as a Conservative to the Congress of 1909, Restrepo strongly opposed the dictatorship of Rafael REYES. These personal and political credentials won him election to the presidency in 1910—the first Antioquian

to hold the office for a full term. His term coincided with a boom in coffee exports that made possible expansion in educational and transportation infrastructure, legal codification, and pensions for schoolteachers. Colombia's territories were also reorganized, and the Thomson–Urrutia Treaty with the United States was negotiated in 1914. Restrepo's Unión Republicana, an effort at bipartisanship, ceased to exist after he left office. Back in Antioquia, he became a spokesperson for the region's interests and, in 1930, for the presidential candidacy of the Liberal Enrique OLAYA HERRERA. Restrepo served Olaya as minister of interior (1930) and as ambassador to the Holy See (1931–1934). He died in Medellín.

– J. LEÓN HELGUERA

RESTREPO, JOSÉ MANUEL

José Manuel Restrepo (*b.* 30 December 1781; *d.* 1 April 1863), Colombian public official and historian. Born in Envigado in the province of Antioquia, Restrepo studied law in Bogotá and participated in the scientific and intellectual ferment of the late colonial period. He was active in the independence movement, for example, as secretary to the dictator Juan del Corral in his native province. During the Spanish reconquest he was allowed to stay in Antioquia as a tithe official (*juez de diezmos*), but fearing reprisals, he fled to Jamaica (1816) and then the United States (1817). After the victory at Boyacá he returned to New Granada, where he served as governor of Antioquia and deputy to the Congress of Cúcuta.

Restrepo's highest official position was minister of the interior of Gran Colombia (1821–1830). He assisted Vice President Francisco de Paula SANTANDER while he was acting chief executive, and then Simón BOLÍVAR once he assumed the presidency. As a political moderate, Restrepo exercised a restraining influence on the two leaders when a bitter feud arose between them. After the breakup of Gran Colombia, he held various positions in independent New Granada, most notably that of director of the Bogotá mint.

The lasting importance of Restrepo is due above all to his stature as the classic historian of Colombian independence. With unrivaled access to official documentation and personal knowledge of people and events, he produced the ten-volume *Historia de la revolución de la República de Colombia,* published in Paris in 1827. An expanded second edition appeared in 1858. A sequel, the two-volume *Historia de la Nueva Granada,* was published posthumously (1952–1963). He also left a four-volume *Diario político y militar* (1954) relating all manner of developments in Gran Colombia and New

Granada. Though Restrepo eschewed blatant partisanship, his perspective is clearly conservative, distrustful of rapid innovation, and disdainful of the lower social orders.

— DAVID BUSHNELL

REVERÓN, ARMANDO

Armando Reverón (*b*. 10 May 1889; *d*. 18 September 1954), Venezuelan artist. A delicate child raised by a foster family in Valencia, near Caracas, Reverón's health was permanently damaged by an attack of typhoid contracted in his youth. His formal education began at home and he received art lessons from his maternal uncle, Ricardo Montilla. In 1908 he went to Caracas and entered the Academy of Fine Arts, where he began painting still lifes. He was expelled from school for participating in a strike against the director, the painter Antonio Herrera Toro. But he returned the following year and in 1911 graduated with distinction as well as with a scholarship to Europe. That same year after his first exhibition, Reverón went to Spain to study at the Academy of San Fernando in Madrid. During his stay in Europe, he became interested in impressionism, pointillism, and the paintings of Francisco Goya. Upon his return to Caracas in 1915, he joined the Fine Arts Circle, a group of landscape painters strongly influenced by the Russian artist Nicolas Ferdinandov, who organized an exhibition of Reverón's work at the Academy of Fine Arts in 1919. Ferdinandov also encouraged Reverón to move to the coastal village of Macuto near Caracas, where the painter constructed a *castillete* ("little castle") that served as his home for the rest of his life. There he began his seascapes, which capture the bright light of the sun heating the sea.

His work falls into three periods. First, the blue period (1919–1924), featuring street scenes, portraits of common people, urban landscapes, and seascapes. Then the white period (1925–1929), which includes near monochrome white paintings of the sea, portraits of his friends, his Muse Juanita, and life-size rag dolls. Finally, his sepia period (1936–1949), in which his painting of female nudes and seascapes becomes much more transparent. In 1940 he won the first prize at the Official Salon of Venezuelan Art. After 1950 his mental health deteriorated and he entered the Sanatoria San Jorge in 1953, where he died the following year. His work found a much greater audience after his death.

— BÉLGICA RODRÍGUEZ

REVILLAGIGEDO, CONDE DE

Conde de Revillagigedo (Juan Vicente de Güemes-Pacheco y Padilla; *b*. 1740; *d*. 1799), one of New Spain's greatest viceroys. Born in Havana, Revillagigedo gained firsthand knowledge of Mexico as a youth, during the viceregal administration of his father (1746–1755). Appointed viceroy himself in 1789, he initiated many new projects and reforms, including a large-scale road-building program, the development of more efficient and regular mail service, the construction of many primary schools, the founding of the Archivo General, and the marked improvement of public facilities in Mexico City, making the capital cleaner, healthier, and better policed. He also sponsored artistic, scientific, and scholarly endeavors, providing patronage to the Academy of San Carlos and inaugurating the Museum of Natural History in 1793.

The epitome of an enlightened Bourbon administrator, Revillagigedo sought to bring New Spain under more efficient bureaucratic control and to increase its yield to the crown. Toward these ends, he established a new system of intendancies, initiated an overhaul of the treasury department, and reorganized and reduced Mexican militia units. He also attempted, with less success, to weaken the power of the church, the Audiencia of Mexico, and the Mexico City merchants' guild. Though many of his reforms were undermined by entrenched bureaucratic opposition, or by later viceroys, Revillagigedo demonstrated what could be accomplished by a government leader who combined energy, scope, and attention to detail in planning with pragmatism and flexibility in execution. He died in Madrid.

— R. DOUGLAS COPE

REVUELTAS, JOSÉ

José Revueltas (*b*. 20 November 1914; *d*. 14 April 1976), Mexican writer and activist. Revueltas was born in the state of Durango to an exceptional family in which all the children were outstanding artists: Silvestre, a musician; Fermin, a painter; and Rosaura, an actress. José mastered the novel and the short story like few others. *El luto humano* (1943), *Los errores* (1964), and *El apando* (1969) are outstanding works in Mexican and Latin American literature due to their rigorous style and uncommon ambition as well as their austere, anecdotal expression of the great ideological conflicts of our time. He also wrote dramas and screenplays and some of the most important essays in twentieth-century Mexico.

But Revueltas's work cannot be reduced merely to his literary production. He was also one of the most intense, honest, and contradictory personalities in twentieth-century Mexico. A militant Marxist from adolescence until death, Revueltas was imprisoned several times for his ideas. The last time, from 1968 to 1971, was for his role as a leader of the student movement of 1968 that resulted in the massacre of Tlatelolco. Even his very funeral was an unforgettably moving political act. At the cemetery the mostly young crowd sang "The International" and other revolutionary songs. When the minister of education tried to speak, he was shouted down and forced to leave—very much in keeping with Revueltas's opposition to hypocrisy and illegitimate power.

Revueltas's work is a vast drama in which is represented the struggle to make public and private life, art and the exercise of thought, one singular and great undertaking of redemption and sacrifice for those oppressed in "this somber period in history," as he himself called our era. With such a messianic sensibility, it is not strange that his dramas combine the biblical and the mundane, the prophetic and the grotesque, the degraded and the sublime. He considered his life and his writing to be examples, nothing more and nothing less, of the simple destiny of a human being.

– JORGE AGUILAR MORA

REVUELTAS, SILVESTRE

Silvestre Revueltas (*b.* 31 December 1899; *d.* 5 October 1940), Mexican violinist, composer, and conductor from Santiago Papasquiaro, Durango. He started violin lessons at age eight in Colima, and continued in Mexico City in 1913. His high school years at St. Edwards College in Austin, Texas (1916–1918), were followed with advanced training at the Chicago Music College (1918–1920; 1922–1924). He worked as a free-lance violinist and conductor in the United States and Mexico before settling permanently in Mexico City, where he was appointed Carlos CHÁVEZ's assistant conductor of the Symphony Orchestra of Mexico in 1928. Revueltas also taught violin and chamber music at the National Conservatory, serving as its interim director briefly in 1933. In 1937 Revueltas went to Spain to join the Loyalists in the Civil War.

Revueltas's compositions embody the Mexican spirit in their vigorous, indigenous rhythms and bracing dissonances, taking on in some instances the character of musical landscapes (*Janitzio,* 1933). He was one of the first in Mexico to compose for films in the emerging sound cinema industry (*Redes,* 1935). His substantial and colorful output and its universal appeal have made him perhaps the most revered Mexican composer of the twentieth century.

– ROBERT L. PARKER

REYES, ALFONSO

Alfonso Reyes (*b.* 17 May 1889; *d.* 27 December 1959), Mexican essayist, poet, literary scholar, educator, and diplomat. Alfonso Reyes was born in Monterrey, Mexico, where his father, General Bernardo REYES, was governor of the state of Nuevo León (later minister of war and rival of Porfirio DÍAZ for the presidency). Reyes went to Mexico City in 1906 and received a law degree from the National University of Mexico in 1913. He was active with the literary society Ateneo de la Juventud, which on the eve of the Mexican Revolution of 1910 initiated a cultural renewal and educational reform at the National Preparatory School and the National University. Following his father's tragic death in a failed counterrevolutionary coup (February 1913), Reyes embarked on a diplomatic career taking him to France (1913–1914, 1924–1927), Spain (1914–1924), and as ambassador to Argentina (1927–1930, 1936–1937) and Brazil (1930–1935, 1938–1939). Returning to Mexico, he cofounded two institutes of advanced studies: the Colegio de México (1940), originally established as the Casa de España in 1939 to welcome numerous Spaniards exiled from the Spanish Civil War; and the Colegio Nacional, founded in 1943. He became president of the Mexican Academy of the Language in 1957. Throughout his career he was a fervent cultural missionary imbued with the aspiration for Mexico and the Americas to play a significant role in universal culture.

Reyes's Última Tule *(1942) focuses through the Columbus and Vespucci discovery voyages on the concept of America as Utopia.*

Reyes's vast literary works include lyric and dramatic poetry; short narrative fiction; familiar essays, memoirs, monographs of literary theory, and criticism. In the poetic essay *Visión de Anáhuac* (1917), a historical evocation of Cortés's encounter with Montezuma in the Aztec city of Tenochtitlán leads to a meditation on the destiny of Mexico, the product of three successive civilizations. *Última Tule* (1942) focuses through the Columbus and Vespucci discovery voyages on the concept of America as Utopia. The dramatic poem *Ifigenia cruel* (1924), through the myth of Iphigenia, embodies a literary catharsis of the author's sense of exile and search for liberation from the political curse associated with the trauma of his father's death. Other works include *The Position of America and Other Essays,* translated by Harriet de Onís (1950); *Obras completas,* 26 vols. (1955–1993); and *Prosa y poesía,* edited by J. W. Robb, 3d ed. (1984). Reyes died in Mexico City.

– JAMES W. ROBB

REYES, RAFAEL

Rafael Reyes (*b.* 5 December 1849; *d.* 18 February 1921), president of Colombia (1904–1909). A native of Boyacá, Reyes made a fortune in the quinine boom of the 1870s, and later explored the Putumayo region. His prominence within the Conservative Party began with the civil war of 1885, and peaked in 1895 when he led government forces at Enciso, Santander. Reyes opposed the governing Nationalist wing of the Conservatives in the 1890s, and sat out the War of the Thousand Days (1899–1902) abroad. In 1904 Reyes won the presidency in a tight election plagued by fraud. His administration, known as the *quinquenio,* reformed public administration and fostered economic recovery through tariff protection and amortization of paper money; his generous policy toward the defeated Liberals won him widespread support from that party. But his authoritarian style, particularly his dissolution of Congress in 1905, eventually alienated political elites of both parties. In June 1909, following street demonstrations in Bogotá, Reyes secretly boarded a ship for Europe, to the surprise of guests expecting him at a Santa Marta dinner.

– RICHARD J. STOLLER

REYES OCHOA, ALFONSO

Alfonso Reyes Ochoa (*b.* 17 May 1889; *d.* 27 December 1959), Mexican essayist and intellectual. The son of prominent nineteenth-century politician General Bernardo REYES, Alfonso studied in Mexico City. In 1909 he cofounded the famous Ateneo de la Juventud, an intellectual society, and in 1913 he graduated from the National University, where he had served as secretary of the graduate school and where he later became a founding professor of Spanish language and literature. To survive financially as a writer, Reyes pursued a career in the foreign service, occupying posts in France, Spain, Argentina, and Brazil, and spent most of his life abroad, at one time working under José Ortega y Gasset. Although lacking a political or ideological focus, his writing helped develop the intellectually inward concentration on Mexican identity continued by Samuel RAMOS and Octavio PAZ. He was a candidate for the Nobel Prize in literature, and was awarded Mexico's National Prize of Arts and Sciences in 1945. Reyes contributed to Mexican intellectual institutional development as first president of the Colegio de México (1939–1959). He presided over Mexico's prestigious Academy of Language shortly before his death.

– RODERIC AI CAMP

REYES OGAZÓN, BERNARDO

Bernardo Reyes Ogazón (*b.* 30 August 1850; *d.* 9 February 1913), Mexican military officer and politician. Bernado Reyes, governor of the important northern state of Nuevo León and a leading contemporary of Porfirio DÍAZ, began campaigning for the presidency in 1909 to replace Díaz. Forced to leave the country, he lived in exile from 1909 to 1911. He returned in 1911, and, in 1913, with Félix Díaz, led a counterrevolutionary movement against President MADERO known as the Tragic Ten Days, during which he was killed leading an attack on the national palace.

Born in Guadalajara, Jalisco, he was the father of Alfonso REYES, a notable poet, and Rodolfo Reyes, a public figure. In 1865 he left school to fight against the French, becoming an aide to General Ramón CORONA. He remained loyal to President Sebastián LERDO DE TEJADA in 1877 but continued his military career under Porfirio Díaz, rising to chief of military operations in Nuevo León and, ultimately, to secretary of war. He later served as governor of Nuevo Léon from 1889 to 1900 and from 1902 to 1909. Reyes had reached the rank of division general (three stars) in 1900.

– RODERIC AI CAMP

REYNA BARRIOS, JOSÉ MARÍA

José María Reyna Barrios (*b.* 24 December 1854; *d.* 8 February 1898), president of Guatemala (1892–1898). Born in San Marcos, he was a nephew of the revered father of Guatemalan Liberalism, Justo Rufino BARRIOS (1873–1885). At the age of seventeen, he joined his uncle and father in the Liberal Revolt of 1871. He studied at the Escuela Politécnica, the Guatemalan military college. After reaching the rank of general, Reyna Barrios easily defeated his Conservative opponent in the 1892 presidential election. The republic's incipient coffee elite expected the new president to capitalize on the successes of the nation's rapidly expanding agricultural exports in order to secure continued prosperity and enlightened government indefinitely. During the first four years of his administration, several contemporary Guatemalan authors described Reyna Barrios as a "young military officer, filled with prestige, educated in the Liberal School, [a] brave son of the 1871 [Liberal] revolution," "a sincere republican," "fully democratic," and "committed to sustaining the Reforma inaugurated in 1871."

These glowing accounts of the Liberal virtues of Reyna Barrios and his administration ended in the summer of 1897. Increasingly dictatorial in nature and under assault from a significant fraction of the nation's coffee planters, Reyna Barrios responded by ruthlessly crushing a regional Liberal revolt in the fall of 1897 that was led by caudillos in Los Altos. Faced with a severe economic and monetary crisis and increasingly assailed by the criticisms of coffee growers from the highlands, Reyna Barrios received the support necessary from the National Assembly to extend his government until 15 March 1902—four years beyond his constitutionally recognized tenure. Nonetheless, for Reyna Barrios, this proved to be an empty victory. On 8 February 1898, he was assassinated in the capital by a mysterious single gunman. On that same evening, the cabinet met and acknowledged Manuel Estrada CABRERA'S (1898–1920) constitutional claim to the presidency as first designate.

— WADE A. KIT

RIANI, CLODSMITH

Clodsmith Riani (*b*. 15 October 1920), Brazilian trade unionist and president of the National Confederation of Workers in Industry (CNTI) and of the Commando Geral dos Trabalhadores (CGT). Born in Minas Gerais, Riani went to work as an apprentice electrician in 1936 for a utility company in Juiz de Fora, where he emerged in 1949 as a key labor leader. He forged close ties with João "Jango" GOULART, the national leader of the Brazilian Labor Party (PTB), and was elected PTB state deputy several times between 1954 and 1964. Joining the CNTI, Riani led the opposition to its conservative president whom he defeated in an upset election in 1961. Elected vice president of the CGT in 1962 and president in 1963, Riani played a central role in the tumultuous struggles prior to the military coup of 31 March 1964. With the CGT dissolved and the CNTI taken over by the government, he was arrested and sentenced to a total of nineteen years in prison, of which he served six. After his release, he returned to his original job in Juiz de Fora, finished secondary school, and went on to earn a law degree. In 1982, Riani was elected state deputy of the Party of the Brazilian Democratic Movement (PMDB), thus continuing the fight, in Riani's words, for "democratic, progressive, and nationalist ideals."

— JOHN D. FRENCH

RIAÑO Y BÁRCENA, JUAN ANTONIO

Juan Antonio Riaño y Bárcena (*b*. 1757; *d*. 28 September 1810), intendant of Guanajuato and defender of the Alhóndiga in the Hidalgo revolt (1810). A native of Santander, Spain, Riaño served as a frigate captain in the Spanish navy. In 1792, he was appointed intendant

of the important Mexican mining province of Guanajuato, a position he held until his death in defense of the *alhóndiga* (granary) against the rebel forces of Father Miguel HIDALGO. A true product of the Spanish Enlightenment, Riaño studied mathematics, astronomy, literature, languages, drawing, and architecture. Unlike many other intendants, he surveyed his province thoroughly and sought to introduce new industries and agricultural crops. He stimulated the planting of olive groves and vineyards.

Despite his popularity and recognized honesty, Riaño was ineffective in defending Guanajuato against Hidalgo's Indian and mestizo rebels. Convinced that the city was indefensible, he moved valuables and members of the Spanish elite into the fortified granary. The populace felt abandoned, and many from the lower classes joined the rebel assault. When Riaño was killed by a musket ball, the defenses collapsed and the garrison of the granary was massacred.

— CHRISTON I. ARCHER

RIBAS, JOSÉ FÉLIX

José Félix Ribas (*b*. 19 September 1775; *d*. 31 January 1815), officer in the Venezuelan Liberating Army. Ribas was connected to Simón Bolívar's family by his marriage to the Liberator's aunt. He was an outstanding participant in the declaration of a *cabildo abierto* and in the ouster of the Spanish governor, Emparán, on 19 April 1810 in Caracas. Ribas was a member of the Junta Suprema de Caracas and participated in the military campaign in defense of the republic under the orders of Francisco de MIRANDA. When the First Republic fell,

---

After Ribas was executed by the royalist troops, his head was sent to Caracas and placed in a cage at the entrance to the city as a warning.

---

he traveled to New Granada in 1813 and then returned with Bolívar as a troop commander in the Admirable Campaign. Bolívar appointed Ribas military chief of Caracas and commander of the province of Caracas. Ribas was successful in various military campaigns in the central area of the republic. With the fall of the Second Republic and the defeat of the republican forces, he was captured and executed by the royalist troops. His head was sent to Caracas and placed in a cage at the entrance to the city as a warning.

— INÉS QUINTERO

RIBEIRO, DARCY

Darcy Ribeiro (*b.* 26 November 1922), Brazilian anthropologist. Born in Montes Claros, Minas Gerais, Ribeiro did fieldwork among Indians in Amazonas and central Brazil. He also studied Indian acculturation with the support of UNESCO and organized the Indian Museum in Rio de Janeiro (1953). Interested in public education, Ribeiro became the first rector of the Universidade de Brasília (1961–1962) and served as minister of education and culture (1962–1963) during João GOULART's presidency. When the military seized power in 1964, Ribeiro, who was a member of the Executive Office of President Goulart, went into exile in Montevideo, Uruguay, where he taught anthropology at the Universidad de la República Oriental del Uruguay. He returned to Brazil in 1974 and resumed his political activity. From 1983 to 1987 he was governor of the state of Rio de Janeiro. His works on cultural anthropology treat the differences between American societies and the effects of civilization on Indian populations. Among the most notable are *Religião e mitologia Kadiwéu* (1950), *Línguas e culturas indígenas no Brasil* (1957), *A política indigenista brasileira* (1962), *O processo civilizatório* (1968), *As Américas e a civilização* (1970), *Os índios e a civilização* (1970), *Os brasileiros* (1972), *O dilema da América latina* (1978). He wrote also a novel, *Maíra* (1977).

— ELIANA MARIA REA GOLDSCHMIDT

RIBEIRO, JOÃO UBALDO

João Ubaldo Ribeiro (*b.* 1941), Brazilian author. Born on the island of Itaparica, off the coast of Bahia, Ribeiro spent his childhood in the state of Sergipe. Though he graduated from law school, he never pursued a legal career, becoming a journalist before turning to writing full time. A man of the world, he has lived in Bahia, as a university professor and editor of the *Tribuna da Bahia;* in Rio de Janeiro, as a journalist; in the United States, where he earned a master's degree in political sciences from the University of Southern California; in Portugal, as a recipient of a Gulbenkian scholarship; and in Germany, as a fellow of the Deutscher Akademicher Austranschdiens. Upon returning to Brazil shortly after celebrating his fortieth birthday, and feeling pressured by urban life, he moved back to his hometown in Itaparica, where he found the spiritual peace he craved to continue writing his books.

At age twenty-one Ribeiro published *Semana da Pátria* (National Week, 1962), which was followed by *Sargento Getúlio* (1971), the novel that earned him not only Brazilian fame but also world recognition. Its subject focuses on the paradoxical personality and isolation of a "strongman." With more than ten editions, the novel was the theme of a motion picture in Brazil and has been translated into more than six languages. Ribeiro's later books also received critical acclaim and high public praise: *Viva o povo brasileiro* (1984; *An Invincible Memory,* 1989) and *O sorriso do lagarto* (1989; The Iguana's Smile), which became a television miniseries in Brazil.

— REGINA IGEL

RIBERA Y ESPINOSA, LÁZARO DE

Lázaro de Ribera y Espinosa (*d.* 1824), penultimate colonial governor of Paraguay. This Spanish-born hidalgo, soldier, and engineer, served as *gobernador-intendente* of Paraguay from 1795 to 1806. A prolix memorialist, contentious, and touchy about his "honor," he nonetheless was representative of the best type of authoritarian, efficient Bourbon administrator. During his eleven-year service he conducted a census of the province, improved public education, encouraged shipbuilding, and energetically promoted the export commerce of the province.

The War of Oranges with Portugal in the first years of the century caught Ribera in the midst of a reorganization of Paraguay's militia. He led an unsuccessful expedition up the Paraguay River to eject the Portuguese from Coimbra. Around the same time Ribera incurred the wrath of the viceroy, the Marqués de Avilés, by objecting to the military exemption for growers who contracted with the Real Renta de Tabacos in Paraguay and opposing the extinction of the communal property system in the Guaraní missions. In both cases Ribera was correct, but his contentious nature was noted in Spain and in 1806 he was relieved of his post. In 1812 he was appointed intendant of Huancavelica.

— JERRY W. COONEY

RIBEYRO, JULIO RAMÓN

Julio Ramón Ribeyro (*b.* 31 August 1929), Peruvian fiction writer. Ribeyro is known for his short stories, more than one hundred in all, most of which have been published collectively in four volumes, *La palabra del mudo* (1972–1992). He has also written successful novels, plays, and literary criticism. Ribeyro especially captures a unique perspective on contemporary life in *Prosas apátridas* (1975; 3d ed., 1986), a combination of pithy but ironic philosophical vignettes, intimate diary, and brief thought pieces. Ribeyro began writing in 1952; shortly afterward he moved to Europe, where he has lived ever since. His fiction reflects this separation from Peru, and writing from a marginalized position of self-imposed exile, Ribeyro's sharp observation and minute detail bring biting irony to his social commentary and give it life by enveloping his characters in fantastic elements—enigma, the double, the eccentric, and the bizarre. His characters suffer the anonymity of urban life in Lima or Paris, where their simple lives are played out in private and public places. Ribeyro probes his characters' psyches from a position of compassionate skepticism; hence, the stories have a tone of melancholic pessimism that captures in ironic fashion the banality, absurdity, and anguish of a fake bourgeoisie that lacks any history, future, or identity. The subtle combination of social commentary and fantasy in Ribeyro's narrative is what makes the stories distinct, readable, and contemporary.

— DICK GERDES

RICCHIERI, PABLO

Pablo Ricchieri (b. 1859; d. 1936), Argentine military leader. Born in Santa Fe Province, Argentina, Ricchieri was the son of Italian immigrants. He studied in the Franciscan College, San Lorenzo, and entered the Military Academy, graduating in 1879. Between 1883 and 1886 Ricchieri studied at the Belgium War College. He was then assigned to the Argentine military legation in Germany. He returned to Argentina in 1886 and served on the general staff. Between 1890 and 1898 Ricchieri made numerous trips to Europe to purchase arms. Returning to Argentina, he was designated director general of arsenals and later chief of staff of the army. In 1900 he was named minister of war and on 12 October 1904 he was designated director of the Military Academy.

Ricchieri is credited for having modernized the Argentine army. In 1901 he approved Law 4301 (known as the Ricchieri Law), which created obligatory military service (conscription). He divided Argentina into seven military districts and reorganized the War Department. In 1910 Ricchieri was promoted to division general and in 1916 commissioned as an observer to the fighting on the Western Front. On 7 August 1922 he retired with the rank of lieutenant general. After retiring, General Ricchieri served on numerous commissions.

— ROBERT SCHEINA

RIEGO Y NÚÑEZ, RAFAEL DEL

Rafael del Riego y Núñez (b. 24 October 1785; d. 7 November 1823), leader of a revolt (pronunciamiento) against Ferdinand VII (1820) and president of the Cortes (1822–1823) in Spain. Riego y Núñez was an army officer stationed in Cádiz on the eve of Spain's Great Expedition to quell rebellion in the New World. Dis-

affected with Ferdinand's treatment of the army and the proposed American campaign, Riego y Núñez and his troops proclaimed their support for the Constitution of 1812 on 1 January 1820. In February, the military uprising spread to royal armies stationed at La Coruña, Saragossa, and Barcelona. Ferdinand accepted the constitutional restoration in March and, for the next three years, presided over increasingly liberal governments led by men he had persecuted in 1814.

In Spain, the revolt established a pattern for future liberal revolutions, which would begin with an army revolt followed by provincial support and, finally, government response in Madrid. In the New World, the revolt signified the end of any chance of sending a large army to reinforce royalist forces and practically guaranteed independence for the various colonies.

— SUZANNE HILES BURKHOLDER

RIESCO ERRÁZURIZ, GERMÁN

germán Riesco Errázuriz (b. 18 May 1854; d. 8 December 1916), president of Chile (1901–1906). A lawyer and professional bureaucrat, Riesco served for almost twenty years as a judge before entering the Senate. Apparently selected as a presidential candidate because he did not threaten the political order, Riesco fulfilled his backers' expectations by essentially doing nothing. His inactivity proved grievous, because the nation suffered from mounting social unrest as well as bitter labor disputes during his tenure. His government's response was to crush outbreaks brutally.

Although Riesco's internal policies lacked both compassion and vision, he did manage to end an extremely costly naval arms race and to avoid war with Argentina by seeking a negotiated settlement to a long-festering border problem. In 1902 he signed the May Pacts (Pactos de Mayo), which, while limiting Chile's sphere of influence to the Southern Hemisphere's Pacific Coast, ended open hostility with Buenos Aires. Riesco's government also negotiated a peace treaty with Bolivia in 1904 which granted Chile the Atacama region but obliged Santiago to finance a railroad from Arica, where the Bolivians would enjoy a duty-free zone, to La Paz.

— WILLIAM F. SATER

RIGAUD, ANDRÉ

André Rigaud (b. 1761; d. 18 September 1811), Haitian general. A mulatto born in Les Cayes, Haiti, and educated in Bordeaux, France, Rigaud trained as a goldsmith and began his military career serving the French during the American Revolution. At the height of the Haitian Revolution, he was appointed commander in the South, where he reestablished prosperity and gained mulatto support through harsh but effective rule. His superiors in Port-au-Prince found him resistant to their direction, but depended heavily on his control over mulattoes and his excellent military skills against the British. In 1799 he entered into a power struggle with the black leader and national hero Toussaint L'OUVERTURE that resulted in Rigaud's defeat and exile to France. He returned to Haiti in 1810.

— PHILIPPE L. SEILER

RIO BRANCO, BARÃO DO

Barão do Rio Branco (José Maria da Silva Paranhos Junior; *b.* 20 April 1845; *d.* 9 February 1912), Brazilian foreign minister. Rio Branco's prestige was founded on his successful settlement of frontier disputes. He was influenced forcefully by his father and namesake, the Viscount do Rio Branco, who was a noted diplomat and Conservative statesman. As a law student at São Paulo (1862) and Recife (1866) as secretary to his father during delicate diplomacy in the Río de la Plata (1869, 1870–1871), Rio Branco acquired a taste for diplomatic and military history not only of that area but of Brazil generally. He cultivated this taste over decades, first as a political journalist and deputy, then in his quiet diplomatic routine as consul in Liverpool (1876–1893). He pursued his studies and bibliophilia in the Parisian home he maintained for his family.

While Argentina saw itself as a hemispheric rival of the United States, Brazil preferred the role of junior partner.

Rio Branco's erudition gradually became well known among cognoscenti; when a representative for the arbitration with Argentina over the Missions area was required, Rio Branco was remembered. His celebrated commitment to painstaking research and analysis was first remarked in this case (1893–1895). Victory dispelled obscurity; first named to a more prestigious European post, he was then sent to contest Gallic claims associated with French Guiana (1898–1900). A second victory was rewarded with the ministerial position in Berlin (1900–1902), after which he became the minister of foreign affairs in the dynamic administration of RODRIGUES ALVES (1902–1906).

Rio Branco was a member of that administration and those that followed for an unprecedented ten years, comprising the golden age of Brazil's diplomatic prestige. From Itamaratí Palace, Rio Branco continued to orchestrate the peaceful settlement of various frontier disputes from Dutch Guiana to Uruguay. He is noted, for example, for negotiating the end to the confrontation over the upper-Amazon sources of natural rubber, a negotiation that led to the origins of the present state of Acre (1904). Rio Branco also oversaw Brazil's developing relationship with the United States. He raised the diplomatic status of Brazil's representation in Washington, D.C., and he appointed Joaquim NABUCO as the first ambassador (1905–1910) to signal appreciation of the relationship's importance.

While Argentina saw itself as a hemispheric rival of the United States, Brazil preferred the role of junior partner. Brazil supported the Pan-American movement, whose Third Conference was held in Rio de Janeiro in 1906. Rio Branco is famed for his successful projection of Brazil's image as a "civilized" nation during this era of Eurocentric imperialism. He did this by attracting the nation's cultivated elite to diplomacy, by ensuring Brazil's inclusion at international meetings, by encouraging celebrated foreigners to travel to Brazil, and by promoting positive reports of the country and its past. His triumphs brought him a singular popularity which, like his books and maps, surrounded him in the cluttered Itamaratí apartment in which he died.

— JEFFREY D. NEEDELL

RIO BRANCO, VISCONDE DO

Visconde do Rio Branco (José Maria da Silva Paranhos; *b.* 16 March 1819; *d.* 1 November 1880), Brazilian statesman and diplomat. Paranhos, father of the Barão do RIO BRANCO, was a foremost statesman of the monarchy (1822–1889), celebrated for his Platine diplomacy and the Free Birth Law (1871), the first direct attack on Brazilian slave holding.

Born in Bahia and orphaned early, Paranhos escaped poverty through scholarship at Rio's navy and army academies, where he studied and then taught. Literary skill brought him early prominence as a journalist and as a Liberal deputy (1848). He caught the attention of Honório Hermeto Carneiro Leão, later Marquês de PARANÁ, a powerful chief of the Conservative Party. Leão was entrusted by his old ally, Paulino José Soares de Sousa, later Visconde do URUGUAI, with the diplomacy in Uruguay that would lead to the victorious alliance against Argentina's Juan Manuel de ROSAS in 1850. In Paranhos, Leão hoped for an able lieutenant, and he was vindicated. Both Soares de Sousa and Leão were impressed enough to champion Paranhos's entry into the Conservative Party and his election as Conservative deputy for Rio de Janeiro province in 1853.

Paranhos, despite his relative youth, was next appointed a minister in the celebrated *Conciliação* (Conciliation) Cabinet organized by Paraná in 1853. He served in several posts from 1853 to 1871, including minister of foreign affairs. Other portfolios followed in the 1850s and 1860s, as did the presidency of Rio de Janeiro Province (1858), ascension to the Senate (for Mato Grosso in 1862) and to the Council of State (1866), and several controversial missions to the Río de la Plata republics (1857, 1864–1865, 1869–1870, and 1870–1871), involving negotiations leading up to and ending the War of the Triple Alliance.

In 1871 the emperor picked him as prime minister to organize a cabinet to address the question of slavery. Rio Branco did so, at the beginning of the longest ministry (1871–1875) of the monarchy. He also defended the crown's prerogatives vis-à-vis the church in the Religious Question, a dispute sparked by two bishops' decision to condemn the participation of Brazilian Catholics in freemasonry. And he introduced many reforms on elections, education, justice, and the infrastructure. But his greatest accomplishment was the passage of the Free Birth Law in 1871, which, like earlier Spanish and English colonial legislation, declared all children of slave mothers free upon majority and provided for self-manumission and apprenticeship. A consummate politician and orator, Rio Branco successfully isolated and then dominated the fierce and able resistance to slavery's reform, led by the namesake and son of his old protector, Paulino José Soares de Sousa. Although its ultimate failure figured in the struggle for complete abolition begun less than a decade later, Rio Branco's legislation was a hard-won and politically crucial step and thus remains his great claim upon posterity.

– JEFFREY D. NEEDELL

RIO, JOÃO DO

João Do Rio (pseudonym of Paulo Barreto; (*b.* 5 August 1880; *d.* 23 June, 1921), Brazilian writer. João do Rio—reporter, short story writer, and man about town—enjoyed a tremendous reputation during his brief lifetime; he was regarded as the personification of Brazilian culture at the turn of the century and was elected to the Brazilian Academy of Letters before he reached age thirty. While one or two of his short stories (particularly the grotesque carnival tale "O bebê de Tarlatana Rosa") are still anthologized, his fame dissipated within a few years after his death. That fame depended, in large measure, upon his public persona, which João do Rio carefully modeled on Oscar Wilde; the persona is also the focus of much of the bibliography on his life and work, although few biographers and critics have directly ad-

dressed the central issue of his homosexuality. His stories and nonfiction accounts of Rio de Janeiro, such as *A alma encantadora das ruas* (1908), are now read primarily as social documents, for they provide more or less realistic descriptions of the city's underworld of brothels and cabarets, a world in which perversion, cruelty, disease, and suffering reigned.

– DAVID T. HABERLY

RÍOS MONTT, JOSÉ EFRAÍN

José Efraín Ríos Montt (*b.* 16 June 1926), president of Guatemala (23 March 1982–9 August 1983). General Ríos Montt came to power in the 23 March 1982 coup that overthrew then president General Fernando Romeo LUCAS GARCÍA. The military-instigated coup named a three-man junta consisting of Ríos Montt, General Horatio Maldonado Schad, and Colonel Francisco Gordillo to head the government. In June 1982, Ríos Montt dismissed his fellow junta members and named himself president of the republic.

At the time Ríos Montt took office, significant portions of the western highlands, particularly in the department of El Quiché and the northern Transversal along the Mexican border, were controlled by or sympathetic to Guatemala's armed resistance, which had united in 1980 to form the Guatemalan National Revolutionary Unity (URNG). Ríos Montt launched a massive counterinsurgency campaign, known as "rifles and beans," to drive the insurgents from the largely Indian highlands. This effort was a military success in that it greatly reduced rebel power; but thousands of civilian lives were lost, and the United Nations estimated that as many as 1 million Guatemalans were forced into exile during this period.

From 1 July 1982 until 23 March 1983, Ríos Montt declared a nationwide state of siege, banning all union and political activity, granting arresting powers to the armed forces, nullifying guarantees of privacy, eliminating writs of habeas corpus, and enforcing strict press censorship. Ríos Montt also established "special tribunals" in which suspected guerrillas and criminals were prosecuted without trial by jury.

Ríos Montt attracted a great deal of attention outside of Guatemala during his term of office, in part because he was an evangelical Protestant and publicly associated himself with his church, the Church of the Word (*Verbo*), which had its home office in California. Ríos Montt's strong reliance on advisers from his church displeased the Guatemalan military, which forced his ouster in 1983. Other reasons for the military's dissatisfaction with Ríos Montt included his failure to shore up the nation's faltering economy, and his reluctance to set a date for new national presidential elections.

On 9 August 1983, Ríos Montt was overthrown in a military coup led by his own minister of defense, Oscar Humberto MEJÍA VICTORES.

– VIRGINIA GARRARD-BURNETT

RÍOS MORALES, JUAN ANTONIO

Juan Antonio Ríos Morales (*b.* 1888; *d.* 27 June 1946), president of Chile (1942–1946). In 1924, Ríos, a lawyer and businessman, won his first election to Congress, where he quickly became a leading member of the Radical party and a contender for the party's presidential nomination in 1938. With the death of Radical president Pedro AGUIRRE CERDA in November 1941, Ríos was elected his successor with 56 percent of the vote. He continued Aguirre Cerda's policies but focused on the principal issue of the time, Chile's neutrality in World War II. Chile finally broke off relations with the Axis in January 1943. Ríos subsequently became the first Chilean president to make an official visit to the United States (October 1945). His health, however, was failing, and, like his predecessor, he died before the end of his term.

– SIMON COLLIER

RIPSTEIN, ARTURO

Arturo Ripstein (*b.* 13 December 1943), Mexican film director. Ripstein studied law, art, and Mexican history at the National University of Mexico, the Universidad Iberoamericana, and El Colegio de México. He made his directorial debut at the age of twenty-one with the film *Tiempo de morir* (1965), which he followed with a number of noted films in the 1970s. He is one of the most respected directors of the post-1968 generation. Almost all his films have been financed by the state. Many of his best films are adaptations of literary works. His favorite cinematic themes are moral decay and social crises; he is also known for unique character studies. Among his critical successes are *El castillo de la pureza* (1972), *La viuda negra* (1977), *La tía Alejandra* (1978), *El lugar sin límites* (1977), *El otro* (1984), *El imperio de la fortuna* (1985), and *Mentiras piadosas* (1988). Ripstein received the Ariel for best direction from the Mexican film academy for *Cadena perpetua* and *El imperio de la fortuna*.

– DAVID MACIEL

RIUS

Rius (pen name of Eduardo del Río; *b.* 20 July 1934), Mexican comic-book writer and cartoonist. Eduardo del Río, more popularly known to millions of his readers by his pen name Rius, is the creator of the most explicitly political comic books and illustrated books in Mexico and perhaps in all of Latin America. As a young man he worked briefly as a cartoonist for the Mexico City newspaper *Ovaciones,* but was dismissed because of the controversial nature of his political cartoons. During the 1950s and early 1960s, he alternately was unemployed and worked for several Mexico City publications. He soon became known to his readers for his outspoken criticism of social customs and prominent political figures, including the Mexican president.

In 1966, Rius made the switch from cartoonist to comic-book writer with the creation of his first comic book, Los supermachos.

In 1966, Rius made the switch from cartoonist to comic-book writer with the creation of his first comic book, *Los supermachos,* for Editorial Meridiano. Unable to tolerate the censorship of his publisher, he abandoned that series. In 1968, Rius created a second comic book, *Los agachados,* which he continued to write and illustrate until 1977. Since the early 1970s he has also written and illustrated over thirty-five books.

Rius's overtly political criticism of Mexican institutions has frequently angered government officials, even to the point of threatening his life. Nonetheless, he has continued to issue sharply satirical attacks against some of Mexico's most sacrosanct beliefs and institutions: the Catholic church, the Revolution, and machismo. Rius is an unabashed admirer of socialism and has devoted many comic-book issues and books to instructing his readers about its basic tenets.

– CHARLES TATUM

RIVA AGÜERO Y OSMA, JOSÉ DE LA

José de la Riva Agüero y Osma (*b.* 26 February 1885; *d.* 26 October 1944), Peruvian historian, literary scholar, and politician. Born in Lima, Riva Agüero attended schools in his native city, receiving degrees in literature and law at the University of Lima. In 1907 he advocated military service for Peruvian students, and he himself enlisted when war with Ecuador and Bolivia appeared imminent. He then wrote an article in which he demanded amnesty for all political prisoners, a work for which he himself was imprisoned. Students rallied on his behalf, and he and all other prisoners were released.

Riva Agüero traveled widely in Latin America and Europe and in the process attended historical and literary conferences. In 1915 he returned to political activity and helped establish the National Democratic Party. Later he was elected mayor of Lima. As the young democrat aged, however, his political philosophy became more conservative. Eventually, he concluded that an enlightened elite should lead the nation rather than trust control to the masses, a belief that eventually led him to accept Fascism in the 1930s.

Riva Agüero focused his historical work on the general history of Peru and on the growth of the Inca Empire in the pre-Hispanic period. Historiographically, he advocated careful research and evaluation of sources. He also believed that history could be used to expand patriotism.

– JACK RAY THOMAS

RIVA PALACIO, VICENTE

Vicente Riva Palacio (*b.* 16 October 1832; *d.* 22 November 1896), Mexican military, political, and literary figure. Born in Mexico City, the son of Mariano Riva Palacio, governor of the state of Mexico, Riva Palacio was educated at the Literary Institute in Toluca and qualified in law in 1854. He was a Liberal deputy in the Constituent Congress of 1856–1857. Though a civilian, he commanded a section of the Liberal army during the Civil War of the Reform (1858–1861). It was in 1861, while a deputy in the federal Congress, that Riva Palacio became known as a skillful satirist and a playwright. His literary proclivities notwithstanding, he fought under Ignacio ZARAGOZA at the battle of Puebla in May 1862. He remained loyal to President Benito JUARÉZ, whom he followed to San Luis Potosí in 1863. As governor of Mexico and later of Michoacán (1865) under Juaréz, he became known for his generous treatment of enemy prisoners, and in 1867 took part in the capture of Querétaro.

After election to the Supreme Court of Justice (1868–1870), he dedicated himself increasingly to writing. With his friend Ignacio ALTAMIRANO, Riva Palacio stood for the creation of a national literature. From 1888 he oversaw the publication of the multivolume *Mexico a través de los siglos.* He founded *El Ahuizote* (1874–1876), a satirical newspaper, which attacked the administration of President Sebastián LERDO DE TEJADA (1872–1876). He supported Portfirio DÍAZ's Plan of Tuxtepec in 1876 and served as secretary for development from 1877 to 1880. For attacks in the Chamber of Deputies on the administration of General Manuel GONZÁLEZ (1880–1884), he was sent to the Santiago Tlatelolco Military Prison in 1883. Upon returning to power in 1884, Porfirio Díaz sent him in 1886 as minister plenipotentiary to Spain and Portugal. Riva Palacio died in Madrid; his remains were brought back to Mexico in 1936.

– BRIAN HAMNETT

RIVADAVIA, BERNARDINO

Bernardino Rivadavia (*b.* 20 May 1780; *d.* 2 September 1845), Argentine statesman, liberal, and unitarist. Born in Buenos Aires, son of a wealthy Spanish merchant, Rivadavia was educated at the Real Colegio de San Carlos; subsequently he married the daughter of Viceroy Joaquín del Pino. He served as an officer in the Galician Corps, which fought against the British invaders in 1806–1807. An active supporter of the Revolution of May 1810, Rivadavia thenceforth made his career as a professional politician of independence. After some vacillation, he supported the Liberal side of the independence movement. As secretary of the First Triumvirate (1811–1812), he was the driving force behind its liberal policies in education, civil rights, and the slave trade. He also showed his commitment to strong central government, marginalizing the agents and agencies of provincial representation, and provoking opposition from federalists and the military. The First Triumvirate was overthrown in October 1812, and Argentina entered a period of acute instability, as unitarists and federalists fought for control.

Rivadavia was a distant observer of these events, being absent on a diplomatic mission in Europe from 1814 to 1820. His own interest lay in the transfer of ideas and resources. In London he visited Jeremy Bentham and became one of his leading disciples. Rivadavia saw that utilitarianism offered a new philosophy in the aftermath of independence and could give liberal republicanism a moral legitimacy in the gap left by the Spanish crown and church. Liberal institutions in turn would be the framework of economic growth, in which British capital, shipping, goods, and immigrants would play an indispensable part.

Rivadavia seized his opportunity in July 1821, when he became chief minister in the government of Martín Rodríguez in Buenos Aires and gave an instant display of applied liberalism. Drawing on previous planning, he established the University of Buenos Aires. He curtailed the temporal power of the church, extended religious freedom, abolished the ecclesiastical *fuero* and the tithe, and suppressed some religious orders. His plan of modernization included the promotion of a mining industry and improvement of transport; the federalization of Buenos Aires and its customhouse; the expansion of agriculture through immigration and land distribution; and a plan of colonization which he promoted in London. Economic development depended on British capital, trade, and markets, and Rivadavia offered his partners generous terms in Argentina. To Argentines themselves, outside the merchant and landed groups, he offered little; vagrants were pursued with ruthless disregard for traditional usages and swept into the army or labor gangs.

Rivadavia sought to extend modernization beyond the province of Buenos Aires and to create a united and centralized Argentina; on 7 February 1826 he was named president of the United Provinces of the Río de la Plata. But his policy was premature and in many respects ineffective. He alienated traditional interest groups, and these came together under Juan Manuel de ROSAS to force his resignation in July 1827. He retired to his country estate and then, in 1829, to Spain. He attempted to return in 1834 but was not permitted to disembark. He died in modest circumstances in Cádiz.

— JOHN LYNCH

RIVAROLA, CIRILO ANTONIO

Cirilo Antonio Rivarola (*b.* 1836; *d.* 31 December 1879), Paraguayan president (1870–1871). Born into a distinguished elite family, Rivarola began his career as an attorney in Asunción in the period just before the War of the Triple Alliance (1864–1870). He soon ran afoul of the autocratic regime of Francisco Solano LÓPEZ for daring to advocate liberal reform, and was briefly imprisoned. Early in the war, López had him sent to the front as a sergeant. Rivarola acquitted himself well in battle, but after his capture by the Allies in 1869, he cooperated with his captors, who discovered in him the perfect puppet.

After his capture by the Allies in 1869, Rivarola cooperated with his captors, who discovered in him the perfect puppet.

With Carlos Loizaga and José Díaz de Bedoya, Rivarola was named to preside over a provisional administration in Asunción that favored Brazilian interests. This government abolished slavery, fostered freedom of the press, arranged for loans from Britain, and held a convention in 1870 to establish a new constitution. By then, Rivarola's two colleagues had resigned, and he stayed on as president. His base of popular support, however, was extremely weak, and he antagonized many of the politicians around him. He went so far as to close

Congress in October 1870. A year later his congressional opponents forced him to step down in favor of his vice president, Salvador JOVELLANOS.

Over the next seven years, Rivarola figured in many political intrigues in a vain effort to recapture the presidential sash (and with it, he hoped, the support of Brazil's minister in Asunción). He continued to be involved in various conspiracies after the Brazilian army evacuated Paraguay in 1876, which brought him still more enemies. He was assassinated on the street in Asunción, in full view of many passersby.

— THOMAS L. WHIGHAM

RIVAROLA, RODOLFO

Rodolfo Rivarola (*b.* 18 December 1857; *d.* 10 November 1942), Argentine jurist and intellectual. Founder in 1910 of the influential *Revista Argentina de Ciencias Políticas,* Rivarola was a strong advocate of political reform in pre–World War I Argentina. After studying law at the University of Buenos Aires, he specialized in criminal law; he was one of the precursors of the Italian school of positivist criminology in Argentina. In 1888, with José Nicolás MATIENZO and José María RAMOS MEJÍA, among others, Rivarola founded the Sociedad de Antropología Jurídica, following the teachings of the Italian psychiatrist Cesare Lombroso.

Rivarola wrote extensively on Argentine judicial institutions: *Orígenes y evolución del derecho penal argentino* (1900) and *Proyecto de Código penal para la República Argentina* (1891), a project for a code drafted in collaboration with Norberto Piñero and Matienzo, deal with criminal law. *Instituciones del derecho civil argentino* (1901) deals with civil law.

In politics, Rivarola became an advocate of centralization against the federalist system, as can be seen in his *Partidos políticos unitario y federal* (1905) and especially in *Del régimen federativo al unitario* (1908). But he was mostly concerned, as exemplified in his writings for the *Revista,* with the reform of the political practices of the liberal-conservative regime that governed the country between 1880 and 1916.

— EDUARDO A. ZIMMERMANN

RIVAS, PATRICIO

Patricio Rivas, provisional president of Nicaragua (October 1855–1857). Although he had served in several governmental capacities, including senator, interim chief of state (1838), and customs officer, Rivas is most remembered for his role in Nicaragua's National War. In October 1855, the American filibuster William WALKER chose Rivas as his president, under the assumption that he could control the relatively inexperienced old man. In February 1856, Rivas signed Walker's revocation of the Accessory Transit Company's canal charter, a popular action, but protested the next day when Walker presented him with a charter for the Morgan and Garrison Company. The terms of this contract gave away much more than had its predecessor, and Rivas would not sign it without modifying its worst clauses. In June 1856, Rivas defected from the Walker government altogether to join the patriot forces that had opposed the foreign invasion. Although he was known to his contemporaries as "Patas Arriba" ("Feet-Up" or "Topsy-Turvy") for his supposed lack of mettle, subsequent generations have come to regard Rivas as a courageous patriot. He is buried in a place of honor in the cemetery in León.

— KAREN RACINE

RIVERA, DIEGO

Diego Rivera (*b.* 13 December 1886; *d.* 24 November 1957), Mexican artist, known primarily for the many murals he painted in Mexico and the United States from the early 1920s through the early 1950s. Over a period of more than fifty years Rivera also produced an extraordinary number of easel paintings, drawings, watercolors, illustrations for books and other publications, and designs for theater productions. A number of his easel paintings and murals, dating from every period of his life, stand out for their artistic quality and thematic coherence.

Rivera was born in Guanajuato. During his formative years in Paris from 1911 to 1921, he experimented with a number of styles before returning to Mexico in 1921 to begin his muralist career. Among the many exemplary works dating from his stay in Paris are *Zapatista Landscape—The Guerilla* (1915) and *The Mathematician* (1918). Rivera expressed his feeling for his native land in the *Zapatista Landscape,* a major cubist work, by including references to the mountains surrounding the Valley of Mexico, the Revolution of 1910 (a sombrero, a serape, and a rifle), and traditional Spanish and Mexican painting (with the realistic depiction of a small piece of paper identifying the subject "nailed" to the lower right of the canvas). *The Mathematician* represents Rivera's deep involvement and assimilation of the work of Paul Cézanne. Rivera depicted a lone figure seated at a small table on which are placed two books. The sitter appears lost in thought. The artist defined every part of the picture with intersecting lines and angles that correspond to several eye levels consistent with Cézanne's approach to painting. He used all of these in

a series of linear connections to create a spare yet visually cohesive composition.

One of the most important easel paintings dating from Rivera's mature period is the portrait *Lupe Marín* (1938), which demonstrates his continuing interest in formal and spatial problems. Marín is shown seated on a backless Mexican chair in a corner of the artist's studio. There is a mirror propped up against the wall behind her, in which she and the window she faces are reflected. Rivera paid homage to several artists he admired in this portrait: El Greco, in the exaggerated proportions and pose of the sitter; Velázquez, in the mirrored image; and Cézanne, in the complex structure of the composition.

Rivera's great artistic achievement is also seen in a few mural panels that form part of larger programs and in several mural cycles that have to be considered as a unit. Among the single panel masterpieces are *The Deliverance of the Peon* (1926), from the Ministry of Education in Mexico City (1923–1928); *Germination,* from the Chapingo Chapel mural cycle *The Land Liberated* (1926–1927); and *Production of Automobile Bodies and*

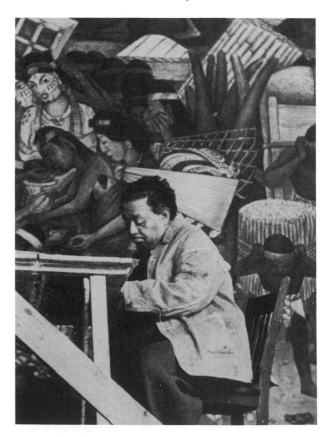

Market at Tlatelolco, *painting by Diego Rivera, 1945. Painting is now housed in the Palacio Nacional. Reproduced from* Rivera: Iconografía personal *(Mexico City: Fondo de Cultura Económica, 1986). (Cenidiap)*

Final Assembly, from the mural *Detroit Industry* (1932–1933), in the Detroit Institute of Arts. Each of these encapsulates the artist's deep involvement with formalist as well as thematic concerns.

Rivera used the Christian theme of "the descent from the cross" for *The Deliverance of the Peon,* in which the dead figure echoes the lowering of the figure of Christ onto a shroud. The scene is filled with tenderness and compassion. It is also a powerful image of a martyr of the Revolution.

Germination has a number of beautifully rendered nude figures that represent various stages from gestation to near birth. It is one of four panels on the right wall of the chapel that focus on the forces of nature. The process begins with chaos and ends with fruition. Comparable forces in society leading to revolutionary action are represented in four panels on the left wall. A synthesis of these forces is represented on the end wall with man at the center in control of nature for the benefit of humankind.

Rivera carried his positive view of technology further in his Detroit mural cycle, in which he devised a complex iconographic program to extoll its virtues. He merged U.S. technology with Mexican mythology on the south wall (*Production of Automobile Bodies and Final Assembly*) by including a reference to the Aztec earth goddess Coatlicue as a fender-stamping machine. The deity, not immediately discernible, is seen to the right of the men working on the assembly line with an automotive chassis. The Coatlicue-like machine retains the silhouette of the deity but not its component parts. The artist's belief in material progress and the benefits to be derived from technology are evident in this panel and the many others that comprise the entire mural cycle. The other panels include the origins of human life and technology on the east wall; the industries of the air (aviation) and water (shipping) on the west wall; the production, manufacture, and assembly of the automobile, and the other industries of Detroit (medical, chemical, and pharmaceutical) on the north and south walls.

Rivera's roles as a political activist, lecturer, and writer pitted him against other artists, art critics, the Communist Party (which expelled him several times), his biographers, Frida KAHLO and his other three wives, and the general public. At the core of these many battles were his views regarding the essence, purpose, and function of art; his views on politics; his love of the Mexican Indian; and his belief that the pre-Columbian past had to be accepted before a true Mexican art and identity could be attained. These battles and controversies, as well as his art, have provided material for numerous articles, monographs, books, exhibition catalogues, and other publications by biographers, journalists, art critics, art historians, and others.

– JACINTO QUIRARTE

RIVERA, FRUCTUOSO

Fructuoso Rivera (*b.* ca. 1784; *d.* 13 January 1854), president of Uruguay (1830–1835 and 1839–1843), around whom the Colorado party, one of the two traditional parties in the country, was formed. When the movement for independence began in 1810, he joined immediately and soon became one of José Gervasio ARTIGAS's most trusted lieutenants, supporting him against the attempts of Buenos Aires to control the region. Rivera played a key role in the fight against Portuguese domination (1816–1820), holding out until March 1820, when he was defeated. As a result of his defeat, he came to terms with the Portuguese invaders and signed the charter of incorporation of Uruguay into the United Kingdom of Portugal and Brazil. In 1822, as a result of Brazil's declaration of independence, Rivera joined the Brazilians against the Portuguese in Uruguay. The Brazilian emperor, Dom PEDRO I, promoted him to brigadier general, and in 1824 he was named commander of all the forces in the countryside. However, when Juan Antonio LAVALLEJA, a leading Uruguayan independence leader and an old friend and collaborator, invaded in 1825, he was captured by Lavalleja's troops, apparently in agreement with Lavalleja himself, and soon became his second in command. But in 1826, he broke off with Lavalleja and moved to Santa Fe, Argentina. While in Santa Fe, with the help of Estanislao LÓPEZ, a prominent regional military leader, Rivera prepared and launched an invasion against the Brazilian territory of Misiones in February 1828. This military feat increased his prestige.

On 28 August 1829, Rivera became minister of war of the provisional government, and on 24 October 1830, he became the first elected president of independent Uruguay. As president, Rivera did not carry out a specific program and was very disorganized, acting more like a caudillo than a president of a country and paying no attention to the affairs of government. Rivera helped General Manuel ORIBE get elected president in 1835 with the hope that he could influence him, but when Oribe wanted to pass a series of laws that affected the interior, which Rivera considered his fiefdom, he rose in revolt on 16 July 1836, forcing Oribe's resignation on 23 October 1838. Rivera was then elected president. His second presidential term was disastrous for the country, for he turned an internal political dispute into a regional conflict with his alliances and intrigues with Argentine Unitarians and the Brazilian *farrapos* (ragamuffins). The affair became an international conflict when France and England intervened in favor of Rivera's Colorados and Argentine Unitarians.

Ten days after he had begun his second term (1839–1843), Rivera declared war on Juan Manuel de ROSAS of Argentina, who had given asylum to Oribe, and plunged Uruguay into a conflict that did not end until 1852. Rivera did have some initial success, but between 1842 and 1845, Oribe and the Argentines had the upper hand. In 1845, Rivera sought refuge in Brazil and in 1846 went back to Uruguay and organized an unsuccessful campaign. He was removed from his command on 3 October 1847 because he had started secret negotiations with Oribe. Sentenced to four years in exile, he left for Brazil. In 1851, when the ban was lifted, he tried to go back to Uruguay. However, the Brazilian government blocked his return and kept him a virtual prisoner. He was not allowed to leave Brazil until 20 January 1853. On his way back to Uruguay, he learned that he had been named as a member of a triumvirate, but he died en route.

— JUAN MANUEL PÉREZ

RIVERA, JOAQUÍN

Joaquín Rivera (b. 26 July 1796; d. 6 February 1845), head of state of Honduras (1833–1836). Born in Tegucigalpa, Rivera was elected head of state of Honduras in 1830 but declined the office because it was not the result of a popular election. Elected again in 1832, this time in a popular election, he accepted the position. Rivera concentrated on improving the educational system, reducing the debt, and developing commerce and industry. He was particularly concerned with maintaining the relationship between Honduras and the other members of the Central American Federation and was a close ally of Francisco MORAZÁN. Rivera's term of office ended in 1836.

Rivera returned to private life but was forced to leave the country when his former "vice president" and main political detractor, Francisco FERRERA, rose to power. While in exile in El Salvador, Rivera aided Morazán in his efforts to restore the disintegrated Central American Federation. In 1844, Rivera was captured in Danlí while leading a rebellion against Ferrera. He was condemned to death and was executed.

— SARA FLEMING

RIVERA, JOSÉ EUSTASIO

José Eustasio Rivera (b. 1888; d. 1 December 1928), Colombian poet and novelist. Born of a poor family in Neiva, in southeastern Colombia, Rivera was a difficult child both at home and at school. Expelled from three schools, he made his family's economic situation yet more precarious. But he had a natural inclination for literature, and during his best days at school, he was called upon to give speeches, recitals, and even poetry improvisations.

Rivera's life was marked by suffering that was both personal and a reflection of Colombia's condition at the end of the nineteenth century.

Rivera studied to become a teacher at the Escuela Normal in Bogotá, attending an extra year to apply for the position of school inspector. In 1910 he was finally appointed inspector of Tolima, a province in central Colombia. Rivera took up his work zealously and conscientiously, but was frustrated at having to slow down and accept routine procedures and traditional methods. On top of this frustration came the sudden death of his sister at seventeen years of age. Rivera's life was marked by suffering that was both personal and a reflection of Colombia's condition at the end of the nineteenth and beginning of the twentieth centuries, when the country was in the midst of civil war and beset by rancorous party politics.

Despite his surroundings, this poor, unknown Colombian became a renowned Latin American figure as a poet and a novelist. In poetry, laurels were bestowed on his volume *Tierra de promisión* (1921), and he achieved his right to sit among the great novelists of America for *La vorágine* (1924; *The Vortex,* 1935). The former, a collection of fifty-five sonnets, won him the stature of national poet; the latter made him famous even outside the boundaries of the Hispanic world when it was published in other countries in translation. In fact, *The Vortex* is a breathtaking romantic vision of the Colombian llanos (plains), a bold encounter with the "green inferno," an exhilarating display of the beauty of the tropics. But most of all, it is a tragic document of the dehumanizing influence of the jungle and *caucherías* (rubber-collecting sites) on the souls and lives of those lured by the promise of fast wealth, who were doomed to endless suffering and often merciless death by the savagery of the *enganchador* (recruiting man). Only five years after the publication of his novel, Rivera died in Bogotá.

— J. DAVID SUÁREZ-TORRES

RIVERA, PEDRO DE

Pedro De Rivera (d. 1744), reformer of Mexico's northern frontier military system. In 1724 Pedro de Rivera was the commander of the garrison of San Juan de Ulua, the fort that guarded the port of Veracruz. In that year Viceroy Juan de Acuña Casafuerte commissioned Rivera to inspect the twenty-three presidios in northern New Spain and in particular to report on fiscal irregularities in their administration. The members of presidio garrisons received a flat salary from which they had to buy their own horses, equipment, and uniforms. The administration in Mexico City had been receiving reports of graft by presidio commanders. The commanders were charging inflated prices not only for the three types of necessities mentioned but also for other items.

Rivera inspected the presidios in 1724 and submitted suggestions that were implemented in 1729 as a comprehensive *reglamento* for the garrisons. The new set of rules reduced the number of presidios from 23 to 19, and the size of the garrisons from 1,006 to 734 soldiers. The *reglamento* also lowered the salary of most common soldiers. The reduction in the number of presidios and soldiers decreased the government's expenditures for frontier defense from 444,883 pesos prior to Rivera's inspection to 381,930 pesos following it. However, his reforms did not improve frontier security, and in the face of continued hostility from tribes beyond Spanish control, the number of presidios and soldiers and the amount of government expenditures grew during the eighteenth century.

– ROBERT H. JACKSON

RIVERA CABEZAS, ANTONIO

Antonio Rivera Cabezas (*b.* 1784; *d.* 8 May 1851), a radical liberal leader in early independent Central America. Born in Guatemala City to a prominent creole family, Rivera was a lawyer by profession. He also served as an officer in the colonial militia and as a member of the *diputación provincial* (regional council) established by the Cortes of Cádiz in 1812. A signer of the declaration of Guatemalan independence on 15 September 1821, Rivera was allied politically with radical liberals (*fiebres*) Pedro MOLINA and José Francisco BARRUNDIA and was a member of the Mexican Congress during Agustín de ITURBIDE's empire.

After Central America separated from Mexico (1 July 1823), Rivera became a member (substituting for Manuel José ARCE, who was in the United States), with Molina and Juan Vicente Villacorta, of the triumvirate that directed the United Provinces of Central America. He was its provisional president from 9 July to 4 October 1823, served as *jefe político* of Guatemala in 1824, and then held the post of intendant of El Salvador. Known for his witty political satire in the press, he edited *El Melitón* in 1825. Elected lieutenant governor of Guatemala in 1829, Rivera became its governor from 9

March 1830 to 10 February 1831 after the legislature pressured Governor Pedro Molina to resign. During his brief administration, he launched anticlerical reforms, established schools (including Lancastrian model schools in Quezaltenango and Guatemala City), worked for judicial reform, and established a highway department. Francisco MORAZÁN defeated him in the 1830 Central American presidential election, but he served as Morazán's finance minister in 1835 and as a district judge in 1832 and 1837. After the 1839 conservative victory, he went into exile and conspired with Pedro Molina against the Guatemalan conservatives.

– RALPH LEE WOODWARD, JR.

RIVERA CARBALLO, JULIO ADALBERTO

Julio Adalberto Rivera Carballo (*b.* 1921; *d.* 29 July 1973), army officer and president of El Salvador (1962–1967). Lieutenant Colonel Rivera headed the provisional government established on 25 January 1961, when a military coup d'état overthrew a leftist junta that had been in power since October 1960. Later, he resigned in order to assume leadership of the National Conciliation Party (PCN). In 1962, he was elected to the presidency as the PCN candidate, following a campaign boycotted by the opposition parties.

Although an outspoken anti-Communist, Rivera appeared to accept the Kennedy administration's argument that the best way to defeat communism was to attack poverty, injustice, and tyranny at home. An enthusiastic supporter of the Alliance for Progress, Rivera initiated a number of significant reforms in El Salvador, including a rural minimum wage. He also liberalized the political system, a policy that encouraged the development of opposition parties. In pushing reforms over conservative objections, Rivera benefited from the country's rapid economic growth in the early 1960s. Later, however, a downturn caused problems for his handpicked successor, Colonel Fidel SÁNCHEZ HERNÁNDEZ (1967–1972). Rivera was serving as ambassador to the United States at the time of his death.

– STEPHEN WEBRE

RIVERA DAMAS, ARTURO

Arturo Rivera Damas (*b.* 30 September 1923), archbishop of San Salvador. Born in San Esteban Catarina and ordained a Salesian priest in 1953, Rivera, who holds a degree in canon law, was consecrated auxiliary bishop of San Salvador in 1960. His support of progressive clergy soon gained him the enmity of the conservative oligarchy, especially when, in January 1970, he refused to leave the Ministry of Defense building until the government released Father José Alas, who had been arrested for advocating land reform.

When Oscar ROMERO was named archbishop of San Salvador in 1977, Rivera was made bishop of Santiago de María, Usulután. He was the only Salvadoran bishop to back Romero consistently in his struggle against government-sponsored represssion and in his actions on behalf of Christian base communities.

After Romero's assassination in March 1980, the Vatican named Rivera apostolic administrator. Nearly three years later, he was made archbishop. As leader of the Salvadoran church, Rivera has not totally followed in his predecessor's footsteps. Although he consistently denounces the brutalities of the security forces and opposes U.S. military aid, he has been less sympathetic than Romero to popular organizations. He tried to take a neutral position in the civil war, calling for dialogue and a negotiated solution, while sometimes acting as a mediator.

– EDWARD T. BRETT

RIVERA MAESTRE, MIGUEL

Miguel Rivera Maestre (*b.* 1806; *d.* 1888), prominent architect in nineteenth-century Guatemala. Together with his brother, Julián Rivera Maestre, also an architect, or individually, the two designed and planned most of the major public buildings of the era, including the Sociedad Económica building, which later became the home of the national congress. Miguel was in charge of the planning and construction of the Teatro Carrera, the national theater in Guatemala City, until he resigned for political reasons and was replaced by the German architect José Beckers. Miguel also drew the first detailed maps of Guatemala City and was responsible for the country's first atlas, *Atlas del Estado de Guatemala* (1832).

– SUE DAWN MCGRADY

RIVERA PAZ, MARIANO

Mariano Rivera Paz. (*b.* 24 September 1804; *d.* 22 February 1849), chief of state of Guatemala (1838–1839, 1839–1841, 1842–1844). The son of a creole family of modest means, Rivera rose to the rank of lieutenant colonel in the federal army during the civil war of 1826–1829. After the army's defeat by Francisco MORAZÁN, Rivera went to Cobán, and during the administration of Mariano GÁLVEZ (1831–1838) he represented Verapaz in the legislature and acquired considerable property. Rivera was an active member of the conservative faction led by Juan José de AYCINENA, and following Rafael Carrera's overthrow of Gálvez in 1838,

served as chief of state of Guatemala for most of the subsequent five years. In collaboration with Carrera, he presided over restoration of Hispanic values and institutions in Guatemala. Rivera later served as alcalde of Guatemala City, director of the Sociedad Económica, and corregidor of the Department of Guatemala. In 1849 President Mariano PAREDES named him *corregidor* of Jutiapa, with orders to pacify that rebellious *montaña* department. Guerrillas ambushed and killed him as he traveled to his new post.

– RALPH LEE WOODWARD, JR.

RIVERA Y MONCADA, FERNANDO DE

Fernando de Rivera y Moncada (*b.* 1711; *d.* 18 July 1781), Spanish commandant of the Californias. Rivera y Moncada, a native of Compostela, Nayarit, served in the military at Loreto, Baja California, in 1742. He explored the Bahía de Sebastián Vizcaíno with the Jesuit Fernando Consag in 1751. As commandant, he aided in the founding of missions at Santa Gertrudis (1752) and San Francisco Borja (1762). With the Jesuit Wenceslaus Linck, Rivera y Moncada explored as far as the Sierra San Pedro Mártir in 1766. In January 1768 he aided Gaspar de PORTOLÁ in the expulsion of the Jesuits from California, and in May of that year he and the Franciscan Juan Crespí led the first land party to San Diego. With Portolá he explored as far as San Francisco and Monterey from July 1769 to January 1770, and from Baja California he supplied Alta California in 1770–1771. Rivera y Moncada retired to Guadalajara in 1772, but by 1774 he was back in service as military commandant of Alta California, where he put down the San Diego revolt in 1775. He was commandant of Loreto from 1777 to 1779, and in 1781 he led Sonoran colonists to Alta California. He was massacred in an uprising by the Yuma Indians near La Concepción on the Colorado River.

– W. MICHAEL MATHES

ROA BASTOS, AUGUSTO

Augusto Roa Bastos (*b.* 13 June, 1917), Paraguayan novelist. Born in Iturbe, Guairá, Roa was raised from age ten by his uncle, a bishop in the country's jungle region. In 1930 he wrote a play, *La carcajada,* and his first short story, "Lucha hasta el alba." Fighting in the Chaco War (1932–1935) while still in his teens left an indelible mark on Roa's writing. After the war he never returned to school and instead became a crime reporter for the newspaper *El País* (Asuncíon). In 1937 his first novel, *Fulgencio Miranda* (unpublished), was awarded the Ateneo Paraguayo Prize, and a book of poems, *El ruiseñor de la aurora* (1942), earned him the National Prize for Poetry. Roa went to England in 1944 to cover the European war for *El País*. He was in France for the Liberation, returning to Paraguay in 1945. Exiled for political reasons, Roa became a journalist in Brazil and then moved to Buenos Aires, where he taught literature at the Argentine Writers' Society at the urging of Ernesto SÁBATO. A collection of poetry, *El naranjal ardiente* appeared in 1960, and his novel *El trueno entre las hojas* (1953) became a motion picture. His collaboration with Armando Bó led to a long association with the Argentine film industry. Roa's novel *Hijo de hombre* (1960; *Son of Man*, 1965) won first prize in the Losada publishing house's international literary competition. Set against the backdrop of the Chaco War, this book reflects on the individual's awakening to freedom and stresses solidarity in the midst of adversity. In 1966 Roa published a collection of short stories, *El baldío*, and in 1967 appeared *Los pies sobre el agua* and *Madera quemada*. Roa held a Guggenheim Fellowship in 1971 and published *Cuerpo presente y otros cuentos* in 1972. In his masterpiece, the monumental novel *Yo el Supremo* (1974; *I the Supreme*, 1986), based on the life of nineteenth-century dictator José Gaspar de FRANCIA, Roa explores the intricate relations between history and fiction. From 1976 to 1985 Roa taught Guaraní and Spanish American studies at the University of Toulouse in France. In 1982 the first Roa symposium was held at the University of Maryland and the same year he published the definitive version of *Hijo*. Augusto Roa Bastos conveyed the culture and history of Paraguay better than any other author. While maintaining his residence in Toulouse, Roa began spending more time in Paraguay after the overthrow of President Alfredo STROESSNER.

– SAÚL SOSNOWSKI

ROBLES, FRANCISCO

Francisco Robles (*b.* 5 May 1811; *d.* 11 March 1893), president of Ecuador (1856–1859). Robles, born in Guayaquil, served as deputy from Manabí Province

---

In 1857 Robles moved to abolish Indian tribute but took no steps to make up for lost revenues.

(1852) and as governor of Guayas Province (1854–1856) prior to assuming the presidency, the successor selected by departing president José María URBINA (1851–1856). In 1857 Robles moved to abolish Indian tribute but took no steps to make up for lost revenues.

As a result, government revenues fell sharply. Not a strong leader, his presidency was further compromised by his serious illness in 1858. Later that year Peru threatened to invade Ecuador, and opponents in Congress, led by the Conservative Gabriel GARCÍA MORENO and the Liberal Pedro Moncayo y Esparsa, refused to cooperate in establishing necessary defenses. Peru blockaded Guayaquil in 1858 and invaded in 1859, effectively cutting off Ecuador from its sole remaining source of revenue, the Guayaquil customs house. The nation quickly disintegrated into civil war: Loja and Cuenca declared their independence, Guayaquil annexed itself to Peru, and in Quito, Gabriel García Moreno selected former president Juan José FLORES to battle Robles. Flores won, and Robles fled into exile in Peru. He died in Guayaquil.

– RONN F. PINEO

ROBLES, MARCOS AURELIO

Marcos Aurelio Robles (*b.* 8 November 1905), president of Panama (1964–1968). A native of Aguadulce, Robles was an active National Liberal Party (PLN) legislator and was appointed minister of the interior and justice in 1960. After being elected to the presidency as the candidate of the National Opposition Union (UNO), composed of the PLN and seven smaller parties, Robles took office 1 October 1964.

Robles, a banker, represented the business-planter elite that had dominated Panama since independence and, in many ways, since the Spanish conquest. He sought new economic development and especially promoted Panama as a Latin American banking center. He encouraged partial incorporation of Panama into the Central American Common Market, but his moderate efforts at tax reform and agrarian reform divided the Liberal Party. His unsuccessful attempt to secure a better treaty with the United States vis-à-vis the Panama Canal following the 1964 flag riots, charges of corruption, and failure to represent a wider constituency led to his impeachment by the National Assembly in 1968. Although the Supreme Court overturned the impeachment, Robles had become unpopular. After his coalition lost the 1968 election to Arnulfo ARIAS, Robles went into voluntary exile in the United States.

– RALPH LEE WOODWARD, JR.

ROBLES, WENCESLAO

Wenceslao Robles (*d.* January 1866), Paraguayan general. At the outbreak of the War of the Triple Alliance in 1864, Robles was a ranking army officer stationed at the fortress of Humaitá, in southern Paraguay. Less than a year later, he was chosen by President Francisco Solano LÓPEZ to command a large force sent to invade the neighboring Argentine province of Corrientes. After the surprise capture of the port of Corrientes on 13 April 1865, Robles disembarked with 3,000 men and immediately pushed southward along the east bank of the Paraná. Reinforcements amounting to another 22,000 men reached Robles en route, and permitted him to advance as far as Goya.

Diversionary attacks by the Argentines in late May and the disastrous naval engagement at Riachuelo in June caused Robles to falter, however, and by the end of the year, the Paraguayans had evacuated Corrientes, leaving much destruction behind. Robles had been relieved of command in July. López later had him arrested and charged with dereliction of duty and possible collusion with the enemy. Despite the lack of evidence against him, a military court found Robles guilty, and he was executed at Humaitá.

– THOMAS L. WHIGHAM

ROCA, BLAS

Blas Roca (Francisco Calderío; *b.* 1898; *d.* 1987), Cuban union organizer and politician. Roca was born in Manzanillo, Oriente Province. A shoemaker by trade, he changed his name to Blas Roca and fought to unionize his fellow workers before joining the Cuban Communist Party in 1929. Five years later he was elected secretary general of the party. Roca held many important positions in the party and government. He helped form the new Cuban Communist Party (PCC) in 1965, served on the central committee, politburo, council of state, and in the National Assembly, of which he was president from 1976 to 1981. Roca played a decisive role in consolidating and institutionalizing the control of the Communist Party. His writings include *The Fundamental Principles of Socialism in Cuba* (1962) and *The Cuban Revolution: Report to the Eighth National Congress of the Popular Socialist Party of Cuba* (1961).

– TODD LITTLE-SIEBOLD

ROCA, JULIO ARGENTINO

Julio Argentino Roca (*b.* 1843; *d.* 20 October 1914), president of Argentina (1880–1886, 1898–1904). Roca, a clever politician who dominated Argentina from 1880 to 1904, represents the predominance of rural landowners. He presided over a period of political order as well as spectacular economic growth until overtaken by reformist opponents.

Roca's rise to power began in the army. As an officer from Tucumán, Roca viewed the army as an agent of national unification. At the age of sixteen, he completed his formal education at the Colegio Nacional de Concepción del Uruguay. He then participated in the battle of Cepeda as a lieutenant in José de URQUIZA's army. Roca became popular after successfully completing his military campaigns along the pampas. He won the support of cattlemen, politicians, and farmers in the interior because he protected and enriched them. Through his military career, Roca broadened his understanding of Argentina and of the provincial upper class.

Roca began to consider himself a viable presidential candidate during the AVELLANEDA regime, in which he served as minister of war. In 1879, he began his desert campaign against the Ranqueles Indians. The government transferred 35 percent of the national territory from the Indians to local caudillos between 1876 and 1893. The provincial *estancieros* (hacienda owners) became part of a capitalistic oligarchy. Land speculation increased as landowners borrowed on the basis of higher land values. Many of these landowners urged Roca to seize power. By January 1880, he had selected candidates and discussed the possibility of their election to the presidency.

Turmoil surrounding the 1880 presidential election enabled Roca to become chief executive. When Carlos TEJEDOR became the Autonomist leader of Buenos Aires province, he provoked the conservative interior because he was a representative of the liberal tradition of Bartolomé MITRE. Roca articulated provincial resentment at the unfair distribution of tariff revenues by officials in Buenos Aires, demanding that the city be federalized as the national capital. The interior wanted to operate the port in order to benefit the other provinces. With friendly governors behind him throughout Argentina, Roca defeated Tejedor in the presidential balloting. Avellaneda lost his nerve when Tejedor revolted in June 1880, but Roca's popularity in the army enabled him to crush the dissidents.

Roca's first regime was generally successful. His program of order appealed to many because Argentina needed economic growth. Landed interests appreciated Roca's railroad construction. Anticlericals within the Partido Autonomista Nacional approved of his secular outlook. Roca was not an idealist and had few scruples about his cynical use of power. A shrewd politician known as "the fox," he used his authority to ensure peace in the interior. Well organized and a prolific correspondent with local supporters, he allowed few details to escape his attention.

The economic boom of the 1880s established Roca's authority. Exports grew tremendously, to the point that Argentina eventually became the world's leading corn exporter and second in wheat exports. Wool, mutton, sheepskin, and beef exports enabled the pastoral sector to retain a slim lead over agriculture. Roca also supported the sugar industry and presided over the best railroad system in Latin America. Foreign capital poured in, to the extent that by 1889, British capital in Argentina represented about half of British overseas investments. Unwisely, however, Roca allowed mortgage banks to sell notes using land as collateral. Meanwhile, the Roca regime encouraged massive European immigration to Argentina despite its lack of a consistent land policy. Fine shops, a wonderful opera theater, and pleasant surroundings led Buenos Aires to become known as the Paris of the Americas.

Roca played a strong role in the PELLEGRINI government. He controlled the countryside as interior minister. At this time Roca formulated a famous *acuerdo* with Mitre and the moderate faction of the Unión Cívica. As Roca probably anticipated, a radical faction of the Unión Cívica split off in protest. Hipólito YRIGOYEN began a long struggle to unseat Pellegrini's and subsequent governments until he triumphed in 1916.

Roca established several local regimes that were improvements over preceding administrations. Elected as head of the national Senate, he imposed Luis SÁENZ PEÑA as Argentina's next president in 1892. Once again, Roca controlled politics. When Sáenz Peña would not allow him to dominate his government, however, Roca and Mitre turned Congress against the president. Using his network, Roca was reelected president in 1898.

Roca's second regime was unsatisfying. He nearly went to war with Chile. Anarchists and socialists established powerful working-class movements. Therefore Roca attempted to repatriate critical immigrants by means of a foreigners' residence law. Economic growth continued, but the foreign debt remained high. For the first time in two decades, Roca discovered that he could not mandate who would become president. Manuel Quintana, Roca's successor, was a compromise selection. But the vice president, José Figueroa Alcorta, was Carlos Pellegrini's choice. When the elderly Quintana died in 1906, Roca quickly lost influence.

After retiring from politics, Roca regretted the imbalance of wealth and power between Buenos Aires and the rest of the country. Although he was the symbol of provincial resentments, he became a classic elite figure. Roca spent many of his later years in Europe and died in Buenos Aires.

— DOUGLAS W. RICHMOND

ROCA RODRÍGUEZ, VICENTE RAMÓN

Vicente Ramón Roca Rodríguez (*b.* 2 September 1792; *d.* 23 February 1858), member of ruling triumvirate (March 1845–October 1845), president of Ecuador (1846–1849). A coastal businessman born in Guayaquil, Roca helped lead the 9 October 1820 uprising that brought independence to Guayaquil. He served as a deputy to the Riobamba convention of 1830 that separated Ecuador from Gran Colombia. Roca held several posts in the new government: vice president of the Congress (1833), governor of Guayas (1835), and senator from Guayas (1837–1839). Roca played a leading role in the 6 March 1845 overthrow of President Juan José FLORES. The subsequent Roca administration faced serious financial problems and repeated coup attempts.

Roca raised money through forced contributions and the advance collection of the Indian tribute, both extremely unpopular measures.

As Congress was pondering impeachment in 1846, news arrived of a planned invasion by former president Flores, backed by 30 million pesos from the Spanish government. South America rallied to Ecuador's side, and Spain withdrew its support for Flores. But if the Spanish threat had temporarily united Ecuador, the cost of building defenses had diverted scarce resources away from urgent domestic concerns, thus weakening the young nation in the long run. Roca raised money through forced contributions and the advance collection of the Indian tribute, both extremely unpopular measures. When Roca left office in 1849, Ecuador fell into fractious dispute, and drifted into a disastrous civil war. He died in Guayaquil.

— RONN F. PINEO

ROCAFUERTE, VICENTE

Vicente Rocafuerte (*b.* 1 May 1783; *d.* 16 May 1847), Ecuadorian independence leader, diplomat, and statesman. Born in Guayaquil to one of the region's wealthiest families, Rocafuerte studied at the Colegio de Nobles Americanos in Granada, Spain, and at the Collège de Saint Germain-en-Laye in France. Returning to Guayaquil in 1807, he devoted himself to family affairs; three years later he was elected *alcalde ordinario* (city magistrate) of Guayaquil. In 1812 he traveled to England, then to the Continent as far as Russia. Elected to the Cortes, he arrived in Madrid in April 1814 in time to witness the abolition of that parliament. Thereafter, he devoted his efforts and his fortune to the interests of the new American nations, serving Colombia, Cuba, and Mexico during 1820–1824.

An advocate of republicanism, Rocafuerte wrote extensively on its behalf and opposed the Mexican empire of ITURBIDE. From 1824 to 1830, he served as Mexico's representative to England and continental Europe. Returning to Mexico in 1830, he advocated social reforms and religious freedom as well as opposition to the conservative regime of Anastasio BUSTAMANTE. Upon his return to Guayaquil in 1833, he joined the opposition to President Juan José FLORES, was elected to Congress, and led a revolt against the president. After reaching an understanding with Flores, however, he later served as president (1835–1839) and then as governor of Guayas (1839–1843), while Flores served another term. But when the president sought to retain power, Rocafuerte opposed him. After Flores's ouster in 1845, Rocafuerte served as president of the Senate in 1846 and accepted a diplomatic mission to Lima, where he died.

In addition to his political and diplomatic activities, Rocafuerte's writings on political systems, social reform, religious toleration, and economic development had significant influence on liberals in several Spanish American nations.

– JAIME E. RODRÍGUEZ O.

ROCHA, DARDO

Dardo Rocha (*b.* 1 September 1838; *d.* 6 September 1921), Argentine jurist and politician. Born in Buenos Aires, Rocha obtained a doctorate in law at the university in 1863. Gravitating to politics, he became known as an orator. He was elected to the Chamber of Deputies in 1873 and to the Senate in 1874, becoming its presiding officer in 1877. In 1881 he was elected governor of the province of Buenos Aires. In that post he is best remembered as the founder of La Plata, designed to be the provincial capital city following the federalization of the city of Buenos Aires in 1882, when the latter became the national capital. Following his unsuccessful bid for the national presidency in 1884, Rocha served on the national Supreme Court and the Superior Court of Buenos Aires Province.

– RONALD C. NEWTON

ROCHA, JUSTINIANO JOSÉ DA

Justiniano José Da Rocha (*b.* 8 November 1812; *d.* 10 July 1862), Brazilian political journalist, litterateur, and Conservative polemicist. Born in Rio de Janeiro, Rocha, a mulatto, was schooled in France and at the São Paulo faculty of law. He taught at the Colégio Pedro II and the military school in Rio, and represented Minas Gerais thrice in the Chamber of Deputies (1843–1844, 1850–1852, 1853–1856). He was also the first in Brazil

to write and translate serial novels as a minor figure in the first Romantic generation. His greatness, however, lay in being the heir (and counterpoise) to the political journalism tradition associated with Evaristo da VEIGA (1799–1837), the liberal who had dominated so many of the First Empire and Regency debates.

Rocha wrote polemics with a celebrated clarity and facility as the servant of the Conservative Party from its beginnings, writing or editing in the Rio press as the party's voice until the era of the Conciliação. He presided over *O Chronista* (1836–1839), *O Brasil* (1840–1852), as well as a number of more ephemeral periodicals, and from 1839 to 1862 he took the Conservative's part in pieces for the *Jornal do Commércio*. Protégé and partisan of Bernardo Pereira de VASCONCELOS (1795–1850) and partisan of the saguarema reactionary leadership of the party in its years of struggle, Rocha is most justly remembered for his incisive analysis in the pamphlet "Ação; reação; transação" (1855).

– JEFFREY D. NEEDELL

ROCHA, MANOEL RIBEIRO

Manoel Ribeiro Rocha, eighteenth-century Portuguese writer and priest. Very little is known about Rocha's life. He was born in Lisbon and after completing his studies at Coimbra University, he moved to Brazil and worked there as a lawyer in Bahia. A specialist in canon and civil law, Rocha wrote three books, all published in 1758: *Socorro dos fiéis aos clamores das almas santas, Nova prática dos oratórios particulares,* and *Etíope resgatado, empenhado, sustentado, corregido, instruido, e libertado.* Whether he died in Bahia is an unsolved question.

Recent analysis of *Etíope resgatado* questions previous studies, by Robert Walsh in *Notícias do Brasil* and Francisco Adolfo de Varnhagen in *História geral do Brasil* (2 vols., 1854), that regarded Rocha as an abolitionist on the basis of his treatment of the slave traffic and compulsory labor. The new perspective considers this book to be a guide for use by slave masters and merchants interested in finding solutions to their problems, and not as an argument in favor of abolishing slavery as an institution.

– ELIANA MARIA REA GOLDSCHMIDT

ROCHA PITA, SEBASTIÃO

Sebastião Rocha Pita (*b.* 3 May 1660; *d.* 2 November 1738), Brazilian historian and member of the Royal Academy of Portuguese History. Born in Bahia, Rocha Pita wrote *Tratado, político* around 1715, but it remained unpublished until 1972. Best known to historians but seldom quoted is his *História da América por-*

tuguesa, desde ano de 1500 do seu descobrimento até o de 1724, published in 1730. The author's purpose was to narrate the events that had taken place in Brazil with the help of "truthful reports" and "modern information" given by those who had traveled in the vast Brazilian territory. This was the only history of Brazil available to his contemporaries, since most of the others composed in the first two centuries of colonization remained in manuscript until the nineteenth century.

According to the model then followed by historians, Rocha Pita wrote a political and natural history, where human events took the same place and aroused the same interest as the description of the productions of nature. Sugarcane, tobacco, manioc, rice, and medicinal plants occupy a large place in the book, and the information on them is mostly the result of direct observation. Although Rocha Pita pays little attention to the academic discussion of the origin of America's inhabitants, the Indians of Portuguese and Spanish America are compared.

– MARIA BEATRIZ NIZZA DA SILVA

ROCHAMBEAU, DONATIEN MARIE JOSEPH DE VIMEUR DE

Donatien Marie Joseph de Vimeur de Rochambeau (*b.* 7 April 1755; *d.* 20 October 1813), French general and last colonial governor of Saint-Domingue. Born at the Rochambeau estate near Vendôme, Rochambeau entered the army at fourteen and accompanied his father, Jean Baptiste de Vimeur de Rochambeau, commander of French troops, to America during the War of Independence. In the early 1790s he was commandant of the Windward Islands and in 1793 was in Martinique. From January to May 1796, he was governor-general of Saint-Domingue. He returned to Saint-Domingue, serving as captain-general from January to November 1803, during which time he helped to put down the revolt led by Toussaint L'OUVERTURE.

On the return voyage to France, Rochambeau's ship was seized by the British, who imprisoned him until 1811. He then resumed his military career. He died of wounds suffered at the Battle of Leipzig.

– ANNE GREENE

RODAS ALVARADO, MODESTO

Modesto Rodas Alvarado (*d.* ca. 1978), a charismatic Honduran political leader. The Liberal Party in Honduras had been out of power since 1932 when its leader, Ramón VILLEDA MORALES, became president in 1957. Rodas Alvarado, who had been provisional secretary of the Liberal Party in 1954, was president of the National

Congress during Villeda Morales's period in office (1957–1963). Rodas Alvarado became the Liberal candidate to replace Villeda Morales in the election of 1963. All signs pointed toward his probable victory. During the campaign he talked about ending the military's budget autonomy and restricting its ability to nominate candidates for the position of chief of staff. Had he been elected he probably would have carried forward the land reforms and other measures opposed by landholders, fruit companies, and conservative military elements.

U.S. President John F. Kennedy refused to recognize the new government, but in December 1963 President Lyndon B. Johnson granted it recognition.

A few days before the scheduled election, the military under General Oswaldo LÓPEZ ARELLANO took over. U.S. President John F. Kennedy refused to recognize the new government, but in December 1963 President Lyndon B. Johnson granted it recognition. In retrospect, the 1963 coup was a major setback for Honduran political development. After the coup, Rodas dropped completely out of public life. His contribution was symbolically recognized by the continuation of the Rodista Liberal Movement, the faction of the Liberal Party led by President Roberto Suazo Córdova in the 1980s.

– DAVID L. JICKLING

RODÓ, JOSÉ ENRIQUE

José Enrique Rodó (*b.* 15 July 1871; *d.* 1 May 1917), Uruguayan writer and literary critic. Rodó was born in Montevideo. In secondary school and at the University of Montevideo he was weak in the sciences but excelled in literature and history. As professor of literature at the University of Montevideo (1898–1902), deputy in Congress for the Colorado Party (1902–1905, 1908–1914), and essayist, he was the spokesman for intellectual motivation, moderation, and good taste—in public life as well as in literature. His principal books are *Ariel* (1900), his first and best-known work; the much longer and less-structured spiritual quest *Motivos de Proteo* (1909; *The Motives of Proteus,* 1928); and a collection of essays, vignettes, and literary criticism, *El mirador de Próspero* (1913; Prospero's Balcony). His writings are collected in *Obras completas,* edited by Emir Rodríguez Monegal, 2d ed. (1967).

Like José MARTÍ in Cuba and Rubén DARÍO in Nicaragua, Rodó was a leading exponent of modernism in

Hispanic American literature in the late nineteenth and early twentieth centuries. As the symbolic name Proteus in one of his titles suggests, change was a fundamental virtue for Rodó: "To change is to live," the first sentence of *The Motives of Proteus,* reflects the indirect but vital influence of Charles Darwin's and Herbert Spencer's evolutionary thought on Rodó's essentially aesthetic view of the world.

Ariel and most of the rest of Rodó's work were composed with clearly didactic intentions and in a refined rhetorical manner. Writing for him was a vocation more than a profession, a quiet endeavor that seemed to symbolize his solitary and meditative way of life. In *The Motives of Proteus* the author extends and elaborates on the encouragement of individualism, expounded before in *Ariel,* and underscores the energy of youth and the importance of self-education and self-knowledge. In his repeated mention of the need for intellectual heroism, which he divides into "wisdom," "art," and "action," he shows congeniality with Carlyle, Emerson, and Nietzsche.

Rodó was writing in an era of transition for Latin America. The war of 1898 between the United States and Spain awoke a new Latin American consciousness of cultural ties to Spain and sharpened awareness of North American hegemony in the Western Hemisphere. In those circumstances he called consistently for a reaffirmation of Hispanic American "spiritual" values as distinct from allegedly more pragmatic North American values. All his written work was an elegant elaboration of that point of view.

— PETER G. EARLE

RODRIGUES, JOSÉ HONÓRIO

José Honório Rodrigues (*b.* 20 September 1913; *d.* 6 April 1987), Brazilian historian. Soon after graduating from the National Law School in his native city of Rio de Janeiro in 1937, José Honório Rodrigues embarked on his chosen career as a historian. His first major work, *Civilização holandesa no Brasil* (Dutch Civilization in Brazil) was written in collaboration with Joaquím Ribeiro and appeared in 1940, before Rodrigues had received any academic training in historical methodology. A fellowship from the Rockefeller Foundation enabled him to study historical theory and methods at Columbia University in 1943–1944 and put him in touch with the main currents of world historiography. Returning to Brazil, he promoted the use of advanced techniques in the researching and writing of Brazilian history, urged the creation of graduate programs in history at Brazilian universities, campaigned for the opening of government archives to scholars and for the publication of important

source material, and developed his own *visão* (perception) of Brazilian history.

As curator of rare books at the Brazilian National Library (1946–1958) and director of the National Archives (1958–1964), Rodrigues made these institutions more responsive to the needs of professional historians. Removed from his directorship as a result of the military coup of 1964, he had more time for writing and lecturing at Brazilian and foreign universities. For Rodrigues, a committed liberal and acute observer of the contemporary scene, writing history was more important than political activism. In his landmark *Independência: revolução e contrarevolução* (5 vols., 1975–1976), he argues that a traditionalist elite has consistently thwarted liberal movements in Brazil and crushed the aspirations of the Brazilian people. In historiographical works like *História da história do Brasil* (4 vols., 1979–1988), Rodrigues exposes the biases of conservative historians who, he charges, have served the ruling class and perpetuated its myths of "nonviolence" and "conciliation." Rodrigues's works translated into English include *Brazil and Africa* (1965) and *The Brazilians: Their Character and Aspirations* (1967).

— NEILL MACAULAY

RODRIGUES, NELSON

Nelson Rodrigues (*b.* 23 August 1912; *d.* 22 December 1980), Brazilian dramatist and journalist. Rodrigues's plays deal with the lives of the bourgeoisie and the lower classes—including slum dwellers and prostitutes—who see themselves as victims of oppression. He described his dramas as "pestilent," fetid" and his characters as "monsters." His exaggerated preoccupations with Brazilian machismo and sex brought him great popularity. His plays were brought to the stage by Brazil's leading directors, including Zbigniew Ziembinski and Antunes Filho. Artistically, Rodrigues singlehandedly brought Brazilian drama into the twentieth century with *O vestido de noiva* (1943; *The Wedding Dress,* 1980), an innovative play for its time owing to its complex narrative levels: the past, the present, and the plane of hallucinations. Other works include *O beijo no asfulta* (1961) and *Toda nudez será castigada* (1965).

— IRWIN STERN

RODRIGUES, RAIMUNDO NINA

Raimundo Nina Rodrigues (*b.* 4 December 1862; *d.* 17 July 1906), founder of Afro-Brazilian studies and anthropology. Trained in Bahia as a physician, he began around 1888 to study Brazilian blacks from the perspective of criminological psychiatry. His work diagnosed Afro-Brazilian culture as the manifestation of racial evolutionary backwardness, yet it pioneered the empirical study of that culture.

His most important contribution was *O animismo fetichista dos negros bahianos* (1896; The Fetishist Animism of Bahian Blacks). This book describes the divinities and rituals of the Candomblé religion and classifies its beliefs as animism, higher on the evolutionary scale than fetishism. *Os africanos no Brasil* (1932; Africans in Brazil), a posthumous collection of articles, includes studies on the regional origins of African slaves in Brazil and on the history of slavery.

Nina Rodrigues's ethnological research was always an adjunct to his primary interest in criminology. His major work was *As raças humanas e a responsabilidade penal no Brasil* (1894; Human Races and Criminal Accountability), but he also published on such diverse topics as the diagnoses of wounds and the nature of criminal crowds. Rodrigues trained or influenced many of the next generation of physician-anthropologists, including Afrânio Peixoto and Artur RAMOS. His disciples continued the study of Afro-Brazilian culture but repudiated his racial theories.

— DAIN BORGES

RODRIGUES ALVES, FRANCISCO DE PAULA

Francisco de Paula Rodrigues Alves (*b.* 7 July 1848; *d.* 16 January 1919), president of Brazil (1902–1906). Allied by birth and through marriage with the coffee-producing elites of São Paulo, Rodrigues Alves graduated from São Paulo Law School in 1870. A Conservative in his youth, he joined the Republican Party after the 1889 overthrow of the monarchy and helped to write the 1891 constitution. He later served as senator, minister of finance, and governor of São Paulo.

Rodrigues Alves's presidency exemplified both positive and negative aspects of the Brazilian drive for "order and progress." A sound treasury and the appointment of men of ability to office enabled a successful campaign to transform Rio de Janeiro into a beautiful and healthful capital. A central boulevard and new municipal buildings, including the Municipal Theater and National Library, were built. Port facilities and rail lines were modernized. Oswaldo CRUZ, director of public health, waged a vigorous campaign to improve sanitation and eradicate pestilence; by 1906 yellow fever deaths had dropped to zero in the city.

Resistance to the sanitation and reconstruction campaigns, in which poor inhabitants of the central city were displaced, was reinforced by the regime's political opponents. In November 1904 the issue of compulsory vaccination for smallpox precipitated riots. Several hundred people suspected of participating in the riots were summarily rounded up and sent to the new Brazilian territory of Acre. Opposition leaders and students from the Praia Vermelha Military School who were involved were arrested but later granted amnesty.

Brazil enjoyed increased international prestige during Rodrigues Alves's administration. In 1903 Foreign Minister Barão do RIO BRANCO resolved the dispute with Bolivia over the territory of Acre in Brazil's favor; in 1905 the first cardinal in Latin America was appointed to Rio de Janeiro; and the Third International Conference of American States convened there in 1906. After leaving the presidency, Rodrigues Alves served again as governor of São Paulo (1912–1916), and in 1918 he was reelected to the presidency, but was too ill to assume office.

— FRANCESCA MILLER

RODRÍGUEZ, ANDRÉS

Andrés Rodríguez (*b.* 19 June 1923), Paraguayan president (1989–1993). Born in the small town of San Salvador de Guairá, Rodríguez entered the army at an early age. He participated in the 1947 civil war, but came into prominence only after the rise to power of his mentor, General Alfredo STROESSNER, in 1954. Seven years later, Rodríguez was promoted to full colonel and given command of the Cavalry Division, after which he became a general and head of the First Army Corps.

Rodríguez prospered tremendously under the corrupt Stroessner dictatorship. Long the number-two man in the army, Rodríguez cemented his relationship with the president when his daughter Marta married Stroessner's youngest son. In turn, this loyalty was rewarded with many concessions. Rodríguez built up major interests in banking and currency exchange, flour milling, brewing, real estate, ranching, and construction—not to mention near-monopoly control of cigarette, liquor, and luxury car imports. By the late 1980s, his personal fortune was estimated at over $1 billion.

On the night of 2 February 1989, Rodríguez launched a coup d'état that toppled Alfredo Stroessner's thirty-five-year dictatorship.

At this time, however, the Stroessner regime was visibly weakening. Fairly open arguments concerning who would succeed the old president broke out among his various henchmen, and Rodríguez decided not to wait any longer. On the night of 2 February 1989, he launched a coup d'état that toppled the thirty-five-year dictatorship. Rodríguez announced that the new government would abandon the old ways in favor of a political democracy. Much to the surprise of many, he did precisely that, freeing the press, permitting the return of exiles, removing the most corrupt and brutal of Stroessner's associates, even saddling a few with long prison terms. In May 1989, a presidential election—arguably the fairest ever held in Paraguay—placed Rodríguez in the presidential palace for a four-year term with 75 percent of the popular vote.

Skeptics still doubted his commitment to democracy, but Rodríguez's liberalization program was nonetheless applauded by the majority of Paraguayans.

– THOMAS L. WHIGHAM

RODRÍGUEZ, CARLOS RAFAEL

Carlos Rafael Rodríguez (*b.* 23 May 1913), Cuban revolutionist. Born in Cienfuegos, Cuba, Rodríguez became actively involved in 1930 with the student movement against Gerardo MACHADO, soon heading the student movement in Cienfuegos. At this time he began meeting with a small nucleus of Communists. For the next two decades, he remained active in political affairs, becoming a member of the Popular Socialist Party (PSP) and editing numerous political publications. In 1958, along with the PSP, he allied with Fidel CASTRO. In postrevolutionary Cuba, Rodríguez devised agrarian reforms and published the official socialist periodical *Hoy.* He often represented Cuba at international meetings. In 1976, the Cuban government named him to several ministries, where he played a vital role in establishing Cuba's foreign policy.

By the early 1980s, Rodríguez ranked behind only Fidel and Raúl Castro within the Cuban hierarchy. He also held numerous administrative posts, including fourth secretary of the Cuban Communist Party.

– ALLAN S. R. SUMNALL

RODRÍGUEZ, LORENZO

Lorenzo Rodríguez (*b.* 1704; *d.* 1774), innovative colonial architect. Born in Gaudix, Andalusia, Rodríguez was in New Spain in 1731 and was examined as an architect in Mexico City in 1740. Despite competition from native architects, his career advanced. In 1744 he was an inspector of the architects' guild, and between 1749 and 1768 he was the architect of the Sagrario Metropolitano of Mexico City Cathedral, a very important commission, which is the basis of his reputation. In 1758 he was also named *maestro mayor* (chief

architect) of the Royal Palace, a post he held until his death. During the last years of his life, Rodríguez wrote an architectural treatise, only recently discovered, in which he stresses the importance of mathematics for his profession.

Rodríguez is considered to have been responsible for introducing the *estípite* (architectural support whose main element is an elongated inverted pyramid) on church exteriors in New Spain. Previously, the *estípite* had been used only in retablos. At the Sagrario, Rodríguez combined a sober, centralized plan and classicistic interior with elaborate *estípite* portals full of figures. Most *estípite* façades in and near Mexico City have been attributed to him in the past, although now these attributions are rejected or considered doubtful. He died in Mexico City.

– CLARA BARGELLINI

RODRÍGUEZ, SIMÓN

Simón Rodríguez (*b.* 28 October 1769; *d.* 28 February 1854), Venezuelan educator and teacher of Simón BOLÍVAR. Rodríguez began life in Caracas as a foundling. He became well educated largely through his own efforts. From an early age Rodríguez was teaching and articulating an educational philosophy that stressed the need for practical studies as well as for making education available to all sectors of society, including women. In his belief in human perfectibility through schooling, he was undoubtedly influenced by Rousseau, but his ideas also bore the stamp of his own highly original personality.

Rodríguez's most famous pupil was Bolívar, who at one time lived with Rodríguez, with the latter serving as guardian, and who conceived a deep admiration for his teacher's "genius." About 1796, Rodríguez left Caracas, traveling first to the United States (where he worked for a time in Baltimore as a printer) and then to France, where he taught and traveled widely. In 1804, in Paris, he renewed his relationship with Bolívar, and he was with him at Rome the next year when Bolívar took an oath to liberate Spanish America.

Rodríguez returned to America in 1823, intending to help in the construction of a republican new order. In Peru he again joined Bolívar, who gave him the task of organizing schools there and, later, in Bolivia. However, his insistence on mixing youths from different social backgrounds and teaching useful crafts to all in his model school at Chuquisaca (later Sucre) aroused much strong criticism, as did his disregard for personal appearance and social conventions.

After a falling out with Bolivia's first president, Antonio José de SUCRE, Rodríguez moved on. For the next three decades he divided his time among Peru, Chile, Ecuador, and Colombia. In all of these nations he was a teacher who won warm admiration from some and harsh rejection from others. He continually publicized his educational ideas, his social egalitarianism, and such pet causes as the simplification of Spanish spelling. Best known of his writings is *Sociedades americanas en 1828,* first published in Arequipa (1840) and then in an expanded version in Lima (1842). He died in Amotape, Peru.

– DAVID BUSHNELL

RODRÍGUEZ-ALCALÁ, HUGO

Hugo Rodríguez-Alcalá (*b.* 25 November 1917), Paraguayan poet, short story writer, and literary critic. Rodríguez-Alcalá is the son of José Rodríguez Alcalá and Teresa Lamas Carísimo, both established writers. Born in Asunción, Hugo studied at the National College and obtained a doctorate from the National University. His *Poemas* appeared in 1938, followed by *Estampas de la guerra,* based on his experiences in the Chaco War, in 1939. In 1947 he moved to the United States and earned a second Ph.D., after which he taught literature at several universities, most notably the University of California at Riverside. He has directed and advised many literary journals, including *Hispanic Review* and *Revista Iberoamericana.*

Rodríguez-Alcalá is perhaps best known for his poetry and his numerous studies in the area of literary criticism. Most of his poetry and short stories revolve around the theme of childhood innocence and contain nostalgic and vivid images in the manner of the Spanish poet Antonio Machado and other members of the Generation of 1898, of which he was a specialist. Rodríguez-Alcalá's critical studies include stylistic analyses of the works of Juan RULFO and Roa Bastos. His *Historia de la literatura paraguaya* (1970) has become a standard reference manual.

Other works include *Abril, que cruza el mundo* (1960); *El arte de Juan Rulfo* (1965); *Relatos de norte al sur* (1985); and *Augusto Roa Bastos, Premio Cervantes 1989* (1990).

– THOMAS E. CASE

RODRÍGUEZ CABRILLO, JUAN

Juan Rodríguez Cabrillo (*b. ca.* 1498; *d.* 3 January 1543), first European explorer to reach California. Rodríguez Cabrillo, probably born in Seville, Spain, participated in the conquest of Cuba and served in the conquest of Mexico as a crossbowman and sailor under Hernán CORTÉS (1485–1547) in 1519. He joined Pedro de Alvarado (ca. 1485–1541) in the conquest of Guatemala in 1523. After settling there as a mine owner and *encomendero,* he traveled to Seville to marry Beatríz Sánchez de Ortega about 1532. Subsequently, Rodríguez Cabrillo ran a shipyard and led an expedition of three ships to the North Pacific on 27 June 1542. After exploring the Baja California coast, he entered the present bay of San Diego on 28 September 1542 and named it San Miguel. He claimed the area for Spain and later explored the coastal areas of California. He died on one of the Santa Barbara Channel Islands as a result of complications from a broken bone.

– IRIS H. W. ENGSTRAND

RODRÍGUEZ CERNA, JOSÉ

José Rodríguez Cerna (*b.* 18 September 1885; *d.* 20 July 1952), Guatemalan novelist, poet, and journalist. Rodríguez is considered the first Guatemalan modernist poet and novelist. He graduated from the University of San Carlos with a legal degree in 1904 but never practiced law professionally. Among his literary works are *El poema de la Antigua* (1915), *Tierra de sol y de montaña* (1930), and *Bajo las alas del águila* (1942). Rodríguez's career in journalism included service as the editor-in-chief of the newspaper *La República* and the magazine *Centro América.* He was a contributing writer for other Guatemalan and Salvadoran newspapers. Rodríguez at times wrote under the pseudonyms Hernani, Barba Azul, Martín Paz, Casa Roja, and Juan Chapin.

– STEVEN S. GILLICK

RODRÍGUEZ DE VELASCO Y OSORIO BARBA, MARÍA IGNACIA

María Ignacia Rodríguez de Velasco y Osorio Barba (*b.* 20 November 1778; *d.* 29 October 1851). Born in Mexico City, "La Güera Rodríguez" (Rodríguez the Blond) was a member of a distinguished aristocratic family of New Spain and a partisan of the insurgents who became notorious for her great beauty as well as for her several love affairs. Rodríguez was a friend of important personages of the era, among them Baron Alexander von HUMBOLDT and Agustín de ITURBIDE, with whom she was said to have had a love affair. During the struggle for independence, La Güera corresponded with the insurgents and sent them money and other forms of aid. Two of her haciendas were in the hands of the insurgent chiefs José Sixto Verduzco and José María Liceaga from the beginning of 1813, but no harm came to her properties. She died in Mexico City.

– VIRGINIA GUEDEA

RODRÍGUEZ DEMORIZI, EMILIO

Emilio Rodríguez Demorizi (*b.* 14 April 1908), Dominican historian. Rodríguez earned a law degree at the University of Santo Domingo and served as ambassador to Colombia, Spain, and Italy as well as in government positions. He was secretary of state, secretary of state for education and fine arts, rector of the Universidad Autónoma de Santo Domingo, and director of the National Archive. He has been president of the Academia Dominicana de la Historia since 1965. While director of the National Archive, he made his greatest contribution in terms of collecting and editing Dominican historical documents. Many of the documents were made available for the first time, and many were found when Rodríguez visited all the major European archives. The series *Documentos para la historia de la República Dominicana* and *Relaciones históricas de Santo Domingo* exceeded 100 volumes. Rodríguez also wrote *Fábulas dominicanas* (1946), *El cancionero de Lilís: Poesía, dictadura y libertad* (1962), and several works on Columbus.

– LARMAN C. WILSON

RODRÍGUEZ ERDOIZA, MANUEL

Manuel Rodríguez Erdoiza (*b.* 25 February 1785; *d.* 26 May 1818), legendary Chilean guerrilla chief. A lawyer by training and a fervent partisan of José Miguel CARRERA during the Chilean *Patria Vieja* (the period,

---

His audacious comings and goings were an irritant to the Spanish forces and won Rodríguez a place in Chilean folk memory that he has never lost.

1810–1814, before the Spanish reconquest), Rodríguez fled to Argentina after the collapse of Chilean independence in October 1814. He soon recrossed the mountains at the head of a guerrilla band. His audacious comings and goings were an irritant to the Spanish forces and won Rodríguez a place in Chilean folk memory that he has never lost. For Chileans he is the guerrilla. Unfortunately, the Bernardo O'Higgins–José Miguel Carrera feud meant that Chile, ruled after 1817 by Bernardo O'HIGGINS, was a less than safe place for the guerrilla hero. Though he rallied the panic-stricken citizenry of Santiago magnificently after the royalist victory at the second battle of Cancha Rayada (19 March 1818) and fought at the battle of Maipú (5 April 1818), he could not escape imprisonment. While on his way to Valparaíso, ostensibly to be sent into exile, he was treacherously murdered at Tiltil, whether on O'Higgins's direct orders or not is still debated.

– SIMON COLLIER

RODRÍGUEZ FREILE, JUAN

Juan Rodríguez Freile (*b.* 15 April 1566; *d.* ca. 1642), Colombian chronicler. The son of a conquistador, Rodríguez Freile studied for the priesthood in his native Bogotá, learning Chibcha as well as Latin and attaining minor orders by 1585. Abandoning clerical life, he took service in an *oidor*'s household and spent the years 1585–1569 as a soldier/clerk in Spain and various parts of the Indies. Back in Bogotá, Freile married Francisca Rodríguez, a mestiza, about 1600, and in 1608 fought against Indians in the Neiva Valley; thereafter he settled as a farmer near Bogotá. Between 1636 and 1638, he wrote his masterpiece, *El carnero,* a racy, sprightly (occasionally fictionalized) firsthand account of colonial Colombia's first century. Considered too salacious for publication, *El carnero* circulated in manuscript. The original was lost after 1850, but a later copy served as the basis for the first printed version (1859).

– J. LEÓN HELGUERA

RODRÍGUEZ JUÁREZ, JUAN

Juan Rodríguez Juárez (*b.* 1675; *d.* 1728), Mexican painter. Grandson of José JUÁREZ, son of Antonio Rodríguez, and brother of Nicolás Rodríguez Juárez, Juan Rodríguez Juárez is the principal artist of the transition from the Zurbaranesque baroque tradition of VILLALPANDO and CORREA to eighteenth-century baroque and rococo tendencies in New Spain. His first known work was done in 1694. In 1719 he was given a major commission, the canvases for the Retablo de los Reyes of the cathedral of Mexico City. In his works one sees the softer coloring, more spacious compositions, and gentler expressions of Bartolomé Murillo. Besides his religious paintings, Rodríguez Juárez produced excellent portraits and an extraordinary self-portrait, symptomatic of the changing role of the artist in the colony in the eighteenth century.

– CLARA BARGELLINI

RODRÍGUEZ JULIÁ, EDGARDO

Edgardo Rodríguez Juliá (*b.* 6 October 1946), Puerto Rican novelist and essayist. Born in Río Piedras and educated at the University of Puerto Rico and New York University, from which he received a master's degree in Spanish literature, Rodríguez Juliá came to public attention in the early 1970s as one of the most strikingly versatile talents of an innovative, historically revisionist generation of young Puerto Rican writers. An exceptionally gifted writer of historical fiction, his two novels, *La renuncia del héroe Baltasar* (1974) and *La noche oscura del Niño Avilés* (1984) re-create, with considerable formal ingenuity, the sociopolitically fraught, baroque ambience of colonial life in eighteenth-century Puerto Rico. Probing that epoch's formative impact on the equivocal character of contemporary life on the island, each work examines the decisive centrality of "white lies" or calculated mythogenesis of an officialdom that, forever fearful of imminent (especially slave) disorder and the revolutionary potential of a populace of ex-slaves and their variously hued creole descendants, is intent to guarantee the colony's uncertain, fragile stability. *La renuncia del héroe Baltasar* offers the reader a fictitious series of lectures on the colonial authorities' co-optation of the mulatto son of a venerated leader of revolted slaves in the 1750s, as observed by a Spanish academic speaking before members of the traditionalist Puerto Rican Antheneum in the turning-point year of 1938. Giving more epic extension to this historicist line of fictional inquiry, *La noche oscura del Niño Avilés* has the same provocative academic prefacing a polyphonic, multivocal collection of allegedly suppressed, still controversial documents of disputed authenticity. These concerned the long-forgotten city of Nueva Venecia, a bawdy and vital would-be utopia of runaway slaves, which was burned to the ground by the colonial church and state and thereafter deliberately erased from the national consciousness. Skillfully blending elements of fact and invention, each novel proposes a revised canvas of island history, intimating that inherited colonial dilemmas of race, caste, and class remain a powerful aspect of contemporary Puerto Rico's historical subsoil.

The island's most accomplished and popular practitioner of the essay-cum-chronicle, Rodríguez Juliá's meditations on the contradictory vivacity of Puerto Rican art, history, contemporary popular culture, thought, and feeling are available in *Campeche o Los diablejos de la melancolía* (1986), *Las tribulaciones de Jonás* (1981), *El entierro de Cortijo* (1983), *Una noche con Iris Chacón* (1986), *Puertorriqueños: Album de la sagrada familia puertorriqueña a partir de 1898* (1988), and *El cruce de la Bahía de Guánica* (*cinco crónicas playeras y un ensayo* [1989]). He currently holds a faculty appointment at the Río Piedras campus of the University of Puerto Rico.

— ROBERTO MÁRQUEZ

RODRÍGUEZ LARA, GUILLERMO

Guillermo Rodríguez Lara (*b.* 4 November 1923; *d.* 1988), president of Ecuador (1972–1976). Born of a modest family in the provincial town of Pujilí, Rodríguez Lara became a career army officer; his training included study at Fort Leavenworth, Kansas, as well as military courses in Argentina and Colombia. During thirty-three years of service he rose to become director of the Army War Academy and eventually commanding general of the army in April of 1971. When a series of events provoked the ouster of José María VELASCO IBARRA on 15 February 1972, Rodríguez Lara became head of the new, self-styled "national revolutionary government."

At the outset of his administration, an explicit program for socioeconomic reform and modernization was outlined, but the military leadership was somewhat ambivalent. Traditionalists fought to block agrarian and tax reforms while opposing a nationalistic policy toward the new petroleum industry. Other officers fought for such measures, while Rodríguez Lara sought with increasing difficulty to maintain a position of compromise. Not a persuasive or crowd-pleasing personality, he lacked a popular movement of his own. In September 1975 an uprising by rightist officers was put down, but Rodríguez's position had been fatally damaged. He was forced to resign on 11 January 1976 and was succeeded by a three-man military junta that eventually returned Ecuador to elected government. Rodríguez Lara retired to his farm outside Pujilí and lived there quietly until his death.

— JOHN D. MARTZ

RODRÍGUEZ LUJÁN, ABELARDO

Abelardo Rodríguez Luján (*b.* 12 May 1889; *d.* 13 February 1967), president of Mexico (1932–1934). Last of the troika of presidents during the 1928–1934 administration, General Rodríguez replaced Pascual ORTIZ RUBIO when he resigned. As chief executive, he is generally considered to have been a caretaker, subordinate to his mentor, General Plutarco ELÍAS CALLES. He was a major stockholder in many incipient Mexican industries, including Portland Cement and La Suiza.

From a humble family in Guaymas, Sonora, and with little formal education, Rodríguez worked at many unskilled jobs before joining the Constitutionalists in 1913. He made the military his career, rising through the ranks to division general (three stars) in 1928. He became governor and military commander of Baja California del Norte (1923–1929), a post he used to develop his personal financial holdings in the fishing and packing industries. Rodríguez held several cabinet posts, including secretary of industry and commerce (1932) and secretary of war and the navy (1932). He served as a regional military commander during World War II and as governor of his home state (1943–1948).

— RODERIC AI CAMP

RODRÍGUEZ MONEGAL, EMIR

Emir Rodríguez Monegal (*b.* 28 July 1921; *d.* 14 November 1985), Uruguayan literary critic. Rodríguez Monegal was a prodigious literary critic, author of forty books and countless articles, and "maker of writers," whose controversial career spanned five decades and three continents. He began publishing in 1943 in *Marcha,* a Uruguayan magazine for which he wrote until 1959. Some of his early pieces appear in *Narradores de esta América,* a collection of his essays published in 1969 (2d ed., 2 vols., 1974). A writer of books as well as articles, he published *El juicio de los parricidas: La nueva generación argentina y sus maestros* in 1956, a work that demonstrated Jorge Luis BORGES's importance and also identified themes that would dominate literary debate in Latin America for the next thirty years. Other book-length studies include works on Andrés Bello, Pablo Neruda, José Enrique Rodó, and Horacio Quiroga. After an acrimonious separation from *Marcha,* Rodríguez Monegal left Uruguay for Paris, where in 1966 he founded *Mundo Nuevo,* a magazine credited with initiating the so-called boom that brought world attention to such writers as Borges, Julio Cortázar, Gabriel García Márquez, Carlos Fuentes, and Mario Vargas Llosa. Despite the magazine's extraordinary effectiveness, its Ford Foundation support led pro-Castro intellectuals to accuse Rodríguez Monegal of fronting for the U.S. Central Intelligence Agency. After a bitter exchange with his accusers, he resigned his position with *Mundo Nuevo,* thus hastening the demise of the magazine, and accepted an influential position at Yale University in 1968. In 1984 he finally returned to Uruguay, where he received a presidential award for his intellectual contributions. He died and is buried in New Haven, Connecticut.

— NICOLAS SHUMWAY

RODRÍGUEZ SANDOVAL, LUIS ARSENIO

Luis Arsenio Rodríguez Sandoval (*b.* 21 June 1898; *d.* 21 November 1977), Ecuadoran military officer and defender of Ecuador during the Peruvian invasion of 1941. Born into a prominent conservative highland family, Rodríguez was among the early graduates of Ecuador's military academy. In October 1924 he and other lieutenants formed a military league to reform the nation. On 9 July 1925 the officers overthrew the government of Gonzalo CÓRDOVA, thereby initiating a period of social change designed to modernize the nation. When the military installed the progressive dictator Isidro AYORA CUEVA to carry out reforms, Rodríguez was named aide-de-camp.

Disillusioned by politicization of the military and the failure of reform, Rodríguez thereafter became a supporter of the constitutional order. During the 1930s he opposed military intervention in national politics and supported the government. During those years, he devoted himself to the improvement of the armed forces, publishing several pamphlets on the future of the army and the need for professionalization. Rodríguez was one of the founders of the air corps and one of the highest-ranking army officers when Peru invaded Ecuador in July 1941. He voluntarily left command of the military zone of Guayaquil to defend the nation with small frontier garrisons while the regular army moved to the border. The government, however, failed to send forces, and the nation suffered a crushing defeat.

Abandoned in the jungle, Rodríguez became a "nonperson" until 1944, when a revolt overthrew the Ecuadoran government.

Abandoned in the jungle, Rodríguez became a "nonperson" until 1944, when a revolt overthrew the government. He was imprisoned for the national defeat, but was ultimately exonerated. Nevertheless, Rodríguez was blackballed for many years, finding it difficult to obtain employment. With the passage of time and the publication of the second edition of his book *La invasión peruana* (1955), public opinion changed. In particular the new military leaders came to admire his patriotism. His book was studied at the War College. In recognition of his earlier service, he was appointed to the High Court of Military Justice, where he served from 1963 to 1965. In 1965 the military government awarded him the Order of Abdón Calderón in recognition of his actions in 1941.

Rodríguez devoted his later years to helping organize the archives of the army and to historical research on the military. Of the many important works he published during his life, the most significant for him was his account of the 1941 conflict.

— JAIME E. RODRÍGUEZ O.

ROGATIS, PASCUAL DE

Pascual de Rogatis (*b.* 17 May 1880; *d.* 2 April 1980), Argentine composer. Born in Teora, Italy, Rogatis came to Argentina when he was very young. He began his musical studies at the National Conservatory in Buenos Aires, where he studied under Pietro Melani and Rafael Díaz Albertini (violin) and Alberto WILLIAMS (composition). During his studies he was awarded the gold medal in violin (1899), first prize in ensemble performance (1902), and the first award in composition (1906). He was a nationalist composer, attracted by the exotic and mythical stories of the indigenous peoples of America. His first works included piano pieces, songs, and orchestral compositions. Among them were the *Suite árabe* (1902) for strings, and three symphonic poems, *Marko y el hada* (1905), *Belkiss en la selva* (1906), and *Zupay* (1910). His opera *Anfión y Zeto,* a Greek tragedy, premiered at the Teatro Colón in Buenos Aires with the Gustavo Salvini Company and the celebrated baritone Titta Ruffo (1877–1953) in 1915. Two orchestral works, *Atipac* (1931) and *Estampas Argentinas* (1942), were awarded, respectively, the Municipal Prize and the National Award for Composition. In his seventies, he produced three works for piano: one in 1952; two in 1957.

Rogatis's best-known work is his opera *Huemac,* based on a Mexican legend; it premiered at the Teatro Colón in 1916 and was conducted by the composer. It was later performed in Rome at the Teatro Costanzi. *Huemac* was awarded the Municipal Prize of Buenos Aires in 1916. Another opera, *La Novia del hereje,* was performed in 1935 in Buenos Aires. Rogatis was professor of chamber music at the National Conservatory and a member of the Argentine Commission of Fine Arts. He died in Buenos Aires.

– SUSANA SALGADO

ROIG DE LEUCHSENRING, EMILIO

Emilio Roig de Leuchsenring (*b.* 23 August 1889; *d.* 8 August 1964), Cuban journalist and historian. Roig, a native of Havana, is best known as one of the founders and leaders of the Cuban revisionist school of historians, a group of writers and scholars, some of them Marxists, who distinguished themselves by their negative appraisal of U.S. influence on Cuban affairs. His work began to reflect this view as early as 1922. In 1933 he was appointed historian of the city of Havana, a position that he used to launch the journal *Cuadernos de historia habanera.* In 1940 he was instrumental in forming the Cuban Society of Historical and International Studies, and two years later he began to promote, with the help of the society, a series of National Historic Congresses, the thirteenth of which met in 1960. Among Roig's favorite theses were that the Cuban struggle for independence was not a series of wars but one continuous war that lasted thirty years, and that U.S. entry into the struggle in 1898 was not necessary for Cuban victory.

– JOSÉ M. HERNÁNDEZ

ROJAS, ISAAC

Isaac Rojas (*b.* 3 December 1906), Argentine naval officer. Born in Buenos Aires, Rojas was a staunch anti-Peronist and one of the organizers of the 1955 coup d'état that overthrew the government of Juan Domingo PERÓN. Rojas was won over to the coup plot after serving as defense counsel for Rear Admiral Aníbal Olivieri in a conspiracy trial. Rojas's threat that the navy would bombard oil storage facilities in Buenos Aires and the national oil refinery in La Plata contributed greatly to the success of the uprising against Perón. Made a full admiral of the navy in 1955, Rojas was prominent in Argentine public life from 1955 to 1958, when he served as the vice president in the governments of both Eduardo LONARDI and Pedro ARAMBURU and became renowned for the ferocity of his anti-Peronist sentiments. Rojas dealt harshly with the participants of the abortive June 1956 uprising of military officers sympathetic to Perón led by Major General Juan José Valle, and supported the execution of Valle and some twenty-six coconspirators.

– JAMES P. BRENNAN

ROJAS, MANUEL

Manuel Rojas (*b.* 8 January 1896; *d.* 11 March 1973), Chilean novelist. The most important storyteller and novelist of his generation, Rojas received the National Award of Literature in 1957. His early work pays tribute to Latin American regionalism, but from the beginning his narratives reveal an anarchist view of the world and demonstrate an awareness of the literary avant garde. The values and experience of laborers and outcasts are represented in Rojas's fiction in terms of pristine anarchism and emotive humanism that are difficult to find in the works of any of his contemporaries. *Lanchas en la bahía* (1932) is the story of a young man's initiation into adult life. Rojas's most important novel is *Hijo de ladrón* (1951), a masterwork of Latin American narrative. It is part of a tetralogy formed by *Mejor que el vino* (1958), *Sombras contra el muro* (1964), and *La oscura vida radiante* (1971), which traces four steps in the life of one man, exploring both personal and social struggles. Rojas also wrote *La ciudad de los Césares* (1936), based on a legend of a Spanish utopia in southern Chile, and *Punta de rieles* (1960), a counterpoint of two defeated men told in thoughts and speech. Among his short stories, closer to Horacio QUIROGA's than to Jorge Luis BORGES's, are the collections *Hombres del sur* (1926), *El delincuente* (1929), and *Travesía* (1934). Rojas also wrote poetry and numerous essays.

– CEDOMIL GOIC

ROJAS, PEDRO JOSÉ

Pedro José Rojas (*b.* 1818; *d.* 1874), Venezuelan politician and journalist. Rojas began his journalistic career as an editor for the weekly *El Manzanares* (1843–1845). He traveled to Caracas in 1846 and was chosen representative to Congress from Cumaná in 1848. He opposed President José Tadeo MONAGAS and left the country for the United States, where he connected with General José Antonio PÁEZ, whom he served as personal secretary. With the fall of Monagas in 1858, Rojas returned to Venezuela. After another period of exile, he returned during the days of the Federal War (1859–1863). Rojas promoted the dictatorship of General Páez and, together with Antonio GUZMÁN BLANCO, was one of the principal protagonists of the 1863 Treaty of Coche, which ended the Federal War. After yet another period of exile in the United States and Europe, he returned to Venezuela, where he was imprisoned in 1871 by Guzmán Blanco and later expelled from the country once again. He died in exile.

– INÉS QUINTERO

ROJAS, RICARDO

Ricardo Rojas (*b.* 16 September 1882; *d.* 29 July 1957), Argentine intellectual, historian, and educator. Born in the northern provincial city of Tucumán, Rojas came to Buenos Aires in 1899 to study law, as did many other provincial intellectuals of his generation. He never completed his studies at law school but began to devote himself exclusively to literature, publishing his first poems in 1903.

The patriarch of Argentine letters, Rojas cultivated all literary genres, with the grandeur and uniqueness of the Americas as a common thread. Yet it is as a humanist that he made his most lasting contribution to an understanding of Argentina at the deepest intellectual and cultural levels. The spirit of *argentinidad,* or awareness of a national identity within the wider context of the Americas as a civilization, dominated his thinking. In such works as *Blasón de plata* (Silver Blazon, 1912) and *Eurindia* (1924), Rojas proclaimed the essential greatness of Argentina and all Hispanic America as deriving from a symbiosis of European and indigenous cultures.

In 1912 Rojas became the first professor of Argentine literature at the University of Buenos Aires. Then, in 1922, he founded the Instituto de Literatura Argentina, and for twenty-five years was its inspiration and guiding force. He served as chancellor of the university from 1926 to 1930. Between 1917 and 1921, Rojas published his monumental *Historia de la literatura Argentina,* which is as much an exegesis of Argentine culture as a remarkable account of Argentine literature from colonial times to the modern period.

Rojas also played an important role in Argentine politics. It was through his efforts to form a new political party that the Liga Patriótica was formed in 1919. In 1930, with the fall of President Hipólito YRIGOYEN, Rojas supported the Unión Cívica Radical (Popular Radical Party) in its struggle against the power of the oligarchy. As a consequence of his outspoken opposition to the Juan PERÓN regime (1946–1955), Rojas suffered persecution and the loss of his university position.

– MYRON I. LICHTBLAU

ROJAS PAÚL, JUAN PABLO

Juan Pablo Rojas Paúl (*b.* 1829; *d.* 1905), Liberal president of Venezuela (1888–1890). Following a failed coup attempt by General Joaquín CRESPO, Rojas Paúl was selected as the presidential candidate by former dictator Antonio GUZMÁN BLANCO. Rojas Paúl took office heading a divided Liberal Party and facing serious civil strife in Venezuela. Nevertheless, his progressive attitudes and generosity soon won over even former enemies, including Crespo. Rojas Paúl reinstated freedom of the press, resurrected the idea of responsible government, and created the National Academy of History in 1888. His efforts to achieve a modicum of liberal democracy were rewarded in 1890 when he successfully and peacefully transferred power to Raimundo ANDUEZA PALACIO. He then served as a senator but was exiled by Andueza in 1891.

– KAREN RACINE

ROJAS PINILLA, GUSTAVO

Gustavo Rojas Pinilla (*b.* 12 March 1900; *d.* 17 January 1975), president of Colombia (1953–1957). Born in Tunja, Boyacá, Rojas attended the Colombian military academy in Bogotá and later studied engineering in the United States. After a stint as a road engineer he rejoined the army in 1932, rising to the rank of lieutenant general by 1949. Despite his Conservative sympathies,

---

Rojas's pledge to end the disastrous Violencia and establish political peace was initially well received by both parties.

---

on 13 June 1953 Rojas deposed Laureano GÓMEZ in a bloodless coup; his pledge to end the disastrous Violencia and establish political peace was initially well received by both parties. However, by 1956 renewed violence, an economic downturn, and bipartisan opposition to Rojas's own political ambitions had weakened his position, and on 10 May 1957 he was forced out by the military. In the 1960s Rojas was a constant thorn in the side of the bipartisan National Front, with his hazily populist and nationalist National Popular Alliance (ANAPO). In April 1970 he narrowly lost the presidential election against the Front candidate, Misael PASTRANA BORRERO. Rojas's ANAPO has continued, under the leadership of his daughter María Eugenia Rojas, but its importance is minimal.

— RICHARD J. STOLLER

ROJAS URTUGUREN, JOSÉ ANTONIO DE

José Antonio de Rojas Urtuguren (*b.* 1732; *d.* 1817), a precursor of Chilean independence. Educated at the University of San Felipe in Santiago, Rojas spent the 1770s in Spain, where he eagerly imbibed the ideas of the Enlightenment. His involvement in a desultory plot against Spanish rule in Chile in 1780 was never proved, but he remained suspect, and in 1810 was arrested and deported to Peru. Too old to play much of a part in the independence governments of 1810–1814, Rojas, nonetheless, was one of those imprisoned on the Juan Fernández Islands in the South Pacific during the restored colonial regime (1814–1817), which hastened his death.

— SIMON COLLIER

ROJO, MARÍA

María Rojo (*b.* 15 August 1946), Mexican actress. As a child, Rojo debuted in the film *Besos prohibidos*. She later studied acting at the University of Veracruz. Her first starring role was in the film *El apando*. Among her other important feature performances are: *Naufragio, Bajo la metralla, María de mi corazón, Confesiones, Las Poquianchis, Lo que importa es vivir, Rojo amanecer, La tarea,* and *Danzón.* Her acting style lends itself to a wide range of roles. One of the finest dramatic actresses in Mexico, Rojo has received more film awards than any actress in the history of the Mexican cinema.

— DAVID MACIEL

ROJO, VICENTE

Vicente Rojo (*b.* 1932), Spanish painter working in Mexico. Born in Barcelona, Rojo moved in 1949 to Mexico, where he has lived ever since. He is one of the most important exponents of geometric art in Mexico. He studied painting at the Escuela de Pintura y Escultura (La Esmeralda) in Mexico City, and privately with

Arturo Souto. He also worked as an assistant for the exiled Spanish artist Miguel Prieto. Rojo's works are in series. From 1966 to 1981 he created the series *Señales* (Signs), *Negaciones* (Negations), *Recuerdos* (Memories), and *Mexico bajo la lluvia* (Mexico Under the Rain). From the late 1980s dates the series *Códices* (Codices), in which Rojo incorporates symbols used in pre-Columbian writing. *Escenas* (Scenes), a series that draws on pre-Columbian imagery, dates from 1992–1993. Rojo's work has been featured in numerous group and solo exhibitions in Mexico, the United States, and Europe.

— ILONA KATZEW

ROKHA, PABLO DE

Pablo de Rokha (*b.* 17 October 1894; *d.* 10 September 1968), Chilean poet. Born Carlos Díaz Loyola but taking the pen name Pablo de Rokha, this writer is seen by some critics as one of the main figures of the Chilean avantgarde. He had a tempestuous personality that put him in frequent conflict with Vicente HUIDOBRO and Pablo NERUDA (*Neruda y yo* [1955]). Rokha's poetic voice was one of ideological and socialist bias; his inordinate epic tone encompassed both the revolutionary facts and figures of world history and the daily life of the local peasant. The hypertrophic "I" of his poetry takes on Nietzschean dimensions in its Dionysian exultation and sensual enjoyment. His poetic diction has its distinct features in verbal violence, lexical creativity, prosaism, and materialist images; Rokha's verse is full of vital gestures and Pantagruelian rural meals. A Marxist, Rokha never accepted the party discipline or espoused any official party line. His huge number of works include *Los quemidos* (1922), *Escritura de Raimondo Contreras* (1929), *Jesucristo* (1933), *Gran temperatura* (1937), *Morfología del espanto* (1942), *Canto al ejército rojo* (1944), *Fuego negro* (1953), and *Canto de fuego a China Popular* (1963). Although addressed to the popular reader, his works, due to their baroque poetic diction and mixture of cosmopolitanism and popular culture, were largely inaccessible to the masses. In 1965 he received the National Literary Award. Two years later, he shot himself.

— CEDOMIL GOIC

ROKHA, WINÉTT DE

Winétt de Rokha (*b.* 7 July 1894; *d.* 7 August 1951), Chilean poet. Born Luisa Anabalón Sanderson, de Rokha published her first poetic works under the pseudonym Juana Inés de la Cruz, a seventeenth-century Mexican poet. After her marriage to the poet Pablo de

ROKHA, she adopted the literary name Winétt de Rokha. Her poetic works include, in a romantic first stage, *Lo que me dijo el silencio* (1915) and *Horas de sol* (1915). In a second stage, she appropriated the Spanish-American avant garde's poetic diction, as shown in *Formas del sueño* (1927). A new stage began with *Cantoral* (1936), followed by *Oniromancia* (1945), *El valle pierde su atmósfera* (1949), which was included in Pablo de Rokha's *Arenga sobre el arte,* and *Suma y destino* (1951). *Antología* (1953) is a selection of her poetry published posthumously. The main characteristic of de Rokha's poetry in its final form is the adoption of a social and revolutionary hyperbolic tone, in permanent dialogue with Pablo de Rokha.

— CEDOMIL GOIC

ROLDÁN, AMADEO

Amadeo Roldán (*b.* 12 July 1900; *d.* 2 March 1939), Cuban composer, conductor, and violinist. Born in Paris of Cuban parents, Roldán settled in Havana in 1921 after studying with A. F. Bordas and Conrado del Campo in Spain. He continued his studies with Pedro Sanjuan in Cuba and established the Society of Chamber Music in 1921. First appointed concertmaster of the Havana Philharmonic Orchestra in 1924, he rose to conductor in 1932. He served as director and taught at the Havana Conservatory from 1934 until his death.

Among the first to bring elements of African Cuban folklore to the concert hall, his works are filled with African Cuban mythology and his collaboration with Alejo CARPENTIER brought forth the first African Cuban ballet on the island. Associated with the group of intellectuals who invigorated Cuban artistic life in the 1920s and 1930s, he was a guiding spirit for the younger generation of Cuban composers.

— JACQUELYN BRIGGS KENT

ROLDÁN, FRANCISCO

Francisco Roldán (*d.* 1502), a native of Donjimeno, Spain; appointed *alcalde mayor* (chief justice) in Hispaniola by Christopher COLUMBUS. Poverty and the harsh, inept government of Bartholomew and Diego Columbus led to discontent among the Spanish settlers. In 1497 they rallied to the sympathetic Roldán, who rebelled with some ninety men, a number perhaps greater than those reliably loyal to the Columbus brothers. Withdrawing to the interior of the island, the rebels pursued lives of idleness, rape, and pillage. When Christopher Columbus returned to Hispaniola in 1498, having been absent for two years, he found the colony in chaos; after weighing the gravity of the situation, he

acceded to the rebels' demands in 1499. In addition to amnesty, each was to have an allotment of Indian labor, which, with some modifications, became known as a *repartimiento* and, eventually, as *encomienda*. Roldán, once again loyal to Columbus, assisted in subduing other revolts. He was lost at sea in 1502.

— WILLIAM L. SHERMAN

ROLDÓS AGUILERA, JAIME

Jaime Roldós Aguilera (*b.* 5 November 1940; *d.* 24 May 1981), president of Ecuador (1979–1981). While a student at the University of Guayaquil, Roldós became a political activist. After completing a law degree, he entered private practice, taught at the University of Guayaquil, and was active in the Concentration of Popular Forces (CFP) led by Asaad BUCARAM. Elected deputy from Guayas in 1968 and 1970, he became a member of the Comisión Legislativa Permanente and headed a second commission appointed by the military government in 1978 to prepare for the return to civilian rule. That same year the CFP selected him to run for the presidency after the party's leader, Asaad Bucaram, was disqualified as a candidate by the military.

Roldós represented a new generation of political leaders who were committed to significant social and economic reform. The reformist program was doomed, however, when the CFP split into factions supporting Roldós and his former mentor Asaad Bucaram. Bucaram used his position as president of the Chamber of Representatives to block presidential initiatives to implement structural change, to maintain fiscal restraint, and to adopt a development program that subordinated regional demands to national objectives. Public support for the government eroded as a result of the legislative impasse. Even the renewed threat of a border conflict with Peru in January 1981 failed to provide the administration sustained public support. Growing economic problems resulting from declines in the world-market price for petroleum, budget deficits, and rising international interest rates forced the government to adopt austerity measures that alienated large segments of the public. The administration was facing growing challenges to its authority when Jaime Roldós died in the crash of a military plane while touring the contested border with Peru.

— LINDA ALEXANDER RODRÍGUEZ

ROLÓN, RAIMUNDO

Raimundo Rolón (*b.* 1903), a prominent Paraguayan soldier and politician. During the Chaco War (1932–1935), he served as General José Félix ESTIGARRIBIA's chief of operations. Following the February Revolution (17 February 1936) he retired from the army. With the overthrow of Rafael FRANCO by a conservative military faction on 13 August 1937, Rolón was reinstated as the chief of staff. During 1949 he served as the ambassador to Brazil and as the minister of defense. Between 30 January and 27 February 1949 he was the provisional president of Paraguay. Rolón wrote numerous books on the Chaco War, the most important being *La guerra del Chaco, campaña de 1934,* 2 vols. (1962–1963).

– ROBERT SCHEINA

ROMÁN DE NÚÑEZ, SOLEDAD

Soledad Román de Núñez (*b.* 6 October 1835; *d.* 19 October 1924), second wife of Colombian president Rafael NÚÑEZ. Román became a controversial figure in strongly Catholic Colombia because she married Núñez in a civil ceremony in 1877 while his first wife was still alive. She is also believed to have influenced his political opinions.

Catholics could not regard Núñez's marriage to Román as valid, and some women boycotted her when she traveled to Bogotá as first lady in 1884.

A native of Cartagena like Núñez, Román was the daughter of a prominent pharmacist. She became acquainted with Núñez as a girl and renewed the friendship upon his return to Colombia in 1874 after a long absence abroad. Because Núñez was divorced from Dolores Gallego, whom he had wed in a Catholic ceremony in 1851, Catholics could not regard his marriage to Román as valid, and some women boycotted her when she traveled to Bogotá as first lady in 1884. After Gallego's death in 1889, she and Núñez were remarried in a religious ceremony. A staunch Conservative, Román is credited with encouraging Núñez, a Liberal, to move toward an accommodation with the Conservative Party.

– HELEN DELPAR

ROMAY Y VALDÉS CHACÓN, TOMÁS

Tomás Romay y Valdés Chacón (*b.* 21 December 1764; *d.* 30 March 1849), Cuban physician and scientist. Romay, a native of Havana, achieved prominence in Cuba between 1790 and 1830, a period of transition during which Cubans discovered their own national identity. A writer, orator, and poet, he was one of the founders in 1790 of *Papel Periódico,* the first Cuban newspaper. He was also a professor of philosophy at the University of Havana and a mentor of students and patron of the arts. Probably Romay's greatest achievement was to introduce in Cuba the vaccine against smallpox and to initiate early investigations into the causes of yellow fever. He was also a founding member of the Sociedad Patriótica, one of the key institutions in the development of colonial Cuba. In a very real sense he was the initiator of the scientific movement in Cuba. Romay died in Havana.

– JOSÉ M. HERNÁNDEZ

ROMERO, CARLOS HUMBERTO

Carlos Humberto Romero (*b.* 1924), president of El Salvador (1977–1979). Educated at the National Military Academy, Romero rose through the ranks to become minister of defense during the presidency of Arturo Armando MOLINA (1972–1977). He resigned that post to become the military-backed PCN (Partido de Conciliación Nacional) candidate in 1977.

Aligned with the agro-exporting wing of the PCN, Romero ended the mild reformism of the Julio A. RIVERA, Fidel SÁNCHEZ HERNÁNDEZ and Arturo Armando Molina administrations (1960–1977), thereby galvanizing the guerrilla and urban popular organizations into mass action. Responding to appeals by business and agro-export groups to curb the agitation, Romero's repressive policies alienated both the Roman Catholic Church (producing the so-called war of the Romeros—a reference to the struggle between President Romero and Oscar Arnulfo ROMERO, archbishop of El Salvador, who was assassinated by a right-wing death squad in 1980) and the Jimmy Carter administration (1977–1981). With the tacit approval of the United States, he was overthrown by a group of progressive officers on 15 October 1979 and went into exile.

– ROLAND H. EBEL

ROMERO, EMILIO

Emilio Romero (*b.* 16 February 1899), Peruvian geographer, economist, lawyer, and writer. Born in Puno, Romero was the son of Eladio and Honorata Padilla Romero. He studied at schools in Arequipa and Lima, receiving his doctorate at the National University of Arequipa in 1932. Between 1920 and 1933, Romero taught school at the secondary and university levels and, beginning in the 1930s, began a government career while continuing to hold academic positions. After holding a ministerial post as chief of the Bureau of Colonization and Mountain Lands, he was elected deputy to the Constituent Congress in 1932–1933. In 1939, he became director of commerce and finance and continued his political career as a senator from Puno from 1945 to 1948.

In the 1950s, Romero wrote essays on the Indian practice of chewing coca leaves, claiming that the Indian use of the hallucinogen coca was similar to, but no more damaging than, the North American practice of chewing gum or smoking cigarettes. In a 1955 book, *Perú por los senderos de América,* he also praised the Incas for their religion and way of life, insisting that their idea of love and marriage surpassed that of the Spaniards who had conquered them.

– JACK RAY THOMAS

ROMERO, FRANCISCO

Francisco Romero (*b.* 19 June 1891; *d.* 7 October 1962), Argentine philosopher who is recognized as one of the most important philosophers in Latin America and the Spanish-speaking world in general. Romero was born in Seville, Spain, and attended a military school in Argentina. He became a disciple of Alejandro KORN, and was professor of philosophy at the Universities of Buenos Aires and La Plata. The German philosophy that flourished during the first three decades of the twentieth century, represented in the writings of Wilhelm Dilthey, Edmund Husserl, Nicolai Hartmann, and Max Scheler, had a great influence on the maturation of Romero's philosophical thought. Within this framework, he made original contributions in his chief work, *Theory of Man* (1964), a philosophical anthropology based on the concept of "intentionality" as a characteristic distinguishing the human psyche from that of animals. *Theory of Man* is also the outline of a metaphysics founded on the idea of the spirit as an absolute transcendence.

Part of Romero's work concerned itself with the diffusion—as well as the interpretation—of philosophy from the Renaissance to the twentieth century. Unlike most other Latin American philosophers, he was interested in the history and structure of philosophy, as can be seen in *Sobre la historia de la filosofía* (1943) and *La estructura de la historia de la filosofía y otros ensayos* (1967). Through his writings and personal activities, he became one of the great inspirations to the development of professional philosophy in Latin American and to the study of Latin American thought.

– JUAN CARLOS TORCHIA ESTRADA

ROMERO, JOSÉ LUIS

José Luis Romero (*b.* 24 March 1909; *d.* 2 March 1977), Argentine historian. Romero was born in Buenos Aires and earned a doctorate in history at the University of La Plata. His work developed in the areas of social history and the history of culture and ideas. As a medievalist, he studied the formation and development of the bourgeoisie in *La revolución burguesa en el mundo feudal* (1967) and *Crisis y orden en el mundo feudoburgués* (1980). He also wrote works interpreting Latin American and Argentine history, the most important of which is *Latinoamérica: Las ciudades y las ideas* (1976). In this book, he tries to understand the role urban societies played in the Latin American historical process from colonial days to the twentieth century. He pursued the relationships between ideologies and historical reality in Latin America in *El pensamiento político de la derecha latinoamericana* (1970) and *Latinoamérica: Situaciones e ideologías* (1967).

Romero's classic work on Argentina is *A History of Argentine Political Thought* (1963), an accurate and widely read synthesis. He investigated ideas in relation to societal changes in *El desarrollo de las ideas en la sociedad argentina del siglo XX* (1965).

Possessed of a great talent for historical interpretation, Romero also considered the history of historiography itself in *De Herodoto a Pobilio* (1952) and *Maquiavelo historiador,* 3d ed. (1986). In *La historia y la vida* (1945), he expressed his views on the theory of history.

– JUAN CARLOS TORCHIA ESTRADA

ROMERO, JOSÉ RUBÉN

José Rubén Romero (*b.* 25 September 1890; *d.* 4 July 1952), Mexican writer. Although he wrote poetry and served as a diplomat, Romero's reputation rests upon his achievements as a novelist of the Mexican Revolution. Born in Cotija, Michoacán, Romero took a nostalgic, humorous, and often satirical view of provincial life during the early decades of the twentieth century. He is most famous for a picaresque novel, *La vida inútil de Pito Pérez* (The Futile Life of Pito Pérez, 1938). In addition, two autobiographical novels, *Apuntes de un lugareño* (Notes of a Villager, 1932) and *Desbandada* (Disbandment, 1934), recount Romero's experience of the Mexican Revolution as it arrived in small provincial towns, and serve as vehicles for his trademark irony as a social critic. He was named to the Mexican Academy of Language in 1941. Romero died in Mexico City.

– DANNY J. ANDERSON

ROMERO, MATÍAS

Matías Romero (*b.* 24 February 1837; *d.* 30 December 1898), Mexican politician and diplomat. Romero was born in Oaxaca, in southwestern Mexico, the birthplace of fellow Mexican liberal leaders Benito Pablo JUÁREZ, Porfirio DÍAZ, and Ignacio Mariscal. Romero filled important posts in the Mexican government for thirty-eight years of his life, beginning with the Foreign Relations Ministry in 1857. Romero's service included a total of twenty-six years as secretary of the legation, chargé, or minister to the United States (1859–1868, 1882–1892, 1893–1898), a total of about seven years as secretary of the treasury (1868–1872, 1877–1879, 1892–1893), and two years in the Mexican Senate (1875–1877).

During the American Civil War, Romero labored tirelessly in establishing personal contacts with U.S. political, military, and business leaders.

Educated as a lawyer, Romero joined the Liberal government under President Benito JUÁREZ during La Reforma (1857–1861). As a protégé of Juárez, he served some time as an unpaid employee in the Ministry of Foreign Relations before being given a salaried post. When the outbreak of the American Civil War thrust considerable responsibility upon the twenty-four-year-old Romero, he already had acquired two years of experience in the United States as secretary of the legation and chargé d'affaires. During the American Civil War and early Reconstruction, he labored tirelessly in establishing personal contacts with U.S. political, military, and business leaders such as Montgomery Blair, Benjamin Wade, Henry Winter Davis, Ulysses S. Grant, and John Schofield. Romero returned to Mexico briefly in late 1867, but was picked to negotiate the U.S.–Mexican Claims Agreement of 1868 in order to facilitate Mexico's credit rating with potential American investors. He married Lucretia Allen on 16 July 1868 just before becoming, at thirty-one, Juárez's secretary of the treasury.

Juárez's decision to seek reelection in 1872 displeased Romero, who resigned to pursue coffee culture in southern Mexico. This activity lasted only three years, in part because of the hostility of the Guatemalan president, Justo Rufino BARRIOS, and in part because Romero was elected to the Mexican Senate in 1875. After serving two years as senator, he became Porfirio Díaz's secretary of the treasury.

In 1879 failing health compelled Romero to resign. Battling recurring stomach problems, which had plagued him since his youth, he traveled to the United States to consult medical specialists. In 1880 and 1881, while recuperating, he was involved in several railroad schemes with former U.S. President Ulysses S. Grant, Albert K. Owen, Hiram Barney, and others. Then, from 1882 until his death, Romero served as minister to the United States, except for a short period from mid-1892 until early 1893, when he returned to Mexico for his third period as secretary of the treasury. He died in Washington on 30 December 1898, after an attack of appendicitis.

– THOMAS SCHOONOVER

ROMERO, OSCAR ARNULFO

Oscar Arnulfo Romero (*b.* 15 August 1917; *d.* 24 March 1980), archbishop of El Salvador (1977–1980). Born in Ciudad Barrios and originally apprenticed as a carpenter, Romero's early religious inclinations won him over and in 1931 he enrolled in San Miguel seminary. In 1937 he progressed to the National Seminary, then proceeded to Rome to study at the Gregorian University. He was ordained in 1942 and began a doctorate in ascetic theology, but World War II curtailed his studies. He returned to El Salvador and served his home parish until he was elevated to monsignor in 1967. Shortly thereafter, Romero was appointed to the National Bishops' Conference and quickly earned additional responsibilities, including auxiliary bishop (1970), editor of the archdiocesan newspaper *Orientación* (1971), bishop of Santiago de María (1974), and membership on the Pontifical Commission for Latin America (1975). Even at this late date, Romero still clung to a moderate, traditional interpretation of Catholic doctrines. He warned against the dangers of a politicized priesthood and instead advocated the higher ideals of brotherhood, faith, and charity. Although he frequently quoted the teachings of the Second Vatican Council, he refrained from mentioning those of the more radical conference of Catholic bishops at Medellín in 1968.

To the surprise of many, Romero was chosen over the equally qualified Arturo Rivera y Damas as archbishop of El Salvador in February 1977. The shy, retiring new archbishop faced growing tensions between church and state, and within the church itself. Shortly after his installation, Romero's close friend Father Rutilio Grande was murdered on his way to visit parishioners. When the government failed to investigate and instead stepped up its attacks on the church by expelling several priests, Archbishop Romero withdrew his support for the government and refused to attend the presidential inauguration of Carlos Humberto ROMERO (no relation) in 1977. Despite the rising tide of violence, Romero still tried to distance the church from the new liberation theology and denied the priests permission to participate in political organizations. As the situation deteriorated, Romero's position became untenable and the moderate archbishop metamorphosed into an impassioned crusader against the violation of human rights in El Salvador. He used his sermons to preach the equality and dignity of all peoples and set up a commission to monitor and document the abuses of power by governmental authorities.

For Romero's efforts the British Parliament nominated him for the Nobel Peace Prize. In February 1980 Romero angered the Vatican by speaking out against U.S. military aid to El Salvador, which he claimed would lead to further human rights abuses. On 24 March he was assassinated while saying evening mass. His death removed a powerful voice for peace in El Salvador and contributed to the bitterness of the struggle. Archbishop Romero remains a powerful symbol of the new direction of the Catholic church in Latin America.

— KAREN RACINE

ROMERO, SÍLVIO

Sílvio Romero (*b.* 21 April 1851; *d.* 18 June 1914), Brazilian critic and historian of literature. Silvio Vasconcelos da Silveira Ramos Romero was born in Lagarto, Sergipe, and began his intellectual life in Recife, Pernambuco, where he was the leader, with Tobias BARRETO, of the Escola de Recife, a group advocating a change from romanticism to realism. Romero criticized Antônio Federico de CASTRO ALVES, one of the most important Brazilian romantic poets; he debated Joaquin Maria MACHADO DE ASSIS, the great novelist of realism; and he opposed José Veríssimo, who studied Brazilian literature from the artistic point of view. Romero followed the sociological method in his literary criticism and was one of the most significant members of the Brazilian naturalistic movement, searching in social life for the source of literary creation.

Mourners in cathedral plaza during the funeral of Archbishop Oscar Romero, San Salvador, 30 March 1980. (Photo by Harry Mattison)

Romero's books include *Cantos do fim do século* (1878), poetry; *Introdução à história da literatura brasileira* (1882) and *Estudos de literatura contemporânea* (1885), criticism; *Contos populares do Brasil* (1883) and *Estudos sobre a poesia popular no Brasil* (1888), folklore; and *Doutrina contra doutrina: O evolucionismo e o positivismo no Brasil* (1894) and *As oligarquias e sua classificação* (1908), sociological meditation. His most important book as a critic is *História da literatura brasileira* (1888), the first systematization of Brazilian literature. He died in Rio de Janeiro, where he had lived since 1876.

— ELIANA MARIA REA GOLDSCHMIDT

ROMERO BARCELÓ, CARLOS

Carlos Romero Barceló (*b.* 4 September 1932), governor of Puerto Rico (1977–1980; 1981–1984). Romero Barceló was educated at Phillips Exeter Academy and at Yale University. He earned a law degree from the University of Puerto Rico in 1956. Romero Barceló helped found the nonpartisan coalition *Ciudadanos Pro Estada 51* (Citizens for State 51), and in 1968 he was elected mayor of San Juan. First elected governor in 1976, he was an advocate of statehood for Puerto Rico. He believed that Puerto Rico as a commonwealth could not compete for federal funds, equal citizenship, and security from the United States government.

On 25 July 1978, Commonwealth Day, two dissidents were assassinated by police, and five years later a cover-up of the incident was exposed. Romero Barceló lost the 1984 elections in the aftermath of the investigations.

— CHRISTOPHER T. BOWEN

ROMERO DE TERREROS, PEDRO

Pedro Romero de Terreros (*b.* 28 June 1710; *d.* 27 November 1781), mining entrepreneur. One of the outstanding miners of eighteenth-century New Spain, Pedro Terreros was born in western Andalucia (modern Huelva) in Spain and before 1733 migrated to the Mexican city of Querétaro, where he became a manager of the business of a maternal uncle. In 1735, upon the death of his uncle, Terreros expanded this already substantial wholesale-retail business. By 1741 he had become the financier (*aviador*) and then the partner in a silver mine near Pachuca. When his partner, José Alejandro Bustamante, died in 1750, Terreros inherited the mines, and within fifteen years, became the principal entrepreneur in the region. When miners were unable to repay loans from Terreros, he became the owner of their mines. Beyond his abundant financial resources

and managerial skills, he displayed considerable talent in the construction of refining haciendas and the planning of drainage works that permitted the exploitation of rich veins of ore. His success as an entrepreneur was soured by troubled relations with workers in the mines and refining haciendas.

In 1775 Terreros founded in Mexico City the first Monte de Piedad—a credit institution that loaned money for pawned articles. As early as the 1750s, donations of dowries for nuns and the financing of the missions of San Saba in Texas (1756–1758) and many other Franciscan projects established his reputation as a generous supporter of ecclesiastical projects. His contributions to the government included money to construct warships and loans to establish a lottery. He also purchased the former JESUIT haciendas that had belonged to the novitiate of Tepozotlán and the Colegio de San Pedro y San Pablo, which made him one of the leading landowners in New Spain. He died in San Miguel Regla.

— EDITH COUTURIER

ROMERO ROSA, RAMÓN

Ramón Romero Rosa (R. de Romeral; *b.* 30 August 1863; *d.* 25 April 1907), Puerto Rican labor organizer, essayist, and dramatist. Romero Rosa was a leading spokesman of the movement to create a national labor union in the years between 1896 and 1907, which led eventually to the formation and political centrality of Santiago IGLESIAS PANTIN's Federación Libre de Trabajadores (Free Federation of Labor) from 1899 to 1930. A typesetter by trade, he served as president of the San Juan Union of Typographers and cofounded the pioneering weekly *Ensayo Obrero* (1897). A charter member of the Federación Regional de los Trabajadores (Regional Federation of Workers, 1897–1899) and a firm supporter of SANTIAGO IGLESIAS, he was twice (1904 and 1906) elected to the Puerto Rican House of Delegates. Affirming "no homeland but the workplace and no religion but labor," as the masthead of *Ensayo Obrero* expressed it, Romero was equally certain that "the triumph of the cause of labor will be the triumph of the *homeland* in Puerto Rico." (Angel G. Quintero Rivera, *Patricios y plebeyos,* p. 258).

Occasionally writing under the pseudonym R. de Romeral, his incisive commentaries on the class structure and exploitative character of Puerto Rican society embodied a novel, anarchist-influenced, and socialist-oriented analytical break with a patrician-dominated discourse as well as the most broadly inclusive expression of the period's emerging working-class consciousness. In addition to writing articles for such periodicals as *El Porvenir Social* (1898–1899), *La Miseria* (1901), and *El Pan del Pobre* (1901), his published works include *La cuestión social en Puerto Rico* (1904), *Musarañas*

"No homeland but the workplace

and no religion but labor."

(1904), *Catecismo Socialista* (1905), *Entre Broma y Vera* (1906), and the allegorical play *La emancipación del obrero* (1903).

— ROBERTO MÁRQUEZ

ROMERO RUBIO, MANUEL

Manuel Romero Rubio (*b.* 1828; *d.* 3 October 1895), Mexican Liberal and public figure. A native of Mexico City, Romero Rubio attended the Conciliar Seminary before completing his legal studies at the Colegio de San Gregorio. He began his career as a practicing lawyer before becoming an active supporter of Benito JUÁREZ during the Revolution of Ayutla (1855). He served as a constitutional deputy from Puebla in the 1856–1857 convention and became governor of Mexico City in 1857. During the French invasion, he was captured and exiled to France (1863). In 1876, he supported Sebastián LERDO DE TEJADA for the presidency and subsequently became his secretary of foreign relations. Although exiled after Porfirio DÍAZ's rebellion, he returned to establish an opposition newspaper and became a senator from the state of Tabasco from 1880 to 1895. He eventually collaborated with his former political opponent by serving in the key post of secretary of government (1884–1895). During these years he became financially and politically prominent, establishing personal and economic ties with other leading figures. His daughter, Carmen, married Díaz in 1881.

— RODERIC AI CAMP

RONDEAU, JOSÉ

José Rondeau (*b.* 4 March 1773; *d.* 18 November 1844), military and political leader of the independence period in Argentina and Uruguay. Born in Buenos Aires, Rondeau was educated in Montevideo, where he spent his early years. His military career included appointments as commander in chief of the Argentine patriot army that fought against Upper Peru (1814), inspector general of Argentine troops (1820), and minister of the navy and of war in Uruguay in 1839. He also held numerous political offices, such as supreme director (1819–1820) in Buenos Aires and captain-general and governor (1828–1830) in Montevideo during the period of Uruguay's transition to independent statehood. Rondeau was thus instrumental in Platine independence and early nation building. Viewed as a native and patriot on both banks of the Río de la Plata, his remains were eventually entombed in the National Pantheon in the Uruguayan capital after negotiations with the Argentines. Rondeau was eulogized as a perfect gentleman by General José María PAZ and as a just and honest man by Bartolomé MITRE.

— FIDEL IGLESIAS

RONDON, CÂNDIDO MARIANO DA SILVA

Cândido Mariano da Silva Rondon (*b.* 5 May 1865; *d.* 19 January 1958), Brazilian general and first director of the Indian Protection Service (SPI). At the beginning of the twentieth century, when the Brazilian government was considering large-scale army intervention to halt episodes of violence between settlers and native peoples along frontiers, Rondon was a principal spokesman for adoption of a humanistic attitude toward indigenous peoples. Influenced by the positivist writings of Auguste Comte, Rondon believed that indigenous peoples were neither savage nor barbarian. He advanced the theory that their societies represented an earlier stage in the development of human civilization and, therefore, deserved governmental protection against exploitation and destruction caused by expansion. Together with a number of other young army officers who shared his philosophy, Rondon successfully convinced the government to establish a special agency to protect Brazil's native peoples and in 1910 the government founded the Indian Protection Service. Rondon maintained that Indian peoples would eventually become members of the national society.

Since 1890 Rondon had headed a governmental commission charged with conducting military and scientific expeditions in Brazil's unexplored interior. The Rondon Commission laid over 1,362 miles of telegraph lines, mapped more than 20,000 square miles of land, and discovered twelve new rivers in the Amazon and Mato Grosso regions. During these expeditions Rondon contacted the Bororo, Nambikuara, and Paresí Indians and developed the strategy for peacefully contacting "hostile" groups that was employed by the SPI and later by National Indian Foundation (FUNAI) pacification teams. In 1913–1914 Rondon also accompanied Theodore Roosevelt on his geographical expedition throughout the Brazilian interior.

— LAURA GRAHAM

ROSA DE LIMA

Rosa de Lima (Rosa de Santa María; *b.* 20 April 1586; *d.* 24 August 1617), first American saint. Rosa was born in Lima, Peru, one of twelve children of Puerto Rican Gaspar de Flores and his Peruvian wife, María de Oliva. The future saint was christened Isabel de Flores. In 1597 she took first communion from Archbishop Alfonso de Toribio de Mogrovejo (1538–1606). She spent her early years helping her mother care for the family; at first her parents discouraged her from entering church service because she was needed in the household. But she demonstrated profound religious convictions, fasting and exercising corporal penitence. At the age of twenty (10 August 1606) she entered the third order of the Dominicans. Her model may have been Saint Catherine of Siena.

Rosa frequently entered the state of ecstasy, reaching a high degree of mystical union with God, and produced small miracles related to nature.

Rosa frequently entered the state of ecstasy, reaching a high degree of mystical union with God, and produced small miracles related to nature, similar to those of Saint Francis. In her devotion she frequently enacted the passion of Christ, having made a crown of thorns and a cross. She helped cure the ill, setting up a small hospital next to her house, and she provided a Christian education for neighborhood children. Rosa spent the last three years of her life, most of the time ill, in the home of Gonzalo de la Maza and María de Uzategui.

Rose was much admired, and civil and ecclesiastical authorities were present at her death. She was beatified on 12 March 1668, named patroness of Lima and Peru in 1669, and patroness of America and the Philippines the following year. On 12 April 1671 she became the first American saint. Her remains lie next to those of Saint Martín de PORRES in a chapel of the Dominican church in Lima. Her nearby house and rose-filled garden are a popular site for the many pilgrims who visit Lima. First captured on canvas just after her death by Angelino Medoro, she is a favorite subject for religious painters.

— NOBLE DAVID COOK

ROSA, JOÃO GUIMARÃES

João Guimarães Rosa (*b.* 27 June 1908; *d.* 19 November 1967), Brazilian fiction writer. A native of the rural town of Cordisburgo in the central Brazilian state of Minas Gerais, Guimarães Rosa enjoyed a multifaceted career as medical doctor, international diplomat, and premier Brazilian writer of prose fiction in the twentieth century. His published works include *Sagarana* (1946),

Corpo de baile (1956), *Grande sertão: veredas* (1956), *Primeiras estórias* (1962), *Tutaméia* (1967), *Estas estórias* (1969), and *Ave, palavra!* (1970). He was elected to the Brazilian Academy of Letters in 1961.

Guimarães Rosa appeared on the Brazilian literary scene as a kind of independent successor to modernist Mário de ANDRADE in the scope, spirit, and innovative form of his fictional works. The short-story collection *Sagarana,* his first published volume, challenged the Brazilian tradition of regionalist fiction based on quaint pictorial re-creation of rural life and a crude theoretical framework, established during the 1930s and still predominant in the mid-1940s. Rosa flouted these stereotypes while remaining faithful to the most ancient and enduring qualities of regionalism. Early commentators likened him to Herman Melville because of his simultaneous treatment of inner/outer realities, and he was compared to James Joyce in his linguistic innovations, which include creation of neologisms, lexical borrowing from classical and modern languages, syntactic inversion and the introduction of a "telegraphic" syntax, and the preference for an orally based storytelling style reminiscent of medieval archetypes and conveying simultaneously a popular and an epic tone.

Sagarana's nine stories, all set in the backlands of central Brazil, depict a fairly primitive level of existence: protagonists include a small donkey, a prodigal husband, two old friends dying of malaria, a witch doctor and his "educated" neighbor, a town bully, a pair of vengeful men in a love triangle, a timid rival who emerges victorious with the help of a spell, talking oxen, and a bully-turned-saint. The author's empathy for his characters is evident, as is his use of what may be called "redemptive analogy" in the Judeo-Christian tradition. *Corpo de baile,* a series of seven novelettes of varying length, exemplifies Rosa's skill in creating the perception and worldview of childhood in terms adult readers can appreciate without condescension. His psychological insight is revealed in the text's treatment of fantasies, fears, forebodings, tenderness, suspense, and erotic tensions in an atmosphere bordering at times on the surrealistic.

Grande sertão: veredas, a 600-page novel in first-person monologue, is considered the author's masterpiece in its epic proportions and theme: the working out of a metaphysical *chanson de geste* in the backlands of Brazil through a plot involving warring bandits, a disguised female warrior, a possible pact with the Devil, a democratic "kangaroo court," herculean trials and travels, and the triumph of Good over Evil. The twenty-one short stories of *Primeiras estórias* are exceeded in brevity only by the forty minuscule narratives of *Tutaméia.* The first of these works structures most of its episodes around "epiphanies" in the lives of children

João Guimarães Rosa. (Iconographia)

and other marginal or powerless members of society, while the second is a series of "anecdotes of abstraction" interspersed with four longer essays of a theoretical, though fanciful, nature.

Guimarães Rosa's two posthumous works echo the style of *Sagarana* but incorporate a more cosmopolitan cast of characters and concerns. The oral quality diminishes over the author's 35-year literary career, although each of his works may be read from a tripartite perspective in terms of form/sound, semantic value, and metaphysical meaning. This multifaceted layering of his fiction explains at once its continuing challenge and attraction for readers and listeners.

— MARY L. DANIEL

ROSA, NOEL

Noel Rosa (Noel de Medeiros Rosa; *b.* 11 December 1910; *d.* 4 May 1937), Brazilian songwriter. Rosa was born in Rio de Janeiro; complications at birth left him disfigured and partly paralyzed. Raised in the neighborhood of Vila Isabel in São Paulo, Rosa began to play the mandolin by ear at the age of thirteen and later took up the guitar. Together with friends from his high school, Colégio Batista, Rosa formed the band Flor do Tempo. Invited to record in 1929, the group renamed themselves the Bando de Tangarás. That same year, Rosa composed his first pieces, "Minha viola" (My Viola) and "Festa no céu" (Party in the Sky), both of which he recorded in 1930.

Rosa's first hit came in 1930 with the samba "Com qué roupa?" (With What Clothes?), featuring humorous observations of life in Rio de Janeiro that would characterize his future work. He was a prolific songwriter; in 1933, his best year, he recorded more than thirty pieces. Beyond the successes of Carnival such as "Até amanhã" (Until Tomorrow) and "Fita amarela" (Yellow Ribbon), other major works of that year included the sambas "Onde está a honestidade?" (Where Is the Honesty?), "O orvalho vem caindo" (The Dew Is Falling), and "Três apitos" (Three Whistles).

Rosa's bohemian life-style and his frequenting of bars and nightclubs had a deleterious effect on his health. After years of intense composing, performing, and traveling, Rosa died in 1937 at the age of twenty-six. Since 1950, when his music was rediscovered through the recordings of singer Araci de Almeida, Rosa is always included in any retrospective collections of Brazilian popular music.

— LISA MARIĆ

ROSA, RAMÓN

Ramón Rosa (*b.* 1848; *d.* 1893), Honduran statesman. Born in Tegucigalpa, Rosa studied law at the University of San Carlos in Guatemala and began his law career in 1869. He took part in the military victory over the Conservatives in 1871.

Rosa is known for his participation in Honduran political and intellectual life during the late nineteenth century. He was a member of the Council of Ministers, exercising executive authority from 10 June 1880 to 30 July 1880. More importantly, Rosa reflected the positivist intellectual currents of his time. This intellectual trend manifested itself throughout Latin America as political leaders sought to develop their societies through a combination of education, training, and agro-export economies. Rosa wrote on the effects of positivism in Honduras, emphasizing the need for material progress and scientific education. He and Honduran president Marco Aurelio SOTO were protégés of Guatemalan intellectuals at the University of San Carlos and of the Guatemalan dictator Justo Rufino BARRIOS. Together, these Liberal "positivists" transformed Honduran society from one characterized by isolation and Liberal-Conservative rivalry to one more open to international commerce and, eventually, the banana trade.

— JEFFREY D. SAMUELS

ROSÁINS, JUAN NEPOMUCENO

Juan Nepomuceno Rosáins (*b.* 13 February 1782, *d.* 27 September 1830), Mexican insurgent leader. Born in

San Juan de los Llanos, Rosáins was a lawyer who joined the insurgency in 1812 and eventually became the auditor general of the army. After Mariano MATAMOROS (1770–1814) was captured, José María MORELOS Y PAVÓN (1765–1815) named Rosáins his second in command (1814). From the outset, Rosáins had conflicts with other insurgents and acted arbitrarily. Defeated and imprisoned by his companions in the Barranca de Jamapa, he escaped and won amnesty from the colonial regime. In 1815, he presented the viceroy, Félix María CALLEJA DEL REY, with a report on the insurgency with recommendations for defeating it. In 1821 he supported the Plan of Iguala promulgated by Agustín de ITURBIDE (1783–1824), and in 1824 he was elected senator from Puebla. He later conspired against President Anastasio BUSTAMANTE (1780–1853) and was shot as a traitor.

— VIRGINIA GUEDEA

ROSAS, JUAN MANUEL DE

Juan Manuel de Rosas (*b.* 30 March 1793; *d.* 14 March 1877), Argentine dictator.

ROAD TO POWER. Rosas was born in Buenos Aires to a creole family of landowners and officeholders, a characteristic beginning for an Argentine caudillo. He himself was a landowner and military commander. He acquired his education mainly on his parents' *estancia* before striking out on his own account, first in the meat-salting industry, then in the accumulation of land in the south of the province of Buenos Aires, where he developed his principal cattle *estancias* and those of his cousins, the Anchorenas. Rosas was thus at the leading edge of Argentina's new frontier of settlement and helped to promote the transition of Buenos Aires from viceregal capital to export center. It was on the *estancia* that he first practiced his principles of government. There, on an anarchic population of peons, gauchos, Indians, and vagrants Rosas imposed respect for authority, social order, and private property; by a mixture of discipline and example he exacted subordination and created a work force and a following. In 1820 he turned his peons into patriots and led a cavalry force to rescue Buenos Aires from the caudillos of the interior, a further victory over anarchy and another tribute to the military power of the southern caudillo.

The next objective was to raise his political profile. From his *estancia* Rosas observed the course of government in Buenos Aires with growing concern. In February 1826 Bernardino RIVADAVIA was appointed president of the United Provinces of the Río de la Plata, and came to power with a unitarist constitution and a modernizing program. The entire package was rejected by Rosas and his associates, who represented a more primitive economy—cattle production for export of hides and salt meat—and objected to sharing their provincial resources with a greater Argentina. In the latter half of 1826, at the head of a network of friends, relations, and clients, Rosas allied himself to the federalist party. Rivadavia bowed to the combined force of his opponents and resigned, and in August 1827 the veteran federalist, Manuel DORREGO, was elected governor. Federalist government in itself was not the political solution sought by Rosas. To secure the hegemony of the *estancia,* the dominance of the export economy, security on the frontier and in the countryside, it was necessary to establish direct control of policy: the time had come for those who possessed economic power, the *estancieros,* to displace the professional politicians of independence and take possession of government through their representative Rosas.

As militia commander, frontiersman, and rancher, Rosas had unique qualifications to assume leadership. He was already a caudillo in his own right with access to land, men, and resources, and the ability to mobilize them for armed action. The opportunity came in 1828, when a unitarist coup engineered by General Juan LAVALLE overthrew and assassinated Dorrego, leaving a gap in the federalist leadership which was instantly filled by Rosas. He had the support of militiamen, *estancieros,* and friendly Indians. He also had a power base among the popular forces of the countryside who looked to him as their *patrón* and protector. In the course of 1829 he waged a guerrilla war on his unitarist enemies and defeated the regular army of Lavalle; on 3 November he entered Buenos Aires at the head of a force which only he could control, and virtually dictated his own terms. On 6 December 1829 he was elected governor of Buenos Aires with absolute powers (*facultades extraordinarias*). From these beginnings he dominated Argentina for the next two decades and beyond.

CONSERVATIVE DICTATOR. Rosas divided society into those who commanded and those who obeyed. He abhorred democracy and liberalism, and the reason why he detested unitarists was not that they wanted a united Argentina but that they were liberals who believed in humanism and progress. The constitutional doctrines of the two parties did not interest him, and he was never a true federalist. He thought and ruled as a centralist, and he insisted on the supremacy of Buenos Aires. This was *rosismo,* and there was nothing quite like it anywhere else in Spanish America. Its power base was the *estancia,* a focus of economic resources and a system of social control.

The domination of the economy by the *estancia* was continued and completed under Rosas. He stood for a policy of territorial settlement and expansion, conquering land from the Indians, rewarding his followers with land, selling public land and eventually giving it away. The trend of his regime was toward greater concentration of property in the hands of a small elite. The *estancia* gave Rosas the sinews of war, the alliance of fellow *estancieros,* and the means of recruiting an army of peons, gauchos, and vagrants. In December 1829 he claimed that, unlike his predecessors, he had cultivated the common people, and had become a gaucho himself in order to control them. To identify with gaucho culture was not necessarily to represent the gauchos or to receive their spontaneous support. The core of Rosas's forces were his own peons and dependents, who were obliged to follow him in war as they worked for him in peace.

Rosas divided society into those who commanded

and those who obeyed.

Rural uprisings occurred in times of exceptional crisis, such as in 1829 and 1835, when Rosas deliberately raised popular forces in order to counter his unitarist enemies. The gaucho forces lasted only as long as Rosas needed them; once he controlled the bureaucracy, the police, the death squads, and the regular army, his rural followers had to return to their *estancias.* Finally, in many cases these informal troops were mobilized not directly by Rosas but by their own *patrón,* who was usually commander of the local militia; this meant that Rosas received his support not from free gaucho hordes but from other *estancieros* leading their peon conscripts.

Another popular sector, the artisans of Buenos Aires and the interior, also looked to Rosas for protection, in this case against the competition of foreign imports. In the Customs Law of December 1835 he introduced higher import duties, giving greater protection to more vulnerable products, and actually prohibiting the import of a large number of articles such as textiles, hardware, and, depending on the domestic price, wheat. The tariff was designed to relieve distress in the industrial and farming sectors without subverting the livestock export economy. In any event, national industries failed to respond, and within five years Rosas was forced to relax protection in the interests of consumers.

TERRORIST STATE. Rosas ruled from 1829 to 1832 with absolute power. After an interregnum during which anarchy once more raised its head, he returned to the governorship in March 1835 and ruled for the next seventeen years with total and unlimited power.

The House of Representatives remained a creature of the governor, whom it formally "elected." It consisted of forty-four deputies, half of whom were annually renewed by election. But only a small minority of the electorate participated, and it was the duty of the justices of the peace to deliver these votes to the regime. The Assembly, lacking legislative function and financial control, was largely an exercise in public relations for the benefit of foreign and domestic audiences.

Propaganda was an essential ingredient of *rosismo,* and conformity in dress, language, and behavior was imposed. The church rallied to the cause, supported the dictator, and extolled the federal system. But the ultimate sanction of the regime was force, controlled by Rosas and applied by the military and the police. The enemy within, conflict with other provinces and with foreign powers, and the obligation to support his allies in the interior caused Rosas to maintain a large defense budget, to recruit a large standing army, and to press the rural areas to increase their militias. One way or another, the people were forced to conform, at every level of society and in every aspect of life. There was a totalitarian character to the regime, untypical of contemporary Spanish America. The government of Rosas responded in some degree to conditions inherent in Argentine society. He offered an escape from anarchy and a promise of peace, on condition that he was granted total power.

To exercise his sovereignty, Rosas personally administered justice and kept the bureaucracy, the military, and the police under close control. Even so, there was resistance. Internally he faced an ideological opposition, partly from unitarists and partly from younger reformists; this came to a head in an abortive conspiracy in 1839 and continued to function throughout the regime from its base in Montevideo. A second focus of opposition formed among the landowners of the south; they were particularly hit by the French blockade which cut off their export outlets and for which they blamed Rosas. But their rebellion of 1839 did not synchronize with the political conspiracy, and they, too, were crushed. Finally, there was external opposition, partly from other provinces and partly from foreign powers. If the external opposition could link up with internal dissidents, Rosas would be in real danger.

Rosas therefore held in reserve another weapon, terror. He used it as an instrument of government, to eliminate enemies and control his own supporters. The special agent of terrorism was the Sociedad Popular Restauradora (Popular Society of the Restorer), a political club and a paramilitary organization. The Society had an armed wing, commonly called the *mazorca,* whose members were the terrorists on the streets. The incidence of terrorism varied according to the pressures on the regime, rising to a peak in 1839–1842, when French intervention, internal rebellion, and unitarist invasion threatened to destroy the Rosas state and produced violent countermeasures. The use of state terrorism was an essential and unique feature of the Rosas regime.

DECLINE AND FALL. The system gave Rosas hegemony in Buenos Aires for over twenty years. But he could not apply the same strategy in the whole of Argentina. He did not govern "Argentina." The thirteen provinces governed themselves independently, though they were grouped in one general Confederation of the United Provinces of the Río de la Plata. Even without a constitution and formal union, however, the provinces were forced to delegate certain common matters to the government of Buenos Aires, partly to secure a broad base for economic and foreign policy and partly to acquire a national dimension for the regime. Rosas tamed the interior in the years between 1831 and 1841 by a mixture of diplomacy and coercion, establishing a series of client caudillos who recognized his informal sovereignty.

But Rosas could not impose these methods on the Littoral provinces, where economic grievances coincided with powerful foreign interests. These provinces wanted trading rights for the river ports of the Paraná and the Uruguay; they wanted a share in customs revenue; and they wanted local autonomy. With outside assistance they could become the Achilles' heel of Rosas. Brazil had its own account to settle with the dictator. Determined to prevent satellites of Buenos Aires from becoming entrenched in Uruguay and the Littoral, and anxious to secure free navigation of the river complex from Matto Grosso to the sea, Brazil was ready to move. An ally was at hand in Entre Ríos, where Justo José de URQUIZA, a powerful *estanciero* and caudillo, placed himself at the head of provincial interests, liberal exiles, and Uruguayan patriots, in an alliance backed by enough Brazilian money and naval force to tip the balance against Rosas. The Triple Alliance of Entre Ríos, Brazil, and Montevideo went into action in May 1851.

In Buenos Aires itself enthusiasm for the regime waned. The economy was no longer dominated exclusively by Rosas's allies, the cattle *estancieros,* but now also contained sheep farms, whose owners were less militarized and less committed to the regime. Rosas had taxed and conscripted more than the *estancieros* could bear. And by his terrorist methods he had depoliticized Buenos Aires, destroying in the process whatever existed of "popular" support for the government. When the army of the Triple Alliance invaded, his troops fled and the people in the town and country did not rise in his

support. On 3 February 1852, at Monte Caseros, he was defeated. He rode alone from the field of battle, took refuge in the house of the British minister, boarded a British vessel, and sailed for England and exile. He died in Southampton in 1877, in his eighty-fourth year.

– JOHN LYNCH

ROSAS, JUVENTINO

Juventino Rosas (*b.* 23 or 25 January 1868; *d.* 13 July 1894), Mexican (Otomi Indian) violinist and composer. At age six Rosas's father brought him and two brothers from their native Santa Cruz de Galeana to Mexico City to perform as a family quartet. He later joined the orchestra of San Sebastian church and toured with the orchestra of legendary opera singer Angela PERALTA. He died in Cuba while on tour with a traveling zarzuela company. Best known for his set of waltzes entitled *Sobre las olas,* he also composed numerous other waltzes, mazurkas, and schottisches, many of them published.

– ROBERT L. PARKER

ROSAS DE TERRERO, MANUELA

Manuela Rosas de Terrero (*b.* 24 May 1817; *d.* 17 September 1898), daughter of Argentine dictator Juan Manuel de ROSAS and Encarnación Ezcurra de Rosas.

> *"For all who appealed to General Rosas in an extra-judicial character, his daughter Doña Manuelita was the universal intercessor."*

After her mother's death in 1838, "Manuelita" served as her father's hostess and confidante. Poorly educated and socially awkward, she was ridiculed as provincial by the liberal intellectuals of Buenos Aires, but as English merchant William MacCann wrote, "For all who appealed to General Rosas in an extra-judicial character, his daughter Doña Manuelita was the universal intercessor." According to John Lynch "she was an intermediary between client and patron, a channel of grace and favor." In 1852 she accompanied her father into exile in England, where she married longtime suitor Máximo Terrero on 23 October 1852. Her father considered her marriage a betrayal and attempted to sever relations with Manuela; for Manuela the marriage was what she described as "an emancipation."

– FRANCESCA MILLER

ROSCIO, JUAN GERMÁN

Juan Germán Roscio (*b.* 27 May 1763; *d.* 10 March 1821), Venezuelan political activist and ideologue in the movement for independence. Roscio earned doctorates in canonical and civil law from the University of Caracas, where he was later a professor, and held the post of provisional treasurer in the Audiencia of Caracas. He played a role in the declaration of a *cabildo abierto* and in the ouster of the Spanish governor on 19 April 1810 in Caracas and was a member of the Junta Suprema de Caracas, secretary of foreign affairs, and representative to the Constituent Congress of 1811. Roscio helped draw up the Declaration of Independence and the Constitution of 1811, distinguishing himself as one of the foremost publicists regarding the American right to independence.

With the fall of the First Republic in 1812, Roscio was sent to the military prison in Ceuta, Africa. When released, he traveled to Jamaica in 1816 and later to Philadelphia, where he published his principal work, *El triunfo de la libertad sobre el despotismo* (1817). In 1818 he returned to Venezuela, became editor of *El Correo del Orinoco,* presided at the Congress of Angostura in 1819, and was appointed vice president of the department of Venezuela. Later that year, when Gran Colombia was formed (17 December 1819), he was appointed vice president of that new republic.

– INÉS QUINTERO

ROSENBLUETH, ARTURO STEARNS

Arturo Stearns Rosenblueth (*b.* 2 October 1900; *d.* 19 September 1970), Mexican educator and physiologist. Born in Chihuahua, Chihuahua, Rosenblueth studied in Monterrey and Mexico City, where he graduated from the National School of Medicine in 1921. He did advanced work in Berlin and at the University of Paris before returning to the National University to teach in 1927. He obtained a Guggenheim fellowship to study under Walter Cannon at Harvard (1930–1932) and stayed to teach physiology until 1944, earning in the process an international reputation in neurophysiology. His work was published by the Massachusetts Institute of Technology, and on his return to Mexico, he mentored a select group of prominent future scientists. He was chief of the department of physiology at the National Polytechnic Institute and directed the physiology laboratory under Ignacio Chávez at the National Institute of Cardiology (1944–1960). He became a member of the National College in 1947, and received Mexico's National Prize in Sciences in 1966.

– RODERIC AI CAMP

ROSS SANTA MARÍA, GUSTAVO

Gustavo Ross Santa María (*b.* June 1879; *d.* 5 April 1961), Chilean financier, businessman, and government minister. Born in Valparaíso, Ross, who supported the efforts to depose President Carlos IBÁÑEZ DEL CAMPO, served as minister of finance during Arturo ALESSANDRI PALMA's second term of office. Through a variety of sometimes controversial methods, he successfully renegotiated Chile's foreign debt. He also engineered Chile's economic recovery during the Great Depression by stimulating local industries, asserting state control over certain utilities as well as the nitrate industry, and restricting the profits of foreign businesses, particularly the American-owned copper mines. Singularly uncharismatic and identified with the nation's most conservative elements, Ross sought the presidency in 1938. Only the abortive Nazi putsch, which led to Ibáñez's support of Pedro AGUIRRE CERDA, prevented him from winning the Moneda.

– WILLIAM F. SATER

ROSSELL Y ARELLANO, MARIANO

Mariano Rossell y Arellano (*b.* 18 July 1894; *d.* 10 December 1964), archbishop of Guatemala (1939–1964). A native Guatemalan, Rossell y Arellano became a priest in 1918. He served as the private secretary of Archbishop Luis Javier Muñoz y Capurón and held the posts of secretary and chancellor in the metropolitan curia. In 1935 he became vicar-general under archbishop Luis Durou y Sure, upon whose death in 1939, Rossell became archbishop. The arrival of foreign missionaries and Rossell's active promotion of the lay apostolate helped to relieve a long-standing clerical shortage in Guatemala.

During the administrations of Juan José ARÉVALO and Jacobo ARBENZ, the archbishop and lay Catholic leaders promoted social-justice teachings and criticized the government for its failure to stem the growth of communism. Their anticommunist crusade played a role in the downfall of Arbenz in 1954. Under the conservative leadership of president Carlos CASTILLO ARMAS, Rossell worked for the reversal of nineteenth-century liberal anticlerical laws, the repeal of which was achieved in the constitutions of 1956 and 1965.

– HUBERT J. MILLER

ROUMAIN, JACQUES

Jacques Roumain (Jean-Baptiste; *b.* 4 June 1907; *d.* 18 August 1944), Haitian poet, novelist, essayist, ethnographer, political leader. In the early and mid-1920s Roumain studied in Switzerland and Spain. The broadly cosmopolitan experience and revisionist outlook he brought home from overseas, the conventional elite's political insolvency, and a national crisis of political leadership in the context of the U.S. occupation all combined in Roumain's rejection of the values and traditional solutions of the mulatto aristocracy into which he was born. Upon returning home he helped found and edit *La Revue Indigène* (1927) and *La Trouée* (1927), and was chief editor of *Le Petit Impartial: Journal de la Masse* (1928). He quickly emerged as an important voice of the indigenous cultural movement and nationalist populism for which these journals spoke during the height of the U.S. occupation (1915–1934) of Haiti. Scion of the mulatto aristocracy, Roumain renounced his class origins and, in June 1934, became founder of the Haitian Communist Party. His *L'Analysis schématique, 1932–1934,* its inaugural document, and "Le Grief de l'homme noir" (1939) anticipated more recent critiques of neocolonial racism and the political dangers of *noiriste* (black) cultural nationalism articulated by, among others, René DEPESTRE, Frantz Fanon, and Walter Rodney. His political activism resulted in arrests for conspiracy and a period of exile in Europe.

Scion of the mulatto aristocracy, Roumain renounced his class origins and, in June 1934, became founder of the Haitian Communist Party.

In October 1941, Roumain returned to Haiti and joined Jean PRICE-MARS and other anthropologists in creating a national Bureau d'Ethnologie. As its first director, he authored several highly technical ethnological studies. His signature collection of poetry, *Bois d'ébène* (1939), and the much-acclaimed posthumous novel *Gouverneurs de la rosée* (1944) epitomize the synthesis of negritude, Marxist internationalism, lyrical realism, and the figurative evocation of human solidarity, voodoo ritual, and popular belief and expression characteristic of Roumain's most accomplished verse and fiction. His lesser known works include the short stories of *La Proie et l'ombre* (1930) and *Les Fantoches* (1931), and the novels *La Montagne ensorcelée* (1931) and *Le Champ de Potier* (unpublished).

Roumain's cultivation of the peasant novel and proletarian fiction, suggesting their unexplored thematic and formal possibilities, proved a stimulus and precursor to the "marvelous realism" of later Haitian novelists such as Jacques Stéphen ALEXIS and Pierre Clitandre. A premature death, while on a visit home from his post

as President Élie LESCOT's (1883–1974) consul to Mexico, deprived Haiti of arguably the most important writer of his generation and its most prominent and influential socialist intellectual.

– ROBERTO MÁRQUEZ

ROY, EUGÈNE

Eugène Roy (*d.* 27 October 1939), president of Haiti (15 May–18 November 1930). In 1918, President Philippe Sudre Dartiguenave (1915–1922) appointed Roy to several government positions. Because of the high esteem in which many held Roy, who was by profession an exchange broker and a member of the elite, he was selected in April 1930 as provisional president. He was then elected by the council of state as the neutral, interim president who then arranged and presided over the election of the legislative chambers, which then elected the new president. This arrangement was designed to carry out the recommendations of U.S. president Herbert Hoover's Forbes Commission, which had investigated the unpopular U.S. occupation (1915–1934), which was forced upon the Louis Borno government (1922–1930) and its opposition. The opposition's landslide victory in the legislature resulted in the election in November 1930 of Sténio VINCENT as president (1930–1941).

– LARMAN C. WILSON

RUBÍ, MARQUÉS DE

Marqués de Rubí (Cayetano María Pignatelli Rubí Corbera y San Climent), Spanish inspector (*visitador*). Rubí arrived in New Spain in November 1764 as part of the Juan de Villalba military mission charged with reorganizing New Spain's defenses. Rubí's assignment was to inspect New Spain's northern presidio system. He left Mexico City in March 1766 with a small entourage that included the expedition's diarist and cartographer, Nicolás de Lafora and draftsman José de Urrutia. Over the next twenty-three months the expedition traveled 7,500 miles from Louisiana to California and visited twenty-three presidio companies. Rubí's report revealed the lamentable condition of the presidio system. His proposals included a realignment of the presidio defenses to reflect New Spain's actual territory rather than its imagined domain. Rubí suggested the creation of a line of fifteen presidios across the frontier with only Santa Fe and San Antonio beyond the line. He also suggested that the danger of Comanche attacks in Texas could best be eliminated by creating alliances with them against the Apache tribes in the area. In response, the king issued the Reglamento of 1772, which incorporated most of Rubí's recommendations.

— AARON PAINE MAHR

RUBIÃO, MURILO

Murilo Rubião (*b.* 1 July 1916; *d.* 16 September 1991), Brazilian author. Born in Carmo, Minas Gerais, Rubião earned a degree in law and in 1939 became an editor at the newspaper *Folha de Minas.* One year later, with the publication of his short story "Elvira e outros mistérios" (Elvira and Other Mysteries), he initiated his literary career, which was to be interrupted several times by his many other activities. He became a cabinet officer for Juscelino KUBITSCHEK at the time the future president of Brazil was governor of Minas Gerais. In 1947 Rubião published his first book of short stories, *O exmágico* (The Ex-Magician); after six years a second book appeared, *A estrela vermelha* (The Red Star). Subsequent publications followed at extended intervals. Among the reasons given by the author for the sparsity of his creative output was his own dissatisfaction with his work; he apparently destroyed many pieces before they were sent to print.

In 1956 Rubião was nominated cultural attaché for the Brazilian embassy in Madrid, where he served for four years. Returning to Brazil, he resumed his duties with the state government, and in 1966 became editor in chief of the literary supplement to the newspaper *Minas Gerais.* Rubião published a total of six books during his lifetime. The most prominent was *O pirotécnico Zacarias* (Zacarias, the Fireworks Maker, 1974). Rubião's work contains elements of the surreal and the fantastic. His fictional construct leans to a great extent upon dreams and hallucinations; his characters are most often presented as victims of insanity. Through portrayals of extreme isolation, his work conveys a critical sense of life's absurdities.

— REGINA IGEL

RUEDA, MANUEL

Manuel Rueda (*b.* 27 August 1921), Dominican musician, playwright, folklorist, and poet. Born in Montecristi, Rueda has received his country's National Book Award four times, and in 1994 he won the Fundación Corripio's National Prize in Literature for a life's work, the highest literary distinction in the Dominican Republic. Associated in the 1940s and 1950s with the Poesía Sorprendida movement, Rueda also spent 14 years studying music in Chile, where he began publishing his work and befriended Vicente HUIDOBRO, Chilean poet and theorist. From his first book, *Las noches*

(1949), Rueda has demonstrated a commitment to enhancing the possibilities of his craft through formal explorations. In February 1974, he presented a lecture, "Claves para una poesía plural," whereby he launched an aesthetic creed called *pluralismo,* which sought to liberate the poetic text by turning it into an interactive, open artifact for both the poet and the reader. His text *Con el tambor de las islas* (1975) exemplifies the aesthetics of *pluralismo,* which, despite the uproar it provoked initially, did not produce notable followers. His mature poetic work appears in *Por los mares de la dama: Poesía 1970–1975* (1976), *Las edades del viento: Poesía inédita 1947–1979* (1979), and *Congregación del cuerpo único: Poesía 1980–1989* (1989). Rueda has also received numerous honors for his musical accomplishments, including the directorship of his country's National Conservatory of Music.

— SILVIO TORRES-SAILLANT

RUELAS, JULIO

Julio Ruelas (*b.* 21 June 1870; *d.* 16 September 1907), Mexican artist. Born in Zacatecas, Ruelas is one of the precursors of modernism in Mexico and the most important representative of symbolism in that country. In 1885 he enrolled at the National School of Fine Arts in Mexico City, where he received an academic training. In 1892 he traveled to Germany and studied at the Academy of Arts in Karlsruhe, where he became interested in the works of Arnold Boeklin. After his return to Mexico in 1895, Ruelas published his works in the *Revista moderna,* founded by the poet Jesús E. Valenzuela; this publication was extremely influential in disseminating the aesthetic of Latin American symbolists. In 1904 Ruelas went to Paris to perfect his etching technique. He also traveled to Belgium, where he may have seen the works of Félicien Rops. Although Ruelas created a number of paintings, he is basically known as an engraver and draftsman. He died in Paris, having produced a small but highly inventive body of work.

— ILONA KATZEW

RUIZ, ANTONIO

Antonio Ruiz (*b.* 1897; *d.* 9 October 1964), Mexican painter, muralist, theater and movie set designer, art teacher, and arts administrator. Ruiz was born in Texcoco and studied at the National School of Fine Arts in Mexico City. In 1926 he went to Hollywood to study set design, and he assisted in painting four murals for Pacific House, in San Francisco. Returning to Mexico in 1929, in 1932 he founded the first workshop on technical maquettes at the School of Engineering and

Architecture. In 1938 he became professor of set design and perspective in the National School of the Plastic Arts. From 1942 to 1954 he designed sets for Mexico City theaters, a film company, and some ballets. He died in Mexico City.

Ruiz is known for his very small, carefully composed, and meticulously painted pictures. Each is full of details that add to the meaning of the subjects portrayed. His use of perspective in some of his pictures to create illusions of great depth demonstrates his knowledge of architecture and stage design. As a painter of the Mexican School, he depicted the people of Mexico at work, at leisure, window shopping, performing, courting, and commemorating national holidays. In some cases, the Mexicans are presented as part of a complex world in which the modern mingles with the past. Ruiz also satirized, in a humorous way, the failings of those who cannot overcome their limitations, for example, the nouveau riche who acquire worldly possessions but not good taste, an aspiring opera singer without talent, and an orator without an audience or a message to deliver.

– JACINTO QUIRARTE

RUIZ, HENRY

Henry Ruiz (*b*. January 1940), Nicaraguan leader and member of the Sandinista National Directorate. Ruiz was born into a poor family in Jinotepe. As a child, he sold tortillas on the street to augment his parents' income. He joined the Nicaraguan Socialist Party as a teenager in the 1950s and went to the Soviet Union as a member of a Socialist Party exchange program. He studied mathematics and physics at Patrice Lumumba University in Moscow, where he also learned the tenets of Marx and Lenin and came to believe that guerrilla warfare was the only viable means of political change in Latin America. This led to philosophical conflicts with his Soviet colleagues. Back in Nicaragua, Ruiz joined the Sandinistas after their debacle at Pancasán in 1967. He was one of the few pure Marxist-Leninists in the revolutionary movement. When the Sandinistas debated their future in Costa Rica in 1968, Ruiz supported the strategy of a prolonged popular war waged by volunteers.

In 1969, just as the movement was broadening its membership, the Nicaraguan government deported Ruiz for his political activities. He returned to Nicaragua in 1971 and became high commander of guerrilla forces in rural areas, using the code name Modesto. (He was so named for his understated demeanor toward the combatants.) Ruiz was one of the principal advocates of rural-based struggle and spent several years hiding in the northern mountains. In December 1974, he participated in a raid on the Christmas party of a wealthy cotton exporter that gained the release of several Sandinistas and fetched $5 million in ransom. Throughout the late 1970s, Ruiz advanced the theoretical principles of Mao Zedong and Vo Nguyen Giap relating to the importance of peasant revolt. However, he encouraged peasants to join the urban insurrection and left the mountains in late 1978 as the war mounted in the cities. He was part of the unified Sandinista leadership that orchestrated the fall of Somoza in July 1979.

> *Throughout the late 1970s, Ruiz advanced the theoretical principles of Mao Zedong and Vo Nguyen Giap relating to the importance of peasant revolt.*

After the victory, Ruiz became minister of planning and developed several schemes for a mixed economy. In 1985, President Daniel ORTEGA abolished the Ministry of Planning after Ruiz voluntarily resigned from the post. Economic policy was subsequently concentrated in the office of the president. Ruiz became minister of external cooperation and managed the Department of International Relations for the Sandinistas, traveling to Eastern Europe and North Africa on diplomatic missions for them.

After the electoral defeat of the revolutionary government in February 1990, Ruiz continued to influence Sandinista political relations. He was a signer of the Protocol of Transition that finalized the transfer of power to the government of Violeta BARRIOS DE CHAMORRO. At the first Sandinista party congress in July 1991, Ruiz was retained on the National Directorate and elected treasurer.

– MARK EVERINGHAM

RUIZ, TOMÁS

Tomás Ruiz (*b*. 10 January 1777; *d*. ca. 1820), Central American priest and patriot. An Indian born in Chinandega, Nicaragua, Tomás Ruiz received a doctoral degree in canon law from the University of San Carlos in Guatemala in 1804. He was the only Indian in Central America to receive this degree. Ruiz was a founder of the University of León in Nicaragua. He taught there and served as vice-rector of the seminary where he himself had studied.

Tomás Ruiz was active in modernizing the curriculum of the University of León; Ruiz stressed mathematics, which he taught. He became involved in disputes and rivalries, and was denied the position of *canongía* (a professorship of holy law) in León in 1807 and then at Comayagua, Honduras, a year later. Racial prejudice and nepotism seem to have been the reasons. His frustration at having suffered discrimination as an Indian probably led to his involvement in the conspiracy at the Belén monastery in Guatemala in December 1813, which anticipated an armed revolt for independence from Spain.

The Belén Conspiracy was quashed; Padre Ruiz was arrested and spent a number of years in confinement. He remained a part of the reformist faction as independence loomed. His main biographer, the Nicaraguan Jorge Eduardo Arellano, argues that Ruiz should be regarded as his country's primary *prócer* (founding father), rather than the conservative Miguel Larreynaga, who signed the independence document. Padre Ruiz may have gone to Chiapas, Mexico, after his release in 1819, but there is no further record of his activities beyond that point.

– GARY G. KUHN

RUIZ CORTINES, ADOLFO

Adolfo Ruiz Cortines (*b.* 30 December 1890; *d.* 3 December 1973), president of Mexico (1952–1958). The administration of Ruiz Cortines is best known for the stabilizing effect it produced in the wake of the political and economic excesses of his predecessor, Miguel ALEMÁN. In terms of political leadership, Ruiz Cortines provided the last hurrah for the revolutionary generation, of which he himself was part. His selection as president, in fact, represented a generational reversal of political trends after Alemán. Socially, like Lázaro CÁRDENAS, he served as an apt personal model of presidential integrity, nationalizing the properties of some of Alemán's more corrupt collaborators. His administration offered no major political innovations but provided a transition for economic growth known as the "stabilizing period."

From a modest family, Ruiz Cortines left school at an early age in the port city of Veracruz to help support his widowed mother. After holding a series of unskilled jobs, he joined the Revolution in 1914 as a second captain during the U.S. invasion of Veracruz, during which he served as an assistant to two major revolutionary figures, generals Heriberto Jara and Jacinto B. Treviño. After holding a number of minor administrative posts in the military, he joined the office of social statistics in the 1920s.

His political career did not prosper until 1934, when he became secretary general of his home state of Veracruz, after which he served as the *oficial mayor* of the

Department of the Federal District (1934–1937). In 1937, he represented his home state in the Chamber of Deputies. During the late 1930s, he became friends with Miguel Alemán, who, based on Ruiz's reputation for integrity, appointed him treasurer of Manuel ÁVILA CAMACHO's presidential campaign in 1945. When Alemán, his political mentor, was appointed secretary of government in 1940, he brought Ruiz Cortines with him as his *oficial mayor* (1940–1944). In 1944, Ruiz Cortines left the executive branch to serve as governor of his home state of Veracruz. After serving four years, Alemán brought him back into the cabinet as his secretary of government, a position he served in until his candidacy as president was announced in 1952.

Alemán's designation of Ruiz Cortines as the government party's (PRI) candidate provoked the last major political opposition from a group of revolutionary generals disappointed in the direction of Mexico's leadership. Their removal from decision-making authority led to the formation of an intense opposition campaign under the leadership of General Miguel Henríquez Guzmán and the lowest reported vote tallies for a government presidential candidate in many years. After his election, Ruiz Cortines did succeed in mollifying those elements and in restoring unity to his party. After leaving office in 1958, he lived modestly in Veracruz, serving as a minor consultant to the government.

– RODERIC AI CAMP

RUIZ DE ALARCÓN Y MENDOZA, JUAN

Juan Ruiz de Alarcón y Mendoza (*b.* 1581?; *d.* 4 August 1639), one of the four great dramatists of the Spanish Golden Age, which reached its peak in the first half of the seventeenth century. Born in Mexico City to an illustrious family, Ruiz de Alarcón studied canon and civil law at the Royal Pontifical University of Mexico (1596–1600) and at the University of Salamanca in Spain (1600–1605). As a lawyer, Alarcón served as assistant to the *corregidor* (mayor) in Mexico City and advisor to the city council. He litigated at the royal court in Madrid and the Audiencia of Mexico, sought and obtained public offices, was financial adviser to those in debt, and in 1610 investigating judge in Veracruz, Mexico. He crossed the Atlantic three times, but he lived most of his life in Spain. He died in Madrid.

Alarcón wrote drama mainly for his own enjoyment, but it was lucrative. *Las paredes oyen* was first performed in 1617. Envious of the success of his plays, his rivals ridiculed him for his physical deformity as a hunchback with bow legs. The Spanish critic Mendéndez y Pelayo described Alarcón as the classic dramatist of a romantic theater. His plays are humorous, subdued, and clever and illustrate moral truths. *La verdad sospechosa* (1619) condemns lying, *Las paredes oyen* (1617) illustrates the evils of slander, and *Mudarse para mejorarse* (1622) deals with inconstancy in love. Alarcón wrote twenty-four plays published under *Parte primera de las comedias de don Juan Ruiz de Alarcón y Mendoza* (1628) and *Parte segunda de las comedias del Licenciado Don Juan Ruiz de Alarcón* (1634). *La prueba de las promesas* is considered by many to be Alarcón's masterpiece, along with *Las paredes oyen* and *La verdad sospechosa*. Alarcón's plays influenced Corneille, Molière, and Goldoni.

– GEORGETTE MAGASSY DORN

RUÍZ DE APODACA, JUAN, CONDE DE VENADITO

Juan Ruíz de Apodaca, Conde de Venadito, (*b.* 3 February 1754; *d.* 11 January 1835), viceroy of New Spain (1816–1821). Born in Cádiz, Apodaca joined the Spanish navy in 1767 and distinguished himself during wartime service against Great Britain and France. When France invaded Spain in 1808, Apodaca commanded a squadron of five warships. During the government of the Junta Central, he served in London as the Spanish plenipotentiary until 1811, then returned to Cádiz. In 1812, he was appointed captain-general of Cuba, a post he held with success until 1816.

Named viceroy of New Spain in 1816, Apodaca renewed and expanded amnesty programs, granting insurgent leaders and their followers resettlement and entry into royalist military forces. Although these policies restored the appearance of peace in some Mexican regions and the invasion of Javier MINA was crushed in 1817, Apodaca understood that victory against the dispersed guerrilla forces was not complete. By 1820, burdensome wartime taxation and the exhaustion of the Mexican royalists made the war impossible to sustain. The restoration of the Spanish constitution and Apodaca's appointment of Agustín de ITURBIDE to quell the guerrilla activities of Vicente GUERRERO and other insurgents destroyed the will of the royalists. Iturbide's rebellion and Plan of Iguala attracted many royalist army officers, and Mexicans invoked the constitution to suspend onerous taxes that supported the counterinsurgency system. During 1821, loyalist officers in Mexico City deposed the viceroy.

King Ferdinand VII granted Apodaca recognition, honors, and high offices. He was named viceroy of Navarre and later was appointed to the Council of State and as captain-general of the Spanish navy. Under Queen Isabel II, Apodaca served as the senior member of the Council of War.

– CHRISTON I. ARCHER

RUIZ DE MONTOYA, ANTONIO

Antonio Ruiz de Montoya (*b.* 11 November 1583; *d.* 11 April 1653), JESUIT missionary who worked among the GUARANÍ Indians. Ruiz was born in Lima, Peru, and entered the Society of Jesus in 1606. He completed his novitiate in Córdoba, Argentina, two years later. After ordination he was sent to the Guaraní missions along the Paraná River and was superior there from 1623 to 1637. He was deeply involved in opposing the Paulista raids on the missions. His writings include the *Conquista espiritual* (1639), which describes the natural features and peoples of the mission area; the *Tesoro de la lengua guaraní* (1639), a catechism and grammar of the Guaraní language; and *Arte y vocabulario de la lengua guaraní* (1640). Ruiz died in Lima and was buried in the reduction of Loreto.

– NICHOLAS P. CUSHNER

RUÍZ TAGLE PORTALES, FRANCISCO

Francisco Ruíz Tagle Portales (*d.* 23 March 1860), Chilean political figure. A prominent creole landowner, Ruíz Tagle played several public roles as a patriot during the Chilean *Patria Vieja* (the period, 1810–1814, before the Spanish reconquest). He nevertheless found no difficulty accepting municipal office under the restored Spanish colonial regime (1814–1817), although his collaborationism won him a 12,000-peso fine after the liberation of Chile. In the 1820s, easily adapting to the new order, he served as a member of the legislature and as a minister during the presidency of Francisco Antonio PINTO. When the Conservatives seized power in 1829–1830, Ruíz Tagle became interim president of Chile (18 February 1830). But his ruthless cousin Diego PORTALES, leader of the Conservative regime, found him insufficiently zealous and forced him to resign only a few weeks after he assumed office (31 March 1830). Ruíz Tagle's days as a trimmer were over: he played no further public role.

– SIMON COLLIER

RULFO, JUAN

Juan Rulfo (*b.* 16 May 1918; *d.* 7 January 1986), Mexican writer. Born in Sayula, Jalisco, Rulfo was a man of vast culture and a writer of extreme economy, despite the fact that his literary aptitude became apparent during childhood. His first works were published while he was still very young in a literary magazine in his native province, where he met Juan José ARREOLA. Arreola and Rulfo became friends as well as representatives of the two most influential styles—both opposing and complementary—in the 1950s and 1960s in Mexico. In 1934, Rulfo moved to Mexico City, where he lived until his death, although in his varied career he traveled throughout the entire country. He came to know intimately the local dialects of many rural areas, which he put to brilliant use in his works. In a period of two years, Rulfo published his only two books: the collection of short stores *El llano en llamas* in 1953 and the novel *Pedro Páramo* in 1955. The revised edition (1970) of the former consists of seventeen stories. All the stories are set in rural Mexico, and in all of them the most diverse possibilities of the genre, ranging from narration in the first person to the objective and impersonal, are developed to perfection.

Pedro Páramo makes use of brief passages of extremely diverse narrative techniques in a disconcerting arrangement. It describes a world in which appear all aspects of human life and death, a world that is at the same time merely a town. This town, in the author's own words, "is dying of itself." It is the symbol of a country and of the myth of paradise lost (Pedro Páramo is the overlord of a paradise-in-reverse called Comala, and it is also desolation, devastation, the desert).

The silence in Rulfo's work is always murmuring and the dead never stop manifesting their vitality.

In his works Rulfo also displayed the best of the large, complex tradition of realist prose in Mexico, one phase of which is known as Mexican Revolution novels. At the same time, since their publication, his works have been enormously influential, not only in Mexico but in all of Latin America. Rulfo knew how to portray with linguistic precision the radiant universality that dwelled within the lives of the poorest, most anonymous campesinos as well as within the most renowned leaders. Through the most mundane acts, each of Rulfo's characters embodies and expresses the essential truths and myths of humanity. A father carries his agonizing son, reproducing an inverted version of the myth of Saint Christopher; a son travels in search of his father, who has never left the place of his birth, and repeats in reverse the story of Telemachus and Ulysses. Rulfo's world is a world in reverse, where extremes touch. Thus, the silence in his work is always murmuring and the dead never stop manifesting their vitality. Rulfo never forgot that in order to be authentic the universality of his imagination had to be rooted in the most profound interconnections of Mexican reality.

Several things stand out about these interconnections: the discreet omnipotence of language which, without great fanfare and with simple, fleeting metaphors, gets to the bottom of the daily miracles of life; the complicity between humankind and nature, which, in Rulfo's eyes, makes the rustic Mexican world an environment full of movement, of animism, where each object and act provides a unique means of seeing the universe; and the vitality that makes his protagonists unforgettable because they are not moved by psychological motives but rather by intense, sanguine convictions. This transforms his characters into human beings whose singular "Mexicanness" is startling, whose fondness for the earthy forces of passion, obsession, and vengeance is disturbing to many foreign readers. With his vision, Rulfo was able to influence Mexican as well as Latin American literature. He created the basic characteristics of "magic realism" and has become a primary source of the universal modern narrative.

— JORGE AGUILAR MORA

S

SÁ, ESTÁCIO DE

Estácio de Sá (*b.* ca. 1520; *d.* 20 February 1567), nephew of Mem de Sá, Brazil's third governor-general, who had initially expelled French intruders from Guanabara Bay. In January 1565, Estácio sailed from Bahia de Todos os Santos to Guanabara Bay, where he found

---

In March 1565, Sá founded a fortified outpost near the base of Sugar Loaf Hill, the nucleus of the future city of Rio de Janeiro.

---

that the French had returned and were too strongly entrenched to be dislodged by his forces. Accordingly, he withdrew to Santos to await reinforcements. Upon his return to Guanabara Bay in March 1565, he founded a fortified outpost near the base of Sugar Loaf Hill, the nucleus of the future city of Rio de Janeiro. A year later Sá was wounded while leading his forces on Glória Hill. He died of his wounds just as Mem de Sá was refounding the city on Castle Hill, opposite the island of Villegaignon.

— DAURIL ALDEN

SÁ, MEM DE

Mem de Sá (*b. ca.* 1500; *d.* 1572), Brazilian high magistrate. Nominated third governor-general of Brazil, he arrived in Salvador, Bahia, on 28 December 1557. During his administration he fought the usury of merchants who sold slaves on credit with a gain of 100 percent a year, controlled the excessive enslavement of the Indians by the Portuguese colonists, and expanded the number of Jesuit *aldeias* (villages) from two or three to around eleven. Mem de Sá helped the chief-captain of Espirito Santo, Vasco Fernandes Coutinho, and the settlers of the captaincy of São Vicente in wars with the Indians. He attacked the French of the so-called Antarctic France who had built the Coligny fort on an island in Rio de Janeiro Bay. The fortress was taken in 1560, but the French took shelter in some Indian villages around the bay. As Sá lacked men to occupy the fort, it was abandoned, and a second attack on the French survivors was led by Sá's nephew, Estácio de Sá (ca. 1526–1567), who

established a military base at the foot of Sugarloaf Mountain in 1565. The primitive settlement was transferred to its current site in 1567 by Mem de Sá, who, in a letter to the king, considered himself the true founder of Rio de Janeiro. In 1569 he asked to be replaced as governor-general; he died in Salvador.

— MARIA BEATRIZ NIZZA DA SILVA

SÁ E BENAVIDES, SALVADOR CORREIA DE

Salvador Correia de Sá e Benavides (*b.* 1602; *d.* 1 January 1681), one of the most important figures in the seventeenth-century Portuguese South Atlantic Empire. Born in Cádiz, Spain, Salvador Correia de Sá e Benavides was the son of Martim de Sá, governor of Rio de Janeiro in 1602–1608 and 1623–1632.

In 1615 Salvador sailed with his father to Brazil for the first time. Back in the Iberian Peninsula by early 1618, he was again in Brazil with his father by the end of the year, searching for minerals in Bahia and Rio de Janeiro. Salvador returned to Portugal about 1623 and sailed to Brazil for the third time in 1624 to help defend it against the Dutch in Espírito Santo and Bahia.

Sá returned to Europe and in 1627 received the title of Admiral of the Southern Coast and Rio de la Plata. He was back in Rio de Janeiro by 1628. In the early 1630s, Sá pacified Payaguá and Guaicurú Indians in the Paraguayan Chaco and Calchaquis Indians in Tucumán Province in Argentina. Sá returned to Portugal and in 1637 was appointed governor and *capitão-mor* of Rio de Janeiro, where he fought attempts by the colonists to expel the Jesuits. Two years later he succeeded his grandfather as administrator of the mines of São Paulo and Santos. Sá returned to Portugal in 1643 and the next year was appointed to the Overseas Council. In 1645 he began leading convoys to and from Portuguese America.

Named governor and captain-general of Angola in 1647, Sá was given the task of driving the Dutch from that captaincy. In November 1647 Sá sailed from Lisbon. After picking up additional men and supplies in Rio de Janeiro, he arrived off the coast of Angola in July 1648. Dutch authorities in Luanda surrendered to him on 21 August 1648 and Benguela fell soon after. To contemporaries, his successes in Angola were Sá's greatest achievements.

In 1652 Sá left Luanda for Brazil but soon returned to Portugal. He was put in charge of the defense of the port of Lisbon in 1654. In September 1658 he was named governor and captain general of the Repartição do Sul–Rio de Janeiro and the captaincies to the south plus Espírito Santo to the north. Sá put down a revolt in 1661 but was relieved of his governorship in 1662 for his harshness in doing so. Returning to Portugal, Sá fell in and out of favor with the crown between 1663 and 1669, until he finally was restored to the good graces of the court in the latter year.

— FRANCIS A. DUTRA

SAAVEDRA, CORNELIO DE

Cornelio de Saavedra (*b.* 15 September 1759; *d.* 29 March 1829), landowner and merchant who played a leading role in the first phase of Argentine independence. Born in Potosí of creole parents, Saavedra moved with his family to Buenos Aires, where he was educated at the Real Colegio de San Carlos. Alongside his merchant career he gained experience in public office, serving on the cabildo and as grain administrator during the last decade of Spanish rule. He also demonstrated

Cornelio de Saavedra. (Archivo General de la Nación, Buenos Aires)

military leadership when he organized a creole militia unit, the Patricios, and commanded them in action against the British invaders in 1807. From his military power base Saavedra intervened decisively in the events of May 1810, voted for a change of government, and became president of the patriotic junta which prepared the way for full independence. Saavedra led the conservative wing of the movement, favoring gradual change and representation of the provinces, against Mariano MORENO and the radical reformists who wanted to impose instant revolution and sought a unified as well as an independent Argentina.

The conservatives ousted the radicals in April 1811 but were themselves weakened by internal opposition and military defeat in Upper Peru. Saavedra went personally to reorganize the Army of the North, but while absent from Buenos Aires (September 1811) he was ousted from government and deprived of his army command. He then suffered political persecution and periods of exile, until in 1818 the national Congress cleared his name and the Supreme Director, Juan Martín de PUEYRREDÓN, restored his military rank and appointed him chief of staff. He spent the year of anarchy (1820) in Montevideo but returned to Buenos Aires during the government of Martín Rodríguez. He retired to private life and died in Buenos Aires.

— JOHN LYNCH

SAAVEDRA LAMAS, CARLOS

Carlos Saavedra Lamas (*b.* 1 November 1878; *d.* 5 May 1959), statesman and Nobel Prize–winning Argentine diplomat. Born in Buenos Aires, Saavedra Lamas received a law degree from the University of Buenos Aires in 1903. He began his career as a professor, but he turned to politics in 1912. As a national deputy he authored the tariff law that protected Argentina's sugar industry in Salta Province. In 1915, he served as President Victorino de la Plaza's (1914–1916) minister of the interior and as minister of justice and public instruction.

It was as a member of the Concordancia that he achieved international prominence. Between 1932 and 1938 he served under President Agustín P. JUSTO (1932–1938) as minister of foreign affairs. Conservative and nationalistic, he represented Argentina at numerous international conferences. In particular, he challenged efforts to establish the hegemony of the United States in hemispheric affairs. He was instrumental in obtaining Latin American support for the Anti-War Pact (1933). His efforts to find a negotiated settlement to the Chaco War (1932–1935) between Bolivia and Paraguay earned him the Nobel Peace Prize in 1936. Although he remained active in national affairs, Saavedra Lamas retired from public service after 1938. He returned to teaching and became the rector of the University of Buenos Aires in 1941.

— DANIEL LEWIS

SAAVEDRA MALLEA, BAUTISTA

Bautista Saavedra Mallea (*b.* 30 August 1870; *d.* 1 March 1939), president of Bolivia (January 1921–September 1925). Born in Sorata, La Paz Province, Saavedra was a lawyer, journalist, and author. Following a peaceful palace revolt that ended several decades of government by the Liberal Party and installed the Republican Party, which appealed more to the literate, lower middle class, Saavedra became head of a governing junta in July 1920. In January 1921 he was elected president. He is considered one of the strongest civilian presidents of Bolivia, having captured the leadership of his party from the venerable Daniel SALAMANCA.

Although Saavedra's presidency was stormy, it also boasted solid achievements, including the first social and labor legislation and construction of direct rail links to Argentina. Saavedra left office in September 1925, turning it over to the president of the Senate, Felipe Segundo Guzmán. A year later, annoyed at postelection statements by the president-elect, Gabino Villanueva, Saavedra had the election annulled on a technicality and imposed Hernando Siles Reyes as his successor in the presidency. Saavedra died in Santiago, Chile.

— CHARLES W. ARNADE

SABAT ERCASTY, CARLOS

Carlos Sabat Ercasty (*b.* 1887; *d.* 1982), Uruguayan poet, literary critic, and educator. Before teaching literature and mathematics in Montevideo and serving as administrator of the Young Women's Teachers College, he worked as a reporter for *El Día* and *La Razón,* both in Montevideo. Sabat Ercasty's prolific poetic production includes more than forty published collections. Early verses—such as the eight volumes of *Poemas del hombre* (1921–1958)—were characterized by Wagnerian thematic shifts from sensuality to mysticism, with traces of pantheistic musings. Later poetry, dramatic and fluid, treated philosophical issues and Oriental myths; at times a sense of abstract and conceptual stoicism predominated.

Works by Sabat Ercasty that were inspired by historical themes include *El charrúa* (1957) and *Himno a Artigas e Himno de mayo* (1964). His major works of poetry are *Sonetos de las agonías y los extásis* (1977), *Parábolas* (1978), *Cánticos a Euridice* (2 vols., 1978–1980),

and *Antología* (2 vols., 1982). His major works of literary criticism are *Retratos del fuego: José Zorrilla de San Martín* (1958), *Retratos del fuego: Carlos Vaz Ferreira* (1958), and *Retratos del fuego: María Eugenia Vaz Ferreira* (1953).

— WILLIAM H. KATRA

SÁBATO, ERNESTO

Ernesto Sábato (*b.* 24 June 1911), Argentine novelist, essayist, and thinker. The years during which Sábato studied at the University of La Plata, where he received a Ph.D. in physics, were crucial in the political life of Argentina. Since he felt great concern for the social problems of his country, Sábato embraced communism for five years, and as a spokesman for the party he suffered personal persecution. In 1934 he traveled secretly to Europe as a representative of the Argentine Communist Youth Organization to attend an antifascist congress in Brussels. However, after suffering a spiritual and ideological crisis, he severed his relationship with the party, refusing a trip to Moscow for indoctrination. In 1938, on a fellowship at the Joliot-Curie Laboratory in Paris, he became acquainted with the surrealists and began writing. This was a turning point in his life since, at that moment, Sábato understood his deeply felt interest in and aptitude for literature.

After a stay at MIT (1939), he taught at the University of La Plata and in Buenos Aires, and contributed to the newspaper *La Nación* and the literary journal *Sur.* At the end of 1945, with the Perón government securely in power, Sábato was fired from both of his teaching jobs because he was an enemy of the dictatorship and dared to proclaim this publicly. This precipitated a second crisis that ended his career in the sciences. Thus was born Sábato-the-writer and his public persona. For the next ten years he earned his livelihood with articles and conferences and as a consultant for the publishing houses Raigal, Codex, and Emecé. In 1947 he worked for two months as an assistant officer of the executive committee of UNESCO in Paris and Rome. In 1955, after Perón's fall and with a de facto government in power, Sábato showed his idealistic nature by accepting the directorship of the important weekly *Mundo Argentino.* But the relationship was short-lived when he resigned for not acquiescing to press censorship. Between 1958 and 1959 he served as director of cultural relations at the Foreign Ministry.

Sábato's scientific education together with his literary passion created an Apollonian and Dionysian personality. Like Sartre, Sábato is a thinker who uses fiction to fully express his ideas. To him, today's novel is closer to metaphysics than to literature. His novels and essays revolve around obsessive ideas that have conditioned his works and his social conduct: a deep existential preoccupation with humanity, literary creation, and his country. In some essays, Sábato emphasized that a writer should be at the service of truth and freedom. Of his three novels, the first, *El túnel* (1948; *The Tunnel,* 1988), could be considered a psychological, existential thriller. The second, *Sobre héroes y tumbas* (1961; *On Heroes and Tombs,* 1981), remains a veritable fresco of modern Argentina, a synthesis of his surrealistic imagination and speculative thinking. The third, *Abaddón, el Exterminador* (1974; *The Angel of Darkness,* 1991), is a "gnostic eschatology" showing that the prophecies of Apocalypse 9:11 are about to become a reality: our materialistic civilization will end and the human race will be renewed on the basis of a new principle that will reestablish the divine order.

The ideas that are the foundation of Sábato's fiction are expressed in five books of essays that must be read to fully understand him. He has also written numerous articles and has presided over the compilation of one of the most heinous texts in the letters of his country and of the world: *Nunca más* (1984), which was the report, based on the testimony of survivors and relatives, of the commission that he chaired to investigate the tragedy of the Argentine *desaparecidos* ("disappeared" persons). Sábato's texts are full of antidogmatic, testimonial, and denunciatory passages, which have revitalized Argentine letters. He has received numerous international awards and honors. At home Sábato was given the prestigious Prize of National Consecration for making the greatest contribution to the enrichment of Argentina's cultural heritage.

– ANGELA B. DELLEPIANE

SABOGAL, JOSÉ

José Sabogal (*b.* 11 March 1888; *d.* 15 December 1956), Peruvian artist. A native of Cajabamba, Sabogal was a prominent member of the Generation of 1919. He began to use indigenous people as subjects of his paintings while he was studying and teaching in Argentina. In Cuzco, he produced paintings with indigenous themes. Because he was heavily influenced by the famed Mexican revolutionary muralists, Sabogal soon attracted many students. José Carlos MARIÁTEGUI, who called him the first truly Peruvian painter, became a close friend. Sabogal suggested the name *Amauta* for Mariátegui's new journal. The name referred to the thinkers of the Incan Empire. Therefore, it won favor for conveying the idea of a uniquely Peruvian form of socialism linked to the nation's original Inca culture. Sabogal also taught at the Escuela de Bellas Artes in

Lima. He died in Lima. *Del arte en el Perú y otros ensayos* (1975), a collection of his writings, was published posthumously.

– VINCENT PELOSO

SACASA, JUAN BAUTISTA

Juan Bautista Sacasa (*b.* 21 December 1874; *d.* 17 April 1946), president of Nicaragua (1933–1936). Born in León, Sacasa rose to prominence in the volatile politics of Nicaragua as a leading member of the Liberal Party during the early twentieth century. He served as vice president in Carlos SOLORZANO's shaky coalition government in 1926 but was ousted after a coup by discontented Conservatives led by Emilano CHAMORRO VARGAS. Sacasa became the leader of Liberal opposition and along with General José María MONCADA led subsequent Liberal uprisings. The U.S. government opposed Sacasa's claim to the Nicaraguan presidency because of his ties with the Liberal Party and his support from Mexican president Plutarco Elías CALLES. The United States placed Adolfo DÍAZ, a Conservative, in the presidency and backed him up with marines. After successfully splitting the Liberal forces of Sacasa and Moncada, the United States supervised the 1928 elections. Moncada became president and Sacasa served as Nicaraguan minister to Washington, D.C. Sacasa ultimately came to power in 1932, in the midst of guerrilla commander Augusto César SANDINO's war against the U.S. Marines. During this period, the United States established the Nicaraguan National Guard and placed Anastasio SOMOZA GARCÍA in its command. Sacasa attempted to negotiate a peace accord with Sandino in good faith, but Sandino was assassinated by the National Guard, leaving Sacasa locked in a power struggle with Somoza (his nephew-in-law). The increasing power and influence of Somoza and his National Guard soon decreased the de facto power of the president. Somoza forced Sacasa to resign from the presidency in June 1936, at which time he went into exile in the United States. He died in Los Angeles.

– HEATHER K. THIESSEN

SACO, JOSÉ ANTONIO

José Antonio Saco (*b.* 7 May 1797; *d.* 26 September 1879), Cuban writer, editor, and statesman. Born in Bayamo, Cuba, Saco studied philosophy and politics and became a professor of philosophy at the San Carlos Seminary in Havana. In 1828 he traveled to New York, where he founded the *Mensajero Quincenal* (Quarterly Messenger), a liberal publication that stressed the evils of slavery. Four years later, back in Havana, Saco founded a similar publication, the *Revista Bimestre Cubana* (Cuban Bimonthly Review). In 1830 Saco wrote *Memoria sobre la vagancia* (On Vagrancy), a subtle attack on many aspects of Cuban government and society,

---

Saco published an article arguing for U.S. annexation of Cuba.

---

which was still under Spanish colonial rule. In 1834 Saco was exiled to Trinidad for writing *Justa defensa de la Academia Cubana de literatura,* a piece that marked his emergence as one of the leading spokespersons for the progressive Cuban creoles. Two years later Saco returned from exile and was named the Cuban representative in the Spanish Cortes. He traveled throughout Europe and while in Paris published an article arguing for U.S. annexation of Cuba. His greatest literary work was his monumental *Historia de la esclavitud* (History of Slavery) (2 vols., 1875–1879). Saco died in Barcelona, Spain.

— MICHAEL POWELSON

SÁENZ, JAIME

Jaime Sáenz (*b.* 8 October 1921; *d.* 1986), Bolivian poet and novelist. Sáenz is one of the most original poets of contemporary Bolivia. Oblivious to common sense, his works reject the construction of clear and well-defined meanings. Syllogistic, closer to concept than to image, Sáenz's poetry is made up of syntactic torsions, paradoxes, and tautologies. From *El escalpelo* (1955), *Muerte por el tacto* (1957), *Aniversario de una visión* (1960), and *Visitante profundo* (1963) to *El frío* (1967), *Recorrer esta distancia* (1973), and *Bruckner: Las tinieblas* (1978), this poetic universe follows a spiral movement, in search of the unity of being. This search, which places Sáenz within the tradition of German romanticism, is markedly subjective. For Sáenz, the human body, the corporeal, is merely an "instrument of living" with little influence on the routines of everyday life. This eccentric view of the world is also present in his novel, *Felipe Delgado* (1979), a challenging exploration of the modern grotesque.

— JAVIER SANJINÉS C.

SÁENZ, MOISÉS

Moisés Sáenz (*b.* 1888; *d.* 1941), Mexican educator. Sáenz was born in Monterrey and studied at a Presbyterian preparatory school in Coyoacán. He received his teaching degree from the Escuela Normal of Jalapa,

studied at the Sorbonne, and completed his graduate studies at Columbia Teachers College in New York, where he became a disciple of John Dewey. He was influential in Mexican revolutionary education when, as undersecretary of education in the Plutarco Elías CALLES government (1924–1928), he fleshed out a program of rural education based on Dewey's notions of action education. The Casa del Pueblo, as the rural school was called by the then *secretaría de educación pública,* was designed to teach farming, hygiene, horticulture, apiculture, aviculture, and civics through student-operated gardens, beehives, orchards, chicken coops, and producer and consumer cooperatives. Sáenz was a strong advocate of indigenous and rural integration into a modernizing, Western society.

Sáenz was known for promoting North American ideas in Mexican education and was singled out by some Catholics as a propagandist for Protestantism. Nonetheless, after José VASCONCELOS, no other Mexican has had as much influence on rural education. Sáenz was also influential in the creation of Mexico's system of secondary schools and the Casa de Estudiante Indígena. He held many educational posts in Mexico, organized the Primer Congreso Indigenista Interamericano, and served as Mexican ambassador to Denmark, Ecuador, and Peru, where he died in 1941. He was the author of several books, including *Sobre el indio peruano y su incorporación al medio nacional* (Mexico, 1933); *Carapán: Bosquejo de una experiencia* (Lima, 1936); *México íntegro* (Lima, 1939); and, with Herbert J. Priestley, *Some Mexican Problems* (Chicago, 1926).

— MARY KAY VAUGHAN

SÁENZ DE THORNE, MANUELA

Manuela Sáenz de Thorne (*b.* 1797; *d.* 23 November 1856), best known as the lover of Simón BOLÍVAR, but also a political figure in her own right. Though she was of illegitimate birth, her parents belonged to the upper class of late colonial Quito. At age twenty she was given in an arranged marriage to an English merchant, James Thorne. However, the enduring passion of her life was for Bolívar, whom she met in 1822, when he first came to Ecuador.

Abandoning her husband, Sáenz followed Bolívar to Peru. She was with him on campaign and subsequently in Lima, where she assumed a prominent role in social and political life. But her most controversial role was in Bogotá, where she arrived in late 1827. There she showed uninhibited vigor in defending Bolívar against his opponents, especially the faction of Vice President Francisco de Paula SANTANDER, at one point having Santander shot in effigy. When an attempt was made on Bolívar's life in September 1828, she was in the palace with him and helped him escape.

Sáenz remained in Bogotá after the final departure of Bolívar in 1830. She continued to be active in politics on behalf of the Bolivarian party and was implicated in a conspiracy against her old enemy Santander after he became president of New Granada. Exiled in 1833, she eventually settled in Paita, on the Peruvian coast, where she lived until her death.

— DAVID BUSHNELL

SÁENZ GARZA, AARÓN

Aarón Sáenz Garza (*b.* 1 June 1891; *d.* 26 February 1983), Mexican politician and entrepreneur. A native of Monterrey, Nuevo León, Sáenz was trained as a lawyer at the National University. He joined the revolutionary army of General Álvaro OBREGÓN in 1913 and thereafter steadily rose in national politics. He was minister of foreign relations from 1924 to 1927, manager of Obregón's successful presidential campaign in 1928, a founder of the National Revolutionary Party in 1928–1929, and minister of public education in 1930. A powerful ally of Obregón (who was assassinated after his election in 1928), Sáenz was a prime contender for the presidential nomination of the National Revolutionary Party in 1929 but lost it to Pascual ORTIZ RUBIO. Although he remained active in politics, Sáenz focused on his business ventures, particularly a multimillion-dollar system of sugar mills. With the help of his sons he expanded the family business interests into paper manufacturing and aviation during the 1950s and 1960s to become one of the nation's leading entrepreneurs.

— JOHN A. BRITTON

SÁENZ PEÑA, LUIS

Luis Sáenz Peña (*b.* 2 April 1822; *d.* 4 December 1907), Argentine politician. Born and raised in Buenos Aires, Sáenz Peña received his law degree from the University of Buenos Aires in 1845. He entered politics in 1860 as a deputy to the Constitutional Convention, thereafter serving in both Buenos Aires provincial assemblies and the national assembly. He also held posts in the provincial Supreme Court, the Provincial Bank, and the General Council on Education. In the wake of the 1890 uprising of the Civic Union and the stock market crash, Sáenz Peña became the compromise candidate for president in 1892. In that post he served the interests of the National Autonomist Party of Julio A. ROCA and Carlos PELLEGRINI, but he never succeeded in emerging from their shadows. Afflicted by ill health and an indecisive temper, Sáenz Peña served a two-year term

marred by strong opposition in Congress, an uprising by the new Radical Civic Union led by Leandro ALEM and future president Hipólito YRIGOYEN, and a worsening economic situation after the Baring Brothers crisis. He submitted his resignation in January 1895 and was replaced by the equally ill-fated José Evaristo URIBURU. Argentine politics did not settle down until Roca reassumed the presidency in 1898. Sáenz Peña's son, ROQUE, followed in his father's footsteps. Elected in 1910, he was best known for the electoral reform law of 1912.

— JEREMY ADELMAN

SÁENZ PEÑA, ROQUE

Roque Sáenz Peña (*b.* 19 March 1851; *d.* 9 August 1914), president of Argentina (1910–1914) who in 1912 initiated an electoral reform law that made voting compulsory and provided for the secret ballot and minority political representation in Congress. The law is known as the Sáenz Peña Law. Sáenz Peña belonged to the Argentine upper class. His father, Luis, was president of Argentina (1892–1895). Roque Sáenz Peña studied law at the University of Buenos Aires, but in 1874 he discontinued his studies for a brief period to join the forces that were suppressing a rebellion led by former President Bartolomé MITRE. He graduated in 1875 and a year later was elected to the Buenos Aires legislature representing the Partido Autonomista Nacional. When the War of the Pacific broke out in 1879, Sáenz Peña moved to Lima and joined the alliance of Peru and Bolivia against Chile. He became known for his bravery and participated in the battles of San Francisco and Tarapacá and also in the heroic defense of Arica, where he was taken prisoner in 1880.

After his return to Argentina, he was named undersecretary of the Ministry of Foreign Relations. In August 1887 he was appointed special envoy and minister plenipotentiary to Uruguay. In 1888 he served as a member of the delegation representing Argentina at the South American Conference of Private International Law held in Montevideo. A year later, he participated in the Pan-American Conference in Washington, D.C. In 1890, he served briefly as minister of foreign relations, having to resign as a consequence of the revolution of 26 July 1890. In 1891, Sáenz Peña became a presidential candidate but withdrew when Julio A. ROCA and Bartolomé Mitre engineered his own father's candidacy. He resigned from the Senate in December 1892 to avoid a confrontation with his father and retired for three years to an *estancia* in the province of Entre Ríos. He returned to Buenos Aires in 1895 after his father's resignation. From that moment on he began attacking the corrupt, personalistic political system. The Reformista faction of the Partido Autonomista Nacional, headed by Carlos PELLEGRINI until his death in 1906, supported Sáenz Peña in the congressional elections of 1906 and 1908. In 1910, he was elected president.

— JUAN MANUEL PÉREZ

SAHAGÚN, BERNARDINO DE

Bernardino de Sahagún (*b.* 1499/1500; *d.* 1590), a Franciscan friar who went to New Spain in 1529 and quickly became one of the key interpreters of the Nahuatl language and Nahua culture of all time. Born Bernardino de Ribeira in Sahagrin, Spain, he was a pioneer ethnographer and devoted messenger of the Gospel, studying Aztec culture with the goal of deepening the indigenous people's conversion to Christianity. He understood that the best pedagogy required an exchange and that a two-way encounter demanded serious language study. It was Franciscan policy to teach both Latin and Nahuatl to the elite indigenous boys of Mexico who would later, ideally, instruct their parents and future generations. The Royal College or Colegio of Santa Cruz, in Tlatelolco, was established for this purpose, and Sahagún and Fray Andrés de Olmos, another renowned *nahuatlato,* were among the instructors.

Sahagún was a devoted messenger of the Gospel, studying Aztec culture with the goal of deepening the indigenous people's conversion to Christianity.

While teaching at the Colegio (1536–1540), Sahagún began collaborating with some of his best students in producing Nahuatl manuscripts. They started with Christian sermons but shifted to the philosophy and oratory of the Nahua elders, indigenous versions of the Spanish conquest, native religious beliefs and practices, calendar, social and political organization, economic production and exchange, daily life, and environment as Sahagún compiled in his magnum opus of twelve parts, the *Historia general de las cosas de Nueva España,* or *Florentine Codex* (so called for the locale where it was preserved). Based on testimony and *códices* (paintings/writings) made by people born and raised prior to European contact, this spectacular work has immense value for ethnohistorians trained to detect what might be the Nahua voice and what has been filtered by the priest-interpreter.

— STEPHANIE WOOD

SÁINZ, GUSTAVO

Gustavo Sáinz (*b.* 13 July 1940), Mexican fiction writer and critic. Born in Mexico City, Sáinz is known as a writer of Mexican "urban picaresque." *Gazapo* (1965), *Obsesivos días circulares* (1969), *La princesa del Palacio de Hierro* (1974), and *Compadre Lobo* (1977) are his best-known novels. Other works include *Fantasmas aztecas* (1982), *Paseo en trapecio* (1985), and *Muchacho en llamas* (1988). Together with José AGUSTÍN, Sáinz is associated with the generation of "La Onda," a group of young Mexican writers who published in the 1960s and 1970s and whose literature was characterized by attention to an urban adolescent subculture, the use of colloquial language and the oral quality of the text, and the characters' self-centered, nonconformist attitudes toward established social codes. In Sáinz's fiction Mexico City is a constant, autobiographically based reference, a voracious space intimately experienced by his characters, where language acts, in his words, "as the major protagonist of history."

— LAURA GARCÍA-MORENO

SALAMANCA, DANIEL

Daniel Salamanca (*b.* 8 July 1868; *d.* 17 July 1935), president of Bolivia (1931–1934). Blamed for Bolivia's defeat by Paraguay in the Chaco War (1932–1935), Salamanca may be the most controversial figure of twentieth-century Bolivian history. A wealthy Cochabamba landowner and eloquent congressional deputy and senator for thirty years, he served as secretary of treasury in the cabinet of President José Manuel PANDO (1899–1904). In 1914 he broke with the conservative Liberal Party and helped found the Republican Party, only to break away again in 1921 to form the Genuine Republican Party. Hailed as the "new messiah" and *hombre símbolo* (human symbol) because of his fierce nationalism and scrupulous integrity in an era of political corruption, Salamanca was the establishment's popular choice for president in March 1931. However, his economic austerity, political repression of the opposition (particularly leftists and Communists), and failed Chaco policy soon left him one of the most unpopular of Bolivian presidents. In November 1934, while he was visiting the Chaco command in Villa Montes, the military seized and deposed him.

— WALTRAUD QUEISER MORALES

SALAS, MANUEL DE

Manuel de Salas (*b.* 19 June 1754; *d.* 28 November 1841), Chilean reformer and patriot, and one of the best-loved Chileans of his time. From a rich creole family, Salas studied law at the University of San Marcos, Lima, from which he graduated in 1774. In the later 1770s he paid a long visit to Spain, taking great interest in economic reforms and education. Superintendent of public works under the governorship of Ambrosio O'HIGGINS, he was named a member of the newly founded *consulado* (merchant guild) of Santiago in 1795. The following year he wrote a classic report on the economy and society of Chile for the Spanish finance minister. In 1798 he founded the Academia de San Luis, a college which aimed to introduce stronger technical education in Chile. He also played an active part in introducing vaccination into the colony in 1806.

Salas's early hopes for reform rested in the Spanish crown, but from 1810 onward he was a patriot, a member of the first national congress (1811), and, briefly, foreign minister (1812–1813). He was exiled to Juan Fernández (an island prison for exiled political prisoners) during the Spanish reconquest (1814–1817). The first director of Chile's National Library, Salas retained a strong interest in educational matters, often visiting schools and advising them.

— SIMON COLLIER

SALAVARRIETA, POLICARPA

Policarpa Salavarrieta (*b.* 26 January 1795; *d.* 14 November 1817), heroine of Colombian independence. Born into a respectable creole family, Policarpa Salavarrieta ("La Pola") grew up in Guaduas, a way station between Bogotá and the Magdalena River. When the independence movement started, she became a strong sympathizer, and the flow of traffic through her town kept her well informed. With the Spanish reconquest of New Granada in 1816, Salavarrieta began providing information and other assistance to the patriot underground, first in Guaduas and then in Bogotá, where it was easier for her to remain inconspicuous. Nevertheless, her key role in the urban network of the resistance was discovered, and she was condemned to death. She went to her execution shouting a tirade against Spanish oppression. Salavarrieta's place in the pantheon of patriot martyrs is indicated by the fact that she was the first Latin American woman commemorated on a postage stamp, one of Colombia's 1910 independence-centennial issue.

— DAVID BUSHNELL

SALAVERRY, FELIPE SANTIAGO

Felipe Santiago Salaverry (*b.* 6 March 1805; *d.* 18 February 1836), Conservative caudillo who became presi-

dent of Peru (1835–1836). A participant in the final battles against the Spanish in 1824, Salaverry, a native of Lima, was promoted to general by President Luis José Orbegoso in 1834. In February 1835, however, the twenty-nine-year-old Salaverry denounced the government of the Liberal Orbegoso and took power in Lima. By the middle of the year, he had allied with Agustín GAMARRA against General Andrés de SANTA CRUZ and Orbegoso, who still claimed the presidency. Salaverry imposed an authoritarian government that gained broad support in Lima and along the coast. In February 1836, his forces finally squared off against those of Santa Cruz. Salaverry was taken prisoner in the battle of Socabaya and, in an unusual action for the period, was executed at Arequipa, setting the stage for the Peru-Bolivia Confederation.

— CHARLES F. WALKER

SALAZAR, MATÍAS

Matías Salazar (*b.* 1828; *d.* 17 May 1872), Venezuelan caudillo. Salazar participated in the Federal War (1859–1863) as a military chief of the central region. After the Federalist triumph he fought in several local armed controversies. When President Juan Crisóstomo FALCÓN was deposed in 1868, Salazar joined the April Revolution of 1870 led by Antonio GUZMÁN BLANCO, becoming an important military leader for Yellow Liberalism, second only to Guzmán. When Guzmán took control of the government, Salazar was named second appointee to the presidency of the republic and later president of the state of Carabobo. He gradually distanced himself from Guzmán and organized a conspiracy against the government but was discovered and expelled from the country. From abroad Salazar instigated a new armed movement in 1872. He was defeated, tried by the War Council, convicted of treason, and sentenced to death by firing squad.

— INÉS QUINTERO

SALAZAR ARRUÉ, SALVADOR EFRAÍN (SALARRUÉ)

Salvador Efraín (Salarrué) Salazar Arrué (*b.* 22 October 1899; *d.* 27 November 1975), Salvadoran writer and painter who used the pseudonym Salarrué. A native of Sonsonate, he became the most popular literary figure of mid-twentieth-century El Salvador. After education in San Salvador and at the Corcoran Art Academy in Washington, D.C. (1917–1919), Salazar produced short stories, novels, poems, and paintings that reflected the Salvadoran common people; helped to preserve Salvadoran folk culture; and awakened a social consciousness in the country. In the late 1920s he was an important contributor to Alberto MASFERRER's *Patria,* and he continued to be an influential writer and intellectual force in El Salvador until his death in 1975. Rural Salvadoran themes dominate Salazar's major novel, *El señor de la burbuja* (1927), and his classic collection of stories, *Cuentos de barro* (1933).

— RALPH LEE WOODWARD, JR.

SALAZAR BONDY, SEBASTIÁN

Sebastián Salazar Bondy (*b.* 4 February 1924; *d.* 4 July 1965), Peruvian writer and journalist. Salazar Bondy, born in Lima, began publishing his poetry while studying literature at San Marcos University. His artistic interest led him to work in Buenos Aires (1948–1951) and study in Paris (1956–1957). Twice he received the Peruvian national prize for theater (1948, 1952) and once the national prize for journalism (1958). Although he earned his living as a newspaperman, briefly directed the Institute of National Art, and participated in politics as an activist member of the Movimiento Social Progresista (Social Progressionist Movement) he had helped to found, Salazar Bondy devoted most of his time to creative writing, purportedly divested of social and ideological content. He is remembered for his strong opposition to pro-Indianist literary trends and advocacy of art for art's sake. His play *Amor, gran laberinto* (1948), his short stories *Pobre gente de París* (1958), and his essay *Lima la horrible* (1964) are among

---

Salazar Bondy is remembered for his strong opposition to pro-Indianist literary trends and advocacy of art for art's sake.

---

his best books. In collaboration with other writers, he edited *La poesía contemporánea del Perú* (1946), *Antología general de la poesía peruana* (1957), and *Cuentos infantiles peruanos* (1958).

— EUGENIO CHANG-RODRÍGUEZ

SALDANHA DA GAMA, LUÍS FELIPE DE

Luís Felipe de Saldanha da Gama (*b.* 7 April 1846; *d.* 24 June 1895), Brazilian admiral and principal figure in a revolt of the fleet during the civil war of 1893. Gama had been the navy's chief representative in the court of Dom PEDRO I because he was cultured, brave,

well traveled, and of noble ancestry. Although a monarchist by preference, he acknowledged the republic as an accomplished fact.

Gama and two other Brazilian admirals, Custódio José de MELO and Eduardo Wandenkolk, became unhappy over the way that the new government had placed the army over the navy in terms of prestige and material benefits. Wandenkolk wasted his prestige in aborted political adventures. Melo, having successfully led a naval revolt against President Deodoro da FONSECA, then tried the same maneuver against Vice President Floriano PEIXOTO, but without success. Gama opposed Melo's revolt and declared his neutrality. Then head of the Naval Academy, Gama was offered the vacated position of minister of the navy, which he refused. He felt that once the fighting was over his mission would be to rebuild the navy using the Naval Academy. His position of neutrality eventually became unbearable since he could not declare loyalty to Peixoto. Finally, despite the evidence that the Federalist and naval revolts would fail, Gama joined the losing cause, and, along with Federalist leader Gaspar da Silveira Martins, called for a plebiscite on the issue of the restoration of the monarchy. That stand ensured their defeat, since the pro-Republican forces by then were strong enough to win the war. Gama was killed in fighting while trying to reach neutral territory (Uruguay).

— ROBERT A. HAYES

SALES, EUGÊNIO DE ARAÚJO

Eugênio de Araújo Sales (*b.* 8 November 1920), archbishop and cardinal of Rio de Janeiro. For decades, Sales has been one of the most important and visible leaders of the Brazilian Catholic church. Ordained as a priest in 1942, Sales became bishop of Natal, Rio Grande do Norte, in 1954. In the 1950s and 1960s, he was known as a leader of the moderately progressive faction within the Brazilian church. As archbishop of Natal, he promoted radio schools as a means of working with the poor, and he supported the creation of the Basic Education Movement in 1958 and of rural Catholic unions in the late 1950s and early 1960s. Both initiatives became important within the Brazilian church and in national politics.

After the coup in 1964, Sales was less critical of the military government and more willing to work with it than most other prominent church leaders. For this reason, he became identified as a leader of the moderately conservative faction of the Brazilian hierarchy. He was named archbishop of Salvador in 1968 and of Rio de Janeiro in 1971. As archbishop of Rio, convinced that the church needed to focus on religious issues, he became one of Brazil's most prominent critics of liberation theology. His theological and ecclesiastical positions made him a favorite of Pope John Paul II after 1978.

– SCOTT MAINWARING

SALGADO, PLINIO

Plinio Salgado (*b.* 22 January 1895; *d.* 7 December 1975), Brazilian politician and journalist. Salgado was born in São Bento de Sapucaí, São Paulo and died in São Paulo. As a youth, he began his long and prolific career as a writer when he founded the hometown paper *O Correio de São Bento.* After moving to the state capital, Salgado began contributing regularly to nationwide newspapers and magazines. In 1931, he launched an integralist campaign and made himself the movement's supreme authority. One year later, the writer and politician founded the Ação Integralista Brasileira. On May 10, 1937, a group of anti-Vargas and integralist demonstrators attacked the presidential palace in Rio de Janeiro. The attack was repulsed and Salgado was exiled to Portugal until 1945. After returning to Brazil, he founded the Partido de Representação Popular (PRP) and became its presidential candidate in 1955. From 1958 to 1966, he served as a federal deputy representing the PRP and, later, the ARENA party from 1966 to 1974.

Salgado was a member of the Academia Paulista de Letras and authored numerous political, fictional, and poetic works such as *Tabor, O estrangeiro, O cavaleiro de Itararé, Literatura e política, A psicologia da revolução, O que é integralismo, Cartas aos camisas-verdes, A doutrina do sigma, O conceito cristão da democracia, Extremismo e democracia, Direitos e Deveres do homem,* and *Espírito de burguesia.* His integralist movement (or *camisas verdes*— green shirts) envisaged an integral state under a single authoritarian head of government patterned after European corporatist movements. Using the motto "God, country, and family," the movement sought to enlist the middle classes who feared communism.

– IÊDA SIQUEIRA WIARDA

SALGADO, SEBASTIÃO

Sebastião Salgado (*b.* 8 February 1944), Brazilian photographer. Born in Minas Gerais, Salgado was the only son among eight children of the owners of a large cattle farm. In 1963, he began studying law, and later switched to economics. Around this time, he married the architect Lélia Deluiz Wanick; they had two children. In 1968, Salgado obtained two master's degrees in economics: one from São Paulo University, and one

from Vanderbilt University; in 1971, he received a doctorate in agricultural economy from the Sorbonne. Immediately thereafter he went to work in Africa for the London-based International Coffee Organization. In 1973, Salgado changed careers once again and became a free-lance photojournalist documenting the drought in the Sahel region of Africa for the World Council of Churches. The following year he joined the Paris-based Sygma agency and covered the coup in Portugal and the revolutions in its colonies of Mozambique and Angola. In 1975, he switched to the Gamma agency, covering stories in Africa, Europe, and Latin America. He began the work on peasants that was featured in his 1986 book *Other Americas* started around this time. Three years later, Salgado joined Magnum, a cooperative agency founded in 1947 by Henri Cartier-Bresson, Robert Capa, and others. In 1982 he received the W. Eugene Smith grant in humanistic photography and an award from the French Ministry of Culture to continue his work in Latin America. Working with a French humanitarian aid group, Médecins sans Frontières, he returned to the Sahel to photograph the calamitous effects of famine in 1984. After the publication of his book *Sahel: L'homme en détresse,* Salgado was internationally recognized as a leading photojournalist. His most ambitious project, on workers and the end of manual labor, was completed in 1992 and published as *Workers: An Archeology of the Industrial Age* (1993). Salgado's work has gone beyond the printed page and onto the walls of galleries and museums. Controversy has arisen over the alleged "beautification of tragedy" in his work, and in an attempt to understand it, critics have variously labeled it "lyric documents," "mannerist documents," or "documentary photography."

– FERNANDO CASTRO

SALGAR, EUSTORGIO

Eustorgio Salgar (*b.* 1 November 1831; *d.* 25 November 1885), president of Colombia (1870–1872). Scion of prominent Santander families, he was born in Bogotá, where he received his law doctorate in 1851. Salgar's talents and Liberal affiliation brought him responsible posts in Cundinamarca. He went on to govern portions of Santander (1853–1855, 1856–1857), was elected a senator (1858–1859), was governor of Cundinamarca (1859), and was a delegate to the Rionegro Convention (1863). He served as Colombian minister in Washington, D.C., (1865–1866) and was elected president in 1870 (nominated in part to attract votes away from General Tomás CIPRIANO MOSQUERA). A devout Catholic and friend of Archbishop Vincente Arbeláez, Salgar won easily. His administration sponsored educational expansion at the primary and secondary levels and established normal schools. Other notable achievements during Salgar's presidency were the chartering of the Banco de Bogotá, Colombia's first successful bank (1870); a reduction of the army by 29 percent; and the construction of roads and of asylums for the insane and leprous. Salgar's elegant personal style and courtesy won him plaudits from both parties. After his term as president, he was governor of Cundinamarca (1874–1876), minister of war (1876), minister of foreign affairs (1878), and minister of the interior (1884). Salgar died in Bogotá.

– J. LEÓN HELGUERA

SALINAS DE GORTARI, CARLOS

Carlos Salinas de Gortari (*b.* 3 April 1948), president of Mexico (1988–1994). After taking office in 1988, Carlos Salinas established himself as a major figure in contemporary Mexican presidential history. Elected in the most disputed presidential campaign since the government party's (PRI) formation in 1929, Salinas came into office with barely a simple majority of the officially tallied vote, the lowest figure ever in a successful presidential campaign. With little legitimacy, outside of and within his own party, he took charge of the presidency in a dynamic, decisive manner. The major leitmotif of his ideology was economic liberalization and political modernization. Building on the legacy of his predecessor, Miguel de la MADRID, in whose administration Salinas himself played a major role as secretary of budgeting and planning, Salinas sought to engineer a reversal of the growing role of the state in Mexican economic life. His administration sold off hundreds of state-owned enterprises, allowed North American firms to participate in the exploration of oil for the first time since 1938, significantly denationalized the banking industry, and advocated the establishment of a regional free trade block among Mexico, the United States, and Canada, thereby significantly reducing many of Mexico's traditional trade barriers. He continued to renegotiate the debt, while keeping up payments, and implemented policies to attract large amounts of foreign capital. As of 1994, those policies had yet to succeed in bringing economic benefits to the working and lower middle classes, who saw their standard of living decline markedly after 1980.

Salinas's promises of political modernization were not fulfilled. Although some structural reforms were implemented during the 1990 PRI convention, and the government successfully legislated political reform through Congress in 1989, elections were characterized by excessive fraud and poliltical violence. The government pursued a political strategy of co-opting the traditional right, represented by the National Action Party (PAN), and implementing an uncompromising, repressive policy toward the new middle left, represented by Cuauhtémoc CÁRDENAS and the Democratic Revolutionary Party (PRD). This strategy was reflected in the 1989 and 1990 state and local elections, in which the National Action Party won its first gubernatorial race since 1929, but in which the PRD fared badly in every contest. This failure of political reform was a factor in the sudden emergence of a revolutionary peasant movement (the Zapatista Army of National Liberation) in Chiapas at the start of 1994. That uprising, together with a series of political assassinations (including that of the PRI's presidential candidate, Luis Donaldo COLOSIO), dominated the troubled close of the Salinas administration. When economic collapse ensued in December 1994 and Salinas's own brother, Raúl, was implicated in one of the assassinations, Carlos Salinas left Mexico with his reputation in considerable disarray.

Salinas also adopted a controversial policy toward the Catholic church, appointing an official representative to the Vatican, consulting the hierarchy on numerous matters, inviting clergy to his inauguration, and welcoming Pope John Paul II to Mexico in 1990. Human rights organizations, including Americas Watch and Amnesty International, severely criticized his administration for the increase in human rights violations and abuses. In response, the government established a new Human Rights Commission in the summer of 1990, but its impact remains to be seen. On other bilateral fronts, especially in drug eradication, Salinas increased cooperation with the United States and took a hard-nosed approach toward this problem within Mexico.

Human rights organizations, including Americas Watch and Amnesty International, severely criticized the Salinas administration for an increase in human rights violations.

Born in Mexico City, the son of Raúl Salinas Lozano, a former cabinet secretary, and Margarita de Gortari Carvajal, a teacher, Salinas pursued an economics degree at the National University. After graduating in 1971, he earned three degrees from Harvard, two M.A.'s in public administration and political economy, and a Ph.D. in political economy and government (1978). In 1966 he began his political career in the PRI under Gonzalo Martínez Corbalá, but quickly entered the public financial sector on completion of his first master's degree. After serving in several posts in the 1970s, Salinas became director general of social and economic policy under Miguel de la MADRID in the secretariat of planning and budgeting (1979–1981). When de la Madrid was selected as the PRI presidential candidate, he asked Salinas to serve as director of the PRI's Institute of Political, Economic, and Social Studies during the campaign of 1981–1982. He also served as de la Madrid's secretary of budgeting and planning, following in his mentor's footsteps, until his own designation as the PRI candidate for president in 1987. His designation, and the economic policies he represented, helped provoke a split within his party, in which Cuauhtémoc Cárdenas and Porfirio MUÑOZ LEDO bolted the organization to form their own political movement in support of political reforms and more populist economic policies. Another group of reformers, calling themselves the "Critical Current," remained within the party, adopting a new structure in 1990, in hopes of exerting further pressure favoring internal reforms.

— RODERIC AI CAMP

SALNAVE, SYLVAIN

Sylvain Salnave (*b.* 1827; *d.* 15 January 1870), president of Haiti (1867–1869). Sylvain Salnave's presidency was marked by civil unrest that threatened to tear the country apart and tempted foreign powers to intervene, once again, in Haitian affairs. Tensions produced in part by the collapse of cotton exports to the United States contributed to the problems Salnave faced. Yet, Salnave's seizure of power through a military rebellion backed by U.S. and Dominican elements also provoked angry reactions from other Haitian leaders. Salnave faced a general uprising in the countryside as various chieftains from the provinces refused to recognize his regime. This led to a state of chronic civil war in which the country became divided into the northern, southern, and central regions. While Salnave faced opposition from armed peasants in the North, the Cacos, and peasant bands in the South, the *piquets,* most of his support came from the center, especially the capital. Salnave became quite popular among the black urban masses, who appreciated his populist economic policies, including the establishment of state-run food stores where basic goods could be bought at low prices. Because of this black support and despite his status as a mulatto, he has been viewed as a founder of Haiti's National Party, which has claimed to speak for the interests of the ordinary black Haitian.

— PAMELA MURRAY

SALOMON, LOUIS ÉTIENNE LYSIUS FÉLICITÉ

Louis Étienne Lysius Félicité Salomon (*b.* 1820; *d.* 1888), Haitian president (1879–1888) and polemicist. He was born to an elite black landowning family in Les Cayes, and after a brief period in the army, turned while still young to politics. He became known as a *noiriste,* an advocate of black dominance, and an opponent of the mulatto elite.

Salomon served as minister of finance and commerce under Faustin SOULOUQUE (1785–1867) and tried to emphasize state ownership of coffee exports. When Fabre Nicolas GEFFRARD (1806–1878) overthrew Soulouque, Salomon left for Jamaica, and from there he bitterly opposed Geffrard.

After his election to the presidency in 1879, many Liberals were exiled or fled. In 1880 Salomon founded the National Bank with foreign capitalization. Some have argued that he thus opened the way for foreign interference and, perhaps, the nineteen-year U.S. occupation that began in 1915. He gave some state land to the peasantry, but he was permissive toward foreign ownership. He was overthrown by a northern coalition in 1888, and he died soon after in exile.

— MURDO J. MACLEOD

SALVADOR, VICENTE DO

Vicente do Salvador (*b.* 1564; *d.* 1639), Portuguese historian and member of the Franciscan order. At the age of sixty-three he wrote a *History of Brazil* that was more concerned with human events than with Brazilian fauna and flora as had been the case with his sixteenth-century predecessors. The first chapter was still devoted to nature and to Brazil's original inhabitants, but all the others narrated the main events of Portuguese colonization in America from 1500 until 1627. In his dedication to the Portuguese scholar Manuel Severim de Faria, the author wrote that he expected his work to be printed at this patron's expense. However, his *History* remained unpublished until the nineteenth century, and some chapters were lost.

Written in Bahia, Salvador's opus is a general history, rather than a local one. The Franciscan does not reveal his sources, but João Capistrano de Abreu, the nineteenth-century historian, proved that Frei Vicente had read Simão Estácio da Silveira's *Relação sumária das cousas do Maranhão* (1624) and Pero de Magalhaes GANDAVO's *História da Província de Santa Cruz* (1576). Wars against the Indians, the French pirate attacks, and the Dutch invasions are narrated. Military actions of governors-general attract his attention more than the colonists and their agricultural and mercantile activities.

— MARIA BEATRIZ NIZZA DA SILVA

SAM, JEAN VILBRUN GUILLAUME

Jean Vilbrun Guillaume Sam (*d.* 28 July 1915), president of Haiti (March–July 1915). Sam's presidency was marked by mounting chaos and violence that resulted in the occupation of the country by U.S. Marines. While responding to U.S. pressures to arrange a customs receivership similar to the one the Americans had created for the Dominican Republic, Sam spent most of his time fighting his political enemies, who were led by the virulently anti-American Rosalvo BOBO. Sam ordered the execution of 167 prisoners, many of them Bobo's supporters. In retaliation, on 28 July 1915, he was lynched and butchered by a mob in Port-au-Prince. Shortly thereafter, the U.S. Marines occupied Haiti.

– PAMELA MURRAY

SAM, TIRÉSIAS AUGUSTIN SIMON

Tirésias Augustin Simon Sam (dates unknown), president of Haiti (31 March 1896–12 May 1902). Military potentate of his native North, minister of war and marine under the presidency of Lysius SALOMON (1879–1888), Sam had strong ties within the then dominant dark-skinned faction of the oligarchy. He offered the Haitian elites the combination of force and compromise they expected. With limited formal training, he used his contacts to bring competence to the service of government. He encouraged the construction of railroads around Cap Haïtien and Port-au-Prince. Financial scandals, factionalism, and the renewed bullying of Haiti by foreign powers, notably Germany, France, and the United States, distracted him from an already loose agenda. Forced out of power when he tried to prolong his constitutional mandate, he predicted an endless civil war: "I am the last president of Haiti."

– MICHEL-ROLPH TROUILLOT

SAMANEZ OCAMPO, DAVID

David Samanez Ocampo (*b.* 1866; *d.* 1947), landowner, provincial leader of Nicolás de PIÉROLA's Democratic Party, and president of a provisional government in Peru between March and December 1931. Born in Huambo, Samanez Ocampo was elected deputy of the province of Antabamba, Apurímac. In 1909 he rebelled against the first government of Augusto B. LEGUÍA and later supported President Guillermo BILLINGHURST (1912–1914). In political retirement by the time Colonel Luis M. SÁNCHEZ CERRO was forced to resign as de facto president in March 1931, Samanez Ocampo was selected to head a transitional government that held presidential and congressional elections in October 1931. Samanez Ocampo's government partially adopted some of adviser Edwin W. Kemmerer's economic recommendations. Samanez Ocampo retired again from national politics when Sánchez Cerro assumed power after the contested elections of 1931.

– ALFONSO W. QUIROZ

SAMAYOA CHINCHILLA, CARLOS

Carlos Samayoa Chinchilla (*b.* 10 December 1898; *d.* 14 February 1973), Guatemalan writer. A member of the same generation as Miguel Ángel ASTURIAS and Luis CARDOZA Y ARAGÓN, he is especially famous for his nativist short stories collected in *Madre Milpa* (1934).

Samayoa published a book of memoirs about his experience working with the most feared man in the country, El dictador y yo.

Born in Guatemala City, the son of wealthy landowners, Samayoa traveled extensively throughout Europe in the 1920s. Forced to return to his native country after the stock market crash of 1929, he served as a minor bureaucrat in the Jorge UBICO administration (1931–1944). While traveling with the dictator throughout the country, he developed his ideas for *Madre Milpa.* The Ubico dictatorship collapsed in 1944, and Samayoa published a book of memoirs about his experience working with the most feared man in the country, *El dictador y yo* (1945). During the 1940s he was director of the National Library and was active in founding several museums. As the new democratic administration became more liberal, Monterroso became a bitter critic of its progressive tendencies and joined in red-baiting the Arbenz government (1951–1954). In his later years he published books of short stories, but none were as accomplished as his original success. Other books by Samayoa are *Cuatro suertes* (1936); *Estampas de la costa grande* (1954); *El quetzal no es rojo* (1956); and *Chapines de ayer* (1957).

– ARTURO ARIAS

SAMBUCETTI, LUIS (NICOLÁS)

Luis (Nicolás) Sambucetti (*b.* 29 July 1860; *d.* 7 September 1926), Uruguayan composer, conductor, violinist, and teacher. Born in Montevideo, Sambucetti first studied with his father, a musician, and later with Luigi Preti, who instructed him in violin, and José Strigelli, in counterpoint. He enrolled at the National Conservatory in Paris in 1885, where he studied violin with Hubert Léonard, harmony with Théodore Dubois, and composition under Ernest Guiraud, Jules Massenet, and

Léo Delibes for three years. For two years he was the concertmaster of the Chatelet Théâtre Orchestra under the baton of Édouard Colonne. In 1890 he returned to Montevideo, where he founded the Instituto Verdi, one of the major conservatories of Uruguay. He also started three chamber groups: the Cuarteto Sambucetti (1891), a second Cuarteto Sambucetti (1900), and the Sociedad de Conciertos (1911). As founder, organizer, and conductor of the Orquesta Nacional (1908), he introduced to Montevideo the contemporary symphonic repertoire, especially that of the French impressionists.

As a composer Sambucetti is considered the master of early Uruguayan symphonism. Besides his lyric poem, *San Francesco d'Assisi,* winner of a first prize and gold medal at the Milan International Fair Competition (1906), his *Suite d'orchestre*—a symphonic triptych performed at the Teatro Solís on 29 September 1899—has unique shades of orchestral color, particularly in the use of woodwind instruments. It is considered the best Uruguayan symphonic work of the nineteenth century. As a teacher and educator Sambucetti guided a whole generation of Uruguayan composers in the early twentieth century. He also wrote three operettas, orchestral and chamber music, and works for voice and piano and for violin. With his wife, the pianist María Verninck, he translated Reber-Dubois's *Harmony Treatise* and other didactic music books into Spanish. He died in Montevideo.

– SUSANA SALGADO

SAMPER, JOSÉ MARÍA

José María Samper (*b.* 31 March 1828; *d.* 22 July 1888), Colombian writer. Samper came from a mercantile family of Honda, Tolima. He received his law doctorate in Bogotá, in 1846, and plunged into politics. In his early years a Liberal with romantic socialist ideas, he began, after his second marriage (1855), to move toward more traditional political views, culminating in his return to Catholicism in 1865. Samper's abandonment of his earlier principles (added to a difficult personality) resulted in his effective exclusion from major political office until a decade before his death. It also meant that he had to earn a living by writing. His production was enormous. Poetry, drama, essays, editorials, novels, travel accounts, history, and legal treatises flowed from his pen. His autobiography, *Historia de un alma . . . 1834 a 1881* (1881), remains a classic; so does his play *Un alcalde a la antigua y dos primos a la moderna* (1856). His reportage, *El sitio de Cartagena de 1885* (1885), and his *Ensayos sobre las revoluciones políticas de las repúblicas colombianas* (1861) are Colombian literary treasures. Samper represented Colombia in the Neth-

erlands and Belgium (1858–1863) and in Argentina (1884). He also served several terms as a congressman. He died in Anapaima, Cundinamarca.

– J. LEÓN HELGUERA

SAMPER AGUDELO, MIGUEL

Miguel Samper Agudelo (*b.* 24 October 1825; *d.* 16 March 1899), Colombian Liberal economist and politician. Samper's devotion to liberal economic principles distinguishes him as one of Colombia's leading nineteenth-century Liberals. Born to a modest family in Guaduas, Cundinamarca, Samper was trained as a lawyer at San Bartolomé College in Bogotá. He dedicated his energies to business rather than politics and invested profitably in tobacco production and trade in the Magdalena Valley during the 1850s. His brothers, José María, Silvestre, Antonio, and Manuel, were also active in politics and commerce. Samper's liberalism is apparent in his noted social commentary *La miseria en Bogotá* (1867), his fervent support of lower tariff rates (1880), and his staunch opposition to the monetary policies of the Regeneration. Despite his economic beliefs, his social conservatism is evident in his increased devotion to Catholicism later in his life. Samper's political roles included positions in the national congress, minister of finance under two administrations, and the Liberal presidential candidate in 1897.

– DAVID SOWELL

SAMUDIO, JUAN A.

Juan A. Samudio (*b.* 21 April 1879; *d.* 1936), Paraguayan artist. Often considered the finest Paraguayan painter of the twentieth century, Samudio was a native-born Asunceño. Though he received his early education in the capital city, he was irresistibly drawn to painting—an interest that he could little hope to pursue if he stayed in Paraguay. Thanks to a scholarship, he went to Rome in 1903 for five years of study.

In Italy, Samudio developed a painting style characterized by a careful interplay of shadows. He limited himself to traditional subjects and avoided the avant garde, but his work nonetheless received a measure of acclaim. He was already winning prizes while still a student in Rome. In 1910 he exhibited two canvasses at the International Exposition of Art in Buenos Aires. One of these, entitled *Noche de luna,* brought the artist a bronze medal and was later acquired by the National Museum in Asunción.

After his return to Paraguay, Samudio dedicated himself as much to teaching and to artistic theory as to painting. He became director of the Paraguayan Academy of Fine Arts, a position he held throughout the 1920s. He also cooperated with the municipal government of Asunción in the design of public parks and gardens.

— THOMAS L. WHIGHAM

SAN MARTÍN, JOSÉ FRANCISCO DE

José Francisco de San Martín (*b.* 25 February 1778; *d.* 17 August 1850), the liberator of three South American countries who aspired to create the United States of South America. San Martín was born in Yapeyú, in the province of Corrientes, Argentina. His Spanish parents took him to Spain in 1784, where he studied at the Seminary of Nobles in Madrid. In 1789 he joined the Murcia Regiment as a cadet, and later participated in military campaigns in Africa, the Iberian Peninsula, and France. His first combat experience was at Oran (25 June 1791), where he fought the Moors. In 1793 he served under General Ricardos, the tactician who had led his troops across the Pyrenees to attack the French enemies of Louis XVI. At Bailén he fought under General Castaños and later was an aide to the Marquess of Coupigny.

In 1811, San Martín retired from the army without a pension, and although authorized to go to Lima, he sailed instead for London. Before leaving Spain, however, San Martín was initiated into the Caballeros Racionales No. 3, which sought the independence of South America. He later joined a similarly inspired secret organization, the Great American Assembly of Francisco de MIRANDA in London, where he met the Venezuelan Andrés BELLO and the Argentines Manuel Moreno and Tomás Guido. Bello was the teacher of General Simón BOLÍVAR, and Moreno and Guido were the brother and secretary, respectively, of Mariano MORENO, a prominent leader of the independence movement in Buenos Aires. In January 1812, San Martín sailed for Buenos Aires aboard the British frigate *George Canning*, with fellow passengers Carlos de ALVEAR and his young wife, José Zapiola, and Francisco Chilavert.

In Buenos Aires, Alvear introduced San Martín to the most influential members of *porteño* society. The ruling triumvirate recognized his Spanish military grade of lieutenant colonel and asked him to organize the Regimiento de Granaderos a Caballo (Mounted Grenadier Regiment). Alvear was second in command. Its personnel eventually consisted of veteran officers of the revolutionary war, young men drawn from the leading families of the city of Buenos Aires, and the provinces of La Rioja, Córdoba, Banda Oriental del Uruguay, and the Guaraní of Corrientes. San Martín taught them military tactics and the use of different weapons. The grenadiers became a model for other regiments.

On 12 September 1812, with Alvear and his wife, María del Carmen Quintanilla, as witnesses, San Martín married fifteen-year-old María de los Remedios de Escalada de la Quintana, daughter of a wealthy Spanish merchant. On 8 October, he and his regiment participated in the military movement that replaced the existing triumvirate with another. This revolution bolstered the independence movement. Four months later he commanded the troops that repulsed superior Spanish numbers seeking to land at San Lorenzo.

In December 1813, San Martín replaced Manuel BELGRANO as commander of the Expeditionary Force to liberate Upper Peru at Posta de Yatasto. In March 1814 he proposed that the best way to win independence was to take Lima by way of Chile, not Bolivia, believing that a small, well trained army invading Chile from Mendoza would prevail in ending Spanish rule on the continent. At his request Supreme Director Gervasio Antonio de POSADAS appointed him intendant governor of the province of Cuyo (14 August 1814), with an annual salary of 300 pesos and instructions to prepare the defenses of Mendoza against any possible Spanish invasion. San Martín established himself at Plumerillo, outside Mendoza, and took steps to provide smallpox vaccinations for all the inhabitants of Cuyo, to help Chilean émigrés arriving after Rancagua, and to persuade those not in militia units to join one or be called traitors to the fatherland. Among the Chilean émigrés were Bernardo O'HIGGINS and the CARRERA brothers. In February 1815 he declined promotion to major colonel in the Armies of the United Provinces of the Río de la Plata, saying that he expected to withdraw from military service once independence was won, and the order relieving him of his command was revoked at the request of the local *cabildo*.

To support San Martín, the local people freed their slaves on the condition that they enlist in the army. The labor guilds took up voluntary contributions, and women offered their jewels.

In 1816, San Martín informed the Supreme Director that he needed an army of 4,000 to invade Chile, and with the aid of the Cuyo deputies, and especially of Tomás GODOY CRUZ, he obtained from the Tucumán Congress a declaration of the independence of the

United Provinces of South America. On 21 July 1816 he and the new Supreme Director Juan Martín de PUEYRREDÓN met in Córdoba, completing arrangements for the liberation of Chile. Pueyrredón agreed to send him more men, armaments, and supplies, and he appointed San Martín commanding general of the Army of the Andes. The army then took an oath to defend the independence of the United Provinces of South America. San Martín now trained his troops and the local militia in basic military tactics and maneuvers, personally instructed the officers in military subjects, and invited neutral foreigners to join him. One of his students was José María PAZ, later a prominent leader in Argentine civil wars. The local people freed their slaves on the condition that they enlist in the army. They supplied San Martín with provisions and transported military goods without charge. The labor guilds took up voluntary contributions, and women offered their jewels. San Martín levied forced loans on the royalists and extracted extraordinary contributions from wealthy natives. The Army of the Andes made its own armaments, ammunition, guns, gunpowder, saddles, bayonets, cannons, and cannonballs. The provincial women sewed military uniforms without charge.

San Martín was named captain-general so that he could have both military and political authority, but he delegated the political functions to Colonel Toribio Luzuriaga, who was ably assisted by the lieutenant governors of San Juan and San Luis. The commander of the general staff was Brigadier General Miguel Estanislao Soler, and the battalion commanders were Juan Gregorio de LAS HERAS, Rudecindo Alvarado, Pedro Conde, and Ambrosio Crámer. The five squadrons of the Granaderos a Caballo were under Mariano Necochea, and among its officers were Juan LAVALLE, Federico de Brandzen, Manuel Medina y Escalada, and Domingo Arcos. The Patriotic Legion of the South was formed primarily by Chilean émigrés who supported O'Higgins. Another Chilean émigré, José Ignacio Zenteno, was the military secretary.

San Martín inaugurated the so-called *guerra de zapa* by placing spies in the enemy camps, spreading false rumors, sending secret emissaries to collect information throughout Chile, and encouraging uprisings. Field Marshal Francisco Marcó del Pont, in charge of the Chilean government, reacted by increasing political repression and stationing his forces at possible invasion points along the Andes. Replying to his request for military and political guidance, Supreme Director Pueyrredón sent San Martín his instructions on 24 December 1816, setting forth in fifty-nine articles how he was to conduct the war, deal with political parties and governments, and pay all expenses of the expeditionary force.

The sole purpose of the campaign, he emphasized, was to secure American independence and the glory of the United Provinces. San Martín was to avoid favoring any of the political groups dividing Chile, to seek to improve the condition of the people, and to negotiate a perpetual alliance between the two nations.

Once the Army of the Andes was fully organized and trained, San Martín named the Virgin of Carmen del Cuyo as its patron and gave it a flag that his wife and other patriots embroidered. He also provided it with a printing press, which was to spread revolutionary ideas and publish battle bulletins. At San Martín's suggestion Brigadier O'Higgins was to become the temporary governor of Chile once Santiago was free.

The Army of the Andes that moved out of Mendoza on 18–19 January 1817 consisted of 4,000 soldiers, over 1,000 militiamen to transport munitions and a twenty-day supply of provisions, muleteers, and laborers to repair the roads. The Andean passes had been surveyed in advance by the engineer Álvarez Condarco. The bulk of the army, under San Martín, used Los Patos pass to cross the Andes to the valley of Putaendo, in the province of Aconcagua. An army division under General Soler formed the vanguard; O'Higgins commanded the reserve division. A column of 800 men under Las Heras used the Uspallata Pass to Chile. It had the ammunition train, the dismounted artillery, and the arsenal, with workers armed with long poles and ropes so that they could suspend the cannons on litters. Once across the peak of the Andes, they defeated the royalists at Guardia Vieja and took Santa Rosa de los Andes. A northern column under Commandant Cabot, crossing the Andes in fourteen days, defeated the royalists at Salala, and took the province of Coquimbo, while a detachment from La Rioja took Copiapó. A southern column under the Chilean Captain Freyre used the Planchón pass to cross the Andes, defeated the royalists at Vega del Campeo, and entered Talca. All the soldiers were mounted on mules, and moved slowly according to the availability of pasture, water, and wood.

The entire army reached San Felipe, from which it dominated the valley of Aconcagua, and its forward units made contact with the royalists at Chacabuco. The Spanish army of 2,500 under Brigadier Rafael Maroto occupied advantageous positions on the hill of Chacabuco, which blocked the road to Santiago. When his army was assembled, San Martín attacked in two corps: the one on the left, under O'Higgins, was to distract the enemy until the corps on the right, under Soler, could attack the enemy from the rear. O'Higgins advanced without waiting for Soler to complete his maneuver, but reinforced by cavalry troops under Zapiola and Necochea, he was able to destroy the royalist squadrons. The retreating Spaniards were routed by Soler. The patriots captured all the enemy artillery, its ammunition train, and 600 prisoners. The battle of Chacabuco (12 February) marked the beginning of the patriot offensive.

On 14 February, the patriot army entered Santiago. An assembly convoked by San Martín elected him governor of Chile, a position he declined, and it then named O'Higgins. Marcó del Pont and other Spanish leaders were captured and sent to San Luis. On 10 March, the Santiago *cabildo* presented San Martín with 10,000 gold pesos, which he donated for the establishment of the national library. An overjoyed directorate in Buenos Aires rewarded him the title of brigadier general of the Armies of the Fatherland (26 February 1817), which he did not accept. San Martín went to Buenos Aires with his aide, John T. O'Brien, to settle military problems and to obtain the resources needed to organize the expedition to Peru. He entered the city disguised, hoping to avoid a public demonstration, but he was detected, and the *cabildo* honored him on 9 April 1817. San Martín discussed the forthcoming campaign to liberate Peru with Pueyrredón, and then left for Santiago.

On 20 June, O'Higgins appointed San Martín as commanding general of the Chilean army, and on 12 February 1818, he and San Martín proclaimed the independence of Chile. Meanwhile, the Spanish forces under Colonel José ORDÓÑEZ, which had not been involved in any battle, gathered in the plaza of Talcahuano. Las Heras and O'Higgins unsuccessfully attacked the town fortifications. General Mariano Osorio then arrived with 3,000 men, stationing them in the town of Talca. San Martín went to help O'Higgins, and while he was repositioning the troops, he was attacked on 19 March at Cancha Rayada by Ordóñez, and was forced to retreat. Las Heras alone kept his division intact. The patriots regrouped and, 5,000 strong, attacked and defeated the royalists under Osorio at Maipú (5 April). San Martín was compelled to use his reserves in the battle. Osorio and his escort abandoned the battlefield, leaving Ordóñez to negotiate surrender. One thousand Spaniards were killed and 3,000 taken prisoners. Victory established the independence of Chile, and provided for Argentina's security by giving it a base of operations on the Pacific. Argentina and Chile concluded an alliance to liberate Peru, while San Martín asked Great Britain to persuade Spain to grant independence to South America.

With the Spaniards now on the defensive, San Martín left for Buenos Aires to obtain the support needed for invading Peru. On 4 May, Congress congratulated O'Higgins, awarded a prize to San Martín and the army, and authorized a loan of 500,000 pesos to finance the expedition to Peru and the formation of a naval unit. It also ordered the erection of a statue to commemorate Chacabuco and Maipú and recognized the officers and soldiers of the Army of the Andes as "heroic defenders of the nation." San Martín asked Congress to prevent Pueyrredón from promoting him, saying that the army alone deserved praise for the victories. On 14 May, Congress appointed him Brigadier of the Armies of the Fatherland. Three days later Congress celebrated in extraordinary session the victories of Chacabuco and Maipú. After Congress authorized a personal coat of arms for him on 20 October, San Martín left for Santiago de Chile. The Buenos Aires government later informed him that it was unable to fulfill its promise of aid.

San Martín assumed political and military command of the new nation as "protector of a free Peru."

At the end of 1818, Commandant Manuel BLANCO ENCALADA, an Argentine serving Chile, doubled the size of the Chilean navy by capturing first a Spanish frigate in the Bay of Talcahuano and then five Spanish transports with 700 men bound for the city with abundant military supplies. He relinquished command of the fleet to Lord Thomas Alexander Cochrane, who had signed a contract in London with the agents of O'Higgins and San Martín. In January 1819, Cochrane attacked the Spanish fleet in Callao, but he was unable to destroy it. Early in 1820, San Martín refused the request of Director José RONDEAU to concentrate his troops in Buenos Aires in order to fight the caudillos. However, he did send a division to Mendoza and San Juan, but he soon withdrew half of it for his campaign to liberate Peru. San Martín went to Mendoza to recover his health, returning to Chile in a litter in January, still expecting to unite Argentina, Chile, and Peru as one nation. On 20 August 1820 the liberating expedition of 2,300 Argentines and 2,100 Chileans sailed from Valparaiso. Most of the officers were Argentines. The fleet consisted of eight warships and sixteen troop transports with a crew of 1,600 men under Cochrane. The cargo of the transports consisted of rifles, swords, cannons, ammunition, artillery shells, grenades, gunpowder, and horses with their feed. San Martín commanded the expedition as captain-general, and he informed the *cabildo* of Buenos Aires of his departure for Peru.

The royal armies San Martín faced consisted of 23,000 men in Upper and Lower Peru. San Martín disembarked in the port of Paracas and established his headquarters at Pisco. His aim was to avoid battle and to provoke rebellions among the people and desertions in the Spanish troops by spreading revolutionary propaganda. Desertions among Spanish commanders and officers did increase, and an entire battalion surrendered. He moved to Ancón, then to Huaura, and finally to Huamanga, from which he could dominate the valley of Huancayo. He negotiated an armistice of short duration with Viceroy Pezuela at Miraflores (26 September). He assured the success of the expedition when he defeated Brigadier Alejandro O'REILLY at Cerro de Pasco (6 December 1820), and captured both O'Reilly and Mayor Andrés de SANTA CRUZ. On 2 June 1821, San Martín met Viceroy Pezuela at Punchauca and asked him to recognize Peru as a sovereign nation, to approve a junta which would write a temporary constitution, and to join him in naming a commission that would ask Ferdinand VII to select a son to become king of Peru after accepting a constitution. The vacillating viceroy agreed only to another armistice. On 19 July, San Martín entered Lima and called a council of notables, which voted for independence. Peruvian independence was declared on 28 July.

San Martín assumed political and military command of the new nation as "protector of a free Peru." He thus prevented Simón Bolívar from seizing Peru. Then, through his secretary, Dr. Bernardo MONTEAGUDO, he abolished the personal service of the Indians (the tributes, the *mitas*, and *encomiendas*); declared the freedom of the newborn children of slaves; established a free press and the sanctity of the home; and ended torture in judicial proceedings. He fought gambling and maintained security and order in town. On 21 November, Lima awarded 500,000 pesos to the officers and commissioned officers of the liberating army. The reward was distributed by lot among the twenty officers named by San Martín. The officers who were ignored probably participated in the conspiracy that led to the downfall of San Martín.

With the bulk of the royalist army, Canterac was in the valley of Jauja, controlling the sierra and suppressing Indian revolts supporting the revolution. Bolívar sent General Antonio José de SUCRE with a division to liberate Quito Province. This inadequate force sought reinforcements from San Martín, who sent Santa Cruz with 1,000 men. The war ended when the Argentine granaderos under Lavalle destroyed the Spanish cavalry at Riobamba and Sucre and the Argentine Manuel de Olazábal defeated the royalists at Pichincha (24 May 1822). By that time the port of Guayaquil had declared its independence, and Peru wanted to annex it. On 13 July, Bolívar placed the port under the protection of Colombia.

San Martín landed at Guayaquil on 25 July, and held three interviews with Bolívar. What transpired at these meetings is still disputed, but the two men evidently discussed the form of government the new nations should have and the military operations required to end the war. San Martín favored a constitutional monarchy for South America, Bolívar a republic. Both men sought the formation of something like the United States of America, a goal which would be reached by first uniting the former viceroyalties, now republics, in a South American Confederation and then fusing them in a federation, the United States of South America. With too meager a force to end the war alone, San Martín asked for help and reminded Bolívar of the aid he had given to Sucre. Bolívar declined to place a substantial Colombian force under his command, and refused San Martín's offer to serve under him. San Martín returned to Lima, and at the meeting of the Constituent Congress on 20 September 1822 he resigned as Protector. He then sailed for Chile, where he was no longer popular, and crossed the Andes to his small farm in Mendoza. In late 1823 he learned that his ailing wife had died on 3 August.

San Martín enjoyed the support of the federalists and the provincial governors, especially that of Governor Estanislao LÓPEZ of Santa Fe, but Bernardino RIVADAVIA was his enemy. He left for Buenos Aires in November to see Rivadavia, who already had negotiated a preliminary peace treaty with Spain (4 July 1823). On 7 February he sailed with his daughter Mercedes for Le Havre and from there to Southampton, England, finally settling in Brussels. In 1828 San Martín briefly returned to Buenos Aires, but he never landed and instead stayed for two months in Montevideo. He declined an invitation from Juan Lavalle to assume command of the government and army of Buenos Aires. He returned to Brussels. In 1834 the wealthy Spaniard Alejandro Aguado helped San Martín purchase a house in Grand Bourges. In 1838, when France was blockading Buenos Aires, San Martín offered his services to Juan Manuel de ROSAS, who declined. Attacks against him appeared in the Buenos Aires press, but Domingo F. SARMIENTO and later Bartolomé MITRE rose to his defense. He was restored to his former rank of captain-general, and Chile awarded him a lifelong pension in 1842.

San Martín died in Boulogne-sur-Mer. He bequeathed his sword to Rosas. At the suggestion of Sarmiento a statue in his honor was erected in Buenos Aires in 1862. In 1880 his remains were moved from the cemetery in Brunoy to the cathedral in Buenos Aires.

— JOSEPH T. CRISCENTI

SANABRIA MARTÍNEZ, VÍCTOR M.

Víctor M. Sanabria Martínez (*b.* 17 January 1898; *d.* 8 June 1952), archbishop of San José, Costa Rica (1940–1952).

Archbishop Sanabria's advocacy of social justice and his political role in the 1940s make him the most famous, popular, and controversial twentieth-century Costa Rican prelate. He rose from humble beginnings to become a well-educated, "people's" priest who addressed the issues that moved his nation during the tumultuous decade 1940–1950. As the established leader of the Costa Rican church, he committed his institution to the social reforms called for in the papal encyclical *Rerum Novarum*. He studied civil and canon law in Rome and returned to San José with an earned doctorate in canon law.

Sanabria wrote extensively on church history. He also produced a multivolume genealogy of Cartago that elicited almost as much controversy as his social activism because it brought to light so many details that the residents of that patriarchal city wished to maintain in obscurity.

Sanabria was appointed the second archbishop of San José in March 1940, the same year in which his friend Dr. Rafael Ángel CALDERÓN GUARDIA (1940–1944) was inaugurated. These two young leaders shared the deep conviction that their nation needed profound social change based on church teachings in order to ensure social justice and progress. Somewhat the older, Sanabria came to political prominence as a mentor to the president. Together they worked to pass a sweeping program of legislation that culminated in the amendment of the constitution to include social guarantees, such as social security insurance, an eight-hour workday, minimum wage, the right to organize trade unions and to form cooperatives, and the basic right to human dignity.

Sanabria publicly advocated the government's reform program and indirectly sanctioned its political alliance with the Popular Vanguard Party (PVP), a communist party. Sanabria was criticized by conservative Catholics at home, and he was denied entry to Guatemala because of his political orientation. He played an active role in organizing Catholic labor unions to rival those organized by the communists.

Sanabria tried valiantly but in vain to mediate the political crisis following the 1948 election. He helped protect president-elect Otilio ULATE BLANCO (1949–1953) and he participated in the mediations that led to the cessation of the armed conflict.

His active role in a time of change and conflict made Sanabria a towering but controversial personage. His accomplishments were recognized after his death, when he was named Benemérito de la Patria by the national congress in 1959.

– JOHN PATRICK BELL

SÁNCHEZ, FLORENCIO

Florencio Sánchez (*b.* 17 January 1875; *d.* 2 November 1910), Uruguayan playwright. Born in Montevideo and raised in the interior, Sánchez, one of eleven children, left high school to help support his family. He worked as a clerk, wrote theater reviews and articles for small-town newspapers, and acted in amateur plays. He fought with the caudillo Aparicio SARAVIA against President Juan Idiarte Borda, an experience that inspired his work *El caudillaje criminal en Sudamérica* (Criminal Caudillo Rule in South America [1914]). Disillusioned with traditional politics, Sánchez became interested in the anarchist movement; his earliest plays were presented in anarchist recreation centers.

Working for newspapers such as *La República* in Rosario, Argentina, Sánchez attained recognition with his muckraking play *El canillita* (The Newspaperboy), which was performed on 2 October 1904. He lost his job as a result of his anarchist activities. In ill health, he accepted a friend's invitation to spend time in the Argentine countryside. The sojourn inspired Sánchez's famous rural plays *La gringa* (The Immigrant Girl [1904]), *M'hijo el dotor* (My Son the Lawyer [1903]), and *Barranca abajo* (Down the Gully [1905]). He then moved to Buenos Aires, where he worked feverishly on a succession of plays and married, but he continued his bohemian life of much drinking and little sleep.

With a sharp ear for dialogue, Sánchez's plays depicted racial antagonism between the native *criollos* and the immigrants. A social activist, Sánchez used theater as a vehicle to educate the public about poverty and the plight of people in urban tenements. His play, *Nuestros hijos* (Our Children [1907]), influenced progressive legislation enacted in Uruguay. On the verge of bankruptcy and struggling with depression and tuberculosis, Sánchez received a grant from the Uruguayan government to survey Italian theater. He died in Milan shortly after his arrival.

– GEORGETTE MAGASSY DORN

SÁNCHEZ, LUIS ALBERTO

Luis Alberto Sánchez (*b.* 12 October 1900; *d.* 6 February 1994), Peruvian literary historian and politician. Sánchez received doctorates in literature (1922) and law (1925) from the University of San Marcos, where he taught Latin American literature for forty years and served three times as president (1946–1949, 1961–

1963, 1966–1969). After joining the Peruvian Aprista Party in 1931, he was elected to two Constituent Assemblies (1932, 1978–1979), the Chamber of Deputies (1945–1948), the Senate (1963–1968, 1980–1992), and the vice presidency of the Republic (1985–1990), and served as acting president of the country on several occasions from 1985 to 1990. During two decades as a political exile, Sánchez was literary editor of *Ercilla* in Chile and visiting professor in several universities, including Columbia and the Sorbonne. In 1980 he was elected a member of the Peruvian Academy of the Spanish Language and corresponding member of the Spanish Royal Academy. Sánchez, one of the most prolific Peruvian writers of his time, wrote more than sixty books, including *La literatura peruana* (5 vols., 1982), *Historia comparada de las literaturas americanas* (4 vols., 1973–1976), and *Perú: Nuevo retrato de un país adolescente* (Lima, 1981). He died in Lima.

— EUGENIO CHANG-RODRÍGUEZ

SÁNCHEZ, LUIS RAFAEL

Luis Rafael Sánchez (*b.* 1936), Puerto Rican playwright, story writer, essayist, and novelist. Born in Humacao and educated at the University of Puerto Rico (B.A., 1960), Columbia University (M.A., 1963), and the Central University of Mexico (Ph.D., 1966), Sánchez was recognized as a talented young actor and playwright in the late 1950s and early 1960s. He emerged shortly thereafter, the first major voice of a new literary generation, as an equally inventive and critically probing fictional observer of contemporary Puerto Rican life and experience. Beginning with *La espera* (1958; The Wait), *Los ángeles se han fatigado* (1960; The Angels Have Become Weary), *La hiel nuestra de cada día* (1962; Our Daily Bile), and more recently, with *Quíntuples* (1985), he examines the insular and more broadly Hispanic American predicament of a dependent society confronted by an often fraudulent and lethal "modernity" as well as the delusions, poses, moral complicity, and uncertain personas assumed by different participants in a poignant national drama. His most widely celebrated play, *La pasión según Antígona Pérez: Crónica americana en dos actos* (1968), reimagines the classical Greek heroine as a twenty-five-year-old mestiza condemned to death by the dictator of a paradigmatic Latin American republic for her dissenting ideas and identification with "those of us growing up in a harsh America, a bitter America, a captured America" (*La pasión según Antígona Pérez* [1973], p. 14).

Sánchez's first collection of stories, *En cuerpo de camisa* (1966), demonstrates his singularly keen ear and eye for the various inflections and social and psycho-logical textures of island life. He especially captures the furtive, taboo worlds of the delinquent, socially alienated, sexually outcast, misfit, and derelict that are produced by a still-colonial society, its failed social policies, clash of classes, prudishness, crude machismo, and pretentious mimicry. *La guaracha del Macho Camacho* (1976) and *La importancia de llamarse Daniel Santos* (1989), his only published novels to date, confirm their author's analytical acuity, thematic daring, and linguistic and formal virtuosity. Powerful repositories of his characters' universe of meaning and an irrepressible popular ethos, language and music ultimately emerge as organizing metaphors for a miscegenated, culturally syncretic creole sensibility of stubborn ubiquity and resilience, despite both internal and external assault. Empathetic recognition of this defining resilience in the "commuting" experience and shifting spaces of Puerto Rican (im)migrants to (and from) the United States is more evident in his later than in his earlier essays and short fiction.

Sánchez describes "those of us growing up in a harsh America, a bitter America, a captured America."

A member of the faculty of the University of Puerto Rico and the most celebrated Puerto Rican writer of his generation, Sánchez has produced many other works, including the plays *Farsa del amor compradito* (1960), *Sol 13, interior* (1961), and *O casi el alma* (1969); the popular short story "La guagua aérea," (1983) (made into an equally popular film in the early 1990s); *Ventana interior,* an unpublished book of verse; the monograph *Fabulación e ideología en la cuentística de Emilio S. Belaval* (1979); and a collection of selected essays, commentaries, and reviews also entitled *La guagua aérea* (1994).

— ROBERTO MÁRQUEZ

SÁNCHEZ, PRISCILIANO

Prisciliano Sánchez (*b.* 4 January 1783; *d.* 30 December 1826), Mexican federalist leader and first governor of Jalisco. Born in the village of Ahuacatlán, Nueva Galicia province, Sánchez's parents died when he was young. After largely educating himself, Sánchez entered Guadalajara's Conciliary Seminary (1804). He briefly took the Franciscan habit, later studying law. During Hidalgo's revolution (1810), Sánchez served in various municipal positions in Compostela, where he was known to sympathize with the insurgent cause.

After independence Sánchez helped make Jalisco a federalist center. He served in the first Mexican congress (Iturbide period) and in 1823 published his influential Federal Pact (Pacto Federal de Anáhuac). In the Constitutional Congress (1823–1824) and as Jalisco's governor (1826), Sánchez helped frame federalist measures, notably Article 7, which made Catholicism the state religion, and the personal contribution tax.

– STANLEY GREEN

SÁNCHEZ CERRO, LUIS MANUEL

Luis Manuel Sánchez Cerro (*b.* 1889; *d.* 1933), military officer and president of Peru (1930–1931, 1931–1933). The politically ambitious Sánchez Cerro, who was born in Piura, participated in three military uprisings between 1914 and 1931. The first ousted President Guillermo BILLINGHURST. The second, in 1922, was an unsuccessful rebellion against President Augusto LEGUÍA in Cuzco. Imprisoned for his participation, Sánchez Cerro later was allowed to serve in the Ministry of War and to advance his training in Spain. Finally, Lieutenant Colonel Sánchez Cerro led the military putsch that ousted Leguía in August 1930. Opposition within the armed forces, however, forced Sánchez Cerro to resign in March 1931. Back from exile and embracing the support of the fascist Revolutionary Union, he claimed victory after the general elections of October 1931. As constitutional president he unleashed a harsh political and military repression of the opposition Aprista Party led by Víctor Raúl HAYA DE LA TORRE. Aprista members conspired to assassinate Sánchez Cerro, failing in 1932 and succeeding in Lima in 1933.

– ALFONSO W. QUIROZ

SÁNCHEZ DE BUSTAMANTE Y SIRVEN, ANTONIO

Antonio Sánchez de Bustamante y Sirven (*b.* 13 April 1865; *d.* 24 August 1951), Cuban jurist and politician. A professor of international law at the University of Havana, Bustamante achieved widespread prestige and distinction as an orator and the author of numerous scholarly books that were translated into many languages, including Turkish and modern Greek. Upon the inauguration of the Cuban republic in 1902, he was elected to the Cuban Senate, serving several terms. In 1922 he was chosen as one of the first eleven justices who sat on the Permanent Court of International Justice established at The Hague, and in 1929 he was chosen for a second term. His most celebrated contribution to international law, however, was the Code of International Private Law (known as the Bustamante Code),

approved by the Sixth International Conference of American States that met in Havana in 1928 and subsequently ratified by fifteen member states. Accused of supporting the Machado dictatorship (1925–1933), he was exonerated and continued to teach international law until his death.

– JOSÉ W. HERNÁNDEZ

SÁNCHEZ DE LOZADA BUSTAMANTE, GONZALO

Gonzalo Sánchez de Lozada Bustamante (*b.* 1930), president of Bolivia (1993–). Born in La Paz, Sánchez de Lozada studied at the University of Chicago, receiving a bachelor's degree in philosophy in 1951. Wealthy from mining interests, he rapidly established himself as a promising political leader, first as an outspoken leader of the opposition in the Chamber of Deputies, later as president of the Senate, and then as minister of planning and coordination in the PAZ ESTENSSORO government. He was one of the principal architects of that government's economic stabilization and reactivation programs. A strong believer in privatization, his views prevailed, and he received the support necessary to turn the economic system away from state capitalism.

Sánchez de Lozada was chosen as the Nationalist Revolutionary Movement (MNR) candidate for the May 1989 elections and won a small plurality with 23.07 percent of the vote. It was presumed that he would be named president in the congressional runoff, but he and the MNR failed to work out a satisfactory arrangement with the Nationalist Democratic Action (ADN). Bitterly disappointed, he became the outspoken head of the opposition. He charged the government with undermining the New Economic Policy and was critical of the natural gas agreements with Argentina.

Sánchez de Lozada was elected party chief at the MNR's national convention in August 1990, and went on to win the 1993 presidential election.

– EDUARDO A. GAMARRA

SÁNCHEZ DE TAGLE, FRANCISCO MANUEL

Francisco Manuel Sánchez de Tagle (*b.* 11 January 1782; *d.* 17 December 1847), a politician. In 1794 Sánchez, a native of Valladolid, entered the Colegio de San Juan de Letrán in Mexico City. He received a bachelor's degree in philosophy and theology and was appointed to the chair of philosophy in 1803. He was active in politics, becoming *regidor perpetuo* of the Ayuntamiento of Mexico from 1805 to 1812 and from 1815 to 1820. Because of his autonomist leanings, Sánchez became a member of the secret society Los Guadalupes, and he participated in the elections resulting from the Constitution of Cádiz; he was elected constitutional *regidor* in 1813 and in 1820. In 1821 he signed the Declaration of Independence, and he was a member of the Provisional Governing Junta. Sánchez remained active in politics after independence; he was elected deputy on various occasions as well as senator, vice governor of the state of Mexico, governor of the state of Michoacán, and secretary of the Supreme Conservative Power. In addition, he was one of the best-known members of the *escocés* (Scottish rite Masons) party. At his death, he was director of the national pawnbrokerage.

— VIRGINIA GUEDEA

SÁNCHEZ DE THOMPSON, MARÍA

María Sánchez de Thompson (*b.* 1 November 1786; *d.* 23 October 1868), author, social reformer. "Mariquita" Sánchez de Thompson was born in Buenos Aires, the daughter of a prominent local merchant. As a young woman she showed herself to be headstrong and independent, going as far as marrying the man of her choice, Martín J. Thompson y López Cárdenas, over parental objections in 1805. Thompson, a career naval officer, died in 1817, while returning from a diplomatic mission to the United States. A widow with five small children, Mariquita soon remarried (1820); her second husband was the young French consul in Buenos Aires, Jean-Baptiste Washington de Mendeville.

As a young woman Mariquita showed herself to be headstrong and independent, going as far as marrying the man of her choice.

Her position in society secure, Mariquita then formed a salon that served as a meeting place for liberal politicians, poets, and other literary figures such as her friends Bernardino RIVADAVIA, Juan María Gutiérrez, Esteban ECHEVERRÍA, and Juan Bautista ALBERDI. A leading member of *porteño* society, Mariquita took a commanding role in the founding of the Sociedad de Beneficencia, and served as the organization's secretary and president. She pressed for elementary education for girls, founding schools in Buenos Aires and the surrounding towns.

Although her second husband was forced from his diplomatic post by Juan Manuel de ROSAS and returned to France in 1835, Mariquita continued to live in Buenos Aires, serving as a magnet for the defeated *unitarios*. An outspoken foe of her childhood friend Rosas,

Mariquita was alternately forced into exile in Montevideo and allowed to return to Buenos Aires between 1836 and 1852. After Rosas's downfall, Mariquita once again established herself in Buenos Aires, befriending a new generation of reformers, such as Domingo SARMIENTO. She died in Buenos Aires just short of her eighty-second birthday.

Throughout her life Mariquita had been an avid letter writer, and her published letters, *Cartas de Mariquita Sánchez* (1952), provide an interesting view of daily life, politics, and society under Rosas. Her reminiscences of life in preindependence Buenos Aires, *Recuerdos de Buenos Aires virreynal* (1953), give a valuable albeit pointed view of late colonial society.

— SUSAN M. SOCOLOW

SÁNCHEZ HERNÁNDEZ, FIDEL

Fidel Sánchez Hernández (*b.* 1917), president of El Salvador (1967–1972). Born in San Miguel, Sánchez Hernández graduated from the National Military Academy. He was minister of the interior when he was tapped by outgoing president Julio A. RIVERA (1962–1967), to be the candidate of the military-backed National Conciliation Party (PCN) in 1967. Although winning easily nationwide, the PCN won only 41 percent of the votes in San Salvador. As a result, Sánchez Hernández felt pressed to continue the mild reformism of his predecessor, pushing through a rural minimum-wage law.

Falling coffee and cotton prices in 1968 stimulated trade union militancy and the congressional elections brought the opposition parties within two seats of the PCN. However, success in fighting in the 1969 "Football War" with Honduras (a conflict over borders, trade relations, and immigration policy triggered by the actions of unruly fans at two preliminary World Cup soccer matches held in Tegucigalpa and San Salvador in June 1969) restored the popularity of the government.

— ROLAND H. EBEL

SÁNCHEZ MANDULEY, CELIA

Celia Sánchez Manduley (*b.* 1920; *d.* 11 January 1980), Cuban revolutionary and adviser to Fidel CASTRO. A dentist's daughter born in Oriente Province, Celia Sánchez Manduley was a leader of the Twenty-Sixth of July Movement. She helped to organize the shipment of arms and material to the forces fighting against Fulgencio BATISTA in the Sierra Maestra. At El Uvero (a battle fought on 28 May 1957), she became the first woman combatant in the revolutionary army; subsequently she formed the Mariana Granjales Platoon for women. She held the position of secretary of the Council of State, and she was a member of both the Communist Party Central Committee and the National Assembly. Her most influential position was as secretary and lifelong companion to Fidel Castro. After her death from cancer, she was given a state funeral and buried in the Mausoleum of the Revolutionary Armed Forces.

— DANIEL P. DWYER, O.F.M.

SÁNCHEZ VILELLA, ROBERTO

Roberto Sánchez Vilella (*b.* 19 February 1913), governor of Puerto Rico (1965–1969). Born in Ponce, Sánchez Vilella studied civil engineering at Ohio State University, graduating in 1934. He was one of the founders of the Partido Democrático Popular (PDP). From 1940 on, he occupied important posts in the public administration of Puerto Rico. Sánchez became governor in 1965 and interpreted his victory as a mandate for change. Because of his governing style, however, he soon ran into problems with the old guard of the party. Although for personal reasons he announced that he would retire from politics upon completing his term as governor in 1969, he nevertheless sought reelection in 1968. When he was unsuccessful, however, he left the PDP and joined the Partido del Pueblo (PP). Because of the PP's inability to become a registered party, Sánchez failed to be elected a member of the legislature in 1972.

— OSCAR G. PELÁEZ ALMENGOR

SANCHO DE HOZ, PEDRO

Pedro Sancho de Hoz (also Pero; *d.* December 1547), Spanish conquistador, secretary to Francisco PIZARRO, and author (at Pizarro's request) of a valuable account of the first phase of the conquest of Peru. He secured from Emperor Charles V the right to conquer territory south of the Strait of Magellan, which conflicted with the claim to Chile then being made by Pedro de VALDIVIA. At Cuzco, in December 1539, Pizarro persuaded the two men to jointly undertake the conquest of Chile. Sancho de Hoz, frustrated in an effort to assassinate Valdivia in the Atacama Desert, was permitted to remain with the expedition, with the Cuzco agreement rescinded. A plot to seize control of the newly established Chilean colony (1547) was also treated leniently. A third plot, soon thereafter, when Valdivia had left Santiago for Peru, caused Valdivia's lieutenant, Francisco de VILLAGRA, to have Sancho de Hoz beheaded without trial.

— SIMON COLLIER

SANDI, LUIS

Luis Sandi (*b.* 22 February 1905), Mexican composer, music teacher, administrator, and critic. When Carlos CHÁVEZ was appointed director of the National Conservatory in 1929, he named Sandi head of choral activities. Sandi also assisted Chávez in reforming public music education within the department of fine arts of the Ministry of Public Education in 1933. He was later chief music administrator in the Ministry of Public Education (1946–1951) and the National Institute of Fine Arts (1959–1963). His *Yaqui Music* for Mexican orchestra, performed at the Museum of Modern Art in New York in 1940, brought him international attention. Other works include the opera *Carlotta,* about the wife of Emperor Maximilian; the Mayan ballet *Bonampak;* and a number of didactic and critical writings.

— ROBERT L. PARKER

SANDINO, AUGUSTO CÉSAR

Augusto César Sandino (*b.* 18 May 1895; *d.* 21 February 1934), general of guerrilla liberation army and Nicaraguan hero. Sandino was the illegitimate son of Gregorio Sandino, a small businessman, and Margarita Calderón, a coffee picker, in the town of Niquinohomo. From an early age he was exposed to bitter human experiences and poverty. At the age of ten, he witnessed his mother's miscarriage while she was imprisoned for debt. He also toiled in the coffee fields with his mother before returning to live with his father in Niquinohomo in 1906. However, his life was not much better with his father. His half brother Socrates received all the attention and benefits while Augusto worked and ate with the servants. He began to question the fairness of society, life, and God. In school, he learned the principles of capitalism and the meaning of exploitation. His education ended in 1910, when he was forced to work in his father's grain business.

In 1916, Sandino left Nicaragua to work as a mechanic in Costa Rica, then returned three years later to start his own grain business. Despite some success, he had to abandon the enterprise after shooting a man during an argument. Between 1920 and 1923, he worked odd jobs until he found employment as a mechanic with the Southern Pennsylvania Oil Company in Tampico, Mexico. There he acquired an eclectic political and spiritual philosophy and an understanding of social revolution.

POLITICAL THOUGHT AND LIBERAL REVOLT. In Mexico, Sandino absorbed a wide range of political ideologies in the midst of revolutionary change. Anarchism, socialism, and communism competed in the workers' unions in the oil fields of Tampico and Veracruz. Sandino grasped the unconditional opposition of government, church, and capitalist institutions advanced by the anarchists; he learned the importance of strategies of social change from the socialists; and he endorsed the Communists' demand for proletarian revolution. In addition, Sandino immersed himself in theological doctrines that attempted to explain the human relationship to God. Mexican Freemasonry and spiritualism penetrated his thinking by 1926, when he returned to Nicaragua to join the Liberal opposition to the Conservative government. Sandino's expectations upon his arrival on the Atlantic coast, to join the constitutionalist army of General José María MONCADA, are conjecture. Moncada espoused classical liberal values of law, property, and limited government.

At the behest of the U.S. government, Emiliano CHAMORRO yielded the presidency to his Conservative colleague Adolfo DÍAZ at the end of 1926. Concurrently, the Liberals formed a provisional government in Puerto Cabezas. Sandino continued to press Moncada for stronger and faster action. Moncada rejected Sandino's request for arms in their only face-to-face meeting in late December. When U.S. Marines landed at the Pacific coast port of Corinto in January 1927, Sandino decided to go to San Juan del Norte in the northern mountains and establish his own military command.

The Liberal-Conservative conflict continued until May 1927, when U.S. envoy Henry Stimson arranged a truce between Moncada and Díaz. Both agreed that Díaz would serve until the 1928 election. The Liberal troops voluntarily disarmed, and the U.S. Marine Corps took control of the Nicaraguan National Guard on 16 May 1927. Moncada sent a telegram to Sandino, asking him to give up the fight. Sandino responded bluntly: "Now I want you to come and disarm me. . . . You will not make me cede by any other means. I am not for sale. I do not give up. You will have to defeat me" (Ramírez, p. 85).

In September 1927, in the village of El Chipote, Sandino promulgated the Articles of Incorporation of the Defending Army of the National Sovereignty of Nicaragua. The Chilean poet Gabriela Mistral later called Sandino's guerrilla band "the crazy little army." The army launched attacks against the marines and the Conservative government, each time retreating to El Chipote. Gradually, the general achieved a mystical quality in Latin America, the United States, and Europe. The marines constantly searched for El Chipote, often interrogating uncooperative peasants in the dense jungle of Las Segovias. The secret camp was discovered in January 1928 by air reconnaissance. Intense bombings began immediately, and the marines entered El Chipote on 3 February, to find only stuffed "soldiers."

Augusto César Sandino (center). (Archivo General de la Nación, México)

Over the next few years, Sandino rejected compromises with the Liberal government that came to power in 1928. His army achieved many small victories, such as downing a U.S. bomber. Carleton Beals of *The Nation* provided an inside look at Sandino's life for the North American public. However, a review of recent literature does not reveal a consensus on Sandino's political thought and revolutionary intentions. The eclectic mix of socialism, nationalism, and theosophy has created disagreement about Sandino's intelligence and ability to apply abstract ideas to the Nicaraguan reality. He insisted on social justice for workers and peasants, often using deeply philosophical and sometimes confusing language to explain his motivation.

TRUCE AND DEATH. In 1932, political conditions in the United States and Nicaragua changed. Franklin D. Roosevelt succeeded the conservative Herbert Hoover. Roosevelt promulgated the Good Neighbor Policy, which redirected resources away from U.S. political adventures abroad. And Liberal candidate Juan Batista SACASA triumphed over Adolfo Díaz in the 1932 presidential election. Thus, the U.S. Department of State laid the groundwork for the withdrawal of the marines and the installation of the National Guard with Anastasio SOMOZA GARCÍA as chief. One of Sacasa's first actions was to send a peace delegation to San Rafael del Norte, to negotiate a truce with Sandino. On 23 January 1933, an agreement was reached that facilitated the departure of the marines on 1 February. Three weeks later, the Defending Army was disarmed.

From this point Sandino's life took a severe turn for the worse. In June 1933 his wife, Blanca, died giving birth to their daughter; in August the National Guard attacked Sandinistas in Las Segovias, which prompted Sandino to request that President Sacasa declare the Guard unconstitutional. Sacasa invited Sandino to come to Managua in late February 1934. Sandino met with Sacasa and Somoza on the evening of 21 February. Upon leaving the presidential house, apparently satisfied with the result, Sandino, his brother Socrates, and two Sandinista generals were kidnapped by the National Guard. They were murdered in an open field. Sandino's remains have never been found.

– MARK EVERINGHAM

SANDOVAL, JOSÉ LEÓN

José León Sandoval (*b.* 1789, *d.* October 1854), supreme director (chief of state) of Nicaragua (4 April 1845–24 July 1846). A mestizo descendant of the conquistador Gonzalo de Sandoval, Sandoval was a justice of the peace at the close of the colonial period in his native Granada, but he also worked in transporting goods on Lake Nicaragua and the Río San Juan. Resentful of the privileges of Spanish officials and wealthier creoles, Sandoval supported independence from Spain and then opposed Nicaraguan incorporation into ITURBIDE's Mexican Empire. In 1825 he became *jefe político* of Granada and later served in other government positions while rising in military rank.

A fervent unionist, he also served Francisco MORAZÁN's federal government in San Salvador. He was supreme director of Nicaragua during the violent struggles among the caudillos Francisco MALESPÍN, José María Valle, José Trinidad MUÑOZ, and Bernabé Somoza. Although a liberal, Sandoval remained loyal to the elected governments, and under the conservative Fruto CHAMORRO, he directed Granada's defense against the siege begun in May 1854 by Máximo JÉREZ. Brigadier General Sandoval died in this defense and was buried in Granada.

– RALPH LEE WOODWARD, JR.

SANDOVAL VALLARTA, MANUEL

Manuel Sandoval Vallarta (*b.* 11 February 1899; *d.* 18 April 1977), Mexican physicist and educator. A graduate of the Massachusetts Institute of Technology in 1921, Sandoval Vallarta later became a disciple of Albert Einstein and other scientists of that time, as well as a costudent and collaborator of Robert Oppenheimer. He received a Guggenheim fellowship to study in Berlin in 1927–1928 and was an exchange professor at Louvain University, Belgium. He began teaching at MIT in 1926 and left his position in 1943 to return to Mexico, where he became director of the National Polytechnic Institute in 1944 and assistant secretary of education in 1953. An internationally recognized physicist, he produced many students who formed the next generation of important Mexican scientists, including Carlos GRAEF FERNÁNDEZ. The Mexican government selected him as one of the original members of the National College and awarded him its National Prize in Sciences in 1959.

– RODERIC AI CAMP

SANFUENTES ANDONAEGUI, JUAN LUIS

Juan Luis Sanfuentes Andonaegui (*b.* 27 December 1858; *d.* 1930), president of Chile (1915–1920). The younger brother of Enrique Sanfuentes (whom President José Manuel BALMACEDA FERNÁNDEZ had tapped as his successor in 1891), Juan Luis Sanfuentes was a supporter of Balmaceda in the civil war of 1891 and later led the Liberal Democratic Party, which nominally espoused Balmaceda's principles. Sanfuentes held several ministerial posts and was a prominent figure during the "parliamentary republic" period in Chile. His main achievement was to uphold Chile's neutrality in World War I. His administration marked the end of the oligarchic era in Chilean politics.

— SIMON COLLIER

SANGUINETTI, JULIO MARÍA

Julio María Sanguinetti (*b.* 1936), president of Uruguay (1985–1989). Sanguinetti was the first president to be elected following the 1973 coup. A forty-eight-year-old lawyer at the time of his election, he had thirty years of experience in the Colorado Party. He was elected to the Chamber of Deputies in 1962 and reelected in 1966 and 1971. He served as minister of education and culture under President Juan María BORDABERRY in 1972 but resigned in early 1973 in protest over the increasing political role of the military. An erudite speaker and skilled negotiator, Sanguinetti was general secretary of the Colorado Party during the negotiations in 1983 and 1984 that led to the Pact of the Naval Club, which paved the way for the November 1984 elections. Building on the success of his newspaper, *Correo de los Viernes,* Sanguinetti ran a skillful campaign for president, putting several young newcomers on his ticket and making effective use of television. His party received 41 percent of the vote to 35 percent for the Blancos (National Party).

Sanguinetti inherited a country mired in recession and still traumatized by the repression and torture that were the hallmarks of military rule.

Sanguinetti inherited a country mired in recession and still traumatized by the repression and torture that were the hallmarks of military rule. He immediately released the remaining political prisoners and restored all constitutional rights. He made the economist and diplomat Enrique Iglesias his minister of foreign affairs and gave him the leeway to develop an active trade policy. The years 1986 and 1987 were a period of economic recovery but growing political controversy. The stated refusal of the military to participate in any civilian trials concerning human-rights abuses led the government to sponsor and pass an amnesty law. This law was challenged in 1989 by a plebiscite that divided the country. Although the vote ultimately upheld the amnesty for the military, it cost the government much political goodwill.

A stagnant economy in the last two years of his administration and a bitter struggle for the presidential nomination of the Batllist wing of the party, with Jorge Batlle prevailing over Sanguinetti's choice, vice president Enrique Tarigo, led to a Colorado defeat in the November 1989 elections. Sanguinetti, who could not succeed himself, was eligible to run for president in future elections. Head of the Colorado faction known as the Batllist Forum and the major Colorado presidential candidate, Sanguinetti won the election of 1994.

— MARTIN WEINSTEIN

SANTA ANNA, ANTONIO LÓPEZ DE

Antonio López de Santa Anna (*b.* 21 February 1794; *d.* 21 June 1876), president of Mexico (nine times, 1833–1855). Santa Anna was the most important political figure in Mexico between 1821 and 1855. He was in many ways a quintessential caudillo, one of the regional military leaders who played such important roles in nineteenth-century Latin America. With a strong base in the Veracruz region in eastern Mexico, Santa Anna was consistently able to recruit and finance an army, which brought him to national power nine times. He never remained in the capital long, however, and often abdicated his authority soon after gaining executive office, only to return. Over the course of his career, Santa Anna became increasingly conservative. His first ascension to the presidency was as an ostensible federalist, his last as an ostentatious dictator. He was known as an untrustworthy but sometimes necessary political ally and a military tactician with an uncanny knack for survival.

Santa Anna was born in Jalapa, Veracruz, and began his military career in 1810 with the Fixed Infantry Regiment of Veracruz. During most of the War of Independence, he was involved in royalist counterinsurgency. However, in March 1821, the young lieutenant colonel switched sides in support of Agustín de ITURBIDE's plan to achieve independence. Upon Iturbide's victory, Santa Anna was awarded a political-military position in his native region.

Santa Anna, whose relationship with Iturbide quickly soured, was instrumental in overthrowing the infant monarchy in 1823. For the rest of the decade, he played an intermittent role in national politics from his Veracruz stronghold, but it was not until the very end of the decade that the first of several military engagements with foreign troops greatly elevated his national stature.

In 1829 Spanish troops made an ill-fated attempt to reconquer Mexico. Santa Anna's victory against the invasion force at Tampico earned him popular approval and a certain cachet as a nationalist and military strategist. He would capitalize on this reputation often in the following twenty-five years.

Santa Anna gained the presidency for the first time on 1 April 1833, in a coalition with federalists who needed his military support to oust a conservative regime. However, he quickly turned the government over to his vice president, the ardent reformer Valentín GÓMEZ FARÍAS. At this point in his career, Santa Anna's political affiliations turned away from the federalist-liberal camp. Conservative leaders convinced him to oust Gómez Farías, whose proposed reforms were deemed a threat to both the Catholic church and the military. Santa Anna thus began his next presidential term in April 1834 on the opposite end of the political spectrum from his first.

In the last half of the 1830s, Santa Anna's career was almost ended, and then resurrected, by international conflicts. He chose to lead the Mexican army sent to squelch the Texas Revolution. In 1836, after a number of early victories, including the infamous battle at the Alamo, Santa Anna was captured. He conceded Texas independence and then retired in defeat from public life. However, in 1838, French troops invaded Mexico to collect indemnities from the government. Santa Anna lost a leg in battle against the French and was once again proclaimed a hero. His role in national politics resumed when he was declared president in March 1839, and in the early 1840s his now familiar oscillation between power (1841, 1843, 1844) and exile was repeated.

Santa Anna's conduct during the Mexican-American War formed another controversial episode in the general's life. Although in exile when the war broke out in 1846, he managed to slip through a U.S. naval blockade, an act that spurred accusations he had secretly agreed to peace terms with the United States. Once back in Mexico, however, Santa Anna took up arms, was appointed president by the congress in December 1846, and for a time bravely led his troops before experiencing defeat and exile once again.

The war with the United States brought Mexico to the brink of disintegration. The political situation in the late 1840s and early 1850s was more chaotic than ever. Santa Anna was in and out of office in 1847. Finally, in 1853 a fragile conservative coalition formed to bring him back to Mexico, and he was granted extraordinary powers in the hope that he might somehow hold the nation together. From 1853 to 1855, as a military dictator he ruled imperiously, the coalition that had brought him to power disintegrated, and he was forced yet again into exile by the liberal leaders of the Revolution of Ayutla. From 1855 until his death in 1876,

Santa Anna played only a marginal role in Mexican politics.

Santa Anna was known as an untrustworthy but sometimes necessary political ally with an uncanny knack for survival.

What are we to make of the "age of Santa Anna's revolutions"? The traditional view of Mexican history portrays his greed and fickleness as one of the main causes of the nation's instability. However, Santa Anna's role must be placed within the broader context of Mexican society during this era. He was an important military leader at a time when military power was the key to political control in Mexico. His unique asset was his ability to present himself as a necessary ally to extraordinarily different political factions. Ultimately, though, his career was more a symptom of Mexico's deeper political, social, and economic problems than the cause of them.

– RICHARD WARREN

SANTA CRUZ, ANDRÉS DE

Andrés de Santa Cruz (*b.* 30 November 1792; *d.* 25 September 1865), president of Peru (1827), president of Bolivia (1829–1836), and president of the Peru-Bolivia Confederation (1836–1839).

A royalist officer who switched to the patriot side in 1820, Santa Cruz distinguished himself in the Wars of Independence and later became one of the longest lasting and most able presidents of Bolivia. His reorganization of governmental institutions on the Napoleonic model provided the basis for republican government for over a century. However, his attempt in 1836 to reunite Peru and Bolivia engendered a Chilean invasion that led to his downfall in 1839.

The son of a minor Spanish colonial official and the wealthy heiress of an Indian chieftainship, Santa Cruz was born in La Paz to wealth and received a good education in Cuzco, though he left school before graduating. He first joined his father's regiment in 1811, and in 1817 fought against the invading Argentine armies. Taken prisoner the same year, Santa Cruz was sent to a prison close to Buenos Aires but managed to escape and return to Peru. Recaptured in 1820, he decided to become a patriot. In 1822, Santa Cruz distinguished himself in the battle of Pichincha, Ecuador, under Antonio José de SUCRE, achieving the rank of brigadier general in both the Colombian and Peruvian patriot armies.

Despite a victory in Zepita over the Spanish army (for which he was promoted to grand marshal), Santa Cruz was unable to liberate his home territory.

After Peru and Bolivia achieved independence, Santa Cruz briefly became president of Peru in 1827 under the auspices of Simón BOLÍVAR. Voted out in the anti-Bolivarian reactions of 1827, Santa Cruz went to Chile on a diplomatic mission. Wanting to reunite Peru and Bolivia, Santa Cruz was convinced that Antonio José de Sucre should be ousted from the Bolivian presidency because his presence made the reunification impossible. In 1828, in the wake of Agustín GAMARRA's invasion of Bolivia, Sucre resigned and Santa Cruz was elected president. He took power in 1829.

Santa Cruz was a mercantilist and favored domestic industries, particularly textiles, over foreign products. Nevertheless, he developed the port of Cobija on the Pacific coast by building a road and providing import tax relief as a way of achieving sovereignty over this sparsely populated desert region.

Santa Cruz also lowered mining taxes, but this action did not stimulate silver mining sufficiently to provide enough government revenues. In 1830 he resorted to minting debased silver currency as a way of covering the fiscal deficit, thereby setting a pattern that would continue into the 1860s and provide a relatively high indirect tariff that protected domestic production from foreign competition.

Recognizing the lack of government revenue and forever a pragmatist, Santa Cruz formally reinstituted the payment of Indian tribute in return for which the state guaranteed the Indians' possession of community lands for ten years. Although this went against the president's otherwise Bolivarian ideas (Bolívar had abolished tribute payments in 1824 and 1825), Santa Cruz recognized the crucial economic role of the Indian communities' economies and the benefits of a regular and substantial income for the fiscally strapped government.

This legislation also provided resources and a stable home base for his other projects, most notably the reunification of Peru and Bolivia. In 1836, Santa Cruz briefly tried to take advantage of the political chaos in Argentina and attempted unsuccessfully to annex Jujuy to Bolivia. More successful, at least temporarily, were Santa Cruz's expansionist plans toward Peru. In 1835 he moved against the divided Peruvian leadership and was able to defeat his rival, Agustín Gamarra, and by 1836 the Peruvian president, Felipe Santiago SALAVERRY.

Once Santa Cruz had conquered Peru, he reorganized the two states into three units, Northern Peru, Southern Peru, and Bolivia. Each unit elected its own president, and Santa Cruz named himself the confederation's protector. As a result, Santa Cruz dropped his efforts at developing the port of Cobija and encouraged trade between the more easily accessible southern Peruvian ports of Arica and Tacna.

Both Chile and Argentina feared a powerful northern neighbor and did everything in their power to eliminate the confederation. While Argentina was suffering from its own internal problems, Chile actively aided Peruvian dissidents, finally invading the confederation in 1838. In 1839 the Chileans won a major battle outside Lima, and Santa Cruz fled into exile in Ecuador. However, in 1841 pro–Santa Cruz forces overthrew the Bolivian president, General José Miguel de VELASCO, precipitating the invasion of Peruvian General Agustín Gamarra. When it became clear that Gamarra intended to annex parts of Bolivia to Peru, Bolivian forces united under the anti–Santa Cruz General José BALLIVIÁN and, in the battle of Ingaví in 1841, defeated the Peruvian army and killed the Peruvian leader. As a result, Santa Cruz was prevented from returning to Bolivia. More important, the battle of Ingaví signaled the end of overt Peruvian and Bolivian intervention into each other's affairs and the end of Bolivia's dominance as a regional power. Santa Cruz was exiled for life and died in Nantes, France.

— ERICK D. LANGER

SANTA CRUZ PACHACUTI YAMQUI SALCAMAYGUA, JOAN DE

Joan de Santa Cruz Pachacuti Yamqui Salcamaygua, writer. Not much is known about the life of Santa Cruz Pachacuti other than that he lived in the first part of the seventeenth century in the region between Cuzco and Lake Titicaca in Peru. But his importance grows day by day because of the information contained in his work *Relación de la antigüedades de este reyno del Pirú* (1613; An Account of the Antiquities of Peru), one of

---

Santa Cruz Pachacuti attempts to explain his native religion in the framework of the Christianity brought by the Spaniards.

---

the most interesting views of the Inca world. The text includes several drawings that have served as clues to the interpretation of the Quechua cosmological view of the world. At the time, Spanish culture, which emphasized writing as its privileged system of recording and as the mark of civilization, coexisted with Quechua culture, based on oral and visual systems of signification.

Santa Cruz Pachacuti attempts to explain his native religion in the framework of the Christianity brought by the Spaniards, and in doing so he discovers that language is limited and must employ visual images. From this tension emerges the force of the *Relación*. Together with the works of El Inca GARCILASO DE LA VEGA and Felipe GUAMÁN POMA DE AYALA, that of Santa Cruz Pachacuti is one of the most important indigenous sources of Inca society as well as of the conflicts of acculturation during the colonial period in the Andean region.

– LEONARDO GARCÍA PABÓN

SANTA CRUZ Y ESPEJO, FRANCISCO JAVIER EUGENIO DE

Francisco Javier Eugenio de Santa Cruz y Espejo (*b*. 21 February 1747; *d*. 27 December 1795), Ecuadorian writer. Born in Quito to a Quechua father and a mulatto mother, Espejo rose from humble origins to become one of Ecuador's leading intellects. Although mostly self-taught through first-hand observation at a women's hospital, he received the degree of doctor of medicine in July 1767 from the Colegio de San Fernando, and later obtained degrees in civil and canon law.

Espejo became most widely known for his diverse writings on economics, medicine, pedagogy, politics, sociology, and theology. In a frequently satirical tone he criticized the clergy and Ecuador's backwardness. His most famous works are *El nuevo Luciano o despertador de ingenios* (1779), which aimed at educational reform, and *Reflexiones . . . acerca de un método seguro para preservar a los pueblos de las viruelas* (1785), which proposed ways to prevent smallpox and received international recognition.

In 1788 Espejo successfully defended himself in Bogotá against charges of having written and circulated *El retrato de Golilla,* which ridiculed both Charles III and José de GÁLVEZ, minister of the Indies. While in Bogotá, Espejo met such New Granadan firebrands as Antonio NARIÑO and Francisco Antonio Zea, who radicalized his thought. Upon returning to Quito, he helped establish the Sociedad Patriótica de Amigos del País de Quito on 30 November 1791. He also edited the society's newspaper, Ecuador's first, the short-lived *Primicias de la Cultura de Quito* in 1792. At the same time he became director of Ecuador's first public library and was founder of the National Library.

Espejo was tried and imprisoned on charges of sedition in January 1795. He became ill while in jail and died shortly after being released.

– PHILIPPE L. SEILER

SANTA MARÍA, ANDRÉS DE

Andrés de Santa María (*b*. 10 December 1860; *d*. 29 April 1945), Colombian artist. Born to a wealthy family that left Colombia for Europe during the civil war of 1862, Santa María spent most of his life in Europe. In 1882 he studied at the École des Beaux Arts in Paris and in 1887 his work *Seine Laundresses* was exhibited at the Salon des Artistes Français and the Salon des Tuileries. He returned to Bogotá in 1893 and was appointed professor of landscape painting at the School of Fine Arts the following year. He went back to Europe in 1901, but returned to Colombia in 1904 and was appointed director of the School of Fine Arts. He generally painted landscapes and scenes of daily life in an impressionist style. His work was shown at the School of Fine Arts, the Teatro Colón (1906), and the Exposición del Centenario (1910). Criticism of his work at the School of Fine Arts prompted his return to Brussels, where he lived for the rest of his life.

His paintings were shown in Paris, Brussels, and Bogotá. In 1923 the French government made him a chevalier of the Legion of Honor and in 1930 he was named academic correspondent of the Academy of San Fernando in Madrid. His later work had richer colors as well as chiaroscuro. Santa María had retrospective exhibitions in Bogotá (1931), Brussels (1936), and London (1937). In 1971 the Museum of Modern Art in Bogotá honored him with a posthumous exhibition of 126 works.

– BÉLGICA RODRÍGUEZ

SANTA MARÍA GONZÁLEZ, DOMINGO

Domingo Santa María González (*b*. 4 August 1825; *d*. 18 July 1889), president of Chile (1881–1886). The early political activities of this attorney, professor, and civil servant twice forced him into exile. Following his second return to Chile in 1862, he served numerous terms in both houses of the legislature and as a justice of the Supreme Court, a cabinet minister, and a diplomat. Elected president in 1881, he led the nation to triumph over Peru and Bolivia in the War of the Pacific.

Apparently a haughty, if not arrogant, man, Santa María launched his own *Kulturkampf,* forcing the legislature to remove the cemeteries from the control of the Roman Catholic church, make marriage a civil contract, and have the state—not the church—keep the civil registry. Violently anticlerical, Santa María supposedly improved the political environment by limiting the power of provincial officials, increasing individual freedoms, and extending suffrage by ceasing to demand that voters possess property. Paradoxically, he shamelessly manipulated the 1882 congressional and 1886 presidential elections.

Ending the War of the Pacific constituted Santa María's greatest achievement. Chile had to withstand pressure from the United States to abandon its demands for territorial concessions and wage a prolonged guerrilla war before forcing Peru to cede to Chile the province of Tarapacá. The following year, in 1884, Bolivia agreed to an armistice.

Santa María concluded his term by pacifying the Araucanian Indians in the south. By 1886, when he left office, Chile had increased its size by approximately a third, controlled the world's supply of nitrates, and dominated the Southern Hemisphere's Pacific coast.

– WILLIAM F. SATER

SANTAMARÍA, HAYDÉE

Haydée Santamaría (*b.* 1927; *d.* 26 July 1980), Cuban revolutionary and cultural director. Haydée Santamaría was one of two women who participated in the 1953 attack on Cuba's Moncada army barracks in Santiago. Arrested and imprisoned, she was released on 20 February 1954. She met with Fidel CASTRO in Mexico, and then returned to Cuba to organize resistance to the BATISTA government in Santiago. Santamaría was a founding member of the national directorate of the Twenty-sixth of July Movement. She was a member of the Central Committee of the Cuban Communist Party, and the director of the Casa de las Américas, an institution for the study of popular culture. Santamaría was married to Minister of Education Armando Hart. She died from a self-inflicted gunshot wound.

– DANIEL P. DWYER, O.F.M.

SANTANA, PEDRO

Pedro Santana (*b.* 29 June 1801; *d.* 14 June 1864), cattle rancher, general, and president of the Dominican Republic (1844–1848, 1853–1856, and 1857–1861). Santana was a wealthy landowner from the eastern part of Hispaniola known as El Seibo, where he organized the armed forces at the time of the Dominican Republic's declaration of independence from Haiti on 27 February 1844. Heading the victorious Dominican troops during the battle of 19 March 1844 at Azua, he emerged as one of the heroes of the war of liberation against Haiti as well as the commander in chief of the liberation forces.

After becoming the first president of the Dominican Republic, Santana ruled as a caudillo with an iron hand, suppressing all opposition and exiling many of his former associates, including the "father of the Dominican

Republic," Juan Pablo DUARTE. Santana executed many Dominican patriots, including María Trinidad Sánchez, who had sewn the first Dominican flag; the brothers José Joaquín and Gabiño Puello, who had distinguished themselves in the war against Haiti; General Antonio Duvergé, victor of many battles against the Haitians; and the national hero, Francisco del Rosario Sánchez, who along with Duarte and Ramón Matias MELLA is regarded as one of the three founding fathers of the Dominican Republic.

Throughout his terms as president, Santana faced Haitian invasions that were organized by the Haitian ruler Faustin SOULOUQUE. In the battles of Santomé (1845), Las Carreras (1845), Cambronal (1855), and Sabana Larga (1856), Santana nullified all Haitian attempts to reconquer the Dominican Republic. However, the frequent Haitian incursions convinced Santana that his country should be annexed by a larger nation. His efforts to persuade France or the United States to annex the Dominican Republic proved futile.

In 1861, Santana made arrangements with the government of Queen Isabel II for the reannexation of the Dominican Republic by Spain and was rewarded with the title of Marqués de Las Carreras. The majority of Dominicans opposed the renewal of Spanish control and fought the successful War of Restoration (1863–1865) against Spain. By the time Santana died at Santo Domingo in 1864, he was no longer regarded by most Dominicans as the hero of the fight against Haiti but as the traitor in the War of Restoration against Spain. His reburial in the Pantheon of Dominican Heroes by order of President Joaquín Balaguer stirred up the controversy over Santana's ambivalent role in the history of his country.

– KAI P. SCHOENHALS

SANTANDER, FRANCISCO DE PAULA

Francisco de Paula Santander (*b.* 2 April 1792; *d.* 6 May 1840), vice president of Gran Colombia and later president of New Granada. Born at Cúcuta, on the New Granada-Venezuela border, to a locally prominent family of cacao planters, Santander was sent at age thirteen to Bogotá to complete his education. He studied for a law degree, but after the independence movement began, he enlisted in the armed forces of the revolution without completing his studies.

In the civil warfare that soon broke out between centralists in Bogotá and the federalist United Provinces of New Granada, Santander, a junior officer, sided with the latter and in 1813 joined the patriot army defending northeastern New Granada against the royalists. Victory alternated with defeat until the patriots suffered a crushing setback at the battle of Cachirí in February 1816. Santander was among the survivors who made their way to relative safety on the eastern llanos, the lowland plains stretching from the foothills of the Andes to the Orinoco Basin.

Santander helped defend the llanos against royalist incursions, ultimately winning promotion to general. It was also in the llanos that he first displayed his talents as an administrator by organizing the province of Casanare as a base of patriot resistance. His success in this effort was one reason Simón BOLÍVAR decided in 1819 to strike westward from the llanos of Venezuela into the heart of New Granada. He picked Santander to lead the vanguard of his army as he invaded the Andean highlands and won the decisive battle of Boyacá on 7 August.

Although Santander played an important part in that victory, Boyacá was the last battle he fought, for Bolívar placed him in charge of organizing all the liberated ter-

Portrait of Francisco de Paula Santander. Oil on canvas by José María Espinosa, 1853. (Museo Nacional de Colombia)

ritories of New Granada. Santander put government on a sound footing and raised troops and supplies for the armies still fighting. When, in 1821, Gran Colombia was formally constituted by the Congress of Cúcuta, Santander was elected vice president. Since the president, Bolívar, was still leading the military struggle against Spain, Santander became acting chief executive and as such again provided an effective administrator. He also endeavored to implement the liberal reforms adopted by the Congress of Cúcuta and subsequent legislatures, which ranged from a free-birth law to tax reforms and various measures curbing the traditional wealth and power of the church.

The government of Santander faced growing disaffection especially in Venezuela, which resented subordination to authorities in Bogotá. These feelings came to a head with the revolt of José Antonio PÁEZ in 1826, just as Bolívar prepared to return home from Peru. Santander was disappointed when Bolívar proceeded to pardon Páez and to work towards revamping the new nation's institutions as a way of preventing future upheavals. Bolívar wanted a moratorium on liberal reform and strengthening of the national executive, policies that, combined with personal and factional rivalry, produced an open split with Santander. Following an unsuccessful attempt at constitutional reform, Bolívar assumed dictatorial powers and stripped Santander of the vice presidency. When liberal supporters of the latter attempted to assassinate Bolívar in September 1828, Santander himself was charged with complicity. Although the charge was never substantiated, the former vice president was exiled.

From 1829 to 1832 Santander traveled in Europe and the United States. He was still in exile at the final breakup of Gran Colombia and the reorganization of its central core as the Republic of New Granada. He returned in 1832 to become the first elected president of New Granada, a position he held until 1837. Once again exercising his administrative talents, he consolidated public order and even produced a balanced budget. Now more cautious than before, he did not push for sweeping reforms, although he did work hard to expand public education.

Santander was succeeded as president by José Ignacio de MÁRQUEZ, a one-time collaborator of Santander who had forged an alliance with his main political adversaries, the former supporters of Bolívar. As ex-president, Santander won election to the Chamber of Representatives, where he was a leader of congressional opposition to Márquez until his death in 1840.

Santander has been revered as "Man of Laws" and "Civil Founder of the Republic" in token of his lasting commitment to constitutional government. He received special honor from members of Colombia's Liberal Party, whose principal founders had been among his strongest supporters. Proclerical conservatives were less enthusiastic, and in recent years they have been joined by new detractors on the left who depict Santander as a spokesman for creole oligarchs and friend to the United States. Nevertheless, among the founders of the Colombian nation he has no close rival apart from Bolívar himself.

– DAVID BUSHNELL

SANTORO, CLAUDIO

Claudio Santoro (*b.* 23 November 1919; *d.* 27 March 1989), Brazilian composer, conductor, violinist, and teacher. Santoro studied composition with Hans Joachim KOELLREUTTER, a pupil of Paul Hindemith. Through his studies with Koellreutter, he was introduced to serial compositional techniques, which, according to Santoro, were the most significant single influence on the works he produced between 1939–1947. His *Impressions of a Steel Mill* (1943), an orchestral composition, won a competition sponsored by the Orquestra Sinfônica Brasileira, and his First String Quartet won the Chamber Music Guild Award, Washington, D.C.

From 1950 to 1960 Santoro focused on national subjects for his compositions. The period after 1960 represents a return to serialism and the beginnings of electro-acoustical writing. In 1962 Santoro became director of the department of music of the University of Brasília, a post he held until 1964, when political changes in the government resulted in resignations at the university. Following his departure from Brasília, Santoro went to Germany, where he did research in Heidelberg on electronic music and experiments in aleatoric sketches combining painting and aleatoric sound.

Santoro returned to Brazil in 1978 as professor of composition at the University of Brasília. He founded the Orquestra Sinfônica do Teatro Nacional and worked tirelessly to establish a national center for theater. Santoro's final Symphony no. 14, first performed eight months after his death, is one of his best works.

– DAVID P. APPLEBY

SANTOS, EDUARDO

Eduardo Santos (*b.* 28 August 1888; *d.* 27 March 1974), president of Colombia (1938–1942). A lawyer by training, Santos entered Liberal politics through journalism; in the 1920s he built Bogotá's *El Tiempo,* which he owned and directed, into one of the continent's most important newspapers and a force in the

Liberal Party. In 1938 he succeeded Alfonso LÓPEZ PUMAREJO in the presidency, abandoning his predecessor's vocal reformism but laying the institutional basis for much of Colombia's modern economic structure. The Industrial Development Institute, the Municipal Development Institute, and the Territorial Credit Institute, among others, were created during his regime. Santos was among the most pro–United States leaders of Latin America, for which he was attacked by the pro-Axis Conservative leader Laureano GÓMEZ. During his administration the Conservatives returned to Congress after four years' absence, and political life was relatively normal. Santos's battles to publish *El Tiempo* during the military regime of the mid-1950s attracted world attention.

– RICHARD J. STOLLER

SANTOS, MARQUESA DE

Marquesa de Santos (Domitila de Castro Canto e Melo; *b.* March 1797; *d.* 13 November 1867), Emperor Pedro I's Brazilian mistress. Domitila was Pedro I's lover from 1822 to 1831. She was one of many Castro women who were chosen to be the mistresses of PEDRO I of Castile and PEDRO II of Portugal. A striking beauty with ivory skin and dark hair, the marquesa was married at age fourteen. She bore three children during her first marriage. Unknown to her spouse, they were actually Pedro's. Eventually, her deranged and jealous husband drove her out of their home. Pedro I arranged an ecclesiastical divorce for his lover. Domitila and the emperor had four children during this often stormy love affair. After Pedro left Brazil, the marquesa married for a second time. She was one of the richest women in Brazil when she died, leaving a fortune of over 1 million *milréis,* the equivalent of $1 million U.S.

– EUL-SOO PANG

SANTOS, SÍLVIO

Sílvio Santos (Senhor Abravanel; *b.* 1931), Brazilian television variety show host, network owner, and 1989 presidential candidate, represents one of the major rags-to-riches stories of Brazil. He started as a street peddler (*camelô*) and developed a Sunday afternoon television variety show that is still one of the most popular in Brazil, featuring games, amateur performances, music, and sensational interviews, such as an adaptation of *Queen for a Day,* in which poor women vie to tell the most pathetic life story. In 1976, he purchased TV Record (São Paulo), and in 1978, TV Rio. In 1981, Santos was awarded four licenses for Rio de Janeiro, São Paulo, Belém, and Pôrto Alegre that belonged to TV Tupi, the earliest Brazilian network, which had gone bankrupt. Within two years, his SBT/TVS network had twenty-one affiliates and roughly 25 percent of the audience, ranking second after TV Globo, which often had 60–80 percent of the audience. The network followed the pattern of Santos's own programs, emphasizing four or five live variety shows, lowbrow comedies, imported series and films from the United States, and *telenovelas* and comedies from Mexico. Santos's programming aimed at a "popular" (lower-middle-class to lower-class) audience and was very successful. He briefly tried to compete for a broader audience with more news and his own *telenovelas,* but returned to "popular" programming. In 1989, after creating an empire of over forty businesses, including some in agriculture, real estate, and sales, Santos made a late entry into the 1989 Brazilian presidential race. His personal popularity put him high in polls, but the party that nominated him was found to be improperly registered and his candidacy was quickly canceled.

– JOSEPH STRAUBHAAR

SANTOS-DUMONT, ALBERTO

Alberto Santos-Dumont (*b.* 20 July 1873; *d.* 23 July 1932), pioneer aviator, inventor, and engineer. Known internationally as the "father of aviation," Santos-Dumont was born on his family's coffee plantation in Palmira (now Santos Dumont), Minas Gerais, Brazil. His engineer father encouraged the young man's passion for mechanics and interest in flying machines, and supported his move in 1891 to Paris, where Santos-Dumont joined an international coterie of aviators experimenting with all manner of aircraft.

During the next three decades Santos-Dumont won international renown for his achievements. He was the first person to turn the internal combustion engine to practical use for aviation (1897). In 1901, flying a dirigible of his own design, he won the coveted Deutsch Prize for being the first to navigate a set-time course, from Saint-Cloud, around the Eiffel Tower, and back. He subsequently turned his attention to the development of heavier-than-air machines and in 1906 piloted his *14-Bis* to claim the Archdeacon Award. The European press proclaimed him the first man to conquer the air, a title immediately disputed by the Wright Brothers, who were conducting their experiments in secrecy in North Carolina. Santos-Dumont, who believed that his designs belonged to the world, began work on a new model. In 1908 he constructed a waterplane, the *Santos Dumont 18,* that is regarded as the precursor of the hydroplane. His *Demoiselle,* completed in 1909, became the world's first successful monoplane, the prototype of the modern airplane.

Santos-Dumont's interests and inventions were broad. He designed the model from which the French jeweler Cartier constructed the first wristwatch, and he wrote three books: *A Conquista do ar* (1901), *Os meus baloẽs* (1903), and *O que eu vi o que nós veremos* (1918). At the outbreak of World War I, he denounced the employment of aircraft for the purposes of war. The Allied governments accused him of espionage, and the French government stripped him of the Legion of Honor it had awarded him in 1909. In poor health, he

Alberto Santos-Dumont with an electric car and a dirigible balloon, two of his creations. (Iconographia)

returned to São Paulo in 1928. During the 1932 Constitutional Revolt, the federal government of Brazil sent planes to bomb the city of São Paulo. Horrified that bombs were being dropped by Brazilians on their fellow countrymen, Santos-Dumont committed suicide.

– FRANCESCA MILLER

SÃO VICENTE, JOSÉ ANTÔNIO PIMENTA BUENO, MARQUÊS DE

José Antônio Pimenta Bueno, Marquês de São Vicente (*b.* 4 December 1803; *d.* 19 February 1878), Brazilian jurist and statesman. Born in São Paulo, São Vicente earned a doctorate from the São Paulo faculty of law and went on to judicial appointments in that province. He represented São Paulo in the Chamber of Deputies (after 1845), the Senate (after 1853), and served on the Council of State (after 1859). There, with José Tomás Nabuco de Araújo (1813–1878), he shared the task imposed by PEDRO II of researching and writing (1866–1868) a legislative project to effect the gradual abolition of slavery. His political career included portfolios for foreign affairs and justice in the Liberal cabinets of 1847 and 1848 and the provincial presidencies of Mato Grosso (1836) and Rio Grande do Sul (1850); he also dabbled in Paraguayan diplomacy in the 1840s. His most important position, however, was as prime minister of a moderate Conservative cabinet in 1870, when he tried, and failed, to marshal the political support for the abolitionist legislation he had helped author in the Council of State; it was the Visconde do RIO BRANCO (1819–1880), a consummate politician, who realized the project instead in 1871. São Vicente's greatest legacy is his widely read discussion of the monarchy's charter: *Direito publico brazileiro e analyse da Constituição do Império* (1857).

– JEFFREY D. NEEDELL

SARAIVA, JOSÉ ANTÔNIO

José Antônio Saraiva (*b.* 1 March 1823; *d.* 23 July 1895), prime minister of Brazil (1880–1882, 1885). After beginning his political career in the judiciary and the provincial legislature of his native Bahia, Saraiva quickly rose to national prominence in the Liberal Party. Between 1850 and 1858 he served as president of the provinces of Piauí, Alagoas, São Paulo, and Pernambuco. In the first of these he ordered the construction of a new capital city, Teresina. In the same years he won election to the national Chamber of Deputies. His success continued in the Congress; in 1857 and in 1865 he held cabinet posts in Liberal ministries.

Saraiva's greatest fame came during his tenure as prime minister. Showing tremendous political skills, he oversaw the passage of important reform laws in both of his administrations. In 1880 he proposed an electoral reform bill that became known as the Saraiva Law after its passage the following year. By mandating direct elections for the two houses of Congress and easing income criteria for voters, this law ostensibly expanded suffrage. Its provisions dealing with how voters were to prove their qualifications were, however, restrictive. In practice, the law ensured that the wealthy and politically powerful would retain control of Brazil's electoral politics.

When Saraiva became prime minister in 1885, after the fall of the Manuel DANTAS regime, he once more proposed a key reform bill. This bill was a more conservative version of Dantas's proposal to free all slaves over sixty years of age and to increase the effectiveness of the system of buying slaves' emancipation. In Saraiva's legislation, only slaves aged sixty-five or over would receive freedom immediately; those between sixty and sixty-five would have to continue in their masters' service for up to three more years. By making such concessions to slaveholding interests, Saraiva managed to have his bill passed by the Chamber of Deputies. In the partisan confusion that this reform provoked, approval by the Senate seemed in doubt. In response, Saraiva dissolved his cabinet, thus clearing the way for the Conservative Cotegipe ministry to achieve final passage of the bill, now known as the Saraiva–Cotegipe Law (Sexagenarian Law), in the Senate.

After the advent of the republic in 1889, Saraiva withdrew from politics for two years. He was elected to the new regime's first Senate in 1891, but soon resigned from office.

– ROGER A. KITTLESON

SARAVIA, APARICIO

Aparicio Saravia (*b.* 1856; *d.* 1 September 1904), leader of the last of Uruguay's many uprisings of mounted insurgents. Born near Santa Clara de Olimar in northern Uruguay, the son of a Brazilian-born landowner, Saravia was not a member of the country's traditional ruling groups. Most Brazilian-born landowning families in northern Uruguay maintained social and political contacts in Brazil, which explains the Saravias' involvement in the Brazilian civil war of 1893–1895. Aparicio's oldest brother, Gumercindo Saravia, rose to the rank of general during the fighting, and Aparicio won fame leading the charges of his brother's horsemen. At Gumercindo's death in 1894, Aparicio inherited his army. Meanwhile, the Blancos (National Party) of Uruguay had begun to reorganize after many years of proscription. When Saravia returned from the Brazilian war with the rank of general, many young Blancos saw in him the leader they awaited. An "armed demonstration" led by Saravia in 1896 galvanized Blancos all over the country to rebel in 1897, and Saravia was acclaimed the party's new caudillo. Unable to subdue them, the government made some power-sharing concessions to the Blancos, and Saravia emerged from the war a symbol of Blanco unity and pride. Within a few years, the Colorado government tried to withdraw the concessions, and Saravia mobilized the Blanco militia again in 1903 and 1904. Though bloodier and on a larger scale, this second period of fighting might have resulted in another standoff if not for Saravia's death in Masoller.

— JOHN CHARLES CHASTEEN

SARDÁ, JOSÉ

José Sardá (*d*. 22 October 1834), Colombian military officer and conspirator. Born in Catalonia (or possibly Navarra), José Sardá fought in the Napoleonic wars in Europe and later joined the 1817 expedition of Francisco Javier MINA in the fight for Mexican independence. Escaping from capture, he eventually joined the patriots in Gran Colombia, where he was a strong supporter of Simón BOLÍVAR and of the short dictatorship of Rafael URDANETA. With the latter's fall in 1831, liberal supporters of Francisco de Paula SANTANDER purged Sardá from the army. After Santander became president of New Granada in 1832, Sardá and other malcontents turned to plotting against him, but they were discovered and Sardá, along with other ringleaders, was condemned to death. He again escaped but was tracked down and killed by loyal officers, whose alleged "assassination" of Sardá gave rise to bitter criticism of Santander.

— DAVID BUSHNELL

SARDANETA Y LLORENTE, JOSÉ MARIANO DE

José Mariano de Sardaneta y Llorente (Second Marqués de San Juan de Rayas; *b*. 1761; *d*. 1835), a politician. Sardaneta was a rich miner and landowner from Guanajuato, who served as *regidor* (alderman), magistrate, and administrator in Guanajuato, as well as administrator of mining in Mexico City. In 1808 he favored the establishment of a governing junta in New Spain. After the coup d'état of that year, Sardaneta, who was a friend of the deposed viceroy José de ITURRIGARAY, tried to vindicate him. A well-known autonomist, he was denounced in 1809 as disaffected with the colonial re-

gime, but nothing was proved against him. In 1811 he was accused of corresponding with the insurgent leader Ignacio ALLENDE, and he was listed as an accomplice of the conspiracy in April of that year. As a member of the secret society of Los Guadalupes, Sardaneta corresponded with José María MORELOS and with Carlos María de BUSTAMANTE and participated in the arrangements to buy a printing press for Morelos. In 1813 he was elected to the Cortes, although he did not occupy his seat. That same year he voted for Morelos as generalísimo in the insurgent elections. Imprisoned by the authorities in February 1816, Sardaneta was sentenced to be deported to Spain, but after reaching Veracruz, he was able to remain. He was one of the signers of the Declaration of Independence in 1821 and a member of the Provisional Governing Junta. He was elected to the Constituent Congress in 1822, and became a member of the Junta Nacional Instituyente during 1822 and 1823. Sardaneta died in Guanajuato.

— VIRGINIA GUEDEA

SARDUY, SEVERO

Severo Sarduy (*b*. 25 February 1937; *d*. 8 June 1993), Cuban novelist, poet, and essayist. Sarduy was born in Camagüey. In 1956 he moved to Havana, where he came in contact with the vital community of writers associated with the literary magazine *Ciclón* and where he began to publish poetry. He studied medicine for two years at the University of Havana, but left to concentrate on writing. After the Cuban Revolution of 1959, he became a contributor to *Lunes de Revolución,* a literary weekly edited by Guillermo Cabrera Infante.

In 1960 Sarduy left for France to study art history at the École du Louvre. From 1964 to 1967 he continued his studies in Paris and became a member of two influential literary groups associated with the publications *Mundo Nuevo,* edited by the critic Emir Rodríguez Monegal, and *Tel quel,* the most influential French publication of the 1960s and 1970s, where he collaborated with Roland Barthes. As editor of the Latin American collection of Éditions du Seuil since 1966, Sarduy has been responsible for launching the writers Gabriel GARCÍA MÁRQUEZ, José LEZAMA LIMA, Jorge Luis BORGES, and Guillermo CABRERA INFANTE into the French arena. In 1971 he was awarded the Prix Paul Gilson for his radio play *La playa* (The Beach). The following year his novel *Cobra* received the prestigious Prix Médici, and another radio play, *Relato,* won the Prix Italia.

Sarduy's work has received enormous critical acclaim, as he is one of the most innovative of Latin American writers. An aesthetic heir of Cuban master José Lezama Lima, for whom he professes great admiration, he uses a rich, elaborately baroque style to combine such seemingly disparate elements as Cuban folklore and music and the art, philosophy, and religion of the Far East. His work has been translated into many languages.

Sarduy's best-known works are *De dónde son los cantantes* (From Cuba with a Song [novel, 1967]), *La playa* (play, 1971), *Cobra* (novel, 1972), *Relato* (play, 1972), and *Maitreya* (novel, 1980; trans. 1987). He died of AIDS in Paris.

— ROBERTO VALERO

SARMIENTO, DOMINGO FAUSTINO

Domingo Faustino Sarmiento (*b.* 15 February 1811; *d.* 11 September 1888), writer, educator, journalist, historian, linguist, and president of Argentina (1868–1874). According to Mary Peabody Mann, Sarmiento was "not a man but a nation." Born in the frontier city of San Juan, near the Andes, he was the son of a soldier who fought in the wars of independence and a mother who supported the family by weaving. An early intellectual influence was a maternal uncle and private tutor, the priest José de Oro. Steeped in the classics, the Bible, Latin, and French, Sarmiento began teaching elementary school in his teens. Post-Independence chaos and anarchy awakened his interest in orderly government. By 1829 he fought with the unitarists against caudillo rule. When the federalists gained control of San Juan, he fled to Chile to the town of Los Andes, where he taught school and worked in a store. Upon returning to San Juan in 1836, he started the newspaper, *El Zonda,* in which he expounded his ideas about education, agriculture, and modernization. Ahead of his time, Sarmiento advocated educating women. In 1839 he founded a secondary school for girls in San Juan (Colegio de Santa Rosa de América), for which he wrote the by-laws. Facing jail because of political activities against tyrant Juan Manuel de ROSAS, Sarmiento fled to Chile in 1840.

Sarmiento said that he "only dreamed of founding schools and teaching the masses to read."

In contrast to Argentina, Chile was developing peacefully under a government framework organized by Diego PORTALES. In Santiago, Sarmiento rose to a position of prestige and influence; he befriended educator and writer Andrés BELLO, director of education (and later president of Chile) Manuel MONTT, historian José Victorino LASTARRIA, and political activist Francisco BILBAO. Sarmiento pursued his twin interests—education

and journalism—and he contributed articles to the influential newspapers *El Mercurio, El Nacional,* and *El Progreso.* He believed that Argentina's problems were "rooted in barbarism," and he said that he "only dreamed of founding schools and teaching the masses to read." For him, universal education was the key to defeating backwardness, and he thought he could transform the gaucho. In 1845 he serialized and also published in book form the work for which he is best known: *Civilización i barbarie: Vida de Juan Facundo Quiroga. I aspecto físico, costumbres, i ámbitos de la República Argentina* (translated by Mary Mann as *Life in the Argentine Republic in the Days of the Tyrants; or, Civilization and Barbarism* [1868]). In this work, also known as *Facundo,* Sarmiento expounded penetrating observations about the Argentine countryside and gaucho life and about the depredations caused by caudillo warfare, and he described the career of the federalist caudillo Juan Facundo QUIROGA. The book represented a passionate indictment of Rosas, which the tyrant perceived as a threat.

In Santiago, Sarmiento served as the head of a new normal school (teacher training institute). He prepared textbooks, school programs, and curricula. Many of his progressive ideas were adopted in Chilean elementary and secondary education. Following the lead of preeminent thinker and educator Andrés Bello, Sarmiento tried to simplify Spanish orthography and render it more phonetic. He published *Memoria sobre ortografía americana* (Compendium of American Orthography [1843]), and all his writings used the new phonetic spelling. He tirelessly advocated universal education—the cornerstone of a true democracy—believing that an educated electorate is the best antidote to anarchy and tyranny.

Rosas dispatched a diplomatic mission to Chile to secure the extradition of the man who wrote *Facundo.* Coincidentally, the Chilean government sent Sarmiento to Europe and the United States to survey various educational methods. Disappointed in the rigid social class system, the lack of democratic governments, and the stultifying educational methods he saw in Spain, France, Germany, Holland, and Switzerland, Sarmiento did not think the fledgling American republics should emulate European models. In England, Sarmiento chanced upon a report written by Horace Mann to the Massachusetts Board of Education. During his stay in the United States, he met in Boston with educators Horace Mann and Mary Peabody Mann, who influenced his ideas about public education. His visit to the Boston area and other parts of the United States convinced Sarmiento of the importance of strong, representative, local government for a meaningful democracy on the national level. He also visited public libraries; elementary, secondary, and normal schools; and universities.

Upon returning to Chile he married his common-law wife Benita Martínez (1848), and he wrote *Viajes en Europa, Africa, i América, 1845–1847* (2 vols., 1849–1851). The portion relating to the United States was translated by Michael Rockland as *Sarmiento's Travels in the United States in 1847* (1970). Like Alexis de Tocqueville before him, Sarmiento perceptively analyzed life in the United States. His *Travels* remains a timeless classic. In addition to his two popular works, *Facundo* and *Travels,* Sarmiento also produced the romantic prose masterpiece *Recuerdos de provincia* (Provincial recollections [1850]); *De la educación popular* (About public education [1849]), which was revised as *Memoria sobre educación común* (Report on public education [1856]); and *Las escuelas: Base de prosperidad i de la república en los Estados Unidos* (Schools as the basis of prosperity and republican government in the United States [1866]).

When General Justo José de URQUIZA successfully rallied the remaining caudillos against Rosas in 1851, Sarmiento traveled to Montevideo to join the armed struggle. After the defeat of Rosas at the Battle of Caseros (1852), and as a result of disagreements with Urquiza, Sarmiento returned to Chile. He moved permanently to Argentina in 1855, where he became the director of the department of education in Buenos Aires Province and threw himself into reforming education with his accustomed energy. Juana Manso de Noronha, an Argentine educator, became his closest assistant and confidante. He founded the journal *Anales de la educación común* (Annals of public education) in 1858; he wrote for the newspaper *El Nacional;* and he continued to promulgate ideas about universal public education with a modern curriculum that included science, practical learning, and gymnastics for both men and women. The proposed reforms met the stiff resistance of the Sociedad de la Beneficiencia (Society for Charity), which had been in charge of women's education since the 1820s. Sarmiento was prevented from reforming women's education. Between 1856 and 1861 Sarmiento founded thirty-four new schools, and he ordered the publication of new textbooks.

Following national unification in 1882, Sarmiento played an important role in bringing peace and order to the provinces. He served as senator and later as governor of San Juan Province (1862–1864), where he tried to implement programs of education reforms and economic development; he also continued writing for newspapers. His projects for land reform were relentlessly opposed by the caudillo Angel Vicente PEÑALOZA

(El Chacho). Federal forces defeated El Chacho on 12 November 1863, and his severed head was displayed on a pike, as was the custom of the times.

By 1862 Sarmiento had separated from his wife Benita and was engaged in a long-term liaison with Aurelia Vélez. In 1864 he became minister plenipotentiary first to Peru, then to the United States. Finding Washington provincial, Sarmiento settled in New York, where he saw greater opportunities to learn about educational innovations and business practices. He reacquainted himself with Mary Mann (Horace Mann died in 1859) and other educators and intellectuals he had met during his previous trip. He visited teachers' colleges and universities in Boston, New York, and Chicago, always helped by Mary Mann. He lectured on North and South America to the Rhode Island Historical Society (1865). The talk was translated into English by the young Bartolomé MITRE, the Argentine president's son. In 1866 Sarmiento's only son, twenty-year-old Dominguito, was killed in the Battle of Curupaití in the War of the Triple Alliance.

In 1868 Sarmiento was elected the second president of a newly unified Argentina. His presidency was the culmination of his tireless struggle to transform Argentina into a modern nation. As president he vigorously promoted economic, social, and cultural development. Following the ideas of Juan Bautista ALBERDI and Bartolomé Mitre, Sarmiento fostered European immigration and encouraged the establishment of agricultural colonies. He worked to expand railways and roads; he promoted shipping, commerce, and advances in public health; and he modernized and beautified the city of Buenos Aires. To further educational reforms, he established public libraries throughout the country, and he recruited North American schoolteachers. More than eighty-eight teachers came to Argentina between 1867 and 1889. In 1869 he mandated the establishment of a normal-school network. He introduced advanced teaching techniques, added foreign languages to curricula, and founded kindergartens. Many of the reforms were implemented by Sarmiento's successor, President Nicolás AVELLANEDA. As a result of their efforts, Argentine schools became the best in Latin America. Sarmiento ordered the first national census of Argentina in 1869; he founded the Colegio Militar (National Military Academy), the first astronomical observatory, and trade and technical schools; he fostered the modernization of agriculture, mining, and industry; and he established the Sociedad Rural to improve livestock breeds.

After leaving the presidency, Sarmiento served in the Senate (1875–1880), held the office of interior minister, visited Chile, was once again superintendent of education of Buenos Aires Province (1879–1882), and founded the journal *La educación común* (Public Education) in 1876 and the newspaper *El Censor* in 1885. Quite ill during the last three years of his life, he died in Asunción, Paraguay.

Political and historical writings of Sarmiento include: *Comentarios de la constitución de la Confederación Argentina* (1853), *Arjirópolis: O la capital de los estados confederados del Río de la Plata* (1850), *Discursos parlamentarios* (2 vols. [1933]), *Emigración alemana al Río de la Plata* (1851), *Condición del extranjero en América* (The Foreigner's Condition in the Americas [1888]), and studies about the War of the Triple Alliance.

Published correspondence includes: *Sarmiento-Mitre: Correspondencia, 1846–1868* (1911), *Epistolario íntimo* (1963), and Julia Ottolenghi's *Sarmiento a través de un epistolario* (Sarmiento Through His Correspondence [1940]). Sarmiento's last publication was *La vida de Dominguito* (1886), which mourned his son Domingo Fidel. Posterity harshly criticized him for the 1883 book *Conflicto y armonías de las razas* (Conflict and Harmony in the Races), in which he largely repeats the prevalent theories about race mixing and racial purity. His *Obras completas* in fifty-three volumes were published in 1888.

During his presidency, Sarmiento dealt with the last of the caudillos. Despite his lifelong opposition to caudillo rule, Sarmiento governed as a personalist and strengthened the power of the executive. As president he used the central government's power to crush political opposition in the interior provinces, and he imposed sieges to quell uprisings. When the law seemed inadequate, he ruled by decree. Viewed by some of his contemporaries as an egotist ("don Yo" or "Mr. Me"), Sarmiento nevertheless looms as a protean figure: a visionary, an educator, a writer, and a seminal nation-builder.

– GEORGETTE MAGASSY DORN

SARMIENTO DE GAMBOA, PEDRO

Pedro Sarmiento de Gamboa (*b.* ca. 1530; *d.* 1608), Spanish admiral and chronicler of South America. Born in Pontevedra, in northwestern Spain, Sarmiento served in the navy of Philip II, reaching the rank of admiral. Combining his maritime profession with the writing of history, he researched the history of the Incas before the Conquest, pursuing his work on *Historia índica* (History of the Incas, 1572) while Viceroy Francisco de TOLEDO ruled Peru. He voyaged to the Strait of Magellan, becoming the first to enter from the west, and attempted to found a colony there. Lacking the enthusiastic backing of the king, the colony failed and its inhabitants perished while Sarmiento was imprisoned in Europe. He described his experience in *Derrotero al Es-*

trecho de Magallanes (Voyage to the Straits of Magellan, 1580).

Arguing against the claims of native Andeans to self-government, Sarmiento promoted a view of Spain's role as Christianizer of the New World.

Among the chroniclers of sixteenth-century Peru, Sarmiento stands out for these two works. The *Historia* is an example of the efforts of Viceroy Toledo and those around him to establish a historiographic record that would confirm the justification for Spanish dominance of the Andean peoples. Arguing against the claims of native Andeans to self-government, chroniclers such as Sarmiento promoted a providentialist view of Spain's role as Christianizer of the New World.

– KATHLEEN ROSS

SARMIENTO DE SOTOMAYOR, GARCÍA

García Sarmiento de Sotomayor (count of Salvatierra), viceroy of Peru (1648–1654). Faced with the continuing decline in crown revenues, Salvatierra initiated various policies to increase state income. Citing weaknesses in the official trade system of the *consulado* (merchant guild), Salvatierra proposed altering that system to reduce smuggling and collect more taxes. Salvatierra wanted to increase Indian tribute payments as well, but his inconsistent policies, including initiating and then suspending a census of the Indian community, failed. Although not as effective as his predecessor, the marquis of Mancera, Salvatierra did raise some crown revenues through *composiciones de tierras,* the practice of declaring Indian lands depopulated or abandoned and thus the property of the crown, subject to sale to private investors. His efforts to tighten control over the regional treasuries were less successful.

– ANN M. WIGHTMAN

SARMIENTOS DE LEÓN, JORGE ALVARO

Jorge Alvaro Sarmientos de León (*b.* 1933), Guatemalan composer, conductor, and percussionist. Born in San Antonio Suchitepéquez, Sarmientos began his training at the National Conservatory of Music in Guatemala City under Ricardo Castillo, José Arévalo Guerra, and other distinguished Guatemalan musicians. He continued his studies in Paris and later at the Instituto Torcuato di Tella in Buenos Aires. Sarmientos returned to Guatemala, where he taught at the National Conservatory and served as musical and artistic director of the National Symphony Orchestra. He has composed over sixty works, among them film scores, chamber music, orchestral works, and a ballet. His music often features indigenous themes, as in his *Las estampas del Popol Vuh*.

– STEVEN S. GILLICK

SARNEY, JOSÉ

José Sarney (*b.* 24 April 1930), president of Brazil (1985–1990) and writer. José Ribamar Ferreira Araújo Costa was born in Pinheiro, Maranhão, and received a law degree in 1953. From childhood he was referred to as Zé do Sarney. For electoral purposes, in 1958 he adopted the name José Sarney and legally changed his name to José Sarney da Costa in 1965.

Sarney began his political career in 1954 as an alternate federal deputy from the National Democratic Union (UDN) and assumed the deputy position in 1956. He was reelected in 1958 and 1962, and in 1965 he became the governor of his home state on the Arena ticket, the same party that brought him to the federal senate in 1970 and 1978. He was a founder of the Social Democratic Party (PDS) and twice its president. Asked by President FIGUEIREDO to coordinate the presidential succession with the goal of finding a national union candidate within the PDS, Sarney failed and renounced the party presidency at that time. Subsequently he ran for vice president on the Democratic Alliance ticket of the PMDB–PFL (Brazilian Democratic Movement Party–Liberal Front Party) in the indirect elections won by Tancredo NEVES in January 1985.

When Neves fell ill on the eve of his inauguration in March 1985, Sarney became interim president and reaffirmed the ministerial choices made by Neves. With the death of Neves in April, Sarney was sworn in as president and governed until March 1990. He helped to lead the country toward direct elections and a new constitution in 1988. In November 1990 he was elected senator from Amapá on the PMDB ticket. His attempts to become a presidential candidate in 1994 were frustrated even though polls indicated he still retained a small but solid following.

Sarney became a member of the Brazilian Academy of Letters in 1980. He has written several books, including *Norte das águas* (1969), *Marimbondos de fogo* (1980), *Brejaldos guajas* (1985), and *Sentimento do mundo* (1985).

– IÊDA SIQUEIRA WIARDA

SARRATEA, MANUEL DE

Manuel de Sarratea (*b.* 13 August 1774; *d.* 21 September 1849), Argentine statesman of the independence and early national periods. Born in Buenos Aires into a distinguished family that eventually included Santiago de LINIERS Y BREMOND as his brother-in-law, Sarratea spent much of his early life in Spain but returned in time to take part in the independence movement. Though Sarratea received important government positions (such as president of the First Triumvirate in 1811 and captain-general and governor of Buenos Aires Province in 1820), he seldom retained any post for long. Some authors have focused on these career changes and his friendship with British merchants to dismiss him as an intriguer, yet he made numerous contributions during three decades of public service. During the second regime of Juan Manuel de ROSAS, for example, Sarratea was named special envoy and minister plenipotentiary to Brazil (in 1838) and France (in 1841). He died in Limoges and his remains were transported to Buenos Aires in 1850.

– FIDEL IGLESIAS

SAS, ANDRÉS

Andrés Sas (*b.* 6 April 1900; *d.* 26 August 1967), Peruvian musicologist and composer. Born in Paris, Sas grew up in Brussels, where from 1918 to 1923 he studied at the Royal Conservatory under Fernand Bauvais (theory), Alfred Marchot (violin), Paul Miry (chamber music), and Ernest Closson (music history). He took private lessons in fugue and counterpoint with Maurice Imbert. In 1920 he began studies in harmony at the Anderlecht Academy in Brussels. Soon afterward he started a teaching career as a violin instructor at the Forest Music School in Brussels. In 1924 the Peruvian government invited him to direct violin classes and chamber music concerts at the National Academy of Music in Lima. The following year he was appointed an instructor in music history at the academy. He returned to Belgium, where he founded and directed the Municipal School of Music in Ninove (1928–1929). Again in Lima, he established the Sas-Rosay Academy with his wife, the pianist Lily Rosay, in 1930. With María Wiesse de Sabogal, he started the *Antara/Revista Musical* (1935). Sas was director of Lima's Bach Institute (1931–1933) and vice president of the Lima Orchestral Society (1932).

Sas was known for his studies of pre-Columbian instruments such as the clay syrinx of the Nazca tribe; his numerous writings on the music of the Nazca and other indigenous groups made him a leading authority on the history of Peruvian music. In addition to his research, Sas was active as an editor of music magazines, lecturer, conductor, recitalist, and teacher. Sas composed symphonic pieces (*Recuerdos* for violin or piano and orchestra [1927]) and choral works (the triptych *Ollantai*

[1933]), ballets (*Sueño de Zamba* [1943]), music for the stage, chamber music (*Cuarteto de cuerdas* [1938]) and songs (*Seis canciones indias del Perú* [1946]). Although some of his songs used French texts, most of his works were inspired by Indian themes and display the pentatonic melodies of the Andean region, but were written with an almost impressionist technique. He died in Lima.

— SUSANA SALGADO

SCALABRINI ORTIZ, RAÚL

Raúl Scalabrini Ortiz (*b.* 14 April 1898; *d.* 30 May 1959), Argentine nationalist writer and historian. Although trained in the physical sciences, Scalabrini early showed literary talent in his collection of short stories, *La manga* (1923). In 1931 he published a famous analysis of the Argentine mind-set *El hombre que está solo y espera,* from which emerge two key ideas. First, echoing nationalist thinkers from Johann Gottfried von Herder to Charles Maurras, Scalabrini holds that authentic Argentines uncontaminated by foreign ideas find their real identity in "the spirit of the land." Second, he argues that nineteenth-century Argentine liberalism, by failing to understand the country's true spirit, had built a country at cross-purposes with its true destiny. Scalabrini's increasing nationalist militance eventually produced two famous revisionist studies, *Política británica en el Río de la Plata* (1940) and *Historia de los ferrocarriles argentinos* (1940), which argue that British imperialists

---

Scalabrini holds that authentic Argentines uncontaminated by foreign ideas find their real identity in "the spirit of the land."

---

in cahoots with Argentine liberals had dispossessed Argentines of their rightful patrimony. Distrusting the British, Scalabrini supported Argentine neutrality during World War II, a position that led to charges of pro-Nazi sympathies. While he never became a Peronist functionary, his rhetoric and ideas became staples of Peronist thinking. Scalabrini's sympathy for Peronism emerges most powerfully in his book of poetry, *Tierra sin nada, tierra de profetas* (1946). His other writings include *Historia del primer empréstito* (1939), *Cuatro verdades sobre nuestras crisis* (1948; 2d ed. 1985), and *Bases para la reconstrucción nacional* (1965). After Juan PERÓN's ouster in 1955, Scalabrini fought until his death for the president's return and vindication.

— NICOLAS SHUMWAY

SCHAERER, EDUARDO

Eduardo Schaerer (*b.* 2 December 1873; *d.* 12 November 1941), Paraguayan statesman and president (1912–1916). Schaerer was related to German colonists who came to Paraguay in the wake of the disastrous War of the Triple Alliance. Though he was born in Caazapá, a small hamlet in the Paraguayan interior, Schaerer displayed distinctly urban ambitions and efficiency, which stood him in good stead at the Colegio Nacional and ultimately in his business affairs.

Politically, Schaerer was a Liberal, and after the Liberal Party came to power after the 1904 revolution, he held a variety of important government posts, including director general of the Customs House, mayor of Asunción, and interior minister. Schaerer's business acumen had already made him a wealthy man, and he used his money to promote his candidacy for president. During his administration, considerable progress was made in the modernization of Asunción, an undertaking highlighted by the inauguration of a tramway system. In foreign relations, he kept Paraguay neutral during World War I.

Schaerer remained influential in Liberal circles after his term of office had expired. For a time he was a national senator and eventually became president of the Senate. He provided financial backing for various Liberal newspapers and remained an important force in the party into the 1930s.

— THOMAS L. WHIGHAM

SCHENDEL, MIRA

Mira Schendel (*b.* 1919; *d.* 1988), graphic artist, painter, and sculptor. Swiss born, Schendel lived in Italy until age thirty, when she emigrated to Brazil. Abstract art with minimalist overtone dominated her repertory until the 1960s, when her work took on constructivist influences, with a monumentality of void characterizing her graphic works. In one piece, simply entitled *Drawing,* for example, linguistic and mathematical signs and scratches are drawn on inked glass and are then transferred onto delicate Japanese paper. The visual result recalls Chinese painting. In 1964 Schendel represented Brazil in the Second Biennial of American Art of Córdoba, Argentina, She had solo exhibitions at the Museum of Modern Art in São Paulo in 1964, at a London gallery in 1965, and in 1971 at the Brazilian-American Cultural Institute in Washington, D.C. In 1975 she was one of twelve artists selected to participate in a nationally sponsored traveling exhibition and discussion series.

— CAREN A. MEGHREBLIAN

SCHICK GUTIÉRREZ, RENÉ

René Schick Gutiérrez (*b.* 1909; *d.* 1966), president of Nicaragua from 1963 to 1966. A close associate of the Somoza family, Schick served as Anastasio SOMOZA GARCÍA's personal secretary and was named minister of education and of foreign relations during the presidency of Luis SOMOZA DEBAYLE. Long portrayed as a quiet "yes-man" and Somoza puppet, Schick proved to be more independent. His term in office was relatively peaceful and he followed Luis Somoza's lead in liberalizing Nicaragua. The Nicaraguan state and economy boomed as government expenditure and entrepreneurial activity increased. Schick, who died in office, was succeeded by Vice President Lorenzo Guerrero Gutiérrez.

— HEATHER K. THIESSEN

SCHNEIDER, RENÉ

René Schneider (*b.* 31 December 1913; *d.* 22 October 1970), Chilean military officer. A graduate of the Chilean military school, Schneider became the army's top-ranking officer in 1968. Appointed by Eduardo FREI to end unrest in the army, Schneider quickly restored discipline and reinforced the principle of civilian supremacy over the armed forces. He also indicated that, regardless of its outcome, the military would not intervene in the 1970 election. This promise became known as the Schneider Doctrine. Forces hostile to the Popular Unity Party (*Unidad Popular*) wanted the army to launch a preventive coup to prevent Salvador ALLENDE from taking office. When it became clear that Schneider would neither countenance nor cooperate with a putsch, the anti-Allende forces, under the leadership of an ex-general, tried to neutralize Schneider by kidnapping him. The conspirators, however, bungled the attempt, in the process mortally wounding Schneider, who put up unexpected resistance. Schneider's death precluded future military participation in an anti-Allende movement, thus ensuring that Allende would take office.

— WILLIAM F. SATER

SCHWARZ-BART, SIMONE

Simone Schwarz-Bart (*b.* 8 January 1938), Guadeloupean novelist and dramatist. Schwarz-Bart was born in Charente-Maritime, where her father was serving in the army. Her mother returned to Guadeloupe with her daughter, whose early schooling took place in Trois-Rivières. Schwarz-Bart began the lycée in Point-à-Pitre and finished in Paris. Married in Paris, Simone and André Schwarz-Bart spent a year in Dakar, and then settled in Switzerland, where Simone began writing short stories. Returning to Guadeloupe, she was instrumental in editing the encyclopedic *Hommage à la femme noire*, 6 vols. (1988–1989).

Schwarz-Bart has been compared with writers as diverse as Antonine Maillet and Toni Morrison. Through her presentation of various insular experiences (a Haitian sugarcane worker, an elderly Martinican woman in a French hospice) she would seem to be in the process of creating a Caribbean mythology in her dramatic and fictional writing. In 1973, she won the Grand Prize of the magazine *Elle* for her novel *Pluie et vent sur Télumée-Miracle* (1972)/ *The Bridge of Beyond* (1982). All of her individually authored works have appeared in English.

— CARROL F. COATES

SCLIAR, MOACYR

Moacyr Scliar (*b.* 23 March 1937), Brazilian author. Born in Pôrto Alegre, Rio Grande do Sul, Scliar studied medicine and has worked in the public health field for most of his life. As a fiction writer, he has published more than twenty books, including novels, collections of short stories, and chronicles. Many of his works have been translated into English and other languages. He has also written stories for children and short novels for young adults. A descendant of Russian Jews, Scliar is internationally recognized as having raised Jewish consciousness in Latin American fiction, focusing on the Jewish immigrant in Brazil. Scliar's writings are characterized by a subtle irony; his short stories have been widely anthologized. He has received prestigious prizes for his fiction in Brazil and elsewhere, and is known as a gifted lecturer. Scliar's works include *O carnaval dos animais* (1968; *The Carnival of Animals,* 1985); *A guerra do Bom Fim* (1972); *O exército de um homem só* (1973); *Os deuses de Raquel* (1975; *The Gods of Raquel,* 1986); *O ciclo das águas* (1977); *Mês de cães danados* (1977); *O centauro no jardim* (1980; *The Centaur in the Garden,* 1985); *A estranha nação de Rafael Mendes* (1983; *The Strange Nation of Rafael Mendes,* 1988); and *Cenas da vida minúscula* (1991).

— REGINA IGEL

SEDEÑO, ANTONIO DE

Antonio de Sedeño (*d.* 1539), conquistador of Tierra Firme, *adelantado* of Trinidad. In 1531 Sedeño, a *contador* of San Juan, Puerto Rico, was granted the title of *adelantado* for the island of Trinidad. Sedeño's original assault of the island with eighty men was repulsed by hostile Arawaks. In spite of the tenacity of the island's native population, a second attempt by Sedeño to conquer the island proved successful. Drawn to the wealth of the South American mainland, Sedeño proceeded to the Gulf of Paria, where he competed with Jerónimo de Alderete and Martín Nieto for conquest of the coastal region in open rebellion of the legitimate governor, Jerónimo de Ortal. The Audiencia of Santo Domingo sent its *fiscal* Juan de Frías to bring Sedeño to trial, but Sedeño captured the royal official and proceeded inland along the Orinoco River. During his escape, Sedeño was poisoned by one of his own men.

— MICHAEL A. POLUSHIN

SEGALL, LASAR

Lasar Segall (*b.* 1891; *d.* 2 August 1957), Brazilian painter considered the pioneer of expressionism in Brazil. Born in Vilna, Lithuania, Segall moved to Berlin at the age of fifteen and studied at the Imperial Academy of Fine Arts from 1907 to 1909, the year he was expelled for participating in the Freie Sezession, an exhibition by artists opposed to official aesthetics. In 1910 he moved to Dresden to study at the Meisterschüle (Art Academy). A year later he joined the German expressionist movement, and in 1912 made his first trip to Brazil.

In Brazil from 1912 to 1914, Segall prompted controversy over expressionism when his work was displayed in 1913 at solo exhibitions in São Paulo and Campinas. In 1923 he returned to Brazil and became a citizen. His paintings of Brazilian themes (1923–1926) were exhibited in 1926 in Dresden, Stuttgart, and Berlin. From 1928 to 1932 he lived in Paris. Segall returned once again to Brazil in 1932, when he cofounded the São Paulo Society of Modern Art.

In 1935, Segall completed a series of Campos de Jordão landscape paintings of Brazil and his *Portraits of Lucy* series. From 1936 to 1950, he produced paintings like *Concentration Camp* (1945) that focused on such social themes as the suffering and plight of Jews in Europe. He also participated in the Brazilian People's Graphics Workshop, a collective work center for artists founded first in Mexico in 1937, producing a series of

---

Segall produced paintings like Concentration Camp *(1945) that focused on such social themes as the suffering and plight of Jews in Europe.*

---

linocut and woodcut prints published in an album entitled *Mangue* (1944), in which he depicted the theme of prostitution. In 1938, he represented Brazil at the International Congress of Independent Arts (Paris) and

had a solo exhibition at the Renou et Colle Gallery in Paris. In the 1940s, his work was exhibited in New York and Rio de Janeiro, and in 1951 and 1953, he had special exhibitions at the São Paulo Biennial. He died in São Paulo.

— MARY JO MILES

SEGUÍN, JUAN JOSÉ MARÍA ERASMO

Juan José María Erasmo Seguín (*b.* 26 May 1782; *d.* 30 October 1857), Texas political figure. A merchant, farmer, and rancher, Seguín served as San Antonio postmaster and held other municipal posts in the 1810s and 1820s. During the Mexican War of Independence he apparently remained loyal to Spain.

Seguín undertook special assignments for the government. In 1821 the governor of Texas sent him to inform Moses Austin of approval of the latter's colonization plan. Elected Texas representative to the Constituent Congress of 1823–1824, Seguín spent much time in Mexico City advocating Anglo immigration to Texas.

Closely identified with the Anglos, Seguín was removed from government office at the outbreak of the Texas rebellion in 1835. Following the war he served briefly as county judge. He soon retired to rebuild his farm and ranch, where he died.

— JESÚS F. DE LA TEJA

SEGUÍN, JUAN NEPOMUCENO

Juan Nepomuceno Seguín (*b.* 27 October 1806; *d.* 27 August 1890), Texas political and military figure. Son of the politically prominent Erasmo Seguín, he served in a number of political posts between 1829 and 1835, including *alcalde* and interim *jefe político* in 1834. Like his father, he was a strong supporter of Anglo settlement.

Seguín, a federalist, involved himself in the 1834–1835 dispute with the centralists over control of the state government. At the outbreak of the Texas revolt, he was commissioned a captain of the Texas forces, and he led the only Mexican-Texan company at the Battle of San Jacinto, 21 April 1836. In the late 1830s Seguín served as senator from Bexar County in the Texas Congress and as mayor of San Antonio.

Compromised by political enemies in early 1842, Seguín was forced to flee to Mexico, where he apparently was given a choice of joining the army or going to prison. He participated in General Adrián Woll's invasion of Texas later that year and remained in the Mexican service through the end of the Mexican-American War. He subsequently returned to San Antonio, and again entered politics in the 1850s, serving as a justice of the peace and as one of the founders of the Bexar County Democratic Party. Increasingly alienated by conditions in Texas, Seguín took his family to Nuevo Laredo, Mexico, where he lived with one of his sons until his death.

– JESÚS F. DE LA TEJA

SENDIC, RAÚL

Raúl Sendic (*b*. 1925; *d*. 28 April 1989), Uruguayan politician and guerrilla leader. As a prominent young socialist, Sendic worked as a legal adviser for rural labor unions in the northern region of Uruguay during the late 1950s. In 1961, he participated in the foundation of the sugarcane workers' union. Due to the lack of response from political institutions to the workers' request for land distribution, Sendic became disappointed with legal procedures as a means to achieve social justice. Starting in 1962, Sendic and other members of the Uruguayan left formed the National Liberation Movement, Tupamaros, one of Latin America's most important urban guerrilla organizations. As a Tupamaro leader, Sendic was captured in December 1964, released, and captured again in 1970. In September 1971 he escaped in a massive jail break. In September 1972, Sendic was shot in the face and captured and the Tupamaros were destroyed by the armed forces. For twelve years Sendic was imprisoned and tortured at various military units. In 1985 Sendic and other Tupamaro leaders were freed by an amnesty granted by the new democratic government. After 1985, Sendic remained a leader of the Tupamaros, as they reentered the political arena on peaceful and legal terms. As a consequence of his torture, Sendic became sick with Charcot's disease and died in France in 1989. While in prison he wrote *Cartes desde la prisión* (1984) and *Reflexiones sobre política económica: Apuntes desde la prisión* (1984).

– ASTRID ARRARÁ

SEOANE, MANUEL

Manuel Seoane (*b*. 1900; *d*. 10 September 1963), Peruvian journalist, author, and politician, one of the most conspicuous leaders of the Aprista Party. Born in Lima, Seoane was educated in a Jesuit school and at San Marcos University. In 1922 he was elected vice president of the Student Federation led by Víctor Raúl HAYA DE LA TORRE. In 1924, President Augusto B. LEGUÍA deported Seoane to Buenos Aires, where he engaged in journalism. After the fall of Leguía, Seoane returned to Lima to found the newspaper *La Tribuna* and to activate the Aprista political campaign for the 1931 elections. Elected deputy for the Constituent Assembly, he was

forced into exile by President Luis M. SÁNCHEZ CERRO in 1932.

Seoane lived mostly in exile until 1945, when he was elected senator for Lima and vice president of the Chamber of Senators. General Manuel ODRÍA exiled him again after the 1948 coup against President BUSTAMANTE Y RIVERO, who had governed with initial Aprista support. Although Seoane criticized Haya on several ideological and political points in 1954 and 1957, he participated once more as first vice-presidential candidate in the nullified elections of 1962. Retired from politics, he died in Washington, D.C., while working for the Alliance for Progress.

– ALFONSO W. QUIROZ

SEPP, ANTON

Anton Sepp (*b*. 21 November 1655; *d*. 13 January 1733), Tyrolean-born Jesuit active in the missions of Paraguay. Of noble birth, Sepp dedicated himself early to various scholarly pursuits. For a time, he taught rhetoric at Augsburg. Then, in 1674, he entered the Society of Jesus, hoping to be sent to missionary fields in South America. Being a non-Spaniard, however, Sepp encountered many obstacles in securing permission to travel in the New World. Only in 1690 was permission finally granted.

Being a non-Spaniard, Sepp encountered many

obstacles in securing permission to travel

in the New World.

A cloud of unwarranted suspicion followed Sepp throughout his labors. He spent forty-one years in the Jesuit *reducciones* of Paraguay, yet he never held high office, nor was his ordination as priest ever confirmed. Still, he had a claim on being the most important cleric in the lives of thousands of Guaraní Indians. His talent and energy seemed boundless. He founded one major mission, San Juan Bautista, in 1698. He designed buildings for several more missions, and organized workshops for the manufacture of musical instruments. He wrote poetry, sermons, and musical compositions that became well known in the region. The schools that he operated at Yapeyú gave the Indians access to many aspects of Western culture. The Indians, in turn, made the Jesuit missions so prosperous and so famous that Voltaire later described them as a sort of Utopia in his classic, *Candide*.

Sepp's own role in giving life to this image was revealed in a series of copious letters he wrote to European relatives. These were published in two volumes between 1696 and 1709, and still constitute a key source for historians studying the Jesuit missions. Sepp died at San José, in what later became the Argentine Misiones.

— THOMAS L. WHIGHAM

SEREBRIER, JOSÉ

José Serebrier (b. 3 December 1938), Uruguayan composer and conductor. Of Russian and Polish descent, Serebrier was born in Montevideo, where he studied violin with Juan Fabbri. At Montevideo's Municipal School of Music his instructors were Miguel Pritsch (violin) and Vicente Ascone (harmony). He also took lessons in composition, fugue, and counterpoint with Guido Santórsola, and piano with Sarah Bourdillon. After attending counterpoint and composition classes at the National Conservatory with Carlos ESTRADA, he moved to the United States to enter the Curtis Institute in Philadelphia (1956), where he studied composition under Vittorio Giannini. He has resided in the United States ever since. Serebrier attended Aaron Copland's classes at Tanglewood, and Antal Dorati and Pierre Monteux coached him in conducting. When he was only seventeen Leopold Stokowski chose him to be associate conductor of the American Symphony Orchestra (1962–1967). He received scholarships and grants from the Organization of American States, and the Guggenheim, Rockefeller, and Koussevitsky foundations. Serebrier served as conductor of the Utica Symphony (1960–1962) and composer-in-residence with the Cleveland Orchestra (1968–1971). At eighteen Serebrier composed his *Leyenda de Fausto Overture,* which won the Uruguayan National Award. He experimented with mixed media, adding lighting to his works, as in *Colores mágicos,* premiered by him at the Fifth Inter-American Music Festival in Washington, D.C., in 1971. In his later works, he explored more advanced composition techniques.

Since 1989 Serebrier has conducted the Scottish Chamber Orchestra and frequently has been guest conductor of the Royal Philharmonic. Many of his compositions have been performed, among them Concerto for Violin and Orchestra (Winter), which premiered March 1994 in New York and which he later recorded with the Royal Philharmonic. In addition to his recordings, Serebrier also has numerous film scores to his credit. In 1984 he founded the Miami Music Festival. He is the recipient of the Alice Ditson Award for his achievements in contemporary music. He conducts and records frequently in the United States and London.

— SUSANA SALGADO

SEREGNI, LÍBER

Líber Seregni (b. 3 December 1917), Uruguayan military leader and politician. The son of an anarchist father, Seregni opted paradoxically for a military career and achieved the rank of general. Toward the end of his military career, he was known to be sympathetic to progressive elements in the Colorado Party. By 1971 he had distanced himself from this position to become a founding member and presidential candidate of the Frente Amplio, receiving 18 percent of the national vote. With the coup d'état of 1973, the leftist coalition and its political leaders were outlawed. Seregni was imprisoned until 1984.

Both in freedom and from prison, Seregni was a central proponent of democratization. He defended the blank ballot in the internal elections of 1982, which left the Frente outlawed. He later promoted and supported the strategy of negotiation that led to the legalization of many of the Frente's political forces and from which came the final formula for the democratic movement. Prevented from running for president in the November 1984 elections, Seregni assumed the presidency of the Frente Amplio. He did run for president of Uruguay again in 1989 and received 21 percent of the vote.

— FERNANDO FILGUEIRA

SERRA, JUNÍPERO

Junípero Serra (b. 24 November 1713; d. 28 August 1784), Franciscan missionary in New Spain. The founder of Mission San Diego de Alcalá, Serra was born in Petra, on the Spanish island of Mallorca, to Antonio and Margarita Ferrer de Serra. Christened Miguel José, he attended a Franciscan primary school in Petra until age fifteen, when he traveled to Palma, the capital of Mallorca, to study theology. Serra took the name Junípero upon joining the Order of Friars Minor (Franciscans) in 1730; he was ordained a priest in 1738. Serra received a doctorate in theology in 1742 and served as a professor of philosophy at Palma's Lullian University until 1749, when he decided to leave Spain and become a missionary among the Indians in the Americas.

Serra began his new career in 1750, working among the natives in the Sierra Gorda region north of Mexico City until 1758. He then returned to the Mexican capital and, although suffering at times from asthma and a painful leg injury, assumed the duties of a traveling missionary priest. In 1768 Serra was placed in charge of former Jesuit missions in Baja (Lower) California, and from there helped plan the occupation of Alta (Upper) California.

Serra, at age fifty-six, accompanied a Spanish overland expedition led by Gaspar de PORTOLÁ that reached

San Diego in the summer of 1769 and founded the first mission there on 16 July. His second mission, San Carlos Borromeo, founded at Monterey on 3 June 1770, served, with the adjoining presidio, as capital of California. The Franciscans, under Serra's direction as father president for the next fourteen years, founded nine missions; taught the Indians Christian doctrine, agricultural techniques, pottery making, and other useful arts; and helped in the settlement of California.

Serra served and protected the Indians until his death at Mission San Carlos Borromeo, by then located on the Carmel River. Because of his accomplishments and exemplary life, he is known as "the Apostle of California." He was declared venerable by Pope John Paul II in May 1986, beatified in Rome on 25 September 1988, and is under consideration for canonization as a saint.

Serra's treatment of his Indian charges is a topic that has aroused much debate. Native Americans claim he enslaved their ancestors. It must be admitted that the mission system did at times result in harsh treatment of Native Americans. Attracted to the missions with offerings of food and gifts, they were given religious instruction, but they also were often pressed into ar-

duous work in the fields. Unmarried Indians were housed separately by sex and punished for attempting to leave the mission or for other infractions. Punishments included whipping and shackling—common disciplinary measures in the eighteenth century. European diseases spread through the confined areas and killed many Native Americans. The natural hunting-and-gathering economy and loose social organization of the Indians were replaced by a more structured, paternalistic administration. Serra's defenders claim that despite its failings, the Spanish mission system was humanitarian in its intent and sought to prepare Indians to live a settled, church-oriented, European way of life. Serra followed the teachings of his order and the goals of Catholic Spain. The California missions prospered and paved the way for a lasting agricultural economy on the Pacific Coast.

– IRIS H. W. ENGSTRAND

SERRANO, JOSÉ

José Serrano (*b.* 1634; *d.* 1713), Spanish missionary and translator. Serrano, born in Andalusia, entered the Society of Jesus and arrived in the Río de la Plata in 1658. In order to be appointed parish priest in the reductions, he had to take an examination in the Guaraní language. He passed the examination, and began mission work in 1665. Serrano is credited with the translation of two Spanish books into the Guaraní language: *De la diferencia entre lo temporal y eternal,* by Jesuit Juan Eusebio Nieremberg, and *Flos sanctorum.* The former was subsequently published and printed with illustrations in 1705, the first book printed in Argentina. Serrano was the rector of the Jesuit college in Buenos Aires in 1696. He died in the Guaraní mission town of Loreto.

– NICHOLAS P. CUSHNER

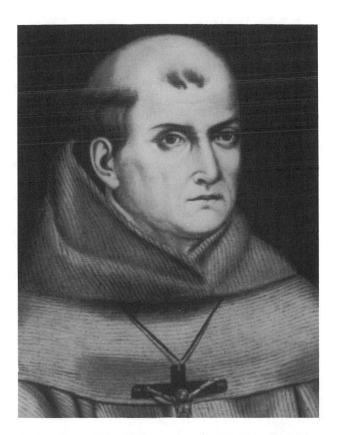

Junípero Serra, from a painting preserved at Mission Santa Barbara. Copied by Rev. José Mosqueda from a now-unknown original. (Benson Latin American Collection, University of Texas at Austin)

SERRANO ELÍAS, JORGE ANTONIO

Jorge Antonio Serrano Elías (*b.* 26 April 1945), president of Guatemala (1991–1993), the first active Protestant to be elected president of a Latin American nation. Born in Guatemala City and educated at the University of San Carlos and at Stanford, Serrano became an evangelical Protestant in 1975. He served as president of the Council of State under the administration of General Efraín RÍOS MONTT (1982–1983). Serrano then formed the Solidary Action Movement (MAS) and placed third among eight candidates in the 1985 presidential election. In 1990, after the Court of Constitutionality ruled Ríos Montt ineligible for another term, most of his electoral support switched to Serrano. This propelled Serrano into the January 1991 runoff election in which he defeated National Center

Union (UCN) candidate Jorge CARPIO in a landslide. Serrano's administration was neoliberal and private-sector oriented. With army support, he suspended the Constitution on 25 May 1993 to quell rising social unrest. In the face of widespread domestic and international pressure, however, the military removed Serrano on 1 June 1993 and allowed the Congress to elect a successor, Ramiro de León Carpio.

— RALPH LEE WOODWARD, JR.

SHARP, BARTHOLOMEW

Bartholomew Sharp (late 1600s), one of the last of the buccaneers. In 1679, Captain Bartholomew Sharp and other buccaneers from Jamaica raided the Caribbean ports of Honduras, plundering royal storehouses and carrying off some 500 chests of indigo, as well as cocoa, cochineal, tortoiseshell, money, and silver plate.

Later that year the same buccaneers, including Sharp and Captain John Coxon, set out upon a plan of much larger design. Six captains met at Point Morant, Jamaica, and on 7 January 1680, set sail for Porto Bello. They entered the town on 17 February. Meeting little resistance, they pillaged it, took prisoners and booty, and departed just after the arrival of Spanish troops. Then they captured two Spanish vessels headed for the port and divided their large haul of plunder. Finally, Sharp and the other buccaneers marched across the Isthmus of Darién to the coasts of Panama and the Pacific, wreaking havoc as they went.

In May 1680, Lord Charles Carlisle, governor of Jamaica, put out a warrant for the apprehension of Sharp and his associates. On 1 July, Henry MORGAN issued a similar arrest order. Sharp eventually returned to England, where he was charged with committing piracy on the South Seas, but he was acquitted because of a reported lack of evidence.

— BLAKE D. PATTRIDGE

SHIMOSE, PEDRO

Pedro Shimose (b. 1940), Bolivian poet. Shimose also sketches and composes popular music. Born in Riberalta del Beni, Bolivia, to Japanese immigrants, Shimose received a degree in communication sciences from the Universidad Complutense in Madrid. He worked as columnist and editor for the daily *Presencia* of La Paz and later taught literature at the Universidad Mayor de San Andrés in La Paz. In the early 1990s he was working at the Institute of Spanish-American Cooperation in Madrid. His poetry has received various prizes: Bolivia's National Poetry Prize in 1960 and 1966, Cuba's House

of the Americas Prize in 1972, and Spain's Olive Prize in 1974 and Leopoldo Panero Prize in 1975.

Shimose's early poetry (*Triludio del exilio* [1961], *Sardonia* [1967], *Poemas para un pueblo* [1968], and *Quiero escribir, pero me sale espuma* [1972]) is characterized by a humanist social commitment of a mythico-religious nature, which evolves into a definitive denunciation of those who perpetuate the conditions causing misery and pain in Latin America. In *Caducidad del fuego* (1975), *Al pie de la letra* (1976), *Reflexiones maquiavélicas* (1980), and *Poemas* (1988), the tone changes. The violence is transformed into a bitter irony mixed with tenderness and humor. Shimose also published a book of stories, *El Coco se llama Drilo* (1976), and *Diccionario de autores iberoamericanos* (1982).

— SILVIA M. NAGY

SIERRA, STELLA

Stella Sierra (b. 5 July 1917), Panamanian poet. Sierra was born in Aguadulce, Panama. In 1936, she graduated from the Colegio Internacional de María Inmaculada, and in 1954 she received a degree in education with specialization in Spanish from the University of Panama.

Her first two books, *Sinfonía jubilosa en doce sonetos* (1942; Joyful Symphony in Twelve Sonnets) and *Canciones de mar y luna* (1944; Songs of Sea and Moon), confirmed her place in Panamanian letters. Her later publications, *Libre y cautiva* (1947; Free and Captive), *Cinco poemas* (1949; Five Poems), *Poesía* (1962; Poetry), and *Presencia del recuerdo* (1965; Presence of Memory) revealed her control over her poetic resources and the universality of her poetry.

Sierra has won many awards for both her poetry and her fiction. Among them the Demetrio H. Brid Prize for her short story *Con los pies descalzos* (1944; Barefooted), the Miró Prize for *Sinfonía jubilosa*, and a first prize from the Chancellery of Uruguay for her *Himno para la glorificación de Franklin D. Roosevelt* (1946; Hymn in Homage of Franklin D. Roosevelt). She has contributed to the weekly *Semanario Mundo Gráfico*, to *Correo Literario*, and to such literary magazines as *Poesía de América*, *Cultura*, and *Épocas*. Sierra has taught at the National Institute of Panama and at the University of Panama and has been a delegate at various international conferences.

— ELBA D. BIRMINGHAM-POKORNY

SIERRA MÉNDEZ, JUSTO

Justo Sierra Méndez (b. 26 January 1848; d. 13 September 1912), Mexican writer, political thinker, historian, and educational leader. Sierra was born in Campeche, the son of prominent Yucatecan politician, writer, and jurist Justo SIERRA O'REILLY, and after 1861 lived and was educated in Mexico City, receiving a law degree in 1871 from the Escuela de Derecho. A protégé of Ignacio M. ALTAMIRANO, in 1868 Sierra began to write poetry, short stories, plays, and a novel. His career as a political journalist and thinker began in 1874 and reached a climax in the important newspaper *La Libertad* (1878–1884), which he directed until 1880, and which was an exponent of a "new" or transformed liberalism that called for a strong government and economic development. Of several histories, his most important was *Evolución política del pueblo mexicano,* first published under another title in 1900–1902. He was a deputy to Congress from 1880 until 1894, when he was appointed to the Supreme Court. As an educator, he taught at the National Preparatory School after 1877 and led the First and Second National Congresses of Public Instruction in 1889 and 1891, which established the principle of free obligatory primary education and reaffirmed the positivist preparatory curriculum. In 1901 he became subsecretary of public instruction, and then secretary from 1905 to 1911. He founded the National Autonomous University of Mexico (UNAM) in 1910. In 1912 he was appointed minister to Spain, where he died.

Sierra was the major Mexican intellectual of his era. His political and educational thought was characterized by a continuing tension between classic liberal principles, including French spiritualism, and positivism. Though an adherent of the regime of Porfirio DÍAZ (1877–1880, 1884–1911), Sierra led the effort (1892–1893) by the *científicos* to limit presidential authority.

— CHARLES A. HALE

SIERRA O'REILLY, JUSTO

Justo Sierra O'Reilly (*b.* 24 September 1814; *d.* 15 January 1861); Yucatecan jurist, journalist, novelist, and historian. The illegitimate son of a parish priest, Sierra grew up in Mérida and was educated first at the local seminary. Later he studied law in Mexico City (1838). After graduation he returned to Yucatán and practiced as a lawyer before turning to politics (serving as judge, ambassador, and congressman) and literary pursuits. He founded newspapers and wrote books on history and literature. He also composed fiction, his most famous novel probably being *La hija del judío* (The Jew's Daughter), a romance. He is the author of the Mexican republic's civil code (1860) and the father of Justo SIERRA MÉNDEZ (1847–1912).

— ROBERT W. PATCH

SIGAUD, EUGENIO DE PROENÇA

Eugenio de Proença Sigaud (*b.* 1889; *d.* 1979) Brazilian architectural engineer and painter. Born in the interior of the state of Rio de Janeiro, Sigaud moved to Rio in the early 1920s to study architecture at the National School of Fine Arts. While there, the artist Modesto Brocos helped perfect Sigaud's drawing skills. In 1931 Sigaud joined Edson Mota, João Rescala, José Pancetti, Milton Dacosta, and other young artists to form the Núcleo Bernardelli, a group that sought to counter the aesthetic traditionalism of the National School of Fine Arts. The Núcleo came to represent a moderate wing of the Brazilian modernist movement.

Sigaud's career consisted of two parallel aspects: he owned an architectural engineering and construction company, and he achieved prominence as a painter of social themes. His canvases and murals depict urban construction workers on scaffolding as well as rural coffee pickers. His most celebrated works include a painting entitled *Work Accident,* an architectural and interior design project for the church of São Jorge, and mural paintings for the cathedral of Jacarèzinho. He also dabbled in printing and book illustration.

— CAREN A. MEGHREBLIAN

SIGÜENZA Y GÓNGORA, CARLOS DE

Carlos de Sigüenza y Góngora (*b.* 20 August 1645; *d.* 22 August 1700), premier intellectual of seventeenth-century Mexico. Born in Mexico City, Sigüenza y Góngora was the son of a former tutor to the Spanish royal family; on his mother's side, he was distantly related to the poet Luís de Góngora. As a youth, he entered the Jesuit order, but curfew violations led to his expulsion in 1668. He then resumed theological and secular studies at the University of Mexico, where, in 1672, he gained the chair of mathematics and astrology. Over time, he accumulated several other important positions, including those of royal cosmographer of New Spain, chaplain of the Amor de Dios Hospital, and almoner to the archbishop of Mexico.

Sigüenza y Góngora argued that comets were a natural phenomenon rather than an omen of divine displeasure.

This talented polymath wrote extensively on a wide variety of subjects, but most of his works were not published. Despite his official capacity as an astrologer, Sigüenza y Góngora roundly belabored contemporary "superstitions." His scientific endeavors reached their summit with the *Libra astronómica y filosófica* (1690), an astronomical treatise in which he argued that comets were a natural phenomenon rather than an omen of divine displeasure; the work also attacked Aristotelian orthodoxy and upheld the validity of Mexican scholarship. In a more journalistic vein, Sigüenza y Góngora chronicled the triumph of Spanish arms in New Mexico and the Caribbean and wrote the finest eyewitness account of the Mexico City riot of 1692.

Sigüenza y Góngora devoted much scholarly energy to the study of Mexico's pre-Hispanic past. More important, he acquired and preserved the magnificent Ixtlilxochitl collection of codices and manuscripts. However, while he glorified the Aztec Empire, even claiming it as Mexico's version of classical antiquity, he despised the Indian masses of his own day. This contradiction ultimately proved fatal to his studies of indigenous peoples, which (along with a projected Indian museum) he abandoned after the 1692 riot.

His intellectual activities were further curtailed after 1694, when failing health forced him to resign his university post. Assailed by numerous ailments, he died in Mexico City. In retrospect, Sigüenza y Góngora appears as a precursor of both the Mexican Enlightenment and Mexican nationalism. Throughout his writings, he sought to delineate, praise, and defend the emerging creole *patria,* particularly as exemplified in its greatest center, Mexico City.

— R. DOUGLAS COPE

SILES ZUAZO, HERNÁN

Hernán Siles Zuazo (*b.* 21 March 1914), president of Bolivia (1956–1960, 1982–1985). Born in La Paz, the son of Hernando Siles Reyes, president of Bolivia (1926–1930), Siles Zuazo studied there at the American Institute and the National University. One of the founders of the Nationalist Revolutionary Movement (MNR) in 1941, he personally commanded the MNR forces in the April 1952 revolution. That year Siles became vice president of Bolivia, and in 1956 he was elected president. His principal task in office was to control the high inflation rate set off by the revolutionary process. Confronting organized labor, a faction of which supported the MNR, he was responsible for the implementation of an International Monetary Fund stabilization program. In 1960 he stepped down and was named Bolivian ambassador to Uruguay.

When the military overthrew the MNR in 1964, Siles became the consummate opponent of the authoritarian rulers, searching for ways to restore civilian rule.

Unlike other founders of the MNR, Siles never allied himself with any faction of the military; instead he suffered imprisonment on several occasions and exile in Uruguay. In 1972 Siles founded a leftist offshoot of the MNR, which he called the MNR de Izquierda (MNRI). When the military convoked elections in the late 1970s, Siles led his MNRI into a coalition dubbed the Popular and Democratic Union (Unidad Democrática y Popular—UDP) that included the Communist Party and the young Movimiento de Izquierda Revolucionaria (MIR). As the UDP's presidential candidate, Siles won three consecutive elections in 1978, 1979, and 1980; each time he was denied victory either because his coalition did not achieve the 50 percent plus required or because the military prevented him from taking power.

In October 1982, Siles Zuazo was elected president of Bolivia by the Congress. Over the next three years, he presided over one of the most difficult periods in Bolivian history. His government faced the impossible task of both resolving the country's worst economic crisis, caused by years of military mismanagement, and responding to the pent-up demands of social groups. At the same time, Siles faced extreme pressure from international financial institutions to implement harsh austerity measures and from the United States to combat the booming cocaine industry. Governing Bolivia under these circumstances proved to be a daunting task. By late 1984, the economy had fallen to a historic low, reaching a yearly hyperinflation rate of 26,000 percent. Faced with tremendous pressure from every sector of Bolivian society, Siles was forced to convoke elections for July 1985 and step down one year before his term expired.

Siles retired from politics in 1985 and returned to Uruguay, where he has lived ever since. Siles was largely responsible for launching Bolivia on the route to democracy.

SILVA, BENEDITA DA

Benedita da Silva (Benedita Souza da Silva; *b.* 11 March 1942), first Afro-Brazilian woman to be elected to Brazil's congress. Da Silva, known as Bené, was one of thirteen children born to a poor Rio de Janeiro family. Married at sixteen, she had five children in rapid succession, of whom only two survived. She was an early member of the newly formed Worker's Party (Partido dos Trabalhadores—PT), and in 1982 successfully ran on the PT ticket for Rio's city council. In 1986, having campaigned largely in Rio's *favelas* (slums), she was elected as a federal deputy to the Chamber of Deputies, Brazil's lower house, becoming one of only nine blacks and twenty-five women in Brazil's 559-member Congress.

Reelected in 1990, she continues to live in Chapéu da Mangueira, the Rio *favela* that is her home.

An energetic supporter of the rights of the oppressed, da Silva describes herself as "three times a minority," stating: "As a black, a woman, and a *favelada* [slum dweller], I have a special responsibility to speak out on the subjects that I know about—against racial discrimination, against the unequal rights of women, and against the injustices suffered by the poor." An evangelical Christian, da Silva is a member of Brazil's rapidly growing Assembly of God Church. She ran unsuccessfully for mayor of Rio de Janeiro in 1992. In 1994 she was elected senator from Rio de Janeiro, becoming the first black woman to serve in the Senate.

— DAPHNE PATAI

SILVA, CLARA

Clara Silva (*b.* 1907; *d.* 1976), Uruguayan poet, novelist, and critic. Silva was born in Montevideo and began writing poetry early on. Her first book, *La cabellera oscura* (The Dark Mane, 1945), showed a mature writer. It was followed by *Memoria de la nada* (1948). A second phase in her work began with *Los delirios* (1954), a collection of sonnets on human and divine love. *Las bodas* (The Wedding, 1960) is a collection of poems that deal with religion, a preoccupation that continued in *Preludio indiano y otros poemas* (1960) and more pointedly in *Guitarra en sombra* (1964). *Juicio final* (1971) is her last book of poems. Her fiction included *El alma y los perros* (The Soul and the Dogs, 1962), *Aviso a la población* (Warning to the Population, 1964), *Habitación testigo* (A Room as Witness, 1967), *Prohibido pasar* (1969), a collection of short stories, and *Las furias del sueño* (The Furies of Dreaming, 1975).

An active participant in the cultural and literary life of Montevideo, she was married to Alberto ZUM FELDE, a prominent critic and writer. She wrote two books on the life and work of the modernist Uruguayan poet Delmira AGUSTINI and elaborated an idealist vision of America through three universal themes: nature, love, and death. In 1976 she received the Grand National Prize of Literature of Uruguay. Silva died in Montevideo.

— MAGDALENA GARCÍA PINTO

SILVA, FRANCISCO MANUEL DA

Francisco Manuel da Silva (*b.* 21 February 1795; *d.* 18 December 1865), Brazilian conductor, cellist, teacher, and composer. Silva studied at the music school in which Padre José Maurício Nunes GARCIA taught children who were unable to pay for musical instruction.

At the age of ten he began to study cello and shortly thereafter was accepted as a boy soprano in the Royal Chapel Choir. He studied counterpoint and composition with Sigismund Neukomm, the Austrian composer who had been lured to Brazil by the promises of Dom João VI, the reigning monarch intent on establishing a school of fine arts. Although Silva wrote considerable sacred music, several art songs, and some instrumental and piano music, he is remembered principally for his patriotic songs and especially for composing the Brazilian national anthem.

— DAVID P. APPLEBY

SILVA, JOSÉ ANTÔNIO DA

José Antônio da Silva (*b.* 1909), Brazilian painter. Born in the interior of the state of São Paulo, Silva gave up his life as a rural agricultural laborer and at the age of thirty-seven, moved to São José do Rio Prêto, where he taught himself painting. Iconoclastic, with a contempt for art critics, Silva did a painting entitled *Hanging the Critics*. For his first three compositions, he won the first prize at a local exhibition whose jury, ironically, was composed of several important art critics.

While early works such as *Houses in the Rain* have an impressionistic look, later paintings were more radical and expressionistic. Examples of these latter include *Roundup, Crucifixion, Swimmers,* and *Demon Stampeding the Herd.* In his best-known work, *The Cotton Harvest,* for instance, painted in 1949, Silva attained dramatic effects by his unconventional use of color and bold composition. His paintings document his own life as well as that of the history of Brazil. He participated in a number of São Paulo biennials and exhibited his works outside of Brazil, including the 1954 Hispano-American Biennial in Havana and two Venice bienalles. In 1967 he founded a museum in São José do Rio Prêto in which he housed old baroque artwork from the local area, paintings of other artists, and those of his own. Silva is the author of *The Romance of My Life* (1949) and two novels, *Alice* and *Maria Clara.*

— CAREN A. MEGHREBLIAN

SILVA, JOSÉ ASUNCIÓN

José Asunción Silva (*b.* 26 November 1865; *d.* 24 May 1896), Colombian poet and important precursor of Spanish modernism. Silva was born into wealth, but left school early due to difficulties with his fellow students. He continued to read the classics (French, English, and Spanish) with other young literati and traveled extensively in Europe (1884–1886), where he met Oscar Wilde and Stéphane Mallarmé. His family's ruin in the

1885 civil war forced his return. He attempted to establish a business career, but failed. His lack of success and his sister's death forced him to work as secretary of the Colombian Legation in Venezuela (1894). He lost his manuscripts in a shipwreck on his return trip to Colombia and committed suicide upon failing to rebuild his career a second time. Silva's works are the posthumous *De sobremesa* (1925), a partly autobiographical novel, and *Poesías* (1910). Despite their brevity, both are revolutionary in theme and technique. His

---

Silva lost his manuscripts in a shipwreck on his return trip to Colombia and committed suicide upon failing to rebuild his career.

---

poems rate among the most musical and rhythmic in the Spanish language. Most notable are "Nocturno III," on the death of his sister Elvira, "Día de difuntos," "Los maderos de San Juan," and "Vejeces."

— MARÍA A. SALGADO

SILVA, LINDOLFO

Lindolfo Silva (*b.* 25 November 1924), rural labor spokesman of the Brazilian Communist Party (PCB). Born on a farm in Rio de Janeiro State, he worked as a tailor until hired by the PCB in 1952. In 1954, he helped found the semiclandestine Union of Farmers and Agricultural Laborers of Brazil (ULTAB), becoming its first secretary. He traveled the nation to address farm workers, published regularly on rural labor matters, and led delegations of workers to lobby officials and attend Soviet-bloc conferences on peasants. Silva's 1963 election as president of the government-sanctioned National Confederation of Agricultural Laborers demonstrated PCB strength in the countryside and in national politics. With the coup d'état of 1964, the military suppressed the PCB, and Silva went into hiding. He did, however, remain a party bureaucrat into the 1990s.

— CLIFF WELCH

SILVA, LUÍS INÁCIO LULA DA

Luís Inácio Lula da Silva (b. 6 October 1945), Brazilian politician. Luís Inácio Lula da Silva (popularly known as Lula) was born in Garanhuns, Pernambuco, the son of Aristides Inácio da Silva and Euridice Ferreira de Melo. A lathe operator, he became a prominent labor leader of the *novo sindicalismo* labor movement that emerged after the Getúlio Vargas era.

From 1979 to 1981, he was president of the São Bernardo do Campo Metallurgical Workers Union of São Paulo and led several strikes in the São Paulo industrial area. In 1986, he received the most votes in the parliamentary elections of the state of São Paulo and was elected federal deputy. In that capacity, he was a participant in the *constituinte* (constitutional convention) that drafted the 1988 constitution. During this constitutional convention, he voted in favor of nationalization of the country's mineral reserves, agrarian reform, protection of national enterprises, and a forty-hour work week. He continued to serve in the federal congress until 1990.

After founding the Partido dos Trabalhadores (Workers' Party, or PT) in 1980, he ran for the presidency of the republic in 1989 and again in 1994. In the runoff elections, Lula lost to Fernando COLLOR DE MELLO and to Fernando Henrique Cardova, respectively. He remains a major political figure in Brazil and frequently travels and lectures abroad where he is a well-known socialist labor leader.

— IÊDA SIQUEIRA WIARDA

SILVA, ORLANDO

Orlando Silva (Orlando Garcia da Silva; *b.* 3 October 1915; *d.* 1978), Brazilian singer and songwriter. As a youngster, Silva loved to sing, carrying leaflets of popular songs with him everywhere. Despite his lack of formal training either in music or voice, Silva received an invitation from Francisco ALVES to sing in his program on Rádio Cajuti in 1934. That same year, Silva starred in radio shows under the pseudonym Orlando Navarro and made his first recordings, "Olha a baiana" (Look at the Girl of Bahia) and "Ondas curtas" (Short Waves). Throughout his career, Silva appeared in various films, including *Cidade-mulher* (City Woman, 1934), *Banana da terra* (Banana of the Earth, 1938), and *Segura essa mulher* (Hold That Woman, 1946). In 1936 he participated in the inauguration of Rádio Nacional, where he became the first singer to have his own show. The following year he recorded one of his greatest hits, "Lábios que beijei" (Lips That I Kissed). Silva was the first singer to interpret PIXINGUINHA's famous "Carinhoso" (Darling). In 1939, four of his productions received prizes: "A jardineira" (The Gardener), "Meu consolo é você" (You Are My Solace), "História antiga" (Ancient History), and "O homem sem mulher não vale nada" (A Man Is Worthless Without a Woman). In 1954, while broadcasting his midday radio program Doze Badaladas, which boasted a huge audience, Silva was awarded the title *rei do rádio* (king of radio). A few years later, he released the record *Carinhoso,* a recording of his greatest hits.

— LISA MARIĆ

SILVA, XICA DA

Xica da Silva (*b.* ca. 1745; *d.* ca. 1796), mulatto mistress of the fantastically rich João Fernandes de Oliveira the younger, a diamond contractor in Minas Gerais from 1759 to 1771. Oliveira was so deeply in love with the slave Francisca (her baptismal name) that he convinced her owner to set her free. The story of Xica da Silva is a mixture of fact and legend. Apparently, Oliveira lavished a fortune on her, including building an artificial lake complete with sailing vessels.

Xica da Silva, the daughter of a Portuguese man and an African slave, has assumed an enduring place in the history of Brazil as a personification of the slave woman whose beauty and charms permit her to gain power over her master and lover. For some, her stature is a reflection of the cult of *mulata* beauty. For others, she represents a nationalist anti-imperialist statement. This latter perspective is evident in the film *Xica da Silva* (directed by Carlos Diegues, 1976; released in the United States, 1982), in which Xica da Silva uses her wiles to combat the Portuguese imperial authorities.

— DONALD RAMOS

SILVA HENRÍQUEZ, RAÚL

Raúl Silva Henríquez (*b.* 27 September 1907), archbishop of Santiago, Chile (1961–1983), during a period of intensifying political struggle between the Left, Right, and Center, which culminated in the 1973 right-wing military coup that brought General Augusto PINOCHET to power.

Unlike the majority of Chilean bishops, Silva was a member of the Salesians, a religious order dedicated primarily to missionary and educational work. Trained as a lawyer at the Catholic University in Santiago, Silva studied philosophy and theology in Italy, where he was ordained in 1938. Upon his return to Chile, he served as a professor and administrator in the Salesian major seminary and secondary schools. In the 1950s he became the director of Cáritas, a church-sponsored social welfare agency that focused on the urban and rural poor.

Silva was appointed to the archbishopric of Santiago in 1961 as a compromise between ostensibly more liberal and conservative candidates. The prelate soon became identified with the progressive sector and was particularly active in promoting workers' rights and agrarian reform, in part through divestment of some of the Catholic church's own properties. He was made a cardinal in 1962.

Silva maintained courteous relations with the Socialist government of Salvador ALLENDE (1970–1973), repeatedly serving as a mediator between it and the centrist Christian Democratic opposition. Eventually he came to accept military intervention as necessary in view of escalating public chaos and a deepening economic crisis. After the coup that ousted Allende, as the extent of assassinations, torture, and disappearances, as well as generalized repression became apparent, Silva helped organize the ecumenical Committee of Cooperation for Peace. When Pinochet forced that institution to close in 1975, the prelate created the Vicariate of Solidarity to provide legal, medical, and social services to victims of the Pinochet regime. He also supported the creation of the Academy of Christian Humanism to analyze public policy issues and assess government responses. By the time of his retirement in 1983, he had become one of the most outspoken critics of the military government.

— MARGARET E. CRAHAN

SILVA HERZOG, JESÚS

Jesús Silva Herzog (*b.* 14 November 1892; *d.* 14 March 1985), leading Mexican economist, author, intellectual, and public figure. Born in San Luis Potosí, he was the son of a German immigrant mother and Mexican engineer. Silva Herzog began his career as a teacher at the National Teachers School in 1919 and rose to prominence in the Secretariat of Education. After serving as ambassador to the Soviet Union, he managed Pemex, the national petroleum concern, for Lázaro Cárdenas in 1939. He served many years as a professor of economics at the National University, where he trained many disciples, and founded and directed *Cuadernos Americanos,* a leading interdisciplinary, intellectual journal. A recipient of the National Prize in Arts and Sciences (1962), Silva Herzog died in Mexico City.

— RODERIC AI CAMP

SILVA LISBOA, JOSÉ DA

José da Silva Lisboa (Visconde de Cairú; *b.* 16 July 1756; *d.* 20 August 1835), Brazilian political economist and politician. Born in Brazil of a Portuguese father and Bahian mother, Silva Lisboa, completed his education at the University of Coimbra in Portugal, then taught Greek, Hebrew, and moral philosophy at Coimbra and in Bahia. Influenced especially by Adam Smith, he published *Princípios de direito mercantil* (1798, 1801) and *Princípios de economia política* (1804), the first major works in Portuguese about liberal political economic theory.

When the Portuguese court, fleeing Napoleon's invasion of the Iberian Peninsula, arrived in Bahia in 1808, Silva Lisboa inspired Emperor João VI's first decree in Brazil, which opened Brazilian ports to direct commerce with foreign nations. Serving as government spokesman, he argued in *Observações sobre o comércio franco do Brasil* (1808) that his free-trade measure would increase government revenues and revive Portuguese manufacturing by forcing it to compete with other nations' industries. Although it did not remove all monopolies and special privileges, the decree that opened Brazil's ports represented a major shift away from mercantilist colonial policies.

In the last years before independence, Silva Lisboa defended the idea of constitutional monarchy and opposed the reimposition of mercantilism but did not call for Brazil's separation from Portugal. After that separation came to pass, his loyalty to the first emperor of independent Brazil marked him as a political conservative. Through his career, Silva Lisboa held high political offices, including member of the 1823 Constituent Assembly and senator from Bahia (1826–1835).

— ROGER A. KITTLESON

SILVA XAVIER, JOAQUIM JOSÉ DA

Joaquim José da Silva Xavier (Tirantendes; *b.* 1746; *d.* 21 April 1792), a participant in the Inconfidência Mineira. Silva Xavier was born near São João del Rei, Minas Gerais, Brazil. His father was a Portuguese-born gold miner important enough to be elected to the town council of São João del Rei; his mother was a native of Minas Gerais. Orphaned at an early age, Silva Xavier was raised by his brother, a priest. It is probable that his godfather, a dentist, provided Silva Xavier with the skills of what became his occasional trade and thus was the source of his nickname, Tiradentes (Toothpuller).

Silva Xavier has become a symbol of opposition to

Portuguese imperialism and of advocacy of

Brazilian independence.

After an unsuccessful career as a muleteer and gold miner, Silva Xavier joined the royal dragoons as an *alferes* (ensign). He became the commander of the troops guarding a crucial portion of the Caminho Novo, the road between the mining district and Rio de Janeiro—

an important post because gold and diamonds were shipped over this road.

Silva Xavier became involved in plotting independence after meeting José Álvares Maciel, newly returned from Portugal and England and imbued with the ideas of the French Enlightenment. The serious planning took shape in late 1788. Silva Xavier's motives for participating were probably a mixture of personal frustration at repeatedly being passed over for promotion and ideological commitment to ending Portuguese domination. Of the central group of plotters, Silva Xavier was the least important socially but perhaps was the most active in spreading their ideas. Under questioning he was unique in assuming sole responsibility for the plot. He was the only plotter to be executed by the state.

Silva Xavier has become one of the major heroic figures of Brazil's past—a symbol of opposition to Portuguese imperialism and of advocacy of Brazilian independence. While his role in the Inconfidência Mineira has often been controversial, he now is a significant symbol of Brazilian nationalism, reflecting the need for a national hero with strong republican roots.

— DONALD RAMOS

SIMON, ANTOINE

Antoine Simon (*b.* ca. 1844; *d.* ca. 1923), president of Haiti (1908–1911). Simon overthrew Pierre NORD-ALEXIS and became the first black since Lysius SALOMON to occupy the president's chair. From southern Haiti, uneducated, and with real sympathy for common folk and folk culture, Simon exhibited populist qualities. But overwhelming problems isolated him from those whom he might have served well.

Growing U.S. capitalist interests burdened his administration. The City Bank of New York extended its interests in the Bank Nationale d'Haiti and financed the McDonald contract—based on grants to James P. McDonald to build a railroad from Port-au-Prince to Cap Haitien. The McDonald contract especially irked rural *cacos* of northern Haiti, who envisioned the confiscation of their small farms to build the hated American railroad. German and French capitalists also were active in the Haitian economy.

Simon's oppression of mulattoes, arbitrary arrests of protesting schoolteachers, and mass slaughter of a *caco* town in northeastern Haiti focused foreign scorn on him. In August 1911 he went into exile.

— THOMAS O. OTT

SIMONSEN, MÁRIO HENRIQUE

Mário Henrique Simonsen (*b.* 19 February 1935), Brazilian minister of finance (1974–1979) and of planning

(1979). Economist, professor, public official, and business administrator, Simonsen served as Brazil's principal economic minister following the high-growth period known as the Economic Miracle (1968–1974). Relatively orthodox in his economic thinking, Simonsen joined the faculty of the Instituto Brasileiro de Economia of the Fundação Getúlio Vargas in Rio de Janeiro in 1961, acted as director of the Graduate School of Economics (1965–1974), and became vice president of the institute (1979). In the mid-1960s, as a staff member in the planning ministry led by Roberto CAMPOS, he designed the wage policy formula and participated in the creation of the housing finance system. In addition to his term as minister, he served as the president of the Brazilian Literacy Movement Foundation (Fundação Movimento Brasileiro de Alfabetização—MOBRAL) from 1970 to 1974 and as director of Citicorp (since 1979) and of other companies.

As minister of finance, Simonsen organized Brazil's response to the increase in world oil prices in 1973 and the adjustment to its spectacular growth in manufacturing capacity during the Economic Miracle. His program, reflected in the Second National Development Plan (Il Plano Nacional de Desenvolvimento), attempted to reduce dependence on external energy and other imports through large public investment projects in basic industry and infrastructure, including transportation and communications. Brazilian private and state companies as well as foreign firms participated in the program, which was financed in part with petrodollars. At the same time, to control inflation and to deal with recurring problems in Brazil's balance of payments and foreign reserves, Simonsen often resorted to restrictive macroeconomic policies in spite of their recessionary impact, although growth during the period was still substantial. In 1979, he resigned as planning minister in the new president's cabinet, owing to public resistance to the prospect of even harsher macroeconomic policies in response to rising inflation; he was replaced by Antônio DELFIM NETO.

– RUSSELL E. SMITH

SIMONSEN, ROBERTO COCHRANE

Roberto Cochrane Simonsen (*b.* 18 February 1889; *d.* 25 May 1948), Brazilian economist and industrialist. Raised in the port city of Santos, Simonsen studied engineering at São Paulo's Escola Politécnica. He graduated in 1909. In the 1910s, as director of a construction company in Santos, Simonsen experimented with methods of scientific management as well as with new forms of labor negotiation.

In the 1920s and 1930s, Simonsen became Brazil's most prominent advocate of industrialization, and emerged as the leading spokesman for São Paulo's powerful industrialist federation. In 1933 he founded the Escola Livre de Sociologia e Política; his appointment as professor of economic history at this institution for advanced study in the social sciences led him to compose his most famous work, *História econômica do Brasil, 1500–1820* (1937).

By the late 1930s Simonsen had become a supporter of the authoritarian regime of Getúlio VARGAS, participating in several national economic commissions in which he called for protective tariffs, state intervention, and economic planning to promote industrial development. Simonsen energetically defended this position at the end of World War II, when Brazil faced intensified foreign competition and U.S. pressure for a return to liberal trade policies.

With the transition to electoral politics, Simonsen successfully ran for the federal senate in 1947. As senator he continued to promote the interests of industry, calling for the suppression of the newly legalized Communist Party, which he considered the chief threat to "social peace." Simonsen died while delivering an address to the Brazilian Academy of Letters, to which he had been elected in 1946.

– BARBARA WEINSTEIN

SINÁN, ROGELIO

Rogelio Sinán (Bernardo Domínguez Alba; *b.* 25 April 1902; *d.* 1993), Panamanian writer and diplomat. Sinán was born on the island of Taboga in the Gulf of Panama. After graduating from the National Institute of Panama in 1923, he attended the Pedagogical Institute in Santiago, Chile, the University of Rome, and was awarded a degree in dramatic arts from the National University of Mexico.

With the appearance, in 1929, of his first book, *Onda* (Wave), Sinán became known as the initiator of the vanguard movement in Panama. *Plenilunio* (1947; Full Moon), *A la orilla de las estatuas maduras* (1946; At the Edge of the Aged Statues), *La boina roja* (1954; The Red Beret), *La isla mágica* (1979; The Magic Island), *La cucarachita Mandinga* (1937; Mandinga, the Little Cockroach), and *Chiquilinga* established his impact on the renewal of the short story, the novel, and theater in Panama, and earned him the title of "Sinán the Magician." He received various literary prizes: first prize in the Inter-American short-story competition sponsored by the Mexican newspaper *El Nacional* (1953) for *La boina roja,* and the 1943, 1949, and 1977 Miró Prize for *Plenilunio* (novel), *Semana Santa en la niebla* (poetry), and *La isla mágica* (novel).

He taught Spanish literature at the National Institute of Panama. He was also director of the department of fine arts and professor of theater at the University of Panama and a member of the Panamanian Academy of the Spanish Language, as well as consul for Panama in India.

— ELBA D. BIRMINGHAM-POKORNY

SINCLAIR, ALFREDO

Alfredo Sinclair (*b.* 8 December 1914), Panamanian painter. After working as a neon sign technician, Sinclair studied under Humberto IVALDI in Panama and then at the Escuela Superior de Bellas Artes E. de la Cárcova in Buenos Aires until 1950. Upon his return to Panama, he became an art professor at the Escuela Nacional de Artes Plásticas and later at the National University.

Initially a figurative painter, in the 1950s Sinclair was influenced by abstract expressionism, which led to the development of a personal style dominated by color and light. His paintings fluctuate from a semi-abstraction with references to the real world, as exemplified by his numerous collages and cityscapes like *La Ciudad* (1962), to a complete lyrical abstraction, as in his series *Movimientos de un río* (1981).

— MONICA E. KUPFER

SINHÔ

Sinhô (José Barbosa da Silva; *b.* 18 September 1888; *d.* 4 August 1930), Brazilian songwriter. Born on Rua do Riachuelo, Rio de Janeiro, Sinhô was encouraged to study the flute by his father, who revered *chôro* performers. Sinhô (his family nickname) eventually abandoned the flute in favor of the piano and guitar. To earn a living, Sinhô played the piano at the society balls and in the dance clubs of Cidade Nova. At twenty-six, he was well regarded as a professional pianist.

His samba "Quem são eles?" (Who Are They?) of 1918 won immediate attention for its innovative rhythm and sparked a musical debate about the samba that soon became tradition in Rio de Janeiro. Organizing a group by the same name, Sinhô and his Quem São Eles? provoked traditional *sambistas,* who were devoted to their folkloric roots and resented Sinhô's urban melodies. He won tremendous success at Carnival in 1920 with "Fala, meu louro" (Speak, My Parrot), a parody of Rui BARBOSA, and "O pé de anjo" (Angel's Foot). Persecuted by the police for his political satire, such as in "Fala baixo" (Speak Softly), a title alluding to gov-

ernment censorship, Sinhô was temporarily forced into hiding. He was named the *rei do samba* (king of the samba) in 1927 and reached the height of his popularity in 1928 with "Jura" (Promise) and "Gosto que me enrosco" (I Like to Swing), the latter coauthored by Heitor dos Prazeres. Although diagnosed with tuberculosis, Sinhô continued to write music intensively until his death in 1930. Numbering almost 150 published compositions, of which more than 100 have been recorded, Sinhô's music is remembered for its urban character, providing a chronicle of daily life and customs.

— LISA MARIĆ

SKÁRMETA, ANTONIO

Antonio Skármeta (*b.* 7 November 1940), Chilean novelist and short story writer. The relevant literary figure of a generation of Chileans who lived under the military dictatorship of 1973–1990, Skármeta went into voluntary exile in 1975. He lived in Argentina and Germany and returned to Chile in 1989. Skármeta is the author of the short story collections *El entusiasmo* (1967), *Desnudo en el tejado* (1969), *Tiro libre* (1973), and *Novios y solitarios* (1975). His novel *Soñé que la nieve ardía* (1975) (*I Dreamt the Snow Was Burning* [1985]) attests to the social and political aspirations and frustrations of the Salvador ALLENDE years. *No pasó nada* (1980) is a short novel of the experience of exile, and *Insurrección* (1982) (*The Insurrection* [1983]), describes the eve of the Sandinista revolution in Nicaragua. *Ardiente paciencia* (1986) (*Burning Patience* [1987]), a humorous novel portraying Pablo NERUDA as matchmaker, was also presented as a drama and a video-film, and *Match Ball* (1989) is a satirical novel of the world of tennis. Skármeta's narrative style mixes the nostalgia of a young generation's dream of social revolution with the experience of exile, parodying many literary genres from poetry to popular fiction to drama to journalism. Skármeta has also written a number of dramatic scripts besides *Ardiente paciencia,* among them *Si viviéramos juntos* (If We Lived Together) and *Permiso de residencia* (Residence Permit).

— CEDOMIL GOIC

SOBREMONTE, RAFAEL DE

Rafael de Sobremonte (*b.* 27 November 1745; *d.* 14 January 1827), intendant of Córdoba (1783–1797), viceroy of Río de la Plata (1804–1807). Born in Seville to a noble family, Sobremonte trained for a military career. After service in Ceuta and Puerto Rico, he arrived in Buenos Aires in 1779 as viceregal secretary under Viceroy VÉRTIZ. Three years later he married Juana

María de Larrazábal, the daughter of a prominent local family. With Vértiz's patronage, he secured the post of intendant of Córdoba (1783), where he served as a dynamic, model administrator. In 1797 Sobremonte was promoted to subinspector general of the military within the viceroyalty, and seven years later was named viceroy.

Sobremonte is best remembered for his ignominious flight to Córdoba during the English invasion of 1806.

Although he was well-known and respected throughout the region, Sobremonte's tenure as viceroy proved to be deeply disappointing. He is best remembered for his ignominious flight to Córdoba (ostensibly to raise fresh troops) during the English invasion of 1806, leaving the city of Buenos Aires to defend itself as best it could. Sobremonte was deposed by the Buenos Aires *cabildo* in 1807 and arrested shortly thereafter. He was allowed to return to Spain in 1809. Exonerated of any wrongdoing in 1813, he was allowed to continue his military career. Named to the Council of the Indies in 1814, he retired the next year, dying in Cádiz after a long illness.

— SUSAN M. SOCOLOW

SODRÉ, NELSON WERNECK

Nelson Werneck Sodré (*b.* 27 April 1911), retired Brazilian army officer, historian, and intellectual. Son of a lawyer-businessman, Sodré, a native of Rio de Janeiro, attended the Colegio Militar (1924–1930) and the Escola Militar in Rio de Janeiro (1931–1934). He was a career army officer until his retirement in 1961. He was a professor of military history at the Escola do Estado Maior do Exército (Army General Staff School) from 1948 to 1950. In 1955 and 1956 Sodré was editorial editor at the center-left Rio newspaper *Última Hora*. In 1954 he became chairman of the history department at the Instituto Superior de Estudos Brasileiros (ISEB), a position he held until the military government closed the ISEB in the immediate aftermath of the coup in 1964. Since 1964 he has lived in Rio de Janeiro, devoting himself to intellectual pursuits.

Sodré participated in the Brazilian nationalist movement of the 1950s and early 1960s. During the 1950s he was influential in the Military Club, a group that generally sought to represent the interests of army officers, and played a role in the successful campaign to nationalize Brazilian oil. He also participated in ISEB's

efforts to articulate a "national-developmentalist" ideology, which sought to overcome Brazil's colonial economic structure through national capitalist development.

Though never a political militant, Sodré has been a lifelong Marxist, and in addition to his other works, he has written texts on Marxist theory. He was imprisoned for several months after the coup of 1964 and for a time thereafter was prohibited from public speaking and writing in the press.

— BRIAN OWENSBY

SOJO, FELIPE

Felipe Sojo (*d.* 1869), Mexican sculptor. At the Academy of San Carlos in Mexico City, Sojo was a part of the first generation of students to leave behind the colonial technique of sculpture in wood and color, replacing it with white marble. In 1853 students under the Catalán master Manuel VILAR presented a biennial exhibition of their work. Sojo's contributions, a relief entitled *La degollación de San Juan Bautista* and the portrait *Señorita Barreiro,* are representative of two of the most common forms of sculpture at the time: the religious theme and the portrait. Sojo later took up another theme in sculpture: allegory. After the death of Manuel Vilar in 1860, Sojo was named director of sculpture at the academy.

The variety of patrons with whom Sojo became connected is notable. In 1853 he sculpted an industrial allegory for the Spanish architect Don Lorenzo de la Hidalga's private residence. As director at the academy during the reign of MAXIMILIAN, he undertook two projects commissioned by the emperor himself: a sarcophagus for the emperor Agustín de Iturbide, which was never completed, and whose plaster model was destroyed by the new republican regime after its triumph over the French, and a portrait in marble of Maximilian, which resides at the Mexican Museum of National History.

— ESTHER ACEVEDO

SOLANO, FRANCISCO

Francisco Solano (*b.* March 1549; *d.* 14 July 1610), Franciscan missionary. Born in Montilla, Spain, Solano studied at the Jesuit college in that country, took minor orders, and was professed as a Franciscan in 1570. For twenty years he worked in Spain as a preacher and a novice master. In 1589 he arrived in America, where he worked principally with the Calchaquí Indians of central Argentina. Solano was the superior of all Franciscan houses and missions in the area and established houses and missions throughout Tucumán. He was noted for his compassion, patience, and love of the Indians. Solano died in Lima and was buried in the Franciscan church there. He was beatified in 1675 and canonized in 1726.

— NICHOLAS P. CUSHNER

SOLDI, RAÚL

Raúl Soldi (*b.* 27 March 1905; *d.* 21 April 1994), Argentine painter, printmaker, and muralist. Soldi was born in Buenos Aires and studied there, at the National Academy of Fine Arts, as well as at the Brera Royal Academy in Milan. He had a strict figurative training in drawing; later, in contact with the school of light devotees (Chiaristi), he developed his own technique and style. In 1938–1939 he worked in theater design and on numerous films. In 1953 he began painting murals in the chapel of Santa Ana in Glew, a small village in the province of Buenos Aires. Working there only in the summer, he finished in 1976. He painted the dome of the Teatro Colón in Buenos Aires in 1966 and a mural at the basilica of the Annunciation in Nazareth, Israel, in 1968. Soldi received numerous awards, including the Palanza Prize from the National Academy of Fine Arts (1952). In 1993 he had a retrospective of his work at the Salas Nacionales de Exposición.

— AMALIA CORTINA ARAVENA

SOLER, ANDRÉS, DOMINGO, AND FERNANDO

Andrés, Domingo, and Fernando Soler (*b.* 1899, 1902, 24 May 1900; *d.* 1969, 1961, 25 October 1979), Mexican film and stage actors. Three pillars of Mexican theater, altogether, the Soler brothers starred in over 200 films. They were key players in the "golden age" of Mexican cinema. Andrés and Domingo Soler served as character and secondary actors in such films as *Doña Bárbara* (1943), *Historia de un gran amor* (1942), *La barraca* (1944), and *Si yo fuera diputado* (1951). Fernando Soler had leading roles in the films *Rosenda* (1948), *La oveja negra* (1949), *México de mis recuerdos* (1943), *Una familia de tantas* (1948), and *Sensualidad* (1950), and received the Ariel from the Mexican film academy in 1951 for best performance by an actor. The Solers constitute one of the few family dynasties of Mexican cinema.

— DAVID MACIEL

SOLÍS, JUAN DÍAZ DE

Juan Díaz de Solís (*b.* mid-1400s; *d.* 1516), navigator who explored the Río de la Plata estuary. The birthplace of Díaz is unclear. Some think it was Lebrija (Seville); others argue that his family migrated from Asturias to Portugal, where he was born. He voyaged to India for Portugal several times, served French corsairs, then moved to Spain in late 1505. He met Juan de la Cosa and Amerigo VESPUCCI at a conference summoned by King Ferdinand in Burgos in 1508, and was commissioned on 23 March 1508 to search for a passage to the Orient along with Vicente Yáñez PINZÓN. The exact itinerary is debated; it seems there was a coastal reconnaissance from central America north to the Yucatán, then Mexico's central Gulf coast.

Díaz de Solís returned to Spain and was serving in the Casa de Contratación in Seville in the late summer of 1509. When Amerigo Vespucci died (22 February 1512), Díaz de Solís was named *piloto mayor* (chief pilot) and commissioned to head two voyages, both of which came to naught. He was encharged with another expedition, which left Sanlúcar on 8 October 1515. This group explored the Río de la Plata estuary in early 1516. When Solís and his party disembarked to take possession of the left bank of the estuary, at a place before the confluence of the Uruguay and Paraná rivers, they were attacked. Indians wielding bows and arrows killed Solís and several companions.

— NOBLE DAVID COOK

SOLÍS FOLCH DE CARDONA, JOSÉ

José Solís Folch de Cardona (*b.* 4 February 1716; *d.* 27 April 1770), viceroy of the New Kingdom of Granada (1753–1761). Born in Madrid into a prestigious and noble family, Solís arrived in New Granada as one of the youngest American viceroys yet appointed. He was accused by contemporaries and modern historians of having a youthful and dissipate moral character, as evidenced by the notorious Marichuela liaison, which created a scandal in Bogotá. But his political administration has generally been judged one of the best in the eighteenth century. Solís is especially known for his promotion of transportation improvements throughout the viceroyalty.

Solís was accused by contemporaries and modern historians of having a youthful and dissipate moral character.

As with his predecessors, complaints of poor health led him in 1757 to request a replacement. Two years later Ferdinand VI tapped Pedro MESSÍA DE LA CERDA

(1761–1772) as the next viceroy. Surprisingly, after he stepped down, Solís entered the Franciscan order and gave much of his personal fortune to the church. He remained in a Santa Fe de Bogotá monastery until his death.

— LANCE R. GRAHN

SOLOGUREN, JAVIER

Javier Sologuren (*b.* 19 January 1921), Peruvian poet, publisher, and essayist. His father was the cousin of the poets Ricardo and Enrique Peña Barrenechea. Javier Sologuren studied literature and humanities in Peru, Mexico, and Belgium. He began publishing in the 1940s. In the 1950s, he lived in Sweden for seven years. Upon returning to Peru, Sologuren undertook the publication of his Ediciones de La Rama Florida, printing Peruvian and foreign literatures on a manual press. In 1960, he received the National Poetry Award. Later, Sologuren organized his poetry architectonically under the title *Vida continua* (1944, 1971, 1980, 1989, 1992).

Sologuren's essays on pre-Columbian and contemporary Peruvian arts, crafts, and literature, reformulating national Andean tradition, link him to such writers as Emilio Adolfo Westphalen, José María Arguedas, and Jorge Eduardo Eielson, and to the painter Fernando de Szyszlo. He also worked with European and Asian literatures, translating Swedish, French, Italian, and Brazilian poetry into Spanish and collaborating in the translation of classical Japanese works.

— LUIS REBAZA-SORALUZ

SOLÓRZANO, CARLOS

Carlos Solórzano (*b.* 1 May 1922), Mexican playwright, director, professor, critic, historian, and governmental impresario. Born in Guatemala City, Solórzano moved to Mexico in 1939 to pursue studies in architecture and literature. In 1948 he received a degree from the National Autonomous University of Mexico. He studied dramatic art in Paris until 1951. Solórzano's exposure to French existentialism resulted in a successful three-act play, *Las manos de Dios* (1956), in which the protagonist chooses personal freedom and metaphorically the freedom of humanity over the repressive forces of church and state. Two earlier full-length plays and several one-acters deal with similar issues. Solórzano was the first critic to deal with twentieth-century Latin American theater on a hemispheric scale; his two books present overviews of major currents and comparative views by country. For years Solórzano was artistic director of the University Theater, taught classes, and wrote reviews and criticism; during the presidency of

José López Portillo, he promoted theater under a project called Teatro de la Nación (1977–1981). He is married to Beatriz Caso de Solórzano, a sculptor and artist.

— GEORGE WOODYARD

SOLÓRZANO PEREIRA, JUAN DE

Juan de Solórzano Pereira (*b.* 1575; *d.* 1655), Spanish jurist and author. Solórzano studied civil and canon law at the University of Salamanca and taught there before being named oidor of the Audiencia of Lima in 1609. In Peru he oversaw the rehabilitation of the Huancavelica mercury mine, married a creole woman from Cuzco, and mastered legislation related to the Indies. By the time he returned from what he considered exile in the New World as *fiscal* of the Council of the Indies in 1627, he was the foremost authority on the laws of the Indies. He published *De Indiarum iure* from 1629 to 1639 and, in 1647, a modified five-volume version, *Política indiana,* for readers of Spanish. Solórzano also was a major contributor, in 1636, to the final draft of the *Recopilación de leyes de los reynos de las Indias,* which was finally published in 1681. Unlike many of his contemporaries, Solórzano considered public office to be a public trust rather than a piece of property.

— MARK A. BURKHOLDER

SOMERS, ARMONÍA

Armonía Somers (Armonía Etchepare de Henestrosa; *b.* 1914; *d.* 1994), Uruguayan writer, educator, and critic. Born in Montevideo, Somers taught elementary school for many years and served in various capacities in the Montevideo school system. She has written on subjects related to the education of adolescents. Her literary career began in 1950 with the publication of her first novel, *La mujer desnuda.*

From the beginning, Somers has been considered one of the major fiction writers of Uruguay, together with Juan Carlos ONETTI and Felisberto HERNÁNDEZ. She is known for the innovative narrative style that she incorporates in her novels, considered by many as a fundamental break with the Uruguayan novel of the 1950s. In 1953 she published her first collection of short stories, in which a nightmarish and erotic atmosphere becomes almost unbearable to the alienated characters. *La calle del viento norte y otros cuentos* (The North Wind Street and Other Stories, 1963), her second collection of short stories, shows a more mature writer in style and depth, one who works slowly and patiently on the margins of literary circles.

Two novels followed, *De miedo en miedo* (From Fear to Fear, 1965) and *Un retrato para Dickens* (1969). *Todos los cuentos* (1967) included the two earlier collections of stories plus two unpublished ones. In these works Somers continued to elaborate the fictional world created in her previous works, emphasizing cruelty and loneliness as central elements that shape the lives of her protagonists.

After a silence of nine years, Somers published a second edition of her short stories. By that time her work had begun to be noticed by critics and readers in several countries. In 1986 she published *Viaje al corazón del día* and *Sólo los elefantes encuentran mandrágora* (Only Elephants Encounter Mandragora), the latter being her most ambitious and difficult text. She also published two additional anthologies of her work, *Muerte por alacrán* (1979; Death by Scorpion) and *La rebelión de la flor* (1988).

— MAGDALENA GARCÍA PINTO

SOMOZA DEBAYLE, ANASTASIO

Anastasio Somoza Debayle (*b*. 5 December 1925; *d*. 17 September 1980), president and dictator of Nicaragua (1967–1979). "Tachito" Somoza was the younger son of Anastasio SOMOZA GARCÍA. Unlike his older brother, Luis, Tachito rose to power through the Nicaraguan military. A graduate of West Point (1948), he returned to Nicaragua to take on a number of high-ranking positions in the National Guard. His father, while president, made him commander of the Guard. Like his father, Tachito believed the National Guard was the only reliable constituency of support for the Somoza family. While Luis, as president, implemented liberal policies and moderate social reform, Anastasio provided the muscle to maintain control over Nicaraguan society.

The human-rights abuses of the Somoza regime caused U.S. President Jimmy Carter to cool relations with the once favorite son.

He used the National Guard to quell minor outbreaks of social unrest. During his brother's presidency (1956–1963), Tachito increasingly came into conflict with Luis on the issue of his own presidential ambitions. His brother's death in 1967 removed a restraining influence over Tachito, who engineered his temporary resignation from the National Guard to be eligible constitutionally to run for president. In 1967, the third Somoza was "elected" to the presidency of Nicaragua.

Tachito proved to be much more his father's son than did his older brother. He has been characterized as greedy, cruel, repressive, and inhuman. He continued his father's methods in maintaining Conservative compliance by raising the party's congressional seat allocation to 40 percent. He continued the pro-U.S. policy of his father and brother (his father had allowed the CIA to use the Managua airport in 1954 for bombing raids against the Arbenz government in Guatemala) and even offered Nicaraguan troops for Vietnam. Strict and repressive control kept him in power, and the stable economy initially kept discontent in check. The middle sectors of Nicaraguan society were weak and divided, and Somoza still represented order in a country where a small guerrilla group, the Sandinista National Liberation Front (FSLN), was beginning to cause political concern.

On 23 December 1972 a massive earthquake hit Managua and Somoza reclaimed the presidency under the auspices of a state of emergency. The corruption that characterized this period included the diversion of international relief funds and the private access to relief supplies of Somoza, his cronies, and the National Guard. Such behavior alienated the Nicaraguan upper classes and resulted in the formation of a broad opposition front, which was formed to challenge Somoza in the 1974 elections and led by *La Prensa* editor Pedro Joaquín CHAMORRO CARDENAL. Increasing numbers of young Nicaraguans from all classes were joining the FSLN in its struggle against the Somoza dictatorship. As the success of FSLN attacks increased, Somoza used the National Guard to repress violently any form of perceived opposition. The human-rights abuses caused U.S. President Jimmy Carter to cool relations with the once favorite son.

In 1977 Somoza suffered a heart attack but did not relinquish power. In 1978 Chamorro was assassinated. Somoza and the guard were blamed, and Somoza's violent repression of the ensuing demonstrations solidified opposition forces on the left and the right. Washington attempted to negotiate, offering "Somocismo without Somoza," but with Somoza's own intransigence and the opposition's strength, the mediation was rejected. An Organization of American States resolution demanded his resignation, and Tachito was forced to leave Nicaragua on 17 July 1979.

On the invitation of President General Alfredo STROESSNER, Somoza ultimately went into exile to Paraguay. On 17 September 1980 he was killed in Asunción when a bomb exploded in the car he was driving. An Argentine guerrilla organization was initially held responsible, but subsequently the FSLN military was connected to the assassination.

— HEATHER K. THIESSEN

SOMOZA DEBAYLE, LUIS

Luis Somoza Debayle (*b.* 18 November 1922; *d.* 13 April 1967), president of Nicaragua (1956–1963). Son of Nicaraguan dictator Anastasio SOMOZA GARCÍA, Luis Somoza was the elder and more liberal brother of Anastasio SOMOZA DEBAYLE. He attended a number of universities in the United States and returned to Nicaragua to sit as a member of the Nationalist Liberal Party (PLN) in Congress while his father was president. Although Luis had an officer's commission in the National Guard, he chose the path of politics and became the president of the PLN, the president of Congress, and the first designate to the Nicaraguan presidency. Upon his father's assassination, Luis assumed the presidency. He served out his father's term and then was elected to the presidency in his own right.

Luis Somoza is best known for relaxing the political repression that characterized his father's time in power. Social reforms of his term included housing development, social-security legislation, limited land reform, and university autonomy. He allowed some measure of freedom of the press and released political detainees, measures that were aimed at improving the regime's image. His liberal social policy notwithstanding, four out of his seven years in office were conducted under martial law, and a number of abortive uprisings were repressed. His goal in liberalizing Nicaragua's political environment was the removal of the Somoza family from obvious political power, making them less vulnerable to attack and opposition. It has been suggested that Luis Somoza envisioned a role for the PLN based on the corporate political model of Mexico. Moreover, he sought a way for his family to exercise "discreet control" through the PLN, a plan that brought him into direct conflict with his younger brother, Anastasio ("Tachito"), who had assumed control of the National Guard under their father's last term in office. Luis's moderate approach was rejected by Tachito, who, like his father, felt control could be maintained only through the National Guard and a hard-line military style. Luis restored the constitutional articles banning the immediate reelection or succession to the presidency by any relative of the incumbent or by the incumbent himself. He reinforced this legislation by stepping down at the end of his term. Luis did not intend to remove the Somozas from power, however, and engineered the selection and election of PLN candidate René SCHICK GUTIÉRREZ, a close Somoza associate, in 1963.

During his time in office, Luis attempted to reestablish friendly relations with Nicaragua's neighbors and supported the establishment of the Central American Common Market (CACM). Despite the variance in political style, Luis maintained the strong pro–United States stance of his father, allowing the ill-fated Bay of Pigs Invasion to be launched from Nicaragua's eastern coast. His last years were spent in conflict with his younger brother over the latter's aspirations to the presidency. Luis's death from a heart attack in 1967 removed a moderating influence from the Somoza family.

– HEATHER K. THIESSEN

SOMOZA GARCÍA, ANASTASIO

Anastasio Somoza García (*b.* 1 February 1896; *d.* 29 September 1956), Nicaraguan dictator (1936–1956) and patriarch of the Somoza dynasty. Born in San Marcos, "Tacho" Somoza dominated Nicaragua from 1930 to 1956. Born in Carazo, department of San Marcos, Tacho was the grandnephew of Bernabé Somoza, Nicaragua's most notorious outlaw. He attended school in Philadelphia, where he gained an excellent command of English. Upon returning to Nicaragua, Somoza embarked upon a military career that would result, with the support of the U.S. representatives in Nicaragua, in his meteoric and violent rise to the presidency. He married Salvadora Debayle, the niece of leading Liberal and President Juan Bautista SACASA, and gained entrance to the upper circles of Nicaraguan society and politics. During the 1927–1933 U.S. military occupation of Nicaragua, Somoza came to the attention of U.S. Secretary of State Henry Stimson. Based on his command of English and charismatic enthusiasm for the United States, he was named Stimson's envoy and also nicknamed "el yanqui." In 1927 the United States gave him command of the newly created National Guard. The guard was created to maintain order in the violent world of Nicaraguan politics, thus allowing the withdrawal of the U.S. Marines.

Under Somoza's tutelage, the guard became increasingly powerful, placing him in a position to challenge and surpass even the political and legal authority of the Nicaraguan president. Not surprisingly, he became embroiled in a struggle for political power with President Sacasa, his uncle-in-law, and increasingly used the guard to exert his influence and control over Nicaragua. In 1934, after Sacasa had completed peace negotiations with the guerrilla commander Augusto César SANDINO, Somoza arranged for Sandino's murder. It has been suggested that he was forced into the plot to maintain his control over the guard. Somoza's authorization for the murder, however, was representative of his methods. Using the guard as a power base, Somoza ousted Sacasa from the presidency in 1936.

Backed by the guard, Somoza came to the presidency with more personal power than any other president in

Nicaraguan history. Despite legal blocks to his becoming president—he was barred from the position as a relation of Sacasa and as commander of the National Guard—Somoza was "elected" to the presidency in December 1936. Although described as charming, astute, and ambitious, Tacho Somoza used guile, opportunism, and ruthlessness to maintain and build a political and economic dynasty. As president he maintained supreme command of the National Guard. He reestablished the Nationalist Liberal Party as a personal political machine, dusted off at election time to ensure his candidacy. The Conservative opposition was bought off with the 1948 and 1950 political pacts that guaranteed them one-third of congressional seats and a place on the Supreme Court while ensuring their compliance with Somoza's domination of Nicaragua.

His economic control of the country increased steadily. He came to power with the proverbial "ruined coffee finca," and died leaving personal wealth estimated between $100 and $150 million. His attitude toward Nicaragua was summed up in a single line, "Nicaragua es mi finca" (Nicaragua is my farm). His exploitation of foreign aid and technical assistance (a substantial amount due to his very pro-U.S. stance) and his opportunism during World War II increased his private holdings dramatically. Under the pretext of combating Nazism, he confiscated German and Italian-owned properties. By 1944 Somoza was the largest private landowner and the leading producer of sugar in the country. His holdings soon expanded to include meat and mining companies, cement works, textile mills, milk processing, and state transport facilities, many of which were monopolies. There were also the "dirty" businesses of gambling, brothels, racketeering, illegal alcohol production, and monopoly control of export-import licensing, much of which occurred with National Guard participation.

Somoza's ability to stay in power stemmed from his control over the National Guard but also from political astuteness. When the winds of political change began to favor prodemocracy movements and rising discontent resulted in democratically elected governments in Guatemala and El Salvador in the 1940s, Somoza enacted a new labor code in 1944 and an income tax law in 1952, and established a development institute in 1953. This "social progress" coincided with an economic boom from the expansion of the cotton industry. Somoza's support was also bolstered by Washington. His pro-U.S. line brought funding for infrastructure development. Despite increasing discontent with his economic and political domination and repressive tactics, the United States saw him as a staunch ally in a region that was fast becoming a concern for U.S. policy. His heavy-handed methods were cause for President Franklin D. Roosevelt's famous description of Somoza as "a son of a bitch, but our son of a bitch." Other Central American leaders became increasingly concerned with his power. In 1954 the Organization of American States (OAS) had to intervene to prevent Somoza from supporting Costa Rican exiles in launching a coup attempt on President José FIGUERES FERRER from Nicaraguan soil.

Ultimately, the repressive nature of Somoza's economic, political, and military dictatorship resulted in his assassination. On 21 September 1956, a young Nicaraguan poet, Rigoberto López Pérez, shot Somoza in León. Somoza had been in the city

Anastasio Somoza García (left) and U.S. President Franklin D. Roosevelt. (Organization of American States)

to receive the presidential nomination from the Nationalist Liberal Party. U.S. Ambassador Thomas Wheaton, with support from President Dwight D. Eisenhower, airlifted Somoza to the American military hospital in Panama, where he died. He was survived by his wife, a daughter, and three sons (one illegitimate). Two of his sons, Luis and Anastasio, would continue the dynasty for another twenty-three years.

— HEATHER K. THIESSEN

SONTHONAX, LÉGER FÉLICITÉ

Léger Félicité Sonthonax (*b.* 17 March 1763; *d.* 28 July 1813), French politician and lawyer. Sonthonax, a native of Oyonnax, France, was a controversial figure whose actions led to profoundly important but unintended results. Appointed commissioner of Saint-Domingue by Louis XVI in June 1792, with the mandate to halt revolutionary activity in the French colony, he implemented the 1792 decree that gave civil rights to coloreds (persons of mixed black and white heritage) and outlawed slavery. The decree had been designed to quell the frustration of blacks and win their support against the British. Instead, revolutionary momentum continued to increase. In 1794 irate white landowners and the revolutionary leader Toussaint L'OUVERTURE forced Sonthonax out of Saint-Domingue and into the hands of the British. He returned to France but two years later was sent back to Haiti, where he undertook an unsuccessful campaign to eradicate voodoo (*vodun*) culture. Sonthonax retired to France in 1797 and died at Oyonnax.

— ANNE GREENE

SORIANO, JUAN

Juan Soriano (*b.* 18 August 1920), Mexican painter and sculptor. Born in Guadalajara, Jalisco, Mexico, he studied with Roberto MONTENEGRO and Jesús (Chucho) Reyes Ferreira. In 1934, Soriano participated in the first one-person show of his paintings in the Guadalajara Museum. He left Guadalajara for Mexico City in 1935 and became affiliated with the Primary School of Art, where he later taught, and the Group of Revolutionary Writers and Artists (LEAR). In the 1950s, Soriano was at the forefront of the Mexican avant-garde movement. He lived for several periods in Rome: 1951–1952, 1956, and 1970–1974. Beginning in 1975 he lived in both Paris and Mexico City.

While Soriano has, throughout his career, associated with all of the great Latin American artists of his time, he has never been identified as a member of a particular group or school. His lyrical and idiosyncratic style does not lend itself easily to classification. He possesses a distinct quality of "Mexican-ness," which is graphically reflected in his works of the 1940s. Since the 1950s his work has reflected a more international scope. With Rufino TAMAYO, Soriano has had a major impact on the internationalization of Mexican art, and his own work has been exhibited internationally since the 1970s. In 1991, the Museum of Modern Art in Mexico City presented a major retrospective exhibition of his work.

— CLAYTON KIRKING

SORIANO, OSVALDO

Osvaldo Soriano (*b.* 1943; *d.* 29 January 1997), Argentine writer. Born in Mar del Plata, Soriano is perhaps best known for the film adaptations of several of his novels, especially *No habrá más penas ni olvido* (1980; *A Funny Dirty Little War,* 1986), which uses the microcosm of a small town in the province of Buenos Aires as the arena for the bloody internal conflicts within the Peronist Party during its brief return to power (1973–1976). The events described in the novel become an allegory of Argentine sociopolitical violence and the irrational yet deadly forces it unleashes. *Cuarteles de invierno* (1982)—the film version starred the actor, psychiatrist, and dramatist Eduardo Pavlovsky, whose own works constitute a prominent entry in contemporary Argentine culture—focuses on the arbitrary exercise of violent power as yet another microcosmic example (it too takes place in a small town on the pampas) of a constant in Argentine history and life.

Soriano, as a significant example of the generation of writers in Argentina to emerge during the neofascist tyranny of the 1976–1983 period, has shown a particular talent for using a narrative voice colored by an intense black humor to describe common men (his narrative world is resolutely sexist) enmeshed in a horrendously violent political process. In his first novel, *Triste, solitario y final* (1976), an acerbic attack on U.S. culture is an oblique condemnation of Argentine cultural dependency.

— DAVID WILLIAM FOSTER

SOTO, HERNANDO DE

Hernando de Soto (*b.* ca. 1496/1497; *d.* 21 May 1542), Spanish explorer and conquistador. Born in Villanveva de Barcarrota, Soto came to America in 1514 as a member of the Pedro Arias de ÁVILA expedition to Darién. By 1520, Soto had acquired substantial wealth from the slave trade in Central America. In 1532, he joined Francisco PIZARRO in the conquest of Peru, and after accumulating significant wealth from the spoliation of Peru, returned to Spain in 1536. Soto had been present at the capture of ATAHUALPA at Cajamarca and afterward had taken Cuzco. Although Soto was at this time one of the richest conquistadores, on his return he sought the governorship of Florida. His expedition landed in Florida near modern Tampa in May 1539. Soto's search for a kingdom as wealthy as Tenochtitlán and Cuzco led his group from Tampa Bay to the modern states of Tennessee and Arkansas. The armada then moved to northwest Texas, and after traveling east to modern Georgia, marched west again to the Mississippi River,

---

Soto's corpse was thrown into the Mississippi River

to keep the Indians from learning that he had died.

---

reaching Pánuco after crossing the Gulf of Mexico in makeshift boats. Soto died in Guachoya in present-day Louisiana. His corpse was thrown into the Mississippi River to keep the Indians from learning that he had died. Only his cruelty toward Indians compares with his foolhardy pursuit of the mirage of a flourishing city in the hinterland.

— JOSÉ RABASA

SOTO, JESÚS RAFAEL

Jesús Rafael Soto (*b*. 5 June 1923), Venezuelan artist. Born in Ciudad Bolívar to a peasant family living on the edge of the Orinoco River, Soto spent his youth in the countryside with Indian companions. He began his career by painting posters for the local movie house. At age nineteen he won a scholarship to study at the Cristóbal Rojas School of Fine and Applied Arts in Caracas, where he met Alejandro OTERO and Carlos CRUZ DIEZ. He became interested in synthetic and geometric forms in the manner of Cézanne and the cubists. In 1947 he was named director of the School of Fine Arts in Maracaibo and held his first exhibition two years later at the Taller Libre de Arte in Caracas. In 1950 he traveled to Paris, where he became friendly with Vasarely, Duchamp, and Calder and exhibited at the Salon des Réalités Nouvelles in 1951 and 1954. In 1955 his relief *Spiral* (composed of a sheet of plexiglass separated from the background, which by repeating the same thumblike fingerprint pattern produced visual movement) was included in the exhibition The Movement, which officially launched the kinetic art movement. In 1958 he launched his *Vibration* series (formed by a black and white thin-striped surface in which twisted wires or squares were hung in front, producing a visual vibration whenever the viewer moved in front of them). That

same year he created two kinetic murals for the Venezuelan Pavilion at the Brussels International Exposition.

In 1963 Soto's work in the São Paulo Bienal was awarded the Grand Wolf Prize. The following year he won the David Bright Prize at the Venice Biennale and the second place at the American Bienal in Córdoba, Argentina. In 1965 he received the first prize at the first Salón Pan-Americano of Painting in Cali, Colombia. He had major retrospectives at the Stedelijk Museum, Amsterdam (1968), and at the Museum of Modern Art of Paris, where he presented his *Penetrable* (1969), an environment constructed out of plastic wires in which the viewer could play.

In 1969 the Venezuelan government created the Jesús Soto Foundation. Four years later the Museum of Modern Art Jesús Soto opened in Ciudad Bolívar filled with Soto's own private collection, which he had donated to his native city. Soto has also completed many public commissions, including kinetic murals for UNESCO in Paris (1970), and the *Esfera Virtual* for the Hilton Hotel in Caracas and the Olympic Sculpture Park in Seoul, South Korea (1988).

— BÉLGICA RODRÍGUEZ

SOTO, MARCO AURELIO

Marco Aurelio Soto (*b*. 13 November 1846; *d*. 25 February 1908), president of Honduras (1876–1883). Born in Tegucigalpa, the son of Máximo Soto and Francisca Martínez, Soto studied at universities in Honduras and Guatemala. Soto represented the best of the second generation of Liberal politicians who governed in Central America beginning in the 1870s. The Soto administration was characterized by an emphasis on scientific progress, education, foreign investment, and infrastructural development typical of the positivist governments that came to power after overthrowing Conservative regimes.

Soto had very strong connections to the Liberal Guatemalan government of Justo Rufino BARRIOS, whom he served at the cabinet level as minister of foreign affairs in the mid-1870s. In addition, he and Ramón ROSA had studied together with Barrios at the University of San Carlos in Guatemala. It was natural for Barrios to support Soto in his efforts to remove Ponciano Leiva and José María Medina as contenders for the presidency of Honduras, and at the second Conference of Chingo on 17 February 1876, Barrios and Andrés Valle of El Salvador signed a pact to do so. Meanwhile, Medina defeated Leiva at the Battle of El Naranjo on 22 February 1876, and on 8 June 1876 Medina and Soto signed the Convenio de Cedros, agreeing to name General Marcelino Mejía interim president. (Mejía served as president one week.) Soto followed as provisional president on 27 August 1876 and became constitutional president on 30 May 1877. He remained in power until 9 May 1883, when he resigned because of differences with Barrios.

Soto's administration dedicated itself to the economic progress and developmental goals espoused by Comtian positivism. The political and philosophical strength of the Liberal regime was sufficient to allow Soto to be relatively lenient with his former Conservative enemies. He was politically tolerant as a statesman, yet he did not apply this tolerance to people belonging to the lower sector of society, whom he considered lazy and without motivation. He did open a national library and initiate free public education, which had been previously decreed several times but never implemented. At the same time, Soto lamented the military interventionism in Central American civilian governments and institutionalized the armed forces on 21 December 1876 in an effort to check the military's power while defining its social and political role. These and other policies culminated in a new Liberal constitution in 1880 and the establishment of Liberal Tegucigalpa as the permanent national capital the same year.

There was also substantial economic progress during Soto's presidency. He personally helped revive the declining silver-mining industry of Tegucigalpa, particularly the El Rosario mine (Rosario Mining Co.). The government also founded a mint (Casa de la Moneda), which acted as a central bank. Soto opened up the country to foreign investment as a matter of policy, a liberal practice that paved the way for the banana boom of the early twentieth century. Infrastructural improvements accompanied economic reforms, and Soto's regime created a national postal service and a national telegraph service that provided relatively rapid and often instant communication in a country known for its regional isolation. Soto resigned in 1883, having asserted both Tegucigalpa's primacy over Comayagua and the Liberal Party's agenda as national policy. His chosen successor, Luis Bográn Baraona, continued to support Liberal oligarchical interests.

— JEFFREY D. SAMUELS

SOTO, PEDRO JUAN

Pedro Juan Soto (*b.* 11 July 1928), Puerto Rican short-story writer, playwright, novelist, and essayist. After finishing grade and secondary schools in Puerto Rico, Soto went to New York City, where, in 1950, he received a B.A. degree in English literature and language from Long Island University, and a master's degree in art from Columbia University in 1953. He divided his life

between Puerto Rico and New York City, and his works show the clash between Puerto Rico and North American cultures through his characters, humble Puerto Ricans, as they struggle with life in New York City. He published articles in *El Diario de Nueva York, Temas,* and *Ecos de Nueva York.* He was a member of a group of writers who from the 1940s on renovated the short story through new techniques and styles, such as the use of stream of consciousness, interior monologues, and a boldness in the treatment of sexual topics. Faulkner, Hemingway, Joyce, and other modern writers inspired him to break away in his own narratives from the mere depiction of rural life and customs of the Puerto Rican man of the times. Among his most known works are *Spiks* (1956), a collection of short stories, *Usmaíl* (1959), and *Las máscaras* (1958), a three-act play.

— MAYRA FELICIANO

SOTO ALFARO, BERNARDO

Bernardo Soto Alfaro (*b.* 12 February 1854; *d.* 28 January 1931), president of Costa Rica (1885–1889). As first designate, Soto assumed the presidency in 1885 following the death of Próspero Fernández, and a year later he was elected to a full four-year term. Continuing the liberal policies of his two immediate predecessors, Fernández and Tomás Guardia, Soto emphasized educational and social reforms. His Fundamental Law of Public Instruction (1886) committed the nation to free, compulsory, and secular education. The education budget was tripled during his administration. Other notable achievements included the construction of the National Library and the Asilo Chapuí mental hospital. Soto demanded complete separation of church and state, which resulted in the closing of the Jesuit University of Santo Tomás.

— THOMAS M. LEONARD

SOUBLETTE, CARLOS

Carlos Soublette (*b.* 15 December 1789; *d.* 11 February 1870), president of Venezuela (1837–1839, 1843–1847). Between 1810 and 1869, Soublette served Venezuelan governments as a soldier and a civilian. Perhaps no other military officer of his generation equaled his reputation for honesty and efficiency. Soublette served twice as president, between 1837 and 1839, following the resignation of José María VARGAS, and between 1843 and 1847. A staunch ally of José Antonio PÁEZ and a Conservative oligarch, he earned a reputation as a cautious but able administrator. His career as a politician included other important positions: vice president (1821, 1836–1837, 1839–1841), minister of war and marine (1825–1827, 1841–1842), and minister plenipotentiary to Europe (1835–1836). Forced into exile in 1848 as a result of the collapse of the Páez faction, Soublette returned in 1858, after the downfall of the Monagas regime, and served in various capacities as a military officer and as a senator, deputy, and minister between 1859 and 1869.

— WINTHROP R. WRIGHT

SOULOUQUE, FAUSTIN ÉLIE

Faustin Élie Soulouque (*b.* 1785; *d.* 1867) President of Haiti (1 March 1847–28 August 1849), emperor of Haiti (29 August 1849–15 January 1859). Faustin Soulouque was the fourth president selected to govern by the Haitian army between 1844 and 1859. Faustin, an illiterate, conducted an extremely incompetent administration. In 1847 he was elected by the Assembly to succeed President Jean-Baptiste Riché because he was perceived as being docile, and thus easily manipulated. Once in power, however, he began a twelve-year regime of terror conducted by his secret police.

A plot to eliminate him in his first year in office failed. Following the example of DESSALINES, in his second year in office, Soulouque named himself Emperor

Faustin Soulouque. (Library of Congress)

Faustin I and created a peerage drawn from black generals that included 4 princes, 59 dukes, 90 counts, 215 barons and 30 knights. These men had no governmental or bureaucratic functions to perform; they were merely reflections of Soulouque's desire for grandeur.

To legitimate his empire, in 1849 Soulouque created his own constitution. Under Soulouque, the Haitian economy was completely destroyed. He lived like an over-indulgent aristocrat, defaulting on the national debt and increasing the deficit of the Haitian government. Soulouque's desire for more power motivated him to lead costly wars against the Dominican Republic, which resulted in the intermittent occupation of Dominican territory. During his reign, Soulouque openly practiced and encouraged voodoo (*vodun*). It was the first time in Haitian history that voodoo flourished openly, with official approval. Nevertheless, his unpopularity and the opposition to his regime increased until the end of 1858. In January 1859 he fled Haiti to escape the forces of General Nicholas GEFFRARD, who became his successor.

— DARIÉN DAVIS

SOUSA, GABRIEL SOARES DE

Gabriel Soares de Sousa (*b.* ca. 1540s; *d.* 1592), Brazilian colonist. Nineteenth-century historian Francisco Adolfo de VARNHAGEN (1816–1878) determined that Sousa was the author of the seminal work *Tratado descriptivo do Brasil em 1587.* The original manuscript was lost, but with more than twenty copies, Varnhagen was able to establish the text and the identity of its author. In 1569, Sousa went to Bahia, where he acquired ownership of a sugar mill as well as several other rural estates. He lived in Brazil for seventeen years, during which he took note of everything he thought worth remembering. While in Madrid in March 1587, Sousa offered his work to Cristóvão de Moura. This manuscript was known in Portugal as early as 1589, when Pedro de Mariz (*d.* 1615) quoted it in the second edition of his *Diálogos de varia historia.*

Sousa's treatise is divided into two parts. In the first one, *Roteiro geral da costa brasílica,* he describes the Brazilian coast from the Amazon to the Río de la Plata; in the second part, *Memorial e declaração das grandezas da Bahia,* he analyzes the Government General in Salvador. This second part, the most frequently quoted by historians, documents the establishment of the colonial government by Tomé de SOUSA, describes the city of Salvador, and enumerates all the sugar mills located in the Bahian Reconcavo.

— MARIA BEATRIZ NIZZA DA SILVA

SOUSA, MARTIM AFONSO DE

Martim Afonso de Sousa (*b.* 1500; *d.* 1564), Portuguese navigator and explorer. In 1531 he was the commander in chief of a naval and military expedition to Brazil whose purpose was fighting the French who were trying to settle along the Brazilian coast. Sousa also intended to explore the rivers and the hinterland and to create Portuguese settlements. He was given full jurisdiction: power to appoint governors, to choose notaries and justice officials, and to grant land under the Portuguese formula of *sesmarias*. He left Lisbon with five ships and approximately five hundred men (sailors, troops, and settlers). He fought the French on the Pernambuco coast and, sailing south, stayed three months in Rio de Janeiro Bay in order to acquire food supplies and two more ships. The expedition went as far as Río dc la Plata. Pero de Sousa (ca. 1500–ca. 1539), Martim's brother, went up this river with thirty men to take possession of the territory for the Portuguese crown.

Returning to São Vicente, Pero de Sousa was sent to Portugal with news for King João III. Martim Afonso returned to Portugal later in July or August 1533, after having created the first *vila* of São Vicente, where the sugar enterprise was begun. Sousa received a donation from the king of one hundred leagues on the Brazilian coast.

– MARIA BEATRIZ NIZZA DA SILVA

SOUSA, OTÁVIO TARQÜÍNIO DE

Otávio Tarqüínio de Sousa (*b.* 7 September 1889; *d.* 22 December 1959), Brazilian historian. Born in Rio de Janeiro, Sousa graduated from Rio's Faculdade de Ciências Jurídicas e Sociais in 1907. He held high positions in public bureaucracies from the 1910s to 1932, after which he turned earlier interests into a career in literary journalism, publishing, and historiography, achieving his reputation in the latter two. He succeeded Gilberto de Melo FREYRE and preceded Afonso Arinos de MELO FRANCO in the direction (1939–1959) of the Coleção Documentos Brasileiros, the pivotal nationalist series published by José Olympio. He also edited the *Revista do Brasil* (1938–1943).

Sousa's own works, devoted to the key statesmen of the era from 1822 to 1850, suggest the preoccupation with the nation-state common to the period. During his Coleção stewardship over ninety volumes were published by such figures as Freyre, Jõao Camilo de Oliveira Torres, Cassiano Ricardo, Luís Viana Filho, Nelson Werneck SODRÉ, Luís da Câmara Cascudo, Afonso de E. TAUNAY, Afonso Arinos de Melo Franco, and Sérgio Buarque de HOLANDA. Sousa's role in the nationalist milieu was central to the reconstruction and rehabilitation of Brazilian studies from the 1930s through the 1950s.

– JEFFREY D. NEEDELL

SOUSA, TOMÉ DE

Tomé de Sousa (*b.* ca. 1502; *d.* 1579) first governor-general of Brazil. Of noble birth, Sousa was the illegitimate son of a prior. A descendant of King Afonso III, he spent his youth at the royal court under the patronage of his cousin, the count of Castenheira, Antônio de Ataíde. As a soldier he fought in Morocco and participated in the spice trade with India. Appointed the first governor-general of Brazil, he arrived in Brazil in 1549 with six ships and one thousand settlers, including sailors, soldiers, six Jesuit missionaries, artisans, carpenters, stone masons, and criminals. His job was to centralize royal control over Brazil, defend the territory from French pirates, and pacify and Christianize the Indians. The Portuguese settler CARAMURÚ met the new governor and promised an Indian alliance.

Sousa purchased land from the heirs of Francisco Pereira Coutinho, the Donatário of Bahia for the seat of a new capital and center of royal government in Brazil. Salvador, the new capital, was built on a location more suitable for defense. The governor provided a good example by helping personally with the construction. He then sent the chief justice and treasurer to the other captaincies to check on abuses and regularize administration, but he also went on an inspection tour of all the captaincies except Pernambuco. The new governor made land grants to settlers and expelled hostile Indians to make the settlement more attractive for European colonization. Livestock was introduced from the Atlantic islands, while *engenhos* (sugar mills) were built and fortified. Market days were established to facilitate trade with the Indians. A customhouse was erected in Salvador. Sousa fortified unprotected towns and patrolled the coastal waters to keep them free of foreign interlopers.

Tomé de Sousa had a close relationship with Manuel da NÓBREGA and the Jesuits. He relied on Jesuit reports for information and sent Jesuits on inspection tours of the captaincies. During his governorship, forts and courts were established, new towns were laid out, and missions, churches, and schools were founded.

– PATRICIA MULVEY

SOUZA, LUIZA ERUNDINA DE

Luiza Erundina de Souza (*b.* 30 November 1934), Brazilian political figure and first woman mayor of South America's largest city, São Paulo, which has a population of 12 million (1989) and provides one-third of Brazil's GNP. Born in the small town of Uiraúna, in the backlands of the northeastern state of Paraíba, Erundina, as she is known, was one of ten children. An unmarried Catholic who considered becoming a nun, she trained as a social worker and in 1971 moved to São Paulo (which, despite its location in the southeast of Brazil, has the largest concentration of Northeasterners of any Brazilian city, the result of migration due to drought and unemployment in the Northeast). Politically active first in the struggle to unionize social workers, in 1979 she became a founding member of the opposition Worker's Party (Partido dos Trabalhadores—PT), which she later represented on the São Paulo City Council and then as a state assemblywoman. A self-proclaimed Marxist who has described capitalism as "unjust and inhuman by nature," Erundina successfully ran for mayor of São Paulo in 1988 on a platform defending the rights of the landless, the working class, and the poor. She held office until 1992, when she served briefly in the cabinet of President Itamar FRANCO but experienced constant conflict with her own party, the PT. Always outspoken, she denounced corruption within the government. In 1994 she ran for a Senate seat, once again without proper support of her party, and was not elected.

— DAPHNE PATAI

SOUZA, MÁRCIO GONÇALVES BENTES

Márcio Gonçalves Bentes Souza (*b.* March 1946), Brazilian writer. A native of the state of Amazonas, Souza has been one of the most influential Brazilian writers since 1977, when his best-selling *Galvez, imperador do Acre* (*The Emperor of the Amazon,* 1980) was first published. Before then he had been a movie critic in his hometown of Manaus (early 1960s), a journalist in São Paulo (1965–1973), and a filmmaker, theater director, and playwright again in Manaus in the mid-1970s. A highly politicized author, Souza belongs to the generation of Brazilian artists who struggled under the constraints imposed by the military dictatorship between 1964 and the early 1980s. Although his reputation is due mostly to the sarcastic tone of his novels of Amazonian inspiration, including *Mad Maria* (1980; Eng. transl. 1985) and *A resistível ascensão do Boto Tucuxi* (1982), the core of his ideological and aesthetic beliefs can be found in *A expressão amazonense: Do colonialismo ao neocolonialismo* (1978). In this history of the literature of his native state, Souza develops the concept of cultural extractivism, according to which Amazonia has always been exploited aesthetically by authors in search

of the exotic for its own sake, without any commitment to the region's social or political realities.

— PEDRO MALIGO

STEFANICH, JUAN

Juan Stefanich (*b.* 3 May 1889; *d.* 1975), Paraguayan politician. Born in Asunción, Stefanich first came to public notice during the 1910s, when, as a brilliant law student, he won a series of prizes in literature and philosophy. Awarded a doctorate in law in 1920, he had already become a well-known professor, author, and political commentator.

In 1928 Stefanich helped found the National Independence League, a radical pressure group that offered a strong nationalist response to Bolivian incursions in the Gran Chaco region. After full-fledged war with Bolivia became a reality in 1932, Stefanich pushed for the strongest possible territorial gains for Paraguay, becoming disappointed when his country had to settle for less.

Stefanich drew his inspiration from an eclectic mix of Italian and Spanish fascism, German nazism, Soviet communism, and individualist democracy.

The fall of the Liberal government in 1936 gave Stefanich an opportunity to try to transform these attitudes into reality. Allying himself with Colonel Rafael Franco and the military insurgents who had seized power, he became the main spokesman for their quasi-authoritarian ideology of *febrerismo*. In this, he drew his inspiration from an eclectic mix of Italian and Spanish fascism, German nazism, Soviet communism, and individualist democracy. He argued that the new Paraguay presented the chance for a new kind of democracy (*democracia solidarista*) in which all class conflicts would cease and be replaced by a dynamic sense of community. Some elements of *febrerista* thinking, especially those that stressed firm executive power, found their way into the 1940 constitution.

Stefanich himself became foreign minister in the Franco government, but when the latter regime was overthrown in 1937, he fled into exile. He continued to participate in party politics and publish *febrerista* tracts and philosophical works from exile, and periodically reappeared in Asunción. He later came to repudiate his earlier extremism, however, in favor of a social-democratic model.

— THOMAS L. WHIGHAM

STEIMBERG, ALICIA

Alicia Steimberg (*b.* 1933), Argentine fiction writer, born in Buenos Aires. Her first novel, *Músicos y relojeros* (Musicians and Watchmakers, 1971), was a finalist in two major literary contests. Her second novel, *La loca 101* (Insane Prisoner 101, 1973), won the Satiricón de Oro Award from Argentina. In the 1980s she published several novels and a collection of short stories. The short stories are in *Como todas las mañanas* (1983), and the novels are *Su espíritu inocente* (1981), which is set in the Buenos Aires of the 1940s, *El árbol del placer* (1986; The Tree of Pleasures), and *Amatista* (1989), a humorous erotic novel that portrays the apprenticeship of a serious gentleman in the practice of erotic games. This book came out in the series La Sonrisa Vertical by Tusquets of Barcelona as the result of winning an award as the best erotic novel of the year. That same year she also published *Salirse de madre*. In 1991 she published a "gastronomic novel" for adolescents, *El mundo no es polenta* (The World Is Not Humor).

The humor and wit of the female protagonists is an important feature of Steimberg's fiction. Her novel *Cuando digo Magdalena* (1992; When I Pronounce Magdalena) won the distinguished Premio Planeta Biblioteca del Sur for 1992. It describes the daily life of a group of people confined on a ranch while practicing "mental control," a technique that became popular in Argentina in the 1990s.

— MAGDALENA GARCÍA PINTO

STORM, RICARDO

Ricardo Storm (*b.* 14 March 1930), Uruguayan composer. Storm was born in Montevideo and began his musical education while very young. He studied piano under Wilhelm Kolischer and composition with the Spanish composer Enrique Casal Chapí, who was living in Montevideo at that time. Storm's initial works, dating from the early 1950s, already showed the composer's preferred style: vocal pieces in the form of songs, lieder and opera. His compositions for piano include a suite (1949), *Fantasía* (1950), several fugues (1950–1951), and a Sonata (1963). *Introducción y allegro,* Storm's first orchestral work, was premiered in 1954 by the OSSODRE (national public broadcast symphony orchestra) under Juan Protasi. His opera *El regreso* is an intensive work, substantial in scope, based on Aeschylus's *Choephoroi,* with a libretto written by the composer. It premiered at the SODRE theater on 17 April 1958. The music is in universalist style, sober in its musical language but distinctly Italian in its dramatic vocal treatment. Among Storm's vocal and choral productions is *Tres canciones para mezzosoprano y orquesta,* on texts by the Nicaraguan poet Rubén DARÍO, performed by Matilde Siano and the OSSODRE under Antonio Pereira Arias in February 1963. Other works of his include *Música para cuerdas, piano y timbales* (1959) and a symphony (1989), both premiered by the OSSODRE.

— SUSANA SALGADO

STORNI, ALFONSINA

Alfonsina Storni (*b.* 29 May 1892; *d.* 25 October 1938), Argentine poet, teacher, and journalist. Born in Switzerland, Storni emigrated to Argentina with her prosperous Italian Swiss family when she was four. Losing most of their possessions shortly thereafter owing to bad management, they lived in San Juan Province until 1901, when they moved to Rosario, in Santa Fe Province. Storni went to work when she was ten, washing dishes and serving tables in a short-lived family restaurant, helping her mother with sewing, and taking care of her youngest brother. Her father died young in 1906, and his death changed the family's fate. Storni began to work in a factory and became interested in anarchist ideas. This background gave her the knowledge and motivation for her later work as a journalist and a feminist.

Storni joined a theatrical company that performed around the country and then taught in a rural school for two years. In 1910 she completed her degree and began a new teaching career in Rosario. She also began to write steadily. In Rosario she met a married man with whom she had a child in April 1912. She remained a single mother for the rest of her life, thus confronting the code of moral behavior of her time.

In 1912 Storni arrived in Buenos Aires, then a city of 1.5 million people. It was a booming city built after the image of Paris. At first she held small jobs and had to compete with male workers until she found a teaching position. In 1916 she published her first collection of poems, *La inquietud del rosal* (The Disquiet of the Rosebush). She also began to write articles for the magazine *Caras y Caretas*. Being a single woman, the self-supporting mother of a child, and a published poet made Storni a symbol of the rebel, the revolutionary, the feminist, and the fighter against a male-dominated society. She published *El dulce daño* (Sweet Harm) in 1918 and *Irremediablemente* the following year.

Storni began writing articles for the daily *La Nación* with the pen name of Tao-Lao. *Languidez* (1920; Languor) was received with great acclaim and won two important literary awards. That same year she was invited to Montevideo to speak about the Uruguayan poet Delmira AGUSTINI. She published *Ocre,* her major collection of poems, in 1925, and the following year *Poemas de amor* appeared in the journal *Nosotros.* She also wrote for children's theater and the play *El amo del mundo* (1927).

In 1930 Storni traveled to Europe where she met many writers, including Federico García Lorca and Ramón Gómez de la Serna. She underwent surgery for breast cancer in 1935, from which she recovered only partially. In 1938 she was honored in a ceremony along with Gabriela MISTRAL of Chile and Juana de IBARBOUROU of Uruguay. That fateful year she published her last book of poems, *Mascarilla y trébol,* and she took her life in Mar del Plata.

— MAGDALENA GARCÍA PINTO

STROESSNER, ALFREDO

Alfredo Stroessner (*b.* 3 November 1912), president of Paraguay (1954–1989). Alfredo Stroessner ruled Paraguay for thirty-five years, becoming thereby the most durable dictator in Latin America's history. The secret of his success was not to be found in any personal charisma, for he had none, nor in the support of a mass revolutionary movement, because he ruled in favor of the status quo. Nevertheless, he was more than a mere army strongman. Stroessner's longevity in power was due to an extraordinary capacity for work, an attention

Alfredo Stroessner during Independence Day ceremonies, 15 May 1986. (Reuters/Bettmann)

to detail, and a genius for organization. Behind a dull, plodding appearance he created a system of rule that approached totalitarian thoroughness, reaching into every corner of the republic and tying every significant social group to his political machine.

Little is known of his early life except that he was born in Encarnación, a southern border town on the Paraná River, to a German immigrant father and a Paraguayan mother. In 1929, at the age of sixteen he entered the Military Academy in Asunción. Three years later the Chaco War broke out and, even though his studies were not completed, Stroessner was sent to the front. Decorated for bravery at the battle of Boquerón (1932), he was awarded his commission as a second lieutenant and given an artillery command. He won a second medal after the battle of El Carmen (1934). By the end of the war (1935) he was a first lieutenant.

After the war Stroessner continued to receive favorable notice from his commanding officers, rising to captain in 1936 and major in 1940. In October 1940 he was selected as one of a group of junior officers to go to Brazil for special artillery training. After returning to Paraguay, Stroessner continued to rise in the military hierarchy. President Higínio MORÍNIGO rewarded him for staying loyal during an abortive coup in 1943 by sending him to the Superior War School; upon graduating he was appointed commander of Paraguay's main artillery unit. In 1946 Stroessner was assigned to the army's General Staff Headquarters.

The civil war of 1947 brought Stroessner to real prominence because he was one of the few officers who remained loyal to the government. Morínigo ordered him to use his artillery to smash a revolt by the navy, which had taken over the Asunción shipyards in the name of the rebel cause. Next, Stroessner took command of the southern front and successfully prevented two heavily armed rebel gunboats from ascending the Paraguay River to bombard the capital. When the rebels were finally defeated, in August 1947, he was one of a handful of officers heading a purged and reorganized army.

Post-civil war Paraguay was dominated by the Colorado Party, one of Paraguay's two traditional parties, which had provided mass support for Morínigo. With their rivals eliminated, the Colorados had a clear political field, which they took advantage of by removing Morínigo in 1948 and seizing power for themselves. Soon afterward, however, the Colorados divided into factions whose leaders struggled for the presidency. From the end of the civil war until May 1954, Paraguay had five different presidents. Stroessner was deeply involved in all the plotting. On 25 October 1948 he backed the wrong side in a coup and had to escape the country hidden in the trunk of a car; three months later he slipped back into Paraguay and rallied his artillery regiment to support the winning side in a new coup. After that he rose rapidly to the top, becoming army commander in chief in April 1951. In May 1954 he ousted the Colorados' Federico CHAVES, who still headed a faction-ridden administration, and seized the presidency for himself.

Stroessner based his government on two pillars: the army and the Colorado Party. As a much-decorated veteran of two wars he enjoyed great prestige among the soldiers. The few officers who opposed him were soon eliminated, with major purges taking place in February 1955 and June 1959. Those coincided with upheavals inside the Colorado Party, for Stroessner encouraged party bickering that allowed him to play the factions off against each other. By mid-1959 factional purges had eliminated all independent spirits among the Colorados, leaving Stroessner with a docile organization that he could dominate.

The control of a political party with a mass following made Stroessner's right-wing military dictatorship unique. By manipulating party symbols and patronage he was able to generate mass demonstrations in support of his policies. Businessmen, professionals, youth, women, veterans, and peasants were tied to the regime through the Colorados' ancillary organizations, and party cells (*seccionales*) reached into every village and every city block. Though his economic policies tended to favor large landowners and foreign investors, Stroessner was able to reward his followers through public works projects that generated jobs and contracts. Up to about 1981 steady economic growth and material improvements made the regime popular. Stroessner also permitted widespread smuggling and racketeering among top military and Colorado Party officials, with benefits trickling down through the clientele system. Those who refused to conform, however, such as the opposition Liberal and Febrerista parties and the Catholic church, were ruthlessly persecuted.

Stroessner's regime began to crumble during the 1980s. Inflation became unmanageable, capital dried up for new public works projects, and the emergence of a new middle class—the fruit of previous economic growth—challenged the regime's rigid structure. Above all, Stroessner was aging, and those around him began jockeying over the question of succession. Some of his cabinet ministers and presidential aides, calling themselves "the militants," wanted to name Stroessner's son, Gustavo, as his successor; but opposing them were the Colorado "traditionalists," who saw their chance to regain the party's independence. The feud split the military as well. When Stroessner backed the "militants"

and plotted to remove General Andrés RODRÍGUEZ as army commander, the latter struck first. During the night of 2 February 1989 Rodríguez's tanks forced Stroessner to relinquish power and leave the country for Brazilian exile.

– PAUL H. LEWIS

SUÁREZ, INÉS DE

Inés de Suárez (*b.* 1512?; *d.* 1580?), Spanish woman who played a forceful and colorful part in the conquest of Chile. In her twenties she went to America, where she became the mistress of Pedro de VALDIVIA (1500–1553). She accompanied him on his expedition to Chile in 1540, and was well liked by the conquistadores. In September 1541, during Valdivia's temporary absence, the newly founded settlement at Santiago was attacked by large numbers of natives. With the inadequate Spanish force facing total defeat, Inés de Suárez suggested the murder of seven captive caciques (chiefs) as a means of instilling terror among the natives. It is generally accepted that she did (or helped with) the killing herself. After the heads (or possibly the corpses) of the dead caciques were thrown into the crowd of attackers, Suárez donned a coat of mail and led the fighting during the remainder of the battle. The only Spanish woman in the settlement, she devoted herself to caring for the wounded and supervising food supplies.

In recognition of her contributions, Valdivia granted her an *encomienda*. When the king's representative in Lima, Pedro de la GASCA, heard charges against Valdivia in November 1548, he advised him to terminate his liaison with Suárez. (Valdivia's wife, who was in Spain, traveled to Chile soon afterward, but arrived there only after his death.) Valdivia complied with La Gasca's suggestion, and married Suárez off to one of his most trusted lieutenants, Rodrigo de Quiroga, who himself later became governor of Chile (1565–1567 and 1575–1580). As an act of penitence, Suárez maintained a small church on the Cerro Blanco in Santiago. In 1553 she and Quiroga presented it to the Dominican order. The present church near the site dates from the 1830s.

– SIMON COLLIER

SUÁREZ, MARCO FIDEL

Marco Fidel Suárez (*b.* 23 April 1855; *d.* 3 April 1927), Colombian man of letters and president (1918–1921). Suárez was born out of wedlock in Hatoviejo (now Bello), Antioquia. Although his mother, a washerwoman, was very poor, a visiting priest recognized his intellectual ability and secured his admission to the seminary in Medellín. Suárez left the seminary in 1877 before ordination and found employment as a teacher in Antioquia and Bogotá. He first gained notice in 1881, when he won a contest sponsored by the Colombian Academy to commemorate the centenary of the birth of philologist Andrés Bello. His winning essay, *Ensayo sobre la "Gramática castellana de D. Andrés Bello,"* was published, and he became a member of the academy in 1883.

In the 1880s and 1890s Suárez held increasingly important government positions and was an articulate spokesman for the Nationalist wing of the Conservative Party. As a cabinet member under President Manuel A. Sanclemente, he protested the latter's removal on 31 July 1900. Returning to public life in 1910, Suárez defeated two other candidates in the presidential election of 1917. Critics charged that his victory was fraudulent, and he had to contend with bitter opposition during his administration.

In 1919 workers who erroneously believed that the government planned to buy army uniforms abroad staged a demonstration in Bogotá. When the crowd prevented Suárez from speaking, there was an outbreak of violence in which seven persons were killed. There was also controversy over ratification of the Thomson–Urrutia Treaty, which aimed at restoring harmonious relations between Colombia and the United States. On 26 October 1921 Laureano GÓMEZ, then a Conservative deputy, directed a vitriolic attack at Suárez, accusing him of various financial improprieties. Suárez denied any misconduct but resigned the following month. He spent his remaining years writing his memoirs in dialogue form. These were published in twelve volumes as *Sueños de Luciano Pulgar* (1925–1940).

— HELEN DELPAR

SUASSUNA, ARIANO VILAR

Ariano Vilar Suassuna (*b.* 16 June 1927), poet, playwright, and novelist from João Pessoa, Paraíba, in northeastern Brazil. Suassuna received an informal education during the years he lived in the *sertão* among ballad singers, puppeteers, and storytellers whose themes, poetic forms, and language would be the substance of his writing. In 1946 Suassuna enrolled at the university in Recife, Pernambuco. With Hermilo Borba Filho and others, he founded in 1948 the Teatro do Estudante de Pernambuco, whose purpose was to bring literature to the masses through theater. Performances were given in parks, factories, churches, and squares. The same year, Suassuna received the prestigious Carlo Magno Prize for *Uma mulher vestida de sol,* a play written in 1947.

His next important work for the theater was *O auto da compadecida* (1957). No other Brazilian play has become as nationally and internationally well known as *The Rogue's Trial,* first presented in Recife. Its novelty was in the revelation of Northeastern Brazil's harsh reality, with its social problems and cultural values. The author incorporates this reality into the traditions of European theater, medieval liturgical drama, and the religious theater of the Golden Age. Suassuna was inspired by the *romanceiro popular do nordeste,* as he called the literature of the cordel.

Suassuna founded the Teatro do Estudante de Pernambuco, whose purpose was to bring literature to the masses through theater.

Suassuna dedicated himself to the theater until 1971. Not only *O auto da compadecida* but *O casamento suspeitoso, O santo e a porca,* and *A pena e a lei* were awarded prizes in Brazil and abroad. From 1971 to 1977 he wrote a novel in two parts, *Romance d'a pedra do reino,* based on ten years of historical and literary research and announced as the first volume of a trilogy. Enthusiastically received, it is an extremely ambitious work in which Suassuna, through a main character representing earlier real or fictional heroes, attempts to create an epic according to armorial or formulaic patterns. After 1977, Suassuna abandoned the theater and the novel, and returned to writing poetry. He also took up painting, illustrating *A pedra do reino,* and taught at the Federal University of Pernambuco.

— RICHARD A. MAZZARA

SUAZO CÓRDOVA, ROBERTO

Roberto Suazo Córdova (*b.* 17 March 1927), president of Honduras (1982–1986). Suazo was born in the small town of La Paz, where he practiced medicine for twenty-five years. Active in the Liberal Party for a number of years, Suazo succeeded Modesto RODAS ALVARADO in 1979 as general coordinator of the Liberal Party and leader of its conservative Rodista wing. After the military rulers agreed in 1980 to restore civilian government, Suazo was elected president in November 1981 and took office on 27 January 1982. He promoted the democratic process and moderate economic reform while cooperating with a U.S. military buildup in response to the Sandinista rise in Nicaragua, which included a substantial increase in the Honduran military as well as support of the Nicaraguan contras in Honduras. In collaboration with U.S. ambassador John Negroponte, the Honduran military, led by Colonel Gustavo ÁLVAREZ MARTÍNEZ, retained much power, thereby creating considerable anti-Americanism and internal criticism of Suazo. Suazo, however, successfully reasserted civilian authority when he dismissed Álvarez in March 1984 and replaced him with Air Force General Walter López Reyes as commander in chief of the armed forces. The FBI arrested Álvarez in Miami in November 1984 in connection with a plot to murder Suazo. Despite this shakeup in the military, there was no reversal of the trend toward greater militarization of Honduras.

– RALPH LEE WOODWARD, JR.

SUBERO, EFRAÍN

Efraín Subero (*b.* 16 October 1931), Venezuelan scholar, critic, and poet. Professor of literature at the Universidad Católica Andrés Bello and the Universidad Simón Bolívar, Subero has been a prolific writer and an important scholar in the fields of literary history and criticism, cultural criticism, and folklore. His poetry, most of which was published between 1956 and 1974, reflects his interest in popular expression and his concern for accessibility even when his writing is of private or intimate content. *Matarile* (1968) is a charming collection of poetry, stories, and one Christmas play for children. *La décima popular en Venezuela* (1977; 2d ed. 1991) is a major contribution to folklore scholarship, an extensive study and presentation of texts of this ancient traditional Hispanic form. He is also noted for his editions and bibliographical work on such figures as Rómulo GALLEGOS, Miguel Otero Silva, Arturo USLAR PIETRI, Teresa de la PARRA, Aquiles Nazoa, Andrés Eloy BLANCO, and Manuel Vicente Romero García.

– MICHAEL J. DOUDOROFF

SUBIRANA, MANUEL DE JESÚS

Manuel de Jesús Subirana (*b.* 1807; *d.* 27 November 1864), Spanish missionary in Cuba and Honduras. Born in Manresa and educated in the seminary in nearby Vich, Subirana was ordained in 1834. He left Spain in 1850 for Cuba, where he worked in El Cobre. In 1856 he was sent to Christianize the Indians of Honduras. Finding them exploited, he struggled to alleviate their misery while catechizing them. He won land and ownership titles for the Jicaque Indians of Yoro and the Paya Indians of Olancho. Subirana's protests to the central government succeeded in mitigating the widespread practices of debt peonage and forced labor. He ended the practice of paying lower prices to Indians for their sarsaparilla than was paid to ladinos. Such efforts won the trust of the Indians, enabling Subirana to baptize

thousands. After his death his work passed on to less zealous priests, and past abuses were soon revived.

– EDWARD T. BRETT

SUCRE ALCALÁ, ANTONIO JOSÉ DE

Antonio José de Sucre Alcalá (*b.* 3 February 1795; *d.* 4 June 1830), Venezuelan military officer in the Wars of Independence, Simón BOLÍVAR's trusted lieutenant, statesman, and the first constitutionally elected president of Bolivia. Sucre's parents were descended from well-to-do Europeans established in the coastal town of Cumaná. When news of the Napoleonic invasion of Spain reached Venezuela, Sucre was studying military engineering in Caracas. In July 1810 he joined the patriotic militia in Cumaná, launching a distinguished military career that culminated in the 9 December 1824 final victory of patriot forces over the Spanish at the battle of Ayacucho (Peru).

Sucre saw active service under the first and second Venezuelan republics but was forced to flee to the Antilles in 1814. After a brief effort to join patriot forces in New Granada (Colombia) at the end of 1815, he again went into exile. Aligning himself with Bolívar, who by 1816 was beginning to succeed in his campaign against loyalists in Venezuela, Sucre undertook a number of successful military assignments for the Liberator and by late 1820 had become his chief of staff. As such, Sucre undertook a delicate mission as head of an expeditionary force sent to Guayaquil (Ecuador) to aid local patriots following their October 1819 uprising against royal authority. Success in Guayaquil was followed by an expedition to liberate Quito, aided by auxiliary forces sent from Peru, which culminated in a patriot victory at the pivotal battle of Pichincha (24 May 1822) on the outskirts of Quito.

With virtually all of Gran Colombia liberated, Bolívar and Sucre turned their attention southward to Peru, where the army of José de SAN MARTÍN and its Peruvian allies were engaged in a bitter struggle against the Spanish army and royalists for possession of Lima and the once-rich viceroyalty. After Bolívar's arrival in Lima, Sucre took charge of the military campaign in the Andean highlands, achieving a crucial victory at the battle of Junín (6 August 1824) and final victory at Ayacucho in December. Sucre was the author of a brilliant strategy that led to the humiliating defeat of the royalist forces, and dictated generous, humanitarian terms of surrender.

After Ayacucho the only serious obstacle to the liberation of Spanish South America was the ragtag army of royalist General Pedro de Olañeta in Upper Peru (today Bolivia). With Sucre in hot pursuit, Olañeta's forces melted away early in 1825, leaving the twenty-five-year-old Venezuelan with the responsibility for creating a republican form of government in the former Audiencia of Charcas. Two days after his triumphant arrival in La Paz, Upper Peru's largest and economically most important city, Sucre issued a decree (9 February 1825) convoking a constituent assembly of delegates from the audiencia's five former *intendencias* to decide whether they wished to ally themselves with the former viceroyalty of the Río de la Plata, with that of Lima, or to become an independent nation. Sucre, without explicit authorization from Bolívar (who had returned to Lima after the victory at Junín) pledged to respect the wishes of the Upper Peruvian delegates.

The assembly, which met during July and August 1825 in Chuquisaca (renamed Sucre in honor of the victor of Ayacucho), voted overwhelmingly to create an independent state. Anticipating Bolívar's unhappiness, the delegates also voted to call the new nation the "Republic of Bolívar" and to name the Liberator its first constitutional president. Reluctantly accepting this fait accompli, during his visit to Upper Peru (July–December 1825) Bolívar acted as president of the infant nation, but most of the routine details of government were left to Sucre. Sucre's presidency ended when he was seriously wounded in a barracks revolt in the Bolivian capital and was forced to delegate his powers (April 1828). He left Bolivia in August of the same year for Quito, to join the woman to whom he had been married by proxy while still in Chuquisaca, Mariana Carcelén y Larrea, the Marquesa de Solanda, one of the wealthiest women in the former Audiencia of Quito.

Sucre's tenure as president of Bolivia (December 1825–April 1828) was marked by a revolutionary effort to impose economic and social reform upon a racially divided, geographically dispersed, and economically weak society led by a traditionalist elite that was jealous of its prerogatives and in time became very resentful of outside political and military influence. This effort included a wholesale reform of the Upper Peruvian church and the liquidation of most of its assets in favor of public education. Sucre created and funded a network of public secondary schools, for which he dictated a modern curriculum, recruited teachers, and provided books and supplies. New primary schools, orphanages, and asylums for the destitute were part of this reform, as were efforts to provide the principal cities with better water supplies, new public markets, street lighting, and public cemeteries. Sucre created a new port for the infant nation at Cobija, on the Atacama coast, in territory that would eventually become part of Chile. He tried to revive silver mining, the traditional mainstay of the Upper Peruvian economy, by attracting European in-

vestment, employing new technology, and reforming colonial institutions. Finally, Sucre tried to impose a revolutionary new experiment in public financing, eliminating the Indian tribute and the tithe and creating in their stead a system of taxes on wealth and income, and a universal head tax. Financially, the experiment was a dismal failure. The negative reaction toward this radical reform effort and toward the continued presence in Bolivia of large numbers of Colombian troops, along with growing hostility from Peru, eventually provoked Sucre's downfall.

The delegates also voted to call the new nation the "Republic of Bolívar" and to name the Liberator its first constitutional president.

Returning to Quito in September 1828, Sucre hoped to dedicate himself to family life and the administration of his wife's estate. But with the outbreak of hostilities between Peru and Gran Colombia, his military services were again needed. In February 1829 an army under his command defeated Peruvian invaders at the battle of Tarqui, in what is today southern Ecuador. Fresh from the victory at Tarqui, in 1830 Sucre served as president of the Congreso Admirable meeting in Bogotá, a last-ditch effort to preserve Gran Colombian unity. The Congreso failed, despite Sucre's prestige, and Bolívar's creation broke up into three independent republics. On his way back to Quito, Sucre was killed at Berruecos, near Pasto. The identity of the assassins remains the object of historical speculation.

– WILLIAM LOFSTROM

SUMAC, YMA

Yma Sumac (*b.* 10 September 1927), Peruvian-born singer, noted for the extraordinary range of her voice and her exotic stage presence. Sumac was born in Ichocan, a small mountain village in Peru. Her parents named her Emperatriz Chavarri, but she chose a variation of her mother's name when she began her singing career.

When she was little more than a child she was heard singing in a local festival by an official from Lima. He persuaded her parents to bring her to the capital, where she could be presented in concert while continuing her education at a convent school. In Lima Sumac met her husband, Moises Vivanco, a composer, musician, and the director of the Peruvian National Board of Broadcasting. He cast her as the star of his musical group, the

Compania Peruana de Arte. After a successful career in Latin America, in 1946 Sumac and Vivanco moved to the United States. Sumac became a naturalized U.S. citizen in 1955.

Sumac struggled to advance her career in the United States. With the 1950 release of her first album for Capitol Records, *Voice of Xtabay* (a nonsense word coined by the recording company to underscore Sumac's Incan roots), she caught the public's attention. Her popularity reached its climax in the early 1950s. Her records sold over a million copies. She appeared on television, in a minor Broadway musical, and appeared in the films *Secret of the Incas* (1954) and *Omar Khayyam* (1957).

Sumac's music, much of it written by her husband, was based on ancient Peruvian folk music. It was adapted to showcase her remarkable four-octave voice, and her ability to evoke the sounds of jaguars and Andean birds. Sumac also performed in opera houses in Europe and South America, singing roles in *The Magic Flute, Lakmé,* and *La Traviata.* After a hiatus of several years, Sumac returned to American music clubs in the 1970s and 1980s. She received good reviews and a modest popularity that did not match her earlier acclaim.

— SHEILA HOOKER

SZYSZLO, FERNANDO DE

Fernando de Szyszlo (*b.* 1925), Peruvian artist. Szyszlo was born in Lima. His father was a Polish geographer, his mother a native Peruvian of Spanish-Indian descent. He studied at the school of fine arts at Lima's Catholic University with Austrian artist Adolfo Winternitz (1944–1946). Soon after, he joined *Espacio* (Space), a group of painters and architects who addressed nativism—indigenous cultures—and sought renewal in their disciplines. His early paintings were figurative; after his first trip to Europe in 1949, he turned to abstraction. Szyszlo studied the lore, language, and arts of Peruvian pre-Conquest cultures. He experimented with plastic symbols derived from these cultures as they appear in architecture, ceramics, and textiles. He traveled to the United States in 1953 and remained in Washington, D.C., to serve as a visual arts unit consultant to the Organization of American States (1957–1960). He eventually settled permanently in Lima in 1970.

In the 1960s, Szyszlo worked on a series of thirteen paintings inspired by a Quechua elegy on the death of ATAHUALPA, the last ruling Inca. Each painting was inspired by an image or a phrase in the elegy. By the late 1960s, Szyszlo had created a personal style called "abstract nativism." He was artist in residence at Cornell University in 1962 and a visiting lecturer at Yale University in 1966. He received several Guggenheim Fellowships and won the first national prize for painting at the Esson Salon of Young Artists in Lima in 1964. He began to incorporate shapes suggestive of knives, ceremonial tables, and mummies wrapped in sacred gowns in his abstract paintings of the 1970s. In the 1980s he painted totemic forms in closed three-dimensional spaces that suggest chambers. Szyszlo has had a powerful influence on Peruvian painting.

— MARTA GARSD

T

TÁBARA, ENRIQUE

Enrique Tábara (*b.* 1930), Ecuadorian artist. Tábara studied painting at the School of Fine Arts in Guayaquil, his native city, and began to paint abstract compositions in 1954. With the aid of a fellowship from the Ecuadorian House of Culture the following year, he moved to Barcelona, where he studied at the School of Fine Arts and participated in the city's Hispanic-American Biennial (1955). He was influenced by Spanish informalism, from which he derived heavy impastos and textures, applying them to a repertoire of pre–Conquest-inspired themes: Ecuadorian Indian traditions, including rattlesnakes, mirrors, feathers, hieroglyphics, pyramids, and other motifs.

Returning to Ecuador in 1964, Tábara founded VAN, an Ecuadorian artists' movement against figurative indigenist art (1968). In the early 1970s he turned to a new figuration, often depicting human limbs across his canvases. He won a gold medal at the First Salon of Drawing, Watercolor, and Tempera at the House of Culture in Quito (1970).

— MARTA GARSD

TABLADA, JOSÉ JUAN

José Juan Tablada (*b.* 3 April 1871; *d.* 2 August 1945), Mexican writer. Born in Mexico City, José Juan de Aguilar Acuña Tablada y Osuna first published in *El Universal* in 1892; by the time of his death, more than

---

A trip to Japan in 1900 led to Tablada's introduction of the Japanese haiku into Spanish.

10,000 of his poems, essays, chronicles, novels, works of literary criticism, memoirs, and diaries had appeared under more than fifteen pseudonyms. Founder of *La Revista Moderna,* Tablada was strongly influenced by the French poet Charles Baudelaire. A trip to Japan in 1900 led to his introduction of the Japanese haiku into Spanish, influencing Ezra Pound and the Anglo-American imagist group, as well as poets in his own language. From 1911 to 1912 Tablada lived in Paris. When he returned to Mexico he became a supporter of Victoriano HUERTA, for which he was forced into exile in New York in 1914.

Tablada was the first to publish ideographic poems in Spanish; his book *Li-Po y otros poemas: Poemas ideográficos* appeared in 1920, following closely upon Guillaume Apollinaire's *Calligrammes.* Mexican president Venustiano CARRANZA named Tablada a member of the diplomatic service in Colombia and Venezuela, but Tablada soon resigned and returned to New York in 1920. He went back to Mexico in 1935, but spent his last years in New York, where he died. His inventive, often ingenious imagery, anticipating vanguard tendencies, gave new life to widely varied but common poetic themes, including Mexican landscapes, natural elements, and travel impressions. Tablada's reputation was solidly reestablished in the mid-twentieth century by a new generation of Mexican writers and critics, including Octavio PAZ.

— KEITH MCDUFFIE

TAJES, MÁXIMO

Máximo Tajes (*b.* 23 November 1852; *d.* 21 November 1912), military leader and president of Uruguay (1886–1890). Tajes began his military career as a distinguished soldier in the army while it was at war with Paraguay. He rose rapidly to the rank of captain (1875) and lieutenant colonel (1880), became minister of war and the navy in 1882, and assumed the presidency in 1886. Tajes pursued the course that had moved Colonel Lorenzo LATORRE, who became dictator in 1876, and General Máximo Santos (president, 1882–1886), two men who implanted what has come to be known in Uruguayan history as "militarism." After the resignation of Santos in 1886, however, Tajes followed the advice of Dr. Julio HERRERA Y OBES and offered himself as constitutionally elected president in order to manage peacefully the transition from militarism to "civilism," a task he fulfilled satisfactorily. His administration took place during the "era of Reus," named after Emilio Reus, a young Spanish financier widely known at the time.

— JOSÉ DE TORRES WILSON

TALAMANTES, MELCHOR DE

Melchor de Talamantes (*b.* 10 January 1765; *d.* 3 May 1809), Mercedarian friar, precursor of Mexican independence. Born in Lima, Talamantes earned his doctorate in theology at the University of San Marcos. In 1807, Viceroy José de ITURRIGARAY (1742–1815) charged him with establishing the boundaries of Texas. He gained prestige and influence with important people in the capital. In 1808 he supported the proposal of the *ayuntamiento* (city council) to establish a junta of authorities and submitted a plan to form a national congress. He was imprisoned during the 1808 coup; among his papers was found a plan for independence. He died in San Juan de Ulúa, while on his way to Spain, the victim of yellow fever.

– VIRGINIA GUEDEA

TALAVERA, MANUEL

Manuel Talavera (*b*. 8 December 1875; *d*. 27 July 1950), Paraguayan politician and businessman. Talavera was a dynamic member of the Colorado Party after the 1947 civil war where the Colorados emerged victorious. A member of the right-wing *Guion rojo* (Red Banner), Talavera led his faction to victory in the aftermath of the Colorado Party convention in November 1947. The Guionists had actually lost the internal election by two votes, but Talavera's friend and presidential candidate, Natalicio González, also a *Guion rojo,* took control of the Colorado Party by force. After winning the February 1948 elections without opposition, González was sworn in as president on 15 August 1948. In February 1949 a group of dissenters in the party, led by Felipe Molas López, succeeded in overthrowing Gonzalez. Talavera's political career ended after the coup.

– MIGUEL A. GATTI

TALAVERA, NATALÍCIO

Natalício Talavera (*b*. 1839; *d*. 14 October 1867), Paraguayan poet and journalist. Born in Villarrica, Talavera became independent Paraguay's first published poet. He studied in his native town and in Asunción, where he

---

Paraguayan soldiers, it was said,

set Talavera's verses to music and sang them in the

trenches to taunt the enemy.

---

came to the attention of Ildefonso Bermejo, a Spanish publicist who had been contracted by the Carlos Antonio LÓPEZ government to launch a new state newspaper and other cultural projects. Under Bermejo's tutelage, Talavera became a first-rate writer. He con-

tributed poems and literary essays to Asunción's cultural journal, *La Aurora,* and translated Lamartine's poem *Graciela* from the French.

It was in the field of journalism, however, that Talavera most distinguished himself, regularly producing articles and essays for the state newspaper, *El Semanario de Avisos y Conocimientos Utiles.* More important, after the beginning of the War of the Triple Alliance (1864–1870), Talavera was chosen to edit *Cabichuí,* a satirical newspaper written mostly in the Guaraní Indian language. His own contributions to this periodical included biting accounts of Allied cowardice as well as clever ditties attacking the character of Emperor Dom PEDRO II and his consort. Paraguayan soldiers, it was said, set these verses to music and sang them in the trenches to taunt the enemy, who lay just beyond gunshot range.

Talavera wrote a series of chronicles from the battlefield that were serialized in *El Semanario* and much later published as a book, *La guerra del Paraguay.* He himself did not survive the war, becoming ill with what was probably pneumonia as a result of hard campaigning, and died at the Paraguayan army camp of Paso Pucu.

– THOMAS L. WHIGHAM

TALLET, JOSÉ ZACARÍAS

José Zacarías Tallet (*b*. 18 October 1893; *d*. 1985), Cuban journalist. Born in Matanzas, Cuba, Tallet moved to the United States with his family in 1912. He graduated with a bachelor's degree in accounting from the Heffly Institute of Commerce in New York City. Upon his return to Cuba in 1923, he participated in the Protesta de los Trece and the Grupo Minorista, both consisting of disenchanted intellectuals who called for change in Cuban letters and politics in the 1920s. He was instrumental in the formation of several leftist organizations, including the Falange de Acción Cubana, the Movimiento de Veteranos y Patriotas, and the Universidad Popular José Martí, of which he was first president. An ardent Marxist, Tallet expressed his ideas in such journals and newspapers as *Social, Alma Mater, Carteles,* and *Revista de La Habana.* In 1927–1928, he was editor of the journal *Revista de avance,* director of the magazine *El Mundo* from 1928 to 1933, and subdirector of the daily newspaper *Ahora* from 1933 to 1935.

For seventeen years Tallet taught world and Cuban history at the Escuela Profesional de Periodismo "Manuel Márquez Sterling," of which he was director (1959–1960). He is best known for his poetry, in which he treated both the social relevance and the aesthetic contribution of all sectors to Cuban culture. He received the Bonifacio Byrne Prize in Poetry (1944). His first book of poetry was *La semilla estéril* (1951) and his best-known poem is "La rumba."

After 1959 he became an enthusiastic supporter of the Castro revolution. He was a frequent contributor to *Bohemia,* one of Cuba's major journals, until his death.

— DARIÉN DAVIS

TAMARÓN Y ROMERAL, PEDRO

Pedro Tamarón y Romeral (*b.* ca. 1695; *d.* 21 December 1768), bishop in colonial Mexico. Tamarón was born in Villa de la Guardia, in the archdiocese of Toledo, but nothing more is known of him until 1719, when he was in Caracas with Bishop Juan José de Escalona y Calatayud. In 1758 he became bishop of Durango in Mexico. Besides some religious tracts, he wrote a long description of his bishopric (1765), based on firsthand knowledge of practically every settlement of the diocese. Because of the amount of detailed information it contains, it is one of the principal sources for colonial Nueva Vizcaya. Tamarón died in Bamos, Sinaloa, while on the first leg of a general pastoral visit.

— CLARA BARGELLINI

TAMAYO, FRANZ

Franz Tamayo (*b.* 29 February 1879; *d.* 29 July 1956), Bolivian poet and politician. Sophisticated and well educated (he spoke several languages and was an accomplished pianist), Tamayo is considered the dominant intellectual figure of the first half of the twentieth century in Bolivia. His ideas on education and the importance of the Indian culture in Bolivia, expressed in *Creación de la pedagogía nacional* (1910), are still relevant today. But it is his poetry that secured his place in Bolivian literature. Tamayo's work is the last major example of the poetic movement of *modernismo.* With his mix of musical verse, baroque erudition (mainly classical Greek and Roman literature), and German philosophy, he created a poetry strongly metaphysical in nature. Tamayo idealized the Indian, the Andes, and the poet as transcendental entities. During the years of Bolivia's war with Paraguay (1932–1935), Tamayo was a strong supporter of Daniel SALAMANCA's government. In 1934 he was Salamanca's chosen candidate in the national election. Tamayo won the election but never became president because of a coup d'état at the war front.

— LEONARDO GARCÍA PABÓN

TAMAYO, RUFINO

Rufino Tamayo (*b.* 26 August 1899; *d.* 24 June 1991), Mexican painter. Tamayo was born in Oaxaca, with its strong pre-Hispanic cultural heritage and Indian population. In 1907 his mother died and the family moved to a different neighborhood, where he began a very intense Catholic and musical education. In 1910–1911, Tamayo lived in Mexico City with his aunt. There he discovered a profound interest in drawing. He earned his living selling fruit. In 1917 he entered the National School of Fine Arts, which he abandoned because of its mediocrity and his lack of interest. Tamayo received almost no formal artistic training, but he acquired a fundamental education from drawing the pre-Hispanic objects and folk art in the Ethnographic Section of the National Museum of Archaeology.

His first solo show took place in 1926 in Mexico City. The twenty paintings and watercolors in that show already displayed his personal use of color and the peculiar images and iconography that characterized his future work. Immediately after, he moved to New York City and became acquainted with and lived near Marcel Duchamp, Stuart Davis, and Reginald Marsh. In October 1926 he opened an exhibition that was well received. In fact, Tamayo was first recognized in the United States and Europe, and only later in his own country. In 1928 he returned to Mexico and began to participate in group shows with Mexican artists. He taught painting at the National School of Fine Arts

Rufino Tamayo drawing on the lithographic stone for Dos personajes atacados por perros. *(Courtesy of Mixografia Workshop/Remba Gallery, photo by Isaias Remba)*

(1928–1930). Tamayo painted a series of still lifes, although in 1938 his themes centered on portraits and the feminine figure.

The 1930s were important in Tamayo's life. He painted his first mural, *The Music and the Song,* for the National School of Music (1933). In 1936 he again moved to New York, where he lived until 1944. He participated in a New York City project for the Works Progress Administration, which he never completed. At the end of the 1930s his painting began to be acclaimed because of its universal and Mexican meanings. He taught at the Dalton School in New York City and showed his paintings in several galleries. In 1949 he made his first trip to Europe, where he visited France, Spain, Holland, England, and Italy. He lived in Paris for several months. In the later decades of his life, Tamayo worked on his paintings, exploring the richness of the texture of canvas and working with sand, marble powder, and other material.

— BÉLGICA RODRÍGUEZ

TANNENBAUM, FRANK

Frank Tannenbaum (*b.* 4 March 1893; *d.* 1 June 1969), pioneering Latin Americanist in the United States. The son of Austrian immigrants who arrived in the United States in 1904, Tannenbaum did graduate work at the Brookings Institution, receiving his doctorate there in 1927. Subsequently, he was an internationally recognized historian at Columbia University from 1935 until his death. A versatile scholar in a time of narrow specialization, he wrote on topics ranging from prison reform to international relations to the history of slavery, arguing that Latin American slavery was more benign than slavery in the United States. His chosen area of concentration, however, was the Mexican Revolution and its consequences. His ground-breaking study of land reform, *The Mexican Agrarian Revolution* (1929), established the focus for his research: village Mexico and its struggle to adjust to the modern world.

Tannenbaum was highly skeptical of large organizations—whether governmental or private sector—and wrote provocative critiques of various theories and plans for large-scale industrialization in Latin America. Often in disagreement with other scholars, he was one of the few leftists to criticize Fidel CASTRO's government in Cuba in the early 1960s.

— JOHN A. BRITTON

TAUNAY, AFFONSO D'ESCRAGNOLLE

Affonso d'Escragnolle Taunay (*b.* 11 July 1876; *d.* 20 March 1958), Brazilian historian and educator. Taunay's historical studies centered on his adopted city and state of São Paulo. He wrote extensive multivolume works on the early history of that city, on São Paulo's *bandeirantes* (colonial explorers of Brazil's interior), and on the history of Brazilian coffee. He was the son of Alfredo d'Escragnolle Taunay, the Viscount Taunay, a distinguished novelist, historian, and statesman. Educated in Rio de Janeiro as an engineer, the younger Taunay settled in the city of São Paulo to teach science, but soon gravitated to history. He was the director of the

---

Taunay wrote extensive works on the early history of São Paulo and on the history of Brazilian coffee.

Paulista Museum there from 1917 until his retirement in 1945. In 1934 he was named to the first chair of Brazilian history at the University of São Paulo. In addition to history, Taunay's writings include studies on philology and lexicography, and translations of history and literature. He was extremely prolific, authoring an estimated 1,500 books and articles. He also located and edited numerous descriptive works by foreign travelers on Brazil. Taunay's writing tended to be prolix and short on interpretation, but his research was distinguished by solid archival documentation, much of which he himself discovered and published. He pioneered in the history of the city and state of São Paulo and of coffee and is credited with establishing the exploits of the *bandeirantes* as part of the Brazilian historical consciousness.

— EUGENE RIDINGS

TAUNAY, ALFREDO D'ESCRAGNOLLE, VICOMTE DE

Alfredo d'Escragnolle, Vicomte de Taunay (*b.* 22 February 1843; *d.* 25 January 1899), Brazilian author and politician. Taunay, born in Rio de Janeiro, was the son of Félix Émile de Taunay, a French painter who came to Brazil in 1816 as a member of the French Artistic Mission, with Jean-Baptiste DEBRET. Taunay enlisted in the army in 1861, graduated from the Military Academy in 1864, and served in the War of the Triple Alliance (1864–1870), in particular at the heroic retreat from Laguna. Soon afterward he wrote an account of the latter, *La retraite de la Lagune* (1871), which was translated into Portuguese a year later by his son, Affonso d'Escragnolle TAUNAY. He published some seven novels, often under pseudonyms, and several travel books. As a deputy for Goiás (1872–1875) and a senator for Santa Catarina (1886–1889), Taunay was active in politics during the last years of the Brazilian Empire, particularly in the cause of immigration. He remained a monarchist during the first years of the Republic. He died in Rio de Janeiro.

The quality of Taunay's fiction varies. The only novel that has been republished, *Inocência* (1872), his second, is the story of an itinerant doctor who falls in love with the young daughter of a landowner in the distant interior of Mato Grosso and of their tragic death while being pursued by her jealous father. Its most notable quality is its realism: Taunay knew this remote area well, and his descriptions of it are much more authentic than those of his contemporary José Martiniano de ALENCAR. Two other novels are *A mocidade de Trajano* (1871), his first, which is set in the coffee-growing area of Campinas, São Paulo, and combines romantic plot and realistic setting, and *O encilhamento* (1893), a rather clumsy but interesting roman à clef about the scandal-ridden boom and bust of 1890–1891. His *Memórias,* up to 1870, published (according to his wishes) a century after his birth, in 1943, is one of the few valuable personal reminiscences written in nineteenth-century Brazil.

– JOHN GLEDSON

TAURIELLO, ANTONIO

Antonio Tauriello (*b.* 20 March 1931), Argentine composer, pianist, and conductor. Born in Buenos Aires, he studied composition with Alberto GINASTERA at the National Conservatory and piano with Walter Gieseking in Tucumán. A resident conductor with the opera and ballet at the Teatro Colón, he worked extensively in the United States as assistant director and conductor of the New York City Opera, the American Opera Theater at the Juilliard School of Music, and the Chicago Lyric Opera. Tauriello has been a member of the Agrupación Música Viva (AMV) in Buenos Aires, a group founded by Gerardo GANDINI, Alcides LANZA, and Armando Krieger. The AMV ensemble presented premieres of his works, and with it Tauriello conducted performances of contemporary music in Argentina and New York. He has also appeared as conductor at the Inter-American Music Festivals in Washington, D.C. In 1968 his Piano Concerto was premiered there, a work in which Tauriello sought to explore freer relationships between the soloist and the orchestra, with the piano part existing as an independent entity. Except for some synchronization cues, the pianist can choose the speed and pacing of musical phrases and the duration of individual notes.

Other works by Antonio Tauriello: *Obertura Sinfónica* (1951); *Ricercari 1 à 6* (1963); *Transparencias* for six orchestral groups (1964); *Música* no. 3 for piano and orchestra (1965); *Canti* for violin and orchestra (1967); and *La mansión de Tlaloc* (1969), which premiered during the Third Festival of Music of the Americas and Spain in Madrid in 1970.

Among his chamber music compositions Tauriello has written *Ilynx* for clarinet, double bass, piano, and percussion (1968); *Diferencias* for flute and piano (1969); *Signos de los tiempos* for flute, violin, clarinet, violoncello, and piano (1969); Serenade no. 2 for eight instruments (1966), written to celebrate Alberto Ginastera's fiftieth birthday and *Diferencias* no. 2 for piano (1969).

– ALCIDES LANZA

TÁVARA Y ANDRADE, SANTIAGO

Santiago Távara y Andrade (*b.* 1790; *d.* 28 January 1874), a major liberal intellectual and politician in the mid-nineteenth century. Távara, a native of Piura, received a degree from the Royal Medical College of San Fernando in 1819. He contributed two widely read works to the formation of a liberal outlook in Peru. *Historia de los partidos políticos* was a series of articles explaining the Peruvian political situation in 1851 that appeared in the Lima newspaper *El Comercio.* The articles were collected and edited in 1951 by Jorge BASADRE. Távara also wrote against slavery. His writings formed part of the campaign conducted by a small antislavery movement in Peru. A staunch supporter of Ramón CASTILLA, Távara penned the only coherent argument for the abolition of black slavery in Peru, *Abolición de la esclavitud en el Perú* (1855), which attacked those who argued that abolition would mean a great increase in crime. He won a seat in the National Convention, serving in 1855–1857, and in the national Chamber of Deputies, which he held from the mid-1860s until his defeat in the hotly contested election of 1868. Távara long had fought electoral corruption, but in this instance both he and his opponent were accused of fraud. After his defeat Távara retired from politics. He died in Piura.

– VINCENT PELOSO

TAVARES, ANTÔNIO RAPÔSO

Antônio Rapôso Tavares (*b.* 1598; *d.* 1658), backwoodsman of São Paulo, born in São Miguel de Beja, Portugal. In 1628, Tavares commanded a powerful military force of several hundred *paulistas* (residents of São Paulo) and about 2,000 Indians that crushed the Jesuit reductions of Guairá and transferred at least 30,000 Guaraní slaves to the farms and plantations of São Paulo. Tavares himself set up a wheat farm along the

Tietê River with over 100 of the Indian slaves. In search of new captives, he led another large expedition to the Tape missions along the Uruguay River in 1636, again capturing thousands of Guaraní slaves.

In 1648, in his most ambitious adventure, Tavares set out from São Paulo in search of the Serranos (possibly Guaraní) Indians of the Andean foothills. Repelled by Spanish and Jesuit forces in Paraguay and weakened by hunger and disease, the expedition disbanded, with Tavares and a few followers plunging forward through the heart of the Amazon, finally reaching the Portuguese fort of Gurupá in 1651. Though acclaimed subsequently by historians as a great exploratory venture that contributed to the territorial formation of modern Brazil, the expedition was a resounding failure in its time.

Tavares wandered aimlessly through the forests of South America for over three years in search of Indian slaves.

After wandering aimlessly through the forests of South America for over three years in search of Indian slaves, Tavares returned to São Paulo, where he died a shattered and impoverished man.

– JOHN M. MONTEIRO

TAVARES BASTOS, AURELIANO CÂNDIDO

Aureliano Cândido Tavares Bastos (*b.* 20 April 1839; *d.* 3 December 1875), Brazilian legislator and publicist. Tavares Bastos was Brazil's leading exponent of the precepts of nineteenth-century liberalism, promoting them in newspaper articles, books, and parliamentary speeches. Intellectually precocious, he received a doctorate in law at the age of twenty from the law school at São Paulo and was elected imperial deputy of his native province of Alagôas the following year. He served the Liberal Party in Parliament from 1861 until 1868. Tavares Bastos ascribed most of the problems of nineteenth-century Brazil to the heritage of Portuguese absolutism, which he said had bequeathed a deficiency of individual liberty and public spirit. His goal was the modernization of Brazil, based on the examples of the United States and Great Britain. He argued for individual liberty, the usefulness of competition, religious freedom, and administrative decentralization. Among the modernizing measures he advocated were the lessening of government restrictions on business enterprise, the lowering of tariffs, the gradual abolition of slavery, the encouragement of immigration (particularly from

northern Europe), the reform of education at all levels, and the creation of competent statistical services. He also called for constitutional change in the form of an independent judiciary, direct elections, and a lessening of the power of the emperor. Based on familiarity with British and French liberal thought, Tavares Bastos's proposals for reform were characterized by thorough research and investigation. The most famous of the legislative measures he fostered was Brazil's opening of the Amazon river system to international commerce in 1866. Many other changes he advocated came to fruition after his premature death from pneumonia.

– EUGENE RIDINGS

TÁVORA, JUAREZ

Juarez Távora (*b.* 14 January 1898; *d.* 18 July 1975), Brazilian military officer, *tenente* leader, and 1955 presidential candidate.

Fifteenth son of a politically active family in Ceará, Távora attended school in nearby towns and then went to Rio and Pôrto Alegre with his brothers to complete high school. In 1916 he began army officer training. After commissioning, he met other junior officers and cadets with whom he would later revolt.

After participating in the 1922 *tenente* rebellion, Távora helped capture São Paulo in 1924. Upon abandoning the city, he assumed greater responsibility for leading the rebels and joined forces with Luís Carlos PRESTES. He gained a lasting reputation for calm, courageous behavior. Captured in 1925, he was sent to prison and began writing a memoir about the revolt.

Escaping in 1927, Távora fled the country and resumed the conspiracy. Eventually he and most of the others joined the Revolution of 1930, which was organized by Getúlio VARGAS's supporters. Távora assumed command of the Northeast and managed to gain control of the entire region within days. Afterward, he was appointed "Viceroy of the North" to oversee security in that region and became active in the Club 3 de Outubro. He formulated vaguely socialist goals for the movement, some of which he pursued in various administrative posts, including minister of agriculture (1932–1934). When his party failed to win a majority in Ceará in 1934, he returned to active duty as road engineer in the south.

In 1945 Távora joined the National Democratic Union party to support fellow *tenente* Eduardo GOMES. Throughout the coming years Távora acted as senior statesman of the officer corps concerned with petroleum, electric power, steel, and national defense. Finally he ran for president in 1955 but came in second to Juscelino KUBITSCHEK. Mostly retired, Távora remained on the political sidelines until becoming congressman from Rio de Janeiro. His last post was minister of transport under Humberto de Alencar CASTELLO BRANCO (1964–1967).

— MICHAEL L. CONNIFF

TEIXEIRA, ANISIO ESPINOLA

Anisio Espinola Teixeira (*b.* 12 June 1900; *d.* 11 March 1971), rector of the University of Brasília (1963–1964) and one of Brazil's most influential educational reformers. In his career as educational administrator he took steps to expand, democratize, and secularize public education. He was born to a landowning family in Caetité, Bahia. After working in Bahia from 1924 to 1927, Teixeira, an admirer of John Dewey and aspects of the North American educational system, earned an M.A. in 1928 from Columbia University's Teachers' College. Moving in 1931 to Rio de Janeiro, Teixeira became a leader of a group known as the Pioneers of New Education. Accused of being a subversive, a populist, and an atheist by various conservative groups, he lost his administrative post in 1935 because of political purges and stayed out of government work, alternately managing a prosperous export business in Bahia and living in Europe, until the end of Getúlio VARGAS's Estado Novo in 1945. He then resumed work as a high-level educational administrator, running two national institutes—the Coordination of Training for Advanced Scholars (Coordenação de Aperfeiçoamento de Pessoa de Nivel Superior—CAPES) and the Instituto Nacional de Estudos Pedagógicos (INEP)—and earning the wrath of conservative political groups and the support of intellectuals.

In 1963 Teixeira became rector of the University of Brasília, only to be ousted by the military coup a year later. When the new government threatened to prosecute him for alleged administrative irregularities, a wave of protests from international academic circles came to his defense. Granted special permission to leave Brazil by President Humberto Castelo Branco, Teixeira traveled to the United States, where he accepted university teaching positions. He returned to Brazil in 1966.

— SUEANN CAULFIELD

TEJADA SORZANO, JOSÉ LUIS

José Luis Tejada Sorzano (*b.* 12 January 1882; *d.* 4 October 1938), president of Bolivia (27 November 1934–17 May 1936). A lawyer by profession, Tejada Sorzano was an expert in banking and a diplomat. He was a legislator from 1914 to 1918 and was minister of finance (Hacienda) during the government of José GU-

TIÉRREZ GUERRA. He was elected vice president in 1931 and assumed the presidency when President Daniel SALAMANCA was forced to resign.

The Chaco War with Paraguay was the main preoccupation of Tejada Sorzano. There were genuine attempts to secure peace for the beleaguered nation, but Tejada Sorzano had little support and was overthrown by frustrated military officers.

— CHARLES W. ARNADE

TEJEDA, LEONOR DE

Leonor de Tejeda (*b.* 1574; *d.* ca. 1640), educator and nun. Born in Córdoba to a prominent conquistador family, Leonor de Tejeda was married to general Manuel de Fonseca y Contreras when she was twenty years old. While her husband was serving as lieutenant governor of Buenos Aires (1594–1598), Leonor began to see a need for an institution to harbor elite women with a religious vocation. When her husband returned to Córdoba, she began a school for gentlewomen in her home. The childless couple soon petitioned the crown to allow them to undertake the foundation of the first convent in Córdoba. Widowed in 1612, Tejeda continued to use her fortune and her influence with the bishop to press for the convent, which was finally created on the site of her home in 1613. Among the first group of sixteen women who entered the convent of Santa Catalina de Sena was Tejeda, who took the name of Mother Catalina de Sena and served as prioress until 1627. In 1628 she moved to the city's newly founded second convent, that of Santa Teresa de Jesús, where she served as prioress until 1637. She returned to the Sena convent sometime before her death.

— SUSAN M. SOCOLOW

TEJEDA OLIVARES, ADALBERTO

Adalberto Tejeda Olivares (*b.* 28 March 1883; *d.* 8 September 1960), military figure and governor of the state of Veracruz (1920–1924 and 1928–1932). Adalberto Tejeda Olivares was a well-known Mexican statesman of the 1920s who strove to implement the Constitution of 1917 through radical political, economic, social, and anticlerical reforms.

Tejeda grew up in the predominantly Indian canton of Chicontepec, Veracruz, and attended engineering school in Mexico City. With the outbreak of the Mexican Revolution in 1910, he enlisted in the forces of Venustiano CARRANZA (1859–1920) and rose to the rank of colonel. While serving as state delegate to the Constitutional Convention of 1916–1917, he advocated strong anticlerical measures and stringent limits on foreign ownership of subsoil rights. The two-time governor of Veracruz championed the rights of the urban and rural lower classes by supporting their efforts to organize, strike, obtain land, and enter into politics. President Plutarco E. CALLES (1877–1945) appointed him to serve as minister of government from 1925–1928, during which time he pursued an active anticlerical policy against the Catholic rebels, the *cristeros*. In 1934 the ex-governor ran for the presidency as an independent socialist, defying the official revolutionary party. He was subsequently politically ostracized by his assignment to diplomatic posts in France (1935–1937), Spain (1937–1939), and Peru. In 1948 he became a brigadier general. He died in Mexico City.

– HEATHER FOWLER SALAMINI

TEJEDOR, CARLOS

Carlos Tejedor (*b.* 4 November 1817; *d.* 3 January 1903), Argentine educator, journalist, lawyer, and politician of the national period. Born in Buenos Aires, Tejedor studied law at its university and graduated in 1837. His academic and judicial pursuits included appointments as professor of criminal and mercantile law at his alma mater in 1856 and government counsel two years later. Tejedor also edited the local *El Nacional* (1852). His greatest contribution, however, was in politics. An opponent of Juan Manuel de ROSAS, the Federalist caudillo of Buenos Aires, Tejedor returned from Chilean exile after the dictator's overthrow in 1852. He later became a representative to the Buenos Aires provincial legislature (1853). Tejedor was also minister to Brazil (1875) and governor of Buenos Aires Province (1878–1880). As governor, he opposed federalization of the city of Buenos Aires, which was accomplished only after his defeat by General Julio Argentino ROCA in the presidential election of 1880 and in the civil war that accompanied it. Tejedor justified his role in that bloody conflict by writing *La defensa de Buenos Aires* (1881). He died in the capital and his statue was erected in Palermo in 1909.

– FIDEL IGLESIAS

TELLES, LYGIA FAGUNDES

Lygia Fagundes Telles (*b.* 19 April 1923), Brazilian fiction writer. As a law student in São Paulo, Telles published a short story collection, *Praia viva* (Living Beach), in 1944. In 1949 her collection of short stories *O cacto vermelho* (The Red Cactus) received the Brazilian Academy of Letters prize for fiction, marking the beginning of a distinguished literary career that includes four novels, seven short-story collections, and eight prizes. Telles's fiction exhibits both modern literary techniques and knowledge of Brazilian life, with emphasis on the female psyche. Her most celebrated novel, *As meninas* (1973; *The Girl in the Photograph,* 1982), re-creates aspects of the 1964–1984 military regime. Telles's forte is the short story; she is known for her use of the fantastic. Her fiction reflects her era, attracting both readers and critics. Female readers recognize themselves in her strong characterizations of urban women. Her 1990 novel, *As horas nuas* (Naked Hours), follows previous directions in presenting an actress's existential concerns in present-day São Paulo. Politically outspoken, Telles participated in protests against the military regime. In 1985 she became the third woman elected to the Brazilian Academy of Letters.

– MARIA ANGÉLICA LOPES

TELLO, JULIO CÉSAR

Julio César Tello (*b.* 11 April 1880; *d.* 3 June 1947), Peruvian who played a central role in initiating the scientific study of Andean prehistory and establishing the institutional framework for protecting and conserving the Peruvian archaeological patrimony. A native Quechua speaker from Huarochirí, in the highlands east of Lima, Tello brought to his research an indigenous perspective and a passionate commitment to uncovering and elucidating the accomplishments of Andean cultures before the Spanish conquest.

Tello brought to his research a passionate commitment to uncovering the accomplishments of Andean cultures before the Spanish conquest.

Tello studied science and medicine at the Universidad Nacional Mayor de San Marcos and wrote his doctoral dissertation on the antiquity of syphilis in Peru. With support from the Peruvian government he subsequently attended Harvard, where he studied archaeology and anthropology at the Peabody Museum and completed a master's degree in anthropology. Tello then studied at London University before returning to Peru as that nation's first professional archaeologist. He immediately became the director of archaeology at the Museo Histórico Nacional and launched a series of expeditions that made him world famous.

By 1924 Tello had been appointed director of both archaeological museums in Lima while introducing the teaching of archaeology and anthropology into the Peruvian university system. During a remarkable career that spanned four decades, Tello founded anthropological journals including *Chaski, Inca,* and *Wira-kocha,* as well as Peru's principal archaeological museum, the Museo Nacional de Antropología y Arqueología.

Concurrent with these academic activities, Tello carried on a political career dedicated to the defense of Peru's indigenous population. In 1917 he was elected as Haurochirí's representative to Congress, where he served for the next eleven years.

Tello's explorations and discoveries covered much of the Peruvian coast and highlands. He identified the Chavín civilization as the matrix out of which later Peruvian cultures developed, and he considered the highland site of Chavín de Huántar as its center. Many of Tello's most important investigations—including those at Paracas on the south coast; Ancón on the central coast; Cerro Sechín, Moxeke, and Cerro Blanco (Nepeña) on the north-central coast; and Kuntur Wasi and Cumbemayo in the northern highlands—demonstrated the existence, temporal priority, and panregional extent of what is now known as the Chavín horizon. By establishing that highland Chavín civilization preceded the better-known coastal cultures such as Moche and Nasea, Tello was able to demonstrate the autochthonous character of Andean civilization and disprove Max Uhle's hypothesis of Mesoamerican and Asian origins of Peruvian high culture. Tello's contention that the roots of Andean civilization lay in still earlier developments within the tropical forest, bolstered by his research at the site of Kotosh, also proved to be influential. His contributions to later Peruvian prehistory include his excavations of the Inca occupation at Pachacamac. Tello's theoretical orientation differed significantly from the approach advocated by his North American colleagues, and in many respects his publications anticipated the ecological and structuralist approaches that became popular many decades later in U.S. and European archaeology.

Tello's publications include "Wira-Kocha," in *Inka,* 1, no. 1 (1923): 94–320, and 1, no. 3 (1923): 583–606; "Discovery of the Chavín Culture in Peru," in *American Antiquity,* 9, no. 1 (1942): 35–66; *Origen y desarrollo de las civilizaciones prehistóricas andinas* (1942); *Arqueología del Valle de Casma* (1956); *Paracas,* 2 vols. (1959–1979); *Chavín, cultura matriz de la civilización andina* (1960); *Páginas escogidas* (1967).

– RICHARD L. BURGER

TERESA CRISTINA

Teresa Cristina (*b.* 14 March 1822; *d.* 30 December 1889), empress of Brazil, youngest daughter of Francis I, king of Naples, and María Isabel, princess of Spain.

Raised in a traditionalist court, Teresa Cristina was notable for her kindness but not for looks or intelligence. When her wedding to her cousin PEDRO II was arranged, she wrote promising to do everything to assure his happiness and to follow his counsels, a promise she faithfully kept. They were married on 4 September 1843. Her patience and good humor overcame Pedro's initial disappointment and coldness, and the birth of children finally aroused affection on her husband's part. Closing her eyes to his subsequent infidelities, she kept as close to him as he would allow. She avoided all involvement in public affairs and devoted her time and income to charity. Sickness plagued her final years. Following the empire's overthrow, she could not adjust to her sudden exile from Brazil. She died in Pôrto, Portugal.

– RODERICK J. BARMAN

TERRA, GABRIEL

Gabriel Terra (*b.* 1873; *d.* 1942), president of Uruguay (1931–1938). Terra was a Colorado Party political leader who ostensibly considered himself a Batllist, that is, a follower of the great political leader and two-time Colorado president José BATLLE Y ORDÓÑEZ. By late 1932, Terra had moved ideologically to the right and became increasingly frustrated with the fact that he had to share decision making with a National Council of Administration under the partially collegial executive structure established by the 1918 Constitution. Amid the economic turmoil brought on by the depression, Terra joined forces with the Blanco (National Party) leader, Luis Alberto de HERRERA, in a nonviolent coup on 13 March 1933, taking total control of the government. The regime drafted a new constitution that returned Uruguay to a full presidential system and left the Senate in total control of the procoup factions of the Colorados and Blancos. Terra repressed the labor movement and devalued the peso in an attempt to help exporters of livestock. He served a full term under the 1934 Constitution, turning the presidency over to his elected successor, his brother-in-law Alfredo BALDOMIR.

– MARTIN WEINSTEIN

TERRAZAS, LUIS

Luis Terrazas (*b.* 20 July 1829; *d.* 15 June 1923), governor of the state of Chihuahua, Mexico (1860–1873, 1879–1884, 1903–1904). A hero of the wars against the northern Indians and the French Intervention (1861–1867), General Terrazas was the political boss and governor of Chihuahua for much of the period from 1860 to 1910. He and his family came to own more than 10 million acres of land in Chihuahua with a half million head of cattle. He was also one of Mexico's foremost bankers and industrialists.

During the French Intervention, Terrazas stood with President Benito JUÁREZ in Mexico's darkest hours, leading the forces that eventually pushed the French from the state. He maintained his alliance with Juárez, defending him against the revolt of La Noria, led by Porfirio DÍAZ, in 1872. Terrazas continued to oppose Díaz during the first decade of the latter's dictatorship. Díaz forced him out of power in Chihuahua from 1884 to 1892, but the overwhelming economic resources of the Terrazas family produced a stalemate. A reconciliation was achieved with the return of Terrazas to the governorship in 1903.

Because he and his sons and sons-in-law ran the state as a family fiefdom, occupying nearly all the important government posts, and used their positions to further their economic interests, they became the lightning rod for the discontent that erupted in the Mexican Revolution of 1910. After Terrazas fled to the United States, Pancho VILLA confiscated his properties in 1913. The old general returned to Mexico in 1920 and two years later the federal government gave him 13 million pesos as compensation for the loss of his lands.

– MARK WASSERMAN

THIEL, BERNARDO AUGUSTO

Bernardo Augusto Thiel (*b.* 1 April 1850; *d.* 9 September 1901), bishop of Costa Rica (1880–1901). Thiel was born in Elberfeld, Germany, and was ordained in Paris in 1874. He became a seminary professor in Costa Rica in 1877. He was named to a politically controversial and vacant bishopric by the anticlerical Liberal president Tomás GUARDIA GUTIÉRREZ as a moderate candidate but was subsequently expelled, along with the Jesuits, by Liberal authorities in 1884. After his return in 1886, Thiel became involved in electoral politics, and in 1889 founded the Catholic Union Party, which campaigned actively against the Liberal regime in 1894. Thiel also made several doctrinal statements on labor's right to organize and to receive "just salaries" in the face of widespread recession during the crisis in world coffee prices, which reduced real wages by 50 percent from 1870 to 1930. He founded a clerical newspaper, *El Mensajero del Clero,* in 1897, and was extremely active in national cultural life. His classic work, "Monografía de la Poblacíon de Costa Rica en el Siglo XIX," in *Revista de Costa Rica en el siglo XIX* (1902), remains a standard source. Thiel died in San José, Costa Rica.

– LOWELL GUDMUNDSON

THOMPSON, GEORGE

George Thompson (*b.* 1839; *d.* 1876), British military engineer active in Paraguay. Coming to Asunción in 1858 under a contractual agreement with the government of Carlos Antonio LÓPEZ, Thompson helped design and build the Paraguay Central Railroad. He remained in the country after the beginning of the War of the Triple Alliance in 1864, serving the regime of Field Marshal Francisco Solano LÓPEZ as colonel and commander of engineers. His preparation of trenches and defensive earthworks made a critical difference in the early stages of the conflict, particularly at Curupayty (September 1866), where the Brazilians and Argentines were repulsed with extremely heavy losses.

Thompson's spirited defense at Angostura in December 1868 facilitated Solano López's escape northward with what remained of the Paraguayan army. After López's subsequent surrender to the Brazilians, Thompson was permitted to return to Britain, where he wrote *The War in Paraguay* (1869), a highly detailed account of his experiences that was also highly critical of López. After the war, Thompson returned to Asunción, married into the local elite, and became an important official in the Paraguay Central Railway. He died in Asunción.

– THOMAS L. WHIGHAM

THOMSON PORTO MARIÑO, MANUEL TOMÁS

Manuel Tomás Thomson Porto Mariño (*b.* 1839; *d.* 1880), Chilean military leader. He entered the Chilean navy during the early 1850s. During the war against Spain (1865–1866) he commanded the captured Spanish warship *Covadonga* and served as its captain during the Battle of Abtao (7 February 1866), the only battle between opposing fleets. During the early days of the War of the Pacific (1879–1883), Thomson commanded the *Esmeralda, Abtao,* and *Amazonas.* In September 1879 the *Amazonas* was dispatched to the Atlantic to intercept the fast Peruvian transport *Oroya* but failed to find the enemy. On 22 December the *Amazonas* captured the Peruvian torpedo launch *Alay* at Ballenitas in northern Peru. In late January 1880 Thomson was given command of the former Peruvian seagoing monitor *Huáscar,* which had been captured at the battle of Angamos (8 October 1879). The *Huáscar* took part in the attack on Arica on 27 February 1880. While engaging the Peruvian coastal monitor *Manco Capac,* Thomson attempted to maneuver between the *Manco Capac* and the Peruvian shore batteries in order to deprive the enemy of its anchorage. At a critical moment the *Huáscar's* engine failed, and the ship became an easy target. The *Huáscar* was hit by a large-caliber shell and Thomson was killed instantly.

— ROBERT SCHEINA

TIMERMAN, JACOBO

Jacobo Timerman (*b.* 6 January 1923) Argentine journalist, publisher, editor, and writer. Jacobo Timerman was born in Bar, Ukraine (then, the USSR). When he was five years old, his family emigrated to Argentina. He began his career in journalism in 1944. Timerman founded the newsweeklies *Primera Plana* (1962) and

---

Timerman's Prisoner Without a Name,

Cell Without a Number, *is a forceful*

account of repression and the violation of human

rights in Argentina.

Confirmado (1969) and became a radio and television commentator. He was a political columnist at the Argentine daily *La Razón,* one of the most widely read papers in the nation during the late 1950s and the 1960s. From 1971 to 1977 he was editor and publisher of the influential Argentine daily *La Opinión.* He was imprisoned by the Argentine military dictatorship from 1977 to 1979. International pressures, as well as internal dissension among the military, gained his freedom. He left Argentina for Israel in 1979, and subsequently lived in Madrid and New York. The story of his imprisonment and torture by the military, *Prisoner Without a Name, Cell Without a Number* (1981), is a forceful account of repression and the violation of human rights in Argentina. The book became an international bestseller. In *The Longest War: Israel in Lebanon* (1982), Timerman expresses his anguish over actions taken by the Israeli armed forces in Lebanon. Upon his return to Argentina in 1984, Timerman became editor-in-chief of *La Razón* for a brief period. His book *Cuba: A Journey* (1990) is based upon a trip that he made to the island in 1987. He has written for the *New Yorker* magazine and in 1987 he published an account of Chile under General Pinochet, *Chile: Death in the South.*

— DANUSIA L. MESON

TIN-TAN

Tin-Tan (Germán Valdés Castillo; *b.* 1915; *d.* 29 June 1973), Mexican comedian and film star. In 1943, Tin-Tan began a radio career in Ciudad Juárez. Turning to comedy, he performed in various border cities of Mexico and the United States. He made his film debut in 1945 with *El hijo desobediente.* He went on to star in thirty-eight films and acted in over 100 more. His unique style incorporated slapstick, satire, musical and dance numbers, and a peculiar manner of speech. Among his classic films are *Calabacitas tiernas* (1948), *El rey del barrio* (1949), *El revoltoso* (1951), and *El campeón ciclista* (1956). Tin-Tan was one of the greatest Mexican film comedians and remains one of the most popular entertainers of all time.

— DAVID MACIEL

TINOCO GRANADOS, FEDERICO

Federico Tinoco Granados (*b.* 1870; *d.* 1931), the extraconstitutional president of Costa Rica (1917–1919) following the overthrow of President Alfredo GONZÁLEZ FLORES (1914–1917). As the last military figure to seize power in modern Costa Rica, Tinoco is still a controversial figure. He was minister of war and the navy, commandant of San José, and head of the police at the time of the coup against González. Faced with crushing economic difficulties as a consequence of World War I, González had attempted a series of progressive tax measures in the face of inflationary pressures. Both wealthy and popular interests welcomed his overthrow, but the popularity of the Tinoco regime, led by Federico and his brother José Joaquín, faded quickly. U.S. president Woodrow Wilson chose to make an example of Tinoco and refused to recognize his regime, both on principle and out of a partisan Democratic suspicion that Republican investors such as Minor Keith (United Fruit) and Luis Valentine (Rosario Mining of Honduras) were in league with Tinoco, expecting to conduct oil exploration and to receive investment incentives. Once Costa Rica was isolated internationally, popular living standards suffered even more under Tinoco, and his occasionally bloody repression of would-be rebellions and exile invasions caused his regime's early popularity to evaporate. Just as he was turning power over to his successor, Vice President Juan Bautista Quirós Segura, on 10 August 1919, his brother Joaquín, the war minister, was assassinated in San José. Tinoco left power two days later. Elections were held later that year, and Julio ACOSTA GARCIA was elected president. Tinoco died in Paris.

— LOWELL GUDMUNDSON

TOCORNAL, JOAQUÍN

Joaquín Tocornal (*b.* 1788; *d.* 1865), Chilean Conservative politician. Tocornal was the youngest man invited to the *cabildo abierto* (open town meeting) that elected Chile's first national junta on 18 September 1810. He became politically prominent with the Conservative rebellion of 1829–1830, serving as vice president of the Congress of Plenipotentiaries, the body that was chiefly instrumental in establishing the new Conservative regime. During the presidency of Joaquín PRIETO (1831–1841), he acted as minister of the interior (1832–1835) and as finance minister (1835–1841). He assumed the interior ministry again (1837–1840) following the murder of Diego PORTALES (1793–1837).

Tocornal played a key part in ensuring the continuity of government. Despite his ministerial eminence, however, he was unable to win Prieto's approval for his own presidential candidacy in 1841. Prieto preferred the war hero General Manuel BULNES (1799–1866): Tocornal did not obtain a single vote in the electoral college. He did retain his influence in the Conservative Party, however, and in January 1858 he helped negotiate the formation of the Liberal-Conservative Fusion. His son Manuel Antonio Tocornal (1817–1867) played a prominent part in politics in 1849–1850 and again in the 1860s as a Fusion leader. Had he not died prematurely, he might well have been the Fusion's presidential candidate in 1871.

– SIMON COLLIER

TOLEDO, FRANCISCO

Francisco Toledo (*b.* 7 July 1940), Mexican artist. Francisco Toledo was born in the Zapotec town of Juchitán, Oaxaca. From Zapotec folklore his paintings, drawings, prints, sculptures, and ceramics re-create the Zapotec world in which reptiles, amphibians, fish, insects, and human beings exude sexuality. Toledo studied five years in Europe, including some time in William Stanley Hayter's print workshop, and has lived in New York City and Mexico City.

– SHIFRA M. GOLDMAN

TOLEDO Y FIGUEROA, FRANCISCO DE

Francisco de Toledo y Figueroa (*b.* 10 July 1515; *d.* 21 April 1582), viceroy of Peru (1569–1581). Don Francisco de Toledo, as he signed himself, was born in Oropesa, New Castile, the third son of the third Count of Oropesa. Through his mother he was closely related to the dukes of Alba and distantly to Emperor Charles V. In 1535 he became a member of the Order of Alcántara.

After many years in the crown's military and diplomatic service, Toledo was appointed viceroy of Peru in 1568. The journey to his new post took him from February to September of 1569. He left ship in the extreme

north of Peru and traveled by land to Lima, the capital, inspecting settlements on the desert coast as he progressed.

Peru had a thirty-five-year history of interrupted government and rebellion. Toledo immediately showed himself to be suspicious of any group with power on whatever level: the *audiencias* (courts) of Lima and La Plata, the secular and regular clergy, the *encomenderos,* the *cabildos* (town councils), and, of course, the independent Inca state of Vilcabamba. After a critical examination of their actions during his administration, he attacked, and generally managed to reduce, their authority and autonomy.

Among his other duties, Toledo was ordered to make a *Visita General* (general inspection) of his viceroyalty. To visit the entire territory, from New Granada (now Colombia) to Chile, was clearly impossible. But in October 1570 Toledo began a tour of the heartland of his jurisdiction that lasted more than five years and took him through the major administrative, economic, and population centers of the Central Andes: Huamanga, Cuzco, Potosí, La Plata, and Arequipa. No other viceroy in the Spanish Empire ever knew his territory as intimately as Toledo came to know his through this exacting personal inspection.

During the *visita,* Toledo achieved the elimination of Inca resistance at Vilcabamba and the execution of the last independent Inca ruler, TÚPAC AMARU; the *reducción* (resettlement) of many native people in new towns for more efficient government, evangelization, and extraction of their labor; the final formulation of the *mita* supplying workers to Spanish mercury and silver mines at Huancavelica and Potosí; and full adoption of a silver-refining process utilizing mercury. These last two measures stimulated a vast growth in silver production. Toledo also issued a multitude of regulations on other administrative, economic, and social matters.

Toledo gathered evidence designed to show that the Incas had been tyrants and that therefore Spaniards were fully justified in destroying them.

Much of what is attributed to Toledo alone, such as the *reducción* program and the mining *mita,* had origins in earlier administrations, but he certainly gave final and legal form to such schemes. Many of his actions seemed, then and later, highly damaging to the native people. For them, he was, and still is, criticized. He was determined that Peru should submit to firm Spanish control and serve Spain's purposes. To those ends, he used whatever means seemed necessary, enforcing the rules with an intolerant and impatient authoritarianism. He enthusiastically praised the efforts of the first inquisitors in Peru, who had traveled with him to Lima. To justify his attacks on Vilcabamba, Túpac Amaru, and other descendants of Inca rulers and nobles, he gathered evidence designed to show that the Incas had been tyrants and that therefore Spaniards had been, and were, fully justified in destroying them.

The rigors of the *Visita General* left Toledo tired and ill. The final five years of his administration were far less active than its first half. Nevertheless, he laid a solid foundation for future Spanish administration of South America. His legislation became a model for governors throughout the empire. He was in a substantial sense the organizer of Spanish Peru, comparable to Viceroy Antonio de MENDOZA in Spanish Mexico.

– PETER BAKEWELL

TOLEDO Y LEYVA, PEDRO DE

Pedro de Toledo y Leyva (Marqués de Mancera; *b.* 1585; *d.* 9 March 1654), viceroy of Peru (1639–1648). Designated the first marqués de Mancera in 1633, former governor of Galicia, and a member of Philip IV's Council of War, Mancera took office as viceroy of Peru in December 1639. He was a vigorous administrator with a mixed reputation. On the one hand he was known for his charity, piety, and Christian fervor. A special friend to the Dominicans, he established a chair of Thomistic theology at the University of San Marcos in Lima exclusively for a Dominican and supported construction of a Dominican church and the school of Santo Tomás. Also in Lima he helped to found a Carmelite nunnery, a hospice and hermitage for the Franciscans, and hospitals for Indians, blacks (San Bartolomé), and the poor. In addition he assisted Franciscan missions in Panataguas with public funds.

Mancera was an efficient but oftentimes arbitrary administrator. On one occasion he ordered the expulsion of all Portuguese Jews living in Peru—6,000 by one estimate—and on another the removal of Lima prostitutes to Valdivia, Chile, to stimulate population growth in that remote region. Imposing a highly unpopular tax on meat and wine to pay the costs, he strengthened fortifications at the port of Callao, where his son Antonio Sebastián was commandant, and built two new galleons for the Pacific fleet (*Armada del Sur*). He also suppressed sixteen holidays, opened new veins at the mercury mine of Huancavelica, and revamped the tribute system. Anxious to immortalize himself, Mancera gave his name to the new fort at Valdivia and to the

town of Pisco (San Clemente de Mancera). He stepped down as viceroy on 20 September 1648.

– JOHN JAY TEPASKE

TOLSÁ, MANUEL

Manuel Tolsá (*b.* 4 May 1757; *d.* 24 December 1816), sculptor and architect. Tolsá was trained in Valencia and at the Academia de San Fernando in Madrid. In 1791 he arrived in New Spain as director of sculpture at the Academia de San Carlos, bringing with him an important collection of plaster casts of classical works. His activity in New Spain soon included architectural as well as sculptural projects. His best-known work is the equestrian statue of King Charles IV of Spain (1796, cast in bronze in 1803). Popularly known as the "Caballito," it was inspired by the Roman Capitol with its sculpture of Emperor Marcus Aurelius, and was the focal point of the 1796 renovation of the Plaza Mayor of Mexico City. Tolsá also worked on the completion of Mexico City's cathedral, on the baldachin (an ornamental structure over the central altar) of the cathedral of Puebla, on the house of the count of Buenavista (today Museo de San Carlos), and on the Palacio de Minería in Mexico City, as well as on many other projects. Because of his energetic participation in so many endeavors, Tolsá is considered largely responsible for the definitive entry of academic neoclassicism into New Spain.

– CLARA BARGELLINI

TOMIC, RADOMIRO

Radomiro Tomic (*b.* 7 May 1914), Chilean politician and former ambassador to the United States. Tomic, born in the Yugoslav enclave in Antofagasta, helped form the Partido Demócrata Cristiano (PDC). In 1968, after serving as ambassador to the United States, he returned to Chile, where he emerged as one of the leaders of the PDC's progressive wing. Selected as the Christian Democratic candidate for president in 1970, Tomic attempted to hold onto the Christian Democratic faithful while reaching out to the leftist vote by advocating more radical agrarian reform, nationalization of the copper mines, and massive state involvement in economic development. Tomic's tactics failed. Unable to retain the vote of those who had voted for Eduardo FREI six years earlier and often ridiculed for being bombastic, he came in a distant third, winning but 27 percent of the vote.

True to an earlier promise, Tomic endorsed the election of Salvador ALLENDE to the presidency. But the Christian Democrat did not abandon his party and even repudiated those who did leave to join the Movimiento de Acción Popular Unitaria (MAPU) or the Christian Left. Tomic, moreover, became increasingly discontented when it became clear that the Unidad Popular (UP) government would refuse to cooperate with the PDC and that it would not moderate its more radical policies. So much so, apparently, that Tomic, like Frei, supported the 1973 anti-Allende coup. He subsequently fled Chile, later returning to join the anti-PINOCHET movement and to act as an elder statesman of the Christian Democratic Party.

— WILLIAM F. SATER

TORNEL Y MENDÍVIL, JOSÉ MARÍA

José María Tornel y Mendívil (*b.* 1794?; *d.* 11 September 1853), Mexican politician and general. Born in Orizaba, Veracruz, Tornel joined the insurgency in 1813. Captured and sentenced to death, he survived the War of Independence, becoming private secretary to Antonio López de SANTA ANNA (1821) and to President Guadalupe Victoria (1824–1829). In his later career, Tornel occupied many other posts, serving as governor of the Federal District (1833–1834) and as minister of war on several occasions. One of Santa Anna's most devoted supporters, Tornel was always closely associated with him and often acted as his spokesman. A man of great energy, he instituted many reforms in the army and was a prolific author on political issues, a translator of Byron, and a playwright. Fervently interested in education, Tornel promoted the Lancasterian system (involving advanced students as monitors) and was director of the Colegio de Minería from 1843 to 1853.

— MICHAEL P. COSTELOE

TORNQUIST, ERNESTO

Ernesto Tornquist (*b.* 31 December 1842; *d.* 17 June 1908), founder of one of the first and most important industrial investment banks in Latin America. Tornquist played a major part in the financial development of Argentina in the last quarter of the nineteenth century. Born in Buenos Aires into a mercantile family of Swedish origin, he studied in a German-speaking school and entered the family firm of Altgelt, Ferber, and Co. in 1859. In 1874 he became the senior partner in the firm, which was henceforth called Ernesto Tornquist and Co. The history of the company was marked by steady growth over fifty years, leading the way in Buenos Aires in the fields of international and industrial finance. Tornquist and Co. was the agent for Baring Brothers in Buenos Aires from the 1880s until 1902, as well as representative for prominent Belgian, German, and French banks. Tornquist personally promoted the establishment of the first sugar refinery in Argentina, established in the city of Rosario in 1887; the largest Argentine meat-packing firm, the Sansinena Company; and several of the first metallurgical and chemical firms in the Argentine capital. He was a close financial adviser to the governments of Julio ROCA, Carlos PELLEGRINI, and other conservative leaders at the turn of the century, participating in most of the important monetary and financial reforms of the time. His firm today is a prominent commercial bank in Buenos Aires.

— CARLOS MARICHAL

TORO, DAVID

David Toro (*b.* 24 June 1898; *d.* 25 July 1977), president of Bolivia (1936–1937). Born in Sucre, Toro rose from military cadet to chief of staff during the Chaco War. Together with army officer Germán BUSCH he overthrew the civilian president José Luis Tejada SORZANO in May 1936, and Toro became president. Toro initiated a nationalistic government of "state syndicalism" and "military socialism," which included tax and banking reforms and the establishment of syndicates (unions) that all interest groups were expected to join. The possessions of the Standard Oil Company of New Jersey were nationalized and the Bolivian state oil monopoly (Yacimientos Petroliferos Fiscales Bolivianos— YPFB), still an important Bolivian agency, was established. Nearly all other social and economic changes were unsuccessful, but a pivotal accomplishment of the Toro period was a decree granting women total equality in all endeavors. The Toro presidency was the very beginning of the great changes that took place in Bolivia after the Chaco War. In July 1937 Busch took over the presidency in a bloodless coup. As ex-president, Toro remained moderately active in government and civic affairs.

— CHARLES W. ARNADE

TORO, FERMÍN

Fermín Toro (*b.* 14 June 1806; *d.* 23 December 1865), Venezuelan intellectual, politician, and diplomat. Toro entered public life as a functionary in the ministry of finance in 1828. In 1831 he was a representative in Congress. He was appointed by the regime of José Antonio PÁEZ to preside over the commission charged with bestowing funerary honors on Simón Bolívar's remains when they were repatriated to Caracas. He provided an important synthesis of his economic ideas in his *Reflexiones sobre la ley del 10 de abril de 1834* (1845). He was the secretary of Alejo Fortique, Venezuela's minister plenipotentiary to Great Britain (1839–1846), in London (1839–1841) as well as minister plenipotentiary in New Granada and then in Spain, France, and England in 1846–1847.

During the first years of the José Tadeo MONAGAS regime, Toro was minister of finance. But as a representative in Congress, he confronted Monagas after the January 1848 assault on Congress. When Monagas was overthrown in 1858, Toro again became politically active, assuming the posts of minister of finance and minister of foreign affairs under President Julián CASTRO. He was a member of the Valencia Convention in 1858 before retiring from public life and devoting himself to his research in botany, anthropology, and linguistics.

– INÉS QUINTERO

TORO ZAMBRANO, MATEO DE

Mateo de Toro Zambrano (*b*. 20 September 1727; *d*. 26 February 1811), president of the first national government of Chile (1810–1811). One of the great creole magnates of eighteenth-century Chile, and certainly one of the richest, Toro Zambrano played a full part in the public life of the colony, as militia officer, *alcalde* (mayor) and *corregidor* (municipal magistrate) of Santiago, lieutenant to the governor (1768), and as a member of the committee that disposed of the expropriated properties of the Jesuits after their expulsion in 1767 (he acquired one of the largest Jesuit haciendas). King Charles III conferred on him the title of Conde de la Conquista in 1770.

Toro Zambrano played little part in the work of Chili's new government, and sometimes fell asleep at its meetings.

The crisis of the Spanish empire after 1808 thrust Toro Zambrano into an unexpected role: in July 1810, following the deposition of the Spanish governor Francisco Antonio García Carrasco (1742–1813), Toro Zambrano became interim governor of the colony. Creole patriots agitating for a national junta persuaded him (partly through his confessor) to agree to a *cabildo abierto* (open town meeting) on 18 September 1810. At this historic assembly a junta was elected with Toro Zambrano as president. He played little part in the work of the new government, and sometimes fell asleep at its meetings. Greatly affected by his wife's death (January 1811), he died soon after.

– SIMON COLLIER

TORQUEMADA, JUAN DE

Juan de Torquemada (*b*. ca. 1562; *d*. 1 January 1624), Franciscan missionary and historian. Passages in Torquemada's major work, *Monarquía indiana* (Indian Monarchy), lead us to believe that he was born in Spain. He was ordained around 1587 and held several important positions in the Franciscan order. Torquemada was the chronicler of the order, a guardian in Santiago de Tlatelolco and Tlaxcala, and provincial of the Holy Gospel. The *Monarquía indiana* comprises observations on the daily life of the colony and descriptions of NEZAHUALPILLI's and MOTECUHZOMA's palaces and other archaeological remains, as well as writings on the pre-Hispanic period that built on the work of such Franciscan historians and linguists as Andrés de Olmos, Bernardino de SAHAGÚN, and Jerónimo de Mendieta. Torquemada also consulted Indian codices and maps and the work of the mestizo historians Fernando de Alva Ixtlilxóchitl and Diego Muñoz Camargo; he followed the ethnographic tradition of Olmos and Sahagún of drawing testimonies from Indian informants. This variety of sources has led critics to refer to Torquemada as the "chronicler of chroniclers."

– JOSÉ RABASA

TORRE, LISANDRO DE LA

Lisandro de la Torre (*b*. 6 December 1868; *d*. 5 January 1939), Argentine statesman, political leader, advocate of popularly elected local government. De la Torre was born in Rosario, Sante Fe, to a landowner father and a mother who descended from one of Argentina's oldest families. After finishing secondary school in Rosario, he studied law at the University of Buenos Aires during a time of political ferment, graduating in 1886. In 1888 he published a thesis comparing models of municipal government in the western world, entitled *El régimen municipal*. He participated in the political demonstration at El Parque in 1889, organized by students and reform-minded youths. He joined the Civic Union (soon to become the Unión Cívica Radical [UCR] of Leandro ALEM and Aristóbulo DEL VALLE, in the three aborted revolutions of 1890, 1891, and 1893, undertaken to reform Argentine politics. De la Torre broke with the UCR over political strategy, and fought a duel with Hipólito YRIGOYEN in 1895, after which the two remained lifelong antagonists. In 1908 de la Torre, a successful cattle breeder in Sante Fe, founded the Liga del Sur (League of the South), an agrarian political party, to reform local government. In Argentina's first truly democratic by-elections of 1911, he won a seat in the Sante Fe legislature. In 1914 he founded the Partido

Demócrata Progresista (Progressive Democratic Party [PDP]) as an alternative to Yrigoyen's UCR, which in some provinces was gaining on the entrenched oligarchic governments. As presidential candidate for the PDP in the 1916 national elections, de la Torre tried to unite reform-minded conservatives and progressives against Yrigoyen's populist campaign. At the last minute, in a three-way race, de la Torre was abandoned by key conservatives, and Yrigoyen won the election by the narrowest of margins. De la Torre served in the Chamber of Deputies from 1912 to 1916 and from 1922 to 1926, and in the Senate from 1932 to 1937. A spellbinding orator, he fought for land reform, separation of church and state, female suffrage, civil divorce, and for the production of domestic industries. He is best remembered for his passionate defense of Argentine meat-packing plants.

In 1932 de la Torre was defeated in his quest for the presidency as candidate of the Democratic Alliance (PDP and Socialist Party). Defeats suffered in the Senate at the hands of conservatives, the assassination in the Senate chamber of his close political ally Enzo Bordabehere, and the failure of his ranch in the arid western province of La Rioja led de la Torre to despondency. He resigned his seat in the Senate, and ultimately he committed suicide in Buenos Aires. His writings are collected in the seven-volume *Obras* (5th ed., 1952). De la Torre, the uncompromising politician and indefatigable champion of social justice, remains an icon for nationalists and the left alike.

– GEORGETTE MAGASSY DORN

TORRE, MIGUEL DE LA

Miguel de la Torre (*d.* 1838), Spanish general. Torre led Spanish troops against Simón BOLÍVAR and revolutionary armies in the wars for Venezuelan and Colombian independence. Following a six-month armistice between General Pablo MORILLO Y MORILLO and Bolívar, the Spanish crown gave Torre command of royalist troops. The two sides fought at the Battle of CARABOBO, in Venezuela on 24 June 1821. The deaths of between 1,000 and 1,500 Spanish soldiers assured Venezuelan and Colombian independence; historians called it the "Colombian Waterloo." Torre fled to Puerto Cabello where he surrendered two years later. He was appointed civil and military governor of Puerto Rico in 1823 and named count of Torrepando.

– CHRISTOPHER T. BOWEN

TORRE TAGLE Y PORTOCARRERO, JOSÉ BERNARDO DE

José Bernardo de Torre Tagle y Portocarrero (fourth marqués of Torre Tagle; *b.* 1779; *d.* 1825), president of Peru in 1823. He inherited several royal positions, including a seat on the Lima city council. Elected *alcalde* of Lima (1811–1812), he became a deputy to the Spanish Cortes in 1813. In late 1820, as governor of Trujillo, he announced in favor of José de SAN MARTÍN, who was advocating a monarchy for independent Peru. When Peru's first president, José de la RIVA AGÜERO, began acting independently of Congress, that body moved to replace him with the very conservative Torre Tagle (1823). Peru was then left with two governments: Riva Agüero's stood for interests in northern Peru, while Torre Tagle's represented Lima. Neither had much support or lasted very long.

Torre Tagle presided over a weak, bankrupt state. When it appeared on the verge of collapse, he committed treason by negotiating secretly with the Spaniards against Simón BOLÍVAR, to whom Torre Tagle had given full control of the army in 1823. Surrendering to the royal army, Torre Tagle presided over the last year of Spanish rule in Peru.

– VINCENT PELOSO

TORRE Y HUERTA, CARLOS DE LA

Carlos de la Torre y Huerta (*b.* 15 May 1858; *d.* 1950), Cuban naturalist, educator, writer, and public figure. Born in Matanzas, de la Torre was the son of a professor. He began his studies under his father, who instilled in him a love of science and objective methodology. De la Torre earned his baccalaureate from the Instituto de La Habana, and then moved on to study zoology and mineralogy at the university under the famous scientist Felipe Poey. There young Carlos's enthusiasm for mollusks quickly earned him the nickname Carlos Caracol, or Charles the Snail. In 1879 he discovered a new species of mollusk and earned a master's degree. In 1881 de la Torre earned his doctorate from the University of Madrid and moved to Puerto Rico. For several years he was on tenuous terms with the scientific community in Cuba, but he finally returned in 1892 and served as director of two reviews: *La enciclopedia* and *La revista enciclopédica*. During the Cuban War of Independence (1895–1898), de la Torre fled to Paris, where he worked closely with naturalists at the Museum of Natural History and across the Channel at the British Museum. In 1900 he returned to Cuba and cofounded the Cuban National Party, on whose platform he was elected to the Havana City Council. De la Torre continued to write on many subjects, including ethnohistory and anthropology in his later years. He received honorary doctorates from Harvard and Jena universities and was considered a pioneering member of the international community of naturalists.

– KAREN RACINE

TORREJÓN Y VELASCO, TOMÁS DE

Tomás de Torrejón y Velasco (baptized 23 December 1644; *d.* 23 April 1728), Spanish composer active in Peru. Torrejón y Velasco may have been born in Villarrobledo, Albacete, Spain. He was the son of one of Philip IV's huntsmen and spent his childhood in Fuencarral, becoming a page in the palace of Don Pedro Fernández de Castro, the count of Lemos. Named viceroy of Peru in 1667, the count brought the twenty-three-year-old Torrejón with him to America. From 1667 until 1672 Torrejón worked in Lima's armory as superintendent and later as magistrate and chief justice of Chachapoyas Province. Torrejón's musical career in Lima started on 1 January 1676, when he was named *maestro de capilla* of Lima's cathedral, a position he retained until his death fifty-two years later. Lima was the center of South America's musical life at that time and Torrejón became its leading figure. To celebrate the installation of the second grand organ of the cathedral, eight polychoral *villancicos* composed by Torrejón were performed. His fame spread to Cuzco, Trujillo, and Guatemala, and was enhanced after the premiere of his memorial vespers for Charles II in June 1701. That same year his opera *La púrpura de la rosa,* with a libretto by Pedro Calderón de la Barca, was lavishly premiered at the viceroyal palace on 19 October. It had been commissioned by the new viceroy, the count of Monclova, to celebrate Philip V's eighteenth birthday. As the first operatic work written and produced in the New World, *La púrpura de la rosa* is of great musicological significance. It has a semimythological plot, based on the story of Venus and Adonis but with popular Spanish characters added. The vast collection of Torrejón's religious music is kept in the archives in Lima, Cuzco, and Guatemala. He died in Lima.

– SUSANA SALGADO

TORRES, JUAN JOSÉ

Juan José Torres (*b.* 1921; *d.* 1976), army officer and president of Bolivia (1970–1971). Born in Cochabamba, Torres was a career soldier. He stayed in the

---

Torres cancelled the U.S. Steel concession on the Matilda zinc mine and expelled the Peace Corps from Bolivia.

---

armed forces even during the 1952–1964 rule of the Movimiento Nacionalista Revolucionario (MNR) following the Bolivian National Revolution, in spite of the fact that in his youth he had belonged to the Bolivian Socialist Falange (FSB), a fascist-oriented party and bitter enemy of the MNR. Torres was a co-conspirator in the overthrow of MNR leader President Víctor PAZ ESTENSSORO in November 1964, and held important posts in the succeeding military regime. He was in command of the army unit that in 1967 suppressed the guerrilla operation of Ernesto "Che" GUEVARA.

When General Alfredo OVANDO overthrew President Luis Adolfo Siles Salinas in September 1969, General Torres became commander in chief of the armed forces. In that position, he supported the "nationalist" position of Ovando. However, in July 1970 he was forced to resign the post because of pressure from right-wing army leaders. When right-wing officers forced the resignation of President Ovando early in October 1970, General Torres emerged as president, with the support of the leadership of the Central Obrera Boliviana (COB), the national labor confederation. Torres presided over a "nationalist" and "leftist" regime. He cancelled the U.S. Steel concession on the Matilda zinc mine and expelled the Peace Corps from Bolivia.

The COB and leftist parties organized the so-called Popular Assembly, which sought to play the role of the 1917 Russian soviets, but it was not granted any official power by Torres. The COB refused several official invitations from Torres to join his administration. In August 1971, Colonel Hugo BANZER SUÁREZ, former head of the Military College, led a conspiracy that ousted Torres, who fled to Argentina, where he was assassinated in 1976.

– ROBERT J. ALEXANDER

TORRES, LUIS EMETERIO

Luis Emeterio Torres (*b.* 1844; *d.* 1935), governor and military commander. A veteran of the war against the French intervention and postwar political revolts in Sinaloa, Torres used the ties he cultivated with the notables of Álamos (southern Sonora) and with Porfirio DÍAZ (while a federal deputy) to secure leadership of a political circle that rose to power in Sonora in the late 1870s and controlled the state until 1911. Though he was elected governor five times (uniquely retaining alternation during the Porfiriato), his principal associates—Ramón CORRAL and Rafael Izábal—were the administrative and legislative directors. Torres managed political relations within the state and with Mexico City; after 1887 he served as commander of Baja California and then of the entire Northwest military zone. Torres embodied the Porfirista ideal of promoting progress and order: Apache raids were terminated; Yaqui Indian autonomy ended (partly through the use of deportation); economic activity markedly expanded; all political opposition was suppressed.

— STUART F. VOSS

TORRES, TORIBIO

Toribio Torres, early-nineteenth-century Honduran religious painter, known especially for his classical realist portraits. Torres painted many of the bishops of Comayagua as well as many biblical scenes for Honduran churches. Reflecting the predominant style of painters of the early independent period, most of his paintings are serious portraits of leading personages, although he painted few of the political leaders of the independence movement in Honduras.

— RALPH LEE WOODWARD, JR.

TORRES BELLO, DIEGO DE

Diego De Torres Bello (*b.* 1551; *d.* 1638), Jesuit founder and first provincial of the Paraguay missions. Born in Villalpando, Castile, Torres joined the Society of Jesus and in 1581 was sent to work in Peru. He served for a few years as superior of the mission in Juli, near Lake Titicaca, then as superior of the Jesuit colleges in Cuzco, Quito, and Potosí. The Juli mission later served as a model for the Paraguay missions. In 1604 Paraguay and Chile were created as a separate Jesuit province, and Torres Bello was designated the first provincial. He set up his residence in Córdoba, Argentina, where he founded the novitiate as well as a seminary, which later became a university. Determined to protect the Indians from the Spaniards, he won approval for his plan to gather the former into mission towns, or "reductions." The first of these missions was founded in 1609; by the eighteenth century there were thirty. Torres Bello laid out the basic norms for the missions in a list of eighteen recommendations. Proficient in Aymara, Quechua, and Guaraní, he personally oversaw the building of the first missions. He finished his term as provincial in 1615, and spent his latter days working in the colleges of Buenos Aires and Chuquisaca, and in the missions among the Indians. He died in Chuquisaca.

— JEFFREY KLAIBER

TORRES BODET, JAIME

Jaime Torres Bodet (*b.* 17 April 1902; *d.* 15 May 1974), Mexican poet and public figure. Torres Bodet, who published his first book at age sixteen, distinguished himself as a preparatory student and became a protégé of José VASCONCELOS at nineteen. He joined the Ateneo de la Juventud in 1918 with other budding intellectual figures, many of whom established the major literary circle known as the "Contemporáneos" in the late 1920s. The prototypical Mexican intellectual of his age, Torres Bodet became a major figure in the public world of international and educational affairs. A professor at the National University, he twice served as secretary of education (1943–1946 and 1958–1964). In foreign affairs, after a long career in the diplomatic service, including posts as ambassador to France and Italy, he became secretary of foreign relations (1946–1948) and secretary general of UNESCO in 1948. Awarded the National Prize for Literature in 1966, he left a monumental four-volume memoir.

— RODERIC AI CAMP

TORRES GARCÍA, JOAQUÍN

Joaquín Torres García (*b.* 25 July 1874; *d.* 8 August 1949), Uruguayan painter and sculptor. Born in Montevideo, Torres García lived in France, Spain, and New York City from 1892 to 1932. He executed a number of murals and the stained-glass windows of the cathedral of Palma de Mallorca. He was a founding member of both the Cercle et Carré in Paris (1930) and the Asociación de Arte Constructivo in Montevideo (1935). Torres García considered himself a realist. Because of his passion for geometry, order, synthesism, construction, and rhythm, Angel Kalenberg spoke of the linguistic quality of Torres García's art, characterizing his creations as ideograms. His work provides an interesting example of pictorial duality, purely plastic elements being sensitively and skillfully fused with the expression of personal feeling. Among his publications are *Structure* (1935), *The Tradition of Abstract Man* (1938), *The Metaphysics of Indo-American Prehistory* (1940), and *Universal Constructivism* (1944).

— AMALIA CORTINA ARAVENA

TORRES RESTREPO, CAMILO

Camilo Torres Restrepo (*b.* 2 February 1929; *d.* 15 February 1966), Colombian revolutionary priest. From an upper-class (though not particularly wealthy) Bogotá family, Camilo Torres began the study of law at the Universidad Nacional in Bogotá, but in 1947 abruptly changed his career goals and entered the Roman Catholic seminary. His vocation was not grounded in traditional religiosity; rather, he was attracted to the progressive social Catholicism that was a strong current in postwar Europe and would gain added impetus from the reforms of the Second Vatican Council and from the movement of liberation theology. After his 1954 ordination he studied sociology at Louvain, in Belgium; taught sociology at the Universidad Nacional; served as university chaplain; and worked with Colombia's agrarian reform agency and other social programs. Like many Colombian intellectuals of the 1960s, he was influenced by the Cuban Revolution and felt increasingly alienated from his country's political and socioeconomic establishment.

Torres's social activism and willingness to work with Marxists troubled his ecclesiastical superiors, who ordered him to choose between priestly duties and secular concerns. In response he abandoned the active priesthood and in 1965 launched a new leftist coalition known as Frente Unido (United Front). His acknowledged charisma attracted followers, but he felt frustration over the difficulty of organizing a viable movement with any chance of implementing radical reform by peaceful means. He therefore gave up the legal struggle and joined the Ejército de Liberación Nacional (Army of National Liberation), which of all the guerrilla organizations operating in Colombia was the one most closely associated with the Cuban model.

Torres died in the first military engagement in which he took part. Nevertheless, his memory and his writings continued to exert strong influence on Colombian leftists, for many of whom his personal example legitimated the recourse to violent action.

– DAVID BUSHNELL

TORRES Y PORTUGAL, FERNANDO DE

Fernando de Torres y Portugal (sixteenth c.), seventh viceroy of Peru. Born in Jaén, Torres y Portugal received the title of conde de Villardompardo in 1576. In 1585 he was appointed viceroy of Peru, where he served until 1584. His rule was marred by conflict with the Inquisition over the activities of his son, don Jerónimo de Torres; nephew, don Diego de Portugal; and secretary, Juan Bello. Torres y Portugal also granted a Peruvian *encomienda* to his grandson, don Francisco de Torres y Portugal. During his rule, Torres y Portugal focused on the silver production of Potosí. After Thomas Cavendish ravaged the coast during his viceregency, Torres y Portugal became concerned with the defenses of the Pacific coast. In an effort to protect the realm he ordered the purchase of five galeons, two smaller ships for coastal service, and two galleys, along with fifty-four pieces of artillery. He returned to Spain in 1592.

– JOHN F. SCHWALLER

TORRIJOS HERRERA, OMAR

Omar Torrijos Herrera (*b*. 13 February 1929; *d*. 31 July 1981), maximum leader and supreme chief of the Panamanian Revolution, chief of state, and commander in chief of the Panamanian National Guard (1968–1981). Born in Santiago de Veraguas, he entered a military academy in El Salvador after attending public schools in Panama.

A career military man, General Omar Torrijos Herrera rose through the ranks of the Panamanian National Guard, joining several other colonels in leading a coup on 11 October 1968 that removed President Arnulfo ARIAS MADRID after only ten days in office. Unsuccessful efforts by his colleagues to secure power left Torrijos as the sole leader of the guard.

Torrijos is most remembered for his successful campaign to establish Panamanian control and sovereignty over the canal, a

Omar Torrijos Herrera shaking hands with U.S. President Jimmy Carter at the signing of the Panama Canal Treaty. (Jimmy Carter Library)

popular cause in Panama, which represented the fulfillment of a longtime national ambition. The general skillfully orchestrated popular sentiment and focused world opinion through a meeting of the U.N. Security Council in March 1993. The Security Council met in the Legislative Palace in Panama City, very close to the frontier separating the Canal Zone from Panama. The Torrijos–Carter Treaty, signed 7 September 1977, established a gradual transition process, assuring U.S. operation of the canal until 31 December 1999 but guaranteeing Panamanian control of the canal on 1 January 2000, thus ending U.S. jurisdiction over Panama's economic resource. The treaty also eliminated the Canal Zone and its special privileges for U.S. citizens three years hence and brought Panama a dramatic increase in canal revenues.

Torrijos's contribution to Panamanian politics, however, was far more significant, for his revolution changed his nation's political institutions and extended political participation to previously excluded and ignored ethnic groups and social classes. A self-made man of the middle class, he focused on ending the dominance of the elite of Spanish ancestry and on opening the political system to the urban masses of laborers and the middle class, which consisted largely of mulattoes and blacks, groups that had previously been denied even citizenship, much less political participation. In this sense, Torrijos permanently changed the nation's politics by opening the system, increasing participation, and ending segregation—an achievement similar to that of neighboring Costa Rica in the 1948 revolution.

The guard represented the main avenue of advance for these classes, and hence led the way to changes placing them in the political mainstream. The Constitution of 1972, which institutionalized Torrijos's personal control of the state, also expanded the National Assembly to 505 members, theoretically making it more representative of the nation, though all key powers resided in the hands of the maximum leader.

Shifting the nation from import substitution to export-oriented economic growth, Torrijos focused on banking, services, and transportation. The Banking Law of 1970 removed all reserve requirements and all limits on the movement of funds into and out of the country, and allowed establishment of secret accounts while virtually eliminating taxation on bank transactions. These provisions made Panama the "Switzerland of Latin America" overnight, establishing it as an international financial center of convenience and leading to a vast expansion in the banking sector. Construction of new roads, a transisthmian oil pipeline, and a new international airport, as well as new container ports, made the nation a focal point of transportation and transfer that complemented the canal.

Torrijos' reforms included the Labor Code of 1972, which instituted a minimum wage, compulsory arbitration, and the principle of state control of the economy, theoretically establishing the state as the protector of the masses and further weakening the power of the oligarchy. A housing code established the principle of government-subsidized public housing and launched a massive housing and public works construction effort in the cities. Reaching out to the equally neglected peasant masses, he increased government spending for rural access roads and promoted peasant settlements through land acquisitions to increase grain production. Between 1969 and 1973, some 260 farm settlements were formed. Covering 540,000 acres, most were acquired through expropriation in return for long-term bonds or for payment of overdue back taxes.

A fervent nationalist, Torrijos restored pride to his nation by resisting U.S. pressures and joining the nonaligned movement as part of the resistance to the United States. He led the nation in confronting the age-old nemesis, the United Fruit Company, regarding taxes and land ownership; opposed the U.S. blockade of Fidel Castro's Cuba; and allowed the use of Panama as a conduit for Cuban arms supplied to the Sandinista rebels in Nicaragua. Yet he also cooperated with the United States in security matters, accepted compromises regarding the canal, sharing responsibilities for its defense, and provided shelter to the exiled Shah of Iran. His willingness to accept gradual change regarding canal jurisdiction ended an era of violent confrontations and enabled the peaceful settlement of a volatile dispute. Torrijos's death in an unexplained airplane crash cut his tenure and revolution short.

– KENNETH J. GRIEB

TOSAR, HÉCTOR ALBERTO

Héctor Alberto Tosar (*b.* 18 July 1923), Uruguayan composer, pianist, and conductor. Born in Montevideo, Tosar began his studies in that city with Wilhelm Kolischer (piano), Tomás Mujica (harmony), and Lamberto Baldi (composition and orchestration). When he was seventeen, his Toccata for orchestra was premiered in Montevideo by maestro Baldi. In 1946 Tosar received a Guggenheim fellowship and went to the United States to study composition with Aaron Copland. With a grant from the French government in 1948 he went to France, where he remained for three years studying under Darius Milhaud, Jean Rivier, and Arthur Honegger (composition), and Eugène Bigot and Jean Fournet (conducting). In 1951 he won the

SODRE first composition award for *Oda a Artigas,* a cantata for speaker and orchestra. He also won first prize at the First Inter-American Music Festival (Montevideo) in 1957 for his Divertimento for strings. He composed a Te Deum in 1960 commissioned by the Koussevitsky Foundation.

Tosar was chairman of the composition department at the Puerto Rico Conservatory (1974) and professor (1983–1984) and director of Montevideo's Escuela Universitaria de Música (1985–1987) and Conservatorio Nacional. From 1987 to 1991 he was composer-in-residence at the SODRE. He was also professor of composition and analysis at the Instituto Simón Bolívar in Caracas, and later taught composition at Indiana University (1981–1982). His early works, which combine contrapuntal and harmonic structures in free forms, are dramatic and rarely nationalistic. In his later works Tosar has experimented with jazz rhythms, new forms of instrumentation, as in his aleatoric composition for thirteen instruments, *A-13,* and serial structures. His *Recitativo y variaciones para orquesta* was commissioned by the Fourth Inter-American Music Festival and premiered in Washington, D.C., in 1968. In the 1980s several of his works were premiered in the United States, Mexico, and Venezuela. Tosar has also composed music for the synthesizer.

— SUSANA SALGADO

TRABA, MARTA

Marta Traba (*b.* 25 January 1930; *d.* 27 November 1983), Argentine-Colombian novelist, art critic, and university professor. Traba earned a degree in literature from the Universidad Nacional de Buenos Aires (1948) and took courses with art critic Jorge Romero Brest. In 1949–1950, she studied art history with Pierre Francastel at the Sorbonne and René Huyghe at L'école du Loure. In Paris she met and married Alberto Zalamea, a Colombian intellectual. She left Europe for Colombia with her family in 1954. In 1958 Traba published her first study on modern art, *El museo vacío.* In 1961 she published an important and pioneering study on Latin American painting, *La pintura nueva en Latinoamérica,* in which she offered a critique of the Mexican muralists and Argentine painting, among other topics, that generated considerable controversy. She taught art history at the Universidad de América and the Universidad de los Andes in Bogotá and became a strong advocate for the creation of the Museum of Modern Art in Bogotá, which was constituted in 1962. She was its director from 1964 to 1967. In 1965 Traba moved the museum to the Universidad Nacional de Bogotá, where she joined the faculty. That year she also published her most important study on Latin American art, *Los cuatro monstruos cardinales.* Although Traba published a book of poems in 1952, *Historia natural de la alegría,* it was not until 1966 that her writing of fiction began in earnest. She received the prestigious Cuban Casa de las Américas prize for her first novel, *Las ceremonias del verano* (1966). *Los laberintos insolados,* another novel, was published in 1967. Both novels explore the possibilities of interior growth and exposure to foreign cultures. *Pasó así* (1968), *La jugada del sexto día* (1970), and *Homérica latina* (1979) followed.

Traba's fiction portrayed political turmoil, repression, persecution, and horror in countries under military regimes.

Increasingly, Traba's fiction portrayed political turmoil, repression, persecution, and horror in countries under military regimes (Argentina, Uruguay, and Chile). These are the central themes in *Conversación al sur* (1981; Mothers and Shadows, 1986) and *En cualquier lugar* (1984). *De la mañana a la noche: Cuentos norteamericanos* (1986) and *Casa sin fin* (1988) were published posthumously. In 1969, after divorcing her first husband, Traba married the Uruguayan critic and writer Angel Rama. They lived in Montevideo, Puerto Rico, Caracas, and Washington, D.C., between 1969 and 1982. Traba and Rama were forced to leave the United States in 1982 when the U.S. Department of State denied them resident visas, a decision that generated heated controversy. They set up residence in Paris, France, where they lived until their death in an airplane crash near Madrid.

— MAGDALENA GARCÍA PINTO

TREJOS FERNÁNDEZ, JOSÉ JOAQUÍN

José Joaquín Trejos Fernández (*b.* 18 April 1916), president of Costa Rica (1966–1970), professor, dean, and vice rector of the University of Costa Rica.

José Joaquín Trejos Fernández came to national prominence only after being nominated as a presidential candidate in 1965 when the former presidents and political adversaries Rafael Ángel CALDERÓN GUARDIA (1940–1944) and Otilio ULATE BLANCO (1949–1953) joined their forces in opposition to the ever more dominant National Liberation Party (PLN). Trejos, although a Calderonist, had little prior political experience but was widely known and respected as a professional of great integrity and rectitude.

After his surprise victory, Trejos's administration distinguished itself in several areas. Among its most notable accomplishments were the sustained growth in the gross national product and the development of the infrastructure on the Atlantic coast with the construction of a highway to Puerto Limon and new wharfage facilities for the port, and the extension of the Tortuguero Canal.

– JOHN PATRICK BELL

TRESGUERRAS, FRANCISCO EDUARDO DE

Francisco Eduardo de Tresguerras (*b.* 13 October 1759; *d.* 3 August 1833), Mexican painter and architect. In contrast to most well-known artists of his time, Tresguerras pursued his career not in Mexico City but in Querétaro, Celaya, and San Luis Potosí. He dedicated himself to painting, music, architecture, engraving, and writing in turn, and can be considered a particularly interesting example of the self-conscious and confident eighteenth-century New World artist. His most famous creation is the church of Nuestra Señora del Carmen in Celaya, with a single tower over the entrance (1802–1807). In painting and drawing his style is rococo, but in architecture he is neoclassical. Although Tresguerras sought recognition from the Academia de San Carlos, he seems never to have been accepted by the Mexico City art establishment.

– CLARA BARGELLINI

TRIANA, JOSÉ

José Triana (*b.* 4 January 1931) Cuban playwright, was born in Hatüey, Camagüey. He returned to Cuba when Fidel Castro came to power in order to support the building of a new society. His early plays captured the nuances and the traditions of the humble classes. The violence inherent in the society is reflected in plays that explore struggles for power, sometimes in mythical terms (*Medea en el espejo,* 1960) or godlike terms (*El general mayor hablará de teogonía,* 1960). These early plays established the bases for his ludic experiments that resonated of Antonin Artaud or Jean Genet. When his masterpiece, *La noche de los asesinos* (1966), won the coveted Casa de las Américas Prize in 1965, it earned him both international recognition and eventually the enmity of the Castro regime. The allusions to generational conflict within a destabilized society attributed to Fulgencio Batista were veiled to obscure a more virulent criticism of the Revolution itself. Triana was not allowed to publish or to present plays again in Cuba.

Triana sought asylum in Paris in 1980 and resumed his theatrical activities. *Worlds Apart,* performed in English by the Royal Shakespeare Company in 1986, was the translation of *Palabras comunes,* itself an adaptation of his earlier *Diálogo para mujeres.* Set in Cuba at the turn of the century, this semihistorical play examines the hypocrisy in sexual and racial attitudes in the Cuban society of the time as a metaphor for the years of the Castro Revolution. *Revolico en el Campo de Marte* (1971) is a verse play with folkloric touches; *Ceremonial de guerra* (1968–1973) is another historical play set in 1895 during the struggle for Cuban independence. In this case the metaphor serves for a society that has lost its direction in its search for truth. Triana's latest play is a monologue, *Cruzando el puente* (1991), in which an abused and abusive character "crosses the bridge" into a world of madness.

Triana is clearly one of the most accomplished playwrights of his generation in terms of dramatic technique and his commitment to a theater that engages important political and social issues with human interest. He manipulates elements of Cuban folklore and culture, even in exile, with great dexterity to achieve one of the most elusive and difficult features of the theater—plays of local interest that transcend their time and space to speak to international audiences.

– GEORGE WOODYARD

TRISTAN, FLORA

Flora Tristan (*b.* 7 April 1803; *d.* 14 November 1844), French social critic and utopian socialist who left important writings on mid-nineteenth-century Europe and Peru. In 1833–1834, fleeing a disastrous marriage, the Paris-born Tristan sought the support of her deceased father's family in Peru, the aristocratic Tristans. Unable to convince them that she was a legitimate member of the family, she traveled extensively in the midst of a civil war. Her travels culminated in the insightful 1838 travelogue *Pérégrinations d'une paria.* Her subsequent publications in Europe dealt with such major issues as living conditions in London, feminism, and socialism. Her intellectual and political activities continued until her death in Bordeaux. The painter Paul Gauguin was her grandson.

– CHARLES F. WALKER

TRONCOSO DE LA CONCHA, MANUEL DE JESÚS

Manuel de Jesús Troncoso de la Concha (*b.* 3 April 1878; *d.* 30 May 1955), Dominican lawyer, university professor, and president (1940–1942). A native of Santo Domingo, Troncoso de la Concha received a licentiate in law from the University of Santo Domingo in 1899 and taught civil law there. From 1911 until his death in 1955, he held many important government positions, such as minister of justice, interior and police; development and communication; and war and naval affairs. During the era of Rafael Trujillo (1930–1961), he served as vice president (1938–1942). After the death of Jacinto B. Peynado in 1940, Troncoso de la Concha also became the nominal head of state. (In reality, Trujillo continued to run the Dominican Republic.)

Of his historical works, the most important is *Genesis de la Ocupación Norteamericana de Santo Domingo,* in which he analyzed the political and economic motives for the U.S. occupation of the Dominican Republic. Another one of his important historical writings is *La Ocupación de Santo Domingo por Haití* (1942), in which he made the unorthodox assertion that the Dominican population actually welcomed the Haitian occupation. Among his literary works, the *Narraciones Dominicanas* (1953) occupies a leading position. He died in Santo Domingo.

– KAI P. SCHOENHALS

TRUJILLO, GUILLERMO

Guillermo Trujillo (*b.* 1927), Panamanian artist. Trujillo completed a degree in architecture in Panama in 1953 and continued his studies in Spain at the San Fernando Academy, the Moncloa School of Ceramics, and the Escuela Superior de Arquitectura. From 1959 to 1988, he was a professor in the School of Architecture at the University of Panama.

Trujillo is an accomplished painter, sculptor, ceramist, printmaker, and draftsman, with a personal style and iconography rooted in the indigenous cultures and traditions of Panama. Initially he was influenced by Spanish informalism and considered part of the Latin American neofigurative movement, and his paintings cover a wide range, from social satires such as *Los Comisionados* (1964) to landscapes and semi-abstractions based on botanical or archaeological themes, like *Paisaje No. 3* (1972).

– MONICA E. KUPFER

TRUJILLO, JULIÁN

Julián Trujillo (*b.* 28 January 1828; *d.* 18 July 1883), president of Colombia (1878–1880). Born into the Popayán gentry, he attended the university there, receiving his law doctorate in 1849. Trujillo fought in the civil wars of 1854 and 1859–1863 in the army of General Tomás Cipriano de MOSQUERA, becoming a colonel in 1861 and a general in 1863. He was noted for his cour-

age, and his military prowess in defeating the Antioquian Conservatives in 1877 brought him the presidency. Trujillo's term was marred by a deteriorating economy and deepening dissention among the ruling Liberals. In his quest for an accommodation with the church and the Conservatives, Trujillo was thwarted by the Radical Liberal Congress. His developmental policies were regionally oriented. He contracted for a canal across Panama and negotiated with Francisco Javier CISNEROS for a railway from the Pacific to the Cauca Valley. A transitional figure holding moderate Liberal views, Trujillo was caught between the Radicals and Rafael NÚÑEZ's Nationalists, toward whom he leaned. He served as general in chief of the army in 1881 and was elected a senator in 1882. He died in Bogotá.

– J. LEÓN HELGUERA

TRUJILLO, MANUEL

Manuel Trujillo (*b.* 1846; *d.* 1945), Paraguayan naval officer and memorialist. Born in Asunción, Trujillo entered the armed forces at an early age, joining in the military buildup ordered by President Francisco Solano LÓPEZ in the early 1860s. He was stationed at the state shipyard and arsenal, working under the direction of British engineers hired by the government to help construct a Paraguayan navy.

During the War of the Triple Alliance (1864–1870), Trujillo fought in half a dozen battles, from the seizure of the port of Corrientes (April 1865) to the fall of Angostura (December 1868). He served aboard several Paraguayan steamers, including the *Yporá* and the *Igurey,* and thus was in a good position to observe naval tactics after the disastrous experience at Riachuelo in June 1865.

Trujillo published a brief account of his war experiences, *Gestas guerreras,* in 1911. Owner of a general store in later life, he was much in demand at veterans' conventions as one of the oldest survivors of the conflict.

– THOMAS L. WHIGHAM

TRUJILLO MOLINA, RAFAEL LEÓNIDAS

Rafael Leónidas Trujillo Molina (*b.* 24 October 1891; *d.* 30 May 1961), military officer and ruler of the Dominican Republic (1930–1961). In 1918 Trujillo, a native of San Cristóbal who had been a telegraph operator and security guard, joined the National Guard that had been established by the U.S. occupation forces in the Dominican Republic. His obedience, discipline, and organizational talents, as well as his enthusiastic participation in the suppression of a guerrilla movement in the eastern part of the country, endeared him to the occupiers, who promoted him rapidly. In 1924, when the National Guard was transformed into the Dominican National Police, Trujillo became its chief officer. When the National Police became the National Armed Forces in 1928, Trujillo emerged as its commander in chief. By using his power as military chief in the maneuverings of Dominican politics, Trujillo became president by 1930.

---

*In order to "whiten" (*blanquear*) his country,*

Trujillo ordered the massacre of all Haitians in the

Dominican Republic.

THE ESTABLISHMENT OF SUPREME POWER (1930–1940). During the next decade, Trujillo established the most totalitarian control over his people that any Latin American country had theretofore experienced. All political parties, newspapers, radio stations, trade unions, and private associations that did not agree with him ceased to exist. Persistent opponents were bribed, jailed, murdered, or driven into exile. In order to "whiten" (*blanquear*) his country, Trujillo ordered the massacre of all Haitians in the Dominican Republic. In October 1937, an estimated 25,000 Haitians were slain by his agents. After the completion of this slaughter, the Dominican ruler encouraged the immigration of European Jews and refugees from the Spanish Civil War, as well as Japanese and Hungarians after 1956.

During the first decade of his rule, Trujillo converted much of the Dominican Republic into his private fief by acquiring immense landholdings and monopolies over the export-import trade. Primarily in order to increase his personal fortune (estimated by 1960 to have been U.S.$800 million), Trujillo modernized his country by the introduction of agricultural machinery, new industrial plants, and a paved road system. Impressed by the modernity, cleanliness, and stability of his country, foreign journalists and politicians heaped praise on the Dominican dictator, who launched a campaign of self-glorification. Santo Domingo became Ciudad Trujillo, and Pico Duarte, the highest mountain in the Caribbean (10,500 feet) was renamed Monte Trujillo. The province in which he had been born was named for his father, José Trujillo Valdez, and a western province became known as El Benefactor, a title the dictator had bestowed on himself.

After having himself fraudulently reelected in 1934 for another four years, Trujillo began in 1938 the practice of installing puppet presidents whom he could con-

trol from behind the scenes. The first of these presidents was a professor of law, Jacinto B. Peynardo, one of whose first actions was to appoint Trujillo's nine-year-old son, Rafael Trujillo Martínez (Ramfis), brigadier general. Upon Peynado's death in 1940, Manuel de Jesús TRONCOSO DE LA CONCHA became president of the Dominican Republic.

By means of various austerity measures, Trujillo succeeded in making regular payments on the Dominican Republic's debt to the United States, which pleased U.S. President Franklin D. Roosevelt so much that he invited Trujillo and his family for a White House visit in 1939. One year later, the Trujillo–Hull Treaty went into effect, ending the collection of Dominican customs duties by the United States. Trujillo hailed the closing of this humiliating chapter in Dominican history as his personal triumph and erected a monument commemorating the treaty along Santo Domingo's waterfront, where it still stands.

WORLD WAR II AND THE COLD WAR (1940–1955). When the United States became involved in World War II, the Dominican Republic was one of the first Latin American countries to declare war on the Axis. The conflict proved to be a great boon for the export of Dominican coffee, cocoa, tobacco, and sugar. When it became clear by 1944 that the democracies would triumph over the fascist powers, Trujillo thought it wise to create a "political opening" by permitting the organization of a number of opposition parties. The Dominican ruler used the start of the cold war in 1947 to put an end to this experiment by arresting, torturing, and killing the leaders of the opposition that he had allowed to emerge only three years before. Trujillo portrayed himself as the staunchest anticommunist leader of Latin America and in 1955 convoked a Fair of Peace and Brotherhood of the Free World that cost the then astronomical sum of U.S.$50 million. The fair, which was only sparsely attended by foreign dignitaries, represented the apogee of Trujillo's power.

SANCTIONS, DECLINE, AND DEATH (1956–1961). After the twenty-fifth anniversary of his rule in 1955, Trujillo was beset by both external and internal challenges. The era of dictators in Latin America seemed to draw to a close. In 1955, Juan Perón was toppled in Argentina. Two years later, Gustavo Rojas Pinilla fled Colombia, and in 1958 Marcos Pérez Jiménez was overthrown in Venezuela. By 1959 Trujillo was the unwilling host to Fulgencio Batista, who had fled to Santo Domingo when the triumphant guerrillas of Fidel Castro entered the Cuban capital on 1 January of that year. Venezuela's new president, Rómulo Betancourt, and Fidel Castro of Cuba assisted in the launching of an anti-Trujillo expedition by Dominican exiles on 14 June 1959. The revolutionaries, who returned to their native land by both air drops and coastal landings, were either killed or captured. Although this expedition met with disaster, it inspired some domestic enemies of Trujillo's to form a secret Castroite organization called the Fourteenth of June Movement, which was led by the charismatic lawyer, Manolo Tavarez.

When Trujillo retaliated by bombing Rómulo Betancourt's car, injuring the Venezuelan president and killing a number of his advisers, the Organization of American States imposed severe economic sanctions in 1960 on the Dominican Republic. The administration of Dwight D. Eisenhower, already displeased over Trujillo's 1956 kidnapping and murder of Columbia University instructor Jesús de GALÍNDEZ, dealt a crippling blow to the dictator by imposing a special excise tax on Dominican sugar. Domestically, Trujillo aroused a wave of opposition from all segments of society, including the Roman Catholic hierarchy, when it was learned that his secret police had waylaid, raped, and then murdered the three young daughters (Patria, Minerva, and Maria Teresa Mirabel) of a prominent merchant. When a desperate Trujillo dispatched agents to Communist eastern Europe to seek help against the United States, the CIA sent arms to opposition elements in Santo Domingo; they attacked and killed Trujillo on the night of 30 May 1961. Thus the aging dictator was removed after an iron rule of thirty-one years, but the legacy of his reign loomed over his nation for decades to come.

– KAI P. SCHOENHALS

TSUCHIYA, TILSA

Tilsa Tsuchiya (*b.* 1932; *d.* 23 September 1984), Peruvian painter. Tsuchiya, a native of Supe, created in her paintings a personal mythology inspired in part by her country's Chavín, Nazca, and Inca cultures. She studied at the National School of the Fine Arts in Lima (1954–1959) and at the workshops of Fernando de SZYSZLO, Carlos Quisquez Asin, Manuel Zapata Orihuela, and Ricardo Grau. From 1960 to 1964 she studied painting and engraving at the École des Beaux Arts in Paris. Her artistic training in Peru and France exposed her to diverse styles of painting: muralism, indigenism, abstract expressionism, and surrealism. She represented Peru at the XV Bienal de São Paulo (1979). Her work has been exhibited throughout Europe, Latin America, and the United States. She died in Lima.

– MIRIAM BASILIO

TUGWELL, REXFORD GUY

Rexford Guy Tugwell (*b.* 10 July 1891; *d.* 21 July 1979), governor of Puerto Rico (1941–1946). In 1932, Tugwell became one of the original members of Franklin Roosevelt's brain trust. He later served as the assistant secretary of agriculture, the director of the Resettlement Administration, chairman of the city planning commission of New York, and chancellor at the University of Puerto Rico. Republicans and big sugar businesses opposed his appointment to the governorship.

Tugwell favored home rule for Puerto Rico and continued economic development through such institutions as the Development Company, the Development Bank, and the Water Resources Authority. He served as the last federally appointed governor of Puerto Rico.

– CHRISTOPHER T. BOWEN

TÚPAC AMARU

Túpac Amaru (*b.* ca. 1554; *d.* 1572), Inca emperor during early colonial period (1571–1572). Túpac Amaru, the third son of MANCO INCA, reigned briefly as emperor of the Inca rump state in the last Inca capital of Vilcabamba, in the *montaña* region of eastern Peru. He was crowned in 1571; the next year the Spanish took the city of Vilcabamba, and Túpac Amaru and his family were captured. Taken to Cuzco, he was condemned to death and executed in the main plaza before a huge crowd of Indians. He was the last of the Inca emperors, and his death extinguished the dynasty. He has remained, nevertheless, a potent symbol of resistance and rebellion in Peru even to the present day. His name has been used by various left-wing guerrilla groups.

– GORDON F. MCEWAN

TÚPAC AMARU (JOSÉ GABRIEL CONDORCANQUI)

Túpac Amaru (José Gabriel Condorcanqui) (*b.* March 1738; *d.* 18 May 1781), the most famous leader and martyr of the Great Andean Rebellion of 1780–1783. Born in Surimana, Canas y Canchis (Tinta), José Gabriel was the son of Miguel Condorcanqui and Rosa Noguera and a descendant of Inca TÚPAC AMARU, executed by Viceroy Francisco de TOLEDO in 1572. Orphaned in 1750, José Gabriel was raised by an aunt and uncle. As heir to the *cacicazgo* (chieftainship) of Tungasuca, Pampamarca, and Surimana, he attended Cuzco's San Francisco de Borja school. In 1760 he married Micaela Bastidas Puyucahua, and they had three sons: Hipólito, Mariano, and Fernando.

At age twenty-five José Gabriel claimed the *cacicazgo* and also became a successful teamster on the route linking Cuzco to Potosí. His travels made him aware of mounting dissatisfaction with colonial rule. The *repartos* (distributions of merchandise), whereby *corregidores* (provincial governors) forced Indians to purchase costly, unwanted goods, caused great discontent. Indians also resented the abusive *mita* (draft labor) for the mines of Potosí. The government's failure to correct the corruption and abuse of the colonial system proved increasingly galling to José Gabriel. Empowered by other caciques from Tinta, he spent 1777 and part of the following year in Lima, attempting to secure the province's exemption from the *mita*. When Visitador José Antonio de Areche rejected his suit, the cacique considered traveling to Spain to press his case. Meanwhile, he unsuccessfully petitioned the government to recognize him as the marquis of Oropesa, the vacant title that belonged to the heir of the original Incas.

Frustrated at each turn, he returned to Tinta in mid-1778, encouraged by influential friends in Lima to act against the illegality and abuse that the regime allowed to flourish. During the following two years, he conspired and planned. Sporadic local revolts independently erupted throughout the Andes. Areche's policies heightened tensions. He established new customhouses to collect higher taxes and intended to force mestizos to pay tribute. Dissatisfaction extended beyond the Indian population to include many creoles and mestizos.

On 4 November 1780, José Gabriel, taking the name Túpac Amaru, struck, arresting Antonio de Arriaga, the *corregidor* of Tinta. A convenient target, Arriaga had openly feuded with local clergy and had been excommunicated by the bishop of Cuzco, Juan Manuel Moscoso y Peralta. Túpac Amaru transported Arriaga to Tungasuca, where he tried Arriaga for corruption and abuse of the *repartos* and hanged him on 10 November. As the news spread, both rebels and royalists gathered forces. Many caciques of Tinta joined Túpac Amaru, whose relatives provided most of the movement's leadership. Building support, Túpac Amaru decreed the emancipation of slaves on 16 November. At Sangarara two days later, the rebels defeated a force sent out from Cuzco. Nonetheless, the mounting violence in the wake of Sangarara caused many creoles and mestizos to withdraw their support for the rebellion.

Túpac Amaru witnessed the torture and execution of his wife and other captive family members and then was pulled apart by four horses.

In early December, Túpac Amaru captured Lampa and Azángaro, and his influence threatened both southern and Upper Peru. Viceroy Augustín de JÁUREGUI and Areche mobilized reinforcements and supplies for the defense of Cuzco. News of their imminent arrival brought Túpac Amaru's forces north from Callao to attack Cuzco. With 40,000 to 60,000 troops, he besieged Cuzco from 2 to 9 January 1781. Aid from royalist caciques helped prevent Cuzco's fall, and Túpac Amaru retreated. Defeated in Tinta, he was betrayed and captured in Langui on 6 April 1781. While the rebellion continued, his captors took him to Cuzco for interrogation and trial. On 18 May he witnessed the torture and execution of his wife and other captive family members and then was pulled apart by four horses.

Although the Great Andean Rebellion comprised more than Túpac Amaru's revolt, other insurgents looked to his leadership. For many Indians his ancestry allowed him to carry the banner of Inca legitimacy, and his violent protest against Spanish colonialism won broad sympathy. Yet his rebellion failed owing to the massive mobilization carried out by the government, his inability to win lasting support from mestizos and creoles, and opposition from many caciques.

– KENDALL W. BROWN

TÚPAC CATARI (JULIÁN APAZA)

Túpac Catari (Julián Apaza) (*b.* ca. 1750; *d.* 14 November 1781), leader of an Aymara insurrection in 1781, which laid siege to La Paz for six months. A commoner born in Ayoayo, Sicasica, Julián Apaza was orphaned at age twelve. He worked in the mines, traded coca leaves and cloth, and married Bartolina Sisa, with whom he had three children. Contemporaries described him as lighter in complexion than most Aymaras and of medium height.

Apaza first came to public notice in early 1781, when insurrection convulsed the provinces of Sicasica, Yungas, and Pacajes. Spanish officials mistakenly blamed the turmoil on TÚPAC AMARU, who rebelled in November 1780 near Cuzco. Ambitious, charismatic, and messianic, Apaza quickly rose to command the Aymara rebels north of La Paz. Speaking only Aymara, he combined Christian and native rhetoric and claimed to receive messages from God through a small silver box he carried. On some occasions he dressed like the Inca, at others like a Spanish official. He also changed his name to Túpac Catari, associating himself with the great indigenous leaders Túpac Amaru and Tomás Catari. Lacking any traditional claim to leadership, he proclaimed himself viceroy, saying he had received authority from Túpac Amaru.

Túpac Catari's greatest undertaking was the siege of La Paz, which began on 14 March 1781. With an army numbering from 10,000 to 40,000, he controlled access to the city and brutally killed those captured while trying to escape. On 18 July, General Ignacio Flores's army temporarily broke the siege but then had to withdraw. Thereupon Túpac Catari joined his forces with those of Andrés Túpac Amaru and again besieged La Paz. Unable to breach the defenses, they dammed the Choqueyapu River above La Paz to unleash a destructive flood on the city. The approach of another royal column under José de Resequín saved La Paz. Túpac Catari may have lost 5,000 at La Paz, while the besieged suffered two or three times more deaths, many from starvation and disease.

Túpac Catari withdrew toward the north, rejecting offers of pardon. At Peñas on 9 November, Tomás Inga Lipe, a former ally, betrayed him, and he was taken into government hands. Quickly interrogated and condemned, on 14 November he was tied to four horses and cruelly torn apart.

Lack of artillery handicapped Túpac Catari at La Paz, and rivalry between the Aymaras and Quechuas prevented successful integration of the rebel movements, although they occasionally cooperated. Túpac Catari declared his intention of driving the Spanish from Peru, but he also talked of liberating the Aymaras from Inca oppression.

— KENDALL W. BROWN

TURBAY, GABRIEL

Gabriel Turbay (*b.* 28 January 1901; *d.* 17 November 1946), Colombian Liberal leader. Of Syrian-Lebanese descent, he was trained in medicine at the Universidad Nacional in Bogotá, but devoted little time to its practice. He attracted attention during the 1920s as a member of a circle of young socialist intellectuals. After the Liberal Party's return to power in 1930, he occupied a series of responsible government positions, and in 1946 he was the official Liberal candidate for president, opposing the dissident Liberal Jorge Eliécer GAITÁN and Conservative Mariano OSPINA PÉREZ. The latter won as a result of the Liberals' division. Turbay then left Colombia for a European tour; he died suddenly in Paris.

— DAVID BUSHNELL

TURBAY AYALA, JULIO CÉSAR

Julio César Turbay Ayala (*b.* 18 June 1916), Colombian Liberal Party politician and president (1978–1982). Turbay was born in Bogotá and received a bachelor's degree from the Escuela Nacional de Comercio. Amid growing public dissatisfaction over the Liberal–Conservative

power-sharing arrangement known as the Frente Nacional (National Front), then in its twentieth year, he won the presidential election of 1978, in which only 41 percent of the electorate voted. Antigovernment guerrilla groups subsequently intensified their operations, attempting to assassinate the president in 1978, staging an audacious theft of army weapons in 1979, and holding a score of diplomats hostage in the Dominican embassy in 1980. Turbay responded by stepping up military antiguerrilla operations, which soon produced an outcry against numerous arbitrary arrests and the physical abuse of detainees. Colombia was economically stable under Turbay, and government authority was never seriously threatened by the extralegal armed forces. Yet criticism of the political status quo, which Turbay represented, signaled an impending opening of the Colombian political system.

Since 1982 Turbay has been a senior member of the Liberal Party, leading a group known as the Turbayistas. However, his following is modest at best, owing to the unpopularity of his presidency and to personal shortcomings.

— JAMES D. HENDERSON

TURCIOS LIMA, LUIS AGOSTO

Luis Agosto Turcios Lima (*b.* 1941; *d.* 2 October 1966), Guatemalan guerrilla leader. On 13 November 1960, Turcios Lima led young military officers in rebellion against the corrupt government of Miguel YDÍGORAS FUENTES (1958–1963). In the aftermath of a coup that lacked ideological direction, Turcios Lima became an advocate of communist revolution through guerrilla warfare and organized the Rebel Armed Forces (FAR) with fellow officer Marco Antonio YON SOSA in 1962. Although Yon Sosa broke from the Communist Party and the FAR in 1965, Turcios Lima reluctantly accepted its decision to suspend military activity in order to give civilian president Julio César MÉNDEZ MONTENEGRO (1966–1970) an opportunity to bring the reactionary military under control. The military, trained and supplied by the United States, rejected Méndez's reformist policies and launched a brutal campaign against the FAR following the accidental death of Turcios Lima. From the devastating losses suffered in the late 1960s, the rebel leaders of the 1970s concluded that there was no democratic alternative to armed revolution.

— PAUL J. DOSAL

U

UBICO Y CASTAÑEDA, JORGE

Jorge Ubico y Castañeda (*b.* 10 November 1878; *d.* 14 June 1946), military figure and president of Guatemala (1931–1944). Born in Guatemala City, Ubico was educated at schools in the United States before entering the military academy in Guatemala (1894), where he remained for three years. He entered the military in 1897, and fought in the border war with El Salvador in 1906, attaining the rank of colonel by the age of twenty-eight.

Ubico served as governor of two states, and, beginning in 1922, as minister of war under President José María ORELLANA until 1926. The regime of General Ubico remains controversial in spite of considerable economic accomplishments, due to his repressive methods and the popularity of the 1944 revolution that overthrew his regime. Coming to power as president by unanimous election during the turbulent years of the Great Depression, Ubico promoted economic stabilization through frugal policies that restricted government spending while imposing law and order through a restrictive and harsh security apparatus.

Jorge Ubico y Castañeda, ca. 1939. (UPI/Bettmann)

Ubico's primary legacy to his nation was the establishment of a systematic infrastructure network, which constituted the basis of the modern Guatemalan economy. By constructing the nation's first highway and telegraph networks, he brought about national unity by linking previously remote parts of the republic with the central core. Ubico considered the Petén highway his greatest accomplishment. Though never quite reaching that distant frontier region, this highway extended the first links from the capital into the northern highlands and the Verapaz region in central Guatemala. The caudillo left the nation with 6,330 miles of road, almost five times the amount that existed when he assumed office. Most were dirt roads constructed by hand.

Ubico's extensive public-works projects included the first paved streets in Guatemala City, the capital, with accompanying sewers, and facilities to house government offices. Construction during his tenure included virtually all the ministry buildings, the National Palace, the Presidential Palace, the legislative building, the Supreme Court building, the post office, and the telegraph office. His efforts extended to a sports stadium, racetrack, public bandstands and parks, public bathhouses, and an aqueduct to bring fresh water to the capital.

Significantly, Ubico's program extended into the nation's smaller cities and remote hamlets. The effort provided virtually all provincial capitals with government buildings, telegraph offices, and military barracks, while extending limited water and electricity service into small towns throughout the nation, following the newly built roads. This marked a clear departure from practices of previous central governments. As a result, the regime and the caudillo enjoyed considerable popularity in the countryside. Construction, however, was done primarily by hand by poorly paid laborers. These efforts promoted economic revival and expansion, while serving to facilitate control from the capital.

Ubico directed a *personalista* regime in which all government actions required his personal approval and all officials took their orders directly from the chief executive. Those in remote regions received authorizations via telegraph. Military officers held key government positions, and his Progressive Party controlled all aspects of government and the legislature, conducting two plebiscites that reelected Ubico without opposition.

Ubico's regime used harsh methods to maintain internal order. Security forces kept a watchful eye on the populace, and political opposition was ruthlessly suppressed. The government controlled the only radio stations and carefully monitored the press. The only facilities to receive external news reports were housed in the National Palace.

Ubico sought to revive agriculture by promoting the cultivation of unused land and to integrate the Indians into the mainstream of the national economy by drawing them from subsistence agriculture into commercial farming. The Vagrancy Law of 1934 abolished debt peonage and substituted a labor obligation to the state, under which all citizens who did not cultivate their own plot of land of a minimum size were considered vagrant unless they were employed for a minimum of 150 days per year. While this constituted the first change in the rural labor system since colonial days, the requirement was long enough to supply labor for the harvesting and planting of export crops. Ubico sought to promote crop diversification, and the highway system enabled an expansion in food production by opening new areas to cultivation and linking once remote regions to the national market.

All citizens who did not cultivate their own plot

of land of a minimum size were considered vagrant

unless they were employed for a minimum of

150 days per year.

Ubico sought to promote Guatemalan dominance in Central America, conducting a diplomatic rivalry with his counterpart in El Salvador and seeking to reassert Guatemalan claims to British Honduras (Belize). Ubico maneuvered carefully to influence domestic politics in Nicaragua and Honduras. While his efforts were initially directed toward promoting the rise of the Liberal Party in neighboring nations, he later sought to promote stability in the isthmus through rapprochement with the incumbent regimes of the other Central American countries. Although this was a time-honored policy, it produced rumors of a so-called Dictators League during the late 1930s and early 1940s. The Belize question also resulted in an acrimonious and protracted dispute with Great Britain.

The advent of World War II proved particularly trying, given the importance of the large German community that constituted a significant part of the Guatemalan economy. Until the mid-1930s most Guatemalan coffee was sold on the Hamburg market. Though

attracted by German investment and the strong centrist policies of national socialism, Ubico remained a staunch nationalist, rejecting outside influence. Ubico supported the United States as soon as it became involved in World War II, despite his dispute with England regarding Belize, and he supplied agricultural products, such as quinine, to the United States to offset the loss of Asian sources.

The Ubico regime was overthrown in 1944 by a revolt led by students, junior military officers, and disgruntled members of the urban middle class who felt his policies favored the landowners. Ubico went into exile to the United States, where he died.

– KENNETH J. GRIEB

UGARTE, MANUEL

Manuel Ugarte (*b.* 1878; *d.* 2 December 1951), Argentine diplomat and writer. Born in Buenos Aires, Ugarte as a young man joined the Socialist Party. A prolific writer, he founded the daily *La Patria* and the review *Vida de Hoy* and became a prominent member of progressive literary and journalistic circles in the capital. A passionate anti-imperialist and pan-Hispanist, Ugarte served during Juan D. PERÓN's first presidency as Argentine ambassador to Mexico (1946–1948), Nicaragua (1949), and Cuba (1950). He formulated Pan-Hispanism in opposition to U.S.-backed Pan-Americanism. His diplomatic career was cut short by failing health, however. He died in Nice, France, in 1951, and three years later was buried in La Recoleta cemetery in Buenos Aires. His writings include travel books (*Visiones de España*, 1904), novels (*La venganza del capataz*, 1925), short stories, poems, and political essays (*El porvenir de la América latina*, 1911; *El destino de un continente*, 1923; and *La nación latinoamericana*, 1978).

– RONALD C. NEWTON

UGARTE, MARCELINO

Marcelino Ugarte (*b.* 1860; *d.* 1929), Argentine provincial politician, one of the last of the old-regime potentates. A product of the Colegio Nacional and the law faculty of the University of Buenos Aires (from which he did not graduate), Ugarte entered Buenos Aires provincial politics in 1888 and rose to governor in 1902. His administration founded schools, built canals and railroads, opened farmlands in the south of the province, and reduced the public debt. In 1913, in the aftermath of the passage of the Sáenz Peña Law, he became a national senator. His power declined with the growth of Radical strength, however, and he resigned in 1914 to reclaim the provincial governorship. In 1916, balked by political opponents and at odds with President Hipólito YRIGOYEN, he withdrew to private life—a withdrawal hastened by Yrigoyen's intervention in the provincial government.

– RONALD C. NEWTON

ULATE BLANCO, OTILIO

Otilio Ulate Blanco (*b.* 25 August 1891; *d.* 27 October 1973), president of Costa Rica (1949–1953) and founder of the National Union Party (PUN).

Otilio Ulate Blanco came early to an exciting and sometimes turbulent life of journalism and politics when he left high school at age seventeen following his father's premature death. He worked for and invested in a number of daily newspapers until he became the owner and publisher of the premier Costa Rican newspaper *El Diario de Costa Rica.* He was the founder of *La Hora.*

His long involvement in political affairs came to dominate his life from the time he was chosen (1947) as the presidential candidate of the united opposition parties (made up of the National Unification Party, the Democratic Party, and the Social Democratic Party) to oppose the progovernment candidate, former president Rafael Ángel CALDERÓN GUARDIA (1940–1944). The government's effort to deny Ulate's victory in the 1948 election served as the catalyst for revolution. Ulate was inaugurated in 1949 following eighteen months of de facto government by the Junta Fundadora de la Segunda República headed by José FIGUERES FERRER.

Ulate's administration emphasized fiscal restraint and pacification. He ran unsuccessfully in the presidential election of 1962. In 1965 Ulate allied the PUN with Calderón Guardia's National Republican Party to support what was to be the successful candidacy of José Joaquín TREJOS FERNÁNDEZ (1966–1970).

– JOHN PATRICK BELL

ULLOA, ANTONIO DE

Antonio de Ulloa (*b.* 12 January 1716; *d.* 5 July 1795), naval officer, scientist, and royal bureaucrat. Born in Seville, Antonio de Ulloa was educated in his native city and subsequently, like his compatriot Jorge JUAN Y SANTACILIA, at the new Spanish naval academy (Guardia Marina) in Cádiz. In 1734, at eighteen, Ulloa was chosen to accompany Juan and the French expedition going to the Indies to measure the exact length of a degree on the equator. Ulloa spent the next ten years (1735–1744) in South America, first assisting Charles Marie de la Condamine at some thirty-five different locations near

Quito, then in Lima advising the viceroy on shoring up the coastal defenses of Peru. The two officers finally left for Spain in October 1744 on separate ships, but not before returning to Quito to make new observations with their own instruments. Reunited in Spain in 1746, Ulloa and Juan wrote *Relación histórica del viaje a la America Meridiónal* (Historical Report on the Voyage to America), a four-volume descriptive account of the various places they had visited in the Indies. They also wrote for crown officials a secret report exposing corruption, inefficiency, fraud, and abuses in the Indies that was published later in England in 1826 as an anti-Spanish tract entitled *Noticias secretas de America* (Secret Information on America).

Ulloa remained in the royal service for the next forty-five years. In the early 1750s he traveled about Europe garnering information on road and canal building and dredging harbors, and seeking to attract skilled artisans to migrate to Spain. In 1757 he assumed the governorship of the mercury mine at Huancavelica in Peru. Although he disliked that post intensely, he increased mercury production a bit, reduced the debt of the mine by 200,000 pesos to 77,000 pesos and exposed fraud in the royal treasuries of Peru, which led to a falling out with Viceroy Manuel de AMAT Y JUNIENT in Lima. Leaving Peru in 1764 to return to Spain, Ulloa found himself sidetracked in Havana by a royal order to go to Spanish Louisiana as governor. His tenure in New Orleans from March 1766 until his forced flight on 1 November 1768 was as stormy as his time in Huancavelica, as he once again proved an unpopular, irascible administrator, especially with the French residents.

Back in Spain, Ulloa returned to Cádiz to teach and do research, his true forté.

CHARLES III called him back into the royal service— in the 1770s as a naval commander and in the 1780s as chief of Spanish naval operations—but Ulloa was always more content engaged in experiments in science or applied science: astronomy, navigation, bookbinding, metallurgy, printing inks, engraving, electricity and magnetism, surgical techniques, weaving, and agriculture. A representative figure of the Spanish Enlightenment, Ulloa remained intellectually vigorous until his death in 1795, the same year he published the most up-to-date guide in Europe on the latest navigational techniques.

– JOHN JAY TEPASKE

UMAÑA BERNAL, JOSÉ

José Umaña Bernal (*b.* 18 December 1899; *d.* 1 August 1982), Colombian poet and politician. A member of the Los Nuevos generation, Umaña studied with the

Jesuits and attended law school at the National University. A multifaceted man, he was a professional reporter, collaborating on newspapers and journals. As a man of the theater, he wrote the prize-winning play *El buen amor* (1927) and directed Bogotá's Municipal Theater in the 1930s. As a politician, he served in parliament, became Colombia's consul to Chile (1927), and traveled throughout Europe, the United States, and Latin America. As a poet, Umaña was rooted in Parnassian and Symbolist esthetics. True to his heritage, he maintained an intellectual approach to poetry, adhering to formal precision, musicality, and purity of language. After translating Rainer Maria Rilke's works, his own earlier emphasis on love and sadness became tinged with introspection and concern for his own death. His best poetry collections are: *Décimas de luz y yelo* (1942), *Poesía 1918–1945* (1951), and *Diario de Estoril* (1948).

— MARÍA A. SALGADO

UNANUE, HIPÓLITO

Hipólito Unanue (*b.* 13 August 1755; *d.* 15 July 1833), Peruvian physician, academician, and author. Unanue was born in Arica, Peru. He studied medicine at the University of San Marcos and became a doctor in 1786. In 1789 he won the chair of anatomy at San Marcos, initiating a long and illustrious academic career there.

Unanue first achieved recognition as a principal author for the *Mercurio Peruano,* the voice of enlightened Peruvians in the early 1790s. His international reputation, however, rested on *Observaciones sobre el clima de Lima* (1806; revised 1815), in which he outlined and documented his theory that climate was primarily responsible for disease.

Unanue brought eighteenth-century medicine to Peru. Through his efforts, Lima secured first an anatomical amphitheater (1792) and then the San Fernando College of Medicine and Surgery, which began functioning in 1811.

With the coming of independence, Unanue served briefly as a government minister. He died amid the instability of early Republican Peru, his contributions to Peruvian intellectual life largely forgotten.

— MARK A. BURKHOLDER

UNGO, GUILLERMO MANUEL

Guillermo Manuel Ungo (*b.* 1931; *d.* 28 February 1991), leader of the Democratic Revolutionary Front (FDR) of El Salvador. Son of Guillermo Ungo, the founder of the Christian Democratic Party of El Salvador (PDC), Ungo taught law at the University of Central America (UCA). In 1964 he helped found the

National Revolutionary Movement (MNR), which, with the proscription of the left-leaning PAR (Party of Renovating Action) in 1967, became the major social democratic party in the nation. He was chosen by José Napoleón DUARTE to be his vice-presidential running mate when the United National Opposition (UNO) coalition was formed to contest the 1972 presidential elections. After the fraudulent defeat of UNO and the exile of Duarte by the military in 1972, Ungo remained in the country as head of the MNR and as a law professor at UCA.

With the overthrow of President Carlos Humberto ROMERO on 15 October 1979, Ungo became a member of the First Junta of the Revolution. However, when he resigned in January 1980 because of the junta's inability to control the army, the government collapsed. In 1980 Ungo brought the MNR into the newly formed Democratic Revolutionary Front (FDR) and became its president after the murder of its six leaders on 28 November 1980. When the FDR and the guerrilla alliance, the Farabundo Martí National Liberation Front (FMLN), joined forces in October 1980, Ungo and the other members of the Diplomatic-Political Commission (the civilian leadership of the FDR-FMLN, headquartered in Mexico City) were forced to live in exile. Living alternately in Mexico City and Panama City, Ungo became the major spokesman for the democratic forces supporting the guerrilla insurgency.

Ungo took advantage of the political opening afforded by the plan for settling the insurgency wars in Central America proposed by President Oscar ARIAS SÁNCHEZ of Costa Rica in February 1987 (known as the Arias peace plan) and returned to El Salvador in late 1987 to help found the Democratic Convergence, a coalition of the MNR, the Popular Social Christian Movement (MPSC), and the Social Democratic Party (PSD). He ran as its presidential candidate in the elections of 1989, and received a surprisingly low 3.9 percent of the vote.

— ROLAND H. EBEL

URBINA, JOSÉ MARÍA

José María Urbina (*b.* March 1808; *d.* 4 September 1891), *jefe supremo* (supreme leader) of Ecuador (1851–1852) and president (1852–1856). Born in Ambato, Urbina attended the Naval School at Guayaquil briefly but left early to participate in military actions (siege of Callao, 1824–1826; Malpelo, 1828; defense of Ecuadorian independence, 1830). Rising rapidly through military ranks, he became aide-de-camp to President Juan José FLORES. On a diplomatic mission to Bogotá for President Vicente ROCAFUERTE, he committed a serious indiscretion and was recalled in 1837. Caught plotting against the government, he was banished but returned in 1839 to enter politics under the tutelage of President Flores. For his political loyalty to Flores, Urbina was rewarded with the governorship of Manabí. In 1845 he joined rebels to topple Flores from power. He was promoted to brigadier general and rose to high posts in the provisional government.

In 1851, Urbina led a revolt and proclaimed himself jefe supremo. *He would dominate Ecuadorian politics for the rest of the decade.*

President Vicente Ramón ROCA (1845–1849) named Urbina chief of the general staff, which enormously increased his political and military power. In 1851, Urbina led a revolt and proclaimed himself *jefe supremo.* He would dominate Ecuadorian politics for the rest of the decade.

As *jefe supremo* Urbina abolished slavery and repelled an armed invasion by Flores from Peru. Under a new constitution he was elected president in 1852 and served a four-year term that was characterized by vigorous executive domination, glib assertions of liberal principles, stern control of the press, and the expulsion of the Jesuits. He severed relations with the Vatican, quarreled with Peru over asylum given to Flores and over Ecuador's southern boundary, and sought unsuccessfully to establish a U.S. protectorate over Ecuador.

From 1856 to 1859, Urbina was the *éminence grise* of the Francisco ROBLES administration, which collapsed in 1859 after a Peruvian attack at Guayaquil. Urbina fled into exile, plotted in Peru to regain power in Ecuador, but did not return until 1876. He helped place Ignacio VEINTEMILLA in power, but his influence diminished rapidly thereafter. He died in Guayaquil, forgotten by friends and denounced by liberal leaders.

– MARK J. VAN AKEN

URBINA, LUIS GONZAGA

Luis Gonzaga Urbina (*b.* 8 February 1864; *d.* 18 November 1934), Mexican journalist and poet. Born in Mexico City, Urbina studied at the National Preparatory School before launching his career as a journalist. He began composing poetry before the age of sixteen. In 1881 he published some of his verses in *La patria ilustrada.* In 1887 he met his mentor, Justo SIERRA MÉNDEZ. Thanks to that friendship, Urbina obtained various government positions as well as posts at peri-

odicals, where he wrote theater criticism and some of the first movie reviews in Mexico. Under Sierra's direction and with the cooperation of Pedro HENRÍQUEZ UREÑA and Nicolás Rangel, Urbina compiled the two volumes of Mexican literature, *Antología del centenario* (1910), produced for the centenary celebrations of that year. Although he is considered a poet of the *modernismo* movement, Urbina represents the persistence of romanticism with his *vespertinas,* poems that reflect upon love and melancholy. In 1913 he was appointed director of the National Library, but two years later he left Mexico to live first in Cuba and then in Spain.

– JOHN WALDRON

URDANETA, ANDRÉS DE

Andrés de Urdaneta (*b.* 1508; *d.* 3 June 1568), Spanish navigator and explorer. A native of Villafranca de Oria, Guipúzcoa, Urdaneta served as a page on the circumnavigation of García Jofre de Loaysa in 1525. After being shipwrecked in the Moluccas, he returned to Spain in 1536. Urdaneta journeyed to Guatemala in 1538, and in 1541 he went to New Galicia with Pedro de ALVARADO. He was *corregidor* of the province of Ávalos in 1543, and visitor of that province until 1545. He became a novice in the Augustinians in 1552 and was named pilot-missionary to the Philippines under Miguel LÓPEZ DE LEGAZPI in 1559. He sailed from Navidad, Jalisco, in November 1564, reached the Philippines in February 1565, and returned to New Spain 8 October 1565. On his return voyage he established the eastbound route, via Japan and California, to Acapulco that was used by the Manila Galleon. Urdaneta retired in 1566 to a monastery in Mexico City, where he died.

– W. MICHAEL MATHES

URDANETA, RAFAEL

Rafael Urdaneta (*b.* 24 October 1788; *d.* 23 August 1845), Venezuelan independence leader and Colombian president. Born in Maracaibo, Venezuela, Rafael Urdaneta studied in Bogotá and at the start of the independence movement joined the patriots of New Granada. He took part in the first civil conflicts (as a federalist) as well as in the struggle against Spain, serving as Bolívar's second in command in the Admirable Campaign (1813). Following the Spanish reconquest of 1815–1816, he was one of those who kept resistance alive in the plains of the Orinoco Basin and later took part in the final liberation of Venezuela.

Urdaneta filled important positions in the government and congress of Gran Colombia. As minister of war in 1828–1829, he was military strongman of Simón

BOLÍVAR's final dictatorship. With Bolívar gone, in 1830 he became president-dictator in a last-ditch effort to preserve the power of the Bolivarian party and the unity of Gran Colombia. Forced to step down early in 1831, he returned to Venezuela, where he continued to play a key political role. He was on a diplomatic mission to Spain when he died in Paris.

— DAVID BUSHNELL
WINFIELD J. BURGGRAAFF

UREÑA, FELIPE

Felipe Ureña (*d.* after 1773), Mexican sculptor, retablo master. Ureña was largely responsible for the spreading of *estípite* baroque throughout New Spain, in places very distant from Mexico City. His decoration of the sacristy of the Church of San Francisco in Toluca, dedicated in 1729, is the first native work in the style. Ureña had what must have been a sizable workshop in Mexico City, but he also executed retablos and architectural projects in Guanajuato, Aguascalientes, Durango, Oaxaca, and elsewhere. His most famous work, still extant, is the Jesuit church La Compañía in Guanajuato, on which he labored between 1747 and 1765, with interruptions for other projects. Fragments of his wood sculpture exist in Durango.

— CLARA BARGELLINI

UREÑA DE HENRÍQUEZ, SALOMÉ

Salomé Ureña de Henríquez (*b.* 21 October 1850; *d.* 6 March 1897), Dominican educator and poet. Ureña de Henríquez was born in Santo Domingo. Her father, Nicolás Ureña de Mendoza, was a distinguished politician, lawyer, and poet who provided her with an excellent education. Together with her husband, Francisco HENRÍQUEZ Y CARVAJAL, she implemented important education reforms in the Dominican Republic, stressing the significance of women's education. Ureña de Henríquez was the founder of the Instituto de Señoritas. She was profoundly influenced by the Puerto Rican educator Eugenio María de HOSTOS (1839–1903), who resided in Santo Domingo for over a decade. A fervent liberal, she supported the Blue Party of Gregorio LUPERÓN and opposed presidents Buenaventura BÁEZ and Ulises HEUREAUX. Beset by frequent illness and faced with the civil wars and dictatorships of one of the most turbulent epochs of Dominican history, she never lost faith in the positivist creed of order and progress.

Ureña de Henríquez was regarded as one of the finest Dominican poets and her writings became known throughout Latin America. Her poetry takes up a variety of themes, such as patriotism ("A Quisqueya," "En defensa de la sociedad," "Anacaona"), sentimentality ("La llegada del invierno," "Tristezas," "Horas de angustias," "El ave y el nido"), and social and political reform ("Ruinas," which is regarded as one of her best poems). She was the mother of the educator and literary critic Camila Henríquez Ureña; the writer, teacher, and diplomat Max HENRÍQUEZ UREÑA; and the writer, philosopher, and educator Pedro HENRÍQUEZ UREÑA. She died in Santo Domingo.

— KAI P. SCHOENHALS

URETA, ELOY G.

Eloy G. Ureta (*b.* 1892; *d.* 1965), Peruvian military leader, presidential candidate, and diplomat. Ureta was born in Chiclayo and educated in Chorrillos Military Academy (1909–1913) and the Advanced War School (1922). As brigadier general in 1941, Ureta was in charge of the military operations during the war with Ecuador. He became a popular military figure especially after the victory achieved in the battle of Zarumilla (24 July 1941). He was promoted to division general in 1941. He retired from the army to run unsuccessfully for the presidency in 1945. He was awarded the honorary rank of marshal in 1946. Between 1949 and 1955 he was the Peruvian ambassador to Spain. He died in Madrid.

— ALFONSO W. QUIROZ

URIBE, JUAN CAMILO

Juan Camilo Uribe (*b.* 20 February 1941), Colombian artist. Born in Medellín, Uribe is known for his conceptualist and experimental work, which uses popular, religious, and historical icons from Colombian culture. He has participated in group shows since 1968. In 1972 he won first prize at the National Independent Salon, and first prize at the Third Salon of Young Artists in Bogotá, where he had his first solo exhibit three years later at the Galería Oficina. He went to Paris on a grant from the Colombian government in 1977, the same year he represented Colombia at the São Paulo Biennial. His work was shown at the Museum of Contemporary Art in Caracas and at the Primera Bienal del Grabado de América in Maracaibo, Venezuela. Uribe's installation *Arte Telescopio* (1979) featured numerous individual slide viewers hanging from the ceiling throughout the room, documenting bits of his personal life, his exhibits, his friends, and his work.

— BÉLGICA RODRÍGUEZ

URIBE HOLGUÍN, GUILLERMO

Guillermo Uribe Holguín (*b.* 17 March 1880; *d.* 26 June 1971), Colombian composer. Guillermo Uribe

Holguín began the study of music in Bogotá, where he was born, and continued his studies in New York and at the Schola Cantorum in Paris. He conducted, taught, served as director of Colombia's Conservatorio Nacional (1910–1935, 1942–1947), and wrote a work on harmony as well as an autobiography. But he is best known as a composer, generally considered Colombia's greatest. His extensive body of works includes eleven symphonies, concerti and chamber music, numerous piano pieces, and songs. In style and technique he was strongly influenced by French impressionism, and for many years he disdained the use of elements from popular Colombian musical culture. Starting with his second symphony (*Del terruño*) in 1924, however, he turned increasingly to national rhythms and melody in his composing, thus giving qualified expression to musical nationalism.

– DAVID BUSHNELL

URIBE URIBE, RAFAEL

Rafael Uribe Uribe (*b.* 12 April 1859; *d.* 15 October 1914), Colombian political caudillo, one of the leaders of the Liberal Party between 1880 and his assassination in 1914. Born on an estate in Antioquia, Uribe was the son of a wealthy landowner. He was educated at the Colegio del Estado (the present-day University of Antioquia).

Due to the singular nature of Colombian politics, Uribe was a political leader who had to do double duty as a military leader, like many others of his generation, in the all-too-frequent civil wars between Liberals and Conservatives. He participated in the civil wars of 1876, 1885, 1895, and 1899.

A charismatic caudillo, he never reached the presidency of the nation because he attained political leadership when the Liberal Party had been displaced by a coalition dominated by the Conservative Party; this group established a hegemony over the country until 1930. Uribe and the rest of the Liberal leadership had to labor under political persecution and even exile, a situation that eventually led to the most traumatic of civil wars, the War of the Thousand Days (1899–1902).

As an ideological leader, Uribe is reputed to have been instrumental in a major ideological shift of his party after 1904, when, in the short article "Socialismo de Estado," he exhorted the Liberals to move away from laissez-faire economics and espoused state intervention in economic and social welfare. His platform is reminiscent of the measures then being implemented in Uruguay by President José BATLLE Y ORDÓÑEZ (1903–1907), rather than the socialism his enemies accused

him of. However, in the Colombia of the 1900s, it was considered subversive to ask the wealthy to pay taxes.

– JOSÉ ESCORCIA

URIBURU, JOSÉ EVARISTO

José Evaristo Uriburu (*b.* 19 November 1831; *d.* 25 October 1914), Argentine statesman, president of Argentina (1895–1898), and senator (1901–1910). Scion of an aristocratic Salta family, Uriburu was part of the so-called Generation of 1880 and one of the most representative figures in the oligarchic politics of the late nineteenth and early twentieth centuries. A leading member of the elite's political machine, the National Autonomist Party (PAN), Uriburu assumed the presidency of the nation after the sudden resignation of Luis SÁENZ PEÑA. Like his predecessor, Uriburu had to deal with the great 1890 depression and he continued Sáenz Peña's policy of consolidating the national and provincial debts. Though brief, his presidency nonetheless produced a number of notable accomplishments. Uriburu's resolution of the ongoing dispute with the British railroad companies over profit guarantees as well as other measures restored investor confidence and led to a return of British capital. In his diplomatic career, Uriburu was one of the principal mediators of the treaty between Chile and Peru that ended the War of the Pacific.

– JAMES P. BRENNAN

URIBURU, JOSÉ FÉLIX

José Félix Uriburu (*b.* 20 July 1868; *d.* 29 April 1932), leader of the army's first military coup and Argentine president (1930–1932). Born in Salta and a nephew of Argentine President José E. URIBURU, Uriburu initially chose a career in the military rather than politics. Rising

---

Uriburu's government intervened in the country's universities, censored the national press, and imprisoned or exiled leaders of the political opposition.

---

through the ranks, he became director of the War College (Escuela Superior de Guerra) in 1907. After serving as a military attaché in Germany and England prior to World War I, he attained the rank of general in 1921. Under President Marcelo T. de ALVEAR (1922–1928), he served as inspector general of the army (1923–1926).

Disaffection with President Hipólito YRIGOYEN's second administration (1928–1930) encouraged conservatives to rebel against the elected government. Although retired from active service, Uriburu led the coup that toppled Yrigoyen on 6 September 1930 and inaugurated Argentina's Infamous Decade.

As provisional president, Uriburu attempted to establish a quasi-fascist regime. His government intervened in the country's universities, censored the national press, and imprisoned or exiled leaders of the political opposition. When the ousted Radical Party swept the April 1931 elections in Buenos Aires Province, his government intensified the repression of political opponents. Dwindling support among conservatives and the military forced him to abandon his plans. His government supervised a second election that gave Agustín P. JUSTO the presidency (1932–1938) and brought the Concordancia to power.

— DANIEL LEWIS

URQUIZA, JUSTO JOSÉ DE

Justo José de Urquiza (*b.* 18 October 1801; *d.* 11 April 1870), Argentine soldier and statesman. Urquiza was born in Talar de Arroyo Largo, Entre Ríos, the son of a merchant and landowner. He studied at the Colegio de San Carlos in Buenos Aires and in 1821 became a lieutenant in the militia. In 1826–1827 he served in the Entre Ríos congress, where he argued for democracy, federalism, and educational improvements; he also persuaded the congress to reject the 1826 Constitution. Urquiza expanded his business activities and became a follower of Ricardo LÓPEZ JORDÁN, who was defeated by a revolution supported by Santa Fe Governor Estanislao López. Urquiza fled to Uruguay, and in 1831 he returned to Entre Ríos to take command of the Army of Observation. In 1837 he was again elected to serve in the provincial congress. In 1838 he was with the Entre Ríos army massed to oppose an attack by Fructuoso RIVERA of Uruguay and Berón de Astrada of Corrientes. The attack was repulsed, thanks largely to Urquiza's cavalry. Urquiza continued fighting interprovincial battles. In 1845 he was named governor of Entre Ríos, a province where the dictator and governor of Buenos Aires, Juan Manuel de ROSAS, had little influence.

Urquiza established a well-equipped militia composed primarily of landowners, and he financed progressive programs in public education. In 1848 he began building the Palacio San José, his residence, and founded the Colegio del Uruguay. Urquiza was reelected governor in 1849, and in 1851 he announced to the provincial governments and the exiles in Montevideo that he would undertake a campaign against Rosas. To further that goal, he negotiated an alliance with Brazil and Uruguay.

Urquiza opened his campaign by raising the siege of Montevideo by Manuel ORIBE. When his forces crossed into Uruguay, many of Oribe's troops and some from Buenos Aires joined them. Meanwhile, Rosas had declared war on Brazil. Urquiza was to command a combined force of Argentine, Brazilian, and Uruguayan troops. Rosas took no defensive measures to stop Urquiza's advance but assembled his army at Santos Lugares. Rosas was defeated at nearby Caseros on 3 February 1852 by a superior cavalry. He fled to Buenos Aires, where he and his daughter sought refuge in the home of the British minister and a few days later sailed for England.

Urquiza appointed Vicente López y Planes as interim governor. In May 1852, at a meeting of provincial governors, at San Nicolás de los Arroyos, Urquiza was named temporary director of the Argentine Confederation. Buenos Aires disapproved, however, and in September it seceded from the confederation. All the provinces except Buenos Aires approved the constitution in 1853, Paraná became the capital of the confederation, and Urquiza was elected president (1854–1860). The new government lacked adequate resources to create the institutions that would further national integration and economic development. Several military invasions were launched to bring Buenos Aires into the union, and in 1859 Congress authorized Urquiza, governor of Entre Ríos since 1 May 1860, to use military force to subdue the rebellious province. The armies of the confederation under Urquiza clashed with the Buenos Aires army, led by Bartolomé MITRE, at Pavón on 17 September 1861. Urquiza's cavalry won, but the infantry was defeated. Urquiza left the battlefield. Some maintain that he was ill, others that he realized that Buenos Aires could not be defeated, and still others that he was disgusted with the disputes among military and civilian leaders. Urquiza, constitutionally prohibited from succeeding himself, secured the election of José María Dominguez as governor in 1864, and in 1865 he sought—unsuccessfully—to prevent war with Paraguay. Francisco Solano LÓPEZ attacked Corrientes, thus compelling Urquiza to support the unified Argentine government of Mitre.

On 11 April 1870, a group of conspirators assassinated Urquiza at his home. Two of his sons were killed in Concordia, Entre Ríos. Urquiza had amassed a considerable fortune in land, cattle, and meat-salting plants. He and his wife had eleven children, and he legitimized twelve of his natural children.

— JOSEPH T. CRISCENTI

URRACÁ

Urracá (*d.* 1531), Panamanian indigenous leader, one of the most romanticized figures in the country, and a symbol of Panamanian patriotism. For nine years he fought the Spaniards Gaspar de Espinosa and Pedrarias Dávila in what is now Veraguas and Natá. Although he was captured once by the Spaniards, he was able to escape. His encounters with the Spaniards are described in Antonio de HERRERA Y TORDESILLAS's *Historia general de los hechos de los castellanos en las islas y tierra firme del mar océano* (1549–1625).

– JUAN MANUEL PÉREZ

URREA, JOSÉ DE

José de Urrea (*b.* 1797; *d.* August 1849), Mexican general. A fourth-generation frontier military officer, Urrea was born in the presidio of Tucson. He followed in his father's footsteps: commanding frontier garrisons; fighting insurgents; seconding Agustín de ITURBIDE's plan for independence, but supporting the republicans against the empire. The involvement of both father and son in the rebellion of the Plan of Montaño led to his father's exile and José's dismissal. He reentered the army two years later (1829), rising to the rank of general in 1835 as a protégé of SANTA ANNA. He distinguished himself in opposing the independence of Texas. As military commander of Sonora and Sinaloa, Urrea launched a series of unsuccessful revolts to reestablish the Federal Constitution of 1824, first in that region in 1837, and then nationally in 1839, 1840, and 1841. With Santa Anna's return to power that latter year, Urrea returned to Sonora as governor and commander general (1842–1844). His aggressive policies against the economic interests and political power of centralist sympathizers, and against the autonomy of the Yaqui and Mayo Indians, provoked a civil war in the state that continued for three years, until a new national government forced him to yield his command. He then fought under Santa Anna in the war with the United States (1846). He died in Durango, of cholera.

– STUART F. VOSS

URREA, TERESA

Teresa Urrea (*b.* 1873; *d.* 1906), popular figure among Mexican revolutionaries. A mestiza born in Ocorini, Sinaloa, Mexico, Teresa Urrea began, around 1890, to claim divine guidance and to preach social reform from her father's rancho at Cabora in the southern part of the state of Sonora. Thousands of Yaqui and Mayo Indians, along with mestizos and whites of various social groups, flocked to hear and revere her as la Santa (saint) de Cabora. In 1892, when armed movements in her name began to wrack the region, the government deported her and her father to Nogales, Arizona, where she continued to inspire armed forays into Mexico. As fame for her healings spread, she traveled from New York to California, performing her "miracles." She died at age thirty-two, in Clifton, Arizona. Throughout her "mission" she denied fomenting revolution, although hundreds of rebels died in her name.

– PAUL J. VANDERWOOD

URRIOLAGOITÍA, MAMERTO

Mamerto Urriolagoitía (*b.* 5 December 1895; *d.* 4 June 1974), president of Bolivia (1949–1951). Born in Sucre, Urriolagoitía became a lawyer and specialized in international law. From 1919 to 1937, he served as Bolivia's Consul General in Great Britain. At the conclusion of his diplomatic career, he returned to Sucre and won election to Bolivia's Senate in the early 1940s. Urriolagoitía became a leading member of a conservative Republican party coalition (Partido de la Unión Republicana Socialista—PURS). In the election of 1947, the PURS candidate Enrique HERTZOG was elected president and Mamerto Urriolagoitía, vice president. Hertzog resigned in May 1949, a few days after the mid-term election resulted in a vote that favored the middle-class reformist Nationalist Revolutionary Movement (MNR). As president Urriolagoitía repeatedly used military intervention to put down worker uprisings in the mining areas and cities. After the MNR won the May 1951 presidential elections, Urriolagoitía resigned on 16 May 1951. He handed over the government to General Hugo BALLIVIÁN, who, a few days later, abrogated the elections.

– ERWIN P. GRIESHABER

URRUTIA LLEÓ, MANUEL

Manuel Urrutia Lleó (*b.* 1901; *d.* 5 July 1981), Cuban lawyer and judge, appointed president after the Cuban Revolution of 1959 and dismissed six months later by Fidel CASTRO. Born in Las Villas province, Urrutia received a law degree in 1923 from the University of Havana and was appointed municipal judge of Oriente Province in 1928. He was later named the magistrate of the district of Santiago. Urrutia first gained national recognition in 1957, when he ruled for the dismissal of 100 youths charged with rebellion against the Batista dictatorship for their involvement in Castro's 1953 attack on the Moncada barracks. Castro's decision to appoint Urrutia as president was apparently based on the assumption that Urrutia would be a compromise candidate acceptable to both radicals and moderates who supported Batista's overthrow. Yet from his first days in office, Urrutia showed little ability in the art of politics practiced amid a volatile revolutionary movement. After attacking growing Communist influence within the government, Urrutia was forced to resign on 17 July 1959, and public sentiment against him was so great that he had to take refuge in the Venezuelan embassy. Urrutia later fled to the United States, where he became a university professor and organizer of an anti-Castro movement. He wrote *Fidel Castro and Co., Inc: Communist Tyranny in Cuba* (1964), his account of the revolution. Urrutia died in Queens, New York.

— MICHAEL POWELSON

URSÚA, PEDRO DE

Pedro De Ursúa (*b.* ca. 1511–1516; *d.* 1 January 1561), leader of the search for El Dorado, the "Land of Cinnamon." Born in Navarre, Spain, Ursúa reached Cartagena de Indias on Colombia's coast in 1545. He served as administrator and military leader, pacified the Chitarero and Muso Indians, and founded the cities of Pamplona and Tudela. As *justicia mayor* (municipal deputy) of Santa Marta in the early 1550s, he brought the Tairona Indians under Spanish domination. Subsequently he undertook the task of subduing runaway slaves on the Isthmus of Panama and succeeded in capturing "King" Bayamo, thus ending a threat to intercolonial trade.

Lope de Aguirre was at the head of the mutinous group that assassinated Ursúa as he rested in his hammock.

The Peruvian viceroy Andrés HURTADO DE MENDOZA, marqués de Cañete, authorized Ursúa's search for El Dorado, reputed to be in the upper Amazon basin. Ursúa collected about 370 Europeans, from 20 to 30 blacks, and from 600 to 2,000 Indian auxiliaries from several Andean cities in February 1559. They constructed several brigantines, flatboats, rafts, and canoes on the upper Huallaga River, setting forth in September 1560. Pedro de Ursúa faced discontent from the start: some were bothered by the presence of his mestiza mistress, Inés de Atienza; others chafed at the hard work and difficult conditions en route downriver. Lope de AGUIRRE was at the head of the mutinous group that assassinated Ursúa as he rested in his hammock near the juncture of the Putumayo and Amazon rivers.

The tale of Aguirre's bloody descent to the Atlantic is one of the most tragic in the era of discovery. Over a hundred of his fellow explorers were killed as Aguirre rebelled against all authority, save that of the sword. Survivors sailed out of the Amazon northwestwardly to the island of Margarita, then headed back toward Peru. Aguirre was finally surrounded by a group of royalists in Venezuela and killed on 27 October 1561.

— NOBLE DAVID COOK

URUGUAI, VISCONDE DO

Visconde do Uruguai (Paulino José Soares de Sousa; *b.* 4 October 1807; *d.* 15 July 1866), Brazilian statesman. Born in Paris, Uruguai was a key spokesman for the early Conservative Party and the driving force in the diplomacy leading to the overthrow of Argentina's dictator, Juan Manuel de ROSAS in 1852. Uruguai began his studies at Coimbra and completed them in São Paulo in 1831. His brilliance and character attracted support and early promotion as a magistrate in São Paulo, and then in Rio de Janeiro. His marriage into an established provincial planter clan brought political entrée through his brother-in-law, Joaquim José Rodrigues Tôrres (later Viscount de ITABORAÍ). In 1834, he was elected to the assembly of Rio de Janeiro Province, which in turn elected him a provincial vice president. In 1836, he was appointed president of the province; that same year the province elected him a national deputy. In the chamber of deputies, with Tôrres and Eusébio de QUEIRÓS, Uruguai led the Saquaremas. The latter were the *fluminense* radical reactionaries of the Conservative Party, which had been created in 1837, in an era of reaction, and was directed by Bernardo Pereira de VASCONCELOS, Honório Hermeto Carneiro Leão, and Tôrres. Uruguai's role was that of jurist and orator. He and Vasconcelos formulated the positions that halted the Regency's liberal momentum and shored up the authoritarian centralization that was identified with the monarchy. His son and namesake, known as Paulino, maintained this legacy against the reformism of Uruguai's former protégé, the Viscount do RIO BRANCO, in the 1870s.

Uruguai, increasingly disgusted with politics, was proudest of his role as foreign minister (1849–1853). He earned his title by defending the empire's perennially insecure southern interests from Rosas's Uruguayan ambitions. It was Uruguai, aided in the field by Honório Hermeto Carneiro Leão (later Viscount de PARANÁ) and Viscount do Rio Branco, who secured Uruguay and the Urquiza alliance that defeated Rosas. Subsequently, Uruguai, after accepting a brief diplomatic mission to Europe, began a retreat from politics.

Although meeting responsibilities as a senator (1849) and councillor of state (1853), he gradually sought the solace of study. The *Ensaio sôbre direito administrativo* was published in 1862 and *Estudos práticos sobre a administração das provincias do império* was published in 1865.

— JEFFREY D. NEEDELL

URVINA JADO, FRANCISCO

Francisco Urvina Jado, from 1902 to 1925 the director of the Banco Comercial y Agrícola, the leading financial institution of Guayaquil—the national commercial center and entrepôt for Ecuador's lucrative cacao bean export trade. Government spending relied heavily on funds borrowed from the Banco Comercial y Agrícola. Critics of this arrangement, such as the sierra (highland) businessman and politician Luis N. Dillon, claimed that the mounting debt gave the bank power to dictate terms to the government. Dillon and others believed that Director Urvina secretly ran Ecuador from behind the scenes. In 1922 Ecuador's monoculture export economy collapsed. The ensuing crisis led to public disclosure of the bank's unsound currency emissions, which had been largely necessitated by government borrowing. Urvina served as a convenient target for popular anger. Following a coup led by young military officers on 9 July 1925, the government seized the assets of the Banco Comercial y Agrícola, arrested Urvina, and sent him into exile.

— RONN F. PINEO

URZAGASTI, JESÚS

Jesús Urzagasti (*b.* October 1941), Bolivian poet, writer, and journalist. Urzagasti, one of the most important writers in Bolivia today, was born in Gran Chaco Province, in a small cattle-raising town, and emigrated to La Paz as a young man. Having decided to become a writer, he abandoned plans for a career in geology. He now works for *Presencia,* a leading Bolivian newspaper.

Urzagasti's first novel, *Tirinea,* was published in 1969; next was *Cuaderno de Lilino* (1972), a book of prose dedicated to a child. *Yerubia* (1978) is his only book of poetry. *En el país del silencio* (1987), Urzagasti's major novel, deals autobiographically with three decades of historical turmoil viewed through the eyes of a narrator who has maintained a sense of solidarity with society and a perception of man's relationship with nature. *De la ventana al parque* (1992), a shorter novel, explores the possibilities of cultural survival and of communication in a country marked by cultural diversity and by verticality of power.

— ANA REBECA PRADA

USIGLI, RODOLFO

Rodolfo Usigli (*b.* 17 November 1905; *d.* 18 June 1979), Mexican writer. Born in Mexico City, Usigli was the child of European immigrants. His father died when he was young and his ambitious mother raised four children in the difficult period of the Mexican Revolution. Belonging to the lower-middle-class and suffering from extremely poor vision, Usigli was unable to finish secondary school. In spite of his lack of social status and formal education, however, by the 1940s Usigli emerged as one of the leading innovators in Mexican drama and a major advocate for the establishment of a national theatrical tradition. In his efforts to modernize Mexican dramaturgy, he frequently interpreted the symbols and historical events that contributed to the formation of a Mexican national identity. The plays *El gesticulador* (The Imposter [written 1937, staged 1947]) and *Corona de sombra* (Crown of Shadow [written 1943, staged 1947]) attest to his concern with understanding Mexico's national cultural identity. In addition to his numerous plays, Usigli also published a psychological-detective novel, *Ensayo de un crimen* (Trial Run for a Murder [1944]), which was filmed by Luis BUÑUEL in 1955. Besides being a dramatist, Usigli also worked as a drama historian, university teacher, and diplomat. He died in Mexico City.

— DANNY J. ANDERSON

USLAR PIETRI, ARTURO

Arturo Uslar Pietri (*b.* 16 May 1906), Venezuelan writer and politician born in Caracas. Uslar Pietri epitomizes the Latin American writer and intellectual who participates in political life. After obtaining a doctorate in political science (1929), he joined the diplomatic corps and was sent to Paris. He returned to Venezuela in 1934, and taught political economy at the Universidad Central; later he held high positions in several Venezuelan ministries and was a delegate to the League of Nations. After the government fell in 1945, Uslar Pietri went to the United States as an exile and taught at Columbia University. He returned to Venezuela in 1950, reentering political life in 1959 as a senator.

In 1969, Uslar Pietri dedicated himself more to literature and teaching. His essays and fictional works evidence his interest in Venezuela's political and economic problems. Currents of democratic thought run through this concern for the national. The first volume of Uslar

Pietri's ample and wide-ranging literary output, *Barrabás y otros relatos,* was published in 1928. Written in a modernist prose style, *Barrabás* introduces elements of vanguardism by developing the inner voices of the characters. His novel *Las lanzas coloradas* (1931) brought him fame and was his most important contribution to Spanish American letters. The novel's plot centers on the violence and chaos in the Venezuelan countryside resulting from the military and ideological confusion during the Wars of Independence. This work is a "novel of the land" or a "novel of national interpretation."

Uslar Pietri's most important short-story collection, *Red* (1936), retains the same vanguardist elements initiated in *Barrabás,* but in this work the author shifts his attention to the vernacular life by using techniques of magical surrealism. Of this collection, "La lluvia" is considered a masterpiece of the genre. Less important works are *El camino de El dorado* (1947), a novel about the conqueror Lope de AGUIRRE; *El laberinto de fortuna: Un retrato en la geografía* (1962), a political work focusing on the epoch of the Juan Vincente GÓMEZ dictatorship (1908–1935). Essay collections include *Letras y hombres de Venezuela* (1948), *De una a otra Venezuela* (1950), *Breve historia de la novela hispanoamericana* (1954), *En busca del Nuevo Mundo* (1969), and *Bolívar Hoy* (1983). Uslar Pietri has also written about theater in *Teatro* (1958), a work in which plays of his appear, and has turned his hand to poetry in *El hombre que voy siendo* (1986).

— JUAN CARLOS GALEANO

V

VACA DE CASTRO, CRISTÓVAL

Cristóval Vaca de Castro (*b.* ca. 1492; *d.* after 1576), governor of Peru (1541–1544). Born in a small town (Izagre) near León, Spain, Vaca de Castro served as *oidor* (judge) of the Audiencia of Valladolid (1536). Recognizing his administrative abilities, Charles I appointed him (September 1540) for a three-year term to investigate Peru's chaotic political situation. Vaca de Castro reached Panama in January 1541, and because of difficult weather decided to travel overland rather than sail. From coastal Buenaventura in present-day Colombia, he proceeded to Cali, where he recuperated for three months from an illness. In Popayán he learned Francisco PIZARRO had been assassinated and Peru was under the control of Diego de ALMAGRO the Younger. Vaca de Castro then moved southward, collecting an army to oust Almagro.

Early in 1542 he left Quito, marched to Piura in northwest Peru, then to Trujillo, back into the highlands, then on to Huamanga. By then Vaca de Castro had the aid of Lima and letters of support from Gonzalo PIZARRO in the south. Almagro had been staying in Cuzco and had been negotiating with royalists. The administration of Peru was settled on 16 September 1542 at the battle of Chupas, one of the bloodiest battles of Peru's civil wars. Almagro fled, but was soon captured. He was executed in Cuzco and buried alongside his father.

A threat of a newly revived Inca state was lessened when the energetic and highly capable leader Manco Inca was assassinated by a group of Spaniards.

Vaca de Castro undertook to defuse Peru's turmoil by removing its cause—the large number of discontented soldiers. He supported three major expeditions: In 1543, Captain Juan de Porcel entered the Bracamoros in northwest Peru; Diego de Rojas began the exploration and settlement of the Tucumán region in present-day northwest Argentina; and Captain Juan Pérez de Vergara initiated the conquest of the Moyobamba and Rupa-Rupa in the upper jungle in 1544. A threat of a newly revived Inca state was lessened when the energetic and highly capable leader MANCO INCA was assassinated by a group of Spaniards the same year.

The arrival of Peru's first viceroy, Blasco NÚÑEZ VELA, brought the end of Vaca de Castro's tenure. The viceroy was welcomed into Lima (15 May 1544) but refused to take advice from the ex-governor. Believing Vaca de Castro to be a member of a conspiracy against him, the new viceroy imprisoned the official and charged him with forcing Indians to work in the mines without salary, authorizing their employment as beasts of burden, and selling *encomiendas*. Before hearings got under way, the viceroy himself was jailed by adherents of Gonzalo Pizarro. Vaca de Castro escaped to Spain, only to face charges there. Caught between the Pizarrist and Almagrist factions at court, he found himself in jail again, in Valladolid, Arévalo, and later Simancas. It was not until 1555 that the court freed and rehabilitated him.

In 1556 he returned to the Council of Castile and in 1559 received back salary. He served on the council until his retirement in 1566. Thereafter, he lived in the convent of San Agustín in Valladolid. After his death, his remains were transferred by order of his second son, Pedro de Castro, Archbishop of Granada, to the Colegiata del Sacro-Monte of Granada.

— NOBLE DAVID COOK

VACCARO BROTHERS

Vaccaro Brothers (Joseph, Luca, and Felix), three Sicilian Americans who, with a son-in-law, Salvador D'Antoni, engaged in the produce business in New Orleans at the close of the nineteenth century. In 1899 a severe freeze destroyed their orange groves, and of necessity they began the importation of bananas from Honduras. Building railroads, wharves, and Honduras's first bank and hospital, Vaccaro Brothers and Company modernized the banana trade and became Honduras's largest investor and exporter before World War I, and second only to the older United Fruit Company in the international banana trade. The need for capital for research, and expansion to other nations, caused this family company to go public in 1925.

— THOMAS L. KARNES

VALCÁRCEL ARCE, EDGAR

Edgar Valcárcel Arce (*b.* 4 Dec. 1932), Peruvian composer. He was born in Puno and studied in Lima at the

National Conservatory with Andrés SAS and at Hunter College in New York City with Donald Lybbert. With a fellowship from the Torcuato Di Tella Institute, Valcárcel studied in Buenos Aires at the Centro Latinoamericano de Altos Estudios Musicales (1963–1964). He studied there with Alberto GINASTERA, director of the center, and Olivier Messiaen, Luigi Dallapiccola, Gerardo GANDINI, Riccardo Malipiero, and Bruno Maderna. He was in New York City in 1966 with a Guggenheim Foundation fellowship to do graduate work on electronic music under the guidance of Vladimir Ussachevsky and Alcides LANZA. In 1986 he became a professor at the National School of Music in Lima and in 1989 the director of that institution. In 1976 he was a visiting professor of composition at the Faculty of Music, McGill University, Montreal. Valcárcel has received the National Music Prize in 1956 and 1965, the State Choir Prize in 1965, the Composition Prize of the Grand Masonic Lodge in 1971, and the Inocente Carreño Prize, Caracas, in 1981.

His principal works include *Variaciones* for piano (1963); *Espectros* no. 1 for flute, viola, and piano (1964); *Cantata para la noche inmensa* for men's choir and orchestra (1964); *Canto coral a Tupac Amaru* no. 1 for soprano, baritone, chorus, and orchestra (1968); Sonata no. 1 for piano (1965); *Dicotomías* nos. 1 and 2 for piano (1966) and no. 3 for chamber ensemble (1966); *Invención* (1966), electronic sounds; *Fisiones* for chamber ensemble (1967); *Hiwaña uru* for winds, strings, and piano (1967), in memory of Andrés Sas; Piano Concerto (1968); *Canto Coral a Tupac Amaru* no. 2 for chorus and electronic sounds on tape (1968); *Antaras* for flute and electronic sounds (1968); *Checán* no. 1 for flute, oboe, clarinet, bassoon, horn, and piano (1969), no. 2 for orchestra (1970), and no. 3 for nineteen instruments (1971); Sonata no. 2 for piano (1971); *Karabotasat Cutintapata* for orchestra (1977); *Zampoña sónica* for flute and tape (1976); *Retablo* no. 2 (*Flor de Sancayo*) for piano and electronic sounds (1975); *Antimemorias* no. 2 for orchestra (1980); *Checán* no. 4 for choir (1981); *Homenaje a Stravinsky* for two pianos, flute, French horn and percussion (1982); *Andahuaylillas* for organ (1983); *Concierto para guitarra y orquesta* (1984); and *A Theodoro* for soprano and three French horns (1986).

— ALCIDES LANZA

VALDÉS, GABRIEL DE LA CONCEPCIÓN

Gabriel de la Concepción Valdés (pseud. Plácido; *b.* 18 March 1809; *d.* 26 June 1844), Cuban poet. Plácido, the pseudonym he adopted and through which he became known, was born in Havana, the illegitimate son of a mulatto hairdresser and a Spanish dancer. Shortly after birth he was left at a home for illegitimate childen, but when he was a few months old, he was retrieved by his father's family, who raised him. He received no schooling until the age of ten, and then his education was haphazard, as was his lifelong economic situation (he was occasionally jailed for indebtedness).

Plácido's poetic talent did not earn him money—he worked as a silversmith and a maker of tortoiseshell combs—but it earned him the admiration of the established poets of the day, including José María HEREDIA. His ability to improvise verse on the spot for various occasions spread his fame and created a great demand for his attendance at all manner of social activities. Eventually his popularity came to be his undoing, however, as the Spanish authorities became suspicious of his active social life and arrested him for conspiracy. Although there was then as later no evidence of his participation in any conspiracy, he was shot by a firing squad in Matanzas. Thus martyred, he became a symbol of the cause of independence.

Plácido's poetry incorporates into traditional Spanish lyrical forms tropical imagery and the romantic themes of intense pathos and the urge for freedom. Although Plácido is not considered a poet of the first rank, many of his poems are recited by heart by Cubans of all ages and have come to form part of popular folklore.

— ROBERTO VALERO

VALDÉZ, JUAN

Juan Valdéz, fictitious Colombian coffee grower, created in 1959 by the National Coffee Growers Federation of Colombia for its advertising campaigns in the United States. Valdéz and his donkey have proven remarkably durable in both print and electronic advertising; a stylized logo was introduced in 1981, and mere invocation of his name is considered sufficient in recent campaigns.

Valdéz does not figure in Colombian domestic advertising, but his name is familiar to Colombians, who consider him a caricature for foreign consumption.

Valdéz does not figure in Colombian domestic advertising (where individual brands, rather than the federation, are in control), but his name is familiar to Colombians, who consider him a caricature for foreign consumption, albeit a positive one. While the Valdéz image of a grower lovingly scrutinizing each coffee bean is, to put it mildly, idealized—the western Colombian coffee harvest is a fast-paced affair increasingly reliant upon tens of thousands of migrant wage-laborers—it does suggest the continuing predominance of independent small- and medium-sized producers in Colombia, as opposed to the larger agribusiness-style operations that characterize Brazil.

— RICHARD J. STOLLER

VALDIVIA, LUIS DE

Luis de Valdivia (*b.* 1561; *d.* 5 November 1642), Spanish JESUIT who spent much of his life in Chile defending and protecting the rights of Indians. In 1589, shortly after entering the Society of Jesus, Valdivia was assigned to the province of Peru, where he remained until 1593, when he was assigned to Chile. There he dedicated himself to Christianizing and protecting the Indians against the Spaniards, for which he gained many enemies.

Valdivia believed that waging war on the Indians to subjugate and Christianize them was not morally right. The Indians were free beings and had control over their lives; therefore, they should become Christians or crown subjects of their own free will. At the insistence of the viceroy of Peru, the count of Montesclaros, Valdivia went to Spain in 1609 to inform the crown about the conditions in the region and the efforts to pacify it. He was heard by the Council of the Indies, and after about a year and a half, on 8 December 1610, a royal *cédula* (decree) ordered a change from offensive to defensive methods in the war against the Indians of Chile. In 1611 he went back to Chile, where he gained many more enemies as a result of the new policy. His enemies tried to thwart his efforts by complaining to royal officials and even to the crown. But a *cédula* of 21 November 1615 reiterated the policy. In 1620 Valdivia returned to Spain permanently.

— JUAN MANUEL PÉREZ

VALDIVIA, PEDRO DE

Pedro de Valdivia (*b.* ca. 1500; *d.* 1553), Spanish conquistador and founder of Chile. Before undertaking the expedition to Chile, Valdivia had already acquired extensive military experience. He entered the army in 1521, participated in the Spanish campaigns in Flanders and Italy, and fought in the battle of Pavia (24 February 1525). He returned to Spain and married Marina Ortíz de Gaete, a native of Salamanca. The sources available contain conflicting information about this union. Some sources say that he was married before the

Italian campaigns, while others say he married after. From 1525, when he was in Milan, to 1535, when he embarked on his voyage to the New World, not much is known about his life.

Valdivia probably sailed for Venezuela in an expedition led by Jerónimo de Alderete. He remained in Venezuela for a year or a year and a half, another period in his life for which there is not too much information. He then went to Peru as a member of an expedition to help Francisco PIZARRO suppress an Indian rebellion led by MANCO CAPAC. His experience in the military served him well, and in 1537, Pizarro named him his aide-de-camp. Valdivia gained a reputation as a brave soldier in the war between Pizarro and Diego de ALMAGRO. He and Gonzalo Pizarro led the infantry against the forces of Almagro in the decisive battle of Salinas on 6 April 1538. As a reward for his services, Francisco Pizarro granted Valdivia an *encomienda* in the valley of La Canela.

Valdivia, however, was a man of adventure, and he asked permission from Pizarro to go to Chile, despite the fact that Almagro had gone before and had come back disappointed because he had not found gold. To finance his expedition, Valdivia sold his lands. In the middle of January 1540, he left for Chile from Cuzco accompanied by twelve Spaniards; one woman, Inés de Suárez (who later became the second of four significant women in Valdivia's life); about one thousand Indians; and a few black slaves. Others joined him as he moved on to Chile. Late in 1540, Valdivia reached the Copiapó Valley and called the new land Nueva Extremadura. He moved farther south to Coquimbo and then to the Mapocho Valley, and on 24 February 1541, near the Mapocho River, Valdivia founded Santiago del Nuevo Extremo, present-day Santiago.

The city endured an Indian siege while Valdivia was absent, and the Spaniards suffered many hardships because reinforcements and supplies did not arrive until two years later, in 1543. With more men and supplies, Valdivia continued exploring and in 1544 founded LA SERENA, halfway between the Copiapó Valley and Santiago. In 1545, he went further south to Quilacura, and at the same time, his lieutenants were exploring other areas.

In 1547, Valdivia left for Peru with the intention of getting more supplies and found himself in the middle of a rebellion led by Gonzalo PIZARRO. He sided with the crown's *visitador,* Pedro de Lagasca, and became an important factor in Pizarro's defeat. He returned to Chile on 21 January 1549, after being cleared by Lagasca of accusations leveled against him by his enemies. Once in Chile, Valdivia continued his explorations and founded more cities: Concepción (1550), VALDIVIA

(1552), and Villarica (1552). He died in 1553 in a battle against the Araucanians led by LAUTARO.

Valdivia symbolizes the spirit of the CONQUISTADORES in his desire for adventure and his drive to explore new lands. He resembles, for example, Alvar Núñez CABEZA DE VACA, Vasco Núñez de BALBOA, and Hernando de SOTO: men who were driven more by the spirit of adventure than by the hope of finding gold.

— JUAN MANUEL PÉREZ

VALENCIA, ANTONIO MARÍA

Antonio María Valencia (*b.* 10 November 1902; *d.* 22 July 1952), Colombian composer, pianist, and teacher. Born in Cali, Valencia began his musical studies with his father, cellist and teacher Julio Valencia Belmonte. Later he entered the Bogotá Conservatory (1917–1919) to study piano with Honorio Alarcón. After concert tours in the southern United States, Valencia moved to Paris and enrolled at the Schola Cantorum (1923–1929), where he studied under Vincent d'Indy (composition), Paul Braud (piano), Paul le Flem (counterpoint and fugue), Louis Saint-Requier (harmony and conducting of vocal and instrumental groups), Gabriel Pierné (chamber music) and Manuel de Falla (orchestration). He was offered a professorship, but at the end of his studies he returned to Colombia, where he gave concerts and pursued a career in composition. His early works show an affinity for national music, though his Paris training later led to a concentration on European forms. In his last years, Valencia returned to the melodies and rhythms of his homeland.

Valencia wrote a considerable number of choral religious works demonstrating a solid technique and exceptional use of counterpoint, as, for example, in his Requiem Mass (1943). Among his chamber music works are *Duo en forma de sonata* (1926), for piano and violin; *Emociones caucanas* (1938), for violin, piano, and cello; songs on French texts; and many piano pieces. He composed *Chirimía y bambuco sotareño* (1942) for orchestra and wrote orchestrations and arrangements of French music. Valencia founded the Conservatory and School of Fine Arts of Cali (1933), remaining as its director until his death. He was also director of the Bogotá Conservatory (1937–1938). He died in Cali.

— SUSANA SALGADO

VALENCIA, GUILLERMO LEÓN

Guillermo León Valencia (*b.* 27 April 1909; *d.* 4 November 1971), president of Colombia (1962–1966). The son of Guillermo Valencia, a celebrated poet and Conservative political leader, Valencia was born in PO-

PAYÁN and studied law at the University of Cauca. Serving in the senate and in the Conservative Party leadership, he became known as a flamboyant orator and impassioned follower of Conservative chieftain Laureano GÓMEZ (president, 1950–1953), who appointed him ambassador to Spain in 1950. Later he moderated his partisanship and distanced himself from Gómez. He was an outspoken critic of President Gustavo ROJAS PINILLA (1953–1957). An order (1 May 1957) that Valencia be placed under house arrest sparked a wave of civic unrest that ended the Rojas regime nine days later. Valencia was slated to be the first presidential candidate of the Frente Nacional (National Front), but he was blackballed by Gómez. Instead, he became the National Front nominee in 1962, winning 62.1 percent of the vote.

As president, Valencia continued many of the policies of his predecessor, Alberto LLERAS CAMARGO (1958–1962), though he is usually considered a less competent chief executive. During his administration the armed forces smashed communist-influenced "republics" in central and southern Colombia. In 1964, however, surviving militants founded a southern guerrilla bloc that became the forerunner of the Fuerzas Armadas Revolucionarias Colombianas (Colombian Revolutionary Armed Force—FARC). Valencia also confronted economic difficulties, notably a fall in coffee prices, balance of payments problems, depreciation of the *peso,* and inflation. Opposition to a new sales tax led to a threatened general strike in January 1965, which was averted partly because of government concessions. Criticism of the government by Minister of War General Alberto Ruiz Novoa, who harbored political ambitions, heightened tensions until he was removed in January 1965. After retiring from the presidency in 1966, Valencia again served as ambassador to Spain.

— HELEN DELPAR

VALENZUELA, LUISA

Luisa Valenzuela (*b.* 26 November 1938), Argentine writer. The daughter of Argentine writer Luisa Mercedes Levinson, Valenzuela was born in Buenos Aires and grew up in Corrientes and Buenos Aires, which provided settings for her later fiction. She began her writing career as a journalist for the newspaper *La Nación* and published her first short story at age seventeen. Between 1956 and 1961 she lived in France, where she wrote her first novel, which was published in 1966. But it was with the publication of *Hay que sonreír* (One Has to Smile, 1966) and a collection of short stories, *Los heréticos* (1967), that she was recognized as a promising young writer. In 1969 she won a Fulbright scholarship to participate in the International Writers Workshop at the University of Iowa, where she wrote *El gato eficaz* (1972), a novel in which language rather than characters is the central concern. Later, she traveled throughout Mexico and became interested in Mexican indigenous cultures. She used some of these experiences in writing the stories in *Donde viven las águilas* (Where Eagles Live, 1983). During 1972 Valenzuela lived in Barcelona, where she wrote *Como en la guerra* (1977). This novel also centers on language and surrealistic experiences.

Returning to Argentina, Valenzuela wrote *Aquí pasan cosas raras* (Strange Things Happen Here, 1975). When she felt that the military government threatened her well-being, she moved to New York City. During her sojourn in the United States, some of her works were translated into English. She was featured in popular magazines like *Time* side-by-side with other well-known Latin American writers, and in 1986 the *Review of Contemporary Fiction,* a scholarly journal published in the United States, dedicated an issue to Valenzuela's fiction. *El libro que no muerde* (1980) and *Cambio de armas* (Other Weapons, 1982) were written during this time. The latter is a collection of five lengthy short stories in which Valenzuela's fiction reaches depth and maturity, where female and male sexuality represents the warped and misunderstood relationship between men and women, who are witness to the disintegration of a reality in which they are victims and victimizers.

In 1983 Valenzuela went back to Argentina, where she published a novel on the political manipulations and sorceries of José López Rega, a picturesque and macabre member of the cabinet of the last Peronist regime, entitled *Cola de lagartija.* Two subsequent novels also deal with Argentina's reality, *Novela negra con argentinos* (Gothic Novel with Argentines, 1990) and *Realidad nacional desde la cama* (National Reality from the Bed, 1990).

— MAGDALENA GARCÍA PINTO

VALERO, ROBERTO

Roberto Valero (*b.* 27 May 1955; *d.* 23 September 1994), Cuban writer. Born in the city of Matanzas, Cuba, Valero studied at the University of Havana (1975–1980). In 1980 he joined the approximately 10,800 Cubans who entered the Peruvian Embassy asking for political asylum, and left the island with the Mariel Boatlift. Valero received a Ph.D. in literature from Georgetown University in 1988 and taught both there and at the George Washington University. During his years in Washington he wrote acclaimed books of poetry, such as *Desde un oscuro ángulo* (From a Dark

Corner) in 1981 and *En fin, la noche* (At Last the Night) in 1984. At the time of his death, Valero had published extensively, had gained wide recognition for his poetry, and had been honored with several prestigious literary

---

Valero's highly lyrical work is marked by a search for the spiritual and a preoccupation with death and man's relationship to God.

---

awards. His highly lyrical work is marked by a search for the spiritual and a preoccupation with death and man's relationship to God. In addition to his poetic output, Valero also published a novel, *Este viento de cuaresma* (This Lenten Wind) a finalist for Spain's Nadal Prize in 1989, and a book of literary criticism, *The Forlorn Humor of Reinaldo Arenas* (1991) for which he received the Letras de Oro award in 1989. Valero's other poetic works include *Dharma* (1985), *Venías* (You Came) (1990), and *No estaré en tu camino* (I Will Not Be in Your Way), a finalist for the Adonais Prize in 1991. He was an editor of the art and literature journal *Mariel.* Valero died in Washington, D.C.

— MARÍA BADÍAS
GEORGETTE MAGASSY DORN

VALLADARES, ARMANDO

Armando Valladares (*b.* 30 May 1937), Cuban poet and prose writer. Valladares was born in Pinar del Río Province. In 1961, while employed by the revolutionary government on the staff of the Cuban postal service, he was arrested and accused of being a counterrevolutionary. After refusing to participate in the government's "rehabilitation" program, he was subjected to severe beatings, torture, forced labor, and twenty-two years of confinement. While in prison he began to write poetry, which he smuggled out of the country in many ingenious ways. His wife, Martha, fought relentlessly to bring international attention to his case, and when his poetry gained recognition outside of Cuba, he became a symbol of the struggle against human rights abuses in that country. When at last Valladares's case was taken up by Amnesty International, which once made him its prisoner of the year, it attracted worldwide attention, dealing a severe blow to the Cuban government's image abroad.

After his release in 1982, Valladares continued to decry the abuses he saw and suffered while in prison in Cuba, and in 1985 he published a memoir of the ordeal, *Contra toda esperanza* (*Against All Hope*), his best-known work, which became a best-seller. He served for a time as U.S. ambassador for human rights to the United Nations. Direct and unpretentious, his poetry is permeated by genuine anguish and the desire to end cruelty. Other works by Valladares include *El corazón en que vivo* (1980).

— ROBERTO VALERO

VALLADARES, TOMÁS

Tomás Valladares (*d.* after 1850), Nicaraguan politician. Active in the confusing era of the breakdown of the United Provinces of Central America, Valladares served as a senator and then president of the Chamber of Deputies in Nicaragua. He was interim chief of state from 1840 to 1841 and subsequently continued to participate in politics. As one of Nicaragua's leading liberals, Valladares served on a junta with Evaristo Rocha, Patricio Rivas, Hilario Ulloa, and Joaquín Caso in the 1840s and was a lieutenant in the wars against José Rafael CARRERA, which tore apart the isthmus at mid-century.

— KAREN RACINE

VALLBONA, RIMA DE

Rima de Vallbona (*b.* 15 March 1931), Costa Rican writer. A professor of Spanish at the University of St. Thomas in Houston, Texas, Vallbona obtained her Ph.D. in modern languages from Middlebury College. She also studied in France and Spain. She has received many Costa Rican and international awards for her fiction, which includes the novels *Noche en vela* (1968), *Las sombras que perseguimos* (1983), and *Mundo, demonio y mujer* (1991); and the collections of short stories *Polvo del camino* (1971), *La salamandra rosada* (1979), *Mujeres y agonías* (1982), *Baraja de soledades* (1983) and *Cosecha de pecadores* (1988). Vallbona has written two scholarly books on her compatriots: *Yolanda Oreamuno* (1972) and *La obra en prosa de Eunice Odio* (1980).

— SUSAN E. CLARK

VALLE, ARISTÓBULO DEL

Aristóbulo del Valle (*b.* 15 March 1845; *d.* 29 January 1896), Argentine politician, journalist, constitutional lawyer, and mentor to reform-minded youth in the 1880s and 1890s. Born in Dolores, Buenos Aires Province, in modest circumstances, he was an early example of the burgeoning Argentine middle class. A veteran of the War of the Triple Alliance, del Valle wrote for the newspapers *El Nacional* and *La Nación,* and served in

the Buenos Aires provincial legislature. Elected to the national Congress in 1872, he was a deputy (1872–1876) and later a senator (1877–1895). He distinguished himself as the Senate's most effective orator and defender of the middle class. He played a leading role in the revolutions of the early 1890s, but when they failed, he worked within the oligarchic government to stave off anarchy. He served for short periods as minister of war, navy, interior, and finance under President Luis SÁENZ PEÑA.

Del Valle is credited as one of the early founders, with Leandro ALEM, of the Unión Cívica Radical. He established the country's first reformist newspaper, *El Argentino,* and taught constitutional law at the University of Buenos Aires, steering a different course from his conservative predecessor José M. ESTRADA. Del Valle's major works include: *Nociones de derecho constitucional* (Aspects of Constitutional Law [1897]), *Cuestión de límites interprovinciales* (Interprovincial Boundary Question [1881]), and *La política económica argentina en la década del 80* (Political Economy of Argentina in the 80s [1955]). De Valle's most influential congressional speeches are gathered in *Discursos selectos* (1922) and *Discursos políticos* (1938). His death at the age of fifty deprived the country of one of its leading reformers and most effective public speakers.

— GEORGETTE MAGASSY DORN

VALLE, JOSÉ CECILIO DEL

José Cecilio del Valle (*b.* 22 November 1776; *d.* 2 March 1834), Honduran scholar and statesman. Born in Choluteca, Honduras, Valle moved with his family to newly established Guatemala City in 1789 and matriculated the next year at the University of San Carlos. With the assistance of his teacher, Fray Antonio de LIENDO Y GOICOECHEA (1735–1814), and Pedro Juan de Lara, he received a degree in philosophy in 1794 and continued to study civil and canon law until he was admitted to the bar in 1803. Enthused by the Enlightenment philosophies of his teachers, he began a pursuit of knowledge that eventually gained him acknowledgment as an authority in economics and as the most prominent scholar of Central America.

Valle's talents and diligence led him to a life of politics at an early age. For almost twenty years, he faithfully served the captaincy general of Guatemala in hopes of obtaining a high official post in Spain. During the turbulent era prior to independence, Valle advanced rapidly in local politics and became the leader of the moderate conservatives. He served as the mayor of Guatemala City in 1820. Reluctant to support independence from Spain, he nonetheless assumed leadership of the apparently inevitable movement in the fear that social revolution, rather than political freedom, would become the focus of the turmoil. Indeed, he was largely responsible for the writing of the declaration of independence. He was a member of the provisional junta that took control of the government of Central America on 15 September 1821 and annexed the region to Mexico under Agustín de ITURBIDE, who later became (1822) Emperor Agustín I.

Valle assumed leadership of the independence movement in the fear that social revolution, rather than political freedom, would become the focus of the turmoil.

Under the empire, he held several official posts. As the representative from the province of Tegucigalpa (Honduras) to the Constituent Congress of Mexico, he served with distinction and rose to become the vice president of the congress. Although Iturbide imprisoned him on false charges of conspiracy, he was exonerated six months later and made secretary of foreign and domestic affairs. After the fall of Iturbide, Valle was appointed secretary of the department of justice and ecclesiastical affairs by the newly formed Mexican Republic.

When Central America decided to seek its own political destiny, Valle returned to Guatemala in January 1824 and was chosen, along with José Manuel de la Cerda and Tomás O'Horan, to be a member of the provisional junta that governed the isthmus until elections for the United Provinces of Central America were held in 1825. In the presidential elections, Valle won a plurality of the electoral votes, but a technicality prevented him from taking office. The federal congress elected instead Manuel José ARCE (1786–1846). Valle responded to the injustice by publishing the *Manifiesto de José del Valle a la nación guatemalteca* (1825), in which he gave an account of the services he had rendered his country and demonstrated the invalidity of Arce's election. During the Arce administration, he represented the department of Guatemala as a deputy to the congress. He ran for the presidency again in 1830 and lost to Francisco MORAZÁN. Finally, Valle was elected president of Central America in 1834, but he became seriously ill on his estate, La Concepción, some

60 miles from Guatemala City, and died en route to his inauguration.

— MICHAEL F. FRY

VALLEJO, CÉSAR

César Vallejo (*b.* 16 March 1892; *d.* 15 April 1938), Peruvian poet. Vallejo is Peru's most renowned poet, and his works are remarkable for their striking originality, lexical complexity, and compressed power. They reveal a profound concern for the suffering of others and nostalgia for his Andean childhood. His journalism, dramas, novels, and short stories gloss the major social, political, and cultural movements of the first third of the century and assert the legitimate, if neglected, place of Latin America in contemporary culture and history.

The youngest of eleven children in a middle-class mestizo family, Vallejo entered the University of Trujillo in 1910 to pursue literary studies, but dropped out. He returned in 1913 and received his B.A. in Spanish literature in 1915, at the same time that he began his study of law. He pursued his legal studies until returning to Lima in 1917 as a schoolteacher. After his return, he experienced two ill-fated love affairs, the second one ending shortly before the death of his lover. In 1918 he suffered the loss of his mother, whose memory remained a recurrent theme in his poetry. Falsely accused of participating in political violence in his Andean hometown of Santiago de Chuco in 1920, he was imprisoned for 112 days (6 November 1920–26 February 1921), to which he alluded in his mature poetry as the "gravest moment" of his life.

Seeking wider cultural and intellectual opportunities, Vallejo left Peru for Europe in 1923, spending most of his final fifteen years of life in self-imposed, impoverished exile in France, with periods in Spain and two influential trips to Russia. Expelled from France for leftist political activities in 1931, he joined the Spanish Communist Party in Madrid. He returned to France in 1932. He died in Paris from an unidentified illness.

Vallejo published two books of poetry before leaving Peru: *Los heraldos negros* (1918) and *Trilce* (1922). The first showed signs of an original poetic voice that emerged powerfully in the irrational and hermetic expression of the second work, which shattered all traditions of poetry written in Spanish. *Poemas humanos* (1939) represented the poet at the height of his power to express the plight of the human animal abandoned in an irrational, absurd world where salvation can come only through fraternal self-sacrifice.

Vallejo worked with other writers and intellectuals to further the Republican cause during the Spanish Civil

War and visited the war front twice. *España, aparta de mí este cáliz* (1938) was first published by Republican soldiers on the front lines. Although in his last years Vallejo sought to inform Europeans about Peruvian culture, he never returned to Peru.

— KEITH MCDUFFIE

VALLEJO, MARIANO GUADALUPE

Mariano Guadalupe Vallejo (*b.* 4 July 1807?; *d.* 18 January 1890), military commander in California. Mariano Vallejo was born in Monterey, son of Ignacio Vallejo, an early settler from Jalisco, and María Antonia Lugo. After joining the Monterey military company at age fifteen, he rose to commandant of the San Francisco presidio by age twenty-four. As military commander and director of colonization of the northern frontier during the 1830s, Vallejo evaluated Russian intentions in California, established the Sonoma colony and organized the civilian government of San Francisco, and pacified Indian tribes. Vallejo was appointed *jefe militar* (military chief) of the revolutionary government of 1836, but soon disengaged himself from the rebel group. After central Mexican authority was reestablished, he was appointed military commander of California, whose prime concern was encroaching foreign influence.

Considered a friend of Americans, Vallejo was a force for moderation among leading Mexican citizens of California during the period leading up to the U.S. conquest. Vallejo's personal collection of eleven thousand documents of early California, a major source for Hubert Bancroft's *History of California* (1884–1890), now resides in the Bancroft Library of the University of California.

— E. JEFFREY STANN

VALLENILLA LANZ, LAUREANO

Laureano Vallenilla Lanz (*b.* 11 October 1870; *d.* 16 November 1936), Venezuelan politician and intellectual. Vallenilla Lanz traveled to Caracas at a very young age to take up engineering, but he did not finish his studies. After a brief stay in Barcelona, Venezuela, he returned to Caracas and mixed with the intellectual circles in the capital. He was a contributor to *El Cojo Ilustrado,* publishing essays on historical themes, which earned him a reputation, to a degree, as an intellectual. Vallenilla Lanz was named Venezuelan consul in Amsterdam in 1904 and remained in Europe for six years. In Paris he attended the Sorbonne and the College de

France, which distinctly influenced his orientation toward the positivist trends of the era.

After his return to Venezuela in 1910, Vallenilla Lanz contributed to important periodicals, met President Juan Vicente GÓMEZ, and became active in politics as a member of the intellectual circle close to the president. He performed important public duties and in 1915 became director of *El Nuevo Diario,* the official government mouthpiece. He conducted an important campaign in defense of the regime and in 1919 published *Cesarismo democrático.* In this work, one of his most important, he used positivist theoretical suppositions as a basis for analyzing the Venezuelan past and concluded by justifying the autocrat as a "Gendarme Necesario," or a natural outgrowth of the collective evolution of Venezuelan society. The work generated contrary opinions. It was translated into several languages and became one of the key works of positivist thought in all of Latin America. Vallenilla Lanz was a member of the Academy of History (1918). In 1931 he was appointed minister of Venezuela in Paris.

— INÉS QUINTERO

VANDOR, AUGUSTO

Augusto Vandor (*b.* 1920; *d.* 30 June 1969), Argentine labor leader. During the early 1960s, exiled past-president Juan D. PERÓN charged the head of the Metal Workers' Union, Augusto Vandor, with promoting the conservative tendency of an increasingly fractious Peronist movement. Vandor's control extended beyond his powerful union. From 1962 until his assassination by the Montoneros in 1969, he controlled what was known as the 62 Organizations (or "62"), the dominant wing of the Peronist General Labor Confederation (CGT).

Vandor and Vandorismo came to define four important developments in Argentine labor. First, Vandor's methods of personalist political control were emulated by subsequent labor bosses, including Lorenzo Miguel (Metal Workers) and Jorge Triaca (Plastics Workers). Second, Vandor's leadership of the 62 marked a transformation in the relationship between the Peronist labor movement and the government from intransigent opposition during the 1950s to a more pragmatic blend of negotiation and conflict in the 1960s. Third, Vandorismo characterized the emergence of an authoritarian and sometimes violent tendency in the labor movement as Vandor set about defeating political opponents within the CGT and in the Peronist movement. Fourth, under Vandor the 62 rose to lead the Peronist movement as the only significant legal component of Peronism. The 62 continued to comprise almost all significant trade unions within the labor movement until the takeover of the CGT by the government after the 1976 coup d'état.

— DAVID M. K. SHEININ

VARAS DE LA BARRA, ANTONIO

Antonio Varas de la Barra (*b.* 13 June 1817; *d.* 3 June 1886), Chilean politician. An outstanding figure of his period, Varas was the closest political associate of the Conservative president Manuel MONTT. Eight times a deputy and twice a senator, he served as minister of the interior from 1850 to 1856, in 1860–1861, and again briefly in 1879. Although he fully supported the authoritarian stance of his intimate friend Montt, Varas was an altogether more attractive character. (In his old age he became quite liberal.) Montt wanted Varas to be his presidential successor in 1861, a prospect that deeply angered the opposition. By accepting the interior ministry again in April 1860, Varas implicitly abandoned all claim to presidential succession. His unselfishness, which won widespread praise, paved the way for the election of the less controversial José Joaquín PÉREZ MOZCAYANO. After 1861, Varas headed the National (or, as it was revealingly nicknamed, Montt-Varista) Party in Congress.

— SIMON COLLIER

VARELA, FELIPE

Felipe Varela (*b.* 1821; *d.* 4 June 1870), Argentine caudillo. Varela was one of the last great regional chieftains of the Argentine interior provinces during the long process of state formation. Born in Huayacama, Catamarca, he moved to La Rioja, where he participated in the civil wars against Buenos Aires. In due course, he

---

Varela was one of the last great regional chieftains

of the Argentine interior provinces during the

long process of state formation.

---

became a close ally of Angel Vicente PEÑALOZA. In 1848 Varela was driven from Argentina to Chile, where he displayed some acumen for business. He became associated with Colonel Tristán Dávila, a local mining magnate, and rose through the ranks of the Chilean military based in Atacama. Ironically, he was promoted to captain in Chile's army for his service in defense of the central government. Varela returned to Argentina

in 1855 and became the President Justo URQUIZA's loyal follower. He participated in the prolonged federalist resistance of the provinces against Buenos Aires, aligning with Governor Juan Sáa of San Luís in the bloody civil war against Buenos Aires-backed forces. Still a loyal Urquizista, Varela joined the last-ditch alliance against Buenos Aires that led to the 1862 mass insurrection in La Rioja. Varela displayed his military prowess, trouncing Buenos Aires forces repeatedly, but the federalists could not overcome the odds. Following the defeat and execution of Peñaloza (1863), Varela fled again to Chile in 1865. He returned to Argentina in 1866, but his distaste for Buenos Aires's plans for the country led him to revolt for the last time in 1867. He could not, however, defeat the combined forces of Buenos Aires and its allies, led by the Taboadas of Tucumán. After a series of bloody encounters, he fled to Bolivia and then to Chile, where he died at Náutico, sick and impoverished.

— JEREMY ADELMAN

VARELA, FLORENCIO

Florencio Varela (*b.* 23 February 1807; *d.* 20 March 1848), Argentine poet and patriot. Brother of the famous neoclassical, civic poet, Juan Cruz Varela, Florencio wrote his first verses at the age of fifteen in celebration of the decisive battle of Ayacucho during the Wars of Independence. Varela studied law at the University of Buenos Aires, graduating in 1827. Following the Argentine revolution of 1828, he fled to Montevideo. In 1830, he published *El día de Mayo* (May Day), a volume containing five poems dedicated to the Uruguayan people. In exile, Varela became a leader of the Unitarian cause against the dictator Juan Manuel de ROSAS. Newspapers supporting Rosas recognized the ardor of Varela's attack, calling him a "savage Unitarian, traitor, and vile slanderer."

In 1841–1842, Varela lived in Río de Janeiro, where he wrote several articles for the *Jornal do Comercio* defending Uruguay against accusations that it had usurped territory from Brazil. While in Río, Varela became friends with Bernardino RIVADAVIA, who furnished Varela with documentary material for a book he was preparing on Argentine history. In 1843, the Uruguayan government sent Varela on an official mission to France and England.

Tireless in his efforts to overthrow Rosas and use the press as a vehicle for shaping public opinion, Varela founded in October 1845 the *Comercio del Plata,* in whose columns he undermined the political and military structure keeping Rosas in power. Varela was also cofounder of a publishing house that brought out works in Spanish translation as well as books by Hispanic-American writers.

— MYRON I. LICHTBLAU

VARELA, JOSÉ PEDRO

José Pedro Varela (*b.* 1845, *d.* 1879), Uruguayan educator. Varela's leadership proved essential in the country's development of free, universal, and secular education. His early contact with educational theory came from his father, who, in 1846, translated from the French the first book on pedagogy to be published in the Plata region. During a trip to the United States in 1867 Varela met Argentine educator and future president Domingo SARMIENTO, whose writings on public education he admired. Under the influence of Sarmiento and the Bostonian educator Horace Mann, Varela decided to dedicate his life to Uruguayan educational reform.

In 1868 Varela published the first of many articles in the Montevidean press promoting free and universal elementary schooling. He became a lecturer on educational reform at the National University that same year. In 1869 he founded Amigos de la Educación Popular, which played a central role in the dissemination of his ideas. Through his newspaper, *La Paz,* he promoted progressive educational ideas and criticized the government of General Lorenzo BATLLE. His most influential writings include *La educación del pueblo* (1874) and *La legislación escolar* (1877). In 1865 the first school with a curriculum designed in accordance with Varela's ideas was founded.

Varela's thinking on education centered on his humanistic beliefs: free and obligatory instruction for all citizens, regardless of sex, race, or social class; the development of a rational and scientific curriculum, as opposed to the traditional, scholastic orientation of the Spanish colony; the central role of the state in training teachers and providing for schools; and the intimate link between educating the populace and the emergence of Uruguay as an independent and prosperous country. The idealistic thrust of his ideas, like those of Sarmiento, was premised on the belief that the individual, empowered through education, would become an agent in the modernization of the region's social and political institutions.

In 1876 Varela was named president of the Comisión de Instrucción Pública, which drafted the important *Ley de educación común* (1877). His death at the age of forty-four did not impede the development of one of the most ambitious and successful systems of public education on the continent, which was based on his ideas.

In addition to his books on education, Varela wrote a volume of lyrical poems, *Ecos perdidos* (1985), which rates among the finest Uruguayan lyrical expressions of the period.

— WILLIAM H. KATRA

VARELA, JUAN CRUZ

Juan Cruz Varela (*b.* 23 November 1794; *d.* 23 January 1839), Argentine journalist, politician, poet. In 1810 Varela, a native of Buenos Aires, entered the Montserrat seminary in Córdoba to study for the priesthood; he graduated in 1816 but did not take holy orders. Varela instead turned to love poetry, writing "La Elvira" (1817), "Mi pasión" (1817), and "El enojo" (1819) among others. In 1818 he returned to Buenos Aires, where he staunchly supported liberal politics. He was a friend of Bernardino RIVADAVIA, becoming his press spokesman and the secretary of the General Congress of 1826. Varela wrote for *El Centinela* and *El Mensajero Argentino* and supported Rivadavia's reforms. He supported the upstart General Juan Gallo Lavalle against the legitimate governor of Buenos Aires, Manuel Dorrego, who was executed in 1828 with the encouragement of Varela among others. This act only served to fortify the very forces Lavalle sought to defeat, and by 1829 Varela had to abandon Buenos Aires for exile in Montevideo. In Uruguay he continued to write articles and poetry opposing Juan Manuel de ROSAS. Varela lived a spartan life in Montevideo and tried unsuccessfully to return to Buenos Aires. He died in Montevideo.

— NICHOLAS P. CUSHNER

VARELA Y MORALES, FÉLIX

Félix Varela y Morales (*b.* 20 November 1788; *d.* 25 February 1853), Cuban priest, thinker, and patriot. Orphaned at an early age, Varela was still a child when he moved to Saint Augustine, Florida. (The area had been returned to Spain by Britain in 1783 under the Treaty of Paris.) There he was consigned to the care of his maternal grandfather, the commander of the city's Spanish garrison. He became the pupil of Fr. Michael O'Reilly, then the vicar of East Florida, who eventually became his role model. It was Fr. O'Reilly who influenced his decision to enter the priesthood rather than become a soldier, as his family traditions called for. "I wish to be a soldier of Jesus Christ," Varela said at the time. "I do not wish to kill men, but to save their souls."

Varela began attending the San Carlos Seminary in Havana in 1803 and was ordained in 1811. By that time he had already started to teach philosophy at the seminary, which in those days was also open to lay students. He thus became the mentor of many of the most distinguished Cuban intellectuals of the period; later they recognized their debt to him, stating that "he was who first taught us to think."

As an opponent of decadent scholasticism and one of the first who wrote philosophical textbooks in Spanish rather than Latin, Varela enjoyed the support of the bishop of Havana, José Díaz de Espada y Landa. The bishop asked him to teach a new course at the seminary on the constitution framed by the Spanish Cortes in 1812. Such was the reputation of his lectures that he was elected to represent Cuba in the Cortes in 1821. While serving, Varela made several significant contributions, advocating a more benign rule over the colonies and submitting a proposal for the abolition of slavery within fifteen years. Unfortunately, the restoration of Spanish absolutism in 1823 made it impossible for the Cortes to discuss these proposals. Forced into exile by this turn of events, he shortly arrived in the United States.

Varela settled in New York, where he soon stood out as a man of irreproachable life, a learned and devoted parish priest, an able administrator, and a wise educator and director of souls. Above all, he was known for his work with the sick and the poor especially during the great cholera epidemic of 1832, when his charity sometimes reached heroic dimensions. As one contemporary put it, his name was "one of benediction in the city of New York." For this reason Varela was admired and respected by everyone. First in 1829, on a temporary basis, and then without interruption from 1837 onward, he held the office of vicar general for New York, a post second in importance only to that of bishop. He attended several of the Baltimore Councils as an advisor to American bishops. Varela also played a leading role as a public defender of the Catholic faith in the violent Catholic–Protestant clashes of the period.

When Varela went to Spain as a member of the

Cortes, he described himself as

"a son of liberty, an American soul."

Varela's achievements as a priest are as much a part of U.S. ecclesiastical history as they are part of Cuba's history. But although he never made any effort to return to his native land, he always regarded it as his country. Cubans, for their part, rightly regard him as the ideological father of their nationality. When Varela went to Spain as a member of the Cortes, he described himself

as "a son of liberty, an American soul." At the time, however, he would have been satisfied with some form of colonial self-government for Cuba. But he soon discovered that most Spanish deputies, including many who enjoyed the reputation of being very liberal, distrusted Spanish Americans and had no faith in their ability to govern themselves. It was then, and most especially after King Ferdinand VII dissolved the Cortes, that he gave up the hope of achieving autonomy for Cuba within the framework of the Spanish monarchy and became the great prophet of Cuban independence.

Varela published his pro-independence articles in the newspaper *El Habanero,* which he founded in the United States. At the time, there were many Cubans who were in favor of Spanish rule, and some of them advocated the annexation of the island to Colombia or Mexico, just as others would support annexation to the United States a few years later. Varela argued against all of these paths. He morally justified rebellion against the oppressive colonial government, saying that it was "inspired by nature and upheld by the sacred laws of self-preservation." As for the idea of Cuba becoming the province of a neighboring state, he wrote: "I am the first to oppose the union of the island to any government. I should wish to see her as much of a political island as she is such in geographical terms."

Ill health eventually led Varela to retire to Saint Augustine, where he died. As a priest, Varela was well ahead of his time; his liberal norms and principles were more in consonance with the orientation of the Second Vatican Council (1962–1965) than with some nineteenth-century Catholic doctrines. As a thinker, he infused new life into philosophical studies in Cuba. As a patriot, he can be justly regarded as the founding father of Cuban nationalism.

– JOSÉ M. HERNÁNDEZ

VARGAS, DIEGO DE

Diego de Vargas (*b.* 1643; *d.* 8 April 1704), Spanish governor and recolonizer of New Mexico (1691–1697; 1703–1704). Heir of a proud but indebted noble house in Madrid, Vargas sailed for New Spain in 1673. Appointed by the viceroy, he was commended for his service as Alcalde Mayor of Teutila (Oaxaca) (1673–1679) and Tlalpujahua (Michoacán) (1679–1687). In 1688 he was appointed governor of New Mexico, a colony in exile since the Pueblo Rebellion of 1680, when the Spaniards fled into the El Paso area. Acceding to office in El Paso in 1691, Vargas led a determined, two-stage reconquest. With the aid of Pueblo Indian auxiliaries, he reoccupied the capital at Santa Fe, reimposing Spanish rule and putting down a second revolt in 1696.

Confined by his successor in 1697 on charges of misgovernment, Vargas returned to Mexico City, stood trial, and was acquitted. The crown, meanwhile, rewarded him with a noble title of Castile—Marqués de la Nava de Barcinas. Reinstated as governor in 1703, he died the following year at Bernalillo while on a campaign against Apaches.

Although Vargas's final resting place is unknown, a shopping mall, bank, and university dormitory bear his name, and he is the central figure in Santa Fe's annual fiestas.

– JOHN L. KESSELL

VARGAS, GETÚLIO DORNELLES

Getúlio Dornelles Vargas (*b*. 19 April 1883; *d*. 24 August 1954), president of Brazil (1930–1945 and 1951–1954). Vargas was the dominant political personality of Brazil for nearly a quarter century, and his legacy persisted after his death by suicide. He is widely regarded as the prime mover of the nationalistic social and economic changes that have prompted the modernization of Brazil since the 1930s.

BACKGROUND. Vargas's personal and political prowess stemmed largely from his family heritage and his experience in the authoritarian political system in the border state of Rio Grande do Sul. The third of five sons of a regionally prominent family, Vargas was born at São Borja, a small town in western Rio Grande do Sul on Brazil's frontier with Argentina. His parents,

Getúlio Vargas announcing the coup d'état in November 1937. (Iconographia)

General Manoel do Nascimento Vargas and Candida Dornelles Vargas, were from rival clans that regularly took opposite sides in armed political contests. In this situation, young Getúlio learned the patience, tact, and tolerance that became the hallmark of his political style. Initially intent on pursuing a military career, he resigned from the army after five years to study law in Pôrto Alegre.

EARLY POLITICAL CAREER. Vargas first became involved in state politics while a law student, campaigning for the gubernatorial candidate of the Republican Party. For this service, when he graduated in 1907, he was appointed to the district attorney's office in Pôrto Alegre, where he remained for two years. He then returned to São Borja to practice law and to run successfully for a seat in the state legislature. The only significant function of that body was to approve periodically the governor's budget. Membership in the legislature, however, assured the political future of those who demonstrated unquestioning support of the Republican governor. The Republican Party regime, based loosely on the hierarchical philosophy of positivism, was a veritable dictatorship in which the governor exercised absolute control over the state administration and party. The perennial governor, BORGES DE MEDEIROS, ruled by decree in all matters except finance, placed maintaining a balanced budget and treasury surplus above building public works and providing social services, and insisted upon personal loyalty from all party officials. In 1912, Vargas learned that even mild criticism of Borges's rule was unacceptable. For such a mistake he was removed from the state legislature and barred from reelection for five years, until he had displayed appropriate contrition and sworn renewed fealty to his party's boss. When he later became political head of the nation, Vargas was never to demand such obeisance from his followers, but he would share Borges's insistence upon keeping the reins of power in his own hands.

Vargas rose to national prominence in the 1920s, a decade of protest and revolts by young military officers (*tenentes*) and disgruntled civilians against corrupt rule by professional politicians in the service of the rural oligarchy. The *tenentes* were eventually defeated— killed, jailed, or exiled by the government—but they remained heroes to much of the press and the urban population. Vargas made no public statements against the young rebels, even though he held increasingly important posts in the established state and national governments. In 1922 he went to Rio de Janeiro as a newly elected congressman and head of his state's congressional delegation. Four years later he was elevated to the cabinet as finance minister of President Washington LUÍS PEREIRA DE SOUSA, and in 1928, following an un-

contested election, Vargas succeeded Borges de Medeiros as governor of Rio Grande do Sul. In contrast to
Borges's rigidly conservative fiscal management, Vargas
secured federal funds for ambitious development projects of value to farmers and urban businessmen. He
also abandoned Borges's strict partisanship, promoting
a policy of collaboration with the opposition party. In
these ways he united Rio Grande do Sul behind his bid
for the presidency of Brazil in the March 1930 elections
or, if that failed, by revolution.

THE RISE TO POWER. Vargas had no scruples against
the use of force for political ends, but preferred to secure
his objectives by nonviolent means, if possible. Because
no opposition candidate had ever been elected president
in Brazil, he first sought to head the administration
ticket, but was rebuffed by President Washington Luís.
In these circumstances, Vargas authorized his colleagues
to make contingency plans for revolution. At the same
time he accepted the nomination of the reformist Liberal Alliance, a coalition formed from Republican Party
regimes in three states and opposition parties elsewhere.
The Vargas campaign was also supported by the *tenentes*
and their civilian followers, who were clamoring for political and social change. Despite his popularity in the
cities, he was badly defeated by the entrenched rural-
based political machines in seventeen of the twenty
states.

While Vargas appeared to accept defeat gracefully, he
was in fact patiently waiting for the propitious moment
to launch a decisive assault on the federal government.
That moment came on 3 October 1930, when the revolution broke out simultaneously in Rio Grande do Sul,
Minas Gerais, and Paraíba, the states that had backed
his presidential campaign. The troops on both sides
were primarily regular army units and militarized state
police. After three weeks, by which time the rebels were
in control of most of the coastal states, the army high
command in Rio de Janeiro staged a coup d'état to halt
the intraservice war. The military junta ordered a cease-
fire, deposed and exiled President Washington Luís, and
agreed to transfer power to the rebel leader when he
reached the capital. On 3 November Getúlio Vargas was
installed as chief of the provisional government for an
unspecified term, with no limitations on his authority.

THE VARGAS ERA. Moving quickly to consolidate
his position, Vargas suspended the 1891 Constitution,
announced the pending reorganization of the judiciary,
dismissed the Congress and all the state legislatures, and
replaced elected state governors with interventors responsible only to him. In response to widespread expectations for social reform, he created new cabinet
ministries for labor and education, and appointed as
their heads civilian reformers with strong ties to state

Republican Party leaders. With regard to the armed
forces, Vargas granted amnesty to the military rebels of
the 1920s, authorized their return to active duty in their
respective units, and appointed regular officers dedicated to the principles of hierarchy and discipline as war
and navy ministers. By these actions Vargas eliminated
constitutional checks on the executive power, deprived
the once-dominant state parties of any legitimate public
functions, and, through the interventors, gained control
over political activity at all levels throughout the nation.
He was now undisputed dictator of Brazil.

There was no protest, because it was widely agreed
that a temporary dictatorship was necessary in order to
carry out the aims of the revolution. Vargas's heterogeneous following, however, could not agree on the nature and extent of those aims or the length of time
required to attain them. Professional politicians and senior military commanders were willing to accept moderate democratic reforms, but they expected the traditional political system to be restored, essentially intact,
within a few months. In contrast, most junior officers
and civilian radicals saw Vargas as the providential
leader who must remain dictator as long as it might
take to secure their goals of order, justice, and honest
government for the Brazilian people.

Vargas did not publicly reject either interpretation of
his role, but most of his actions tended to favor the
radicals. He attempted to placate his conservative allies
by making repeated vows to respect the de facto autonomy long enjoyed by state governments, and to hold
elections to restore constitutional rule as soon as a thorough revision of the electoral laws could be completed.
Eventually, however, he so antagonized the conservatives by ignoring states' rights and refusing to call for
immediate elections that the establishment political
elites in São Paulo and some of his former supporters
in other states tried to overthrow him.

The Constitutionalist Revolution of 1932, which
raged for three months before collapsing, was far costlier
in lives and treasure than the Revolution of 1930. It
was limited chiefly to the state of São Paulo, because
elsewhere all interventors and the armed forces remained loyal to the dictatorship. Although Vargas's national popularity remained high, the São Paulo rebels
claimed a moral victory, for within a year elections were
held for the constituent assembly that wrote the Constitution of 1934. This charter incorporated all reforms
enacted by the provisional government, restored full
civil rights, and provided for the election of a new congress as well as elected state governors and legislatures.
On 17 July 1934, the constituent assembly elected Vargas president of Brazil for a four-year term.

The changes introduced in Brazil under Vargas were expressed in national and often nationalistic terms, but could not fail to reflect the impact of the world economic depression and the struggle between fascism and democracy abroad. The Great Depression cut deeply

---

The incongruity of waging war against dictatorships in Europe while living under a dictator at home was not lost on the Brazilian people.

---

into Brazil's revenues from agricultural exports and exposed the country's great dependence on foreign sources for industrial products. Vargas dealt pragmatically with these problems, nationalizing much of the nation's rail and sea transportation, setting up advisory councils and official agencies to revive the export economy, and promoting the growth of industry in Brazil by private foreign and domestic firms. These essentially economic policies not only enhanced the regulatory powers of the central government but also contributed to a great increase in the size and importance of the federal bureaucracy, the middle class, and the urban labor force, which then became permanent features of Brazilian society.

Vargas had no firm ideological convictions: he was motivated by love of power and what he saw as Brazil's national interests. These qualities determined his responses to the increasingly bitter rivalry among fascist and antifascist political systems in the Western world. Abroad, the United States and Nazi Germany were vying openly for Brazil's support. Within Brazil, neofascist, liberal democratic, and Communist organizations clashed and competed for followers, posing a potential threat to Vargas's rule. Thus, in foreign affairs he pursued a flexible policy seeking advantages for Brazil from both camps. At home, following the abortive Communist-led revolt in November 1935, Vargas relied on his congressional majority to suspend civil rights and strengthen his police powers for most of the remainder of his term. A spurious Communist threat was the avowed justification for the coup d'état of 10 November 1937, which Vargas and the armed forces staged to create the allegedly totalitarian Estado Nôvo (New State).

Ostensibly patterned on the European fascist dictatorships, the Estado Nôvo lacked the usual political party, militia, and national police loyal to the dictator. Vargas saw no role for political parties, and he relied upon the army to maintain order. For more than seven years he ruled Brazil without the constraints of Congress or the distractions of parties and elections. His

domestic policies continued as before to focus chiefly on the urban population and on the need to strengthen the material and human bases for industrialization. Their fruits were seen in large national electrification and steel manufacturing projects, as well as in the great expansion in public health services and in education at all levels. The major social reforms under the Estado Nôvo were enactment of a minimum wage law and codification of all labor legislation enacted since 1930, which had the effect of bringing urban workers into the political arena as staunch supporters of Vargas.

Despite his apparent identification with fascism and the pro-German bias of some Brazilian military commanders, Vargas finally decided that Brazil's interests would best be served by a close relationship with the United States. In 1942 Brazil entered World War II as one of the Allied powers, and in 1944 Brazil sent a substantial expeditionary force to fight in the Italian campaign.

The incongruity of waging war against dictatorships in Europe while living under a dictator at home was not lost on the Brazilian people, who pressed for an early return to democracy. During 1945 Vargas abolished censorship, released political prisoners, issued a new electoral law authorizing political parties (two of which he himself organized), and called for the election of a new government in December. Fearing that he was planning another coup d'état, the army, led by officers recently returned from Italy, deposed Vargas on 29 October 1945, without recriminations, and installed an interim civilian regime to preside over the December elections.

Although he did not participate in the campaign, Vargas was elected to the Senate, but chose not to serve or to comment publicly on national issues. Rather, he spent the next five years quietly at his home in São Borja. He returned to politics as the candidate of his Brazilian Labor Party in the 1950 presidential elections. He waged a vociferously populist campaign and won with a large plurality. With the grudging acceptance of the armed forces, he was installed in office on 31 January 1951. However, as a democratically elected president obliged to share power with a bitterly divided Congress, Vargas proved unable to cope with the soaring inflation that eroded his labor following, or with the widespread ultranationalism to which his past policies had contributed. In mid-1954 he was overwhelmed by a wave of public revulsion caused by exposure of gross corruption and criminal activities within his official entourage. When the military withdrew its support and demanded his resignation, he complied on 24 August 1954; later that day he committed suicide. Vargas left a political testament in which he presented his death as a sacrifice on behalf of Brazilian workers.

– ROLLIE E. POPPINO

VARGAS, JOSÉ MARÍA

José María Vargas (*b.* 10 March 1786; *d.* 13 July 1854), physician and president of Venezuela (1834–1836). Born in Puerto de la Guaira, Venezuela, Vargas excelled in his studies in philosophy, theology, and medicine at the Royal Pontifical University in Caracas. He continued his medical studies at the University of Caracas (1808). With the fall of the First Republic, he was taken prisoner and then released in 1813. In 1814, he traveled to Edinburgh and London to pursue his medical education, becoming proficient in anatomy, surgery, chemistry, and botany. He returned to Venezuela in 1825 and by 1827 was appointed rector of the Central University by Simón BOLÍVAR. While serving as the university's rector, Vargas founded the faculties of anatomy, surgery, and chemistry.

In 1834, he reluctantly accepted the nomination for the nation's presidency, which he won. Several months after he became president, the military's Las Reformas Revolution broke out (June 1835). Vargas was taken prisoner and expelled from the country. But José Antonio PÁEZ defeated the "reformists," and Vargas was returned to power in August.

Vargas is fondly remembered for continuing to see patients on a medical basis while serving as president. During his short term, Vargas extended education to all youngsters, founded a national library, and promulgated a new legal code. Citing poor health, he resigned in 1836. Returning to academia, he traveled to New York, where in 1853 he unsuccessfully sought a cure for an eye ailment. He died while in New York.

– ALLAN S. R. SUMNALL
INÉS QUINTERO

VARGAS LLOSA, MARIO

Mario Vargas Llosa (*b.* 28 March 1936), Peruvian writer and politician. Vargas Llosa is Peru's best-known novelist, one of the creators of the so-called boom in Latin American fiction during the 1960s, and one of the most celebrated Latin American writers of the twentieth century. In addition to novels, he has written short stories, plays, essays, and literary, cultural, and political criticism. In 1990 he undertook a short-lived political career as a candidate for the presidency of Peru. He has taught at various universities, including Washington State University, Harvard, Georgetown, the University of Puerto Rico, the University of London, and Cambridge University. Many of his works have been translated into English and numerous other languages.

Born into a middle-class Peruvian family, Vargas Llosa experienced an idyllic childhood in Bolivia and Piura, Peru, where his grandfather held local political office. There followed a difficult adolescence, spent mainly in Lima, where he coped with his parents' separation and with life in the Leoncio Prado Military School in Lima, an experience he wrote about in his first novel, *La ciudad y los perros* (1963; *The Time of the Hero,* 1966). The military school was viewed by the author as a microcosm of Peruvian society, with all its machismo, prejudices, and hypocrisy. After its publication, a thousand copies of the novel were burned on school grounds.

Vargas Llosa became involved in socialist causes as a student at the National University of San Marcos in the 1950s, but he soon grew disillusioned with the official communist aesthetic of social realism. In the late 1950s his short stories began appearing in Peruvian journals and newspapers. One story won him a brief trip to France in 1958, and he subsequently traveled in the Amazonian jungle of Peru. He later won a scholarship to the University of Madrid, where his doctoral thesis on Gabriel GARCÍA MÁRQUEZ became a major critical study of that writer. In 1959 Vargas Llosa moved to Paris, where he worked for the French radio-television network and came to the attention of several prominent Latin American writers, including Jorge Luis BORGES, Alejo CARPENTIER, Miguel Ángel ASTURIAS, Carlos FUENTES, and Julio CORTÁZAR. His self-imposed exile in Europe and the United States ended only in 1974. Since 1990 he has lived in Spain and England; in 1994 he became a Spanish citizen.

It is Vargas Llosa's belief that literature is larger than politics, that it is born of, and indeed feeds upon, the real world.

Two of Vargas Llosa's most important novels appeared in the 1960s, *La casa verde* (1966; *The Green House,* 1968), and *Conversación en la catedral* (1969; *Conversation in the Cathedral,* 1975), and made him internationally famous. In 1967 he received Venezuela's Rómulo Gallegos prize for *La casa verde.* In his acceptance speech he described the role of Latin American writers as that of maintaining a continuous, never-ending insurrection against ignorance and exploitation. More recent works include *La guerra del fin del mundo*

(1981; *The War of the End of the World,* 1984); *Elogio de la madrastra* (1988; *In Praise of the Stepmother,* 1990); and *El pez en el agua: Memorias* (1994; A Fish in the Water: A Memoir, 1995). In 1993 Vargas Llosa was awarded Spain's prestigious Cervantes Prize in Literature.

Vargas Llosa's novels may be considered a renewal of the nineteenth-century European realist tradition. Like much of the literature of the boom, they are experimental works. His innovative narrative techniques include the structural dispersion of the narrative, the interpenetration of different narrative levels, and the complex juxtaposition of multiple points of view, or dialogic counterpoint (often challenging to the reader because it may involve the presentation of two or more scenes as one). Other innovations include the simultaneous presentation of different temporal sequences (often involving flashbacks or shifts based on analogy); what Vargas Llosa has called the "Chinese boxes" technique, in which narrative elements contain within themselves other narrative elements that reflect the original material; references to popular culture, such as the *telenovela* or soap opera; humor—a rare element in Latin American literature heretofore; the use of slang and taboo language; and the fusion of a "subjective"

psychological reality with a carefully realized "objective" observation of reality.

Narrative innovations aside, Vargas Llosa's work follows a perennial Latin American literary tradition that sees cultural and political criticism as an integral part of fiction, although his sensibilities generally prevented him from sliding into a simplistically Manichaean view of reality. His steadily growing interest in the Peruvian and international political situation during the 1970s and 1980s, as well as his exceptional influence as a public figure both inside and outside of Peru, led him to campaign seriously in the 1990 presidential campaign, which he lost to the independent candidate Alberto Fujimori. Vargas Llosa's campaign, supported by a center-right coalition, dramatized his shift from the left-wing political beliefs he had held as a young man to a more conservative libertarian view.

Despite his participation in Peruvian political and cultural life, Vargas Llosa purports not to use the novel as political statement. It is his belief that literature is larger than politics, that it is born of, and indeed feeds upon, the real world, yet it does not simply reflect that world but embodies a "real dissatisfaction" with it. Literature shows us both what we are and what we would like to have been. To put it another way, perhaps, lit-

Mario Vargas Llosa campaigning at Calca, 1990. (Sygma)

erature supplements, if it does not complete, the human being's capacity for infinite desire.

– KEITH MCDUFFIE

VARNHAGEN, FRANCISCO ADOLFO DE

Francisco Adolfo de Varnhagen (*b.* 17 February 1816; *d.* 29 June 1878), Brazilian historian and viscount of Porto Seguro (1874). The founder of modern historical writing in Brazil, Varnhagen, however, lived most of his life abroad. The son of a German military officer who had been engaged to supervise the recently created ironworks in Sorocaba (São Paulo), he was raised in Portugal, where his family had been established since Brazilian independence. After first receiving military training to become an engineer, he went on to study paleography and political economy. In 1841, he was granted Brazilian citizenship and, in the following year, he obtained a position in the Brazilian army, where he began his diplomatic career, serving in Portugal (1842–1852), Spain (1852–1858), several Latin-American republics (1859–1868), and Austria (1868–1878). He was a member of the Portuguese Royal Academy of Sciences and of the Brazilian Historical and Geographical Institute.

A product of the intellectual climate of Portuguese romanticism, Varnhagen considered the nation to be the natural framework for historical writing but, at the same time, followed the rules of historical research established by German scholars at the beginning of the century. Probing into the archives of Portugal, Spain, and Brazil, he prepared the work for which he is today chiefly known: the *História geral do Brasil antes da sua separação e independência de Portugal* (1856–1857). He also published a study on the Dutch occupation of Brazil (1871), a second, much altered, edition of the *História geral do Brasil* (1877) and, on his death, left unfinished the *História da independência do Brasil* (1916). His interests also included the history of Brazilian literature and Amerindian cultures and languages. Although deprived of literary craftsmanship and tainted by a very conservative outlook, which marred some of his judgments, his work stands, by virtue of the depth and scope of its scholarship, above all others in nineteenth-century Brazilian historical writing.

– GUILHERME PEREIRA DAS NEVES

VARO, REMEDIOS

Remedios Varo (*b.* 16 December 1908; *d.* 8 October 1963), Spanish painter. Born in Anglés, a town in Gerona, Catalonia, Remedios Varo was the daughter of an Andalusian hydraulic engineer and a Basque mother. In 1924 she enrolled at the Academy of San Fernando in Madrid. She moved to Barcelona in 1932 and shared a studio with the Catalan artist Esteban Francés. She participated in the Exposición Logicofobista, organized by ADLAN (Amics de les Arts Nous; Friends of the New Art), in 1936. In Barcelona, Varo met the French surrealist poet Benjamín Péret, with whom she traveled to Paris in 1937, and became involved with the activities of the surrealist circle. Fleeing World War II, Varo immigrated to Mexico in 1942; there she met other exiled artists, including Leonara Carrington, Wolfgang Paalen, José and Kati Horna; with Carrington, Varo established close personal and artistic ties. Most of Varo's works were produced during her stay in Mexico, where she remained until her death. Her works display a range of fantastic subjects, some of which are based on her interest in alchemy and the occult.

– ILONA KATZEW

VARONA Y PERA, ENRIQUE JOSÉ

Enrique José Varona y Pera (*b.* 13 April 1849; *d.* 19 November 1933) Cuban philosopher, intellectual, and vice president (1913–1916). A native-born Cuban, Varona earned a Ph.D. from the University of Havana and became a representative from Cuba to the Spanish Cortes, where he strongly supported Cuban autonomy. He called for independence, moved to New York, and joined José MARTÍ's independence movement, editing the revolutionary paper, *La Patria Libre*. After Martí's death, he became Cuba's most influential polemicist. While a member of the cabinet of Governor Leonard Wood during the U.S. occupation, he directed the reopening and reorganization of the University of Havana. Although serving as vice president under General Mario García MENOCAL, he opposed the president's reelection bid and joined the conservative cause. An opponent of the corruption in post-occupation regimes, he served as a vice president of the National Association of Veterans and Patriots against the government of Alfredo ZAYAS and led students against faculty improprieties at the University of Havana under Zayas and against the repression of opposition by Gerardo MACHADO.

Varona led the positivist movement in Cuba, blending the teachings of Auguste Comte with those of other European positivists. A fervent nationalist, he died lonely and unsatisfied. However, his voice and his writings served to lead Cubans during the turbulence of the 1920s and 1930s, and his philosophical and political contributions helped forge the reality of Cuban nationhood.

– JACQUELYN BRIGGS KENT

VASCONCELOS, BERNARDO PEREIRA DE

Bernardo Pereira de Vasconcelos (*b.* 27 August 1795; *d.* 1 August 1850), Brazilian statesman. Born in Ouro Preto, Vasconcelos took his degree in Coimbra (1818) and returned to Brazil in 1820, soon beginning a career as a crown magistrate in São Paulo and Maranhão. He began his political career in the first legislature (1826). He achieved prominence in the conflicts of the Regency period (1831–1840). He helped lead the opposition to the First Reign's absolutist centralism, a struggle that led to PEDRO I's abdication in 1831. Vasconcelos, a minister in the Regency's first cabinet, also figured importantly in the triumph of liberal moderates and consequent decentralizing reforms, notably the Additional Act of 1834. Later, ambition, social unrest, and secessionism thrust him into opposition to moderate Diogo Antônio FEIJÓ, who was then serving as regent. He sought social order and national unity by identifying the crown's central power with the interests of the propertied classes. After Pedro I's death (1834), Vasconcelos allied the more conservative moderates to the first emperor's reactionary supporters. They formed a parliamentary majority that triumphed with the ascension of Regent Pedro de Araújo Lima (later Marqués de OLINDA) and the birth of the Conservative Party (1837).

This movement, known as the *Regresso* (reaction), pitted itself against the decentralist liberalism Vasconcelos had once championed. In conservative cabinets (1837 and 1839) and the Senate (after 1838), Vasconcelos, with Paulino José Soares de SOUSA (later Viscount do URUGUAI), reversed the earlier reforms. They promoted the Interpretation of the Additional Act (1840), reforms of the Criminal Code, and restoration of the Council of State (1841). The Liberal minority attempted to thwart this Conservative reversal by forcing the early majority of PEDRO II, who then called them to power (1840). However, the Liberals' cabinet soon imploded, and the Conservative march resumed until the early 1850s, despite brief Liberal administrations and revolts. Vasconcelos, as a senator and councillor of state (1841), remained a preeminent conservative chieftain until his untimely death in 1850.

– JEFFREY D. NEEDELL

VASCONCELOS CALDERÓN, JOSÉ

José Vasconcelos Calderón (*b.* 28 February 1882; *d.* 30 June 1959), Mexican philosopher and politician. Vasconcelos, a multifaceted intellectual and political figure, had a significant impact on intellectual thought in Latin America and on higher education and political behavior in Mexico. Intellectually, his work on the "cosmic race" (1925), which maintained that the mestizo race combined the best of indigenous and European qualities, was a great contribution to the growing literature of the region. His multivolume autobiography (1935–1939) is a classic in acerbic, intellectual literature. During his tenure as education minister in Mexico in the 1920s, he provided an important refuge for many radical students from South America, exposing them to the dynamic undercurrents of Mexico in the postrevolutionary era. At the same time he also attempted to bring art, music, and classical literature to the Mexican masses, fostering a flowering of the arts most notable for its painting, made world-famous by a generation of muralists that included Diego RIVERA, David ALFARO SIQUEIROS, and José Clemente OROZCO. And although he opposed political centralism, Vasconcelos helped to centralize the educational system as it is organized today.

Vasconcelos' work on the "cosmic race" maintains that the mestizo race combined the best of indigenous and European qualities.

As a moral leader of students and intellectuals, he ran against Pascual ORTIZ RUBIO, the first official party candidate for the presidency of Mexico, in 1929. His campaign was innovative in that it drew many young female activists into politics. Although he abandoned his supporters in defeat, his essays and articles, written in exile but published in *El Universal,* were among the most widely read in Mexico. He remained in Europe until 1940. While many of his supporters, embittered by the experience, rejected politics altogether after his defeat, others joined the government party, hoping to bring about change from within. These activists, among them Adolfo LÓPEZ MATEOS (president 1958–1964), dominated Mexican politics for many years but ignored their original goals.

Vasconcelos was born in Oaxaca, the son of Ignacio Vasconcelos and Carmen Calderón. His grandparents had ties to Porfirio DÍAZ, whom Vasconcelos later opposed. After completing his education at the National Preparatory School and the National University in 1905, he joined the intellectual circle of the Ateneo de la Juventud. He became interested in political reform when Francisco I. MADERO began his anti-reelectionist activity against Porfirio Díaz. He served as Madero's confidential agent in Washington, D.C., and became vice president of the Progressive Constitution Party. Although he never taught a single class, he became rector of the National University (1920–1921) and then secretary of public education (1921–1924). While in exile in Europe from 1924 to 1928, he founded *Antorcha* (1924–1925), an intellectual magazine he used to oppose the Calles regime. In later life, he lost touch with his generation and his disciples, becoming an apologist for fascism.

— RODERIC AI CAMP

VÁSQUEZ, FRANCISCO DE ASÍS

Francisco de Asís Vásquez (also Vázquez; *b.* 10 October 1647; *d.* 1713) Guatemalan chronicler of Franciscan colonial church history. Vásquez is best known for writing the carefully detailed, *Crónica de la provincia del santísmo nombre de Jesús de Guatemala* in two volumes, the first appearing in 1714, the second one in 1716, edited and printed by the San Franciscan Monastery in Antigua, Guatemala. He is also the author of *Historia del venerable hermano Pedro de José de Bethancourt* and *Historia lauretana.* The latter narrates the vicissitudes of the Virgin of Loreto, who is venerated in the San Francisco Church in Antigua.

As well as being a renowned professor of philosophy and theology, Vásquez was deputy of the Third Order and superior of the Franciscan monasteries of Guatemala and San Salvador. He became the bishop's representative for the province of Nicaragua and held the titles of examiner of curates and confessors, and censor of the Inquisition. He became the chronicler and custodian of the Franciscan province of Guatemala, a position of supreme prominence in the Franciscan order.

— JANE EDDY SWEZEY

VÁSQUEZ, HORACIO

Horacio Vásquez (*b.* 1860; *d.* 1936), president of the Dominican Republic (1899, 1902–1903, 1924–1930). Horacio Vásquez came to be recognized as the last president of the Dominican Republic's oligarchic era. He had been very active in plots to overthrow the Dominican dictator Ulises HEUREAUX during the 1890s and ultimately came to power after Heureaux's assassination in 1899. His supporters came to be known as *Horacistas* and soon grew to become a major political party.

Characterized as inept and chaotic and yet as the most democratic of the period, the Vásquez era government was marked by severe political factionalism and increasing U.S. involvement in Dominican affairs. At the same time, the republic experienced accelerated economic growth and the emergence of a wealthy merchant and planter class. This era was most known, however,

for the evolution of U.S. involvement, from customs collection to controlling national elections, and finally to outright occupation in 1916. Vásquez played a major role during the 1916–1924 occupation as a member of the negotiating committee that effected the withdrawal of the U.S. Marines. Supported by Washington in his 1924 presidential bid, he came to be seen as a puppet of the U.S. government. This perception and economic hardship brought on by the Great Depression resulted in increasing political factionalism, which led to his ouster in 1930 by the army commander Rafael Leónidas TRUJILLO MOLINA, who symbolized a new era of dictatorship for the Dominican Republic. Vásquez died in exile in the United States.

— HEATHER K. THIESSEN

VÁSQUEZ DE ARCE Y CEBALLOS, GREGORIO

Gregorio Vásquez de Arce y Ceballos (*b.* 9 May 1638; *d.* 1711), Colombia's major colonial painter. Vásquez, a native of Bogotá, studied under Gaspar de Figueroa (1594–1658) and his son Baltasar (1629–1667), both celebrated locally for their canvases. About 1657 Vásquez set up his own studio. With him worked his two children, Feliciana and Bartolomé-Luis, and his brother, Juan Bautista. His patrons were mainly local religious communities. Vásquez's best oeuvre (1680–1705) is religious in theme. Some four hundred paintings are attributed to Vásquez. Many display mediocre composition and perspective and occasional poor figure rendition. These faults have perhaps unfairly been blamed on Vásquez, since there is no agreement regarding the attribution of numerous works.

Vásquez's real forte was drawing. Over one hundred drawings survive, and are truly masterpieces. In 1701, Vásquez was accused of rape and imprisoned for a time. This experience caused him severe economic loss and mental anguish. He died, insane, in Bogotá.

— J. LEÓN HELGUERA

VÁZQUEZ DE AYLLÓN, LUCAS

Lucas Vázquez de Ayllón (*b.* ca. 1475; *d.* 18 October 1526), judge and leader of an ill-fated colony in La Florida. Vázquez de Ayllón, an official in the Audiencia of Santo Domingo, sponsored two exploratory voyages to the Atlantic coast of La Florida. The earlier one, led by Pedro de Quejo and Francisco Gordillo in 1521, gave rise to the legend of Chicora, a fabled land of riches in the Carolina region.

In 1523 Vázquez de Ayllón was granted a royal charter to establish a colony on the southeast Atlantic coast. Named San Miguel de Gualdape, the colony of six hundred, including African slaves, lasted only for three months in 1526. Many of the colonists, along with Vázquez de Ayllón, lost their lives. It is believed that the African slaves were abandoned when the colony withdrew. The exact location of the colony has not been established.

— JERALD T. MILANICH

VAZ FERREIRA, CARLOS

Carlos Vaz Ferreira (*b.* 15 October 1872; *d.* 3 January 1958); Uruguayan educator, writer, and philosopher. Trained as an attorney, he became a professor of philosophy at the age of twenty-three and later taught legal philosophy at the University of the Republic, where from 1913 until his death he organized and taught seminars. He held directorships in primary-, secondary-, and university-level education. In 1933, during the coup d'état of Gabriel TERRA, he was rector of the university. Later, he inspired and founded the College of Humanities and Sciences and served as its first dean.

Vaz Ferreira produced most of his writings between the years 1905 and 1910. He published *Los problemas de la libertad* (1907), *Conocimiento y acción* (1908), *Moral para intelectuales* (1908), *El pragmatismo* (1909), and *Lógica viva* (1910). A good part of these are based on notes from his conferences, and his later work undertaken while at the university basically develops these themes and their pedagogical derivations, which are an essential part of all of his work. With Vaz Ferreira, the sharp polemics of the 1870s and 1880s between different schools of philosophy were brought to a close. He initiated a postpositivist neospiritualism that would characterize Uruguayan thought in the first half of the twentieth century.

— JOSÉ DE TORRES WILSON

VÁZQUEZ DE CORONADO, FRANCISCO

Francisco Vázquez de Coronado (*b.* 1510; *d.* 22 September 1554), Spanish explorer. Vázquez de Coronado was born in Salamanca, second son of nobleman Juan Vázquez de Coronado and Isabel de Lujan. In 1535, he arrived in Mexico with the newly appointed viceroy, Antonio de MENDOZA. As the viceroy's protégé, he was appointed a member of the *cabildo* of Mexico City. A short time after his arrival, Vázquez de Coronado had become an important landowner and had married Beatriz de Estrada, daughter of the royal treasurer, Alonso de Estrada. In 1539, he succeeded to the governorship of Nueva Galicia, due to the imprisonment of his predecessor, Nuño de GUZMÁN. In 1540, Mendoza selected him to lead a massive expedition to explore an unknown

area of North America that Fray Marcos de NIZA claimed was CÍBOLA, one of seven cities of untold wealth. The group included over 300 potential conquistadores from Spain, 1,000 Indians, Fray Marcos

---

Vázquez de Coronado's expedition was responsible for the European discoveries of the Grand Canyon, the Continental Divide, and the Great Plains.

---

and five other Franciscans, at least three women, and well over 1,000 pack animals. Vázquez de Coronado's explorers marched from Compostela on the west coast of Mexico through Sonora, eastern Arizona, New Mexico, and the panhandles of Texas and Oklahoma to the Great Bend of the Arkansas River in central Kansas. The expedition was a disaster; it found no wealth, and Vázquez de Coronado and his party destroyed as many as thirteen Pueblo villages in New Mexico while putting down an indigenous uprising against Spanish maltreatment. However, it was responsible for the European discoveries of the Grand Canyon, the Continental Divide, and the Great Plains as well as the people, flora, and fauna of those regions. Its members influenced the cartography of the area and established a written heritage for northwestern Mexico and the southwestern portion of present-day United States. Vázquez de Coronado lived for another twelve years after the expedition's return in 1542. A broken man, he died in Mexico City and was buried in the Church of Santo Domingo.

— JOSEPH P. SÁNCHEZ

VEDIA Y MITRE, MARIANO

Mariano Vedia y Mitre (*b.* 1881; *d.* 19 February 1958) Argentine politician and writer. Born and raised in Buenos Aires, Vedia y Mitre earned a law degree from the University of Buenos Aires. He entered education administration, becoming supervisor of secondary schools (1909–1911) and rector of the Colegio Bernardino Rivadavia (1910–1916). At the same time, from 1908, he was professor of history at the University of Buenos Aires and wrote a series of lesser historical works dealing with nineteenth-century Argentine history. Vedia y Mitre entered municipal politics dramatically in November 1932 when he was made *intendente* (mayor) of Buenos Aires, a position he occupied until February 1938. A controversial administrator, he ran roughshod over the city council, signed many contracts with foreign transport and public works companies, and ruled in an autocratic style befitting the conservative and fraudulent political spirit of the decade.

Vedia y Mitre made his mark by breaking the political logjam blocking Argentina's transportation system. The Buenos Aires Transport Corporation was set up to regulate all public transportation (subways, buses, tramways, and local railways). He resolved a long-standing dispute with electricity companies over service charges, had major soccer stadiums and a riverside bathing zone and promenade built, and widened the celebrated Avenida Corrientes. He crowned his achievements with a massive obelisk, modeled on that in the Place de la Concorde in Paris, built in the center of a construction project for the city's widest avenue to commemorate the four-hundredth anniversary of the founding of Buenos Aires in 1536. Vedia y Mitre oversaw one of the last major public works and construction waves in Buenos Aires, in an effort to fulfill the Argentine elite's ambitions to inhabit one of the world's great capitals. He died in Montevideo.

– JEREMY ADELMAN

VEGA, AURELIO DE

Aurelio de Vega (*b.* 28 November 1925). Born in Havana, Vega is one of Cuba's most prominent composers of the twentieth century. He received his bachelor's degree in humanities from De La Salle College in Havana in 1944, then went on to complete a doctorate in diplomacy at the University of Havana in 1947. His musical training began with private lessons from Frederick Kramer (1942–1946).

In 1947 Vega was appointed cultural attaché to the Cuban consulate in Los Angeles. There he studied composition with Ernest Toch. Upon his return to Cuba in 1949, Vega became editorial secretary of *Conservatorio,* the official publication of the Havana Municipal Conservatory. The following year he composed *Legend of the Creole Ariel* for piano and cello.

From 1953 to 1959 Vega was dean of the MUSIC department of the University of Oriente in Santiago. In the latter year he returned to Los Angeles. He became professor of music at San Fernando Valley State College (now California State University at Northridge), and has continued to produce a variety of musical works.

– DARIÉN DAVIS

VEGA, JORGE LUIS DE LA

Jorge Luis de la Vega (*b.* 27 March 1930; *d.* 26 August 1971), Argentine painter and draftsman. Vega was born in Buenos Aires and studied architecture at the National University. Believing that nonrepresentational art had

reached a dead end, he helped to form the New Figuration Group in 1960. In his work Vega depicts violence with a passionate eloquence that stands in marked contrast to the formal refinement of lyrical abstraction and geometrical art. Over the years he had numerous exhibitions in North and South America.

– AMALIA CORTINA ARAVENA

VEIGA, EVARISTO FERREIRA DA

Evaristo Ferreira da Veiga (*b.* 8 October 1799; *d.* 12 May 1837), Brazilian journalist and politician. Veiga was a newspaper owner, writer, and congressional deputy elected for three consecutive terms to represent the state of Minas Gerais. As a political propagandist he was influential in promoting the cause of Brazil's independence from Portugal, declared by PEDRO I in 1822. Famed for his comment, "We want a constitution, not a revolution," Veiga represented the nationalist interests of Brazil's agro-exporting sector. Once the constitution was promulgated in 1824, Veiga pressed for its execution, arguing that it would be interpreted from a liberal standpoint. Veiga supported independence and the abdication of Pedro I in favor of Pedro's native-born son as measures that would increase the political power of the Brazilian elite and ensure ready access to international markets. His views were propagated through his newspaper *Aurora Fluminense* (1827–1835). Veiga was also the founder of the Sociedade Defensora da Liberdade e da Independência Nacional (Society for the Defense of National Liberty and Independence), one of three major political groups during the regency that followed the abdication of Pedro I in favor of six-year-old PEDRO II in 1831. Veiga is held to have been responsible for many of the regents' decisions, most notably the creation of the National Guard as a force that could confront local armies and militias and contain regional unrest.

– SUEANN CAULFIELD

VEIGA VALE, JOSÉ JOAQUIM DA

José Joaquim da Veiga Vale (*b.* 1806; *d.* 1874), Brazilian sculptor. Veiga Vale spent most of his adult life in the state of Goiás. Lacking formal artistic training, he early began to experiment with woodcarving. Although born in the nineteenth century, his art appears to have remained virtually unaffected by the then popular neoclassical tradition taught at the Imperial Academy of Fine Arts in Rio de Janeiro. Rather, his carvings display an archaic quality that firmly embeds them in the eighteenth-century baroque tradition. His best-known work, the *Santíssima Trindade,* still holds a place of honor in an important religious procession in Vila Boa de Goiás, Veiga Vale's hometown. His series of carved religious figures, housed today in the Museu de Arte Sacra da Boa Morte in Goiás, gained recognition in 1940, when an exhibition of his works took place in Vila Boa de Goiás.

— CAREN A. MEGHREBLIAN

VEINTEMILLA, JOSÉ IGNACIO DE

José Ignacio de Veintemilla (also spelled Veintimilla; *b.* 31 July 1828; *d.* 19 July 1908), president of Ecuador (1878–1883). Born in Quito, Veintemilla studied at the Military College and was commissioned second lieutenant in 1847. He rose rapidly through the ranks, partly through involvement in politics, and became brigadier general in 1866. Under President Jerónimo CARRIÓN (1865–1867) he became minister of war. After narrowly escaping execution by President GARCÍA MORENO in 1869, he fled into exile.

Veintemilla returned from exile in 1875, ostensibly to support the liberal administration of President Antonio BORRERO. However, with support from coastal liberals, he seized power in 1876 and arranged his own election in 1878. His presidency was plagued by great tension and violence between liberals and clerical conservatives, provoked in part by the government's suspension of the ultramontane concordat and by the mysterious poisoning of the archbishop of Quito.

Veintemilla claimed credit for reopening the University of Quito, providing free elementary schools, promoting railroad construction, and maintaining prudent neutrality during the War of the Pacific. He governed arbitrarily and in 1882 sought to perpetuate his rule through dictatorship, but he was forced from office and exiled the next year.

— MARK J. VAN AKEN

VELASCO, JOSÉ MARÍA

José María Velasco (*b.* 6 July 1840; *d.* 26 August 1912), Mexican painter. Velasco, a major landscape painter, is the foremost Mexican painter of the nineteenth century. He was the favorite pupil of the Italian landscapist Eugenio Landesio, who taught at the Academia de San Carlos between 1855 and 1873. Velasco succeeded him in 1875 and remained on the staff for the rest of his life. In *Excursion in the Environs of Mexico City* (1866), an early work, small figures from different walks of life, against a background of enormous trees and a distant landscape, suggest historical and social commentary. Velasco never ignored the human presence in landscape, but with time that presence became less anecdotal. In 1873 he executed the first of several large canvases titled *Valley of Mexico,* his most famous works.

Although he painted elsewhere in the country (Oaxaca, Veracruz) and produced views of buildings, self-portraits, and portraits, the broad vistas and the clear light of central Mexico were Velasco's favorite subjects. In *The Bridge of Metlac* (1881) he celebrates the modernity of the age of Porfirio DÍAZ by depicting a train moving through a tropical landscape. *Hacienda of Chimalpa* (1893), a vast, simplified landscape in silvery tonalities, is his most important late work.

Although Velasco traveled to international exhibitions where his paintings received prizes (Philadelphia in 1876, Paris in 1889, and Chicago in 1893), his style was hardly affected by these contacts. Velasco had a strong scientific bent, and he executed many drawings and paintings of plants, animals, and archaeological objects and sites for scientific institutions and publications, as well as meticulous studies of rocks and vegetation.

— CLARA BARGELLINI

VELASCO, JOSÉ MIGUEL DE

José Miguel de Velasco (*b.* 29 September 1795; *d.* 13 October 1859), president of Bolivia (1829, 1839–1841, 1848). Velasco was born in Sucre. In 1815 he joined the royalist army. After five years of service and promotion to lieutenant colonel, Velasco defected to the

---

While Santa Cruz was absent from Bolivia,

uprisings by other caudillos led to Velasco's ascension

to the presidency in 1829.

Republican cause. He fought under José de San Martín, Simón Bolívar, and Antonio José de Sucre Alcalá, and participated at the battle of Ayacucho in 1824. After Sucre departed Bolivia in 1828, the new congress elected Andrés de SANTA CRUZ president and Velasco vice president. While Santa Cruz was absent from Bolivia, uprisings by other caudillos led to Velasco's ascension to the presidency in January 1829. Six months later, at the request of Congress, Velasco relinquished the presidency to Santa Cruz. During the latter period of the Peru-Bolivian Confederation, Velasco took advantage of the growing unpopularity of Santa Cruz, whose meddling in Peru had become very expensive for Bolivia. Velasco deposed Santa Cruz in 1839, but he in turn was overthrown by another ambitious general, José BALLIVIÁN, in 1841. Velasco returned to the presidency in 1848 after the populace of Bolivia became disenchanted with Ballivián. Lacking any coherent program and without widespread support in the army, Velasco was overthrown by Manuel Isidoro BELZÚ later the same year.

— ERWIN P. GRIESHABER

VELASCO, LUIS DE

Luis de Velasco (*b.* ca. 1511; *d.* 1564), second viceroy of Mexico. Velasco was born in Carrión de los Condes, Palencia, in Spain, into the extended family of the constables of Castile. His early career included service in France and Navarre (viceroy, 1547–1548). In 1549 he was appointed the viceroy of Mexico. He served from his arrival in 1550 until his death. Central to his rule was the implementation of the New Laws, which placed restrictions on the *encomienda.* The discovery of silver mines on the northern frontier caused a need for protection from the nomadic Indians. Velasco helped to define the military policy. He also supported expeditions, specifically to Florida under don Tristán de Luna. His son, don Luis de Velasco (the Younger), daughter, and half-brother married into the creole elite. The latter years of his rule were marred by the visitation of Licentiate Jerónimo de Valderrama and by an upsurge of creole animosity toward Spain due to the implementation of the New Laws.

— JOHN F. SCHWALLER

VELASCO, LUIS DE ("THE YOUNGER")

Luis de ("The Younger") Velasco (*b.* 1538; *d.* 1617), viceroy of Mexico and of Peru. Born in Carrión de los Condes, Palencia, in Spain, Velasco first went to Mexico in 1560 to join his father, who was the second viceroy. Earlier he had gone with his brother, don Antonio de Velasco, as a member of the party which accompanied Philip II to England for his marriage to Queen Mary. In Mexico, Velasco married doña María de Ircio, daughter of a conquistador. In 1565 he assisted in the uncovering of the "Cortes Conspiracy." After returning to Spain in 1585, he served as ambassador to Florence. In 1589 he was appointed viceroy of Mexico, where he served until becoming viceroy of Peru in 1595. In 1604 he retired to his estates in Mexico only to be reappointed viceroy of Mexico in 1607 and eventually president of the Council of the Indies in Spain in 1611. He was granted the title of marqués de las Salinas del Río Pisuerga in 1609.

Velasco is credited with the successful pacification of the northern Mexican frontier, reorganization of the textile mills, and the initiation of the drainage of the Valley of Mexico. In Peru he reorganized the system of Indian labor, regulated the textile mills, and reorganized the mercury mines of Huancavelica.

— JOHN F. SCHWALLER

VELASCO ALVARADO, JUAN

Juan Velasco Alvarado (*b.* 16 June 1910; *d.* 24 December 1977), military officer and president of Peru (1968–1975), leader of a radical nationalist government that introduced a number of reforms and increased state intervention in economic, social, and political affairs. Velasco was born in Piura and entered the army as a private in 1929. In 1930 he was accepted to the officers' military school, from which he graduated first in his class. After serving as army officer in the Peruvian jungle, he continued his military training in the Advanced War School. In 1959 he was promoted to the rank of brigadier general, and in 1962–1963 he was the military attaché in Paris. In 1963 he was promoted to division general and served in Washington, D.C.

In 1968, Velasco and twelve other army officers plotted to oust President Fernando BELAÚNDE TERRY. They allegedly elaborated the Plan Inca, a blueprint for introducing strategic reforms intended to modernize the country and avoid leftist and social uprisings. Soon after the coup of 3 October 1968, Velasco and his government team initiated a process of nationalization of the petroleum, mining, fishing, and agrarian industries. A vast agrarian reform was implemented, and in 1974 the press was nationalized. With initial popular support, Velasco's popularity had declined considerably by 1975. In 1973 he suffered a stroke that led to the amputation of his left leg. General Francisco MORALES BERMÚDEZ CERRUTI led a 1975 coup that ousted Velasco and prepared for the return of democracy in 1980. Velasco died in Lima.

— ALFONSO W. QUIROZ

VELASCO IBARRA, JOSÉ MARÍA

José María Velasco Ibarra (*b.* 19 March 1893; *d.* 30 March 1979), president of Ecuador (1934–1935, 1944–1947, 1952–1956, 1960–1961, 1968–1972). Trained in law at the Central University in Quito, Velasco began his long and remarkable political career at an early age. He was elected to Congress in 1932, became president of the Chamber of Deputies in 1933, and replaced the president of the republic a year later. He attained the presidency five times but was forcibly removed on four occasions. Only his third presidency (1952–1956) was completed in accordance with constitutional provisions.

A spellbinding orator and charismatic figure of the first order, Velasco dominated national politics for nearly five decades. When out of office he was busily planning a return to power, and few prominent public figures were not associated with him at one time or another. A lifelong critic of political parties, Velasco won power through a personal electoral machine, which was dismantled once he left office. Unable to delegate authority, Velasco was a disastrous administrator whose authoritarian proclivities encouraged political unrest.

A widely read intellectual, Velasco had minimal comprehension of economic issues and was inclined toward short-term opportunistic policies. By nature a conservative, Velasco nonetheless put forward a populist image throughout his career. During his 1960 presidential campaign his views were avowedly leftist in character, reflecting the impact of the Cuban Revolution.

Velasco's fifth and final term, after a narrow victory in 1968, was characteristic of his earlier terms in office. The constitution was eventually suspended, and ultimately the military intervened. Velasco went into exile, returning in 1979 to bury his wife; he died a month later. With his demise, the remaining Velasquista forces disintegrated.

– JOHN D. MARTZ

VELÁSQUEZ, DIEGO DE

Diego de Velásquez (*b.* ca. 1465; *d.* 11/12 May 1524) Spanish explorer, conqueror, and first governor of Cuba (1514–1524). Born in the region of Segovia, in Old Castile, Velásquez left few records of his early life. He won early acclaim fighting with the Spanish forces in Italy and his reputation grew when he traveled to the New World on COLUMBUS's second voyage in 1494. For his active role in the conquest of the natives on Hispaniola, he received land and *encomiendas,* amassing great wealth in agriculture. He served as lieutenant governor before being named to lead the expedition to conquer Cuba. Velásquez and three hundred men sailed for Cuba in 1511 and, upon arrival, founded Baracoa, establishing it as the island's first administrative headquarters. The conquest of the island, renowned for its barbarity, lasted three years and decimated the native population.

In 1515, Velásquez moved the capital to Santiago de Cuba. During his government, the center of Spanish activities in the New World shifted to Cuba and the island prospered under his capable leadership. In his latter years, dissension arose over many of his activities, including the use of Indian labor, leading to his dismissal as governor in 1521, though he regained the position in 1523. He died unexpectedly the next year. His

wealth diminished with his losses from investments in exploration expeditions, like those of Francisco HERNÁNDEZ DE CÓRDOBA and of Hernán CORTÉS, yet at his death he was the richest Spaniard in the Americas. He created and organized a profitable and successful colony in Cuba; founded many towns whose names remain today; established a strong Spanish presence in the region, implanting her administration and her culture; and made Cuba a launching point for expeditions throughout the Western Hemisphere.

– JACQUELYN BRIGGS KENT

VELÁSQUEZ, JOSÉ ANTONIO

José Antonio Velásquez (*b.* 8 February 1906; *d.* 14 February 1983), the first and foremost Honduran primitivist painter. Born in Caridad, department of Valle, Velásquez was a barber by profession, without formal artistic training. He began to paint in 1927, and after working at various places throughout Honduras, he moved in 1930 to the village of San Antonio de Oriente, where in addition to being the barber and telegraph operator, he painted scenes of the village. His unique, primitive paintings, reflect the innocence and tranquility of that Honduran village where he spent the next thirty years of his life.

His paintings were discovered in 1943 by Doctor Wilson POPENOE, director of the Agriculture School at El Zamorano, and his wife. Popenoe hired Velásquez as a barber at his school, but he and his wife encouraged Velásquez to market his paintings in Tegucigalpa. They sold there only at low prices until 1954, when the Popenoes arranged for an exhibition of his work at the Pan American Union in Washington, D.C. This event catapulted Velásquez to international recognition, and in 1955 he was awarded Honduras's most prestigious art award, the Pablo ZELAYA SIERRA National Prize for Art. Among many other honors, he was elected mayor of San Antonio de Oriente. Now famous, he moved in 1961 to Tegucigalpa and in 1971 was the subject of a movie produced by Shirley Temple Black and filmed in San Antonio de Oriente.

– RALPH LEE WOODWARD, JR.

VELÁZQUEZ CÁRDENAS DE LEÓN, JOAQUÍN

Joaquín Velázquez Cárdenas de León (*b.* 12 June 1732; *d.* 7 March 1786), Mexican lawyer, mathematician, and miner. Velázquez de León was born near Tizicapán (state of Mexico) where his father and uncle were miners. After his father's death he was tutored in native languages by Manuel Asensio. Later he was placed in the care of his uncle, Carlos Celedonia Velázquez de

León, vice-rector of the Colegio Seminario de México, who encouraged his nephew to study science and mathematics. In 1765, Velázquez de León became an instructor at the Real y Pontífica Universidad. From 1765 to 1768, Velázquez de León and Juan Lucas de Lassaga (a Spaniard) studied various aspects of mining and mineralogy, especially smelting methods. In 1766 they presented a plan to the Spanish crown for separating gold from silver. After experimenting for two years, however, the plan proved to be flawed.

In 1766 Velázquez de León presented a plan to the Spanish crown for separating gold from silver.

In the early 1770s, Velázquez de León visited Europe, where he was already known for his astronomical observations and maps. Upon his return he and Lucas de Lassaga published the *Representación que a nombre de la minería de ésta Nueva España* (1774). It portrayed a deteriorating mining industry that should be reorganized to include a guild and a tribunal to give overall direction, a bank to provide credit and loans, and a mining college to teach modern techniques. Its most important finding was that the industry would benefit from miners supplementing their practical knowledge with scientific knowledge. Some reforms were implemented during the next decade, although the college was not launched until after Velázquez de León's death in 1786. How much the reforms contributed to the acceleration in output of silver remains open to debate. As director general of the Mining Tribunal, Velázquez de León was also in charge of technical education and experimentation. He helped to write the new mining code (1783), which tried to bring mining laws into conformity with mining practices, and he participated in the founding of the tribunal's bank.

— RICHARD L. GARNER

VELÁZQUEZ SÁNCHEZ, FIDEL

Fidel Velázquez Sánchez (*b.* 14 April 1900), Mexican labor leader. Velázquez Sánchez is probably the longest-lived top labor union official in Latin America, having served continuously as secretary general of the Mexican Federation of Labor (CTM) from 1950 to the 1990s. His notoriety comes from his long continuity rather than from any dramatic ideological or structural contributions to the Mexican or Latin American labor movement. Velázquez Sánchez's influence stems from his reputation for being indispensable to the control of numerous affiliated unions and to their acceptance of their status as a co-opted member of the dominant political coalition in Mexico. Because he has been so successful at this task, no president has either wanted to remove him, or has had the political courage to do so. This perception of his power has gained him a measure of autonomy from Mexico's president, making him the only Mexican official to have enjoyed this advantage for so long. Since the 1970s, it has led Velázquez, on occasion, to take stronger, more independent positions for labor vis-à-vis the executive branch, sometimes bringing his vision of politics into conflict with that of the incumbent president. However, because of Mexico's declining economic fortunes during most of the 1970s and 1980s, and the consequent high levels of unemployment, Velázquez has not been able to translate his potential power into much political influence. Although the PRI's perpetuation of electoral fraud in the 1990s had made it more dependent on the support of the CTM as the major member of the labor sector, the number of PRI candidates from that sector continues to decline. Velázquez is considered to be representative of the old-style politicians or "dinosaur" faction in contemporary political life.

Velázquez was born in Villa Nicolás, state of México, the son of poor farmers. He completed primary school while working in the fields. It is likely that Velázquez entered the union movement because his father, Gregorio Velázquez Reyna, was killed defending his farm, and Fidel was wounded in the shoulder during the incident. Velázquez began work as a dairyman in the 1920s, and became a labor activist at that time. He assumed his first union post in 1921 and became secretary general of the Milk Industry Workers Union in 1929. Originally a member of the executive committee of the CTM (1936–1940), he became secretary general of the major federation from 1940 to 1946. He, in collaboration with other labor union leaders, succeeded in wresting control away from Vicente LOMBARDO TOLEDANO. That success eventually led to his domination of the union after 1950. In his capacity as secretary general of the CTM, and dean of Mexico's union leaders, Velázquez served as senator from the Federal District (1946–1952 and 1958–1964) and has represented the labor sector on the National Executive Committee of the PRI on several occasions. Many observers speculate about the ability of the CTM to remain united after Velázquez's death.

— RODERIC AI CAMP

VÉLEZ DE ESCALANTE, SILVESTRE

Silvestre Vélez de Escalante (*b.* ca. 1750; *d.* April 1780), Franciscan missionary and explorer. Born in Santander,

Spain, Escalante joined the Franciscan order at age seventeen and served among the Pueblo Indians of New Mexico. In 1776 he accompanied Fray Francisco Atanasio Domínguez in an attempt to find a northwesterly route from New Mexico to Monterey. Although the Domínguez-Escalante expedition failed to open a new road to the Pacific coast, it was the earliest known European exploration of the Four Corners area. Escalante's journal provided the earliest written description of this region. Escalante returned to Santa Fe in 1777 and remained in New Mexico for several more years, serving as a missionary and ecclesiastical official.

– SUZANNE B. PASZTOR

VÉLEZ SARSFIELD, DALMACIO

Dalmacio Vélez Sarsfield (*b.* 18 February 1800; *d.* 30 March 1875), perhaps the greatest Argentine jurist of the nineteenth century. Vélez Sarsfield was born in the city of Córdoba and studied law at the law faculty of the university there, graduating in 1823. From 1824 to 1827 he was a deputy in the Constituent Congress in Buenos Aires and was briefly one of the first professors of political economy of the period. During the 1830s he practiced law, wrote important juridical works that included *Instituciones reales de España* and *Prontuario de práctica forense,* and was named president of the Academy of Jurisprudence in 1835. In the 1850s Vélez Sarsfield was deputy and senator in the local legislatures of the province of Buenos Aires and an adviser to the provincial government. In 1863 he was named minister of finance of Argentina by President Bartolomé MITRE, and from 1868 to 1873, was minister of the interior under President Domingo SARMIENTO. He is perhaps best known for his work as coauthor, with Eduardo ACEVEDO, of the Commercial Code of Argentina (1857) and as author of the Civil Code (1864).

– CARLOS MARICHAL

VELOSO, CAETANO

Caetano Veloso (*b.* 7 August 1942), Brazilian singer-songwriter. Veloso was the principal figure, along with Gilberto GIL, of *tropicalismo,* a dadaist-like late 1960s Brazilian movement of cultural and musical renovation, which included Torquato Neto, Helio OITICICA, José Carlos Capinam, Tom Zé, Gal Costa, and others. As performer, cultural agitator, and composer of numerous songs, including the 1960s classic "Alegria, alegria" (1967, Happiness, Happiness) and tropicalismo's manifesto "Tropicália" (1968), he and Gil are almost universally credited with redefining the aesthetics of Brazilian popular music through the incorporation of foreign elements such as rock, dismantling existing barriers between popular and "high" culture forms such as concrete poetry, and reelaborating folk forms.

Since his 1972 return to Brazil from England, where he had been forced into exile by the military government in 1969 (probably because he was a prominent proponent of *tropicalismo*), Veloso has continued a prolific career as a singer-songwriter, utilizing genres as diverse as samba, rap, and reggae to produce hybrid compositions with broad popular appeal. "His importance in Brazil," writes Perrone, "can be compared with that of Bob Dylan and John Lennon in the Anglo-American sphere."

– ROBERT MYERS

VENEGAS DE SAAVEDRA, FRANCISCO JAVIER

Francisco Javier Venegas de Saavedra (*b.* 1760, *d.* 1838), viceroy of Mexico (1810–1813). Venegas distinguished himself in 1808 as an officer fighting the French in Spain. Named to govern New Granada (Bogotá) by the Spanish regency (of which his uncle was a member), he was instead diverted to serve in Mexico, where he assumed office as viceroy just two days before the outbreak of Father Miguel HIDALGO's rebellion in September 1810. Venegas responded skillfully to the crisis in the colony, confronting and partially containing the military threat from the rapidly growing insurgency, creating new militia units, imposing a series of wartime revenue measures, instituting an internal security system for the capital and other cities, and abolishing Indian tributes. In attempting to maintain his own authority, Venegas effectively abrogated much of the liberal Spanish Constitution of 1812, though he quarreled with the ultraroyalist faction in the colony. Noted for his personal integrity, Venegas retired in relative poverty to Spain, where he was eventually ennobled (1816). He later served in a series of high political posts.

– ERIC VAN YOUNG

VERA CRUZ, ALONSO DE LA

Alonso de la Vera Cruz (also Veracruz or Gutiérrez de Veracruz; *b.* ca. 1507; *d.* 1584), Augustinian friar and distinguished philosopher, theologian, and educator in early colonial Mexico. Born in Caspueñas, Toledo, Spain, he studied grammar, literature, and rhetoric at the University of Alcalá. Afterward he pursued philosophy and theology at the University of Salamanca, where he was a pupil of the famous Dominican Francisco de Vitoria. He traveled to Mexico in 1536 at the invitation of Francisco de la Cruz and took the Augustinian habit in 1537. The long, varied list of Vera Cruz's accomplishments includes serving as missionary to the Tarasacan Indians, whose language he mastered; teaching in the Augustinian *colegio* in Michoacán, where he

---

Vera Cruz endowed the College of San Pablo with a fine collection of books that he had transported from Spain in sixty boxes.

---

established one of the earliest New World libraries; founding the monasteries of Cuitzeo, Yuririapúndaro, Cupándaro, and Charo in Michoacán; and founding the College of San Pablo in Mexico City in 1575 and endowing it with a fine collection of books that he had transported from Spain in sixty boxes. In 1553, Vera Cruz was appointed first rector and professor of Scripture and Thomistic theology at the newly established University of Mexico. A preeminent orator and classic writer in the Spanish language, Vera Cruz was an eloquent voice of Scholastic theology in Mexico and has been called the "father of Mexican philosophy." He died in Mexico City.

— J. DAVID DRESSING

VERGARA, MARTA

Marta Vergara (*b.* 1898; *d.* after 1948), leader of the Chilean women's movement, founding member of the Comité Pro Derecho de las Mujeres (1933) and, with other members of the Asociación de Mujeres Universitarias, of the Movimiento Pro Emancipación de la Mujer Chilena (MEMCH) (1935). Vergara edited the MEMCH journal, *La Mujer Nueva.* Her political sympathies were with the Chilean left and the Chilean Communist Party, though she was not a party member. Vergara lived and traveled abroad much of her life and was connected to the international diplomatic and intellectual communities. From 1941 to 1948, she lived in Washington, D.C., where she served as Chilean representative to the Inter-American Commission of Women.

— CORINNE ANTEZANA-PERNET

VERGARA ECHEVEREZ, JOSÉ FRANCISCO

José Francisco Vergara Echeverez (*b.* 10 October 1833; *d.* 15 February 1889), late-nineteenth-century Chilean statesman. A prominent politician, Vergara, the son of an army officer, was educated as an engineer. While holding public office, including a ministerial portfolio,

he was particularly recognized for his service during the War of the Pacific. Beginning his career as a nursemaid for an indecisive and perhaps senescent general, Vergara, a colonel of a National Guard cavalry unit, first served in the Tarapacá campaign. Landing with the troops at Pisagua, he fought at San Francisco and participated in the ill-fated attack on Tarapacá.

Although Vergara resigned from active military service, he continued to advise the army's general staff, often suggesting well-conceived plans which, unfortunately, the military commander rejected. Vergara subsequently held the post of minister of the interior in the Domingo SANTA MARÍA government. Although he was a brilliant and dedicated administrator, he failed to win the Conservative Party's nomination for the 1886 presidential campaign. Upon retiring to his farm in what is now Viña del Mar, he unexpectedly died.

— WILLIAM F. SATER

VERÍSSIMO, ÉRICO

Érico Veríssimo (*b.* 17 December 1905; *d.* 1975), Brazilian novelist. Born in Cruz Alta, Rio Grande do Sul, Veríssimo belonged nonetheless to the later modernist novelists of Brazil, who at first preferred the *novela,* a short novel emphasizing one character and limited space and time. One of his first such fictional efforts, *Clarissa,* was an immediate success. The youthful Veríssimo was fascinated by the plastic arts, but he left painting with colors for painting with words. Counterpoint, flashbacks, montage, simultaneity, telescoping, diary, and documentary are only a few of the devices he used in his broad, cosmopolitan view of the world. Veríssimo wrote in the first person and expressed details so convincingly that the reader readily becomes absorbed in the characters; yet psychological development and philosophy are subordinate to the story.

Veríssimo's humanistic and ideological themes were often conveyed by symbols and portrayed in characters. Music is often found in his works as allusions and symphonic structures, for instance, in *Música ao longe* (1935). Dialogue, used sparingly in his early novels, becomes increasingly important in his great multivolume work, *O tempo e o vento.*

Veríssimo quickly developed the novel as his preferred genre. He was the first in Brazil to make effective use of the point-counterpoint novel. He focused on urban life and immediately became a best-selling novelist, the first writer in Brazil to live by the pen. Other novels, *Caminhos cruzados* (1935), *Um lugar ao sol* (1936), *Olhai os lírios do campo* (1938), and *O resto é silêncio* (1943), followed in rapid succession, each a result of Veríssimo's continuing experimentation in his medium.

In *O tempo e o vento,* Veríssimo gives his broad, penetrating view of the history of his home state. On a wide panoramic screen developed in three volumes (the third of which has three parts), Veríssimo chronicles the vicissitudes of two families. He presents in human and symbolic terms the rise of Rio Grande do Sul from the mythical past and its history from the founding of its society in the middle of the eighteenth century to the dictatorship of Getúlio VARGAS in the first half of the twentieth. The principal subject of this great work is the evolution of the urban middle class, along with all the inherent issues, both in the state and in the nation. Volume 1, *O continente,* appeared in 1949 and volume 2, *O retrato,* in 1951; the first two books of volume 3, *O arquipélago,* were published in 1961, and the third, the following year.

– RICHARD A. MAZZARA

VERNET, LOUIS

Louis Vernet (*b.* 1792; *d.* 1871), first governor of the Islas Malvinas (Falkland Islands) under the authority of Buenos Aires (1829–1831). Vernet was a central figure in the incidents that led to the establishment of continuous British possession of the islands. He was born in France but he had lived in Hamburg and the United States before coming to Buenos Aires in 1817. In 1826 he set up a cattle business on the islands that provisioned passing ships with fresh and salted beef before they rounded Cape Horn. His presence and activities were challenged by seal hunters (mainly from the United States), so in 1829 the Buenos Aires government appointed him governor and gave him exclusive control of fishing and hunting in the area, an act that was protested by the British. In 1831, after several warnings against unlawful hunting, Vernet seized the *Harriet,* a U.S. sealing vessel, and took it to Buenos Aires. George W. Slacum, the U.S. consul in Buenos Aires, reacted strongly, called Vernet a pirate, and demanded payment for damages. The U.S. Navy corvette *Lexington* was in the Río de la Plata at the time, and at Slacum's instigation its captain, Silas Duncan, sailed to the islands in late 1831, destroyed Vernet's settlement, and declared the islands *res nullis* (property of no one). A little over a year later the British expelled the remaining Argentines and began their century and a half of continuous occupation of the islands.

– JACK CHILD

VÉRTIZ Y SALCEDO, JUAN JOSÉ DE

Juan José de Vértiz y Salcedo (*b.* 11 July 1719; *d.* 1799), governor of Buenos Aires (1770–1777), viceroy of Río de la Plata (1778–1784). Born in Mérida, Yucatán, while his father was serving as governor, Vértiz was trained as a military man in Spain and later participated in the Italian campaigns. He arrived in Río de la Plata as governor in 1770. Although he was forced to step aside during the brief viceroyalty in Cevallos, he soon succeeded him. As second viceroy of Río de la Plata, Vértiz was the true architect of viceregal government in the Río de la Plata. While governor and later viceroy, Vértiz was a very successful leader: he implemented a series of far-reaching reforms, including the creation of the intendency system; free trade; improvement of public services, education, and welfare; geographical exploration; construction of forts; and agricultural experimentation. Vértiz returned to Spain in 1784.

– SUSAN M. SOCOLOW

VESCO, ROBERT LEE

Robert Lee Vesco (*b.* 4 Dec. 1935), U.S. financial manipulator and white-collar thief. Born into a lower-class Detroit neighborhood to immigrant parents, Vesco achieved wealth with his International Controls Corporation (ICC). An investigation of ICC's takeover of International Overseas Services (IOS) by the U.S. Securities and Exchange Commission in the early 1970s led to a protracted hearing in 1973 that revealed many of Vesco's questionable financial activities. These ventures included $250,000 in illegal contributions to President Richard Nixon's 1972 reelection campaign, for which Vesco was indicted twice. Vesco, in the meantime, transferred his operations to the Bahamas and to Costa Rica, where he had cultivated a close relationship with José FIGUERES. While remaining in Costa Rica, he evaded U.S. extradition attempts but eventually became the source of such a political scandal there that he was forced to retire to the Bahamas after the Costa Rican government refused his request for citizenship in 1978. Seeking again to evade U.S. extradition, he filed for political asylum in the Bahamas in 1980. When the Bahamas, under intense U.S. pressure refused, Vesco found refuge in Antigua in 1981, promising to invest heavily in that newly independent island. In 1982, however, U.S. pressure forced that government to renounce Vesco, who then fled to Costa Rica and in 1983 to Nicaragua, where Tomás BORGE arranged asylum for him in Cuba.

– RALPH LEE WOODWARD, JR.

VESPUCCI, AMERIGO

Amerigo Vespucci (*b.* 18 March 1454; *d.* 22 February 1512), Florentine navigator and cosmographer. Vespucci came from a merchant family engaged in the trade of wine, silk, and woolens as well as in other commercial and banking interests. He was very well educated by his uncle Guido Antonio and traveled with him to Paris as a secretary on a diplomatic mission during 1481–1483. In 1489 he went briefly to Seville to examine the accounts of Florentine agents. He returned to Spain in 1492 and in a letter to Italy in December referred to himself as a Florentine merchant resident there. Vespucci was clearly aware of the return of COLUMBUS from the "Indies" and of the preparations for the great second fleet.

Vespucci joined an expedition of four ships that left Cádiz on 10 May 1497. Its purpose was to test the theories of Columbus, especially the physical configuration of Cuba. The leadership of the expedition is unclear, but Vespucci kept a record and may have acted as a navigator. From the Canaries they entered the Caribbean between Puerto Rico and the Virgin Islands, and sailed westward to Costa Rica. It is likely they continued north along the Mexican Gulf coast and the southern United States and sailed around Florida as far north as Chesapeake Bay. Vespucci provides the only account of this voyage, tracing the outlines of a northern continental mass in a report to Piero Soderini in 1504. The group returned to Cádiz on 15 October 1498.

The next year Vespucci joined another fleet of three or four ships that included Juan de la Cosa and Alonso de Hojeda. They left Cádiz 16 May 1499, touched the African coast, the Canaries, and Cape Verdes, and split up. Amerigo's ship went south, landing on Cape St. Vincent in Brazil on 27 June 1499, ten months before Pedro Alvares CABRAL's discovery. Returning to Seville, he received letters from Italian merchant friends in Lisbon with an invitation from King Manuel I to explore under Portugal's flag.

In May 1501, with orders to explore from Cape St. Agustín southward, Vespucci left Lisbon to examine lands mentioned by Cabral. The group passed the Canaries and stopped at Dakar, on the African coast, where they met Cabral's fleet returning from India. They touched Brazil and sailed to the south. When the land seemed to aim westward, Gonzalo Coehlo, the commander of the expedition, resigned, and Amerigo Vespucci assumed leadership, obviously to avoid problems regarding the division between Portuguese and Spanish spheres of influence as established by the Treaty of Tordesillas. In the search for a southwest passage to the Orient, they touched what became Montevideo, and passed the La Plata estuary (Río Jordán). They continued sailing to the south; in the first week of April, approaching the straits later discovered by MAGELLAN, they planted a flag in Patagonia. They returned to Lisbon via Sierra Leone and the Azores, reaching home port in September 1502.

After returning, Vespucci composed letters to Lorenzo di Pier Francesco de'Medici that were ultimately published. These, in somewhat garbled form, announced the discovery of a continent, *Mundus Novus.*

A variation of his name, America, was included on the new continent of the Martin Waldseemüller map printed on 25 April 1507.

Vespucci undertook a fourth voyage in 1503–1504. He left Lisbon on 10 May 1503, passed through the Cape Verdes and Sierra Leone, and reached Bahia on 20 August 1503. The leader of the group was Captain Gonzalo Coelho; Vespucci captained one of the six vessels. They explored to the south of San Vicente and traded for logwood. Vespucci later wrote Soderini in Florence reporting the details of the fourth voyage. Vespucci wished to return to his wife María as well as to his relatives and associates in Seville. Taking leave of Portugal, he returned to Seville in 1505. He journeyed to court, where King Ferdinand naturalized him as a citizen of Castile. In 1508 he joined Juan de la Cosa and Juan DÍAZ DE SOLÍS and was appointed *piloto mayor* (chief pilot) in Burgos on 22 March. This office combined trade, administration, and science. Vespucci headed the University of Mariners and collected and prepared composite maps or master charts on the basis of the most accurate knowledge then available. He died childless in Seville with wife María Cerezo and nephew Giovanni at his side. A variation of his name, America, was included on the new continent of the Martin Waldseemüller map printed on 25 April 1507 in the small printing house in the Monastery of Sainte-Dié in Lorraine.

– NOBLE DAVID COOK

VIAL, PEDRO

Pedro Vial (*b.* ca. 1746; *d.* 1814), explorer and pathfinder of the Spanish Southwest. A native of Lyons, France, Vial spent his first years in the New World on the Missouri River, working as a gunsmith for various southwestern tribes. As part of the Spanish attempt to protect and strengthen the northern frontier, he was recruited to open three new roads connecting Santa Fe with Spanish outposts to the east. Commissioned by the Spanish governor of Texas, Vial established an overland communication route between San Antonio and

Santa Fe in 1787. Under the auspices of the governor of New Mexico, he opened a second road from Santa Fe to Natchitoches, Louisiana, in 1788. From 1792 to 1793 Vial blazed a third trail from Santa Fe to Saint Louis, traveling what later became the Santa Fe Trail. After these trailblazing excursions, Vial continued to work for the Spanish crown. He was enlisted to help protect Spain's claims to Texas and New Mexico against Anglo-American encroachment, and he led an unsuccessful attempt to intercept the Lewis and Clark expedition of 1804–1806. With his extensive knowledge of the Southwest, including its native tribes and languages, Vial was also a valuable guide and interpreter, serving in this capacity until his death in Santa Fe.

– SUZANNE B. PASZTOR

VIAMONTE, JUAN JOSÉ

Juan José Viamonte (*b.* 9 February 1774; *d.* 31 March 1843), Argentine military officer and governor of Buenos Aires. Born in Buenos Aires, Viamonte began a professional military career in the late colonial period. He opposed the British Invasions of 1806–1807, and after the May Revolution of 1810 he joined the first disastrous expedition of the Argentine patriots to Upper Peru. He later took part in the struggle against Federalist dissidents of the littoral provinces and their Uruguayan protector, José Gervasio ARTIGAS.

Viamonte retired from the military in 1822 but remained active in public life, serving as acting governor of Buenos Aires in 1829, just before the first governorship of Juan Manuel de ROSAS. He became governor again in 1833, but his essential moderation and evenhanded treatment of Rosas's enemies infuriated the latter's supporters, who unleashed a campaign of terrorism. In 1834 Viamonte resigned, paving the way for Rosas to return to office. Increasingly disaffected, he moved in 1840 to Uruguay, where he died in Montevideo.

– DAVID BUSHNELL

VIANA, FRANCISCO JOSÉ DE OLIVEIRA

Francisco José de Oliveira Viana (*b.* 20 June 1883; *d.* 28 March 1951), Brazilian social theorist. Born in Saquarema, Viana was a major figure in the alienated first generation of the Old Republic (1889–1930). Viana was a publicist and jurist whose legacies are the tradition of authoritarian nationalism and the Estado Novo's *trabalhista* (corporativist sindicalist) legislation. Viana, trained at the Faculty of Law in Rio de Janeiro, was influenced by Serzedelo Correia and Sílvio ROMERO. A disciple of Alberto Tôrres in the 1910s, he first gained

prestige writing critical essays, which were an established genre in the era's journalism. His greatest work, *Populações meridionais do Brasil* (1920), was followed by other studies on Brazilian society, history, and politics, the best of which were written before 1940.

With the Revolution of 1930, analysis began to give way to application, as Viana served President Getúlio VARGAS as consultant, jurist, and minister. His most notable impact was on constitutional law and corporativist legislation that successfully helped contain and co-opt the political potential of the emerging urban proletariat. His direct influence on the intellectual milieu of the 1920s and 1930s was enormous, especially his analysis of Brazil's social, racial, and political evolution. He asserted that Brazil, hindered by mass degradation, racial inferiority, and tendencies toward disaggregation and clientelism, was historically predisposed toward enlightened, centralized, authoritarian government and endangered by liberalism. Although his ideas derived from European positivist and corporativist theorists from the 1880s to the 1920s, he remains indirectly influential today. He died in Niterói.

– JEFFREY D. NEEDELL

VICARIO FERNÁNDEZ, [MARÍA] LEONA

[María] Leona Vicario Fernández (*b.* 10 April 1789; *d.* 21 August 1842), Mexican insurgent heroine. A rich heiress, Vicario Fernández lived under the care of her uncle, Agustín Fernández de San Salvador. Working in her uncle's law office was Andrés QUINTANA ROO (1787–1851), with whom she was betrothed. After Quintana Roo joined the movement in 1812, she decided to help the insurgents. Affiliated with the secret society, Los Guadalupes, she received and distributed insurgent correspondence. She also sent the insurgents money, arms, and weapons, and helped several individuals to join them. She fled in March 1813, when she was discovered in San Antonio Huixquiluean on her way to Tlalpujahua. Her uncle convinced her to return, and she was detained in the College of Belén. Although the authorities prosecuted her, she did not inform on the conspirators. When she was rescued and taken to Oaxaca by the insurgents in April 1813, the authorities confiscated her property. The insurgent Congress granted her a pension that same year. She married Quintana Roo, whom she followed in his travels as deputy of the Congress. They were discovered in 1817 and she was captured in the sierra of Tlatlaya; both accepted amnesty from the royalists. Her remains rest in the Column of Independence.

– VIRGINIA GUEDEA

VICTORIA, GUADALUPE

Guadalupe Victoria (*b.* 29 September 1785; *d.* 21 March 1842), Mexican revolutionary leader and president (1824–1829). Born in Tamazula, Durango, under the name Miguel Fernández y Félix, he studied law at the College of San Ildefonso but abandoned his studies in 1811 to join MORELOS's forces, changing his name to Guadalupe Victoria in honor of the Mexican Virgin and for victory. He emerged as one of the major insurgent leaders after Morelos was killed.

Accepting the Plan of Iguala in 1821, Victoria was soon jailed for his opposition to Emperor ITURBIDE. In 1824 he became Mexico's first president. Although he attempted to consolidate the new government by avoiding excesses and refusing to side with either the *Escoceses* (Scottish rite Masons) or the *Yorkinos* (York rite Masons), he proved unable to transfer his office peacefully to Manuel GÓMEZ PEDRAZA in 1829. Victoria's administration suffered from lack of funds and an inability to control the radical mass politics that divided the nation. Thereafter, he retired from public life because of chronic illness.

— JAIME E. RODRÍGUEZ O.

VICTORIA, MANUEL

Manuel Victoria (*d.* after 1832), governor of Baja California (1829–1831) and Alta California (1831–1832). Lieutenant Colonel Victoria was very unpopular during his brief administration for seeking to abolish the *ayuntamientos* (town councils) in Alta California and to replace the local politicians with military rule. Victoria was overthrown in a revolt of his own troops and immediately recalled to Mexico. His overthrow led to greater autonomy in Alta California.

— ROBERT H. JACKSON

VICUÑA LARRAÍN, FRANCISCO RAMÓN

Francisco Ramón Vicuña Larraín (*b.* 1775?; *d.* 13 January 1849), Chilean Liberal politician. A prominent personality in the congresses and governments of the 1820s, Vicuña Larraín was president of the Senate in 1829 and in that capacity was the first to become acting president of the republic while President Francisco Antonio PINTO (1775–1858) recuperated from an illness (July 1829). In September 1829 an irregularity in the election of the vice president by congress (which selected a Liberal in spite of the fact that a Conservative had won a plurality of votes) provoked the successful Conservative rebellion that over the next few months destroyed the Liberal regime and inaugurated a long period of Conservative hegemony (1830–1857). Vicuña Larraín, who continued as acting president following Pinto's final withdrawal from office, was powerless to stem the tide: on 7 November 1829 a public tumult in Santiago forced him to hand power over to a junta headed by General Ramón FREIRE (1787–1851). With the presidential sash hidden in a hat, Vicuña Larraín withdrew to Valparaíso and from there to Coquimbo, where he was captured when the province fell into Conservative hands. He was the brother of Manuel Vicuña Larraín (1777?–1843), first archbishop of Santiago; father of the Liberal politician Pedro Félix Vicuña Aguirre (1806–1874); and grandfather of the brilliant writer-politician Benjamín VICUÑA MACKENNA (1831–1886).

— SIMON COLLIER

VICUÑA MACKENNA, BENJAMIN

Benjamin Vicuña Mackenna (*b.* 25 August 1831; *d.* 25 January 1886), Chilean lawyer, politician, and historian. The son of an eccentric intellectual father, Vicuña Mackenna was educated at the University of Chile. He became involved in politics while still a student, achieving the distinction of being jailed by the Manuel MONTT administration for participating in the 1851 revolution. Following that abortive struggle, Vicuña Mackenna traveled abroad, then returned to Chile, only to be exiled a second time. Following the 1861 conclusion of Montt's administration, Vicuña Mackenna successfully ran for the legislature, where he served as both a deputy and a senator.

During Chile's ill-fated war against Spain in the mid-1860s, Vicuña Mackenna traveled to the United States, where he attempted to purchase weapons. In the early 1870s, as the provincial governor of Santiago, he instituted various programs to beautify the city. After Federico ERRÁZURIZ prevented him from receiving the Liberal Party's 1876 nomination for president, Vicuña Mackenna ran as a candidate of the Liberal Democratic Party, an organization he created. Although he campaigned throughout the country, it became clear that the Liberal political machine had rigged the election in favor of Aníbal PINTO. Consequently, Vicuña Mackenna withdrew his nomination, although he continued to serve in the Senate.

An avowed nationalist, Vicuña Mackenna had many firm opinions, which he never hesitated to share, either in the press or the halls of Congress. In addition to his political career, he proved to be an extremely prolific writer. He wrote for numerous newspapers as well as authored dozens of books, many of them valuable monographs, on a variety of economic and historical topics.

— WILLIAM F. SATER

VIDAURRI, SANTIAGO

Santiago Vidaurri (*b.* 25 July 1808; *d.* 8 July 1867), governor of the state of Nuevo León–Coahuila, Mexico (1855–1865). Born in Lampazos (Nuevo León) near the United States border, Vidaurri was one of the most outstanding leaders of northern Mexico. While secretary of the Nuevo León government in 1855, he rebelled against President Antonio López de SANTA ANNA and became one of the stalwarts of liberalism in the northeast. On 23 May 1855 he occupied Monterrey, the capital of Nuevo León. Two days later he revealed the Plan Restaurador de la Libertad (Plan for the Restoration of Freedom), which announced his support for the republican cause. On orders from the Northern Army, he took possession of Saltillo, the capital of Coahuila, on 23 July 1855. From then until his dismissal by President Benito JUÁREZ, he governed both states, which he formally united on 19 February 1856. His military and political hegemony extended to Tamaulipas, where the border and maritime customhouses proved to be strategic. During his administration, he furnished customhouses on the Río Bravo, instituted the so-called Vidaurri tariff, and maintained strong liberal trade policies. This program won him the support of merchants from Monterrey, other areas of the northeast, and from Texas, and helped him amass substantial resources for supporting armed forces under his control, which he used to defend liberalism and maintain his own regional power.

The Vidaurri era, which coincided with the Civil War in the United States, laid the foundation for the future development of Monterrey.

The Vidaurri era, which coincided with the Civil War in the United States, laid the foundation for the future economic and industrial development of Monterrey. Vidaurri's autocratic behavior and harsh exploitation of the customhouses provoked a crisis with Juárez, which exploded in the beginning of 1864. In order to subdue Vidaurri, Juárez decreed the separation of Nuevo León and Coahuila on 16 February and imposed martial law. In March, Vidaurri abdicated and left the country. Some time later he joined the empire of MAXIMILIAN. He was named *consejero* (adviser), *ministro de hacienda* (chancellor of the exchequer), and commander of one of Maximilian's brigades. Vidaurri was captured in Mexico City when the French forces were defeated. Porfirio DÍAZ ordered his execution by firing squad.

— MARIO CERUTTI

VIDELA, JORGE RAFAEL

Jorge Rafael Videla (*b.* 2 August 1925), military leader and president of Argentina (1976–1981). Born in Mercedes, province of Buenos Aires, he graduated from the Military Academy (Colegio Militar) in 1944. During his early career he was rewarded with assignments of significant responsibility and educational opportunity. In 1954 he graduated from the Senior War College, and he became the director of the Military Academy in 1971. Two years later Videla was promoted to chief of the General Staff, the number two position in the army. In 1975, General Videla was elevated to commander in chief of the Argentine Army.

These were trying times for Argentina. Juan PERÓN died on 1 July 1974 and his wife, María Estela Martínez de PERÓN, political novice, succeeded him. Urban guerrilla violence increased significantly; kidnappings, assassinations, and car bombings were common. Also, the country was staggering under triple-digit inflation. On 24 March 1976 the Argentine armed forces seized control of the government. General Videla emerged as its leader and was declared president of the republic.

Videla carried out an aggressive war against the guerrillas. He retired in 1981, turning the government over to his handpicked successor, General Roberto VIOLA. Videla and other members of the military juntas that ruled between 1976 and 1982 were tried for excesses committed during what became known as the Dirty War. The defendants were charged with imprisonment without charge, torture, and executions. On 9 December 1985, Videla was convicted and sentenced to life in prison. In December 1990 he was released under a general amnesty.

— ROBERT SCHEINA

VIEIRA, ANTÔNIO

Antônio Vieira (*b.* 6 February 1608; *d.* 18 July 1697), Jesuit missionary, preacher, writer, and diplomat. Born in Lisbon and taken as a child to Bahia, Vieira went to live in that city's Jesuit college at the age of fifteen. Ten years later he delivered his first sermon, to an audience of black slaves at a Bahian sugar mill.

In 1641, Vieira was sent to Lisbon by the viceroy in Bahia to express the support of the Brazilian colony for King João IV following the Portuguese Restoration. He soon became the court preacher and a confidant of the king, who dispatched him on a series of diplomatic missions to Amsterdam and Rome. Among the ideas for which he was attacked during the 1640s were proposals to limit the power of the Inquisition, to encourage New Christian merchants to invest in Portuguese commercial enterprises, and to cede Pernambuco to the Dutch, for which he was vilified as "the Judas of Brazil."

Vieira returned to Brazil in 1653 as superior of the Jesuit missions in the Amazon. Relations between the Jesuits and settlers there were strained by the missionaries' control over the distribution of Indian workers to Europeans. João IV gave Vieira the additional task of curbing the notorious slaving expeditions the Portuguese were conducting in the Amazon. From his base in São Luís do Maranhão, Vieira sought to improve relations between the Jesuits and the settlers while leading a series of highly successful missionary expeditions in the hinterlands. Unable to enforce crown legislation protecting the Indians, Vieira returned briefly to Portugal in 1655 to present his case against the settlers at court. Soon after his arrival in Lisbon, Vieira preached his most famous sermon, the "Sermão da Sexagésima," from the pulpit of the royal chapel. In it he attacked the homiletic conventions of the day and the idleness of the clergy in Portugal, particularly that of the Jesuits' rivals, the Dominicans. Sounding one of the central themes of his writings, Vieira argued that work in the overseas missions was the highest service a religious could render to the church.

Tensions with the settlers persisted after Vieira's return to Maranhão. In what proved to be the turning point of his missionary career, rebellious settlers expelled Vieira and his fellow Jesuits from the Amazon in 1661 and sent them back to Lisbon. Vieira gradually abandoned his effort to promote the peaceful incorporation of the Indians into colonial society. During the latter part of his career Vieira worked to protect the Indians by separating them from the settler communities as completely as possible.

While in the Amazon, Vieira wrote *Esperanças de Portugal* (1659), a privately circulated prophetic treatise that was to provide the pretext for his arrest in 1663 by the Inquisition. Vieira for many years criticized the Inquisition on both religious and socioeconomic grounds. He was an equally vigorous critic of the church hierarchy, and with the death of João IV in 1656 he was no longer protected from retribution. Drawing on traditional Jewish messianism and apocalyptic folk beliefs then current in Portugal, Vieira developed—in *Esperanças* and his subsequent defense before the tribunal, as well as in later writings such as *História do futuro*—a millenarian interpretation of Portuguese history that placed ever-greater emphasis on the crown and the Jesuits as agents of divine providence. Vieira spent five years in prison and under house arrest. Following his release by the Inquisition in 1668, he had a successful sojourn as a preacher in Rome before returning to Brazil in 1681. During the last years of his life he served again as a Jesuit administrator, edited his sermons for publication, and wrote *Clavis Prophetarum,* a treatise left unfinished at his death. Vieira continues to be considered one of the greatest writers in the Portuguese language and a central figure in the religious and political history of the Luso-Brazilian world.

– THOMAS M. COHEN

VIEIRA, JOSÉ CARLOS DO AMARAL

José Carlos do Amaral Vieira (*b.* 2 March 1952), Brazilian composer and pianist. Amaral Vieira was better known as a pianist until 1984, when an Amaral Vieira Festival featuring an amazing diversity of musical works by the young composer was held in São Paulo. The festival included fourteen concerts during which 157 works by Vieira were performed. When Vieira later announced his intention to record the complete piano works and transcriptions of Franz Liszt, a project that would require seventy compact discs to complete, and it became obvious that no commercial company would undertake this vast project, Vieira established Scorpio, his own recording label. New musical works and vast projects appear to blossom forth from his fertile mind and nimble fingers with incredible rapidity. In a nation in which Heitor VILLA-LOBOS established a tradition of explosive creativity with more than one thousand musical works, Vieira is attempting to surpass his predecessors. Vieira's compositional style in works such as *Elegy, Nocturne and Toccata* (for piano [1980]), and *Variações Fausto* (a set of variations in fantasia form on a theme of Franz Liszt's *Faust Symphony* [1985]) shows his ability to write brilliantly for the piano and his intense involvement with the compositional style of Franz Liszt.

– DAVID P. APPLEBY

VIERA, FELICIANO

Feliciano Viera (*b.* 8 November 1872; *d.* 13 November 1927), president of Uruguay (1915–1919). Viera was the son of a veteran colonel of the Colorados who fought in the internal wars of Uruguay. At first a proponent of BATLLISMO, he separated from the main body of this group and gave rise to a splinter faction known as Vierismo. More conservative than José BATLLE and his reformist followers, Viera maintained a popular and charismatic style. After the failure of the Batllist constitutional project at the polls in 1916, Viera became the main force behind a movement to halt the social reforms that had characterized previous periods. In this way, Viera obtained a vote of confidence from the conservatives, which he in fact never betrayed. The political faction his actions had generated lost relevance with his death.

— FERNANDO FILGUEIRA

VIEYTES, HIPÓLITO

Hipólito Vieytes (*b.* 12 August 1762; *d.* 5 October 1815), journalist and political figure of Argentine independence. Born in San Antonio de Areco, Buenos Aires Province, Vieytes attended the well-known Real Colegio de San Carlos, where he studied law and philosophy. Committed to physiocratic doctrines and to the promotion of useful works, he spread his views by establishing various newspapers, including the *Semanario de Agricultura, Industria y Comercio* in 1802, and collaborated with Manuel BELGRANO on *El Correo de Comercio* in 1810. Many scholars credit Vieytes with the inception of modern journalism in his country. Vieytes served in the capital as police superintendent and representative to the General Constituent Assembly in 1813. Though he is regarded as one of the intellectual authors of the Argentine independence movement, he eventually succumbed to the political instabilities of the time. Vieytes was arrested and exiled in 1815 after the overthrow of Supreme Director Carlos María de AL-VEAR. He died in San Fernando shortly thereafter.

— FIDEL IGLESIAS

VIGIL, DONACIANO

Donaciano Vigil (*b.* 6 September 1802; *d.* 11 August 1877), governor of New Mexico (1847–1848). Vigil was a popular and well-educated native New Mexican. In New Mexico's Revolution of 1837, Vigil was captured at La Cañada by the revolutionists and appointed secretary for the rebel government. While questions were raised about his loyalty, he was later cleared of any misconduct. In the 1830s and 1840s, Vigil served as a member of the departmental assembly, editor of a Spanish newspaper in New Mexico, and military secretary under governor Manuel Armijo. When the United States occupied New Mexico in 1846, General Stephen W. KEARNY appointed him secretary of the territory and upon the assassination of Charles Bent (*d.* 1847) in Taos, Vigil became governor. An antimilitarist, Vigil proclaimed the first elections in the territory under U.S. rule. Later, he served in the territorial legislature.

— AARON PAINE MAHR

VIGIL, FRANCISCO DE PAULA GONZÁLEZ

Francisco de Paula González Vigil (*b.* 13 September 1792; *d.* 9 June 1875), Peruvian priest, liberal politician, and author. Vigil rose to prominence in the early post-Independence era for his 1832 attack on presidential usurpation of constitutional authority. In 1834 he presided over the liberal National Convention, and in 1836 he helped prevent Bolivian annexation of his native Tacna. From 1845, Vigil served as director of Peru's National Library, writing voluminously on church-state relations and national reform. Influenced by Enlightenment thought, Vigil extolled the virtues of reason, freedom of conscience, republicanism, education, and work. His religious dissertations provoked condemnation by the church for their assertion of the authority of national churches over the Roman Curia.

— MATTHEW J. O'MEAGHER

VILAR, MANUEL

Manuel Vilar (*b.* 15 November 1812; *d.* 25 November 1860), sculptor. Trained in his native Barcelona and Rome, Vilar was chosen as director of sculpture when the Academia de San Carlos in Mexico City was reestablished. He arrived in 1846. Vilar had studied with Pietro Tenerani and was sympathetic to the ideals of the Nazarenes (a group of German painters who sought to revitalize Christian art). He brought to Mexico an important collection of plaster casts acquired in Rome, and worked with the energy of a believer in the redemptive value of art to revive monumental sculpture in Mexico. He produced work with themes that were classical, religious, and secular, as well as portraits. Probably his most ambitious work was a full-size bronze statue of a pre-Columbian hero, *Tlahuicole* (1851). Autographed manuscripts and many documents provide information about his life and career.

— CLARA BARGELLINI

VILARIÑO, IDEA

Idea Vilariño (*b.* 1920), Uruguayan poet and critic. She taught literature in the high school system of Montevideo, where she was born, as did many other women of her generation. She began teaching in 1984 as a humanities faculty member at the University of the Republic in Montevideo. She has written critical studies of the poetry of the Spaniard Antonio Machado, *Grupos simétricos en poesía de Antonio Machado* (1951), and the Uruguayan Julio HERRERA Y REISSIG, *Julio Herrera y Reissig* (1950), as well as many articles on other Spanish poets. She published a thorough study on TANGO lyrics in *Las letras de tango* (1965). Her critical essays have appeared in *Clinamen, Asir, Hiperión, Marcha, Puente, Carte Segrete, Texto Crítico, La Opinión, Revista del Sur,* and *Brecha.* She is also an accomplished translator of Shakespeare into Spanish.

Vilariño's poetic expression is concise, with minimal utilization of rhetorical devices, and expresses a dark world, where the vital elements fail to survive. In form, her poetry is also brief, without much artifice. She has published *La suplicante* (1945), *Cielo, cielo* (1947), *Paraíso perdido* (1949), *Nocturnos* (1955), *Poemas de amor* (1957), *Pobre mundo* (1966), *Treinta poemas* (1967), *Poesía* (1970), and *Segunda antología* and *No* (1980).

— MAGDALENA GARCÍA PINTO

VILLA, FRANCISCO "PANCHO"

Francisco "Pancho" Villa (*b.* 5 June 1878; *d.* 20 July 1923), Mexican revolutionary, general, governor of Chihuahua (1913–1915). Christened Doroteo Arango, one-time bandit and muleteer, Villa became one of the most important and controversial leaders of the Mexican Revolution (1910–1920).

The history of Villa's youth is masked in legend. He was by occupation a hacienda peon, miner, bandit, and merchant. There is a colorful story of his killing a *hacendado* who had raped his sister and his subsequent escape to banditry. Most certainly, according to biographer Friedrich Katz, he was a cattle rustler, which far from branding him an outlaw brought him a degree of popular renown. Villa eventually settled in San Andrés, Chihuahua, a village in the throes of violent protest against taxes imposed by the Chihuahua state government controlled by the TERRAZAS family.

In 1910 Villa joined the revolution led by Francisco I. MADERO in Chihuahua. After Madero's victory in May of 1911, Villa retired to Chihuahua City, using his mustering-out money to begin a meat-packing business. He returned to military duty in 1912 to fight against the counterrevolution of Pascual OROZCO, Jr. His commander, General Victoriano HUERTA, ordered him executed for insubordination, but Madero intervened, sending him to prison, from which he escaped shortly thereafter. Following a few months in exile in the United States, Villa returned to avenge the overthrow and assassination of Madero by Huerta in February 1913. In March 1913 Villa crossed the Rio Grande from Texas with a handful of men. His key lieutenants came from the northern villages that had once been military colonies in the Indian wars of the eighteenth and nineteenth centuries. Toribio Ortega and Porfirio Talamantes, for example, had led their Chihuahuan villages, Cuchillo Parado and Janos, respectively, in protests against land expropriations. With his peasant-worker army, Villa conquered Chihuahua in the name of the Constitutionalist movement in 1913.

In control of Chihuahua from late 1913 through 1915, Villa expropriated the estates of the landed oligarchy and used the revenues they produced to finance his army and government. His rule in Chihuahua was an ingenious compromise between the need to satisfy the demands of the revolutionary masses for land reform and the immediate necessity of obtaining funds to win the war first against Huerta and then against his despised rival, Venustiano CARRANZA. He promised to distribute the confiscated properties after the triumph of the Revolution. In the meantime, these estates, some

Francisco "Pancho" Villa. (La Fototeca del Inah)

managed by his generals and others by a state agency, supported the widows and orphans of veterans and the starving unemployed of the mining and timber regions of Chihuahua, and provided the necessary funds for supplying the Villista army.

His Division of the North, led by an elite corps, the *dorados,* paved the way to Huerta's defeat. Along the way south from his initial victories in Chihuahua, Villa fought bloody battles, first at Torreón in April and then at Zacatecas in June 1914. His split with Carranza widened, however, and Villa withdrew from the campaign.

It was during the fight against Huerta that Villa first manifested his hatred for Spaniards. In Torreón he rounded them up and shipped them across the U.S. border, in the meantime confiscating their property. Later he would commit additional atrocities against them.

The Constitutionalists defeated Huerta in 1914 but almost immediately split into two factions, one led by Villa and the other by Carranza. One of the crucial issues between the two leaders was Carranza's intention to return the landed estates confiscated by the Villistas to their owners. This would have undercut much of Villa's support by depriving him of the main symbol of reform and the main source of his funds.

When a revolutionary convention met in Aguascalientes in the fall of 1914, Villa, allied with Emiliano ZAPATA, the peasant leader from the state of Morelos, demanded that Carranza abdicate as leader of the Revolution. When Carranza refused, Villa and Zapata declared themselves to be in armed opposition under the provisions of the convention. In November 1914 the Conventionist armies of Villa and Zapata occupied Mexico City. The Constitutionalists were in apparent disarray. The Conventionist alliance between Villa and Zapata dissipated, however, because neither of their regionally based, popular movements could sustain long-term military or political success outside its home area.

In a series of brutal battles in the center of the country in 1915 (Celaya, 6–7 April and 13–16 April; León, throughout May; Aguascalientes, 10 July), however, Villa suffered major defeats at the hands of the Carrancista general Alvaro OBREGÓN SALIDO. Villa's tactics of unrelenting attack were disastrous in the face of Obregón's entrenched troops. Villa's once mighty army disintegrated. The crucial battle took place at León (also called Trinidad), where over thirty-eight days at least five thousand men died.

Villa, though badly defeated and eliminated as a major military force, stayed in the field. His prestige was irretrievably damaged and his allies rapidly defected. In late 1915 he made a desperate effort to establish a foothold in Sonora but failed when Obregón dispatched troops through the United States to reinforce Constitutionalist troops in Agua Prieta. A series of defeats followed, sending Villa back across the Sierra Madre to Chihuahua.

Villa was forced once again to adopt guerrilla tactics. Many of his aides, especially the more respectable former Maderistas, went into exile in the United States. Villa stayed and tormented the national and state governments for four years. This "second wind" of Villismo brought it back to its roots as a local, popular movement based in the sierras of Chihuahua.

In 1916 Villa responded to U.S. recognition of and cooperation with Carranza by viewing Americans with increasing hostility. One of his lieutenants murdered seventeen American engineers at Santa Isabel, Chihuahua, in January. On 8–9 March several hundred Villista raiders crossed the border into Columbus, New Mexico. Although his motives for the attack are much debated, there is some evidence Villa sought to precipitate a military intervention by the United States in order to prevent an agreement with Carranza that would have rendered Mexico a virtual protectorate of the United States.

A force led by U.S. general John J. Pershing futilely chased Villa from mid-March 1916 until early February 1917, nearly a year. After Pershing's withdrawal, for the next two years Villa periodically occupied Chihuahua's major cities, Ciudad Juárez and Hidalgo de Parral. He was able to raise armies of from one thousand to two thousand men.

A force led by U.S. general John J. Pershing futilely chased Villa from mid-March 1916 until early February 1917, nearly a year.

Shortly after the 1920 overthrow and murder of Carranza by his own army, led by Alvaro Obregón, the interim president of Mexico, Adolfo DE LA HUERTA, negotiated Villa's amnesty and retirement. As part of the bargain, the general obtained a large hacienda in northern Durango, Canutillo, and a substantial subsidy for himself and a retinue of his troops. In 1923 Villa was assassinated in Hidalgo de Parra, perhaps because the national regime feared he would join de la Huerta, who would rebel some months later.

– MARK WASSERMAN

VILLA-LOBOS, HEITOR

Heitor Villa-Lobos (*b.* 5 March 1887; *d.* 17 November 1959), Latin America's most famous twentieth-century composer. Born in Rio de Janeiro, Heitor Villa-Lobos was the son of a minor library official and amateur musician, Raul Villa-Lobos, and Noemia Villa-Lobos. The composer's earliest childhood recollections were of Saturday evenings when friends came to the household for music making. Villa-Lobos's first musical instruction was from his father, who taught him to play the cello and provided him with ear training. When Villa-Lobos was asked if he considered himself to be self-taught, he often replied that he received such a complete musical foundation from his father that further instruction was unnecessary.

In 1899 Raul Villa-Lobos died during a smallpox epidemic, leaving the family in desperate financial circumstances. Noemia Villa-Lobos attempted to provide for the needs of the family by taking in laundry. Although she enrolled Tuhú, as she called young Heitor, in classes that would prepare him for a medical career, he was much more interested in all-night music-making sessions with young improvisers of popular music, the *chorões*. He frequently missed school, and when his mother tearfully objected, he ran away from home to live with an aunt who was more sympathetic to his musical interests and who played Bach preludes and fugues in a manner that never ceased to amaze him.

At eighteen Villa-Lobos traveled in the northern and northeastern parts of Brazil, an area rich in folk traditions. After selling some rare books that had belonged to his father, Villa-Lobos embarked on a journey through Brazil that lasted several years. He was gone such a long time that his mother assumed, not unreasonably, that he had been killed. Although Villa-Lobos frequently cited the period of his travels as one of collecting folk melodies which he subsequently used in his major works, there is little evidence that he made a systematic effort to collect folk materials firsthand. However, he did acquire an extensive knowledge of his native country—its folk traditions, customs, and various kinds of musical styles.

Back in Rio de Janeiro by 1911, he began to establish himself as a musician and composer. In 1913 he married Lucilia Guimarães, a pianist and teacher at the National Institute of Music. Limited financial resources necessitated their moving into the small house of the Guimarães family. Villa-Lobos kept the family awake most of the night as he composed, usually beginning after the evening meal and working at the piano throughout the night. By 1915 he had collected a portfolio of works and arranged several concerts, the first of which was held in Nova Friburgo, a town in the state of Rio de Janeiro. By November of the same year he was ready for a complete program of his works in the the capital city of Rio de Janeiro.

The first review of Villa-Lobos's works were mixed. While recognizing a significant original talent, all the critics noted his lack of traditional training and disregard of conventional harmonic and formal principles of writing. In his attempt to find more acceptable expression for some of his musical ideas, Villa-Lobos was supported by his friend Darius Milhaud, who joined the staff of the French embassy in Rio in 1917. Milhaud encouraged Villa-Lobos to find his own way rather than imitate European models. With a recommendation from Arthur Rubinstein, Villa-Lobos secured funds in 1923 for a short trip to Europe, where he presented a few concerts of his music. In 1927 he obtained assistance for a longer stay, and with the help of Rubinstein and several Brazilian musicians in Paris, he performed several works at the Salle Gaveau, in Paris, on 24 October and 5 December 1927. With these performances Heitor Villa-Lobos established himself as a talented and original composer, and soon thereafter received invitations to present his music and conduct orchestras in London, Amsterdam, Vienna, Berlin, Brussels, Madrid, Liège, Lyon, and other European cities.

Villa-Lobos remained in Europe until 1930. With the country in a state of intense political disruption, Villa-Lobos decided to return to Europe to resume his career shortly after his arrival. In the meantime, however, he wrote a memorandum to the state government in São Paulo, expressing his distress at the condition of musical training and proposing a program of universal music education. He was summoned to appear at the governor's palace to defend his proposal. The next years were the busiest of Villa-Lobos's life. He postponed his plans to return to Europe and remained in São Paulo, and later Rio de Janeiro, as organizer and director of a program of choral singing, music education, and mass choral performances intended to instill patriotism. All of these programs were supported by the Getúlio VARGAS government. In 1944 Villa-Lobos visited the United States for the first time and during the final years of his life, he spent several months each year in Paris and New York.

Villa-Lobos wrote a torrent of musical works, variously estimated at two or three thousand, including arrangements and adaptations. Although he is recognized for his incredible fecundity and facility of musical writing, most of his music is unknown and has not been performed internationally, despite worldwide performances during the Villa-Lobos Centennial Celebrations in 1987 and 1988, which gave a broader representation of his life work. His sixteen *Choros* are a microcosm of the riches of Brazilian rhythmic invention and the diversity of its folk music. His *Nonetos,* although frequently referred to as chamber music, call for a gigantic percussion section. His late string quartets, written when the composer was near death, represent some of his finest writing. Individual works such as *Uirapurú* (The Magic Bird) draw their inspiration from various Brazilian myths and show the composer's mastery of orchestration. The best-known work of Villa-Lobos is the aria from *Bachianas brasileiras* no. 5, written in 1938. Because of his use of national and regional materials, he is regarded as a crucial figure in the development of Brazilian musical nationalism. Capturing, and building on, the urban salon music tradition of Ernesto Nazareth, Villa-Lobos molded diverse elements into a musical language that has been internationally recognized as an expression of both individual genius and the spirit of Brazilian music.

– DAVID P. APPLEBY

VILLACORTA CALDERÓN, JOSÉ ANTONIO

José Antonio Villacorta Calderón (*b.* 1879; *d.* unknown), Guatemalan historian, anthropologist, and bibliographer. Villacorta Calderón is particularly noted for his general histories of Guatemala and his important editorial work. Significantly, he edited the Maya sacred book *Anales de los Cakchiqueles* (1937). He also compiled in his *Bibliografía guatemalteca* (1944) a complete listing of bibliographic information for all the volumes exhibited at a national exposition in honor of the anniversary of printing in Guatemala in 1939. His most famous and widely read work, *Historia de la República de Guatemala* (1960), is a detailed survey of Guatemala, from political independence from Spain to 1885, based on extensive research in secondary and archival sources. Often used as a textbook in schools, the book has been influential in shaping the historical views of countless Guatemalans. Villacorta Calderón was one of the most significant and prestigious of the shapers of academic life in twentieth-century Guatemala.

– MICHAEL F. FRY

VILLAGRA, FRANCISCO DE

Francisco de Villagra (Villagrán; *b.* 1512?; *d.* 22 June 1563), Spanish conquistador. A soldier with experience in North Africa, Villagra went to America in 1537, and accompanied Pedro de VALDIVIA (1500–1553) on his expedition to Chile in 1540. During Valdivia's absence from the new colony in 1547–1548, he acted as interim governor, and in that capacity ordered the execution of Pedro SANCHO DE HOZ, who had plotted to seize control. In 1549 Valdivia sent him to fetch reinforcements from Peru, a mission he eventually completed after many adventures. Early in 1552, again on Valdivia's in-

structions, he attempted an overland expedition to the Strait of Magellan by way of the eastern side of the Andes, only to turn back at the Río Negro.

After Valdivia's death (December 1553), Villagra unsuccessfully claimed the governorship of Chile: his forcible seizure of the government was firmly resisted by the *cabildo* (municipal council) of Santiago. He remained an active leader in the warfare against the Araucanians, bringing about the defeat of the *toqui* (chief) LAUTARO in 1557. It was not until the departure of governor García HURTADO DE MENDOZA (1535–1609) that Villagra finally secured the governorship (1561–1563). On his death it passed to his cousin Pedro de Villagra (1563–1565), a brilliant tactician, who was eventually dismissed by the viceroy of Peru.

– SIMON COLLIER

VILLAGRÁ, GASPAR PÉREZ DE

Gaspar Pérez de Villagrá (*b.* 1555; *d.* 1620), soldier and chronicler. Born in New Spain, Villagrá was one of the few early creoles to study at the University of Salamanca. After his return to New Spain he was appointed *procurador general* (solicitor general) and captain in Juan de OÑATE's 1596 conquest and colonization expedition to New Mexico, where Villagrá participated in many operations, including the battle of Ácoma (1599). After a visit to Spain, Villagrá published his epic poem *Historia de la Nueva México* (1610), which related the history of the Oñate expedition. Although sometimes marked by hyperbole and heroic vision, Villagrá's *Historia* remains valuable today as an eyewitness account of the conquest of New Mexico.

His literary achievement notwithstanding, shortly afterward he was found guilty of executing two deserters in New Mexico and forcibly bringing dozens of Ácoman women to convents in Spain, for which he was banished from the province for six years and from Mexico City for two years. In 1620, en route from Spain to fill a bureaucratic position in Guatemala, Villagrá died at sea.

– AARON PAINE MAHR

VILLAGRÁN, JULIÁN AND JOSÉ MARÍA ("EL CHITO")

Julián and José María ("El Chito") Villagrán, Mexican insurgents. Julián Villagrán (*b.* 1760; *d.* 21 June 1813), his son Chito (*b.* ca. 1780; *d.* 14 May 1813), and their kinsmen, clients, and allies were in many ways typical of the great creole clans of lower and middling economic position who led the insurgency in the Mexican provinces in the period 1810–1821. Julián was a muleteer, minor landowner, and sometime militia officer; Chito, a delinquent and estate foreman in their native town of Huichapán in central Mexico. Chito joined the rebellion to escape legal charges against him for the murder of a local landowner and town official with

---

Chito joined the rebellion to escape legal charges against him for the murder of a local landowner.

---

whose wife he had been amorously involved; Julián, to protect his son and to pursue vague political and economic goals. Their forces attacked or occupied a number of important provincial towns from late 1810 through mid-1813, including Huichapán, Ixmiquilpán, Zimapán, and Tulancingo. Both refused to acknowledge any higher insurgent authority in their spheres of influence; both rejected royalist pardons; and both were captured and executed in 1813.

— ERIC VAN YOUNG

VILLAGRÁN KRAMER, FRANCISCO

Francisco Villagrán Kramer (*b.* 5 April 1922), vice president of Guatemala (1977–1980). Born in Guatemala City into a Protestant family, Francisco Villagrán earned his law degree at the University of San Carlos in 1951. Active in the October Revolution (1944), he served both Juan José ARÉVALO (1945–1951) and Jacobo ARBENZ (1950–1954) at international conferences. He helped Mario MÉNDEZ MONTENEGRO (1912–1965) found the Partido Revolucionario (PR) in 1957, but broke with the PR to organize the more leftist Revolutionary Unity Party (URD) in 1958.

Considered a radical, he was exiled by the Enrique PERALTA AZURDIA military regime (1963–1966) in 1965. The new constitution drafted that year raised the minimum age for the presidency from thirty-five to forty to specifically bar him from the 1966 elections.

Concerned about growing political polarization and violence, Villagrán returned to the PR in 1978 to become General Romeo LUCAS GARCÍA's (1978–1982) running mate in order to, in his words to a *Washington Post* reporter, "avoid a Custer's last stand in Guatemala." Failing to moderate the repressive character of the regime, he helped organize the Democratic Front Against Repression in 1979. He resigned as vice president in September 1980. He subsequently became a leader in the Christian Democratic Party (DCG), and also worked for the World Bank.

— ROLAND H. EBEL

VILLALBA, JÓVITO

Jóvito Villalba (*b.* 23 March 1908), Venezuelan political leader. A native of Nueva Esparta State, Villalba attended the Central University of Venezuela, where he became one of the most prominent members of the student Generation of 1928 as leader of the Venezuelan Students Federation. His eloquent oratory in opposition to the dictatorship of Juan Vicente GÓMEZ resulted in his imprisonment from 1928 to 1934. After 1935 the young lawyer was a founder and leader of influential political organizations. In 1946 he joined a new political party, the Republican Democratic Union (Unión Republicana Democrática—URD), and quickly rose to be its secretary-general, a post he held for decades. In 1952 he ran for president in a military-sponsored election, but his apparent victory over the official candidate was nullified by the military authorities, who promptly deported him. After his return from exile in the United States in 1958, Villalba became a principal architect of the new democratic political system. He headed the URD, served in Congress, and ran unsuccessfully as his party's presidential candidate in 1963 and 1973.

— WINFIELD J. BURGGRAAFF

VILLALONGA, JORGE

Jorge Villalonga (Conde de la Cueva; *b.* ca. 1665; active late seventeenth and early eighteenth centuries), viceroy of the New Kingdom of Granada (1719–1724). Philip V named Villalonga the first viceroy of the newly established Viceroyalty of New Granada in June 1717. Promoted from his position as governor of the Callao presidio, Villalonga was to effect the political reform program established by Antonio de la PEDROSA Y GUERRERO at the king's behest (1718–1719). Specifically, metropolitan officials expected Villalonga to solidify the Caribbean defenses of New Granada, curb smuggling, quell political infighting, promote economic development and so increase crown revenues, and project royal authority. From his very arrival in Santa Fe in November 1719 with demands for pomp, however, Villalonga provoked much internal opposition to his policies and demeanor. While Villalonga's *residencia* (end-of-tenure review) generally praised him, the king and his ministers judged his rule to be ineffective at best, for in late 1723 they decided to extinguish the viceroyalty and return the colony to *audiencia* rule. Villalonga returned to Spain in 1724 and became minister of war.

— LANCE R. GRAHN

VILLALPANDO, CRISTÓBAL DE

Cristóbal de Villalpando (*b.* ca. 1650; *d.* 20 August 1714), painter. Villalpando is responsible for the most agitated of Mexican colonial baroque paintings; he was also for many years an official of the painters' guild of Mexico City. There is considerable discussion about his training. Suggestions include study with José JUÁREZ, Antonio Rodríguez, and his father-in-law, Diego Mendoza of Puebla. Much is also made of the influence on his work of Baltasar de Echave Rioja. His works are found throughout Mexico and many are of enormous size, decorating vaults and entire walls. His earliest known paintings were for a retablo at Huaquechula, Puebla, signed and dated in 1675. Between 1684 and 1686 he executed four huge canvases for the sacristy of the cathedral of Mexico City, and in 1688 he painted the dome of the Capilla de los Reyes of Pueblo Cathedral. Often inventive in their iconography, his compositions recall Peter Paul Rubens and Juan de Valdés Leal. His brilliant coloring is sometimes shrill, and he makes generous use of shadow for dramatic effects. His production is uneven.

— CLARA BARGELLINI

VILLANUEVA, CARLOS RAÚL

Carlos Raúl Villanueva (b. 30 May 1900; d. October 1976), Venezuelan architect. Villanueva was educated in Paris at the Lycée Condorcet and the school of architecture of the École Nationale des Beaux-Arts, where he studied with Gabriel Héraud. Villanueva's projects were numerous and demonstrated a long-term vision devoted to re-creating the landscape of Caracas. In addition to acting as an architectural consultant to the Worker's Bank of Venezuela, he was a pioneer of urban renewal, planning El Silencio in Caracas, and the low-cost General Rafael Urdaneta housing developments in Maracaibo during the 1940s. Between 1944 and 1957 he designed several buildings for the University of Caracas, among them the library and the medical school. Villanueva is known for his design of "floating structures," which include his crowning achievements: the university's Olympic Stadium (1950) and the Olympic Swimming Pool (1957). Villanueva was the founder and first president of the Venezuelan Society of Architects; he was also a professor of ARCHITECTURE at the Central University of Venezuela.

— MICHAEL A. POLUSHIN

VILLARÁN, MANUEL VICENTE

Manuel Vicente Villarán (b. 11 October 1873; d. 21 February 1958), a leading authority on constitutional issues in early-twentieth-century Peru. Villarán was born in Lima. At the age of twenty-three, having received a degree in law, he joined the department of sociology at the University of San Marcos. In 1904 he

led the progressive Civilista faction that supported José PARDO Y BARREDA for president. He argued passionately for education, saying that Peru needed well-educated middle and working classes to forge a modern nation. But he also agreed with Javier PRADO Y UGARTECHE that the laziness and mental inertia of the indigenous people were the cause of the country's low level of development. He was minister of justice, religion, and instruction during Augusto LEGUÍA's first government (1908–1910) and helped to bring the first U.S. educators to Peru. In 1918 he wrote a newspaper essay, "Costumbres electorales," decrying the sorry state of political maturity of the Peruvian masses in the nineteenth century. In 1922 he became the rector of San Marcos and held that post until early 1924. Subsequently, he taught law and advised various governments during the 1920s and 1930s. After World War II he lived in virtual obscurity. Villarán's books include *El arbitraje de Washington en la cuestión peruanochilena* (1925), *Bosquejo histórico de la constitución inglesa*, 2d ed. (1935), and *La Universidad de San Marcos de Lima: Los orígenes, 1548–1577* (1938).

— VINCENT PELOSO

VILLARROEL LÓPEZ, GUALBERTO

Gualberto Villarroel López (b. 1908; d. 21 July 1946), president of Bolivia (1943–1946). Villarroel was a virtually unknown military officer when he came to power in a coup against the administration of General Enrique PEÑARANDA. An instructor in the reformist military college and a key figure in the secret nationalist military lodge Razón de Patria (the Nation's Right, known as RADEPA), Villarroel allied himself with the leftist-fascist Nationalist Revolutionary Movement (Movimiento Nacionalista Revolucionario—MNR) during the coup.

Under his government, largely dependent upon the MNR for popular support, important mine labor legislation was passed. In 1945 the government organized the First National Indian Congress, during which a thousand Indian leaders met. As a result, *pongueaje,* or free-labor services to the hacienda owners, was abolished, and other reforms were advanced, though the legislation was never enacted.

Despite its attempt at reform, the Villarroel regime brutally suppressed the opposition, executing various opposition leaders after a failed coup in 1944. Villarroel himself went to his death in 1946, when a teacher's strike turned violent. A mob stormed the presidential palace and hanged the president from a lamppost in the adjoining plaza.

The Villarroel regime is noted for its attempts at social reform and for the participation of the MNR, which in 1952 would lead Latin America's second social revolution.

— ERICK D. LANGER

VILLAS BÔAS BROTHERS

Villas Bôas Brothers, rights activists who became internationally known during the 1960s and 1970s for their defense of Brazilian Indians. Orlando (*b.* 1914), Cláudio (*b.* 1916), and Leonardo (*b.* 1918; *d.* 1961) Villas Bôas opposed the policy of the Brazilian government, which at that time favored rapid integration of Indians into the national society and economy. They argued strongly that reservations should be protected from outside influences for an indefinite period to protect Indian cultures and ways of life.

The brothers were members of the Roncador-Xingu expedition of 1943 sent to survey unexplored regions of central Brazil. Their experience with unacculturated Indians of the Upper Xingu River Basin convinced them to remain there and devote their lives to the welfare and protection of Indians. In 1954, when a devastating measles epidemic struck the Upper Xingu tribes, the Villas Bôas brothers mobilized the support of the Medical School of São Paulo, which set up a model program of medical assistance for the Indians.

Anthropologists, journalists, and other visitors were

impressed with the well-being and peace in which

the Indians of the park lived.

In 1961 the Villas Bôas brothers were instrumental in persuading the Brazilian government to set aside most of the Upper Xingu region (8,800 square miles) as a national park for protection of the Indians and wildlife preservation. The two surviving brothers, Orlando and Cláudio, became the administrators of the Xingu National Park. Anthropologists, journalists, and other visitors were impressed with the well-being and peace in which the Indians of the park lived. In 1967 the Villas Bôas brothers received the Founders' Gold Medal of the Royal Geographical Society and in 1971 they were nominated for the Nobel Peace Prize.

Some supporters of Indian self-determination have criticized the Villas Bôases' administration of the Xingu Park as overly protective and paternalistic. It has also been pointed out that idyllic images of the park disseminated in Brazil and abroad tend to mask the much less favorable conditions under which many Indians in other parts of the country live.

— NANCY M. FLOWERS

VILLAURRUTIA, JACOBO DE

Jacobo de Villaurrutia (*b.* May 1757; *d.* 23 August 1833), judge and journalist in Central America and Mexico. Jacobo de Villaurrutia López Osorio was born in the city of Santo Domingo on the island of Hispaniola. His father was Antonio Villaurrutia, a native of Mexico; his mother was María Antonieta López de Osorio. In his youth, he moved to Spain, where, as part of the family, he was a page for Francisco LORENZANA, archbishop of Mexico and later cardinal and archbishop of Toledo. Under Lorenzana's protection, Villaurrutia began his studies, completing the equivalent of a master's degree on 14 May 1781, and a doctorate in law four days later from the University of Toledo.

Villaurrutia began a successful career in public administration. On 2 November 1782 he was appointed magistrate and chief justice for Alcalá de Henares, a post he held for five years. In May 1792 he was named judge of the Audiencia of Guatemala, and later became a founder of the Sociedad Económica de Amigos del País (Economic Society of Friends of the Country). The purpose of this organization and similar ones in the Spanish dominions was to promote industry and the arts. They also promulgated the ideas of Spanish intellectuals through journalism.

Villaurrutia's innovative ideas led to his removal from his post in 1808 and transfer as a criminal court magistrate to Mexico City, where he continued his work in journalism, aided by Carlos María de BUSTAMANTE. His periodical was finally suppressed by Viceroy José de ITURRIGARAY. When problems arose as a result of Napoleon's invasion of Spain, Villaurrutia played an important role in opposing the Spanish authorities in Mexico, for which he was expelled from Mexico in 1814. Upon returning to Spain, he was appointed judge in Barcelona and became dean and internal regent. When Mexican independence was declared in 1821, he resigned and returned to Mexico, where he was appointed regent of the *audiencia* in 1822 and president of the Supreme Court of Justice in 1824. In 1827 he was circuit judge for the Federal District, the state of Mexico, and the territory of Tlaxcala. In November of the same year he was elected minister of the Supreme Court, and in 1831 he became its president. He died of cholera in Mexico City.

— OSCAR G. PELÁEZ ALMENGOR

VILLAURRUTIA, XAVIER

Xavier Villaurrutia (*b.* 27 March 1903; *d.* 25 December 1950), Mexican poet, critic, and playwright. Villaurrutia was born and died in Mexico City. He belonged to the generation known as the Contemporaries. With

Salvador NOVO, he participated in the review and theatrical group Ulises. He studied drama at Yale (1935–1936) and was one of the first professional writers of his country. He wrote an avant-garde novel (*Dama de corazones,* 1928) and the plays *Parece mentira* (1934), *¿En qué piensas?* (1938), and *La hiedra* (1941). His screenplays include *Vámonos con Pancho Villa* (1934) and *Distinto amanecer* (1943). He translated William Blake, André Gide, and many others and was a critic of literature, film, and the fine arts (*Textos y pretextos,* 1940). The most notable of his work, however, is his brief and rigorous poetry: *Reflejos* (1926), *Nocturnos* (1933), *Décima muerte* (1941), *Canto a la primavera* (1948), and especially *Nostalgia de la muerte* (Buenos Aires, 1938), in which the verbal creativity of the avant-garde is united with classic Spanish lyricism and a reflection on mortality reminiscent of Nahuatl poetry. His works were collected by Alí Chumacero, Luis Mario Schneider, and Miguel Capistrán (*Obras,* 2d ed. 1966). Eliot Weinenberg has translated *Nostalgia for Death* (1992), which includes an essay by Octavio PAZ.

                  — J. E. PACHECO

VILLAVERDE, CIRILO

Cirilo Villaverde (*b.* 28 October 1812; *d.* 20 October 1894), Cuban writer. Villaverde was born on a sugar plantation and, as a young writer and lawyer in Havana, he wrote romantic stories and accounts of his travels in his home province, Pinar del Río. Dedicated to freeing Cuba from Spanish control, Villaverde favored annexation by the United States and, to that end, worked as a secretary for General Narciso LÓPEZ. Because of his conspiratorial activities, Villaverde was imprisoned by the Spaniards in 1848. One year later, he escaped to the United States, where he worked as a teacher, married fellow Cuban Emilia Casanova, and continued contributing to Spanish-speaking publications.

    Villaverde resided in the United States until 1858, and then again from 1861 until his death. In 1882 he published *Cecilia Valdés,* a novel about Spanish colonialism and slavery in early-nineteenth-century Cuba. It shows how the Cuban oligarchy's push toward modernization of the sugar industry had dramatic consequences for the slaves, symbolized by the book's eponymous female protagonist. With this novel of manners, more than with any other work, Villaverde secured his place in Cuban literary history.

                  — INEKE PHAF

VILLAZÓN, ELIODORO

Eliodoro Villazón (*b.* 22 January 1848; *d.* 14 September 1940), president of Bolivia (1909–1913). Born in Sacaba in the department of Cochabamba, Villazón was trained as a lawyer. He entered politics and became deputy from Cochabamba to the Assembly of 1871 when he was only twenty-three years old. At the National Convention of 1880 he caught the attention of Narciso CAMPERO, the recently installed president (1880–1884). Under Campero, Villazón was appointed minister of finance and later financial agent in Europe. After returning from abroad, Villazón joined the Liberal Party and became one of its most loyal members. When the Liberals came to power after the Federal War of 1898, Villazón became minister of foreign affairs. In 1909 the leader of the Liberals, Ismael MONTES, who had been president from 1904 to 1908, selected Villazón to be the party's presidential candidate in a special election made necessary by the death of Montes's successor. Elected overwhelmingly, Villazón, as caretaker for Montes, continued government support for railroad construction and successfully negotiated loans with Europeans that led to the formation of the Banco de la Nación.

                  — ERWIN P. GRIESHABER

VILLEDA MORALES, RAMÓN

Ramón Villeda Morales (*b.* 1908; *d.* 8 October 1971), Honduran president (1957–1963). Villeda Morales studied medicine in Europe and Honduras. Called the "Little Bird" for his small stature and oratorical prowess, he was also known for his cosmopolitan polish, rare in Honduran politicians. He dominated the Liberal Party as chairman and founded the party newspaper, *El Pueblo.* Although he won a plurality in the 1954 presidential election, a subsequent coup deprived him of office.

    In 1957 Villeda Morales came to power after a military coup overthrew Julio LOZANO DÍAS. Between the coup and his inauguration, Villeda Morales seems to have participated in a pact of the Blue Water (named after the United Fruit Company villa where the clandestine pact was apparently devised). He agreed to conform radical agrarian and labor reforms to Alliance for Progress ideology in return for ample U.S. aid and Honduran military support. The 1958 labor code brought realistic worker benefits. The 1962 Agrarian Reform Law nationalized, with compensation, undeveloped land for peasants. In response to the 1954 United Fruit strike, peasant organizations were legalized. However, Villeda Morales's close relationship with Serafino Remauldi, a Central Intelligence Agency (CIA) operative and labor representative, assured that an AFL-CIO alliance of peasant and labor organizations dominated labor.

The limited reforms of Villeda Morales nonetheless brought conservative opposition and charges of Communist infiltration. Afraid that the 1963 Liberal presidential candidate would make good on Villeda Morales's "second republic" rhetoric, military chief Oswaldo LÓPEZ ARELLANO staged a successful coup two months before the election.

Several factors point to CIA involvement in the Arellano coup. Villeda Morales, who had CIA links through Remauldi, piqued the agency by pushing for a more radical successor. This apparently prompted CIA endorsement of Arellano's coup. Also, CIA backing is indicated by the quick commendation of the coup by the U.S. ambassador and the Voice of America, although this support was repudiated by the U.S. State Department.

Arriving in New York in 1971 as Honduran ambassador to the United Nations, Villeda Morales suffered a fatal heart attack. The Honduran Liberal Party continues to invoke the memory of Villeda Morales as a Kennedyesque figure.

— EDMOND KONRAD

VILLEGAIGNON, NICOLAS DURAND DE

Nicolas Durand de Villegaignon (*b.* 1510; *d.* 29 January 1572), French colonizer in Brazil. Born in Provins, Villegaignon was a knight of Malta and nephew of the Grand Master. He served under Emperor Charles V at Algiers and fought the Turks in Hungary and at Tripoli. An experienced seaman, Villegaignon defied the English fleet by escorting Mary Stuart (later called Mary Queen of Scots) to France to marry the dauphin. Villegaignon, a warrior and humanist, anguished over spiritual matters and at one point embraced Calvinism.

As vice-admiral of Brittany, he interested Admiral Gaspard de Coligny in using Brazil, a land already visited by Normans and Bretons, as a sanctuary for Protestant refugees. In November 1555, with three boats manned by Catholics and Protestants, Villegaignon arrived at Guanabara Bay. He fortified a small island as a base for further exploration, naming the colony La France Antarctique. Encouraged by the reformer John Calvin, three hundred Protestants arrived in March 1557. Villegaignon, noted for his generous treatment of the native peoples, was less forgiving to the Protestants, whom he punished harshly for even slight transgressions. He returned to France in 1559, leaving his nephew in charge.

The newly arrived French colonists encountered resistance from the established Portuguese settlers in Brazil. Deemed heretics by the Portuguese, they supported the indigenous peoples against their colonial overlords.

With only seventy-four men, the French held out for twenty days until the Portuguese (led by Mem de Sá) took the island and razed the fort. Survivors fled to the mainland to live among the native people. Villegaignon finally conceded the colonial rights to Portugal, and he remained in France until his death.

— PHILIPPE BONNICHON

VILLEGAS, OSCAR

Oscar Villegas (*b.* 18 March 1943), Mexican playwright. Villegas, a native of Ciudad del Maíz and a graduate of the directing program of the National Institute of Fine Arts, is generally considered to be the most talented playwright of his generation. His inveterate experimentation produces plays rich in interesting techniques, including one, *El señor y la señora* (1969), in which the speeches are not identified by character. His themes are contemporary and sometimes shocking: youth, love, sex, myths, values, and traditions, presented most often in one-act plays. Villegas's two major plays are *Atlántida* (1976), which takes place in a declining society without values, and *Mucho gusto en conocerlo* (1985), which also paints the hypocrisy and perversions that assault human sensibilities. Difficult economic and theatrical conditions in Mexico have hindered productions of Villegas's works; by occupation he is a ceramicist.

— GEORGE WOODYARD

VINCENT, STÉNIO JOSEPH

Sténio Joseph Vincent (*b.* 1874; *d.* 1959), president of Haiti (1930–1941). A member of the mulatto elite, Vincent was a lawyer, diplomat, and politician. He served as the mayor of Port-au-Prince and went on several diplomatic missions to Paris, Berlin, and the

Vincent declared the Haitian Senate "in rebellion to the will of the people" and expelled its members from the chamber.

Hague. Vincent headed both the anti-interventionist Nationalist Party and the Patriotic Union and gained the presidency on the basis of his opposition to the U.S. occupation. Vincent was elected president by the National Assembly in November 1930. Although he entered office committed to the principle of parliamentary government, he based his power on officially controlled plebiscites.

As president, Vincent was widely regarded as partial toward mulattoes. He was particularly suspicious of the *Garde d'Haiti,* a predominantly black national guard organized by the U.S. Marines. As such he built up his own special presidential guard, which kept its weapons in the National Palace. In 1934 Vincent visited the United States and convinced President Franklin D. Roosevelt to withdraw the U.S. Marines. Thereafter, Vincent's fervent nationalism abated somewhat. In 1935 Vincent extended his tenure in office by five years. In addition, he declared the Senate "in rebellion to the will of the people" and expelled its members from the chamber. He then made several overtures to improve U.S.-Haitian relations and to attract U.S. tourists, such as offering to amend a law that would have facilitated casino gambling.

Vincent's popularity waned, however, because of his antipathy toward blacks and his weak reaction to the Dominican massacre of Haitians in 1937. In 1941 Vincent decided against having his term in office extended again and instead retired peaceably. He died in Port-au-Prince.

— DOUGLAS R. KEBERLEIN

VIÑES Y MARTORELL, BENITO

Benito Viñes y Martorell (*b.* 19 September 1837; *d.* 23 July 1893), pioneer of hurricane forecasting. A Jesuit priest born in Catalonia, Spain, Viñes was sent to Havana to take charge of the Belén Observatory (Belén was a Jesuit preparatory school), where he carried out his scientific work for the rest of his life. He was well acquainted with all that was then known about hurricanes, which amounted to very little as far as the signs announcing their coming or their passing were concerned. He devoted his life to finding a way to detect these signs.

Viñes began by studying the movements of the clouds that he called "featherlike cirrostratus." He then combined the data he gathered with information about the relationship between changes in barometric pressure and the paths of hurricanes that had blown through at the same time in previous years. After a while, he found it possible to predict, within certain limits, the path that a hurricane would follow. On 11 September 1875 he was able to make the first accurate hurricane forecast in history. A year later, again in September, the only sea captain who did not heed his warning lost his ship in the Straits of Florida.

In time Viñes was able to establish a network of information sources in the Caribbean. But he never had at his disposal the sophisticated observing tools that are available today, and thus his "laws of the hurricanes"

(which also explained the structure of these tropical storms) have been superseded by researchers. This does not mean, however, that the essential validity of his observations has been proved erroneous. On the contrary, according to Dr. Neil L. Frank, director of the U.S. National Hurricane Center, they have been rediscovered and confirmed. Viñes's work is a historical landmark in the field of hurricane forecasting. Viñes died in Havana.

— JOSÉ M. HERNÁNDEZ

VIOLA, ROBERTO EDUARDO

Roberto Eduardo Viola (*b.* 13 October 1924; *d.* 10 October 1994), military leader and president of Argentina (1981). Born in the city of Buenos Aires, he graduated from the Military Academy (Colegio Militar) in 1944. While a colonel, Viola served as an Argentine representative to the Inter-American Defense Board in Washington, D.C. (1967–1968). In 1975 he was promoted to chief of the General Staff, the number two position in the army. He was deeply involved in the Dirty War (1970–82) against the urban guerrillas. On 31 July 1978 he was promoted to commander in chief of the Argentine Army. In 1981 he succeeded General Jorge VIDELA as the senior member of the military junta and president of the republic. In early November, Viola fell ill. Although he recovered, General Leopoldo GALTIERI politically outmaneuvered him in the ruling military junta and by 29 December had seized the presidency, forcing Viola into retirement. On 9 December 1985 Viola was sentenced to seventeen years in prison for his participation in the Dirty War. In December 1990 he was released under a general amnesty.

— ROBERT SCHEINA

VISCARDO Y GUZMÁN, JUAN PABLO

Juan Pablo Viscardo y Guzmán (*b.* 20 June 1748; *d.* February 1798), Peruvian Jesuit. Viscardo was born in Pampacolca (region of Arequipa) into a long-established creole family. He entered the Society of Jesus in 1761 and, although still a novice, was affected by the expulsion of the Jesuits ordered by Charles III in 1767. Early the following year Viscardo went to Cádiz, a trip which marked the beginning of an exile that took him to Italy, France, and England, where he died.

Viscardo is best known for his inflammatory "Letter to Spanish Americans," published in French in 1799 and in a Spanish translation in London in 1801. In it, Viscardo cataloged the alleged tyranny of colonial Spanish rule for three centuries and forcefully outlined why the colonies should be independent. Some historians consider him the "first and most important ideological precursor of Hispanic American independence." It has yet to be demonstrated, however, that his "Letter" was a significant stimulus for independence.

— MARK A. BURKHOLDER

VISCONTI, ELISEU D'ANGELO

Eliseu d'Angelo Visconti (*b.* 1866; *d.* 1944) Brazilian painter. Born in Italy, Visconti came to Brazil as an infant with his family. Although he studied music during his youth, he chose painting over the violin. He took his first art classes at the Liceu de Artes e Ofícios (School of Arts and Crafts) in Rio de Janeiro. Then in 1885 he enrolled in Brazil's Imperial Academy of Fine Arts, where his talents were quickly recognized. During the first artistic competition of the republic, Visconti won a travel award that allowed him to study in Europe. While there, he won prizes and recognition as a student at the École des Beaux Arts in Paris and took classes at the School Guérin, where he studied decorative art under the tutelage of Eugène Grasset.

He returned to Brazil in 1897 and by 1901 had his first individual exhibition, showing eighty-eight works. In 1905, while in Paris, he received a governmental commission from Brazil, the first of many, to execute a panel painting destined for the entrance of the Municipal Theater in Rio de Janeiro. For the foyer, ceiling, and proscenium of the theater, he also did paintings celebrating the arts through allegorical themes.

In 1946 Brazil's National Museum of Fine Arts organized a retrospective of his works that included 285 oil paintings as well as watercolors, drawings, and decorative pieces. Visconti's work is stylistically eclectic with influences drawn from impressionism and realism. He once referred to himself as a "presentist" who produces an art that is constantly changing and modifying.

— CAREN A. MEGHREBLIAN

VITALINO PEREIRA DOS SANTOS, MESTRE

Mestre Vitalino Pereira dos Santos (*b.* 1909; *d.* 1963), Brazilian sculptor. Mestre Vitalino's work was virtually unknown until 1947 when the Pernambucan painter and illustrator Augusto Rodrigues saw his art and recognized that his miniature clay figurines represented a new popular ceramic tradition for Brazil. The sculptures recount daily life among the inhabitants and their animals in the backlands of Vitalino's home state of Pernambuco. Unlike other popular ceramicists of his time, Vitalino sculpted them with a softness of line and curve, and imbued them with wit and subtle irony. His work was included in the 1948 Exposição de Arte Popular in

Rio de Janeiro. Prior to 1953 Vitalino grouped together and painted his subjects. Later, his compositions focused on single figures, which he left unpainted. He influenced the popular artists Nó Caboclo and Zé Rodriguez. Vitalino's sons continued the tradition popularized by their father.

— CAREN A. MEGHREBLIAN

VITERI Y UNGO, JORGE

Jorge Viteri y Ungo (*b.* 23 April 1802; *d.* 25 July 1853), bishop of El Salvador and Nicaragua. Born in San Salvador of Spanish parents and educated in Guatemala, Viteri was active in the politics of Central America following the collapse of the federation. A noted orator and a leading adviser to Rafael CARRERA, who was close to the Guatemalan conservative elite, he became a member of the Guatemalan Council of State in 1840. In 1842 he visited the Vatican, where he secured establishment of a separate diocese of El Salvador, to which Pope Gregory XVI named him the first bishop. Viteri also arranged for appointment of Francisco de Paula GARCÍA PELÁEZ as archbishop of Guatemala.

Viteri was an active force in Salvadoran politics in alliance with General Francisco MALESPÍN, but when Malespín ordered the execution of a priest, Pedro Crespín, in 1845, Viteri excommunicated Malespín. Opposition to Viteri's meddling in politics forced him out of El Salvador in 1846. He went to Nicaragua, where the Vatican formally named him bishop of Nicaragua and Costa Rica on 5 November 1849. He was active in the politics of Nicaragua until his death.

— RALPH LEE WOODWARD, JR.

VITIER, CINTIO

Cintio Vitier (*b.* 25 September 1921), Cuban essayist, poet, and literary critic. The son of prominent Cuban educator Medardo Vitier, Cintio Vitier was born in Key West and spent most of his childhood in Matanzas, Cuba. In 1935 he moved to Havana, where from 1942 to 1947 he was editor of the literary journal *Clavileño*. Although he received a law degree from the University of Havana, he never entered the profession. During his student years he became part of the literary group that revolved around the magazine *Orígenes*, through which he befriended the founder, José LEZAMA LIMA, as well as the poets Eliseo DIEGO and Fina García Marruz, whom he married in 1947. Between 1947 and 1961 he taught French and compiled key anthologies of Cuban poetry, including *Diez poetas cubanos, 1937–1947* (1948), *Cincuenta años de poesía cubana, 1902–1952* (1952), and *Los grandes románticos cubanos* (1960).

Vitier is best known for his literary analysis. One of his books on this subject, *Lo cubano en la poesía* (1957, repr. 1970), is still considered one of the most sensitive, authoritative works defining the Cuban poetic sensibility.

Vitier has edited critical editions of the complete works of José MARTÍ and, along with Fina García Marruz, is the recognized authority on Martí within the island. (He was director of the José Martí wing of the National Library from 1968 to 1973 and a researcher at the Centro Martiano from 1987 to 1988.) He has edited several literary publications, including *La Nueva Revista Cubana, Anuario Martiano,* and *Revista de la Biblioteca Nacional "José Martí."* Since 1959 he has represented Cuba at numerous international cultural activities. As of the mid-1990s, he was retired and living in Cuba.

— ROBERTO VALERO

VITORIA, FRANCISCO DE

Francisco de Vitoria (*b.* 1486; *d.* 12 August 1546), one of the founders of international law. Francisco de Vitoria, a Dominican friar, was the *prima* (senior) professor of theology at the University of Salamanca (1526–1546). His published works include *De Indis I* (1537/1538) and *De Indis II* or *Dure jure belli* (1538/1539), collections of lectures published posthumously. Vitoria outlined the rights of Spaniards in the New World and

---

Vitoria argued that Spaniards should respect the political sovereignty and property rights of the native peoples they found in the Indies.

---

wrestled with the moral questions raised when a government founded on Christian principles imposes its will on pagans. Subscribing to the Thomistic theory that all men (including pagans) are rational beings who belong to a worldwide community based on natural law and a law of nations (*jus gentium*), Vitoria argued that Spaniards should respect the political sovereignty and property rights of the native peoples they found in the Indies. Thus, Spaniards did not have any inherent rights over subjects in the New World based on jurisdiction. War was justified only if natives prevented Spaniards from trading and living with them in peace, practiced cannibalism, refused to allow missionaries to preach, or discouraged conversion to Christianity.

— SUZANNE HILES BURKHOLDER

VIVANCO, MANUEL IGNACIO

Manuel Ignacio Vivanco (*b.* 1806; *d.* 1873), conservative Peruvian military caudillo. Born in Lima, the son of a Spanish merchant, Vivanco was educated in the traditional San Carlos school. He joined the independence forces to fight the decisive battles of Junín and Ayacucho. After Independence Vivanco sided with several military leaders, including Pedro Bermúdez, the conservative Felipe Santiago SALAVERRY, and Agustín GAMARRA, who opposed the Peru-Bolivia Confederation. In 1841, Vivanco campaigned on behalf of his own "regenerating" movement with the undemocratic intent of strong government to end the caudillo struggle.

Especially strong in the southern provinces of Arequipa, Vivanco was able to control power during the multiple military uprisings of the early 1840s. However, in 1844, his archenemy, General Ramón CASTILLA, was able to defeat Vivanco's forces and initiate a gradual reorganization of the Peruvian state. Vivanco continued to oppose Castilla. In the elections of 1850 he ran against Castilla's official candidate, José R. ECHENIQUE. In 1856 he started a revolution against Castilla in Arequipa. During the beleaguered regime of Juan Antonio PEZET, Vivanco was the Peruvian representative who in 1865 signed the popularly repudiated Vivanco-Pareja Treaty that led to the ousting of Pezet and the decline of Vivanco's popularity. He died in Valparaíso, Chile.

— ALFONSO W. QUIROZ

VIZCAÍNO, SEBASTIÁN

Sebastián Vizcaíno (*b.* 1548; *d.* 1623), Spanish explorer and cartographer of the Californias. A native of Estremadura, Vizcaíno was a cavalry commander in the invasion of Portugal in 1580. He went to New Spain in 1583 and became merchant-militia commander at Manila in 1586. He conducted explorations in connection with his pearl-fishing monopoly, in the Gulf of California, from June to November 1596, founding La Paz on 13 September. Vizcaíno was general of an expedition that charted and mapped the Pacific coast of the Californias from 5 May 1602 to 21 February 1603; it also gave place-names from Cabo San Lucas to Cabo Blanco (in present-day Oregon). He was chief magistrate of Tehuantépec in 1604 and opened a supply route from Coatzocoalcos to the Pacific in 1606. After being granted an *encomienda* in the province of Ávalos in 1607, Vizcaíno served as the first European ambassador and cartographer in Japan (March 1611–January 1614). In October–November 1615 Vizcaíno repelled Dutch corsairs led by Joris von Spilbergen in Colima. After serving as chief magistrate of Acapulco (1616), he retired in 1619 to Mexico City, where he died.

— W. MICHAEL MATHES

VOLIO JIMÉNEZ, JORGE

Jorge Volio Jiménez (*b.* 26 August 1882; *d.* 20 October 1955), Costa Rican politician. Volio Jiménez was born in Cartago, Costa Rica, to a bourgeois family. From a young age, he held Christian and reformist ideas, in pursuit of which he formed study groups and in 1902 created the daily *La Justicia Social.* In 1903 he went to the University of Lovain in Belgium to study for the priesthood. He was ordained in 1909, at which time he also received a master's degree in philosophy. He then took his Christian-socialist ideas back to his country and worked as priest and professor. In 1911, his fighting spirit took him to Nicaragua, where he participated in the resistance against the U.S. intervention. In 1915, he left the priesthood in order to work as a journalist and professor. Between 1917 and 1919 he fought against the dictatorship of General Federico TINOCO in Costa Rica, whose defeat in the battle of El Jobo led to the reestablishment of a liberal democracy. In 1920 Volio Jiménez received the rank of major general. In 1922 he was elected to Congress and in 1923 he formed the Reformist Party, of which he was a candidate for president.

During the 1920s, Volio Jiménez outlined a reformist ideology that questioned the liberal system and the dominant oligarchy and advocated reforms favoring the working class. His program called for state intervention to obtain agrarian reform, civil rights, tax reform, political democracy, a public university, and protection of the nation's resources. He played an important role in awakening the workers, peasants, and middle class to political participation, and several of his ideas were later put into practice, especially during the 1940s. Owing to his alliance with the liberals, he served as vice president of the republic from 1924 to 1926. In 1932 he participated in a failed coup d'état and later retired from politics. Between 1940 and 1948, he was dean of Philosophy and Letters at the University of Costa Rica. From 1954 until his death in San José, Costa Rica, he served in Congress.

— JORGE MARIO SALAZAR

VON VACANO, ARTURO

Arturo Von Vacano (*b.* 1938), Bolivian writer and journalist born in La Paz. Except for *El apocalipsis de Antón* (1972), an allegorical novel dealing with the violence and contradictions of a drastically stratified society in a setting marked by native cultural sacredness, the narrative of Von Vacano is highly autobiographical. *Sombra de exilio* (1970) concerns the reaching of adulthood during the Revolution of 1952 and the following years. *Morder el silencio* (1980) continues the experience of the man in *Sombra de exilio* and sets forth the impossibility of a literary vocation in a social context paralyzed by military dictatorship, violence, and the predominance of utilitarian values. All of Von Vacano's narrative strongly criticizes power and is characterized by a sense of blocked social redemption. *Morder el silencio* has been published in English as *Biting Silence* (1987), with the translation by Von Vacano himself. Von Vacano has published short pieces in Bolivian literary magazines and newspapers. Fleeing Bolivia in 1980, he lived as an exile in the United States, working as a writer, editor, and translator for United Press International in New York and Washington, D.C.

— ANA REBECA PRADA

WALCOTT, DEREK

Derek Walcott (*b.* 23 January 1930), poet, playwright, and painter from Saint Lucia in the Lesser Antilles. Winner of the 1992 Nobel Prize for literature, Walcott was the first native of the Caribbean to win this prestigious award. Given the award for, among other works, his book *Omeros* (1990), an epic poem divided into sixty-four chapters, the academy cited Walcott for his "historical vision, the outcome of a multi-cultural commitment." Walcott has been described as "the best poet the English language has today." Of both African and European ancestry, Walcott describes himself as "the divided child of the wrong color," and much of Walcott's artistic efforts have concentrated on his own multiethnic heritage.

Of both African and European ancestry,

Walcott describes himself as

"the divided child of the wrong color."

Born in 1930 in Castries, Saint Lucia, his grandmothers on both sides were descended from slaves, while both of his grandfathers were European. Walcott's parents were both educators, and he grew up amid books and received strong encouragement to pursue his education. Walcott's father died when the younger Walcott was only one year old, and along with his twin brother and sister, Walcott was raised by his mother. His first published work, *25 Poems* (1948), appeared when he was only eighteen years old. He was denied a scholarship to study in England, so in 1950 he went to Jamaica to study on scholarship at the University of the West Indies, where he majored in French, Latin, and Spanish. In 1953 Walcott moved to Trinidad, and in the late 1950s he left there for New York City, where he founded his own repertory company, the Trinidad Theatre Workshop.

The book that first brought Walcott recognition was a collection of his poems entitled *In a Green Night* (1962). In 1986 Walcott won the Los Angeles Times Book Prize for his *Collected Poems* (1986), which includes selections from all his major works, especially *Sea Grapes* (1975), as well as the entire text of *Another Life*

(1973) and his autobiography in verse. In 1988 he became the first Commonwealth citizen to be awarded the Queen's Gold Medal for Poetry. In 1991 he was awarded the W. H. Smith Literary Award in Britain. Also a noted playwright, Walcott won an Obie Award in 1971 for his play, *Dream on Monkey Mountain* (1970), which in 1994 was produced in Sweden. But Walcott's expression of the Caribbean experience through poetry was what brought him the Nobel Prize. Most recently, Walcott has worked to produce his play *Odyssey,* a retelling of the Homeric epic using Walcott's store of characters, images, and slang from his own Caribbean background.

Walcott's life has not been devoid of controversy. In 1981, while teaching at Harvard University, a student of Walcott's accused him of sexual harassment. After looking into the charges, the university wrote a letter of reproachment to Boston University, where Walcott had begun teaching.

From the early 1980s, Walcott taught poetry and creative writing at Boston University, while dividing his time between Trinidad and the United States. In 1994 he was working on a stage translation of Homer's *Odyssey* for the Royal Shakespeare Company. Married three times, Walcott had three children by the early 1990s.

– MICHAEL POWELSON

WALKER, WILLIAM

William Walker (*b.* 8 May 1824; *d.* 12 September 1860). The most famous American filibuster, Walker conquered Nicaragua in 1855–1856. His various expeditions to Mexico and Central America from 1853 to 1860 fostered anti-Americanism in the region. In particular his impact upon Nicaragua, which suffered extensive property destruction and much loss of life because of his involvement there, was especially profound and lingers to this day. Walker's expeditions interrupted normal transit across Nicaragua's isthmus and embroiled the United States in disputes with Mexico, the countries of Central America, Colombia, and Great Britain.

EARLY LIFE. Walker was born in Nashville, Tennessee, and graduated from the University of Nashville in 1838. He received an M.D. degree from the University of Pennsylvania in 1843 and furthered his medical education in Europe, after which he spent several years in law, journalism, and politics in New Orleans and California. Perhaps curiously, given his later military escapades, surviving documents describe the slightly built Walker as a shy, somewhat effeminate youth. Several scholars have argued that the death in 1849 of Ellen Galt Martin, a deaf mute with whom he had fallen in love, radically transformed Walker's personality and paved the way for his filibustering career.

EXPEDITION TO MEXICO. The self-proclaimed "Colonel" Walker's filibusters began on October 1853, when, aboard the schooner *Caroline,* he departed San Francisco with forty-five followers bound for Mexico's Baja (Lower) California but actually intending the eventual conquest of the Mexican state of Sonora. Walker captured La Paz on 3 November, raised a flag with two stars signifying Lower California and Sonora, proclaimed the creation of the Republic of Lower California, and soon announced himself president. Mexican resistance forced Walker to flee to Ensenada, which he proclaimed his capital. Reinforcements from California arrived there, but Walker experienced supply deficiencies and made the mistake of provoking resistance from Antonio María Melendrez by attacking the ranch of Melendrez's father.

On 18 January 1854, Walker proclaimed the formation of the Republic of Sonora, consisting of the states of Sonora and Lower California. In March, Walker and about one hundred filibusters set out for Sonora. He crossed the Colorado River into Sonora on 4 April but soon returned to Lower California. Harassed by Mexican guerrillas, Walker retreated northward, crossing the U.S. border with his thirty-three remaining followers on 8 May and surrendered to U.S. military authorities. In October, a jury in San Francisco acquitted Walker of violating American neutrality laws. By threatening Mexico with uncompensated territorial losses, however, Walker's expedition may have helped persuade Mexico to cede, in a treaty signed on 30 December 1853, the territory which became known as the Gadsden Purchase.

EXPEDITIONS TO CENTRAL AMERICA. Though Walker became one of the most despised figures in Central American history, he initially entered Nicaragua's affairs by invitation. Locked in conflict with the Legitimist, or Conservative, ruling party in Nicaragua, that country's Democrats, or Liberals, contracted in 1854 for Walker to bring three hundred filibusters (described as colonists, to avoid flagrantly violating U.S. neutrality statutes) to Nicaragua and occupy 52,000 acres of land. Walker and fifty-seven men calling themselves the Immortals departed San Francisco on 4 May 1855 and arrived in Nicaragua in June. As colonel of *La Falange*

Americana (the American phalanx), Walker captured Granada, the Legitimist capital, on 13 October.

In a subsequently negotiated agreement, Walker became commander in chief of the Nicaraguan army under a coalition government. When he came into possession of letters by Minister of War Ponciano Corral, the former Legitimist Army commander, soliciting intervention from other Central American states to oust Walker, he had an excuse to eliminate his most formidable rival by having him executed for treason. From November 1855 to June 1856, Walker ruled Nicaragua through a figurehead, President Patricio RIVAS. Walker received reinforcements, assisted by the Accessory Transit Company, an American enterprise holding a monopoly over isthmian transit across Nicaragua. The weekly English- and Spanish-language publication *El Nicaragüense* testified to Walker's Americanization of the country. To encourage native support, the paper dubbed Walker the Gray-eyed Man, after a Mosquito Indian legend.

In May 1856, the United States recognized Rivas's government. Following Rivas's break with Walker that June, the filibuster was elected president on June 29 in a controlled election. Inaugurated on 12 July, Walker entertained visions of one day ruling all Central America. However, the loss of U.S. recognition, growing U.S. interference with his supply of reinforcements, armed interventions by other Central American states receiving support from Great Britain, the opposition of shipping magnate Cornelius Vanderbilt, and epidemic disease combined to undermine Walker's cause. His reestablishment of slavery in a 22 September decree won him increased favor in the slave states of the American Union, but this move could not save his regime. Forced to evacuate Granada, Walker had the city destroyed.

On 1 May 1857, Walker surrendered to U.S. naval captain Charles H. Davis and subsequently returned to the United States. Still claiming the presidency of Nicaragua, Walker devoted the rest of his life to filibustering schemes.

In 1860, landing at Trujillo, Honduras, by way of Ruatán and Cozumel, Walker eventually surrendered to British naval commander Norvell Salmon, who in turn handed him over to Honduran authorities. He was executed at Trujillo by a local firing squad on 12 September 1860.

— ROBERT E. MAY

WALLACE, PETER

Peter Wallace (*fl.* 1630s), Scottish buccaneer. According to popular legend, Captain Peter Wallace (Willis) was the first European to harbor inside the barrier reef along the coast of present-day Belize. His base of operations was said to be founded in 1638 near the mouth of the Belize River. Wallace captained the *Swallow*, out of Tortuga Island, and Swallow Cay off the coast of Belize City is said to have been named after his ship. His name in Spanish became "Wallix" and later "Valis" or "Ballese" and was used as the name for the settlement at the mouth of the Belize River. Emory King, president of the Belize Historical Society, favors this thesis and notes that recently discovered documents from the Bay Islands refer to the area as "Wallix" or "Wallis."

His name in Spanish became "Wallix" and later "Valis" or "Ballese" and was used as the name for the settlement at the mouth of the Belize River.

Other theories suggest that Belize may be of Maya origin from the word *belix,* meaning "muddy water" or *belakin,* meaning "land that looks toward the sea." It is also possible that the name Belize is derived from the Spanish term *baliza* or the French term *balise,* meaning "lighthouse" or other sea marker indicating dangerous conditions, the mouth of an important river, or the site of previous wrecks. In the eighteenth century, for example, the Spanish referred to a small settlement at the mouth of the Mississippi River as the *belize.*

— BRIAN E. COUTTS

WEFFORT, FRANCISCO CORREIA

Francisco Correia Weffort (*b.* 17 May 1937), one of Brazil's leading political scientists, known for his probing analysis of populism, syndicalism, and the role of leftist- and labor-based political movements in the consolidation of democracy in Brazil and other Latin American nations with a history of authoritarian and corporatist regimes. A 1962 graduate of the University of São Paulo, Weffort has taught in Brazil and abroad. He is a faculty member of the Political Science Department of the University of São Paulo and a founding member of the Center for the Study of Contemporary Culture. Weffort was one of the original founders of the Workers Party (PT), serving as its secretary-general in the early 1980s. In 1995 he became minister of culture under President Fernando Henrique Cardoso.

— DARYLE WILLIAMS

WEINGÄRTNER, PEDRO

Pedro Weingärtner (*b.* 1853; *d.* 1929), Brazilian painter. Born in Pôrto Alegre, Weingärtner did not take up painting until he went to Germany in 1879. After four years in Hamburg and Karlsruhe, he moved to Paris, where he studied under the painters Tony Robert-Fleury and Adolphe Bouguereau. In 1885 he received a travel award from the personal coffers of the Brazilian emperor Dom Pedro II that allowed him to continue his artistic training in Italy. Before leaving for Rome, however, he had his first exhibition. The ten paintings he showed were received favorably, and one critic was so impressed with Weingärtner's drawing abilities that he declared him "Brazil's first painter." While in Rome, he executed genre paintings and paintings with themes drawn from classical subject matter. Examples include *Bad Harvest, Jealousies, Bacanal,* and *Cock Fights.* The French press criticized *Cock Fights* when it was shown at the Paris Salon because it was a copy of Jean-Léon Gérôme's painting of the same title. Weingärtner's first gaucho paintings were exhibited in 1892. Paintings such as *Late Arrival* and *Tangled Threads* affirmed his talent.

Throughout his later life, Weingärtner spent many years living and painting in Rome. In spite of the winds of modernism, he remained devoted to themes of daily life, classical subject matter, and life among the gauchos in Pôrto Alegre.

— CAREN A. MEGHREBLIAN

WEYLER Y NICOLAU, VALERIANO

Valeriano Weyler y Nicolau (*b.* 17 September; *d.* 20 October 1930), captain-general of Cuba (1896–1898) who supervised the Spanish war effort to subdue the independence movement on that island. His mission was twofold: to end the Cuban conflict by military means and to restore colonial consensus through political methods. He instituted what would become the model by which colonial powers responded in their colonies: the reconcentration policy.

The reconcentration policy divided Cuba into war zones. In these zones the entire population was ordered into concentration camps located in the major cities. The Spanish Army then assumed that all those found in these areas were rebels and dealt with them accordingly. The concentration camps were not meant to punish their residents, but Spanish and local officials were not prepared to care for the displaced peasants. Inadequate food supplies and sanitary facilities led to the spread of disease and the death of tens of thousands of the 300,000 inhabitants.

Under General Weyler the royalist army inflicted widespread destruction of life and property. In addition to the reconcentration policy and the attacks on the rebels, the army burned entire villages, homes, fields, and food reserves. They also slaughtered the livestock. Vast stretches of the countryside were reduced to wasteland. The new offensive led by Weyler succeeded in containing the revolutionaries but was unable to defeat them. Weyler's tactics proved to be counterproductive, as the atrocities resulted in more Cubans supporting the revolution and caused a public outcry in the United States and even in Spain. In January 1898 Weyler was replaced and a more conciliatory Spanish policy was adopted.

— DAVID CAREY, JR.

WHEELOCK ROMÁN, JAIME

Jaime Wheelock Román (*b.* 30 May 1947), Nicaraguan leader and member of the Sandinista National Directorate. Jaime Wheelock was born in Managua. His family owned a large coffee farm in the fertile region of Carazo, near the town of Jinotepe. Wheelock gained firsthand knowledge of large agro-export operations that would influence his politics later in life. He attended the best schools in Managua and traveled abroad frequently.

Wheelock met several Sandinista leaders in the 1960s but did not join the movement until 1969. In 1970 he was accused of killing a National Guardsman and fled to Chile, where he studied politics, sociology, and agricultural law. Considered brilliant by his professors, he has been described by both friends and enemies as vain, materialistic, and intellectually arrogant. During his studies in Germany in 1972 and 1973, Wheelock applied Marxist-Leninist thought to Nicaraguan politics and society. This resulted in his *Imperialismo y dictadura* (1975), a historical survey of coffee farming and agro-export industrialization since the nineteenth century. He identified what he thought was a large rural proletariat exploited by large landowners and banking interests in agriculture. The argument follows Marx's prediction that in the transition from feudalism to capitalism the emerging bourgeoisie would experience internal crisis and the working masses would develop class consciousness. However, this thesis has been sharply criticized by scholars of political and economic development in Nicaragua. Much of the research was based on Wheelock's dogmatic bias for proletarian revolution.

Wheelock published the book in Nicaragua and injected his ideological and theoretical perspective into the Sandinista debate over tactics and strategy. A clash between Wheelock's "Proletarian Tendency" and the prevailing doctrine of prolonged popular war was inevitable. The Proletarians considered the Maoist, voluntarist approach of Carlos FONSECA, Henry RUÍZ, and Tomás BORGE to be a waste of time. This view was borrowed directly from Marx's conclusion that peasants were incapable of self-mobilization and revolt. The internecine struggle of the Sandinista leadership reached a pinnacle with bitter exchanges. Borge threatened Wheelock with physical harm, which caused him to take refuge in the house of a priest. The Proletarians were purged from the guerrilla organization in October 1975.

However, Wheelock pressed forward with his notion of how revolution would come about in Nicaragua. He organized labor strikes among poor barrio dwellers as the national crisis worsened in 1977 and 1978. Wheelock, Luis Carrión, and Carlos Núñez focused their attention on the vast settlements on the outskirts of Managua, where they gained a substantial following. This contributed to the reunification of the Proletarians with the Sandinista directorate in March 1979. Wheelock helped coordinate the final offensive against the SOMOZA regime in urban slums.

Wheelock became minister of agriculture and agrarian reform after the insurrection. He directed the redistribution of land confiscated from Somoza and his associates to peasants. However, Wheelock was an exponent of pragmatic, gradualist policies that were reflected in the 1981 agrarian reform law. He recognized the dangers of encouraging invasions of non-Somocista estates by rapidly distributing land confiscated by decrees 3 and 38, which affected only Somocista properties. Wheelock favored creating large-scale, capital-intensive state farms that would facilitate a centralized economy. This position contradicted that of many officials who wanted to allow peasants to determine agricultural policies. Thus, the proletarian tendency that dominated the Ministry of Agriculture divided along these lines, putting distance between Wheelock and supporters of Luis Carrión and Carlos Núñez.

By 1983 the Sandinista agrarian program was threatened by the influence of counterrevolutionary forces in rural areas. Many peasants in the northeast had not benefited from the government's strategy, and they began to join the contras. Wheelock therefore decided to increase the pace of land distribution. He oversaw the creation of an extensive cooperative system known as the Area of People's Property, which gave more control over planting and harvesting to individual farmers. In 1984 the Ministry of Agriculture handed out titles to over 2 million acres. Furthermore, Wheelock supported the expansion of the National Union of Farmers and Cattlemen, an organization of small and medium producers who accounted for a large percentage of agro-exports and basic grains.

A new agrarian reform law was passed in January 1986. Wheelock used some of its provisions to expropriate the property of several large exporters of coffee and cotton, accusing them of sending bank credit out of the country instead of using it for production. The objective was to demonstrate Sandinista resolve to support small private farmers and peasant cooperatives. Nevertheless, the general failure of agrarian reform was one of the contributing factors to the electoral defeat of the regime in February 1990. The Nicaragua Opposition Union and Violeta BARRIOS DE CHAMORRO received majorities in most rural areas. Wheelock has written several articles in the postelection period justifying the actions of the Ministry of Agriculture. He blames aggression from the Reagan administration and decapitalization of the banking system by "unpatriotic" producers for the Sandinistas' inability to secure property rights and, thus, the loyalty of peasants.

Wheelock blames aggression from the Reagan administration and decapitalization of the banking system for the Sandinistas' inability to secure the loyalty of peasants.

As of 1993, Wheelock retains his post on the Sandinista National Directorate. At the party congress in July 1991, the debate over agrarian reform intensified and Wheelock was the target of much criticism. Several social scientists and political figures opened a public dialogue about the plight of the peasant in the Nicaraguan revolution. Wheelock responded in the newspaper *Barricada,* explaining his views about agricultural policy in the 1980s. He also denied the rumor that he controls several properties confiscated from Somocistas. He continues to live in a large farmhouse outside of Managua.

– MARK EVERINGHAM
– WILLIAM F. SATER

WHITE Y LAFITTA, JOSÉ

José White y Lafitta (*b.* 31 December 1835; *d.* 15 March 1918), Cuban violinist and composer. A world-famous black musician, White was born in Matanzas, Cuba. There he met the renowned American composer Louis M. Gottschalk, who in 1855 persuaded White's family to send him to study at the Paris Conservatory. There he worked under the master violinist Jean-Delphin Alard, whom he temporarily replaced at the Conservatory when Alard was away.

White was highly praised by the critics and musicians of his time. He traveled throughout the world, playing for royalty and receiving standing ovations from the most sophisticated audiences. He may have been the first black musician to appear with an American orchestra. At home he sympathized with the Cuban insurgents in the Ten Years' War (1868–1878) against Spain. He composed a popular piece for violin and orchestra titled "La bella cubana," for which he was expelled from Cuba in 1875 when his playing it in a Havana theater caused a patriotic disturbance. Most of his works, however, are classic compositions. His Violin Concerto was played for the first time in the United States in New York City in 1974.

– JOSÉ M. HERNÁNDEZ

WILDE, EDUARDO

Eduardo Wilde (*b.* 15 June 1844; *d.* 5 September 1913), Argentine statesman, diplomat, and writer. Wilde, born in Tupiza, Bolivia, became a symbol of the liberal "Generación del Ochenta" (Generation of 1880) that came to power with President Julio Argentino ROCA in 1880. Wilde graduated from the Medical School of the University of Buenos Aires in 1870 and made an outstanding contribution during the yellow fever epidemic that scourged that city in 1871. In 1875 he was appointed professor of forensic medicine and toxicology at the University of Buenos Aires and professor of anatomy at the Colegio Nacional. He became interested in issues of public health and in 1878 published his *Curso de higiene pública.* He served in Congress as a national deputy for Buenos Aires (1874–1876, 1876–1880). President Roca chose him as his minister of justice and education, and it was in that post that Wilde made his mark. In the early 1880s, a series of laws gave the national government jurisdiction over primary education and the Civil Register of Births and Marriages (Office of Vital Statistics), which had been in the hands of the Catholic church. After successfully defending the secularizing laws, Wilde remained at the forefront in the ensuing confrontations with militant Catholics, which continued during his service as minister of the interior under President Miguel JUÁREZ CELMAN (1886–1889). During this period he returned to his concern with public health, pushing forward a project for the construction of a drainage and sewage system for the city of Buenos Aires that would produce a dramatic improvement in sanitary conditions. In 1898 he was appointed president of the National Department of Health and was later chosen to represent his country in Madrid and Brussels. He published several collections of articles and short stories, such as *Tiempo perdido* (1878) and *La lluvia* (1880).

– EDUARDO A. ZIMMERMANN

WILLIAMS, ALBERTO

Alberto Williams (*b.* 23 November 1862; *d.* 17 June 1952), Argentine composer, conductor, pianist, and teacher. Born in Buenos Aires into a family of musicians, Williams's first teacher was Pedro Beck (piano). Later he studied with Nicolás Bassi (harmony) and Luis Bernasconi (piano) at the Escuela de Música in Buenos Aires. While very young he gave piano recitals at the Teatro Colón. Williams published his first piece, the mazurka *Ensueño de juventud,* in 1881. At age twenty he received a government scholarship and went to Paris, where he enrolled at the National Conservatory and studied under Georges Mathias (piano), Auguste Durand (harmony), and Benjamin Godard (counterpoint). He was also a pupil of César Franck's and Charles de Bériot's in composition. After publishing a number of piano pieces in Paris, he returned in 1889 to Argentina, where he gave recitals and began incorporating into his works tunes, rhythms, and forms derived from native folklore. In Argentina, he became a pioneer of the nationalist style, which began with his *El rancho abandonado* (1890), a piano work. From 1892 on, he promoted nationalism in music, founding performance series such as the Concerts of the Athenaeum, National Library Concerts, Popular Concerts, and the Buenos Aires Conservatory Concerts. He was also active in the field of music education, where he could apply the modern methods he'd learned in Paris. In 1893 he founded the Buenos Aires Conservatory of Music, later renamed the Conservatorio Williams, which he directed until 1941. He conducted in Buenos Aires and Europe, where, in performances of his own work, he led the Berlin Philharmonic in 1900 and gave three concerts in Paris during the 1930 season.

Williams's works can be divided into three periods: the first, marked by a European influence, runs through 1890; the second, for which he is known as the progenitor of Argentine nationalism, covers 1890–1910; and the third, which dates from the publication of his Symphony no. 2 (1910), was nationalist but with an international character. Williams wrote nine symphonies and other orchestral works, chamber music, choral and vocal works, and several piano pieces, as well as several pedagogical and technical books. He died in Buenos Aires.

— SUSANA SALGADO

WILLIAMS CALDERÓN, ABRAHAM

Abraham Williams Calderón (*b.* 16 March 1896; *d.* 24 March 1986), Honduran military figure and politician. In 1954, Honduras suffered directly the political results of the coup d'état in Guatemala in the form of a large strike against the United Fruit Company in the North Coast region. The strike was due in part to the perception of the company as dominating Central American politics. Political unrest, exacerbated by the strike, culminated in a split within the National Party (PNH) when it became clear that the party would nominate former President Tiburcio CARÍAS ANDINO (president 1933–1949), who owed his political career to United Fruit. Former vice president Williams Calderón is known primarily for leading the newly organized National Reformist Movement (MNR) splinter group in the 10 October 1954 presidential election. He lost to Ramón Villeda Morales, who obtained 121,213 votes. The aging Carías Andino received 77,041 votes, and Williams Calderón received 53,041. Despite his poor showing in the polls, Williams Calderón and the MNR continued to play an active political role. However, with the National Party splintered, the Liberal Party (PLH) won the 1957 elections as well.

— JEFFREY D. SAMUELS

WILLIAMS REBOLLEDO, JUAN

Juan Williams Rebolledo (1826–1910), Chilean naval officer who commanded his country's fleet in 1865 during its difficult struggle against the Spanish navy. The son of an English officer who had helped Chile win its independence and a resourceful officer himself, Williams not only attempted to hold off the Spanish—an impossible task, given the small size of Chile's fleet—but managed to capture one of Madrid's vessels, the *Covadonga.* Williams again served as commander of the Chilean flotilla during the War of the Pacific. By then an old man and perhaps ill, Williams seemed incapable of waging as aggressive a war as he had decades earlier. Obsessed with the idea of winning the Conservative Party's nomination for the 1881 presidential campaign, Williams acted cautiously to avoid any disasters which might wreck his political career. His failure to blockade Callao and his overall incompetence, which resulted in the capture of the *Rimac,* as well as his refusal to cooperate with the Aníbal PINTO government eventually led to his dismissal. As a pro-BALMACEDA officer he refused to join his naval colleagues in launching the 1891 revolution. Williams also worked as a hydrographer, fixing the borders between Chile and Bolivia, and served as the maritime governor of Atacama.

— WILLIAM F. SATER

WILLIMAN, CLAUDIO

Claudio Williman (*b.* 2 September 1863; *d.* 9 February 1934), president of Uruguay (1907–1911). After graduating with a degree in law in 1888, Williman taught courses in mathematics and physics at the University of the Republic. From 1902 to 1924 he served as rector of the university. He was one of the founders of the College of Mathematics and the School of Commerce, today called the College of Economic Sciences. Between 1904 and 1907, he served as minister of government in the administration of President José BATLLE Y ORDÓÑEZ. After this term, Williman was nominated as a candidate for the presidency by the Colorado Party. He won the election and served from 1907 to 1911.

Williman's administration was characterized by meticulousness and strict control over public spending, and is often considered conservative when compared to that of Batlle y Ordóñez. Throughout the Williman administration, Batlle stayed in Europe with his family, but in 1910 he returned to Uruguay to take up the role of chief of the Colorado Party, and in 1911 he succeeded Williman as president.

— JOSÉ DE TORRES WILSON

WISNER VON MORGENSTERN, FRANZ

Franz Wisner von Morgenstern (*b.* 1800; *d.* 1878), Hungarian military officer active in Paraguay. Coming to South America in 1845 after minor service in the Austrian army, Wisner was contacted by Paraguayan president Carlos Antonio LÓPEZ, who wished to train his rustic battalions in modern European military techniques. For a time, Wisner commanded the tiny state flotilla stationed on the Paraguay River. He later headed an expeditionary force that intervened in the Argentine province of Corrientes in 1849. During the 1850s, Wisner gained a trusted position within the Paraguayan hierarchy and played a key role in obtaining the services of British military engineers who supervised the modernizing of the national army, which later effectively resisted the Brazilians and Argentines for six years during the War of the Triple Alliance (1864–1870).

Wisner, meanwhile, wrote an official biography of the Paraguayan dictator José Gaspar Rodríguez de FRANCIA. He also accepted a commission as chief military engineer on the state railway project, and later at the fortress of Humaitá. Captured at the 1868 battle of Lomas Valentinas (also called Pikysyry), Wisner returned to Paraguay after the war to prepare a major cartographical survey of the country; published in Vienna in 1873, it was easily the best complete map of Paraguay to appear up to that time. In his later years, Wisner, now the patriarch of a large Asunción family, was head of Paraguay's national railroad, and of the Immigration Office.

— THOMAS L. WHIGHAM

WOLFF, EGON

Egon Wolff (*b.* 13 April 1926), Chilean playwright. Wolff is the most staged—both in his own country and abroad—award-honored, and translated of Chilean dramatists; his plays have been performed in thirty countries, translated into twenty languages, and produced as films in Mexico and England. The son of German immigrants, Wolff pursued a parallel career as an engineer, in the manufacture and sale of chemical products. Unlike many artists and intellectuals of his generation, he steered clear of self-serving political posturing. Similarly, his plays are largely devoid of partisan didacticism. He focused instead on the social issues at work in the rapidly changing Chilean society of his day. In terms of form he preferred the fourth-wall theater (in which the proscenium arch represents a "fourth wall" to the audience) and complied with the classical Aristotelian dramatic unities. Stylistically, he favored social and psychological realism, with doses of poetry and humor.

Unlike many artists and intellectuals of his generation, he steered clear of self-serving political posturing.

His plays *Mansión de lechuzas* (*Mansion of Owls,* 1958), *Discípulos del miedo* (*Disciples of Fear,* 1958), *Niñamadre* (*A Touch of Blue,* 1960), and his most discussed work *Los invasores* (*The Invaders,* 1963) exemplify his characteristic probing into snobbery, prejudice, and the clash between social classes. He portrays the tension between traditional values—dictated by a crumbling ruling class—and those of the emerging middle class, including the heritage of postwar non-Spanish European immigrants. *El signo de Caín* (*The Sign of Cain,* 1969), *Flores de papel* (*Paper Flowers,* 1970), and *Kindergarten* (1977) explore the concepts of freedom and commitment on an individualistic level. In *Espejismos* (*Mirages,* 1978), *El sobre azul* (*The Blue Envelope,* 1978), *José* (1980), *Álamos en la azotea* (*Poplars on the Roof Terrace,* 1981), *La balsa de la Medusa* (*Medusa's Barge,* 1984), and *Háblame de Laura* (*Tell Me About Laura,* 1986), Wolff deftly and poetically plumbs the depths of personal relationships.

— ELENA CASTEDO

WOOSTER, CHARLES WHITING

Charles Whiting Wooster (*b.* 1780; *d.* 1848), officer in the Chilean navy. Born in New Haven, Connecticut, he was the nephew of David Wooster, hero of the Battle of Danbury during the American Revolution. Wooster went to sea at an early age. During the War of 1812 he served on board the U.S. privateer *Saratoga.* Having earned substantial prize money and gained significant influence, he was named captain of the Port of New York after the war. With the death of his young wife he chose to join the fight for independence in Chile.

Investing his entire fortune, Wooster purchased the brigantine *Columbus,* which he outfitted with sixteen guns. He carried a cargo of rifles to Chile, arriving 25 April 1818. Wooster was commissioned into the Chilean navy as a commander and put in charge of the frigate *Lautaro.* The *Lautaro* along with the *San Martín* intercepted a Spanish squadron on 25 October at Talcahuano and captured the frigate *Reina María Isabel,* which was escorting reinforcements for the royalist army in Peru. The following day the Chilean squadron captured the transports one by one. This was a significant victory for the patriots.

When Thomas A. Cochrane was hired by the Chileans to command their fleet, Wooster resigned rather than serve under the British officer, a former enemy. Between 1818 and 1822 Wooster engaged in commercial pursuits, including whaling. When Cochrane resigned from the Chilean navy, Wooster was recommissioned with the rank of captain and again took command of the *Lautaro.* Between 1822 and 1826 he campaigned against the royalists in Chiloé and southern Peru. In 1829 he was promoted to rear admiral.

Following the capture of Chiloé, the Chilean navy, except for the *Aquiles,* was sold off. In 1829, while Wooster was ashore, the crew mutinied against the selection of Joaquín Vicuña as vice president. At the direction of the Chilean government, Wooster boarded the British frigate *Thesis,* which captured the *Aquiles* and returned it to Chilean control. However, on 8 December Vicuña was driven from the capital and took refuge on the *Aquiles.* The forts at Valparaíso, also in the hands of the rebels, drove the ship out of port. Wooster sailed to Coquimbo, where Vicuña surrendered. These events ended Wooster's career in the navy. Wooster settled in California, where he had become one of the most powerful property owners in San Francisco.

— ROBERT SCHEINA

WYLD OSPINA, CARLOS

Carlos Wyld Ospina (*b.* 19 June 1891; *d.* 17 June 1956), Guatemalan writer and journalist, member of the influential Generation of 1920. Wyld was born in Antigua to wealthy parents, Guillermo Wyld and Soledad Ospina. Largely self-taught, he began to write romantic poetry at an early age. As a novelist he is regarded as a chief exponent of *criollismo,* a literary movement devoted to denouncing social evils and to promoting national regeneration. Among his most notable works in this vein are *El solar de los Gonzaga* (1924; Ancestral Home) and *La gringa* (1935). In his short stories, such as "La tierra de las Nahuyacas" (1933; "The Land of the Nahuyacas"), he was among the first to depict realistically the wretched condition of the Indian majority, thus becoming a precursor of the Indigenista movement.

It was in Mexico that Wyld established himself as a journalist of note, becoming the editor of the paper *El Independiente* (1913–1914). Upon his return to Guatemala, he settled in Quetzaltenango, where he taught literature and worked as the editor of *Diario de Los Altos.* In 1920 he founded, in association with the writer Alberto Vásquez, *El Pueblo,* the organ of the Unionist Party in which he bitterly criticized the Guatemalan dictator Manuel ESTRADA CABRERA. He also founded the cultural magazines *Estudio* (1922) and *Semana* (1939), and from 1922 to 1925 worked as the editor of the prominent newspaper *El Imparcial.* He married Amalia Cheves, a noted poet from Cobán. From 1937 to 1942, he served as deputy in the National Assembly. He died in Quetzaltenango while serving as director of the Bank of the West.

— JORGE H. GONZÁLEZ

X

XIMÉNEZ, FRANCISCO

Francisco Ximénez (*b.* 28 November 1666; *d.* between 11 May 1729 and mid-1730), a Dominican priest who translated the *Popol Vuh*, the Maya–K'iche' story of creation.

Born in Écija, Andalusia, Ximénez joined the Dominican order in 1688 and was sent to Guatemala to continue his religious studies. He was ordained in 1690. His facility for learning the Indian languages soon became evident, and he was assigned as parish priest in San Juan Sacatepéquez to learn the Kaqchikel language. Under the guidance of another friar who knew Kakchikel, he prepared a grammar in that language and went on to master the K'iche' and Tz'utujil languages.

While serving in Chichicastenango from 1701 to 1703, Ximénez found a manuscript of the ancient book of the K'iche' people, the *Popol Vuh*. He translated into Spanish its story of creation and the history of the K'iche' nation. The *Popol Vuh* is now considered the national book of Guatemala.

Later Ximénez founded a hospital for Indians in Rabinal and developed a treatment for rabies. During his stay at Rabinal he also began a careful study of bees. Ximénez became interested in the flora and fauna of Guatemala. His work as a naturalist was recorded in *Historia natural del Reino de Guatemala*. About 1715 he began writing the history of the Dominican order in Guatemala, *Historia de la provincia de San Vicente de Chiapa y Guatemala de la Orden de Predicadores*. His writings were often critical of the Spaniards. He died in the convent of Santo Domingo in Santiago de Guatemala.

— DAVID L. JICKLING

XUL SOLAR

Xul Solar (Oscar Agustín Alejandro Schulz Solari; *b.* 14 December 1888; *d.* 10 April 1963). Argentine painter and illustrator who also made musical instruments and toys. Xul Solar was born in San Fernando, Buenos Aires Province. He studied engineering and architecture at the University of Buenos Aires. He left school and traveled to Paris, where he studied drawing and painting with Emilio Pettorutti in 1908. His first artistic attempts, in 1917, related to art nouveau forms. The art of Xul Solar possesses an esoteric flavor of deep religious

and metaphysical suggestion. In an imaginary space, Xul Solar combines faces, magical elements, and fragmentary objects, treating his material in a schematic, planimetric way with dynamic action and an exceptional refinement of color.

— AMALIA CORTINA ARAVENA

XUXA

Xuxa (*b.* 1963), Brazilian model, actress, singer, and children's television show host. Born Maria da Graça Meneghel in Santa Rosa, Rio Grande do Sul, Brazil, Xuxa (pronounced "shoo-sha") was the highest-paid Brazilian performer even before her children's show "Xou da Xuxa" was picked up by the Fox Network in 1992 for broadcast in the United States. Xuxa first

---

In 1983 Xuxa hosted a children's television show in which she was presented as a sex symbol, wearing miniskirts and short shorts.

---

came to public attention in Brazil in 1978 as a model for the national photo magazine *Manchete* (Headline), in which she, a tall blonde, was a striking contrast to most Brazilian models. In 1980 she made further headlines as the girlfriend of soccer star Pelé and by appearing nude in the Brazilian edition of *Playboy* and in films such as *Amor Estranho Amor* by Walter Khoury (1982), which features Xuxa in a sex scene with a young boy. At about this time, the Brazilian press began comparing her with Marilyn Monroe. In 1983 she hosted a children's television show called "Clube da Criança" (Children's Club) for the Manchete Television Network, in which she was presented as a sex symbol, wearing miniskirts and short shorts. As a television personality, she is known for her ingenuousness, spontaneity, and what critics call a permissive approach to children's entertainment. She moved to Brazil's TV Globo in 1986 to obtain broader exposure on a much more widely watched network. The "Xou da Xuxa" show became slicker, and certain trademarks, like Xuxa blowing kisses (*beijinhos*) to the audience increased. As with other Globo stars, her records, concerts, and movies were cross-marketed by Globo television and radio stations. She also began merchandizing a wide variety of products under her name and image. In 1990 production of her show moved to Argentina for the Latin American and Hispanic U.S. markets. Then in 1992, her show was packaged for syndication in English in the United States and was picked up by the Fox Network for early-morning daily broadcast in 1993. For many critics, Xuxa symbolizes a Brazilian ethnic and sexual identity contradiction between a blond ideal and a brown reality.

— JOSEPH D. STRAUBHAAR

Y

YANES, FRANCISCO JAVIER

Francisco Javier Yanes (*b.* 12 May 1776; *d.* 17 June 1842), political activist and historian of the Venezuelan independence movement. Yanes was born in Cuba but moved to Venezuela at a very young age. He studied law at the University of Caracas. He was connected with the independence movement from its start. Yanes was a member of the Sociedad Patriótica de Caracas and of the Constituent Congress of 1811; he was also a censor at *El Publicista,* the official publication of the Congress. He left the country at the fall of the First Republic in 1812, returning in 1813. The Congress of Angostura designated him a member of the Supreme Court of Justice of Venezuela in 1819 and in 1820 as president of the Court of Almirantazgo.

With the creation of Gran Colombia, Yanes was appointed a member of the Superior Court of Justice of Venezuela (1821), which was subordinate to the government in Bogotá. He worked on the publication of the periodical *El Observador Caraqueño* (1824–1825) with Cristóbal Mendoza, historian, journalist, and first president of Venezuela (1811), with whom he also collaborated on an important collection of twenty-two volumes of documents concerning Venezuela's emancipation [FRANCISCO JAVIER YANES and Cristóbal Mendoza, *Colección de documentos relativos a la vida pública del Libertador de Colombia y del Perú, Simón Bolívar,* 22 vols. (1983)]. Yanes was a member of the Sociedad Económica de Amigos del País (1829) and of the Constituent Congress of 1830. After 1830 he devoted himself to judicial activities and to his private life. His personal archive can be found in the National Academy of History in Caracas.

— INÉS QUINTERO

YÁÑEZ SANTOS DELGADILLO, AGUSTÍN

Agustín Yáñez Santos Delgadillo (*b.* 4 May 1904; *d.* 17 January 1980), Mexican novelist and public figure. Of the many novels and literary studies Agustín Yáñez produced, he is best remembered for his focus on the regional qualities of his native culture in the small, rural towns of Jalisco, in western Mexico. *Al filo del agua* (*On the Edge of the Storm*), his best-known work in this genre, was first published in 1947 and is considered an outstanding example of a historical novel depicting, in the words of critic John Brushwood, "the reality of Mexico on the edge of the Revolution." Brushwood considers it a turning point in Mexican literature.

The writings of Yáñez focus on the regional qualities of his native culture in the small, rural towns of Jalisco, in western Mexico.

Yáñez was born in Guadalajara, Jalisco, the child of modest, extremely religious parents. A law school graduate, he quickly joined the intellectual scene, after first involving himself with the Cristero Rebellion, a religious uprising against the government. He moved to Mexico City, where he taught at the National University and served at a number of administrative posts. After holding several minor posts in the federal government, he became governor of his home state (1953–1959). He became a speech writer for President Adolfo LÓPEZ MATEOS, who appointed him assistant secretary of the presidency (1962–1964). In 1964, he became secretary of public education. Unlike many intellectuals, Yáñez did not surround himself with disciples, although he gave his time to intellectual institutions as president of the Seminar of Mexican Culture (1949–1952) and the Mexican Academy of Language (1973–1977).

— RODERIC AI CAMP

YDÍGORAS FUENTES, MIGUEL

Miguel Ydígoras Fuentes (*b.* 17 October 1895; *d.* 6 October 1982), president of Guatemala (1958–1963). Born in Pueblo Nuevo, Retalhuleu, to a family of Basque ancestry, Ydígoras pursued a military career, rising to the rank of general. He served as a departmental governor and as the head of the department of highways during the dictatorship of General Jorge UBICO (1931–1944), when he developed a reputation in the countryside as a tough but fair administrator. As a reward for supporting the new junta of the October Revolution (1944), he was named ambassador to Great Britain, where he became impressed by British parliamentary democracy.

In 1950 he ran for the presidency of Guatemala against Jacobo ARBENZ (1950–1954), but was forced into hiding during much of the campaign. Exiled to El Salvador, he helped organize the U.S.–backed insurrection that toppled Arbenz in 1954.

After the assassination of President Carlos CASTILLO ARMAS in July 1957, Ydígoras reorganized his political party, Reconciliación Democrática Nacional, and campaigned for the presidency against Miguel Ortiz Passarelli, the official candidate. When the government declared Ortiz the winner in a disputed election, Ydígoras launched the massive street demonstrations that succeeded in overturning the election. In January 1958 he defeated Colonel José Luis Cruz Salazar in what was considered to be a fair and free election.

The Ydígoras Fuentes regime was a peculiar mixture of populism, economic conservatism, and nationalism. Thus, he strongly supported the creation of the Central American Common Market and pushed through an industrial incentives law, a law protecting foreign investment, a limited agrarian reform law, and an income-tax law. Ydígoras also permitted substantial personal liberty.

Faced with the threat of Castroite subversion and the need for support from the United States, Ydígoras secretly provided a base for the Bay of Pigs Invasion. Reaction by nationalist officers led to a military uprising in November 1960 that was put down by loyal army units with U.S. assistance. In 1961 several of the rebellious officers launched the guerrilla movement that has continued into the 1990s.

In March 1962 charges of electoral manipulation, administrative incompetence, and corruption precipitated a student-led protest movement that forced Ydígoras to install a military cabinet in order to retain power. But the military turned against him when he permitted their old nemesis (and also that of the United States), former president Juan José ARÉVALO (1945–1951), to return to Guatemala to contest the 1963 elections. Ydígoras was overthrown on 30 March 1963 in a coup led by his defense minister, General Enrique PERALTA AZURDIA (1963–1966).

Ydígoras lived in exile in Nicaragua, Costa Rica, and El Salvador until the early 1970s, when he returned to Guatemala under an amnesty offered to all ex-presidents living abroad by President Carlos ARANA OSORIO (1970–1974). He commented extensively in the press on Guatemalan affairs. In 1980 he traveled to the Vatican to see fulfilled a goal for which he had worked many years—the beatification of Hermano Pedro de BETHANCOURT.

– ROLAND H. EBEL

YEGROS, FULGENCIO

Fulgencio Yegros (b. 1780; d. 17 July 1821), Paraguayan militiaman and political figure. Born into a well-established and wealthy creole family, Yegros chose a career with the colonial militia at an early age. During the first decade of the nineteenth century, he commanded troops against the Portuguese and their Indian allies. His chief claim to military fame, however, came in 1811, when his cavalry defeated a *porteño* expeditionary force at the battles of Paraguarí and Tacuarí. The vanquished *porteño* commander, Manuel BELGRANO, invited Yegros to a parley after the conclusion of the fighting, and convinced him to join the patriot cause. Soon thereafter, Yegros joined with other militia leaders in a *cuartelazo* (barracks revolt) against the colonial governor, which led to independence shortly thereafter.

Though ill at ease in the political realm, Yegros joined the junta together with fellow officer Pedro Juan CABALLERO, cleric Francisco Xavier Bogarín, businessman Fernando de la Mora, and a distant relative, José Gaspar de FRANCIA. The latter quickly eclipsed the other members of the junta and began formulating Paraguayan policy without much consulting of his associates. In October 1813 an extraordinary congress assembled in Asunción and replaced the junta with a two-man consular government led by Francia and Yegros. It was clear from the beginning that Francia held all the real power. Yegros's tenure was brief; within a year, Francia abolished the consulate and founded a "supreme dictatorship" that lasted until his death in 1840.

Yegros, who had hoped to retire peacefully to his ranch at Quyquyó, found himself implicated in an antigovernment conspiracy in 1820. Fearing that this might signal the beginning of a revolt, Francia had his old associate arrested, tortured, and finally shot, less than 100 yards from the government house.

– THOMAS L. WHIGHAM

YERMO, GABRIEL DE

Gabriel de Yermo (b. 1757; d. 1813), leader of the Mexican coup d'état of 1808. The Sodupe-born Yermo was a rich Spanish merchant and landowner who became the enemy of Viceroy José de ITURRIGARAY (1742–1815) because of financial matters, specifically, the taxes levied on products Yermo imported. Backed by the Audiencia of Mexico, Yermo and 300 armed men apprehended the viceroy and his family on the night of 15 September 1808. By so doing, they successfully prevented the establishment of the governing junta that the *ayuntamiento* (city council) proposed and that Iturrigaray appeared to support. Also detained were several members of the *ayuntamiento* and Fray Melchor de TALAMANTES (1765–1809).

— VIRGINIA GUEDEA

YNSFRÁN, EDGAR L.

Edgar L. Ynsfrán (*b.* 1920; *d.* 1991), Paraguayan politician. When General Alfredo STROESSNER seized power in 1954, he needed competent allies to give his regime a veneer of legitimacy and respectability. In this effort it was natural that he would turn to Edgar L. Ynsfrán, a talented young intellectual who had made a name for himself in Colorado Party circles ever since the 1947 civil war. A protégé of the right-wing former president Juan Natalicio González, Ynsfrán was a lawyer by training. He had already served as a Colorado deputy, police official, and member of the Junta de Gobierno. He was also a much read essayist, an indefatigable worker, and a shrewd party organizer. Most important of all, he was willing to act as Stroessner's agent in political matters.

Though Ynsfrán gave the impression of being a tranquil, austere scholar, in fact he filled Paraguay's jails with hundreds of political prisoners.

The general made Ynsfrán his interior minister in the mid-1950s at precisely the time when the democratic opposition—as well as the left-leaning guerrilla groups—were actively seeking the dictator's ouster. Ynsfrán took energetically to combating these threats. Though he gave the impression of being a tranquil, austere scholar, in fact he filled Paraguay's jails with hundreds of political prisoners, many of whom were tortured.

By the mid-1960s, Ynsfrán's repressive apparatus had destroyed nearly all of Stroessner's enemies in the country. The very success of his campaign, however, gave Ynsfrán a measure of power uncomfortably close to that of the president himself. Not wishing to place too much temptation before his minister's eyes, Stroessner abruptly dropped Ynsfrán from the cabinet in 1966. Thereafter the former interior minister devoted himself to business matters and to the building of a magnificent library of Paraguayan books, documents, and memorabilia, much of which was donated to the nation just before his death. In the last two years of his life, he attempted a political comeback, but his unsavory past

prevented him from making much headway, even within his own Colorado Party.

— THOMAS L. WHIGHAM

YNSFRÁN, PABLO MAX

Pablo Max Ynsfrán (*b.* 30 June 1894; *d.* 2 May 1972), Paraguayan educator and historian. Born in Asunción, Ynsfrán received formal training as a diplomat during the 1920s and 1930s, but early on expressed as much interest in the study of history as in the practical application of politics. From 1923 to 1928 he taught philosophy and Roman history at the Colegio Nacional de la Capital (Asunción) at the same time as he served as a congressional deputy.

The Chaco War of 1932–1935 found Ynsfrán in Washington, D.C., as Paraguay's chargé d'affaires. There he participated in the 1938 Chaco peace conference and was subsequently chosen to be public works minister by President José Félix ESTIGARRIBIA.

With the start of the Higínio MORÍNIGO dictatorship in 1940, Ynsfrán went into exile in the United States. He became a professor of Latin American history at the University of Texas at Austin, where he remained until his death.

Ynsfrán wrote two finely detailed studies, *The Epic of the Chaco: Marshal Estigarribia's Memoirs of the Chaco War, 1932–1935* (1950), and *La expedición norteamericana contra el Paraguay, 1858–1859* (1954), as well as many articles and polemical pieces.

— MARTA FERNÁNDEZ WHIGHAM

YON SOSA, MARCO ANTONIO

Marco Antonio Yon Sosa (*b.* 1932; *d.* June 1970), Guatemalan guerrilla leader. On 13 November 1960, Yon Sosa led a revolt of nationalist army officers against the corrupt government of Miguel YDÍGORAS FUENTES (1958–1963). After a brief exile, he returned to eastern Guatemala as a proponent of radical revolution through guerrilla warfare, and organized the Rebel Armed Forces (FAR) with Luis TURCIOS LIMA and the Communist Party. Yon Sosa broke from the FAR in 1965 over ideological issues, but he continued the guerrilla struggle as leader of the Revolutionary Movement of November 13 (MR-13). An advocate of immediate socialist revolution through general insurrection, Yon Sosa rejected the electoral strategies of the FAR, although the two guerrilla movements forged a tenuous alliance during the devastating counterinsurgency program supported by the United States in the late 1960s. After a confrontation with the army, he fled Mexico, where he was killed by Mexican authorities. The FAR and MR-13 provided the training ground for the rebel leaders of the 1970s.

— PAUL J. DOSAL

YRIGOYEN, HIPÓLITO

Hipólito Yrigoyen (Irigoyen; *b.* 12 July 1852; *d.* 3 July 1933), president of Argentina (1916–1922, 1928–1930). Controversial, charismatic, and enigmatic, Hipólito Yrigoyen was Argentina's most popular president before Juan Domingo PERÓN. As leader of the Unión Cívica Radical (UCR), or Radical Party, he built a populist organization driven by patronage and run by an efficient urban-based political machine. In 1930 a deteriorating economy, charges of political corruption, and a loss of support by the military sparked a coup that removed Yrigoyen from power.

In the words of Yrigoyen, on the occasion of the failed uprising of 1905: "Revolutions are an integral part of the moral law of society."

Born the illegitimate son of a blacksmith in provincial Buenos Aires, Yrigoyen developed a personality that defies easy explanation. Virtually every author or biographer who assumed the task resorted to the term "enigmatic." That he was a remarkable character lies beyond doubt. Over the masses he exercised an extraordinary fascination and displayed a quiet charisma despite poorly developed oratorical abilities. Indeed, except for a single instance in the 1880s, he never made a public speech. Yrigoyen preferred bargains struck in the background and cultivated an air of mystery. His political mission was buried in the moralistic rhetoric of his manifestos; Yrigoyen's philosophy, derived partly from the works of the minor German philosopher Karl Krause, was equally obscure and stressed a mystical belief in a God-given harmony and in moral living. Even in later life, he continued to wear suits of somber shades, lived in modest dwellings in the poorer districts of Buenos Aires, and shunned photographers. Much of this reflects his personal history of political conspiracy.

Yrigoyen's public career began in 1872, when his uncle, Leandro ALEM, secured for him the position of police superintendent in a district of Buenos Aires. The appointment was lost, however, when Yrigoyen was accused of participation in a scheme to rig elections. In 1877 Yrigoyen, together with Alem and Artistóbulo del VALLE, helped to form the short-lived Republican Party,

which supported provincial rights and attacked corrupt politics. In 1879 he successfully ran for a seat in Congress and in 1880 was chosen for a high position on the National Council for Education. When his term of office ended in 1882, he bought land and entered the cattle-fattening business.

In 1890 Yrigoyen joined the Unión Cívica and participated in "El Noventa," an armed insurrection that toppled the government of Miguel JUÁREZ CELMAN. Following a struggle over leadership, the party split in 1891 into two factions. One, the Unión Cívica Nacionál, was led by Bartolomé MITRE and the other, the Unión Cívica Radical, was initially guided by Leandro Alem. Yrigoyen worked successfully to wrest control of the UCR from Alem, who committed suicide in 1896. By 1898 Yrigoyen was the acknowledged leader of radicalism. Holding vague populist ideals and driven more by emotion than careful attention to issues, the UCR continued, unsuccessfully, to play at revolution. From the UCR's perspective, illegitimate government legitimized insurrection. In the words of Yrigoyen, on the occasion of the failed uprising of 1905: "Revolutions are an integral part of the moral law of society." According to Manuel GÁLVEZ, his biographer, Yrigoyen realized that he had a mission and destiny that called for the moral and political regeneration of the nation. At any rate, after 1900 he cultivated an air of mystery that he effectively combined with a remarkable behind-the-scenes personal persuasiveness.

Argentina's political scene shifted fundamentally in 1912, when an electoral reform law that provided for universal male suffrage and obligatory and secret voting took effect. Offered a long-awaited political opening, the UCR ran candidates for elected office. In 1916 Yrigoyen won the presidency of Argentina.

Yrigoyen's first term (1916–1922) was marked by contradiction. While the UCR purported to stand for open and honest politics, Yrigoyen did not hesitate to use his executive powers for narrow political ends to "intervene" in provincial elections to assure Radical victories. Yrigoyen's noisy economic nationalism, which targeted foreign capital invested in Argentina, contained more rhetoric than substance and was particularly strident at election time. While the UCR attempted to forge an alliance with organized labor, Yrigoyen readily authorized the use of violence against strikers when they demanded more than Radicals were willing to concede.

Ostensibly a party of the middle class, Yrigoyen's personalist rule, according to Susan and Peter Calvert, "failed to build up a middle-class political philosophy or establish viable institutions for the continued political involvement of newly mobilised groups" (*Argentina: Political Culture and Instability*, p. 97). Lacking programmatic unity, the UCR of Yrigoyen acted pragmatically as it played to the wide range of interests and coalitions that had to be rewarded for their political support. State patronage at a local level took the form of dispersals of free bread, milk, meat, and seed, which wed the electorate to the party. Importantly, the focus of the party's unity became its leader, Yrigoyen. Personalism, patronage, and political loyalty rather than open participation came to typify the years of Radical control.

Yrigoyen's most telling failure was his politicization of the Argentine military. He offended their sense of professionalism when he promoted officers dropped from military service for their participation in the uprising of 1905. He challenged their perceived sense of mission when he used troops to break strikes or to monitor federal interventions in elections; he became deeply involved in the army's inner institutional life. After Yrigoyen won a second term as president in 1928, his meddling in military matters became intolerable,

helping to lay the groundwork for the military coup of 1930 that removed him from power.

Yrigoyen died in 1933 and became a myth,

a symbol of the aspirations of the middle class.

To military unrest must be added spreading economic dislocation occasioned by world depression. The depression destroyed the ability of the state to grant patronage and undermined the UCR's popular base of support. As the party disintegrated and economic conditions worsened, Yrigoyen lost prestige. He died in 1933 and, in the words of the Calverts, "was accorded the spontaneous tribute of a splendid funeral and became a myth, a symbol of the aspirations of the middle class."

– PAUL B. GOODWIN

Z

ZACHRISSON, JULIO

Julio Zachrisson (*b.* 1930), Panama's foremost print-maker. Zachrisson studied in Panama under Juan Manuel CEDEÑO at the Instituto Nacional de Bellas Artes in Mexico (1953–1959), at the Vanucci Academy in Perugia (1959–1960), and at the San Fernando Academy in Madrid.

The grotesque characters in Zachrisson's fantastic

world are drawn from urban Panamanian folklore,

Spanish literature, classical mythology, and

personal experience.

Zachrisson's prints, which include etchings, drypoints, woodcuts, and lithographs, are characterized by a unique sense of satire and sociopolitical commentary. The grotesque characters in his fantastic world are drawn from urban Panamanian folklore, Spanish literature, classical mythology, and personal experience. Since the 1970s, he has also painted these subjects in oil on wood or canvas. He now lives in Spain.

— MONICA E. KUPFER

ZAID, GABRIEL

Gabriel Zaid (*b.* 14 October 1934), Mexican poet and essayist. Although an engineer by training, Zaid has become one of the Mexican literary establishment's most active members, recognized as a poet, essayist, literary critic, translator, editor, and researcher. He is a member of El Colegio Nacional and the Mexican Language Academy. Zaid won the Xavier Villaurrutia Prize (1972) and the Magda Donato Prize (1986) for his poetry, which has been described as meticulously structured, refined, concise, and as the antithesis of the confessional and exuberant poetry of Jaime Sabines, his contemporary. His literary criticism has concentrated on poetic theory and practice. Besides editing the work of renowned poets, Zaid has promoted the work of young writers in several anthologies. In *Asamblea de poetas jóvenes de México* (1980), he identified a new generation of poets among the ever-increasing numbers who pub-

lished in small presses and/or literary journals and supplements in the 1970s. As a cultural critic, his books, such as *La economía presidencial* and *De los libros al poder,* and his articles, appearing regularly in *Vuelta,* engage the current political debates.

— NORMA KLAHN

ZALDÚA, FRANCISCO JAVIER

Francisco Javier Zaldúa (*b.* 3 December 1821; *d.* 21 December 1882), Colombian president. Born in Bogotá, Francisco Javier Zaldúa was a distinguished professor of law and an active member of the Liberal Party. He served frequently in Congress and in other positions, and presided over the constituent convention of Ríonegro in 1863. In the subsequent division of the party between the more doctrinaire Radicals and the Independents who followed Rafael NÚÑEZ, Zaldúa initially aligned himself with the latter, even though he was essentially a moderate. Thus both factions accepted him as their presidential candidate in 1881. Despite that consensus, however, his term was marked by bitter wrangling with Congress, cut short by his death after less than a year as president.

— DAVID BUSHNELL

ZAMORA, RUBÉN

Rubén Zamora (*b.* 9 November 1942), Salvadoran political leader. Born in Cojutepeque, Zamora received his law degree from the University of El Salvador in 1968; at about the same time, he joined the Christian Democratic Party (PDC). In 1969 he moved to England to pursue graduate studies in political science at the University of Essex. He returned to El Salvador after an army-led reformist coup d'état overthrew the repressive government of General Carlos Humberto ROMERO on 15 October 1979. Zamora was appointed secretary of the presidency (chief of staff) to the newly created civilian-military junta. When conservative army officers blocked political and economic reforms that the junta intended to implement, Zamora and most members of the junta and cabinet resigned on 31 December 1979. The PDC made a pact with the military and joined it in a second junta. Zamora's older brother, Mario, the attorney general for the poor, was assassinated by a death squad in late February 1980. Appalled by the increasing human rights violations and the PDC's insistence on continuing its coalition with the military, Zamora and several other leading Christian Democrats resigned from the party on 9 March. Zamora and his family went into exile in Nicaragua.

In April 1980 Zamora helped found the Democratic Revolutionary Front (FDR), a coalition of political parties, unions, and mass organizations. Together with an influential group of former PDC members, he founded the Popular Social Christian Movement (MPSC) in May 1980, and was its secretary-general until 1993. From January 1981 to December 1986 Zamora served as an MPSC member of the Political-Diplomatic Commission of the FDR and Farabundo Martí Front for National Liberation (FMLN). In October and November 1984 he returned to El Salvador as a member of the FDR-FMLN negotiating team for the first two meetings between the government and revolutionary organizations.

In November 1987 Zamora returned to El Salvador to help build the MPSC. With Guillermo Manuel UNGO and Enrique Roldán, the leaders of the two social democratic parties, Zamora organized the Democratic Convergence on 27 November 1987, which began to participate in national elections with the 1989 presidential elections. Publicly threatened with death on armed forces radio during the 1989 FMLN offensive, Zamora remained in El Salvador. In 1993 he became the coalition candidate for president of the republic of the Democratic Convergence and the FMLN, which had become a legal political party following the 1992 Salvadoran peace accords that ended the eleven-year civil war. He lost the April 1994 election to ARENA candidate Armando Calderon Sol in a run-off. Zamora continues to live in El Salvador and owns a consulting firm. He has consistently described himself politically as a "social Christian." In practice, this has meant embracing socioeconomic policies that are close to the Social Democrats but are informed by progressive, Roman Catholic theology.

– TOMMIE SUE MONTGOMERY

ZAMORANO, AGUSTÍN JUAN VICENTE

Agustín Juan Vicente Zamorano (*b.* 1798; *d.* 1842), Spanish military officer in California and printer. A native of Saint Augustine, Florida, Zamorano served as a royalist cadet in the Mexican Wars of Independence. As a lieutenant of engineers, he went to California with Governor José María Escheandía in February 1825. While commandant of the presidio at Monterey (1831–1836), Zamorano ordered (from Boston) the first printing press in California in 1834; the first work printed

on it, in the same year, was a set of regulations. Zamorano surveyed the Santa Rosa settlement for Governor José FIGUEROA in 1834, and the following year he printed Figueroa's *Manifesto a la República mejicana,* which concerned colonization. He served as commandant of Loreto in 1839–1840 and was named inspector of Alta California in 1842. He died shortly after his arrival in San Diego.

– W. MICHAEL MATHES

ZAPATA, EMILIANO

Emiliano Zapata (*b.* ca. 8 August 1879; *d.* 10 April 1919), Mexican revolutionary. Born and raised in the village of Anenecuilco in the small south-central state of Morelos, in 1911 Zapata took up arms against the regime of long-time president Porfirio DÍAZ, and quickly became one of the most prominent leaders of the Mexican Revolution (1910–1920). He is most often remembered for voicing rural demands for land and local liberties.

Zapata was the ninth of ten children of a *campesino* (peasant) family. He received little schooling, though he did learn to read and write. During his early years, the centuries-long struggle between Morelian villages and haciendas for land and water was becoming increasingly tense as the haciendas sought to expand. Like other young men raised in this environment, Zapata had trouble with the law from an early age: in 1897 he fled Morelos to avoid arrest for a minor infraction at a fiesta. By 1906 he was helping to defend Anenecuilco's land in the courts, and in 1909 he was elected president of the village council.

Meanwhile, national politics were becoming unsettled. In 1910, after an aborted campaign for the presidency, Francisco MADERO called for a revolution against the dictatorship of Porfirio Díaz. In March 1911 Zapata responded by helping form a small guerrilla band. He soon attained leadership of this group, which grew large enough by May to capture the regional center of Cuautla, Morelos. The taking of Cuautla, only about 50 miles south of Mexico City, was an important factor in forcing Díaz from power.

Zapata soon discovered, however, that the new national leadership was more dedicated to democracy than to land reform. The large landowners of Morelos immediately maneuvered to preserve their power in the state, and it gradually became clear that Madero, a hacienda owner himself, identified with them. Zapata was attacked by the conservative Mexico City press, which began calling him the "Attila of the South" in June for the real and imagined atrocities committed by his followers. Under these circumstances he was reluctant to disarm his forces. After weeks of negotiations, in August 1911 troops were sent against him under the command of General Victoriano HUERTA. Zapata returned to the mountains, now to fight an ostensibly revolutionary regime.

To explain their cause to the nation, Zapata and a local schoolmaster named Otilio Montaño composed the Plan of Ayala in November. This document was a remarkable expression of the goals of many of Mexico's peasant rebels. It clarified Zapata's demands for land, calling not only for the return of lands the haciendas had stolen, but for the expropriation of one-third of all hacienda holdings for villages without land titles, and the confiscation of the property of those who opposed Zapata's rebellion. It also insisted on the rule of law and the right of the people to choose their own leaders.

The struggle against Madero lasted until Huerta deposed and assassinated him in a February 1913 coup. Huerta sought to make peace with Zapata, but Zapata did not trust his promises, and the fighting continued. Zapatismo grew as peasants from Morelos, Mexico

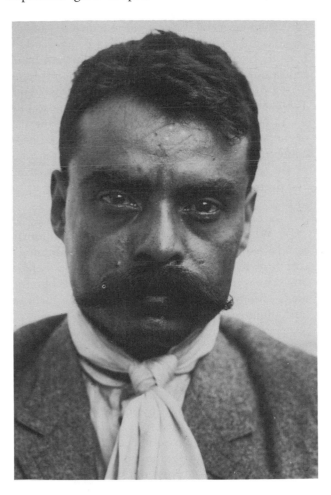

Emiliano Zapata. (Archivo Histórico Fotográfico Inah-Sep)

State, the Federal District, Puebla, Guerrero, and farther afield joined Zapata against the new and in some ways more oppressive regime. As the movement expanded it became more heterogeneous, and it was Zapata's task to discipline it enough to make it a force on the national scene. One measure of his success was that by the summer of 1914 he controlled Morelos and large parts of neighboring states, and threatened Mexico City.

In July 1914 Huerto followed Díaz into exile, and Zapata's forces soon came into contact with the troops of two northern revolutionaries who had also opposed Huerta: Venustiano CARRANZA and Francisco "Pancho" VILLA. Zapata was now confronted with a crucial decision about what kind of alliances, if any, would be most useful to the pursuit of his agenda. Consulting closely with Manuel Palafox, his most prominent intellectual adviser at the time, he eventually sided with the popular Chihuahuan rebel Villa against Carranza, a hacienda owner like Madero who gave little indication that he favored land reform.

By November 1914 the war started again. On 4 December Zapata and Villa met at Xochimilco in the Federal District to firm up their alliance. Two days later they made their official entry into Mexico City, which the Zapatistas had actually occupied in late November. When Zapata captured Puebla on 16 December, it looked as though he and Villa would quickly defeat Carranza, but a series of assassinations in the capital strained relations between the two leaders. Moreover, there was conflict among the urban intellectuals they had put in charge of their national government.

Just before Christmas, Zapata returned to Morelos. With the aid of Palafox, who was minister of agriculture in the new government, he began to carry out the land reform he had promised. In some respects 1915 was a utopian period in Morelos, a time in which Zapata helped the *campesinos* act on their hopes for change in a way that they have seldom been able to do in Mexican history. But internal tensions limited what Zapata could accomplish. Neighboring villages often fought over land and other resources, and differences between Zapatista guerrillas and the civilian population were becoming more evident.

In mid-1915 Villa lost the biggest battles of the revolution to Carrancista general Álvaro OBREGÓN. In early August Zapata's army was driven out of Mexico City, and in the spring of 1916 Carranza's troops invaded Morelos. There was no longer any realistic hope that Zapata might defeat the forces arrayed against him. Some historians contend that this failure was inevitable given the nature of the various revolutionary factions; others have argued that Zapata might have better supported Villa's military effort, or that he might have negotiated a more successful national alliance. In any event, Zapatismo now entered a long decline.

Still Zapata did not give up. With the help of a new chief adviser, Gildardo Magaña, he began to seek alliances with anyone who might help him fight Carranza. But conflict within Zapatismo now reached its highest level, and several prominent leaders defected. The most striking case was that of Otilio Montaño, coauthor of the Plan of Ayala, who was implicated in an uprising against Zapata in May 1917. Zapata ordered Montaño executed to send a message to other would-be traitors, but there was no way to counter the centrifugal forces at work. Zapata's efforts to lure supporters from other revolutionary camps thus became increasingly desperate. Finally, he invited a supposedly disaffected Carrancista colonel named Jesús Guajardo to join him. After exchanging a few letters, on 10 April 1919 Guajardo and Zapata met at a place called Chinameca. With a handful of men Zapata rode through the gate of the hacienda there and Guajardo's troops, assembled as if to give him military honors, shot him dead.

Some in Morelos still claim that Zapata is not dead,

that a man who looked like him took his place at

Chinameca and Zapata is hiding in the mountains

until the people need him again.

Zapata left a deep mark on Mexican life. Some in Morelos still claim that he is not dead, that a man who looked like him took his place at Chinameca and Zapata is hiding in the mountains until the people need him again. Meanwhile, for both the government of the institutionalized revolution and many of those who have opposed that government over the years, the figure of Zapata has become an enduring symbol of rural Mexico's struggle for justice.

– SAMUEL BRUNK

ZAPATA, FELIPE

Felipe Zapata (*b.* 24 May 1838; *d.* 28 July 1902), Colombian Liberal journalist and politician. He was born in Bogotá to a family of the Santander elite and attended the Colegio de Piedecuesta in his home region. He was imprisoned after the Liberals' defeat at Oratorio (1860). As a delegate to the Rionegro Convention (1863), Zapata resisted the extreme federalists and the anticlericals among his colleagues. He was a leading opponent of General Tomás Cipriano de MOSQUERA's increasing authoritarianism, a position revealed in articles

published in *La Unión* (March–June 1866) and *El Mensagero* (November 1866–March 1867). In both these Bogotá newspapers, Zapata chipped away at his opponent with calm logic. He later served in several Liberal governments in ministerial roles and was minister plenipotentiary to Great Britain and France in 1874. Zapata did not hesitate to criticize the foibles of his fellow Liberals. He opposed Rafael NÚÑEZ but condemned the Liberal revolutionaries in 1885. He moved to London in that year, becoming a liaison with Francisco Javier CISNEROS and British financiers. He died in London.

– J. LEÓN HELGUERA

ZARACONDEGUI, JULIÁN DE

Julián de Zaracondegui (*d.* 1873), Peruvian merchant. Heavily involved in lending activities in Lima in the 1850s, Zaracondegui had excellent political connections. By 1860 he had established himself in a variety of enterprises. Owner of a major export-import business in Lima, he was also a member of the Tribunal del Consulado (the merchant regulatory board), a guano consignee, a general director of the Banco de Lima, and an officer of the welfare agency called Beneficiencia Pública de Lima. He also served a term in the Chamber of Deputies. In the 1850s Zaracondegui founded a marketing firm to sell Peruvian cotton in Europe, and in 1859 he formed a partnership with the ASPÍLLAGA FAMILY to purchase a cotton plantation in the Saña Valley of the north coast. He put up the necessary cash—the equivalent of $120,000—and the Aspíllagas managed production on the plantation. Soon the cotton failed and the owners turned to sugar, thereafter the main crop in that region.

Zaracondegui's fortunes began to deteriorate after 1870. When one of his partners, Manuel de Argumániz, scandalized Lima by accusing him of undermining the cotton merchandising operation, difficulties befell his other enterprises. The financial crisis of 1873 blindsided many entrepreneurs, Zaracondegui among them, and he committed suicide.

– VINCENT PELOSO

ZARAGOZA, IGNACIO

Ignacio Zaragoza (*b.* 1829; *d.* 8 September 1862), Mexican military officer and hero of the battle of Puebla (5 May 1862). Born in Bahía de Espíritu Santo, in the Mexican province of Texas, and educated in Matamoros and Monterrey, Zaragoza hoped to pursue a career in business but found his opportunities limited by the devastated condition of the Mexican economy and his status as a mestizo. Zaragoza turned to a traditional occupation in his family—the military. He first joined the militia as a sergeant, and later was accepted into the regular army as a captain in 1853.

Zaragoza supported the Plan of Ayutla in 1854 and spent the rest of his life fighting on the side of the liberals. He fought against Santa Anna's army at Saltillo and in defense of Monterrey. When President Ignacio Comonfort supported the Plan of Tacubaya, Zaragoza organized riflemen in the capital against the conservative forces and in defense of the Constitution of 1857. With Leandro Valle, he led the liberal forces that took Guadalajara from Severo del Castillo and defeated Leonardo Márquez. Zaragoza served as quartermaster under Jesús GONZÁLEZ ORTEGA during the battle of Calpulalpán, where the liberal victory over the conservatives ended the War of the Reform.

In April 1861 President Benito JUÁREZ named Zaragoza his minister of war, replacing González Ortega, who had resigned in protest of Juárez's policies. Zaragoza held this post until December, when he resigned to take command of the Army of the East, confronting the forces of England, France, and Spain, which had landed in Veracruz that month to force payment of Mexico's foreign debt. After the English and Spanish forces withdrew and the French began their march on Mexico City, Zaragoza lost a battle at Azcultzingo and was forced to retreat. He quickly ordered fortifications built on the small hills of Loreto and Guadalupe that overlooked the city of Puebla. Mexican troops, armed with muskets the British had captured from Napoleon I at Waterloo and had sold to the Mexican government in the 1820s, faced roughly equal numbers of better-equipped and professionally trained French soldiers commanded by General Charles Fernand Latrille, Count of Lorencez. On 5 May 1862, the French made repeated assaults up the slopes of the Cerro de Guadalupe but were beaten back by Zaragoza's army. French casualties numbered roughly one thousand of a force of six thousand. The French retreated to Orizaba to await reinforcements, delaying their invasion of central Mexico for a year and giving Juárez's government time to organize resistance.

The moral and political effects of the victory far outweighed its importance in military terms. Zaragoza's victory over the French at Puebla became a powerful symbol of Mexico's national defiance of foreign interference and the occasion of one of Mexico's most important national holidays, Cinco de Mayo. Zaragoza died a few months later of typhoid in Puebla.

– D. F. STEVENS

ZÁRATE WILLKA, PABLO

Pablo Zárate Willka (*d.* 1903), an Aymara Indian from the Bolivian Altiplano who led an Indian uprising that grew out of the Bolivian Civil War (1899). *Willka* is an archaic Aymara word, meaning "greatness" or "eminence," that had previously been used by Indian protest leaders, including Luciano Willka in 1870–1871. We now know that the more important Willka of 1899 was Pablo Zárate, born on an unknown date in Imillaimilla, between Sicasica, La Paz, and Eucaliptus, Oruro.

Zárate, assuming the name *Willka,* originally joined the federalist cause led by José Manuel PANDO, later president of Bolivia, whose main preoccupation was to move the capital from Sucre to La Paz. But Zárate Willka and his Indian contingents soon demanded social changes, including the return of Indian communal lands lost several decades earlier. The uprising turned violent and became extensive. After Zárate Willka's capture in April 1899, the revolt collapsed. He died either while escaping from jail or being transported to another location. However, other versions of his death have some currency.

– CHARLES W. ARNADE

ZARCO, FRANCISCO

Francisco Zarco (*b.* 1829; *d.* 1869), Mexican journalist and politician. Born in Durango's capital, where his father was a minor bureaucrat in the state government and a colonel in the military, Zarco was largely self-educated because his family could not pay for his education. Luis de la Rosa named Zarco to a post in his foreign relations ministry in 1847. Zarco soon turned to journalism, writing political, literary, and biographical articles, some of which earned him the antipathy of President Mariano ARISTA, who had Zarco jailed, and of President Antonio López de SANTA ANNA, who forced him into exile. With the triumph of the Revolution of Ayutla, Zarco was able to return to Mexico and in 1855 was named editor of *El Siglo XIX,* a journal in which he continued to publish until shortly before his death. Representing Durango at the Constituent Congress of 1856–1857, Zarco was elected secretary by acclamation. His history of the congressional debates is a classic work on Mexico's political history. Zarco served as floor manager for the provisions of Constitution, known as the Ley Lerdo, that would force the church to sell its real estate. He defended the law as a prudent measure that would save the government from bankruptcy and benefit the clergy as well as the government. Later events pushed Zarco to recommend the confiscation of clerical property on the grounds that the clergy, by supporting the Rebellion of the Polkos in 1847 and the French Intervention after 1861, had proven to be disloyal to the nation and an "enemy of the people."

At the beginning of the War of the Reform in 1858, Zarco was arrested by the conservative government but managed to escape. In hiding, he continued to publish for two years, until he was discovered and jailed again. The liberal victory brought his release in December 1860, and the following month, President Benito JUÁREZ asked Zarco to serve as his minister of government and minister of foreign relations. Zarco negotiated a settlement of French claims but resigned when the Mexican congress rejected the proposed treaty.

Zarco turned to journalism, writing political, literary, and biographical articles, some of which earned him the antipathy of President Arista, who had Zarco jailed.

Zarco remained a supporter of Juárez in congress and his adviser. He continued publishing in Mexico City until May 1863, when the French forces approached, then moved north to San Luis Potosí and later to the United States, where he kept the international community informed about Mexico's struggle for national sovereignty and resistance to monarchy and aristocracy. After the defeat of the Empire, Zarco returned to Mexico and was again elected to the national legislature.

– D. F. STEVENS

ZAVALA, JOAQUÍN

Joaquín Zavala (*b.* 30 November 1835; *d.* 30 November 1906), president of Nicaragua (1879–1883, 1893). Zavala, a native of Managua, continued work on the Pacific Railroad, extended telegraph lines to Las Segovias, favored public education, founded the National Library, and continued the process of secularization by decreasing church influence in both government and education. In addition, he maintained peace in the country.

Zavala, a Conservative, was reelected to the presidency in 1893 when acting President Salvador Machado stepped down in the face of a rebellion led by the Genuines, a splinter group of the Conservative Party, and by Liberals commanded by José Santos ZELAYA. Zavala, however, was an ally and friend of Zelaya's and thought Zelaya could bring modernity to Nicaragua. Nonetheless, Zavala and Zelaya engaged in two battles to determine their country's future. Zavala lost both of these crucial battles, and his administration quickly fled Managua, leaving the government to Zelaya.

– SHANNON BELLAMY

ZAVALA, JOSÉ VÍCTOR

José Víctor Zavala (*b.* 1815; *d.* 1886), Guatemalan military leader. As a young corregidor, Zavala provided aid that was crucial to José Rafael CARRERA's 1848 return to power. By 1854 Zavala was a core member of Carrera's new government, which also included Zavala in-laws José Najera, Manuel Francisco PAVÓN AYCIENA, and Luís BATRES JUARROS.

Zavala continued his military climb with the successful 1854 siege of Omoa and with the command of Guatemalan troops during the National War (1856–1857) against William WALKER. Zavala returned to Guatemala as a national hero and proven Carrera ally. His general popularity as a moderate progressive led to public outrage over his loss in the 1869 presidential election. Zavala climaxed his career as commander in chief of the army of Liberal Justo RUFINO BARRIOS, who attempted to unify Central America.

– EDMOND KONRAD

ZAVALA, LORENZO DE

Lorenzo de Zavala (*b.* 3 October 1788; *d.* 15 November 1836), Mexican politician and writer. Born in Mérida, Yucatán, Zavala distinguished himself as a liberal member of the San Juan group in Mérida during the first constitutional period (1810–1814). Incarcerated in 1814, he spent three years in prison. Elected deputy to the restored Spanish Cortes in 1820, Zavala joined other American deputies in favoring home rule. He returned to Mexico in 1822 and was elected to the First Constituent Congress. He sided with Mexico's emperor, Agustín de ITURBIDE, when he dissolved the congress.

After the fall of the monarchy Zavala was elected to Congress once again, this time as a federalist. He joined the *yorkinos* (York Rite Masons) in 1825, becoming a leading radical. In 1827, Zavala was elected governor of the state of Mexico, where he introduced legislation to disentail church property and to break up village lands to encourage private ownership. The following year he joined the revolt of Acordada, eventually becoming minister of the treasury in the Vicente GUERRERO administration. In that capacity he had the temerity to levy new taxes in a vain attempt to restore sound fiscal policy. Driven out of office in 1829, Zavala traveled to the United States and Europe, where he wrote *Ensayo histórico de las revoluciones de Mégico*. He returned to Mexico and to politics in 1832; the following year he was elected to Congress once again. Shortly thereafter, he accepted the post of minister to France, where he remained until 1835.

With the collapse of federalism, Zavala returned to Texas, where he owned vast properties as a result of many years of land speculation. When Texas declared independence, he joined the separatists, becoming the first vice president of that republic. Suffering from poor health, he died in 1836, apparently from pneumonia.

– JAIME E. RODRÍGUEZ O.

ZAVALA, SILVIO

Silvio Zavala (*b.* 7 February, 1909), Mexican historian known for his work on the economic history of sixteenth-century Mexico, the political philosophy of the Spanish Conquest, and the nature of colonial economic institutions. Born in Mérida, Yucatán, he received a doctorate in law from the Universidad Central de Madrid in 1931. Zavala founded and served as director of the *Revista de historia de América* (1938–1965). He was also director of the National History Museum (1946–1954) and president of the Historical Commission of the Pan-American Institute of Geography and History (1947–1965). Zavala founded and was director of the Centro de Estudios Históricos at El Colegio de México (1940–1956) and was president of the college from 1963 to 1966. On the diplomatic front, he represented Mexico as permanent delegate to the United Nations for Education, Science and Culture (1956–1963) and as ambassador to France (1966–1975).

Zavala's scholarly work includes a pioneering study on the nature of the colonial labor systems, *La encomienda indiana* (1935), and one on colonial law, *Las instituciones jurídicas en la conquista de América* (1935). He published eight volumes of documents on labor, *Fuentes para la historia del trabajo en Nueva España* (1939–1946). His work is wide-ranging and includes *Francisco del Paso y Troncoso: Su misión en Europa, 1892–1916* (1938) and other substantial contributions to the study of colonial institutions in Spanish America.

– CARMEN RAMOS-ESCANDÓN

ZAYAS Y ALFONSO, ALFREDO

Alfredo Zayas y Alfonso (*b.* 21 September 1861; *d.* 11 April 1934), president of Cuba (1921–1925). An urban leader of the struggle against Spanish domination, Zayas held many offices after independence: president of the Senate (1905), revolutionary leader (1906), and adviser to the occupation authorities during the second U.S. intervention in Cuba (1906–1909). In 1909–1913 he was vice president and in 1921 finally succeeded in ascending to the presidency.

Historians usually focus on the nepotism, graft, and corruption that characterized Zayas's administration and tend to underemphasize his achievements. Nevertheless, despite his mismanagement, Zayas reestablished Cuba's international credit, which had been suffering from a sugar crisis. He succeeded in keeping within certain bounds the interference of U.S. envoy General Enoch Crowder. And he secured title to the Isle of Pines in 1925 after twenty years of U.S. procrastination. Above all, Zayas recognized that Cuba was undergoing a period of transition and that new social and political forces were emerging in the country. While in office, he had to face increasing student turbulence at the University of Havana, numerous bitter strikes, and even an uprising organized by the Veterans' and Patriots' Association. But Zayas preferred compromise to violence and managed to keep the peace. He always respected the right to dissent. In 1925, unable to secure his own reelection, he ceded the presidency to General Gerardo MACHADO Y MORALES and retired to private life.

– JOSÉ M. HERNÁNDEZ

ZEA AGUILAR, LEOPOLDO

Leopoldo Zea Aguilar (*b.* 30 June 1912), Mexican philosopher and scholar. One of the leading intellectual historians and philosophers in Latin America, Zea obtained undergraduate and graduate degrees from the National Autonomous University of Mexico (UNAM). His distinguished career has included important administrative positions, an impressive publication record, and the mentorship of generations of Latin American students. Among his most celebrated books are: *El apogeo y decadencia del positivismo en Mexico* (1944), *Dos etapas del pensamiento hispanoamericano* (1949), *América en la historia* (1957), and *Filosofía de la historia de América* (1976). He has received numerous academic awards from all over the world and has been instrumental in the development of Latin American intellectual centers and scholarship throughout Latin America.

– DAVID MACIEL

ZEBALLOS, ESTANISLAO

Estanislao Zeballos (*b.* 22 July 1854; *d.* 4 October 1923), Argentine statesman and intellectual. As minister of foreign affairs under presidents Miguel JUÁREZ CELMAN (1888–1890), Carlos PELLEGRINI (1891–1892), and José FIGUEROA ALCORTA (1906–1908), and minister to the U.S. government between 1893 and 1896, Zeballos played a key role in determining Argentine foreign policy during the liberal-conservative era.

Zeballos began his political career as a provincial deputy in Buenos Aires in 1879; he was elected in 1880 and again in 1884 to the National Congress. During his periods as minister of foreign affairs, Zeballos continued the line adopted by the Argentine delegation to the 1889 Pan-American Conference in Washington D.C.: a rejection of any hemispheric economic agreement that could jeopardize Argentine connections with European markets. Also of great consequence for Latin American international relations at the turn of the century was Zeballos's personal feud with José Maria da Silva Paranhos, Barão de RIO BRANCO, a Brazilian diplomat. After 1906, as President Figueroa Alcorta's foreign minister, Zeballos embarked upon an arms race with Brazil which—although Zeballos resigned in 1908—continued until 1914. In 1910, Zeballos became one of the delegates to the fourth Pan-American Conference in Buenos Aires. He was reelected to Congress for the 1912–1916 period and continued to influence public life through his writings on international relations. He wrote frequently for the press, mainly *El Nacional,* which he founded, and *La Prensa.* He also founded and directed a prestigious academic journal, *Revista de Derecho, Historia y Letras.* Professor of international law, he was appointed dean of the University of Buenos Aires Law School in 1910 and 1918. Zeballos was also a founder of the Sociedad Científica Argentina and president of the Sociedad Rural Argentina.

— EDUARDO A. ZIMMERMANN

ZELAYA, JOSÉ SANTOS

José Santos Zelaya (*b.* 31 October 1853; *d.* 17 May 1919), president of Nicaragua (1893–1909). Zelaya came to the presidency of Nicaragua in September 1893 by means of a revolution. His presidency was important to Nicaragua from several points of view. Politically, Zelaya's presidency constitutes the only substantial interval of rule by the Liberal Party in Nicaragua's history until the 1930s and the arrival of the Somozas. Liberal rule

---

In his first year in office Zelaya determined to

recapture Nicaraguan sovereignty over the

Miskito Coast.

---

resulted in several important measures to secularize and modernize Nicaraguan society. Economically, Zelaya presided over a commercial expansion that had considerable effect on Nicaragua's citizens. Internationally, his administration coincided with the period of Nicaragua's greatest influence on its Central American neighbors.

Although critics often make light of the ideological commitments of Central American political figures,

there is no doubt that Zelaya was committed to Liberal reforms. The Constitution of 1893 strengthened municipal government, separated church and state, prohibited convents and monasteries, guaranteed lay education, established a unicameral legislature, and abolished the death penalty. Like other positivist Latin American leaders, Zelaya was dedicated to bringing economic progress to his country, even by authoritarian methods. He undertook measures to promote export agriculture and granted concessions for the purpose of exploiting natural resources. Railway construction and the building of steamships for use on lakes Managua and Nicaragua received particular attention. Zelaya's zeal for reform, his commitment to economic progress and education, and his youthful cabinet contributed to making Managua an important headquarters for Liberals from northern South America and Central America during his presidency.

Despite democratic procedures outlined in the Constitution of 1893, Zelaya managed elections and ruled as a dictator. He faced approximately fifteen serious efforts by Conservatives to overthrow him. Having modernized and strengthened the Nicaraguan army, Zelaya had little difficulty suppressing his opponents. Unsuccessful rebels were jailed, received amnesty, and often fought again. He was not unusually repressive compared with other Central American presidents of the time.

It was in the field of international affairs that Zelaya made his most significant mark. Sympathetic to the alluring idea of restoring the Central American confederation, he lent his support in 1895 to the creation of the República Mayor, a union of Nicaragua, El Salvador, and Honduras. Although he was an admirer of Justo Rufino BARRIOS, the Guatemalan president who attempted to restore the confederation by force in 1885, Zelaya took no military measures to preserve the union of the three states. When a coup in El Salvador threatened the union, Zelaya counseled nonintervention, and the union collapsed. During the period 1902–1905, he promoted numerous international peace conferences among the Central American states.

Nicaraguan relations with Honduras and Costa Rica, Nicaragua's immediate neighbors, were primarily peaceful in the early years of Zelaya's presidency, although they deteriorated in 1907–1909. Zelaya initiated negotiations resulting in the signing of a treaty that, when it was finally accepted long after Zelaya's presidency, ended a border dispute between Honduras and Nicaragua. The border with Costa Rica, which had been determined by treaty in 1858 but was not marked, also occupied Zelaya's attention. Negotiations with Costa Rica led to the marking of the border in 1898.

neers preferred a Nicaraguan route for the proposed isthmian canal, negotiations stalled over Zelaya's resistance to Washington's demand for extraterritorial jurisdiction over the canal zone. When canal construction began in 1904 in Panama, the United States closely watched Zelaya, who was rumored to be courting other nations for possible construction of a rival canal. In 1907, when rivalry between Nicaragua and Guatemala spilled over into Honduras and El Salvador, threatening the stability of the Central American isthmus, Washington began to consider Zelaya a meddler and a threat to peace. An incident in 1909 involving the execution of two U.S. mercenaries led to a decision by Washington to support a rebellion against Zelaya. Recognizing that he could not stay in office against the opposition of the United States, Zelaya resigned and went into exile in December 1909.

– CHARLES L. STANSIFER

ZELAYA SIERRA, PABLO

Pablo Zelaya Sierra (*b.* 1896; *d.* 1933), twentieth-century Honduran painter. Zelaya studied at the Academy of Fine Arts of Costa Rica and subsequently at the San Fernando Academy in Madrid, where he came under the strong influence of Daniel Vásquez Díaz before returning to Honduras. His painting of *Las Monjas* was especially praised and was representative of his paintings while at San Fernando Academy. Although he died young, his neorealist painting made a strong impression in Honduras. His formal style exhibited strong technical perfection, but he often emphasized the figurative rather than the literal. He is credited with applying the Spanish style of Vásquez Díaz to Honduran motifs. His paintings *La muchacha del huacal* and *Dos campesinas* are especially fine examples of this.

– RALPH LEE WOODWARD, JR.

ZELEDÓN, BENJAMÍN FRANCISCO

Benjamín Francisco Zeledón (*b.* 4 October 1879; *d.* 4 October 1912), Nicaraguan Liberal general. The Liberal–Conservative coalition formed in the wake of the overthrow of dictator José Santos ZELAYA (1909) proved to be extremely unstable. In July 1912, Minister of War Luis Mena revolted against Conservative President Adolfo DÍAZ. Mena's chief lieutenant, Benjamín Zeledón, followed suit, to protect the coffee interests. Zeledón quickly seized Managua, Granada, and Masaya. Díaz grew increasingly concerned and requested military assistance from U.S. President William Howard Taft, who dispatched a Marine contingent on 4 August 1912. The marines soon numbered 2,700. Mena, out-

José Santos Zelaya, ca. 1906. (Latin American Library, Tulane University)

Problems with Great Britain and the United States were not so easily resolved. In his first year in office Zelaya determined to recapture Nicaraguan sovereignty over the Miskito Coast, which had been yielded formally by Great Britain over thirty years earlier but which was still subject to British influence over the Miskito Indians. Zelaya sent troops to Bluefields, headquarters for the Miskitos, and expelled the British consul, provoking British wrath and a brief British blockade of the port of Corinto. In the end Zelaya prevailed. A treaty accepting full Nicaraguan sovereignty was signed by Great Britain in 1904. The Miskito Coast was appropriately named the Department of Zelaya in recognition of his bold action.

The United States sided with Nicaragua on the issue of Miskito sovereignty, but other problems steered Nicaraguan relations with the United States on a perilous course. In the late 1890s, when it appeared that engi-

numbered and overwhelmed, fled the country, leaving the struggle to Zeledón. Both marines and Nicaraguan troops loyal to Díaz pursued Zeledón, who was killed at El Arroyo while attempting to break out of a U.S. encirclement. The victors paraded Zeledón's body on horseback in order to discourage further rebellions.

– SHANNON BELLAMY

ZENIL, NAHUM BERNABÉ

Nahum Bernabé Zenil (*b.* 1 January 1947), Mexican painter. Zenil, a native of Chicontepec, Veracruz, graduated from the National Teachers School in 1964 and began to teach primary school. In 1972 he completed studies at the National School of Painting and Sculpture, then continued to teach and paint until the late 1980s, when he dedicated himself to painting full time. Zenil's mixed-media paintings, generally self-portraits done on paper, address social circumstances and traditions in contemporary Mexican society, such as sexual identity, religion, and the family. His paintings are highly personal and autobiographical. Zenil is much influenced by the work of Frida KAHLO and popular painting of the nineteenth century, including the traditional *ex-voto* and *retablo* formats. He often incorporates text into his compositions. Zenil's work is consistently imbued with a profound gay sensibility. His first important exhibitions were held at the Galería de Arte Mexicano, in Mexico City, in 1985. Since that time he has been exhibited and collected internationally.

– CLAYTON C. KIRKING

ZENO GANDÍA, MANUEL

Manuel Zeno Gandía (*b.* 10 January 1855; *d.* 30 January 1930), Puerto Rican writer and politician. Zeno Gandía was born in Arecibo, Puerto Rico, where he attended elementary school. He did undergraduate and graduate work in medicine in Barcelona and Madrid, respectively. During this time he met the Cuban José MARTÍ, with whom he established a friendship that influenced him in literature and politics. Through his novels, newspaper articles, and poetry Zeno Gandía exposed the major social, economic, ethical, and political problems that afflicted Puerto Rico during the nineteenth and early twentieth centuries. In the political arena he fought for Puerto Rican independence from Spain and from the United States. In 1902 Zeno Gandía bought *La Correspondencia,* a newspaper in which he criticized public officials. Because of this criticism he was sued for libel by a U.S. representative, a case he won in the U.S. Supreme Court. In 1904 Zeno Gandía participated in the founding of the Partido de Unión

de Puerto Rico, which remained dominant in Puerto Rican politics until the mid-1920s.

Zeno Gandía is considered by many to be Puerto Rico's most important novelist of the nineteenth century, because his works represent the first serious realization of the genre in his country. His novels *La charca* (1894), *Garduña* (1896), *El negocio* (1922), and *Redentores* (1925) were grouped together under the series title of *Crónicas de un mundo enfermo.* In *La charca,* his best-known novel, which richly portrays the rural nineteenth-century Puerto Rican, he expressed all of his theories on naturalism and determinism.

– MAYRA FELICIANO

ZEPEDA, ERACLIO

Eraclio Zepeda (*b.* 24 March 1937), Mexican author. Born in Chiapas, Zepeda was educated at the Universidad Veracruzana, where he also taught. Considered the premier writer and storyteller in Mexico, Zepeda concentrates mostly on the indigenous culture of Chiapas. In 1959, he gained national prominence with the publication of *Benzulul,* a book of indigenous stories. Most of his work is socially oriented, speaking of humanity's basic needs and its relationship to nature. *Asalto nocturno* (1973; Nocturnal Assault) won Mexico's national prize for the best short-story collection in 1974. Also a renowned poet and member of La Espiga Amotinada, Zepeda, with four friends, published the collective work *La espiga amotinada* (1960) and *Ocupación de la palabra* (1965). These anthologies collected the works of a generation of Mexican poets who grounded their poetry in the social reality of the country. Other members of La Espiga Amotinada were Juan Banuelos, Oscar Oliva, Jaime Augusto Shelley, and Jaime Labastida. As a political activist, actor, and popular television personality, Zepeda is a forceful and affirmative figure, having earned worldwide respect and recognition. Other major works are *Andando el tiempo* (1982; Time Marching On), *Relación de travesía* (1985; Cross-Street Story), and *Confrontaciones* (1985; Confrontations).

– JEANNE C. WALLACE

ZEPEDA Y ZEPEDA, JUAN DE JESÚS

Juan de Jesús Zepeda y Zepeda (*b.* 20 November 1808; *d.* 20 April 1885), bishop of Comayagua, Honduras (1861–1885). Zepeda was born in San Antonio de Oriente and ordained a Franciscan priest in 1832. He became Guatemalan auxiliary bishop in 1859 and in 1861 was named bishop of Comayagua, where he soon distinguished himself as a friend of the needy and as a peacemaker. When Liberal President Marco Aurelio

SOTO initiated anticlerical legislation in 1879–1880, Zepeda, in poor health, complained but promised not to resist if the state provided funds to partly compensate for the loss of the tithe. Soto evidently complied, but when Luis Bográn Baraona became president in 1883, the church was treated more harshly. Financially weakened, it was unable to carry out even basic programs. Consequently, its role in Honduran society was reduced.

— EDWARD T. BRETT

ZIPOLI, DOMENICO

Domenico Zipoli (*b.* 16 or 17 October 1688; *d.* 2 January 1726), Italian organist and composer. Born in Prato, Tuscany, Zipoli commenced musical studies early. At the age of twenty-one, he moved to Naples to

---

While remembered particularly for his harpsichord works, Zipoli composed sonatas and toccatas for various instruments.

---

study with Alessandro Scarlatti. Later teachers included Lavinio Felice Vannucci and Bernardo Pasquini. Zipoli became choirmaster and organist of the Church of the Jesuits in Rome in 1715. He joined the Society of Jesus in 1716, and the following year traveled to Argentina, where he became choirmaster and organist in the Cathedral of Córdoba. His fame as a composer was established in 1716 with the publication of the *Sonate d'intavolatura,* a collection of keyboard music, the first part for organ and the second for harpsichord. Not much survives of the music he composed while in Argentina, and for many years his contribution to Argentine music was primarily thought to consist of his having brought to it music in the style of Scarlatti and Pasquini. But in 1959, in the Sucre Cathedral archives, a copy made at Potosí in 1784 of one of his masses was discovered. In 1966, the compositions *Tantum Ergo* and *Letania* were found in Beni, Bolivia, by Samuel Claro Valdés. While remembered particularly for his harpsichord works, Zipoli composed sonatas and toccatas for various instruments. He died in Córdoba.

— SERGIO BARROSO

ZORITA, ALONSO DE

Alonso de Zorita (Zurita; *b.* 1511/12; *d.* ca. 1585), judge of the Audiencia of Mexico (1556–1564). Zorita held various legal posts in the Caribbean and South America before reaching New Spain and, after ten years there, returned to Spain. Zorita's early career experiences in the fringe areas influenced the direction he took in Mexico attacking the *encomienda* system and promoting the role of the regular clergy, particularly the Franciscans, in dealings with the indigenous peoples.

Zorita left writings on New Spain's indigenous cultures, Nahua government and tribute systems, the Spanish invasion and post-Conquest Christianization efforts, published partly in his *Breve y sumaria relación de los señores de la Nueva España.* Although portions of his writings are based on earlier (now lost) sources, making them especially valuable, controversy nevertheless exists regarding some of his interpretations of the meaning of terms such as *mayeque* and *calpulli* and his remarks about Nahua nobility and municipal officers.

— STEPHANIE WOOD

ZORRILLA DE SAN MARTÍN, JUAN

Juan Zorrilla de San Martín (*b.* 28 December 1855; *d.* 3 November 1931), Uruguayan statesman and poet. Zorrilla de San Martín received his early education in Jesuit schools in Montevideo and in Santa Fe, Argentina. He received his law degree in 1877 from the university in Santiago de Chile. Returning to Montevideo in 1878, he took a position in the federal courts. In 1880, Zorrilla was appointed professor of aesthetics at the National University in Montevideo.

Zorrilla is best known as the author of the epic poem *Tabaré* (1888), an homage to the Charrúa Indians and an exaltation of the fusion of Hispanic and indigenous races. The postromantic verses of *Tabaré* recite the story of Uruguay—its people, its civilization, its spirit, and its aspirations. A dynamic orator, Zorrilla was also one of the most revered public figures in Uruguay: a defender of his country's democratic institutions and the voice of Uruguay in its art and music, its heritage and traditions.

In 1878, Zorrilla founded *El bien público,* a Catholic periodical. In 1885, his opposition to President Máximo Santos forced him to resign his position as professor of aesthetics at the National University and take refuge in Argentina, where he joined other Uruguayans in unsuccessful efforts to overthrow Santos.

Zorrilla was elected to Congress by the National Party in 1886. In 1892 he went to Madrid as Uruguayan representative to celebrate the four-hundredth anniversary of Columbus's arrival in the New World, and in 1894 served as Uruguayan ambassador in Paris. In 1899, Zorrilla edited *El Bien,* the new name of the journal he had founded. In recognition of his many years of public service, the National University in 1899 conferred on Zorrilla the title of professor of international law.

Zorrilla's political views apparently clashed with the policies of the liberal government of José BATLLE Y ORDÓÑEZ during the years 1903–1904. Despite this opposition, Zorrilla was appointed treasurer of the Bank of the Republic and was reelected as a government delegate every three years thereafter until his death.

– MYRON I. LICHTBLAU

ZUBIRÁN ANCHONDO, SALVADOR

Salvador Zubirán Anchondo (*b.* 23 December 1898), Mexican physician, educator, and nutritional expert. A 1923 graduate of the National University, Zubirán was one of an important generation of medical students. A disciple of Gastón Melo, he continued his medical studies at Harvard University, and in 1925 joined the medical faculty at the National University, where he taught for many years. He served as first head of the Child Welfare Department (1937), before becoming assistant secretary of health (1938–1943). Appointed rector of the National University in 1946, he resigned in 1948 after a violent student protest. Following his resignation, he directed programs in nutrition, and his efforts contributed substantially to Mexican knowledge in this field. He served as president of the Mexican Academy of Medicine (1947), and received Mexico's National Prize in Sciences (1968).

– RODERIC AI CAMP

ZUBIRÍA, JOSÉ ANTONIO LAUREANO DE

José Antonio Laureano de Zubiría (*b.* ca. 1780; *d.* after 1845), bishop of Durango, Mexico. Zubiría's pronouncements outlined the canonical justification for bringing the new Mexican church back under episcopal control and curbing aspects of folk piety that Catholic orthodoxy deemed harmful. Although Zubiría could not enforce his decrees, he laid the foundation for the reforms instituted by the first bishops of Santa Fe under American control.

Many of the criticisms that Zubiría leveled against the churches and Franciscan missions in New Mexico reflected the innovations and improvisations that New Mexicans had adopted since the 1760s, when the Spanish province found itself virtually isolated from the rest of Mexico by Comanche, Apache, and Ute raids. Symbolic of his view of New Mexican religious devotion, Zubiría criticized the crude pictures of the saints that some Franciscan missionaries had painted on animal hides because they had little access to religious art imported from Mexico. The combination of episcopal disapproval and the rise of an indigenous style of Santos carved from pine wood and decorated with brightly colored tempera on a coat of gesso led to the loss of most hide paintings from the missions during the Mexican period. Zubiría described even the new devotional art as "ugly images."

Zubiría's denunciation of the Brotherhood of Penitentes during the 1833 visitation is one of the few descriptions of the confraternity during its formative period. He mentioned that the organization had existed "for a good number of years, but without any authorization or even the knowledge of the bishops." He ordered the clergy in New Mexico to forbid Penitente meetings and ritual, because of "the excesses of very indiscreet corporal punishment which they are accustomed to practice . . . even publicly."

Zubiría's condemnation of the Penitentes had little effect. The church failed in its attempt to exert control over the brotherhood until the reforms of 1851–1852 promulgated by Bishop Jean Baptiste Lamy, first bishop of Santa Fe under the jurisdiction of the United States.

– ROSS H. FRANK

ZUBIZARRETA, GERÓNIMO

Gerónimo Zubizarreta (*b.* 9 October 1880; *d.* 14 May 1952), Paraguayan politician and university professor. Zubizarreta studied and later taught law at the National University in Asunción. After joining the Liberal Party in 1909, he occupied various positions in the party as well as in the Paraguayan Congress. Zubizarreta was highly respected for defending Paraguay's legal position before the Chaco War erupted between Paraguay and Bolivia in 1932. In 1937 he headed the Paraguayan delegation at the Buenos Aires Peace Conference but resigned in 1938 after losing in a power struggle with Paraguay's leader of the armed forces, General José Félix ESTIGARRIBIA. He was elected president of the Liberal Party in 1946, but he was forced into exile the following year after his arrest under President Higínio MORÍNIGO's regime. He returned to Paraguay in 1951 and remained president of his party until his death.

– MIGUEL A. GATTI

ZULEN, PEDRO S. AND DORA MAYER DE ZULEN

Pedro S. Zulen (*b.* 1889; *d.* 1925) and Dora Mayer de Zulen (*b.* 1868; *d.* 1957), Peruvian intellectuals and leaders of the *indigenismo* movement. *Indigenismo* has been one of the most controversial aspects of social reform in modern Peru. Alive since the 1880s in the essays of writers like Ricardo PALMA, Clorinda MATTO DE

TURNER, and Manuel GONZÁLEZ PRADA, the movement rests on the idea that the culture of the indigenous Andean population is at the core of the country's culture and should receive its due recognition. Several strategies were developed in the early twentieth century to make this idea a reality. Some of the proponents of *indigenismo* worked directly in the highland center of Cuzco, where under the leadership of men like archaeologist

---

The indigenismo *movement rests on the idea that the culture of the indigenous Andean population is at the core of Peru's culture and should receive its due recognition.*

Luis E. Valcárcel, the movement became intertwined with the drive to end the abuse of villagers at the hands of landlords. In Lima early-twentieth-century intellectuals, under the leadership of Pedro Zulen and Dora Mayer, sought to unify urban, sophisticated culture with their Andean roots. To do this they founded the Pro-Indigenous Association in 1909. In a weekly newsletter, *El Deber Pro-Indígena,* they fought for legal relief of Andean misery. Senator Joaquín CAPELO and José Antonio ENCINAS later joined their legal struggle. Soon delegates of the Pro-Indigenous Association throughout the country began reporting in the press and in the association newsletter injustices committed against indigenous people. The association recruited lawyers to defend villagers, and to arouse public opinion it sponsored public debates. The Zulens hoped thus to prod the legislature into passing remedial legislation. After 1919 the government of President Augusto LEGUÍA undermined the effectiveness of the association by absorbing its more important efforts into government programs. Laws, decrees, and resolutions reflecting the influence of the *indigenistas* were passed, but Leguía did not try to enforce them against the opposition of major highland landowners. Many highland villagers thereafter became more aware of their legal rights, and by the mid-1920s the *indigenista* movement had been absorbed into the revolutionary and reformist political movements taking shape in Peru.

— VINCENT PELOSO

ZULOAGA, FÉLIX MARÍA

Félix María Zuloaga (*b.* 1813; *d.* 1898), Mexican military officer and president of Mexico (January 1858–January 1859). Born in Álamos, Sonora, Zuloaga was raised in Chihuahua. He studied for a time in Mexico City but returned to the north, where he began a military career by joining the civic militia of Chihuahua in 1834 and fighting the Apaches and Comanches. He then returned to Mexico City, where he passed the engineering exam in 1838 and received a commission as second lieutenant in an engineering battalion of the regular army. He fought against the separatists in Yucatán, and was raised to the rank of lieutenant colonel in 1841. During the war with the United States, Zuloaga directed the fortifications at Monterrey in 1846 and fought in defense of Mexico City in 1847. After the war he returned to Chihuahua, where he held posts in the city government before returning to the army in 1851. He served as President of the Council of War of the Plaza of Mexico under President SANTA ANNA in 1853. Zuloaga fought against the Revolution of Ayutla in 1854 and was raised to the rank of brigadier general before being taken prisoner by the liberals.

After President Ignacio COMONFORT reintegrated him into the army, Zuloaga fought against a conservative rebellion in Puebla before supporting the Plan of Tacubaya in December 1857. The Plan of Tacubaya backed President Comonfort in the struggle between *puros* and *moderados,* and called for a new congress to write a new constitution "more in harmony with the will of the Nation." At first Comonfort supported the plan; then he organized against it and was deposed by General José de la Parra in January 1858. Benito JUÁREZ, head of the supreme court and next in legal succession to the presidency, assumed that office with the support of the liberals. Zuloaga, however, was elected president by the conservative Council of Representatives of the Departments (22 January 1853). This political clash began the War of the Reform. By presidential decree, Zuloaga annulled the Ley Iglesias, the Ley Juárez, and the Ley Lerdo, and reinstated all government employees who had lost their jobs for failing to swear allegiance to the Constitution of 1857. For his part in the execution of Melchor OCAMPO, Zuloaga was declared an outlaw by the liberals. He spent the years of the French Intervention in Cuba but returned to Mexico before his death.

— D. F. STEVENS

ZUM FELDE, ALBERTO

Alberto Zum Felde (*b.* 1889; *d.* 1976), Uruguayan poet, literary critic, and essayist. Alberto Zum Felde was born in Bahía Blanca, Argentina, but his parents moved to Uruguay when he was a young child. He joined the intellectual circle headed by Roberto de las Carreras. His poetry was first published under a pseudonym in

La Razón and *El Siglo*. In 1908 Zum Felde selected the name Aurelio del Hebrón as his pseudonym and his first book, *Domus aurea* (1908), a collection of sonnets and plays, was published under that name. These modernist sonnets and plays reflect both his talent and the influence that Nietzsche and Ibsen had on his writings.

With the publication of *El huanakauri* (1917), Zum Felde began to distance himself from modernist influences. The book, a didactic poem, argues for the autonomous cultural development of the Americas based upon tradition and historical reality. From 1919 until 1929, he worked as a literary critic for the afternoon edition of the newspaper *El Día* (later called *El Ideal*). He served as secretary, assistant director, and director (1940–1944) of the National Library. During the 1920s he also directed the literary magazine *La Pluma*. One of his notable books, *Proceso histórico del Uruguay* (1919) analyzes the sociopolitical evolution of the country. *Crítica de la literatura uruguaya* (1921) is a collection of weekly articles that were published in 1919–1920 in *El Día*. One of his most important books, *Proceso intelectual del Uruguay y crítica de su literatura* (1930), evaluates intellectual and literary production in the country beginning with the colonial period.

Zum Felde has been credited with the professionalization of literary studies in Uruguay. After his conversion to Catholicism, he published *Cristo y nosotros* (1959) and *Diálogo Cristo-Marx* (1971). Zum Felde was one of nine writers who founded the National Academy of Letters in 1943. In 1957 he won the National Literature Prize, and in 1968 he was awarded Uruguay's Grand Prize for Literature.

— DANUSIA L. MESON

ZUMÁRRAGA, JUAN DE

Juan de Zumárraga (*b.* ca. 1468; *d.* 3 June 1548), first bishop (1528–1547) and archbishop (1547–1548) of Mexico. Fray Juan de Zumárraga was born in Durango, near Bilbao, Spain; his birthdate is unknown but he was said to have been over eighty at death. Impressed by Zumárraga's campaign against alleged Basque witches, Charles V appointed him bishop of Mexico City. Zumárraga arrived in Mexico in 1528 as bishop-elect and Protector of the Indians. Zumárraga went to Spain in 1532 to report to the emperor; he was consecrated as bishop there in 1534. In 1535 Zumárraga joined forces with Don Antonio de MENDOZA, newly arrived first viceroy, to stabilize colonial rule and promote Indian education and Christianization. In 1536 they founded the Colegio de Santa Cruz, a Franciscan college for indigenous nobles. Zumárraga imported a printing press in 1536 and authored or sponsored a number of imprints, including Erasmian tracts. Zumárraga's think-

ing, typical of Spanish Franciscans, combined Renaissance humanism with mysticism and militant religious zeal. He conducted inquisitorial proceedings against Indians suspected of religious violations; the trials culminated with the 1539 burning at the stake of Don Carlos Mendoza Ometochtzin, native ruler of Texcoco. In 1547 Zumárraga was named archbishop of a new archdiocese comprising the bishoprics of México, Oaxaca, Michoacán, Tlaxcala, Guatemala, and Chiapas; he died soon after receiving the news.

— LOUISE M. BURKHART

ZUMAYA, MANUEL DE

Manuel de Zumaya (*b.* ca. 1678; *d.* between 12 March and 6 May 1756), Mexican composer and the first Mexican-born chapelmaster of the cathedral of Mexico City. Zumaya was a choirboy at the cathedral and became a pupil of the chapelmaster, the composer and organist Antonio Salazar. At sixteen he began lessons with the principal organist, José de Ydíaquez. Zumaya was ordained a priest in 1700 and a few years later was appointed one of three organists of the cathedral and polyphony teacher of the choirboys; he served as assistant to and substitute for Salazar. At Salazar's death in 1715, Zumaya was designated his successor as cathedral chapelmaster. To celebrate his twenty-four years at the cathedral, a new great organ was installed, considered the best of its kind in the Americas; its inauguration (15 August 1735) was commemorated with lavish festivities.

As a church composer Zumaya followed the traditional Spanish religious music style, but in some of his *villancicos* and in all his stage works he was strongly influenced by Italian opera. The music of the church at that time was not only for organ; strings and wind instruments accompanied the choirs with embellished melodic lines, strongly resembling operatic arias. In 1708 Zumaya had composed the music for *Don Rodrigo* [*El Rodrigo*], a play performed at the viceroyal palace; the manuscript, however, has been lost. The duke of Linares, the viceroy, made possible the performance of Zumaya's opera *La parténope* at the palace in May 1711. After Tomás de TORREJÓN Y VELASCO's *La púrpura de la rosa*, this opera was the second premiered in the New World and the first written by an American-born composer. In 1739 Zumaya moved to Oaxaca, where he became chapelmaster in 1745. He remained in that position until his death in Oaxaca.

— SUSANA SALGADO

ZUMBI

Zumbi (*b.* 1655?; *d.* 20 November 1695), organizer and leader of the free black republic (*quilombo*) of Palmares, in Alagoas state, northeastern Brazil. Little information is available concerning the early life of Zumbi and that which is known is subject to speculation. In 1685 he murdered his uncle Ganga Zumba, who had attempted to live in peace with the Portuguese, and proclaimed himself king of Palmares. He was responsible for the strengthening of a series of fortifications that made Palmares almost invincible to attackers. Zumbi's leadership proved effective in defeating a Portuguese expedition against the *quilombo* in 1686. When the forces of the *bandeirante* Domingos Jorge Velho attacked Palmares

---

Zumbi was decapitated and his head displayed in public in order to prevent any legends of his immortality.

---

in 1691, Zumbi's ambushes and counterattacks devastated them. In 1692 attempts were initiated to surround the *quilombo,* but Zumbi's forces were able to hold out until 1694, when a Luso-Brazilian expedition backed by artillery and reinforcements was finally able to destroy Palmares. Zumbi was decapitated and his head displayed in public in order to prevent any further legends of his immortality, but tradition grew about a heroic suicide in which he threw himself off a cliff rather than surrender and submit to enslavement. The actions of Zumbi forced the Portuguese to change their military strategy with regard to Maroon communities; henceforth, special military units were given the task of finding and destroying potentially dangerous fugitive Maroon settlements. Zumbi is considered an African Brazilian hero; his date of death is commemorated each year.

— MICHAEL L. JAMES

ZÚÑIGA, IGNACIO

Ignacio Zúñiga, nineteenth-century frontier military officer and politician. Zúñiga rose in the colonial army to command a series of presidio garrisons on Mexico's northwestern frontier, beginning with that of Tucson in 1809. As senator and then deputy in the national congress in the late 1820s, he unsuccessfully opposed the division of the state of Occidente into Sonora and Sinaloa. His 1835 treatise (*Rápida ojeada . . .*) detailed the problems of Sonora and proposed measures to alleviate public insecurities and promote enterprise. He supported the federalist revolts of José de URREA in 1837 and SANTA ANNA in 1841, and served as a federal deputy in 1842.

— STUART F. VOSS

ZÚÑIGA FIGUEROA, CARLOS

Carlos Zúñiga Figueroa (*b.* 1884; *d.* 1964), Honduran neorealist painter. Zúñiga studied during the 1920s at the San Fernando Academy in Madrid, where he received wide acclaim. He returned to Honduras to become one of Central America's leading painters in the following decades. His work was exhibited widely in Central America and the United States. He specialized in realistic portraits of ordinary people, but he also painted many contemporary Honduran leaders of society and politics. His series of historical paintings of Honduras's independence leaders, especially his *Glorification of General Morazán,* received favorable recognition. Toward the end of his life he began to focus his work on those at the bottom of the society—vagabonds, beggars, the mentally ill, and the poor. Unfortunately, a great many of these paintings were destroyed in a 1959 fire.

— RALPH LEE WOODWARD, JR.

Appendix: Biographies by Category

The encyclopedia contains biographies of nearly 3000 persons who have affected the course of Latin American history or culture. The present listing attempts a rough classification of these persons according to occupation or field of activity. The division of human endeavor into twenty-one overlapping fields is necessarily imperfect: many individuals have contributed to several areas, and not all activities are included in our categories. Nevertheless, the editors believe this listing offers a convenient starting point for research on the range of human enterprise in Latin America.

The final category ("Women") merely identifies the female subjects treated herein. Many of them have been neglected in previous compendiums. Although comparable treatments of African and indigenous origin would be of considerable interest, the editors did not attempt such classification on the grounds that the American complex of race mixtures and attitudes is not susceptible to schematic breakdown.

BUSINESS, FINANCE, TRADE, AND INDUSTRY

Aldama y González, Ignacio de
Álvarez, Manuel
Andresote
Antuñano, Estevan de
Aramayo Family
Billinghurst, Guillermo Enrique
Brión, Luis
Bunau-Varilla, Philippe Jean
Camacho Roldán, Salvador
Candamo, Manuel
Escandón, Manuel
Farquhar, Percival
Fernández, Max
Fernandini, Eulogio E.
Ferré Aguayo, Luis Antonio
Ibarra, Diego
Ibarra, José de Pineda
Irisarri y Larraín, Juan Bautista
Kinney, Henry L.
Krieger Vasena, Adalberto
Lagos, Ricardo
Le Bretón, Tomás Alberto
Leguía, Augusto Bernardino
Limantour, José Yves
López de Quiroga, Antonio
Maluf, Paulo Salim

Marinho, Roberto
Martínez de Hoz, José Alfredo
Mauá, Visconde de
Menocal, Mario García
Mindlin, José E.
Molina Solís, Olegario
Monte Alto
Mora Porrás, Juan Rafael
Noriega Moreno, Manuel Antonio
Noronha, Fernão de
Orlich Bolmarcich, Francisco José
Ottoni, Teofilo Benedito
Pacheco, Gregorio
Palenque, Carlos
Pardo y Lavalle, Manuel
Parra, Aquileo
Pastrana Borrero, Misael
Patiño, Simón Iturri
Pearson, Weetman Dickinson
Pelé (Edson Arantes do Nascimento)
Piérola, Nicolás de
Pinedo, Federico
Piñol y Sala, José
Porras, José Basilio
Prado, Paulo
Prado y Ugarteche, Javier
Prado y Ugarteche, Manuel
Prat Echaurren, Jorge

Prebisch, Raúl
Quijano, Carlos
Ramos Mejía, Ezequiel
Rengifo Cárdenas, Manuel
Ríos Morales, Juan Antonio
Robles, Marcos Aurelio
Romero de Terreros, Pedro
Rosas, Juan Manuel de
Roy, Eugène
Ruíz Tagle Portales, Francisco
Sacasa, Juan Bautista
Samper Agudelo, Miguel
Sancho de Hoz, Pedro
Santos, Sílvio
Sardaneta y Llorente, José Mariano de
Simonsen, Mário Henrique
Terrazas, Luis
Tornquist, Ernesto
Trejos Fernández, José Joaquín
Uribe Uribe, Rafael
Vaccaro Brothers
Velázquez Cárdenas de León, Joaquín
Vergara Echeverez, José Francisco
Vernet, Louis
Vesco, Robert Lee
Villanueva, Carlos Raúl
Yermo, Gabriel de
Zamorano, Agustín Juan Vicente

Zaracondegui, Julián de
Zavala, Lorenzo de
Zemurray, Samuel

CINEMA, THEATER, TELEVISION, SPORTS, AND RECREATION

Acevedo Hernández, Antonio
Alcoriza, Luis
Álvarez Armellino, Gregorio Conrado
Amorim, Enrique
Armendáriz, Pedro
Arnaz, Desi
Arriví, Francisco
Arrufat, Antón
Castro, Juan José
Chocrón, Isaac
Clair, Janete
Clemente Walker, Roberto
Córdova, Arturo de
Cugat, Xavier
Del Río, Dolores
Denevi, Marco
Fernández, Emilio "El Indio"
Figueroa, Gabriel
Galindo, Alejandro
Gambaro, Griselda
García, Sara
Garmendia, Salvador
Gavidia, Francisco Antonio
Gómez-Cruz, Ernesto
Marqués, René
Miranda, Carmen
Monterroso, Augusto
Nalé Roxlo, Conrado
Negrete, Jorge
Pardavé, Joaquín
Pelé
Perricholi, La
Prado y Ugarteche, Mariano Ignacio
Ripstein, Arturo
Rojo, María
Sánchez, Florencio
Santos, Sílvio
Sarduy, Severo
Silva, Orlando
Skármeta, Antonio
Soler, Andrés, Domingo, and Fernando
Steimberg, Alicia
Sumac, Yma
Tin-Tan
Triana, José

Uslar Pietri, Arturo
Valle, Rafael Heliodoro
Wolff, Egon
Xuxa
Zorilla de San Martín, Juan

EDUCATION AND SCHOLARSHIP

Aceval, Benjamín
Acosta, José de
Adem Chahín, José
Adem Chahín, Julián
Alcorta, Diego
Alegre, Francisco Javier
Alemán Valdés, Miguel
Alfaro, Ricardo Joaquín
Alonso, Amado
Alvarado, Lisandro
Álvarez Armellino, Gregorio Conrado
Álvarez Gardeazábal, Gustavo
Amorim, Enrique
Amunátegui Aldunate, Miguel Luis
Anchieta, José de
Anderson Imbert, Enrique
Andreoni, João Antônio
Angelis, Pedro de
Arboleda, Carlos
Argüello, Leonardo
Arosemena, Justo
Arzáns Orsúa y Vela, Bartolomé
Ávila, Julio Enrique
Ayala, Eligio
Ayala, Eusebio
Ayala, José de la Cruz
Ayora Cueva, Isidro
Azara, Félix de
Azevedo, Fernando de
Azevedo, Thales de
Bachiller y Morales, Antonio
Baldorioty de Castro, Ramón
Baptista, Mariano
Baquedano, Manuel
Baquíjano y Carrillo de Córdoba, José de
Baralt, Rafael María
Barbero, Andrés
Barnola, Pedro Pablo
Barreda, Gabino
Barreto de Menezes, Tobias, Jr.
Barros, João de
Barros Arana, Diego
Basadre, Jorge

Bassols, Narciso
Bellegarde, Luis Dantès
Bello, Andrés
Benítez, Jaime
Bermejo, Ildefonso
Bernal y García Pimentel, Ignacio
Bingham, Hiram
Bolaños, Luis de
Bolton, Herbert Eugene
Borges, Jorge Luis
Box, Pelham Horton
Bray, Arturo
Brenner, Anita
Bresser Pereira, Luiz Carlos
Brum, Baltasar
Bunge, Alejandro
Bunge, Carlos Octavio
Bustamante y Rivero, José Luis
Caballero y Rodríguez, José Agustín
Cabrera, Lydia
Calcaño, José Antonio
Caldera Rodríguez, Rafael
Calógeras, João Pandiá
Calvo, Carlos
Campos, Francisco Luiz da Silva
Campos, Roberto (de Oliveira)
Cañas, José Simeón
Cané, Miguel
Capelo, Joaquín
Capistrano de Abreu, João
Cardim, Frei Fernão
Cardoso, Felipe Santiago
Cardoso, Fernando Henrique
Caro, Miguel Antonio
Carrillo Flores, Antonio
Carrillo Flores, Nabor
Caso y Andrade, Alfonso
Caso y Andrade, Antonio
Castañeda, Francisco de Paula
Castillo, Jesús
Castillo Ledón, Amalia
Castro Madriz, José María
Centurión, Carlos R.
Cerezo Arévalo, Marco Vinicio
Cervantes, Vicente
Chávez Sánchez, Ignacio
Clavigero, Francisco Javier
Cobo, Bernabé
Coldazzi, Agustín
Coni, Emilio R.
Constant Botelho de Magalhães, Benjamin
Cordero Crespo, Luis

Cornejo, Mariano H.
Corona, Ramón
Correoso, Buenaventura
Corvalán Lepe, Luis
Cosío Villegas, Daniel
Coutinho, José Joaquim da Cunha de Azeredo
Couto, José Bernardo
Covarrubias, Miguel
Cuervo, Rufino José
Delfim Neto, Antônio
Deustua, Alejandro O.
Di Tella, Torcuato
Dias, Antônio Gonçalves
Díaz de Guzmán, Ruy
Díaz Soto y Gama, Antonio
Dobles Segreda, Luis
Dobrizhoffer, Martín
Domínguez, Manuel
Drago, Luis María
Durão, José de Santa Rita
Elhuyar, Juan José de
Elhuyar y Zúbice, Fausto de
Encina, Francisco Antonio
Escalada, Asunción
Esquiú, Mamerto
Estimé, Dumarsais
Etchepareborda, Roberto
Facio Brenes, Rodrigo
Falcón, José
Faoro, Raymundo
Feijóo, Benito Jerónimo
Fernandes, Florestan
Fernández Artucio, Hugo
Figueiredo, Afonso Celso de Assis
Figueroa Gajardo, Ana
Figueroa Larraín, Emiliano
Francia, José Gaspar Rodríguez de
Freire, Paulo
Freyre, Gilberto (de Mello)
Frías, Antonio
Frigerio, Rogelio
Frondizi, Risieri
Fuentes, Manuel Atanasio
Fúrlong Cárdiff, Guillermo
Furtado, Celso
Galindo, Juan
Gallegos, Rómulo
Galván Rivera, Mariano
Gamio Martínez, Manuel
Gandavo, Pero de Magalhães
Garay, Blas
García, Genaro

García de Castro, Lope
García Diego y Moreno, Francisco
García Icazbalceta, Joaquín
García Robles, Alfonso
García Salinas, Francisco
Garibay Kintana, Ángel María
Gavidia, Francisco Antonio
Gelly, Juan Andrés
Gil Fortoul, José
Golbery do Couto e Silva
Gómez, Benígno
Gondra, Manuel
González, Joaquín Victor
González, Juan Natalicio
Gonález Casanova, Pablo
González Prada, Manuel
González Suárez, (Manuel María) Federico
Gorostiza, Manuel Eduardo de
Gorriti, Juan Ignacio de
Graef Fernández, Carlos
Grau San Martín, Ramón
Groussac, Paul
Guamán Poma de Ayala, Felipe
Guerra y Sánchez, Ramiro
Guevara Arze, Walter
Halperín-Donghi, Tulio
Haro Barraza, Guillermo
Henríquez Ureña, Max
Henríquez Ureña, Pedro
Henry the Navigator
Hernández Colón, Rafael
Herrera, Bartolomé
Holanda, Sérgio Buarque de
Hostos y Bonilla, Eugenio María de
Ianni, Octavio
Ibarguren, Carlos
Incháustegui Cabral, Héctor
Ingenieros, José
Ivaldi, Humberto
Jaguaribe Gomes de Matos, Hélio
James, Cyril Lionel Robert
Jerez, Francisco de
Justo, Juan B.
Koellreutter, Hans Joaquim
Korn, Alejandro
Kumate Rodríguez, Jesús
Labarca Hubertson, Amanda
Landívar, Rafael
Las Casas, Bartolomé de
Lastarria, José Victorino
León-Portilla, Miguel
Lescot, Élie

Letelier Madariaga, Valentín
Lewis, Roberto
Ley, Salvador
Lida, Raimundo
Liendo y Goicoechea, José Antonio
Lima, Alceu Amoroso
Lindo Zelaya, Juan
Liscano Velutini, Juan
Llorente y Lafuente, Anselmo
López, Vicente Fidel
López Michelsen, Alfonso
Lozano, Pedro
Luna Pizarro, Francisco Javier de
Luz y Caballero, José de la
Maldonado, Francisco Severo
Mansilla, Lucio Victorio
Margil de Jesús, Antonio
Marroquín, Francisco
Masferrer, Alberto
Massera, José Pedro
Matienzo, José Nicolás
Maza, Manuel Vicente de
Medina, José Toribio
Mejía del Valle y Llequerica, José Joaquín
Mello, Zélia Maria Cardoso de
Mendes, Gilberto
Méndez Montenegro, Julio César
Mendiburu, Manuel de
Mendieta y Montefur, Carlos
Millas Jiménez, Jorge
Mir, Pedro
Mitre, Bartolomé
Mogrovejo, Toribio Alfonso de
Molina Garmendia, Enrique
Monteiro, Tobias do Rêgo
Montt Torres, Manuel
Moog, Vianna
Mora Porrás, Juan Rafael
Morales Carrión, Arturo
Moreau de Justo, Alicia
Moreno, Fulgencio
Moreno, Mariano
Moscote, José Dolores
Moshinsky Borodiansky, Marcos
Moziño, José Mariano
Munguía, Clemente de Jesús
Mutis, José Celestino
Nabuco de Araújo, Joaquim
Nascimento, Abdias do
Nimuendajú, Curt
Nóbrega, Manuel de
Novo, Salvador

Núñez Vargas, Benjamin
Nusdorffer, Bernardo
O'Gorman, Edmundo
Oliveria, Willy Correia de
Oliveira Lima, Manuel de
Oré, Luis Gerónimo de
Orozco y Berra, Manuel
Ortiz, Fernando
Oviedo y Valdés, Gonzalo Fernández
Pacheco, José Emilio
País, Frank
Palafox y Mendoza, Juan de
Pane, Ignacio Alberto
Pardo y Aliaga, Felipe
Paso y Troncoso, Francisco del
Paterson, William
Paz Soldán Family
Peixoto, Júlio Afrânio
Peláez, Amelia
Pellicer Cámara, Carlos
Pena, Afonso Augusto Moreira
Peralta Azurdia, Enrique
Peralta Barnuevo y Rocha, Pedro de
Pérez Acosta, Juan Francisco
Pérez Aguirre, Luis
Pinheiro, José Feliciano Fernandes
Pinho, José Wanderley de Araújo
Popenoe, Frederick Wilson
Porras Barrenechea, Raúl
Prado, João Fernando de Almeida
Prado, Paulo
Prado da Silva Júnior, Caio
Prieto Rodríguez, Sotero
Querino, Manoel Raimundo
Quesada, Ernesto
Quiroga, Vasco de
Rabasa, Emilio
Rama, Angel
Ramírez, José Fernando
Ramírez Vázquez, Pedro
Ramos, Artur
Ramos Mejía, José María
Ramos y Magaña, Samuel
Ravignani, Emilio
Rebouças, André
Restrepo, Carlos Eugenio
Reyes, Rafael
Reyes Ochoa, Alfonso
Ribeiro, Darcy
Ribera y Espinosa, Lázaro de
Riva Agüero y Osma, José de la
Rivarola, Rodolfo
Rocafuerte, Vicente

Rocha, Justiniano José da
Rocha, Manoel Ribeiro
Rocha Pita, Sebastião
Rodrigues, José Honório
Rodrigues, Raimundo Nina
Rodríguez, Simón
Rodríguez Lara, Guillermo
Rodríguez Monegal, Emir
Roig de Leuchsenring, Emilio
Romay y Valdés Chacón, Tomás
Romero, Emilio
Romero, Sílvio
Romero Rubio, Manuel
Rosenblueth, Arturo Stearns
Ruiz de Montoya, Antonio
Saco, José Antonio
Sáenz, Moisés
Salvador, Vicente do
Sánchez, Luis Alberto
Sánchez, Prisciliano
Sánchez de Bustamante y Sirven, Antonio
Sánchez de Tagle, Francisco Manuel
Sandoval Vallarta, Manuel
Santamaría, Haydée
Sarmiento, Domingo Faustino
Sepp, Anton
Serrano, José
Sierra O'Reilly, Justo
Sigüenza y Góngora, Carlos de
Silva Herzog, Jesús
Silva Lisboa, José da
Simonsen, Mário Henrique
Simonsen, Roberto Cochrane
Sodré, Nelson Werneck
Solano, Francisco
Solórzano Pereira, Juan de
Soto Alfaro, Bernardo
Sousa, Gabriel Soares de
Sousa, Otávio Tarqüínio de
Stefanich, Juan
Suárez, Marco Fidel
Tallet, José Zacarías
Tamayo, Franz
Tannenbaum, Frank
Taunay, Affonso d'Escragnolle
Tavares Bastos, Aureliano Cândido
Teixeira, Anisio Espinola
Tello, Julio César
Toledo y Figueroa, Francisco de
Torres Bello, Diego de
Torres Bodet, Jaime
Torre y Huerta, Carlos de la

Trejos Fernández, José Joaquín
Tugwell, Rexford Guy
Unanue, Hipólito
Uribe Uribe, Rafael
Uruguai, Visconde do
Valdivia, Luis de
Valencia, Guillermo León
Valle, José Cecilio del
Varela, José Pedro
Varela y Morales, Félix
Varnhagen, Francisco Adolfo de (Visconde de Porto Seguro)
Varona y Pera, Enrique José
Vasconcelos Calderón, José
Vaz Ferreira, Carlos
Velázquez Cárdenas de León, Joaquín
Vélez Sarsfield, Dalmacio
Vera Cruz, Alonso de la
Viana, Francisco José de Oliveira
Vieira, Antônio
Vigil, Francisco de Paula González
Villacorta Calderón, José Antonio
Villanueva, Carlos Raúl
Villarán, Manuel Vicente
Vitoria, Francisco de
Weffort, Francisco Correia
Wilde, Eduardo
Ximénez, Francisco
Yáñez Santos Delgadillo, Agustín
Ynsfrán, Pablo Max
Zaldúa, Francisco Javier
Zavala, Joaquín
Zavala, Silvio
Zayas y Alfonso, Alfredo
Zea Aguilar, Leopoldo
Zubirán Achondo, Salvador
Zubiría, José Antonio Laureano de
Zulen, Pedro S. [and] Dora Mayer de Zulen
Zum Felde, Alberto

EXPLORATION AND CONQUEST (including *bandeirantes*)

Abreu, Diego de
Aguayo, Marqués de
Aguilar, Jerónimo de
Aguilar, Martín de
Aguirre, Lope de
Alarcón, Martín de
Alberni, Pedro de
Almagro, Diego de

Alvarado y Mesía, Pedro de
Álvarez de Pineda, Alonso
Ampíes, Juan de
Andagoya, Pascual de
Anza, Juan Bautista de
Arias de Saavedra, Hernando
Ávila, Pedro Arias de
Balboa, Vasco Núñez de
Bastidas, Rodrigo de
Bazaine, François Achille
Belalcázar, Sebastián de
Bodega y Quadra, Juan Francisco de la
Borba Gato, Manuel de
Brasseur de Bourbourg, Charles
    Étienne
Cabeza de Vaca, Alvar Núñez
Cabot, Sebastian
Cabral, Pedro Álvares
Castellanos, Juan de
Cavallón, Juan de
Columbus, Christopher
Coronado, Juan Vázquez de
Cortés, Hernán
Díaz del Castillo, Bernal
Elcano, Juan Sebastián de
Enciso, Martín Fernández de
Escandón, José de
Espejo, Antonio de
Esteban
Fajardo, Francisco
Féderman, Nicolás
Fernández, Juan
Fernández de Córdoba, Diego
Frémont, John Charles
Galindo, Juan
Gama, Vasco da
Garay, Juan de
Garcés, Francisco Tomás Hermenegildo
García, Aleixo
Girón, Francisco Hernández
González Dávila, Gil
Grijalva, Juan de
Guzmán, Nuño Beltrán de
Henry the Navigator
Heredia y Heredia, José M.
Hurtado de Mendoza, Andrés
Hurtado de Mendoza, García
Ibarra, Diego
Irala, Domingo Martínez de
Jiménez de Quesada, Gonzalo
Juan y Santacilia, Jorge
Kinney, Henry L.
Kino, Eusebio Francisco

La Salle, René-Robert Cavelier, Sieur
    de
Lasuén, Fermín Francisco de
León, Alonso de
Lepe, Diego de
López, Narciso
López de Legazpi y Gurruchátegui,
    Miguel
Losada, Diego de
Luna y Arellano, Tristán de
Luque, Hernando de
Magellan, Ferdinand
Malinche
Manso de Velasco, José Antonio
Martínez, Esteban José
Melgares, Facundo
Mendoza, Pedro de
Menéndez de Avilés, Pedro
Montejo, Francisco de
Narváez, Pánfilo de
Nicuesa, Diego
Niño, Pedro Alonso
Niza, Marcos de
Ojeda, Alonso de
Olid, Cristóbal de
Oña, Pedro de
Oñate, Juan de
Orellana, Francisco de
Oriz de Zárate, Juan and Juana
Pardo, Juan
Pérez, Juan
Pérez de Tolosa, Juan
Pinzón, Martín Alonso
Pinzón, Vicente Yáñez
Pizarro, Francisco
Pizarro, Gonzalo
Pizarro, Hernando
Ponce de León, Juan
Portolá, Gaspar de
Ramalho, João
Reyes, Rafael
Rivera, Pedro de
Rivera y Moncada, Fernando de
Rodríguez Cabrillo, Juan
Rodríguez Freile, Juan
Rondon, Cândido Mariano da Silva
Sarmiento de Gamboa, Pedro
Sedeño, Antonio de
Serra, Junipero
Solís, Juan Díaz de
Soto, Hernando de
Sousa, Martim Afonso de
Talamantes, Melchor de

Tavares, Antônio Rapôso
Ulloa, Antonio de
Urdaneta, Andrés de
Ursúa, Pedro de
Valdivia, Pedro de
Vargas, Diego de
Vázquez de Ayllón, Lucas
Velázquez, Diego de
Vélez de Escalante, Silvestre
Vespucci, Amerigo
Vial, Pedro
Villagra, Francisco de
Villagrá, Gaspar Pérez de
Villas Bôas Brothers
Vizcaíno, Sebastián

JOURNALISM (including polemicists)

Acosta, José de
Alamán, Lucas
Alberdi, Juan Bautista
Alencar, José Martiniano de
Alzate y Ramírez, José Antonio de
Amaral, Antônio José Azevedo do
Andrade, Carlos Drummond de
Andreve, Guillermo
Andueza Palacio, Raimundo
Ângelo, Ivan
Antuñano, Estevan de
Arango y Parreño, Francisco de
Arboleda, Julio
Arce Castaño, Bayardo
Arciniegas, Germán
Arguedas, Alcides
Ayala, José de la Cruz
Aycinena Piñol, Juan José de
Azevedo, Fernando de
Báez, Cecilio
Baldorioty de Castro, Ramón
Barreda y Loas, Felipe
Barreiro, Antonio
Barrett, Rafael
Barros Arana, Diego
Barroso, Gustavo Dodt
Bedoya Reyes, Luis
Belaúnde, Víctor Andrés
Beltrán, Pedro
Bergaño y Villegas, Simón
Berges, José
Betances, Ramón Emeterio
Betancourt, Rómulo
Betancourt Cisneros, Gaspar

Blanco, Andrés Eloy
Blanco Acevedo, Eduardo
Blanco Galdós, Hugo
Bocaiúva, Quintino
Brandão, Ignácio de Loyola
Bravo, Mario
Bray, Arturo
Brenner, Anita
Bulnes, Francisco
Bustamante, Carlos María de
Bustamante y Rivero, José Luis
Cabrera Lobato, Luis
Callado, Antônio
Capistrano de Abreu, João
Cárcano, Miguel Ángel
Cárcano, Ramón José
Caro, José Eusebio
Caro, Miguel Antonio
Carpio Nicolle, Jorge
Caso y Andrade, Antonio
Castelli, Juan José
Castro Madriz, José María
Centurión, Carlos R.
Centurión, Juan Crisóstomo
Chamorro Cardenal, Pedro Joaquín
Coelho Neto, Henrique
Coll y Toste, Cayetano
Cooke, John William
Correoso, Buenaventura
Corvalán Lepe, Luis
Cos y Pérez, José María
Cosío Villegas, Daniel
Costa, Hipólito José da
Creydt, Oscar
Cuadra, Pablo Antonio
Cumplido, Ignacio
Cunha, Euclides da
Darío, Rubén
Dávila Espinoza, Carlos Guillermo
Debray, [Jules] Régis
Del Prado, Jorge
Deustua, Alejandro O.
Dickmann, Adolfo
Dickmann, Enrique
Dobles Segreda, Luis
Echeverría, Esteban
Egaña Fabres, Mariano
Escalante, Aníbal
Estrada, José Manuel
Etchepareborda, Roberto
Faoro, Raymundo
Fernández Artucio, Hugo
Fernández Madrid, José

Fernández Retamar, Roberto
Figueiredo, Afonso Celso de Assis
Flores Magón, Ricardo
Fortuny, José Manuel
Francia, José Gaspar Rodríguez de
Frondizi, Risieri
Fuentes, Manuel Atanasio
Gainza Paz, Alberto
Gaitan, Jorge Eliécer
Galeano, Eduardo Hughes
Gálvez, Manuel
Gama, Luís
Garay, Blas
Garcilaso de la Vega, El Inca
Garvey, Marcus
Gelly, Juan Andrés
Ghioldi, Américo
Ghioldi, Rodolfo
Gil Fortoul, José
Girri, Alberto
Gómez, Eugenio
Gómez, Juan Gualberto
Gómez Carrillo, Enrique
Gómez Castro, Laureano
González, Florentino
González, Joaquín Victor
González, Juan Natalicio
Gorostiza, Manuel Eduardo de
Groussac, Paul
Guardia, Ricardo Adolfo de la
Gutiérrez, Gustavo
Gutiérrez, José María
Gutiérrez Estrada, José María
Gutiérrez Nájera, Manuel
Guzmán, Antonio Leocadio
Guzmán, Martín Luis
Haya de la Torre, Víctor Raúl
Henríquez Ureña, Max
Henríquez Ureña, Pedro
Hernández, José
Herrera, Bartolomé
Herrera, Luis Alberto de
Herrera y Obes, Julio
Herzog, Vladimir
Hidalgo, Bartolomé
Hidalgo, Enrique Agustín
Hidalgo y Costilla, Miguel
Holanda, Sérgio Buarque de
Ibarguren, Carlos
Iglesias Pantin, Santiago
Infante, José Miguel
Ingenieros, José
Irisarri y Larraín, Juan Bautista

James, Cyril Lionel Robert
Justo, Juan B.
Krauze, Enrique
Lacerda, Carlos Frederico Werneck de
Larrea, Juan
Las Casas, Bartolomé de
Lastarria, José Victorino
Lida, Raimundo
Lima, Alceu Amoroso
Lima Barreto, Afonso Henriques de
Liscano Velutini, Juan
Lleras Restrepo, Carlos
Lombardo Toledano, Vicente
López Michelsen, Alfonso
López Pumarejo, Alfonso
López Trujillo, Alfonso
López Vallecillos, Italo
López y Fuentes, Gregorio
Lugones, Leopoldo
Luisi, Luisa
Luna Pizarro, Francisco Javier de
Machado, Gustavo
Machado de Assis, Joaquim Maria
Maldonado, Francisco Severo
Mallea, Eduardo
Mañach y Robato, Jorge
Mansilla, Lucio Victorio
Mariátegui, José Carlos
Marinho, Roberto
Martínez Estrada, Ezequiel
Masferrer, Alberto
Massera, José Pedro
Matto de Turner, Clorinda
Mendieta y Montefur, Carlos
Mier Noriega y Guerra, José Servando
   Teresa de
Milla y Vidaurre, José
Miranda, Francisco de
Miro Quesada Family
Mitre, Bartolomé
Molina, Pedro
Molina Enríquez, Andrés
Monsiváis, Carlos
Montalvo, Juan
Monte Alto
Monteiro, Tobias do Rêgo
Monteiro Lobato, José Bento
Moog, Vianna
Mora, José María Luis
Mora Fernández, Juan
Morales Lemus, José
Moreno, Fulgencio
Moreno, Mariano

Moshinsky Borodianksky, Marcos
Munguía, Clemente de Jesús
Muñoz Marín, Luis
Muñoz Rivera, Luis
Nardone, Benito
Nariño, Antonio
Novás Calvo, Lino
Novo, Salvador
Núñez Moledo, Rafael
Ocampo, Melchor
Ocampo, Victoria
O'Gorman, Edmundo
Olaya Herrera, Enrique
Olmedo, José Joaquín
Ortiz, Fernando
Ospina Rodríguez, Mariano
Otero, Mariano
Ottoni, Teofilo Benedito
Pacheco, José Emilio
Palma, Ricardo
Pardo y Aliaga, Felipe
Paso y Troncoso, Francisco del
Patrocínio, José do
Payno y Flores, Manuel
Paz, Octavio
Paz Soldán Family
Perera, Víctor
Pérez, Carlos Andrés
Pérez Esquivel, Adolfo
Picón Salas, Mariano
Porras Barrenechea, Raúl
Posada, José Guadalupe
Prado, João Fernando de Almeida
Prado da Silva Júnior, Caio
Prieto, Guillermo
Puig Casauranc, José Manuel
Quesada, Ernesto
Rama, Angel
Ramírez, Ignacio
Ramírez, José Fernando
Ramos Mejía, José María
Real de Azúa, Carlos
Rebouças, André
Restrepo, Carlos Eugenio
Ribeiro, João Ubaldo
Rio Branco, Barão do
Rio Branco, Visconde do
Rio, João do
Rius
Riva Palacio, Vicente
Roca, Blas
Rocafuerte, Vicente
Rocha, Justiniano José da

Rodó, José Enrique
Rodríguez, Carlos Rafael
Rodríguez, Simón
Rodríguez Cerna, José
Rodríguez Monegal, Emir
Roig de Leuchsenring, Emilio
Rojas, Ricardo
Romay y Valdés Chacón, Tomás
Rubião, Murilo
Saco, José Antonio
Salazar Bondy, Sebastián
Salgado, Plinio
Sánchez, Luis Alberto
Sánchez de Bustamante y Sirven,
    Antonio
Sanguinetti, Julio María
Santa Cruz y Espejo, Francisco Javier
    Eugenio de
Santos, Eduardo
Sarmiento, Domingo Faustino
Sarmiento de Gamboa, Pedro
Scalabrini Ortiz, Raúl
Sierra O'Reilly, Justo
Silva Herzog, Jesús
Sodré, Nelson Werneck
Solórzano Pereira, Juan de
Sousa, Otávio Tarqüínio de
Souza, Márcio Gonçalves Bentes
Talavera, Natalício
Tallet, José Zacarías
Távara y Andrade, Santiago
Timerman, Jacobo
Torre, Lisandro de la
Torres Bodet, Jaime
Traba, Marta
Tristan, Flora
Trujillo, Manuel
Turbay Ayala, Julio César
Ugarte, Manuel
Ulate Blanco, Otilio
Urbina, Luis Gonzaga
Valencia, Guillermo León
Valle, Artistóbulo del
Valle, José Cecilio del
Varela, José Pedro
Varela y Morales, Félix
Vargas Llosa, Mario
Varona y Pera, Enrique José
Vasconcelos Calderón, José
Vedia y Mitre, Mariano
Veiga, Evaristo Ferreira da
Villarán, Manuel Vicente
Villaurrutia, Jacobo de

Villeda Morales, Ramón
Walker, William
Wyld Ospina, Carlos
Zapata, Felipe
Zarco, Francisco
Zavala, Lorenzo de
Zavala, Silvio
Zayas y Alfonso, Alfredo
Zeballos, Estanislao
Zulen, Pedro S. [and] Dora Mayer de
    Zulen

LABOR AND LABOR RELATIONS (excluding slavery)

Abadía Méndez, Miguel
Aguirre Cerda, Pedro
Alem, Leandro
Allende Gossens, Salvador
Arcos, Santiago
Arismendi, Rodney
Arze, José Antonio
Bilbao Barquín, Francisco
Bravo, Mario
Campa Salazar, Valentín
Cano, María de los Ángeles
Chonchol, Jacques
Collor, Lindolfo
Corral Verdugo, Ramón
Del Prado, Jorge
Eder, Santiago Martín
Fallas Sibaja, Carlos Luis
Flores Magón, Ricardo
Ghioldi, Américo
Ghioldi, Rodolfo
Guevara, Ernesto "Che"
Guiérrez Garbín, Víctor Manuel
Iglesias Pantin, Santiago
Julião Arruda de Paula, Francisco
Justo, Juan B.
Lacerda, Maurício Pavia de
Lechín Oquendo, Juan
Lombardo Toledano, Vicente
López, Ambrosio
Machado, Gustavo
Mendes Filho, Francisco "Chico" Alves
Molina Solís, Olegario
Monge Álvarez, Luis Alberto
Morones, Luis
Núñez Vargas, Benjamin
Pacheco da Silva, Osvaldo
Palacios, Alfredo L.
Pellacani, Dante

Peña, Lázaro
Prieto Figueroa, Luis Beltrán
Querino, Manoel Raimundo
Recabarren Serrano, Luis Emilio
Riani, Clodsmith
Roca, Blas
Romero Rosa, Ramón
Seoane, Manuel
Siles Zuazo, Hernán
Silva, Lindolfo
Silva, Luis Inácio Lula da
Torre, Lisandro de la
Velázquez Sánchez, Fidel

LAND OWNERSHIP (including *encomenderos, hacendados,* agriculturalists, etc.)

Abasolo, Mariano
Agramonte y Loynaz, Ignacio
Aguayo, Marqués de
Álzaga, Martín de
Arana, Felipe de
Arana, Julio César
Arango y Parreño, Francisco de
Argüello, Santiago
Aspíllaga Family
Aycinena, Juan Fermín de
Bemberg, Otto
Bulnes Prieto, Manuel
Carvajal, Luis de
Cedillo Martínez, Saturnino
Chiari, Rodolfo E.
Chiari Remón, Roberto Francisco
Cisneros Betancourt, Salvador
Cortés, Hernán
Cortés, Martín
de León, Martín
Dellepiane, Luis J.
Egaña Fabres, Mariano
Elías, Domingo
Figueres Ferrer, José
Galindo, Juan
Garay, Juan de
Gildermeister Family
Gómez, Juan Vicente
Guerra, Ramón
Güiraldes, Ricardo
Irala, Domingo Martínez de
Lacalle Herrera, Luis Alberto
Leguía, Augusto Bernardino
López de Quiroga, Antonio
López de Romaña, Eduardo

Machado y Morales, Gerardo
Madero, Francisco Indalecio
Miro Quesada Family
Monte Alto
Mora, Fernando de la
Nicuesa, Diego
Orlich Bolmarcich, Francisco José
Paz Soldán Family
Pétion, Alexandre Sabès
Romero, Matías
Rosáins, Juan Nepomuceno
Ruíz Tagle Portales, Francisco
Sousa, Gabriel Soares de
Terrazas, Luis
Toro Zambrano, Mateo de
Torre Tagle, José Bernardo de Tagle y Portocarrero
Uribe Uribe, Rafael
Vallejo, Mariano Guadalupe
Zaracondegui, Julián de

LITERATURE, BELLES LETTRES, AND PHILOSOPHY

Abadía Méndez, Miguel
Abbad y Lasierra, Íñigo
Abente y Lago, Victorino
Abril, Xavier
Acevedo Díaz, Eduardo Inés
Acevedo Hernández, Antonio
Acosta, José de
Aguiar, Adonias
Aguilera Malta, Demetrio
Aguirre, Nataniel
Agustín, José
Agustini, Delmira
Alamán, Lucas
Albán, Laureano
Alegre, Francisco Javier
Alegría, Ciro
Alegría, Claribel
Alegría, Fernando
Alencar, José Martiniano de
Alexis, Jacques Stéphen
Alfaro, Ricardo Joaquín
Allende, Isabel
Almafuerte
Almeida, José Américo de
Almeida, Manuel Antônio de
Almonte, Juan Nepomuceno
Alonso, Amado
Alonso, Manuel A.
Altamirano, Ignacio Manuel

Alvarado, Lisandro
Alvarado, Salvador
Álvarez Gardeazábal, Gustavo
Alzate y Ramírez, José Antonio de
Amado, Jorge
Ambrogi, Arturo
Amorim, Enrique
Anchieta, José de
Andagoya, Pascual de
Anderson Imbert, Enrique
Andrade, Carlos Drummond de
Andrade, Jorge
Andrade, Mário de
Andrade, Oswald de
Andreve, Guillermo
Ángel, Albalucía
Angelis, Pedro de
Ângelo, Ivan
Appleyard, José Luis
Arboleda, Julio
Arciniegas, Germán
Arcos, Santiago
Arenas, Reinaldo
Arévalo Bermejo, Juan José
Arévalo Martínez, Rafael
Arguedas, Alcides
Arguedas, José María
Argüelles, Hugo
Arias, Arturo
Arias Sánchez, Oscar
Aridjis, Homero
Arlt, Roberto
Arosemena, Justo
Arreola, Juan José
Arriví, Francisco
Arrufat, Antón
Ascasubi, Hilario
Assunção, Leilah
Asturias, Miguel Ángel
Ávila, Julio Enrique
Azar, Héctor
Azcárate y Lezama, Juan Francisco de
Azevedo, Aluísio
Azuela, Mariano
Bachiller y Morales, Antonio
Balbuena, Bernardo de
Ballagas y Cubeñas, Emilio
Balseiro, José Agustín
Bandiera, Manuel Carneiro de Souza
Baquerizo Moreno, Alfredo
Baralt, Rafael María
Barbosa, Domingos Caldas
Barnet, Miguel

Barnola, Pedro Pablo
Barreiro, Antonio
Barreto de Menezes, Tobias, Jr.
Barrios, Eduardo
Barroso, Gustavo Dodt
Basso Maglio, Vicente
Basurto, Luis
Batlle y Ordóñez, José
Batres Montúfar, José
Bedregal de Conitzer, Yolanda
Bélance, René
Bellegarde, Luis Dantès
Belli, Gioconda
Bello, Andrés
Beltrán, Washington
Benedetti, Mario
Benítez, Gregorio
Benítez-Rojo, Antonio
Bermejo, Ildefonso
Betances, Ramón Emeterio
Bianco, José
Bilbao Barquín, Francisco
Bioy Casares, Adolfo
Blanco, Andrés Eloy
Blanco Fombona, Rufino
Blest Gana, Alberto
Bombal, María Luisa
Bonifaz Nuño, Rubén
Borge, Tomás
Borges, Jorge Luis
Borno, Joseph Louis E. Antoine
    François
Bosch Gaviño, Juan
Brañas Guerra, César
Brandão, Ignácio de Loyola
Brannon de Samayoa Chinchilla,
    Carmen
Brasseur de Bourbourg, Charles
    Étienne
Brathwaite, Edward Kamau
Brenner, Anita
Brierre, Jean-Fernand
Britto García, Luis
Brull, Mariano
Brunet, Marta
Bryce Echenique, Alfredo
Bulnes, Francisco
Burgos, Julia de
Bustamante, Carlos María de
Caballero y Rodríguez, José Agustín
Caballero Calderón, Eduardo
Cabeza de Vaca, Alvar Núñez
Cabral, Manuel del

Cabrera, Lydia
Cabrera Infante, Guillermo
Cáceres, Esther de
Calcaño, José Antonio
Callado, Antônio
Cambaceres, Eugenio
Camille, Roussan
Camões, Luís Vaz de
Campo, Estanislao del
Campos, Julieta
Campos Cervera, Hérib
Canales, Nemesio Rosario
Candanedo, César
Cané, Miguel
Cantón, Wilberto
Capelo, Joaquín
Cardenal, Ernesto
Cardoza y Aragón, Luis
Caro, José Eusebio
Caro, Miguel Antonio
Carpentier, Alejo
Carranza Fernández, Eduardo
Carrasquilla, Tomás
Carrera Andrade, Jorge
Carrión, Alejandro
Carrión, Manuel Benjamín
Carvajal, Luis de
Casal, Julián del
Casanova y Estrada, Ricardo
Caso y Andrade, Antonio
Castellanos, Juan de
Castellanos, Rosario
Castillo, Jesús
Castillo, Otto René
Castillo y Guevara, Francisca Josefa de
    la Concepción de
Castro Alves, Antônio de
Caviedes, Juan del Valle y
Centurión, Roque Miranda
Cerruto, Óscar
Césaire, Aimé
Céspedes y Quesada, Carlos Manuel de
Charry Lara, Fernando
Chauvet, Marie Vieux
Chávez Sánchez, Ignacio
Chimalpahin
Chocano, José Santos
Chumacero, Alí
Cieza de León, Pedro de
Clavigero, Francisco Javier
Cobo, Bernabé
Coelho Neto, Henrique
Coicou, Massillon

Coll y Toste, Cayetano
Colmán, Narciso
Condé, Maryse
Constant Botelho de Magalhães,
    Benjamin
Coronel Urtecho, José
Correa, Julio Myzkowsky
Cortázar, Julio
Cortés, Hernán
Cosío Villegas, Daniel
Costa, Cláudio Manuel da
Couto, José Bernardo
Cruz e Sousa, João da
Cuadra, Pablo Antonio
Cuevas, Mariano
Cunha, Euclides da
Cunha Dotti, Juan
Dalton García, Roque
Darío, Rubén
Debray, [Jules] Régis
Dellepiane, Luis J.
Denevi, Marco
Depestre, René
D'Escoto Brockmann, Miguel
Desnoes, Edmundo Pérez
Dias, Antônio Gonçalves
Dias Gomes, Alfredo
Díaz, José Pedro
Díaz Lozano, Argentina
Díaz Soto y Gama, Antonio
Diego, Eliseo
Diego, José de
Donoso, José
Dragún, Osvaldo
Durán, Diego
Durand, Oswald
Durão, José de Santa Rita
Echeverría, Esteban
Edwards, Agustín
Edwards, Jorge
Edwards Bello, Joaquín
Eguren, José María
Elizondo, Salvador
Encisco, Martín Fernández de
Enríquez de Guzmán, Alonso
Ercilla y Zúñiga, Alonso de
Estrada, José Manuel
Facio Brenes, Rodrigo
Fallas Sibaja, Carlos Luis
Fariña Núñez, Eloy
Féderman, Nicolás
Feijóo, Benito Jerónimo
Fernandes, Millôr

Fernández de Lizardi, José Joaquín
Fernández Madrid, José
Fernández Retamar, Roberto
Figueiredo, Afonso Celso de Assis
Florit, Eugenio
Fortuny, José Manuel
Franco, Rafael
Freire, Paulo
Freyre, Gilberto (de Mello)
Frondizi, Risieri
Fuentes, Carlos
Fuentes y Guzmán, Francisco Antonio
  de
Funes, Gregorio
Gaitán Durán, Jorge
Galeano, Eduardo Hughes
Galindo, Sergio
Gallego, Laura
Gallegos, Rómulo
Galván, Manuel de Jesús
Gálvez, Manuel
Gama, José Basilio da
Gama, Luís
Gambaro, Griselda
Gamboa Iglesias, Federico
Gaos, José
García, Genaro
García Icazbalceta, Joaquín
García Márquez, Gabriel
García Peláez, Francisco de Paula
Garcilaso de la Vega, El Inca
Garmendia, Salvador
Garro, Elena
Gatón Arce, Freddy
Gavidia, Francisco Antonio
Girri, Alberto
Glantz, Margo
Glissant, Édouard
Goldemberg, Isaac
Gómez, Juan Carlos
Gómez Carrillo, Enrique
Gómez de Avellaneda y Arteaga,
  Gertrudis
Gonzaga, Tomás Antônio
González, Joaquín Victor
González, Juan Natalicio
González, Juan Vicente
González Casanova, Pablo
González León, Adriano
González Martínez, Enrique
González Prada, Manuel
Gorodischer, Angélica
Gorostiza, Manuel Eduardo de

Grimard, Luc
Groussac, Paul
Guarnieri, Gianfrancesco
Gudiño Kieffer, Eduardo
Guerra y Sánchez, Ramiro
Guido, Beatriz
Guillén, Nicolás
Güiraldes, Ricardo
Guirao, Ramón
Gutiérrez González, Gregorio
Gutiérrez Nájera, Manuel
Guzmán, Augusto
Guzmán, Enrique
Guzmán, Martín Luis
Haro Barraza, Guillermo
Henríquez Ureña, Max
Henríquez Ureña, Pedro
Heredia y Heredia, José M.
Hernández, Felisberto
Hernández, José
Hernández, Luisa Josefina
Herrera, Flavio
Herrera y Reissig, Julio
Herrera y Tordesillas, Antonio de
Hidalgo, Bartolomé
Hidalgo, Enrique Agustín
Hippolyte, Dominique
Holguín, Jorge
Huidobro Fernández, Vicente
Ibáñez, Roberto
Ibáñez, Sara de
Ibarbouro, Juana de
Ibargüengoitia, Jorge
Icaza Coronel, Jorge
Iglesias, José María
Illescas, Carlos
Incháustegui Cabral, Héctor
Isaacs, Jorge
James, Cyril Lionel Robert
Jaramillo Levi, Enrique
Jesus, Carolina Maria de
Juana Inés de la Cruz, Sor
Korn, Alejandro
Krauze, Enrique
Labrador Ruiz, Enrique
Laguerre, Enrique Arturo
Laleau, Léon
Lame, Manuel Quintín
Landa, Diego de
Landívar, Rafael
Larreta, Enrique Rodríguez
Las Casas, Bartolomé de
Leante, César

Leñero, Vicente
Levinson, Luisa Mercedes
Lezama Lima, José
Lida, Raimundo
Liendo y Goicoechea, José Antonio
Lihn, Enrique
Lima, Alceu Amoroso
Lima, Jorge de
Lima Barreto, Afonso Henriques de
Lins, Osman da Costa
Lins do Rego, José
Liscano Velutini, Juan
Lispector, Clarice
Llorens Torres, Luis
López, Willebaldo
López de Cogolludo, Diego
López Portillo, José
López Vallecillos, Italo
López Velarde, Ramón
López y Fuentes, Gregorio
Lorenzana y Buitrón, Francisco
  Antonio de
Lugones, Leopoldo
Luz y Caballero, José de la
Lynch, Benito
Lynch, Marta
Macedo, Joaquim Manuel de
Machado de Assis, Joaquim Maria
Magalhães, Domingos José Gonçalves
  de
Magaña, Sergio
Magdelano, Mauricio
Maíz, Fidel
Mallea, Eduardo
Mañach y Robato, Jorge
Manzano, Juan Francisco
Marechal, Leopoldo
Marinello, Juan
Mármol, José Pedro Crisólogo
Marqués, René
Marroquín, José Manuel
Martínez Estrada, Ezequiel
Masferrer, Alberto
Massera, José Pedro
Matos, Gregório de
Matto de Turner, Clorinda
Meireles, Cecília
Melo Franco, Afonso Arinos de
Melo Neto, João Cabral de
Méndez Ballester, Manuel
Méndez Pereira, Octavio
Milla y Vidaurre, José
Mir, Pedro

Miró, César
Mistral, Gabriela
Mitre, Bartolomé
Molina, Juan Ramón
Molina Bedoya, Felipe
Molinari, Ricardo E.
Montalvo, Juan
Monteiro Lobato, José Bento
Monterroso, Augusto
Montúfar, Lorenzo
Morais, Vinícius de
Morales, Beltrán
Morales, Mario Roberto
Morales Carrión, Arturo
Morejón, Nancy
Moscote, José Dolores
Moshinsky Borodianksky, Marcos
Motecuhzoma II
Motolinía, Toribio de
Munguía, Clemente de Jesús
Muñoz Marín, Luis
Muñoz Rivera, Luis
Mutis, Albaro
Naipaul, V. S.
Nalé Roxlo, Conrado
Naranjo, Carmen
Nascimento, Abdias do
Neruda, Pablo
Nervo, Amado
Nezahualcoyotl
Novás Calvo, Lino
Novo, Salvador
Núñez Moledo, Rafael
Obaldía, María Olimpia de
Ocampo, Victoria
Odio, Eunice
O'Gorman, Edmundo
O'Leary, Daniel Florencio
Oliveira, Manuel Botelho de
Olmedo, José Joaquín
Onetti, Juan Carlos
Oreamuno, Yolanda
Oribe, Emilio
Orozco, Olga
Orozco y Berra, Manuel
Orphée, Elvira
Ortiz, Fernando
Ortiz de Ayala, Simón Tadeo
Otero, Mariano
Ovando, Nicolás de
Oviedo y Valdés, Gonzalo Fernández
Pacheco, José Emilio
Padilla, Heberto

Palacios, Antonia
Palés Matos, Luis
Palma, Ricardo
Pani Arteaga, Alberto J.
Pardo y Aliaga, Felipe
Pareja Diezcanseco, Alfredo
Parra, Nicanor
Parra, Teresa de la
Paso, Fernando del
Paso y Troncoso, Francisco del
Paterson, William
Patrocínio, José do
Payno y Flores, Manuel
Paz, Octavio
Peixoto, Júlio Afrânio
Pellicer Cámara, Carlos
Pena, Luís Carlos Martins
Peralta Barnuevo y Rocha, Pedro de
Perera, Víctor
Peri Rossi, Cristina
Phelps, Anthony
Picón Salas, Mariano
Piñera, Virgilio
Piñon, Nélida
Pita Rodríguez, Félix
Pitol, Sergio
Pizarnik, Alejandra
Plá, Josefina
Pompéia, Raúl
Poniatowska, Elena
Porras Barrenechea, Raúl
Pôrto Alegre, Manuel Araújo
Prado, Pedro
Prieto, Guillermo
Puga, María Luisa
Puig, Manuel
Puig Casauranc, José Manuel
Queiroz, Dinah Silveira de
Queiroz, Rachel de
Quintana Roo, Andrés
Quiroga, Horacio
Rabasa, Emilio
Rada, Manuel de Jesús
Ramírez, Ignacio
Ramírez, José Fernando
Ramírez Mercado, Sergio
Ramos, Graciliano
Ramos Arizpe, José Miguel
Ramos y Magaña, Samuel
Rego Monteiro, Vicente do
Restrepo, José Manuel
Revueltas, José
Reyes, Alfonso

Reyes, Rafael
Reyes Ochoa, Alfonso
Ribeiro, João Ubaldo
Ribeyro, Julio Ramón
Rio, João do
Riva Agüero y Osma, José de la
Riva Palacio, Vicente
Rivera, José Eustasio
Rivera, Pedro de
Roa Bastos, Augusto
Rodó, José Enrique
Rodrigues, Nelson
Rodríguez-Alcalá, Hugo
Rodríguez Cerna, José
Rodríguez Freile, Juan
Rodríguez Juliá, Edgardo
Roig de Leuchsenring, Emilio
Rojas, Manuel
Rojas, Ricardo
Rokha, Pablo de
Rokha, Winétt de
Romay y Valdés Chacón, Tomás
Romero, Emilio
Romero, Francisco
Romero, José Luis
Romero, José Rubén
Romero, Matías
Romero, Sílvio
Romero Rosa, Ramón
Rosa, João Guimarães
Rosáins, Juan Nepomuceno
Roscio, Juan Germán
Rosenblueth, Arturo Stearns
Roumain, Jacques
Rubião, Murilo
Rueda, Manuel
Ruiz de Alarcón y Mendoza, Juan
Rulfo, Juan
Sabat Ercasty, Carlos
Sábato, Ernesto
Sáenz, Jaime
Sahagún, Bernardino de
Sáinz, Gustavo
Salazar Arrué, Salvador Efraín
Salazar Bondy, Sebastián
Salgado, Plinio
Samayoa Chinchilla, Carlos
Samper, José María
Sánchez, Luis Rafael
Sánchez, Prisciliano
Sánchez de Bustamante y Sirven,
  Antonio
Sánchez de Tagle, Francisco Manuel

Santa Cruz y Espejo, Francisco Javier
Eugenio de
Sarduy, Severo
Sarmiento, Domingo Faustino
Sarmiento de Gamboa, Pedro
Sarney, José
Schwarz-Bart, Simone
Scliar, Moacyr
Shimose, Pedro
Sierra, Stella
Sierra Méndez, Justo
Sierra O'Reilly, Justo
Sigüenza y Góngora, Carlos de
Silva, Clara
Silva, José Asunción
Sinán, Rogelio
Skármeta, Antonio
Sologuren, Javier
Solórzano, Carlos
Solórzano Pereira, Juan de
Somers, Armonía
Soriano, Osvaldo
Soto, Pedro Juan
Souza, Márcio Gonçalves Bentes
Squier, Ephraim George
Steimberg, Alicia
Storni, Alfonsina
Suárez, Marco Fidel
Suassuna, Ariano Vilar
Subero, Efraín
Tablada, José Juan
Talamantes, Melchor de
Talavera, Natalício
Tallet, José Zacarías
Tamayo, Franz
Taunay, Alfredo d'Escragnolle, Vicomte
de
Távara y Andrade, Santiago
Telles, Lygia Fagundes
Tello, Julio César
Thiel, Bernardo Augusto
Toro, Fermín
Torres Bodet, Jaime
Torre y Huerta, Carlos de la
Traba, Marta
Triana, José
Tristan, Flora
Trujillo, Manuel
Umaña Bernal, José
Unanue, Hipólito
Urbina, Luis Gonzaga
Urzagasti, Jesús
Usigli, Rodolfo

Uslar Pietri, Arturo
Valdés, Gabriel de la Concepción
Valenzuela, Luisa
Valero, Roberto
Vallbona, Rima de
Vallejo, César
Vallenilla Lanz, Laureano
Varela, Florencio
Vargas Llosa, Mario
Varona y Pera, Enrique José
Vasconcelos Calderón, José
Vásquez, Francisco de Asís
Vega, Aurelio de
Vera Cruz, Alonso de la
Veríssimo, Érico
Vespucci, Amerigo
Vial, Pedro
Vieira, Antônio
Vigil, Francisco de Paula González
Vilariño, Idea
Villacorta Calderón, José Antonio
Villagrá, Gaspar Pérez de
Villarán, Manuel Vicente
Villaurrutia, Xavier
Villaverde, Cirilo
Villegas, Oscar
Vitier, Cintio
Vizcaíno, Sebastián
Von Vacano, Arturo
Walcott, Derek
Wheelock Román, Jaime
Wyld Ospina, Carlos
Ximénez, Francisco
Yanes, Francisco Javier
Yáñez Santos Delgadillo, Agustín
Ydígoras Fuentes, Miguel
Zaid, Gabriel
Zavala, Lorenzo de
Zavala, Silvio
Zayas y Alfonso, Alfredo
Zea Aguilar, Leopoldo
Zelaya, José Santos
Zeno Gandía, Manuel
Zepeda, Eraclio
Zorita, Alonso de

THE MILITARY

Abascal y Souza, José Fernando
Acevedo Díaz, Eduardo Inés
Achá, José María
Acosta, Tomás
Agramonte y Loynaz, Ignacio

Aguayo, Marqués de
Aguilar, Jerónimo de
Aguirre, Juan Francisco de
Alarcón, Martín de
Alberni, Pedro de
Alberto, João
Albuquerque, Antônio Francisco de
Paula
Aldama y González, Juan de
Alfaro Delgado, José Eloy
Allende, Ignacio
Almazán, Juan Andréu
Almonte, Juan Nepomuceno
Alonso, Mariano Roque
Alvarado, Lisandro
Alvarado, Salvador
Alvarado y Mesía, Pedro de
Álvarez, Juan
Álvarez Armellino, Gregorio Conrado
Álvarez Martínez, Gustavo
Amat y Juniet, Manuel de
Ampíes, Juan de
Ampudia y Grimarest, Pedro de
Anaya, Pedro María de
Andrade, Gomes Freire de
Andresote
Ángeles, Felipe
Anza, Juan Bautista de
Anzoátegui, José Antonio
Aramburu, Pedro Eugenio
Arana, Francisco J.
Arana Osorio, Carlos
Arbenz Guzmán, Jacobo
Arenales, Juan Antonio Álvarez de
Argüello, Santiago
Arias, Desiderio
Arismendi, Juan Bautista
Arista, Mariano
Armijo, Manuel
Artigas, José Gervasio
Ávila, Pedro Arias de
Ávila Camacho, Manuel
Avilés, Gabriel
Axayacatl
Ayolas, Juan de
Azcuénaga, Miguel de
Balboa, Vasco Núñez de
Balcarce, Mariano
Baldomir, Alfredo
Ballivián, José
Balta, José
Banzere Suárez, Hugo
Barrientos Ortuño, René

Barrios, Justo Rufino
Batista y Zaldívar, Fulgencio
Bazaine, François Achille
Belgrano, Manuel
Belzu, Manuel Isidoro
Bermúdez, José Francisco
Bermúdez Varela, Enrique
Beruti, Antonio Luis
Bignone, Reynaldo
Blanco, José Félix
Blanco Encalada, Manuel
Blanco Galindo, Carlos
Bodega y Quardra, Juan Francisco de la
Bolívar, Simón
Bolognesi, Francisco
Bordaberry, Juan María
Borge, Tomás
Bouchard, Hipólito
Boves, José Tomás
Boyer, Jean-Pierre
Bravo, Leonardo
Bravo, Nicolás
Brión, Luis
Brizuela, Francisco
Busch Becerra, Germán
Bustamante, Anastasio
Bustamante y Guerra, José
Caamaño Deñó, Francisco
Caamaño y Gómez Cornejo, José
   María Plácido
Caballero, Pedro Juan
Cabañas, José Trinidad
Cáceres, Andrés Avelino
Cajeme
Calfucurá
Calleja del Rey, Félix María
Calles, Plutarco Elías
Campero, Narciso
Campos, Luis María
Campos, Manuel Jorge
Cañas, José María
Candioti, Francisco Antonio
Cárdenas del Río, Lázaro
Cardozo, Efraím
Carondelet, François-Louis Hector
Carrera, José Miguel
Carrera, José Rafael
Carrión, Jerónimo
Carvalho, Antônio de Albuquerque
   Coelho de
Castañeda Castro, Salvador
Castello Branco, Humberto de Alencar
Castilla, Ramón

Castillo Armas, Carlos
Castro, Julián
Castro Jijón, Ramón
Castro Ruz, Fidel
Castro Ruz, Raúl
Caupolicán
Cazneau, William Leslie
Cedillo Martínez, Saturnino
Cerna, Vicente
Chacón, Lázaro
Chamorro Vargas, Emiliano
Chávez, Mariano
Chirino, José Leonardo
Christmas, Lee
Christophe, Henri
Cienfuegos, Camilo
Cieza de León, Pedro de
Cochrane, Lord Thomas Alexander
Codazzi, Agustín
Comonfort, Ignacio
Constant Botelho de Magalhães,
   Benjamin
Córdoba, José María
Corona, Ramón
Coronado, Juan Vázquez de
Cortés, Hernán
Cortés, Martín
Cos, Martín Perfecto de
Cos y Pérez, José María
Costa e Silva, Artur da
Crespo, Joaquín
Croix, Marqués de
Croix, Teodoro de
Cruz, Serapio
Cruz, Vicente
Cuauhtemoc
Cuitlahuac
d'Aubuisson, Roberto
Dávila, Miguel R.
Daza, Hilarión
Degray, [Jules] Régis
Degollado, Santos
Delgado Chalbaud, Carlos
Dessalines, Jean Jacques
Di Tella, Torcuato
Dias, Henrique
Díaz, Félix, Jr.
Díaz, José Eduvigis
Díaz, Porfirio
Dorrego, Manuel
Drake, Francis
Duarte, Juan Pablo
Duarte, Pedro

Dutra, Eurico Gaspar
Echeandía, José María de
Enríquez de Guzmán, Alonso
Enríquez Gallo, Alberto
Escobedo, Mariano
Estigarribia, Antonio de la Cruz
Estrada, José Dolores
Facio Segreda, Gonzalo
Fages, Pedro
Falcón, Juan Crisóstomo
Fallas Sibaja, Carlos Luis
Farrell, Edelmiro
Febres-Cordero Ribadeneyra, León
Fernández de Castro Andrade y
   Portugal, Pedro Antonio
Fernández (Hernández) de Córdoba,
   Francisco
Fernández Oreamuno, Próspero
Ferreira, Benigno
Ferrera, Francisco
Figueiredo, João Baptista de Oliveira
Figueroa, José
Filísola, Vicente
Flores, Juan José
Flores, Venancio
Fonseca, Hermes Rodrigues da
Fonseca, Manoel Deodoro da
Fonseca Amador, Carlos
Francia, José Gaspar Rodríguez de
Franco, Guillermo
Frémont, John Charles
Fuentes y Guzmán, Francisco Antonio
   de
Gaínza, Gabino
Galán, Luis Carlos
Galeana, Hermenegildo
Galindo, Juan
Galtieri, Leopoldo Fortunato
Galvarino
Gálvez, Bernardo de
Gálvez, Matías de
Gama, Vasco da
Gamarra, Agustín
Gándara Enríquez, Marcos
Garay, Eugenio
Garcés, Francisco Tomás Hermenegildo
García, Calixto
García Conde, Pedro
García y González, Vicente
Garibay, Pedro
Garro, José de
Geffrard, Fabre Nicolas
Geisel, Ernesto

Gelly y Obes, Juan Andrés
Gestido, Oscar Daniel
Girón, Francisco Hernández
Golbery do Couto e Silva
Gomes, Eduardo
Gómez, José Miguel (d. 1805)
Gómez, José Miguel (d. 1921)
Gómez, Juan Vicente
Gómez Pedraza, Manuel
Gómez y Báez, Máximo
González, Manuel
González, Pablo
González Dávila, Gil
González Ortega, Jesús
Gorostiza, Manuel Eduardo de
Grau, Miguel
Grijalva, Juan de
Guardia Gutiérrez, Tomás
Guardiola, Santos
Güemes, Martín
Guerra, Ramón
Guerrero, Vicente
Guevara, Ernesto "Che"
Gutiérrez, Eulalio
Gutiérrez Brothers
Guitérrez de Lara, José Bernardo
Guzmán, Nuño Beltrán de
Haro y Tamariz, Antonio de
Hernández, José Manuel
Hernández Martínez, Maximiliano
Herrán, Pedro Alcántara
Herrera, Benjamín
Herrera, José Joaquín Antonio
 Florencio
Herrera, Tomás
Heureaux, Ulises
Holguín, Jorge
Huascar
Huerta, Victoriano
Huertas, Esteban
Ibáñez del Campo, Carlos
Ibarra, Juan Felipe
Iglesias, Miguel
Irala, Domingo Martínez de
Iturbide, Agustín de
Itzcoatl
Jerez, Máximo
Jiménez de Quesada, Gonzalo
Julião, Carlos
Justo, José Agustín Pedro
Kearny, Stephen W.
Körner, Emil

La Salle, René-Robert Cavelier, Sieur
 de
Lamadrid, Gregorio Aráoz de
Lanusse, Alejandro Augusto
Laprida, Francisco Narciso de
Laredo Bru, Federico
Larrazábal Ugueto, Wolfgang
Las Heras, Juan Gregorio de
Lavalle, Juan Galo
Lavalleja, Juan Antonio
Leclerc, Charles Victor Emmanuel
Leighton Guzmán, Bernardo
Lemus, José María
León, Alonso de
Levingston, Roberto Marcelo
Leyva Solano, Gabriel
Lima e Silva, Luís Alves de
Linares, José María
Linares Alcántara, Francisco
Lindley López, Nicolás
Lisboa, Joaquim Marques
Lonardi, Eduardo
López, Enrique Solano
López, Estanislao
López, Francisco Solano
López, José Hilario
López, Narciso
López Arellano, Oswaldo
López Contreras, Eleázar
López Jordán, Ricardo
López y Fuentes, Gregorio
Lorenzo Troya, Victoriano
Lott, Henrique Batista Duffles Teixeira
L'Ouverture, Toussaint
Lozada, Manuel
Luperón, Gregorio
Maceo, Antonio
Machado, Gustavo
Machado y Morales, Gerardo
Madureira, Antônio de Sena
Magloire, Paul Eugène
Majano, Adolfo Arnoldo
Maldonado, Francisco Severo
Malespín, Francisco
Manco Capac
Mandu Ladino
Manso de Maldonado, Antonio
Manso de Velasco, José Antonio
Mar, José de la
Mariño, Santiago
Márquez, Leonardo

Martínez, Esteban José
Martínez, Juan José
Martínez, Tomás
Matamoros y Guridi, Mariano
Maurits, Johan
Médici, Emílio Garrastazú
Medina Angarita, Isaías
Mejía, Tomás
Mejía Victores, Oscar Humberto
Melgarejo, Mariano
Melgares, Facundo
Melo, Custódio José de
Melo, José María
Mendiburu, Manuel de
Mendieta y Montefur, Carlos
Menéndez de Avilés, Pedro
Menocal, Mario García
Merino Castro, José Toribio
Mier y Terán, Manuel
Mina y Larrea, Javier
Miramón, Miguel
Mitre, Bartolomé
Molina, Arturo Armando
Molina Enríquez, Andrés
Molony, Guy
Monagas, José Gregorio
Moncada, José María
Montalvo y Ambulodi Arriola y
 Casabente Valdespino, Francisco
Monteiro, Pedro Aurélio de Góis
Montes, César
Montes, Ismael
Montt Álvarez, Jorge
Montúfar Montes de Oca, Lorenzo
Mora, Fernando de la
Mora Porrás, Juan Rafael
Morales, Agustín
Morales, Francisco Tomás
Morales Bermúdez Cerruti, Francisco
Morales Lemus, José
Morazán, Francisco
Morelos y Pavón, José María
Morgan, Henry
Morillo, Pablo
Mosquera, Tomás Cipriano de
Motecuhzoma I
Motecuhzoma II
Múgica, Francisco José
Muñoz, José Trinidad
Nariño, Antonio
Narváez, Pánfilo de
Navarro Wolff, Antonio

Neve, Felipe de
Nezahualcoyotl
Nord, Pierre Alexis
Noriega Moreno, Manuel Antonio
Nufio, José Dolores
Núñez Vela, Blasco
O, Genovevo de la
Obando, José María
Obregón Salido, Álvaro
O'Donojú, Juan
Odría, Manuel Apolinario
Ogé, Jacques Vicente
O'Higgins, Ambrosio
O'Higgins, Bernardo
O'Leary, Daniel Florencio
O'Leary, Juan Emiliano
Olid, Cristóbal de
Olivares, Conde-Duque de
Onganía, Juan Carlos
Orbegoso, Luis José de
Ordóñez, José
O'Reilly y McDowell, Alejandro
Orlich Bolmarcich, Francisco José
Orozco, Pascual, Jr.
Ortega Saavedra, Daniel
Ortega Saavedra, Humberto
Ortiz de Zárate, Juan and Juana
Osório, Manuel Luís
Ospina, Pedro Nel
Ovando Candía, Alfredo
Páez, José Antonio
País, Frank
Palacio Fajardo, Manuel
Palafox y Mendoza, Juan de
Pando, José Manuel
Pardo, Juan
Paredes, Mariano
Paredes y Arrillaga, Mariano
Pastora Gómez, Edén
Patiño, José de
Pavón Aycinena, Manuel Francisco
Paz, José María
Paz García, Policarpo
Pedreira, Antonio S.
Peixoto, Floriano Vieira
Peñalosa Briceño, Diego Dionisio de
Peñaloza, Ángel Vicente
Peñaranda del Castillo, Enrique
Peralta Azurdia, Enrique
Péralte, Charlemagne Masséna
Pérez, Albino
Pérez, Juan

Pérez Godoy, Ricardo
Pérez Jiménez, Marcos
Perón, Juan Domingo
Pétion, Alexandre Sabès
Pinochet Ugarte, Augusto
Pizarro, José Alonso
Plaza Gutiérrez, Leonidas
Ponce de León, Juan
Portolá, Gaspar de
Prado, Mariano Ignacio
Prats González, Carlos
Prestes, Luís Carlos
Pueyrredón, Honorio
Pueyrredón, Juan Martín de
Ramírez, Francisco
Ramírez, Pedro Pablo
Ramírez Mercado, Sergio
Raousset-Boulbon, Gaston Raul de
Rayón, Ignacio
Regalado, Tomás
Remón Cantera, José Antonio
Reyes, Rafael
Reyes Ogazón, Bernardo
Riaño y Bárcena, Juan Antonio
Ribas, José Félix
Ricchieri, Pablo
Riego y Núñez, Rafael del
Rigaud, André
Ríos Montt, José Efraín
Riva Palacio, Vicente
Rivera, Pedro de
Rivera Carballo, Julio Adalberto
Rivera y Moncada, Fernando de
Robles, Francisco
Robles, Wenceslao
Roca, Julio Argentino
Rochambeau, Donatien Marie Joseph
    de Vimeur de
Rodríguez, Andrés
Rodríguez Cabrillo, Juan
Rodríguez Erdoiza, Manuel
Rodríguez Lara, Guillermo
Rodríguez Luján, Abelardo
Rodríguez Sandoval, Luis Arsenio
Rojas, Isaac
Rojas Pinilla, Gustavo
Rolón, Raimundo
Romero, Carlos Humberto
Romero Rubio, Manuel
Rosa, Ramón
Rosáins, Juan Nepomuceno
Ruíz, Henry

Ruíz de Apodaca, Juan
Sá, Estácio de
Sá, Mem de
Sá e Benavides, Salvador Correia de
Salaverry, Felipe Santiago
Salazar, Matías
Saldanha da Gama, Luís Felipe da
Salgar, Eustorgio
Salnave, Sylvain
Sam, Tirésias Augustin Simon
Samanez Ocampo, David
San Martín, José Francisco de
Sánchez Cerro, Luis Manuel
Sánchez Hernández, Fidel
Sandino, Augusto César
Santa Anna, Antonio López de
Santa Cruz, Andrés de
Santamaría, Haydée
Santana, Pedro
Santander, Francisco de Paula
Sardá, José
Schneider, René
Sedeño, Antonio de
Seguín, Juan Nepomuceno
Sodré, Nelson Werneck
Solís, Juan Díaz de
Somoza Debayle, Anastasio
Somoza García, Anastasio
Sonthonax, Léger Félicité
Soto, Hernando de
Soto Alfaro, Bernardo
Soublette, Carlos
Soulouque, Faustin Élie
Sousa, Martim Afonso de
Sousa, Tomé de
Stroessner, Alfredo
Sucre Alcalá, Antonio José de
Tavares, Antônio Rapôso
Távora, Juárez
Tejeda Olivares, Adalberto
Thomson Porto Mariño, Manuel Tomás
Tinoco Granados, Federico
Tornel y Mendívil, José María
Toro, David
Torre, Miguel de la
Torre Tagle, José Bernardo de Tagle y
    Portocarrero
Torres, Juan José
Torres, Luis Emeterio
Torrijos Herrera, Omar
Trujillo, Julián
Trujillo Molina, Rafael Leónidas

Túpac Amaru
Túpac Catari, Julián Apaza
Turcios Lima, Luis Agosto
Ubico y Castañeda, Jorge
Urbina, José María
Urdaneta, Andrés de
Urdaneta, Rafael
Ureta, Eloy G.
Uribe Uribe, Rafael
Urracá
Urrea, José de
Valdivia, Pedro de
Vallejo, Mariano Guadalupe
Varela, Felipe
Vargas, Diego de
Veintimilla, José Ignacio de
Velasco, José Miguel de
Velasco Alvarado, Juan
Velázquez, Diego de
Venegas de Saavedra, Francisco Javier
Vernet, Louis
Vértiz y Salcedo, Juan José de
Vial, Pedro
Victoria, Guadalupe
Victoria, Manuel
Vidaurri, Santiago
Videla, Jorge Rafael
Viera, Feliciano
Villa, Francisco "Pancho"
Villagrá, Gaspar Pérez de
Villagrán, Julián and José María ("El Chito")
Villarroel López, Gualberto
Villegaignon, Nicolas Durand de
Viola, Roberto Eduardo
Vivanco, Manuel Ignacio
Walker, William
Weyler y Nicolau, Valeriano
Williams Rebolledo, Juan
Wisner von Morgenstern, Franz
Wooster, Charles Whiting
Ydígoras Fuentes, Miguel
Yegros Fulgencio
Yon Sosa, Marco Antonio
Zamorano, Agustín Juan Vicente
Zapata, Emiliano
Zaragoza, Ignacio
Zavala, José Victor
Zelaya, José Santos
Zeledón, Benjamín Francisco
Zuloaga, Félix María
Zumbi
Zúñiga, Ignacio

MONARCHS AND ROYALTY
(including indigenous leaders)

Agüeybana II
Alvarado Xicotencatl, Leonor
Amélia, Empress
Atahualpa (Juan Santos)
Axayacatl
Cajeme
Calfucurá
Cuauhtemoc
Cuitlahuac
Dessalines, Jean Jacques
Henry the Navigator
Huascar
Huayna Capac
Isabel of Brazil, Princess
Itzcoatl
Leopoldina, Empress
Manco Capac
Manco Inca
Maximilian
Montalvo y Ambulodi Arriola y Casabente Valdespino, Francisco
Motecuhzoma I
Motecuhzoma II
Nezahualcoyotl
Nezahualpilli
Pedro I of Brazil
Pedro II of Brazil
Túpac Amaru
Zumbi

MUSIC AND DANCE

Aguirre, Julián
Alcaraz, José Antonio
Aldana, José María
Allende-Sarón, Pedro Humberto
Alomía Robles, Daniel
Alves, Francisco
Amenábar, Juan
Aponte-Ledée, Rafael
Araujo, Juan de
Archila, Andrés
Ardévol, José
Arnaz, Desi
Arrau, Claudio León
Asur, José Vicente
Barroso, Ary
Becerra-Schmidt, Gustavo
Bernal Jiménez, Miguel
Berutti, Arturo

Blanco, Juan
Boero, Felipe
Bolaños, César
Broqua, Alfonso
Brouwer, Leo
Buarque, Chico
Calcaño, José Antonio
Callado Junior, Joaquim Antônio da Silva
Campos-Parsi, Héctor
Carlos, Roberto
Carrillo, Julián [Antonio]
Castellanos, Gonzalo
Castillo, Jesús
Castro, Ricardo
Caymmi, Dorival
Ceruti, Roque
Cervantes y Kawanagh, Ignacio
Cervetti, Sergio
Chacrinha
Chávez, Carlos
Cluzeau-Mortet, Luis [Ricardo]
Cordero, Roque
Cotapos Baeza, Acario
Cugat, Xavier
de Jesus, Clementina
Dianda, Hilda
Discépolo, Enrique Santos
Duprat, Rogério
Elizaga, José María
Enríquez, Manuel
Escobar, Luis Antonio
Fabini, [Felix Eduardo]
Fernandez, Oscar Lorenzo
Fernández Hidalgo, Gutierre
Ficher, Jacobo
Franco, Hernando
Gaito, Constantino
Galindo, Blas
Gallet, Luciano
Gandini, Gerardo
Gante, Pedro de
Garcia, José Maurício Nunes
García Caturla, Alejandro
García Morillo, Roberto
Gardel, Carlos
Garrido-Lecca Seminario, Celso
Gil, Gilberto
Gilardi, Gilardo
Gilberto, João
Ginastera, Alberto Evaristo
Giribaldi, (Vicente) Tomás E.
Gismonti, Egberto

Goicuría y Cabrera, Domingo
Gomes, Antônio Carlos
Gonzaga, Francisca Hedwiges
Gonzaga, Luiz
González Ávila, Jorge
Guarnieri, M[ozart] Camargo
Gutiérrez de Padilla, Juan
Gutiérrez y Espinosa, Felipe
Halffter, Rodolfo
Hernández Moncado, Eduardo
Holzmann, Rodolfo
Infante, Pedro
Isamitt Alarcón, Carlos
Jara, Víctor
Jobim, Antônio Carlos "Tom"
Kagel, Mauricio Raúl
Koellreutter, Hans Joaquim
Krieger, Edino
Lacerda, Osvaldo
Lamarque Pons, Jaurés
Lanza, Alcides
Lara, Agustín
Lavista, Mario
Lecuona y Casado, Ernesto
Leng, Alfonso
Letelier Valdés, Miguel
Levy, Alexandre
Ley, Salvador
López Buchardo, Carlos
López Capillas, Francisco
Mastrogiovanni, Antonio
Mata, Eduardo
Mendes, Gilberto
Mignone, Francisco
Miranda, Carmen
Mojica, José de Jesús
Moncayo García, José Pablo
Morais, Vinícius de
Morales, Melesio
Nascimento, Milton
Nazareth, Ernesto
Negrete, Jorge
Nepomuceno, Alberto
Nobre, Marlos
Oliveira, Willy Correia de
Orbón, Julián
Orejón y Aparicio, José de
Orellana, Joaquín
Orrego-Salas, Juan Antonio
Ortega del Villar, Aniceto
Paniagua y Vasques, Cenobio
Pardavé, Joaquín
Parra, Violeta

Pasta, Carlos Enrico
Paz, Juan Carlos
Peixe, César Guerra
Peralta, Angela
Pineda-Duque, Roberto
Pinilla, Enrique
Pixinguinha
Ponce, Manuel
Portugal, Marcos Antônio da Fonseca
Quintanar, Hector
Revueltas, Silvestre
Riva Palacio, Vicente
Rogatis, Pascual de
Roldán, Amadeo
Rosa, Noel
Rosas, Juventino
Sambucetti, Luís Nicolás
Sandi, Luis
Santoro, Claudio
Sarmientos de León, Jorge Alvaro
Sas, Andrés
Sepp, Anton
Serebrier, José
Silva, Francisco Manuel da
Silva, Orlando
Sinhô
Storm, Ricardo
Tauriello, Antonio
Torrejón y Velasco, Tomás de
Tosar, Héctor Alberto
Uribe Holguín, Guillermo
Valcárcel Arce, Edgar
Valencia, Antonio María
Vega, Aurelio de
Veloso, Caetano
Vieira, Amaral
Villa-Lobos, Heitor
White y Lafitta, José
Williams, Alberto
Zipoli, Domenico
Zumaya, Manuel de

OUTLAWRY (including pirates, filibusters, freebooters, privateers, and bandits)

Alvarado Xicotencatl, Leonor
Bonnet, Stede
Bonny, Anne
Crabb, Henry A.
Drake, Francis
Hawkins, John
Kinney, Henry L.

Lampião
L'Olonnais, Francis
López, Narciso
Morgan, Henry
Raousset-Boulbon, Gaston Raul de
Read, Mary
Sharp, Bartholomew
Walker, William
Wallace, Peter

POLITICAL LEADERS: THE COLONIAL ERA

Abalos, José de
Abascal y Souza, José Fernando
Acosta, Tomás
Alarcón, Martín de
Alberro, Francisco de
Alvarado y Mesía, Pedro de
Álvarez, Manuel
Álzaga, Martín de
Amar y Borbón, Antonio
Amat y Junient, Manuel de
Andrade, Gomes Freire de
Arenales, Juan Antonio Álvarez de
Arias de Saavedra, Hernando
Artigas, José Gervasio
Ávila, Pedro Arias de
Avilés, Gabriel
Aycinena, Juan Fermín de
Aycinena Piñol, Juan José de
Ayolas, Juan de
Azara, Félix de
Azcárate y Lezama, Juan Francisco de
Balboa, Vasco Núñez de
Baldorioty de Castro, Ramón
Barros, João de
Bobadilla, Francisco de
Borja y Aragón, Francisco de
Boves, José Tomás
Bucareli y Ursúa, Antonio María
Bucareli y Ursúa, Francisco de Paula
Caballero y Góngora, Antonio
Cabeza de Vaca, Alvar Núñez
Calchaquí, Juan
Calleja del Rey, Félix María
Camacho Roldán, Salvador
Cañedo, Juan de Dios
Caramurú
Cárdenas, Bernardino de
Carlota
Carondelet, François-Louis Hector
Carrera, José Miguel

Carvalho, Antônio de Albuquerque
   Coelho de
Caupolicán
Cavallón, Juan de
Cevallos, Pedro Antonio de
Cisneros, Baltasar Hidalgo de
Coelho, Jorge de Albuquerque
Coelho Pereira, Duarte
Coronado, Juan Vázquez de
Cortés, Hernán
Coutinho, José Joaquim da Cunha de
   Azeredo
Croix, Marqués de
Croix, Teodoro de
Cueva, Francisco de la
Cueva de Alvarado, Beatriz de la
Cueva Enríquez y Saavedra, Baltásar de
   la
Díaz Vélez, José Miguel
Domínguez, Miguel
Elío, Francisco Javier
Enríquez de Almansa, Martín
Eslava y Lazaga, Sebastián de
Espeleta y Galdeano Dicastillo y del
   Prado, Viceroy
Esquiú, Mamerto
Fages, Pedro
Fagoaga y Lizaur, José María
Fernández de Cabrera, Bobadilla, Cerda
   y Mendoza,
Fernández de Córdoba, Diego
Flores Maldonado Martínez y Bodquín,
   Manuel Anton
Funes, Gregorio
Gaínza, Gabino
Gálvez, Bernardo de
Gálvez, José de
Gálvez, Matías de
Gama, Vasco da
Garay, Francisco de
García de Castro, Lope
Garibay, Pedro
Garro, José de
Gasca, Pedro de la
Gelves, Marqués de
Gil de Taboada y Lemos, Francisco
Girón, Francisco Hernández
Godoy Cruz, Tomás
Güemes, Martín
Guirior, Manuel
Gutiérrez de Piñeres, Juan Francisco
Guzmán, Nuño Beltrán de
Herrera, Tomás

Huascar
Hurtado de Mendoza, Andrés
Hurtado de Mendoza, García
Iturrigaray, José de
Jáuregui, Agustín de
Ladrón de Guevara, Diego
Lamar, Mirabeau Buonaparte
Las Casas, Bartolomé de
Lasuén, Fermín Francisco de
Lavradio, Marquês do
León, Alonso de
López, Narciso
López de Cerrato, Alonso
López de Cogolludo, Diego
Lorenzana y Buitrón, Francisco
   Antonio de
Luna y Arellano, Tristán de
Maldonado, Rodrigo de Arias
Manco Inca
Manrique de Zúñiga, Alvaro
Manso de Velasco, José Antonio
Marroquín, Francisco
Martínez, Padre Antonio J.
Maurits, Johan
Mendinueta y Múzquiz, Pedro de
Mendoza, Antonio de
Mendoza Caamaño y Sotomayor, José
   Antonio de
Mendoza y Luna, Juan Manuel de
Messía de la Cerda, Pedro de
Mompox de Zayas, Fernando
Mon y Velarde, Juan Antonio
Montejo, Francisco de
Morga Sánchez Garay y López,
   Antonio de
Morgan, Henry
Morillo, Pablo
Moya de Contreras, Pedro
Muñoz Rivera, Luis
Namuncurá, Ceferino
Namuncurá, Manuel
Navarra y Rocaful, Melchor de
Navarro Wolff, Antonio
Neve, Felipe de
Núñez Vela, Blasco
O'Donojú, Juan
Ogé, Jacques Vicente
O'Higgins, Ambrosio
O'Higgins, Bernardo
O'Leary, Juan Emiliano
Olivares, Conde-Duque de
Oliveira, Manuel Botelho de
Oñate, Juan de

O'Reilly y McDowell, Alejandro
Ovando, Nicolás de
Palafox y Mendoza, Juan de
Palou, Francisco
Pardo Leal, Jaime
Parish, Woodbine
Paso, Juan José
Pedrosa y Guerrero, Antonio de la
Peñalosa Briceño, Diego Dionisio de
Pérez de Tolosa, Juan
Pizarro, Francisco
Pizarro, Gonzalo
Pizarro, José Alonso
Ponce de León, Juan
Porras, José Basilio
Portocarrero y Lasso de la Vega,
   Melchor
Portolá, Gaspar de
Prado y Ugarteche, Jorge
Primo de Verdad y Ramos, Francisco
Quiroga, Vasco de
Rada, Manuel de Jesús
Ramalho, João
Ramírez y Blanco, Alejandro
Ramos Arizpe, José Miguel
Revillagigedo, Conde de
Rivera, Pedro de
Rochambeau, Donatien Marie Joseph
   de Vimeur de
Roldán, Francisco
Rondeau, José
Rosas, Juan Manuel de
Ruíz de Apodaca, Juan
Sá, Mem de
Sá e Benavides, Salvador Correia de
Saco, José Antonio
Sarmiento de Sotomayor, García
Seguín, Juan José María Erasmo
Seguín, Juan Nepomuceno
Sobremonte, Rafael de
Solís Folch de Cardona, José
Solórzano Pereira, Juan de
Sonthonax, Léger Félicité
Sousa, Martim Afonso de
Sousa, Tomé de
Suárez, Inés de
Talamantes, Melchor de
Toledo y Figueroa, Francisco de
Toledo y Leyva, Pedro de
Torre, Miguel de la
Torres y Portugal, Fernando de
Túpac Amaru

Túpac Amaru (José Gabriel
 Condorcanqui)
Urdaneta, Andrés de
Ursúa, Pedro de
Vaca de Castro, Cristóval
Valdivia, Pedro de
Velasco, Luis de
Velázquez, Diego de
Venegas de Saavedra, Francisco Javier
Vértiz y Salcedo, Juan José de
Viamonte, Juan José
Vicuña Larraín, Francisco Ramón
Vicuña Mackenna, Benjamin
Villagrá, Gaspar Pérez de
Villalonga, Jorge
Villegaignon, Nicolas Durand de
Weyler y Nicolau, Valeriano
Yegros, Fulgencio
Yermo, Gabriel de
Zapata, Felipe
Zorita, Alonso de
Zumbi

POLITICAL LEADERS: THE NATIONAL ERA

Abadía Méndez, Miguel
Aceval, Benjamín
Acevedo Díaz, Eduardo Inés
Achá, José María
Acosta García, Julio
Agüero Rocha, Fernando
Aguilar Vargas, Cándido
Aguirre Cerda, Pedro
Aguirre y Salinas, Osmín
Alamán, Lucas
Alambert, Zuleika
Alberdi, Juan Bautista
Alberto, João
Albizu Campos, Pedro
Albuquerque, Antônio Francisco de
 Paula
Alem, Leandro
Alemán Valdés, Miguel
Alencar, José Martiniano de
Alessandri Palma, Arturo
Alessandri Rodríguez, Jorge
Alexis, Jacques Stéphen
Alfaro, Ricardo Joaquín
Alfaro Delgado, José Eloy
Alfonsín, Raúl Ricardo
Allende Gossens, Salvador
Almazán, Juan Andréu

Almeida, José Américo de
Alonso, Mariano Roque
Alsina, Adolfo
Alsina, Valentín
Alsogaray, Alvaro
Alvarado, Salvador
Álvarez, Juan
Alvear, Carlos María de
Alvear, Marcelo Torcuato de
Amador Guerrero, Manuel
Amézaga, Juan José de
Amunátegui Aldunate, Miguel Luis
Andrada, Antônio Carlos de and
 Martim Francisco
Andrada, José Bonifácio de
Andrade, Oswald de
Andueza Palacio, Raimundo
Aramburu, Pedro Eugenio
Arana, Felipe de
Arana, Francisco J.
Arana Osorio, Carlos
Aranha, Oswaldo
Araujo, Arturo
Arbenz Guzmán, Jacobo
Arboleda, Julio
Arce, Aniceto
Arce, Manuel José
Arce Castaño, Bayardo
Arévalo Bermejo, Juan José
Argüello, Leonardo
Arias, Desiderio
Arias Calderón, Ricardo
Arias Madrid, Arnulfo
Arias Madrid, Harmodio
Arias Sánchez, Oscar
Arismendi, Juan Bautista
Arista, Mariano
Aristide, Jean-Bertrand
Armijo, Manuel
Arosemena, Florencio Harmodio
Arosemena, Juan Demóstenes
Arosemena, Pablo
Arosemena Gómez, Otto
Arosemena Monroy, Carlos Julio
Arosemena Quinzada, Albacíades
Arrais, Miguel
Arroyo del Río, Carlos Alberto
Arze, José Antonio
Aspíllaga Family
Avellaneda, Nicolás
Ávila Camacho, Manuel
Ayala, Eligio
Ayala, Eusebio

Aycinena, Mariano de
Aycinena, Pedro de
Aylwin Azócar, Patricio
Ayora Cueva, Isidro
Azcona Hoyo, José Simón
Báez, Buenaventura
Báez, Cecilio
Balaguer, Joaquín
Balbín, Ricardo
Baldomir, Alfredo
Ballivián, José
Balmaceda Fernández, José Manuel
Balta, José
Banzer Suárez, Hugo
Baquerizo Moreno, Alfredo
Barbosa, Francisco Villela
Barbosa y Alcalá, José Celso
Barco Vargas, Virgilio
Bareiro, Cándido
Barrientos Ortuño, René
Barrillas, Manuel Lisandro
Barrios, Gerardo
Barrios, Gonzalo
Barrios de Chamorro, Violeta
Barros, Adhemar de
Barroso, Gustavo Dodt
Barrundia, José Francisco
Barrundia, Juan
Batista, Cícero Romão
Batista y Zaldívar, Fulgencio
Batlle, Lorenzo
Batlle Berres, Luis Conrado
Batlle y Ordóñez, José
Baltres Juarros, Luis
Bazaine, François Achille
Bedoya de Molina, Dolores
Bedoya Reyes, Luis
Béjar, Héctor
Belaúnde, Victor Andrés
Belaúnde Terry, Fernando
Belgrano, Manuel
Bellegarde, Luis Dantès
Belzu, Manuel Isidoro
Benavides, Oscar Raimundo
Benítez, Jaime
Bernardes, Artur da Silva
Berreta, Tomás
Berrío, Pedro Justo
Berro, Carlos
Bertrand, Francisco
Betancourt, Rómulo
Betancur Cuartas, Belisario
Bignone, Reynaldo

Billinghurst, Guillermo Enrique
Blanco Acevedo, Eduardo
Blanco Galindo, Carlos
Bocaiúva, Quintino
Bolívar, Simón
Bonifaz Ascasubi, Neptalí
Bonilla, Policarpo
Bonilla Chirinos, Manuel
Bordaberry, Juan María
Borge, Tomás
Borges de Medeiros, Antônio Augusto
Borja Cevallos, Rodrigo
Borno, Joseph Louis E. Antoine
    François
Borrero y Cortázar, Antonio
Bosch Gaviño, Juan
Boyer, Jean-Pierre
Bramuglia, Juan Atilio
Branco, Manuel Alves
Brás Pereira Gomes, Wenceslau
Bravo, Nicolás
Bray, Arturo
Brizola, Leonel
Brum, Baltasar
Bucaram Elmhalin, Asaad
Bulnes Prieto, Manuel
Bunau-Varilla, Philippe Jean
Busch Becerra, Germán
Bustamante, Anastasio
Bustamante y Rivero, José Luis
Caamaño Deñó, Francisco
Caamaño y Gómez Cornejo, José
    María Plácido
Caballero, Bernardino
Cabañas, José Trinidad
Cáceres, Andrés Avelino
Cáceres, Ramón
Café Filho, João
Caldera Rodríguez, Rafael
Calderón Fournier, Rafael Ángel
Calderón Guardia, Rafael Ángel
Callejas Romero, Rafael Leonardo
Calles, Plutarco Elías
Calógeras, João Pandiá
Campero, Narciso
Campisteguy, Juan
Campo, Rafael
Cámpora, Héctor José
Campos, Francisco Luiz da Silva
Campos, Roberto (de Oliveira)
Campos Sales, Manuel Ferraz de
Candamo, Manuel
Caneca, Frei Joaquím do Amor Divino

Cañedo, Francisco
Cañedo, Juan de Dios
Cantilo, José Luis
Capelo, Joaquín
Carazo Odio, Rodrigo
Cárcano, Ramón José
Cárdenas del Río, Lázaro
Cárdenas Solorzano, Cuauhtémoc
Cardoso, Fernando Henrique
Cardozo, Efraím
Carías Andino, Tiburcio
Carneiro de Campos, José Joaquim
Caro, Miguel Antonio
Carpio Nicolle, Jorge
Carranza, Venustiano
Carrera, José Rafael
Carrillo Colina, Braulio
Carrillo Puerto, Felipe
Carrión, Jerónimo
Castañeda Castro, Salvador
Castelli, Juan José
Castello Branco, Humberto de Alencar
Castilhos, Júlio de
Castilla, Ramón
Castillo, Ramón S.
Castillo Armas, Carlos
Castillo Ledón, Amalia
Castro, Cipriano
Castro, Julián
Castro Madriz, José María
Castro Pozo, Hildebrando
Castro Ruz, Fidel
Castro Ruz, Raúl
Centurión, Carlos R.
Centurión, Juan Crisóstomo
Cerezo Arévalo, Marco Vinicio
Cerna, Vicente
Céspedes, Carlos Manuel de (the Elder)
Céspedes y Quesada, Carlos Manuel de
Chacón, Lázaro
Chamorro, Fruto
Chamorro Cardenal, Pedro Joaquín
Chamorro Vargas, Emiliano
Chaves, Federico
Chaves, Francisco C.
Chaves, Julio César
Chiari, Rodolfo E.
Chiari Remón, Roberto Francisco
Chibás, Eduardo
Christophe, Henri
Cisneros Betancourt, Salvador
Clouthier del Rincón, Manuel J.
Coll y Toste, Cayetano

Collor, Lindolfo
Collor de Mello, Fernando Affonso
Colosio Murrieta, Luis Donaldo
Colunje, Gil
Comonfort, Ignacio
Concha, José Vicente
Cooke, John William
Cordero Crespo, Luis
Córdova, Jorge
Córdova Rivera, Gonzalo S.
Corral Verdugo, Ramón
Cortés Castro, León
Costa e Silva, Artur da
Cotegipe, Barão de
Creel, Enrique Clay
Crespo, Joaquín
Cristiani, Alfredo
Cruz, Arturo
Cruz, Vicente
Cruz Ucles, Ramón Ernesto
Cuestas, Juan Lindolfo
Dantas, Manuel Pinto de Souza
Dartiguenave, Philippe-Sudré
d'Aubuisson, Roberto
Dávila, Miguel R.
Dávila Espinoza, Carlos Guillermo
Daza, Hilarión
de la Huerta, Adolfo
Decoud, Hector Francisco
Decoud, José Segundo
Del Prado, Jorge
Delfim Neto, Antônio
Delgado, José Matías
Derqui, Santiago
D'Escoto Brockmann, Miguel
Díaz Arosemena, Domingo
Díaz, Adolfo
Díaz, Porfirio
Díaz Ordaz, Gustavo
Dickmann, Enrique
Domínguez, Manuel
Dorrego, Manuel
Dorticós Torrado, Osvaldo
Duarte, Juan Pablo
Duarte Fuentes, José Napoleón
Dueñas, Francisco
Dutra, Eurico Gaspar
Duvalier, François
Duvalier, Jean-Claude
Echenique, José Rufino
Echeverría Álvarez, Luis
Echeverría Bianchi, José Antonio
Egaña Fabres, Mariano

Egaña Risco, Juan
Elías, Domingo
Emparán, Vicente
Enríquez Gallo, Alberto
Errázuriz Echaurren, Federico
Errázuriz Zañartu, Federico
Erro, Enrique
Escobar, Patricio
Espaillat, Ulises Francisco
Espinosa y Espinosa, (Juan) Javier
Esquivel, Manuel Amadeo
Estigarribia, José Félix
Estimé, Dumarsais
Estrada, José María (d. 1856)
Estrada Cabrera, Manuel
Estrada Palma, Tomás
Falcón, Juan Crisóstomo
Faoro, Raymundo
Farrell, Edelmiro
Feijó, Diogo Antônio
Fernandes, Florestan
Fernández Alonso, Sévero
Fernández Crespo, Daniel
Fernández Madrid, José
Fernández Oreamuno, Próspero
Fernández y Medina, Benjamín
Ferré Aguayo, Luis Antonio
Ferreira, Benigno
Ferreira Aldunate, Wilson
Ferrera, Francisco
Figueiredo, Afonso Celso de Assis
Figueriedo, Jackson de
Figueiredo, João Baptista de Oliveira
Figueres Ferrer, José
Figueroa Alcorta, José
Filísola, Vicente
Flores, Juan José
Flores, Luis A.
Flores, Venancio
Flôres da Cunha, José Antônio
Flores Jijón, Antonio
Fonseca, Manoel Deodora da
Fortuny, José Manuel
Francia, José Gaspar Rodríguez de
Franco, Guillermo
Franco, Itamar Augusto Cautiero
Franco, Wellington Moreira
Frei Montalva, Eduardo
Freire Serrano, Ramón
Freyre, Gilberto (de Mello)
Frondizi, Arturo
Fujimori, Alberto Keinya
Gabeira, Fernando Nagle

Gallegos, Rómulo
Galtieri, Leopoldo Fortunato
Galván, Manuel de Jesús
Gálvez, Juan Manuel
Gálvez, Mariano
Gamarra, Agustín
Gamarra, Francisca Zubiaga Bernales de (La Mariscala)
Garay, Blas
García Calderón, Francisco
García Godoy, Héctor
García Granados, Miguel
García Meza, Luis
García Moreno, Gabriel
García Pérez, Alan
García Salinas, Francisco
Gaviria Trujillo, César Augusto
Geffrard, Fabre Nicolas
Geisel, Ernesto
Gestido, Oscar Daniel
Gill, Juan Bautista
Girón de León, Andrés de Jesús
Godoi, Juan Silvano
Golbery do Couto e Silva
Gomes, Eduardo
Gómez, Indalecio
Gómez, José Miguel (d. 1921)
Gómez, Juan Vicente
Gómez, Miguel Mariano
Gómez Castro, Laureano
Gómez Farías, Valentín
Gómez Hurtado, Alvaro
Gómez Morín, Manuel
Gómez Pedraza, Manuel
González, Manuel
González Flores, Alfredo
González Ortega, Jesús
González Videla, Gabriel
González Viquez, Cleto
Grau San Martín, Ramón
Grove Vallejo, Marmaduke
Guardia, Ricardo Adolfo de la
Guardia Gutiérrez, Tomás
Guardia Navarro, Ernesto de la
Guardiola, Santos
Gueiler Tejada, Lidia
Guerra, Ramón
Guerrero, Vicente
Guevara, Ernesto "Che"
Guevara Arze, Walter
Guggiari, José Patricio
Guido, José María
Guimarães, Ulysses Silveira

Gutiérrez, José María
Gutiérrez Brothers
Gutiérrez Garbín, Víctor Manuel
Gutiérrez Guerra, José
Guzmán, Enrique
Guzmán Blanco, Antonio Leocadio
Haya de la Torre, Victor Raúl
Henríquez, Camilo
Henríquez y Carvajal, Francisco
Hernández, José Manuel
Hernández Colón, Rafael
Hernández Martínez, Maximiliano
Herrán, Pedro Alcántara
Herrera, Benjamín
Herrera, Carlos
Herrera, Dionisio de
Herrera, José Joaquín Antonio Florencio
Herrera, Luis Alberto de
Herrera Campins, Luis
Herrera y Obes, Julio
Hertzog Garaizabal, Enrique
Heureaux, Ulises
Holguín, Jorge
Huerta, Victoriano
Hurtado Larrea, Osvaldo
Hyppolite, Louis Modestin Florville
Ibáñez del Campo, Carlos
Ibarra, Juan Felipe
Iglesias, Miguel
Iglesias Castro, Rafael
Iglesias Pantin, Santiago
Illia, Arturo Umberto
Infante, José Miguel
Irigoyen, Bernardo de
Irisarri, Antonio José de
Iturbide, Agustín de
Jiménez, Enrique A.
Jiménez Oreamuno, Ricardo
Jovellanos, Salvador
Juárez, Benito
Juárez Celman, Miguel
Julião Arruda de Paula, Francisco
Justo, José Agustín Pedro
Justo, Juan B.
Kinney, Henry L.
Kubitschek, Marcia
Kubitschek de Oliveira, Juscelino
La Serna, José de
Labistida y Dávalos, Pelagio Antonio de
Lacalle Herrera, Luis Alberto
Lacerda, Carlos Frederico Werneck de
Lacerda, Maurício Pavia de

Lagos, Ricardo
Lanusse, Alejandro Augusto
Laredo Bru, Federico
Larrazábal Ugueto, Wolfgang
Larrea, Juan
Las Heras, Juan Gregorio de
Latorre, Lorenzo
Laugerud García, Eugenio Kjell
Lavelleja, Juan Antonio
Lechín Oquendo, Juan
Leconte, Michel Cincinnatus
Leguía, Augusto Bernardino
Lemus, José María
Lencinas, Carlos Washington
León de la Barra, Francisco
Leoni, Raúl
Lerdo de Tejada, Sebastián
Lescot, Élie
Lesseps, Ferndinand Marie, Vicomte de
Levingston, Roberto Marcelo
Lima, Alceu Amoroso
Lima, Pedro de Araújo
Linares, José María
Linares Alcántara, Francisco
Lindo Zelaya, Juan
Liniers y Bremond, Santiago de
Lleras, Lorenzo María
Lleras Camargo, Alberto
Lleras Restrepo, Carlos
Lombardo Toledano, Vicente
Lonardi, Eduardo
López, Carlos Antonio
López, Enrique Solano
López, Estanislao
López, Francisco Solano
López, José Hilario
López, Vicente Fidel
López Arellano, Oswaldo
López Contreras, Eleázar
López de Romaña, Eduardo
López Jordán, Ricardo
López Mateos, Adolfo
López Michelsen, Alfonso
López Portillo, José
López Pumarejo, Alfonso
L'Ouverture, Toussaint
Lozano Díaz, Julio
Lucas García, Fernando Romeo
Luís Pereira de Sousa, Washington
Luna Pizarro, Francisco Javier de
Luperón, Gregorio
Lusinchi, Jaime
Lutz, Bertha Maria Julia

Lynch, Elisa Alicia
Machado, Gustavo
Machado y Morales, Gerardo
Mac-Iver Rodríguez, Enrique
Madero, Francisco Indalecio
Madrazo, Carlos A.
Madrid Hurtado, Miguel de la
Magloire, Paul Eugène
Maldonado, Francisco Severo
Malespín, Francisco
Maluf, Paulo Salim
Mar, José de la
Mariátegui, José Carlos
Marighela, Carlos
Mariño, Santiago
Márquez, José Ignacio de
Marroquín, José Manuel
Martí, Agustín Farabundo
Martínez, Tomás
Mauá, Visconde de
Maza, Manuel Vicente de
Médici, Emílio Garrastazú
Medina, Hugo
Medina Angarita, Isaías
Mejía Victores, Oscar Humberto
Meléndez Chaverri, Carlos
Meléndez Family
Melgarejo, Mariano
Mella, Julio Antonio
Melo, José María
Menchú Tum, Rigoberta
Méndez Fleitas, Epifanio
Méndez Montenegro, Julio César
Méndez Montenegro, Mario
Méndez Pereira, Octavio
Mendieta, Salvador
Mendieta y Montefur, Carlos
Mendoza, Carlos Antonio
Menem, Carlos Saúl
Menocal, Mario García
Merino Castro, José Toribio
Michelina, Santos
Michelini, Zelmar
Miró Cardona, José
Miro Quesada Family
Mitre, Bartolomé
Molina, Arturo Armando
Molina, Marcelo
Molina, Pedro
Molina Ureña, José Rafael
Monagas, José Gregorio
Monagas, José Tadeo
Moncada, José María

Monge Álvarez, Luis Alberto
Monte Alegre, José da Costa Carvalho, Marquís de
Monteagudo, Bernardo de
Montealegre Fernández, José María
Monteiro, Pedro Aurélio de Góis
Montes, Ismael
Montt Torres, Manuel
Montúfar, Lorenzo
Mora Fernández, Juan
Mora Porrás, Juan Rafael
Mora Valverde, Manuel
Morais Barros, Prudente José de
Morales, Agustín
Morales, Eusebio A.
Morales Bermúdez, Remigio
Morales Bermúdez Cerruti, Francisco
Morazán, Francisco
Moreira da Costa Ribeiro, Delfim
Morelos y Pavón, José María
Moreno, Mariano
Morínigo, Higínio
Mosquera, Manuel José
Mosquera, Tomás Cipriano de
Mosquera y Arboleda, Joaquín
Muñoz Ledo Lazo de la Vega, Porfiro
Muñoz Marín, Luis
Muñoz Rivera, Luis
Murillo Toro, Manuel
Murtinho, Joaquim Duarte
Nabuco de Araújo, Joaquim
Nardone, Benito
Nascimento, Abdias do
Neruda, Pablo
Neves, Tancredo de Almeida
Noboa y Arteta, Diego
Nord, Pierre Alexis
Noriega Moreno, Manuel Antonio
Núñez Moldeo, Rafael
Núñez Vargas, Benjamin
Obando, José María
Obando y Bravo, Miguel
Obregón Salido, Álvaro
Odría, Manuel Apolinario
Oduber Quirós, Daniel
Olañeta, José Joaquín Casimiro
Olaya Herrera, Enrique
Olmedo, José Joaquin
Onganía, Juan Carlos
Orbegoso, Luis José de
Orellana, José María
Oribe, Manuel
Orlich Bolmarcich, Francisco José

Ortega Saavedra, Daniel
Ortega Saavedra, Humberto
Ortiz, Roberto Marcelino
Ortiz Rubio, Pascual
Osório, Manuel Luís
Osorio, Oscar
Ospina, Pedro Nel
Ospina Pérez, Mariano
Ospina Rodríguez, Mariano
Ottoni, Teofilo Benedito
Ovando Candía, Alfredo
Pacheco, Gregorio
Pacheco Areco, Jorge
Pacheco da Silva, Osvaldo
Páez, Federico
Páez, José Antonio
Palacio Fajardo, Manuel
Palacios, Alfredo L.
Palenque, Carlos
Pando, José Manuel
Paraná, Honôrio Hermeto Carneiro
    Leão, Marquês de
Pardo y Barreda, José
Pardo y Lavalle, Manuel
Paredes, Mariano
Paredes y Arrillaga, Mariano
Parra, Aquileo
Pascal-Trouillot, Ertha
Paso, Juan José
Passarinho, Jarbas Gonçalves
Pastora Gómez, Edén
Pastrana Borrero, Misael
Patrón Costas, Robustiano
Pavón Aycinena, Manuel Francisco
Paz, José María
Paz Baraona, Miguel
Paz Estenssoro, Victor
Paz García, Policarpo
Paz Zamora, Jaime
Peçanha, Nilo Procópio
Pedreira, Antonio S.
Peixoto, Floriano Vieira
Peixoto, Júlio Afrânio
Pellacani, Dante
Pellegrini, Carlos
Pena, Afonso Augusto Moreira
Peña, Manuel Pedro de
Peña Gómez, José Francisco
Peñaloza, Ángel Vicente
Peñaranda del Castillo, Enrique
Pcralta Azurdia, Enrique
Pereira, José Clemente
Pérez, Carlos Andrés

Pérez Jiménez, Marcos
Pérez Mascayano, José Joaquín
Pérez Salas, Francisco Antonio
Perón, Juan Domingo
Perón, María Estela Martínez de
Perón, María Eva Duarte de
Pessoa, Epitácio da Silva
Pessoa Cavalcanti de Albuquerque, João
Pétion, Alexandre Sabès
Pezet, Juan Antonio
Picado Michalski, Teodoro
Piérola, Nicolás de
Pinedo, Federico
Pinheiro, José Feliciano Fernandes
Pinheiro Machado, José Gomes
Pinho, José Wanderley de Araújo
Pino Suárez, José María
Pinochet Ugarte, Augusto
Pinto Díaz, Francisco Antonio
Pinto Garmendia, Aníbal
Plaza, Victorino de la
Plaza Gutíerrez, Leonidas
Plaza Lasso, Galo
Ponce Enríquez, Camilo
Porras, Belisario
Portes Gil, Emilio
Posadas, Gervasio Antonio de
Prado, Mariano Ignacio
Prado y Ugarteche, Javier
Prado y Ugarteche, Manuel
Prat Echaurren, Jorge
Prestes, Luís Carlos
Prestes de Albuquerque, Julio
Price, George Cadle
Prieto, Guillermo
Prieto Figueroa, Luis Beltrán
Prío Socarrás, Carlos
Puente Uceda, Luis de la
Pueyrredón, Honorio
Pueyrredón, Juan Martín de
Quadros, Jânio da Silva
Queirós Coutinho Matoso da Câmara,
    Eusébio de
Quiñones Molina, Alfonso
Quintana, Manuel
Quintana Roo, Andrés
Quiroga, Juan Facundo
Quiroga Santa Cruz, Marcelo
Ramírez, Francisco
Ramírez, Pedro Pablo
Ramos Mejía, Ezequiel
Regalado, Tomás
Remón Cantera, José Antonio

Restrepo, Carlos Eugenio
Restrepo, José Manuel
Revueltas, José
Reyes, Rafael
Reyes Ogazón, Bernardo
Reyna Barrios, José María
Riani, Clodsmith
Riesco Errázuriz, Germán
Rio Branco, Barão do
Rio Branco, Visconde do
Ríos Montt, José Efraín
Ríos Morales, Juan Antonio
Rivadavia, Bernardino
Rivarola, Cirilo Antonio
Rivas, Patricio
Rivera, Fructuoso
Rivera, Joaquín
Rivera Cabezas, Antonio
Rivera Carballo, Julio Adalberto
Rivera Maestre, Miguel
Rivera Paz, Mariano
Robles, Francisco
Robles, Marcos Aurelio
Roca, Julio Argentino
Roca Rodríguez, Vicente Ramón
Rocha, Dardo
Rocha, Justiniano José da
Rodas Alvarado, Modesto
Rodrigues Alves, Francisco de Paula
Rodríguez, Andrés
Rodrígucz, Carlos Rafael
Rodríguez Demorizi, Emilio
Rodríguez Lara, Guillermo
Rodríguez Luján, Abelardo
Rojas, Isaac
Rojas, Pedro José
Rojas Paúl, Juan Pablo
Rojas Pinilla, Gustavo
Roldós Aguilera, Jaime
Romero, Carlos Humberto
Romero, Oscar Arnulfo
Romero Barceló, Carlos
Rosa, Ramón
Rosas, Juan Manuel de
Roy, Eugène
Ruiz Cortines, Adolfo
Saavedra, Cornelio de
Saavedra Lamas, Carlos
Saavedra Mallea, Juan Bautista
Sacasa, Juan Batista
Sáenz Peña, Luis
Sáenz Peña, Roque
Salamanca, Daniel

Salas, Manuel de
Salaverry, Felipe Santiago
Salazar, Matías
Salgado, Plinio
Salgar, Eustorgio
Salinas de Gortari, Carlos
Salnave, Sylvain
Salomon, Étienne Lysius Félicité
Sam, Jean Villbrun Guillaume
Sam, Tirésias Augustin Simon
Samanez Ocampo, David
Samper Agudelo, Miguel
Sanabria Martínez, Víctor M.
Sánchez, Luis Alberto
Sánchez Cerro, Luis Manuel
Sánchez de Lozada Bustamante,
    Gonzalo
Sánchez Hernández, Fidel
Sánchez Vilella, Roberto
Sandino, Augusto César
Sandoval, José León
Sanfuentes Andonaegui, Juan Luis
Sanguinetti, Julio María
Santa Anna, Antonio López de
Santa Cruz, Andrés de
Santa María González, Domingo
Santana, Pedro
Santos, Eduardo
São Vicente, José Antônio Pimenta
    Bueno, Marquês de
Saraiva, José Antônio
Saravia, Aparicio
Sarmiento, Domingo Faustino
Sarney, José
Schaerer, Eduardo
Schick Gutiérrez, René
Sendic, Raúl
Seoane, Manuel
Seregni, Líber
Serrano Elías, Jorge Antonio
Siles Zuazo, Hernán
Silva, Benedita da
Silva, Lindolfo
Silva, Luis Inácio Lula da
Silva Lisboa, José da
Simon, Antoine
Somoza Debayle, Anastasio
Somoza Debayle, Luis
Somoza García, Anastasio
Soto, Marco Aurelio
Soto Alfaro, Bernardo
Soublette, Carlos
Soulouque, Faustin Élie

Souza, Luiza Erundina de
Stefanich, Juan
Stroessner, Alfredo
Suárez, Marco Fidel
Suazo Córdova, Roberto
Sucre Alcalá, Antonio José de
Tajes, Máximo
Talavera, Manuel
Taunay, Alfredo d'Escragnolle, Vicomte
    de
Tavares Bastos, Aureliano Cândido
Tejada Sorzano, José Luis
Tejedor, Carlos
Terra, Gabriel
Thompson, George
Tocornal, Joaquín
Tomic, Radomiro
Toro, David
Toro Zambrano, Mateo de
Torre, Lisandro de la
Torre Tagle, José Bernardo de Tagle y
    Portocarrero
Torres, Juan José
Torrres, Luis Emeterio
Torrijos Herrera, Omar
Trejos Fernández, José Joaquín
Tronscoso de la Concha, Manuel de
    Jesús
Trujillo, Julián
Trujillo Molina, Rafael Leónidas
Turbay, Gabriel
Turbay Ayala, Julio César
Ubico y Casteñeda, Jorge
Ugarte, Marcelino
Ulate Blanco, Otilio
Ungo, Guillermo Manuel
Urbina, José María
Urdaneta, Rafael
Ureta, Eloy G.
Uriburu, José Evaristo
Uriburu, José Félix
Urquiza, Justo José de
Urriolagoitía, Mamerto
Urrutia Lleó, Manuel
Uruguai, Visconde do
Valencia, Guillermo León
Valladares, Tomás
Valle, José Cecilio del
Vallejo, Mariano Guadalupe
Vallenilla Lanz, Laureano
Varas de la Barra, Antonio
Varela, Felipe
Vargas, Getúlio Dornelles

Vargas, José María
Vargas Llosa, Mario
Varona y Pera, Enrique José
Vasconcelos, Bernardo Pereira de
Vásquez, Horacio
Veiga, Evaristo Ferreira da
Veintimilla, José Ignacio de
Velasco, José Miguel de
Velasco Alvarado, Juan
Velasco Ibarra, José María
Velázquez Sánchez, Fidel
Victoria, Guadalupe
Victoria, Manuel
Videla, Jorge Rafael
Viera, Feliciano
Vieytes, Hipólito
Vigil, Donaciano
Villa, Francisco "Pancho"
Villagrán Kramer, Francisco
Villalba, Jóvito
Villarroel López, Gualberto
Villazón, Eliodoro
Villeda Morales, Ramón
Vincent, Sténio Joseph
Viola, Roberto Eduardo
Viteri y Ungo, Jorge
Vivanco, Manuel Ignacio
Volio Jiménez, Jorge
Walker, William
Weffort, Francisco Correia
Williams Calderón, Abraham
Williman, Claudio
Ydígoras Fuentes, Miguel
Ynsfrán, Edgar L.
Yrigoyen, Hipólito
Zaldúa, Francisco Javier
Zavala, Lorenzo de
Zayas y Alfonso, Alfredo
Zeballos, Estanislao
Zelaya, José Santos
Zubizarreta, Gerónimo
Zuloaga, Félix María
Zúñiga, Ignacio

PUBLIC ADMINISTRATION, CIVIL SERVICE, AND DIPLOMACY

Acosta García, Julio
Aguilar Vargas, Cándido
Albán, Laureano
Alberdi, Juan Bautista
Alberto, João

Albuquerque, Antônio Francisco de
  Paula
Alcorta, Diego
Alfaro, Ricardo Joaquín
Almonte, Juan Nepomuceno
Altamirano, Ignacio Manuel
Alvarado, Salvador
Amador, Manuel E.
Andrade, Carlos Drummond de
Andrade, Gomes Freire de
Andueza Palacio, Raimundo
Angelis, Pedro de
Arana, Felipe de
Arana Osorio, Carlos
Arango y Parreño, Francisco de
Arciniegas, Germán
Arévalo Bermejo, Juan José
Arévalo Martínez, Rafael
Arguedas, Alcides
Argüello, Leonardo
Argüello, Santiago
Arias Sánchez, Oscar
Armijo, Manuel
Arosemena, Justo
Arriaga, Ponciano
Azcuénaga, Miguel de
Balcarce, Mariano
Baptista, Mariano
Baquíjano y Carrillo de Córdoba, José
  de
Barbosa, Francisco Villela
Barbosa de Oliveira, Rui
Barreda y Laos, Felipe
Barreiro, Antonio
Barrios, Gonzalo
Barros, João de
Barroso, Gustavo Dodt
Barrundia, José Francisco
Barrundia, Juan
Bassols, Narciso
Batres Juarros, Luis
Bedoya Reyes, Luis
Benítez, Jaime
Berges, José
Bernardes, Artur da Silva
Betancourt, Rómulo
Blanco, José Félix
Bonifaz Ascasubi, Neptalí
Borba Gato, Manuel de
Borge, Tomás
Borges, Jorge Luis
Borno, Joseph Louis E. Antoine
  François

Borrero y Cortázar, Antonio
Cabeza de Vaca, Alvar Núñez
Caldera Rodríguez, Rafael
Calderón Fournier, Rafael Ángel
Calderón Guardia, Rafael Ángel
Callejas Romero, Rafael Leonardo
Calógeras, João Pandiá
Calvo, Carlos
Campero, Narciso
Campo, Rafael
Campos, Francisco Luiz da Silva
Campos, Roberto (de Oliveira)
Campos Sales, Manuel Ferraz de
Cañas, José Simeón
Cañedo, Juan de Dios
Carazo Odio, Rodrigo
Carbo y Noboa, Pedro José
Cárcano, Miguel Ángel
Cárdenas Solorzano, Cuauhtémoc
Carneiro de Campos, José Joaquim
Caro, José Eusebio
Caro, Miguel Antonio
Carondelet, François-Louis Hector
Carrillo Colina, Braulio
Carrillo Flores, Antonio
Carrillo Flores, Nabor
Carvalho, Antônio de Albuquerque
  Coelho de
Caso y Andrade, Alfonso
Casteñeda Castro, Salvador
Castillo Ledón, Amalia
Castro Madriz, José María
Castro Ruz, Raúl
Cazneau, William Leslie
Cedillo Martínez, Saturnino
Chamorro Vargas, Emiliano
Chávez, Mariano
Chonchol, Jacques
Christmas, Lee
Cobos, Francisco de los
Coelho, Jorge de Albuquerque
Coelho Pereira, Duarte
Coll y Toste, Cayetano
Collor, Lindolfo
Colosio Murrieta, Luis Donaldo
Colunje, Gil
Concha, José Vicente
Constant Botelho de Magalhães,
  Benjamin
Córdova Rivera, Gonzalo S.
Corona, Ramón
Cortés Castro, León
Costa, Hipólito José da

Cotegipe, Barão de
Coutinho, Rodrigo Domingos Antonio
  de Sousa
Couto, José Bernardo
Creel, Enrique Clay
Cruz, Arturo
Dantas, Manuel Pinto de Souza
de la Huerta, Adolfo
Del Monte, Domingo
Delfim Neto, Antônio
Delgado Chalbaud, Carlos
D'Escoto Brockmann, Miguel
Díaz, Félix, Jr.
Díaz Vélez, José Miguel
Dobles Segreda, Luis
Domínguez, Miguel
Dorticós Torrado, Osvaldo
Drago, Luis María
Durán, Fray Narciso
Dutra, Eurico Gaspar
Echeandía, José María de
Echeverría Álvarez, Luis
Emparán, Vicente
Encinas, José Antonio
Ensenada, Cenón de Somodevilla,
  Marqués de la
Escalante, Aníbal
Escobedo, Mariano
Estimé, Dumarsais
Fabela Alfaro, Isidro
Facio Brenes, Rodrigo
Facio Segreda, Gonzalo
Falcón, José
Fallas Sibaja, Carlos Luis
Feijó, Diogo Antônio
Fernández, Max
Ferré Aguayo, Luis Antonio
Ferrera, Francisco
Figueroa, José
Figueroa Larraín, Emiliano
Finlay, Carlos Juan
Floridablanca, Conde de
Fonseca, Juan Rodríguez de
Fuentes, Carlos
Fuentes, Manuel Atanasio
Gallegos, Rómulo
Galván Rivera, Mariano
Gálvez, José de
Gamboa Iglesias, Federico
Gamio Martínez, Manuel
García Calderón, Francisco
García Godoy, Héctor
García Robles, Alfonso

García Salinas, Francisco
Garrido Canabal, Tomás
Gastão d'Orléans
Gelly, Juan Andrés
Gelly y Obes, Juan Andrés
Golbery do Couto e Silva
Gomes, Eduardo
Gómez, Indalecio
Gómez, José Valentín
Gómez, Juan Gualberto
Gómez, Miguel Mariano
Gómez Pedraza, Manuel
Gondra, Manuel
Gonzaga, Tomás Antônio
González, Abraham
González, Florentino
González, Manuel
González Ortega, Jesús
Gorostiza, Manuel Eduardo de
Gorostiza Alcalá, José
Graef Fernández, Carlos
Guardia, Ricardo Adolfo de la
Guevara, Ernesto "Che"
Gutiérrez, Eulalio
Gutiérrez Estrada, José María
Gutiérrez Garbín, Victor Manuel
Guzmán, Antonio Leocadio
Haro Barraza, Guillermo
Haro y Tamariz, Antonio de
Hawkins, John
Hernández, José
Hernández Colón, Rafael
Herrán, Pedro Alcántara
Herrera Campins, Luis
Herrera Lane, Felipe
Holguín, Jorge
Iglesias, José María
Jiménez, Enrique A.
Juan y Santacilia, Jorge
Kubitschek, Marcia
Kubitschek de Oliveira, Juscelino
Kumate Rodríguez, Jesús
Larrazábal Ugueto, Wolfgang
Lavalle Urbina, María
Lavradio, Marquês do
Le Bretón, Tomás Alberto
Lencinas, Carlos Washington
León de la Barra, Francisco
Leoni, Raúl
Lerdo de Tejada, Miguel
Lerdo de Tejada, Sebastián
Lescot, Élie
Letelier de Solar, Orlando

Lewis, Roberto
Lima, Alceu Amoroso
Lima, Pedro de Araújo
Limantour, José Yves
Lisboa, Joaquim Marques
Lleras, Lorenzo María
Lleras Camargo, Alberto
Lleras Restrepo, Carlos
López, Vicente Fidel
López Arellano, Oswaldo
López Mateos, Adolfo
López Michelsen, Alfonso
López Portillo, José
López Rega, José
Lott, Henrique Batista Duffles Teixeira
Lutzenberger, José
Machado, Gustavo
Machado de Assis, Joaquim Maria
Machado y Morales, Gerardo
Madrazo, Carlos A.
Madrid Hurtado, Miguel de la
Magalhães, Domingos José Gonçalves de
Maluf, Paulo Salim
Mansilla, Lucio Victorio
Manso de Maldonado, Antonio
Mariño, Santiago
Márquez, José Ignacio de
Masferrer, Alberto
Maurits, Johan
Médici, Emílio Garrastazú
Mello, Zélia Maria Cardoso de
Melo, Leopoldo
Melo e Castro, Martinho de
Melo Franco, Afonso Arinos de
Melo Franco, Afrânio de
Melo Neto, João Cabral de
Méndez Pereira, Octavio
Mendiburu, Manuel de
Mendieta, Salvador
Mendieta y Montefur, Carlos
Mendoza, Antonio de
Michelina, Santos
Mindlin, José E.
Miró Cardona, José
Mistral, Gabriela
Molina, Marcelo
Molina Bedoya, Felipe
Molina Enríquez, Andrés
Monge Álvarez, Luis Alberto
Monte Alegre, José da Costa Carvalho, Marquís de
Monteagudo, Bernardo de

Montealegre Fernández, José María
Monteiro, Pedro Aurélio de Góis
Monteiro, Tobias do Rêgo
Montt Torres, Manuel
Montúfar, Lorenzo
Montúfar Montes de Oca, Lorenzo
Moog, Vianna
Mora, José María Luis
Mora Otero, José Antonio
Mora Porrás, Juan Rafael
Mora Valverde, Manuel
Morales Carrión, Arturo
Morales Lemus, José
Moreno, Fulgencio
Morones, Luis
Moshinsky Borodiansksy, Marcos
Mosquera, Tomás Cipriano de
Mosquera y Arboleda, Joaquín
Moya de Contreras, Pedro
Múgica, Francisco José
Muñoz Ledo Lazo de la Vega, Porfirio
Murillo Toro, Manuel
Murtinho, Joaquim Duarte
Nabuco de Araújo, Joaquim
Naón, Rómulo S.
Neves, Tancredo de Almeida
Novo, Salvador
Núñez Moledo, Rafael
Ocampo, Melchor
Oduber Quirós, Daniel
Olaya Herrera, Enrique
Olivares, Conde-Duque de
Oliveira Lima, Manuel de
Orfila, Washington Alejandro José Luis
Orlich Bolmarchich, Francisco José
Orozco y Berra, Manuel
Ortiz, Fernando
Ortiz de Ayala, Simón Tadeo
Ortiz Mena, Antonio
Osório, Manuel Luís
Ospina, Pedro Nel
Ospina Pérez, Mariano
Otero, Mariano
Padilla Peñalosa, Ezequiel
Páez, Federico
Páez, José Antonio
Palacio Fajardo, Manuel
Pani Arteaga, Alberto J.
Paraná, Honôrio Hermeto Carneiro Leão, Marquês de
Pareja Diezcanseco, Alfredo
Parra, Aquileo
Passarinho, Jarbas Gonçalves

Pastrana Borrero, Misael
Paterson, William
Patiño, José de
Patiño, Simón Iturri
Payno y Flores, Manuel
Paz, Octavio
Paz Soldán Family
Peçanha, Nilo Procópio
Peixoto, Júlio Afrânio
Pellacani, Dante
Pellegrini, Carlos
Pellicer Cámara, Carlos
Pena, Afonso Augusto Moreira
Pena, Luís Carlos Martins
Peña Gómez, José Francisco
Peña y Peña, Manuel de la
Peralta Azurdia, Enrique
Pereira, José Clemente
Pérez, Albino
Pérez, Carlos Andrés
Pérez Jiménez, Marcos
Pérez Mascayano, José Joaquín
Pessoa, Epitácio da Silva
Pessoa Cavalcanti de Albuquerque, João
Picado Michalski, Teodoro
Pinedo, Federico
Pinheiro, José Feliciano Fernandes
Pinho, José Wanderley de Araújo
Piñol y Sala, José
Plaza Gutiérrez, Leonidas
Plaza Lasso, Galo
Poinsett, Joel Roberts
Pombal, Marquês de (Sebastião José de Carvalho e Melo)
Porras, Belisario
Porter, David
Portes Gil, Emilio
Prebisch, Raúl
Prieto, Guillermo
Prieto Figueroa, Luis Beltrán
Puig Casauranc, José Manuel
Queirós Coutinho Matoso da Câmara, Eusébio de
Queiroz, Dinah Silveira de
Quiñones Molina, Alfonso
Quintana Roo, Andrés
Quintero, Ángel
Rabasa, Emilio
Ramírez, Ignacio
Ramírez, José Fernando
Ramírez Vázquez, Pedro
Ramírez y Blanco, Alejandro
Ramos Arizpe, José Miguel

Ramos Mejía, Ezequiel
Ramos y Magaña, Samuel
Rayón, Ignacio
Rejón, Manuel Crescencio
Rengifo Cárdenas, Manuel
Restrepo, Carlos Eugenio
Reyes, Rafael
Reyes Ochoa, Alfonso
Reyes Ogazón, Bernardo
Ribeiro, Darcy
Rio Branco, Barão do
Rio Branco, Visconde do
Rivarola, Rodolfo
Robles, Marcos Aurelio
Roca, Blas
Roca Rodríguez, Vicente Ramón
Rodríguez, Carlos Rafael
Rodríguez Demorizi, Emilio
Rodríguez Erdoiza, Manuel
Rodríguez Luján, Abelardo
Rojas, Pedro José
Rojas Paúl, Juan Pablo
Rojas Urtuguren, José Antonio de
Romero, Matías
Romero Barceló, Carlos
Romero Rubio, Manuel
Rondon, Cândido Mariano da Silva
Rosáins, Juan Nepomuceno
Roscio, Juan Germán
Rubí, Marqués de
Rubião, Murilo
Ruiz Cortines, Adolfo
Ruiz de Alarcón y Mendoza, Juan
Sá, Mem de
Sá e Benavides, Salvador Correia de
Saavedra Lamas, Carlos
Saco, José Antonio
Sáenz, Moisés
Sáenz Garza, Aaron
Salgar, Eustorgio
Salinas de Gortari, Carlos
Sánchez, Prisciliano
Sánchez de Bustamante y Sirven, Antonio
Sánchez de Tagle, Francisco Manuel
Sánchez Hernández, Fidel
Sánchez Vilella, Roberto
Sandoval Vallarta, Manuel
Santamaría, Haydée
Santos, Eduardo
São Vicente, José Antônio Pimenta Bueno, Marquês de
Schaerer, Eduardo

Schick Gutiérrez, René
Scliar, Moacyr
Seguín, Juan José María Erasmo
Sierra Méndez, Justo
Sierra O'Reilly, Justo
Silva Herzog, Jesús
Simonsen, Mário Henrique
Soto Alfaro, Bernardo
Soublette, Carlos
Sousa, Otávio Tarquínio de
Suárez, Marco Fidel
Távara y Andrade, Santiago
Teixeira, Anisio Espinola
Tinoco Granados, Federico
Tocornal, Joaquín
Toro, Fermín
Torres, Luis Emeterio
Torres Bodet, Jaime
Tronscoso de la Concha, Manuel de Jesús
Trujillo, Julián
Tugwell, Rexford Guy
Turbay, Gabriel
Ugarte, Manuel
Urbina, José María
Urbina, Luis Gonzaga
Uribe Uribe, Rafael
Urrea, José de
Urrutia Lleó, Manuel
Uruguai, Visconde do
Urvina Jado, Francisco
Valle, Artistóbulo del
Valle, José Cecilio del
Varas de la Barra, Antonio
Vargas, Getúlio Dornelles
Varnhagen, Francisco Adolfo de (Visconde de Porto Seguro)
Vasconcelos Calderón, José
Vázquez de Ayllón, Lucas
Velázquez Sánchez, Fidel
Vélez Sarsfield, Dalmacio
Vidaurri, Santiago
Vieira, Antônio
Villanueva, Carlos Raúl
Villas Bôas Brothers
Villaurrutia, Jacobo de
Villeda Morales, Ramón
Vincent, Sténio Joseph
Volio Jiménez, Jorge
Wheelock Román, Jaime
Wilde, Eduardo
Yáñez Santos Delgadillo, Agustín
Ynsfrán, Pablo Max

Zaldúa, Francisco Javier
Zamora, Rubén
Zaragoza, Ignacio
Zarco, Francisco
Zavala, Joaquín
Zavala, Lorenzo de
Zavala, Silvio
Zayas y Alfonso, Alfredo
Zeballos, Estanislao
Zubirán Achondo, Salvador
Zubizarreta, Gerónimo

RELIGION (including saints, shamans, missionaries, and clerical leaders)

Abad y Queipo, Manuel
Abbad y Lasierra, Íñigo
Acosta, José de
Alegre, Francisco Javier
Anchieta, José de
Andreoni, João Antônio
Antequera y Castro, José de
Aparecida, Nossa Senhora da
Aristide, Jean-Bertrand
Arns, Paulo Evaristo
Balbuena, Bernardo de
Batista, Cícero Romão
Bazán, Juan Gregorio
Beltrán, Luis
Beltrán, Luis (Saint)
Benavides, Alonso de
Bethancourt, Pedro de San José de
Blanco, José Félix
Boff, Leonardo
Bolaños, Luis de
Bonfim, Nosso Senhor do
Brasseur de Bourbourg, Charles
    Étienne
Caballero y Góngora, Antonio
Câmara, Hélder
Cañas, José Simeón
Caneca, Frei Joaquím do Amor Divino
Cardenal, Ernesto
Cárdenas, Bernardino de
Cardim, Frei Fernão
Carney, James "Guadalupe"
Casaldáliga, Pedro
Casanova y Estrada, Ricardo
Casáus y Torres, Ramón
Castañeda, Francisco de Paula
Castillo y Guevara, Francisca Josefa de
    la Concepción de

Claver, Pedro
Clavigero, Francisco Javier
Cobo, Bernabé
Conselheiro, Antônio
Cortés de Madariaga, José
Cos y Pérez, José María
Coutinho, José Joaquim da Cunha de
    Azeredo
Cuadra, Pablo Antonio
Cuevas, Mariano
Delgado, José Matías
Díaz de Guzmán, Ruy
Dobrizhoffer, Martín
Donovan, Jean
Durán, Diego
Durán, Fray Narciso
Durão, José de Santa Rita
Errázuriz Valdivieso, Crescente
Esquiú, Mamerto
Feijóo, Benito Jerónimo
Figueiredo, Jackson de
Fonseca, Juan Rodríguez de
Fresno Larraín, Juan Francisco
Frías, Antonio
Funes, Gregorio
Fúrlong Cárdiff, Guillermo
Gallo Goyenechea, Pedro León
Gante, Pedro de
Garcés, Francisco Tomás Hermenegildo
García, Diego
García Diego y Moreno, Francisco
García Peláez, Francisco de Paula
Gasca, Pedro de la
Girón de León, Andrés de Jesús
Godoy, Manuel
Gómez, José Valentín
González de Santa Cruz, Roque
González Suárez, (Manuel María)
    Federico
Gorriti, Juan Ignacio de
Gutiérrez, Gustavo
Henríquez, Camilo
Herrán y Zaldúa, Antonio Saturnino
Herrera, Bartolomé
Hidalgo y Costilla, Miguel
Jerez, Francisco de
Juan Diego
Juana Inés de la Cruz, Sor
Kino, Eusebio Francisco
Labastida y Dávalos, Pelagio Antonio
    de
Landa, Diego de
Landázuri Ricketts, Juan

Landívar, Rafael
Las Casas, Bartolomé de
Lasuén, Fermín Francisco de
Liendo y Goicoechea, José Antonio
Lima, Alceu Amoroso
Llorente y Lafuente, Anselmo
López de Cogolludo, Diego
López Trujillo, Alfonso
Lorenzana y Buitrón, Francisco
    Antonio de
Lozano, Pedro
Luna Pizarro, Francisco Javier de
Luque, Hernando de
Maldonado, Francisco Severo
Maldonado, Rodrigo de Arias
Margil de Jesús, Antonio
Marroquín, Francisco
Martínez, Padre Antonio J.
Martyr, Peter
Matamoros y Guridi, Mariano
Melville, Thomas and Margarita
Menininha do Gantois, Mãe
Mier Noriega y Guerra, José Servando
    Teresa de
Mogrovejo, Toribio Alfonso de
Montesinos, Antonio de
Mora, José María Luis
Mora y del Río, José
Morelos y Pavón, José María
Mosquera, Manuel José
Motolinía, Toribio de
Moya de Contreras, Pedro
Munguía, Clemente de Jesús
Niza, Marcos de
Nóbrega, Manuel da
Núñez Vargas, Benjamín
Nusdorffer, Bernardo
Obando y Bravo, Miguel
Oré, Luis Gerónimo de
Oro, Justo Santa María de
Palafox y Mendoza, Juan de
Palou, Francisco
Pérez Aguirre, Luis
Piñol y Aycinena, Bernardo
Porres, Martín de
Quiroga, Vasco de
Rada, Manuel de Jesús
Ramos Arizpe, José Miguel
Rivera Damas, Arturo
Rocha, Manoel Ribeiro
Romero, Oscar Arnulfo
Rosa de Lima
Rossell y Arellano, Mariano

Ruiz de Montoya, Antonio
Sahagún, Bernardino de
Sales, Eugênio de Araújo
Salvador, Vicente do
Sanabria Martínez, Victor M.
Sepp, Anton
Serra, Junipero
Serrano, José
Silva Henríquez, Raúl
Solano, Francisco
Solís Folch de Cardona, José
Subirana, Manuel de Jesús
Talamantes, Melchor de
Thiel, Bernardo Augusto
Torquemada, Juan de
Torres Bello, Diego de
Torres Restrepo, Camilo
Urdaneta, Andrés de
Urrea, Teresa
Valdivia, Luis de
Varela y Morales, Félix
Vásquez, Francisco de Asís
Vélez de Escalante, Silvestre
Vera Cruz, Alonso de la
Vieira, Antônio
Vigil, Francisco de Paula González
Viñes y Martorell, Benito
Viscardo y Guzmán, Juan Pablo
Viteri y Ungo, Jorge
Vitoria, Francisco de
Ximénez, Francisco
Zepeda y Zepeda, Juan de Jesús
Zubiría, José Antonio Laureano de
Zumárraga, Juan de

REVOLUTIONARY LEADERSHIP (including guerrillas)

Abasolo, Mariano
Agramonte y Loynaz, Ignacio
Agüeybana II
Albizu Campos, Pedro
Aldama y González, Ignacio de
Aldama y González, Juan de
Alem, Leandro
Alfaro Delgado, José Eloy
Alfaro Siqueiros, David
Allende, Ignacio
Allende Gossens, Salvador
Alvarado, Salvador
Andresote
Anzoátegui, José Antonio

Aramburu, Pedro Eugenio
Arce Castaño, Bayardo
Arcos, Santiago
Arias Madrid, Harmodio
Arismendi, Juan Bautista
Arismendi, Rodney
Atahaulpa
Ávila, Alonso de
Azcárate y Lezama, Juan Francisco de
Barrett, Rafael
Barrios, Gonzalo
Barrios, Justo Rufino
Barrundia, José Francisco
Bedoya de Molina, Dolores
Bello, Andrés
Berbco, Juan Francisco
Bermúdez, José Francisco
Bertoni, Moisés
Bilbao Barquín, Francisco
Blanco Galdós, Hugo
Bobo, Rosalvo
Bolívar, Simón
Borge, Tomás
Bravo, Leonardo
Brión, Luis
Caamaño Deñó, Francisco
Caballero, Pedro Juan
Caldas, Francisco José de
Campos, Luis María
Campos, Manuel Jorge
Candioti, Francisco Antonio
Canek, Jacinto
Carlés, Manuel
Carranza, Venustiano
Castro, Julián
Castro Ruz, Fidel
Castro Ruz, Raúl
Céspedes, Carlos Manuel de (the Elder)
Chibás, Eduardo
Chirino, José Leonardo
Cienfuegos, Camilo
Cisneros Betancourt, Salvador
Contreras Brothers
Cortés de Madariaga, José
Cos y Pérez, José María
Creydt, Oscar
Cruz, Serapio
de la Huerta, Adolfo
Debray, [Jules] Régis
Delgado, José Matías
D'Escoto Brockmann, Miguel
Dessalines, Jean Jacques
Díaz Soto y Gama, Antonio

Domínguez, Miguel
Dorticós Torrado, Osvaldo
Duarte, Juan Pablo
Echeverría Bianchi, José Antonio
Erro, Enrique
Escalante, Aníbal
Estrada Palma, Tomás
Facio Segreda, Gonzalo
Falcón, Juan Crisóstomo
Febres-Cordero Ribadeneyra, León
Fernández Madrid, José
Flores, Juan José
Flores Magón, Ricardo
Fonseca Amador, Carlos
Freire Serrano, Ramón
Gabeira, Fernando Nagle
Galeana, Hermenegildo
Gallo Goyenechea, Pedro León
Gálvez, Mariano
Gamarra, Agustín
García, Calixto
García Granados, Miguel
Garibaldi, Giuseppe
Godoi, Juan Silvano
Godoy Cruz, Tomás
Gómez, Eugenio
Gómez, José Miguel (d. 1805)
Gómez, José Miguel (d. 1921)
Gómez, José Valentín
José y Báez, Máximo
González, Abraham
González, Pablo
González Prada, Manuel
Grove Vallejo, Marmaduke
Guerrero, Vicente
Guevara, Ernesto "Che"
Gutiérrez, Eulalio
Gutiérrez Brothers
Gutiérrez de Lara, José Bernardo
Guzmán, Martín Luis
Hernández, José Manuel
Herrera, Tomás
Hidalgo y Costilla, Miguel
Hostos y Bonilla, Eugenio María de
James, Cyril Lionel Robert
Jauretche, Arturo M.
Justo, Juan B.
La Serna, José de
Laprida, Francisco Narciso de
Laredo Bru, Federico
Larrazábal Ugueto, Wolfgang
Lautaro
Leyva Solano, Gabriel

López, Narciso
López Trujillo, Alfonso
López y Fuentes, Gregorio
L'Ouverture, Toussaint
Maceo, Antonio
Machado, Gustavo
Machado y Morales, Gerardo
Madero, Francisco Indalecio
Mandu Ladino
Marighela, Carlos
Mariño, Santiago
Martí, Agustín Farabundo
Martínez, Juan José
Matamoros y Guridi, Mariano
Mayorga, Silvio
Mella, Julio Antonio
Mella, Ramón Matías
Melo, José María
Mendieta y Montefur, Carlos
Menocal, Mario García
Mina y Larrea, Javier
Miranda, Francisco de
Miró Cardona, José
Molina, Pedro
Molina Ureña, José Rafael
Monagas, José Gregorio
Monagas, José Tadeo
Monteagudo, Bernardo de
Montes, César
Montt Álvarez, Jorge
Montúfar y Larrea, Juan Pío de
Morales Lemus, José
Morelos y Pavón, José María
Morínigo, Higínio
Múgica, Francisco José
Nariño, Antonio
Navarro Wolff, Antonio
Nufio, José Dolores
O, Genovevo de la
Obregón Salido, Álvaro
Oduber Quirós, Daniel
Olañeta, José Joaquín Casimiro
Orozco, Pascual, Jr.
Ortega Saavedra, Daniel
Ortega Saavedra, Humberto
Ortiz de Ayala, Simón Tadeo
Ortiz de Domínguez, Josefa
Padilla Peñalosa, Ezequiel
Páez, José Antonio
País, Frank
Palacio Fajardo, Manuel
Pani Arteaga, Alberto J.
Pastora Gómez, Edén

Peimbert, Margarita
Peña, Antonia
Peña, Lázaro
Péralte, Charlemagne Masséna
Pérez Salas, Francisco Antonio
Piérola, Nicolás de
Pinto Díaz, Francisco Antonio
Portes Gil, Emilio
Prestes, Luís Carlos
Prieto Figueroa, Luis Beltrán
Puente Uceda, Luis de la
Quintana Roo, Andrés
Ramírez Mercado, Sergio
Rayón, Ignacio
Recabarren Serrano, Luis Emilio
Rejón, Manuel Crescencio
Reyes Ogazón, Bernardo
Ribas, José Félix
Riego y Núñez, Rafael del
Rigaud, André
Roca, Blas
Rodríguez, Carlos Rafael
Rosáins, Juan Nepomuceno
Roscio, Juan Germán
Ruíz, Henry
Ruiz, Tomás
Ruiz Cortines, Adolfo
San Martín, José Francisco de
Sánchez, Prisciliano
Sandino, Augusto César
Santa Cruz y Espejo, Francisco Javier
   Eugenio de
Santamaría, Haydée
Saravia, Aparicio
Sardaneta y Llorente, José Mariano de
Sendic, Raúl
Seregni, Líber
Siles Zuazo, Hernán
Silva Xavier, Joaquim José da
Sucre Alcalá, Antonio José de
Tallet, José Zacarías
Tejeda Olivares, Adalberto
Torres Restrepo, Camilo
Túpac Amaru (José Gabriel
   Condorcanqui)
Turcios Lima, Luis Agosto
Urracá
Urrea, José de
Urrutia Lleó, Manuel
Varona y Pera, Enrique José
Vasconcelos Calderón, José
Velasco Alvarado, Juan
Vicario Fernández, [María] Leona

Victoria, Guadalupe
Vidaurri, Santiago
Villa, Francisco "Pancho"
Villagrán, Julián and José María ("El
   Chito")
Villagrán Kramer, Francisco
Wheelock Román, Jaime
Yanes, Francisco Javier
Yon Sosa, Marco Antonio
Zamora, Rubén
Zapata, Emiliano
Zaragoza, Ignacio
Zárate Willka, Pablo
Zayas y Alfonso, Alfredo
Zeledón, Benjamín Francisco

SCIENCE AND MEDICINE

Adem Chahín, José
Adem Chahín, Julián
Alcorta, Diego
Alexis, Jacques Stéphen
Almonte, Juan Nepomuceno
Alonso, Manuel A.
Alzate y Ramírez, José Antonio de
Amador Guerrero, Manuel
Ameghino, Florentino
Ávila, Julio Enrique
Azara, Félix de
Barbero, Andrés
Barbosa y Alcalá, José Celso
Bertoni, Moisés
Betances, Ramón Emeterio
Bunge, Alejandro
Bunge, Augusto
Caldas, Francisco José de
Calderón Guardia, Rafael Ángel
Carrillo Flores, Nabor
Cervantes, Vicente
Chagas, Carlos Ribeiro Justiniano
Clavigero, Francisco Javier
Codazzi, Agustín
Coni, Gabriela Laperrière de
Cordero Crespo, Luis
Cruz, Oswaldo Gonçalves
Dobrizhoffer, Martín
Duvalier, François
Elhuyar, Juan José de
Elhuyar y Zúbice, Fausto de
Finlay, Carlos Juan
Frías, Antonio
Fuentes, Manuel Atanasio
García, Diego

García Conde, Pedro
González de Santa Cruz, Roque
Graef Fernández, Carlos
Grau San Martín, Ramón
Haro Barraza, Guillermo
Hernández, Francisco
Houssay, Bernardo A.
Kubitschek de Oliveira, Juscelino
Kumate Rodríguez, Jesús
Leloir, Luis F.
Liendo y Goicoechea, José Antonio
Longinos Martínez, José
Magalhães, Domingos José Gonçalves de
Malaspina, Alessandro
Mejía del Valle y Llequerica, José Joaquín
Mendinueta y Múzquiz, Pedro de
Messía de la Cerda, Pedro de
Montealegre Fernández, José María
Moreau de Justo, Alicia
Moshinsky Borodiansky, Marcos
Moziño, José Mariano
Murtinho, Joaquim Duarte
Mutis, José Celestino
Nezahualcoyotl
Niza, Marcos de
Nusdorffer, Bernardo
Paterson, William
Peixoto, Júlio Afrânio
Peralta Barnuevo y Rocha, Pedro de
Popenoe, Frederick Wilson
Prieto Rodríguez, Sotero
Ramos, Artur
Ramos Mejía, José María
Rawson, Guillermo
Rodrigues, Raimundo Nina
Romay y Valdés Chacón, Tomás
Romero, Emilio
Rosenblueth, Arturo Stearns
Ruiz de Montoya, Antonio
Sandoval Vallarta, Manuel
Santa Cruz y Espejo, Francisco Javier Eugenio de
Scliar, Moacyr
Torres Bello, Diego de
Torre y Huerta, Carlos de la
Unanue, Hipólito
Vargas, José María
Velasco, José María
Velázquez Cárdenas de León, Joaquín
Villeda Morales, Ramón
Viñes y Martorell, Benito

Wilde, Eduardo
Zubirán Achondo, Salvador

SOCIAL PROTEST AND REFORM

Abad y Queipo, Manuel
Albizu Campos, Pedro
Alem, Leandro
Allende Gossens, Salvador
Alvarado, Salvador
Arguedas, José María
Arismendi, Rodney
Arriaga, Ponciano
Arze, José Antonio
Atahualpa
Bachiller y Morales, Antonio
Barrios, Justo Rufino
Bassols, Narciso
Benedetti, Mario
Betances, Ramón Emeterio
Betancourt Cisneros, Gaspar
Bilbao Barquín, Francisco
Bonilla, Policarpo
Bonilla Chirinos, Manuel
Bravo, Mario
Caballero y Rodríguez, José Agustín
Calderón Guardia, Rafael Ángel
Campa Salazar, Valentín
Cañas, José Simeón
Caneca, Frei Joaquím do Amor Divino
Canek, Jacinto
Carlés, Manuel
Carrillo Puerto, Felipe
Casaldáliga, Pedro
Castro Alves, Antônio de
Castro Pozo, Hildebrando
Castro Ruz, Fidel
Caupolicán
Chibás, Eduardo
Chonchol, Jacques
Cisneros Betancourt, Salvador
Clouthier del Rincón, Manuel J.
Coni, Emilio R.
Coni, Gabriela Laperrière de
Conselheiro, Antônio
Corona, Ramón
Degollado, Santos
Del Prado, Jorge
Díaz Soto y Gama, Antonio
Donovan, Jean
Dorticós Torrado, Osvaldo
Escalante, Aníbal

Escobedo, Mariano
Estrada Palma, Tomás
Fernández Oreamuno, Próspero
Figueres Ferrer, José
Flores Magón, Ricardo
Fonseca Amador, Carlos
Fresno Larraín, Juan Francisco
Frugoni, Emilio
Gabeira, Fernando Nagle
Gaitan, Jorge Eliécer
Galán, Luis Carlos
Galeano, Eduardo Hughes
Gallo Goyenechea, Pedro León
Gama, Luís
Gamarra, Francisca Zubiaga Bernales de (La Mariscala)
García Granados, Miguel
García Salinas, Francisco
Garrido Canabal, Tomás
Ghioldi, Américo
Ghioldi, Rodolfo
Gómez, Juan Gualberto
Gómez Farías, Valentín
Gonzaga, Tomás Antônio
González, Pablo
González Víquez, Cleto
Grau San Martín, Ramón
Guevara, Ernesto "Che"
Gutiérrez Estrada, José María
Gutiérrez Garbín, Víctor Manuel
Guzmán, Antonio Leocadio
Haro y Tamariz, Antonio de
Haya de la Torre, Víctor Raúl
Hertzog Garaizabal, Enrique
Hidalgo y Costilla, Miguel
Iglesias, José María
Iglesias Pantin, Santiago
James, Cyril Lionel Robert
Jara, Víctor
Jauretche, Arturo M.
Juárez, Benito
Julião Arruda de Paula, Francisco
Justo, Juan B.
Kahlo, Frida
Labarca Hubertson, Amanda
Landázuri Ricketts, Juan
Las Casas, Bartolomé de
Lerdo de Tejada, Miguel
Letelier de Solar, Orlando
Leyva Solano, Gabriel
Lima, Alceu Amoroso
Lima Barreto, Afonso Henriques de
Lleras Restrepo, Carlos

Lombardo Toledano, Vicente
López, Ambrosio
López, José Hilario
López Pumarejo, Alfonso
L'Ouverture, Toussaint
Lozada, Manuel
Luisi, Luisa
Lutz, Bertha Maria Julia
Lutzenberger, José
Luz y Caballero, José de la
Madero, Francisco Indalecio
Madrazo, Carlos A.
Maldonado, Francisco Severo
Mariátegui, José Carlos
Martí, Agustín Farabundo
Medeiros da Fonseca, Romy Martins
Mejía, Tomás
Mejía del Valle y Llequerica, José Joaquín
Mella, Julio Antonio
Mier Noriega y Guerra, José Servando Teresa de
Miramón, Miguel
Miró Cardona, José
Molina Enríquez, Andrés
Mon y Velarde, Juan Antonio
Mora, José María Luis
Mora Valverde, Manuel
Morales Lemus, José
Moreau de Justo, Alicia
Morelos y Pavón, José María
Múgica, Francisco José
Muñoz Ledo Lazo de la Vega, Porfirio
Muñoz Marín, Luis
Nabuco de Araújo, Joaquim
Nascimento, Abdias do
Neruda, Pablo
O, Genovevo de la
Ocampo, Melchor
Orozco, José Clemente
Ortega Saavedra, Daniel
Ortega Saavedra, Humerto
Ortiz de Ayala, Simón Tadeo
Ortiz de Domínguez, Josefa
Osorio, Oscar
Otero, Mariano
Palacios, Alfredo L.
Pani Arteaga, Alberto J.
Paso, Fernando del
Patrocínio, José do
Paz Estenssoro, Víctor
Peimbert, Margarita
Peña, Antonia

Peña, Lázaro
Péralte, Charlemagne Masséna
Pérez Esquivel, Adolfo
Piérola, Nicolás de
Poblete Poblete de Espinosa, Olga
Portes Gil, Emilio
Prieto, Guillermo
Primo de Verdad y Ramos, Francisco
Prío Socarrás, Carlos
Puente Uceda, Luis de la
Quintana Roo, Andrés
Quiroga, Vasco de
Rabasa, Emilio
Ramírez, Ignacio
Ramírez, José Fernando
Rayón, Ignacio
Rebouças, André
Recabarren Serrano, Luis Emilio
Rejón, Manuel Crescencio
Revueltas, José
Reyes Ogazón, Bernardo
Riaño y Bárcena, Juan Antonio
Riego y Núñez, Rafael del
Rius
Riva Palacio, Vicente
Rivera, Diego
Roca, Blas
Rodríguez, Carlos Rafael
Rodríguez de Velasco y Osorio Barba, María Ignacia
Rodríguez Luján, Abelardo
Roig de Leuchsenring, Emilio
Romero, Oscar Arnulfo
Rosáins, Juan Nepomuceno
Roumain, Jacques
Ruiz, Tomás
Ruiz Cortines, Adolfo
Sábato, Ernesto
Sáenz de Thorne, Manuela
Salavarrieta, Policarpa
Sanabria Martínez, Víctor M.
Sánchez, Prisciliano
Sánchez Cerro, Luis Manuel
Sandino, Augusto César
Sardaneta y Llorente, José Mariano de
Seoane, Manuel
Sierra Méndez, Justo
Siles Zuazo, Hernán
Silva Henríquez, Raúl
Tejeda Olivares, Adalberto
Torres, Luis Emeterio
Torres Restrepo, Camilo
Torre y Huerta, Carlos de la

Tristan, Flora
Ulate Blanco, Otilio
Urrea, Teresa
Valladares, Armando
Vallejo, César
Vandor, Augusto
Vasconcelos Calderón, José
Velázquez Sánchez, Fidel
Vergara, Marta
Vicario Fernández, [María] Leona
Vieira, Antônio
Vigil, Francisco de Paula González
Villa, Francisco "Pancho"
Villalba, Jóvito
Viscardo y Guzmán, Juan Pablo
Volio Jiménez, Jorge
Wyld Ospina, Carlos
Yon Sosa, Marco Antonio
Zamora, Rubén
Zapata, Emiliano
Zarco, Francisco
Zavala, Lorenzo de
Zulen, Pedro S. [and] Dora Mayer de Zulen

TECHNOLOGY AND INVENTION

Adem Chahín, Julián
Alvear, Marcelo Torcuato de
Arnaz, Desi
Belly, Félix
Bunau-Varilla, Philippe Jean
Cisneros, Francisco Javier
Codazzi, Agustín
Cos y Pérez, José María
Elhuyar, Juan José de
Elhuyar y Zúbice, Fausto de
Enciso, Martín Fernández de
Escandón, Antonio
Galindo, Juan
Goethals, George Washington
Graef Fernández, Carlos
Lesseps, Ferdinand Marie, Vicomte de
Matienzo, Benjamín
Orozco y Berra, Manuel
Pani Arteaga, Alberto J.
Porras, Diego
Pueyrredón, Prilidiano
Ramírez Vázquez, Pedro
Rebouças, André
Reed, Walter
Riaño y Bárcena, Juan Antonio

Rivera, Pedro de
Rivera Maestre, Miguel
Santos-Dumont, Alberto
Velázquez Cárdenas de León, Joaquín
Vergara Echeverez, José Francisco
Vieytes, Hipólito

THE VISUAL ARTS (including architecture)

Acosta León, Ángel
Aizenberg, Roberto
Aleijadinho
Alfaro Siqueiros, David
Almeida Júnior, José Ferraz de
Alonso, Raúl
Alvarado, Antonio
Álvarez Bravo, Lola
Álvarez Bravo, Manuel
Amador, Manuel E.
Amaral, Tarsila do
Americo de Figuereido e Melo, Pedro
Antúnez, Nemesio
Apolinar
Arango, Débora
Arboleda, Carlos
Arciniega, Claudio de
Arden Quin, Carmelo
Arrieta, José Agustín
Arrieta, Pedro de
Atl, Dr.
Baca Flor, Carlos
Balbás, Jerónimo de
Barradas, Rafael
Barragán Morfin, Luis
Basaldúa, Hector
Berni, Antonio
Bicalho Oswald, Henrique Carlos
Bigaud, Wilson
Blanes, Juan Manuel
Bonpland, Aimé Jacques
Borges, Jacobo
Botero, Fernando
Bravo, Claudio
Brecheret, Vítor
Burle Marx, Roberto
Bustos, Hermenegildo
Cabrera, Miguel
Camargo, Sergio de
Camnitzer, Luis
Cantú, Federico
Carballo, Aída
Cárdenas Arroyo, Santiago

Carreño, Mario
Casasola, Agustín
Castro, José Gil de
Cavalcanti, Newton
Cerezo Arévalo, Marco Vinicio
Chambi, Martín
Chávez Morado, José
Chong Neto, Manuel
Clark, Lygia
Clavé, Pelegrín
Codesido, Julia
Concha, Andrés de la
Cordero, Juan
Coronel, Pedro
Correa, Juan
Costa, Lúcio
Covarrubias, Miguel
Cruz Diez, Carlos
Cuevas, José Luis
Cúneo Perinetti, José
Daríe, Sandu
Davidovsky, Mario
Debret, Jean-Baptiste
Deira, Ernesto
di Cavalcanti, Emiliano
Díaz, Gonzalo
Diomede, Miguel
Dittborn, Eugenio
Duarte, Augusto Rodrigues
Dutary, Alberto
Echave Orio, Baltasar de
Egas, Camilo Alejandro
Enríquez, Carlos
Espinosa, José María
Estrada, José María (d. ca. 1862)
Euceda, Maximiliano
Felguérez, Manuel
Fernandes, Millôr
Ferrer, Rafael
Ferrez, Marc
Fierro Rimac, Francisco
Figari, Pedro
Figueroa, Pedro José
Fonseca, Gonzalo
Fonseca e Silva, Valentim da
Fontana, Lucio
Forner, Raquel
Gahona, Gabriel Vicente
Galán, Julio
Gamarra, José
Garay, Carlos
Garay, Epifanio
Gego

Gerzso, Gunther
Gil, Jerónimo Antonio
Gironella, Alberto
Goeritz, Mathias
Gómez, Benigno
González, Beatriz
González, Carlos
González Camarena, Jorge
González Goyri, Roberto
Grandjean de Montigny, Auguste Henri Victor
Grau, Enrique
Grilo, Sarah
Grippo, Víctor
Guayasamín, Oswaldo
Guerrero, Xavier
Guerrero y Torres, Francisco
Herrán, Saturnino
Herrerabarría, Adriano
Homar, Lorenzo
Hyppolite, Hector
Iturbide, Graciela
Ivaldi, Humberto
Izquierdo, María
Jaar, Alfredo
Jimeno y Planes, Rafael
Joaquim, Leandro
Juárez, José
Juárez, Luis
Julião, Carlos
Kahlo, Frida
Kosice, Gyula
Lam y Castilla, Wifredo
Landaluze, Víctor Patricio de
Laplante, Eduardo
Laso, Francisco
Leal, Fernando
Lewis, Roberto
Liautaud, Georges
Linares, Pedro
López de Arteaga, Sebastián
Lozza, Raúl
Macció, Rómulo
Mac Entyre, Eduardo
Malfatti, Anita Catarina
Marisol
Martorell, Antonio
Matta Echaurren, Roberto Sebastián Antonio
Meireles de Lima, Vítor
Mele, Juan N.
Mérida, Carlos
Minujin, Marta

Montenegro y Nervo, Roberto
Montes de Oca, Confucio
Morales, Armando
Nascimento, Abdias do
Niemeyer Soares Filho, Oscar
Noé, Luis Felipe
Obin, Philomé
Obregón, Alejandro
Obregón, José
O'Gorman, Juan
O'Higgins, Pablo
Oiticica, Hélio
Oliviera, Geraldo Teles de
Orozco, José Clemente
Ortiz, Rafael Montáñez
Otero, Alejandro
Pacheco, María Luisa
Pape, Lygia
Parra, Félix
Peláez, Amelia
Pereyns, Simon
Pettoruti, Emilio
Pingret, Édouard Henri Théophile
Pinto, Joaquín
Ponce de León, Fidelio
Porter, Liliana
Portillo, Efraín
Portinari, Cândido Torquato
Pôrto Alegre, Manuel Araújo
Portocarrero, René
Posada, José Guadalupe
Post, Frans Jansz
Prado, Vasco
Pueyrredón, Prilidiano
Quinquela Martín, Benito
Quirós, Cesáreo Bernaldo de
Ramírez Villamizar, Eduardo
Rego Monteiro, Vicente do
Reverón, Armando
Rius
Rivera, Diego
Rodríguez, Lorenzo
Rodríguez Juárez, Juan
Rojo, Viente
Rueda, Manuel
Ruelas, Julio
Ruiz, Antonio
Sabogal, José
Salazar Arrué, Salvador Efraín
Salgado, Sebastião
Santa María, Andrés de
Schendel, Mira
Segall, Lasar

Sigaud, Eugenio de Proença
Silva, José Antonio da
Sinclair, Alfredo
Sojo, Felipe
Soldi, Raúl
Soriano, Juan
Soto, Jesús Rafael
Szyszlo, Fernando de
Tábara, Enrique
Tamarón y Romeral, Pedro
Tamayo, Rufino
Toledo, Francisco
Tolsá, Manuel
Torres, Toribio
Torres García, Joaquín
Tresguerras, Francisco Eduardo de
Trujillo, Guillermo
Tsuchiya, Tilsa
Ureña, Felipe
Urie, Juan Camilo
Varo, Remedios
Vásquez de Arce y Ceballos, Gregorio
Vega, Jorge Luis de la
Veiga Vale, José Joaquim da
Velasco, José María
Velásquez, José Antonio
Vilar, Manuel
Villalpando, Cristóbal de
Villanueva, Carlos Raúl
Visconti, Eliseu d'Angelo
Vitalino Pereira dos Santos, Mestre
Weingärtner, Pedro
Xul Solar
Zachrisson, Julio
Zelaya Sierra, Pablo
Zenil, Nahum Bernabé
Zúñiga Figueroa, Carlos

WOMEN

Aguilar, Rosario Fiallos de
Agustini, Delmira
Alambert, Zuleika
Alegría, Claribel
Allende, Isabel
Amaral, Tarsila do
Amélia, Empress
Ángel, Albalucía
Arango, Débora
Assunção, Leliah
Barrios de Chamorro, Violeta
Bedoya de Molina, Dolores
Bedregal de Conitzer, Yolanda

Belli, Gioconda
Beltrán, Manuela
Berenguer, Amanda
Berman, Sabina
Bombal, María Luisa
Bonny, Anne
Brannon de Samayoa Chinchilla,
  Carmen
Brenner, Anita
Brunet, Marta
Burgos, Julia de
Cabrera, Lydia
Cáceres, Esther de
Calderón de la Barca, Fanny
Campos, Julieta
Cano, María de los Ángeles
Carballo, Aída
Castellanos, Rosario
Castillo Ledón, Amalia
Castillo y Guevara, Francisca Josefa de
  la Concepción de
Clair, Janete
Clark, Lygia
Codesido, Julia
Condé, Maryse
Coni, Gabriela Laperrière de
Cueva de Alvarado, Beatriz de la
de Jesus, Clementina
Del Río, Dolores
Dianda, Hilda
Díaz Lozano, Argentina
Espín de Castro, Vilma
Félix, María
Figueroa Gajardo, Ana
Gallego, Laura
Gamarra, Francisca Zubiaga Bernales
  de (La Mariscala)
Gambaro, Griselda
García, Sara
Garro, Elena
Gego
Glantz, Margo
Gómez de Avellaneda y Arteaga,
  Gertrudis
Gonzaga, Francisca Hedwiges
González, Beatriz
Gorodischer, Angélica
Grilo, Sarah
Gueiler Tejada, Lidia
Guido, Beatriz
Hernández, Luisa Josefina
Ibáñez, Sara de
Ibarbourou, Juana de

Isabel of Brazil, Princess
Iturbide, Graciela
Izquierdo, María
Jesus, Carolina Maria de
Juana Inés de la Cruz, Sor
Kahlo, Frida
Kosice, Gyula
Kubitschek, Marcia
Labarca Hubertson, Amanda
Lavalle Urbina, María
Levinson, Luisa Mercedes
Lispector, Clarice
Luisi, Luisa
Luisi, Paulina
Lutz, Bertha Maria Julia
Lynch, Elisa Alicia
Lynch, Marta
Malfatti, Anita Catarina
Malinche
Marisol
Matto de Turner, Clorinda
Medeiros da Fonseca, Romy Martins
Meireles, Cecília
Menchú Tum, Rigoberta
Menininha do Gantois, Mãe
Minujin, Marta
Miranda, Carmen
Mistral, Gabriela
Moreau de Justo, Alicia
Morejón, Nancy
Naranjo, Carmen
Obaldía, María Olimpia de
Ocampo, Victoria
Odio, Eunice
O'Gorman, Camila

Oreamuno, Yolanda
Orozco, Olga
Orphée, Elvira
Ortiz de Domínguez, Josefa
Pacheco, María Luisa
Palacios, Antonia
Pape, Lygia
Parra, Teresa de la
Parra, Violeta
Pascal-Trouillot, Ertha
Peimbert, Margarita
Peláez, Amelia
Peña, Antonia
Peralta, Angela
Peri Rossi, Cristina
Perón, María Estela Martínez de
Perón, María Eva Duarte de
Perricholi, La
Piñon, Nélida
Pizarnik, Alejandra
Plá, Josefina
Poblete Poblete de Espinosa, Olga
Poniatowska, Elena
Porter, Liliana
Puga, María Luisa
Queiroz, Dinah Silveira de
Queiroz, Rachel de
Read, Mary
Rodríguez de Velasco y Osorio Barba,
    María Ignacia
Rojo, María
Rokha, Winétt de
Román de Núñez, Soledad
Rosa de Lima
Rosas de Terrero, Manuela

Sáenz de Thorne, Manuela
Salavarrieta, Policarpa
Sánchez de Thompson, María
Sánchez Manduley, Celia
Santamaría, Haydée
Santos, Marquesa de
Schendel, Mira
Sierra, Stella
Silva, Benedita da
Silva, Clara
Silva, Xica da
Somers, Armonía
Souza, Luiza Erundina de
Steimberg, Alicia
Storni, Alfonsina
Suárez, Inés de
Sumac, Yma
Tejeda, Leonor de
Telles, Lygia Fagundes
Teresa Christina, Empress
Traba, Marta
Tristan, Flora
Tsuchiya, Tilsa
Ureña de Henríquez, Salomé
Valenzuela, Luisa
Vallbona, Rima de
Varo, Remedios
Vergara, Marta
Vicario Fernández, [María] Leona
Vilariño, Idea
Xuxa
Zulen, Pedro S. [and] Dora Mayer de
    Zulen

Index

A

Abadía Méndez, Miguel, 1, 279
Abad y Queipo, Manuel, 1
Abalos, José de, 1–2
Abascal y Souza, José Fernando, 2
Abasolo, Mariano, 2
Abbad y Lasierra, Íñigo, 2
Abente y Lago, Victorino, 2–3
Abertura, 391
Abreau, Diego de, 3
Abrego, Gonzalo de, 71
Abreu, Casimiro de, 456
Abreu, Isabel López de, 266
Abreu, João Capistrano de, 825
Abril, Xavier, 3
Academia Brasileira de Letras, 377
Academia de la Lengua y Cultura Guaraní, 250
Academia Nacional de Pintura, 573
Academia Universitaria del Paraguay, 58
Ação Integralista Brasileira, 195
Acción Democrática, 115, 143, 361, 569, 604, 790–791, 793, 800, 830
Acción Democrática y Nacionalista (ADN), 106, 778
Acción Nacional, 826
Aceval, Benjamín, 3
Acevedo Díaz, Eduardo Inés, 3–4, 1044
Acevedo Hernández, Antonio, 4
Achá, José María, 4, 284, 647
Acindar, 635
Acosta, José de, 730
Acosta, José Julián, 2
Acosta, Mariano, 35
Acosta, Tomás, 5
Acosta García, Julio, 5, 989
Acosta León, Ángel, 5
Action for National Liberation (ALN), 627
Acuerdo de San Nicolás, 35
Adem Chahín, José, 5, 6
Adem Chahín, Julián, 5–6
ADLAN (Amics de les Arts Nous; Friends of the New Art), 1035
Afonso Arinos Law (1951), 708
Afro-Brazilian Studies and Research Institute (IPEAFRO), 708
Agramonte, Ignacio, 253, 852
Agramonte y Loynaz, Ignacio, 6
Agrarian Reform Law (1961), 584
Agrarian Reform Law (1962), 1060
Agrarian Reform Law (1964), 241
Agrarian Reform Training and Research Institute, 392
Agreement of Toledo, 811

Agrupación Música Viva (AMV), 415, 554, 983
Agrupación Nueva Música (ANM), 775
Aguado, Juan, 277
Agua Prieta Revolt, 726
Aguascalientes Convention (1914), 725
Aguayo, Marqués de, 6
Agüero, Leopoldo Torres, 311
Agüero Rocha, Fernando, 6–7
Agüeybana I, 7
Agüeybana II, 7
Aguiar, Adonias, 7
Aguilar, Jerónimo de, 7
Aguilar, Manuel de, 226, 684–685
Aguilar, Martín de, 7
Aguilar, Rosario Fiallos de, 8
Aguilar Vargas, Cándido, 8
Aguilar y Maya, José, 751
Aguilera, Francisco Vicente, 253
Aguilera Malta, Demetrio, 8
Aguirre, Atanásio Cruz, 582
Aguirre, Juan Francisco de, 8–9
Aguirre, Julián, 9
Aguirre, Lope de, 9
Aguirre, Nataniel, 9–10
Aguirre Cerda, Pedro, 10, 28, 863, 898
Aguirre y Salinas, Osmín, 10
Agustín, José, 10–11, 911
Agustini, Delmira, 11, 321, 953, 971–972
Ahora, Teatro de, 618
Ainsa, Filomena, 294
Aizenberg, Roberto, 11
Alamán, Lucas, 11–12, 488, 684
Alambert, Zuleika, 12
Alarcón, Martín, de, 11
Alard, Jean-Delphin, 1071
Alba, Esther, 764
Alba, Luis Larrea, 107
Albán, Laureano, 12
Alberdi, Juan Bautista, 12–15, 18, 449, 629, 840, 926, 941
Alberni, Pedro de, 15
Alberro, Francisco de, 15
Albertini, Rafael Díaz, 220, 222, 779, 882
Alberto, João, 15
Albizu Campos, Pedro, 16
Albuquerque, Antônio Francisco de Paula, 16
Albuquerque, Dona Brites de, 272
Albuquerque, Jerónimo de, 272
Albuquerque, Jorge de, 272
Albuquerque, Matias de, 17–18, 272
Albuquerque Coehlo, Duarte de, 17

Albuquerque Coelho, Jorge de, 17
Alcalá, José Rodríguez, 879
Alcántara, Francisco Linares, 54
Alcántara, Francisco Martín de, 810
Alcántara Herrán, Pedro, 753
Alcaraz, José Antonio, 18
Alcoriza, Luis, 18
Alcorta, Diego, 18
Alcorta, José Figueroa, 602, 873
Aldama, Doña Rosa de, 677
Aldama, Juan, 503
Aldama y González, Ignacio de, 19
Aldama y González, Juan de, 19
Aldana, José Maria, 19
Aldana, Lorenzo de, 442
Aldao, José Félix, 445
Aldea, José Antonio Rodríguez, 731
Alderete, Jerónimo de, 946, 1021
Alegre, Francisco Javier, 19
Alegría, Ciro, 20
Alegría, Claribel, 20
Alegría, Fernando, 20–21
Aleijadinho, 21–22
Aleixo, Pedro, 292, 643
Alem, Leandro, 22–23, 34, 42, 200, 669, 910, 993, 1024,
      1080
Alemán Valdés, Miguel, 23, 94, 213, 227, 232, 260, 594, 902
Alencar, José Martiniano de, 23–24, 609, 983
Alende, Oscar, 199
Alenquer, Joâo de, 491
Alessandri Palma, Arturo, 10, 24–25, 514, 547, 566, 898
Alessandri Rodríguez, Jorge, 25
Alexandrino, Pedro, 45
Alexis, Jacques Stéphen, 25, 899
Alexis, Nord, 273
Alfaro, David, 223
Alfaro, Eloy, 283, 813
Alfaro, Guadalupe, 361
Alfaro, Ricardo Joaquín, 26, 817
Alfaro Delgado, José Eloy, 26
Alfaro Siqueiros, David, 26–27, 140, 475, 1036
Alfaro y Arosemena, Eloy, 462–463
Alfinger, Ambrosio, 366
Alfonsín, Raúl, 100, 635
Alfonso XIII, 263
Aliança Nacional Libertadora, 550, 847
Aliança Renovadora Nacional (ARENA), 394
Alianza Popular Revolucionaria Americana (APRA), 20, 83,
      426, 441, 791
Alkimin, José Maria, 390
Allegretti, Mary, 653
Allen, Lucretia, 889
Allende, Humberto, 746
Allende, Ignacio, 19, 27–28, 503, 504, 648, 750, 939
Allende, Isabel, 28
Allende, Pedro Humberto, 127, 521
Allende Gossens, Salvador, 25, 28–29, 92, 309, 391–392, 499,
      526, 572, 659, 804, 827, 955, 991

Allende-Sarón, Pedro Humberto, 29–30
Alliance for Production, 595
Alliance Française of Port-au-Prince, 504
Almafuerte (Pedro Bonifacio Palacios), 30
Almagro, Diego de, 30–31, 38, 86, 347, 604, 756, 809, 810,
      811, 1019, 1021
Almazán, Andréu, 213
Almazán, Juan Andréu, 31
Almeida, Araci de, 894
Almeida, Guilherme de, 53
Almeida, José Américo de, 31–32
Almeida, Manuel Antônio de, 32
Almonte, Juan Nepomuceno, 32–33
Alomía Robles, Daniel, 33
Alonso, Amado, 33, 575
Alonso, Juan Carlos, 34
Alonso, Manuel A., 33–34
Alonso, Mariano Roque, 34, 587
Alsina, Adolfo, 34–35, 36, 203, 669, 706
Alsina, Juan de, 35
Alsina, Valentín, 34, 35–36
Alsogaray, Alvaro, 36
Alsonso, Raúl, 34
Altamirano, Ignacio M., 864, 951
Althusser, Louis, 309
Alvarado, Antonio, 36
Alvarado, Camilo Mora, 686
Alvarado, Lisandro, 36
Alvarado, Modesto Rodas, 590
Alvarado, Pedro de, 270, 288, 630, 1011
Alvarado, Rudecindo, 920
Alvarado, Salvador, 37
Alvarado, Velasco, 689
Alvarado Xicotencatl, Leonor, 37
Alvarado y Mesía, Pedro de, 37–38, 300
Álvarez, Ignacio, 142
Álvarez, Juan, 39, 278, 534, 693, 726, 830
Álvarez, Luis Héctor, 39
Álvarez, Manuel, 39–40
Álvarez Armellino, Gregorio Conrado, 40
Álvarez Bravo, Lola, 40
Álvarez Bravo, Manuel, 40–41, 523
Álvarez de Pineda, Alonso, 41, 417
Álvarez Gardeazábal, Gustavo, 41
Álvarez Martínez, Gustavo, 41, 974–975
Alvear, Carlos María de, 41–42, 770, 824, 919, 1052
Alvear, Marcelo Torcuato de, 42, 217, 537, 638, 750, 832,
      1013
Alves, Francisco Rodrigues, 42, 297, 954
Álzaga rebellion (1809), 580
Alzate y Ramírez, José Antonio de, 42–43
Amado, Jorge, 43–44, 248, 313, 581, 658
Amador, Manuel E., 44
Amador Guerrero, Manuel, 44
Amaral, Antônio José Azevedo do, 44
Amaral, Tarsila do, 44–45, 621
Amar y Borbón, Antonio, 44, 656
Amat y Junient, Manuel de, 45, 797, 1009

Amaya, Ramón G., 509
Ambrogi, Arturo, 45
Ameghino, Florentino, 45–46
Amélia, Empress, 46
Amenábar, Juan, 46
American Fur Company, 39
American Popular Revolutionary Alliance, 20, 83, 426, 441, 791
Americas Watch, 915
Americo de Figuereido e Melo, Pedro, 46–47
Amézaga, Juan José de, 47, 140
Amics de les Arts Nous (ADLAN), 1035
Amigos de la Educación Popular, 1028
Amnesty International, 915, 1023
Amorim, Enrique, 47
Ampíes, Juan de, 47
Amplio, Frente, 74, 948
Ampudia y Grimarest, Pedro de, 47–48
Amunátegui Aldunate, Miguel Luis, 48
Anastasio Somoza García Institute, 845
Anaya, Pedro María de, 48
Anchieta, José de, 48–49
Ancón, Treaty of (1883), 187, 420, 517
Andagoya, Pascual de, 49
Anderson, Charles, 752
Anderson Imbert, Enrique, 49
Andino, Carías, 1072
Andrada, Antônio Carlos Ribeiro de, 49–50, 218
Andrada, José Bonifácio de, 49, 50, 218, 780
Andrada, Martim Francisco Ribeiro de, 49–50, 218
Andrada e Silva, José Bonifácio de, 46, 570, 779
Andrade, Carlos Drummond de, 513, 550
Andrade, Drummond de, 456
Andrade, Fernáo Álvares de, 118
Andrade, Gomes Freire de, 51–52
Andrade, Ignacio, 493
Andrade, Jorge, 52
Andrade, Maria, 232
Andrade, Mário de, 45, 52–53, 406–407, 472, 621, 661, 893
Andrade, Oswald de, 45, 51, 53, 169, 621
Andrade Carlos Drummond de, 50–51
Andrades, Freire de, 51
André, José, 426, 441
Andreoni, João Antônio, 53–54
Andresote (Andrés López Del Rosario), 54
Andreve, Guillermo, 54
Andueza Palacio, Raimundo, 54, 884
Angel, Albalucía, 54–55
Angelis, Pedro de, 55
Ângelo, Ivan, 55–56
Angostura Congress (1819), 761
Anísio, Chico, 649
Ansermet, Ernest, 9, 240
Antequera y Castro, José de, 56, 75, 674
Anti-Güemes Patria Nueva movement, 474
Antioquian Assembly, 141
Anti-Personalist Radicals, 750
Anti-Reelectionist Center of Mexico, 614

Anti-War Pact (1933), 906
Antoñanzas, Eusebio, 164
Antonio Alzate Science Society, 830
Antropofagia movement, 53
Antuñano, Estevan de, 56–57
Antúnez, Nemesio, 57
Anza, Juan Bautista de, 57, 418
Anzoátegui, José Antonio, 57–58
Aparicio, Timoteo, 124, 560
Apolinar (Pablo Livinalli Santaella), 58
Apollinaire, Guillaume, 509
Aponte-Ledée, Rafael, 58
Appleyard, José Luis, 58
Aprista movement, 179
Aprista Party, 728, 729
Aragón, Luis Valesco, 256, 761
Aramayo, Diego Ortiz de, 58–59
Aramayo, Francisco Ortiz de, 58–59
Aramayo, Isidoro Ortiz de, 58–59
Aramburu, Pedro Eugenio, 36, 59, 586, 737, 883
Arana, Beatriz Enríquez de, 276
Arana, Felipe de, 59
Arana, Francisco Javier, 59–60, 62, 68, 238
Arana, Julio César, 60
Arana Osorio, Carlos, 60, 85, 561, 654, 1078
Arango, Débora, 60
Arango y Parreño, Francisco de, 60–61, 182
Aranguren, José María, 9
Aranha, Oswaldo, 61, 651
Arano, Hugo, 643
Aráoz, Bernabé, 516
Araújo, Arturo, 10, 61, 632, 636
Araújo, José Ribamar Ferreira, 943
Araújo, José Tomás Nabuco de, 412, 938
Araujo, Juan de, 61–62
Araújo, Sampaio, 710
Arbenz Guzmán, Jacobo, 62–63, 68, 238, 250, 388, 409, 518, 898, 1057, 1078
Arboleda, Carlos, 63
Arboleda, Julio, 63, 505
Arce, Aniceto, 63–64
Arce, Bayardo, 159
Arce, Manuel José, 64, 91, 120, 202, 312, 381, 497, 621, 869
Arce Castaño, Bayardo, 64
Archdiocesan Justice and Peace Commission, 76
Archila, Andrés, 64
Archivo General de la Nación, 11
Archuleta, Diego, 843
Arciniega, Claudio de, 65
Arciniega, Luis de, 790
Arciniegas, Germán, 65
Arcos, Domingo, 920
Arcos, Santiago, 65–66
Ardao, Arturo, 837
Arden Quin, Carmelo, 66
Ardévol, Fernando, 66
Ardévol, José, 66, 147
Area of People's Property, 1070

Areche, José Antonio de, 480, 1004
Arellano, J. E., 299
Arenales, Juan Antonio Álvarez de, 66–67
ARENA party, 914
Arenas, Reinaldo, 67
Arévalo, Cerezo, 238
Arévalo Bermejo, Juan José, 59, 67–68, 84, 250, 324, 654, 789, 898, 1057, 1078
Arévalo Martínez, Rafael, 68
Argentine Association of Composers, 151
Argentine Association of Writers, 622
Argentine Chapter of the International Society for Contemporary Music (ISCM), 442
Argentine Cinematography Academy, 440
Argentine Commission, 35
Argentine Composers' League (1947), 376
Argentine Patriotic League, 216–217
Argentine Radical Party, 22
Argentine Revolution, 737
Argentine School of Music, 9
Argentino, Teatro, 403
Argüedas, Alcides, 68–69, 113
Arguedas, José María, 69, 480, 961
Argüelles, Hugo, 69, 138
Argüello, Leonardo, 69–70
Argüello, Santiago, 70
Arias, Arnulfo, 78, 871
Arias, Arturo, 70
Arias, Céleo, 157
Arias, Desiderio, 70
Arias, Harmodio, 817
Arias, Juan Ángel, 157
Arias, Madrid, Harmodio, 77
Arias, Oscar, 748
Arias Calderón, Ricardo, 70–71
Arias de Saavedra, Hernando, 71, 152
Arias Madrid, Arnulfo, 70, 71–72, 470, 528
Arias Madrid, Harmodio, 72
Arias peace plan, 72, 1010
Arias Sánchez, Oscar, 72–73, 721, 1010
Aridjis, Homero, 73, 265
Arismendi, José, 99
Arismendi, Juan Bautista, 73
Arismendi, Rodney, 73–74
Arista, Mariano, 74, 351, 830, 1087
Aristide, Jean-Bertrand, 74, 769
Arlt, Roberto, 74–75
Armendáriz, José de, 75
Armendáriz, Pedro, 75
Armijo, Manuel, 39–40, 75, 261, 1052
Army of National Liberation, 997
Army of National Liberation (ELN), 128
Army of the Andes, 743
Arnaz, Desi, 75–76
Arns, Paulo Evaristo, 76
Arosemena, Carlos Julio, 174
Arosemena, Florencio Harmodio, 71, 72, 76
Arosemena, Juan Demóstenes, 76–77, 323

Arosemena, Justo, 77
Arosemena, Pablo, 77, 656
Arosemena Gómez, Otto, 77
Arosemena Monroy, Carlos Julio, 77–78, 241
Arosemena Quinzada, Albacíades, 78
Arp, Jean, 66, 196
Arrábida, António de, 779
Arraes, Miguel, 235
Arrais, Miguel, 78
Arrau, Claudio León, 78–79
Arredondo, Inés, 808
Arreola, Juan José, 73, 79, 567, 903
Arriaga, Camillo, 325
Arriaga, Ponciano, 79, 534
Arrieta, José Agustín, 79
Arrieta, Pedro de, 79–80
Arriví, Francisco, 80
Arroyo, Antonio Vanegas, 823
Arrufat, Antón, 81
Arteaga, Sebastián López, 535
Artes, Escola de Belas, 836
Arteta, Pedro José, 228
Artigas, José Gervasio, 81–82, 203, 214, 329, 399, 502, 562, 588, 743, 844, 867, 1048
Arzáns Orsúa y Vela, Bartolomé, 82
Arze, José Antonio, 82–83
Ascasubi, Hilario, 83, 161, 198, 516
Ascásubi, Manuel de, 716
Ascone, Vicente, 948
Asin, Carlos Quisquez, 1003
Asociación de Arte Concreto-Invención, 601, 646
Asociación de Arte Constructivo, 996
Asociación de Mayo, 340
Asociación de Mujeres Universitarias, 1045
Asociación Nacional Republicana, 182
Asociación Uruguaya de Música de Cámara, 269–270
Asonal, 766
Aspíllaga, Antero, 83
Aspíllaga, Baldomero, 83
Aspíllaga, Ismael, 83
Aspíllaga, Ramón, 83
Aspíllaga Family, 83–84
Associação Gaúcha de Proteção Ambiente Natural (AGAPAN), 605
Association for the Protection of the Natural Environment of Rio Grande de Sul, 605
Assunção, Leilah, 84
Asturias, Miguel Ángel, 68, 84–85, 165, 388, 661, 671, 917, 1033
Asturias y Arroyve, Mario Álvarez de las, 817
Asuaje y Vargas Machuca, Pedro Manuel de, 531
Asuar, José Vicente, 46, 85
Asunción, 3
Atahualpa Capac, 623
Atahualpa (Juan Santos), 85–86, 86, 299, 507, 508, 810, 811, 966, 977
Ataíde, Manoel da Costa, 21
Ateneo de Lima, 55, 618, 639

Athenaeum of Buenos Aires, 9
Atl, Dr., 86–87
Atondo, Isidro de, 541
Audiencia of Quito, 219
Auer, Leopold, 376
Augier, Ángel, 478
Aury, Louis-Michael, 170
Austin, Moses, 946
Authentic Revolutionary Party, 476
Ávalos y Mendoza, José de, 56
Avant-garde movement, 509
Avellaneda, Nicolás, 14, 34, 87, 198, 469, 520, 669, 872, 941
Ávila, Alonso de, 87
Ávila, Julio Enrique, 87
Ávila, Pedro Arias de, 87–88, 101, 281, 372, 459, 680, 809
Avila, Rosa Quiroz, 514
Ávila Camacho, Manuel, 31, 88–89, 194, 211, 586, 902
Avilés, Gabriel, 89
Avilés, Pedro Menéndez de, 765
Avril, Prosper, 769
Axayacatl, 89
Ayala, Daniel, 676
Ayala, Eligio, 89–90
Ayala, Eusebio, 90, 355, 391, 417
Ayala, José de la Cruz, 90
Ayala, Ramón Pérez de, 65
Aycinena, Juan Fermín de, 90–91
Aycinena, Mariano de, 91, 671
Aycinena, Pedro de, 91
Aycinena Piñol, Juan José de, 91–92, 426, 870
Aycinena y Micheo, Dolores, 91
Aylwin Azócar, Patricio, 92, 550, 805
Ayolas, Juan de, 92–93, 519
Ayora Cueva, Isidro, 93, 882
Ayutla, Revolution of, 488, 645, 726, 931, 1095
Azar, Héctor, 93, 138
Azara, Félix de, 93–94
Azcárate y Lezama, Juan Francisco de, 94
Azcárraga Milmo, Emilio, 94
Azcárraga Vidaurreta, Emilio, 94
Azcona Hoyo, José Simón, 94
Azcuénaga, Miguel de, 94–95
Azevedo, Aluísio, 95
Azevedo, Fernando de, 95
Azevedo, João de, 272
Azevedo, Luiz Heitor Correa de, 661
Azevedo, Thales de, 95–96
Aznar, Juan Manuel Figueroa, 256
Azpurua, Ramón, 147
Azuela, Mariano, 96
Azuero, Vicente, 630
Azul, Partido, 501
Azurara, Gomes Eanes de, 491

B
Baca, Bartolomé, 843
Baca Flor, Carlos, 97
Bachiller y Morales, Antonio, 97

Bacon, Francis, 183, 606
Badechi, Master, 264
Badía, Manuel Pérez, 361
Báez, Buenaventura, 97–98, 352, 501, 1012
Báez, Cecilio, 98
Baião, 455
Baily, John, 126
Bairros, Angela de, 229
Balaguer, Joaquín, 98, 163, 787, 934
Balaiada Rebellion (1838–1841), 582
Balbás, Jerónimo de, 99
Balbín, Ricardo, 99, 395–396
Balboa, Vasco Núñez de, 8, 41, 88, 100–101, 129, 346, 459, 604, 714, 809, 1022
Balbuena, Bernardo de, 101
Balcarce, Antonio González, 101
Balcarce, Mariano, 101, 770
Baldi, Lamberto, 998
Baldomir, Alfredo, 47, 101–102, 148, 987
Baldorioty de Castro, Ramón, 102
Baliño, Carlos, 648
Ballagas, Emilio, 478
Ballagas y Cubeñas, Emilio, 102–103
Ballivián, Hugo, 1015
Ballivián, José, 103, 579, 687, 932, 1040
Balmaceda Fernández, José Manuel, 48, 103–104, 106, 349, 542, 572, 613, 644, 681, 929
Balmaseda, Pedro, 306
Balmes, James, 416
Balseiro, José Agustín, 104
Balta, José, 104–105, 481, 763
Baltimore Incident, 682
Balzac, Honoré de, 96, 149
Balzo, Hugo, 252
Banco Comercial y Agrícola, 1017
Banco de Avio, 11
Banco de Santa Fe, 230
Banco Nacional de Desenvolvimento Econômico (BNDE), 201
Bandeira, Manuel Carneiro de Souza, 105, 513
Bando de Tangarás, 894
Bañuelos, Baltazar de Temiño de, 516
Banuelos, Juan, 1092
Banville, Théodore de, 306
Banzer Suárez, Hugo, 105–106, 777, 840, 995
Baptista, João, 21
Baptista, Mariano, 106, 757
Baquedano, Manuel, 106
Baquerizo Moreno, Alfredo, 106–107
Baquero, Gastón, 172
Baquíjano y Carrillo de Córdoba, José de, 107
Barahona, Leonor de, 248
Baralt, Rafael María, 107
Baraona, Luis Bográn, 967
Barbara de Noronha, Dona Catarina, 18
Barbero, Andrés, 107–108
Barbosa, Beatríz, 618
Barbosa, Domingos Caldas, 108
Barbosa, Francisco Villela, 108

Barbosa de Oliveira, Rui, 108–109, 412, 785–786
Barbosa y Alcalá, José Celso, 109
Barco Vargas, Virgilio, 109, 404, 434
Bareiro, Cándido, 109–110, 182, 310, 332, 352, 441
Barillas, Manuel, 231
Barnet, Miguel, 110
Barney, Hiram, 889
Barnola, Pedro Pablo, 110
Barquisimeto, Nueva Segovia de, 598
Barradas, Rafael, 110–111
Barragán, Juan José, 111
Barragán Morfín, Luis, 111
Barreda, Gabino, 111–112
Barreda y Laos, Felipe, 112
Barreiro, Antonio, 112
Barrenechea, Enrique Peña, 961
Barrenechea, Ricardo, 961
Barreto de Menezes, Tobias, Jr., 112–113, 890
Barrett, Rafael, 113
Barrientos, José Luis, 631
Barrientos Ortuño, René, 105, 113–114, 476, 755, 777
Barrillas, Manuel Lisandro, 114
Barrios, Agustín, 114
Barrios, Eduardo, 114–115
Barrios, Gerardo, 115, 199, 202, 225, 251, 333, 621, 720
Barrios, Gonzalo, 115–116
Barrios, Ignacio, 116
Barrios, Justo Rufino, 114, 116–117, 231, 358, 373, 422, 471, 529, 683, 857, 889, 894, 966, 1090
Barrios de Chamorro, Violeta, 117–118, 257, 724, 748, 749, 901, 1071
Barrón, Catalina, 350
Barros, Adhemar de, 835
Barros, João de, 118
Barros, Josue de, 664
Barros, Ademar de, 188
Barros, Adhemar de, 118
Barros Arana, Diego, 48, 118–119
Barroso, Ary, 119
Barroso, Gustavo Dodt, 119
Barrundia, José Francisco, 119–120, 120, 224, 312, 381, 528, 720, 869
Barrundia, Juan, 120
Barrundia, Martín, 119
Barthe, Obdulio, 295
Barthes, Roland, 939
Barzin, Leon, 282
Basadre, Jorge, 120–121, 983
Basaldúa, Hector, 121
Bases Orgánicas (1843), 845
Bassi, Nicolás, 142, 1072
Bassols, Narciso, 121, 453
Basso Maglio, Vicente, 121
Bastidas, Rodrigo de, 100, 121–122
Bastide, Roger, 214
Bastos, Roa, 879
Basurto, Luis, 122
Bataille, Georges, 808

Batallion, Marcel, 730
Batista, Cícero Romão, 122–123, 553
Batista, Julián, 554–555
Batista y Zalvídar, Fulgencio, 67, 110, 123, 242, 246, 266, 379, 450, 467, 555, 628, 655, 786, 832, 926, 1000
Batlle, Jorge, 930
Batlle, Lorenzo, 123–124, 429, 1028
Batlle Berres, Luis Conrado, 124, 707
Batlle y Ordóñez, José, 47, 124–126, 198, 274, 373, 498, 499, 987, 1013, 1073
Batllismo, 370–371, 1051
Batllist Forum, 930
Batraville, Benoît, 789
Batres Juarros, Luís, 126, 1088
Batres Montúfar, José, 126–127
Battle Planas, Juan, 11
Baudot, Georges, 730
Bautista Gill, Juan, 3
Bauvais, Fernand, 943
Bayley, Edgar, 66
Bay of Pigs (1961), 244, 246
Bayón, Damián, 467
Bazaine, François Achille, 127, 548, 641, 664
Bazán, Juan Gregorio, 127
Beals, Carleton, 929
Beaubien-Miranda Grant, 261
Beauharnais, Eugène de, 46
Beauvoir, Simone de, 758
Becerra-Schmidt, Gustavo, 127–128
Beck, Pedro, 9, 1072
Becker, Jean, 226
Beckers, José, 870
Beckman Revolt, 51
Becknell, William, 843
Bécquer, Gustavo Adolfo, 306, 321
Bedoya, José Díaz de, 865
Bedoya de Molina, Dolores, 128, 672
Bedoya Reyes, Luis, 128
Bedregal de Conitzer, Yolanda, 128
Behaim, Martin, 491
Béjar, Héctor, 128, 832
Belalcázar, Sebastián de, 49, 128–129, 367, 442, 529, 721
Belaúnde, Víctor Andrés, 129–130
Belaúnde Terry, Fernando, 128, 130, 489, 580, 689, 729, 1041
Belén Conspiracy, 902
Belgrano, Manuel, 67, 82, 130–131, 182, 203, 551, 833, 919, 1052, 1078
Béliardi, Abbé, 408
Bellegarde, Luis Dantès, 131
Belli, Gioconda, 131
Bello, Andrés, 48, 131–132, 342, 520, 662, 736, 882, 919, 940, 974
Bello, Daniel J., 617
Bello de Carvalho, Hermínio, 308
Belloso, Ramón, 199
Belmonte, Julio Valencia, 1022
Beloff, Angelina, 816

Belo Horizonte, 199
Beltrán, Luis (Saint), 132–133
Beltrán, Manuela, 133
Beltrán, Pedro, 133, 728, 826
Beltrán, Washington, 133
Belucci, Héctor, 590
Belzú, Manuel Isidoro, 4, 58–59, 284, 579, 647, 687
Bemberg, María Luisa, 729
Benário, Olga, 828
Benavides, Oscar Raimundo, 83, 135, 146, 383, 826
Benavídez, Nazario, 788
Benedetti, Mario, 135, 837
Beneficiencia Pública de Lima, 1086
Benegas, Treaty of (1820), 588
Beneyto, Antonio, 809
Benítez, Gregorio, 135–136
Benítez, Jaime, 136
Benítez Rojo, Antonio, 136–137, 478
Bennett, Marshall, 137
Bennett, Michèle, 337
Bent, Charles, 39, 40, 261
Berbeo, Juan Francisco, 137
Berenguer, Amanda, 137
Bergamín, José, 220
Bergaño y Villegas, Simón, 137–138
Berges, José, 138
Bergson, Henri, 316, 541
Berio, Luciano, 572
Berman, Sabina, 138
Bermejo, Ildefonso, 138–139, 980
Bermúdez, José Francisco, 139
Bermúdez, Pedro, 738
Bermúdez, Remigio Morales, 187, 689
Bermúdez Varela, Enrique, 139
Bernal, Francisca, 193
Bernal Jiménez, Miguel, 139
Bernal y García Pimentel, Ignacio, 139–140
Bernardes, Artur da Silva, 140, 386
Bernardo, Don (de Yrigoyen), 23
Bernasconi, Luis, 1072
Berni, Antonio, 140
Berreta, Tomás, 124, 140
Berrío, Eufemia, 806
Berrío, Pedro Justo, 140–141
Berro, Bernardo Prudencio, 383
Berro, Carlos, 141
Bertoni, Guillermo Tell, 107
Bertoni, Moisés, 141
Bertrand, Francisco, 141–142
Beruti, Antonio Luis, 142
Berutti, Arturo, 142
Betancourt, Rómulo, 142–144, 379, 406, 449, 556, 569, 791, 793, 800, 1002
Betancourt, Salvador Cisneros, 253
Betancourt Cisneros, Gaspar, 144
Betancur Cuartas, Belisario, 144, 595
Beteta, José, 120
Bethancourt, Hermano Pedro de, 620, 1078

Bethancourt, Pedro de San José de, 144
Bethania, Maria, 658
Betrayed Generation of the 1960s, 688
Beviláqua, Clóvis, 113
Bianchetti, Glenio, 825
Biano, José, 144–145
Biassou, Georges, 599
Biblioteca Nacional, 3
Bicalho Oswald, Henrique Carlos, 145
Bidart, Andrés Etchebarne, 456
Biedma, María de, 811
Bienal de San Juan del Grabado Latinoamericano, 506
Bienvenido, Héctor, 99
Bigaud, Wilson, 145, 724
Bignone, Reynaldo, 145
Bigot, Eugène, 998
Bilac Pinto, Olavo, 145–146, 236
Bilbao Barquín, Francisco, 66, 146, 940
Billinghurst, Guillermo Enrique, 135, 146, 826, 917, 925
Bioy Casares, Adolfo, 146–147, 161
Bischoff-Culm, 621
Bishop, Elizabeth, 51
Bisquertt, Próspero, 568
Bistolfi, Leonardo, 302
Blacher, Boris, 85, 351, 803
Blackbeard, 157
Black Spartacus, 599, 600
Blair, Montgomery, 889
Blanchot, Maurice, 808
Blanco, Andrés Eloy, 147
Blanco, Antonio Guzmán, 54, 579
Blanco, Hugo, 580
Blanco, José Félix, 147
Blanco, Juan, 147–148
Blanco Acevedo, Eduardo, 101, 148
Blanco Encalada, Manuel, 148, 921
Blanco Fombona, Rufino, 148–149
Blanco Galdós, Hugo, 149
Blanco Galindo, Carlos, 149
Blanco (National Party), 141, 938–939, 987
Blanes, Juan Manuel, 149
Blaszko, Martin, 66
Blest Gana, Alberto, 149
Blest Gana, Guillermo, 150
Bloc, Victory, 800
Bloch, Ernest, 292
Bloc of Revolutionary Youth of the Red Shirts, 616
Blondel, Jorge Urrutia, 46
Bloque de Obreros y Campesinos (BOC), 362
Blue Revolution, 364
Boas, Franz, 414
Bobadilla, Francisco de, 150, 277, 754
Bobo, Rosalvo, 150, 917
Bocaiúva, Quintino, 150–151
Bodega y Quadra, Juan Francisco de la, 151, 700–701
Boeck, Auguste de, 361
Boeklin, Arnold, 900
Boero, Felipe, 151

Boettiger, Rafael Fuentes, 397
Boff, Leonardo, 151–152
Bogarín, Francisco Xavier, 1078
Bolanños, César, 152
Bolaños, Luis de, 152
Bolívar, Simón, 131, 132, 139, 147, 153–155, 170, 218, 239,
    263, 264, 270, 290, 325, 399, 413, 424, 498, 626, 628,
    672, 696, 708, 732, 733, 738, 759, 761, 799, 854, 878,
    919, 922, 932, 935, 939, 975, 994, 1011–1012, 1033
Bolivian National Brewery, 369
Bolivian National Revolution, 113
Bolivian Socialist Falange (FSB), 840, 995
Bolivian Workers Center (COB), 564
Bolognesi, Francisco, 155–156
Bombal, María Luisa, 156
Bonaparte, Joseph, 439
Bonaparte, Napoleon, 153, 523, 564, 823
Bonaparte, Pauline, 564
Bonfá, Luís, 291, 530
Bonifácio, José, 50
Bonifaz Ascasubi, Neptalí, 156
Bonifaz Nuño, Rubén, 156–157
Bonilla, Manuel, 142, 216, 264, 307
Bonilla, Policarpo, 157, 671
Bonilla, Ronald, 12
Bonilla Chirinos, Manuel, 157
Bonnard, Pierre, 467
Bonnat, Leon, 573
Bonnet, Stede, 157
Bonny, Anne, 158, 851
Bonny, James, 158
Bonpland, Aimé Jacques, 158
Borba Gato, Manuel de, 158–159
Borda, Juan Idiarte, 300, 923
Bordaberry, Domingo R., 707
Bordaberry, Juan María, 159, 758, 930
Borge, Tomás, 64, 159–160, 642, 1046, 1070
Borges, Jacobo, 160
Borges, Jorge Luis, 33, 74, 84, 111, 146, 160–161, 492, 509,
    573, 575, 674, 794, 820, 882, 883, 939, 1033
Borges de Medeiros, Antônio Augusto, 161, 236, 273, 1030,
    1031
Borja Cevallos, Rodrigo, 161–162
Borja y Aragón, Francisco de, 162
Borno, Joseph Louis E. Antoine François, 162
Borno, Louis, 899
Bórquez, Josefina, 816
Borrero, Manuel María, 348
Borrero y Cortázar, Antonio, 162–163, 1040
Bosch Gaviño, Juan, 99, 163, 181, 422, 674
Boscovich, Roger, 395
Bosque, Pío Romero, 61
Boss, Homer, 621
Botero, Fernando, 163–164, 466
Bottesini, Giovanni, 442, 764
Bouchard, Hipólito, 164
Bouguereau, Adolphe, 1069
Boulanger, Nadia, 201, 803

Boulez, Pierre, 652, 735
Bourbon Reforms, 5
Bourdillon, Sarah, 948
Bóveda y Savavia, Felipa, 593
Boves, José Tomás, 164, 688
Boyd, Augusto S., 77
Boyer, Jean-Pierre, 164–165, 332, 648
Bradbury, Ray, 794
Brady, Matthew, 231
Bramuglia, Juan Atilio, 165
Brañas Guerra, César, 165
Branco, Humberto Castelo, 985
Branco, Manuel Alves, 165–166
Branco, Viscount do Rio, 1016
Brancusi, Constantin, 66, 196, 285, 368, 646
Brandão, Ignácio de Loyola, 166
Brandzen, Federico de, 920
Brannon de Samayoa Chinchilla, Carmen, 166
Brasil, Música Viva, 541
Brasileira, Ação Integralista, 914
Brasil Novo (New Brazil) plan, 649
Brasil's National Security Law, 230
Brás Pereira Gomes, Wenceslau, 166–167
Brasseur de Bourbourg, Charles Étienne, 167
Brathwaite, Edward Kamau, 167
Braud, Paul, 1022
Brauner, Victor, 285
Bravo, Claudio, 167
Bravo, Ignacio A., 508
Bravo, Leonardo, 168
Bravo, Mario, 168
Bravo, Nicolás, 168, 851
Bravo, Pedro Espinoza, 572
Bray, Arturo, 168–169
Brazilian Academy of Letters (1897), 705
Brazilian Communist Party (PCB), 12, 627, 784, 827–828
Brazilian Conservatory, 370
Brazilian Democratic Movement (MDB), 390, 391, 479, 643,
    713
Brazilian Democratic Movement Party (PMDB), 274, 391, 479,
    713, 943
Brazilian Expeditionary Force (FEB), 335
Brazilian Federation of Feminine Progress (Federação Brasileira
    pelo Progresso Feminino-FBPF), 605
Brazilian Historical and Geographical Institute, 803
Brazilian Labor Party (PTB), 390, 544, 784, 858
Brazilian Literacy Movement Foundation, 957
Brazilian National Bank for Economic Development, 400
Brazilian Society of Anthropology and Ethnology, 847
Brazil Railway Company, 365
Brazilwood Manifesto, 53
Brecheret, Vítor, 45, 169, 316, 621
Bresser Pereira, Luiz Carlos, 169
Brest, Jorge Romero, 999
Breton, André, 219, 511, 540
Brierre, Jean-Fernand, 169–170
Brión, Luis, 170
Britto García, Luis, 170

Brizola, Leonel, 170–171, 235, 465, 708
Brizuela, Francisco, 171
Broqua, Alfonso, 171, 270, 361
Brotherhood of Penitentes, 1094
Brotherhood of St. Cecilia, 419
Brouwer, Leo, 171–172
Brown, William, 392, 429, 556
Brull, Mariano, 172, 219
Brum, Baltasar, 172–173
Brunet, Marta, 173
Brunnet, Louis-Jacques, 46
Brushwood, John, 1077
Bryan, William Jennings, 258
Bryan-Chamorro Treaty (1913), 646
Bryce Echenique, Alfredo, 173
Buarque, Chico, 173–174
Bucaram Elmhalin, Asaad, 174, 886
Bucareli, Antonio María de, 174–175, 791
Bucareli Treaty (1923), 726
Bucareli y Ursúa, Antonio María, 174
Bucareli y Ursúa, Francisco de Paula, 174–175
Buen Aire, Santa María del, 3
Buenaventura, Alonso de, 152
Buenos Aires Conservatory of Music, 1072
Buenos Aires Transport Corporation, 1039
Bujones, Fernando, 543
Bukovsky, Vladimir, 290
Bulhões, Octavio, 235
Bullrich, Adolfo, 279
Bulnes, Francisco, 112, 175, 302
Bulnes Prieto, Manuel, 175, 732, 806, 990
Bunau-Varilla, Philippe Jean, 44
Bunge, Alejandro, 175
Bunge, Augusto, 175
Bunge, Carlos Octavio, 176
Bunker, Ellsworth, 422
Buñuel, Luis, 18, 176–177, 380
Burger, Fritz, 621
Burgos, Julia de, 177
Burle Marx, Roberto, 177, 268, 291, 714
Burnier, João Bosco Penido, 230
Busch, Alberto Natusch, 473
Busch Becerra, Germán, 177–178, 505, 788
Bush, George, 374
Busser, Henri, 356
Bustamante, Anastasio, 79, 178, 422, 475, 660, 684, 767, 774, 830, 874, 895
Bustamante, Carlos María de, 178, 939, 1059
Bustamante, José Alejandro, 891
Bustamante, Mariano Montealegre, 678
Bustamante Code, 925
Bustamante y Guerra, José de, 119, 178–179, 671
Bustamante y Rivero, José Luis, 128, 130, 179, 489, 728, 947
Bustamente, José de, 128
Bustos, Hermenegildo, 179
Bustos, Juan Bautista, 774
Buzzati, Dino, 794

C

Caamaño, Roberto, 415
Caamaño Deño, Francisco, 181
Caamaño Medina, Fausto, 181
Caamaño y Gómez Cornejo, José María Plácido, 181, 384
Caballero, Agustín, 689
Caballero, Bernardino, 90, 109, 181–182, 250, 310, 332, 351
Caballero, Pedro Juan, 182, 1078
Caballero Calderón, Eduardo, 183
Caballeros Orientales, 743
Caballero y Góngora, Antonio, 137, 182, 675
Caballero y Rodríguez, José Augustín, 182–183
Cabañas, José María, 183
Cabañas, José Trinidad, 183–184, 376, 528, 621, 720
Cabañas, Lucio, 340
Cabeza de Vaca, Alvar Núñez, 3, 71, 184, 355, 520, 708, 1022
Caboclo, Nó, 1063
Cabot, John, 184
Cabot, Sebastián, 184–185, 419
Cabral, Donald Reid, 99, 674
Cabral, Manuel de, 185
Cabral, Pedro Álvares, 185, 570, 1047
Cabrales, Luís Alberto, 285
Cabrera, Daniel, 384
Cabrera, Estrada, 359
Cabrera, Guillermo, 939
Cabrera, Lydia, 185–186, 574
Cabrera, Manuel Estrada, 231, 264, 655, 853, 858
Cabrera, Miguel, 186
Cabrera, Nicolás, 806
Cabrera Infante, Guillermo, 186–187
Cabrera Lobato, Luis, 187
Cabrujas, José Ignacio, 263
Cacama, 714
Caca Revolt (1915–1920), 789–790
Cáceres, Andrés Avelino, 146, 187, 420, 517, 689
Cáceres, Esther de, 187–188, 513
Cáceres, Ramón, 188
Café Filho, João, 188, 447
Cafiero, Antonio, 657
Cajeme, 188–189
Cajigal, Juan Manuel de, 696
Calabi, André, 649
Calcaño, José Antonio, 189
Calchaquí, Juan, 189
Caldas, Francisco José de, 189, 696
Caldeira, Francisco Xavier Cardoso Caldeira, 388
Caldera, Rafael, 604
Caldera Rodríguez, Rafael, 189–190
Calderón, Arias, 70
Calderón, Francisco García, 187, 527
Calderón, José, 432
Calderón, Margarita, 927
Calderón, Matilde, 539
Calderón, Rafael Angel, 362
Calderón, Williams, 1072
Calderón Fournier, Rafael Ángel, 73, 190

Calderón Guardia, Rafael Ángel, 190–191, 289, 339, 378, 686, 923, 999, 1009
Calfucurá, 191, 706
Calicanto, 761
Callado, Antônio, 84, 191–192
Callado Junior, Joaquim Antônio da Silva, 192, 455
Calleja del Rey, Félix María (Conde de Calderón), 192, 504, 637, 693, 895
Callejas Romero, Rafael Leonardo, 192–193
Calles, Juan B., 193
Calles, Plutarco Elías, 121, 193–194, 228, 686, 697, 834, 908, 986
Callis, Eulalia, 362
Callot, Jacques, 806
Calógeras, João Pandiá, 194–195
Calvert, Peter, 1080
Calvert, Susan, 1080
Calvo, Carlos, 195
Calvo, Carmelo, 442
Calvo Doctrine, 330
Camacho, Eufrosina, 89
Camacho, Tomás, 806
Camacho Roldán, Salvador, 195
Câmara, Eugênia, 241
Câmara, Hélder, 195–196, 236
Camarasa, Hermenegildo Anglada, 302
Camarena, Ignacio, 347
Camargo, Diego Muñoz, 993
Camargo, Iberé, 413
Camargo, Sergio de, 196
Cambaceres, Eugenio, 196–197
Camille, Roussan, 197
Camilo, José Luis, 572
Caminha, Pero Vaz de, 185
Camnitzer, Luis, 197, 820
Camões, Luís vaz de, 197, 334
Campa, Valentín, 594
Campa Salazar, Valentín, 197–198
Campero, Narciso, 198, 1060
Campisteguy, Juan, 198
Campo, Estanislao Del, 198–199
Campo, Rafael, 199
Campobello, Nellie, 96
Campomar, Jaime, 566
Cámpora, Héctor José, 199, 554, 796
Campos, Francisco Luiz da Silva, 199–200
Campos, Julieta, 200
Campos, Luis María, 200
Campos, Manuel Jorge, 200
Campos, Roberto (de Oliveira), 200–201, 235, 957
Campos Cervera, Hérib, 201
Campos-Parsi, Héctor, 201
Campos Sales, Manuel Ferraz de, 201–202, 679, 703
Camus, Albert, 574, 727
Canales, Nemesio Rosario, 202, 585
Cañas, José María, 202
Cañas, José Simeón, 202
Candamo, Manuel, 203, 566, 593, 766

Candanedo, César, 203
Candido, Antônio, 847
Candioti, Francisco Antonio, 203
Cané, Miguel, 203–204
Caneca, Joaquím do Amor Divino, 204
Cañedo, Francisco, 204
Cañedo, Juan de Dios, 204
Canek, Jacinto, 204–205
Cañete, José, 56
Cañete, Pedro Vicente, 56
Cannibal Manifesto, 53
Canning, George, 577
Cannon, Walter, 898
Cano, María de los Ángeles, 205
Cansinos-Asséns, 509
Cantilo, José Luis, 205
Cantinflas, 205–206
Cantón, Wilberto, 206
Cantoni, Federico, 742
Cantú, Federico, 206
Capa, Robert, 914
Capablanca, José Raúl, 206
Capelo, Joaquín, 206–207, 1095
Caperton, William B., 150
Capinam, José Carlos, 1044
Capistrano de Abreu, João, 207
Caramurú, 207, 969
Carazo Odio, Rodrigo, 190, 207–208, 362
Carballido, Emilio, 208, 618
Carballo, Aida, 208
Carbo y Noboa, Pedro José, 208–209, 228
Cárcano, Miguel Ángel, 209
Cardenal, Ernesto, 209–210, 286, 314
Cárdenas, Bernardino de, 210
Cárdenas, Cuauhtémoc, 585, 616, 702, 915, 916
Cárdenas, Lázaro, 31, 89, 121, 194, 249, 309, 340, 701, 821, 834
Cárdenas, Román, 450
Cárdenas Arroyo, Santiago, 210–211
Cárdenas del Río, Lázaro, 211
Cárdenas Solorano, Cuauhtémoc, 213–214
Cardim, Frei Fernão, 214
Cardoso, Felipe Santiago, 214
Cardoso, Fernando Henrique, 214–215, 368, 513, 1069
Cardova, Fernando Henrique, 954
Cardoza y Aragón, Luis, 215, 917
Cardozo, Efraím, 215
Carías, Calixto, 215
Carías, Sara Andino de, 215
Carías Andino, Tiburcio, 215–216, 409, 601, 674, 1072
Caribbean Legion, 378
Carillo, Juana Pabla, 587
Carísimo, Teresa Lamas, 879
Carlés, Manuel, 216–217
Carlisle, Charles, 950
Carlos, Antônio, 50
Carlos, Erasmo, 217
Carlos, Roberto, 217

Carlos IV, 217
Carlota, 217–218, 641
Carneiro, Francisco Xavier, 21
Carneiro de Campos, José Joaquím, 218
Carney, James "Guadalipe," 218
Caro, José Eusebio, 218–219
Caro, Miguel Antonio, 219, 279, 299, 505
Carondelet, François-Louis Hector, 219
Carpentier, Alejo, 84, 219–220, 421, 574, 886, 1033
Carpio, Jorge, 950
Carpio, Ramiro de León, 950
Carpio Nicolle, Jorge, 220
Carranza, Venustiano, 8, 37, 55, 86, 187, 194, 220–222, 249,
    309, 320, 361, 458, 480, 508, 697, 701, 724, 725, 726,
    745, 764, 843, 979, 985, 1053, 1085
Carranza Fernández, Eduardo, 222–223
Carrasco, Francisco Antonio García, 793, 993
Carrasquilla, Tomás, 223
Carreño, Mario, 223
Carrera, José Miguel, 132, 223–224, 520, 731, 793, 880
Carrera, José Rafael, 91, 115, 117, 120, 184, 199, 224–225,
    231, 251, 297, 333, 375, 411, 422, 426, 620, 661, 671,
    683, 691, 767, 774, 805, 1024, 1063, 1088
Carrera, Juan José, 224
Carrera, Luis, 224
Carrera Andrade, Jorge, 225–226
Carrera Fontecilla, José Miguel, 224
Carrillo, Braulio, 5
Carrillo, Enrique Gómez, 68
Carrillo, Julián (Antonio), 226, 227
Carrillo Colina, Braulio, 226–227, 685
Carrillo Flores, Antonio, 227
Carrillo Flores, Nabor, 227
Carrillo Puerto, Felipe, 227–228
Carrington, Leonara, 1035
Carrión, Alejandro, 228
Carrión, Jerónimo, 228, 1040
Carrión, Luis, 1070
Carrión, Manuel Benjamín, 228–229
Carter, Jimmy, 163, 601, 887, 962
Cartier-Bresson, Henri, 914
Carvajal, Francisco de, 266, 433
Carvajal, José María, 540
Carvajal, Juan de, 792
Carvajal y de la Cueva, Luis de, 229
Carvalho, Antônio de Albuquerque Coelho de, 229–230
Carvalho, Celi Elizabeth Monteiro de, 274
Carvalho, Feliciano Coelho de, 229
Carvalho, Francisco de Albuquerque Coelho de, 229, 230
Carvalho, João Souza de, 823
Casa de Contratación, 386
Casa de la Cultura Ecuatoriana, 229
Casa de las Américas, 314, 808
Casa del Obrero Mundial, 697
Casado, Carlos, 230
Casafuerte, Juan de Acuña, 869
Casal, Julián del, 230, 783
Casaldáliga, Pedro, 230–231

Casals, Felipe, 231
Casals, Pablo, 240
Casanova, Emilia, 1060
Casanova, Mariano, 104
Casanova y Estrada, Ricardo, 231
Casariego, Mario, 60, 654
Casas, Bartolomé de las, 500
Casas, Francisco de las, 734–735
Casasola, Agustín, 231
Casasús, Joaquín, 112
Casáus y Torres, Ramón, 231, 426
Casement, Roger, 60
Caso, Alfonso, 139, 453, 586
Caso, Antonio, 490, 541, 849
Caso, Joaquín, 1024
Caso y Andrade, Alfonso, 121, 231–232, 232
Caso y Andrade, Antonio, 232, 361
Caso y Morali, Antonio, 232
Castañeda, Francisco de Paula, 232
Castañeda, 741
Castañeda Castro, Salvador, 232–233
Castaños, General, 919
Castellanos, Aarón González, 233
Castellanos, Gonzalo, 233
Castellanos, Juan de, 233
Castellanos, Rosario, 156, 233–234
Castelli, Juan José, 234
Castello Branco, Dom Rodrigo de, 158
Castello Branco, Humberto de Alencar, 234–236, 291, 446,
    447, 985
Castellón, Francisco, 528
Casteñeda Castro, Salvador, 752
Castera, Eugenio, 789
Caste War of Yucatán, 673
Castilhos, Júlio de, 161, 236, 274
Castilla, José María, 120, 661
Castilla, Ramón, 155, 187, 236–237, 339, 344, 412, 466, 654,
    763, 778, 799, 983, 1064
Castilla del Oro, 88
Castillo, Heberto, 213
Castillo, Jesús, 237
Castillo, José Guillermo, 820, 821
Castillo, José Videla, 445
Castillo, Otto René, 237
Castillo, Ramón S., 237–238, 773, 801, 845
Castillo, Ricardo, 942
Castillo Armas, Carlos, 63, 238, 898, 1078
Castillo Ledón, Amalia, 238
Castillo y Guevara, Francisco Josefa de la Concepción de, 239
Castro, Cipriano, 239, 449, 474, 591
Castro, José Gil de, 239–240
Castro, José María, 672, 775
Castro, Juan José, 240, 775
Castro, Julián, 240, 675
Castro, Lina Ruz, 242
Castro, Melgar, 778
Castro, Pedro Fernández de, 995, 1019
Castro, Ricardo, 240–241

Castro Alves, Antônio Federico de, 113, 241, 456, 890

Castro Jijón, Ramón, 241

Castro Madriz, José María, 242

Castro Pozo, Hildebrando, 242

Castro Ruz, Fidel, 67, 123, 143, 159, 242–246, 266, 341, 350, 353, 379, 402, 475, 628, 760, 786, 878, 926, 927, 934, 982, 1000, 1002, 1015

Castro Ruz, Raúl, 246, 353, 475

Catalonian Volunteers, 15

Catamarca, 788

Catari, Tomás, 1004

Catavi Massacre (1942), 772, 777

Catherine the Great, 664

Catholic Left, 576

Catholic Union Party, 988

Cató, 9

Caupolicán, 247

Cavalcanti, Newton, 247

Cavallón, Juan de, 248

Cavañas, Manuel Atanasio, 182

Cavendish, Thomas, 997

Caviedes, Juan del Valle y, 248

Caymmi, Dorival, 248, 439

Cazalla, Leonor de, 266

Cazneau, William Leslie, 248–249

Cea, José Manuel, 818

Ceballos, Santos, 806

Cedeño, Juan Manuel, 249, 1083

Cedillo Martínez, Saturnino, 249

Cedras, Raoul, 74

Celibidache, Sergiu, 233

Celman, Miguel Juárez, 22, 23, 200, 209, 594

Cendrars, Blaise, 53

Center for Atmospheric Sciences, 5–6

Center for Puerto Rican Art (CAP), 506

Center for Study of National Problems, 361, 729

Central American Common Market (CACM), 743, 963

Central American Socialist Party, 631

Central Auténtica Nacional (CAN), 60

Central Obrera Boliviano (COB), 995

Centro de Arte Dramático (CADAC), 93

Centro de Arte y Cultura, 63

Centro Dom Vital, 377–378

Centro Tecnológico-Cultural, 364

Centurión, Carlos R., 249

Centurión, Juan Crisóstomo, 249–250

Centurión, Roque Miranda, 250

Cepeda y Coronado, Teresa, 119

Cercle et Carré (Paris), 996

Cerda, Durán, 4

Cerda, José Manuel de la, 1025

Cerda, Pedro Aguirre, 463

Cerezo, María, 1047

Cerezo Arévalo, Marco Vinicio, 250–251, 646

Cerna, Vicente, 91, 116, 117, 251, 297

Cernuda, Luis, 779

Cerro, Luis Sánchez, 489

Cerruti, Ernesto, 341

Cerruto, Óscar, 251

Ceruti, Roque, 251–252

Cervantes, Vicente, 252

Cervantes Kawanagh, Ignacio, 252

Cervera, Andrés Campos, 812

Cervetti, Sergio, 252–253

Césaire, Aimé, 253, 313, 444

Césped, Lucila, 46

Céspedes, Augusto, 777

Céspedes y Quesada, Carlos Manuel de (The Elder), 6, 123, 253–254, 454, 467

Cevallos, Pedro Antonio de, 254

Cevallos expedition (1776), 580

Chacón, Jerónima Fernández, 678

Chacón, Lázaro, 254–255

Chaco War (1932–1935), 90, 98, 215, 260, 286, 295, 417, 484, 697, 734, 755, 777, 812, 906, 911, 972, 985, 1094

Chacrinha, 255

Chagas, Carlos Ribeiro Justiniano, 255

Chalbaud, Román, 263

Chalicuchima, 507

Chamber Orchestra of Havana (1934), 66

Chambi, Martín, 255–256

Chamorro, Emialiano, 319

Chamorro, Fruto, 256–257, 357, 527, 528, 929

Chamorro, Pedro José, 256

Chamorro Cardenal, Pedro Joaquín, 117, 257, 298, 962

Chamorro Vargas, Emiliano, 257–259, 908

Chamuscado, Francisco Sánchez, 353

Chandler, David L., 92

Change 1990, 399

Chanis, Daniel, 262

Chapí, Enrique Casal, 971

Charles I (Spain), 270, 618, 1019

Charles III (Spain), 1, 56, 219, 408, 554, 704, 740, 933, 993, 1009, 1062

Charles IV (Spain), 523, 597

Charles V (Spain), 65, 557, 558, 680, 990, 1096

Charles X (France), 577

Charlot, Jean, 563

Charry Lara, Fernando, 259

Chatfield, Frederick, 774

Chauvet, Marie Vieux, 259

Chaves, Federico, 259, 653

Chaves, Francisco C., 259–260

Chaves, Julio César, 260

Chávez, Carlos, 260–261, 405, 495, 637, 676, 838, 856, 927

Chávez, Héctor Cornejo, 128

Chávez, Mariano, 261

Chávez Morado, José, 261

Chávez Sánchez, Ignacio, 261, 898

Cherkov, Fenia, 691

Cherkov, Mariana, 692

Chiari, Rodolfo E., 76, 261–262

Chiari Remón, Roberto Francisco, 262

Chibás, Eduardo, 262, 266

Chibata Revolt, 386

Chibchas, 367

Chilavert, Francisco, 919
Chilean Development Corporation (CORFO), 10
Chilean Wars of Independence (1814–1817), 392
Chimalpahin, 262–263
Chimalpopoca, 523
Chirico, Giorgio de, 140
Chirino, José Leonardo, 263
Chocano, José Santos, 263, 343, 514
Chocrón, Isaac, 263–264
Chomón, Fauré, 341
Chonchol, Jacques, 264
Chong Neto, Manuel, 264
Christian Democratic Party of El Salvador (PDC), 92, 128,
    510, 566, 1010, 1083
Christian Democratic Party of Guatemala (DCG), 1057
Christian Left, 264
Christian Popular Party, 128
Christmas, Lee, 157, 264, 674
Christophe, Henri, 164, 264–265
Chumacero, Alí, 265
Churata, Gamaliel, 256
Cid, Miguel del, 471
Cienfuegos, Camilo, 265–266, 266
Cienfuentes, Miguel Venegas, 167
Cieza de León, Pedro de, 266–267
Cipriano Mosquera, Tomás, 914
Círculo Literario, 639
Círculos de Obreros Católicos, 175
Cisneros, Baltasar Hidalgo de, 267, 694
Cisneros, Francisco Javier, 267
Cisneros, Guy Pérez, 574
Cisneros Betancourt, Salvador, 267
Ciudad Juárez, Treaty of (1911), 220, 323, 614
CivicADO (Democratic Alliance of Civic Opposition), 70–71
Civic Solidarity Unity, 369
Civil Code (1917), 167
Civil Code Commission, 785
Civilista Alliance, 262
Civilista Party, 203
Clair, Janette, 267–268
Claridad, Escuela, 68
Clark, Lygia, 268, 732, 765
Clarkson, Thomas, 729
Clavé, Pelegrín, 268, 282
Claver, Pedro, 268–269
Clavijero, Francisco Javier, 269, 621
Clemente Walker, Roberto, 269
Clement X (Pope), 133
Cleveland, Grover, 258
Clitandre, Pierre, 899
Closson, Ernest, 943
Clouthier del Rincón, Manuel J., 39, 269
Clube de Gravura, 825
Club Liberal Ponciano Arriaga, 325
Cluzeau-Mortet, Luis (Ricardo), 171, 269–270, 361
Coalición Institucionalista Democrática (CID), 77
Cobo, Bernabé, 270
Cobos, Alonso, 363

Cobos, Francisco de Los, 270
Coche, Treaty of (1863), 485
Cochrane, Thomas Alexander, 148, 405, 626, 665, 921, 1074
Codazzi, Agustín, 107, 270–271
Code of International Private Law, 925
Codesido, Julia, 271
Codovilla, Victoria, 438
Coelho, Gonçalo, 272, 1047
Coelho, Jorge de Albuquerque, 271–272, 273
Coelho de Albuquerque, Duarte, 271, 273
Coelho Neto, Henrique, 272, 577
Coelho Pereira, Duarte, 271, 272–273
Coen, Hans, 640
Coicou, Massillon, 273, 504
Coicuría y Cabrera, Domingo, 445
Cole, Byron, 357
Cole, Hubert, 265, 315
Colegio de Santa Cruz de Tlatelolco, 416
Colegio Nacional of Asunción, 3, 363
Colina, José de la, 808
Collivadino, Pío, 838
Collor, Lindolfo, 273–274
Collor de Mello, Fernando Affonso, 274, 390, 479, 605, 649,
    954
    impeachment of, 215
Collor de Mello, Leda, 274
Coll y Toste, Cayetano, 273
Colmán, Narciso, 274–275
Colombian Revolutionary Armed Forces (FARC), 1022
Colombo, Domenico, 275
Colón, Diego, 754
Colonne, Édouard, 918
Colorado Front of Unity, 438
Colorado Party, 375, 659–660, 930, 948, 973
Colorados, 697
Colosio, Luis Donaldo, 915
Colosio Murrieta, Luis Donaldo, 275
Columbus, Bartholomew, 277
Columbus, Christopher, 275–278, 386, 417, 557, 732, 807,
    886, 1042
Columbus, Diego, 275, 277, 681
Columbus, Hernando, 559
Colunje, Gil, 278
Comibol, 773
Comisión Corográfica, 270
Comité Democrático Afro-Brasileiro, 708
Comité de Organización Política Electoral Independiente
    (COPEI), 190
Comité Pro Derecho de las Mujeres, 1045
Commando Geral dos Trabalhadores (CGT), 784, 858
Committee on Cooperation for Peace, 955
Communist Party of El Salvador, 632
Community of Solidarity, 737
Comonfort, Ignacio, 278, 534, 548, 570, 571, 663, 726, 1087,
    1095
Compactacíon Obreta Nacional, 156
Compagnie Aramayo des Mines Bolivie in Geneva (1916), 59
Compañía Unida de Minas (United Mining Company), 11

Comte, Auguste, 112, 207, 236
Comunero Revolt (1781), 182, 385, 482
Concentración de Fuerzas Populares (CFP), 174, 511, 886
Concepción, José de la, 678
Concha, Andrés de la, 278–279, 790
Concha, José Vicente, 279
Conciencia de la Patria, 762
Condamine, Charles Marie de la, 531, 1009
Condarco, Álvarez, 920
Condé, Maryse, 279
Conde, Pedro, 920
Condillac, Étienne Bonnot de, 183, 606
Confederación de Trabajadores de Cuba (CTC), 786
Confederación Revolucionaria Michoacana de Trabajo, 211
Confederation of Equator, 582
Confederation of Guatemalan Workers, 482
Confederation of Mexican Workers (CROM), 212
Confederation of the United Provinces of the Río de la Plata, 897
Conference of Latin American Bishops (CELAM), 393
Congress for the Colorado Party, 875
Congress of Tucumán, 743
Coni, Emilio R., 279
Coni, Gabriela Laperrière de, 279–280
Consag, Fernando, 870
Conselheiro, Antônio, 280–281, 302, 687
Conservatorio López Buchardo, 591
Conservatorio Nacional, 1013
Conspiracy of the Cuban Rose Mine, 589
Constant, Benjamin, 97
Constant Botelho de Magalhães, Benjamin, 150, 280
Constitutional Convention (1917), 725
Constitutionalist Progressive Party (PCP), 615
Constitutionalist Revolution (1932), 1031
Contreras, Eleázar López, 406
Contreras, Hernando, 281–282
Contreras, Jerónima, 71
Contreras, Pedro, 281–282
Contreras, Rafaela, 306
Contreras, Rodrigo de, 88
Contreras, Salvador, 676
Convention of Aguascalientes (1914–1915), 458
Cooke, John William, 282
Coordenação da Mobilização Econômica, 15
Coordinating Commission of the Committee of Peasant Unity (CUC), 652
Coordination of Training for Advanced Scholars, 985
Copland, Aaron, 260, 292, 405, 543, 550, 738, 948, 998
Copland, Maderna, 554
Coppée, François, 334
Cordero, Juan, 282
Cordero, Roque, 282–283
Cordero Crespo, Luis, 283
Córdoba, Gonzalo Fernández de, 263, 755
Córdoba, Hernández de, 288
Córdoba, José María, 283, 698
Córdoba, Marcos Paz of, 788
Córdoba, Treaty of (1821), 522, 728

Córdova, Arturo de, 283
Córdova, Gonzalo, 882
Córdova, Jorge, 4, 283–284
Córdova, Roberto Suazo, 41, 875
Córdova Rivera, Gonzalo S., 284
Cori, Carl F., 507
Cori, Gerty T., 507
Corinth, Lovis, 621
Cornejo, José María, 115
Cornejo, Mariano H., 284
Corona, Ramón, 284
Coronado, Francisco Vázquez de, 284, 355, 716
Coronado, Juan Vázquez de, 5, 248, 284–285
Coronel, Paraíban, 798
Coronel, Pedro, 285
Coronel Urtecho, José, 209, 285–286
Corral, Juan del, 854
Corral Verdugo, Ramón, 579, 614, 995
Correa, Juan, 286
Correa, Julio Myzkowsky, 286
Correa, 880
Correia, Diogo Álvares, 334
Correia, Serzedelo, 1048
Correoso, Buenaventura, 286
Cortázar, Julio, 49, 287, 403, 626, 794, 882, 1033
Cortes, Araci, 308
Cortés, Martín, 289, 622
Cortés, Hernán, 38, 270, 287–289, 299, 372, 386, 417, 459, 603, 621, 622, 656, 680, 708, 734, 810, 879, 1042
Cortés Castro, León, 289, 686
Cortés de Madariaga, José, 289–290
Cortina, Juan, 541
Corvalán Lepe, Luis, 290
Cos, Martín Perfecto de, 290
Cosa, Juan de la, 570, 807, 1047
Cosío Villegas, Daniel, 290, 542
Cosmes, Francisco G., 112
Cossa, Roberto, 330
Costa, Andrés, 806
Costa, Cláudio Manuel da, 290–291, 455
Costa, Duarte da, 207
Costa, Gal, 248, 455, 1044
Costa, Hipólito José da, 291
Costa, Lúcio, 177, 291, 545, 714
Costa, Olga, 261
Costa e Silva, Artur da, 235, 236, 291–292, 446, 623, 643, 770
Costa Rican Communist Party (PC), 686
Costa Rican Writers Circle, 12
Cos y Pérez, José María, 290, 693
Cotapos Baeza, Acario, 292, 568
Cotegipe, Barão de, 292, 803
Council of Latin American Bishops (CELAM), 596
Council of the Indies, 409
Coupigny, Marquess of, 919
Coutinho, Dom Alvaro, 17
Coutinho, Dom Fernando, 272
Coutinho, Francisco Pereira, 207

Coutinho, José Joaquim da Cunha de Azeredo, 292–293
Coutinho, Rodrigo Domingos Antonio de Sousa, 293
Coutinho, Vasco Fernandes, 905
Coutinho, 292–293
Couto, José Bernardo, 293
Covarrubias, Miguel, 293–294
Cowan, Rosemonde, 293
Cowell, Henry, 292
Coxon, John, 950
Cozzella, Damiano, 333, 652, 735
Crabb, Henry A., 294
Crámer, Ambrosio, 920
Creel, Enrique Clay, 294
Creelman, James, 323
Creixell, José Luis, 111
Crespo, Joaquín, 54, 294–295, 474, 485–486, 884
Creydt, Oscar, 295
Cristero Rebellion (1926–1929), 194
Cristiani, Alfredo, 295, 307, 333
Cristina, María, 589
Croix, Marqués de, 295–296
Croix, Teodoro de, 296, 527
Crowder, Enoch, 1089
Cruz, Arturo, 296
Cruz, José María de la, 175
Cruz, Oswaldo Gonçalves, 255, 296–297, 877
Cruz, Ramón Ernesto, 590
Cruz, Rodrigo de la, 620
Cruz, Serapio, 116, 297
Cruz, Vicente, 297
Cruz, Victoria Maria de, 419
Cruzado Plan II, 274
Cruz Diez, Carlos, 196, 297–298, 966
Cruz e Sousa, João da, 298
Cruz Ucles, Ramón Ernesto, 298
Cry of Montán, 517
Cuadra, Pablo Antonio, 285, 298–299
Cuauhtemoc, 299, 700
Cuauhtlehuanitzin, Domingo Chimalpahin, 621
Cuban Alliance for a Free World Against Fascism, 749
Cuban Communist Party (PCC), 243, 872
Cuban Missile Crisis (1962), 244, 246
Cuban Revolution (1959), 628
Cuban Revolutionary Party, 454, 633
Cuban Union of Writers and Artists (UNEAC), 220, 326, 373, 808
Cuban War of Independence, 658
Cuenca, Alejandro Martínez, 748
Cuervo, Rufino José, 219, 299
Cuestas, Juan Lindolfo, 125, 198, 299–300
Cueva, Francisca de la, 37, 38, 300
Cueva de Alvarado, Beatriz de la, 37, 38, 300
Cueva Enríquez y Saavedra, Baltásar de la, 300
Cuevas, Alejandro, 670
Cuevas, José Luis, 300–301, 445
Cuevas, Mariano, 301
Cugat, Xavier, 76, 301
Cuitlahuac, 288, 301, 700

Cuitlahua (Cuitlahuac), 288, 301, 700
Cumplido, Ignacio, 301–302
Cúneo Perinetti, José, 302
Cunha, Aires da, 118
Cunha, Euclides da, 280–281, 302–303
Cunha, Higinho, 113
Cunha, Pedro da, 271
Cunha Dotti, Juan, 303
Cunha e Meneses, Luís da, 455, 456

D
D'Abuisson, Roberto, 295
Dacosta, Milton, 951
Da Gama, Vasco, 185
Dalí, Salvador, 140, 176
Dallas-Clarendon Convention (1856), 471
Dalton García, Roque, 237, 305
Damas, Léon, 313
Dantas, Audálio, 528
Dantas, João, 798
Dantas, Manuel Pinto de Souza, 305, 938
D'Antoni, Salvador, 1019
Dardón, Manuel, 116
Darié, Sandu, 305
Darío, Andrés, 560
Darío Paredes, Rubén, 45, 68, 285, 305–307, 434, 450, 560, 575, 633, 670–671, 671, 718, 844, 875
Dartiguenave, Philippe-Sudré, 150, 307, 899
D'Aubuisson, Roberto, 307, 332
Davertige, 800
David, Jacques-Louis, 802
Davidovsky, Mario, 252, 307
Dávila, María Antonia, 824
Dávila, Miguel R., 142, 307–308
Dávila, Pedrarias, 49, 1015
Dávila, Tristán, 1027
Dávila Espinoza, Carlos Guillermo, 308
Davis, B. Lynch, 146
Davis, Charles H., 1068
Davis, Stuart, 981
Davis, Winter, 889
Daza, Hilarión, 198, 308
Debayle, Salvadora, 963
Debravo, Jorge, 12
Debray, [Jules] Régis, 305, 309
Debret, Jean-Baptiste, 309–310, 822, 982
Decoud, Hector Francisco, 310
Decoud, José Segundo, 310
Degollado, Santos, 310–311, 462
Deilers, Leonore Niessen, 837
Deira, Ernesto, 311
Déjoie, Louis, 336
Delaroche, Hippolyte, 559
Delauney, Robert, 285, 646
Del Castillo, Bernal Díaz, 324
Delfim Neto, Antônio, 312
Delgado, José Matías, 64, 202, 312
Delgado Chalbaud, Carlos, 312–313

Dellepiane, Luis J., 313, 527
Del Monte, Domingo, 625
Del Prado, Jorge, 311
Del Rio, Dolores, 311–312
Del Valle, Aristóbulo, 469, 993
Delvalle, Eric Arturo, 719
Demetrio, Pedro, 732
Democractic Left, 162
Demócrata Progresista, 994
Democratic Convergence, 1010
Democratic Labor Party (PDT), 171
Democratic Progressive Party, 515
Democratic Renovation Party, 207
Democratic Republican Union, 793
Democratic Revolutionary Front (FDR), 1010, 1084
Democratic Revolutionary Party (PRD), 915
Democratic Society of Artisans, 586
Democratic Union of Liberation (UDEL), 257
Democratic Vanguard, 388
Denevi, Marco, 313
Depestre, René, 25, 313–314
Dermée, Paul, 509
Derqui, Santiago, 314
Descartes, René, 532, 606
D'Escoto Brockmann, Miguel, 314
Desilu, 76
Desnoes, Edmundo Pérez, 314
Dessalines, Jean Jacques, 314–315, 564–565, 599, 799
Deustua, Alejandro O., 315–316, 541
Deutsch, Max, 572
Dewey, John, 909, 985
Dianda, Hilda, 317, 415
Dias, Antônio Gonçalves, 317–318
Dias, Henrique, 318
Días, Daniel Vásquez, 757
Dias Gomes, Alfredo, 318–319
Díaz, Adolfo, 258, 319, 676, 908, 928, 929, 1091
Díaz, César, 593
Díaz, Félix, Jr., 319–320, 615, 857
Díaz, Gonzalo, 320
Díaz, Jorge, 320, 489
Díaz, José Eduvigis, 320–321
Díaz, José Pedro, 321
Díaz, Manuel, 786
Díaz, Miguel Arriaga, 786
Díaz, Porfirio, 37, 204, 220, 320, 321–323, 352, 449, 457–458, 458, 508, 509, 517, 535, 571, 578, 614, 630, 673, 751, 770, 845, 856, 857, 864, 889, 892, 951, 988, 995, 1036, 1050, 1084
Díaz Arosemena, Domingo, 323, 528
Díaz-Balart, Mirta, 245
Díaz Castro, Eugenio, 323
Díaz de Guzmán, Ruy, 323–324
Díaz del Castillo, Bernal, 88, 324, 398, 621
Díaz de Solís, Juan, 807, 1047
Díaz Lozano, Argentina, 324
Díaz Ordaz, Gustavo, 324–325, 340, 594, 616
Díaz Soto y Gama, Antonio, 325

Díaz Vélez, José Miguel, 325
Di Cavalcanti, Emiliano, 45, 169, 316, 621
Dickens, Charles, 111
Dickmann, Adolfo, 325–326
Dickmann, Enrique, 326, 437, 537
Diego, Eliseo, 326, 574
Diego, Gerardo, 222, 509
Diego, José de, 326–327
Diego Padró, José I. de, 762
Diegues, Carlos, 955
Diepalismo movement, 762
Dillon, Luis N., 1017
Dilthey, Wilhelm, 541, 888
D'Indy, Vincent, 240, 1022
Diomede, Miguel, 327
Dirección Nacional de Inteligencia (DINA), 572
Dirty War, 607, 1050, 1062
Discépolo, Enrique Santos, 327
Di Tella, Torcuato, 316–317
Dittborn, Eugenio, 327
Doblado, Manuel, 311
Dobles, Julieta, 12
Dobles Segreda, Luis, 327–328
Dobrizhoffer, Martín, 328
Doctrinary Liberal Party, 323
Domecq, H. Bustos, 146
Domela, Cesar, 646
Domeyko, Ignacio, 132
Domingo, Plácido, 565
Domínguez, Alfonso Martínez, 340
Domínguez, José María, 1014
Domínguez, Manuel, 328
Domínguez, Miguel, 328–329, 750
Domínguez, Oscar, 223
Dominican Revolutionary Party (PRD), 163, 673–674, 787
Dongen, Kees van, 302
Donoso, José, 329
Dorantes de Carranza, Andrés, 184, 355
Dorati, Antal, 948
Dorfman, Ariel, 84
Dorrego, Manuel, 329–330, 436, 562, 895, 1028
Dorticós Torrado, Osvaldo, 330
Douglass, Frederick, 511
Downing, Luís, 285
Drago, Luis María, 330
Drago Doctrine, 330
Dragún, Osvaldo, 330
Drake, Francis, 330–331, 331
Dreyfus Company, 104–105
Duarte, Augusto Rodrigues, 331
Duarte, Juan Pablo, 331–332, 796, 934
Duarte, Pedro, 332
Duarte Fuentes, José Napoleón, 332, 670, 1010
Dubois, Albert, 573
Dubois, Théodore, 917
Duchamp, Marcel, 981
Duclos, Jean Jacques, 314
Dueñas, Francisco, 199, 333

Duguay-Trouin, René, 229
Dukas, Paul, 815
Duprat, Rogério, 333, 652, 735
Dupuy, Vicente, 738
Durán, Diego, 333–334
Durán, Fray Narciso, 334
Durán Cerda, 4
Durand, Auguste, 1072
Durand, Oswald, 334
Durão, José de Santa Rita, 334
Durate, Pedro, 355
Durou y Sure, Luis, 898
Dutary, Alberto, 36, 334–335
Dutra, Eurico Gaspar, 234, 335
Duvalier, François, 170, 259, 335–336, 830
Duvalier, Jean-Claude, 74, 336–337
Duvergé, Antonio, 934

E

Echandi Jiménez, Mario, 339
Echave Orio Baltasar de, 339
Echeandía, José María de, 339
Echenique, José Rufino, 155, 187, 339–340, 345, 496, 654,
    824, 1064
Echeverría, Esteban, 13, 161, 340, 590, 629, 926
Echeverría Álvarez, Luis, 340, 595
Echeverría Bianchi, José Antonio, 340–341
Eckhout, Albert, 640–641
Economic Action Plan of the Government, 201
Eder, Santiago Martín, 341
Edmundo, Raúl, 488
Edwards, Agustín, 341
Edwards, Jorge, 341–342
Edwards Bello, Joaquín, 342
Egaña Fabres, Mariano, 342
Egaña Risco, Juan, 342
Egas, Camilo Alejandro, 342–343
Eguren, José María, 3, 343
Eichelbaum, Samuel, 343
Eielson, Jorge Eduardo, 961
Eight Contemporaries, 757
Einstein, Albert, 929
Eisenhower, Dwight D., 545, 965
Eisenhower-Remón Treaty (1955), 854
Ejército de Liberación Nacional (Army of National Liberation),
    997
Elbrick, Charles, 401
Elcano, Juan Sebastián de, 344, 618, 755
Elhuyar, Juan José de, 344
Elhuyar y Zúbice, Fausto de, 344
Elías Calles, Plutarco, 193, 211, 309, 725, 751, 764, 820, 881
Elías Domingo, 344–345
Elío, Francisco Javier, 345
Eliot, T. S., 209
Elizaga, José María, 345
Elizondo, Salvador, 345
Ellis, Keith, 478
El Noventa, 22–23

Elpons, Georg Fischer, 45
El Salvador del Mundo schools, 457
Éluard, Paul, 219
Emparán, Vicente, 345
Encilhamentol, 202
Encina, Francisco Antonio, 345–346
Encinas, José Antonio, 346, 1095
Encisco, Martín Fernández de, 100, 346, 714, 809
Enríquez, Carlos, 347
Enríquez, Manuel, 347
Enríquez de Almansa, Martín, 347, 460
Enríquez de Guzmán, Alonso, 347–348
Enríquez Gallo, Alberto, 348, 759
Ensenada, Cenón de Somodevilla, Marqués de la, 348
Ercilla y Zúñiga, Alonso de, 247, 348–349, 408, 736
Ernest, Max, 539
Errázuriz Echaurren, Federico, 349
Errázuriz Valdivieso, Crescente, 349
Errázuriz Zañartu, Federico, 349
Erro, Enrique, 349–350
Escalada, Asunción, 350
Escalada, Gustavo Sosa, 114
Escalada, Juan Pedro, 350
Escalada de la Quintana, María de los Remedios de, 919
Escalante, Aníbal, 350
Escalón, Pedro José, 853
Escalona y Calatayud, Juan José de, 981
Escandón, Antonio, 350
Escandón, José de, 351
Escandón, Manuel, 350, 351
Escheandía, José María, 1084
Escobar, Luis Antonio, 351
Escobar, Marisol, 628
Escobar, Patricio, 90, 109, 310, 332, 351–352
Escobedo, Mariano, 352
Escola de Recife, 890
Escuela, Agrícola Panamericana, 816–817
Escuela Municipal de Declamación y Arte Escénico, 250
Eslava y Lazaga, Sebastián de, 352, 812
Esmeraldas affair, 181
Espada y Landa, José Díaz, 1029
Espaillat, Ulises Francisco, 352–353, 603
Espejo, Antonio de, 353
Espejo, Bartolomé Blanche, 308
Espeleta y Galdeano Dicastillo y del Prado, José Manuel de, 353
Espín de Castro, Vilma, 353
Espinosa, Gaspar de, 1015
Espinosa, José Ignacio, 782
Espinosa, José María, 353–354
Espinosa y Espinosa, (Juan) Javier, 354
Espionage Ace (1917), 385
Espira, Féderman, 367
Espira, Jorge, 367
Espiro, Manuel Fernández, 356
Esquipulas II, 72
Esquiú, Mamerto, 354
Esquivel, Manuel Amadeo, 354–355, 829
Estado Novo, 43, 651

Estadual Orchestra, 333
Esteban, 355
Estenssoro, Paz, 113
Estero, Santiago del, 788
Estigarribia, Antonio de la Cruz, 332, 355
Estigarribia, José Félix, 169, 260, 355–356, 697, 886–887, 1079, 1094
Estimé, Dumarsais, 197, 335, 355, 356, 619
Estrada, Beatriz de, 1038
Estrada, Carlos, 252, 356–357, 636, 948
Estrada, Emilio, 813
Estrada, José Dolores, 357, 358
Estrada, José Manuel, 357, 469, 1024
Estrada, José María, 357–358
Estrada, Juan José, 258, 319, 358
Estrada Cabrera, Manuel, 84, 307, 358–359, 497, 742, 853, 1074
Estrada Palma, Tomás, 359–360, 448
Estridentism, 509
Etchepareborda, Roberto, 360
Euceda, Maximiliano, 360, 447
European Committee of Brazilian Women, 12
Ewald, Georg von, 113
Exposición Logicofobista, 1035

F

Fabbri, Juan, 948
Fabela, Francisco Trinidad, 361
Fabela Alfaro, Isidro, 361
Fabini, Eduardo, 270, 361
Facio Brenes, Rodrigo, 361–362
Facioli, Valentim, 847
Facio Segreda, Gonzalo, 362
Fages, Pedro, 362
Fagoaga y Lizaur, José María, 363
Faillos, Juana María, 183
Fajardo, Francisco, 363
Falange Nacional, 566
Falco, Angel, 11
Falcón, Jose, 363
Falcón, Juan Crisóstomo, 54, 364, 457, 485, 912
Faletto, Enzo, 214
Falkland Islands, 407
Falla, Manuel de, 487, 1022
Fallas Sibaja, Carlos Luis, 364, 686
Fangio, Juan Manuel, 364
Faoro, Raymundo, 364–365
Farabundo Martí Front for National Liberation (FMLN), 632, 1010, 1084
Faras, Mestre João, 185
Farías, Gómez, 464, 848
Farías, Victoria, 848
Fariña Núñez, Eloy, 365
Farquhar, Percival, 365–366
Farrell, Edelmiro, 366, 795, 845
Febreristas, 697
Febres-Cordero Ribadeneyra, León, 8, 228, 366
Federación Chilena de Instituciones Femeninas (FECHIF), 381

Federación Nacional Velasquista, 77
Federación Obrera Marítima, 447
Federación Sindical de Trabajodores Mineros de Bolivia, 564
Federalist Pact, 588
Federalist Party, 702
Federalist Revolt (1893–1895), 161, 783, 803
Federalist War (1898–1899), 370, 764
Federal League of Rural Action (LFAR), 707
Federal War (1859–1863), 364, 579, 760, 839, 884, 1060
Federation of Latin American Workers, 586
Federation of Miners, 564
Féderman, Nicolás, 129, 366–367, 529
Feijó, Diogo Antônio, 367, 678, 765, 1036
Feijóo, Benito Jerónimo, 183, 367–368
Felde, Alberto Zum, 500
Felguérez, Manuel, 368
Félix, María, 368
Feo, José Rodríguez, 574, 802
Ferdinadov, Nicolas, 855
Ferdinand II (Aragon), 276
Ferdinand VI, 348, 368, 625
Ferdinand VII, 1, 27, 44, 91, 107, 154, 439, 503, 589, 662, 683, 696, 831, 903, 1029
Fernandes, Florestan, 214, 368, 513
Fernandes, Millôr, 368–369
Fernández, Emilio, 75, 311, 369, 380
Fernández, Félix, 250
Fernández, Francisco F., 593
Fernández, Juan, 369
Fernández, Max, 369–370
Fernandez, Oscar Lorenzo, 370
Fernández, Padre Rufo, 102
Fernández, Pedro, 528–529
Fernández, Próspero, 967
Fernández Alonso, Sévero, 370, 764
Fernández Artucio, Hugo, 370
Fernández Crespo, Daniel, 370–371
Fernández de Cabrera Bobadilla Cerda y Mendoza, Luis Gerónimo, 371
Fernández de Castro Andrade y Portugal, Pedro Antonio, 371
Fernández de Córdoba, Diego, 371–372
Fernández de Lizardi, José Joaquín, 372
Fernández (Hernández) de Córdoba, Francisco, 372, 459, 467, 494
Fernández Hidalgo, Gutierre, 372–373
Fernández Madrid, José, 373
Fernández Oreamuno, Próspero, 373
Fernández Retamar, Roberto, 373
Fernández y Medina, Benjamín, 373
Fernandini, Eulogio E., 373–374
Fernando, Carlos, 257
Fernando, Claudia, 257
Fernando VII (King of Spain), 217
Ferrara, Vicente, 432
Ferré, Pedro, 35
Ferré Aguayo, Luis Antonio, 374
Ferreira, Benigno, 374
Ferreira, Jesús (Chucho) Reyes, 111, 965

Ferreira Aldunate, Wilson, 159, 374–375, 548
Ferreira Brêtas, Rodrigo José, 22
Ferreiro, Oscar, 201
Ferrer, Rafael, 375
Ferrera, Francisco, 375–376, 868
Ferrer de Serra, Antonio, 948
Ferrer de Serra, Margarita, 948
Ferrez, Gilberto, 376
Ferrez, Marc, 376
Ferrocarriles Nacionales de Mexico, 578
Ferrocarril Interoceánico de Honduras, 471
Feuerbach, Ludwig, 113
Ficher, Jacobo, 376
Fidelito, Castro, 245
Fierro Rimac, Francisco, 376–377
Fierro y Acero, Fundidora de, 432
Figari, Pedro, 377
Fignolé, Daniel, 335
Figueiredo, Afonso Celso de Assis, 377
Figueiredo, Euclides de Oliveira, 378
Figueiredo, Guilherme de, 378
Figueiredo, Jackson de, 377–378
Figueiredo, João Baptista de Oliveira, 378, 392, 394, 436, 446, 771
Figueredo, Pedro, 253
Figueres Ferrer, José, 72, 73, 207, 339, 361, 362, 378–380, 676, 686, 706–707, 721, 729, 743, 800, 964, 1009, 1046
Figueroa, Gabriel, 380
Figueroa, Gaspar de, 1037
Figueroa, José, 380, 1084
Figueroa, José Miguel y Santos, 380
Figueroa, Pedro José, 380
Figueroa Alcorta, José, 380–381, 848, 1089, 1090
Figueroa Gajardo, Ana, 381
Figueroa Larraín, Emiliano, 381
Filho, Antunes, 876
Filho, Hermilo Borba, 974
Filho, João Café, 598
Filísola, Vicente, 64, 120, 381, 401
Fine Arts Circle, 855
Finlay, Carlos Juan, 382
First Company of Catalonian Volunteers, 362
Fischer, Bobby, 206
Flag riots (1964), 871
Flakoll, Darwin, 20
Fleitas, Eduardo, 477
Flem, Paul le, 1022
Flores, Antonio, 7
Flores, Ignacio, 1004–1005
Flores, Juan José, 382–383, 384, 390, 425, 716, 736, 871, 873, 874, 1010
Flores, Luis A., 383
Flores, Matías Delgado, 71
Flores, Venancio, 124, 383, 499, 560
Flores da Cunha, José Antônio, 383–384
Flores Jijón, Antonio, 384
Flores Magón, Enrique, 384
Flores Magón, Jesús, 384

Flores Magón, Ricardo, 325, 384–385, 458
Flores Maldonado Martínez y Bodquín, Manuel Antonio, 385, 482
Floridablanca, Conde de, 385
Florit, Eugenio, 385, 574
Fluxus group, 58
Fonseca, Carlos, 159, 642, 748, 845, 1070
Fonseca, Deodora da, 150, 617, 783
Fonseca, Gonzalo, 385–386
Fonseca, Hermes Rodrigues da, 386, 803
Fonseca, Juan Rodríguez de, 386, 570
Fonseca, Manuel Deodora da, 202, 280, 386–387, 649
Fonseca, Marechal Deodora da, 236
Fonseca, Marshal Hermes da, 779
Fonseca Amador, Carlos, 387
Fonseca e Silva, Valentim da, 387–388, 530
Fonseca Martins, Climéria da, 642
Fonseca y Contreras, Manuel de, 985
Fontana, Lucio, 196, 388
Foraker Act, 109
Forbes Commission, 899
Ford, Guillermo, 70
Ford, Henry, 540
Ford, John, 380
Foreign Agents Registration Act, 405
Forey, Élie-Frédéric, 127, 548
Forino, Luis, 590
Fornarini, Eduardo, 240
Forner, Raquel, 388
Fortes, Bias, 390
Fortuny, José Manuel, 63, 68, 388–389
Fouché, Franck, 197
Foulkes, Richard, 27
Fournet, Jean, 998
Fournier, Rafael Angel Calderón, 362
Fourteenth of June Movement, 1003
Fowler, Amy, 604
Frageiro, Clemente L., 850
França, Agnelo, 406
Francés, Esteban, 1035
Francia, José, 233
Francia, José Gaspar Rodríguez de, 34, 82, 158, 182, 260, 363, 389, 436, 587, 684, 871, 1073, 1078
Francisca, Doña, 413
Francisca Lopes, Joana, 22
Francisco, Carlos, 296
Francisco, Juan, 310
Francisco, Martim, 50
Francisco Lisbôa, Manuel, 22
Francis I (Emperor of Austria), 569
Francis I (King of Naples), 987
Franco, Guillermo, 390
Franco, Hernando, 390
Franco, Itamar Augusto Cautiero, 274, 390, 970
Franco, Rafael, 390–391, 697, 887
Franco, Wellington Moreira, 391
Franco-Prussian War (1870), 127
Frank, Neil L., 1062

Frank, Waldo, 727
Free Birth Law (1871), 861, 862
Frei Montalva, Eduardo, 29, 92, 391–392, 566, 945, 991
Freire, Paulo, 392
Freire Serrano, Ramón, 392–393, 731, 806, 1049
French Artistic Mission, 309
Frente Amplio, 375
Frente de la Izquierda Democrática (FID), 174
Frente do Recife, 78
Frente Nacional, 826, 1005
Frente Popular Libertador (FPL), 654
Frente Sandinista de Liberación Nacional, 258
Frente Unido, 997
Fresno Larraín, Juan Francisco, 393
Freyre, Gilberto (de Mello), 393–395, 581, 969
Freyre, Ricardo Jaimes, 306
Frías, Antonio, 395
Frías, Felix, 18
Friedeberg, Petro, 445
Friedlaender, John, 413
Friends of America, 651
Friends of the New Art, 1035
Friesz, Othon, 121, 140
Frigerio, Rogelio, 395
Frondizi, Arturo, 36, 99, 360, 395–396, 396, 518, 635
Frondizi, Risieri, 396
Front Antillo-Guyanais pour l'Indépendance, 444
Front of Democratic Youth, 130
Front of the Democratic Left, 174
Frost, Robert, 776
Frugoni, Emílio, 396–397, 447
Fuentes, Carlos, 329, 397, 403, 882, 1033
Fuentes, Manuel Atanasio, 398
Fuentes, Miguel Ydígoras, 63, 68, 1078
Fuentes y Guzmán, Francisco Antonio de, 398
Fuerzas Armadas Revolucionarias Colombianas, 1022
Fuerzas Democráticas Nicaragüenses (FDN), 139, 179, 771
Fujimori, Alberto Keinya, 398–399
Funaro, Dilson, 169, 649
Fundação Movimento Brasileiro de Alfabetização (MOBRAL), 957
Funes, Gregorio, 35, 399–400
Fúrlong Cárdiff, Guillermo, 400
Furtado, Celso, 214, 400

G
Gabeira, Fernando Nagle, 401
Gadsden Purchase, 726
Gaete, Marina Ortíz de, 1021
Gahona, Gabriel Vicente, 401
Gaínza, Gabino, 312, 401, 731
Gainza Paz, Alberto, 401–402
Gaitán, Jorge Eliécer, 65, 242, 402–403, 753, 1005
Gaitán Durán, Jorge, 403
Gaito, Constantino, 240, 403, 426, 590
Galán, José María Garza, 220
Galán, Julio, 403
Galán Sarmiento, Luis Carlos, 109, 403–404, 434

Galavís, Félix, 450
Galeana, Hermenegildo, 168, 404, 693
Galeano, Eduardo Hughes, 404
Galíndez, Jesús de, 404–405, 1003
Galindo, Alejandro, 405
Galindo, Blás, 405, 676
Galindo, Juan, 405
Galindo, Philemon, 405
Galindo, Sergio, 405–406
Galindo y Villa, Jesús, 414
Gallego, Laura, 406
Gallegos, José María, 786
Gallegos, Rómulo, 143, 147, 406, 569, 791, 793
Gallet, Luciano, 406–407
Gallo Goyenechea, Pedro León, 407, 682
Galtieri, Leopoldo Fortunato, 407, 1062
Galván, Manuel de Jesús, 407
Galván Rivera, Mariano, 407–408
Galvarino, 408
Gálvez, Bernardo de, 408, 411, 709
Gálvez, José de, 296, 344, 362, 408–409, 411, 481, 823, 933
Gálvez, Juan Manuel, 409–410, 437, 514, 601
Gálvez, Mariano, 120, 137, 224, 410–411, 671, 672, 690, 767, 870
Gálvez, Matías de, 411
Gálvez, Pedro, 237
Gálvez Durón, Juan Manuel, 216
Gama, José Basilio da, 411–412
Gama, Luís, 412
Gama, Vasco da, 334, 412
Gamarra, Agustín, 103, 236, 412–413, 413, 738, 912, 932, 1064
Gamarra, Francisca Zubiaga Bernales de (la Mariscala), 413
Gamarra, José, 413
Gambaro, Griselda, 413–414
Gamboa, Federico, 618
Gamboa, Manuel, 414
Gamboa Iglesias, Federico, 414
Gamio, Gabriel, 414
Gamio Martínez, Manuel, 414
Gándara, María Francisca de la, 192
Gándara Enríquez, Marcos, 414–415
Gandavo, Pero de Magalhães, 415
Gandini, Gerardo, 58, 152, 415–416, 637, 983
Gante, Pedro de, 416
Gaos, José, 416
Garay, Blas, 416
Garay, Carlos, 417
Garay, Epifanio, 417
Garay, Eugenio, 417
Garay, Francisco de, 41, 417–418
Garay, Juan de, 71, 152, 418
Garcés, Francisco Tomás Hermenegildo, 418
Garcés, Isabel, 592
Garcés, Julián, 592
García, Aleixo, 418–419
García, Apolinário Nunes, 419–420
García, Calixto, 419, 658

García, Diego, 419
García, Joaquín Torres, 66
García, José Maurício Nunes, 419–420, 711, 823, 953
García, José Uriel, 256
García, Juan Agustín, 850
García, Lizardo, 26
García, Lucas, 250
García, Pablo Antonio, 380
García, Petrona, 224
García, Sara, 420
García, Genaro, 419
García Calderón, Francisco, 420
García Caturla, Alejandro, 420–421
García Conde, Pedro, 421
García de Castro, Lope, 421
García Diego y Moreno, Francisco, 421–422
García-Godoy, Héctor, 181, 422
García Granados, Miguel, 251, 422
García-Guerrero, 568
García Icazbalceta, Joaquín, 422–423
García Márquez, Gabriel, 54, 329, 403, 423–424, 758, 939, 1033
García Meza, Luis, 424–425, 840
García Moreno, Gabriel, 162, 181, 208, 228, 354, 382, 384, 425, 871
García Morillo, Roberto, 426
García Peláez, Francisco de Paula, 426, 1063
García Pérez, Alan, 426–427
García Robles, Alfonso, 427
García Salinas, Francisco, 427
García y García, Aurelio, 466
García y González, Vicente, 427
Garcilaso de la Vega, El Inca, 427–428, 739, 933
Gardel, Carlos, 161, 428–429
Gari, Juan José, 707
Garibaldi, Domenico, 429
Garibaldi, Giuseppe, 429
Garibay, Pedro, 429
Garibay Kintana, Ángel María, 429–430
Garín, José León, 375
Garmendia, Francisco, 430
Garmendia, Salvador, 430
Garrido Canabal, Tomás, 430, 616
Garrido-Lecca Seminario, Celso, 430–431
Garro, Elena, 431
Garro, José de, 431
Garvey, Marcus, 431–432
Garza, Patricia de la, 309
Garza Sada Family, 432
Garzón, Eugenio, 593
Gasca, Pedro de la, 281, 432–433, 973
Gasset, José Ortega y, 65
Gastão D'Orléans, 433–434, 521
Gatón Arce, Freddy, 434
Gauguin, Paul, 1000
Gavidia, Francisco Antonio, 434
Gaviría, César, 710
Gaviria Trujillo, César Augusto, 434–435

Gaztelu, Ángel, 574
Geffrard, Fabre Nicolas, 435, 916, 968
Gego, 435
Geisel, Ernesto, 378, 435–436
Gelly y Obes, Juan Andrés, 436–437
Gelves, Marqués de, 437
Generación Comprometida, 596
General Association of Latin American Students (AGELA), 837
General Confederation of Guatemalan Workers, 482
General Confederation of Workers (CGT), 518
General Federation of Workers, 627
General Labor Command (CGT), 758
General Labor Confederation, 794
General Strike Command, 758
Generation of '45, 851
Generation of 1940, 744–745
Generative Art, 609
Gerchunoff, Alberto, 437
Gérôme, Jean-Léon, 331
Gerzso, Gunther, 437–438
Gestido, Oscar Daniel, 370, 438, 758
Ghioldi, Américo, 438
Ghioldi, Rodolfo, 438
Giannini, Vittorio, 550
Gil, Gilberto, 248, 438–439, 455
Gil, Jerónimo Antonio, 439, 530
Gil, José, 426, 441
Gilardi, Gilardo, 440
Gilberto, João, 248, 439, 440, 531
Gildemeister Family, 440–441
Gil de Taboada y Lemos, Francisco, 182, 439
Gil Fortoul, José, 439–440
Gill, Juan Bautista, 441
Ginastera, Alberto Evaristo, 58, 152, 415, 441–442, 554, 572, 717, 1020
Giribaldi, (Vicente) Tomás E., 442
Giró, Juan Francisco, 383
Girón, Francisco Hernández, 442–443
Girón de León, Andrés de Jesús, 443
Gironella, Alberto, 443
Girri, Alberto, 443
Gismonti, Egberto, 443–444
Giuffra, Giuseppe, 442
Glantz, Margo, 444
Gleizes, Albert, 45
Gleyre, Marc Gabriel Charles, 559
Glissant, Édouard, 444
Gobierno, Junta de, 439
Gobineau, Joseph-Arthur, 346
Godard, Benjamin, 1072
Godin, Louis, 531
Godinho, Vitorino Magalhães, 492
Godoi, Juan Silvano, 444–445
Godoy, Manuel de, 385, 523
Godoy, Pérez, 580
Godoy, Sebastiana, 33
Godoy Cruz, Tomás, 445, 919
Goeritz, Mathias, 111, 445

Góes, Zacarias de, 305
Golbery do Couto e Silva, 445–446
Goldemberg, Isaac, 446
Gómara, Francisco López de, 500, 621
Gombrowicz, Witold, 802
Gomes, Antônio Carlos, 142, 446
Gomes, Dias, 267
Gomes, Diogo, 491
Gomes, Eduardo, 447, 984
Gómez, Benigno, 447, 821
Gómez, Emilio Vázquez, 615
Gómez, Eugenio, 74, 447
Gómez, Francisco Sada, 432
Gómez, Francisco Vázquez, 615
Gómez, Indalecio, 447–448
Gómez, José Miguel, 448, 450, 555, 658
Goméz, José Valentín, 448
Gómez, Juan Carlos, 448–449
Gómez, Juan Gualberto, 449
Gómez, Juan Vicente, 143, 148, 440, 449–450, 474, 493, 569, 610, 644, 791, 800, 1026
Gómez, Laureano, 584, 753, 884, 936, 1022
Gómez, Miguel Mariano, 450
Gómez, Peña, 787
Gómez Carrillo, Enrique, 450–451
Gómez Castro, Laureano, 451, 453
Gómez-Cruz, Ernesto, 451
Gómez de Avellaneda y Arteaga, Gertrudis, 451–452
Gómez Farías, Valentín, 380, 452–453, 684, 931
Gómez Hurtado, Alvaro, 453
Gómez Morín, Manuel, 121, 453, 585
Gómez Pedraza, Manuel, 453, 848, 1049
Gómez y Báez, Máxino, 453–454
Gonçalves, Danúbio, 825
Gondra, Manuel, 90, 454, 477
Góngora, Diego de, 71
Góngora, Luís de, 951
Gonzaga, Chiquinha, 192
Gonzaga, Francisca Hedwiges, 454–455
Gonzaga, José Basileu Neves, 454
Gonzaga, Luís, 439, 455
Gonzaga, Tomás Antônio, 455–456
Gonzaga, Vespasiano, 500
Gonzaguinha, 455
González, Abraham, 456
González, Beatriz, 456
González, Carlos, 456
González, Florentino, 456–457, 584
González, Francisca, 809
González, Ignacio María, 352
González, Joaquín Víctor, 457
González, José Caridad, 263
González, Juan Gualberto, 141
González, Juan Natalicio, 259, 457, 1079
González, Juan Vicente, 457
González, Lina Ruz, 246
González, Manuel, 322, 323, 457–458, 864
González, Natalicio, 980

González, Pablo, 458, 509
González Ávila, Jorge, 458–459
González Camarena, Jorge, 459
González Casanova, Pablo, 459
González Dávila, Gil, 87, 372, 459, 734–735
González de Eslava, Fernán, 460
González de Santa Cruz, Roque, 460
González Echevarría, Roberto, 478
González Flores, Alfredo, 460–461, 463, 989
González Goyri, Roberto, 461
González León, Adriano, 461
González Martínez, Enrique, 461–462
González Ortega, Jesús, 311, 462, 571, 645, 830, 1087
González Prada, Manuel, 462, 639, 1095
González Suárez, (Manuel María) Federico, 462–463
González Videla, Gabriel, 25, 391, 463, 566, 673
González Víquez, Cleto, 463
Good Neighbor Policy, 929
Gordillo, Francisco, 601, 862, 1037
Górecki, Henryk, 172
Gorodischer, Angélica, 463–464
Gorostiza, Carlos, 330
Gorostiza, José, 265, 464
Gorostiza, Manuel Eduardo de, 464
Gorriarán, Osmani Cienfuegos, 245
Gorriti, Juana Manuela, 638
Gorriti, Juan Ignacio de, 464
Gortari, Elí de, 487
Gortari, Margarita de, 915
Gottschalk, Louis M., 252, 1071
Goulart, João Belchior Marques, 78, 170, 234, 235, 291, 378, 400, 464–465, 544, 549, 599, 643, 650, 713, 784, 828, 835, 859
Gouveia, Cristóvão de, 214
Goya, Francisco, 855
Goyeneche, José Manuel, 412
Graça Aranha, José Pereira da, 465
Graef Fernández, Carlos, 465–466, 929
Graetzer, Guillermo, 307
Graiver, David, 554
Grajales, Mariana, 610
Gramatges, Harold, 147
Grammont, François, 15
Granados, Federico Tinoco, 289
Granados, Miguel García, 116
Grandjean de Montigny, Auguste Henri Victor, 309, 466
Grant, Ulysses S., 889
Grau, Enrique, 466
Grau, Miguel, 466
Grau, Ricardo, 1003
Grau San Martín, Ramón, 123, 262, 466–467, 786, 831, 832
Graves, Robert, 20
Great Andean Rebellion, 1004
Greene, Graham, 430, 727
Green Party, 401
Gregory XVI (Pope), 1063
Grieder, Terence, 294
Grijalva, Juan de, 37, 288, 324, 467

Grilo, Sarah, 467–468
Grimard, Luc, 468
Grippo, Víctor, 468
Gris, Juan, 509
Groot, José Manuel, 417
Group of Revolutionary Writers and Artists (LEAR), 965
Groussac, Paul, 468–469
Grové, Stefan, 252
Grove Vallejo, Marmaduke, 469
Grünenwald, Jean-Jacques, 572
Grupo de los Cuatro, 676
Grupo de los Trece, 468
Grupo de Renovación Musical, 66
Grupo Industrial AIFA, 595
Grupo Obra de Unificación, 845
Grupo Renovación, 440, 738
Guadalupe Hidalgo, Treaty of (1848), 453, 517, 726, 754, 787, 853
Guajardo, Jesús, 1086
Guamán Poma de Ayala, Felipe, 469–470, 933
Guanabarino, Oscar, 710
Guaraní War (1752–1756), 51–52
Guardia, Calderón, 686
Guardia, Fernández, 967
Guardia, Ricardo Adolfo de la, 470
Guardia Gutiérrez, Tomás, 373, 470–471, 678, 967, 988
Guardia Navarro, Ernesto de la, 471
Guardiola, Santos, 184, 471–472, 580
Guarnieri, Camargo, 541, 550, 717
Guarnieri, Gianfrancesco, 472
Guarnieri, M[ozart] Camargo, 472
Guatemalan Communist Party (PCG), 388
Guatemalan Labor Party (PGT), 388
Guatemalan National Revolutionary Union (URNG), 251, 862
Guatemalan Union of Educational Workers, 482
Guayasamín, Oswaldo, 472–473
Gudiño Kieffer, Eduardo, 473
Gueiler Tejada, Lidia, 424, 473
Gúemes, Martín, 474
Guérin, Charles, 121
Guerra, José Arévalo, 942
Guerra, Ramón, 474
Guerra, Ruy, 173
Guerra y Sánchez, Ramiro, 474
Guerrero, Francisco, 372
Guerrero, José, 528
Guerrero, Vicente, 474–475, 693, 814, 903
Guerrero, Xavier, 26, 475
Guerrero y Torres, Francisco Antonio, 475
Guerrilla Army of the Poor (EGP), 601
Guevara, Ángel, 789
Guevara, Ernesto "Che," 114, 244, 245, 246, 305, 309, 627, 760, 995
Guevara Arze, Walter, 473, 476, 777
Guevara y Lira, Silvestre, 485
Guggiari, José Patricio, 90, 476–477
Guido, Beatriz, 477
Guido, José María, 477, 635, 801

Guido, Tomás, 919
Guignard, Alberto da Veiga, 268
Guillén, Jorge, 776
Guillén, Nicolás, 197, 220, 421, 477–479
Guillermo, Cesareo, 501
Guimarães, Lucilia, 1055
Guimarães, Ulysses Silveira, 479
Guipuzcoana, Compañía, 2
Güiraldes, Ricardo, 479
Guirao, Ramón, 479–480
Guirior, Manuel de, 480, 527, 659
Gullar, Ferreira, 268
Gumucio, Rafael Agustín, 566
Gutiérrez, Elvira, 30
Gutiérrez, Ernesto, 286
Gutiérrez, Eulalio, 480
Gutiérrez, Francisco, 261
Gutiérrez, Gustavo, 480, 554
Gutiérrez, José María, 480–481
Gutiérrez, Juan María, 18, 926
Gutiérrez, Lorenzo Guerrero, 945
Gutiérrez, Luis, 480
Gutiérrez, Rafael, 635–636
Gutiérrez, Victor Manuel, 63
Gutiérrez de Lara, José Bernardo, 481
Gutiérrez del Arroyo, Isabel, 2
Gutiérrez de Padilla, Juan, 481
Gutiérrez de Piñeres, Juan Francisco, 385, 481–482
Gutiérrez Estrada, José María, 302, 482
Gutiérrez Garbín, Víctor Manuel, 68, 482
Gutiérrez González, Gregorio, 482–483
Gutiérrez Guerra, José, 483, 985
Gutiérrez Nájera, Manuel, 230, 483
Gutiérrez y Espinosa, Felipe, 483
Guzmán, Antonio Leocadio, 483, 485, 787
Guzmán, Augusto, 484
Guzmán, Enrique, 484
Guzmán, Felipe Segundo, 907
Guzmán, Jacobo Arbenz, 59
Guzmán, Juan José, 620
Guzmán, Martín Luís, 96, 484
Guzmán, Miguel Henríquez, 213, 701, 902
Guzmán, Nuño Beltrán de, 484
Guzmán, Nuño de, 1038
Guzmán Blanco, Antonio Leocadio, 239, 240, 294, 474, 483, 484–486, 734, 884, 912

H
Hadju, Étienne, 825
Haines, Ricardo, 35
Hait, M. T., 376
Haitian Commission of Intellectual Co-operation, 504
Haitian Revolution, 860–861
Halac, Ricardo, 330
Halffter, Cristóbal, 58
Halffter, Rodolfo, 458, 487, 838
Halperín-Donghi, Tulio, 487

Hanneken, Herman H., 789
Hapsburg, Leopoldina de, 779–780
Hardy, Jean, 265
Hari, Mata, 450–451
Haro, González López de, 634
Haro Barraza, Guillermo, 487
Haro y Tamariz, Antonio de, 351, 487–488
Hart, Armando, 934
Hartmann, Nicolai, 888
Hartt, Charles Fredrick, 376
Haslam de Borges, Fanny, 161
Hassler, Emilio, 107
Hawkins, John, 331, 488
Haya de la Torre, Víctor Raúl, 129, 311, 488–489, 580, 728, 925, 947
Hay-Bunau-Varilla Treaty (1903), 44, 854
Hayes, Rutherford B., 3, 322
Hay-Herran Treaty (1902), 279
Hayter, Stanley W., 57
Heidegger, Martin, 622
Heinl, Robert D., 336
Heiremans, Luis Alberto, 489
Henderson, Fanny, 283
Henderson, James, 283
Henri, Robert, 44
Henríque y Carvajal, Francisco, 491
Henríquez, Camilo, 489–490
Henríquez Ureña, Camila, 1012
Henríquez Ureña, Max, 490, 1012
Henríquez Ureña, Pedro, 33, 49, 172, 290, 490–491, 575, 586, 849, 1012
Henríquez y Carvajal, Francisco, 490, 1012
Henry the Navigator, 491–492
Henze, Emil Körner, 542
Henze, Hans Werner, 172
Hérard, Charles, 648
Héraud, Gabriel, 1058
Heraud, Javier, 580
Herbin, Auguste, 66
Herder, Johann Gottfried von, 944
Heredia y Heredia, José M., 492
Heredia y Mieses, José Francisco, 492
Hereñú, José Eusebio, 203
Hermosillo, Jaime-Humberto, 492
Hernández, Angélica, 692
Hernández, Felisberto, 321, 492, 961
Hernández, Fidel Sánchez, 670
Hernández, Francisco, 492–493, 614, 703–704
Hernández, José, 34, 493
Hernández, José Zuno, 340
Hernández, Luisa Josefina, 493–494
Hernández, José Manuel, 239, 493
Hernández Colón, Rafael, 494
Hernández de Córdoba, Francisco, 88, 324, 372, 494, 1042
Hernández Martínez, Maximiliano, 20, 61, 216, 232, 494–495, 636, 838
Hernández Matos, Rafael, 494
Hernández Moncada, Eduardo, 495, 676

Herold, J. Christopher, 600
Heroles, Jesús Reyes, 595
Herrán, Pedro Alcántara, 495–496
Herrán, Saturnino, 496
Herrán y Zaldúa, Antonio Saturnino, 496
Herrara Campíns, Luis, 499, 791
Herrera, Bartolomé, 496–497
Herrera, Benjamín, 497, 598, 752
Herrera, Carlos, 497, 742
Herrera, Dionisio de, 497
Herrera, Flavio, 497–498
Herrera, Luis Alberto de, 101–102, 124, 498, 548, 987
Herrera, Tomás, 498–499
Herrera, José Joaquín Antonio Florencio, 498
Herrerabarría, Adriano, 501
Herrera Lane, Felipe, 499
Herrera y Obes, Julio, 125, 141, 499–500, 500, 979
Herrera y Reissig, Julio, 11, 500, 1052
Herrera y Tordesillas, Antonio de, 500, 1015
Herrería, Julián de la, 812
Hertzog Garaizabal, Enrique, 501
Herzog, Vladimir, 472, 501
Heureaux, Ulises, 188, 501–502, 507, 1012, 1037
Hidalga, Don Lorenzo de la, 959
Hidalgo, Bartolomé, 502
Hidalgo, Enrique Agustín, 502
Hidalgo, Mariano, 503
Hidalgo y Costilla, Miguel, 1, 2, 19, 27, 329, 481, 502–504, 522, 620, 634, 637, 648, 692, 693, 750, 850, 858, 1044
Higgins, Ambrose, 730
Hill, Benjamin, 725
Hindemith, Paul, 542, 782, 936
Hinestrosa, Gregorio de, 210
Hippolyte, Dominique, 504
Hochschild, Mauricio, 504–505
Hockney, David, 403
Hofmann, Hans, 628
Hojeda, Alonso de, 1047
Holanda, Sérgio Buarque de, 173, 505
Holguín, Carlos, 505
Holguín, Cecilia, 505
Holguín, Jorge, 505
Holzmann, Rodolfo, 430, 505–506
Homar, Lorenzo, 506, 635
Homem, Alberto Torres, 617
Honduran Liberal Party, 216
Honduras, Ferrocarril Interoceánico de, 184
Honegger, Arthur, 219, 998
Hoover, Herbert, 899, 929
Hopkins, Frederick Gowland, 566
Hopkinson, Amanda, 20
Horenstein, Jasha, 270
Horna, José, 1035
Horna, Kati, 1035
Hostos y Bonilla, Eugenio María de, 506–507, 1012
House of the World Worker, 697
Houssay, Bernardo A., 507, 566

Houston, Sam, 541
Huallpa, Topa, 623
Huanchaca Company, 63
Huarte, Doña Ana María, 345
Huascar Capac, 507–508, 623, 810
Huayna Capac, 85, 266, 507, 508, 623
Hubertson, Guillermo Labarca, 547
Huerta, Adolfo de la, 8, 37, 194, 308–309, 453, 725, 751
Huerta, Epitacio, 701
Huerta, Victoriano, 37, 55, 211, 221, 414, 508–509, 568, 595, 614, 615, 745, 751, 804, 843, 979, 1053, 1085
Huertas, Esteban, 509
Huete, José Ángel Zúñiga, 216
Hughes, Langston, 197
Huidobro, Vicente, 768, 885, 900
Huidobro Fernández, Vicente, 509–510
Huitzilihuitl, 699
Huízar, Candelario, 676
Hull, Cordell, 834
Hull-Alfaro Treaty (1936), 26
Humboldt, Alexander von, 112, 189, 704, 879
Hurtado de Mendoza, Andrés, 510, 1016
Hurtado de Mendoza, García, 247, 408, 510, 736, 1056
Hurtado Larrea, Osvaldo, 366, 510–511
Husserl, Edmund, 888
Huston, John, 380
Huxley, Aldous, 727
Hyppolite, Hector, 511
Hyppolite, Louis Modestin Florville, 511
Hyslop, Maxwell, 170

I

Ianni, Octávio, 368, 513
Ibáñez, Roberto, 513
Ibáñez, Sara de, 513
Ibáñez del Campo, Carlos, 24, 381, 469, 513–514, 898
Ibara, Velasco, 80
Ibarbourou, Juana de, 514–515
Ibarbourou, Lucas, 514
Ibargüengoitia, Jorge, 515
Ibarguren, Carlos, 515
Ibarguren, Juana, 796
Ibarra, Diego, 515–516
Ibarra, Francisco, 516
Ibarra, José de Pineda, 516
Ibarra, Juan Felipe, 516
Icaza, Jorge, 8, 113, 516–517
Icazbalceta, Joaquín García, 19, 139
Iglesias, José María, 322, 414, 517, 571, 830
Iglesias, Ley, 1095
Iglesias, Lugarda, 414
Iglesias, Miguel, 187, 517, 689
Iglesias Castro, Rafael, 517–518
Iglesias Pantin, Santiago, 518, 891
Ignacio de Loyola, Martín, 152
Illescas, Carlos, 518
Illia, Arturo Umberto, 518, 737
Imagism, 509

Import-substitution industrialization (ISI), 214
Incháustegui Cabral, Héctor, 518
Inconfidência Mineira, 455, 956
Independent Political Electoral Organization Committee, 190
Independent Revolutionary Party (PRI), 787
Independent Socialist Party (PSI), 176
Indian Protection Service, 892
Infante, Guillermo Cabrera, 939
Infante, José Miguel, 518–519
Infante, Pedro, 519, 710
Infazón, María Pilar, 625
Inferno, Anjos do, 248
Ingenieros, José, 519
Institutional Democratic Party (PID), 789
Institutional Revolutionary Party (PRI), 213, 616
Instituto de Ciências Sociais, 95
Instituto Histórico e Geográfico Brasileiro, 377
Instituto Joaquim Nabuco de Pesquisas Sociais, 394
Instituto Nacional de Estudos Pedagógicos (INEP), 985
Intendancy System, 1
Inter-American Commission of Women, 238
Inter-American Development Bank, 361
Inter-American Institute of Political Education, 676
Inter-American Regional Organization of Workers (ORIT), 676
International Controls Corporation (ICC), 1046
International Court of Justice, 109
Internationalist Socialist Party (PSI), 438
International Overseas Services (IOS), 1046
Interoceanic Railway Company, 471
Intransigent Radical Civic Union, 395, 396
IPEAFRO (Afro-Brazilian Studies and Research Institute), 708
Irala, Domingo Martínez de, 519–520
Irigoyen, Bernardo de, 520, 669
Irisarri, Antonio José de, 520
Irisarri y Larraín, Antonio José, 520
Irisarri y Larraín, Juan Bautista, 520
Isaacs, Jorge, 520–521
Isabel, Princess of Brazil, 521
Isabel II, 903
Isabella I (Castile), 276
Isabella (Queen), 386, 589
Isamitt Alarcón, Carlos, 521–522
Itaboraí, Visconde de, 522
Iturbide, Agustín de, 64, 74, 94, 168, 290, 345, 363, 381, 522–523, 660, 750, 767, 814, 848, 853, 869, 874, 879, 895, 903, 930, 1015, 1025
  fall of, 410
Iturbide, Graciela, 523
Iturrigaray, José de, 328, 429, 502, 523, 660, 939, 980, 1059, 1078
Itzcoatl, 89, 523
Ivaldi, Humberto, 249, 523–524, 958
Ixtlilxóchitl, Fernando de Alva, 714, 993
Izábal, Rafael, 995
Izquierda Democrática, 162
Izquierdo, María, 524

J

Jaar, Alfredo, 525
Jachino, Carlo, 801
Jackson, William Henry, 376
Jacob, Max, 509
Jadassohn, Salomon, 142, 226
Jaguaribe Gomes de Matos, Héllo, 525
Jamaica Letter (1815), 264
James, Cyril Lionel Robert, 315, 525–526, 599
James, Henry, 808
Jan-Jan movement, 784
Jara, Heriberto, 902
Jara, Víctor, 526
Jaramillo, Juan, 622
Jaramillo Levi, Enrique, 526
Jáuregui, Agustín de, 526–527, 1004
Jauretche, Arturo M., 527
Jean-François, 599
Jentel, Francisco, 230
Jerez, Francisco de, 527
Jerez, Máximo, 357, 527–528, 701, 929
Jesus, Carolina María de, 528
Jesus, Clementina de, 308
Jijón, Modesto Larrea, 156
Jijón y Vivanco, Mercedes, 382
Jiménez, Enrique A., 470, 528
Jiménez, José Olivio, 385
Jiménez, Juan I., 70
Jiménez, Juan Ramón, 136, 222, 306, 385, 574
Jiménez, Marcos Pérez, 379, 1002
Jiménez, Mariano, 504
Jiménez de Quesada, Gonzalo, 129, 367, 528–529
Jiménez Oreamuno, Ricardo, 289, 529–530, 800
Jimeno y Planes, Rafael, 530
João, Prince, 217
João II, 276, 412
João III, 273, 412, 969
João IV, 17, 18, 1050, 1051
João VI, 218, 419–420, 779, 953, 956
Joaquim, Leandro, 388, 530
Joaquín, José, 685, 934
Joaquina, Carlota, 131
Jobim, Antônio Carlos, 291, 440, 530–531
Job Reyes, Enrique, 11
Jodorowsky, Alexandro, 368
Johann VI, 640
Johann VII, 640
John I (Portugal), 491
John Paul II (Pope), 914, 915, 949
Johnson, Lyndon Baines, 875
Joliver, André, 572
Jones Act (1917), 702
Jordán, López, 593–594
Jordan, Thomas, 852
Joseph, Francis, 641
Jovellanos, Salvador, 531, 865
Juana Inés de la Cruz, Sor, 460, 531–533
Juan Diego, 531

Juan Fernández Islands, 369
Juan y Santacilia, Jorge, 531, 1009
Juárez, Benito Pablo, 39, 79, 112, 175, 220, 251, 278, 322,
    462, 517, 533–535, 570–571, 571, 641, 650, 726, 830,
    844–845, 864, 889, 988, 1087, 1088, 1095
Juárez, José, 535, 880, 1058
Juárez, Ley, 1095
Juárez, Luis, 535
Juárez, Nicolás Rodríguez, 880
Juárez Celman, Miguel, 535–536, 669, 784, 837, 848, 1071,
    1080
Juàzeiro do Norte, 122–123
Judd, Donald, 525
Julião, Carlos, 536
Julião Arruda de Paula, Francisco, 536
Justiz, Beatriz de, 625
Justo, Juan B., 326, 537, 691
Justo, José Agustín Pedro, 536–537, 563, 638, 650, 750, 795,
    801, 906, 1014
Juventud, Ateneo de la, 361

K

Kagel, Mauricio Raúl, 539
Kahlo, Frida, 403, 539–540, 540, 730, 867, 1092
Kahlo, Guillermo, 539
Kalenberg, Angel, 996
Katz, Alex, 210
Katz, Kriedrich, 1053
Kearny, Stephen Watts, 40, 75, 1052
Keith, Minor, 989
Keller, Franz, 376
Kemmerer, Edwin W., 93, 752, 917
Kempeneer, Peter, 278
Kennedy, John F., 690, 875
Khrushchev, Nikita, 244
King, Emory, 1069
Kinney, Henry L., 540–541
Kino, Eusebio Francisco, 541
Kircher, Athanasius, 532
Klarén, Peter, 488
Klein, Jacques, 443
Klein, Julius, 728
Klossowski, Pierre, 808
Knox, Philander, 308, 565
Koellreutter, Hans Joachim, 541, 542, 717, 782, 936
Kolischer, Wilhelm, 971, 998
Korguyev, S., 376
Korn, Alejandro, 49, 541–542
Körner, Emil, 542
Korngold, Ralph, 265, 599–600
Kosice, Gyula, 66, 542
Kramer, Luis Gudiño, 473
Kraus, Karl Christian Friedrich, 124
Krause, Karl, 316
Krause, Martin, 78
Krauze, Enrique, 542
Krenek, Ernst, 252, 282

Krieger, Aldo, 542
Krieger, Armando, 415, 983
Krieger, Daniel, 236
Krieger, Edino, 542–543
Krieger, Gertrudes, 542
Krieger Vasena, Adalberto, 543
Kröpfl, Francisco, 637
Krug, Jorge, 621
Kubitschek, Márcia, 543
Kubitschek de Oliveira, Juscelino, 188, 235, 390, 400, 465, 543–545, 549, 599, 650, 714, 900, 984
Kumate Rodríguez, Jesús, 545
Kupia-Kumi Pact (1971), 7
Kutzinski, Vera, 478

L ————————————————————

Labarca Hubertson, Amanda, 547–548
Labastida, Jaime, 1092
Labastida, Archbishop, 641
Labastida y Dávalos, Pelagio Antonio de, 548
Labor Code (1972), 998
Labrador Ruíz, Enrique, 548
Lacalle Herrera, Luis Alberto, 498, 548–549, 758
Lacerda, Carlos Frederico Werneck de, 549
Lacerda, Maurício Paiva de, 549–550
Lacerda, Osvaldo, 550
La Cruzada de los Treinta y Tres, 743
Ladder Conspiracy (1844), 626, 678
Ladrón de Guevara, Diego, 550
La Espiga Amotinada, 1092
Lafaye, Frederico, 688
La Florida, 765–766
Lafontant, Roger, 74
Lafora, Nicolás de, 899
Lagasca, Pedro de, 1021
Lagos, Hilario, 35
Lagos, Ricardo, 550
Laguerre, Enrique Arturo, 550–551
La Hora del Pueblo, 100
La Huella, 792
Laleau, Léon, 551
La Libertadora Revolution (1901–1903), 474
Lam, Wilfredo, 574
La Madrid, Aráoz de, 840
Lamadrid, Gregorio Aráoz de, 551, 839
Lamar, Mirabeau Buonaparte, 551–552
Lamarque Pons, Jaurés, 552
Lambert, Lucien, 710
Lame, Manuel Quintín, 552
Lamennais, Hugh-Félicité-Robert, 146
Lampião, 552–553
Lamprecht, Karl, 837
Lamy, Jean-Baptiste, 634
Lam y Castilla, Wifredo, 551
Lancaster, James, 271
Landa, Diego de, 500, 553
Landaluze, Víctor Patricio de, 553
Landázuri Ricketts, Juan, 553–554

Landesio, Eugenio, 1040
Landívar, Rafael, 554
Land Law 200 (1936), 596
Lanusse, Alejandro Augusto, 199, 554, 572
Lanza, Alcides, 252, 415, 554–555, 803, 983, 1020
"La Onda," 10
La Pérouse, Jean François de, 634
La Piedad, 108
Laplante, Eduardo, 555
Laprida, Cayetano, 35
Laprida, Francisco Narciso de, 555
Lara, Agustín, 555
Lara, Pedro Juan de, 1024
Laredo Bru, Federico, 555
La Réforme, 600, 648
Lares, Grito de, 142
La Revista de América, 65
Larios, Felipe, 689
Larrave, Miguel, 497
Larrazábal, Juana María, 958–959
Larrazábal Ugueto, Wolfgang, 555–556
Larrea, Juan, 509, 556
Larreta, Enrique Rodríguez, 556
LaSalle, René-Robert Cavelier, Sieur de, 547
Las Casas, Bartolomé de, 47, 324, 556–559, 592, 681, 730, 754
Las Casas, Luis de, 60
Las Casas, Pedro de, 557
La Serna, José de, 547
Las Heras, Juan Gregorio de, 559, 920
Lasker, Emanuel, 206
Laso, Francisco, 559–560
Las Reformas Revolution (1835), 1033
Lassaga, Juan Lucas de, 1043
Lastarria, José Victorino, 560, 940
Lastiri, Raúl, 199
Lasuén, Fermín Francisco de, 560
Latorre, Lorenzo, 125, 499, 560–561, 979
Latorre, Roberto, 256
Latrille, Charles Fernand, 1087
La Trinitaria, 331–332, 648
Laugerud, Kjell, 601
Laugerud García, Eugenio Kjell, 561
Laurens, Jean-Paul, 97
Lautaro, 247, 561
Lavalle, Juan Gallo, 561–562, 1028
Lavalleja, Juan Antonio, 383, 562, 867
Lavalle Urbina, María, 562
Laveaux, Etienne, 599
Lavín, Carlos, 521, 568
Lavista, Mario, 562
Lavradio, Marquês do, 562–563
Law 4301, 860
Law of the Free Womb (1871), 521
Law Students Cultural Association, 361
League of Political Action, 121
Leal, Fernando, 563
Leante, César, 563–564

Leão, Carlos, 714
Leão, Honório Hermeto Carneiro, 861, 1016
Lebreton, Joaquim, 466
Le Bretón, Tomás Alberto, 563
Lechín Oquendo, Juan, 564
Leclerc, Charles Victor Emmanuel, 315, 564–565, 600, 799
Leconte, Michel Cincinnatus, 565
Le Corbusier, 714
Lecuona y Casado, Ernesto, 565
Ledo, Porfirio Muñoz, 213
Leduc, Paul, 565
Legagneur, Serge, 800
Léger, Ferdinand, 45, 268, 825
Léger, Georges, 551
Legión Paraguaya, 374
Leguía, Augusto Bernardino, 83, 130, 133, 135, 242, 489, 565–566, 666, 917, 925, 947, 1058
Leighton Guzmán, Bernardo, 566
Leinsdorf, Eric, 637
Leite da Fonseca, José Gomes, 642
Leiva, Ponciano, 157, 966
Lejarza, José Mariano Martínez, 786
Leloir, Luis F., 566–567
Leme, Sebastião, 195
Lemos, Sarah Gomes de, 543
Lemus, José María, 567
Lencinas, Carlos Wáshington, 567
Lencinas, José Néstor, 567
Lencinista Radical Civic Union, 567
Leñero, Vicente, 567–568
Leng, Alfonso de, 568
Leo XII (Pope), 744
Leo XIII (Pope), 721
Leocádia, Anita, 828
León, Alonso de, 568
León, Antonio, 533
León, Lope de, 266
León, Martín de, 309
León, Nicolás, 414
León, Nuevo, 508, 579
Léonard, Hubert, 917
León de la Barra, Francisco, 568, 614
Leongómez, Carlos Pizarro, 710
Leoni, Raúl, 143, 406, 569
León-Portilla, Miguel, 568–569, 730
Leopold I, 641
Leopoldina, Empress, 569–570
Le Parc, Julio, 196
Lepe, Diego de, 570, 807
Lerdo, Ley, 1095
Lerdo, Sebastián, 352
Lerdo de Tejada, Miguel, 278, 534, 570–571, 571, 727
Lerdo de Tejada, Sebastián, 121, 322, 517, 535, 571, 830, 857, 864, 892
Lerma, Hernando de, 71
Lescot, Élie, 468, 571, 619
Letelier del Solar, Orlando, 571–572
Letelier Madariaga, Valentín, 572, 613

Letelier Valdés, Miguel Francisco, 572
Letellier, Graciela, 514
Leuchtenberg, Amélia Augusta, 780
Levingston, Roberto Marcelo, 572, 738
Levinson, Luisa Mercedes, 572–573, 1022
Levy, Alexandre, 573
Lewis, Roberto, 249, 523, 573
Ley, Salvador, 573
Leyburn, James, 264, 315
Leyva Solano, Gabriel, 573–574
Lezama Lima, José, 67, 172, 574, 822, 939, 1063
Lezo, Blas de, 352
Lhote, André, 45
Liautaud, Georges, 574–575
Liberal Alliance, 349
Liberal Laws (1884), 373
Liberal Party, 612, 1060, 1072
Liberal revolts (1842), 765
LIberal Revolution (1860–1862), 589
Liberal Revolutionary Movement (MRL), 594–595
Liberation Theology movement, 480, 554, 576, 996
Libertad, Bayou de, 599
Liceaga, José María de, 634, 693, 879
Lichthart, Jan Corneliszoon, 640
Lida, Raimundo, 575
Liendo y Goicoechea, Antonio de, 671, 1024
Liendo y Goicoechea, José Antonio, 575
Liga de Escritores y Artistas Revolucionarios, 732
Liga Patriótica, 884
Ligeti, György, 562, 572
Lihn, Enrique, 575–576
Lima, Alceu Amoroso, 576
Lima, Brasilina Laurentina de, 280
Lima, Jorge de, 576
Lima, José Lezama, 341
Lima, José María, 497
Lima, Pedro de Araújo, 576–577, 1036
Lima Barreto, Afonso Henriques de, 577
Lima e Silva, Francisco de, 577
Lima e Silva, Luís Alves de, 577–578
Limantour, José Yves, 112, 294, 323, 578–579
Limits, Treaty of (1750), 721
Linares, David, 579
Linares, José María, 579, 687
Linares, Leonardo, 579
Linares, Pedro, 579
Linares, Ricardo, 579
Linares Alcántara, Francisco, 485, 579
Linck, Wenceslaus, 870
Lincoln, Abraham, 435
Lindley López, Nicolás, 580
Lindo, Joaquín Fernández, 580
Lindo Zelaya, Juan, 580
Liniers, Santiago de, 474, 694
Liniers y Bremond, Santiago de, 42, 345, 580, 943
Lins, Osman da Costa, 580–581
Lins Do Rego, José, 581–582
Lisbôa, Antônio Francisco, 21

Lisboa, Joaquim Marques, 582
Lisbôa, Manuel Francisco, 21
Liscano Velutini, Juan, 147, 582–583
Lispector, Clarice, 583–584
List 99, 659–660
Littéraire, Haïti, 800
Little War (1878–1880), 419
Liverpool, Lord, 577
Livingston Codes, 410
Lizardo, Antón, incident, 534
Lleras, Lorenzo María, 584
Lleras Camargo, Alberto, 584, 1022
Lleras Restrepo, Carlos, 404, 584, 771
Llerena, Juan de, 266
Llorens Torres, Luis, 585
Llorente y Lafuente, Anselmo, 585, 685
Llosa, Mario Vargas, 20, 882
Loaysa, Francisco García de, 630
Lobo, Manuel, 431
Locke, John, 183, 606
Lockhart, James, 811
Loizaga, Carlos, 865
L'Olonnais, Francis, 585
Lombardo Toledano, Vicente, 121, 212, 232, 453, 585–586
Lombroso, Cesare, 865
Lonardi, Eduardo, 59, 586, 883
Longinos Martínez, José, 586
López, Ambrosio, 586
López, Carlos Antonio, 34, 135, 138, 363, 374, 436, 441, 587, 588, 606, 786, 980, 988, 1073
López, Enrique Solano, 587
López, Estanislao, 82, 587–588, 844, 867, 922
López, Esteban, 7
López, Felipe Molas, 259, 980
López, Francisco Solano, 135, 138, 139, 181–182, 249, 310, 320, 351, 355, 363, 374, 383, 436, 444, 587, 588, 619, 669, 764, 786, 872, 988, 1014
López, Jerónimo, 586
López, José Hilario, 63, 219, 496, 499, 589, 703
López, José María, 649
López, Marshal, 734
López, Narciso, 589–590, 1060
López, Solano, 606, 669
López, Vicente Fidel, 590
López, Wilebaldo, 590
Lopez, Vicente Fidel, 82
López Arellano, Oswaldo, 298, 590, 875, 1061
López Buchardo, Carlos, 590–591
López Capillas, Francisco, 591
López Contreras, Eleázar, 569, 591–592, 644, 791
López de Arteaga, Sebastián, 592
López de Cerrato, Alonso, 592
López de Cogolludo, Diego, 592
López de Gómara, Francisco, 484
López de Legazpi, Miguel, 1011
López de Legazpi y Gurruchátegui, Miguel, 592
López de Osorio, María Antonieta, 1059
López de Quiroga, Antonio, 592–593

López de Romaña, Eduardo, 593
López Jordán, Ricardo, 35, 200, 493, 593–594, 1014
López Mateos, Adolfo, 325, 594, 1077
López Michelsen, Alfonso, 594–595
López Portillo, José, 340, 595–596, 617, 702, 751
López Pumarejo, Alfonso, 451, 584, 586, 594, 596, 936
López Pumarejo, José, 584
López Rayón, Ignacio, 290
López Rega, José, 596
López Trujillo, Alfonso, 596
López Vallecillos, Italo, 596–597
López Velarde, Ramón, 597
López y Fuentes, Gregorio, 597
López y Planes, Vicente, 35, 590, 1014
Lorca, Federico García, 111, 176, 201, 219–220, 666, 779, 972
Lorenzana, Manuel de, 152
Lorenzana y Buitrón, Francisco Antonio de, 597
Lorenzo Troya, Victoriano, 597–598
Loriod, 554
Losada, Diego de, 598
Los Guadalupes, 1048
Lothe, André, 121, 140
Lott, Henrique Batista Duffles Teixeira, 188, 598–599
Louis XVI, 919
L'Ouverture, Toussaint, 164, 265, 315, 564, 599–600, 799, 861, 875, 965
Lowell, Amy, 209
Lowie, Robert, 716
Lozada, Manuel, 284, 600
Lozano, Pedro, 600–601
Lozano, Raúl Salinas, 915
Lozano Díaz, Julio, 409, 601
Lozza, Raúl, 601
Lucas García, Fernando Romeo, 561, 601, 862, 1057
Luco, Ramón Barros, 381
Luftalla, Silvia, 623
Lugones, Leopoldo, 86, 437, 556, 597, 601–602, 606
Luís, Afonso, 271
Luís, Washington, 1031
Luisi, Clotilde, 603
Luisi, Luisa, 602–603
Luisi, Paulina, 603
Luís Pereira de Sousa, Washington, 602
Lumbroso, Joseph, 229
Luna, Carlos Correa, 356
Luna, Tristán de, 1041
Luna, Enfraín González, 111
Luna Pizarro, Francisco Javier de, 603
Luna y Arellano, Tristán de, 603
Luperón, Gregorio, 352, 501, 603–604
Luque, Hernando de, 31, 604, 809
Lusinchi, Jaime, 604
Lusotropicalism, 394–395
Lutz, Adolfo, 604
Lutz, Bertha María Julia, 604–605
Lutzenberger, José Antônio, 605–606
Luz, Carlos, 390

Luz y Caballero, José de la, 606
Lyall Plan, 777
Lybbert, Donald, 1020
Lynch, B. Suárez, 146
Lynch, Benito, 20, 606
Lynch, John, 897
Lynch, Marta, 607
Lynch, Elisa Alicia, 587, 588, 606–607
Lyra, Carlos, 440

M ————————————————————————
M-19 Party, 453
MacCann, William, 897
Macchiaioli, 302
Macció, Rómulo, 609
Macedo, Joaquim Manuel de, 609
Macedo, Miguel, 112
Macedo, Pablo, 112
Mac Entyre, Eduardo, 609
Maceo, Antonio, 609–610
Machado, Antonio, 306, 779
Machado, Gerardo, 76, 123, 262, 467, 623, 628, 786, 831,
    878, 1035
Machado, Gustavo, 610–611
Machado, Manuel, 306
Machado, Pinheiro, 161
Machado de Assis, Joaquim María, 577, 611–612, 890
Machado y Morales, Gerardo, 254, 450, 612–613
Maciel, António Vicente Mendes, 280–281
Maciel, José Álvares, 956
Mac-Iver Rodríguez, Enrique, 613
Madden, Richard, 625
Madeira, Eduardo, 710
Madeira-Mamoré Railroad, 365
Madero, Evaristo, 614
Madero, Francisco, 220, 323, 361, 480, 568, 574, 686, 701,
    725, 1084
Madero, Rafael Hernández, 112
Madero, Francisco Indalecio, 613–616
Madious, Thomas, 315
Madrazo, Carlos A., 325, 616
Madrid, Treaty of (1750), 8, 51
Madrid Hurtado, Miguel de la, 595, 616–617, 915, 916
Madureira, Antônio de Sena, 617
Maestre, Julián Rivera, 870
Maetzu, Ramiro de, 65
Magalhães, Antonio Carlos, 658
Magalhães, Domingos José Gonçalves de, 617–618, 786
Magalhães, Juracy, 236
Magaña, Gildardo, 1086
Magaña, Sergio, 618
Magdaleno, Mauricio, 618
Magellan, Ferdinand, 344, 369, 386, 419, 618, 1047
Maggi, Carlos, 843
Magloire, Paul Eugène, 170, 336, 619
Magritte, René, 820
Maíz, Fidel, 619
Majano, Adolfo Arnoldo, 619–620

Majluta, Jacobo, 787
Malaspina, Alejandro, 620
Maldonado, Alonso del Castillo, 184, 355
Maldonado, Francisco Severo, 620
Maldonado, Juan Álvarez, 421
Maldonado, Rodrigo de Arias, 144, 620
Maldonado, Tomás, 66
Malé, Belkis Cuza, 758
Malespín, Francisco, 64, 183, 376, 620–621, 929, 1063
Malfatti, Anita Catarina, 45, 621
Malfatti, Paulistas Anita, 316
Malinche, 621–622
Malipiero, Gian Francesco, 317
Mallarino, Manuel María, 505
Mallarmé, Stéphane, 953
Mallea, Eduardo, 622–623, 727
Malta, Aguilera, 8
Malta, Rosane, 274
Maluf, Maria Estefano, 623
Maluf, Paulo Salim, 623
Maluf, Salim Farah, 623
Malvinas Islands, 407
Mama Ocllo, 623
Mañach y Robato, Jorge, 623
Manco Capac, 623, 1021
Manco Inca, 623–624, 812
Mandu Ladino, 624
Mango Inca, 1003
Manifesto of Monte Christi, 454
Mann, Horace, 940, 1028
Mann, Mary Peabody, 940–941
Mann, Thomas, 808
Mano Blanca, 60, 654
Manoilesco, Mihail, 44
Manosalvas, Juan, 806
Mañozca, Juan de, 695
Manrique de Zúñiga, Alvaro, 624
Mansilla, Lucio Victorio, 469, 624–625
Manso de Maldonado, Antonio, 625
Manso de Velasco, José Antonio, 625
Mantuan War (1628–1631), 735
Manuel I, 412, 1047
Manuilski, Dmitri, 827
Manzano, Juan Francisco, 625–626
Manzano, Toribio, 625
Mar, José de la, 413, 626
Marcgraf, Georg, 640
Marchot, Alfred, 943
Marcó del Pont, Francisco, 920, 921
Marcy, William L., 249
Marechal, Leopoldo, 626
Margaretha, 640
Margarita Island, 363
Margil de Jesús, Antonio, 626
Maria, Ángela, 248
María Cristina, 589
María de Alvear, Carlos, 556
María de Alvear, Larrea, 556

María II (Queen of Portugal), 218, 570
María Isabel (Princess of Spain), 987
María Luisa (Queen of Spain), 217
Mariana Granjales Platoon, 926
Marianello, Juan, 220
Mariátegui, José Carlos, 129, 242, 311, 480, 489, 626–627, 666, 908
Mariel Boatlift, 67, 1023
Marighela, Carlos, 627
Marília, 455
Marín, Luis Muñoz, 136
Marinello, Juan, 627–628
Mariño, Santiago, 107, 628
Mariscal, Ignacio, 889
Marisol, 628
Maritime Workers Federation, 447
Mariz, Pedro de, 968
Markham, Catherine, 629
Markham, Clements Robert, 629
Markham, David F., 629
Mármol, José Pedro Crisólogo, 18, 629
Mármol, Miguel, 632
Maroto, Rafael, 920
Marqués, René, 629–630
Márquez, Gabriel García, 402, 844, 882
Márquez, José Ignacio de, 218, 630
Márquez, Leonardo, 630, 641, 664, 727
Married Woman's Statute, 642
Marroquín, Francisco, 300, 630–631
Marroquín, José Manuel, 279, 631, 752
Marruz, Fina García, 1064
Marsh, Reginald, 981
Marshall, Frank J., 206
Marshall, George, 402
Martí, Agustín Farabundo, 631–632
Martí, José, 102, 230, 252, 306, 359, 449, 454, 623, 628, 631, 831, 844, 875, 1035, 1064
Martin, Ellen Galt, 1068
Martin, Gerald, 84
Martínez, Alfredo Ramos, 563
Martínez, Ángel, 189
Martínez, Antonio José, 261, 634
Martínez, Arévalo, 68
Martínez, Benita, 941
Martínez, Coronel Pascual, 73
Martínez, Esteban José, 634
Martínez, Hernández, 232
Martínez, Juan José, 634
Martínez, Marina, 414
Martínez, Rafael Trujillo, 1002
Martínez, Tomás, 528, 634
Martínez Corbalá, Gonzalo, 916
Martínez de Hoz, José Alfredo, 635
Martínez de Irala, Domingo, 3
Martinó, José A. Torres, 506
Martins, Gaspar da Silveira, 913
Martins, Wilson, 735
Martí y Pérez, José, 68

Martí y Pérez, José Julián, 632–633
Martorell, Antonio, 635
Martos, Marco, 446
Masferrer, Alberto, 61, 166, 635–636, 913
Masi, Romeo, 361
Masó, Bartolomé, 253
Massacre de Yáñez, 4
Massenet, Jules, 917
Massera, José Pedro, 636
Masson, Ernst, 802
Mastrogiovanni, Antonio, 636–637
Mata, Eduardo, 487, 562, 637
Matamoros y Guridi, Mariano, 637, 693, 745, 895
Mateos, Adolfo López, 1036
Matheu, Rosa Ascásubi, 425
Mathew, George W., 311
Mathias, Georges, 1072
Matienzo, Benjamín, 637
Matienzo, José Nicolás, 637–638, 865
Matos, Gregório de, 638, 735
Matos, Hubert, 245
Matos, Juan Francisco Torres, 580
Matta, Manuel Antonio, 407
Matta Echaurren, Roberto Sebastián Antonio, 638
Matto de Turner, Clorinda, 113, 638–639, 1094–1095
Mauá, Visconde de, 639–640
Maurits, Johan, 640–641
Maurras, Charles, 944
Maximilian, 33, 352, 571, 630, 641–642, 664, 746, 959
May Association, 13
Mayer de Zulen, Dora, 207, 1095
Mayorga, Silvio, 159, 642
May Pacts, 860
May Revolution (1810), 232
Maytorena, José M., 194
Maza, Antonia, 34, 35
Maza, Manuel Vicente de, 35, 642
Maza, Margarita, 533
McCloy, Shelby, 600
McDonald, James P., 956
McKinley, William, 507
McLane, Robert M., 534
McLane-Ocampo Treaty (1859), 534, 726
McLeod, Hugh, 75
Medaglia, Júlio, 652, 735
Medeiros da Fonseca, Arnoldo, 642
Medeiros da Fonseca, Romy Martins, 642
Medellín Cartel, 404
Médici, Emílio Garrastazú, 292, 446, 642–643, 771
Medici, Lorenzo di Pier Francesco de, 1047
Medicina, Faculdade de, 44
Medina, Antonio, 89
Medina, Elvira, 836
Medina, Hugo, 643
Medina, José María, 966
Medina, José Toribio, 643–644
Medina Angarita, Isaías, 644, 793
Medina y Escalada, Manuel, 920

Mee, Margaret, 662
Meiggs, Henry, 105
Meireles, Cecília, 644–645
Meireles de Lima, Vítor, 32, 46, 331, 645
Mejía, Marcelino, 966–967
Mejía, Ramos, 848
Mejía, Tomás, 645, 664
Mejía del Valle y Llequerica, José Joaquín, 645
Mejía Victores, Oscar Humberto, 645–646, 863
Melani, Pietro, 882
Melé, Juan N., 646
Meléndez, Jorge, 646
Meléndez Chavetti, Carlos, 646, 837
Meléndez Doctrine, 646
Meléndez Family, 646–647
Melgarejo, Mariano, 4, 59, 308, 647, 687
Melgares, Facundo, 647–648
Mella, Duarte, 934
Mella, Julio Antonio, 648
Mella, Ramón Matías, 331, 648, 934
Mello, Arnon de, 274
Mello, Auzélia Cardoso de, 649
Mello, Zélia María Cardoso de, 649
Melo, Custódio José de, 649, 783
Melo, Euridice Ferreira de, 954
Melo, Gastón, 1094
Melo, José de, 913
Melo, José María, 63, 496, 586, 649–650, 698, 723
Melo, Juan Vicente, 808
Melo, Leopoldo, 650
Melo e Castro, Martinho de, 293, 650
Melo Franco, Afonso Arinos de, 650–651, 969
Melo Franco, Afrânio de, 650, 651, 692
Melo Franco, Virgílio de, 44
Melo Franco, Virgílio Martins de Melo Franco, 650
Melo Maldonado, Diego de, 15
Melo Neto, João Cabral de, 651
Melo Revolt (1854), 589
Melville, Margarita (Marjorie), 651–652
Melville, Thomas, 651–652
Mena, Juan de, 56
Mena, Luis, 258, 319
Menchú, Vicente, 652
Menchú Tum, Rigoberta, 652
Mencos, Martín Carlos, 516
Mendaña, Álvaro de, 421
Mendes, Gilberto, 652, 735
Mendes Filho, Francisco "Chico" Alves, 652–653
Méndez, Julio César, 60
Méndez, Miguel A. García, 374
Méndez Ballester, Manuel, 653
Méndez Fleitas, Epifanio, 653
Méndez Montenegro, Julio César, 85, 653–654, 789, 1005
Méndez Montenegro, Mario, 654, 1057
Méndez Pereira, Octavio, 654
Mendiburu, Manuel de, 654–655
Mendieta, Salvador, 655
Mendinueta y Múzquiz, Pedro de, 655–656

Mendive, Rafael María, 632
Mendonça, Luisa Antônia de, 230
Mendonça, Newton, 530
Mendonça Furtado, Diogo de, 17
Mendoza, Antonio de, 38, 516, 558, 592, 656, 1038, 1096
Mendoza, Carlos Antonio, 77, 656, 817
Mendoza, Cristóbal, 1077
Mendoza, Diego, 1058
Mendoza, Palafox y, 481
Mendoza, Pedro de, 92, 656
Mendoza Caamaño y Sotomayor, José Antonio de, 657
Mendoza y Luna, Juan Manuel de, 657
Menem, Carlos Saúl, 27, 657
Menéndez, Andrés I., 10
Menéndez de Avilés, Pedro, 657–658
Menininha do Gantois, Mãe, 658
Mennin, Peter, 543
Menocal, Ancieto G., 658
Menocal, Mario García, 658, 1035
Menton, Seymour, 689
Mercado, Alberto Vázquez del, 585
Mercier, Louis-Sébastien, 490
Mérida, Carlos, 658–659
Meriño, Fernando Arturo de, 501, 604
Merino Castro, José Toribio, 659
Merton, Thomas, 209
Mesquita, Henrique Alves de, 455
Mesquita, Jeronyma, 642
Messervy, William, 40
Messía de la Cerda, Pedro de, 659, 703, 960–961
Messiaen, 554
Mexican-American War, 946
Mexican Communist Party (PCM), 212
Mexican Federation of Labor (CTM), 212, 585, 1043
Mexican Regional Labor Confederation (CROM), 222
Mexican Revolution (1910–1920), 1084
Mexican Society of Landscape Architects, 111
Mexican War of Independence, 946
Meyer-Eppler, Werner, 46, 539
Miahuaxihuitl, 699
Michalski, Cado, 362
Michelet, Jules, 146
Michelina, Rafael, 660
Michelina, Santos, 659
Michelini, Zelmar, 659–660
Micrópera de Mexico, 18
Mier, Fray Servando Teresa de, 662
Mier y Terán, Manuel, 660–661
Mignone, Francisco, 661
Miguel, Lorenzo, 1026
Milhaud, Darius, 292, 543, 998, 1055
Militar, Colegio, 941
Military Question, 387
Milk Industry Workers Union, 1043
Milla, José, 450
Milla, Justo, 661
Milla, Santiago, 661
Millas Jiménez, Jorge, 662

Milla y Vidaurre, José, 661–662
Milmo, Laura, 94
Mina, Francisco Javier, 939
Minardi, Tommaso, 268
Minas Conspiracy (1788–1789), 650
Minas Gerais, 602, 692, 709
Mina y Larrea, Javier, 662
Mindlin, Ephim Henrique, 662
Mindlin, Fanny, 662
Mindlin, Guita Kaufman, 662
Mindlin, José E., 662–663
Minujin, Marta, 663
Mir, Pedro, 663
Miramón, Miguel, 352, 641, 663–664
Miranda, Carmen, 248, 664
Miranda, Francisco de, 153, 197, 664–666, 731, 858, 919
Miró, César, 666
Miró Cardona, José, 666
Miró Quesada, José Antonio, 666
Miró Quesada de la Guerra, Antonio, 666
Miró Quesada de la Guerra, Luis, 666
Miró Quesada Family, 666
Miró Quesada Garland, Alejandro, 666
Miró Quesada Sosa, Aurelio, 666
Miry, Paul, 943
Missionary Council to Indigenous Peoples, 230
Mission San Antonio de Valero (the Alamo), 12
Mission San Diego de Alcalá, 948
Mistral, Gabriela, 65, 187–188, 513, 574, 575, 666–667, 928, 972
Mitre, Bartolomé, 14, 23, 35, 36, 82, 87, 161, 200, 203, 380, 383, 436, 448, 493, 590, 668–669, 752, 788, 824, 850, 872, 892, 910, 922, 941, 1014, 1044, 1080
Mitropoulos, Dimitri, 282
MNR de Izquierda (MNRI), 952
Mochi, Giovanni, 97
Moctezuma, Isabel, 299
Modotti, Tina, 540
Modyford, Thomas, 695
Moffitt, Ronni, 572
Mogrovejo, Toribio Alfonso de, 669–670
Mojica, José de Jesús, 670
Molina, Arturo Armando, 332, 670, 887
Molina, Enrique, 729
Molina, Juan Ramón, 670–671
Molina, Marcelo, 671
Molina, Pedro, 64, 120, 128, 312, 671–672, 869
Molina Bedoya, Felipe, 672
Molina Enríquez, Andrés, 672
Molina Garmendia, Enrique, 662, 672–673
Molinari, Ricardo E., 674
Molina Solís, Olegario, 673
Molina Ureña, José Rafael, 673–674
Molony, Guy, 264, 674
Mompox de Zayas, Fernando, 674
Monagas, José Gregorio, 628, 675
Monagas, José Tadeo, 240, 457, 483, 485, 675, 760, 839, 884, 993

MONARCA (Rafael Callejas National Renovation Movement), 193
Moncada, José María, 258, 319, 675–676, 928
Moncayo García, José Pablo, 676
Moncayo y Esparsa, Pedro, 871
Mondragón, Manuel, 615
Monegal, Emir Rodríguez, 186, 837, 939
Monge, Carlos Francisco, 12
Monge, Joaquín García, 327
Monge Álvarez, Luis Alberto, 73, 676
Moniz, Felipa, 275
Monroe Doctrine, 157, 203
Monsiváis, Carlos, 676–677
Montalvo, Juan, 425, 677
Montalvo y Ambulodi Arriola y Casabente Valdespino, Francisco, 677
Montaño, Otilio, 1086
Monte, Domingo del, 677–678
Monteagudo, Bernardo de, 678, 922
Monte Alegre, José da Costa Carvalho, Marquis de, 678
Montealegre Fernández, José María, 678, 685
Monteau, Pierre, 948
Monte de Piedad, 891
Monteiro, Pedro Aurélio de Góis, 678–679
Monteiro, Tobias do Rêgo, 679
Monteiro Lobato, José Bento, 679
Montejo, Francisco de, 38, 680
Montejo y León, Franciso, 680
Montenegro, Carlos, 777
Montenegro, Juan de, 30
Montenegro, Roberto, 475, 965
Montenegro y Nervo, Roberto, 680
Montero, Adelina Pérez, 356
Montero Rodríguez, Juan Esteban, 24
Monterroso, Augusto, 680
Montes, Avelino, 673
Montes, César, 680–681
Montes, Ismael, 681, 1060
Montes de Oca, Confucio, 681
Montes de Oca, Zoroastro, 681
Montesinos, Antonio de, 681
Monteverde, Juan Domingo, 665
Montiel y Duarte, Julián, 789
Montilla, Ricardo, 855
Montoro, André Franco, 649
Montt, Efrain Ríos, 645
Montt, Manuel, 106, 118, 407, 793, 940, 1027
Montt, Pedro, 341
Montt, Ríos, 645
Montt Álvarez, Jorge, 681–682
Montt Torres, Manuel, 682
Montúfar, Lorenzo, 682–683
Montúfar, Manuel, 120
Montúfar Montes de Oca, Lorenzo, 683
Montúfar y Coronado, Manuel, 682, 683
Montúfar y Coronado, Rafael, 682
Montúfar y Larrea, Juan Pío de, 683
Mon y Velarde, Juan Antonio, 675

Moog, Clodomiro Vianna, 683
Mora, Fernando de la, 684
Mora, José Joaquín de, 806
Mora, José María Luis, 452, 684
Mora, Juan Rafael, 225, 585
Moraes, Vinícius de, 440, 530
Mora Fernández, Juan, 684–685
Morais, Vinícius de, 687
Morais Barros, Prudente José de, 687
Morales, Agustín, 59, 687–688
Morales, Andrés, 754
Morales, Armando, 688
Morales, Beltrán, 688
Morales, Carlos, 188
Morales, Cristóbal de, 372
Morales, Eusebio A., 688
Morales, Francisco de, 790
Morales, Francisco Tomás, 688
Morales, Mario Roberto, 688–689
Morales, Melesio, 226, 689
Morales, Ramiro Condarco, 64
Morales, Ramón Villeda, 1072
Morales Bermúdez, Remigio, 689
Morales Bermúdez Cerruti, Francisco, 689, 1041
Morales Carrión, Arturo, 690
Morales Lemus, José, 690
Moran, Jaime Cerdas, 686
Mora Otero, José Antonio, 685
Mora Porrás, Juan Rafael, 202, 678, 685–686
Mora Valverde, Manuel, 686
Moravia, Charles, 197
Mora y Del Río, José, 686
Morazán, Francisco, 64, 91, 115, 120, 126, 127, 137, 183,
    224, 226, 231, 375, 620, 661, 672, 690–691, 868, 869,
    1025
Morcillo, Diego, 75
Moreas, Jean, 306
Moreau de Justo, Alicia, 603, 691–692
Moreira, Juan, 142
Moreira da Costa Ribeiro, Delfim, 692
Morejón, Felipe, 692
Morejón, Nancy, 478, 692
Morelos y Pavón, José María, 32, 39, 168, 192, 404, 474, 637,
    660, 662, 692–694, 850, 895, 939
Moreno, Carlos Guevara, 80
Moreno, Fulgencio, 694
Moreno, García, 677, 1040
Moreno, Lucas, 593
Moreno, Manuel, 919
Moreno, Mariano, 556, 694–695, 770, 906, 919
Morente, Manuel García, 416
Morgan, Henry, 695–696, 950
Morgan, John Pierpont, 97
Morga Sánchez Garay y López, Antonio de, 695
Morillo y Morillo, Pablo, 170, 677, 696, 733, 994
Morínigo, Higínio, 169, 215, 259, 391, 696–697, 972, 1079
Morisseau, Roland, 800
Morones, Luis, 697

Morphy, Paul, 206
Morris, Robert, 525
Morse, Wayne, 405
Moscoso y Peralta, Juan Manuel, 1004
Moscote, José Dolores, 697–698
Moshinsky Borodianksky, Marcos, 698
Mosquera, Manuel José, 496, 589, 698
Mosquera, Tomás Cipriano de, 63, 219, 283, 457, 495, 496,
    498, 586, 589, 649, 698–699, 723, 1001, 1086
Mosquera y Arboleda, Joaquín, 699
Mota, Edson, 951
Motecuhzoma, 89, 810, 993
Motecuhzoma I, 523, 699
Motecuhzoma II, 288, 301, 699–700, 714, 734
Motolinía, Toribio de, 700, 730
Moura, Emílio, 51
Movement for a People's Government, 659–660
Movement for Integration and Development, 395
Movement of the Revolutionary Left (MIR), 106, 778
Movimiento Chileno de Partidarios de la Paz, 814
Movimiento Cívico Democrático Nacional (MCDN), 813
Movimiento de Acción Popular Unitaria (MAPU), 992
Movimiento de Conciliación Nacional (MCN), 422
Movimiento de Intransigencia y Renovación (MIR) (1945),
    99
Movimiento de Liberación Nacional, 213
Movimiento Nacionalista Revolucionario (MNR), 473, 476,
    564, 762, 777–778, 925, 952. 1015, 995, 1058
Movimiento Popular Colorado (MOPOCO), 653
Movimiento Pro-Emancipación de la Mujer Chilena
    (MEMCH), 814, 1045
Movimiento Social Cristiano (MSC), 816
Moya de Contreras, Pedro, 460, 700
Moyse Rebellion (1801), 265
Moziño, José Mariano, 700–701
Mucchi, Anton, 302
Múgica, Francisco José, 701
Muguerza, Consuelo Sada, 432
Muguerza, José A., 432
Mujeres de Chile, 547
Mujica, Tomás, 552, 998
Munguía, Clemente de Jesús, 701
Muñiz de Pineda, Juana, 516
Muñoz, José Trinidad, 701–702, 929
Muñoz, Rafael F., 96
Muñoz Ledo Lazo de la Vega, Porfirio, 616, 702, 916
Muñoz Marín, Luis, 16, 374, 702
Muñoz Rivera, Luis, 702
Muñoz-Vernaza-Suarez Treaty (1916), 107
Muñoz y Capurón, Luis Javier, 898
Munro, Dana G., 358
Murillo, Bartolomé, 880
Murillo Toro, Manuel, 496, 702–703
Muró, Antonio, 575
Muro, José Fernández, 467
Murphy, Gerald, 405
Murtinho, Joaquim Duarte, 703
Museo de Antigüedades e Historia Nacional, 11

Museo del Automovilismo Juan Manuel Fangio, 364
Musical Indianism, 522
Música Popular Brasileira, 651
Música Viva group, 782
Mutis, Alvaro, 703
Mutis, José Celestino, 189, 659, 703–704
Muybridge, Eadweard, 376

N

Nabokov, Nicholas, 351
Nabuco, Joaquim, 412, 861
Nabuco de Araújo, Joaquim, 705
Nabuco de Araújo, José Tomás, 705
Naipaul, V. S., 705
National Liberation Party (PLN), 676
Najera, José, 1088
Nájera, Maria Micaela Aycinena, 774
Nalé Roxlo, Conrado, 705–706
Namuncurá, Ceferino, 706
Namuncurá, Manuel, 706
Naón, Rómulo S., 706
Napoleon Bonaparte, 153, 523, 564, 823
Napoleon III, 33, 641, 642
Naranjo, Carmen, 706–707
Nardone, Benito, 707
Nariño, Antonio, 353, 707–708, 933
Narváez, Aurelio Mosquera, 80
Narváez, Pánfilo de, 288, 467, 557, 700, 708
Nascimento, Abdias do, 708
Nascimento, João Ramos do, 784
Nascimento, Milton, 308, 455, 708–709
National Academy of History, 884
National Action Party (PAN), 212, 453, 915
National Association of Composers, 46
National Association of Honduran Peasants (ANACH), 218
National Autonomist Party (PAN), 1013
National Autonomous University of Mexico (UNAM), 1089
National Bank, 182
National Campesino Federation (CNC), 212
National Cancer Institute, 107
National Civic Union (UCN), 23
National Coalition, 133
National Coffee Growers Federation of Colombia, 1020
National Conciliation Party (PCN), 869, 926
National Confederation of Guatemalan Campesinos (CNCG), 62
National Confederation of Workers in Industry (CNTI), 784, 858
National Conference of Brazilian Bishops (CNBB), 196
National Conservatory of Music, 345, 403, 440
National Council of Administration, 172–173
National Council of Brazilian Women (CNMB), 642
National Council of Production, 379
National Council of Rubber Tappers (CNS), 653
National Council on Culture, 220
National Cultural Commission, 440
National Democratic Movement, 238
National Democratic parties, 804

National Democratic Party, 115
National Democratic Union (UDN), 384, 447, 544, 835, 943
National Economic Development Bank, 201
National Federation of Printing Workers, 784
National Front, 451
National Herrerist Council, 548
National Independent Convention of Anti-Reelectionist Parties, 804
National Indian Foundation (FUNAI), 892
National Intelligence Agency (SNI), 378
Nationalist Democratic Action, 106, 778, 925
Nationalist Popular Front, 105
Nationalist Republican Alliance, 307
Nationalist Revolutionary Movement, 473, 476, 564, 762, 777–778, 925, 952, 1015
National Law School, 182
National Liberation Movement, 238, 721, 947
National Liberation Party (PLN), 207, 361, 362, 378, 379, 721, 729, 743, 871, 963, 964, 999
National Movement, 396
National Music Committee, 66
National Music Society, 151
National Opposition Union (Unión Nacional Opositora-UNO), 6, 117, 871
National Peasants' Association for Land, 443
National Popular Alliance (ANAPO), 885
National Reformist Movement, 1072
National Renovating Alliance (ARENA), 274, 643
National Revolutionary Movement, 82, 105–106, 113, 1010
National Salvation Movement, 453
National Sinarquista Union (UNS), 212
Nationalsozialistische Deutsche Arbeiter-Partei, 370
National Student Federation (FUB), 82
National Student Union (Unión Nacional Estudiantil), 189
National Union of Cuban Writers and Artists (UNEAC), 574
National Union of Farmers and Cattlemen, 1070
National Union of Popular Action and Justice (UNAP), 257
National Union Party (PUN), 1009
National Unity Front (FUN), 789
National War, 634
Nationa Union of Popular Action, 296
Nation's Right, 1058
Navarra y Rocaful, Melchor de, 709
Navarro, Martín Antonio (Félix), 709–710
Navarro Wolf, Antonio, 434, 710
Nazareth, Ernesto, 710
Nazareth, María Julia da Conceição, 658
Nazareth, Vasco Lourenzo da Silva, 710
Negra, Guarda, 773
Negret, Edgar, 466
Negrete, Jorge, 710
Negrista Movement, 478
Nepomuceno, Alberto, 710–711
Neruda, Pablo, 127, 222, 320, 513, 540, 666, 711–712, 761, 769, 882, 885
Nervo, Amado, 712–713
Neto, João Cabral de Melo, 173
Neto, Torquato, 438, 1044

Neukomm, Sigismund, 309, 953
Neve, Felipe de, 713
Neves, Risoleta Tolentino, 713
Neves, Tancredo de Almeida, 390, 623, 713, 943
New Brazil plan, 649
New Chilean Song movement, 526, 769
New Economic Policy (NPE), 778
New Figuration Group, 1039
New Liberalism movement, 404
New Mexico's Revolution (1837), 1052
New Nicaragua Movement, 387, 642
New Progressive Party (PNP), 374
Nezahualcoyotl, 523, 713–714
Nezahualpilli, 714, 993
Nicaraguan Democratic Forces, 139, 179, 771
Nicaraguan Opposition Union (UNO), 748, 1071
Nicaraguan Patriotic Youth organization, 747
Nicaraguan Socialist Party, 901
Nicuesa, Diego de, 100, 714
Niemeyer Soares Filho, Oscar, 196, 291, 544, 714–715
Nieto, Andrés F. Córdova, 174
Nieto, Martín, 946
Nikisch, Arthur, 226
Nilsson, Leopoldo Torre, 477
Nimuendajú, Curt, 715–716
Ninan Cuyochi, 508
Niño, Pedro Alonso, 716
Nixon, Richard, 1046
Niza, Marcos de, 716
Noboa y Arteta, Diego, 716
Nobre, Manuel Antônio Ferreira, 280
Nobre, Marlos, 717
Nóbrega, Manuel da, 48, 717, 969
Noé, Luis Felipe, 717–718
Noguchi, Isamu, 540
Nono, Luigi, 172
Nootka Sound Convention, 15
Nord, Pierre Alexis, 718, 956
Noriega Moreno, Manuel Antonio, 70, 72, 718–719
Noronha, Fernão de, 719
Noronha, Juana Manso de, 941
North, John Thomas, 103
Northeastern Generation (1930), 581
Nova Arcádia literary club, 108
Novais, Faustino Xavier de, 611
Novás Calvo, Lino, 719
Novo, Salvador, 719–720
Novoa, Alberto Ruiz, 1022
Nuclear Arms Treaty of Tlatelolco, 427
Núcleo Bernardelli, 951
Nufio, José Dolores, 720
Núñez, Carlos, 1070
Núñez, Rafael, 219, 887, 1001, 1083, 1086
Núñez, Roberto, 112
Núñez Moledo, Rafael, 720
Núñez Vargas, Benjamin, 720–721
Núñez Vela, Blasco, 129, 432, 721, 750, 811, 1019
Nusdorffer, Bernardo, 721–722

O

O, Genovevo de la, 723
Oaxaca, Antequera de, 693
Obaldía, José Domingo de, 77, 656
Obaldía, María Olimpia de, 723
Obando, José María, 584, 589, 630, 698, 723
Obando y Bravo, Miguel, 723–724, 747, 749
Obin, Othan, 724
Obin, Philomé, 724
Obin, Senêque, 724
Obregón, Alejandro, 466, 724
Obregón, Álvaro, 86, 309, 458, 509, 697, 764, 834, 910, 1085
Obregón, Francisco, 725
Obregón, José, 724
Obregón Salido, Alvaro, 37, 228, 294, 667, 724–726 1054
O'Brien, John T., 921
Ocampo, Melchor, 79, 310, 534, 630, 726–727, 1095
Ocampo, Miguel, 467
Ocampo, Sebastián de, 754
Ocampo, Victoria, 65, 626, 692, 727
Ocaña Convention (1828), 589
Oceransky, Abraham, 138
Ochoa, Pedro, 356
Ocllo, Ragua, 85, 507
Odio, Eunice, 727–728
O'Donnell, Leopoldo, 589
O'Donojú, Juan, 522, 728
Odría, Manuel Apolinario, 128, 179, 489, 580, 728–729, 832, 947
Odría, María Delgado de, 728
Odriista National Union, 729
Oduber Quirós, Daniel, 362, 729
Oello, Chimpu, 427
O'Farrill, Rómulo, 94
Ogazón, Luis, 260
Ogé, Jacques Vicente, 729
Ogé, Vincent, 264–265
O'Gorman, Camila, 729
O'Gorman, Edmundo, 729–730
O'Gorman, Juan, 730
O'Higgins, Ambrosio, 89, 730
O'Higgins, Bernardo, 224, 239, 490, 519, 730–732, 743, 831, 880, 919, 920, 921
O'Higgins, Pablo, 732
O'Higgins, Rosa, 732
O'Horan, Tomás, 1025
Oiticica, Hélio, 268, 732, 765, 1044
Ojeda, Alonso de, 732–733
Olañeta, Josef Joaquín Casimiro, 733
Olañeta, Pedro Antonio de, 733, 975–976
Olaya Herrera, Enrique, 451, 733, 854
Olazábal, Manuel de, 922
O'Leary, Daniel Florencio, 733–734
O'Leary, Juan Emiliano, 328, 457, 734, 764
Olid, Cristóbal de, 734–735
Oliva, Oscar, 1092
Olivares, Conde-Duque de, 735
Oliveira, Geraldo Teles de, 735

Oliveira, João Fernandes de, 955
Oliveira, Manuel Bothelho de, 735
Oliveira, Maria Guilhermina de, 785
Oliveira, Willy Correia de, 333, 652, 735–736
Oliveira Lima, Manuel de, 736
Olivieri, Aníbal, 883
Olmedo, José Joaquín, 382, 736
Olmos, Andrés de, 911
Olsen, José María Figueres, 190
Olympio, José, 969
Ometochtzin, Carlos Mendoza, 1096
Oña, Pedro de, 736
Oñate, Cristóbal de, 516, 736
Oñate, Juan de, 736–737, 1056
Onetti, Juan Carlos, 135, 737, 794, 837, 844, 961
Onganía, Juan Carlos, 487, 572, 737–738
Opera de Cámara of the National Institute of Fine Arts (INBA), 18
Operation Pan American, 545
Oppenheimer, Robert, 929
Orbegoso, Luis José de, 236, 413, 738, 912
Orbigny, Alcide Dessalines D', 738
Orbón, Julián, 738
Ordaz, Gustavo Díaz, 340, 594
Ordem dos Advogados, 365
Order of Christ, 17
Ordóñez, José, 738, 921
Oré, Antonio de, 739
Oré, Luis Gerónimo de, 739
Oreamuno, Yolanda, 739
O'Reilly, Alejandro, 408, 922
O'Reilly, Code, 740
O'Reilly, Michael, 1028
O'Reilly y McDowell, Alejandro, 740
Orejón y Aparicio, José de, 740–741
Orellana, Francisco de, 741, 811
Orellana, Joaquín, 741
Orellana, José María, 254, 497, 741–742, 1007
Orfila, Washington Alejandro José Luis, 742
Organization of American States (OAS), 379, 964
Oribe, Emilio, 742
Oribe, Manuel, 35, 429, 562, 593, 668, 742–743, 1014
Orihuela, Manuel Zapata, 1003
Orixá Oxum, 658
Orizaba, 404
Orlando, Artur, 113
Orlich Bolmarcich, Francisco José, 207, 676, 743
Orloff, Abraham, 437
Oro, José de, 940
Oro, Juan Bustillo, 618
Oro, Justo Santa María de, 743–744
Orozco, José Clemente, 473, 744, 1036
Orozco, Olga, 744–745
Orozco, Pascual, 249, 458, 509, 614, 615
Orozco, Pascual, Jr., 456, 745, 1053
Orozco Revolt (1912), 725
Orozco y Berra, Manuel, 745–746
Orozquistas, 615

Orphée, Elvira, 746
Orquesta Renacimiento, 240
Orrego-Salas, Juan Antonio, 85, 746
Ortega, Daniel, 296, 901
Ortega, Humberto, 845
Ortega, Jesús González, 535, 1087
Ortega, Pilar, 70
Ortega, Toribio, 1053
Ortega del Villar, Aniceto, 299, 747
Ortega Saavedra, Daniel, 747–748
Ortega Saavedra, Humberto, 747, 748–749
Ortega y Fonseca, Francisco, 226
Ortega y Gasset, José, 416, 727, 857
Ortiz, Fernando, 749
Ortiz, Josefa, 328
Ortiz, Pascual, 751
Ortiz, Rafael Montáñez, 749–750
Ortiz, Roberto Marcelino, 238, 563, 750
Ortiz de Ayala, Simón Tadeo, 750
Ortiz de Domínguez, Josefa, 750
Ortiz de Zárate, Juan, 750–751
Ortiz de Zárate, Juana, 751
Ortiz Mcna, Antonio, 594, 751
Ortiz Rubio, Pascual, 751, 910
Osorio, Diego de Escobar, 210
Osório, Manuel Luís, 751–752
Osorio, Mariano, 738, 921
Osorio, Oscar, 233, 567, 752
Ospina, Pedro Nel, 497, 752
Ospina, Soledad, 1074
Ospina Pérez, Mariano, 451, 584, 752–753, 771, 1005
Ospina Rodríguez, Mariano, 219, 698, 752, 753
Osver, Arthur, 506
Oswald, Henrique, 406
Otazo, Rafael, 777
Otero, Alejandro, 753, 966
Otero, Mariano, 753–754
Ott, Thomas O., 599, 600
Ottoni, Teofilo Benedito, 754
Ovando, Juan de, 700
Ovando, Nicolás de, 277, 754, 809
Ovando, Alfredo, 113, 995
Ovando Candía, Alfredo, 755
Overá, Cacique, 152
Ovide, François, 309
Oviedo, Gonzalo Fernández, 500
Oviedo, José Miguel, 446
Oviedo y Valdés, Gonzalo Fernández de, 88, 755–756
Owen, Albert K., 889

P

Paalen, Wolfgang, 1035
Pablo Livinalli Santaella. See Apolinar (Pablo Livinalli Santaella)
Pacelli, Cardinal Eugenio, 97
Pacheco, Eleonora, 836
Pacheco, Gregorio, 63, 106, 757
Pacheco, José Emilio, 265, 757
Pacheco, María Luisa, 757–758

Pacheco Areco, Jorge, 159, 758
Pacheco da Silva, Osvaldo, 758
Pact of San José de Flores, 35, 668
Pact of the Naval Club, 375, 930
Pact of Unity and Action (PUA), 758
Pact of Zanjón, 454, 610
Padilla, Heberto, 341, 758–759, 843
Padilla, Mario, 821
Padilla Affair, 758
Padilla Peñalosa, Ezequiel, 759
Páenz, José Antonio, 992
Páez, Federico, 348, 759
Páez, José Antonio, 154, 457, 675, 759–760, 839, 884, 935,
    967, 1033
Paganini, Niccolò, 114
Pais, Fernão Dias, 158
País, Frank, 760
Palacio, Andueza, 148
Palacio Fajardo, Manuel, 760–761
Palacios, Alfredo L., 65, 437, 761
Palacios, Antonia, 761
Palacios, Juana Castillo, 684
Palacios, Nicolás, 346
Palacios, Pedro Bonifacio. See Almafuerte (Pedro Bonifacio
    Palacios)
Palafox, Manuel, 1085
Palafox y Mendoza, Juan de, 761–762
Palenque, Carlos, 762
Palés Matos, Luis, 762–763
Palma, Arturo Alessandri, 381
Palma, Athos, 441
Palma, Ramón de, 625
Palma, Ricardo, 105, 376, 639, 763, 1094
Palos, José de, 56
Palou, Francisco, 763–764
Panameñismo, 71
Pan American Conference of Women, 605
Pan-American movement, 861, 1008
Pancetti, José, 951
Pando, José Manuel, 764, 911, 1087
Pane, Ignacio Alberto, 764
Pan-Hispanism, 1008
Paniagua, Cenobio, 689
Paniagua y Vasques, Cenobio, 764–765
Pani Arteaga, Alberto J., 764
Paniza, Endara, 70
Panizo, Cruz, 33
Panizza, Ettore, 151
Pape, Lygia, 268, 732, 765
Paraguayan Communist Party (PCP), 295
Paraguayan Comunero Revolt (1721–1735), 674
Paraguayan Red Cross, 107
Paraguayan War (1865–1870), 14, 578, 803
Paraná, Honôrio Hermeto Carneiro Leão, Marqués de, 765
Pardavé, Joaquín, 765
Pardo, Emilio, 112
Pardo, Felipe, 766
Pardo, José, 566

Pardo, Juan, 658, 765–766
Pardo, Manuel, 187, 481, 801
Pardo, Rafael, 112
Pardo Leal, Jaime, 766
Pardo y Aliaqa, Felipe, 766
Pardo y Barreda, Alliaga, 766
Pardo y Barreda, José, 766, 1058
Pardo y Lavalle, Manuel, 766–767
Pardo y Ugarteche, Javier, 1058
Paredes, Pancho Arias, 528
Paredes y Arrillaga, Mariano, 297, 533, 767, 870
Pareja Diezcanseco, Alfredo, 767–768
Paris, Treaty of (1763), 740
Parra, Ángel, 526, 769
Parra, Aquileo, 768
Parra, Félix, 768
Parra, Isabel, 526, 769
Parra, José de la, 1095
Parra, Nicanor, 768–769, 769
Parra, Porfirio, 112
Parra, Teresa de la, 769
Parra, Violeta, 769
Partido Colorado, 182
Partido Comunista del Uruguay (PCU), 447
Partido da Social Democracia Brasileira (PSDB), 215
Partido de la Revolución Democrática, 213
Partido de la Unión Republicana Socialista (PURS), 1015
Partido del Pueblo (PP), 927
Partido Demócrata Cristiano (PDC), 991
Partido Democrático, 825
Partido Democrático Nacional (PDN), 115
Partido Democrático Popular (PDP), 927
Partido Democrático Trabalhista (PDT), 708
Partido de Representação Popular (PRP), 914
Partido dos Trabalhadores (PT), 952, 954, 970, 1069
Partido Nacionalista Revolucionario (PNR), 78, 211
Partido Obrero Socialista (POS), 852
Partido Popular, 585
Partido Renovador, 528
Partido Republicano Paulista (PRP), 602
Partido Revolucionario, 654
Partido Revolucionario de Unificación (PRUN), 31
Partido Revolucionario Febretista, 390–391
Partido Socialista del Uruguay (Socialist Party-PSU), 447
Partido Social Progressista (PRP), 188
Partido Social Revolucionario, 205
Partido Union Nacional, 601
Party of Dominican Liberation (PLD), 163
Party of Mexican Revolution (PRM), 212, 616
Party of the Brazilian Democratic Movement (PMDB), 858
Party of the Revolutionary Left (PIR), 82
Pascal-Trouillot, Ertha, 769
Paso, Fernando del, 769–770
Paso, Juan José, 770
Pasos, Joaquín, 285
Paso y Troncoso, Francisco Del, 770
Pasquini, Bernardo, 1093
Passarelli, Miguel Ortíz, 1078

Passarinho, Jarbas Gonçalves, 770–771
Pasta, Carlo Enrico, 771
Pastana Borrero, Misael, 885
Pastor, Mateo, 818
Pastora Gómez, Edén, 771
Pastrana Borrero, Misael, 771
Paterson, William, 771–772
Patiño, José de, 772
Patiño, Simón Iturri, 483, 772–773
Patriotic Military Union (Unión Patriótica Militar-UPM), 793
Patrocínio, José do, 773
Patrón Costas, Robustiano, 773
Paucarpata, Treaty of (1837), 520
Paul III (Pope), 558
Paul V (Pope), 133
Paul VI (Pope), 393
Paunero, Wenceslao, 788
Pauw, Corneille de, 269
Paves, Cesare, 808
Pavón, Manuel José, 774
Pavón Aycinena, Manuel Francisco, 774, 1088
Payno y Bustamante, Manuel, 302, 774
Payno y Flores, Manuel, 774
Payró, Robert J., 437
Paz, José María, 429, 551, 588, 774–775, 839, 892, 920
Paz, Juan Carlos, 539, 775
Paz, Marcos, 36, 668
Paz, Mariano Rivera, 224
Paz, Octavio, 403, 464, 542, 574, 730, 757, 775–777, 809, 857, 979
Paz Baraona, Miguel, 216, 777
Paz Estenssoro, Víctor, 564, 755, 777–778, 925, 995
Paz García, Policarpo, 778
Paz Soldán, José Gregorio, 778
Paz Soldán, Mariano Felipe, 778
Paz Soldán Family, 778
Paz Soldán y Unanue, Pedro, 778
Paz Zamora, Jaime, 106, 778–779
Peçanha, Nilo Procópio, 779
Pedreira, Antonio S., 779
Pedro, Hermano, 144
Pedro I (Brasil), 46, 108, 367, 420, 466, 569, 577, 678, 779–780, 803, 867, 913, 936, 1036
Pedro II (Brazil), 108, 166, 280, 376, 521, 570, 576, 578, 582, 617, 678, 765, 780–782, 851, 938, 980, 1039, 1069
Pedrosa y Guerrero, Antonio de la, 782, 1057
Peel, Robert, 577
Peimbert, Margarita, 782
Peimbert y Hernández, Juan Nazario, 782
Peixe, César Guerra, 541, 782–783
Peixoto, Floriano Vieira, 577, 649, 773, 783, 913
Peixoto, Inácio José de Alvarenga, 455
Peixoto, Júlio Afrânio, 783
Peixoto, Marshal Floriano, 387
Peláez, Amelia, 574, 783–784
Peláez, Carlos, 703
Pelayo, Mendéndez y, 902
Pelé (Edson Arantes do Nascimento), 784

Pellacani, Dante, 784
Pellegrini, Carlos, 200, 380, 447, 469, 784–785, 848, 873, 910, 911, 1089
Pellicer Cámara, Carlos, 785
Pena, Afonso Augusto Moreira, 779, 785–786
Peña, Antonia, 786
Peña, Feliciano, 261
Peña, Lázaro, 786
Pena, Luís Carlos Martins, 786
Peña, Manuel Pedro de, 786–787
Peña Gómez, José Francisco, 787
Peñalba, Rodrigo, 688
Peñalosa Briceño, Diego Dionisio de, 787–788
Peñaloza, Ángel Vicente, 788, 941
Peñaranda del Castillo, Enrique, 777, 788
Peña y Peña, Manuel de la, 764, 787
Peralta, Ángela, 747, 788–789, 897
Peralta Azurdia, Enrique, 601, 789, 1057, 1078
Peralta Barnuevo y Rocha, Pedro de, 789
Péralte, Charlemagne Masséna, 789–790
Peraza, Manuel Cepeda, 673
Pereda, Fernando de, 513
Pereira, Gabriel Antonio, 124
Pereira, José Clemente, 790, 798
Pereira, Nuño Vaz, 618
Pereira de Sousa, Luís, 828, 1030–1031
Perera, Víctor, 790
Pereyns, Simón, 790
Pérez, Albino, 261, 790
Pérez, Carlos Andrés, 143, 790–791
Pérez, Jaime, 74
Pérez, José Joaquín, 175, 682
Pérez, Juan, 791
Pérez, Rigoberto López, 964
Pérez Acosta, Juan Francisco, 791
Pérez Aguirre, Luis, 791–792
Pérez de Tolosa, Alonso, 792
Pérez de Tolosa, Juan, 598, 792
Pérez Esquivel, Adolfo, 792
Pérez Firmat, Gustavo, 478
Pérez Godoy, Ricardo, 580, 792–793
Pérez Jiménez, Marcos, 143, 555, 569, 582, 791, 793
Pérez Mascayano, José Joaquín, 793
Pérez Salas, Francisco Antonio, 793–794
Peri Rossi, Cristina, 794, 837
Pernambuco, João, 576, 808
Perón, Eva, Foundation, 797
Perón, Evita, 165, 364
Perón, Isabel, 199, 657
Perón, Juan Domingo, 59, 74, 99, 160, 165, 199, 282, 326, 364, 366, 395, 396, 401, 438, 507, 527, 586, 635, 727, 761, 794–796, 883, 884, 1002, 1008, 1026, 1050, 1080
Perón, María Estela Martínez de, 796, 1050
Perón, María Eva Duarte de, 796–797
Peronist General Labor Confederation (CGT), 1026
Peronist movement, 1026
Perricholi, La, 797–798
Pershing, John, 725, 1054

Persichetti, Vincent, 171–172
Peru-Bolivia Confederation (1836–1839), 413, 654, 687, 738, 1064
Peruvian Communist Party (PCP), 311
Peruvuan Aprista Party (PAP), 488
Pessoa, Epitácio da Silva, 195, 798
Pessoa Cavalcanti de Albuquerque, João, 798
Peters, DeWitt, 511, 574
Pétion, Alexandre Sabès, 58, 164, 315, 799
Petróleos Mexicanos (PEMEX), 212
Petrópolis, Treaty of (1903), 59
Pettoruti, Emilio, 196, 799, 1075
Peurifoy, 238
Peynado, Jacinto B., 1001, 1002
Pezet, Juan Antonio, 237, 799–800, 1064
Pezuela, Joaquín de la, 547
Phelps, Anthony, 800
Philip II (Spain), 348, 492, 510, 657, 658, 942
Philip IV (Spain), 210, 735, 991
Philip V (Spain), 352, 531, 625, 657, 772
Philippa (Lancaster), 491
Philoctète, René, 800
Picado Michalski, Teodoro, 191, 289, 686, 800
Picasso, Pablo, 219, 223, 509
Picchia, Menotti del, 45, 169, 621
Picón Salas, Mariano, 800–801
Pierné, Gabriel, 1022
Piérola, Nicolás de, 104, 420, 593, 689, 767, 801
Pike, Zebulon, 648
Pilar, Treaty of (1820), 82, 844
Pimentel, Luis García, 139–140
Pineda, José Laureano, 701
Pineda, Leonardo Ruiz, 791
Pineda-Duque, Roberto, 801
Pinedo, Federico, 801–802
Pinedo Plan, 537, 801
Piñera, Virgilio, 67, 574, 802
Piñeres, Gutiérrez de, 133
Piñero, Norberto, 637, 865
Pingret, Édouard Henri Théophile, 802
Pinheiro, José Feliciano Fernandes, 802–803
Pinheiro Machado, José Gomes, 803
Pinho, José Wanderley de Araújo, 803
Pinilla, Enrique, 803
Pinilla, Gustavo Rojas, 1002
Pino, Joaquín del, 864
Pinochet Ugarte, Augusto, 92, 327, 392, 393, 550, 572, 659, 804–805
Piñol y Aycinena, Bernardo, 805
Piñol y Sala, José, 805
Piñon, Nélida, 805–806
Pino Suárez, José María, 508, 616, 803–804
Pinto, André Teixeira, 45
Pinto, Aníbal, 1049, 1072
Pinto, Joaquín, 806
Pinto, Onofre, 547
Pinto, Sabina, 547
Pinto Díaz, Francisco Antonio, 806

Pinto Garmendia, Aníbal, 806–807
Pinzón, Martín Alonso, 276, 807
Pinzón, Rosa, 586
Pinzón, Vicente Yáñez, 570, 807
Pious Fund, 422
Pirovano, Igancio, 609
Pita Rodríguez, Félix, 220, 808
Pitol, Sergio, 808
Pius VI (Pope), 597
Pius VII (Pope), 597
Pius IX (Pope), 426, 641, 701
Pius X (Pope), 377
Pius XII (Pope), 97, 393
Pixinguinha, 664, 808
Pizarnik, Alejandra, 808–809
Pizarro, Francisco, 31, 38, 49, 86, 88, 100, 442, 508, 604, 733, 809–810, 811, 812, 965, 1019, 1021
Pizarro, Gonzalo, 266, 433, 442, 721, 809, 810–811, 1019, 1021
Pizarro, Hernando Alonso, 86, 809, 811–812
Pizarro, José Alonso, 812
Plá, Josefina, 201, 812
Plan de Guadalupe, 508
Plan de Tomé, 261
Plan Inca, 1041
Plano de Ação Econômica do Governo (PAEG), 201
Plan of Agua Prieta, 194
Plan of Ayala (1911), 723, 1086
Plan of Ayutla (1854), 278, 845
Plan of Casa Mata, 522, 848
Plan of Cuernavaca, 74
Plan of Iguala (1821), 381, 498, 522, 767, 1049
Plan of La Noria, 458
Plan of Montaño, 1015
Plan of San Luis Potosí (1910), 614, 745
Plan of Tacubaya, 1087, 1095
Plan of Tuxtepec (1876), 458, 845, 864
Plan of Zacapoaxtla (1855), 488
Platania, Pietro, 403
Platt Amendment (1901), 449, 655
Plaza, Leonidas, 26
Plaza, Victorino de la, 813
Plaza Gutiérrez, Leonidas, 813
Plaza Lasso, Galo, 813–814
Pluchon, Pierre, 600
Poblete Poblete de Espinoza, Olga, 814
Poe, Edgar Allan, 839
Poesía Sorprendida movement, 900
Poinsett, Joel Roberts, 814
Polanco, Gaspar, 352
Poliakoff, Serge, 66
Pombal, Francisco, 815
Pombal, Henrique, 815
Pombal, Marquês de (Sebastião José de Carvalho e Mello), 814–815
Pombal, Paulo, 815
Pompéia, Raúl, 815
Ponce, Juan García, 808

Ponce, Manuel, 260, 815
Ponce de León, Fidelio, 815
Ponce de León, Juan, 754, 815–816
Ponce Enríquez, Camilo, 816
Ponce Massacre, 16
Ponciano Corral, 1068
Poniatowska, Elena, 816
Poniatowski, Estanislau, 816
Poor Clares Convent, 739
Popenoe, Frederick Wilson, 816–817
Popenoe, Wilson, 1042
Popular Action, 130
Popular and Democratic Union, 778, 952
Popular Democratic Party (PPD), 702
Popular Liberation Front, 388, 654
Popular Library of Colombian Culture, 65
Popular Nationalist Front (FPN), 778
Popular Revolutionary Alliance of America (APRA), 488
Popular Social Christian Movement (MPSC), 1084
Popular Socialist Party, 585
Popular Vanguard Party (PVP), 362, 686, 923
Porcel, Juan de, 1019
Porfiriato (1876–1911), 220
Porrás, Ana María Mora, 678, 686
Porras, Belisario, 76–77, 262, 598, 817
Porras, Diego, 817
Porras, José Basilio, 817
Porras, Micaela, 817
Porras Barrencchca, Raúl, 818
Porres, Juan de, 818
Porres, Martín de, 818
Porres, Saint Martín de, 893
Portales, Diego, 393, 831, 854, 903, 940
Portales Palazuelos, Diego José Pedro Víctor, 818–820
Portales y Larraín, Josefa, 818
Porter, Charles, 405
Porter, Liliana, 820
Portes Gil, Emilio, 759, 820–821
Portillo, Efraín, 821
Portillo y Weber, José López, 595
Portinari, Cândido Torquato, 544, 821–822
Porto Alegre, Manuel de Araújo, 617, 822
Portocarrero, Alonso Hernández, 622
Portocarrero, Pedro de, 37
Portocarrero, René, 822
Portocarrero y Lasso de la Vega, Melchor, 822–823
Portolá, Gaspar de, 823, 870, 948–949
Portugal, Diego de, 997
Portugal, Marcos Antônio da Fonseca, 420, 823
Posada, José Guadalupe, 579, 744, 823–824
Posadas, Felipe Santiago de, 824
Posadas, Gervasio Antonio de, 556, 824, 919
Posadas, Manuel, 240
Positivist movement, 1035
Pound, Ezra, 209, 979
Pousseur, Henri, 652
Prada, Pedro Vargas, 580
Pradier, Charles S., 309

Prado, Antônio, 825
Prado, João Fernando de Almeida, 824
Prado, Manuel Ignacio, 149, 179, 466, 489, 728
Prado, Mariano Ignacio, 104, 187, 237, 799, 824, 826
Prado, Paulo, 825
Prado, Pedro, 825
Prado, Vasco, 825
Prado da Silva Júnior, Caio, 825–826
Prado y Ugarteche, Javier, 826
Prado y Ugarteche, Jorge, 826
Prado y Ugarteche, Manuel, 826
Praieira Revolt (1848–1849), 582, 765
Prat Echaurren, Jorge, 826–827
Prati, Lidy, 66
Prats González, Carlos, 804, 827
Prebisch, Raúl, 586, 827
Presas, Leopoldo, 311
Presidio Bahía del Espíritu Santo, 6
Presidio de los Texas, 6
Prestes, Júlio, 798
Prestes Column, Luís Carlos, 140, 234, 549, 550, 553, 827–828, 984
Prestes de Albuquerque, Julio, 828
Price, George Cadle, 828–829
Price-Mars, Jean, 829–830, 899
Prieto, Guillermo, 302, 830, 844
Prieto, Joaquín, 732, 819, 820
Prieto, Raúl, 830
Prieto, Sotero, 830
Prieto Figueroa, Luis Beltrán, 830
Prieto Rodríguez, Sotero, 830–831
Prieto Vial, Joaquín, 831
Primer Congreso Indigenista Interamericano, 909
Primo de Verdad y Ramos, Francisco, 831
Prío Socarrás, Carlos, 262, 831–832
Pritsch, Miguel, 948
Progressive Democratic Party (PDP), 994
Projeto Seringueiro (Rubber Tapper Project), 653
Protasi, Juan, 971
Protest of Baraguá, 610
Puello, Gabiño, 934
Puente Uceda, Luis de la, 832
Puerto Rican Autonomist Party, 102
Puerto Rico Nationalist Party, 16
Puerto Rico's Liberal Reformist Party, 102
Pueyrredón, Honorio, 706, 832
Pueyrredón, Juan Martín de, 329, 448, 832–833, 833, 906, 920
Pueyrredón, Prilidiano, 833
Puga, María Luisa, 833
Puig, Manuel, 833–834
Puig Casauranc, José Manuel, 834
Puyucahua, Micaela Bastidas, 1003

Q ————————————————————
Quadrilateral Treaty (1822), 588
Quadros, Jânio da Silva, 118, 235, 400, 446, 465, 545, 549, 599, 650, 784, 835

Quatrefages, Xavier, 606
Quebracho Revolution, 124, 125
Queirós, Eusébio de, 1016
Queirós Coutinho Matoso da Câmera, Eusébio de, 835
Queiroz, Dinah Silveira de, 835–836
Queiroz, Rachel de, 836
Quejo, Pedro de, 1037
Querino, Manoel Raimundo, 836
Quesada, Ernesto, 836–837, 850
Quesada, Vicente G., 836
Quevedo, Francisco de, 575
Quevedo, Juan de, 88
Quijano, Carlos, 837, 843
Quijano, Manuel, 226
Quinet, Edgar, 146
Quiñones Molina, Alfonso, 631, 646–647, 837–838
Quinquela Martín, Benito, 838
Quintana, Andrés, 1048
Quintana, Doña Ysabel de la, 344
Quintana, Manuel, 447, 457, 838
Quintanar, Héctor, 487, 838
Quintana Roo, Andrés, 830, 838
Quintanilla, María del Carmen, 919
Quintero, Ángel, 838–839
Quintinar, Hector, 562
Quiroga, Horacio, 839, 844, 882, 883
Quiroga, Juan Facundo, 551, 642, 774, 788, 839–840, 940
Quiroga, Rodrigo de, 973
Quiroga, Vasco de, 840
Quiroga Santa Cruz, Marcelo, 840
Quirós, Cesáreo Bernaldo de, 840–841
Quirós, Francisco, 236
Quito and Guayaquil Railroad, 26
Quizquiz, 507–508

R

Rabasa, Emilio, 843
Rackam, "Calico Jack," 158
Rada, Manuel de Jesús, 843
Radical Civic Union of the People, 100, 217, 396, 518, 567
Radical Olympus, 768
Radical Orientation Force of Argentine Youth (FORJA), 527
Radical Party, 395–396, 407, 1080
Radio, rural, 707
Rafael Callejas National Renovation Movement, 193
Ragiundo, Rosa, 429
Raimondi, Giuseppina, 429
Rama, Ángel, 837, 843–844, 999
Ramalho, Elba, 455
Ramalho, João, 844
Ramañach, Leopoldo, 815
Ramírez, Bernarda Sarmiento, 306
Ramírez, Bruno Carranza, 470
Ramírez, Francisco, 82, 588, 593, 844
Ramírez, Ignacio, 302, 844–845
Ramírez, José Fernando, 745, 845
Ramírez, Juan Pérez, 460
Ramírez, María Montez, 516

Ramírez, Pedro Pablo, 238, 366, 795, 845
Ramírez Mercado, Sergio, 748, 845–846
Ramírez Vázquez, Pedro, 846
Ramírez Villamizar, Eduardo, 846
Ramírez y Blanco, Alejandro, 846–847
Ramón, Corral Verdugo, 286
Ramón Emeterio, Betances, 142
Ramón I, 215
Ramos, Artur, 847
Ramos, Graciliano, 847–848
Ramos, Nereu, 598
Ramos, Samuel, 487, 857
Ramos Arizpe, José Miguel, 728, 848
Ramos Mejía, Ezequiel, 848–849
Ramos Mejía, José María, 849, 865
Ramos y Magaña, Samuel, 849
Ranney, Edward, 256
Raoul, Nicolás, 64
Raousset-Boulbon, Gaston Raul de, 849–850
Rathaus, Karol, 505
Ratton, Jacome, 650
Ratzinger, Joseph, 230
Raúl Ricardo, Alfonsín, 27
Rávago, Juan de Estrada, 248
Ravel, Maurice, 565
Ravignani, Emilio, 850
Rawson, Arturo, 238, 366
Rawson, Guillermo, 850
Raya, Antonio de la, 739
Raynal, Guillaume-Thomas-François de, 490
Raynaud, Georges, 215
Rayón, Ignacio, 693, 782, 850–851
Rayón, Ramón, 851
Razón de Patria, 1058
Razzano, José, 428
Read, Mary, 158, 851
Readjustment Obligations of the National Treasury (ORTN), 201
Real de Azúa, Carlos, 837, 851
Rebagliati, Claudio, 33
Rebel Armed Forces (FAR), 1005
Rebouças, André, 851–852
Recabarren Serrano, Luis Emilio, 852
Recco, Nardo Antonio, 493
Reclus, Elisée, 141
Redman, Sofia Matilde Joy, 678
Reed, Walter, 382
Reeve, Henry M., 852
Rega, José López, 1023
Regalado, Tomás, 852–853
Regimiento de Dragones Provinciales de la Reina, 19
Regina, Elis, 248
Regional Confederation of the Mexican Worker, 697
Region-Tradition movement, 581
Rego Monteiro, Vicente do, 853
Regresso movement (1835–1839), 522
Rein, Mercedes, 837
Reinecke, Carl, 142, 226

Rejón, Manuel Crescencio, 853
Remauldi, Serafino, 1060
Remón Cantera, José Antonio, 262, 471, 528, 853–854
Renard, Émile, 45
Rendón, César, 821
Rendón, Ricardo, 60
René, Bélance, 129
Rengifo, Manuel, 819
Rengifo, Ramón, 854
Rengifo Cárdenas, Manuel, 854
Repetto, Nicolás, 537
Republican Statehood Party (PER), 374
Rescala, João, 951
Restrepo, Carlos Eugenio, 733, 854
Restrepo, José Manuel, 854–855
Reuss, Emilio, 979
Reverdy, Pierre, 509
Reverón, Armando, 855
Revillagugedo, Segundo Conde de, 385, 855
Revindicating Revolution (1878), 579
Revolutionary Action Party (PAR), 388, 654
Revolutionary Democratic Alliance (ARDE), 771
Revolutionary Movement (October, 8), 401
Revolutionary Party of Democratic Unification–National
    Coalition Party, 752
Revolutionary Party of Nationalist Left, 564
Revolutionary Party of National Unification, 31
Revolutionary Sandinista Front (FRS), 771
Revolutionary Unity Party (URD), 1057
Revolutionary Workers Party (POR), 473
Revolution of 1859–1861, 723
Revolution of Ayutla, 488, 645, 726, 931, 1095
Revueltas, José, 79, 855–856
Revueltas, Silvestre, 856
Reyes, Alfonso, 65, 172, 265, 490, 514, 575, 757, 856, 857
Reyes, Bernardo, 220, 320, 323, 508, 615–616, 856, 857
Reyes, Hernando Siles, 907, 952
Reyes, Rafael, 279, 505, 854, 857
Reyes, Vicente, 349
Reyes, Walter López, 975
Reyes Ochoa, Alfonso, 857
Reyes Ogazón, Bernardo, 578–579, 857
Reyna Barrios, José María, 857–858
Reza, Jorge de la, 757
Rhet, William, 157
Riani, Clodsmith, 858
Riaño, Juan Antonio, 503
Riaño y Bárcena, Juan Antonio, 858
Ribas, José Félix, 858
Ribeiro, Darcy, 859
Ribeiro, João Ubaldo, 859
Ribera y Espinosa, Lázaro de, 859
Ribeyro, Julio Ramón, 859–860
Ribot, 636
Ricardos, General, 919
Ricchieri, Pablo, 860
Ricchieri Law, 860
Riché, Jean-Baptiste, 968

Riego y Núñez, Rafael del, 860
Riesco Errázuriz, Germán, 860
Rigaud, André, 600, 860–861
Riggs, Francis, 16
Rio, João do, 44, 862
Rio Branco, Barão do, 861, 877, 1089
Rio Branco, Visconde do, 861–862, 938
Rio Grande do Sul, 602
Rionegro Convention (1863), 589, 698
Ríos Montt, José Efraín, 561, 601, 789, 862–863, 949
Ríos Morales, Juan Antonio, 863
Ripari, Virgilio, 377
Ripstein, Arturo, 863
Riquelme, Isabel, 730
Riscos, Juan de, 591
Risler, Edouard, 240
Rius (Eduardo del Río), 863
Riva Agüero y Osma, José de la, 863–864, 994
Rivadavia, Bernardino, 13, 42, 67, 158, 232, 329, 555, 559,
    839, 864–865, 895, 926, 1027, 1028
Riva Palacio, Vicente, 864
Rivarola, Cirilo Antonio, 441, 531, 865
Rivarola, Rodolfo, 637, 865
Rivas, Berta Macías, 397
Rivas, Carlos Martínez, 286
Rivas, Patricio, 865–866, 1024, 1068
Rivera, Diego, 380, 539, 730, 732, 744, 816, 866–867, 1036
Rivera, Fructuoso, 82, 383, 562, 743, 867–868, 1014
Rivera, Joaquín, 375, 868
Rivera, José Eustasio, 868
Rivera, Julio A., 887, 926
Rivera, Payo Enríquez de, 516
Rivera, Pedro De, 868–869
Rivera Cabezas, Antonio, 869
Rivera Carballo, Julio Adalberto, 869
Rivera Damas, Arturo, 869–870
Rivera Maestre, Miguel, 870
Rivera Paz, Mariano, 870
Rivera y Damas, Arturo, 889
Rivera y Moncada, Fernando de, 870
Rivero, Agustín P., 785
Rivero, Marcelo, 818
Rivier, Jean, 998
Roa Bastos, Augusto, 201, 870–871
Robels, Francisco, 228
Robert-Fleury, Tony, 1069
Roberts Group, 635
Robitschek, Robert, 505
Robledo, Jorge, 129, 266
Robles, Francisco, 871, 1011
Robles, Marcos Aurelio, 262, 871
Robles, Wenceslao, 871–872
Roca, Blas, 872
Roca, Julio Argentino, 200, 380, 457, 515, 520, 535, 593, 706,
    784, 838, 848, 872–873, 910, 986, 992, 1071
Rocafuerte, Vicente, 382, 425, 873–874, 1010
Roca Rodríguez, Vicente Ramón, 873, 1011
Roca-Runciman Pact (1933), 209, 537

Rocha, Dardo, 874
Rocha, Evaristo, 1024
Rocha, Justiniano José Da, 874
Rocha, Manoel Ribeiro, 874
Rochambeau, Donatien Marie Joseph de Vimeur de, 875
Rochambeau, Jean Baptiste de Vimeur de, 875
Rocha Pita, Sebastião, 874–875
Rockefeller, John D., 540
Rockefeller, Nelson, 540
Rockland, Michael, 941
Rodas Alvarado, Modesto, 875, 974
Rodista Dissent Movement, 94
Rodó, José Enrique, 65, 851, 875–876, 882
Rodrigues, Augusto, 1063
Rodrigues, Glauco, 825
Rodrigues, José Honório, 549, 876
Rodrigues, Nelson, 876
Rodrigues, Raimundo Nina, 836, 876–877
Rodrigues Alves, Francisco de Paula, 831, 877
Rodríguez, Agustín, 353
Rodríguez, Andrés, 877–878, 973
Rodríguez, Antonio, 880, 1058
Rodríguez, Carlos Rafael, 878
Rodríguez, Emir, 875
Rodríguez, Joaquín, 529
Rodríguez, Jorge Alessandri, 514
Rodríguez, José Joaquín, 517
Rodríguez, Lorenzo, 878
Rodríguez, Mariano, 574
Rodríguez, Martín, 864
Rodríguez, Roque J., 601
Rodríguez, Simón, 153, 263, 878–879
Rodriguez, Zé, 1063
Rodríguez-Alcalá, Hugo, 201, 879
Rodríguez Cabrillo, Juan, 879
Rodríguez Cerna, José, 879
Rodríguez de Fonseca, Juan, 88, 716
Rodríguez Demorizi, Emilio, 880
Rodríguez de Toro, María Teresa, 153
Rodríguez de Velasco y Osorio Barba, María Ignacia, 879
Rodríguez Erdoiza, Manuel, 880
Rodríguez Freile, Juan, 880
Rodríguez Juárez, Juan, 880
Rodríguez Juliá, Edgardo, 880–881
Rodríguez Lara, Guillermo, 881
Rodríguez Luján, Abelardo, 881
Rodríguez Monegal, Emir, 329, 882
Rodríguez Sandoval, Luis Arsenio, 882
Rogatis, Pascual de, 882–883
Roger-Ducasse, Jean-Jules Aimable, 356
Rogers, Woodes, 158
Roig de Leuchsenring, Emilio, 883
Roja, Liga, 646
Rojas, Cecilio Guzmán de, 757
Rojas, Diego de, 1019
Rojas, Isaac, 883
Rojas, Manuel, 883
Rojas, Pedro José, 884

Rojas, Ricardo, 324, 606, 884
Rojas Paúl, Juan Pablo, 54, 486, 884
Rojas Pinilla, Gustavo, 451, 884–885, 1022
Rojas Urtuguren, José Antonio de, 885
Rojas y Borgia, Luis de, 17
Rojo, Antonio Benítez, 478
Rojo, María, 885
Rojo, Partido, 501
Rojo, Vicente, 885
Rokha, Pablo de, 885
Rokha, Winétt de, 885–886
Roldán, Amadeo, 219, 421, 886
Roldán, Enrique, 1084
Roldán, Francisco, 886
Roldán, Salvador Camacho, 768
Roldós Aguilera, Jaime, 174, 366, 511, 886
Rolón, Raimundo, 886–887
Román de Núñez, Soledad, 887
Romano, Diego, 624
Romay y Valdés Chacón, Tomás, 887
Romero, Carlos Humberto, 332, 620, 887, 890, 1083
Romero, Emilio, 887–888
Romero, Francisco, 888
Romero, José Luis, 23, 888
Romero, José Rubén, 888
Romero, Matías, 578, 889
Romero, Oscar Arnulfo, 231, 870, 887, 889–890
Romero, Sílvio, 890–891, 1048
Romero Barceló, Carlos, 891
Romero de Terreros, Pedro, 891
Romero Rosa, Ramón, 891–892
Romero Rubio, Manuel, 892
Roncador-Xingu Expedition (1943), 1059
Rondeau, José, 551, 892, 921
Rondon, Cândido Mariano da Silva, 892
Roo, Quintana, 1048
Roosevelt, Franklin Delano, 585, 613, 929, 964, 1002
Rops, Félicien, 900
Roque, Vicente Menéndez, 477
Ros, Baltasar García, 56
Rosa, João Guimarães, 893–894
Rosa, Luis da Fonseca, 387
Rosa, Noel, 894
Rosa, Ramón, 894
Rosa de Lima, 892–893
Rosáins, Juan Nepomuceno, 894–895
Rosas, José Manuel de, 624
Rosas, Juan Manuel Ortiz de, 13, 18, 23, 55, 59, 83, 138, 142, 161, 176, 191, 314, 410, 436, 448, 474, 551, 562, 578, 588, 590, 629, 642, 668, 678, 729, 743, 752, 765, 774, 788, 840, 850, 861, 865, 868, 895–897, 922, 926, 940, 943, 986, 1014, 1016–1017, 1028, 1048
Rosas, Juventino, 897
Rosas de Terrero, Manuela, 897
Rosay, Lily, 943
Roscio, Juan Germán, 898
Rosenblat, Ángel, 110
Rosenblueth, Arturo Stearns, 898

Ross, Gustavo, 10
Rossell y Arellano, Mariano, 898
Ross Santa María, Gustavo, 898
Rothfuss, Kosice, 66
Rothfuss, Rhod, 66
Roumain, Jacques, 898–899
Rousseau, Jean-Jacques, 490
Roussel, Albert, 591
Roxas y Rivera, Luisa Dias de, 739
Roy, Eugène, 899
Ruano, María Pastora, 35
Rubí, Marqués de, 899–900
Rubião, Murilo, 900
Rubio, Leonor, 751
Rudolf, Max, 637
Rueda, Manuel, 900
Ruelas, Julio, 900
Ruffinelli, Jorge, 837
Ruffo, Titta, 883
Rufino Barrios, Justo, 1088
Ruiz, Antonio, 900–901
Ruíz, Henry, 159, 901, 1070
Ruiz, Tomás, 901–902
Ruiz Cortines, Adolfo, 594, 751, 902
Ruiz de Alcarcón y Mendoza, Juan, 902–903
Ruíz de Apodaca, Juan, Conde de Venadito, 903
Ruiz de Montoya, Antonio, 903
Ruíz Tagle Portales, Francisco, 903
Rulfo, Juan, 79, 96, 567, 879, 903–904
Rusiñol, Santiago, 302

S

Sá, Estácio de, 905
Sá, Martim de, 905
Sá, Mem de, 905, 1061
Sáa, Juan, 1027
Saavedra, Cornelio de, 42, 694, 906
Saavedra Lamas, Carlos, 906–907
Saavedra Mallea, Bautista, 907
Sabat Ercasty, Carlos, 907
Sábato, Ernesto, 871, 907–908
Sabines, Jaime, 156
Sabogal, José, 271, 908
Sabogal, María Wiesse de, 943
Sacasa, José, 528
Sacasa, Juan Bautista, 258, 319, 675, 908, 929, 963
Saco, José Antonio, 492, 606, 908–909
Sada, Eugenio Garza, 432
Sada, Francisco, 432
Sada, Isaac Garza, 432
Sada, Roberto Garza, 432
Sá e Benavides, Salvador Correia de, 905–906
Sáenz, Aniceto Esquivel, 470
Sáenz, Jaime, 909
Sáenz, Moisés, 909
Sáenz de Thorne, Manuela, 909–910
Sáenz Garza, Aarón, 910
Sáenz Peña, Luis, 669, 838, 873, 910, 1013, 1024

Sáenz Peña, Roque, 209, 217, 381, 447, 515, 813, 849, 910–911
Sáenz Peña Law, 910
Sahagún, Bernardino de, 770, 911
Saint-Requiet, Louis, 1022
Sáinz, Gustavo, 911
Sakai, Kasuya, 467
Salamanca, Daniel, 177, 501, 907, 911, 981, 985
Salanueva, Antonio, 533
Salas, Esteban, 220
Salas, José González, 745
Salas, Manuel de, 911–912
Salavarrieta, Policarpa, 912
Salaverry, Felipe Santiago, 236, 738, 912, 932, 1064
Sálazar, Alonso Pérez de, 71
Salazar, Antonio, 1096
Salazar, José Luis Cruz, 1078
Salazar, Juan, 19
Salazar, Matías, 912–913
Salazar Arrué, Salvador Efraín (Salarrué), 912–913
Salazar Bondy, Sebastián, 913
Salazar y Ezpinosa, Juan de, 3
Salbach, Vicente Lecuna, 450
Salcedo, Gaspar, 371
Salcedo, José Antonio, 352, 371
Saldanha da Gama, Luís Felipe de, 913
Sales, Eugênio de Araújo, 913–914
Salgado, Plinio, 914
Salgado, Sebastião, 914
Salgar, Eustorgio, 914–915
Salinas, Antonio Ortiz, 751
Salinas, Carlos, 269, 325, 545, 617, 751
Salinas, Luis Adolfo Siles, 755, 995
Salinas, Pedro, 136, 220, 779
Salinas de Gortari, Carlos, 915–916
Salinas de Gortari, Raul, 915
Salinas Grandes, 191
Salmon, Norvell, 1068
Salnave, Sylvain, 435, 916
Salomini, Tomás, 114
Salomon, Louis Étienne Lysius Félicité, 916
Salomon, Lysius, 917, 956
Salvador, Vicente do, 271, 916
Sam, Jean Vilbrun Guillaume, 150, 917
Sam, Tirésias Augustin Simon, 917
Samane Ocampo, David, 917
Sámano, Juan, 677
Samayoa Chinchilla, Carlos, 917
Sambucetti, Luis (Nicolás), 917–918
Samper, José María, 918
Samper Agudelo, Antonio, 918
Samper Agudelo, José María, 918
Samper Agudelo, Manuel, 918
Samper Agudelo, Miguel, 918
Samper Agudelo, Silvestre, 918
Samudio, Juan A., 918–919
Sanabria, María, 71
Sanabria Martínez, Victor M., 686, 720, 923

Sanabria y Mencia Calderón, Juan, 71
San Carlos Borromeo, 949
Sánchez, Florencio, 552, 923
Sánchez, Francisco de Rosario, 331, 934
Sánchez, Luis Alberto, 923–924
Sánchez, Luis Rafael, 924
Sánchez, Prisciliano, 924–925
Sánchez Cerro, Luis Manuel, 135, 179, 383, 566, 917, 925
Sánchez de Bustamante y Sirven, Antonio, 925
Sánchez de Lozada Bustamante, Gonzalo, 925
Sánchez de Tagle, Francisco Manuel, 925–926
Sánchez de Thompson, María, 926
Sánchez Hernández, Fidel, 869, 887, 926
Sánchez Manduley, Celia, 245–246, 926–927
Sánchez Vilella, Roberto, 374, 927
Sancho de Hoz, Pedro, 927, 1056
Sanclemente, Manuel Antonio, 279, 505, 752, 974
Sandi, Luis, 927
Sandinista National Directorate, 64, 747, 748
Sandinista National Liberation Front (FSLN), 117, 159, 210, 257, 387, 642, 748, 771, 845, 962
Sandinista Popular Army, 749
Sandino, Augusto César, 387, 632, 676, 747, 908, 927–929, 963
Sandino, Gregorio, 927
Sandoval, Alonso, 268
Sándoval, José León, 527, 929
Sandoval Vallarta, Manuel, 465, 929
Sanfuentes, Enrique, 929
Sanfuentes, Juan Luis, 10, 349
Sanfuentes Andonaegui, Juan Luis, 929–930
Sanguily, Julio, 6
Sanguinetti, Julio María, 40, 375, 643, 930
San José de los Naturales, 416
Sanjuán, Pedro, 421
San Martín, Cosme, 97
San Martín, José de Francisco de, 13, 67, 87, 101, 131, 142, 154, 224, 236, 239, 413, 474, 547, 551, 559, 561, 603, 626, 678, 731, 738, 743, 833, 919–922, 975, 994
San Martín, Juan Zorrilla de, 4
San Martín, Mercedes de, 101
San Miguel el Grande, 27
Sannbria, Victor Manuel, 190
San Salvador, Agustín Fernández de, 1048
Santa Anna, Antonio López de, 39, 48, 74, 79, 278, 290, 351, 452, 482, 488, 517, 534, 570, 663, 701, 767, 787, 790, 830, 930–931, 992, 1015, 1050, 1087, 1095, 1097
Santa Coloma, Gaspar de, 42
Santa Cruz, Andrés de, 236, 283–284, 382, 412, 520, 654, 687, 738, 820, 912, 922, 931–932, 1040
Santa Cruz, Domingo, 127, 746
Santa Cruz Pachacuti Yamqui Salcamaygua, Joan de, 932–933
Santa Cruz y Espejo, Francisco Javier Eugenio de, 933
Santa María, Andrés de, 933
Santa María, Domingo, 103
SantaMaría, Haydée, 934
Santa María de la Antigua del Darién, 100
Santa María González, Domingo, 933–934

Santana, Pedro, 332, 648, 934
Santander, Francisco de Paula, 154, 218, 495, 496, 584, 586, 630, 698, 699, 703, 708, 854, 909, 934–936, 939
Santiago Iglesias, 891
Santillana, Isabel Ramírez de, 531
Santo, Colegio Mayor de Espíritu, 584
Santoro, Claudio, 333, 541, 936
Santórsola, Guido, 252, 552, 948
Santos, Eduardo, 451, 584, 936
Santos, Juan, 625, 657
Santos, Marquesa de, 936
Santos, Máximo, 124, 125, 198, 499, 561
Santos, Sílvio, 936–937
Santos, Turíbio, 308
Santos-Dumont, Alberto, 937–938
São Bernardo do Campo Metallurgical Workers Union of São Paulo, 954
São Paulo Chamber Orchestra, 333
São Paulo revolt (1842), 367
São Paulo School of Sociology, 368
São Paulo's State Council on the Status of Women, 12
São Vicente, José Antônio Pimenta Bueno, Marquês de, 938
Saraiva, José Antônio, 582, 938
Saraiva-Cotegipe Law (1885), 292
Saravia, Aparicio, 125, 141, 396, 923, 938–939
Saravia, Gumercindo, 938
Saravia, Nepomuceno, 396
Saravia-Cotegipe Law, 938
Sardá, José María, 496, 939
Sardaneta y Llorente, José Mariano de, 939
Sarduy, Severo, 446, 939–940
Sarmiento, Domingo Faustino, 14, 35, 66, 82, 87, 176, 448, 493, 593, 635, 668, 669, 774, 788, 850, 922, 940–942, 1028, 1044
Sarmiento de Gamboa, Pedro, 942
Sarmiento de León, Jorge Alvaro, 942–943
Sarmiento de Sotomayor y Luna, García, 592, 762, 942
Sarney, José, 169, 274, 649, 651, 943
Sarratea, Manuel de, 943
Sarratea, María Marina de, 580
Sarratea, Martín de, 580
Sartre, Jean-Paul, 622
Sas, Andrés, 943–944, 1020
Saumell, Manuel, 220
Saussure, Ferdinand de, 33
Scalabrini Ortiz, Raúl, 527, 944
Scarabelli, Virgilio, 361
Scarlatti, Alessandro, 1093
Schad, Horacio Maldonado, 601, 862
Schaerer, Eduardo, 944
Schäffer, Bogustaw, 172
Scheler, Max, 888
Schendel, Mira, 944
Scherchen, Hermann, 66, 317, 505
Schick Gutiérrez, René, 6, 945
Schneider, René, 827, 945
Schofield, John, 889
School for Rural Obstetrics, 107

School of Fine Arts of the National University, 440
Schoppe, Sigismund von, 640
Schwartz, Francis, 58
Schwarz-Bart, André, 945
Schwarz-Bart, Simone, 945
Scliar, Carlos, 825
Scliar, Moacyr, 945
Second Company of Catalonian Volunteers, 362
Second Conference of Latin American Bishops (CELAM), 553
Second International Peace Conference, 109
Second Vatican Council (1962–1965), 480, 1029
Sedeño, Antonio de, 945–946
Sedeño, Arévalo, 390
Seelinger, Hélios, 169
Segall, Lasar, 946
Segovia, Andrés, 114
Seguín, Juan José María Erasmo, 946
Seguín, Juan Nepomuceno, 946–947
Segura, Juan Bautista Quirós, 989
Segura, Vicente, 844
Selva, Salomón de la, 166
Seminario Conciliar de San Luis, 372
Seminar of Scientific and Philosophical Problems, 487
Sendic, Raúl, 947
Senghor, Léopold Sédar, 170, 313
Seoane, Manuel, 947
Sepp, Anton, 947–948
Sepúlveda, Juan Ginés de, 558
Sepúlveda, Manuel Contreras, 572
Serdán, Aquiles, 614
Serebrier, José, 948
Seregni, Líber, 948
Serna, Juan Pérez de la, 437
Serna, Ramón Gómez de la, 972
Serpa, Ivan, 732
Serra, Junípero, 763, 823, 948–949
Serrano, José, 949
Serrano, María Pilar, 329
Serrano Elías, Jorge Antonio, 251, 949–950
Serrat, Joan Manuel, 135
Service for Peace and Justice (SERPAJ), 792
Servicio Aereo de Honduras, S.A., 590
Seuphor, Michel, 66
Severim de Faria, Manuel, 916
Seward, William H., 98
Sexagenarian Law, 938
Sharp, Bartholomew, 950
Sharpless, Richard, 402
Shavitch, Vladimir, 361
Shelley, Jaime Augusto, 1092
Sheppard, Meg, 554
Shimose, Pedro, 950
Shining Path, 130, 399
Shubert, Lee, 664
Sicre, José Gómez, 300
Sierra, Justo, 112
Sierra, Stella, 950
Sierra Méndez, Justo, 950–951, 951, 1011

Sierra O'Reilly, Justo, 951
Sigaud, Eugenio de Proença, 951
Sigüenza y Góngora, Carlos de, 951–952
Siles Zuazo, Hernán, 777, 778, 952
Silva, Ana María Ribeiro da, 429
Silva, Aristides Inácio da, 954
Silva, Aurelio, 30
Silva, Benedita la, 952–953
Silva, Clara, 953
Silva, Darly Alves da, 653
Silva, Francisco Gomes da, 779
Silva, Francisco Manuel da, 953
Silva, José Antônio da, 953
Silva, José Asunción, 953–954
Silva, Lavinia Ferreira da, 199
Silva, Lindolfo, 954
Silva, Luís Inácio Lula da, 274, 954
Silva, Maria Joaquina Xavier da, 650
Silva, Orlando, 954–955
Silva, Xica da, 955
Silva Henríquez, Raúl, 955
Silva Herzog, Jesús, 955
Silva Paranhos, José Maria da, 1089
Silva Xavier, Joaquim José da, 956
Silveira, Aurelio, 443
Silveira, Simão Estácio da, 916
Silvestre, Gonzalo, 428
Silv Lisboa, José da, 955–956
Simon, Antoine, 718, 956
Simon-Baptiste, Suzanne, 599
Simone, Antoine, 565
Simonetti, 403
Simonsen, Mário Henrique, 956–957
Simonsen, Roberto Cochrane, 957
Sinán, Rogelio, 526, 957–958
Sinclair, Alfredo, 958
Sinclair, Enrique, 35
Sindicato Unitario Mexicano, 197
Sinhô, 958
Siqueiros, David Alfaro, 744
62 Organizations, 1026–1027
Skármeta, Antonio, 958
Smith, Adam, 955
Smith, Sidney, 217
Soares, Frei Henrique, 185
Sobremonte, Rafael de, 580, 832, 958
Sobrinho, José Cardoso, 196
Socarrás, Carlos Prío, 123, 163
Social Christian COPEI, 604
Social Christian Party, 190
Social Democratic Party (PDS), 361, 391, 544, 713, 943
Socialist Party of Peru, 627
Socialist Party of the Southwest, 227
Social Progressive Party (PSP), 118
Sociedad Amigos del Arte, 377
Sociedad Chilena de Filosofia, 673
Sociedad Científica del Paraguay, 107
Sociedad de Antropología Jurídica, 865

Sociedad de la Beneficiencia (Society of Charity), 941
Sociedad de la Igualdad (Society for Equality), 66
Sociedad Económica de Amigos del País (Economic Society of Friends of the Country), 1059
Sociedade Defensora da Liberdade e da Independéncia Nacional (Society for the Defense of National Liberty and Independence), 1039
Sociedad Elemental de Medicina, 18
Sociedade Pró-Arte Moderna, 169
Sociedad Filarmónica Mexicana, 747
Sociedad Patriótica de Amigos del País de Quito, 933
Sociedad Popular Restauradora, 896
Société Américaine de France, 167
Société de Géographie of Paris, 167
Société d'Ethnographie, 167
Société Haïtienne-Américaine du Développement Agricole (SHADA), 571
Society of Afro-Cuban Studies, 749
Soderini, Piero, 1047
Sodré, Nelson Werneck, 959
Sojo, Felipe, 959
Sol, Armando Calderon, 1084
Solano López, Francisco, 98, 149, 739, 781, 959–960
Soldi, Raúl, 960
Soler, Andrés, 960
Soler, Domingo, 960
Soler, Fernando, 960
Soler, Miguel Angel, 295
Solidary Action Movement (MAS), 949
Solís, Juan Díaz de, 418, 960
Solís Folch de Cardona, José, 812, 960–961
Sologuren, Javier, 961
Solórzano, Beatriz Caso de, 961
Solórzano, Carlos, 258, 908, 961
Solórzano, Octavio Paz, 775
Solórzano Pereira, Juan de, 961
Somers, Armonía, 961–962
Sommavilla, Godofredo, 377
Somoza, Bernabé, 929
Somoza Debayle, Anastasio, 6–7, 64, 191, 379, 655, 962, 963
Somoza Debayle, Luis, 963
Somoza García, Anastasio, 69–70, 159, 209, 257, 296, 747, 908, 929, 945, 962, 963–965
Somoza García, Luis, 962
Sonora Expedition (1767–1771), 15
Sontag, Henrietta, 788
Sonthonax, Léger Félicité, 965
Sorbonne Group, 598
Soriano, Juan, 965
Soriano, Osvaldo, 965
Soroeta, Ignacio, 674
Sosa, Francisco, 302
Soto, Hernando de, 86, 88, 766, 965–966
Soto, Jesús Rafael, 966
Soto, Marco Aurelio, 157, 966–967, 1092–1093
Soto, Pedro Juan, 967
Soto Alfaro, Bernardo, 967

Soto-Hall, Máximo, 68
Sotomayor, Cristóbal de, 7
Soublette, Carlos, 675, 967–968
Soulouque, Faustin Élie, 435, 916, 968
Sousa, Gabriel Soares de, 968
Sousa, Martim Afonso de, 969
Sousa, Otávio Tarqüínio de, 969
Sousa, Paulino José Soares de, 835, 861, 862, 1036
Sousa, Tomé de, 207, 968, 969
Sousa Coutinho, Rodrigo de, 802
Souza, Luiza Erundina de, 969–970
Souza, Márcio Gonçalves Bentes, 970
Souza, Raymond, 8
Spanish Armada, 331
Spanish Civil War, 1025–1026
Spanish Constitution of Cádiz, 2
Spencer, Herbert, 207
Spíndola, Rafael Reyes, 112
Squier, Ephraim George, 184
Ssarney, José, 605
Staël, Nicolas de, 66
Stalinist Party of the Revolutionary Left, 777
Stefanich, Juan, 970
Steimberg, Alicia, 971
Stimson, Henry L., 676, 928, 963
Stockhausen, Karlheinz, 562, 652, 735
Stokowski, Leopold, 948
Stolyarsky, Pyotr Solomonovich, 376
Storm, Ricardo, 971
Storni, Alfonsina, 161, 971–972
Strauss, Richard, 361
Stroessner, Alfredo, 259, 260, 295, 391, 653, 734, 877, 962, 972–973, 1079
Student Revolutionary Front, 845
Suárez, González, 806
Suárez, Inés de, 973
Suárez, Joaquín, 123
Suárez, Marco Fidel, 451, 505, 973–974
Suárez y Romero, Anselmo, 625, 677
Suassuna, Ariano Vilar, 974
Suazo Córdova, Roberto, 974–975
Subero, Efraín, 147, 975
Subirana, Manuel de Jesús, 975
Sucre, Antonio José de, 154, 382, 399, 547, 733, 878, 922, 931
Sucre Alcalá, Antonio José de, 283, 975–976
Sumac, Yma, 976–977
Suprema Junta Nacional Americana, 850
Sur, 727
Suzigan, Wilson, 703
Syndicate of Technical Workers, Painters, and Sculptors, 26
Szyszlo, Fernando de, 961, 977, 1003

T

Tábara, Enrique, 979
Tablada, José Juan, 776, 979
Tacoma Pact (1911), 142
Tadeo, José, 675

Taft, William Howard, 319, 1091
Tagore, Rabindranath, 727
Tajes, Máximo, 499, 561, 979
Taki Onqoy movement, 421
Talamantes, Melchor de, 523, 979–980, 1079
Talamantes, Porfirio, 1053
Talavera, Manuel, 980
Talavera, Natalício, 980
Taller Alacrán, 635
Taller de Gráfica Popular, 732
Taller Torres García (TTG), 386
Tallet, José Zacarías, 478, 980–981
Tamandaré, 582
Tamante y Rivero, José Luis, 133
Tamarón y Romeral, Pedro, 981
Tamayo, Franz, 981
Tamayo, Rufino, 93, 506, 524, 965, 981–982
Tamberlik, Enrico, 747
Tanco y Bosmeniel, Félix, 677
Tanguy, Ives, 219
Tannenbaum, Frank, 393, 982
Tapia, Francisca Xaviera, 726
Tapuia, 624
Tarigo, Enrique, 930
Taunay, Affonso d'Escragnolle, 982
Taunay, Alfredo d'Escragnolle, Vicomte de, 982–983
Taunay, Auguste Marie, 309
Taunay, Félix Émile de, 982
Taunay, Nicolas Antoine, 309
Tauriello, Antonio, 415, 983
Távara y Andrade, Santiago, 983
Tavares, Antônio Rapôso, 983–984
Tavares Bastos, Aureliano Cândido, 984
Tavarez, Manolo, 1003
Távora, Juarez, 984–985
Taylor, Zachary, 74, 540
Teatro de la Nación (1977–1981), 961
Teatro do Estudante de Pernambuco, 974
Teatro Experimental do Negro (TEN), 708
Teixeira, Anisio Espinola, 985
Teixeira, Humberto, 455
Tejada, Andrés Archila, 64
Tejada Sorzano, José Luis, 177
Tejeda, Adalberto, 211
Tejeda, Leonor de, 985
Tejeda Olivares, Adalberto, 985–986
Tejedor, Carlos, 669, 872, 986
Tellería, José, 263
Telles, Lygia Fagundes, 986
Tello, Julio César, 986–987
Tello, Rafael, 495
Tenants Revolt, 262
Tenochtitlán, 89
Ten Years' War (1868–1878), 6, 97, 242, 419, 427, 448, 449,
    454, 610, 632, 633, 690, 1071
Teresa Cristina Matia of Bourbon, 521, 780, 987
Terra, Gabriel, 47, 101, 148, 172, 447, 987, 1038
Terrazas, Luis, 294, 987–988

Terrazas-Creel clan, 615
Terrero, Máximo, 897
Terres, Jaime García, 156
Testa, Clorindo, 467
Texas Revolution, 931
Thibaud, Alfonso, 590
Thiel, Bernardo Augusto, 988
Third Church Council of Lima, 739
Thomas, Victor, 49
Thompson, George, 988
Thompson y López Cárdenas, Martín J., 926
Thomson, César, 361
Thomson Porto Mariño, Manuel Tomás, 988–989
Thomson-Urrutia Treaty (1914), 854, 974
Thorne, James, 909
Timerman, Jacobo, 989
Tinglado Puertorriqueño, 80
Tinoco de Contreras, José Gregorio, 580
Tinoco Granados, Federico, 461, 989, 1065
Tin-Tan, 989
Tipitapa Agreements, 676
Tizoc, 89
Tlacaelel, 699
Tobajara, 624
Tobar, Juan B., 509
Toch, Ernest, 1039
Tocornal, Joaquín, 819, 989–990
Tocornal, Manuel Antonio, 990
Toledano, Vicente Lombardo, 89, 121
Toledo, Agreement of, 811
Toledo, Martín Juárez de, 71
Toledo y Figueroa, Francisco de, 421, 428, 942, 990–991,
    1003
Toledo y Leyva, Pedro de, 991
Tolosa, Diego de, 792
Tolosa, Juan de, 516
Tolsá, Manuel, 530, 991
Tomic, Radomiro, 29, 392, 566, 991–992
Toni, Olivier, 333
Toribio de Mogrovejo, Alfonso de, 893
Tornel y Mendívil, José María, 992
Tornquist, Ernesto, 992
Toro, Antonio Herrera, 855
Toro, David, 177, 777, 992
Toro, Fermín, 992–993
Toro, Manuel Murillo, 141
Toro Zambrano, Mateo de, 993
Torquemada, Juan de, 993
Torre, Guillermo de, 509
Torre, Lisandro de la, 993–994
Torre, Miguel de la, 994
Torrejón y Velasco, Tomás de, 61, 251–252, 740, 995, 1096
Tôrres, Alberto, 1048
Torres, Camilo, 696
Torres, Gumersindo, 450
Torres, Jerónimo de, 997
Tôrres, Joaquim José Rodrigues, 835, 1016
Torres, José Antonio, 662

Torres, Juan José, 755, 995
Torres, Luis Emeterio, 286, 995–996
Torres, Toribio, 996
Torres Bello, Diego de, 996
Torres Bodet, Jaime, 464, 996
Torres García, Joaquín, 386, 837, 996
Torres Restrepo, Camilo, 996–997
Torres y Portugal, Fernando de, 997
Torre Tagle y Portocarrero, José Bernardo de, 994
Torre y Huerta, Carlos de la, 994
Torrico, Juan Crisóstomo, 236
Torrijos Herrera, Omar, 718, 997–998
Tosar, Héctor Alberto, 636, 998–999
Toscanelli, Paulo de Pozzo, 276
Townley, Michael, 572
Traba, Marta, 843, 999
Treaty to End Traffic in Women and Children (1922), 603
Trejos Fernández, José Joaquín, 999–1000, 1009
Tresguerras, Francisco Eduardo de, 1000
Treviño, Jacinto B., 902
Triaca, Jorge, 1026
Triana, Clotilde, 584
Triana, José, 1000
Tridentine Reforms, 421
Triple A (Alianza Anticomunista Argentina), 596
Triple Alliance, Treaty of, 669
Triple Alliance of Entre Ríos, Brazil, and Montevideo, 897
Tristan, Flora, 1000
Tristán, Pío, 412
Troncoso de la Concha, Manuel de Jesús, 1000–1001, 1002
Trotsky, Leon, 539
Trouillot, Ertha Pascal, 74
Troup, George M., 552
Trujano, Valerio, 693
Trujillo, Guillermo, 1001
Trujillo, Julián, 1001
Trujillo, Manuel, 1001
Trujillo, Rafael Leónidas, 143, 163, 181, 242, 379, 404, 490, 518, 663, 1001
Trujillo, Torcuato, 503
Trujillo-Hull Treaty, 1002
Trujilloism, 99
Trujillo Molina, Rafael Leónidas, 70, 99, 163, 1001–1003, 1037
Truman, Harry S, 335
Tsuchiya, Tilsa, 1003
Tufiño, Rafael, 506
Tugwell, Rexford Guy, 1003
Tum, Juana, 652
Túpac Amaru (José Gabriel Condorcanqui), 428, 527, 810, 1003–1004
Túpac Amaru Rebellion (1780–1783), 89, 296, 399, 409
Túpac Catari (Julián Apaza), 1004–1005
Tupamaros, 309
Tupi-Guaraní Indian mission, 411
Turbay, Gabriel, 1005
Turbay Ayala, Julio César, 434, 584, 1005
Turcios, Froylan, 671

Turcios Lima, Luis, 681, 1005, 1079
Turner, Joseph, 638
Turrialba group, 12
Turton, Robert, 829
Tutt, Ernest, 563
Twelve in the Broad Opposition Front (1978), 845
Twenty-sixth of July Movement, 244, 246, 266, 330, 350, 760, 926, 934
Twiggs, David E., 48
Tworkov, Jack, 210

U
Ubico, Jorge, 62, 84, 216, 250, 388, 495, 917, 1077
Ubico y Castañeda, Jorge, 215, 254, 1007–1008
Ugarte, Alfonso, 155
Ugarte, Floro, 426
Ugarte, Manuel, 1008
Ugarte, Marcelino, 1008–1009
Ulate, Otilio, 191
Ulate Blanco, Otilio, 339, 378, 686, 923, 999, 1009
Ulloa, Antonio de, 45, 531, 740, 1009
Ulloa, Hilario, 1024
Ultraist school of literature, 513
Umaña, Lucía Encarnación Fernández, 684
Umaña Bernal, José, 1009–1010
Unanue, Hipólito, 1010
Ungo, Guillermo Manuel, 1010, 1084
União Democrática Nacional (UDN), 140, 650
Unidad Democrática y Popular (UDP), 778, 952
Unión Cívica, 22
Unión Cívica de la Juventud (Youth Civic Union), 22
Unión Cívica Nacionál, 1080
Unión Cívica Radical del Pueblo, 100, 217, 396, 518, 567
Unión Cívica Radical (UCR), 22, 884, 993, 1080
Unión Latino Americana, 519
Unión Nacional Izquierdista Revolucionaria (UNIR), 402
Unión Nacional Opositora (UNO), 6, 117, 871
Union of Farmers and Agricultural Laborers of Brazil (ULTAB), 954
Union of the Democratic Center (UCD), 36
Union of the National Center (UCN), 220
Unión Republicana Democrática (URD), 793
Unitarios, 629
Unitarist faction, 67
United Democratic Party (UDP), 354
United Front, 997
United Fruit Company, 62–63, 409, 998
United Mining Company, 11
United Movement of Popular Action (MAPU), 264
United National Opposition (UNO), 1010
United Nations
  Commission on Juridical and Social Condition of Women, 381
  Economic Commission for Latin America (ECLA), 400
United Officers Group, 845
United Representation of the Guatemalan Opposition (RUOG), 652
U.S.-Mexican Claims Agreement (1868), 889

Universal Negro Improvement Association (UNIA), 431–432

Urban VIII (Pope), 210

Urbina, José María, 716, 871, 1010–1011

Urbina, Luis Gonzaga, 1011

Urdaneta, Andrés de, 592, 1011–1012

Urdaneta, Rafael, 589, 699, 939, 1011, 1058

Ureña, Felipe, 1012

Ureña, Molina, 674

Ureña, Rafael Estrella, 99

Ureña de Henríquez, Salomé, 490, 1012

Ureta, Eloy G., 1012

Ureta, Manuel Toribio, 237

Uribe, Juan Camilo, 1012

Uribe Holguín, Guillermo, 1012–1013

Uribe Uribe, Rafael, 497, 768, 1013

Uriburu, José Evaristo, 669, 910, 1013

Uriburu, José Félix, 217, 515, 537, 795, 1013–1014

Urquiza, Justo José de, 14, 34, 35, 314, 493, 593, 629, 668, 743, 774, 872, 941, 1014, 1027

Urracá, 1015

Urrea, José de, 452, 1015, 1097

Urrea, Teresa, 1015

Urriolagoitía, Mamerto, 501, 1015

Urrutia, José de, 899

Urrutia, Manuel, 330

Urrutia, Wenceslao, 675

Urrutia-Blondel, Jorge, 85

Urrutia Lleó, Manuel, 244, 1015–1016

Urrutia y Montoya, Carlos Luis de, 401

Ursúa, Pedro de, 9, 1016

Urtecho, Coronel, 286

Uruguai, Visconde do, 1016–1017

Uruguayan Press Association, 349

Urvina, José María, 26

Urvina Jado, Francisco, 1017

Urzagasti, Jesús, 1017

Usigli, Rodolfo, 515, 719, 1017

Uslar Pietri, Arturo, 591, 1017–1018

Ussachevsky, Vladimir, 803, 1020

V

Vaca de Castro, Cristóval, 31, 1019

Vaccaro, Felix, 1019

Vaccaro, Joseph, 1019

Vaccaro, Luca, 1019

Vaccine Revolt (1904), 386

Vadillo, Juan de, 266

Vagrancy Law (1934), 1008

Vaides, Federico Ponce, 62

Valadares, Benedito, 543

Valasco y Castilla, Luis de, 516

Valásquez, José Antonio, 817

Valcárcel, Luis E., 256, 1095

Valcárcel Arce, Edgar, 1019–1020

Valderrama, Jerónimo de, 1041

Valdés, Gabriel de la Concepción, 626, 1020

Valdés, Gerónimo, 589

Valdés, Letelier, 572

Valdés, Ramiro, 245

Valdés, Ramón Maximiliano, 817

Valdés, Samuel Claro, 1093

Valdez, José Trujillo, 1002

Valdéz, Juan, 1020–1021

Valdivia, Luis de, 1021

Valdivia, Pedro de, 433, 561, 927, 973, 1021–1022, 1056

Valdivieso, Antonio de, 281

Valencia, Antonio María, 801, 1022

Valencia, Guillermo, 222, 1022

Valencia, Juan Galdós de, 695

Valentim, Mestre, 388

Valentine, Luis, 989

Valenzuela, Jesús, 712

Valenzuela, Luisa, 573, 1022–1023

Valenzuela, Pedro, 224

Valério, João, 847

Valero, Roberto, 1023

Valéry, Paul, 172, 574

Valladares, Armando, 1023–1024

Valladares, Martha, 1023

Valladares, Tomás, 1024

Vallbona, Rima de, 1024

Valle, Andrés, 966

Valle, Antonio, 689

Valle, Aristóbulo del, 22, 1024, 1080

Valle, Barrios, 966

Valle, José Cecilio del, 64, 312, 690, 1024–1025

Valle, José María, 929

Valle, Juan José, 883

Valle, Leandro, 630

Vallejo, César, 152, 711, 761, 1025–1026

Vallejo, Mariano Guadalupe, 1026

Vallenilla Lanz, Laureano, 1026

Valverde, Mateo Mora, 684

Valverde, Vicente de, 86, 810

VAN, 979

Van Buren, Martin, 814

Vancouver, George, 151

Vandor, Augusto, 1026–1027

Vanegas, Rafael, 806

Vanguardia movement, 285

Van Horne, William, 365

Vannucci, Lavinio Felice, 1093

Vantongerloo, Georges, 196, 646

Varacchi, Nieves, 636

Varas de la Barra, Antonio, 682, 793, 1027

Varela, Felipe, 1027

Varela, Felix, 492

Varela, Florencio, 1027–1028

Varela, José Pedro, 1028

Varela, Juan Cruz, 629, 1027, 1028

Varela, María Victorio, 552

Varela y Morales, Félix, 182–183, 606, 1028–1029

Varèse, Edgard, 260, 292

Vargas, Alonso de, 428

Vargas, Candida Dornellas, 1030

Vargas, Diego de, 1029–1030

Vargas, Getúlio Dornelles, 15, 32, 43, 61, 118, 188, 195, 199, 234, 274, 291, 383, 394, 447, 464, 543–544, 544, 549, 581, 598, 602, 650, 651, 679, 827–828, 828, 984, 1030–1033, 1046

Vargas, José María, 628, 967, 1033

Vargas, Manoel do Nascimento, 1030

Vargas, Max T., 255

Vargas, Ramón, 806

Vargas, Riograndense Getúlio, 273

Vargas Llosa, Mario, 446, 1033–1035

Varnhagen, Francisco Adolfo de, 874, 968, 1035

Varo, Remedios, 1035

Varona y Pera, Enrique José, 1035

Vasconcellos, Luiz de, 388

Vasconcelos, Bernardo Pereira de, 765, 874, 1016, 1036

Vasconcelos Calderón, José, 84, 148, 290, 361, 489, 541, 563, 594, 597, 667, 744, 785, 849, 909, 996, 1036–1037

Vásquez, Francisco de Asís, 1037

Vásquez, Horacio, 99, 1037

Vásquez de Arce y Ceballos, Gregorio, 1037

Vatican Council II (1962–1965), 480, 1029

Vaughan, John, 695

Vaz de Melo, Clélia, 140

Vaz Ferreira, María Eugenia, 11

Vaz Ferreira, Carlos, 541, 636, 1038

Vázquez de Ayllón, Lucas, 1037–1038

Vázquez de Coronado, Francisco, 1038

Vedia y Mitre, Mariano, 1038–1039

Vega, Aurelio de, 1039

Vega, Jorge Luis de la, 1039

Vega, Sebastián Garcilaso de la Vega, 427

Veiga, Evaristo Ferreira da, 1039

Veiga Vale, José Joaquim da, 1039–1040

Veintemilla, Ignacio, 1011

Veintimilla, José Ignacio de, 162, 181, 208–209, 384, 1040

Velarde, López, 597

Velasco, José María, 730, 1040

Velasco, José Miguel de, 932, 1040–1041

Velasco, Luis de ("The Younger"), 65, 87, 516, 736–737, 1041

Velasco Alvarado, Juan, 666, 689, 1041

Velasco Ibarra, José María, 77, 80, 813, 816, 881, 1041–1042

Velázquez, Ana, 818

Velázquez, Diego de, 287–288, 467, 494, 557, 680, 1042

Velázquez, José Antonio, 1042

Velázquez Cárdenas de León, Joaquín, 1042–1043

Velázquez de León, Carlos Celedonia, 1042–1043

Velázquez Sánchez, Fidel, 1043

Vélez, Aurelia, 941

Vélez, José Miguel Díaz, 203

Vélez de Escalante, Silvestre, 1043–1044

Vélez of Tepic, Juana, 15

Vélez Sarsfield, Dalmacio, 1044

Veloso, Carybé Caetano, 248, 438, 455, 658, 1044

Venegas de Saavedra, Francisco Javier, 1044

Venezuelan Communist Party, 610–611

Venezuelan Democratic Party, 644

Venezuelan National Theater Company, 263

Venezuelan Organization (Organización Venezolana-ORVE), 115

Vera Cruz, Alonso de la, 1044–1045

Verapaz, Alta, 561

Vera y Aragón, Alonso de, 71

Vera y Aragón, Juan Torres de, 71, 751

Verde, Cuerno, 57

Verdi, Giuseppe, 403

Verdugo, Domingo, 451–452

Verduzco, José Sixto, 693, 879

Vergara, Juan Pérez de, 1019

Vergara, Margarita de, 755

Vergara, Marta, 1045

Vergara Echeverez, José Francisco, 1045

Vergara y Vergara, José María, 323

Veríssimo, Érico, 1045–1046

Veríssimo, José, 890

Verlaine, Paul, 306, 450

Vernet, Louis, 1046

Verninck, María, 918

Vértiz, Viceroy, 958

Vértiz y Salcedo, Juan José de, 1046

Vesco, Robert Lee, 380, 1046

Vespucci, Amerigo, 732, 960, 1046–1047

Vial, Pedro, 1047–1048

Viamonte, Juan José, 1048

Viana, Francisco José de Oliveira, 1048

Vicanco Pareja Treaty (1865), 799

Vicario, Leona, 838

Vicario Fernández, [María] Leona, 1048

Vicente, Juan, 406

Victores, Mejía, 645

Victoria, Guadalupe, 427, 453, 992, 1049

Victoria, Manuel, 339, 1049

Victorio, Tomás Luis de, 372

Vicuña, Joaquín, 1074

Vicuña Aguirre, Pedro Félix, 1049

Vicuña Larraín, Francisco Ramón, 1049

Vicuña Larraín, Manuel, 1049

Vicuña Mackenna, Benjamin, 1049

Vidal, Francisco A., 236, 561

Vidal, Miguel Angel, 609

Vidaurre, Mercedes, 661

Vidaurri, Santiago, 352, 1050

Videla, Jorge Rafael, 1050, 1062

Vidrios y Cristales, Fábrica de, 432

Vieira, Antônio, 54, 1050–1051

Viera, Decio, 268

Viera, Feliciano, 1051–1052

Viera, José Carlos do Amaral, 1051

Vieytes, Hipólito, 1052

Vigil, Donaciano, 1052

Vigil, Francisco de Paula González, 1052

Vijil, Diego, 691

Vilanova, María Cristina, 62

Vilar, Manuel, 268, 959, 1052

Vilariño, Idea, 500, 837, 1052–1053

Vilches, Luis, 46
Villa, Francisco "Pancho," 221, 231, 509, 725, 759, 988, 1053–1054, 1085
Villacorta, Juan Vicente, 869
Villacorta Calderón, José Antonio, 1056
Villa de la Navidad, 276
Villagra, Francisco de, 561, 927, 1056
Villagrá, Gaspar Pérez de, 1056
Villagra, Pedro de, 561
Villagrán, José María ("El Chito"), 1056–1057
Villagrán, Julian, 1056–1057
Villagrán Kramer, Francisco, 1057
Villalba, Jóvito, 1057
Villalba, Juan de, 899
Villa-Lobos, Heitor, 45, 370, 621, 661, 710, 1051, 1054–1056
Villa-Lobos, Lucília Guimarães, 45, 621
Villa-Lobos, Noemia, 1055
Villa-Lobos, Raul, 1055
Villalonga, Jorge de, 352, 625, 782, 1057
Villalpando, Cristóbal de, 286, 880, 1057–1058
Villamizar, Eduardo Ramírez, 466
Villanueva, Carlos Raúl, 1058
Villanueva, Gabino, 907
Villarán, Manual Vicente, 1058
Villarino, J., 677
Villarroel López, Gualberto, 113, 505, 777, 1058–1059
Villas Bôas, Cláudio, 1059
Villas Bôas, Leonardo, 1059
Villas Bôas, Orlando, 1059
Villaurrutia, Antonio, 1059
Villaurrutia, Jacobo de, 1059
Villaurrutía, Xavier, 265, 719, 1059–1060
Villaverde, Cirilo, 1060
Villazón, Eliodoro, 1060
Villeda Morales, Ramón, 409, 601, 875, 1060–1061
Villegaignon, Nicolas Durand de, 1061
Villegas, Juan de, 598
Villegas, Oscar, 1061
Vincent, Sténio Joseph, 829, 1061–1062
Viñes y Martorell, Benito, 1062
Viola, Paulinho da, 308
Viola, Roberto Eduardo, 1050, 1062
Visca, María, 269
Viscardo y Guzmán, Juan Pablo, 1062–1063
Visconti, Eliseu d'Angelo, 1063
Vitale, Ida, 843
Vitalino Pereira dos Santos, Mestre, 1063
Viteri y Ungo, Jorge, 426, 620, 1063
Vitier, Cintio, 172, 1063–1064
Vitier, Medardo, 1063
Vitoria, Francisco de, 1064
Viva, Música, 542
Vivanco, Manuel Ignacio, 155, 187, 236, 466, 1064
Vivanco, Moises, 976
Viza, Manuela López, 255
Vizcaíno, Sebastián, 7, 1064–1065
Vogel, Wladimir, 505

Volio Jiménez, Jorge, 1065
Von Reichenbach, 637
Von Vacano, Arturo, 1065

W

Wade, Benjamin, 889
Wagener, Zacharias, 641
Wagnerian Association, 591
Walcott, Derek, 1067
Walker, William, 115, 199, 225, 248, 257, 357, 445, 471, 520, 528, 634, 685, 701–702, 767, 865–866, 1067–1068, 1088
Wallace, Peter, 1068–1069
Walsh, Robert, 874
Wandenkolk, Eduardo, 913
Wanick, Lélia Deluiz, 914
Ward, Henry George, 814
Warhol, Andy, 403
War of Independence (1813), 731, 819
War of Jenkins's Ear, 531, 657
War of Oranges, 859
War of Restoration (1863–1865), 501, 603, 934
War of the Emboabas, 229
War of the Knives (1799–1800), 600
War of the Mascates, 230
War of the Pacific (1879–1884), 4, 9, 63, 106, 155–156, 187, 308, 420, 483, 517, 638, 654–655, 689, 764, 801, 807, 824, 910, 933–934, 1072
War of the Reform (1857–1860), 33, 457, 488, 517, 534, 568, 1087–1088
War of the Seven Reductions (1752–1756), 411
War of the Supremes (1839–1842), 218, 496, 630, 649, 698, 723
War of the Thousand Days (1899–1903), 219, 497, 509, 597, 631, 768, 854, 857, 1013
War of the Triple Alliance (1864–1870), 2, 98, 109, 136, 138, 181, 200, 259–260, 280, 286, 310, 320, 328, 332, 350, 351, 355, 363, 365, 374, 383, 387, 433, 436, 449, 468, 499, 522, 531, 560, 587, 588, 593, 606–607, 617, 619, 640, 645, 668, 734, 764, 781, 783, 786–787, 803, 851, 862, 865, 941, 944, 980, 982, 988, 1001, 1024, 1073
Washington de Mendeville, Jean-Baptiste, 926
Watermelon Riot (1856), 286
Weffort, Francisco Correia, 1069
Weingartner, Felix, 591
Weingärtner, Pedro, 1069
Welles, Sumner, 613
Welliver, Neil, 210
Wessín y Wessín, Elías, 163
Westphalen, Emilio Adolfo, 961
Weyler y Nicolau, Valeriano, 1069–1070
Wheelock Román, Jaime, 747, 1070–1071
White, Guillermo Pio, 556
White, José, 252
White Hand, 60, 654
White y Lafitta, José, 1071
Widt, Adolfo, 388

Wildberger, Jacques, 85
Wilde, Eduardo, 469, 1071
Wilde, Oscar, 953
Williams, Alberto, 9, 882, 1072
Williams, Andy, 248
Williams Calderón, Abraham, 601, 1072
Williams Rebolledo, Juan, 1072
William the Silent of Orange, 640
Williman, Claudio, 1072–1073
Willka, Luciano, 1087
Wilson, Henry Lane, 508–509, 616
Wilson, Woodrow, 157, 258, 461, 508–509
Winter, Paul, 248
Wisner von Morgenstern, Franz, 1073
Wolf, Winfried, 505
Wolff, Egon, 489, 1073
Woll, Adrián, 946
Wolpe, Stefan, 171–172
Wood, Leonard, 382, 448
Wooster, Charles Whiting, 1073–1074
Wooster, David, 1074
Workers and Peasants Bloc, 686
Worker's Party, 952, 970, 1069
Wyke-Aycinena Treaty (1859), 91
Wyld, Guillermo, 1074
Wyld Ospina, Carlos, 1074

X

Xapuri Rural Workers' Union, 652–653
Xavier, Francisco dos Santos, 388
Xaviera Echeverz Subiza y Yaldés, Ignacia, 6
Xenakis, Iannis, 562
Xicoténcatl, Luisa de, 37, 300
Ximénez, Francisco, 1075
Ximeno, Fabián, 591
Xul Solar, 1075
XuXa, 1075–1076

Y

Yacimientos Petrolíferos Fiscales Bolivianos (YPFB), 992
Yanes, Francisco Javier, 1077
Yáñez, Plácido, 4
Yáñez Santos Delgadillo, Agustín, 1077
Yasao Kuniyoshi, 628
Ydíaquez, José de, 1096
Ydígoras Fuentes, Miguel, 654, 789, 1005, 1077–1078, 1079
Yegros, Fulgencio, 182, 389, 1078
Yellow fever, 382
Yellow Liberalism, 912
Yermo, Gabriel de, 523, 1078–1079
Ynsfrán, Edgar L., 1079
Ynsfrán, Pablo Max, 1079
Yon Sosa, Marco Antonio, 681, 1005, 1079–1080
Young Argentine Generation, 629
Yrigoyen, Hipólito, 22, 23, 27, 42, 205, 217, 313, 537, 602, 650, 706, 795, 801, 832, 873, 884, 910, 993, 1009, 1014, 1080–1081
Yupanqui, Leonor, 751

Z

Zacapoaxtla, 548
Zachrisson, Julio, 1083
Zadkine, Ossip, 368
Zaid, Gabriel, 1083
Zalamea, Alberto, 999
Zaldívar, Rafael, 306
Zaldúa, Francisco Javier, 1083
Zambrana, Luis Pérez de, 452
Zamor, Oreste, 789
Zamora, Ezequiel, 483
Zamora, Manuel Gutiérrez, 534
Zamora, Mario, 1083
Zamora, Rubén, 1083–1084
Zamorano, Agustín Juan Vicente, 1084
Zapata, Emiliano, 227, 231, 249, 325, 458, 480, 509, 614, 723, 725, 1054, 1084–1086
Zapata, Felipe, 1086
Zapatista Army of National Liberation, 915
Zapatistas, 221, 615
Zapiola, José, 919
Zaracondegui, Julián de, 83, 1086
Zaragoza, Ignacio, 864, 1086–1087
Zárate, Ortiz de, 418
Zárate Wilka, Pablo, 1087
Zarco, Francisco, 302, 1087–1088
Zavala, Joaquín, 484, 1088
Zavala, José Víctor, 1088
Zavala, Lorenzo de, 452, 1088–1089
Zavala, Silvio, 730, 1089
Zayas y Alfonso, Alfredo, 555, 648, 1035, 1089
Zé, Tom, 1044
Zea, Francisco Antonio, 933
Zea, Leopoldo, 416
Zea Aguilar, Leopoldo, 1089
Zebadúa, Marcial, 120
Zeballos, Estanislao, 849, 1089–1090
Zé Dantas, 455
Zelaya, Barbara, 580
Zelaya, José Santos, 157, 257–258, 307, 358, 634, 655, 675, 853, 1088, 1090–1091, 1091
Zelaya Sierra, Pablo, 1042, 1091
Zeledón, Benjamin Francisco, 1091–1092
Zemurray, "Banana Man," 264
Zemurray, Samuel, 157, 216, 816
Zenil, Nahum Bernabé, 1092
Zeno Gandía, Manuel, 1092
Zenteno, José Ignacio, 920
Zepeda, Eraclio, 1092
Zepeda y Zepeda, Juan de Jesus, 1092–1093
Zevada, Ricardo J., 617
Ziembinski, Zbigniew, 876
Zimmer, Albert, 226
Zimmerman telegram, 222
Zipoli, Domenico, 1093
ZLC-Consultores Associados, 649
Zola, Émile, 95, 96, 196
Zorita, Alonso de, 1093

Zorrilla de San Martín, Juan, 171, 514, 1093–1094
Zuazo, Siles, 476
Zubirán Anchondo, Salvador, 1094
Zubiri, Xavier, 416
Zubiría, José Antonio Laureano de, 1094
Zubizarreta, Gerónimo, 1094
Zulen, Dora Mayer de, 1094–1095
Zulen, Pedro S., 207, 1094–1095, 1095
Zuloaga, Félix María, 534, 1095
Zumárraga, Juan de, 484, 630, 1096
Zumaya, Francisco de, 339
Zumaya, Manuel de, 1096

Zumba, Ganga, 1097
Zumbi, 1096–1097
Zum Felde, Alberto, 11, 953, 1095–1096
Zúñiga, Ángel, 216
Zúñiga, Diego López de, 421
Zúñiga, Ercilla, 644
Zúñiga, Ignacio, 1097
Zúñiga Figueroa, Carlos, 360, 1097
Zúñiga y Velasco, Diego López de, 750
Zurbarán, Francisco de, 167, 535, 592
Zweig, Stefan, 65